TESTS IN PRINT V

VOLUME II

S-Indexes

EARLIER PUBLICATIONS IN THIS SERIES

EDUCATIONAL, PSYCHOLOGICAL, AND PERSONALITY TESTS OF 1933 AND 1934

EDUCATIONAL, PSYCHOLOGICAL, AND PERSONALITY TESTS OF 1933, 1934, AND 1935

EDUCATIONAL, PSYCHOLOGICAL, AND PERSONALITY TESTS OF 1936

THE NINETEEN THIRTY-EIGHT MENTAL MEASUREMENTS YEARBOOK

THE NINETEEN FORTY MENTAL MEASUREMENTS YEARBOOK

THE THIRD MENTAL MEASUREMENTS YEARBOOK

THE FOURTH MENTAL MEASUREMENTS YEARBOOK

THE FIFTH MENTAL MEASUREMENTS YEARBOOK

TESTS IN PRINT

THE SIXTH MENTAL MEASUREMENTS YEARBOOK

THE SEVENTH MENTAL MEASUREMENTS YEARBOOK

TESTS IN PRINT II

THE MONOGRAPH SERIES

THE EIGHTH MENTAL MEASUREMENTS YEARBOOK

TESTS IN PRINT III

THE NINTH MENTAL MEASUREMENTS YEARBOOK

THE SUPPLEMENT TO THE NINTH MENTAL MEASUREMENTS YEARBOOK

THE TENTH MENTAL MEASUREMENTS YEARBOOK

THE SUPPLEMENT TO THE TENTH MENTAL MEASUREMENTS YEARBOOK

THE ELEVENTH MENTAL MEASUREMENTS YEARBOOK

TESTS IN PRINT IV

THE SUPPLEMENT TO THE ELEVENTH MENTAL MEASUREMENTS YEARBOOK

BUROS DESK REFERENCE: PSYCHOLOGICAL ASSESSMENT IN THE SCHOOLS

BUROS DESK REFERENCE: ASSESSMENT OF SUBSTANCE ABUSE

THE TWELFTH MENTAL MEASUREMENTS YEARBOOK

THE SUPPLEMENT TO THE TWELFTH MENTAL MEASUREMENTS YEARBOOK

THE THIRTEENTH MENTAL MEASUREMENTS YEARBOOK

TESTS
IN PRINT V

AN INDEX TO TESTS, TEST REVIEWS, AND THE LITERATURE ON SPECIFIC TESTS

Edited by

LINDA L. MURPHY
JAMES C. IMPARA
BARBARA S. PLAKE

Volume II
S-Indexes
(Tests 2263-2939)

The Buros Institute of Mental Measurements
The University of Nebraska-Lincoln
Lincoln, Nebraska

1999
Distributed by The University of Nebraska Press

LC 83-18866
ISBN 910674-51-5

Manufactured in the United States of America.

The paper used in this publication meets the minimum requirements of American National Standard for Information Sciences—Permanence of Paper for Printed Library Materials, ANSI Z39.48-1984.

Note to Users

The staff of the Buros Institute of Mental Measurements has made every effort to ensure the accuracy of the test information included in this work. However, the Buros Institute of Mental Measurements and the Editors of *Tests in Print V* do not assume, and hereby expressly and absolutely disclaim, any liability to any party for any loss or damage caused by errors or omissions or statements of any kind in *Tests in Print V*.

All material included in *Tests in Print V* is intended solely for the use of our readers. None of this material may be used in advertising or for any other commercial purpose.

TABLE OF CONTENTS

	Page
INTRODUCTION	ix
TESTS IN PRINT	1
MMY TEST REVIEWERS	1083
INDEX OF TITLES	1109
INDEX OF RECENTLY OUT-OF-PRINT TESTS	1157
INDEX OF ACRONYMS	1165
CLASSIFIED SUBJECT INDEX	1193
PUBLISHERS DIRECTORY AND INDEX	1249
INDEX OF NAMES	1285
SCORE INDEX	1577

Tests in Print

(Continued)

[2263]

S-D Proneness Checklist.

Purpose: "Intended to be used for the measurement of depression and suicide-proneness."
Population: Depressed or suicidal clients.
Publication Dates: 1970-1972.
Scores, 3: Suicide, Depression, Total.
Administration: Individual.
Price Data, 1989: $8.25 per 25 rating forms; $5 per specimen set.
Time: (5) minutes.
Comments: Checklist completed by interviewer.
Author: William T. Martin.
Publisher: Psychologists and Educators, Inc.
Cross References: For a review by Charles Neuringer, see 8:664.

[2264]

Safran Student's Interest Inventory, Third Edition.

Purpose: Developed to identify occupational interests.
Population: Grades 5-9, 9-12.
Publication Dates: 1960-1985.
Scores, 7: Economic, Technical, Outdoor, Service, Humane, Artistic, Scientific.
Administration: Group.
Levels, 2: One, Two.
Price Data, 1999: $53.50 per 35 test booklets (select level); $32 per student's manual ('85, 8 pages); $32 per counsellor's manual ('85, 39 pages); $33 per examination kit.
Time: Administration time not reported.
Comments: Self-administered.
Authors: Carl Safran, Douglas W. Feltham, and Edgar N. Wright.
Publisher: ITP Nelson Canada [Canada].
Cross References: For reviews by Albert M. Bugaj and Caroline Manuele-Adkins, see 12:336; for a review by Thomas T. Frantz of an earlier edition, see 7:1035; see also 6:1069 (1 reference).

[2265]

Sales Achievement Predictor.

Purpose: Constructed to assess "characteristics that are critical for success in sales."
Population: Adults.
Publication Date: 1995.
Acronym: Sales AP.
Scores, 21: Validity Scores (Inconsistent Responding, Self-Enhancing, Self-Critical), Special Scores (Sales Disposition, Initiative-Cold Calling, Sales Closing), Basic Domain Scores (Achievement, Motivation, Competitiveness, Goal Orientation, Planning, Initiative-General, Team Player, Managerial, Assertiveness, Personal Diplomacy, Extroversion, Cooperativeness, Relaxed Style, Patience, Self-Confidence).
Administration: Group.
Price Data, 1999: $175 per kit including manual (73 pages), 2 mail-in answer sheets, 2-use disk for on-site computer scoring, and 2 PC answer sheets; $45 per mail-in answer sheet; $50 per manual; $360 per 25-use computer disk (PC with Windows); $15 per 100 PC answer sheets; $39.50 per FAX service scoring.
Time: (20–25) minutes.
Comments: Microsoft Windows 3.1 or above required for computer scoring.

Authors: Jotham G. Friedland, Sander I. Marcus, and Harvey P. Mandel.
Publisher: Western Psychological Services.

[2266]
Sales Aptitude Test: ETSA Test 7A.

Purpose: Designed to measure a person's likelihood of success in sales positions.
Population: Job applicants.
Publication Dates: 1960-1984.
Scores, 8: Sales Judgement, Interest in Selling, Personality Factors, Identification of Self with Selling Occupation, Level of Aspiration, Insight into Human Nature, Awareness of Sales Approach, Total.
Administration: Group.
Price Data, 1998: $15 per 10 tests and scoring key.
Time: (60) minutes.
Author: Psychological Services Bureau.
Publisher: Educators'/Employers' Tests and Services Associates.
Cross References: For reviews by Marvin D. Dunnette and Raymond A. Katzell of an earlier version of the ETSA Tests, see 6:1025.

[2267]
Sales Attitude Check List.

Purpose: To measure attitudes toward selling and habits in the sales situation.
Population: Applicants for sales positions.
Publication Dates: 1960-1992.
Acronym: SACL.
Scores: Total score only.
Administration: Individual or group.
Price Data, 1998: $77 per start-up kit including 25 test booklets and examiner's manual; $66 per 25 test booklets (quantity discounts available); $19.75 per examiner's manual.
Time: No limit (approximately 10–15 minutes).
Author: Erwin K. Taylor.
Publisher: NCS (Rosemont).
Cross References: For reviews by Walter C. Borman and Stephan J. Motowidlo, see 9:1066 (1 reference); for a review by John P. Foley, Jr., see 6:1177.

[2268]
Sales Competency Inventory.

Purpose: Designed to measure the frequency with which respondents display certain competencies associated with effective sales performance.
Population: Salespeople.
Publication Date: 1996.
Scores, 5: Achievement Orientation, Customer Service Orientation, Impact and Influence, Initiative, Interpersonal Understanding.
Administration: Group.
Price Data, 1998: $65 per 10 Profile and Interpretive Notes (22 pages) and 10 questionnaires.
Time: Administration time not reported.
Comments: Self-scoring and interpretive information provided.
Author: Hay/McBer.
Publisher: Hay/McBer.

[2269]
Sales Comprehension Test.

Purpose: "Designed to aid in the appraisal of sales ability and potential."
Population: Sales applicants.
Publication Dates: 1947-1994.
Acronym: SCT.
Scores: Total score only.
Administration: Group.
Price Data, 1998: $77.40 per tests; $3.75 per key; $35.40 per profiles; $52.65 per manual ('76, 20 pages), manuals supplement ('84, 17 pages), manual supplement ('85, 4 pages), and norms supplement ('94, 4 pages); $4.20 per norms supplement ('88, 1 page); $55.95 per specimen set.
Foreign Language Editions: Spanish, Dutch, French, German, and Italian editions available.
Time: (15-20) minutes.
Comments: Revision of the Aptitudes Associates Test of Sales Aptitude.
Author: Martin M. Bruce.
Publisher: Martin M. Bruce, Ph.D.
Cross References: See T2:2406 (3 references) and 6:1178 (7 references); for a review by Raymond A. Katzell, see 5:947 (10 references).

[2270]
Sales Effectiveness Analysis.

Purpose: Designed to identify an individual's strengths and weaknesses in the area of sales.
Population: Salespeople.
Publication Dates: 1985-1999.
Acronym: SEA.
Scores, 25: Market Awareness, Technical, Strategic, Structure, Sales Focus, Prospecting, Entrepreneurship, Communication, Outgoing, Optimistic, Excitement, Persuasive Negotiation, Insight, Aggressiveness, Tactical, Empathy, Customer Identification, Team Player, Persistence, Production, Management Focus, Idealism, Ego Drive, Materialism, Exaggeration.
Administration: Group.
Price Data: Available from publisher.
Time: (45) minutes.
Comments: Purchase and use requires training by publisher.

Authors: James T. Mahoney (test) and Management Research Group Staff (manual).
Publisher: Management Research Group.

[2271]

Sales Effectiveness Survey.

Purpose: "Designed to help salespeople and others responsible for business development assess their effectiveness."
Population: Sales and business development professionals.
Publication Date: 1996.
Scores: Total score only.
Administration: Group.
Manual: No manual.
Price Data, 1998: $99 per set including questionnaires and answer sheets for 1 self-assessment, 6 others, 6 customers, and 1 feedback report.
Time: [30] minutes.
Author: Terry R. Bacon.
Publisher: International LearningWorks®.

[2272]

Sales Motivation Inventory, Revised.

Purpose: Designed for "assessment of interest in, and motivation for, sales work."
Population: Prospective and employed salespeople.
Publication Dates: 1953-1988.
Acronym: SMI.
Scores: Total score only.
Administration: Group.
Price Data, 1998: $77.40 per test package; $52.65 per manual/manuals supplement; $4.20 per norms supplement; $35.40 per profile sheet package; $3.75 per scoring key; $55.95 per specimen set.
Time: (20-30) minutes.
Author: Martin M. Bruce.
Publisher: Martin M. Bruce, Ph.D.
Cross References: For a review by Leo M. Harvill, see 11:338; for reviews by Robert M. Guion and Stephan J. Motowidlo of an earlier edition, see 9:1067; see also T2:2408 (5 references); for a review by S. Rains Wallace, see 5:948 (2 references).

[2273]

Sales Motivation Survey.

Purpose: Designed to assess the kinds of needs and values salespeople see as important considerations in making decisions about their work.
Population: Salespeople.
Publication Dates: 1972–1995.
Scores, 5: Basic Creative Comfort, Safety and Order, Belonging and Affiliation, Ego-Status, Actualization and Self-Expression.
Administration: Group.
Price Data, 1995: $7.95 per survey.
Time: Administration time is not reported.
Comments: Self-administered; self-scored.
Authors: Jay Hall and Norman J. Seim.
Publisher: Teleometrics International.

[2274]

Sales Personality Questionnaire.

Purpose: Developed to assess personality characteristics necessary for sales success.
Population: Sales applicants.
Publication Dates: 1987-1990.
Acronym: SPQ.
Scores, 12: Interpersonal (Confidence, Empathy, Persuasive), Administration (Systematic, Conscientious, Forward Planning), Opportunities (Creative, Observant), Energies (Relaxed, Resilient, Results Oriented), Social Desirability.
Administration: Group.
Price Data: Available from publisher.
Time: (20-30) minutes.
Author: Saville & Holdsworth Ltd.
Publisher: Saville & Holdsworth.
Cross References: For reviews by Wayne J. Camara and Michael J. Roszkowski, see 12:337.

[2275]

Sales Relations Survey.

Purpose: Designed to assess the interpersonal practices and customer orientation of salespeople.
Population: Salespeople.
Publication Dates: 1972–1995.
Scores, 2: Exposure, Feedback.
Administration: Group.
Price Data, 1995: $8.95 per survey.
Time: Administration time not reported.
Comments: Self-administered; self-scored.
Author: Jay Hall.
Publisher: Teleometrics International.

[2276]

The Sales Sentence Completion Blank.

Purpose: "Designed to aid in the selection of competent sales personnel."
Population: Applicants for sales positions.
Publication Dates: 1961-1982.
Acronym: SSCB.
Scores: Total score only.
Administration: Group.
Price Data, 1998: $65.95 per test package; $19.50 per manual ('61, 25 pages); $28.05 per specimen set.
Time: (20-35) minutes.
Author: Norman Gekoski.
Publisher: Martin M. Bruce, Ph.D.

Cross References: For a review by William E. Kendall, and an excerpted review by John O. Crites, see 6:1181.

[2277]

Sales Staff Selector.

Purpose: "Evaluates the suitability of candidates of all levels of experience for the position of Sales Representative."
Population: Candidates for sales representative positions.
Publication Date: 1984.
Scores: 5 tests: Numerical Skills, Problem Solving Ability, Fluency, Sales Comprehension, Sales Motivation.
Administration: Group.
Price Data, 1999: $355 per candidate.
Foreign Language Edition: French edition available.
Time: (120) minutes.
Comments: Information on scoring service available from publisher; detailed report provided on each candidate.
Authors: Walden Personnel Performance, Inc.
Publisher: Walden Personnel Performance, Inc.
Cross References: For reviews by Philip G. Benson and Richard W. Johnson, see 10:319.

[2278]

Sales Style Diagnosis Test.

Purpose: Designed to assess the degree of task and relationship orientations in selling.
Population: Salespeople.
Publication Date: 1975.
Scores, 12: Dimension Scores (Task Orientation, Relationships Orientation, Effectiveness), Sales Style Scores (Deserter, Missionary, Autocrat, Compromiser, Bureaucrat, Developer, Benevolent Autocrat, Executive), Sales Style Synthesis.
Administration: Group.
Manual: No manual.
Price Data, 1998: $40 per complete kit including 10 test booklets and user's guide.
Time: (20-40) minutes.
Comments: Self-administered, self-scored.
Authors: W. J. Reddin and David Forman.
Publisher: Organizational Tests Ltd. [Canada].

[2279]

Sales Style Indicator.

Purpose: To assist individuals and sales teams to identify strengths and weaknesses, and to help develop a plan to increase sales style flexibility.
Population: Sales personnel.
Publication Date: 1991.
Acronym: SSI.
Scores, 4: Behavioral Action, Cognitive Analysis, Interpersonal Harmony, Affective Expression.
Administration: Group.
Price Data, 1993: $15 per test booklet; $10 per interpretations booklet (41 pages).
Time: (90) minutes.
Comments: Self-administered, self-scored, self-interpreted.
Authors: Terry D. Anderson and Bruce R. Wares.
Publisher: Consulting Resource Group International, Inc.
Cross References: For reviews by Wayne J. Camara and Gerald A. Rosen, see 13:271.

[2280]

Sales Transaction Audit.

Purpose: Intended as an assessment of sales style and its impact on salesperson-customer transactions.
Population: Salespeople.
Publication Dates: 1972–1980.
Acronym: STA.
Scores, 3: Parent, Adult, Child.
Administration: Group.
Manual: No manual.
Price Data, 1997: $8.95 per test booklet.
Time: Administration time not reported.
Authors: Jay Hall and C. Leo Griffith.
Publisher: Teleometrics International.
Cross References: For a review by Stephen L. Cohen, see 8:1127.

[2281]

Salford Sentence Reading Test.

Purpose: To assess level of oral reading achievement.
Population: Ages 6-0 to 10-6.
Publication Date: 1976.
Acronym: SSRT.
Scores: Total score only.
Administration: Individual.
Forms, 3: A, B, C.
Price Data, 1999: £6.99 per set of 3 test cards (A, B, C); £4.99 per manual (11 pages).
Time: [2-3] minutes.
Author: G. E. Bookbinder.
Publisher: Hodder & Stoughton Educational [England].
Cross References: See T4:2320 (1 reference); for a review by J. Douglas Ayers, see 8:791.

[2282]

The Salience Inventory.

Purpose: Assesses an individual's "participation in, commitment to, and value expectations of five major life roles."
Population: Upper elementary through adult.

Publication Date: 1985–1987.
Acronym: SI.
Scores, 15: 5 roles (Homemaker, Worker, Student, Citizen, and Leisure) on 3 scales (Commitment, Participation, Value Expectations).
Administration: Group.
Price Data, 1999: $16.50 per 25 reusable test booklets; $14.50 per 50 answer sheets; price data per 50 profiles available from publisher; $10 per manual (41 pages); $11 per specimen set; price data for scoring service available from publisher.
Time: (30-45) minutes.
Comments: Developed as part of the international Work Importance Study; the Work Importance Study has inventories in 7 different languages.
Authors: Dorothy D. Nevill and Donald E. Super.
Publisher: Consulting Psychologists Press.
Cross References: See T4:2321 (3 references); for reviews by Rosa A. Hagin and Timothy M. Osberg, see 11:339 (1 reference).

TEST REFERENCES

1. Nevill, D., & Super, D. E. (1988). Career maturity and commitment to work in university students. *Journal of Vocational Behavior, 32,* 139-151.
2. Krau, E. (1989). The transition in life domain salience and the modification of work values between high school and adult employment. *Journal of Vocational Behavior, 34,* 100-116.
3. Sverko, B. (1989). Origin of individual differences in importance attached to work: A model and a contribution to its evaluation. *Journal of Vocational Behavior, 34,* 28-39.
4. Biller, E. F., & Horn, E. E. (1991). A career guidance model for adolescents with learning disabilities. *The School Counselor, 38,* 279–286.
5. Camp, C. C., & Chartrand, J. M. (1992). A comparison and evaluation of interest congruence indices. *Journal of Vocational Behavior, 41,* 162-182.
6. Munson, W. W. . (1992). Self-esteem, vocational identity, and career salience in high school students. Career *Development Quarterly, 40,* 361-368.
7. Munson, W. W., & Strauss, C. F. (1993). Career salience of institutionalized adolescent offenders. *Career Development Quarterly, 41,* 246-256.
8. Luzzo, D. A. (1994). An analysis of gender and ethnic differences in college students' commitment to work. *Journal of Employment Counseling, 31,* 38-45.
9. Niles, S. G., Sowa, C. J., & Laden, J. (1994). Life role participation and commitment as predictors of college student development. *Journal of College Student Development, 35,* 159-163.
10. Duarte, M. E. (1995). Career concerns, values, and role salience in employed men. *Career Development Quarterly, 43,* 338–349.
11. Jackson, G. C., & Healy, C. C. (1996). Career development profiles and interventions for underrepresented college students. *The Career Development Quarterly, 44,* 258–269.
12. Hartung, P. J. (1998). Assessing Ellenore Flood's roles and values to focus her career shopping. *Career Development Quarterly, 46,* 360–366.

[2283]

Sand: Concepts About Print Test.

Purpose: "The early detection of reading difficulties."
Population: Ages 5-0 to 7-0.
Publication Date: 1972.
Scores: Total score only.
Administration: Individual.
Price Data: Available from publisher.
Time: Administration time not reported.
Comments: Combined manual (31 pages) for this and other diagnostic measures.
Author: Marie M. Clay.
Publisher: Heinemann.
Cross References: See T4:2322 (1 reference).

[2284]

SAQ-Adult Probation [Substance Abuse Questionnaire].

Purpose: "Designed specifically for adult probation department and corrections use as a risk and needs assessment instrument."
Population: Adult probationers.
Publication Dates: 1989-1992.
Acronym: SAQ.
Scores: Behaviors/characteristics relevant to probation risk and needs assessment in 6 areas: Validity/Truthfulness Scale, Alcohol Scale, Drug Scale, Aggressivity Scale, Resistance Scale, Stress Coping Abilities.
Administration: Individual or group.
Price Data: $5-7 per test; other price data available from publisher.
Time: (25-30) minutes.
Comments: Self-administered, computer-scored test.
Author: Behavior Data Systems, Ltd.
Publisher: Behavior Data Systems, Ltd.
Cross References: For a review by Tony Toneatto, see 12:338.

[2285]

SAQ-Adult Probation III.

Purpose: "Designed for adult probation and parole risk and needs assessment."
Population: Adult offenders.
Publication Dates: 1985–1997.
Acronym: SAQ.
Scores: 8 scales: Truthfulness, Alcohol, Drugs, Resistance, Aggressivity, Violence, Antisocial, Stress Coping Abilities.
Administration: Group.
Price Data: Available from publisher.
Time: (30) minutes.
Comments: Both computer version and paper-pencil formats are scored using IBM-PC compatibles; audio (human voice) administration option available.
Author: Risk & Needs Assessment, Inc.
Publisher: Risk & Needs Assessment, Inc.

[2286]

SAQS Chicago Q Sort.

Purpose: Developed to "describe people to be sorted out in terms of continuum of applicability about self or others" to obtain a measure of similarity.
Population: College and adults.
Publication Dates: 1956-1957.
Acronym: SAQS.
Scores: Total score only.
Administration: Group.
Price Data: Available from publisher.

Time: (10-15) minutes.
Author: Raymond Corsini.
Publisher: Psychometric Affiliates.
Cross References: See T2:1358 (5 references) and P:232 (2 references); for reviews by William Stephenson and Clifford H. Swenson, Jr., see 5:103 (2 references).

[2287]
Scale for Assessing Emotional Disturbance.

Purpose: Designed to assist in "the identification of children who qualify for the federal special education category of emotional disturbance."
Population: Students ages 5-0 to 18-11.
Publication Date: 1998.
Acronym: SAED.
Scores, 7: Inability to Learn, Relationship Problems, Inappropriate Behavior, Unhappiness or Depression, Physical Symptoms or Fears, Socially Maladjusted, Overall Competence.
Administration: Individual.
Price Data, 1999: $79 per complete kit.
Time: (10) minutes.
Comments: Should be "completed ... by teachers or other school personnel who have had substantial contact with the student."
Authors: Michael H. Epstein and Douglas Cullinan.
Publisher: PRO-ED.

[2288]
Scale for the Assessment of Negative Symptoms.

Purpose: To assess negative symptoms of schizophrenia.
Population: Psychiatric inpatients and outpatients of all ages.
Publication Dates: 1981-1984.
Acronym: SANS.
Scores: 25 behavioral rating scores within 5 areas: Affective Flattening or Blunting, Alogia, Avolition-Apathy, Anhedonia-Asociality, Attention.
Administration: Individual.
Price Data: Available from publisher.
Foreign Language Editions: Available in Spanish, French, Italian, German, Portuguese, Japanese, Chinese, and Greek.
Time: [15-30] minutes.
Comments: May be used in conjunction with the Scale for the Assessment of Positive Symptoms (SAPS; 2289).
Author: Nancy C. Andreasen.
Publisher: Nancy C. Andreasen.
Cross References: For reviews by Suzanne King and Niels G. Waller, see 12:339 (75 references); see also T4:2325 (37 references); for information on an earlier edition, see 9:1069 (2 references).

TEST REFERENCES

1. Andreasen, N. C. (1987). The diagnosis of schizophrenia. *Schizophrenia Bulletin, 13,* 9–22.
2. Tienari, P., Sorri, A., Lahti, I., Naarala, M., Wahlberg, K., Moring, J., Pohjola, J., & Wynne, L. C. (1987). Genetic and psychosocial factors in schizophrenia: The Finnish adoptive family study. *Schizophrenia Bulletin, 13,* 477–484.
3. Barchas, J. D., Hadley, S. W., Detre, T., Endicott, J., Glover, R., King, R., Meltzer, H. Y., Sackeim, H., Strauss, J. S., Wahl, P., & Williams, D. (1988). Research resources. *Schizophrenic Bulletin, 14,* 439–484.
4. DeMyer, M. K., Gilmor, R. L., Hendrie, H. C., DeMyer, W. E., Augustyn, G. T., & Jackson, R. K. (1988). Magnetic resonance brain images in schizophrenic and normal subjects: Influence of diagnosis and education. *Schizophrenic Bulletin, 14,* 21–37.
5. Harvey, P. D., Earle-Boyer, E. A., & Levinson, J. C. (1988). Cognitive deficits and thought disorder: A retest study. *Schizophrenic Bulletin, 14,* 57–66.
6. Brenner, H. D., Dencker, S. J., Goldstein, M. J., Hubbard, J. W., Keegan, D. L., Kruger, G., Kulhanek, F., Liberman, R. P., Malm, V., & Midha, K. K. (1990). Defining treatment refractoriness in schizophrenia. *Schizophrenia Bulletin, 16,* 551–561.
7. Harvey, P. D., Docherty, N. M., Serper, M. R., & Rasmussen, M. (1990). Cognitive deficits and thought disorder: II. An 8-month follow-up study. *Schizophrenia Bulletin, 16,* 147–156.
8. Sullivan, G., Marder, S. R., Liberman, R. P., Donahoe, C. P., & Mintz, J. (1990). Social skills and relapse history in outpatient schizophrenics. *Psychiatry, 53,* 340–345.
9. Van Kammen, D. P., Peters, J., Yao, J., van Kammen, W. B., Neylan, T., Shaw, D., & Linnoila, M. (1990). Norepinephrine in acute exacerbations of chronic schizophrenia. *Archives of General Psychiatry, 47,* 161–168.
10. Andreasen, N. C. (1991). Assessment issues and the cost of schizophrenia. *Schizophrenia Bulletin, 17,* 475–481.
11. Andreasen, N. C., & Flaum, M. (1991). Schizophrenia: The characteristic symptoms. *Schizophrenia Bulletin, 17,* 27–49.
12. Christison, G. W., Kirch, D. G., & Wyatt, R. J. (1991). When symptoms persist: Choosing among alternative somatic treatments for schizophrenia. *Schizophrenia Bulletin, 17,* 217–245.
13. Keith, S. J., & Matthews, S. M. (1991). The diagnosis of schizophrenia: A review of onset and duration issues. *Schizophrenia Bulletin, 17,* 51–67.
14. Moscarelli, M., Capri, S., & Neri, L. (1991). Cost evaluation of chronic schizophrenia patients during the first 3 years after the first contact. *Schizophrenia Bulletin, 17,* 421–426.
15. Attkisson, C., Cook, J., Karno, M., Lehman, A., McGlashan, T. H., Meltzer, H. Y., O'Connor, M., Richardson, D., Rosenblatt, A., Wells, K., Williams, J., & Hohmann, A. A. (1992). Clinical services research. *Schizophrenia Bulletin, 18,* 561–626.
16. Bromet, E. J., Schwartz, J. E., Fennig, S., Geller, L., Jandorf, L., Kovasznay, B., Lavelle, J., Miller, A., Pato, C., Ram, R., & Rich, C. (1992). The epidemiology of psychosis: The Suffolk County Mental Health Project. *Schizophrenia Bulletin, 18,* 243–255.
17. David, A. S., & Appleby, L. (1992). Diagnostic criteria in schizophrenia: Accentuate the positive. *Schizophrenia Bulletin, 18,* 551–557.
18. Dworkin, R. H. (1992). Affective deficits and social deficits in schizophrenia: What's what? *Schizophrenia Bulletin, 18,* 59–64.
19. Glynn, S. M., Randolph, E. T., Eth, S., Paz, G. G., Leong, G. B., Shaner, A. L., & VanWort, W. (1992). Schizophrenic symptoms, work adjustment, and behavioral family therapy. *Rehabilitation Psychology, 37,* 323–338.
20. Haas, G. L., & Sweeney, J. A. (1992). Premorbid and onset features of first-episode schizophrenia. *Schizophrenia Bulletin, 18,* 373–386.
21. Hoff, A. L., Riordan, H., O'Donnell, D., Stritzke, P., Neale, C., Boccio, A., Anand, A. K., & DeLisi, L. E. (1992). Anomalous lateral sulcus asymmetry and cognitive function in first-episode schizophrenia. *Schizophrenia Bulletin, 18,* 257–273.
22. Keshavan, M. S., & Schooler, N. R. (1992). First-episode studies in schizophrenia: Criteria and characterization. *Schizophrenia Bulletin, 18,* 491–513.
23. Kojima, T., Matsushima, E., Ando, K., Ando, H., Sakurada, M., Ohta, K., Moriya, H., & Shimazono, Y. (1992). Exploratory eye movements and neuropsychological tests in schizophrenia patients. *Schizophrenia Bulletin, 18,* 85–94.
24. Ram, R., Bromet, E. J., Eaton, W. W., Pato, C., & Schwartz, J. E. (1992). The natural course of schizophrenia: A review of first-admission studies. *Schizophrenia Bulletin, 18,* 185–207.
25. Shtasel, D. L., Gur, R. E., Gallacher, F., Heimberg, C., Cannon, T., & Gur, R. C. (1992). Phenomenology and functioning in first-episode schizophrenia. *Schizophrenia Bulletin, 18,* 449–462.
26. Sweeney, J. A., Haas, G. L., & Li, S. (1992). Neuropsychological and eye movement abnormalities in first-episode and chronic schizophrenia. *Schizophrenia Bulletin, 18,* 283–293.
27. Heresco-Levy, V., Greenberg, D., Lerer, B., Dasberg, H., & Brown, W. A. (1993). Trial of maintenance neuroleptic dose reduction in schizophrenic outpatients: Two-year outcome. *Journal of Clinical Psychiatry, 54,* 59–62.
28. Jeste, D. V., Lacro, J. P., Gilbert, P. L., Kline, J., & Kline, N. (1993). Treatment of late-life schizophrenia with neuroleptics. *Schizophrenia Bulletin, 19,* 817–830.
29. Lohr, J. B., & Flynn, K. (1993). Minor physical anomalies in schizophrenia and mood disorders. *Schizophrenia Bulletin, 19,* 551–556.
30. McDowd, J. M., Filion, D. L., Harris, M. J., & Braff, D. L. (1993). Sensory gating and inhibitory function in late-life schizophrenia. *Schizophrenia Bulletin, 19,* 733–746.

31. Andreasen, N. C., & Carpenter, W. T. (1994). Diagnosis and classification of schizophrenia. *Schizophrenia Bulletin, 20,* 199–214.

32. Benedict, R. H. B., Harris, A. E., Markow, T., McCormick, J. A., Nuechterlein, K. H., & Asarnow, R. F. (1994). Effects of attention training on information processing in schizophrenia. *Schizophrenia Bulletin, 20,* 537–546.

33. Blanchard, J. J., Kring, A. M., & Neale, J. M. (1994). Flat affect in schizophrenia: A test of neuropsychological models. *Schizophrenia Bulletin, 20,* 311–325.

34. Cuesta, M. J., & Peralta, V. (1994). Lack of insight in schizophrenia. *Schizophrenia Bulletin, 20,* 359–366.

35. Lieberman, J. A., & Koreen, A. R. (1994). Neurochemistry and neuroendocrinology of schizophrenia: A selective review. *Schizophrenia Bulletin, 19,* 371–429.

36. McGlashan, T. H., & Fenton, W. S. (1994). Subtype progression and pathophysiologic deterioration in early schizophrenia. *Schizophrenia Bulletin, 20,* 71–84.

37. Russell, A. T. (1994). The clinical presentation of childhood-onset schizophrenia. *Schizophrenia Bulletin, 20,* 631–646.

38. Schooler, N. R. (1994). Negative symptoms in schizophrenia: Assessment of the effect of risperidone. *The Journal of Clinical Psychiatry, 55:5 (supp),* 22–28.

39. Strauss, M. E. (1994). Relations of symptoms to cognitive deficits in schizophrenia. *Schizophrenia Bulletin, 19,* 215–231.

40. Torrey, E. F., Taylor, E. H., Bracha, H. S., Bowler, A. E., McNeil, T. F., Rawlings, R. R., Quinn, P. O., Bigelow, L. B., Rickler, K., Sjostrom, K., Higgins, E. S., & Gottesman, I. I. (1994). Prenatal origin of schizophrenia in a subgroup of discordant monozygotic twins. *Schizophrenia Bulletin, 20,* 423–432.

41. Walker, E. F., Savoie, T., & Davis, D. (1994). Neuromotor precursors of schizophrenia. *Schizophrenia Bulletin, 20,* 441–452.

42. Andia, A. M., Zissok, S., Heaton, R. K., Hesselink, J., Jernigan, T., Kuck, J., Moranville, J., & Braff, D. L. (1995). Gender differences in schizophrenia. *The Journal of Nervous and Mental Disease, 183,* 522–528.

43. Andreasen, N. C., Arndt, S., Alliger, R., Miller, D., & Flaum, M. (1995). Symptoms of schizophrenia: Methods, meanings, and mechanisms. *Archives of General Psychiatry, 52,* 341–351.

44. Arndt, S., Andreasen, N. C., Flaum, M., Miller, D., & Nopoulos, P. (1995). A longitudinal study of symptom dimensions in schizophrenia: Prediction and patterns of change. *Archives of General Psychiatry, 52,* 352–360.

45. Chatterjee, A., Chakos, M., Koreen, A., Geisler, S., Sheitman, B., Woerner, M., Kane, J. M., Alvir, J., & Lieberman, J. A. (1995). Prevalence and clinical correlates of extrapyramidal signs and spontaneous dyskinesia in never-medicated schizophrenic patients. *American Journal of Psychiatry, 152,* 1724–1729.

46. Crawford, T. J., Haeger, B., Kennard, C., Reveley, M. A., & Henderson, L. (1995). Saccadic abnormalities in psychotic patients. I. Neuroleptic-free psychotic patients. *Psychological Medicine, 25,* 461–471.

47. Crawford, T. J., Haegger, B., Kennard, C., Reveley, M. A., & Henderson, L. (1995). Saccadic abnormalities in psychotic patients. II. The role of neuroleptic treatment. *Psychological Medicine, 25,* 473–483.

48. Gur, R. E., Mozley, D., Resnick, S. M., Mozley, L. H., Shtasel, D. L., Gallacher, F., Arnold, S. E., Karp, J. S., Alavi, A., Reivich, M., & Gur, R. C. (1995). Resting cerebral glucose metabolism in first-episode and previously treated patients with schizophrenia relates to clinical features. *Archives of General Psychiatry, 52,* 657–667.

49. Huron, C., Danion, J.-M., Giacomoni, F., Grange, D., Robert, P., & Rizzo, L. (1995). Impairment of recognition memory with, but not without, conscious recollection in schizophrenia. *American Journal of Psychiatry, 152,* 1737–1742.

50. Kotrla, K. J., Chacko, R. C., Harper, R. G., & Doody, R. (1995). Clinical variables associated with psychosis in Alzheimer's disease. *American Journal of Psychiatry, 152,* 1377–1379.

51. Landre, N. A., & Taylor, M. A. (1995). Formal thought disorder in schizophrenia: Linguistic, attentional, and intellectual correlates. *The Journal of Nervous and Mental Disease, 183,* 673–680.

52. McFarlane, W. R., Lukens, E., Link, B., Dushay, R., Deakins, S. A., Newmark, M., Dunne, E. J., Horen, B., & Toran, J. (1995). Multiple-family groups and psychoeducation in the treatment of schizophrenia. *Archives of General Psychiatry, 52,* 679–687.

53. Peralta, V., & Cuesta, M. J. (1995). Negative symptom in schizophrenia: A confirmatory factor analysis of competing models. *American Journal of Psychiatry, 152,* 1450–1457.

54. Serper, M. R., Alpert, M., Richardson, N. A., Dickson, S., Allen, M. H., & Werner, A. (1995). Clinical effects of recent cocaine use on patients with acute schizophrenia. *American Journal of Psychiatry, 152,* 1464–1469.

55. Stanley, J. A., Williamson, P. C., Drost, D. J., Carr, T. J., Rylett, J., Malla, A., & Thompson, T. (1995). An in vivo study of the prefrontal cortex of schizophrenic patients at different stages of illness via phosphorous magnetic resonance spectroscopy. *Archives of General Psychiatry, 52,* 399–406.

56. Susser, E., Fennig, S., Jandorf, L., Amador, X., & Bromet, E. (1995). Epidemiology, diagnosis, and course of brief psychoses. *American Journal of Psychiatry, 152,* 1743–1748.

57. Turetsky, B., Cowell, P. E., Gur, R. C., Grossman, R. I., Shtasel, D. L., & Gur, R. E. (1995). Frontal and temporal lobe brain volumes in schizophrenia: Relationship to symptoms and clinical subtypes. *Archives of General Psychiatry, 52,* 1061–1070.

58. van Kammen, D. P., Kelley, M. E., Gurklis, J. A., Gilbertson, M. W., Yao, J. K., & Peters, J. L. (1995). Behavioral vs. biochemical prediction of clinical stability following haloperidol withdrawal in schizophrenia. *Archives of General Psychiatry, 52,* 673–678.

59. Vazquez-Barquero, J. L., Nunez, M. J. C., Pando, F. Q., DeLaVarga, M., Castanedo, S. H., & Dunn, G. (1995). Structural abnormalities of the brain in schizophrenia: Sex differences in the Cantabria First Episode of Schizophrenia study. *Psychological Medicine, 25,* 1247–1257.

60. Wible, C. G., Shenton, M. E., Hokama, H., Kikinis, R., Jotesz, F. A., Metcalf, D., & McCarley, R. W. (1995). Prefrontal cortex and schizophrenia: A quantitative magnetic resonance imaging study. *Archives of General Psychiatry, 52,* 279–288.

61. Zisook, S., Byrd, D., Kuck, J., & Jeste, D. V. (1995). Command hallucinations in outpatients with schizophrenia. *Journal of Clinical Psychiatry, 56,* 462–465.

62. Bastillo, J. R., Buchanan, R. W., Irish, D., & Breier, A. (1996). Differential effect of clozapine on weight: A controlled study. *American Journal of Psychiatry, 153,* 817–819.

63. Capleton, R. A. (1996). Cognitive function in schizophrenia: Association with negative and positive symptoms. *Psychological Reports, 78,* 123–128.

64. Chakos, M. H., Alvir, J. M. J., Woerner, M. G., Koreen, A., Geisler, S., Mayerhoff, D., Sobel, S., Kane, J. M., Borenstein, M., & Lieberman, J. A. (1996). Incidence and correlates of Tardive Dyskinesia in first episode of schizophrenia. *Archives of General Psychiatry, 53,* 313–319.

65. Cowell, P. E., Kostianovsky, D. J., Gur, R. C., Turetsky, B. I., & Gur, R. E. (1996). Sex differences in neuroanatomical and clinical correlations in schizophrenia. *American Journal of Psychiatry, 153,* 799–805.

66. Crowe, S. F. (1996). The performance of schizophrenic and depressed subjects on tests of fluency: Support for a compromise in dorsolateral prefrontal functioning. *Australian Psychologist, 31,* 204–209.

67. Flashman, L. A., Flaum, M., Gupta, S., & Andreasen, N. C. (1996). Soft signs and neuropsychological performance in schizophrenia. *American Journal of Psychiatry, 153,* 526–532.

68. Frazier, J. A., Giedd, J. N., Hamburger, S. D., Albus, K. E., Kaysen, D., Vaituzis, A. C., Rajapakse, J. C., Lenaine, M. C., McKenna, K., Jacobsen, L. K., Gordon, C. T., Brier, A., & Rapoport, J. L. (1996). Brain anatomic magnetic resonance imaging in childhood-onset schizophrenia. *Archives of General Psychiatry, 53,* 617–624.

69. Jeste, D. V., Heaton, S. C., Paulsen, J. S., Ercoli, L., Harris, M. J., & Heaton, R. K. (1996). Clinical and neuropsychological comparison of psychotic depression with nonpsychotic depression and schizophrenia. *American Journal of Psychiatry, 153,* 490–496.

70. Keefe, R. S. E., Frescka, E., Apter, S. H., Davidson, M., Macaluso, J. M., Hirschowitz, J., & Davis, K. L. (1996). Clinical characteristics of Kraepelinian schizophrenia: Replication and extension of previous findings. *American Journal of Psychiatry, 153,* 806–811.

71. Kumra, S., Frazier, J. A., Jacobsen, L. K., McKenna, K., Gordon, C. T., Lenane, M. C., Hamburger, S. C., Smith, A. K., Albus, K. E., Alaghband-Rad, J., & Rapoport, J. L. (1996). Childhood-onset schizophrenia: A double-blind clozapine-haloperidol comparison. *Archives of General Psychiatry, 53,* 1090–1097.

72. McAdams, L. A., Harris, M. J., Bailey, A., Fell, R., & Jeste, D. V. (1996). Validating specific psychopathology scales in older patients with schizophrenia. *Journal of Nervous and Mental Disease, 184,* 246–251.

73. Paulus, M. P., Geyer, M. A., & Braff, D. L. (1996). Use of methods from chaos theory to quantify a fundamental dysfunction in the behavioral organization of schizophrenic patients. *American Journal of Psychiatry, 153,* 714–717.

74. Sison, C. E., Alpert, M., Fudge, R., & Stern, R. M. (1996). Constricted expressiveness and psychophysiological reactivity in schizophrenia. *Journal of Nervous and Mental Disease, 184,* 589–597.

75. Szymanski, S. R., Cannon, T. D., Gallacher, F., Erwin, R. J., & Gur, R. E. (1996). Course of treatment response in first-episode and chronic schizophrenia. *American Journal of Psychiatry, 153,* 519–525.

76. Tien, A. Y., Ross, D. E., Pearlson, G., & Strauss, M. E. (1996). Eye movements and psychopathology in schizophrenia and bipolar disorder. *Journal of Nervous and Mental Disease, 184,* 331–338.

77. Williams, L. M. (1996). Cognitive inhibition and schizophrenic symptom subgroups. *Schizophrenia Bulletin, 22,* 139–151.

78. Bartha, R., Williamson, P. C., Drost, D. J., Malla, A., Carr, T. J., Cortese, L., Canaran, G., Rylet, J., & Neufeld, R. W. J. (1997). Measurement of glutamate and glutamine in the medial prefrontal cortex of never-treated schizophrenic patients and healthy controls by proton magnetic resonance spectroscopy. *Archives of General psychiatry, 54,* 959–965.

79. Bartha, R., Williamson, P. C., Drost, D. J., Malla, A., Carr, T. J., Cortese, L., Canaran, G., Rylett, J., & Neufeld, R. W. J. (1997). Measurement of glutamate and glutamine in the medial prefrontal cortex of never-treated schizophrenic patients and healthy controls by proton magnetic reasonance spectroscopy. *Archives of General Psychiatry, 54,* 959–965.

80. Brébion, G., Smith, M. J., Gorman, J. M. & Amador, X. (1997). Discrimination accuracy and decision biases in different types of reality monitoring in schizophrenia. *Journal of Nervous and Mental Disease, 185,* 247–253.

81. Mizuno, M., Kato, M., Sartori, G., Okawaza, H., & Kashima, H. (1997). Performance characteristics of chronic schizophrenia on attention tests sensitive to unilateral brain damage. *Journal of Nervous and Mental Disease, 185,* 427–433.

82. Small, J. G., Hirsh, S. R., Arvanitis, L. A., Miller, B. G., Link, C. G. G., & Seroquel Study Group. (1997). Quetiapine in patients with schizophrenia: A high- and low-dose double-blind comparison with placebo. *Archives of General Psychiatry, 54,* 549–557.

83. Van Ammers, E. C., Sellman, J. D., & Mulder, R. T. (1997). Temperament and substance abuse in schizophrenia: Is there a relationship? *Journal of Nervous and Mental Disease, 185,* 283–288.

84. Hien, D., Haas, G., & Cook, H. (1998). Gender differences in premorbid social adjustment and intimacy motivation in schizophrenia. *Journal of Clinical Psychology, 54,* 35–48.

85. Ratakonda, S., Gorman, J. M., Yale, S. A., & Amador, X. F. (1998). Characterization of psychotic conditions: use of the domains of psychopathology model. *Archives of General Psychiatry, 55,* 75–81.

[2289]

Scale for the Assessment of Positive Symptoms.

Purpose: "Designed to assess positive symptoms, principally those that occur in schizophrenia."

Population: Psychiatric inpatients and outpatients of all ages.

Publication Date: 1984.

Acronym: SAPS.

Scores: 35 behavior ratings within 5 areas: Hallucinations, Delusions, Bizarre Behavior, Positive Formal Thought Disorder, Inappropriate Affect.

Administration: Individual.

Price Data: Available from publisher.

Time: [15-30] minutes.

Comments: Intended to serve as a complementary instrument to the Scale for the Assessment of Negative Symptoms (SANS; 2288).

Author: Nancy C. Andreasen.

Publisher: Nancy C. Andreasen.

Cross References: For reviews by John D. King and Suzanne King, see 12:340 (44 references); see also T4:2326 (24 references).

TEST REFERENCES

1. Andreasen, N. C. (1987). The diagnosis of schizophrenia. *Schizophrenia Bulletin, 13,* 9–22.

2. DeMyer, M. K., Gilmor, R. L., Hendrie, H. C., DeMyer, W. E., Augustyn, G. T., & Jackson, R. K. (1988). Magnetic resonance brain images in schizophrenic and normal subjects: Influence of diagnosis and education. *Schizophrenia Bulletin, 14,* 21–37.

3. Harvey, P. D., Earle-Boyer, E. A., & Levinson, J. C. (1988). Cognitive deficits and thought disorder: A retest study. *Schizophrenia Bulletin, 14,* 57–66.

4. Brenner, H. D., Dencker, S. J., Goldstein, M. J., Hubbard, J. W., Keegan, D. L., Kruger, G., Kulhanek, F., Liberman, R. P., Malm, V., & Midha, K. K. (1990). Defining treatment refractoriness in schizophrenia. *Schizophrenia Bulletin, 16,* 551–561.

5. Harvey, P. D., Docherty, N. M., Serper, M. R., & Rasmussen, M. (1990). Cognitive deficits and thought disorder: II. An 8-month follow-up study. *Schizophrenia Bulletin, 16,* 147–156.

6. Wolters, E. C., Hurwitz, T. A., Mak, E., Teal, P., Peppard, F. R., Remick, R., Calne, S., & Calne, D. B. (1990). Clozapine in the treatment of Parkinsonian patients with dopaminomimetic psychosis. *Neurology, 40,* 832–834.

7. Andreasen, N. C. (1991). Assessment issues and the cost of schizophrenia. *Schizophrenia Bulletin, 17,* 475–481.

8. Andreasen, N. C., & Flaum, M. (1991). Schizophrenia: The characteristic symptoms. *Schizophrenia Bulletin, 17,* 27–49.

9. Moscarelli, M., Capri, S., & Neri, L. (1991). Cost evaluation of chronic schizophrenia patients during the first 3 years after the first contact. *Schizophrenia Bulletin, 17,* 421–426.

10. Attkisson, C., Cook, J., Karno, M., Lehman, A., McGlashan, T. H., Meltzer, H. Y., O'Connor, M., Richardson, D., Rosenblatt, A., Wells, K., Williams, J., & Hohmann, A. A. (1992). Clinical services research. *Schizophrenia Bulletin, 18,* 561–626.

11. Bromet, E. J., Schwartz, J. E., Fennig, S., Geller, L., Jandorf, L., Kovasznay, B., Lavelle, J., Miller, A., Pato, C., Ram, R., & Rich, C. (1992). The epidemiology of psychosis: The Suffolk County Mental Health Project. *Schizophrenia Bulletin, 18,* 243–255.

12. Haas, G. L., & Sweeney, J. A. (1992). Premorbid and onset features of first-episode schizophrenia. *Schizophrenia Bulletin, 18,* 373–386.

13. Hoff, A. L., Riordan, H., O'Donnell, D., Stritzke, P., Neale, C., Boccio, A., Anand, A. K., & DeLisi, L. E. (1992). Anomalous lateral sulcus asymmetry and cognitive function in first-episode schizophrenia. *Schizophrenia Bulletin, 18,* 257–273.

14. Shtasel, D. L., Gur, R. E., Gallacher, F., Heimberg, C., Cannon, T., & Gur, R. C. (1992). Phenomenology and functioning in first-episode schizophrenia. *Schizophrenia Bulletin, 18,* 449–462.

15. Sweeney, J. A., Haas, G. L., & Li, S. (1992). Neuropsychological and eye movement abnormalities in first-episode and chronic schizophrenia. *Schizophrenia Bulletin, 18,* 283–293.

16. deLeon, J., Peralta, V., & Cuesta, M. J. (1993). Negative symptoms and emotional blunting in schizophrenic patients. *Journal of Clinical Psychiatry, 54,* 103–108.

17. Dworkin, R. H., Clark, W. C., Lipsitz, J. D., Amador, X. F., Kaufmann, C. A., Opler, L. A., White, S. R., & Gorman, J. M. (1993). Affective deficits and pain insensitivity in schizophrenia. *Motivation and Emotion, 17,* 245–276.

18. Heresco-Levy, V., Greenberg, D., Lerer, B., Dasberg, H., & Brown, W. A. (1993). Trial of maintenance neuroleptic dose reduction in schizophrenic outpatients: Two-year outcome. *Journal of Clinical Psychiatry, 54,* 59–62.

19. Jeste, D. V., Lacro, J. P., Gilbert, P. L., Kline, J., & Kline, N. (1993). Treatment of late-life schizophrenia with neuroleptics. *Schizophrenia Bulletin, 19,* 817–830.

20. Lohr, J. B., & Flynn, K. (1993). Minor physical anomalies in schizophrenia and mood disorders. *Schizophrenia Bulletin, 19,* 551–556.

21. McDowd, J. M., Filion, D. L., Harris, M. J., & Braff, D. L. (1993). Sensory gating and inhibitory function in late-life schizophrenia. *Schizophrenia Bulletin, 19,* 733–746.

22. Pearlson, G. D., Tune, L. E., Wong, D. F., Aylward, E. H., Barta, P. E., Powers, R. E., Tien, A. Y., Chase, G. A., Harris, G. J., & Rabins, P. V. (1993). Quantitative D2 dopamine receptor PET and structural MRI changes in late-onset schizophrenia. *Schizophrenia Bulletin, 19,* 783–795.

23. Andreasen, N. C., & Carpenter, W. T. (1994). Diagnosis and classification of schizophrenia. *Schizophrenia Bulletin, 20,* 199–214.

24. Benedict, R. H. B., Harris, A. E., Markow, T., McCormick, J. A., Nuechterlein, K. H., & Asarnow, R. F. (1994). Effects of attention training on information processing in schizophrenia. *Schizophrenia Bulletin, 20,* 537–546.

25. Cuesta, M. J., & Peralta, V. (1994). Lack of insight in schizophrenia. *Schizophrenia Bulletin, 20,* 359–366.

26. Lieberman, J. A., & Koreen, A. R. (1994). Neurochemistry and neuroendocrinology of schizophrenia: A selective review. *Schizophrenia Bulletin, 19,* 371–429.

27. McGlashan, T. H., & Fenton, W. S. (1994). Subtype progression and pathophysiologic deterioration in early schizophrenia. *Schizophrenia Bulletin, 20,* 71–84.

28. Russell, A. T. (1994). The clinical presentation of childhood-onset schizophrenia. *Schizophrenia Bulletin, 20,* 631–646.

29. Schooler, N. R. (1994). Negative symptoms in schizophrenia: Assessment of the effect of risperidone. *The Journal of Clinical Psychiatry, 55:5 (supp),* 22–28.

30. Strauss, M. E. (1994). Relations of symptoms to cognitive deficits in schizophrenia. *Schizophrenia Bulletin, 19,* 215–231.

31. Walker, E. F., Savoie, T., & Davis, D. (1994). Neuromotor precursors of schizophrenia. *Schizophrenia Bulletin, 20,* 441–451.

32. Andia, A. M., Zissok, S., Heaton, R. K., Hesselink, J., Jernigan, T., Kuck, J., Moranville, J., & Braff, D. L. (1995). Gender differences in schizophrenia. *The Journal of Nervous and Mental Disease, 183,* 522–528.

33. Andreasen, N. C., Arndt, S., Alliger, R., Miller, D., & Flaum, M. (1995). Symptoms of schizophrenia: Methods, meanings, and mechanisms. *Archives of General Psychiatry, 52,* 341–351.

34. Arndt, S., Andreasen, N. C., Flaum, M., Miller, D., & Nopoulos, P. (1995). A longitudinal study of symptom dimensions in schizophrenia: Prediction and patterns of change. *Archives of General Psychiatry, 52,* 352–360.

35. Crawford, T. J., Haeger, B., Kennard, C., Reveley, M. A., & Henderson, L. (1995). Saccadic abnormalities in psychotic patients. I. Neuroleptic-free psychotic patients. *Psychological Medicine, 25,* 461–471.

36. Crawford, T. J., Haegger, B., Kennard, C., Reveley, M. A., & Henderson, L. (1995). Saccadic abnormalities in psychotic patients. II. The role of neuroleptic treatment. *Psychological Medicine, 25,* 473–483.

37. Gur, R. E., Mozley, D., Resnick, S. M., Mozley, L. H., Shtasel, D. L., Gallacher, F., Arnold, S. E., Karp, J. S., Alavi, A., Reivich, M., & Gur, R. C. (1995). Resting cerebral glucose metabolism in first-episode and previously treated patients with schizophrenia relates to clinical features. *Archives of General Psychiatry, 52,* 657–667.

38. Huron, C., Danion, J.-M., Giacomoni, F., Grange, D., Robert, P., & Rizzo, L. (1995). Impairment of recognition memory with, but not without, conscious recollection in schizophrenia. *American Journal of Psychiatry, 152,* 1737–1742.

39. Keck, P. E., Jr., McElroy, S. L., Strakowski, S. M., West, S. A., Hawkins, J. M., Huber, T. J., Newman, R. M., & DePriest, M. (1995). Outcome and comorbidity in first-compared with multiple-episode mania. *The Journal of Nervous and Mental Disease, 183,* 320–324.

40. Landre, N. A., & Taylor, M. A. (1995). Formal thought disorder in schizophrenia: Linguistic, attentional, and intellectual correlates. *The Journal of Nervous and Mental Disease, 183,* 673–680.

41. Serper, M. R., Alpert, M., Richardson, N. A., Dickson, S., Allen, M. H., & Werner, A. (1995). Clinical effects of recent cocaine use on patients with acute schizophrenia. *American Journal of Psychiatry, 152,* 1464–1469.

42. Stanley, J. A., Williamson, P. C., Drost, D. J., Carr, T. J., Rylett, J., Malla, A., & Thompson, T. (1995). An in vivo study of the prefrontal cortex of schizophrenic patients at different stages of illness via phosphorous magnetic resonance spectroscopy. *Archives of General Psychiatry, 52,* 399–406.

43. Susser, E., Fennig, S., Jandorf, L., Amador, X., & Bromet, E. (1995). Epidemiology, diagnosis, and course of brief psychoses. *American Journal of Psychiatry, 152,* 1743–1748.

44. Turetsky, B., Cowell, P. E., Gur, R. C., Grossman, R. I., Shtasel, D. L., & Gur, R. E. (1995). Frontal and temporal lobe brain volumes in schizophrenia: Relationship to symptoms and clinical subtypes. *Archives of General Psychiatry, 52,* 1061–1070.

45. Vazquez-Barquero, J. L., Nunez, M. J. C., Pando, F. Q., DeLaVarga, M., Castanedo, S. H., & Dunn, G. (1995). Structural abnormalities of the brain in schizophrenia: Sex differences in the Cantabria First Episode of Schizophrenia study. *Psychological Medicine, 25,* 1247–1257.

46. Wible, C. G., Shenton, M. E., Hokama, H., Kikinis, R., Jotesz, F. A., Metcalf, D., & McCarley, R. W. (1995). Prefrontal cortex and schizophrenia: A quantitative magnetic resonance imaging study. *Archives of General Psychiatry, 52,* 279–288.

47. Zisook, S., Byrd, D., Kuck, J., & Jeste, D. V. (1995). Command hallucinations in outpatients with schizophrenia. *Journal of Clinical Psychiatry, 56,* 462–465.

48. Capleton, R. A. (1996). Cognitive function in schizophrenia: Association with negative and positive symptoms. *Psychological Reports, 78,* 123–128.

49. Cowell, P. E., Kostianovsky, D. J., Gur, R. C., Turetsky, B. I., & Gur, R. E. (1996). Sex differences in neuroanatomical and clinical correlations in schizophrenia. *American Journal of Psychiatry, 153,* 799–805.

50. Crowe, S. F. (1996). The performance of schizophrenic and depressed subjects on tests of fluency: Support for a compromise in dorsolateral prefrontal functioning. *Australian Psychologist, 31,* 204–209.

51. Flashman, L. A., Flaum, M., Gupta, S., & Andreasen, N. C. (1996). Soft signs and neuropsychological performance in schizophrenia. *American Journal of Psychiatry, 153,* 526–532.

52. Frazier, J. A., Giedd, J. N., Hamburger, S. D., Albus, K. E., Kaysen, D., Vaituzis, A. C., Rajapakse, J. C., Lenaine, M. C., McKenna, K., Jacobsen, L. K., Gordon, C. T., Brier, A., & Rapoport, J. L. (1996). Brain anatomic magnetic resonance imaging in childhood-onset schizophrenia. *Archives of General Psychiatry, 53,* 617–624.

53. Jeste, D. V., Heaton, S. C., Paulsen, J. S., Ercoli, L., Harris, M. J., & Heaton, R. K. (1996). Clinical and neuropsychological comparison of psychotic depression with nonpsychotic depression and schizophrenia. *American Journal of Psychiatry, 153,* 490–496.

54. Keck, P. E., McElroy, S. L., Strakowski, S. M., Balistreri, T. M., Kizer, D. L., & West, S. A. (1996). Factors associated with maintenance antipsychotic treatment of patients with bipolar disorder. *Journal of Clinical Psychiatry, 57,* 147–151.

55. Keefe, R. S. E., Frescka, E., Apter, S. H., Davidson, M., Macaluso, J. M., Hirschowitz, J., & Davis, K. L. (1996). Clinical characteristics of Kraepelinian schizophrenia: Replication and extension of previous findings. *American Journal of Psychiatry, 153,* 806–811.

56. Kumra, S., Frazier, J. A., Jacobsen, L. K., McKenna, K., Gordon, C. T., Lenane, M. C., Hamburger, S. C., Smith, A. K., Albus, K. E., Alaghband-Rad, J., & Rapoport, J. L. (1996). Childhood-onset schizophrenia: A double-blind clozapine-haloperidol comparison. *Archives of General Psychiatry, 53,* 1090–1097.

57. McAdams, L. A., Harris, M. J., Bailey, A., Fell, R., & Jeste, D. V. (1996). Validating specific psychopathology scales in older patients with schizophrenia. *Journal of Nervous and Mental Disease, 184,* 246–251.

58. McElroy, S. L., Keck, P. E., Stanton, S. P., Tugral, K. C., Bennett, J. A., & Strakowski, S. M. (1996). A randomized comparison of divalproex oral loading versus haloperidol in the initial treatment of acute psychotic mania. *Journal of Clinical Psychiatry, 57,* 142–146.

59. Paulus, M. P., Geyer, M. A., & Braff, D. L. (1996). Use of methods from chaos theory to quantify a fundamental dysfunction in the behavioral organization of schizophrenic patients. *American Journal of Psychiatry, 153,* 714–717.

60. Strakowski, S. M., McElroy, S. L., Keck, P. E., Jr., & West, S. A. (1996). Racial influence on diagnosis in psychotic mania. *Journal of Affective Disorders, 39,* 157–162.

61. Strakowski, S. M., McElroy, S. L., Keck, P. E., Jr., & West, S. A. (1996). Suicidality among patients with mixed and manic bipolar disorder. *American Journal of Psychiatry, 153,* 674–676.

62. Szymanski, S. R., Cannon, T. D., Gallacher, F., Erwin, R. J., & Gur, R. E. (1996). Course of treatment response in first-episode and chronic schizophrenia. *American Journal of Psychiatry, 153,* 519–525.

63. Tien, A. Y., Ross, D. E., Pearlson, G., & Strauss, M. E. (1996). Eye movements and psychopathology in schizophrenia and bipolar disorder. *Journal of Nervous and Mental Disease, 184,* 331–338.

64. Williams, L. M. (1996). Cognitive inhibition and schizophrenic symptom subgroups. *Schizophrenia Bulletin, 22,* 139–151.

65. Bartha, R., Williamson, P. C., Drost, D. J., Malla, A., Carr, T. J., Cortese, L., Canaran, G., Rylet, J., & Neufeld, R. W. J. (1997). Measurement of glutamate and glutamine in the medial prefrontal cortex of never-treated schizophrenic patients and healthy controls by proton magnetic resonance spectroscopy. *Archives of General Psychiatry, 54,* 959–965.

66. Brébion, G., Smith, M. J., Gorman, J. M. & Amador, X. (1997). Discrimination accuracy and decision biases in different types of reality monitoring in schizophrenia. *Journal of Nervous and Mental Disease, 185,* 247–253.

67. Mizuno, M., Kato, M., Sartori, G., Okawaza, H., & Kashima, H. (1997). Performance characteristics of chronic schizophrenia on attention tests sensitive to unilateral brain damage. *Journal of Nervous and Mental Disease, 185,* 427–433.

68. Van Ammers, E. C., Sellman, J. D., & Mulder, R. T. (1997). Temperament and substance abuse in schizophrenia: Is there a relationship? *Journal of Nervous and Mental Disease, 185,* 283–288.

69. Ratakonda, S., Gorman, J. M., Yale, S. A., & Amador, X. F. (1998). Characterization of psychotic conditions: use of the domains of psychopathology model. *Archives of General Psychiatry, 55,* 75–81.

[2290]

Scale for the Assessment of Thought, Language, and Communication.

Purpose: Designed to assess clinical and pathological characteristics of language behavior.

Population: Manics, depressives, and schizophrenics.

Publication Date: 1980.

Acronym: TLC.

Scores: 19 ratings: Poverty of Speech, Poverty of Content of Speech, Pressure of Speech, Distractible Speech, Tangentiality, Derailment, Incoherence, Illogicality, Clanging, Neologisms, Word Approximations, Circumstantiality, Loss of Goal, Perseveration, Echolalia, Blocking, Stilted Speech, Self-Reference, Global Rating.

Administration: Individual.

Price Data: Price data for materials including manual (19 pages) available from publisher.

Time: [45-60] minutes.

Author: Nancy C. Andreasen.

Publisher: Nancy C. Andreasen.

Cross References: See T4:2327 (4 references).

TEST REFERENCES

1. Szor, H., Meilijson, S., & Meilijson, I. (1988). Letters to editor: A comment on Andreason and Grove. *Schizophrenic Bulletin, 14,* 17–18.

2. Harvey, P. D., & Serper, M. R. (1990). Linguistic and cognitive failures in schizophrenia: A multivariate analysis. *The Journal of Nervous and Mental Disease, 178,* 487-493.

[2291]

Scale of Feelings and Behavior of Love: Revised.

Purpose: Designed to "identify the patterns of behavior and feelings people exhibit and experience in their love relationships."

Population: College and adults.

Publication Dates: 1973-1992.

Scores, 8: Verbal Expression of Affection, Self-Disclosure, Toleration of Loved Ones' Bothersome Aspects, Moral Support/Encouragement and Interest, Feelings Not Expressed, Material Evidence of Affection, Total Love Scale, Love Scale Index.

Administration: Group.

Price Data: Available from publisher.

Time: (30) minutes.

Comments: Separate answer sheets may be used; current edition now included in Innovations in Clinical Practice: A Source Book (Vol. II).

Authors: Clifford H. Swensen, Michele Killough Nelson, Jan Warner, and David Dunlap.

Publisher: Clifford H. Swensen.

Cross References: See T4:2328 (1 reference); for a review by H. Thompson Prout of an earlier edition, see 9:1072.

[2292]

Scale of Marriage Problems: Revised.

Purpose: Designed to measure marital conflicts.
Population: Couples.
Publication Dates: 1975–1992.
Scores, 7: Problem-Solving, Childrearing, Relatives, Personal Care, Money, Outside Relationships, Total.
Administration: Group.
Price Data: Available from publisher.
Time: Administration time not reported.
Comments: Current edition now included in Innovations in Clinical Practice: A Source Book (Vol. II).
Authors: Clifford H. Swensen, Michele Killough Nelson, Jan Warner, and David Dunlap.
Publisher: Clifford H. Swensen.

[2293]

Scaled Curriculum Achievement Levels Test.

Purpose: Assesses individual and group achievement in mathematics computation, reading, and language usage.
Population: Grades 3-8.
Publication Date: 1992.
Acronym: SCALE.
Administration: Group.
Levels: 9 levels in each of 3 subtests: Mathematics Computation (M1-M9), Reading (R1-R9), Language Usage (L1-L9).
Price Data, 1999: $92.50 per complete kit including 6 reusableadministration booklets (2 each for Mathematics Computation, Reading, and Language Usage), 10 class placement/record sheets; 30 answer forms (10 each for Mathematics Computation, Reading, and language Usage), and manual (135 pages); $15 per 100 class placement/record sheets; $47.50 per manual.
Authors: Victor W. Doherty and Gale H. Roid.
Publisher: Western Psychological Services.

a) MATHEMATICS COMPUTATION.
Scores: Total score only.
Price Data: $24.50 per 10 reusable administration booklets; $15 per 10 AutoScore™ answer forms.
Time: (20-25) minutes.

b) READING.
Scores: Same as *a* above.
Price Data: $34.50 per 10 reusable administration booklets; $15 per 10 AutoScore™ answer forms.
Time: Same as *a* above.

c) LANGUAGE USAGE.
Scores: Sames as *a* above.
Price Data: $31.50 per 10 reusable administration booklets; $15 per 10 AutoScore™ answer forms.
Time: (15-20) minutes.

Cross References: For reviews by Russell N. Carney and Robert K. Gable, see 12:341.

[2294]

Scales for Predicting Successful Inclusion.

Purpose: Designed to identify students with disabilities for potential for success in general education classes.
Population: Ages 5–18.
Publication Date: 1997.
Acronym: SPSI.
Scores: 4 scales: Work Habits, Coping Skills, Peer Relationships, Emotional Maturity.
Administration: Group.
Price Data, 1999: $79 per complete kit including manual (47 pages) and 50 summary/response forms; $39 per 50 summary/response forms; $42 per manual.
Time: (5–10) minutes.
Comments: Ratings by teachers, parents, and/or assistants.
Authors: James E. Gilliam and Kathleen S. McConnell.
Publisher: PRO-ED.

[2295]

Scales for Rating the Behavioral Characteristics of Superior Students.

Purpose: Designed to aid teachers in the identification of gifted children.
Population: Population unspecified, developed from research with students in grades 4-6.
Publication Date: 1976.
Acronym: SRBCSS.
Scores, 10: Learning, Motivational, Creativity, Leadership, Artistic, Musical, Dramatics, Communication (Precision, Expressiveness), Planning.
Administration: Group.
Price Data: Available from publisher.
Time: Administration time not reported.
Comments: Scales for rating by teachers.
Authors: Joseph S. Renzulli, Linda H. Smith, Alan J. White, Carolyn M. Callahan, and Robert K. Hartman.
Publisher: Creative Learning Press, Inc.
Cross References: For reviews by Edward N. Argulewicz and James O. Rust, see 9:1073 (1 reference).

TEST REFERENCES

1. Banbury, M. M., & Wellington, B. (1989). Designing and using peer nomination forms. *Gifted Child Quarterly, 33,* 160–164.

2. Carter, K. R. (1992). A model for evaluating programs for the gifted under non-experimental conditions. *Journal for the Education of the Gifted, 15,* 266-283.

3. Cornell, D. G., Delcourt, M. A. B., Goldberg, M. D., & Bland, L. C. (1992). Characteristics of elementary students entering gifted programs: The Learning Outcomes Project at the University of Virginia. *Journal for the Education of the Gifted, 15,* 309-331.

4. Roberts, C., Ingram, C., & Harris, C. (1992). The effect of special versus regular classroom programming on higher cognitive processes of intermediate elementary aged gifted and average ability students. *Journal for the Education of the Gifted, 15,* 332-343.

5. Callahan, C. M., Lundberg, A. C., & Hunsaker, S. L. (1993). The development of the Scale for the Evaluation of Gifted Identification Instruments (SEGII). *Gifted Child Quarterly, 37,* 133-140.
6. Huchingson, R., & Huchingson, J. (1993). Waldorf education as a program for gifted students. *Journal for the Education of the Gifted, 16,* 400-419.
7. Hunsaker, S. L., & Callahan, C. M. (1995). Creativity and giftedness: Published instrument uses and abuses. *Gifted Child Quarterly, 39,* 110–114.
8. Oakland, T., Falkenberg, B. A., & Oakland, C. (1996). Assessment of leadership in children, youth, and adults. *Gifted Child Quarterly, 40,* 138–146.
9. Hunsaker, S. L., Finley, V. S., & Frank, E. L. (1997). An analysis of teacher nominations and student performance in gifted programs. *Gifted Child Quarterly, 41,* 19–24.

[2296]

Scales of Adult Independence, Language and Recall.

Purpose: By "assessing the domains of functional independence, language, and recall of adults with neurogenically based communication and cognitive disorders," the SAILR is "designed to differentiate between the communication and related deficits associated with stroke, dementia, and depression."
Population: Adults with dementia.
Publication Date: 1997.
Acronym: SAILR.
Scores, 8: Self-Care, Daily Living, Social Interaction, Client Interview, Word Retrieval, Sentence Comprehension, Paragraph Recall, Standard Score.
Administration: Individual.
Forms, 2: A, B.
Price Data, 1999: $189 per complete kit including examiner's manual (42 pages), stimulus manual (66 pages), 25 caretaker/relative interviews, and 25 record forms; $44 per examiner's manual; $44 per stimulus manual; $29 per 25 each of interview and record.
Time: Administration time varies.
Author: Barbara C. Sonies.
Publisher: PRO-ED.

[2297]

Scales of Cognitive Ability for Traumatic Brain Injury.

Purpose: To "provide a systematic method of assessing cognitive deficits associated with traumatic brain injury."
Population: Patients with acquired brain damage.
Publication Date: 1992.
Acronym: SCATBI.
Scores, 46: Perception and Discrimination (Sound Recognition, Shape Recognition, Word Recognition [no distraction], Word Recognition [with distraction], Color Discrimination, Shape Discrimination, Size Discrimination, Discrimination of Color/Shape/Size, Discrimination of Pictured Objects, Auditory Discrimination [real words], Auditory Discrimination [nonsense], Total); Orientation (Premorbid Questions, Postmorbid Questions, Total); Organization (Identifying Pictured Categories, Identifying Pictured Category Members, Word Associations, Sequencing Objects [size], Sequencing Words [alphabetical], Sequencing Events [time of year], Sequencing Events [pictured task steps], Sequencing Events [recall task steps], Total); Recall (Memory for Graphic Elements, Naming Pictures, Immediate Recall of Word Strings, Delayed Recall of Word Strings, Cued Recall of Words, Cued Recall of Words in Discourse, Word Generation, Immediate Recall of Oral Directions, Recall of Oral Paragraphs, Total); Reasoning (Figural Reasoning: Matrix Analogies, Convergent Thinking: Central Theme, Deductive Reasoning: Elimination, Inductive Reasoning: Opposites, Inductive Reasoning: Analogies, Divergent Thinking: Homographs, Divergent Thinking: Idioms, Divergent Thinking: Proverbs, Divergent Thinking: Verbal Absurdities, Multiprocess Reasoning: Task Insight, Multiprocess Reasoning: Analysis, Total).
Administration: Individual.
Price Data, 1999: $249 per complete kit; $54 per 25 record forms; $49 per card set; $64 per picture book; $64 per manual; $24 per cassette.
Time: Administration time not reported.
Authors: Brenda Adamovich and Jennifer Henderson.
Publisher: PRO-ED.
Cross References: For reviews by Charles J. Long and Faith Gunning and by Deborah D. Roman, see 13:273.

[2298]

Scales of Early Communication Skills for Hearing-Impaired Children.

Purpose: "Designed to evaluate speech and language development of hearing-impaired children between the ages of two and eight years."
Population: Ages 2-0 to 8-11.
Publication Date: 1975.
Acronym: SECS.
Scores, 4: Receptive Language Skills, Expressive Language Skills, Nonverbal Receptive Skills, Nonverbal Expressive Skills.
Administration: Individual.
Price Data, 1998: $12 per manual (42 pages); $10 per 25 rating forms.
Time: [60] minutes (through observation).
Comments: Ratings by teachers.
Authors: Jean S. Moog and Ann E. Geers.
Publisher: Central Institute for the Deaf.
Cross References: For reviews by Vincent J. Samar and Marc Marschark and E. W. Testut, see 12:342.

TEST REFERENCES

1. Geers, A., & Moog, J. (1994). Description of the CID sensory aids study. *Volta Review, 96,* 1–11.
2. Geers, A., & Moog, J. (1994). Spoken language results: Vocabulary, syntax, and communications. *Volta Review, 96,* 131–148.
3. Nicholas, J. G. (1994). Sensory aid use and the development of communicative function. *Volta Review, 96,* 181–198.

[2299]

Scales of Independent Behavior—Revised.

Purpose: "Designed to measure functional independence and adaptive functioning in school, home, employment, and community settings."

Population: Infants to adults, with or without developmental disabilities.

Publication Dates: 1984–1997.

Acronym: SIB-R.

Scores, 24: Full Scale (Gross-Motor Skills, Fine Motor Skills, Social Interaction, Language Comprehension, Language Expression, Eating and Meal Preparation, Toileting, Dressing, Personal Self-Care, Domestic Skills, Time and Punctuality, Money and Value, Work Skills, Home/Community Orientation), Problem Behavior Scale [optional] (Hurtful to Self, Unusual or Repetitive habits, Withdrawal or Inattentive Behavior, Socially Offensive Behavior, Uncooperative Behavior, Hurtful to Others, Destructive to Property, Disruptive Behavior).

Administration: Individual.

Forms, 3: Comprehensive, Short Form, Early Development Form.

Price Data, 1999: $175 per kit including all test materials, 15 Full Scale Response Booklets, 5 Short Form Response Booklets, and 5 Early Development Form Response Booklets; $44.50 per 25 Full Scale Response Booklets; $28 per 25 Short Form Booklets; $28 per 25 Early Development Response Booklets; $34 per 25-item package (15 Full Scale, 5 Short Form, and 5 Early Development Booklets); $63 per comprehensive manual ('96, 287 pages); $79.50 per Interview Book.

Time: (60) minutes.

Comments: SIB-R in conjunction with the Woodcock-Johnson Psychoeducational Battery—Revised can be used as a comprehensive diagnostic system for measuring adaptive behavior, problem behavior, cognitive ability, language proficiency, and achievement; can be administered either via interview or checklist; short and early development forms available as part of test kit; computerized DOS-based scoring system available.

Authors: Robert H. Bruininks, Richard W. Woodcock, Richard F. Weatherman, and Bradley K. Hill.

Publisher: The Riverside Publishing Company.

Cross References: See T4:2335 (6 references); for reviews by Bonnie W. Camp and Louis J. Heifetz of the earlier version, see 10:321.

TEST REFERENCES

1. MacMillan, D. L., Gresham, F. M., & Siperstein, G. N. (1993). Conceptual and psychometric concerns about the 1992 AAMR definition of mental retardation. *American Journal on Mental Retardation, 98,* 325–335.

2. McDonnell, J., Hardman, M. L., Hightower, J., Keifer-O'Donnel, R., & Drew, C. (1993). Impact of community-based instruction on the development of adaptive behavior of secondary-level students with mental retardation. *American Journal on Mental Retardation, 97,* 575-584.

3. Widaman, K. F., Stacy, A. W., & Borthwick-Duffy, S. A. (1993). Construct validity of dimensions of adaptive behavior: A multitrait-multimethod evaluation. *American Journal on Mental Retardation, 98,* 219–234.

4. Merrell, K. W., & Popinga, M. R. (1994). The alliance of adaptive behavior and social competence: An examination of relationships between the Scales of Independent Behavior and the Social Skills Rating System. *Research in Development Disabilities, 15,* 39-47.

5. Barnett, W. S., & Boyce, G. C. (1995). Effects of children with Down Syndrome on parents' activities. *American Journal on Mental Retardation, 100,* 115–127.

6. Maisto, A. A., & Hughes, E. (1995). Adaptation to group home living for adults with mental retardation as a function of previous residential placement. *Journal of Intellectual Disability Research, 39,* 15–18.

7. Newton, J. S., Olson, D., Horner, R. H., & Ard, W. R., Jr. (1996). Social skills and the stability of social relationships between individuals with intellectual disabilities and other community members. *Research in Developmental Disabilities, 17,* 15–26.

[2300]

SCAN: A Screening Test for Auditory Processing Disorders.

Purpose: "To identify children who have auditory processing problems which may complicate or compound language or learning problems."

Population: Ages 3-11.

Publication Date: 1986.

Acronym: SCAN.

Scores, 3: Filtered Words, Auditory Figure Ground, Competing Words.

Administration: Individual.

Price Data, 1999: $121 per complete kit including 25 record forms, test audiocassette, and examiner's manual (107 pages); $28.50 per 25 record forms; $64 per test audiocassette; $47.50 per examiner's manual.

Time: (20) minutes.

Comments: Stereo cassette player necessary for administration.

Author: Robert W. Keith.

Publisher: The Psychological Corporation.

Cross References: For a review by Sami Gulgoz, see 11:341 (2 references).

TEST REFERENCE

1. Keith, R. W., & Engineer, P. (1991). Effects of methylphenidate on the auditory processing abilities of children with attention deficit-hyperactivity disorder. *Journal of Learning Disabilities, 24,* 630–363; 640.

[2301]

SCAN-A: A Test for Auditory Processing Disorders in Adolescents and Adults.

Purpose: Used to identify adolescents and adults who have auditory processing disorders and who may benefit from intervention.

Population: Ages 12 to 50.

Publication Dates: 1986–1994.

Acronym: SCAN-A.

Scores, 6: Filtered Words, Auditory Figure-Ground, Competing Words, Competing Sentences, Total Test, Competing Words Ear Advantage.

Administration: Individual.

Price Data, 1999: $104 per complete kit including examiner's manual ('94, 69 pages), test audiocassette,

and 12 record forms; $15 per 12 record forms; $49.50 per examiner's manual; $64 per test audiocassette.
Time: (20–25) minutes.
Comments: SCAN-A requires an audiocassette player, two sets of stereo headphones, and a "Y" adapter.
Author: Robert W. Keith.
Publisher: The Psychological Corporation.
Cross References: For reviews by William R. Merz, Sr., and Jaclyn B. Spitzer, see 13:275.

[2302]

SCC Clerical Skills Series.

Purpose: Assess clerical skills needed in various public service positions.
Population: Job applicants.
Publication Dates: 1975-1976.
Scores: 6 tests in series: 361.1 Clerical Skills Series (Punctuation, Vocabulary, Filing, Reading Skills, Grammar, Spelling); 362.1 Clerical Skills Series (Name and Number Checking, Vocabulary, Reading Skills, Numerical Skills, Coding Part I, Coding Part II); 363.1 Clerical Skills Series (Name and Number Checking, Vocabulary, Filing, Coding Part I, Coding Part II); Oral Instructions; Typing Test; Dictation/Transcription.
Administration: Group.
Restricted Distribution: Restricted to public personnel agencies who have completed a Test Security Agreement and returned it to the publisher.
Price Data, 1994: $40 basic rental fee; $8.25 per test booklet (agency member); $8.50 per test booklet (non-agency member); $9.75 per manual (member); $30 per manual; $30 per set scoring fee plus $.25 per answer sheet.
Time: (5-87) minutes; varies by test.
Author: Selection Consultation Center.
Publisher: International Personnel Management Association.
Cross References: For a review by Lorraine D. Eyde, see 9:1074.

[2303]

The Scenotest: A Practical Technique for Understanding Unconscious Problems and Personality Structure.

Purpose: A projective instrument intended "to help very quickly assess emotional problems in children."
Population: Children and adolescents.
Publication Dates: 1971–1998.
Scores: Score information available from publisher.
Administration: Individual.
Price Data, 1998: $775 per complete test kit and manual ('98, 120 pages).
Time: Administration time not reported.
Comments: Material in the test kit consists of flexible human figures and accessories including animals, trees, symbolic figures, and items from everyday life.
Author: G. von Staabs.
Publisher: Hogrefe & Huber Publishers.

[2304]

Schaie-Thurstone Adult Mental Abilities Test.

Purpose: Designed to "measure the mental abilities of adults."
Population: Ages 22-84.
Publication Date: 1985.
Acronym: STAMAT.
Scores: 7 scale scores: Recognition Vocabulary (V), Figure Rotation (FR), Object Rotation (OR, Form OA only), Letter Series (LS), Word Series (WS, Form OA only), Number Addition (N), Word Fluency (W).
Administration: Group.
Forms, 2: Form A (for "Adult," essentially the Thurstone Primary Mental Abilities Test Form II-17 (PMA) with new adult norms), Form OA (for "Older Adult," large-type version of the original plus two additional scales for adults over age 55).
Price Data, 1990: $55 per 25 Form OA expendable test booklets; $39 per 25 Form A booklets; $12 per 50 Form A answer sheets; $6 per Form A scoring key; $7 per 25 profiles for both OA and A; $18 per manual (86 pages); $27 per specimen set.
Time: (50-60) minutes.
Author: K. Warner Schaie.
Publisher: K. Warner Schaie (the author).
Cross References: See T4:2339 (3 references); for a review by Eric F. Gardner, see 10:322.

TEST REFERENCES

1. Willis, S. L., & Schaie, K. W. (1986). Training the elderly on the ability factors of spatial orientation and inductive reasoning. *Psychology and Aging, 1,* 239-247.
2. Salthouse, T. A., & Prill, K. A. (1987). Inferences about age impairments in inferential reasoning. *Psychology and Aging, 2,* 43-51.
3. Lynn, R. (1989). A nutrition theory of the secular increases in intelligence; (sic) positive correlations between height, head size and IQ. *British Journal of Educational Psychology, 59,* 372–377.
4. Gruber-Baldini, A. L., Schaie, K. W., & Willis, S. L. (1995). Similarity in married couples: A longitudinal study of marital abilities and rigidity-flexibility. *Journal of Personality and Social Psychology, 69,* 191–203.

[2305]

Schedule for Affective Disorders and Schizophrenia, Third Edition.

Purpose: "To record information regarding a subject's functioning and psychopathology."
Population: Adults.
Publication Dates: 1977-1988.
Acronym: SADS.
Administration: Individual.
Price Data, 1998: $.50 per SADS/SADS-L suggested procedures; $2.50 per SADS/SADS-L instructions and clarifications ('85, 24 pages).

Time: [30–120] minutes.
Authors: Robert L. Spitzer, Jean Endicott, Jo Ellen Loth (SADS-LB, SADS-LI), Patricia McDonald-Scott (SADS-LI), and Patricia Wasek (SADS-LI).
Publisher: Department of Research Assessment and Training.

a) SCHEDULE FOR AFFECTIVE DISORDERS AND SCHIZOPHRENIA.

Scores, 24: Current Syndromes (Depressive Mood/Ideation, Endogenous Features, Depressive-Associated Features, Suicidal Ideation/Behavior, Anxiety, Manic Syndrome, Delusions-Hallucinations, Formal Thought Disorder, Impaired Functioning, Alcohol or Drug Abuse, Behavioral Disorganization, Miscellaneous Psychopathology, GAS [worst period], Extracted Hamilton); Past Week Functioning (Depressive Syndrome, Endogenous Features, Manic Syndrome, Anxiety, Delusions-Hall-Disorganization, GAS rating, Extracted Hamilton, Miscellaneous Psychopathology); Past Other than Diagnosis (Social Functioning, Suicidal Behavior).

Price Data: $3 per SADS booklet; $.50 per SADS score sheet; $1.50 per SADS summary scales scores; $.25 per editing and coding instructions; $2.50 per instructions/clarifications.

b) SCHEDULE FOR AFFECTIVE DISORDERS AND SCHIZOPHRENIA LIFETIME (VARIOUS VERSIONS).

1) *SADS-L.*

Purpose: To record information regarding a subject's functioning and psychopathology; includes current disturbance.

Price Data: $2 per SADS-L booklet; $.50 per SADS-L score sheet.

2) *SADS-LB.*

Purpose: To record information regarding a subject's functioning and psychopathology; includes current disturbance and additional items related to bipolar affective disorder.

Price Data: $2 per SADS-LB booklet; $.50 per SADS-LB score sheet.

3) *SADS-LI.*

Purpose: To record information regarding a subject's functioning and psychopathology; specifies follow-up interval.

Price Data: $2 per SADS-LI booklet; $.50 per SADS-LI score sheet.

Cross References: For reviews by Paul A. Arbisi and James C. Carmer, see 12:343 (414 references); see also T4:2340 (152 references).

TEST REFERENCES

1. Chapman, L. J., & Chapman, J. P. (1987). The search for symptoms predictive of schizophrenia. *Schizophrenia Bulletin, 13,* 497–503.

2. Erlenmeyer-Kimling, L., & Cornblatt, B. (1987). The New York high-risk project: A followup report. *Schizophrenia Bulletin, 13,* 451–461.

3. Fish, B. (1987). Infant predictors of the longitudinal course of schizophrenic development. *Schizophrenia Bulletin, 13,* 395–409.

4. Freedman, R., Adler, L. E., Gerhardt, G. A., Waldo, M., Baker, N., Rose, G. M., Drebing, C., Nagamoto, H., Bickford-Wimer, P., & Franks, R. (1987). Neurobiological studies of sensory gating in schizophrenia. *Schizophrenia Bulletin, 13,* 669–678.

5. Marcus, J., Hans, S. L., Nagler, S., Auerbach, J. G., Mirsky, A. F., & Aubrey, A. (1987). Review of the NIMH Israeli Kibbutz-City study and the Jerusalem infant development study. *Schizophrenia Bulletin, 13,* 425–438.

6. Weintraub, S. (1987). Risk factors in schizophrenia: The Stony Brook high risk project. *Schizophrenia Bulletin, 13,* 439–450.

7. DeMyer, M. K., Gilmor, R. L., Hendrie, H. C., DeMyer, W. E., Augustyn, G. T., & Jackson, R. K. (1988). Magnetic resonance brain images in schizophrenic and normal subjects: Influence of diagnosis and education. *Schizophrenic Bulletin, 14,* 21–37.

8. Harvey, P. D., Earle-Boyer, E. A., & Levinson, J. C. (1988). Cognitive deficits and thought disorder: A retest study. *Schizophrenia Bulletin, 14,* 57–66.

9. Lin, K., & Kleinman, A. M. (1988). Psychopathology and clinical course of schizophrenia: A cross-cultural perspective. *Schizophrenia Bulletin, 14,* 555–567.

10. Prezant, D. W., & Neimeyer, R. A. (1988). Cognitive predictors of depression and suicide ideation. *Suicide and Life-Threatening Behavior, 18,* 259–264.

11. Wielgus, M. S., & Harvey, P. D. (1988). Dichotic listening and recall in schizophrenia and mania. *Schizophrenia Bulletin, 14,* 689–700.

12. Asnis, G. M., Friedman, J. M. H., Miller, A. H., Iqbal, N., Lo, E. S., Cooper, T. B., Halbreich, U., Lemus, C. Z., vanPraag, H. M., & Robinson, E. (1989). Plasma dexamethasone and cortisol levels in depressed outpatients. *Journal of Affective Disorders, 16,* 5–10.

13. Banks, R. E., Aiton, J. F., Naylor, G. J., Cramb, G., Wright, A. F., Griffith, R. C., & Reich, T. (1989). Cation transport in lymphoblastoid cell lines established from bipolar manic-depressive patients. *Journal of Affective Disorders, 16,* 259–267.

14. Charles, G. A., Schittecatte, M., Rush, A. J., Panzer, M., & Wilmotte, J. (1989). Persistent cortisol non-suppression after clinical recovery predicts symptomatic relapse in unipolar depression. *Journal of Affective Disorders, 17,* 271–278.

15. Cutting, J., & Dunne, F. (1989). Subjective experience of schizophrenia. *Schizophrenia Bulletin, 15,* 217–231.

16. Emery, O. B., & Breslau, L. D. (1989). Language deficits in depression: Comparisons with SDAT and normal aging. *Journal of Gerontology, 44,* 85–92.

17. Garvey, M., Cook, B., & Noyes, R., Jr. (1989). Comparison of major depressive patients with a predominantly sad versus anxious mood. *Journal of Affective Disorders, 17,* 183–187.

18. Hirschfeld, R. M. A., Kosier, T., Keller, M. B., Lavori, P. W., & Endicott, J. (1989). The influence of alcohol on the course of depression. *Journal of Affective Disorders, 16,* 151–158.

19. Hopkins, J., Campbell, S. B., & Marcus, M. (1989). Postpartum depression and postpartum adaption: Overlapping constructs? *Journal of Affective Disorders, 17,* 251–254.

20. Kaufmann, C. A., DeLisi, L. E., Lehner, T., & Gilliam, T. C. (1989). Physical mapping, linkage analysis of a putative schizophrenia locus on chromosome 5q. *Schizophrenia Bulletin, 15,* 441–452.

21. Kendler, K. S., Lieberman, J. A., & Walsh, D. (1989). The structured interview for schizotypy (SIS): A preliminary report. *Schizophrenia Bulletin, 15,* 559–571.

22. Kennedy, J. L., Giuffra, L. A., Moises, H. W., Wetterberg, L., Sjögren, B., Cavalli-Sforza, L. L., Pakstis, A. J., Kidd, J. R., & Kidd, K. K. (1989). Molecular genetic studies in schizophrenia. *Schizophrenia Bulletin, 15,* 383–391.

23. Lahmeyer, H. W., Reynolds, C. F., III, Kupfer, D. J., & King, R. (1989). Biologic markers in borderline personality disorder: A review. *The Journal of Clinical Psychiatry, 50,* 217–225.

24. Robbins, D. R., Alessi, N. E., & Colfer, M. V. (1989). Treatment of adolescents with major depression: Implications of the DST and the milancholic clinical subtype. *Journal of Affective Disorders, 17,* 99–104.

25. Robins, C. J., Block, P., & Peselow, E. D. (1989). Specificity of symptoms in RDC endogenous depression. *Journal of Affective Disorders, 16,* 243–248.

26. Surtees, P. G., & Duffy, J. C. (1989). Binary and rate measures of life event experience: Their association with illness onset in Edinburgh and London community surveys. *Journal of Affective Disorders, 16,* 139–149.

27. Adinoff, B., Martin, P. R., Bone, G. H. A., Eckardt, M. J., Roehrich, L., George, D. T., Moss, H. B., Eskay, R., Linnoila, M., & Gold, P. W. (1990). Hypothalamic-pituitary-adrenal axis functioning and cerebrospinal fluid corticotropin releasing hormone and corticotropin levels in alcoholics after recent and long-term abstinence. *Archives of General Psychiatry, 47,* 325–330.

28. Bauer, M. S., Whybrow, P. C., & Winokur, A. (1990). Rapid cycling bipolar affective disorder. *Archives of General Psychiatry, 47,* 427–432.

29. Berrettini, W. H., Goldin, L. R., Gelernter, J., Gejman, P. V., Gershon, E. S., & Detera-Wadleigh, S. (1990). X-chromosome markers and manic-depressive illness. *Archives of General Psychiatry, 47,* 366–373.

30. Davidson, J., Kudler, H., Smith, R., Mahorney, S. L., Lipper, S., Hammett, E., Saunders, W. B., & Cavenar, J. O., Jr. (1990). Treatment of posttraumatic stress disorder with amitriptyline and placebo. *Archives of General Psychiatry, 47,* 259–266.

31. Depue, R. A., Arbisi, P., Krauss, S., Iacono, W. G., Leon, A., Muir, R., & Allen, J. (1990). Seasonal independence of low prolactin concentration and high spontaneous eye blink rates in unipolar and bipolar III seasonal affective disorder. *Archives of General Psychiatry, 47,* 356–364.

32. Dupont, R. M., Jernigan, T. L., Butters, N., Delis, D., Hesselink, J. R., Heindel, W., & Gillin, J. C. (1990). Subcortical abnormalities detected in bipolar affective disorder using magnetic resonance imaging. *Archives of General Psychiatry, 47,* 55–59.

33. Duval, F., Macher, J., & Mokrani, M. (1990). Difference between evening and morning thyrotropin responses to protirelin in major depressive episode. *Archives of General Psychiatry, 47,* 443–448.

34. Fyer, A. J., Mannuzza, S., Gallops, M. S., Martin, L. Y., Aaronson, C., Gorman, J. M., Liebowitz, M. R., & Klein, D. F. (1990). Familial transmission of simple phobias and fears. *Archives of General Psychiatry, 47,* 252–256.

35. Grillon, C., Courchesne, E., Ameli, R., Geyer, M. A., & Braff, D. L. (1990). Increased distractibility in schizophrenic patients. *Archives of General Psychiatry, 47,* 171–179.

36. Harrington, R., Fudge, H., Rutter, M., Pickles, A., & Hill, J. (1990). Adult outcomes of childhood and adolescent depression. *Archives of General Psychiatry, 47,* 465–473.

37. Harvey, P. D., Docherty, N. M., Serper, M. R., & Rasmussen, M. (1990). Cognitive deficits and thought disorder: II. An 8-month follow-up study. *Schizophrenia Bulletin, 16,* 147–156.

38. Holmes-Eber, P., & Riger, S. (1990). Hospitalization and the composition of mental patients' social networks. *Schizophrenia Bulletin, 16,* 157–164.

39. Jarrett, D. B., Miewald, J. M., & Kupfer, D. J. (1990). Recurrent depression is associated with a persistent reduction in sleep-related growth hormone secretion. *Archives of General Psychiatry, 47,* 113–118.

40. Lewinsohn, P., Clarke, G. N., Hops, H., & Andrews, J. (1990). Cognitive-behavioral treatment for depressed adolescents. *Behavior Therapy, 21,* 385–401.

41. McGory, P. D., Copolov, D. L., & Singh, B. S. (1990). Royal Park multidiagnostic instrument for psychosis: Part 1. Rationale and review. *Schizophrenia Bulletin, 16,* 501–515.

42. Mueser, K. T. Yarnold, P. R., Levinson, D. F., Singh, H., Bellack, A. S., Kee, K., Morrison, R. L., & Yadalam, K. G. (1990). Prevalence of substance abuse in schizophrenia: Demographic and clinical correlates. *Schizophrenia Bulletin, 16,* 31–56.

43. Neimeyer, R. A., & Feixas, G. (1990). The role of homework and skill acquisition in the outcome of group cognitive therapy for depression. *Behavior Therapy, 21,* 281–292.

44. Sack, R. L., Lewy, A. J., White, D. M., Singer, C. M., Fireman, M. J., & Vandiver, R. (1990). Morning vs. evening light treatment for winter depression. *Archives of General Psychiatry, 47,* 343–351.

45. Sackeim, H. A., Prohovnik, I., Moeller, J. R., Brown, R. P., Apter, S., Prudic, J., Devanand, D. P., & Mukherjee, S. (1990). Regional cerebral blood flow in mood disorders. *Archives of General Psychiatry, 47,* 60–70.

46. Schuckit, M. A., Irwin, M., & Brown, S. A. (1990). The history of anxiety symptoms among 171 primary alcoholics. *Journal of Studies on Alcohol, 51,* 34–41.

47. Turner, W. M., & Tsuang, M. T. (1990). Impact of substance abuse on the course and outcome of schizophrenia. *Schizophrenia Bulletin, 16,* 87–95.

48. van Kammen, D. P., Peters, J., Yao, J., van Kammen, W. B., Neylan, T., Shaw, D., & Linnoila, M. (1990). Norepinephrine in acute exacerbations of chronic schizophrenia. *Archives of General Psychiatry, 47,* 161–168.

49. Weeks, D. E., Brzustowicz, L., Squires-Wheeler, E., Cornblatt, B., Lehner, T., Stefanovich, M., Bassett, A., Gilliam, T. C., Ott, J., & Erlenmeyer-Kimling, L. (1990). Report of a workshop on genetic linkage studies in schizophrenia. *Schizophrenia Bulletin, 16,* 673–686.

50. Young, E. A., Watson, S. J., Koton, J., Haskett, R. F., Grunhaus, L., Murphy-Weinberg, V., Vale, W., Rivier, J., & Akil, H. (1990). B-lipotropin-B-endorphin response to low-dose ovine corticotropin releasing factor in endogenous depression. *Archives of General Psychiatry, 47,* 449–457.

51. Andreasen, N. C. (1991). Assessment issues and the cost of schizophrenia. *Schizophrenia Bulletin, 17,* 475–481.

52. Andreasen, N. C., & Flaum, M. (1991). Schizophrenia: The characteristic symptoms. *Schizophrenia Bulletin, 17,* 27–49.

53. Garbutt, J. C., Mayo, J. P., Jr., Gillette, G. M., Little, K. Y., Hicks, R. E., Mason, G. A. & Prange, A. J. (1991). Dose-response studies with thyrotropin-releasing hormone (TRH) in abstinent male alcoholics: Evidence for selective thyrotroph dysfunction. *Journal of Studies on Alcohol, 52,* 275–280.

54. Kochanska, G. (1991). Socialization and temperament in the development of guilt and conscience. *Child Development, 62,* 1379–1392.

55. Kochanska, G., & Kuczynski, L. (1991). Maternal autonomy granting: Predictors of normal and depressed mothers' compliance and noncompliance with the requests of five-year-olds. *Child Development, 62,* 1449–1459.

56. Levinson, D. F., & Mowry, B. J. (1991). Defining the schizophrenia spectrum: Issues for genetic linkage studies. *Schizophrenia Bulletin, 17,* 491–514.

57. Mueser, K. T., Douglas, M. S., Bellack, A. S., & Morrison, R. L. (1991). Assessment of enduring deficit and negative symptom subtypes in schizophrenia. *Schizophrenia Bulletin, 17,* 565–582.

58. Plasky, P. (1991). Antidepressant usage in schizophrenia. *Schizophrenia Bulletin, 17,* 649–657.

59. Raine, A. (1991). The SPQ: A scale for the assessment of schizotypal personality based on DSM-III-R criteria. *Schizophrenia Bulletin, 17,* 555–564.

60. Silverstein, M. L., Marengo, J. T., & Fogg, L. (1991). Two types of thought disorder and lateralized neuropsychological dysfunction. *Schizophrenia Bulletin, 17,* 679–687.

61. Thase, M. E., Simons, A. D., Cahalane, J. F., & McGeary, J. (1991). Cognitive behavior therapy of endogenous depression: Part 1: An outpatient clinical replication series. *Behavior Therapy, 22,* 457–467.

62. Attkisson, C., Cook, J., Karno, M., Lehman, A., McGlashan, T. H., Meltzer, H. Y., O'Connor, M., Richardson, D., Rosenblatt, A., Wells, K., Williams, J., & Hohmann, A. A. (1992). Clinical services research. *Schizophrenia Bulletin, 18,* 561–626.

63. Ganguli, R., & Brar, J. S. (1992). Generalizability of first-episode studies in schizophrenia. *Schizophrenia Bulletin, 18,* 463–469.

64. Hans, S. L., Marcus, J., Henson, L., Auerbach, J. G., & Mirsky, A.F. (1992). Interpersonal behavior of children at risk for schizophrenia. *Psychiatry, 55,* 314–335.

65. Heimburg, R. G., Mueller, G. P., Holt, C. S., Hope, D. A., & Liebowitz, M. R. (1992). Assessment of anxiety in social interaction and being observed by others: The social interaction anxiety scale and the social phobia scale. *Behavior Therapy, 23,* 53–73.

66. Hoff, A. L., Riordan, H., O'Donnell, D., Stritzke, P., Neale, C., Boccio, A., Anand, A. K., & DeLisi, L. E. (1992). Anomalous lateral sulcus asymmetry and cognitive function in first-episode schizophrenia. *Schizophrenia Bulletin, 18,* 257–273.

67. Keshavan, M. S., & Schooler, N. R. (1992). First-episode studies in schizophrenia: Criteria and characterization. *Schizophrenia Bulletin, 18,* 491–513.

68. Kochanska, G., & Radke-Yarrow, M. (1992). Inhibition in toddlerhood and the dynamics of the child's interaction with an unfamiliar peer at age five. *Child Development, 63,* 325–335.

69. Kojima, T., Matsushima, E., Ando, K., Ando, H., Sakurada, M., Ohta, K., Moriya, H., & Shimazono, Y. (1992). Exploratory eye movements and neuropsychological tests in schizophrenia patients. *Schizophrenia Bulletin, 18,* 85–94.

70. Lieberman, J. A., Alvir, J. M. J., Woerner, M., Degreef, G., Bilder, R. M., Ashtari, M., Bogerts, B., Mayerhoff, D. I., Geisler, S. H., Loebel, A., Levy, D. L., Hinrichsen, G., Szymanski, S., Chakos, M., Koreen, A., Borenstein, M., & Kane, J. M. (1992). Prospective study of psychobiology in first-episode schizophrenia at Hillside Hospital. *Schizophrenia Bulletin, 18,* 351–371.

71. McKnight, D. L., Nelson-Gray, R. O., & Barnhill, J. (1992). Dexamethasone suppression test and response to cognitive therapy and antidepressant medication. *Behavior Therapy, 23,* 99–111.

72. Meltzer, H. Y. (1992). Treatment of the neuroleptic-nonresponsive schizophrenic patient. *Schizophrenia Bulletin, 18,* 515–542.

73. Nuechterlein, K. H., Dawson, M. E., Gitlin, M., Ventura, J., Goldstein, M. J., Snyder, K. S., Yee, C. M., & Mintz, J. (1992). Developmental processes in schizophrenia disorders: Longitudinal studies of vulnerability and stress. *Schizophrenia Bulletin, 18,* 387–425.

74. Ram, R., Bromet, E. J., Eaton, W. W., Pato, C., & Schwartz, J. E. (1992). The natural course of schizophrenia: A review of first-admission studies. *Schizophrenia Bulletin, 18,* 185–207.

75. Brekke, J. S., Levin, S., Wolkon, G. H., Sobel, E., & Slade, E. (1993). Psychosocial functioning and subjective experience in schizophrenia. *Schizophrenia Bulletin, 19,* 599–608.

76. Carroll, K. M., Rounsaville, B. J., & Bryant, K. J. (1993). Alcoholism in treatment seeking cocaine abusers: Clinical and prognostic significance. *Journal of Studies on Alcohol, 54,* 199–208.

77. Dworkin, R. H., Clark, W. C., Lipsitz, J. D., Amador, X. F., Kaufmann, C. A., Opler, L. A., White, S. R., & Gorman, J. M. (1993). Affective deficits and pain insensitivity in schizophrenia. *Motivation and Emotion, 17,* 245–276.

78. Dworkin, R. H., Cornblatt, B. A., Friedmann, R., Kaplansky, L. M., Lewis, J. A., Rinaldi, A., Shilliday, C., & Erlenmeyer-Kimling, L. (1993). Childhood precursors of affective vs. social deficits in adolescents at risk for schizophrenia. *Schizophrenia Bulletin, 19,* 563–577.

79. Leung, P. K., Kinzie, J. D., Boehnlein, J. K., & Shore, J. H. (1993). A prospective study of the natural course of alcoholism in a native American village. *Journal of Studies on Alcohol, 54,* 733–738.

80. Nathan, M., Frenkel, E., & Kugelmass, S. C. (1993). From adolescence to adulthood: Development of psychopathology in kibbutz and town subjects. *Journal of Youth and Adolescence, 22,* 605–621.

81. Paveza, G. J. (1993). Social services and the Alzheimer's disease patient: An overview. *Neurology, 43,* 11–15.

82. Pisani, V. D., Fawcett, J., Clark, D. C., & McGuire, M. (1993). The relative contributions of medication adherence and AA meeting attendence to abstinent outcome for chronic alcoholics. *Journal of Studies on Alcohol, 54,* 115–119.

83. Raskin, A., Pelchat, R., Sood, R., Alphs, L. D., & Levine, J. (1993). Negative symptom assessment of chronic schizophrenia patients. *Schizophrenia Bulletin, 19,* 627–635.

84. Rosenblatt, A., & Attkisson, C. C. (1993). Assessing outcomes for sufferers of severe mental disorder: A conceptual framework and review. *Evaluation and Program Planning, 16,* 347–363.

85. Seilhamer, R. A., Jacob, T., & Dunn, N. J. (1993). The impact of alcohol consumption on parent-child relationship in families of alcoholics. *Journal of Studies on Alcohol, 54,* 189–198.

86. Steinhauer, S. R., & Hill, S. Y. (1993). Auditory event-related potentials in children at high risk for alcoholism. *Journal of Studies on Alcohol, 54,* 408–421.

87. Torrey, E. F., Bowler, A. E., Rawlings, R., & Terrazas, A. (1993). Seasonality of schizophrenia and stillbirths. *Schizophrenia Bulletin, 19,* 557–562.

88. Virkkunen, M., & Linnoila, M. (1993). Brain serotonin, Type II alcoholism and impulsive violence. *Journal of Studies on Alcoholism, Sup. 11,* 163–169.

89. Andreasen, N. C., & Carpenter, W. T. (1994). Diagnosis and classification of schizophrenia. *Schizophrenia Bulletin, 20,* 199–214.

90. Beck, J. G., & Zebb, B. J. (1994). Behavioral assessment and treatment of panic disorder: Current status, future directions. *Behavior Therapy, 25,* 581–611.

91. Benedict, R. H. B., Harris, A. E., Markow, T., McCormick, J. A., Nuechterlein, K. H., & Asarnow, R. F. (1994). Effects of attention training on information processing in schizophrenia. *Schizophrenia Bulletin, 20,* 537–546.

92. Blanchard, J. J., Kring, A. M., & Neale, J. M. (1994). Flat affect in schizophrenia: A test of neuropsychological models. *Schizophrenia Bulletin, 20,* 311–325.

93. Burke, P. M., Kocoshis, S., Neigut, D., Sauer, J., Chandra, R., & Orenstein, D. (1994). Maternal psychiatric disorders in pediatric inflamatory bowel disease and cystic fibrosis. *Child Psychiatry and Human Development, 25,* 45–52.

94. Burke, P. M., Neigut, D., Kocoshis, S., Chandra, R., & Saver, J. (1994). Correlates of depression in new onset pediatric inflammatory bowel disease. *Child Psychiatry and Human Development, 24,* 275–283.

95. Casper, R. C., Katz, m. M., Bowden, C. L., Davis, J. M., Koslow, S. H., & Hanin, I. (1994). The pattern of physical symptom changes in major depressive disorder following treatment with antriptyline or imipramine. *Journal of Affective Disorders, 31,* 151–164.

96. Cornblatt, B. A., & Keilp, J. G. (1994). Impaired attention, genetics, and the pathophysiology of schizophrenia. *Schizophrenia Bulletin, 20,* 31–46.

97. Coryell, W., Winokur, G., Maser, J. D., Akiskal, H. S., Keller, M. B., & Endicott, J. (1994). Recurrently situational (reactive) depression: A study of cource, phenomenology and familial psychopathology. *Journal of Affective Disorders, 31,* 203–210.

98. DeLisi, L. E., Friedrich, V., Wahlstrom, J., Boccio-Smith, A., Forsman, A., Eklund, K., & Crow, T. J. (1994). Schizophrenia and sex chromosome anomalies. *Schizophrenia Bulletin, 20,* 495–505.

99. Erlenmeyer-Kimling, L., Cornblatt, B. A., Rock, D., Roberts, S., Bell, M., & West, A. (1994). The New York high-risk project: Anhedonia, attentional deviance, and psychopathology. *Schizophrenia Bulletin, 20,* 141–153.

100. Freedman, M. (1994). Frontal and parietal lobe dysfunction in depression: Delayed alternation and tactile learning deficits. *Neuropsychologia, 32,* 1015–1025.

101. Gladis, M. M., Levinson, D. F., & Mowry, B. J. (1994). Delusions in schizophrenia spectrum disorders: Diagnostic issues. *Schizophrenia Bulletin, 20,* 747–754.

102. Goodman, A. B. (1994). Medical conditions in Ashkenazi schizophrenic pedigrees. *Schizophrenia Bulletin, 20,* 507–517.

103. Gordon, C. T., Frazier, J. A., McKenna, K., Giedd, J., Zametkin, A., Zahn, T., Hommer, D., Hong, W., Kaysen, D., Albus, K. E., & Rapoport, J. L. (1994). Childhood-onset schizophrenia: An NIMH study in progress. *Schizophrenia Bulletin, 20,* 697–712.

104. Green, M. F., Satz, P., & Christenson, C. (1994). Minor physical anomalies in schizophrenia patients, bipolar patients, and their siblings. *Schizophrenia Bulletin, 20,* 433–440.

105. Harrow, M., Yonan, C. A., Sands, J. R., & Marengo, J. (1994). Depression in schizophrenia: Are neuroleptics, akinesia, or anhedonia involved. *Schizophrenia Bulletin, 20,* 327–338.

106. Johnson, S. L., Monroe, S., Simons, A., & Thase, M. E. (1994). Clinical characteristics associated with interpersonal depression: Symptoms, course and treatment response. *Journal of Affective Disorders, 31,* 97–109.

107. Lieberman, J. A., & Koreen, A. R. (1994). Neurochemistry and neuroendocrinology of schizophrenia: A selective review. *Schizophrenia Bulletin, 19,* 371–429.

108. Maier, W., Lichterman, D., Minges, J., & Heun, R. (1994). Personality disorders among the relatives of schizophrenia patients. *Schizophrenia Bulletin, 20,* 481–493.

109. Pettegrew, J. W., Keshavan, M. S., & Minshew, N. J. (1994). 31P nuclear magnetic resonance spectroscopy: Neurodevelopment and schizophrenia. *Schizophrenia Bulletin, 20,* 35–53.

110. Pini, S., Goldstein, R. B., Wickramaratne, P. J., & Weissman, M. M. (1994). Phenomenology of panic disorder and major depression in a family study. *Journal of Affective Disorders, 30,* 257–272.

111. Rice, J. P., & Todorov, A. A. (1994). Stability of diagnosis: Application to phenotype definition. *Schizophrenia Bulletin, 20,* 185–190.

112. Richter, M. A., Cox, B. J., & Direnfeld, D. M. (1994). A comparison of three assessment instruments for obsessive-compulsive symptoms. *Journal of Behavior Therapy and Experimental Psychiatry, 25,* 143–147.

113. Strauss, M. E. (1994). Relations of symptoms to cognitive deficits in schizophrenia. *Schizophrenia Bulletin, 19,* 215–231.

114. Uhde, T. W., Tancer, M. E., Gelernter, C. S., & Vittone, B. J. (1994). Normal urinary fue cortisol and postdexamethasone cortisol in social phobia: Comparison to normal volunteers. *Journal of Affective Disorders, 30,* 155–161.

115. Urquiza, A. J., Wirtz, S. J., Peterson, M. S., & Singer, V. A. (1994). Screening and evaluating abused and neglected children entering protective custody. *Child Welfare, 73,* 155–171.

116. Walker, E. F., Savoie, T., & Davis, D. (1994). Neuromotor precursors of schizophrenia. *Schizophrenia Bulletin, 20,* 441–451.

117. Abbar, M., Courlet, P., Amadéo, S., Caer, Y., Mallet, J., Baldy-Moulinier, M., Castelnau, D., & Malafosse, A. (1995). Suicidal behaviors and the tryptophan hydroxylase gene. *Archives of General Psychiatry, 52,* 846–849.

118. Aizenborg, D., Zemishlany, Z., Dorfman-Etrog, P., & Waizman, A. (1995). Sexual dysfunction in male schizophrenic patients. *Journal of Clinical Psychiatry, 56,* 137–141.

119. Akiskal, H. S., Maser, J. D., Zeller, P. J., Endicott, J., Coryell, W., Keller, M., Warshaw, M., Clayton, P., & Goodwin, F. (1995). Switching from "unipolar" to bipolar II: An 11-year prospective study of clinical and tempermental predictors in 559 patients. *Archives of General Psychiatry, 52,* 114–123.

120. Altshuler, L. L., Curran, J. G., Hauser, P., Mintz, J., Denicoff, K., & Post, R. (1995). T2 hyperintensities in bipolar disorder: Magnetic resonance imaging comparison and literature meta-analysis. *American Journal of Psychiatry, 152,* 1139–1144.

121. Biederman, J., Santangelo, S. L., Faraone, S. V., Kiely, K., Guite, J., Mick, E., Reed, E. D., Kraus, I., Jellinek, M., & Perrin, J. (1995). Clinical correlates of enuresis in ADHD and non-ADHD children. *Journal of Child Psychology and Psychiatry and Allied Disciplines, 36,* 865–877.

122. Castonguay, L. G., Hayes, A. M., Goldfried, M. R., & DeRubeis, R. J. (1995). The focus of therapist interventions in cognitive therapy for depression. *Cognitive Therapy and Research, 19,* 485–503.

123. Chatterjee, A., Chakos, M., Koreen, A., Geisler, S., Sheitman, B., Woerner, M., Kane, J. M., Alvir, J., & Lieberman, J. A. (1995). Prevalence and clinical correlates of extrapyramidal signs and spontaneous dyskinesia in never-medicated schizophrenic patients. *American Journal of Psychiatry, 152,* 1724–1729.

124. Chochinou, H. M., Wilson, K. G., Enns, M., Mowchun, N., Lander, S., Levitt, M., & Clinch, J. J. (1995). Desire for death in the terminally ill. *American Journal of Psychiatry, 152,* 1185–1191.

125. Coryell, W., Endicott, J., Winokur, G., Akiskal, H., Solomon, D., Leon, A., Mueller, T., & Shea, T. (1995). Characteristics and significance of untreated major depressive disorder. *American Journal of Psychiatry, 152,* 1124–1129.

126. Crawford, T. J., Haeger, B., Kennard, C., Reveley, M. A., & Henderson, L. (1995). Saccadic abnormalities in psychotic patients. I. Neuroleptic-free psychotic patients. *Psychological Medicine, 25,* 461–471.

127. Crawford, T. J., Haegger, B., Kennard, C., Reveley, M. A., & Henderson, L. (1995). Saccadic abnormalities in psychotic patients. II. The role of neuroleptic treatment. *Psychological Medicine, 25,* 473–483.

128. Dobson, K. S., & Pusch, D. (1995). A test of the depressive realism hypothesis in clinically depressed subjects. *Cognitive Therapy and Research, 19,* 179–194.

129. Duggan, C., Sham, P., Lee, A., Minne, C., & Murray, R. (1995). Neuroticism: A vulnerability marker for depression evidence from a family study. *Journal of Affective Disorders, 35,* 139–143.

130. Dupont, R. M., Jernigan, T. L., Heindel, W., Butters, N., Shafer, K., Wilson, T., Hesselink, J., & Gillin, J. C. (1995). Magnetic resonance imaging and mood disorders: Localization of white matter and other subcortical abnormalities. *Archives of General Psychiatry, 52,* 747–755.

131. Erlemeyer-Kimling, L., Squires-Wheeler, E., Adamo, V. H., Bassett, A. S., Cornblatt, B. A., Kestenbaum, C. J., Rock, D., Roberts, S. A., & Gottesman, I. I. (1995). The New York high-risk project: Psychoses and cluster A personality disorders in offspring of schizophrenic parents at 23 years of follow-up. *Archives of General Psychiatry, 52,* 857–865.

132. Fyer, A. J., Mannuzza, S., Chapman, T. F., Martin, L. Y., & Klein, D. F. (1995). Specificity in familial aggregation of phobic disorders. *Archives of General Psychiatry, 52,* 564–573.

133. Gangoli, R., Brar, J. S., Chengappa, K. N. R., DeLeo, M., Yang, Z. W., Shonn, G., & Rabin, B. S. (1995). Mitogen-stimulated interleukin-z production in never-medicated, first-episode schizophrenic patients. *Archives of General Psychiatry, 52,* 668–672.

134. Geller, B., Sun, K., Zimerman, B., Luby, J., Frazier, J., & Williams, M. (1995). Complex and rapid-cycling in bipolar children and adolescents: A preliminary study. *Journal of Affective Disorders, 34,* 259–268.

135. Goisman, R. M., Warshaw, M. G., Steketee, G. S., Fierman, E. J., Rogers, M. P., Goldenberg, I., Weishenker, N. J., Vasile, R. G., & Keller, M. B. (1995). DSM-IV and the disappearance of agoraphobia without a history of panic disorder: New data on a controversial diagnosis. *American Journal of Psychiatry, 152,* 1438–1443.

136. Goodnick, P. J., Henry, J. H., & Buki, V. M. V. (1995). Treatment of depression in patients with diabetes mellitus. *Journal of Clinical Psychiatry, 56,* 128–136.

137. Gordon, C. T., Cotelingam, G. M., Stager, S., Ludlow, C. L., Hamburger, S. D., & Rapoport, J. L. (1995). A double-blind comparison of clomipramine and desipramine in the treatment of developmental stuttering. *Journal of Clinical Psychiatry, 56,* 238–242.

138. Hayward, C., Taylor, C. B., Blair-Greiner, A., Strachoski, D., Killen, J. D., Wilson, D. M., & Hammer, L. D. (1995). School refusal in young adolescent girls with nonclinical panic attacks. *Journal of Anxiety Disorders, 9,* 329–338.

139. Hedlund, S., & Rude, S. S. (1995). Evidence of latent depressive schemas in formerly depressed individuals. *Journal of Abnormal Psychology, 104,* 517–525.

140. Horwath, E., Wolk, S. I., Goldstein, R. B., Wickramarante, P., Sobin, C., Adams, P., Lish, J. D., & Weissman, M. M. (1995). Is the comorbidity between social phobia and panic disorder due to familial cotransmission or other factors? *Archives of General Psychiatry, 52,* 574–582.

141. Kalsi, G., Mankoo, B. S., Curtis, D., Brynjolfsson, J., Read, T., Sharma, T., Murphy, P., Petursson, H., & Gurling, H. M. D. (1995). Exclusion of linkage of schizophrenia to the gene for the dopamine D2 receptor (DRD2) and chromosome 11q translocation sites. *Psychological Medicine, 25,* 531–537.

142. Koenig, L. J., Ragin, A. B., & Harrow, M. (1995). Accuracy and bias in depressives' judgments for self and other. *Cognitive Therapy and Research, 19,* 505–517.

143. Landre, N. A., & Taylor, M. A. (1995). Formal thought disorder in schizophrenia: Linguistic, attentional, and intellectual correlates. *The Journal of Nervous and Mental Disease, 183,* 673–680.

144. Links, P. S., Hesbegrave, R. J., Mitton, J. E., VanReekum, R., & Patrick, J. (1995). Borderline psychopathology and recurrences of clinical disorders. *The Journal of Nervous and Mental Disease, 183,* 582–586.

145. Maier, W., Minges, J., Lichtermann, D., & Heun, R. (1995). Personality disorders and personality variations in relatives of patients with bipolar affective disorders. *Journal of Affective Disorders, 35,* 173–181.

146. Maj, M., Pirozzi, R., & Magliano, L. (1995). Nonresponse to reinstituted lithium prophylaxis in previously responsive bipolar patients: prevalence and predictors. *American Journal of Psychiatry, 152,* 1810–1811.

147. Mannuzza, S., Schneier, F. R., Chapman, T. F., Liebowitz, M. R., Klien, D. F., & Fyer, A. J. (1995). Generalized social phobia: Reliability and validity. *Archives of General Psychiatry, 52,* 230–237.

148. McDougle, C. J., Barr, L. C., Goodman, W. K., Pelton, G. H., Aronson, S. C., Anand, A., & Price, L. H. (1995). Lack of efficacy of clozapine monotherapy in refractory obsessive-compulsive disorder. *American Journal of Psychiatry, 152,* 1812–1814.

149. Miller, T. W. & Veltkamp, L. J. (1995). Assessment of sexual abuse and trauma: Clinical measures. *Child Psychiatry and Human Development, 26,* 3–10.

150. O'Donnell, B. F., Faux, S. F., McCarley, R. W., Kimble, M. O., Salisbury, D. F., Nestor, P. G., Kikinis, R., Jolesz, F. A., & Shenton, M. E. (1995). Increased rate of P3000 latency prolongation with age in schizophrenia. *Archives of General Psychiatry, 52,* 544–549.

151. Perry, W., Moore, D., & Braff, D. (1995). Gender differences on thought disturbance measures among schizophrenic patients. *American Journal of Psychiatry, 152,* 1298–1301.

152. Rutherford, M. J., Alterman, A. I., Cacciola, J. S., & Snider, E. C. (1995). Gender differences in diagnosing antisocial personality disorder in methadone patients. *American Journal of Psychiatry, 152,* 1309–1316.

153. Schexnayder, L. W., Hirschowitz, J., Sautter, F. J., & Garver, D. L. (1995). Predictors of response to lithium in patients with psychoses. *American Journal of Psychiatry, 152,* 1511–1513.

154. Schuckit, M. A., Klein, J. L., & Twitchell, G. R. (1995). The misclassification of family history status in studies of children of alcoholics. *Journal of Studies on Alcohol, 56,* 47–50.

155. Spencer, T., Biederman, J., Wilens, T., Guite, J., & Harding, M. (1995). ADHD and thyroid abnormalities: A research note. *Journal of Child Psychology and Psychiatry and Allied Disciplines, 36,* 879–885.

156. Swann, A. C. (1995). Mixed or dysphoric manic states: psychopathology and treatment. *Journal of Clinical Psychiatry, 56,* 6–10.

157. White, P. D., Grover, S. A., Kangro, H. O., Thomas, J. M., Amess, J., & Clare, A. W. (1995). The validity and reliability of the fatigue syndrome that follows glandular fever. *Psychological Medicine, 25,* 917–924.

158. White, P. D., Thomas, J. M., Amess, J., Grover, S. A., Kangro, H. O., & Clare, A. W. (1995). The existence of a fatigue syndrome after glandular fever. *Psychological Medicine, 25,* 907–916.

159. Wible, C. G., Shenton, M. E., Hokama, H., Kikinis, R., Jotesz, F. A., Metcalf, D., & McCarley, R. W. (1995). Prefrontal cortex and schizophrenia: A quantitative magnetic resonance imaging study. *Archives of General Psychiatry, 52,* 279–288.

160. Winokur, G., Coryell, W., Endicott, J., Akiskal, H., Keller, M., Maser, J. D., & Warshaw, M. (1995). Familial depression versus depression identified in a control group: Are they the same? *Psychological Medicine, 25,* 797–806.

161. Winokur, G., Coryell, W., Keller, M., Endicott, J., & Leon, A. (1995). A family study of manic-depressive (bipolar I) disease: Is it a distinct illness separable from primary unipolar depression? *Archives of General Psychiatry, 52,* 367–373.

162. Woody, G. E., McLellan, A. T., Luborsky, L., & O'Brien, C. P. (1995). Psychotherapy in community methadone programs: A validation study. *American Journal of Psychiatry, 152,* 1302– 1308.

163. Allen, L. A., Woolfolk, R. L., Gara, M. A., & Apter, J. T. (1996). Possible selves in major depression. *Journal of Nervous and Mental Disease, 184,* 739–745.

164. Bagby, R. M., Schuller, D. R., Levitt, A. J., Joffe, R. T., & Harkness, K. L. (1996). Seasonal and non-seasonal depression and the five-factor model of personality. *Journal of Affective Disorders, 38,* 89–95.

165. Biederman, J., Faraone, S., Milberger, S., Guite, J., Mick, E., Chen, L., Mennin, D., Marrs, A., Quellette, C., Moore, P., Spencer, T., Norman, D., Wilens, T., Kraus, I., & Perrin, J. (1996). A prospective 4-year follow-up study of attention-deficit hyperactivity and related disorders. *Archives of General Psychiatry, 53,* 437–446.

166. Bowden, C. L., Janicak, P. G., Orsulak, P., Swann, A. C., Davis, J. M., Calabrese, J. R., Goodnick, P., Small, J. G., Rush, A. J., Kimmel, S. E., Risch, S. C., & Morris, D. D. (1996). Relation of serum valproate concentration to response in mania. *American Journal of Psychiatry, 153,* 765– 770.

167. Brent, D. A., Bridge, J., Johnson, B. A., & Connolly, J. (1996). Suicidal behavior runs in families: A controlled family study of adolescent suicide victims. *Archives of General Psychiatry, 53,* 1145–1152.

168. Calabrese, J. R., Kimmel, S. E., Woyshville, M. J., Rapport, D. J., Faust, C. J., Thompson, P. A., & Meltzer, H. Y. (1996). Clozapine for treatment-refractory mania. *American Journal of Psychiatry, 153,* 759–764.

169. Castellanos, F. X., Ritchie, G. F., Marsh, W. L., & Rapoport, J. L. (1996). DSM-IV stereotypic movement disorder: Persistance of stereotypies of infancy in intellectually normal adolescents and adults. *Journal of Clinical Psychiatry, 57,* 116–122.

170. Chakos, M. H., Alvir, J. M. J., Woerner, M. G., Koreen, A., Geisler, S., Mayerhoff, D., Sobel, S., Kane, J. M., Borenstein, M., & Lieberman, J. A. (1996). Incidence and correlates of Tardive Dyskinesia in first episode of schizophrenia. *Archives of General Psychiatry, 53,* 313–319.

171. Cooke, R. G., Robb, J. C., Young, L. T., & Joffe, R. T. (1996). Well-being and functioning in patients with bipolar disorder assessed using the MOS 20-Item short form (SF-20). *Journal of Affective Disorders, 39,* 93–97.

172. Coryell, W., Leon, A., Winokur, G., Endicott, J., Keller, M., Akiskal, H., & Solomon, D. (1996). Importance of psychotic features to long-term course in major depressive disorder. *American Journal of Psychiatry, 153,* 483–489.

173. Dew, M. A., Reynolds, C. F., III, Buysse, D. J., Houck, P. R., Hoch, C. C., Monk, T. H., & Kupfer, D. J. (1996). Electroencephalographic sleep profiles during depression: Effects of episode duration and other clinical and psychosocial factors in older adults. *Archives of General Psychiatry, 53,* 148–156.

174. Docherty, N. M., Hawkins, K. A., Hoffman, R. E., Quinlan, D. M., Rakfeldt, J., & Sledge, W. H. (1996). Working memory, attention, and communication disturbances in schizophrenia. *Journal of Abnormal Psychology, 105,* 212–219.

175. Farren, C. K., & Dinan, T. G. (1996). Alcoholism and typology: Findings in an Irish private hospital population. *Journal of Studies on Alcohol, 57,* 249–252.

176. Fils-Aime, M-L., Eckardt, M. J., George, D. T., Brown, G. L., Mefford, I., & Linnoila, M. (1996). Early-onset alcoholics have lower cerebrospinal fluid 5-hydroxindoleacetic acid levels than late-onset alcoholics. *Archives of General Psychiatry, 53,* 211–216.

177. Giancola, P. R., Martin, C. S., Tarter, R. E., Pelham, W. E., & Moss, H. B. (1996). Executive cognitive functioning and aggressive behavior in preadolescent boys at high risk for substance abuse/dependence. *Journal of Studies on Alcohol, 57,* 352–359.

178. Goldenberg, I. M., White, K., Yonkers, K., Reich, J., Warshaw, M. G., Goisman, R. M., & Keller, M. B. (1996). The infrequency of "pure culture" diagnoses among the anxiety disorders. *Journal of Clinical Psychiatry, 57,* 528–533.

179. Hasin, D. S., Tsai, W-Y., Endicott, J., Mueller, t. I., Coryell, W., & Keller, M. (1996). Five-year course of major depression: Effects of comorbid alcoholism. *Journal of Affective Disorders, 41,* 63–70.

180. Kalsi, G., Sherrington, R., Mankoo, B. S., Brynjoffsson, J., Sigmundsson, T., Curtis, D., Read, T., Murphy, P., Butler, R., Petursson, H., & Gurling, H. M. D. (1996). Linkage study of the D5 dopamine receptor gene (DRD5) in multiplex Icelandic and English schizophrenia pedigrees. *American Journal of Psychiatry, 153,* 107–109.

181. Keefe, R. S. E., Frescka, E., Apter, S. H., Davidson, M., Macaluso, J. M., Hirschowitz, J., & Davis, K. L. (1996). Clinical characteristics of Kraepelinian schizophrenia: Replication and extension of previous findings. *American Journal of Psychiatry, 153,* 806–811.

182. Klein, D. N., Lewinsohn, P. M., & Seeley, J. R. (1996). Hypomanic personality traits in a community sample of adolescents. *Journal of Affective Disorders, 38,* 135–143.

183. Kring, A. M., & Neale, J. M. (1996). Do schizophrenic patients show a disjunctive relationship among expressive, experiential, and psychophysiological components of emotion? *Journal of Abnormal Psychology, 105,* 249–257.

184. Kwapil, T. R. (1996). A longitudinal study of drug and alcohol use by psychosis-prone and impulsive-nonconforming individuals. *Journal of Abnormal Psychology, 105,* 114–123.

185. Levitt, A. J., Wesson, V. A., Joffe, R. T., Maunder, R. G., & King, E. F. (1996). A controlled comparison of light box and head-mounted units in the treatment of seasonal depression. *Journal of Clinical Psychiatry, 57,* 105–110.

186. Maj, M., Pirozzi, R., & Magliano, L. (1996). Late non-response to lithium prophylaxis in bipolar patients: Prevalence and predictors. *Journal of Affective Disorders, 39,* 39–42.

187. Manfro, G. G., Otto, M. W., McArdle, E. T., Worthington, J. J., III, Rosenbaum, J. F., & Pollack, M. H. (1996). Relationship of antecedent stressful life events to childhood and family history of anxiety and the course of panic disorder. *Journal of Affective Disorders, 41,* 135–139.

188. McIvor, R. J., Davies, R. A., Wieck, A., Marks, M. N., Brown, N., Campbell, I. C., Checkley, S. A., & Kumar, R. (1996). The growth hormone response to apomorphine at 4 days postpartum in women with a history of major depression. *Journal of Affective Disorders, 40,* 131–136.

189. Mueller, T. I., Goldenberg, J. M., Gordon, A. L., Keller, M. B., & Warshaw, M. G. (1996). Benzodiazepine use in anxiety disordered patients with and without a history of alcoholism. *Journal of Clinical Psychiatry, 57,* 83–89.

190. O'Donnell, B. F., Swearer, J. M., Smith, L. T., Nestor, P. G., Shenton, M. E., & McCarley, R. W. (1996). Selective deficits in visual perception and recognition in schizophrenia. *American Journal of Psychiatry, 153,* 687–692.

191. Raheja, S. K., King, E. A., & Thompson, C. (1996). The seasonal pattern questionnaire for identifying seasonal affective disorders. *Journal of Affective Disorders, 41,* 193–199.

192. Rintelmann, J. W., Emslie, G. J., Rush, A. J., Varghese, T., Gullion, C. M., Kowatch, R. A., & Hughes, C. W. (1996). The effects of extended evaluation on depressive symptoms in children and adolescents. *Journal of Affective Disorders, 41,* 149–156.

193. Rosenbaum, M., Lewinsohn, P. M., & Gotlib, I. H. (1996). Distinguishing between state-dependent and non-state-dependent depression-related psycholosocial variables. *British Journal of Clinical Psychology, 35,* 341–358.

194. Rotheram-Borus, M. J., Walker, J. U., & Ferns, W. (1996). Suicidal behavior among middle-class adolescents who seek crisis services. *Journal of Clinical Psychology, 52,* 137–143.

195. Schuckit, M. A., Tipp, J. E., Anthenelli, R. M., Bucholz, K. K., Hesselbrock, V. M., & Nurnberger, J. I. (1996). Anorexia nervosa and bulimia nervosa in alcohol-dependent men and women and their relatives. *American Journal of Psychiatry, 153,* 74–82.

196. Servan-Schreiber, D., Cohen, J. D., & Steingard, S. (1996). Schizophrenic deficits in the processing of context: A test of a theoretical model. *Archives of General Psychiatry, 53,* 1105–1112.

197. Shaffer, D., Gould, M. S., Fisher, P., Trautman, P., Moreau, D., Kleinman, M., & Flory, M. (1996). Psychiatric diagnosis in child and adolescent suicide. *Archives of General Psychiatry, 53,* 339–348.

198. Sherbourne, C. D., Wells, K. B., & Judd, L. L. (1996). Functioning and well-being of patients with panic disorder. *American Journal of Psychiatry, 153,* 213–218.

199. Smyth, C., Kalsi, G., Brynjolfsson, J., O'Neill, J., Curtis, D., Rifkin, L., Moloney, E., Murphy, P., Sherrington, R., Petursson, H., & Gurling, H. (1996). Further tests for linkage of bipolar affective disorder to the tyrosine hydroxylase gene locus on chromosome 11p15 in a new series of multiplex British affective disorder pedigrees. *American Journal of Psychiatry, 153,* 271–274.

200. Solomon, D. A., Shea, M. T., Leon, A. C., Mueller, T. I., Coryell, W., Maser, J. D., Endicott, J., & Keller, M. B. (1996). Personality traits in subjects with bipolar I disorder in remission. *Journal of Affective Disorders, 40,* 41–48.

201. Strober, M., Freeman, R., Bowen, S., & Riguls, J. (1996). Binge eating in anorexia nervosa predicts later onset of substance use disorder: A ten-year, prospective, longitudinal follow-up of 95 adolescents. *Journal of Youth and Adolescence, 25,* 519–532.

202. Swann, A. C., Bowden, C. L., Morris, D., Calabrese, J. R., Petty, F., Small, J., Dilsaver, S. C. & Davis, J. M. (1996). Depression during mania: Treatment response to lithium or divalproex. *Archives of General Psychiatry, 53,* 37–42.

203. Thaker, G. K., Cassady, S., Adami, H., Moran, M., & Ross, D. E. (1996). Eye movements in spectrum personality disorders: Comparison of community subjects and relatives of schizophrenic patients. *American Journal of Psychiatry, 153,* 362–368.

204. Tulen, J. H. M., Bruijn, J. A., de Man, K. J., van der Velden, E., Pepplinkhuizen, L., & Man in 't Veld, A. J. (1996). Anxiety and autonomic regulation in major depressive disorder: An exploratory study. *Journal of Affective Disorders, 40,* 61–71.

205. Vostanis, P., Feehan, C., Grattan, E., & Bickerton, W-L. (1996). A randomised controlled out-patient trial of cognitive-behavioural treatment for children and adolescents with depression: 9-month follow-up. *Journal of Affective Disorders, 40,* 105–116.

206. Warshaw, M. G., & Keller, M. B. (1996). The relationship between fluoxetine use and suicidal behavior in 654 subjects with anxiety disorders. *Journal of Clinical Psychiatry, 57,* 158–166.

207. Watkins, P. C., Vache, K., Verney, S. P., Muller, S., & Mathews, A. (1996). Unconscious mood-congruent memory bias in depression. *Journal of Abnormal Psychology, 105,* 34–41.

208. Wisner, K. L., Peindl, K. S., & Hanusa, B. H. (1996). Effects of child bearing on the natural history of panic disorder with comorbid mood disorder. *Journal of Affective Disorders, 41* 173–180.

209. Young, L. T., Li, P. P., Kamble, A., Siu, K. P., & Warsh, J. J. (1996). Lack of effect of antidepressants on mononuclear leukocyte G-protein levels or function in depressed outpatients. *Journal of Affective Disorders, 39,* 201–207.

210. Young, M. A., Fogg, L. F., Scheftner, W., Fawcett, J., Akiskal, H., & Maser, J. (1996). Stable trait components of hopelessness: Baseline and sensitivity to depression. *Journal of Abnormal Psychology, 105,* 155–165.

211. Agosti, V., & Ocepek-Welikson, K. (1997). The efficacy of imipramine and psychotherapy in early-onset chronic depression: A reanalysis of the National Institute of Mental Health treatment of depression collaborative research program. *Journal of Affective Disorders, 43,* 181–186.

212. Alda, M., Grof, E., Cavazzoni, P., Duffy, A., Martin, R., Ravindran, L., & Grof, P. (1997). Autosomal recessive inheritance of affective disorders in families of responders to lithium prophylaxis? *Journal of Affective Disorders, 44,* 153–157.

213. Bagby, R. M., Kennedy, S. H., Schuller, D. R., Dickens, S. E., Minifie, C. E., Levitt, A., & Joffe, R. (1997). Differential pharmacological treatment response in high angry hostile and low angry hostile depressed patients: A retrospective analysis. *Journal of Affective Disorders, 45,* 161–166.

214. Bennett, D. S., Ambrosini, P. J., Bianchi, M., Barnett, D., Metz, C., & Rabinovich, H. (1997). Relationship of Beck Depression Inventory factors to depression among adolescents. *Journal of Affective Disorders, 45,* 127–134.

215. Biederman, J., Faranoe, S. V., Hatch, M., Mennin, D., Taylor, A., & George, P. (1997). Conduct disorder with and without mania in a referred sample of ADHD children. *Journal of Affective Disorders, 44,* 177–188.

216. Birmaher, B., Kaufman, J., Brent, D. A., Dahl, R. E., Perel, J. M., Al-Shabbout, M., Nelson, B., Stull, S., Rao, U., Waterman, G. S., Williamson, D. E. & Ryan, N. D. (1997). Neuroendocrine response to 5-hydroxy-L-tryptophan in prepubertal children at high risk of major depressive disorder. *Archives of General Psychiatry, 54,* 1113–1119.

217. Blacker, C. V. R., Thomas, T. M., & Thompson, C. (1997). Seasonality prevalence and incidence of depressive disorder in a general practice sample: Identifying differences in thinking by caseness. *Journal of Affective Disorders, 43,* 41–52.

218. Cohen, Y., Spirito, A., Apter, A., & Saini, S. (1997). A cross-cultural comparison of behaviior disturbance and suicidal behavior among psychiatrically hospitalized adolescents in Israel and the United States. *Child Psychiatry and Human Development, 28,* 89–102.

219. Coryell, W. (1997). Do psychotic, minor and intermittent depressive disorders exist on a continuum? *Journal of Affective Disorders, 45,* 75–83.

220. Erlenmeyer-Kimling, L., Adamo, U. H., Rock, D., Roberts, S. A., Bassett, A. S., Squires-Wheeler, E., Cornblatt, B. A., Endicott, J., Pape, S., & Gottesman, I. I. (1997). The New York high-risk project: Prevalence and comorbidity of Axis I disorders in offspring of schizophrenic parents at 25-year follow-up. *Archives of General Psychiatry, 54,* 1096–1102.

221. Faraone, F. V., Biederman, J., & Mick, E. (1997). Symptom reports by adults with attention deficit hyperactivity disorder: Are they influenced by attention deficit hyperactivity disorder in their children? *Journal of Nervous and Mental Disease, 185,* 583–584.

222. Filipek, P. A., Semrud-Clikeman, M., Steingard, R. J., Renshaw, P. F., Kennedy, D. N., & Biederman, J. (1997). Volumetric MRI analysis comparing subjects having attention-deficit hyperactivity disorder with normal controls. *Neurology, 48,* 589–601.

223. Goldstein, R. B., Wickramaratne, P. J., Horwath, E., & Weissman, M. M. (1997). Familial aggregation and phenomenology of "early"-onset (at or before age 20 years) panic disorder. *Archives of General Psychiatry, 54,* 271–278.

224. Harrington, R., Rutter, M., Weissman, m., Fudge, H., Groothues, C., Bredenkamp, D., Pickles, A., Rende, R., & Wickramaratne, P. (1997). Psychiatric disorders in the relatives of depressed probands I. Comparison of prepubertal, adolescent and early adult onset cases. *Journal of Affective Disorders, 42,* 9–22.

225. Keefe, R. S. E., Silverman, J. M., Mohs, R. C., Siever, L. J., Harvey, P. D., Friedman, L., Roitman, S. E. L., DuPre, R. L., Smith, C. J., Schmeidler, J., & Davis, K. L. (1997). Eye tracking, attention, and schizotypal symptoms in nonpsychotic relatives of patients with schizophrenia. *Archives of General Psychiatry, 54,* 169–176.

226. Kentros, M., Smith, T. E., Hull, J., McKee, M., Terkelsen, K., & Capalbo, C. (1997). Stability of personality traits in schizophrenia and schizoaffective disorder: A pilot project. *Journal of Nervous and Mental Disease, 185,* 549–555.

227. Klein, D. N., Lewinsohn, P. M., & Seeley, J. R. (1997). Psychosocial characteristics of adolescents with a past history of dysthymic disorder: Comparison with adolescents with past histories of major depressive and non-affective disorders and never mentally ill controls. *Journal of Affective Disorders, 42,* 127–135.

228. Max, J. E., Lindgren, S. D., Robin, D. A., Smith, W. L., Jr., Sato, Y., Matheis, P. J., Castillo, C. S., & Stierwalt, J. A. G. (1997). Traumatic brain injury in children and adolescents: psychiatric disorders in the second three months. *Journal of Nervous and Mental Disease, 185,* 394–401.

229. Miner, C. R. Rosenthal, R. N., Hellerstein, D. J., & Muenz, L. R. (1997). Prediction of compliance with outpatient referral in patients with schizophrenia and psychoactive substance use disorders. *Archives of General Psychiatry, 54,* 706–712.

230. Orvaschel, H., Beeferman, D., & Kabacoff, R. (1997). Depression, self-esteem, sex, and age in a child and adolescent clinical sample. *Journal of Clinical Child Psychology, 26,* 285–289.

231. Perrin, S., & Last, C. G. (1997). Worrisome thoughts in children clinically referred for anxiety disorder. *Journal of Clinical Child Psychology, 26,* 181–189.

232. Rapoport, J. L., Giedd, J., Kumra, S., Jacobsen, L., Smith, A., Lee, P., Nelson, J., & Hamburger, S. (1997). Childhood-onset schizophrenia: Progressive ventricular change during adolescence. *Archives of General Psychiatry, 54,* 897–903.

233. Riso, L. P., Thase, m. E., Howland, R. H., Friedman, E. S., Simons, A. D., & Tu, X. M. (1997). A prospective test of criteria for response, remission, relapse, recovery, and recurrence in depressed patients treated with cognitive behavior therapy. *Journal of Affective Disorders, 43,* 131–142.

234. Robin, R. W., Chester, B., Rasmussen, J. K., Jaranson, J. M., & Goldman, D. (1997). Prevalence, characteristics, and impact of childhood sexual abuse in a southwestern American Indian tribe. *Child Abuse & Neglect, 21,* 769–787.

235. Silverstein, M. L., Harrow, M., Mavroleft-Eros, G. & Close, D. (1997). Neuropsychological dysfunction and clinical outcome in psychiatric disorders: A two-year follow-up study. *Journal of Nervous and Mental Disease, 185,* 722–729.

236. Simpson, H. B., Nee, J. C., & Endicott, J. (1997). First-episode major depression: Few sex differences in course. *Archives of General Psychiatry, 54,* 633–639.

237. Steinhauer, S. R., Locke, J., & Hill, S. Y. (1997). Vigilance and iconic memory in children at high risk for alcoholism. *Journal of Studies on Alcohol, 58,* 428–434.

238. Vieta, E., Benabarre, A., Colom, F., Gastó, C. Nieto, E., Otero, A., & Vallejo, J. (1997). Suicidal behavior in bipolar I and bipolar II disorder. *Journal of Nervous and Mental Disease, 185,* 407–409.

239. Warshaw, M. G., Massion, A. O., Shea, M. T., Allsworth, J., & Keller, M. B. (1997). Predictors of remission in patients with panic with and without agoraphobia: Prospective 5-year follow-up data. *Journal of Nervous and Mental Disease, 185,* 517–519.

240. Wilens, T. E., Biederman, J., Mick, E., Faraone, S. V., & Spencer, T. (1997). Attention Deficit Hyperactivity Disorder (ADHD) is associated with early onset substance use disorders. *Journal of Nervous and Mental Disease, 185,* 475–482.

241. Yoshida, K., Marks, M. N., Kibe, N., Kumar, R., Wakano, H., & Tashiro, N. (1997). Postnatal depression in Japanese women who have given birth in England. *Journal of Affective Disorders, 43,* 69–77.

242. Zahn, T. P., Jacobsen, L. K., Gordon, C. T., McKenna, K., Frazier, J. A., & Rapoport, J. L. (1997). Autonomic nervous system markers of psychopathology in childhood-onset schizophrenia. *Archives of General Psychiatry, 54,* 904–912.

243. Ghaziuddin, M., Weidmer-Mikhail, E., & Ghaziuddin, N. (1998). Comorbidity of Asperger syndrome: A preliminary report. *Journal of Disability Research, 42,* 279–283.

244. Giancola, P. R., Mezzich, A. C., & Tarter, R. E. (1998). Disruptive, delinquent and aggressive behavior in female adolescents with a psychoactive substance use disorder: Relation to executive cognitive functioning. *Journal of Studies on Alcohol, 59,* 560–567.

245. Kaufman, J., Birmaher, B., Brent, D., Dahl, R., Bridge, J., & Ryan, N. D. (1998). Psychopathology in the relatives of depressed-abused children. *Child Abuse & Neglect, 22,* 171–181.

246. Pfeffer, C. R. Normandin, L., & Kakuma, T. (1998). Suicidal children grow up: Relations between family psychopathology and adolescents' lifetime suicidal behavior. *Journal of Nervous and Mental Disease, 186,* 269–275.

247. Ring, A., Stein, D., Barak, Y., Teicher, A., Hadjez, J., Elizur, A., & Weizman, A. (1998). Sleep disturbances in children with attention-deficit/hyperactivity disorder: A comparative study with healthy siblings. *Journal of Learning Disabilities, 31,* 572–578.

248. Tamplin, A., Goodyer, I. M., & Herbert, J. (1998). Family functioning and parent general health in families of adolescents with major depressive disorder. *Journal of Affective Disorders, 48,* 1–13.

[2306]

Schedule for Nonadaptive and Adaptive Personality.

Purpose: "Designed to assess trait dimensions in the domain of personality disorders."

Population: Ages 18 and older.

Publication Date: 1993.

Acronym: SNAP.

Scores: 34 scales: Trait (Mistrust, Manipulativeness, Aggression, Self-Harm, Eccentric Perceptions, Dependency, Exhibitionism, Entitlement, Detachment, Impulsivity, Propriety, Workaholism), Temperament (Negative Temperament, Positive Temperament, Disinhibition), Diagnostic (Paranoid, Schizoid, Schizotypal, Antisocial, Borderline, Histrionic, Narcissistic,

Avoidant, Dependent, Obsessive-Compulsive, Passive-Aggressive, Sadistic, Self-Defeating), Validity (Variable Response Inconsistency, True Response Inconsistency, Desirable Response Inconsistency, Deviance, Rare Virtues, Invalidity Index).
Administration: Individual or group.
Price Data, 1993: $50 per starter kit including test booklet, answer sheet, set of scoring keys, and manual for administration, scoring, and interpretation (92 pages); $10 per 10 test booklets; $15 per 100 answer sheets; $25 per set of 34 scoring keys; $15 per manual for administration, scoring, and interpretation; price data for scoring disks available from publisher.
Time: Administration time not reported.
Author: Lee Anna Clark.
Publisher: University of Minnesota Press.
Cross References: See T4:2341 (1 reference).

TEST REFERENCE

1. Gibbs, N. A., & Oltmanns, T. F. (1995). The relation between obsessive-compulsive personality traits and subtypes of compulsive behavior. *Journal of Anxiety Disorders, 9,* 397–410.

[2307]

A Schedule of Adaptive Mechanisms in CAT Response.

Purpose: "Designed to aid in qualitative evaluation of C.A.T. stories."
Population: Children.
Publication Date: [ca. 1963].
Scores: 12 categories: Defense Mechanisms (Reaction-Formation, Undoing and Ambivalence, Isolation, Repression and Denial, Deception, Symbolization, Projection and Introjection, Fear and Anxiety, Regression, Controls Weak or Absent), Identification (Adequate/Same-Sex, Confused/or Opposite Sex).
Administration: Individual.
Manual: No manual.
Price Data, 1998: $9.50 per 30 forms.
Time: Administration time not reported.
Comments: See Children's Apperception Test (466).
Author: Mary Haworth.
Publisher: C.P.S., Inc.

[2308]

The Schedule of Growing Skills: Second Edition.

Purpose: Designed as an assessment of child development.
Population: Ages 0–5 years.
Publication Dates: 1987–1996.
Acronym: SGS II.
Scores, 9: Passive Posture, Active Posture, Locomotor, Manipulative, Visual, Hearing and Language, Speech and Language, Interactive Social, Self-Care Social.
Administration: Individual.
Price Data, 1998: £120 per starter set including 10 child records, 50 profiles, user's guide ('96, 109 pages), and all stimulus materials; £40 per conversion kit including user's guide, picture book, shape formboard, fish formboard, pegboard and pegs, STYCAR distant vision card B and key card, pom pom, and baby rattle; £65 per 10 record forms; £40 per 50 profiles; £30 per reference manual.
Time: (20) minutes.
Authors: Martin Bellman, Sundara Lingam, and Anne Aukett.
Publisher: NFER-Nelson Publishing Co., Ltd. [England].
Cross References: For reviews by Michelle M. Creighton and Scott R. McConnell and by Donna Spiker of an earlier edition, see 11:342.

TEST REFERENCE

1. Clegg, J. A., Standen, P. J., & Jones, G. (1996). Striking the balance: A grounded theory analysis of staff perspectives. *British Journal of Clinical Psychology, 35,* 249–264.

[2309]

Scholastic Abilities Test for Adults.

Purpose: "Designed to be a general measure of scholastic accomplishment."
Population: Ages 16 through 70.
Publication Date: 1991.
Acronym: SATA.
Scores: 9 subtest scores: Verbal Reasoning, Nonverbal Reasoning, Quantitative Reasoning, Reading Vocabulary, Reading Comprehension, Math Calculation, Math Application, Writing Mechanics, Writing Composition, and 9 composite scores: Scholastic Abilities, General Aptitude, Total Achievement, Verbal, Quantitative, Reading, Mathematics, Writing, Achievement Screener.
Administration: Group.
Price Data, 1999: $154 per complete kit including 10 test books, 25 response booklets, 25 profile/examiner record forms, and manual (102 pages); $51 per 10 test books; $39 per 25 response booklets; $24 per 25 profile/examiner record forms; $244 per manual.
Time: (60-120) minutes.
Authors: Brian R. Bryant, James R. Patton, and Caroline Dunn.
Publisher: PRO-ED.
Cross References: For reviews by Nambury S. Rau and Douglas K. Smith, see 12:344.

TEST REFERENCES

1. Dunn, C. (1995). A comparison of three groups of academically at-risk college students. *Journal of College Student Development, 36,* 270–279.
2. Schiefele, V. (1996). Topic interest, test representation, and quality of experience. *Contemporary Educational Psychology, 21,* 3–18.

[2310]

School-Age Care Environment Rating Scale.

Purpose: Designed to assess the quality of center-based child care for school-aged children.

Population: Child care programs.
Publication Dates: 1980–1996.
Acronym: SECERS.
Scores, 7: Space and Furnishings, Health and Safety, Activities, Interactions, Program Structure, Staff Development, Total.
Administration: Group.
Price Data, 1998: $10.95 per test booklet/manual ('96, 44 pages).
Time: (120) minutes.
Comments: An adaptation of the Early Childhood Environment Rating Scale (9:365); for use with center-based care (not family child care homes); respondents cue evaluators of the child-care environment; "Also includes a set of 6 supplementary items for centers that include children with special needs."
Authors: Thelma Harms, Ellen Vineberg Jacobs, and Donna Romano White.
Publisher: Teachers College Press.

[2311]

School Archival Records Search.

Purpose: ""Designed to overlay existing school records so that they can be coded and quantified systematically."
Population: Grades 1–12.
Publication Date: 1991.
Acronym: SARS.
Scores: 11 archival variables: Demographics, Attendance, Achievement Test Information, School Failure, Disciplinary Contacts, Within-School Referrals, Certification for Special Education, Placement Out of Regular Classroom, Receiving Chapter I Services, Out-of-School Referrals, Negative Narrative Comments.
Administration: Group.
Price Data, 1993: $35 per complete kit including user's guide, technical manual (86 pages), and 50 instrument packets.
Time: Administration time varies.
Authors: Hill M. Walker, Alice Block-Pedego, Bonnie Todis, and Herbert H. Severson.
Publisher: Sopris West.
Cross References: For reviews by John Crawford and Robert Fitzpatrick, see 13:275 (1 reference).

[2312]

School Assessment Survey.

Purpose: "Designed to measure schoolwide characteristics."
Population: Elementary through senior high school teachers and administrators.
Publication Date: 1985.
Acronym: SAS.
Scores, 9: Goal Consensus, Facilitative Leadership, Centralization of Influence: Classroom Instruction, Centralization of Influence: Curriculum and Resources, Vertical Communication, Horizontal Communication, Staff Conflict, Student Discipline, Teaching Behavior.
Administration: Group.
Price Data, 1998: $9.99 per kit including manual (69 pages).
Time: [30-40] minutes.
Authors: Bruce L. Wilson and William A. Firestone.
Publisher: Research for Better Schools, Inc.
Cross References: For reviews by LeAnn M. Gamache and Dean Nafziger and Joanne L. Jensen, see 12:345 (1 reference); see also T4:2355 (1 reference).

TEST REFERENCE

1. Olenchak, F. R. (1995). Effects of enrichment on gifted/learning-disabled students. *Journal for the Education of the Gifted, 18,* 385–399.

[2313]

School Attitude Measure, Second Edition.

Purpose: "To evaluate students' views of their academic environment and of themselves as competent students."
Population: Grades 1-2, 3-4, 5-6, 7-8, 9-12.
Publication Date: 1989.
Acronym: SAM.
Scores: 5 scales: Motivation for Schooling, Academic Self-Concept—Performance Based, Academic Self-Concept—Reference Based, Student's Sense of Control over Performance, Student's Instructional Mastery.
Administration: Group.
Levels, 6: C/D, E2, E/F, G/H, I/J, K/L.
Price Data, 1999: $55 per 25 machine-scorable booklets; $43 per 25 reusable booklets; $18.30 per 35 answer sheets; $43.50 per 100 answer sheets; $4.50 per directions for administration; $17 per Technical Manual ('90, 55 pages); $25 per norms booklet; $29.75 per grades 1-8 test review kit; $9 per high school level test review kit.
Foreign Language Editions: Spanish edition available.
Time: (30-40) minutes.
Comments: Level E is a machine-scorable version of Level E/F.
Authors: Lawrence J. Dolan and Marci Morrow Enos.
Publisher: ACT, Inc.
Cross References: See T4:2357 (1 reference); for a review by Dan Wright, see 11:344 (2 references).

TEST REFERENCES

1. Hess, R. S., & D'Amato, R. C. (1996). High school completion among Mexican-American children: Individual and family background variables. *School Psychology Quarterly, 11,* 353–368.
2. Dev, P. C. (1998). Intrinsic motivation and the student with learning disabilities. *Journal of Research and Development in Education, 31,* 98–108.

[2314]

School Effectiveness Questionnaire.

Purpose: Assesses variables that have an impact on school effectiveness.

Population: Students, teachers, parents.
Publication Date: 1993.
Acronym: SEQ.
Scores, 11: Effective Instructional Leadership, Clear and Focused Mission, Safe and Orderly Environment, Positive School Climate, High Expectations, Frequent Assessment/Monitoring of Student Achievement, Emphasis on Basic Skills, Maximum Opportunities for Learning, Parent/Community Involvement, Strong Professional Development, Teacher Involvement in Decision Making.
Administration: Group.
Forms, 4: Level 1 Students (Elementary), Level 2 Students (High School), Teachers, Parents.
Price Data, 1999: $11.25 per 10 reusable questionnaires (Teacher Form); $27.75 per 10 reusable questionnaires (Level 1, Level 2, Parent Forms); $15 per manual (45 pages); $71.25 per 100 Type 2 machine-scorable answer documents; $19.75 per examination kit including manual, one each of all four questionnaires, and one answer document.
Time: (15–20) minutes.
Comments: Optional data analysis software available from publisher.
Authors: Lee Baldwin, Freeman Coney III, Diane Färdig, and Roberta Thomas.
Publisher: The Psychological Corporation.
Cross References: For reviews by Robert Fitzpatrick and Michael Harwell, see 13:276.

[2315]

School Environment Preference Survey.

Purpose: "Designed to measure the student's commitment to the set of attitudes, values and behaviors that have been characteristically fostered and rewarded in traditional school environments."
Population: Grades 4-12.
Publication Date: 1978.
Acronym: SEPS.
Scores, 5: Self-Subordination, Traditionalism, Rule Conformity, Uncriticalness, Structured Role Orientation.
Administration: Group.
Price Data, 1998: $9 per 25 SEPS forms (machine form for hand scoring or computer processing by EdITS) [$35.75 per 100, $143.75 per 500]; $14.75 per hand-scoring keys; $4 per manual (17 pages); $7.50 per specimen set.
Time: (10-15) minutes.
Author: Leonard V. Gordon.
Publisher: EdITS/Educational and Industrial Testing Service.
Cross References: See T4:2360 (1 reference); for a review by Joan Silverstein, see 10:324.

TEST REFERENCE

1. Austin, J. S., & Martin, N. K. (1992). College-bound students: Are we meeting their needs? *Adolescence, 27,* 115-121.

[2316]

School Function Assessment.

Purpose: Designed to "measure a student's performance of functional tasks that support his or her participation in the academic and social aspects of an elementary school program."
Population: Grades K–6.
Publication Date: 1998.
Acronym: SFA.
Scores, 26: Participation, Task Supports (Physical Tasks Assistance, Physical Tasks Adaptations, Cognitive/Behavioral Tasks Assistance, Cognitive/Behavioral Tasks Adaptations), Activity Performance (Travel, Maintaining and Changing Positions, Recreational Movement, Manipulation with Movement, Using Materials, Setup and Cleanup, Eating and Drinking, Hygiene, Clothing Management, Up/Down Stairs, Written Work, Computer and Equipment Use, Functional Communication, Memory and Understanding, Following Social Conventions, Compliance with Adult Directives and School Rules, Task Behavior/Completion, Positive Interaction, Behavior Regulation, Personal Care Awareness, and Safety).
Administration: Individual.
Price Data, 1999: $134 per complete kit including 25 record forms with 3 rating scale guides and user's manual (136 pages); $51.50 per 25 record forms with 3 rating scale guides.
Time: Administration time not reported.
Comments: Ratings to be completed by an educational and therapeutic professional who is familiar with the child's typical performance.
Author: Wendy Coster, Theresa Deeney, Jane Haltiwanger, and Stephen Haley.
Publisher: Therapy Skills Builders—A Division of The Psychological Corporation.

[2317]

School Leaders Licensure Assessment.

Purpose: To provide an assessment for states to use as part of the licensure process for school principals.
Population: Prospective school principals.
Publication Date: 1998.
Scores: Total score only.
Administration: Group.
Restricted Distribution: Secure instruments administered three time annually at centers established by the publisher.
Price Data, 1999: $400 examination fee.
Time: 360 minutes in three 120-minute modules.
Comments: State department of education for a particular state should be consulted to determine whether the School Leaders Licensure Assessment is required.

Author: Educational Testing Service.
Publisher: Educational Testing Service.

[2318]

The School Motivation Analysis Test.

Purpose: Designed to assess motivation and interest.
Population: Ages 12-17.
Publication Dates: 1961-1976.
Acronym: SMAT.
Scores, 45: 4 motivation scores (Unintegrated, Integrated, Total, Difference [Conflict]) for each of 6 drives (Assertiveness, Mating, Fear, Narcism, Pugnacity-Sadism, Protectiveness) and each of 4 sentiments (Self-Sentiment, Superego, School, Home) plus 5 derived scores (Total Autism-Optimism, General Information-Intelligence, Total Integration, Total Personal Interest, Total Conflict).
Administration: Group.
Price Data, 1999: $20.50 per 10 reusable test booklets; $18 per 3 scoring keys; $12.75 per 25 answer sheets; $22.25 per 25 profile sheets; $15 per administration manual ('76, 38 pages); $17.25 per specimen set including test booklet, manual, answer sheet, and profile sheet.
Foreign Language Edition: Castillian Spanish edition available from TEA Ediciones (Madrid, Spain).
Time: (50-60) minutes.
Comments: Downward extension of the Motivation Analysis Test (1721).
Authors: Arthur B. Sweney, Raymond B. Cattell, and Samuel E. Krug.
Publisher: Institute for Personality and Ability Testing, Inc.
Cross References: See T4:2362 (3 references) and T3:2087 (2 references); for reviews by Jacob Cohen and Paul McReynolds, see 8:668 (11 references); see also T2:1367 (2 references) and 7:135 (10 references).

TEST REFERENCE

1. Boyle, G. J., & Houndoulesi, V. (1993). Utility of the School Motivation Analysis Test in predicting second language acquisition. *British Journal of Educational Psychology, 63,* 500–512.

[2319]

School-Readiness Evaluation by Trained Teachers.

Purpose: To screen all school entrants to identify different levels of school-readiness.
Population: South African school beginners.
Publication Date: 1984.
Acronym: SETT.
Scores, 9: Language and General Development (Basic Level, Potential Level, Total), Physical Motor Development (Motor Ability, Integration, Total), Emotional Social Development (Sociability, Emotionality, Total).
Administration: Individual.
Price Data: Available from publisher.
Time: (30) minutes.
Comments: Parent Questionnaire for the Evaluation of School-Readiness and Nursery-School Questionnaire for the Evaluation of School-Readiness may be used in conjunction with this test.
Author: Marianne Joubert.
Publisher: Human Sciences Research Council [South Africa].

[2320]

School Readiness Test.

Purpose: Designed to test the student's readiness for first grade academics.
Population: End of Kindergarten through first 3 weeks of Grade 1.
Publication Dates: 1974-1990.
Acronym: SRT.
Scores, 9: Vocabulary, Identifying Letters, Visual Discrimination, Auditory Discrimination, Comprehension and Interpretation, Number Knowledge, Handwriting Ability, Developmental Spelling Ability, Total.
Administration: Group.
Price Data, 1993: $41.60 per 35 test booklets, scoring key, class record sheet, and manual ('90, 26 pages); $4.15 per scoring key; $9.95 per manual; $2.15 per class record sheet; $20 per specimen set.
Time: (90) minutes.
Comments: Subtest scores convert to "OK," "Probably Needs Help," "Definitely Needs Help"; total score converts to "Gifted Ready," "Superior Ready," "Average Ready," "Marginal," "Short Delay," "Long Delay."
Authors: O. F. Anderhalter and Jan Perney.
Publisher: Scholastic Testing Service, Inc.
Cross References: For reviews by Esther Stavrou Toubanos and Larry Weber, see 12:346; for a review of an earlier edition by Thorsten R. Carlson, see 8:808.

[2321]

School Situation Survey.

Purpose: Designed to measure "school-related student stress."
Population: Grades 4-12.
Publication Date: 1989.
Acronym: SSS.
Scores, 7: Sources of Stress (Teacher Interactions, Academic Stress, Peer Interactions, Academic Self-Concept), Manifestations of Stress (Emotional, Behavioral, Physiological).
Administration: Group.
Price Data, 1999: $25 per sampler set containing each test component: $125 per permission set including sampler set along with agreement that allows purchaser

to reproduce up to 200 copies of the instrument in one year; $25 per 25 test booklets; $10 per scoring key.
Time: (10-15) minutes.
Authors: Barbara J. Helms and Robert K. Gable.
Publisher: Mind Garden, Inc.
Cross References: For reviews by Theodore Coladarci and LeAdelle Phelps, see 12:347; see also T4:2368 (1 reference).

[2322]

School Social Behavior Scales.

Purpose: Provides rating of both social skills and antisocial problem behaviors.
Population: Grades K–12.
Publication Date: 1993.
Acronym: SSBS.
Scores, 8: Social Competence (Interpersonal Skills, Self-Management Skills, Academic Skills, Total), Antisocial Behavior (Hostile-Irritable, Antisocial-Aggressive, Disruptive-Demanding, Total).
Administration: Individual.
Price Data, 1999: $42 per complete kit; $25 per manual (38 pages); $19 per 20 test booklets.
Time: (5–10) minutes.
Author: Kenneth W. Merrell.
Publisher: PRO-ED.
Cross References: For reviews by Stephen R. Hooper and Lesley A. Welsh, see 13:277 (2 references); see also T4:2369 (1 reference).

[2323]

School Social Skills Rating Scale.

Purpose: Developed to assess social skills exhibited in a school setting.
Population: Elementary school and junior high school and high school.
Publication Date: 1984.
Acronym: S3 Rating Scale.
Scores: Ratings in 4 categories: Adult Relations, Peer Relations, School Rules, Classroom Behaviors.
Administration: Individual.
Price Data, 1992: $40 per complete kit including manual (25 pages); $22 per 50 rating scales.
Time: (10) minutes.
Comments: Ratings by teachers.
Authors: Laura J. Brown, Donald D. Black, and John C. Downs.
Publisher: Slosson Educational Publications, Inc.
Cross References: For reviews by Beth D. Bader and William K. Wilkinson, see 12:348; see also T4:2370 (1 reference).

[2324]

Schubert General Ability Battery.

Purpose: Developed as a test of an individual's ability to understand and think in terms of words, numbers, and ideas.
Population: Grades 12-16 and adults.
Publication Dates: 1946-1965.
Acronym: SGAB.
Scores, 5: Vocabulary, Analogies, Arithmetic Problems, Syllogisms, Total.
Administration: Group.
Price Data, 1988: $37 per complete kit including 25 tests and manual ('65, 24 pages); $16 per 25 tests.
Time: 16(25) or 32(40) minutes.
Authors: Herman J. P. Schubert and Daniel S. P. Schubert (test).
Publisher: Slosson Educational Publications, Inc.
Cross References: See 7:386 (1 reference); for a review by William B. Schrader, see 5:382.

[2325]

Scientific Orientation Test.

Purpose: "Designed to measure a range of affective outcomes for students of science or science-related subjects."
Population: Students in school years 5 to 12.
Publication Date: 1995.
Acronym: S.OR.T.
Scores, 4: Interest in Science, Scientific Attitude, Attitude to School Science, Total.
Administration: Group or individual.
Price Data, 1995: $120 per complete kit including manual (153 pages), 10 test booklets, and 10 response folios; $25 per 10 test booklets; $25 per 10 response folios; $75 per manual.
Time: (40) minutes.
Comments: Includes 5 subtests yielding 13 subscores; formerly titled A Test of Interests.
Author: G. Rex Meyer.
Publisher: GRM Educational Consultancy [Australia].

[2326]

SCL—90—Analogue.

Purpose: A brief rating scale "for collecting observer data on a patient's psychological symptomatic distress."
Population: Adults and adolescents.
Publication Date: 1976.
Scores, 10: Primary Dimensional Scales (Somatization, Obsessive Compulsive, Interpersonal Sensitivity, Depression, Anxiety, Hostility, Phobic Anxiety, Paranoid Ideation, Psychoticism), Global Psychopathology Scale.
Administration: Group.
Price Data, 1994: $30 per 100 forms.
Time: (1–3) minutes.
Comments: Designed for use by health professionals without in-depth training or knowledge of psychopathology.

Author: Leonard R. Derogatis.
Publisher: NCS (Minnetonka).

TEST REFERENCES

1. Simons, R. L., Beaman, J., Conger, R. D., & Chao, W. (1993). Stress, support, and antisocial behavior trait as determinants of emotional well-being and parenting practices among single mothers. *Journal of Marriage and the Family, 55,* 385–398.
2. Winston, A., Laikin, M., Pollack, J., Samstag, L. W., McCullough, L., & Muran, C. (1994). Short-term psychotherapy of personality disorders. *American Journal of Psychiatry, 151,* 190-194.
3. Bunce, D. (1997). What factors are associated with the outcome of individual-focused worksite stress management interventions? *Journal of Occupational and Organizational Psychology, 70,* 1–17.

[2327]
Scorable Self-Care Evaluation (Revised).

Purpose: To assess clients' motivation and performance of self-care tasks and identify problems in basic living skills.
Population: Adolescent and adult occupational therapy clients.
Publication Date: 1993.
Acronym: SSCE.
Scores, 23: Subtasks divided among 4 subscales: Personal Care (Initial Appearance, Orientation, Hygiene, Communications, First Aid, Total), Housekeeping (Foods Selection, House Chores, Safety, Laundry, Total), Work and Leisure (Leisure Activity, Transportation, Job-Seeking Skills, Total), Financial Management (Making Change, Checking, Paying Personal Bills, Budgeting, Procurement of Supplemental Income, Source of Income, Total), Total Score.
Administration: Individual.
Price Data, 1999: $36 per manual (90 pages).
Time: (40–50) minutes.
Comments: Administrator must provide pencils, map of the local area, 16 3-inch cards, telephone book with yellow pages, and play money.
Authors: E. Nelson Clark and Mary Peters.
Publisher: Therapy Skill Builders—A Division of The Psychological Corporation.

[2328]
Screening Assessment for Gifted Elementary Students.

Purpose: "To obtain information that is helpful in identifying children for gifted classes that emphasize aptitude, achievement, and/or creativity."
Population: Ages 7-0 to 12-11.
Publication Date: 1987.
Acronym: SAGES.
Scores, 4: Reasoning, School-Acquired Information, Divergent Production, SAGES Quotient.
Administration: Individual in part.
Price Data, 1999: $119 per complete kit including examiner's manual (61 pages), picture book, and 50 profile and response sheets; $24 per 50 profile and response sheets; $59 per picture book; $39 per examiner's manual.
Time: (30-50) minutes.
Authors: Susan K. Johnsen and Anne L. Corn.
Publisher: PRO-ED.
Cross References: For a review by E. Scott Huebner, see 10:327.

TEST REFERENCE

1. Tallent-Runnells, M. K., & Martin, M. R. (1992). Identifying Hispanic gifted children using the Screening Assessment for Gifted Elementary Students. *Psychological Reports, 70,* 939-942.

[2329]
Screening Assessment for Gifted Elementary Students–Primary.

Purpose: Assesses a child's aptitude and achievement level in order to identify academically gifted students.
Population: Ages 5-0 to 8-11.
Publication Date: 1992.
Acronym: SAGES-P.
Scores, 3: General Information, Reasoning, Total.
Administration: Group or individual.
Price Data, 1999: $104 per complete kit including examiner's manual (40 pages), 25 student response booklets, and 25 profile and summary sheets; $44 per examiner's manual; $49 per 25 student response booklets; $14 per 25 profile and summary sheets.
Time: (30-45) minutes.
Authors: Susan K. Johnsen and Anne L. Corn.
Publisher: PRO-ED.
Cross References: For reviews by Lewis R. Aiken and Susana Urbina, see 12:349.

[2330]
Screening Form for District Manager Selection.

Purpose: "Developed to help newspapers select the best candidates for district manager positions."
Population: Applicants for newspaper district manager positions.
Publication Date: 1982.
Scores: Total score only.
Administration: Group.
Price Data: Not available.
Time: Administration time not reported.
Author: Newspaper Advertising Bureau, Inc.
Publisher: Newspaper Advertising Bureau, Inc. [No reply from publisher; Status unknown].

[2331]
Screening Kit of Language Development.

Purpose: Assesses preschool language development in order to identify language disorders/delays.
Population: Ages 2-5.
Publication Date: 1983.
Acronym: SKOLD.
Scores, 6: Vocabulary, Comprehension, Story Completion, Individual and Paired Sentence Repeti-

tion with Pictures, Individual Sentence Repetition without Pictures, Comprehension of Commands.
Administration: Individual.
Editions, 2: Standard English, Black English.
Price Data, 1992: $55 per complete kit including manual (37 pages), stimulus book, and 1 set of standard English scoring forms or 1 set of Black English scoring forms; $20 per 25 standard English scoring forms; $20 per 25 Black English scoring forms.
Time: (15) minutes.
Authors: Lynn S. Bliss and Doris V. Allen.
Publisher: Slosson Educational Publications, Inc.
Cross References: See T4:2381 (1 reference).

[2332]

Screening Test for Developmental Apraxia of Speech.

Purpose: "To assist in the differential diagnosis of developmental apraxia of speech."
Population: Ages 4-12.
Publication Date: 1980.
Scores, 9: Expressive Language Discrepancy, Vowels and Diphthongs, Oral-Motor Movement, Verbal Sequencing, Articulation, Motorically Complex Words, Transpositions, Prosody, Total.
Administration: Individual.
Price Data, 1999: $79 per complete test including 50 test forms and manual (42 pages); $39 per 50 test forms.
Time: (10) minutes.
Author: Robert W. Blakeley.
Publisher: PRO-ED.
Cross References: See T4:2383 (3 references); for a review by Ronald K. Sommers, see 11:347.

TEST REFERENCES

1. Hargrove, P. M., Roetzel, K., & Hoodin, R. B. (1989). Modifying the prosody of a language-impaired child. *Language, Speech, and Hearing Services in Schools, 20,* 245–258.

2. Marion, M. J., Sussman, H. M., & Marquardt, T. P. (1993). The perception and production of rhyme in normal and developmentally apraxic children. *Journal of Communication Disorders, 26,* 129–160.

[2333]

Screening Test for Educational Prerequisite Skills.

Purpose: Developed to screen for skills needed for beginning kindergarten.
Population: Ages 4-0 to 5-11.
Publication Dates: 1976-1990.
Acronym: STEPS.
Scores: 5 areas: Motor Skills, Intellectual Skills, Verbal Information Skills, Cognitive Strategies, Attitudes.
Administration: Individual.
Price Data, 1999: $139.95 per complete kit including test materials (pictures, bears, pencil), 25 AutoScore™ forms, 25 AutoScore™ home questionnaires, and manual ('90, 68 pages); $35 per set of test materials; $49.50 per 25 AutoScore™ forms; $26 per 25 AutoScore™ home questionnaires; $39.50 per manual; $99.50 per 50-use IBM microcomputer disk; $15 per 100 microcomputer answer sheets for use with disk.
Time: (8-10) minutes.
Author: Frances Smith.
Publisher: Western Psychological Services.
Cross References: For reviews by John Christian Busch, M. Elizabeth Graue, and Jeffrey K. Smith, see 12:351.

[2334]

Screening Test for the Luria-Nebraska Neuropsychological Battery: Adult and Children's Forms.

Purpose: Screening tests for "predicting which individuals would probably show 'normal' or 'clinical' patterns if they were administered the appropriate form of the full Luria-Nebraska Neuropsychological Battery."
Population: Ages 8-12, 13 and older.
Publication Date: 1987.
Acronym: ST-LNNB-C, ST-LNNB-A.
Scores: Running total score.
Administration: Individual.
Forms, 2: Children's Form, Adult Form.
Price Data, 1999: $135 per complete set including 25 administration and scoring booklets for children, 25 administration and scoring booklets for adults, set of stimulus cards, and manual; $25 per 25 administration and scoring booklets (specify adult or children's form); $47.50 per set of stimulus cards; $45 per manual.
Time: (20) minutes.
Comments: For screening purposes only.
Author: Charles J. Golden.
Publisher: Western Psychological Services.
Cross References: For reviews by Arlene Coopersmith Rosenthal and W. Grant Willis, see 11:348.

[2335]

Screening Test of Spanish Grammar.

Purpose: To be used as a syntax screening device to identify "Spanish-speaking children who do not demonstrate native syntactic proficiency commensurate with their age."
Population: Spanish-speaking children ages 3-6.
Publication Date: 1973.
Acronym: STSG.
Scores, 2: Receptive, Expressive.
Administration: Individual.
Price Data: Not available.
Time: (15-25) minutes.
Author: Allen S. Toronto.

Publisher: Northwestern University Press [No reply from publisher; status unknown].
Cross References: See T4:2388 (1 reference) and T3:2109 (1 reference); for a review by Diana S. Natalicio and excerpted reviews by Alex Bannatyne and Huberto Molina, see 8:171 (3 references).

TEST REFERENCE

1. Gutierrez-Clellen, V. F., & Hofstetter, R. (1994). Syntactic complexity in Spanish narratives: A developmental study. *Journal of Speech and Hearing Research, 37*, 645–654.

[2336]

Search Institute Profiles of Student Life: Attitudes and Behaviors.

Purpose: Designed to "assist ... school officials ... in monitoring a series of indicators related to student well-being."
Population: Grades 6–12.
Publication Dates: 1989–1996.
Scores: Total score only.
Administration: Group.
Price Data, 1996: $2 per survey; $700 per 80-page report.
Time: (30–40) minutes.
Author: Search Institute.
Publisher: Search Institute.
Cross References: For reviews by Ernest A. Bauer and Sharon Johnson-Lewis of an earlier edition, see 11:350.

[2337]

Second Language Oral Test of English.

Purpose: "To assess the ability of non-native English speakers to produce standard English grammatical structures."
Population: Child and adult nonnative English speakers.
Publication Date: 1983.
Acronym: SLOTE.
Scores, 21: Affirmative Declarative, Articles, Present Participle, Possessive, Present Tense (third person-regular), Comparative, Superlative, Present Tense (third person-irregular), Preposition, Past Participle (regular), Negative, Past Participle (irregular), Subject Pronoun, Object Pronoun, Possessive Pronoun, Plural (irregular), Imperative, Yes/No Question, Wh Question, Plural (regular), Total.
Administration: Individual.
Price Data: Not available.
Time: (15) minutes.
Author: Ann K. Fathman.
Publisher: The Alemany Press [No reply from publisher; status known].
Cross References: For a review by Alex Voogel, see 11:351.

[2338]

Secondary & College Reading Inventory, Second Edition.

Purpose: "To help ... place students in appropriate reading materials."
Population: Grades 7 through college.
Publication Dates: 1981–1990.
Scores, 9: 3 reading level scores (Independent, Frustration, Instructional) for each of 3 subtests (Word Recognition in Isolation, Word Recognition in Context, Comprehension).
Administration: Individual or group.
Forms, 2: A, B.
Price Data: Available from publisher.
Time: Administration time not reported.
Author: Jerry L. Johns.
Publisher: Kendall/Hunt Publishing Company.
Cross References: For reviews by Hoi K. Suen and Sandra Ward, see 13:278 (1 reference).

[2339]

Secondary Level English Proficiency Test.

Purpose: "A measure of ability in two primary areas: understanding spoken English and understanding written English."
Population: Grades 7-12.
Publication Dates: 1980-1994.
Acronym: SLEP.
Scores, 3: Listening Comprehension, Reading Comprehension, Total.
Administration: Group.
Forms, 3: 1, 2, 3.
Price Data, 1998: $155 per complete set including 20 tests, 100 answer sheets, cassette tape, test manual ('97, 31 pages); $55 per 10 testbooks; $55 per 100 2-play answer sheets; $10 per cassette tape; $6 per test manual.
Time: 85(90) minutes.
Author: Educational Testing Service.
Publisher: Educational Testing Service.
Cross References: See T4:2393 (2 references); for reviews by Brenda H. Loyd and Michael J. Subkoviak, see 9:1090.

[2340]

Secondary-School Record.

Purpose: "Designed to present a summary of the student's academic record and summarize ratings by several teachers."
Population: Grades 9-12.
Publication Dates: 1941-1964.
Acronym: SSR.
Price Data: Available from publisher.
Time: Administration time not reported.
Comments: Transcript form only still available.

Author: National Association of Secondary School Principals.
Publisher: National Association of Secondary School Principals.
Cross References: See 4:516 (1 reference).

[2341]

Secondary Screening Profiles.

Purpose: Designed to help "identify pupils' individual strengths and weaknesses upon entry to secondary school (junior high)," and also as a "standardised basis for screening special education needs."
Population: Junior high students, ages 10–13 years.
Publication Dates: 1995–1999.
Acronym: SSP.
Scores, 3: Reasoning, Reading, Mathematical.
Administration: Group.
Forms, 6: Reading, Forms A and B; Mathematics, Forms A and B; Reasoning, Forms A and B.
Price Data, 1999: £9.99 per 20 test forms; £10.50 per manual; £12.99 per specimen set.
Time: (20–40) minutes for each form.
Authors: Centre for Research on Learning and Instruction, University of Edinburgh.
Publisher: Hodder & Stoughton Educational [England].

[2342]

SEED Developmental Profiles.

Purpose: Functional assessment designed to be used to establish a developmental profile of a child's performance.
Population: Birth to 72 months.
Publication Date: 1976.
Scores, 9: 8 developmental profile areas: Social-Emotional, Gross Motor, Fine Motor, Adaptive-Reasoning, Receptive Language, Expressive Language, Feeding, Dressing and Simple Hygiene, plus a Master Developmental Profile.
Administration: Individual.
Price Data, 1990: $6 per manual (52 pages) including record forms, material lists, source list, and instructions; $4 per set of profile/record forms.
Time: Administration time not reported.
Authors: Joan Herst, Sheila Wolfe, Gloria Jorgensen, and Sandra Pallon.
Publisher: Sewall Early Education Developmental (SEED) Program [No reply from publisher; status unknown].
Cross References: For reviews by Bob Algozzine and Johnny L. Matson, see 9:1091.

[2343]

The Seeking of Noetic Goals Test.

Purpose: Constructed "to measure the strength of motivation to find life meaning."
Population: Adolescents and adults.
Publication Date: 1977.
Acronym: SONG.
Scores: Total score only.
Administration: Group.
Price Data, 1985: $5 per 25 test booklets; $4 per specimen set.
Time: (10) minutes.
Comments: Complementary scale to the Purpose in Life Test.
Author: James C. Crumbaugh.
Publisher: Psychometric Affiliates.
Cross References: For reviews by Brenda Bailey-Richardson and Kevin L. Moreland, see 9:1092, see also T3:2124 (1 reference).

[2344]

Seguin-Goddard Formboards.

Purpose: Designed for testing spatial perception and motor coordination.
Population: Age 4 to adult.
Publication Date: [1911].
Scores: No scores.
Price Data, 1998: $185 per "flush" formboard; $340 per "raised" formboard.
Time: [5-10] minutes.
Comments: Used in the Halstead-Reitan Neuropsychological Test Battery (1164, Merrill-Palmer Scale of Mental Tests (1653), and Arthur Point Scale of Performance Tests (182).
Authors: E. Seguin, H. H. Goddard, and N. Norsworthy.
Publisher: Stoelting Co.
Cross References: See T4:2397 (1 reference), T3:2125 (1 reference), and T2:578 (25 references).

[2345]

Selby MillSmith Adaptive Ability Tests.

Purpose: "For use in the selection, training, and career development of personnel in the UK."
Population: Junior school–adult.
Publication Dates: 1988–1990.
Administration: Individual.
Price Data: Available from publisher.
Time: [15] minutes per subtest.
Comments: All subtests are computer administered.
Author: Selby MillSmith, Ltd.
Publisher: Selby MillSmith, Ltd. [England].

a) NUMERIC ABILITY TEST.
Purpose: "To assess basic numeracy and numerical skills at all levels of the organisation."
Scores: Total score only.

b) LANGUAGE ABILITY TEST.
Purpose: "Assesses the individual's range and clarity in the use of vocabulary."
Scores: Total score only.

c) ADMINISTRATIVE ABILITY TEST.
Purpose: "To assess the speed and accuracy of an individual's administrative capabilities."
Scores, 3: Numbers, Addresses, Codes.
Cross References: For reviews by Colin Cooper and Glen Fox, see 13:279.

[2346]

Selby MillSmith Values Indices.

Purpose: "A measure of personal values associated with work and the working environment."
Population: Adults.
Publication Dates: 1985–91.
Administration: Individual or group.
Editions, 2: Management Values Index, Supervisory Values Index.
Price Data: Available from publisher.
Comments: Test may be paper-and-pencil or computer administered.
Author: Adrian W. Savage.
Publisher: Selby MillSmith [England].
a) MANAGEMENT VALUES INDEX.
Purpose: "For selection, assessment and training and development at managerial and senior levels within an organisation."
Population: Managers.
Acronym: MVI.
Scores, 27: Core Scales [Achievement Values (Work Ethic, Responsibility, Risk Taking, Task Orientation, Leadership, Activity, Need for Status, Self Esteem), Expertise Values (Need for Mental Challenge, Innovation, Analysis, Attention to Detail), Consolidation Values (Need for Stability, Need for Structure, Career Development), Interpersonal Values (Sociability, Inclusion, Personal Warmth, Tactfulness, Tolerance)], [Second Order Indices (Executive Index, Stability Index, Conscientiousness Index, Expert Orientation Index, Team Orientation Index, Empathy Index, Motivational Distortion Index)].
Time: (30–45) minutes.
b) SUPERVISORY VALUES INDEX.
Purpose: "For selection, assessment and training and development at supervisory and 'A' level standard."
Scores, 26: Core Scales [Achievement Values (Work Ethic, Responsibility, Risk Taking, Task Orientation, Leadership, Activity, Need for Status, Self Esteem), Expertise Values (Need for Mental Challenge, Innovation, Analysis, Attention to Detail), Consolidation Values (Need for Stability, Need for Structure, Career Development), Interpersonal Values (Sociability, Inclusion, Personal Warmth, Tactfulness, Tolerance)], Second Order Indices (Initiative Index, Team Orientation Index, Stability Index, Enquiry Index, Conscientiousness Index, Motivational Distortion Index).
Time: (30–45) minutes.

[2347]

SELECT Associate Screening System.

Purpose: Designed to assist organizations in making effective employee selection decisions.
Publication Dates: 1995–1998.
Acronym: SELECT.
Administration: Individual or group.
Price Data, 1998: $189 per one-time purchase of Initial System including HASP key preloaded with units for 10–12 surveys, SELECT software, and user's guide ('98, 90 pages); $50 per additional HASPs for satellite sites; $12 or less per report.
Time: (20–45) minutes depending on survey.
Author: Bigby, Havis, & Associates, Inc.
Publisher: Bigby, Havis, & Associates, Inc.
Comments: A software platform that combines seven screening tools; computer administered, scored, and interpreted; reports include results, recommendations, and interview questions.
a) SELECT FOR CONVENIENCE STORES.
Purpose: Designed to "measure characteristics and abilities important in most convenience store jobs."
Population: Applicants for positions in convenience stores.
Scores, 3: Provides Overall Performance, Integrity, and Retail Math indices with recommended ranges; subscale results for Energy, Frustration Tolerance, Self-Control, Accommodation to Others, Acceptance of Diversity, Positive Service Attitude; also includes self-report of Counterproductive Work Behaviors, Willingness to Do Common C-Store Tasks.
b) SELECT FOR CUSTOMER SERVICE.
Purpose: Designed as an associate-level pre-employment test for positions in customer service.
Population: Job Applicants for customer service positions.
Scores, 2: Provides Overall Performance and Integrity indices with recommended ranges; subscale results for Energy, Frustration Tolerance, Accommodation to Others, Acceptance of Diversity, and Positive Service Attitude; optional modules available for Counterproductive Behaviors, Retail Math.
c) SELECT FOR HEALTH CARE.
Purpose: Designed to "measure characteristics important in most health care provider jobs."
Population: Applicants for health care positions.
Scores, 2: Provides Overall Performance and Integrity indices with recommended ranges;

subscale results for Energy, Frustration Tolerance, Accommodation to Others, Acceptance of Diversity, Positive Service Attitude, Accountability, Rapport, Empathy, Multi-Tasking.

d) SELECT FOR PRODUCTION AND DISTRIBUTION.

Purpose: Designed to "measure characteristics important to team-oriented manufacturing and distribution jobs."

Population: Applicants for production and distribution positions.

Scores, 2: Provides Overall Performance and Integrity indices with recommended ranges; subscale results for Energy, Frustration Tolerance, Acceptance of Diversity, Self-Control, Acceptance of Structure, Productive Attitude; optional module is available for Counterproductive Behaviors.

e) SELECT FOR ADMINISTRATIVE SUPPORT.

Purpose: Designed "as a personality-based survey for measuring characteristics that have been found to predict job effectiveness in administrative or clerical positions."

Population: Applicants for administrative support positions.

Scores, 2: Provides Overall Performance and Integrity indices with recommended ranges; subscale results for Energy, Multi-Tasking, Attention to Detail, Self-Reliance, Task Focus, Interpersonal Insight, Criticism Tolerance, Acceptance of Diversity, Self-Control, Productive Attitude.

f) SELECT FOR PERSONAL SERVICES.

Purpose: Designed "as a personality-based survey for measuring characteristics that have been found to predict job effectiveness for those employed in personal-care-type positions."

Population: Applicants for personal services positions (i.e., hairstylists/photographers).

Scores, 2: Provides Overall Performance and Integrity indices with recommended ranges; subscale results for Energy, Frustration Tolerance, Accommodation to Others, Acceptance of Diversity, Social Comfort, Positive Service Attitude.

g) SELECT FOR CALL CENTERS—INBOUND SERVICE.

Purpose: Designed to help screen applicants for inbound service positions at call centers.

Population: Applicants for inbound sales positions at call centers.

Scores, 2: Provides Overall Performance and Integrity indices with recommended ranges; subscale results for Energy, Frustration Tolerance, Accommodation to Others, Acceptance of Diversity, Positive Service Attitude.

h) SELECT FOR CALL CENTERS—INBOUND SALES.

Purpose: Designed to help screen applicants for inbound sales positions at call centers.

Population: Applicants for inbound sales positions at call centers.

Scores, 2: Provides Overall Performance and Integrity indices with recommended ranges; subscale results for Energy, Frustration Tolerance, Accountability, Preference for Structure, Influence, Social Comfort, Productive Attitude.

i) SELECT FOR CALL CENTERS—OUTBOUND SALES.

Purpose: Designed to help screen applicants for outbound sales positions at call centers.

Population: Applicants for outbound sales positions at call centers.

Scores, 2: Provides Overall Performance and Integrity indices with recommended ranges; subscale results for Energy, Multi-Tasking Ability, Accountability, Assertiveness, Social Comfort, Diplomacy, Acceptance of Diversity, Frustration Tolerance, Criticism Tolerance, Productive Attitude.

[2348]

[Selection Interview Forms].

Purpose: Designed to help interviewers obtain appropriate and valid information from job applicants.

Population: Business and industry.

Publication Date: 1962.

Scores: Ratings in 8 areas (Motivation for the Job, Adequacy of Work Experience, Supervisory Experience and Ability, Achievements at School, Vocational Adjustment, Family Background and Personal Adjustments, Wife's and Family's Role, Health) plus Total.

Administration: Individual.

Author: Benjamin Balinsky.

Publisher: Martin M. Bruce, Ph.D.

a) SELECTION INTERVIEW FORM.

Price Data, 1998: $13.75 per specimen set; $26.40 per package of forms.

Time: [60-90] minutes.

b) INTERVIEW RATING FORM.

Price Data: $10.45 per specimen set; $19.80 per package of forms.

Time: [15] minutes.

[2349]

Self-Actualization Test.

Purpose: Designed to measure the degree to which six needs related to self-actualization are met.

Population: Managers and students of administration.

Publication Dates: 1970–1994.

Scores, 6: Physical, Security, Relationship, Respect, Independence, Self-Actualization.

Administration: Group.

Price Data, 1998: $40 per 10 tests including fact sheet and administration guide.

Time: (10–20) minutes.
Comments: A 28-item self-administered, self-scored inventory; formerly listed as the Self-Actualization Inventory.
Authors: W. J. Reddin and Ken Rowell.
Publisher: Organizational Tests Ltd. [Canada].
Cross References: For a review by Thomas F. Cash of the earlier edition, see 9:1093 (1 reference).

[2350]

Self-Administered Dependency Questionnaire.

Purpose: Constructed to identify dependency in mother/child relationships.
Population: Ages 8-15.
Publication Dates: 1973-1974.
Acronym: SADQ.
Scores, 4: Affection, Assistance, Communication, Travel.
Administration: Individual.
Manual: No manual.
Price Data: Not available.
Time: [10-30] minutes.
Comments: Revision of Highlands Dependency Questionnaire; title on test booklet is The Self-Administered HDQ; self-administered.
Author: Ian Berg.
Publisher: Ian Berg [England] [No reply from publisher; status unknown].
Cross References: See T4:2403 (1 reference), T3:2128 (2 references), and 8:669 (6 references).

[2351]

A Self-Appraisal Scale for Teachers.

Purpose: Developed as a self-help device that allows instructors to appraise themselves.
Population: Teachers.
Publication Date: 1957.
Scores: 6 appraisal areas: Person, Specialist and Educator, Relations With Students, Course, Classroom Performance, Student's Appraisal.
Administration: Group.
Manual: No manual.
Price Data: Not available.
Time: [30-40] minutes.
Author: Howard Wilson.
Publisher: Administrative Research Associates [No reply from publisher; status unknown].

[2352]

Self-Assessment in Writing Skills.

Purpose: Developed as a self-assessment tool to assess writing skills.
Population: Clerical, managerial, and sales employees.
Publication Date: 1990.
Scores, 3: Content and Style, Organization and Format, Total.
Administration: Group or individual.
Price Data, 1990: $60 per complete kit including 20 inventories, 20 scoring sheets for part 1, and 20 scoring sheets for part 2.
Time: [90-120] minutes.
Comments: Self-administered, self-scored.
Authors: Training House, Inc.
Publisher: Training House, Inc.
Cross References: For reviews by Gabriel M. Della-Piana and Stephen Jurs, see 12:352.

[2353]

Self-Awareness Profile.

Purpose: "This self-assessment provides insight into the basic personality attributes that influence the way we behave."
Population: Industry.
Publication Dates: 1980-1987.
Scores, 4: Dominance, Influence, Conformity, Evenness.
Administration: Individual or group.
Price Data, 1988: $80 per 20 complete sets including 16-item inventory, interpretation sheet, planning sheet, and 20 sets of cards containing profiles on 10 different personalities, to be sorted by participants ("most like me, next most," etc.).
Time: (80-100) minutes.
Author: Scott B. Parry.
Publisher: Training House, Inc.
Cross References: For a review by Timothy M. Osberg, see 11:353.

[2354]

Self-Concept Adjective Checklist.

Purpose: Developed to assess self-concept.
Population: Grades K-8.
Publication Dates: 1971-1972.
Acronym: SCAC.
Scores: Total score only.
Administration: Group.
Price Data, 1987: $15 per 25 rating checklists including manual ('72, 4 pages); $5 per specimen set.
Time: [10] minutes.
Author: Alan J. Politte.
Publisher: Psychologists and Educators, Inc.

[2355]

The Self-Concept and Motivation Inventory: What Face Would You Wear?

Purpose: To assess motivation and academic self-concept.

Population: Age 4-kindergarten, grades 1-3, 3-6, 7-12.
Publication Dates: 1967-1977.
Acronym: SCAMIN.
Administration: Group.
Price Data: Not available.
Authors: Norman J. Milchus, George A. Farrah, and William Reitz.
Publisher: Person-O-Metrics, Inc.

a) PRE-SCHOOL/KINDERGARTEN FORM.
Population: Age 4-kindergarten.
Scores, 14: Motivation (Goal and Achievement Needs, Achievement Investment, Self-Concept), Total (optional).
Time: (25-30) minutes.

b) EARLY ELEMENTARY FORM.
Population: Grades 1-3.
Scores, 5: Motivation (Goal and Achievement Needs, Achievement Investment), Self-Concept (Role Expectations, Self-Adequacy), Total (optional).
Time: (25-30) minutes.

c) LATER ELEMENTARY FORM.
Population: Grades 3-6.
Scores, 10: Same as *b* above plus 6 optional Sources of Support Climate scores (Parents, Teachers, Peers and Siblings, Academic Self, Academic Activity Climate, School Climate), Total (optional).
Time: (30-35) minutes.

d) SECONDARY FORM.
Population: Grades 7-12.
Scores, 20: Same as *b* above plus 16 optional scores: Sources of Support Climate (Parents, Teachers, Peers, Academic Self, Physical and Social Self, Adults and Counselors, Academic Activity Climate, School Climate), Immediate-Intrinsic Orientation (Evaluated Competition, Tasks and Projects, Discovery and Creativity, Skills), Fulfillment Orientation (Aspiration, Cooperation and Conformity, Responsibility, Acceptance and Praise).
Time: (40) minutes.

Cross References: See T4:2408 (3 references); for a review by Lorrie Shepard, see 8:670 (4 references).

TEST REFERENCES

1. Karnes, M. B., & Johnson, L. J. (1987). Bringing out Head Start talents: Findings from the field. *Gifted Child Quarterly, 31,* 174–179.
2. Richert, E. S. (1987). Rampant problems and promising practices in the identification of disadvantaged gifted students. *Gifted Child Quarterly, 31,* 149–154.
3. Finn, J. D., & Achilles, C. M. (1990). Answers and questions about class size: A statewide experiment. *American Educational Research Journal, 27,* 557-577.

[2356]

Self-Concept as a Learner Scale.

Purpose: Designed to measure "one's self-concept as a learner in the school context."
Population: Grades 4-12.
Publication Dates: 1967-1972.
Acronym: SCAL.
Scores, 5: Motivation, Task Orientation, Problem Solving, Class Membership, Total.
Administration: Group.
Manual: No manual.
Price Data: Available from publisher.
Time: (20) minutes.
Author: Walter B. Waetjen.
Publisher: Walter B. Waetjen.
Cross References: See T4:2409 (2 references), T3:2132 (2 references), and 8:671 (1 reference).

TEST REFERENCE

1. Jarvis, P. A., & Justice, E. M. (1992). Social sensitivity in adolescents and adults with learning disabilities. *Adolescence, 27,* 977-988.

[2357]

Self Concept Scale, Secondary Level.

Purpose: To measure self concepts in basic living skills.
Population: Grades 7-12.
Publication Dates: 1980-1982.
Scores, 6: Decision Making, Interpersonal Relationships, Responsibility, Citizenship, Career Planning, Total.
Administration: Group.
Price Data, 1996: $35.80 per kit including manual ('82, 14 pages), 35 pupil record forms and profile sheets; $35.75 per 50 pupil record forms/profile sheets; $3.85 per manual; $1 per pupil for machine scoring.
Time: (15-20) minutes.
Author: Bob Percival.
Publisher: Dallas Educational Services.

[2358]

Self-Description Questionnaire—I, II, III.

Purpose: To measure aspects of self-concept.
Population: Ages 5–12, 13–17, 16–Adult.
Publication Dates: 1987–1992.
Acronym: SDQ.
Administration: Group.
Price Data, 1998: A$150 per complete kit including SDQ-I manual ('92, 171 pages), SDQ-II manual ('92, 118 pages), and SDQ-III manual ('89, 114 pages), master copy of each instrument, master copy of each scoring profile, and scoring program; A$120 per materials for two instruments; A$75 per materials for one instrument.
Comments: Self-report measures.
Author: Herbert W. Marsh.
Publisher: SDQ Instruments, Publication Unit [Australia].

a) SELF-DESCRIPTION QUESTIONNAIRE—I.
Population: Ages 8–12.
Scores, 11: Academic (Mathematics, Reading, General—School, Total), Non-Academic (Physical Abilities, Physical Appearance, Peer Relations,

Parent Relations, Total), Global (General—Self, Total—Self).
Time: (15–20) minutes.
b) SELF-DESCRIPTION QUESTIONNAIRE—II.
Population: Ages 13–17.
Scores, 12: Academic (Mathematics, Verbal, General—School), Non-Academic (Physical Abilities, Physical Appearance, Same Sex Peer Relations, Opposite Sex Peer Relations, Parent Relations, Emotional Stability, Honesty/Trustworthiness), Global (General—Self, Total—Self).
Time: (20–25) minutes.
c) SELF-DESCRIPTION QUESTIONNAIRE—III.
Population: Ages 16–Adult.
Scores, 14: Academic (Mathematics, Verbal, Problem-Solving, General—Academic), Non-Academic (Physical Abilities, Physical Appearance, Same Sex Peer Relations, Opposite Sex Peer Relations, Parent Relations, Spiritual Values/Religion, Honesty/Trustworthiness, Emotional Stability), Global (General—Self, Total—Self).
Time: (20–25) minutes.
Cross References: For reviews by Jeffrey A. Atlas, Robert K. Gable, and Steven Isonio, see 13:280 (42 references); see also T4:2412 (10 references).

TEST REFERENCES

1. Marsh, H. W., & Richards, G. E. (1990). Self-other agreement and self-other differences on multidimensional self-concept ratings. *Australian Journal of Psychology, 42,* 31–45.
2. McInman, A. D., & Grove, J. R. (1991). Multidimensional self-concept, cigarette smoking, and intentions to smoke in adolescents. *Australian Psychologist, 26,* 192–196.
3. Marsh, H. W., & Byrne, B. M. (1993). Do we see ourselves as others infer: A comparison of self-other agreement on multiple dimensions of self-concept from two continents. *Australian Journal of Psychology, 45,* 49–58.
4. McInman, A. D., & Berger, B. G. (1993). Self-concept and mood changes associated with aerobic dance. *Australian Journal of Psychology, 45,* 134–140.
5. Hatzichriston, C., & Hopf, D. (1995). School adaptation of Greek children after immigration: Age differences in multiple domains. *Journal of Cross-Cultural Psychology, 26,* 505–522.
6. Orr, E., & Dinur, B. (1995). Social setting effects on gender differences in self-esteem: Kibbutz and urban adolescents. *Journal of Youth and Adolescence, 24,* 3–27.
7. Watkins, D., & Cheung, S. (1995). Culture, gender, and response bias: An analysis of responses to the self-description questionnaire. *Journal of Cross-Cultural Psychology, 26,* 490–504.
8. Hatzichriston, C., & Hopt, D. (1996). A multiperspective comparison of peer sociometric status groups in childhood and adolescence. *Child Development, 67,* 1085–1102.
9. Tafarodi, R. W., & Swann, W. B., Jr. (1996). Individualism-collectivison and global self-esteem: Evidence for a cultural trade-off. *Journal of Cross-Cultural Psychology, 27,* 651–672.
10. Hay, I., Shaman, A., & Van Kraayenoord, C. E. (1997). Investigating the influence of achievement on self-concept using an intra-class design and a comparison of the PASS and SDQ-1 self-concept tests. *British Journal of Educational Psychology, 67,* 311–321.
11. Hodge, G. M., McCormick, J., & Elliott, R. (1997). Examination-induced distress in a public examination at the completion of secondary schooling. *British Journal of Educational Psychology, 67,* 185–197.
12. Hunter, J. A., Platon, M. J., Bell, L. M., Kypri, K., & Lewis, C. A. (1997). Intergroup bias and self-evaluation: Domain-specific self-esteem, threats to identify and dimensional importance. *British Journal of Social Psychology, 36,* 405–426.
13. Marsh, H. W., Roche, L. A., Pajares, F., & Miller, D. (1997). Item-specific efficacy judgments in mathematical problem solving: The downside of standing too close to trees in a forest. *Contemporary Educational Psychology, 22,* 363–377.
14. Plucker, J. A., Taylor, J. W., V, Callahan, C. M., & Tomchin, E. M. (1997). Mirror, mirror, on the wall: Reliability and validity evidence for the Self-Description Questionnaire—II with gifted students. *Educational and Psychological Measurement, 57,* 704–713.
15. Bear, G. G., Minke, K. M., Griffin, S. M., & Deemer, S. A. (1998). Achievement-related perceptions of children with learning disabilities and normal achievement: Group and developmental differences. *Journal of Learning Disabilities, 31,* 91–104.
16. Lopez, M. A., & Heffer, R. W. (1998). Self-concept and social competence of university student victims of childhood physical abuse. *Child Abuse & Neglect, 22,* 183–195.
17. McDougall, P., & Hymel, S. (1998). Moving into middle school: Individual differences in the transition experience. *Canadian Journal of Behavioural Science, 30,* 108–120.

[2359]

Self-Directed Learning Readiness Scale.

Purpose: Assesses "learning preferences and attitudes towards learning, which result in readiness for self-directed learning."
Population: Age 15 and over.
Publication Dates: 1977-1982.
Acronym: SDLRS.
Scores: Total score only.
Administration: Individual or group.
Price Data, 1999: $3.95 each (quantity discounts available).
Time: Administration time not reported.
Comments: A self-scoring form, entitled the Learning Preference Assessment, is available for use in workshops.
Authors: Lucy M. Guglielmino.
Publisher: Guglielmino and Associates.

TEST REFERENCES

1. Carter, K. R. (1992). A model for evaluating programs for the gifted under non-experimental conditions. *Journal for the Education of the Gifted, 15,* 266-283.
2. Confessore, G. (1992). What became of the kids who participated in the 1981 Johnson Early College Summer Arts Program? *Journal for the Education of the Gifted, 15,* 64-82.

[2360]

Self-Directed Search, 4th Edition [Forms R, E, and CP].

Purpose: A vocational inventory designed to identify "a person's particular activities, competencies, and self-estimates compared with various occupational groups."
Population: Ages 12 and above.
Publication Dates: 1970–1997.
Acronym: SDS.
Scores, 6: Realistic, Investigative, Artistic, Social, Enterprising, Conventional.
Administration: Group.
Editions, 3: Form R (Regular), Form E (Easy), Form CP (Career Planning).
Price Data: Price information available from publisher for kit (Form R) including manuals, 25 booklets and occupational finders, 25 "You and Your Career" booklets, 10 leisure activity finders, and 10 educational opportunities finders; for kit (Form E) including manuals, 25 assessment booklets, 25 job finders, and 25 "You and Your Job" booklets; for per kit (Form CP) including manuals, 25 assessment booklets, 25 career options finders, and 25 exploring career options booklets; various combinations of components available in varied-priced kits; price information for additional versions and computer software also available from publisher.

Foreign Language Editions: "Adaptations available in the following countries/continents: Australia, Canada, China, Finland, France, Greece, Guyana, Hungary, Indonesia, Israel, Italy, Japan, Netherlands, New Zealand, Nigeria, Norway, Poland, Portugal, Russia, Saudi Arabia, Slovenia, South Africa, South America, Spain, Switzerland"; English-Canadian, Spanish, Vietnamese, and Braille editions also available.
Time: (40–50) minutes.
Comments: Self-administered, -scored, and -interpreted; computer software available; based on the Holland typology of vocational preferences.
Authors: John L. Holland (test and manuals), Amy B. Powell (manuals), and Barbara A. Fritzsche (manuals).
Publisher: Psychological Assessment Resources, Inc.
Cross References: For reviews by Joseph C. Ciechalski and Esther E. Diamond of an earlier edition, see 13:281 (48 references); see also T4:2414 (23 references); for reviews by M. Harry Daniels and Caroline Manuele-Adkins, see 10:330 (19 references); for a review by Robert H. Dolliver, see 9:1098 (12 references); see also T3:2134 (55 references); for a review by John O. Crites and excerpted reviews by Fred Brown, Richard Seligman, Catherine C. Cutts, Robert H. Dolliver, and Robert N. Hanson, see 8:1022 (88 references); see also T2:2211 (1 reference).

TEST REFERENCES

1. Domenci, L. (1995). Construct validity of the Self-Directed Search using hierarchically nested structural models. *Journal of Vocational Behavior, 47,* 21–34.
2. Ohler, D. L., Levinson, E. M., & Hays, G. M. (1995). The relationship between career maturity and congruence consistency, and differentiation among individuals with and without learning disabilities. *Journal of Employment Counseling, 33,* 50–60.
3. Sutherland, L. F., Fogarty, G. J., & Pithers, R. T. (1995). Congruence as a predictor of occupational stress. *Journal of Vocational Behavior, 46,* 292–309.
4. Glidden-Tracey, C. E., & Parraga, M. I. (1996). Assessing the structure of vocational interests among Bolivian university students. *Journal of Vocational Behavior, 48,* 96–106.
5. Nordick, H. (1996). Relationships between Holland's vocational typology, Schein's career anchors and Myers-Briggs' types. *Journal of Occupational and Organizational Psychology, 69,* 263–275.
6. Reardon, R., Lenz, J., & Strausberger, S. (1996). Integrating theory, practice, and research with the Self-Directed Search: Computer Version Form R. *Measurement and Evaluation in Counseling and Development, 28,* 211–218.
7. Betsworth, D. G. & Fouad, N. A. (1997). Vocational interests: A look at the past 70 years and a glance at the future. *Career Development Quarterly, 46,* 23–47.
8. Carless, S. A., & Allwood, V. E. (1997). Managerial assessment centres: What is being rated? *Australian Psychologist, 32,* 101–105.
9. Luzzo, D. A., McWhirter, E. H., & Hutcheson, K. G. (1997). Evaluating career decision-making factors associated with employment among first-year college students. *Journal of College Student Development, 38,* 166–172.
10. Miller, M. J. (1997). Error rates on two forms of the Self-Directed Search and satisfaction with the results. *Journal of Employment Counseling, 34,* 98–103.
11. Wilkinson, L. J. (1997). Generalizable biodata: An application to the vocational interests of managers. *Journal of Occupational and Organizational Psychology, 70,* 49–69.
12. Miller, M. J., & Cowger, E. L., Jr. (1998). Degree of the relationship between the college majors finder and anticipated college majors among high school students. *College Student Journal, 32,* 311–314.
13. Rayman, J. R., (1998). Interpreting Ellenore Flood's Self-Directed Search. *Career Development Quarterly, 46,* 330–338.

[2361]

Self-Esteem Index.

Purpose: "Designed to measure the way individuals perceive themselves."
Population: Ages 7-0 to 18-11.
Publication Dates: 1990-1991.
Acronym: SEI.
Scores, 5: Familial Acceptance, Academic Competence, Peer Popularity, Personal Security, Self-Esteem Quotient.
Administration: Group.
Price Data, 1999: $119 per complete kit including 50 student response booklets, 50 profile/record forms, and manual ('91, 51 pages); $39 per 50 student response booklets; $39 per 50 profile/record forms; $44 per manual.
Time: (30-35) minutes.
Authors: Linda Brown and Jacquelyn Alexander.
Publisher: PRO-ED.
Cross References: For reviews by E. Scott Huebner and by Ralph O. Mueller and Paula J. Dupuy, see 11:354.

TEST REFERENCES

1. Waterman, J., & Lusk, R. (1993). Psychological testing in evaluation of child sexual abuse. *Child Abuse & Neglect, 17,* 145-159.
2. Bracken, B. A., & Mills, B. C. (1994). School counselors' assessment of self-concept: A comprehensive review of 10 instruments. *The School Counselor, 42,* 14–31.
3. Brooke, S. L. (1996). Critical analysis of the Self-Esteem Index. *Measurement and Evaluation in Counseling and Development, 28,* 233–238.
4. King, D. A., & Daniel, L. G. (1996). Psychometric integrity of the Self-Esteem Index: A comparison of normative and field study results. *Educational and Psychological Measurement, 56,* 537–550.

[2362]

The Self-Esteem Inventory.

Purpose: Developed to examine an individual's self-esteem.
Population: Adolescents and adults.
Publication Date: 1995.
Scores: Total score only.
Administration: Group.
Manual: No manual.
Price Data: Available from publisher.
Time: Administration time not reported.
Author: Millard J. Bienvenu.
Publisher: Millard J. Bienvenu, Northwest Publications.

[2363]

Self-Esteem Questionnaire.

Purpose: Measures self esteem and satisfaction with self esteem.
Population: Ages 9 and over.
Publication Dates: 1971-1976.
Acronym: SEQ.
Scores, 2: Self-Esteem, Self-Other Satisfaction.
Administration: Group.
Price Data: Not available.
Time: (15-20) minutes.
Author: James K. Hoffmeister.
Publisher: Test Analysis & Development Corporation.
Cross References: See T4:2416 (3 references).

[2364]

Self-Motivated Career Planning Guide.

Purpose: To help the individual develop vocational objectives through self-administered exercises.
Population: High school and college and adults.
Publication Dates: 1978–1984.
Acronym: S-MCP.
Scores: 7 pencil/paper exercises (Personal Orientation Survey, Education Summary, Career Experience Summary, Personal Career Life Summary, Career Strengths and Interests, Next Career Steps, Personal Development Summary) plus a 16PF personality assessment and interpretive report (Personal/Career Development Profile).
Administration: Group.
Price Data, 1999: $25 per self-motivated Career Planning Guide ('84, 126 pages).
Time: (50-120) minutes per exercise.
Authors: Verne Walter and Melvin Wallace.
Publisher: Institute for Personality and Ability Testing, Inc.
Cross References: For reviews by Larry Cochran and Samuel Juni, see 11:355; for reviews by Robert H. Dolliver and Kevin W. Mossholder of an earlier edition, see 9:1099.

[2365]

Self Observation Scales.

Purpose: Designed as a measure of self-concept.
Population: Grades K-3, 4-6, 7-9, 10-12.
Publication Dates: 1974-1979.
Acronym: SOS.
Administration: Group.
Forms: 1 or 2 for each of 4 levels.
Price Data: Available from publisher.
Time: (20-30) minutes.
Comments: Publisher recommends use of local norms; self-report; interactive computer version of the SOS available.
Authors: A. Jackson Stenner and William G. Katzenmeyer.
Publisher: NTS Research Corporation.

a) PRIMARY LEVEL.
Population: Grades K-3.
Scores: 4 scales: Self Acceptance, Self Security, Social Maturity, School Affiliation.
Forms, 2: A, C.
Comments: Orally administered.

b) INTERMEDIATE LEVEL.
Population: Grades 4-6.
Scores: 7 scales: Same as *a* above plus Social Confidence, Teacher Affiliation, Peer Affiliation.
Forms, 2: A, C.

c) JUNIOR HIGH LEVEL.
Population: Grades 7-9.
Scores: 7 scales: Same as *a* above except include Self Assertion in place of Social Maturity.

d) SENIOR HIGH LEVEL.
Population: Grades 10-12.
Scores: 7 scales: Same as *c* above.

Cross References: See T4:2418 (2 references); see 9:1100 (3 references).

[2366]

Self-Perception Inventory: Nursing Forms.

Purpose: "The primary purpose of the SPI is research."
Population: Student nurses and professional staff.
Publication Dates: 1967-1985.
Acronym: SPI.
Scores: 7 scales: Self-Concept, Self-Concept/Nurse, Ideal Concept/Nurse, Reflected Self/Supervisors, Nurse-Rating Scale/Students, Nurse-Rating Scale/Professionals, Nurse-Rating Scale/Patient.
Administration: Group.
Price Data: Not available.
Time: (5-20) minutes per scale.
Authors: Anthony T. Soares and Louise M. Soares.
Publisher: Soares Associates.
Cross References: For reviews by Gerald E. DeMauro and Michael R. Harwell, see 11:356. For additional information on other forms and a review by Janet Morgan Riggs of other forms, see 9:1101 (2 references); see also T3:2139 (1 reference); for a review by Lorrie Shepard of other forms, see 8:673 (2 references).

[2367]

Self Perception Inventory.

Purpose: Designed to determine subject's perceptions of self, how other perceive him/her, and perceptions others have of him/her.
Population: Ages 12 and over.
Publication Dates: 1967-1969.
Acronym: SPI.
Scores, 12: General Adjustment (Consistency, Self-Actualization, Supervision, Total), General Maladjustment (Uncommon Response, Rigidity-Dogmatism, Authoritarianism, Anxiety, Depression, Paranoia, Total), Time.
Administration: Group.
Price Data, 1987: $27.50 per 25 tests; $9 per 9 score keys; $6.75 per 25 answer sheets; $6.75 per 25 profile sheets; $40 per examiner's set including 10 tests, 25 answer sheets, 25 profile sheets, score keys, and manual ('69, 14 pages); $12 per specimen set.
Time: (5-20) minutes.
Author: William T. Martin.
Publisher: Psychologists and Educators, Inc.
Cross References: For additional information and a review by John R. Braun, see 8:674 (1 reference); see also 7:136 (3 references).

[2368]

Self-Perception Inventory [SOARES Associates].

Purpose: "Designed to measure subjects' self-concept and subjects' perception of how significant others perceive him/her."
Publication Dates: 1965-1989.
Acronym: SPI.
Administration: Group.
Price Data: Available from publisher.
Foreign Language Editions: Spanish, Italian, and French Editions available.
Time: (5-20) minutes per test.
Authors: Anthony T. Soares and Louise M. Soares.
Publisher: SOARES Associates [No reply from publisher; status unknown].

a) STUDENT FORMS.
Population: Grades 1-12.
Scores, 8: Self Concept, Reflected Self/Classmates, Reflected Self/Teachers, Reflected Self/Parents, Ideal Self, Others' Perceptions, Student Self, Others' Perceptions of Student Self.
Forms: 1 form for tests 1-5 and 7; separate forms for males and females for tests 6 and 8.

b) ADULT FORMS.
Population: Grades 9-12 and adults.
Scores, 9: Self Concept, Reflected Self/Friends, Reflected Self/Teachers or Professors, Reflected Self/Parents, Reflected Self/Partners, Ideal Self, Others' Perceptions, Student Self, Others' Perceptions of Student Self.
Forms: 1 form for tests 1-6 and 8; separate forms for males and females for tests 7 and 9.

c) TEACHER FORMS.
Population: Student teachers.
Scores, 9: Self Concept/Teacher, Reflected Self/Cooperating Teacher, Reflected Self/Supervisor, Reflected Self/Professionals, Ideal Concept/Teacher, Teacher Perceptions, Student Teacher Ratings, Reflected Teacher Perceptions, Student Perceptions.
Forms: 1 form for tests 1-8; separate forms for males and females for test 9.

d) NURSING FORMS.
Population: Nurses.
Scores, 5: Self Concept, Self Concept/Nurse, Ideal Concept/Nurse, Reflected Self/Supervisor, Nurse-Rating Forms.
Forms: 1 form for tests 1-4; separate forms for students, professionals, and patients.

Cross References: See T4:2421 (1 reference); for a review by Janet Morgan Riggs, see 9:1101; see also T3:2139; for a review by Lorrie Shepard, see 8:673 (2 references).

[2369]

Self-Perception Profile for College Students.

Purpose: To measure college students' self-concept.
Population: College students.
Publication Date: 1986.
Scores: 13 domains: Creativity, Intellectual Ability, Scholastic Competence, Job Competence, Athletic Competence, Appearance, Romantic Relationships, Social Acceptance, Close Friendships, Parent Relationships, Finding Humor in One's Life, Morality, Global Self-Worth.
Administration: Group.
Price Data, 1989: $9 per manual (84 pages).
Time: 30(40) minutes.
Authors: Jennifer Neemann and Susan Harter.
Publisher: Susan Harter, University of Denver.
Cross References: For reviews by Robert D. Brown and Stephen F. Davis, see 11:357 (1 reference).

TEST REFERENCES

1. Van Tassel-Baska, J., & Kulieke, M. J. (1987). The role of community-based scientific resources in developing scientific talent: A case study. *Gifted Child Quarterly, 31,* 111–115.
2. McGregor, L. N., Mayleben, M. A., Buzzanga, V. L., Davis, S. F., & Becker, A. H. (1991). Selected personality characteristics of first-generation college students. *College Student Journal, 25,* 231-234.
3. Hopkins, H. R., & Klein, H. A. (1993). Multidimensional self-perception: Linkages to parental nurturance. *The Journal of Genetic Psychology, 154,* 465-473.
4. Okun, M. A., & Fournet, L. M. (1993). Academic self-esteem and perceived validity of grades: A test of self-verification theory. *Contemporary Educational Psychology, 18,* 414-426.
5. Meltzer, L., & Reid, D. K. (1994). New directions in the assessment of students with special needs: The shift toward a constructivist perspective. *The Journal of Special Education, 28,* 338–355.
6. Brooks, J. H., II, & DuBois, D. L. (1995). Individual and environmental predictors of adjustment during the first year of college. *Journal of College Student Development, 36,* 347–360.
7. Klein, H. A. (1995). Self-perception in late adolescence: An interactive perspective. *Adolescence, 30,* 579–591.
8. Paul, E. L., & Kelleher, M. (1995). Precollege concerns about losing and making friends in college. *Journal of College Student Development, 36,* 513–521.
9. Phares, V. (1995). Fathers' and mothers' participation in research. *Adolescence, 30,* 593–602.
10. Berlant, A. R., & Weiss, M. R. (1997). Goal orientation and the modeling process: An individual's focus on form and outcome. *Research Quarterly for Exercise & Sport, 68,* 317–330.
11. Curry, L. A., Rehm, M., & Bernuth, C. (1997). Participation in Division I athletics: Self-perception differences in athletes and nonathletes. *College Student Journal, 31,* 96–103.
12. Eidson, T. A. (1997). Assessment of hearing-impaired athletes anxiety and self-perceptions. *Perceptual and Motor Skills, 85,* 491–496.

[2370]

Self Profile Q-Sort.

Purpose: Designed to assess self-concepts of children.
Population: Grades 2-8.
Publication Dates: 1972-1974.
Acronym: SPQS.
Scores: No scores; examiners may develop their own criteria for evaluation of items.
Administration: Individual or group.
Price Data, 1987: $6.75 per 25 forms and manual ('72, 1 page); $4.50 per specimen set.
Time: [5-10] minutes.
Author: Alan J. Politte.
Publisher: Psychologists and Educators, Inc.

Cross References: For a review by Stanley E. Ridley, see 9:1102.

[2371]

Self Worth Inventory.

Purpose: "Helps respondents increase their understanding of self-worth and how it is developed."
Population: Adults.
Publication Date: 1990.
Acronym: SWI.
Scores, 8: Self, Family, Peers, Work, Projected Self, Self-Concept, Self-Esteem, Self-Worth.
Administration: Group.
Manual: No manual.
Price Data, 1993: $10 per inventory.
Time: Administration time not reported.
Comments: May be self-administered.
Author: Everett Robinson.
Publisher: Consulting Resource Group International, Inc.
Cross References: For reviews by Jayne E. Stake and Norman D. Sundberg, see 13:282.

[2372]

The Senior Apperception Technique [1985 Revision].

Purpose: A projective instrument to gather information on forms of depression, loneliness, or rage in the elderly.
Population: Ages 65 and over.
Publication Dates: 1973–1985.
Acronym: S.A.T.
Scores: No scores.
Administration: Individual.
Price Data, 1993: $19.75 per manual ('85, 12 pages) and set of picture cards.
Time: Administration time not reported.
Author: Leopold Bellak.
Publisher: C.P.S., Inc.
Cross References: For reviews by Paul A. Arbisi and Michael G. Kavan, see 13:283; see also T3:2148 (2 references); for a review by K. Warner Schaie of an earlier edition, see 8:676 (1 reference).

[2373]

Senior Aptitude Tests.

Purpose: Constructed "to measure a number of aptitudes of pupils . . . for the purpose of guidance and selection."
Population: Standards 8-10 in South African schools, college, and adults.
Publication Dates: 1969-1970.
Acronym: SAT.
Scores, 12: Verbal Comprehension, Numerical Fluency, Word Fluency, Visual Perception Speed, Reasoning (Deductive, Inductive), Spatial Visualization (2 Dimensional, 3 Dimensional), Memory (Paragraphs, Symbols), Psychomotor Coordination, Writing Speed.
Administration: Group.
Price Data: Available from publisher.
Time: 88(120) minutes.
Comments: Test materials in English and Afrikaans.
Authors: F. A. Fouche and N. F. Alberts.
Publisher: Human Sciences Research Council [South Africa].
Cross References: See T4:2430 (1 reference).

TEST REFERENCE

1. Dunn, A., & Eliot, J. (1996). Spatial intelligence and the six-factor personality questionnaire. *Perceptual and Motor Skills, 82,* 1235–1240.

[2374]

Senior Clerical Skills Test.

Purpose: "Evaluates the suitability of candidates for all levels of experience for the position of clerk."
Population: Candidates for clerical positions.
Publication Dates: 1954-1984.
Acronym: PRCLERIC.
Scores: 5 tests: Problem Solving Ability, Numerical Skills, Attention to Detail, Coding, Alphabetizing & Filing.
Administration: Group.
Price Data, 1999: $230 per candidate.
Foreign Language Edition: French edition available.
Time: (25) minutes.
Authors: Walden Personnel Performance, Inc.
Publisher: Walden Personnel Performance, Inc.
Cross References: For a review by Ruth G. Thomas, see 10:62.

[2375]

Senior South African Individual Scale—Revised.

Purpose: Measures general intelligence.
Population: Ages 7-0 to 16-11.
Publication Dates: 1964–1991.
Acronym: SSAIS-R.
Scores: 11 tests: Verbal (Vocabulary, Comprehension, Similarities, Number Problems, Story Memory, Memory for Digits), Nonverbal (Pattern Completion, Block Designs, Missing Parts, Form Board, Coding).
Administration: Individual.
Price Data: Available from publisher.
Time: Tests 1–9: (75) minutes; Tests 10–11: (10) minutes; Tests 3, 4, 7, and 8 (Abbreviated Scale): (45) minutes.
Comments: Developed for Afrikaans-speaking and English-speaking South African students.
Author: Human Sciences Research Council.

Publisher: Human Sciences Research Council [South Africa].
Cross References: See T3:2153 (1 reference) and 7:413 (1 reference).

[2376]

Sensory Evaluation Kit.

Purpose: "Designed to increase functional performance through the primary use of smell."
Population: Ages 2 to adult.
Publication Date: 1991.
Scores, 20: Motor, Tactile, Visual, Auditory, Olfactory, Gustatory, Problem Solving, Attention Span, Directions (2-Step, No Cuing), Interpretation of Signs/Symbols, Memory, Body Scheme (Body Parts, R/L Discrimination), Motor Planning, Stereognosis, Figure/Ground, Color Perception, Form Constancy, Position in Space.
Administration: Individual.
Price Data: Available from publisher.
Time: Administration time not reported.
Author: Bonnye S. Klein.
Publisher: Maddak, Inc.
Cross References: For reviews by J. Jeffrey Grill and Ellen Weissinger, see 13:284.

[2377]

Sensory Integration and Praxis Tests.

Purpose: Designed to assess several practic abilities, various aspects of sensory processing status, and behavioral manifestations of deficits in integration of sensory inputs from these systems.
Population: Ages 4-8.11.
Publication Date: 1989.
Acronym: SIPT.
Scores: 17 tests: Space Visualization, Figure-Ground Perception, Standing and Walking Balance, Design Copying, Postural Praxis, Bilateral Motor Coordination, Praxis Verbal Command, Constructional Praxis, Postrotary Nystagmus, Motor Accuracy, Sequencing Praxis, Oral Praxis, Manual Form Perception, Kinesthesia, Finger Identification, Graphesthesia, Localization of Tactile Stimuli.
Administration: Individual.
Price Data, 1999: $1,155 per set for mail-in scoring including all test materials, 25 copies of each consumable test form, 10 complete sets of all 17 computer-scored answer sheets with 10 transmittal sheets, manual (307 pages), and carrying case; $1,150 per set for PC scoring including all test materials, 25 copies of each consumable test form, 1 disk, 10 PC answer booklets, manual, and carrying case; $29.50 per one each of 17 test answer sheets and 1 transmittal sheet; $14.50 per transmittal sheet; $3.90 per individual test answer sheet; $250 per 10-use disk (PC with Microsoft Windows) with 10 PC answer booklets; $16.50 per 25 test booklets (specify Design Copying, Motor Accuracy, or Kinesthesia); $70 per manual; $129.95 per training administration video (VHS); $179.50 per training administration 2 CD-ROM set.
Time: (10) minutes or less per individual test.
Comments: Extension and revision of the Southern California Sensory Integration Tests (SCSIT) and the Southern California Postrotary Nystagmus Test (SCPNT); computer-scoring only; stopwatch capable of recording 1/10 seconds needed (available from publisher).
Author: A. Jean Ayres.
Publisher: Western Psychological Services.
Cross References: For a review by James E. Ysseldyke, see 12:353 (18 references); see also T4:2433 (9 references). For a review by Byron P. Rourke of the SCPNT, see 9:1157 (20 references); for information on the SCSIT, see 9:1158 (5 references) and T3:2244 (21 references); for reviews by Homer B. C. Reed, Jr. and Alida S. Westman of the SCSIT, see 8:875 (5 references); see also T2:1887 (18 references).

TEST REFERENCES

1. Butler, R., & Marinor-Glassman, D. (1994). The effects of educational placement and grade level on the self-perceptions of low achievers and students with learning disabilities. *Journal of Learning Disabilities, 27,* 325–334.
2. Case-Smith, J. (1996). Fine motor outcomes in preschool children who receive occupational therapy services. *American Journal of Occupational Therapy, 50,* 52–61.
3. Mulligan, S. (1996). An analysis of score patterns of children with attention disorders on the Sensory Integration and Praxis Tests. *American Journal of Occupational Therapy, 50,* 647–654.
4. Cross, L. A., & Coster, W. J. (1997). Symbolic play language during sensory integration treatment. *American Journal of Occupational Therapy, 51,* 808–814.

[2378]

Sensory Integration Inventory—Revised for Individuals with Developmental Disabilities.

Purpose: "Designed to screen for [occupational therapy] clients who might benefit from a sensory integration treatment approach."
Population: Developmentally disabled occupational therapy clients school aged to adults, including autism spectrum and PDD.
Publication Dates: 1990–1992.
Acronym: SI Inventory.
Scores, 111: Item scores in each of 4 sections interpreted individually: Tactile, Vestibular, Proprioception, General Reactions.
Administration: Individual.
Price Data: Available from publisher.
Time: Administration time not reported.
Comments: A semistructured interview of a person who works/lives closely with the client (e.g., parent or therapeutic staff member); space also provided for qualitative comments.
Authors: Judith E. Reisman and Bonnie Hanschu.
Publisher: P.D.P. Press, Inc.

[2379]
Sentence Completion Series.

Purpose: Constructed as a "semiprojective method of gathering client information" for personality and psychodiagnostic assessment.
Population: Adolescents and adults.
Publication Dates: 1991–1992.
Acronym: SCS.
Scores: No scores.
Administration: Group.
Forms, 8: Adult, Adolescent, Family, Marriage, Parenting, Work, Illness, Aging.
Price Data: Price information available from publisher for complete kit including manual and 15 of each form
Time: [10–45] minutes.
Comments: Forms may be administered alone or in any combination.
Authors: Larry H. Brown and Michael A. Unger.
Publisher: Psychological Assessment Resources, Inc.

[2380]
Sentence Completion Test.

Purpose: Developed to assess examinee's feelings, urges, beliefs, attitudes, and desires.
Population: High school and college.
Publication Date: 1972.
Acronym: SCT.
Scores: 35 item scores in 6 areas: Self Concept, Parental Attitude, Peer Attitude, Need for Achievement, Learning Attitude, Body Image.
Administration: Group or individual.
Price Data, 1987: $8.25 per 25 tests; $6.75 per specimen set.
Time: [15] minutes.
Author: Floyd S. Irvin.
Publisher: Psychologists and Educators, Inc.
Cross References: See T4:2434 (19 references), T3:2155 (9 references), and T2:1057 (5 references).

TEST REFERENCES

1. Blanchard-Fields, F. (1986). Reasoning on social dilemmas varying in emotional saliency: An adult developmental perspective. *Psychology and Aging, 1,* 325-333.
2. Armstrong, J. G., & Loewenstein, R. J. (1990). Characteristics of patients with multiple personality and dissociative disorders on psychological testing. *The Journal of Nervous and Mental Disease, 178,* 448-454.
3. Noam, G. G., & Dill, D. L. (1991). Adult development and symptomatology. *Psychiatry, 54,* 208–217.
4. Sakheim, G. A., Osborn, E., & Abrams, D. (1991). Toward a clearer differentiation of high-risk from low-risk fire-setters. *Child Welfare, 70,* 489–503.
5. Hayamizu, T. (1992). Spontaneous causal attributions: A cross-cultural study using the Sentence Completion Test. *Psychological Reports, 71,* 715-720.
6. Luthar, S. S., & Zigler, E. (1992). Intelligence and social competence among high-risk adolescents. *Development and Psychopathology, 4,* 287-299.
7. Piotrowski, C., Keller, J. W., & Ogawa, T. (1993). Projective techniques: An international perspective. *Psychological Reports, 72,* 179-182.
8. Rierdan, J., & Koff, E. (1993). Developmental variables in relation to depressive symptoms in adolescent girls. *Development and Psychopathology, 5,* 485-496.
9. Szajnberg, M. D., Krall, V. K., Davis, P., Treem, W., & Hyams, J. (1993). Psychopathology and relationship measures in children with inflammatory bowel disease and their parents. *Child Psychiatry and Human Development, 23,* 215–232.
10. Waterman, J., & Lusk, R. (1993). Psychological testing in evaluation of child sexual abuse. *Child Abuse & Neglect, 17,* 145-159.
11. Helson, R., & Roberts, B. W. (1994). Ego development and personality change in adulthood. *Journal of Personality and Social Psychology, 66,* 911-920.

[2381]
Sentence Completion Tests.

Purpose: "These tests provide a projective technique for individuals to express in their own way their own unique feelings, behaviors, attitudes, assets, needs, problems, thoughts, opinions of self, relationships, likes, dislikes, moods, frustrations, inhibitions, fantasies, backgrounds, responses from others, desires, mistakes, habits, secrets, idiosyncrasies, dreams, attitudes toward the test, etc."
Publication Dates: 1989-1995.
Administration: Group.
Price Data, 1998: $10 per 20 tests; $95 for 2 copies of all tests and Lifetime License to copy for personal or institutional use.
Time: Administration time not reported.
Comments: Master List includes sentence completion stems and alternatives used in the development of all the tests.
Author: Allan Roe.
Publisher: Diagnostic Specialists, Inc.

a) GENERAL INCOMPLETE SENTENCES TEST.
Population: General including college, clinical, hospitalized, and private practice adults.
Acronym: GIST.
Foreign Language Editions: Spanish GIST is available.

b) SHORT INCOMPLETE SENTENCES.
Population: Adult and adolescent clients.
Acronym: SIS.

c) FULL INCOMPLETE SENTENCES TEST.
Purpose: To be used for courts, custody, and diagnostic decisions.
Acronym: FIST.

d) FULL I AM TEST.
Purpose: "Helpful for eliciting identity problems."
Acronym: FIAT.

e) KIDS INCOMPLETE SENTENCES TEST.
Population: Ages 5-12.
Acronym: KIST.

f) TEENAGE SENTENCE COMPLETION.
Population: Ages 13-19.
Acronym: TASC.

g) MARRIAGE INCOMPLETE SENTENCES TEST.
Population: Married couples.
Acronym: MIST.

h) RELATIONSHIP INCOMPLETE SENTENCES TEST.
Population: Any relationship.
Acronym: RIST.

i) FULL LENGTH ALCOHOL SENTENCE COMPLETION.
Population: Alcohol users.
Acronym: FLASC.
j) DRUG INQUIRY SENTENCE COMPLETION.
Population: Drug users.
Acronym: DISC.
k) TALKING HONESTLY AND OPENLY ABOUT OUT RELATIONSHIP.
Population: Sex offenders.
Acronym: THOR.
l) SEXUAL ABUSE SURVIVOR'S TEST.
Populaton: Sex abuse victim.
Acronym: SAST.

[2382]

Sequenced Inventory of Communication Development, Revised Edition.

Purpose: Designed as a diagnostic assessment to evaluate the communication abilities of normal and retarded children.
Population: Ages 4 months through 4 years.
Publication Dates: 1975-1984.
Acronym: SICD-R.
Administration: Individual.
Price Data, 1999: $385 per complete kit (includes instruction manual ['84, 79 pages], test manual ['84, 117 pages], 50 record booklets/profile forms, and over 100 items used in the test administration); $45 per 25 scales (Expressive and Receptive); $32.50 per instruction manual; $32.50 per test manual.
Foreign Language Edition: Cuban-Spanish edition available; Spanish translation included in test manual and separate Spanish-language forms with pictures are available.
Time: (30-75) minutes.
Comments: Some test accessories (e.g., paper, coins, and picture book) must be assembled locally.
Authors: Dona Lea Hedrick, Elizabeth M. Prather, and Annette R. Tobin, with contributions by Doris V. Allen, Lynn S. Bliss, and Lillian R. Rosenberg.
Publisher: Western Psychological Services.
a) RECEPTIVE SCALE.
Scores, 3: Awareness, Discrimination, Understanding.
b) EXPRESSIVE SCALE.
Scores, 4: Imitating, Initiating, Responding, Verbal Output.
Cross References: See T4:2438 (21 references); for reviews by Carol Mardell-Czudnowski and Mary Ellen Pearson, see 10:331 (6 references); for reviews by Barbara W. Hodson and Joan I. Lynch of the earlier edition, see 9:1109 (4 references); see also T3:2159 (4 references).

TEST REFERENCES

1. Kelly, D. J., & Rice, M. L. (1986). A strategy for language assessment of young children: A combination of two approaches. *Language, Speech, and Hearing Services in Schools, 17,* 83–94.
2. Landry, S. H., & Loveland, K. A. (1989). The effect of social context on the functional communication skills of autistic children. *Journal of Autism and Developmental Disorders, 19(2),* 283-299.
3. Roberts, J. M. A. (1989). Echolalia and comprehension in autistic children. *Journal of Autism and Developmental Disorders, 19(2),* 271-281.
4. Olswang, L. B., & Bain, B. A. (1991). Clinical Forum: Treatment efficacy when to recommend intervention. *Language, Speech, and Hearing Services in Schools, 22,* 255–263.
5. Abkarian, G. G. (1992). Communication effects of prenatal alcohol exposure. *Journal of Communication Disorders, 25,* 221–240.
6. Emde, R., Plomin, R., Robinson, J., Corley, R., DeFries, J., Fulker, D. W., Reznick, J. S., Campos, J., Kagan, J., & Zahn-Waxler, C. (1992). Temperament, emotion, and cognition at fourteen months: The MacArthur longitudinal twin study. *Child Development, 63,* 1437–1455.
7. Feldman, H. M., Evans, J. L., Brown, R. E., & Wareham, N. L. (1992). Early language and communicative abilities of children with periventricular leukomalacia. *American Journal on Mental Retardation, 97,* 222-234.
8. Feldman, H. M., Holland, A. L., & Brown, R. E. (1992). A fluent language disorder following antepartum left-hemisphere brain injury. *Journal of Communication Disorders, 25,* 125–142.
9. Gravel, J. S., & Wallace, I. F. (1992). Listening and language at 4 years of age: Effects of early otitis media. *Journal of Speech and Hearing Research, 35,* 588–595.
10. Lewy, A. L., & Dawson, G. (1992). Social stimulation and joint attention in young autistic children. *Journal of Abnormal Child Psychology, 20,* 555-566.
11. Ogletree, B. T., Wetherby, A. M., & Westling, D. L. (1992). Profile of the prelinguistic intentional communicative behaviors of children with profound mental retardation. *American Journal on Mental Retardation, 97,* 186-196.
12. Restrepo, M. A., Swisher, L., Plante, E., & Vance, R. (1992). Relations among verbal and nonverbal cognitive skills in normal language and specifically language-impaired children. *Journal of Communication Disorders, 25,* 205–219.
13. Tannock, R., Girolametto, L., & Siegal, L. S. (1992). Language intervention with children who have developmental delays: Effects of an interactive approach. *American Journal on Mental Retardation, 97,* 145-160.
14. Johnston, J. R., Miller, J. F., Curtiss, S., & Tallal, P. (1993). Conversations with children who are language impaired: Asking questions. *Journal of Speech and Hearing Research, 36,* 973–978.
15. Lipkens, R., Hayes, S. C., & Hayes, L. J. (1993). Longitudinal study of the development of derived relations in an infant. *Journal of Experimental Child Psychology, 56,* 201-239.
16. Plomin, R., Kagan, J., Emoe, R. N., Reznick, J. S., Braungart, J. M., Robinson, J., Campos, J., Zahn-Waxler, C., Corley, R., Fulker, D. W., & DeFries, J. C. (1993). Genetic change and continuity from fourteen to twenty months: The MacArthur longitudinal twin study. *Child Development, 64,* 1354–1376.
17. Weismer, S. E., Murray-Branch, J., & Miller, J. F. (1993). Comparison of two methods for promoting productive vocabulary in late talkers. *Journal of Speech and Hearing Research, 36,* 1037–1050.
18. Yoder, P. J., Kaiser, A. P., Alpert, C., & Fischer, R. (1993). Following the child's lead when teaching nouns to preschoolers with mental retardation. *Journal of Speech and Hearing Research, 36,* 158–167.
19. Bendersky, M., & Lewis, M. (1994). Environment risk, biological risk, and developmental outcome. *Developmental Psychology, 30,* 484-494.
20. Feagans, L. V., Kipp, E., & Blood, I. (1994). The effect of otitis media on the attention skills of day-care-attending toddlers. *Developmental Psychology, 30,* 701-708.
21. Feldman, H. M., Janosky, J. E., Scher, M. S., & Wareham, N. L. (1994). Language abilities following prematurity, periventricular brain injury, and cerebral palsy. *Journal of Communication Disorders, 27,* 71–90.
22. Girolametto, L., & Tannock, R. (1994). Correlates of directiveness in the interactions of fathers and mothers of children with developmental delays. *Journal of Speech and Hearing, 37,* 1178–1192.
23. Kaiser, A. P., & Hester, P. P. (1994). Generalized effects of enhanced milieu teacher. *Journal of Speech and Hearing, 37,* 1320–1340.
24. Leadbeater, B. J., & Bishop, S. J. (1994). Predictors of behavioral problems in preschool children of inner-city African-American and Puerto Rican adolescent mothers. *Child Development, 65,* 638–648.
25. Plante, E., & Vance, R. (1994). Selection of preschool language tests: A data-based approach. *Language, Speech, and Hearing Services in Schools, 25,* 15–24.
26. Roberts, J. E., Burchinal, M. R., & Bailey, D. B. (1994). Communication among preschoolers with and without disabilities in same-age and mixed-age classes. *American Journal on Mental Retardation, 99,* 231–249.
27. Warren, S. F., Gazdag, G. E., Bambara, L. M., & Jones, H. A. (1994). Changes in the generativity and use of semantic relationships concurrent with milieu language intervention. *Journal of Speech and Hearing, 37,* 924–934.
28. Weismer, S. E., Murray-Branch, J., & Miller, J. F. (1994). A prospective longitudinal study of language development in late talkers. *Journal of Speech and Hearing, 37,* 852–867.
29. Yoder, P. J., Davies, B., & Bishop, K. (1994). Adult interaction style effects on the language sampling and transcription process with children who have developmental disabilities. *American Journal on Mental Retardation, 99,* 270–282.
30. Yoder, P. J., Davies, B., Bishop, K., & Munson, L. (1994). Effect of adult continuing wh-questions on conversational participation in children with developmental disabilities. *Journal of Speech and Hearing Research, 37,* 193–204.
31. Cooper, S. A., & Collacott, R. A. (1995). The effect of age on language in people with Down's syndrome. *Journal of Intellectual Disability Research, 39,* 197–200.
32. Schwartz, R. G. (1995). Effect of familiarity on word duration in children's speech: A preliminary investigation. *Journal of Speech and Hearing, 38,* 76–84.

33. Burchimal, M. R., Roberts, J. E., Nabors, L. A., & Bryant, D. M. (1996). Quality of center child care and infant cognitive and language development. *Child Development, 67,* 606–620.
34. Clark, M. G., & Leonard, L. B. (1996). Lexical comprehension and grammatical deficits in children with specific language impairment. *Journal of Communication Disorders, 29,* 95–105.
35. Smith, K. E., Landry, S. H., Swank, P. R., Baldwin, C. D., Denson, S. E., & Wildin, S. (1996). The relation of medical risk and maternal stimulation with preterm infants' development of cognitive, language and daily living skills. *Journal of Child Psychology and Psychiatry, 37,* 858–864.
36. Vernon-Feagans, L., Manlove, E. E., & Volling, B. L. (1996). Otitis media and the social behavior of day-care-attending children. *Child Development, 67,* 1528–1539.
37. Waterhouse, L., Morris, R., Allen, D., Dunn, M., Fein, D., Feinstein, C., Rapin, I., & Wing, L. (1996). Diagnosis and classification in autism. *Journal of Autism and Developmental Disorders, 26,* 59–86.
38. Johnson, J. M., Seikel, J. A., Madison, C. L., Foose, S. M., & Rinard, K. D. (1997). Standardized test performance of children with a history of prenatal exposure to multiple drugs/cocaine. *Journal of Communication Disorders, 30,* 45–73.
39. Kiernan, B., Snow, D., Swisher, L., & Vance, R. (1997). Another look at nonverbal rule induction in children with SLI: Test a flexible reconceputalization hypothesis. *Journal of Speech, Language, and Hearing Research, 40,* 75–82.
40. Kiernam, B., & Gray, S. (1998). Word learning in a supported-learning context by preschool children with specific language impairment. *Journal of Speech, Language, and Hearing Research, 41,* 161–171.

[2383]

Sequential Assessment of Mathematics Inventories: Standardized Inventory.

Purpose: "To differentiate among students in terms of their overall performance in mathematics and to measure an individual student's particular strengths and weaknesses in learning the mathematics curriculum."
Population: Grades K-8.
Publication Date: 1985.
Acronym: SAMI.
Scores, 9: Mathematical Language (Grades K-3 only), Ordinality (Grades K-3 only), Number/Notation, Computation, Measurement, Geometric Concepts, Mathematical Applications (Grades 4-8 only), Word Problems, Total.
Administration: Individual.
Price Data, 1994: $95.95 per complete program including easel, 12 student response booklets, 12 record forms, examiner's manual (95 pages), and case; $29.50 per 12 each of student response booklets and record forms; $56 per easel; $24.50 per manual.
Time: (20-60) minutes.
Comments: May be used in conjunction with the SAMI Informal Inventory.
Authors: Fredricka K. Reisman and Thomas A. Hutchinson (manual).
Publisher: The Psychological Corporation.
Cross References: For reviews by John W. Fleenor and Sylvia T. Johnson, see 11:359.

TEST REFERENCE

1. Vaidya, S. R. (1994). Diagnostic assessments and consideration of learning styles and lows of control characteristics—How do they impact teaching and learning? *College Student Journal, 27,* 159-162.

[2384]

Service Animal Adaptive Intervention Assessment.

Purpose: Constructed for "evaluating predispositions to and outcomes of service animal use."
Population: Occupational, physical, and recreational therapists, assistive technology professionals, and animal assisted therapy specialists.
Publication Date: 1998.
Acronym: SAAIA.
Scores, 5: Knowledge and Experience of Animals, Typical Activities/Skills, Personal/Social Characteristics, Requirements of Service Animal Compared to Resources of Person, Total Predisposition Score.
Administration: Group or individual.
Price Data, 1998: $29.95 per complete kit including all assessments as masters for photocopying and manual (10 pages).
Time: (90–120) minutes.
Comments: Ratings by professionals; also includes qualitative information.
Author: Susan A. Zapf.
Publisher: The Institute for Matching Person & Technology.

[2385]

Service Excellence.

Purpose: Designed to provide "customer service personnel with a diagnostic 'snapshot' of their individual approaches" to their roles.
Population: Customer service personnel.
Publication Dates: 1990-1999.
Scores, 19: Market Awareness, Technical, Strategic, Taking Initiative, Optimism, Outgoing, Customer Focus, Empathy, Communication, Sales Focus, Insight, Using Resources, Tactical, Structuring, Team Player, Quality Focus, Relaying Customer Views, Following Through, Exaggeration.
Administration: Group.
Price Data: Available from publisher.
Time: (30) minutes.
Comments: Purchase and use requires training by publisher.
Authors: James T. Mahoney (test), Thomas M. Rand (manual), and F. Carl Mahoney (manual).
Publisher: Management Research Group.

[2386]

Service First.

Purpose: Constructed to measure "customer service orientation or potential."
Population: Employees in service-oriented positions.
Publication Dates: 1990–1995.
Scores, 5: Active Customer Relations, Polite Customer Relations, Helpful Customer Relations, Personalized Customer Relations, Total.
Administration: Group.
Price Data, 1996: $25 per test kit including sample test booklet, sample answer sheet, test manual ('95, 47 pages), administration and scoring manual, and dem-

onstration administration and scoring manual; $5 per administrator's manual; $3 per test booklet; scoring service $5 to $7.50 per applicant.
Time: (20) minutes.
Author: CORE Corporation.
Comments: Scoring is done via telephone by publisher or on site with a DOS-compatible disk; paper-and-pencil and computer administration.
Publisher: CORE Corporation.

[2387]

Severe Cognitive Impairment Profile.

Purpose: Designed to measure and monitor the cognitive performance of patients previously diagnosed with dementia.
Population: Severely demented patients.
Publication Dates: 1995–1998.
Acronym: SCIP.
Scores, 9: Comportment, Attention, Language, Memory, Motor, Conceptualization, Arithmetic, Visuospatial, Total.
Administration: Individual.
Price Data, 1998: $349 per complete kit including manual ('98, 67 pages), leather carrying case with secure lock, 25 record forms, and all other test materials.
Time: (30–45) minutes.
Author: Guerry M. Peavy.
Publisher: Psychological Assessment Resources, Inc.

[2388]

The Severity and Acuity of Psychiatric Illness Scales—Adult Version.

Purpose: Designed to assess the severity and acuity of psychiatric illness in adult mental health service recipients.
Population: Adults.
Publication Date: 1998.
Scores, 6: Severity (Complexity Indicator, Probability of Admission, Total), Acuity (Clinical Status, Nursing Status, Total).
Administration: Individual.
Price Data, 1999: $65 per starter kit including training manual (52 pages), 10 reusable Severity item booklets, 25 Severity scale rating sheets, 10 reusable Acuity item booklets, and 25 Acuity scale rating sheets; $15 per 10 Severity scale item booklets; $12.50 per 25 Severity scale rating sheets; $15 per 10 Acuity scale item booklets; $12.50 per 25 Acuity scale rating sheets; $17 per training manual.
Time: (5) minutes.
Comments: Computer versions available; two scales (Severity and Acuity) can be used separately or together; results to be used as an "integrated outcomes-management and decision-support system for assisting treatment decision-making"; ratings are done by caregivers about clients/patients.
Author: John S. Lyons.
Publisher: The Psychological Corporation.

[2389]

Sex-Role Egalitarianism Scale.

Purpose: "Developed to measure attitudes toward the equality of men and women."
Population: High school to adult.
Publication Date: 1993.
Acronym: SRES.
Scores, 6: Marital Roles, Parental Roles, Employment Roles, Social-Interpersonal-Heterosexual Roles, Educational Roles, Total.
Administration: Group.
Price Data, 1999: $31 per examination kit including manual ('93, 58 pages), 10 question-and-answer documents, and 10 profile sheets; $24 per test manual; $36 per 25 Form B question-and-answer documents; $23 per 25 Form K Research Forms; $9–$11 (depending on volume) per 25 profile sheets; $11–$13 (depending on volume) per 25 Short Form BB or KK Question-and-answer sheets; $24 per researcher's kit including one each of manual, Form B question-and-answer documents, Research Form, Form B profile sheet, and one each of Form BB and KK Short Forms.
Time: (25–35) minutes.
Comments: Two full forms, B and K; two abbreviated forms, BB and KK.
Authors: Lynda A. King and Daniel W. King.
Publisher: Sigma Assessment Systems, Inc.
Cross References: For a review by Carol Collins, see 13:285.

TEST REFERENCE

1. Scandura, T. A., Tejeda, M. J., & Lankau, M. J. (1995). An examination of the validity of the Sex-Role Egalitarianism Scale (SRES-KK) using confirmatory factor analysis procedures. *Educational and Psychological Measurement, 55,* 832–840.

[2390]

Sexometer.

Purpose: Designed to measure one's sex information.
Population: Adolescents and adults.
Publication Date: 1974.
Scores: Total score only.
Administration: Group.
Price Data, 1998: $1 per scale.
Time: [20] minutes.
Comments: Manual is a reprint of a journal article by the author.
Author: Panos D. Bardis.
Publisher: Donna Bardis.
Cross References: See 8:353 (1 reference).

[2391]

Sexual Abuse Screening Inventory.

Purpose: For routine sex abuse screenings on children.
Population: Preschool through adolescence.

Publication Date: 1987.
Acronym: SASI.
Scores: 8 categories: School, Peer Relations, Adult Relations, Bedtime, Hygiene, Behavioral/Emotional, Medical, Miscellaneous.
Administration: Individual.
Price Data, 1996: $20 per 50 Sexual Abuse Screening Checklists.
Time: Administration time not reported.
Author: Diana L. McCoy.
Publisher: Magic Lantern Publications [No reply from publisher; status unknown].

[2392]

Sexual Adaptation and Functioning Test.

Purpose: Designed "as an aid in the planning of psychotherapeutic intervention techniques and to gain insight into an individual's sexual adaptation and sexual functioning."
Population: White adults ages 16 and over.
Publication Dates: 1985-1986.
Acronym: SAFT.
Scores: Total score only.
Administration: Individual.
Restricted Distribution: Distribution restricted to psychologists registered with the South African Medical and Dental Council.
Foreign Language Edition: Afrikaans edition available.
Price Data: Available from publisher.
Time: (90-100) minutes.
Comments: Projective test; self-administered using audiotaped instructions.
Author: Louise Olivier.
Publisher: Human Sciences Research Council [South Africa].

[2393]

Sexual Adjustment Inventory.

Purpose: "Designed to identify sexually deviate and paraphiliac behavior."
Population: People accused or convicted of sexual offenses.
Publication Date: 1991.
Acronym: SAI.
Scores: 13 scales: Test Item Truthfulness, Sex Item Truthfulness, Sexual Adjustment, Child Molest, Sexual Assault, Exhibitionism, Incest, Alcohol, Drugs, Violence, Antisocial, Distress, Judgment.
Administration: Group.
Forms, 2: Adult, Juvenile.
Price Data: Available from publisher.
Time: (35–40) minutes.
Comments: Both computer version and paper-pencil format are scored using IBM-PC compatibles.
Author: Risk & Needs Assessment, Inc.
Publisher: Risk & Needs Assessment, Inc.

[2394]

Sexual Communication Inventory.

Purpose: Designed to help couples develop their skills for communicating about sexual matters in their relationship.
Population: Premarital and marital counselees.
Publication Date: 1980.
Acronym: SCI.
Scores: Overall score.
Administration: Group.
Price Data, 1993: $.75 per inventory; $2 per manual (6 pages).
Time: (20) minutes
Author: Millard J. Bienvenu.
Publisher: Millard J. Bienvenu, Northwest Publications.
Cross References: For a review by Richard B. Stuart, see 9:1118.

[2395]

Sexual Violence Risk-20.

Purpose: Designed as a "method" (not a test or scale) of assessing an individual's risk for committing sexual violence.
Population: Individuals suspected to be at-risk for committing sexual violence.
Publication Dates: 1997–1998.
Acronym: SVR-20.
Scores: Not scored; ratings in five areas: Psychosocial Adjustment, Sexual Offenses, Future Plans, Other Considerations, Summary Risk Rating.
Administration: Individual.
Price Data, 1999: $44 per kit including manual ('98, 99 pages) and 50 coding sheets; $32 per manual; $19 per 50 coding sheets.
Time: Administration time not reported.
Comments: "Designed to assist evaluations of risk for sexual violence"; administration and coding by trained professionals only; rating done by the professional about a client/offender.
Authors: Douglas P. Boer, Stephen P. Hart, P. Randall Kropp, and Christopher D. Webster.
Publisher: British Columbia Institute Against Family Violence [Canada].

[2396]

Sexuality Experience Scales.

Purpose: To be used in sex counseling as an aid in interviewing, diagnosis of sexual dysfunction, and evaluation of therapy, as well as in research.
Population: Adults.
Publication Date: 1981.
Acronym: SES.
Scores: 4 scales: Sexual Morality, Psychosexual Stimulation, Sexual Motivation, Attraction to Marriage.

Administration: Group.
Editions, 2: Female, Male.
Price Data: Available from publisher.
Time: Administration time not reported.
Authors: J. Frenken and P. Vennix.
Publisher: Swets Test Publishers [The Netherlands].
Cross References: See T4:2449 (2 references).

TEST REFERENCE

1. Faith, M. S., & Schare, M. L. (1993). The role of body image in sexually avoidant behavior. *Archives of Sexual Behavior, 22,* 345-356.

[2397]

SF-36 Health Survey.

Purpose: Designed as a "survey of general health concepts."
Population: Ages 14 and older.
Publication Dates: 1989–1993.
Acronym: SF-36.
Scores: 8 scales: Physical Functioning, Role-Physical, Bodily Pain, General Health, Vitality, Social Functioning, Role-Emotional, Mental Health.
Administration: Group.
Price Data: Available from publisher; administration and scoring software available from CogniSyst, Inc.
Time: Administration time not reported.
Author: John E. Ware, Jr.
Publisher: The Health Institute, New England Medical Center.

TEST REFERENCE

1. Perry, W., McDougall, A., & Viglione, D. (1995). A five-year follow-up on the temporal stability of the ego impairment index. *Journal of Personality Assessment, 64,* 112–118.

[2398]

Shapes Analysis Test.

Purpose: Designed as a test of spatial perception.
Population: Ages 14 and over.
Publication Date: 1972.
Acronym: SAT.
Scores, 3: 2-Dimensional, 3-Dimensional, Total.
Administration: Group.
Price Data, 1993: £53.50 per 25 booklets; £35 per 50 answer sheets; £12.50 per manual (20 pages); £15 per specimen set.
Time: 25(35) minutes.
Authors: A. W. Heim, K. P. Watts, and V. Simmonds.
Publisher: The Test Agency Ltd. [England].
Cross References: For a review by Charles T. Myers, see 8:1046 (2 references).

[2399]

Shapiro Control Inventory.

Purpose: Designed to "categorize, refine, and articulate a person's state of consciousness regarding control."
Population: Ages 14–88.
Publication Date: 1994.
Acronym: SCI.
Scores, 9: General Domain (Overall Sense of Control, Positive Sense of Control, Negative Sense of Control), Modes of Control (Positive Assertive, Positive Yielding, Negative Assertive, Negative Yielding), Domain-Specific Sense of Control, Overall Desire for Control.
Administration: Group or individual.
Price Data: Available from publisher.
Foreign Language Editions: Spanish, Japanese, and Polish editions under development.
Time: (20–30) minutes.
Author: Deane H. Shapiro, Jr.
Publisher: Behaviordata, Inc.
Cross References: For reviews by Wesley E. Sime and Claudia R. Wright, see 13:286.

TEST REFERENCE

1. Gottschack, L. A., Stein, M. K., & Shapiro, D. H. (1997). The application of computerized content analysis of speech to the diagnostic process in a psychiatric outpatient clinic. *Journal of Clinical Psychology, 53,* 427–441.

[2400]

Sheltered Employment Work Experience Program.

Purpose: Evaluation of specific vocational competency.
Population: Mentally retarded teenagers and adults.
Publication Dates: 1975-1982.
Acronym: SEWEP.
Scores, 12: Factory Work Training, Carpentry, Print Shop, Laundry, Building Maintenance, General and Outdoor Maintenance, Transportation Aide, Library Aide, Food Service, Housekeeping, Personal/Social Development, General Vocational Development.
Administration: Group.
Price Data, 1987: $6 per manual ('75, 57 pages including scales).
Time: Administration time not reported.
Author: The Barber Center Press, Inc.
Publisher: The Barber Center Press, Inc.
Cross References: For reviews by Edwin L. Herr and David P. Wacker, see 9:1121.

[2401]

Ship Destination Test.

Purpose: Constructed to measure "general reasoning."
Population: Grades 9 and over.
Publication Dates: 1955-1956.
Scores: Total score only.
Administration: Group.
Price Data: Available from publisher.
Time: 15(20) minutes.
Authors: Paul R. Christensen and J. P. Guilford.
Publisher: Mind Garden.

Cross References: See T2:457 (13 references); for a review by William B. Schrader, see 6:500 (8 references); for a review by C. J. Adcock, see 5:383.

TEST REFERENCE

1. Brown, N. W. (1994). Cognitive, interest, and personality variables predicting first-semester GPA. *Psychological Reports, 74,* 605-606.

[2402]

Shipley Institute of Living Scale.

Purpose: "Designed to assess general intellectual functioning in adults and adolescents and to aid in detecting cognitive impairment in individuals with normal original intelligence."

Population: Ages 14 and over.

Publication Dates: 1939-1986.

Acronym: SILS.

Scores, 6: Vocabulary, Abstraction, Combined Total, Conceptual Quotient, Abstraction Quotient, Estimated WAIS or WAIS-R IQ.

Administration: Group.

Price Data, 1999: $99.50 per complete kit including 100 test forms, hand-scoring key, 2 AutoScore™ test forms, and manual ('86, 100 pages); $18.50 per hand-scoring key; $35 per 100 test forms; $39.95 per 25 AutoScore™ test forms; $47.50 per manual; $225 per 25-use IBM Shipley microcomputer disk (PC with DOS).

Time: 20 minutes.

Comments: Formerly called Shipley-Hartford Retreat Scale for Measuring Intellectual Impairment and Shipley-Institute of Living Scale for Measuring Intellectual Impairment.

Authors: Walter C. Shipley (test and original manual) and Robert A. Zachary (revised manual).

Publisher: Western Psychological Services.

Cross References: See T4:2453 (63 references); for a review by William L. Deaton, see 11:360 (56 references); see also 9:1122 (13 references), T3:2179 (64 references), 8:677 (39 references), and T2:1380 (34 references); for a review by Aubrey J. Yates, see 7:138 (21 references); see also P:244 (38 references), 6:173 (13 references), and 5:111 (23 references); for reviews by E. J. G. Bradford, William A. Hunt, and Margaret Ives, see 3:95 (25 references).

TEST REFERENCES

1. Hartley, J. T. (1986). Reader and text variables as determinants of discourse memory in adulthood. *Psychology and Aging, 1,* 150-158.

2. Die, A. H., Seelbach, W. C., & Shenman, G. D. (1987). Achievement, motivation, achieving styles, and morale in the elderly. *Psychology and Aging, 2,* 407-408.

3. Erickson, R. C. (1989). Applications of cognitive testing to group therapies with the chronically mentally ill. *International Journal of Group Psychotherapy, 39,* 223–235.

4. Carey, M. P., Carey, K. B., Meisler, A. W. (1990). Training mentally ill chemical abusers in social problem solving. *Behavior Therapy, 21,* 511–518.

5. Haertzen, C. A., Hickey, J. E., Rose, M. R., & Jaffe, J. H. (1990). The relationship between a diagnosis of antisocial personality and hostility: Development of an antisocial hostility scale. *Journal of Clinical Psychology, 46,* 679–686.

6. London, E. D., Broussolle, E. D. M., Links, J. M., Wong, D. F., Cascella, N. G., Dannals, R. F., Sano, M., Herning, R., Snyder, F. R., Rippetoe, L. R., Toong, T. J. K., Jaffe, J. H., & Wagner, H. N., Jr. (1990). Morphine-induced metabolic changes in human brain. *Archives of General Psychiatry, 47,* 73–81.

7. Gacono, C. B., & Meloy, J. R. (1991). A Rorschach investigation of attachment and anxiety in antisocial personality disorder. *The Journal of Nervous and Mental Disease, 179,* 546-552.

8. Parker, E. S., Parker, D. A., & Harford, T. C. (1991). Specifying the relationship between alcohol use and cognitive loss: The effects of frequency of consumption and psychological distress. *Journal of Studies on Alcohol, 52,* 366–373.

9. Svanum, S., & McAdoo, W. G. (1991). Parental alcoholism: An examination of male and female alcoholics in treatment. *Journal of Studies on Alcohol, 52,* 127–132.

10. Bates, M. E., & Pandina, R. J. (1992). Familial alcoholism and premorbid cognitive deficit: A failure to replicate subtype differences. *Journal of Studies on Alcohol, 53,* 320–327.

11. Cynn, V. E. H. (1992). Persistence and problem solving skills in young male alcoholics. *Journal of Studies on Alcohol, 53,* 57–62.

12. Francis, C. R., Hughes, H. M., & Hitz, L. (1992). Physically abusive parents and the 16-PF: A preliminary psychological topology. *Child Abuse & Neglect, 16,* 673-691.

13. O'Connor, M. J., Sigman, M., & Kasari, C. (1992). Attachment behavior of infants exposed prenatally to alcohol: Mediating effects of infant affect and mother-infant interaction. *Development and Psychopathology, 4,* 243-256.

14. Andrews, J. A., Lewinsohn, P. M., Hops, H., & Roberts, R. E. (1993). Psychometric properties of scales for the measurement of psychosocial variables associated with depression in adolescence. *Psychological Reports, 73,* 1019-1046.

15. Baldwin, A. L., Baldwin, C. P., Kasser, T., Zax, M., Sameroff, A., & Seifer, R. (1993). Contextual risk and resiliency during late adolescence. *Development and Psychopathology, 5,* 741-761.

16. Beatty, W. W., Katzung, V. M., Nixon, S. J., & Moreland, V. J. (1993). Problem-solving deficits in alcoholics: Evidence from California Card Sorting Test. *Journal of Studies on Alcohol, 54,* 687–692.

17. Bishop, D. R. (1993). Validity issues in using the Millon-II with substance abusers. *Psychological Reports, 73,* 27-33.

18. Haller, D. L., Knisely, J. S., Dawson, K. S., & Schnoll, S. H. (1993). Perinatal substance abusers: Psychological and social characteristics. *The Journal of Nervous and Mental Disease, 181,* 509-513.

19. Holmstrom, R. W., Karp, S. A., & Siber, D. E. (1993). Relationship between the Apperceptive Personality Test and verbal intelligence in a university sample. *Psychological Reports, 73,* 575-578.

20. Johnson, D. L., Howie, V. M., Owen, M., Baldwin, C. D., & Luttman, D. (1993). Assessment of three-year-olds with the Stanford-Binet Fourth Edition. *Psychological Reports, 73,* 51-57.

21. Rosenfarb, I. S., Burker, E. J., Morris, S. A., & Cush, D. T. (1993). Effects of changing contingencies on the behavior of depressed and nondepressed individuals. *Journal of Abnormal Psychology, 102,* 642-646.

22. Sameroff, A. J., Seifer, R., Baldwin, A., & Baldwin, C. (1993). Stability of intelligence from preschool to adolescence: The influence of social and family risk factors. *Child Development, 64,* 80-97.

23. Schuldberg, D. (1993). Personal resourcefulness: Positive aspects of functioning in high-risk research. *Psychiatry, 56,* 137–152.

24. Wong, J. L. (1993). Comparison of the Shipley versus the WAIS-R subtests and summary scores in predicting college grade point average. *Perceptual and Motor Skills, 76,* 1075–1078.

25. Dalton, J. G. (1994). MMPI-168 and Marlowe-Crowne profiles of adoption applicants. *Journal of Clinical Psychology, 50,* 863-866.

26. Erber, J. T., Caiola, M. A., & Pupo, F. A. (1994). Age and forgetfulness: Managing perceivers' impressions of targets' capability. *Psychology and Aging, 9,* 554-561.

27. Gottschalk, L. A. (1994). The development, validation, and applications of a computerized measurement of cognitive impairment from the content analysis of verbal behavior. *Journal of Clinical Psychology, 50,* 349-361.

28. Harnish, M. J., Beatty, W. W., Nixon, S. J., & Parsons, O. A. (1994). Performance by normal subjects on the Shipley Institute of Living Scale. *Journal of Clinical Psychology, 50,* 881-888.

29. Horton, A. M., Jr. (1994). Identification of neuropsychological deficit: Levels of assessment. *Perceptual and Motor Skills, 79,* 1251-1255.

30. Moore, R. H. (1994). Underage female DUI offenders: Personality characteristics, psychological stressors, alcohol and other drug use, and driving-risk. *Psychological Reports, 74,* 435-445.

31. Munley, P. H., & Busby, R. (1994). MMPI-2 Negative Treatment Indicators scale and irregular discharge. *Psychological Reports, 74,* 903-906.

32. Rudd, M. D., Rajab, M. H., & Dahm, F. (1994). Problem-solving appraisal in suicide ideators and attempters. *American Journal of Orthopsychiatry, 64,* 136–149.

33. Spicer, K. B., Brown, G. G., & Gorell, J. M. (1994). Lexical decision in Parkinson disease: Lack of evidence for generalized bradyphrenia. *Journal of Clinical and Experimental Neuropsychology, 16,* 457-471.

34. Stone, J., Morin, C. M., Hart, R. P., Remsberg, S., & Mercer, J. (1994). Neuropsychological functioning in older insomniacs with or without obstructive sleep apnea. *Psychology and Aging, 9,* 231-236.

35. Tracy, J. I., & Bates, M. E. (1994). Models of functional organization as a model for detecting cognitive deficits: Data from a sample of social drinkers. *Journal of Studies on Alcohol, 55,* 726–738.

36. Baker, J. D., Williamson, D. A., & Syloe, C. (1995). Body image disturbance, memory bias, and body dysphoria: Effects of negative mood induction. *Behavior Therapy, 26,* 747–759.

37. Beatty, W. W., Paul, R. H., Wilbanks, S. L., Hames, K. A., Blanco, C. R., & Goodkin, D. E. (1995). Identifying multiple sclerosis patients with mild or global cognitive impairment using the Screening Examination for Cognitive Impairment (SEFCI). *Neurology, 45,* 718–723.

38. Hall, G. C. N., Hirschman, R., & Oliver, L. L. (1995). Sexual arousal and arousability to pedophilic stimuli in a community sample of normal men. *Behavior Therapy, 26,* 681–694.
39. Hays, J. R. (1995). Trail Making Test norms for psychiatric patients. *Perceptual and Motor Skills, 80,* 187-194.
40. Lundy, A., Gottheil, E., Serota, R. D., Weinstein, S. P., & Sterling, R. C. (1995). Gender differences and similarities in African-American crack cocaine abusers. *The Journal of Nervous and Mental Disease, 183,* 260–266.
41. Martin, R. A., Kazarian, S. S., & Breiter, H. J. (1995). Perceived stress, life events, dysfunctional attitudes, and depression in adolescent psychiatric inpatients. *Journal of Psychopathology and Behavioral Assessment, 17,* 81–95.
42. McDowd, J. M., & Filion, D. L. (1995). Aging and negative priming in a location suppression task: The long and short of it. *Psychology and Aging, 10,* 34-47.
43. McNally, R. J., & Shin, L. M. (1995). Association of intelligence with severity of posttraumatic stress disorder symptoms in Vietnam combat veterans. *American Journal of Psychiatry, 152,* 936-938.
44. Munley, P. H., Bains, D. S., Bloem, W. D., Busby, R. M., & Pendziszewski, S. (1995). Posttraumatic stress disorder and the MCMI-II. *Psychological Reports, 76,* 939-944.
45. Murphy, M. A., & Tosi, D. J. (1995). Typological description of the chronic low back-pain syndrome using the Millon Behavioral Health Inventory. *Psychological Reports, 76,* 1227–1234.
46. Smith, R. L., Goode, K. T., La Marche, J. A., & Boll, T. J. (1995). Selective Reminding Test short form administration: A comparison of two through twelve trials. *Psychological Assessment, 7,* 177-182.
47. Sutker, P. B., Davis, J. M., Uddo, M., & Ditta, S. R. (1995). Assessment of psychological distress in Persian Gulf troops: Ethnicity and gender comparisons. *Journal of Personality Assessment, 64,* 415-427.
48. Sutker, P. B., Davis, J. M., Uddo, M., & Ditta, S. R. (1995). War zone stress, personal resources, and PTSD in Persian Gulf War returnees. *Journal of Abnormal Psychology, 104,* 444–452.
49. Tarter, R. E., Switalz, J., Lu, S., & Van Thiel, D. (1995). Abstracting capacity in cirrhotic alcoholics: Negative findings. *Journal of Studies on Alcohol, 56,* 99–103.
50. Tivis, L. J., & Parsons, O. A. (1995). An investigation of verbal spatial functioning in chronic alcoholics. *Assessment, 2,* 285–292.
51. Toomey, R., & Schuldberg, D. (1995). Recognition and judgement of facial stimuli in schizotypal subjects. *Journal of Communication Disorders, 28,* 193–203.
52. Woody, G. E., McLellan, A. T., Luborsky, L., & O'Brien, C. P. (1995). Psychotherapy in community methadone programs: A validation study. *American Journal of Psychiatry, 152,* 1302–1308.
53. Ammerman, R. T., & Patz, R. J. (1996). Determinants of child abuse potential: Contribution of parent and child factors. *Journal of Clinical Child Psychology, 25,* 300–307.
54. Beatty, W. W., Hames, K. A., Blanco, C. R., Nixon, S. J., & Tivis, L. J. (1996). Visuospatial perception, construction and memory in alcoholism. *Journal of Studies on Alcohol, 57,* 136–143.
55. Burns, B., & Viglione, D. J., Jr. (1996). The Rorschach human experiences variable, interpersonal relatedness, and object representation in nonpatients. *Psychological Assessment, 8,* 92–99.
56. Ellis, T. E., Rudd, M. D., Rajab, M. H., & Wehrly, T. E. (1996). Cluster analysis of MCMI scores of suicidal psychiatric patients: Four personality profiles. *Journal of Clinical Psychology, 52,* 411–422.
57. Haines, M. E., Norris, M. P., & Kashy, D. A. (1996). The effects of depressed mood on academic performance in college students. *Journal of College Student Development, 37,* 519–526.
58. Hodgins, D. C., Pennington, M., el-Guebaly, N., & Dufour, M. (1996). Correlates of dissociative symptoms in substance abusers. *Journal of Nervous and Mental Disease, 184,* 636–639.
59. Murphy, K. R., & Barkley, R. A. (1996). Parents of children with attention-deficit/hyperactivity disorder: Psychological and attentional impairment. *American Journal of Orthopsychiatry, 66,* 93–102.
60. Tien, A. Y., Ross, D. E., Pearlson, G., & Strauss, M. E. (1996). Eye movements and psychopathology in schizophrenia and bipolar disorder. *Journal of Nervous and Mental Disease, 184,* 331–338.
61. Bates, M. E. (1997). Stability of neuropsychological assessments early in alcoholism treatment. *Journal of Studies on Alcohol, 58,* 617–621.
62. Downey, K. K., Stelson, F. W., Pomerleau, O. F. & Giordani, B. (1997). Adult attention deficit hyperactivity disorder: Psychological test profiles in a clinical population. *Journal of Nervous and Mental Disease, 185,* 32–38.
63. Gottschack, L. A., Stein, M. K., & Shapiro, D. H. (1997). The application of computerized content analysis of speech to the diagnostic process in a psychiatric outpatient clinic. *Journal of Clinical Psychology, 53,* 427–441.
64. Ham, H. P., & Parsons, O. A. (1997). Organization of psychological functions in alcoholics and nonalcoholics: A test of the compensatory hypothesis. *Journal of Studies on Alcohol, 58,* 67–74.
65. Kosson, D. S., Steverwald, B. L., Forth, A. E., & Kirkhart, K. J. (1997). A new method for assessing interpersonal behavior of psychopathic individuals: Preliminary validation studies. *Psychological Assessment, 9,* 89–101.
66. Lakein, D. A., Fantie, B. D., Grafman, J., Ross, S., O'Fallon, A., Dale, J., & Straus, S. E. (1997). Patients with chronic fatigue syndrome and accurate feeling-of-knowing judgments. *Journal of Clinical Psychology, 53,* 635–645.
67. McCarthy, C. J., Liu, H. T., Ghormley, M. R., Brack, G., & Brack, C. J. (1997). The relationship of beliefs about mood to coping resource effectiveness. *Journal of College Student Development, 38,* 157–165.
68. Pulos, S. (1997). Adolescents' implicit theories of physical phenomena: A matter of gravity. *International Journal of Behavioral Development, 20,* 493–507.
69. Tivis, L. J., & Parsons, O. A. (1997). Assessment of prose recall performance in chronic alcoholics: Recall of essential versus detail propositions. *Journal of Clinical Psychology, 53,* 233–242.
70. Wilhelm, S., McNally, R. J., Baer, L., & Florine, I. (1997). Autobiographical memory in obsessive-compulsive disorder. *British Journal of Clinical Psychology, 36,* 21–31.
71. Putzke, J. D., Williams, M. A., & Boll, T. J. (1998). A defensive response set and the relation between cognitive and emotional functioning: A replication. *Perceptual and Motor Skills, 86,* 251–257.

[2403]

Shoplifting Inventory.

Purpose: "Designed to evaluate people charged or convicted of shoplifting."
Population: Shoplifting offenders.
Publication Date: 1995.
Acronym: SI.
Scores: 9 scales: Truthfulness, Entitlement, Shoplifting, Antisocial, Peer Pressure, Self-Esteem, Impulsiveness, Alcohol, Drugs.
Administration: Group.
Price Data: Available from publisher.
Time: (35) minutes.
Comments: Both computer version and paper-pencil format are scored on IBM-PC compatibles.
Author: Risk & Needs Assessment, Inc.
Publisher: Risk & Needs Assessment, Inc.

[2404]

Shorr Imagery Test.

Purpose: "Designed to elicit and score the degree of conflict in the visual images projected by the subject."
Population: College students and adults.
Publication Dates: 1974-1977.
Acronym: SIT.
Scores, 6: Item scores in 5 areas (Human, Animal, Inanimate, Botanical, Others) plus Total score for Conflict.
Administration: Individual.
Price Data: Not available.
Time: (15-40) minutes.
Comments: For information for Group Shorr Imagery Test, see 1149.
Author: Joseph E. Shorr.
Publisher: Institute for Psycho-Imagination Therapy [Status unknown; no reply from publisher].

[2405]

Short Category Test, Booklet Format.

Purpose: A sensitive indicator of brain damage measuring an individual's ability to solve problems requiring careful observation, development of organizing principles, and responsiveness to feedback.
Population: Ages 15 and over.
Publication Dates: 1986-1987.
Acronym: SCT.
Scores: Total score only.

Subtests, 5: 1, 2, 3, 4, 5.
Administration: Individual.
Price Data, 1999: $175 per complete kit including 100 answer sheets, set of stimulus cards, and manual ('87, 40 pages); $115 per set of stimulus cards, 5 booklets ('86, 20 cards per booklet); $19.50 per 100 answer sheets; $45 per manual.
Time: (15-30) minutes.
Comments: Revision of the Halstead-Reitan Category Test.
Authors: Linda Wetzel and Thomas J. Boll.
Publisher: Western Psychological Services.
Cross References: For reviews by Scott W. Brown and Hope J. Hartman, see 11:361.

TEST REFERENCE

1. Downey, K. K., Stelson, F. W., Pomerleau, O. F. & Giordani, B. (1997). Adult attention deficit hyperactivity disorder: psychological test profiles in a clinical population. *Journal of Nervous and Mental Disease, 185,* 32–38.

[2406]

Short Employment Tests, Second Edition.

Purpose: "Measures verbal, numerical, and clerical skills."
Population: Adults.
Publication Dates: 1951–1993.
Acronym: SET.
Scores, 4: Verbal, Numerical, Clerical, Total.
Administration: Group or individual.
Forms, 4: 1, 2, 3, 4.
Price Data, 1999: $72 per 25 test booklets (specify test and form) including directions for administering, test booklets, and key; $23 per keys; $38 per examination kit including 1 booklet per test and manual ('93, 71 pages) (Form 1); $42 per examination kit (Forms 2, 3, 4); $253 per 100 test booklets (specify test and form) including directions for administering booklet and key.
Time: 5(10) minutes.
Comments: Distribution of Form 1 restricted to banks that are members of the American Banking Association.
Author: George K. Bennett and Marjorie Gelink.
Publisher: The Psychological Corporation.
Cross References: For reviews by Caroline Manuele-Adkins and by Bert W. Westbrook and Michael C. Hansen, see 13:287; see also T4:2456 (3 references); for reviews by Samuel Juni, Ronald Baumanis, and Leonard J. West of an earlier edition, see 9:1124 (1 reference); see also T3:2180 (1 reference); for reviews by Ronald N. Taylor and Paul W. Thayer, see 8:1037 (4 references); see also T2:2151 (6 references); for a review by Leonard W. Ferguson, see 6:1045 (9 references); for a review by P. L. Mellenbruch, see 5:854 (16 references).

[2407]

Short Imaginal Processes Inventory.

Purpose: Designed to "measure aspects of daydreaming style and content, mental style, and general inner experience."
Population: Adolescents and adults.
Publication Dates: 1982-1983.
Acronym: SIPI.
Scores, 3: Positive-Constructive Daydreaming, Guilt and Fear-of-Failure Daydreaming, Poor Attentional Control.
Administration: Group.
Price Data, 1998: $26 per examination kit including manual ('82, y pages), 10 question-and-answer booklets, 10 profile sheets and one set of templates; $12 per test manual; $18.50 per 25 question-and-answer booklets; $11 per 25 profile sheets; $11 per set of four scoring templates.
Time: (10) minutes.
Authors: George J. Huba, Jerome L. Singer, Carol S. Aneshensel, and John S. Antrobus.
Publisher: Sigma Assessment Systems, Inc.
Cross References: See T4:2457 (3 references); for reviews by Clifford V. Hatt and Laura Hines, see 9:1125.

TEST REFERENCES

1. Hurlburt, R. T., & Melancon, S. M. (1987). P-technique factor analyses of individuals' thought- and mood-sampling data. *Cognitive Therapy and Research, 11(4),* 487–500.
2. Holdt, P. A., & Stone, G. L. (1988). Needs, coping strategies, and coping outcomes associated with long-distance relationships. *Journal of College Student Development, 29,* 136–141.
3. Purifoy, F. E., Grodsky, A., & Giambra, L. M. (1992). The relationship of sexual daydreaming to sexual activity, sexual drive, and sexual attitudes for women across the life-span. *Archives of Sexual Behavior, 21,* 369–385.
4. Brannigan, G. G., Schaller, J. A., & McGarva, A. (1993). Approval motivation and sexual daydreaming. *The Journal of Genetic Psychology, 154,* 383–387.

[2408]

Short Tests of Clerical Ability.

Purpose: Designed to measure aptitudes and abilities in tasks common to various office jobs.
Population: Applicants for office positions.
Publication Dates: 1959-1997.
Acronym: STCA.
Administration: Individual or group.
Price Data, 1998: $55.50 per start-up kit including 25 test booklets and examiner's manual (specify Arithmetic, Business Vocabulary, Checking, Coding, Directions—Oral and Written, Filing, or Language); $42 per 25 test booklets (specify test; quantity discounts available); $89 per Quanta Computer Administration and Scoring software (DOS).
Author: Science Research Associates.
Publisher: NCS (Rosemont).

a) ARITHMETIC.
Scores, 3: Computation, Business Arithmetic, Total.
Time: 6 minutes.

b) BUSINESS VOCABULARY.
Time: 5 minutes.
c) CHECKING.
Time: 5 minutes.
d) CODING.
Time: 5 minutes.
e) DIRECTIONS—ORAL AND WRITTEN.
Time: 5 minutes.
f) FILING.
Time: 5 minutes.
g) LANGUAGE.
Time: 5 minutes.
Cross References: For reviews by Lorraine D. Eyde and Dean R. Malsbary, see 8:1039 (1 reference); for reviews by Philip H. Kriedt and Paul W. Thayer, see 6:1046.

[2409]

Shortened Edinburgh Reading Test.

Purpose: Designed as a survey measure of children's reading skills in the upper primary school, and as a screening instrument to detect children who might need remedial help in reading.
Population: Ages 10-0 to 11-6.
Publication Date: 1985.
Scores, 5: Vocabulary, Syntax, Comprehension, Retention, General Reading Quotient.
Administration: Group.
Price Data, 1999: £13.99 per 20 test booklets; £12.99 per manual; £13.99 per specimen set.
Time: (40–45) minutes.
Authors: The Godfrey Thomson Unit, University of Edinburgh.
Publisher: Hodder & Stoughton [England].

[2410]

Silver Drawing Test of Cognition and Emotion [Third Edition Revised].

Purpose: Designed as a nonverbal measure of ability in three areas of cognition: sequential concepts, spatial concepts, and association and formation of concepts; and to screen for depression.
Population: Ages 5 and over.
Publication Dates: 1983–1998.
Acronym: SDT.
Scores, 5: Predictive Drawing, Drawing from Observation, Drawing from Imagination, Self-Image, Projection.
Administration: Individual or group.
Price Data, 1998: $10 per set of 10 test booklets, layout sheet, and scoring forms; $32 per manual ('96, 147 pages); $15 per manual entitled "Updating the Silver Drawing Test and Draw A Story Manuals" ('98, 32 pages).
Foreign Language Edition: Brazilian translation and standardization available.
Time: (12–15) minutes.
Comments: Revision of Silver Drawing Test of Cognitive Skills and Adjustment.
Author: Rawley Silver.
Publisher: Ablin Press Distributors.
Cross References: See T4:2462 (1 reference); for reviews by Kevin D. Crehan and Annie W. Ward of an earlier edition, see 11:362; for reviews by Clinton I. Chase and David J. Mealor of the original edition, see 10:333.

[2411]

The Singer-Loomis Type Deployment Inventory.

Purpose: Designed to assess "personality factors that may help an individual in self-understanding and in utilizing skills, talents, and abilities to better deal with interactions between the self and the environment."
Population: High school and college and adults.
Publication Date: 1984–1996.
Acronym: SL-TDI.
Scores: Profile of 8 scores: Introverted, Extroverted, for each of 4 functions (Thinking, Feeling, Sensing, Intuition), plus Extraversion, Introversion, Judging, Perceiving.
Administration: Group.
Price Data, 1998: $430 per 12 test booklets; $18 per 12 answer sheets/scoring forms; $17 per manual ('96, 20 pages); $9.95 per interpretive guide ('96, 53 pages); $24.95 per manual and guide; $15 per specimen set.
Time: (30-40) minutes.
Comments: Self-report type profile based on Jung's typology.
Authors: June Singer, Mary Loomis, Elizabeth Kirkhart, and Larry Kirkhart.
Publisher: Moving Boundaries [No reply from publisher; status unknown].
Cross References: For a review by Richard B. Stuart of the earlier edition, see 10:334 (1 reference).

[2412]

SIPOAS: Styles in Perception of Affect Scale.

Purpose: "Measures the preferred style in the awareness of, and response to, the minute changes in bodily feelings that lead to emotions and responses."
Population: Age 18 to adult.
Publication Date: 1995.
Acronym: SIPOAS.
Scores: 3 styles: BB (Based on Body), EE (Emphasis on Evaluation), LL (Looking to Logic).
Administration: Individual or group.
Price Data, 1996: $20 per 25 copies of questionnaire; $22.50 per complete research report (203 pages).
Time: [20–30] minutes.

Author: Michael Bernet.
Publisher: Institute for Somat Awareness.

[2413]
Situational Attitude Scale.
Purpose: "Measures the attitudes of whites toward blacks."
Population: College and adults.
Publication Dates: c1969-1972.
Acronym: SAS.
Scores, 11: 10 situation scores, Total.
Administration: Group.
Forms, 2: A, B.
Price Data: Available from publisher.
Time: Untimed.
Authors: William E. Sedlacek and Glenwood C. Brooks, Jr.
Publisher: University of Maryland, University Counseling Center.
Cross References: See T4:2466 (2 references); for reviews by Ralph Mason Dreger and Marvin E. Shaw, see 8:678 (1 reference); see also T2:1381 (3 references).

TEST REFERENCE
1. Engstrom, C. M., Sedlacek, W. E., & McEwen, M. K. (1995). Faculty attitudes toward male revenue and nonrevenue student athletes. *Journal of College Student Development, 36,* 217–227.

[2414]
Situational Confidence Questionnaire.
Purpose: Designed to help clients identify high-risk drinking relapse situations.
Population: Adult alcoholics.
Publication Dates: 1987–1988.
Administration: Group.
Editions, 2: Computerized, print.
Authors: Helen M. Annis and J. Martin Graham.
Publisher: Addiction Research Foundation [Canada].
a) SITUATIONAL CONFIDENCE QUESTIONNAIRE.
Acronym: SCQ-39.
Scores, 9: Unpleasant Emotions/Frustrations, Physical Discomfort, Social Problems at Work, Social Tension, Pleasant Emotions, Positive Social Situations, Urges and Temptations, Testing Personal Control, Average.
Price Data, 1993: $14.75 per 25 questionnaires; $13.50 per user's guide ('88, 49 pages); $70 per 50 uses software edition (includes user's guide); $225 per 200 uses software edition (includes user's guide); $25 per specimen set including user's guide and 25 questionnaires.
Time: (10–15) minutes.
b) ALCOHOL CONFIDENCE QUESTIONNAIRE.
Acronym: ACQ-16.
Scores: Total score only.
Time: Administration time not reported.
Comments: Brief version of the Situational Confidence Questionnaire; test items listed in SCQ user's guide.
Cross References: For reviews by Merith Cosden and Cecil R. Reynolds, see 13:288 (4 references); see also T4:2467 (1 reference).

TEST REFERENCES
1. Greeley, J. D., Swift, W., Prescott, J., & Heather, N. (1993). Reactivity to alcohol-related cues in heavy and light drinkers. *Journal of Studies on Alcohol, 54,* 359–368.
2. Sobell, L. C., Sobell, M. B., Toneatto, T., & Leo, G. I. (1993). Severely dependent alcohol abusers may be vulnerable to alcohol cues in television programs. *Journal of Studies on Alcohol, 54,* 85–91.
3. Brown, S. A., Vik, P. W., Patterson, T. L., Grant, I., & Schuckit, M. A. (1995). Stress, vulnerability and adult alcohol relapse. *Journal of Studies on Alcohol, 56,* 538–545.
4. Evans, D. M., & Dunn, N. J. (1995). Alcohol expectancies, coping responses and self-efficacy judgments: A replication and extension of Cooper et al.'s 1988 study in a college sample. *Journal of Studies on Alcohol, 56,* 186–193.
5. Timko, C., Finney, J. W., Moos, R. H., & Moos, B. S. (1995). Short-term treatment careers and outcomes of previously untreated alcoholics. *Journal of Studies on Alcohol, 56,* 597–610.
6. Sklar, S. M., Annis, H. M., & Turner, N. E. (1997). Development and validation of the drug-taking confidence questionnaire: A measure of coping self-efficacy. *Addictive Behaviors, 22,* 655–670.
7. Maisto, S. A., McKay, J. R., & O'Farrell, T. J. (1998). Twelve-month abstinence from alcohol and long-term drinking and marital outcomes in men with severe alcohol problems. *Journal of Studies on Alcohol, 59,* 591–598.

[2415]
Situational Leadership®.
Purpose: Designed to identify successful leaders as "those who can adapt their behavior to meet the demands of their own unique situation."
Population: Managers, leaders, administrators, supervisors, and staff.
Publication Dates: 1973-1998.
Acronym: SL.
Administration: Group.
Manual: No manual.
Price Data: Available from publisher.
Time: Administration time not reported.
Comments: Related programs, Situational Leadership Simulator and Situational Leadership: Leveraging Human Performance, and Situational Leadership One-Day, also available.
Authors: Paul Hersey and Joseph W. Keilty.
Publisher: Leadership Studies, Inc.
a) LEADER EFFECTIVENESS AND ADAPTABILITY.
Publication Dates: 1973–1998.
Acronym: LEAD.
Comments: Ratings of self and others.
Forms, 2: LEAD Self, LEAD Other.
b) READINESS STYLE MATCH.
Publication Date: 1979.
Acronym: RSM.
Scores: Ratings in 4 areas: Major Objectives, Readiness, Integration of Style and Readiness, Readiness Style Match Matrix.
Forms, 2: Staff Member Rating Form, Manager Rating Form.

c) READINESS SCALE.
Publication Date: 1977.
Acronym: MS.
Scores: 2 scores (Task Readiness, Psychological Readiness) for each of 5 major objectives or responsibilities.
Forms, 2: Self Rating Form, Manager Rating Form.
d) POWER PERCEPTION PROFILE.
Publication Date: 1979–1998.
Acronym: PPP.
Scores, 7: Coercive, Connection, Expert, Information, Legitimate, Referent, Reward.
Forms, 2: Perception of Self, Perception of Other.
e) LEADERSHIP SCALE.
Publication Date: 1980–1997.
Acronym: LS.
Scores: 2 scores (Total Task-Behavior, Total Relationship-Behavior) for each of 5 major objectives or responsibilities.
Forms, 2: Staff Member Form, Manager Form.
Cross References: For reviews by Bruce J. Eberhardt and Sheldon Zedeck, see 9:1133.

[2416]

Situational Preference Inventory.

Purpose: "Designed to assess individual styles of social interaction."
Population: Grades 9-16 and adults.
Publication Dates: 1968-1973.
Acronym: SPI.
Scores, 3: Cooperational, Instrumental, Analytic.
Administration: Group.
Price Data: Available from publisher.
Time: (10-15) minutes.
Comments: Self-administered.
Author: Carl N. Edwards.
Publisher: Carl N. Edwards.
Cross References: See T2:1382 (2 references).

[2417]

Sixteen Personality Factor (16PF®) Questionnaire, Fifth Edition.

Purpose: Designed to measure personality traits.
Population: Ages 16 and over.
Publication Dates: 1949-1994.
Acronym: 16PF.
Scores, 24: 16 primary factor scores: Warm vs. Reserved (A), Abstract-Reasoning vs. Concrete-Reasoning (B), Emotionally Stable vs. Reactive (C), Dominant vs. Deferential (E), Lively vs. Serious (F), Rule-Conscious vs. Expedient (G), Socially Bold vs. Shy (H), Sensitive vs. Utilitarian (I), Vigilant vs. Trusting (L), Abstracted vs. Grounded (M), Private vs. Forthright (N), Apprehensive vs. Self-Assured (0), Open to Change vs. Traditional (Q1), Self-Reliant vs. Group-Oriented (Q2), Perfectionistic vs. Tolerates Disorder (Q3), Tense vs. Relaxed (Q4); 5 global factor scores: Extraverted vs. Introverted (EX), High Anxiety vs. Low Anxiety (AX), Tough-Minded vs. Receptive (TM), Independent vs. Accommodating (IN), Self-Controlled vs. Unrestrained (SC); 3 response style indices: Impression Management (IM), Infrequency (INF), Acquiescence (ACQ).
Administration: Group or individual.
Price Data, 1999: $107 per complete kit including 10 test booklets, 25 answer sheets, 25 individual record forms, scoring keys, administrator's manual ('94, 162 pages), and one prepaid processing certificate for a basic interpretive report (BIR); $15 per 10 test booklets; $27.50 per scoring keys and norms tables; $12.50 per 25 answer sheets; $8 per 25 individual record forms; $40 per administrator's manual; $46 per trial packet including test booklet, answer sheet, administrator's manual, and certificate for a Basic Interpretive Report (BIR); $10–$25 for Basic Interpretive Report including profiles, scores, and descriptive comments; $6.50–$25 per Basic Score Report (includes scores only); $55 per technical manual ('94, 279 pages).
Time: (35-50) minutes.
Comments: Computer administration, interpretative reports, and scoring available.
Authors: Raymond B. Cattell, A. Karen S. Cattell, Heather E. P. Cattell (16PF), Mary Russell, Darcie Karol (manual).
Publisher: Institute for Personality and Ability Testing, Inc.
a) 16PF BASIC SCORE REPORT.
Comments: Most concise 16PF report.
b) 16PF DATA SUMMARY REPORT.
Comments: Developed to provide standard output for researchers providing profiles on individual test takers as well as group average profile.
c) 16PF BASIC INTERPRETIVE REPORT.
Comments: A multipurpose, computerized interpretation of the 16PF providing the basic 16 personality scores and other information about characteristics relevant to personal and vocational counseling.
d) 16PF TEAMWORK DEVELOPMENT REPORT.
Comments: Intended to evaluate personality implications for performance in teamwork settings, for development of either individual and/or teams.
e) 16PF CATTELL COMPREHENSIVE PERSONALITY INTERPRETATION.
Comments: Provides 8–10 pages of comprehensive narrative covering a number of diverse areas of functioning and offering multi-trait com-

binations and interactions to provide an in-depth understanding of the client's whole personality. The narrative also discusses therapeutic considerations and approaches.

f) 16PF KARSON CLINICAL REPORT.

Comments: Provides 2–3 pages of descriptive narrative intended for professional use only. Contains sections describing basic areas of functioning, including: emotional adjustment, interpersonal issues, self-control, cognitive style, and areas to explore in couseling.

g) 16PF COUPLE'S COUNSELING REPORT.

Comments: A computer-interpreted report for paired 16PF profiles that examines the personality organization of two people, and compares the profiles.

h) 16PF INDIVIDUALIZED STRESS MANAGEMENT PROGRAM.

Comments: An assessment and training package using 16PF data plus a stress evaluation inventory to yield a computer-generated, book length report providing an individualized prescription plan for participants in a stress management program.

Cross References: For reviews by Mary J. McLellan and Pamela Carrington Rotto, see 12:354 (38 references); see also T4:2470 (140 references); for reviews of an earlier edition by James N. Butcher and Marvin Zuckerman, see 9:1136 (67 references); see also T3:2208 (182 references); for reviews by Bruce M. Bloxam, Brian F. Bolton, and James A. Walsh, see 8:679 (619 references); see also T2:1383 (244 references); for reviews by Thomas J. Bouchard, Jr. and Leonard G. Rorer, see 7:139 (295 references); see also P:245 (249 references); for a review by Maurice Lorr, see 6:174 (81 references); for a review by C. J. Adcock, see 5:112 (21 references); for reviews by Charles M. Harsh, Ardie Lubin, and J. Richard Wittenborn, see 4:87 (8 references).

TEST REFERENCES

1. Gerber, K. E., Nehemkis, A. M., Farberow, N. L., & Williams, J. (1981). Indirect self-destructive behavior in chronic hemodialysis patients. *Suicide and Life-Threatening Behavior, 11,* 31–42.

2. Gott, P. S., Hughes, E. C., & Whipple, K. (1984). Voluntary control of two lateralized conscious states: Validation by electrical and behavioral studies. *Neuropsychologia, 22,* 65–72.

3. Chubon, R. A. (1986). Genesis II: A computer-based case management simulation. *Rehabilitation Counseling Bulletin, 30,* 25–32.

4. Livneh, H. (1988). Assessing outcome criteria in rehabilitation: A multi-component approach. *Rehabilitation Counseling Bulletin, 32,* 72–94.

5. Argentero, P. (1989). Second-order factor structure of Cattell's 16 Personality Factor Questionnaire. *Perceptual and Motor Skills, 68,* 1043–1047.

6. Kocsis, J. H., Mason, B. J., Frances, A. J., Sweeney, J., Mann, J. J., & Marin, D. (1989). Prediction of response of chronic depression to imipramine. *Journal of Affective Disorders, 17,* 255–260.

7. Grant, V. J. (1990). Maternal personality and sex of infant. *British Journal of Medical Psychology, 63,* 261–266.

8. Kaplan, S. P. (1990). Social support, emotional distress, and vocational outcomes among persons with brain injuries. *Rehabilitation Counselor Bulletin, 34,* 16–23.

9. Spiro, A., III, Aldwin, C. M., Levenson, M. R., & Bosse, R. (1990). Longitudinal findings from the normative aging study: Do emotionality and extraversion predict symptom change? *Journal of Gerontology, 45,* 136°144.

10. Tammany, J. M., Evans, R. G., & Barnett, R. W. (1990). Personality and intellectual characteristics of adult male felons as a function of offence category. *Journal of Clinical Psychology, 46,* 906–911.

11. Whitworth, R. H. & Perry, S. M. (1990). Comparison of Anglo- and Mexican-Americans on the 16PF administered in Spanish and English. *Journal of Clinical Psychology, 46,* 847–863.

12. Gerbing, D. W., & Tuley, M. R. (1991). The 16PF related to the five-factor model of personality: Multiple-indicator measurement versus the a priori scales. *Multivariate Behavioral Research, 26,* 271–289.

13. Whipple, S. C., & Noble, E. P. (1991). Personality characteristics of alcoholic fathers and their sons. *Journal of Studies on Alcohol, 52,* 331–337.

14. Zhang, H., & Zhang, Y. (1991). Psychological consequences of earthquake disaster survivors. *International Journal of Psychology, 26,* 613–621.

15. Farberow, N. L., Gallagher-Thompson, D., Gilewski, M., & Thompson, L. (1992). Changes in grief and mental health of bereaved spouses of older suicides. *Journal of Gerontology, 47,* 357–366.

16. Nosek, M. A., Fuhrer, M. J., & Howland, C. A. (1992). Independence among people with disabilities: II. Personal independence profile. *Rehabilitation Counselor Bulletin, 36,* 21–36.

17. Atwater, L. E., & Yammarino, F. J. (1993). Personal attributes as predictors of superiors' and subordinates' perceptions of military academy leadership. *Human Relations, 46,* 645–668.

18. Kurian, M., Caterino, L. C. & Kulhavy, R. W. (1993). Personality characteristics and duration of ATA Taekwondo training. *Perceptual and Motor Skills, 76,* 363–366.

19. Oei, T. P. S., Hansen, J., & Miller, S. (1993). The empirical status of irrational beliefs in rational emotive therapy. *Australian Psychologist, 28,* 195–200.

20. Grant, V. J. (1994). Maternal dominance and the conception of sons. *British Journal of Medical Psychology, 67,* 343–351.

21. Novy, D. M., Frankiewicz, R. G., Francis, D. J., Liberman, D., Overall, J. E., & Vincent, K. R. (1994). An investigation of the structural validity of Loevinger's Model and measure of ego development. *Journal of Personality, 62,* 87–118.

22. Baker, D. E., & Stephenson, L. A. (1995). Personality characteristics of adult children of alcoholics. *Journal of Clinical Psychology, 51,* 694–702.

23. Ben-Porath, Y. S., Almagor, M., Hoftman-Chemi, A., & Tellegen, A. (1995). A cross-cultural study of personality with the multidimensional personality questionnaire. *Journal of Cross-Cultural Psychology, 26,* 360–373.

24. Byravan, A., & Ramanaiah, N. V. (1995). Structure of the 16PF Fifth Edition from the perspective of the five-factor model. *Psychological Reports, 76,* 555–560.

25. Cattell, R. B., & Cattell, H. E. P. (1995). Personality structure and the new fifth edition of the 16PF. *Educational and Psychological Measurement, 55,* 926–937.

26. Kowner, R., & Ogawa, T. (1995). The role of raters' sex, personality, and appearance in judgments of facial beauty. *Perceptual and Motor Skills, 81,* 339–349.

27. Melamed, T. (1995). Career success: The moderating effect of gender. *Journal of Vocational Behavior, 47,* 35–60.

28. Shaughnessy, M. F., Self, E., Schwartz, G., & Naylor, K. (1995). Personality characteristics of outstanding teachers. *Psychological Reports, 76,* 1035–1038.

29. Smith, D. W., & Saunders, B. E. (1995). Personality characteristics of father/perpetrators and nonoffending mothers in incest families: Individual and dyadic analyses. *Child Abuse & Neglect, 19,* 607–617.

30. Spiro, A., Ward, K. D., Mroczek, D. K., & Aldwin, C. M. (1995). Personality and the incidence of hypertension among older men: Longitudinal findings from the normative aging study. *Health Psychology, 14,* 563–569.

31. Williams, L. M., & Finkelhor, D. (1995). Paternal caregiving and incest: Test of a biosocial model. *American Journal of Orthopsychiatry, 65,* 101–113.

32. Accardo, C. M., Aboyoun, D. C., Alford, B. A., & Cannon, J. T. (1996). Diaries: Who keeps them and why. *Perceptual and Motor Skills, 82,* 559–562.

33. Deary, I. J. (1996). A (latent) big five personality model in 1915? A reanalysis of Webb's data. *Journal of Personality and Social Psychology, 71,* 992–1005.

34. Holliday, G. A., Koller, J. R., & Kunce, J. T. (1996). Personality attributes of high IQ/high achieving gifted adolescents: Implications of the personal styles model. *Journal for the Education of the Gifted, 20,* 84–102.

35. Melamed, T. (1996). Career success: An assessment of a gender-specific model. *Journal of Occupational and Organizational Psychology, 69,* 217–242.

36. Ones, D. S., Viswesvaran, C., & Reiss, A. D. (1996). Role of social desirability in personality testing for personnel selection: The red herring. *Journal of Applied Psychology, 81,* 660–679.

37. Summers, M., Anderson, J. L., Hines, A. R., Gelder, B. C., & Dean, R. S. (1996). The camera adds more than pounds: Gender differences in course satisfaction for campus and distance learning students. *Journal of Research and Development in Education, 29,* 212–219.

38. Narayan, R., Shams, G. K., Jain, R., & Gupta, B. S. (1997). Personality characteristics of persons addicted to heroin. *The Journal of Psychology, 131,* 125–127.

39. Broucek, W. G. & Randell, G. (1998). An assessment of the construct validity of the Belbin Self-Perception Inventory and Observer's Assessment from the perspective of the two-factor model. *Journal of Occupational and Organizational Psychology, 69,* 389–405.

40. Fisher, S. G., Hunter, T. A., & Macrosson, W. D. K. (1998). The structure of Belbin's team roles. *Journal of Occupational and Organizational Psychology, 71,* 283–288.

41. Huang, C-Y., Liao, H-Y., & Chang, S-H. (1998). Social desirability and the clinical self-report inventory: Methodological reconsideration. *Journal of Clinical Psychology, 54,* 517–528.

42. Magids, D. M. (1998). Personality comparison between children of hidden Holocaust survivors and American Jewish parents. *Journal of Psychology, 132,* 245–254.

43. Paunonen, S. V., & Ashton, M. C. (1998). The structured assessment of personality across cultures. *Journal of Cross-Cultural Psychology, 29,* 150–170.

[2418]

16PF® Human Resource Development Report.

Purpose: Assesses an individual's management potential and style, provides insights into the individual's personality, and focuses on five management dimesnions frequently identified in research on successful managers.
Population: Managerial candidates.
Publication Dates: 1982-1997.
Acronym: HRDR.
Scores: 5 dimensions: Leadership, Interaction with Others, Decision-Making Abilities, Initiative, Personal Adjustment.
Administration: Group or individual.
Price Data, 1999: $34 per introductory kit including 16 PF test booklet, answer sheet, prepaid processing form to receive Human Resource Development Report, and user's guide ('87, 47 pages); $15 per 10 16PF reusable test booklets; $12.50 per 25 16PF machine-scorable answer sheets; $28 per user's guide; $15.50 to $25 per Human Resource Development Report available from publisher scoring service.
Time: 35–50 minutes.
Comments: Based on the Sixteen Personality Factor Questionnaire (2417); mail-in, fax, and on-site software delivery options available; can be generated from 4th or 5th edition of 16PF questionnaire.
Author: IPAT staff.
Publisher: Institute for Personality and Ability Testing, Inc.
Cross References: For reviews by S. Alvin Leung and Mary A. Lewis, see 11:169.

[2419]

16PF® Personal Career Development Profile.

Purpose: A consulting tool designed to provide insight into a person's behavioral and career strengths; "commonly used as part of personnel selection and job placement programs, career transition consulting, and career and personal life planning."
Population: Ages 16 and over.
Publication Dates: 1977-1998.
Acronym: PCDP.
Scores: 7 Narrative paragraphs: Orientation to the 16PF Questionnaire, Problem-Solving Patterns, Patterns for Coping with Stressful Conditions, Patterns of Interpersonal Interaction, Organizational Role and Work-Setting Patterns, Patterns for Career Activity Interests, Personal Career Life-Style Effectiveness Considerations plus 7 score summary pages.
Administration: Group or individual.
Parts, 3: Narrative Paragraphs, Occupational Data, Score Profile Pages.
Price Data, 1999: $40 per introductory kit with PCDP+ including Technical & Interpretive Manual ('95, 70 pages) with manual supplement ('98, 32 pages), 16PF test booklet, answer sheet, and prepaid processing form for one individual to receive both the PCDP and PCDP+; $30 per manual; $16 to $25 per PCDP report; $18 to $27 per PCDP+ report; $22 per 10 performance effectiveness planning booklets; $25 per Self-Motivated Career Planning Guide.
Foreign Language Edition: Australian English adaptation available; information regarding other non-English-language adaptations available from publisher.
Time: 35–50 minutes.
Comments: Computer-interpreted report of the Sixteen Personality Factor Questionnaire; PCDP+ is available as optional supplement to the PCDP; mail-in, fax, and on-site software delivery options available.
Author: Verne Walter.
Publisher: Institute for Personality and Ability Testing, Inc.
Cross References: For a review by Kevin M. Mossholder, see 9:939.

[2420]

Skills and Attributes Inventory.

Purpose: Assesses the relative importance of job-related skills and attributes for a position as well as the degree to which an individual possesses thos skills and attributes.
Population: Non-management positions.
Publication Dates: 1976-1979.
Acronym: SAI.
Scores, 13: General Functioning Intelligence, Visual Acuity, Visual and Coordination Skills, Physical Coordination, Mechanical Skills, Graphic and Clerical Skills, General Clerical Skills, Leadership Ability, Tolerance in Interpersonal Relations, Organization Identification, Conscientiousness and Reliability, Efficiency Under Stress, Solitary Work.
Administration: Individual or group.
Forms, 2: Ability Rating, Importance Rating.
Price Data, 1998: $79.50 per start-up kit (specify Importance or Ability) including 25 test booklets, 25 score sheets, and interpretation and research manual; $44 per 25 test booklets (specify Importance or Ability); $25 per 25 score sheets; $19.75 per interpretation and research manual.
Time: No limit (approximately 30–45 minutes).
Author: Melany E. Baehr.
Publisher: NCS (Rosemont).
Cross References: For a review by Lenore W. Harmon, see 9:1137.

[2421]

Skills Assessment Module.

Purpose: To assess a student's affective, cognitive, and manipulative strengths and weaknesses in relation to vocational skills required in various training programs within a school system.

Population: Average, handicapped, and disadvantaged vocational training school students ages 14-18.
Publication Date: 1985–1994.
Acronym: SAM.
Scores, 13: Digital Discrimination, Clerical Verbal, Motor Coordination, Clerical Numerical, Following Written Directions, Finger Dexterity, Aiming, Reading a Ruler (Measurement), Manual Dexterity, Form Perception, Spatial Perception, Color Discrimination, Following Diagrammed Instructions.
Administration: Individual in part.
Price Data, 1998: $2,495 for complete test including all subtests.
Time: (90-150) minutes.
Comments: Module includes Basic Skills Locater Test (259), Learning Styles Inventory (1476), and Auditory Directions Screen.
Author: Michele Rosinek.
Publisher: Piney Mountain Press, Inc.
Cross References: For reviews by Jean Powell Kirnan and Wilbur L. Layton, see 11:364.

[2422]

Skills for Independent Living.

Purpose: Resource kit "developed for use in instructional programs addressing survival skills, daily living skills, or social and prevocational skills."
Population: Educable mentally retarded secondary students and low-achieving nonretarded secondary school students.
Publication Date: 1981.
Acronym: SIL.
Scores: 9 areas: Purchasing Habits, Budgeting, Banking, Job Search Skills, Job-Related Behavior, Home Management, Health Care, Hygiene and Grooming, Functional Signs.
Administration: Individual.
Price Data: Available from publisher.
Time: Administration time not reported.
Comments: Curriculum guide for use with the Social and Prevocational Information Battery (2443) and Tests for Everyday Living (2734).
Authors: Larry K. Irvin, Andrew S. Halpern, and Jacqueline D. Becklund.
Publisher: CTB/McGraw-Hill.
Cross References: For a review by Reece L. Peterson, see 9:1138.

[2423]

Skills Inventory for Teams.

Purpose: To aid early intervention practitioners to "evaluate their ability to work as part of a team."
Population: Early intervention practitioners.
Publication Dates: 1978–1992.
Acronym: SIFT.
Scores, 12: Clarity of Purpose, Cohesion, Clarity of Roles, Communication, Use of Resources, Decision Making/Problem Solving, Responsibility Implementation, Conflict Resolution, View of Family Role, Evaluation, External Support, Internal Support.
Administration: Group.
Price Data, 1993: $24.95 per administration guide and inventory ('92, 66 pages) (volume discount available).
Time: Administration time not reported.
Comments: Previously called Skills Inventory for Teachers; self-administered inventory.
Authors: Corinne Garland, Adrienne Frank, Deana Buck, and Patti Seklemian.
Publisher: Child Development Resources.
Cross References: For reviews by Robert Johnson and E. Lea Witta, see 13:289.

[2424]

SkillScan for Management Development.

Purpose: "A 360-degree diagnostic feedback tool that helps field managers understand how they can be more effective managers, and helps organizations understand the strengths and weaknesses of their managers."
Population: Sales managers.
Publication Date: 1994.
Scores: 8 Tasks: Staffing (Recruiting and Selecting), Training, Field Office Development, Administration, Performance Management (Supervision), Business Management, Sales Assistance, Management Development; 12 Behaviors: Communicating, Counseling, Planning, Delegating, Coordinating, Team Building, Supporting, Rewarding, Motivating, Networking, Monitoring, Problem Solving and Decision Making; 5 Personal Attributes: Ethics and Professionalism, Stress Tolerance, Achievement Motivation, Self Improvement, Other Orientation.
Administration: Individual or group.
Forms, 2: Form O (Assessment by Others) and Form S (Self-Assessment by the Manager).
Price Data, 1996: $110 per SkillScan kit including 1 Form S and 7 Form O questionnaires, instructions, and 8 postage-paid envelopes addressed to LIMRA; $3 per additional Form O questionnaire and envelope; $10 per manual (no publication date, 25 pages).
Time: Administration time not reported.
Comments: Replacement for the Management Development Profile (T4:1507); Manager development workshops available.
Authors: LIMRA International.
Publisher: LIMRA International.
Cross References: For a review by Richard M. Wolf of the Management Development Profile, see 12:225.

[2425]

SKILLSCOPE for Managers.

Purpose: Assesses managerial strengths and developmental needs from managers and coworkers perspectives.
Population: Managers.
Publication Dates: 1988-1993.
Scores: 15 Skill Areas: Getting Information, Communication, Taking Action, Risk Taking, Administration, Conflict Management, Relationships, Selecting/Developing, Influencing, Flexibility, Knowledge of Job, Energy/Drive, Time Management, Coping With Pressure, Self-Management.
Administration: Group.
Price Data, 1993: $125 per complete set including 9 survey instruments, The Results computer scoring, The Summary, The Action Plan, and The Trainer's Guide ('93, 22 pages).
Time: Administration time not reported.
Comments: SKILLSCOPE questionnaires are returned to the Center for Creative Leadership for confidential scoring; managers are rated by self and by coworkers.
Authors: Robert E. Kaplan (survey), Maxine Dalton (Trainer's Guide), Bob Kaplan, Jean Leslie, Russ Moxley, Patricia Ohlott, and Ellen VanVelsor.
Publisher: Center for Creative Leadership.
Cross References: For a review by Linda F. Wightman, see 12:355.

[2426]

Sklar Aphasia Scale, Revised 1983.

Purpose: "Developed as a clinical procedure to provide systematic information about the severity and nature of language disorders following brain damage in adults."
Population: Brain-damaged adults.
Publication Dates: 1966-1983.
Acronym: SAS.
Scores, 5: Auditory Decoding, Visual Decoding, Oral Encoding, Graphic Encoding, Total Impairment.
Administration: Individual.
Price Data, 1999: $75 per kit including 25 protocol booklets, stimulus cards, and manual ('83, 25 pages); $18.50 per 25 protocol booklets; $27 per manual.
Time: [15–20] minutes.
Author: Maurice Sklar.
Publisher: Western Psychological Services.
Cross References: For reviews by Linda Crocker and Lawrence J. Turton, see 10:336 (1 reference); see also T3:2213 (1 reference); for a review by Manfred J. Meier, see 8:976 (1 reference); for reviews by Arthur L. Benton and Daniel R. Boone of the original edition, see 7:970; see also P:247 (2 references).

[2427]

Slingerland College-Level Screening for the Identification of Language Learning Strengths and Weaknesses.

Purpose: Developed to screen for strengths and weaknesses in language learning.
Population: College or college graduates.
Publication Date: 1991.
Scores, 10: Visual to Kinesthetic-Motor I, Visual to Kinesthetic-Motor II, Visual Perception-Memory, Visual Discrimination, Visual Perception and Memory to Kinesthetic-Motor, Auditory to Visual-Kinesthetic I, Auditory to Visual-Kinesthetic II, Auditory to Visual, Comprehension, Auditory to Kinesthetic.
Administration: Group.
Price Data: Available from publisher.
Time: (45-50) minutes.
Comments: Upward extension of the Slingerland Screening Tests (2428).
Author: Carol Murray.
Publisher: Educators Publishing Service, Inc.
Cross References: For reviews by Mary Anne Bunda and Thomas W. Guyette, see 12:356; see T4:2478 (2 references).

[2428]

Slingerland Screening Tests for Identifying Children with Specific Language Disability.

Purpose: "To screen from among a group of children those with potential language difficulties and those with already present specific language disabilities who are in need of special attention."
Population: Grades 1-2.5, 2.5-3.5, 3.5-4, 5-6.
Publication Dates: 1962-1984.
Administration: Group (Echolalia test individually administered).
Subtests, 8 or 9: Copying-Chart, Copying-Page, Visual Perception-Memory, Visual Discrimination, Visual Perception-Memory with Kinesthetic Memory, Auditory Recall, Auditory Sounds, Auditory Association, Orientation (Form D only); plus individual Echolalia test.
Price Data, 1999: $3.70 (6+ copies) or $5.55 (1-5) per technical manual ('80, 24 pages).
Author: Beth H. Slingerland.
Publisher: Educators Publishing Service, Inc.

a) FORMS A, B, C, REVISED EDITION.
Population: Grades 1-2.5, 2.5-3.5, 3.5-4.
Publication Dates: 1962-1970.
Scores, 13 (8 tests): Visual Copying Far Point, Visual Copying Near Point, Total, Visual Perception-Memory, Visual Discrimination, Visual Perception-Memory with Kinesthetic Memory, Auditory Recall (Letters, Numbers, Spelling), Au-

ditory Discrimination of Sounds, Auditory-Visual Association, Total Errors (excluding Visual Copying), Total Errors plus Self-Corrections and Poor Formations.
Price Data: $5.40 per 12 tests (A, B, or C); $3.30 (6+ copies) or $4.95 (1-5 copies) per directions for administration (A, B, or C); $10.95 (6+) or $16.45 (1-5) per cards and charts (A, B, or C); $9.85 (6+) or $14.80 (1-5) per teacher's manual ('70, 172 pages); $9.85 (6+ sets) or $14.80 (1-5 sets) per specimen set (manual and one each of above tests).
Time: 56(66) minutes in 2 or 3 sessions.
Authors: Revisions by Beth H. Slingerland and Alice S. Ansara.
1) *Form A.*
Population: Grades 1-2.5.
2) *Form B.*
Population: Grades 2.5-3.5.
3) *Form C.*
Population: Grades 3.5-4.
b) FORM D.
Population: Grades 5-6.
Publication Date: 1974.
Scores, 14 (9 tests): Visual Copying Far Point, Visual Copying Near Point, Total, Visual Perception-Memory, Visual Discrimination, Visual Perception-Memory with Kinesthetic Memory, Auditory Recall (Letters, Numbers, Spelling), Auditory Discrimination of Sounds, Auditory-Visual Association, Auditory Perception and Individual Orientation, Total Errors (excluding Visual Copying), Total Errors and Confusions.
Price Data: $13.65 (6+ sets) or $20.50 (1-5 sets) per 12 tests and 12 summary sheets; $12.55 (6+) or $18.80 (1-5) per cards and charts (including directions for administration and scoring); $7.80 (6+) or $11.70 (1-5) per teacher's manual; $7.80 (6+ sets) or $11.70 (1-5 sets) specimen set including teacher's manual, test, summary sheet, and list of material needed..
Time: (110-125) minutes in 2 sessions.

[2429]

Slosson Articulation, Language Test with Phonology.

Purpose: Measures the communicative competence of a child by combining into a single score the assessment of articulation, phonology and language.
Population: Ages 3-0 to 5-11.
Publication Date: 1986.
Acronym: SALT-P.
Scores, 4: Consonants + Vowels/Diphthongs, Phonological Processes, Language Errors, Composite Score.
Administration: Individual.
Price Data, 1992: $50 per complete kit; $14 per examiner's manual (12 pages); $20 per 50 scoring forms; $18 per test book/picture plates; $70 per video tape.
Time: (7-10) minutes.
Comments: Instructional video tape with taped administration of test available.
Author: Wilma Jean Tade.
Publisher: Slosson Educational Publications, Inc.
Cross References: For reviews by Clinton W. Bennett and Robert A. Reineke, see 12:357.

[2430]

Slosson Drawing Coordination Test.

Purpose: "Designed to identify individuals with various forms of brain dysfunction or perceptual disorders where eye-hand coordination is involved."
Population: Ages 1-adult.
Publication Dates: 1962-1971.
Acronym: SDCT.
Scores: Accuracy Score.
Administration: Group.
Price Data, 1992: $40 per complete kit including manual ('71, 46 pages), scoring procedures, and 2 score sheets; $14 per 50 score sheets.
Time: (10-15) minutes.
Comments: Previously known as Slosson Drawing Coordination Test for Children and Adults.
Author: Richard L. Slosson.
Publisher: Slosson Educational Publications, Inc.
Cross References: See T3:2216 (1 reference); for reviews by Arthur L. Benton and James C. Reed, see 7:140.

[2431]

Slosson Full-Range Intelligence Test.

Purpose: Constructed as a "quick estimate of general cognitive ability."
Population: Ages 5–21.
Publication Dates: 1988–1994.
Acronym: S-FRIT.
Scores, 8: General Cognition (Full-Range Intelligence Quotient, Rapid Cognitive Index, Best g Index), Cognitive Subdomains (Verbal Index, Abstract Index, Quantitative Index, Memory Index, Performance Index).
Administration: Individual.
Forms, 2: Item Profiles/Score Summaries Form, Brief Score Form.
Price Data, 1996: $115 per complete kit including examiner's manual ('94, 80 pages), normative/technical manual ('94, 93 pages), picture book, 50 motor response forms, 50 brief score forms, and 50 item profiles/score summaries: $20 per 50 forms (specify Motor response, brief score, or item profiles/score summaries); $26 per examiner's manual; $24 per normative/technical manual; $22 per picture book.

Time: (20–35) minutes.
Authors: Bob Algozzine, Ronald C. Eaves, Lester Mann, H. Robert Vance, and Steven W. Slosson (Brief Score Form).
Publisher: Slosson Educational Publications, Inc.

[2432]

Slosson Intelligence Test [1991 Edition].

Purpose: Designed for use as a "quick estimate of general verbal cognitive ability."
Population: Ages 4-0 and over.
Publication Dates: 1961-1991.
Acronym: SIT-R.
Scores: Total score only.
Administration: Individual.
Price Data, 1992: $57 per complete kit including 50 test forms, manual ('91, 45 pages), and norms tables/technical manual ('91, 39 pages); $16 per 50 test forms; $21 per norms tables/technical manual; $23 per manual.
Time: (10-20) minutes.
Authors: Richard L. Slosson, Charles L. Nicholson (revision), and Terry H. Hibpshman (revision).
Publisher: Slosson Educational Publications, Inc.
Cross References: For reviews by Randy W. Kamphaus and T. Steuart Watson, see 12:358 (16 references); see also T4:2482 (43 references); for reviews by Thomas Oakland and William M. Reynolds of an earlier edition, see 9:1142 (11 references); see also T3:2217 (82 references), 8:227 (62 references), and T2:524 (12 references); for reviews by Philip Himelstein and Jane V. Hunt, see 7:424 (31 references).

TEST REFERENCES

1. Swift, C. (1984). Sentence imitation in kindergarten children at risk for learning disability: A comparative study. *Language, Speech, and Hearing Services in Schools, 15,* 10–15.
2. Fagan, W. T. (1988). Concepts of reading and writing among low-literate adults. *Reading Research and Instruction, 27,* 47–60.
3. Cornell, D. G. (1989). Child adjustment and parent use of the term "gifted." *Gifted Child Quarterly, 33,* 59–64.
4. Graham, S., & Harris, K. R. (1989). Components analysis of cognitive strategy instruction: Effects on learning disabled students' compositions and self-efficacy. *Journal of Educational Psychology, 81,* 353–361.
5. Graham, S., & Harris, K. R. (1989). Improving learning disabled students' skills at composing essays: Self-instructional strategy training. *Exceptional Children, 56,* 201–214.
6. Lewis, B. A., Aram, D. M., & Horwitz, S. J. (1989). Language and motor findings in benign megalencephaly. *Perceptual and Motor Skills, 68,* 1051–1054.
7. Nelson, R., & Lignugaris/Kraft, B. (1989). Postsecondary education for students with learning disabilities. *Exceptional Children, 56,* 246–265.
8. Weinberg, W. A., McLean, A., Snider, R. L., Rintelmann, J. W., & Brumback, R. A. (1989). Comparison of reading and listening-reading techniques for administration of SAT reading comprehension subtest: Justification for the bypass approach. *Perceptual and Motor Skills, 68,* 1015–1018.
9. Eichinger, J. (1990). Goal structure effects on social interaction: Nondisabled and disabled elementary students. *Exceptional Children, 56,* 408–416.
10. Elliott, D., Weeks, D. J., & Gray, S. (1990). Manual and oral praxis in adults with Down's syndrome. *Neuropsychologia, 28,* 1307–1315.
11. Graham, S. (1990). The role of production factors in learning disabled students' composition. *Journal of Educational Psychology, 82,* 781–791.
12. Kanevsky, L. (1990). Pursuing qualitative differences in the flexible use of problem-solving strategy by young children. *Journal for the Education of the Gifted, 13,* 115–140.
13. Dyer, K., Williams, L., & Luce, S. C. (1991). Training teachers to use naturalistic communication strategies in classrooms for students with autism and other severe handicaps. *Language, Speech, and Hearing Services in Schools, 22,* 313–321.
14. Swanson, H. L., & Ramalgia, J. M. (1992). The relationship between phonological codes on memory and spelling tasks for students with and without learning disabilities. *Journal of Learning Disabilities, 25,* 396–407.
15. Graham, S., Schwartz, S. S., & MacArthur, C. A. (1993). Knowledge of writing and the composing process, attitude toward writing, and self-efficacy for students with and without learning disabilities. *Journal of Learning Disabilities, 26,* 237–249.
16. Kaplan, B. J., Polatajko, H. J., Wilson, B. N., & Faris, P. D. (1993). Reexamination of sensory integration treatment: A combination of two efficacy studies. *Journal of Learning Disabilities, 26,* 342–347.
17. Hoehn, T. P., & Baumeister, A. A. (1994). A critique of the application of sensory integration therapy to children with learning disabilities. *Journal of Learning Disabilities, 27,* 338–350.
18. Lysaker, P., & Bell, M. (1994). Insight and cognitive impairment in schizophrenia. *The Journal of Nervous and Mental Disease, 182,* 656–660.
19. Lysaker, P., Bell, M., Milstein, R., Bryson, G., & Beam-Goulet, J. (1994). Insight and psychosocial treatment compliance in schizophrenia. *Psychiatry, 57,* 307–315.
20. Reid, R., Maag, J. W., Vasa, S. F., & Wright, G. (1994). Who are the children with attention deficit-hyperactivity disorder? A school-based survey. *The Journal of Special Education, 28,* 117–137.
21. Turner, L. A., Matherne, J. L., III, & Heller, S. S. (1994). The effects of performance feedback on memory strategy use and recall accuracy in students with and without mild mental retardation. *Journal of Experimental Education, 62,* 303–315.
22. Bender, B. (1995). Are asthmatic children educationally handicapped? *School Psychology Quarterly, 10,* 274–291.
23. Campbell, C. A., & Ashmore, R. J. (1995). The Slosson Intelligence Test-Revised. *Measurement and Evaluation in Counseling and Development, 28,* 116–118.
24. Hoba, M. E., & Ramisetty-Mikler, S. (1995). The language skills and concepts of early and nonearly readers. *The Journal of Genetic Psychology, 156,* 313–331.
25. Lysaker, P. H., Bell, M. D., Zito, W. S., & Bioty, S. M. (1995). Social skills at work: Deficits and predictors of improvement in schizophrenia. *The Journal of Nervous and Mental Disease, 183,* 688–697.
26. Perez, E., Slate, J. R. Neeley, R., McDaniel, M., Briggs, T., & Layton, K. (1995). Validity of the CELF-R, TONI, and SIT for children referred for auditory processing problems. *Journal of Clinical Psychology, 51,* 540–543.
27. Simon, E. W., Rappaport, D. A., Papka, M., & Woodruff-Pak, D. S. (1995). Fragile-X and Down's syndrome: Are there syndrome-specific cognitive profiles at low IQ levels. *Journal of Intellectual Disability Research, 39,* 326–330.
28. Wilson, B. N., Polatajko, H. J., Kaplan, B. J., & Faris, P. (1995). Use of Bruininks-Oseretsky Test of Motor Proficiency in occupational therapy. *The American Journal of Occupational Therapy, 49,* 8–17.
29. Baumann, J. F. (1996). "Coping with reading disability"—12 years later. *Journal of Adolescent & Adult Literacy, 39,* 532–535.
30. Lysaker, P. H., Bell, M. D., Bioty, S. M., & Zito, W. S. (1996). Cognitive impairment and substance abuse history as predictors of the temporal stability of negative symptoms in schizophrenia. *Journal of Nervous and Mental Disease, 184,* 21–26.
31. McFadden, T. V. (1996). Creating language impairments in typically achieving children: The pitfalls of "normal" normative sampling. *Language, Speech, and Hearing Services in Schools, 27,* 3–9.
32. Simon, E. W., Rosen, M., & Ponpipom, A. (1996). Age and IQ as predictors of emotion identification in adults with mental retardation. *Research in Developmental Disabilities, 17,* 383–389.
33. Chaffin, M., Wherry, J. N., & Dykman, R. (1997). School age children's coping with sexual abuse: Abuse stresses and symptoms associated with four coping strategies. *Child Abuse & Neglect, 21,* 227–240.

[2433]

Slosson Oral Reading Test [Revised].

Purpose: Designed as a "quick estimate to target word recognition levels for children and adults."
Population: Preschool-adult.
Publication Dates: 1963-1990.
Acronym: SORT-R.
Scores: Total score only.
Administration: Individual.
Price Data, 1992: $32 per complete kit; $14 per manual ('90, 38 pages); $16 per 50 score sheets; $7 per bound word lists; $3 per large print word lists.
Special Editions: Large print edition available for individuals with visual handicaps.
Time: (3-5) minutes.
Comments: Grade equivalent (GE) and age equivalent (AE) scores are also available.
Authors: Richard L. Slosson and Charles L. Nicholson.
Publisher: Slosson Educational Publications, Inc.

Cross References: For reviews by Steven R. Shaw and Carol E. Westby, see 12:359 (4 references); see T4:2483 (16 references), T3:2218 (15 references), T2:1688 (5 references), and 6:844.

TEST REFERENCES

1. Reynolds, C. A., Hewitt, J. K., Erickson, M. T., Silberg, J. L., Rutter, M., Simonoff, E., Meyer, J., & Eaves, J. (1996). The genetics of children's oral reading performance. *Journal of Child Psychology and Psychiatry, 37,* 425–434.

2. Burns, K. A., Chethik, L., Burns, W. J., & Clark, R. (1997). The early relationship of drug abusing mothers and their infants: An assessment at eight to twelve months of age. *Journal of Clinical Psychology, 53,* 279–287.

3. Roberts, R. L., Harper, R., & Preszler, B. (1997). The effects of the Fresh Start program on Native Americans parolees' job placement. *Journal of Employment Counseling, 34,* 115–122.

4. Rounsaville, B. J., Kranzler, H. R. Ball, S., Tennen, H., Poling, J., & Triffleman, E. (1998). Personality disorders in substance abusers: Relation to substance use. *Journal of Nervous and Mental Disease, 186,* 87–95.

[2434]

Slosson Test of Reading Readiness.

Purpose: "Designed to identify children who are at risk of failure in programs of formal reading instruction."
Population: Latter kindergarten-grade 1.
Publication Date: 1991.
Acronym: STRR.
Scores, 12: Visual Skills (Recognition of Capital Letters, Recognition of Lower Case Letters, Matching Capital and Lower Case Letters, Visual Discrimination-Matching Word Forms, Total), Auditory Skills (Auditory Discrimination-Rhyming Words, Auditory Discrimination and Memory—Recognition of Beginning Sounds, Total), Cognitive Skills (Sequencing, Opposites, Total), Total Inventory.
Administration: Individual.
Price Data, 1992: $48 per complete kit; $18 per manual (24 pages); $12 per test stimulus booklet; $16 per 50 scoring booklets; $6 per 50 letter to parent.
Time: (15) minutes.
Authors: Leslie Anne Perry and Gary J. Vitali.
Publisher: Slosson Educational Publications, Inc.
Cross References: For reviews by Gerald S. Hanna and Diane J. Sawyer, see 12:360.

[2435]

Small Business Assessment.

Purpose: Provides information "about how people in the company work together."
Population: Small businesses.
Publication Date: 1984.
Acronym: SBA.
Scores: 4 areas: Organizational Climate, Supervisory Leadership, Peer Relationships, Outcomes.
Administration: Group.
Price Data: Not available.
Time: Administration time not reported.
Comments: Scored by publisher.
Author: Rensis Likert Associates, Inc.
Publisher: Rensis Likert Associates, Inc. [No reply from publisher; status unknown].
Cross References: For a review by Robert W. Hiltonsmith, see 13:290.

[2436]

Smedley Hand Dynamometer.

Purpose: Developed to "measure the muscular torque (grip) of the hand and forearm."
Population: Ages 6-18.
Publication Dates: [1920-1953].
Scores: Total score only.
Administration: Individual.
Price Data, 1998: $190 per hand dynamometer.
Time: Administration time not reported.
Author: F. Smedley.
Publisher: Stoelting Co.
Cross References: See T2:1901 (10 references).

[2437]

Smell Identification Test™ [Revised].

Purpose: Designed to measure an individual's ability to "identify a number of odorants at the suprathreshold level."
Population: People 5 years and up with suspected olfactory dysfunction.
Publication Dates: 1981–1995.
Acronym: SIT; UPSIT.
Scores: Total score only.
Administration: Individual.
Price Data, 1998: $169.50 per introductory/combination package including 50 Pocket Smell Tests, 3 Smell Identification Tests, administration manual ('95, 51 pages), and scoring keys; $26.95 per Smell Identification Test; $135 per Pocket Smell Test (75 Pocket Smell Tests); $12.95 per Cross-Cultural Smell Identification Test (must order at least 10); $19.50 per administration manual with scoring keys; $14.95 per Picture Identification Test; $3.50 per scoring key for Smell Identification Test, Picture Identification Test, or Cross-Cultural Smell Identification Test.
Time: [10–15] minutes.
Comments: A 40-item forced-choice questionnaire; also known as University of Pennsylvania Smell Identification Test; for use only by individuals "professionally engaged in the scientific or medical evaluation of smell function"; related versions include the Pocket Smell Test, the Cross-Cultural Smell Identification Test, and the Picture Identification Test (equivalent to the SIT except stimuli are pictures rather than odors).
Author: Richard L. Doty.
Publisher: Sensonics, Inc.

TEST REFERENCES

1. Breckler, S. J., & Fried, H. S. (1993). On knowing what you like and liking what you smell: Attitudes depend on the form in which the object is represented. *Personality and Social Psychology Bulletin, 19,* 228-240.

2. Madigan, N. K., Ehrlichman, H., & Borod, J. C. (1994). Hedonic ratings of odors as a function of odor sequence in older adults. *Perceptual and Motor Skills, 79,* 27-32.

3. Bromley, S. M., & Doty, R. L. (1995). Odor recognition memory is better under bilateral than unilateral test conditions. *Cortex, 31,* 25-40.
4. Pierce, J. D., Jr., Doty, R. L., & Amoore, J. E. (1996). Analysis of position of trial sequence and type of diluent on the detection threshold for phenylethyl alcohol using a single staircase method. *Perceptual and Motor Skills, 82,* 451–458.

[2438]
Smit-Hand Articulation and Phonology Evaluation.

Purpose: Designed to assess a child's level of phonology.
Population: Ages 3–9.
Publication Date: 1997.
Acronym: SHAPE.
Scores, 11: Total, Weak Syllable Deletion, Final Consonant Deletion, Reduction of /lrw/ Clusters, Reduction of /s/ Clusters, Stopping of Initial Fricatives, Voicing of Initial Voiceless Obstruents, Fronting of Velars, Depalatalization, Gliding of Liquid Singletons, Vocalization of Liquids.
Administration: Individual.
Price Data, 1999: $125 per kit including 10 record booklets, 10 autoscore answer forms, manual (63 pages), and 1 picture set; $29.50 per 10 record booklets; $14.50 per 10 autoscore forms; $35 per manual; $65 per picture set; $135 per computerized scoring system (IBM with Windows).
Time: (30) minutes.
Authors: Ann B. Smit and Linda Hand.
Publisher: Western Psychological Services.

[2439]
Smith-Johnson Nonverbal Performance Scale.

Purpose: For "evaluating the language- and/or hearing-impaired child."
Population: Ages 2-4.
Publication Date: 1977.
Scores, 14: Formboard, Block Building, Pencil Drawing, Bead Stringing, Knot Tying, Color Items, Scissors, Paper Folding, Cube Tapping, Form Discrimination, Completion Items, Manikin, Block Patterns, Sorting.
Administration: Individual.
Price Data, 1999: $198 per complete kit including 1 set of test materials, 100 record sheets, and manual (38 pages); $19.50 per 100 record sheets; $22.50 per manual (38 pages).
Time: (30-45) minutes.
Authors: Alathena J. Smith and Ruth E. Johnson.
Publisher: Western Psychological Services.
Cross References: For a review by Patricia M. Sullivan, see 9:1145.

[2440]
Smoker Complaint Scale.

Purpose: Designed to measure changes in physiological/emotional/craving states as a function of smoking cessation.
Population: Persons quitting smoking.
Publication Date: 1984.
Acronym: SCS.
Scores: Total score and item scores only.
Administration: Individual or group.
Manual: No manual.
Price Data, 1989: Instrument available without charge from publisher.
Time: (1-5) minutes.
Comments: Self-administered.
Author: Nina G. Schneider.
Publisher: Nina G. Schneider.

TEST REFERENCE

1. Spring, B., Wurtman, J., Gleason, R., Wurtman, R., & Kessler, K. (1991). Weight gain and withdrawal symptoms after smoking cessation: A preventive intervention using d-finfluramine. *Health Psychology, 10,* 216-233.

[2441]
Snijders-Oomen Non-Verbal Intelligence Test—Revised.

Purpose: Developed as an untimed, nonverbal test of intelligence.
Publication Dates: 1939-1997.
Administration: Individual.
Price Data: Available from publisher.
Foreign Language Edition: Dutch and German editions available.
Comments: Administered in pantomime (for hearing impaired) or orally.
Publisher: Swets Test Publishers [The Netherlands].

a) SNIJDERS-OOMEN NON-VERBAL INTELLIGENCE SCALE FOR YOUNG CHILDREN.
Population: Dutch children ages 2-6 to 7-0.
Acronym: SON-R 2 1/2-7.
Scores, 6: Sorting, Mosaic, Combination, Memory, Copying, Total.
Time: (45-50) minutes.
Comments: Also called Non-Verbal Intelligence Scale S.O.N. 2 1/2-7.
Authors: J. T. Snijders and N. Snijders-Oomen.

b) SON-R.
Population: Dutch children ages 5-6 to 17-0.
Acronym: SON-R 5 1/2-17.
Scores, 8: Categories, Mosaics, Hidden Pictures, Patterns, Situations, Analogies, Stories, Total.
Time: (60-120) minutes.
Comments: Revised version of the SON-'58 and SSON; older versions out-of-print.
Authors: J. T. Snijders, P. J. Tellegen, J. A. Laros, N. Snijders-Oomen (test), and M. A. H. Huijnen (test).

Cross References: See T4:2491 (2 references); for reviews by Douglas K. Detterman and Timothy Z. Keith of an earlier edition, see 9:1146; see also T3:2221 (1 reference) and T2:512 (5 references); for a review by J. S. Lawes of the 1958 edition, see 6:529 (2 references).

TEST REFERENCES

1. Schaper, M. W., & Reitsma, P. (1993). The use of speech-based recording in reading by prelingually deaf children. *American Annals of the Deaf, 138,* 46-54.
2. Roeden, J. M., & Zitman, F. G. (1995). Ageing in adults with Down's syndrome in institutionally-based and community-based residences. *Journal of Intellectual Disability Research, 39,* 399–497.

[2442]

Social Adjustment Scale—Self Report.

Purpose: Designed to assess "the ability of an individual to adapt to, and derive satisfaction from, their social roles."
Population: Adults.
Publication Date: 1999.
Acronym: SAS-SR.
Scores: 7 areas: Work, Social and Leisure Activities, Relations with Extended Family, Primary Relationship, Parenthood, Family Life, Economic.
Administration: Group.
Price Data, 1999: $125 per complete kit including 25 interview guides, 25 QuikScore™ forms, and manual; $60 per 25 interview guides; $35 per 25 QuikScore™ forms; $45 per manual; $55 per specimen set including 3 interview guides, 3 QuikScore™ forms, and manual.
Foreign Language Editions: Available in Afrikaans, Cantonese, Czech, Danish, Dutch, Finnish, French (European), French-Canadian, German, Greek, Hebrew, Hungarian, Italian, Japanese, Mandarin, Norwegian, Portuguese, Russian, Spanish (European), Spanish (South American), and Swedish.
Time: Administration time not reported.
Author: Myrna Weissmann.
Publisher: Multi-Health Systems, Inc.

[2443]

Social and Prevocational Information Battery—Revised.

Purpose: "To assess knowledge of certain skills and competencies regarded as important for the community adjustment of students with mild mental retardation."
Population: Mildly mentally retarded students in grades 7-12.
Publication Dates: 1975-1986.
Acronym: SPIB-R.
Scores, 10: Purchasing Habits, Budgeting, Banking, Job Related Behavior, Job Search Skills, Home Management, Health Care, Hygiene and Grooming, Functional Signs, Total.
Administration: Group.
Price Data: Available from publisher.
Time: (20-30) minutes per test.
Comments: Orally administered.
Authors: Andrew S. Halpern, Larry K. Irvin, and Arden W. Munkres (design).
Publisher: CTB/McGraw-Hill.
Cross References: See T4:2492 (1 reference); for reviews by Terry Overton and Terry A. Stinnett, see 11:367; for reviews by M. Harry Daniels and Carol Kehr Tittle of an earlier edition, see 9:1147; see also T3:2224 (7 references); for a review by C. Edward Meyers of the original edition, see 8:984 (2 references).

[2444]

Social Behavior Assessment Inventory.

Purpose: Assesses social skill levels in students.
Population: Grades K-9.
Publication Dates: 1978-1992.
Acronym: SBAI.
Scores, 30: Environmental Behaviors (Care for the Environment, Dealing with Emergencies, Lunchroom Behavior, Movement Around Environment), Interpersonal Behaviors (Accepting Authority, Coping with Conflict, Gaining Attention, Greeting Others, Helping Others, Making Conversation, Organized Play, Positive Attitude Toward Others, Playing Informally, Property: Own and Others), Self-Related Behaviors (Accepting Consequences, Ethical Behavior, Expressing Feelings, Positive Attitude Toward Self, Responsible Behavior, Self-Care), Task-Related Behaviors (Asking and Answering Questions, Attending Behavior, Classroom Discussion, Completing Tasks, Following Directions, Group Activities, Independent Work, On-Task Behavior, Performing Before Others, Quality of Work).
Administration: Individual or group.
Price Data: Price information available from publisher for complete kit including Social Skills in the Classroom–2nd ed., manual ('92, 34 pages), and 25 rating booklets.
Time: (30-45) minutes.
Comments: Observations made by teacher or trained paraprofessional.
Authors: Thomas M. Stephens and Kevin D. Arnold.
Publisher: Psychological Assessment Resources, Inc.
Cross References: For reviews by Kathryn A. Hess and David MacPhee, see 12:361; see also T4:2493 (1 reference); for a review by Ronald S. Drabman of an earlier edition, see 9:1148; see also T3:2226 (1 reference).

TEST REFERENCE

1. Demaray, M. K., Ruffalo, S. L., Carlson, J., Busse, R. T., Olson, A. E., McManus, S. M., & Leventhal, A. (1995). Social skills assessment: A comparative evaluation of six published rating scales. *School Psychology Review, 24,* 648- 671.

[2445]

The Social Climate Scales.

Purpose: Developed to assess measures of environmental or social climate.
Population: Members of various groups.

Comments: For reviews and additional references and information, see the separate test entries.
Author: Rudolf Moos and Associates.
Publisher: Consulting Psychologists Press, Inc.

a) CLASSROOM ENVIRONMENT SCALE, SECOND EDITION.

b) COMMUNITY ORIENTED PROGRAMS ENVIRONMENT SCALE.

c) FAMILY ENVIRONMENT SCALE, SECOND EDITION.

d) GROUP ENVIRONMENT SCALE, SECOND EDITION.

e) UNIVERSITY RESIDENCE ENVIRONMENT SCALE.

f) WARD ATMOSPHERE SCALE.

g) WORK ENVIRONMENT SCALE, SECOND EDITION.

Cross References: For a review by James M. Richards, Jr., see 8:681 (84 references).

TEST REFERENCE

1. Stevenson, J. C., & Evans, G. T. (1994). Conceptualization and measurement of cognitive holding power. *Journal of Educational Measurement, 31,* 161–181.

[2446]

Social Competence and Behavior Evaluation, Preschool Edition.

Purpose: "Designed to assess patterns of social competence, affective expression, and adjustment difficulties."
Population: Children aged 30 months to 76 months.
Publication Date: 1995.
Acronym: SCBE.
Scores: 8 Basic scales (Depressive-Joyful, Anxious-Secure, Angry-Tolerant, Isolated-Integrated, Aggressive-Calm, Egotistical-Prosocial, Oppositional-Cooperative, Dependent-Autonomous); 4 Summary scales (Social Competence, Internalizing Problems, Externalizing Problems, General Adaptation).
Administration: Group.
Price Data, 1999: $75 per complete kit including 25 AutoScore™ forms and manual (67 pages); $33.50 per 25 AutoScore™ forms; $45 per manual.
Time: (15) minutes.
Comments: Ratings by teachers or other child care professionals.
Authors: Peter J. LaFreniere and Jean E. Dumas.
Publisher: Western Psychological Services.

[2447]

Social-Emotional Dimension Scale.

Purpose: Provides a means for rating nonacademic student behaviors "which may be judged by teachers as problems in the classroom setting."
Population: Ages 5.5-18.5.
Publication Date: 1986.
Acronym: SEDS.
Scores: 6 scores (Avoidance of Peer Interaction, Aggressive Interaction, Avoidance of Teacher Interaction, Inappropriate Behavior, Depressive Reaction, Physical/Fear Reaction) plus a Behavior Quotient and a Behavior Observation Web.
Administration: Individual.
Price Data, 1999: $76 per complete kit including 50 profile/examiner record forms and examiner's manual (54 pages); $39 per 50 profile/examiner record forms; $39 per examiner's manual.
Time: Administration time not reported.
Comments: Behavior checklist for ratings by school personnel.
Authors: Jerry B. Hutton and Timothy G. Roberts.
Publisher: PRO-ED.
Cross References: For a review by Jean Powell Kirnan, see 11:368.

[2448]

Social Phobia and Anxiety Inventory.

Purpose: Constructed for assessment of the "somatic, cognitive and behavioral aspects of social phobia."
Population: Ages 14 and older.
Publication Date: 1996.
Acronym: SPAI.
Scores, 3: Social Phobia, Agoraphobia, Difference.
Administration: Individual or group.
Price Data, 1999: $55 per complete kit including manual and 25 QuikScore™ forms; $30 per 25 QuikScore™ forms; $30 per manual; $33 per specimen set including manual and 3 QuikScore™ forms.
Time: (15) minutes.
Comments: Self-report.
Authors: Samuel M. Turner, Deborah C. Beidel, and Constance V. Dancu.
Publisher: Multi-Health Systems, Inc.

[2449]

Social Reticence Scale.

Purpose: To assess an individual's shyness.
Population: High school and college and adults.
Publication Date: 1986.
Acronym: SRS.
Scores: Total score only.
Administration: Individual or group.
Price Data, 1998: $25 per sampler set including test booklet, scoring key, and manual; $100 per permission set including sampler set and permission to reproduce 200 administrations of the test.
Time: (5-10) minutes.
Author: Warren H. Jones and Stephen Briggs.
Publisher: Mind Garden, Inc.
Cross References: See T4:2499 (1 reference); for reviews by Owen Scott, III and William K. Wilkinson, see 11:370 (1 reference).

[2450]

Social Skills for Adults with Severe Retardation–An Inventory and Training Program.

Purpose: "Designed to establish an avenue for moving toward culturally appropriate behaviors in residential, school, and activity settings."
Population: Severely or profoundly handicapped adolescents and adults.
Publication Date: 1980.
Scores: 10 areas of social behavior: Appropriate Physical Interaction, Touching/Manipulating Objects, Reacts to Name, Social Smiling, Eye Contact, Social Interaction with Training, Traveling with Trainer, Group Interaction, Development of Leisure Skills, Waiting.
Administration: Individual.
Price Data, 1988: $49.95 per manual (284 pages in a 3-ring binder, including instructions for administration, inventory, training program, and forms for record keeping).
Time: Administration time not reported.
Comments: Previously listed as Social Skills for Severely Retarded Adults–An Inventory and Training Program.
Authors: Sandra E. McClennen, Ronald R. Hoekstra, and James E. Bryan.
Publisher: Research Press.
Cross References: For a review by Joel Hundert, see 9:1151.

[2451]

Social Skills Inventory, Research Edition.

Purpose: "To assess basic social communication skills."
Population: Ages 14 and over reading at or above the eighth grade level.
Publication Date: 1989.
Acronym: SSI.
Scores, 7: Emotional Expressivity, Emotional Sensitivity, Emotional Control, Social Expressivity, Social Sensitivity, Social Control, Total.
Administration: Group and individual.
Price Data, 1999: $49.50 per 25 test booklets; $10.50 per scoring key; $49.75 per 25 answer sheets; $26.25 per manual (21 pages), $41 per preview kit including item booklet, non-prepaid answer sheet, scoring key, and manual; scoring service offered by publisher.
Time: (30-45) minutes.
Comments: Test booklet title is Self-Description Inventory; self-administered.
Authors: Ronald E. Riggio.
Publisher: Consulting Psychologists Press, Inc.
Cross References: See T4:2501 (4 references); for reviews by Judith C. Conger and Susan M. Sheridan, see 11:371 (3 references).

TEST REFERENCES

1. Luthar, S. S., & Blatt, S. J. (1993). Dependent and self-critical depressive experiences among inner-city adolescents. *Journal of Personality, 61,* 365–386.
2. James, K., Lovato, C., & Khoo, G. (1994). Social identity correlates of minority workers' health. *Academy of Management Journal, 37,* 383–396.
3. Miller, R. S. (1995). On the nature of embarrassability, shyness, social evaluation, and social skill. *Journal of Personality, 63,* 315–339.
4. Wompold, B. E., Ankarb, G., Mondin, G., Trinidad-Carrillo, M., Baumler, B., & Prater, K. (1995). Social skills of and environments produced by different Holland Types: A social perspective on person-environment fit models. *Journal of Counseling Psychology, 42,* 365–379.

[2452]

Social Skills Rating System.

Purpose: Constructed to screen and classify children suspected of having social behavior problems and to assist in the development of appropriate interventions for identified children.
Publication Date: 1990.
Acronym: SSRS.
Administration: Individual or group.
Price Data, 1999: $129.95 per preschool/elementary levels starter set including 10 copies of each form and level questionnaires, 10 assessment-intervention records, and manual (207 pages); $119.95 per secondary level starter set; $24.95 per 30 questionnaires (select level and form); $33.95 per 30 assessment-intervention records; $39.95 per manual.
Time: (15-25) minutes.
Comments: Ratings by teachers and parents as well as student self-ratings; expanded version of the Teacher Ratings of Social Skills; hand scored or computer scores; computer-scored report options: individual or group summary reports, teacher and parent letters, suggested intervention activities.
Authors: Frank M. Gresham and Stephen N. Elliott.
Publisher: American Guidance Service, Inc.

a) PRESCHOOL.
Population: Ages 3-0 to 4-11.
Scores, 6: Social Skills, Cooperation, Assertion, Problem Behaviors, Internalizing, Externalizing.
Forms, 2: Parent, Teacher.

b) ELEMENTARY.
Population: Grades K-6.
Scores, 11: Social Skills, Cooperation, Assertion, Responsibility, Empathy, Self-Control, Problem Behaviors, Externalizing, Internalizing, Hyperactivity, Academic Competence.
Forms, 3: Student, Parent, Teacher.

c) SECONDARY.
Population: Grades 7-12.
Scores, 3: Same as *b* above except no Hyperactivity subscale.
Forms, 3: Same as *b* above.

Cross References: For reviews by Kathryn M. Benes and Michael Furlong and Mitchell Karno, see 12:362 (10 references); see also T4:2502 (4 references).

TEST REFERENCES

1. Gresham, F. M. (1993). Social skills and learning disabilities as a type III error: Rejoinder to Conte and Andrews. *Journal of Learning Disabilities, 26,* 154–158.

2. Vaughn, S., Zaragoza, N., Hogan, A., & Walker, J. (1993). A four-year longitudinal investigation of the social skills and behavior problems of students with learning disabilities. *Journal of Learning Disabilities, 26,* 404–412.

3. Vaughn, S., & Hogan, A. (1994). The social competence of students with learning disabilities over time: A within-individual examination. *Journal of Learning Disabilities, 27,* 292–303.

4. August, G. J., Realmuto, G. M., Crosby, R. D., & MacDonald, A. W. (1995). Community-based multiple-gate screening of children at risk for conduct disorder. *Journal of Abnormal Child Psychology, 23,* 521–544.

5. Bell, S. M., & McCallum, R. S. (1995). Development of a scale reasoning student attributions and its relationship to self-concept and social functioning. *School Psychology Review, 24,* 271–286.

6. Demaray, M. K., Ruffalo, S. L., Carlson, J., Busse, R. T., Olson, A. E., McManus, S. M., & Leventhal, A. (1995). Social skills assessment: A comparative evaluation of six published rating scales. *School Psychology Review, 24,* 648– 671.

7. Frankel, F., Myatt, R., & Cantwell, D. P. (1995). Training outpatient boys to conform with the social ecology of popular peers: Effects on parent and teacher ratings. *Journal of Clinical Child Psychology, 24,* 300–310.

8. Haager, D., & Vaughn, S. (1995). Parent, teacher, peer, and self-reports of the social competence of students with learning disabilities. *Journal of Learning Disabilities, 28,* 205–215, 231.

9. Margalit, M., & Ben-Dov, I. (1995). Learning disabilities and social environments: Kibbutz versus city comparisons of loneliness and social competence. *International Journal of Behavioral Development, 18,* 519–536.

10. Feng, H., & Carledge, G. (1996). Social skills assessment of inner city Asian, African, and European American students. *School Psychology Review, 25,* 228–239.

11. Flanagan, D. P., Alfonso, V. C., Primavera, L. H., Povall, L., & Higgins, D. (1996). Convergent validity of the BASC and SSRS: Implications for social skills assessment. *Psychology in the Schools, 33,* 13–23.

12. Fujiki, M., Brinton, B., & Todd, C. M. (1996). Social skills of children with specific language impairment. *Language, Speech, and Hearing Services in Schools, 27,* 195– 202.

13. Gresham, F. M., Noell, G. H., & Elliott, S. N. (1996). Teachers as judges of social competence: A conditional probability analysis. *School Psychology Review, 25,* 108–117.

14. MacMillan, D. L., Gresham, F. M., Lopez, M. F., & Bocian, K. M. (1996). Comparison of students nominated for prereferral interventions by ethnicity and gender. *The Journal of Special Education, 30,* 133–151.

15. MacMillan, D. L., Gresham, F. M., Siperstein, G. N., & Bocian, K. M. (1996). The labyrinth of IDEA: School decisions on referred students with subaverage general intelligence. *American Journal on Mental Retardation, 101,* 161–174.

16. Walker, K. C., & Bracken, B. A. (1996). Inter-parent agreement on four preschool behavior rating scales: Effects of parents and child gender. *Psychology in the Schools, 33,* 273–283.

17. Agostin, T. M., & Bam, S. K. (1997). Predicting early school success with developmental and social skills screeners. *Psychology in the Schools, 34,* 219–228.

18. Caldarella, P., & Merrell, K. W. (1997). Common dimensions of social skills of children and adolescents: A taxonomy of positive behaviors. *School Psychology Review, 26,* 264–278.

19. Gresham, F. M., MacMillan, D. L., & Bocian, K. M. (1997). Teachers as "tests": Differential validity of teacher judgements in identifying students at-risk for learning disabilities. *School Psychology Review, 26,* 47–60.

20. Phelps, L., Wallace, N. V., & Bontrager, A. (1997). Risk factors in early child development: Is prenatal cocaine/polydrug exposure a key variable? *Psychology in the Schools, 34,* 245–252.

21. Ruffalo, S. L., & Elliott, S. N. (1997). Teachers' and parents' ratings of children's social skills: A closer look at cross-informant agreements through an item analysis protocol. *School Psychology Review, 26,* 489–501.

22. Sheridan, S. M. (1997). Conceptual and empirical bases of conjoint behavioral consultation. *School Psychology Quarterly, 12,* 119–133.

23. Vallance, D. D., & Wintre, M. G. (1997). Discourse processes underlying social competence in children with language learning disabilities. *Development and Psychopathology, 9,* 95–108.

24. Gresham, F. M., MacMillan, D. L., Bocian, K. M., Ward, S. L., & Forness, S. R. (1998). Comorbidity of hyperactivity-impulsivity-inattention and conduct problems: Risk factors in social, affective, and academic domains. *Journal of Abnormal Child Psychology, 26,* 393–406.

[2453]

Social Styles Analysis.

Purpose: Constructed to identify a person's social style of presentation and interaction.
Population: Adults.
Publication Date: 1989.
Scores: 4 categories: Analytical, Driver, Amiable, Expressive.
Administration: Group.
Editions, 2: Self, Other.
Manual: No manual.
Price Data, 1991: $25 per package for self analysis (5.25-inch or 3.5-inch diskette); $50 per package for other analyses (5.25-inch or 3.5-inch diskette).
Time: Administration time not reported.
Comments: IBM microcomputer necessary for scoring.
Authors: Wilson Learning Corporation.
Publisher: Jossey-Bass/Pfeiffer.
Cross References: For a review by C. Dale Carpenter, see 11:372.

[2454]

Socio-Sexual Knowledge & Attitudes Test.

Purpose: Designed to assess sex knowledge and attitudes of individuals with development disabilities.
Population: Developmentally disabled ages 18-42 and non-retarded persons of all ages.
Publication Dates: 1976-1980.
Acronym: SSKAT.
Scores: 14 topic areas: Anatomy Terminology, Menstruation, Dating, Marriage, Intimacy, Intercourse, Pregnancy and Childbirth, Birth Control, Masturbation, Homosexuality, Venereal Disease, Alcohol and Drugs, Community Risks and Hazards, Terminology Check.
Administration: Individual.
Price Data, 1998: $150 per complete kit including stimulus picture book, manual ('80, 59 pages), and 10 record forms; $44.50 per 10 record forms including student profile and response summary; $25 per manual.
Time: Administration time not reported.
Comments: Criterion-referenced.
Authors: Joel R. Wish, Katherine Fiechtl McCombs, and Barbara Edmonson.
Publisher: Stoelting Co.
Cross References: For a review by Edward S. Herold, see 9:1152; see also T3:2237 (1 reference).

[2455]

Softball Skills Test.

Purpose: "To improve teaching and evaluation of softball skills."
Population: Grades 5-12 and college.
Publication Date: 1991.
Scores, 4: Batting, Fielding Ground Balls, Overhand Throwing, Baserunning.
Administration: Individual.
Price Data, 1999: $14 per manual (64 pages).
Time: Administration time not reported.
Author: Roberta E. Rikli, Editor.
Publisher: American Association for Active Lifestyles and Fitness.
Cross References: For a review by Don Sebolt, see 12:363.

[2456]

Solid Geometry: National Achievement Tests.

Purpose: To measure achievement in solid geometry.
Population: High school students.
Publication Dates: 1958-1960.
Scores: Total score only.
Administration: Group.
Forms, 2: A, B.
Price Data, 1985: $8.75 per 25 tests; $4 per specimen set.
Time: 40 minutes.
Comments: No specific manual; combined manual ('58, 12 pages) for this test and following tests: Plane Trigonometry (1999), Plane Geometry (1998), and First Year Algebra Test (1038).
Authors: Ray Webb and Julius H. Hlavaty (manual).
Publisher: Psychometric Affiliates.
Cross References: For a review by Sheldon S. Myers, see 6:653.

[2457]

Somatic Inkblot Series.

Purpose: "A projective test for personality, diagnostic, and clinical assessment."
Population: Ages 3 and over.
Publication Dates: 1969-1990.
Acronym: SIS.
Scores: 4 scales: Pathologic Anatomy Score, Depression, Hostility and Aggression Scale, Paranoia Scale.
Administration: Individual or group.
Forms, 3: SIS-I, SIS-II, SIS-II Video.
Price Data: Not available.
Time: (30) minutes for SIS-I; (60) minutes for SIS-II or SIS-II Video.
Author: Wilfred A. Cassell.
Publisher: Wilfred A. Cassell [No reply from publisher; status unknown].
Cross References: See T3:2239 (1 reference) and 8:518 (2 references).

[2458]

South African Written Language Test.

Purpose: To evaluate the written language ability of English-speaking pupils.
Population: South African pupils in Grade II to Standard 5.
Publication Date: 1981.
Acronym: SAWLT.
Scores, 7: Total Words, Total Sentences, Words per Sentence, Sentence Complexity, Correctness, Abstract-Concrete Content, Total.
Administration: Group.
Price Data: Available from publisher.
Time: (30-35) minutes.
Comments: Adaptation of Die Suid-Afrikaanse Skryftaaltoets.
Authors: Marita Brink, Italia Boninelli, and Jan Vorster.
Publisher: Human Sciences Research Council [South Africa].

[2459]

The Southern California Ordinal Scales of Development.

Purpose: To provide "differential assessment of educational needs and abilities."
Population: Multihandicapped, developmentally delayed, and learning disabled children.
Publication Dates: 1977-1985.
Acronym: SCOSD.
Scores: 6 scales: Cognition, Communication, Social-Affective Behavior, Practical Abilities, Fine Motor Abilities, Gross Motor Abilities.
Administration: Individual.
Price Data, 1998: $130 per complete instrument.
Time: (60-120) minutes per scale.
Comments: A Piagetian-based assessment system.
Authors: Donald I. Ashurst, Elaine Bamberg, Julika Barrett, Ann Bisno, Artice Burke, David C. Chambers, Jean Fentiman, Ronald Kadish, Mary Lou Mitchell, Lambert Neeley, Todd Thorne, and Doris Wents.
Publisher: Foreworks.
Cross References: For reviews by Cameron J. Camp and Arlene C. Rosenthal, see 10:338.

TEST REFERENCE

1. Schery, T. K., & O'Connor, L. C. (1992). The effectiveness of school-based computer language intervention with severely handicapped children. *Language, Speech, and Hearing Services in Schools, 23,* 43–47.

[2460]

Space Thinking (Flags).

Purpose: To measure the ability to visualize a stable figure, drawing or diagram when it is moved into different positions.
Population: Industrial employees.
Publication Date: 1959–1984.
Scores: Total score only.
Administration: Individual or group.
Price Data, 1998: $70.50 per start-up kit including 25 test booklets, score key, and interpretation and research manual; $44 per 25 test booklets (quantity discounts available); $14.75 per score key; $19.75 per interpretation and research manual.
Time: 5 minutes.
Authors: L. L. Thurstone and T. E. Jeffrey.
Publisher: NCS (Rosemont).
Cross References: See T4:2515 (1 reference), T3:898 (1 reference), and T2:2245 (1 reference); for a review by I. Macfarlane Smith, see 6:1086.

[2461]

Spadafore Attention Deficit Hyperactivity Disorder Rating Scale.

Purpose: Designed "to examine the wide range of behaviors that are frequently associated with ADHD symptoms."
Population: Ages 5–19.
Publication Date: 1997.
Acronym: S-ADHD-RS.
Scores, 4: Impulsivity/Hyperactivity, Attention, Social Adjustment, ADHD Index.
Administration: Individual.
Price Data, 1999: $65 per test kit including 25 scoring protocols, 25 observation forms, 25 medication tracking forms, and manual (80 pages); $20 per 25 scoring protocols; $10 per 25 observation forms; $10 per 25 medication tracking forms; $22 per manual.
Time: Untimed.
Comments: Rating scale to be completed by classroom teachers about a child; also included in kit: behavioral observation form and medication monitoring form.
Authors: Gerald J. Spadafore and Sharon J. Spadafore.
Publisher: Academic Therapy Publications, Inc.

[2462]

Spadafore Diagnostic Reading Test.

Purpose: Constructed to assess decoding and comprehension skills in reading.
Population: Grades 1-12 and adults.
Publication Date: 1983.
Acronym: SDRT.
Scores, 15: 3 performance levels (Independent, Instructional, Frustration) for each of 5 subtests (Decoding [Word Recognition, Oral Reading], Comprehension [Oral Reading, Silent Reading, Listening]).
Administration: Individual.
Price Data, 1999: $60 per complete kit including test plates, 10 test booklets, and manual (60 pages); $25 per set of test plates; $15 per 10 test booklets; $17 per manual; $17 per specimen set.
Time: (30-60) minutes.
Comments: "Criterion-referenced."
Authors: Gerald J. Spadafore.
Publisher: Academic Therapy Publications.
Cross References: See T4:2516 (1 reference); for a review by James R. Sanders and Blaine R. Worthen, see 9:1159.

[2463]

Spanish Assessment of Basic Education, Second Edition.

Purpose: "Designed to measure achievement in the basic skills ... with students for whom Spanish is the language of instruction."
Population: Grades 1.0–1.9, 1.6–2.9, 2.6–3.9, 3.6–4.9, 4.6–6.9, 6.6–8.9.
Publication Dates: 1991–1994.
Acronym: SABE/2.
Administration: Group.
Price Data, 1993: $9.45 per 35 practice tests (select level); $29 per 100 student diagnostic profiles (select level); $9.45 per 35 parent reports (select level); $1.20 per class record sheet; $8.35 per examiner's manual ('91, 41–57 pages) (select level); $11.45 per user's guide ('91, 64 pages); $11.45 per technical report ('94, 43 pages); $8.35 per norms book ('94, 159 pages); scoring service available from publisher.
Author: CTB Macmillan/McGraw-Hill.
Publisher: CTB/McGraw-Hill.

a) LEVEL 1.
Population: Grades 1.0–1.9.
Scores, 11: Word Attack, Vocabulary, Reading Comprehension, Mechanics, Expression, Mathematics Computation, Mathematics Concepts and Applications, Total Reading, Total Mathematics, Total Language, Total Battery.
Price Data: $99.75 per 35 machine-scorable consumable test books; $71.75 per 35 hand-scorable consumable test books.
Time: (205) minutes.

b) LEVEL 2.
Population: Grades 1.6–2.9.
Scores: Same as *a* above.
Price Data: Same as *a* above.
Time: (219) minutes.

c) LEVEL 3.
Population: Grades 2.6–3.9.
Scores: Same as *a* above.
Price Data: Same as *a* above.
Time: (255) minutes.

d) LEVEL 4.
Population: Grades 3.6–4.9.
Scores, 12: Vocabulary, Reading Comprehension, Spelling, Mechanics, Expression, Mathematics Computation, Mathematics Concepts and Applications, Study Skills, Total Reading, Total Mathematics, Total Language, Total Battery.
Price Data: $71.75 per 35 reusable test books; $22 per 50 answer sheets (for CompuScan® or hand-scoring); $31.95 per set of 3 hand-scoring stencils.
Time: (249) minutes.

e) LEVEL 5.
Population: Grades 4.6–6.9.
Scores: Same as *d* above.
Price Data: Same as *d* above.
Time: (260) minutes.

f) LEVEL 6.
Population: Grades 6.6–8.9.
Scores: Same as *d* above.

Price Data: Same as *d* above.
Time: (259) minutes.
Cross References: For reviews by Maria Prendes Lintel and Emelia C. Lopez, see 13:291.

[2464]

A Spanish Computerized Adaptive Placement Exam.

Purpose: Designed to assist appropriate placement into college-level Spanish courses.
Population: College students.
Publication Dates: 1986-1988.
Acronym: S-CAPE.
Scores: Total score only.
Administration: Individual.
Price Data: Available from publisher.
Time: (20-25) minutes.
Comments: IBM-PC or compatible computer necessary for administration.
Authors: Jerry W. Larson and Kim L. Smith.
Publisher: Brigham Young University, Humanities Research Center.
Cross References: For reviews by G. Gage Kingsbury and Steven L. Wise, see 12:364.

[2465]

Spanish/English Reading Comprehension Test [Revised].

Purpose: Designed to "determine the degrees of bilingualism."
Population: Grades 1–6.
Publication Dates: 1974–1993.
Scores: Total score and grade level equivalents.
Administration: Group or individual.
Forms, 2: English, Spanish.
Price Data, 1999: $20 per packet including manual ('93, 42 pages) and 1 English and 1 Spanish rating/answer sheet (permission to copy answer sheets is included).
Time: (30) minutes.
Comments: Spanish Reading based on Mexican curriculum materials; English Reading based on U.S.A. curriculum materials; English Reading Comprehension Test is translated from the Spanish version; pretesting and posttesting used.
Author: Steve Moreno.
Publisher: Moreno Educational Co.
Cross References: For reviews by Esteban L. Olmedo and David T. Sanchez, see 9:1161.

[2466]

Spanish Structured Photographic Expressive Language Test.

Purpose: Assessment of "the monolingual or bilingual child's generation of specific morphological and syntactical structures."
Population: Ages 3-0 to 5-11, 4-0 to 9-5.
Publication Date: 1989.
Acronym: SPELT.
Scores: Item scores only.
Administration: Individual.
Time: Administration time not reported.
Comments: The design of the Spanish SPELT tests is patterned after the original SPELT-II and SPELT-P (9:1198), however, it is not a direct translation of them. Many of the grammatical structures in the English edition were not able to be translated into Spanish. When necessary, to allow for differences in the two languages, grammatical structures were either deleted or added.
Authors: Ellen O'Hara Werner and Janet Dawson Kresheck.
Publisher: Janelle Publications, Inc.

a) SPANISH STRUCTURED PHOTOGRAPHIC EXPRESSIVE LANGUAGE TEST-II.
Population: Ages 4-0 to 9-5.
Acronym: SPELT-II.
Price Data, 1998: $99 per 10 response forms, 50 color photographs, and manual ('89, 39 pages); $20 per 50 response forms.

b) SPANISH STRUCTURED PHOTOGRAPHIC EXPRESSIVE LANGUAGE TEST-PRESCHOOL.
Population: Ages 3-0 to 5-11.
Acronym: SPELT-P.
Price Data: $89 per 10 response forms, 37 color photographs, and manual ('89, 34 pages); $12 per 50 response forms.

Cross References: For a review by Ronald B. Gillam and Linda S. Day, see 11:373; for a review by Joan D. Berryman of the original SPELT, see 9:1198 (2 references).

[2467]

SPAR Spelling and Reading Tests, Third Edition.

Purpose: Designed as a "group test of literacy."
Population: Ages 7-0 to 12-11 years.
Publication Dates: 1976–1998.
Acronym: SPAR.
Scores, 2: Reading Total Score, Spelling Total Score.
Administration: Group.
Parts, 2: Reading Test, Spelling Test.
Price Data, 1999: £5.99 per 20 For A or Form B; £8.99 per manual ('76, 32 pages) including photocopiable version of spelling test; £4.99 per scoring template (A or B); £9.99 per specimen set including 1 copy each of Test Forms A and B, and manual.
Time: 13 minutes for Spelling Test; (20–25) minutes for Reading Test.
Comments: Reading Test is available in parallel Forms (A and B); Spelling Test is created from three parallel banks of items found in the manual.

Author: Dennis Young.
Publisher: Hodder & Stoughton Educational [England].
Cross References: For reviews by Cleborne D. Maddux and William R. Merz of the second edition, see 12:365 (2 references); see also T4:2520 (3 references); for reviews by J. Douglas Ayers of earlier editions of the Spelling Test and the Reading Test, see 8:76 and 8:742.

TEST REFERENCE

1. Treiman, R., Goswami, V., Tincoff, R., & Leevers, H. (1997). Effects on dialect on American and British children's spelling. *Child Development, 68,* 229–245.

[2468]

Spatial Orientation Memory Test.

Purpose: "Assesses the development of a child's ability to retain and recall the orientation of visually presented forms."
Population: Ages 5-10.
Publication Dates: 1971-1985.
Scores: Total score only.
Administration: Individual.
Forms, 2: Form 1, Form 2.
Price Data, 1999: $75 per complete kit including stimulus cards ('71, 44 cards), 25 score sheets ('85, 2 pages), and manual ('75, 4 pages); $19.50 per pad of 100 score sheets; $14.50 per manual.
Time: (10) minutes.
Comments: Orally administered.
Authors: Joseph M. Wepman and Dainis Turaids.
Publisher: Western Psychological Services.
Cross References: For reviews by Deborah Erickson and Nora M. Thompson, see 11:374 (1 reference); see also T3:2251 (2 references).

[2469]

Specific Language Disability Test.

Purpose: Aims to "identify children who have some degree of specific language disability."
Population: "Average to high IQ" children in grades 6-8.
Publication Dates: 1967-1968.
Acronym: SLDT.
Scores: 10 tests (Visual Copying Far Point, Visual Copying Near Point, Visual Discrimination, Visual Perception Memory for Words, Visual Perception Memory in Association with Kinesthetic Memory, Auditory Discrimination, Auditory Perception and Recall, Auditory-Visual Discrimination, Comprehension, Spelling) with 4 scores (Omissions, Errors, Self-Corrections, Reversals) for each.
Administration: Group.
Price Data, 1999: $14.10 (6+ sets) or $21.15 (1-5 sets) per 12 tests; $14.10 or $21.15 (1-5 sets) per 12 charts and cards; $1.90 (6+) or $2.85 (1-5) per teacher's manual ('67, 16 pages) including instructions for test administration and evaluation; $2.10 (6+ sets) or $3.15 (1-5 sets) per specimen set (teacher's manual and 1 test booklet).
Time: 5-8(10-15) minutes.
Comments: Upward extension of Screening Tests for Identifying Children With Specific Language Disability.
Author: Neva Malcomesius.
Publisher: Educators Publishing Service, Inc.
Cross References: See T4:2522 (1 reference); for reviews by S. Alan Cohen and Robert E. Valett, see 7:971.

[2470]

Speech and Language Evaluation Scale.

Purpose: "Designed for in-school screening and referral of students with speech and language problems."
Population: Ages 4.5-18.
Publication Dates: 1989-1990.
Acronym: SLES.
Scores, 7: Speech (Articulation, Voice, Fluency), Language (Form, Content, Pragmatics), Total.
Administration: Individual.
Price Data, 1999: $117.50 per complete kit including 50 pre-referral checklist forms, 50 pre-referral intervention strategies documentation forms, technical manual ('89, 47 pages), 50 rating forms, and Speech and Language Classroom Intervention Manual ('90, 205 pages); $26 per 50 pre-referral checklist forms; $26 per 50 pre-referral intervention strategies documentation forms; $12.50 per technical manual; $31 per 50 rating forms; $22 per Speech and Language Intervention Manual; $20 per quick score (IBM).
Time: (15-20) minutes.
Comments: Ratings by teachers.
Authors: Diane R. Fressola, Sandra Cipponeri-Hoerchler, Jacquelyn S. Hagan, Steven B. McDannold, Jacqueline Meyer (manual), and Stephen B. McCarney (technical manual).
Publisher: Hawthorne Educational Services, Inc.
Cross References: For reviews by Katharine G. Butler and Penelope K. Hall, see 12:367.

[2471]

Speech-Ease Screening Inventory (K-1).

Purpose: "Designed to screen the articulation, language development," and auditory comprehension of kindergartners and first-graders.
Population: Grades K-1.
Publication Date: 1985.
Scores: Item scores only in 5 areas (Articulation, Language Association, Auditory Recall, Vocabulary, Basic Concepts) and in 4 optional areas (Auditory,

Similarities and Differences, Language Sample, Linguistic Relationships) plus 5 observational ratings (Voice Quality, Fluency, Syntax, Oral-Peripheral, Hearing).
Administration: Individual.
Price Data, 1999: $98 per complete kit; $29 per 100 screening forms; $23 per 50 summary sheets (specify kindergarten or first grade); $29 per manual (32 pages).
Time: (7-10) minutes.
Authors: Teryl Pigott, Jane Barry, Barbara Hughes, Debra Eastin, Patricia Titus, Harriett Stensel, Kathleen Metcalf, and Belinda Porter.
Publisher: PRO-ED.
Cross References: For reviews by Kris L. Baack and Eleanor E. Sanford, see 12:368.

[2472]

Speech Evaluation of the Patient with a Tracheostomy Tube.

Purpose: Designed to help speech-language pathologists "assess the potential of an adult patient with an artificial airway to use a device that promotes phonation."
Population: Adults with artificial airways.
Publication Dates: 1994–1997.
Scores: 6 evaluative areas: Current Airway Assessment Information, Ventilation Status, Nutritional and Swallowing Status, Clinical Observations/Assessment, Patient Goals, Recommendations.
Administration: Individual.
Price Data, 1998: $44.95 per kit including manual ('97, 124 pages) and reproducible report form.
Time: Administration time not reported.
Comments: Not a standardized test but author provides clinical recommendations based on the information provided on a patient's report form.
Author: Nancy Conway.
Publisher: Imaginart International, Inc.

[2473]

Spelling Test: National Achievement Tests.

Purpose: Assesses achievement in the spelling of common words.
Population: Grades 3-4, 5-8, 7-9, 10-12.
Publication Dates: 1936-1957.
Scores: Total score only.
Administration: Group.
Manual: No manual.
Price Data, 1985: $2.75 per 25 tests (specify grade level); $3.50 per specimen set (specify grade level).
Time: (25) minutes.
Comments: 1956-57 tests identical to tests copyrighted 1939.
Authors: Robert K. Speer and Samuel Smith.
Publisher: Psychometric Affiliates.
Cross References: For a review by James A. Fitzgerald, see 5:230; for a review by W. J. Osburn, see 1:1161.

[2474]

Spiritual Well-Being Scale.

Purpose: "Developed as a general indicator of the subjective state of religious and existential well-being."
Population: Adults.
Publication Dates: 1982-1991.
Acronym: SWBS.
Scores, 3: Religious Well-Being, Existential Well-Being, Total Spiritual Well-Being.
Administration: Individual or group.
Price Data, 1992: $12 per specimen set including scale, manual ('91, 6 pages), and scoring and research information; $2.25 or less per scale; volume discounts and student discounts available.
Time: (10-15) minutes.
Comments: Even-numbered items produce Existential Well-Being Scale (EWB); odd-numbered items produce Religious Well-Being Scale (RWB).
Authors: Craig W. Ellison and Raymond F. Paloutzian.
Publisher: Life Advance, Inc.
Cross References: For reviews by Ayres D'Costa and Patricia Schoenrade, see 12:369 (1 reference); see also T4:2529 (1 reference).

TEST REFERENCE

1. Rasmussen, C. H., & Johnson, M. E. (1994). Spirituality and religiosity: Relative relationships to death anxiety. *Omega, 29,* 313–318.

[2475]

Sports Emotion Test.

Purpose: "Designed to show how an athlete responds affectively to a competition."
Population: High school through adult athletes.
Publication Dates: 1980-1983.
Acronym: SET.
Scores, 24: 4 scores (Intensity, Concentration, Anxiety, Physical Readiness) for 6 different points in time (24 Hours Before, At Breakfast, Just Before, After Start, At Peak, Something Wrong).
Administration: Group.
Price Data: License to reproduce for Ph.Ds and Ed.D.s available from publisher.
Time: (10-20) minutes.
Authors: E. R. Oetting and C. W. Cole (profile).
Publisher: E. R. Oetting (the author), Colorado State University.
Cross References: For reviews by Robert D. Brown and Robert P. Markley, see 10:339.

[2476]

Spousal Assault Risk Assessment Guide.

Purpose: "Helps criminal justice professionals predict the likelihood of domestic violence."
Population: Individuals suspected of or being treated for spousal or family-related assault.
Publication Date: 1999.

Acronym: SARA.
Scores: Total score only.
Administration: Individual.
Price Data, 1999: : $45 per complete kit including 25 assessment forms and manual; $22 per 25 assessment forms; $27 per manual; $30 per specimen set including 3 assessment forms and manual.
Time: Administration time not reported.
Comments: Completed by criminal justice professional after all available sources of information from suspect/offender, victim, etc. are gathered.
Authors: P. Randall Kropp, Stephen D. Hart, Christopher D. Webster, and Derek Eaves.
Publisher: Multi-Health Systems, Inc.

[2477]

Standard Progressive Matrices [Australian Edition].

Purpose: "Intended as a test of non-verbal reasoning ability."
Population: Students in years 3-11 (ages 8.3 to 17.2).
Publication Dates: 1955-1989.
Scores: Total score only.
Administration: Group.
Price Data, 1994: A$15.50 per reusable test booklet; $4.10 per scoring key; $4.20 per 10 answer sheets; $40 per Australian manual ('89, 67 pages); $42 per specimen set.
Time: 20(25) minutes.
Comments: 1986 Australian norms are based on the 1958 version of the test; norms are available for timed and for untimed administration.
Authors: Marion M. deLemos (manual) and J. C. Raven (test).
Publisher: The Australian Council for Educational Research Ltd. [Australia].
Cross References: For information on all editions of the Progressive Matrices, see 9:1007 (67 references), T3:1914 (200 references), 8:200 (190 references), T2:439 (122 references), and 7:376 (194 references); for a review by Morton Bortner, see 6:490 (78 references); see also 5:370 (62 references); for reviews by Charlotte Banks, W. D. Wall, and George Westby, see 4:314 (32 references); for reviews by Walter C. Shipley and David Wechsler of the 1938 edition, see 3:258 (13 references); for a review by T. J. Keating, see 2:1417 (8 references).

TEST REFERENCE

1. Light, J., & Lindsay, P. (1992). Message-encoding techniques for augmentative communication systems: The recall performances of adults with severe speech impairments. *Journal of Speech and Hearing Research, 35,* 853–864.

[2478]

Standard Progressive Matrices, New Zealand Standardization.

Purpose: Designed as a measure of nonverbal reasoning skills.
Population: New Zealand children ages 8-15.
Publication Dates: 1955-1991.
Acronym: SPM.
Scores: Total score only.
Administration: Group.
Price Data: Available from publisher.
Time: (30) minutes.
Authors: J. Raven (manual), J. C. Raven (manual), J. H. Court (manual), and New Zealand Council for Educational Research.
Publisher: New Zealand Council for Educational Research [New Zealand].
Cross References: For information on all editions of the Progressive Matrices, see 9:1007 (67 references), T3:1914 (200 references), 8:200 (190 references), T2:439 (122 references), and 7:376 (194 references); for a review by Morton Bortner, see 6:490 (78 references); see also 5:370 (62 references); for reviews by Charlotte Banks, W. D. Wall, and George Westby, see 4:314 (32 references); for reviews by Walter C. Shipley and David Wechsler of the 1938 edition, see 3:258 (13 references); for a review by T. J. Keating, see 2:1417 (8 references).

TEST REFERENCES

1. Luthar, S. S., & Ripple, C. H. (1994). Sensitivity to emotional distress among intelligent adolescents: A short-term prospective study. *Development and Psychopathology, 6,* 343-357.
2. Hodgson, C., & Ellis, A. W. (1998). Last in, first to go: Age of acquisition and naming in the elderly. *Brain and Language, 64,* 146–163.

[2479]

The Standard Timing Model.

Purpose: "Designed to simulate the motions, functions and operations of automatic production machines" for use in selection, evaluation, and training of employees.
Population: Mechanics.
Publication Date: 1971.
Scores: 4 tasks: Cam "F" Retarded, Rod "C" Lengthened 1/16 inch, Rod "E" Shortened 1/16 inch Spring "E" Disconnected at Lever "E", Cam "D" Retarded.
Administration: Individual.
Price Data: Available from publisher.
Time: [60] minutes.
Author: Scientific Management Techniques, Inc.
Publisher: Scientific Management Techniques, Inc.
Cross References: For reviews by Sami Gulgoz and Gary L. Marco, see 12:370.

[2480]

Standardized Bible Content Tests.

Purpose: Aims to assess "general familiarity with the Bible."
Population: Bible college students.
Publication Dates: 1956–1993.
Acronym: SBCT.
Scores: Total score only.
Administration: Group.
Forms, 6: A (Bible Major), B (Bible Major), G, H, HS (short form), GS (short form).

Price Data, 1994: $1 per test booklet [$75 per 100]; $.40 per Short Form test booklet [$30 per 100]; $.10 per answer sheet; $2 per scoring key; $1 per instructions; $5 per manual.
Time: 45(50) minutes.
Comments: Special form (Form SP) available for administration in missionary organizations, Christian high schools, and churches; information concerning foreign language editions available from publisher.
Author: Commission on Professional Development of the Accrediting Association of Bible Colleges.
Publisher: Accrediting Association of Bible Colleges.
Cross References: See 7:651 (1 reference).

[2481]

Standardized Reading Inventory, Second Edition.

Purpose: Designed to evaluate students' reading abilities.
Population: Children with reading ability not exceeding eighth grade level.
Publication Date: 1999.
Acronym: SRI-2.
Scores, 2: Word Recognition, Comprehension.
Administration: Individual.
Forms, 2: A, B.
Price Data, 1999: $214 per complete kit; $39 per examiner's manual; $36 per student booklet; $13 per 25 summary/record sheets.
Time: (15-60) minutes.
Comments: "Criterion-referenced" and norm-referenced.
Author: Phyllis L. Newcomer.
Publisher: PRO-ED.
Cross References: For reviews by Kenneth W. Howell and Cleborne D. Maddux, see 10:340.

[2482]

Standardized Test of Computer Literacy and Computer Anxiety Index (Version AZ), Revised.

Purpose: To measure general computer literacy and identify students who have computer-related anxieties.
Population: Students in introductory computer literacy courses.
Publication Date: 1984.
Acronym: STCL and CAIN.
Administration: Group.
Price Data: Available from publisher.
Authors: Michael Simonson, Mary Montag (manual and achievement test), and Matt Maurer (manual and anxiety survey).
Publisher: Iowa State University Research Foundation, Inc.

a) STANDARDIZED TEST OF COMPUTER LITERACY (VERSION AZ), REVISED.
Purpose: Measures achievement in computer literacy.
Scores, 3: Computer Systems, Computer Applications, Computer Programming.
Time: 90(105) minutes.
Comments: May be administered in one session or in separate sessions for each of 3 sections.

b) COMPUTER ANXIETY INDEX.
Time: Administration time not reported.
Comments: Test booklet title is Computer Opinion Survey.

Cross References: For reviews by Ron Edwards and Kevin L. Moreland, see 10:341.

[2483]

Stanford Achievement Test—Abbreviated Version—8th Edition.

Purpose: "Measures student achievement in reading, mathematics, language, spelling, study skills, science, social science, and listening."
Population: Primary (1.5-4.5), Intermediate (4.5-7.5), Advanced (7.5-9.9), TASK (9.0-12.9).
Publication Dates: 1989-1992.
Administration: Group.
Price Data, 1999: $39.75 per examination kit (for preview only) including complete battery test booklet, directions for administering, practice test with directions (Primary 1 through Advanced 2 only), and hand-scorable answer document (Primary 3 through TASK 3 only); $97.25–$101.25 per 25 complete/partial battery hand-scorable test booklets; $16 per copy of directions for administration (specify level); $5.75 per copy of class records; $50 per fall or spring national norms booklet (1988), and $80 per SAT abbreviated national norms booklet (1991).
Comments: For fall testing, the publisher recommends the use of the previous grade level test.
Author: The Psychological Corporation.
Publisher: The Psychological Corporation.

a) PRIMARY 1.
Population: Grades 1.5-2.5.
Scores, 12: Word Study Skills, Word Reading, Reading Comprehension, Total Reading, Language/English, Spelling, Listening, Concepts of Number, Mathematics Computation, Mathematics Applications, Total Mathematics, Environment.
Price Data: $122 per 25 complete battery Type 2 machine-scorable test booklets; $101.25 per 25 hand-scorable test booklets; $31 for keys for hand scoring (hand scoring requires Norms Booklets)

complete/partial battery hand-scorable test booklets (Primary 1–Primary 3).
Time: 167 minutes for Partial battery; 187 minutes for Basic battery; 210 minutes for Complete battery.
b) PRIMARY 2.
Population: Grades 2.5-3.5.
Scores, 12: Word Study Skills, Reading Vocabulary, Reading Comprehension, Total Reading, Language/English, Spelling, Listening, Concepts of Numbers, Mathematics Computation, Mathematics Applications, Total Mathematics, Environment.
Price Data: Same as *a* above.
Time: 160 minutes for Partial battery; 180 minutes for Basic battery; 203 minutes for Complete battery.
c) PRIMARY 3.
Population: Grades 3.5-4.5.
Scores, 16: Word Study Skills, Reading Vocabulary, Reading Comprehension, Total Reading, Language Mechanics, Language Expression, Total Language, Study Skills, Spelling, Listening, Concepts of Number, Mathematics Computation, Mathematics Applications, Total Mathematics, Science, Social Science.
Price Data: $122 per 25 complete battery machine-scorable test booklets; $101.25 per 25 complete battery hand-scorable test booklets; $117.75 per 25 Type 2 partial battery machine-scorable test booklets; $97.25 per 25 partial battery hand-scorable test booklets; $101.25 per 25 complete battery reusable test booklets; $97.25 per 25 partial battery reusable test booklets; $91.50 per 100 complete/partial battery Type 2 machine-scorable answer folders; $22.50 per 25 Form J complete/partial battery hand-scorable answer folders; $35.75 per keys for hand scoring complete battery hand-scorable answer folders (Primary 3–TASK 3).
Time: 152 minutes for Partial battery; 197 minutes for Basic battery; 233 minutes for Complete battery.
d) INTERMEDIATE 1-3.
Population: Grades 4.5-7.5.
Scores, 15: Reading Vocabulary, Reading Comprehension, Total Reading, Language Mechanics, Language Expression, Total Language, Study Skills, Spelling, Listening, Concepts of Numbers, Mathematics Computation, Mathematics Applications, Total Mathematics, Science, Social Science.
Price Data: $101.25 per 25 complete battery reusable test booklets; $97.25 per 25 partial battery reusable test booklets; $91.50 per 100 complete/partial battery Type 2 machine-scorable answer folders; $22.50 per 25 Form J complete/partial battery hand-scorable answer folders; $35.75 per keys for hand scoring complete battery hand-scorable answer folders (Primary 3–TASK 3); see *c* above for additional price information.
Time: 142 minutes for Partial battery; 187 minutes for Basic battery; 223 minutes for Complete battery.
e) ADVANCED 1-2.
Population: Grades 7-8.
Scores, 15: Reading Vocabulary, Reading Comprehension, Total Reading, Language Mechanics, Language Expression, Total Language, Study Skills, Spelling, Listening, Concepts of Numbers, Mathematics Computation, Mathematics Applications, Total Mathematics, Science, Social Science.
Price Data: Same as *d* above.
Time: 142 minutes for Partial battery; 186 minutes for Basic battery; 222 minutes for Complete battery.
f) TASK 1-3.
Population: Grades 9-12.
Scores, 9: Reading Vocabulary, Reading Comprehension, Total Reading, Language/English, Study Skills, Spelling, Mathematics, Science, Social Science.
Price Data: $101.25 per 25 complete battery reusable test booklets; $91.50 per 100 complete/partial battery Type 2 machine-scorable answer folders; $22.50 per 25 Form J complete/partial battery hand-scorable answer folders.
Time: 95 minutes for Partial battery; 119 minutes for Basic battery; 155 minutes for Complete battery.
Cross References: For reviews by Stephen N. Elliott, James A. Wollack, and Kevin L. Moreland, see 12:371.

TEST REFERENCE

1. Agostin, T. M., & Bam, S. K. (1997). Predicting early school success with developmental and social skills screeners. *Psychology in the Schools, 34,* 219–228.

[2484]

Stanford Achievement Test, Ninth Edition.

Purpose: Measures student achievement in reading, language, spelling, study skills, listening, mathematics, science, and social science.
Population: Grades K.0–13.0.
Publication Dates: 1923–1997 .
Acronym: Stanford 9.
Forms, 5: Multiple Choice (Complete Battery, Form S; Complete Battery, Form SA; Basic Battery, Form S; Abbreviated Battery, Form S); Open-Ended.
Administration: Group.
Levels, 13: Stanford Early School Achievement Test 1, Stanford Early School Achievement Test 2, Primary 1, Primary 2, Primary 3, Intermediate 1, Inter-

mediate 2, Intermediate 3, Advanced 1, Advanced 2, Stanford Test of Academic Skills 1, Stanford Test of Academic Skills 2, Stanford Test of Academic Skills 3.
Comments: A variety of assessment options are available including full-length and abbreviated batteries, customized content modules (with locally developed items), and open-ended assessments.
Author: Harcourt Brace Educational Measurement.
Publisher: Harcourt Brace Educational Measurement—the educational testing division of The Psychological Corporation.

a) STANFORD EARLY SCHOOL ACHIEVEMENT TEST 1.
Population: Grades K.0–K.5.
Acronym: SESAT 1.
Scores, 6: Reading (Sounds and Letters, Word Reading, Total Reading), Mathematics, Listening to Words and Stories, Environment.
Price Data, 1999: $29.50 per Exam Kits (Forms S and SA) including Complete Battery Test Booklet, Directions for Administering, and Practice Test with Directions (SESAT 1 through Advanced 2 only), separate Answer Document (Primary 3–TASK 3 only), open-ended Assessment Preview Brochure (Primary 1–TASK 3 only), and Reviewer's Edition; $15 per 25 Practice Tests, Form S; $110.75 per 25 Complete Battery Type 1 Machine-Scorable Test Booklets (Forms S and SA); $73.25 per 25 Complete Battery Hand-Scorable Test Booklets, Form S; $31 per Side-by-Side Keys for Scoring Hand-Scorable Booklets, Forms S and SA (hand-scoring requires Norms Books); $24.50 per Response Keys, Forms S and SA; $61 per Norms Book including scoring tables for both Multiple-Choice and Open-Ended Assessments (all levels; separate Norms Book published for fall and spring); $11.25 per Directions for Administering (Forms S and SA); $18.25 per 25 Multiple-Choice Complete Battery Preview for Parents; $18.25 per 25 Understanding Test Results, appropriate for all forms and batteries; $4.50 per Class Record, appropriate for all forms and batteries; $5.75 per 25 Stanford Markers for all levels, appropriate for all forms and batteries; $19.25 per Compendium of Instructional Objectives, Forms S and SA, all levels; $23 per Strategies for Instruction: A Handbook of Performance Activities, appropriate for all forms and batteries; $29.50 per Guide for Organizational Planning, all levels, appropriate for all forms and batteries; $17 per Guide for Classroom Planning, appropriate for all forms and batteries; $4.75 per Directions for Administering Practice Tests, Forms S and SA; $55 per Technical Data Report for all levels, Forms S and SA.
Time: (105) minutes for Basic Battery; (135) minutes for Complete Battery.

b) STANFORD EARLY SCHOOL ACHIEVEMENT TEST 2.
Population: Grades K.5–1.5.
Acronym: SESAT 2.
Scores, 7: Reading (Sounds and Letters, Word Reading, Sentence Reading, Total Reading), Mathematics, Listening to Words and Stories, Environment.
Price Data: Same as *a* above.
Time: (140) minutes for Basic Battery; (170) minutes for Complete Battery.

c) PRIMARY 1.
Population: Grades 1.5–2.5.

1) *Multiple-Choice and Abbreviated Multiple-Choice.*
Scores, 11: Reading (Word Study Skills, Word Reading, Reading Comprehension, Total Reading), Mathematics (Mathematics: Problem Solving, Mathematics: Procedures, Total Mathematics), Language Form S, Spelling, Listening, Environment.
Price Data: Same as *a* above; $29.50 per Exam Kit, Multiple-Choice Assessment Abbreviated Battery, Form S including Abbreviated Battery Test Booklet, Directions for Administering, Practice Test with Directions and Open-Ended Assessment Preview Brochure; $15 per 25 Practice Tests, Form S; $86.25 per 25 Multiple-Choice Abbreviated Battery Type 1 Machine-Scorable Test Booklets, Form S; $24.50 per Multiple-Choice Abbreviated Battery Response Keys, Form S; $4.75 per Directions for Administering Practice Tests, Form S; $9.75 per Directions for Administering, Form S.
Time: (260) minutes for Basic Battery; (290) minutes for Complete Battery; (143) minutes for Abbreviated Battery.

2) *Open-Ended.*
Scores, 4: Reading, Mathematics, Science, Social Science.
Price Data: Same as *a* above; $9.75 per Open-Ended Reading Exam Kit including Open-Ended Test Booklet and Directions for Administering; $9.75 per Open-Ended Mathematics Exam Kit including Open-Ended Test Booklet and Directions for Administering; $9.75 per Open-Ended Science Exam Kit including Open-Ended Test Booklet and Directions for Administering; $9.75 per Open-Ended Social Science Exam Kit including Open-Ended Test Booklet and Directions for Administering; $24 per 25 Open-Ended Reading Test Booklets, Form S including Directions for Administering; $24 per 25 Open-Ended Mathematics Test Booklets, Form S including

Directions for Administering; $24 per 25 Open-Ended Science Test Booklets, Form S including Directions for Administering; $24 per 25 Open-Ended Social Science Test Booklets, Form S including Directions for Administering; $19.25 per Scoring Guide for Open-Ended Reading Assessment; $19.25 per Scoring Guide for Open-Ended Mathematics Assessment; $19.25 per Scoring Guide for Open-Ended Science Assessment; $19.25 per Scoring Guide for Open-Ended Social Science Assessment; $7.50 per Directions for Administering Open-Ended Reading Assessment; $7.50 per Directions for Administering Open-Ended Mathematics Assessment; $7.50 per Directions for Administering Open-Ended Science Assessment; $7.50 per Directions for Administering Open-Ended Social Science Assessment.

Time: (50) minutes.

d) PRIMARY 2.

Population: Grades 2.5–3.5.

1) *Multiple-Choice and Abbreviated Multiple-Choice.*

Scores, 11: Reading (Word Study Skills, Reading Vocabulary, Reading Comprehension, Total), Mathematics (Mathematics: Problem Solving, Mathematics: Procedures, Total), Language Form S, Spelling, Listening, Environment.

Price Data: Same as *a* and *c*1 above.

Time: (260) minutes for Basic Battery; (290) minutes for Complete Battery; (137) minutes for Abbreviated Battery.

2) *Open-Ended.*

Scores, 4: Reading, Mathematics, Science, Social Science.

Price Data: Same as *a* and *c*2 above.

Time: (50) minutes.

e) PRIMARY 3.

Population: Grades 3.5–4.5.

1) *Multiple-Choice and Abbreviated Multiple-Choice.*

Scores, 11: Reading (Reading Vocabulary, Reading Comprehension, Total), Mathematics (Mathematics: Problem Solving, Mathematics: Procedures, Total), Language Form S, Spelling, Listening, Science, Social Science.

Price Data: Same as *a* and *c*1 above; $90.50 per 25 Complete Battery Hand-Scorable Test Booklets, including Science and Social Science, Form S subtests; $90.50 per 25 Complete Battery Reusable Test Booklets, Form S, including Science and Social Science subtests; $90.50 per 25 Complete Battery Reusable Test Booklets, Form SA, including Alternate Language, Science, and Social Science subtests (does not include separate Spelling and Study Skills subtests); $70.50 per 25 Abbreviated Battery Reusable Test Booklets, Form S; $42.75 per Stencil Keys for Scoring Hand-Scorable Answer Documents, Form S; $36.50 per Overlay Keys for Scoring Machine-Scorable Answer Documents, Form S; $67.50 per 100 Complete Battery Type 1 Machine-Scorable Answer Documents, Forms S and SA; $918.50 per 1,250 Continuous Form Type 1 Machine-Scorable Answer Documents, Form S; $22.50 per 25 Hand-Scorable Answer Folders, Form S; $55 per 100 Abbreviated Battery Type 1 Machine-Scorable Answer Documents, Form S.

Time: (250) minutes for Basic Battery; (300) minutes for Complete Battery; (123) minutes for Abbreviated Battery.

2) *Open-Ended.*

Scores, 5: Reading, Mathematics, Science, Social Science, Writing.

Price Data: Same as *a* and *c*2 above; $9.75 per Writing Exam Kit including 1 Prompt each of Descriptive, Narrative, Expository, and Persuasive, Directions for Administering, and Response Form; $24 per Writing Prompts: Descriptive, Form S including 25 Writing Prompts, 25 Response Forms, and Directions for Administering; $24 per Writing Prompts: Narrative, Form S including 25 Writing Prompts, 25 Response Forms, and Directions for Administering); $24 per Writing Prompts: Expository, Form S including 25 Writing prompts, 25 Response Forms, and Directions for Administering; $24 per Writing Prompts: Persuasive, Form S including 25 Writing Prompts, 25 Response Forms, and Directions for Administering; $19.25 per Manual for Interpreting Writing Assessment, all forms and levels; $16 per Anchor Papers, Descriptive, Form S; $7.50 per Directions for Administering, Descriptive, Form S; $7.50 per Directions for Administering, Narrative, Form S; $7.50 per Directions for Administering, Expository, Form S; $7.50 per Directions for Administering, Persuasive, Form S.

Time: (50) minutes.

f) INTERMEDIATE 1.

Population: Grades 4.5–5.5.

1) *Multiple-Choice and Abbreviated Multiple-Choice.*

Scores, 12: Reading (Reading Vocabulary, Reading Comprehension, Total); Mathematics (Mathematics: Problem Solving, Mathematics: Procedures, Total), Language Form S, Spelling, Study Skills, Listening, Science, Social Science.

Price Data: Same as *a*, *c*1, and *e*1 above.
Time: (275) minutes for Basic Battery; (325) minutes for Complete Battery; (121) minutes for Abbreviated Battery.
2) *Open-Ended.*
Scores, 5: Same as *e*2 above.
Price Data: Same as *a*, *c*2, and *e*2 above.
Time: (50) minutes.

g) INTERMEDIATE 2.
Population: Grades 5.5–6.5.
1) *Multiple-Choice and Abbreviated Multiple-Choice.*
Scores, 12: Same as *f*1 above.
Price Data: Same as *a*, *c*1, and *e*1 above.
Time: (275) minutes for Basic Battery; (325) minutes for Complete Battery; (121) minutes for Abbreviated Battery.
2) *Open-Ended.*
Scores, 5: Same as *e*2 above.
Price Data: Same as *a*, *c*2, and *e*2 above.
Time: (50) minutes.

h) INTERMEDIATE 3.
Population: Grades 6.5–7.5.
1) *Multiple-Choice and Abbreviated Multiple-Choice.*
Scores, 12: Same as *f*1 above.
Price Data: Same as *a*, *c*1, and *e*1 above.
Time: (275) minutes for Basic Battery; (325) minutes for Complete Battery; (121) minutes for Abbreviated Battery.
2) *Open-Ended.*
Scores, 5: Same as *e*2 above.
Price Data: Same as *a*, *c*2, and *e*2 above.
Time: (50) minutes.

i) ADVANCED 1.
Population: Grades 7.5–8.5.
1) *Multiple-Choice and Abbreviated Multiple-Choice.*
Scores, 12: Same as *f*1 above.
Price Data: Same as *a*, *c*1, and *e*2 above; $20 each per Strategies for Instruction: A Handbook of Performance Activities for Reading, Mathematics, Language/Spelling/Listening, and/or Science/Social Science.
Time: (270) minutes for Basic Battery; (320) minutes for Complete Battery; (120) minutes for Abbreviated Battery.
2) *Open-Ended.*
Scores, 5: Same as *e*2 above.
Price Data: Same as *a*, *c*2, and *e*2 above.
Time: (50) minutes.

j) ADVANCED 2.
Population: Grades 8.5–9.9.
1) *Multiple-Choice and Abbreviated Multiple-Choice.*
Scores, 12: Same as *f*1 above.
Price Data: Same as *a*, *c*1, *e*1, and *i*1 above.
Time: (270) minutes for Basic Battery; (320) minutes for Complete Battery; (119) minutes for Abbreviated Battery.
2) *Open-Ended.*
Scores, 5: Same as *e*2 above.
Price Data: Same as *a*, *c*2, and *e*2 above.
Time: (50) minutes.

k) STANFORD TEST OF ACADEMIC SKILLS 1.
Population: Grades 9.0–9.9.
Acronym: TASK 1.
1) *Multiple-Choice and Abbreviated Multiple-Choice.*
Scores, 9: Reading (Reading Vocabulary, Reading Comprehension, Total), Mathematics, Language Form S, Spelling, Study Skills, Science, Social Science.
Price Data: Same as *a*, *c*1, *e*1, and *i*1 above; $86.25 per 25 Complete Battery Reusable Test Booklets, Form S including Science and Social Science subtests; $86.25 per Complete Battery Reusable Test Booklets, Form SA including Alternate Language, Science, and Social Science subtests (does not include separate Spelling and Study Skills subtests).
Time: (185) minutes for Basic Battery; (225) minutes for Complete Battery; (95) minutes for Abbreviated Battery.
2) *Open-Ended.*
Scores, 5: Same as *e*2 above.
Price Data: Same as *a*, *c*2, and *e*2 above.
Time: (50) minutes.

l) STANFORD TEST OF ACADEMIC SKILLS 2.
Population: Grades 10.0–10.9.
Acronym: TASK 2.
1) *Multiple-Choice and Abbreviated Multiple-Choice.*
Scores, 9: Same as *k*1 above.
Price Data: Same as *a*, *c*1, *e*1, *i*1, and *k*1 above.
Time: Same as *k*1 above.
2) *Open-Ended.*
Scores, 5: Same as *e*2 above.
Price Data: Same as *a*, *c*2, and *e*2 above.
Time: (50) minutes.

m) STANFORD TEST OF ACADEMIC SKILLS 3.
Population: Grades 11.0–13.0.
Acronym: TASK 3.
1) *Multiple-Choice and Abbreviated Multiple-Choice.*
Scores, 9: Same as *k*1 above.
Price Data: Same as *a*, *c*1, *e*1, *i*1, and *k*1 above.
Time: Same as *k*1 above.
2) *Open-Ended.*
Scores, 5: Same as *e*2 above.
Price Data: Same as *a*, *c*2, and *e*2 above.
Time: (50) minutes.

Cross References: For reviews by Ronald A. Berk and Thomas M. Haladyna, see 13:292 (80 references). For reviews of the Stanford Achievement Test—Abbreviated—8th Edition by Stephen N. Elliott and James A. Wollack and by Kevin L. Moreland, see 12:371; for information on an earlier edition of the Stanford Achievement Test, see T4:2551 (44 references); for reviews by Frederick G. Brown and Howard Stoker, see 11:377 (78 references); for reviews by Mark L. Davison and Michael J. Subkoviak and Frank H. Farley of the 1982 Edition, see 9:1172 (19 references); see also T3:2286 (80 references); for reviews by Robert L. Ebel and A. Harry Passow and an excerpted review by Irvin J. Lehmann of the 1973 edition, see 8:29 (51 references); see also T2:36 (87 references); for an excerpted review by Peter F. Merenda of the 1964 edition, see 7:25 (44 references); for a review by Miriam M. Bryan and an excerpted review by Robert E. Stake (with J. Thomas Hastings), see 6:26 (13 references); for a review by N. L. Gage of an earlier edition, see 5:25 (19 references); for reviews by Paul R. Hanna (with Claude E. Norcross) and Virgil E. Herrick, see 4:25 (20 references); for reviews by Walter W. Cook and Ralph C. Preston, see 3:18 (33 references). For reviews of subtests, see 9:1173 (1 review), 9:1174 (1 review), 9:1175 (1 review), 8:291 (2 reviews), 8:745 (2 reviews), 7:209 (2 reviews), 7:527 (1 review), 7:708 (1 review), 7:802 (1 review), 7:895 (1 review), 6:637 (1 review), 5:656 (2 reviews), 5:698 (2 reviews), 5:799 (1 review), 4:419 (1 review), 4:555 (1 review), 4:593 (2 reviews), 3:503 (1 review), and 3:595 (1 review); for a review of the Stanford Test of Academic Skills [1982 Edition] by John C. Ory, see 9:1182; see also T3:2298 (3 references); for reviews by Clinton I. Chase and Robert L. Thorndike of an earlier edition, see 8:31.

TEST REFERENCES

1. Weinberg, W. A., McLean, A., Snider, R. L., Rintelmann, J. W., & Brumback, R. A. (1989). Comparison of reading and listening-reading techniques for administration of SAT reading comprehension subtest: Justification for the bypass approach. *Perceptual and Motor Skills, 68,* 1015–1018.

2. Busch, K. G., Zagar, R., Hughes, J. R., Arbit, J., & Russell, R. E. (1990). Adolescents who kill. *Journal of Clinical Psychology, 46,* 472–485.

3. Allinder, R. M., Fuchs, L. S., Fuchs, D., & Hamlett, C. L. (1992). Effects of summer break on method spelling performance as a function of grade level. *The Elementary School Journal, 92,* 451–460.

4. Rust, J. O., & Wallace, K. A. (1993). Effects of grade level retention for four years. *Journal of Instructional Psychology, 20,* 162–166.

5. Mantzicopoulos, P. Y., & Morrison, D. (1994). A comparison of boys and girls with attention problems: Kindergarten through second grade. *American Journal of Orthopsychiatry, 64,* 522–533.

6. Satake, E., & Amato, P. P. (1995). Mathematics anxiety and achievement among Japanese elementary school studies. *Educational and Psychological Measurement, 55,* 1000–1007.

7. Galotti, K. M., & Kozberg, S. F. (1996). Adolescents' experience of a life-framing decision. *Journal of Youth and Adolescence, 25,* 3–16.

8. Jefferson, J. W. (1996). Social phobia: Everyone's disorder? *Journal of Clinical Psychiatry, 57,* 28–32.

9. Vaughn, S., Elbaum, B. E., & Schumm, J. S. (1996). The effects of inclusion on the social functioning of students with learning disabilities. *Journal of Learning Disabilities, 29,* 598–608.

10. Wu, P., & Campbell, D. T. (1996). Extending latent variable Lisrel analysis of the 1969 Westinghouse Head Start evaluation to Blacks and full year Whites. *Evaluation and Program Planning, 19,* 183–191.

11. Yoshinaga-Itano, C. Snyder, L. S., & Mayberry, R. (1996). Can lexical/semantic skills differentiate deaf or hard-of-hearing readers and nonreaders? *Volta Review, 98,* 39–61.

12. Buntaine, R. L., & Costenbader, V. K. (1997). The effectiveness of a transitional prekindergarten program on later academic achievement. *Psychology in the Schools, 34,* 41–50.

13. Hartman, J. M., & Fuller, M. L. (1997). The development of curriculum-based measurement norms in literature-based classrooms. *Journal of School Psychology, 35,* 377–389.

14. Jordan, N. C., & Montani, T. O. (1997). Cognitive arithmetic and problem solving: A comparison of children with specific and general mathematics difficulties. *Journal of Learning Disabilities, 30,* 624–634.

15. Badian, N. A. (1998). A validation of the role of preschool phonological and orthographic skills in the prediction of reading. *Journal of Learning Disabilities, 31,* 472–481.

[2485]

Stanford-Binet Intelligence Scale, Fourth Edition.

Purpose: Designed as "an instrument for measuring cognitive abilities that provides an analysis of pattern as well as the overall level of an individual's cognitive development."

Population: Ages 2-adult.

Publication Dates: 1916-1986.

Acronym: S-B.

Scores, 20: Verbal Reasoning (Vocabulary, Comprehension, Absurdities, Verbal Relations, Total), Abstract/Visual Reasoning (Pattern Analysis, Copying, Matrices, Paper Folding and Cutting, Total), Quantitative Reasoning (Quantitative, Number Series, Equation Building, Total), Short-Term Memory (Bead Memory, Memory for Sentences, Memory for Digits, Memory for Objects, Total), Total.

Administration: Individual.

Price Data, 1999: $675 per complete examiner's kit; $71 per 35 record booklets; $63 per guide for administrating and scoring ('86, 196 pages); $37 per examiner's handbook ('87, 171 pages); $29 per technical manual ('86, 142 pages).

Time: Administration time varies.

Comments: Third revision still available.

Authors: Robert L. Thorndike, Elizabeth P. Hagen, Jerome M. Sattler, Elizabeth A. Delaney (Examiner's Handbook), and Thomas F. Hopkins (Examiner's Handbook).

Publisher: Riverside Publishing.

Foreign Adaptation: Australian adaptation available from Australian Council for Educational Research Ltd., 9 Frederick St., P.O. Box 210, Hawthorn, Victoria 3122, Australia. Australian adaptations include a manual supplement, stick-on labels for all modified test items, and an Australian record booklet.

Cross References: See T4:2553 (120 references); for reviews by Anne Anastasi and Lee J. Cronbach, see 10:342 (89 references); see also 9:1176 (41 references), T3:2289 (203 references), 8:229 (176 references), and T2:525 (428 references); for a review by David Freides, see 7:425 (258 references); for a review by Elizabeth D. Fraser and excerpted reviews by Benjamin Balinski, L.

B. Birch, James Maxwell, Marie D. Neale, and Julian C. Stanley, see 6:536 (110 references); for reviews by Mary R. Haworth and Norman D. Sundberg of the second revision, see 5:413 (121 references); for a review by Boyd R. McCandless, see 4:358 (142 references); see also 3:292 (217 references); for excerpted reviews by Cyril Burt, Grace H. Kent, and M. Krugman, see 2:1420 (132 references); for reviews by Francis W. Maxfield, J. W. M. Rothney, and F. L. Wells, see 1:1062.

TEST REFERENCES

1. Pipe, M.-E., & Beale, I. L. (1983). Hemispheric specialization for speech in retarded children. *Neuropsychologia, 21,* 91–98.

2. Siegel, L. S. (1984). A longitudinal study of a hyperlexic child: Hyperlexia as a language disorder. *Neuropsychologia, 22,* 577–585.

3. Glass, M. R., Franks, J. R., & Potter, R. E. (1986). A comparison of two tests of auditory selective attention. *Language, Speech, and Hearing Services in Schools, 17,* 300–306.

4. Burns, J. M., & Collins, M. D. (1987). Parents' perceptions of factors affecting the reading development of intellectually superior accelerated readers and intellectually superior nonreaders. *Reading Research and Instruction, 26,* 239–246.

5. Cornell, D. G., & Grossberg, I. W. (1987). Family environment and personality adjustment in gifted program children. *Gifted Child Quarterly, 31,* 59–64.

6. Hall, P. K., & Jordan, L. S. (1987). An assessment of a controlled association task to identify word-finding problems in children. *Language, Speech, and Hearing Services in Schools, 18,* 99–111.

7. Spicker, H. H., Southern, W. T., & Davis, B. I. (1987). The rural gifted child. *Gifted Child Quarterly, 31,* 155–157.

8. Gallucci, N. T. (1988). Emotional adjustment of gifted children. *Gifted Child Quarterly, 32,* 273–276.

9. Karnes, F. A., & D'Ilio, V. R. (1988). Comparison of gifted children and their parents' perception of the home environment. *Gifted Child Quarterly, 32,* 277–279.

10. Kistner, J. A., Osborne, M., & LeVerrier, L. (1988). Causal attributions of learning-disabled children: Developmental patterns and relation to academic progress. *Journal of Educational Psychology, 80,* 82–89.

11. McNally, R. J., Calamari, J. E., Hansen, P. M., & Kaliher, C. (1988). Behavioral treatment of psychogenic polydipsia. *Journal of Behavior Therapy and Experimental Psychiatry, 19,* 57–61.

12. Torgesen, J. K., Rashotte, C. A., & Greenstein, J. (1988). Language comprehension in learning disabled children who perform poorly on memory span tests. *Journal of Educational Psychology, 80,* 480–487.

13. Broderick, P., & Laszlo, J. I. (1989). The copying of upright and tilted squares by Swazi children and adults. *International Journal of Psychology, 24,* 333–350.

14. Burns, J. M., & Richgels, D. J. (1989). An investigation of task requirements associated with the invented spellings of 4-year-olds with above average intelligence. *Journal of Reading Behavior, 21,* 1-14.

15. Cornell, D. G. (1989). Child adjustment and parent use of the term "gifted." *Gifted Child Quarterly, 33,* 59–64.

16. Karnes, F. A., & D'Ilio, V. R. (1989). Leadership positions and sex role stereotyping among gifted children. *Gifted Child Quarterly, 33,* 76–78.

17. Kistner, J. A., & Gatlin, D. F. (1989). Sociometric differences between learning-disabled and nonhandicapped students: Effects of sex and race. *Journal of Educational Psychology, 81,* 118–120.

18. Power, T. J., & Radcliffe, J. (1989). The relationship of play behavior to cognitive ability in developmentally disabled preschoolers. *Journal of Autism and Developmental Disorders, 19(1),* 97-107.

19. Szatmari, P., Bartolucci, G., Bremner, R., Bond, S., & Rich, S. (1989). A follow-up study of high-functioning autistic children. *Journal of Autism and Developmental Disorders, 19(2),* 213-225.

20. Banich, M. T., Levine, S. C., Kim, H., & Huttenlocher, P. (1990). The effects of developmental factors on IQ in hemiplegic children. *Neuropsychologia, 28,* 35–47.

21. Burns, J. M., Mathews, F. N., & Mason, A. (1990). Essential steps in screening and identifying preschool gifted children. *Gifted Child Quarterly, 34,* 102-107.

22. Carvajal, H., & McKnab, P. (1990). Relationships between scores of gifted students on Stanford-Binet IV and the SRA Educational Ability Series. *Gifted Child Quarterly, 34,* 80-82.

23. Chase, C. H., & Tallal, P. (1990). A developmental, interactive activation model of the Word Superiority Effect. *Journal of Experimental Child Psychology, 49,* 448-487.

24. Duffy, F. H., & McAnulty, K. (1990). Neurophysiological heterogeneity and the definition of dyslexia: Preliminary evidence for plasticity. *Neuropsychologia, 28,* 555–571.

25. Eichinger, J. (1990). Goal structure effects on social interaction: Nondisabled and disabled elementary students. *Exceptional Children, 56,* 408–416.

26. Kanevsky, L. (1990). Pursuing qualitative differences in the flexible use of problem-solving strategy by young children. *Journal for the Education of the Gifted, 13,* 115–140.

27. Kochanek, T. T., Kabacoff, R. I., & Lipsitt, L. P. (1990). Early identification of developmentally disabled and at-risk preschool children. *Exceptional Children, 56,* 528–538.

28. Moss, E. (1990). Social interaction and metacognitive development in gifted preschoolers. *Gifted Child Quarterly, 34,* 16-20.

29. Schulte, A. C., Osborne, S. S., & McKinney, J. D. (1990). Academic outcomes for students with learning disabilities in consultation and resource programs. *Exceptional Children, 57,* 162-172.

30. Sowell, E. J., Zeigler, A. J., Bergwall, L., & Cartwright, R. M. (1990). Identification and description of mathematically gifted students: A review of empirical research. *Gifted Child Quarterly, 34,* 147-154.

31. Vaillant, G. E., & Vaillant, C. O. (1990). Determinants and consequences of creativity in a cohort of gifted women. *Psychology of Women Quarterly, 14,* 607-616.

32. Alessandri, S. M. (1991). Play and social behavior in maltreated preschoolers. *Development and Psychopathology, 3,* 191-205.

33. Clark, J., & Tollefson, N. (1991). Differences in beliefs and attitudes toward the improvability of writing skills of gifted students who exhibit mastery-oriented and helpless behaviors. *Journal for the Education of the Gifted, 14,* 119-133.

34. Demb, J. M. (1991). Reported hyperphagia in foster children. *Child Abuse & Neglect, 15,* 77-88.

35. Dyer, K., Williams, L., & Luce, S. C. (1991). Training teachers to use naturalistic communication strategies in classrooms for students with autism and other severe handicaps. *Language, Speech, and Hearing Services in Schools, 22,* 313–321.

36. Handleman, J. S., Harris, S. L., Kristoff, B., Fuentes, F., & Alessandri, M. (1991). A specialized program for preschool children with autism. *Language, Speech, and Hearing Services in Schools, 22,* 107–110.

37. Harris, S. L., Handleman, J. S., Gordon, R., Kristoff, B., & Fuentes, F. (1991). Changes in cognitive and language functioning of preschool children with autism. *Journal of Autism and Developmental Disorders, 21(3),* 281-290.

38. Haskett, M. E., & Kistner, J. A. (1991). Social interactions and peer perceptions of young physically abused children. *Child Development, 62,* 979–990.

39. Karnes, M. B., & Johnson, L. J. (1991). The preschool/primary gifted child. *Journal for the Education of the Gifted, 14,* 267-283.

40. Rescoria, L., Parker, R., & Stolley, P. (1991). Ability, achievement, and adjustment in homeless children. *American Journal of Orthopsychiatry, 61,* 210–220.

41. Salyer, K. M., Holmstrom, R. W., & Noshpitz, J. D. (1991). Learning disabilities as a childhood manifestation of severe psychopathology. *American Journal of Orthopsychiatry, 61,* 230–240.

42. Stanley, J. C. (1991). Critique of "Socioemotional adjustment of adolescent girls enrolled in a residential acceleration program." *Gifted Child Quarterly, 35,* 67-70.

43. Abkarian, G. G. (1992). Communication effects of prenatal alcohol exposure. *Journal of Communication Disorders, 25,* 221–240.

44. Alessandri, S. M. (1992). Mother-child interactional correlates of maltreated and nonmaltreated children's play behavior. *Development and Psychopathology, 4,* 257-270.

45. Anastopoulos, A. D., Goevremont, D. C., Shelton, T. L., & DuPaul, G. J. (1992). Parenting stress among families of children with attention deficit hyperactivity disorder. *Journal of Abnormal Child Psychology, 20,* 503-520.

46. Aram, D. M., Morris, R., & Hall, N. E. (1992). The validity of discrepancy criteria for identifying children with developmental language disorders. *Journal of Learning Disabilities, 25,* 549–554.

47. Barker, T. A., Torgesen, J. K., & Wagner, R. K. (1992). The role of orthographic processing skills on five different reading tasks. *Reading Research Quarterly, 27,* 335-345.

48. Benson, M. J. (1992). Beyond the reaction range concept: A developmental, contextual, and situational model of the heredity-environment interplay. *Human Relations, 45,* 937–956.

49. Burack, J. A., & Volkmar, F. R. (1992). Development of low- and high-functioning autistic children. *Journal of Child Psychology and Psychiatry and Allied Disciplines, 33,* 607-616.

50. Burd, L., Kauffman, D. W., & Kerbeshian, J. (1992). Tourette syndrome and learning disabilities. *Journal of Learning Disabilities, 25,* 598–604.

51. Gerken, K. C., & Hodapp, A. F. (1992). Assessment of preschoolers at-risk with the WPPSI-R and the Stanford-Binet L-M. *Psychological Reports, 71,* 659-664.

52. Gowen, J. W., Johnson-Martin, N., Goldman, B. D., & Hussey, B. (1992). Object-play and exploration in children with and without disabilities: A longitudinal study. *American Journal on Mental Retardation, 97,* 21-38.

53. Gravel, J. S., & Wallace, I. F. (1992). Listening and language at 4 years of age: Effects of early otitis media. *Journal of Speech and Hearing Research, 35,* 588–595.

54. Gross, M. U. M. (1992). The use of radical acceleration in cases of extreme intellectual precocity. *Gifted Child Quarterly, 36,* 91-99.

55. Janelle, S. (1992). Locus of control in nondisabled versus congenitally physically disabled adolescents. *The American Journal of Occupational Therapy, 46,* 334-342.

56. Karsh, K. G., & Repp, A. C. (1992). The task demonstration model: A concurrent model for teaching groups of students with severe disabilities. *Exceptional Children, 59,* 54-67.

57. Kline, R. B., Snyder, J., Guilmette, S., & Castellanos, M. (1992). Relative usefulness of elevation, variability, and shape information from WISC-R, K-ABC, and Fourth Edition Stanford-Binet profiles in predicting agreement. *Psychological Assessment, 4,* 426–432.

58. Koller, H., Richardson, S. A., & Katz, M. (1992). Families of children with mental retardation: Comprehensive view from an epidemiologic perspective. *American Journal on Mental Retardation, 97,* 315-332.

59. Louis, B., & Lewis, M. (1992). Parental beliefs about giftedness in young children and their relation to actual ability level. *Gifted Child Quarterly, 36,* 27-31.

60. Malone, L. D., & Mastropieri, M. A. (1992). Reading comprehension instruction: Summarization and self-monitoring training for students with learning disabilities. *Exceptional Children, 58,* 270-279.

61. Marcell, M. M., & Cohen, S. (1992). Hearing abilities of Down syndrome and other mentally handicapped adolescents. *Research in Development Disabilities, 13,* 533-551.

62. Matthew, J. L., Golin, A. K., Moore, M. W., & Baker, C. (1992). Use of SOMPA in identification of gifted African-American children. *Journal for the Education of the Gifted, 15,* 344-356.

63. McGee, R., Williams, S., & Feehan, M. (1992). Attention defcit disorder and age of onset of problem behaviors. *Journal of Abnormal Child Psychology, 20,* 487-502.

64. McInerney, C. A., & McInerney, M. (1992). A mobility skills training program for adults with developmental disabilities. *The American Journal of Occupational Therapy, 46,* 233-239.

65. Merril, E. C. (1992). Attentional resource demands of stimulus encoding for persons with and without mental retardation. *American Journal on Mental Retardation, 97,* 87-98.

66. Noble, K. D., & Drummond, J. E. (1992). But what about the prom? Students' perceptions of early college entrance. *Gifted Child Quarterly, 36,* 106-111.

67. Paul, S. (1992). Test-retest reliability study of the Pennsylvania Bi-Manual Worksample. *The American Journal of Occupational Therapy, 46,* 809-812.

68. Prior, M., Smart, D., Sanson, A., Pedlow, R., & Oberklaid, F. (1992). Transient versus stable behavior problems in a normative sample: Infancy to school age. *Journal of Pediatric Psychology, 17,* 423–443.

69. Scarr, S. (1992). Developmental theories for the 1990s: Development and individual differences. *Child Development, 63,* 1–19.

70. Tannenbaum, A. (1992). Early signs of giftedness: Research and commentary. *Journal for the Education of the Gifted, 15,* 104-133.

71. Abbott, R. D., & Berninger, V. W. (1993). Structural equation modelling of relationships among developmental skills and writing skills in primary- and intermediate-grade writers. *Journal of Educational Psychology, 85,* 478-508.

72. Abel, T., & Karnes, F. A. (1993). Self-perceived strengths in leadership abilities between suburban and rural gifted students using the Leadership Strengths Indicator. *Psychological Reports, 73,* 687-690.

73. Aman, M. G., Kern, R. A., McGhee, D. E., & Arnold, L. E. (1993). Fenfluramine and methylphenidate in children with mental retardation and attention deficit hyperactivity disorder: Laboratory effects. *Journal of Autism and Developmental Disorders, 23(3),* 491-506.

74. Aram, D. M., Morris, R., & Hall, N. E. (1993). Clinical and research congruence in identifying children with specific language impairment. *Journal of Speech and Hearing Research, 36,* 580–591.

75. Brooks-Gunn, J., Klebanov, P. K., Liaw, F., & Spiker, D. (1993). Enhancing the development of low-birthweight, premature infants: Changes in cognition and behavior over the first three years. *Child Development, 64,* 736-753.

76. Carvajal, H. H., Hayes, J. E., Lackey, K. L., Rathke, M. L., Wiebe, D. A., & Weaver, K. A. (1993). Correlations between scores on the Wechsler Intelligence Scale for Children-III and the General Purpose Abbreviated Battery of the Stanford-Binet IV. *Psychological Reports, 72,* 1167-1170.

77. Celiberti, D. A., & Harris, S. L. (1993). Behavioral intervention for siblings of children with autism: A focus on skills to enhance play. *Behavior Therapy, 24,* 573–599.

78. Clarke, G. N., Sack, W. H., Ben, R., Lanham, K., & Him, C. (1993). English language skills in a group of previously traumatized Khmer adolescent refugees. *The Journal of Nervous and Mental Disease, 181,* 454-456.

79. de Cubas, M. M., & Field, T. (1993). Children of methadone-dependent women: Developmental outcomes. *American Journal of Orthopsychiatry, 63,* 266–276.

80. Doll, B. (1993). Evaluating parental concerns about children's friendships. *Journal of School Psychology, 31,* 431-447.

81. Ducharme, J. M., & Popynick, M. (1993). Errorless compliance to parental requests: Treatment effects and generalization. *Behavior Therapy, 24,* 209–226.

82. Eberlin, M., McConnachie, G., Ibel, S., & Volpe, L. (1993). Facilitated communication: A failure to replicate the phenomenon. *Journal of Autism and Developmental Disorders, 23(3),* 507-530.

83. Fitzgerald, H. E., Sullivan, L. A., Ham, H. P., Zucker, R. A., Bruckel, S., Schneider, A. M., & Noll, R. B. (1993). Predictors of behavior problems in three-year-old sons of alcoholics: Early evidence for the onset of risk. *Child Development, 64,* 110-123.

84. Floyd, F. J., & Phillippe, K. A. (1993). Parental interactions with children with and without mental retardation: Behavior management, coerciveness, and positive exchange. *American Journal on Mental Retardation, 97,* 673-684.

85. Flynn, J. R. (1993). Skodak and Skeels: The inflated mother-child IQ gap. *Intelligence, 17,* 557-561.

86. Fuchs-Beauchamp, K. D., Karnes, M. B., & Johnson, L. J. (1993). Creativity and intelligence in preschoolers. *Gifted Child Quarterly, 37,* 113-117.

87. Hall, N. E., Yamashita, T. S., & Aram, D. M. (1993). Relationship between language and fluency in children with developmental language disorders. *Journal of Speech and Hearing Research, 36,* 568–579.

88. Hayes, B. K., & Taplin, J. E. (1993). Development of conceptual knowledge in children with mental retardation. *American Journal on Mental Retardation, 98,* 293–303.

89. Hodapp, A. F. (1993). Correlation between Stanford-Binet IV and PPVT-R scores for young children. *Psychological Reports, 73,* 1152-1154.

90. Johnson, D. L., Howie, V. M., Owen, M., Baldwin, C. D., & Luttman, D. (1993). Assessment of three-year-olds with the Stanford-Binet Fourth Edition. *Psychological Reports, 73,* 51-57.

91. Kasari, C., Sigman, M., & Yirmiya, N. (1993). Focused and social attention of autistic children in interactions with familiar and unfamiliar adults: A comparison of autistic, mentally retarded, and normal children. *Development and Psychopathology, 5,* 403-414.

92. Kasari, C., Sigman, M. D., Baumgartner, P., & Stipek, D. J. (1993). Pride and mastery in children with autism. *Journal of Child Psychology and Psychiatry and Allied Disciplines, 34,* 353-362.

93. Kenny, D. T., & Chekaluk, E. (1993). Early reading performance: A comparison of teacher-based and test-based assessments. *Journal of Learning Disabilities, 26,* 227–236.

94. Kline, R. B., Snyder, J., Guilmette, S., & Castellanos, M. (1993). External validity of the profile variability index for the K-ABC, Stanford-Binet, and WISC-R: Another cul-de-sac. *Journal of Learning Disabilities, 26,* 557–567.

95. Macmann, G. M., & Barnett, D. W. (1993). Reliability of psychiatric and psychological diagnoses of mental retardation severity: Judgements under naturally occurring conditions. *American Journal on Mental Retardation, 97,* 559-567.

96. Masciuch, S., & Kienapple, K. (1993). The emergence of jealousy in children 4 months to 7 years of age. *Journal of Social and Personal Relationships, 10,* 431–435.

97. McCall, R. B., & Carriger, M. S. (1993). A meta-analysis of infant habituation and recognition memory performance as predictors of later IQ. *Child Development, 64,* 57-79.

98. McDonnell, J., Hardman, M. L., Hightower, J., Keifer-O'Donnel, R., & Drew, C. (1993). Impact of community-based instruction on the development of adaptive behavior of secondary-level students with mental retardation. *American Journal on Mental Retardation, 97,* 575-584.

99. McEvoy, R. E., Rogers, S. J., & Pennington, B. F. (1993). Executive function and social communication deficits in young autistic children. *Journal of Child Psychology and Psychiatry and Allied Disciplines, 34,* 563-578.

100. Morris, C. D., Niederbuhl, J. M., & Mahr, J. M. (1993). Determining the capability of individuals with mental retardation to give informed consent. *American Journal on Mental Retardation, 98,* 263–272.

101. Morris, R. D., Krawiecki, N. S., Wright, J. A., & Walter, L. W. (1993). Neuropsychological, academic, and adaptive functioning in children who survive in-hospital cardiac arrest and resuscitation. *Journal of Learning Disabilities, 26,* 46–51.

102. Nagle, R. J., & Bell, N. L. (1993). Validation of Stanford-Binet Intelligence Scale: Fourth Edition abbreviated batteries with college students. *Psychology in the Schools, 30,* 227-231.

103. Prewett, P. N., & McCaffery, L. K. (1993). A comparison of the Kaufman Brief Intelligence Test (K-BIT) with the Stanford-Binet, a two-subtest short form, and the Kaufman Test of Educational Achievement (K-TEA) Brief Form. *Psychology in the Schools, 30,* 299-304.

104. Reid, R., & Harris, K. R. (1993). Self-monitoring of attention versus self-monitoring of performance: Effects on attention and academic performance. *Exceptional Children, 60,* 29-40.

105. Waterman, J., & Lusk, R. (1993). Psychological testing in evaluation of child sexual abuse. *Child Abuse & Neglect, 17,* 145-159.

106. Weismer, S. E., Murray-Branch, J., & Miller, J. F. (1993). Comparison of two methods for promoting productive vocabulary in late talkers. *Journal of Speech and Hearing Research, 36,* 1037–1050.

107. Yoder, P. J., Kaiser, A. P., Alpert, C., & Fischer, R. (1993). Following the child's lead when teaching nouns to preschoolers with mental retardation. *Journal of Speech and Hearing Research, 36,* 158–167.

108. Arbelle, S., Sigman, M. D., & Kasari, C. (1994). Compliance with parental prohibition in autistic children. *Journal of Autism and Developmental Disorders, 24,* 693-702.

109. Bagnato, S. J., & Neisworth, J. T. (1994). A national study of the social and treatment "invalidity" of intelligence testing for early intervention. *School Psychology Quarterly, 9,* 81-102.

110. Bird, E. K., & Chapman, R. S. (1994). Sequential recall in individuals with Down Syndrome. *Journal of Speech and Hearing, 37,* 1369–1380.

111. Borland, J. H., & Wright, L. (1994). Identifying young, potentially gifted, economically disadvantaged students. *Gifted Child Quarterly, 38,* 164-171.

112. Bradely, R. H., Whiteside, L., Mundform, D. J., Casey, P. H., Caldwell, B. M., & Barrett, K. (1994). Impact of the infant health and development program (IHDP) on the home environments of infants born prematurely and with low birthweights. *Journal of Educational Psychology, 86,* 531-541.

113. Bradely, R. H., Whiteside, L., Mundfrom, D. J., Casey, P. H., Kelleher, K. J., & Pope, S. K. (1994). Contribution of early intervention and early caregiving experiences to resilience in low-birthweight, premature children living in poverty. *Journal of Clinical Child Psychology, 23,* 425-434.

114. Bradley, R. H., Mundfrom, D. J., Whiteside, L., Caldwell, B. M., Casey, P. H., Kirby, R. S., & Hansen, S. (1994). A reexamination of the association between HOME scores and income. *Nursing Research, 43,* 260–266.

115. Bradley, R. H., Whiteside, L., Mundfrom, D. J., Casey, P. H., Kelleher, K. J., & Pope, S. K. (1994). Early indicators of resilience and their relation to experiences in the home environments of low birthweight, premature children living in poverty. *Child Development, 65,* 346–360.

116. Brown, D. T. (1994). Review of the Kaufman Adolescent and Adult Intelligence Test (KAIT). *Journal of School Psychology, 32,* 85-99.

117. Brugge, K. L., Nichols, S. L., Salmon, D. P., Hill, L. R., Delis, D. C., Aaron, L., & Trainer, D. A. (1994). Cognitive impairment in adults with Down's Syndrome: Similarities to early cognitive changes in Alzheimer's disease. *Neurology, 44,* 232–238.

118. Campbel, S. B. (1994). Hard-to-manage preschool boys: Externalizing behavior, social competence, and family context at two-year followup. *Journal of Abnormal Child Psychology, 22,* 147-166.

119. Campbell, S. E., Pierce, E. W., March, C. L., Ewing, L. J., & Szumowski, E. K. (1994). Hard-to-manage preschool boys: Symptomatic behavior across contexts and time. *Child Development, 65,* 836-851.

120. Carpenter, P. K. (1994). Prader-Willi syndrome in old age. *Journal of Intellectual Disability Research, 38,* 529–531.

121. Carr, J. (1994). Annotation: Long term outcome for people with Down's syndrome. *Journal of Child Psychology and Psychiatry and Allied Disciplines, 35,* 425-439.

122. Cohen, R., Duncan, M., & Cohen, S. (1994). Classroom peer relations of children participating in a pull-out enrichment program. *Gifted Child Quarterly, 38,* 33-37.

123. Ducharme, J. M., Lucas, H., & Pontes, E. (1994). Errorless embedding in the reduction of severe maladaptive behavior during interactive and learning tasks. *Behavior Therapy, 25,* 489–501.

124. Ducharme, J. M., Pontes, E., Guger, S., Crozier, K., Lucas, H., & Popynick, M. (1994). Errorless compliance to parental requests II: Increasing clinical practicality through abbreviations of treatment parameters. *Behavior Therapy, 25,* 469–487.

125. Eaves, L. C., Ho, H. H., & Eaves, D. M. (1994). Subtypes of autism by cluster analyses. *Journal of Autism and Developmental Disorders, 24,* 3-22.

126. Fields, J. H., Grochowski, S., Lindenmayer, J. P., Kay, S. R., Grosz, D., Hyman, R. B., & Alexander, G. (1994). Assessing positive and negative symptoms in children and adolescents. *American Journal of Psychiatry, 151,* 249-253.

127. Flanagan, D. P., Alfonso, V. C., & Flanagan, R. (1994). A review of the Kaufman Adolescent and Adult Intelligence Test: An advancement in cognitive assessment? *School Psychology Review, 23,* 512–525.

128. Freeman, J. (1994). Some emotional aspects of being gifted. *Journal for the Education of the Gifted, 17,* 180-197.

129. Gagné, F. (1994). Are teachers really poor talent detectors? Comments on Pegnato and Birch's (1959) study of the effectiveness and efficiency of various identification techniques. *Gifted Child Quarterly, 38,* 124-126.

130. Grantham-McGregor, S., Powell, C., Walker, S., Chang, S., & Fletcher, P. (1994). The long-term follow-up of severely malnourished children who participated in an intervention program. *Child Development, 65,* 428–439.

131. Gyurke, J. S. (1994). A reply to Bagnato and Neisworth: Intelligent versus intelligence testing of preschoolers. *School Psychology Quarterly, 9,* 109-112.

132. Jensen, A. R., & Johnson, F. W. (1994). Race and sex differences in head size and IQ. *Intelligence, 18,* 309-333.

133. Kelly, D. J., & Rice, M. L. (1994). Preferences for verb interpretation in children with specific language impairment. *Journal of Speech and Hearing Research, 37,* 182–192.

134. Kobe, F. H., Mulick, J. A., Rash, T. A., & Martin, J. (1994). Nonambulatory persons with profound mental retardation: Physical, developmental, and behavioral characteristics. *Research in Developmental Disabilities, 15,* 413-423.

135. Liaw, F., & Brooks-Gunn, J. (1994). Cumulative familial risks and low-birthweight children's cognitive and behavioral development. *Journal of Clinical Child Psychology, 23,* 360-372.

136. Loehlin, J. C., Horn, J. M., & Willerman, L. (1994). Differential inheritance of mental abilities in the Texas Adoption Project. *Intelligence, 19,* 325-336.

137. Lynn, R. (1994). Some reinterpretations of the Minnesota transracial adoption study. *Intelligence, 19,* 21-27.

138. Molfese, V. J., Holcomb, L., & Helwig, S. (1994). Biomedical and social-environmental influences cognitive and verbal abilities in children 1 to 3 years of age. *International Journal of Behavioral Development, 17,* 271-287.

139. Mundy, P., Sigman, M., & Kasari, C. (1994). Joint attention, developmental level, and symptom representation in autism. *Development and Psychopathology, 6,* 389-401.

140. Osterling, J., & Dawson, G. (1994). Early recognition of children with autism: A study of first birthday home videotapes. *Journal of Autism and Developmental Disorders, 24,* 247-257.

141. Pearson, D. A., & Aman, M. G. (1994). Rating hyperactivity and developmental indices: Should clinicians correct for developmental level. *Journal of Autism and Developmental Disorders, 24,* 395-411.

142. Poehlmann, J. A., & Fiese, B. H. (1994). The effects of divorce, maternal employment, and maternal social support on toddlers' home environments. *Journal of Divorce & Remarriage, 22(1/2),* 121-135.

143. Prewett, P. N., & Farhney, M. R. (1994). The concurrent validity of the Matrix Analogies Test—Short Form with the Stanford-Binet: Fourth Edition and KTEA-BF (Academic Achievement). *Psychology in the Schools, 31,* 20-25.

144. Reid, R., Maag, J., Vasa, S. F., & Wright, G. (1994). Who are the children with attention deficit-hyperactivity disorder? A school-based survey. *The Journal of Special Education, 28,* 117–137.

145. Reid, R., Maag, J. W., Vasa, S. F., & Wright, G. (1994). Who are the children with attention deficit-hyperactivity disorder? A school-based survey. *The Journal of Special Education, 28,* 117–137.

146. Rice, M. L., Oetting, J. B., Marquis, J., Bode, J., & Pae, S. (1994). Frequency of input effects on word comprehension of children with specific language impairment. *Journal of Speech and Hearing Research, 37,* 106–122.

147. Roberts, J. E., Burchinal, M. R., & Campbell, F. (1994). Otitis media in early childhood and patterns of intellectual development and later academic performance. *Journal of Pediatric Psychology, 19,* 347–367.

148. Romski, M. A., Sevcik, R. A., Robinson, B., & Bakeman, R. (1994). Adult-directed communications of youth with mental retardation using the system for augmenting language. *Journal of Speech and Hearing Research, 37,* 617–628.

149. Ruth, W. J. (1994). Goal setting, responsibility training, and fixed ratio reinforcement: Ten-month application to students with emotional disturbance in a public school setting. *Psychology in the Schools, 31,* 146-155.

150. Stewart, S. M., Kennard, B. D., Waller, D. A., & Fixler, D. (1994). Cognitive function in children who receive organ transplantation. *Health Psychology, 13,* 3-13.

151. Summers, J. A., & Craik, F. I. M. (1994). The effects of subject-performed tasks on the memory performance of verbal autistic children. *Journal of Autism and Developmental Disorders, 24,* 773-783.

152. Walker, D., Greenwood, C., Hart, B., & Carter, J. (1994). Prediction of school outcomes based on early language production and socioeconomic factors. *Child Development, 65,* 606–621.

153. Warren, S. F., Gazdag, G. E., Bambara, L. M., & Jones, H. A. (1994). Changes in the generativity and use of semantic relationships concurrent with milieu language intervention. *Journal of Speech and Hearing Research, 37,* 924–934.

154. Weismer, S. E., Murray-Branch, J., & Miller, J. F. (1994). A prospective longitudinal study of language development in late talkers. *Journal of Speech and Hearing, 37,* 852–867.

155. Yoder, P. J., Davies, B., & Bishop, K. (1994). Adult interaction style effects on the language sampling and transcription process with children who have developmental disabilities. *American Journal on Mental Retardation, 99,* 270–282.

156. Yoder, P. J., Davies, B., Bishop, K., & Munson, L. (1994). Effect of adult continuing wh-questions on conversational participation in children with developmental disabilities. *Journal of Speech and Hearing Research, 37,* 193–204.

157. Zucco, G. M., & Negrin, N. S. (1994). Olfactory deficits in down subjects: A link with Alzheimer disease. *Perceptual and Motor Skills, 78,* 627–631.

158. Belfiore, P. J., & Toro-Zambrana, W. (1995). Programming for efficiency: The effects of motion economy on vocational tasks for adults with severe and profound mental retardation. *Research in Developmental Disabilities, 16,* 205–220.

159. Bisanz, J., Morrison, F. J., & Dunn, M. (1995). Effects of age and schooling on the acquisition of elementary quantitative skills. *Developmental Psychology, 31,* 221-236.

160. Bower, A., & Hayes, A. (1995). Relations of scores on the Stanford Binet, Fourth Edition and Form L–M: Concurrent validation study with children who have mental retardation. *American Journal on Mental Retardation, 99,* 555–558.

161. Burt, D. B., Loveland, K. A., Chen, Y-W., Chuang, A., Lewis, K. R., & Cherry, L. (1995). Aging in adults with Down Syndrome: Report from a longitudinal study. *American Journal on Mental Retardation, 100,* 262–270.

162. Campbell, F. A., & Ramey, C. T. (1995). Cognitive and school outcomes for high-risk African-American students at middle adolescence: Positive effects of early intervention. *American Educational Research Journal, 32,* 743–772.

163. Carlson-Greene, B., Morris, R. D., & Krawiecki, N. (1995). Family and illness predictors of outcome in pediatric brain tumors. *Journal of Pediatric Psychology, 20,* 769–784.

164. Das, J. P., Divis, B., Alexander, J., Parrila, R. K., & Naglieri, J. A. (1995). Cognitive decline due to aging among persons with Down Syndrome. *Research in Developmental Disabilities, 16,* 461–478.

165. Everington, C., & Dunn, C. (1995). A second validation study of the Competence Assessment for Standing Trial for Defendants with mental Retardation (CAST-MR). *Criminal Justice and Behavior, 22,* 44–59.

166. Graham, S., MacArthur, C., & Schwartz, S. (1995). Effects of goal setting and procedural facilitation on the revising behavior and writing performance of students with writing and learning problems. *Journal of Educational Psychology, 87,* 230-240.

167. Hannan, C. L., & Shore, B. M. (1995). Metacognition and high intellectual ability: Insights from the study of learning-disabled gifted students. *Gifted Child Quarterly, 39,* 95.

168. Hauck, M., Fein, D., Waterhouse, L., & Feinstein, C. (1995). Social initiations by autistic children to adults and other children. *Journal of Autism and Developmental Disorders, 25,* 579–595.

169. Holmbeck, G. N., & Faier-Routman, J. (1995). Spinal lesion level, shunt status, family relationships, and psychosocial adjustment in children and adolescents with spina bifida myelomeningocele. *Journal of Pediatric Psychology, 20,* 817–832.

170. Katusic, S. K., Colligan, R. C., Beard, C. M., O'Fallon, W. M., Bergstralli, E. J., Jacobsen, S. J., & Kurland, L. T. (1995). Mental retardation in a birth cohort, 1976–1980, Rochester, Minnesota. *American Journal on Mental Retardation, 100,* 335–344.

171. Marcell, M. M., Ridgeway, M. M., Sewell, D. H., & Whelan, M. L. (1995). Sentence imitation by adolescents and young adults with Down's syndrome and other intellectual disabilities. *Journal of Intellectual Disability Research, 39,* 215–232.

172. McBride, J. A., & Panksepp, J. (1995). An examination of the phenomenology and the reliability of ratings of compulsive behavior in autism. *Journal of Autism and Developmental Disorders, 25,* 381–396.

173. Mills, P. E., Dale, P. S., Cole, K. N., & Jenkins, J. R. (1995). Follow-up of children from academic and cognitive preschool curricula at age 9. *Exceptional Children, 61,* 378–393.

174. Moon, S. M., & Dillon, D. R. (1995). Multiple exceptionalities: A case study. *Journal for the Education of the Gifted, 18,* 111-130.

175. Morrison, F. J., Smith, L., & Dow-Ehrensberger, M. (1995). Education and cognitive development: A natural experiment. *Developmental Psychology, 31,* 789–799.

176. Nagle, R. J., & Bell, N. L. (1995). Validation of an item-reduction short form of the Stanford-Binet Intelligence Scale: Fourth Edition with college students. *Journal of Clinical Psychology, 51,* 63-70.

177. Nippold, M. A. (1995). School-age children and adolescents: Norms for word definition. *Language, Speech, and Hearing Services in Schools, 26,* 320–325.

178. Peoples, C. E., Fagan, J. F., III., & Drotar, D. (1995). The influence of race on 3-year-old children's performance on the Stanford-Binet Fourth Edition. *Intelligence, 21,* 69–82.

179. Porretta, D. L., & Surburg, P. R. (1995). Imagery and physical practice in the acquisition of gross motor timing of coincidence by adolescents with mild mental retardation. *Perceptual and Motor Skills, 80,* 1171–1183.

180. Schweitzer, J. B., & Sulzer-Azaroff, B. (1995). Self-control in boys with Attention Deficit Hyperactivity Disorder: Effects of added stimulation and time. *Journal of Child Psychology and Psychiatry and Allied Disciplines, 36,* 671-686.

181. Slater, A. (1995). Individual differences in infancy and later IQ. *Journal of Child Psychology and Psychiatry and Allied Disciplines, 36,* 69-112.

182. Stahmer, A. C. (1995). Teaching symbolic play skills to children with autism using pivotal response training. *Journal of Autism and Developmental Disorders, 25,* 123–141.

183. Sullivan, G. S., Mastropieri, M. A., & Scruggs, T. E. (1995). Reasoning and remembering: Coaching students with learning disabilities to think. *The Journal of Special Education, 29,* 310–322.

184. Thorp, D. M., Stahmer, A. C., & Schreibman, L. (1995). Effects of sociodramatic play training on children with autism. *Journal of Autism and Developmental Disorders, 25,* 265–282.

185. Wisniewski, J. J., Andrews, T. J., & Mulick, J. A. (1995). Objective and subjective factors in the disproportionate referral of children for academic problems. *Journal of Consulting and Clinical Psychology, 63,* 1032–1076.

186. Young, R. L., & Nettelbeck, T. (1995). The abilities of a musical savant and his family. *Journal of Autism and Developmental Disorders, 25,* 231–248.

187. Zigmond, N. (1995). Including in Pennsylvania: Educational experiences of students with learning disabilities in one elementary school. *The Journal of Special Education, 29,* 124–132.

188. Abell, S. C., Von Brieson, P. D., & Watz, L. S. (1996). Intellectual evaluations of children using human figure drawings: An empirical investigation of two methods. *Journal of Clinical Psychology, 52,* 67–74.

189. Baumeister, A. A., & Baeharach, V. R. (1996). A critical analysis of the Infant Health and Development Program. *Intelligence, 23,* 79–104.

190. Benasich, A. A., & Brooks-Gunn, J. (1996). Maternal attitudes and knowledge of child-rearing: Associations with family and child outcomes. *Child Development, 67,* 1185–1205.

191. Bennetto, L., Pennington, B. F., & Rogers, S. J. (1996). Infant and impaired memory functions in autism. *Child Development, 67,* 1816–1835.

192. Brooks-Gunn, J., Klebanov, P. K., & Duncan, G. J. (1996). Ethic differences in children's intelligence test scores: Role of economic deprivation, home environment, and maternal characteristics. *Child Development, 67,* 396–408.

193. Burchinal, M. R., Follmer, A., & Bryant, D. M. (1996). The relations of maternal social support and family structure with maternal responsiveness and child outcomes among African American families. *Developmental Psychology, 32,* 1073–1083.

194. Dissanayake, C., Sigman, M., & Kasari, C. (1996). Long-term stability of individual differences in the emotional responsiveness of children with autism. *Journal of Child Psychology and Psychiatry, 37,* 461–467.

195. Dittrichová, J., Brichácek, V., Mandys, F., Paul, K., Sobotková, D., Tautermannová, M., Vondrácek, J., & Zezuláková, J. (1996). The relationship of early behaviour to later developmental outcome for preterm children. *International Journal of Behavioral Development, 19,* 517–532.

196. Ducharme, J. M., Popynick, M., Pontes, E., & Steele, S. (1996). Errorless compliance to parental requests III: Group parent training with parent observational data and long-term follow-up. *Behavior Therapy, 27,* 353–372.

197. Dunn, M., Flax, J., Sliwinski, M., & Aram, D. (1996). The use of spontaneous language measures as criteria for identifying children with specific language impairment: An attempt to reconcile clinical and research in congruence. *Journal of Speech and Hearing Research, 39,* 643–654.

198. Einfeld, S. L., & Tonge, B. J. (1996). Population prevalence of psychopathology in children and adolescents with intellectual disability: I. Rationale and methods. *Journal of Disability Research, 40,* 91–98.

199. Ferro, J., Foster-Johnson, L., & Dunlap, G. (1996). Relation between curricular activities and problem behaviors of students with mental retardation. *American Journal on Mental Retardation, 101,* 184–194.

200. Fornham, A., & Weir, C. (1996). Lay theories of child development. *The Journal of Genetic Psychology, 157,* 211–226.

201. Glover, D., Maltzman, I., & Williams, C. (1996). Food preferences among individuals with and without Prader-Willi Syndrome. *American Journal on Mental Retardation, 101,* 195–205.

202. Harris, S., Kasari, C., & Sigman, M. D. (1996). Joint attention and language gains in children with Down Syndrome. *American Journal on Mental Retardation, 100,* 608–619.

203. Hughes, C., Hugo, K., & Blatt, J. (1996). Self-instructional intervention for teaching generalized problem-solving within a functional task sequence. *American Journal on Mental Retardation, 100,* 565–579.

204. Jenkins, J. M., & Astington, J. W. (1996). Cognitive factors and family structure associated with theory of mind development in young children. *Developmental Psychology, 32,* 70–78.

205. Leffert, J. S., & Siperstein, G. N. (1996). Assessment of social-cognitive processes in children with mental retardation. *American Journal on Mental Retardation, 100,* 441–455.

206. Livingston, J. A., & Gentile, J. R. (1996). Mastery learning and the decreasing variability hypothesis. *Journal of Educational Research, 90,* 67–86.

207. Lovrich, D., Cheng, J. C., & Velting, D. M. (1996). Late cognitive brain potentials, phonological and semantic classification of spoken words, and reading ability in children. *Journal of Clinical and Experimental Neuropsychology, 18,* 161–177.

208. Lukens, J., & Hurrell, R. M. (1996). A comparison of the Stanford-Binet IV and the WISC-III with mildly retarded children. *Psychology in the Schools, 33,* 24–27.

209. Mayes, S. D., Handford, H. A., Schaefer, J. H., Scogno, C. A., Neagley, S. R., Michael-Good, L., & Pelco, L. E. (1996). The relationship of HIV status, type of coagulation disorder, and school absenteeism to cognition, educational performance, mood, and behavior of boys with hemophilia. *The Journal of Genetic Psychology, 157,* 137–151.

210. McFadden, T. V. (1996). Creating language impairments in typically achieving children: The pitfalls of "normal" normative sampling. *Language, Speech, and Hearing Services in Schools, 27,* 3–9.

211. Pearson, D. A., Yaffee, L. S., Loveland, K. A., & Lewis, K. R. (1996). Comparison of sustained and selective attention in children who have mental retardation with and without attention deficit hyperactivity disorder. *American Journal on Mental Retardation, 100,* 592–607.

212. Rideout, B. E., & Lauibach, C. M. (1996). EEG correlates of enhanced spatial performance following exposure to music. *Perceptual and Motor Skills, 82,* 427–432.

213. Ross, G., Lipper, E., & Auld, P. A. M. (1996). Cognitive abilities and early precursors of learning disabilities in very-low-birthweight children with normal intelligence and normal neurological status. *International Journal of Behavioral Development, 19,* 563–580.

214. Sansavini, A., Rizzardi, M., Alessandroni, R., & Giovanelli, G. (1996). The development of Italian low- and very-low-birthweight infants from birth to 5 years: The role of biological and social risks. *International Journal of Behavioral Development, 19,* 533–547.

215. Scarvie, K. M., Ballantyne, A. O., & Trauner, D. A. (1996). Visuomotor performance in children with infantile nephropathic cystinosis. *Perceptual and Motor Skills, 82,* 67–75.

216. Spruill, J. (1996). Composite SAS of the Stanford-Binet Intelligence Scale, Fourth Edition: Is it determined by only one area of SAS? *Psychological Assessment, 8,* 328–330.

217. Vig, S., & Jedryoek, E. (1996). Stanford Binet Fourth Edition: Useful for young children with language impairment. *Psychology in the Schools, 33,* 124–131.

218. Waterhouse, L., Morris, R., Allen, D., Dunn, M., Fein, D., Feinstein, C., Rapin, I., & Wing, L. (1996). Diagnosis and classification in autism. *Journal of Autism and Developmental Disorders, 26,* 59–86.

219. Werts, M. G., Wolery, M., Venn, M. L., Deinblowski, D., & Doren, H. (1996). Effects of transition-based teaching with instructive feedback on skill acquisition by children with and without disabilities. *Journal of Educational Research, 90,* 75–86.

220. Whiteside-Mansell, L., Pope, S. K., & Bradley, R. H. (1996). Patterns of parenting behavior in young mothers. *Family Relations, 45,* 273–281.

221. Aman, M. G., Kern, R. A., Osborne, P., Tumuluru, R., Rojahn, J., & del Medico, V. (1997). Fenfluramine and methylphenidate in children with mental retardation and borderline IQ: Clinical effects. *American Journal on Mental Retardation, 101,* 521–534.

222. Burchinal, M. R., Campbell, F. A., Bryant, D. M., Wasik, H., & Ramey, C. T. (1997). Early intervention and mediating processes in cognitive performance of children of low-income African American families. *Child Development, 68,* 935–954.

223. Elder, G. H., Jr., Shanahan, M. J., & Clipp, E. C. (1997). Linking combat and physical health: The legacy of World War II in men's lives. *American Journal of Psychiatry, 154,* 330–336.

224. Girolametto, L., Pearce, P. S., & Weitzman, E. (1997). Effects of lexical intervention on the phonology of late talkers. *Journal of Speech, Language, and Hearing Research, 40,* 333–348.

225. Handen, B. L., Janosky, J., & McAuliffe, S. (1997). Long-term follow-up of children with mental retardation/borderline intellectual functioning and ADHD. *Journal of Abnormal Child Psychology, 25,* 287–295.

226. Harden, A., & Sahl, R. (1997). Psychopathology in children and adolescents with developmental disorders. *Research in Developmental Disabilities, 18,* 369–382.

227. Johnston, J. R., Smith, L. B., & Box, P. ((1997). Cognition and communication: Referential strategies used by preschoolers with specific language impairment. *Journal of Speech, Language, and Hearing Research, 40,* 964–974.

228. Keogh, B. K., Bernheimer, L. P., & Guthrie, D. (1997). Stability and change over time in cognitive level of children with delays. *American Journal on Mental Retardation, 101,* 365–373.

229. Matson, J. L., & Smiroldo, B. B. (1997). Validity of the mania subscale of the diagnostic assessment for the severely handicapped-II (DASH-II). *Research in Developmental Disabilities, 18,* 221–225.

230. McGrew, K. S., Keith, T. Z., Flanagan, D. P., & Vanderwood, M. (1997). Beyond g: The impact of gf-gc specific cognitive abilities research on the future use and interpretation of intelligence tests in the schools. *School Psychology Review, 26,* 189–210.

231. Molfese, V. J., & Acheson, S. (1997). Infant and preschool mental and verbal abilities: How are infant scores related to preschool scores? *International Journal of Behavioral Development, 20,* 595–607.

232. Molfese, V. J., DiLalla, L. F., & Bunce, D. (1997). Prediction of the intelligence test scores of 3- to 8-year-old children by home environment, socioeconomic status, and biomedical risks. *Merrill-Palmer Quarterly, 43,* 219–234.

233. Phelps, L., Wallace, N. V., & Bontrager, A. (1997). Risk factors in early child development: Is prenatal cocaine/polydrug exposure a key variable? *Psychology in the Schools, 34,* 245–252.

234. Pietrini, P., Dani, A., Furey, M. L., Alexander, G. E., Freo, U., Grady, C. L., Mentis, M. J., Mangot, D., Simon, E. W., Horwitz, B., Haxby, J. V., & Schapiro, M. B. (1997). Low glucose metabolism during brain stimulation in older Down's Syndrome subjects a risk for Alzheimer's Disease prior to dementia. *American Journal of Psychiatry, 154,* 1063–1069.

235. Rideout, B. E., & Taylor, J. (1997). Enhanced spatial performance following 10 minutes exposure to music: A replication. *Perceptual and Motor Skills, 85,* 112–114.

236. Rosenbaum, J. L., Almli, C. R., Yunot, K. D., Altman, D. I., & Powers, W. J. (1997). Higher neonatal cerebral blood flow correlates with worse childhood neurologic outcome. *Neurology, 49,* 1035–1041.

237. Tasbihsazan, R., Nettelbeck, T., & Kirby, N. (1997). Increasing mental development index in Australian children: A comparative study of two versions of the Bayley mental scale. *Australian Psychologist, 32,* 120–125.

238. Abrams, E. Z. & Goodman, J. F. (1998). Diagnosing developmental problems in children: Parents and professionals negotiate bad news. *Journal of Pediatric Psychology, 23,* 87–98.

239. Bacharach, V. R., & Baumeister, A. A. (1998). Effects of maternal intelligence, marital status, income, and home environment on cognitive development of low birthweight infants. *Journal of Pediatric Psychology, 23,* 197–205.

240. Bear, G. G., Minke, K. M., Griffin, S. M., & Deemer, S. A. (1998). Achievement-related perceptions of children with learning disabilities and normal achievement: Group and developmental differences. *Journal of Learning Disabilities, 31,* 91–104.

241. Burns, G. L., & Kondrick, P. A. (1998). Psychological behaviorisms reading therapy program: Parents as reading therapists for their children's reading disability. *Journal of Learning Disabilities, 31,* 278–285.

242. Cherkes-Julkowski, M. (1998). Learning disability, attention-deficit disorder, and language impairment as outcomes of prematurity: A longitudinal descriptive study. *Journal of Learning Disabilities, 31,* 294–306.

243. Macias, M., Saylor, C., Watson, M., & Spratt, E. (1998). Children with both developmental and behavioral needs: Profile of two clinic populations. *Child Psychiatry and Human Development, 28,* 135–148.

244. Petrill, S. A., Saundino, K., Cherny, S. S., Emde, R. N., Fulker, D. W., Hewitt, J. K., & Plomin, R. (1998). Exploring the genetic and environmental etiology of high general cognitive ability in fourteen- to thirty-six-month-old twins. *Child Development, 69,* 68–74.

245. Vigneau, F., Lavergne, G., & Brault, M. (1998). Automaticité du traitement de l'information et évaluation du retard mental. *Canadian Journal of Behavioural Science, 3,* 99–107.

[2486]

Stanford Diagnostic Mathematics Test, Fourth Edition.

Purpose: Designed to measure "competence in the basic concepts and skills that are prerequisite to problem solving in mathematics."

Publication Dates: 1976–1996.

Acronym: SDMT.

Administration: Group.

Parts, 2: Multiple Choice, Free Response.

Forms: 1 for Red, Orange, and Green levels; 2 (J, K) for Purple, Brown, and Blue levels.

Price Data, 1997: $27 per examination kit including multiple-choice test booklet and free-response test booklet (specify level) and directions for administering for each, answer document, practice test and practice test directions for administering, and ruler/marker; $12 per 25 practice tests and directions (specify level); $85.50 per 25 machine-scorable multiple-choice test booklets (specify Red, Orange, or Green level); $59 per 25 hand-scorable multiple-choice test booklets (specify Red, Orange, or Green level), directions for administering, and class record; $59 per 25 free-response test booklets (specify Red, Orange, or Green level) and directions for administering; $85.50 per hand-scorable multiple-choice/free-response combination kit including 25 hand-scorable multiple-choice test booklets and directions for administering, 25 free-response test booklets and directions for administering, and class record (specify Red, Orange, or Green level); $107 per machine-scorable multiple-choice/free response combination kit including 25 machine-scorable multiple-choice test booklets and directions for administering and 25 free-response test booklets and directions for administering (specify Red, Orange, or Green level); $59 per 25 reusable multiple-choice test booklets and directions for administering (specify Purple, Brown, or Blue level and Form J or K); $59 per 25 free response test booklets and directions for administering (specify Purple, Brown, or Blue level and Form J or K); $85.50 per reusable multiple-choice/free-response combination kit including 25 reusable multiple-choice test booklets and directions for administering and 25 free-response test booklets and directions for administering (specify Purple, Brown, or Blue level and Form J or K); $11 per set of response keys for multiple-choice tests (specify level and form); $11 per side-by-side keys for hand-scorable test booklets including blackline master of student record form (specify Red, Orange, or Green level); $11 per scoring guide for free-response tests including blackline master of student record form (specify level and form); $16 per stencil keys for hand-scorable answer documents (specify Purple, Brown, or Blue level and Form J or K); $21.50 per 25 hand-scorable answer documents with blackline master of student record form and class record (specify Purple, Brown, or Blue level); $27 per 25 Purple/Brown/Blue level machine-scorable answer documents type I; $4.50 per 25 ruler/markers; $37.50 per Fall ('96, 166 pages) or Spring ('96, 166 pages) multilevel norms booklet; $16 per teacher's manual for interpreting (specify Level Red/Orange ['96, 61 pages], Green/Purple ['96, 64 pages], or Brown/Blue ['96, 63 pages]); $7.50 per directions for administering (specify multiple-choice or free-response, and Level Red, Orange, Green, or Purple/Brown/Blue); $4.50 per practice test directions for administering (specify Red, Orange, Green, Purple, or Brown Level); $4.50 per class record (specify Red, Orange, Green, or Purple/Brown/Blue level); prince information for various scoring services available from publisher.

Author: Harcourt Brace Educational Measurement.

Publisher: Harcourt Brace Educational Measurement—the educational testing division of The Psychological Corporation.

a) RED LEVEL.

Population: Grades 1.5–2.5.

Scores, 9: Concepts and Applications (Number Systems and Numeration, Patterns and Functions, Graphs and Tables, Problem Solving, Geometry and Measurement, Total), Computation (Addition of Whole Numbers, Subtraction of Whole Numbers, Total).

Time: 65 minutes for multiple choice; 90 minutes for free response.
b) ORANGE LEVEL.
Population: Grades 2.5–3.5.
Scores, 9: Same as for Red level.
Time: Same as for Red level.
c) GREEN LEVEL.
Population: Grades 3.5–4.5.
Scores, 11: Concepts and Applications (Number Systems and Numeration, Patterns and Functions, Graphs and Tables, Problem Solving, Geometry and Measurement, Total), Computation (Addition of Whole Numbers, Subtraction of Whole Numbers, Multiplication of Whole Numbers, Division of Whole Numbers, Total).
Time: Same as for Red level.
d) PURPLE LEVEL.
Population: Grades 4.5–6.5.
Scores, 12: Concepts and Applications (Number Systems and Numeration, Statistics and Probability, Graphs and Tables, Problem Solving, Geometry and Measurement, Patterns and Functions [free response only], Total), Computation (Addition of Whole Numbers, Subtraction of Whole Numbers, Multiplication of Whole Numbers, Division of Whole Numbers, Total).
Time: 65 minutes for multiple choice; 80 minutes for free response.
e) BROWN LEVEL.
Population: Grades 6.5–8.9.
Scores, 15: Concepts and Applications (Number Systems and Numeration, Patterns and Functions [free response only], Statistics and Probability, Graphs and Tables, Problem Solving, Geometry and Measurement, Total), Computation (Addition and Subtraction of Whole Numbers, Multiplication of Whole Numbers [multiple choice only], Division of Whole Numbers [multiple choice only], Multiplication and Division of Whole Numbers [free response only], Operations with Fractions and Mixed Numbers, Operations with Decimals and Percents, Equations, Total).
Time: Same as Purple level.
f) BLUE LEVEL.
Population: Grades 9.0–13.0.
Scores, 12: Concepts and Applications (Number Systems and Numeration, Patterns and Functions [free response only], Statistics and Probability, Graphs and Tables, Problem Solving, Geometry and Measurement, Total), Computation (Operations with Whole Numbers, Operations with Fractions and Mixed Numbers, Operations with Decimals and Percents, Equations, Total).
Time: Same as Purple level.

Cross References: For reviews by Irvin J. Lehmann, Philip Nagy, and G. Michael Poteat, see 13:293; see also T4:2554 (5 references); for reviews by Bruce G. Rogers and Lorrie A. Shepard of an earlier edition, see 9:1177 (2 references); see also T3:2291 (1 reference); for reviews by Glenda Lappan and Larry Souder, see 8:292.

TEST REFERENCES

1. Goh, D. S., & McElheron, D. (1992). Another look at the aptitude-achievement distinction. *Psychological Reports, 70,* 833-834.
2. Heller, L. R., & Fantuzzo, J. W. (1993). Reciprocal peer tutoring and parent partnership: Does parent involvement make a difference? *School Psychology Review, 22,* 517-534.
3. Fantuzzo, J. W., Davis, G. Y., & Ginsburg, M. D. (1995). Effects of parent involvement in isolation or in combination with peer tutoring on student self-concept and mathematics achievement. *Journal of Educational Psychology, 87,* 272-281.

[2487]

Stanford Diagnostic Reading Test, Fourth Edition.

Purpose: "Intended to diagnose students' strengths and weaknesses in the major components of the reading process."
Publication Dates: 1978–1996.
Acronym: SDRT4.
Administration: Group.
Forms, 2: J, K (for Purple, Brown, and Blue levels).
Price Data, 1999: $31 per examination kit including multiple-choice test booklet and directions for administering, practice test and directions for administering, answer document, class record form, Reading Questionnaire, Reading Strategies Survey, Story Retelling (Story and Response Form), and directions for each (specify level); $14 per 25 practice tests and directions for administering (specify Red, Orange, Green, Purple, or Brown level); $98 per 25 machine-scorable test booklets type 1 and directions for administering (specify Red, Orange, or Green level); $67.50 per 25 hand-scorable test booklets, directions for administering, and class record (specify Red, Orange, or Green level); $67.50 per 25 reusable test booklets and directions for administering (specify level and form); $31 per 25 Reading Questionnaires and directions for administering (specify level and form); $31 per 25 Reading Strategies Surveys and directions for administering (specify Level Red/Orange, Green/Purple, or Brown/Blue); $36.50 per Story Retelling manual ('95, 15 pages) and 25 Story and Response forms (specify Level Red/Orange, Green/Purple, or Brown/Blue); $31 per 25 machine-scorable answer documents type 1 (for Purple/Brown/Blue levels); $24.50 per 25 hand-scorable answer documents with blackline master of student record form and class record (for Purple/Brown/Blue levels); $12.75 per side-by-side keys for hand-scorable test booklets including blackline master of student record form (specify Red, Orange, or Green level); $12.75 per response keys (specify Purple, Brown, or Blue level and Form J or K); $18.25 per stencil keys for hand-scorable

answer documents (specify Purple, Brown, or Blue level and Form J or K); $5.25 per class record (specify Level Red, Orange, Green, or Purple/Brown/Blue); $5.75 per 25 row markers; $42.75 per Fall or Spring Multilevel norms booklet ('96, 103 pages); $18.25 per teacher's manual for interpreting (specify Level Red/Orange ['96, 67 pages], Green/Purple ['96, 68 pages], or Brown/ Blue ['96, 62 pages]); $8.50 per test directions for administering (specify Level Red, Orange, Green, or Purple/Brown/Blue); $5.25 per practice test directions for administering (specify Level Red, Orange, Green, Purple, or Brown); $5.25 per Reading Questionnaire directions for administering; $5.25 per Reading Strategies Survey directions for administering; $7.50 per Story Retelling manual; price information for scoring services available from publisher.

Authors: Bjorn Karlsen and Eric F. Gardner.

Publisher: Harcourt Brace Educational Measurement—the educational testing division of The Psychological Corporation.

a) RED LEVEL.

Population: Grades 1.5–2.5.

Scores, 19: Phonetic Analysis (Consonants-Single, Consonants-Blends, Consonants-Digraphs, Consonants Total, Vowels-Short, Vowels-Long, Vowels Total, Total), Vocabulary (Word Reading, Listening Vocabulary, Nouns, Verbs, Others, Total), Comprehension (Sentences, Riddles, Cloze, Total), Paragraphs with Questions.

Time: 105(110) minutes.

b) ORANGE LEVEL.

Population: Grades 2.5–3.5.

Scores, 19: Phonetic Analysis (Consonants-Single, Consonants-Blends, Consonants-Digraphs, Consonants Total, Vowels-Short, Vowels-Long, Vowels Total, Total), Vocabulary (Listening Vocabulary, Reading Vocabulary, Synonyms, Classification, Total), Comprehension (Cloze, Total), Paragraphs with Questions, Recreational Reading, Textual Reading, Functional Reading.

Time: 100(105) minutes.

c) GREEN LEVEL.

Population: Grades 3.5–4.5.

Scores, 25: Phonetic Analysis (Consonants-Single, Consonants-Blends, Consonants-Digraphs, Consonants Total, Vowels-Short, Vowels-Long, Vowels-Other, Vowels Total, Total), Vocabulary (Listening Vocabulary, Reading Vocabulary, Synonyms, Classification, Word Parts, Content Area Words, Total), Comprehension, Paragraphs with Questions, Recreational Reading, Textual Reading, Functional Reading, Initial Understanding, Interpretation, Critical Analysis and Reading Strategies.

Time: 100(105) minutes.

d) PURPLE LEVEL.

Population: Grades 4.5–6.5.

Scores, 16: Vocabulary (Reading Vocabulary, Synonyms, Classification, Word Parts, Content Area Words, Total), Comprehension, Paragraphs with Questions, Recreational Reading, Textual Reading, Functional Reading, Initial Understanding, Interpretation, Critical Analysis, Reading Strategies, Scanning.

Time: 85(90) minutes.

e) BROWN LEVEL.

Population: Grades 6.5–8.9.

Scores, 16: Same as Purple Level.

Time: 85(90) minutes.

f) BLUE LEVEL.

Population: Grades 9.0–12.9.

Scores, 16: Same as Purple Level.

Time: 85(90) minutes.

Cross References: For reviews by George Engelhard, Jr. and by Mark E. Swerdlik and Jayne E. Bucy, see 13:294 (9 references); see also T4:2555 (24 references); for reviews by Robert J. Tierney and James E. Ysseldyke of an earlier edition, see 9:1178 (7 references); see also T3:2292 (15 references); for a review by Bryon H. Van Roekel, see 8:777 (13 references); see T2:1651 (2 references); for a review by Lawrence M. Kasdon of Levels 1–2 of an earlier edition, see 7:725 (3 references).

TEST REFERENCES

1. Lewandowski, L. J., & Martens, B. K. (1989). Selecting and evaluating standardized reading tests. *Journal of Reading, 33,* 384-388.
2. Moore, D., & Zabrucky, K. (1989). Verbal reports as measures of comprehension evaluation. *Journal of Reading Behavior, 21,* 295-307.
3. Schumm, J. S., & Baldwin, R. S. (1989). Cue system usage in oral and silent reading. *Journal of Reading Behavior, 21,* 141-154.
4. Wepner, S. B., Feeley, J. T., & Minery, B. (1989). Do computers have a place in college reading courses? *Journal of Reading, 33,* 348-354.
5. Zabrucky, K., & Moore, D. (1989). Children's ability to use three standards to evaluate their comprehension of text. *Reading Research Quarterly, 24,* 336-352.
6. Gordon, C. J. (1990). Contexts for expository test structure use. *Reading Research and Instruction, 29(2),* 55-72.
7. Sadoski, M., Goetz, E. T., Olivarez, A., Jr., Lee, S., & Roberts, N. M. (1990). Imagination in story reading: The role of imagery, verbal recall, story analysis, and processing levels. *Journal of Reading Behavior, 22,* 55-70.
8. Nolan, T. E. (1991). Self-questioning and prediction: Combining metacognitive strategies. *Journal of Reading, 35,* 132-138.
9. Wesson, C. L. (1991). Curriculum-based measurement and two models of follow-up consultation. *Exceptional Children, 57,* 246-256.
10. Cipielewski, J., & Stanovich, K. E. (1992). Predicting growth in reading ability from children's exposure to print. *Journal of Experimental Child Psychology, 54,* 74-89.
11. Marmurek, H. H. C. (1992). The development of letter and syllable effects in categorization, reading aloud, and picture naming. *Journal of Experimental Child Psychology, 53,* 277-299.
12. Zabrucky, K., & Ratner, H. H. (1992). Effects of passage type on comprehension monitoring and recall in good and poor readers. *Journal of Reading Behavior, 24,* 373-391.
13. Nagy, W. E., Diakidoy, I. N., & Anderson, R. C. (1993). The acquisition of morphology: Learning the contribution of suffixes to the meanings of derivatives. *Journal of Reading Behavior, 25,* 155-170.
14. Spedding, S., & Chan, L. K. S. (1993). Metacognition, word identification, and reading competence. *Contemporary Educational Psychology, 18,* 91-100.
15. Spires, H. A. (1993). Learning from a lecture: Effects of comprehension monitoring. *Reading Research and Instruction, 32(2),* 19-30.
16. Morton, L. L. (1994). Interhemispheric balance patterns detected by selective phonemic dichotic laterality measures in four clinical subtypes of reading-disabled children. *Journal of Clinical and Experimental Neuropsychology, 16,* 556-567.
17. Renzulli, J. S., & Reis, S. M. (1994). Research related to the schoolwide enrichment triad model. *Gifted Child Quarterly, 38,* 7-20.
18. Siegel, L. S. (1994). Working memory and reading: A life-span perspective. *International Journal of Behavioral Development, 17,* 109-124.
19. Fuchs, L. S., Fuchs, D., Kazdan, S., & Allen, S. (1999). Effects of peer-assisted learning strategies in reading with and without training in elaborated help giving. *The Elementary School Journal, 99,* 201–219.

[2488]

Stanford Early School Achievement Test, Third Edition.

Purpose: Measures school achievement.
Population: Grades K.0-K.5, K.5-1.5.
Publication Dates: 1969-1991.
Acronym: SESAT.
Administration: Group.
Forms, 2: J, L.
Price Data, 1999: $144.25 per 25 machine-scorable tests (Type 1, Form J; Type 2, Form L) (scored by publisher) (select level); $18.50 per 25 practice tests and one directions for administering (select level); $5.75 per class record form; $27.50 per 25 previews for parents (select level); $16 per administration directions (select level and form); $5.75 per administration directions for practice test (select level); $52.25 per norms booklet (1988, Form J Only; 1991, Forms J and L) (select level); $36.75 per coordinator's handbook; $39.75 per examination kit including test booklet, administration directions, and practice test with directions (select level and form).
Comments: Downward extension of the Stanford Achievement Test Series.
Author: The Psychological Corporation.
Publisher: The Psychological Corporation.

a) LEVEL 1.
Population: Grades K.0-K.5.
Scores, 8: Sounds and Letters, Word Reading, Total, Mathematics, Listening to Words and Stories, Total for Basic Battery, Environment, Total for Complete Battery.
Price Data: $144.25 per 25 machine-scorable test booklets (Type 1, Form J; Type 2, Form L); $92.50 per 25 hand-scorable test booklets (select form); $135.75 per set of scoring keys (select form).
Time: (190) minutes over 9 sessions.

b) LEVEL 2.
Population: Grades K.5-1.5.
Scores, 9: Sounds and Letters, Word Reading, Sentence Reading, Total, Mathematics, Listening to Words and Stories, Basic Battery Total, Environment, Complete Battery Total.
Price Data: $144.25 per 25 machine-scorable test booklets (Tye 1, Form J; Type 2, Form L); $97.25 per 25 hand-scorable test booklets (select form); 4141.50 per set of scoring keys (select form).
Time: (225) minutes over 9 sessions.

Cross References: See T4:2556 (2 references); for reviews by Phillip L. Ackerman and C. Dale Carpenter, see 11:378 (8 references); for a review by Mary J. Allen of an earlier edition, see 9:1179 (1 reference); see also T3:2293 (9 references); for a review by Courtney B. Cazden of an earlier edition, see 8:30 (6 references); see also T2:38 (1 reference); for reviews by Elizabeth Hagen and William A. Mehrens of Level 1, see 7:28.

TEST REFERENCES

1. Valencia, R. R. (1988). The McCarthy Scales and Hispanic children: A review of psychometric research. *Hispanic Journal of Behavioral Sciences, 10,* 81–104.
2. Mantzicopoulos, D., Morrison, D. C., Hinshaw, S. D., & Carte, E. T. (1989). Nonpromotion in kindergarten: The role of cognitive, perceptual, visual-motor, behavioral, achievement, socioeconomic, and demographic characteristics. *American Educational Research Journal, 26,* 107–121.
3. Scarborough, H. S. (1989). Prediction of reading disability from familial and individual differences. *Journal of Educational Psychology, 81,* 101–108.
4. Vaughn, S., Hogan, A., Kouzekanani, K., & Shapiro, S. (1990). Peer acceptance, self-perceptions, and social skills of learning disabled students prior to identification. *Journal of Educational Psychology, 82,* 101–106.
5. May, D. C., & Kundert, D. K. (1993). Pre-first placements: How common and how informed? *Psychology in the Schools, 30,* 161-167.
6. Vaughn, S., Schumm, J. S., & Gordon, J. (1993). Which motoric condition is most effective for teaching spelling to students with and without learning disabilities? *Journal of Learning Disabilities, 26,* 191–198.
7. Vaughn, S., Zaragoza, N., Hogan, A., & Walker, J. (1993). A four-year longitudinal investigation of the social skills and behavior problems of students with learning disabilities. *Journal of Learning Disabilities, 26,* 404–412.
8. Mantzicopoulos, P. Y., & Morrison, D. (1994). A comparison of boys and girls with attention problems: Kindergarten through second grade. *American Journal of Orthopsychiatry, 64,* 522–533.
9. Pasnak, R., Madden, S. E., Malabonger, V. A., Holt, R., & Martin, J. W. (1996). Persistance of gains from instruction in classification, seriation, and conservation. *Journal of Educational Research, 90,* 87–92.
10. Sénéchal, M., LeFevre, J-A., Thomas, E. M., & Daley, K. E. (1998). Differential effects of home literacy experiences on the development of oral and written language. *Reading Research Quarterly, 33,* 96–116.

[2489]

Stanford Writing Assessment Program, Third Edition.

Purpose: Provides for the direct assessment of written expression in four modes: Descriptive, Narrative, Expository, and Persuasive.
Population: Grades 3–12.
Publication Dates: 1982–1997.
Scores: 4 writing modes: Descriptive, Narrative, Expository, Persuasive.
Administration: Group.
Levels, 9: Primary 3, Intermediate 1, Intermediate 2, Intermediate 3, Advanced 1, Advanced 2, TASK 1, TASK 2, TASK 3.
Forms, 2: S, T (Form T is a secure form).
Price Data, 1999: $24 per 25 writing prompts, 25 response forms, and Directions for Administering (specify Descrptive, Narrative, Expository, or Persuasive); $7.50 per Directions for Administering (specify Descriptive, Narrative, Expository, or Persuasive); $9.75 per writing exam kit including 1 prompt each of Descriptive, Narrative, Expository and Persuasive, 1 Directions for Administering, 1 response form, and Reviewer's Edition; $61 per norms book; $19.25 per manual for interpreting ('97, 70 pages) (all forms and levels); scoring prices available from publisher.
Time: (50) minutes.
Comments: Holistic and analytic scoring available; computer scoring available; Form T is a secure form; Third edition provides information about student strengths and weaknesses, which can assist in instructional planning.

Authors: Harcourt Brace Educational Measurement—the educational testing division of The Psychological Corporation.
Publisher: Harcourt Brace Educational Measurement—the educational testing division of The Psychological Corporation.
Cross References: For reviews by Philip Nagy and Wayne H. Slater of an earlier editions, see 13:295.

[2490]

The Stanton Profile.

Purpose: Designed to provide "pre-employment personality and attitudinal pre-employment assessments."
Population: Employment applicants.
Publication Dates: 1987–1995.
Scores, 6: 4 content scores (Work Motivation, Adaptability/Flexibility, Service Orientation, Trustworthiness), 2 validity checks (Social Desirability Bias, Infrequent Response Patterns).
Administration: Group or individual.
Manual: No manual.
Price Data: Available from the publisher.
Time: Untimed, generally requiring approximately 20 minutes.
Author: William G. Harris.
Publisher: Pinkerton Services Group.

[2491]

The Stanton Survey and the Stanton Survey Phase II.

Purpose: Provides indications of previous counterproductive work behavior and attitudes toward honesty.
Population: Applicants for employment.
Publication Dates: 1964–1995.
Scores: Total score only.
Administration: Individual or group.
Price Data: Available from publisher.
Time: Untimed.
Comments: Available in hard copy or via telephonic IVR.
Authors: Carl S. Klump, Homer B. C. Reed, Jr., and Sherwood Perman.
Publisher: Pinkerton Services Group.

a) THE STANTON SURVEY.

b) THE STANTON SURVEY PHASE II.

Cross References: For reviews by H. C. Ganguli and Kenneth G. Wheeler, see 9:1185. (An additional review by William G. Harris is available from the Buros Institute national database: available from SilverPlatter.)

[2492]

STAR Math™.

Purpose: Designed as a computer-adaptive math test and database to place students at the appropriate math level.
Population: Grades 3–12.
Publication Date: 1998.
Scores: Total score only (grade-equivalent and percentile scores).
Administration: Individual.
Price Data, 1998: $1,499 per school license for up to 200 students, installation guide, instruction manual, 10 Quick Reference cards, technical manual, 1-year Expert Support Plan, and Pre-Test Instruction Kit; $399 per single-computer license, Quick Install card, instruction manual, Quick Reference card; 1-year Expert Support Plan, and Pre-Test Instruction Kit.
Time: Untimed, (15) minutes.
Comments: Available for Macintosh and IBM-compatible computers; can be repeated at no extra cost through school year to track growth.
Author: Advantage Learning Systems, Inc.
Publisher: Advantage Learning Systems, Inc.

[2493]

STAR Reading™.

Purpose: A computer-adaptive reading test and database designed "to quickly and accurately place students in books at the appropriate reading level."
Population: Grades 1–12.
Publication Date: 1997–1998.
Scores: Total score only.
Administration: Individual.
Price Data, 1998: $1,499 per school license for up to 200 students, including administrator's manual (173 pages), 5 teacher's guides, norms/technical manual (94 pages), 1-year Expert Support Plan, and pre-test instruction kit; $399 per single-computer license, including administrator's manual, Quick Install card, 1-year Expert Support Plan, and pretest instruction kit.
Time: [10] minutes.
Comments: Provides grade equivalents, percentile scores, and instructional reading level; available for both Macintosh and IBM/Windows computers; can be repeated through school year to track growth at no extra cost.
Author: Advantage Learning Systems, Inc.
Publisher: Advantage Learning Systems, Inc.

[2494]

STARS Test (Short Term Auditory Retrieval and Storage).

Purpose: "Designed to assess short term auditory retrieval and storage function in children."
Population: Grades 1-6.
Publication Date: 1972.
Acronym: STARS.
Scores: Total score only.
Administration: Group.
Price Data: Available from publisher.

Time: (20-30) minutes.
Author: Arthur Flowers.
Publisher: Perceptual Learning Systems [No reply from publisher; status unknown].

[2495]
START—Strategic Assessment of Readiness for Training.

Purpose: Designed to diagnose adult's learning strengths and weaknesses.
Population: Adults.
Publication Date: 1994.
Acronym: START.
Scores, 8: Anxiety, Attitude, Motivation, Concentration, Identifying Important Information, Knowledge Acquisition Strategies, Monitoring Learning, Time Management.
Administration: Group.
Price Data, 1996: $19.95 per user's manual (21 pages); $9.95 per assessment and learner's guide (volume discounts available).
Time: (15) minutes.
Comments: Self-administered; self-scored.
Authors: Claire E. Weinstein and David R. Palmer.
Publisher: H & H Publishing Co., Inc.

[2496]
State-Trait Anger Expression Inventory.

Purpose: Designed to measure "the experience and expression of anger."
Population: Ages 13 and up.
Publication Dates: 1979–1996.
Acronym: STAXI.
Scores, 8: State Anger, Trait Anger (Angry Temperament, Angry Reaction), Anger-in, Anger-out, Anger Control, Anger Expression.
Administration: Group or individual.
Editions, 2: Hand-scored, machine-scored.
Price Data: Price information available from publisher for kit including manual ('96, 46 pages), 50 item booklets, and 50 rating sheets.
Time: (10–12) minutes.
Comments: Test forms are entitled Self-Rating Questionnaire; Self-rating; Form G recommended for large scale research.
Author: Charles D. Spielberger.
Publisher: Psychological Assessment Resources, Inc.
Cross References: For reviews by David J. Pittenger and Alan J. Raphael of the Revised Research Edition, see 13:296 (52 references); see also T4:2562 (12 references); for reviews by Bruce H. Biskin and Paul Retzlaff of the STAXI-Research Edition, see 11:379 (8 references).

TEST REFERENCES

1. Leonard, K. E., & Senchak, M. (1993). Alcohol and premarital aggression among newlywed couples. *Journal of Studies on Alcohol, Sup. 11,* 96–108.
2. Tucker, J. S., & Friedman, H. S. (1993). Sex differences in nonverbal expressiveness: Emotional expression, personality, and impressions. *Journal of Nonverbal Behavior, 17,* 103–117.
3. Banks, R., Hogue, A., & Timberlake, T. (1996). An afrocentric approach to group social skills training with inner-city African American adolescents. *Journal of Negro Education, 65,* 414–423.
4. Vandell, D. L., Hyde, J. S., Plant, E. A., & Essex, M. J. (1997). Fathers and "others" as infant-care providers: Predictors of parent's emotional well-being and marital satisfaction. *Merrill-Palmer Quarterly, 43,* 361–385.
5. Pithers, W. D., Gray, A., Busconi, A., & Houchens, P. (1998). Caregivers of children with sexual behavior problems: Psychological and familial functioning. *Child Abuse & Neglect, 22,* 129–141.
6. Siegman, A. W., Townsend, S. T., Blumenthal, R. S., Sorkin, J. D., & Civelek, A. C. (1998). Dimensions of anger and CHD in men and women: Self-ratings versus spouse ratings. *Journal of Behavioral Medicine, 21,* 315–336.

[2497]
State-Trait Anxiety Inventory.

Purpose: Designed to assess anxiety as an emotional state (S-Anxiety) and individual differences in anxiety proneness as a personality trait (T-Anxiety).
Population: Grades 9-16 and adults.
Publication Dates: 1968-1984.
Acronym: STAI.
Scores, 2: State Anxiety, Trait Anxiety.
Administration: Group.
Forms, 2: X, Y.
Parts, 2: 2 parts for each form labeled Form 1 (State), Form 2 (Trait).
Price Data: Available from publisher.
Foreign Language Edition: Spanish edition available.
Time: (10-20) minutes.
Comments: Title on test is Self-Evaluation Questionnaire.
Authors: Charles D. Spielberger; Form Y and manual prepared in collaboration with R. L. Gorsuch, R. Lushene, P. R. Vagg, and G. A. Jacobs.
Publisher: Mind Garden.
Cross References: See T4:2563 (646 references), 9:1186 (158 references), and T3:2300 (277 references); for reviews by Ralph Mason Dreger and Edward S. Katkin, see 8:683 (268 references); see also T2:1391 (45 references) and 7:141 (20 references).

TEST REFERENCES

1. Sugalski, T. D. & Greenhaus, J. H. (1986). Career exploration and goal setting among managerial employees. *Journal of Vocational Behavior, 29,* 102-114.
2. Wilkinson, H. J., & Wilkinson, J. W. (1986). Evaluation of a hospice volunteer training program. *Omega, 17,* 263–275.
3. Ahles, T. A., Cassens, H. L., & Stalling, R. B. (1987). Private body consciousness, anxiety and the perception of pain. *Journal of Behavior Therapy and Experimental Psychiatry, 18,* 215–222.
4. Calvo, M. G., & Alamo, L. (1987). Test anxiety and motor performance: The role of muscular and attentional demands. *International Journal of Psychology, 22,* 165–178.
5. Carlson, C. R., Ventrella, M. A., & Sturgis, E. T. (1987). Relaxation training through muscle stretching procedures: A pilot case. *Journal of Behavior Therapy and Experimental Psychiatry, 18,* 121–126.
6. Fuqua, D. R., Seaworth, T. B., & Newman, J. L. (1987). The relationship of career indecision and anxiety: A multivariate examination. *Journal of Vocational Behavior, 30,* 175-186.
7. Hamilton, S. B., Keilin, W. G., & Know, T. A. (1987). Thinking about the unthinkable: The relationship between death anxiety and cogntive/emotional responses to the threat of nuclear war. *Omega, 18,* 53–61.

8. Harlan, C., & Jansen, M. A. (1987). The psychological and physical well-being of women in sex-stereotyped occupations. *Journal of Employment Counseling, 24,* 31–39.

9. Kaplan, D. M., & Brown, D. (1987). The role of anxiety in career indecisiveness. *Career Development Quarterly, 36,* 148-162.

10. Allen, J. L., & Schroeder, D. A. (1988). Anxiety, cognitive development, and correspondence: Attributions and behavioral prescriptions. *Personality and Social Psychology Bulletin, 14,* 221–230.

11. Braith, J. A., McCullough, J. P., & Bush, J. P. (1988). Relaxation-induced anxiety in a subclinical sample of chronically anxious subjects. *Journal of Behavior Therapy and Experimental Psychiatry, 19,* 193–198.

12. Fuqua, D. R., Blum, C. R., & Hartman, B. W. (1988). Empirical support for the differential diagnosis of career indecision. *Career Development Quarterly, 36,* 364-373.

13. Livneh, H. (1988). Assessing outcome criteria in rehabilitation: A multi-component approach. *Rehabilitation Counseling Bulletin, 32,* 72–94.

14. McMenamy, C. J., Katz, R. C., & Gipson, M. (1988). Treatment of eczema by EMG biofeedback and relaxation training: A multiple baseline analysis. *Journal of Behavior Therapy and Experimental Psychiatry, 19,* 221–227.

15. Anderson, N. B., Lane, J. O., Taguchi, F., & Williams, R. B., Jr. (1989). Patterns of cardiovascular responses to stress as a function of race and parental hypertension in men. *Health Psychology, 8,* 525–540.

16. Arena, J. G., Goldberg, S. J., Saul, D. L., & Hobbs, S. H. (1989). Temporal stability of psychophysiological response profiles: Analysis of individual response stereotypy and stimulus response specificity. *Behavior Therapy, 20,* 609–618.

17. Barlow, D. H., Craske, M. G., Cerny, J. A., & Klasko, J. S. (1989). Behavioral treatment of panic disorder. *Behavior Therapy, 20,* 261–282.

18. Beidel, D. C., Turner, S. M., Stanley, M. A., & Dancu, C. V. (1989). The Social Phobia and Anxiety Inventory: Concurrent and external validity. *Behavior Therapy, 20,* 417–427.

19. Blanchard, E. B., Kolb, L. C., Taylor, A. E., & Wittrock, D. A. (1989). Cardiac response to relevant stimuli as an adjunct in diagnosing post-traumatic stress disorder: Replication and extension. *Behavior Therapy, 20,* 535–543.

20. Blanchard, E. B., McCoy, G. C., Berger, M., Musso, A., Pallmeyer, T. P., Gerardi, R., Gerardi, M. A., & Pangburn, L. (1989). A controlled comparison of thermal biofeedback and relaxation training in the treatment of essential hypertensional IV: Prediction of short-term clinical outcome. *Behavior Therapy, 20,* 405–415.

21. Blumenthal, J. A., Emery, C. F., Madden, D. J., George, L. K., Coleman, R. E., Riddle, M. W., McKee, D. C., Reasoner, J., & Williams, R. S. (1989). Cardiovascular and behavioral effects of aerobic exercise in healthy older men and women. *Journal of Gerontology, 44,* 147–157.

22. Bosley, F., & Allen, T. W. (1989). Stress management training for hypertensives: Cognitive and physiological effects. *Journal of Behavioral Medicine, 12,* 77-89.

23. Chibnall, J. T., & Tait, R. C. (1989). The Psychosomatic Symptom Checklist revisited: Reliability and validity in a chronic pain population. *Journal of Behavioral Medicine, 12,* 297-307.

24. Christensen, A. P., Oei, T. P. S., & Callan, V. J. (1989). The relationship between premenstrual dysphoria and daily ratings dimensions. *Journal of Affective Disorders, 16,* 127–132.

25. Cosyns, P., Maes, M., Vandewoude, M., Stevens, W. J., DeClerck, L. S., & Schotte, C. (1989). Impaired nitrogen-induced lymphocyte responses and the hypothalmic-pituitary-adrenal axis in depressive disorders. *Journal of Affective Disorders, 16,* 41–48.

26. Craske, M. G., & Barlow, D. H. (1989). Nocturnal panic. *The Journal of Nervous and Mental Disease, 177,* 160-167.

27. Deffenbacher, J. L., & Shepard, J. M. (1989). Evaluating a seminar on stress management. *Teaching of Psychology, 16,* 79-81.

28. Ditto, B., France, C., & Miller, S. (1989). Spouse and parent-offspring similarities in cardiovascular response to mental arithmetic and isometric handgrip. *Health Psychology, 8,* 159–173.

29. Dreman, S., Orr, E., & Aldor, R. (1989). Competence or dissonance? Divorce mothers' perceptions of sense of competence and time perspective. *Journal of Marriage and the Family, 51,* 405-415.

30. Durel, L. A., Carver, C. S., Spitzer, S. B., Llabre, M. M., Weintraub, J. K., Saab, P. G., & Schneiderman, N. (1989). Associations of blood pressure with self-report measures of anger and hostility among Black and White men and women. *Health Psychology, 8,* 557–575.

31. Feehan, M., & Marsh, N. (1989). The reduction of bruxism using contingent EMG audible biofeedback: A case study. *Journal of Behavior Therapy and Experimental Psychiatry, 20,* 179–183.

32. Fox, E., O'Boyle, C., Barry, H., & McCreary, C. (1989). Repressive coping style and anxiety in stressful dental surgery. *British Journal of Medical Psychology, 62,* 371–380.

33. Greenberger, E., Goldberg, W. A., Hamill, S., O'Neil, R., & Payne, C. K. (1989). Contributions of a supportive work environment to parents' well-being and orientation to work. *American Journal of Community Psychology, 17,* 755-783.

34. Hatfield, E., Brinton, C., & Cornelius, J. (1989). Passionate love and anxiety in young adolescents. *Motivation and Emotion, 13,* 271–289.

35. Kalter, N., Kloner, A., Schreier, S., & Okla, K. (1989). Predictors of children's postdivorce adjustment. *American Journal of Orthopsychiatry, 59,* 605–618.

36. Keane, T. M., Fairbank, J. A., Caddell, J. M., & Zimering, R. T. (1989). Implosive (flooding) therapy reduces symptoms of PTSD in Vietnam combat veterans. *Behavior Therapy, 20,* 245–260.

37. Kulik, J. A., & Mahler, H. I. M. (1989). Social support and recovery from surgery. *Health Psychology, 8,* 221–238.

38. LaKey, B. (1989). Personal and environmental antecedents of perceived social support developed at college. *American Journal of Community Psychology, 17,* 503-519.

39. Long, B. C. (1989). Sex-role orientation, coping strategies, and self-efficacy of women in traditional and nontraditional occupations. *Psychology of Women Quarterly, 13,* 307-324.

40. Lopez, F. G. (1989). Current family dynamics, trait anxiety, and academic adjustment: Test of a family-based model of vocational identity. *Journal of Vocational Behavior, 35,* 76-87.

41. Lynch, P. M., & Zamble, E. (1989). A controlled behavioral treatment study of Irritable Bowel Syndrome. *Behavior Therapy, 20,* 509–523.

42. MacIntyre, P. D., & Gardner, R. C. (1989). Anxiety and second-language learning: Toward a theoretical clarification. *Language Learning, 39,* 251–275.

43. Morin, C. M., Kowatch, R. A., & Wade, J. B. (1989). Behavioral management of sleep disturbances secondary to chronic pain. *Journal of Behavior Therapy and Experimental Psychiatry, 20,* 295–302.

44. Nelson, R. A., & Borkovec, T. D. (1989). Relationship of client participation to psychotherapy. *Journal of Behavior Therapy and Experimental Psychiatry, 20,* 155–162.

45. Norbeck, J. S., & Anderson, N. J. (1989). Psychosocial predictors of pregnancy outcomes in low-income Black, Hispanic, and White women. *Nursing Research, 38,* 204–209.

46. Nouri, S., & Beer, J. (1989). Relations of moderate physical exercise to scores on hostility, aggression, and trait-anxiety. *Perceptual and Motor Skills, 68,* 1191–1194.

47. Pendleton, M., Stotland, E., Spiers, P., & Kirsch, E. (1989). Stress and strain among police, firefighters, and government workers: A comparative analysis. *Criminal Justice and Behavior, 16,* 196–210.

48. Phifer, J. F., & Norris, F. H. (1989). Psychological symptoms in older adults following natural disaster: Nature, timing, duration, and course. *Journal of Gerontology, 44,* 207–217.

49. Smith, T. W., O'Keeffe, J. L., & Allred, K. D. (1989). Neuroticism, symptom reports and Type A behavior: Interpretive cautions for the Framingham Scale. *Journal of Behavioral Medicine, 12,* 1-11.

50. Terry, D. J. (1989). Coping resources and adaptation: Main or buffering effects? *Australian Journal of Psychology, 41,* 159–173.

51. Tiller, J., Schweitzer, I., Maguire, K., & Davies, B. (1989). A sequential double-blind controlled study of moclobemide and diazepan in patients with atypical depression. *Journal of Affective Disorders, 16,* 181–187.

52. Bertolotti, G., Zotti, A. M., Michielin, P., Vidotto, G., & Sanavio, E. (1990). A computerized approach to cognitive behavioral assessment: An introduction to CBA-2.0 primary scales. *Journal of Behavior Therapy and Experimental Psychiatry, 21,* 21–27.

53. Brown, T. A., & Cash, T. F. (1990). The phenomenon of nonclinical panic: Parameters of panic, fear, and avoidance. *Journal of Anxiety Disorders, 4,* 15-29.

54. Bystritsky, A., Linn, L. S., & Ware, J. E. (1990). Development of a multidimensional scale of anxiety. *Journal of Anxiety Disorders, 4,* 99-115.

55. Callanan, G. A., & Greenhaus, J. H. (1990). The career indecision of managers and professionals: Development of a scale and test of a model. *Journal of Vocational Behavior, 37,* 79-103.

56. Carlson, C. R., Collins, F. L., Nitz, A. J., Sturgis, E. T., & Rogers, J. L. (1990). Muscle stretching as an alternative relaxation training procedure. *Journal of Behavior Therapy and Experimental Psychiatry, 21,* 29–38.

57. Craske, M. G., & Krueger, M. T. (1990). Prevalence of nocturnal panic in a college population. *Journal of Anxiety Disorders, 4,* 125-139.

58. Czajkowski, S. M., Hindelang, R. D., Dembroski, T. M., Mayerson, S. E., Parks, E. B., & Holland, J. C. (1990). Aerobic fitness, psychological characteristics, and cardiovascular reactivity to stress. *Health Psychology, 9,* 676-692.

59. Dreman, S., Orr, E., & Aldor, R. (1990). Sense of competence, time perspective, and state-anxiety of separated versus divorced mothers. *American Journal of Orthopsychiatry, 60,* 77–85.

60. Eisen, A. R., Rapee, R. M., & Barlow, D. H. (1990). The effects of breathing rate and pCO-2 levels on relaxation and anxiety in a non-clinical population. *Journal of Anxiety Disorders, 4,* 183-190.

61. Elias, M. F., Robbins, M. A., Schultz, N. R., & Pierce, T. W. (1990). Is blood pressure an important variable in research on aging and neuropsychological test performance? *Journal of Gerontology, 45,* 128–135.

62. Engle, P. L., Scrimshaw, S. C. M., Zambrana, R. E., & Dunkel-Schetter, C. (1990). Prenatal and postnatal anxiety in Mexican women giving birth in Los Angeles. *Health Psychology, 9,* 285-299.

63. French, C. C., & Richards, A. (1990). The relationship between handedness, anxiety, and questionnaire response patterns. *British Journal of Psychology, 81,* 457-61.

64. Genest, M., Bowen, R. C., Dudley, J., & Keegan, D. (1990). Assessment of strategies for coping with anxiety: Preliminary investigations. *Journal of Anxiety Disorders, 4,* 1-14.

65. Greenberger, E., & O'Neil, R. (1990). Parents' concern about their child's development: Implications for fathers' and mothers' well-being and attitudes toward work. *Journal of Marriage and the Family, 52,* 621–635.

66. Hale, V. E., & Strassberg, D. S. (1990). The role of anxiety on sexual arousal. *Archives of Sexual Behavior, 19,* 569-581.

67. Hartley, L., Lebovits, A. H., Paddison, P. L., & Strain, J. J. (1990). Issues in the identification of premenstrual syndromes. *The Journal of Nervous and Mental Disease, 178,* 228-234.

68. Heimberg, R. G., Hope, D. A., Dodge, C. S., & Becker, R. E. (1990). DSM-III-R subtypes of social phobia: Comparison of generalized social phobics and public speaking phobics. *The Journal of Nervous and Mental Disease, 178,* 172-179.

69. Jacobsen, P. B., Manne, S. L., Gorfinkle, K., Schorr, O., Rapkin, B., & Redd, W. H. (1990). Analysis of child and parent behavior during painful medical procedures. *Health Psychology, 9,* 559-576.

70. Kalichman, S. C. (1990). Affective and personality characteristics of MMPI profile subgroups of incarcerated rapists. *Archives of Sexual Behavior, 19,* 443-459.

71. Kearney, C. A., & Silverman, W. K. (1990). Treatment of an adolescent with obsessive-compulsive disorder by alternating response prevention and cognitive therapy: An empirical analysis. *Journal of Behavior Therapy and Experimental Psychiatry, 21,* 39–47.

72. Kilborn, L. C., & Labbé, F. E. (1990). Magnetic resonance imaging scanning procedures: Development of phobic response during scan and at one-month follow-up. *Journal of Behavioral Medicine, 13,* 391-401.

73. Matthews, D. B. (1990). A comparison of burnout in selected occupational fields. *Career Development Quarterly, 38,* 230-239.

74. McCaffrey, R. J., Rapee, R. M., Gansler, D. A., & Barlow, D. H. (1990). Interaction of neuropsychological and psychological factors in two cases of "space phobia." *Journal of Behavior Therapy and Experimental Psychiatry, 21,* 113–120.

75. Meir, E. I., Melamed, S., & Abu-Freha, A. (1990). Vocational, avocational, and skill utilization congruences and their relationship with well-being in two cultures. *Journal of Vocational Behavior, 36,* 153-165.

76. Mercer, R. T., & Ferketich, S. L. (1990). Predictors of family functioning eight months following birth. *Nursing Research, 39,* 76–82.

77. Middleton, H. C. (1990). An enhanced hypotensive response to clonidine can still be found in panic patients despite psychological treatment. *Journal of Anxiety Disorders, 4,* 213-219.

78. Middleton, H. C. (1990). Cardiovascular dystonia in recovered panic patients. *Journal of Affective Disorders, 19,* 229-236.

79. Moss, M., Frank, E., & Anderson, B. (1990). The effects of marital status and partner support on rape trauma. *American Journal of Orthopsychiatry, 60,* 379–391.

80. Newman, J. L., Fuqua, D. R., & Minger, C. (1990). Further evidence for the use of career subtypes in defining career status. *Career Development Quarterly, 39,* 178-188.

81. Oei, T. P. S., Foley, J., & Young, R. McD. (1990). The in vivo manipulation of alcohol-related beliefs in male social drinkers in a naturalistic setting. *British Journal of Medical Psychology, 63,* 279–286.

82. Oei, T. P. S., Wanstall, K., & Evans, L. (1990). Sex differences in panic disorder with agoraphobia. *Journal of Anxiety Disorders, 4,* 317-324.

83. Orr, E., & Aronson, E. (1990). Relationships between orthopedic disability and perceived social support: Four theoretical hypotheses. *Rehabilitation Psychology, 35,* 29–42.

84. Petzel, T. P., & Rado, E. D. (1990). Divergent validity evidence for Eckblad and Chapman's Hypomanic Personality Scale. *Journal of Clinical Psychology, 46,* 43–46.

85. Rainwater, A. J., III, & McNeil, D. W. (1990). Behavioral Assessment Test with Video (BATV): Assessment of phobic disorders. *Journal of Anxiety Disorders, 4,* 163-170.

86. Renneberg, B., Goldstein, A. J., Phillips, D., & Chambless, D. L. (1990). Intensive behavioral group treatment of avoidant personality disorder. *Behavior Therapy, 21,* 363–377.

87. Robiner, W. N. (1990). Psychological and physical reactions to whirlpool baths. *Journal of Behavioral Medicine, 13,* 157-173.

88. Schneider, H. G., & Shugar, G. J. (1990). Audience and feedback effects in computer learning. *Computers in Human Behavior, 6,* 315–321.

89. Shapiro, D. A., Barkham, M., Hardy, G. E., & Morrison, L. A. (1990). The second Sheffield psychotherapy Project: Ratinale, design and preliminary outcome data. *British Journal of Medical Psychology, 63,* 97–108.

90. Shek, D. T. L. (1990). Reliability and factorial structure of the Chinese version of the Beck Depression Inventory. *Journal of Clinical Psychology, 46,* 35–43.

91. Spence, S. H. (1990). Psychopathology amongst acute and chronic patients with occupationally related upper limb pain versus accident injuries of the upper limbs. *Australian Psychologist, 25,* 293–305.

92. Steketee, G. (1990). Personality traits and disorders in obsessive-compulsiveness. *Journal of Anxiety Disorders, 4,* 351-364.

93. Swartzman, L. C., Edelberg, R., & Kemmann, E. (1990). Impact of stress on objectively recorded menopausal hot flushes and on flush report bias. *Health Psychology, 9,* 529-545.

94. Thompson, S. C., Nanni, C., & Schwankovsky, L. (1990). Patient-oriented interventions to improve communication in a medical office visit. *Health Psychology, 9,* 390-404.

95. Wood, F. B., & Flowers, D. L. (1990). Hypofrontal vs. hypo-sylvian blood flow in schizophrenia. *Schizophrenia Bulletin, 16,* 413–424.

96. Young, R. M., Knight, R. D., & Oei, T. P. S. (1990). The stability of alcohol—related expectancies in social drinking situations. *Australian Journal of Psychology, 42,* 321–330.

97. Abelson, J. L., Glitz, D., Cameron, O. G., Lee, M. A., Bronzo, M., & Curtis, G. C. (1991). Blunted growth hormone response to clonidine in patients with generalized anxiety disorder. *Archives of General Psychiatry, 48,* 157-162.

98. Adler, R., Hayes, M., Nolan, M., Lewin, T., & Raphael, B. (1991). Antenatal prediction of mother-infant difficulties. *Child Abuse & Neglect, 15,* 351-361.

99. Barnett, B., Schaafsma, M. F., Guzman, A. M., & Parker, G. B. (1991). Maternal anxiety: A 5-year review of an intervention study. *Journal of Child Psychology and Psychiatry and Allied Disciplines, 32,* 423-438.

100. Barone, C., Aguirre-Deandreis, A. I., & Trickett, E. J. (1991). Means-ends problem-solving skills, life stress, and social support as mediators of adjustment in the normative transition to high school. *American Journal of Community Psychology, 19,* 207-225.

101. Barth, R. P. (1991). An experimental evaluation of in-home child abuse prevention services. *Child Abuse & Neglect, 15,* 363-375.

102. Beaton, A. A., & Moseley, L. G. (1991). Hand preference scores and completion of questionnaires: Another look. *British Journal of Psychology, 82,* 521-525.

103. Bernstein, J., & Carmel, S. (1991). Gender differences over time in medical school stressors, anxiety and the sense of coherence. *Sex Roles, 24,* 335-344.

104. Blumenthal, J. A., Emery, C. F., Madden, D. J., Schniebolk, S., Walsh-Riddle, M., George, L. K., McKee, D. C., Higginbotham, M. B., Cobb, F. R., & Coleman, R. E. (1991). Long-term effects of exercise on psychological functioning in older men and women. *Journal of Gerontology, 46,* 352–361.

105. Brown, S. A., Irwin, M., & Schuckit, M. A. (1991). Changes in anxiety among abstinent male alcoholics. *Journal of Studies on Alcohol, 52,* 55–61.

106. Burnette, M. M., Koehn, K. A., Kenyon-Jump, R., Hutton, K., & Stark, C. (1991). Control of genital herpes recurrences using progressive muscle relaxation. *Behavior Therapy, 22,* 237–247.

107. Christensen, L., Miller, J., & Johnson, D. (1991). Efficacy of caffeine versus expectancy in altering caffeine-related symptoms. *The Journal of General Psychology, 118,* 5-12.

108. Clifford, P. A., Tan, S. Y., & Gorsuch, R. L. (1991). Efficacy of a self-directed behavioral health change program: Weight, body composition, cardiovascular fitness, blood pressure, health risk, and psychosocial mediating variables. *Journal of Behavioral Medicine, 14,* 303-323.

109. Craske, M. G., Brown, T. A., & Barlow, D. H. (1991). Behavioral treatment of panic disorder: A two-year follow-up. *Behavior Therapy, 22,* 289–304.

110. Davison, G. C., Williams, M. E., Nezami, E., Bice, T. L., & DeQuattro, V. L. (1991). Relaxation, reduction in angry articulated thoughts, and improvements in borderline hypertension and heart rate. *Journal of Behavioral Medicine, 14,* 453-468.

111. Eisen, A. R., & Silverman, W. K. (1991). Treatment of an adolescent with bowel movement phobia using self-control therapy. *Journal of Behavior Therapy and Experimental Psychiatry, 22,* 45–51.

112. Fariña, F., Arce, R., Sobral, J., & Carames, R. (1991). Predictors of anxiety toward computers. *Computers in Human Behavior, 7,* 263–267.

113. Fowler-Kerry, S., & Lander, J. (1991). Assessment of sex differences in children's and adolescents' self-reported pain from venipuncture. *Journal of Pediatric Psychology, 16,* 783–793.

114. Gelernter, C. S., Uhde, T. W., Cimbolic, P., Arnkoff, D. B., ViHone, B. H., Tancer, M. E., & Bartko, J. J. (1991). Cognitive-behavioral and pharmacological treatments of social phobia. *Archives of General Psychiatry, 48,* 938-945.

115. Gift, A. G. (1991). Psychologic and physiologic aspects of acute dyspnea in asthmatics. *Nursing Research, 40,* 196–199.

116. Head, L. Q., Engley, E., & Knight, C. B. (1991). The effects of trait anxiety on state anxiety and perception of test difficulty for undergraduates administered high and low difficulty tests. *Journal of Instructional Psychology, 18,* 65-68.

117. Johansson, N., & Lally, T. (1991). Effectiveness of a death-education program in reducing death anxiety among nursing students. *Omega, 22,* 25–33.

118. Kalichman, S. C. (1991). Psychopathology and personality characteristics of criminal sexual offenders as a function of victim age. *Archives of Sexual Behavior, 20,* 187-197.

119. Kerns, R. D., Haythronthwaite, J., Rosenberg, R., Southwick, S., Giller, E. L., & Jacob, M. C. (1991). The Pain Behavior Checklist (PBCL): Factor structure and psychometric properties. *Journal of Behavioral Medicine, 14,* 155-167.

120. Kessler, J., Herholz, K., Grond, M., & Heiss, W. D. (1991). Impaired metabolic activation in Alzheimer's disease: A PET study during continuous visual recognition. *Neuropsychologia, 29,* 229–243.

121. Lesch, K. P., Hoh, A., Disselkamp-Tietze, J., Wiesmann, M., Osterheider, M., & Schulte, H. M. (1991). 5-hydroxytryptamine receptor responsivity in obsessive-compulsive disorder. *Archives of General Psychiatry, 48,* 540-547.

122. Lucas, J. A., Telch, M. J., & Bigler, E. D. (1991). Memory functioning in panic disorder: A neuropsychological perspective. *Journal of Anxiety Disorders, 5,* 1-20.

123. Lucic, K. S., Steffen, J. J., Harrigan, J. A., & Stuebing, R. C. (1991). Progressive relaxation training: Muscle contraction before relaxation? *Behavior Therapy, 22,* 249–256.

124. MacCleod, A. K., & Williams, j. M. G. (1991). Moderate levels of chronic mood disturbance are associated with increased cognitive complexity about the self. *British Journal of Medical Psychology, 64,* 179–188.

125. MacIntyre, P. D., & Gardner, R. C. (1991). Language anxiety: Its relationship to other anxieties and to processing in native and second languages. *Language Learning, 41,* 513–534.

126. MacIntyre, P. D., & Gardner, R. C. (1991). Methods and results in the study of anxiety and language learning: A review of the literature. *Language Learning, 41,* 85–117.

127. Maes, M., Vandewoude, M., Scharpé, S., Clercq, L. D., Stevens, W., Lepoutre, L., & Schutte, C. (1991). Anthropometric and biochemical assessment of the nutritional state in depression: Evidence for lower visceral protein plasma levels in depression. *Journal of Affective Disorders, 23,* 25-33.

128. Martin, J. B., Ahles, T. A., Jeffery, R. (1991). The role of private body consciousness and anxiety in the report of somatic symptoms during magnetic resonance imaging. *Journal of Behavior Therapy and Experimental Psychiatry, 22,* 3–7.

129. Moore, R., Brodsgaard, I., Berggren, V., & Carlsson, S. (1991). Generalization of effects of dental fear treatment in a self-referred population of odontophobics. *Journal of Behavior Therapy and Experimental Psychiatry, 22,* 243–253.

130. Morse, C. A., Dennerstein, L., Farrell, E., & Varnavides, R. (1991). A comparison of hormone therapy, coping skills training, and relaxation for the relief of premenstrual syndrome. *Journal of Behavioral Medicine, 14,* 469-489.

131. Ollendick, T. H., Hagopian, L. P., & Huntzinger, R. M. (1991). Cognitive-behavior therapy with nighttime fearful children. *Journal of Behavior Therapy and Experimental Psychiatry, 22,* 113–121.

132. Ollo, C., Johnson, R., & Grafman, J. (1991). Signs of cognitive change in HIV disease: An event-related brain potential study. *Neurology, 41,* 209–215.

133. Öst, L. G., Salkovskis, P. M., & Hellström, K. (1991). One-session therapist-directed exposure vs. self-exposure in the treatment of spider phobia. *Behavior Therapy, 22,* 407–422.

134. Piper, W. E., Azim, H. F. A., Joyce, A. S., McCallum, M., Nixon, G. W. H., & Segal, P. S. (1991). Quality of object relations versus interpersonal functioning as predictors of therapeutic alliance and psychotherapy outcome. *The Journal of Nervous and Mental Disease, 179,* 432-438.

135. Radford, M. H. B., Nakane, Y., Ohta, Y., Mann, L., Kalucy, R. S. (1991). Decision making in clinically depressed patients: A transcultural social psychological study. *The Journal of Nervous and Mental Disease, 179,* 711-719.

136. Rao, S. M., Leo, G. J., Ellington, L., Navertz, T., Bernardin, L., & Unverzagt, F. (1991). Cognitive dysfunction in multiple sclerosis. II. Impact on employment and social functioning. *Neurology, 41,* 692–696.

137. Reed, D. L., Thompson, J. K., Brannick, M. T., & Sacco, W. P. (1991). Development and validation of the Physical Appearance State and Trait Anxiety Scale (PASTAS). *Journal of Anxiety Disorders, 5,* 323-332.

138. Robbins, R. A. (1991). Bugen's coping with death scale: Reliability and further validation. *Omega, 22,* 287–299.

139. Robinson, P. J., & Kobayashi, K. (1991). Development and evaluation of a presurgical preparation program. *Journal of Pediatric Psychology, 16,* 193–212.

140. Schneider, M. S., Friend, R., Whitaker, P., & Wadhwa, N. K. (1991). Fluid noncompliance and symptomatology in end-stage renal disease: Cognitive and emotional variables. *Health Psychology, 10,* 209-215.

141. Shear, M. K., Ball, G., Fitzpatrick, M., Josephson, S., Klosko, J., & Frances, A. (1991). Cognitive-behavioral therapy for panic: An open study. *The Journal of Nervous and Mental Disease, 179,* 468-472.

142. Silverman, I. W., & Dubow, E. F. (1991). Looking ahead to parenthood: Nonparents' expectations of themselves and their future children. *Merrill-Palmer Quarterly, 37,* 231–250.

143. Stein, M. B., & Uhde, T. W. (1991). Endocrine, cardiovascular, and behavioral effects of intravenous protirelin in patients with panic disorder. *Archives of General Psychiatry, 48,* 148-156.

144. Steketee, G., Quay, S., & White, K. (1991). Religion and guilt in OCD patients. *Journal of Anxiety Disorders, 5,* 359-367.

145. Taylor, S., & Rachman, S. J. (1991). Fear of sadness. *Journal of Anxiety Disorders, 5,* 375-381.

146. Taylor, S., Koch, W. J., & Crockett, D. J. (1991). Anxiety sensitivity, trait anxiety, and the anxiety disorders. *Journal of Anxiety Disorders, 5,* 293-311.

147. Terry, D. J. (1991). Predictors of subjective stress in a sample of new patients. *Australian Journal of Psychology, 43,* 29–36.

148. Thomas, S. P., & Williams, R. L. (1991). Perceived stress, trait anger, modes of anger expression, and health status of college men and women. *Nursing Research, 40,* 303–307.

149. Van Ameringen, M., Mancini, C., Styan, G., & Donison, D. (1991). Relationship of social phobia with other psychiatric illness. *Journal of Affective Disorders, 21,* 93-99.

150. Webster-Stratton, C., & Spitzer, A. (1991). Development, reliability, and validity of the Daily Telephone Discipline Interview. *Behavioral Assessment, 13,* 221-239.

151. Whipple, E. E., & Webster-Stratton, C. (1991). The role of parental stress in physically abusive families. *Child Abuse & Neglect, 15,* 279-291.

152. Wilson, C. C. (1991). The pet as an anxiolytic intervention. *The Journal of Nervous and Mental Disease, 179,* 482-489.

153. Barlow, D. H., Rapee, R. M., & Brown, T. A. (1992). Behavioral treatment of generalized anxiety disorder. *Behavior Therapy, 23,* 551–570.

154. Baron, R. S., Inman, M. L., Kao, C. F., & Logan, H. (1992). Negative emotion and superficial social processing. *Motivation and Emotion, 16,* 323–346.

155. Bartrop, R. W. Hancock, K., Craig, A., & Porritt, D. W. (1992). Psychological toxicity of bereavement: Six months after the event. *Australian Psychologist, 27,* 192–196.

156. Baum, B. E., & Gray, J. J. (1992). Expert modeling, self-observation using videotype, and acquisition of basic therapy skills. *Professional Psychology: Research and Practice, 23,* 220–225.

157. Belfer, P. L., & Glass, C. R. (1992). Agoraphobic anxiety and fear of fear: Test of a cognitive-attentional model. *Journal of Anxiety Disorders, 6,* 133-146.

158. Berenbaum, J., & Hatcher, J. (1992). Emotional distress of mothers of hospitalized children. *Journal of Pediatric Psychology, 17,* 359–372.

159. Brown, T. A., & Deagle, E. A. (1992). Structured interview assessment of nonclinical panic. *Behavior Therapy, 23,* 75–85.

160. Callanan, G. A., & Greenhaus, J. H. (1992). The career indecision of managers and professionals: An examination of multiple subtypes. *Journal of Vocational Behavior, 41,* 212-231.

161. Carter, R. T., & Helms, J. E. (1992). The counseling process as defined by relationship types: A test of Helm's interactional model. *Journal of Multicultural Counseling and Development, 20,* 181-201.

162. Challis, G. B., & Stam, H. J. (1992). A longitudinal study of the development of anticipatory nausea and vomiting in cancer chemotherapy patients: The role of absorption and autonomic perception. *Health Psychology, 11,* 181–189.

163. Chambless, D. L., Renneberg, B., Goldstein, A., & Graceley, E. J. (1992). MCMI-diagnosed personality disorders among agoraphobic outpatients: Prevalence and relationship to severity and treatment outcome. *Journal of Anxiety Disorders, 6,* 193-211.

164. Cole, P. M., Barrett, K. C., & Zahn-Waxler, C. (1992). Emotion displays in two-year-olds during mishaps. *Child Development, 63,* 314–324.

165. Deane, F. P., Leathem, J., & Spicer, J. (1992). Clinical norms, reliability and validity for the Hopkins Symptom Checklist-21. *Australian Journal of Psychology, 44,* 21–25.

166. Denollt, J., & De Potter, B. (1992). Coping subtypes for men with coronary heart disease: Relationship to well-being, stress and type A behaviour. *Psychological Medicine, 22,* 667-684.

167. Firth-Cozens, J., & Hardy, G. E. (1992). Occupational stress, clinical treatment and changes in job perceptions. *Journal of Occupational and Organizational Psychology, 65,* 81-88.

168. Fydrich, T., Dowdall, D., & Chambless, D. L. (1992). Reliability and validity of the Beck Anxiety Inventory. *Journal of Anxiety Disorders, 6,* 55-61.

169. Geisser, M. E., Robinson, M. E., & Pickren, W. E. (1992). Differences in cognitive coping strategies among pain-sensitive and pain-tolerant individuals on the cold-pressor test. *Behavior Therapy, 23,* 31–41.

170. George, C. E., Lankford, J. S., & Wilson, S. E. (1992). The effects of computerized versus paper-and-pencil administration on measures of negative affect. *Computers in Human Behavior, 8,* 203–209.

171. Gift, A. G., Moore, T., & Soeken, K. (1992). Relaxation to reduce dyspnea and anxiety in COPD patients. *Nursing Research, 41,* 242–246.

172. Glenn, S. W., & Parsons, O. A. (1992). Neuropsychological efficiency measures in male and female alcoholics. *Journal of Studies on Alcohol, 53,* 546–552.

173. Gur, R. C., Erwin, R. J., & Gur, R. E. (1992). Neurobehavioral probes for physiologic neuroimaging studies. *Archives of General Psychiatry, 49,* 409-414.

174. Hatch, J. P., Moore, P. J., Bocherding, S., Cyr-Provost, M., Boutros, N. N., & Seleshi, E. (1992). Electromyographic and affective responses of episodic tension-type headache patients and headache-free controls during stressful task performance. *Journal of Behavioral Medicine, 15,* 89-112.

175. Johnson, E. H., Collier, P., Nazzaro, P., & Gilbert, D. C. (1992). Psychological and physiological predictors of lipids in black males. *Journal of Behavioral Medicine, 15,* 285-298.

176. Kay, J. A., & Carlson, C. R. (1992). The role of stretch-based relaxation in the treatment of chronic neck tension. *Behavior Therapy, 23,* 423–431.

177. Khawaja, N. G., & Oei, T. P. S. (1992). Development of a Catastrophic Cognition Questionnaire. *Journal of Anxiety Disorders, 6,* 305-318.

178. King, N. J., Gullone, E., & Ollendick, T. H. (1992). Manifest anxiety and fearfulness in children and adolescents. *The Journal of Genetic Psychology, 153,* 63-73.

179. Konefal, J., & Duncan, R. C. (1992). Neurolinguistic programming training, trait anxiety, and locus of control. *Psychological Reports, 70,* 819-832.

180. Kumari, N., & Blackburn, I-M. (1992). How specific are negative automatic thoughts to a depressed population? An explanatory study. *British Journal of Medical Psychology, 65,* 167–176.

181. Labrecque, M. S., Peak, T., & Toseland, R. W. (1992). Long-term effectiveness of a group program for caregivers of frail elderly veterans. *American Journal of Orthopsychiatry, 62,* 575–588.

182. Landsbergis, P. A., Schnall, P. L., Deitz, D., Friedman, R., & Pickering, T. (1992). The patterning of psychological attributes and distress by "job strain" and social support in a sample of working men. *Journal of Behavioral Medicine, 15,* 379-405.

183. Lauver, D. (1992). Psychosocial variables, race, and intention to seek care for breast cancer symptoms. *Nursing Research 41,* 236–241.

184. Lobel, M., Dunkel-Schetter, C., & Scrimshaw, S. C. M. (1992). Prenatal maternal stress and prematurity: A prospective study of socioeconomically disadvantaged women. *Health Psychology, 11,* 32-40.

185. Lortie-Lussier, M., Simond, S., Rinfret, N., & DeKoninck, J. (1992). Beyond sex differences: Family and occupational roles' impact on women's and men's dreams. *Sex Roles, 26,* 79-96.

186. Maller, R. G., & Reiss, S. (1992). Anxiety sensitivity in 1984 and panic attacks in 1987. *Journal of Anxiety Disorders, 6,* 241-247.

187. Masters, R. S. W. (1992). Knowledge, knerves, and know-how: The role of explicit versus implicit knowledge in the breakdown of a complex motor skill under pressure. *British Journal of Psychology, 83,* 343-358.

188. Miller, S., & Watson, B. C. (1992). The relationship between communication attitude, anxiety, and depression in stutterers and nonstutterers. *Journal of Speech and Hearing Research, 35,* 789–798.

189. Moleman, P., Tulen, J. H. M., Blankestijn, P. J., Man in't Veld, A. J., & Boomsma, F. (1992). Urinary excretion of catecholamines and their metabolites in relation to circulating catecholamines: Six-hour infusion of epinephrine and norepinephrine in healthy volunteers. *Archives of General Psychiatry, 49,* 568-572.

190. Morrow, G. R., Asbury, R., Hammon, S., Dobkin, P., Caruso, L., Pandya, K., & Rosenthal, S. (1992). Comparing the effectiveness of behavioral treatment for chemotherapy-induced nausea and vomiting when administered by oncologists, oncology nurses, and clinical psychologists. *Health Psychology, 11,* 250–256.

191. Passchier, J., Verheij, R., Tulen, J. H. M., Timmerman, L., & Pepplinkhuizen, L. (1992). Positive association between anticipatory anxiety and needle pain for subjective but not for physiological measures of anxiety. *Psychological Reports, 70,* 1059-1062.

192. Perry, S., Fishman, B., Jacobsberg, L., & Francis, A. (1992). Relationships over 1 year between lymphacyte subsets and psychosocial variables among adults with infection of Human Immunodeficiency Virus. *Archives of General Psychiatry, 49,* 396-401.

193. Philips, H. C., Fensta, H. N., & Samson, D. (1992). An effective treatment for urinary incoordination. *Journal of Behavioral Medicine, 15,* 45-63.

194. Politano, P. M., Stapleton, L. A., & Correll, J. A. (1992). Differences between children of depressed and non-depressed mothers: Locus of control, anxiety and self esteem: A research note. *Journal of Child Psychology and Psychiatry and Allied Disciplines, 33,* 451-455.

195. Reznick, L. S., Hegeman, I. M., Kaufman, E. R., Woods, S. W., & Jacobs, M. (1992). Retrospective and concurrent self-report of behavioral inhibition and their relation to adult mental health. *Development and Psychopathology, 4,* 301-321.

196. Rubin, S. S. (1992). Adult child loss and the two-track model of bereavement. *Omega, 24,* 183–202.

197. Schultz, C. L., Schultz, N. C., & Greenwood, K. M. (1992). Caring for family caregivers: A replication study. *Australian Psychologist, 27,* 181–185.

198. Sears, H. A., & Galambos, N. L. (1992). Women's work conditions and marital adjustment in two-earner couples: A structural model. *Journal of Marriage and the Family, 54,* 789–797.

199. Shalev, A. Y., Orr, S. P., Peri, T., Schreiber, S., & Pitman, R. K. (1992). Physiologic responses to loud tones in Israeli patients with posttraumatic stress disorder. *Archives of General Psychiatry, 49,* 870-875.

200. Shapiro, D. E., Boggs, S. R., Melamed, B. G., & Graham-Pole, J. (1992). The effect of varied physician affect on recall, anxiety, and perceptions in women at risk for breast cancer: An analogue study. *Health Psychology, 11,* 61-66.

201. Sheeber, L. B., & Johnson, J. H. (1992). Child temperament, maternal adjustment, and changes in family life style. *American Journal of Orthopsychiatry, 62,* 178–185.

202. Shek, D. T. L. (1992). Meaning in life and psychological well-being: An empircial study using the Chinese version of the purpose in life questionnaire. *The Journal of Genetic Psychology, 153,* 185-200.

203. Siblerud, R. L. (1992). A comparison of mental health of multiple sclerosis patients with silver/mercury dental fillings and those with fillings removed. *Psychological Reports, 70,* 1139-1151.

204. Speechley, K. N., & Noh, S. (1992). Surviving childhood cancer, social support, and parents' psychological adjustment. *Journal of Pediatric Psychology, 17,* 15–31.

205. Stanfeld, S. A., Sharp, D. S., Gallacher, J. E. J., & Yarnell, J. W. G. (1992). A population survey of ischaemic heart disease and minor psychiatric disorder in men. *Psychological Medicine, 22,* 939-949.

206. Stein, M. B., Tanar, M. E., & Uhde, T. W. (1992). Heart rate and plasma norepinephrine responsivity to orthostatic challenge in anxiety disorders: Comparison of patients with panic disorder and social phobia and normal control subjects. *Archives of General Psychiatry, 49,* 311-317.

207. Taylor, D. N., & Pilar, J. D. (1992). Self-esteem, anxiety, and drug use. *Psychological Reports, 71,* 896-898.

208. Taylor, S., Koch, W., & McNally, R. J. (1992). How does anxiety sensitivity vary across the anxiety disorders? *Journal of Anxiety Disorders, 6,* 249-259.

209. Teichman, Y., Rabinovitz, D., & Rabinovitz, Y. (1992). Gender preferences of pregnant women and emotional reaction to information regarding fetal gender and postpartum: An examination of Freud's view about motivation for motherhood. *Sex Roles, 26,* 175-195.

210. Valliant, P. M., & Blasutti, B. (1992). Personality differences of sex offenders referred for treatment. *Psychological Reports, 71,* 1067-1074.

211. Vealey, R. S., Udry, E. M., Zimmerman, V., & Soliday, J. (1992). Intrapersonal and situational predictors of coaching burnout. *Journal of Sport and Exercise Psychology, 14,* 40-58.

212. Waddington, S. R., & Busch-Rossnagel, N. A. (1992). The influence of a child's disability on mother's role functioning and psychological well-being. *Genetic Psychology Monographs, 118,* 293–311.

213. Webster, A. (1992). The effect of pre-assessment information on clients' satisfaction, expectations and attendance at a mental health day center. *British Journal of Medical Psychology, 65,* 89–93.

214. Williams, P. G., Wiebe, D. J., & Smith, T. W. (1992). Coping processes as mediators of the relationship between hardiness and health. *Journal of Behavioral Medicine, 15,* 237-255.

215. Zamble, E. (1992). Behavior and adaptation in long-term prison inmates. *Criminal Justice and Behavior, 19,* 409–425.

216. Zeidner, M., & Hammer, A. L. (1992). Coping with missile attack: Resources, strategies, and outcomes. *Journal of Personality, 60,* 709–746.

217. Ahles, T. A. (1993). Cancer pain: Research from multidimensional and illness representation models. *Motivation and Emotion, 17,* 225–243.

218. Allen, B. G., Calhoun, L. G., Cann, A., & Tedeschi, R. G. (1993). The effect of cause of death on responses to the bereaved: Suicide compared to accident and natural causes. *Omega, 28,* 39–48.

219. Andersson, L., & Stevens, N. (1993). Associations between early experiences with parents and well-being in old age. *Journal of Gerontology, 48,* 109–116.

220. Andrews, J. A., Lewinsohn, P. M., Hops, H., & Roberts, R. E. (1993). Psychometric properties of scales for the measurement of psychosocial variables associated with depression in adolescence. *Psychological Reports, 73,* 1019-1046.

221. Archer, J., & Rhodes, V. (1993). The grief process and job loss: A cross-sectional study. *British Journal of Psychology, 84,* 395-410.

222. AuBuchon, P. G. (1993). Formulation-based treatment of a complex phobia. *Journal of Behavior Therapy and Experimental Psychiatry, 24,* 63–71.

223. Bachar, E., Peri, T., Halamish, R., & Shalev, A. Y. (1993). Auditory startle response in blind subjects. *Perceptual and Motor Skills, 76,* 1251–1256.

224. Baron, R. S., Logan, H., & Hoppe, S. (1993). Emotional and sensory focus as mediators of dental pain among patients differing in desired and felt dental control. *Health Psychology, 12,* 381-389.

225. Bauer, M., Priebe, S., Haring, B., & Adamczak, K. (1993). Long-term mental sequelae of political imprisonment in East Germany. *The Journal of Nervous and Mental Disease, 181,* 257-262.

226. Benson, M. J., Larson, J., Wilson, S. M., & Demo, D. H. (1993). Family of origin influences on late adolescent romantic relationships. *Journal of Marriage and the Family, 55,* 663–672.

227. Bleiker, E. M. A., Van Der Ploeg, H. M., Mook, J., & Kleijn, W. C. (1993). Anxiety, anger, and depression in elderly women. *Psychological Reports, 72,* 567-574.

228. Blood, D. J., & Ferriss, S. J. (1993). Effects of background music on anxiety, satisfaction with communication, and productivity. *Psychological Reports, 72,* 171-177.

229. Bond, A. J., & Silverira, J. C. (1993). The combination of alprazolan and alcohol on behavioral aggression. *Journal of Studies on Alcoholism, Sup. 11,* 30–39.

230. Britt, T. W., & Blumenthal, T. D. (1993). Social anxiety and latency of response to startle stimuli. *Journal of Research in Personality, 27,* 1-14.

231. Buchanan, L. M., Cowan, M., Burr, R., Waldron, C., & Kogan, H. (1993). Measurement of recovery from myocardial infarction using heart rate variability and psychological outcomes. *Nursing Research, 42,* 74–78.

232. Burling, J. W. (1993). Death concerns and symbolic aspects of the self: The effects of mortality salience on status concern and religiosity. *Personality and Social Psychology Bulletin, 19,* 100-105.

233. Calvo, M. G., & Carreiras, M. (1993). Selective influence of test anxiety on reading processes. *British Journal of Psychology, 84,* 375-388.

234. Carmel, S., & Glick, S. M. (1993). Compassionate physicians: Personality traits and prosocial attitudes. *Psychological Reports, 73,* 1362.

235. Channon, S., Baker, J. E., & Robertson, M. M. (1993). Working memory in clinical depression: An experimental study. *Psychological Medicine, 23,* 87-91.

236. Channon, S., Jones, M., & Stephenson, S. (1993). Cognitive strategies and hypothesis testing during discrimination learning in Parkinson's disease. *Neuropsychologia, 31,* 75-82.

237. Cox, W. J., & Kenardy, J. (1993). Performance anxiety, social phobia, and setting effects in instrumental music students. *Journal of Anxiety Disorders, 7,* 49-60.

238. Dahlquist, L. M., Czyewski, D. I., Copeland, K. G., Jones, C. L., Taub, E., & Vaughan, J. K. (1993). Parents of children newly diagnosed with cancer: Anxiety, coping, and marital distress. *Journal of Pediatric Psychology, 18,* 365–376.

239. deBoer, M. C., Schippers, G. M., & van der Staak, C. P. F. (1993). Alcohol and social anxiety in women and men: Pharmacological and expectancy effects. *Addictive Behaviors, 18,* 117-126.

240. Denollet, J. (1993). Emotional distress and fatigue in coronary heart disease: The Global Mood Scale (GMS). *Psychological Medicine, 23,* 111-121.

241. Dixon, D. C., Talcott, G. W., & Kelleher, W. J. (1993). Habit reversal treatment of temporomandibular disorders: A pilot investigation. *Journal of Behavior Therapy and Experimental Psychiatry, 24,* 49–55.

242. Donovan, J. M. (1993). Validation of a Portuguese form of Templer's Death Anxiety Scale. *Psychological Reports, 73,* 195-200.

243. Errico, A. L., Parsons, O. A., King, A. C., & Lovallo, W. R. (1993). Attenuated cortisol response to biobehavioral stressors in sober alcoholics. *Journal of Studies on Alcohol, 54,* 393–398.

244. Flick, S. N., Roy-Byrne, P. P., Cowley, D. S., Shores, M. M., & Dunner, D. L. (1993). DSM-III-R personality disorders in a mood and anxiety disorders clinic: Prevalence, comorbidity, and clinical correlates. *Journal of Affective Disorders, 27,* 71-79.

245. Ford, J. G., Lawson, J., & Hook, M. (1993). Further development of the public-private congruence technique. *Psychological Reports, 73,* 872-874.

246. Gillis, J. S. (1993). Effects of life stress and dysphoria on complex judgements. *Psychological Reports, 72,* 1355-1363.

247. Godfrey, H. P. D., Partridge, F. M., Knight, R. G., & Bishara, S. (1993). Course of insight disorder and emotional dysfunction following closed head injury: A controlled cross-sectional follow-up study. *Journal of Clinical and Experimental Neuropsychology, 15,* 503-515.

248. Gossette, R. L., & O'Brien, R. M. (1993). Efficacy of rational emotive therapy (RET) with children: A critical re-appraisal. *Journal of Behavior Therapy and Experimental Psychiatry, 24,* 15–25.

249. Greene, A. F., Sears, S. F., Jr., & Clark, J. E. (1993). Anger and sports participation. *Psychological Reports, 72,* 523-529.

250. Greenglass, E. R. (1993). Structural and social-psychological factors associated with job functioning by women managers. *Psychological Reports, 73,* 979-986.

251. Hatcher, J. W., Powers, L. L., & Richtsmeier, A. J. (1993). Parental anxiety and response to symptoms of minor illness in infants. *Journal of Pediatric Psychology, 18,* 397–408.

252. Hoffart, A., Due-Madsen, J., Lande, B., Gude, T., Bille, H., & Torgersen, S. (1993). Clomipramine in the treatment of agoraphobic inpatients resistant to behavioral therapy. *Journal of Clinical Psychiatry, 54,* 481–487.

253. Huntington, D. D., & Bender, W. N. (1993). Adolescents with learning disabilities at risk? Emotional well-being, depression, suicide. *Journal of Learning Disabilities, 26,* 159–166.

254. Huzel, L. L., Delaney, S. M., & Stein, M. B. (1993). Lymphocyte A B-adrenergic receptors in panic disorder: Findings with a highly selective ligand and relationship to clinical parameters. *Journal of Anxiety Disorders, 7,* 349-357.

255. Jacobs, G. D., Benson, H., & Friedman, R. (1993). Home-based central nervous system assessment of a multifactor behavioral intervention for chronic sleep-onset insomnia. *Behavior Therapy, 24,* 159–174.

256. Jacobsen, P. B., Boubjerg, D. H., & Redd, W. H. (1993). Anticipatory anxiety in women receiving chemotherapy for breast cancer. *Health Psychology, 12,* 469-475.

257. James, L. D., Thorn, B. E., & Williams, D. A. (1993). Goal specification in cognitive-behavioral therapy for chronic headache pain. *Behavior Therapy, 24,* 305–320.

258. Kenardy, J., & Dei, T. P. S. (1993). Phobic anxiety in panic disorder: Cognition, heart rate, and subjective anxiety. *Journal of Anxiety Disorders, 7,* 359-371.

259. Koenders, M. E. F., Passchier, J., Teuns, G., Harskamp, F. V., Cammen, T. J. M. V. D., & Schudel, W. J. (1993). Trait-anxiety and achievement motivation are positively correlated with memory performance in patients who visit a geriatric outpatient clinic with amnestic symptoms. *Psychological Reports, 73,* 1227-1231.

260. Kubitz, K. A., & Landers, D. M. (1993). The effects of aerobic training on cardiovascular responses to mental stress: An examination of underlying mechanisms. *Journal of Sport and Exercise Psychology, 15,* 326-337.

261. Lai, J., & Linden, W. (1993). The smile of Asia: Acculturation effects on symptom reporting. *Canadian Journal of Behavioural Science, 25,* 303-313.

262. Linehan, M. M., Heard, H. L., & Armstrong, H. E. (1993). Naturalistic follow-up of a behavioral treatment for chronically parasuicidal borderline patients. *Archives of General Psychiatry, 50,* 971-974.

263. Markland, D., & Hardy, L. (1993). Anxiety, relaxation and anaesthesia for day-case surgery. *British Journal of Clinical Psychology, 32,* 493-504.

264. Melnyk, B. M. (1993). Coping with unplanned childhood hospitalization: Effects of informational interventions on mothers and children. *Nursing Research, 42,* 50–55.

265. Mennemeier, M., Garner, R. D., & Heilman, K. M. (1993). Memory, mood, and measurement in hypothyroidism. *Journal of Clinical and Experimental Neuropsychology, 15,* 822-831.

266. Mercer, R. T., & Ferketich, S. L. (1993). Predictors of maternal role competence by risk status. *Nursing Research, 42,* 38–43.

267. Mijares-Colmenares, B. E., Masten, W. G., & Underwood, J. R. (1993). Effects of trait anxiety and the scamper technique on creative thinking of intellectually gifted students. *Psychological Reports, 72,* 907-912.

268. Morrison, M., de Man, A. F., & Drumheller, A. (1993). Correlates of socially restrictive and authoritarian attitudes toward mental patients in university students. *Social Behavior and Personality, 21,* 333-338.

269. Mueller, J. H., Grove, T. R., & Thompson, W. B. (1993). Text anxiety and handedness. *Bulletin of the Psychonomic Society, 31,* 461–464.

270. Nicholson, N. L., & Blanchard, E. B. (1993). A controlled evaluation of behavioral treatment of chronic headache in the elderly. *Behavior Therapy, 24,* 395–408.

271. Nivison, M. E., & Endresen, I. M. (1993). An analysis of relationships among environmental noise, annoyance and sensitivity to noise, and the consequences for health and sleep. *Journal of Behavioral Medicine, 16,* 257-276.

272. Ollendick, T. H., Lease, C. A., & Cooper, C. (1993). Separation anxiety in young adults: A preliminary examination. *Journal of Anxiety Disorders, 7,* 293-305.

273. Osman, A., Barrios, F. X., Aukes, D., Osman, J. R., & Markway, K. (1993). The Beck Anxiety Inventory: Psychometric properties in a community population. *Journal of Psychopathology and Behavioral Assessment, 15,* 287–297.

274. Osterhaus, S. O. L., Passchier, J., van der Helm-Hylkema, H., de Jong, K. T., Orlebeke, J. F., DeGrauw, A. J. C., & Dekker, P. H. (1993). Effects of behavioral psychophysiological treatment on school children with migraine in a nonclinical setting: Predictors and process variables. *Journal of Pediatric Psychology, 18,* 697–715.

275. Pierce, T. W., Madden, D. J., Siegel, W. C., & Blumenthal, J. A. (1993). Effects of aerobic exercise on cognitive and psychosocial functioning in patients with mild hypertension. *Health Psychology, 12,* 286–291.

276. Powell, J., Dame, S., Richards, D., Gossop, M., Marks, I., Strang, J., & Gray, J. (1993). Can opiate addicts tell us about their relapse risk? Subjective predictors of clinical prognosis. *Addictive Behaviors, 18,* 473-490.

277. Pretorius, T. B. (1993). Assessing the problem-solving appraisal of black South African students. *International Journal of Psychology, 28,* 861–870.

278. Rebeta, J. L., Brooks, C. I., O'Brien, J. P., & Hunter, G. A. (1993). Variations in trait-anxiety and achievement motivation of college students as a function of classroom seating position. *Journal of Experimental Education, 61,* 257–267.

279. Schmidt, P. J., Grover, G. N., & Rubinow, D. R. (1993). Alprazolam in the treatment of premenstrual syndrome. *Archives of General Psychiatry, 50,* 467-473.

280. Schultz, C. L., Smyrnios, K. X., Schultz, N. C., & Grisich, C. F. (1993). Longitudinal outcomes of psychoeducational support for family cargivers of dependent elderly persons. *Australian Psychologist, 28,* 21–24.

281. Schultz, G., & Melzack, R. (1993). Visual hallucinations and mental state: A study of 14 Charles Bonnet Syndrome hallucinators. *The Journal of Nervous and Mental Disease, 181,* 639-643.

282. Semenchuk, E. M., & Larkin, K. T. (1993). Behavioral and cardiovascular responses to interpersonal challenges among male offspring of essential hypertensives. *Health Psychology, 12,* 416-419.

283. Smith, A. P., Behan, P. O., Bell, W., Millar, K., & Bakheit, M. (1993). Behavioural problems associated with the chronic fatigue syndrome. *British Journal of Psychology, 84,* 411-423.

284. Stein, M. B., Enns, M. W., & Kryger, M. H. (1993). Sleep in nondepressed patients with panic disorder: II. Polysomnographic assessment of sleep architecture and sleep continuity. *Journal of Affective Disorders, 28,* 1-6.

285. Stronks, D. L., Rijpma, S. E., Passchier, J., Verhage, F., Meijden, W. V. D., & Stolz, E. (1993). Psychological consequences of genital herpes, an exploratory study with a gonorrhea control-group. *Psychological Reports, 73,* 395-400.

286. Talbot, K. F., & Haude, R. H. (1993). The relation between sign language skill and spatial visualization ability: Mental rotation of three-dimensional objects. *Perceptual and Motor Skills, 77,* 1387–1391.

287. Taylor, S. (1993). The structure of fundamental fears. *Journal of Behavior Therapy and Experimental Psychiatry, 24,* 289–299.

288. Teichman, Y., Shenhar, S., & Segal, S. (1993). Emotional distress in Israeli women before and after abortion. *American Journal of Orthopsychiatry, 63,* 277–288.

289. Thompson, T. (1993). Characteristics of self-worth protection in achievement behaviour. *British Journal of Educational Psychology, 63,* 469–488.

290. Timko, C., Moos, R. H., & Michelson, D. J. (1993). The contexts of adolescents' chronic life stressors. *American Journal of Community Psychology, 21,* 397-420.

291. Tucker, J. S., & Friedman, H. S. (1993). Sex differences in nonverbal expressiveness: Emotional expression, personality, and impressions. *Journal of Nonverbal Behavior, 17,* 103–117.

292. Van Den Bergh, O., Vandenriessche, F., De Broeck, K., & Van De Woestijne, K. P. (1993). Predictability and perceived control during 5.5% CO2-enriched air inhalation in high and low anxious subjects. *Journal of Anxiety Disorders, 7,* 61-73.

293. VanAmeringen, M., Mancini, C., & Streiner, D. L. (1993). Fluoxetine efficacy in social phobia. *Journal of Clinical Psychiatry, 54,* 27–32.

294. Acierno, R., Tremont, G., Last, C., & Montgomery, D. (1994). Tripartite assessment of the efficacy of eye-movement desensitization in a multi-phobic patient. *Journal of Anxiety Disorders, 8,* 259-276.

295. Altchiler, L., & Motta, R. (1994). Effects of aerobic and nonaerobic exercise on anxiety, absenteeism, and job satisfaction. *Journal of Clinical Psychology, 50,* 829-840.

296. Asmundson, G. J. G., & Stein, M. B. (1994). A preliminary analysis of pulmonary function in panic disorder: Implications for the dyspnea-fear theory. *Journal of Anxiety Disorders, 8,* 63-69.

297. Asmundson, G. J. G., & Stein, M. B. (1994). Selective processing of social threat in patients with generalized social phobia: Evaluation using a dot-probe paradigm. *Journal of Anxiety Disorders, 8,* 107-117.

298. Auerbach, S. M., Kiesler, D. J., Strentz, T., Schmidt, J. A., & Serio, C. D. (1994). Interpersonal impacts and adjustment to the stress of simulated captivity: An empirical test of the Stockholm syndrome. *Journal of Social and Clinical Psychology, 13,* 207–221.

299. Baron, R., Logan, H., Lilly, J., Inman, M., & Brennan, M. (1994). Negative emotion and message processing. *Journal of Experimental Social Psychology, 30,* 181–201.

300. Barsky, A. J., Cleary, P. D., Sarnie, M. K., & Ruskin, J. N. (1994). Panic disorder, palpitations, and the awareness of cardiac activity. *The Journal of Nervous and Mental Disease, 182,* 63-71.

301. Basoglu, M., Paker, M., Paker, O., Ozmen, E., Marks, I., Incesu, C., Sahin, D., & Sarimurat, N. (1994). Psychological effects of torture: A comparison of tortured with nontortured political activists in Turkey. *American Journal of Psychiatry, 151,* 76-81.

302. Beck, J. G., & Zebb, B. J. (1994). Behavioral assessment and treatment of panic disorder: Current status, future directions. *Behavior Therapy, 25,* 581–611.

303. Beck, J. G., Stanley, M. A., Baldwin, L. E., Deagle, E. A., III, & Averill, P. M. (1994). Comparison of cognitive therapy and relaxation training for panic disorder. *Journal of Consulting and Clinical Psychology, 62,* 818-826.

304. Becker, E., Rinck, M., & Margraf, J. (1994). Memory bias in panic disorder. *Journal of Abnormal Psychology, 103,* 396-399.

305. Behen, J. M., & Rodrigue, J. R. (1994). Predictors of coping strategies among adults with cancer. *Psychological Reports, 74,* 43-48.

306. Benkelfat, C., Ellenbogen, M. A., Dean, P., Palmour, R. M., & Young, S. N. (1994). Mood-lowering effect of tryptophan depletion: Enhanced susceptibility of young men at genetic risk for major affective disorders. *Archives of General Psychiatry, 51,* 687-697.

307. Berman, W. H., Heiss, G. E., & Sperling, M. B. (1994). Measuring continued attachment to parents: The Continued Attachment Scale—Parent Version. *Psychological Reports, 75,* 171-182.

308. Borden, J. W. (1994). Panic disorder and suicidality: Prevalence and risk factors. *Journal of Anxiety Disorders, 8,* 217-225.

309. Borden, J. W., & Lister, S. C. (1994). The anxiety sensitivity construct: Cognitive reactions to physiological change. *Journal of Anxiety Disorders, 8,* 311-321.

310. Calamari, J. E., Faber, S. D., Hitsman, B. L., & Poppe, C. J. (1994). Treatment of obsessive compulsive disorder in the elderly: A review and case example. *Journal of Behavior Therapy and Experimental Psychiatry, 25,* 95–104.

311. Carey, M. P., Faulstick, M. E., & Carey, T. C. (1994). Assessment of anxiety in adolescents: Concurrent and factorial validities of the Trait Anxiety scale of Spielberger's State-Trait Anxiety Inventory for Children. *Psychological Reports, 75,* 331–338.

312. Chemtob, C. M., Hamada, R. S., Roitblat, H. L., & Muraoka, M. Y. (1994). Anger, impulsivity, and anger control in combat-related posttraumatic stress disorder. *Journal of Consulting and Clinical Psychology, 62,* 827-832.

313. Christenson, G. A., Faber, R. J., deZwaan, M., Raymond, N. C., Specker, S. M., Ekern, M. D., Mackenzie, T. B., Crosby, R. D., Crow, S. J., Eckert, E. D., Mussell, M. P., & Mitchell, J. E. (1994). Compulsive buying: Descriptive characteristics and psychiatric comorbidity. *The Journal of Clinical Psychiatry, 55,* 5–11.

314. Christo, G., & Sutton, S. (1994). Anxiety and self-esteem as a function of abstinence time among recovering addicts attending Narcotics Anonymous. *British Journal of Clinical Psychology, 33,* 198-200.

315. Clark, K., Dinsmore, S., Grafman, J., & Dalakas, M. C. (1994). A personality profile of patients diagnosed with post-polio syndrome. *Neurology, 44,* 1809–1811.

316. Clark, M. E. (1994). Interpretive limitations of the MMPI-2 anger and cynicism content scales. *Journal of Personality Assessment, 63*, 89-96.

317. Cloitre, M., Shear, M. K., Cancienne, J., & Zeitlin, S. B. (1994). Implicit and explicit memory for catastrophic associations to bodily sensation words in panic disorder. *Cognitive Therapy and Research, 18*, 225-240.

318. Comunian, A. L. (1994). Self-Consciousness Scale dimensions: An Italian adaptation. *Psychological Reports, 74*, 483-489.

319. Craig, A. (1994). Anxiety levels in persons who stutter: Comments on the research of Miller and Watson (1992). *Journal of Speech and Hearing Research, 37*, 90–92.

320. Crews, W. D., Jr., & Harrison, D. W. (1994). Cerebral asymmetry in facial affect perception by women: Neuropsychological effects of depressed mood. *Perceptual and Motor Skills, 79*, 1667-1679.

321. Crews, W. D., Jr., & Harrison, D. W. (1994). Functional assymetry in the motor performance of women: Neuropsychological effects of depression. *Perceptual and Motor Skills, 78*, 1315-1322.

322. Davey, G. C. L., & Matchett, G. (1994). Unconditioned stimulus rehearsal and the retention and enhancement of differential "fear" conditioning: Effects of trait and state anxiety. *Journal of Abnormal Psychology, 103*, 708-718.

323. de Boer, M., Schippers, G. M., & van der Stark, C. P. F. (1994). The effects of alcohol, expectancy, and alcohol beliefs on anxiety and self-disclosure in women: Do beliefs moderate alcohol effects? *Addictive Behaviors, 19*, 509–520.

324. DeBono, K. G., & McDermott, J. B. (1994). Trait anxiety and persuasion: Individual differences in information processing strategies. *Journal of Research in Personality, 28*, 395-407.

325. Deffenbacher, J. L., Thwaites, G. A., Wallace, T. L., & Oetting, E. R. (1994). Social skills and cognitive-relaxation approaches to general anger reduction. *Journal of Counseling Psychology, 41*, 386-396.

326. Delignieres, D., Marcellini, A., & Brisswalter, J. (1994). Self-perception of fitness and personality traits. *Perceptual and Motor Skills, 78*, 843-851.

327. Derryberry, D., & Reed, M. A. (1994). Temperament and attention: Orienting toward and away from positive and negative signals. *Journal of Personality and Social Psychology, 66*, 1128-1139.

328. Dreman, S., & Aldor, R. (1994). A comparative study of custodial mothers and fathers in the stabilization phase of the divorce process. *Journal of Divorce & Remarriage, 21(3/4)*, 59-79.

329. Dreman, S., & Aldor, R. (1994). Work or marriage? Competence in custodial mothers in the stabilization phase of the divorce process. *Journal of Divorce & Remarriage, 22(1/2)*, 3-22.

330. Durham, R. C., Murphy, T., Allan, T., Richard, K., Treliving, L. R., & Fenton, G. W. (1994). Cognitive therapy, analytic psychotherapy and anxiety management training for generalized anxiety disorder. *British Journal of Psychiatry, 165*, 315-323.

331. Eells, G. T., & Boswell, D. L. (1994). Validity of Rorschach inanimate movement and diffuse shading responses as measures of frustration and anxiety. *Perceptual and Motor Skills, 78*, 1299-1302.

332. Engel, N. A., Rodrigue, J. R., & Geffken, G. R. (1994). Parent-child agreement on ratings of anxiety in children. *Psychological Reports, 75*, 1251-1260.

333. Ferketich, S. L., & Mercer, R. T. (1994). Predictors of paternal role competence by risk status. *Nursing Research, 43*, 80–85.

334. Fuller, K. H., Waters, W. F., & Scott, O. (1994). An investigation of slow-wave sleep processes in chronic PTSD patients. *Journal of Anxiety Disorders, 8*, 227-236.

335. Gamble, W. C. (1994). Perceptions of controllability and other stressor event characteristics as determinant of coping among young adolescents and young adults. *Journal of Youth and Adolescence, 23*, 65–84.

336. Gerlsma, C., Kramer, J. J., Scholing, A., & Emmelkamp, P. M. (1994). The influence of mood on memories of parental rearing practices. *British Journal of Clinical Psychology, 33*, 159-172.

337. Goldman, S. L., & Owen, M. T. (1994). The impact of parental trait anxiety on the utilization of health care services in infancy: A prospective study. *Journal of Pediatric Psychology, 19*, 369–381.

338. Gournay, K., & Brooking, J. (1994). Community psychiatric nurses in primary health care. *British Journal of Psychiatry, 165*, 231-238.

339. Greene, B., & Blanchard, E. B. (1994). Cognitive therapy for irritable bowel syndrome. *Journal of Consulting and Clinical Psychology, 62*, 576-582.

340. Grunseit, A. C., Perdices, M., Dunbar, N., & Cooper, D. A. (1994). Neuropsychological function in asymptomatic HIV-1 infection: Methodological issues. *Journal of Clinical and Experimental Neuropsychology, 16*, 898-910.

341. Hadjistavropoulos, T., & Genest, M. (1994). The underestimation of the role of physical attractiveness in dating preferences: Ignorance or taboo? *Canadian Journal of Behavioural Science, 26*, 298-318.

342. Hains, A. A. (1994). The effectiveness of a school-based, cognitive-behavioral stress management program with adolescents reporting high and low levels of emotional arousal. *The School Counselor, 42*, 114–125.

343. Harger, G. J., & Raglin, J. S. (1994). Correspondence between actual and recalled precompetition anxiety in collegiate track and field athletes. *Journal of Sport and Exercise Psychology, 16*, 206-211.

344. Harrigan, J. A., Suarez, I., & Hartman, J. S. (1994). Effect of speech errors on observers' judgements of anxious and defensive individuals. *Journal of Research in Personality, 28*, 505-529.

345. Hayward, P., Ahmad, T., & Wardle, J. (1994). Into the dangerous world: An in vivo study of information processing in agoraphobics. *British Journal of Clinical Psychology, 33*, 307-315.

346. Hegel, M. T., Ravaris, C. L., & Ahles, T. A. (1994). Combined cognitive-behavioral and time-limited alprazolam treatment of panic disorder. *Behavior Therapy, 25*, 183–195.

347. Hertel, P. T., & Milan, S. (1994). Depressive deficits in recognition: Dissociation of recollection and familiarity. *Journal of Abnormal Psychology, 103*, 736-742.

348. Hiss, H., Foa, E. B., & Kozak, M. J. (1994). Relapse prevention program for treatment of obsessive-compulsive disorder. *Journal of Consulting and Clinical Psychology, 62*, 801-808.

349. Hobfoll, S. E., Dunahoo, C. L., Ben-Porath, Y., & Monmer, J. (1994). Gender and coping: The dual-axis model of coping. *American Journal of Community Psychology, 22*, 49-82.

350. Hovens, J. E., Falger, P. R. J., Den Velde, W. O., & DeGroen, J. H. M. (1994). Posttraumatic stress disorder in male and female Dutch resistance veterans of World War II in relation to trait anxiety and depression. *Psychological Reports, 74*, 275-285.

351. Intrieri, R. C., Jones, G. E., & Alcorn, J. D. (1994). Masseter muscle hyperactivity and myofascial pain dysfunction syndrome: A relationship under stress. *Journal of Behavioral Medicine, 17*, 479–500.

352. Joseph, S. (1994). Subscales of the Automatic Thoughts Questionnaire. *The Journal of Genetic Psychology, 155*, 367-368.

353. Katz, R. C., Wilson, L., & Frazer, N. (1994). Anxiety and its determinants in patients undergoing magnetic resonance imaging. *Journal of Behavior Therapy and Experimental Psychiatry, 25*, 131–134.

354. Khawaja, N. G., Oei, T. P. S., & Baglioni, A. J. (1994). Modification of the catastrophic cognitions questionnaire (CCQ-M) for normals and patients: Exploratory and LISREL analyses. *Journal of Psychopathology and Behavioral Assessment, 16*, 325–342.

355. Kirkby, R. J. (1994). Changes in premenstrual symptoms and irrational thinking following cognitive-behavioral coping skills training. *Journal of Consulting and Clinical Psychology, 62*, 1026-1032.

356. Kiselica, M. S., Baker, S. B., Thomas, R. N., & Reedy, S. (1994). Effects of stress inoculation training on anxiety, stress, and academic performance among adolescents. *Journal of Counseling Psychology, 41*, 335-342.

357. Kranzler, H. R., Kadden, R. M., Babor, T. F., & Rounsaville, B. J. (1994). Longitudinal, expert, all data procedure for psychiatreic diagnosis in patients with psychoactive substance use disorders. *The Journal of Nervous and Mental Disease, 182*, 277-283.

358. Kugler, J., Seelbach, H., & Kruskemper, G. M. (1994). Effects of rehabilitation programmes on anxiety and depression in coronary patients: A meta-analysis. *British Journal of Clinical Psychology, 33*, 401-410.

359. Lakey, B., & Dickinson, L. G. (1994). Antecedents of perceived support: Is perceived family environment generalized to new social relationships? *Cognitive Therapy and Research, 18*, 39-53.

360. Lankford, J. S., Bell, R. W., & Elias, J. W. (1994). Computerized versus standard personality measures: Equivalency, computer anxiety, and gender differences. *Computers in Human Behavior, 10*, 497–510.

361. Law, W. A., Martin, A., Mapou, R. L., Roller, T. L., Salazar, A. M., Temoshok, L. R., & Rundell, J. R. (1994). Working memory in individuals with HIV infection. *Journal of Clinical and Experimental Neuropsychology, 16*, 173-182.

362. Leddy, M. H., Lambert, M. J., & Ogles, B. M. (1994). Psychological consequences of athletic injury among high-level competitors. *Research Quarterly for Exercise and Sport, 65*, 347–354.

363. Lee, H. B., & Oei, T. P. S. (1994). Factor structure, validity, and reliability of the Fear Questionnaire in a Hong Kong Chinese population. *Journal of Psychopathology and Behavioral Assessment, 16*, 189–199.

364. Lenehan, M. C., Dunn, R., Ingham, J., Signer, B., & Murray, J. B. (1994). Effects of learning-style intervention on college students' achievement, anxiety, anger, and curiosity. *Journal of College Student Development, 35*, 461–466.

365. Lenzenweger, M. F., & Korfine, L. (1994). Perceptual aberrations, schizotypy, and the Wisconsin Card Sorting Test. *Schizophrenia Bulletin, 20*, 345–357.

366. Lewinsohn, P. M., Roberts, R. E., Seeley, J. R., Rohde, P., Gotlib, I. H., & Hops, H. (1994). Adolescent psychopathology: II. Psychosocial risk factors for depression. *Journal of Abnormal Psychology, 103*, 302-315.

367. Loosen, P. T., Purdon, S. E., & Pavlou, S. N. (1994). Effects on behavior of modulation of gonadal function in men with gonadotropin-releasing hormone antagonists. *American Journal of Psychiatry, 151*, 271-273.

368. MacLeod, A. K., & Tarbuck, A. F. (1994). Explaining why negative events will happen to oneself: Parasuicides are pessimistic because they can't see any reason not to be. *British Journal of Clinical Psychology, 33*, 317-326.

369. Maruff, P., Wood, S., Currie, J., McArthur-Jackson, C., Malone, V., & Benson, E. (1994). Computer-administered visual analogue mood scales: Rapid and valid assessment of mood in HIV positive individuals. *Psychological Reports, 74*, 39-42.

370. McAuley, E., & Courneya, K. S. (1994). The Subjective Exercise Experiences Scale (SEES): Development and preliminary validation. *Journal of Sport and Exercise Psychology, 16*, 163-177.

371. Mehta, M. D., & Simpson-Housley, P. (1994). Trait anxiety and perception of a potential nuclear power plant disaster. *Psychological Reports, 74*, 291-295.

372. Mogg, K., Bradley, B. P., Miller, T., Potts, H., Glenwright, J., & Kentish, J. (1994). Interpretation of homophones related to threat: Anxiety or response bias effects? *Cognitive Therapy and Research, 18*, 461-477.

373. Moore, R. G., & Blackburn, I-M. (1994). The relationship of sociotropy and autonomy to symptoms, cognition, and personality in depressed patients. *Journal of Affective Disorders, 32*, 239-245.

374. Morin, C. M., Stone, J., McDonald, K., & Jones, S. (1994). Psychological management of insomnia: A clinical replication series with 100 patients. *Behavior Therapy, 25*, 291–309.

375. Newman, M. G., Hofmann, S. G., Trabert, W., Roth, W. T., & Taylor, C. B. (1994). Does behavioral treatment of social phobia lead to cognitive changes? *Behavior Therapy, 25,* 503–517.
376. O'Neil, R., & Greenberger, E. (1994). Patterns of commitment to work and parenting: Implications for role strain. *Journal of Marriage and the Family, 56,* 101–118.
377. Orbach, I., Shopen-Kofman, R., & Mikulincer, M. (1994). The impact of subliminal symbiotic vs. identification messages in reducing anxiety. *Journal of Research in Personality, 28,* 492-504.
378. Orsillo, S. M., Lilienfield, S. O., & Heimberg, R. G. (1994). Social phobia and response to challenge procedures: Examining the interaction between anxiety sensitivity and trait anxiety. *Journal of Anxiety Disorders, 8,* 247-258.
379. Osseiran-Waines, N., & Elmacian, S. (1994). Types of social support: Relation to stress and academic achievement among prospective teachers. *Canadian Journal of Behavioural Science, 26,* 1-20.
380. Oz, S., & Eden, D. (1994). Restraining the golem: Boosting performance by changing the interpretation of low scores. *Journal of Applied Psychology, 79,* 744-754.
381. Payne, R. B., & Corley, T. J. (1994). Motivational effects of anxiety of psychomotor performance. *Perceptual and Motor Skills, 79,* 1507-1521.
382. Pearl, J. H., & Carlozzi, A. F. (1994). Effect of meditation on empathy and anxiety. *Perceptual and Motor Skills, 78,* 297–298.
383. Polivy, J., Herman, C. P., & McFarlane, T. (1994). Effects of anxiety on eating: Does palatability moderate distress-induced overeating in dieters. *Journal of Abnormal Psychology, 103,* 505-510.
384. Pugh, K., Riccio, M., Jadresic, D., Burgess, A. P., Baldeweg, T., Catalan, J., Lovett, E., Hawkins, D. A., Gruzelier, J., & Thompson, C. (1994). A longitudinal study of the neuropsychiatric consequences of HIV-1 infection of gay men. II. Psychological and health status at baseline and at 12-month follow-up. *Psychological Medicine, 24,* 897-904.
385. Rapee, R. M., & Medoro, L. (1994). Fear of physical sensations and trait anxiety as mediators of the response to hyperventilation in nonclinical subjects. *Journal of Abnormal Psychology, 103,* 693-699.
386. Rawson, H. E., Bloomer, K., & Kendall, A. (1994). Stress, anxiety, depression, and physical illness in college students. *The Journal of Genetic Psychology, 155,* 321-330.
387. Richman, H., & Nelson-Gray, R. (1994). Nonclinical panicker personality: Profile and discriminative ability. *Journal of Anxiety Disorders, 8,* 33-47.
388. Rocha-Singh, I. A. (1994). Perceived stress among graduate students: Development and validation of the Graduate Stress Inventory. *Educational and Psychological Measurement, 54,* 714-727.
389. Roemer, L., & Borkovec, T. D. (1994). Effects of suppressing thoughts about emotional material. *Journal of Abnormal Psychology, 103,* 467-474.
390. Rogler, L. H., Cortes, D. E., & Malgady, R. G. (1994). The mental health relevance of idioms of distress: Anger and perceptions of injustic among New York Puerto Ricans. *The Journal of Nervous and Mental Disease, 182,* 327-330.
391. Scheier, M. F., Carver, C. S., & Bridges, M. W. (1994). Distinguishing optimism from neuroticism (and trait anxiety, self-mastery, and self-esteem): A reevaluation of the Life Orientation Test. *Journal of Personality and Social Psychology, 67,* 1063-1078.
392. Schiff, B. B., & Gagliese, L. (1994). The consequences of experimentally induced and chronic unilateral pain: Reflections of hemispheric lateralization of emotion. *Cortex, 30,* 255-267.
393. Schuckit, M. A., Klein, J., Twitchell, G., & Smith, T. (1994). Personality test scores as predictors of alcoholism almost a decade later. *The American Journal of Psychiatry, 151,* 1038-1042.
394. Sheebar, L. B., & Johnson, J. H. (1994). Evaluation of a temperament-focused, parent-training program. *Journal of Clinical Child Psychology, 23,* 249-259.
395. Siblerud, R. L., Motl, J., & Kienholz, E. (1994). Psychometric evidence that mercury from silver dental fillings may be an etiological factor in depression, excessive anger, and anxiety. *Psychological Reports, 74,* 67-80.
396. Spector, P. E., & O'Connell, B. J. (1994). The contribution of personality traits, negative affectivity, locus of control and Type A to the subsequent reports of job stressors and job strains. *Journal of Occupational and Organizational Psychology, 67,* 1-11.
397. Stein, M. B., Asmundson, G. J. G., & Chartier, M. (1994). Antonomic responsivity in generalized social phobia. *Journal of Affective Disorders, 31,* 211–221.
398. Stoltenberg, C. D., McNeill, B. W., & Crethar, H. C. (1994). Changes in supervision as counselors and therapists gain experience: A review. *Professional Psychology: Research and Practice, 25,* 416–449.
399. Sugiyama, Y., & Ichimura, S. (1994). Preference for practicing location in table tennis classes and students' personalities. *Perceptual and Motor Skills, 79,* 195-199.
400. Sugiyama, Y., Shiraki, H., & Ichimura, S. (1994). Relation of preference for location with scores on anxiety and on visibility in golf practice. *Perceptual and Motor Skills, 79,* 812-814.
401. Sutker, P. B., Uddo, M., Brailey, K., Vasterling, J. J., & Errera, P. (1994). Psychopathology in war-zone deployed and nondeployed Operation Desert Storm troops assigned graves registration duties. *Journal of Abnormal Psychology, 103,* 383-390.
402. Taylor, K. A., Purser, K. C. D., & Baluch, B. (1994). Could popping air capsules affect state anxiety? *Psychological Reports, 75,* 161-162.
403. Tomarken, A. J., & Davidson, R. J. (1994). Frontal brain activation in repressors and nonrepressors. *Journal of Abnormal Psychology, 103,* 339-349.
404. Trinder, J., Kleiman, J., & Chaffer, D. (1994). The effect of presleep anxiety on respiratory instability during sleep. *Australian Journal of Psychology, 46,* 81–86.
405. Uhde, T. W., Tancer, M. E., Gelernter, C. S., & Vittone, B. J. (1994). Normal urinary fue cortisol and postdexamethasone cortisol in social phobia: Comparison to normal volunteers. *Journal of Affective Disorders, 30,* 155–161.
406. Valentiner, D. P., Holahan, C. J., & Moos, R. H. (1994). Social support, appraisals of event controllability, and coping: An integrative model. *Journal of Personality and Social Psychology, 66,* 1094-1102.
407. Valliant, P. M., & Raven, L. M. (1994). Management of anger and its effect on incarcerated assaultive and nonassaultive offenders. *Psychological Reports, 75,* 275-278.
408. Van Ameringen, M., Mancini, C., & Streiner, D. (1994). Sertraline in social phobia. *Journal of Affective Disorders, 31,* 141–145.
409. van Elderen-van Kemenade, T., Maes, S., & van den Broek, Y. (1994). Effects of a health education programme with telephone follow-up during cardiac rehabilitation. *British Journal of Clinical Psychology, 33,* 367-378.
410. Vaughan, K., Armstrong, M. S., Gold, R., O'Connor, N., Jenneke, W., & Tarrier, N. (1994). A trial of eye movement desensitization compared to image habituation training and applied muscle relaxation in post-traumatic stress disorder. *Journal of Behavior Therapy and Experimental Psychiatry, 25,* 283–291.
411. Vera, M. N., Vila, J., & Godovy, J. F. (1994). Cardiovascular effects of traffic noise: The role of negative self-statements. *Psychological Medicine, 24,* 817-827.
412. Watson, B. C., & Miller, S. (1994). Response to Craig. *Journal of Speech and Hearing Research, 37,* 92–95.
413. Wegner, D. M., & Zanakos, S. (1994). Chronic thought suppression. *Journal of Personality, 62,* 615–640.
414. Weizman, R., Laor, N., Yerachmiel, B., Selman, A., Schudovizky, A., Wolmer, L., Laron, Z., & Gil-Ad, I. (1994). Impact of the Gulf War on the anxiety, cortisol, and growth hormone levels of Israeli civilians. *American Journal of Psychiatry, 151,* 71-75.
415. Wendt, P. E., & Risberg, J. (1994). Cortical activation during visual spatial processing: Relation between hemispheric asymmetry of blood flow and performance. *Brain and Cognition, 24,* 87-103.
416. Whittal, M. L., Suchday, S., & Goetsch, V. L. (1994). The Panic Attack Questionnaire: Factor analysis of symptom profiles and characteristics of undergraduates who panic. *Journal of Anxiety Disorders, 8,* 237-245.
417. Wiebe, D. J., Alderfer, M. A., Palmer, S. C., Lindsay, R., & Jarrett, L. (1994). Behavioral self-regulation in adolescents with Type I diabetes: Negative affectivity and blood glucose symptom perception. *Journal of Consulting and Clinical Psychology, 62,* 1204-1212.
418. Wise, S. L., Roos, L. L., Plake, B. S., & Nebelsick-Gullet, L. J. (1994). The relationship between examinee anxiety and preference for self-adapted testing. *Applied Measurement in Education, 7,* 81-91.
419. Yee, C. M., & Miller, G. A. (1994). A dual-task analysis of resource allocation in dysthymia and anhedonia. *Journal of Abnormal Psychology, 103,* 625-636.
420. Akillas, E., & Efran, J. S. (1995). Symptom prescription and reframing: Should they be combined? *Cognitive Therapy and Research, 19,* 263–279.
421. Althof, S. E., Levine, S. B., Corty, E. W., Risen, C. B., Stern, E. B., & Kurit, D. M. (1995) A double-blind crossover trial of clomipramine for rapid ejaculation in 15 couples. *Journal of Clinical Psychiatry, 56,* 402–407.
422. Arroyo, C. G., & Zigler, E. (1995). Racial identity, academic achievement, and the psychological well-being of economically disadvantages adolescents. *Journal of Personality and Social Psychology, 69,* 903–914.
423. Baran, S. A., Weltzin, T. E., & Kaye, W. H. (1995). Low discharge weight and outcome in anxorexia nervosa. *American Journal of Psychiatry, 152,* 1070-1072.
424. Barnett, R. C., Raudenbush, S. W., Brennan, R. T., Pleck, J. H., & Marshall, N. L. (1995). Change in job and marital experiences and change in psychological distress: A longitudinal study of dual-earner couples. *Journal of Personality and Social Psychology, 69,* 839–850.
425. Basoglu, M., & Parker, M. (1995). Severity of trauma as predictor of long-term psychological status in survivors of torture. *Journal of Anxiety Disorders, 9,* 339–350.
426. Betz, N. E., Wohlegmuth, E., Serling, D., Harshbarger, J., & Klein, K. (1995). Evaluation of a measure of self-esteem based on the concept of unconditional positive regard. *Journal of Counseling and Development, 74,* 76–83.
427. Blanchard, E. B., Hickling, E. J., Taylor, A. E., & Loos, W. (1995). Psychiatric morbidity associated with motor vehicle accidents. *The Journal of Nervous and Mental Disease, 183,* 495–504.
428. Bond, A. J., Curran, H. V., Bruce, m. S., O'Sullivan, G., & Shine, P. (1995). Behavioural aggression in panic disorder after 8 weeks' treatment with alprazolam. *Journal of Affective Disorders, 35,* 117–123.
429. Bradley, B. P., Mogg, K., Millar, N., & White, J. (1995). Selective processing of negative information: Effects of clinical anxiety, concurrent depression, and awareness. *Journal of Abnormal Psychology, 104,* 532–536.
430. Brand, E. F., LaKey, B., & Buman, S. (1995). A preventative, psychoeducational approach to increased perceived social support. *American Journal of Community Psychology, 23,* 117–135.
431. Brown, E. J., Heimberg, R. G., & Juster, H. R. (1995). Social phobia subtype and avoidant personality disorder: Effect on severity of social phobia, impairment, and outcome of cognitive behavioral treatment. *Behavior Therapy, 26,* 467–486.
432. Bruchon-Schweitzer, M., Quintard, B., Paulhan, I., Nuissier, J., & Cousson, F. (1995). Psychological adjustment to hospitalization: Factorial structure, antecedents, and outcome. *Psychological Reports, 76,* 1091–1100.
433. Bryant, R. A., & Harvey, A. G. (1995). Acute stress response: A comparison of head injured and nonhead injured patients. *Psychological Medicine, 25,* 869–873.

434. Bryant, R. A., & Harvey, A. G. (1995). Processing threatening information in posttraumatic stress disorder. *Journal of Abnormal Psychology, 104,* 537–541.
435. Burger, J. M. (1995). Individual differences in preference for solitude. *Journal of Research in Personality, 29,* 85-108.
436. Burker, E. J., Blumenthal, J. A., Feldman, M., Burnett, R., White, W., Smith, R. L., Croughwell, N., Schnell, R., Newman, M., & Reves, J. G. (1995). Depression in male and female patients undergoing cardiac surgery. *British Journal of Clinical Psychology, 34,* 119-128.
437. Campbell, L. A., Kirkpatrick, S. E., Berry, C. C., & Lamberti, J. J. (1995). Preparing children with congenital heart disease for cardiac surgery. *Journal of Pediatric Psychology, 20,* 313–328.
438. Carter, M. M., Hollon, S. D., Carson, R., & Shelton, R. C. (1995). Effects of a safe person on induced distress following a biological challenge in panic disorder with agoraphobia. *Journal of Abnormal Psychology, 104,* 156-163.
439. Christensen, A. P., & Oei, T. P. S. (1995). The efficacy of cognitive behaviour therapy in treating premenstrual dysphoric changes. *Journal of Affective Disorders, 33,* 57-63.
440. Christensen, A. P., & Oli, T. P. S. (1995). Correlates of premenstrual dysphoria in help-seeking women. *Journal of Affective Disorders, 33,* 47-55.
441. Colpin, H., Demyttenaese, K., & Vandemeulebroecke, L. (1995). New reproductive technology and the family: The parent-child relationship following in vitro fertilization. *Journal of Child Psychology and Psychiatry, 36,* 1429–1441.
442. Cook, R., Golombok, S., Bish, A., & Murray, C. (1995). Disclosure of donor insemination: Parental attitudes. *American Journal of Orthopsychiatry, 65,* 549–559.
443. Cooke, D. K., Sims, R. L., & Peyrefitte, J. (1995). The relationship between graduate student attitudes and attrition. *The Journal of Psychology, 129,* 677–688.
444. Corrigan, P. W., Holmes, E. P., & Luchins, D. (1995). Burnout and collegial support in state psychiatric hospital staff. *Journal of Clinical Psychology, 51,* 703–710.
445. Coughlan, G. M., Ridout, K. L., & Williams, A. C. de C. (1995). Situation from a pain management programme. *British Journal of Clinical Psychology, 34,* 471–479.
446. Cournoyer, R. J., & Mahalik, J. R. (1995). Cross-sectional study of gender role conflict examining college-aged and middle-aged men. *Journal of Counseling Psychology, 42,* 11-19.
447. Craig, A. R., & Kearns, M. (1995). Results of a traditional acupuncture intervention for stuttering. *Journal of Speech and Hearing, 38,* 572–578.
448. Cramer, D., & Buckland, N. (1995). Effect of rational and irrational statements and demand characteristics on task anxiety. *The Journal of Psychology, 129,* 269–275.
449. Craske, M. G., Brown, T. A., Meadows, E. A., & Barlow, D. H. (1995). Uncued and cued emotions and associated distress in a college sample. *Journal of Anxiety Disorders, 9,* 125-137.
450. Dalack, G. W., Glassman, A. H., Rivelli, S., Covey, L., & Stetner, F. (1995). Mood, major depression, and fluoxetine response in cigarette smokers. *American Journal of Psychiatry, 152,* 398-403.
451. Dalgleish, T., Cameron, C. M., Power, M. J., & Bond, A. (1995). The use of an emotional priming paradigm with clinically anxious subjects. *Cognitive Therapy and Research, 19,* 69-89.
452. Deffenbacher, J. L., Oetting, E. R., Huff, M. E., & Thwaites, G. A. (1995). Fifteen-month follow-up of social skills and cognitive-relaxation approaches to general anger reduction. *Journal of Counseling Psychology, 42,* 400–405.
453. Diener, M. L., Goldstein, L. H., & Mangelsdorf, S. C. (1995). The role of prenatal expectations in parents' report of infant temperament. *Merrill-Palmer Quarterly, 41,* 172–190.
454. Doby, V. J., & Caplan, R. D. (1995). Organizational stress as threat to reputation: Effects on anxiety at work and at home. *Academy of Management Journal, 38,* 1105–1123.
455. Dvir, T., Eden, D., & Banjo, M. L. (1995). Self-fulfilling prophecy and gender: Can women be Pygmalion and Galatea? *Journal of Applied Psychology, 80,* 253-270.
456. Eckhardt, M. J., Stapleton, J. M. , Rawlings, R. R., Davis, E. Z., & Grodin, D. M. (1995). Neuropsychological functioning in detoxified alcoholics between 18 and 35 years of age. *American Journal of Psychiatry, 152,* 53-59.
457. Ehlers, A. (1995). A 1-year prospective study of panic attacks: Clinical course and factors associated with maintenance. *Journal of Abnormal Psychology, 104,* 164-172.
458. Ehlers, A., & Breuer, P. (1995). Selective attention to physical threat in subjects with panic attacks and specific phobias. *Journal of Anxiety Disorders, 9,* 11-31.
459. Everson, S. A., Matthews, K. A., Guzick, D. S., Wing, R. R., & Kuller, L. H. (1995). Effects of surgical menopause on psychological characteristics and lipid levels: The healthy women study. *Health Psychology, 14,* 435–443.
460. Farmer, R. F., & Nelson-Gray, R. O. (1995). Anxiety, impulsivity, and the anxious-fearful and erratic-dramatic personality disorders. *Journal of Research in Personality, 29,* 189-207.
461. Fergusson, L. C., Bonshek, A. J., & Boudigues, J-M. (1995). Personality and health characteristics of Cambodian undergraduates: A case for student development. *Journal of Instructional Psychology, 22,* 308–319.
462. Feske, U., & Chambless, D. L. (1995). Cognitive behavioral versus exposure only treatment for social phobia: A meta-analysis. *Behavior Therapy, 26,* 695–720.
463. Foa, E. B., Riggs, D. S., & Gershuny, B. S. (1995). Arousal, numbing, and intrusion: Symptom structure of PTSD following assault. *American Journal of Psychiatry, 152,* 116-120.
464. Foa, E. B., Riggs, D. S., Massle, E. D., & Yacczower, M. (1995). The impact of fear activation and anger on the efficacy of exposure treatment for posttraumatic stress disorder. *Behavior Therapy, 26,* 487–499.
465. Frank, N. C., Blount, R. L., Smith, A. J., Manimala, M. R., & Martin, J. K. (1995). Parent and staff behavior, previous child medical experience, and maternal anxiety as they relate to child procedural distress and coping. *Journal of Pediatric Psychology, 20,* 277–289.
466. Frasure-Smith, N., Lespérance, F., & Talajic, M. (1995). The impact of negative emotions on prognosis following myocardial infarction: Is it more than depression? *Health Psychology, 14,* 388–398.
467. Gershuny, B. S., & Sher, K. J. (1995). Compulsive checking and anxiety in a nonclinical sample: Differences in cognition, behavior, personality and affect. *Journal of Psychopathology and Behavioral Assessment, 17,* 19–38.
468. Glass, C. R., Arnkoff, D. B., Wood, H., Meyerhoff, J. L., Smith, H. R., Oleshansky, M. A., & Hedges, S. M. (1995). Cognition, anxiety, and performance on a career-related oral examination. *Journal of Counseling Psychology, 42,* 47-54.
469. Glass, C. R., Arnkoff, D. B., Wood, H., Meyerhoff, T. L., Smith, H. R., Oleshansky, M. A., & Hedges, S. M. (1995). Cognition, anxiety, and performance on a career-related oral examination. *Journal of Counseling Psychology, 42,* 47-54.
470. Golombok, S., Cook, R., Bish, A., & Murray, C. (1995). Families created by the new reproductive technologies: Quality of parenting and social and emotional development of the children. *Child Development, 66,* 285-298.
471. Good, M. (1995). A comparison of the effects of jaw relaxation and music on postoperative pain. *Nursing Research, 44,* 52–57.
472. Green, M. W., & Rogers, P. J. (1995). Impaired cognitive functioning during spontaneous dieting. *Psychological Medicine, 25,* 1003–1010.
473. Griffin, K. W., Friend, R., & Wadhwa, N. K. (1995). Measuring disease severity in patients with end-stage renal disease: Validity of the Craven et al. ESRD Severity Index. *Psychological Medicine, 25,* 189-193.
474. Gudjonsson, G. H., Rutter, S. C., & Clare, I. C. H. (1995). The relationship between suggestibility and anxiety among suspects detained at police stations. *Psychological Medicine, 25,* 875–878.
475. Halberstadt, A. G., Cassidy, J., Stifter, C. A., Parke, R. D., & Fox, N. A. (1995). Self-expressiveness within the family context: Psychometric support for a new measure. *Psychological Assessment, 7,* 93-103.
476. Halvari, H., & Gjesme, T. (1995). Trait and anxiety before and after competitive performance. *Perceptual and Motor Skills, 81,* 1059–1074.
477. Handlin, D., & Levin, R. (1995). Dreams of traditional and nontraditional women: Are dream aggression and hostility related to higher levels of waking well-being? *Sex Roles, 33,* 515–530.
478. Heller, W., Etienne, M. A., & Miller, G. A. (1995). Patterns of perceptual asymmetry in depression and anxiety: implications for neuropsychological models of emotion and psychopathology. *Journal of Abnormal Psychology, 104,* 327-333.
479. Hoffart, A. (1995). Psychoanalytical personality types and agoraphobia. *The Journal of Nervous and Mental Disease, 183,* 139-144.
480. Hofmann, S. G., Newman, M. G., Becker, E., Taylor, C. B., & Roth, W. T. (1995). Social phobia with and without avoidant personality disorder: Preliminary behavior therapy outcome findings. *Journal of Anxiety Disorders, 9,* 427–438.
481. Hofmann, S. G., Newman, M. G. , Ehlers, A., & Roth, W. T. (1995). Psychophysiological differences between subgroups of social phobia. *Journal of Abnormal Psychology, 104,* 224-231.
482. Hyde, J. S., Klein, M. H., Essex, M. J., & Clark, R. (1995). Maternity leave and women's mental health. *Psychology of Women Quarterly, 19,* 257-285.
483. Jussim, L., Yen, H., & Aiello, J. R. (1995). Self-consistency, self-enhancement, and accuracy in reactions to feedback. *Journal of Experimental Social Psychology, 31,* 322–356.
484. Kagan, N. I., Kagan, (K). H., & Watson, M. G. (1995). Stress reduction in the workplace: The effectiveness of psychoeducational programs. *Journal of Counseling Psychology, 42,* 71-78.
485. Kalichman, S. C., Sikkema, K. J., & Somlai, A. (1995). Assessing persons with human immunodeficiency virus (HIV) infection using the Beck Depression Inventory: Disease processes and other potential confounds. *Journal of Personality Assessment, 64,* 86-100.
486. Kaplan, D. M., Smith, T., & Coons, J. (1995). A validity study of the Subjective Unit of Discomfort (SUD) score. *Measurement and Evaluation in Counseling and Development, 27,* 195-199.
487. Kavussanu, M., & McAuley, E. (1995). Exercise and optimism: Are highly active individuals more optimistic. *Journal of Sport and Exercise Psychology, 17,* 246–258.
488. Kennedy, P., Lowe, R., Grey, N., & Short, E. (1995). Traumatic spinal cord injury and psychological impact: A cross-sectional analysis of coping strategies. *British Journal of Clinical Psychology, 34,* 627–639.
489. Levin, R., & Masling, J. (1995). Relations of oral imagery to thought disorder in subjects with frequent nightmares. *Perceptual and Motor Skills, 80,* 1115–1120.
490. Lindström, T. C. (1995). Experiencing the presence of the dead: Discrepencies in "the sensing experience" and their psychological concomitants. *Omega, 31,* 11–21.
491. Mancini, C., Van Ameringen, M., & Macmillan, H. (1995). Relationship of childhood sexual and physical abuse to anxiety disorders. *The Journal of Nervous and Mental Disease, 183,* 309–314.
492. McCabe, S. B., & Gotlib, I. H. (1995). Selective attention and clinical depression: Performance on a deployment-of-attention task. *Journal of Abnormal Psychology, 104,* 241-245.
493. McWhirter, B. T., Okey, J., Roth, S., & Herlache, L. (1995). Evaluation of a college level stress management course. *College Student Journal, 29,* 227–233.
494. Meir, E. I., Melamed, S., & Dinur, C. (1995). The benefits of congruence. *Career Development Quarterly, 43,* 257-266.
495. Melnyk, B. M. (1995). Coping with unplanned childhood hospitalization: The mediating functions of parental beliefs. *Journal of Pediatric Psychology, 20,* 299–312.

496. Mocellin, J. S. P. (1995). Levels of anxiety aboard two expeditionary ships. *The Journal of General Psychology, 122,* 317–324.

497. Munday, R., Windham, R., Cartwright, C., & Bodenhamer, R. (1995). Stress management training for preservice secondary teachers. *Journal of Instructional Psychology, 22,* 141–145.

498. Novy, D. M., Nelson, D. V., Smith, K. G., Rogers, P. A., & Rowzee, R. D. (1995). Psychometric comparability of the English- and Spanish-language versions of the State-Trait Anxiety Inventory. *Hispanic Journal of Behavior Sciences, 17,* 209–224.

499. Orr, E., Thein, R. D., & Aronson, E. (1995). Orthopedic disability, conformity, and social support. *The Journal of Psychology, 129,* 203–219.

500. Orr, S. P., Lasko, N. B., Shalev, A. Y., & Pitman, R. K. (1995). Physiologic responses to loud tones in Vietnam veterans with posttraumatic stress disorder. *Journal of Abnormal Psychology, 104,* 75-82.

501. Osato, E., Ogawa, N., & Takaoka, N. (1995). Relations among heart rate, immediate memory, and time estimation under two different instructions. *Perceptual and Motor Skills, 80,* 831–842.

502. Palace, E. M. (1995). Modification of dysfunctional patterns of sexual response through autonomic arousal and false physiological feedback. *Journal of Consulting and Clinical Psychology, 63,* 604–615.

503. Park, S., Holzman, P. S., & Lenzenweger, M. F. (1995). Individual differences in spatial working memory in relation to schizotypy. *Journal of Abnormal Psychology, 104,* 355-363.

504. Payne, A., & Blanchard, E. B. (1995). A controlled comparison of cognitive therapy and self-help support groups in the treatment of irritable bowel syndrome. *Journal of Consulting and Clinical Psychology, 63,* 779–786.

505. Perna, G., Barbini, B., Cocchi, S., Bertani, A., & Gasperini, M. (1995). 35% CO2 challenge in panic and mood disorders. *Journal of Affective Disorders, 33,* 189-194.

506. Perry, O. E., III, & Daugherty, T. K. (1995). Trait anxiety of college males who witnessed murder or injury as a child. *College Student Journal, 29,* 243–245.

507. Pickens, J., Field, T., Prodromidis, M., Pelaez-Nogueras, M., & Hossain, Z. (1995). Posttraumatic stress, depression, and social support among college students after Hurricane Andrew. *Journal of College Student Development, 36,* 152-161.

508. Reed, M. A., & Derryberry, D. (1995). Temperament and response processing: Facilitatory and inhibitory consequences of positive and negative motivational states. *Journal of Research in Personality, 29,* 59-84.

509. Richards, A., French, C. C., & Dowd, R. (1995). Hemisphere asymmetry and the processing of emotional words in anxiety. *Neuropsychologia, 33,* 835–841.

510. Robinson, L. C., Garthoeffner, J. L., & Henry, C. S. (1995). Family structure and interpersonal relationship quality in young adults. *Journal of Divorce and Remarriage, 23,* 23–43.

511. Robinson, M. D., Anastasio, G. D., Little, J. M., Sigmon, J. L., Jr., Menscer, D., Pettice, Y. J., & Norton, H. J. (1995). Ritalin™ for nicotine withdrawal: Nesbitt's paradox revisited. *Addictive Behaviors, 20,* 481–490.

512. Romach, M., Busto, U., Somer, G., Kaplan, H. L., & Sellers, E. (1995). Clinical aspects of chronic use of alprazolam and lorazepan. *American Journal of Psychiatry, 152,* 1161–1167.

513. Saam, R. H., Hodtke, K. H., & Hains, A. A. (1995). A cognitive reduction program for recently unemployed managers. *The Career Development Quarterly, 44,* 43–51.

514. Schiff, B. B., & Romp, S. A. (1995). Asymmetrical hemispheric activation and emotion: The effects of unilateral forced nostril breathing. *Brain and Cognition, 29,* 217–231.

515. Sharpe, M. J., Heppner, P. P., & Dixon, W. A. (1995). Gender role conflict, instrumentality, expressiveness, and well-being in adult men. *Sex Roles, 33,* 1–18.

516. Shek, D. T. L. (1995). Chinese adolescents' perceptions of parenting styles of fathers and mothers. *The Journal of Genetic Psychology, 156,* 175–190.

517. Smith, W. P., Comptn, W. C., & West, W. B. (1995). Meditation as an adjunct to a happiness enhancement program. *Journal of Clinical Psychology, 51,* 269-273.

518. Stein, M. B., Millar, T. W., Larsen, D. K., & Kryger, M. H. (1995). Irregular breathing during sleep in patients with panic disorder. *American Journal of Psychiatry, 152,* 1168–1173.

519. Stewart, S. H., & Zeitlin, S. B. (1995). Anxiety sensitivity and alcohol use motives. *Journal of Anxiety Disorders, 9,* 229-240.

520. Sullivan, M. J. L., Bishop, S. R., & Pivik, J. (1995). The Pain Catastrophizing Scale: Development and validation. *Psychological Assessment, 7,* 524–532.

521. Sutker, P. B., Davis, J. M., Uddo, M., & Ditta, S. R. (1995). Assessment of psychological distress in Persian Gulf troops: Ethnicity and gender comparisons. *Journal of Personality Assessment, 64,* 415-427.

522. Tasker, F., & Golombok, S. (1995). Adults raised as children in lesbian families. *American Journal of Orthopsychiatry, 65,* 203–215.

523. Taylor, D. N. (1995). Effects of a behavioral stress-management program on anxiety, mood, self-esteem, and T-cell count in HIV-positive men. *Psychological Reports, 76,* 451–457.

524. Tivis, L. J., & Parsons, O. A. (1995). An investigation of verbal spatial functioning in chronic alcoholics. *Assessment, 2,* 285–292.

525. Totten, G. L., & France, C. R. (1995). Physiological and subjective anxiety responses to caffeine and stress in nonclinical panic. *Journal of Anxiety Disorders, 9,* 473–488.

526. Trent, N. H., III, Templer, D. I., Gandolfo, R., Corgiat, M., & Trent, A. P. (1995). Multivariate investigation of anxiety in a psychiatric population. *Journal of Clinical Psychology, 51,* 196-201.

527. Tsuang, D., Cowley, D., Ries, R., Dunner, D. L., & Roy-Burne, P. P. (1995). The effects of substance use disorder on the clinical presentation of anxiety and depression in an outpatient psychiatric clinic. *Journal of Clinical Psychiatry, 56,* 549–555.

528. Valliant, P. M., Maksymchuk, L. L., & Antonowicz, D. (1995). Attitudes and personality traits of female adult victims of childhood abuse: A comparison of university students and incarcerated women. *Social Behavior and Personality, 23,* 205–216.

529. Van Dulmen, A. M., Fennis, J. F. M., Mokkink, H. G. A., Van Der Velden, H. G. M., & Bleijenberg, G. (1995). Doctor-dependent changes in complaint-related cognitions and anxiety during medical consultations in functional abdominal complaints. *Psychological Medicine, 25,* 1011–1018.

530. Verburg, K., Griez, E., Meijer, J., & Pols, H. (1995). Discrimination between panic disorder and generalized anxiety disorder by 35% carbon dioxide challenge. *American Journal of Psychiatry, 152,* 1081-1083.

531. Vrana, S. R., Roodman, A. & Beckham, J. C. (1995). Selective processing of trauma-relevant words in posttraumatic stress disorder. *Journal of Anxiety Disorders, 9,* 515–530.

532. Weekes, J. R., Morison, S. J., Millson, W. A., & Fettig, D. M. (1995). A comparison of native, metis, and caucasian offender profiles on the MCMI. *Canadian Journal of Behavioural Science, 27,* 187–1908.

533. Wilson, S. A., Becker, L. A., & Tinker, R. H. (1995). Eye movement desensitization and reprocessing (EMDR) treatment for psychologically traumatized individuals. *Journal of Consulting and Clinical Psychology, 63,* 923–937.

534. Zeitlin, S. B., & Polivy, J. (1995). Coprophagia as a manifestation of obsessive-compulsive disorder: A case report. *Journal of Behavior Therapy and Experimental Psychiatry, 26,* 57–63.

535. Agras, W. S. Berkowitz, R. I., Arnow, B. A., Telch, C. F., Marnell, M., Henderson, J., Morris, Y., & Wilfley, D. E. (1996). Maintance following a very-low-calorie diet. *Journal of Consulting and Clinical Psychology, 64,* 610–613.

536. Ballard, J. C. (1996). Computerized assessment of sustained attention: Interactive effects of task demand, noise, and anxiety. *Journal of Clinical and Experimental Neuropsychology, 18,* 846–882.

537. Beatty, W. W., Hames, K. A., Blanco, C. R., Nixon, S. J., & Tivis, L. J. (1996). Visuospatial perception, construction and memory in alcoholism. *Journal of Studies on Alcohol, 57,* 136–143.

538. Bish, A., Golombok, S., Hallstrom, C., & Fawcett, S. (1996). The role of coping strategies in protecting individuals against long-term tranquillizer use. *British Journal of Medical Psychology, 69,* 101–115.

539. Blazina, C., & Watkins, C. E., Jr. (1996). Masculine gender role conflict: Effects on college men's psychological well-being, chemical substance usage, and attitudes toward help-seeking. *Journal of Counseling Psychology, 43,* 461–465.

540. Bleau, R. (1996). Dietary restraint and anxiety in adolescent girls. *British Journal of Clinical Psychology, 35,* 573–583.

541. Bowman, B. J. (1996). Cross-cultural validation of Antonovsky's Sense of Coherence Scale. *Journal of Clinical Psychology, 52,* 547–549.

542. Catanzaro, S. J. (1996). Negative mood regulation expectancies, emotional distress, and examination performance. *Personality and Social Psychology Bulletin, 22,* 1023–1029.

543. Clark, M. E. (1996). MMPI-2 negative treatment indicators content and content component scales: Clinical correlates and outcome prediction for men with chronic pain. *Psychological Assessment, 8,* 32–38.

544. Coleman, M. J., Levy, D. L., Lenzenweger, M. F & Holzman, P. S. (1996). Thought disorder, perceptual aberrations, and schizotypy. *Journal of Abnormal Psychology, 105,* 469–473.

545. Corr, P. J., & Gray, J. A. (1996). Structure and validity of the attributional style questionnaire: A cross-sample comparison. *The Journal of Psychology, 130,* 645–657.

546. Dahlquist, L. M., Czyzewski, D. I., & Jones, C. L. (1996). Parents of children with cancer: A longitudinal study of emotional distress, coping style, and marital adjustment two and twenty months after diagnosis. *Journal of Pediatric Psychology, 21,* 541–554.

547. Davey, G. C. L., Tallis, F., & Capuzzo, N. (1996). Beliefs about the consequences of worrying. *Cognitive Therapy and Research, 20,* 499–520.

548. Davis, J. M., Adams, H. E., Uddo, M., Vasterling, J. J., & Sutker, P. B. (1996). Physiological arousal and attention in veterans with posttraumatic stress disorder. *Journal of Psychopathology and Behavioral Assessment, 18,* 1–20.

549. de Jong, G. M., Timmerman, I. G. H., & Emmelkamp, P. M. G. (1996). The survey of recent life experiences: A psychometric evaluation. *Journal of Behavioral Medicine, 19,* 529–542.

550. Deffenbacher, J. L., Lynch, R. S., Oetting, E. R., & Kemper, C. C. (1996). Anger reduction in early adolescents. *Journal of Counseling Psychology, 43,* 149–157.

551. Deffenbacher, J. L., Oetting, E. R., Thwaites, G. A., Lynch, R. S., Baker, D. A., Stark, R. S., Tacker, S., & Elswerth-Cox, L. (1996). State-trait anger theory and the utility of the Trait Anger Scale. *Journal of Counseling Psychology, 43,* 131–148.

552. Fastenau, P. S., Denburg, N. L., & Abeles, N. (1996). Age differences in retrieval: Further support for the resource-reduction hypothesis. *Psychology and Aging, 11,* 140–146.

553. Fisher, B. L., Allen, R., & Kose, G. (1996). The relationship between anxiety and problem-solving skills in children with and without learning disabilities. *Journal of Learning Disabilities, 29,* 439–446.

554. Fonagy, P., Leigh, T., Steele, M., Steele, H., Kennedy, R., Mattoon, A., Target, M., & Gerter, A. (1996). The relation of attachment status, psychiatric classification, and response to psychotherapy. *Journal of Consulting and Clinical Psychology, 64,* 22–31.

555. French, C. C., Richards, A., & Scholfield, E. J. (1996). Hypomania, anxiety and the emotional Stroop. *British Journal of Clinical Psychology, 35,* 617–626.

556. Gullone, E., King, N. J., & Cummins, R. A. (1996). Fears of youth with mental retardation: Psychometric evaluation of the Fear Survey Schedule for Children-II (FSSC-II). *Research in Developmental Disabilities, 17,* 269–284.

557. Hardy, L., Mullen, R., & Jones, G. (1996). Knowledge and conscious control of motor actions under stress. *British Journal of Psychology, 87,* 621–636.

558. Harrigan, J. A., Harrigan, K. M., Sale, B. A., & Rosenthal, R. (1996). Detecting anxiety and defensiveness from visual and auditory cues. *Journal of Personality, 64,* 675–709.

559. Hill, C. A. (1996). Interpersonal and dispositional influences on problem-related interactions. *Journal of Research in Personality, 30,* 1–22.

560. Hutri, M. (1996). When careers reach a dead end: Identification of occupational crisis states. *The Journal of Psychology, 130,* 383–399.

561. Hyer, L., Boyd, S., Scurfield, R., Smith, D., & Burke, J. (1996). Effects of outward bound experience as an adjunct to inpatient PTSD treatment of war veterans. *Journal of Clinical Psychology, 52,* 263–278.

562. Jacob, R. G., Furman, J. M., Durrant, J. D., & Turner, S. M. (1996). Panic, agoraphobia, and vestibular dysfunction. *American Journal of Psychiatry, 153,* 503–512.

563. Johnson, D. P., & Slaney, R. B. (1996). Perfectionism: Scale development and a study of perfectionistic clients in counseling. *Journal of College Student Development, 37,* 29–41.

564. Joyce, A. S., & Piper, W. E. (1996). Interpretive work in short-term individual psychotherapy: An analysis using hierarchical linear modeling. *Journal of Consulting and Clinical Psychology, 64,* 505–512.

565. Kopper, B. A., & Epperson, D. L. (1996). The experience and expression of anger: Relationships with gender, gender role socialization, depression, and mental health functioning. *Journal of Counseling Psychology, 43,* 158–165.

566. Kroeze, S., van den Hout, M., Haenen, M-A., & Schmidt, A. (1996). Symptom reporting and interoceptive attention in panic patients. *Perceptual and Motor Skills, 82,* 1019–1026.

567. Kumari, V. (1996). Eysenck Personality Inventory: Impulsivity/neuroticism and social desirability response set. *Psychological Reports, 78,* 35–40.

568. Kushner, M. G., Mackenzie, T. B., Fiszdon, J., Valentiner, D. P., Foa, E., Anderson, N., & Wangensteen, D. (1996). The effects of alcohol consumption on laboratory-induced panic and state anxiety. *Archives of General Psychiatry, 53,* 264–270.

569. LaMontagne, L. L., Hepworth, J. T., Johnson, B. D., & Cohen, F. (1996). Children's preoperative coping and its effects on postoperative anxiety and return to normal activity. *Nursing Research, 45,* 141–147.

570. Lee, P. W. H., Leung, P. W. L., Fung, A. S. M., Low, L. C. K., Tsang, M. C., & Leung, W. C. (1996). An episode of syncope attacks in adolescent schoolgirls: Investigations, intervention and outcome. *British Journal of Medical Psychology, 69,* 247–257.

571. Malgady, R. G., Rogler, L. H., & Cortés, D. E. (1996). Cultural expression of psychiatric symptoms: Idioms of anger among Puerto Ricans. *Psychological Assessment, 8,* 265–268.

572. Mancini, C., & Van Ameringen, M. (1996). Paroxetine in social phobia. *Journal of Clinical Psychiatry, 57,* 519–522.

573. Mann, B. J., Sylvester, C. E., & Chen, R. (1996). Reliability and validity of the Retrospective Childhood and Current Adult Fear Survey (RCCAFS). *Journal of Anxiety Disorders, 10,* 59–72.

574. McDermott, P. A., Alterman, A. I., Brown, L., Zaballero, A., Snider, E. C., & McKay, J. R. (1996). Construct refinement and confirmation for the addiction severity index. *Psychological Assessment, 8,* 182–189.

575. McNally, R. J., Amir, N., & Lipke, H. J. (1996). Subliminal processing of threat cues in posttraumatic stress disorder. *Journal of Anxiety Disorders, 10,* 115–128.

576. Mednick, B. R., Hocevar, D., Baker, R. L., & Scholsinger, C. (1996). Personality and demographic characteristics of mothers and their ratings of child difficulties. *International Journal of Behavioral Development, 19,* 121–140.

577. Mednick, B. R., Hocevar, D., Schulsinger, C., & Baker, R. L. (1996). Personality and demographic characteristics of mothers and their ratings of their 3- to 10-year-old children's temperament. *Merrill-Palmer Quarterly, 42,* 397–417.

578. Nunn, K. P., Lewin, T. J., Walton, J. M., & Carr, V. J. (1996). The construction and characteristics of an instrument to measure personal hopefulness. *Psychological Medicine, 26,* 531–545.

579. O'Neil, H. F., & Abedi, J. (1996). Reliability and validity of a state metacognitive inventory: Potential for alternative assessment. *Journal of Educational Research, 89,* 234–245.

580. Orsillo, S. M., Weathers, F. W., Litz, B. T., Steinberg, H. R., Huska, J. A., & Keane, T. M. (1996). Current and lifetime psychiatric disorders among veterans with war zone-related posttraumatic stress disorder. *Journal of Nervous and Mental Disease, 184,* 307–313.

581. Patrick, C. J., Berthot, B. D., & Moore, J. D. (1996). Diazepam blocks fear-potentiated startle in humans. *Journal of Abnormal Psychology, 105,* 89–96.

582. Pedersen, F. A., Huffman, L. C., del Carmen, R., & Bryan, Y. E. (1996). Prenatal maternal reactivity to infant cries predicts postnatal perceptions of infant temperament and marriage appraisal. *Child Development, 67,* 2541–2552.

583. Pols, H. J., Hauzer, R. C., Meijer, J. A., Verburg, K., & Griez, E. J. (1996). Fluvoxamine attenuates panic induced by 35% CO2 challenge. *Journal of Clinical Psychiatry, 57,* 539–542.

584. Power, M. J., Cameron, C. M., & Dalgleish, T. (1996). Emotional priming in clinically depressed subjects. *Journal of Affective Disorders, 38,* 1–11.

585. Radcliffe, J., Bennett, D., Kazak, A. E., Foley, B., & Phillips, P. C. (1996). Adjustment in childhood brain tumor survival: Child, mother, and teacher report. *Journal of Pediatric Psychology, 21,* 529–539.

586. Reed, M. K., McLeod, S., Randall, Y., & Waller, B. (1996). Depressive symptoms in African-American women. *Journal of Multicultural Counseling and Development, 24,* 6–14.

587. Reed, M. K., Walker, B., Williams, G., McLeod, S., & Jones, S. (1996). MMPI-2 patterns in African-American females. *Journal of Clinical Psychology, 52,* 437–441.

588. Richards, A., French, C. C., & Randall, F. (1996). Anxiety and the use of strategies in the performance of sentence-picture verification task. *Journal of Abnormal Psychology, 105,* 132–136.

589. Robinson, J. R., Rankin, J. L., & Drotar, D. (1996). Quality of attachment as a predictor of maternal visitation to young hospitalized children. *Journal of Pediatric Psychology, 21,* 401–417.

590. Ross, M. J., & Berger, R. S. (1996). Effects of stress inoculation training on athletes' postsurgical pain and rehabilitation after orthopedic injury. *Journal of Consulting and Clinical Psychology, 64,* 406–410.

591. Roth, R. M., & Baribeau, j. (1996). Performance of subclinical compulsive checkers on putative tests of frontal and temporal lobe memory functions. *Journal of Nervous and Mental Disease, 184,* 411–416.

592. Sanna, L. J. (1996). Defensive pessimism, optimision, and simulating alternatives: Some ups and downs of prefactual and counterfactual thinking. *Journal of Personality and Social Psychology, 71,* 1020–1036.

593. Shalev, A., Peri, T., Canetti, L., & Schreiber, S. (1996). Predictors of PTSD in injured trauma survivors: A prospective study. *American Journal of Psychiatry, 153,* 219–225.

594. Sherman, M. D., & Thelen, M. H. (1996). Fear of intimacy scale: Validation and extension with adolescents. *Journal of Social and Personal Relationships, 13,* 507–521.

595. Silvestri, L., Dantonio, M., & Eason, S. (1996). The effects of a self development program and relaxation/imagery training on the anxiety levels of at-risk fourth grade students. *Journal of Instructional Psychology, 23,* 167–173.

596. Stanley, M. A., Beck, J. G., & Glassco, J. D. (1996). Treatment of generalized anxiety disorder in older adults: A preliminary comparison of cognitive-behavioral and supportive approaches. *Behavior Therapy, 27,* 565–581.

597. Stanley, M. A., Beck, J. G., Averill, P. M., Baldwin, L. E., Deagle, D. A., & Stadler, J. G. (1996). Patterns of change during cognitive behavioral treatment for panic disorder. *Journal of Nervous and Mental Disease, 184,* 567–572.

598. Timmons, P. L., Oehlet, M. E., Sumerall, S. W., Timmons, C. W., & Borgers, S. B. (1996). Stress inoculation training for maladaptive anger: Comparison of group counseling versus computer guidance. *Computers in Human Behavior, 12,* 51–64.

599. Troisi, A., Delle Chiaie, R., Russo, F., Russo, M. A., Mosco, C., & Pasini, A. (1996). Nonverbal behavior and alexithymic traits in normal subjects: Individual differences in encoding emotions. *Journal of Nervous and Mental Disease, 184,* 561–566.

600. Van Ameringen, M., Mancini, C., & Wilson, C. (1996). Buspirone augmentation of selective serotonin reuptake inhibitors (SSRIs) in social phobia. *Journal of Affective Disorders, 39,* 115–121.

601. Varni, J. W., & Setoguchi, Y. (1996). Perceived physical appearance and adjustment of adolescents with congenital/acquired limb deficiencies: A path-analytic model. *Journal of Clinical Child Psychology, 25,* 201–208.

602. Veltman, D. J., van Zijderveld, G., & van Dyck, R. (1996). Epinephrine infusions in panic disorder: A double-blind placebo-controlled study. *Journal of Affective Disorders, 39,* 133–140.

603. Waldstein, S. R., Polefrone, J. M., Fazzari, T. V., Manuck, S. B., Jennings, J. R., Ryan, C. M., Muldoon, M. F., & Shapiro, A. P. (1996). Hypertension and neuropsychological performance in men: Interactive effects of age. *Health Psychology, 15,* 102–109.

604. Watson, J. C. (1996). The relationship between vivid description, emotional arousal, and in-session resolution of problematic reactions. *Journal of Consulting and Clinical Psychology, 64,* 459–464.

605. Yuen, N., Andrade, N., Nahulu, L., Makini, G., McDermott, J. F., Danko, G., Johnson, R., & Waldron, J. (1996). The rate and characteristics of suicide attempters in the native Hawaiian adolescent population. *Suicide and Life-Threatening Behavior, 26,* 27–36.

606. Zeidner, M. (1996). How do high school and college students cope with test situations. *British Journal of Educational Psychology, 66,* 115–128.

607. Abdel-Khalek, A. M. (1997). Death, anxiety, and depression. *Omega, 35,* 219–229.

608. Ball, S., Robinson, A., Shekhar, A., & Walsh, K. (1997). Dissociative symptoms in panic disorder. *Journal of Nervous and Mental Disease, 185,* 755–760.

609. Barakat, L. P., Kazak, A. E., Meadows, A. T., Casey, R., Meeske, K., & Stuber, M. L. (1997). Families surviving childhood cancer: A comparison of posttraumatic stress symptoms with families of healthy children. *Journal of Pediatric Psychology, 22,* 843–859.

610. Beck, J. G., & Stanley, M. A. (1997). Anxiety disorders in the elderly: The emerging role of behavior therapy. *Behavior Therapy, 28,* 83–100.

611. Bjorck, J. P., Lee, Y. S., & Cohen, L. H. (1997). Control beliefs and faith as stress moderators for Korean American versus Caucasian American Protestants. *American Journal of Community Psychology, 25,* 61–72.

612. Bowman, D., Scogin, F., Floyd, M., Patton, E., & Gist, L. (1997). Efficacy of self-examination therapy in the treatment of generalized anxiety disorder. *Journal of Counseling Psychology, 44,* 267–273.

613. Braaten, E. B., & Handelsman, M. M. (1997). Client preferences for informed consent information. *Ethics & Behavior 7,* 311–328.

614. Brock, K. J., Mintz, L. B., & Good, G. E. (1997). Differences among sexually abused and nonabused women from functional and dysfunctional families. *Journal of Counseling Psychology, 44,* 425–432.

615. Bunce, D. (1997). What factors are associated with the outcome of individual-focused worksite stress management interventions? *Journal of Occupational and Organizational Psychology, 70,* 1–17.

616. Cheng, C. (1997). Assessment of major life events for Hong Kong adolescents: The Chinese Adolescent Life Event Scale. *American Journal of Community Psychology, 25,* 17–33.

617. Christensen, A. J., Moran, P. J., Lawton, W. J., Stallman, D., & Voigts, A. L. (1997). Monitoring attentional style and medical regimen adherence in hemodialysis patients. *Health Psychology, 16,* 256–262.

618. Croyle, R. T., Smith, K. R., Botkin, J. R., Baty, G., & Nash, J. (1997). Psychological responses to BRACA 1 mutation testing. *Health Psychology, 16,* 63–72.

619. Durham, R. C., Allan, T., & Hackett, C. A. (1997). On predicting improvement and relapse in generalized anxiety disorder following psychotherapy. *British Journal of Clinical Psychology, 36,* 101–119.

620. Evers, A. W. M., Kraaimaat, F. W., Geenan, R., & Bijlsma, J. W. J. (1997). Determinants of psychological distress and its course in the first year after diagnosis in rheumatoid arthritis patients. *Journal of Behavioral Medicine, 20,* 489–504.

621. Faravelli, C., Marinoni, M., Spiti, R., Ginanneschi, A., Serena, A., Fabbri, C., Dimatteo, C., Delmastio, M., & Inzitari, D. (1997). Abnormal brain hemodynamic responses during passive orthostatic challenge in panic disorder. *American Journal of Psychiatry, 154,* 378–383.

622. Fastenau, P. S., Denburg, N. L., & Domitrovic, L. A. (1997). Intentional and incidental memory: Order effects in clinical testing. *Professional Psychology: Research and Practice, 28,* 32–35.

623. Ferguson, K. S., & Dacey, C. M. (1997). Anxiety, depression, and dissociation in women health care providers reporting a history of childhood psychological abuse. *Child Abuse & Neglect, 21,* 941–952.

624. Fiset, L., LeRoux, B., Rothen, M., Prall, C., Zhu, C., & Ramsay, D. S. (1997). Pain control in recovering alcoholics: Effects of local anesthesia. *Journal of Studies on Alcohol, 58,* 291–296.

625. Foster, Y. A. (1997). Brief Aikido training versus karate and golf training and university students' scores on self-esteem, anxiety, and depression of anger. *Perceptual and Motor Skills, 84,* 609–610.

626. George, D. T., Benkelfat, C., Rawlings, R. R., Eckardt, M. J., Phillips, M. J., Nutt, D. J., Wynne, D., Murphy, D. L., & Linnoila, M. (1997). Behavioral and neuroendocrine responses to m-chlorophenylpiperazine in subtypes of alcoholics and in healthy comparison subjects. *American Journal of Psychiatry, 154,* 81–87.

627. Greenfield, S., & Thelen, M. (1997). Validation of the Fear of Intimacy Scale with a lesbian and gay male population. *Journal of Social and Personal Relationships, 14,* 707–716.

628. Gump, B. B., & Kulik, J. A. (1997). Stress, affiliation, and emotional contagion. *Journal of Personality and Social Psychology, 72,* 305–319.

629. Hains, A. A., Davies, W. H., Behrens, D., & Biller, J. A. (1997). Cognitive behavioral interventions for adolescents with cystic fibrosis. *Journal of Pediatric Psychology, 22,* 669–687.

630. Hart, D., Field, N. P., Garfinkle, J. R., & Singer, J. L. (1997). Representations of self and other: A semantic space model. *Journal of Personality, 65,* 77–105.

631. Hatzitaskos, P. K., Soldatos, C. R., Sakkas, P. N., & Stefanis, C. N. (1997). Discriminating borderline from antisocial personality disorder in male patients based on psychopathology patterns and type of hostility. *Journal of Nervous and Mental Disease, 185,* 442–446.

632. Herschbach, P., Duran, G., Waadts, S., Zettler, A., Amm, C., & Marten-Mittage, B. (1997). Psychometric properties of the Questionnaire on Stress in Patients with Diabetes—Revised (QSD-R). *Health Psychology, 16,* 171–174.

633. Hittner, J. B. (1997). A preliminary analysis of the perceived risks of misusing multiple substances, trait anxeity, and approval motivation. *The Journal of Psychology, 131,* 501–511.

634. Hoffart, A. (1997). Interpersonal problems among patients suffering from panic disorder with agoraphobia before and after treatment. *British Journal of Medical Psychology, 70,* 149–157.

635. Johnston, W. M., & Davey, G. C. L. (1997). The psychological impact of negative TV news bulletins: The catastrophizing of personal worries. *British Journal of Psychology, 88,* 85–91.

636. Joseph, S., Dalgleish, T., Williams, R., Yule, W., Thrasher, S., & Hodgkinson, P. (1997). Attitudes towards emotional expression and post-traumatic stress in survivors of the Herald of Free Enterprise disaster. *British Journal of Clinical Psychology, 36,* 133–138.

637. Kassel, J. D., & Shiffman, S. (1997). Attentional mediation of cigarette smoking's effect on anxiety. *Health Psychology, 16,* 359–368.

638. Kassinove, H., Sukhodolsky, D. G., Eckhardt, C. I., & Tsytsarev, S. V. (1997). Development of a Russian State-Trait Anger Expression Inventory. *Journal of Clinical Psychology, 53,* 543–557.

639. Kazak, A. E., & Barakat, L. P. (1997). Brief report: Parenting stress and quality of life during treatment for childhood leukemia predicts child and parent adjustment after treatment ends. *Journal of Pediatric Psychology, 22,* 749–758.

640. Kochanska, G., Clark, L. A., & Goldman, M. S. (1997). Implications of mother's personality for their parenting and their young children's developmental outcomes. *Journal of Personality, 65,* 387–420.

641. Laughrea, K., Bélanger, C., & McDuff, J. W. et P. (1997). L'Étude de la colère au sein des relations conjugales. *International Journal of Psychology, 32,* 155–167.

642. Marteau, T. M., Dundas, R., & Axworthy, D. (1997). Long-term cognitive and emotional impact of genetic testing for carriers of cystic fibrosis: The effects of test result and gender. *Health Psychology, 16,* 51–62.

643. McCarthy, C. J., Liu, H. T., Ghormley, M. R., Brack, G., & Brack, C. J. (1997). The relationship of beliefs about mood to coping resource effectiveness. *Journal of College Student Development, 38,* 157–165.

644. Middleton, W., Raphael, B., Burnett, P., & Martinek, N. (1997). Psychological distress and bereavement. *Journal of Nervous and Mental Disease, 185,* 447–453.

645. Narayan, R., Shams, G. K., Jain, R., & Gupta, B. S. (1997). Personality characteristics of persons addicted to heroin. *The Journal of Psychology, 131,* 125–127.

646. Negy, C., Woods, D. J., & Carlson, R. (1997). The relationship between female inmates' coping and adjustment in a minimum-security prison. *Criminal Justice and Behavior, 24,* 224–233.

647. Nouwen, A., Gingas, J., Talbot, F., & Bouchard, S. (1997). The development of an empirical psychosocial taxonomy for patients with diabetes. *Health Psychology, 16,* 263–271.

648. Osman, A., Kopper, B. A., Barrios, F. X., Osman, J. R., & Wade, T. (1997). The Beck Anxiety Inventory: Reexamination of factor structure and psychometric properties. *Journal of Clinical Psychology, 53,* 7–14.

649. Patton, D., Barnes, G. E., & Murray, R. P. (1997). A personality typology of smokers. *Addictive Behaviors, 22,* 269–273.

650. Richardson, F. J., Jr., & Weinfurt, K. P. (1997). Death education: A comparison of two programs for mothers of young children. *Omega, 34,* 149–162.

651. Rodriguez, C. M., & Green, A. J. (1997). Parenting stress and anger expression as predictors of child abuse potential. *Child Abuse & Neglect, 21,* 367–377.

652. Roos, L. L., Wise, S. L., & Plake, B. S. (1997). The role of item feedback in self-adapted testing. *Educational and Psychological Measurement, 57,* 85–98.

653. Sapp, M., Farrell, W. C., Johnson, J. H., & Ioannidis, G. (1997). Utilizing the PK scale of the MMPI-2 to detect posttraumatic stress disorder in college students. *Journal of Clinical Psychology, 53,* 841–846.

654. Schafer, J., & Fals-Stewart, W. (1997). Spousal violence and cognitive functioning among men recovering from multiple substance abuse. *Addictive Behaviors, 22,* 127–130.

655. Schippers, G. M., DeBoer, M., & van der Staak, C. P. F. (1997). Effects of alcohol and expectancy on self-disclosure and anxiety in male and female social drinkers. *Addictive Behaviors, 22,* 305–314.

656. Schmidt-Traub, S., & Bamler, K. (1997). The psychoimmunological association of panic disorder and allergic reaction. *British Journal of Clinical Psychology, 36,* 51–62.

657. Sigmon, S. T., Rohan, K. J., Dorhofer, D., Hotovy, L. A., Trask, P. C., & Boulard, N. (1997). Effects of consent form information on self-disclosure. *Ethics & Behavior, 7,* 299–310.

658. Thorpe, S. J., & Salkovskis, P. M. (1997). The effects of one-session treatment for spider phobia on attentional bias and beliefs. *British Journal of Clinical Psychology, 36,* 225–241.

659. Tyc, V. L., Mulhern, R. K., Barclay, D. R., Smith, B. F., & Bieberich, A. A. (1997). Variables associated with anticipatory nausea and vomiting in pediatric cancer patients receiving ondansetron antiemetic therapy. *Journal of Pediatric Psychology, 22,* 45–58.

660. Van der Does, A. J. W., Van Dyck, R., & Spinhoven, P. (1997). Accurate heartbeat perception in panic disorder: Fact and artefact. *Journal of Affective Disorders, 43,* 121–130.

661. Vandell, D. L., Hyde, J. S., Plant, E. A., & Essex, M. J. (1997). Fathers and "others" as infant-care providers: Predictors of parent's emotional well-being and marital satisfaction. *Merrill-Palmer Quarterly, 43,* 361–385.

662. Vernon, S. W., Gritz, E. R., Peterson, S. K., Amos, C. I., Perz, C. A., Baile, W. F., & Lynch, P. M. (1997). Correlates of psychologic distress in colorectal cancer patients undergoing genetic testing for hereditary colon cancer. *Health Psychology, 16,* 73–86.

663. Williams, E. N., Judge, A. B., Hill, C. E., & Hoffman, M. A. (1997). Experiences of novice therapists in prepracticum: Trainees', clients', and supervisors' perceptions of therapists' personal reactions and management strategies. *Journal of Counseling Psychology, 44,* 390–399.

664. Williams, R. B., Barefoot, J. C., Blumenthal, J. A., Helms, M. J., Luecken, L., Pieper, C. F., Siegler, I. C., & Suarez, E. C. (1997). Psychosocial correlates of job strain in a sample of working women. *Archives of General Psychiatry, 54,* 543–548.

665. Bartholomew, J. B., & Linder, D. E. (1998). State anxiety following resistance exercise: The role of gender and exercise intensity. *Journal of Behavioral Medicine, 21,* 205–219.

666. Classen, C., Field, N. P., Atkinson, A., & Spiegel, D. (1998). Representations of self in women sexually abused in childhood. *Child Abuse and Neglect, 22,* 997–1004.

667. Dent, O. F., Tennant, C., Fairley, J. J., Sulway, M-R., Broe, G. A., Jorm, A. F., Creasey, H., & Allen, B. A. (1998). Prisoner of war experience: Effects on wives. *Journal of Nervous and Mental Disease, 186,* 231–237.

668. Haslett, T., Smyrnios, K. X., & Osborne, C. (1998). A cusp catastrophe analysis of anxiety levels in pre-university students. *Journal of Psychology, 132,* 5–24.

669. Haycock, L. A., McCarthy, P., & Skay, C. L. (1998). Procrastination in college students: The role of self-efficacy and anxiety. *Journal of Counseling & Development, 76,* 317–324.

670. Hoekstra-Weebers, J. E. H. M., Heuvel, F., Jaspers, J. P. C., Kamps, W. A., & Klip, E. C. (1998). An intervention program for parents of pediatric cancer patients: A randomized controlled trial. *Journal of Pediatric Psychology, 23,* 207–214.

671. Jaycox, L. H., Foa, E. B., & Morral, A. R. (1998). Influence of emotional engagement and habituation on exposure therapy to PISD. *Journal of Consulting and Clinical Psychology, 66,* 185–192.

672. McNeil, D. W., & Rainwater, A. J., III. (1998). Development of the Fear of Pain Questionnaire—III. *Journal of Behavioral Medicine, 21,* 389–410.
673. Moser, M., Lehofer, M., Hoehn-Saric, R., McLeod, D. R., Hildebrandt, G., Steinbrenner, B., Voica, M., Lebmann, P., & Zapotoczky, H-G. (1998). Increased heart rate in depressed subjects inspite of unchanged autonomic balance? *Journal of Affective Disorders, 48,* 115–124.
674. Nayak, M. B., & Milner, J. S. (1998). Neuropsychological functioning: Comparison of mothers at high- and low-risk for child physical abuse. *Child Abuse & Neglect, 22,* 687–703.
675. Pithers, W. D., Gray, A., Busconi, A., & Houchens, P. (1998). Caregivers of children with sexual behavior problems: Psychological and familial functioning. *Child Abuse & Neglect, 22,* 129–141.
676. Sears, H. A., & Armstrong, V. H. (1998). A prospective study of adolescents' self-reported depressive symptoms: Are risk behaviours a stronger predictor than anxiety symptoms? *Canadian Journal of Behavioural Science, 30,* 225–233.
677. Sharkansky, E. J., & Finn, P. R. (1998). Effects of outcome expectancies and disinhibition on ad lib alcohol consumption. *Journal of Studies on Alcohol, 59,* 198–206.
678. Steptoe, A., Kimbell, J., & Basford, P. (1998). Exercise and the experience and appraisal of daily stressors: A naturalistic study. *Journal of Behavioral Medicine, 21,* 363–374.
679. Symons, D. K. (1998). Post-partum employment patterns, family-based care arrangements, and the mother-infant relationship at age two. *Canadian Journal of Behavioural Science, 30,* 121–131.
680. Trenholm, P., Trent, J., & Comptom, W. C. (1998). Negative religious conflict as a predict of panic disorder. *Journal of Clinical Psychology, 54,* 59–65.

[2498]

State-Trait Anxiety Inventory for Children.

Purpose: Designed "as a research tool for the study of anxiety in elementary school children."
Population: Grades 4-6.
Publication Dates: 1970-1973.
Acronym: STAIC.
Scores, 2: State Anxiety, Trait Anxiety.
Administration: Group.
Price Data: Available from publisher.
Time: (20) minutes.
Comments: Downward extension of State-Trait Anxiety Inventory (2497); title on test is "How-I-Feel Questionnaire"; self-administering.
Authors: Charles D. Spielberger, C. Drew Edwards, Robert E. Lushene, Joseph Montuori, Denna Platzek.
Publisher: Mind Garden.
Cross References: See T4:2564 (58 references) and T3:2301 (15 references); for a review by Norman S. Endler, see 8:684 (19 references); see also T2:1392 (2 references).

TEST REFERENCES

1. Glyshaw, K., Cohen, L. H., & Towbes, L. C. (1989). Coping strategies and psychological distress: Prospective analyses of early and middle adolescents. *American Journal of Community Psychology, 17,* 607-624.
2. Kane, M. T., & Kendall, P. C. (1989). Anxiety disorders in children: A multiple-baseline evaluation of a cognitive-behavioral treatment. *Behavior Therapy, 20,* 499–508.
3. Wolfe, V. V., Gentile, C., & Wolfe, D. A. (1989). The impact of sexual abuse on children: A PTSD formulation. *Behavior Therapy, 20,* 215–228.
4. Cowen, E. L., Pedro-Carroll, J. L., & Alpert-Gillis, L. J. (1990). Relationships between support and adjustment among children of divorce. *Journal of Child Psychology and Psychiatry and Allied Disciplines, 31,* 727-735.
5. Hagopian, L. P., Weist, M. D., & Ollendick, T. H. (1990). Cognitive-behavioral therapy with an 11-year-old girl fearful of AIDS infection, other diseases, and poisoning: A case study. *Journal of Anxiety Disorders, 4,* 257-265.
6. Costantino, G., Malgady, R. G., Casullo, M. M., & Castillo, A. (1991). Cross-cultural standardization of TEMAS in three Hispanic subcultures. *Hispanic Journal of Behavioral Sciences, 13,* 48-62.
7. Edwards, M. C., Finney, J. W., & Bonner, M. (1991). Matching treatment with recurrent abdominal pain symptoms: An evaluation of dietary fiber and relaxation treatments. *Behavior Therapy, 22,* 257–267.
8. Fowler-Kerry, S., & Lander, J. (1991). Assessment of sex differences in children's and adolescents' self-reported pain from venipuncture. *Journal of Pediatric Psychology, 16,* 783–793.
9. Hazzard, A., Webb, C., Kleemeier, C., Angert, L., & Pohl, J. (1991). Child sexual abuse prevention: Evaluation and one-year follow-up. *Child Abuse & Neglect, 15,* 123-138.
10. Kendall, P. C., & Chansky, T. E. (1991). Considering cognition in anxiety-disordered children. *Journal of Anxiety Disorders, 5,* 167-185.
11. Last, C. G. (1991). Somatic complaints in anxiety disordered children. *Journal of Anxiety Disorders, 5,* 125-138.
12. Rosenbaum, T., McMurray, N. E., & Campbell, I. M. (1991). The effects of rational emotive education on locus of control, rationality and anxiety in primary school children. *Australian Journal of Education, 35,* 187-200.
13. Turner, S. M., Beidel, D. C., & Epstein, L. H. (1991). Vulnerability and risk for anxiety disorders. *Journal of Anxiety Disorders, 5,* 151-166.
14. Walker, L. S., & Greene, J. W. (1991). Negative life events and symptom resolution in pediatric abdominal pain patients. *Journal of Pediatric Psychology, 16,* 341–360.
15. Walker, L. S., & Greene, J. W. (1991). The Functional Disability Inventory: Measuring a neglected dimension of child health status. *Journal of Pediatric Psychology, 16,* 39–58.
16. Cauce, A. M., Hannan, K., & Sargeant, M. (1992). Life stress, social support, and locus of control during early adolescence: Interactive effects. *American Journal of Community Psychology, 20,* 787-798.
17. Dawson, G., Klinger, L. G., Panagiotides, H., Hill, D., & Spieker, S. (1992). Frontal lobe activity and affective behavior of infants of mothers with depressive symptoms. *Child Development, 63,* 725–737.
18. Perrin, S., & Last, C. G. (1992). Do childhood anxiety measures measure anxiety? *Journal of Abnormal Child Psychology, 20,* 567-578.
19. Rossman, B. B. R., & Rosenberg, M. S. (1992). Family stress and functioning in children: The moderating effects of children's beliefs about their control over parental conflict. *Journal of Child Psychology and Psychiatry and Allied Disciplines, 33,* 699-715.
20. Varni, J. W., Setoguchi, Y., Rappaport, L. R., & Talbot, D. (1992). Psychological adjustment and perceived social support in children with congenital/acquired limb deficiencies. *Journal of Behavioral Medicine, 15,* 31-44.
21. Kearney, C. A., & Silverman, W. K. (1993). Measuring the function of school refusal behavior: The School Refusal Assessment Scale. *Journal of Clinical Child Psychology, 22,* 85-96.
22. Labbé, E. E., Delaney, D., Olson, K., & Hickman, H. (1993). Skin-temperature biofeedback training: Cognitive and developmental factors in a non-clinical child population. *Perceptual and Motor Skills, 76,* 955–962.
23. Rankin, E. J., Gilner, F. H., Gfeller, J. D., & Katz, B. M. (1993). Efficacy of progressive muscle relaxation for reducing state anxiety among elderly adults on memory tasks. *Perceptual and Motor Skills, 77,* 1395–1402.
24. Ross, C. K., Lavigne, J. V., Hayford, J. R., Berry, S. L., Sinacore, J. M., & Pachman, L. M. (1993). Psychological factors affecting reported pain in juvenile rheumatoid arthritis. *Journal of Pediatric Psychology, 18,* 561–573.
25. Varni, J. W., Katz, E. R., Colegrove, R., Jr., & Dolgin, M. (1993). The impact of social skills training on the adjustment of children with newly diagnosed cancer. *Journal of Pediatric Psychology, 18,* 751–767.
26. Waterman, J., & Lusk, R. (1993). Psychological testing in evaluation of child sexual abuse. *Child Abuse & Neglect, 17,* 145-159.
27. Wyman, P. A., Cowen, E. L., Work, W. C., & Kerley, J. H. (1993). The role of children's future expectations in self-system functioning and adjustment to life stress: A prospective study of urban at-risk children. *Development and Psychopathology, 5,* 649-661.
28. Beidel, D. C., Turner, M. W., & Turner, K. N. (1994). Test anxiety and childhood anxiety disorders in African American and White school children. *Journal of Anxiety Disorders, 8,* 169-179.
29. Blood, G. W., Blood, I. M., Bennett, S., Simpson, K. C., & Susman, E. J. (1994). Subjective anxiety measurements and cortisol responses in adults who stutter. *Journal of Speech and Hearing, 37,* 760–768.
30. Borchardt, C. M., Giesler, J., Bernstein, G. A., & Crosby, R. D. (1994). A comparison of inpatient and outpatient school refusers. *Child Psychiatry and Human Development, 24,* 255–264.
31. Campbell, M. A., & Rapee, R. M. (1994). The nature of feared outcome representations in children. *Journal of Abnormal Child Psychology, 22,* 99-111.
32. Carey, M. P., Faulstick, M. E., & Carey, T. C. (1994). Assessment of anxiety in adolescents: Concurrent and factorial validities of the Trait Anxiety scale of Spielberger's State-Trait Anxiety Inventory for Children. *Psychological Reports, 75,* 331-338.
33. Clark, D. B., Turner, S. M., Beidel, D. C., Donovan, J. E., Kirischi, L., & Jacob, R. G. (1994). Reliability and validity of the Social Phobia and Anxiety Inventory for adolescents. *Psychological Assessment, 6,* 135-140.
34. Dreman, S., & Aldor, R. (1994). Work or marriage? Competence in custodial mothers in the stabilization phase of the divorce process. *Journal of Divorce & Remarriage, 22(1/2),* 3-22.
35. Engel, N. A., Rodrigue, J. R., & Geffken, G. R. (1994). Parent-child agreement on ratings of anxiety in children. *Psychological Reports, 75,* 1251-1260.
36. Gfeller, J. D., & Katz, B. M. (1994). Anxiety states and sustained attention in a cognitively intact elderly sample: Preliminary results. *Psychological Reports, 75,* 1176-1178.
37. Levy-Shiff, R., Einat, G., Har-Even, D., Mogilner, M., Mogilner, S., Lerman, M., & Krikler, R. (1994). Emotional and behavioral adjustment in children born prematurely. *Journal of Clinical Child Psychology, 23,* 323-333.
38. Mannarino, A. P., Cohen, J. A., & Berman, S. R. (1994). The Children's Attributions and Perceptions Scale: A new measure of sexual abuse-related factors. *Journal of Clinical Child Psychology, 23,* 204-211.
39. Mannarino, A. P., Cohen, J. A., & Berman, S. R. (1994). The relationship between preabuse factors and psychological symptomatology in sexually abused girls. *Child Abuse & Neglect, 18,* 63-71.

40. Nelson, C. C., & Allen, J. (1994). Effects of maternal hospitalization in early childhood: Anticipated anxiety associated with an analog separation for childbirth and surgery. *Journal of Pediatric Psychology, 19,* 629-642.

41. Peterson, L., Gillies, R., Cook, S. C., Schick, B., & Little, T. (1994). Developmental patterns of expected consequences for simulated bicycle injury events. *Health Psychology, 13,* 218-223.

42. Ronan, K. R., Kendall, P. C., & Rowe, M. (1994). Negative affectivity in children: Development and validation of a self-statement questionnaire. *Cognitive Therapy and Research, 18,* 509528.

43. Shear, M. K., Pilkonis, P. A., Cloitre, M., & Leon, A. C. (1994). Cognitive behavioral treatment compared with nonprescriptive treatment of panic disorders. *Archives of General Psychiatry, 51,* 395-401.

44. Utz, S. W. (1994). The effect of instructions on cognitive strategies and performance in biofeedback. *Journal of Behavioral Medicine, 17,* 291-308.

45. Virella, B., Arbona, C., & Novy, D. M. (1994). Psychometric properties and factor structure of the Spanish version of the State-Trait Anxiety Inventory. *Journal of Personality Assessment, 63,* 401-412.

46. Wachtel, J., Rodrigue, J. R., Geffken, G. R., Graham-Pole, J., & Turner, C. (1994). Children awaiting invasive medical procedures: Do children and their mothers agree on child's level of anxiety? *Journal of Pediatric Psychology, 19,* 723-735.

47. Weiss, B., & Catron, T. (1994). Specificity of the comorbidity of aggression and depression in children. *Journal of Abnormal Child Psychology, 22,* 389-401.

48. Albano, A. M., Marten, P. A., Holt, C. S., Heimberg, R. G., & Barlow, D. H. (1995). Cognitive-behavioral group treatment for social phobia in adolescents. *The Journal of Nervous and Mental Disease, 183,* 649–656.

49. Beidel, D. C., Turner, S. M., & Morris, T. L. (1995). A new inventory to assess childhood social anxiety and phobia: The Social Phobia and Anxiety Inventory for Children. *Psychological Assessment, 7,* 73-79.

50. Campbell, L. A., Kirkpatrick, S. E., Berry, C. C., & Lamberti, J. J. (1995). Preparing children with congenital heart disease for cardiac surgery. *Journal of Pediatric Psychology, 20,* 313–328.

51. Holahan, C. J., Valentiner, D. P., & Moos, R. H. (1995). Parental support, coping strategies, and psychological adjustment: An integrative model with late adolescents. *Journal of Youth and Adolescence, 24,* 633–648.

52. King, N. J., Mietz, A., Tinney, L., & Ollendick, T. H. (1995). Psychopathology and cognition in adolescents experiencing severe test anxiety. *Journal of Clinical Child Psychology, 24,* 49-54.

53. Miller, T. W. & Veltkamp, L. J. (1995). Assessment of sexual abuse and trauma: Clinical measures. *Child Psychiatry and Human Development, 26,* 3–10.

54. Mullins, L. L., Chaney, J. M., Hartman, V. L., Olson, R. A., Youll, L. K., Reyes, S., & Blackett, P. (1995). Child and maternal adaptation to cystic fibrosis and insulin-dependent diabetes mellitus: Differential patterns across disease states. *Journal of Pediatric Psychology, 20,* 173–186.

55. Treadwell, K. R. H., Flannery-Schroeder, E. C., & Kendall, P. C. (1995). Ethnicity and gender in relation to adaptive functioning, diagnostic status, and treatment outcome in children from an anxiety clinic. *Journal of Anxiety Disorders, 9,* 373-384.

56. Vasey, M. W., Daleiden, E. L., Williams, L. L., & Brown, L. M. (1995). Biased attention in childhood anxiety disorders: A preliminary study. *Journal of Abnormal Child Psychology, 23,* 267-279.

57. Beidel, D. C., Fink, C. M., & Turner, S. M. (1996). Stability of anxious symptomatology in children. *Journal of Abnormal Child Psychology, 24,* 257–269.

58. Beidel, D. C., Silverman, W. K., & Hammond-Lawrence, K. (1996). Overanxious disorder: Subsyndromal state or specific disorder? A comparison of clinic and community samples. *Journal of Clinical Child Psychology, 25,* 25–32.

59. Chorpita, B. F., Albano, A. M., & Barlow, D. H. (1996). Child anxiety sensitivity index: Considerations for children with anxiety disorders. *Journal of Clinical Child Psychology, 25,* 77–82.

60. Chorpita, B. F., Albano, A. M., & Barlow, D. H. (1996). Cognitive processing in children: Relation to anxiety and family influences. *Journal of Clinical Child Psychology, 25,* 170–176.

61. Crowley, S. L., & Emerson, E. N. (1996). Discriminant validity of self-reported anxiety and depression in children: Negative effectivity or independent constructs? *Journal of Clinical Child Psychology, 25,* 139–146.

62. Drotar, D., Agle, D. P., Eckl, L., & Thompson, P. A. (1996). Impact of the repressive personality style on the measurement of psychological distress in children and adolescents with chronic illness: An example from hemophilia. *Journal of Pediatric Psychology, 21,* 283–293.

63. Gullone, E., Cummins, R. A., & King, N. J. (1996). Self-reported fears: A comparison study of youths with and without an intellectual disability. *Journal of Disability Research, 40,* 227–240.

64. Howard, B. L., & Kendall, P. C. (1996). Cognitive-behavioral family therapy for anxiety-disordered children: A multiple evaluation. *Cognitive Therapy and Research, 20,* 423–443.

65. Oldfield, D., Hays, B. J., & Megel, M. E. (1996). Evaluation of the effectiveness of project trust: An elementary school-based victimization prevention strategy. *Child Abuse & Neglect, 20,* 821–832.

66. Saigh, P. A., Yule, W., & Inamdar, S. C. (1996). Imaginal flooding of traumatized children and adolescents. *Journal of School Psychology, 34,* 163–183.

67. Field, T., Hernandez-Reif, M., Seligman, S., Kraswegor, J., Sunshine, W., Rivas-Chacon, R., Schanberg, S., & Kuhn, C. (1997). Juvenile rheumatoid arthritis: Benefits from massage therapy. *Journal of Pediatric Psychology, 22,* 607–617.

68. Levy-Shiff, R., Zoran, N., & Shulman, S. (1997). International and domestic adoption: Child, parents, and family adjustment. *International Journal of Behavioral Development, 20,* 109–129.

69. Lovejoy, M. C., Verda, M. R., & Hays, C. E. (1997). Convergent and discriminant validity of measures of parenting efficacy and control. *Journal of Clinical Child Psychology, 26,* 366–376.

70. Moisan, P. A., Sanders-Phillips, K., & Moisan, P. M. (1997). Ethnic differences in circumstances of abuse and symptoms of depression and anger among sexually abused Black and Latino boys. *Child Abuse & Neglect, 21,* 473–488.

71. Nagel, D. E., Putnam, F. W., Noll, J. G., & Trickett, P. K. (1997). Disclosure patterns of sexual abuse and psychological functioning at a 1-year follow-up. *Child Abuse & Neglect, 21,* 137–147.

72. Perrin, S., & Last, C. G. (1997). Worrisome thoughts in children clinically referred for anxiety disorder. *Journal of Clinical Child Psychology, 26,* 181–189.

73. Ronan, K. R., & Kendall, P. C. (1997). Self-talk in distressed youth: States-of-mind and content specificity. *Journal of Clinical Child Psychology, 26,* 330–337.

74. Stilley, C. S., Miller, D. J., & Tarter, R. E. (1997). Measuring psychological distress in candidates for liver transplantation: A pilot study. *Journal of Clinical Psychology, 53,* 459–464.

75. Kendall, P. C., & Flannery-Schroeder, E. C. (1998). Methodological issues in treatment research for anxiety disorders in youth. *Journal of Abnormal Child Psychology, 26,* 27–38.

76. Pargament, K. I., Zinnbauer, B. J., Scott, A. B., Butter, E. M., Zerowin, J., & Stanik, P. (1998). Red flags and religious coping: identifying some religious warning signs among people in crisis. *Journal of Clinical Psychology, 54,* 77–89.

77. Savard, J., Laberge, B., Gauthier, J. G., ivers, H., & Bergeron, M. G. (1998). Evaluating anxiety and depression in HIV-infected patients. *Journal of Personality Assessment, 71,* 349–367.

78. Weems, C. F., Hammond-Laurence, K., Silverman, W. K., & Ginsburg, G. S. (1998). Testing the utility of the anxiety sensitivity construct in children and adolescents referred for anxiety disorders. *Journal of Clinical Child Psychology, 27,* 69–77.

[2499]

State Trait-Depression Adjective Check Lists.

Purpose: "Measures depressed mood and feelings in a form that neither implies pathology nor is judgmental."

Population: Ages 14 and older.

Publication Dates: 1967–1994.

Acronym: ST-DACL.

Scores, 6: State-Positive Mood, State-Negative Mood, State Mood-Total, Trait-Positive Mood, Trait-Negative Mood, Trait Mood-Total.

Administration: Group.

Forms, 4: 1, 2, A-B, C-D.

Price Data: Price information available from publisher for introductory kit including manual ('94, 117 pages), 25 Forms 1 & 2, 25 Forms A-B, 25 Forms C-D, and 25 profile forms.

Time: (8) minutes per list (A–G).

Comments: Developed from the Depression Adjective Check Lists (T4:742); Forms 1 and 2 are used to measure state and trait depressed mood, Forms A-B and C-D are used to measure only state depressed mood.

Author: Bernard Lubin.

Publisher: Psychological Assessment Resources, Inc.

Cross References: For reviews by Andres Barona and by Janet F. Carlson and Betsy Waterman, see 13:297 (21 references); see also T4:742 (79 references), 9:315 (21 references), T3:681 (46 references), 8:536 (20 references), and T2:1154 (2 references); for reviews of the earlier edition by Leonard D. Goodstein and Douglas M. McNair, see 7:65 (3 references); see also P:57 (4 references).

TEST REFERENCE

1. Whitlock, R. V., Lulun, B., & Noble, E. (1995). Factor structure of the state and trait versions of the Depression Adjective Check Lists. *Journal of Clinical Psychology, 51,* 614–625.

[2500]

The Steenburgen Diagnostic-Prescriptive Math Program.

Purpose: "Designed to assess computational skills."
Population: Grades 1-3, 4-6.
Publication Date: 1978.
Scores: Item scores only.
Administration: Group.
Levels, 2: Level I, Level II.
Price Data, 1999: $18 per test kit including Quick Math Screening Test and answer key, Diagnostic-Prescriptive Guide, Prescriptive Worksheets and answer key for Levels I and II; $18 per 25 test forms and 25 profile sheets (specify level).
Time: (20-30) minutes.
Comments: "Criterion-referenced"; title on tests is The Steenburgen Quick Math Screening Test.
Author: Fran Steenburgen Gelb.
Publisher: Academic Therapy Publications.
Cross References: For review by Ronald K. Hambleton and John R. Hills, see 9:1191.

[2501]

Stenographic Skills Test: ETSA Test 4A.

Purpose: Designed "to measure typing and/or shorthand and the general skills required of secretaries and stenographers."
Population: Job applicants.
Publication Dates: 1960-1984.
Scores: Total score only.
Administration: Group.
Price Data, 1998: $15 per 10 tests and scoring key; $15 per ETSA Test Administrator's Manual; $15 per Tests Technical Manual.
Time: 45 minutes.
Author: Psychological Services Bureau.
Publisher: Educators'/Employers' Tests and Services Associates.
Cross References: For reviews by Marvin D. Dunnette and Raymond A. Katzell of an earlier version of the ETSA Tests, see 6:1025.

[2502]

Stephens Oral Language Screening Test.

Purpose: To screen children "for potential problems in syntax and/or articulation associated with their production of standard American English dialects."
Population: Prekindergarten-grade 1.
Publication Date: 1977.
Acronym: SOLST.
Scores, 2: Syntax, Articulation.
Administration: Individual.
Price Data: Available from publisher.
Time: (9) minutes.
Author: M. Irene Stephens.
Publisher: Interim Publishers.
Cross References: See 9:1193 (2 references).

[2503]

The Stieglitz Informal Reading Inventory: Assessing Reading Behaviors from Emergent to Advanced Levels.

Purpose: Designed to provide educators with information about students' reading behaviors.
Population: Grades 1–9.
Publication Date: 1992.
Acronym: SIRI.
Scores, 7: Graded Words in Context (Independent, Instructional, Frustration), Graded Reading Passages (Word Recognition, Oral Comprehension, Prior Knowledge, Interest).
Administration: Individual.
Price Data: Available from publisher.
Time: (20–30) minutes.
Author: Ezra L. Stieglitz.
Publisher: Allyn & Bacon.
Cross References: For reviews by Koressa Kutsick Malcolm and Stephanie Stein, see 13:298.

[2504]

STIM/CON: Prognostic Inventory for Misarticulating Kindergarten and First Grade Children.

Purpose: "Measures stimulability for defective sounds and the consistency of error of defective sounds."
Population: Grades K-3.
Publication Date: 1987.
Scores, 4: Stimulability Percentage (for phonemes tested), Inconsistency Percentage (for phonemes tested), Stimulability/Inconsistency Average, Overall Prognostic Score.
Administration: Individual.
Price Data: Not available.
Time: (5-20) minutes.
Comments: 3 forms: Form for Stimulability Assessment, Predictive Summary for Kindergarten Children, Predictive Summary for First Grade Children; orally administered.
Author: Ronald K. Sommers.
Publisher: United/DOK Publishers [No reply from publisher; status unknown].
Cross References: For reviews by Nicholas W. Bankson and Allan O. Diefendorf and Kathy S. Kessler, see 11:380.

[2505]

Stokes/Gordon Stress Scale.

Purpose: Developed to measure stressors in healthy individuals over age 65.
Population: Healthy individuals over age 65.

Publication Date: 1987.
Acronym: SGSS.
Scores: Total stress score.
Administration: Group.
Price Data, 1993: $30 per 100 scales.
Time: (15–30) minutes.
Comments: Self-administered in person or by mail.
Authors: Shirlee A. Stokes and Susan E. Gordon.
Publisher: Lienhard School of Nursing.
Cross References: For a review by Sharon L. Weinberg, see 13:299; see also T4:2572 (1 reference).

[2506]

Strategic Decision Making Inventory.

Purpose: Designed as a guide to business managers to help them think strategically in their decision making process (deciding how to decide).
Population: Business managers.
Publication Date: 1983.
Scores, 2: Flexibility, Appropriateness.
Administration: Group.
Price Data, 1998: $7.50 per inventory (volume discounts available).
Time: [15–20] minutes.
Comments: Self-administered; self-scored.
Author: Herbert S. Kindler.
Publisher: The Center for Management Effectiveness.

[2507]

Strength Deployment Inventory.

Purpose: Designed to assess "personal strengths in relating to others" under two conditions: when things are going well, and when there is conflict.
Population: Adults.
Publication Dates: 1973–1996.
Acronym: SDI®.
Scores: 7 Motivational Values Systems: (Altruistic-Nurturing, Assertive-Directing, Analytic-Autonomizing, Flexible-Cohering, Assertive-Nurturing, Judicious-Competing, Cautious-Supporting); 13 scores reflecting progression through stages of conflict.
Administration: Group or individual.
Price Data, 1999: $20 per Premier Edition including Standard Edition of the Strength Deployment Inventory, interpretive charts, and 2 exercises; Portrait of Personal Strengths and Portrait of Overdone Strengths; $5 per either Portrait available separately: $9 per Standard Edition; $30 per manual ('96, 146 pages).
Foreign Language Editions: Standard Edition available in French, German, and Spanish.
Time: (20–40) minutes for Premier Edition; (20–40) minutes per exercise.
Comments: Self-scorable; for corporate (e.g., team building), clinical (e.g., relationship counseling), and career development (e.g., outplacement and welfare-to-work) uses; Feedback Edition uses self-rating and ratings of a significant other person.
Author: Elias H. Porter.
Publisher: Personal Strengths Publishing, Inc.

[2508]

Stress Audit.

Purpose: "Samples the magnitude and types of stress [and stress symptoms] experienced by the respondent and assesses relative vulnerability to stress."
Population: Adults.
Publication Dates: 1983-1987.
Scores, 16: Situational (Family, Individual Roles, Social Being, Environment, Financial, Work/School), Symptom (Muscular System, Parasympathetic Nervous System, Sympathetic Nervous System, Emotional, Cognitive System, Endocrine, Immune System), Vulnerability, Total Situational Stress, Total Symptoms.
Administration: Group.
Price Data: Available from publisher.
Time: [20-30] minutes.
Comments: Self-administered; v5.0 is available in paper-and-pencil format (optically scannable for computer scoring and interpretation), PC format (computer administration, scoring, and interpretation), and on the World Wide Web (http://www.bbinst.org/).
Authors: Lyle H. Miller, Alma Dell Smith, and Bruce L. Mehler (manual only).
Publisher: Biobehavioral Associates.
Cross References: For a review by Rolf A. Peterson, see 10:347.

[2509]

Stress in General Scale.

Purpose: Designed as a global measure of job stress.
Population: Employees.
Publication Date: 1992.
Acronym: SIG.
Scores: Total score only.
Administration: Individual or group.
Price Data, 1997: $7 per 100 test booklets; $1 per scoring key.
Time: Administration time not reported.
Authors: Patricia C. Smith, William K. Balzer, Gail H. Ironson, Karen B. Paul, Bob Hayes, Sarah Moore-Hirschl, Luis Fernando Parra.
Publisher: Bowling Green State University, Department of Psychology.

[2510]

Stress Index for Parents of Adolescents.

Purpose: Designed to assess the level of stress in parents of adolescents.
Population: Parents of 11–19-year-olds.

Publication Date: 1998.
Scores, 11: Adolescent Domain (Moodiness/Emotional Lability, Social Isolation/Withdrawal, Delinquency/Antisocial, Failure to Achieve or Persevere), Parent Domain (Life Restrictions, Relationship with Spouse/Partner, Social Alienation, Incompetence/Guilt), Adolescent-Parent Relationship Domain, Life Stressors, Total Parenting Stress.
Administration: Group.
Price Data: Price information available from publisher for introductory kit including 25 reusable item booklets, 25 hand-scorable answer sheet/profile forms, and professional manual (76 pages).
Time: (20) minutes.
Authors: Peter L. Sheras, Richard R. Abidin, and Timothy R. Konold.
Publisher: Psychological Assessment Resources, Inc.

[2511]

Stress Indicator & Health Planner.

Purpose: "Assists people to identify their present health practices, pinpoint problem areas and plan for improved health, productivity and well-being."
Population: Adults.
Publication Dates: 1990–1993.
Acronym: SIHP.
Scores, 10: Physical Distress, Psychological Distress, Behavioral Distress, Total Distress Assessment, Interpersonal Stress Assessment, Nutritional Assessment, Health Assessment, Total Wellness Assessment, Time-Stress Assessment, Occupational Stress Assessment.
Administration: Group.
Price Data, 1993: $12 per test booklet; $12 per Professional's Guide ('93, 12 pages); $15 per Releasing Relaxation: Mind and Body audiotape.
Time: (30) minutes for Basic; (180–360) minutes for Facilitated/Advanced.
Comments: Self-administered and self-scored.
Authors: Gwen Faulkner and Terry Anderson.
Publisher: Consulting Resource Group International, Inc.
Cross References: For reviews by Dennis C. Harper and Barbara L. Lachar, see 13:300.

[2512]

Stress Management Questionnaire [Revised].

Purpose: Identifies how one responds to life stressors and copes with stress.
Population: Adults and adolescents.
Publication Dates: 1980–1999.
Acronym: SMQ.
Scores, 11: Warning Signs (Hostility/Anger, Perfectionism, Time Orientation, Disappointment, Negative Mood, Underachievement, Tension), Stress Effects (Physical, Live Work Satisfaction), Stressors (Life Events, Hassles).
Administration: Group or individual.
Forms, 2: Participant, Companion.
Price Data, 1999: $14 per questionnaire (discounts available).
Time: (20–25) minutes.
Comments: Manual title is "Stressmaster Trainer's Manual"; questionnaire completed by self and by a close companion; self-scored.
Author: James C. Peterson.
Publisher: The Assessment and Development Centre.
Cross References: For a review by Jayne E. Stake of an earlier version, see 10:348.

[2513]

Stress Resiliency Profile.

Purpose: Designed to identify some ways individuals unintentionally contribute to their own stress levels.
Population: Employees.
Publication Date: 1992.
Acronym: SRP.
Scores, 3: Deficiency Focusing, Necessitating, Skill Recognition.
Administration: Group or individual.
Price Data, 1993: $5.50 per test booklet/manual (23 pages).
Time: (15) minutes.
Comments: Self-administered and self-scored.
Authors: Kenneth W. Thomas and Walter G. Tymon, Jr.
Publisher: XICOM.
Cross References: For reviews by John A. Mills and William A. Merz, Sr., see 13:301.

[2514]

Stress Response Scale.

Purpose: A measure of children's emotional status "designed for children referred for possible emotional adjustment problems or behavior problems."
Population: Ages 5-14.
Publication Dates: 1979-1993.
Acronym: SRS.
Scores, 6: Impulsive (Acting Out), Passive-Aggressive, Impulsive (Overactive), Repressed, Dependent, Total.
Administration: Individual or group.
Price Data: Price information available from publisher for professional kit including manual ('86, 26 pages), rating forms, and profiles; $20 per manual.
Special Edition: The Stress Response Scale for Children: A Profile Analysis Program. 1985; "a program for scoring SRS data"; 2 modes: clinical applications, research applications; Apple II/II+/IIe/IIc (64K RAM) or IBM-PC/XT/AT (or 100% compatibles) required; price information for program and manual available from Mark Shermis; Mark D. Shermis and

Louis A. Chandler (authors); Mark D. Shermis (publisher).
Time: (5) minutes.
Comments: Ratings by parents or teachers; manual title is The Stress Response Scale, 1993 Revision.
Author: Louis A. Chandler.
Publisher: Psychological Assessment Resources, Inc.
Cross References: For reviews by Mary Lou Kelley and William K. Wilkinson, see 11:381 (2 references).

TEST REFERENCE

1. Larson, D. K., & Bittner, M. T. (1994). Temperament and school-aged children's coping abilities and responses to stress. *The Journal of Genetic Psychology, 155,* 289–302.

[2515]

Stromberg Dexterity Test.

Purpose: "Developed as an aid in choosing workers for jobs which require speed and accuracy of arm and hand movement."
Population: Trade school and adults.
Publication Dates: 1945-1981.
Acronym: SDT.
Scores: Total score only.
Administration: Individual.
Price Data, 1999: $556.50 per complete set including all necessary equipment and manual ('81, 12 pages) in case; $16.50 per manual.
Time: (5-10) minutes.
Author: Eleroy L. Stromberg.
Publisher: The Psychological Corporation.
Cross References: See T3:2317 (2 references) and T2:2235 (8 references); for a review by Julian C. Stanley, see 4:755 (1 reference).

[2516]

Stroop Color and Word Test.

Purpose: Designed "for the evaluation of brain dysfunction or for an evaluation of psychopathology in general."
Population: Ages 7 and over.
Publication Date: 1978.
Scores, 3: Word, Color, Color-Word.
Administration: Group.
Price Data, 1998: $75 per complete kit including manual (97 pages) and 25 tests; $55 per 25 tests; $30 per manual.
Time: 2.25(5) minutes.
Author: Charles J. Golden.
Publisher: Stoelting Co.
Cross References: See T4:2582 (40 references); for reviews by James R. Evans and George W. Hynd, see 9:1196 (15 references); see also T3:2319 (1 reference).

TEST REFERENCES

1. Bentall, R. P., & Kaney, S. (1989). Content specific information processing and persecutory delusions: An investigation using the emotional Stroop test. *British Journal of Medical Psychology, 62,* 355–364.

2. Blumenthal, J. A., Emery, C. F., Madden, D. J., George, L. K., Coleman, R. E., Riddle, M. W., McKee, D. C., Reasoner, J., & Williams, R. S. (1989). Cardiovascular and behavioral effects of aerobic exercise in healthy older men and women. *Journal of Gerontology, 44,* 147–157.

3. Everett, J., Laplante, L., & Thomas, J. (1989). The selective attention deficit in schizophrenia: Limited resources or cognitive fatigue? *The Journal of Nervous and Mental Disease, 177,* 735–738.

4. Kelly, M. S., Best, C. T., & Kirk, U. (1989). Cognitive processing deficits in reading disabilities: A prefrontal cortical hypothesis. *Brain and Cognition, 11,* 275–293.

5. Rapesak, S. Z., Kaszniak, A. W., & Rubens, A. B. (1989). Anomia for facial expressions: Evidence for a category specific visual-verbal disconnection syndrome. *Neuropsychologia, 27,* 1031–1041.

6. Streufert, S., DePadova, A., McGlynn, T., Piasecki, M., & Pogash, R. (1989). Effects of Beta blockade with Metoprolol on simple and complex task performance. *Health Psychology, 8,* 143–158.

7. Tipper, S. P., Bourque, T. A., Anderson, S. H., & Brehaut, J. C. (1989). Mechanisms of attention: A developmental study. *Journal of Experimental Child Psychology, 48,* 353–378.

8. Batson, C. D. (1990). Good Samaritans—or priests and levites?: Using William James as a guide in the study of religious prosocial motivation. *Personality and Social Psychology Bulletin, 16,* 758–768.

9. Stern, Y., Tetrud, J. W., Martin, W. R. W., Kutner, S. J., & Langston, J. W. (1990). Cognitive change following MPTP exposure. *Neurology, 40,* 261–264.

10. Dodrill, C. B., & Troupin, A. S. (1991). Neuropsychological effects of carbamazepine and phenytoin: A reanalysis. *Neurology, 41,* 141–143.

11. Everett, J., Thomas, J., Cote, F., Levesque, J., & Michaud, D. (1991). Cognitive effects of psychostimulant medication in hyperactive children. *Child Psychiatry and Human Development, 22,* 79–87.

12. Matthews, K. A., Davis, M. C., Stoney, C. M., Owens, J. F., & Caggiula, A. R. (1991). Does the gender relevance of the stressor influence sex differences in psychophysiological responses? *Health Psychology, 10,* 112–120.

13. Miller, B. L., Cummings, J. L., Villanueva-Meyer, J., Boone, K., Mehringer, C. M., Lesser, I. M., & Mena, I. (1991). Frontal lobe degeneration: Clinical, neuropsychological, and SPECCT characteristics. *Neurology, 41,* 1374–1382.

14. Rao, S. M., Leo, G. J., Bernardin, L., & Unverzagt, F. (1991). Cognitive dysfunction in multiple sclerosis. I. Frequency, patterns, and prediction. *Neurology, 41,* 685–691.

15. Scheltens, P., Visscher, F., VanKeimpema, A. R. J., Lindeboom, J., Taphoorn, M. J. B., & Wolters, E. C. (1991). Sleep apnea syndrome presenting with cognitive impairment. *Neurology, 41,* 155–156.

16. Stern, Y., Marder, K., Bell, K., Chen, J., Dooneief, G., Goldstein, S., Mindry, D., Richards, M., Sano, M., Williams, J., Gorman, J., Ehrhardt, A., & Mayeux, R. (1991). Multidisciplinary baseline assessment of homosexual men with and without human immonodeficiency virus infection. *Archives of General Psychiatry, 48,* 131–138.

17. Dustman, R. E., Emmerson, R. Y., Steinhaus, L. A., Shearer, D. E., & Dustman, T. J. (1992). The effects of videogame playing on neuropsychological performance of elderly individuals. *Journal of Gerontology, 47,* 168–171.

18. Mayberg, H. S., Starkstein, S. E., Peyser, C. E., Brandt, J., Dannals, R. F., & Folstein, S. E. (1992). Paralimbic frontal lobe hypomentabolism in depression associated with Huntington's disease. *Neurology, 42,* 1791–1797.

19. Nemeth, C., Mosier, K., & Chiles, C. (1992). When convergent thought improves performance: Majority versus minority influence. *Personality and Social Psychology Bulletin, 18,* 139–144.

20. Bohnen, N. I., Twijnstra, A., & Jolles, J. (1993). A controlled trial with vasopression analogue (DGAVP) on cognitive recovery immediately after head trauma. *Neurology, 43,* 103–106.

21. Crockett, D. J. (1993). Cross-validation of WAIS-R prototypical patterns of intellectual functioning using neuropsychological test scores. *Journal of Clinical and Experimental Neuropsychology, 15,* 903–920.

22. Dodrill, C. B., Arnett, J. L., Sommerville, K. W., & Sussman, N. M. (1993). Evaluation of the effects of vigabatrin on cognitive abilities and quality of life epilepsy. *Neurology, 43,* 2501–2507.

23. Girdler, S. S., Pedersen, C. A., Stern, R. A., & Light, K. C. (1993). Menstrual cycle and premenstrual syndrome: Modifiers of cardiovascular reactivity in women. *Health Psychology, 12,* 180–192.

24. Goldberg, T. E., Hyde, T. M., Kleinman, J. E., & Weinberger, D. R. (1993). Course of schizophrenia: Neuropsychological evidence for a static encephalopathy. *Schizophrenia Bulletin, 19,* 797–804.

25. Kenner, A. N. (1993). A cross-cultural study of body-focused hand movement. *Journal of Nonverbal Behavior, 17,* 263–279.

26. Krupp, L. B., Masur, D. M., & Kaufman, L. D. (1993). Neurocognitive dysfunction in the eosinophilia-myalgia syndrome. *Neurology, 43,* 931–936.

27. Kuschè, C. A., Cook, E. T., & Greenberg, M. T. (1993). Neuropsychological and cognitive functioning in children with anxiety, externalizing, and comorbid psychopathology. *Journal of Clinical Child Psychology, 22,* 172–195.

28. Mayeux, R., Stern, Y., Tang, M.-X., Todak, G., Marder, K., Sano, M., Richards, M., Stein, Z., Ehrhardt, A. A., & Gorman, J. M. (1993). Mortality risks in gay men with human immunodeficiency virus infection and cognitive impairment. *Neurology, 43,* 176–182.

29. Meneilly, G. S., Cheung, E., Tessier, D., Yakura, C., & Tuokko, H. (1993). The effect of improved glycemic control on cognitive functions in the elderly patient with diabetes. *Journal of Gerontology, 48,* 117–121.

30. Pierce, T. W., Madden, D. J., Siegel, W. C., & Blumenthal, J. A. (1993). Effects of aerobic exercise on cognitive and psychosocial functioning in patients with mild hypertension. *Health Psychology, 12,* 286–291.

31. Ray, C., Phillips, L., & Weir, W. R. C. (1993). Quality of attention in chronic fatigue syndrome: Subjective reports of everyday attention and cognition difficulty, and performance on tasks of focused attention. *British Journal of Clinical Psychology, 32,* 357–364.

32. Rothlind, J. C., Bylsma, F. W., Peyser, C., Folstein, S. E., & Brandt, J. (1993). Cognitive and motor correlates of everyday functioning in early Huntington's disease. *The Journal of Nervous and Mental Disease, 181,* 194–199.

33. Berti, A., Frassinetti, F., & Umilta, C. (1994). Nonconscious reading? Evidence from neglect dyslexia. *Cortex, 30,* 181–197.

34. Buchanan, R. W., Strauss, M. E., Kirkpatrick, B., Holstein, C., Breier, A., & Carpenter, W. T., Jr. (1994). Neuropsychological impairments in deficit vs. nondeficit forms of schizophrenia. *Archives of General Psychiatry, 51,* 804-811.

35. Buytenhuijs, E. L., Berger, H. J. C., Van Spaendonck, K. P. M., Horstink, M. W. I. M., Borm, G. F., & Cools, A. R. (1994). Memory and learning strategies in patients with Parkinson's disease. Neuropsychologia, 32, 335–342.

36. Chemtob, C. M., Hamada, R. S., Roitblat, H. L., & Muraoka, M. Y. (1994). Anger, impulsivity, and anger control in combat-related posttraumatic stress disorder. *Journal of Consulting and Clinical Psychology, 62,* 827–832.

37. Damos, D. L., & Parker, E. S. (1994). High false alarm rates on a vigilance task may indicate recreational drug use. *Journal of Clinical and Experimental Neuropsychology, 16,* 713–722.

38. Davidson, K. W., Prkachin, K. M., Mills, D. E., & Lefcourt, H. M. (1994). Comparison of three theories relating facial expressiveness to blood pressure in male and female undergraduates. *Health Psychology, 13,* 404–411.

39. Feinstein, A., Brown, R., & Ron, M. (1994). Effects of practice of serial tests of attention in healthy subjects. *Journal of Clinical and Experimental Neuropsychology, 16,* 436–447.

40. Hayward, P., Ahmad, T., & Wardle, J. (1994). Into the dangerous world: An in vivo study of information processing in agoraphobics. *British Journal of Clinical Psychology, 33,* 307–315.

41. Kamarck, T. W., Jennings, J. R., Pogue-Geile, M., & Manuck, S. B. (1994). A multidimensional measurement model for cardiovascular reactivity: Stability and cross-validation in two adult samples. *Health Psychology, 13,* 471–478.

42. Kremen, W. S., Seidman, L. J., Pepple, J. R., Lyons, M. J., Tsuang, M. T., & Faraone, S. V. (1994). Neuropsychological risk indicators for schizophrenia: A review of family studies. *Schizophrenia Bulletin, 20,* 103–119.

43. Lavoie, M. E., & Charlebois, P. (1994). The discriminant validity of the Stroop Color and Word Test: Toward a cost-effective strategy to distinguish subgroups of disruptive preadolescents. *Psychology in the Schools, 31,* 98–107.

44. Malapani, C., Pillon, B., Dubois, B., & Agid, Y. (1994). Impaired simultaneous cognitive task performance in Parkinson's disease: A dopamine-related dysfunction. *Neurology, 44,* 319–326.

45. Merrill, L. L., Lewandowski, L. J., & Kobus, D. A. (1994). Selective attention skills of experienced sonar operators. *Perceptual and Motor Skills, 78,* 803–812.

46. Motta, R. W., Suozzi, J. M., & Joseph, J. M. (1994). Assessment of secondary traumatization with an emotional Stroop task. *Perceptual and Motor Skills, 78,* 1274.

47. Murphy, D. G. M., Allen, G., Haxby, J. V., Largay, K. A., Daly, E., White, B. J., Powell, L. M., & Schapiro, M. B. (1994). The effects of sex steroids and the X chromosome on female brain function: A study of the neuropsychology of adult Turner syndrome. *Neuropsychologia, 32,* 1309–1323.

48. Orsillo, S. M., Lilienfield, S. O., & Heimberg, R. G. (1994). Social phobia and response to challenge procedures: Examining the interaction between anxiety sensitivity and trait anxiety. *Journal of Anxiety Disorders, 8,* 247–258.

49. Palmer, B. W., Boone, K. B., Chang, L., Lee, A., & Black, S. (1994). Cognitive deficits and personality patterns in maternally versus paternally inherited myotonic dystrophy. *Journal of Clinical and Experimental Neuropsychology, 16,* 784-795.

50. Patterson, S. M., Zakoroski, S. G., Hall, M. H., Cohen, L., Wollman, K., & Baum, A. (1994). Psychological stress and platelet activation: Differences in platelet reactivity in healthy men during active and passive stressors. *Health Psychology, 13,* 34-38.

51. Persinger, M. A. (1994). Sense of a presence and suicidal ideation following traumatic brain injury: Indications of right-hemispheric intrusions from neuropsychological profiles. *Psychological Reports, 75,* 1059–1070.

52. Pomerleau, C. S., Teuscher, F., Goeters, S., & Pomerleau, O. F. (1994). Effects of nicotine abstinence and menstrual phase on task performance. *Addictive Behaviors, 19,* 357–362.

53. Shum, D. H. K., McFarland, K., & Bain, J. D. (1994). Assessment of attention: Relationship between psychological testing and information processing approaches. *Journal of Clinical and Experimental Neuropsychology, 16,* 531–538.

54. Stracciari, A., Ghidoni, E., Guarino, M., Poletti, M., & Pazzaglia, P. (1994). Post-traumatic retrograde amnesia with selective impairment of autobiographical memory. *Cortex, 30,* 459–468.

55. Strauss, M. E., & Summerfelt, A. (1994). Response to Serper and Harvey. *Schizophrenia Bulletin, 20,* 13–21.

56. Van der Linden, M., Meulemans, T., & Lorrain, D. (1994). Acquisition of new concepts by two amnesic patients. *Cortex, 30,* 305–317.

57. Vernoy, M. W. (1994). A computerized Stroop experiment that demonstrates the interaction in a 2 x 3 factorial design. *Teaching of Psychology, 21,* 186–189.

58. Vilkki, J., Ahola, K., Holst, P., Öhman, J., Servo, A., & Heiskanen, O. (1994). Prediction of psychosocial recovery after head injury with cognitive tests and neurobehavioral ratings. *Journal of Clinical and Experimental Neuropsychology, 16,* 325–338.

59. White, J. L., Moffitt, T. E., Caspi, A., Bartusch, D. J., Needles, D. J., & Stouthamer-Loeber, M. (1994). Measuring impulsivity and examining its relationship to delinquency. *Journal of Abnormal Psychology, 103,* 192–205.

60. Zesiger, P., Pegna, A., & Rilliet, B. (1994). Unilateral dysgraphia of the dominant hand in a left-hander: A disruption of graphic motor pattern selection. *Cortex, 30,* 673–683.

61. Binetti, G., Magni, E., Padovani, A., Coppan, S. F., Bianchetti, A., & Trabucchi, M. (1995). Release from proactive interference in early Alzheimer's disease. *Neuropsychologia, 33,* 379–384.

62. Brandt, J., Bylsma, F. W., Aylward, E. H., Rothlind, J., & Gow, C. A. (1995). Impaired source memory in Huntington's Disease and its relation to basal ganglia atrophy. *Journal of Clinical and Experimental Neuropsychology, 17,* 868–877.

63. Britton, J. W., Vitti, R. J., Ahlskog, J. E., Robinson, R. G., Kremor, B., & Hayden, M. R. (1995). Hereditary late-onset chorea without significant dementia: Genetic evidence for substantial phenotypic variation in Huntington's disease. *Neurology, 45,* 443–447.

64. Eustache, F., Rioux, P., Desgranges, B., Marchal, G., Taboue, M. C. P., Dary, M., Lechevalier, B., & Baron, J.-C. (1995). Healthy aging, memory subsystemy and regional cerebral oxygen consumption. *Neuropsychologia, 33,* 867–887.

65. Faraone, S. V., Seidman, L. J., Kremen, W. S., Pepple, J. R., Lyons, M. J., & Tsuang, M. T. (1995). Neuropsychological functioning among the nonpsychotic relatives of schizophrenic patients: A diagnostic efficiency analysis. *Journal of Abnormal Psychology, 104,* 286–304.

66. Graf, P., Uttle, B., & Tuokko, H. (1995). Color- and Picture-Word Stroop Tests: Performance changes in old age. *Journal of Clinical and Experimental Neuropsychology, 17,* 390–415.

67. Hunkin, N. M., & Parkin, A. J. (1995). The method of vanishing cues: An evaluation of its effectiveness in teaching memory-impaired individuals. *Neuropsychologia, 33,* 1255–1279.

68. Kindlon, D., Mezzacappa, E., & Earls, F. (1995). Psychometric properties of impulsivity measures: Temporal stability, validity and factor structure. *Journal of Child Psychology and Psychiatry and Allied Disciplines, 36,* 645–661.

69. Kosslyn, S. M., Hamilton, S. E., & Bernstein, J. H. (1995). The perception of curvature can be selectively disrupted by prosopagnosia. *Brain and Cognition, 27,* 36–58.

70. McNeil, D. W., Ries, B. J., Taylor, L. J., Boone, M. L., Carter, L. E., Turk, C. L., & Lewin, M. R. (1995). Comparison of social phobia subtypes using Stroop tests. *Journal of Anxiety Disorders, 9,* 47–57.

71. Mirsky, A. F. (1995). Perils and pitfalls of the path to normal potential: The role of impaired attention. Homage to Herbert G. Birch. *Journal of Clinical and Experimental Neuropsychology, 17,* 481–498.

72. Peyser, C. E., Folstein, M., Chase, G. A., Starkstein, S., Brandt, J., Cockrell, J. R., Bylsma, F., Coyle, J. T., McHugh, P. R., & Folstein, S. E. (1995). Trial of d-2-Tocopherol in Huntington's disease. *American Journal of Psychiatry, 152,* 1771–1775.

73. Trichard, C., Martinot, J. L, Alagille, M., Masure, M. C., Hardy, P., Ginestet, D., & Feline, A. (1995). Time course of prefrontal lobe dysfunction in severely depressed in-patients: A longitudinal neuropsychological study. *Psychological Medicine, 25,* 79–85.

74. Tryon, W. W. (1995). Neural networks for behavior therapists: What are they and why are they important. *Behavior Therapy, 26,* 295–318.

75. van Spaendonck, K. P. M., Berger, H. J. C., Horstink, M. W. I. M., Borm, G. F., & Cools, A. R. (1995). Card sorting performance in Parkinson's Disease: A comparison between acquisition and shifting performance. *Journal of Clinical and Experimental Neuropsychology, 17,* 918–925.

76. Waller, G., & Ruddock, A. (1995). Information-processing correlates of reported sexual abuse in eating-disordered and comparison women. *Child Abuse & Neglect, 19,* 745–759.

77. Azouvi, P., Jokic, C., Van Der Linden, M., Marlier, N., & Bussel, B. (1996). Working memory and supervisory control after severe closed-head injury. A study of dual task performance and random generation. *Journal of Clinical and Experimental Neuropsychology, 18,* 317–337.

78. Flashman, L. A., Flaum, M., Gupta, S., & Andreasen, N. C. (1996). Soft signs and neuropsychological performance in schizophrenia. *American Journal of Psychiatry, 153,* 526–532.

79. Hall, M., Whaley, R., Robertson, K., Hamby, S., Wilkins, J., & Hall, C. (1996). The correlation between neuropsychological and neuroanatomic changes over time in asymptomatic and symptomatic HIV-1-infected individuals. *Neurology, 46,* 1697–1702.

80. Hogervorst, E., Riedel, W., Jeukendrop, A., & Jolles, J. (1996). Cognitive performance after strenuous physical exercise. *Perceptual and Motor Skills, 83,* 479–488.

81. Palmer, B. W., Boone, K. B., Lesser, I. M., Wohl, M. A., Berman, N., & Miller, B. L. (1996). Neuropsychological deficits among older depressed patients with predominently psychological or vegatative symptoms. *Journal of Affective Disorders, 41,* 17–24.

82. Pillon, B., Ertle, S., Deweer, B., Sarazin, M., Agid, Y., & Dubois, B. (1996). Memory for spatial location is affected in Parkinson's disease. *Neuropsychologia, 34,* 77–85.

83. Pliskin, N. H., Hamer, D. P., Goldstein, D. S., Towle, V. L., Reder, A. T., Noronha, A., & Arnason, B. G. W. (1996). Improved delayed visual production test performance in multiple sclerosis patients receiving interferon B-1b. *Neurology, 47,* 1463–1468.

84. Salthouse, T. A. (1996). General and specific speed mediation of adult age differences in memory. *Journal of Gerontology, 51,* 30–42.

85. Simpson, D. M., Dorfman, D., Olney, R. K., Mckinley, G., Dobkin, J., So, Y., Berger, J., Ferdon, M. B., Fiedman, B., & The Peptide Neuropathy Study Group. (1996). Peptide T in the treatment of painful distal neuropathy associated with AIDS: Results of a placebo-controlled trial. *Nursing Research, 47,* 1254–1259.

86. Spikman, J. M., van Zomeren, A. H., & Deelman, B. G. (1996). Deficits of attention after closed-head injury: Slowness only? *Journal of Clinical and Experimental Neuropsychology, 18,* 755–767.
87. Van Spaendonck, K. P. M., Berger, H. J. C., Horstink, M. W. I. M., Borm, G. F., & Cools, A. R. (1996). Memory performance under varying cueing conditions in patients with Parkinson's disease. *Neuropsychologia, 34,* 1159–1164.
88. Van Spaendonek, K. P. M., Berger, H. J. C., Horstink, M. W. I. M., Buytenhuijs, E. L., & Cools, A. R. (1996). Executive functions and disease characteristics in Parkinson's Disease. *Neuropsychologia, 34,* 617–626.
89. Waldstein, S. R., Polefrone, J. M., Fazzari, T. V., Manuck, S. B., Jennings, J. R., Ryan, C. M., Muldoon, M. F., & Shapiro, A. P. (1996). Hypertension and neuropsychological performance in men: Interactive effects of age. *Health Psychology, 15,* 102–109.
90. Bahri, T., & Bendania, A. (1997). Effect of language dominance on cognitive processes in a Stroop task. *Perceptual and Motor Skills, 84,* 979–988.
91. Bates, M. E. (1997). Stability of neuropsychological assessments early in alcoholism treatment. *Journal of Studies on Alcohol, 58,* 617–621.
92. Brand, N., Verspui, L., & Oving, A. (1997). Induced mood and selective attention. *Perceptual and Motor Skills, 84,* 455–463.
93. Bruggemans, E. F. Van de Vijver, F. J. R., & Huysmans, H. A. (1997). Assessment of cognitive deterioration in individual patients following cardiac surgery: Correcting for measurement error and practice effects. *Journal of Clinical and Experimental Neuropsychology, 19,* 543–559.
94. Chen, J-Y. (1997). How should the Stroop interference effect be measured? Further evidence from alternative versions of the Stoop task. *Perceptual and Motor Skills, 84,* 1123–1133.
95. Cunningham, J. M., Pliskin, N. H., Cassisi, J. E., Tsang, B., & Rao, S. M. (1997). Relationship between confabulation and measures of memory and executive function. Journal of Clinical and Experimental *Neuropsychology, 19,* 867–877.
96. Dodrill, C. B., Arnett, J. L., Sommerville, K. W., & Shu, V. (1997). Cognitive and quality of life effects of differing dosages of tiagabine in epilepsy. *Neurology, 48,* 1025–1031.
97. Downey, K. K., Stelson, F. W., Pomerleau, O. F. & Giordani, B. (1997). Adult attention deficit hyperactivity disorder: psychological test profiles in a clinical population. *Journal of Nervous and Mental Disease, 185,* 32–38.
98. Griffiths, P., Tarrini, M., & Robinson, P. (1997). Executive functional psychosocial adjustment in children with early treated phenylketonuria: Correlation with historical and concurrent phenylalanine levels. *Journal of Disability Research, 41,* 317–323.
99. Hänninen, T., Hallikainen, M., Koivisto, K., Partanen, K., Laakso, M. P., Riekkinen, P. J., Sr., & Soininen, H. (1997). Decline of frontal lobe functions in subjects with age-associated memory impairment. *Neurology, 48,* 148–153.
100. Jurado, M. A., Junquê, C., Pujol, J., Oliver, B., & Vendrell, P. (1997). Impaired estimation of word occurrence frequency in frontal lobe patients *Neuropsychologia, 35,* 635–641.
101. Kessler, J., Markowitsch, H. J., Huber, M., Kalbe, E., Weber-Luxenburger, G., & Kock, P. (1997). Massive and persistent antugrade amnesia in the absence of detectable brain damage: Anterograde psychogenic amnesia or gross reduction in sustained effort? *Journal of Clinical and Experimental Neuropsychology, 19,* 604–614.
102. Klein, M., Ponds, R. W. H. M., Houx, P. J., & Jolles, J. (1997). Effect of test duration on age-related differences in Stroop interference. *Journal of Clinical and Experimental Neuropsychology, 19,* 77–82.
103. Lemelin, S., Baruch, P., Vincent, A., Everett, J., & Vincent, P. (1997). Distractibility and processing resource deficit in major depression. Evidence for two deficient attentional processing models. *Journal of Nervous and Mental Disease, 185,* 542–548.
104. McDowell, S., Whyte, J., & D'Esposito, M. (1997). Working memory impairments in traumatic brain injury: Evidence from a dual-task paradigm. *Neuropsychologia, 35,* 1341–1353.
105. McFetridge, J. A., & Yarandi, h. N. (1997). Cardiovascular function during cognitive stress in men before and after coronary artery bypass grafts. *Nursing Research, 46,* 188–194.
106. Motta, R. W., Joseph, J. M., Rose, R. D., Suozzi, J. M., & Leiderman, L. J. (1997). Secondary trauma: Assessing inter-generational transmission of war experiences with a modified Stroop procedure. *Journal of Clinical Psychology, 53,* 895–903.
107. Paradiso, S., Lamberty, G. J., Garvey, M. J. & Robinson, R. G. (1997). Cognitive impairment in the euthymic phase of chronic unipolar depression. *Journal of Nervous and Mental Disease, 185,* 748–754.
108. Porterfield, T., Cook, M., Deary, I. J., & Ebmeier, K. P. (1997). Neuropsychological function and diurnal variation in depression. *Journal of Clinical and Experimental Neuropsychology, 19,* 906–913.
109. Robertson, I. H., Manly, T., Andrade, J., Baddeley, B. T., & Yiend, J. (1997). "Oops!": Performance correlates of everyday attentional failures in traumatic brain injured and normal subjects. *Neuropsychologia, 35,* 747–758.
110. Schagen, S., Schmand, B., de STerke, S., & Lindeboom, J. (1997). Amsterdam Short-Term Memory Test: A new procedure for detection of feigned memory deficits. *Journal of Clinical and Experimental Neuropsychology, 19,* 43–51.
111. Siegrist, M. (1997). Test-retest reliability of different versions of the Stroop test. *The Journal of Psychology, 131,* 299–306.
112. Troster, A. I., Fields, J. A., Wilkinson, S. B., Pahwa, R., Miyawaki, E., Lyons, K. E., & Koller, W. C. (1997). Unilateral pallidal stimulation for Parkinson's disease: Neurobehavioral functioning before and 3 months after electrode implantation. *Neurology, 49,* 1078–1083.
113. Uttl, B., & Graf, P. (1997). Color-Word Stroop Test performance across the adult life span. *Journal of Clinical and Experimental Neuropsychology, 19,* 405–420.
114. Verstraeton, E., Cluydts, R., Verbraecken, J., & DeRoeck, J. (1997). Psychomotor and cognitive performance in nonapneic snorers: Preliminary findings. *Perceptual and Motor Skills, 84,* 1211–1222.
115. Aylward, E. H., Anderson, N. B., Bylsma, F. W., Wagster, M. V., Barta, P. E., Sherr, M., Feeney, J., Davis, A., Rosenblatt, A., Pearlson, G. D., & Ross, C. A. (1998). Frontal lobe volume in patients with Huntington's disease. *Neurology, 50,* 252–258.
116. Brown, T. L., Gore, C. L., & Pearson, T. (1998). Visual half-field Stroop effects with spatial separation of words and color targets. *Brain and Language, 63,* 122–142.
117. Giancola, P. R., Mezzich, A. C., & Tarter, R. E. (1998). Disruptive, delinquent and aggressive behavior in female adolescents with a psychoactive substance use disorder: Relation to executive cognitive functioning. *Journal of Studies on Alcohol, 59,* 560–567.
118. Hale, J. B., Hoeppner, J. B., DeWitt, M. B., Coury, D. L., Ritacco, D. G., & Trommer, B. (1998). Evaluating medication response in ADHD: Cognitive, behavioral, and single-subject methodology. *Journal of Learning Disabilities, 31,* 595–607.
119. Handwerk, M. L., & Marshall, R. M. (1998). Behavioral and emotional problems of students with learning disabilities, serious emotional disturbance, or both conditions. *Journal of Learning Disabilities, 31,* 327–338.
120. Miller, B. L., Cummings, J., Mishkin, F., Boone, K., Prince, F., Penton, M., & Cotman, C. (1998). Emergence of artistic talent in frontotemporal dementia. *Neurology, 51,* 978–982.
121. Nayak, M. B., & Milner, J. S. (1998). Neuropsychological functioning: Comparison of mothers at high- and low-risk for child physical abuse. *Child Abuse & Neglect, 22,* 687–703.
122. van Gorp, W, G., Altshuler, L., Theberge, D. C., Wilkins, J., & Dixon, W. (1998). Cognitive impairment in euthymic bipolar patients with and without prior alcohol dependence: A preliminary study. *Archives of General Psychiatry, 55,* 41–46.

[2517]

Stroop Neuropsychological Screening Test.

Purpose: Provides "an efficient and sensitive neuropsychological screening measure based on the Stroop procedure."
Population: Ages 18 and over.
Publication Date: 1989.
Acronym: SNST.
Scores, 2: Color, Color-Word.
Administration: Individual.
Price Data: Available from publisher.
Time: 4(9) minutes.
Authors: Max R. Trenerry, Bruce Crosson, James DeBoe, and William R. Leber.
Publisher: Psychological Assessment Resources, Inc.
Cross References: See T4:2583 (3 references); for reviews by Manfred J. Meier and Cecil R. Reynolds, see 11:382 (1 reference).

TEST REFERENCES

1. Seilhean, D., Duyckaerts, C., Vazeux, R., Bolgert, F., Brunet, P., Katlama, C., Gentilini, M., & Hauxn, J.-J. (1993). HIV-1-associated cognitive/motor complex: Absence of neuronal loss in the cerebral neocortex. *Neurology, 43,* 1492–1499.
2. Bamford, K. A., Caine, E. D., Kido, D. K., Cox, C., & Shoalson, I. (1995). A prospective evaluation of cognitive decline in early Huntington's disease: Functional and radiographic correlates. *Neurology, 45,* 1867–1873.
3. Caselli, R. J., Smith, B. E., & Osborne, D. (1995). Primary lateral sclerosis: A neuropsychological study. *Neurology, 45,* 2005–2009.
4. Meador, K. J., Loring, D. W., Moore, E. E., Thompson, W. O., Nichols, M. E., Oberzan, R. E., Durking, M. W., Gallagher, B. B., & King, D. W. (1995). Comparative cognitive effects of phenobarbital, phenytoin, and valproate in healthy adults. *Neurology, 45,* 1494–1499.
5. Swoboda, K. J., & Jenike, M. A. (1995). Frontal abnormalities in a patient with obsessive-compulsive disorder: The role of structural lesions in obsessive-compulsive behavior. *Neurology, 45,* 2130–2134.
6. Weyandt, L. L., Linterman, I., & Rice, J. A. (1995). Reported prevalence of attentional difficulties in a general sample of college students. *Journal of Psychopathology and Behavioral Assessment, 17,* 293–304.
7. Pillon, B., Dubois, B., & Agid, Y. (1996). Testing cognition may contribute to the diagnosis of movement disorders. *Neurology, 46,* 329–334.
8. Putzke, J. D., Williams, M. A., & Boll, T. J. (1998). A defensive response set and the relation between cognitive and emotional functioning: A replication. *Perceptual and Motor Skills, 86,* 251–257.

[2518]

Structure of Intellect Learning Abilities Test.

Purpose: "Designed to assess a wide variety of cognitive abilities or factors of intelligence in children and adults."

Population: Preschool-adult.

Publication Dates: 1975-1985.

Acronym: SOI-LA.

Administration: Group or individual.

Price Data, 1999: $210 per complete kit including 10 standard test booklets (5 Form A and 5 Form B), set of scoring keys, set of stimulus cards, 10 worksheets/ profiles, and manual ('85, 165 pages); $19.90 per 5 standard test booklets (specify Form A or B); $40 per scoring keys for Forms A, B, and G; $78 per manual ('85, 165 pages).

Authors: Mary Meeker, Robert Meeker, and Gale H. Roid (manual).

Publisher: Western Psychological Services.

a) FORM A.

Population: Grade 2-adult.

Scores: 26 subtests in 5 test areas: Cognition (Cognition of Figural Units, Cognition of Figural Classes, Cognition of Figural Systems, Cognition of Figural Transformations, Cognition of Symbolic Relations, Cognition of Symbolic Systems, Cognition of Semantic Units, Cognition of Semantic Relations, Cognition of Semantic Systems), Memory (Memory of Figural Units, Memory of Symbolic Units—Visual, Memory of Symbolic Systems—Visual, Memory of Symbolic Units—Auditory, Memory of Symbolic Systems—Auditory, Memory of Symbolic Implications), Evaluation (Evaluation of Figural Units, Evaluation of Figural Classes, Evaluation of Symbolic Classes, Evaluation of Symbolic Systems), Convergent Production (Convergent Production of Figural Units, Convergent Production of Symbolic Systems, Convergent Production of Symbolic Transformations, Convergent Production of Symbolic Implications), and Divergent Production (Divergent Production of Figural Units, Divergent Production of Semantic Units, and Divergent Production of Symbolic Relations) yielding 14 general ability scores: Cognition, Memory, Evaluation, Convergent Production, Divergent Production, Figural, Symbolic, Semantic, Units, Classes, Relations, Systems, Transformations, Implications.

Time: (150-180) minutes.

b) FORM B.

Purpose: Alternative to Form A.

c) GIFTED SCREENING FORM (FORM G).

Population: Grade 2-adult.

Subtests, 12: From Form A which best predict gifted status.

Price Data: $22 per 5 test booklets.

Time: (60-90) minutes.

d) PRIMARY FORM (FORM P).

Population: Grades K-3.

Subtests, 11: Similar to Form A, 5 measuring figural abilities, 3 measuring symbolic abilities, and 3 measuring semantic abilities.

Price Data: $26.50 per 5 test booklets; $45 per scoring key.

Time: (60-90) minutes.

Comments: Formerly called Process and Diagnostic Screening Test.

Cross References: For reviews by Jack A. Cummings and Dianna L. Newman, see 10:349 (5 references); for reviews by William E. Coffman and Donald A. Leton of an earlier form, see 9:1197 (2 references); see also T3:2320 (2 references).

TEST REFERENCES

1. O'Tuel, F. S. (1989). Sex differences on the Structure of Intellect (SOI-LA) Gifted Screening Form. *Gifted Child Quarterly, 33,* 73–75.

2. Cooper, E. (1991). A critique of six measures for assessing creativity. *Journal of Creative Behavior, 25,* 194-204.

3. Clapham, M. M., & Schuster, D. H. (1992). Can engineering students be trained to think more creatively. *Journal of Creative Behavior, 26,* 156–162.

4. Clapham, M. M. (1996). The construct validity of divergent scores in the Structure-of-Intellect Learning Abilities Test. *Educational and Psychological Measurement, 56,* 287–292.

[2519]

Structured Clinical Inverview for DSM-IV Axis I Disorders: Clinician Version.

Purpose: Constructed as "a semistructured interview for making the major DSM-IV Axis I diagnoses."

Population: Psychiatric or general medical patients ages 18 or older.

Publication Date: 1997.

Acronym: SCID-CV.

Scores, 6: Mood Episodes, Psychotic Symptoms, Psychotic Disorders, Mood Disorders, Substance Use Disorders, Anxiety and Other Disorders.

Administration: Individual.

Price Data, 1998: $65 per complete kit including user's guide (138 pages), administration booklet (84 pages), and 5 score sheets; $21.95 per packet of 5 score sheets; $27.50 per user's guide; $24 per administration booklet.

Time: (45–90) minutes.

Comments: Shortened, clinician version of the Structured Clinical interview for DSM-IV Axis I Disorders: Research Version.

Authors: Michael B. First, Robert L. Spitzer, Miriam Gibbon, and Janet B. W. Williams.

Publisher: American Psychiatric Press, Inc.

TEST REFERENCES

1. Eisen, J. L., & Rasmussen, S. A. (1989). Coexisting obsessive compulsive disorder and alcoholism. *Journal of Clinical psychiatry, 50,* 96–98.

2. Reich, J., Noyes, R., Jr., & Yates, W. (1989). Alprazolam treatment of avoidant personality traits in social phobic patients. *Journal of Clinical Psychiatry, 50,* 91–95.

3. Reich, J. H. (1989). Familiality of DSM-III dramatic and anxious personality clusters. *The Journal of Nervous and Mental Disease, 177,* 96–100.

4. Reich, J. H. (1989). Update on instruments to measure DSM-III and DSM-III-R personality disorders. *The Journal of Nervous and Mental Disease, 177,* 366–370.

5. Sokol, L., Beck, A. T., Greenberg, R. L., Wright, F. D., & Berchick, R. J. (1989). Cognitive therapy of panic disorder: A nonpharmacological alternative. *The Journal of Nervous and Mental Disease, 177,* 711–716.

6. Alnaes, R., & Torgersen, S. (1990). DSM-III personality disorders among patients with major depression, anxiety disorders, and mixed conditions. *The Journal of Nervous and Mental Disease, 178,* 693–698.

7. Beitman, B. D., Kushner, M., Lamberti, J. W., & Mokerji, V. (1990). Panic disorder without fear in patients with angiographically normal coronary arteries. *The Journal of Nervous and Mental Disease, 178,* 307–312.

8. Buydens-Branchey, L., Noumair, D., & Brancheu, M. (1990). Duration and intensity of combat exposure and posttraumatic stress disorder in Vietnam veterans. *The Journal of Nervous and Mental Disease, 178,* 582–587.

9. Christensen, L., & Burrows, R. (1990). Dietary treatment of depression. *Behvior Therapy, 21,* 183–193.

10. Kleinman, P. H., Miller, A. B., Millman, R. B., Woody, G. E., Todd, T., Kemp, J., & Lipton, D. S. (1990). Psychopathology among cocaine abusers entering treatment. *The Journal of Nervous and Mental Disease, 178,* 442–447.

11. Morrison, R. L., Bellack, A. S., Wixted, J. T., & Mueser, K. T. (1990). Positive and negative symptoms in schizophrenia: A cluster-analytic approach. *The Journal of Nervous and Mental Disease, 178,* 377–384.

12. Nelson, G. M., & Beach, S. R. H. (1990). Sequential interaction in depression: Effects of depressive behavior on spousal aggression. *Behavior Therapy, 21,* 167–182.

13. Reich, J. (1990). The effect of personality on placebo response in panic patients. *The Journal of Nervous and Mental Disease, 178,* 699.

14. Yehuda, R. Southwick, S. M., Nussbaum, G., Wahby, V., Giller, E. L., & Mason, J. W. (1990). Low urinary cortisol excretion in patients with posttraumatic stress disorder. *The Journal of Nervous and Mental Disease, 178,* 366–369.

15. Zimmerman, M., & Coryell, W. H. (1990). DSM-III personality disorder dimensions. *The Journal of Nervous and Mental Disease, 178,* 686–692.

16. Corrigan, P. W., & Green, M. F. (1991). Signal detection analysis of short-term recall in schizophrenia. *The Journal of Nervous and Mental Disease, 179,* 495–498.

17. Goff, D. C., Brotman, A. W., Kindlon, D., Waites, M., & Amico, E. (1991). The delusion of possession in chronically psychotic patients. *The Journal of Nervous and Mental Disease, 179,* 567–571.

18. Lin, K., Miller, M. H., Poland, R. E., Nuccio, I., & Yamaguchi, M. (1991). Ethnicity and family involvement in the treatment of schizophrenic patients. *The Journal of Nervous and Mental Disease, 179,* 631–633.

19. Townsley, R. M., Beach, S. R. H., Fincham, F. D., & O'Leary, K. D. (1991). Cognitive specificity for marital discord and depression: What types of cognition influence discord? *Behavior Therapy, 22,* 519–530.

20. Beach, S. R. H., & O'Leary, K. D. (1992). Treating depression in the context of marital discord: outcome and predictors of response of marital therapy versus cognitive therapy. *Behavior Therapy, 23,* 507–528.

21. Adams, S. G., & Howe, J. T. (1993). Predicting medication compliance in a psychotic population. *The Journal of Nervous and Mental Disease, 181,* 558–560.

22. Beatty, W. W., Jooc, Z., Monson, N., & Staton, R. D. (1993). Memory and frontal lobe dysfunction in schizophrenia and schizoaffective disorder. *The Journal of Nervous and Mental Disease, 181,* 448–453.

23. Brooner, R. K., Herbst, J. H., Schmidt, C. W., Bigelow, G. E. & Costa, P. T. (1993). Antisocial personality disorder among drug abusers: Relations to other personality diagnoses and the five-factor model of personality. *The Journal of Nervous and Mental Disease, 181,* 313–319.

24. Christensen, L., Bourgeois, A., & Cockroft, R. (1993). Electroencephalographic concomitants of a caffeine-induced panic reaction. *The Journal of Nervous and Mental Disease, 181,* 327–330.

25. Cox, B. J., Swinson, R. P., & Fergus, K. D. (1993). Changes in fear versus avoidance ratings with behavioral treatments for agoraphobia. *Behavior Therapy, 24,* 619–624.

26. Haller, D. L., Knisely, J. S., Dawson, K. S., & Schnoll, S. (1993). Perinatal substance abusers: Psychological and social characteristics. *The Journal of Nervous and Mental Disease, 181,* 509–513.

27. Haslam, N., & Beck, A. T. (1993). Categorization of major depression in an outpatient sample. *The Journal of Nervous and Mental Disease, 181,* 725–731.

28. Kinney, D. K., Yurgelun-Todd, D. A., & Woods, B. T. (1993). Neurological hand signs in schizophrenia and major mood disorders. *The Journal of Nervous and Mental Disease, 181,* 202–204.

29. Kosten, T. R., Schottenfeld, R., Ziedonis, D., & Falcioni, J. (1993). Buprenorphine versus methadone maintenance for Opioid dependence. *The Journal of Nervous and Mental Disease, 181,* 358–364.

30. Lehman, A. F., Myers, C. D., Thompson, J. W., & Corty, E. (1993). Implications of mental and substance use disorders: A comparison of single and dual diagnosis patients. *The Journal of Nervous and Mental Disease, 181,* 365–370.

31. Phillips, K. A., & McElroy, S. L. (1993). Insight, overvalued ideation, and delusional thinking in body dysmorphic disorder: Theoretical and treatment implications. *The Journal of Nervous and Mental Disease, 181,* 699–702.

32. Rund, B. R., Landro, N. I., & Orbeck, A. L. (1993). Stability in backward-masking performance in schizophrenics, affectively disturbed patients and normal subjects. *The Journal of Nervous and Mental Disease, 181,* 233–237.

33. Smith, J. E., Waldorf, V. A., & McNamara, C. L. (1993). Use of implosive therapy scenes to assess the fears of women with bulimia in two response modes. *Behavior Therapy, 24,* 601–618.

34. Turner, S. M., Beidel, D. C., Long, P. J., Turner, M. W., & Townsley, R. M. (1993). A composite measure to determine the functional status of treated social phobics: The Social Phobia Endstate Functioning Index. *Behavior Therapy, 24,* 265–275.

35. Beck, J. G., & Zebb, B. J. (1994). Behavioral assessment and treatment of panic disorder: Current status, future directions. *Behavior Therapy, 25,* 581–611.

36. Cloitre, M., Shear, m. K., Cancienne, J., & Zeitlin, S. B. (1994). Implicit and explicit memory for catastrophic associations to bodily sensation words in panic disorder. *Cognitive Therapy and Research, 18,* 225–240.

37. Côté, G., Gauthrer, J. G., Laberge, B., Cormier, H. J., & Plamondon, J. (1994). Reduced therapist contact in the cognitive behavioral treatment of panic disorder. *Behavior Therapy, 25,* 123–145.

38. Famularo, R., Fenton, T., Kinscherff, R., Ayoub, C., & Barnum, R. (1994). Maternal and child posttraumatic stress disorder in cases of child maltreatment. *Child Abuse & Neglect, 18,* 27–36.

39. Fava, M., Bless, E., Otto, M. W., Pava, J. A., & Rosenbaum, J. F. (1994). Dysfunctional attitudes in major depression: Changes with pharmacotherapy. *The Journal of Nervous and Mental Disease, 182,* 45–49.

40. Hegel, M. T., Ravaris, C. L., & Ahles, T. A. (1994). Combined cognitive-behavioral and time-limited alprazolam treatment of panic disorder. *Behavior Therapy, 25,* 183–195.

41. Ingram, R. E., Bernet, C. Z., & McLaughlin, S. C. (1994). Attentional allocation processes in individuals at risk for depression. *Cognitive Therapy and Research, 18,* 317–332.

42. Keller, M. B., Yonkers, K. A., Warshaw, M. G., Pratt, L. A., Gollan, J. K., Massion, A. O., White, K., Swartz, A. R., Reich, J., & Lavori, P. W. (1994). Remission and relapse in subjects with panic disorder and panic with agoraphobia: A prospective short-interval naturalistic follow-up. *The Journal of Nervous and Mental Disease, 182,* 290–296.

43. Kidorf, M., Stitzer, M. L., & Brooner, R. K. (1994). Characteristics of methadone patients responding to take-home incentives. *Behavior Therapy 25,* 109–121.

44. Lehman, A. F., Myers, C. D., Corty, E., & Thompson, J. (1994). Severity of substance use disorders among psychiatric inpatients. *The Journal of Nervous and Mental Disease, 182,* 164–167.

45. Organista, K. C., Muñoz, R. F., & González, G. (1994). Cognitive-behavioral therapy for depression in low-income and minority medical outpaitents: Description of a program and exploratory analyses. *Cognitive Therapy and Research, 18,* 241–259.

46. Reich, J., Goldenberg, I., Goisman, R., Vasile, R., & Keller, M. (1994). A prospective, follow-along study of the course of social phobia: II. Testing for basic predictors of course. *The Journal of Nervous and Mental Disease, 182,* 297–301.

47. Rowan, A. B., Foy, D. W., Rodriguez, N., & Ryan, S. (1994). Posttraumatic stress disorder in a clinical sample of adults sexually abused as children. *Child Abuse & Neglect, 18,* 51–61.

48. Shearer, S. L. (1994). Phenomenology of self-injury among inpatient women with borderline personality disorder. *The Journal of Nervous and Mental Disease, 182,* 524–526.

49. Sonne, S. C., Brady, K. T., & Morton, W. A. (1994). Substance abuse and bipolar affective disorder. *The Journal of Nervous and Mental Disease 182,* 349–352.

50. Starcevic, V., Fallon, S., & Uhlenhuth, E. H. (1994). The frequency and severity of generalized anxiety disorder symptoms: Toward a less cumbersome conceptualization. *The Journal of Nervous and Mental Disease, 182,* 80–84.

51. Steketee, G. (1994). Behavioral assessment and treatment planning with obsessive compulsive disorder: A review emphasizing clinical application. *Behavior Therapy, 25,* 613–633.

52. Sullivan, P. F., Joyce, P. R., & Mulder, R. T. (1994). Borderline personality disorder in major depression. *The Journal of Nervous and Mental Disease, 182,* 508–511.

53. Chambless, D. L., & Williams, K. E. (1995). A preliminary study of African Americans with agoraphobia: Symptom severity and outcome of treatment with in vivo exposure. *Behavior Therapy, 26,* 501–515.

54. Foa, E. B., Riggs, D. S., Massle, E. D., & Yarczower, M. (1995). The impact of fear activation and anger on the efficacy of exposure treatment for posttraumatic stress disorder. *Behavior Therapy, 26,* 487–499.

55. Lawrence, K. J., Cozolino, L., & Foy, D. W. (1995). Psychological sequelae in adult females reporting childhood ritualistic abuse. *Child Abuse & Neglect, 19,* 975–984.

56. Wells, A., Clark, D. M., Salkovskis, P., Ludgate, J., Hackmann, A., & Gelder, M. (1995). Social phobia: The role of in-situation safety behaviors in maintaining anxiety and negative beliefs. *Behavior Therapy, 26,* 153–161.

[2520]

Structured Clinical Interview for DSM-IV Axis II Personality Disorders.

Purpose: Designed as "a semistructured diagnostic interview for assessing the 10 DSM-IV Axis II personality disorders as well as Depressive Personality Disorder and Passive-Aggressive Personality Disorder."

Population: Adults receiving psychiatric or general medical care.

Publication Date: 1997.
Acronym: SCID-II.
Scores, 13: Avoidant, Dependent, Obsessive-Compulsive, Passive-Aggressive, Depressive, Paranoid, Schizotypal, Schizoid, Histrionic, Narcissistic, Borderline, Antisocial, Not Otherwise Specified.
Administration: Individual.
Price Data, 1998: $46 per complete kit including user's guide and packet of 5 interviews and questionnaire; $21.95 per 5 interviews and questionnaires; $29.95 per user's guide.
Time: Administration time not reported.
Comments: Also includes optional, self-report SCID-II Personality Questionnaire.
Authors: Michael B. First, Miriam Gibbon, Robert L. Spitzer, Janet B. W. Williams, and Lorna Smith Benjamin.
Publisher: American Psychiatric Press, Inc.

TEST REFERENCES

1. Eisen, J. L., & Rasmussen, S. A. (1989). Coexisting obsessive compulsive disorder and alcoholism. *Journal of Clinical psychiatry, 50,* 96–98.
2. Reich, J., Noyes, R., Jr., & Yates, W. (1989). Alprazolam treatment of avoidant personality traits in social phobic patients. *Journal of Clinical Psychiatry, 50,* 91–95.
3. Reich, J. H. (1989). Familiality of DSM-III dramatic and anxious personality clusters. *The Journal of Nervous and Mental Disease, 177,* 96–100.
4. Reich, J. H. (1989). Update on instruments to measure DSM-III and DSM-III-R personality disorders. *The Journal of Nervous and Mental Disease, 177,* 366–370.
5. Sokol, L., Beck, A. T., Greenberg, R. L., Wright, F. D., & Berchick, R. J. (1989). Cognitive therapy of panic disorder: A nonpharmacological alternative. *The Journal of Nervous and Mental Disease, 177,* 711–716.
6. Alnaes, R., & Torgersen, S. (1990). DSM-III personality disorders among patients with major depression, anxiety disorders, and mixed conditions. *The Journal of Nervous and Mental Disease, 178,* 693–698.
7. Beitman, B. D., Kushner, M., Lamberti, J. W., & Mokerji, V. (1990). Panic disorder without fear in patients with angiographically normal coronary arteries. *The Journal of Nervous and Mental Disease, 178,* 307–312.
8. Buydens-Branchey, L., Noumair, D., & Brancheu, M. (1990). Duration and intensity of combat exposure and posttraumatic stress disorder in Vietnam veterans. *The Journal of Nervous and Mental Disease, 178,* 582–587.
9. Christensen, L., & Burrows, R. (1990). Dietary treatment of depression. *Behvior Therapy, 21,* 183–193.
10. Kleinman, P. H., Miller, A. B., Millman, R. B., Woody, G. E., Todd, T., Kemp, J., & Lipton, D. S. (1990). psychopathology among coccaine abusers entering treatment. *The Journal of Nervous and Mental Disease, 178,* 442–447.
11. Morrison, R. L., Bellack, A. S., Wixted, J. T., & Mueser, K. T. (1990). Positive and negative symptoms in schizophrenia: A cluster-analytic approach. *The Journal of Nervous and Mental Disease, 178,* 377–384.
12. Nelson, G. M., & Beach, S. R. H. (1990). Sequential interaction in depression: Effects of depressive behavior on spousal aggression. *Behavior Therapy, 21,* 167–182.
13. Reich, J. (1990). The effect of personality on placebo response in panic patients. *The Journal of Nervous and Mental Disease, 178,* 699.
14. Renneberg, B., Goldstein, A. J., Phillips, D., & Chambless, D. L. (1990). Intensive behavioral group treatment of avoidant personality disorder. *Behavior Therapy, 21,* 363–377.
15. Yehuda, R. Southwick, S. M., Nussbaum, G., Wahby, V., Giller, E. L., & Mason, J. W. (1990). Low urinary cortisol excretion in patients with posttraumatic stress disorder. *The Journal of Nervous and Mental Disease, 178,* 366–369.
16. Zimmerman, M., & Coryell, W. H. (1990). DSM-III personality disorder dimensions. *The Journal of Nervous and Mental Disease, 178,* 686–692.
17. Corrigan, P. W., & Green, M. F. (1991). Signal detection analysis of short-term recall in schizophrenia. *The Journal of Nervous and Mental Disease, 179,* 495–498.
18. Goff, D. C., Brotman, A. W., Kindlon, D., Waites, M., & Amico, E. (1991). The delusion of possession in chronically psychotic patients. *The Journal of Nervous and Mental Disease, 179,* 567–571.
19. Lin, K., Miller, M. H., Poland, R. E., Nuccio, I., & Yamaguchi, M. (1991). Ethnicity and family involvement in the treatment of schizophrenic patients. *The Journal of Nervous and Mental Disease, 179,* 631–633.
20. Townsley, R. M., Beach, S. R. H., Fincham, F. D., & O'Leary, K. D. (1991). Cognitive specificity for marital discord and depression: What types of cognition influence discord? *Behavior Therapy, 22,* 519–530.
21. Beach, S. R. H., & O'Leary, K. D. (1992). Treating depression in the context of marital discord: outcome and predictors of response of marital therapy versus cognitive therapy. *Behavior Therapy, 23,* 507–528.
22. Adams, S. G., & Howe, J. T. (1993). Predicting medication compliance in a psychotic population. *The Journal of Nervous and Mental Disease, 181,* 558–560.
23. Beatty, W. W., Jooc, Z., Monson, N., & Staton, R. D. (1993). Memory and frontal lobe dysfunction in schizophrenia and schizoaffective disorder. *The Journal of Nervous and Mental Disease, 181,* 448–453.
24. Brooner, R. K., Herbst, j. H., Schmidt, C. W., Bigelow, G. E. & Costa, P. T. (1993). Antisocial personality disorder among drug abusers: Relations to other personality diagnoses and the five-factor model of personality. *The Journal of Nervous and Mental Disease, 181,* 313–319.
25. Christensen, L., Bourgeois, A., & Cockroft, R. (1993). Electroencephalographic concomitants of a caffeine-induced panic reaction. *The Journal of Nervous and Mental Disease, 181,* 327–330.
26. Cox, B. J., Swinson, R. P., & Fergus, K. D. (1993). Changes in fear versus avoidance ratings with behavioral treatments for agoraphobia. *Behavior Therapy, 24,* 619–624.
27. Haller, D. L., Knisely, J. S., Dawson, K. S., & Schnoll, S. (1993). Perinatal substance abusers: Psychological and social characteristics. *The Journal of Nervous and Mental Disease, 181,* 509–513.
28. Haslam, N., & Beck, A. T. (1993). Categorization of major depression in an outpatient sample. *The Journal of Nervous and Mental Disease, 181,* 725–731.
29. Kinney, D. K., Yurgelun-Todd, D. A., & Woods, B. T. (1993). Neurological hand signs in schizophrenia and major mood disorders. *The Journal of Nervous and Mental Disease, 181,* 202–204.
30. Kosten, T. R., Schottenfeld, R., Ziedonis, D., & Falcioni, J. (1993). Buprenorphine versus methadone maintenance for Opioid dependence. *The Journal of Nervous and Mental Disease, 181,* 358–364.
31. Lehman, A. F., Myers, C. D., Thompson, J. W., & Corty, E. (1993). Implications of mental and substance use disorders: A comparison of single and dual diagnosis patients. *The Journal of Nervous and Mental Disease, 181,* 365–370.
32. Phillips, K. A., & McElroy, S. L. (1993). Insight, overvalued ideation, and delusional thinking in body dysmorphic disorder: Theoretical and treatment implications. *The Journal of Nervous and Mental Disease, 181,* 699–702.
33. Rund, B. R., Landro, N. I., & Orbeck, A. L. (1993). Stability in backward-masking performance in schizophrenics, affectively disturbed patients and normal subjects. *The Journal of Nervous and Mental Disease, 181,* 233–237.
34. Smith, J. E., Waldorf, V. A., & McNamara, C. L. (1993). Use of implosive therapy scenes to assess the fears of women with bulimia in two response modes. *Behavior Therapy, 24,* 601–618.
35. Turner, S. M., Beidel, D. C., Long, P. J., Turner, M. W., & Townsley, R. M. (1993). A composite measure to determine the functional status of treated social phobics: The Social Phobia Endstate Functioning Index. *Behavior Therapy, 24,* 265–275.
36. Anand, A., Wales, R. J., Jackson, H. J., & Copolov, D. L. (1994). Linguistic impairment in early psychosis. *The Journal of Nervous and Mental Disease, 182,* 488–493.
37. Cloitre, M., Shear, M. K., Cancienne, J., & Zeitlin, S. B. (1994). Implicit and explicit memory for catastrophic associations to bodily sensation words in panic disorder. *Cognitive Therapy and Research, 18,* 225–240.
38. Côté, G., Gauthrer, J. G., Laberge, B., Cormier, H. J., & Plamondon, J. (1994). Reduced therapist contact in the cognitive behavioral treatment of panic disorder. *Behavior Therapy, 25,* 123–145.
39. Famularo, R., Fenton, T., Kinscherff, R., Ayoub, C., & Barnum, R. (1994). Maternal and child posttraumatic stress disorder in cases of child maltreatment. *Child Abuse & Neglect, 18,* 27–36.
40. Fava, M., Bless, E., Otto, M. W., Pava, J. A., & Rosenbaum, J. F. (1994). Dysfunctional attitudes in major depression: Changes with pharmacotherapy. *The Journal of Nervous and Mental Disease, 182,* 45–49.
41. Ingram, R. E., Bernet, C. Z., & McLaughlin, S. C. (1994). Attentional allocation processes in individuals at risk for depression. *Cognitive Therapy and Research, 18,* 317–332.
42. Keller, M. B., Yonkers, K. A., Warshaw, M. G., Pratt, L. A., Gollan, J. K., Massion, A. O., White, K., Swartz, A. R., Reich, J., & Lavori, P. W. (1994). Remission and relapse in subjects with panic disorder and panic with agoraphobia: A prospective short-interval naturalistic follow-up. *The Journal of Nervous and Mental Disease, 182,* 290–296.
43. Kidorf, M., Stitzer, M. L., & Brooner, R. K. (1994). Characteristics of methadone patients responding to take-home incentives *Behavior Therapy, 25,* 109–121.
44. Lehman, A. F., Myers, C. D., Corty, E., & Thompson, J. (1994). Severity of substance use disorders among psychiatric inpatients. *The Journal of Nervous and Mental Disease, 182,* 164–167.
45. Lyness, S. A., Eaton, E. M., & Schneider, L. S. (1994). Cognitive performance in older and middle-aged depressed outpatients and controls. *Journal of Gerontology: Psychological Sciences, 49* (Pt.1), P129–P136.
46. Newman, M. G., Hofmann, S. G., Trabert, W., Roth, W. T., & Taylor, C. B. (1994). Does behavioral treatment of social phobia lead to cognitive changes? *Behavior Therapy, 25,* 503–517.
47. Reich, J., Goldenberg, I., Goisman, R., Vasile, R., & Keller, M. (1994). A prospective, follow-along study of the course of social phobia: II. Testing for basic predictors of course. *The Journal of Nervous and Mental Disease, 182,* 297–301.
48. Rowan, A. B., Foy, D. W., Rodriguez, N., & Ryan, S. (1994). Posttraumatic stress disorder in a clinical sample of adults sexually abused as children. *Child Abuse & Neglect, 18,* 51–61.

49. Sonne, S. C., Brady, K. T., & Morton, W. A. (1994). Substance abuse and bipolar affective disorder. *The Journal of Nervous and Mental Disease 182,* 349–352.

50. Starcevic, V., Fallon, S., & Uhlenhuth, E. H. (1994). The frequency and severity of generalized anxiety disorder symptoms: Toward a less cumbersome conceptualization. *The Journal of Nervous and Mental Disease, 182,* 80–84.

51. Sullivan, P. F., Joyce, P. R., & Mulder, R. T. (1994). Borderline personality disorder in major depression. *The Journal of Nervous and Mental Disease, 182,* 508–511.

52. Chambless, D. L., & Williams, K. E. (1995). A preliminary study of African Americans with agoraphobia: Symptom severity and outcome of treatment with in vivo exposure. *Behavior Therapy, 26,* 501–515.

53. Foa, E. B., Riggs, D. S., Massle, E. D., & Yarczower, M. (1995). The impact of fear activation and anger on the efficacy of exposure treatment for posttraumatic stress disorder. *Behavior Therapy, 26,* 487–499.

54. Lawrence, K. J., Cozolino, L., & Foy, D. W. (1995). Psychological sequelae in adult females reporting childhood ritualistic abuse. *Child Abuse & Neglect, 19,* 975–984.

55. Wells, A., Clark, D. M., Salkovskis, P., Ludgate, J., Hackmann, A., & Gelder, M. (1995). Social phobia: The role of in-situation safety behaviors in maintaining anxiety and negative beliefs. *Behavior Therapy, 26,* 153–161.

[2521]

Structured Interview for Disorders of Extreme Stress & Traumatic Antecedents Questionnaire—Self Report.

Purpose: Designed to assist "in the initial assessment, treatment planning, and progress measurement of clients potentially affected with Post Traumatic Stress Disorder."
Population: Adults potentially affected with Post Traumatic Stress Disorder.
Publication Date: 1999.
Administration: Individual.
Price Data: Available from publisher.
Time: Administration time not reported.
Comments: Computerized.
Authors: Bessel A. van der Kolk.
Publisher: Multi-Health Systems, Inc.

a) STRUCTURED INTERVIEW FOR DISORDERS OF EXTREME STRESS.
Acronym: SIDES.
Scores, 9: Affect Regulation, Modulation of Anger, Self Destructiveness, Suicide Preoccupation, Sexual Involvement, Risk Taking, Amnesia, Transient Dissociative Episodes, Depersonalization.

b) TRAUMATIC ANTECEDENTS QUESTIONNAIRE—SELF REPORT.
Acronym: TAQ-S.
Scores, 10: Competence, Safety, Neglect, Separation, Family Secrets, Conflict Resolution, Physical Trauma, Sexual Trauma, Witnessing Trauma, Exposure to Drugs.

[2522]

Structured Interview of Reported Symptoms.

Purpose: Designed to "detect malingering and other forms of feigning of psychological symptoms."
Population: Ages 18 and over.
Publication Dates: 1986-1992.
Acronym: SIRS.
Scores, 13: Primary Scales (Rare Symptoms, Symptom Combinations, Improbable or Absurd Symptoms, Subtle Symptoms, Blatant Symptoms, Severity of Symptoms, Selectivity of Symptoms, Reported vs. Observed Symptoms), Supplementary Scales (Direct Appraisal of Honesty, Defensive Symptoms, Symptom Onset and Resolution, Overly Specified Symptoms, Inconsistency of Symptoms).
Administration: Individual.
Price Data: Price information available from publisher for complete kit including manual ('92, 47 pages) and 10 interview booklets.
Time: (30-45) minutes.
Authors: Richard Rogers, R. Michael Bagby, and Susan E. Dickens.
Publisher: Psychological Assessment Resources, Inc.
Cross References: For reviews by David N. Dixon and Ronald J. Ganellen, see 12:375.

[2523]

Structured Photographic Articulation Test Featuring Dudsberry.

Purpose: Designed to assess the child's articulation and phonological skills.
Population: Ages 3-9.
Publication Date: 1989.
Acronym: SPAT-D.
Scores: Total score only.
Administration: Individual.
Price Data, 1998: $89 per SPAT-D kit including 48 color photographs, 25 response forms, and manual (24 pages); $10 per 25 response forms.
Time: [10-15] minutes.
Comments: Forty-eight photographs are used to assess 59 consonant singletons and 21 consonant blends.
Authors: Janet D. Kresheck and Pat Tattersall.
Publisher: Janelle Publications, Inc.
Cross References: For reviews by Clinton W. Bennett and Susan Felsenfeld, see 12:376.

[2524]

Structured Photographic Expressive Language Test.

Purpose: Designed "to assess ... production of expressive morphology and syntax."
Publication Date: 1983.
Acronym: SPELT II.
Scores: Total score only.
Administration: Individual.
Comments: Includes a system of alternative response structures for assessment of the Black population.
Authors: Ellen O'Hara Werner and Janet Dawson Kresheck.
Publisher: Janelle Publications, Inc.

a) STRUCTURED PHOTOGRAPHIC EXPRESSIVE LANGUAGE TEST—PRESCHOOL.
Population: Ages 3-0 to 5-11.

Acronym: SPELT-P.
Price Data, 1998: $89 per complete kit including 37 color photos, 10 response forms, and manual (27 pages); $8 per 50 response forms; $12 per 50 articulation forms.
Time: (3-10) minutes.
b) STRUCTURED PHOTOGRAPHIC EXPRESSIVE LANGUAGE TEST—II.
Population: Ages 4-0 to 9-5.
Acronym: SPELT-II.
Price Data: $99 per complete kit including 50 color photos, 10 response forms, and manual (51 pages); $20 per 50 response forms.
Cross References: See T4:2588 (1 reference); for a review by Joan D. Berryman, see 9:1198 (2 references).

TEST REFERENCES

1. Wilson, K. S., Blackmon, R. C., Hall, R. E., & Elcholtz, G. E. (1991). Methods of language assessment: A survey of California public school clinicians. *Language, Speech, and Hearing Services in Schools, 22,* 236–241.
2. Eiserman, W. D., Weber, C., & McCoun, M. (1992). Two alternative program models for serving speech disordered preschoolers: A second follow-up. *Journal of Communication Disorders, 25,* 77–106.
3. Weiss, A. L., & Zebrowski, P. M. (1992). Disfluencies in the conversations of young children who stutter: Some answers about questions. *Journal of Speech and Hearing Research, 35,* 1230–1238.
4. Catts, H. W. (1993). The relationship between speech-language impairments and reading disabilities. *Journal of Speech and Hearing Research, 36,* 948–958.
5. Swisher, L., & Plante, E. (1993). Nonverbal IQ tests reflect different relations among skills for specifically language-impaired and normal children: Brief report. *Journal of Communication Disorders, 26,* 65–71.
6. Plante, E., & Vance, R. (1994). Selection of preschool language tests: A data-based approach. *Language, Speech, and Hearing Services in Schools, 25,* 15–24.
7. Eiserman, W. D., Weber, C., & McCan, M. (1995). Parent and professional roles in early intervention: A longitudinal comparison of the effects of two intervention configurations. *The Journal of Special Education, 29,* 20–44.
8. Gilbertson, M., & Kamhi, A. G. (1995). Novel word learning in children with language impairment. *Journal of Speech and Hearing Research, 38,* 630–642.
9. Kamhi, A. G., Ward, M. F., & Mills, E. A. (1995). Hierarchical planning abilities in children with specific language impairments. *Journal of Speech and Hearing Research, 38,* 1108–1116.
10. Swisher, L., Restrepo, M. A., Plante, E., & Lowell, S. (1995). Effect of implicit and explicit "rule" presentation on bound-morpheme generalization in specific language impairment. *Journal of Speech and Hearing Research, 38,* 168–173.
11. Tomblin, J. B., Records, N. L., & Zhang, X. (1996). A system for the diagnosis of specific language impairment in kindergarten children. *Journal of Speech and Hearing Research, 39,* 1284–1294.
12. Kiernan, B., Snow, D., Swisher, L., & Vance, R. (1997). Another look at nonverbal rule induction in children with SLI: Test a flexible reconceputalization hypothesis. *Journal of Speech, Language, and Hearing Research, 40,* 75–82.
13. Kiernan, B., & Gray, S. (1998). Word learning in a supported-learning context by preschool children with specific language impairment. *Journal of Speech, Language, and Hearing Research, 41,* 161–171.

[2525]

Student Adaptation to College Questionnaire.

Purpose: "Designed to assess how well a student is adapting to the demands of the college experience."
Population: College freshmen.
Publication Date: 1989.
Acronym: SACQ.
Scores, 5: Academic Adjustment, Social Adjustment, Personal Emotional Adjustment, Attachment, Full Scale.
Administration: Group or individual.
Price Data, 1999: $89.50 per complete kit including 25 hand-scorable questionnaires and manual (76 pages) plus 2 prepaid mail-in answer sheets for computer scoring and interpretation; $36 per 25 hand-scorable questionnaires; $45 per manual; $11 per computer-scored mail-in answer sheet (quantity discounts available); $165 per IBM computer disk (25 uses).
Time: (20) minutes.
Authors: Robert W. Baker and Bohdan Siryk.
Publisher: Western Psychological Services.
Cross References: See T4:2590 (9 references); for a review by E. Jack Asher, Jr., see 11:383 (4 references).

TEST REFERENCES

1. Lopez, F. G., Campbell, V. L., & Watkins, C. E., Jr. (1988). The relation of parental divorce to college student development. *Journal of Divorce, 12*(1), 83–98.
2. Montgomery, R. L., & Haemmerlie, F. M. (1993). Undergraduate adjustment to college, drinking behavior, and fraternity membership. *Psychological Reports, 73,* 801–802.
3. Ollendick, T. H., Lease, C. A., & Cooper, C. (1993). Separation anxiety in young adults: A preliminary examination. *Journal of Anxiety Disorders, 7,* 293–305.
4. Haemmerlie, F. M., Steen, S. C., & Benedicto, J. A. (1994). Undergraduates' conflictual independence, adjustment, and alcohol use: The importance of the mother-student relationship. *Journal of Clinical Psychology, 50,* 644–650.
5. Hammerlie, F. M., Montgomery, R. L., & Saling, C. (1994). Age of first use and present use of alcohol by undergraduates. *Psychological Reports, 75,* 1268–1270.
6. Rice, K. G., & Whaley, T. J. (1994). A short-term longitudinal study of within-semester stability and change in attachment and college student adjustment. *Journal of College Student Development, 35,* 324-330.
7. Solberg, V. S., Valdez, J., & Villarreal, P. (1994). Social support, stress, and Hispanic college adjustment: Test of diathesis-stress model. *Hispanic Journal of Behavioral Sciences, 16,* 230-239.
8. Tomlinson-Clarke, S., & Clarke, D. (1994). Predicting social adjustment and academic achievement for college women with and without precollege leadership. *Journal of College Student Development, 35,* 120-124.
9. Brooks, J. H., II, & DuBois, D. L. (1995). Individual and environmental predictors of adjustment during the first year of college. *Journal of College Student Development, 36,* 347–360.
10. Low, C. A., & Handal, P. J. (1995). The relationship between religion and adjustment to college. *Journal of College Student Development, 36,* 406–412.
11. Silverthorn, N. A., & Gekoski, W. L. (1995). Social desirability effects on measures of adjustment to university, independence from parents, and self-efficacy. *Journal of Clinical Psychology, 51,* 244-251.
12. Kenny, M. E., & Stryker, S. (1996). Social network characteristics and college adjustment among racially and ethnically diverse first-year students. *Journal of College Student Development, 37,* 649–658.
13. Shilkret, R., & Nigrosh, E. E. (1997). Assessing students' plans for college. *Journal of Counseling Psychology, 44,* 222–231.

[2526]

Student Adjustment Inventory.

Purpose: Designed as "an instrument for identifying common affective-social problems."
Population: Upper elementary, junior high, senior high, and beginning college students.
Publication Dates: 1975-1989.
Acronym: SAI.
Scores, 7: Self-Esteem, Group Interaction, Self-Discipline, Communication, Energy/Effort, Learning/Studying, Attitude Towards Learning Environment.
Administration: Group or individual.
Forms, 2: Available in pencil and paper or microcomputer versions.
Price Data, 1998: $34 per report kit including manual ('89, 23 pages); $10 per 10 reusable test booklets; $8 per 50 answer sheets; $10 per manual; $5.45-$6.35 per mail-in report; $225 per SAI microcomputer version (unlimited usage, specify IBM 5.25 or 3.5).
Time: (30) minutes.
Author: James R. Barclay.

Publisher: MetriTech, Inc.
Cross References: For reviews by Philip Ash and Mark J. Benson, see 12:377.

[2527]

Student Developmental Task and Lifestyle Inventory.

Purpose: "Assisting students in understanding their own development and establishing goals and plans to shape their own futures."
Population: College students ages 17-24.
Publication Date: 1987.
Acronym: SDTLI.
Scores, 12: Establishing and Clarifying Purpose Task (Educational Involvement Subtask, Career Planning Subtask, Life Management Subtask, Lifestyle Planning Subtask, Cultural Participation Subtask), Developing Mature Interpersonal Relationships Task (Peer Relationships Subtask, Tolerance Subtask, Emotional Autonomy Subtask), Academic Autonomy Task, Salubrious Lifestyle Scale, Intimacy Scale, Response Bias Scale.
Administration: Group.
Price Data, 1987: $45 per 50 reusable test booklets; $20 per 50 answer sheets; $12.50 per 50 Understanding and Using the SDTLI: A Guide for Students (6 pages); $9 per manual (50 pages).
Time: (30-40) minutes.
Comments: Revision of the Student Developmental Task Inventory, Revised, Second Edition.
Authors: Roger B. Winston, Jr., Theodore K. Miller, and Judith S. Prince.
Publisher: Student Development Associates, Inc.
Cross References: See T4:2592 (9 references); for reviews by Mary Henning-Stout and Willam D. Porterfield, see 11:384 (13 references); for reviews by Fred H. Borgen and Steven D. Brown of the Second Edition, see 9:1199 (5 references).

TEST REFERENCES

1. Benshoff, J. J., Fried, J. H., & Roberto, K. A. (1990). Developmental skill attainment among college students with disabilities. *Rehabilitation Counselor Bulletin, 34,* 44–52.
2. Cooper, D. L., Healy, M. A., & Simpson, J. (1994). Student development through involvement: Specific changes over time. *Journal of College Student Development, 35,* 98–102.
3. Eschbach, L., & Morgan, O. J. (1994). The freshman goal-setting program: Implementing an integrated student development project. *Journal of College Student Development, 35,* 385–386.
4. Hunt, S., & Rentz, A. L. (1994). Greek-letter social group members' involvement and psychosocial development. *Journal of College Student Development, 35,* 289–295.
5. Niles, S. G., Sowa, C. J., & Laden, J. (1994). Life role participation and commitment as predictors of college student development. *Journal of College Student Development, 35,* 159–163.
6. Strange, C. (1994). Student development: The evolution and status of an essential idea. *Journal of College Student Development, 35,* 399–412.
7. Upcraft, M. L. (1994). The dilemmas of translating theory to practice. *Journal of College Student Development, 35,* 438–443.
8. Cornelius, A. (1995). The relationship between athletic identity, peer and faculty socialization, and college student development. *Journal of College Student Development, 36,* 560–573.
9. Harris, S. M. (1995). Body image attitudes and the psychosocial development of college women. *The Journal of Psychology, 129,* 315–329.
10. Hess, W. D., & Winston, R. B., Jr. (1995). Developmental task achievement and students' intentions to participate in developmental activities. *Journal of College Student Development, 36,* 314–321.
11. Johnson, L. S. (1995). The psychosocial development of academically talented college students: An exploratory investigation. *College Student Journal, 29,* 278–289.
12. Long, B. E., Sowa, C. J., & Niles, S. G. (1995). Differences in student development reflected by the career decisions of college seniors. *Journal of College Student Development, 36,* 47–52.
13. Rochey, H. E. (1995). A profile of collegiate black adult children of alcoholics. *Journal of College Student Development, 36,* 228–235.
14. Sheehan, O. T. O., & Pearson, F. (1995). Asian international and American students' psychosocial development. *Journal of College Student Development, 36,* 522–530.
15. Dawson-Threat, J., & Huba, M. E. (1996). Choice of major and clarity of purpose among college seniors as a function of gender, type of major, and sex-role identification. *Journal of College Student Development, 37,* 297–308.
16. Greene, D. (1997). The use of service learning in client environments to enhance ethical reasoning in students. *American Journal of Occupational Therapy, 51,* 844–852.
17. Taub, D. J. (1997). Autonomy and parental attachment in traditional-age undergraduate women. *Journal of College Student Development, 38,* 645–654.

[2528]

Student Educational Assessment Screening.

Purpose: "A developmental assessment tool."
Population: Pre-kindergarten-grade 9.
Publication Date: 1991.
Acronym: SEAS.
Scores: 9 ratings: Social Emotional, Gross Motor, Fine Motor, Receptive Speech, Expressive Speech, Writing, Auditory Perception, Visual Perception, Self-Help.
Administration: Individual.
Price Data: Available from publisher.
Time: Administration time not reported.
Comments: Observations made by teachers.
Author: Enid G. Wolf-Schein.
Publisher: Psychometrics Canada Ltd. [Canada] [No reply from publisher; status unknown].

[2529]

Student Evaluation Scale.

Purpose: To assess children's academic and social-emotional behaviors.
Population: Grades 1-12.
Publication Date: 1970.
Acronym: SES.
Scores, 3: Educational Response, Social Emotional Response, Total.
Administration: Individual.
Price Data, 1987: $6.75 per 25 rating forms; $6.75 per 25 profiles; $5 per specimen set including manual (4 pages).
Time: Administration time not reported.
Comments: Ratings by teachers.
Authors: William T. Martin and Sue Martin.
Publisher: Psychologists and Educators, Inc.

[2530]

Student Goals Exploration.

Purpose: "Designed to help researchers better understand the academic goals of college students."
Population: College.
Publication Date: 1990.
Acronym: SGE.

Scores: 46 scales in 7 sections: Goals in Attending College (Prepare for Career and/or Graduate Professional School, Acquire a General Education, Nondirected), Educational Purpose (Social Change, Effective Thinking, Systematic Instruction, Vocational Orientation, Personal Enrichment, Great Ideas, Values Clarification), General Academic Orientation (Develop Creativity, Increase Self-Understanding, Improve Speaking Skills, Improve Reasoning Skills, Develop a Life Philosophy, Understand the World Around Me, Work for Social Causes, Develop Scientific Inquiry Skills, Prepare for a Career, Gain Expertise, Develop Human Relations, Improve Numerical Ability, Understand Cultural Diversity, Value Learning for Its Own Sake, Improve Basic Skills), Subject-Specific Goals (English, History, Sociology, Psychology, Biology, Mathematics, Fine Arts, Romance Languages, Introductory Business, Universally Endorsed), Feelings About Studying (Goal Time Frame [Long-Range], Goal Time Frame [Short-Range], Goal Clarity, Goal Source [Expectations], Goal Source [Self], Expectations and Study Skills (Self-Confident Scholar, Anxious Student), Types of Activities Scales (Relates and Applies Coursework, Interacts About Coursework, Explores Beyond Assignments, Concentrates on Task).
Administration: Group.
Forms, 6: Version IR-1 (to be completed early in academic term); Version IR-2 (to be completed late in academic term); Version IR-M (for students who have chosen a field of study); Version CR-1 ("examines goals that students bring to their college courses"); Version CR-2 ("examines students' goals as they complete college courses"); Version CR-M ("examines goals that students hope to achieve in their chosen major").
Price Data, 1993: $15 per user's manual (Institutional Research Guide, 1991, 149 pages; Classroom Research Guide, 1991, 117 pages) and 300 forms; $.50 per additional copy.
Time: (45) minutes for SGE-IR version; (30) minutes for SGE-CR version.
Authors: Joan S. Stark, Malcolm A. Lowther, Kathleen M. Shaw, and Paula L. Sossen.
Publisher: National Center for Research to Improve Postsecondary Teaching and Learning.
Cross References: For reviews by Robert D. Brown and by Steven R. Shaw and Nicholas Benson, see 13:302.

[2531]

Student Instructional Report II.

Purpose: Provides a means for students to "describe and assess their courses and instruction."
Population: College teachers.
Publication Dates: 1971–1996.
Acronym: SIR II.
Scores: 45 item scores plus up to 10 optional locally prepared items.
Administration: Group.
Price Data: Available from publisher.
Time: (10–15) minutes.
Comments: Ratings and background data by students concerning the instructor, course, and student.
Author: Educational Testing Service.
Publisher: Educational Testing Service.
Cross References: See T4:2597 (1 reference) and T3:2334 (3 references); for reviews by Frank Costin and William C. McGaghie of the earlier edition, see 8:398 (16 references); see also T2:894 (1 reference).

TEST REFERENCES

1. Baba, V. V., & Ace, M. E. (1989). Serendipity in leadership: Initiating structure and consideration in the classroom. *Human Relations, 42,* 509–525.
2. Follman, J. (1992). Secondary school students' ratings of teacher effectiveness. *The High School Journal, 75,* 168–178.
3. Glenwick, D. S., & Busch-Rossnagel, N. A. (1993). Co-teaching a joint graduate practicum in community and applied developmental psychology. *Teaching of Psychology, 20,* 141–143.

[2532]

Student Opinion Inventory, Revised Edition.

Purpose: To assess students' opinions concerning many facets of the school and to "solicit students' recommendations for improvement."
Population: Grades 5–12.
Publication Dates: 1974-1995.
Scores: 4 subscales: Quality of the Instructional Program, Support for Student Learning, School Climate/Environment for Learning, Student Activities/Intervention in School.
Administration: Group.
Parts, 2: A (Likert-scale items), B (customize up to 20 local questions).
Price Data, 1998: $15 per 25 inventories; $6.50 per manual ('95, 26 pages).
Time: (35-40) minutes.
Author: National Study of School Evaluation.
Publisher: National Study of School Evaluation.
Cross References: See T3:2335 (1 reference).

[2533]

Student Referral Checklist.

Purpose: Assesses behavioral and emotional signs of developmental or emotional problems.
Population: Grades K-6, 7-12.
Publication Date: 1985-1988.
Scores: Unscored.
Administration: Individual.
Levels, 2: Grades K-6, Jr.-Sr. High.
Manual: No manual.
Price Data: Available from publisher.
Time: Administration time not reported.
Comments: Reliability and validity data not reported; problems checklist.

Author: John A. Schinka.
Publisher: Psychological Assessment Resources, Inc.
Cross References: For a review by Ayres G. D'Costa, see 11:386.

TEST REFERENCE

1. King, G. A., Shultz, I. Z., Steel, K., Gilpin, M., & Cathers, T. (1993). Self-evaluation and self-concept of adolescents with physical disabilities. *The American Journal of Occupational Therapy, 47,* 132–140.

[2534]

Student Rights Scales.

Purpose: Designed to determine student and teacher perceptions of student rights in junior and senior high school.
Population: Grades 7-12.
Publication Dates: 1982-1986.
Acronym: SRS.
Scores, 5: General Rights, Due Process, Academic Self Determination, Freedom of Expression, Personal Conduct.
Administration: Group.
Price Data: Available from publisher.
Time: Administration time not reported.
Comments: For research use only.
Author: Thomas R. Oaster.
Publisher: Thomas R. Oaster.
Cross References: For reviews by Steven W. Lee and David Moshman, see 10:351.

[2535]

Student Self-Concept Scale.

Purpose: Designed as a "multidimensional self-report measure of self-concept and related psychological constructs."
Population: Grades 3–12.
Publication Date: 1993.
Acronym: SSCS.
Scores, 13: Self-Confidence (Self-Image, Academic, Social, Lie, Composite), Importance (Self-Image, Academic, Social, Lie), Outcome Confidence (Self-Image, Academic, Social, Composite).
Administration: Group.
Levels, 2: Grades 3–6, grades 7–12.
Price Data, 1999: $31.95 per 25 record booklets (specify Level 1 or Level 2); $39.95 per manual (82 pages).
Time: (20–30) minutes.
Authors: Frank M. Gresham, Stephen N. Elliott, and Sally E. Evans-Fernandez.
Publisher: American Guidance Service, Inc.
Cross References: For reviews by Jeri Benson and Frederick T. L. Leong, see 13:303.

[2536]

Student Styles Questionnaire™.

Purpose: "Designed to detect individual differences students display in their preferences, temperaments, and personal styles."
Population: Ages 8–13.
Publication Date: 1996.
Acronym: SSQ.
Scores, 8: Extroverted, Introverted, Practical, Imaginative, Thinking, Feeling, Organized, Flexible.
Administration: Group or individual.
Price Data, 1999: $80 per starter kit including manual (241 pages), classroom applications booklet, 5 Ready Score™ answer documents, and question booklet; $54 per 25 question booklets; $28.50 per 25 Ready Score™ answer documents; $15 per 25 record forms; $51 per manual; $15 per classroom applications booklet; $90.50 per microcomputer kit including 3.5-inch diskette, user's guide, and 25 record forms (Windows only).
Time: (30) minutes.
Authors: Thomas Oakland, Joseph Glutting, and Connie Horton.
Publisher: The Psychological Corporation.

[2537]

Student Talent and Risk Profile.

Purpose: To identify talented students as well as students "at-risk" for counseling, guidance, and special teaching strategies.
Population: Grades 5-12.
Publication Date: 1990.
Acronym: STAR Profile.
Scores, 7: Academic Performance, Creativity, Artistic Potential, Leadership, Emotional Maturity, Educational Orientation, At Risk.
Administration: Group.
Price Data, 1990: $40 per 35 test booklets; $.05 per NCS answer sheet; $8 per manual (21 pages); $10 per specimen set; scoring service offered by publisher ($160 minimum charge plus $1.60 or less per subject over 100).
Time: (60-65) minutes.
Comments: Revision of Biographical Inventory Form U.
Author: The Institute for Behavioral Research in Creativity.
Publisher: The Institute for Behavioral Research in Creativity.
Cross References: For reviews by Barbara Kerr and John W. Shepard, see 12:378; for reviews by Christopher Borman and Courtland C. Lee of Biographical Inventory Form U, see 9:150.

[2538]

Study Attitudes and Methods Survey [Revised Short Form].

Purpose: "Developed to measure non-cognitive factors associated with success in school."
Population: Junior high, high school, college.
Publication Dates: 1972–1985.

Acronym: SAMS.
Scores, 6: Academic Interest-Love of Learning, Academic Drive-Conformity, Study Methods, Study Anxiety, Manipulation, Alienation Toward Authority.
Administration: Group.
Price Data, 1998: $13.50 per 25 machine-scoring booklets and answer sheets [$47.50 per 100, $223.50 per 500]; $4.75 per 25 profile and interpretation guides (specify high school or college norms); $14.75 per set of hand-scoring keys; $7.75 per specimen set including test booklet, answer sheet, profile sheet, and manual ('88, 12 pages); $4 per manual.
Time: (20–25) minutes.
Authors: William B. Michael, Joan J. Michael, and Wayne S. Zimmerman.
Publisher: EdITS/Educational and Industrial Testing Service.
Cross References: See T4:2604 (6 references) and T3:2340 (2 references); for reviews by Allen Berger and John W. Lombard of an earlier edition, see 8:818 (6 references); see also T2:1766 (4 references).

TEST REFERENCE

1. Austin, J. S., & Martin, N. K. (1992). College-bound students: Are we meeting their needs? *Adolescence, 27,* 115–121.

[2539]

Study of Values: British Edition, 1965.

Purpose: "Aims to measure the relative importance of six basic interests or motives in personality."
Population: College and adults.
Publication Date: 1965.
Acronym: SOV.
Scores, 6: Theoretical, Economic, Aesthetic, Social, Political, Religious.
Administration: Group.
Price Data, 1989: £15.55 per 25 booklets; £9.20 per manual (microfiche) (20 pages).
Time: (20) minutes.
Comments: Self-administering; adaptation of Study of Values: A Scale for Measuring the Dominant Interests in Personality, Third Edition.
Authors: Original test by Gordon W. Allport, Philip E. Vernon, and Gardner Lindzey; adaptation by Sylvia Richardson.
Publisher: NFER-Nelson Publishing Co., Ltd. [England].
Cross References: See T3:2344 (2 references), T2:1404 (4 references), and P:259A.

TEST REFERENCE

1. Achter, J. A., Lubinski, D., & Benbow, C. P. (1996). Multipotentiality among the intellectually gifted: "It was never there and already it's vanishing." *Journal of Counseling Psychology, 43,* 65–76.

[2540]

Study Process Questionnaire.

Purpose: "To assess the extent to which a tertiary student at college or university endorses different approaches to learning and the more important motives and strategies comprising those approaches."
Population: College students.
Publication Dates: 1985-1987.
Acronym: SPQ.
Scores, 10: Surface Motive, Surface Strategy, Deep Motive, Deep Strategy, Achieving Motive, Achieving Strategy, Surface Approach, Deep Approach, Achieving Approach, Deep-Achieving Approach.
Administration: Individual or group.
Price Data, 1994: A$5.75 per 10 questionnaires, $4.20 per 10 answer sheets; $4.10 per score key; $29.95 per monograph entitled Student Approaches to Learning and Studying ('87, 151 pages); $16 per manual ('87, 44 pages).
Time: 20(40) minutes.
Comments: Secondary counterpart of the Learning Process Questionnaire (1466).
Author: John Biggs.
Publisher: Australian Council for Educational Research Ltd. [Australia].
Cross References: See T4:2608 (1 reference); for a review by Cathy W. Hall, see 11:389 (2 references). For a review by Robert D. Brown of both the Learning Process Questionnaire and the Study Process Questionnaire and a review by Cathy W. Hall of the Learning Process Questionnaire, see 11:202.

TEST REFERENCES

1. Biggs, J. (1993). What do inventories of students' learning processes really measure? A theoretical review and clarification. *British Journal of Educational Psychology, 63,* 3–19.
2. Gow, L., & Kember, D. (1993). Conceptions of teaching and their relationship to student learning. *British Journal of Educational Psychology, 63,* 20–33.
3. Dyne, A. M., Taylor, P. G., & Boulton-Lewis, G. M. (1994). Information processing and the learning context: An analysis from recent perspectives in cognitive psychology. *British Journal of Educational Psychology, 64,* 359–372.
4. Murray-Harvey, R. (1994). Learning styles and approaches to learning: Distinguishing between concepts and instruments. *British Journal of Educational Psychology, 64,* 373–388.
5. Volet, S. E., Renshaw, P. D., & Tietzel, K. (1994). A short-term longitudinal investigation of cross-cultural differences in study approaches using Biggs' SPQ questionnaire. *British Journal of Educational Psychology, 64,* 301–318.
6. Watkins, D., & Regmi, M. (1996). Toward the cross-cultural validation of a western model of student approaches to learning. *Journal of Cross-Cultural Psychology, 27,* 547–560.
7. Wilson, K. L., Smart, R. M., & Watson, R. J. (1996). Gender differences in approaches to learning in first year psychology students. *British Journal of Educational Psychology, 66,* 59–71.
8. Bessant, K. C. (1997). The development and validation of scores on the Mathematics Information Processing Scale (MIPS). *Educational and Psychological Measurement, 57,* 841–857.

[2541]

The Study Skills Counseling Evaluation.

Purpose: "Developed to enable students ... to identify ... their study weaknesses."
Population: High school and college.
Publication Date: 1962.
Scores: 5 areas: Time Distribution, Examinations, Study Conditions, Habits and Attitudes, Taking Notes.
Administration: Group.
Price Data, 1999: $36.50 per complete kit including 25 forms and manual; $17.50 per 25 forms; $19.50 per manual (6 pages).

Time: (10-20) minutes.
Author: George D. Demos.
Publisher: Western Psychological Services.
Cross References: For reviews by Stanley E. Davis and W. G. Fleming, see 6:865.

[2542]

Stuttering Prediction Instrument for Young Children.

Purpose: Designed to "measure severity and predict chronicity."
Population: Ages 3-8.
Publication Date: 1981.
Acronym: SPI.
Scores, 5: Reactions, Part-Word Repetitions, Prolongations, Frequency, Total.
Administration: Individual.
Price Data, 1999: $84 per complete kit including 50 tests, picture plates, and manual (45 pages); $39 per 50 test forms.
Time: Administration time not reported.
Comments: Information taken from parent interview, observation and tape recording of the child's speech, and analysis of the tape recording.
Author: Glyndon D. Riley.
Publisher: PRO-ED.
Cross References: See T4:2612 (1 reference).

TEST REFERENCES

1. Zebrawski, P. M. (1994). Duration of sound prolongation and sound/syllable repetition in children who stutter: Preliminary observations. *Journal of Speech and Hearing Research, 37,* 254–263.
2. Zebrawski, P. M. (1995). The topography of beginning stuttering. *Journal of Communication Disorders, 28,* 75–91.

[2543]

Stuttering Severity Instrument for Children and Adults, Third Edition.

Purpose: "Measures stuttering severity for both children and adults."
Population: School-age children and adults.
Publication Dates: 1980–1994.
Acronym: SSI-3.
Scores, 8: Frequency, Duration, Physical Concomitants (Distracting Sounds, Facial Grimaces, Head Movements, Movements of the Extremities, Total), Total.
Administration: Individual.
Forms, 2: Reading, Nonreading.
Price Data, 1999: $89 per complete kit; $39 per 50 test record and frequency computation forms; $52 per examiner's manual ('94, 48 pages) and picture plates.
Time: Administration time not reported.
Comments: Tape recorder necessary for speech sample.
Author: Glyndon D. Riley.
Publisher: PRO-ED.
Cross References: For reviews by Ronald B. Gillam and Rebecca McCauley, see 13:304 (21 references); see also T4:2613 (5 references).

TEST REFERENCES

1. Kelly, E. M., Smith, A., & Goffman, L. (1995). Orofacial muscle activity of children who stutter: A preliminary study. *Journal of Speech and Hearing Research, 38,* 1025–1036.
2. Logan, K. J., & Conture, E. G. (1997). Selected temporal, grammatical, and phonological characteristics of conventional utterances produced by children who stutter. *Journal of Speech, Language, and Hearing Research, 40,* 107–120.
3. Silverman, S. W., & Ratner, N. B. (1997). Syntactic complexity, fluency, and accuracy of sentence imitation in adolescents. *Journal of Speech, Language, and Hearing Research, 40,* 95–106.

[2544]

Stycar Vision Tests.

Purpose: Designed "to assess visual competence during infancy and early childhood."
Population: Normal and handicapped children 6 months and over.
Publication Dates: 1958-1981.
Acronym: SVT.
Administration: Individual.
Price Data, 1999: £210 per complete kit; £25 per manual ('81, 53 pages).
Author: Mary D. Sheridan.
Publisher: NFER-Nelson Publishing Co., Ltd. [England].

a) MINIATURE TOYS TEST.
Population: Nonspeaking handicapped children mental ages 21 months and over who are unable to recognize letters.
Publication Dates: 1958-1976.
Price Data: £11 per 25 record forms; £27.50 per set of toys (A); £25 per set of toys (B).
Time: [5-10] minutes.

b) GRADED BALLS TEST.
Population: Ages 6-30 months (also handicapped children with mental ages within this range).
Publication Dates: 1968-1976.
Price Data: Record forms same as for *a*; £25 per set of graded balls and rods.
Time: [5] minutes.

c) AGES 3, 4-5.
Publication Dates: 1958-76.
Levels, 2: 5-letter booklet for 3-year-olds, 7-letter booklet for 4-5-year-olds.
Price Data: £11 per 25 record forms for charts and card tests; £25 per set of distant vision cards and 9 letter cards; £35 per envelope of cards.
Time: [5-10] minutes.

d) AGES 5-7.
Publication Dates: 1958-1976.
Price Data: Record forms same as for *c*; Set C must be purchased to obtain 9-letter key card.
Time: (4) minutes.

e) PANDA TEST.
Population: Severely visually handicapped children ages 6-30 months (also handicapped children with mental ages within this range).

Publication Dates: 1973-1976.
Price Data: £27.50 per set of test cards; £45 per set of plastic letters.
Time: [10] minutes.
Cross References: See T3:2350 (1 reference), 8:884 (8 references), and T2:1931 (5 references).

TEST REFERENCE

1. Burch, H. (1995). Medical aspects of ageing in a population with intellgectual disability: I. Visual impairment. *Journal of Intellectual Disability Research, 39,* 19–25.

[2545]

Style of Learning and Thinking.

Purpose: To indicate a student's learning strategy and brain hemisphere preference in problem solving.
Population: Grades K-5, 6-12.
Publication Date: 1988.
Acronym: SOLAT.
Scores, 3: Whole Brain, Left Brain, Right Brain.
Administration: Group.
Forms, 2: Elementary, Youth.
Price Data, 1993: $28.50 per 35 tests (specify Elementary or Youth Form); $17.50 per Administrator's manual (46 pages); $27 per specimen set including manual and 1 each Elementary and Youth Form questionnaires.
Time: [30-40] minutes.
Comments: Self-scored.
Author: E. Paul Torrance.
Publisher: Scholastic Testing Service, Inc.
Cross References: For reviews by Kenneth A. Kiewra and Damian McShane and by Donald U. Robertson and Virginia L. Brown, see 11:390 (2 references).

TEST REFERENCES

1. Stice, C. F., Bertrand, N. P., Leuder, D. C., & Dunn, M. B. (1989). Personality types and theoretical orientation to reading: An exploratory study. *Reading Research and Instruction, 29*(1), 39–51.
2. Zalewski, L. J., Sink, C. A., & Yachimowicz, D. J. (1992). Using cerebral dominance for education programs. *The Journal of General Psychology, 119,* 45–57.
3. Albaili, M. A. (1993). Inferred hemispheric thinking style, gender, and academic major among United Arab Emirates college students. *Perceptual and Motor Skills, 76,* 971–977.
4. Roig, M., & Ryan, R. (1993). Hemisphercity style, sex, and performance on a letter-detection task. *Perceptual and Motor Skills, 77,* 831–834.
5. Smith, B. D., Miller, C., Grossman, F., & Gold, M. V. (1994). Vocabulary retention: Effects of using spatial imaging on hemispheric-preference thinking. *Journal of Research and Development in Education, 27,* 244–252.
6. Kim, J., & Michael, W. B. (1995). The relationship of creativity measures to school achievement and to preferred learning and thinking style in a sample of Korean high school students. *Educational and Psychological Measurement, 55,* 60–74.

[2546]

Styles of Conflict Inventory.

Purpose: "Designed to aid in the assessment of couples' conflict."
Population: Heterosexual couples.
Publication Date: 1992–1993.
Acronym: SCI.
Scores, 6: Appraisal of Conflict, Styles of Conflict, Comparison of Partners' Styles of Conflict, Differences Between Behaviors and Perceptions, Critical Items, Total.
Administration: Group.
Price Data, 1999: $50 per preview kit including manual ('93, 83 pages), and prepaid combined item booklet/answer sheet; $110.80 per 10 prepaid combined item booklet/answer sheet; $38.75 per manual.
Time: (15–20) minutes.
Comments: Self-administered test; mail-in scoring.
Author: Michael E. Metz.
Publisher: Consulting Psychologists Press, Inc.
Cross References: For reviews by Julie A. Allison and Judy L. Elliott, see 13:305.

[2547]

Styles of Leadership Survey.

Purpose: Assesses individual leadership skills under a variety of conditions.
Population: Adults.
Publication Dates: 1968-1986.
Scores, 5: Philosophy, Planning and Goal Setting, Implementation, Performance and Evaluation, Total.
Administration: Group.
Price Data, 1993: $6.95 per survey.
Time: Untimed.
Comments: Self-administered survey.
Authors: Jay Hall, Jerry B. Harvey, and Martha S. Williams.
Publisher: Teleometrics International.
Cross References: For reviews by Kenneth N. Anchor and Norman Sundberg, see 12:379 (1 reference); see T3:2351 (1 reference); for a review by Abraham K. Korman of [Styles of Leadership and Management], see 8:1185 (8 references).

TEST REFERENCE

1. Oakland, T., Falkenberg, B. A., & Oakland, C. (1996). Assessment of leadership in children, youth, and adults. *Gifted Child Quarterly, 40,* 138–146.

[2548]

Styles of Management Inventory.

Purpose: Assesses individual management style under a variety of conditions.
Population: Adults.
Publication Dates: 1964-1986.
Scores, 5: Philosophy, Planning and Goal Setting, Implementation, Performance Evaluation, Total.
Administration: Group.
Price Data, 1993: $6.95 per inventory.
Time: Untimed.
Comments: Self-administered survey.
Authors: Jay Hall, Jerry B. Harvey, and Martha S. Williams.
Publisher: Teleometrics International.
Cross References: For reviews by Richard W. Faunce and Linda F. Wightman, see 12:380; see T3:2351 (1 reference); for a review by Abraham K. Korman of [Styles of Leadership and Management], see 8:1185 (8 references).

[2549]

Styles of Teamwork Inventory.

Purpose: Assess individual feelings about working in teams and the behaviors one typically employs in work-team situations.
Population: Individuals whose work responsibilities require work-team cooperation.
Publication Date: 1963-1987.
Acronym: STI.
Scores, 5: Synergistic, Compromise, Win-Lose, Yield-Lose, Lose-Leave.
Administration: Group.
Price Data, 1990: $6.95 per manual ('87, 28 pages).
Time: Administration time not reported.
Comments: Based on Team Behaviors Model of analysis of individual behaviors in a team setting; self ratings; self scored; formerly called Group Encounter Survey (T3:1014).
Authors: Jay Hall.
Publisher: Teleometrics International.
Cross References: See 8:1048 (2 references).

[2550]

Substance Abuse Life Circumstance Evaluation.

Purpose: "Designed to assess alcohol and drug use/abuse behavior, as well as the role that attitude and stress may play in this use/abuse."
Population: Adults.
Publication Date: 1988.
Acronym: SALCE.
Scores, 6: Test-Taking Attitude, Life Circumstance Evaluation, Drinking Evaluation Category, Alcohol Addiction Evaluation, Drug Use Evaluation, Summary Score.
Administration: Individual or group.
Manual: No manual.
Price Data, 1998: $4.50 per evaluation.
Time: (20) minutes.
Comments: Self-administered; computer scored, IBM compatible with either DOS or Windows required; provides both DSM-IV classification and ASAM patient placement criteria.
Author: ADE Incorporated.
Publisher: ADE Incorporated.

[2551]

Substance Abuse Relapse Assessment.

Purpose: Designed to assess and monitor relapse prevention and coping skills.
Population: Adolescents and adults.
Publication Date: 1993.
Acronym: SARA.
Scores: 4 parts: Substance Abuse Behavior, Antecedents of Substance Abuse, Consequences of Substance Abuse, Responses to Slips.
Administration: Individual.
Price Data: Price information available from publisher for introductory kit including 25 interview record forms, 25 each of 3 relapse prevention planning forms, and manual (31 pages) with stimulus card.
Time: (60) minutes.
Authors: Lawrence Schonfeld, Roger Peters, and Addis Dolente.
Publisher: Psychological Assessment Resources, Inc.
Cross References: For reviews by Michael G. Kavan and Jeffrey S. Rain, see 13:306.

[2552]

Substance Abuse Screening Test.

Purpose: "Designed to screen-out those students who are unlikely to have a substance abuse problem."
Population: Ages 13–adult.
Publication Date: 1993.
Acronym: SAST.
Scores: Total Level of Risk.
Administration: Group.
Forms, 2: Response Form, Observation Report.
Price Data, 1996: $55 per complete kit including 50 Response Forms, 50 Observation Reports, and manual (34 pages); $22 per 50 Response Forms; $14 per 50 Observation Reports; $25 per manual.
Time: (5) minutes.
Authors: Terry Hibpshman and Sue Larson.
Publisher: Slosson Educational Publications, Inc.
Cross References: For reviews by Mary Lou Kelley and Mariela C. Shirley, see 13:307.

[2553]

Substance Abuse Subtle Screening Inventory.

Purpose: To "identify individuals who have a high probability of having a substance dependence disorder."
Population: Ages 12-18, adults.
Publication Dates: 1983-1997.
Acronym: SASSI.
Administration: Individual or group.
Levels, 2: Adult, Adolescent.
Price Data, 1998: $75–$95 per starter kit; $1.50 per test and profile; $10 per scoring key; $5–$7 per computer test and report; $55 per manual ('85, 242 pages); $20 per User's Guide ('97, 67 pages).
Time: [10-15] minutes.
Author: Glenn A. Miller.
Publisher: The SASSI Institute.

a) ADULT FORM.

Scores, 10: Symptoms, Obvious Attributes, Subtle Attributes, Defensiveness, Supplemental Addiction Measure, Family vs. Controls, Correctional, Random Answering Pattern, Face Valid Alcohol, Face Valid Other Drug.

b) ADOLESCENT FORM.

Scores, 8: Obvious Attributes, Subtle Attributes, Defensiveness, Defensive Abuser vs. Defensive Non-Abuser, Correctional, Random Answering Pattern, Face Valid Alcohol, Face Valid Other Drug.

Cross References: For reviews by Barbara Kerr and Nicholas A. Vacc of an earlier edition, see 12:381 (1 reference); see also T4:2623 (1 reference).

TEST REFERENCES

1. Karacostas, D. D., & Fisher, G. L. (1993). Chemical dependency in students with and without learning disabilities. *Journal of Learning Disabilities, 26,* 491–495.

2. Yeh, L. S., & Hedgespeth, J. (1995). A multiple case study comparison of normal private preparatory school and substance abusing/mood disordered adolescents and their families. *Adolescence, 30,* 413–428.

3. Blazina, C., & Watkins, C. E., Jr. (1996). Masculine gender role conflict: Effects on college men's psychological well-being, chemical substance usage, and attitudes toward help-seeking. *Journal of Counseling Psychology, 43,* 461–465.

4. Rogers, R. Cashel, M. L., Johansen, J., Sewell, K. W., & Gonzalez, C. (1997). Evaluation of adolescent offenders with substance abuse: Validation of the SASSI with conduct-disordered youth. *Criminal Justice and Behavior, 24,* 114–128.

5. Lazowski, L. E., Miller, F. G., Boye, M. W., & Miller, G. A. (1998). Efficacy of the Substance Abuse Subtle Screening Inventory-3 (SASSI-3) in identifying substance dependence disorders in clinical settings. *Journal of Personality Assessment, 71,* 114–128.

6. Myerholtz, L., & Rosenberg, H. (1998). Screening college students for alcohol problems: Psychometric assessment of the SASSI-2. *Journal of Studies on Alcohol, 59,* 439–446.

[2554]

Substance Use Disorders Diagnosis Schedule.

Purpose: Designed to elicit information related to the diagnosis of substance use disorders.

Population: Suspected alcohol or drug abusers.

Publication Date: 1989.

Acronym: SUDDS.

Scores: Scores for 12 substances (Alcohol, Marijuana, Cocaine, Sedatives, Tranquilizers, Stimulants, Heroin, Other Opioids, Hallucinogens, PCP, Inhalants, Other/Mixed); ratings for Stress; and a Depression Screen.

Administration: Individual.

Price Data: Available from publisher.

Time: (30–45) minutes.

Comments: Structured diagnostic interview; also available as a computer-administered interview.

Authors: Patricia Ann Harrison and Norman G. Hoffmann.

Publisher: New Standards, Inc.

Cross References: For reviews by Andres Barona and Steven I. Pfeiffer, see 13:308 (2 references).

[2555]

Subsumed Abilities Test.

Purpose: Designed "to determine an individual's or group's ability to learn or to use a previously learned written language, system of mathematics, coding system, or other visual symbol system."

Population: Ages 9 and over.

Publication Dates: 1957-1984.

Acronym: SAT.

Scores, 5: Recognition, Abstraction, Conceptualization, Total (Demonstrated Abilities), Potential Abilities.

Administration: Individual or group.

Price Data, 1998: $79 per test package; $39.50 per manual ('63, 12 pages) and manuals supplement ('84, 17 pages); $39 per key-tabulation sheet package; $46.50 per specimen set.

Time: 30(40) minutes.

Comments: Subtitle on manual is A Measure of Learning Efficiency.

Author: Joseph R. Sanders.

Publisher: Martin M. Bruce, Ph.D.

Cross References: See T2:582 (2 references); for a review by Naomi Stewart, see 6:560.

[2556]

Suffolk Reading Scale.

Purpose: "To provide a standardized measure of reading attainment and to monitor the progress of individuals and groups."

Population: Ages 6-12.

Publication Dates: 1986-1987.

Scores: Total score only.

Administration: Group.

Levels: 3 overlapping levels: Level 1 (ages 6-7), Level 2 (ages 8-10), Level 3 (ages 10-12); 2 parallel forms: A, B.

Price Data, 1987: £5.20 per set of 10 Level 1A booklets or Level 1B booklets or Level 2A booklets or Level 2B booklets; £6.35 per set of 10 Level 3A booklets or Level 3B booklets; £5.75 per set of 25 Level 3 answer sheets; £6.90 per Teacher's Guide ('87, 48 pages); scoring service for Level 3 offered by publisher.

Time: (35-45) minutes per level.

Author: Fred Hagley.

Publisher: NFER-Nelson Publishing Co., Ltd. [England].

Cross References: For reviews by Robert B. Cooter, Jr. and Richard Lehrer, see 11:392.

TEST REFERENCES

1. Schagen, I. P. (1990). A method for the age standardization of test scores. *Applied Psychological Measurement, 14,* 387–393.

2. Beech, J. R., & Keys, A. (1997). Reading, vocabulary and language preference in 7- to 8-year-old bilingual Asian children. *British Journal of Educational Psychology, 67,* 405–414.

3. Nation, K., & Snowling, M. (1997). Assessing reading difficulties: The validity and utility of current measures of reading skill. *British Journal of Educational Psychology, 67,* 359–370.

[2557]

Suicidal Ideation Questionnaire.

Purpose: To measure suicidal ideation.

Population: Grades 7-9, 10-12.

Publication Dates: 1987-1988.

Acronym: SIQ.

Scores: Total Suicidal Ideation.

Administration: Individual or group.

Levels, 2: SIQ (senior high school), SIQ-JR (junior high school).

Forms, 2: G (machine-scored), HS (hand-scored).

Price Data: Price information available from publisher for introductory kit including manual ('88, 47 pages), 25 each SIQ and SIQ-JR hand-scorable answer sheets, and scoring keys for SIQ and SIQ-JR; $18 per 25 hand-scorable answer sheets (specify SIQ or SIQ-JR).
Time: (5-10) minutes.
Author: William M. Reynolds.
Publisher: Psychological Assessment Resources, Inc.
Cross References: See T4:2627 (1 reference); for reviews by James C. Carmer and Collie W. Conoley, see 11:393 (2 references).

TEST REFERENCES

1. Morano, C. D., Cisler, R. A., & Lemerond, J. (1993). Risk factors for adolescent suicidal behavior: Loss, insufficient familial support, and hopelessness. *Adolescence, 28,* 851–865.
2. Siemen, J. R., Warrington, C. A., & Mangano, E. L. (1994). Comparison of the Millon Adolescent Personality Inventory and the Suicide Ideation Questionnaire-Junior with an adolescent inpatient sample. *Psychological Reports, 75,* 947–950.
3. Baker, J. A. (1995). Depression and suicidal ideation among academically gifted adolescents. *Gifted Child Quarterly, 39,* 218–223.
4. King, C. A., Radpour, L., Naylor, M. W., Segal, H. G., & Jouriles, E. N. (1995). Parents' marital functioning and adolescent psychopathology. *Journal of Consulting and Clinical Psychology, 63,* 749–753.
5. King, C. A., Segal, H., Kaminski, K., Naylor, M. W., Ghaziuddin, N., & Radpour, L. (1995). A prospective study of adolescent suicidal behavior following hospitalization. *Suicide and Life-Threatening Behavior, 25,* 327–338.
6. Levy, S. R., Jurkovic, G. L., & Spirito, A. (1995). A multisystems analysis of adolescent suicide attempters. *Journal of Abnormal Child Psychology, 23,* 221–234.
7. Adams, J., & Adams, M. (1996). The association among negative life events, perceived problem solving alternatives, depression, and suicidal ideation in adolescent psychiatric patients. *Journal of Child Psychology and Psychiatry, 37,* 715–720.
8. Keane, E. M., Dick, R. W., Bechtold, D. W., & Manson, S. M. (1996). Predictive and concurrent validity of the Suicidal Ideation Questionnaire among American Indian adolescents. *Journal of Abnormal Child Psychology, 24,* 735–747.
9. Hewitt, P. L., Newton, J., Flett, G. L., & Callander, L. (1997). Perfectionism and suicide ideation in adolescent psychiatric patients. *Journal of Abnormal Child Psychology, 25,* 95–101.
10. King, C-A., Katz, S. H., Chaziuddin, N., Brand, E., Hill, E., & McGovern, L. (1997). Diagnosis and assessment of depression and suicidality using the NIMH Diagnostic Interview Schedule for Children (DISC-2.3). *Journal of Abnormal Child Psychology, 25,* 173–181.
11. Pinto, A., Whisman, M. A., & McCoy, K. J. M. (1997). Suicidal ideation in adolescents: Psychometric properties of the Suicidal Ideation Questionnaire in a clinical sample. *Psychological Assessment, 9,* 63–66.

[2558]

Suicide Intervention Response Inventory [Revised].

Purpose: Designed to assess "the paraprofessional's ability to select an appropriate response to the self-destructive client."
Population: Mental health paraprofessionals.
Publication Dates: 1980–1997.
Acronym: SIRI.
Scores: Total score only.
Administration: Group.
Price Data: Available from publisher.
Time: (15) minutes.
Author: Robert A. Neimeyer.
Publisher: Robert A. Neimeyer, Ph.D.

TEST REFERENCES

1. Neimeyer, R. A., & Neimeyer, G. J. (1984). Death anxiety and counseling skill in the suicide interventionist. *Suicide and Life-Threatening Behavior, 14,* 126–131.
2. Neimeyer, R. A., & Hartley, R. E. (1986). Factorial structure of the Suicide Intervention Response Inventory. *Suicide and Life-Threatening Behavior, 16,* 434–447.
3. Abbey, K. J., Madsen, C. H., Jr., & Polland, R. (1989). Short-term suicide awareness curriculum. *Suicide and Life-Threatening Behavior, 19,* 216–227.

[2559]

Suicide Probability Scale.

Purpose: Designed to "measure an individual's self-reported attitudes and behaviors which have a bearing on suicide risk."
Population: Ages 14 and over.
Publication Date: 1982.
Acronym: SPS.
Scores, 5: Hopelessness, Suicide Ideation, Negative Self-Evaluations, Hostility, Total.
Administration: Group or individual.
Price Data, 1999: $85 per kit including 25 tests, 25 profiles, and manual (73 pages plus test and profile); $35.50 per 25 tests; $22.50 per 100 profiles; $44 per manual; $215 per microcomputer disk (IBM, 25 uses); $15 per 100 answer sheets for use with disk; $8.50 per FAX Service scoring charge.
Time: (5-10) minutes.
Authors: John G. Cull and Wayne S. Gill.
Publisher: Western Psychological Services.
Cross References: See T4:2629 (6 references); for a review by Stephen L. Golding, see 9:1210.

TEST REFERENCES

1. Ramsay, R., & Bagley, C. (1984). The prevalence of suicidal behaviors, attitudes and associated social experiences in an urban population. *Suicide and Life-Threatening Behavior, 14,* 151–167.
2. VonCleve, E., Jamelka, R., & Trupin, E. (1991). Reliability of psychological test scores for offenders entering a state prison system. *Criminal Justice and Behavior, 18,* 159–165.
3. Teare, J. F., Furst, D. W., Peterson, R. W., & Arthier, K. (1992). Family reunification following shelter placement: Child, family, and program correlates. *American Journal of Orthopsychiatry, 62,* 142–146.
4. Boone, D. E. (1994). Validity of the MMPI-2 depression content scale with psychiatric inpatients. *Psychological Reports, 74,* 159–162.
5. Dancer, L. S., Anderson, A. J., & Derlin, R. L. (1994). Use of log-linear models for assessing differential item functioning in a measure of psychological functioning. *Journal of Consulting and Clinical Psychology, 62,* 710–717.
6. Osman, A., Barrios, F. X., Panak, W. F., & Osman, J. R. (1994). Validation of the multi-attitude suicide tendency scale in adolescent samples. *Journal of Clinical Psychology, 50,* 847–855.
7. Boone, D. (1995). Differential validity of the MMPI-2 subtle and obvious scales with psychiatric inpatients: Scale 2. *Journal of Clinical Psychology, 51,* 526–531.
8. Eskin, M. (1995). Suicidal behavior as related to social support and assertiveness among Swedish and Turkish high school students: A cross-cultural investigation. *Journal of Clinical Psychology, 51,* 158–172.
9. Rudd, M. D., & Rajab, M. H. (1995). Use of the modified scale for suicidal ideation with suicide ideators and attempters. *Journal of Clinical Psychology, 51,* 632–635.
10. Rudd, M. D., Joiner, T. E., Jr., & Rajab, M. H. (1995). Help negation after acute suicidal crisis. *Journal of Consulting and Clinical Psychology, 63,* 499–503.
11. Valliant, P. M., Maksymchuk, L. L., & Antonowicz, D. (1995). Attitudes and personality traits of female adult victims of childhood abuse: A comparison of university students and incarcerated women. *Social Behavior and Personality, 23,* 205–216.
12. Ellis, T. E., Rudd, M. D., Rajab, M. H., & Wehrly, T. E. (1996). Cluster analysis of MCMI scores of suicidal psychiatric patients: Four personality profiles. *Journal of Clinical Psychology, 52,* 411–422.
13. Osman, A., Kopper, B. A., Barrios, F. X., Osman, J. R., Besett, T., & Linehan, M. M. (1996). The Brief Reasons for Living Inventory for Adolescents (BRFL-A). *Journal of Abnormal Child Psychology, 24,* 433–443.

[2560]

SUPERA.

Purpose: Designed to measure students' understanding of concepts, processes, and skills in the areas of Reading, Language Arts, and Mathematics.
Population: Spanish-speaking students, grades 1–11.
Publication Date: 1997.

Administration: Group.
Levels, 9: Level 11 (1.6–2.6), Level 12 (2.0–3.2), Level 13 (2.6–4.2), Level 14 (3.6–5.2), Level 15 (4.6–6.2), Level 16 (5.6–7.2), Level 17 (6.6–8.2), Level 18 (7.6–9.2), Levels 19/20 (8.6–11.2).
Price Data, 1998: $13 per 30 practice activities booklets (specify edition and level); $2.60 per practice activities directions 9specify edition and level); $24.25 per 30 locator tests (specify Test 1 or Test 2); $21.50 per 50 locator test answer sheets: $16.50 per technical manual; $11.25 per additional test directions for teachers (specify battery and level); $8.50 per locator manual.
Time: Administration time not reported.
Comments: Spanish-language version of TerraNova (2654); test is in Spanish, instructions are in Spanish and English; a standardized test that evaluates "performance growth and institutional effectiveness over a period of time"; Survey Edition is a brief form, Multiple Assessments Edition is longer and more involved, SUPERA Plus can be used with either edition and adds supplemental tests.
Author: CTB/McGraw-Hill.
Publisher: CTB/McGraw-Hill.

a) SUPERA SURVEY EDITION.
Scores, 3: Reading/Language Arts, Mathematics, Total.
Price Data: $103 per 30 consumable test booklets (specify level); $81.25 per 30 reusable test booklets (specify level); $30.75 per 50 answer sheets; $1,540 per 2,500 continuous feed answer sheets; $23.05 per 25 SCOREZE answer sheets; $2.85 per student for basic service scoring.

b) SUPERA MULTIPLE ASSESSMENTS EDITION.
Scores, 3: Reading/Language Arts, Mathematics, Total.
Price Data: $87.50 per 30 consumable image-scorable test booklets (specify level); $6.35 per student for basic service scoring.

c) SUPERA PLUS.
Scores, 5: Word Analysis, Language Mechanics, Vocabulary, Math Computation, Spelling.
Price Data: $30 per 30 test booklets (specify level); $30.75 per 50 answer sheets (specify regular or survey); $11.25 per manual (specify level).

[2561]

Supervisory Change Relations.

Purpose: "To measure knowledge about change relations."
Population: Supervisors and prospective supervisors.
Publication Dates: 1970-1978.
Scores: Total score only.
Administration: Group.
Manual: No manual; fact sheet and administration guide available.
Price Data, 1998: $30 per complete kit including 10 test inventories, fact sheet, and administration guide.
Time: (20-25) minutes.
Comments: Self-administered.
Authors: W. J. Reddin and E. Keith Stewart.
Publisher: Organizational Tests Ltd. [Canada].

[2562]

Supervisory Coaching Relations.

Purpose: Measures "knowledge of sound methods of coaching subordinates."
Population: Supervisors and potential supervisors.
Publication Dates: 1970-1978.
Acronym: SCORE.
Scores: Total score only.
Administration: Group.
Manual: No manual; fact sheet available.
Price Data, 1998: $30 per complete kit including 10 test booklets, fact sheet, and user's guide.
Time: (15-20) minutes.
Comments: Self-administered.
Authors: W. J. Reddin and E. Keith Stewart.
Publisher: Organizational Tests Ltd. [Canada].

[2563]

Supervisory Communication Relations.

Purpose: "To measure knowledge about communications relations."
Population: Supervisors and potential supervisors.
Publication Dates: 1970-1981.
Acronym: SCOM.
Scores: Total score only.
Administration: Group.
Manual: No manual; fact sheet available.
Price Data, 1998: $30 per complete kit including 10 test booklets, fact sheet, and user's guide.
Time: (15-20) minutes.
Comments: Self-administered.
Authors: E. Keith Stewart, W. J. Reddin, and K. J. Rowell.
Publisher: Organizational Tests Ltd. [Canada].
Cross References: For a review by Niels G. Waller, see 11:396.

[2564]

Supervisory Human Relations.

Purpose: Measures "attitudes toward others."
Population: Supervisors and potential supervisors.
Publication Dates: 1970-1981.
Acronym: SHR.
Scores: Total score only.
Administration: Group.
Manual: No manual; fact sheet available.
Price Data, 1998: $30 per complete kit including 10 test booklets, fact sheet, and user's guide.

Time: (15-20) minutes.
Comments: Self-administered.
Authors: W. J. Reddin and E. Keith Stewart.
Publisher: Organizational Tests Ltd. [Canada].
Cross References: For a review by Niels G. Waller, see 11:397.

[2565]

Supervisory Inventory on Communication.

Purpose: Designed to assess supervisor's knowledge of certain principles, facts, and techniques of communication.
Population: Supervisors and prospective supervisors.
Publication Dates: 1965-1979.
Acronym: SIC.
Scores: Total score only.
Administration: Group.
Price Data, 1998: $40 per 20 SIC tests and answer booklets; $5 per instructor's manual ('79, 11 pages); $10 per specimen set (including test, answer booklet, manual and leader's guide).
Time: (20) minutes.
Author: Donald L. Kirkpatrick.
Publisher: Donald L. Kirkpatrick.
Cross References: For a review by Joyce L. Carbonell, see 9:1211; see also 7:1152 (1 reference).

[2566]

Supervisory Inventory on Human Relations.

Purpose: Designed to assess supervisors' knowledge of human relations principles, facts, and techniques.
Population: Supervisors and prospective supervisors.
Publication Dates: 1960-1982.
Acronym: SIHR.
Scores: Total score only.
Administration: Group.
Price Data, 1998: $40 per 20 tests and answer booklets; $5 per instructor's manual ('82, 12 pages); $10 per specimen set (including test, answer booklet, and manual).
Time: (15-20) minutes.
Authors: Donald L. Kirkpatrick and Earl Planty (test).
Publisher: Donald L. Kirkpatrick.
Cross References: See T2:2463 (1 reference); for a review by Seymour Levy of the original edition, see 6:1193 (1 reference).

[2567]

Supervisory Job Discipline.

Purpose: Measures knowledge of disciplinary techniques.
Population: Supervisors and potential supervisors.
Publication Dates: 1970-1978.
Acronym: SJD.
Scores: Total score only.
Administration: Group.
Manual: No manual; fact sheet available.
Price Data, 1998: $30 per complete kit including 10 test booklets, fact sheet, and user's guide.
Time: (15-20) minutes.
Comments: Self-administered.
Author: E. Keith Stewart.
Publisher: Organizational Tests Ltd. [Canada].

[2568]

Supervisory Job Instruction.

Purpose: Measures "knowledge of sound job instruction techniques."
Population: Supervisors and potential supervisors.
Publication Dates: 1970-81.
Acronym: SJI.
Scores: Total score only.
Administration: Group.
Manual: No manual; fact sheet available.
Price Data, 1998: $30 per complete kit including 10 test booklets, fact sheet, and user's guide.
Time: (15-20) minutes.
Comments: Self-administered.
Authors: W. J. Reddin and E. Keith Stewart.
Publisher: Organizational Tests Ltd. [Canada].

[2569]

Supervisory Job Safety.

Purpose: Measures "knowledge of and attitudes toward safety practices."
Population: "Blue-collar" supervisors and potential supervisors.
Publication Dates: 1970-1981.
Acronym: SJS.
Scores: Total score only.
Administration: Group.
Manual: No manual; fact sheet available.
Price Data, 1998: $30 per complete kit including 10 test booklets, fact sheet, and user's guide.
Time: (15-20) minutes.
Comments: Self-administered.
Author: E. Keith Stewart.
Publisher: Organizational Tests Ltd. [Canada].

[2570]

Supervisory Potential Test.

Purpose: "To measure supervisory potential."
Population: Supervisors or potential supervisors.
Publication Dates: 1970-1981.
Acronym: SPT.
Scores, 9: New Role Clarity, Productivity, Superior Relationship, Change Introduction, Subordinate Motivation, Subordinate Development, Subordinate Evaluation, Discipline, Total.

Administration: Group.
Manual: No manual; fact sheet available.
Price Data, 1998: $30 per complete kit including 10 test booklets, fact sheet, and user's guide.
Time: (15-20) minutes.
Comments: Self-administered.
Authors: W. J. Reddin and J. Brian Sullivan.
Publisher: Organizational Tests Ltd. [Canada].

[2571]

Supervisory Practices Inventory.

Purpose: To measure what employees want their supervisor to do and what they perceive their supervisor does.
Population: Managers or administrators.
Publication Date: 1981.
Acronym: SPI.
Scores, 8: 3 emphasis scale scores (People, Tasks, Results), Emphasis Dissonance Score, 3 methods scale scores (Group Interaction, Individual Initiation, Supervisor Initiation), Methods Dissonance Score, covering 10 areas: Setting Objectives, Planning, Organizing, Delegating, Problem Identification, Decision Making, Subordinate Development, Performance Evaluation, Conflict Resolution, Team Building.
Administration: Group or individual.
Price Data, 1999: $39.50 per complete kit including 10 inventories and manual ('81, 18 pages); $25.50 per 10 inventories; $16.50 per manual.
Time: (45-65) minutes.
Comments: Self-scoring.
Authors: Judith S. Canfield and Albert A. Canfield.
Publisher: Western Psychological Services.
Cross References: For reviews by Gregory H. Dobbins and Robert M. McIntire, see 9:1214.

[2572]

Supervisory Practices Test, Revised.

Purpose: "Designed to aid in appraising supervisory ability and potential."
Population: Supervisors.
Publication Dates: 1957-1984.
Acronym: SPT.
Scores: Total score only.
Administration: Group.
Price Data, 1998: $55.95 per specimen set; $77.40 per test package; $52.65 per manual ('74, 14 pages), manuals supplement ('84, 17 pages), and norms supplement; $35.40 per profile sheet package; $3.75 per key.
Foreign Language Editions: French and German editions available.
Time: (20-30) minutes.
Author: Martin M. Bruce.
Publisher: Martin M. Bruce, Ph.D.
Cross References: See T3:2363 (1 reference), T2:2466 (2 references), and 6:1194 (4 references); for reviews by Clifford E. Jurgensen and Mary Ellen Oliverio, see 5:955.

[2573]

Supervisory Profile Record.

Purpose: "To identify candidates with a high potential for success in first-line supervisory classifications."
Population: Prospective supervisors.
Publication Dates: 1981-1985.
Acronym: SPR.
Scores, 10: Judgment Record (Employee Communication-Motivation, Employee Training-Evaluation, Problem-Resolution, Disciplinary Practices, General Style-Practices, Total), Background Record (Present Self Concept-Evaluation, Present Work Values-Orientation, Total), Total.
Administration: Individual or group.
Price Data: Not available.
Time: (180) minutes.
Author: Richardson, Bellows, Henry & Co., Inc.
Publisher: Richardson, Bellows, Henry & Co., Inc. [No reply from publisher; status unknown].
Cross References: See T4:2646 (1 reference); for a review by Sheldon Zedeck, see 11:402.

[2574]

Supervisory Simulator.

Purpose: "Designed to assess supervisory skills of first-level supervisors and/or forepersons independent of any particular job classification; may be used for selection and/or career development."
Population: First-level supervisors and/or forepersons.
Publication Dates: 1991–1994.
Acronym: SupSim.
Scores, 3: Leadership/Decision Making, Team Relations, Total.
Administration: Group.
Forms, 4: Public and private sector forms include Standard Version, Police Version, Fire Version, and Transportation Version.
Restricted Distribution: Clients must pay a one-time overhead/sign-up fee of $100–$200.
Price Data, 1993: $75 per candidate for rental/scoring and bar chart; $50 for optional Supervisory Simulator Feedback Report.
Time: (75) minutes.
Author: Richard C. Joines.
Publisher: Management & Personnel Systems, Inc.

[2575]

Supervisory Skills Inventory.

Purpose: Developed to assess a supervisor's day-to-day, on-the-job behavior as seen by self and collectively by five other people.
Population: First-line supervisors.

Publication Date: 1982.
Acronym: SSI.
Scores: 2 scores (Self, Other) in 12 supervisory skill areas: Setting Goals, Planning and Organizing, Directing and Delegating, Solving Problems, Enforcing Work Rules, Relating to and Supporting Staff, Maintaining and Controlling Materials and Equipment, Building Teams, Assuring Safety, Evaluating Performance, Training and Coaching, Reacting to Stress, plus 5 summary perception scores.
Administration: Group.
Price Data, 1990: $45 per SSI, 5 Description by Others Inventories, Self-Development Guide, and scorers worksheet; $15 per leader's manual (62 pages); can be scored locally, information available for scoring by publisher.
Comments: Administered to supervisor and 4 or 5 workers.
Authors: Human Synergistics.
Publisher: Human Synergistics.

[2576]

Supervisory Union Relations.

Purpose: "To measure attitude about union relations."
Population: Supervisors and potential supervisors.
Publication Dates: 1970-1981.
Acronym: SUR.
Scores: Total score only.
Administration: Group.
Manual: No manual; fact sheet available.
Price Data, 1998: $30 per complete kit including 10 test booklets, fact sheet, and user's guide.
Time: (15-20) minutes.
Comments: Self-administered; may be self-scored.
Authors: W. J. Reddin and E. Keith Stewart.
Publisher: Organizational Tests Ltd. [Canada].

[2577]

SUP'R Star Profiles.

Purpose: Designed to identify an individual's dominant personality type.
Population: Adults.
Publication Date: 1994.
Scores: 4 personality types: Self-Reliant, Upbeat, Patient, Reasoning.
Administration: Group.
Price Data, 1994: $5.95 per test; price information for user's guide available from publisher.
Time: (15–20) minutes.
Author: James H. Brewer.
Publisher: Associated Consultants in Education.
Cross References: For reviews by Jeffrey B. Brookings and Carol Collins, see 13:309.

[2578]

Survey of Employee Access.

Purpose: Measures effective managerial behavior.
Population: Adults.
Publication Date: 1989.
Acronym: SEA.
Scores, 5: Access to the Problem, Access to People, Access to Information and Resources, Access to Emotional/Procedural Supports, Access to Solution.
Administration: Group.
Price Data, 1993: $6.95 per survey.
Time: Untimed.
Comments: Self-administered survey.
Author: Jay Hall.
Publisher: Teleometrics International.
Cross References: For reviews by Marcia J. Belcher and Robert Fitzpatrick, see 12:383.

[2579]

Survey of Functional Adaptive Behaviors.

Purpose: To assess an individual's skill level of adaptive behavior.
Population: Ages 16 and over.
Publication Date: 1986.
Acronym: SFAB.
Scores, 5: Residential Living Skills, Daily Living Skills, Academic Skills, Vocational Skills, SFAB Total Score.
Administration: Individual.
Manual: No manual.
Price Data, 1999: $48.25 per 25 surveys.
Authors: Jack G. Dial, Carolyn Mezger, Theresa Massey, Steve Carter, and Lawrence T. McCarron.
Publisher: McCarron-Dial Systems.
Cross References: For reviews by Steven W. Lee and Steven I. Pfeiffer, see 11:404.

[2580]

Survey of Influence Effectiveness.

Purpose: "Designed to help business and government professionals determine how they are at influencing others with integrity."
Population: Business and government professionals.
Publication Date: 1994.
Administration: Group.
Forms, 2: Self, Other.
Manual: No Manual.
Price Data, 1998: $99 per set including questionnaires and answer sheets for 1 self-assessment, 6 others, 6 customers, and 1 feedback report.
Time: [30] minutes.
Comments: Computer scored and interpreted by publisher.
Author: Terry R. Bacon.
Publisher: International LearningWorks®.

a) SELF FORM.
Scores, 4: Influence Tactic Frequency, Influence Tactic Appropriateness, Influence Tactic Skills and Effectiveness, Source of Power.
b) OTHER FORM.
Scores, 7: Positive Influence Tactic Frequency, Negative Influence Tactic Frequency, Influence Tactic Appropriateness, Influence Tactic Skills and Effectiveness, Overall Influence Assessment, Sources of Power Recommendations.
Comments: A 128-item rating form.

[2581]

Survey of Interpersonal Values.

Purpose: Designed to measure certain values involving an individual's relationships with others.
Population: Individuals in a variety of occupations and job levels.
Publication Dates: 1960-1993.
Acronym: SIV.
Scores, 6: Support, Conformity, Recognition, Independence, Benevolence, Leadership.
Administration: Individual or group.
Price Data, 1998: $131.50 per start-up kit including 25 test booklets, 100 profile sheets, scoring stencil, and examiner's manual; $52 per 25 test booklets (quantity discounts available); $59.75 per 100 profile sheets; $14.75 per scoring stencil; $19.75 per examiner's manual.
Time: No limit (approximately 15 minutes).
Author: Leonard V. Gordon.
Publisher: NCS (Rosemont).
Cross References: See T4:2653 (3 references) and T3:2366 (14 references); for reviews by John D. Black and Allan L. LaVoie, see 8:688 (51 references); see also T2:1407 (78 references) and P:261 (48 references); for reviews by Lee J. Cronbach, Leonard D. Goodstein, and John K. Hemphill and an excerpted review by Laurence Siegel, see 6:184 (12 references).

TEST REFERENCES

1. Testerman, M., Keim, M., & Karmos, J. (1994). Values differences in Greek affiliation and gender. *College Student Journal, 28,* 486–491.
2. Baron, H. (1996). Strengths and limitations of ipsative measurement. *Journal of Occupational and Organizational Psychology, 69,* 49–56.
3. Hofstede, G. (1996). Gender stereotypes and partner preferences of Asian women in masculine and feminine cultures. *Journal of Cross-Cultural Psychology, 27,* 533–546.

[2582]

Survey of Management Perception.

Purpose: Designed to identify supervisors' and executives' perceptions about the "Gist" (Groups, Individual, Structure, Technology) dimensions of management.
Population: Supervisors and executives.
Publication Dates: 1956-1958.
Acronym: SMP.
Scores: Card sort on 20 management qualities.
Administration: Group.
Price Data: Not available.
Time: (45) minutes.
Comments: A projective test requiring the subject to write stories (setting, characters, plot, outcome) about 9 pictures and a story "that could happen in your own company"; clinical analysis training (workshops) needed in projective stories and the 20 card sort descriptions.
Author: Charles W. Nelson.
Publisher: Management Research Associates [No reply from publisher; status unknown].

[2583]

Survey of Management Practices.

Purpose: To assess a manager's organizational practices, and whether they enhance employee productivity.
Population: Subordinates of managers.
Publication Date: 1987.
Acronym: SMP.
Scores, 12: Dimension I (Management Values, Support Structure, Managerial Credibility, Total), Dimension II (Impact, Relevance, Community, Total), Dimension III (Task Environment, Social Context, Problem Solving, Total).
Administration: Group.
Price Data, 1990: $6.95 per manual (21 pages); $15 per Leader's Guide (18 pages).
Time: Administration time not reported.
Comment: Manager behavior rated by subordinates.
Authors: Jay Hall.
Publisher: Teleometrics International.

TEST REFERENCES

1. Shipper, F. (1991). Mastery and frequency of managerial behaviors relative to sub-unit effectiveness. *Human Relations, 44,* 371–388.
2. Shipper, F. (1995). A study of the psychometric properties of the managerial skill scales of the Survey of Management Practices. *Educational and Psychological Measurement, 55,* 468–479.

[2584]

Survey of Organizational Climate.

Purpose: To assess an individual's opinion of his/her organizational climate.
Population: Employees.
Publication Dates: 1977-1985.
Scores, 12: Clarity of Goals, Job Interest and Challenge, Rewards and Satisfactions, Standards of Excellence, Degree of Responsibility, Personal Development, Working Relationships, Advancement/Mobility, Job Security, Management's Credibility, Personnel Policies and Procedures, Self-Confidence.
Administration: Group or individual.
Manual: No manual.
Price Data, 1993: $60 per kit including 20 copies of survey, 20 answer sheets, and 20 interpretation sheets.
Time: (20) minutes.
Comments: Self-scored.
Author: Training House, Inc.

Publisher: Training House, Inc.
Cross References: For a review by Charles K. Parsons, see 11:406.

[2585]

Survey of Organizational Culture.

Purpose: Identification of organizational purpose and mission, perception of customers, and interrelationships of organization members.
Population: Employees of organizations.
Publication Dates: 1987-1989.
Acronym: SOC.
Scores: 15 scales: Culture (Orientation to Customers, Orientation to Employees, Orientation to Stakeholders, Impact of Mission, Managerial Depth, Decision Level/Autonomy, Communication/Openness, Human Scale, Incentive/Motivation, Cooperation/Competition, Organizational Congruence, Behavior Under Pressure, Theory-S/Theory-T, 13 Scales Aggregated), Job Characteristics (Job Satisfaction, Organizational Commitment).
Administration: Group.
Editions, 2: Select Items, Professional.
Manual: No manual.
Price Data: Available from publisher.
Time: (20-25) minutes.
Authors: Robert W. Tucker and Walt J. McCoy.
Publisher: Human Services Resource Group.
Cross References: For a review by Bertram C. Sippola, see 11:407.

[2586]

Survey of Organizational Stress.

Purpose: To "provide a comprehensive anonymous analysis and feedback for both individuals and management as they jointly pursue a program of Health Maintenance to reduce stress-related illness."
Population: High school and college, government and private enterprise.
Publication Dates: 1981-1986.
Acronym: SOS.
Scores, 5: 4 Life Style Needs (Security, Achievement, Recognition, Belonging) and Total Stress.
Administration: Group.
Forms, 2: Quality of Life Survey in Your Educational Setting, Quality of Life Survey in Your Organizational Setting.
Price Data: Not available.
Time: Administration time not reported.
Comments: Not available without special preparation including workshop training.
Author: Charles W. Nelson.
Publisher: Management Research Associates [No reply from publisher; status unknown].

a) QUALITY OF LIFE SURVEY IN YOUR EDUCATIONAL SETTING.
Population: High school and college.
Publication Date: 1985.
b) QUALITY OF LIFE SURVEY IN YOUR ORGANIZATIONAL SETTING.
Population: Government and private enterprise.
Publication Date: 1981.
Cross References: For reviews by Philip G. Benson and David M. Saunders, see 11:408.

[2587]

Survey of Organizations.

Purpose: "Describes conditions and practices" in an organization "to determine specific opportunities for improvement."
Population: Employees.
Publication Dates: 1967–1988.
Acronym: SOO-2000.
Scores, 28: Organization Climate (Communication Flow, Decision Making Practices, Concern for People, Influence and Control, Job Challenge, Job Reward, Job Clarity, Organization of Work, Absence of Bureaucracy, Coordination, Work Interdependence), Supervisory Leadership (Support, Team Building, Goal Emphasis, Work Facilitation, Encouragement of Participation, Interpersonal Competence, Involvement, Administrative Scope), Peer Relationships (Support, Team Building, Goal Emphasis, Work Facilitation), End Results (Group Functioning, Goal Integration, Satisfaction, Group Performance, Individual Performance).
Administration: Group.
Price Data: Not available.
Foreign Language Edition: Available in Spanish, French, Finnish, Norwegian, and Swedish.
Time: Administration time not reported.
Comments: For measurement of groups rather than individuals.
Author: Rensis Likert Associates, Inc.
Publisher: Rensis Likert Associates, Inc. [No reply from publisher; status unknown].
Cross References: For reviews by John M. Enger and John W. Fleenor, see 13:310; see alsof T3:2369 (2 references); for reviews by Robert Fitzpatrick and Stephan J. Motowidlo, and an excerpted review by John Toplis of an earlier edition, see 8:985 (12 references).

[2588]

Survey of Personal Values.

Purpose: To "measure certain critical values that help to determine the manner in which individuals cope with the problems of everyday living."
Population: Individuals in a variety of occupations, high school and college students.

Publication Dates: 1964-1992.
Acronym: SPV.
Scores, 6: Practical Mindedness, Achievement, Variety, Decisiveness, Orderliness, Goal Orientation.
Administration: Individual or group.
Price Data, 1998: $131.50 per start-up kit including 25 test booklets, 100 profile sheets, scoring stencil, and examiner's manual: $52 per 25 test booklets (quantity discount available); $59.75 per 100 profile sheets; $14.75 per scoring stencil; $19.75 per examiner's manual.
Time: No limit (approximately 15 minutes).
Author: Leonard V. Gordon.
Publisher: NCS (Rosemont).
Cross References: For reviews by William P. Erchul and Rodney L. Lowman, see 10:354; see also T3:2370 (5 references) and T2:1409 (5 references); for a review by Gene V Glass, see 7:148 (6 references); see also P:263 (3 references).

[2589]

Survey of Student Assessment of Study Behaviors.

Purpose: Designed to help students understand their current study behaviors.
Population: Grades 6–13.
Publication Date: 1991.
Scores, 6: Positive Attitudes, Useful Work Habits, Efficient Learning Tools, Good Comprehension, High Performance Writing, Effective Test Taking.
Administration: Individual.
Price Data, 1991: $3 per survey.
Time: Administration time not reported.
Comments: Self-report survey.
Author: The Cambridge Stratford Study Skills Institute.
Publisher: The Cambridge Stratford Study Skills Institute.

[2590]

Survey of Student Opinion of Instruction.

Purpose: For "obtaining student opinion of instruction for use in instructional development and faculty evaluation."
Population: High school systems.
Publication Date: 1985.
Scores: 6 Factors: Instructor Commitment to Student Learning, Instructor's Communication Skills, Testing and Evaluation, Learning and Understanding, Classroom Supervision and Organization, Instructor Preparation and Enthusiasm.
Administration: Group.
Price Data: Available from publisher.
Time: (20) minutes.
Comments: Separate questionnaires to be completed by students and instructor; provides Class Summary, Instructor Summary, Unit Summary Report, and Comprehensive Summary; 9-track magnetic tape or 8-inch diskette containing all local data may be provided as part of standard report package.
Authors: Summa Information Systems, Inc.
Publisher: Summa Information Systems, Inc. [No reply from publisher; status unknown].
Cross References: For reviews by Kathryn Clark Gerken and Richard A. Saudargas, see 10:355.

[2591]

Survey of Study Habits and Attitudes.

Purpose: Developed to assess "study methods, motivation for studying, and certain attitudes toward scholastic activities."
Population: Grades 7-12, 12-14.
Publication Dates: 1953-1967.
Acronym: SSHA.
Scores, 7: Study Habits (Delay Avoidance, Work Methods, Total), Study Attitudes (Teacher Approval, Education Acceptance, Total), Total.
Administration: Group.
Levels, 2: H (Grades 7-12), C (Grades 12-14).
Price Data, 1999: $58.25 per 25 survey booklets (select level); $34.25 per 50 IBM 805 hand-scorable answer documents; $41.25 per set of keys and manual ('67, 30 pages); $41.25 per examination kit including survey booklets, IBM 805 answer document and key, and manual.
Foreign Language Edition: Spanish edition available.
Time: (20-35) minutes.
Authors: William F. Brown and Wayne H. Holtzman.
Publisher: The Psychological Corporation.
Cross References: See T4:2663 (14 references), 9:1218 (8 references), T3:2374 (26 references), 8:820 (45 references), and T2:1772 (33 references); for a review by Carleton B. Shay and excerpts by Martin J. Higgins and Albert E. Roark (with Scott A. Harrington), see 7:782 (69 references); see also 6:856 (12 references); for reviews by James Deese and C. Gilbert Wrenn and Roy D. Lewis of the original edition, see 5:688 (14 references).

TEST REFERENCES

1. Peterson, A. V., & Peppas, G. J. (1988). Trained peer helpers facilitate student adjustment in an overseas school. *The School Counselor, 36,* 67–73.
2. Olszewski-Kubilins, P., Kulieke, M. J., Shaw, B., Willis, G. B., & Krasney, N. (1990). Predictors of achievement in mathematics for gifted males and females. *Gifted Child Quarterly, 34,* 64-71.
3. Turner, G. Y. (1992). College students' self-awareness of study behaviors. *College Student Journal, 26,* 129-134.
4. Swanson, S., & Howell, C. (1996). Test anxiety in adolescents with learning disabilities and behavior disorders. *Exceptional Children, 62,* 389–397.

[2592]

Survey of Work Styles.

Purpose: A "measure of six components of the Type A behavior pattern."
Population: Adults.

Publication Dates: 1988–1993.
Acronym: SWS.
Scores, 8: Impatience, Anger, Time Urgency, Work Involvement, Job Dissatisfaction, Competitiveness, Scale A, Total.
Administration: Group.
Price Data, 1999: $44 per research test kit including manual, 2nd edition ('93, 22 pages), 25 hand-scorable question-and-answer documents, 25 scoring sheets, and one set of templates; $13 per test manual; $15 per 25 question-and-answer documents; $11 per 25 scoring sheets; $13 per set of four templates; $12 per machine-scorable question-and-answer document for a Developmental Report; $6 per machine-scorable question-and-answer document for a Basic Report; $99 per software package including disks, software manual for Windows, test manual, and 10 coupons for computer reports.
Time: (15–20) minutes.
Authors: Douglas N. Jackson and Anna Mavrogiannis Gray.
Publisher: Sigma Assessment Systems, Inc.
Cross References: For a review by Peggy A. Hicks, see 13:311 (1 reference); see also T4:2664 (1 reference).

TEST REFERENCE

1. Monforton, M., Helmes, E., & Deathe, A. B. (1993). Type A personality and marital intimacy in amputees. *British Journal of Medical Psychology, 66,* 275–280.

[2593]

Survey of Work Values, Revised, Form U.

Purpose: Constructed to identify attitudes toward work.
Population: Employees.
Publication Dates: 1975-1976.
Scores, 6: Social Status, Activity Preference, Upward Striving, Attitude Toward Earnings, Pride in Work, Job Involvement.
Administration: Group.
Manual: No manual.
Price Data, 1997: $21 per 100 test booklets; $5 per 100 answer sheets; $5 per 100 hand-scoring sheets; general instructions, free.
Time: [15] minutes.
Authors: Bowling Green State University.
Publisher: Bowling Green State University.
Cross References: For reviews by Julie A. Allison and H. John Bernardin and Donna K. Cooke, see 12:383 (1 reference); see also T4:2665 (1 reference).

[2594]

Surveys of Research Administration and Environment.

Purpose: Designed "to gather both facts and opinions on a variety of factors related to the jobs of scientists, engineers, and technicians."
Population: Research and engineering and scientific firms.
Publication Dates: 1959-1960.
Scores: No scores.
Administration: Group.
Price Data: Available from publisher.
Author: Morris I. Stein.
Publisher: The Mews Press.

a) STEIN SURVEY FOR ADMINISTRATION.
Population: Supervisors and administrators.
Comments: Also part of Technical Personnel Recruiting Inventory (2711).
Time: (30-40) minutes.

b) STEIN RESEARCH ENVIRONMENTAL SURVEY.
Population: Research and technical personnel.
Time: (90-120) minutes.

[2595]

Sutter-Eyberg Student Behavior Inventory.

Purpose: "Constructed to provide a comprehensive, narrow-band measure of conduct problem behaviors."
Population: Ages 2-17.
Publication Date: [1984].
Acronym: SESBI.
Scores, 2: Intensity, Problem.
Administration: Individual.
Price Data: No charge for one copy; may be photocopied for research or clinical use.
Time: [5] minutes.
Comments: Ratings by teachers.
Author: Joseph Sutter and Sheila M. Eyberg.
Publisher: Sheila M. Eyberg, Ph.D.
Cross References: See T4:2668 (1 reference); for a review by T. Steuart Watson, see 11:410 (2 references).

TEST REFERENCES

1. Burns, G. L., Walsh, J. A., & Owen, S. M. (1995). Twelve-month stability of descriptive classroom behavior as measured by the Sutter-Eyberg Student Behavior Inventory. *Journal of Clinical Child Psychology, 24,* 453–462.
2. Rayfield, A., Eyberg, S. M., & Foote, R. (1998). Revision of the Sutter-Eyberg Student Behavior Inventory: Teacher ratings of conduct problem behavior. *Educational and Psychological Measurement, 58,* 88–98.

[2596]

Swanson-Cognitive Processing Test.

Purpose: Designed to assess "different aspects of mental processing ability and potential."
Population: Ages 5 to adult.
Publication Date: 1996.
Acronym: S-CPT.
Scores: 11 subtest scores: Rhyming Words, Visual Matrix, Auditory Digit Sequence, Mapping and Directions, Story Retelling, Picture Sequence, Phrase Recall, Spatial Organization, Semantic Association, Semantic Categorization, Nonverbal Sequence; 3 composite scores: Semantic, Episodic, Total; 4 component scores: Audi-

tory, Visual, Prospective, Retrospective; 4 supplementary scores: Strategy Efficiency Index, Processing Difference Index, Instructional Efficiency Index, Stability Index.
Administration: Individual.
Price Data, 1999: $184 per complete kit including manual (183 pages), 25 profile/examiner record booklets, picture book, card decks, and strategy cards in storage box; $54 per 25 profile/examiner record booklets; $49 per manual; $24 per picture book; $43 per card deck; $19 per strategy cards.
Time: (120) minutes.
Author: H. Lee Swanson.
Publisher: PRO-ED.
Cross References: For reviews by Carolyn M. Callahan and Ralph F. Darr, Jr., see 13:312.

TEST REFERENCE

1. Turkstra, L. S., & Holland, A. L. (1998). Assessment of syntax after adolescent brain injury: Effects of memory on test performance. *Journal of Speech, Language, and Hearing Research, 41,* 137–149.

[2597]

Swassing-Barbe Modality Index.

Purpose: To identify an individual's "most efficient learning mode."
Population: Children and adults.
Publication Dates: 1979–1998.
Scores, 4: Visual, Auditory, Kinesthetic, Total.
Administration: Individual.
Price Data, 1998: $213.32 per complete kit ($159.99 school price); $4.99 per 100 scoring sheets.
Time: (20–25) minutes.
Comments: Also known as Zaner-Bloser Modality Index.
Author: Walter B. Barbe and Raymond H. Swassing.
Publisher: Zaner-Bloser Educational Publishers.
Cross References: See T4:2669 (1 reference); for a review by Barbara A. Kerr and Roberta S. Myers, see 9:1219.

[2598]

Sweet Technical Information Test.

Purpose: "Designed to assess the suitability of students for technical and subprofessional occupations."
Population: Ages 14-17.
Publication Dates: 1973-1975.
Acronym: STIT.
Scores: Total score only.
Administration: Group.
Price Data, 1994: A$2.75 per test booklet; $4.20 per 10 answer sheets; $4.10 per score key; $15.50 per manual ('73, 66 pages).
Time: 20(25) minutes.
Author: R. Sweet.
Publisher: Australian Council for Educational Research Ltd. [Australia].

[2599]

Symbol Digit Modalities Test.

Purpose: Designed as an early screening of cerebral dysfunction.
Population: Ages 8 and over.
Publication Date: 1973.
Acronym: SDMT.
Scores: Total score only.
Administration: Group or individual.
Forms, 2: Written, Oral.
Price Data, 1999: $65 per complete kit including 25 WPS AutoScore™ test forms and manual (10 pages plus test); $34.50 per 25 AutoScore™ test forms; $32.50 per manual.
Time: 1.5(10) minutes.
Author: Aaron Smith.
Publisher: Western Psychological Services.
Cross References: See T4:2671 (20 references) and T3:2380 (2 references); for reviews by Brad S. Chissom and James C. Reed, see 8:878; see also T2:1889 (4 references).

TEST REFERENCES

1. Asbury, C. A., Stokes, A., Adderly-Kelly, B., & Knuckle, E. P. (1989). Effectiveness of selected neuropsychological, academic, and sociocultural measures for predicting Bannatyne pattern categories in black adolescents. *Journal of Negro Education, 58,* 177–188.

2. Jongbloed, L., Stacey, S., & Brighton, C. (1989). Stroke rehabilitation: Sensorimotor integrative treatment versus functional treatment. *The American Journal of Occupational Therapy, 43,* 391–397.

3. Beatty, W. W., Wonderlich, S. A., Staton, R. D., & Ternes, L. A. (1990). Cognitive functioning in bulimia: Comparison with depression. *Bulletin of the Psychonomic Society, 28,* 289–292.

4. Miller, E. N., Selnes, O. A., McArthur, J. C., Satz, P., Becker, J. T., Cohen, B. A., Sheridan, K., Machado, A. M., Van Gorp, W. G., & Visscher, B. (1990). Neuropsychological performance in HIV-I-infected homosexual men: The Multicenter AIDS Cohort Study (MACS). *Neurology, 40,* 197–203.

5. Selnes, O. A., Miller, E., McArthur, J., Gordon, B., Muñoz, A., Sheridan, K., Fox, R., Saah, A. J., & the Multicenter AIDS Cohort Study. (1990). HIV-I infection: No evidence of cognitive decline during the asymptomatic stages. *Neurology, 40,* 204–208.

6. Brown, W. S., Marsh, J. T., Wolcott, D., Takushi, R., Carr, C. R., Higa, J., & Nissenson, A. R. (1991). Cognitive function, mood and P3 latency: Effects of the amelioration of anemia in dialysis patients. *Neuropsychologia, 29,* 35–45.

7. Meador, K. J., Loring, D. W., Allen, M. E., Zamrini, E. Y., Moore, E. E., Abney, O. L., & King, D. W. (1991). Comparative cognitive effects of carbamazepine and phenytoin in healthy adults. *Neurology, 41,* 1537–1540.

8. Miller, E. N., Satz, P., & Visscher, B. (1991). Computerized and conventional neuropsychological assessment of HIV-1-infected homosexual men. *Neurology, 41,* 1608–1616.

9. Selrees, O. A., McArthur, J. C., Royal, W., Updike, M. L., Nance-Sproson, T., Concha, M., Gordon, B., Solomon, L., & Vlahor, D. (1992). HIV-I infection and intravenous drug use: Longitudinal neuropsychological evaluation of asymptomatic subjects. *Neurology, 42,* 1924–1930.

10. Swirsky-Sacchetti, T., Mitchell, D. R., Seward, J., Gonzales, C., Lublin, F., Knobler, R., & Field, H. L. (1992). Neuropsychological and structural brain lesions in multiple sclerosis: A regional analysis. *Neurology, 42,* 1291–1295.

11. Bird, M., & Luszcz, M. (1993). Enhancing memory performance in Alzheimer's disease: Acquisition assistance and cue effectiveness. *Journal of Clinical and Experimental Neuropsychology, 15,* 921–932.

12. Dodrill, C. B., Arnett, J. L., Sommerville, K. W., & Sussman, N. M. (1993). Evaluation of the effects of vigabatrin on cognitive abilities and quality of life epilepsy. *Neurology, 43,* 2501–2507.

13. Fitzgerald, H. E., Sullivan, L. A., Ham, H. P., Zucker, R. A., Bruckel, S., Schneider, A. M., & Noll, R. B. (1993). Predictors of behavior problems in three-year-old sons of alcoholics: Early evidence for the onset of risk. *Child Development, 64,* 110–123.

14. Krupp, L. B., Masur, D. M., & Kaufman, L. D. (1993). Neurocognitive dysfunction in the eosinophilia-myalgia syndrome. *Neurology, 43,* 931–936.

15. Christensen, H., Mackinnon, A., Jorm, A. F., Henderson, A. S., Scott, L. R., & Korten, A. E. (1994). Age differences and interindividual variation in cognition in community-dwelling elderly. *Psychology and Aging, 9,* 381–390.

16. Farlow, M., Murrell, J., Ghetti, B., Unverzagt, F., Zeldenrust, S., & Benson, M. (1994). Clinical characteristics in a kindred with early-onset Alzheimer's

disease and their linkage to a G->T change at position 2149 of the amyloid percursor protein gene. *Neurology, 44,* 105–111.

17. Feinstein, A., Brown, R., & Ron, M. (1994). Effects of practice of serial tests of attention in healthy subjects. *Journal of Clinical and Experimental Neuropsychology, 16,* 436–447.

18. Hillbrand, M., & Waite, B. M. (1994). The everyday experience of an institutionalized sex offender: An idiographic application of the experience sampling method. *Archives of Sexual Behavior, 23,* 453–463.

19. Hiscock, C. K., Branham, J. D., & Hiscock, M. (1994). Detection of feigned cognitive impairment: The two-alternative forced-choice method compared with selected conventional tests. *Journal of Psychopathology and Behavioral Assessment, 16,* 95–110.

20. Lyness, S. A., Eaton, E. M., & Schneider, L. S. (1994). Cognitive performance in older and middle-aged depressed outpatients and controls. *Journal of Gerontology: Psychological Sciences, 49*(1), 129–136.

21. Shum, D. H. K., McFarland, K., & Bain, J. D. (1994). Assessment of attention: Relationship between psychological testing and information processing approaches. *Journal of Clinical and Experimental Neuropsychology, 16,* 531–538.

22. Smits, R. C. F., Emmen, H. H., Bertelsmann, F. W., Kulig, B. M., vanLoenen, A. C., & Polman, C. H. (1994). The effects of 4-aminopyridine on cognitive function inpatients with multiple sclerosis: A pilot study. *Neurology, 44,* 1701–1705.

23. Sobell, L. C., Toneatto, T., & Sobell, M. (1994). Behavioral assessment and treatment planning for alcohol, tobacco, and other drug problems: Current status with an emphasis on clinical applications. *Behavior Therapy, 25,* 533–580.

24. Thompson, N. J., & Morris, R. D. (1994). Predicting injury risk in adolescent football players: The importance of psychological variables. *Journal of Pediatric Psychology, 19,* 415–429.

25. van Gorp, W. G., Miller, E. N., Marcotte, T. D., Dixon, W., Paz, D., Selnes, O., Wesch, J., Becker, J. T., Hinkin, C. H., Mitrushina, M., Satz, P., Weisman, J. D., Buckingham, S. L., & Stenquist, P. K. (1994). The relationship between age and cognitive impairment in HIV-I infection: Findings from the Multicenter AIDS Cohort Study and a clinical cohort. *Neurology, 44,* 929–935.

26. Beatty, W. W., Paul, R. H., Wilbanks, S. L., Hames, K. A., Blanco, C. R., & Goodkin, D. E. (1995). Identifying multiple sclerosis patients with mild or global cognitive impairment using the Screening Examination for Cognitive Impairment (SEFCI). *Neurology, 45,* 718–723.

27. Creighton, C. (1995). Effects of afternoon rest on the performance of geriatric patients in a rehabilitation hospital: A pilot study. *The American Journal of Occupational Therapy, 49,* 775–779.

28. Hannon, R., Adams, P., Harrington, S., Fries-Dias, C., & Gipson, M. T. (1995). Effects of brain injury and age on prospective memory self-rating and performance. *Rehabilitation Psychology, 40,* 289–298.

29. Kinsella, G., Prior, M., Sawyer, M., Murtagh, D., Eisenmajer, R., Anderson, J., Bryan, D., & Klug, G. (1995). Neuropsychological deficit and academic performance in children and adolescents following traumatic brain injury. *Journal of Pediatric Psychology, 20,* 753–767.

30. Meador, K. J., Loring, D. W., Moore, E. E., Thompson, W. O., Nichols, M. E., Oberzan, R. E., Durking, M. W., Gallagher, B. B., & King, D. W. (1995). Comparative cognitive effects of phenobarbital, phenytoin, and valproate in healthy adults. *Neurology, 45,* 1494–1499.

31. Morgan, S. F., & Wheelock, J. (1995). Comparability of WAIS-R digit symbol and the Symbol Digit Modalities Test. *Perceptual and Motor Skills, 80,* 631–634.

32. Selnes, O. A., Galai, N., Bacellar, H., Miller, E. N., Becker, J. T., Wesch, J., VanGorp, W., & McArthur, J. C. (1995). Cognitive performance after progression to AIDS: A longitudinal study from the Multicenter AIDS Cohort Study. *Neurology, 45,* 267–275.

33. Aarsland, D., Hoien, T., Larsen, J. P., & Oftedal, M. (1996). Lexical and nonlexical spelling deficits in dementia of the Alzheimer type. *Brain and Language, 52,* 551–563.

34. Bird, M., & Kinsella, G. (1996). Long-term cued recall of tasks in senile dementia. *Psychology and Aging, 11,* 45–46.

35. Galloway, S., Malloy, P., Kohn, R., Gillard, E., Duffy, J., Rogg, J., Tung, G., Richardson, E., Thomas, C., & Westlake, R. (1996). MRI and neuropsychological differences in early- and late-life-onset geriatric depression. *Neurology, 46,* 1567–1574.

36. Verhaeghen, P., & Marcoen, A. (1996). On the mechanisms of plasticity in young and older adults after instruction in the method of loci: Evidence for an amplification model. *Psychology and Aging, 11,* 165–178.

37. Bruggemans, E. F. Van de Vijver, F. J. R., & Huysmans, H. A. (1997). Assessment of cognitive deterioration in individual patients following cardiac surgery: Correcting for measurement error and practice effects. *Journal of Clinical and Experimental Neuropsychology, 19,* 543–559.

38. Ferraro, F. R., Wonderlich, S., & Jocic, Z. (1997). Performance variability as a new theoretical mechanism regarding eating disorders and cognitive processing. *Journal of Clinical Psychology, 53,* 117–121.

39. Hinton-Bayre, A. D., Geffen, G., & McFarland, K. (1997). Mild head injury and speed of information processing: A prospective study of professional rugby league players. *Journal of Clinical and Experimental Neuropsychology, 19,* 275–289.

40. Llorente, A. M., Miller, E. N., D'Elia, L. F., Selnes, O. A., Wesch, J., Becker, J. T., & Satz, P. (1998). Slowed information processing in HIV-1 disease. *Journal of Clinical and Experimental Neuropsychology, 20,* 60–72.

41. Putzke, J. D., Williams, M. A., & Boll, T. J. (1998). A defensive response set and the relation between cognitive and emotional functioning: A replication. *Perceptual and Motor Skills, 86,* 251–257.

42. Swan, G. E., DeCarli, C., Miller, B. L., Reed, T., Wolf, P. A., Jack, L. M., & Carmelli, D. (1998). Association of midlife blood pressure to late-life cognitive decline and brain morphology. *Neurology, 51,* 986–993.

43. van Buchem, M. A., Grossman, R. I., Armstrong, C., Polansky, M., Miki, Y., Heyning, F. H., Boncoeur-Martel, M. P., Wei, L., Udupa, J. K., Grossman, M., Kolson, D. L., & McGowan, J. C. (1998). Correlation of volumetric magnetization transfer imaging with clinical data in MS. *Neurology, 50,* 1609–1617.

[2600]

Symbol Elaboration Test.

Purpose: Projective instrument designed to assess personality.

Population: Ages 6 and over.

Publication Dates: 1950-1953.

Acronym: SET.

Scores: Item scores only.

Administration: Individual.

Price Data: Available from publisher.

Time: [40-50] minutes.

Authors: Johanna Krout [Tabin].

Publisher: Johanna Krout Tabin [No reply from publisher; status unknown].

Cross References: For a review by Richard H. Dana, see 5:160 (1 reference).

[2601]

Symbolic Play Test, Second Edition.

Purpose: Developed to assess early concept formation and symbolization based on a child's spontaneous nonverbal play.

Population: Ages 1-3.

Publication Dates: 1976-1988.

Scores: Total score only.

Administration: Individual.

Price Data, 1999: £145 per complete set including toys, 25 record forms, and manual ('88, 39 pages); £14.50 per 25 record forms; £25 per manual.

Time: (10-15) minutes.

Authors: Marianne Lowe and Anthony J. Costello.

Publisher: NFER-Nelson Publishing Co., Ltd. [England].

Cross References: For reviews by Anthony W. Paolitto and Harvey N. Switzky, see 12:384; see also T4:2673 (2 references) and T3:2383 (1 reference).

TEST REFERENCES

1. Weismer, S. E., Murray-Branch, J., & Miller, J. F. (1993). Comparison of two methods for promoting productive vocabulary in late talkers. *Journal of Speech and Hearing Research, 36,* 1037–1050.

2. Weismer, S. E., Murray-Branch, J., & Miller, J. F. (1994). A prospective longitudinal study of language development in late talkers. *Journal of Speech and Hearing, 37,* 852–867.

3. Girolametto, L., Pearce, P. S., & Weitzman, E. (1997). Effects of lexical intervention on the phonology of late talkers. *Journal of Speech, Language, and Hearing Research, 40,* 333–348.

[2602]

Symptom Assessment-45 Questionnaire.

Purpose: Designed as a "brief yet comprehensive general assessment of psychiatric symptomalogy."

Population: Ages 13 and over, reading at the 6th grade level or higher.

Publication Dates: 1996–1998.
Acronym: SA-45.
Scores, 11: 9 subscales (Anxiety, Depression, Hostility, Interpersonal Sensitivity, Obsessive-Compulsive, Paranoid Ideation, Phobic Anxiety, Psychoticism, Somatization), 2 composite scores (Global Severity Index, Positive Symptom Total).
Administration: Group.
Price Data: Available from publisher.
Time: (10–15) minutes.
Comments: Derived from the Symptom Checklist—90 (SCL-90; 2603); self-report inventory.
Author: Strategic Advantage, Inc.
Publisher: Multi-Health Systems, Inc.

[2603]

Symptom Checklist-90-Revised.

Purpose: "Designed primarily to reflect the psychological symptom patterns of psychiatric and medical patients," as well as nonpatients.
Population: Adults and adolescents age 13 and older.
Publication Dates: 1975.
Acronym: SCL-90-R.
Scores: 9 primary symptom dimensions: Somatization, Obsessive-Compulsive, Interpersonal Sensitivity, Depression, Anxiety, Hostility, Phobic Anxiety, Paranoid Ideation, Psychoticism; plus 3 indices of distress: Global Severity Index, Positive Symptom Distress Index, Positive Symptom Total.
Administration: Group.
Price Data, 1994: $75 per hand-scoring starter kit including manual, 50 answer sheets, 50 profile forms, 2 worksheets, answer keys, and bibliography (specify Nonpatient Adult, Nonpatient Adolescent, Outpatient Psychiatric, or Inpatient Psychiatric); $32.50 per 50 hand-scoring answer sheets; $17.50 per 50 profile forms and 2 worksheets (specify Nonpatient Adult, Nonpatient Adolescent, Outpatient Psychiatric, or Inpatient Psychiatric); $18 per answer keys; $19.50 per manual; price information for Interpretive Report and Profile Report scoring and software available from publisher.
Time: (12–15) minutes.
Comments: Self-report test; companion clinician and observer rating forms also available.
Authors: Leonard R. Derogatis.
Publisher: NCS (Minnetonka)
Cross References: See T4:2674 (318 references); for reviews by Jerome D. Pauker and Robert W. Payne, see 9:1082 (61 references); see also T3:2100 (13 references).

TEST REFERENCES

1. Shanfield, S. B., Swain, B. J., & Benjamin, G. A. H. (1986). Parents' responses to the death of adult children from accidents and cancer: A comparison. *Omega, 17,* 289–297.

2. Bossé, R., Aldwin, C. M., Levenson, M. R., & Ekerdt, D. J. (1987). Mental health differences among retirees and workers: Findings from the normative aging study. *Psychology and Aging, 2,* 383-389.

3. Beck, J. G., Scott, S. K., Teague, R. B., Perez, F. I., & Brown, G. A. (1988). Correlates of daily impairment in COPD. *Rehabilitation Psychology, 33,* 77–84.

4. Buckelew, S. P., Burk, J. P., Brownlee-Deffeck, M., Frank, R. G., & DeGood, D. (1988). Cognitive and somatic aspects of depression among a rehabilitation sample: Reliability and validity of SCL-90-R research subscales. *Rehabilitation Psychology, 33,* 67–75.

5. Strauman, T. J., & Higgins, E. T. (1988). Self-discrepancies as predictor of vulnerability to distinct syndromes of chronic emotional distress. *Journal of Personality, 56,* 685–707.

6. Benjamin, J., Silk, K. R., Lohr, N. E., & Westen, D. (1989). The relationship between borderline personality disorder and anxiety disorders. *American Journal of Orthopsychiatry, 59,* 461–467.

7. Blanchard, E. B., McCoy, G. C., Berger, M., Musso, A., Pallmeyer, T. P., Gerardi, R., Gerardi, M. A., & Pangburn, L. (1989). A controlled comparison of thermal biofeedback and relaxation training in the treatment of essential hypertensional IV: Prediction of short-term clinical outcome. *Behavior Therapy, 20,* 405–415.

8. Blumenthal, J. A., Emery, C. F., Madden, D. J., George, L. K., Coleman, R. E., Riddle, M. W., McKee, D. C., Reasoner, J., & Williams, R. S. (1989). Cardiovascular and behavioral effects of aerobic exercise in healthy older men and women. *Journal of Gerontology, 44,* 147–157.

9. Braver, S. L., Gonzalez, N., Wolchik, S. A., & Sandler, I. N. (1989). Economic hardship and psychological distress in custodial mothers. *Journal of Divorce, 12*(4), 19–34.

10. Brook, J. S., Gordon, A. S., Brook, A., & Brook, D. W. (1989). The consequences of marijuana use on intrapersonal and interpersonal functioning in Black and White adolescents. *Genetic Psychology Monographs, 115,* 349–369.

11. Budman, S. H., Soldz, S., Demby, A., Feldstein, M., Springer, T., & Davis, M. S. (1989). Cohesion, alliance and outcome in group psychotherapy. *Psychiatry, 52,* 339–350.

12. Campbell, J. C. (1989). A test of two explanatory models of women's responses to battering. *Nursing Research, 38,* 18–24.

13. Canetto, S. S., Feldman, L. B., & Lupei, R. L. (1989). Suicidal persons and their partners: Individual and interpersonal dynamics. *Suicide and Life-Threatening Behavior, 19,* 237–248.

14. Dakof, G. A., & Mendelsohn, G. A. (1989). Patterns of adaptation to Parkinson's disease. *Health Psychology, 8,* 355–372.

15. Downey, J., Ehrhardt, A. A., Gruen, R., Bell, J. J., & Morishima, A. (1989). Psychopathology and social functioning in women with Turner syndrome. *The Journal of Nervous and Mental Disease, 177,* 191-201.

16. Fontana, A. F., Kerns, R. D., Rosenberg, R. L., & Colonese, K. L. (1989). Support, stress, and recovery from coronary heart disease: A longitudinal causal model. *Health Psychology, 8,* 175–193.

17. Frone, M. R., & McFarlin, D. B. (1989). Chronic occupational stressors, self-focused attention, and well-being: Testing a cybernetic model of stress. *Journal of Applied Psychology, 74,* 876-883.

18. Grady, D. A., Woolfork, R. L., & Budney, A. J. (1989). Dimensions of war zone stress: An empirical analysis. *The Journal of Nervous and Mental Disease, 177,* 347-350.

19. Gunderson, J. G., Frank, A. F., Ronningstam, E. F., Wachter, S., Lynch, V. J., & Wolf, P. J. (1989). Early discontinuance of borderline patients from psychotherapy. *The Journal of Nervous and Mental Disease, 177,* 38-42.

20. Johnson, C., Tobin, D., & Enright, A. (1989). Prevalence and clinical characteristics of borderline patients in an eating-disordered population. *The Journal of Clinical Psychiatry, 50,* 9–15.

21. Johnson, V., & White, H. R. (1989). An investigation of factors related to intoxicated driving behaviors among youth. *Journal of Studies on Alcohol, 50,* 320–330.

22. Jones, D. N., & Reznikoff, M. (1989). Psychosocial adjustment to a mastectomy. *The Journal of Nervous and Mental Disease, 177,* 624-631.

23. Kurdek, L. A. (1989). Social support and psychological distress in first-married and remarried newlywed husbands and wives. *Journal of Marriage and the Family, 51,* 1047-1052.

24. Lesser, I. M., Rubin, R. T., Rifkin, A., Swinson, R. P., Ballenger, J. C., Burrows, G. D., DuPont, R. L., Noyes, R., & Pecknold, J. C. (1989). Secondary depression in panic disorder and agoraphobia II. Dimensions of depressive symptomatology and their response to treatment. *Journal of Affective Disorders, 16,* 49–58.

25. Martin, F., Sabourin, S., & Gendreau, P. (1989). Les dimensions de la detresse psychologique: Analyse factorielle confirmatoire de type hierarchique. *International Journal of Psychology, 24,* 571–584.

26. Miller, I. W., Norman, W. H., Keitner, G. I., Bishop, S. B., & Dow, M. G. (1989). Cognitive-behavioral treatment of depressed inpatients. *Behavior Therapy, 20,* 25–47.

27. Pope, R., & Whitmarsh, G. A. (1989). A clinical study of patients who manifest early change in a private psychiatric hospital. *The Journal of Nervous and Mental Disease, 177,* 305-306.

28. Sohlberg, S., Norring, C., Holmgren, S., & Rosmark, B. (1989). Impulsivity and long-term prognosis of psychiatric patients with anorexia nervosa/bulimia nervosa. *The Journal of Nervous and Mental Disease, 177,* 249-258.

29. Vitaliano, P. D., Maiuro, R. D., Russo, J., & Mitchell, E. S. (1989). Medical student distress: A longitudinal study. *The Journal of Nervous and Mental Disease, 177,* 70-76.

30. Warrenburg, S., Levine, J., Schwartz, G. E., Fontana, A. F., Kerns, R. D., Delaney, R., & Mattson, R. (1989). Defensive coping and blood pressure reactivity in medical patients. *Journal of Behavioral Medicine, 12,* 407-424.

31. Westermeyer, J., Neider, J., & Callies, A. (1989). Psychosocial adjustment of Hmong refugees during their first decade in the United States. *The Journal of Nervous and Mental Disease, 177,* 132-139.

32. Alford, B. A., & Jaremko, M. E. (1990). Behavioral design of a positive verbal community: A preliminary experimental analysis. *Journal of Behavior Therapy and Experimental Psychiatry, 21,* 173–184.
33. Angst, J., Merikangas, K., Scheidegger, P., & Wicki, W. (1990). Recurrent brief depression: A new subtype of affective disorder. *Journal of Affective Disorders, 19,* 87-98.
34. Armstrong, J. G., & Loewenstein, R. J. (1990). Characteristics of patients with multiple personality and dissociative disorders on psychological testing. *The Journal of Nervous and Mental Disease, 178,* 448-454.
35. Baum, A. (1990). Stress, intrusive imagery, and chronic distress. *Health Psychology, 9,* 653-675.
36. Biedel, D. C., & Bulik, C. M. (1990). Flooding and response prevention as a treatment for bowel obsessions. *Journal of Anxiety Disorders, 4,* 247-256.
37. Brennan, J., Andrews, G., Morris-Yates, A., & Pollock, C. (1990). An examination of defense style in parents who abuse children. *The Journal of Nervous and Mental Disease, 178,* 592-595.
38. Buckelew, S. P., Baumstark, K. E., Frank, R. G., & Hewett, J. E. (1990). Adjustment following spinal cord injury. *Rehabilitation Psychology, 35,* 101–109.
39. Bulik, C. M., Carpenter, L. L., Kupfer, D. J., & Frank, E. (1990). Features associated with suicide attempts in recurrent major depression. *Journal of Affective Disorders, 18,* 29-37.
40. Cervantes, R. C., Padilla, A. M., & deSnyder, N. S. (1990). Reliability and validity of the Hispanic Stress Inventory. *Hispanic Journal of Behavior Sciences, 12,* 76–82.
41. Christensen, L., & Burrows, R. (1990). Dietary treatment of depression. *Behavior Therapy, 21,* 183–193.
42. Compas, B. E., & Williams, R. A. (1990). Stress, coping and adjustment in mothers and young adolescents in single- and two-parent families. *American Journal of Community Psychology, 18,* 525-545.
43. Dew, M. A., Ragni, M. V., & Nimorwicz, P. (1990). Infection with human immunodeficiency virus and vulnerability to psychiatric distress. *Archives of General Psychiatry, 47,* 737-744.
44. Dworkin, S. F., Von Korff, M., & LeResche, L. (1990). Multiple pains and psychiatric disturbance. *Archives of General Psychiatry, 47,* 239–244.
45. Elsenga, S., & Emmelkamp, E. M. G. (1990). Behavioral treatment of an incest-related trauma in an agoraphobic client. *Journal of Anxiety Disorders, 4,* 151-162.
46. Gil, K. M., Williams, D. A., Keefe, F. J., & Beckham, J. C. (1990). The relationship of negative thoughts to pain and psychological distress. *Behavior Therapy, 21,* 349–362.
47. Green, B. L., Lindy, J. D., Grace, M. C., Gleser, G. C., Leonard, A. C., Korol, M., & Winget, C. (1990). Buffalo Creek survivors in the second decade: Stability of stress symptoms. *American Journal of Orthopsychiatry, 60,* 43–54.
48. Haertzen, C. A., Hickey, J. E., Rose, M. R., & Jaffe, J. H. (1990). The relationship between a diagnosis of antisocial personality and hostility: Development of an antisocial hostility scale. *Journal of Clinical Psychology, 46,* 679–686.
49. Holmes, J. A., & Stevenson, C. A. Z. (1990). Differential effects of avoidant and attentional coping strategies on adaptation to chronic and recent-onset pain. *Health Psychology, 9,* 577-584.
50. Kedem, D., Mikulincer, M., Nathanson, Y. E., & Bartoov, B. (1990). Psychological aspects of male infertility. *British Journal of Medical Psychology, 63,* 73–80.
51. Keefe, F. J., & Williams, D. A. (1990). A comparison of coping strategies in chronic pain patients in different age groups. *Journal of Gerontology, 45,* 161–165.
52. Kelley, S. J. (1990). Parental stress response to sexual abuse and ritualistic abuse of children in day-care centers. *Nursing Research, 39,* 25–29.
53. Kleinman, P. H., Miller, A. B., Millman, R. B., Woody, G. E., Todd, T., Kemp, J., & Lipton, D. S. (1990). Psychopathology among cocaine abusers entering treatment. *The Journal of Nervous and Mental Disease, 178,* 442-447.
54. Koeske, G. F., & Koeske, R. D. (1990). The buffering effect of social support on parental stress. *American Journal of Orthopsychiatry, 60,* 440–451.
55. Kurdek, L. A. (1990). Divorce history and self-reported psychological distress in husbands and wives. *Journal of Marriage and the Family, 52,* 701–708.
56. Kurdek, L. A. (1990). Effects of child age on the marital quality and psychological distress of newly married mothers and stepfathers. *Journal of Marriage and the Family, 52,* 81–85.
57. Leroux, M. D., Vincent, K. R., McPherson, R. H., & Williams, W. (1990). Construct validity of the Diagnostic Inventory of Personality and Symptoms: External correlates. *Journal of Clinical Psychology, 46,* 285–291.
58. Montgomery, D. E., Fine, M. A., & James-Myers, L. (1990). The development and validation of an instrument to assess an optimal Afrocentric world view. *The Journal of Black Psychology, 17,* 37-54.
59. Nelson, D. L., & Sutton, C. (1990). Chronic work stress and coping: A longitudinal study and suggested new directions. *Academy of Management Journal, 33,* 859–869.
60. Richman, J. A., & Flaherty, J. A. (1990). Alcohol-related problems of future physicians prior to medical training. *Journal of Studies on Alcohol, 51,* 296–300.
61. Schag, C. A. C., Heinrich, R. L., Aadland, R. L., & Ganz, P. A. (1990). Assessing problems of cancer patients: Psychometric properties of the Cancer Inventory of Problem Situations. *Health Psychology, 9,* 83-102.
62. Schultz, R., Visintainer, P., & Williamson, G. M. (1990). Psychiatric and physical morbidity effects of caregiving. *Journal of Gerontology, 45,* 181–191.
63. Shapiro, D. A., Barkham, M., Hardy, G. E., & Morrison, L. A. (1990). The second Sheffield psychotherapy Project: Ratinale, design and preliminary outcome data. *British Journal of Medical Psychology, 63,* 97–108.
64. Sheehan, D. Y., Raj, A. B., Harnett-Sheehan, K., Soto, S., & Lewis, C. P. (1990). Adinazolam sustained release formulation in the treatment of generalized anxiety disorder. *Journal of Anxiety Disorders, 4,* 239-246.
65. Shutty, M. S., Jr., & DeGood, D. E. (1990). Patient knowledge and beliefs about pain and its treatment. *Rehabilitation Psychology, 35,* 43–54.
66. Smith, L. W., Patterson, T. L., & Grant, I. (1990). Avoidant coping predicts psychological disturbance in the elderly. *The Journal of Nervous and Mental Disease, 178,* 525-530.
67. Soldz, S., Budman, S., Demby, A., & Feldstein, M. (1990). Patient activity and outcome in group psychotherapy: New findings. *International Journal of Group Psychotherapy, 40,* 53–62.
68. Soloman, Z., Mikulincer, M., & Habershaim, N. (1990). Life-events, coping strategies, social resources, and somatic complaints among combat stress reaction casualties. *British Journal of Medical Psychology, 63,* 137–148.
69. Solomon, Z., Oppenheimer, B., Elizur, Y., & Waysman, M. (1990). Exposure to recurrent combat stress: Can successful coping in a second war heal combat-related PTSD from the past? *Journal of Anxiety Disorders, 4,* 141-145.
70. Steinberger, L. G., & Burns, G. L. (1990). Compulsive Activity Checklist and the Maudsley Obsessiona-Compulsive Inventory: Psychometric properties of two measures of obsessive-compulsive disorder. *Behavior Therapy, 21,* 117–127.
71. Surrey, J., Swett, C., Michaels, A., & Levin, S. (1990). Reported history of physical and sexual abuse and severity of symptomatology in women psychiatric outpatients. *American Journal of Orthopsychiatry, 60,* 412–417.
72. Tate, D. G., Kewman, D. G., & Maynard, F. (1990). The Brief Symptom Inventory: Measuring psychological distress in spinal cord injury. *Rehabilitation Psychology, 35,* 211–216.
73. Tiedje, L. B., Wortman, C. B., Downey, G., Emmons, C., Biernat, M., & Lang, E. (1990). Women with multiple roles: Role-compatibility perceptions, satisfaction, and mental health. *Journal of Marriage and the Family, 52,* 63–72.
74. VanPutten, T., Marder, S. R., & Mintz, J. (1990). A controlled dose comparison of haloperidol in newly admitted schizophrenia patients. *Archives of General Psychiatry, 47,* 754-758.
75. Vitaliano, P. P., Maiuro, R. D., Russo, J., Katon, W., DeWolfe, D., & Hall, G. (1990). Coping profiles associated with psychiatric, physical health, work, and family problems. *Health Psychology, 9,* 348-376.
76. Wagner, B. M., & Compas, B. E. (1990). Gender, instrumentality, and expressivity: Moderators of the relation between stress and psychological symptoms during adolescence. *American Journal of Community Psychology, 18,* 383-406.
77. Weddington, W. W., Brown, B. S., Haertzen, C. A., Cone, E. J., Dax, E. M., Herring, R. I., & Michaelson, B. S. (1990). Changes in mood, craving, and sleep during short-term abstinence reported by male cocaine addicts. *Archives of General Psychiatry, 47,* 861-868.
78. Westermeyer, J., Callies, A., & Neider, J. (1990). Welfare status and psychosocial adjustment among 100 Hmong refugees. *The Journal of Nervous and Mental Disease, 178,* 300-306.
79. Barnas, M. V., Pollina, L., & Cummings, E. M. (1991). Life-span attachment: Relations between attachment and socioemotional functioning in adult women. *Genetic Psychology Monographs, 117,* 175–202.
80. Barnett, R. C., Kibria, N., Baruch, G. K., & Pleck, J. H. (1991). Adult daughter-parent relationships and their association with daughter's subjective well-being and psychological distress. *Journal of Marriage and the Family, 53,* 29–42.
81. Barton, J., & Folkard, S. (1991). The response of day and night nurses to their work schedules. *Journal of Occupational Psychology, 64,* 207-218.
82. Berg, B. J., & Wilson, J. F. (1991). Psychological functioning across stages of treatment for infertility. *Journal of Behavioral Medicine, 14,* 11-25.
83. Blumenthal, J. A., Emery, C. F., Madden, D. J., Schniebolk, S., Walsh-Riddle, M., George, L. K., McKee, D. C., Higginbotham, M. B., Cobb, F. R., & Coleman, R. E. (1991). Long-term effects of exercise on psychological functioning in older men and women. *Journal of Gerontology, 46,* 352–361.
84. Burnette, M. M., Koehn, K. A., Kenyon-Jump, R., Hutton, K., & Stark, C. (1991). Control of genital herpes recurrences using progressive muscle relaxation. *Behavior Therapy, 22,* 237–247.
85. Carey, M. D., Carey, K. B., & Meisler, A. W. (1991). Psychiatric symptoms in mentally ill chemical abusers. *The Journal of Nervous and Mental Disease, 179,* 136-138.
86. Davis, R. C., Brickman, E., & Baker, T. (1991). Supportive and unsupportive responses of others to rape victims: Effects on concurrent victim adjustment. *American Journal of Community Psychology, 19,* 443-451.
87. de Bonis, M., Lebeaux, M. O., de Boeck, P., Simon, M., & Pichot, P. (1991). Measuring the severity of depression through a self-report inventory. *Journal of Affective Disorders, 22,* 55-64.
88. Deltito, J. A., Moline, M., Pollak, C., Martin, L. Y., & Manemmani, I. (1991). Effects of phototherapy on non-seasonal unipolar and bipolar depressive spectrum disorders. *Journal of Affective Disorders, 23,* 231-237.
89. Dozier, M., Stevenson, A. L., Lee, S. W., & Velligan, D. I. (1991). Attachment organization and familial overinvolvement for adults with serious psychopathological disorders. *Development and Psychopathology, 3,* 475-489.
90. Dyck, M. J. (1991). Positive and negative attitudes mediating suicide ideation. *Suicide and Life-Threatening Behavior, 21,* 360–373.
91. Easley, M. J., & Epstein, N. (1991). Coping with stress in a family with an alcoholic parent. *Family Relations, 40,* 218-224.
92. Ellwood, M. S., & Stolberg, A. L. (1991). A preliminary investigation of family systems' influences on individual divorce adjustment. *Journal of Divorce & Remarriage, 15*(1/2), 157-174.
93. Fairburn, C. G., Jones, R., Peveler, R. C., Carr, S. J., Solomon, R. A., O'Connor, M. E., Burton, J., & Hope, R. A. (1991). Three psychological treatments for bulimia nervosa. *Archives of General Psychiatry, 48,* 463-469.
94. Fitzgerald, T. E., & Phillips, W. (1991). Attentional bias and agoraphobic avoidance: The role of cognitive style. *Journal of Anxiety Disorders, 5,* 333-341.

95. Gallant, S. J., Hamilton, J. A., Popiel, D. A., Morokoff, P. J., & Chakraborty, P. K. (1991). Daily moods and symptoms: Effects of awareness of study focus, gender, menstrual-cycle phase, and day of the week. *Health Psychology, 10,* 180-189.

96. Gibbs, J. J. (1991). Environmental congruence and symptoms of psychopathology: A further exploration of the effects of exposure to the jail environment. *Criminal Justice and Behavior, 18,* 351–374.

97. Gil, K. M., Williams, D. A., Thompson, R. J., Jr., & Kinney, T. R. (1991). Sickle cell disease in children and adolescents: The relation of child and parent pain coping strategies to adjustment. *Journal of Pediatric Psychology, 16,* 643–663.

98. Girodo, M. (1991). Symptomatic reactions to undercover work. *The Journal of Nervous and Mental Disease, 179,* 626-630.

99. Greenberg, M. T., Speltz, M. L., Derlyen, M., & Endriga, M. C. (1991). Attachment security in preschoolers with and without externalizing behavior problems: A replication. *Development and Psychopathology, 3,* 413-430.

100. Hagen, J. W. (1991). Psychological adjustment following coronary artery bypass graft surgery. *Rehabilitation Counseling Bulletin, 35,* 97–104.

101. Herbert, T. B., Silver, R. C., & Ellard, J. H. (1991). Coping with an abusive relationship: I. How and why do women stay? *Journal of Marriage and the Family, 53,* 311–325.

102. Holloway, S. D., & Machida, S. (1991). Child-rearing effectiveness of divorced mothers: Relationship to coping strategies and social support. *Journal of Divorce & Remarriage, 14*(3/4), 179-201.

103. Hsu, L. K. G., Clement, L., Santhouse, R., & Ju, E. S. Y. (1991). Treatment of bulimia nervosa with lithium carbonate: A controlled study. *The Journal of Nervous and Mental Disease, 179,* 351-355.

104. Johnson, B. K., & Kenkel, M. B. (1991). Stress, coping, and adjustment in female adolescent incest victims. *Child Abuse & Neglect, 15,* 293-305.

105. Kalus, O., Asnis, G. M., Rubinson, E., Kahn, R., Friedman, J. M. K., Iqbal, N., Grosz, D., van Praag, H., & Cahn, W. (1991). Desipramine treatment in panic disorder. *Journal of Affective Disorders, 21,* 239-244.

106. Kaminer, H., & Lavie, P. (1991). Sleep and dreaming in Holocaust survivors: Dramatic decrease in dream recall in well-adjusted survivors. *The Journal of Nervous and Mental Disease, 179,* 664-669.

107. Kirmayer, L. J., & Robbins, J. M. (1991). Three forms of somatization in primary care: Prevalence, co-occurrence, and sociodemographic characteristics. *The Journal of Nervous and Mental Disease, 179,* 647-655.

108. Lesser, I. M., & Rubin, R. T. (1991). Adinazolam-SR in the treatment of generalized anxiety disorder and panic disorder. *Journal of Anxiety Disorders, 5,* 255-265.

109. Liskow, B., Powell, B. J., Nickel, E., & Povick, E. (1991). Antisocial alcoholics: Are there clinically significant diagnostic subtypes? *Journal of Studies on Alcoholism, 52,* 62–69.

110. Lunn, S., Skydsbjerg, M., Schulsinger, H., Parnas, J., Pedersen, C., & Mathiesen, L. (1991). A preliminary report on the neuropsychologic sequelae of human immunodeficiency virus. *Archives of General Psychiatry, 48,* 139-142.

111. Macnee, C. L. (1991). Perceived well-being of persons quitting smoking. *Nursing Research, 40,* 200–203.

112. Munjack, D. J., Bruns, J., Baltazar, P. L., Brown, R., Leonard, M., Nagy, R., Koek, R., Crocker, B., & Schafer, S. (1991). A pilot study of buspirone in the treatment of social phobia. *Journal of Anxiety Disorders, 5,* 87-98.

113. Noam, G. G., & Dill, D. L. (1991). Adult development and symptomatology. *Psychiatry, 54,* 208–217.

114. Norvell, N., Martin, D., & Salamon, A. (1991). Psychological and physiological benefits of passive and aerobic exercise in sedentary middle-aged women. *The Journal of Nervous and Mental Disease, 179,* 573-574.

115. Parks, S. H., & Pilisuk, M. (1991). Caregiver burden: Gender and the psychological costs of caregiving. *American Journal of Orthopsychiatry, 61,* 501–509.

116. Perconte, S. T., & Griger, M. L. (1991). Comparison of successful, unsuccessful, and relapsed Vietnam veterans treated for posttraumatic stress disorder. *The Journal of Nervous and Mental Disease, 179,* 558-562.

117. Piper, W. E., Azim, H. F. A., Joyce, A. S., & McCallum, M. (1991). Transference interpretations, therapeutic alliance, and outcome in short-term individual psychotherapy. *Archives of General Psychiatry, 48,* 946-953.

118. Piper, W. E., Azim, H. F. A., Joyce, A. S., McCallum, M., Nixon, G. W. H., & Segal, P. S. (1991). Quality of object relations versus interpersonal functioning as predictors of therapeutic alliance and psychotherapy outcome. *The Journal of Nervous and Mental Disease, 179,* 432-438.

119. Shear, M. K., Ball, G., Fitzpatrick, M., Josephson, S., Klosko, J., & Frances, A. (1991). Cognitive-behavioral therapy for panic: An open study. *The Journal of Nervous and Mental Disease, 179,* 468-472.

120. Spinhoven, P., Methorst, G. J., van Grieken, N., & Mulder, A. (1991). An abbreviated questionnaire for quantifying treatment requests for Dutch outpatients. *The Journal of Nervous and Mental Disease, 179,* 502.

121. Stanton, A. L., Burker, E. J., & Kershaw, D. (1991). Effects of resercher follow-up of distressed subjects: Tradeoff between validity and ethical responsibility? *Ethics & Behavior, 1,* 105–112.

122. Tambs, K. (1991). Transmission of symptoms of anxiety and depression in nuclear families. *Journal of Affective Disorders, 21,* 117-126.

123. Taylor, J., & Jackson, B. B. (1991). Evaluation of a holistic model of mental health symptoms in African American women. *The Journal of Black Psychology, 18*(1), 19-45.

124. Toro, P. A., & Wall, D. D. (1991). Research on homeless persons: Diagnostic comparisons and practice implications. *Professional Psychology: Research and Practice, 22,* 479–488.

125. Tttle, D. H., Shutty, M. S., & DeGood, D. E. (1991). Empirical dimensions of coping in chronic pain patients: A factorial analysis. *Rehabilitation Psychology, 36,* 179–188.

126. Turner, J. B., Kessler, R. C., & House, J. S. (1991). Factors facilitating adjustment to unemployment: Implications for intervention. *American Journal of Community Psychology, 19,* 521-542.

127. van Gent, E. M., & Zwart, F. M. (1991). Psychoeducation of partners of bipolar-manic patients. *Journal of Affective Disorders, 21,* 15-18.

128. Wilson, K. G., Sandler, L. S., Asmundson, G. J. G., Larsen, D. K., & Ediger, J. M. (1991). Effects of instructional set on self-reports of panic attacks. *Journal of Anxiety Disorders, 5,* 43-63.

129. Winston, A., Pollack, J., McCullough, L., Flegenheimer, W., Kestenbaum, R., & Trujillo, M. (1991). Brief psychotherapy of personality disorders. *The Journal of Nervous and Mental Disease, 179,* 188-193.

130. Anastopoulos, A. D., Goevremont, D. C., Shelton, T. L., & DuPaul, G. J. (1992). Parenting stress among families of children with attention deficit hyperactivity disorder. *Journal of Abnormal Child Psychology, 20,* 503-520.

131. Barkley, R. A., Anastopoulos, A. D., Goevremont, D. C., & Fletcher, K. E. (1992). Adolescents with attention deficit hyperactivity: Mother-adolescent interactions, family beliefs and conflicts and maternal psychopathology. *Journal of Abnormal Child Psychology, 20,* 263-288.

132. Barnett, R. C., & Marshall, N. L. (1992). Men's job and partner roles: Spillover effects and psychological distress. *Sex Roles, 27,* 455-472.

133. Barnett, R. C., Marshall, N. L., & Pleck, J. H. (1992). Men's multiple roles and their relationships to men's psychological distress. *Journal of Marriage and the Family, 54,* 358–367.

134. Budd, K. S., McGraw, T. E., Farbisz, R., Murphy, T. B., Hawkins, D., Heilman, N., Werle, M., & Hochstadt, N. J. (1992). Psychosocial concomitants of children's feeding disorders. *Journal of Pediatric Psychology, 17,* 81–94.

135. Cassano, G. B., Akiskal, H. S., Savino, M., Musetti, L., & Perugi, G. (1992). Proposed subtypes of bipolar II and related disorders: With hypomanic episodes (or cyclothymia) and with hyperthymic temperament. *Journal of Affective Disorders, 26,* 127-140.

136. Conger, R. D., Conger, K. J., Elder, G. H., Jr., Lorenz, F. O., Simons, R. L., & Whitbeck, L. B. (1992). A family process model of economic hardship and adjustment of early adolescent boys. *Child Development, 63,* 526–541.

137. Cook, J. A., Hoffschmidt, S., Cohler, B. J., & Pickett, S. (1992). Marital satisfaction among parents of the severly mentally ill living in the community. *American Journal of Orthopsychiatry, 62,* 552–563.

138. Deal, J. E., Wampler, K. S., & Halverson, C. F., Jr. (1992). The importance of similarity in the marital relationship. *Family Process, 31,* 369-382.

139. Dew, M. A., Bromet, E. J., & Penkower, L. (1992). Mental health effects of job loss in women. *Psychological Medicine, 22,* 751-764.

140. Diamond, R., White, R. F., Myers, R. H., Mastromauro, C., Koroshetz, W. J., Butters, N., Rothstein, D. M., Moss, M. B., & Vasterling, J. (1992). Evidence of presymptomatic cognitive decline in Huntington's disease. *Journal of Clinical and Experimental Neuropsychology, 14,* 961-975.

141. Diedrich, G. K., Stock, W., & LoPiccolo, J. (1992). A study on the mechanical reliability of the dacomed snap gauge: Implications for the differentiation between organic and psychogenic impotence. *Archives of Sexual Behavior, 21,* 509-523.

142. Firth-Cozens, J., & Hardy, G. E. (1992). Occupational stress, clinical treatment and changes in job perceptions. *Journal of Occupational and Organizational Psychology, 65,* 81-88.

143. Holmlund, V. (1992). Psychogenic needs and psychiatric symptoms in young Swedish women. *British Journal of Medical Psychology, 65,* 27–38.

144. Irvine, A. A., Cox, D., & Gonder-Frederick, L. (1992). Fear of hypoglycemia: Relationship to physical and psychological symptoms in patients with insulin-dependent diabetes mellitus. *Health Psychology, 11,* 135–138.

145. Koeter, M. W. J. (1992). Validity of the GHQ and SCL anxiety and depression scales: A comparative study. *Journal of Affective Disorders, 24,* 271-280.

146. Koslowsky, M., Bleich, A., Apter, A., Solomon, Z., Wagner, B., & Greenspoon, A. (1992). Structural equation modelling of some of the determinants of suicide risk. *British Journal of Medical Psychology, 65,* 157–165.

147. Kronenberger, W. G., & Thompson, R. J., Jr. (1992). Psychological adaptation of mothers of children with spina bifida: Association with dimensions of social relationships. *Journal of Pediatric Psychology, 17,* 1–14.

148. Leo, D. D., Capodieci, S., & Villa, A. (1992). Personality factors in monozygotic and dizygotic twins: A comparative study. *Psychological Reports, 71,* 1115-1122.

149. Litt, M. D., Babor, T. F., DelBoca, F. K., Kadden, R. M., & Cooney, N. L. (1992). Types of alcoholics, II: Application of an empirically derived typology to treatment matching. *Archives of General Psychiatry, 49,* 609-614.

150. Miller, D. J., Goreczny, A. J., & Perconte, S. T. (1992). Comparison of symptom distress between World War II ex-POWs and Vietnam combat veterans with post-traumatic stress disorder. *Journal of Anxiety Disorders, 6,* 41-46.

151. O'Brien, K. (1992). Primary relationships affect the psychological health of homosexual men at risk for AIDS. *Psychological Reports, 71,* 147-153.

152. Osman, A., Markway, K., & Osman, J. R. (1992). Psychometric properties of the Social Interaction Self-Statement Test in a college sample. *Psychological Reports, 71,* 1171-1177.

153. Pop, V. J., Komproe, I. H., & van Son, M. J. (1992). Characteristics of the Edinburgh Post Natal Depression Scale in the Netherlands. *Journal of Affective Disorders, 26,* 105-110.

154. Quittner, A. L., DiGirolamo, A. M., Michel, M., & Eigen, H. (1992). Parental response to cystic fibrosis: A contextual analysis of the diagnosis phase. *Journal of Pediatric Psychology, 17,* 683–704.

155. Rhodes, J. E., Ebert, L., & Fischer, K. (1992). Natural mentors: An overlooked resource in the social networks of young, African American mothers. *American Journal of Community Psychology, 20,* 445-461.

156. Richman, J. A., Flaherty, J. A., & Pyskoty, C. (1992). Shifts in problem drinking during a life transition: Adaptation to medical school training. *Journal of Studies on Alcohol, 53,* 17–24.

157. Sandler, L. S., Wilson, K. G., Asmundson, G. J. G., Larsen, D. K., & Ediger, J. M. (1992). Cardiovascular reactivity in nonclinical subjects with infrequent panic attacks. *Journal of Anxiety Disorders, 6,* 27-39.

158. Schaufeli, W. B., & Van Yperen, N. W. (1992). Unemployment and psychological distress among graduates: A longitudinal study. *Journal of Occupational and Organizational Psychology, 65,* 291-305.

159. Siblerud, R. L. (1992). A comparison of mental health of multiple sclerosis patients with silver/mercury dental fillings and those with fillings removed. *Psychological Reports, 70,* 1139-1151.

160. Simon, P. M., Morse, E. V., Osofsky, H. J., Balson, P. M., & Gaumer, H. R. (1992). Psychological characteristics of a sample of male street prostitutes. *Archives of Sexual Behavior, 21,* 33-44.

161. Solomon, Z., Waysman, M., Levy, G., Fried, B., Mikulincer, M., Benbenishty, R., Florian, V., & Bleich, A. (1992). From front line to home front: A study of secondary traumatization. *Family Process, 31,* 289-302.

162. Stanton, A. L. (1992). Downward comparison in infertile couples. *Basic and Applied Social Psychology, 13,* 389-403.

163. Starcevic, V., Kellner, R., Uhlenhuth, E. H., & Pathak, D. (1992). Panic disorder and hypochondriacal fears and beliefs. *Journal of Affective Disorders, 24,* 73-85.

164. Stewart, S. H., Knize, K., & Pihl, R. O. (1992). Anxiety sensitivity and dependency in clinical and non-clinical panickers and controls. *Journal of Anxiety Disorders, 6,* 119-131.

165. Strauman, T. J., & Wetzler, S. (1992). The factor structure of SCL-90 and MCMI scale scores: Within measure and interbattery analyses. *Multivariate Behavioral Research, 27,* 1–20.

166. Thompson, R. J., Jr., Gustafson, K. E., Hamlett, K. W., & Spock, A. (1992). Psychological adjustment of children with cystic fibrosis: The role of child cognitive processes and maternal adjustment. *Journal of Pediatric Psychology, 17,* 741–755.

167. Thompson, R. J., Jr., Gustafson, K. E., Hamlett, K. W., & Spock, A. (1992). Stress, coping, and family functioning in the psychological adjustment of mothers of children and adolescents with cystic fibrosis. *Journal of Pediatric Psychology, 17,* 573–585.

168. Unger, D. G., Wandersman, A., & Hallman, W. (1992). Living near a hazardous waste facility: Coping with individual and family distress. *American Journal of Orthopsychiatry, 62,* 55–70.

169. Volpicelli, J. R., Alterman, A. I., Hayashida, M., & O'Brien, C. P. (1992). Naltrexone in the treatment of alcohol dependence. *Archives of General Psychiatry, 49,* 876-880.

170. Von Korff, M., Ormel, J., Katon, W., & Lin, E. H. B. (1992). Disability and depression among high utilizers of health care: A longitudinal analysis. *Archives of General Psychiatry, 49,* 91-100.

171. Zakowski, S. G., McAllister, C. G., Deal, M., & Baum, A. (1992). Stress, reactivity, and immune function in healthy men. *Health Psychology, 11,* 223–232.

172. Ahles, T. A. (1993). Cancer pain: Research from multidimensional and illness representation models. *Motivation and Emotion, 17,* 225–243.

173. Ankuta, G. Y., & Abeles, N. (1993). Client satisfaction, clinical significance, and meaningful change in psychotherapy. *Professional Psychology: Research and Practice, 24,* 70–74.

174. Baldwin, A. L., Baldwin, C. P., Kasser, T., Zax, M., Sameroff, A., & Seifer, R. (1993). Contextual risk and resiliency during late adolescence. *Development and Psychopathology, 5,* 741-761.

175. Brent, D. A., Perper, J. A., Moritz, G., Liotus, L., Schweers, J., Roth, C., Balach, L., & Allman, C. (1993). Psychiatric impact of the loss of an adolescent sibling to suicide. *Journal of Affective Disorders, 28,* 249-256.

176. Christensen, L., Bourgeois, A., & Cockroft, R. (1993). Electroencephalographic concomitants of a caffeine-induced panic reaction. *The Journal of Nervous and Mental Disease, 181,* 327-330.

177. De Beurs, E., Lange, A., Koele, P., & Van Dyck, R. (1993). Frequency of panic as an outcome measure in agoraphobia research: Latent effects of exposure on panic. *Journal of Anxiety Disorders, 7,* 307-319.

178. deBears, E., Lange, A., Blonk, R. W. B., Koele, P., van Balkom, A. J. L. M., & van Dyck, R. (1993). Goal attainment scaling: An idiosyncratic method to assess treatment effectiveness in agoraphobia. *Journal of Psychopathology and Behavioral Assessment, 15,* 357–373.

179. Fairburn, C. G., Jones, R., Peveler, R. C., Hope, R. A., & O'Connor, M. (1993). Psychotherapy and bulimia nervosa: Longer-term effects of interpersonal psychotherapy, behavior therapy, and cognitive behavior therapy. *Archives of General Psychiatry, 50,* 419-428.

180. Fitzgibbon, M. L., Stolley, M. R., & Kirschenbaum, D. S. (1993). Obese people who seek treatment have different characteristics than those who do not seek treatment. *Health Psychology, 12,* 342-345.

181. Floyd, F. J., & Phillippe, K. A. (1993). Parental interactions with children with and without mental retardation: Behavior management, coerciveness, and positive exchange. *American Journal on Mental Retardation, 97,* 673-684.

182. Gerlsma, C., Das, J., & Emmelkamp, P. M. G. (1993). Depressed patients' parental representations: Stability across changes in depressed mood and specificity across diagnosis. *Journal of Affective Disorders, 27,* 173-181.

183. Giunta, C. T., & Compas, B. E. (1993). Coping in marital dyads: Patterns and associations with psychological symptoms. *Journal of Marriage and the Family, 55,* 1011–1017.

184. Gold, J. M., & Scanlon, C. R. (1993). Psychological distress and counseling duration of career and noncareer clients. *Career Development Quarterly, 42,* 186-191.

185. Handal, P. J., Gist, D., Gilner, F. H., & Searight, H. R. (1993). Preliminary validity for the Langner Symptom Survey and the Brief Symptom Inventory as mass-screening instruments for adolescent adjustment. *Journal of Clinical Child Psychology, 22,* 382-386.

186. Hazzard, A., Rogers, J. H., & Angert, L. (1993). Factors affecting group therapy outcome for adult sexual abuse survivors. *International Journal of Group Psychotherapy, 43,* 453–468.

187. Horowitz, M., Stinson, C., Fridhandler, B., Milbrath, C., Redington, D., & Ewert, M. (1993). Vivid representation of psychotherapeutic processes: Pathological grief: An intensive case study. *Psychiatry, 56,* 356–374.

188. Hull, J. W., Clarkin, J. F., & Alexopoulos, G. S. (1993). Time series analysis of intervention effects: Fluoxetine therapy as a case illustration. *The Journal of Nervous and Mental Disease, 181,* 48-53.

189. Hull, J. W., Clarkin, J. F., & Kakuma, T. (1993). Treatment response of borderline inpatients: A growth curve analysis. *The Journal of Nervous and Mental Disease, 181,* 503-508.

190. James, L. D., Thorn, B. E., & Williams, D. A. (1993). Goal specification in cognitive-behavioral therapy for chronic headache pain. *Behavior Therapy, 24,* 305–320.

191. Katz, M. M., Wetzler, S., Cloitre, M., Swann, A., Secunda, S., Mendels, J., & Robins, E. (1993). Expressive characteristics of anxiety in depressed men and women. *Journal of Affective Disorders, 28,* 267-277.

192. Kelley, S. J., Brant, R., & Waterman, J. (1993). Sexual abuse of children in day care centers. *Child Abuse & Neglect, 17,* 71-89.

193. Kolko, D. J., & Kazdin, A. E. (1993). Emotional/behavioral problems in clinic and nonclinic children: Correspondence among children, parent and teacher reports. *Journal of Child Psychology and Psychiatry and Allied Disciplines, 34,* 991-1006.

194. Krakow, B., Kellner, R., Neidhardt, J., Pathak, D., & Lambert, L. (1993). Imagery rehearsal treatment of chronic nightmares: With a thirty month follow-up. *Journal of Behavior Therapy and Experimental Psychiatry, 24,* 325–330.

195. Lefley, H. P., Scott, C. S., Llabre, M., & Hicks, D. (1993). Cultural beliefs about rape and victims' response in three ethnic groups. *American Journal of Orthopsychiatry, 63,* 623–632.

196. Long, B. C. (1993). Coping strategies of male managers: A prospective analysis of predictors of psychosomatic symptoms and job satisfaction. *Journal of Vocational Behavior, 42,* 184-199.

197. Louie, A. K., Lewis, T. B., & Lannon, R. A. (1993). Use of low-dose fluoxetine in major depression and panic disorder. *Journal of Clinical Psychiatry, 54,* 435–438.

198. Maddock, R. J., Carter, C. S., Blacker, K. H., Beitman, B. D., Krishnan, K. R. R., Jefferson, J. W., Lewis, C. P., & Liebowitz, M. R. (1993). Relationship of past depressive episodes to symptom severity and treatment response in panic disorder with agoraphobia. *Journal of Clinical Psychiatry, 54,* 88–95.

199. Markt, C., & Johnson, M. (1993). Transitional objects, pre-sleep rituals, and psychopathology. *Child Psychiatry and Human Development, 23,* 161–173.

200. McCarroll, J. E., Ursano, R. J., Fullerton, C. S., & Lundy, A. (1993). Traumatic stress of a wartime mortuary: Anticipation of exposure to mass death. *The Journal of Nervous and Mental Disease, 181,* 545-551.

201. Mills, J. K., & Andrianopoulos, G. D. (1993). The relationship between childhood onset obesity and psychopathology in adulthood. *The Journal of Psychology, 127,* 547-551.

202. Mroczek, D. K., Spiro, A., III, Aldwin, C. M., Ozir, D. J., & Bossé, R. (1993). Construct vallidation of optimism and pessimism in older men: Findings from the normative aging study. *Health Psychology, 12,* 406-409.

203. Noyes, R., Clancy, J., Woodman, C., Holt, C. S., Suelzer, M., Christiansen, J., & Anderson, D. J. (1993). Environmental factors related to the outcome of panic disorder: A seven-year follow-up study. *The Journal of Nervous and Mental Disease, 181,* 529-538.

204. Osman, A., Barrios, F. X., Aukes, D., Osman, J. R., & Markway, K. (1993). The Beck Anxiety Inventory: Psychometric properties in a community population. *Journal of Psychopathology and Behavioral Assessment, 15,* 287–297.

205. Overholser, J. C., Schubert, D. S. P., Foliart, R., & Frost, F. (1993). Assessment of emotional distress following a spinal cord injury. *Rehabilitation Psychology, 38,* 187–198.

206. Penn, D. L., Van Der Does, A. J. W., Spaulding, W. D., Garbin, C. D., Linszen, D., & Dingemans, P. (1993). Information processing and social cognitive problem solving in schizophrenia. *The Journal of Nervous and Mental Disease, 181,* 13-20.

207. Persons, J. B., Burns, D. D., Perloff, J. M., & Miranda, J. (1993). Relationships between symptoms of depression and anxiety and dysfunctional beliefs about achievement and attachment. *Journal of Abnormal Psychology, 102,* 518-524.

208. Pickett, S. A., Vraniak, D. A., Cook, J. A., & Choler, B. J. (1993). Strength in adversity: Blacks bear burden better than whites. *Professional Psychology: Research and Practice, 24,* 460–467.

209. Rhodes, J. E., Fischer, K., Ebert, L., & Meyers, A. B. (1993). Patterns of service utilization among pregnant and parenting African American adolescents. *Psychology of Women Quarterly, 17,* 257-274.

210. Rosenblatt, A., & Attkisson, C. C. (1993). Assessing outcomes for sufferers of severe mental disorder: A conceptual framework and review. *Evaluation and Program Planning, 16,* 347–363.

211. Savino, M., Perugi, G., Simonini, E., Soriani, A., Cassano, G. B., & Akiskal, H. S. (1993). Affective comorbidity in panic disorder: Is there a bipolar connection? *Journal of Affective Disorders, 28,* 155-163.

212. Schneider, S. E., & Phillips, W. M. (1993). Depression and anxiety in medical, surgical, and pediatric interns. *Psychological Reports, 72,* 1145-1146.

213. Simons, R. L., Beaman, J., Conger, R. D., & Chao, W. (1993). Childhood experience, conceptions of parenting, and attitudes of spouse as determinants of parental behavior. *Journal of Marriage and the Family, 55,* 91–106.

214. Simons, R. L., Johnson, C., Beaman, J., & Conger, R. D. (1993). Explaining women's double jeopardy: Factors that mediate the association between harsh treatment as a child and violence by a husband. *Journal of Marriage and the Family, 55,* 713–723.

215. Soloff, P. H., Cornelius, J., George, A., Nathan, S., Perel, J. M., & Ulrich, R. F. (1993). Efficacy of phenelzine and haloperidol in borderline personality disorder. *Archives of General Psychiatry, 50,* 377-385.

216. Starcevic, V., Uhlenhuth, E. H., Kellner, R., & Pathak, D. (1993). Comparison of primary and secondary panic disorder: A preliminary report. *Journal of Affective Disorders, 27,* 81-86.

217. Steer, R. A., Ranieri, W. F., Beck, A. T., & Clark, D. A. (1993). Further evidence for the validity of the Beck Anxiety Inventory with psychiatric outpatients. *Journal of Anxiety Disorders, 7,* 195-205.

218. Steiger, H., Leung, F., Thibaudeau, J., & Houle, L. (1993). Prognostic utility of subcomponents of the borderline personality construct in bulimia nervosa. *British Journal of Clinical Psychology, 32,* 187-197.

219. Stinson, C. H., & Horowitz, M. J. (1993). Psyclops: An exploratory graphical system for clinical research and education. *Psychiatry, 56,* 375–389.

220. Swann, A. C., Secunda, S. K., Katz, M. M., Croughan, J., Bowden, C. L., Koslow, S. H., Berman, N., & Stokes, P. E. (1993). Specificity of mixed affective states: Clinical comparison of dysphoric mania and agitated depression. *Journal of Affective Disorders, 28,* 81-89.

221. Terkuile, M. M., Linssen, A. C. G., & Spinhoven, P. (1993). The development of the Multidimensional Locus of Pain Control Questionnaire (MLPC): Factor structure, reliability, and validity. *Journal of Psychopathology and Behavioral Assessment, 15,* 387–404.

222. Thompson, R. J., Merritt, K. A., Keith, B. R., Murphy, L. B., & Johndrow, D. A. (1993). The role of maternal stress and family functioning in maternal distress and mother-reported and child-reported psychological adjustment of nonreferred children. *Journal of Clinical Child Psychology, 22,* 78-84.

223. Thompson, R. J., Jr., Gil, K. M., Burbach, D. J., Keith, B. R., & Kinney, T. R. (1993). Psychological adjustment of mothers of children and adolescents with sickle cell disease: The role of stress, coping methods, and family functioning. *Journal of Pediatric Psychology, 18,* 549–559.

224. Yama, M. F., Fogas, B. S., Teegarden, L. A., & Hastings, B. (1993). Childhood sexual abuse and parental alcoholism: Interactive effects in adult women. *American Journal of Orthopsychiatry, 63,* 300–305.

225. Abramis, D. J. (1994). Relationship of job stressors to job performance: Linear or an inverted-u? *Psychological Reports, 75,* 547-558.

226. Agnew, R. M., Harper, H., Shapiro, D. A., & Barkham, M. (1994). Resolving a challenge to the therapeutic relationship: A single-case study. *British Journal of Medical Psychology, 67,* 155–170.

227. Aldwin, C. M., Levenson, M. R., & Spiro, A. (1994). Vulnerability and resilience to combat exposure: Can stress have lifelong effects? *Psychology and Aging, 9,* 34-44.

228. Anderson, C. A., Hinshaw, S. P., & Simmel, C. (1994). Mother-child interactions in ADHD and comparison boys: Relationships with overt and covert externalizing behavior. *Journal of Abnormal Child Psychology, 22,* 247-265.

229. Auerbach, S. M., Kiesler, D. J., Strentz, T., Schmidt, J. A., & Serio, C. D. (1994). Interpersonal impacts and adjustment to the stress of simulated captivity: An empirical test of the Stockholm syndrome. *Journal of Social and Clinical Psychology, 13,* 207–221.

230. Barkham, M., Hardy, G. E., & Startup, M. (1994). The structure, validity and clinical relevance of the Inventory of Interpersonal Problems. *British Journal of Medical Psychology, 67,* 171–185.

231. Barnett, R. C. (1994). Home to work spillover revisited: A study of full-time employed women in dual-earner couples. *Journal of Marriage and the Family, 56,* 647–656.

232. Barnett, R. C., Bronnan, R. T., Raudenbush, S. W., & Marshall, N. L. (1994). Gender and the relationship between marital-role quality and psychological distress. *Psychology of Women Quarterly, 18,* 105-127.

233. Basoglu, M., Marks, I. M., Kilic, C., Swinson, R. P., Noshirvani, H., Kuch, K., & O'Sullivan, G. (1994). Relationship of panic, anticipatory anxiety, agoraphobia, and global improvement in panic disorder with agoraphobia treated with alprazolam and exposure. *British Journal of Psychiatry, 164,* 647-652.

234. Basoglu, M., Marks, I. M., Swinson, R. P., Noshirvani, H., O'Sullivan, G., & Kuch, K. (1994). Pre-treatment predictors of treatment outcome in panic disorder and agoraphobia treated with alprazolam and exposure. *Journal of Affective Disorders, 17,* 123–132.

235. Beck, J. G., Stanley, M. A., Baldwin, L. E., Deagle, E. A., III, & Averill, P. M. (1994). Comparison of cognitive therapy and relaxation training for panic disorder. *Journal of Consulting and Clinical Psychology, 62,* 818-826.

236. Beers, S. R., Goldstein, G., & Katz, L. J. (1994). Neuropsychological differences between college students with learning disabilities and those with mild head injury. *Journal of Learning Disabilities, 27,* 315–324.

237. Behen, J. M., & Rodrigue, J. R. (1994). Predictors of coping strategies among adults with cancer. *Psychological Reports, 74,* 43-48.

238. Beiser, M., Bean, G., Erickson, D., Zhang, J., Iacono, W. G., & Rector, N. A. (1994). Biological and psychosocial predictors of job performance following a first episode of psychosis. *American Journal of Psychiatry, 151,* 857-863.

239. Bell, I. R., Schwartz, G. E., Amend, D., Peterson, J. M., Kaszniak, A. W., & Miller, C. S. (1994). Psychological characteristics and subjective intolerance for xenobiotic agents of normal young adults with trait shyness and defensiveness: A Parkinsonian-like personality type? *The Journal of Nervous and Mental Disease, 182,* 367-374.

240. Benkelfat, C., Ellenbogen, M. A., Dean, P., Palmour, R. M., & Young, S. N. (1994). Mood-lowering effect of tryptophan depletion: Enhanced susceptibility of young men at genetic risk for major affective disorders. *Archives of General Psychiatry, 51,* 687-697.

241. Biernat, M., & Herkov, M. J. (1994). Reactions to violence: A campus copes with serial murder. *Journal of Social and Clinical Psychology, 13,* 309–334.

242. Borden, J. W. (1994). Panic disorder and suicidality: Prevalence and risk factors. *Journal of Anxiety Disorders, 8,* 217-225.

243. Burnett, P. L., Galletly, C. A., Moyle, R. J., & Clark, C. R. (1994). Low-dose depot medication in schizophrenia. *Schizophrenia Bulletin, 20,* 155–164.

244. Conger, R. D., Ge, X., Elder, G. H., Jr., Lorenz, F. O., & Simons, R. L. (1994). Economic stress, coercive family process, and developmental problems of adolescents. *Child Development, 65,* 541–561.

245. Costantino, G., Malgady, R. G., & Rogler, L. H. (1994). Storytelling through pictures: Cultural sensitivity psychotherapy for Hispanic children and adolescents. *Journal of Clinical Child Psychology, 23,* 13-20.

246. Cozzarelli, C., & Major, B. (1994). The effects of anti-abortion demonstrators and pro-choice escorts on women's psychological responses to abortion. *Journal of Social and Clinical Psychology, 13,* 404–427.

247. deBeurs, E., Van Dyck, R., van Balkom, A. J. L. M., Lange, A., & Koele, P. (1994). Assessing the clinical significance of outcome in agoraphobia research: A comparison of two approaches. *Behavior Therapy, 25,* 147–158.

248. Dew, M. A., Simmons, R. G., Roth, L. H., Schulberg, H. C., Thompson, M. E., Armitage, J. M., & Griffith, B. P. (1994). Psychosocial predictors of vulnerability to distress in the year following heart transplantation. *Psychological Medicine, 24,* 929-945.

249. Eells, T. D., Lacefield, P., & Maxey, J. (1994). Symptom correlates and factor structure of the Health Professions Stress Inventory. *Psychological Reports, 75,* 1563-1568.

250. Emmelkamp, P. M. G., & Gerlsma, C. (1994). Marital functioning and the anxiety disorders. *Behavior Therapy, 25,* 407–429.

251. Engels, M-L., & Moisan, D. (1994). The Psychological Maltreatment Inventory: Development of a measure of psychological maltreatment in childhood for use in adult clinical settings. *Psychological Reports, 74,* 595-604.

252. Fichter, M. M., Quadflieg, N., & Rief, W. (1994). Course of multi-impulsive bulimia. *Psychological Medicine, 24,* 591-604.

253. Fifer, S. K., Mathias, S. D., Patrick, D. L., Mazonson, P. D., Lubeck, D. P., & Buesching, D. P. (1994). Untreated anxiety among adult primary care patients in a health maintenance organization. *Archives of General Psychiatry, 51,* 740-750.

254. Forbes, D., Creamer, M., & Rycroft, P. (1994). Eye movement desensitization and reprocessing in posttraumatic stress disorder: A pilot study using assessment measures. *Journal of Behavior Therapy and Experimental Psychiatry, 25,* 113–120.

255. Franchini, L., Gasperini, M., & Smeraldi, E. (1994). A 24-month follow-up study of unipolar subjects: A comparison between lithuim and fluroxamine. *Journal of Affective Disorders, 32,* 225-231.

256. Ge, X., Lorenz, F. O., Conger, R. D., Elder, G. H., Jr., & Simons, R. L. (1994). Trajectories of stressful life events and depressive symptoms during adolescence. *Developmental Psychology, 30,* 467-483.

257. Giunta, C. T., & Compas, B. E. (1994). Adult daughters of alcoholics: Are they unique? *Journal of Studies on Alcohol, 55,* 600–606.

258. Glover, H., Ohlde, C., Silver, S., Packard, P., Goodnick, P., & Hamlin, C. L. (1994). Vulnerability scale: A preliminary report of psychometric properties. *Psychological Reports, 75,* 1651-1668.

259. Hardy, G. E., & Barkham, M. (1994). The relationship between interpersonal attachment styles and work difficulties. *Human Relations, 47,* 263–281.

260. Hauff, E., & Vaglum, P. (1994). Chronic posttraumatic stress disorder in Vietnamese refugees: A prospective community study of prevalence, course, psychopathology, and stressors. *The Journal of Nervous and Mental Disease, 182,* 85-90.

261. Heppner, P. P., Kivlighan, D. M., Good, G. E., Roehlke, H. J., Hills, H. I., & Ashby, J. S. (1994). Presenting problems of university counseling center clients: A snapshot and multivariate classification scheme. *Journal of Counseling Psychology, 41,* 315-324.

262. Herrero, M. E., Hechtman, L., & Weiss, G. (1994). Antisocial disorders in hyperactive subjects from childhood to adulthood: Predictive factors and characterization of subgroups. *American Journal of Orthopsychiatry, 64,* 510–521.

263. Hill, C. R., & Safran, J. D. (1994). Assessing interpersonal schemas: Anticipated responses of significant others. *Journal of Social and Clinical Psychology, 13,* 366–379.

264. Hiller, W., Goebel, G., & Rief, W. (1994). Reliability of self-rated tinnitus distress and association with psychological symptom patterns. *British Journal of Clinical Psychology, 33,* 231-239.

265. Hoencamp, E., Haffmans, P. M. J., Duiven-voorden, H., Knegtering, H., & Dijken, W. A. (1994). Predictors of (non-) response in depressed outpaients treated with a three-phase sequential medication strategy. *Journal of Affective Disorders, 31,* 235–246.

266. Horowitz, M. J., Milbrath, C., Jordan, D. S., Stinson, C. H., Ewert, M., Redington, D. J., Fridhandler, B., Reidbord, S. P., & Hartley, D. (1994). Expressive and defensive behavior during discourse on unresolved topics: A single case study of pathological grief. *Journal of Personality, 62,* 527–563.

267. Hudiburg, R. A., Ahrens, P. K., & Jones, T. M. (1994). Psychology of computer use: XXXI. Relating computer users' stress, daily hassles, somatic complaints, and anxiety. *Psychological Reports, 75,* 1183-1186.

268. Huselid, R. F., & Cooper, M. L. (1994). Gender roles as mediators of sex differences in expressions of pathology. *Journal of Abnormal Psychology, 103,* 595-603.

269. Jolly, J. B., & Kramer, T. A. (1994). The hierarchical arrangement of internalizing cognitions. *Cognitive Therapy and Research, 18,* 1-14.

270. Jolly, J. B., Dyck, M. J., Kramer, T. A., & Wherry, J. N. (1994). Integration of positive and negative affectivity and cognitive content-specificity: Improved discrimination of anxious and depressive symptoms. *Journal of Abnormal Psychology, 103,* 544-552.

271. Joyce, P. R., Mulder, R. T., & Cloninger, C. R. (1994). Temperament predicts clomipramine and desipramine response in major depression. *Journal of Affective Disorders, 30,* 35–46.

272. Kazdin, A. E., & Mazurick, J. L. (1994). Dropping out of child psychotherapy: Distinguishing early and late dropouts over the course of treatment. *Journal of Consulting and Clinical Psychology, 62,* 1069-1074.

273. Kendler, K. S., Walters, E. E., Truett, K. R., Heath, A. C., Neale, M. C., Martin, N. G., & Eaves, L. J. (1994). Sources of individual differences in depressive symptoms: Analysis of two samples of twins and their families. *American Journal of Psychiatry, 151,* 1605-1614.

274. Kopta, S. M., Howard, K. I., Lowry, J. L., & Beutler, L. E. (1994). Patterns of symptomatic recovery in psychotherapy. *Journal of Consulting and Clinical Psychology, 62,* 1009-1016.

275. Kotler, T., Buzwell, S., Romeo, Y., & Bowland, J. (1994). Avoidant attachment as a risk factor for health. *British Journal of Medical Psychology, 67,* 237–245.

276. Kugler, J., Seelbach, H., & Kruskemper, G. M. (1994). Effects of rehabilitation programmes on anxiety and depression in coronary patients: A meta-analysis. *British Journal of Clinical Psychology, 33,* 401-410.

277. Laraia, M. T., Stuart, G. W., Frye, L. H., Lydiard, R. B., & Ballenger, J. C. (1994). Childhood environment of women having panic disorder with agoraphobia. *Journal of Anxiety Disorders, 8,* 1-17.

278. Lee, S. (1994). The heterogeneity of stealing behaviors in Chinese patients with anorexia nervosa in Hong Kong. *The Journal of Nervous and Mental Disease, 182,* 304-307.

279. Lipsitz, J. D., Williams, J. B. W., Rabkin, J. G., Remien, R. H., Bradbury, M., el Saor, W., Goetz, R., Sorrell, S., & Gorman, J. M. (1994). Psychopathology in male and female intravenous drug users with and without HIV infection. *American Journal of Psychiatry, 151,* 1662-1668.

280. Lu, L. (1994). University transition: Major and minor life stressors, personality characteristics and mental health. *Psychological Medicine, 24,* 81-87.

281. Lutzky, S. M., & Knight, B. G. (1994). Explaining gender differences in caregiver distress: The roles of emotional attentiveness and coping styles. *Psychology and Aging, 9,* 513-519.

282. McCullough, J. D., McCune, K. J., Kaye, A. L., Braith, J. A., Friend, R., Roberts, W. C., Belyea-Caldwell, S., Norris, S. L. W., & Hampton, C. (1994). Comparison of community dysthymia sample at screening with a matched group of nondepressed community controls. *The Journal of Nervous and Mental Disease, 182,* 402-407.

283. McCullough, J. D., McCune, K. J., Kaye, A. L., Braith, J. A., Friend, R., Roberts, W. C., Belyea-Caldwell, S., Norris, S. L. W., & Hampton, C. (1994). One-year prospective replication study of an untreated sample of community dysthymia subjects. *The Journal of Nervous and Mental Disease, 182,* 396-401.

284. Merikangas, K., & Angst, J. (1994). Neurasthenia in a longitudinal cohort study of young adults. *Psychological Medicine, 24,* 1013-1024.

285. Merikangas, K. R., Wicki, W., & Angst, J. (1994). Heterogeneity of depression. Classification of depressive subtypes by longitudinal course. *British Journal of Psychiatry, 164,* 342-348.

286. Muran, J. C., Segal, Z. V., & Samstag, L. W. (1994). Self-scenarios as a repeated measures outcome measurement of self-schemas in short-term cognitive therapy. *Behavior Therapy, 25,* 255–274.

287. Niedemann, G., Hahlweg, K., Hank, G., Feinstein, E., Müller, V., & Dose, M. (1994). Deliverability of psychoeducational family management. *Schizophrenia Bulletin, 20,* 547-556.

288. O'Sullivan, G. H., Noshirvani, H., Basoglua, M., Marks, I. M., Swinson, R., Kuch, K., & Kirby, M. (1994). Safety and side-effects of alprazolam: Controlled study in agoraphobia with panic disorder. *British Journal of Psychiatry, 165,* 79-86.

289. Ornduff, S. R., Freedenfeld, R. N., Kelsey, R. M., & Critelli, J. W. (1994). Object relations of sexually abused female subjects: A TAT analysis. *Journal of Personality Assessment, 63,* 223-238.

290. Piper, W. E., Joyce, A. A., Rosie, J. S., & Hassan, F. A. A. (1994). Psychological mindedness, work, and outcome in day treatment. *International Journal of Group Psychotherapy, 44,* 291–311.

291. Piper, W. E., Joyce, A. S., Azim, H. F. A., & Rosie, J. S. (1994). Patient characteristics and success in day treatment. *The Journal of Nervous and Mental Disease, 182,* 381-386.

292. Porter, J., Wilson, C., & Frisch, G. R. (1994). Psychotherapy and symptom change. *Psychological Reports, 75,* 1313-1314.

293. Prinz, R. J., & Miller, G. E. (1994). Family-based treatment for childhood antisocial behavior: Experimental influences on dropout and engagement. *Journal of Consulting and Clinical Psychology, 62,* 645-650.

294. Renfrey, G., & Spates, C. R. (1994). Eye movement desensitization: A partial dismantling study. *Journal of Behavior Therapy and Experimental Psychiatry, 25,* 231–239.

295. Rhodes, J. E., Contreras, J. M., & Mangelsdorf, S. C. (1994). Natural mentor relationships among Latina adolescent mothers: Psychological adjustment, moderating processes, and the role of early parental acceptance. *American Journal of Community Psychology, 22,* 211-227.

296. Rickels, K., Schweizer, E., Clary, C., Fox, I., & Weise, C. (1994). Nefazodone and imipramine in major depression: A placebo-controlled trial. *British Journal of Psychiatry, 164,* 802-805.

297. Rojder, R., Nelson, W. M., III, Hart, K. J., & Fercho, M. C. (1994). Criterion-related validity and stability: Equivalence of the MMPI and the MMPI-2. *Journal of Clinical Psychology, 50,* 361-367.

298. Rosenbaum, A., Hoge, S. K., Adelman, S. A., Warnken, W. J., Fletcher, K. E., & Kane, R. L. (1994). Head injury in partner-abusive men. *Journal of Consulting and Clinical Psychology, 62,* 1187-1193.

299. Sahs, J. A., Goetz, R., Reddy, M., Rabkin, J. G., Williams, J. B. W., Kertzner, R., & Gorman, J. M. (1994). Psychological distress and natural killer cells in gay men with and without HIV infection. *American Journal of Psychiatry, 151,* 1479-1484.

300. Salzer, M. S., & Berenbaum, H. (1994). Somatic sensations, anxiety, and control in panic disorder. *Journal of Behavior Therapy and Experimental Psychiatry, 25,* 75–80.

301. Shapiro, D. A., Barkham, M., Rees, A., Hardy, G. E., Reynolds, S., & Startup, M. (1994). Effects of treatment duration and severity of depression on the effectiveness of cognitive-behavioral and psychodynamic-interpersonal psychotherapy. *Journal of Consulting and Clinical Psychology, 62,* 522-534.

302. Shear, M. K., Pilkonis, P. A., Cloitre, M., & Leon, A. C. (1994). Cognitive behavioral treatment compared with nonprescriptive treatment of panic disorders. *Archives of General Psychiatry, 51,* 395-401.

303. Sheldon, K. M. (1994). Emotionality differences between artists and scientists. *Journal of Research in Personality, 28,* 481-491.

304. Simons, R. L., Johnson, C., & Conger, R. D. (1994). Harsh corporal punishment versus quality of parental involvement as an explanation of adolescent maladjustment. *Journal of Marriage and the Family, 56,* 591–607.

305. Simons, R. L., Whitbeck, L. B., Beaman, J., & Conger, R. D. (1994). Impact of mothers' parenting, involvement by nonresidential fathers, and parental conflict on the adjustment of adolescent children. *Journal of Marriage and the Family, 56,* 356–374.

306. Sobell, L. C., Toneatto, T., & Sobell, M. (1994). Behavioral assessment and treatment planning for alcohol, tobacco, and other drug problems: Current status with an emphasis on clinical applications. *Behavior Therapy, 25,* 533–580.

307. Soloff, P. H., Liss, J. A., Kelly, T., Cornelius, J., & Ulrich, R. (1994). Risk factors for suicidal behavior in borderline personality disorder. *American Journal of Psychiatry, 151,* 1316-1323.

308. Spiro, A., Schnurr, P. P., & Aldwin, C. M. (1994). Combat-related posttraumatic stress disorder symptoms in older men. *Psychology and Aging, 9,* 17-26.

309. Stanley, M. A., & Borden, J. W. (1994). Nonclinical hair pulling: Phenomenology and related psychopathology. *Journal of Anxiety Disorders, 8,* 119-130.

310. Steer, R. A., Clark, D. A., & Ranieri, W. F. (1994). Symptom dimensions of the SCL-90-R: A test of the tripartite model of anxiety and depression. *Journal of Personality Assessment, 62,* 525-536.

311. Stein, A., Woolley, H., Cooper, S. D., & Fairburn, C. G. (1994). An observational study of mothers with eating disorders and their infants. *Journal of Child Psychology and Psychiatry and Allied Disciplines, 35,* 733-748.

312. Steketee, G. (1994). Behavioral assessment and treatment planning with obsessive compulsive disorder: A review emphasizing clinical application. *Behavior Therapy, 25,* 613–633.

313. Sterling, R. C., Gottheil, E., Weinstein, S. P., & Shannon, D. M. (1994). Psychiatric symptomatology in crack cocaine abusers. *The Journal of Nervous and Mental Disease, 182,* 564–569.

314. Stiles, W. B., & Shapiro, D. A. (1994). Disabuse of the drug metaphor: Psychotherapy process-outcome correlations. *Journal of Consulting and Clinical Psychology, 62,* 942-948.

315. Stoltenberg, C. D., McNeill, B. W., & Crethar, H. C. (1994). Changes in supervision as counselors and therapists gain experience: A review. *Professional Psychology: Research and Practice, 25,* 416–449.

316. Strauman, T. J., & Glenberg, A. M. (1994). Self-concept and body-image disturbance: Which self-beliefs predict body size overestimation? *Cognitive Therapy and Research, 18,* 105-125.

317. Streufert, S., Pogash, R., Roache, J., Severs, W., Gingrich, D., Landis, R., Lonardi, L., & Kantner, A. (1994). Alcohol and managerial performance. *Journal of Studies on Alcohol, 55,* 230–238.

318. Sullivan, P. F., Joyce, P. R., & Mulder, R. T. (1994). Borderline personality disorder in major depression. *The Journal of Nervous and Mental Disease, 182,* 508-516.

319. Tasca, G. A., Russell, V., & Busby, K. (1994). Characteristics of patients who choose between two types of group therapy. *International Journal of Group Psychotherapy, 44,* 499–508.

320. Thompson, J., Chung, M. C., & Rosser, R. (1994). The marchioness disaster: Preliminary report of psychological effects. *British Journal of Clinical Psychology, 33,* 75-77.

321. Thompson, R. J., Jr., Gil, K. M., Gustafson, K. E., George, L. K., Keith, B. R., Spock, A., & Kinney, T. R. (1994). Stability and change in the psychological adjustment of mothers of children and adolescents with cystic fibrosis and sickle cell disease. *Journal of Pediatric Psychology, 19,* 171–188.

322. Thompson, R. J., Jr., Gil, K. M., Keith, B. R., Gustafson, K. E., George, L. K., & Kinney, T. R. (1994). Psychological adjustment of children with sickle cell disease: Stability and change over a 10-month period. *Journal of Consulting and Clinical Psychology, 62,* 856-860.

323. Tschuschke, V., & Dies, R. R. (1994). Intensive analysis of therapeutic factors and outcome in long-term inpatient groups. *International Journal of Group Psychotherapy, 44,* 185–208.
324. Van den Broucke, S., Vandereycken, W., & Vertommen, H. (1994). Psychological distress in husbands of eating disorder patients. *American Journal of Orthopsychiatry, 64,* 270–279.
325. Veeninga, A. T. (1994). The relationship between late luteal phase dysphoric disorder and anxiety disorders (1994). *Journal of Anxiety Disorders, 8,* 207–215.
326. Waldinger, R. J., Swett, C., Frank, A., & Miller, K. (1994). Levels of dissociation and histories of reported abuse among women outpatients. *The Journal of Nervous and Mental Disease, 182,* 625–630.
327. Walker, L. S., Garber, J., & Greene, J. W. (1994). Somatic complaints in pediatric patients: A prospective study of the role of negative life events, child social and academic competence, and parental somatic symptoms. *Journal of Consulting and Clinical Psychology, 62,* 1213-1221.
328. Woodman, C. L., Noyes, R., Jr., Ballenger, J. C., Lydiard, R. B., Sievers, G., & Mihalko, D. (1994). Predictors of response to alprazolan and placebo in patients with panic disorder. *Journal of Affective Disorders, 30,* 5–13.
329. Agras, W. S., Telch, C. F., Arnow, B., Eldredge, K., Detzer, M. J., Henderson, J., & Marnell, M. (1995). Does interpersonal therapy help patients with binge eating disorder who fail to respond to cognitive-behavioral therapy? *Journal of Consulting and Clinical Psychology,* 63, 356-360.
330. Althof, S. E., Levine, S. B., Corty, E. W., Risen, C. B., Stern, E. B., & Kurit, D. M. (1995) A double-blind crossover trial of clomipramine for rapid ejaculation in 15 couples. *Journal of Clinical Psychiatry, 56,* 402–407.
331. Asnis, G. M., McGinn, L. K., & Sanderson, W. C. (1995). Atypical depression: Clinical aspects and noradrenergic function. *American Journal of Psychiatry, 152,* 31-36.
332. Baker, D. B., Taylor, C. J., & Leyva, C. (1995). Continuous performance tests: A comparison of modalities. *Journal of Clinical Psychology, 51,* 548–551.
333. Barnett, R. C., Raudenbush, S. W., Brennan, R. T., Pleck, J. H., & Marshall, N. L. (1995). Change in job and marital experiences and change in psychological distress: A longitudinal study of dual-earner couples. *Journal of Personality and Social Psychology, 69,* 839–850.
334. Bell, I. R., Peterson, J. M., & Schwartz, G. E. (1995). Medical histories and psychological profiles of middle-aged women with and without self-reported illness from environmental chemicals. *Journal of Clinical Psychiatry, 56,* 151–160.
335. Blatt, S. J., Quinlan, D. M., Pilkonis, P. A., & Shea, M. T. (1995). Impact of perfectionism and need for approval on the brief treatment of depression: The National Institute of Mental Health Treatment of Depression Collaborative Research Program revisited. *Journal of Consulting and Clinical Psychology, 63,* 125-132.
336. Bonanno, G. A., Keltner, D., Holen, A., & Horowitz, M. J. (1995). When avoiding unpleasant emotions might not be such a bad thing: Verbal-autonomic response dissociation and midlife conjugal bereavement. *Journal of Personality and Social Psychology, 69,* 975–989.
337. Bordiun, C. M., Mann, B. J., Cone, L. T., Henggeler, S. W., Fucci, B. R., Blaske, D. M. & Williams, R. A. (1995). Multisystemic treatment of serious juvenile offenders: Long-term prevention of criminality and violence. *Journal of Consulting and Clinical Psychology, 63,* 569–578.
338. Brewlin, F. C., Hayward, M., & Baum, A. S. (1995). Stress and alcohol: The moderating effect of chronic stress on the acute stress-intoxication relationship. *Journal of Studies on Alcohol, 56,* 546–552.
339. Brook, R. J., & Brook, J. A. (1995). Sequential tree method of examining the relationship between job stress and mental health. *Perceptual and Motor Skills, 80,* 287-290.
340. Burker, E. J., Wong, H., Sloane, P. D., Mattingly, D., Preisser, J., & Mitchell, C. M. (1995). Predictors of fear of falling in dizzy and nondizzy elderly. *Psychology and Aging, 10,* 104-110.
341. Carpenter, K. M., & Hittner, J. B. (1995). Dimensional characteristics of the SCL-90-R: Evaluation of gender differences in dually diagnosed inpatients. *Journal of Clinical Psychology, 51,* 383-390.
342. Carter, C. S., Faucett, J., Hertzman, M., Papp, L. A., Jones, W., Patterson, W. M., Swimson, R. P., Weise, C. C., Maddock, R. J., Denahan, A., & Liebowitz, M. (1995). Adinazolam-SR in panic disorder with agoraphobia: Relationship of daily dose to efficacy. *Journal of Clinical Psychiatry, 56,* 202–210.
343. Cinciripini, P. M., Lapitsky, L., Seay, S., Wallfisch, A., Kitchens, K., & Vunakis, H. V. (1995). The effects of smoking schedules on cessation outcome: Can we improve on common methods of gradual and abrupt nicotine withdrawal? *Journal of Consulting and Clinical Psychology, 63,* 388-399.
344. Clay, D. L., Wood, P. K., Frank, R. G., Hagglund, K. J., & Johnson, J. C. (1995). Examining systematic differences to chronic illness: A growth modeling approach. *Rehabilitation Psychology, 40,* 61–70.
345. Conger, R. D., Patterson, G. R., & Ge, X. (1995). It takes two to replicate: A mediational model for the impact of parents' stress on adolescent adjustment. *Child Development, 66,* 80-97.
346. Craighead, W. E., Curry, J. F., & Ilardi, S. S. (1995). Relationship of Children's Depression Inventory factors to major depression among adolescents. *Psychological Assessment, 7,* 171-176.
347. David, D., Giron, A., & Mellman, T. A. (1995). Panic-phobic patients and developmental trauma. *Journal of Clinical Psychiatry, 56,* 113–117.
348. Davis, C. G., Lehman, D. R., Wortman, C. B., Silver, R. C., & Thompson, S. C. (1995). The undoing of traumatic life events. *Personality and Social Psychology Bulletin, 21,* 109-124.
349. De Beurs, E., van Balkom, A. J. L. M., Lange, A., Koele, P., & van Dyck, R. (1995). Treatment of panic disorder with agoraphobia: Comparison of fluvoxamine, placebo, and psychological panic management combined with exposure and of exposure in vivo alone. *American Journal of Psychiatry, 152,* 683-691.
350. Dozois, D. J. A., Dobson, K. S., Wong, M., Hughes, D., & Long, A. (1995). Factors associated with rehabilitation outcome in patients with low back pain (LBP): Prediction of employment outcome at 9-month follow-up. *Rehabilitation Psychology, 40,* 243–259.
351. Fann, J. R., Katon, W. J., Uomoto, J. M., & Esselman, P. C. (1995). Psychiatric disorders and functional disability in outpatients with traumatic brain injuries. *American Journal of Psychiatry, 152,* 1493–1499.
352. Feske, U., & Chambless, D. L. (1995). Cognitive behavioral versus exposure only treatment for social phobia: A meta-analysis. *Behavior Therapy, 26,* 695–720.
353. France, A-C. I., & Alper, V. S. (1995). Structural analysis of social behavior and perceptions of caregiving. *The Journal of Psychology, 129,* 375–388.
354. Garlinski, J. H., Safyer, A. W., Hauser, S. T., & Allen, J. P. (1995). Self-cognitions and expressed negative emotions during midadolescence: Contributions to young adult psychological adjustment. *Development and Psychopathology, 7,* 193-216.
355. Ge, X., Conger, R. D., Lorenz, F. O., Shanahan, M., & Elder, G. H., Jr. (1995). Mutual influences in parent and adolescent psychological distress. *Developmental Psychology, 31,* 406-419.
356. Gleaves, D. H., & Eberenz, K. P. (1995). Validating a multidimensional model of the psychopathology of bulimia nervosa. *Journal of Clinical Psychology, 51,* 181-189.
357. Good, G. E., Robertson, J. M., O'Neil, J. M., Fitzgerald, L. F., Stevens, M., DeBord, K. A., & Bartels, K. M. (1995). Male gender role conflict: Psychometric issues and relations to psychological distress. *Journal of Counseling Psychology, 42,* 3-10.
358. Gracia, E. (1995). Visible but unreported: A case for the "not serious enough" cases of child maltreatment. *Child Abuse & Neglect, 19,* 1083–1093.
359. Hardy, G. E., Barkham, M., Shapiro, D. A., Reynolds, S., & Rees, A. (1995). Credibility and outcome of cognitive-behavioural and psychodynamics-interpersonal psychotherapy. *British Journal of Clinical Psychology, 34,* 555–569.
360. Hardy, G. E., Barkham, M., Shapiro, D. A., Stiles, W. B., Rees, A., & Reynolds, S. (1995). Impact of cluster C personality disorders on outcomes of contrasting brief psychotherapies for depression. *Journal of Consulting and Clinical Psychology, 63,* 997–1004.
361. Haskett, M. E., Myers, L. W., Pirrello, V. E., & Dombalis, A. O. (1995). Parenting style as a mediating link between parental emotional health and adjustment of maltreated children. *Behavior Therapy, 26,* 625–642.
362. Hays, P. A., & Zouari, J. (1995). Stress, coping, and mental health among rural, village, and urban women in Tunisia. *International Journal of Psychology, 30,* 69–90.
363. Heersink, N., & Strassberg, D. S. (1995). A normative and descriptive study of the MMPI with acknowledged child molesters. *Journal of Psychopathology and Behavioral Assessment, 17,* 377–391.
364. Hill, A. L., & Spokane, A. R. (1995). Career counseling and possible selves: A case study. *Career Development Quarterly, 3,* 221-232.
365. Himle, J. A, Bordnick, P. S., & Thyer, B. A. (1995). A comparison of trichotillomania and obsessive-compulsive disorder. *Journal of Psychopathology and Behavioral Assessment, 17,* 251–260.
366. Johnson, J. G., Williams, J. B. W., Rabkin, J. G., Goetz, R. R., & Remien, R. H. (1995). Axis I psychiatric symptoms associated with HIV infection and personality disorder. *American Journal of Psychiatry, 152,* 551-554.
367. Johnson, W. G., Schlundt, D. G., Barclay, D. R., Carr-Nangle, R. E., & Engler, L. B. (1995). A naturalistic functional analysis of binge eating. *Behavior Therapy, 26,* 101–108.
368. Kendall, J. C., Sherman, M. F., & Bigelow, G. E. (1995). Psychiatric symptoms in polysubstance abusers: Relationship to race, sex, and age. *Addictive Behaviors, 20,* 685–690.
369. Kim-Goh, M., Suh, C., Blake, D. D., & Hiley-Young, B. (1995). Psychological impact of the Los Angeles riots on Korean-American victims. *American Journal of Orthopsychiatry, 65,* 138–146.
370. Kirkorian, R., Kay, J., & Liang, W. M. (1995). Emotional distress, coping, and adjustment in human immunodeficiency virus infection and acquired immune deficiency syndrome. *The Journal of Nervous and Mental Disease, 183,* 293–298.
371. Kuch, K., Cox, B. J., & Direnfeld, D. M. (1995). A brief self-rating scale for PTSD after road vehicle accident. *Journal of Anxiety Disorders, 9,* 503–514.
372. Larigneur, S., Sauier, J., & Tremblay, R. E. (1995). Supporting fathers and supported mothers in families with disruptive boys: Who are they? *Journal of Child Psychology and Psychiatry, 36,* 1003–1018.
373. Lindsay, K. A., & Widiger, T. A. (1995). Sex and gender bias in self-report personality disorder inventories: Item analyses of the MCMI–II, MMPI, and PDQ-R. *Journal of Personality Assessment, 65,* 1–20.
374. Lohr, J. M., Tolin, D. F., & Kleinknecht, R. A. (1995). Eye movement desensitization of medical phobias: Two case studies. *Journal of Behavior Therapy and Experimental Psychiatry, 26,* 141–151.
375. Lundy, A., Gottheil, E., Serota, R. D., Weinstein, S. P., & Sterling, R. C. (1995). Gender differences and similarities in African-American crack cocaine abusers. *The Journal of Nervous and Mental Disease, 183,* 260–266.
376. Mann, B. J. (1995). The North Carolina Dissociation Index: A measure of dissociation using items from the MMPI-2. *Journal of Personality Assessment, 64,* 349-359.
377. Mavissakalian, M. R., Hamann, M. S., Haidar, S. A., & De Groot, C. M. (1995). Correlates of DSM-III personality disorder in generalized anxiety disorder. *Journal of Anxiety Disorders, 9,* 103-115.

378. McCarroll, J. E., Ursano, R. J., & Fullerton, C. S. (1995). Symptoms of PTSD following recovery of war dead: 13–15-month follow-up. *American Journal of Psychiatry, 152,* 939-941.

379. McKenry, P. C., Julian, T. W., & Gavazzi, S. M. (1995). Toward a biopsychosocial model of domestic violence. *Journal of Marriage and the Family, 57,* 307–320.

380. Mellman, T. A., David, D., Kulick-Bell, R., Hebding, J., & Nolan, B. (1995). Sleep disturbance and its relationship to psychiatric morbidity after Hurricane Andrew. *American Journal of Psychiatry, 152,* 1659–1663.

381. Meyers, A. B., & Rhodes, J. E. (1995). Oral contraceptive use among African-American adolescents: Individual and community influences. *American Journal of Community Psychology, 23,* 99–115.

382. Mills, J. K. (1995). A note on interpersonal sensitivity and psychotic symptomatology in obese adult outpatients with a history of childhood obesity. *The Journal of Psychology, 129,* 345–348.

383. Morrow, K. A., Thoreson, R. W., & Penney, L. L. (1995). Predictors of psychological distress among infertility clinic patients. *Journal of Consulting and Clinical Psychology, 63,* 163-167.

384. Mouanoutouna, V. L., & Brown, L. G. (1995). Hopkins Symptom Checklist-25, Hmong Version: A screening instrument for psychological distress. *Journal of Personality Assessment, 64,* 376–383.

385. Mullin, C. R., & Linz, D. (1995). Desensitization and resensitization to violence against women: Effects of exposure to sexually violent films on judgment of domestic violence victims. *Journal of Personality and Social Psychology, 69,* 449–459.

386. Muran, J. C., Gorman, B. S., Safran, J. D., Twining, L., Samstag, L. W., & Winston, A. (1995). Linking in-session change to overall outcome in short-term cognitive therapy. *Journal of Consulting and Clinical Psychology, 63,* 651–657.

387. Nussbaum, P. D., & Goreczny, A. J. (1995). Self-appraisal of stress level and related psychopathology. *Journal of Anxiety Disorders, 9,* 463–472.

388. Ogles, B. M., Lambert, M. J., & Sawyer, J. D. (1995). Clinical significance of the National Institute of Mental Health Treatment of Depression Collaborative Research Program Data. *Journal of Consulting and Clinical Psychology, 63,* 321-326.

389. Paivio, S. C., & Greenberg, L. S. (1995). Resolving "unfinished business": Efficacy of experiential therapy using empty-chair dialogue. *Journal of Consulting and Clinical Psychology, 63,* 419-425.

390. Parra, E. B., Arkowitz, H., Hannah, M. T., & Vasquez, A. M. (1995). Coping strategies and emotional reactions to separation and divorce in Anglo, Chicana, and Mexicana women. *Journal of Divorce & Remarriage, 23,* 117–129.

391. Plante, T. G., Manuel, G. M., Menendez, A. V., & Marcotte, D. (1995). Coping with stress among Salvadoran immigrants. *Hispanic Journal of Behavior Sciences, 17,* 471–479.

392. Potts, S. G., & Bass, C. M. (1995). Psychological morbidity in patients with chest pain and normal or near-normal coronary arteries: A long-term follow-up study. *Psychological Medicine, 25,* 339-347.

393. Prigerson, H. G., Frank, E., Kasl, S. V., Reynolds, C. F., Anderson, B., Zubenko, G. S., Houck, P. R., George, C. J., & Kupfer, D. J. (1995). Complicated grief and bereavement-related depression as distinct disorders: Preliminary empirical validation in elderly bereaved spouses. *American Journal of Psychiatry, 152,* 22-30.

394. Riesenmy, K. R., Lubin, B., Van Whitlock, R., & Penick, E. C. (1995). Psychometric characteristics of the trait version of the Depression Adjective Check Lists (DACL) in adult psychiatric outpatients. *Journal of Clinical Psychology, 51,* 13-17.

395. Rogers, J. H., Widiger, T. A., & Krupp, A. (1995). Aspects of depression associated with borderline personality disorder. *American Journal of Psychiatry, 152,* 268-270.

396. Romach, M., Busto, U., Somer, G., Kaplan, H. L., & Sellers, E. (1995). Clinical aspects of chronic use of alprazolam and lorazepan. *American Journal of Psychiatry, 152,* 1161–1167.

397. Rotheram-Borus, M. J., Rosario, M., Reid, H., & Koopman, C. (1995). Predicting patterns of sexual acts among homosexual and bisexual youths. *American Journal of Psychiatry, 152,* 588-595.

398. Rotheram-Borus, M. J., Rosario, M., Rossem, R. V., Reid, H., & Gillis, R. (1995). Prevalence, course, and predictors of multiple problem behaviors among gay and bisexual male adolescents. *Developmental Psychology, 31,* 75-85.

399. Rubenstein, C. S., Altemus, M., Pigott, T. A., Hess, A., & Murray, D. L. (1995). Symptom overlap between OCD and bulimia nervosa. *Journal of Anxiety Disorders, 9,* 1-9.

400. Savournin, R., Evans, C., Hirst, J. F., & Watson, J. P. (1995). The elusive factor structure of the Inventory of Interpersonal Problems. *British Journal of Medical Psychology, 68,* 353–369.

401. Schmitter-Edgecombe, M., Fahy, J. F., Whelan, J. P., & Long, C. J. (1995). Memory remediation after severe closed head injury: Notebook training versus supportive therapy. *Journal of Consulting and Clinical Psychology, 63,* 484-489.

402. Sequin, M., Lesage, A., & Kiely, M. C. (1995). Parental bereavement after suicide and accident: A comparative study. *Suicide and Life-Threatening Behavior, 25,* 489–498.

403. Shapiro, D. A., Rees, A., Barkham, M., Hardy, G., Reynolds, S., & Startup, M. (1995). Effects of treatment duration and severity of depression on the maintenance of gains after cognitive-behavioral and psychodynamic-interpersonal psychotherapy. *Journal of Consulting and Clinical Psychology, 63,* 378-387.

404. Sigmon, S. T., Stanton, A. L., & Snyder, C. R. (1995). Gender differences in coping: A further test of socialization and role constraint theories. *Sex Roles, 33,* 565–587.

405. Snell, W. E., Jr., Gum, S., Shuck, R. L., Mosley, J. A., & Hite, T. L. (1995). The Clinical Anger Scale: Preliminary reliability and validity. *Journal of Clinical Psychology, 51,* 215-226.

406. Solomon, Z. (1995). The effect of prior stressful experience on coping with war trauma and capacity. *Psychological Medicine, 25,* 1289–1294.

407. Spanos, N. P., McNulty, S. A., DuBreuil, S. C., Pires, M., & Burgress, M. F. (1995). The frequency and correlates of sleep paralysis in a university sample. *Journal of Research in Personality, 29,* 285–305.

408. Spates, C. R., & Burnette, M. M. (1995). Eye movement desensitization: Three unusual cases. *Journal of Behavior Therapy and Experimental Psychiatry, 26,* 51–55.

409. Steer, R. A., Kumar, G., Ranieri, W. F., & Beck, A. T. (1995). Use of the Beck Anxiety Inventory with adolescent psychiatric outpatients. *Psychological Reports, 76,* 459–465.

410. Stein, D. J., Simeon, D., Freukel, M., Islam, M. N., & Hollander, E. (1995). An open trial of valproute in borderline personality disorder. *Journal of Clinical Psychiatry, 56,* 506–510.

411. Stiles, W. B., & Shapiro, D. A. (1995). Verbal exchange structure of brief psychodynamic-interpersonal and cognitive-behavioral psychotherapy. *Journal of Consulting and Clinical Psychology, 63,* 15-27.

412. Stiles, W. B., Shapiro, D. A., Harper, H., & Morrison, L. A. (1995). Therapist contributions to psychotherapeutic assimilation: An alternative to the drug metaphor. *British Journal of Medical Psychology, 68,* 1–13.

413. Stinson, C. H., Milbrath, C., & Horowitz, M. J. (1995). Dysfluency and topic orienttion and bereaved individuals: Bridging individual and group studies. *Journal of Consulting and Clinical Psychology, 63,* 37-45.

414. Sutker, P. B., Davis, J. M., Uddo, M., & Ditta, S. R. (1995). Assessment of psychological distress in Persian Gulf troops: Ethnicity and gender comparisons. *Journal of Personality Assessment, 64,* 415-427.

415. Sutker, P. B., Davis, J. M., Uddo, M., & Ditta, S. R. (1995). War zone stress, personal resources, and PTSD in Persian Gulf War returnees. *Journal of Abnormal Psychology, 104,* 444–452.

416. Svartberg, M., Seltzer, M. H., Stiles, T. C., & Khoo, S. (1995). Symptom improvement and its temporal course in short-term dynamic psychotherapy. *The Journal of Nervous and Mental Disease, 183,* 242–248.

417. Taylor, S. (1995). Assessment of obsessions and compulsions: Reliability, validity, and sensitivity to treatment effects. *Clinical Psychology Review, 15,* 261–296.

418. Thompson, J. A., Charlton, P. F. C., Kerry, R., Lee, D., & Turner, S. W. (1995). An open trial of exposure therapy based on deconditioning for post-traumatic stress disorder. *British Journal of Clinical Psychology, 34,* 407–416.

419. Toro, P. A., Bellavia, C. W., Daeschler, C. V., Owens, B. J., Wall, D. D., Passero, J. M., & Thomas, D. M. (1995). Distinguishing homelessness from poverty: A comparative study. *Journal of Consulting and Clinical Psychology, 63,* 280-289.

420. Ursano, R. J., Fullerton, C. S., Kao, T. C., & Bhartiya, V. R. (1995). Longitudinal assessment of posttraumatic stress disorder and depression after exposure to traumatic death. *The Journal of Nervous and Mental Disease, 183,* 36-42.

421. Van den Broucke, S., Vandereycken, W., & Vertommen, H. (1995). Conflict management in married eating disorder patients: A controlled observational study. *Journal of Social and Personal Relationships, 12,* 27–48.

422. Van den Broucke, S., Vandereycken, W., & Vertommen, H. (1995). Marital intimacy in patients with an eating disorder: A controlled self-report study. *British Journal of Clinical Psychology, 34,* 67-78.

423. van Knippenberg, F. C. E., Passchier, J., Heysteck, D., Shackleton, D., Schmitz, P., Poublon, R. M. L., & Van Der Mache, F. (1995). The Rotterdam Daytime Sleepiness Scale: A new daytime sleepiness scale. *Psychological Reports, 76,* 83-87.

424. Wanigaratne, S., & Barker, C. (1995). Clients' preferences for styles of therapy. *British Journal of Clinical Psychology, 34,* 215-222.

425. Watson, D., Weber, K., Assenheimer, J. S., Clark, L. A., Strauss, M. E., & McCormick, R. A. (1995). Testing a tripartite model: I. Evaluating convergent and discriminant validity of Anxiety and Depression Symptom Scales. *Journal of Abnormal Psychology, 104,* 3-14.

426. Weine, S. M., Becker, D. F., McGlashan, T. H., Laub, D., Lazrove, S., Vojvoda, D., & Hyman, L. (1995). Psychiatric consequences of "ethnic cleansing": Clinical assessments and trauma testimonies of newly resettled Bosnian refugees. *American Journal of Psychiatry, 152,* 536-542.

427. Weiss, D. S., Marmar, C. R., Metzler, T. J., & Ronfeldt, H. M. (1995). Predicting symptomatic distress in emergency services personnel. *Journal of Consulting and Clinical Psychology, 63,* 361-368.

428. Westermeyer, J., Schaberg, L., & Nugent, S. (1995). Anxiety symptoms in Hmong refugees 1.5 years after migration. *The Journal of Nervous and Mental Disease, 183,* 342–344.

429. Wichstrom, L. (1995). Harter's Self-Perception Profile for Adolescents: Reliability, validity, and evaluation of the question format. *Journal of Personality Assessment, 65,* 100–116.

430. Wilson, S. A., Becker, L. A., & Tinker, R. H. (1995). Eye movement desensitization and reprocessing (EMDR) treatment for psychologically traumatized individuals. *Journal of Consulting and Clinical Psychology, 63,* 923–937.

431. Woody, G. E., McLellan, A. T., Luborsky, L., & O'Brien, C. P. (1995). Psychotherapy in community methadone programs: A validation study. *American Journal of Psychiatry, 152,* 1302–1308.

432. Allen, J. P., & Hauser, S. T. (1996). Autonomy and relatedness in adolescent-family interactions as predictors of young adults' states of mind regarding attachment. *Development and Psychopathology, 8,* 793–809.

433. Allen, J. P., Hauser, S. T., & Borman-Spurell, E. (1996). Attachment theory as a framework for understanding sequelae of severe adolescent psychopathology: An 11-year follow-up study. *Journal of Consulting and Clinical Psychology, 64,* 254–263.

434. Amir, M., Kaplan, Z., & Kotler, M. (1996). Type of trauma, severity of posttraumatic stress disorder core symptoms, and associated features. *The Journal of General Psychology, 123,* 341–351.

435. Ammerman, R. T., & Patz, R. J. (1996). Determinants of child abuse potential: Contribution of parent and child factors. *Journal of Clinical Child Psychology, 25,* 300–307.

436. Baker-Pierce, L. A., & Persinger, M. A. (1996). Weak, but complex pulsed magnetic fields may reduce depression following traumatic brain injury. *Perceptual and Motor Skills, 83,* 491–498.

437. Ballard, E., Butzer, J. F., & Donders, J. (1996). Susac's syndrome: neuropsychological characteristics in a young man. *Neurology, 47,* 266–268.

438. Berent, S., Giordani, B., Gilman, S., Junck, L., Klurn, K. J., & Koeppe, R. A. (1996). Psychological factors and PET measured glucose matabolism in olivopontocerebellar atrophy. *Assessment, 3,* 339–349.

439. Bernstein, G. A., & Borchardt, C. M. (1996). School refusal: Family constellation and family functioning. *Journal of Anxiety Disorders, 10,* 1–19.

440. Bowman, V., Ward, L. C., Bowman, D., & Scogin, F. (1996). Self-examination therapy as an adjunct treatment for depressive symptoms in substance abusing patients. *Addictive Behaviors, 21,* 129–133.

441. Budman, S. H., Demby, A., Soldz, S., & Merry, J. (1996). Time-limited group psychotherapy for patients with personality disorders: Outcomes and drop-outs. *International Journal of Group Psychotherapy, 46,* 357–377.

442. Burgess, E., Dorn, L. D., Haaga, D. A. F., & Chrousos, G. (1996). Sociotropy, autonomy, stress, and depression in Cushing syndrome. *Journal of Nervous and Mental Disease, 184,* 362–367.

443. Burlingame, G. M., & Barlow, S. H. (1996). Outcome and process differences between professional and nonprofessional therapists in time-limited group psychotherapy. *International Journal of Group Psychotherapy, 46,* 455–478.

444. Capps, L., Sigman, M., Sena, R., & Henker, B. (1996). Fear, anxiety and perceived control in children of agoraphobic parents. *Journal of Child Psychology and Psychiatry, 37,* 445–452.

445. Charlton, P. F. C., & Thompson, J. A. (1996). Ways of coping with psychological distress after trauma. *British Journal of Clinical Psychology, 35,* 517-530.

446. Cheung, E. C. (1996). Cultural differences in optimism, pessimism, and coping: Predictors of subsequent adjustment in Asian American and Caucasian American college students. *Journal of Counseling Psychology, 43,* 113–123.

447. Chwalisz, K. (1996). The perceived stress model of a caregiver burden: Evidence from spouses of persons with brain injuries. *Rehabilitation Psychology, 41,* 91–114.

448. Cincirpini, P. M., Cincirpini, L. G., Wallfisch, A., Haque, W., & Van Vunakis, H. (1996). Behavior therapy and the transdermal nicotine patch: Effects on cessation outcome, affect, and coping. *Journal of Consulting and Clinical Psychology, 64,* 314–323.

449. Cloitre, M., Cancienne, J., Brodsky, B., Dulit, R., & Perry, S. W. (1996). Memory performance among women with parental abuse histories: Enhanced directed forgetting or directed remembering? *Journal of Abnormal Psychology, 105,* 204–211.

450. Debats, D. L. (1996). Meaning in life: Clinical relevance and predictive power. *British Journal of Clinical Psychology, 35,* 503–516.

451. Derecho, C. N., Wetzler, S., McGinn, L. K., Sanderson, W. C., & Asnis, G. M. (1996). Atypical depression among psychiatric inpatients: Clinical features and personality traits. *Journal of Affective Disorders, 39,* 55–59.

452. Downey, G., & Feldman, S. I. (1996). Implications of rejection sensitivity for intimate relationships. *Journal of Personality and Social Psychology, 70,* 1327–1343.

453. Fairburn, C. G., Welch, S. L., Norman, P. A., O'Connor, M. E., & Doll, H. A. (1996). Bias and bulimia nervosa: How typical are clinic cases? *American Journal of Psychiatry, 153,* 386–391.

454. Fonagy, P., Leigh, T., Steele, M., Steele, H., Kennedy, R., Mattoon, A., Target, M., & Gerter, A. (1996). The relation of attachment status, psychiatric classification, and response to psychotherapy. *Journal of Consulting and Clinical Psychology, 64,* 22–31.

455. Gauthier, L., Stollack, G., Messé, L., & Aronoff, J. (1996). Recall of childhood neglect and physical abuse as differential predictors of current psychological functioning. *Child Abuse & Neglect, 20,* 549–559.

456. Ge, X., Best, K. M., Conger, R. D., & Simons, R. L. (1996). Parenting behaviors and the occurrence and co-occurrence of adolescent depressive symptoms and conduct problems. *Developmental Psychology, 32,* 717–731.

457. Ge, X., Conger, R. D., & Elder, G. H., Jr. (1996). Coming of age too early: Pubertal influences on girls' vulnerability to psychological distress. *Child Development, 67,* 3386–3400.

458. Ge, X., Conger, R. D., Cadoret, R. J., Neiderhiser, J. M., Yates, W., Troughton, E., & Stewart, M. A. (1996). The developmental interface between nature and nurture: A mutual influence model of child antisocial behavior and parent behaviors. *Developmental Psychology, 32,* 574–589.

459. Good, G. E., Robertson, J. M., Fitzgerald, L. F., Stevens, M., & Bartels, K. M. (1996). The relation between masculine role conflict and psychological distress in male university counseling center clients. *Journal of Counseling and Development, 75,* 44–49.

460. Gotham, H. J., & Sher, K. J. (1996). Do codependent traits involve more than basic dimensions of personality and psychopathology? *Journal of Studies on Alcohol, 57,* 34–39.

461. Greenberg, M. A., Wortman, C. B., & Stone, A. A. (1996). Emotional expression and physical health: Revising traumatic memories or fostering self-regulation? *Journal of Personality and Social Psychology, 71,* 588–602.

462. Grenyer, B. F. S., & Luborsky, L. (1996). Dynamic change in psychotherapy: Mastery of interpersonal conflicts. *Journal of Consulting and Clinical Psychology, 64,* 411–416.

463. Grissett, N. I., & Fitzgibbon, M. L. (1996). The clinical significance of binge eating in an obese population: Support for BED and questions regarding its criteria. *Addictive Behaviors, 21,* 57–66.

464. Himelein, M. J., & McElrath, J. A. V. (1996). Resilient child sexual abuse survivors: Cognitive coping and illusions. *Child Abuse & Neglect, 20,* 747–758.

465. Horowitz, M., Sonneborn, D., Sugahara, C., & Maercker, A. (1996). Self-regard: A new measure. *American Journal of Psychiatry, 153,* 382–385.

466. Horwitz, A. V., White, H. R., & Howell-White, S. (1996). Becoming married and mental health: A longitudinal study of a cohort of young adults. *Journal of Marriage and the Family, 58,* 895–907.

467. Hraba, J., Lorenz, F. O., Lee, G., & Pechacová, Z. (1996). Gender and well-being in the Czech Republic. *Sex Roles, 34,* 517–533.

468. Hyer, L., Boyd, S., Scurfield, R., Smith, D., & Burke, J. (1996). Effects of outward bound experience as an adjunct to inpatient PTSD treatment of war veterans. *Journal of Clinical Psychology, 52,* 263–278.

469. Janssen, H. J. E. M., Cuisinier, M. C. J., Hoodguin, K. A. L., & deGraauw, K. P. H. M. (1996). Controlled prospective study on the mental health of women following pregnancy loss. *American Journal of Psychiatry, 153,* 226–230.

470. Johnson, J. G., Bornstein, R. F., & Sherman, M. F. (1996). A modified scoring algorithm for the PDQ-R: Psychiatric symptomatology and substance use in adolescents with personality disorders. *Educational and Psychological Measurement, 56*(1), 76–89.

471. Johnson, M. E., Brems, C., & Fisher, D. G. (1996). Self-reported levels of psychopathology of drug abusers not currently in treatment. *Journal of Psychopathology and Behavioral Assessment, 18,* 21–34.

472. Johnston, C. (1996). Parent characteristics and parent-child interactions in families of nonproblem children and ADHD children with higher and lower levels of oppositional-defiant behavior. *Journal of Abnormal Child Psychology, 24,* 85–104.

473. Jolly, J. B., Dyck, M. J., Kramer, T. A., & Wherry, J. N. (1996). The relations between sociotropy and autonomy, positive and negative affect and two proposed depression subtypes. *British Journal of Clinical Psychology, 35,* 91–101.

474. Katon, W., Robinson, P., VonKorff, M., Lin, E., Bush, T., Ludman, E., Simon, G., & Walker, E. (1996). A multifaceted intervention to improve treatment of depression in primary care. *Archives of General Psychiatry, 53,* 924–932.

475. Laor, N., Wolmer, L., Mayes, L. C., Golomb, A., Silverberg, D. S., Weizman, R., & Cohen, D. J. (1996). Israeli preschoolers under scud missile attacks: A developmental perspective on risk-modifying factors. *Archives of General Psychiatry, 53,* 416–423.

476. Layman, M. J., Gidycz, C. A., & Lynn, S. J. (1996). Unacknowledged versus acknowledged rape victims: Situational factors and posttraumatic stress. *Journal of Abnormal Psychology, 105,* 124–131.

477. Lepore, S. J., Silver, R. C., Wortman, C. B., & Wayment, H. A. (1996). Social constraints, intrusive thoughts, and depressive symptoms among bereaved mothers. *Journal of Personality and Social Psychology, 70,* 271–282.

478. Lohr, J. M., Tolin, D. F., & Kleinknecht, R. A. (1996). An intensive design investigation of eye movement desensitization and reprocessing of claustrophobia. *Journal of Anxiety Disorders, 10,* 73–88.

479. Mahalik, J. R. (1996). Client vocational interests as predictors of client reactions to counselor intentions. *Journal of Counseling and Development, 74,* 416–421.

480. Michiels, V., Cluydts, R., Fischler, B., Hoffmann, G., Le Bon, O., & De Meirleir, K. (1996). Cognitive functioning in patients with chronic fatigue syndrome. *Journal of Clinical and Experimental Neuropsychology, 18,* 666–677.

481. Mulder, R. T., Joyce, P. R., Sullivan, P. F., & Oakley-Browne, M. A. (1996). Intimate bonds in depression. *Journal of Affective Disorders, 40,* 175–178.

482. Murphy, K. R., & Barkley, R. A. (1996). Parents of children with attention-deficit/hyperactivity disorder: Psychological and attentional impairment. *American Journal of Orthopsychiatry, 66,* 93–102.

483. Newmann, J. P., Klein, M. H., Jensen, J. E., & Essex, M. J. (1996). Depressive symptom experiences among older women: A comparison of alternative measurement approaches. *Psychology and Aging, 11,* 112–126.

484. Nunn, K. P., Lewin, T. J., Walton, J. M., & Carr, V. J. (1996). The construction and characteristics of an instrument to measure personal hopefulness. *Psychological Medicine, 26,* 531–545.

485. Parker, W. D. (1996). Psychological adjustment in mathematically gifted students. *Gifted Child Quarterly, 40,* 154–157.

486. Perloff, J. N., & Buckner, J. C. (1996). Fathers of children on welfare: Their impact on child well-being. *American Journal of Orthopsychiatry, 66,* 557–571.

487. Quitkin, F. M., McGrath, P. J., Stewart, J. W., Ocepek-Welikson, K., Taylor, B. P., Nunes, E., Deliyannides, D., Agosti, V., Donovan, S. J., Petkova, E., & Klein, D. F. (1996). Chronological milestones to guide drug change: When should clinicians switch antidepressants? *Archives of General Psychiatry, 53,* 785–792.

488. Rauter, V. K., Leonard, C. E., & Swett, C. P. (1996). SCL-90-R factor structure in an acute, involunatry, adult psychiatric inpatient sample. *Journal of Clinical Psychology, 52,* 625–629.

489. Rief, W., Heuser, J., & Fichter, M. M. (1996). What does the Toronto Alexithymia Scale TAS-R measure? *Journal of Clinical Psychology, 52,* 423–429.

490. Robbins, R. A., Moody, D. S., Hahn, M. B., & Weaver, M. A. (1996). Psychological testing variables as predictors of return to work by chronic pain patients. *Perceptual and Motor Skills, 83,* 1317–1318.

491. Rosenstein, D. S., & Horowitz, H. A. (1996). Adolescent attachment and psychopathology. *Journal of Consulting and Clinical Psychology, 64,* 244–253.

492. Rowe, J. B., Sullivan, P. F., Mulder, R. T., & Joyce, P. R. (1996). The effect of a history of conduct disorder in adult major depression. *Journal of Affective Disorders, 37,* 51–63.

493. Sammallahti, P. R., Holi, M. J., Komulainen, E. J., & Aalberg, V. A. (1996). Compairing two self-report measures of coping—the Sense of Coherence

Scale and the Defense Style Questionnaire. *Journal of Clinical Psychology, 52,* 517–524.

494. Saravay, S. M., Pollack, S., Steinberg, M. D., Weinschel, B., & Herbert, M. (1996). Four-year follow-up of the influence of psychological comorbidity on medical rehospitalization. *American Journal of Psychiatry, 153,* 397–403.

495. Scheidt, C. E., Schuller, B., Rayki, O., Kommerell, G., & Deuschl, G. (1996). Relative absence of psychopathology in benign essential blepharospasm and hemifacial spasm. *Neurology, 47,* 43–45.

496. Seifer, R., Sameroff, A. J., Dickstein, S., Keitner, G., Miller, I., Rasmussen, S., & Hayden, L. C. (1996). Parental psychopathology, multiple contextual risks, and one-year outcomes in children. *Journal of Clinical Child Psychology, 25,* 423–435.

497. Slaap, B. R., van Vliet, I. M., Westenberg, H. G. M., & Den Boer, J. A. (1996). Responders and nonresponders to drug treatment in social phobia: Differences at baseline and prediction of response. *Journal of Affective Disorders, 39,* 13–19.

498. Sledge, W. H., Tebes, J., Rakfeldt, J., Davidson, L., Lyons, L., & Druss, B. (1996). Day hospital/crisis respite care versus inpatient care, Part I: Clinical outcomes. *American Journal of Psychiatry, 153,* 1065–1073.

499. Solomon, Z., & Kleinhauz, M. (1996). War-induced psychic trauma: An 18-year follow-up of Israeli veterans. *American Journal of Orthopsychiatry, 66,* 152–160.

500. Spinhoven, P., & Kooiman, C. G. (1996). Defense style in depressed and anxious psychiatric outpatients: An explorative study. *Journal of Nervous and Mental Disease, 184,* 87–94.

501. Steiger, H., Jabalpurwala, S., & Champagne, J. (1996). Axis II comorbidity and developmental adversity in bulimia nervosa. *Journal of Nervous and Mental Disease, 184,* 555–560.

502. Striegel-Moore, R. H., Goldman, S. L., Garvin, V. & Rodin, J. (1996). A prospective study of somatic and emotional symptoms of pregnancy. *Psychology of Women Quarterly, 20,* 393–408.

503. Thase, M. E., Fava, M., Halbreich, V., Kocsis, J. H., Koran, L., Davidson, J., Rosenbaum, J., & Harrison, W. (1996). A placebo-controlled, randomized clinical trial comparing sectraline and imipramine for the treatment of dysthymia. *Archives of General Psychiatry, 53,* 777–784.

504. Thompson, R. J., Jr., Gil, K. M., Abrams, M. R., & Phillips, G. (1996). Psychological adjustment of adults with Sickle Cell Anemia: Stability over 20 months, correlates, and predictors. *Journal of Clinical Psychology, 52,* 253–261.

505. Thompson, S. C., Collins, M. A., Newcomb, M. D., & Hunt, W. (1996). On fighting versus accepting stressful circumstances: Primary and secondary control among HIV-positive men in prison. *Journal of Personality and Social Psychology, 70,* 1307–1317.

506. Tiemens, B. G., Ormel, J., & Simon, G. E. (1996). Occurrence, recognition, and outcome of psychological disorders in primary care. *American Journal of Psychiatry, 153,* 636–644.

507. Timmons-Mitchell, J., Chandler-Holtz, D., & Semple, W. E. (1996). Post-traumatic stress symptoms in mothers following children's reports of sexual abuse: An exploratory study. *American Journal of Orthopsychiatry, 66,* 463–467.

508. van Balkom, A. J. L. M., de Beurs, E., Koele, P., Lange, A., & van Dyck, R. (1996). Long-term benzodiazepine use is associated with smaller treatment gain in panic disorder with agoraphobia. *Journal of Nervous and Mental Disease, 184,* 133–135.

509. van Widenfelt, B., Hosman, C., Schaap, C., & van der Staak, C. (1996). The prevention of relationship distress for couples at risk: A controlled evaluation with nine-month and two-year follow-ups. *Family Relations, 45,* 156–165.

510. Wetzler, S., Asnis, G. M., Hyman, R. B., Virtue, C., Zimmerman, J., & Rathus, J. H. (1996). Characteristics of suicidality among adolescents. *Suicide and Life-Threatening Behavior, 26,* 37–45.

511. Woessner, R., & Caplan, B. (1996). Emotional distress following stroke: Interpretive limitations of the SCL—90—R. *Assessment, 3,* 291–305.

512. Zelkowitz, P., & Milet, T. (1996). Postpartum psychiatric disorders: Their relationship to psychological adjustment and marital satisfaction in the spouses. *Journal of Abnormal Psychology, 105,* 281–285.

513. Allan, S., & Gilbert, P. (1997). Submissive behaviour and psychopathology. *British Journal of Clinical Psychology, 36,* 467–488.

514. Bagby, R. M., Kennedy, S. H., Dickens, S. E., Minifie, C. E., & Schuller, D. R. (1997). Personality and symptom profiles of the angry hostile depressed patient. *Journal of Affective Disorders, 45,* 155–160.

515. Beckman, H. T., & Lueger, R. J. (1997). Readability of self-report clinical outcome studies. *Journal of Clinical Psychology, 53,* 785–789.

516. Benight, C. C., Antoni, M. H., Kilbourn, K., Ironson, G., Kumar, M. A., Fletcher, M. A., Redwine, L., Baum, A., & Schnetderman, N. (1997). Coping self-efficacy buffers psychological and physiological disturbances in HIV-infected men following a natural disaster. *Health Psychology, 16,* 248–255.

517. Bland, S. H., O'Leary, E. S., Farinaro, E., Jossa, F., Krogh, V., Violanti, J. M., & Trevisan, M. (1997). Social network disturbances and psychological distress following earthquake evacuation. *Journal of Nervous and Mental Disease, 185,* 188–194.

518. Bowman, D., Scogin, F., Floyd, M., Patton, E., & Gist, L. (1997). Efficacy of self-examination therapy in the treatment of generalized anxiety disorder. *Journal of Counseling Psychology, 44,* 267–273.

519. Briggs, L., & Joyce, P. R. (1997). What determines post-traumatic stress disorder symptomatology for survivors of childhood sexual abuse? *Child Abuse & Neglect, 21,* 575–582.

520. Buchman, J. P., Dixon, D. R., & Thyer, B. A. (1997). A preliminary evaluation of treatment outcomes at a veteran's hospital's inpatient psychiatry unit. *Journal of Clinical Psychology, 53,* 853–858.

521. Burns, K. A., Chethik, L., Burns, W. J., & Clark, R. (1997). The early relationship of drug abusing mothers and their infants: An assessment at eight to twelve months of age. *Journal of Clinical Psychology, 53,* 279–287.

522. Castellani, B., Wedgeworth, R., Wootton, E., & Rugle, L. (1997). A bidirectional theory of addiction: Examining coping and the factors related to substance relapse. *Addictive Behaviors, 22,* 139–144.

523. Chaney, J. M., Mullins, L. L., Frank, R. G., Peterson, L., Mace, L. D., Kashani, J. H., & Goldstein, D. L. (1997). Transactional patterns of child, mother, and father adjustment in insulin-dependent diabetes mellitus: A prospective study. *Journal of Pediatric Psychology, 22,* 229–244.

524. Craske, M. G., Rowe, M., Levin, M., & Noriega-Dimitric, R. (1997). Interoceptive exposure versus breathing retraining within cognitive-behavioural therapy for panic disorder with agoraphobia. *British Journal of Clinical Psychology, 36,* 85–99.

525. Fichter, M. S., Gyynn, S. M., Weyerer, S., Liberman, R. P., & Frick, U. (1997). Family climate and expressed emotion in the course of alcoholism. *Family Process, 36,* 203–221.

526. Gall, T. L., Evans, D. R., & Howard, J. (1997). The retirement adjustment process: Changes in the well-being of male retirees across time. *Journal of Gerontology, 52,* 110–117.

527. George, E. L., & Bloom, B. L. (1997). A brief scale for assessing parental child-rearing practices: Psychometric properties and psychosocial correlates. *Family Process, 36,* 63–80.

528. Gest, S. D. (1997). Behavioral inhibition: Stability and associations with adaptation from childhood to early adulthood. *Journal of Personality and Social Psychology, 72,* 467–475.

529. Gick, M., McLeod, C., & Hulittam, D. (1997). Absorption, social desirability, and symptoms in a behavioral medicine population. *Journal of Nervous and Mental Disease, 185,* 454–458.

530. Gottschack, L. A., Stein, M. K., & Shapiro, D. H. (1997). The application of computerized content analysis of speech to the diagnostic process in a psychiatric outpatient clinic. *Journal of Clinical Psychology, 53,* 427–441.

531. Harold, G. T., & Conger, R. D. (1997). Marital conflict and adolescent distress: The role of adolescent awareness. *Child Development, 68,* 333–350.

532. Higgs, M. L., Wade, T., Cescato, M., Atchinson, M., Slavotinek, A., & Higgins, B. (1997). Differences between treatment seekers in an obese population: Medical intervention vs. dietary restriction. *Journal of Behavioral Medicine, 20,* 391–405.

533. Holmbeck, G. N., Gorey-Ferguson, L., Hudson, T., Seefeldt, T., Shapera, W., Turner, T., & Uhler, J. (1997). Maternal, paternal, and marital functioning in families of preadolescents with spina bifida. *Journal of Pediatric Psychology, 22,* 167–181.

534. Huyser, B., Buckelew, S. P., Hewett, J. E., & Johnson, J. C. (1997). Factors affecting adherence to rehabilitation interventions for individuals with fibromyalgia. *Rehabilitation Psychology, 42,* 75–91.

535. Janssen, H. J. E. M., Cuisinier, M. C. J., de Graauw, K. P. H. M., & Hoogduin, K. A. L. (1997). A prospective study of risk factors predicting grief intensity following pregnancy loss. *Archives of General Psychiatry, 54,* 56–61.

536. Jung, J. (1997). Balance and source of social support in relation to well-being. *The Journal of General Psychology, 124,* 77–90.

537. Katerndahl, D. A., & Realini, J. P. (1997). Comorbid psychiatric disorders in subjects with panic attacks. *Journal of Nervous and Mental Disease, 185,* 669–674.

538. Kellett, S., & Beail, N. (1997). The treatment of chronic post-traumatic nightmares using psychodynamic-interpersonal psychotherapy: A single-case study. *British Journal of Medical Psychology, 70,* 35–49.

539. Lecrubier, Y., Boyer, P., Turjanski, S., Rein, W., & Amisulpride Study Group. (1997). Amisulpride versus imipramine and placebo in dysthymia and major depression. *Journal of Affective Disorders, 43,* 95–103.

540. Levy-Shiff, R., Zoran, N., & Shulman, S. (1997). International and domestic adoption: Child, parents, and family adjustment. *International Journal of Behavioral Development, 20,* 109–129.

541. Lindgren, M., österberg, K., ørbæk, P., & Rosén, I. (1997). Solvent-induced toxic encephalopathy: Electrophysiological data in relation to neuropsychological findings. *Journal of Clinical and Experimental Neuropsychology, 19,* 772–783.

542. Marziali, E., Monroe-Blum, H., & McCleary, L. (1997). The contribution of group cohesion and group alliance to outcome of group psychotherapy. *International Journal of Group Psychotherapy, 47,* 475–497.

543. McCallum, M., Piper, W. E., & O'Kelly, J. (1997). Predicting patient benefit from a group-oriented, evening treatment program. *International Journal of Group Psychotherapy, 47,* 291–314.

544. McKay, J. R., Cacciola, J. S., McLellan, A. T., Alterman, A. I., & Wirtz, P. W. (1997). An initial evaluation of the psychosocial dimensions of the American Society of Addiction Medicine Criteria for inpatient versus intensive outpatient substance abuse rehabilitation. *Journal of Studies on Alcohol, 58,* 239–252.

545. Mullins, L. L., Chaney, J. M., Pace, T. M., & Hartman, V. L. (1997). Illness uncertainty, attributional style, and psychological adjustment in older adolescents and young adults with asthma. *Journal of Pediatric Psychology, 22,* 871–880.

546. Muran, J. C., Samstag, L. W., Jilton, R., Batchelder, S., & Winston, A. (1997). Development of a suboutcome strategy to measure interpersonal process in psychotherapy from an observer perspective. *Journal of Clinical Psychology, 53,* 405–420.

547. Newman, M. L., & Greenway, P. (1997). Therapeutic effects of providing MMPI-2 test feedback to clients at a university counseling service: A collaborative approach. *Psychological Assessment, 9,* 122–131.

548. Owens, M. D., & Brome, D. R. (1997). A preliminary examination of family environment and social support among African American nongrandmothers, grandmothers, and grandmothers-to-be. *Journal of Black Psychology, 23,* 74–89.
549. Rabkin, J. G., Goetz, R. R., Remien, R. H., Williams, J. B. W., Todak, G., & Gorman, J. M. (1997). Stability of mood despite HIV illness progression in a group of homosexual men. *American Journal of Psychiatry, 154,* 231–238.
550. Runtz, M. G., & Schallow, J. R. (1997). Social support and coping strategies as mediators of adult adjustment following childhood maltreatment. *Child Abuse & Neglect, 21,* 211–226.
551. Schmitz, J. M., Oswald, L. M., Jacks, S. D., Rustin, T., Rhoades, H. M., & Grabowski, J. (1997). Relapse prevention treatment for cocaine dependence: Group vs. individual format. *Addictive Behaviors, 22,* 405–418.
552. Schonfeld, W. H., Verboncoeur, C. J., Fifer, S. K., Lipschutz, R. C., Lubeck, D. P., & Buesching, D. P. (1997). The functioning and well-being of patients with unrecognized anxiety disorders and major depressive disorder. *Journal of Affective Disorders, 43,* 105–119.
553. Sigmon, S. T., Rohan, K. J., Dorhofer, D., Hotovy, L. A., Trask, P. C., & Boulard, N. (1997). Effects of consent form information on self-disclosrue. *Ethics & Behavior, 7,* 299–310.
554. Sillanpaa, M. C., Agaza, L. M., Milner, I. B., Podany, E. C., Axelrod, B. N., & Brown, G. G. (1997). Gulf War veterans: A neuropsychological examination. *Journal of Clinical and Experimental Neuropsychology, 19,* 211–219.
555. Sklar, S. M., Annis, H. M., & Turner, N. E. (1997). Development and validation of the drug-taking confidence questionnaire: A measure of coping self-efficacy. *Addictive Behaviors, 22,* 655–670.
556. Streufert, S., Satish, V., Pogash, R., Gingrich, D., Landis, R., Roache, J., & Severs, W. (1997). Excess coffee consumption in simulated complex work settings: Detriment or facilitation of performance? *Journal of Applied Psychology, 82,* 774–782.
557. Todd, D. M., Deane, F. P., & McKenna, P. A. (1997). Appropriateness of SCL-90-R adolescent and adult norms for outpatient and nonpatient college students. *Journal of Counseling Psychology, 44,* 294–301.
558. Van Buren, A., & Nowicki, S., Jr. (1997). Awareness of interpersonal style and self-evaluation. *The Journal of Social Psychology, 137,* 429–434.
559. Van Gerwen, L. J., Spinhoven, P., Diekstra, R. F. W., & Van Dyck, R. (1997). People who seek help for fear of flying: Typology of flying phobics. *Behavior Therapy, 28,* 237–251.
560. Van Strien, T. (1997). The concurrent validity of a classification of dieters with low versus high susceptibility toward failure of restraint. *Addictive Behaviors, 22,* 587–597.
561. Volpicelli, J. R., Rhines, K. C., Rhines, J. S., Volpicelli, L. A., Alterman, A. I., & O'Brien, C. P. (1997). Naltrexone and alcohol dependence: Role of subject compliance. *Archives of General Psychiatry, 54,* 737–742.
562. Walsh, B. T., Wilson, G. T., Loeb, K. L., Devlin, M. J., Pike, K. M., Roose, S. P., Fleiss, J., & Waternaux, C. (1997). Medication and psychotherapy in the treatment of bulimia nervosa. *American Journal of Psychiatry, 154,* 523–531.
563. Weidner, G., Boughal, T., Connor, S. L., Pieper, C., & Mendell, N. R. (1997). Relationship of job strain to standard coronary risk factors and psychological characteristics in women and men of the family heart study. *Health Psychology, 16,* 239–247.
564. Whiffen, V. E., Benazon, N. R., & Bradshaw, C. (1997). Discriminant validity of the TSC-40 in an outpaitent setting. *Child Abuse & Neglect, 21,* 107–115.
565. Whiffen, V. E., & Clark, S. E. (1997). Does victimization account for sex differences in depressive symptoms? *British Journal of Clinical Psychology, 36,* 185–193.
566. Wickrama, K. A. S., & Elder, G. H. (1997). Marital quality and physical illness: A latent growth curve analysis. *Journal of Marriage and the Family, 59,* 143–155.
567. Zanis, D. A., Cohen, E., Meyers, K., & Cnaan, R. A. (1997). HIV risks among homeless men differentiated by cocaine use and psychiatric distress. *Addictive Behaviors, 22,* 287–292.
568. Zisook, S., Paulus, M., Shuchter, S. R., & Judd, L. L. (1997). The many faces of depression following spousal bereavement. *Journal of Affective Disorders, 45,* 85–95.
569. Allan, W. D., Kashani, J. H., & Reid, J. C. (1998). Parental hostility: Impact on the family. *Child Psychiatry and Human Development, 28,* 169–178.
570. Ambrose, L. M., Button, E. J., & Ormrod, J. A. (1998). A long-term follow-up study of a cohort of referrals to an adult mental health clinical psychology department. *British Journal of Clinical Psychology, 37,* 113–115.
571. Baker, K. A., Schmidt, M. F., Heinemann, A. W., Langley, M., & Miranti, S. V. (1998). The validity of the Katz Adjustment Scale among people with traumatic brain injury. *Rehabilitation Psychology, 43,* 30–40.
572. Bemak, F., & Chung, R. C-Y. (1998). Vietnamese Amerasians: Predictors of distress and self-destructive behavior. *Journal of Counseling & Development, 76,* 452–458.
573. Biby, E. L. (1998). The relationship between body dysmorphic disorder and depression, self-esteem, somatization, and obsessive-compulsive disorder. *Journal of Clinical Psychology, 54,* 489–499.
574. Blatt, S. J., Zuroff, D. C., Bondi, C. M., Saneslow, C. A.,III, & Pilkonis, P. A. (1998). When and how perfectionism impedes the brief treatment of depression: Further analyses of the National Institute of Nental Health Treatment of Depression Collaborative Research Program. *Journal of Consulting and Clinical Psychology, 66,* 423–428.
575. Chambers, J. W., Jr., Kambon, K., Birdsong, B. D., Brown, J., Dixon, P., & Robbins-Brinson, L. (1998). Africentric cultural identity and the stress experience of African American college students. *Journal of Black Psychology, 24,* 368–396.
576. Chang, E. C., & Bridewell, W. B. (1998). Irrational beliefs, optimism, pessimism, and psychological distress: A preliminary examination of differential effects in a college population. *Journal of Clinical Psychology, 54,* 137–142.
577. Dugbartey, A. T., Dugbartey, M. T., & Apedo, M. Y. (1998). Delayed neuropsychiatric effects of malaria in Ghana. *Journal of Nervous and Mental Disease, 186,* 183–186.
578. Favaro, A., & Santonastaso, P. (1998). Impulsive and compulsive self-injurious behavior in bulimia nervosa: Prevalence and psychological correlates. *Journal of Nervous and Mental Disease, 186,* 157–165.
579. Frone, M. R. (1998). Predictors of work injuries among employed adolescents. *Journal of Applied Psychology, 83,* 565–576.
580. Garber, J., Van Slyke, D. A., & Walker, L. S. (1998). Concordance between mothers' and children's reports of somatic and emotional symptoms in patients with recurrent abdominal pain or emotional disorders. *Journal of Abnormal Child Psychology, 26,* 381–391.
581. Guydish, J., Werdegas, D., Sorensen, J. L., & Clar, W. (1998). Drug abuse day treatment: A randomized clinical trail comapring day and residential treatment programs. *Journal of Consulting and Clinical Psychology, 66,* 280–289.
582. Hardy, G. E., Stiles, W. B., Barkham, M., & Startup, M. (1998). Therapist responsiveness to client interpersonal styles during time-limited treatments for depression. *Journal of Consulting and Clinical Psychology, 66,* 304–312.
583. Heitkemper, M., Charman, A. B. D., Shaver, J., Lentz, M. J., & Jarrett, M. E. (1998). Self-report and polysomnographic measures of sleep in women with irritable bowel syndrome. *Nursing Research, 47,* 270–277.
584. Hoekstra-Weebers, J. E. H. M., Heuvel, F., Jaspers, J. P. C., Kamps, W. A., & Klip, E. C. (1998). An intervention program for parents of pediatric cancer patients: A randomized controlled trial. *Journal of Pediatric Psychology, 23,* 207–214.
585. Hoglend, P., & Perry, J. C. (1998). Defensive functioning predicts improvement in major depressive episodes. *Journal of Nervous and Mental Disease, 186,* 238–243.
586. Holmes, D. T., Tariot, P. N., & Cox, C. (1998). Preliminary evidence of psychological distress among reservists in the Persian Gulf War. *Journal of Nervous and Mental Disease, 186,* 166–173.
587. Horwitz, A. V., & White, H. R. (1998). The relationship of cohabitation and mental health: A study of a young adult cohort. *Journal of Marriage and the Family, 60,* 505–514.
588. Lueger, R. J. (1998). Using feedback on patient progress to predict the outcome of psychotherapy. *Journal of Clinical Psychology, 54,* 383–393.
589. Neria, Y., Solomon, Z., & Dekel, R. (1998). An eighteen-year follow-up study of Israeli prisoners of war and combat veterans. *Journal of Nervous and Mental Disease, 186,* 174–182.
590. Shelton, T. L., Barkley, R. A., Crosswait, C., Moorehouse, M., Fletcher, K., Barrett, S., Jenkins, L., & Metevia, L. (1998). Psychiatric and psychological morbidity as a function of adaptive disability in preschool children with aggressive and hyperactive-impulsive-inattention behavior. *Journal of Abnormal Child Psychology, 26,* 475–494.
591. Thompson, S. C., Thomas, C., Rickabaugh, C. A., Tantamjarik, P., Otsuki, T., Pan, D., Garcia, B. F., & Sinar, E. (1998). Primary and secondary control over age-related changes in physical appearance. *Journal of Personality, 66,* 583–605.
592. Trent, L. K. (1998). Evaluation of a four- versus six-week length of stay in the Navy's alcohol treatment program. *Journal of Studies on Alcohol, 59,* 270–279.
593. Venable, W. M. & Thompson, B. (1998). Caretaker psychological factors predicting premature termination of children's counseling. *Journal of Counseling & Development, 76,* 286–293.

[2604]

Symptom Scale—77.

Purpose: "Designed to reflect specific symptom changes ... capable of modification by psychotherapy or neuropharmacology."

Population: Adolescents and adults.

Publication Dates: 1992–1995.

Acronym: SS-77.

Scores: 10 scales: Somatic Complaints, Depression, Alcohol and Other Drug Abuse, Anxiety, Obsessive–Compulsive Symptoms, Panic Disorder Without and With Agoraphobia, Traumatic Stress, Minimization of Symptoms, Magnification of Symptoms, Guardedness Index.

Administration: Individual or group.

Price Data: Not available.

Time: (15–20) minutes.

Comments: Computer administration requires IBM-compatible with at least 4 MB RAM and 1.4 MB disk drive and mouse and Windows 3.1.

Author: Judith L. Johnson and William McCown
Publisher: DocuTrac, Inc. [No reply from publisher; status unknown].

[2605]

System for Testing and Evaluation of Potential.

Purpose: "To evaluate managerial and professional personnel."
Population: Managerial and professional personnel.
Publication Dates: 1986–1995.
Acronym: LH-STEP.
Administration: Group or individual.
Price Data, 1999: $250 per job analysis kit including 10 job analysis questionnaires, computer scoring, individual and composite reports, and a recommendation regarding which LH-STEP battery to use.
Author: Human Resources Center, The University of Chicago.
Publisher: NCS [Rosemont].

a) LH-STEP (STANDARD REPORT).
Scores: 6 ratings: Potential Estimates (Executive, Middle Manager, Supervisors and Nonsupervisory Professionals), Job Skills (Executive, Middle Manager, Supervisors and Nonsupervisory Professionals); 39 scores: Predictor Profile: (School Achievement, Drive, Vocational Satisfaction, Financial Responsibility, General Family Responsibility, Leadership, Relaxation Pursuits, Non-Verbal Reasoning, Word Fluency, Vocabulary, Closure Flexibility, Creative Potential, Sales Aptitude, Personal Insight, Extroversion, Emotional Responsiveness, Self-Reliance, Ability to Work Under Pressure, Level of Stress Response, Internal Adjustment, External Adjustment, Social Adjustment, General Adjustment), Job Skills: Organization (Setting Organizational Objectives, Financial Planning and Review, Improving Work Procedures and Practices, Interdepartmental Coordination), Leadership (Developing and Implementing Technical Ideas, Judgment and Decision Making, Developing Group Cooperation and Teamwork, Coping With Difficulties and Emergencies, Promoting Safety Attitudes and Practices, Communications), Human Resources (Developing Employee Potential, Supervisory Practices, Self-Development and Improvement, Personnel Practices), Community (Promoting Community/Organization Relations, Handling Outside Contacts).
Price Data: $200 or less per battery.
Time: (190–210) minutes.

b) LH-STEP (EXTENDED REPORT).
Scores: 6 ratings: same as LH-STEP Standard Report; 63 scores: same as LH-STEP Standard Report, plus Calm, Cautious, Composed, Decisive, Demonstrative, Even-Tempered, Persevering, Seeks Company, Self-Confident, Serious, Steady Worker, Talkative, Reaction Time to Verbal Stimuli, Reaction Time to Color Stimuli, Dominance, Independence, Autonomous Work Environment, Pressure Performance, Energy Level, Speed of Reaction, Ideational Spontaneity, Theoretical Interests, Artistic Interests, Mechanical Interests; 12 tests: Managerial and Professional Job Functions Inventory for Ability, Experience and Background Inventory, Word Fluency, Temperament Comparator, Vocabulary Inventory, Non-Verbal Reasoning, Sales Inventory, Cree Questionnaire, The Press Test, Closure Flexibility, EMO Questionnaire, Management Style Questionnaire.
Price Data: $225 or less per battery.
Time: (190–210) minutes.

[2606]

System of Multicultural Pluralistic Assessment.

Purpose: Designed as "a comprehensive system for assessing the level at which children function in cognitive abilities, perceptual motor abilities, and adaptive behavior."
Population: Ages 5–11.
Publication Dates: 1977–1978.
Acronym: SOMPA.
Administration: Individual.
Price Data, 1999: $252.50 per basic kit including parent interview manual ('77, 150 pages), 25 parent interview record forms, 6 ABIC scoring keys, student assessment manual ('78, 125 pages), 25 student assessment record forms, 25 profile folders, and technical manual ('79, 164 pages).
Foreign Language Edition: Spanish edition available.
Authors: Jane R. Mercer and June F. Lewis.
Publisher: The Psychological Corporation.

a) STUDENT ASSESSMENT.
Population: Ages 5–11.
Publication Date: 1978.
Scores: 6 instruments: Physical Dexterity Tasks, Bender Visual Motor Gestalt Test, Weight by Height, Visual Acuity (Snellen Test), Auditory Acuity (audiometer), WISC-R (WPPSI for children under 6 years).
Price Data: $161.50 per SOMPA student assessment kit including 25 record forms, 25 profile folders, and manual.
Time: (60) minutes, several test sessions should be scheduled.
Comments: The following instruments are not available in the SOMPA test kit and must be

obtained by the tester: Bender Gestalt, Snellen Test, audiometer, WISC-R, or WPPSI.

b) PARENT INTERVIEW.

Population: Parents.

Publication Date: 1977.

Scores: 3 instruments: Sociocultural Scales, Adaptive Behavior Inventory for Children (ABIC), Health History Inventory.

Price Data: $204.50 per SOMPA parent interview kit including 25 record forms, 25 profile folders, and manual.

Cross References: See T4:2676 (11 references); for reviews by Lloyd G. Humphreys, Cecil R. Reynolds, and Jonathan Sandoval, see 9:1222 (6 references).

TEST REFERENCES

1. Richert, E. S. (1987). Rampant problems and promising practices in the identification of disadvantaged gifted students. *Gifted Child Quarterly, 31,* 149–154.

2. Figueroa, R. A. (1989). Psychological testing of linguistic-minority students: Knowledge gaps and regulations. *Exceptional Children, 56,* 145–152.

3. Rueda, R. (1989). Defining mild disabilities with language-minority students. *Exceptional Children, 56,* 121–128.

4. Barkley, R. A., Fischer, M., Edelbrock, C., & Smallish, L. (1991). The adolescent outcome of hyperactive children diagnosed by research criteria: III. Mother-child interactions, family conflicts and maternal psychopathology. *Journal of Child Psychology and Psychiatry and Allied Disciplines, 32,* 233-255.

5. Matthew, J. L., Golin, A. K., Moore, M. W., & Baker, C. (1992). Use of SOMPA in identification of gifted African-American children. *Journal for the Education of the Gifted, 15,* 344-356.

[2607]

Systematic Screening for Behavior Disorders.

Purpose: To screen and identify students at risk for developing serious behavior problems.

Population: Grades K–6.

Publication Dates: 1990–1992.

Acronym: SSBD.

Administration: Individual and group.

Price Data, 1993: $195 per complete kit including technical manual ('92, 80 pages), user's guide ('92, 151 pages), observer training manual ('92, 136 pages), videotape, and 25 sets of classroom screening forms.

Authors: Hill M. Walker and Herbert H. Severson.

Publisher: Sopris West.

a) STAGE I.

Scores: 2 rankings: Internalizing, Externalizing.

Time: (30–45) minutes.

Comments: Rankings by teacher.

b) STAGE II.

Scores, 6: 3 scores: Total Critical Events, Total Adaptive Behavior, Total Maladaptive Behavior in two areas: Internalizing, Externalizing.

Time: (30–45) minutes.

Comments: Ratings by teachers.

c) STAGE III.

Scores, 11: Academic Engaged Time (Total); Peer Social Behavior (Social Engagement, Participation, Parallel Play, Alone, No Code, Social Interaction, Negative Interaction, Positive Interaction, Total Positive Behavior, Total Negative Behavior).

Administration: Individual and group.

Time: (60–90) minutes.

Comments: Observations by trained staff member.

Cross References: For reviews by Mary Lou Kelley and by Leland C. Zlomke and Robert Spies, see 13:313.

TEST REFERENCE

1. MacMillan, D. L., Gresham, F. M., Lopez, M. F., & Bocian, K. M. (1996). Comparison of students nominated for prereferral interventions by ethnicity and gender. *The Journal of Special Education, 30,* 133–151.

[2608]

Systems Analysis Aptitude Test.

Purpose: "Measures aptitude for business systems design using a real-life problem."

Population: Applicants for computer systems analyst position.

Publication Dates: 1973.

Acronym: SAAT.

Administration: Group.

Restricted Distribution: Restricted to employers of systems analysts, not available to school personnel.

Price Data, 1999: $455 per candidate.

Time: (240) minutes.

Comments: Detailed report on system designed by each candidate; test previously listed as Wolfe Systems Analysis Aptitude Test.

Author: Jack M. Wolfe.

Publisher: Rose Wolfe.

[2609]

Systems Programming Aptitude Test.

Purpose: "To evaluate the aptitude and potential of systems programming candidates of all experience levels, for work in all types of systems programming tasks."

Population: Systems programmers.

Publication Dates: 1979.

Acronym: SPAT.

Administration: Group.

Price Data, 1999: $430 per person.

Time: Untimed.

Comments: Detailed report provided on each candidate.

Author: Jack M. Wolfe.

Publisher: Rose Wolfe.

Cross References: For reviews by Samuel Juni and David Marshall, see 10:356.

[2610]

T.A. Survey.

Purpose: "Evaluates an individual's trust attitudes which predict trust performance."

Population: Employees.

Publication Dates: 1970-1981.

Scores: Total score only.

Administration: Group or individual.

Price Data, 1990: $7.50 or less per 25 surveys; $5 per year license fee.
Time: (15) minutes.
Comments: Also called Trustworthiness Attitude Survey.
Authors: Alan L. Strand and others.
Publisher: Predictive Surveys Corporation.
Cross References: For reviews by John K. Butler, Jr. and Denise M. Rousseau, see 9:1223.

[2611]

Tapping Students' Science Beliefs: A Resource for Teaching and Learning.

Purpose: Designed to "assess the belief students have about certain natural phenomena and permits appropriate learning experiences to be planned."
Population: Primary grade level students.
Publication Date: 1993.
Acronym: TSSB.
Scores, 5: Skateboard News, What Happened Last Night, The Day We Cooked Pancakes in School, Children's Week, Our School Garden.
Administration: Group.
Price Data, 1993: A$90 per complete kit including manual (77 pages), 5 unit tests with 1 student score sheet and 1 group profile sheet per unit.
Time: (30) minutes per unit.
Authors: Brian Doig and Ray Adams.
Publisher: Australian Council for Educational Research Ltd. [Australia].
Cross References: For reviews by Jerrilyn V. Andrews and James P. Van Haneghan, see 13:314.

[2612]

The Tapping Test: A Predictor of Typing and Other Tapping Operations.

Purpose: Measures the student's ability to learn typing.
Population: High school.
Publication Dates: 1959-1970.
Acronym: TARC.
Scores: Total score only.
Administration: Group.
Price Data, 1998: $1.50 per sample test including felt dots and paint sets; $16 per set of 25 tests, felt dots, and paints; $4 shipping charge.
Time: [30] minutes.
Authors: John C. Flanagan, Grace Fivars (manual), Shirley A. Tuska (manual), and Carol F. Hershey (manual).
Publisher: Grace Fivars.
Cross References: See T2:796 (3 references); for reviews by Ray G. Price and Henry Weitz, see 6:52 (2 references).

[2613]

Target Mathematics Tests.

Purpose: Designed "to provide achievement tests which reflect the content of the National Curriculum in Mathematics" in Great Britain.
Population: Levels 2–5, 2–6.
Publication Date: 1993.
Scores: Total score only.
Administration: Group.
Forms, 2: Test 4, Test 5.
Price Data, 1999: £8.50 per 20 test booklets (specify test); £7.99 per manual; £8.99 per specimen set.
Time: [30] minutes.
Author: D. Young.
Publisher: Hodder & Stoughton Educational [England].

[2614]

Tasks of Emotional Development Test.

Purpose: Assesses "the emotional and social adjustment of children" by means of projective techniques.
Population: Ages 6-11, 12-18.
Publication Dates: 1960-1971.
Acronym: TED.
Scores: LATENCY: 5 scores: (Perception, Outcome, Affect, Motivation, Spontaneity) in each of 12 areas (Peer Socialization, Trust, Aggression Toward Peers, Attitudes For Learning, Respect For Property of Others, Separation From Mother Figure, Identification With Same-Sex Parent, Acceptance of Siblings, Acceptance of Need-Frustration, Acceptance of Parents' Affection to One Another, Orderliness and Responsibility, Self-Image); ADOLESCENCE: 5 scores in each of 13 areas: Same as for Latency plus Heterosexual Socialization.
Administration: Individual.
Levels, 2: Latency (Ages 6-11); Adolescence (Ages 12-18).
Price Data: Available from publisher.
Time: [30-40] minutes.
Authors: Haskel Cohen and Geraldine Rickard Weil.
Publisher: Massachusetts School of Professional Psychology/T.E.D. Associates.
Cross References: See T4:2686 (1 reference); for excerpted reviews by Edward Earl Gates, C. H. Ammons, and R. B. Ammons, see 8:691 (7 references); see also T2:1517 (2 references) and P:481 (1 reference).

TEST REFERENCES

1. Steck, G. M., Anderson, S. A., & Boylin, W. M. (1992). Satanism among adolescents: Empirical and clinical considerations. *Adolescence, 27,* 901-914.
2. McCrone, E. R., Egeland, B., Kalkoske, M., & Carlson, E. A. (1994). Relations between early maltreatment and mental representations of relationships assessed with projective storytelling in middle childhood. *Development and Psychopathology, 6,* 99-120.

[2615]

TAT Analysis Sheet.

Purpose: "Tool to facilitate interpretation and analysis of the TAT protocol."
Population: Ages 4 and over.
Publication Date: 1974.
Scores, 19: Section I (Hero or Heroine, General Theme, Dependency Needs, Specific Drives, Views of Special Figures, Trends and Similarities), Section II (Depression, Mania, Paranoid Ideation, Antisocial Reaction, Schizoid Personality, Paranoid Personality, Anxiety, Conversion Reactions, Obsessive-Compulsive, Schizophrenia, Simple Schizophrenia, Paranoid Schizophrenia, Summary).
Administration: Individual.
Manual: No manual.
Price Data, 1989: $15 per 25 analysis forms; $4.50 per specimen set.
Time: (10-20) minutes.
Author: John A. Blazer.
Publisher: Psychologists and Educators, Inc.

[2616]

TAV Selection System.

Purpose: Constructed to measure "interpersonal reactions" for use in vocational selection and counseling.
Population: Adults.
Publication Dates: 1963-1968.
Acronym: TAV.
Administration: Group.
Price Data: Available from publisher.
Time: (180) minutes for the battery, (15-20) minutes for any one test.
Comments: Self-administered.
Author: R. R. Morman.
Publisher: TAV Selection System.

a) TAV ADJECTIVE CHECKLIST.
Scores, 3: Toward People (T), Away from People (A), Versus People (V).
b) TAV JUDGMENTS.
Scores, 3: Same as *a* above.
c) TAV PERSONAL DATA.
Scores, 3: Same as *a* above.
d) TAV PREFERENCES.
Scores, 3: Same as *a* above.
e) TAV PROVERBS AND SAYINGS.
Scores, 3: Same as *a* above.
f) TAV SALESMAN REACTIONS.
Scores, 3: Same as *a* above.
g) TAV MENTAL AGILITY.
Scores, 3: Follow Directions and Carefulness, Weights and Balances, Verbal Comprehension.

Cross References: For a review by Robert G. Demaree, see 8:986 (1 reference); see also T2:2113 (3 references); for an excerpted review by John O. Crites, see 7:983 (1 reference); see also P:263A (11 references).

[2617]

The Taylor-Helmstadter Pair Comparison Scale of Aesthetic Judgment.

Purpose: Constructed to assess aesthetic judgment.
Population: Ages 4 and over.
Publication Dates: 1973-1976.
Scores: Total score only.
Administration: Group.
Price Data: Available from publisher.
Time: [20-30] minutes.
Comments: Two carousel slide projectors necessary for administration.
Author: Anne P. Taylor.
Publisher: Anne P. Taylor.
Cross References: See T3:2395 (1 reference).

[2618]

Taylor-Johnson Temperament Analysis [1996 Edition].

Purpose: Designed to "measure a number of ... personality variables or attitudes and behavioral tendencies which influence personal, social, marital, parental, family, scholastic, and vocational adjustment."
Population: Ages 13 and up.
Publication Dates: 1941–1996.
Acronym: T-JTA.
Scores, 11: Nervous vs. Composed, Depressive vs. Light-Hearted, Active-Social vs. Quiet, Expressive-Responsive vs. Inhibited, Sympathetic vs. Indifferent, Subjective vs. Objective, Dominant vs. Submissive, Hostile vs. Tolerant, Self-Disciplined vs. Impulsive, Total, Attitude.
Administration: Group.
Forms, 4: Regular Edition (criss-cross and self-report forms); Form "S" for Adolescents (criss-cross and self-report).
Price Data, 1999: $236.50 per comprehensive kit (for handscoring); $92 per computer scoring package (for use with mail-in scoring service); $49 per secondary materials module; $85 per test manual; $36.50 per handbook.
Time: Untimed.
Comments: Can be used as a self-report questionnaire or as a tool for obtaining perceptions of another person (criss-cross form); Form S can be used with adolescents or with adults with poor reading skills; 1996 Edition based upon new norms.
Authors: Original edition by Roswell H. Johnson, revision by Robert M. Taylor, Lucile P. Morrison (manual), W. Lee Morrison (statistical consultant), and Richard C. Romoser (statistical consultant).
Publisher: Psychological Publications, Inc.
Cross References: For reviews by Jeffrey A. Jenkins and Barbara J. Kaplan of an earlier edition, see 13:315;

see also T4:2690 (3 references); for reviews by Cathy W. Hall and Paul McReynolds, see 10:357; see also T3:2396 (1 reference) and T2:840 (3 references); for a review by Robert F. Stahmann, see 8:692 (18 references); for a review by Donald L. Mosher of an earlier edition, see 7:572 (1 reference); see also P:264 (3 references) and 6:130 (10 references); for a review by Albert Ellis of the original edition, see 4:62 (6 references); for a review by H. Meltzer of the original edition, see 3:57.

[2619]

TD (Tardive Dyskinesia) Monitor.

Purpose: "Measures the presence and severity of the tardive dyskinesia movements."
Population: Patients receiving chronic neuroleptic maintenance.
Publication Date: 1999.
Acronym: TD Monitor.
Scores: Total score only.
Administration: Individual.
Price Data, 1999: $95 per complete kit including 25 Modified AIMS QuikScore™ forms, 25 Modified Webster QuikScore™ forms, 25 TD Monitor history forms, and manual; $20 per 25 QuikScore™ forms (specify Modified Webster or Modified AIMS); $30 per 25 history forms; $36 per manual; $40 per specimen set including 1 Modified AIMS QuikScore™ form, 1 Modified Webster QuikScore™ form, 1 history form, and manual.
Time: Administration time not reported.
Comments: Includes the Modified Webster and centers around the Modified Abnormal Involuntary Movement Scale.
Author: William M. Glazer.
Publisher: Multi-Health Systems, Inc.

[2620]

Teacher Assessment of Grammatical Structures.

Purpose: "Developed to evaluate a child's understanding and use of the grammatical structures of English and to suggest a sequence for teaching these structures."
Population: Ages 2-4, 5-9, 9 and over.
Publication Date: 1983.
Acronym: TAGS.
Scores: 3 ratings: Imitated, Prompted, Spontaneous Production.
Administration: Individual.
Price Data, 1998: $10 per 25 rating forms per level; $15 per manual (203 pages).
Time: Administration time not reported.
Comments: Ratings are based on informal administration in classroom or therapy setting.
Authors: Jean S. Moog and Victoria J. Kozak.
Publisher: Central Institute for the Deaf.

a) TAGS-P, PRE-SENTENCE LEVEL.
Population: Ages up to 6 years for hearing-impaired children, ages 2-4 for language-impaired children.
Comments: Assesses receptive and expressive skills.

b) TAGS-S, SIMPLE-SENTENCE LEVEL.
Population: Ages 5-9 years for hearing-impaired children, ages 3 and over for language-impaired children.
Comments: Assesses expressive skills.

c) TAGS-C, COMPLEX SENTENCE LEVEL.
Population: Ages 8 and over for hearing-impaired children, ages 3.5 and over for language-impaired children.

Cross References: See T4:2691 (1 reference); for reviews by Elizabeth M. Prather and Kenneth G. Shipley, see 10:358 (1 reference).

TEST REFERENCE

1. Schneiderman, E. (1995). The effectiveness of an interactive instructional context. *American Annals of the Deaf, 140,* 8–15.

[2621]

A Teacher Attitude Inventory: Identifying Teacher Positions in Relation to Educational Issues and Decisions.

Purpose: Designed as an "Indicator of teacher attitudes regarding philosophical issues and contrasting educational practices."
Population: Teachers.
Publication Date: 1986.
Acronym: TAI.
Scores, 5: Controlling, Rigidity, Individualism, Professionalism, Total.
Administration: Group.
Price Data: Not available.
Time: (10-15) minutes.
Comments: For evaluation and research purposes.
Authors: Joanne Rand Whitmore.
Publisher: United/DOK Publishers [No reply from publisher; status unknown].
Cross References: For reviews by Mary Henning-Stout and Sylvia Rosenfield, see 10:359.

[2622]

Teacher Observation Scales for Identifying Children with Special Abilities.

Purpose: Designed as an assessment instrument for identifying gifted children, tailored to be culturally appropriate for use in New Zealand.
Population: Junior and middle primary school.
Publication Date: 1996.

Scores, 5: Learning Characteristics, Social Leadership Characteristics, Creative Thinking Characteristics, Self-Determination Characteristics, Motivational Characteristics.
Administration: Individual.
Price Data, 1996: NZ$12.50 per 20 observation scales; $12.50 per teacher's handbook (9 pages).
Time: Administration time not reported.
Authors: Don McAlpine and Neil Reid.
Publisher: New Zealand Council for Educational Research [New Zealand].

[2623]

Teacher Opinion Inventory, Revised Edition.

Purpose: To assess teachers' opinions concerning many facets of the school, to "compile teachers' recommendations for improvement," and to provide "data to guide the school's professional staff in decision making relative to program development."
Population: Elementary and secondary school teachers.
Publication Dates: 1975-1995.
Scores: 4 subscales: Quality of the Instructional Program, Support for Student Learning, School Climate/Environment for Learning, School Organization and Administration.
Administration: Group.
Parts, 2: A (Likert-scale items), B (customize up to 20 local questions).
Price Data, 1998: $15 per 25 inventories; $6.50 per Administrator's Manual ('95, 26 pages).
Time: Untimed.
Author: National Study of School Evaluation.
Publisher: National Study of School Evaluation.

[2624]

Teacher Opinionaire on Democracy.

Purpose: Intended as "an objective measure of educational philosophy."
Population: Teachers.
Publication Date: 1949.
Scores: Total score only.
Administration: Group.
Forms, 2: G, H.
Price Data: Available from publisher.
Time: Administration time not reported.
Authors: Enola Ledbetter and Theodore F. Lentz.
Publisher: Lentz Peace Research Laboratory.
Cross References: See T2:901 (2 references); for reviews by George W. Hartmann and C. Robert Pace, see 4:805.

[2625]

Teacher Role Survey (Revised).

Purpose: "To measure teachers' expectancies for internal or external control of important aspects of the work of teaching."
Population: Elementary, secondary, or technical school teachers.
Publication Date: 1986.
Acronym: TRS.
Scores: 3 factors: Recognition, Teaching/Learning Process, Attitudes of Parents and Society.
Administration: Group.
Price Data: Not available.
Time: Administration time not reported.
Authors: Darrell E. Anderson and Wayne R. Maes.
Publisher: Wayne R. Maes [No reply from publisher; status unknown].
Cross References: See T4:2696 (1 reference); for a review by Susan J. Schenck, see 10:360.

[2626]

Teacher Values Inventory.

Purpose: Measures "teacher's preferences and opinions."
Population: Teachers.
Publication Dates: 1980-1981.
Acronym: TVI.
Scores, 6: Theoretical, Economic, Aesthetic, Social, Political, Religious.
Administration: Group.
Price Data: Available from publisher.
Foreign Language Edition: Hindi version also available.
Time: Administration time not reported.
Authors: Harbhajan L. Singh and S. P. Ahluwalia.
Publisher: National Psychological Corporation [India].

[2627]

Teacher's Handbook of Diagnostic Inventories, Second Edition.

Purpose: Developed "to assess the learning needs of individual students."
Population: Grades K-8.
Publication Dates: 1974-1979.
Scores: 4 areas: Spelling, Reading, Handwriting, Arithmetic.
Administration: Individual.
Price Data: Available from publisher.
Authors: Philip H. Mann, Patricia A. Suiter, and Rose Marie McClung.
Publisher: Allyn & Bacon.

[2628]

Teacher's Handbook of Diagnostic Screening, Second Edition.

Purpose: Provides teachers with a series of screening tests to facilitate the assessment of readiness and the identification of preferred learning modalities.

Population: Ages 4, 6, and over.
Publication Dates: 1974-1979.
Scores: 18 areas: Visual Motor, Visual Figure-Ground, Visual Discrimination, Visual Closure, Visual Memory, Auditory Discrimination, Auditory Closure, Auditory Memory (Sentences), Alphabet-Speech (Auditory-Visual Association), Visual Language Classification, Visual Language Association, Auditory Language Classification, Auditory Language Association, Manual Language Expression, Speech, Verbal Language Expression, Written Language Expression, Non-Verbal Language.
Administration: Individual.
Price Data: Available from publisher.
Comments: 2 levels; one form used for both levels.
Authors: Philip H. Mann, Patricia A. Suiter, and Rose Marie McClung.
Publisher: Allyn & Bacon.
Cross References: For a review by J. Manuel Casas, see 9:1229.

[2629]

Teaching Resource and Assessment of Critical Skills.

Purpose: Designed to assist decision making about an individual's skills and potential to live in an unsupervised setting.
Population: People with special needs.
Publication Date: 1989.
Acronym: TRACS.
Scores: Unscored.
Administration: Individual.
Price Data, 1998: $124 per program including resource, assessment and skill log booklets, user's guide (49 pages), master forms, and audio tape.
Time: Administration time not reported.
Authors: Lauren Meiklejohn and Mark Rice.
Publisher: Program Development Associates.

[2630]

Team Competency Assessment.

Purpose: Designed to "evaluate the level at which a team is performing on ten team competencies."
Population: Team members.
Publication Date: Not dated.
Scores, 11: Committing to a Team Approach, Communicating Effectively Within Teams, Utilizing Team Member Abilities, Resolving Team Conflicts, Creating a Shared Team Purpose, Planning for Results, Making Meetings Work, Evaluating Team Process and Performance, Making Team Decisions by Consensus, Solving Team Problems, Climate.
Administration: Group.
Price Data, 1997: $25 per assessment disk; $69.95 per administrator's manual (includes reporting diskette); $10 per performance skills team preview.
Time: Administration time not reported.
Comments: A 65-item questionnaire; can be computer administered, scored, and interpreted (requiring IBM Windows compatible) or available in pencil-paper format; can be used separately or as one component of a team skills workshop.
Author: Human Technology, Inc.
Publisher: Human Resource Development Press.

[2631]

Team-Development Inventory.

Purpose: "A means by which work-team members can give each other feedback concerning how they are working together."
Population: Work-team members.
Publication Date: 1982.
Acronym: TDI.
Scores, 8: Each team member rank orders all members on 8 dimensions: Participation, Collaboration, Flexibility, Sensitivity, Risk Taking, Commitment, Facilitation, Openness.
Administration: Group.
Price Data, 1990: $69.95 per kit including 10 instruments, 10 handouts, and facilitator's guide (16 pages).
Time: (35-50) minutes.
Author: John E. Jones.
Publisher: Jossey-Bass/Pfeiffer.

[2632]

Team Development Survey.

Purpose: A brief assessment tool for work teams.
Population: Work team members.
Publication Date: 1992.
Acronym: TDS.
Scores, 12: Clear Purpose, Informality, Participation, Listening, Civilized Disagreement, Consensus Decisions, Open Communication, Clear Roles and Work Assignments, Shared Leadership, External Relations, Style Diversity, Self-Assessment.
Administration: Group.
Price Data, 1993: $40 per complete kit including leader's guide (18 pages), scoring form, and 10 team member surveys.
Time: Administration time not reported.
Author: Glenn M. Parker.
Publisher: XICOM.
Cross References: For reviews by Gregory J. Cizek and Lynn R. Offermann, see 13:316.

[2633]

Team Effectiveness and Meeting Strategy.

Purpose: "Designed to evaluate the effectiveness of group process."
Population: Groups or teams.

Publication Date: 1977.
Acronym: T.E.A.M.S.
Scores, 18: Skill Factors (Situation Analysis, Purpose and Objectives, Identifying Problems, Generating Alternatives, Evaluating Alternatives and Selection of Solutions, Making Decisions), Quality Factors (Role and Task Definition, Emphasizing Facts, Standards, Judgment, Verification, Total), Acceptance Factors (Group Involvement and Participation, Your Effort Counts, Support Climate, Trust Level, Commitment Level, Total).
Administration: Group.
Price Data: Available from publisher.
Time: [30-60] minutes.
Comments: Ratings by individuals and group of team effectiveness.
Authors: Norman R. F. Maier, J. Clayton Lafferty, Glenn J. Morris, and Janice E. Brown.
Publisher: Human Synergistics.
Cross References: For a review by Lyle F. Schoenfeldt, see 10:361.

[2634]

Team Effectiveness Survey.

Purpose: Designed to assess process issues associated with team dynamics.
Population: Team members.
Publication Dates: 1968-1986.
Acronym: TES.
Scores: 4 scores for each team member: Exposure, Feedback, Defensive, Supportive, plus Total Team Effectiveness score.
Administration: Group.
Price Data, 1991: $6.95 per test booklet/manual.
Time: Administration time not reported.
Author: Jay Hall.
Publisher: Teleometrics International.
Cross References: For reviews by Gregory H. Dobbins and Harrison G. Gough, see 12:388; for a review by William G. Mollenkopf of an earlier version, see 8:1055.

[2635]

The Team Leadership Practices Inventory.

Purpose: Focuses on the behaviors and actions of high-performing teams and self-directed work groups.
Population: Managers.
Publication Date: 1992.
Acronym: LPI.
Scores, 15: 3 scores: Self-Average, Team-Average, Total in each of 5 areas: Challenging the Process, Inspiring a Shared Vision, Enabling Others to Act, Modeling the Way, Encouraging the Heart.
Administration: Group.
Price Data, 1993: $34.95 per trainer's package including 3 booklets, self-assessment, and observer and trainer's manual (47 pages); $59.95 per deluxe trainer's package including the leadership challenge, self-assessment and analysis, and trainer's manual; $195 per IBM scoring program including manual (12 pages); $8.95 per instrument and participant's manual.
Time: (20–140) minutes.
Comments: Self-scored inventory.
Authors: James M. Kouzes and Barry Z. Posner.
Publisher: Jossey-Bass/Pfeiffer.
Cross References: For reviews by Jeffrey B. Brookings and William J. Waldron, see 13:317.

[2636]

Team Process Diagnostic.

Purpose: To analyze and classify group processes according to their implications for member and team effectiveness.
Population: Individuals whose work responsibilities require work-team cooperation.
Publication Date: 1974-1989.
Scores: 9 clusters in 3 modes: Problem Solving (Integrative, Content-Bound, Process-Bound), Fight (Perceptual Difference, Status-Striving, Frustration), Flight (Fear, Indifference, Powerlessness).
Administration: Group.
Price Data, 1990: $6.95 per manual ('89, 21 pages).
Time: Administration time not reported.
Comments: Team associate ratings, self ratings, self scored.
Authors: Jay Hall.
Publisher: Teleometrics International.
Cross References: For a review by Lawrence A. Aleamoni, see 11:416.

[2637]

Teamness Index.

Purpose: To "survey ... conditions of work and the array of feelings that might exist among two or more people as they seek to work together."
Population: Individuals whose work responsibilities require work-team cooperation.
Publication Date: 1988.
Scores: Item scores only.
Administration: Group.
Price Data, 1990: $6.95 per manual (12 pages).
Time: Administration time not reported.
Comments: Self-ratings; self-scored.
Authors: Jay Hall.
Publisher: Teleometrics International.
Cross References: For reviews by Barbara Lachar and Frederick T. L. Leong, see 11:417.

[2638]

Teamwork Appraisal Survey.

Purpose: To assess "an associate's feelings about working in teams and the behaviors he or she employs in work-team situations."

Population: Individuals whose work responsibilities require work-team cooperation.
Publication Date: 1987.
Acronym: TAS.
Scores, 5: Synergistic, Compromise, Win-Lose, Yield-Lose, Lose-Leave.
Administration: Group.
Price Data, 1990: $6.95 per manual (24 pages).
Time: Administration time not reported.
Comment: Based on Team Behaviors Model of analysis of individual behaviors in a team setting; work associates rate each other's behavior.
Authors: Jay Hall.
Publisher: Teleometrics International.

[2639]

Technical Personnel Recruiting Inventory.

Purpose: Intended for use in research and development within industrial organizations; also for use in hiring.
Population: Research, engineering, and scientific firms.
Publication Dates: 1959-1960.
Scores: Item scores only.
Administration: Group.
Price Data: Available from publisher.
Author: Morris I. Stein.
Publisher: The Mews Press.

a) INDIVIDUAL QUALIFICATION FORM.
Population: Supervisors.
Comments: For description of available position.

b) PERSONAL DATA FORM FOR SCIENTIFIC, ENGINEERING, AND TECHNICAL PERSONNEL.
Population: Job applicants.

c) STEIN SURVEY FOR ADMINISTRATORS.
Population: Administrators.
Time: (30-40) minutes.
Comments: Description of company's research environment; also part of Surveys of Research Administration and Environment.

Cross References: For additional information, see 6:1167.

[2640]

Technical Support Staff Selector.

Purpose: To measure knowledge and aptitude for technical support positions.
Population: Candidates for the position of technical support.
Publication Date: 1994.
Acronym: TECHSUP.
Scores: Total score only.
Administration: Group.
Price Data, 1999: $340 per candidate.
Time: (80) minutes.
Author: Bruce A. Winrow.
Publisher: Walden Personnel Performance, Inc.

[2641]

Technical Test Battery.

Purpose: "Designed for occupational selection and placement."
Population: Technical job applicants and incumbents entry level to professional.
Publication Date: 1990.
Acronym: TTB.
Scores: Total score only for each of 9 tests.
Administration: Individual or group.
Price Data: Available from publisher.
Comments: Subtests available as separates.
Author: Saville & Holdsworth Ltd.
Publisher: Saville & Holdsworth.

a) FOLLOWING INSTRUCTIONS (VTS1).
Time: 20(25) minutes.

b) NUMERICAL COMPUTATION (NT2).
Time: 10(15) minutes.

c) MECHANICAL COMPREHENSION (MT4).
Time: 15(20) minutes.

d) NUMERICAL ESTIMATION (NTS2).
Time: 10(15) minutes.

e) MECHANICAL COMPREHENSION (MTS3).
Time: 15(20) minutes.

f) FAULT FINDING (FTS4).
Time: 20(25) minutes.

g) DIAGRAMMATIC THINKING (DTS6).
Time: 20(25) minutes.

h) SPATIAL REASONING (ST7).
Time: 20(25) minutes.

i) DIAGRAMMATIC REASONING (DT8).
Time: 15(20) minutes.

Cross References: For a review by Sami Gulgoz, see 11:419.

[2642]

Technical Test Battery [British Edition].

Purpose: Assess vocational skills and abilities.
Population: Apprentice and technical personnel.
Publication Dates: 1979–1982.
Acronym: TTB.
Administration: Group.
Restricted Distribution: Persons who have completed the publisher's training course or members of the Division of Occupational Psychology of the British Psychological Society.
Price Data: Available from publisher.
Comments: Subtests available as separates.
Authors: David Hawkey, Peter Saville, Robert Page (MT4), and Gill Nyfield (manual).

Publisher: Saville & Holdsworth.

a) LEVEL 1.

Purpose: "Basic skills and comprehension."

Publication Dates: 1979-1981.

1) *Verbal Comprehension.*

Acronym: VT 1.

Time: 10(15) minutes.

2) *Numerical Computation.*

Acronym: NT 2.

Time: 10(15) minutes.

3) *Visual Estimation.*

Acronym: ET 3.

Time: 10(15) minutes.

4) *Mechanical Comprehension.*

Acronym: MT 4.

Time: 15(20) minutes.

b) LEVEL 2.

Purpose: "Higher older reasoning and analytical skills."

Publication Dates: 1979-1981.

1) *Verbal Reasoning.*

Acronym: VT 5.

Time: 10(15) minutes.

2) *Numerical Reasoning.*

Acronym: NT 6.

Time: 10(15) minutes.

3) *Spatial Reasoning.*

Acronym: ST 7.

Time: 20(25) minutes.

4) *Diagrammatic Reasoning.*

Acronym: DT 8.

Time: 15(20) minutes.

5) *Spatial Recognition (optional test for Levels 1 and 2).*

Acronym: ST 9.

Time: 15(20) minutes.

[2643]

Technician Electrical Test—Form A2.

Purpose: "To measure the knowledge and skills required for electrical jobs."

Population: Electrical workers and applicants for electrical jobs.

Publication Dates: 1987–1997.

Scores, 15: Motors, Digital Electronics, Analog Electronics, Schematics and Print Reading, Control Circuits, Power Supplies, Basic AC/DC Theory, Power Distribution, Test Instruments, Mechanical, Computers and PLC, Hand and Power Tools, Electrical Maintenance, Mobile Equipment Operation, Total.

Administration: Group.

Price Data, 1998: $498 per 10 reusable test booklets, administration manual ('97, 14 pages), scoring key, and 100 blank answer sheets.

Time: (120) minutes.

Author: Roland T. Ramsay.

Publisher: Ramsay Corporation.

Cross References: For reviews by John Geisler and Keith Hattrup, see 13:318.

[2644]

Technician Mechanical Test—Form A2.

Purpose: Measures "knowledge and skill in the mechanical area."

Population: Mechanical workers and applicants for mechanical jobs.

Publication Dates: 1987–1997.

Scores, 12: Hydraulics, Pneumatics, Print Reading, Welding, Power Transmissions, Lubrication, Pumps, Piping, Rigging, Mechanical Maintenance, Shop Machines/Tools and Equipment, Total.

Administration: Group.

Price Data, 1998: $498 per 10 reusable test booklets, administration manual ('97, 16 pages), scoring key, and 100 blank answer sheets.

Time: (120) minutes.

Author: Roland T. Ramsay.

Publisher: Ramsay Corporation.

Cross References: For a review by William M. Verdi, see 13:219.

[2645]

Technology and Internet Assessment.

Purpose: Designed to determine strengths and weaknesses in eight areas related to computer, Internet, and information skills.

Population: Middle school, high school, and college students, potential and existing employees.

Publication Date: 1999.

Acronym: TIA.

Scores, 8: Use of Technology, Specific Computer Skills, Acquisition of Technology Knowledge, Basic Internet Knowledge, Internet Information Skills, Adapting to Technological Change, Impact of Technology, Ethics of Technology.

Administration: Individual or group.

Price Data, 1999: $3 per test (100 copies or less); $2.50 per test (over 100 copies); user's manual free.

Time: (20–30) minutes.

Comments: Administration and results via World Wide Web.

Author: Michael Ealy.

Publisher: H & H Publishing Co., Inc.

[2646]

Telemarketing Staff Selector.

Purpose: To evaluate the necessary knowledge and skills needed for the position of telemarketing representative.

Population: Candidates for the position of telemarketing representative.

Publication Date: 1997.

Scores: Total score only.

Administration: Group.
Price Data, 1999: $355 per candidate.
Time: (81) minutes.
Author: Walden Personnel Performance, Inc.
Publisher: Walden Personnel Performance, Inc.

[2647]

TEMAS (Tell-Me-A-Story).

Purpose: Identifies "both strengths and deficits in cognitive, affective, and intrapersonal and interpersonal functioning."
Population: Ages 5-18.
Publication Dates: 1986-1988.
Acronym: TEMAS.
Scores, 34: Quantitative Scales (Cognitive Functions [Reaction Time, Total Time, Fluency, Total Omissions], Personality Functions [Interpersonal Relations, Aggression, Anxiety/Depression, Achievement Motivation, Delay of Gratification, Self-Concept, Sexual Identity, Moral Judgment, Reality Testing], Affective Functions [Happy, Sad, Angry, Fearful]), Qualitative Indicators (Affective Functions [Neutral, Ambivalent, Inappropriate Affect], Cognitive Functions [Conflict, Sequencing, Imagination, Relationships, Total Transformations, Inquiries, Omissions and Transformations scores for each of the following: Main Character, Secondary Character, Event, Setting]).
Administration: Individual.
Forms, 2: Short, Long.
Versions, 2: Minority, Nonminority.
Price Data, 1999: $260 per complete kit including nonminority stimulus cards ('86, 36 cards), minority stimulus cards ('86, 36 cards), 25 record booklets, administration instruction card, and manual ('88, 166 pages); $89 per set of stimulus cards; $17.50 per 25 record booklets; $9.50 per administration instruction card; $62.50 per manual.
Time: (45-60) minutes (short form); (120) minutes (long form).
Authors: Giuseppe Costantino, Robert G. Malgady (manual and record booklet), and Lloyd H. Rogler (manual).
Publisher: Western Psychological Services.
Cross References: See T4:2716 (1 reference); for a review by William Steve Lang, see 11:422.

TEST REFERENCES

1. Costantino, G., Malgady, R. G., Casullo, M. M., & Castillo, A. (1991). Cross-cultural standardization of TEMAS in three Hispanic subcultures. *Hispanic Journal of Behavioral Sciences, 13,* 48–62.
2. Ireland, M. (1997). Death anxiety and self-esteem in young children with AIDS: A sense of hope. *Omega, 36,* 131–145.

[2648]

Temperament Comparator.

Purpose: "Designed to assess the relatively permanent temperament traits which are characteristic of an individual's behavior."
Population: Managers, supervisors, salespeople, and other higher-level professionals.
Publication Dates: 1958-1996.
Acronym: TC.
Scores, 15: Trait Scores (Calm, Cautious, Decisive, Demonstrative, Composed, Even-Tempered, Persevering, Seeks Company, Self-Confident, Serious, Steady Worker, Talkative), Factor Scores (Extroversive/Impulsive vs. Introvertive/Cautious, Emotionally Responsive vs. Non-Emotionally Controlled, Self-Reliant/Self-Oriented vs. Dependent/Group Oriented).
Administration: Individual or group.
Price Data, 1998: $75 per start-up kit including 25 test booklets, 25 score sheets, and interpretation and research manual; $44 per 25 test booklets (quantity discounts available); $19.75 per 25 score sheets; $19.75 per interpretation and research manual.
Time: No limit (approximately 15 minutes).
Author: Melany E. Baehr.
Publisher: NCS (Rosemont).
Cross References: For reviews by Paul M. Muchinsky and Aharon Tziner, see 9:1234; see also T2:1413 (1 reference); for reviews by Lawrence J. Stricker and Robert L. Thorndike, see 6:187 (1 reference).

TEST REFERENCE

1. Baehr, M. E., & Orban, J. A. (1989). The role of intellectual abilities and personality characteristics in determining success in higher-level positions. *Journal of Vocational Behavior, 35,* 270-287.

[2649]

Temperament Inventory.

Purpose: Designed to measure a set of four genetically determined temperaments.
Population: College and adults.
Publication Dates: 1977-1980.
Acronym: TI.
Scores, 4: Phlegmatic, Sanguine, Choleric, Melancholy.
Administration: Group.
Price Data: Available from publisher.
Foreign Language Editions: French, German, Spanish, Portuguese, and Afrikaans editions available.
Time: Administration time not reported.
Authors: Robert J. Cruise, W. Peter Blitchington, and W. G. A. Futcher (manual).
Publisher: Andrews University Press.

a) [GROUP EDITION].
Publication Date: 1977.

b) UNDERSTANDING YOUR TEMPERAMENT.
Publication Date: 1979.
Comments: For self-administering, self-scoring, and self-interpreting the scores from a Christian viewpoint.

Cross References: For reviews by Allan L. Lavoie and Paul McReynolds, see 9:1235 (1 reference); see also T3:2411 (1 reference).

[2650]

Temple University Short Syntax Inventory [Revised].

Purpose: Designed to obtain descriptive information about selected aspects of delayed language.
Population: Ages 3-0 to 4-11.
Publication Dates: 1984-1988.
Acronym: TUSSI.
Administration: Individual.
Price Data, 1992: $44 per complete kit including manual ('84, 29 pages).
Authors: Adele Gerber, Henry Goehl, and Reinhart Heuer (Diagnostic and Screening Test Supplementary Manual).
Publisher: Slosson Educational Publications, Inc.

a) TEMPLE UNIVERSITY SHORT SYNTAX INVENTORY.
Scores, 3: Imitated Response Errors, Elicited Response Errors, Total Errors.
Price Data: $14.95 per 25 scoring sheets/test forms.
Time: (10-15) minutes.

b) TUSSI DIAGNOSTIC AND SCREENING TESTS.
Scores: Total Errors.
Price Data: $12 per supplementary manual ('88, 12 pages) and 25 supplementary test forms; $5 per 25 supplementary test forms.
Time: (2-3) minutes.

Cross References: For reviews by Steven H. Long and Rebecca J. McCauley, see 12:389.

[2651]

Templin-Darley Tests of Articulation, Second Edition.

Purpose: Designed to evaluate articulation proficiency and to identify articulation errors.
Population: Ages 3 and over.
Publication Dates: 1960–1969.
Acronym: TDTA.
Administration: Individual.
Price Data, 1994: $10 per specimen set including test form, scoring overlays, and manual; $.15 per test form; $3 per set of scoring overlays; $7 per manual.
Time: Untimed.
Authors: Mildred C. Templin and Frederic L. Darley.
Publisher: The University of Iowa, Publications Order Service.

a) TEMPLIN-DARLEY SCREENING AND DIAGNOSTIC TESTS OF ARTICULATION.
Population: Ages 3-8.
Publication Date: 1960.
Scores: 2 tests: Screening Test, Total Diagnostic Test.

b) TEMPLIN-DARLEY TESTS OF ARTICULATION [SECOND EDITION].
Population: Ages 3 and over.
Publication Dates: 1960-1969.
Scores, 10: Screening Test, Consonant Singles—Initial and Final, Vowels, Diphthongs and Combination, Clusters (4 scores), Iowa Pressure Articulation Test, Total Diagnostic Test.

Cross References: See T4:2722 (18 references), T3:2412 (14 references), and T2:2095 (8 references); for a review by Raphael M. Haller of *b*, see 7:972 (16 references); for excerpted reviews by Harry Hollien and Al Knox of *a*, see 6:315 (9 references).

TEST REFERENCES

1. Andrews, N., & Fey, M. E. (1986). Analysis of the speech of phonologically impaired children in two sampling conditions. *Language, Speech, and Hearing Services in Schools, 17,* 187–198.
2. Lowe, R. J. (1986). Phonological process analysis using three position tests. *Language, Speech, and Hearing Services in Schools, 17,* 72–79.
3. Westman, M. J., & Broen, P. A. (1989). Preschool screening for predictive articulation errors. *Language, Speech, and Hearing Services in Schools, 20,* 139–148.
4. Felsenfeld, S., Broen, P. A., & McGue, M. (1992). A 28-year follow-up of adults with a history of moderate phonological disorder: Linguistic and personality results. *Journal of Speech and Hearing Research, 35,* 1114–1125.
5. Garn-Nunn, P. G., & Martin, V. (1992). Using conventional articulation tests with highly unintelligible children: identification and programming concerns. *Language, Speech, and Hearing Services in Schools, 23,* 52–60.
6. Washington, J. A., & Craig, H. K. (1992). Articulation test performances of low-income, African-American preschoolers with communication impairments. *Language, Speech, and Hearing Services in Schools, 23,* 203–207.
7. Weiss, A. L., & Zebrowski, P. M. (1992). Disfluencies in the conversations of young children who stutter: Some answers about questions. *Journal of Speech and Hearing Research, 35,* 1230–1238.
8. Craig, C. H., Kim, B. W., Rhyner, P. M. P., & Chirillo, T. K. B. (1993). Effects of word predictability, child development, and aging on time-gated speech recognition performance. *Journal of Speech and Hearing Research, 36,* 832–841.
9. Crary, M. A., & Tallman, V. L. (1993). Production of linguistic prosody by normal and speech-disordered children. *Journal of Communication Disorders, 26,* 245–262.
10. Elfenbein, J. L., Small, A. M., & Davis, J. M. (1993). Developmental patterns of duration discrimination. *Journal of Speech and Hearing Research, 36,* 842–849.
11. Elliot, L. L., & Hammer, M. A. (1993). Fine-grained auditory discrimination: Factor structures. *Journal of Speech and Hearing Research, 36,* 396–409.
12. Marion, M. J., Sussman, H. M., & Marquardt, T. P. (1993). The perception and production of rhyme in normal and developmentally apraxic children. *Journal of Communication Disorders, 26,* 129–160.
13. Sturner, R. A., Heller, J. H., Funk, S. G., & Layton, T. L. (1993). The Fluharty Preschool Speech and Language Screening Test: A population-based validation study using sample-independent decision rules. *Journal of Speech and Hearing Research, 36,* 738–745.
14. Felsenfeld, S., Broen, P. A., & McGue, M. (1994). A 28-year follow-up of adults with a history of moderate phonological disorder: Educational and Occupational results. *Journal of Speech and Hearing, 37,* 1341–1353.
15. Liederman, J., & Flannery, K. A. (1994). Fall conception increases the risk of neurodevelopmental disorder in offspring. *Journal of Clinical and Experimental Neuropsychology, 16,* 754-768.
16. Windsor, J., Doyle, S. S., & Siegel, G. M. (1994). Language acquisition after mutism: A longitudinal case study of autism. *Journal of Speech and Hearing Research, 37,* 96–105.
17. Flannery, K. A., & Liederman, J. (1995). Is there really a syndrome involving the co-occurrence of neurodevelopmental disorder, talent, non-right handedness and immune disorder among children? *Cortex, 31,* 503–515.
18. Ruscello, D. M., Yanero, D., & Ghalichebuf, M. (1995). Cooperative service delivery between a university clinic and a school system. *Language, Speech, and Hearing Services in Schools, 26,* 273–277.
19. Kummer, A. W., & Lee, L. (1996). Evaluation and treatment of resonance disorders. *Language, Speech, and Hearing Services in Schools, 27,* 271–281.
20. Sabers, D. L. (1996). By their tests we will know them. *Language, Speech, and Hearing Services in Schools, 27,* 102–108.

[2652]

Tennessee Self-Concept Scale, Second Edition.

Purpose: Designed as a multidimensional self-concept assessment instrument.

Population: Ages 7 to 90.
Publication Dates: 1964–1996.
Acronym: TSCS: 2.
Scores, 15: Validity scores (Inconsistent Responding, Self-Criticism, Faking Good, Response Distribution); Summary scores (Total Self-Concept, Conflict); Self-Concept scales (Physical, Moral, Personal, Family, Social, Academic/Work); Supplementary scores (Identity, Satisfaction, Behavior).
Administration: Group.
Price Data, 1999: $135 per complete kit including 20 AutoScore™ answer forms (10 for adults and 10 for children), 4 prepaid mail-in answer sheets for computer scoring and interpretation (2 for adults and 2 for children), manual ('96, 141 pages), and a 2-use disk and 2 PC answer sheets for on-site computer scoring and interpretation; $32.50 per 20 AutoScore™ forms (specify Adult of Child); $11.50 per 10 Spanish Research edition answer sheets (specify Adult or Child); $13.50 per mail-in answer sheet (specify Adult or Child); $229 per 25-use disk (PC with Windows; specify Adult or Child form); $15 per 100 answer sheets for use with disk; $9.50 per FAX Service Scoring; $52.50 per manual.
Time: (10–20) minutes.
Comments: Self-administered; WPS TEST REPORT Service available for computerized scoring and test interpretation.
Authors: William H. Fitts and W. L. Warren.
Publisher: Western Psychological Services.

a) TSCS:2 ADULT FORM.
Population: Ages 13 and older.
b) TSCS:2 CHILD FORM.
Population: Ages 7–14.
c) TSCS:2 SHORT FORM.
Population: Adults (13 and older); child (7–14).
Comments: The Short Form consists of the first 20 items on the adult and child forms.

Cross References: For reviews by Ric Brown and John Hattie, see 13:320 (41 references); see also T4:2723 (32 references); for reviews by Francis X. Archambault, Jr. and E. Thomas Dowd, see 11:424 (89 references); see also 9:1236 (60 references), T3:2413 (120 references), 8:693 (384 references), and T2:1415 (80 references); for reviews by Peter M. Bentler and Richard M. Suinn and an excerpted review by John O. Crites of an earlier edition, see 7:151 (88 references); see also P:266 (30 references).

TEST REFERENCES

1. Campbell, J. C. (1989). A test of two explanatory models of women's responses to battering. *Nursing Research, 38,* 18–24.
2. Cullari, S., & Trubilla, R. S. (1989). Body-image distortion in normal-weight college women. *Perceptual and Motor Skills, 68,* 1195–1198.
3. Felsen, I., & Erlich, H. S. (1990). Identification patterns of offspring of Holocaust survivors with their families. *American Journal of Orthopsychiatry, 60,* 506–520.
4. Levy-Shiff, R., Bar, O., & Har-Even, D. (1990). Psychological adjustment of adoptive parents-to-be. *American Journal of Orthopsychiatry, 60,* 258–267.
5. Mock, V. (1993). Body image in women treated for breast cancer. *Nursing Research, 42,* 153–157.
6. Brayden, R. M., Deitrich-MacLean, G., Dietrich, M. S., & Sherrod, K. B. (1995). Evidence for specific effects of childhood sexual abuse on mental well-being and physical self-esteem. *Child Abuse & Neglect, 19,* 1255–1262.
7. Jackson, M. H., & Canada, R. (1995). Self-concept and math among potential school dropouts. *Journal of Instructional Psychology, 22,* 234–237.
8. Lefkowitz, D. M. (1995). Student offenders—a proactive counseling strategy. College Student Journal, 29, 427–429.
9. Abell, S. C., & Richards, m. H. (1996). The relationship between body shape satisfaction and self-esteem: An investigation of gender and class differences. *Journal of Youth and Adolescence, 25,* 691–703.
10. Bishop, S. L., Walling, D. P., & Walker, B. A. (1997). The emperor's clothes: Assessing the validity of score on the Tennessee Self-Concept Scale. *Educational and Psychological Measurement, 57,* 150–163.
11. Groth-Marnat, G., & Roberts, L. (1998). Human figure drawings and house tree person drawings as indictors of self-esteem: A quantitative approach. *Journal of Clinical Psychology, 54,* 219–222.
12. Tam, S-F. (1998). Comparing the self-concepts of persons with and without physical disabilities. *Journal of Psychology, 132, 78–86.*

[2653]

Tennis Skills Test Manual.

Purpose: Designed to assess essential skills needed to play tennis.
Population: High school and college.
Publication Date: 1989.
Scores, 3: Ground Stroke, Serve, Volley.
Administration: Individual.
Price Data, 1999: $14 per manual (50 pages).
Time: Administration time not reported.
Authors: Larry Hensley, Graham Hatcher, Gloria Hook, Paul Hook, Carolyn Lehr, and Jacqueline Shick.
Publisher: American Association for Active Lifestyles and Fitness.
Cross References: For reviews by Claude A. Sandy and William A. Stock, see 12:390; see also T4:2724 (1 reference).

[2654]

TerraNova.

Purpose: Constructed as a "comprehensive modular assessment series" of student achievement.
Population: Grades K–12.
Publication Date: 1997.
Administration: Group.
Levels, 12: 10, 11, 12, 13, 14, 15, 16, 17, 18, 19, 20, 21/22.
Price Data, 1997: $12.50 per practice activities (specify battery and level); $2.70 per directions for practice activities (specify battery and level); $25 per teacher's guide; $11.25 per additional test directions for teachers (specify battery and level); norms book available from publisher.
Foreign Language Edition: Available in English and in Spanish editions.
Time: Administration time varies by test and level.
Comments: Instruments may be administered alone or in any combination.
Author: CTB/McGraw-Hill.
Publisher: CTB/McGraw-Hill.

a) CTBS COMPLETE BATTERY AND COMPLETE BATTERY PLUS.
Population: Grades K–12.
Scores, 10: Complete Battery (Reading, Language Arts, Mathematics, Science, Social Studies), Complete Battery Plus (Word Analysis, Vocabulary, Language Mechanics, Spelling, Mathematics Computation).
Price Data: $115.50 per 30 Complete Battery consumable test booklets (specify level); $122 per 30 Complete Battery Plus consumable test booklets; $86 per 30 Complete Battery reusable test booklets (specify level); $92.50 per 30 Complete Battery Plus reusable test booklets (specify level); $30.75 per 50 reflective answer sheets (specify battery and level); $770 per 1,250 continuous foreign answer sheets (specify battery and level); $3.53 per student basic service scoring for Complete Battery; $3.80 per student basic service scoring for Complete Battery Plus.
b) CTBS BASIC BATTERY AND BASIC BATTERY PLUS.
Population: Grades K–12.
Scores, 8: Basic Battery (Reading, Language Arts, Mathematics), Basic Battery Plus (Word Analysis, Vocabulary, Language Mechanics, Spelling, Mathematics Computation).
Price Data: $108.15 per 30 Basic Battery consumable test booklets (specify level); $114.65 per 30 Basic Battery Plus consumable test booklets (specify level); $83.75 per 30 Basic Battery reusable test booklets (specify level); $90.25 per 30 Basic Battery Plus reusable test booklets (specify level); $30.75 per 50 reflective answer sheets (specify battery and level); $770 per 1,250 continuous form answer sheets (specify battery and level); $3.53 per student for Basic Battery basic service scoring; $3.80 per student for Basic Battery Plus basic service scoring.
c) CTBS SURVEY AND SURVEY PLUS.
Purpose: Designed as a norm-referenced measure of academic achievement.
Population: Grades 2–12.
Scores, 10: Survey (Reading, Language Arts, Mathematics, Science, Social Studies); Survey Plus (Word Analysis, Vocabulary, Language Mechanics, Spelling, Mathematics Computation).
Price Data: $103 per 30 Survey consumable test booklets (specify level); $109.50 per 30 Survey Plus consumable test booklets (specify level); $81.25 per 30 Survey reusable test booklets (specify level); $87.75 per 30 Survey Plus reusable test booklets (specify level); $30.75 per 50 reflective answer sheets (specify battery and level); $770 per 1,250 continuous form answer sheets (specify level); $3.37 per student for Survey basic service scoring; $3.64 per student for Survey Plus basic service scoring.
d) MULTIPLE ASSESSMENTS.
Purpose: Intended to assess academic achievement using "a combination of the selected-response items of the Survey edition and a section of constructed-response items that allow students to produce their own short and extended responses."
Population: Grades 1–12.
Scores, 5: Reading, Language Arts, Mathematics, Science, Social Studies.
Price Data: $125 per 30 consumable test booklets (specify level); $9.80 per student for basic service scoring.
e) SUPERA.
Purpose: Constructed as a "TerraNova Spanish edition."
Price Data: $13 per 30 practice activities (specify battery and level); $2.60 per directions for practice activities (specify battery and level); $24.25 per 30 locator tests (specify test and level); $21.50 per 50 locator answer sheets; $16.50 per SUPERA technical bulletin; $11.25 per SUPERA additional test directions for teachers (specify battery and level); $8.50 per locator manual.

1) *SUPERA Survey.*
Population: Grades 1–10.
Scores, 3: Reading, Language Arts, Mathematics.
Price Data: $103 per 30 consumable test booklets (specify level); $81.25 per 30 reusable test booklets (specify level); $30.75 per 50 answer sheets; $1,540 per 2,500 continuous feed answer sheets; $23.05 per 25 ScorEZE answer sheets; $2.83 per student for basic service scoring.

2) *SUPERA Multiple Assessments.*
Population: Grades 1–10.
Scores, 3: Reading, Language Arts, Mathematics.
Price Data: $87.50 per 30 consumable image-scorable test booklets (specify level); $6.35 per student for basic service scoring.

3) *SUPERA Plus.*
Population: Grades 1–10.
Scores, 5: Word Analysis, Language Mechanics, Vocabulary, Math Computation, Spelling.
Price Data: $30 per 30 test booklets (specify level); $30.75 per 50 answer sheets (specify regular or survey); $11.25 per manual (specify level).
Comments: Intended for use with either SUPERA Multiple Assessments or SUPERA Survey.

f) PERFORMANCE ASSESSMENTS.
Purpose: Constructed to "meet the needs of educators who wish to use context-based tasks or open-ended assessments."

Scores, 4: Communication Arts, Mathematics, Science, Social Studies.
Comments: Available only through contract with publisher; additional scores can be provided for broad competencies such as communication or problem solving.

[2655]

Test Anxiety Profile.

Purpose: Constructed to measure "how much anxiety a person generally experiences in different types of testing situations."
Population: Grades 9–12 and college.
Publication Date: 1980.
Acronym: TAP.
Scores, 12: 2 anxiety scores (Feeling of Anxiety, Thought Interference) for 6 different situations (Multiple Choice Test, Time-Limit Test, "Pop" Quiz, Essay Test, Giving Talk, Math Test).
Administration: Group.
Price Data: License to reproduce for Ph.D.s or Ed.D.s available from publisher.
Time: (20) minutes.
Authors: E. R. Oetting, C. W. Cole (test), and J. L. Deffenbacher (manual).
Publisher: E. R. Oetting (the author), Colorado State University.
Cross References: See T4:2725 (2 references); for reviews by Steven D. Brown and John P. Galassi, see 9:1237.

[2656]

Test Attitude Inventory.

Purpose: "Developed to measure individual differences in test anxiety as a situation-specific personality trait."
Population: High school and college students.
Publication Dates: 1977–1980.
Acronym: TAI.
Scores, 3: Worry, Emotionality, Total.
Administration: Group.
Price Data: Available from publisher.
Time: (5–10) minutes.
Comments: Self-report inventory of test anxiety; title of manual is Test Anxiety Inventory.
Authors: Charles D. Spielberger.
Publisher: Mind Garden.
Cross References: See T4:2726 (16 references); for reviews by John P. Galassi and Thomas R. Knapp, see 9:1238 (3 references); see also T3:2417 (2 references).

TEST REFERENCES

1. Bauermeister, J. J., Huergo, M., Garcia, C. I., & Otero, R. F. (1988). El inventario de autoevaluación sobre exámenes (IDASE) y su aplicabilidad a estudiantes de escuela secundaria. *Hispanic Journal of Behavioral Sciences, 10,* 21–37.
2. Zeidner, M., Klingman, A., & Papko, O. (1988). Enhancing students' test coping skills: Report of a psychological health education program. *Journal of Educational Psychology, 80,* 95–101.
3. El-Zahhar, N. E., & Hocevar, D. (1991). Cultural and sexual differences in test anxiety, trait anxiety and arousability. *Journal of Cross-Cultural Psychology, 22,* 238-249.
4. Head, L. Q., Engley, E., & Knight, C. B. (1991). The effects of trait anxiety on state anxiety and perception of test difficulty for undergraduates administered high and low difficulty tests. *Journal of Instructional Psychology, 18,* 65-68.
5. Shelton, D. M., & Mallinckrodt, B. (1991). Test anxiety, locus of control, and self-efficacy as predictors of treatment preference. *College Student Journal, 25,* 544-551.
6. Calvo, M. G., & Carreiras, M. (1993). Selective influence of test anxiety on reading processes. *British Journal of Psychology, 84,* 375-388.
7. Comunian, A. L. (1993). Anxiety, cognitive interference, and school performance of Italian children. *Psychological Reports, 73,* 747-754.
8. Gossette, R. L., & O'Brien, R. M. (1993). Efficacy of rational emotive therapy (RET) with children: A critical re-appraisal. *Journal of Behavior Therapy and Experimental Psychiatry, 24,* 15–25.
9. Rebeta, J. L., Brooks, C. I., O'Brien, J. P., & Hunter, G. A. (1993). Variations in trait-anxiety and achievement motivation of college students as a function of classroom seating position. *Journal of Experimental Education, 61,* 257–267.
10. Bauman, W., & Melnyk, W. T. (1994). A controlled comparison of eye movements and finger tapping in the treatment of test anxiety. *Journal of Behavior Therapy and Experimental Psychiatry, 25,* 29–33.
11. Comunian, A. L. (1994). Self-Consciousness Scale dimensions: An Italian adaptation. *Psychological Reports, 74,* 483-489.
12. Hall, R. H., & Sidio-Hall, M. A. (1994). The effect of student color coding of knowledge maps and test anxiety on student learning. *Journal of Experimental Education, 62,* 291–302.
13. Neely, D. L., Springston, F. J., & McCann, S. J. H. (1994). Does item order affect performance on multiple-choice exams? *Teaching of Psychology, 21,* 44-45.
14. Sanz, J., & Avia, M. D. (1994). Cognitive specificity in social anxiety and depression: Self-statements, self-focused attention, and dysfunctional attitudes. *Journal of Social and Clinical Psychology, 13,* 105–137.
15. Vispoel, W. D., & Coffman, D. D. (1994). Computerized-adaptive and self-adapted music listening tests: Psychometric features and motivational benefits. *Applied Measurement in Education, 7,* 25-51.
16. Vispoel, W. P., Rocklin, T. R., & Wang, T. (1994). Individual differences and test administration procedures: A comparison of fixed-item, computerized-adaptive, and self-adapted testing. *Applied Measurement in Education, 7,* 53-79.
17. Williams, J. E. (1994). Anxiety measurement: Construct validity and test performance. *Measurement and Evaluation in Counseling and Development, 27,* 302-307.
18. Bandalos, D. L., Yates, K., & Thorndike-Christ, T. (1995). Effects of math self-concept, perceived self-efficacy, and attributions for failure and success on test anxiety. *Journal of Educational Psychology, 87,* 611–623.
19. Rocklin, T. R., O'Donnell, A. M., & Holst, P. M. (1995). Effects and underlying mechanisms of self-adapted testing. *Journal of Educational Psychology, 87,* 103-116.
20. Giegl, M. L., & Rogers, W. T. (1996). A confirmatory factor analysis of the Text Anxiety Inventory using Canadian high school students. *Educational and Psychological Measurement, 56* 315–324.
21. Sapp, M. (1996). Three treatments for reducing the worry and emotionality components of test anxiety with undergraduate and graduate college students: Cognitive behavioral hypnosis, relaxation therapy, and supportive counseling. *Journal of College Student Development, 37,* 79–87.
22. Swanson, S., & Howell, C. (1996). Test anxiety in adolescents with learning disabilities and behavior disorders. *Exceptional Children, 62,* 389–397.
23. Zeidner, M. (1996). How do high school and college students cope with test situations. *British Journal of Educational Psychology, 66,* 115–128.
24. Roos, L. L., Wise, S. L., & Plake, B. S. (1997). The role of item feedback in self-adapted testing. *Educational and Psychological Measurement, 57,* 85–98.
25. Weist, M. D., Paskewitz, D. A., Jackson, C. Y., & Jones, D. (1998). Self-reported delinquent behavior and psychosocial functioning in inner-city teenagers: A brief report. *Child Psychiatry and Human Development, 28,* 241–248.

[2657]

Test for Auditory Comprehension of Language—Third Edition.

Purpose: Designed as a measure of receptive spoken vocabulary, grammar, and syntax.
Population: Ages 3-0 to 9-11.
Publication Dates: 1973–1999.
Acronym: TACL-3.
Scores, 4: Vocabulary, Grammatical Morphemes, Elaborated Phrases and Sentences, Total.
Administration: Individual.
Price Data, 1999: $234 per complete kit.
Time: (15–25) minutes.

Author: Elizabeth Carrow-Woolfolk.
Publisher: PRO-ED.
Cross References: See T4:2727 (20 references); for reviews by Nicholas W. Bankson and William O. Haynes of an earlier edition, see 10:363; see also T3:2472 (25 references); for reviews by John T. Hatten and Huberto Molina of an earlier edition, see 8:454 (6 references); see also T2:997A (2 references).

TEST REFERENCES

1. Fujiki, M., Brinton, B., & Dunton, S. (1987). A grammatical judgement screening test for young elementary school-aged children. *Language, Speech, and Hearing Services in Schools, 18,* 131–143.
2. Alessandri, S. M. (1991). Play and social behavior in maltreated preschoolers. *Development and Psychopathology, 3,* 191-205.
3. Rydell, P. J., & Mirenda, P. (1991). The effects of two levels of linguistic constraint on echolalia and generative language production in children with autism. *Journal of Autism and Developmental Disorders, 21*(2), 131-157.
4. Eiserman, W. D., Weber, C., & McCoun, M. (1992). Two alternative program models for serving speech disordered preschoolers: A second follow-up. *Journal of Communication Disorders, 25,* 77–106.
5. English, K. (1992). Clinical exchange: Sharing Test of Auditory Comprehension results with parents. *Language, Speech, and Hearing Services in Schools, 23,* 88–89.
6. Fey, M. E., Cleave, P. L., Long, S. H., & Hughes, D. L. (1993). Two approaches to the facilitation of grammar in children with language impairment: An experimental evaluation. *Journal of Speech and Hearing Research, 36,* 141–157.
7. Marion, M. J., Sussman, H. M., & Marquardt, T. P. (1993). The perception and production of rhyme in normal and developmentally apraxic children. *Journal of Communication Disorders, 26,* 129–160.
8. Sussman, J. E. (1993). Auditory processing in children's speech perception: Results of selective adaptation and discrimination tasks. *Journal of Speech and Hearing Research, 36,* 380–395.
9. Sussman, J. E. (1993). Perception of format transition cues to place of articulation in children with language impairments. *Journal of Speech and Hearing Research, 36,* 1286–1299.
10. Berhardt, B., & Stoel-Gammon, C. (1994). Nonlinear phonology: Introduction and clinical application. *Journal of Speech and Hearing Research, 37,* 123–143.
11. Bird, E. K., & Chapman, R. S. (1994). Sequential recall in individuals with Down Syndrome. *Journal of Speech and Hearing, 37,* 1369–1380.
12. Camarata, S. M., Nelson, K. E., & Camarata, M. N. (1994). Comparison of conversational-recasting and imitative procedures for training grammatical structures in children with specific language impairment. *Journal of Speech and Hearing, 37,* 1414–1423.
13. Cole, K. N., Mills, P. E., & Kelley, D. (1994). Agreement of assessment profiles used in cognitive referencing. *Language, Speech, and Hearing Services in Schools, 25,* 25–31.
14. Connell, P. J., & Stone, C. A. (1994). The conceptual basis for morpheme learning problems in children with specific language impairment. *Journal of Speech and Hearing Research, 37,* 389–398.
15. Fey, M. E., Cleave, P. L., Ravida, A. I., Long, S. H., Oejmal, A. E., & Easton, D. L. (1994). Effects of grammar facilitation on the phonological performance of children with speech and language impairments. *Journal of Speech and Hearing Research, 37,* 594–607.
16. Plante, E., & Vance, R. (1994). Selection of preschool language tests: A data-based approach. *Language, Speech, and Hearing Services in Schools, 25,* 15–24.
17. Records, N. L., & Tomblin, J. B. (1994). Clinical decision making: Describing the decision rules of practicing speech-language pathologists. *Journal of Speech and Hearing Research, 37,* 144–156.
18. Sommers, R. K., Fragapane, L., & Schmock, K. (1994). Changes in maternal attitudes and perceptions and children's communication skills. *Perceptual and Motor Skills, 79,* 851-861.
19. Wilkinson, K. M., Romski, M. A., & Sevcik, R. A. (1994). Emergence of visual-graphic symbol combinations by youth with moderate or severe mental retardation. *Journal of Speech and Hearing, 37,* 883–895.
20. Windsor, J. (1994). Children's comprehension and production of derivational suffixes. *Journal of Speech and Hearing Research, 37,* 408–417.
21. Windsor, J., Doyle, S. S., & Siegel, G. M. (1994). Language acquisition after mutism: A longitudinal case study of autism. *Journal of Speech and Hearing Research, 37,* 96–105.
22. Eiserman, W. D., Weber, C., & McCan, M. (1995). Parent and professional roles in early intervention: A longitudinal comparison of the effects of two intervention configurations. *The Journal of Special Education, 29,* 20–44.
23. Felsenfeld, S., McGue, M., & Broen, P. A. (1995). Familial aggregation of phonological disorders: Results from a 28-year follow-up. *Journal of Speech and Hearing Research, 38,* 1091–1107.
24. Flipsen, P. (1995). Speaker-listener familiarity: Parents as judges of delayed speech intelligibility. *Journal of Communication Disorders, 28,* 3–19.
25. Guralnick, M. J., Connor, R. T., & Hammond, M. (1995). Parent perspective of peer relationships and friendships in integrated and specialized programs. *American Journal on Mental Retardation, 99,* 457–476.
26. Guralnick, M. J., Connor, R. T., Hammond, M., Gottman, J. M., & Kinnish, K. (1995). Immediate effects of mainstreamed settings on the social interactions and social integration of preschool children. *American Journal on Mental Retardation, 100,* 359–377.
27. Tomblin, J. B., Abbas, P. J., Records, N. L., & Brenneman, L. M. (1995). Auditory evoked responses to frequency-modulated tones in children with specific language impairment. *Journal of Speech and Hearing Research, 38,* 387–392.
28. Williams, J. M., Voelker, S., & Ricciardi, P. W. (1995). Predictive validity of the K-ABC for exceptional preschoolers. *Psychology in the Schools, 32,* 178–185.
29. Guralnick, M. J., Connor, R. T., Hammond, M. A., Gottman, J. M., & Kinnish, K. (1996). The peer relations of preschool children with communication disorders. *Child Development, 67,* 471–489.
30. Leffert, J. S., & Siperstein, G. N. (1996). Assessment of social-cognitive processes in children with mental retardation. *American Journal on Mental Retardation, 100,* 441–455.
31. Weismer, S. E., & Hesketh, L. J. (1996). Lexical learning by children with specific language impairment: Effects of linguistic input presented at varying speaking rates. *Journal of Speech and Hearing Research, 39,* 177–190.
32 Fey, M. E., Cleave, P. L., & Long, S. H. (1997). Two models of grammar facilitation in children with language impairments: Phase 2. *Journal of Speech, Language, and Hearing Research, 40,* 5–19.
33. Gottman, J. M., Guralnick, M. J., Wilson, B., Swanson, C. C., & Murray, J. D. (1997). What should be the focus of emotional regulation in children? A nonlinear dynamic mathematical model of children's peer interaction in groups. *Development and Psychopathology, 9,* 421–452.
34. Guralnick, M. J. (1997). Peer social networks of young boys with developmental delays. *American Journal on Mental Retardation, 101,* 595–612.
35. Rescorla, 1., Roberts, J., & Dahlsgaard, K. (1997). Late talkers at 2: Outcome at age 3. *Journal of Speech, Language, and Hearing Research, 40,* 556–566.
36. Webster, P. E., Plante, A. S., & Couvillion, L. M. (1997). Phonologic impairment and prereading: Update on a longitudinal study. *Journal of Studies on Alcohol, 30,* 365–375.
37. Tomblin, J. B., & Buckwalter, P. R. (1998). Heritability of poor language achievement among twins. *Journal of Speech, Language, and Hearing Research, 41,* 188–199.

[2658]

Test for Colour-Blindness.

Purpose: To identify congenital color vision deficiency.
Population: Ages 4 and over.
Publication Dates: 1917-1970.
Scores: Total score only.
Administration: Individual.
Price Data: Available from distributor.
Time: Administration time not reported.
Author: Shinobu Ishihara.
Publisher: Graham-Field (U.S. Distributor).
Cross References: See T4:2729 (3 references), T3:2419 (1 reference), T2:1932 (29 references), 7:882 (13 references), and 6:962 (58 references).

TEST REFERENCES

1. DeVreese, L. P. (1991). Two systems for colour-naming defects: Verbal disconnection vs. colour imagery disorder. *Neuropsychologia, 29,* 1–18.
2. Shuren, J. E., Brott, T. G., Schefft, B. K., & Houston, W. (1996). Preserved color imagery in an achromatopsic. *Neuropsychologia, 34,* 485–489.

[2659]

Test for Creative Thinking—Drawing Production.

Purpose: "Meant to be a screening instrument which allows for a first rough, simple, and economic assessment of a person's creative potential."
Population: Age 4–adult.
Publication Date: 1996.
Acronym: TCT-DP.
Scores, 15: Continuations, Completions, New Elements, Connections Made with Lines, Connections that Contribute to a Theme, Boundary-Breaking Being

Fragment—Dependent, Perspective, Humour/Affectivity/Emotionality/Expressive Power of the Drawing, Unconventionality A—Uncoventional Manipulation, Unconventionality B—Symbolic/Abstract/Fictional, Unconventionality C—Symbol-Figure-Combinations, Unconventionality D—Nonstereotypical Utilization of Given Fragments/Figures, Speed, Total.
Administration: Group.
Forms, 2: A, B.
Price Data: Available from publisher.
Time: (30) minutes.
Authors: Klaus K. Urban and Hans G. Jellen.
Publisher: Swets Test Publishers [The Netherlands].

[2660]

Test for Examining Expressive Morphology.

Purpose: "Developed to help clinicians evaluate expressive morpheme development with children whose language skills range from three to eight years of age."
Population: Ages 3-0 to 8-12.
Publication Date: 1983.
Acronym: TEEM.
Scores, 7: (6 morphemes plus 1 age level approximation): Present Progressives, Plurals, Possessives, Past Tenses, Third-Person Singulars, Derived Adjectives, Total.
Administration: Individual.
Price Data, 1999: $36 per complete kit including manual (43 pages), test booklet, and 25 scoring forms; $15 per 25 scoring forms.
Time: (5-7) minutes.
Authors: Kenneth G. Shipley, Terry A. Stone, and Marlene B. Sue.
Publisher: Communication Skill Builders—A Division of the Psychological Corporation.
Cross References: See T4:2730 (1 reference); for reviews by Doris V. Allen and Janice A. Dole, see 10:364.

TEST REFERENCES

1. Koenig, L. A., & Biel, C. D. (1989). A delivery system of comprehensive language services in a school district. *Language, Speech, and Hearing Services in Schools, 20,* 338–365.
2. Shipley, K. G., Maddox, M. A., & Driver, J. E. (1991). Children's development of irregular past tense verb forms. *Language, Speech, and Hearing Services in Schools, 22,* 115–122.
3. Wilson, K. S., Blackmon, R. C., Hall, R. E., & Elcholtz, G. E. (1991). Methods of language assessment: A survey of California public school clinicians. *Language, Speech, and Hearing Services in Schools, 22,* 236–241.
4. Plante, E., & Vance, R. (1994). Selection of preschool language tests: A data-based approach. *Language, Speech, and Hearing Services in Schools, 25,* 15–24.

[2661]

Test for Oral Language Production.

Purpose: "Provides measures for 16 facets of language production."
Population: Ages 4-6 to 10-5.
Publication Date: 1980.
Acronym: TOLP.
Scores, 16: Word per T-Unit, Type-Token Ratio, Adverbs per T-Unit, Prepositions per T-Unit, Co-Verbs per T-Unit, Deletions per T-Unit, Substitutions per T-Unit, Permutations per T-Unit, Incomplete T-Units per T-Unit, Sentence Structure Corrections per T-Unit, Choice-of-Word Corrections per T-Unit, Word Repetitions per T-Unit, Labels per T-Unit, Nonsense per T-Unit, Abstract-Concreteness Index, Total Number of Words.
Administration: Individual.
Price Data: Available from publisher.
Time: [90-100] minutes.
Author: Jan Vorster.
Publisher: Human Sciences Research Council [South Africa].

[2662]

Test for the Reception of Grammar.

Purpose: "Designed to assess understanding of grammatical contrasts in English."
Population: Ages 4–12 years and also dysphasic adults.
Publication Dates: 1983–1989.
Acronym: TROG.
Scores, 21: Noun, Verb, Adjective, Two Element Combination, Negative, Three Element Combination, Singular/Plural Personal Pronoun, Reversible Active, Masculine/Feminine Personal Pronoun, Singular/Plural Noun Inflection, Comparative/Absolute, Reversible Passive, In and On, Postmodified Subject, X But Not Y, Above and Below, Not Only X But Also Y, Relative Clause, Neither X nor Y, Embedded Sentence, Total.
Administration: Individual.
Price Data, 1998: £70 per test kit including 25 test forms, manual, stimulus book, and cards.
Time: (10–20) minutes.
Comments: An 80-item, orally administered, multiple-choice test; "suitable for American as well as British subjects."
Author: Dorothy Bishop.
Publisher: Age and Cognitive Performance Research Centre, University of Manchester [England].

TEST REFERENCES

1. Frisk, V., & Milner, B. (1990). The relationship of working memory to the immediate recall of stories following unilateral temporal or frontal lobectomy. *Neuropsychologia, 28,* 121–135.
2. Charman, T., & Baron-Cohen, S. (1994). Another look at imitation in autism. *Development and Psychopathology, 6,* 403–413.
3. Hughes, C., Russell, J., & Robbins, T. W. (1994). Evidence for executive dysfunction in autism. *Neuropsychologia, 32,* 477–492.
4. Montgomery, J. W. (1995). Sentence comprehension in children with specific language impairment: The role of phonological working memory. *Journal of Speech and hearing Research,* 38, 187–199.
5. Hughes, C. (1996). Control of action and thought: Normal development and dysfunction in autism: A research note. *Journal of Child Development and Psychiatry, 37,* 229–236.
6. North, T., & Donlan, C. (1996). Nonword repetition as a behavioural marker for inherited language impairment: Evidence from a twin study. *Journal of Child Psychology and Psychiatry, 37,* 391–403.
7. Karmiloff-Smith, A., Grant, J., Berthoud, I., Davies, M., Howlin, P., & Udivin, O. (1997). Language and Williams syndrome: How intact is "intact"? *Child Development, 68,* 246–262.
8. Leevers, H. J., & Harris, P. L. (1998). Drawing impossible entities: A measure of the imagination in children with autism, children with learning disabilities, and normal 4-year olds. *Journal of Child Psychology and Psychiatry, 39,* 399–410.

[2663]

Test Lessons in Primary Reading, Second Enlarged and Revised Edition.

Purpose: "Designed to evaluate students' reading progress and thinking skills."
Population: Children.
Publication Date: 1980.
Scores: Item scores only.
Administration: Group.
Price Data, 1994: $3.50 per lesson booklet; $2.95 per teacher's manual/answer key (17 pages).
Time: Administration time not reported.
Authors: William A. McCall and Mary Lourita Harby.
Publisher: Teachers College Press.

[2664]

Test Lessons in Reading Figurative Language.

Purpose: To develop students' abilities to recognize and interpret figurative language.
Population: High school and college and adult learners.
Publication Date: 1980.
Scores: Item scores only.
Administration: Group.
Price Data, 1994: $6.95 per lesson booklet; $1.95 per teacher's manual/answer key (8 pages).
Time: (5) minutes per Lesson.
Authors: William A. McCall, Edwin H. Smith, and Barbara C. Palmer.
Publisher: Teachers College Press.

[2665]

Test of Academic Achievement Skills—Reading, Arithmetic, Spelling, and Listening Comprehension.

Purpose: Measures a child's reading, arithmetic, spelling, and listening comprehension skills.
Population: Ages 4-0 to 12-0.
Publication Date: 1989.
Scores, 6: Spelling, Total Reading (Letter/Word Identification, Listening Comprehension, Total), Arithmetic, Total.
Administration: Individual.
Price Data: Not available.
Time: (15–25) minutes.
Author: Morrison F. Gardner.
Publisher: Psychological & Educational Publications, Inc. [No reply from publisher; status unknown].
Cross References: For reviews by C. Dale Carpenter and Steve Graham, see 13:321.

[2666]

Test of Academic Performance.

Purpose: Developed to assess achievement in four curriculum areas: Mathematics, Spelling, Reading, and Writing.
Population: Grades K–12.
Publication Date: 1989.
Acronym: TOAP.
Scores, 6: Basic subtests (Mathematics, Spelling, Reading Recognition, Reading Comprehension), Optional subtests (Written Composition, Copying Rate).
Administration: Individual and group.
Price Data, 1999: $94 per complete set including examiner's manual (182 pages), 25 student response forms, 25 record forms, and package of four reading stimulus cards.
Time: (20–45) minutes.
Authors: Wayne Adams, Lynn Erb, and David Sheslow.
Publisher: The Psychological Corporation.
Cross References: For reviews by Steve Graham and Cleborne D. Maddux, see 13:222.

[2667]

Test of Adolescent/Adult Word Finding.

Purpose: Developed to assess word finding skills.
Population: Ages 12-80.
Publication Date: 1990.
Acronym: TAWF.
Scores: 5 sections (Picture Naming: Nouns, Sentence Completion Naming, Description Naming, Picture Naming: Verbs, Category Naming) yielding 4 scores: Accuracy, Comprehension, Item Response Time, Word Finding Profile.
Administration: Individual.
Forms, 2: Complete, Brief.
Price Data, 1999: $198 per complete kit including test book, 25 response booklets, examiner's manual (204 pages), and technical manual (121 pages); $36 per 25 response forms.
Time: (20-30) minutes for complete test; [10] minutes for brief test.
Comments: Upward extension of the Test of Word Finding (2725); speed can be measured in actual or estimated Item Response Time; tape recorder and stopwatch required on Section 1 only when using Actual Item Response Time Option.
Author: Diane J. German.
Publisher: PRO-ED.
Cross References: For reviews by Ronald B. Gillam and Richard E. Harding, see 12:391.

TEST REFERENCE

1. Ward-Lonergan, J. M., Liles, B. Z., & Anderson, A. M. (1998). Listening comprehension and recall abilities in adolescents with language-learning disabilities and without disabilities for social studies lectures. *Journal of Communication Disorders, 31,* 1–32.

[2668]

Test of Adolescent and Adult Language, Third Edition.

Purpose: Designed "(a) to identify adolescents and adults whose scores are significantly below those of

their peers and who might need interventions designed to improve language proficiency; (b) to determine areas of relative strength and weakness across language abilities; (c) to document overall progress in language development as a consequence of intervention programs; and (d) to serve as a measure for research efforts designed to investigate language characteristics of adolescents and adults."
Population: Ages 12-0 to 24-11.
Publication Dates: 1980–1994.
Acronym: TOAL-3.
Scores, 8: 8 subtest scores (Listening/Vocabulary, Listening/Grammar, Speaking/Vocabulary, Speaking/Grammar, Reading/Vocabulary, Reading/Grammar, Writing/Vocabulary, Writing/Grammar); 10 composite scores (Listening, Speaking, Reading, Writing, Spoken Language, Written Language, Vocabulary, Grammar, Receptive Language, Expressive Language).
Administration: Individual and group.
Price Data, 1999: $169 per complete kit including 50 answer booklets, 10 test booklets, 50 summary/profile sheets, and examiner's manual ('94, 111 pages); $54 per 50 answer booklets; $34 per 10 test booklets; $34 per 50 summary/profile sheets; $46 per examiner's manual; $79 per IBM software scoring system.
Time: (60–180) minutes.
Authors: Donald D. Hammill, Virginia L. Brown, Stephen C. Larsen, and J. Lee Wiederholt.
Publisher: PRO-ED.
Cross References: For reviews by John MacDonald and Roger A. Richards, see 13:323 (6 references); see also T4:2738 (9 references); for reviews by Allen Jack Edwards and David A. Shapiro of an earlier edition, see 10:365; for a review by Robert T. Williams of an earlier edition, see 9:1243.

TEST REFERENCES

1. Klein, S. K., Kurtzberg, D., Brattson, A., Kreuzer, J. A., Stapells, D. R., Dunn, M. A., Rapin, I., & Vaughn, H. G., Jr. (1995). Electrophysiologic manifestations of impaired temporal lobe auditory processing in verbal auditory agnosia. *Brain and Language, 51,* 383–405.
2. Sparks, R., Ganschow, L., & Thomas, A. (1996). Role of intelligence tests in speech/language referrals. *Perceptual and Motor Skills, 83,* 195–204.
3. Wong, B. Y. L., Butler, D. L., Ficzere, S. A., & Kuperis, S. (1996). Teaching low achievers and students with learning disabilities to plan, write, and revise opinion essays. *Journal of Learning Disabilities, 29,* 197–212.
4. Bennett, D., & Dancer, J. (1997). Communication screening in older adults with vision loss. *Perceptual and Motor Skills, 84,* 1097–1098.
5. Tomblin, J. B., & Buckwalter, P. R. (1998). Heritability of poor language achievement among twins. *Journal of Speech, Language, and Hearing Research, 41,* 188–199.
6. Turkstra, L. S., & Holland, A. L. (1998). Assessment of syntax after adolescent brain injury: Effects of memory on test performance. *Journal of Speech, Language, and Hearing Research, 41,* 137–149.
7. Ward-Lonergan, J. M., Liles, B. Z., & Anderson, A. M. (1998). Listening comprehension and recall abilities in adolescents with language-learning disabilities and without disabilities for social studies lectures. *Journal of Communication Disorders, 31,* 1–32.

[2669]

Test of Articulation in Context.

Purpose: Designed to "examine a student's phonological abilities in the contest of spontaneous conversation, and can be used to screen, predict change, diagnose and assess a student's phonological progress following treatment."
Population: Preschool through elementary-school-aged children.
Publication Date: 1998.
Acronym: TAC.
Scores, 4: Sound Production, Speech Mechanism, Intelligibility, Adverse Effect on Educational Performance.
Administration: Individual.
Price Data, 1999: $110 per kit including 25 response forms, 4 laminated test boards, and manual (45 pages).
Time: Untimed.
Author: Teresa Lanphere.
Publisher: Imaginart International, Inc.

[2670]

Test of Attitude Toward School.

Purpose: To assess a student's attitude toward school.
Population: Boys in grades 1, 3, 5.
Publication Dates: 1973-1984.
Acronym: TAS.
Scores, 2: Scholastic Attitude Score, Evaluation by the Teacher.
Administration: Individual.
Price Data, 1998: $20 per set of 16 drawings; $49.95 per 25 teacher questionnaires ('84, 3 pages); $18 per manual ('84, 116 pages).
Time: Administration time not reported.
Comments: Projective test.
Authors: Guy Thibaudeau, Cathy Ingram-LeBlanc (translation from French), and Michael Dewson (verification of technical terms).
Publisher: Institute of Psychological Research, Inc. [Canada].
Cross References: For a review by Bert A. Goldman, see 11:425.

[2671]

Test of Auditory Analysis Skills.

Purpose: Constructed to assess "a child's auditory perceptual skills."
Population: Children.
Publication Date: 1975–1993.
Acronym: TAAS.
Scores: Total score only.
Administration: Individual.
Manual: No manual (Directions on each form).
Price Data, 1999: $14 per 50 test forms.
Time: Administration time not reported.
Comments: "Criterion-referenced"; may be used in conjunction with the Test of Visual Analysis Skills (2721); test is reproduced from author's book Helping Children Overcome Learning Difficulties (1993, Walker Publishing Company, New York).
Author: Jerome Rosner.

Publisher: Academic Therapy Publications.
Cross References: For reviews by Allan O. Diefendorf and Kathy S. Kessler and by Rick Lindskog of the earlier edition, see 11:426.

TEST REFERENCES

1. Felton, R. H., & Pepper, P. P. (1995). Early identification and intervention of phonological deficits in kindergarten and early elementary children at risk for reading disability. *School Psychology Review, 24,* 405–414.
2. O'Connor, R. E., Jenkins, J. R., & Slocum, T. A. (1995). Transfer among phonological tasks in kindergarten: Essential instructional content. *Journal of Educational Psychology, 87,* 202-217.
3. Moore, B. D., Slopis, J. M., Schomer, D., Jackson, E. F., & Levy, B. M. (1996). Neuropsycholgical significance of areas of high signal intensity on brain MRI's of children with neurofibromatosis. *Neurology, 46,* 1660–1668.

[2672]

Test of Auditory Comprehension.

Purpose: Designed to be used for the selection of auditory training objectives and measurement of progress in comprehension.
Population: Hearing impaired ages 4-17.
Publication Dates: 1976-1981.
Acronym: TAC.
Scores, 10: Linguistic vs. Nonlinguistic, Linguistic/Human Nonlinguistic/Environmental, Stereotypic Messages, Single Element Core Noun Vocabulary, Recalls Two Critical Elements, Recalls Four Critical Elements, Sequences Three Events, Recalls Five Details, Sequences Three Events With Competing Message, Recalls Five Details With Competing Message.
Administration: Individual.
Price Data, 1998: $90 per complete test.
Time: (30) minutes.
Comments: Test administered by cassette tape.
Author: Audiologic Services and Southwest School for the Hearing Impaired, Office of the Los Angeles County Superintendent of Schools.
Publisher: Foreworks.
Cross References: See T4:2741 (7 references); for a review by James R. Cox, see 9:1246.

TEST REFERENCES

1. Brown, J. R. (1989). The truth about scores children achieve on tests. *Language, Speech, and Hearing Services in Schools, 20,* 366–371.
2. Bernstein, M. E., & Morrison, M. E. (1992). Are we ready for PL 99-457? *American Annals of the Deaf, 137,* 7-13.

[2673]

Test of Auditory-Perceptual Skills.

Purpose: "To measure a child's functioning in various areas of auditory perception."
Population: Ages 4–12.
Publication Date: 1985.
Acronym: TAPS.
Scores, 7: Auditory Number Memory, Auditory Sentence Memory, Auditory Word Memory, Auditory Interpretation of Directions, Auditory Word Discrimination, Auditory Processing (Thinking and Reasoning), Hyperactivity Index.
Administration: Individual.
Price Data: Not available.
Foreign Language Edition: Spanish version available.
Time: (15–25) minutes.
Comments: The Hyperactivity Index is a parental questionnaire developed by C. Keith Connors.
Author: Morrison F. Gardner.
Publisher: Psychological & Educational Publications, Inc. [Status unknown; no reply from publisher].
Cross References: For reviews by Annabel J. Cohen and by Anne R. Kessler and Jaclyn B. Spitzer, see 13:324 (2 references).

[2674]

Test of Awareness of Language Segments.

Purpose: "Assesses a child's ability to segment the stream of spoken language into words, syllables, and phonemes (sounds)."
Population: Ages 4-6 and over.
Publication Date: 1987.
Acronym: TALS.
Scores, 4: Sentence-to-Words, Words-to-Syllables, Words-to-Sounds, Total.
Administration: Individual.
Levels: 2 overlapping levels (ages 4-6 to 5-6 and 5-7 and over) in a single booklet.
Price Data, 1999: $109 per complete kit including test booklet and manual ('87, 47 pages).
Time: Administration time not reported.
Comments: Orally administered.
Author: Diane J. Sawyer.
Publisher: PRO-ED.
Cross References: For reviews by Carolyn Chaney and Mary E. Huba, see 11:427.

TEST REFERENCES

1. Miller, L. (1989). Classroom-based language intervention. *Language, Speech, and Hearing Services in Schools, 20,* 153–169.
2. Catts, H. W. (1991). Facilitating phonological awareness: Role of speech-language pathologists. *Language, Speech, and Hearing Services in Schools, 22,* 196–203.
3. Peterson, M. E., & Haines, L. D. (1992). Orthographic analogy training with kindergarten children: Effects on analogy use, phonemic segmentation, and letter-sound knowledge. *Journal of Reading Behavior, 24,* 109-127.
4. Ball, E. W. (1993). Assessing phonological awareness. *Language, Speech, and Hearing Services in Schools, 24,* 130–139.
5. Catts, H. W. (1993). The relationship between speech-language impairments and reading disabilities. *Journal of Speech and Hearing Research, 36,* 948–958.

[2675]

Test of Basic Assumptions.

Purpose: "Designed to reveal basic assumptions about reality and provide a means for studying the influence of a philosophical position on behavior."
Population: Adults.
Publication Dates: 1957-1968.
Acronym: TBA.
Scores, 12: 3 attitude scores (Realist, Idealist, Pragmatist) for each of 4 "life areas" (Organization of Effort and Problem Solving, Human Abilities and Individual, General Philosophy of Life, Economics and Business).

Administration: Group.
Price Data: Available from publisher.
Time: (20-30) minutes.
Comments: For experimental and research use.
Authors: James H. Morrison and Martin Levit.
Publisher: James H. Morrison [No reply from publisher; status unknown].

[2676]

Test of Children's Language: Assessing Aspects of Spoken Language, Reading, and Writing.

Purpose: "Designed to measure important aspects of spoken language, reading, and writing."
Population: Ages 5–0 to 8–11.
Publication Date: 1996.
Acronym: TOCL.
Scores, 11: 7 Component Scores (Spoken Language, Knowledge of Print, Word Recognition, Reading Comprehension, Writing Skills, Writing From Memory, Original Writing); 4 Combined Scores (Spoken Language Quotient, Reading Quotient, Writing Quotient, Total Language Quotient).
Administration: Individual.
Price Data, 1999: $139 per complete kit including manual (62 pages), "A Visit with Mr. Turtle" storybook, story picture sheet, 25 student workbooks, and 25 profile/examiner record forms in storage box; $39 per 25 student workbooks; $44 per 25 profile/examiner record forms; $44 per manual; $5 per storybook picture sheet; $12 per "A Visit with Mr. Turtle" storybook.
Time: (30–40) minutes.
Authors: Edna Barenbaum and Phyllis Newcomer.
Publisher: PRO-ED.

[2677]

Test of Cognitive Skills, Second Edition.

Purpose: "Designed to assess the academic aptitude of students in Grades 2–12."
Population: Grades 2–3, 4–5, 6–7, 8–9, 10–11, 11–12.
Publication Dates: 1981–1992.
Acronym: TCS/2.
Scores, 5: Sequences, Analogies, Memory, Verbal Reasoning, Total (Cognitive Skills Index).
Administration: Group.
Price Data, 1994: $9.45 per 35 practice tests; $32 per 100 individual record sheets for hand scoring; $1.15 per class record sheet for hand scoring; $8.35 per norms book ('92, 50 pages); $11.75 per test coordinator's handbook ('92, 41 pages); $11.75 per technical bulletin ('93, 62 pages); $8.35 per examiner's manual ('92, 29 pages) (select Levels 1, 2–6); $12.60 per test organizer; scoring service available from publisher.
Authors: CTB/Macmillan/McGraw-Hill.
Publisher: CTB/McGraw-Hill.

a) LEVEL 1.
Population: Grades 2–3.
Price Data: $50.05 per 35 hand-scorable consumable test books; $63.35 per 35 CompuScan machine-scorable consumable test books.
Time: 50(55) minutes.

b) LEVEL 2.
Population: Grades 4–5.
Price Data: $63.35 per 35 machine-scorable consumable test books; $50.05 per 35 hand-scorable or reusable test books; $13 per 50 CompuScan answer sheets; $23 per 50 hand-scorable answer sheets; $17 per 25 SCOREZE answer sheets; $9.60 per hand-scoring stencil.
Time: 54(59) minutes.

c) LEVEL 3.
Population: Grades 6–7.
Price Data: $45.15 per 35 reusable test books; answer sheet prices same as *b* above.
Time: Same as *b* above.

d) LEVEL 4.
Population: Grades 8–9.
Price Data: Same as *b* above.
Time: Same as *c* above.

e) LEVEL 5.
Population: Grades 10–11.
Price Data: Same as *b* above.
Time: Same as *c* above.

f) LEVEL 6.
Population: Grades 11–12.
Price Data: Same as *b* above.
Time: Same as *c* above.

Cross References: For a review by Randy W. Kamphaus, see 13:325 (8 references); see also T4:2745 (4 references); for reviews by Timothy Z. Keith and Robert J. Sternberg of an earlier edition, see 9:1248; for a review by Lynn H. Fox and an excerpted review by David M. Shoemaker of the Short Form Test of Academic Aptitude, see 8:202 (9 references).

[2678]

Test of Cognitive Style in Mathematics.

Purpose: Identifies preferences in mathematical computation methods and problem solving methods.
Population: Ages 8-adult.
Publication Date: 1986.
Acronym: TCSM.
Scores, 5: Mental Computation, Arithmetic, Geometry/Visual, Algebra, Total.
Administration: Individual.
Price Data, 1992: $54 per complete kit including manual (65 pages); $8 per 50 profile record forms; $15 per 50 worksheets; $15 per 50 observation folders.
Time: (20) minutes.

Authors: John B. Bath, Stephen J. Chinn, and Dwight E. Knox.
Publisher: Slosson Educational Publications, Inc.
Cross References: For reviews by Richard C. Pugh and Dan Wright, see 12:392.

[2679]

Test of Creativity.

Purpose: To gain a quick measure of a person's creativity.
Population: Adolescents and adults.
Publication Date: 1994.
Scores: Total score only.
Administration: Group.
Manual: No manual.
Price Data, 1994: $60 per 20 tests including self-assessment, answer sheet and feedback, and Types of Creativity.
Time: 35(40) minutes.
Comments: Self-administered, self-scored.
Author: Training House, Inc.
Publisher: Training House, Inc.

[2680]

Test of Early Language Development, Third Edition.

Purpose: Designed to measure the early development of spoken language in the areas of receptive and expressive language, syntax, and semantics.
Population: Ages 2-0 to 7-11.
Publication Dates: 1981–1999.
Acronym: TELD-3.
Scores, 3: Receptive Language, Expressive Language, Spoken Language Quotient.
Administration: Individual.
Forms, 2: A, B.
Price Data, 1999: $249 per complete kit.
Time: (15–40) minutes.
Authors: Wayne P. Hresko, D. Kim Reid, and Donald D. Hammill.
Publisher: PRO-ED.
Cross References: See T4:2749 (6 references); for reviews by Javaid Kaiser and David A. Shapiro of an earlier edition, see 12:393 (4 references); for reviews by Janice Arnold Dale and Elizabeth M. Prather of an earlier edition, see 9:1250 (1 reference).

TEST REFERENCES

1. Dale, P. S., & Henderson, V. L. (1987). An evaluation of the Test of Early Language Development as a measure of receptive and expressive language. *Language, Speech, and Hearing Services in Schools, 18,* 179–187.
2. Dale, P. S., & Cole, K. N. (1991). What's normal? Specific language impairment in an individual differences perspective. *Language, Speech, and Hearing Services in Schools, 22,* 80–83.
3. Lewis, B. A. (1992). Pedigree analysis of children with phonology disorders. *Journal of Learning Disabilities, 25,* 586–597.
4. Lewis, B. A., & Freebairn, L. (1992). Residual effects of preschool phonology disorders in grade school, adolescence, and adulthood. *Journal of Speech and Hearing Research, 35,* 819–831.
5. Aram, D. M., Morris, R., & Hall, N. E. (1993). Clinical and research congruence in identifying children with specific language impairment. *Journal of Speech and Hearing Research, 36,* 580–591.
6. Hall, N. E., Yamashita, T. S., & Aram, D. M. (1993). Relationship between language and fluency in children with developmental language disorders. *Journal of Speech and Hearing Research, 36,* 568–579.
7. Swisher, L., & Plante, E. (1993). Nonverbal IQ tests reflect different relations among skills for specifically language-impaired and normal children: Brief report. *Journal of Communication Disorders, 26,* 65–71.
8. Cole, K. N., Mills, P. E., & Kelley, D. (1994). Agreement of assessment profiles used in cognitive referencing. *Language, Speech, and Hearing Services in Schools, 25,* 25–31.
9. McGregor, K. K., & Leonard, L. B. (1994). Subject pronoun and article omissions in the speech of children with specific language impairment: A phonological interpretation. *Journal of Speech and Hearing Research, 37,* 171–181.
10. Plante, E., & Vance, R. (1994). Selection of preschool language tests: A data-based approach. *Language, Speech, and Hearing Services in Schools, 25,* 15–24.
11. Swisher, L., & Snow, D. (1994). Learning and generalization components of morphological acquisition by children with specific language impairment: Is there a functional relation? *Journal of Speech and Hearing, 37,* 1406–1413.
12. Leonard, L. B. (1995). Functional categories in the grammars of children with specific language impairment. *Journal of Speech and Hearing Research, 38,* 1270–1283.
13. Swisher, L., Restrepo, M. A., Plante, E., & Lowell, S. (1995). Effect of implicit and explicit "rule" presentation on bound-morpheme generalization in specific language impairment. *Journal of Speech and Hearing Research, 38,* 168–173.
14. Dunn, M., Flax, J., Sliwinski, M., & Aram, D. (1996). The use of spontaneous language measures as criteria for identifying children with specific language impairment: An attempt to reconcile clinical and research in congruence. *Journal of Speech and Hearing Research, 39,* 643–654.
15. Gierut, J. A., Morrisette, M. L., Hughes, M. T., & Rowland, S. (1996). Phonological treatment of efficacy and developmental norms. *Language, Speech, and Hearing Services in Schools, 27,* 215–230.
16. Jenkins, J. M., & Astington, J. W. (1996). Cognitive factors and family structure associated with theory of mind development in young children. *Developmental Psychology, 32,* 70–78.
17. Miccio, A. W., & Elbert, M. (1996). Enhancing stimulability: A treatment program. *Journal of Communication Disorders, 29,* 335–351.
18. Waterhouse, L., Morris, R., Allen, D., Dunn, M., Fein, D., Feinstein, C., Rapin, I., & Wing, L. (1996). Diagnosis and classification in autism. *Journal of Autism and Developmental Disorders, 26,* 59–86.
19. Cox, B. E., Fang, Z., & Otto, B. W. (1997). Preschoolers' developing ownership of literate register. *Reading Research Quarterly, 32,* 34–53.

[2681]

Test of Early Mathematics Ability, Second Edition.

Purpose: To "identify those children who are significantly behind or ahead of their peers in the development of mathematical thinking."
Population: Ages 3-0 to 8-11.
Publication Dates: 1983-1990.
Acronym: TEMA-2.
Scores: Total score only.
Administration: Individual.
Price Data, 1999: $164 per complete kit; $46 per picture book; $39 per 50 profile/record forms; $39 per Assessment Probes and Instructional Activities manual; $29 per examiner's manual ('90, 48 pages).
Time: (20) minutes.
Authors: Herbert P. Ginsburg and Arthur J. Baroody.
Publisher: PRO-ED.
Cross References: For reviews by Jerry Johnson and Joyce R. McLarty, see 11:428 (1 reference); for a review by David P. Lindeman, see 9:1252.

TEST REFERENCES

1. Borland, J. H., & Wright, L. (1994). Identifying young, potentially gifted, economically disadvantaged students. *Gifted Child Quarterly, 38,* 164-171.
2. Siegal, M., & Smith, J. (1997). Toward making representation count in children's conceptions of fractions. *Contemporary Educational Psychology, 22,* 1–22.

[2682]
Test of Early Reading Ability—2.

Purpose: "Measures children's ability to attribute meaning to printed symbols, their knowledge of the alphabet and its function, and their understanding of the conventions of print."
Population: Ages 3-0 to 9-11.
Publication Dates: 1981-1989.
Acronym: TERA-2.
Scores: Total score with the capability for individual item analysis in the areas of Alphabet Knowledge, Word Meaning, and Reading Conventions.
Administration: Individual.
Forms, 2: A, B.
Price Data, 1999: $169 per complete kit; $56 per administration/picture book; $39 per 50 profile/record forms (specify form A or B); $39 per manual ('89, 50 pages).
Time: (15-30) minutes.
Authors: D. Kim Reid, Wayne P. Hresko, and Donald D. Hammill.
Publisher: PRO-ED.
Cross References: See T4:2751 (2 references); for reviews by Michael D. Beck and Robert W. Hiltonsmith, see 11:429 (1 reference); for reviews by Isabel L. Beck and Janet A. Norris of the original edition, see 9:1253.

TEST REFERENCES

1. Burns, J. M., Mathews, F. N., & Mason, A. (1990). Essential steps in screening and identifying preschool gifted children. *Gifted Child Quarterly, 34,* 102-107.
2. Cole, K. N., Mills, P. E., Dale, P. S., & Jenkins, J. R. (1991). Effects of preschool integration for children with disabilities. *Exceptional Children, 58,* 36-45.
3. Neuman, S. B., & Roskos, K. (1992). Literacy objects as cultural tools: Effects on children's literacy behaviors in play. *Reading Research Quarterly, 27,* 203-225.
4. Cole, K. N., Dale, P. S., Mills, P. E., & Jenkins, J. R. (1993). Interaction between early intervention curricula and student characteristics. *Exceptional Children, 60,* 17-28.
5. O'Connor, R. E., Jenkins, J. R., Cole, K. N., & Mills, P. E. (1993). Two approaches to reading instruction with children with disabilities: Does program design make a difference? *Exceptional Children, 59,* 312-323.
6. Borland, J. H., & Wright, L. (1994). Identifying young, potentially gifted, economically disadvantaged students. *Gifted Child Quarterly, 38,* 164-171.
7. Hoba, M. E., & Ramisetty-Mikler, S. (1995). The language skills and concepts of early and nonearly readers. *The Journal of Genetic Psychology, 156,* 313–331.
8. Mills, P. E., Dale, P. S., Cole, K. N., & Jenkins, J. R. (1995). Follow-up of children from academic and cognitive preschool curricula at age 9. *Exceptional Children, 61,* 378–393.
9. DeBaryshe, B. D., Buell, M. J., & Binder, J. C. (1996). What a parent brings to the table: Young children writing with and without parental assistance. *Journal of Literacy Research, 28,* 71–90.
10. Sacks, C. H., & Mergendoller, J. R. (1997). The relationship between teachers' theoretical orientation toward reading and student outcomes in kindergarten children with different initial reading abilities. *American Educational Research Journal, 34,* 721–739.
11. Saracho, O. N. (1997). Home literacy program and children's development of literacy. *Perceptual and Motor Skills, 85,* 185–186.
12. van Kleeck, A., Gillam, R. B., Hamilton, L., & McGrath, C. (1997). The relationship between middle-class parents' book-sharing discussion and their preschoolers' abstract language development. *Journal of Speech, Language, and Hearing Research, 40,* 1261–1271.
13. Mathes, P. G., Howard, J. K., Allen, S. H., & Fuchs, D. (1998). Peer-assisted learning strategies for first-grade readers: Responding to the needs of diverse learners. *Reading Research Quarterly, 33,* 62–94.

[2683]
Test of Early Reading Ability—Deaf or Hard of Hearing.

Purpose: Designed to measure "children's ability to attribute meaning to printed symbols, their knowledge of the alphabet and its functions, and their knowledge of the conventions of print."
Population: Deaf and hard of hearing children ages 3-0 to 13-11.
Publication Date: 1991.
Acronym: TERA-D/HH.
Scores: Total score only.
Administration: Individual.
Forms, 2: A, B.
Price Data, 1999: $169 per complete kit including picture book, 25 Form A and 25 Form B profile/examiner record forms, and manual (49 pages); $49 per picture book; $39 per 25 profile/examiner record forms (select Form A or B); $46 per manual.
Time: (20-30) minutes.
Comments: Adaptation of the Test of Early Reading Ability-2 (2682).
Authors: D. Kim Reid, Wayne P. Hresko, Donald D. Hammill, and Susal Wiltshire.
Publisher: PRO-ED.
Cross References: For reviews by Barbara A. Rothlisberg and Esther Stavrou Toubanos, see 12:394.

[2684]
Test of Early Written Language, Second Edition.

Purpose: "Measures early writing ability in children."
Population: Ages 3–0 to 10–11.
Publication Dates: 1988–1996.
Acronym: TEWL—2.
Scores, 3: Basic Writing, Contextual Writing, Global Writing.
Administration: Individual or group.
Forms, 2: A, B.
Price Data, 1999: $134 per complete kit including manual ('96, 116 pages), 10 each Form A and Form B student workbooks, 10 each Form A and Form B profile/record booklets in storage box; $39 per 10 student workbooks (specify Form A or B); $19 per 10 profile/record booklets (specify Form A or B); $44 per manual.
Time: (30–45) minutes.
Authors: Wayne P. Hresko, Shelley R. Herron, and Pamela K. Peak.
Publisher: PRO-ED.
Cross References: For reviews by David P. Hurford and Michael S. Trevisan, see 13:326; for a review by Patricia Wheeler of an earlier edition, see 11:430.

[2685]
Test of Economic Knowledge.

Purpose: Measures knowledge of economic concepts.
Population: Grades 8-9.
Publication Date: 1987.
Acronym: TEK.
Scores: Total score only.

Administration: Group.
Forms, 2: A, B.
Price Data: Available from publisher.
Time: (40-45) minutes.
Comments: "Designed to replace the Junior High School Test of Economics."
Authors: William B. Walstad and John C. Soper.
Publisher: National Council on Economic Education.
Cross References: For reviews by William A. Mehrens and Anthony J. Nitko, see 11:431.

[2686]

Test of Economic Literacy, Second Edition.

Purpose: Designed to "evaluate a student's performance and make decisions about economics instruction at the senior high school level."
Population: Grades 11-12.
Publication Dates: 1978-1987.
Acronym: TEL.
Scores: Total score only.
Administration: Group.
Forms, 2: A, B.
Price Data: Price information available from publisher for test materials including examiner's manual ('87, 76 pages).
Time: (40-50) minutes.
Comments: Revision of the Test of Economic Understanding ('64).
Authors: John C. Soper and William B. Walstad.
Publisher: National Council on Economic Education.
Cross References: For reviews by Jennifer J. Fager and Dan Wright, see 12:395; for a review by Anna S. Ochoa, see 9:1256; see also T2:1968 (19 references); for reviews by Edward J. Furst and Christine H. McGuire, and an excerpted review by Robert L. Ebel, see 7:901 (10 references).

TEST REFERENCES

1. Walstad, W. B., & Wcyoc, L. V. (1990). The effects of textbooks on economics understanding and attitudes in high school economics courses. *Journal of Research and Development in Education, 24*(1), 44–52.
2. Stock, P. A. (1997). Level of economic understanding for senior high school students in Ohio. *Journal of Educational Research, 91,* 60–63.

[2687]

Test of English for International Communication (TOEIC).

Purpose: To evaluate the English proficiency of those whose native language is not English.
Population: Adult nonnative speakers of English.
Publication Dates: 1980-1999.
Acronym: TOEIC.
Scores, 3: Listening Comprehension, Reading Comprehension, Total.
Administration: Group.
Price Data, 1999: Price varies for Secure and institutional Programs; price data available from publisher; ICS Program: $175 (plus S & H) per 5 test booklets and answer sheets, audiocassette, and test administration manual ('98, 26 pages); volume discounts available.
Time: (120) minutes.
Comments: Secure Program administered on set dates and scored by TOEIC program office; Institutional and ICS Program administered by the client on-site and/or by TOEIC representative; one-half of test (100 questions) administered by audiocassette tape recording; separate answer sheet.
Author: Educational Testing Service.
Publisher: The Chauncey Group International.
Cross References: For reviews by Dan Douglas and Roger A. Richards, see 11:432.

[2688]

Test of English Proficiency Level.

Purpose: "To determine a student's instructional level for placement in an English as a Second Language Program."
Population: Limited English proficient students in secondary and adult programs.
Publication Date: 1985.
Acronym: TEPL.
Scores: 4 skill area scores: Oral, Structure, Reading, Writing.
Administration: Individual in part.
Price Data: Not available.
Time: Oral Section, (5-20) minutes; Written Section, 60(70) minutes.
Author: George Rathmell.
Publisher: The Alemany Press [No reply from publisher; status unknown].
Cross References: For reviews by Alan Garfinkel and Maurice Tatsuoka, see 11:433.

[2689]

Test of Gross Motor Development.

Purpose: To identify, plan instructional programs, assess individual student progress, evaluate programs, and serve as a measurement instrument in research involving gross motor development.
Population: Ages 3-10.
Publication Date: 1985.
Acronym: TGMD.
Scores, 3: Locomotor Skills, Object Control Skills, Gross Motor Development Quotient.
Administration: Individual.
Price Data, 1999: $74 per complete kit including 50 student record books and examiner's manual (43 pages); $39 per 50 student record books; $37 per examiner's manual.

Time: (15) minutes.
Comments: Additional materials must be supplied by examiner.
Author: Dale A. Ulrich.
Publisher: PRO-ED.
Cross References: See T4:2762 (2 references); for reviews by Linda K. Bunker and Ron Edwards, see 10:370.

TEST REFERENCES

1. Suomi, R., & Suomi, J. (1997). Effectiveness of a training program with physical education students and experienced physical education teachers in scoring the Test of Gross Motor Development. *Perceptual and Motor Skills, 84,* 771–778.
2. Woodard, R. J., & Surburg, P. R. (1997). Fundamental gross motor skill performance by girls and boys with learning disabilities. *Perceptual and Motor Skills, 84,* 867–870.

[2690]

Test of Inference Ability in Reading Comprehension.

Purpose: "Designed to provide diagnostic information about the inference ability of students."
Population: Grades 6–8.
Publication Dates: 1987–1989.
Scores: Total score only.
Administration: Group.
Forms, 2: Multiple-choice, Constructed-response.
Price Data, 1993: $35 per 35 tests (specify multiple-choice or constructed-response); $10 per manual ('89, 24 pages); $12 per technical report ('89, 58 pages).
Time: (40–45) minutes per form.
Authors: Linda M. Phillips and Cynthia C. Patterson (multiple-choice format).
Publisher: Linda M. Phillips [Canada].
Cross References: For reviews by Douglas K. Smith and Robert Wall, see 13:327.

[2691]

Test of Initial Literacy.

Purpose: To provide teachers with diagnostic information about children who have difficulty with reading and writing.
Population: Ages 7-12.
Publication Date: 1989.
Acronym: TOIL.
Scores, 9: Letter Matching, Word Matching, Copying, Grammatical Punctuation, Orthographic Punctuation, Spelling of Homophones, Spelling, Style, Free Writing.
Administration: Group.
Price Data, 1990: £6.70 per 10 test booklets; £8 per teacher's set, including test booklet and manual ('89, 39 pages).
Time: Untimed.
Comments: Complements Reading Ability Series.
Authors: Anne Kispal, Alison Tate, Tom Gorman, and Chris Whetton.
Publisher: NFER-Nelson Publishing Co., Ltd. [England].
Cross References: For reviews by Jerrilyn V. Andrews and Cleborne D. Maddux, see 11:434.

[2692]

Test of Kindergarten/First Grade Readiness Skills.

Purpose: "To assess a child's readiness for kindergarten or for first grade."
Population: Ages 3–6 to 7–0.
Publication Date: 1987.
Acronym: TKFGRS.
Scores, 3: Reading, Spelling, Arithmetic.
Administration: Individual.
Price Data: Not available.
Time: (20–25) minutes.
Author: Karen Gardner Codding.
Publisher: Psychological & Educational Publications, Inc. [No reply from publisher; status unknown].
Cross References: For reviews by D. Joe Olmi and J. Steven Welsh, see 13:328.

[2693]

Test of Language Competence—Expanded Edition.

Purpose: "To evaluate delays in the emergence of linguistic competence and in the use of semantic, syntactic, and pragmatic strategies."
Publication Dates: 1985-1989.
Acronym: TLC-Expanded.
Scores: 5 subtest scores: Ambiguous Sentences, Listening Comprehension: Making Inferences, Oral Expression: Recreating Speech Acts, Figurative Language, Remembering Word Pairs (supplemental subtest for Level 2 only), plus 4 composite scores: Expressing Intents, Interpreting Intents, Screening Composite, TLC-Expanded Composite.
Administration: Individual.
Price Data, 1999: $359.50 per complete kit with briefcase including 25 Level 1 & 2 record forms, Level 1 & 2 stimulus manuals, administration manual ('89, 311 pages), technical manual ('89, 98 pages; $313.50 per complete kit without briefcase; $83.50 per administration manual; $61 per technical manual.
Time: (60-70) minutes per level.
Authors: Elisabeth H. Wiig and Wayne Secord.
Publisher: The Psychological Corporation.

a) LEVEL 1.
Population: Ages 5 through 18.
Price Data: $38 per 25 record forms; $58.50 per stimulus manual.

b) LEVEL 2.
Population: Ages 5 through 18.

Price Data: $38 per 25 record forms; $58.50 per stimulus manual.

Cross References: For reviews by Dolores Kluppel Vetter and Carol E. Westby, see 11:435 (1 reference).

TEST REFERENCES

1. Nippold, M. A. (1991). Evaluating and enhancing idiom comprehension in language-disordered students. *Language, Speech, and Hearing Services in Schools, 22,* 100–106.
2. Mack, A. E., & Warr-Leeper, G. A. (1992). Language abilities in boys with chronic behavior disorders. *Language, Speech, and Hearing Services in Schools, 23,* 214–223.
3. Dennis, M., & Barnes, M. A. (1993). Oral discourse after early-onset hydrocephalus: Linguistic ambiguity, figurative language, speech acts, and script-based inferences. *Journal of Pediatric Psychology, 18,* 639–652.
4. Gillam, R. B., Cowan, N., & Day, L. S. (1995). Sequential memory in children with and without language impairment. *Journal of Speech and Hearing Research, 38,* 393–402.
5. Johnson, C. J. (1995). Expanding norms for narration. *Language, Speech, and Hearing Services in Schools, 26,* 326–341.
6. Sabers, D. L. (1996). By their tests we will know them. *Language, Speech, and Hearing Services in Schools, 27,* 102–108.
7. Sparks, R., Ganschow, L., & Thomas, A. (1996). Role of intelligence tests in speech/language referrals. *Perceptual and Motor Skills, 83,* 195–204.
8. Wiig, E. H., Jones, S. S., & Wiig, E. D. (1996). Computer-based assessment of word knowledge in teens with learning disabilities. *Language, Speech, and Hearing Services in Schools, 27,* 21–28.
9. Vallance, D. D., Cummings, R. L., & Humphries, T. (1998). Mediators of the risk for problem behavior in children with language learning disabilities. *Journal of Learning Disabilities, 31,* 160–171.
10. Ward-Lonergan, J. M., Liles, B. Z., & Anderson, A. M. (1998). Listening comprehension and recall abilities in adolescents with language-learning disabilities and without disabilities for social studies lectures. *Journal of Communication Disorders, 31,* 1–32.

[2694]

Test of Language Development—Intermediate, Third Edition.

Purpose: To determine strengths and weaknesses in language skills.

Population: Ages 8-0 to 12-11.

Publication Dates: 1977–1997.

Acronym: TOLD-I:3.

Scores, 12: General Intelligence/Aptitude Quotient, Spoken Language Quotient (SLQ), Listening Quotient (LiQ), Speaking Quotient (SpA), Semantics Quotient (SeQ), Syntax Quotient (SyQ), Sentence Combining (SC), Picture Vocabulary (PV), Word Ordering (WO), Generals (GL), Grammatic Comprehension (GC), Malapropism (MP).

Administration: Individual

Price Data, 1999: $154 per complete kit.

Time: (30–60) minutes.

Comments: Primary edition also available.

Authors: Donald D. Hammill and Phyllis L. Newcomer.

Publisher: PRO-ED.

Cross References: See T4:2767 (7 references); for reviews by Rebecca McCauley and Kenneth G. Shipley of the TOLD-I:2, see 11:436 (5 references). For a review by Doris V. Allen of an earlier version of the entire Test of Language Development, see 9:1261 (5 references).

TEST REFERENCES

1. Catts, H. W., & Kamhi, A. G. (1986). The linguistic basis of reading disorders: Implications for the speech-language pathologist. *Language, Speech, and Hearing Services in Schools, 17,* 329–341.
2. Fujiki, M., Brinton, B., & Dunton, S. (1987). A grammatical judgement screening test for young elementary school-aged children. *Language, Speech, and Hearing Services in Schools, 18,* 131–143.
3. Koenig, L. A., & Biel, C. D. (1989). A delivery system of comprehensive language services in a school district. *Language, Speech, and Hearing Services in Schools, 20,* 338–365.
4. Miniutti, A. M. (1991). Language deficiencies in inner-city children with learning and behavioral problems. *Language, Speech, and Hearing Services in Schools, 22,* 31–38.
5. Shelton, B. S., Gast, D. L., Wolery, M., & Winterling, V. (1991). The role of small group interaction in facilitating observational and incidental learning. *Language, Speech, and Hearing Services in Schools, 22,* 123–133.
6. Abkarian, G. G. (1992). Communication effects of prenatal alcohol exposure. *Journal of Communication Disorders, 25,* 221–240.
7. Mack, A. E., & Warr-Leeper, G. A. (1992). Language abilities in boys with chronic behavior disorders. *Language, Speech, and Hearing Services in Schools, 23,* 214–223.
8. Shuster, L. I., Ruscello, D. M., & Haines, K. B. (1992). Acoustic patterns of an adolescent with multiple articulation errors. *Journal of Communication Disorders, 25,* 165–174.
9. Masterson, J. J. (1993). The performance of children with language-learning disabilities on two types of cognitive tasks. *Journal of Speech and Hearing Research, 36,* 1026–1036.
10. Masterson, J. J., Evans, L. H., & Aloia, M. (1993). Verbal analogical reasoning in children with language-learning disabilities. *Journal of Speech and Hearing Research, 36,* 76–82.
11. Walker, D., Greenwood, C., Hart, B., & Carter, J. (1994). Prediction of school outcomes based on early language production and socioeconomic factors. *Child Development, 65,* 606–621.
12. Wiig, E. H., & Wilson, C. C. (1994). Is a question a question? Passage understanding by preadolescents with learning disabilities. *Language, Speech, and Hearing Services in Schools, 25,* 241–250.
13. Hedrick, W. B., & Cunningham, J. W. (1995). The relationship between wide reading and listening comprehension of written language. *Journal of Reading Behavior, 27,* 425–438.
14. Klein, S. K., Kurtzberg, D., Brattson, A., Kreuzer, J. A., Stapells, D. R., Dunn, M. A., Rapin, I., & Vaughn, H. G., Jr. (1995). Electrophysiologic manifestations of impaired temporal lobe auditory processing in verbal auditory agnosia. *Brain and Language, 51,* 383–405.
15. Liles, B. Z., Duffy, R. J., Merritt, D. D., & Purcell, S. L. (1995). Measurement of narrative discourse ability in children with language disorders. *Journal of Speech and Hearing Research, 38,* 415–425.
16. Pearl, R., & Donahue, M. (1995). Brief report: Four years after a preterm birth: Children's development and their mother's beliefs and expectations. *Journal of Pediatric Psychology, 20,* 363–370.
17. Scott, C. M., & Stokes, S. L. (1995). Measures of syntax in school-age children and adolescents. *Language, Speech, and Hearing Services in Schools, 26,* 309–319.
18. Stevens, L. J., & Bliss, L. S. (1995). Conflict resolution abilities of children with specific language impairment and children with normal language. *Journal of Speech and Hearing Research, 38,* 599–611.
19. Tomblin, J. B., Abbas, P. J., Records, N. L., & Brenneman, L. M. (1995). Auditory evoked responses to frequency-modulated tones in children with specific language impairment. *Journal of Speech and Hearing Research, 38,* 387–392.
20. Sabers, D. L. (1996). By their tests we will know them. *Language, Speech, and Hearing Services in Schools, 27,* 102–108.
21. Schneider, P., & Watkins, R. V. (1996). Applying Vygotskian developmental theory to language intervention. *Language, Speech, and Hearing Services in Schools, 27,* 157–170.
22. Sparks, R., Ganschow, L., & Thomas, A. (1996). Role of intelligence tests in speech/language referrals. *Perceptual and Motor Skills, 83,* 195–204.
23. Wiig, E. H., Jones, S. S., & Wiig, E. D. (1996). Computer-based assessment of word knowledge in teens with learning disabilities. *Language, Speech, and Hearing Services in Schools, 27,* 21–28.
24. Vallance, D. D., & Wintre, M. G. (1997). Discourse processes underlying social competence in children with language learning disabilities. *Development and Psychopathology, 9,* 95–108.
25. Tomblin, J. B., & Buckwalter, P. R. (1998). Heritability of poor language achievement among twins. *Journal of Speech, Language, and Hearing Research, 41,* 188–199.
26. Vallance, D. D., Cummings, R. L., & Humphries, T. (1998). Mediators of the risk for problem behavior in children with language learning disabilities. *Journal of Learning Disabilities, 31,* 160–171.
27. Ward-Lonergan, J. M., Liles, B. Z., & Anderson, A. M. (1998). Listening comprehension and recall abilities in adolescents with language-learning disabilities and without disabilities for social studies lectures. *Journal of Communication Disorders, 31,* 1–32.

[2695]

Test of Language Development—Primary, Third Edition.

Purpose: To determine children's specific strengths and weaknesses in language skills.

Population: Ages 4-0 to 8-11.

Publication Dates: 1977–1997.

Acronym: TOLD-P:3.

Scores, 15: Subtests (Picture Vocabulary, Relational Vocabulary, Oral Vocabulary, Grammatic Understanding, Sentence Imitation, Grammatic Completion, Word Discrimination [Optional], Phoenemic Analysis [Optional], Word Articulation [Optional]); Composites (Listening, Organizing, Speaking, Semantics, Syntax, Spoken Language).
Administration: Individual.
Parts, 2: Subtests, Composites.
Price Data, 1999: $218 per complete kit.
Time: (60) minutes.
Comments: Intermediate edition also available; orally administered; examiners need formal training in assessment.
Authors: Phyllis L. Newcomer and Donald D. Hammill.
Publisher: PRO-ED.
Cross References: See T4:2768 (21 references); for reviews by Linda Crocker and Carol E. Westby of a previous edition, see 11:437 (20 references).

TEST REFERENCES

1. Catts, H. W., & Kamhi, A. G. (1986). The linguistic basis of reading disorders: Implications for the speech-language pathologist. *Language, Speech, and Hearing Services in Schools, 17,* 329–341.

2. Grossman, F. M. (1986). Statistics for determining relative strengths and weaknesses on the Test of Language Development—Primary. *Language, Speech, and Hearing Services in Schools, 17,* 312–317.

3. Channell, R. W., & Peek, M. S. (1989). Four measures of vocabulary ability compared in older preschool children. *Language, Speech, and Hearing Services in Schools, 20,* 407–419.

4. Hargrove, P. M., Roetzel, K., & Hoodin, R. B. (1989). Modifying the prosody of a language-impaired child. *Language, Speech, and Hearing Services in Schools, 20,* 245–258.

5. Slavin, R. E., Madden, N. A., Kurweit, N. L., Livermon, B. J., & Dolan, L. (1990). Success for all: First-year outcomes of a comprehensive plan for reforming urban education. *American Educational Research Journal, 27,* 255-278.

6. Channell, R. W., & Ford, C. T. (1991). Four grammatic completion measures of language ability. *Language, Speech, and Hearing Services in Schools, 22,* 211–218.

7. Fujiki, M., & Brinton, B. (1991). The verbal noncommunicator: A case study. *Language, Speech, and Hearing Services in Schools, 22,* 322–333.

8. Rubin, H., Patterson, P. A., & Kantor, M. (1991). Morphological development and writing ability in children and adults. *Language, Speech, and Hearing Services in Schools, 22,* 228–235.

9. Shipley, K. G., Maddox, M. A., & Driver, J. E. (1991). Children's development of irregular past tense verb forms. *Language, Speech, and Hearing Services in Schools, 22,* 115–122.

10. Wilson, K. S., Blackmon, R. C., Hall, R. E., & Elcholtz, G. E. (1991). Methods of language assessment: A survey of California public school clinicians. *Language, Speech, and Hearing Services in Schools, 22,* 236–241.

11. Abkarian, G. G. (1992). Communication effects of prenatal alcohol exposure. *Journal of Communication Disorders, 25,* 221–240.

12. Leonard, L. B., McGregor, K. K., & Allen, G. D. (1992). Grammatical morphology and speech perception in children with specific language impairment. *Journal of Speech and Hearing Research, 35,* 1076–1085.

13. Marcell, M. M., & Cohen, S. (1992). Hearing abilities of Down syndrome and other mentally handicapped adolescents. *Research in Development Disabilities, 13,* 533-551.

14. Masterson, J. J., & Kamhi, A. G. (1992). Linguistic trade-offs in school-age children with and without language disorders. *Journal of Speech and Hearing Research, 35,* 1064–1075.

15. McGregor, K. K., & Schwartz, R. G. (1992). Converging evidence for underlying phonological representation in a child who misarticulates. *Journal of Speech and Hearing Research, 35,* 596–603.

16. Catts, H. W. (1993). The relationship between speech-language impairments and reading disabilities. *Journal of Speech and Hearing Research, 36,* 948–958.

17. Masterson, J. J. (1993). The performance of children with language-learning disabilities on two types of cognitive tasks. *Journal of Speech and Hearing Research, 36,* 1026–1036.

18. Masterson, J. J., Evans, L. H., & Aloia, M. (1993). Verbal analogical reasoning in children with language-learning disabilities. *Journal of Speech and Hearing Research, 36,* 76–82.

19. Montgomery, J. W. (1993). Haptic recognition of children with specific language impairment: Effects of response modality. *Journal of Speech and Hearing Research, 36,* 98–104.

20. Paul, R., Lynn, T. F., & Lohr-Flanders, M. (1993). History of middle ear involvement and speech/language development in late talkers. *Journal of Speech and Hearing Research, 36,* 1055–1062.

21. Sturner, R. A., Heller, J. H., Funk, S. G., & Layton, T. L. (1993). The Fluharty Preschool Speech and Language Screening Test: A population-based validation study using sample-independent decision rules. *Journal of Speech and Hearing Research, 36,* 738–745.

22. Sutton, A. E., & Gallagher, T. M. (1993). Verb class distinctions and AAC language-encoding limitations. *Journal of Speech and Hearing Research, 36,* 1216–1226.

23. Weismer, S. E., & Hesketh, L. J. (1993). The influence of prosodic and gestural cues on novel word acquisition by children with specific language impairment. *Journal of Speech and Hearing Research, 36,* 1013–1025.

24. Camarata, S. M., Nelson, K. E., & Camarata, M. N. (1994). Comparison of conversational-recasting and imitative procedures for training grammatical structures in children with specific language impairment. *Journal of Speech and Hearing, 37,* 1414–1423.

25. Haley, K. L., Camarata, S. M., & Nelson, K. E. (1994). Social valence in children with specific language impairment during imitation-based and conversation-based language intervention. *Journal of Speech and Hearing Research, 37,* 378–388.

26. Hansen, J., & Bowey, J. A. (1994). Phonological analysis skills, verbal working memory, and reading ability in second-grade children. *Child Development, 65,* 938-950.

27. Hoehn, T. P., & Baumeister, A. A. (1994). A critique of the application of sensory integration therapy to children with learning disabilities. *Journal of Learning Disabilities, 27,* 338–350.

28. Plante, E., & Vance, R. (1994). Selection of preschool language tests: A data-based approach. *Language, Speech, and Hearing Services in Schools, 25,* 15–24.

29. Records, N. L., & Tomblin, J. B. (1994). Clinical decision making: Describing the decision rules of practicing speech-language pathologists. *Journal of Speech and Hearing Research, 37,* 144–156.

30. Sommers, R. K., Kozarevich, M., & Michaels, C. (1994). Word skills of children normal and impaired in communication skills and measures of language and speech development. *Journal of Communication Disorders, 27,* 223–240.

31. Tyler, A. A., & Sandoval, K. T. (1994). Preschoolers with phonological and language disorders: Treating different linguistic domains. *Language, Speech, and Hearing Services in Schools, 25,* 215–234.

32. Walker, D., Greenwood, C., Hart, B., & Carter, J. (1994). Prediction of school outcomes based on early language production and socioeconomic factors. *Child Development, 65,* 606–621.

33. Windsor, J., Doyle, S. S., & Siegel, G. M. (1994). Language acquisition after mutism: A longitudinal case study of autism. *Journal of Speech and Hearing Research, 37,* 96–105.

34. Bowey, J. A. (1995). Socioeconomic status differences in preschool phonological sensitivity and first-grade reading achievement. *Journal of Educational Psychology, 87,* 476–487.

35. Giddan, J. J., Wahl, J., & Brogan, M. (1995). Importance of communication training for psychiatric residents and mental health trainees. *Child Psychiatry and Human Development, 26,* 19–28.

36. Gilbertson, M., & Kamhi, A. G. (1995). Novel word learning in children with language impairment. *Journal of Speech and Hearing Research, 38,* 630–642.

37. Hulsing, M. M., Luetke-Stahlman, B., Loeb, D. F., Nelson, P., & Wegner, J. (1995). Analysis of successful initiations of three children with hearing loss mainstreamed in kindergarten classrooms. *Language, Speech, and Hearing Services in Schools, 26,* 45–55.

38. Jordan, N. C., Levine, S. C., & Huttenlocher, J. (1995). Calculation abilities in young children with different patterns of cognitive functioning. *Journal of Learning Disabilities, 28,* 53–64.

39. Kamhi, A. G., Ward, M. F., & Mills, E. A. (1995). Hierarchical planning abilities in children with specific language impairments. *Journal of Speech and Hearing Research, 38,* 1108–1116.

40. Lahey, M., & Edwards, J. (1995). Specific language impairment: Preliminary investigation of factors associated with family history and with patterns of language performance. *Journal of Speech and Hearing Research, 38,* 643–657.

41. Lincoln, A. J., Courchesne, E., Harms, L., & Allen, M. (1995). Sensory modulation of auditory stimuli in childeren with autism and developmental language disorder: Event-related brain potential evidence. *Journal of Autism and Developmental Disorders, 25,* 521–539.

42. Marcell, M. M., Ridgeway, M. M., Sewell, D. H., & Whelan, M. L. (1995). Sentence imitation by adolescents and young adults with Down's syndrome and other intellectual disabilities. *Journal of Intellectual Disability Research, 39,* 215–232.

43. Nippold, M. A. (1995). School-age children and adolescents: Norms for word definition. *Language, Speech, and Hearing Services in Schools, 26,* 320–325.

44. Oetting, J. B., Rice, M. L., & Swank, L. K. (1995). Quick incidental learning (QUIL) of words by school-age children with and without SLI. *Journal of Speech and Hearing Research, 38,* 434–445.

45. Tomblin, J. B., Abbas, P. J., Records, N. L., & Brenneman, L. M. (1995). Auditory evoked responses to frequency-modulated tones in children with specific language impairment. *Journal of Speech and Hearing Research, 38,* 387–392.

46. Young, R. L., & Nettelbeck, T. (1995). The abilities of a musical savant and his family. *Journal of Autism and Developmental Disorders, 25,* 231–248.

47. Beitchman, J. H., Brownlie, E. B., Inglis, A., Wild, J., Ferguson, B., Schachter, D., Lancee, W., Wilson, B., & Mathews, R. (1996). Seven-year follow-up of speech/language impaired and control children: Psychiatric outcome. *Journal of Child Psychology and Psychiatry, 37,* 961–970.

48. Clark, M. G., & Leonard, L. B. (1996). Lexical comprehension and grammatical deficits in children with specific language impairment. *Journal of Communication Disorders, 29,* 95–105.
49. Edwards, J., & Lahey, M. (1996). Auditory lexical decisions of children with specific language impairment. *Journal of Speech, Language, and Hearing Research, 39,* 1263–1273.
50. Fazio, B. B. (1996). Mathematical abilities in children with specific language impairment: A 2-year follow-up. *Journal of Speech and Hearing Research, 39,* 839–849.
51. Fazio, B. B., Naremore, R. C., & Connell, P. J. (1996). Tracking children from poverty at risk for specific language impairment: A 3-year longitudinal study. *Journal of Speech and Hearing Research, 39,* 611–624.
52. Fujiki, M., Brinton, B., & Todd, C. M. (1996). Social skills of children with specific language impairment. *Language, Speech, and Hearing Services in Schools, 27,* 195–202.
53. Gierut, J. A., Morrisette, M. L., Hughes, M. T., & Rowland, S. (1996). Phonological treatment of efficacy and developmental norms. *Language, Speech, and Hearing Services in Schools, 27,* 215–230.
54. Lahey, M., & Edwards, J. (1996). Why do children with specific language impairment name pictures more slowly than their peers? *Journal of Speech, Language, and Hearing Research, 39,* 1081–1098.
55. Livingston, J. A., & Gentile, J. R. (1996). Mastery learning and the decreasing variability hypothesis. *Journal of Educational Research, 90,* 67–86.
56. McFadden, T. V. (1996). Creating language impairments in typically achieving children: The pitfalls of "normal" normative sampling. *Language, Speech, and Hearing Services in Schools, 27,* 3–9.
57. Nelson, K. E., Camarata, S. M., Welsh, J., Butkovsky, L., & Camarata, M. (1996). Effects of imitative and conversational recasting treatment on the acquisition of grammar in children with specific language impairment and younger language-normal children. *Journal of Speech and Hearing Research, 39,* 850–859.
58. Paradis, C. M., Gironda, F., & Bennett, M. (1996). Cognitive impairment in Schwartz-Jampel syndrome: A case study. *Brain and Language, 56,* 301–305.
59. Rice, M. L., & Wexler, K. (1996). Toward tense as a clinical marker of specific language impairment in English-speaking children. *Journal of Speech and Hearing Research, 39,* 1239–1257.
60. Sabers, D. L. (1996). By their tests we will know them. *Language, Speech, and Hearing Services in Schools, 27,* 102–108.
61. Smith, L. J., Ross, S. M., & Casey, J. (1996). Multi-site comparison of the effects of success for all on reading achievement. *Journal of Literacy Research, 28,* 329–353.
62. Sparks, R., Ganschow, L., & Thomas, A. (1996). Role of intelligence tests in speech/language referrals. *Perceptual and Motor Skills, 83,* 195–204.
63. Tomblin, J. B., Records, N. L., & Zhang, X. (1996). A system for the diagnosis of specific language impairment in kindergarten children. *Journal of Speech and Hearing Research, 39,* 1284–1294.
64. Werts, M. G., Wolery, M., Venn, M. L., Deinblowski, D., & Doren, H. (1996). Effects of transition-based teaching with instructive feedback on skill acquisition by children with and without disabilities. *Journal of Educational Research, 90,* 75–86.
65. Fazio, B. B. (1997). Learning a new poem: Memory for connected speech and phonological awareness in low-income children with and without specific language impairment. *Journal of Speech, Language, and Hearing Research, 40,* 1285–1297.
66. Gauger, L. M., Lombardino, L. J., & Leonard, C. M. (1997). Brain morphology in children with specific language impairment. *Journal of Speech, Language, and Hearing Research, 40,* 1272–1284.
67. Lewis, B. A., & Freebairn, L. (1997). Subgrouping children with familial phonologic disorders. *Journal of Communication Disorders, 30,* 385–402.
68. Oetting, J. B., & Horohov, J. E. (1997). Past-tense marking by children with and without specific language impairment. *Journal of Speech, Language, and Hearing Research, 40,* 62–74.
69. Paul, R., Murray, C., Clancy, K., & Andrews, D. (1997). Reading and metaphonological outcomes in late talkers. *Journal of Speech, Language, and Hearing Research, 40,* 1037–1047.
70. Spitz, R. V., Tallal, P., Flax, J., & Benasich, A. A. (1997). Look who's talking: A prospective study of familial transmission of language impairments. *Journal of Speech, Language, and Hearing Research, 40,* 990–1001.
71. Tomblin, J. B., Records, N. L., Buckwalter, P., Zhang, X., Smith, E., & O'Brien, M. (1997). Prevalence of specific language impairment in kindergarten children. *Journal of Speech, Language, and Hearing Research, 40,* 1245–1260.
72. Tomblin, J. B., & Buckwalter, P. R. (1998). Heritability of poor language achievement among twins. *Journal of Speech, Language, and Hearing Research, 41,* 188–199.

[2696]

Test of Learning Ability.

Purpose: Constructed to assess spatial, verbal, and numerical ability.
Population: Industrial and business applicants.
Publication Dates: 1947-1989.
Scores: Total score only.
Administration: Group.
Forms, 2: S89, T89.
Price Data: Not available.
Time: 12 minutes.
Comments: Previously known as RBH Test of Learning Ability.
Authors: Richardson, Bellows, Henry & Co., Inc.
Publisher: Richardson, Bellows, Henry & Co., Inc. [No reply from publisher; status unknown].
Cross References: For reviews by Sue M. Legg and Victor L. Willson, see 12:396; see T3:1984 (1 reference) and T2:44 (1 reference); for a review by Erwin K. Taylor, see 7:379 (2 references); see also 6:504 (2 references).

[2697]

Test of Library/Study Skills.

Purpose: Designed to measure the basic essentials of library skills.
Population: Grades 2-5, 4-9, 8-12.
Publication Date: 1975.
Scores: Total score only.
Administration: Group.
Manual: No manual.
Price Data: Not available.
Time: (50) minutes.
Authors: Irene Gullette and Frances Hatfield.
Publisher: Larlin Corporation [No reply from publisher; status unknown].

[2698]

Test of Mathematical Abilities for Gifted Students.

Purpose: "Designed to identify students who have talent or giftedness in mathematics."
Population: Ages 6–12.
Publication Date: 1998.
Acronym: TOMAGS.
Scores: Total score only.
Administration: Group or individual.
Levels, 2: Primary, Intermediate.
Price Data, 1999: $139 per complete kit including manual (53 pages), 25 each Primary Level and Intermediate Level student booklets, and 25 each Primary Level and Intermediate Level profile/scoring sheets; $39 per 25 student booklets (specify level); $14 per 25 profile/scoring sheets (specify level); $40 per manual.
Time: (30–60) minutes.
Authors: Gail R. Ryser and Susan K. Johnsen.
Publisher: PRO-ED.

[2699]

Test of Mathematical Abilities, Second Edition.

Purpose: "A measure of math ability."
Population: Ages 8-0 to 18-11.
Publication Dates: 1984–1994.

Acronym: TOMA-2.
Scores, 6: Vocabulary, Computation, General Information, Story Problems, Attitude Toward Math, Total.
Administration: Group.
Price Data, 1999: $84 per complete kit including 25 Profile/Record forms and Examiner's Manual ('94, 51 pages); $42 per 25 Profile/Record forms; $42 per examiner's manual.
Time: (120–130) minutes.
Authors: Virginia L. Brown, Mary E. Cronin, and Elizabeth McEntire.
Publisher: PRO-ED.
Cross References: For reviews by Delwyn L. Harnisch and Rosemary Sutton, see 13:329 (1 reference); for a review by Mark L. Davison of the earlier edition, see 9:1263.

[2700]

Test of Mechanical Concepts.

Purpose: "Designed to measure an individual's ability to visualize and understand basic mechanical relationships."
Population: Applicants for industrial positions.
Publication Date: 1976–1995.
Scores, 4: Mechanical Interrelationships, Mechanical Tools and Devices, Spatial Relations, Total.
Administration: Individual or group.
Forms, 2: A, B.
Price Data, 1998: $87 per start-up kit including 25 test booklets (specify Form A or Form B) and examiner's manual; $77 per 25 test booklets (quantity discounts available; specify Form A or Form B); $19.75 per examiner's manual.
Time: No limit (approximately 35–45 minutes).
Comments: Previously listed as SRA Test of Mechanical Concepts.
Author: Science Research Associates.
Publisher: NCS (Rosemont).
Cross References: For reviews by Lorraine D. Eyde and Lyle F. Schoenfeldt, see 8:1045.

TEST REFERENCE

1. Pungello, E. P., Kupersmidt, J. B., Patterson, C. J., & Burchinal, M. R. (1996). Environmental risk factors and children's achievement from middle childhood to early adolescence. *Developmental Psychology, 32,* 755–767.

[2701]

Test of Memory and Learning.

Purpose: For "evaluating children or adolescents referred for learning disabilities, traumatic brain injury, neurological diseases, serious emotional disturbance, Attention Deficit-Hyperactivity Disorder."
Population: Ages 5 to 19.
Publication Date: 1994.
Acronym: TOMAL.
Scores, 25: 9 Verbal subtest scores (Memory for Stories, Word Selective Reminding, Object Recall, Digits Forward, Paired Recall, Letters Forward, Digits Backward, Letters Backward, Total); 7 Nonverbal subtest scores (Facial Memory, Visual Selective Reminding, Abstract Visual Memory, Visual Sequential Memory, Memory for Location, Manual Imitation, Total); 4 composite scores (Verbal Memory Index, Nonverbal Memory Index, Composite Memory Index, Delayed Recall Index); 5 Delayed Recall scores (Memory for Stories, Facial Memory, Word Selective Reminding, Visual Selective Reminding, Total).
Administration: Individual.
Price Data, 1999: $209 per complete kit including examiner's manual (105 pages), picture book, 25 record forms and administration booklets, 25 supplementary analysis forms, facial memory picture book, 15 facial memory chips, visual selective reminding test board, and a set of delayed recall cue cards; $44 per examiner's manual; $59 per picture book; $44 per 25 record forms and administration booklets; $14 per 25 supplementary analysis forms; $25 per facial memory picture book; $7 per visual selective reminding test board; $17 per delayed cue card set; $89 per software scoring and report system.
Time: (40–45) minutes.
Authors: Cecil R. Reynolds and Erin D. Bigler.
Publisher: PRO-ED.
Cross References: For reviews by Karen Geller and Susan J. Maller, see 13:330 (1 reference).

[2702]

Test of Memory Malingering.

Purpose: To "assist neuropsychologists in discriminating between bona fide memory-impaired patients and malingerers."
Population: Ages 16 to 84.
Publication Date: 1996.
Acronym: TOMM.
Scores: Total score only.
Administration: Individual
Price Data, 1999: $95 per complete kit including manual (55 pages), 25 recording forms, and 1 set of stimulus booklets; $20 per 25 recording forms; $50 per set of 3 stimulus booklets; $35 per manual; $60 per Computer Program for Windows™ including user's manual, software manual, and 3 uses.
Time: (15) minutes.
Comments: Windows™ computer software available on CD or 3.5-inch disk to administer, score, and report results of TOMM.
Author: Tom N. Tombaugh.
Publisher: Multi-Health Systems, Inc.

[2703]

Test of Minimal Articulation Competence.

Purpose: Assesses articulation performance in children and adults.
Population: Ages 3 to adult.

Publication Date: 1981.
Acronym: T-MAC.
Scores, 3: Vowel/Diphthong, Consonant, Total.
Administration: Individual.
Parts, 3: Complete Test, Screening Test, Rapid Screening Test.
Price Data, 1999: $103.50 per complete program including Examiner's Manual and 25 record forms; $38.50 per 25 record forms; $67 per examiner's manual including administration, scoring, and interpretation information.
Time: Administration time not reported.
Author: Wayne Secord.
Publisher: The Psychological Corporation.
Cross References: For a review by Barbara W. Hodson, see 9:1264.

TEST REFERENCES

1. Montoya, I. D., Haertzen, C., Hess, J. M., Cori, L., Fudala, P. J., Johnson, R. E., & Gorelick, D. A. (1995). Comparison of psychological symptoms between drug abusers seeking and not seeking treatment. *The Journal of Nervous and Mental Disease, 183,* 50-53.

2. Pawluk, L. K., Hurwitz, T. D., Schluter, J. L., Ullevig, C., & Mahowald, M. W. (1995). Psychiatric morbidity in narcoleptics on chronic high dose methylphenidate therapy. *The Journal of Nervous and Mental Disease, 183,* 45-48.

[2704]
Test of Nonverbal Intelligence, Third Edition.

Purpose: "Developed to assess aptitude, intelligence, abstract reasoning, and problem solving in a completely language-free format."
Population: Ages 6-0 through 89-11.
Publication Dates: 1982–1997.
Acronym: TONI-3.
Scores: Total score only.
Administration: Individual.
Price Data, 1999: $229 per complete kit including manual ('97, 160 pages), picture book, and 50 each Form A and Form B answer booklets and record forms; $39 per 50 answer booklet and record forms (specify Form A or B); $96 per picture book; $59 per manual.
Time: (15–20) minutes.
Authors: Linda Brown, Rita J. Sherbenou, and Susan K. Johnson.
Publisher: PRO-ED.
Cross References: See T4:2775 (10 references); for reviews by Kevin K. Murphy and T. Steuart Watson of the Second Edition, see 11:439 (9 references); for reviews by Philip M. Clark and Samuel T. Mayo of the original edition, see 9:1266.

TEST REFERENCES

1. Kowall, M. A., Watson, G. M. W., & Madak, P. R. (1990). Concurrent validity of the Test of Nonverbal Intelligence with referred suburban and Canadian native children. *Journal of Clinical Psychology, 46,* 632–636.

2. Fey, M. E. (1992). Clinical forum: Phonological assessment and treatment. Articulation and phonology: Inextricable constructs in speech pathology. *Language, Speech, and Hearing Services in Schools, 23,* 225–232.

3. Gillam, R. B., & Johnston, J. R. (1992). Spoken and written language relationships in language/learning-impaired and normally achieving school-age children. *Journal of Speech, Language, and Hearing Research, 35,* 1303–1315.

4. Lewis, B. A. (1992). Pedigree analysis of children with phonology disorders. *Journal of Learning Disabilities, 25,* 586–597.

5. Lewis, B. A., & Freebairn, L. (1992). Residual effects of preschool phonology disorders in grade school, adolescence, and adulthood. *Journal of Speech and Hearing Research, 35,* 819–831.

6. Masterson, J. J., & Kamhi, A. G. (1992). Linguistic trade-offs in school-age children with and without language disorders. *Journal of Speech and Hearing Research, 35,* 1064–1075.

7. Shuster, L. I., Ruscello, D. M., & Haines, K. B. (1992). Acoustic patterns of an adolescent with multiple articulation errors. *Journal of Communication Disorders, 25,* 165–174.

8. Valliant, P. M., & Blasutti, B. (1992). Personality differences of sex offenders referred for treatment. *Psychological Reports, 71,* 1067-1074.

9. Fuller, G. B., & Vance, B. (1993). Comparison of the Minnesota Percepto-Diagnostic Test—Revised and Bender-Gestalt in predicting achievement. *Psychology in the Schools, 30,* 220-226.

10. Landry, S. H., Robinson, S. S., Copeland, D., & Garner, P. W. (1993). goal-directed behavior and perception of self-competence in children with spina bifida. *Journal of Pediatric Psychology, 18,* 389–396.

11. Masterson, J. J. (1993). The performance of children with language-learning disabilities on two types of cognitive tasks. *Journal of Speech and Hearing Research, 36,* 1026–1036.

12. Masterson, J. J., Evans, L. H., & Aloia, M. (1993). Verbal analogical reasoning in children with language-learning disabilities. *Journal of Speech and Hearing Research, 36,* 76–82.

13. Nelson, C., & Valliant, P. M. (1993). Personality dynamics of adolescent boys where the father was absent. *Perceptual and Motor Skills, 76,* 435–443.

14. Sutton, A. E., & Gallagher, T. M. (1993). Verb class distinctions and AAC language-encoding limitations. *Journal of Speech and Hearing Research, 36,* 1216–1226.

15. Swisher, L., & Plante, E. (1993). Nonverbal IQ tests reflect different relations among skills for specifically language-impaired and normal children: Brief report. *Journal of Communication Disorders, 26,* 65–71.

16. Cole, K. N., Mills, P. E., & Kelley, D. (1994). Agreement of assessment profiles used in cognitive referencing. *Language, Speech, and Hearing Services in Schools, 25,* 25–31.

17. D'Amato, R. C., Lidiak, S. E., & Lassiter, K. S. (1994). Comparing verbal and nonverbal intellectual functioning with the TONI and WISC-R. *Perceptual and Motor Skills, 78,* 701–702.

18. Gonzalez, V. (1994). A model of cognitive, cultural, and linguistic variables affecting bilingual Hispanic children's development of concepts and language. *Hispanic Journal of Behavioral Sciences, 16,* 396–421.

19. Hillbrand, M., Krystal, J. H., Sharpe, K. S., & Foster, H. G. (1994). Clinical predictors of self-mutilation in hospitalized forensic patients. *The Journal of Nervous and Mental Disease, 182,* 9-13.

20. Niver, J. M., & Schery, T. K. (1994). Deaf children's spoken language output with a hearing peer and with a hearing mother. *American Annals of the Deaf, 139,* 96-103.

21. Swank, L. K., & Catts, H. W. (1994). Phonological awareness and written word decoding. *Language, Speech, and Hearing Services in Schools, 25,* 9–14.

22. Valliant, P. M., & Raven, L. M. (1994). Management of anger and its effect on incarcerated assaultive and nonassaultive offenders. *Psychological Reports, 75,* 275-278.

23. Gilbertson, M., & Kamhi, A. G. (1995). Novel word learning in children with language impairment. *Journal of Speech and Hearing Research, 38,* 630–642.

24. Gillam, R. B., Cowan, N., & Day, L. S. (1995). Sequential memory in children with and without language impairment. *Journal of Speech and Hearing Research, 38,* 393–402.

25. Gillon, G., & Dodd, B. (1995). The effects of training phonological, semantic, and syntactic processing skills in spoken language on reading ability. *Language, Speech, and Hearing Services in Schools, 26,* 58–68.

26. Jordan, N. C., Levine, S. C., & Huttenlocher, J. (1995). Calculation abilities in young children with different patterns of cognitive functioning. *Journal of Learning Disabilities, 28,* 53–64.

27. Kamhi, A. G., Ward, M. F., & Mills, E. A. (1995). Hierarchical planning abilities in children with specific language impairments. *Journal of Speech and Hearing Research, 38,* 1108–1116.

28. Kertoy, M. K., & Goetz, K. M. (1995). The relationship between listening performance on the sentence verification technique and other measures of listening comprehension. *Contemporary Educational Psychology, 20,* 320–339.

29. Lahey, M., & Edwards, J. (1995). Specific language impairment: Preliminary investigation of factors associated with family history and with patterns of language performance. *Journal of Speech and Hearing Research, 38,* 643–657.

30. Montgomery, J. W. (1995). Sentence comprehension in children with specific language impairment: The role of phonological working memory. *Journal of Speech and Hearing Research, 38,* 187–199.

31. Oetting, J. B., Rice, M. L., & Swank, L. K. (1995). Quick incidental learning (QUIL) of words by school-age children with and without SLI. *Journal of Speech and Hearing Research, 38,* 434–445.

32. Perez, E., Slate, J. R. Neeley, R., McDaniel, M., Briggs, T., & Layton, K. (1995). Validity of the CELF-R, TONI, and SIT for children referred for auditory processing problems. *Journal of Clinical Psychology, 51,* 540–543.

33. Ricard, R. J., Miller, G. A., & Heffer, R. W. (1995). Developmental trends in the relation between adjustment and academic achievement for elementary school children in mixed-age classrooms. *School Psychology Review, 24,* 258–270.

34. Stevens, L. J., & Bliss, L. S. (1995). Conflict resolution abilities of children with specific language impairment and children with normal language. *Journal of Speech and Hearing Research, 38,* 599–611.

35. Valliant, P. M., Jensen, B., & Raven-Brook, L. (1995). Brief cognitive behavioural therapy with male adolescent offenders in open custody or on probation: An evaluation of management of anger. *Psychological Reports, 76,* 1056–1058.
36. Valliant, P. M., Maksymchuk, L. L., & Antonowicz, D. (1995). Attitudes and personality traits of female adult victims of childhood abuse: A comparison of university students and incarcerated women. *Social Behavior and Personality, 23,* 205–216.
37. Edwards, J., & Lahey, M. (1996). Auditory lexical decisions of children with specific language impairment. *Journal of Speech, Language, and Hearing Research, 39,* 1263–1273.
38. Frey, P. D. (1996). Comparison of visual-motor performance and nonverbal reasoning among child and adolescent patients in an urban psychiatric hospital. *Perceptual and Motor Skills, 82,* 179–184.
39. Fujiki, M., Brinton, B., & Todd, C. M. (1996). Social skills of children with specific language impairment. *Language, Speech, and Hearing Services in Schools, 27,* 195–202.
40. Lahey, M., & Edwards, J. (1996). Why do children with specific language impairment name pictures more slowly than their peers? *Journal of Speech, Language, and Hearing Research, 39,* 1081–1098.
41. Mauer, D. M., & Kamhi, A. G. (1996). Factors that influence phoneme-grapheme correspondence learning. *Journal of Learning Disabilities, 29,* 259–270.
42. McFadden, T. V. (1996). Creating language impairments in typically achieving children: The pitfalls of "normal" normative sampling. *Language, Speech, and Hearing Services in Schools, 27,* 3–9.
43. McFadden, T. V., & Gillam, R. B. (1996). An examination of the quality of narratives produced by children with language disabilities. *Language, Speech, and Hearing Services in Schools, 27,* 48–56.
44. Wiig, E. H., Jones, S. S., & Wiig, E. D. (1996). Computer-based assessment of word knowledge in teens with learning disabilities. *Language, Speech, and Hearing Services in Schools, 27,* 21–28.
45. Gauger, L. M., Lombardino, L. J., & Leonard, C. M. (1997). Brain morphology in children with specific language impairment. *Journal of Speech, Language, and Hearing Research, 40,* 1272–1284.
46. Grimshaw, G. M., Adelstein, A., Bryden, M. P., & MacKinnon, G. E. (1998). First-language acquisition in adolescence: Evidence for a critical period for verbal language development. *Brain and Language, 63,* 237–255.
47. Comeau, L., Cormier, P., Grandmaison, E., & Lacroix, D. (1999). A longitudinal study of plumological processing skills in children learning to read in a second language. *Journal of Educational Psychology, 91,* 29–43.

[2705]

Test of Oral and Limb Apraxia.

Purpose: "Designed to identify, measure, and evaluate the presence of oral and limb apraxia in individuals with developmental or acquired neurologic disorders."
Population: Ages 20–99.
Publication Date: 1992.
Acronym: TOLA.
Scores, 5: Limb, Oral, Pictures, Command, Imitation, Total.
Administration: Individual.
Price Data, 1999: $59 per complete test; $24 per 25 record forms; $19 per stimulus card set; $19 per manual.
Time: (15–20) minutes.
Author: Nancy Helm-Estabrooks.
Publisher: PRO-ED.
Cross References: For reviews by Peggy A. Hicks and Michael Lee Russell, see 13:331.

[2706]

Test of Oral Structures and Functions.

Purpose: "Assesses oral structures and motor integrity during verbal and nonverbal oral functioning."
Population: Ages 7-Adults.
Publication Date: 1986.
Acronym: TOSF.
Scores, 16: Speech Survey (Articulation, Rate/Prosody, Fluency, Voice, Total); Verbal Oral Functioning (Resonance, Balance, Sequenced Syllables, Mixed Syllable Sequence, Sequenced Vowels, Sequenced Syllable Rates, Total); Nonverbal Oral Functions (Isolated Functioning, Sequenced Functioning); Survey of Orofacial Structures; History-Behavioral Survey.
Administration: Individual.
Price Data, 1992: $60 per TOSF complete kit including manual (36 pages), 25 test booklets, finger cots, tongue blades, penlight, and balloons; $22.50 per examiner's manual; $25 per 25 test booklets; $6 per oroscope penlight.
Time: (20) minutes.
Author: Gary J. Vitali.
Publisher: Slosson Educational Publications, Inc.
Cross References: For reviews by Ronald B. Gillam and Roger L. Towne, see 12:397.

TEST REFERENCES

1. Lewis, B. A. (1992). Pedigree analysis of children with phonology disorders. *Journal of Learning Disabilities, 25,* 586–597.
2. Lewis, B. A., & Freebairn, L. (1992). Residual effects of preschool phonology disorders in grade school, adolescence, and adulthood. *Journal of Speech and Hearing Research, 5,* 819–831.

[2707]

Test of Perceptual Organization.

Purpose: "Designed to measure (1) abstract reasoning, (2) psychomotor functioning, and (3) the ability to follow specific, exacting instructions in an accurate manner."
Population: "Normals and psychiatric patients ages 12 and over."
Publication Dates: 1967-1970.
Acronym: TPO.
Scores: Total score only.
Administration: Group.
Price Data, 1987: $40 per examiner set including 25 tests, 25 profiles, scoring key, and manual ('70, 24 pages); $15 per 25 tests; $2.75 per scoring key; $8.25 per 25 profiles; $6.75 per manual; $9 per specimen set including manual, forms, and scoring key.
Time: 10(15) minutes.
Comments: Formerly called Test of Abstract Reasoning.
Author: William T. Martin.
Publisher: Psychologists and Educators, Inc.
Cross References: For reviews by A. Ralph Hakstian and Robert C. Nichols, and an excerpted review by Barton B. Proger, see 8:203, see also 7:390 (1 reference).

[2708]

Test of Phonological Awareness.

Purpose: "Measures young children's awareness of individual sounds in words."
Population: Ages 5–8.
Publication Date: 1994.
Acronym: TOPA.

Scores: Total score only.
Administration: Group.
Editions, 2: Kindergarten, Early Elementary.
Price Data, 1999: $143 per complete kit including examiner's manual (38 pages), 25 kindergarten student booklets, 25 early elementary student booklets, 25 kindergarten profile/examiner forms, and 25 early elementary profile/examiner forms; $42 per examiner's manual; $39 per 25 student booklets (specify kindergarten or early elementary); $14 per 25 profile/examiner forms (specify kindergarten or early elementary).
Time: (15–20) minutes.
Authors: Joseph K. Torgesen and Brian R. Bryant.
Publisher: PRO-ED.
Cross References: For reviews by Steven H. Long and Rebecca McCauley, see 13:333 (3 references).

[2709]

Test of Pragmatic Language.

Purpose: Designed "to provide an in-depth screening of the effectiveness and appropriateness of a student's pragmatic, or social, language skills."
Population: Ages 5-0 to 13-11.
Publication Date: 1992.
Acronym: TOPL.
Scores, 3: Listening Skills, Speaking Skills, Total.
Administration: Individual.
Price Data, 1999: $124 per complete kit; $44 per examiner's manual (35 pages); $44 per TOPL picture book; $39 per 25 TOPL profile/examiner record forms.
Time: (45) minutes.
Authors: Diana Phelps-Terasaki and Trisha Phelps-Gunn.
Publisher: PRO-ED.
Cross References: For reviews by Salvador Hector Ochoa and William K. Wilkinson, see 12:398.

[2710]

Test of Problem Solving.

Purpose: Designed to assess children's everyday thinking and reasoning skills.
Population: Ages 6-12.
Publication Date: 1984.
Acronym: TOPS.
Scores, 6: Explaining Inferences, Determining Causes, Negative Why Questions, Determining Solutions, Avoiding Problems, Total.
Administration: Individual.
Price Data, 1988: $57.95 per complete kit including 20 test forms, book of visual stimuli, examiner's manual (83 pages), and vinyl folder; $14.95 per 20 test forms.
Time: (20-25) minutes.
Authors: Linda Zachman, Carol Jorgensen, Rosemary Huisingh, and Mark Barrett.
Publisher: LinguiSystems, Inc.

TEST REFERENCES

1. Skarakis-Doyle, E., & Mallet, C. A. (1991). Test-retest reliability: Another evaluation of the Test of Problem Solving. *Language, Speech, and Hearing Services in Schools, 22,* 278–279.
2. Wilson, K. S., Blackmon, R. C., Hall, R. E., & Elcholtz, G. E. (1991). Methods of language assessment: A survey of California public school clinicians. *Language, Speech, and Hearing Services in Schools, 22,* 236–241.
3. Powell, T. W. (1993). Factorial validity of the Test of Problem Solving. *Perceptual and Motor Skills, 76,* 753–754.
4. Ghaziuddin, M., Bolyard, B., & Alessi, N. (1994). Autistic disorder in Noonan syndrome. *Journal of Intellectual Disability Research, 38,* 67–72.
5. Johnson, C. J. (1995). Expanding norms for narration. *Language, Speech, and Hearing Services in Schools, 26,* 326–341.
6. McFadden, T. V. (1996). Creating language impairments in typically achieving children: The pitfalls of "normal" normative sampling. *Language, Speech, and Hearing Services in Schools, 27,* 3–9.
7. Ripich, D. N., Carpenter, B., & Ziol, E. (1997). Comparison of African-American and white persons with Alzheimer's disease on language measures. *Neurology, 48,* 781–783.
8. Ward-Lonergan, J. M., Liles, B. Z., & Anderson, A. M. (1998). Listening comprehension and recall abilities in adolescents with language-learning disabilities and without disabilities for social studies lectures. *Journal of Communication Disorders, 31,* 1–32.

[2711]

Test of Reading and Number: Inter-American Series.

Purpose: Assesses "achievement in reading and in 19 simple numerical operations for placement and guidance."
Population: Grade 4 entrants.
Publication Date: 1969.
Acronym: TRN.
Scores, 3: Reading, Number, Total.
Administration: Group.
Price Data: Not available.
Time: (34) minutes.
Comments: Experimental form.
Author: Herschel T. Manuel.
Publisher: Guidance Testing Associates [No reply from publisher; status unknown].

[2712]

Test of Reading Comprehension, Third Edition.

Purpose: Designed to "quantify the reading comprehension ability of individuals."
Population: Ages 7-0 to 17-11.
Publication Dates: 1978–1995.
Acronym: TORC-3.
Scores: 9 subtests: General Vocabulary, Syntactic Similarities, Paragraph Reading, Sentence Sequencing, Supplementary (Mathematics Vocabulary, Social Studies Vocabulary, Science Vocabulary, Reading the Directions of Schoolwork), Reading Comprehension Quotient.
Administration: Group or individual.
Price Data, 1999: $154 per complete kit including 10 student booklets, 50 answer sheets and subtest 8, 50 profiles, and manual ('95, 91 pages) in storage box; $34 per 10 student booklets; $39 per 50 answer sheets and subtest 8; $39 per 50 profiles; $46 per manual.
Time: (60) minutes.

Authors: Virginia L. Brown, Donald D. Hammill, and J. Lee Wiederholt.
Publisher: PRO-ED.
Cross References: For reviews by Felice J. Green and Carole Perlman, see 13:334 (3 references); see also T4:2785 (3 references); for reviews by James A. Poteet and Robert J. Tierney of an earlier edition, see 10:372 (4 references); for reviews by Brendon John Bartlett and Joyce Hood of the original edition, see 9:1270; see also T3:2456 (1 reference).

TEST REFERENCE

1. Lovett, M. W., Borden, S. L., Warren-Chapman, P. M., Lacerenza, L., DeLuca, T., & Giovinazzo, R. (1996). Text comprehension training for disabled readers: An evaluation of reciprocal teaching and text analysis training programs. *Brain and Language, 54,* 447–480.

[2713]

Test of Retail Sales Insight.

Purpose: "Developed ...primarily for assessing the degree of knowledge that an individual has in relation to retail selling."
Population: Retail clerks and students.
Publication Dates: 1960-1971.
Acronym: TRSI.
Scores, 6: Sales Knowledge, Customer Motivation, Merchandise Procurement, Sales Promotion, Sales Closure, Total.
Administration: Group.
Price Data, 1987: $27.50 per 25 reusable test booklets; $6.75 per scoring key; $6.75 per 25 answer sheets; $8.25 per 25 profiles; $6.75 per manual ('71, 18 pages); $9 per specimen set (manual, forms, keys not included).
Time: (30) minutes.
Comments: Self-administered; earlier form called Test of Sales Insight.
Author: Russell N. Cassel.
Publisher: Psychologists and Educators, Inc.

[2714]

Test of Scholastic Abilities.

Purpose: Designed to "measure verbal and numerical reasoning abilities deemed to be requisites for success in academic aspects of the New Zealand school curriculum."
Population: Ages 9-0 to 14-11.
Publication Date: 1981.
Acronym: TOSCA.
Scores: Total score only.
Administration: Group.
Price Data, 1987: NZ$3 per 20 tests; $.40 per answering key; $3.75 per manual (35 pages); $4.65 per specimen set.
Time: (30-40) minutes.
Authors: Neil Reid, Peter Jackson, Alison Gilmore, and Cedric Croft.
Publisher: New Zealand Council for Educational Research [New Zealand].
Cross References: For reviews by Barry J. Fraser and Cie Taylor, see 9:1271.

TEST REFERENCES

1. Chapman, J. W. (1988). Cognitive-motivational characteristics and academic achievement of learning disabled children: A longitudinal study. *Journal of Educational Psychology, 80,* 357–365.
2. Chapman, J. W., & McAlpine, P. D. (1988). Students' perceptions of ability. *Gifted Child Quarterly, 32,* 222–225.
3. Chapman, J. W. (1992). Learning disabilities in New Zealand: Where Kiwis and kids with LD can't fly. *Journal of Learning Disabilities, 25,* 362–370.
4. Fergusson, D. M., Horwood, L. J., & Lynskey, M. T. (1993). The effects of conduct disorder and attention deficit in middle childhood on offending and scholastic ability at age 13. *Journal of Child Psychology and Psychiatry and Allied Disciplines, 34,* 899-916.
5. Fergusson, D. M., Horwood, L. J., & Lynskey, M. T. (1994). A longitudinal study of early childhood education and subsequent academic achievement. *Australian Psychologist, 29,* 110–115.
6. Fergusson, D. M., & Horwood, L. J. (1995). Early disruptive behavior, IQ, and later school achievement and delinquent behavior. *Journal of Abnormal Child Psychology, 23,* 183-199.

[2715]

Test of Sensory Functions in Infants.

Purpose: Developed to measure "sensory processing and reactivity in infants."
Population: Infants ages 4-18 months with regulatory disorders or developmental delays.
Publication Date: 1989.
Acronym: TSFI.
Scores, 6: Reactivity to Tactile Deep Pressure, Adaptive Motor Functions, Visual-Tactile Integration, Ocular-Motor Control, Reactivity to Vestibular Stimulation, Total.
Administration: Individual.
Price Data, 1999: $165 per complete kit including set of test materials, 100 administration and scoring forms, and manual (45 pages) in carrying case; $22.50 per 100 administration and scoring forms; $38.50 per manual.
Time: (20) minutes.
Authors: Georgia A. DeGangi and Stanley I. Greenspan.
Publisher: Western Psychological Services.
Cross References: For a review by Mark Albanese, see 11:441.

TEST REFERENCE

1. Jirikowie, T. L., Engel, J. M., & Deitz, J. C. (1997). The Test of Sensory Functions in Infants: Test-retest reliability for infants with developmental delays. *American Journal of Occupational Therapy, 51,* 733–738.

[2716]

Test of Social Insight.

Purpose: Designed to "appraise the characteristic mode of reaction the individual uses in resolving interpersonal (social) problems."
Population: Grades 6-12, 13-16 and adults.
Publication Dates: 1959-1984.
Acronym: TSI.
Scores, 6: Withdrawal, Passivity, Cooperation, Competition, Aggression, Total.

Administration: Group.
Levels, 2: Youth Edition, Adult Edition.
Price Data, 1999: $90 per test package; $56.40 per manual ('63, 19 pages) and manual supplement ('84, 19 pages); $83.40 per IBM answer sheet/profile sheet package; $43.20 per set of IBM scoring stencils.
Time: [20-25] minutes.
Author: Russell N. Cassel.
Publisher: Martin M. Bruce, Ph.D.
Cross References: See T3:2461 (1 reference) and T2: 1419 (3 references). For reviews by John D. Black and John Pierce-Jones, and an excerpted review by Edward S. Bordin, see 6:190 (4 references).

[2717]

Test of Spoken English.

Purpose: Measures the ability of nonnative speakers of English to communicate orally in English.
Population: Nonnative speakers of English.
Publication Dates: 1979-1999.
Acronym: TSE.
Scores: Holistic score taking into consideration competence comprising Linguistic, Discourse, Functional, and Sociolinguistic competence.
Administration: Group.
Price Data: Examination fee per candidate available from publisher.
Time: (20-25) minutes.
Comments: Test administered 12 times annually at TSE centers (domestic and foreign) established by publisher; cassette or 3/4 ips test tape and 5-inch reel necessary for administration.
Author: International Language Programs, Educational Testing Service.
Publisher: Educational Testing Service.
Cross References: For reviews by Michael J. Subkoviak and Kikumi K. Tatsuoka, see 9:1273.

TEST REFERENCE

1. Brutten, S. R., Angelis, P. J., & Perkins, K. (1985). Music and memory: Predictors for attained ESL oral proficiency. *Language Learning, 35,* 299–313.

[2718]

Test of Understanding in College Economics, Third Edition.

Purpose: To measure college students' understanding of college economics.
Population: Introductory economics students.
Publication Dates: 1967–1991.
Acronym: TUCE III.
Scores: Total score only.
Administration: Group.
Editions, 2: Microeconomics, Macroeconomics.
Price Data: Available from publisher.
Time: (40–45) minutes per test.
Author: Phillip Saunders.
Publisher: National Council on Economic Education.
Cross References: For reviews by Joseph C. Ciechalski and Jennifer J. Fager, see 13:335; see also T2:1970 (10 references); for a review by Christine H. McGuire of an earlier edition, see 7:902.

[2719]

Test of Understanding in Personal Economics.

Purpose: Designed to measure the individual's understanding of personal economics.
Population: High school.
Publication Date: 1971.
Acronym: TUPE.
Scores: Total score only.
Administration: Group.
Price Data: Available from publisher.
Time: (45) minutes.
Comments: Separate answer sheets must be used.
Author: Joint Council on Economic Education.
Publisher: National Council on Economic Education.
Cross References: See T3:2463 (2 references); for a review by Hulda Grobman, see 8:902 (5 references).

[2720]

Test of Variables of Attention (Version 7.03).

Purpose: "Developed to assess attention and impulse control."
Population: Ages 4–80.
Publication Dates: 1988–1996.
Acronym: TOVA.
Administration: Individual.
Price Data: Available from publisher.
Time: (21.6) minutes.
Comments: Computer administered via separate or combined software; IBM and Macintosh versions available.
Authors: Lawrence M. Greenberg, Clifford L. Corman, and Carol L. Kindschi.
Publisher: Universal Attention Disorders, Inc.

a) T.O.V.A. VISUAL.
Scores, 3: Commission, Omission, Response Time Variability and Signal Detection.
b) T.O.V.A. AUDITORY.
Scores: Same as *a* above.

Cross References: For reviews by Rosa A. Hagin and Peter Della Bella and by Margot B. Stein of an earlier edition, see 13:336 (1 reference).

TEST REFERENCES

1. DeBaun, M. R., Schatz, J., Siegel, M. J., Koby, M., Craft, S., Resar, L., Chu, J.-Y., Launius, G., Dadash-Zadeh, M., Lee, R. B., & Noetzel, M. (1998). Cognitive screening examinations for silent cerebral infarcts in sickle cell disease. *Neurology, 50,* 1678–1682.
2. Forbes, G. B. (1998). Clinical utility of the Test of Variables of Attention (TOVA) in the diagnosis of attention-deficit/hyperactivity disorder. *Journal of Clinical Psychology, 54,* 461–476.

[2721]
Test of Visual Analysis Skills.

Purpose: Constructed to assess "a child's ability to understand the relationship of parts to wholes."
Population: Children.
Publication Date: 1975–1993.
Acronym: TVAS.
Scores: Total score only.
Administration: Group.
Manual: No manual.
Price Data, 1999: $15 per 10 test booklets; $4 per direction card.
Time: Administration time not reported.
Comments: "Criterion-referenced"; may be used in conjunction with the Test of Auditory Analysis Skills (2671); test is reproduced from author's book Helping Children Overcome Learning Difficulties (1993, Walker Publishing Company, New York).
Author: Jerome Rosner.
Publisher: Academic Therapy Publications.

[2722]
Test of Visual-Motor Integration.

Purpose: Constructed as "a standardized norm-referenced test of visual-motor integration."
Population: Ages 4–17.
Publication Date: 1996.
Acronym: TVMI.
Scores: Total score only.
Administration: Individual or group.
Price Data, 1999: $109 per complete kit including manual (75 pages) and 50 summary/response forms in storage box; $69 per 50 summary/response forms; $43 per manual.
Time: (20) minutes.
Authors: Donald D. Hammill, Nils A. Pearson, and Judith K. Voress.
Publisher: PRO-ED.

TEST REFERENCE

1. Handwerk, M. L., & Marshall, R. M. (1998). Behavioral and emotional problems of students with learning disabilities, serious emotional disturbance, or both conditions. *Journal of Learning Disabilities, 31,* 327–338.

[2723]
Test of Visual-Motor Skills.

Purpose: To assess a child's visual-motor functioning.
Population: Ages 2–13.
Publication Date: 1986.
Acronym: TVMS.
Scores: Total score only.
Administration: Group or individual.
Price Data: Not available.
Time: (3–5) minutes.
Author: Morrison F. Gardner.
Publisher: Psychological & Educational Publications, Inc. [Status unknown; no reply from publisher].
Cross References: For reviews by Deborah Erickson and Janet E. Spector, see 13:337 (2 references); see also T4:2791 (1 reference).

[2724]
Test of Visual-Perceptual Skills (Non-Motor).

Purpose: Constructed to "determine a child's visual-perceptual strengths and weaknesses."
Population: Ages 4-12.
Publication Date: 1982.
Acronym: TVPS.
Scores: 7 areas: Visual Discrimination, Visual Memory, Visual-Spatial Relationships, Visual Form Constancy, Visual Sequential Memory, Visual Figure-Ground, Visual Closure.
Administration: Individual.
Price Data: Available from publisher.
Time: (7-15) minutes.
Author: Morrison F. Gardner.
Publisher: Special Child Publications [No reply from publisher; status unknown].
Cross References: For reviews by Nancy A. Busch-Rossnagel and Joseph W. Denison, see 9:1276.

TEST REFERENCES

1. Carr, S. H. (1989). Louisiana's criteria of eligibility for occupational therapy services in the public school system. *The American Journal of Occupational Therapy, 43,* 503-506.
2. Ross, F. L. (1992). The use of computers in occupational therapy for visual-scanning training. *The American Journal of Occupational Therapy, 46,* 314-322.
3. Farrell, W. J., & Muik, E. A. (1993). Computer applications that streamline test scoring and other procedures in occupational therapy. *The American Journal of Occupational Therapy, 47,* 462-465.
4. McFall, S. A., Deitz, J. C., & Crowe, T. K. (1993). Test-retest reliability of the Test of Visual Perceptual Skills with children with learning disabilities. *The American Journal of Occupational Therapy, 47,* 819-824.
5. Tseng, M. H., & Cermak, S. A. (1993). The influence of ergonomic factors and perceptual-motor abilities on handwriting performance. *The American Journal of Occupational Therapy, 47,* 919-926.
6. Butler, R., & Marinor-Glassman, D. (1994). The effects of educational placement and grade level on the self-perceptions of low achievers and students with learning disabilities. *Journal of Learning Disabilities, 27,* 325–334.
7. Cohen, M. J., Branch, W. B., & Hynd, G. W. (1994). Receptive prosody in children with left or right hemisphere dysfunction. *Brain and Language, 47,* 171–181.
8. Sikora, D. M., & Plapinger, D. S. (1994). Using standardized tests to identify learning disabilities in students with sensorineural hearing impairments. *Journal of Learning Disabilities, 27,* 352–359.
9. Branch, W. B., Cohen, M. J., & Hynd, G. W. (1995). Academic achievement and attention-deficit/hyperactivity disorder in children with left- or right-hemisphere dysfunction. *Journal of Learning Disabilities, 28,* 35–43, 64.
10. Plapinger, D. S., & Sikora, D. M. (1995). The use of standardized test batteries in assessing the skill development of children with mild-to-moderate sensorineural hearing loss. *Language, Speech, and Hearing Services in Schools, 26,* 39–44.
11. Watson, C., & Willows, D. M. (1995). Information-processing patterns in specific reading disability. *Journal of Learning Disabilities, 28,* 216–231.
12. Farel, A. M., Hooper, S. R., Teplin, S. W., Henry, M. M., & Kraybill, E. N. (1998). Very-low-birthweight infants at seven years: An assessment of the health and neurodevelopmental risk conveyed by chronic lung disease. *Journal of Learning Disabilities, 31,* 118–126.
13. Parush, S., Yochman, A., Cohen, D., & Gershon, E. (1998). Relation of visual perception and visual-motor integration for clumsy children. *Perceptual and Motor Skills, 86,* 291–295.

[2725]
Test of Word Finding.

Purpose: Designed to assess word-finding disorders.
Population: Grades 1-6.
Publication Dates: 1986-1989.

Acronym: TWF.
Scores: 5 sections (Picture Naming: Nouns, Sentence Completion Naming, Description Naming, Picture Naming: Verbs, Picture Naming: Categories) yielding 4 scores: Accuracy, Item Response Time, Word Finding Profile, Comprehension Summary.
Administration: Individual.
Levels, 2: Primary, Intermediate (on 1 overlapping form).
Price Data, 1999: $164 per complete kit including easel-binder test book, 25 response booklets, administration manual ('89, 173 pages), and technical manual ('86, 127 pages); $34 per 25 response booklets.
Time: (20-30) minutes.
Comments: Prorated accuracy rescoring summary allows for interpretation when comprehension is low; speed can be measured in actual or estimated item response time; estimated response time can be done during testing and eliminates need for stopwatch or tape recorder; if actual response time is desired, a tape recorder and stopwatch are needed.
Author: Diane J. German.
Publisher: PRO-ED.
Cross References: For reviews by Sharon L. Weinberg and Susan Ellis Weismer, see 11:443 (1 reference); for reviews by Mavis Donahue and Priscilla A. Drum, see 10:373.

TEST REFERENCES

1. Tomblin, J. B., Freese, P. R., & Records, N. L. (1992). Diagnosing specific language impairment in adults for the purpose of pedigree analysis. *Journal of Speech and Hearing Research, 35,* 832–843.
2. Weiss, A. L., & Zebrowski, P. M. (1992). Disfluencies in the conversations of young children who stutter: Some answers about questions. *Journal of Speech and Hearing Research, 35,* 1230–1238.
3. Lahey, M., & Edwards, J. (1995). Specific language impairment: Preliminary investigation of factors associated with family history and with patterns of language performance. *Journal of Speech and Hearing Research, 38,* 643–657.
4. Rustin, L., & Cook, F. (1995). Parental involvement in the treatment of stuttering. *Language, Speech, and Hearing Services in Schools, 26,* 127–137.
5. Stevens, L. J., & Bliss, L. S. (1995). Conflict resolution abilities of children with specific language impairment and children with normal language. *Journal of Speech and Hearing Research, 38,* 599–611.
6. Tomblin, J. B., Abbas, P. J., Records, N. L., & Brenneman, L. M. (1995). Auditory evoked responses to frequency-modulated tones in children with specific language impairment. *Journal of Speech and Hearing Research, 38,* 387–392.
7. Lahey, M., & Edwards, J. (1996). Why do children with specific language impairment name pictures more slowly than their peers? *Journal of Speech, Language, and Hearing Research, 39,* 1081–1098.
8. McGregor, K. K., & Windsor, J. (1996). Effects of priming on the naming accuracy of preschoolers with word-finding deficits. *Journal of Speech and Hearing Research, 39,* 1048–1058.
9. McGregor, K. K. (1997). The nature of word-finding errors of preschoolers with and without word-finding deficits. *Journal of Speech, Language, and Hearing Research, 40,* 1232–1244.
10. Stark, R. E., & McGregor, K. K. (1997). Follow-up study of a right- and a left-hemisphere-ctomized child: Implications for localization and impairment of language in children. *Brain and Language, 60,* 222–242.

[2726]

Test of Word Finding in Discourse.

Purpose: Designed to assess children's word-finding skills in discourse.
Population: Ages 6-6 to 12-11.
Publication Date: 1991.
Acronym: TWFD.
Scores, 2: Productivity Index, Word-Finding Behaviors Index.
Administration: Individual.
Price Data, 1999: $98 per complete test including manual (173 pages) and 25 test record forms; $29 per 25 test record forms.
Time: (15-20) minutes.
Author: Diane J. German.
Publisher: PRO-ED.
Cross References: For reviews by James Dean Brown and Rebecca J. Kopriva, see 12:399; see also T4:2800 (1 reference).

[2727]

Test of Word Knowledge.

Purpose: Developed to "assess a student's skill in the reception and expression of ... semantics."
Population: Ages 5–17.
Publication Date: 1991–1992.
Acronym: TOWK.
Scores, 11: Expressive Vocabulary, Receptive Vocabulary, Word Opposites, Word Definitions, Synonyms, Multiple Contexts, Figurative Usage, Conjunctions and Transition Words, Receptive Composite, Expressive Composite, Total.
Administration: Individual.
Levels, 2: Ages 5–8, Ages 8–17.
Price Data, 1999: $155 per complete kit including stimulus manual, examiner's manual (118 pages), and 12 record forms; $83 per stimulus manual; $58.50 per examiner's manual; $28.50 per 12 record forms.
Time: (31) minutes for Level 1; (65) minutes for Level 2.
Authors: Elisabeth H. Wiig and Wayne Secord.
Publisher: The Psychological Corporation.
Cross References: For a review by Rick Lindskog, see 13:338 (3 references).

TEST REFERENCE

1. Ward-Lonergan, J. M., Liles, B. Z., & Anderson, A. M. (1998). Listening comprehension and recall abilities in adolescents with language-learning disabilities and without disabilities for social studies lectures. *Journal of Communication Disorders, 31,* 1–32.

[2728]

Test of Work Competency and Stability.

Purpose: Developed to "measure psychological capacity for work."
Population: Ages 21 and over.
Publication Dates: 1959-1961.
Acronym: TWCS.
Scores, 9 to 11: Negative (Questionnaire, Tremometer, Time for P.A.I., Total), Positive (Tapping, Digits Backward, Picture Arrangement, Total), Level of Work Competency, Mirror Tracing (optional), Digit Symbol (optional).
Administration: Individual.

Price Data, 1998: $350 per complete kit; $10 per 25 record blanks; $10 per 25 interview questionnaire sheets; $6 per 25 mirror tracing patterns; $6 per 25 tapping patterns; $75 per mirror tracing apparatus; $18 per manual ('59, 59 pages).
Foreign Language Edition: French edition available.
Time: (30-40) minutes.
Comments: Stopwatch necessary for administration.
Author: A. Gaston Leblanc.
Publisher: Institute of Psychological Research, Inc. [Canada].
Cross References: For a review by Jerome D. Pauker, see 8:695; see also T2:1420 (1 reference) and 6:191 (2 references).

[2729]

Test of Written English.

Purpose: "Designed to measure a student's performance in written English."
Population: Grades 1-6.
Publication Date: 1979.
Acronym: TWE.
Scores, 4: Capitalization, Punctuation, Written Expression, Total.
Administration: Individual.
Price Data, 1999: $40 per test kit including manual (95 pages) and 50 test forms; $18 per 50 test forms; $19 per manual; $19 per specimen set.
Time: (10-20) minutes.
Comments: Can be adapted for administration to small groups if subjects can read; separate answer sheets (test forms) must be used.
Authors: Velma R. Andersen and Sheryl K. Thompson.
Publisher: Academic Therapy Publications.
Cross References: For reviews by James A. Poteet and Robert E. Shafer, see 9:1277.

TEST REFERENCES

1. Koenig, L. A., & Biel, C. D. (1989). A delivery system of comprehensive language services in a school district. *Language, Speech, and Hearing Services in Schools, 20,* 338–365.

2. Sowell, E. J., Zeigler, A. J., Bergwall, L., & Cartwright, R. M. (1990). Identification and description of mathematically gifted students: A review of empirical research. *Gifted Child Quarterly, 34,* 147-154.

3. Carson, J. E., & Kuehn, P. A. (1992). Evidence of transfer and loss in developing second language writers. *Language Learning, 42,* 157–182.

[2730]

Test of Written Expression.

Purpose: Constructed as a "norm-referenced test of writing."
Population: Ages 6-6 to 14-11.
Publication Date: 1995.
Acronym: TOWE.
Scores, 2: Items, Essay.
Administration: Individual or group.
Price Data, 1999: $124 per complete kit including manual (58 pages), 25 profile/examiner record forms, and 25 student booklets in storage box; $39 per 25 student booklets; $44 per profile/examiner record forms; $44 per examiner's manual.
Time: (60) minutes.
Authors: Ron McGhee, Brian R. Bryant, Stephen C. Larsen, and Diane M. Rivera.
Publisher: PRO-ED.
Cross References: For reviews by Mildred Murray-Ward and Carole Perlman, see 13:339 (1 reference).

[2731]

Test of Written Language—Third Edition.

Purpose: Designed to "(a) identify students who perform significantly more poorly than their peers in writing and who as a result need special help; (b) determine a student's particular strengths and weaknesses in various writing abilities; (c) document a student's progress in a special writing program; and conduct research in writing."
Population: Ages 7-6 to 17-11.
Publication Dates: 1978–1996.
Acronym: TOWL-3.
Scores: 8 subtest scores (Vocabulary, Spelling, Style, Logical Sentences, Sentence Combining, Contextual Conventions, Contextual Language, Story Construction) plus 3 composite scores (Contrived Writing, Spontaneous Writing, Overall Writing).
Administration: Individual or group.
Forms, 2: A, B.
Price Data, 1999: $176 per complete kit including manual ('96, 134 pages), 25 student response booklets Form A, 25 student response booklets Form B, and 50 profile/story scoring forms in storage box; $44 per 25 A or B student response booklets; $39 per 50 profile/story scoring forms; $53 per manual; $98 per Windows or Macintosh PRO-SCORE System; $89 per IBM DOS PRO-SCORE System.
Time: (90) minutes.
Authors: Donald D. Hammill and Stephen C. Larsen.
Publisher: PRO-ED.
Cross References: For reviews by Joe B. Hansen and by Jayne E. Bucy and Mark E. Swerdlik, see 13:340 (16 references); see also T4:2804 (2 references); for reviews by Stephen L. Benton and Joseph M. Ryan of an earlier edition, see 11:444 (6 references); for reviews by Edward A. Polloway and Robert T. Williams of the original edition, see 9:1278.

TEST REFERENCES

1. Ganschow, L., Sparks, R. L., Javorsky, J., Pohlman, J., & Bishop-Marbury, A. (1991). Identifying native language difficulties among foreign language learners in college: A "foreign" language learning disability? *Journal of Learning Disabilities, 24,* 530–541.

2. MacArthur, C. A., Graham, S., Haynes, J. B., & DeLaPaz, S. (1996). Spelling checkers and students with learning disabilities: Performance comparisons and impact on spelling. *The Journal of Special Education, 30,* 35–57.

3. Sparks, R., Ganschow, L., & Thomas, A. (1996). Role of intelligence tests in speech/language referrals. *Perceptual and Motor Skills, 83,* 195–204.
4. Yarger, C. C. (1996). An examination of the Test of Written Language—3. *Volta Review, 98,* 211–215.
5. Yoshinaga-Itano, C., Snyder, L. S., & Mayberry, R. (1996). How deaf and normally hearing students convey meaning within and between written sentences. *Volta Review, 98,* 9–38.
6. McBride, H. E. A., & Siegel, L. S. (1997). Learning disabilities and adolescent suicide. *Journal of Learning Disabilities, 30,* 652–659.
7. Baynes, K., Kegl, J. A., Brentari, D., Kussmaul, C., & Poizner, H. (1998). Chronic auditory agnosia following Landau-Kleffner syndrome: A 23 year outcome study. *Brain and Language, 63,* 381–425.
8. Ward-Lonergan, J. M., Liles, B. Z., & Anderson, A. M. (1998). Listening comprehension and recall abilities in adolescents with language-learning disabilities and without disabilities for social studies lectures. *Journal of Communication Disorders, 31,* 1–32.

[2732]

Test of Written Spelling, Fourth Edition.

Purpose: Designed to assess students' spelling abilities.
Population: Ages 6-0 to 18-11.
Publication Dates: 1976–1999.
Acronym: TWS-4.
Scores: Total score only.
Administration: Group.
Price Data, 1999: $74 per complete kit including manual ('99, 59 pages) and 50 answer sheets; $42 per examiner's manual; $34 per 50 answer sheets.
Time: (15) minutes.
Authors: Stephen C. Larsen, Donald D. Hammill, and Louisa C. Moats.
Publisher: PRO-ED.
Cross References: For reviews by Alfred P. Longo and Hoi K. Suen of an earlier edition, see 13:341 (5 references); see also T4:2805 (4 references); for reviews by Deborah B. Erickson and Ruth M. Noyce of an earlier edition, see 10:374; for reviews by John M. Bradley and Deborah B. Erickson of an earlier edition, see 9:1279.

TEST REFERENCES

1. MacArthur, C. A., Graham, S., Haynes, J. B., & DeLaPaz, S. (1996). Spelling checkers and students with learning disabilities: Performance comparisons and impact on spelling. *The Journal of Special Education, 30,* 35–57.
2. Lewis, B. A., & Freebairn, L. (1997). Subgrouping children with familial phonologic disorders. *Journal of Communication Disorders, 30,* 385–402.

[2733]

Test on Appraising Observations.

Purpose: Designed to test one aspect of critical thinking: judging credibility.
Population: Grade 10 to adult.
Publication Dates: 1983–1990.
Administration: Group.
Price Data: Available from publishers.
Authors: Stephen P. Norris (multiple-choice format and constructed-response format) and Ruth King (multiple-choice format).
Publisher: Faculty of Education, Memorial University of Newfoundland [Canada].

a) MULTIPLE-CHOICE FORMAT.
Publication Date: 1983.
Scores: Total score only.
Parts, 2: A, B.
Time: (40–45) minutes.

b) CONSTRUCTED-RESPONSE VERSION.
Publication Date: 1986.
Scores, 2: Answer-Choice, Justification.
Time: (40–45) minutes.

Cross References: For reviews by Michael Kane and Jeffrey K. Smith, see 13:342; see also T4:2806 (1 reference).

[2734]

Tests for Everyday Living.

Purpose: Designed to "measure achievement in the life skill area."
Population: Junior and senior high school.
Publication Date: 1979.
Acronym: TEL.
Scores, 8: 7 subtest scores (Purchasing Habits, Banking, Budgeting, Health Care, Home Management, Job Search Skills, Job Related Behavior) plus Total.
Administration: Group.
Price Data: Available from publisher.
Time: (20-30) minutes per test, recommended to administer 2 tests per session in 3 sessions.
Comments: Designed for oral administration in order to eliminate reading ability as a determinant of performance.
Authors: Andrew S. Halpern, Larry K. Irvin, and Janet T. Landman.
Publisher: Publishers Test Service [No reply from publisher; status unknown].
Cross References: For a review by William A. Mehrens, see 9:1281; see also T3:2473 (1 reference).

[2735]

Tests of Achievement and Proficiency, Forms K, L, and M.

Purpose: Designed to "provide a comprehensive and objective measure of students' progress in a high school curriculum."
Population: Grades 9–12.
Publication Dates: 1978–1996.
Acronym: TAP.
Forms, 3: K, L, M; 2 batteries: Complete and Survey.
Administration: Group.
Levels, 4: 15, 16, 17, 18.
Price Data, 1999: $17 per 25 practice test booklets including 1 directions for administration; $3 per practice test directions for administration; $7 per Preparing for Testing with the Tests of Achievement and Proficiency; $98 per 25 Form K or L Complete Battery reusable test booklets including 1 directions for administration; $12.50 per Forms K and L Complete Battery

directions for administration; $98 per 25 Form K or L Survey Battery reusable test booklets including 1 directions for administration; $12.50 per Forms K and L Survey Battery directions for administration; $98 per 25 Form M Complete Battery reusable test booklets including 1 directions for administration; $12.50 per Form M Complete Battery directions for administration; $98 per 25 Form M Survey Battery reusable test booklets including 1 directions for administration; $12.50 per Form M Survey Battery directions for administration; $52 per 50 Forms K and l Listening Assessment answer documents including 1 directions for administration and score interpretation; $10 per Forms K and L Listening Assessment directions for administration and score interpretation; $44 per 50 Form M Listening Assessment answer documents including 1 directions of administration and score interpretation; $9.50 per Form M Listening Assessment directions for administration and score interpretation; $99 per Form K Complete Battery Braille Edition test, Braille administration notes, and supplement to the directions for administration; $118 per Form K Survey Battery Braille Edition test, Braille administration notes, and supplement to the direction for administration; $60 per Form K Complete Battery large-print edition including test booklet and general instructions for testing visually impaired students; $42 per Form K Survey Battery large-print edition including test booklet and general instructions for testing visually impaired students; $38 per 50 Forms K and L Complete Battery answer documents; $35 per 50 Forms K and L Survey Battery answer documents; $38 per 50 Form M Complete Battery answer documents; $35 per 50 Form M Survey Battery answer documents; $1,260 per 1,500 Forms K and L Complete Battery continuous-form answer documents; $1,260 per 1,500 Forms K and L Survey Battery continuous-form answer documents; $31 per 25 Form M Survey Battery easy-score answer documents including 1 class record folder; $25 per scoring key; $50 per Forms K and L Complete Battery scoring masks; $50 per Form M Complete Battery scoring masks; $44 per Complete Battery norms and score conversions booklet; $44 per Survey Battery norms and score conversions booklet; $47 per special norms booklets (large city, Catholic, high socioeconomic, international, or low socioeconomic); $120 per Forms K and L keyscore norm look-up software including program disk (3.5-inch) and user's guide; $6 per 5 class record folders (specify form); $9.50 per 25 student profile charts (specify form); $10 per 25 profile charts for averages; $16 per interpretive guide (Form M, '96, 140 pages; Forms K and L, '93, 149 pages) for teachers and counselors; $26 per interpretive guide for school administrators; $15 per 25 report to students and parents; $15 per 25 reporte para estudiantes y padres; $26 per content classifications with item norms booklets; $25 per Technical Summary 1.

Special Editions: Braille and large-print editions available.

Authors: Dale P. Scannell, Oscar M. Haugh, Brenda H. Loyd, and C. Frederick Risinger.

Publisher: Riverside Publishing.

a) COMPLETE BATTERY.

Scores, 15: Vocabulary, Reading Comprehension, Written Expression, Math Concepts and Problem Solving, Math Computation [optional], Social Studies, Science, Information Processing, Reading Total, Math Total, Core Total, Composite, plus Advance Skills Scores for reading, language, and mathematics.

Time: (255) minutes; (275) minutes with optional test.

b) SURVEY BATTERY.

Scores, 10: Reading (Vocabulary, Comprehension, Total), Written Expression, Math Concepts and Problem Solving, Math Computation [optional], Total, plus Advanced Skills Scores for reading, language, and mathematics.

Time: (90) minutes; (100) minutes with optional test.

Cross References: See T4:2810 (1 reference) and 11:445 (4 references); for a review by Elaine Clark of Forms G and H, see 10:375 (2 references); for reviews by John M. Keene, Jr. and James L. Wardrop of an earlier form, see 9:1282.

TEST REFERENCE

1. Carroll, W. M. (1994). Using worked examples as an instructional support in the algebra classroom. *Journal of Educational Psychology, 86*, 360–367.

[2736]

Tests of Achievement in Basic Skills: Mathematics.

Purpose: To assess mathematics achievement.

Population: Preschool-kindergarten, grades 1, 2, 3-4, 4-6, 7-9, 10-adult.

Publication Dates: 1970-1976.

Acronym: TABS-M.

Administration: Group.

Price Data, 1998: $13.50 per 30 tests (specify Level K, 1, 2, or A and Form 1 or 2); $13.50 per 35 tests (specify Level B, C, or D and Form 1 or 2); $5.75 per 35 answer sheets; $3.50 per hand-scoring keys (specify Level A, B, C, or D); $30 per manual K ('76, 11 pages) and 30 tests; $4.50 per specimen set (specify level); price data for Individualized Mathematics Program (IMP) materials available from publisher.

Time: (45-70) minutes.

Comments: May be used separately or as part of instructional Individualized Mathematics Program (IMP); "crite-

rion-referenced tests"; 18-69 item scores, each item measuring a specific objective, and part and total scores; separate answer sheets (Digitek) must be used with Levels B-D.
Authors: James C. Young and Robert R. Knapp (Level C manuals).
Publisher: EdITS/Educational and Industrial Testing Service.

a) LEVEL K.
Population: Preschool-kindergarten.
Publication Date: 1974.
Scores: 18 item scores in 3 areas: Arithmetic Skills, Geometry-Measurement, Modern Concepts.

b) LEVEL 1.
Population: Grade 1.
Publication Date: 1974.
Scores: 36 item scores in 3 areas: same as *a* above.

c) LEVEL 2.
Population: Grade 2.
Publication Date: 1974.
Scores: 41 item scores in 3 areas: same as *a* above.

d) LEVEL A.
Population: Grades 3-4.
Publication Date: 1973.
Scores: 49 item scores in 3 areas: same as *a* above.

e) LEVEL B.
Population: Grades 4-6.
Publication Dates: 1972-1973.
Scores: 73 items and total scores in 3 areas: same as *a* above, plus Total.

f) LEVEL C.
Population: Grades 7-9.
Publication Dates: 1970-1971.
Scores: 68 items and total scores in 3 areas: same as *e* above.

g) LEVEL D.
Population: Grades 10-12.
Publication Dates: 1972-1976.
Scores: 47 items and total scores in 2 areas: Arithmetic Skills, Arithmetic Application, plus Total.

Cross References: For reviews by James Braswell and C. Alan Riedesel, and an excerpted review by Barton B. Proger, see 8:293 (2 references); see also 7:492 (1 reference).

[2737]
Tests of Adult Basic Education, Forms 7 & 8.

Purpose: Designed to measure achievement of basic skills commonly found in adult basic education curricula and taught in instructional programs.
Acronym: TABE.
Administration: Group.
Levels, Editions, and Parts: 2 Forms: 7 & 8, each with 2 editions: Complete Battery and Survey, and 5 Levels: L, E, M, D, A.
Price Data, 1994: $19.08 per review kit including product overview, complete battery test book Levels L, M–7, and A–7, and Survey test book Levels E–8 and D–8, Practice Exercise and Locator test, 2 examiner's manuals ('94, 63 pages [complete battery] and 36 pages [survey battery]), individual diagnostic profile Level M, marker item booklet, examinee record book Level L, SCOREZE answer sheet, CompuScan answer sheet; $30 per 25 Practice exercise and Locator Test booklets; $25 per 25 Complete Battery Test booklets Level L; $54.50 per 25 Complete Battery and Survey Test books E, M, D, and A; $15 per Large Print Edition Practice Exercise and Locator Test; $15 per large print Complete Battery Test book Level L; $31.75 per large print edition Complete Battery or Survey Tests Levels E, M, D, or A; $30.21 per 50 answer sheets; $19 per 25 hand-scorable SCOREZE answer sheets; $15 per 50 machine-scorable answer sheets—Scantron Option 2; $15 per 50 CompuScan 48-column Practice Exercise and Locator Test or Survey Levels E, M, D, A; $29.50 per 50 CompuScan 48-column Complete Battery Levels E, M, D, or A; $11 per scoring stencil for hand-scoring CompuScan answer sheets for Practice Exercise and Locator Test stencil; $22 per scoring stencil for hand-scoring CompuScan answer sheets for Complete Battery and Survey Levels E, M, D, A; $11.95 per word list; $20 per 25 marker item booklets; $8 per individual diagnostic profile Complete Battery and Survey Levels E, M, D, A; $27 per test user's handbook; $9.75 per norms book, Form 7 & 8 ('95, 90 pages); $1.75 per group record sheet; $11 per technical report ('96, 72 pages); $9.75 per Complete Battery or Survey manual; $14 per 25 examinee record book Level L.
Foreign Language Edition and Other Special Editions: Form 7 is available in a large print edition; TABE Español is available.
Comments: Level L is the same for both the Complete Battery and the Survey editions; an interview checklist, a word list to assist determination of appropriate TABE level, and an Individual Diagnostic Profile are available; a Practice Exercise is available in the same booklet as the Locator Test.
Authors: CTB/McGraw-Hill.
Publisher: CTB/McGraw-Hill.

a) FORMS 7 & 8.
Population: Adults in Adult Basic Education programs, vocational-technical centers, and correctional facilities, first and second year college students.
Publication Dates: 1957–1996.
Scores: Level L: 3 scores: Pre-Reading, Reading Skills, Total Reading; Levels E, M, D, and A: 7 scores: Reading, Math Computation, Applied Math, Total Mathematics (Math Computation plus Applied Math), Language, Total Battery, Spelling.
Price Data: $25 per 25 Level L Test books; $54.50 per 25 E, M, D, or A test books; $15 per large print edition test book, Level L; $31.75 per

large print edition test book, Levels E, M, D, or A; $30.21 per 50 large print answer sheets; $19 per 25 hand-scorable SCOREZE answer sheets; $29.50 per 50 CompuScan 48-column answer sheets; $22 per scoring stencil for hand-scoring CompuScan answer sheets; $8 per 25 individual diagnostic profiles; $9.75 per manual ('94, 63 pages).
Time: 154–164 (209) minutes for Levels E, M, D, and A; 35 (65) minutes for Level L.

1) *Locator Test.*
Purpose: "Used to determine the appropriate level of TABE to administer to each examinee."
Scores, 3: Reading, Mathematics, Language (optional).
Time: (35–40) minutes for Reading and Mathematics; (50–55) minutes for Reading, Mathematics, and Language.

b) SURVEY FORM.
Population: Adults in Adult Basic Education programs, vocational-technical centers, and correctional facilities, second year college students.
Publication Dates: 1987–1996.
Scores: Level L: 3 scores: Pre-Reading, Reading Skills, Total Reading; Levels E, M, D, and A: 5 scores: Reading, Mathematics Computation, Applied Mathematics, Language, Spelling.
Price Data: $54 per 25 test books; $31.75 per large print test book; $30.21 per 50 large print answer sheets; $19 per 25 hand-scorable SCOREZE answer sheets; $15 per 50 machine-scorable answer sheets or CompuScan 48-column answer sheets; $11 per survey stencil for hand-scoring CompuScan answer sheets; $9.75 per manual ('94, 36 pages).
Time: (112) minutes.

1) *Locator Test (same as a1 above).*

Cross References: For reviews by Michael D. Beck and Bruce G. Rogers, see 13:343; for reviews by Robert W. Lissitz and Steven J. Osterlind of an earlier edition, see 11:446 (2 references); for reviews by Thomas F. Donlon and Norman E. Gronlund of an earlier edition, see 8:33 (1 reference); for a review by A. N. Hieronymus and an excerpted review by S. Alan Cohen of an earlier edition, see 7:32.

[2738]

Tests of Adult Basic Education Work-Related Foundation Skills.

Purpose: "To provide pre-instructional information about an examinee's level of achievement on basic skills, ... to identify areas of weakness ... measure growth, ... and involve the examinee in appraising his or her learning needs to assist ... [in preparing] an instructional program to meet the examinee's individual needs."
Population: Adults in vocational/technical programs, students in adult basic education programs 2-year colleges, and secondary school ROP & JTPA programs.
Publication Date: 1994–1996.
Acronym: TABE WF.
Scores, 6: Reading, Math Computation, Applied Math, Total Mathematics (Math Computation and Applied Math), Language, Total Battery.
Administration: Group.
Forms, 4: General, Business/Office, Health, Trade/Technical.
Price Data, 1994: $17.97 per review kit including general test book, trade/technical test book, health test book, business/office test book, examiner's manual ('94, 30 pages), and individual diagnostic profile; $30 per manual and 25 locator tests; $54.50 per manual and general trade technical, health, or business/office test book; $14.50 per 25 locator test SCOREZE answer sheets; $19 per general trade/technical, health, or business/office SCOREZE answer sheets; $15 per 50 CompuScan answer sheets; $15 per 50 Scantron Opt. 2 answer sheets; $8 per 25 individual diagnostic profiles; $11 per hand-scoring stencil; $1.75 per group record sheet; $9.75 per examiner's manual; $9.75 per norms book; $8.85 per technical bulletin; price data for technical report ('96, 33 pages) for use with this test and the TABE Work-Related Problem Solving available from publisher.
Time: 120(160) minutes.
Authors: CTB Macmillan/McGraw-Hill.
Publisher: CTB/McGraw-Hill.
Cross References: For reviews by Kurt F. Geisinger and Jeffrey A. Jenkins, see 13:344.

[2739]

Tests of Adult Basic Education Work-Related Problem Solving.

Purpose: "Designed to help employers, educators, and training professionals diagnose how an examinee deals with the different aspects of problem solving."
Population: Students in secondary schools, vocational education programs, adult basic education programs, and junior colleges, and employees in industry.
Publication Date: 1994–1996.
Acronym: TABE-PS.
Scores, 5: Competency scores (Employs Reading and Math Skills to Identify and Define a Problem, Examines Situations Using Problem-Solving Techniques, Makes Decisions About Possible Solutions, Evaluates Outcomes and Effects of Implementing Solutions), Total Number Correct Score.
Administration: Group.
Forms, 2: 7, 8.
Price Data, 1994: $11.50 per review kit including examiner's manual/scoring guide ('94, 56 pages), and

test book; $32 per 25 test books with 1 manual; $19 per 50 practice exercises; $8 per 25 hand-scorable individual diagnostic profiles; $15 per 50 machine-scorable individual diagnostic profiles; $9.75 per examiner's manual/scoring guide; price data for technical report ('96, 33 pages) for use with this test and the TABE Work-Related Foundation Skills available from publisher.
Time: 70(75) minutes for Form 7; 60(65) minutes for Form 8.
Comments: May be administered alone or in conjunction with other TABE materials; test includes a Practice Exercise which was included in the norming studies and so should be administered along with the test; includes Individual Diagnostic Profile, and Interview/Interest Questionnaire.
Authors: CTB Macmillan/McGraw-Hill.
Publisher: CTB/McGraw-Hill.
Cross References: For reviews by Gale M. Morrison and Jerry Tindal, see 13:345.

[2740]

Tests of Basic Experiences 2.

Purpose: Designed to measure children's readiness to engage in a number of academic activities.
Population: PreK-beginning of grade 1, end of K-end of grade 1.
Publication Dates: 1970-1979.
Acronym: TOBE/2.
Subtests, 4: Language, Mathematics, Science, Social Studies.
Administration: Group.
Levels, 2: K, L.
Price Data, 1994: $119 per instructional activities kit; $10.50 per norms and technical data ('79, 61 pages); $1.20 per additional class evaluation records; $8.35 per Spanish directions; $18.90 per 30 individual evaluation records.
Time: (40-50) minutes per test for each level.
Comments: Revision of still-in-print Tests of Basic Experiences; no reading by examinees; Spanish directions available for both levels.
Author: Margaret H. Moss.
Publisher: CTB/McGraw-Hill.

a) LEVEL K.
Population: PreK-end of grade 1.
Price Data: $147.60 per complete battery including 30 hand-scorable booklets for Language, Mathematics, Science, and Social Studies); $48.30 per 30 of each hand-scored subtest; $51.90 per 30 CompuScan test booklets for Language or Mathematics; $18.90 per 30 practice tests; $8.35 per examiner's manual ('78, 44 pages).
Comments: Hand-scored test booklets for each test; combined CompuScan machine-scored test booklets for Language and Mathematics tests.

b) LEVEL L.
Population: End of K-end of grade 1.
Price Data: Same as *a* above.
Comments: Hand-scored test booklets for each test; combined CompuScan test booklets for Language and Mathematics tests.

Cross References: See 9:1283 (1 reference) and T3:2478 (7 references); for a review by Esther E. Diamond and excerpted reviews by Steven Thurber and Barton B. Proger of an earlier edition, see 8:34 (8 references); for a review by Courtney B. Cazdan of an earlier complete edition, see 7:33. For a review by Stephen M. Koziol, Jr. of the language test, see 8:59; for a review by Leroy G. Callahan of the mathematics test, see 8:294; for a review by Arlen R. Gullickson of the science test, see 8:860.

[2741]

Tests of General Ability: Inter-American Series.

Purpose: Measures general and specific ability levels of students.
Population: Grades Kgn-1.5, 2-3, 4-6, 7-9, 10-13.5.
Publication Dates: 1961-1973.
Acronym: TGA.
Scores: Verbal-Numerical, Nonverbal, Verbal, Numerical, Total.
Administration: Group.
Levels, 5: Primary 1, Primary 2, Elementary, Intermediate, Advanced.
Price Data: Not available.
Foreign Language Edition: Parallel editions in English and Spanish.
Time: Administration time not reported.
Author: Herschel T. Manual.
Publisher: Guidance Testing Associates [No reply from publisher; status unknown].
Cross References: See T3:2484 (1 reference) and T2:468 (1 reference); for reviews by Russel F. Green and Richard E. Schutz, see 7:391 (2 references); for reviews by Raleigh M. Drake and Walter N. Durost of the earlier edition, see 4:325 (8 references).

[2742]

Tests of General Educational Development [the GED Tests].

Purpose: To "assess skills representative of the typical outcomes of a traditional high school education" for the purpose of awarding a secondary school level (GED) diploma.
Population: Candidates for high school equivalency diplomas.
Publication Dates: 1944-1998.
Acronym: GED Tests.

Scores, 6: Writing Skills, Social Studies, Science, Interpreting Literature and the Arts, Mathematics, Total.
Administration: Group or individual.
Forms: 17 U.S. English Operational (secure) full-length forms available; 8 U.S. English forms available of Official GED Practice test (7 nonsecure half-length test, 1 nonsecure full-length test).
Price Data, 1998: Operational (secure) forms not available for purchase and are available only to and administered at Official GED Testing Centers; Official GED Practice Tests half-length (available from Steck-Vaughn Co., (800) 531-5015): $37.50 per 10 test batteries; $15.98 per set of 50 universal machine-scorable answer sheets; $12.98 per set of 10 self-scoring answer sheets (for use with half-length practice test U.S. English Form CC only); full-length U.S. English practice test: $36 per set of 5; $14.91 per set of 25 corresponding answer sheets; $24.20 per administrator's set including teacher's manual ('89, 203 pages), scoring materials, and conversion tables, available in U.S. English half-length, U.S. English full-length, Spanish, or French; $40.50 per 10 Spanish-language edition batteries (or $.88 for one test and one univrsal answer sheet); $15.98 per 50 Spanish-language universal answer sheets; $40.50 per 10 French-language edition batteries (or $4.88 for one test and one universal answer sheet); $15.98 per 50 French-language universal answer sheets; $13.80 per 1 Large Print practice test (U.S. English only) and universal answer sheet; $47.87 per 1 audiocassette practice test (U.S. English only) with large print reference copy. Canadian English practice test batteries (2 forms) available from Gage Publishing Ltd., (416) 293-8141: C27.50 per 10 batteries (avalable singly at C$4.98 each); C$13.68 per 50 Canadian English universal answer sheets; C$25.99 per Canadian English administrator's set. U.S. English (4 forms) and Canadian English (2 forms) computer-delivered practice tests available on CD-ROM through NTC/Contemporary Publishing, (800) 621-1918; outside the U.S., Canada, and their territories through Sylvan Learning Systems (800) 627-4276.
Foreign Language and Special Editions: Operational (secure) full length GED batteries: Canadian English (6 forms), Spanish (3 forms), French (2 forms), and U.S. English large print (3 forms), audiocassettte (2 forms), and Braille (2 forms) available. Computer-delivered U.S. English-language tests available only outside U.S., Canada, and their territories. Official GED Practice Tests: Canadian English, Spanish, French, U.S. English large print, and audiocassette.
Time: 120 minutes for Writing Skills, 85 minutes for Social Studies, 95 minutes for Science, 65 minutes for Interpreting Literature and the Arts, 90 minutes for Mathematics [all times are for Operational (secure forms) of the tests and do not include time required to give and clarify verbal test-taking instructions].
Comments: Tests administered throughout the year at official GED centers; tests originated in 1942 for granting high school/college credit for veterans, in mid-1950s GED program extended to all non-high school graduates; extensive 1988 revisions include addition of essay component to Writing Skills test and increased emphasis on higher order cognitive skills (e.g., application, analysis/evaluation, and math problem solving) throughout the battery; new tests scheduled for release in September 2001.
Author: General Educational Development Testing Service of the American Council on Education.
Publisher: General Educational Development Testing Service of the American Council on Education.
Cross References: See T4:2816 (2 references); for reviews by Bruce G. Rogers and Michael S. Trevisan, see 11:447 (2 references); for reviews by J. Stanley Ahmann and A. Harry Passow, see 9:1284 (1 reference); see also T3:2485 (2 references), 8:35 (20 references), and 7:34 (21 references); for a review by Robert J. Solomon of earlier forms, see 5:29 (39 references); for a review by Gustav J. Froehlich, see 4:26 (27 references); for reviews by Herbert S. Conrad and Warren G. Findley, see 3:20 (11 references). For reviews by Charlotte W. Croon of an earlier form of the expression subtest, see 3:122; for reviews by W. E. Hall and C. Robert Pace of an earlier form of the social studies reading subtest, see 3:528.

[2743]

Tests of Reading Comprehension.

Purpose: "They aim at assessing the extent to which readers are able to obtain meaning from text."
Population: Grades 3-7, 6-10.
Publication Date: 1987.
Acronym: TORCH.
Scores, 14: Grasshoppers, The Bear Who Liked Hugging People, Lizards Love Eggs, Getting Better, Feeding Puff, Shocking Things/Earthquakes!, The Swamp-creature, The Cats, A Horse of Her Own, Iceberg Towing, The Accident, The Killer Smog of London, I Want to be Andy, The Red Ace of Spades.
Administration: Individual or group.
Levels: 2 overlapping test booklets: A, B.
Price Data, 1994: A$63 per complete kit including test booklet A, test booklet B, 16 answer sheets, set of photocopy master sheets, and manual (84 pages); $25 per manual.
Time: Untimed.
Comments: "Content-referenced" and/or "norm-referenced."

Authors: Leila Mossenson, Peter Hill, and Geoffrey Masters.
Publisher: Australian Council for Educational Research, Ltd. [Australia].
Cross References: See T4:2817 (1 reference); for reviews by Robert B. Cooter, Jr. and Diane J. Sawyer, see 11:448.

TEST REFERENCES

1. Griffin, P. E. (1990). Profiling literacy development monitoring the accumulation of reading skills. *Australian Journal of Education, 34,* 290–311.
2. Chan, L. K. S. (1994). Relationship of motivation, strategic learning, and reading achievement in grades 5, 7, and 9. *Journal of Experimental Education, 62,* 319–339.
3. Hay, I., Ashman, A., & van Kraayenoord, C. E. (1997). Investigating the influence of achievement on self-concept using an intra-class design and a comparison of the PASS and SDQ-1 self-concept tests. *British Journal of Educational Psychology, 67,* 311–321.

[2744]

Tests of Reading: Inter-American Series.

Purpose: To assess vocabulary and reading comprehension in English or Spanish.
Population: Grades 1-2, 2-3, 4-6, 7-9, 10-12.
Publication Dates: 1950-1973.
Scores: LEVEL 1 (GRADES 1-2): Vocabulary, Comprehension; LEVEL 2 (GRADES 2-3): Level of Comprehension, Speed of Comprehension, Vocabulary; LEVELS 3, 4, 5 (GRADES 4-6, 7-9, 10-12): Vocabulary, Speed of Comprehension, Level of Comprehension.
Administration: Group.
Levels, 5: Parallel editions in English and Spanish.
Price Data: Not available.
Foreign Language Edition: French edition available.
Time: (18-41) minutes.
Author: Herschel T. Manuel.
Publisher: Guidance Testing Association [No reply from publisher; status unknown].

[2745]

TestWell: Health Risk Appraisal.

Purpose: "Designed to provide an awareness of how current behaviors and physical health measurements impact health risks."
Population: Adults ages 18–60 with a minimum of 10th grade education.
Publication Date: 1992.
Scores, 5: Appraised Age, Achievable Age, Positive Lifestyle Behaviors, Top 10 Risks of Death, Suggestions for Improvement.
Administration: Group.
Manual: No manual.
Price Data, 1998: $7 per individual National Wellness Institute scoring; $40 per group report.
Time: (20) minutes.
Comments: Scoring by National Wellness Institute; individual and group reports available.
Author: National Wellness Institute, Inc.
Publisher: National Wellness Institute, Inc.
Cross References: For reviews by Barbara L. Lachar and Steven G. LoBello, see 13:346.

[2746]

TestWell: Wellness Inventory for Windows.

Purpose: Designed to promote awareness of wellness.
Population: Adults with a minimum of 10th grade education.
Publication Date: 1992.
Scores, 11: Physical Fitness and Nutrition, Social Awareness, Medical Self-Care, Spirituality and Values, Emotional Management, Intellectual Wellness, Environmental Wellness, Safety, Occupational Wellness, Sexuality and Emotional Awareness, Total.
Administration: Group.
Manual: No manual.
Price Data, 1998: $399 per interactive version, single user license; $249.95 per interactive version, multiuser license; $695 per group/batch version; $.50 per group/batch entry questionnaire booklet; $750 per reproduction rights (educational institutions only); $395 per scanner support capability.
Time: (20) minutes.
Comments: Requires IBM or compatible computer hardware.
Author: National Wellness Institute, Inc.
Publisher: National Wellness Institute, Inc.
Cross References: For reviews by William W. Deardorff and Theodore L. Hayes, see 13:347; see also T4:2821 (1 reference).

[2747]

TestWell: Wellness Inventory for Windows—College Version.

Purpose: "Designed to address lifestyle choices facing today's college students."
Population: College students.
Publication Date: 1993.
Scores, 11: Physical Fitness, Nutrition, Social Awareness, Self-Care and Safety, Emotional and Sexuality, Intellectual Wellness, Environmental Wellness, Emotional Management, Occupational Wellness, Spirituality and Values, Total.
Administration: Group.
Price Data, 1998: $399 per interactive version, single user license; $599 per interactive version, multiuser license; $695 per group/batch version; $.50 per group/batch entry questionnaire booklet; $750 per reproduction rights (for educational institutions only); $395 per scanner support capability.
Time: (20) minutes.
Author: National Wellness Institute, Inc.

Publisher: National Wellness Institute, Inc.
Cross References: For reviews by David L. Bolton and Richard E. Harding, see 13:348.

[2748]

Thanatometer.

Purpose: Measures attitudes concerning death.
Population: Adults.
Publication Date: 1986.
Scores: Total score only.
Administration: Group or individual.
Manual: No manual.
Price Data, 1998: $1 per scale.
Time: [5-10] minutes.
Author: Panos D. Bardis.
Publisher: Donna Bardis.

[2749]

Thematic Apperception Test.

Purpose: "A method of revealing to the trained interpreter some of the dominant drives, emotions, sentiments, complexes and conflicts of a personality."
Population: Ages 4 and over.
Publication Dates: 1935-1943.
Acronym: TAT.
Scores: Total score only.
Administration: Individual.
Price Data: Available from publisher.
Time: 100(200) minutes in 2 sessions 1 day apart.
Author: Henry A. Murray.
Publisher: Harvard University Press.
Cross References: See T4:2824 (107 references), 9:1287 (51 references), and T3:2491 (105 references); for a review by Jon D. Swartz, see 8:697 (241 references); see also T2:1519 (231 references); for a review by Richard H. Dana and Leonard D. Eron, see 7:181 (297 references); see also P:484 (339 references); for a review by C. J. Adcock, see 6:245 (287 references); for reviews by Leonard D. Eron and Arthur R. Jensen, see 5:164 (311 references); for a review by Arthur L. Benton, see 4:136 (198 references); for reviews by Arthur L. Benton, Julian Rotter, and J. R. Wittenborn and an excerpted review, see 3:103 (102 references).

TEST REFERENCES

1. Richardson, V., & Sands, R. (1986). Death attitudes among mid-life women. *Omega, 17,* 327–341.
2. Cramer, P. (1987). The development of defense mechanisms. *Journal of Personality, 55,* 597–614.
3. Doane, J. A., & Mintz, J. (1987). Communication deviance in adolescence and adulthood: A longitudinal study. *Psychiatry, 50,* 5–13.
4. McAdams, D. P., & Bryant, F. B. (1987). Intimacy motivation and subjective mental health in a nationwide sample. *Journal of Personality, 55,* 395–413.
5. Cramer, P., & Gaul, R. (1988). The effects of success and failure on children's use of defense mechanisms. *Journal of Personality, 56,* 729–742.
6. Biernat, M. (1989). Motives and values to achieve: Different constructs with different effects. *Journal of Personality, 57,* 69–95.
7. O'Connell, M., Cooper, S., Perry, C., & Hoke, L. (1989). The relationship between thought disorder and psychotic symptoms in borderline personality disorder. *The Journal of Nervous and Mental Disease, 177,* 273-278.
8. Schiff, B. B., & Lamon, M. (1989). Inducing emotion by unilateral contraction of facial muscles: A new look at hemispheric specialization and the experience of emotion. *Neuropsychologia, 27,* 923–935.
9. Sommers-Flanagan, J., & Greenberg, R. P. (1989). Psychosocial variables and hypertension: A new look at an old controversy. *The Journal of Nervous and Mental Disease, 177,* 15-24.
10. Wilson, A., Passik, S. D., Faude, J., Abrams, J., & Gordon, E. (1989). A hierarchical model of opiate addiction: Failures of self-regulation as a central aspect of substance abuse. *The Journal of Nervous and Mental Disease, 177,* 390-399.
11. Armstrong, J. G., & Loewenstein, R. J. (1990). Characteristics of patients with multiple personality and dissociative disorders on psychological testing. *The Journal of Nervous and Mental Disease, 178,* 448-454.
12. Ehrenreich, J. H. (1990). Effect of social class of subjects on normative responses to TAT cards. *Journal of Clinical Psychology, 46,* 467–471.
13. Frank, A. F., & Gunderson, J. G. (1990). The role of the therapeutic alliance in the treatment of schizophrenia. *Archives of General Psychiatry, 47,* 228–236.
14. Hodges, W. F., London, J., & Colwell, J. B. (1990). Stress in parents and late elementary age children in divorced and intact families and child adjustment. *Journal of Divorce & Remarriage, 14*(1), 63-79.
15. Lisak, D., & Roth, S. (1990). Motives and psychodynamics of self-reported, unincarcerated rapists. *American Journal of Orthopsychiatry, 60,* . 268–280.
16. Ungar, L., Florian, V., & Zernitsky-Shurka, E. (1990). Aspects of fear of personal death, levels of awareness, and professional affiliation among dialysis unit staff members. *Omega, 21,* 51–67.
17. Webb, N. B., Sakheim, G. A., Towns-Miranda, L., & Wagner, C. R. (1990). Collaborative treatment of juvenile firesetters: Assessment and outreach. *American Journal of Orthopsychiatry, 60,* 305–310.
18. Abramson, L., McClelland, D. C., Brown, D., & Kelner, S. (1991). Alexithymic characteristics and metabolic control in diabetic and healthy adults. *The Journal of Nervous and Mental Disease, 179,* 490-494.
19. Cramer, P. (1991). Anger and the use of defense mechanisms in college students. *Journal of Personality, 59,* 39–55.
20. Kim, W. J., Hahn, S. U., Kish, J., Rosenberg, L., & Harris, J. (1991). Separation reaction of psychiatrically hospitalized children: A pilot study. *Child Psychiatry and Human Development, 22,* 53-67.
21. Koestner, R., Weinberger, J., & McClelland, D. C. (1991). Task-intrinsic and social-extrinsic sources of arousal for motives assessed in fantasy and self-report. *Journal of Personality, 59,* 57–82.
22. Sakheim, G. A., Osborn, E., & Abrams, D. (1991). Toward a clearer differentiation of high-risk from low-risk fire-setters. *Child Welfare, 70,* 489–503.
23. Saunders, E. B., & Awad, G. A. (1991). Male adolescent sexual offenders: Exhibitionism and obscene phone calls. *Child Psychiatry and Human Development, 21,* 169-178.
24. Daie, N., Witztum, E., Mark, M., & Rabinowitz, S. (1992). The belief in the transmigration of souls: Psychotherapy of a Druze patient with severe anxiety reaction. *British Journal of Medical Psychology, 65,* 119–130.
25. Erwin, E. (1992). Current philosophical issues in the scientific evaluation of behavior therapy theory and outcome. *Behavior Therapy, 23,* 151–171.
26. Friedman, A., & Pines, A. M. (1992). Increase in Arab women's perceived power in the second half of life. *Sex Roles, 26,* 1-9.
27. Friedman, A., Tzukerman, Y., Wienberg, H., & Todd, J. (1992). The shift in power with age: Changes in perception of the power of women and men over the life cycle. *Psychology of Women Quarterly, 16,* 513-525.
28. Leigh, J., Westen, D., Barends, A., Mendel, M. J., & Byers, S. (1992). The assessment of complexity of representations of people using TAT and interview data. *Journal of Personality, 60,* 809–837.
29. Oz, S., Tari, A., & Fine, M. (1992). A comparison of the psychological profiles of teenage mothers and their nonmother peers: II. Responses to a set of TAT cards. *Adolescence, 27,* 357-367.
30. Super, J. T., & Block, J. R. (1992). Self-concept and need for achievement of men with physical disabilities. *The Journal of General Psychology, 119,* 73-80.
31. Becker, J. V., & Quinsey, V. L. (1993). Assessing suspected child molestors. *Child Abuse & Neglect, 17,* 169-174.
32. French, L. A. (1993). Adaptive projective tests for minority children. *Psychological Reports, 72,* 15-18.
33. Piotrowski, C., Keller, J. W., & Ogawa, T. (1993). Projective techniques: An international perspective. *Psychological Reports, 72,* 179-182.
34. Szajnberg, M. D., Krall, V. K., Davis, P., Treem, W., & Hyams, J. (1993). Psychopathology and relationship measures in children with inflammatory bowel disease and their parents. *Child Psychiatry and Human Development, 23,* 215–232.
35. Waterman, J., & Lusk, R. (1993). Psychological testing in evaluation of child sexual abuse. *Child Abuse & Neglect, 17,* 145-159.
36. Alvarado, N. (1994). Empirical validity of the Thematic Apperception Test. *Journal of Personality Assessment, 63,* 59-79.
37. Friedman, A., & Todd, J. (1994). Kenyan women tell a story: Interpersonal power of women in three subcultures in Kenya. *Sex Roles, 28,* 533-546.
38. George, B. L., & Waehler, C. A. (1994). The ups and downs of TAT Card 17BM. *Journal of Personality Assessment, 63,* 167-172.
39. Hibbard, S., Farmer, L., Wells, C., Difillipo, E., Barry, W., Korman, R., & Sloan, P. (1994). Validation of Cramer's defense mechanism manual for the TAT. *Journal of Personality Assessment, 63,* 197-210.
40. Keller, D. S., & Wilson, A. (1994). Affectivity in cocaine and opiate abusers. *Psychiatry, 57,* 333–347.
41. Lenzenweger, M. F. (1994). Psychometric high-risk paradigm, perceptual aberrations, and schizotypy: An update. *Schizophrenia Bulletin, 20,* 121–135.

42. Lewis, J. R., Bates, B. C., & Lawrence, S. (1994). Empirical studies of projection: A critical review. *Human Relations, 47,* 1295-1319.

43. Lowe, R. C., & Wilczynski, M. (1994). A cross-cultural study of need for achievement in Italian and American children. *Psychological Reports, 75,* 590.

44. McCrone, E. R., Egeland, B., Kalkoske, M., & Carlson, E. A. (1994). Relations between early maltreatment and mental representations of relationships assessed with projective storytelling in middle childhood. *Development and Psychopathology, 6,* 99-120.

45. Ornduff, S. R., Freedenfeld, R. N., Kelsey, R. M., & Critelli, J. W. (1994). Object relations of sexually abused female subjects: A TAT analysis. *Journal of Personality Assessment, 63,* 223-238.

46. Peterson, C., & Ulrey, L. M. (1994). Can explanatory style be scored from TAT protocols? *Personality and Social Psychology Bulletin, 20,* 102-106.

47. Pistole, D. R., & Ornduff, S. R. (1994). TAT assessment of sexually abused girls: An analysis of manifest content. *Journal of Personality Assessment, 63,* 211-222.

48. Rosenberg, S. D., Blatt, S. J., Oxman, T. E., McHugo, G. J., & Ford, R. Q. (1994). Assessment of object relatedness through a lexical content analysis of the TAT. *Journal of Personality Assessment, 63,* 345-362.

49. Tracey, T. J. (1994). An examination of the complementarilty of interpersonal behavior. *Journal of Personality and Social Psychology, 67,* 864-878.

50. Woike, B. A. (1994). The use of differentiation and integration processes: Empirical studies of "separate" and "connected" ways of thinking. *Journal of Personality and Social Psychology, 67,* 142-150.

51. Woike, B. A. (1994). Vivid recollection as a technique to arouse implicit motive-related affect. *Motivation and Emotion, 18,* 335–349.

52. Acklin, M. W. (1995). Rorschach assessment of the borderline child. *Journal of Clinical Psychology, 51,* 294-302.

53 Ching, J. W. J., McDermott, J. F., Fukunaga, C., Yanagida, E., Mann, E., & Waldron, J. A. (1995). Perceptions of family values and roles among Japanese Americans: Clinical considerations. *American Journal of Orthopsychiatry, 65,* 216–224.

54. Fodor, E. M., & Greenier, K. D. (1995). The power motive, self-affect, and creativity. *Journal of Research in Personality, 29,* 242-252.

55. Freedenfeld, R. N., Ornduff, S. R., & Kelsey, R. M. (1995). Object relations and physical abuse: A TAT analysis. *Journal of Personality Assessment, 64,* 552-568.

56. Hibbard, S., Hilsenroth, M. J., Hibbard, J. K., & Nash, M. R. (1995). A validity study of two projective object representations measures. *Psychological Assessment, 7,* 432–439.

57. James, J. B., Lewkowicz, C., Libhaber, J., & Lachman, M. (1995). Rethinking the gender identity cross over hypothesis: A test of a new model. *Sex Roles, 32,* 185–207.

58. King, L. A. (1995). Wishes, motives, goals, and personal memories: Relations of measures of human motivation. *Journal of Personality, 63,* 986–1007.

59. Pam, A., & Rivera, J. (1995). Sexual pathology and dangerousness from a Thematic Apperception Test protocol. *Professional Psychology: Research and Practice, 26,* 72–77.

60. Porcerelli, J. H., & Sandler, B. A. (1995). Narcissism and empathy in steroid users. *American Journal of Psychiatry, 152,* 1672–1674.

61. Ronan, G. F., Date, A. L., & Weisbrod, M. (1995). Personal problem-solving scoring of the TAT: Sensitivity to training. *Journal of Personality Assessment, 64,* 119-131.

62. Schiff, B. B., & Romp, S. A. (1995). Asymmetrical hemispheric activation and emotion: The effects of unilateral forced nostril breathing. *Brain and Cognition, 29,* 217–231.

63. Smith, S. M., & Petty, R. E. (1995). Personality moderators of mood congruency effects on cognition: The role of self-esteem and negative mood regulation. *Journal of Personality and Social Psychology, 68,* 1092–1107.

64. Welsh, W. M., & Stewart, A. J. (1995). Relationships between women and their parents: Implications for midlife well-being. *Psychology and Aging, 10,* 181-190.

65. Adkins, K. K., & Parker, W. (1996). Perfectionism and suicidal preoccupation. *Journal of Personality, 64,* 529–543.

66. Heinze, M. C., & Grisso, T. (1996). Review of instruments assessing parenting competencies used in child custody evaluations. *Behavior Sciences and the Law, 14,* 293–313.

67. Locraft, C., & Teglasi, H. (1996). Teacher rated emphatic behaviors and children's TAT stories. *Journal of School Psychology, 35,* 217–237.

68. Mansfield, E. D., & McAdams, D. P. (1996). Generativity and themes of agency and communion in adult autobiography. *Personality and Social Psychology Bulletin, 22,* 721–731.

69. McAdams, D. P., Hoffman, B. J., Mansfield, E. D., & Day, R. (1996). Themes of agency and communication in significant autobiographical scenes. *Journal of Personality, 64,* 339–377.

70. McAninch, C. B., Milich, R., & Harris, M. J. (1996). Effects of an academic expectancy and gender on students' interactions. *Journal of Educational Research, 89,* 146–153.

71. Peterson, B. E., & Stewart, A. J. (1996). Antecedents and contexts of generativity motivation at midlife. *Psychology and Aging, 11,* 21–33.

72 Wilson, M. S., & Reschly, D. J. (1996). Assessment in school psychology training and practice. *School Psychology Review, 25,* 9–23.

73. Woike, B. A., Osier, T. J., & Candela, K. (1996). Attachment styles and violent imagery in thematic stories about relationships. *Personality and Social Psychology Bulletin, 22,* 1030–1034.

74. Cramer, P. (1997). Evidence for change in children's use of defense mechanisms. *Journal of Personality, 65,* 233–247.

75. Cruz, E. B., Brier, N. M., & Reznikoff, M. (1997). An examination of the relationship between form level ratings on the Rorschach and learning disability status. *The Journal of Psychology, 131,* 167–174.

76. Lavallee, L. & Suedfeld, P. (1997). Conflict in Clayoquot Sound: Using thematic content analysis to understand psychological aspects of environmental controversy. *Canadian Journal of Behavioural Science, 29,* 194–209.

77. Liem, J. H., James, J. B., O'Toole, J. G., & Boudewyn, A. C. (1997). Assessing resilience in adults with histories of childhood sexual abuse. *American Journal of Orthopsychiatry, 67,* 594–606.

78. McAdams, D. P., Diamons, A., de St. Aubin, E., & Mansfield, E. (1997). Stories of commitment: The psychosocial construction of generative lives. *Journal of Personality and Social Psychology, 72,* 678–694.

79. Nasby, W., & Read, N. W. (1997). The life voyage of a solo circumnavigator: Integrating theoretical and methodological perspectives. *Journal of Personality, 65,* 785–1068.

80. Rossini, E. D., & Moretti, R. J. (1997). Thematic Apperception Test (TAT) interpretation: Practice recommendations from a survey of clinical psychology doctoral programs accredited by the American Psychological Association. *Professional Psychology: Research and Practice, 28,* 393–398.

81. Wodrich, D. L., & Tholl, L. M. (1997). Childhood Tourette's Syndrome and the Thematic Apperception Test: is there a recognizable pattern? *Perceptual and Motor Skills, 85,* 635–641.

82. Cramer, P. (1998). Threeat to gender representation: Identity and identification. *Journal of Personality, 66,* 335–337.

83. Hien, D., Haas, G., & Cook, H. (1998). Gender differences in premorbid social adjustment and intimacy motivation in schizophrenia. *Journal of Clinical Psychology, 54,* 35–48.

84. Litinsky, A. M., & Haslam, N. (1998). Dichotomous thinking as a sign of suicide risk in the TAT. *Journal of Personality Assessment, 71,* 368–378.

85. Porcerelli, J. H., Thomas, S., Hibbard, S., & Cogan, R. (1998). Defense mechanisms development in children, adolescents, and late adolescents. *Journal of Personality Assessment, 71,* 411–420.

86. Silberg, J. L. (1998). Dissociative symptomatology in children and adolescents as displayed on psychological testing. *Journal of Personality Assessment, 71,* 421–439.

87. Winter, D. G. (1998). The contributions of David McClelland to personality assessment. *Journal of Personality Assessment, 71,* 129–145.

[2750]

Themes Concerning Blacks.

Purpose: Designed to measure individual motivation, specific thematic responses, creativity, ingenuity, and problem solving.

Population: Blacks ages 4 and over.

Publication Date: 1972.

Acronym: TCB.

Scores: Total score only.

Administration: Individual.

Price Data, 1985: $30 per complete kit including 20 cards and manual (21 pages); $3.50 per manual.

Time: Administration time not reported.

Author: Robert L. Williams.

Publisher: Robert L. Williams & Associates, Inc. [No reply from publisher; status unknown].

Cross References: For reviews by James M. Daum and Myrna K. Ness, see 9:1288.

[2751]

Theological School Inventory.

Purpose: Assesses motivation for entering the ministry.

Population: Incoming seminary students.

Publication Dates: 1962-1972.

Acronym: TSI.

Scores, 12: Definiteness, Natural Leading, Special Leading, Concept of the Call, Flexibility, Acceptance by Others, Intellectual Concern, Self-Fulfillment, Leadership Success, Evangelistic Witness, Social Reform, Service to Persons.

Administration: Group.
Price Data: Available from publisher.
Time: Administration time not reported.
Authors: James E. Dittes, Frederick Kling, Ellery Pierson, and Harry DeWire.
Publisher: Ministry Inventories.
Cross References: See T2:1028 (7 references) and P:273 (5 references).

[2752]

Therapy Attitude Inventory.

Purpose: Provides ratings of parental satisfaction with training in the behavioral management of their children.
Population: Parents.
Publication Date: 1974.
Scores: Total score only.
Administration: Individual.
Price Data, 1994: No charge for first copy; may photocopy for research or clinical use.
Time: (5) minutes.
Author: Sheila Eyberg.
Publisher: Sheila M. Eyberg.
Cross References: See T4:2827 (1 reference); for a review by Terry B. Gutkin, see 9:1289 (2 references); see also T3:2494 (1 reference).

TEST REFERENCES

1. Eisenstadt, T. H., Eyberg, S., McNeil, C. B., Newcomb, K., & Funderburk, B. (1993). Parent-child interaction therapy with behavior problem children: Relative effectiveness of two stages and overall treatment outcome. *Journal of Clinical Child Psychology, 22,* 42-51.
2. Schuhmann, E. M., Foote, R. C., Eybert, S. M., Boggs, S. R., & Algina, J. (1998). Efficacy of parent-child interaction therapy: Interim report of a randomized trial with short-term maintenance. *Journal of Clinical Child Psychology, 27,* 34-45.

[2753]

Thinking About My School.

Purpose: Designed to measure "student perceptions of the school environment and feelings about their school."
Population: Grades 4-6.
Publication Date: 1985.
Acronym: TAMS.
Scores, 6: Power, Social, Work, Teachers, Liking for School, Total.
Administration: Group.
Price Data: Not available.
Time: (30-60) minutes.
Author: Joanne Rand Whitmore.
Publisher: United/DOK Publishers [No reply from publisher; status unknown].
Cross References: For reviews by S. E. Phillips and Sylvia Rosenfield, see 10:376.

TEST REFERENCE

1. Lupart, J. L., & Pyryt, M. C. (1996). "Hidden gifted" students: Underachiever prevalence and profile. *Journal for the Education of the Gifted, 20,* 36–53.

[2754]

Thinking Creatively in Action and Movement.

Purpose: "Designed to sample . . . creative thinking abilities of preschool children."
Population: Ages 3–8.
Publication Date: 1981.
Acronym: TCAM.
Scores, 3: Fluency, Originality, Imagination.
Administration: Individual.
Price Data, 1992: $33 per 20 tests and manual/scoring guide (34 pages); $16.95 per manual; $24.15 per specimen set; scoring service, $5 per booklet.
Time: (10-30) minutes.
Author: E. Paul Torrance.
Publisher: Scholastic Testing Service, Inc.
Cross References: See T4:2829 (2 references); for reviews by Joseph S. Renzulli and James O. Rust, see 9:1290.

TEST REFERENCES

1. Karnes, M. B., & Johnson, L. J. (1987). Bringing out Head Start talents: Findings from the field. *Gifted Child Quarterly, 31,* 174–179.
2. Cooper, E. (1991). A critique of six measures for assessing creativity. *Journal of Creative Behavior, 25,* 194-204.
3. Meador, K. S. (1992). Emerging rainbows: A review of the literature on creativity in preschoolers. *Journal for the Education of the Gifted, 15,* 163-181.
4. Fuchs-Beauchamp, K. D., Karnes, M. B., & Johnson, L. J. (1993). Creativity and intelligence in preschoolers. *Gifted Child Quarterly, 37,* 113-117.
5. Daugherty, M., White, C. S., & Manning, B. H. (1994). Relationships among private speech and creativity measurements of young children. *Gifted Child Quarterly, 38,* 21-26.

[2755]

Thinking Creatively With Sounds and Words, Research Edition.

Purpose: Developed to assess creative thinking.
Population: Grades 3–12, adults.
Publication Date: 1973.
Acronym: TCSW.
Scores, 2: Sounds and Images, Onomatopoeia and Images.
Administration: Group.
Levels, 2: I, II.
Forms, 2: A, B.
Price Data, 1993: $28.95 per complete kit including 20 test booklets (specify level and form) and manual/scoring guide (20 pages); $31.95 per cassettes; $12.60 per manual/scoring guide; $12.50 per norms/technical manual (65 pages); $24.15 per specimen set; scoring service, $5 or less per booklet.
Time: (30–35) minutes for each test.
Authors: E. Paul Torrance, Joe Khatena, and Bert F. Cunnington (except technical manual).
Publisher: Scholastic Testing Service, Inc.
Cross References: See T4:2830 (5 references); for a review by Lynn H. Fox, see 9:1291 (3 references); see also T3:2496 (5 references); for reviews by Philip M.

Clark and Mary Lee Smith, see 8:248 (6 references); see also T2:587 (17 references).

TEST REFERENCES

1. Cooper, E. (1991). A critique of six measures for assessing creativity. *Journal of Creative Behavior, 25,* 194-204.

2. Coney, J., & Serna, P. (1995). Creative thinking from an information processing perspective: A new approach to Mednick's theory of associative hierarchies. *The Journal of Creative Behavior, 29,* 109–132.

[2756]

Thomas-Kilmann Conflict Mode Instrument.

Purpose: Designed to assess "an individual's behavior in conflict situations."
Population: Managers.
Publication Date: 1974.
Acronym: TKI.
Scores, 5: Competing, Collaborating, Compromising, Avoiding, Accommodating.
Administration: Group or individual.
Price Data, 1993: $5.50 per instrument (16 pages including test and general information).
Time: [15] minutes.
Comments: Self-administered, self-scored.
Authors: Kenneth W. Thomas and Ralph H. Kilmann.
Publisher: XICOM.
Cross References: For reviews by Richard E. Harding and Ronn Johnson, see 10:377 (4 references).

TEST REFERENCES

1. Bond, M. H., Leung, K., & Schwartz, S. (1992). Explaining choices in procedural and distributive justice across cultures. *International Journal of Psychology, 27,* 211–225.

2. Chiu, R. K., & Kosinski, F. A., Jr. (1994). Is Chinese conflict-handling behavior influenced by Chinese values. *Social Behavior and Personality, 22,* 81-90.

[2757]

Thurstone Temperament Schedule.

Purpose: Measures personality traits related to job performance.
Population: Variety of occupations from entry-level to management.
Publication Dates: 1949-1991.
Acronym: TTS.
Scores, 6: Active, Impulsive, Dominant, Stable, Sociable, Reflective.
Administration: Individual or group.
Price Data, 1998: $59 per start-up kit including 25 test booklets and examiner's manual; $46 per 25 test booklets (quantity discount available); $19.75 per examiner's manual; $89 per Quanta Computer administration and scoring software (DOS format).
Time: No limit (approximately 15–20 minutes).
Comments: Can be administered via paper and pencil or computer; hand-scored carbon format or computer scoring.
Author: L. L. Thurstone.
Publisher: NCS (Rosemont).
Cross References: See T4:2833 (6 references), T3:2499 (2 references), T2:1423 (32 references), P:277 (20 references), and 6:192 (17 references); for a review by Neil J. Van Steenberg, see 5:118 (12 references); for reviews by Hans J. Eysenck, Charles M. Harsh, and David G. Ryans, and an excerpted review by Laurance F. Shaffer, see 4:93.

TEST REFERENCE

1. Lee, C., Ashford, S. J., & Bobko, P. (1990). Interactive effects of "Type A" behavior and perceived control on worker performance, job satisfaction, and somatic complaints. *Academy of Management Journal, 33,* 870–881.

[2758]

Thurstone Test of Mental Alertness.

Purpose: Measures general mental ability to learn and comprehend.
Population: Wide variety of occupations.
Publication Dates: 1943-1998.
Acronym: TMA.
Scores, 3: Quantitative, Linguistic, Total.
Administration: Individual or group.
Forms, 2: A, B.
Price Data, 1998: $67 per start-up kit including 25 test booklets and examiner's manual (specify Form A or Form B); $55 per 25 test booklets (quantity discounts available; specify Form A or Form B); $19.75 per examiner's manual; $89 per (DOS version) Quanta computer administration and scoring software (Form A only).
Time: 20 minutes.
Authors: Thelma Gwinn Thurstone and L. L. Thurstone.
Publisher: NCS (Rosemont).
Cross References: See T2:469 (5 references); for a review by Robert D. North, see 7:392 (4 references); for a review by Joshua A. Fishman, see 5:391; see also 4:326 (3 references); for reviews by Anne Anastasi and Emily T. Burr of an earlier edition, see 3:265.

TEST REFERENCE

1. Rossini, E. D., Wygonik, E. J., Barrett, D. E., & Friedman, B. (1994). WAIS-R validation of the Thurstone Test of Mental Alterness. *Psychological Reports, 74,* 1339-1345.

[2759]

Tiffany Control Scales.

Purpose: Designed to evaluate personality problems related to one's experience of control across different situations.
Population: Adolescents and adults.
Publication Dates: 1985–1999.
Acronym: TCS.
Scores, 16: Control from Self/Internal, Control over Self, Control over the Environment, Control from the Environment, Coping Index, Passive/Assertive/Aggressive Index, Extratensive/Intratensive Index, Repression, Expressive, Self-Directed, Non-Self-Directed, and 5 other measures.

Administration: Individual or group.
Editions, 2: Paper and pencil, computer administered.
Price Data, 1998: $12.50 per 25 paper and pencil tests; $695.95 per computer edition, unlimited use; $50 per limited use edition (5 uses); demo and sample report are free; $25 per test for mail-in scoring; $19.95 per manual ('99, 83 pages).
Time: [20] minutes for Standard TCS; varies when customized.
Comments: For research or clinical use or in employment screening; may be customized to fit examiner's needs; self-rating instrument; scoring and interpretation by computer.
Authors: Donald W. Tiffany and Phyllis G. Tiffany.
Publisher: Psychological Growth Associates, Inc.

TEST REFERENCE

1. Gross, W. C., Tiffany, P. G., & Billingham, R. E. (1987). Situation-specific expertise and perceived control. *Perceptual and Motor Skills, 64,* 659–662.

[2760]

The Time of Your Life.

Purpose: Constructed as a self-assessment tool to provide "insight" into time management.
Population: Employees.
Publication Date: 1988.
Scores: Total score only.
Administration: Group or individual.
Price Data, 1990: $40 per complete kit including 20 inventories and 20 scoring and interpretation sheets.
Time: [30] minutes.
Comments: Self-administered, self-scored.
Author: Training House, Inc.
Publisher: Training House, Inc.
Cross References: For reviews by Ralph F. Darr, Jr. and Richard W. Faunce, see 12:400.

[2761]

Time Perception Inventory.

Purpose: Measures perceptions of time use including degree of personal concern about time usage and frame of reference (past, present, future) used.
Population: Students in time management courses.
Publication Dates: 1976-1987.
Scores, 4: Time Effectiveness, Orientation (Past, Present, Future).
Administration: Group.
Price Data, 1999: $38.50 per complete kit including 10 inventories and manual ('87, 8 pages); $24.50 per 10 inventories, including profile; $16.50 per manual.
Time: Administration time not reported.
Comments: Manual has been revised; self-administered.
Author: Albert A. Canfield.
Publisher: Western Psychological Services.
Cross References: For a review by Douglas J. McRae, see 11:449.

[2762]

Time Problems Inventory.

Purpose: Identifies reasons people waste time.
Population: Management and administrative personnel.
Publication Dates: 1980-1987.
Scores, 4: Priorities, Planning, Delegation, Self-Discipline.
Administration: Group.
Price Data, 1999: $38.50 per complete kit including 10 inventories and manual ('87, 8 pages); $24.50 per 10 inventories ('87); $16.50 per manual.
Time: (20-25) minutes.
Comments: Manual has been revised; self-administered.
Author: Albert A. Canfield.
Publisher: Western Psychological Services.
Cross References: For reviews by Jeanette N. Cleveland and Lyle F. Schoenfeldt of an earlier edition, see 9:190.

[2763]

The Time-Sample Behavioral Checklist.

Purpose: Developed to measure the level and nature of functioning of adult residential patients and also used to document how and where residents and staff spend their time.
Population: Adults in residential treatment settings.
Publication Date: 1987.
Acronym: TSBC.
Scores: 7 categories: Location, Position, Awake-Asleep, Facial Expression, Social Orientation, Concurrent Activities, Crazy Behavior combined in a variety of ways to produce 9 higher-order scores: Appropriate Behavior (Interpersonal Interaction, Instrumental Activity, Self-Maintenance, Individual Entertainment, Total), Inappropriate Behavior (Bizarre Motor Behavior, Bizarre Facial & Verbal, Hostile-Belligerence, Total).
Administration: Individual.
Price Data, 1991: $18.95 per manual/checklist (286 pages).
Time: 10 2-second observations.
Comments: Should be used in conjunction with the Staff-Resident Interaction Chronograph.
Authors: Gordon L. Paul, Mark H. Licht, Marco J. Mariotto, Christopher T. Power, and Kathryn L. Engel.
Publisher: Research Press.
Cross References: For reviews by Cynthia Ann Druva-Roush and Susan L. Crowley and Blaine R. Worthen, see 12:402; see also T4:2840 (1 reference).

[2764]

Time Use Analyzer.

Purpose: Designed to "clarify the importance of using time effectively in various aspects of life."
Population: Adults.
Publication Dates: 1981–1990.
Scores: 2 scores (Typicalness, Dissatisfaction) for 8 areas: Work, Sleep, Personal, Personal/Family, Community, Family/Home, Education/Development, Recreation/Hobbies.
Administration: Group.
Price Data, 1999: $38.50 per complete kit including manual ('90, 8 pages), and 10 inventories; $24.50 per 10 inventories; $16.50 per manual.
Time: (5–10) minutes.
Comments: May be used alone or in combination with the Time Perception Inventory (2761) and the Time Problems Inventory (2762).
Author: Albert A. Canfield.
Publisher: Western Psychological Services.

[2765]

Timed Typings for Holidays.

Purpose: To measure typing skill growth, develop fluency, and help reach for new speed goals.
Population: Students in typing classes.
Publication Date: 1988.
Scores: Total score only.
Administration: Group.
Manual: No manual.
Price Data, 1993: $13.95 per 24 blackline masters.
Time: (1-5) minutes per writing.
Authors: Berkley H. Rudd and Carol R. Scott.
Publisher: J. Weston Walch, Publisher.

[2766]

TMJ Scale.

Purpose: "Designed to measure the [clinical significance of] symptom patterns of dental patients with temporomandibular joint disorders and orofacial pain."
Population: TM [temporomandibular] dental patients ages 13 and over.
Publication Dates: 1984-1987.
Scores, 10: Physical Domain (Pain Report, Palpation Pain, Perceived Malocclusion, Joint Dysfunction, Range of Motion Limitation, Non-TM Disorder), Psychosocial Domain (Psychological Factors, Stress, Chronicity), Global Scale.
Administration: Individual.
Price Data, 1994: $20 per specimen set including question booklet, manual ('87, 86 pages), and sample report.
Time: (10-15) minutes.
Comments: Self-administered; self-report.
Authors: Stephen R. Levitt, Tom F. Lundeen, and Michael W. McKinney.
Publisher: Pain Resource Center, Inc.
Cross References: For a review by William W. Deardorff, see 12:402; see also T4:2842 (3 references).

[2767]

Toddler and Infant Motor Evaluation.

Purpose: Designed to be used for "diagnostic, comprehensive assessment of children who are suspected to have motor delays or deviations, the development of appropriate remediation programs, and treatment efficacy research."
Population: Ages 4 months to 3.5 years.
Publication Date: 1994.
Acronym: TIME: Version 1.0.
Scores: 5 Primary Subtests: Mobility, Stability, Motor Organization, Social-Emotional, Functional Performance; 3 Clinical Subtests: Quality Rating, Component Analysis Rating, Atypical Positions.
Administration: Individual.
Price Data, 1999: $395 per complete kit including manual (324 pages), 10 record forms, timer, rattle, 2 balls, squeak toy, toy car, 3 containers, toy telephone, 2 shoelaces, 6 blocks, and nylon tote bag; $35 per 10 record forms; $125 per manual.
Time: (15–40) minutes.
Comments: Diagnostic assessment tool designed to be used by licensed/highly trained physical and occupational therapists, or appropriately trained adaptive physical educators, special education teachers, or others with expertise in the motor domain; administered utilizing a partnership between parent(s) or caretaker(s) and a trained examiner.
Authors: Lucy J. Miller and Gale H. Roid.
Publisher: Therapy Skill Builders—A Division of The Psychological Corporation.

[2768]

The Token Test for Children.

Purpose: Designed to assess receptive language dysfunction.
Population: Ages 3-12.
Publication Date: 1978.
Scores: Total score only.
Administration: Individual.
Parts, 5: I, II, III, IV, V.
Price Data, 1999: $94 per complete kit including 50 scoring forms, 20 tokens, and manual (63 pages); $29 per 20 tokens; $34 per 50 forms; $34 per manual.
Time: (8) minutes.
Author: Frank DiSimoni.
Publisher: PRO-ED.
Cross References: See T4:2846 (24 references); for reviews by William M. Reynolds and John Salvia, see 9:1295 (9 references); see also T3:2509 (1 reference).

TEST REFERENCES

1. Catts, H. W., & Kamhi, A. G. (1986). The linguistic basis of reading disorders: Implications for the speech-language pathologist. *Language, Speech, and Hearing Services in Schools, 17,* 329–341.

2. Fujiki, M., Brinton, B., & Dunton, S. (1987). A grammatical judgement screening test for young elementary school-aged children. *Language, Speech, and Hearing Services in Schools, 18,* 131–143.

3. Lewis, B. A., Aram, D. M., & Horwitz, S. J. (1989). Language and motor findings in benign megalencephaly. *Perceptual and Motor Skills, 68,* 1051–1054.

4. Szatmari, P., Bartolucci, G., Bremner, R., Bond, S., & Rich, S. (1989). A follow-up study of high-functioning autistic children. *Journal of Autism and Developmental Disorders, 19*(2), 213-225.

5. Keith, R. W., & Engineer, P. (1991). Effects of methylphenidate on the auditory processing abilities of children with attention deficit-hyperactivity disorder. *Journal of Learning Disabilities, 24,* 630–636, 640.

6. Rubin, H., Patterson, P. A., & Kantor, M. (1991). Morphological development and writing ability in children and adults. *Language, Speech, and Hearing Services in Schools, 22,* 228–235.

7. Wilson, K. S., Blackmon, R. C., Hall, R. E., & Elcholtz, G. E. (1991). Methods of language assessment: A survey of California public school clinicians. *Language, Speech, and Hearing Services in Schools, 22,* 236–241.

8. Aram, D. M., Morris, R., & Hall, N. E. (1992). The validity of discrepancy criteria for identifying children with developmental language disorders. *Journal of Learning Disabilities, 25,* 549–554.

9. Mack, A. E., & Warr-Leeper, G. A. (1992). Language abilities in boys with chronic behavior disorders. *Language, Speech, and Hearing Services in Schools, 23,* 214–223.

10. Aram, D. M., Morris, R., & Hall, N. E. (1993). Clinical and research congruence in identifying children with specific language impairment. *Journal of Speech and Hearing Research, 36,* 580–591.

11. Barba, G. D. (1993). Different patterns of confabulation. *Cortex, 29,* 567-581.

12. Benke, T. (1993). Two forms of apraxia in Alzheimer's disease. *Cortex, 29,* 715-725.

13. Catts, H. W. (1993). The relationship between speech-language impairments and reading disabilities. *Journal of Speech and Hearing Research, 36,* 948–958.

14. Ehlers, S., & Gillberg, C. (1993). The epidemiology of Asperger syndrome: A total population study. *Journal of Child Psychology and Psychiatry and Allied Disciplines, 34,* 1327-1350.

15. Elliot, L. L., & Hammer, M. A. (1993). Fine-grained auditory discrimination: Factor structures. *Journal of Speech and Hearing Research, 36,* 396–409.

16. Hall, N. E., Yamashita, T. S., & Aram, D. M. (1993). Relationship between language and fluency in children with developmental language disorders. *Journal of Speech and Hearing Research, 36,* 568–579.

17. Johnston, J. R., Miller, J. F., Curtiss, S., & Tallal, P. (1993). Conversations with children who are language impaired: Asking questions. *Journal of Speech and Hearing Research, 36,* 973–978.

18. Rasku-Puttonen, H., Lyytinen, P., Porkkeus, A. M., Laakso, M. L., & Ahonen, T. (1993). Communication deviances and clarity among the mothers of normally achieving and learning-disabled boys. *Family Process, 33,* 71-80.

19. Slaghuis, W. L., Lovegrove, W. J., & Davidson, J. A. (1993). Visual and language processing deficits are concurrent in dyslexia. *Cortex, 29,* 601-615.

20. Sussman, J. E. (1993). Auditory processing in children's speech perception: Results of selective adaptation and discrimination tasks. *Journal of Speech and Hearing Research, 36,* 380–395.

21. Sussman, J. E. (1993). Perception of format transition cues to place of articulation in children with language impairments. *Journal of Speech and Hearing Research, 36,* 1286–1299.

22. Taylor, H. G., Barry, C. T., & Schatschneider, C. (1993). School-age consequences of haemophilus influenzae Type b meningitis. *Journal of Clinical Child Psychology, 22,* 196-206.

23. Vallar, G., & Papagno, C. (1993). Preserved vocabulary acquisition in Down's syndrome: The role of phonological short-term memory. *Cortex, 29,* 467-483.

24. Brazzelli, M., Colombo, N., Della Salla, S., & Spinnler, H. (1994). Spared and impaired cognitive abilities after bilateral frontal damage. *Cortex, 30,* 27-51.

25. Korkman, M., & Häkkinen-Rihu, P. (1994). A new classification of developmental language disorders (DLD). *Brain and Language, 47,* 96–116.

26. Stracciari, A., Ghidoni, E., Guarino, M., Poletti, M., & Pazzaglia, P. (1994). Post-traumatic retrograde amnesia with selective impairment of autobiographical memory. *Cortex, 30,* 459-468.

27. Bastiaanse, R. (1995). Broca's aphasia: A syntactic and/or a morphological disorder? A case study. *Brain and Language, 48,* 1–32.

28. DeVos, K. J., Wyllie, E., Geckler, C., Kotagal, P., & Comair, Y. (1995). Language dominance in patients with early childhood tumors near left hemisphere language areas. *Neurology, 45,* 349–356.

29. Kamhi, A. G., Ward, M. F., & Mills, E. A. (1995). Hierarchical planning abilities in children with specific language impairments. *Journal of Speech and Hearing Research, 38,* 1108–1116.

30. McGuinness, D., McGuinness, C., & Donohue, J. (1995). Phonological training and the alphabet principle: Evidence for reciprocal causality. *Reading Research Quarterly, 30,* 830–852.

31. Stark, R. E., Bleile, K., Brandt, J., Freeman, J., & Vining, E. P. G. (1995). Speech-language outcomes of hemispherectomy in children and young adults. *Brain and Language, 51,* 406–421.

32. Stevens, L. J., & Bliss, L. S. (1995). Conflict resolution abilities of children with specific language impairment and children with normal language. *Journal of Speech and Hearing Research, 38,* 599–611.

33. Cronan, T. A., Cruz, S. G., Arriaga, R. I., & Sarkin, A. J. (1996). The effects of a community-based literacy program on young children's language and conceptual development. *American Journal of Community Psychology, 24,* 251–272.

34. Gallassi, R., Morreale, A., Montagna, P., Cortelli, P., Avoni, P., Castellani, R., Gambetti, P., & Lugaresi, E. (1996). Fatal familial insomnia: Behavioral and cognitive features. *Neurology, 46,* 935–939.

35. Marson, D. C., Chatterjee, A., Ingram, K. K., & Harrell, L. E. (1996). Toward a neurologic model of competency: Cognitive predictors of capacity to consent in Alzheimer's disease using three different legal standards. *Neurology, 46,* 666–672.

36. Paradis, C. M., Gironda, F., & Bennett, M. (1996). Cognitive impairment in Schwartz-Jampel syndrome: A case study. *Brain and Language, 56,* 301–305.

37. Strand, E. A., & McNeil, M. R. (1996). Effects of length and linguistic complexity on temporal acoustic measures in apraxia of speech. *Journal of Speech and Hearing Research, 39,* 1018–1033.

38. Tierney, M. C., Szalai, J. P., Snow, W. G., Fisher, R. H., Nores, A., Nadon, G., Dunn, E., & St. George-Hyslop, P. H. (1996). Prediction of probable Alzheimer's disease in mentally-impaired patients: A prospective longitudinal. *Neurology, 46,* 661–665.

39. Tierney, M. C., Szalai, J. P., Snow, W. G., Fisher, R. H., Tsuda, T., Chi, H., McLachlan, D. R., & St. George-Hyslop, P. H. (1996). A prospective study of the clinical utility of Apo E genotype in the prediction of outcome in patients with memory impairment. *Neurology, 46,* 149–154.

40. Weismer, S. E., & Hesketh, L. J. (1996). Lexical learning by children with specific language impairment: Effects of linguistic input presented at varying speaking rates. *Journal of Speech and Hearing Research, 39,* 177–190.

41. Stark, R. E., & McGregor, K. K. (1997). Follow-up study of a right- and a left-hemisphere-ctomized child: Implications for localization and impairment of language in children. *Brain and Language, 60,* 222–242.

42. Antozzi, C., Granata, T., Aurisano, N., Zardini, G., Confalonieri, P., Airaghi, G., Mantegazza, R., & Spreafico, R. (1998). Long-term selective IgG immuno-absorption improves Rasmussen's encephalitis. *Neurology, 51,* 302–305.

43. Glass, P., Bulas, D. I., Wagner, A. E., Rajasingham, S. R., Civitello, L. A., & Coffman, C. E. (1998). Pattern of neuropsychological deficit at age five years following neonatal unilateral brain injury. *Brain and Language, 63,* 346–356.

[2769]

Tool Room Attendant.

Purpose: "Developed to measure the knowledge and skills required for maintenance jobs."

Population: Applicants for maintenance jobs.

Publication Dates: 1991–1994.

Scores: 10 areas: Electrical, Hydraulics and Pneumatics, Print Reading, Tools/Materials and Equipment, Power Transmission, Pumps and Piping, Rigging, Maintenance Records, Mobile Equipment, Total.

Administration: Group.

Price Data, 1998: $498 per complete kit including manual ('94, 12 pages), scoring key, 10 reusable test booklets, and 100 answer sheets.

Time: (100–120) minutes.

Author: Roland T. Ramsay.

Publisher: Ramsay Corporation.

Cross References: For reviews by Stephen L. Koffler and Eugene (Geno) Pichette, see 13:349.

[2770]

Tooze Braille Speed Test: A Test of Basic Ability in Reading Braille.

Purpose: "A speed test which seeks to give a quick appraisal of the child's ability to read Braille characters."

Population: Students (Ages 7-13) in Grades 1 or 2 Braille.

Publication Date: 1962.

Scores: Total score only.

Administration: Individual.
Price Data: Available from publisher.
Time: 1(5) minutes.
Author: F. H. G. Tooze.
Publisher: Association for the Education and Welfare of the Visually Handicapped [England].

[2771]

Torrance Tests of Creative Thinking.

Purpose: To identify and evaluate creative potential.
Population: Grades K through graduate school.
Publication Dates: 1966–1984.
Acronym: TTCT.
Administration: Individual and group.
Price Data, 1993: $28.95 per 20 scoring worksheets, class record, and directions manual/scoring guide (specify Form A or B and Figural or Verbal); $19.95 per norms/technical manual ('74, 80 pages); $24.15 per specimen set including Figural and Verbal booklets (specify Form A or B); $5.10 per student for scoring service.
Author: E. Paul Torrance.
Publisher: Scholastic Testing Service, Inc.

a) VERBAL TEST.
Scores: 3 for equivalent Forms A and B: Fluency, Flexibility, Originality.
Administration: Individual for Grades K to 3.
Price Data: $37.25 per examiner's kit; $23 per directions/scoring manual ('74, 49 pages) (specify Form A or B).
Time: 45(60) minutes.
Comments: Test booklet is titled Thinking Creatively With Words.

b) FIGURAL TEST.
Scores: 4 for equivalent Forms A and B: Fluency, Flexibility, Originality, Elaboration.
Price Data: $11.95 per directions/scoring manual ('74, 43–48 pages) (specify Form A or B); $20.50 per streamlined manual for Forms A and B ('84, 74 pages).
Time: 30(45) minutes.
Comments: Test booklet is titled Thinking Creatively with Pictures.

Cross References: See T4:2849 (33 references); for reviews by Clinton I. Chase and Donald J. Treffinger, see 9:1296 (20 references); see also T3:2512 (107 references), 8:249 (229 references), and T2:589 (88 references); for reviews by Leonard L. Baird and Robert L. Thorndike, and excerpted reviews by Ralph Hoepfner, John L. Holland, and Michael A. Wallach, see 7:448 (243 references).

TEST REFERENCES

1. Baum, S., & Owen, S. V. (1988). High ability/learning disabled students: How are they different? *Gifted Child Quarterly, 32,* 321–326.
2. Campos, A., & Pérez, M. J. (1989). High and low imagers and their scores on creativity. *Perceptual and Motor Skills, 68,* 403–406.
3. Davis, G. A. (1989). Objectives and activities for teaching creative thinking. *Gifted Child Quarterly, 33,* 81–84.
4. Jackson, L. M., & Gorassni, D. R. (1989). Artifact in the hypnosis-creativity relationship. *The Journal of General Psychology, 116,* 333–344.
5. Torrance, E. P., & Safter, H. T. (1989). The long range predictive validity of the Just Suppose Test. *Journal of Creative Behavior, 23,* 219-223.
6. Harpaz, I. (1990). Asymmetry of hemispheric functions and creativity: An empirical examination. *Journal of Creative Behavior, 24,* 161-170.
7. Luchman, A., & Michels, K. A. (1990). NDN: An outlet for exemplary programs. *Journal for the Education of the Gifted, 13,* 156–167.
8. Sowell, E. J., Zeigler, A. J., Bergwall, L., & Cartwright, R. M. (1990). Identification and description of mathematically gifted students: A review of empirical research. *Gifted Child Quarterly, 34,* 147-154.
9. Toth, L. S., & Baker, S. R. (1990). The relationship of creativity and instructional style preferences to overachievement and underachievement in a sample of public school children. *Journal of Creative Behavior, 24,* 190-198.
10. Clements, D. H. (1991). Enhancement of creativity in computer environments. *American Educational Research Journal, 28,* 173-187.
11. Cooper, E. (1991). A critique of six measures for assessing creativity. *Journal of Creative Behavior, 25,* 194-204.
12. Gruber, E. J., McNinch, G. W., & Cone, A. (1991). The effects of a graduate course in creative arts on the creative test behavior of early childhood teachers. *College Student Journal, 25,* 377-381.
13. McCabe, M. P. (1991). Influence of creativity and intelligence on academic performance. *Journal of Creative Behavior, 25,* 116-122.
14. Niaz, M., & Saud-de-Numez, G. (1991). The relationship of mobility-fixity to creativity, formal reasoning, and intelligence. *Journal of Creative Behavior, 25,* 205-217.
15. Poreh, A. M., & Whitman, R. D. (1991). Creative cognitive processes and hemispheric specialization. *Journal of Creative Behavior, 25,* 169-179.
16. Curnow, K. W., & Turner, E. T. (1992). The effect of exercise and music on the creativity of college students. *Journal of Creative Behavior, 26,* 50-52.
17. Flaherty, M. A. (1992). The effects of a holistic creativity program on the self-concept and creativity of third graders. *Journal of Creative Behavior, 26,* 165-171.
18. Meador, K. S. (1992). Emerging rainbows: A review of the literature on creativity in preschoolers. *Journal for the Education of the Gifted, 15,* 163-181.
19. Patton, J. M. (1992). Assessment and identification of African-American learners with gifts and talents. *Exceptional Children, 59,* 150-159.
20. Strom, R., Johnson, A., Strom, S., & Strom, P. (1992). Designing curriculum for parents of gifted children. *Journal for the Education of the Gifted, 15,* 182-200.
21. Tallent-Runnels, M. K., & Yarbrough, D. W. (1992). Effects of the future problem solving program on children's concerns about the future. *Gifted Child Quarterly, 36,* 190-194.
22. Dudek, S. Z., Strobel, M. G., & Runco, M. A. (1993). Cumulative and proximal influences on the social environment and children's creative potential. *The Journal of Genetic Psychology, 154,* 487-499.
23. Güncer, B., & Oral, G. (1993). Relationship between creativity and nonconformity to school discipline as perceived by teachers of Turkish elementary school children, by controlling for grade and sex. *Journal of Instructional Psychology, 20,* 208–214.
24. Mevarech, Z. R., & Kramarski, B. (1993). Vygotsky and Papert: Social-cognitive interactions within logo environments. *British Journal of Educational Psychology, 63,* 96–109.
25. Mijares-Colmenares, B. E., Masten, W. G., & Underwood, J. R. (1993). Effects of trait anxiety and the scamper technique on creative thinking of intellectually gifted students. *Psychological Reports, 72,* 907-912.
26. Palaniappan, A. K. (1993). Preliminary study of the bilingual version of the Khatena-Torrance Creative Perception Inventory. *Perceptual and Motor Skills, 77,* 948–950.
27. Runco, M. A. (1993). Divergent thinking, creativity, and giftedness. *Gifted Child Quarterly, 37,* 16-22.
28. Clasen, D. R., Middleton, J. A., & Connell, T. J. (1994). Assessing artistic and problem-solving performance in minority and nonminority students using a nontraditional multidimensional approach. *Gifted Child Quarterly, 38,* 27-32.
29. Lowe, G. (1994). Group differences in alcohol-creativity interactions. *Psychological Reports, 75,* 1635-1638.
30. Meador, K. S. (1994). The effect of synectics training on gifted and nongifted kindergarten students. *Journal for the Education of the Gifted, 18,* 55-73.
31. Palaniappan, A. K. (1994). A preliminary study of the bilingual version of Khatena-Morse Multitalent Perception Inventory. *Perceptual and Motor Skills, 78,* 784-786.
32. Taradash, G. (1994). Extending educational opportunities for middle school gifted students. *Gifted Child Quarterly, 38,* 89-94.
33. Yong, L. M. S. (1994). Relations between creativity and intelligence among Malaysian pupils. *Perceptual and Motor Skills, 79,* 739-742.
34. Adaman, J. E., & Blaney, P. H. (1995). The effects of musical mood induction on creativity. *The Journal of Creative Behavior, 29,* 95–108.
35. Bennett, R. E., & Rock, D. A. (1995). Generalizability, validity, and examinee perceptions of a computer-delivered formulating-hypotheses test. *Journal of Educational Measurement, 32,* 19–36.
36. Daugherty, M., White, C. S., & Manning, B. H. (1995). Private speech and creativity. *Contemporary Educational Psychology, 20,* 222-229.
37. Hearne, D., & Stone, S. (1995). Multiple intelligences and underachievement: Lessons from individuals with learning disabilities. *Journal of Learning Disabilities, 28,* 439–448.
38. Hunsaker, S. L., & Callahan, C. M. (1995). Creativity and giftedness: Published instrument uses and abuses. *Gifted Child Quarterly, 39,* 110–114.

39. Kim, J., & Michael, W. B. (1995). The relationship of creativity measures to school achievement and to preferred learning and thinking style in a sample of Korean high school students. *Educational and Psychological Measurement, 55,* 60-74.

40. Young, R. L., & Nettelbeck, T. (1995). The abilities of a musical savant and his family. *Journal of Autism and Developmental Disorders, 25,* 231–248.

41. Blissett, S. E., & McGrath, R. E. (1996). The relationship between creativity and interpersonal problem-solving skills in adults. *Journal of Creative Behavior, 30,* 173–183.

42. King, L. A., Walker, L. M., & Broyles, S. L. (1996). Creativity and the five-factor model. *Journal of Research in Personality, 30,* 189–203.

43. Merarech, Z. R., & Kapa, E. (1996). The effects of problem-solving based logo environment on children's information processing components. *British Journal of Educational Psychology, 66,* 181–195.

44. Upmanyu, V. V., Bhardwaj, S., & Singh, S. (1996). Word-association emotional indicators: Associations with anxiety, psychoticism, neuroticism, extraversion, and creativity. *The Journal of Social Psychology, 136,* 521–529.

45. Palaniappan, A. K. (1998). Figural creativity and cognitive prefrence among Malaysian undergraduate students. *Journal of Psychology, 132,* 387–388.

[2772]

Tower of London: Research Version.

Purpose: "An individually administered neuropsychological instrument designed to assess higher order problem-solving, specifically executive planning abilities."
Population: Children and adolescents and adults.
Publication Date: 1999.
Acronym: TOL:RV.
Scores, 2: Executive Planning, Higher-Order Problem-Solving.
Administration: Individual.
Forms, 2: Adult, Child.
Price Data, 1999: $195 per complete kit including 25 child recording forms, 25 adult recording forms, 2 peg boards with beads, and manual; $24 per 25 recording forms (specify Child or Adult); $45 per manual.
Time: (10–15) minutes.
Authors: William C. Cullbertson and Eric A. Zillmer.
Publisher: Multi-Health Systems, Inc.

[2773]

TQ Manager Inventory and Feedback From Others.

Purpose: To access competency from a Total Quality Management style of leadership approach to managing organizations.
Population: Business managers.
Scores, 5: Openness & Trust, Collaboration & Teamwork, Managing By Fact, Recognition & Reward, Learning Organization.
Administration: Group.
Time: Administration not reported.
Authors: Warren H. Schmidt and Jerome P. Finnigan
Publisher: XICOM.

a) TQ MANAGER INVENTORY.
Publication Date: 1994.
Acronym: TQMI.
Price Data, 1995: $6.75 per inventory.
Comments: Self-assessment.

b) TQ MANAGER INVENTORY: FEEDBACK FROM OTHERS.
Publication Date: 1995.
Acronym: TQMO.
Price Data: $4.50 per inventory.
Comments: Feedback from colleagues to business managers.

[2774]

Trade Aptitude Test Battery.

Purpose: "To select prospective pupils for admission to technical institutes and colleges."
Population: First-year South African students in the technical fields.
Publication Dates: 1981-1983.
Acronym: TRAT.
Scores, 16: Dexterity, Co-ordination, Patterns, Components, Classification, Assembly, Computations, Inspection, Graphs, Mechanical Insight, Mathematics, Spatial Perception/2-D, Vocabulary, Figure Series, Woordeskat, Spatial Perception/3-D.
Administration: Group.
Price Data: Available from publisher.
Time: 288(293) minutes.
Comments: Test materials in both English and Afrikaans.
Authors: J. J. Taljaard and J. W. von Mollendorf (test).
Publisher: Human Sciences Research Council [South Africa].

[2775]

Trainer's Assessment of Proficiency (TAP).

Purpose: Constructed as a "self-assessment exercise that measures relative strengths in twelve instructional skills."
Population: Trainers.
Publication Date: 1991.
Acronym: TAP.
Scores, 12: Assessing Needs and Entering Behavior, Setting Objectives and Terminal Behavior, Analyzing Participants and Situations, Eliciting Relevant Responses and Testing, Applying Classroom Facilitation Skills, Forming Questions and Probes Effectively, Maintaining Adult Relationships, Giving Feedback and Reinforcement, Building Toward Transfer of Training, Getting All Learners to Participate, Managing Classroom Time Effectively, Displaying Good Flow/Logic/Organization.
Administration: Group.
Forms, 2: Long, Short.
Price Data: Available from publisher.
Time: (60) minutes for Short form; (180) minutes for Long form.
Comments: Videocassette recorder necessary for administration of inventory.
Author: Scott B. Parry.
Publisher: Training House, Inc.

Cross References: For reviews by Mark W. Roberts and Daniel E. Vogler, see 12:403.

[2776]

Trait Evaluation Index.

Purpose: "Designed to elicit comprehensive, multidimensional appraisals of 'normal' personality dimensions."
Population: College and adults.
Publication Dates: 1967-1984.
Acronym: TEI.
Scores: 29 scores (Social Orientation, Compliance, Benevolence, Elation, Ambition, Motivational Drive, Self-Confidence, Dynamism, Independence, Personal Adequacy, Caution, Self-Organization, Responsibility, Propriety, Courtesy, Verbal Orientation, Intellectual Orientation, Perception, Self-Control, Fairmindedness, Adaptability, Sincerity) plus 4 general supplementary scores (Overall Adjustment, Masculinity, Femininity, Consistency) and 3 supplementary scores for engineers (Employment Stability, Productivity-Creativity, Job Satisfaction).
Administration: Group.
Price Data, 1999: $77.40 per test package; $83.40 per IBM answer/profile sheet package; $46 per set of IBM scoring stencils; $56.40 per manual ('68, 38 pages) and manual supplement ('84, 17 pages); $74.25 per specimen set; $79 per German edition.
Foreign Language Edition: German edition available.
Time: (30-50) minutes.
Author: Alan R. Nelson.
Publisher: Martin M. Bruce, Ph.D.
Cross References: See T2:1424 (1 reference); for reviews by Harold Borko and Jacob Cohen, see 7:155 (1 reference).

[2777]

The Trait Pleasure-Displeasure Scale.

Purpose: One of three fundamental dimensions of temperament in Mehrabian's Temperament Model; provides a general assessment of psychological adjustment-maladjustment.
Population: Ages 15 and older.
Publication Dates: 1978–1994.
Scores: Total score only.
Administration: Group or individual.
Price Data: Available from publisher for complete kit including scale, scoring directions, norms, manual ('94, 10 pages), and literature review.
Time: (10–15) minutes.
Author: Albert Mehrabian.
Publisher: Albert Mehrabian (the author).
Cross References: For reviews by Thaddeus Rozecki and Chockalingam Viswesvaran, see 13:351 (1 reference).

[2778]

Transdisciplinary Play-Based Assessment, Revised Edition.

Purpose: Constructed as a multidimensional approach to identifying service needs, to developing intervention plans, and to evaluating progress in children.
Population: Children developmentally functioning between infancy and 6 years of age.
Publication Date: 1993.
Acronym: TPBA.
Scores: 4 domains: Cognitive, Social-Emotional, Communication and Language, Sensorimotor Development.
Administration: Individual
Price Data, 1995: $48 per manual (347 pages).
Time: (60–90) minutes.
Comments: Ratings by transdisciplinary team.
Author: Toni W. Linder.
Publisher: Paul H. Brookes Publishing Co., Inc.
Cross References: For reviews by Terry Overton and Gary J. Stainback, see 13:352.

[2779]

Transition Behavior Scale.

Purpose: "Measures student's readiness for transition to employment and independent living."
Population: Grades 11-12.
Publication Date: 1989.
Acronym: TBS.
Scores, 4: Work-Related, Interpersonal Relations, Social/Community Expectations, Total.
Administration: Individual.
Price Data, 1999: $63.50 per complete kit including technical manual (32 pages), 50 rating forms, and IEP and intervention manual (230 pages); $12.50 per technical manual; $31 per 50 rating forms; $20 per IEP and intervention manual.
Time: (15) minutes.
Author: Stephen B. McCarney.
Publisher: Hawthorne Educational Services, Inc.
Cross References: For reviews by Martha Blackwell and David O. Herman, see 12:404.

[2780]

Transition Planning Inventory.

Purpose: To identify and plan for the comprehensive transition needs of students.
Population: High school students with disabilities who need future planning.
Publication Date: 1997.
Acronym: TPI.
Scores: Ratings in 9 areas: Employment, Further Education/Training, Daily Living, Leisure Activities, Community Participation, Health, Self-Determination, Communication, Interpersonal Relationships.

Administration: Individual.
Forms, 4: Student, Home, School, Profile and Further Assessment Recommendations.
Price Data, 1999: $126 per complete kit; $35 per Administration and Resource Guide (232 pages), $24 per 25 Profile and Further Assessment Recommendations Forms; $24 per 25 School Forms; $24 per 25 Home Forms; $24 per 25 Student Forms; $24 per 25 Spanish Home Forms.
Time: Administration time not reported.
Authors: Gary M. Clark and James R. Patton.
Publisher: PRO-ED.

[2781]

Transition-to-Work Inventory: A Job Placement System for Workers with Severe disAbilities.

Purpose: "Designed to assist employers, supported employment counselors, and other transition professionals in identifying the best match between the skills of an individual with disabilities and the requirements of the job."
Population: Individuals with severe disabilities.
Publication Date: 1995–1996.
Acronym: TWI™.
Scores, 3: Job Analysis Rating, Worker Analysis Rating, Difference Score.
Administration: Individual.
Parts, 2: Job Analysis Scale, Worker Analysis Scale.
Price Data, 1999: $86.50 per starter kit including user and accommodation manual, 10 job analysis booklets, 25 worker analysis booklets, and 25 profile sheets; $29 per 25 worker analysis booklets; $15 per 10 job analysis booklets; $14 per individual profile sheets; $52 per manual and accommodation guide ('96, 102 pages).
Time: (30–35) minutes per scale.
Comments: Ratings by transition professionals.
Authors: Lee Friedman, Carl Cameron, and Jennifer Fletcher.
Publisher: The Psychological Corporation.

[2782]

Trauma Symptom Inventory.

Purpose: Designed for the "evaluation of acute and chronic traumatic symptomatology."
Population: Ages 18 and older.
Publication Date: 1995.
Acronym: TSI.
Scores, 13: Validity Scales (Response Level, Atypical Response, Inconsistent Response); Clinical Scales (Anxious Arousal, Depression, Anger/Irritability, Intrusive Experiences, Defensive Avoidance, Dissociation, Sexual Concerns, Dysfunctional Sexual Behavior, Impaired Self-Reference, Tension Reduction Behavior).
Administration: Group.
Price Data: Price information available from publisher for complete kit including manual (67 pages), 10 item booklets, 25 hand-scorable answer sheets, and 25 each of male and female profile forms.
Time: (20) minutes.
Comments: Computer scoring system available from publisher.
Author: John Briere.
Publisher: Psychological Assessment Resources, Inc.

TEST REFERENCES

1. Higgins, D. J., & McCabe, M. P. (1994). The relationship of child sexual abuse and family violence to adult adjustment: Toward an integrated risk-sequelae model. *Journal of Sex Research, 31,* 255–266.
2. Edens, J. F., Otto, R. K., & Dwyer, T. J. (1998). Susceptibility of the Trauma Symptom Inventory to malingering. *Journal of Personality Assessment, 71,* 379–392.
3. Schaaf, K. K., & McCanne, T. R. (1998). Relationship of childhood sexual, physical, and combined sexual and physical abuse to adult victimization and posttraumatic stress disorder. *Child Abuse and Neglect, 22,* 1119–1133.

[2783]

Treatment Intervention Inventory.

Purpose: Designed for intake, referral and post-treatment comparisons of adult counseling clients.
Population: Ages 12–18; Adult counseling clients.
Publication Dates: 1991–1997.
Acronym: TII; TII-J.
Scores, 9: Truthfulness, Anxiety, Depression, Self-Esteem, Distress, Family, Alcohol, Drug, Stress Coping Abilities.
Administration: Group.
Levels, 2: Adult, Juvenile.
Price Data: Available from publisher.
Time: (35) minutes Adult; (25–30) minutes Juvenile.
Comments: "A computerized, self-report assessment"; administration by paper and pencil or by computer; computer scored.
Author: Behavior Data Systems Ltd.
Publisher: Behavior Data Systems Ltd.

[2784]

Triadal Equated Personality Inventory.

Purpose: To measure personality variables.
Population: Adult males.
Publication Dates: 1960-1963.
Acronym: TEPI.
Scores, 22: Dominance, Self-Confidence, Decisiveness, Independence, Toughness, Suspiciousness, Conscientiousness, Introversion, Restlessness, Solemnity, Foresight, Industriousness, Warmth, Enthusiasm, Conformity, Inventiveness, Persistence, Sex Drive, Recognition Drive, Cooperativeness, Humility-Tolerance, Self-Control.
Administration: Group.
Price Data, 1985: $5 per 25 tests; $50 per specimen set.
Time: (50-120) minutes.

Author: Research Staff, United Consultants.
Publisher: Psychometric Affiliates.
Cross References: For a review by Jacob Cohen, see 7:156.

[2785]

Troubled Talk Test.

Purpose: Can be used to present basic principles involved in human communication and human relations.
Population: Adults.
Publication Date: 1973.
Scores: Total score only.
Administration: Group.
Price Data, 1993: $.50 each (minimum of 10).
Time: Administration time not reported.
Comments: Assesses understanding of the companion book Troubled Talk.
Author: James Kubeck.
Publisher: International Society for General Semantics.

[2786]

Typing 5.

Purpose: Assesses typing skills.
Population: Administrative assistants, secretaries, and any position requiring typing ability.
Publication Date: 1975.
Scores, 2: Speed, Accuracy.
Administration: Individual or group.
Price Data, 1998: $70.50 per start-up kit (specify Form A, B, or C) including 25 test booklets, 25 practice sheets, and examiner's manual; $44 per 25 test booklets (specify Form A, B, or C; quantity discounts available); $14.75 per 25 practice sheets (quantity discounts available); $19.75 per examiner's manual.
Time: 5 minutes per test.
Comments: Previously listed as SRA Typing 5.
Author: Science Research Associates.
Publisher: NCS (Rosemont).
a) FORM A—TYPING SPEED.
b) FORM B—BUSINESS LETTER.
c) FORM C—NUMERICAL.
Cross References: For reviews by Charles J. Cranny and Lawrence W. Erickson, see 8:1035.

[2787]

Typing Test for Business.

Purpose: Developed "to assess competence within the various areas of typing."
Population: Applicants for typing positions.
Publication Dates: 1964-1984.
Acronym: TTB.
Administration: Group.
Price Data, 1994: $39 per set of scoring stencils; $22 per manual ('84, 23 pages); $43 per examination kit.
Authors: Jerome E. Doppelt, Arthur D. Hartman, and Fay B. Krawchick.
Publisher: The Psychological Corporation.
a) PRACTICE COPY.
Scores: No scores.
Price Data: $28 per 25 tests.
Time: 2 minutes.
b) STRAIGHT COPY.
Scores, 2: Speed, Accuracy.
Price Data: $46 per 25 test booklets.
Time: 5 minutes.
c) LETTERS.
Scores: Total score only.
Price Data: Same as *b* above.
Time: 10 minutes.
d) REVISED MANUSCRIPT.
Scores: Total score only.
Price Data: Same as *b* above.
Time: 10 minutes.
e) NUMBERS.
Scores: Total score only.
Price Data: Same as *b* above.
Time: 3 minutes.
f) TABLES.
Scores: Total score only.
Price Data: Same as *b* above.
Time: 10 minutes.
Cross References: For reviews by Mary T. Harrison and Leonard J. West, see 7:1007.

[2788]

The Uncritical Inference Test.

Purpose: "Helps students learn to distinguish between observations and inferences."
Population: Adolescents and adults.
Publication Dates: 1955–1982.
Scores: Total score only.
Administration: Group.
Manual: No manual.
Price Data, 1993: $.50 per test (minimum order of 10 tests).
Time: Administration time not reported.
Author: William V. Haney.
Publisher: International Society for General Semantics.

[2789]

Understanding and Managing Stress.

Purpose: Assesses stress level and health-related behaviors.
Population: Adults.
Publication Date: 1989.
Scores: Continuum of risk scores (low, medium, high) for each of 22 areas: Changes on the Job/Total, Changes on the Job/High-Impact, Changes in Personal

Life/Total, Changes in Personal Life/High-Impact, Chronic Stressful Conditions on the Job, Chronic Stressful Conditions in Personal Life, Strain Response, Psychological Outlook, General Lifestyle/Importance to Health, General Lifestyle/Present Effectiveness, Social Support, Nutritional Habits and Awareness/Total, Physical Exercise Habits and Awareness, Drinking Habits, Behavioral Habits, Tobacco, Systolic Blood Pressure Reading, Diastolic Blood Pressure Reading, Total Cholesterol, High-Density Lipoprotein (HDL) Level, Ratio of Total Cholesterol to HDL, Triglyceride Level.
Administration: Group.
Price Data, 1991: $9.95 per handbook (64 pages).
Time: Administration time not reported.
Comments: Self-administered, self-scored.
Author: John D. Adams.
Publisher: Jossey-Bass/Pfeiffer.
Cross References: For reviews by William J. Waldron and William K. Wilkinson and Christopher P. Migotsky, see 12:405.

[2790]
Understanding Communication.

Purpose: Developed "to measure comprehension of verbal material in the form of short sentences and phrases."
Population: Variety of occupations.
Publication Date: 1959–1992.
Scores: Total score only.
Administration: Individual of group.
Price Data, 1998: $70.50 per start-up kit including 25 test booklets, score key, and interpretation and research manual; $44 per 25 test booklets (quantity discounts available); $14.75 per score key; $19.75 per interpretation and research manual.
Time: 15 minutes.
Author: Thelma Gwinn Thurstone.
Publisher: NCS (Rosemont).
Cross References: See T4:2864 (1 reference) and T2:1747 (1 reference); for reviews by C. E. Jurgensen and Donald E. P. Smith, see 6:840.

[2791]
Uniform Child Custody Evaluation System.

Purpose: Constructed as a "uniform custody evaluation procedure."
Population: Professionals involved in custody evaluation.
Publication Date: 1994.
Acronym: UCCES.
Scores: No scores.
Administration: Individual.
Forms, 25: General Data and Administrative Forms (UCCES Checklist, Initial Referral Form, Chronological Record of all Case Contacts Form, Case Notes Form, Consent for Psychological Services to Child(ren) Form, Authorization to Release Information Form, Suitability for Joint Custody Checklist, Collateral Interview Form, Consent for Evaluation of Minor(s) Form, UCCES Summary Chart), Parent Forms (Parent's Family/Personal History Questionnaire, Parent Interview Form, Parenting Abilities Checklist, Suitability for Joint Custody Interview, Analysis of Response Validity Checklist, Behavioral Observations of Parent-Child Interaction Form, Home Visit Observation Form, Agreement Between Parent and Evaluator Form, Explanation of Custody Evaluation Procedures for Parents and Attorneys), Child Forms (Child History Questionnaire, Child Interview Form, Child Abuse Interview Form, Abuse/Neglect Checklist, Child's Adjustment to Home and Community Checklist, Parent-Child Goodness of Fit Observation Form and Checklist).
Price Data: Price information available from publisher for complete kit including manual (47 pages), 2 sets of Parent Forms, 2 sets of Child Forms, and 1 set of Administrative and Data Forms.
Time: Administration time not reported.
Authors: Harry L. Munsinger and Kevin W. Karlson.
Publisher: Psychological Assessment Resources, Inc.
Cross References: For a review by Steven Zucker, see 13:353.

[2792]
Universal Nonverbal Intelligence Test.

Purpose: "Designed to provide a more fair measure of the general intelligence and cognitive abilities of children and adolescents ... who may be disadvantaged by traditional verbal and language-loaded measures."
Population: Ages 5–17.
Publication Date: 1998.
Acronym: UNIT.
Scores, 11: Symbolic Memory, Cube Design, Spatial Memory, Analogic Reasoning, Object Memory, Mazes, Memory Quotient, Reasoning Quotient, Symbolic Quotient, Nonsymbolic Quotient, Full Scale IQ.
Administration: Individual.
Forms: Abbreviated Battery, Standard Battery, Extended Battery.
Price Data, 1999: $460 per complete kit including examiner's manual (334 pages), stimulus book 1 & 2, 16 response chips, response grid, 9 cubes, response mat, 10 symbolic memory cards, 25 record forms, 25 maze response booklets, black pencil, and canvas carrying case; $35 per 25 record forms (specify standard or extended); $17 per 25 abbreviated record forms; $39 per mazes response booklets; $64.50 per manual.
Time: (10–15) minutes, Abbreviated Battery; (30) minutes, Standard Battery; (45) minutes, Extended Battery.
Authors: Bruce A. Bracken and R. Steve McCallum.
Publisher: Riverside Publishing.

[2793]

University Residence Environment Scale [Revised].

Purpose: Designed to "assess the social climate of university student living groups."
Population: University students and staff.
Publication Dates: 1974–1988.
Acronym: URES.
Scores, 10: Involvement, Emotional Support, Independence, Traditional Social Orientation, Competition, Academic Achievement, Intellectuality, Order and Organization, Student Influence, Innovation.
Administration: Group.
Forms, 4: Real (R), Ideal (I), Expectations (E), Short (S).
Price Data, 1997: $25 per sampler set including manual, test booklet (Forms R, I, E, and S), scoring key, and profile sheet; $90 per permission set.
Time: Administration time not reported.
Comments: Part of the Social Climate Scales (2445).
Author: Rudolf H. Moos.
Publisher: Mind Garden, Inc.
Cross References: See T4:2865 (8 references) and T3:2534 (3 references); for reviews by Fred H. Borgen and James V. Mitchell, Jr. of an earlier edition, see 8:700 (12 references).

[2794]

Useful Field of View.

Purpose: Designed as a "computer-administered and computer-scored test of visual attention," which may be used to help predict the degree to which a person may perform some everyday activities, such as driving a motor vehicle, safely.
Population: Adults.
Publication Date: 1998.
Acronym: UFOV.
Scores, 3: Central Vision and Processing Speed, Divided Attention, Selective Attention.
Administration: Individual.
Price Data, 1998: $130 per complete kit including user's manual (106 pages), reference card, CD, and use counter.
Time: (15) minutes.
Comments: Microsoft Windows 95 required with video card and CD ROM drive; not for use with laptops.
Authors: Karlene K. Ball and Daniel L. Roenker.
Publisher: The Psychological Corporation.

[2795]

USES Basic Occupational Literacy Test.

Purpose: "Provides measures of literacy achievement in the areas of reading and arithmetic expressed in terms of occupational requirements for reading and arithmetic" in order to facilitate "vocational counseling and placement by providing direct comparison of a person's literacy skills with literacy skills required for satisfactory performance in various occupations."
Population: Educationally disadvantaged adults.
Publication Dates: 1971-1983.
Acronym: BOLT.
Administration: Group.
Parts: 5 tests: Wide-Range Scale, Reading Vocabulary, Reading Comprehension, Arithmetic Computation, Arithmetic Reasoning.
Price Data: Price data and ordering information for tests, answer sheets, scoring stencils, record card, information brochure, manual and manual revisions, DOT supplements, pretesting orientation booklet, and other materials for use by individuals and organizations must be cleared through appropriate State Employment Security Agencies.
Comments: Each subject matter area test and screening test may be administered and interpreted independently; developed and published for use primarily by State Employment Security Agencies.
Author: U.S. Department of Labor.
Publisher: U.S. Department of Labor, Employment and Training Administration.

a) WIDE-RANGE SCALE.
Purpose: Screening test to determine appropriate level of BOLT to administer.
Scores, 2: Vocabulary, Arithmetic.
Time: (15-25) minutes.

b) READING VOCABULARY.
Acronym: RV.
Levels, 4: Advanced, High Intermediate, Basic Intermediate, Fundamental.
Time: Same as for *a* above.

c) READING COMPREHENSION.
Acronym: RC.
Levels, 4: Same as for *b* above.
Time: Same as for *a* above.

d) ARITHMETIC COMPUTATION.
Acronym: AC.
Levels, 4: Same as for *b* above.
Time: (30-40) minutes.

e) ARITHMETIC REASONING.
Acronym: AR.
Levels, 3: Advanced, Intermediate, Fundamental.
Time: Same as for *d* above.

Cross References: For reviews by Gary L. Marco and by Dean H. Nafziger and Amy H. Shively, see 11:453; for reviews by Lee J. Cronbach and Bruce W. Tuckman, see 8:489.

[2796]

USES Clerical Skills Tests.

Purpose: Designed to measure clerical skills and knowledge.
Population: Applicants for clerical positions.

Publication Dates: 1968-1990.
Scores: 4 tests: Typing, Transcribing Machine Operator, Spelling, Dictation.
Administration: Group.
Restricted Distribution: "Except for the Manual for Clerical Skills Tests, Section II: Development, which is on public sale, Clerical Skills test materials are not available to organizations outside of the State Employment Security Agencies."
Price Data: Available from local State Employment Security Agency.
Author: United States Department of Labor, Employment and Training Administration.
Publisher: United States Department of Labor, Employment and Training Administration.
Cross References: See 7:1009 (1 reference).

[2797]

USES General Aptitude Test Battery.

Purpose: Designed as an aptitude measure for occupational guidance.
Population: Grades 1–12 and adults.
Publication Dates: 1946–1986.
Acronym: GATB.
Administration: Group.
Restricted Distribution: Orders for test materials must be submitted to local State Employment Security Agency for approval of purchase.
Price Data: Available from local State Employment Security Agency; no testing fee for applicants tested through State Employment Service Offices.
Time: Time varies according to test.
Comments: Developed by the United States Employment Service for use in its occupational counseling program and released for use by State Employment Services.
Author: United States Employment Service.
Publisher: U.S. Department of Labor, Employment and Training Administration.

a) GATB-NATB SCREENING.
Purpose: To identify examinees who are deficient in reading skills and should be tested with USES Nonreading Aptitude Test Battery.
Time: (15–20) minutes.
Comments: Consists of the Wide-Range Scale of the USES Basic Occupational Literacy Test.

b) GATB, B-1002.
Population: Grades 9–12 and adults.
Scores, 9: Intelligence, Verbal, Numerical, Spatial, Form Perception, Clerical Perception, Motor Coordination, Finger Dexterity, Manual Dexterity.
Tests: 12 tests.
Forms, 4: A, B, C, D.
Foreign Language Edition: Available in Spanish.
Time: 48(150) minutes.
Cross References: See T4:2868 (10 references); for a review by J. Ward Keesling, see 9:1304; see also T3:2537 (23 references), 8:490 (96 references), and T2:1073 (45 references); for a review by David J. Weiss, see 7:676 (138 references); for reviews by Harold P. Bechtoldt and John B. Carroll of earlier forms, see 6:777 (55 references); for reviews by Andrew L. Comrey, Clifford P. Froehlich, and Lloyd G. Humphreys, see 5:609 (176 references); for reviews by Milton L. Blum, Edward B. Greene, and Howard R. Taylor, see 4:714 (33 references).

TEST REFERENCES

1. Alexander, R. A., Carson, K. D., Alliger, G. M., & Cronshan, S. F. (1989). Empirical distributions of range restricted SD/x in validity studies. *Journal of Applied Psychology, 74,* 253-258.
2. Waldman, D. A., & Avolio, B. J. (1989). Homogeneity of test validity. *Journal of Applied Psychology, 74,* 371-374.
3. Randahl, G. J. (1990). A typological analysis of the relations between measured vocational interests and abilities. *Journal of Vocational Behavior, 38,* 333-350.
4. Janikowski, T. P., Berven, N. L., & Bordieri, J. E. (1991). Validity of the microcomputer evaluation screening and assessment aptitude scores. *Rehabilitation Counseling Bulletin, 35,* 38–51.
5. Janikowski, T. P., Bordieri, J. E., & Musgrave, J. (1992). The impact of vocational evaluation on client self-estimated aptitudes and interests. *Rehabilitation Counselor Bulletin, 36,* 70–83.
6. Bizot, E. B., & Goldman, S. H. (1993). Prediction of satisfactoriness and satisfaction: An 8-year follow up. *Journal of Vocational Behavior, 43,* 19–29.
7. Breeden, S. A. (1993). Job and occupational change as a function of occupational correspondence and job satisfaction. *Journal of Vocational Behavior, 43,* 30-45.
8. Velozo, C. A. (1993). Work evaluations: Critique of the state of the art of functional assessment of work. *The American Journal of Occupational Therapy, 47,* 203-209.

[2798]

USES General Aptitude Test Battery for the Deaf.

Purpose: Used "in vocational counseling and occupational placement."
Population: Hearing impaired adults.
Publication Dates: 1984–1990.
Acronym: GATB for the Deaf.
Scores: Scores are the same as for the USES General Aptitude Test Battery (see 2797).
Administration: Group or individual.
Price Data: Available from publisher.
Time: (150–160) minutes.
Comments: Adaptation of the USES General Aptitude Test Battery (2797).
Author: U.S. Department of Labor.
Publisher: U.S. Department of Labor, Employment and Training Administration.
Cross References: For a review by Ralph G. Leverett, see 13:354.

[2799]

USES Nonreading Aptitude Test Battery, 1982 Edition.

Purpose: Designed as an aptitude measure for occupational guidance.
Population: Disadvantaged grades 9–12 and adults.
Publication Dates: 1965–1982.

Acronym: NATB.
Scores, 9: Intelligence, Verbal, Numerical, Spatial, Form Perception, Clerical Perception, Motor Coordination, Finger Dexterity, Manual Dexterity.
Administration: Group.
Restricted Distribution: Orders for test materials must be submitted to local State Employment Security Agency for approval of purchase.
Price Data, 1993: $1 per pretest booklet; $2 per Book 1 (Tests B-D); $2.75 per Book 2 (Tests E-G); $11 per 100 Part 8 (Mark Making) sheets; $8.50 per 10 sets Oral Vocabulary Flashcards, Pretest Practice (1-8); $12 per set of Oral Vocabulary Flashcards; $2.50 per 10 sets NATB Three-Dimensional Space Demonstration Cutouts; $1 per pretest scoring key; $2.25 per Book 1 scoring key; $2.50 per Book 2 scoring key; $10 per 100 USES NATB/BOLT test record cards; $10 per 100 records of apparatus test scores form; $2.75 per training manual; $6 per manual Section I: Administration, Scoring and Interpretation ('82, 94 pages); $3.50 per manual Section II: Development ('82, 44 pages).
Time: (107) minutes.
Comments: Nonreading adaptation of the USES General Aptitude Test Battery (2797).
Author: United States Employment Service.
Publisher: U.S. Department of Labor, Employment and Training Administration.
Cross References: For reviews by Randy W. Kamphaus and J. Ward Keesling, see 9:1305; see also T3:2539 (2 references); for a review by Bruce W. Tuckman and an excerpted review by Victor Steckler of an earlier edition, see 8:491 (5 references); see also 7:679 (3 references).

[2800]

Uses Test.

Purpose: To assess cross-cultural differences in values.
Population: Ages 11-13.
Publication Date: 1974.
Scores, 8: Sustentative, Benevolent, Malevolent, Hedonistic, Esthetic, Religious, Hierarchical, Not Scorable.
Administration: Group.
Price Data: Available from publisher.
Time: (30-45) minutes.
Comments: Translations must be made locally for use with non-English-speaking children.
Author: Wayne Dennis.
Publisher: Psychological Test Specialists.
Cross References: See 8:701 (15 references).

[2801]

Utah Test of Language Development—3.

Purpose: To assess listening (comprehension) and speaking (expression).
Population: Ages 3-0 to 9-11.
Publication Dates: 1958-1989.
Acronym: UTLD-3.
Scores, 3: Language Comprehension, Language Expression, Language Quotient.
Administration: Individual.
Price Data, 1999: $114 per complete kit including picture book, 50 profile/examiner record forms, and manual ('89, 36 pages); $49 per picture book; $29 per 50 profile/examiner record forms; $39 per manual.
Time: Administration time not reported.
Comments: Revised edition of Utah Test of Language Development; earlier edition called Utah Verbal Language Development Scale.
Author: Merlin J. Mecham.
Publisher: PRO-ED.
Cross References: See T4:2872 (1 reference); for a review by Lynn S. Bliss, see 11:454 (2 references); for reviews by Joan I. Lynch and Michelle Quinn of an earlier edition, see 9:1306 (3 references); see also T3:2541 (5 references) and T2:2097 (4 references); for reviews by Katharine G. Butler and William H. Perkins of an earlier edition, see 7:973.

TEST REFERENCES

1. Fujiki, M., & Brinton, B. (1991). The verbal noncommunicator: A case study. *Language, Speech, and Hearing Services in Schools, 22,* 322–333.
2. Marion, M. J., Sussman, H. M., & Marquardt, T. P. (1993). The perception and production of rhyme in normal and developmentally apraxic children. *Journal of Communication Disorders, 26,* 129–160.
3. Plante, E., & Vance, R. (1994). Selection of preschool language tests: A data-based approach. *Language, Speech, and Hearing Services in Schools, 25,* 15–24.

[2802]

Validity Indicator Profile.

Purpose: "Designed to ... evaluate an individual's motivation and effort during cognitive testing."
Population: Ages 18–69.
Publication Date: 1997.
Acronym: VIP.
Scores, 2: Nonverbal Subtest Response Style, Verbal Subtest Response Style.
Administration: Individual.
Price Data, 1997: $30 per test booklet; $15 per 25 answer sheets; $32 per manual (97 pages); $15 per interpretive report (Microtest Q™ scoring); $16 per interpretive report (mail-in scoring); $98 per preview package including manual, test booklet, 3 answer sheets, and 3 interpretive reports (specify Microtest Q™ scoring or mail-in scoring).
Time: (50) minutes.
Comments: Instrument must be scored by computer.
Author: Richard I. Frederick.
Publisher: NCS (Minnetonka).

[2803]

Values Inventory.

Purpose: Designed to identify managerial value systems.
Population: Managers and students of management.

Publication Dates: 1970-1981.
Acronym: VI.
Scores: 6 scales: Theoretical, Power, Achievement, Human, Industry, Financial.
Administration: Group.
Price Data, 1998: $40 per 10 tests including fact sheet and administration guide.
Time: (10-20) minutes.
Authors: W. J. Reddin and Ken Rowell.
Publisher: Organizational Tests Ltd. [Canada].
Cross References: For reviews by Paul M. Muchinsky and Aharon Tziner, see 9:1308.

[2804]

Values Preference Indicator.

Purpose: "Provides respondents with the tools to examine their values and priorities for the purpose of self-learning, group discussion, team development and gaining insight into corporate culture."
Population: Adults.
Publication Date: 1990.
Acronym: VPI.
Scores, 21: Accomplishment, Acknowledgement, Challenge, Cooperation, Creativity, Expertise, Friendship, Honesty, Independence, Instruction, Intimacy, Organization, Pleasure, Quality, Recognition, Responsibility, Security, Spirituality, Tranquility, Variety, Wealth.
Administration: Group.
Manual: No manual.
Price Data, 1993: $10 per inventory.
Time: (45–60) minutes.
Comments: May be self-administered.
Author: Everett Robinson.
Publisher: Consulting Resource Group International, Inc.

[2805]

The Values Scale, Second Edition.

Purpose: "A cross-cultural measure of values in various life roles."
Population: Junior high school to adult.
Publication Dates: 1986–1989.
Acronym: VS.
Scores, 21: Ability Utilization, Achievement, Advancement, Aesthetics, Altruism, Authority, Autonomy, Creativity, Economic Rewards, Life Style, Personal Development, Physical Activity, Prestige, Risk, Social Interaction, Social Relations, Variety, Working Conditions, Cultural Identity, Physical Prowess, Economic Security.
Administration: Group.
Price Data, 1999: $64.50 per preview kit including item booklet, prepaid answer sheet, and manual; $48.40 per 25 reusable test booklets; $29.70 per 25 non-prepaid answer sheets; $29.70 per 25 report forms; $50.90 per manual.
Time: (30–45) minutes.
Author: Dorothy D. Nevill and Donald E. Super.
Publisher: Consulting Psychologists Press, Inc.
Cross References: For reviews by Kathy E. Green and Patricia Schoenrade, see 13:355 (4 references); see also T4:2876 (1 reference); for reviews by Denise M. Rousseau and Robert B. Slaney of an earlier edition, see 10:379.

TEST REFERENCES

1. Duarte, M. E. (1995). Career concerns, values, and role salience in employed men. *Career Development Quarterly, 43,* 338–349.
2. Walsh, B. D., Vacha-Haase, T., Kapes, J. T., Dresden, J. H., Thomson, W. A., & Ochoa-Shargey, B. (1996). The Values Scale: Differences across grade levels for ethnic minority students. *Educational and Psychological Measurement, 56,* 263–275.
3. Hartung, P. J. (1998). Assessing Ellenore Flood's roles and values to focus her career shopping. *Career Development Quarterly, 46,* 360–366.

[2806]

Vasectomy Scale: Attitudes.

Purpose: To measure attitudes toward vasectomy.
Population: Adults.
Publication Date: 1974.
Scores: Total score only.
Administration: Group.
Price Data, 1998: $1 per scale.
Time: [10] minutes.
Author: Panos D. Bardis.
Publisher: Donna Bardis.

[2807]

Verbal Form.

Purpose: Designed to measure general ability to learn and comprehend.
Population: Employees in a wide variety of occupations.
Publication Dates: 1946-1984.
Scores, 3: Quantitative, Linguistic, Total.
Administration: Individual or group.
Forms, 2: A, B.
Price Data, 1998: $60.50 per start-up kit including 25 test booklets (specify Form A or Form B) and examiner's manual; $48 per 25 test booklets (quantity discounts available; specify Form A or Form B); $19.75 per examiner's manual; $89 per (DOS version) Quanta computer administration and scoring software (Form A only).
Time: 15 minutes.
Comments: Previously listed as SRA Verbal Form.
Authors: Thelma Gwinn Thurstone and L. L. Thurstone.
Publisher: NCS (Rosemont).
Cross References: See T4:2542 (3 references), T3:2276 (3 references), T2:452 (1 reference), and 7:383 (2 references); for reviews by W. D. Commins and Willis C. Schaefer, see 4:319.

[2808]

Verbal Reasoning.

Purpose: To measure the capacity to reason logically based on verbal problems.
Population: Wide variety of occupations and vocational counseling.
Publication Dates: 1958-1961.
Scores: Total score only.
Administration: Individual or group.
Price Data, 1998: $71.50 per start-up kit including 25 test bookets, score key, and interpretation and research manual ('61, 20 pages); $45 per 25 test booklets (quantity discounts available); $14.75 per score key; $19.75 per interpretation and reseach manual ('61, 20 pages).
Time: 15 minutes.
Authors: Raymond J. Corsini and Richard Renck.
Publisher: NCS (Rosemont).
Cross References: See T3:2553 (1 reference); for reviews by James E. Kennedy and David G. Ryans, see 6:509.

[2809]

VESPAR: A Verbal and Spatial Reasoning Test.

Purpose: "Designed to measure fluid intelligence in neurological patients."
Population: People "who have suffered physical or cognitive impairments as a result of neurological illness."
Publication Date: 1995.
Acronym: VESPAR.
Scores: Available from publisher.
Administration: Individual.
Price Data, 1999: $160 per multi-part test.
Time: Administration time not reported.
Authors: Dawn W. Langdon and Elizabeth K. Warrington.
Publisher: Psychology Press.

[2810]

Veterinary College Admission Test.

Purpose: Designed to measure general academic ability and scientific knowledge.
Population: Veterinary college applicants.
Publication Dates: 1951-1991.
Acronym: VCAT.
Scores, 6: Verbal Ability, Biology, Chemistry, Quantitative Ability, Reading Comprehension, Composite.
Administration: Group.
Restricted Distribution: Distribution restricted and test administered at licensed testing centers; details may be obtained from publisher.
Price Data: Available from publisher.
Time: 205 minutes.
Comments: Formerly called the Veterinary Aptitude Test.
Author: The Psychological Corporation.
Publisher: The Psychological Corporation.
Cross References: For reviews by James B. Erdmann and Terry A. Stinnett, see 12:406; see T2:2358 (1 reference), 7:1101, 6:1139 (3 references), and 5:957 (3 references).

[2811]

Victoria Symptom Validity Test.

Purpose: "Designed to provide evidence that can help to confirm or disconfirm the validity of an examinee's reported cognitive impairments."
Population: Ages 18 and over.
Publication Date: 1997.
Acronym: VSVT.
Scores, 6: Total Items Correct, Easy Items Correct, Difficult Items Correct, Easy Items Response Latency, Difficult Items Response Latency, Right-Left Preference.
Administration: Individual.
Price Data: Price information available from publisher for introductory kit including program disk, 3.5-inch disk (10 uses), and professional manual (93 pages).
Time: Administration time not reported.
Comments: Requires IBM of compatible personal computer (80386 required; Pentium recommended) with MS Windows 3.11 or Windows 95; computer administered, scored, and interpreted.
Authors: Daniel Slick, Grace Hopp, Esther Strauss, and Garrie B. Thompson.
Publisher: Psychological Assessment Resources, Inc.

[2812]

Vincent Mechanical Diagrams Test, 1979 Revision.

Purpose: "Assesses the individual's ability to understand the concepts of cog, pulley and lever systems and general mechanical reasoning ability."
Population: Ages 15-adult.
Publication Dates: 1936-1979.
Acronym: VMD.
Scores: Total score only.
Administration: Group.
Price Data, 1987: £10.35 per 10 test booklets ('79, 13 pages); £2.25 per 10 answer sheets; £3.25 per marking key; £1.50 per instruction card (no date, 2 pages).
Time: 12(15) minutes.
Comments: Subtest of NIIP Engineering Selection Test Battery.
Author: National Institute of Industrial Psychology.
Publisher: NFER-Nelson Publishing Co., Ltd. [England].

[2813]

Vineland Adaptive Behavior Scales.

Purpose: To "assess personal and social sufficiency of individuals from birth to adulthood."

Population: Birth through age 18-11 and low-functioning adults, ages 3 through 12-11.

Publication Dates: 1935-1985.

Scores, 13: 3 Communication scores (Receptive, Expressive, Written), 3 Daily Living scores (Personal, Domestic, Community), 3 Socialization scores (Interpersonal Relationships, Play and Leisure Time, Coping Skills), 2 Motor Skills scores (Gross, Fine), Adaptive Behavior Composite, Maladaptive Behavior (optional for Survey and Expanded Forms only).

Administration: Individual.

Foreign Language Edition: Spanish edition available.

Comments: Revision of the Vineland Social Maturity Scale; semistructured interview for Survey and Expanded Forms.

Publisher: American Guidance Service, Inc.

a) INTERVIEW EDITION, SURVEY FORM.

Purpose: General assessment of adaptive strengths and weaknesses.

Population: Birth through age 18-11 and low-functioning adults.

Publication Dates: 1935-1984.

Price Data, 1999: $47.95 per 25 record booklets; $17.95 per 25 reports to parents; $14.95 per Interview Training Audiocassette; $49.955 per manual ('84, 313 pages); $69.95 per starter set including 10 record booklets, manual, and 1 report to parents; $149.95 per scoring and reporting software (DOS version for PCs).

Time: (20-60) minutes.

Authors: Sara S. Sparrow, David A. Balla, and Domenic V. Cicchetti.

b) INTERVIEW EDITION, EXPANDED FORM.

Purpose: Comprehensive assessment of adaptive behavior for program planning.

Population: Birth through age 18-11 and low-functioning adults.

Publication Dates: 1935-1984.

Price Data: $74.95 per 25 item booklets and 25 score summary and profile reports; $17.95 per 25 reports to parents; $27.95 per 25 program planning reports; $99.95 per starter set including 10 item booklets, 10 score summary and profile reports, 1 program planning report, 1 report to parents and manual ('84, 334 pages); $149.95 per scoring and reporting software (DOS version for PCs).

Time: (60-90) minutes.

Authors: Sara S. Sparrow, David A. Balla, and Domenic V. Cicchetti.

c) CLASSROOM EDITION.

Purpose: Assessment of adaptive behavior in the classroom.

Population: Ages 3 through 12-11.

Publication Date: 1985.

Price Data: $44.95 per 25 questionnaire booklets; $17.95 per 25 reports to parents; $47.95 per starter set including 10 questionnaire booklets, manual ('85, 186 pages), and 1 report to parents; $149.95 per scoring and reporting software (DOS version for PCs).

Time: (20) minutes.

Authors: Sara S. Sparrow (test and report), David A. Balla (test and report), Domenic V. Cicchetti (test and report), and Patti L. Harrison (manual).

Cross References: See T4:2882 (62 references); for a review by Jerome M. Sattler, see 10:381 (9 references); for a review by Iris Amos Campbell of the Survey Form and Expanded Form, see 9:1327 (8 references); see T3:2557 (38 references), 8:703 (23 references), T2:1428 (50 references), P:281 (21 references), 6:194 (20 references), and 5:120 (15 references); for reviews by William M. Cruickshank and Florence M. Teagarden of an earlier edition, see 4:94 (21 references); for reviews by C. M. Louttit and John W. M. Rothney and an excerpted review, see 3:107 (58 references); for reviews by Paul H. Furfey, Elaine F. Kinder, and Anna S. Starr, see 1:1143.

TEST REFERENCES

1. Braverman, M., Fein, D., Lucci, D., & Waterhouse, L. (1989). Affect comprehension in children with pervasive developmental disorders. *Journal of Autism and Developmental Disorders, 19*(2), 301-316.

2. Oswald, D. P., & Ollendick, T. H. (1989). Role taking and social competence in autism and mental retardation. *Journal of Autism and Developmental Disorders, 19*(1), 119-127.

3. Perry, A., & Factor, D. C. (1989). Psychometric validity and clinical usefulness of the Vineland Adaptive Behavior Scales and the AAMD Adaptive Behavior Scale for an autistic sample. *Journal of Autism and Developmental Disorders, 19*(1), 41-55.

4. Szatmari, P., Bartolucci, G., Bremner, R., Bond, S., & Rich, S. (1989). A follow-up study of high-functioning autistic children. *Journal of Autism and Developmental Disorders, 19*(2), 213-225.

5. Buitelaar, J., van Engeland, H., van Ree, J. M., & de Wied, D. (1990). Behavioral effects of Org 2766, a synthetic analog of the adrenocorticotrophic hormone (4-9), in 14 outpatient autistic children. *Journal of Autism and Developmental Disorders, 20*(4), 467-478.

6. Eichinger, J. (1990). Goal structure effects on social interaction: Nondisabled and disabled elementary students. *Exceptional Children, 56,* 408–416.

7. Sholle-Martin, S., & Alessi, N. E. (1990). Formulating a role for occupational therapy in child psychiatry: A clinical application. *The American Journal of Occupational Therapy, 44,* 871-882.

8. Asarnow, R. F., Satz, P., Light, R., Lewis, R., & Neumann, E. (1991). Behavior problems and adaptive functioning in children with mild and severe closed head injury. *Journal of Pediatric Psychology, 16,* 543–555.

9. Dyer, K., Williams, L., & Luce, S. C. (1991). Training teachers to use naturalistic communication strategies in classrooms for students with autism and other severe handicaps. *Language, Speech, and Hearing Services in Schools, 22,* 313–321.

10. Leckman, J. F., Hardin, M. T., Riddle, M. A., Stevenson, J., Ort, S. I., & Cohen, D. J. (1991). Clonidine treatment of Gilles de la Tourette's Syndrome. *Archives of General Psychiatry, 48,* 324-328.

11. Murray-Branch, J., Udavari-Solner, A., & Bailey, B. (1991). Textured communication systems for individuals with severe intellectual and dual sensory impairment. *Language, Speech, and Hearing Services in Schools, 22,* 260–268.

12. Perry, A., Sarlo-McGarvey, N., & Haddad, C. (1991). Cognitive and adaptive functioning in 28 girls with Rett syndrome. *Journal of Autism and Developmental Disorders, 21*(4), 551-556.

13. Rodrigue, J. R., Morgan, S. B., & Geffken, G. R. (1991). A comparative evaluation of adaptive behavior in children and adolescents with autism, Down

syndrome, and normal development. *Journal of Autism and Developmental Disorders, 21*(2), 187-196.

14. Sevin, J. A., Matson, J. L., Coe, D. A., Fee, V. E., & Sevin, B. M. (1991). A comparison and evaluation of three commonly used autism scales. *Journal of Autism and Developmental Disorders, 21*(4), 417-432.

15. Barakat, L. P., & Linney, J. A. (1992). Children with physical handicaps and their mothers: The interrelation of social support, maternal adjustment, and child adjustment. *Journal of Pediatric Psychology, 17,* 725–739.

16. Bernstein, M. E., & Morrison, M. E. (1992). Are we ready for PL 99-457? *American Annals of the Deaf, 137,* 7-13.

17. Burack, J. A., & Volkmar, F. R. (1992). Development of low- and high-functioning autistic children. *Journal of Child Psychology and Psychiatry and Allied Disciplines, 33,* 607-616.

18. Lewy, A. L., & Dawson, G. (1992). Social stimulation and joint attention in young autistic children. *Journal of Abnormal Child Psychology, 20,* 555-566.

19. Ogletree, B. T., Wetherby, A. M., & Westling, D. L. (1992). Profile of the prelinguistic intentional communicative behaviors of children with profound mental retardation. *American Journal on Mental Retardation, 97,* 186-196.

20. Perry, A., Sarlo-McGarvey, N., & Factor, D. C. (1992). Stress and family functioning in parents of girls with Rett syndrome. *Journal of Autism and Developmental Disorders, 22*(2), 235-248.

21. Prior, M., Smart, D., Sanson, A., Pedlow, R., & Oberklaid, F. (1992). Transient versus stable behavior problems in a normative sample: Infancy to school age. *Journal of Pediatric Psychology, 17,* 423–443.

22. Schery, T. K., & O'Connor, L. C. (1992). The effectiveness of school-based computer language intervention with severely handicapped children. *Language, Speech, and Hearing Services in Schools, 23,* 43–47.

23. Sokolov, J. L. (1992). Linguistic imitation in children with Down syndrome. *American Journal on Mental Retardation, 97,* 209-221.

24. Taylor, H. G., & Schatschneider, C. (1992). Academic achievement following childhood brain disease: Implications for the concept of learning disabilities. *Journal of Learning Disabilities, 25,* 630–638.

25. Tiedemann, G. L., & Johnston, C. (1992). Evaluation of a parent training program to promote sharing between young siblings. *Behavior Therapy, 23,* 299–318.

26. Tombokan-Runtukohu, J., & Nitko, A. J. (1992). Translation, cultural adjustment, and validation of a measure of adaptive behavior. *Research in Developrnent Disabilities, 13,* 481-501.

27. Van Bourgondien, M. E., Marcus, L. M., & Schopler, E. (1992). Comparison of DSM-III-R and Childhood Autism Rating Scale diagnoses of autism. *Journal of Autism and Developmental Disorders, 22*(4), 493-506.

28. Venter, A., Lord, C., & Schopler, E. (1992). A follow-up study of high-functioning autistic children. *Journal of Child Psychology and Psychiatry and Allied Disciplines, 33,* 489-507.

29. Weber, R. C., & Thorpe, J. (1992). Teaching children with autism through task variation in physical education. *Exceptional Children, 59,* 77-86.

30. Aram, D. M., Morris, R., & Hall, N. E. (1993). Clinical and research congruence in identifying children with specific language impairment. *Journal of Speech and Hearing Research, 36,* 580–591.

31. Castelloe, P., & Dawson, G. (1993). Subclassification of children with autism and pervasive developmental disorder: A questionnaire based on Wing's subgrouping scheme. *Journal of Autism and Developmental Disorders, 23*(2), 229-241.

32. Chiaunza, G. A. (1993). Movement-related brain macropotentials of persons with Down syndrome during skilled performance. *American Journal on Mental Retardation, 97,* 449-467.

33. Cohen, I. L., Sudhalter, V., Landon-Jimenez, D., & Keogh, M. (1993). A neural network approach to the classification of autism. *Journal of Autism and Developmental Disorders, 23*(3), 443-466.

34. DeGangi, G. A., Wietlisbach, S., Goodin, M., & Scheiner, N. (1993). A comparison of structured sensorimotor therapy and child-centered activity in the treatment of preschool children with sensorimotor problems. *The American Journal of Occupational Therapy, 47,* 777-786.

35. Eberlin, M., McConnachie, G., Ibel, S., & Volpe, L. (1993). Facilitated communication: A failure to replicate the phenomenon. *Journal of Autism and Developmental Disorders, 23*(3), 507-530.

36. Ericson, G. D., & Riordan, R. J. (1993). Effects of a psychosocial and vocational intervention on the rehabilitation potential of young adults with end-stage renal disease. *Rehabilitation Counselor Bulletin, 37,* 25–36.

37. Fombonne, E., & Achard, S. (1993). The Vineland Adaptive Behavior Scale in a sample of normal French children: A research note. *Journal of Child Psychology and Psychiatry and Allied Disciplines, 34,* 1051-1058.

38. Hecht, B. F., Levine, H. G., & Mastergeorge, A. B. (1993). Conversational roles of children with developmental delays and their mothers in natural and semi-structured situations. *American Journal on Mental Retardation, 97,* 419-429.

39. Little, S. S. (1993). Nonverbal learning disabilities and socioemotional functioning: A review of recent literature. *Journal of Learning Disabilities, 26,* 653–665.

40. Macmann, G. M., & Barnett, D. W. (1993). Reliability of psychiatric and psychological diagnoses of mental retardation severity: Judgements under naturally occurring conditions. *American Journal on Mental Retardation, 97,* 559-567.

41. MacMillan, D. L., Gresham, F. M., & Siperstein, G. N. (1993). Conceptual and psychometric concerns about the 1992 AAMR definition of mental retardation. *American Journal on Mental Retardation, 98,* 325–335.

42. McEachin, J. J., Smith, T., & Lovaas, O. I. (1993). Long-term outcome for children with autism who received early intensive behavioral treatment. *American Journal on Mental Retardation, 97,* 359-372.

43. Morris, R. D., Krawiecki, N. S., Wright, J. A., & Walter, L. W. (1993). Neuropsychological, academic, and adaptive functioning in children who survive in-hospital cardiac arrest and resuscitation. *Journal of Learning Disabilities, 26,* 46–51.

44. Mundy, P. (1993). Normal versus high-functioning status in children with autism. *American Journal on Mental Retardation, 97,* 381-384.

45. Raggio, D. J., & Massingale, T. W. (1993). Comparison of the Vineland Social Maturity Scale, the Vineland Adaptive Behavior Scales—Survey Four, and the Bayley Scales of Infant Development with infants evaluated for developmental delay. *Perceptual and Motor Skills, 77,* 931–937.

46. Riccio, C. A., & Hynd, G. W. (1993). Developmental language disorders in children: Relationship with learning disability and attention deficit hyperactivity disorder. *School Psychology Review, 22,* 696-709.

47. Rodrigue, J. R., Geffken, G. R., & Morgan, S. B. (1993). Perceived competence and behavioral adjustment of siblings of children with autism. *Journal of Autism and Developmental Disorders, 23*(4), 665-674.

48. Sanson, A., Prior, M., Smart, D., & Oberklaid, F. (1993). Gender differences in aggression in childhood: Implications for a peaceful world. *Australian Psychologist, 28,* 86–92.

49. Smith, S. A. (1993). Confusing the terms "guilty" and "not guilty": Implications for alleged offenders with mental retardation. *Psychological Reports, 73,* 675-678.

50. Smith, T., McEachin, J. J., & Lovaas, O. I. (1993). Comments on replication and evaluation of outcome. *American Journal on Mental Retardation, 97,* 385-391.

51. Szatmari, P., Saigal, J., Rosenbaum, P., & Campbell, D. (1993). Psychopathology and adaptive functioning among extremely low birthweight children at eight years of age. *Development and Psychopathology, 5,* 345-357.

52. Volkmar, F. R., Szatmari, P., & Sparrow, S. S. (1993). Sex differences in pervasive developmental disorder. *Journal of Autism and Developmental Disorders, 23*(4), 579-591.

53. Widaman, K. F., Stacy, A. W., & Borthwick-Duffy, S. A. (1993). Construct validity of dimensions of adaptive behavior: A multitrait-multimethod evaluation. *American Journal on Mental Retardation, 98,* 219–234.

54. Alcantara, P. R. (1994). Effects of videotape instructional package on purchasing skills of children with autism. *Exceptional Children, 61,* 40-55.

55. Antia, S. D., Kreimeyer, K. H., & Eldredge, N. (1994). Promoting social interaction between young children with hearing impairments and their peers. *Exceptional Children, 60,* 262-275.

56. Baranek, G. T., & Berkson, G. (1994). Tactile defensiveness in children with developmental disabilities: Responsiveness and habituation. *Journal of Autism and Developmental Disorders, 24,* 457-471.

57. Brinker, R. P., Seifer, R., & Sameroff, A. J. (1994). Relations among maternal stress, cognitive development, and early intervention in middle- and low-SES infants with developmental disabilities. *American Journal on Mental Retardation, 98,* 463–480.

58. Carpentieri, S. C., & Morgan, S. B. (1994). Brief report: A comparison of patterns of cognitive functioning of autistic and nonautistic retarded children on the Stanford-Binet—Fourth Edition. *Journal of Autism and Developmental Disorders, 24,* 215-223.

59. Davies, P. L., & Gavin, W. J. (1994). Comparison of individual and group/consultation treatment methods for preschool children with developmental delays. *The American Journal of Occupational Therapy, 48,* 155-161.

60. Dykens, E. M., Hodapp, R. M., & Evans, D. W. (1994). Profiles and development of adaptive behavior in children with Down Syndrome. *American Journal on Mental Retardation, 98,* 580–587.

61. Ghaziuddin, M., Butler, E., Tsai, L., & Ghaziuddin, N. (1994). Is clumsiness a marker for Asperger syndrome? *Journal of Intellectual Disability Research, 38,* 519–527.

62. Hollowood, T. M., Salisbury, C. L., Rainforth, B., & Palombarb, M. M. (1994). Use of instructional time in classrooms serving students with and without disabilities. *Exceptional Children, 61,* 242-253.

63. Janniro, F., Sapp, G. L., & Kohler, M. P. (1994). Validating the Street Survival Skills Questionnaire. *Psychological Reports, 74,* 191-194.

64. Kaler, S. R., & Freeman, B. J. (1994). Analysis of environmental deprivation: Cognitive and social development in Romanian orphans. *Journal of Child Psychology and Psychiatry and Allied Disciplines, 35,* 769-781.

65. Kerby, D. S., & Dawson, B. L. (1994). Autistic features, personality, and adaptive behavior in males with the fragile X syndrome and no autism. *American Journal on Mental Retardation, 98,* 455–462.

66. Kobe, F. H., Mulick, J. A., Rash, T. A., & Martin, J. (1994). Nonambulatory persons with profound mental retardation: Physical, developmental, and behavioral characteristics. *Research in Developmental Disabilities, 15,* 413-423.

67. Loveland, K. A., Stehbens, J., Constant, C., Bordeaux, J. D., Sirois, P., Bell, T. S., & Hill, S. (1994). Hemophilia growth and development study: Baseline neurodevelopmental findings. *Journal of Pediatric Psychology, 19,* 223–239.

68. Matese, M., Matson, J. L., & Servin, J. (1994). Comparison of psychotic and autistic children using behavioral observation. *Journal of Autism and Developmental Disorders, 24,* 83-94.

69. Nicholas, J. G. (1994). Sensory aid use and the development of communicative function. *Volta Review, 96,* 181–198.

70. Owen, M. T., & Mulvihill, B. A. (1994). Benefits of a parent education and support program in the first three years. *Family Relations, 43,* 206-212.

71. Pearson, D. A., & Lachar, D. (1994). Using behavior questionnaires to identify adaptive deficits in elementary school children. *Journal of School Psychology, 32,* 33-52.

72. Raggio, D. J., Massingale, T. W., & Bass, J. D. (1994). Comparison of Vineland Adaptive Behavior Scales—Survey Form age equivalent and standard score with the Bayley Mental Development Index. *Perceptual and Motor Skills, 79,* 203-206.

73. Restall, G., & Magill-Evans, J. (1994). Play and preschool children with autism. *The American Journal of Occupational Therapy, 48,* 113-120.

74. Szatmari, P., Archer, L., Fisman, S., & Streiner, D. L. (1994). Parent and teacher agreement in the assessment of pervasive developmental disorders. *Journal of Autism and Developmental Disorders, 24,* 703-717.

75. Taylor, J. C., Ekdahl, M. M., Romanczyk, R. G., & Miller, M. L. (1994). Escape behavior in task situations: Task versus social antecedents. *Journal of Autism and Developmental Disorders, 24,* 331-344.

76. Tingley, E. C., Gleason, J. B., & Hooshyar, N. (1994). Mothers' lexicon of internal state words in speech to children with Down Syndrome and to nonhandicapped children at mealtime. *Journal of Communication Disorders, 27,* 135–155.

77. Torrey, E. F., Taylor, E. H., Bracha, H. S., Bowler, A. E., McNeil, T. F., Rawlings, R. R., Quinn, P. O., Bigelow, L. B., Rickler, K., Sjostrom, K., Higgins, E. S., & Gottesman, I. I. (1994). Prenatal origin of schizophrenia in a subgroup of discordant monozygotic twins. *Schizophrenia Bulletin, 20,* 423–432.

78. Urquiza, A. J., Wirtz, S. J., Peterson, M. S., & Singer, V. A. (1994). Screening and evaluating abused and neglected children entering protective custody. *Child Welfare, 73,* 155–171.

79. Vaughn, B. E., Goldberg, S., Atkinson, L., Marcovitch, S., MacGregor, D., & Seifer, R. (1994). Quality of toddler-mother attachment in children with Down Syndrome: Limits to interpretation of strange situation behavior. *Child Development, 65,* 95-108.

80. Weismer, S. E., Murray-Branch, J., & Miller, J. F. (1994). A prospective longitudinal study of language development in late talkers. *Journal of Speech and Hearing, 37,* 852–867.

81. Wolters, P. L., Brouwers, P., Moss, H. A., & Pizzo, P. A. (1994). Adaptive behavior of children with symptomatic HIV infection before and after zidovudine therapy. *Journal of Pediatric Psychology, 19,* 47–61.

82. Yoder, P. J., Davies, B., & Bishop, K. (1994). Adult interaction style effects on the language sampling and transcription process with children who have developmental disabilities. *American Journal on Mental Retardation, 99,* 270–282.

83. Yoder, P. J., Davies, B., Bishop, K., & Munson, L. (1994). Effect of adult continuing wh-questions on conversational participation in children with developmental disabilities. *Journal of Speech and Hearing Research, 37,* 193–204.

84. Burt, D. B., Loveland, K. A., Chen, Y. W., Chuang, A., Lewis, K. R., & Cherry, L. (1995). Aging in adults with Down Syndrome: Report from a longitudinal study. *American Journal on Mental Retardation, 100,* 262–270.

85. Capps, L., Sigman, M., & Yirmiya, N. (1995). Self-competence and emotional understanding in high-functioning children with autism. *Development and Psychopathology, 7,* 137-149.

86. Carlson-Greene, B., Morris, R. D., & Krawiecki, N. (1995). Family and illness predictors of outcome in pediatric brain tumors. *Journal of Pediatric Psychology, 20,* 769–784.

87. Dykens, E. M. (1995). Measuring behavioral phenotypes: Provocations from the "New Genetics." *American Journal on Mental Retardation, 99,* 522–532.

88. Fletcher, J. M., Brookshire, B. L., Landry, S. H., Bohan, T. P., Davidson, K. C., Francis, D. J., Thompson, N. M., & Miner, M. E. (1995). Behavioral adjustment of children with hydrocephalus: Relationships with etiology, neurological, and family stress. *Journal of Pediatric Psychology, 20,* 109-125.

89. Franco, F., & Wishart, J. G. (1995). Use of pointing and other gestures by young children with Down Syndrome. *American Journal on Mental Retardation, 100,* 160–182.

90. Gaskell, G., Dockrell, J., & Rehman, H. (1995). Community care for people with challenging behaviors and mild learning disability: An evaluation of an assessment and treatment unit. *British Journal of Clinical Psychology, 34,* 383–395.

91. Glick, M., & Zigler, E. (1995). Developmental differences in the symptomatology of psychiatric inpatients with and without mild mental retardation. *American Journal on Mental Retardation, 99,* 407–417.

92. Guralnick, M. J., Connor, R. T., & Hammond, M. (1995). Parent perspective of peer relationships and friendships in integrated and specialized programs. *American Journal on Mental Retardation, 99,* 457–476.

93. Guralnick, M. J., Connor, R. T., Hammond, M., Gottman, J. M., & Kinnish, K. (1995). Immediate effects of mainstreamed settings on the social interactions and social integration of preschool children. *American Journal on Mental Retardation, 100,* 359–377.

94. Hauck, M., Fein, D., Waterhouse, L., & Feinstein, C. (1995). Social initiations by autistic children to adults and other children. *Journal of Autism and Developmental Disorders, 25,* 579–595.

95. Janzen-Wilde, M. L., Duchan, J. F., & Higginbotham, D. J. (1995). Successful use of facilitated communication with an oral child. *Journal of Speech and Hearing Research, 38,* 658–676.

96. Lancioni, G. E., Oliva, D., & Bracalente, S. (1995). An acoustic orientation system to promote independent indoor travel in blind persons with severe mental retardation. *Perceptual and Motor Skills, 80,* 747–754.

97. Linehan, S. L., & Brady, M. P. (1995). Functional versus developmental assessment: Influences on instructional planning decisions. *The Journal of Special Education, 29,* 295–309.

98. Luetke-Stahlman, B. (1995). Social interaction: Assessment and intervention with regard to students who are deaf. *American Annals of the Deaf, 140,* 295–303.

99. Luthar, S. S., Woolston, J. L., Sparrow, S. S., Zimmerman, L. D., & Riddle, M. A. (1995). Adaptive behaviors among psychiatrically hospitalized children: The role of intelligence and related attributes. *Journal of Clinical Child Psychology, 24,* 98-108.

100. Mathias, J. L., Mertin, P., & Murray, A. (1995). The psychological functioning of children for backgrounds of domestic violence. *Australian Psychologist, 30,* 47–56.

101. Roeden, J. M., & Zitman, F. G. (1995). Ageing in adults with Down's syndrome in institutionally-based and community-based residences. *Journal of Intellectual Disability Research, 39,* 399–497.

102. Schatz, J., & Hamdam-Allen, G. (1995). Effects of age and IQ on adaptive behavior domains for children with autism. *Journal of Autism and Developmental Disorders, 25,* 51-60.

103. Schultz, T. M., & Berkson, G. (1995). Definition of abnormal focused affections and exploration of their relation to abnormal stereotyped behaviors. *American Journal on Mental Retardation, 99,* 376–390.

104. Sevin, J. A., Matson, J. L., Coe, D., Love, S. R., Matese, M. J., & Benavidez, D. A. (1995). Empirically derived subtypes of pervasive developmental disorders: A cluster analytic study. *Journal of Autism and Developmental Disorders, 25,* 561–578.

105. Simon, E. W., Rosen, M., Grossman, E., & Pratowski, E. (1995). The relationships among facial emotion recognition, social skills, and quality of life. *Research in Developmental Disabilities, 16,* 383–391.

106. Smith, S. A., & Hudson, R. L. (1995). A quick screening test of competency to stand trial for defendents with mental retardation. *Psychological Reports, 76,* 91-97.

107. Stein, M. A., Szumowski, E., Blondis, T. A., & Roizen, N. J. (1995). Adaptive skills dysfunction in ADD and ADHD children. *Journal of Child Psychology and Psychiatry and Allied Disciplines, 36,* 663-670.

108. Taylor, H. G., Hack, M., Klein, N., & Schatschneider, C. (1995). Achievement in children with birth weights less than 750 grams with normal cognitive abilities: Evidence for specific learning disabilities. *Journal of Pediatric Psychology, 20,* 703–719.

109. Tordjman, S., Anderson, G. M., McBride, P. A., Hertzig, M. E., Snow, M. E., Hall, L. M., Ferrari, P., & Cohen, D. J. (1995). Plasma androgens in autism. *Journal of Autism and Developmental Disorders, 25,* 295–304.

110. Tucker, C. M., Chennault, S. A., Brady, B. A., Fraser, K. P., Gaskin, V. T., Dunn, C., & Frisby, C. (1995). A parent, community, public schools, and university involved partnership education program to examine and boost academic achievement and adaptive functioning skills of African-American students. *Journal of Research and Development in Education, 28,* 174–185.

111. Walters, A. S., Rowland, P. B., Knapp, L. G., & Borden, M. C. (1995). Suicidal behavior in children and adolescents with mental retardation. *Research in Developmental Disabilities, 16,* 85-96.

112. Beange, H., & Taplin, J. E. (1996). Prevalence of intellectual disability in northern Sydney adults. *Journal of Disability Research, 40,* 191–197.

113. Ducharme, J. M., Popynick, M., Pontes, E., & Steele, S. (1996). Errorless compliance to parental requests III: Group parent training with parent observational data and long-term follow-up. *Behavior Therapy, 27,* 353–372.

114. Dunn, M., Flax, J., Sliwinski, M., & Aram, D. (1996). The use of spontaneous language measures as criteria for identifying children with specific language impairment: An attempt to reconcile clinical and research in congruence. *Journal of Speech and Hearing Research, 39,* 643–654.

115. Dykens, E. (1996). The draw-a-person task in persons with mental retardation: What does it measure? *Research in Developmental Disabilities, 17,* 1–13.

116. Dykens, E., Ort, S., Cohen, I., Finucane, B., Spiridigliozzi, G., Lachiewicz, A., Reiss, A., Freund, L., Hagerman, R., & O'Connor, R. (1996). Trajectories and profiles of adaptive behavior in males with Fragile X syndrome: Multicenter studies. *Journal of Autism and Developmental Disorders, 26,* 287-301.

117. Ferro, J., Foster-Johnson, L., & Dunlap, G. (1996). Relation between curricular activities and problem behaviors of students with mental retardation. *American Journal on Mental Retardation, 101,* 184–194.

118. Gallimore, R., Coots, J., Weisner, T., Garnier, H., & Guthrie, D. (1996). Family responses to children with early developmental delays II: Accomodation intensity and activity in early and middle children. *American Journal on Mental Retardation, 101,* 215–232.

119. Guralnick, M. J., Connor, R. T., Hammond, M. A., Gottman, J. M., & Kinnish, K. (1996). The peer relations of preschool children with communication disorders. *Child Development, 67,* 471–489.

120. Hughes, C., Hugo, K., & Blatt, J. (1996). Self-instructional intervention for teaching generalized problem-solving within a functional task sequence. *American Journal on Mental Retardation, 100,* 565–579.

121. Lancioni, G. E., & Boelens, H. (1996). Teaching student with mental retardation and other disabilities to make simple drawings through the computer system and special cards. *Perceptual and Motor Skills, 83,* 401–402.

122. Lancioni, G. E., Oliva, D., & Gnocchini, F. (1996). A visual orientation system for promoting indoor travel in persons with profound developmental disabilities and visual impairment. *Perceptual and Motor Skills, 83,* 619–626.

123. Lyon, M. A., Albertos, C., Birkinbine, J., & Naibi, J. (1996). A validity study of the social skills rating system—teacher version with disabled and nondisabled preschool children. *Perceptual and Motor Skills, 83,* 307–316.

124. Macmillan, D. L., Siperstein, G. N., & Gresham, F. M. (1996). A challenge to the viability of mild mental retardation as a diagnostic category. *Exceptional Children, 62,* 356–371.

125. O'Brien, S. K. (1996). The validity and reliability of the Wing Subgroups Questionnaire. *Journal of Autism and Developmental Disorders, 26,* 321–335.

126. Perloff, J. N., & Buckner, J. C. (1996). Fathers of children on welfare: Their impact on child well-being. *American Journal of Orthopsychiatry, 66,* 557–571.

127. Powell, T. W. (1996). Stimulability considerations in the phonological treatment of a child with a persistant disorder of speech-sound production. *Journal of Communication Disorders, 29,* 315–333.

128. Radcliffe, J., Bennett, D., Kazak, A. E., Foley, B., & Phillips, P. C. (1996). Adjustment in childhood brain tumor survival: Child, mother, and teacher report. *Journal of Pediatric Psychology, 21,* 529–539.

129. Simon, E. W., Rosen, M., & Ponpipom, A. (1996). Age and IQ as predictors of emotion identification in adults with mental retardation. *Research in Developmental Disabilities, 17,* 383–389.
130. Smith, K. E., Landry, S. H., Swank, P. R., Baldwin, C. D., Denson, S. E., & Wildin, S. (1996). The relation of medical risk and maternal stimulation with preterm infants' development of cognitive, language and daily living skills. *Journal of Child Psychology and Psychiatry, 37,* 858–864.
131. Waterhouse, L., Morris, R., Allen, D., Dunn, M., Fein, D., Feinstein, C., Rapin, I., & Wing, L. (1996). Diagnosis and classification in autism. *Journal of Autism and Developmental Disorders, 26,* 59–86.
132. Werts, M. G., Wolery, M., Venn, M. L., Deinblowski, D., & Doren, H. (1996). Effects of transition-based teaching with instructive feedback on skill acquisition by children with and without disabilities. *Journal of Educational Research, 90,* 75–86.
133. Williams, K. C. (1996). Piagetian principles: Simple and affective application. *Journal of Disability Research, 40,* 110–119.
134. Yoshinaga-Itano, C., & Downey, D. M. (1996). The psychoeducational characteristics of school-aged students in Colorado with educationally significant hearing losses. *Volta Review, 98,* 65–96.
135. Yoshinaga-Itano, C. Snyder, L. S., & Mayberry, R. (1996). Can lexical/semantic skills differentiate deaf or hard-of-hearing readers and nonreaders? *Volta Review, 98* 39–61.
136. Baranek, G. T., Foster, L. G., & Berkson, G. (1997). Tactile defensiveness and stereotyped behaviors. *American Journal of Occupational Therapy, 51,* 91–95.
137. Blacher, J., Shapiro, J., Lopez, S., Diaz, L., & Fusco, J. (1997). Depression in Latino mothers of children with mental retardation: A neglected concern. *American Journal on Mental Retardation, 101,* 483–496.
138. Borthwick-Duffy, S. A., Lane, K. L., & Widaman, K. F. (1997). Measuring problem behaviors in children with mental retardation: Dimensions and predictors. *Research in Developmental Disabilities, 18,* 415–433.
139. Dura, J. (1997). Expressive communicative ability, symptoms of mental illness and aggressive behavior. *Journal of Clinical Psychology, 53,* 307–318.
140. Filipek, P. A., Semrud-Clikeman, M., Steingard, R. J., Renshaw, P. F., Kennedy, D. N., & Biederman, J. (1997). Volumetric MRI analysis comparing subjects having attention-deficit hyperactivity disorder with normal controls. *Neurology, 48,* 589–601.
141. Gottman, J. M., Guralnick, M. J., Wilson, B., Swanson, C. C., & Murray, J. D. (1997). What should be the focus of emotional regulation in children? A nonlinear dynamic mathematical model of children's peer interaction in groups. *Development and Psychopathology, 9,* 421–452.
142. Griffiths, D., Feldman, M. A., & Tough, S. (1997). Programming generalization of social skills in adults with developmental disabilities: Effects on generalization and social validity. *Behavior Therapy, 28,* 253–269.
143. Guralnick, M. J. (1997). Peer social networks of young boys with developmental delays. *American Journal on Mental Retardation, 101,* 595–612.
144. Harcovitch, S., Goldberg, S., Gold, A., Washington, J., Wasson, C., Krekewich, K., & Handley-Derry, M. (1997). Determinants of behavioural problems in Romanian children adopted in Ontario. *International Journal of Behavioral Development, 20,* 17–31.
145. Keogh, B. K., Bernheimer, L. P., & Guthrie, D. (1997). Stability and change over time in cognitive level of children with delays. *American Journal on Mental Retardation, 101,* 365–373.
146. Landry, S. H., Denson, S. E., & Swank, P. E. (1997). Effects of medical risk and socioeconomic status on the rate of change in cognitive and social development for low birth weight children. *Journal of Clinical and Experimental Neuropsychology, 19,* 261–274.
147. Matson, J. L., & Smiroldo, B. B. (1997). Validity of the mania subscale of the diagnostic assessment for the severely handicapped-II (DASH-II). *Research in Developmental Disabilities, 18,* 221–225.
148. Matson, J. L., Kiely, S. L., & Bamburg, J. W. (1997). The effect of stereotypes on adaptive skills as assessed with the DASH-II and Vineland Adaptive Behavior Scales. *Research in Developmental Disabilities, 18,* 471–476.
149. Max, J. E., Lindgren, S. D., Robin, D. A., Smith, W. L., Jr., Sato, Y., Matheis, P. J., Castillo, C. S., & Stierwalt, J. A. G. (1997). Traumatic brain injury in children and adolescents: Psychiatric disorders in the second three months. *Journal of Nervous and Mental Disease, 185,* 394–401.
150. Nicholas, J. G., & Geers, A. E. (1997). Communication of oral deaf and normally hearing children at 36 months of age. *Journal of Speech, Language, and Hearing Research, 40,* 1314–1327.
151. Phelps, L., Wallace, N. V., & Bontrager, A. (1997). Risk factors in early child development: Is prenatal cocaine/polydrug exposure a key variable? *Psychology in the Schools, 34,* 245–252.
152. Rescorla, l., Roberts, J., & Dahlsgaard, K. (1997). Late talkers at 2: Outcome at age 3. *Journal of Speech, Language, and Hearing Research, 40,* 556–566.
153. Wallander, J. L., & Marullo, D. S. (1997). Handicap-related problems in mothers of children with physical impairments. *Research in Developmental Disabilities, 18,* 151–165.
154. Whitaker, A. H., Rossem, R. V., Feldman, J. F., Schonfeld, I. S., Pinto-Martin, J. A., Torre, C., Shaffer, D., & Paneth, N. (1997). Psychiatric outcomes in low-birth-weight children at age 6 years: Relation to neonatal cranial ultrasound abnormalities. *Archives of General Psychiatry, 54,* 847–856.
155. Howlin, P., Davies, M., & Udwin, O. (1998). Cognitive functioning in adults with Williams syndrome. *Journal of Child Psychology and Psychiatry, 39,* 183–189.
156. Price, J. M., & Landsverk, J. (1998). Social information-processing patterns as predictors of social adaptation and behavior problems among maltreated children in foster care. *Child Abuse & Neglect, 22,* 845–858.

[2814]

Vineland Social-Emotional Early Childhood Scales.

Purpose: Designed to assess the social and emotional functioning of young children.
Population: Birth to age 5-11.
Publication Date: 1998.
Acronym: SEEC.
Scores, 4: Interpersonal Relationships, Play and Leisure Time, Coping Skills, Composite.
Administration: Individual.
Price Data, 1999: $49.95 per complete kit; $24.95 per 25 record forms; price data available from publisher for scoring and reporting software (Early Childhood Assessment ASSIST).
Foreign Language Edition: Spanish edition available.
Time: (15–25) minutes.
Comments: Administered as a structured oral interview; interviewee should be the person with the most knowledge of the child's social and emotional functioning (e.g., parent, grandparent, legal guardian).
Authors: Sara S. Sparrow, David A. Balla, and Dominic V. Cicchetti.
Publisher: American Guidance Service, Inc.

[2815]

A Violence Scale.

Purpose: Designed to measure attitudes toward violence.
Population: Adolescents and adults.
Publication Date: 1973.
Scores: Total score only.
Administration: Group.
Price Data, 1998: $1 per scale.
Time: [10] minutes.
Comments: The manual is a reprint of a journal article by the author.
Author: Panos D. Bardis.
Publisher: Donna Bardis.
Cross References: See 8:704 (1 reference).

[2816]

The Visual Aural Digit Span Test.

Purpose: Intended as a "standardized test of intersensory integration and short-term memory for school-age children."
Population: Ages 5-6 to 12.
Publication Date: 1977.
Acronym: VADS Test.
Scores, 11: Aural-Oral, Visual-Oral, Aural-Written, Visual-Written, Aural Input, Visual Input, Oral Expression, Written Expression, Intrasensory Integration, Intersensory Integration, Total.

Subtests, 4: Aural-Oral, Visual-Oral, Aural-Written, Visual-Written.
Administration: Individual.
Price Data, 1999: $48 per examination kit including 1 package of stimulus cards, Directions for Administering, and 100 visual scoring forms); $27 per 100 visual scoring forms; $65.50 per manual ('77, 216 pages).
Time: [10-15] minutes.
Author: Elizabeth M. Koppitz.
Publisher: The Psychological Corporation.
Cross References: See T4:2884 (1 reference); for reviews by H. Lee Swanson and Robert H. Zabel, see 9:1329 (2 references); see also T3:2560 (2 references).

TEST REFERENCE

1. Kusché, C. A., Cook, E. T., & Greenberg, M. T. (1993). Neuropsychological and cognitive functioning in children with anxiety, externalizing, and comorbid psychopathology. *Journal of Clinical Child Psychology, 22,* 172-195.

[2817]

Visual Discrimination Test.

Purpose: Measures "ability to discriminate between like non-alphabetic forms."
Population: Ages 5-8.
Publication Date: 1975.
Scores: Total score only.
Administration: Individual.
Price Data, 1999: $19.50 per 100 score sheets; $14.50 per manual (8 pages); $80 per kit including 1 set of reusable stimulus cards, 25 score sheets, and manual.
Time: (5-7) minutes.
Authors: Joseph M. Wepman, Anne Morency, and Marva Seidl.
Publisher: Western Psychological Services.
Cross References: See T4:2885 (3 references); for reviews by Morton Bortner and Mildred H. Huebner, see 8:448.

[2818]

Visual Functioning Assessment Tool.

Purpose: "Assessment of a student's visual functioning in the educational setting."
Population: Visually impaired in grades preschool and over.
Publication Date: 1980.
Acronym: VFAT.
Scores: No scores.
Administration: Individual.
Price Data, 1998: $95 per complete kit; $38 per reproducible recording booklet; $65 per manual (123 pages).
Time: Administration time not reported.
Authors: Kathleen Byrnes Costello, Patricia Pinkney, and Wendy Scheffers.
Publisher: Stoelting Co.

[2819]

Visual Memory Test.

Purpose: Measures "ability to hold in immediate memory visually presented forms of a non-alphabetic nature."
Population: Ages 5-8.
Publication Date: 1975.
Scores: Total score only.
Administration: Individual.
Price Data, 1999: $19.50 per 100 score sheets; $14.50 per manual (8 pages); $85 per kit including 1 set of reusable stimulus cards, 25 score sheets, and manual.
Time: (5-7) minutes.
Authors: Joseph M. Wepman, Anne Morency, and Marva Seidl.
Publisher: Western Psychological Services.
Cross References: See T4:2887 (1 reference).

TEST REFERENCE

1. Stracciari, A., Ghidoni, E., Guarino, M., Poletti, M., & Pazzaglia, P. (1994). Post-traumatic retrograde amnesia with selective impairment of autobiographical memory. *Cortex, 30,* 459-468.

[2820]

Visual Search and Attention Test.

Purpose: Constructed to assess "ability to scan accurately and [to] sustain attention on each of four different visual cancellation tasks."
Population: Ages 18 and over.
Publication Dates: 1987-1990.
Acronym: VSAT.
Scores, 3: Left, Right, Total.
Administration: Individual.
Price Data: Price information available from publisher for complete kit including 25 test booklets and manual ('90, 18 pages).
Time: 4(6) minutes.
Authors: Max R. Trenerry, Bruce Crosson, James DeBoe, and William R. Leber.
Publisher: Psychological Assessment Resources, Inc.
Cross References: For reviews by Stephen R. Hooper and Wilfred G. Van Gorp, see 12:407.

TEST REFERENCE

1. Weyandt, L. L., Linterman, I., & Rice, J. A. (1995). Reported prevalence of attentional difficulties in a general sample of college students. *Journal of Psychopathology and Behavioral Assessment, 17,* 293-304.

[2821]

Visual Skills Appraisal.

Purpose: "Developed to assist teachers and other educators, who may not have specialized training in visual skills assessment, to identify visual inefficiencies that affect school performance."
Population: Grades K-4.
Publication Date: 1984.
Acronym: VSA.
Scores: 6 subtests: Pursuits, Scanning, Aligning, Locating, Eye-Hand Coordination, Fixation Unity.

Administration: Individual.
Price Data, 1999: $65 per complete kit including manual (112 pages), stimulus cards, 25 design completion forms, 25 red/green trail forms, 25 score sheets, and red/green glasses; $8 per stimulus cards; $9 per 25 design completion forms, 25 red/green trail forms, or 25 score sheets; $8 per red/green glasses; $19 per manual; $12 per Classroom Visual Activities optional companion manual.
Time: (10-15) minutes.
Authors: Regina G. Richards and Gary S. Oppenheim in consultation with G. N. Getman.
Publisher: Academic Therapy Publications.
Cross References: See 11:456 (1 reference).

[2822]

Voc-Tech Quick Screener.

Purpose: Designed to identify job interests.
Population: Non-college bound high school students and adults.
Publication Dates: 1984-1990.
Acronym: VTQS.
Scores, 14: Administrative Support/Clerical, Agriculture/Animals and Forestry, Construction Trades, Design/Graphics and Communication, Food/Beverage Services, Health Services, Health Technicians, Industrial Production Trades, Marketing/Sales, Mechanical/Craftsmanship Trades, Personal Services, Protective Services, Science/Engineering Technicians, Transportation/Equipment Operators.
Administration: Group.
Price Data, 1990: $.50 per folder/questionnaire; $89.95 per microcomputer software package (Apple or IBM).
Time: (20-25) minutes.
Authors: Robert Kauk and Robert Robinett.
Publisher: CFKR Career Materials, Inc.
Cross References: For reviews by Albert M. Bugaj and Del Eberhardt, see 12:411.

[2823]

Vocabulary Test: National Achievement Tests.

Purpose: Measures the student's vocabulary and judgment in the choice of effective words.
Population: Grades 3-8, 7-12.
Publication Dates: 1939-1957.
Scores: Total score only.
Administration: Group.
Price Data, 1985: $3.50 per 25 tests (specify grade level); $4 per specimen set.
Time: (15) minutes.
Authors: Robert K. Speer and Samuel Smith.
Publisher: Psychometric Affiliates.
Cross References: For a review by Clifford Woody, see 3:168.

[2824]

Vocational Adaptation Rating Scales.

Purpose: "To measure maladaptive behavior that is likely to occur in a vocational setting for a mentally retarded worker."
Population: Ages 13-50 (mentally retarded individuals).
Publication Date: 1980.
Acronym: VARS.
Scores: Frequency and Severity scores in 7 areas: Verbal Manners, Communication Skills, Attendance and Punctuality, Interpersonal Behavior, Respect for Property and Rules and Regulations, Grooming and Personal Hygiene, Total.
Administration: Group.
Price Data, 1999: $55 per complete kit; $26.50 per rating booklet and 25 profile forms; $32 per manual (31 pages).
Time: (30-40) minutes.
Authors: Robert G. Malgady, Peter R. Barcher, John Davis (test), and George Towner (test).
Publisher: Western Psychological Services.
Cross References: For a review by Michael Ryan, see 9:1334.

[2825]

The Vocational Apperception Test: Advanced Form.

Purpose: Designed as "a test of vocational interests and attitudes, based on interpretation of fantasy material elicited by sets of cards."
Population: College.
Publication Date: 1949.
Acronym: VAT:ADV.
Administration: Individual.
Price Data: Price data available from publisher for set of plates and manual (8 pages).
Time: (25-40) minutes.
Authors: Robert B. Ammons, Margaret N. Butler, and Sam A. Herzig.
Publisher: Psychological Test Specialists.

a) [FORM FOR MEN].
Scores: Preferences in 8 areas: Teacher, Executive or Office Worker, Doctor, Lawyer, Engineer, Personnel or Social Worker, Salesman, Laboratory Technician.

b) [FORM FOR WOMEN].
Scores: Preferences in 10 areas: Laboratory Technician, Dietician, Buyer, Nurse, Teacher, Artist, Secretary, Social Worker, Mother, Housewife.

Cross References: See P:492 (3 references); for reviews by Benjamin Balinsky and William E. Henry and an excerpted review by George S. Rhodes, see 4:146 (1 reference).

[2826]

Vocational Assessment and Curriculum Guide.

Purpose: "Designed to assess and identify skill deficits in terms of competitive employment expectations; to prescribe training goals designed to reduce identified deficits; to evaluate program effectiveness by reassessing the worker after training."
Population: Mentally retarded employees.
Publication Dates: 1982–1993.
Acronym: VACG.
Scores, 10: Attendance/Endurance, Independence, Production, Learning, Behavior, Communication Skills, Social Skills, Grooming/Eating, Reading/Writing, Math.
Administration: Group.
Price Data, 1994: $12 per complete kit including manual (5 pages), 10 test booklets, curriculum guides, and summary profile sheets; $8 per set of 10 extra forms.
Time: (15–20) minutes.
Authors: Frank R. Rusch, Richard P. Schutz, Dennis E. Mithaug, Jeffrey E. Stewart, and Deanna K. Mar.
Publisher: Exceptional Education.
Cross References: For reviews by Hinsdale Bernard and Gerald R. Schneck, see 13:356; see also T4:2898 (1 reference).

[2827]

Vocational Behavior Checklist.

Purpose: Checklist of "vocational skills ... designed for vocational training and on-the-job training programs."
Population: Vocational rehabilitation clients.
Publication Date: 1978.
Acronym: VBC.
Scores: 7 areas: Pre-Vocational Skills, Job-Seeking Skills, Interview Skills, Job-Related Skills, Work Performance Skills, On-the-Job Social Skills, Union-Financial-Security Skills.
Administration: Individual.
Price Data, 1988: $8 per test and manual.
Time: Time varies depending on task being completed.
Comments: Criterion-referenced.
Authors: Richard T. Walls, Thomas Zane, and Thomas J. Werner.
Publisher: West Virginia Rehabilitation Research and Training Center.
Cross References: For reviews by Samuel Juni and Ronald Baumanis and Robert M. McIntyre, see 9:1335.

TEST REFERENCE

1. Livneh, H. (1988). Assessing outcome criteria in rehabilitation: A multicomponent approach. *Rehabilitation Counseling Bulletin, 32,* 72–94.

[2828]

Vocational Decision-Making Interview—Revised.

Purpose: Constructed as a structured interview process to assist persons who have disabilities in making vocational decisions.
Population: Disabled individuals who need to make vocational decisions.
Publication Date: 1993.
Acronym: VDMI-R.
Scores, 4: Decision-Making Readiness, Employment Readiness, Self-Appraisal, Total.
Administration: Individual.
Price Data: Available from publisher.
Time: (20–40) minutes.
Comments: Structured interview administered by vocational rehabilitation workers.
Authors: Thomas Czerlinsky and Shirley K. Chandler.
Publisher: JIST Works, Inc.

[2829]

Vocational Interest and Sophistication Assessment.

Purpose: Constructed "to determine the interest pattern and knowledge mildly retarded adolescents and young adults have for selected job categories."
Population: Retarded adolescents and young adults.
Publication Dates: 1967-1968.
Acronym: VISA.
Administration: Individual.
Price Data: Available from publisher.
Time: (30) minutes.
Authors: Joseph J. Parnicky, Harris Kahn, and Arthur D. Burdett.
Publisher: Ohio State University, Nisonger Center [No reply from publisher; status unknown].

a) MALE FORM.
Scores, 14: Knowledge and Interest scores in each of 7 job areas: Garage, Laundry, Food Service, Maintenance, Farm/Grounds, Materials Handling, Industry.

b) FEMALE FORM.
Scores, 8: Knowledge and Interest scores in each of 4 job areas: Business/Clerical, Housekeeping, Food Service, Laundry/Serving.

Cross References: For reviews by Esther E. Diamond and George Domino, see 8:1024 (3 references); see also T2:2217 (1 reference) and 7:1039 (2 references).

[2830]

Vocational Interest, Experience, and Skill Assessment.

Purpose: "Designed to stimulate and facilitate self/career exploration on the part of persons in the early

stages of educational and vocational planning or replanning."
Population: Grades 8-10, 11-adults.
Publication Dates: 1976-1984.
Acronym: VIESA.
Scores: Scores for the Interest, Experience, and Skill inventories are reported for basic work tasks: Data, Ideas, People, and Things.
Administration: Group.
Levels, 2: 1, 2.
Price Data: Available from publisher including user's handbook ('84, 61 pages).
Time: Untimed.
Comments: Self-scored inventory of career-related interests, experiences, skills, and values with supporting materials for counselors; scores for three inventories are integrated via the World-of-Work Map, an extension of John Holland's hexagon.
Author: ACT, Inc.
Publisher: ACT, Inc.
Cross References: For a review by Charles J. Krauskopf of an earlier edition, see 8:1025.

[2831]

Vocational Interest, Experience and Skill Assessment (VIESA), 2nd Canadian Edition.

Purpose: Designed to stimulate career exploration.
Population: Grades 8-10, 11-adults.
Publication Date: 1985–1992.
Acronym: VIESA, 2nd Canadian Edition.
Scores: Scores for Interests, Skills, and Experiences in 4 areas: People, Data, Things, Ideas.
Administration: Group or individual.
Levels, 2: 1, 2.
Price Data, 1997: $49.50 per 25 guide books and job family charts (specify level); $25 per examination kit level 1 & 2; $24.95 per user's handbook.
Time: (40-45) minutes.
Comments: Self-scored inventory of career-related interests, experiences, skills and values, with supporting materials for counselors; adapted from VIESA, U.S. Edition.
Author: ACT Career Planning Services.
Publisher: ITP Nelson [Canada].
Cross References: For reviews by David J. Bateson and Brenda H. Loyd; see 12:409; for information for VIESA, 2nd Edition, see 9:1338; for a review by Charles J. Krauskopf of an earlier edition, see 8:1025.

[2832]

Vocational Interest Inventory and Exploration Survey.

Purpose: Designed to "assess a student's interest in school based training programs" and provide "information about the training area."
Population: Vocational education students.
Publication Date: 1991.
Scores: 15 vocational training interest areas: Auto Mechanics, Business and Office, Construction, Cosmetology, Drafting, Electromechanics, Electronics, Family and Consumer Science, Food Service, Graphic Arts, Health Services, Horticulture/Agriculture, Marketing, Metals, Technology Education, Home Economics, Technology Education.
Administration: Individual or group.
Price Data, 1991: $495 per set.
Time: (15-20) minutes.
Authors: Nancy L. Scott and Charles Gilbreath.
Publisher: Piney Mountain Press, Inc.
Cross References: For reviews by Larry Cochran and Kevin R. Murphy, see 12:408.

[2833]

Vocational Interest Inventory—Revised.

Purpose: "Measures the relative strength of an individual's interest in eight occupational areas."
Population: High school juniors and seniors.
Publication Dates: 1981–1993.
Acronym: VII-R.
Scores, 8: Service, Business Contact, Organization, Technical, Outdoor, Science, General Culture, Arts and Entertainment.
Administration: Group.
Price Data, 1999: $69.50 per complete kit including manual ('93, 63 pages), 4 test reports and mail-in answer sheets; $40 per manual; $9.80 (or less) per mail-in answer sheet and test report; $155 or less per VII-R disk (IBM; 25 uses); $15 per 100 answer sheets for use with VII-R disk.
Time: (20–25) minutes.
Comments: Based on Ann Roe's occupational classifications.
Author: Patricia W. Lunneborg.
Publisher: Western Psychological Services.
Cross References: For reviews by David O. Herman and Joseph G. Law, Jr., see 13:357 (2 references); for reviews by Jo-Ida Hansen and Richard W. Johnson of an earlier edition, see 9:1339 (2 references).

[2834]

Vocational Opinion Index.

Purpose: Constructed to measure "an individual's attitudes, perceptions and motivations that impact on his/her ability to get and/or hold a job."
Population: Disadvantaged trainees in vocational skills programs.
Publication Dates: 1973-1976.
Acronym: VOI.
Scores, 13: Attractions to Work (Overall, Benefits to Children, Benefits to Worker, Better Life Style, Independence), Losses Associated with Work (Overall,

Personal Freedom, Time for Family), Barriers to Employment (Medical, Child Care and Family, New Situation and People, Ability to Get and Hold a Job, Transportation).
Administration: Group.
Forms, 2: A, B.
Price Data: Available from publisher.
Foreign Language Edition: Spanish edition available.
Time: (20-40) minutes.
Author: Associates for Research in Behavior, Inc.
Publisher: ARBOR, Inc.

[2835]
Vocational Preference Inventory, 1985 Edition.

Purpose: "To assess personality ... also useful for assessing vocational interests."
Population: High school and college and adults.
Publication Dates: 1953-1985.
Acronym: VPI.
Scores: 11 scales: Realistic, Investigative, Social, Conventional, Enterprising, Artistic, Self-Control, Masculinity-Femininity, Status, Infrequency, Acquiescence.
Administration: Individual or group.
Price Data: Price information available from publisher for complete kit including 25 test booklets, scoring key, 50 answer sheets, 50 profiles, and manual ('85, 36 pages); price information for computer version also available from publisher.
Time: (15-30) minutes.
Author: John L. Holland.
Publisher: Psychological Assessment Resources, Inc.
Cross References: See T4:2910 (9 references); for reviews by John W. Shepard and Nicholas A. Vacc, see 10:382 (17 references); for reviews by James B. Rounds and Nicholas A. Vacc and James Pickering of an earlier edition, see 9:1342 (19 references); see also T3:2581 (45 references); for an excerpted review by W. Bruce Walsh of an earlier edition, see 8:1028 (175 references); see also T2:1430 (48 references); for reviews by Joseph A. Johnston and Paul R. Lohnes, see 7:157 (39 references); see also P:283 (31 references); for reviews by Robert L. French and H. Bradley Sagen of an earlier edition, see 6:115 (13 references).

TEST REFERENCES

1. Martin, D. C., & Bartol, K. M. (1986). Holland's Vocational Preference Inventory and the Myers-Briggs Type Indicator as predictors of vocational choice among master's in business administration. *Journal of Vocational Behavior, 29,* 51-65.
2. Walsh, W. B., Bingham, R. P., & Sheffey, M. A. (1986). Holland's theory and college educated working Black men and women. *Journal of Vocational Behavior, 29,* 194-200.
3. Johnson, J. A. (1987). Influence of adolescent social crowds on the development of vocational identity. *Journal of Vocational Behavior, 31,* 182-199.
4. Monahan, C. J. (1987). Construct validation of a modified differentiation index. *Journal of Vocational Behavior, 30,* 217-226.
5. Miller, M. J., Springer, T. P., & Wells, D. (1988). Which occupational environments do black youths prefer? Extending Holland's typology. *The School Counselor, 36,* 103–106.
6. Walsh, W. B., & Huston, R. E. (1988). Traditional female occupations and Holland's theory for employed men and women. *Journal of Vocational Behavior, 32,* 358-365.
7. Jones, L. K., Gorman, S., & Schroeder, C. G. (1989). A comparison between the SDS and the Career Key among career undecided college students. *Career Development Quarterly, 37,* 334-344.
8. Hesketh, B., Durant, C., & Pryor, R. (1990). Career compromise: A test of Gottfredson's (1981) theory using a policy-capturing procedure. *Journal of Vocational Behavior, 36,* 97-108.
9. Nordvik, H. (1990). Work activity and career goals in Holland's and Schein's theories of vocational personalities and career anchors. *Journal of Vocational Behavior, 38,* 165-178.
10. Wiggins, J. D., Evans, G., & Martin, F. (1990). Counselor self-esteem related to personal and demographic values. *The School Counselor, 37,* 213–218.
11. Leong, F. T. L. (1991). Career development attributes and occupational values of Asian American and White American college students. *Career Development Quarterly, 39,* 221-230.
12. Bizot, E. B., & Goldman, S. H. (1993). Prediction of satisfactoriness and satisfaction: An 8-year follow up. *Journal of Vocational Behavior, 43,* 19-29.
13. Jones, L. K. (1993). Two career guidance instruments: Their helpfulness to students and effect on students' career exploration. *The School Counselor, 40,* 191–200.
14. Luzzo, D. A. (1993). A multi-trait, multi-method analysis of three career development measures. *Career Development Quarterly, 41,* 367-374.
15. Miller, M. J., Knippers, J. A., Burley, K., & Tobacyk, J. J. (1993). Relationship between sex-role orientation and Holland's typology: Implications for career counselors. *College Student Journal, 27,* 356-361.
16. Rounds, J., & Tracey, T. J. (1993). Prediger's dimensional representation of Holland's RIASEC circumplex. *Journal of Applied Psychology, 78,* 875-890.
17. Randolph, D. L., & Waldrop, D. G. (1995). Efficacy of the Vocational Preference Inventory as a discriminator of attachment styles. *Psychological Reports, 76,* 1260–1262.
18. Tracey, T. J. G., & Rounds, J. (1995). The arbitrary nature of Holland's RIASEC types: A concentric-circles structure. *Journal of Counseling Psychology, 42,* 431–439.
19. Upperman, P. J., & Church, A. T. (1995). Investigating Holland's typology theory with Army occupational specialties. *Journal of Vocational Behavior, 47,* 61–75.
20. Mobley, M., & Slaney, R. B. (1996). Holland's theory: its relevance for lesbian women and gay men. *Journal of Vocational Behavior, 48,* 125–135.
21. Nordick, H. (1996). Relationships between Holland's vocational typology, Schein's career anchors and Myers-Briggs' types. *Journal of Occupational and Organizational Psychology, 69,* 263–275.
22. Ryan, J. M., Tracey, J. G., & Rounds, J. (1996). Generalizability of Holland's structure of vocational interests across ethnicity, gender, and socioeconomic status. *Journal of Counseling Psychology, 43,* 330–337.
23. Sabers, D. L. (1996). By their tests we will know them. *Language, Speech, and Hearing Services in Schools, 27,* 102–108.
24. Tracey, T. J. G., & Rounds, J. (1996). Contributions of the spherical representation of vocational interests. *Journal of Vocational Behavior, 48,* 85–95.
25. Tracey, T. J. G., & Rounds, J. (1996). The spherical representation of vocational interests. *Journal of Vocational Behavior, 48,* 3–41.
26. Hanson, W. E., Claiborn, C. D., & Kerr, B. (1997). Differential effects of two test-interpretation styles in counseling: A field study. *Journal of Counseling Psychology, 44,* 400–405.
27. Kahn, J. H., & Scott, N. A. (1997). Predictors of research productivity and science-related career goals among counseling psychology doctoral students. *The Counseling Psychologist, 25,* 38–67.
28. Meir, E. I., Rubin, A., Temple, R., & Osipow, S. H. (1997). Examination of interest inventories based on Roe's classification. *Career Development Quarterly, 46,* 48–61.

[2836]
Vocational Research Interest Inventory.

Purpose: To provide accurate and meaningful information about the occupational interests of students and clients in vocational counseling, and rehabilitation and job training program participants.
Population: High school and adults.
Publication Date: 1985.
Acronym: VRII.
Scores, 12: Artistic, Scientific, Plants/Animals, Protective, Mechanical, Industrial, Business Detail, Selling, Accommodating, Humanitarian, Lead/Influence, Physical Performing.
Administration: Group.
Price Data, 1989: $17.25 or less per package including 25 test forms; $12.50 per specimen kit in-

cluding 5 test forms and manual (36 pages); $295 per Apple or IBM software package.
Foreign Language Edition: Spanish edition (entitled Inventario Investigativo de Interés Vocacional) available.
Time: (15-20) minutes.
Comments: Uses idiographic Individual Profile Analysis to determine relatively high interest areas.
Authors: Howard Dansky, Jeffrey A. Harris, and Thomas W. Gannaway.
Publisher: Vocational Research Institute [No reply from publisher; status unknown].
Cross References: For a review by Joseph G. Law, Jr., see 11:458.

[2837]

A Voice Assessment Protocol for Children and Adults.

Purpose: "Assesses five parameters of the voice: pitch, loudness, quality, breath features, and rate/rhythm."
Population: Children and adults.
Publication Date: 1987.
Scores: 5 assessments: Pitch, Loudness, Quality, Breath Features, Rate/Rhythm.
Administration: Individual.
Price Data, 1999: $54 per complete kit including 25 protocols, audiocassette, and manual (24 pages); $24 per 25 protocols; $14 per audiocassette; $19 per manual.
Time: Administration time not reported.
Author: Rebekah H. Pindzola.
Publisher: PRO-ED.
Cross References: For a review by Maynard D. Filter, see 11:459.

TEST REFERENCE

1. Pindzola, R. H., Jenkins, M. M., & Lokken, K. J. (1989). Speaking rates of young children. *Language, Speech, and Hearing Services in Schools, 20,* 133–138.

[2838]

Vulpe Assessment Battery—Revised

Purpose: Designed as "a comprehensive, process-oriented, criterion-referenced assessment that emphasizes children's functional abilities."
Population: Children functioning between full term birth to six years of age.
Publication Date: 1994.
Acronym: VAB-R.
Scores: 8 scales: Basic Senses and Functions, Gross Motor, Fine Motor, Language, Cognitive Processes and Specific Concepts, Adaptive Behaviors, Activities of Daily Living, Environmental Assessment.
Administration: Individual or group.
Price Data, 1994: $65 per complete kit including manual ('94, 480 pages) and 50 record sheets; $12 per 50 record sheets.
Time: Administration time not reported.
Comments: Ratings by person familiar with the child.
Author: Shirley German Vulpe.
Publisher: Slosson Educational Publications, Inc.

[2839]

Wahler Physical Symptoms Inventory.

Purpose: Designed to assist in distinguishing patients with real physical ailments from those with imagined ones.
Population: Adults.
Publication Date: 1973.
Acronym: WPSI.
Scores: Total score only.
Administration: Group.
Price Data, 1999: $45 per complete kit; $22.50 per 100 inventory sheets; $26 per manual (14 pages).
Time: (5-10) minutes.
Author: H. J. Wahler.
Publisher: Western Psychological Services.
Cross References: See T4:2914 (3 references) and T2:1432 (1 reference).

TEST REFERENCES

1. Armistead, L., McCombs, A., Forehand, R., Wierson, M., Long, N., & Fauber, R. (1990). Coping with divorce: A study of young adolescents. *Journal of Clinical Child Psychology, 19,* 79–84.
2. Jackson, J. L., Calhoun, K. S., Amick, A. E., Maddever, H. M., & Habif, V. L. (1990). Young adult women who report childhood intrafamilial sexual abuse: Subsequent adjustment. *Archives of Sexual Behavior, 19,* 211-221.
3. Carstensen, L. L., & Turk-Charles, S. (1994). The salience of emotion across the adult life span. *Psychology and Aging, 9,* 259-264.
4. Faust, J., & Forehand, R. (1994). Adolescents' physical complaints as a function of anxiety due to familial and peer stress: A causal model. *Journal of Anxiety Disorders, 8,* 139-153.
5. Kalichman, S. C., Sikkema, K. J., & Somlai, A. (1995). Assessing persons with human immunodeficiency virus (HIV) infection using the Beck Depression Inventory: Disease processes and other potential confounds. *Journal of Personality Assessment, 64,* 86-100.
6. Wright, L., Nielsen, B. A., Abbanto, K. R., Jackson, T., Lancaster, C., & Son, J. (1995). The relationship of various measures of time urgency to indices of physical health. *Journal of Clinical Psychology, 51,* 610–614.
7. Baker-Pierce, L. A., & Persinger, M. A. (1996). Weak, but complex pulsed magnetic fields may reduce depression following traumatic brain injury. *Perceptual and Motor Skills, 83,* 491–498.
8. Bowman, B. J. (1996). Cross-cultural validation of Antonovsky's Sense of Coherence Scale. *Journal of Clinical Psychology, 52,* 547–549.
9. Moseley, T. H., Jr., Payne, T. J. Plaud, J. J., Johnson, C. A., Wittrock, D. A., Seville, J. L., Penzien, D. B., & Rodriguez, G. (1996). Psychometric properties of the Weekly Stress Inventory (WSI): Extension to a patient sample with coronary heart disease. *Journal of Behavioral Medicine, 19,* 273–287.

[2840]

WAIS-R NI.

Purpose: Constructed as a "process approach to neuropsychological assessment of cognitive functions."
Population: Ages 16–74.
Publication Date: 1991.
Scores, 14: Verbal (Information, Comprehension, Arithmetic, Similarities, Digit Span, Vocabulary, Total), Performance (Digit Symbol, Picture Completion, Block Design, Picture Arrangement, Object Assembly, Total), Total.
Administration: Individual.
Price Data, 1999: $418 per complete kit including manual (153 pages), stimulus booklet, sentence ar-

rangement booklet, 25 response booklets, 25 record forms, 3 puzzles/boxes, spatial span board, object assembly layout shield, and 3 Koh's blocks; $1,050 per combination kit including WAIS-R NI complete kit, WAIS-R complete set and attaché case; $23.50 per 25 digit symbol response booklets; $84.50 per 25 record forms.
Time: Administration time varies by number of supplemental subtests administered.
Comments: It is necessary to have the Wechsler Adult Intelligence Scale—Revised (WAIS-R; T4:2937) complete set in order to administer WAIS-R NI.
Authors: Edith Kaplan, Deborah Fein, Robin Morris, and Dean C. Delis.
Publisher: The Psychological Corporation.

[2841]

Waksman Social Skills Rating Scale.

Purpose: "Developed to assist psychologists, educators, and other clinicians to identify specific and clinically important social skill deficits in children and adolescents."
Population: Grades K-12.
Publication Dates: 1983-1992.
Acronym: WSSRS.
Scores, 3: Aggressive, Passive, Total.
Administration: Individual.
Price Data: Price information available from publisher for complete kit including 50 each of male and female forms, and manual ('92, 10 pages).
Time: Administration time not reported.
Author: Steven A. Waksman.
Publisher: Psychological Assessment Resources, Inc.
Cross References: See T4:2915 (2 references); for reviews by Harold R. Keller and Ellen McGinnis, see 10:383.

TEST REFERENCE

1. Demaray, M. K., Ruffalo, S. L., Carlson, J., Busse, R. T., Olson, A. E., Mcmanus, S. M., & Leventhal, A. (1995). Social skills assessment: A comparative evaluation of six published rating scales. *School Psychology Review, 24,* 648–671.

[2842]

Walden CICS/VS Command Level Proficiency Test.

Purpose: Used to assess the technical capabilities of candidates to effectively use CICS/VS commands.
Population: Applicants for computer training or employment.
Publication Date: 1981.
Scores: Total score only.
Administration: Group.
Price Data, 1999: $40 per candidate.
Time: 35(40) minutes.
Comments: Detailed evaluation report provided on each candidate; test previously listed as Wolfe-Winrow CICS/VS Command Level Proficiency Test.
Author: Bruce A. Winrow.
Publisher: Walden Personnel Performance, Inc.

[2843]

Walden DOS JCL (VS, VSE) Proficiency Test.

Purpose: "Used for assessing the technical capabilities of candidates to effectively use Job Control Language."
Population: Applicants for computer training or employment.
Publication Date: 1982.
Scores: Total score only.
Administration: Group.
Price Data, 1999: $89 per candidate.
Time: 35(40) minutes.
Comments: Detailed evaluation report provided on each candidate; test previously listed as Wolfe-Winrow DOS JCL (VS, VSE) Proficiency Test.
Author: Bruce A. Winrow.
Publisher: Walden Personnel Performance, Inc.

[2844]

Walden OS/JCL Proficiency Test.

Purpose: Designed to appraise proficiency on OS JCL operating systems.
Population: Applicants for computer training or employment.
Publication Date: 1981.
Scores: Total score only.
Administration: Group.
Price Data, 1999: $140 per candidate.
Time: 35(40) minutes.
Comments: Detailed evaluation report provided on each candidate; test previously listed as Wolfe-Winrow OS JCL Proficiency Test.
Author: Bruce A. Winrow.
Publisher: Walden Personnel Performance, Inc.

[2845]

Walden Structured Analysis and Design Concepts Proficiency Test.

Purpose: "Evaluates candidate's knowledge of structured analysis and design methodology, as well as commonly used tools and techniques."
Population: Candidates for EDP systems analysts/designers.
Publication Date: 1983.
Administration: Group.
Price Data, 1999: $140 per candidate.
Time: 35(45) minutes.
Comments: Detailed evaluation report provided on each candidate; test previously listed as Wolfe-Winrow Structured Analysis and Design Concepts Proficiency Test.

Author: Bruce A. Winrow.
Publisher: Walden Personnel Performance, Inc.
Cross References: For reviews by David O. Anderson and Cynthia Ann Druva-Roush, see 11:474.

[2846]

Walden Structured COBOL Proficiency Test.

Purpose: "Used for assessing the technical capabilities of candidates in their ability to effectively use the COBOL programming language."
Population: Applicants for computer training or employment.
Publication Date: 1982.
Scores: Total score only.
Administration: Group.
Price Data, 1999: $140 per candidate.
Time: 35(40) minutes.
Comments: Detailed report provided on each candidate; test previously listed as Wolfe-Winrow Structured COBOL Proficiency Test.
Author: Bruce A. Winrow.
Publisher: Walden Personnel Performance, Inc.

[2847]

Walden TSO/SPF Proficiency Test.

Purpose: "Used for assessing the technical capabilities of candidates in their ability to effectively use the TSO/SPF facility."
Population: Applicants for computer training or employment.
Publication Date: 1982.
Scores: Total score only.
Administration: Group.
Price Data, 1999: $140 per candidate.
Time: 30(35) minutes.
Comments: Detailed evaluation report provided on each candidate; test previously listed as Wolfe-Winrow TSO/SPF Proficiency Test.
Author: Bruce A. Winrow.
Publisher: Walden Personnel Performance, Inc.

[2848]

Walker Problem Behavior Identification Checklist.

Purpose: Tool to assist the elementary teacher in "identifying children with behavior problems who should be referred for further evaluation."
Population: Preschool to grade 6.
Publication Dates: 1970-1983.
Acronym: WPBIC.
Scores, 6: Acting Out, Withdrawal, Distractibility, Disturbed Peer Relations, Immaturity, Total.
Administration: Group.
Forms, 2: Male, Female.
Price Data, 1999: $75 per complete kit including 200 checklists and profiles (100 each of Male and Female Forms) and manual ('83, 19 pages); $27.50 or less per 100 pads of checklist and profile (specify Male or Female form); $26.50 per manual.
Time: (2-5) minutes.
Author: Hill M. Walker.
Publisher: Western Psychological Services.
Cross References: See T4:2923 (18 references); for a review by F. Charles Mace, see 9:1345 (5 references); see also T3:2585 (17 references) and 7:159 (1 reference).

TEST REFERENCES

1. Baum, S., & Owen, S. V. (1988). High ability/learning disabled students: How are they different? *Gifted Child Quarterly, 32,* 321–326.
2. Wood, J. I., & Lewis, G. J. (1990). The coparental relationship of divorced spouses: Its effect on children's school adjustment. *Journal of Divorce & Remarriage, 14*(1), 81-95.
3. Little, S. S. (1993). Nonverbal learning disabilities and socioemotional functioning: A review of recent literature. *Journal of Learning Disabilities, 26,* 653–665.

[2849]

W-APT Programming Aptitude Test.

Purpose: To evaluate the aptitude and potential for computer programming work at all levels of experience.
Population: Programmers and general population.
Publication Date: 1984.
Acronym: W-APT.
Scores: Total score only.
Administration: Group.
Price Data, 1999: $180 per candidate.
Time: (60) minutes.
Comments: Detailed report provided on each candidate.
Author: Jack M. Wolfe.
Publisher: Rose Wolfe [Canada].

[2850]

Ward Atmosphere Scale (Third Edition).

Purpose: Designed to evaluate treatment program social climates in health care settings.
Population: Patients and staff members.
Publication Dates: 1974–1996.
Acronym: WAS.
Scores, 10: Involvement, Support, Spontaneity, Autonomy, Practical Orientation, Personal Problems Orientation, Anger and Aggression, Order and Organization, Program Clarity, Staff Control.
Administration: Group.
Forms, 3: Real, Ideal, Expectations.
Price Data, 1998: $100 per permission set including sampler set plus permission to reproduce up to 200 copies of the instrument; $25 per sampler set including manual ('96, 73 pages), questionnaire/answer sheet, and scoring directions.

Foreign Language Editions: Translations available in Danish, Dutch, Finnish, French, German, Hebrew, Italian, Norwegian, Spanish, and Swedish.
Time: Administration time not reported.
Comments: Used to describe, plan for, and monitor change or improvements in treatment programs by examining patient and staff social climate perceptions.
Author: Rudolph H. Moos.
Publisher: Mind Garden, Inc.
Cross References: See T4:2925 (17 references) and T3:2587 (16 references); for a review by Earl S. Taulbee of an earlier edition, see 8:706 (31 references). For a review of the Social Climate Scales, see 8:681.

TEST REFERENCES

1. Squier, R. W. (1994). The relationship between ward atmosphere and staff attitude to treatment in psychiatric in-patient units. *British Journal of Medical Psychology, 67,* 319–331.
2. Haller, E., McNiel, D. E., & Binder, R. L. (1996). Impact of a smoking ban on a locked psychiatric unit. *Journal of Clinical Psychiatry, 57,* 329–336.
3. Hansen, J. T., & Slevin, C. (1996). The implementation of therapeutic community principles in acute care psychiatric hospital settings: An empirical analysis and recommendations to clinicians. *Journal of Clinical Psychology, 52,* 673–678.

[2851]

Warehouse/Plant Worker Staff Selector.

Purpose: To assess the intellectual skills needed for the position of plant worker.
Population: Applicants for plant work.
Publication Date: 1991.
Acronym: PLANT.
Scores: Total score only.
Administration: Group.
Price Data, 1999: $495 per candidate.
Time: (60) minutes.
Comments: Detailed evaluation report provided on each candidate.
Authors: Walden Personnel Performance, Inc.
Publisher: Walden Personnel Performance, Inc. [Canada].

[2852]

Washer Visual Acuity Screening Technique.

Purpose: To assess visual acuity for near and far vision.
Population: Mental ages 2-6 and over.
Publication Date: 1984.
Acronym: WVAST.
Scores, 6: Farpoint (Both Eyes, Right Eye, Left Eye), Nearpoint (Both Eyes, Right Eye, Left Eye).
Administration: Individual.
Price Data, 1993: $70 per complete set, including manual (15 pages), 20 screening records, symbol cards, stimulus cards, set of equipment; $11 per additional manual; $8.95 per 20 screening records; $59.50 per set of equipment; $20 per specimen set.
Time: Administration time not reported.
Comments: Criterion-referenced scores.
Author: Rhonda Wiczer Washer.
Publisher: Scholastic Testing Service, Inc.

[2853]

The Watkins-Farnum Performance Scale: A Standardized Achievement Test for All Band Instruments.

Purpose: Designed to measure performance and progress on a musical instrument.
Population: Music students.
Publication Dates: 1942-1962.
Scores: Total score only.
Administration: Individual.
Forms, 2: A, B.
Price Data, 1989: $12.95 per Farnum String Scale pad; $6 per Farnum String Scale book; $7 per Watkins Performance pad (A or B); $9 per Watkins Performance book (A or B).
Time: [20-30] minutes.
Authors: John G. Watkins and Stephen E. Farnum.
Publisher: Hal Leonard Publishing Corporation.
Cross References: See T2:216 (4 references); for a review by Herbert D. Wing, see 5:253 (2 references); for related reviews, see 3:1228 (4 excerpts).

[2854]

Watson-Barker Listening Test.

Purpose: To measure adult interpersonal listening abilities.
Population: Adults in business, professions, and college.
Publication Dates: 1984-1994.
Scores, 6: Evaluating Message Content, Understanding Meaning in Conversations, Understanding and Remembering Information in Lectures, Evaluating Emotional Meanings in Messages, Following Instructions and Directions, Total.
Administration: Group.
Forms, 3: A (pre-test), B (post-test), Short Form (for demonstration and listening awareness).
Price Data, 1993: $249.95 per test package (A and B) including 20 test booklets, 20 self-scoring answer sheets, 2 video cassettes, and facilitator's guide (32 pages) for both forms; $179.95 per test package (A or B) including all above listed materials for either Form A or Form B.
Time: (40) minutes.
Comments: Administered by video tape.
Authors: Kittie W. Watson and Larry L. Barker with Charles Roberts and Patrice Johnson.
Publisher: Jossey-Bass/Pfeiffer.
Cross References: For a review by James R. Clopton, see 10:384.

[2855]

Watson-Barker Listening Test—High School Version.

Purpose: "Designed to assess overall listening ability."
Population: Grades 7-12.
Publication Dates: 1985-1991.
Acronym: HS-WBLT.
Scores, 6: Evaluating Message Content, Understanding Meaning in Conversations, Understanding and Remembering Information in Lectures, Evaluating Emotional Meanings in Messages, Following Instructions and Directions, Total.
Administration: Group.
Forms, 2: A (pre-test) and B (post-test).
Price Data, 1994: $229.95 per Form A and B package (including video tape, facilitator's guide ['91, 42 pages], and 20 answer sheets per group [A & B]).
Time: 40 minutes.
Comments: May be self-scored for awareness training; VHS video tape player and 17-inch (minimum size) color TV monitor needed; high school version of Watson-Barker Listening Test (2854).
Authors: Kittie W. Watson, Larry L. Barker, and Charles V. Roberts.
Publisher: SPECTRA Incorporated, Publishers.
Cross References: For reviews by Michael R. Harwell and by Carol Kehr Tittle and Deborah Hecht, see 11:461; for reviews by James R. Clopton and Joseph P. Stokes of the adult version, see 10:384.

[2856]

Watson-Glaser Critical Thinking Appraisal.

Purpose: Constructed to assess critical thinking abilities related to reading comprehension.
Population: Grades 9-12 and college and adults.
Publication Dates: 1942-1980.
Acronym: WGCTA.
Scores, 6: Inference, Recognition of Assumptions, Deduction, Interpretation, Evaluation of Arguments, Total.
Administration: Group or individual.
Forms, 2: A, B.
Price Data, 1999: $111.25 per 25 test booklets including manual ('80, 17 pages) (select form); $24 per set of hand scoring keys (select form); $6 per class record; $32 per manual; $51.25 per examination kit including Form A and B test booklets, answer document, and manual.
Time: (40–60) minutes.
Comments: Revision of Form YM and ZM.
Authors: Goodwin Watson and Edward M. Glaser.
Cross References: See T4:2933 (5 references); for reviews by Allen Berger and Gerald C. Helmstadter, see 9:1347 (4 references); see also T3:2594 (15 references), 8:822 (49 references), and T2:1775 (35 references); for excerpted reviews by John O. Crites and G. C. Helmstadtler, see 7:783 (74 references); see also 6:867 (24 references); ffor reviews by Walker H. Hill and Carl I. Hovland of an earlier edition, see 5:700 (8 references); for a review by Robert H. Thouless and an excerpted review by Harold P. Fawcett, see 3:544 (3 references).

TEST REFERENCES

1. Lowman, R. L., & Williams, R. E. (1987). Validity of self-ratings of abilities and competence. *Journal of Vocational Behavior, 31,* 1-13.
2. Feldt, R. C. (1989). Reading comprehension and critical thinking as predictors of course performance. *Perceptual and Motor Skills, 68,* 642.
3. Hill, O. W., Pettus, W. C., & Hedin, B. A. (1990). Three studies of factors affecting the attitudes of blacks and females toward the pursuit of science and science-related careers. *Journal of Research in Science Teaching, 27,* 289-314.
4. Bitner, B. L. (1991). Formal operational reasoning modes: Predictors of critical thinking abilities and grades assigned by teachers in science and mathematics for students in grades nine through twelve. *Journal of Research in Science Teaching, 28,* 265–274.
5. McMurray, M. A., Beisenherz, P., & Thompson, B. (1991). Reliability and concurrent validity of a measure of critical thinking skills in biology. *Journal of Research in Science Teaching, 28,* 183–192.
6. Reboy, L. M., & Semb, G. B. (1991). PSI and critical thinking: Compatibility or irreconcilable differences? *Teaching of Psychology, 18,* 212-214.
7. McCutcheon, L. E., Apperson, J. M., Hanson, E., & Wynn, V. (1992). Relationships among critical thinking skills, academic achievement, and misconceptions about psychology. *Psychological Reports, 71,* 635-639.
8. Stanovich, K. E. (1993). Dysrationalia: A new specific learning disability. *Journal of Learning Disabilities, 26,* 501–515.
9. White, W. F., & Burke, C. M. (1994). Teacher item behavior influenced by critical thinking and personal social determinants. *College Student Journal, 28,* 141-146.
10. Melamed, T. (1995). Career success: The moderating effect of gender. *Journal of Vocational Behavior, 47,* 35–60.
11. Gadzella, B. M., Ginter, D. W., Masten, W. G., & Guthrie, D. (1997). Predicting students as deep and shallow processors of information. *Perceptual and Motor Skills, 84,* 875–881.
12. Morgan, R. K., & Morgan, D. L. (1998). Critical thinking and belief in the paranormal. *College Student Journal, 32,* 135–139.
13. Witt, L. A. (1998). Enhancing organizational goal congruence: A solution to organizational politics. *Journal of Applied Psychology, 83,* 666–674.

[2857]

Watson-Glaser Critical Thinking Appraisal, Form S.

Purpose: Designed to help "select employees for any job requiring careful, analytical thinking."
Population: Adults with at least a ninth grade education.
Publication Date: 1994.
Acronym: WGCTA-S.
Scores: Composite score derived from following content areas: Inference, Recognition of Assumptions, Deduction, Interpretation, Evaluation of Arguments.
Administration: Group or individual.
Price Data, 1999: $57.25 per examination kit including Form S test booklet, answer document, and manual (87 pages); $90.50 per 25 test booklets including directions for administering; $34.25 per 25 scannable answer documents; $24 per key for hand scoring scannable answer documents; $44.50 per manual; $6 per Directions for Administering.
Time: (30–45) minutes.
Comments: Developed as a shorter version of the WGCTA Form A; Form S norms are developed from norms of original WGCTA (2856).

Authors: Goodwin B. Watson and Edward M. Glaser.
Publisher: The Psychological Corporation.
Cross References: For reviews by Kurt F. Geisinger and Stephen H. Ivens, see 13:358. For information on the original edition of the WGCTA, see T4:2933; for reviews by Allen Berger and Gerald C. Helmstadter, see 9:1347 (4 references); see also T3:2594 (15 references), 8:822 (49 references), and T2:1775 (35 references); for excerpted reviews by John O. Crites and G. C. Helmstadter, see 7:783 (74 references); see also 6:867 (24 references); for reviews by Walker H. Hill and Carl I. Hovland of an earlier edition, see 5:700 (8 references); for a review by Robert H. Thouless and an excerpted review by Harold P. Fawcett, see 3:544 (3 references).

TEST REFERENCE

1. Inlow, F. H., & Chovan, W. (1993). Another search for the effects of teaching thinking and problem solving skills on college students' performance. *Journal of Instructional Psychology, 20,* 215–223.

[2858]

Ways of Coping Questionnaire, Research Edition.

Purpose: "To identify the thoughts and actions an individual has used to cope with a specific stressful encounter."
Population: Adults.
Publication Date: 1988.
Scores, 8: Confrontive Coping, Distancing, Self-Controlling, Seeking Social Support, Accepting Responsibility, Escape-Avoidance, Planful Problem-Solving, Positive Reappraisal.
Administration: Group.
Price Data: Available from publisher.
Time: (10-15) minutes.
Comments: Self-administered.
Authors: Susan Folkman and Richard S. Lazarus.
Publisher: Mind Garden.
Cross References: See T4:2936 (25 references); for reviews by Judith C. Conger and Kathryn D. Hess, see 11:462 (16 references).

TEST REFERENCES

1. Felton, B. J., & Revenson, T. A. (1987). Age differences in coping with chronic illness. *Psychology and Aging, 2,* 164-170.
2. Folkman, S., Bernstein, L., & Lazarus, R. S. (1987). Stress processes and the misuse of drugs in older adults. *Psychology and Aging, 2,* 366-374.
3. Folkman, S., Lazarus, R. S., Pimley, A., & Novacek, J. (1987). Age differences in stress and coping processes. *Psychology and Aging, 2,* 171-184.
4. Labourie-Vief, G., Hakim-Larson, J., & Hobart, C. J. (1987). Age, ego level, and the life-span development of coping and defense processes. *Psychology and Aging, 2,* 286-293.
5. Stumpf, S. A., Brief, A. P., & Hartman, K. (1987). Self-efficacy expectations and coping with career-related events. *Journal of Vocational Behavior, 31,* 91-108.
6. Feeley, N., & Gottlieb, L. N. (1988). Parents' coping and communication following their infant's death. *Omega, 19,* 51–67.
7. Gass, K. A., & Chang, A. S. (1989). Appraisals of bereavement, coping, resources, and psychosocial health dysfunction in widows and widowers. *Nursing Research, 38,* 31–36.
8. Hilton, B. A. (1989). The relationship of uncertainty, control, commitment, and threat of recurrence to coping strategies used by women diagnosed with breast cancer. *Journal of Behavioral Medicine, 12,* 39-54.
9. Vitaliano, P. D., Maiuro, R. D., Russo, J., & Mitchell, E. S. (1989). Medical student distress: A longitudinal study. *The Journal of Nervous and Mental Disease, 177,* 70-76.
10. Borden, W., & Berlin, S. (1990). Gender, coping, and psychological well-being in spouses of older adults with chronic dementia. *American Journal of Orthopsychiatry, 60,* . 603–610.
11. Bruder-Mattson, S. F., & Hovanitz, C. A. (1990). Coping and attributional styles as predictors of depression. *Journal of Clinical Psychology, 46,* 557–565.
12. Buckelew, S. P., Baumstark, K. E., Frank, R. G., & Hewett, J. E. (1990). Adjustment following spinal cord injury. *Rehabilitation Psychology, 35,* 101–109.
13. DeMaio-Esteves, M. (1990). Mediators of daily stress and perceived health status in adolescent girls. *Nursing Research, 39,* 360–364.
14. Edwards, J. R., Baglioni, A. J., Jr., & Cooper, C. L. (1990). Stress, Type-A coping, and psychological and physical symptoms: A multi-sample test of alternative models. *Human Relations, 43,* 919–956.
15. Manne, S. L., & Zaitra, A. J. (1990). Couples coping with chronic illness: Women with rheumatoid arthritis and their healthy husbands. *Journal of Behavioral Medicine, 13,* 327-342.
16. Maxim, P. E., & Hunt, D. D. (1990). Appraisal and coping in the process of patient change during short-term psychotherapy. *The Journal of Nervous and Mental Disease, 178,* 235-241.
17. McCullough, J. P., Braith, J. A., Chapman, R. C., Kasnetz, M. D., Carr, K. F., Cones, J. H., Fielo, J., Shoemaker, O. S., & Roberts, W. C. (1990). Comparison of early and late onset dysthymia. *The Journal of Nervous and Mental Disease, 178,* 577-581.
18. McNaughton, M. E., Smith, L. W., Patterson, T. L., & Grant, I. (1990). Stress, social support, coping resources, and immune status in elderly women. *The Journal of Nervous and Mental Disease, 178,* 460-461.
19. Patterson, T. L., Smith, L. W., Grant, I., Clopton, P., Jospeho, S., & Yager, J. (1990). Internal vs. external determinants of coping responses to stressful life-events in the elderly. *British Journal of Medical Psychology, 63,* 149–160.
20. Smith, L. W., Patterson, T. L., & Grant, I. (1990). Avoidant coping predicts psychological disturbance in the elderly. *The Journal of Nervous and Mental Disease, 178,* 525-530.
21. Soloman, Z., Mikulincer, M., & Habershaim, N. (1990). Life-events, coping strategies, social resources, and somatic complaints among combat stress reaction casualties. *British Journal of Medical Psychology, 63,* 137–148.
22. Vitaliano, P. P., Maiuro, R. D., Russo, J., Katon, W., DeWolfe, D., & Hall, G. (1990). Coping profiles associated with psychiatric, physical health, work, and family problems. *Health Psychology, 9,* 348-376.
23. Bird, G. W., Stith, S. M., & Schladale, J. (1991). Psychological resources, coping strategies, and negotiation styles as discriminators of violence in dating relationships. *Family Relations, 40,* 45-50.
24. Blanchard-Fields, F., Sulsky, L., & Robinson-Whelen, S. (1991). Moderating effects of age and context on the relationship between gender, sex role differences, and coping. *Sex Roles, 25,* 645-660.
25. Easley, M. J., & Epstein, N. (1991). Coping with stress in a family with an alcoholic parent. *Family Relations, 40,* 218-224.
26. Holloway, S. D., & Machida, S. (1991). Child-rearing effectiveness of divorced mothers: Relationship to coping strategies and social support. *Journal of Divorce & Remarriage, 14*(3/4), 179-201.
27. Johnson, B. K., & Kenkel, M. B. (1991). Stress, coping, and adjustment in female adolescent incest victims. *Child Abuse & Neglect, 15,* 293-305.
28. Lu, L. (1991). Daily hassles and mental health: A longitudinal study. *British Journal of Psychology, 82,* 441-447.
29. Mishel, M. H., & Sorenson, D. H. (1991). Uncertainty in gynecological cancer: A test of the mediating functions of mastery and coping. *Nursing Research, 40,* 167–171.
30. Mullins, L. L., Olson, R. A., Reyes, S., Bernardy, N., Huszti, H. C., & Volk, R. J. (1991). Risk and resistance factors in the adaptation of mothers of children with cystic fibrosis. *Journal of Pediatric Psychology, 16,* 701–715.
31. Neundorfer, M. M. (1991). Coping and health outcomes in spouse caregivers of persons with dementia. *Nursing Research, 40,* 260–265.
32. Berzonsky, M. D. (1992). Identity style and coping strategies. *Journal of Personality, 60,* 771–788.
33. Conway, V. J., & Terry, D. J. (1992). Appraised controllability as a moderation of the effectiveness of different coping strategies: A test of the goodness of fit hypothesis. *Australian Journal of Psychology, 44,* 1–7.
34. Dolan, C. A., Sherwood, A., & Light, K. C. (1992). Cognitive coping strategies and blood pressure responses to real-life stress in healthy young men. *Health Psychology, 11,* 233–240.
35. Dunkel-Schetter, C., Feinstein, L. G., Taylor, S. E., & Falke, R. L. (1992). Patterns of coping with cancer. *Health Psychology, 11,* 79–87.
36. Folkman, S., Chesney, M. A., Pallack, L., & Phillips, L. (1992). Stress, coping, and high-risk sexual behavior. *Health Psychology, 11,* 218–222.
37. Knussen, C., Sloper, P., Cunningham, C. C., & Turner, S. (1992). The use of the Ways of Coping (Revised) Questionnaire with parents of children with Down's syndrome. *Psychological Medicine, 22,* 775-786.
38. Miller, A. C., Gordon, R. M., Daniele, R. J., & Diller, L. (1992). Stress, appraisal, and coping in mothers of disabled and nondisabled children. *Journal of Pediatric Psychology, 17,* 587–605.
39. Nakano, K. (1992). Role of personality characteristics in coping behaviors. *Psychological Reports, 71,* 687-690.
40. Posner, C. M., Wilson, K. G., Kral, M. J., Lander, S., & Mellwraith, R. D. (1992). Family psychoeducational support groups in schizophrenia. *American Journal of Orthopsychiatry, 62,* 206–218.

41. Prochaska, J. O., Norcross, J. C., Fowler, J. L., Follick, M. J., & Abrams, D. B. (1992). Attendance and outcome in a work site weight control program: Processes and stages of change as process and predictor variables. *Addictive Behaviors, 17,* 35-45.

42. Smyth, K. A., & Yarandi, H. N. (1992). A path model of Type A and Type B responses to coping and stress in employed Black women. *Nursing Research, 41,* 260–265.

43. Stanton, A. L. (1992). Downward comparison in infertile couples. *Basic and Applied Social Psychology, 13,* 389-403.

44. Stern, M., & Alvarez, A. (1992). Knowledge of child development and caretaking attitudes: A comparison of pregnant, parenting, and nonpregnant adolescents. *Family Relations, 41,* 297–302.

45. Strutton, D., & Lumpkin, J. (1992). Relationship between optimism and coping strategies in the work environment. *Psychological Reports, 71,* 1179-1186.

46. Thompson, R. J., Jr., Gustafson, K. E., Hamlett, K. W., & Spock, A. (1992). Stress, coping, and family functioning in the psychological adjustment of mothers of children and adolescents with cystic fibrosis. *Journal of Pediatric Psychology, 17,* 573–585.

47. Atkinson, M., & Violato, C. (1993). A factor analysis of the Ways of Coping Questionnaire based on data from saddening experiences. *Psychological Reports, 72,* 1159-1164.

48. Folkman, S., Chesney, M., Pollack, L., & Coates, T. (1993). Stress, control, coping, and depressive mood in human immunodeficiency, virus-positive and negative gay men in San Francisco. *The Journal of Nervous and Mental Disease, 181,* 409-416.

49. Girdler, S. S., Pedersen, C. A., Stern, R. A., & Light, K. C. (1993). Menstrual cycle and premenstrual syndrome: Modifiers of cardiovascular reactivity in women. *Health Psychology, 12,* 180-192.

50. Hoffart, A., & Martinsen, E. W. (1993). Coping strategies in major depressed, agoraphobic and comorbid in-patients: A longitudinal study. *British Journal of Medical Psychology, 66,* 143–155.

51. Jung, J. (1993). The relationship of worrying, coping, and symptoms among college men and women. *The Journal of General Psychology, 120,* 139-148.

52. Kuiper, N. A., Martin, R. A., & Olinger, L. J. (1993). Coping humor, stress, and cognitive appraisals. *Canadian Journal of Behavioural Science, 25,* 81-96.

53. Long, B. C. (1993). Coping strategies of male managers: A prospective analysis of predictors of psychosomatic symptoms and job satisfaction. *Journal of Vocational Behavior, 42,* 184-199.

54. Norvell, N. K., Cornell, C. E., & Limacher, M. C. (1993). Emotional and coping responses to serial killings: The Gainesville murders. *The Journal of Nervous and Mental Disease, 181,* 417-421.

55. Scherer, R. F., Drumheller, P. M., & Owen, C. L. (1993). Evaluating differences in cognitive appraisal and coping over stages of a transaction. *The Journal of Psychology, 127,* 435-441.

56. Schuldberg, D. (1993). Personal resourcefulness: Positive aspects of functioning in high-risk research. *Psychiatry, 56,* 137–152.

57. Stanton, A. L., & Snider, P. R. (1993). Coping with a breast cancer diagnosis: A prospective study. *Health Psychology, 12,* 16-23.

58. Thompson, R. J., Jr., Gil, K. M., Burbach, D. J., Keith, B. R., & Kinney, T. R. (1993). Psychological adjustment of mothers of children and adolescents with sickle cell disease: The role of stress, coping methods, and family functioning. *Journal of Pediatric Psychology, 18,* 549–559.

59. Baron-Cohen, S., Cross, P., Crowson, M., & Robertson, M. (1994). Can children with Gilles de la Tourette Syndrome edit their intentions? *Psychological Medicine, 24,* 29-40.

60. Brown, S. L. (1994). Factor structure of a brief version of the Ways of Coping (WOC) Questionnaire: A study with veterinary science students. *Measurement and Evaluation in Counseling and Development, 27,* 308-315.

61. Chan, D. W. (1994). The Chinese Ways of Coping Questionnaire: Assessing coping secondary school teachers and students in Hong Kong. *Psychological Assessment, 6,* 108-116.

62. David, A. S., & Howard, R. (1994). An experimental phenomenological approach to delusional memory in schizophrenia and late paraphrenia. *Psychological Medicine, 24,* 515-524.

63. DeGenova, M. K., Patton, D. M., Jurich, J. A., & MacDermid, S. M. (1994). Ways of coping among HIV-infected individuals. *The Journal of Social Psychology, 134,* 655-663.

64. Duffy, L., & O'Carroll, R. (1994). Memory impairment in schizophrenia—a comparison with that observed in the Alcoholic Korsakoff Syndrome. *Psychological Medicine, 24,* 155-165.

65. Folkman, S., Chesney, M. A., Cooke, M., Boccellari, A., & Collette, L. (1994). Caregiver burden in HIV-positive and HIV-negative partners of men with AIDS. *Journal of Consulting and Clinical Psychology, 62,* 746-756.

66. Frydenberg, E., & Lewis, R. (1994). Coping with different concerns: Consistency and variation in coping strategies used by adolescents. *Australian Psychologist, 29,* 45–48.

67. Grummon, K., Rigby, E. D., Orr, D., Procidano, M., & Reznikoff, M. (1994). Psychological variables that affect the psychological adjustment of IVDU patients with AIDS. *Journal of Clinical Psychology, 50,* 488-502.

68. Hogg, K. E., Goldstein, L. H., & Leigh, P. N. (1994). The psychological impact of motor neurone disease. *Psychological Medicine, 24,* 625-632.

69. Hotopf, M. H., Pollock, S., & Lishman, W. A. (1994). An unusual presentation of multiple sclerosis. *Psychological Medicine, 24,* 515-528.

70. Hurlburt, R. T., Happe, F., & Frith, U. (1994). Sampling the form of inner experience in three adults with Asperger Syndrome. *Psychological Medicine, 24,* 385-395.

71. Kotler, T., Buzwell, S., Romeo, Y., & Bowland, J. (1994). Avoidant attachment as a risk factor for health. *British Journal of Medical Psychology, 67,* 237–245.

72. Kuyken, W., & Brewin, C. R. (1994). Stress and coping in depressed women. *Cognitive Therapy and Research, 18,* 403-412.

73. Law, A., Logan, H., & Baron, R. (1994). Desire for control, felt control, and stress inoculation training during dental treatment. *Journal of Personality and Social Psychology, 67,* 926-936.

74. Lewinsohn, P. M., Roberts, R. E., Seeley, J. R., Rohde, P., Gotlib, I. H., & Hops, H. (1994). Adolescent psychopathology: II. Psychosocial risk factors for depression. *Journal of Abnormal Psychology, 103,* 302-315.

75. Lewis, S., Cooper, C. L., & Bennett, D. (1994). Psychosocial factors and chronic fatigue syndrome. *Psychological Medicine, 24,* 661-671.

76. Ludwig, A. M. (1994). Mental illness and creative activity in female writers. *American Journal of Psychiatry, 151,* 1650-1656.

77. Mayer, J. D., & Stevens, A. A. (1994). An emerging understanding of the reflective (meta-) experience of mood. *Journal of Research in Personality, 28,* 351-373.

78. McCullough, J. D., McCune, K. J., Kaye, A. L., Braith, J. A., Friend, R., Roberts, W. C., Belyea-Caldwell, S., Norris, S. L. W., & Hampton, C. (1994). Comparison of community dysthymia sample at screening with a matched group of nondepressed community controls. *The Journal of Nervous and Mental Disease, 182,* 402-407.

79. McCullough, J. D., McCune, K. J., Kaye, A. L., Braith, J. A., Friend, R., Roberts, W. C., Belyea-Caldwell, S., Norris, S. L. W., & Hampton, C. (1994). One-year prospective replication study of an untreated sample of community dysthymia subjects. *The Journal of Nervous and Mental Disease, 182,* 396-401.

80. Narsavage, G. L., & Weaver, T. E. (1994). Physiologic status, coping, and hardiness as predictors of outcomes in chronic obstructive pulmonary disease. *Nursing Research, 43,* 90–94.

81. Papadatou, D., Anagnostopoulos, F., & Monos, D. (1994). Factors contributing to the development of burnout in oncology nursing. *British Journal of Medical Psychology, 67,* 187–199.

82. Reed, G. M., Kemeny, M. E., Taylor, S. E., Wang, H-Y. J., & Visscher, B. R. (1994). Realistic acceptance as a predictor of decreased survival time in gay men with AIDS. *Health Psychology, 13,* 299-307.

83. Scherer, R. F., Coleman, J. C., Drumheller, P. M., Jr., & Owen, C. L. (1994). Assessment of cognitive appraisal and coping linkages using two forms of canonical correlation. *Perceptual and Motor Skills, 79,* 259-264.

84. Tata, P. R., Rollings, J., Collins, M., Pickering, A., & Jacobson, R. R. (1994). Lack of cognitive recovery following withdrawal from long-term benzodiazepine use. *Psychological Medicine, 24,* 203-213.

85. Terry, D. J. (1994). Determinants of coping: The role of stable and situational factors. *Journal of Personality and Social Psychology, 66,* 895-910.

86. Thompson, R. J., Jr., Gil, K. M., Gustafson, K. E., George, L. K., Keith, B. R., Spock, A., & Kinney, T. R. (1994). Stability and change in the psychological adjustment of mothers of children and adolescents with cystic fibrosis and sickle cell disease. *Journal of Pediatric Psychology, 19,* 171–188.

87. Wineman, N. M., Durand, E. J., & McCulloch, B. J. (1994). Examination of the factor structure of the Ways of Coping Questionnaire with clinical populations. *Nursing Research, 43,* 268–273.

88. Bauman, G. D., & Stern, M. (1995). Adjustment to occupational stress: The relationship of perceived control to effectiveness of coping strategies. *Journal of Counseling Psychology, 42,* 294–303.

89. Breslin, F. C., O'Keeffe, M. K., Burrell, L., Ratliff-Crain, J., & Baum, A. (1995). The effects of stress and coping on daily alcohol consumption. *Addictive Behaviors, 20,* 141-147.

90. Brown, S. A., Vik, P. W., Patterson, T. L., Grant, I., & Schuckit, M. A. (1995). Stress, vulnerability and adult alcohol relapse. *Journal of Studies on Alcohol, 56,* 538–545.

91. Bull, M. J., Maruyama, G., & Luo, D. (1995). Testing a model for posthospital transition of family caregivers for elderly persons. *Nursing Research, 44,* 132–138.

92. Chan, D. W. (1995). Depressive symptoms and coping strategies among Chinese adolescents in Hong Kong. *Journal of Youth and Adolescence, 24,* 267–279.

93. Chan, D. W. (1995). Multidimensional assessment and causal modeling in teacher stress research: A commentary. *British Journal of Educational Psychology, 65,* 381–385.

94. Chan, D. W., & Hui, E. K. P. (1995). Burnout and coping among Chinese secondary school teachers in Hong Kong. *British Journal of Educational Psychology, 65,* 15–25.

95. Christensen, A. J., Benotsch, E. G., Wiebe, J. S., & Lawton, W. J. (1995). Coping with treatment-related stress: Effects on patient adherence in hemodialysis. *Journal of Consulting and Clinical Psychology, 63,* 454-459.

96. Eagan, A. E., & Walsh, W. B. (1995). Person-environment congruence and coping strategies. *Career Development Quarterly, 43,* 246-256.

97. Gotlib, I. H., Lewinsohn, P. M., & Seeley, J. R. (1995). Symptoms versus a diagnosis of depression: Differences in psychosocial functioning. *Journal of Consulting and Clinical Psychology, 63,* 90-100.

98. Hatton, C., Knussen, C., Sloper, P., & Turner, S. (1995). The stability of the Ways of Coping (Revised) Questionnaire over time in parents of children with Down's Syndrome: A research note. *Psychological Medicine, 25,* 419-422.

99. Jelinek, J., & Morf, M. E. (1995). Accounting for variance shared by measures of personality and stress-related variables: A canonical correlational analysis. *Psychological Reports, 76,* 959–962.

100. Kirkorian, R., Kay, J., & Liang, W. M. (1995). Emotional distress, coping, and adjustment in human immunodeficiency virus infection and acquired immune deficiency syndrome. *The Journal of Nervous and Mental Disease, 183,* 293–298.

101. Kolt, G. S., Kirkby, R. J., & Lindner, H. (1995). Coping processes in competitive gymnasts: Gender differences. *Perceptual and Motor Skills, 81,* 1139–1145.

102. Kupst, M. J., Natta, M. B., Richardson, C. C., Schulman, J. L., Lavigne, J. V., & Das, L. (1995). Family coping with pediatric leukemia: Ten years after treatment. *Journal of Pediatric Psychology, 20,* 601–617.

103. Lehmicke, N., & Hicks, R. A. (1995). Relationships of response-set differences on Beck Depression Inventory scores of undergraduate students. *Psychological Reports, 76,* 15-21.

104. Morrow, K. A., Thoreson, R. W., & Penney, L. L. (1995). Predictors of psychological distress among infertility clinic patients. *Journal of Consulting and Clinical Psychology, 63,* 163-167.

105. Patterson, T. L., Semple, S. J., Temoshock, L. R., Atkinson, J. H., McCutchan, J. A., Straits-Tröster, K., Chandler, J. L., Grant, I., & the HIV Neurobehavioral Research Center Group. (1995). Stress and depressive symptoms prospectively predict immune change among HIV-seropositive men. *Psychiatry, 58,* 299–312.

106. Santiago-Rivera, A. L., Bernstein, B. L., & Gard, T. L. (1995). The importance of achievement and the appraisal of stressful events as predictors of coping. *Journal of College Student Development, 36,* 374–383.

107. Sutker, P. B., Davis, J. M., Uddo, M., & Ditta, S. R. (1995). War zone stress, personal resources, and PTSD in Persian Gulf War returnees. *Journal of Abnormal Psychology, 104,* 444–452.

108. Thompson, J. A., Charlton, P. F. C., Kerry, R., Lee, D., & Turner, S. W. (1995). An open trial of exposure therapy based on deconditioning for post-traumatic stress disorder. *British Journal of Clinical Psychology, 34,* 407–416.

109. Vitaliano, P. P., Russo, J., & Niaura, R. (1995). Plasma lipids and their relationships with psychosocial factors in older adults. *Journal of Gerontology: Psychological Sciences, 50B,* P18-P24.

110. Wolf, T. M., Heller, S. S., Camp, C. J., & Faucett, J. M. (1995). The process of coping with a gross anatomy exam during the first year of medical school. *British Journal of Medical Psychology, 68,* 85–87.

111. Aldwin, C. M., Sutton, K. J., Chiara, G., & Spiro, A., III. (1996). Age differences in stress, coping, and appraisal: Findings from the normative aging study. *Journal of Gerontology, 51,* 179–188.

112. Bruchon-Schweitzer, M., Cousson, F., Quintard, B., Nuissier, J., & Rascle, N. (1996). French adaptation of the Ways of Coping Checklist. *Perceptual and Motor Skills, 83,* 104–106.

113. Charlton, P. F. C., & Thompson, J. A. (1996). Ways of coping with psychological distress after trauma. *British Journal of Clinical Psychology, 35,* 517-530.

114. Essan, C. A., & Trommsdorff, A. (1996). Coping with university-related problems: A cross-cultural comparison. *Journal of Cross-Cultural Psychology, 27,* 315–328.

115. Kelly, V. A., & Myers, J. E. (1996). Parental alcoholism and coping: A comparison of female children of alcoholics with female children of nonalcoholics. *Journal of Counseling and Development, 74,* 501–504.

116. Myers, M. G., & Brown, S. A. (1996). The Adolescent Relapse Coping Questionnaire: Psychometric validation. *Journal of Studies on Alcohol, 57,* 40–46.

117. O'Brien, T. B., & DeLongis, A. (1996). The interactional context of problem-, emotion- and relationship-focused coping: The role of the big five personality factors. *Journal of Personality, 64,* 775–813.

118. Reed, M. K., Walker, B., Williams, G., McLeod, S., & Jones, S. (1996). MMPI-2 patterns in African-American females. *Journal of Clinical Psychology, 52,* 437–441.

119. Sloper, P., & Turner, S. (1996). Progress in social-independent functioning of young people with Down's syndrome. *Journal of Disability Research, 40,* 39–48.

120. Smyth, K., & Yarandi, H. N. (1996). Factor analysis of the Ways of Coping Questionnaire for African American women. *Nursing Research, 45,* 25–29.

121. Terry, D. J., Mayocchi, L., & Hynes, G. J. (1996). Depressive symptomatology in new mothers: A stress and coping perspective. *Journal of Abnormal Psychology, 105,* 220–231.

122. Thompson, R. J., Jr., Gil, K. M., Abrams, M. R., & Phillips, G. (1996). Psychological adjustment of adults with Sickle Cell Anemia: Stability over 20 months, correlates, and predictors. *Journal of Clinical Psychology, 52,* 253–261.

123. Aikens, J. E., Fischer, J. S., Namey, M., & Rudick, R. A. (1997). A replicated prospective investigation of life stress, coping, and depressive symptoms in multiple sclerosis. *Journal of Behavioral Medicine, 20,* 433–445.

124. Bouchard, G., Sabourin, S., Lussier, Y., Wright, J., & Richer, C. (1997). Testing the theoretical models underlying the Ways of Coping questionnaire with couples. *Journal of Marriage and the Family, 59,* 409–418.

125. Bowman, B. J. (1997). Cultural pathways toward Antonovsky's sense of coherence. *Journal of Clinical Psychology, 53,* 139–142.

126. Carlier, I. V. E., Lamberts, R. D., & Gersons, B. P. R. (1997). Risk factors for posttraumatic stress symptomatology in police officers: A prospective analysis. *Journal of Nervous and Mental Disease, 185,* 498–506.

127. Kaplan, M. S., Marks, G., & Mertens, S. B. (1997). Distress and coping among women with HIV infection: Preliminary findings from a multiethnic sample. *American Journal of Orthopsychiatry, 67,* 80–91.

128. McKee, K. J., Whittick, J. E., Ballinger, B. B., Gilhooly, M. M. L., Gordon, D. S., Mutch, W. J., & Philp, I. (1997). Coping in family supporters of elderly people with dementia. *British Journal of Clinical Psychology, 36,* 323–340.

129. Wanberg, C. R. (1997). Antecedents and outcomes of coping behaviors among unemployed and reemployed individuals. *Journal of Applied Psychology, 82,* 731–744.

[2859]

Wechsler Abbreviated Scale of Intelligence.

Purpose: Designed as a "short and reliable measure of intelligence."
Population: Ages 6–89.
Publication Date: 1999.
Acronym: WASI.
Administration: Individual.
Price Data, 1999: $185 per complete kit; R30 per 25 record forms; $108 per 100 record forms; $75 per stimulus book; $59 per manual (238 pages).
Author: The Psychological Corporation.
Publisher: The Psychological Corporation.

a) TWO SUBTEST FORM.
Scores, 3: Verbal (Vocabulary), Performance (Matrix Reasoning), Full Scale IQ.
Time: (15) minutes.

b) FOUR SUBTEST FORM.
Scores, 7: Verbal (Vocabulary, Similarities), Performance (Block Design, Matrix Reasoning), Verbal IQ, Performance IQ, Full Scale IQ.
Time: (30) minutes.

[2860]

Wechsler Adult Intelligence Scale—Third Edition.

Purpose: Designed to assess the intellectual ability of adults.
Population: Ages 16–89.
Publication Dates: 1939–1997.
Acronym: WAIS-III.
Scores, 22: Verbal (Vocabulary, Similarities, Arithmetic, Digit Span, Information, Comprehension, Letter-Number Sequencing, Total), Performance (Picture Completion, Digit Symbol-Coding, Block Design, Matrix Reasoning, Picture Arrangement, Symbol Search, Object Assembly, Mazes, Total), Verbal Comprehension Index, Perceptual Organization Index, Working Memory Index, Processing Speed Index, Total.
Administration: Individual.
Price Data, 1999: $682.50 per complete set in attaché case; $625 per complete set in box; $35 per 25 response books; $134 per 100 response books; $68.50 per 25 response forms; $263.50 per 100 response forms; $73.50 per administration and scoring manual ('97, 217 pages); $42 per technical manual ('97, 370 pages).
Time: (60–90) minutes.
Author: David Wechsler.
Publisher: The Psychological Corporation.
Cross References: See T4:2937 (1131 references), 9:1348 (291 references), T3:2598 (576 references), 8:230 (351 references), and T2:529 (178 references); for reviews of the original edition by Alvin G. Burstein and Howard B. Lyman, see 7:429 (538 references); see also

6:538 (180 references); for reviews by Nancy Bayley and Wilson H. Guertin, see 5:414 (42 references).

TEST REFERENCES

1. Pabis, R., Mirza, M. A., & Tozman, S. (1981). Autocastration as a counterphobic focal suicide. *Suicide and Life-Threatening Behavior, 11,* 3–9.
2. Butters, N., Albert, M. S., Sax, D. S., Miliotis, P., Nagode, J., & Sterste, A. (1983). The effect of verbal mediators on the pictorial memory of brain-damaged patients. *Neuropsychologia, 21,* 307–323.
3. Cermak, L. S., & O'Connor, M. (1983). The anterograde and retrograde retrieval ability of a patient with amnesia due to encephalitis. *Neuropsychologia, 21,* 213–234.
4. Cicerone, K. D., Lazar, R. M., & Shapiro, W. R. (1983). Effects of frontal lobe lesions on hypothesis sampling during concept formation. *Neuropsychologia, 21,* 513–524.
5. Haxby, J. V., Lundgren, S. L., & Morley, G. K. (1983). Short-term retention of verbal, visual shape and visuospatial location information in normal and amnesic subjects. *Neuropsychologia, 21,* 25–33.
6. Howes, J. L. (1983). Effects of experimenter- and self-generated imagery on the Korsakoff patient's memory performance. *Neuropsychologia, 21,* 341–349.
7. Larrabee, G. J., & Kane, R. L. (1983). Differential drawing size associated with unilateral brain damage. *Neuropsychologia, 21,* 173–177.
8. Stuss, D. T., Benson, D. F., Kaplan, E. F., Weir, W. S., Naeser, M. A., Lieberman, I., & Ferrill, D. (1983). The involvement of orbitofrontal cerebrum in cognitive tasks. *Neuropsychologia, 21,* 235–248.
9. Zola-Morgan, S., Cohen, N. J., & Squire, L. R. (1983). Recall of remote episodic memory in amnesia. *Neuropsychologia, 21,* 487–500.
10. Bauer, R. M. (1984). Autonomic recognition of names and faces in prosopagnosia: A neuropsychological application of the Guilty Knowledge Test. *Neuropsychologia, 22,* 457–469.
11. Bentin, S., Sahar, A., & Moscovitch, M. (1984). Intermanual information transfer in patients with lesions in the trunk of the corpus callosum. *Neuropsychologia, 22,* 601–611.
12. Gott, P. S., Hughes, E. C., & Whipple, K. (1984). Voluntary control of two lateralized conscious states: Validation by electrical and behavioral studies. *Neuropsychologia, 22,* 65–72.
13. Kee, D. W., Bathurst, K., & Hellige, J. B. (1984). Lateralized interference in finger tapping: Assessment of block design activities. *Neuropsychologia, 22,* 197–203.
14. Kirshner, H. S., Webb, W. G., & Kelly, M. P. (1984). The naming disorder of dementia. *Neuropsychologia, 22,* 23–30.
15. Ogden, J. A. (1984). Dyslexia in a right-handed patient with a posterior lesion of the right cerebral hemisphere. *Neuropsychologia, 22,* 265–280.
16. Sandson, J., & Albert, M. L. (1984). Varieties of perseveration. *Neuropsychologia, 22,* 715–732.
17. Smith, M. L., & Milner, B. (1984). Differential effects of frontal-lobe lesions on cognitive estimation and spatial memory. *Neuropsychologia, 22,* 697–705.
18. Winocur, G., Oxbury, S., Roberts, R., Agnetti, V., & Davis, C. (1984). Amnesia in a patient with bilateral lesions to the thalamus. *Neuropsychologia, 22,* 123–143.
19. Coyne, A. C., Allen, P. A., & Wickens, D. D. (1986). Influence of adult age on primary and secondary memory search. *Psychology and Aging, 1,* 187-194.
20. Hess, T. M., & Slaughter, S. J. (1986). Specific exemplary retention and prototype abstraction in young and old adults. *Psychology and Aging, 1,* 202-207.
21. La Rue, A., D'Elia, L. F., Clark, E. O., Spar, J. E., & Jarvik, L. F. (1986). Clinical test of memory in dementia, depression, and healthy aging. *Psychology and Aging, 1,* 69-77.
22. Lignugaris-Kraft, B., Salzberg, C. L., Stowitschek, J. J., & McConaughy, E. K. (1986). Social interaction patterns among employees in sheltered and nonprofit business settings. *Career Development Quarterly, 35,* 123-135.
23. Nebes, R. D., Boller, F., & Holland, A. (1986). Use of semantic context by patients with Alzheimer's disease. *Psychology and Aging, 1,* 261-269.
24. Parks, C. W., Jr., Mitchell, D. B., & Perlmutter, M. (1986). Cognitive and social functioning across adulthood: Age or student status differences. *Psychology and Aging, 1,* 248-254.
25. Plude, D. J., & Hoyer, W. J. (1986). Age and the selectivity of visual information processing. *Psychology and Aging, 1,* 4-10.
26. Sinnott, J. D. (1986). Prospective/intentional and incidental everyday memory: Effects of age and passage of time. *Psychology and Aging, 1,* 110-116.
27. Stine, E. L., Wingfield, A., & Poon, L. W. (1986). How much and how fast: Rapid processing of spoken language in later adulthood. *Psychology and Aging, 1,* 303-311.
28. Cerella, J., Plude, D. J., & Milberg, W. (1987). Radial localization in the aged. *Psychology and Aging, 2,* 52-55.
29. Chastain, R. L., & Joe, G. W. (1987). Multidimensional relations between intellectual abilities and demographic variables. *Journal of Educational Psychology, 79,* 323–325.
30. Craik, F. I. M., Byrd, M., & Swanson, J. M. (1987). Patterns of memory loss in three elderly samples. *Psychology and Aging, 2,* 79-86.
31. Desrosiers, G. (1987). Emergency telephone calls: A multiple baseline study using instructional programming. *Journal of Behavior Therapy and Experimental Psychiatry, 18,* 373–380.
32. Glisky, E. L., & Schacter, D. L. (1987). Acquisition of domain-specific knowledge in organic amnesia: Training for computer-related work. *Neuropsychologia, 25,* 893–906.
33. Goldstein, M. J. (1987). Psychosocial issues. *Schizophrenia Bulletin, 13,* 157–171.
34. Grady, C. L., Haxby, J. V., Horwitz, B., Berg, G., & Rapoport, S. I. (1987). Neuropsychological and cerebral metabolic function in early vs. late onset dementia of the Alzheimer type. *Neuropsychologia, 25,* 807–816.
35. Grigsby, J. P., Kemper, M. B., & Hagerman, R. J. (1987). Developmental Gerstmann Syndrome without aphasia in Fragile X Syndrome. *Neuropsychologia, 25,* 881–891.
36. Hannay, H. J., Falgout, J. C., Leli, D. A., Katholi, C. R., Halsey, H., Jr., & Willis, E. L. (1987). Focal right temporo-occipital blood flow changes associated with judgment of line orientation. *Neuropsychologia, 25,* 755–763.
37. Hess, T. M., & Wallsten, S. M. (1987). Adult age differences in the perception and learning of artistic style categories. *Psychology and Aging, 2,* 243-253.
38. Jones, M. L., Ulicny, G. R., Czyzewski, M. J., & Plante, T. G. (1987). Employment in care-giving jobs for mentally disabled young adults: A feasability study. *Journal of Employment Counseling, 24,* 122–129.
39. Marcus, J., Hans, S. L., Nagler, S., Auerbach, J. G., Mirsky, A. F., & Aubrey, A. (1987). Review of the NIMH Israeli Kibbutz-City study and the Jerusalem infant development study. *Schizophrenia Bulletin, 13,* 425-438.
40. Mayes, A. R., Pickering, A., & Fairbairn, A. (1987). Amnesic sensitivity to proactive interference: Its relationship to priming and the causes of amnesia. *Neuropsychologia, 25,* 211–220.
41. McAndrews, M. P., Glisky, E. L., & Schacter, D. L. (1987). When priming persists: Long-lasting implicit memory for a single episode in amnesic patients. *Neuropsychologia, 25,* 497–506.
42. McCrae, R. R. Arenberg, D., & Costa, P. T., Jr. (1987). Declines in divergent thinking with age: Cross-sectional, longitudinal, and cross-sequential analyses. *Psychology and Aging, 2,* 130-137.
43. Newcombe, F., Ratcliff, G., & Damasio, H. (1987). Dissociable visual and spatial impairments following right posterior cerebral lesions: Clinical, neuropsychological and anatomical evidence. *Neuropsychologia, 25,* 149–161.
44. Ptito, A., Lassonde, M., Lepore, F., & Ptito, M. (1987). Visual discrimination in hemispherectomized patients. *Neuropsychologia, 25,* 869–879.
45. Rybarczyk, B. D., Hart, R. P., & Harkins, S. W. (1987). Age and forgetting rate with pictorial stimuli. *Psychology and Aging, 2,* 404-406.
46. Salthouse, T. A. (1987). Adult age differences in integrative spatial ability. *Psychology and Aging, 2,* 254-260.
47. Salthouse, T. A. (1987). The role of representations in age differences in analogical reasoning. *Psychology and Aging, 2,* 357-362.
48. Salthouse, T. A., & Prill, K. A. (1987). Inferences about age impairments in inferential reasoning. *Psychology and Aging, 2,* 43-51.
49. Scialfa, C. T., Kline, D. W., & Lyman, B. J. (1987). Age differences in target identification as a function of retinal location and noise level: Examination of the useful field of view. *Psychology and Aging, 2,* 14-19.
50. Squire, L. R., Shimamura, A. P., & Graf, P. (1987). Strength and duration of priming effects in normal subjects and amnesic patients. *Neuropsychologia, 25,* 195–210.
51. Stine, E. L., & Wingfield, A. (1987). Process and strategy in memory for speech among younger and older adults. *Psychology and Aging, 2,* 272-279.
52. Sugishita, M., & Yoshioka, M. (1987). Visual processes in a hemialexic patient with posterior callosal section. *Neuropsychologia, 25,* 329–339.
53. Tienari, P., Sorri, A., Lahti, I., Naarala, M., Wahlberg, K., Moring, J., Pohjola, J., & Wynne, L. C. (1987). Genetic and psychosocial factors in schizophrenia: The Finnish adoptive family study. *Schizophrenia Bulletin, 13,* 477–484.
54. Trope, I., Fishman, B., Grur, R. C., Sussman, N. M., & Gur, R. E. (1987). Contralateral and ipsilateral control of fingers following callosotomy. *Neuropsychologia, 25,* 287–291.
55. Vandergoot, D. (1987). Review of placement research literature: Implications for research and practice. *Rehabilitation Counseling Bulletin, 30,* 243–272.
56. Vilkki, J. (1987). Incidental and deliberate memory for words and faces after focal cerebral lesions. *Neuropsychologia, 25,* 221–230.
57. Wynne, L. C., Cole, R. E., & Perkins, P. (1987). University of Rochester child and family study: Risk research in progress. *Schizophrenia Bulletin, 13,* 463–476.
58. Aggleton, J. P., Nicol, R. M., Huston, A. E., & Fairbairn, A. F. (1988). The performance of amnesic subjects on tests of experimental amnesia in animals: Delayed matching-to-sample and concurrent learning. *Neuropsychologia, 26,* 265–272.
59. Aram, D., & Ekelman, B. L. (1988). Scholastic aptitude and achievement among children with unilateral brain lesions. *Neuropsychologia, 26,* 903–916.
60. Clark, C. M., Klonoff, H., Tyhurst, J. S., Ruth, T., Adam, M., Rogers, J., Harrop, R., Martin, W., & Pate, B. (1988). Regional cerebral glucose metabolism in identical twins. *Neuropsychologia, 26,* 615–621.
61. Corballis, M. C., & Ogden, J. A. (1988). Dichotic listening in commissurotomized and hemispherectomized subjects. *Neuropsychologia, 26,* 565–573.
62. Corballis, M. C., & Sergent, J. (1988). Imagery in a commissurotomized patient. *Neuropsychologia, 26,* 13–26.
63. DeMyer, M. K., Gilmor, R. L., Hendrie, H. C., DeMyer, W. E., Augustyn, G. T., & Jackson, R. K. (1988). Magnetic resonance brain images in schizophrenic and normal subjects: Influence of diagnosis and education. *Schizophrenic Bulletin, 14,* 21–37.
64. Dennis, M., Farrell, K., Hoffman, H. J., Hendrick, E. B., Becker, L. E., & Murphy, E. G. (1988). Recognition memory of item, associative and serial-order information after temporal lobectomy for seizure disorder. *Neuropsychologia, 26,* 53–65.
65. Glisky, E. L., & Schacter, D. L. (1988). Long-term retention of computer learning by patients with memory disorders. *Neuropsychologia, 26,* 173–178.
66. Gurd, J. M., Bessell, N. J., Bladon, R. A. W., & Bamford, J. M. (1988). A case of foreign accent syndrome, with follow-up clinical, neuropsychological and phonetic descriptions. *Neuropsychologia, 26,* 237–251.

67. Jones-Gotman, M., & Zatorre, R. J. (1988). Olfactory identification deficits in patients with focal cerebral excision. *Neuropsychologia, 26,* 387–400.
68. Lee, G. P., Loring, D. W., Flanigin, H. F., Smith, J. R., & Meador, K. J. (1988). Electrical stimulation of the human hippocampus produces verbal intrusions during memory testing. *Neuropsychologia, 26,* 623–627.
69. Leonard, G., Jones, L., & Milner, B. (1988). Residual impairment in handgrip strength after unilateral frontal-lobe lesions. *Neuropsychologia, 26,* 555–564.
70. Leonard, G., Milner, B., & Jones, L. (1988). Performance on unimanual and bimanual tapping tasks by patients with lesions of the frontal or temporal lobe. *Neuropsychologia, 26,* 79–91.
71. Ogden, J. A. (1988). Language and memory functions after long recovery periods in left-hemispherectomized subjects. *Neuropsychologia, 26,* 645–659.
72. Ptito, A., & Zatorre, R. J. (1988). Impaired stereoscopic detection thresholds after left or right temporal lobectomy. *Neuropsychologia, 26,* 547–554.
73. Smith, M. L., & Milner, B. (1988). Estimation of frequency of occurrence of abstract designs after frontal or temporal lobectomy. *Neuropsychologia, 26,* 297–306.
74. Spruill, J., & May, J. (1988). The mentally retarded offender: Prevalence rates based on individual versus group intelligence tests. *Criminal Justice and Behavior, 15,* 484–491.
75. Takahashi, Y. (1988). Aokigahara-jukai: Suicide and amnesia in Mt. Fuji's Black Forest. *Suicide and Life-Threatening Behavior, 18,* 164–180.
76. Trope, I., Rozin, P., & Gur, R. C. (1988). Validation of the lateral limits technique with a callosotomy patient. *Neuropsychologia, 26,* 673–684.
77. Weddell, R. A., Trevarthen, C., & Miller, J. D. (1988). Reaction of patients with focal cerebral lesions to success or failure. *Neuropsychologia, 26,* 373–385.
78. Alivisatos, B., & Milner, B. (1989). Effects of frontal or temporal lobectomy on the use of advance information in a choice reaction time task. *Neuropsychologia, 27,* 495–503.
79. Berger, H. J. C., Van Hoof, J. J. M., Van Spaendonck, K. P. M., Harstink, M. W. I., Van Den Bercken, J. H. L., Jaspers, R., & Cools, A. R. (1989). Haloperidol and cognitive shifting. *Neuropsychologia, 27,* 629–639.
80. Blonder, L. X., Gur, R. E., Gur, R. C., Saykin, A. J., & Hurtig, H. I. (1989). Neuropsychological functioning in hemiparkinsonism. *Brain and Cognition, 9,* 244-257.
81. Blumenthal, J. A., Emery, C. F., Madden, D. J., George, L. K., Coleman, R. E., Riddle, M. W., McKee, D. C., Reasoner, J., & Williams, R. S. (1989). Cardiovascular and behavioral effects of aerobic exercise in healthy older men and women. *Journal of Gerontology, 44,* 147–157.
82. Bolla-Wilson, K., & Bleeker, M. L. (1989). Absence of depression in elderly adults. *Journal of Gerontology, 44,* 53–55.
83. Borod, J. C., Fitzpatrick, P. M., Helm-Estabrooks, N., & Goodglass, H. (1989). The relationship between limb apraxia and the spontaneous use of communicative gesture in aphasia. *Brain and Cognition, 10,* 121-131.
84. Canavan, A. G. M., Passingham, R. E., Marsden, C. D., Quinn, N., Wyke, M., & Polkey, C. E. (1989). Sequencing ability in Parkinsonians, patients with frontal lobe lesions and patients who have undergone unilateral temporal lobectomies. *Neuropsychologia, 27,* 787–798.
85. Canavan, A. G. M., Passingham, R. E., Marsden, C. D., Quinn, N., Wyke, M., & Polkey, C. E. (1989). The performance on learning tasks of patients in the early stages of Parkinson's disease. *Neuropsychologia, 27,* 141–156.
86. Carvajal, H., McKnab, P., Gerber, J., Hewes, P., & Smith, P. (1989). Counseling college bound students: Can ACT scores be predicted? *The School Counselor, 36,* 186–191.
87. Corballis, M. C., & Sergent, J. (1989). Mental rotation in a commissurotomized subject. *Neuropsychologia, 27,* 585–597.
88. Dakof, G. A., & Mendelsohn, G. A. (1989). Patterns of adaptation to Parkinson's disease. *Health Psychology, 8,* 355–372.
89. Dick, M. B., Kean, M., & Sands, D. (1989). Memory for internally generated words in Alzheimer-type dementia: Breakdown in encoding and semantic memory. *Brain and Cognition, 9,* 88-108.
90. Downes, J. J., Roberts, A. C., Sahakian, B. J., Evenden, J. L., Morris, R. G., & Robbins, T. W. (1989). Impaired extra-dimension shift performance in medicated and unmedicated Parkinson's disease: Evidence for a specific attentional dysfunction. *Neuropsychologia, 27,* 1329–1343.
91. Erickson, R. C. (1989). Applications of cognitive testing to group therapies with the chronically mentally ill. *International Journal of Group Psychotherapy, 39,* 223–235.
92. Farah, M. J., Hammond, K. M., Mehta, Z., & Ratcliff, G. (1989). Category-specificity and modality-specificity in semantic memory. *Neuropsychologia, 27,* 193–200.
93. Faust, D., & Fogel, B. S. (1989). The development and initial validation of a sensitive bedside cognitive screening test. *The Journal of Nervous and Mental Disease, 177,* 25-31.
94. Fitzgibbon, M. L., Cella, D. F., Humfleet, G., Griffen, E., & Sheridan, K. (1989). Motor slowing in asymptomatic HIV infection. *Perceptual and Motor Skills, 68,* 1331–1338.
95. Forgatch, M. S. (1989). Pattern and outcome in family problem solving: The disrupting effect of negative emotion. *Journal of Marriage and the Family, 51,* 115-124.
96. Foxx, R. M., Martella, R. C., & Marchand-Martella, N. E. (1989). The acquisition, maintenance, and generalization of problem-solving skills by closed head-injured adults. *Behavior Therapy, 20,* 61–76.
97. Geers, A., & Moog, J. (1989). Factors predictive of the development of literacy in profoundly hearing-impaired adolescents. *Volta Review, 91,* 69–86.
98. Glisky, E. L., & Schacter, D. L. (1989). Extending the limits of complex learning in organic amnesia: Computer training in a vocational domain. *Neuropsychologia, 27,* 107–120.
99. Goldstein, L. H., Canavan, A. G. M., & Polkey, C. E. (1989). Cognitive mapping after unilateral temporal lobectomy. *Neuropsychologia, 27,* 167–177.
100. Gonon, M. A. H., Bruckert, R., & Michel, F. (1989). Lexicalization in an anomic patient. *Neuropsychologia, 27,* 391–407.
101. Green, M. F., Satz, P., Gaier, D. J., Ganzell, S., & Kharabi, F. (1989). Minor physical anomalies in schizophrenia. *Schizophrenia Bulletin, 15,* 91–99.
102. Grosser, G. S., & Spafford, C. S. (1989). Perceptual evidence for an anomalous distribution of rods and cones in the retinas of dyslexics: A new hypothesis. *Perceptual and Motor Skills, 68,* 683–698.
103. Helkala, E.-L., Laulumaa, V., Soininen, H., & Riekkinen, P. (1989). Different error pattern of episodic and semantic memory in Alzheimer's disease and Parkinson's disease with dementia. *Neuropsychologia, 27,* 1241–1248.
104. Janowsky, J. S., Shimamura, A. P., & Squire, L. R. (1989). Source memory impairment in patients with frontal lobe lesions. *Neuropsychologia, 27,* 1043–1056.
105. Jones, L. (1989). Force matching by patients with unilateral focal cerebral lesions. *Neuropsychologia, 27,* 1153–1163.
106. Kashiwagi, A., Kashiwagi, T., Nishikawa, T., & Okuda, J. (1989). Hemispheric asymmetry of processing temporal aspects of repetitive movement in two patients with infarction involving the corpus callosum. *Neuropsychologia, 27,* 799–809.
107. Kesner, R. D., Adelstein, T. B., & Crutcher, K. A. (1989). Equivalent spatial location memory deficits in rats with medial septum or hippocampal formation lesions and patients with dementia of the Alzheimer's type. *Brain and Cognition, 9,* 289-300.
108. Kivlahan, D. R., Sher, K. J., & Donovan, D. M. (1989). The Alcohol Dependence Scale: A validation study among inpatient alcoholics. *Journal of Studies on Alcohol, 50,* 170–175.
109. Klusman, L. E., & Cripe, L. J. (1989). Analysis of errors on the trail making test. *Perceptual and Motor Skills, 68,* 1199–1204.
110. Koeppl, D. M., Bolla-Wilson, K., & Bleecker, M. L. (1989). The MMPI: Regional difference or normal aging. *Journal of Gerontology, 44,* 95–99.
111. Kopelman, M. D. (1989). Remote and autobiographical memory, temporal context memory and frontal atrophy in Korsakoff and Alzheimer patients. *Neuropsychologia, 27,* 437–460.
112. Ladish, C., & Polich, J. (1989). P300 and probability in children. *Journal of Experimental Child Psychology, 48,* 212-223.
113. Levinson, H. N. (1989). Abnormal optokinetic and perceptual span parameters in cerebellar-vestibular dysfunction and learning disabilities or dyslexia. *Perceptual and Motor Skills, 68,* 35–54.
114. Lord, C., Rutter, M., Goode, S., Heemsbergen, J., Jordan, H., Mawhood, L., & Schopler, E. (1989). Autism Diagnostic Observation Schedule: A standardized observation of communicative and social behavior. *Journal of Autism and Developmental Disorders, 19*(2), 185-212.
115. Loring, D. W., Meador, K. J., & Lee, G. P. (1989). Differential-handed response to verbal and visual spatial stimuli: Evidence of specialized hemispheric processing following callosotomy. *Neuropsychologia, 27,* 811–827.
116. Magnussen, S., & Mathiesen, T. (1989). Detection of moving and stationary gratings in the absence of striate cortex. *Neuropsychologia, 27,* 725–728.
117. Malloy, P., Noel, N., Rodgers, S., Longabaugh, R., & Beattie, M. (1989). Risk factors for neuropsychological impairment in alcoholics: Antisocial personality, age, years of drinking and gender. *Journal of Studies on Alcohol, 50,* 422–426.
118. Matteson, R., & Hellige, J. (1989). Lateralized finger-tapping interference produced by block design activities. *Brain and Cognition, 11,* 127-132.
119. Mayes, A. R., & Gooding, P. (1989). Enhancement of word completion priming in amnesics by cueing with previously novel associates. *Neuropsychologia, 27,* 1057–1072.
120. Moskowitz, D. S., & Schwartzman, A. E. (1989). Painting group portraits: Studying life outcomes for aggressive and withdrawn children. *Journal of Personality, 57,* 723–746.
121. Myors, B., Stankov, L., & Oliphant, G. (1989). Competing tasks, working memory, and intelligence. *Australian Journal of Psychology, 41,* 1–16.
122. Nelson, R., & Lignugaris/Kraft, B. (1989). Postsecondary education for students with learning disabilities. *Exceptional Children, 56,* 246–265.
123. Nissen, M. J., Willingham, D., & Hartman, M. (1989). Explicit and implicit remembering: When is learning preserved in amnesia? *Neuropsychologia, 27,* 341–352.
124. O'Connell, M., Cooper, S., Perry, C., & Hoke, L. (1989). The relationship between thought disorder and psychotic symptoms in borderline personality disorder. *The Journal of Nervous and Mental Disease, 177,* 273-278.
125. Obrzut, J. E., Conrad, P. F., & Boliek, C. A. (1989). Verbal and nonverbal auditory processing among left- and right-handed good readers and reading-disabled children. *Neuropsychologia, 27,* 1357–1371.
126. Ogden, J. A. (1989). Visuospatial and other "right-hemispheric" functions after long recovery periods in left-hemispherectomized subjects. *Neuropsychologia, 27,* 765–776.
127. Perini, G. I., Colombo, G., Armani, M., Pellegrini, A., Ermani, M., Miotti, M., & Angelini, C. (1989). Intellectual impairment and cognitive evoked potentials in myotonic dystrophy. *The Journal of Nervous and Mental Disease, 177,* 750-754.
128. Pickering, A. D., Mayes, A. R., & Fairbairn, A. F. (1989). Amnesia and memory for modality information. *Neuropsychologia, 27,* 1249–1259.
129. Rapesak, S. Z., Kaszniak, A. W., & Rubens, A. B. (1989). Anomia for facial expressions: Evidence for a category specific visual-verbal disconnection syndrome. *Neuropsychologia, 27,* 1031–1041.

130. Renault, B., Signoret, J. L., Bebruille, B., Breton, F., & Bolgert, F. (1989). Brain potentials reveal covert facial recognition in prosopagnosia. *Neuropsychologia, 27,* 905–912.

131. Riklan, M., Reynolds, C. M., & Stellar, S. (1989). Correlates of memory in Parkinson's disease. *The Journal of Nervous and Mental Disease, 177,* 237-240.

132. Roberts, R. E., Vernon, S. W., & Rhoades, H. M. (1989). Effects of language and ethnic status on reliability and validity of the Center for Epidemiologic Studies-Depression Scale with psychiatric patients. *The Journal of Nervous and Mental Disease, 177,* 581-592.

133. Robertson, I. (1989). Anomalies in the laterality of omissions in unilateral left visual neglect: Implications for an attentional theory of neglect. *Neuropsychologia, 27,* 157–165.

134. Ross, J. M., & Smith, J. O. (1989). Adult basic educators' perceptions of learning disabilities. *Journal of Reading, 33,* 340-347.

135. Sands, L. P., & Meredith, W. (1989). Effects of sensory and motor functioning on adult intellectual performance. *Journal of Gerontology, 44,* 56–58.

136. Savicki, V. (1989). Computers in the child and youth care field. *Child Welfare, 68,* 505–516.

137. Saykin, A. J., Gur, R. C., Sussman, N. M., O'Connor, M. J., & Gur, R. E. (1989). Memory deficits before and after temporal lobectomy: Effect of laterality and age of onset. *Brain and Cognition, 9,* 191-200.

138. Sayles-Folks, S. L., & Harrison, D. K. (1989). Reflection-impulsivity and work adjustment. *Rehabilitation Counseling Bulletin, 33,* 110–117.

139. Scarborough, H. S. (1989). Prediction of reading disability from familial and individual differences. *Journal of Educational Psychology, 81,* 101–108.

140. Simith, M. L., & Milner, B. (1989). Right hippocampal impairment in the recall of spatial location: Encoding deficit or rapid forgetting? *Neuropsychologia, 27,* 71–81.

141. Spring, B., Chiodo, J., Harden, M., Bourgeois, M. J., Mason, J. D., & Lutherer, L. (1989). Psychobiological effects of carbohydrates. *The Journal of Clinical Psychiatry, 50,* 27–33.

142. Szatmari, P., Bartolucci, G., Bremner, R., Bond, S., & Rich, S. (1989). A follow-up study of high-functioning autistic children. *Journal of Autism and Developmental Disorders, 19*(2), 213-225.

143. Vilkki, J. (1989). Perseveration in memory for figures after frontal lobe lesion. *Neuropsychologia, 27,* 1101–1104.

144. Vilkki, J., & Holst, P. (1989). Deficient programming in spatial learning after frontal lobe damage. *Neuropsychologia, 27,* 971–976.

145. Watkins, C. E., Jr., Edinger, J. D., Shipley, R. H., Reinberg, J. A., Godin, K. W., Hunton-Shoup, J., McKay, B. L., Parra, R., Klaus, A., Polk, N., & Settle, K. (1989). WISC-R and WAIS-R odd- and even-item short forms: Criterion validity in three patient samples. *Rehabilitation Psychology, 34,* 175–183.

146. Wilbur, R., Goodhart, W., & Fuller, D. (1989). Comprehension of English models by hearing-impaired students. *Volta Review, 91,* 5–18.

147. Williams, B. W., Mack, W., & Henderson, V. W. (1989). Boston Naming Test in Alzheimer's disease. *Neuropsychologia, 27,* 1073–1079.

148. Zacker, J., Pepper, B., & Kirshner, M. C. (1989). Neuropsychological characteristics of young adult chronic psychiatric patients: Preliminary observations. *Perceptual and Motor Skills, 68,* 391–399.

149. Zatorre, R. J. (1989). Perceptual asymmetry on the dichotic fused words test and cerebral speech lateralization determined by the carotid sodium amytal test. *Neuropsychologia, 27,* 1207–1219.

150. Andreasen, N. C., Flaum, M., Swayze, V. W., II, Tyrrell, G., & Arndt, S. (1990). Positive and negative symptoms in schizophrenia. *Archives of General Psychiatry, 47,* 615-621.

151. Armstrong, J. G., & Loewenstein, R. J. (1990). Characteristics of patients with multiple personality and dissociative disorders on psychological testing. *The Journal of Nervous and Mental Disease, 178,* 448-454.

152. Aronson, M. K., Ooi, W. L., Morgenstern, H., Hafner, A., Masur, D., Crystal, H., Frishman, W. H., Fisher, D., & Katzman, R. (1990). Women, myocardial infarction, and dementia in the very old. *Neurology, 40,* 1102–1106.

153. Banich, M. T., Levine, S. C., Kim, H., & Huttenlocher, P. (1990). The effects of developmental factors on IQ in hemiplegic children. *Neuropsychologia, 28,* 35–47.

154. Bartfai, A., Winborg, I.-M., Nordstrom, P., & Asberg, M. (1990). Suicidal behavior and cognitive flexibility: Design and verbal fluency after attempted suicide. *Suicide and Life-Threatening Behavior, 20,* 254–266.

155. Benowitz, L. I., Moya, K. L., & Levine, D. N. (1990). Impaired verbal reasoning and constructional apraxia in subjects with right hemisphere damage. *Neuropsychologia, 28,* 231–241.

156. Berk, L. A., & Fekken, G. C. (1990). Person reliability evaluated in the context of vocational interest assessment. *Journal of Vocational Behavior, 37,* 7-16.

157. Bernard, L. C., & Fowler, W. (1990). Assessing the validity of memory complaints: performance of brain-damaged and normal individuals on Rey's task to detect malingering. *Journal of Clinical Psychology, 46,* 432–436.

158. Bolla, K. I., Lindgren, K. N., Bonaccorsy, C., & Bleecker, M. L. (1990). Predictors of verbal fluency (FAS) in the healthy elderly. *Journal of Clinical Psychology, 46,* 623–628.

159. Bondareff, W., Raval, J., Woo, B., Hauser, D. L., & Colletti, P. M. (1990). Magnetic resonance imaging and the severity of dementia in older adults. *Archives of General Psychiatry, 47,* 47–51.

160. Boone, D. E. (1990). Short forms of the WAIS-R with psychiatric inpatients: A comparison of techniques. *Journal of Clinical Psychology, 46,* 197–200.

161. Campbell, R., Heywood, C. A., Cowey, A., Regard, M., & Landis, T. (1990). Sensitivity to eye gaze in prosopagnosic patients and monkeys with superior temporal sulcus ablation. *Neuropsychologia, 28,* 1123–1142.

162. Canavan, A. G. M., Passingham, R. E., Marsden, C. D., Quinn, N., Wyke, M., & Polkey, C. E. (1990). Prism adaptation and other tasks involving spatial abilities in patients with Parkinson's disease, patients with frontal lobe lesions and patients with unilateral temporal lobectomies. *Neuropsychologia, 28,* 969–984.

163. Cappa, S. F., Papagno, C., & Vallar, G. (1990). Language and verbal memory after right hemispheric stroke: A clinical-CT scan study. *Neuropsychologia, 28,* 503–509.

164. Clarkson-Smith, L., & Hartley, A. A. (1990). The game of bridge as an exercise in working memory and reasoning. *Journal of Gerontology, 45,* 233–238.

165. DeLuca, J., Kovaleski, M. E., Burright, R. G., & Donovick, P. J. (1990). Asymmetries in hand movement during block design construction. *Neuropsychologia, 28,* 719–726.

166. Dobbins, C., & Russell, E. W. (1990). Left temporal lobe brain damage pattern on the Wechsler Adult Intelligence Scale. *Journal of Clinical Psychology, 46,* 863–868.

167. Dodrill, C. B., & Wilensky, A. J. (1990). Intellectual impairment as an outcome of status epilepticus. *Neurology, 40*(Supp 2), 23–27.

168. Dubois, B., Pillon, B., Sternic, N., Lhermitte, F., & Agid, Y. (1990). Age-induced cognitive disturbances in Parkinson's disease. *Neurology, 40,* 38–41.

169. Egeland, B., Kalkoske, M., Gottesman, N., & Erickson, M. F. (1990). Preschool behavior problems: Stability and factors accounting for change. *Journal of Child Psychology and Psychiatry and Allied Disciplines, 31,* 891-909.

170. Ehrenreich, J. H. (1990). Effect of social class of subjects on normative responses to TAT cards. *Journal of Clinical Psychology, 46,* 467–471.

171. Eskes, G. A., Bryson, S. E., & McCormick, T. A. (1990). Comprehension of concrete and abstract words in autistic children. *Journal of Autism and Developmental Disorders, 20*(1), 61-73.

172. Fein, G., Van Dyke, C., Davenport, L., Turetsky, B., Brant-Zawadzki, M., Zatz, L., Dillon, W., & Valk, P. (1990). Preservation of normal cognitive functioning in elderly subjects with extensive white-matter lesions of long duration. *Archives of General Psychiatry, 47,* 220–223.

173. Ferrarese, C., Appollonio, J., Frigo, M., Meregalli, S., Piolti, R., Tamma, F., & Frattola, L. (1990). Cerebrospinal fluid levels of diazepam-binding inhibitor in neurodegenerative disorders with dementia. *Neurology, 40,* 632–635.

174. Fowler, P. C., Zillmer, E., & Macciocchi, S. N. (1990). Confirmatory factor analytic models of the WAIS-R for neuropsychiatric patients. *Journal of Clinical Psychology, 46,* 324–333.

175. Frank, A. F., & Gunderson, J. G. (1990). The role of the therapeutic alliance in the treatment of schizophrenia. *Archives of General Psychiatry, 47,* 228–236.

176. Frisk, V., & Milner, B. (1990). The relationship of working memory to the immediate recall of stories following unilateral temporal or frontal lobectomy. *Neuropsychologia, 28,* 121–135.

177. Frisk, V., & Milner, B. (1990). The role of the left hippocampal region in the acquisition and retention of story content. *Neuropsychologia, 28,* 349–359.

178. Gade, A., & Mortensen, E. L. (1990). Temporal gradient in the remote memory impairment of amnesic patients with lesions in the basal forebrain. *Neuropsychologia, 28,* 985–1001.

179. Giordani, B., Boivin, M. J., Hall, A. L., Foster, N. L., Lehtihen, S. J., Bluemlein, L. A., & Berent, S. (1990). The utility and generality of Mini-Mental State Examination scores in Alzheimer's disease. *Neurology, 40,* 1894–1896.

180. Gould, J. H., & Glencross, D. J. (1990). Do children with a specific reading disability have a general serial-ordering deficit? *Neuropsychologia, 28,* 271–278.

181. Graff-Radford, N. R., Damasio, A. R., Hyman, B. T., Hart, M. N., Tranel, D., Damasio, H., Van Hoesen, G. W., & Rezai, K. (1990). Progressive aphasia in a patient with Pick's disease: A neuropsychological, radiologic, and anatomic study. *Neurology, 40,* 620–626.

182. Green, J., Morris, J. C., Sandson, J., McKeel, D. W., & Miller, J. W. (1990). Progressive aphasia: A precursor of global dementia? *Neurology, 40,* 423–429.

183. Hampson, E. (1990). Variations in sex-related cognitive abilities across the menstrual cycle. *Brain and Cognition, 14,* 26-43.

184. Hansen, L., Salmon, D., Galasko, D., Masliah, E., Katzman, R., DeTeresa, R., Thal, L., Pay, M. M., Hofstetter, R., Klauber, M., Rice, V., Butters, N., & Alford, M. (1990). The Lewy body variant of Alzheimer's disease: A clinical and pathologic entity. *Neurology, 40,* 1–8.

185. Harper, R. G., Kotik-Harper, D., & Kirby, H. (1990). Psychometric assessment of depression in an elderly general medical population: Over- or underassessment? *The Journal of Nervous and Mental Disease, 178,* 113-119.

186. Heilman, K. M., Bowers, D., Watson, R. T., Day, A., Valenstein, E., Hammond, E., & Duara, R. (1990). Frontal hypermetabolism and thalamic hypometabolism in a patient with abnormal orienting and retrosplenial amnesia. *Neuropsychologia, 28,* 161–169.

187. Hirt, M., & Pithers, W. (1990). Arousal and maintenance of schizophrenic attention. *Journal of Clinical Psychology, 46,* 15–21.

188. Johnson, M. M. S. (1990). Age differences in decision making: A process methodology for examining strategic information processing. *Journal of Gerontology, 45,* 75–78.

189. Johnson, W. G., Nicholson, R. A., & Service, N. M. (1990). The relationship of competency to stand trial and criminal responsibility. *Criminal Justice and Behavior, 17,* 169–185.

190. Johnstone, E. C., Owens, D. G. C., Lambert, M. T., Crow, T. J., Frith, C. D., & Done, D. J. (1990). Combination tricyclic antidepressant and lithium maintenance medication in unipolar and bipolar depressed patients. *Journal of Affective Disorders, 20,* 225-233.

191. Kim, H., Levine, S. C., & Kertesz, S. (1990). Are variations among subjects in lateral asymmetry real individual differences or random error in measurement?: Putting variability in its place. *Brain and Cognition, 14,* 220-242.

192. Klemchuk, H. P., Bond, L. A., & Howell, D. C. (1990). Coherence and correlates of level 1 perspective taking in young children. *Merrill-Palmer Quarterly, 36,* 369–387.

193. Kurz, A., Romero, B., & Lauter, H. (1990). The onset of Alzheimer's disease: A longitudinal case study and a trial of new diagnostic criteria. *Psychiatry, 53,* 53–61.

194. Lee, G. D., Loring, D. W., Meader, K. J., & Brooks, B. B. (1990). Hemispheric specialization for emotional expression: A reexamination of results from intracarotid administration of sodium amobarbital. *Brain and Cognition, 12,* 267-280.

195. Macciocchi, S. N. (1990). "Practice makes perfect:" Retest effects in college athletes. *Journal of Clinical Psychology, 46,* 628–631.

196. Mann, V. A., Sasanuma, S., Sakuma, N., & Masaki, S. (1990). Sex differences in cognitive abilities: A cross-cultural perspective. *Neuropsychologia, 28,* 1063–1077.

197. Marsico, D. S., & Wagner, E. E. (1990). A comparison of the Lacks and Pascal-Sattell Bender-Gestalt scoring methods for diagnosing brain damage in an outpatient sample. *Journal of Clinical Psychology, 46,* 868–877.

198. Meador, K. J., Loring, D. W., Huh, K., Gallagher, B. B., & King, D. W. (1990). Comparative cognitive effects of anticonvulsants. *Neurology, 40,* 391–394.

199. Mesibov, G. B., & Stephens, J. (1990). Perceptions of popularity among a group of high-functioning adults with autism. *Journal of Autism and Developmental Disorders, 20*(1), 33-43.

200. Miller, E. N., Selnes, O. A., McArthur, J. C., Satz, P., Becker, J. T., Cohen, B. A., Sheridan, K., Machado, A. M., Van Gorp, W. G., & Visscher, B. (1990). Neuropsychological performance in HIV-I-infected homosexual men: The Multicenter AIDS Cohort Study (MACS). *Neurology, 40,* 197–203.

201. Moreno, C. R., Borod, J. C., Welkowitz, J., & Alpert, M. (1990). Lateralization for the expression and perception of facial emotion as a function of age. *Neuropsychologia, 28,* 199–209.

202. Morrell, R. W., Park, D. C., & Poon, L. W. (1990). Effects of labeling techniques on memory and comprehension of prescription information in young and old adults. *Journal of Gerontology, 45,* 166–172.

203. Neistadt, M. E. (1990). A critical analysis of occupational therapy approaches for perceptual deficits in adults with brain injury. *The American Journal of Occupational Therapy, 44,* 299-304.

204. O'Donnell, J. P., Romero, J. J., & Leicht, D. J. (1990). A comparison of language deficits in learning-disabled, head-injured, and nondisabled young adults: Results from an abbreviated aphasia screening test. *Journal of Clinical Psychology, 46,* 310–315.

205. Oscar-Berman, M., Pulaski, J. L., Hutner, N., Weber, D. A., & Freedman, M. (1990). Cross-modal functions in alcoholism and aging. *Neuropsychologia, 28,* 851–869.

206. Owen, A. M., Downes, J. J., Sahakian, B. J., Polkey, C. E., & Robbins, T. W. (1990). Planning and spatial working memory following frontal lobe lesions in man. *Neuropsychologia, 28,* 1021–1034.

207. Perlmutter, M., & Nyquist, L. (1990). Relationships between self-reported physical and mental health and intelligence performance across adulthood. *Journal of Gerontology, 45,* 145–155.

208. Peterson, J. B., Rothfleisch, J., Zelazo, P. D., & Pihl, R. O. (1990). Acute alcohol intoxication and cognitive functioning. *Journal of Studies on Alcohol, 51,* 114–122.

209. Petrides, M. (1990). Nonspatial conditional learning impaired in patients with unilateral frontal but not unilateral temporal lobe excisions. *Neuropsychologia, 28,* 137–149.

210. Rausch, R., & Ary, C. M. (1990). Supraspan learning in patients with unilateral anterior temporal lobe resections. *Neuropsychologia, 28,* 111–120.

211. Ricci, C., & Blundo, C. (1990). Perception of ambiguous figures after focal brain lesions. *Neuropsychologia, 28,* 1163–1173.

212. Robertson, I. H. (1990). Digit span and visual neglect: A puzzling relationship. *Neuropsychologia, 28,* 217–222.

213. Rumsey, J. M., & Hamburger, S. D. (1990). Neuropsychological divergence of high-level autism and severe dyslexia. *Journal of Autism and Developmental Disorders, 20*(2), 155-168.

214. Ryan, J. J., Paolo, A. M., & Brungardt, T. M. (1990). Factor analysis of the Wechsler Adult Intelligence Scale—Revised for persons 75 years and older. *Professional Psychology: Research and Practice, 21,* 177–181.

215. Sahakian, B. J., Downes, J. J., Eagger, S., Evenden, J. L., Levy, R., Philpot, M. P., Roberts, A. C., & Robbins, T. W. (1990). Sparing of attentional relative to mnemonic function in a subgroup of patients with dementia of the Alzheimer type. *Neuropsychologia, 28,* 1197–1213.

216. Sass, K. J., Spencer, D. D., Kim, J. H., Westerveld, M., Novelly, R. A., & Lencz, T. (1990). Verbal memory impairment correlates with hippocampal pyramidal cell density. *Neurology, 40,* 1694–1697.

217. Selnes, O. A., Miller, E., McArthur, J., Gordon, B., Muñoz, A., Sheridan, K., Fox, R., Saah, A. J., & the Multicenter AIDS Cohort Study. (1990). HIV-I infection: No evidence of cognitive decline during the asymptomatic stages. *Neurology, 40,* 204–208.

218. Sevy, S., Kay, S. R., Opler, L. A., & Van Praag, H. M. (1990). Significance of cocaine history in schizophrenia. *The Journal of Nervous and Mental Disease, 178,* 642-648.

219. Shaw, C., Kentridge, R. W., & Aggleton, J. P. (1990). Cross-modal matching by amnesic subjects. *Neuropsychologia, 28,* 665–671.

220. Shimamura, A. P., Janowsky, J. S., & Squire, L. R. (1990). Memory for the temporal order of events in patients with frontal lobe lesions and amnesic patients. *Neuropsychologia, 28,* 803–813.

221. Silverstein, A. B. (1990). Critique of a doppelt-type short form of the WAIS-R. *Journal of Clinical Psychology, 46,* 333–339.

222. Silverstein, A. B. (1990). Notes on the reliability of Wechsler short forms. *Journal of Clinical Psychology, 46,* 194–196.

223. Skuy, M., Gaydon, V., Hoffenberg, S., & Fridjhon, P. (1990). Predictors of performance of disadvantaged adolescents in a gifted program. *Gifted Child Quarterly, 34,* 97-101.

224. Strauss, E., Satz, P., & Wada, J. (1990). An examination of the crowding hypothesis in epileptic patients who have undergone the carotid amytal test. *Neuropsychologia, 28,* 1221–1227.

225. Sullivan, L., & Stankov, L. (1990). Shadowing and target detection as a function of age: Implications for the role of processing resources in completing tasks and in general intelligence. *Australian Journal of Psychology, 42,* 173–185.

226. Tammany, J. M., Evans, R. G., & Barnett, R. W. (1990). Personality and intellectual characteristics of adult male felons as a function of offence category. *Journal of Clinical Psychology, 46,* 906–911.

227. Taylor, A. E., Saint-Cyr, J. A., & Lang, A. E. (1990). Memory and learning in early Parkinson's disease: Evidence for a "frontal lobe syndrome". *Brain and Cognition, 13,* 211-232.

228. Ulicny, G. R., Adler, A. B., & Jones, M. L. (1990). Training effective interview skills to attendent service users. *Rehabilitation Psychology, 35,* 55–66.

229. Verfaellie, M., Cermak, L. S., Blackford, S. D., & Weiss, S. (1990). Strategic and automatic priming of semantic memory in alcoholic Korsakoff patients. *Brain and Cognition, 13,* 178-192.

230. Wallesch, C., & Horn, A. (1990). Long-term effects of cerebellar pathology on cognitive functions. *Brain and Cognition, 14,* 19-25.

231. Watson, C. G., Tilleskjor, C. & Jacobs, L. (1990). The construct validity of an aftereffect-based subtyping system for alcoholics. *Journal of Clinical Psychology, 46,* 507–517.

232. Wetzig, D. L., & Hardin, S. I. (1990). Neurocognitive deficits of alcoholism: An intervention. *Journal of Clinical Psychology, 46,* 219–229.

233. Young, A. W., De Haan, E. H. F., Newcombe, F., & Hay, D. C. (1990). Facial neglect. *Neuropsychologia, 28,* 391–415.

234. Abbey, A., Andrews, F. M., & Halman, L. J. (1991). Gender's role in responses to infertility. *Psychology of Women Quarterly, 15,* 295-316.

235. Berman, A. L. (1991). Suicide cases. *Suicide and Life-Threatening Behavior, 21,* 18–36.

236. Blanchard-Fields, F., Sulsky, L., & Robinson-Whelen, S. (1991). Moderating effects of age and context on the relationship between gender, sex role differences, and coping. *Sex Roles, 25,* 645-660.

237. Blumenthal, J. A., Emery, C. F., Madden, D. J., Schniebolk, S., Walsh-Riddle, M., George, L. K., McKee, D. C., Higginbotham, M. B., Cobb, F. R., & Coleman, R. E. (1991). Long-term effects of exercise on psychological functioning in older men and women. *Journal of Gerontology, 46,* 352–361.

238. Bornstein, R. F., & Greenberg, R. P. (1991). Dependency and eating disorders in female psychiatric inpatients. *The Journal of Nervous and Mental Disease, 179,* 148-152.

239. Braff, D. L., Heaton, R., Kuck, J., Cullom, M., Moranville, J., Grant, I., & Zisook, S. (1991). A generalized pattern of neuropsychological deficits in outpatients with chronic schizophrenia with heterogeneous Wisconsin Card Sorting Test results. *Archives of General Psychiatry, 48,* 891-898.

240. Brown, W. S., Marsh, J. T., Wolcott, D., Takushi, R., Carr, C. R., Higa, J., & Nissenson, A. R. (1991). Cognitive function, mood and P3 latency: Effects of the amelioration of anemia in dialysis patients. *Neuropsychologia, 29,* 35–45.

241. Calev, A., Nigal, D., Shapira, B., Tubi, N., Chazan, S., Ben-Yehuda, Y., Kugelmass, S., & Lerer, B. (1991). Early and long-term effects of electroconvulsive therapy and depression on memory and other cognitive functions. *The Journal of Nervous and Mental Disease, 179,* 526-533.

242. Callahan, C. (1991). Media themes and threads. *Journal for the Education of the Gifted, 14,* 312-341.

243. Cermak, L. S., Verfaellie, M., Milberg, W., Letourneau, L., & Blackford, S. (1991). A further analysis of perceptual identification priming in alcoholic Korsakoff patients. *Neuropsychologia, 29,* 725–736.

244. Claus, J. J., Ludwig, C., Mohr, E., Gioffra, M., Blin, J., & Chase, T. N. (1991). Nootropic drugs in Alzheimer's disease: Symptomatic treatment with pramiracetam. *Neurology, 41,* 570–574.

245. Cullum, C. M., & Bigler, E. D. (1991). Short- and long-term psychological status following stroke: Short form MMPI results. *The Journal of Nervous and Mental Disease, 179,* 274-278.

246. Dennis, M., Spiegler, B. J., Hoffman, H. J., Hendrick, E. B., Humphreys, R. P., & Becker, L. E. (1991). Brain tumors in children and adolescents—I.: Effects on working, associative and serial-order memory of IQ, age of tumor onset and age of tumor. *Neuropsychologia, 29,* 813–827.

247. Dennis, M., Spiegler, C. R., Hoffman, H. J., Hendrick, E. B., Humphreys, R. P., & Chuang, S. (1991). Brain tumors in children and adolescents—II.: The neuroanatomy of deficits in working, associative and serial-order memory. *Neuropsychologia, 29,* 829–847.

248. Dickerson, F. B., Ringel, N. B., & Boronow, J. J. (1991). Neuropsychological deficits in chronic schizophrenics: Relationship with symptoms and behavior. *The Journal of Nervous and Mental Disease, 179,* 744-749.

249. Doyon, J., & Milner, B. (1991). Right temporal-lobe contribution to global visual processing. *Neuropsychologia, 29,* 343–360.

250. Doyon, J., & Milner, B. (1991). Role of the right temporal lobe in visual-cue learning during repeated pattern discriminations. *Neuropsychologia, 29,* 861–876.

251. Dykens, E., Volkmar, F., & Glick, M. (1991). Thought disorder in high-functioning autistic adults. *Journal of Autism and Developmental Disorders, 21*(3), 291-301.

252. Eviator, Z., & Zaidel, E. (1991). The effects of word length and emotionality on hemispheric contribution to lexical decision. *Neuropsychologia, 29,* 415–428.

253. Farah, M. J., McMullen, P. A., & Meyer, M. M. (1991). Can recognition of living things be selectively impaired? *Neuropsychologia, 29,* 185–193.

254. Fitzgerald, T. E., & Phillips, W. (1991). Attentional bias and agoraphobic avoidance: The role of cognitive style. *Journal of Anxiety Disorders, 5,* 333-341.

255. Frisk, V., & Milner, B. (1991). Does left temporal lobectomy adversely affect the rate at which verbal material can be processed. *Neuropsychologia, 29,* 113–123.

256. Gacono, C. B., & Meloy, J. R. (1991). A Rorschach investigation of attachment and anxiety in antisocial personality disorder. *The Journal of Nervous and Mental Disease, 179,* 546-552.

257. Ganschow, L., Sparks, R. L., Javorsky, J., Pohlman, J., & Bishop-Marbury, A. (1991). Identifying native language difficulties among foreign language learners in college: A "foreign" language learning disability? *Journal of Learning Disabilities, 24,* 530–541.

258. Goldman, R. S., Avelrod, B. N., & Tandon, R. (1991). Analysis of executive functioning in schizophrenics using the Wisconsin Card Sorting Test. *The Journal of Nervous and Mental Disease, 179,* 507-508.

259. Grigoroiu-Serbânescu, M., Christodorescu, D., Mâgureanu, S., Jipescu, I., Totoescu, A., Marinescu, E., Ardelean, V., & Popa, S. (1991). Adolescent offspring of endogenous unipolar depressive parents and of normal parents. *Journal of Affective Disorders, 21,* 185-198.

260. Harrington, D. L., & Haaland, K. Y. (1991). Hemispheric specialization for motor sequencing: Abnormalities in levels of programming. *Neuropsychologia, 29,* 147–163.

261. Hartman, M. (1991). The use of semantic knowledge in Alzheimer's disease: Evidence for impairment of attention. *Neuropsychologia, 29,* 213–228.

262. Haut, M. W., Petros, T. V., Frank, R. G., & Haut, J. S. (1991). Speed of processing within semantic memory following severe closed head injury. *Brain and Cognition, 17,* 31-41.

263. Hyyppä, M. T., Kronholm, E., & Mattlar, C-E. (1991). Mental well-being of good sleepers in a random population sample. *British Journal of Medical Psychology, 64,* 25–34.

264. Johnson, R., Litvan, J., & Grafman, J. (1991). Progressive supranuclear palsey: Altered sensory processing leads to degraded cognition. *Neurology, 41,* 1257–1262.

265. Jongbloed, L., & Morgan, D. (1991). An investigation of involvement in leisure activities after a stroke. *The American Journal of Occupational Therapy, 45,* 420-427.

266. Joyce, E. M., & Robbins, T. W. (1991). Frontal lobe function in Korsakoff and non-Korsakoff alcoholics: Planning and spatial working memory. *Neuropsychologia, 29,* 709-723.

267. Kahn, H. J., & Whitaker, H. A. (1991). Acalculia: An historical review of localization. *Brain and Cognition, 17,* 102-115.

268. Kartsounis, L. D., & Warrington, E. K. (1991). Failure of object recognition due to a breakdown of figure-ground discrimination in a patient with normal acuity. *Neuropsychologia, 29,* 969–980.

269. Kester, D. B., Saykin, A. J., Sperling, M. R., O'Connor, M. J., Robinson, L. J., & Gur, R. C. (1991). Acute effect of anterior temporal lobectomy on musical processing. *Neuropsychologia, 29,* 703–708.

270. Klonoff, H., Clark, C., Oger, J., Paty, D., & Li, D. (1991). Neuropsychological performance in patients with mild multiple sclerosis. *The Journal of Nervous and Mental Disease, 179,* 127-131.

271. Knopmon, D., & Nissen, M. J. (1991). Procedural learning is impaired in Huntington's disease: Evidence from the serial reaction time task. *Neuropsychologia, 29,* 245–254.

272. Lassonde, M., Sauerwein, H., Chicoine, A. J., & Geoffroy, G. (1991). Absence of disconnexion syndrome in callosal agenesis and early callosotomy: Brain reorganization or lack of structural specificity during ontogeny? *Neuropsychologia, 29,* 481–495.

273. Lavach, J. F. (1991). Cerebral hemisphericity, college major and occupational choices. *Journal of Creative Behavior, 25,* 218-222.

274. Leonard, G., & Milner, B. (1991). Contribution of the right frontal lobe to the encoding and recall of kinesthetic distance information. *Neuropsychologia, 29,* 47–58.

275. Leonard, G., & Milner, B. (1991). Recall of the end-position of examiner-defined arm movements by patients with frontal- or temporal-lobe lesions. *Neuropsychologia, 29,* 629–640.

276. Levin, B. E., Llabre, M. M., Reisman, S., Weiner, W. J., Sanchez-Ramos, J., Singer, C., & Brown, M. C. (1991). Visuospatial impairment in Parkinson's disease. *Neurology, 41,* 365–369.

277. Loewenstein, D. A., D'Elia, L., Guteman, A., Eisdorfer, C., Wilkie, F., LaRue, A., Mintzer, J., & Duara, R. (1991). The occurrence of different intrusive errors in patients with Alzheimer's disease, multiple cerebral infarctions, and major depression. *Brain and Cognition, 16,* 104-117.

278. Lucas, J. A., Telch, M. J., & Bigler, E. D. (1991). Memory functioning in panic disorder: A neuropsychological perspective. *Journal of Anxiety Disorders, 5,* 1-20.

279. Lunn, S., Skydsbjerg, M., Schulsinger, H., Parnas, J., Pedersen, C., & Mathiesen, L. (1991). A preliminary report on the neuropsychologic sequelae of human immunodeficiency virus. *Archives of General Psychiatry, 48,* 139-142.

280. Lyons-Roth, K., Repacholi, B., McLeod, S., & Silva, E. (1991). Disorganized attachment behavior in infancy: Short-term stability, maternal and infant correlates, and risk-related subtypes. *Development and Psychopathology, 3,* 377-396.

281. Mahurin, R. K., DeBettignies, B. H., & Pirozzolo, F. J. (1991). Structured assessment of independent living skills: Preliminary report of a performance measure of functional abilities in dementia. *Journal of Gerontology, 46,* 58–66.

282. Markham, R., & Darke, S. (1991). The effects of anxiety on verbal and spatial task performance. *Australian Journal of Psychology, 43,* 107–111.

283. Mayes, A. R., Meudell, P. R., & MacDonald, C. (1991). Disproportionate intentional spatial-memory impairments in amnesia. *Neuropsychologia, 29,* 771–784.

284. McAndrews, M. P., & Milner, B. (1991). The frontal cortex and memory for temporal order. *Neuropsychologia, 29,* 849–859.

285. McCloskey, M., Aliminosa, D., & Macaruso, P. (1991). Theory-based assessment of acquired dyscalculia. *Brain and Cognition, 17,* 285-308.

286. Miller, B. L., Cummings, J. L., Villanueva-Meyer, J., Boone, K., Mehringer, C. M., Lesser, I. M., & Mena, I. (1991). Frontal lobe degeneration: Clinical, neuropsychological, and SPECCT characteristics. *Neurology, 41,* 1374–1382.

287. Miller, E. N., Satz, P., & Visscher, B. (1991). Computerized and conventional neuropsychological assessment of HIV-1-infected homosexual men. *Neurology, 41,* 1608–1616.

288. Milner, B., Corsi, P., & Leonard, G. (1991). Frontal-lobe contribution to recency judgements. *Neuropsychologia, 29,* 601–618.

289. Moon, G. W., Blakely, W. A., Gorsuch, R. L., & Fantuzzo, J. W. (1991). Frequent WAIS-R administration errors: An ignored source of inaccurate measurement. *Professional Psychology: Research and Practice, 22,* 256–258.

290. Nestor, P. G., Parasuraman, R., Haxby, J. V., & Grady, C. L. (1991). Divided attention and metabolic brain dysfunction in mild dementia of the Alzheimer's type. *Neuropsychologia, 29,* 379–387.

291. Norman, S., Kemper, S., Kynette, D., Cheung, H., & Anagnopoulos, C. (1991). Syntactic complexity and adults' running memory span. *Journal of Gerontology, 46,* 346–351.

292. Ollo, C., Johnson, R., & Grafman, J. (1991). Signs of cognitive change in HIV disease: An event-related brain potential study. *Neurology, 41,* 209–215.

293. Pakalnis, A., Drake, M. E., & Phillips, B. (1991). Neuropsychiatric aspects of psychogenic status epilepticus. *Neurology, 41,* 1104–1106.

294. Paller, K. A., Mayes, A. R., McDermott, M., Pickering, A. D., & Meudell, P. R. (1991). Indirect measures of memory in a duration-judgment task are normal in amnesic patients. *Neuropsychologia, 29,* 1007–1018.

295. Pawlak, A. E., Boulet, J. R., & Bradford, J. M. W. (1991). Discriminant analysis of a sexual-functioning inventory with intrafamilial and extrafamilial child molesters. *Archives of Sexual Behavior, 20,* 27-34.

296. Perlmuter, L. C. (1991). Choice enhances performance in non-insulin dependent diabetics and controls. *Journal of Gerontology, 46,* 218–223.

297. Peselow, E. D., Corwin, J., Fiere, R. R., Rotrosen, J., & Cooper, T. B. (1991). Disappearance of memory deficits in outpatient depressives responding to imipramine. *Journal of Affective Disorders, 21,* 173-183.

298. Pillon, B., Dubois, B., Ploska, A., & Agid, Y. (1991). Severity and specificity of cognitive impairment in Alzheimer's, Huntington's, and Parkinson's diseases and progressive supranuclear palsy. *Neurology, 41,* 634–643.

299. Piven, J., Tsai, G., Nehme, E., Coyle, J. T., Chase, G. A., & Folstein, S. E. (1991). Platelet serotonin, a possible marker for familial autism. *Journal of Autism and Developmental Disorders, 21*(1), 51-59.

300. Raine, A. (1991). Are lateral eye-movements a valid index of functional hemispheric asymmetries. *British Journal of Psychology, 82,* 129-135.

301. Rao, S. M., Leo, G. J., Bernardin, L., & Unverzagt, F. (1991). Cognitive dysfunction in multiple sclerosis. I. Frequency, patterns, and prediction. *Neurology, 41,* 685–691.

302. Rice, D. M., Buchsbaum, M. S., Hardy, D., & Burgwald, L. (1991). Focal left temporal slow EEG activity in related to a verbal recent memory deficit in a non-demented elderly population. *Journal of Gerontology, 46,* 144–151.

303. Rousselle, C., & Wolff, P. H. (1991). The dynamics of bimanual coordination in developmental dyslexia. *Neuropsychologia, 29,* 907–924.

304. Rozeboom, W. W. (1991). Hyball: A method for subspaced-constrained factor rotation. *Multivariate Behavioral Research, 26,* 163–177.

305. Shapiro, E. S., & Lentz, F. E., Jr. (1991). Vocational-technical programs: Follow-up of students with learning disabilities. *Exceptional Children, 58,* 47-59.

306. Shoqeirat, M. A., & Mayes, A. R. (1991). Disproportionate incidental spatial-memory and recall deficits in amnesia. *Neuropsychologia, 29,* 749–769.

307. Silverstein, M. L., Marengo, J. T., & Fogg, L. (1991). Two types of thought disorder and lateralized neuropsychological dysfunction. *Schizophrenia Bulletin, 17,* 679–687.

308. Simonian, S. J., Tarnowski, K. J., & Gibbs, J. C. (1991). Social skills and antisocial conduct of delinquents. *Child Psychiatry and Human Development, 22,* 17-27.

309. Slate, J. R., Jones, C. H., & Murray, R. A. (1991). Teaching administration and scoring of the Wechsler Adult Intelligence Scale—Revised: An empirical evaluation of practice administrations. *Professional Psychology: Research and Practice, 22,* 375–379.

310. Stern, Y., Marder, K., Bell, K., Chen, J., Dooneief, G., Goldstein, S., Mindry, D., Richards, M., Sano, M., Williams, J., Gorman, J., Ehrhardt, A., & Mayeux, R. (1991). Multidisciplinary baseline assessment of homosexual men with and without human immonodeficiency virus infection. *Archives of General Psychiatry, 48,* 131-138.

311. Titus, M. N. D., Gall, N. G., Yerxa, E. J., Roberson, T. A., & Mack, W. (1991). Correlation of perceptual performance and activities of daily living in stroke patients. *The American Journal of Occupational Therapy, 45,* 410-418.

312. Tramo, M. J., & Bharucha, J. J. (1991). Musical priming by the right hemisphere post-callosotomy. *Neuropsychologia, 29,* 313–325.

313. Tuttle, G. E., & Pillard, R. C. (1991). Sexual orientation and cognitive abilities. *Archives of Sexual Behavior, 20,* 307-318.

314. Verfaellie, M., Cermak, L. S., Letourneau, L., & Zuffante, P. (1991). Repetition effects in a lexical decision task: The role of episodic memory in the performance of alcoholic Korsakoff patients. *Neuropsychologia, 29,* 641–657.

315. Volden, J., & Lord, C. (1991). Neologisms and idiosyncratic language in autistic speakers. *Journal of Autism and Developmental Disorders, 21*(2), 109-130.

316. Walker, R., Findlay, J. M., Young, A. W., & Welch, J. (1991). Disentangling neglect and hemianopia. *Neuropsychologia, 29,* 1019–1027.

317. Weinstein, C. S., Seidman, L. J., Feldman, J. J., & Ratey, J. J. (1991). Neurocognitive disorders in psychiatry: A case example of diagnostic and treatment dilemmas. *Psychiatry, 54,* 65–75.

318. Westermeyer, J. F., Harrow, M., & Marengo, J. T. (1991). Risk for suicide in schizophrenia and other psychotic and nonpsychotic disorders. *The Journal of Nervous and Mental Disease, 179,* 259-266.

319. Williams, K. S., Ochs, J., Williams, J. M., & Mulhern, R. K. (1991). Parental report of everyday cognitive abilities among children treated for acute lymphoblastic leukemia. *Journal of Pediatric Psychology, 16,* 13–26.

320. Witelson, S. F., & McCulloch, P. B. (1991). Premortem and postmortem measurement to study structure with function: A human brain collection. *Schizophrenia Bulletin, 17,* 583–591.

321. Zalewski, C., & Archer, R. P. (1991). Assessment of borderline personality disorder: A review of MMPI and Rorschach findings. *The Journal of Nervous and Mental Disease, 179,* 338-345.

322. Abkarian, G. G. (1992). Communication effects of prenatal alcohol exposure. *Journal of Communication Disorders, 25,* 221–240.

323. Adelstein, T. B., Kesner, R. P., & Strassberg, D. S. (1992). Spatial recognition and spatial order memory in patients with dementia of the Alzheimer's type. *Neuropsychologia, 30,* 59-67.

324. Akshoomoff, N. A., Courchesne, E., Press, G. A., & Iragui, V. (1992). Contribution of the cerebellum to neuropsychological functioning: Evidence from a case of cerebellar degenerative disorder. *Neuropsychologia, 30,* 315-328.

325. Allen, P. A., & Crozier, L. C. (1992). Age and ideal chunk size. *Journal of Gerontology, 47,* 47–51.

326. Atkinson, L. (1992). Mental retardation and the WAIS-R scatter analysis. *Journal of Intellectual Disability Research, 36,* 443-448.

327. Atkinson, L. (1992). The Wechsler Memory Scale—Revised: Abnormality of selected index differences. *Canadian Journal of Behavioural Science, 24,* 537-539.

328. Austin, M. P., Ross, M., Murray, C., O'Carroll, R. E., Ebmeier, K. P., & Goodwin, G. M. (1992). Cognitive function in major depression. *Journal of Affective Disorders, 25,* 21-30.

329. Bachman, D. L., Wolf, P. A., Linn, R., Knoefel, J. E., Cobb, J., Belanger, A., D'Agostino, R. B., & White, L. R. (1992). Prevalence of dementia and probable senile dementia of the Alzheimer type in the Framingham study. *Neurology, 42,* 115–119.

330. Bates, M. E., & Pandina, R. J. (1992). Familial alcoholism and premorbid cognitive deficit: A failure to replicate subtype differences. *Journal of Studies on Alcohol, 53,* 320–327.

331. Bederman, J., Faraone, S. V., Keenan, K., Benjamin, J., Krifcher, B., Moore, C., Sprich-Buckminster, S., Ugaglia, K., Jellinek, M. S., Steingard, R., Spencer, T., Norman, D., Kolodny, R., Kraus, I., Perrin, J., Keller, M. B., & Tsuang, M. T. (1992). Further evidence for family-genetic risk factors in attention deficit hyperactivity disorder: Patterns of comorbidity in probands and relatives in psychiatrically and pediatrically referred samples. *Archives of General Psychiatry, 49,* 728-738.

332. Bigler, E. D. (1992). The neurobiology and neuropsychology of adult learning disorders. *Journal of Learning Disabilities, 25,* 488–506.

333. Bilder, R. M., Lipschutz, L., Reiter, G., Geisler, S. H., Mayerhoff, D. I., & Lieberman, J. A. (1992). Intellectual deficits in first-episode schizophrenia: Evidence for progressive deterioration. *Schizophrenia Bulletin, 18,* 437–448.

334. Bolton, P., Pickles, A., Harrington, R., MacDonald, H., & Rutter, M. (1992). Season of birth: Issues, approaches, and findings for autism. *Journal of Child Psychology and Psychiatry and Allied Disciplines, 33,* 509-530.

335. Bromet, E. J., Schwartz, J. E., Fennig, S., Geller, L., Jandorf, L., Kovasznay, B., Lavelle, J., Miller, A., Pato, C., Ram, R., & Rich, C. (1992). The epidemiology of psychosis: The Suffolk County Mental Health Project. *Schizophrenia Bulletin, 18,* 243–255.

336. Carver, R. P. (1992). The three factors in reading ability: Reanalysis of a study by Cunningham, Stanovich, and Wilson. *Journal of Reading Behavior, 24,* 173-190.

337. Cermak, L. S., Verfaellie, M., Sweeney, M., & Jacoby, L. L. (1992). Fluency versus conscious recollection in the word completion performance of amnesic patients. *Brain and Cognition, 20,* 367-377.

338. Chaffin, M. (1992). Factors associated with treatment completion and progress among intrafamilial sexual abusers. *Child Abuse & Neglect, 16,* 251-264.

339. Daie, N., Witztum, E., Mark, M., & Rabinowitz, S. (1992). The belief in the transmigration of souls: Psychotherapy of a Druze patient with severe anxiety reaction. *British Journal of Medical Psychology, 65,* 119–130.

340. Davidson, R. A., Fedio, P., Smith, B. D., Aureille, E., & Martin, A. (1992). Lateralized mediation of arousal and habituation: Differential bilateral electrodermal activity in unilateral temporal lobectomy patients. *Neuropsychologia, 30,* 1053-1063.

341. DeLuca, J. (1992). Cognitive dysfunction after aneurysm of the anterior communicating artery. *Journal of Clinical and Experimental Neuropsychology, 14,* 924-934.

342. Dennis, M., Spiegler, B. J., Obonsaruin, M. C., Maria, B. L., Cowell, C., Hoffman, H. J., Hendrick, E. B., Humphreys, R. P., Bailey, J. D., & Ehrlich, R. M. (1992). Brain tumors in children and adolescents—III. Effects of radiation and hormone status on intelligence and on working, associative and serial-order memory. *Neuropsychologia, 30,* 257-275.

343. Detterman, D. K., Mayer, J. D., Caruso, D. R., Legree, P. J., Conners, F. A., & Taylor, R. (1992). Assessment of basic cognitive abilities in relation to cognitive deficits. *American Journal on Mental Retardation, 97,* 251-286.

344. Diamond, R., White, R. F., Myers, R. H., Mastromauro, C., Koroshetz, W. J., Butters, N., Rothstein, D. M., Moss, M. B., & Vasterling, J. (1992). Evidence of presymptomatic cognitive decline in Huntington's disease. *Journal of Clinical and Experimental Neuropsychology, 14,* 961-975.

345. Dustman, R. E., Emmerson, R. Y., Steinhaus, L. A., Shearer, D. E., & Dustman, T. J. (1992). The effects of videogame playing on neuropsychological performance of elderly individuals. *Journal of Gerontology, 47,* 168–171.

346. Evenhuis, H. M., van Zanten, G. A., & Brocaar, M. P. (1992). Hearing loss in middle-age persons with Down syndrome. *American Journal on Mental Retardation, 97,* 47-56.

347. Faigel, H. C., Doak, E., Howard, S. D., & Sigel, M. L. (1992). Emotional disorders in learning disabled adolescents. *Child Psychiatry and Human Development, 23,* 31–40.

348. Felsenfeld, S., Broen, P. A., & McGue, M. (1992). A 28-year follow-up of adults with a history of moderate phonological disorder: Linguistic and personality results. *Journal of Speech and Hearing Research, 35,* 1114–1125.

349. Flaum, M. A., Andreasen, N. C., & Arndt, S. (1992). The Iowa prospective longitudinal study of recent-onset psychoses. *Schizophrenia Bulletin, 18,* 481–490.

350. Flint, J., & Goldstein, L. H. (1992). Familial calcification of the basal ganglia: A case report and review of the literature. *Psychological Medicine, 22,* 581-595.

351. Freund, L. S., Reiss, A. L., Hagerman, R., & Vinogradov, S. (1992). Chromosome fragility and psychopathology in obligate female carriers of the fragile X chromosome. *Archives of General Psychiatry, 49,* 54-60.

352. Galski, T., Bruno, R. L., & Ehle, H. T. (1992). Driving after cerebral damage: A model with implications for evaluation. *The American Journal of Occupational Therapy, 46,* 324-332.

353. Geers, A. E., & Moog, J. S. (1992). Speech perception and production skills of students with impaired hearing from oral and total communication education settings. *Journal of Speech and Hearing Research, 35,* 1384–1393.

354. Goh, D. S., & McElheron, D. (1992). Another look at the aptitude-achievement distinction. *Psychological Reports, 70,* 833-834.

355. Gregg, N., Hoy, C., King, M., Moreland, C., & Jagota, M. (1992). The MMPI-2 profile of adults with learning disabilities in university and rehabilitation settings. *Journal of Learning Disabilities, 25,* 386–395.

356. Heinze, H., Münte, T. F., Gobiet, W., Niemann, H., & Ruff, R. M. (1992). Parallel and serial visual search after closed head injury: Electrophysiological evidence for perceptual dysfunctions. *Neuropsychologia, 30,* 495-514.

357. Hibbard, M. R., Gordon, W. A., Stein, P. N., Grober, S., & Sliwinski, M. (1992). Awareness of disability in patients following stroke. *Rehabilitation Psychology, 37,* 103–119.

358. Huebner, R. A. (1992). Autistic disorder: A neuropsychological enigma. *The American Journal of Occupational Therapy, 46,* 487-501.

359. Jack, C. R., Peterson, R. C., O'Brien, P. C., & Tangalos, E. G. (1992). MR-based hippocampal volumetry in the diagnosis of Alzheimer's disease. *Neurology, 42,* 183–188.

360. Jarvis, P. A., & Justice, E. M. (1992). Social sensitivity in adolescents and adults with learning disabilities. *Adolescence, 27,* 977-988.

361. Jorgensen, R. S., Gelling, P. D., & Kliner, L. (1992). Patterns of social desirability and anger in young men with a parental history of hypertension: Association with cardiovascular activity. *Health Psychology, 11,* 403–412.

362. Jurden, F. H., & Reese, H. W. (1992). Educational context differences in prose recall in adulthood. *The Journal of Genetic Psychology, 153,* 275-291.

363. Kaplan, R. F., Meadows, M.-E., Vincent, L. C., Logigan, E. L., & Steere, A. C. (1992). Memory impairment and depression in patients with Lyme encephalopathy: Comparison with fibromyalgia and nonpsychotically depressed patients. *Neurology, 42,* 1263–1267.

364. Karlinsky, H., Vanla, G., Haines, J. L., Ridgley, J., Bergeron, C., Mortilla, M., Tupler, R. G., Percy, M. E., Robitaille, Y., Noldy, N. E., Yip, T. C. K., Tanzi, R. E., Gusella, J. F., Becker, R., Berg, J. M., McLachlan, D. R. C., & St. George-Hyslop, P. H. (1992). Molecular and prospective phenotypic characterization of a pedigree with familial Alzheimer's disease and a missense mutuation in codon 717 of the B-amyloid precursor proteingene. *Neurology, 42,* 1445–1453.

365. Kojima, T., Matsushima, E., Ando, K., Ando, H., Sakurada, M., Ohta, K., Moriya, H., & Shimazono, Y. (1992). Exploratory eye movements and neuropsychological tests in schizophrenia patients. *Schizophrenia Bulletin, 18,* 85–94.

366. Kruesi, M. J. P., Hibbs, E. D., Zahn, T. P., Keyser, C. S., Hamburger, S. D., Bartko, J. J., & Rapoport, J. L. (1992). A 2-year prospective follow-up study of children and adolescents with disruptive behavior disorders: Prediction by cerebrospinal fluid 5-hydroxyindoleacetic acid, homovanillic acid, and autonomic measures? *Archives of General Psychiatry, 49,* 429-435.

367. Lamm, O., & Epstein, R. (1992). Specific reading impairments—Are they to be associated with emotional difficulties? *Journal of Learning Disabilities, 25,* 605–615.

368. Lehman, E. B., Bovasso, M., Grout, L. A., & Happ, L. K. (1992). Orienting task effects on memory for presentation modality in children, young adults, and older adults. *The Journal of General Psychology, 119,* 15-27.

369. Leigh, J., Westen, D., Barends, A., Mendel, M. J., & Byers, S. (1992). The assessment of complexity of representations of people using TAT and interview data. *Journal of Personality, 60,* 809–837.

370. Lynn, R. (1992). Does Spearman's *g* decline at high IQ levels? Some evidence from Scotland. *The Journal of Genetic Psychology, 153,* 229-230.

371. Madison, C. L., & Wong, E. Y. F. (1992). Use of the Clark-Madison Test of Oral Language with the hearing-impaired: A content validity and comparative study. *Journal of Communication Disorders, 25,* 241–250.

372. McCarthy, R. A., & Warrington, E. K. (1992). Actors but not scripts: The dissociation of people and events in retrograde amnesia. *Neuropsychologia, 30,* 633-644.

373. McInerney, C. A., & McInerney, M. (1992). A mobility skills training program for adults with developmental disabilities. *The American Journal of Occupational Therapy, 46,* 233-239.

374. MeKitrick, L. A. Camp, C. J., & Black, F. W. (1992). Prospective memory intervention in Alzheimer's Disease. *Journal of Gerontology, 47,* 337–343.

375. Meyers, C. A., & Abbruzzese, J. L. (1992). Cognitive functioning in cancer patients: Effect of previous treatment. *Neurology, 42,* 434–436.

376. Milgram, N. A., Dangour, W., & Raviv, A. (1992). Situational and personal determinants of academic procrastination. *The Journal of General Psychology, 119,* 123-133.

377. Miller, W. R., Leckman, A. L., Delaney, H. D., & Tinkcom, M. (1992). Long-term follow-up of behavioral self-control training. *Journal of Studies on Alcohol, 53,* 249–261.

378. Misra, A. (1992). Generalization of social skills through self-monitoring by adults with mild mental retardation. *Exceptional Children, 58,* 495-507.

379. Mortimer, J. A., Ebbit, B., Jun, S.-P., & Finch, M. D. (1992). Predictors of cognitive and functional progression in patients with probable Alzheimer's disease. *Neurology, 42,* 1689–1696.

380. Nass, R., Sadler, A. E., & Sidtis, J. J. (1992). Differential effects of congenital versus acquired unilateral brain injury on dichotic listening performance: Evidence for sparing and asymmetric crowding. *Neurology, 42,* 1960–1965.

381. Neistadt, M. E. (1992). Occupational therapy treatments for constructional deficits. *The American Journal of Occupational Therapy, 46,* 141-148.

382. Newcombe, N., & Dubas, J. S. (1992). A longitudinal study of predictors of spatial ability in adolescent females. *Child Development, 63,* 37–46.

383. Norman, S., Kemper, S., & Kynette, D. (1992). Adults' reading comprehension: Effects of syntactic complexity and working memory. *Journal of Gerontology, 47,* 258–265.

384. Nuechterlein, K. H., Dawson, M. E., Gitlin, M., Ventura, J., Goldstein, M. J., Snyder, K. S., Yee, C. M., & Mintz, J. (1992). Developmental processes in schizophrenia disorders: Longitudinal studies of vulnerability and stress. *Schizophrenia Bulletin, 18,* 387–425.

385. O'Carroll, R. E., Moffoot, A., Ebmeier, K. P., & Goodwin, G. M. (1992). Estimating pre-morbid intellectual ability in the alcoholic Korsakoff syndrome. *Psychological Medicine, 22,* 903-909.

386. Paller, K. A., Mayes, A. R., Thompson, K. M., Young, A. W., Roberts, J., & Meudell, P. R. (1992). Priming of face matching in amnesia. *Brain and Cognition, 18,* 46-59.

387. Park, S., & Holzman, P. S. (1992). Schizophrenics show spatial working memory deficits. *Archives of General Psychiatry, 49,* 975-982.

388. Paul, S. (1992). Test-retest reliability study of the Pennsylvania Bi-Manual Worksample. *The American Journal of Occupational Therapy, 46,* 809-812.

389. Peach, R. K. (1992). Factors underlying neuropsychological test performance in chronic severe traumatic brain injury. *Journal of Speech and Hearing Research, 35,* 810–818.

390. Peavy, G. M., Herzog, A. G., Rubin, N. P., & Mesulam, M.-M. (1992). Neuropsychological aspects of dementia of motor neuron disease: A report of two cases. *Neurology, 42,* 1004–1008.

391. Pennington, B. F., Gilger, J. W., Olson, R. K., & DeFries, J. C. (1992). The external validity of age- versus IQ-discrepancy definitions of reading disability: Lessons from a twin study. *Journal of Learning Disabilities, 25,* 562–573.

392. Peterson, J. B., Finn, P. R., & Pihl, R. O. (1992). Cognitive dysfunction and the inherited predisposition to alcoholism. *Journal of Studies on Alcoholism, 53,* 154–160.

393. Pollina, L. K., Greene, A. L., Tunick, R. H., & Puckett, J. M. (1992). Dimensions of everyday memory in young adulthood. *British Journal of Psychology, 83,* 305-321.

394. Rouet, J. F., Ehrlich, R. M., & Sorbara, D. L. (1992). Neurodevelopment in infants and preschool children with congenital hypothyroidism: Etiological and treatment factors affecting outcome. *Journal of Pediatric Psychology, 17,* 187–213.

395. Ryan, J. J, Dai, X., Paolo, A. M., & Harrington, R. G. (1992). Factor analysis of the Chinese WAIS with persons who have mental retardation. *American Journal on Mental Retardation, 97,* 111-114.

396. Sakurai, Y., Kurisaki, H., Takeda, K., Iwata, M., Bandoh, M., Watanabe, T., & Momose, T. (1992). Japanese crossed Wernicke's aphasia. *Neurology, 42,* 144–148.

397. Salthouse, T. A. (1992). What do adult age differences in the digit symbol substitution test reflect? *Journal of Gerontology, 47,* 121–128.

398. Sands, L. P., & Meredith, W. (1992). Blood pressure and intellectual functioning in late midlife. *Journal of Gerontology, 47,* 81–84.

399. Scarr, S. (1992). Developmental theories for the 1990s: Development and individual differences. *Child Development, 63,* 1–19.

400. Scheffers, M. K., Johnson, R., Grafman, J., Dale, J. K., & Straus, S. E. (1992). Attention and short-term memory in chronic fatigue syndrome patients: An event-related potential analysis. *Neurology, 42,* 1667–1675.

401. Selrees, O. A., McArthur, J. C., Royal, W., Updike, M. L., Nance-Sproson, T., Concha, M., Gordon, B., Solomon, L., & Vlahor, D. (1992). HIV-I infection and intravenous drug use: Longitudinal neuropsychological evaluation of asymptomatic subjects. *Neurology, 42,* 1924–1930.

402. Smalley, S. L., Tanguay, P. E., Smith, M., & Gutierrez, G. (1992). Autism and tuberous sclerosis. *Journal of Autism and Developmental Disorders, 22*(3), 339-355.

403. Smith, M. E., & Oscar-Berman, M. (1992). Resource-limited information processing in alcoholism. *Journal of Studies on Alcohol, 53,* 514–518.

404. Stein, P. N., Gordon, W. A., Hibbard, M. R., & Sliwinski, M. J. (1992). An examination of depression in the spouses of stroke patients. *Rehabilitation Psychology, 37,* 121–130.

405. Sullivan, P. M., & Schulte, L. E. (1992). Factor analysis of WISC-R with deaf and hard-of-hearing children. *Psychological Assessment, 4,* 537–540.

406. Suzuki, I., Shimuzu, H., Ishijima, B., Tani, K., Sugishita, M., & Adachi, N. (1992). Aphasic seizure caused by focal epilepsy in the left fusiform gyrus. *Neurology, 42,* 2207–2210.

407. Tatemichi, T. K., Desmond, D. W., Mayeux, R., Paik, M., Stern, Y., Sano, M., Remien, R. H., Williams, J. B. W., Mohr, J. P., Hauser, W. A., & Figueroa, M. (1992). Dementia after stroke: Baseline frequency, risks, and clinical features in a hospitalized cohort. *Neurology, 42,* 1185–1193.

408. Tatemichi, T. K., Desmond, D. W., Prohovnik, I., Cross, D. T., Gropen, T. I., Mohr, J. P., & Stern, Y. (1992). Confusion and memory loss from capsular genu infarction: A thalamocortical disconnection syndrome? *Neurology, 42,* 1966–1979.

409. Tomblin, J. B., Freese, P. R., & Records, N. L. (1992). Diagnosing specific language impairment in adults for the purpose of pedigree analysis. *Journal of Speech and Hearing Research, 35,* 832–843.

410. Turkheimer, E., & Farace, E. (1992). A reanalysis of gender differences in IQ scores following unilateral brain lesions. *Psychological Assessment, 4,* 498–501.

411. Venter, A., Lord, C., & Schopler, E. (1992). A follow-up study of high-functioning autistic children. *Journal of Child Psychology and Psychiatry and Allied Disciplines, 33,* 489-507.

412. Verfaellie, M., Milberg, W. D., Cermak, L. S., & Letourneau, L. L. (1992). Priming of spatial configurations in alcoholic Korsakoff's amnesia. *Brain and Cognition, 18,* 34-45.

413. Vilkki, J. (1992). Cognitive flexibility and mental programming after closed head injuries and anterior or posterior cerebral excisions. *Neuropsychologia, 30,* 807-814.

414. Walsh, A. (1992). The P>V sign in corrections: Is it a useful diagnostic tool? *Criminal Justice and Behavior, 19,* 372–383.

415. Warrington, E. K., & Duchen, L. W. (1992). A re-appraisal of a case of persistant global amnesia following right temporal lobectomy: A clinico-pathological study. *Neuropsychologia, 30,* 437-450.

416. Watkins, C. E., Jr., & Campbell, V. L. (1992). The test-retest reliability and stability of the WAIS-R in a sample of mentally retarded adults. *Journal of Intellectual Disability Research, 36,* 265-268.

417. Williams, D. L., Gridley, B. E., & Fitzhugh-Bell, K. (1992). Cluster analysis of children and adolescents with brain damage and learning disabilities using neuropsychological, psychoeducational, and sociobehavioral variables. *Journal of Learning Disabilities, 25,* 290–299.

418. Wingfield, A., Wayland, S. C., & Stine, E. A. L. (1992). Adult age differences in the use of prosody for syntactic parsing and recall of spoken sentences. *Journal of Gerontology, 47,* 350–356.

419. Wolkin, A., Sanfilipo, M., Wolf, A. D., Angrist, B., Brodie, J. D., & Rotrosen, J. (1992). Negative symptoms and hypofrontality in chronic schizophrenia. *Archives of General Psychiatry, 49,* 959-965.

420. Zipursky, R. B., Lim, K. O., Sullivan, E. V., Brown, B. W., & Pfefferbaum, A. (1992). Widespread cerebral gray matter volume deficits in schizophrenia. *Archives of General Psychiatry, 49,* 195-205.

421. Adams, S. G., & Howe, J. T. (1993). Predicting medication compliance in a psychotic population. *The Journal of Nervous and Mental Disease, 181,* 558-560.

422. Allen, P. A., Weber, T. A., & May, N. (1993). Age differences in letter and color matching: Selective attention or internal noise? *Journal of Gerontology, 48,* 69–77.

423. Almkvist, O., Backman, L., Basun, H., & Wahlund, L. (1993). Patterns of neuropsychological performance in Alzheimer's desease and vascular dementia. *Cortex, 29,* 661-673.

424. Amin, K., Douglas, V. I., Mendelson, M. J., & Dufresne, J. (1993). Separable/integral classification by hyperactive and normal children. *Development and Psychopathology, 5,* 415-431.

425. Aplin, D. Y. (1993). Psychological evaluation of adults in a cochlear implant program. *American Annals of the Deaf,* 138, 415-419.

426. Appollonio, I. M., Grafman, J., Schwartz, V., Massaquoi, S., & Hallet, M. (1993). Memory in patients with cerebellar degeneration. *Neurology, 43,* 1536–1544.

427. Bailey, A., Bolton, P., Butler, L., LeCouteur, A., Murphy, M., Scott, S., Webb, T., & Rutter, M. (1993). Prevalence of the fragile X anomaly amongst autistic twins and singletons. *Journal of Child Psychology and Psychiatry and Allied Disciplines, 34,* 673-688.

428. Bank, L., Forgatch, M. S., Patterson, G. R., & Fetrow, R. A. (1993). Parenting practices of single mothers: Mediators of negative contextual factors. *Journal of Marriage and the Family, 55,* 371–384.

429. Barba, G. D. (1993). Different patterns of confabulation. *Cortex, 29,* 567-581.

430. Beatty, W. W., Jocic, Z., Monson, N., & Staton, R. D. (1993). Memory and frontal lobe dysfunction in schizophrenia and schizoaffective disorder. *The Journal of Nervous and Mental Disease, 181,* 448-453.

431. Bird, M., & Luszcz, M. (1993). Enhancing memory performance in Alzheimer's disease: Acquisition assistance and cue effectiveness. *Journal of Clinical and Experimental Neuropsychology, 15,* 921-932.

432. Bloom, R. L., Borod, J. C., Obler, L. K., & Gerstman, L. J. (1993). Suppression and facilitation of pragmatic performance: Effects of emotional content on discourse following right and left brain damage. *Journal of Speech and Hearing Research, 36,* 1227–1235.

433. Boone, D. E. (1993). WAIS-R scatter with psychiatric inpatients: II. Intersubtest scatter. *Psychological Reports, 73,* 851-860.

434. Borod, J. C., Martin, C. C., Alpert, M., Brozgold, A., & Welkowitz, J. (1993). Perception of facial emotion in schizophrenic and right brain-damaged patients. *The Journal of Nervous and Mental Disease, 181,* 494-502.

435. Canavan, A. G. M., & Beckmann, J. (1993). Deriving principal component IQ scores from the WAIS-R. *British Journal of Clinical Psychology, 32,* 81-86.

436. Casey, B. J., Gordon, C. T., Mannheim, G. B., & Rumsey, J. M. (1993). Dysfunctional attention in autistic savants. *Journal of Clinical and Experimental Neuropsychology, 15,* 933-946.

437. Castelloe, P., & Dawson, G. (1993). Subclassification of children with autism and pervasive developmental disorder: A questionnaire based on Wing's subgrouping scheme. *Journal of Autism and Developmental Disorders, 23*(2), 229-241.

438. Channon, S., Baker, J. E., & Robertson, M. M. (1993). Working memory in clinical depression: An experimental study. *Psychological Medicine, 23,* 87-91.

439. Christianson, S. A., Saisa, J., Garvill, J., & Silfvenius, H. (1993). Hemisphere inactivation and mood-state changes. *Brain and Cognition, 23,* 127-144.

440. Clare, I. C. H., & Gudjonsson, G. H. (1993). Interrogative suggestibility, confabulation, and aquiescence in people with mild learning disabilities (mental handicap): Implications for reliability during police interrogations. *British Journal of Clinical Psychology, 32,* 295-301.

441. Clausen, T., & Scott, R. (1993). Factor analysis of the WAIS-R and verbal memory and visual memory indices of the Wechsler Memory Scale—Revised, for a vocational rehabilitation sample. *Perceptual and Motor Skills, 76,* 907–911.

442. Cornoldi, C., Bertuccelli, B., Rocchi, P., & Sbrana, B. (1993). Processing capacity limitations in pictorial and spatial representations in the totally congenitally blind. *Cortex, 29,* 675-689.

443. Correll, R. E., Brodginski, S. E., & Rokosz, S. F. (1993). WAIS performance during the acute recovery stage following closed-head injury. *Perceptual and Motor Skills, 76,* 99–109.

444. Crawford, J. R., O'Bonsawin, M. C., & Bremner, M. (1993). Frontal lobe impairment in schizophrenia: Relationship to intellectual functioning. *Psychological Medicine, 23,* 787-790.

445. Crockett, D. J. (1993). Cross-validation of WAIS-R prototypical patterns of intellectual functioning using neuropsychological test scores. *Journal of Clinical and Experimental Neuropsychology, 15,* 903-920.

446. Dautrich, B. R. (1993). Visual perceptual differences in the dyslexic reader: Evidence of greater visual peripheral sensitivity to color and letter stimuli. *Perceptual and Motor Skills, 76,* 755–764.

447. DeLuca, J. (1993). Predicting neurobehavioral patterns following anterior communicating artery aneurysm. *Cortex, 29,* 639-647.

448. DeRenzi, E., & Lucchelli, F. (1993). Dense retrograde amnesia, intact learning capability and abnormal forgetting rate: A consolidation deficit? *Cortex, 29,* 449-466.

449. Deweer, B., Pillon, B., Michon, A., & Dubois, B. (1993). Mirror reading in Alzheimer's disease: Normal skill learning and acquisition of item-specific information. *Journal of Clinical and Experimental Neuropsychology, 15,* 789-804.

450. Dodrill, C. B., Arnett, J. L., Sommerville, K. W., & Sussman, N. M. (1993). Evaluation of the effects of vigabatrin on cognitive abilities and quality of life epilepsy. *Neurology, 43,* 2501–2507.

451. Dvara, R., Lopez-Alberola, R. F., Barker, W. W., Loewenstein, D. A., Zatinsky, M., Eisdorfer, C. E., & Weinberg, G. B. (1993). A comparison of familial and sporadic Alzheimer's disease. *Neurology, 43,* 1377–1384.

452. Dworkin, R. H., Cornblatt, B. A., Friedmann, R., Kaplansky, L. M., Lewis, J. A., Rinaldi, A., Shilliday, C., & Erlenmeyer-Kimling, L. (1993). Childhood precursors of affective vs. social deficits in adolescents at risk for schizophrenia. *Schizophrenia Bulletin, 19,* 563–577.

453. Egan, V. G., Chiswick, A., Brettle, R. P., & Goodwin, G. M. (1993). The Edinburgh cohort of HIV-positive drug users: The relationship between auditory P3 latency, cognitive function and self-rated mood. *Psychological Medicine, 23,* 613-622.

454. Elias, M. F., Robbins, M. A., Walter, L. J., & Schultz, N. R., Jr. (1993). The influence of gender and age on Halstead-Reitan neuropsychological Test performance. *Journal of Gerontology, 48,* 278–281.

455. Feingold, A. (1993). Cognitive gender differences: A developmental perspective. *Sex Roles, 29,* 91-112.

456. Fenwick, T. L., & Holmes, C. B. (1993). Effect of visual cues with the WAIS-R digit span subtest. *Perceptual and Motor Skills, 76,* 1025–1026.

457. Fitzgerald, H. E., Sullivan, L. A., Ham, H. P., Zucker, R. A., Bruckel, S., Schneider, A. M., & Noll, R. B. (1993). Predictors of behavior problems in three-year-old sons of alcoholics: Early evidence for the onset of risk. *Child Development, 64,* 110-123.

458. Fujiki, M., & Brinton, B. (1993). Comprehension monitoring skills of adults with mental retardation. *Research in Developmental Disabilities, 14,* 409-421.

459. Goldberg, T. E., Hyde, T. M., Kleinman, J. E., & Weinberger, D. R. (1993). Course of schizophrenia: Neuropsychological evidence for a static encephalopathy. *Schizophrenia Bulletin, 19,* 797–804.

460. Goldberg, T. E., Torrey, E. F., Gold, J. M., Ragland, J. D., Bigelow, L. B., & Weinberger, D. R. (1993). Learning and memory in monozygotic twins discordant for schizophrenia. *Psychological Medicine, 23,* 71-85.

461. Gooding, P. A., van Eijk, R., Mayes, A. R., & Meudell, P. (1993). Preserved pattern completion priming for novel, abstract geometric shapes in amnesics of several aetiologies. *Neuropsychologia, 31,* 789-810.

462. Hart, L. R. (1993). Diagnosis of disruptive behavior disorders using the Millon Adolescent Personality Inventory. *Psychological Reports, 73,* 895-914.

463. Hestad, K., Aukrust, A., Ellersten, B., Klove, H., & Wilberg, K. (1993). Neuropsychological deficits in HIV-1 seropositive and seronegative intravenous drug users. *Journal of Clinical and Experimental Neuropsychology, 15,* 732–742.

464. Hill, L. R., Klauber, M. R., Salmon, D. P., Yu, E. S. H., Liu, W. T., Zhang, M., & Katzman, R. (1993). Functional status, education, and the diagnosis of dementia in the Shanghai survey. *Neurology, 43,* 138–145.

465. Hill, R. D., Storandt, M., & Malley, M. (1993). The impact of long-term exercise training on psychological function in older adults. *Journal of Gerontology, 48,* 12–17.

466. Horton, A. M., Jr. (1993). Posttraumatic stress disorder and mild head trauma: Follow-up of a case study. *Perceptual and Motor Skills, 76,* 243–246.

467. Howe, G. W., Feinstein, C., Reiss, D., Molock, S., & Berger, K. (1993). Adolescent adjustment to chronic physical disorders-I. Comparing neurological and non-neurological conditions. *Journal of Child Psychology and Psychiatry and Allied Disciplines, 34,* 1153-1176.

468. Howieson, D. B., Holm, L. A., Kaye, J. A., Oken, B. S., & Howieson, J. (1993). Neurologic function in the optimally healthy oldest old: Neuropsychological evaluation. *Neurology, 43,* 1882–1886.

469. Hull, J. W., Clarkin, J. F., & Alexopoulos, G. S. (1993). Time series analysis of intervention effects: Fluoxetine therapy as a case illustration. *The Journal of Nervous and Mental Disease, 181,* 48-53.

470. Incisa della Rocchetta, A., & Milner, B. (1993). Strategic search and retrieval inhibition: The role of the frontal lobes. *Neuropsychologia, 31,* 503-524.

471. Inouye, S. K., Albert, M. S., Mohs, R., Sun, K., & Berkman, L. F. (1993). Cognitive performance in a high-functioning community-dwelling elderly population. *Journal of Gerontology, 48,* 146–151.

472. Ishiai, S., Sugishita, M., Idrikawa, T., Gono, S., & Watabiki, S. (1993). Clock-drawing test and unilateral spatial neglect. *Neurology, 43,* 106–110.

473. Jacobson, S. W., Jacobson, J. L., Sokol, R. J., Martier, S. S., & Ager, J. W. (1993). Prenatal alcohol exposure and infant information processing ability. *Child Development, 64,* 1706-1721.

474. Jeste, D. V., Lacro, J. P., Gilbert, P. L., Kline, J., & Kline, N. (1993). Treatment of late-life schizophrenia with neuroleptics. *Schizophrenia Bulletin, 19,* 817–830.

475. Katz, L., & Goldstein, G. (1993). The Luria-Nebraska Neuropsychological Battery and the WAIS-R in assessment of adults with specific learning disabilities. *Rehabilitation Counselor Bulletin, 36,* 190–198.

476. Katz, L., Goldstein, G., Rudisin, S., & Bailey, D. (1993). A neuropsychological approach to the bannatyne recategorization of the Wechsler Intelligence Scales in adults with learning disabilities. *Journal of Learning Disabilities, 26,* 65–72.

477. Katzman, R. (1993). Education and the prevalence of dementia and Alzheimer's disease. *Neurology, 43,* 13–20.

478. Kline, R. B., Snyder, J., Guilmette, S., & Castellanos, M. (1993). External validity of the profile variability index for the K-ABC, Stanford-Binet, and WISC-R: Another cul-de-sac. *Journal of Learning Disabilities, 26,* 557–567.

479. Krupp, L. B., Masur, D. M., & Kaufman, L. D. (1993). Neurocognitive dysfunction in the eosinophilia-myalgia syndrome. *Neurology, 43,* 931–936.

480. Larrabee, G. J., Youngjohn, J. R., Sudilovsky, A., & Crook, T. H. (1993). Accelerated forgetting in Alzheimer-type dementia. *Journal of Clinical and Experimental Neuropsychology, 15,* 701-712.

481. Lindsay, W. R., Howells, L., & Pitcaithly, D. (1993). Cognitive therapy for depression with individuals with intellectual disabilities. *British Journal of Medical Psychology, 66,* 135–141.

482. Lis, A., & Magro, T. (1993). Study of Longeot's test of formal operational thinking in a group of Italian adolescents. *Perceptual and Motor Skills, 76,* 739–752.

483. Little, S. S. (1993). Nonverbal learning disabilities and socioemotional functioning: A review of recent literature. *Journal of Learning Disabilities, 26,* 653–665.

484. Loewenstein, D. A., Argüelles, T., Barker, W. W., & Duara, R. (1993). A comparative analysis of neuropsychological test performance of Spanish-speaking and English-speaking patients with Alzheimer's Disease. *Journal of Gerontology, 48,* 142–149.

485. Luszcz, M. A. (1993). When knowing is not enough: The role of memory beliefs in prose recall of older and younger adults. *Australian Psychologist, 28,* 16–20.

486. Lynn, R., & Dai, X. (1993). Sex differences on the Chinese standardization sample of the WAIS-R. *The Journal of Genetic Psychology, 154,* 459-463.

487. Macmann, G. M., & Barnett, D. W. (1993). Reliability of psychiatric and psychological diagnoses of mental retardation severity: Judgements under naturally occurring conditions. *American Journal on Mental Retardation, 97,* 559-567.

488. MacMillan, D. L., Gresham, F. M., & Siperstein, G. N. (1993). Conceptual and psychometric concerns about the 1992 AAMR definition of mental retardation. *American Journal on Mental Retardation, 98,* 325–335.

489. Mandes, E., & Kellin, J. (1993). Male-female response profile differences on the WAIS-R in clients suffering from borderline personality disorders. *The Journal of Psychology, 127,* 565-572.
490. Mann, V. A. (1993). Phoneme awareness and future reading ability. *Journal of Learning Disabilities, 26,* 259–269.
491. Marcel, B. B., Samson, J., Cole, J. O., & Schatzberg, A. F. (1993). Discrimination of facial emotion in depressed patients with visual-perceptual disturbances. *The Journal of Nervous and Mental Disease, 181,* 583-584.
492. Markowitsch, H. J., Calabrese, P., Haupts, M., Durwen, H. F., Liess, J., & Gehlen, W. (1993). Searching for the anatomical basis of retrograde amnesia. *Journal of Clinical and Experimental Neuropsychology, 15,* 947-967.
493. Martin, R. C., Bolter, J. F., Todd, M. E., Gouvier, W. D., & Niccolls, R. (1993). Effects of sophistication and motivation on the detection of malingered memory performance using a computerized forced-choice task. *Journal of Clinical and Experimental Neuropsychology, 15,* 867-880.
494. Mayberry, R. I. (1993). First-language acquisition after childhood differs from second-language acquisition: The case of American Sign Language. *Journal of Speech and Hearing Research, 36,* 1258–1270.
495. Mayes, A. R., Downes, J. J., Shoqeirat, M., Hall, C., & Sagar, H. J. (1993). Encoding ability is preserved in amnesia: Evidence from a direct test of encoding. *Neuropsychologia, 31,* 745-759.
496. Mayeux, R., Stern, Y., Tang, M. X., Todak, G., Marder, K., Sano, M., Richards, M., Stein, Z., Ehrhardt, A. A., & Gorman, J. M. (1993). Mortality risks in gay men with human immunodeficiency virus infection and cognitive impairment. *Neurology, 43,* 176–182.
497. McCarley, R. W., Shenton, M. E., O'Donnell, B. F., Faux, S. F., Kikinis, R., Nestor, P. G., & Jolesz, F. A. (1993). Auditory P300 abnormalities and left posterior superior temporal gyros volume reduction in schizophrenia. *Archives of General Psychiatry, 50,* 190-197.
498. Meneilly, G. S., Cheung, E., Tessier, D., Yakura, C., & Tuokko, H. (1993). The effect of improved glycemic control on cognitive functions in the elderly patient with diabetes. *Journal of Gerontology, 48,* 117–121.
499. Meyerhoff, P. J., Mackay, S., Bachman, L., Poole, N., Dillon, W. P., Weiner, M. W., & Fein, G. (1993). Reduced brain N-acetylaspartate suggests neuronal loss in cognitively impaired human immunodeficiency virus-seropositve individuals: In viro 1H magnetic resonance spectroscopic imaging. *Neurology, 43,* 509–515.
500. Moore, A. D., Stambrook, M., Gill, D. D., Hawryluk, G. A., Peters, L. C., & Harrison, M. M. (1993). Factor structure of the Wechsler Adult Intelligence Scale—Revised in a traumatic brain injury sample. *Canadian Journal of Behavioural Science, 25,* 605-614.
501. Moriarty, J., Ring, H. A., & Robertson, M. M. (1993). An idiot savant calendrical calculator with Gilles de la Tourette syndrome: Implications for an understanding of the savant syndrome. *Psychological Medicine, 23,* 1019-1021.
502. Murphy, D. G. M., Bottomley, P. A., Salerno, J. A., DeCarli, C., Mentis, M. J., Grady, C. L., Teichberg, D., Giacometti, K. R., Rosenberg, J. M., Hardy, C. J., Schapiro, M. B., Rapoport, S. I., Alger, J. R., & Horwitz, B. (1993). An in vivo study of phosphorus and glucose metabolism in Alzheimer's disease using magnetic resonance spectroscopy and PET. *Archives of General Psychiatry, 50,* 341-349.
503. Nagle, R. J. (1993). The relationship between the WAIS-R and academic achievement among EMR adolescents. *Psychology in the Schools, 30,* 37-39.
504. Naglieri, J. A., & Reardon, S. M. (1993). Traditional IQ is irrelevant to learning disabilities—intelligence is not. *Journal of Learning Disabilities, 26,* 127–133.
505. Persinger, M. A. (1993). Personality changes following brain injury as a grief response to the loss of sense of self: Phenomenological themes as indices of local lability and neurocognitive structuring as psychotherapy. *Psychological Reports, 72,* 1059-1068.
506. Pierce, T. W., & Elias, M. F. (1993). Cognitive function and cardiovascular responsivity in subjects with a parental history of hypertension. *Journal of Behavioral Medicine, 16,* 277-294.
507. Pierce, T. W., Madden, D. J., Siegel, W. C., & Blumenthal, J. A. (1993). Effects of aerobic exercise on cognitive and psychosocial functioning in patients with mild hypertension. *Health Psychology, 12,* 286–291.
508. Prigatano, G. P., & Amin, K. (1993). Digit Memory Test: Unequivocal cerebral dysfunction and suspected malingering. *Journal of Clinical and Experimental Neuropsychology, 15,* 537-546.
509. Raggio, D. J. (1993). Correlations of the Kahn Intelligence Test and the WAIS-R IQs among mentally retarded adults. *Perceptual and Motor Skills, 76,* 252–254.
510. Randolph, C., Gold, J. M., Carpenter, C. J., Goldberg, T. E., & Weinberger, D. R. (1993). Implicit memory in patients with schizophrenia and normal controls: Effects of task demands on susceptibility to priming. *Journal of Clinical and Experimental Neuropsychology, 15,* 853-866.
511. Randolph, C., Mohr, E., & Chase, T. (1993). Assessment of intellectual function in dementing disorders: Validity of WAIS-R short forms for patients with Alzheimer's, Huntington's, and Parkinson's disease. *Journal of Clinical and Experimental Neuropsychology, 15,* 743-753.
512. Richards, M., Bell, K., Dooneief, G., Marder, K., Sano, M., Mayeux, R., & Stern, Y. (1993). Patterns of neuropsychological performance in Alzheimer's disease patients with and without extra pyramidal signs. *Neurology, 43,* 1708–1711.
513. Rodriguez, M. (1993). Cognitive functioning, family history of alcoholism, and antisocial behavior in female polydrug abusers. *Psychological Reports, 73,* 19-26.
514. Rothlind, J. C., Bylsma, F. W., Peyser, C., Folstein, S. E., & Brandt, J. (1993). Cognitive and motor correlates of everyday functioning in early Huntington's disease. *The Journal of Nervous and Mental Disease, 181,* 194-199.
515. Roxborough, H., Muir, W. J., Blackwood, D. H. R., Walker, M. T., & Blackburn, I. M. (1993). Neuropsychological and P300 abnormalities in schizophrenics and their relatives. *Psychological Medicine, 23,* 305-314.
516. Ryan, C. M., & Williams, T. M. (1993). Effects of insulin-dependent diabetes on learning and memory efficiency in adults. *Journal of Clinical and Experimental Neuropsychology, 15,* 685-700.
517. Ryan, L., Clark, C. M., Klonoff, H., & Paty, D. (1993). Models of cognitive deficit and statistical hypotheses: Multiple sclerosis, an example. *Journal of Clinical and Experimental Neuropsychology, 15,* 563-577.
518. Ryan, T. V., Sciara, A. D., & Barth, J. T. (1993). Chronic neuropsychological impairment resulting from disulfirain overdose. *Journal of Studies on Alcohol, 54,* 389–392.
519. Saint-Cyr, J. A., Taylor, A. E., & Lang, A. E. (1993). Neuropsychological and psychiatric side effects in the treatment of Parkinson's disease. *Neurology, 43,* 547–552.
520. Saling, M. M., Berkovic, S. F., O'Shea, M. F., Kalnins, R. M., Darby, D. G., & Bladin, P. F. (1993). Lateralization of verbal memory and unilateral hippocampal sclerosis: Evidence of task-specific effects. *Journal of Clinical and Experimental Neuropsychology, 15,* 608-618.
521. Salthouse, T. A. (1993). Attentional blocks are not responsible for age-related slowing. *Journal of Gerontology, 48,* 263–270.
522. Salthouse, T. A. (1993). Influence of working memory on adult age differences in matrix reasoning. *British Journal of Psychology, 84,* 171-199.
523. Salthouse, T. A. (1993). Speed and knowledge as determinants of adult age differences in verbal tasks. *Journal of Gerontology, 48,* 29–36.
524. Scarr, S., Weinberg, R. A., & Waldman, I. D. (1993). IQ correlations in transracial adoptive families. *Intelligence, 17,* 541-555.
525. Schmidt, R., Fazekas, F., Offenbacher, H., Dusek, T., Zach, E., Reinhart, B., Grieshofer, P., Freidl, W., Eber, B., Schumacher, M., Koch, M., & Lechner, H. (1993). Neuropsychologic correlates of MRI white matter hyperintensities: A study of 150 normal volunteers. *Neurology, 43,* 2490–2494.
526. Schuldberg, D. (1993). Personal resourcefulness: Positive aspects of functioning in high-risk research. *Psychiatry, 56,* 137–152.
527. Seilhean, D., Duyckaerts, C., Vazeux, R., Bolgert, F., Brunet, P., Katlama, C., Gentilini, M., & Hauxn, J. J. (1993). HIV-1-associated cognitive/motor complex: Absence of neuronal loss in the cerebral neocortex. *Neurology, 43,* 1492–1499.
528. Shah, A., & Frith, U. (1993). Why do autistic individuals show superior performance on the block design task? *Journal of Child Psychology and Psychiatry and Allied Disciplines, 34,* 1351-1364.
529. Sharrock, R., & Gudjonsson, G. H. (1993). Intelligence, previous convictions and interrogative suggestibility: A path analysis of alleged false-confession cases. *British Journal of Clinical Psychology, 32,* 169-175.
530. Shuren, J., Geldmacher, D., & Heilman, K. M. (1993). Nonoptic aphasia: Aphasia with preserved confrontation naming in Alzheimer's disease. *Neurology, 43,* 1900–1907.
531. Smith, S. A. (1993). Confusing the terms "guilty" and "not guilty": Implications for alleged offenders with mental retardation. *Psychological Reports, 73,* 675-678.
532. Soloff, P. H., Cornelius, J., George, A., Nathan, S., Perel, J. M., & Ulrich, R. F. (1993). Efficacy of phenelzine and haloperidol in borderline personality disorder. *Archives of General Psychiatry, 50,* 377-385.
533. Stevenson, J., Pennington, B. F., Gilger, J. W., DeFries, J. C., & Gillis, J. J. (1993). Hyperactivity and spelling disability: Testing for shared genetic aetiology. *Journal of Child Psychology and Psychiatry and Allied Disciplines, 34,* 1137-1152.
534. Strandburg, R. J., Marsh, J. T., Brown, W. S., Asarnow, R. F., Guthrie, D., & Higa, J. (1993). Event-related potentials in high-functioning adult autistics: Linguistic and nonlinguistic visual information processing tasks. *Neuropsychologia, 31,* 413-434.
535. Strauss, E., & Hunter, M. (1993). Wisconsin Card Sorting performance: Effects of age of onset of damage and laterality of dysfunction. *Journal of Clinical and Experimental Neuropsychology, 15,* 896-902.
536. Torrey, E. F., Bowler, A. E., Rawlings, R., & Terrazas, A. (1993). Seasonality of schizophrenia and stillbirths. *Schizophrenia Bulletin, 19,* 557–562.
537. Trenerry, M. R., Jack, C. R., Ivnik, R. J., Sharbrough, F. W., Cascino, G. D., Hirschorn, K. A., Marsh, W. R., Kelly, P. J., & Meyer, F. B. (1993). MRI hippocampal volumes and memory function before and after temporal lobectomy. *Neurology, 43,* 1800–1805.
538. Trueblood, W., & Schmidt, M. (1993). Malingering and other validity considerations in the neuropsychological evaluation of mild head injury. *Journal of Clinical and Experimental Neuropsychology, 15,* 578-590.
539. Truscott, D. (1993). Adolescent offenders: Comparison for sexual, violent, and property offences. *Psychological Reports, 73,* 657-658.
540. Turkheimer, E., Farace, E., Yeo, R. A., & Bigler, E. D. (1993). Quantitative analysis of gender differences in the effects of lateralized lesions on verbal and performance IQ. *Intelligence, 17,* 461-474.
541. Vallar, G., & Papagno, C. (1993). Preserved vocabulary acquisition in Down's syndrome: The role of phonological short-term memory. *Cortex, 29,* 467-483.
542. van den Broek, M. D., Bradshaw, C. M., & Szabadi, E. (1993). Utility of the modified Wisconsin Card Sorting Test in neuropsychological assessment. *British Journal of Clinical Psychology, 32,* 333-343.
543. Volkmar, F. R., Szatmari, P., & Sparrow, S. S. (1993). Sex differences in pervasive developmental disorder. *Journal of Autism and Developmental Disorders, 23*(4), 579-591.

544. Wade, J. B., Hart, R. P., & Dougherty, L. M. (1993). Factors related to the severity of Tardive Dyskinesia. *Brain and Cognition, 23,* 71-80.

545. Watson, B. V., & Miller, T. K. (1993). Auditory perception, phonological processing, and reading ability/disability. *Journal of Speech and Hearing Research, 36,* 850–863.

546. Wong, J. L. (1993). Comparison of the Shipley versus the WAIS-R subtests and summary scores in predicting college grade point average. *Perceptual and Motor Skills, 76,* 1075–1078.

547. Wood, D. A., Rosenberg, M. S., & Carran, D. T. (1993). The effects of tape-recorded self-instruction cues on the mathematics performance of students with learning disabilities. *Journal of Learning Disabilities, 26,* 250–258.

548. Woodard, J. L. (1993). Confirmatory factor analysis of the Wechsler Memory Scale—Revised in a mixed clinical population. *Journal of Clinical and Experimental Neuropsychology, 15,* 968-973.

549. Youngjohn, J. R., & Crook, T. H. (1993). Forgetting and retrieval of everyday material across the adult life span. *Journal of Clinical and Experimental Neuropsychology, 15,* 447-460.

550. Zametkin, A. J., Liebenaver, L. L., Fitzgerald, G. A., King, A. C., Minkonas, D. V., Herscovitch, P., Yamada, E. M., & Cohen, R. M. (1993). Brain metabolism in teenagers with attention-deficit hyperactivity disorder. *Archives of General Psychiatry, 50,* 333-340.

551. Zatorre, R. J., & Halpern, A. R. (1993). Effect of unilateral temporal-lobe excision on perception and imagery of songs. *Neuropsychologia, 31,* 221-232.

552. Abell, S. C., Heiberger, A. M., & Johnson, J. E. (1994). Cognitive evaluations of young adults by means of human figure drawings: An empirical investigation of two methods. *Journal of Clinical Psychology, 50,* 900-905.

553. Alderdice, F. A., McGuinness, C., & Brown, K. (1994). Identification of subtypes of problem drinkers based on neuropsychological performance. *British Journal of Clinical Psychology, 33,* 483-498.

554. Alexander, G. E., Prohovnik, I., Stern, Y., & Mayeux, R. (1994). WAIS-R subtest profile and cortical perfusion in Alzheimer's disease. *Brain and Cognition, 24,* 24-43.

555. Allen, P. A., Patterson, M. B., & Propper, R. E. (1994). Influence of letter size on age differences in letter matching. *Journal of Gerontology: Psychological Sciences, 49*(Pt.1), 24-28.

556. Allen, P. A., Weber, T. A., & Madden, D. J. (1994). Adult age differences in attention: Filtering or selection? *Journal of Gerontology: Psychological Sciences, 49*(Pt.2), 213-222.

557. Alpert, M., Clark, A., & Pouget, E. R. (1994). The syntactic role of pauses in the speech of schizophrenic patients with alogia. *Journal of Abnormal Psychology, 103,* 750-757.

558. Anderson, S. W., & Rizzo, M. (1994). Hallucinations following occipital lobe damage: A pathological activation of visual representations. *Journal of Clinical and Experimental Neuropsychology, 16,* 651-663.

559. Aram, D. M., & Eisele, J. A. (1994). Intellectual stability in children with unilateral brain lesions. *Neuropsychologia, 32,* 85–95.

560. Arbuckle, T. Y., Cooney, R., Milne, J., & Melchior, A. (1994). Memory for spatial layouts in relation to age and schema typicality. *Psychology and Aging, 9,* 467-480.

561. Arnett, P. A., Rao, S. M., Bernardin, L., Grafman, J., Yetkin, F. Z., & Lobeck, L. (1994). Relationship between frontal lobe lesions and Wisconsin Card Sorting Test performance in patients with multiple sclerosis. *Neurology, 44,* 420–425.

562. Babcock, R. L. (1994). Analysis of adult age differences on the Raven's Advanced Progressive Matrices Test. *Psychology and Aging, 9,* 303-314.

563. Backman, L., Hill, R. D., Herlitz, A., Fratiglioni, L., & Winblad, B. (1994). Predicting episodic memory performance in dementia: Is severity all there is? *Psychology and Aging, 9,* 520-527.

564. Barch, D., & Berenbaum, H. (1994). The relationship between information processing and language production. *Journal of Abnormal Psychology, 103,* 241-250.

565. Beers, S. R., Goldstein, G., & Katz, L. J. (1994). Neuropsychological differences between college students with learning disabilities and those with mild head injury. *Journal of Learning Disabilities, 27,* 315–324.

566. Bennett, K. M. B., & Castiello, U. (1994). Reach to grasp: Changes with age. *Journal of Gerontology: Psychological Sciences, 49*(Pt.1), 1-7.

567. Bernstein, V. J., & Hans, S. L. (1994). Predicting the developmental outcome of two-year-old children born exposed to methadone: Impact of social-environmental risk factors. *Journal of Clinical Child Psychology, 23,* 349-359.

568. Bieman-Copland, S., & Charness, N. (1994). Memory knowledge and memory monitoring in adulthood. *Psychology and Aging, 9,* 287-302.

569. Blanchard, J. J., Bellack, A. S., & Mueser, K. T. (1994). Affective and social-behavioral correlates of physical and social anhedonia in schizophrenia. *Journal of Abnormal Psychology, 103,* 719-728.

570. Blanchard-Fields, F. (1994). Age differences in causal attributions from an adult developmental perspective. *Journal of Gerontology: Psychological Sciences, 49*(Pt.1), 43-51.

571. Bolton, P., MacDonald, H., Pickles, A., Rios, P., Goode, S., Crowson, M., Bailey, A., & Rutter, M. (1994). A case-control family history study of autism. *Journal of Child Psychology and Psychiatry and Allied Disciplines, 35,* 877-900.

572. Bowler, D. M., & Worley, K. (1994). Susceptibility to social influence in adults with Asperger's syndrome: A research note. *Journal of Child Psychology and Psychiatry and Allied Disciplines, 35,* 689-697.

573. Bowles, N. L. (1994). Age and rate of activation in semantic memory. *Psychology and Aging, 9,* 414-429.

574. Boyle, G. J., Ward, J., & Steindl, S. R. (1994). Psychometric properties of Russell's short form of the Booklet Category Test. *Perceptual and Motor Skills, 79,* 128-130.

575. Breen, K., & Warrington, E. K. (1994). A study of anomia: Evidence for a distinction between nominal and propositional language. *Cortex, 30,* 231-245.

576. Brier, N. (1994). Targeted treatment for adjudicated youth with learning disabilities: Effects on recidivism. *Journal of Learning Disabilities, 27,* 215–222.

577. Brinton, B., & Fujiki, M. (1994). Ability of institutionalized and community-based adults with retardation to respond to questions in an interview context. *Journal of Speech and Hearing Research, 37,* 369–377.

578. Brown, D. T. (1994). Review of the Kaufman Adolescent and Adult Intelligence Test (KAIT). *Journal of School Psychology, 32,* 85-99.

579. Brown, R. G., Scott, L. C., Bench, C. J., & Dolan, R. J. (1994). Cognitive function in depression: Its relationship to the presence and severity of intellectual decline. *Psychological Medicine, 24,* 829-847.

580. Brugge, K. L., Nichols, S. L., Salmon, D. P., Hill, L. R., Delis, D. C., Aaron, L., & Trainer, D. A. (1994). Cognitive impairment in adults with Down's Syndrome: Similarities to early cognitive changes in Alzheimer's disease. *Neurology, 44,* 232–238.

581. Burgess, A. P., Riccio, M., Jadresic, D., Pugh, K., Catalan, J., Hawkins, D. A., Baldeweg, T., Lovett, E., Gruzelier, J., & Thompson, C. (1994). A longitudinal study of the neuropsychiatric consequences of HIV-1 infection in gay men. I. Neuropsychological performance and neurological status at baseline and at 12-month follow-up. *Psychological Medicine, 24,* 885-895.

582. Burton, D. B., Ryan, J. J., Paolo, A. M., & Mittenberg, W. (1994). Structural equation analysis of the Wechsler Adult Intelligence Scale—Revised in a normal elderly sample. *Psychological Assessment, 6,* 380-385.

583. Butter, C. M., & Trobe, J. D. (1994). Integrative agnosia following progressive multifocal leukoencephalopathy. *Cortex, 30,* 145-158.

584. Buytenhuijs, E. L., Berger, H. J. C., Van Spaendonck, K. P. M., Horstink, M. W. I. M., Borm, G. F., & Cools, A. R. (1994). Memory and learning strategies in patients with Parkinson's disease. *Neuropsychologia, 32,* 335–342.

585. Carlesimo, G. A. (1994). Perceptual and conceptual priming in amnesic and alcoholic patients. *Neuropsychologia, 32,* 903–921.

586. Chertkow, H., Bub, D., Bergman, H., Bruemmer, A., Merling, A., & Rothfleisch, J. (1994). Increased semantic priming in patients with dementia of the Alzheimer's type. *Journal of Clinical and Experimental Neuropsychology, 16,* 608-622.

587. Christensen, H., Mackinnon, A., Jorm, A. F., Henderson, A. S., Scott, L. R., & Korten, A. E. (1994). Age differences and interindividual variation in cognition in community-dwelling elderly. *Psychology and Aging, 9,* 381-390.

588. Cipolotti, L., Butterworth, B., & Warrington, E. K. (1994). From "one thousand nine hundred and forty-five" to 1000,945. *Neuropsychologia, 32,* 503–509.

589. Clancy, S. M., & Hoyer, W. J. (1994). Age and skill in visual search. *Developmental Psychology, 30,* 545-552.

590. Clare, I. C. H., Gudjonsson, G. H., Rotter, S. C., & Cross, P. (1994). The inter-rater reliability of the Gudjonsson Suggestibility Scale (Form 2). *British Journal of Clinical Psychology, 33,* 357-365.

591. Cohen, G., Conway, M. A., & Maylor, E. A. (1994). Flashbulb memories in older adults. *Psychology and Aging, 9,* 454-463.

592. Cohen, R. A., Kaplan, R. F., Meadows, M. E., & Wilkinson, H. (1994). Habituation and sensitization of the orienting response following bilateral anterior cingulotomy. *Neuropsychologia, 32,* 609–617.

593. Corballis, M. C. (1994). Can commissurotomized subjects compare digits between the visual fields? *Neuropsychologia, 32,* 1475–1486.

594. Crawford, J. R., & Allan, K. M. (1994). The mahalanobis distance index of WAIS-R subtest scatter: Psychometric properties in a healthy UK sample. *British Journal of Clinical Psychology, 33,* 65-69.

595. Cronin-Golomb, A., Corkin, S., & Growdon, J. H. (1994). Impaired problem solving in Parkinson's disease: Impact of a set-shifting deficit. *Neuropsychologia, 32,* 579–593.

596. Crossen, J. R., & Wiens, A. N. (1994). Comparison of the Auditory-Verbal Learning Test (AVLT) and the California Verbal Learning Test (CVLT) in a sample of normal subjects. *Journal of Clinical and Experimental Neuropsychology, 16,* 190-194.

597. Crossman, L. L., Casey, T. A., & Reilley, R. R. (1994). Influence of cognitive variables on MMPI-2 scale scores. *Measurement and Evaluation in Counseling and Development, 27,* 151-157.

598. Csernansky, J. G., & Newcomer, J. W. (1994). Are there neurochemical indicators of risk for schizophrenia? *Schizophrenia Bulletin, 20,* 75–88.

599. Cuesta, M. J., & Peralta, V. (1994). Lack of insight in schizophrenia. *Schizophrenia Bulletin, 20,* 359–366.

600. Damos, D. L., & Parker, E. S. (1994). High false alarm rates on a vigilance task may indicate recreational drug use. *Journal of Clinical and Experimental Neuropsychology, 16,* 713-722.

601. DCCT Research Group. (1994). A screening algorithm to identify clinically significant changes in neuropsychological functions in the diabetes control and complications trial. *Journal of Clinical and Experimental Neuropsychology, 16,* 303-316.

602. DeLuca, J., Barbieri-Berger, S., & Johnson, S. K. (1994). The nature of memory impairments in multiple sclerosis: Acquisition versus retrieval. *Journal of Clinical and Experimental Neuropsychology, 16,* 183-189.

603. DeRenzi, E., & Lucchelli, F. (1994). Are semantic systems separately represented in the brain? The case of living category impairment. *Cortex, 30,* 3-25.

604. Desmond, D. W., Glenwick, D. S., Stern, Y., & Tatenichi, T. K. (1994). Sex differences in the representation of visuospatial functions in the human brain. *Rehabilitation Psychology, 39,* 3–14.

605. DeWeer, B., Ergis, A. M., Fossati, P., Pillon, B., Boller, F., Agid, Y., & Dubois, B. (1994). Explicit memory, procedural learning, and lexical priming in Alzheimer's disease. *Cortex, 30,* 113-126.

606. Diamond, B. J., Valentine, T., Mayes, A. R., & Sandel, M. E. (1994). Evidence of covert recognition in a prosopagnosic patient. *Cortex, 30,* 377-393.

607. Dopkins, S., Kovner, R., & Goldmeier, E. (1994). Frequency judgements for semantic categories in amnesics and normal controls. *Cortex, 30,* 127-134.

608. Duncombe, M. E., Bradshaw, J. L., Iansek, R., & Phillips, J. G. (1994). Parkinsonian patients without dementia or depression do not suffer from bradyphrenia as indexed by performance in mental rotation tasks with and without advance information. *Neuropsychologia, 32,* 1383–1396.

609. Durlak, C. M., Rose, E., & Bursuck, W. D. (1994). Preparing high school students with learning disabilities for the transition to post-secondary education: Teaching the skills of self-determination. *Journal of Learning Disabilities, 27,* 51–59.

610. Dywan, J., Segalowitz, S. J., & Williamson, L. (1994). Source monitoring during name recognition in older adults: Psychometric and electrophysiological correlates. *Psychology and Aging, 9,* 568-577.

611. Eisele, J. A., & Aram, D. M. (1994). Comprehension and imitation of syntax following early hemisphere damage. *Brain and Language, 46,* 212–231.

612. Eslinger, P. J., & Grattan, L. M. (1994). Altered serial position learning after frontal lobe lesion. *Neuropsychologia, 32,* 729–739.

613. Fals-Stewart, W., & Lucente, S. (1994). The effect of cognitive rehabilitation on the neuropsychological status of patients in drug abuse treatment who display neurocognitive impairment. *Rehabilitation Psychology, 39,* 75–94.

614. Farlow, M., Murrell, J., Ghetti, B., Unverzagt, F., Zeldenrust, S., & Benson, M. (1994). Clinical characteristics in a kindred with early-onset Alzheimer's disease and their linkage to a G->T change at position 2149 of the amyloid percursor protein gene. *Neurology, 44,* 105–111.

615. Faure, S., & Blanc-Garin, J. (1994). Right hemisphere semantic performance and competence in a case of partial interhemispheric disconnection. *Brain and Language, 47,* 557–581.

616. Felsenfeld, S., Broen, P. A., & McGue, M. (1994). A 28-year follow-up of adults with a history of moderate phonological disorder: Educational and Occupational results. *Journal of Speech and Hearing, 37,* 1341–1353.

617. Fenton, W. S., Wyatt, R. J., & McGlashan, T. H. (1994). Risk factors for spontaneous dyskinesia in schizophrenia. *Archives of General Psychiatry, 51,* 643-650.

618. Flanagan, D. P., Alfonso, V. C., & Flanagan, R. (1994). A review of the Kaufman Adolescent and Adult Intelligence Test: An advancement in cognitive assessment? *School Psychology Review, 23,* 512–525.

619. Fletcher, J., & Martinez, G. (1994). An eye-movement analysis of the effects of scotopic sensitivity correction on parsing and comprehension. *Journal of Learning Disabilities, 27,* 67–70.

620. Foundas, A. L., Leonard, C. M., Gilmore, R., Fennell, E., & Heilman, K. M. (1994). Planum temporal asymmetry and language dominance. *Neuropsychologia, 32,* 1225–1231.

621. Friedman, D., Snodgrass, J. G., & Ritter, W. (1994). Implicit retrieval processes in cued recall: Implications for aging effects in memory. *Journal of Clinical and Experimental Neuropsychology, 16,* 921-938.

622. Fuh, J., Liao, K., Wang, S., & Lin, K. (1994). Swallowing difficulty in primary progressive aphasia: A case report. *Cortex, 30,* 701-705.

623. Gabrieli, J. D. E., Keane, M. M., Stanger, B. Z., Kjelgaard, M. M., Corkin, S., & Growdon, J. H. (1994). Dissociations among structural-perceptual, lexical-semantic, and event-fact memory systems in Alzheimer, amnesic, and normal subjects. *Cortex, 30,* 75-103.

624. Garety, P. A., Kuipers, L., Fowler, D., Chamberlain, F., & Dunn, G. (1994). Cognitive behavioural therapy for drug-resistant psychosis. *British Journal of Medical Psychology, 67,* 259–271.

625. Giancola, P. R., & Zeichner, A. (1994). Intellectual ability and aggressive behavior in nonclinical-nonforensic males. *Journal of Psychopathology and Behavioral Assessment, 16,* 121–130.

626. Giancola, P. R., & Zeichner, A. (1994). Neuropsychological performance on tests of frontal-lobe functioning and aggressive behavior in men. *Journal of Abnormal Psychology, 103,* 832-835.

627. Gilinsky, A. S., & Judd, B. B. (1994). Working memory and bias in reasoning across the life span. *Psychology and Aging, 9,* 356-371.

628. Gold, J. M., Hermann, B. P., Randolph, C., Wyler, A. R., Goldberg, T. E., & Weinberger, D. R. (1994). Schizophrenia and temporal lobe epilepsy: A neuropsychological analysis. *Archives of General Psychiatry, 51,* 265-272.

629. Goldman, W. P., Winograd, E., Goldstein, F. C., O'Jile, J., & Green, R. C. (1994). Source memory in mild to moderate Alzheimer's disease. *Journal of Clinical and Experimental Neuropsychology, 16,* 105-116.

630. Goldstein, G., Minshew, N. J., & Siegel, D. J. (1994). Age differences in academic achievement in high-functioning autistic individuals. *Journal of Clinical and Experimental Neuropsychology, 16,* 671-680.

631. Gooding, P. A., Mayes, A. R., & Meudell, P. (1994). Long lasting indirect memory performance for abstract shapes in amnesics and matched controls. *Neuropsychologia, 32,* 1135–1143.

632. Gottschalk, L. A. (1994). The development, validation, and applications of a computerized measurement of cognitive impairment from the content analysis of verbal behavior. *Journal of Clinical Psychology, 50,* 349-361.

633. Goulet, P., Ska, B., & Kahn, H. J. (1994). Is there a decline in picture naming with advancing age? *Journal of Speech and Hearing Research, 37,* 629–644.

634. Green, A., Steiner, R., & White, N. (1994). A follow-up dual-task investigation of lateralized effects in right- and left-handed males. *Brain and Cognition, 25,* 207-219.

635. Grisby, J., Kaye, K., & Busenbark, D. (1994). Alphanumeric sequencing: A report on a brief measure of information processing used among persons with multiple sclerosis. *Perceptual and Motor Skills, 78,* 883-887.

636. Grossi, D., Becker, J. T., & Trojano, L. (1994). Visuospatial imagery in Alzheimer disease. *Perceptual and Motor Skills, 78,* 867-874.

637. Grossman, I., Chan, T., & Parente, A. (1994). Validation of two new brief tests with a WAIS-R short form using a hospitalized depressed sample. *Perceptual and Motor Skills, 78,* 107–111.

638. Haaland, K. Y., & Harrington, D. L. (1994). Limb-sequencing deficits after left but not right hemisphere damage. *Brain and Cognition, 24,* 104-122.

639. Happé, F. (1994). An advanced test of theory of mind: Understanding of story characters' thoughts and feelings by able, autistic, mentally handicapped, and normal children and adults. *Journal of Autism and Developmental Disorders, 24,* 129-154.

640. Happé, F. G. E. (1994). Wechsler IQ profile and theory of mind in autism: A research note. *Journal of Child Psychology & Psychiatry & Allied Disciplines, 35,* 1461-1471.

641. Harvey, M., Milner, A. D., & Roberts, R. C. (1994). Spatial bias in visually-guided reaching and bisection following right cerebral stroke. *Cortex, 30,* 343-350.

642. Hashtroudi, S., Johnson, M. K., Vnek, N., & Ferguson, S. A. (1994). Aging and the effects of affective and factual focus in source monitoring and recall. *Psychology and Aging, 9,* 160-170.

643. Heaton, R., Paulsen, J. S., McAdams, L. A., Kuck, J., Zisook, S., Braff, D., Hams, J., & Jeste, D. V. (1994). Neuropsychological deficits in schizophrenics: Relationships to age, chronicity, and dementia. *Archives of General Psychiatry, 51,* 469-476.

644. Hess, T. M., & Pullen, S. M. (1994). Adult age differences in impression change process. *Psychology and Aging, 9,* 237-250.

645. Hillbrand, M., & Waite, B. M. (1994). The everyday experience of an institutionalized sex offender: An idiographic application of the experience sampling method. *Archives of Sexual Behavior, 23,* 453-463.

646. Hillbrand, M., Krystal, J. H., Sharpe, K. S., & Foster, H. G. (1994). Clinical predictors of self-mutilation in hospitalized forensic patients. *The Journal of Nervous and Mental Disease, 182,* 9-13.

647. Hittmair-Delazer, M., Denes, G., Semenza, C., & Mantovan, M. C. (1994). Anomia for people's names. *Neuropsychologia, 32,* 465–476.

648. Hom, J., Turner, M. B., Risser, R., Bonte, F. J., & Tintner, R. (1994). Cognitive deficits in asymptomatic first-degree relatives of Alzheimer's disease patients. *Journal of Clinical and Experimental Neuropsychology, 16,* 568-576.

649. Hooper, S., Sales, G., & Rysavy, S. D. (1994). Generating summaries and analogies alone and in pairs. *Contemporary Educational Psychology, 19,* 53-62.

650. Horton, A. M., Jr. (1994). Identification of neuropsychological deficit: Levels of assessment. *Perceptual and Motor Skills, 79,* 1251-1255.

651. Hughes, C. A., & Suritsky, S. K. (1994). Note-taking skills of university students with and without learning disabilities. *Journal of Learning Disabilities, 27,* 20–24.

652. Humes, L. E., Watson, B. V., Christensen, L. A., Cokely, C. G., Halling, D. C., & Lee, L. (1994). Factors associated with individual differences in clinical measures of speech recognition among the elderly. *Journal of Speech and Hearing Research, 37,* 465–474.

653. Hunkin, N. M., Parkin, A. J., & Longmore, B. E. (1994). Aetiological variation in the amnesic syndrome: Comparisons using the list discrimination task. *Neuropsychologia, 32,* 819–825.

654. Jaedicke, S., Storoschuk, S., & Lord, C. (1994). Subjective experience and causes of affect in high-functioning children and adolescents with autism. *Development and Psychopathology, 6,* 273-284.

655. Johnsrude, I., & Milner, B. (1994). The effect of presentation rate on the comprehension and recall of speech after anterior temporal-lobe resection. *Neuropsychologia, 32,* 77–84.

656. Jones, P. B., Harvey, I., Lewis, S. W., Toone, B. K., van Os, J., Williams, M., & Murray, R. M. (1994). Cerebral ventricle dimensions as risk factors for schizophrenia and effective psychosis: An epidemiological approach to analysis. *Psychological Medicine, 24,* 995-1011.

657. Juni, S. (1994). Measurement of defenses in special populations: Revision of the Defense Mechanisms Inventory. *Journal of Research in Personality, 28,* 230-244.

658. Kaplan, R. F., Meadows, M. E., Verfaellie, M., Kwan, E., Ehrenberg, B. L., Bromfield, E. B., & Cohen, R. A. (1994). Lateralization of memory for the visual attributes of objects: Evidence from the posterior cerebral artery amobarbital test. *Neurology, 44,* 1069–1073.

659. Kapur, N., Ellison, D., Parkin, A. J., Hunkin, N. M., Burrows, E., Sampson, S. A., & Morrison, E. A. (1994). Bilateral temporal lobe pathology with sparing of medial temperal lobe structures: Lesion profile and pattern of memory disorder. *Neuropsychologia, 32,* 23–38.

660. Kareken, D. A., & Williams, J. M. (1994). Human judgement and estimation of premorbid intellectual function. *Psychological Assessment, 6,* 83-91.

661. Kartsounis, L. D., & Findley, L. J. (1994). Task specific visuospatial neglect related to density and salience of stimuli. *Cortex, 30,* 647-659.

662. Kaufman, A. S. (1994). A reply to Macmann and Barnett. Lessons from the blind men and the elephant. *School Psychology Quarterly, 9,* 199-207.

663. Keith, T. Z. (1994). Intelligence is important. Intelligence is complex. *School Psychology Quarterly, 9,* 209-221.

664. Kemeny, M. E., Werner, H., Taylor, S. E., Schneider, S., Visscher, B., & Fahey, J. L. (1994). Repeated bereavement, depressed mood, and immune parameters in HIV seropositive and seronegative gay men. *Health Psychology, 13,* 14-24.

665. Khan, A., Mirolo, M. H., Claypoole, K., Bhang, J., Cox, G., Horita, A., & Tucker, G. (1994). Effects of low-dose TRH on cognitive deficits in the ECT postictal state. *American Journal of Psychiatry, 151,* 1694-1696.

666. Kobus, D. A., Moses, J. D., & Bloom, F. A. (1994). Effect of multimodal stimulus presentation on recall. *Perceptual and Motor Skills, 78,* 320–322.

667. Kopelman, M. D., Christensen, H., Puffett, A., & Stanhope, N. (1994). The great escape: A neuropsychological study of psychogenic amnesia. *Neuropsychologia, 32,* 675–691.

668. Kopelman, M. D., Green, R. E. A., Guinan, E. M., Lewis, P. D. R., & Stanhope, N. (1994). The case of the amnesic intelligence officer. *Psychological Medicine, 24,* 1037-1045.

669. Kovacs, M., Ryan, C., & Obrosky, D. S. (1994). Verbal intellectual and verbal memory performance of youths with childhood-onset insulin-dependent diabetes mellitus. *Journal of Pediatric Psychology, 19,* 475-483.

670. Kramer, A. F., Humphrey, D. G., Larish, J. F., Logan, G. D., & Strayer, D. L. (1994). Aging and inhibition: Beyond a unitary view of inhibitory processing in attention. *Psychology and Aging, 9,* 491-512.

671. Kremen, W. S., Seidman, L. J., Pepple, J. R., Lyons, M. J., Tsuang, M. T., & Faraone, S. V. (1994). Neuropsychological risk indicators for schizophrenia: A review of family studies. *Schizophrenia Bulletin, 20,* 103–119.

672. Lamborn, S. D., Fischer, K. W., & Pipp, S. (1994). Constructive criticism and social ties: A developmental sequence for understanding honesty and kindness in social interactions. *Developmental Psychology, 30,* 495-508.

673. Levin, M. (1994). Comment on the Minnesota transracial adoption study. *Intelligence, 19,* 13-20.

674. Lindsay, W. R., Fee, M., Michie, A., & Heap, I. (1994). The effects of cue control relaxation on adults with severe mental retardation. *Research in Developmental Disabilities, 15,* 425-437.

675. Loehlin, J. C., Horn, J. M., & Willerman, L. (1994). Differential inheritance of mental abilities in the Texas Adoption Project. *Intelligence, 19,* 325-336.

676. Lyness, S. A., Eaton, E. M., & Schneider, L. S. (1994). Cognitive performance in older and middle-aged depressed outpatients and controls. *Journal of Gerontology: Psychological Sciences, 49*(Pt.1), 129-136.

677. Lynn, R. (1994). Some reinterpretations of the Minnesota transracial adoption study. *Intelligence, 19,* 21-27.

678. MacKay, D. G., Miller, M. D., & Schuster, S. P. (1994). Repetition blindness and aging: Evidence for a binding deficit involving a single, theoretically specified connection. *Psychology and Aging, 9,* 251-258.

679. Macmann, G. M., & Barnett, D. W. (1994). Some additional lessons from the Wechsler scales: A rejoinder to Kaufman and Keith. *School Psychology Quarterly, 9,* 223-236.

680. Macmann, G. M., & Barnett, D. W. (1994). Structural analysis of correlated factors: Lessons from the verbal-performance dichotomy of the Wechsler scales. *School Psychology Quarterly, 9,* 161-197.

681. Marcos, T., Salamero, M., Gutiérrez, F., Catalán, R., Gasto, C., & Lázaro, L. (1994). Cognitive dysfunctions in recovered melancholic patients. *Journal of Affective Disorders, 32,* 133-137.

682. Masur, D. M., Sliwinski, M., Lipton, R. B., Blau, A. D., & Crystal, H. A. (1994). Neuropsychological prediction of dementia and the absence of dementia in healthy elderly persons. *Neurology, 44,* 1427–1432.

683. Mattis, P. J., Hannay, H. J., Plenger, P. M., & Pollock, L. (1994). Head injury and the Satz-Mogel short form WAIS-R. *Journal of Clinical Psychology, 50,* 605-614.

684. Mauri, A., Daum, I., Sartori, G., Riesch, G., & Birbaumer, N. (1994). Category-specific semantic impairment in Alzheimer's disease and temporal lobe dysfunction: A comparative study. *Journal of Clinical and Experimental Neuropsychology, 16,* 689-701.

685. Mayes, A. R., Downes, J. J., Symons, V., & Shoqeirat, M. (1994). Do amnesics forget faces pathologically fast? *Cortex, 30,* 543-563.

686. Maylor, E. A., & Rabbitt, P. M. A. (1994). Applying Brinley plots to individuals: Effects of aging on performance distributions in two speeded tasks. *Psychology and Aging, 9,* 224-230.

687. McArdle, J. J. (1994). Structural factor analysis experiments with incomplete data. *Multivariate Behavioral Research, 29,* 409–454.

688. McCurry, S. M., Fitz, A. G., & Teri, L. (1994). Comparison of age-extended norms for the Wechsler Adult Intelligence Scale—Revised in patients with Alzheimer's disease. *Psychological Assessment, 6,* 231-235.

689. McCusker, P. J. (1994). Validation of Kaufman, Ishikuma, and Kaufman-Packer's Wechsler Adult Intelligence Scale—Revised short forms on a clinical sample. *Psychological Assessment, 6,* 246-248.

690. McGuire, S., Neiderhiser, J. M., Reiss, D., Hetherington, E. M., & Plomin, R. (1994). Genetic and environmental influences on perceptions of self-worth and competence in adolescence: A study of twins, full siblings, and step siblings. *Child Development, 65,* 785-799.

691. McHenry, M. A., Minton, J. T., Wilson, R. L., & Post, Y. V. (1994). Intelligibility and nonspeech orafacial strength and force control following traumatic brain injury. *Journal of Speech and Hearing, 37,* 1271–1283.

692. McNeil, J. E., & Warrington, E. K. (1994). A dissociation between addition and subtraction with written calculation. *Neuropsychologia, 32,* 717–728.

693. Meadows, M. E., Kaplan, R. F., & Bromfield, E. B. (1994). Cognitive recovery with vitamin B12 therapy: A longitudinal neuropsychological assessment. *Neurology, 44,* 1764–1765.

694. Merrill, L. L., Lewandowski, L. J., & Kobus, D. A. (1994). Selective attention skills of experienced sonar operators. *Perceptual and Motor Skills, 78,* 803-812.

695. Meudell, P. R., Mayes, A. R., & MacDonald, C. (1994). Dual task performance in amnesic and normal people: Does resource depletion cause amnesia? *Cortex, 30,* 159-166.

696. Minshew, N. J., Goldstein, G., Taylor, H. G., & Siegel, D. J. (1994). Academic achievement in high functioning autistic individuals. *Journal of Clinical and Experimental Neuropsychology, 16,* 261-270.

697. Mitrushina, M., Drebing, C., Satz, P., Gorp, W. V., Chervinsky, A., & Uchiyama, C. (1994). WAIS-R intersubtest scatter in patients with dementia of Alzheimer's type. *Journal of Clinical Psychology, 50,* 753-758.

698. Mitrushina, M., Drebing, C., Uchiyama, C., Satz, P., Van Gorp, W., & Chervinsky, A. (1994). The pattern of deficit in different memory components in normal aging and dementia of Alzheimer's type. *Journal of Clinical Psychology, 50,* 591-596.

699. Moffoot, A. P. R., O'Carroll, R. E., Bennie, J., Carroll, S., Dick, H., Ebmeier, K. P., & Goodwin, G. M. (1994). Diurnal variation of mood and neuropsychological function in major depression with melancholia. *Journal of Affective Disorders, 32,* 257-269.

700. Morrow, D., Leirer, V., Altieri, P., & Fitzsimmons, C. (1994). When expertise reduces age differences in performance. *Psychology and Aging, 9,* 134-148.

701. Mozingo, D., Ackley, G. B. E., & Bailey, J. S. (1994). Training quality job interviews with adults with developmental disabilities. *Research in Development Disabilities, 15,* 389-410.

702. Munley, P. H., & Busby, R. (1994). MMPI-2 Negative Treatment Indicators scale and irregular discharge. *Psychological Reports, 74,* 903-906.

703. Murphy, D. G. M., Allen, G., Haxby, J. V., Largay, K. A., Daly, E., White, B. J., Powell, L. M., & Schapiro, M. B. (1994). The effects of sex steroids and the X chromosome on female brain function: A study of the neuropsychology of adult Turner syndrome. *Neuropsychologia, 32,* 1309–1323.

704. Mutter, S. A., & Pliske, R. M. (1994). Aging and illusory correlation in judgements of co-occurrence. *Psychology and Aging, 9,* 53-63.

705. Mutter, S. A., Howard, J. H., & Howard, D. V. (1994). Serial pattern learning after head injury. *Journal of Clinical and Experimental Neuropsychology, 16,* 271-288.

706. Neistadt, M. E. (1994). A meal preparation treatment protocol for adults with brain injury. *The American Journal of Occupational Therapy, 48,* 431-438.

707. Neistadt, M. E. (1994). Perceptual retraining for adults with diffuse brain injury. *The American Journal of Occupational Therapy, 48,* 225-233.

708. Neistadt, M. E. (1994). The effect of different treatment activities on functional fine motor coordination in adults with brain injury. *The American Journal of Occupational Therapy, 48,* 877-882.

709. O'Donnell, J. P., Macgregor, L. A., Dabrowski, J. J., Oestreicher, J. M., & Romero, J. J. (1994). Construct validity of neuropsychological tests of conceptual and attentional abilities. *Journal of Clinical Psychology, 50,* 596-600.

710. Olson, S. L., Kieschnick, E., Banyard, V., & Ceballo, R. (1994). Socioenvironmental and individual correlates of psychological adjustment in low-income single mothers. *American Journal of Orthopsychiatry, 64,* 317–331.

711. Paller, K. A., & Mayes, A. R. (1994). New association priming of word identification in normal and amnesic subjects. *Cortex, 30,* 53-73.

712. Palmer, B. W., Boone, K. B., Chang, L., Lee, A., & Black, S. (1994). Cognitive deficits and personality patterns in maternally versus paternally inherited myotonic dystrophy. *Journal of Clinical and Experimental Neuropsychology, 16,* 784-795.

713. Parkin, A. J., Rees, J. E., Hunkin, N. M., & Rose, P. E. (1994). Impairment of memory following discrete thalamic infarction. *Neuropsychologia, 32,* 39–51.

714. Parkin, A. J., Yeomans, J., & Bindschaedler, C. (1994). Further characterization of the executive memory impairment following frontal lobe lesions. *Brain and Cognition, 26,* 23–42.

715. Pedersen, N. L., Plomin, R., & McClearn, G. E. (1994). Is there G beyond *g*? (Is there genetic influence on specific cognitive abilities independent of genetic influence on general cognitive ability?). *Intelligence, 18,* 133-143.

716. Persinger, M. A. (1994). Sense of a presence and suicidal ideation following traumatic brain injury: Indications of right-hemispheric intrusions from neuropsychological profiles. *Psychological Reports, 75,* 1059-1070.

717. Persinger, M. A., Bureau, Y. R. J., Peredery, O. P., & Richards, P. M. (1994). The sensed presence as right hemispheric intrusions into the left hemispheric awareness of self: An illustrative case study. *Perceptual and Motor Skills, 78,* 999-1009.

718. Peterson, R. C., Smith, G. E., Ivnik, R. J., Kokmen, E., & Tangalos, E. G. (1994). Memory function in very early Alzheimer's disease. *Neurology, 44,* 867–872.

719. Pigott, S., & Milner, B. (1994). Capacity of visual short-term memory after unilateral frontal or anterior temporal-lobe resection. *Neuropsychologia, 32,* 969–981.

720. Pillon, B., Deweer, B., Michon, A., Malapani, C., Agid, Y., & Dubois, B. (1994). Are explicit memory disorders of progressive supranuclear palsy related to damage to striatofrontal circuits? Comparison with Alzheimer's, Parkinson's, and Huntington's disease. *Neurology, 44,* 1264–1270.

721. Piven, J., Wzorek, M., Landa, R., Lainhart, J., Bolton, P., Chase, G. A., & Folstein, S. (1994). Personality characteristics of the parents of autistic individuals. *Psychological Medicine, 24,* 783-795.

722. Podraza, A. M., Bornstein, R. A., Whitacre, C. C., Para, M. F., Fass, R. J., Rice, R. R., & Nasrallah, H. A. (1994). Neuropsychological performance and CD4 levels in HIV-1 asymptomatic infection. *Journal of Clinical and Experimental Neuropsychology, 16,* 777-783.

723. Pogge, D. L., Stokes, J. M., & Harvey, P. D. (1994). Empirical evaluation of the factorial structure of attention in adolescent psychiatric patients. *Journal of Clinical and Experimental Neuropsychology, 16,* 344-353.

724. Poole, J. L., & Schneck, C. M. (1994). Developmental differences in praxis in learning-disabled and normal children and adults. *Perceptual and Motor Skills, 78,* 1219-1228.

725. Poreh, A. M., Whitman, R. D., Weber, M., & Ross, T. (1994). Facial recognition in hypothetically schizotypic college students: The role of generalized poor performance. *The Journal of Nervous and Mental Disease, 182,* 503-507.
726. Rains, G. D., & Milner, B. (1994). Right-hippocampal contralateral-hand effect in the recall of spatial location in the tactual modality. *Neuropsychologia, 32,* 1233–1242.
727. Rains, G. D., & Milner, B. (1994). Verbal recall and recognition as a function of depth of encoding in patients with unilateral temporal lobectomy. *Neuropsychologia, 32,* 1243–1256.
728. Rapcsak, S. Z., Polster, M. R., Comer, J. F., & Rubens, A. B. (1994). False recognition and misidentification of faces following right hemisphere damage. *Cortex, 30,* 565-583.
729. Rapport, L. J., Webster, J. S., & Dutra, R. L. (1994). Digit span performance and unilateral neglect. *Neuropsychologia, 32,* 517–525.
730. Records, N. L. (1994). A measure of the contribution of a gesture to the perception of speech in listeners with aphasia. *Journal of Speech and Hearing, 37,* 1086–1099.
731. Ricker, J. H., Keenan, P. A., & Jacobson, M. W. (1994). Visuoperceptual-spatial ability and visual memory in vascular dementia and dementia of the Alzheimer type. *Neuropsychologia, 32,* 1287–1296.
732. Roberts, J. E., Burchinal, M. R., & Campbell, F. (1994). Otitis media in early childhood and patterns of intellectual development and later academic performance. *Journal of Pediatric Psychology, 19,* 347–367.
733. Robertson, I. H., & North, N. T. (1994). One hand is better than two: Motor extinction of left hand advantage in unilateral neglect. *Neuropsychologia, 32,* 1–11.
734. Rodriquez, A. L. T., Marin, P. B., Borrero, I. M. G., Romero-Nieva, F. D., & Alvarez, A. D. (1994). Association between autism and schizophrenia. *The Journal of Nervous and Mental Disease, 182,* 478-479.
735. Roffman, A. J., Herzog, J. E., & Wershba-Gershon, P. M. (1994). Helping young adults understand their learning disabilities. *Journal of Learning Disabilities, 27,* 413–419.
736. Rosenberg, S. D., Blatt, S. J., Oxman, T. E., McHugo, G. J., & Ford, R. Q. (1994). Assessment of object relatedness through a lexical content analysis of the TAT. *Journal of Personality Assessment, 63,* 345-362.
737. Rossini, E. D., Wygonik, E. J., Barrett, D. E., & Friedman, B. (1994). WAIS-R validation of the Thurstone Test of Mental Alterness. *Psychological Reports, 74,* 1339-1345.
738. Rovet, J., Szekely, C., & Hockenberry, M. (1994). Specific arithmetic calculation deficits in children with Turner syndrome. *Journal of Clinical and Experimental Neuropsychology, 16,* 820-839.
739. Ryan, J. J., & Bohac, D. L. (1994). Neurodiagnostic implications of unique profiles of the Wechsler Adult Intelligence Scale—Revised. *Psychological Assessment, 6,* 360-363.
740. Saarnio, P. K. (1994). An asymmetry between the WAIS Digit Symbol and Block Design scores in abstinent alcoholics. *Perceptual and Motor Skills, 78,* 875-880.
741. Sampson, R. J., & Laub, J. H. (1994). Urban poverty and the family context of delinquency: A new look at structure and process in a classic study. *Child Development, 65,* 523–540.
742. Samson, S., & Zatorre, R. J. (1994). Contribution of the right temporal lobe to musical timbre discrimination. *Neuropsychologia, 32,* 231–240.
743. Sands, J. R., & Harrow, M. (1994). Psychotic unipolar depression at follow-up: Factors related to psychosis in the affective disorders. *The American Journal of Psychiatry, 151,* 995-1000.
744. Saykin, A. J., Shtasel, D. L., Gur, R. E., Kester, D. B., Mozley, L. H., Stafiniak, P., & Gur, R. C. (1994). Neuropsychological deficits in neuroleptic naive patients with first-episode schizophrenia. *Archives of General Psychiatry, 51,* 124-131.
745. Schacter, D. L., Osowiecki, D., Kaszniak, A. W., Kihlstrom, J. F., & Valdiserri, M. (1994). Source memory: Extending the boundaries of age-related deficits. *Psychology and Aging, 9,* 81-89.
746. Schinka, J. A., Vanderploeg, R. D., & Curtiss, G. (1994). Wechsler Adult Intelligence Scale—Revised subtest scatter as a function of maximum subtest scaled score. *Psychological Assessment, 6,* 364-367.
747. Schmidt, E., Rupp, A., Burgard, P., Pietz, J., Weglage, J., & de Sonneville, L. (1994). Sustained attention in adult phenylketonuria: The influence of the concurrent phenycalnine-blood-level. *Journal of Clinical and Experimental Neuropsychology, 16,* 681-688.
748. Schretlen, D., Benedict, R. H. B., & Bobholz, J. H. (1994). Composite reliability and standard errors of measurement for a seven-subtest short form of the Wechsler Adult Intelligence Scale—Revised. *Psychological Assessment, 6,* 188-190.
749. Scialfa, C. T., & Thomas, D. M. (1994). Age differences in same-different judgements as a function of multidimensional similarity. *Journal of Gerontology: Psychological Sciences, 49*(Pt.2), 173-178.
750. Sears, L. L., Finn, P. R., & Steinmetz, J. E. (1994). Abnormal classical eye-blink conditioning in autism. *Journal of Autism and Developmental Disorders, 24,* 737-751.
751. Shafrir, V., & Siegel, L. S. (1994). Subtypes of learning disabilities in adolescents and adults. *Journal of Learning Disabilities, 27,* 123–134.
752. Shapiro, E. G., Lockman, L. A., Knopman, D., & Krivit, W. (1994). Characteristics of the dementia in late-onset metachromatic leukodystrophy. *Neurology, 44,* 662–665.
753. Shaw, C., & Aggleton, J. P. (1994). The ability of amnesic subjects to estimate time intervals. *Neuropsychologia, 32,* 857–873.
754. Shum, D. H. K., McFarland, K., & Bain, J. D. (1994). Assessment of attention: Relationship between psychological testing and information processing approaches. *Journal of Clinical and Experimental Neuropsychology, 16,* 531-538.
755. Siscoe, K. L., Segel, M. D., LaGrange, M. R., Templer, D. I., & Richardson, R. L. (1994). Exploration of the neuropsychological spectrum in clients of heterogeneous disabilities. *Perceptual and Motor Skills, 78,* 815-816.
756. Skuse, D., Pickles, A., Wolke, D., & Reilly, S. (1994). Postnatal growth and mental development: Evidence for a "sensitive period." *Journal of Child Psychology and Psychiatry and Allied Disciplines, 35,* 521-545.
757. Smith, J., Staudinger, U. M., & Baltes, P. B. (1994). Occupational settings facilitating wisdom-related knowledge: The sample case of clinical psychologists. *Journal of Consulting and Clinical Psychology, 62,* 989-999.
758. Sobell, L. C., Toneatto, T., & Sobell, M. (1994). Behavioral assessment and treatment planning for alcohol, tobacco, and other drug problems: Current status with an emphasis on clinical applications. *Behavior Therapy, 25,* 533–580.
759. Spencer, W. D., & Raz, N. (1994). Memory for facts, source, and context: Can frontal lobe dysfunction explain age-related differences? *Psychology and Aging, 9,* 149-159.
760. Stewart, S. M., Kennard, B. D., Waller, D. A., & Fixler, D. (1994). Cognitive function in children who receive organ transplantation. *Health Psychology, 13,* 3-13.
761. Stone, J., Morin, C. M., Hart, R. P., Remsberg, S., & Mercer, J. (1994). Neuropsychological functioning in older insomniacs with or without obstructive sleep apnea. *Psychology and Aging, 9,* 231-236.
762. Strauss, E., Wada, J., & Hunter, M. (1994). Callosal morphology and performance on intelligence tests. *Journal of Clinical and Experimental Neuropsychology, 16,* 79-83.
763. Strayer, D. L., & Kramer, A. F. (1994). Aging and skill acquisition: Learning-performance distinctions. *Psychology and Aging, 9,* 589-605.
764. Sunderland, A., Tinson, D., & Bradley, L. (1994). Differences in recovery from constructional apraxia after right and left hemisphere stroke. *Journal of Clinical and Experimental Neuropsychology, 16,* 916-920.
765. Taylor, J. L., Yesavage, J. A., Morrow, D. G., Dolhert, N., Brooks, J. O., III, & Poon, L. W. (1994). The effects of information load and speech rate on younger and older aircraft pilots' ability to execute simulated air-traffic controller instructions. *Journal of Gerontology: Psychological Sciences, 49*(Pt.2), 191-200.
766. Thompson, A., & Hodgins, C. (1994). Evaluation of a checking procedure for reducing clerical and computational errors on the WAIS-R. *Canadian Journal of Behavioural Science, 26,* 492–504.
767. Thompson, A. P., & Bulow, C. A. (1994). Administration error in presenting the WAIS-R blocks: Approximating the impact of scrambled presentations. *Professional Psychology: Research and Practice, 25,* 89-91.
768. Tracy, J. I., & Bates, M. E. (1994). Models of functional organization as a model for detecting cognitive deficits: Data from a sample of social drinkers. *Journal of Studies on Alcohol, 55,* 726–738.
769. Trueblood, W. (1994). Qualitative and quantitative characteristics of malingered and other invalid WAIS-R and clinical memory data. *Journal of Clinical and Experimental Neuropsychology, 16,* 597-607.
770. van der Broek, M. D., & Bradshaw, C. M. (1994). Detection of acquired deficits in general intelligence using the National Adult Reading Test and Raven's Standard Progressive Matrices. *British Journal of Clinical Psychology, 33,* 509-515.
771. Van der Linden, M., Meulemans, T., & Lorrain, D. (1994). Acquisition of new concepts by two amnesic patients. *Cortex, 30,* 305-317.
772. van Gorp, W. G., Miller, E. N., Marcotte, T. D., Dixon, W., Paz, D., Selnes, O., Wesch, J., Becker, J. T., Hinkin, C. H., Mitrushina, M., Satz, P., Weisman, J. D., Buckingham, S. L., & Stenquist, P. K. (1994). The relationship between age and cognitive impairment in HIV-I infection: Findings from the Multicenter AIDS Cohort Study and a clinical cohort. *Neurology, 44,* 929–935.
773. VanderPloeg, R. D., Schinka, J. A., & Retzlaff, P. (1994). Relationships between measures of auditory verbal learning and executive functioning. *Journal of Clinical and Experimental Neuropsychology, 16,* 243-252.
774. Venneri, A., Cubelli, R., & Caffarra, P. (1994). Perseverative dysgraphia: A selective disorder in writing double letters. *Neuropsychologia, 32,* 923–931.
775. Verfaellie, M., & Cermak, L. S. (1994). Acquisition of generic memory in amnesia. *Cortex, 30,* 293-303.
776. Vilkki, J., & Holst, P. (1994). Speed and flexibility on word fluency tasks after focal brain lesions. *Neuropsychologia, 32,* 1257–1262.
777. Vilkki, J., Ahola, K., Holst, P., Öhman, J., Servo, A., & Heiskanen, O. (1994). Prediction of psychosocial recovery after head injury with cognitive tests and neurobehavioral ratings. *Journal of Clinical and Experimental Neuropsychology, 16,* 325-338.
778. Virkkunen, M., Kallio, E., Rawlings, R., Tokola, R., Poland, R. E., Guidotti, A., Nemeroff, C., Bissette, G., Kalogeras, K., Karonen, S., & Linnoila, M. (1994). Personality profiles and state aggressiveness in Finnish alcoholic, violent offenders, fire setters, and healthy volunteers. *Archives of General Psychiatry, 51,* 28-33.
779. Volkow, N. D., Wang, G. J., Hitzemann, R., Fowler, J. S., Overall, J. E., Burr, G., & Wolf, A. P. (1994). Recovery of brain glucose metabolism in detoxified alcoholics. *American Journal of Psychiatry, 151,* 178-183.
780. Warrington, E. K., & McCarthy, R. A. (1994). Multiple meaning systems in the brain: A case for visual semantics. *Neuropsychologia, 32,* 1465–1473.
781. Webster, J. S., Rapport, L. J., Godlewski, M. C., & Abadee, P. S. (1994). Effect of attentional bias to right space on wheelchair mobility. *Journal of Clinical and Experimental Neuropsychology, 16,* 129-137.
782. Weddell, R. A. (1994). Effects of subcortical lesion site on human emotional behavior. *Brain and Cognition, 25,* 161-193.
783. Weinstein, C. S., Seidman, L. J., Ahern, G., & McClure, K. (1994). Integration of neuropsychological and behavioral neurological assessment in psychiatry: A case example involving brain injury and polypharmacy. *Psychiatry, 57,* 62–76.

784. Wiggs, C. L., & Martin, A. (1994). Aging and feature-specific priming of familiar and novel stimuli. *Psychology and Aging, 9,* 578-588.

785. Williams, C. J., Yeomans, J. D. I., & Coughlan, A. K. (1994). Sleep deprivation as a diagnostic instrument. *British Journal of Psychiatry, 164,* 554-556.

786. Wold, D. C., Evans, C. R., Montague, J. C., Jr., & Dancer, J. E. (1994). A pilot study of SPINE test scores and measures of tongue deviancy in speakers with severe-to-profound hearing loss. *American Annals of the Deaf, 139,* 352-357.

787. Yates, B. T., Hecht-Lewis, R., Fritsch, R. C., & Goodrich, W. (1994). Locus of control in severely disturbed adolescents: loci for peers, parents, achievement, relationships, and problems. *Journal of Youth and Adolescence, 23,* 289–314.

788. Young, D. W., & Childs, N. A. (1994). Family images of hospitalized adolescents: The failure to generate shared understandings. *Psychiatry, 57,* 258–267.

789. Zesiger, P., Pegna, A., & Rilliet, B. (1994). Unilateral dysgraphia of the dominant hand in a left-hander: A disruption of graphic motor pattern selection. *Cortex, 30,* 673-683.

790. Zolten, A. J., Bush, L. K., Green, A., & Harrell, E. H. (1994). Comparison of error rates and performance on Wechsler's Coding and Digit Symbol subtests and the Symbol-Symbol test for children and adults. *Perceptual and Motor Skills, 79,* 1627-1631.

791. Allen, S. R., & Thorndike, R. M. (1995). Stability of the WAIS-R and WISC-III factor structure using cross-validation of covariance structures. *Journal of Clinical Psychology, 51,* 648–657.

792. Almeida, D. P., Howard, R. J., Levy, R., David, A. S., Morris, R. G., & Sahakian, B. J. (1995). Cognitive features of psychotic states arising in late life (late paraphrenia). *Psychological Medicine, 25,* 685–698.

793. Anderson, C. V., Bigler, E. D., & Blatter, D. D. (1995). Frontal lobe lesions, diffuse damage, and neuropsychological functioning in traumatic brain injured patients. *Journal of Clinical and Experimental Neuropsychology, 17,* 900–908.

794. Apthorp, H. S. (1995). Phonetic coding and reading in college students with and without learning disabilities. *Journal of Learning Disabilities, 28,* 342–352.

795. Bailey, A., LeCouteur, A., Gottesman, I., Bolton, P., Simonoff, E., Yuzda, E., & Rutter, M. (1995). Autism as a strongly genetic disorder: Evidence from a British twin study. *Psychological Medicine, 25,* 63-77.

796. Bamford, K. A., Caine, E. D., Kido, D. K., Cox, C., & Shoalson, I. (1995). A prospective evaluation of cognitive decline in early Huntington's disease: Functional and radiographic correlates. *Neurology, 45,* 1867–1873.

797. Barba, G. D., & Wong, C. (1995). Encoding specificity and intrusion in Alzheimer's disease and amnesia. *Brain and Cognition, 27,* 1-16.

798. Beatty, W. W., Paul, R. H., Wilbanks, S. L., Hames, K. A., Blanco, C. R., & Goodkin, D. E. (1995). Identifying multiple sclerosis patients with mild or global cognitive impairment using the Screening Examination for Cognitive Impairment (SEFCI). *Neurology, 45,* 718–723.

799. Becker, J. T., Lopex, O. L., & Boller, F. (1995). Understanding impaired analysis of faces by patients with probable Alzheimer's disease. *Cortex, 31,* 129-137.

800. Bennett, K. M. B., & Castiello, U. (1995). Reorganization of prehension components following perturbation of object size. *Psychology and Aging, 10,* 204-214.

801. Biederman, J., Milberger, S., Faraone, S. V., Kiely, K., Guite, J., Mick, E., Ablon, S., Warburton, R., & Reed, E. (1995). Family-environment risk factors for attention-deficit hyperactivity disorder: A test of Rotter's indicators of adversity. *Archives of General Psychiatry, 52,* 464–470.

802. Biederman, J., Milberger, S., Faraone, S. V., Lapey, K. A., Reed, E. D., & Seidman, L. J. (1995). No confirmation of Geschwind's hypothesis of associations between reading disability, immune disorders, and motor preference in ADHD. *Journal of Abnormal Child Psychology, 23,* 545–552.

803. Bigler, E. D., Johnson, S. C., Jackson, C., & Blatter, D. D. (1995). Aging, brain size, and IQ. *Intelligence, 21,* 109–119.

804. Binetti, G., Magni, E., Padovani, A., Coppan, S. F., Bianchetti, A., & Trabucchi, M. (1995). Release from proactive interference in early Alzheimer's disease. *Neuropsychologia, 33,* 379–384.

805. Boatman, D., Lesser, R. P., & Gordon, B. (1995). Auditory speech processing in the left temporal lobe: An electrical interference study. *Brain and Language, 51,* 269–290.

806. Boekamp, J. R., Strauss, M. E., & Adams, N. (1995). Estimating premorbid intelligence in African-American and White elderly veterans using the American version of the National Adult Reading Test. *Journal of Clinical and Experimental Neuropsychology, 17,* 645–653.

807. Boone, D. E. (1995). A cross-sectional analysis of WAIS-R aging patterns with psychiatric inpatients: Support for Horn's hypothesis that fluid cognitive abilities decline. *Perceptual and Motor Skills, 81,* 371–379.

808. Bourg, S., Connor, E. J., & Landis, E. E. (1995). The impact of expertise and sufficient information on psychologists ability to detect malingering. *Behavior Sciences and the Law, 13,* 505–515.

809. Brandt, J., Bylsma, F. W., Aylward, E. H., Rothlind, J., & Gow, C. A. (1995). Impaired source memory in Huntington's Disease and its relation to basil ganglia atrophy. *Journal of Clinical and Experimental Neuropsychology, 17,* 868–877.

810. Bromley, S. M., & Doty, R. L. (1995). Odor recognition memory is better under bilateral than unilateral test conditions. *Cortex, 31,* 25-40.

811. Brown, A. S., Jones, E. M., & Davis, T. L. (1995). Age differences in conversational source monitoring. *Psychology and Aging, 10,* 111-122.

812. Bryant, R. A., & Harvey, A. G. (1995). Processing threatening information in posttraumatic stress disorder. *Journal of Abnormal Psychology, 104,* 537–541.

813. Burton, D. B., Naugle, R. I., & Schuster, J. M. (1995). A structural equation analysis of the Kaufman Brief Intelligence Test and the Wechsler Adult Intelligence Scale—Revised. *Psychological Assessment, 7,* 538–540.

814. Butler, D. L. (1995). Promoting strategic learning by postsecondary students with learning disabilities. *Journal of Learning Disabilities, 28,* 170–190.

815. Byrne, J. M., Dywan, C. A., & Connolly, J. F. (1995). An innovative method to assess the receptive vocabulary of children with cerebral palsy using event-related brain potentials. *Journal of Clinical and Experimental Neuropsychology, 17,* 9-19.

816. Calabrese, P., Markowitsch, H. J., Harders, A. G., Scholz, M., & Gehlen, W. (1995). Fornix damage and memory: A case report. *Cortex, 31,* 555–564.

817. Campbell, F. A., & Ramey, C. T. (1995). Cognitive and school outcomes for high-risk African-American students at middle adolescence: Positive effects of early intervention. *American Educational Research Journal, 32,* 743–772.

818. Campion, D., Brice, A., Hannequin, D., Tardieu, S., Dubois, B., Calenda, A., Brun, E., Penet, C., Tayot, J., Martinez, M., Bellis, M., Mallet, J., Agid, Y., & Clerget-Darpoux, F. (1995). A large pedigree with early-onset Alzheimer's disease: Clinical, neuropathologic, and genetic characterization. *Neurology, 45,* 80–85.

819. Caplan, L. J., & Lipman, P. D. (1995). Age and gender differences in the effectiveness of map-like learning aids in memory for routes. *Journal of Gerontology: Psychological Sciences, 50*B, P126-P133.

820. Carlesimo, G. A., Sabbadini, M., Fadda, L., & Caltagirone, C. (1995). Forgetting from long-term memory in dementia and pure amnesia: Role of task, delay of assessment and aetiology of cerebral damage. *Cortex, 31,* 285-300.

821. Carvajal, H., & Pauls, K. K. (1995). Relationships among graduate record examination scores, Wechsler Adult Intelligence Scale—Revised IQs, and undergraduate grade point average. *College Student Journal, 29,* 414–416.

822. Caselli, R. J., Smith, B. E., & Osborne, D. (1995). Primary lateral sclerosis: A neuropsychological study. *Neurology, 45,* 2005–2009.

823. Christensen, H., Henderson, A. S., Jorm, A. F., MacKinnon, A. J., Scott, R., & Korten, A. G. (1995). ICD-10 mild cognitive disorder: Epidemiological evidence on its validity. *Psychological Medicine, 25,* 105-120.

824. Ciesielski, K. T., Knight, J. E., Prince, R. J., Harris, R. J., & Handmaker, S. D. (1995). Event-related potentials in cross-modal divided attention in autism. *Neuropsychologia, 33,* 225–246.

825. Ciesielski, K. T., Waldorf, A. V., & Jung, R. E. (1995). Anterior brain deficits in chronic alcoholism: Cause and effect? *The Journal of Nervous and Mental Disease, 183,* 756–761.

826. Cipolotti, L., & Costello, A. de-L. (1995). Selective impairment for simple division. *Cortex, 31,* 433–449.

827. Cipolotti, L., Warrington, E. K., & Butterworth, B. (1995). Selective impairment in manipulating Arabic numerals. *Cortex, 31,* 73-86.

828. Cockburn, J. (1995). Task interruption in prospective memory: A frontal lobe function? *Cortex, 31,* 87-97.

829. Cooke, D. L., & Kausler, D. H. (1995). Content memory and temporal memory for actions in survivors of traumatic brain injury. *Journal of Clinical and Experimental Neuropsychology, 17,* 90-99.

830. Corrigan, P. W., & Boican, B. (1995). The construct validity of subjective equality of life for the severely mentally ill. *The Journal of Nervous and Mental Disease, 183,* 281–285.

831. Crawford, J. R., Gray, C. D., & Allan, K. M. (1995). The WAIS-R (UK): Basic psychometric properties in an adult UK sample. *British Journal of Clinical Psychology, 34,* 237-250.

832. Curfs, L. M. G., Hoondert, V., van Lieshout, C. F. M., & Fryns, J. P. (1995). Personality profiles of youngsters with Prader-Willi syndrome and youngsters attending regular schools. *Journal of Intellectual Disability Research, 39,* 241–248.

833. D'Esposito, M., Verfaellie, M., Alexander, M. P., & Katz, D. I. (1995). Amnesia following traumatic bilateral fornix transection. *Neurology, 45,* 1546–1550.

834. Das, J. P., Divis, B., Alexander, J., Parrila, R. K., & Naglieri, J. A. (1995). Cognitive decline due to aging among persons with Down Syndrome. *Research in Developmental Disabilities, 16,* 461–478.

835. Daum, I., Schugens, M. M., Spieker, S., Poser, U., Schonle, P. W., & Birbaumer, N. (1995). Memory and skill acquisition in Parkinson's disease and frontal lobe dysfunction. *Cortex, 31,* 413–432.

836. De Renzi, E., Lucchelli, F., Muggia, S., & Spinnler, H. (1995). Persistent retrograde amnesia following a minor trauma. *Cortex, 31,* 531–542.

837. DeCarli, C., Murphy, D. G. M., Trauh, M., Grady, C. L., Haxby, J. V., Gillette, J. A., Salerno, J. A., Conzales-Aviles, A., Horwitz, B., Rapoport, S. I., & Schapiro, M. B. (1995). The effect of white matter hyperintensity volume on brain structure, cognitive performance, and cerebral metabolism of glucose in 51 healthy adults. *Neurology, 45,* 2077–2084.

838. della Rocchetta, A. I., Gadian, D. G., Connelly, A., Polkey, C. E., Jackson, G. D., Watkins, K. E., Johnson, C. L., Mishkin, M., & Vargha-Khadem, F. (1995). Verbal memory impairment after right temporal lobe surgery: Role of contralateral damage as revealed by 1H magnetic resonance spectroscopy and T2 relaxometry. *Neurology, 45,* 797–802.

839. DeRenzi, E., & di Pellegrino, G. (1995). Sparing of verbs and preserved, but ineffectual reading in a patient with impaired word production. *Cortex, 31,* 619–636.

840. Di Pellegrino, G. (1995). Clock-drawing in a case of left visuo-spatial neglect: A deficit of disengagement? *Neuropsychologia, 33,* 353–358.

841. Digiusto, E., & Bird, K. D. (1995). Matching smokers to treatment: Self control versus social support. *Journal of Consulting and Clinical Psychology, 63,* 290-295.

842. DiPellegrino, G., & De Renzi, E. (1995). An experimental investigation on the nature of extinction. *Neuropsychologia, 33,* 153–170.

843. DiPellegrino, G., Frassinetti, F., & Basso, G. (1995). Coordinate frames for naming misoriented chimerics: A case study of visuo-spatial neglect. *Cortex, 31,* 767–777.

844. Dominey, P., Decety, J., Broussolle, E., Chazot, G., & Jeannerod, M. (1995). Motor imagery of a lateralized sequential task is asymmetrically slowed in hemi-Parkinson's patients. *Neuropsychologia, 33,* 727–741.
845. Drake, A. I., Butters, N., Shear, P. K., Smith, T. L., Bondi, M., Irwin, M., & Schuckit, M. A. (1995). Cognitive recovery with abstinence and its relationship to family history for alcoholism. *Journal of Studies on Alcohol, 56,* 104–109.
846. Duncan, J., Burgess, P., & Emslie, H. (1995). Fluid intelligence after frontal lobe lesions. *Neuropsychologia, 33,* 261–268.
847. Dywan, C. A., McGlone, J., & Fox, A. (1995). Do intracarotid barbiturate injections offer a way to investigate hemispheric models of anosognosia? *Journal of Clinical and Experimental Neuropsychology, 17,* 431-438.
848. Eckhardt, M. J., Stapleton, J. M., Rawlings, R. R., Davis, E. Z., & Grodin, D. M. (1995). Neuropsychological functioning in detoxified alcoholics between 18 and 35 years of age. *American Journal of Psychiatry, 152,* 53-59.
849. Elliot, R., McKenna, P. J., Robbins, T. W., & Sahakian, B. J. (1995). Neuropsychological evidence for frontostriatal dysfunction in schizophrenia. *Psychological Medicine, 25,* 619–630.
850. Elwan, F. Z. (1995). Gender differences on simultaneous and sequential cognitive tasks among Egyptian school children. *Perceptual and Motor Skills, 80,* 119-127.
851. Eronen, M. (1995). Mental disorders and homicidal behavior in female subjects. *American Journal of Psychiatry, 152,* 1216–1218.
852. Everingston, C., & Dunn, C. (1995). A second validation study of the Competence Assessment for Standing Trial for Defendants with Mental Retardation (CAST-MR). *Criminal Justice and Behavior, 22,* 44–59.
853. Fabiano, R. J., & Crewe, N. (1995). Variables associated with employment following severe traumatic brain injury. *Rehabilitation Psychology, 40,* 223–231.
854. Farah, M. J., Levinson, K. L., & Klein, K. L. (1995). Face perception and within-category discrimination in prosopagnosia. *Neuropsychologia, 33,* 661–674.
855. Faraone, S. V., Seidman, L. J., Kremen, W. S., Pepple, J. R., Lyons, M. J., & Tsuang, M. T. (1995). Neuropsychological functioning among the nonpsychotic relatives of schizophrenic patients: A diagnostic efficiency analysis. *Journal of Abnormal Psychology, 104,* 286-304.
856. Feldman, J., Kerr, B., & Streissguth, A. D. (1995). Correlational analyses of procedural and declarative learning performance. *Intelligence, 20,* 87-114.
857. Fery, P., Vincent, E., & Bredart, S. (1995). Personal name anomia: A single case study. *Cortex, 31,* 191-198.
858. Finkel, D., Whitfield, K., & McGue, M. (1995). Genetic and environmental influences on functional age: A twin study. *Journal of Gerontology, 50,* 104–113.
859. Fischer, R. S., Alexander, M. P., D'esposito, M., & Otto, R. (1995). Neuropsychological and neuroanatomical correlates of confabulation. *Journal of Clinical and Experimental Neuropsychology, 17,* 20-28.
860. Fisk, A. D., Cooper, B. P., Hertzog, C., Anderson-Garlach, M. M., & Lee, M. D. (1995). Understanding performance and learning in consistent memory search: An age-related perspective. *Psychology and Aging, 10,* 255-268.
861. Frankle, A. H. (1995). A new method for detecting brain disorder by measuring perseveration in personality inventory responses. *Journal of Personality Assessment, 64,* 63-85.
862. Gershberg, F. B., & Shimamura, A. P. (1995). Impaired use of organizational strategies in free recall following frontal lobe damage. *Neuropsychologia, 33,* 1305–1333.
863. Gfeller, J. D., Meldrum, D. L., & Jacobi, K. A. (1995). The impact of constructional impairment on the WMS-R visual reproduction subtests. *Journal of Clinical Psychology, 51,* 58-63.
864. Ghaziuddin, M., Leininger, L., & Tsai, L. (1995). Brief report: Thought disorder in Asperger syndrome: Comparison with high-functioning autism. *Journal of Autism and Developmental Disorders, 25,* 311–317.
865. Giambra, L. M., Arenberg, D., Zonderman, A. B., Kawas, C., & Costa, P. T. (1995). Adult life span changes in immediate visual memory and verbal intelligence. *Psychology and Aging, 10,* 123-139.
866. Gjerde, P. F. (1995). Alternative pathways to chronic depressive symptoms in young adults: Gender differences in developmental trajectories. *Child Development, 66,* 1277–1300.
867. Glick, M., & Zigler, E. (1995). Developmental differences in the symptomatology of psychiatric inpatients with and without mild mental retardation. *American Journal on Mental Retardation, 99,* 407–417.
868. Godefroy, O., Leys, D., Furby, A., DeReuck, J., Daems, C., Rondepierre, P., Debachy, B., Deleume, J., & Desaulty, A. (1995). Psychoacoustical deficits related to bilateral subcortical hemorrhages: A case with apperceptive auditory agnosia. *Cortex, 31,* 149-159.
869. Goel, V., & Grofman, J. (1995). Are the frontal lobes implicated in "planning" functions? Interpreting data from the Tower of Hanoi. *Neuropsychologia, 33,* 623–642.
870. Gold, M., Adair, J. C., Jacobs, D. H., & Heilman, K. M. (1995). Right-left confusion in Gerstmann's Syndrome: A model of body centered spatial orientation. *Cortex, 31,* 267-283.
871. Goldberg, T. E., Gold, J. M., Torrey, E. F., & Weinberger, D. R. (1995). Lack of sex differences in the neuropsychological performance of patients with schizophrenia. *American Journal of Psychiatry, 152,* 883-888.
872. Goldenberg, G. (1995). Imitating gestures and manipulating a mannikin: The representation of the human body in ideomotor apraxia. *Neuropsychologia, 33,* 63–72.
873. Goldenberg, G., Mullbacher, W., & Nowak, A. (1995). Imagery without perception: A case study of anosognosia for cortical blindness. *Neuropsychologia, 33,* 1373–1382.
874. Goodman, R., Simonoff, E., & Stevenson, J. (1995). The impact of child IQ, parent IQ and sibling IQ on child behavioural deviance scores. *Journal of Child Psychology and Psychiatry and Allied Disciplines, 36,* 409-425.
875. Goren, A. R., Fine, J., Manaim, H., & Apter, A. (1995). Verbal and nonverbal expressions of central deficits in schizophrenia. *The Journal of Nervous and Mental Disease, 183,* 715–719.
876. Graf, P., Uttle, B., & Tuokko, H. (1995). Color- and Picture-Word Stroop Tests: Performance changes in old age. *Journal of Clinical and Experimental Neuropsychology, 17,* 390-415.
877. Greenbaum, B., Graha, S., & Scales, W. (1995). Adults with learning disabilities: Educational and social experiences during college. *Exceptional Children, 56* 460–471.
878. Gresham, K. M., MacMillan, D. L., & Siperstein, G. N. (1995). Critical analysis of the 1992 AAMR definition: Implications for school psychology. *School Psychology Quarterly, 10,* 1-19.
879. Grigsby, J., & Kaye, K. (1995). Alphanumeric sequencing and cognitive impairment among elderly persons. *Perceptual and Motor Skills, 80,* 732–734.
880. Grote, C. L., Pierre-Louis, S. J. C., Smith, M. C., Roberts, R. J., & Varney, N. R. (1995). Significance of unilateral ear extinction on the Dichotic Listening Test. *Journal of Clinical and Experimental Neuropsychology, 17,* 1-8.
881. Gudjonsson, G. H., Rutter, S. C., & Clare, I. C. H. (1995). The relationship between suggestibility and anxiety among suspects detained at police stations. *Psychological Medicine, 25,* 875–878.
882. Gureje, O., Aderibigbe, Y. A., & Obikoya, O. (1995). Three syndromes in schizophrenia: Validity in young patients with recent onset of illness. *Psychological Medicine, 25,* 715–725.
883. Haier, R. J., Chuch, D., Touchette, P., Lott, I., Buchsbaum, M. S., MacMillan, D., Sandman, C., LaCasse, L., & Sosa, E. (1995). Brain size and cerebral glucose metabolic rate in nonspecific mental retardation and Down syndrome. *Intelligence, 20,* 191–210.
884. Hamberger, M. J., Friedman, D., Ritter, W., & Rosen, J. (1995). Event-related potential and behavioral correlates of semantic processing in Alzheimer's patients and normal controls. *Brain and Language, 48,* 33–68.
885. Harris, D. M., & Kay, J. (1995). Selective impairment of the retrieval of people's names: A case of category specificity. *Cortex, 31,* 575–582.
886. Harvey, M., Miller, A. D., & Roberts, R. C. (1995). An investigation of hemispatial neglect using the landmark task. *Brain and Cognition, 27,* 59-78.
887. Hays, J. R. (1995). Trail Making Test norms for psychiatric patients. *Perceptual and Motor Skills, 80,* 187-194.
888. Herlitz, A., Hill, R. D., Fratiglioni, L., & Bäckman, L. (1995). Episodic memory and visuospatial ability in detecting and staging dementia in a community-based sample of very old adults. *Journal of Gerontology: Medical Sciences, 50A,* 107-113.
889. Hermann, B., & Seidenberg, M. (1995). Executive system dysfunction in temporal lobe epilepsy: Effects of nociferous cortex versus hippocampal pathology. *Journal of Clinical and Experimental Psychology, 17,* 809–819.
890. Hibbard, S., Hilsenroth, M. J., Hibbard, J. K., & Nash, M. R. (1995). A validty study of two projective object representations measures. *Psychological Assessment, 7,* 432–439.
891. Hinton, V. J., Halperin, J. M., Dobkin, C. S., Ding, X. H., Brown, W. T., & Miezejeski, C. M. (1995). Cognitive and molecular aspects of fragile X. *Journal of Clinical and Experimental Neuropsychology, 17,* 518–528.
892. Hittmair-Delazer, M., Sailer, U., & Benke, T. (1995). Impaired arithmetic facts but intact conceptual knowledge—a single case study of dyscalculia. *Cortex, 31,* 139-147.
893. Hodapp, R. M. (1995). Definitions in mental retardation: Effects on research, practice, and perceptions. *School Psychology Quarterly, 10,* 24-28.
894. Hogg, J., & Moss, S. (1995). The applicability of the Kaufman Assessment Battery for Children with older adults (50+ years) with moderate, severe and profound intellectual impairment. *Journal of Intellectual Disability Research, 39,* 167–176.
895. Hokkanen, L., Launes, J., Vataja, R., Valanne, L., & Iivanainen, M. (1995). Isolated retrograde amnesia for autobiographical material associated with acute left temporal lobe encephalitis. *Psychological Medicine, 25,* 203-208.
896. Holdstock, J. S., Shaw, C., & Aggleton, J. P. (1995). The performance of amnesic subjects on tests of delayed matching-to-sample and delayed matching-to-position. *Neuropsychologia, 33,* 1583–1596.
897. Holland, D. C., Dollinger, S. J., Holland, C. J., & MacDonald, D. A. (1995). The relationship between psychometric intelligence and the five-factor model of personality in a rehabilitation sample. *Journal of Clinical Psychology, 51,* 79-88.
898. Hugdahl, K., Helland, T., Faerevaag, M. K., Lyssand, E. T., & Asbjornsen, A. (1995). Absence of ear advantage on the consonant-vowel dichotic listening test in adolescent and adult dyslexics: Specific auditory-phonetic dysfunction. *Journal of Clinical and Experimental Neuropsychology, 17,* 833–840.
899. Hunkin, N. M., & Parkin, A. J. (1995). The method of vanishing cues: An evaluation of its effectiveness in teaching memory-impaired individuals. *Neuropsychologia, 33,* 1255–1279.
900. Hunkin, N. M., Parkin, A. J., Bradley, V. A., Burrows, E. H., Aldrich, F. K., Jonsari, A., & Burdon-Cooper, C. (1995). Focal retrograde amnesia following closed head injury: A case study and theoretical account. *Neuropsychologia, 33,* 509–525.
901. Hurford, D. D., & Sanders, R. E. (1995). Phonological recoding ability in young children with reading disabilities. *Contemporary Educational Psychology, 20,* 121-126.
902. Huron, C., Danion, J.-M., Giacomoni, F., Grange, D., Robert, P., & Rizzo, L. (1995). Impairment of recognition memory with, but not without, conscious recollection in schizophrenia. *American Journal of Psychiatry, 152,* 1737–1742.

903. Hütter, B. O., & Gilsbach, J. M. (1995). Introspective capacities in patients with cognitive deficits after subbarachnoid hemorrhage. *Journal of Clinical and Experimental Neuropsychology, 17,* 499–517.

904. Ilsley, J. E., Moffoot, A. P. R., & O'Carroll, R. E. (1995). An analysis of memory dysfunction in major depression. *Journal of Affective Disorders, 35,* 1–9.

905. Ivnik, R. J., Smith, G. E., Malec, J. F., Petersen, R. C., & Tangalos, E. G. (1995). Long-term stability and intercorrelations of cognitive abilities in older persons. *Psychological Assessment, 7,* 155-161.

906. Jacobs, D. M., Marder, K., Cote, L. J., Sano, M., Stern, Y., & Mayeux, R. (1995). Neuropsychological characteristics of preclinical dementia in Parkinson's disease. *Neurology, 45,* 1691–1696.

907. Jacobs, D. M., Sano, M., Dooneief, G., Marder, K., Bell, K. L., & Stern, Y. (1995). Neuropsychological detection and characterization of preclinical Alzheimer's disease. *Neurology, 45,* 957–962.

908. Jeste, D. V., Harris, M. J., Krull, A., Kuck, J., McAdams, L. A., & Heaton, R. (1995). Clinical and neuropsychological characteristics of patients with late-onset schizophrenia. *American Journal of Psychiatry, 152,* 722-730.

909. Jurden, F. H. (1995). Individual differences in working memory and complex cognition. *Journal of Educational Psychology, 87,* 93-102.

910. Katusic, S. K., Colligan, R. C., Beard, C. M., O'Fallon, W. M., Bergstralli, E. J., Jacobsen, S. J., & Kurland, L. T. (1995). Mental retardation in a birth cohort, 1976–1980, Rochester, Minnesota. *American Journal on Mental Retardation, 100,* 335–344.

911. Kershner, J., Kirkpatrick, T., & McLaren, D. (1995). The career success of an adult with a learning disability: A psychosocial study of amnesic-semantic aphasia. *Journal of Learning Disabilities, 28,* 121–126.

912. Klein, S. K., Kurtzberg, D., Brattson, A., Kreuzer, J. A., Stapells, D. R., Dunn, M. A., Rapin, I., & Vaughn, H. G., Jr. (1995). Electrophysiologic manifestations of impaired temporal lobe auditory processing in verbal auditory agnosia. *Brain and Language, 51,* 383–405.

913. Koivisto, K., Reinikainen, K. J., Hänninen, T., Vanhanen, M., Helkala, E.-L., Mykkänen, L., Laakso, M., Pyörälä, K., & Riekkinen, P. J. (1995). Prevalence of age-associated memory impairment in a randomly selected population from eastern Finland. *Neurology, 45,* 741–747.

914. Korhonen, T. T. (1995). The persistance of rapid naming problems in children with reading disabilities: A nine-year follow-up. *Journal of Learning Disabilities, 28,* 232–239.

915. Kreitler, S., Zigler, E., Kagan, S., Olsen, D., Weissler, K., & Kreitler, H. (1995). Cognitive and motivational determinants of academic achievement and behavior in third and fourth grade disadvantaged children. *British Journal of Educational Psychology, 65,* 297–316.

916. Larigneur, S., Sauier, J., & Tremblay, R. E. (1995). Supporting fathers and supported mothers in families with disruptive boys: Who are they? *Journal of Child Psychology and Psychiatry, 36,* 1003–1018.

917. Larrabee, G. J., & Curtiss, G. (1995). Construct validity of various verbal and visual memory tests. *Journal of Clinical and Experimental Neuropsychology, 17,* 536–547.

918. LaRue, A., O'Hara, R., Matsuyama, S. S., & Jarvik, L. F. (1995). Cognitive changes in young-old adults: Effect of family history of dementia. *Journal of Clinical and Experimental Neuropsychology, 17,* 65-70.

919. LaRue, A., Swan, G. E., & Carmelli, D. (1995). Cognition and depression in a cohort of aging men: Results from the western collaborative group study. *Psychology and Aging, 10,* 30-33.

920. Lau, M. A., Pihl, R. O., & Peterson, J. B. (1995). Provocation, acute alcohol intoxication, cognitive performance, and aggression. *Journal of Abnormal Psychology, 104,* 150-155.

921. Leonard, G., & Milner, B. (1995). Recall of self-generated arm movements by patients with unilateral cortical excisions. *Neuropsychologia, 33,* 611–622.

922. Lerer, B., Shapira, B., Calev, A., Tubi, N., Drexler, H., Kindler, S., Lidsky, D., & Schwartz, J. E. (1995). Antidepressant and cognitive effects of twice- versus three-times weekly ECT. *American Journal of Psychiatry, 152,* 564-570.

923. Lernhart, L. A., & Rabiner, D. L. (1995). An integrative approach to the study of social competence in adolescence. *Development and Psychopathology, 7,* 543–561.

924. Levinson, D. F., Simpson, G. M., Lo, E. S., Cooper, T. B., Singh, H., Yadalam, K., & Stephanos, M. J. (1995). Fluphenazine plasma levels, dosage, efficacy, and side effects. *American Journal of Psychiatry, 152,* 765-771.

925. Linnville, S. E. (1995). Are there age-related processing differences in semantic priming? *Perceptual and Motor Skills, 80,* 5858–586.

926. Luszcz, M., & Hinton, M. (1995). Domain- and task-specific beliefs about memory in adulthood: A microgenetic approach. *Australian Journal of Psychology, 47,* 54–59.

927. Maravita, A., Spadoni, M., Mazzucchi, A., & Parma, M. (1995). A new case of retrograde amnesia with abnormal forgetting rate. *Cortex, 31,* 653–667.

928. Marcell, M. M., Ridgeway, M. M., Sewell, D. H., & Whelan, M. L. (1995). Sentence imitation by adolescents and young adults with Down's syndrome and other intellectual disabilities. *Journal of Intellectual Disability Research, 39,* 215–232.

929. Matson, J. L. (1995). Comments on Gresham, MacMillan, and Siperstein's paper "Critical analysis of the 1992 AAMR definition: Implications for school psychology." *School Psychology Quarterly, 10,* 20-23.

930. Mazaux, J. M., Dartigues, J. F., Letenneur, L., Darriet, D., Wiart, L., Gagnon, M., Commenges, D., & Boller, F. (1995). Visuo-spatial attention and psychomotor performance in elderly community residents: Effects of age, gender, and education. *Journal of Clinical and Experimental Neuropsychology, 17,* 71-81.

931. McBride, J. A., & Panksepp, J. (1995). An examination of the phenomenology and the reliability of ratings of compulsive behavior in autism. *Journal of Autism and Developmental Disorders, 25,* 381–396.

932. McDougle, C. J., Kresch, L. E., Goodman, W. K., Naylor, S. T., Volkmar, F. R., Cohen, D. J., & Price, L. H. (1995). A case-controlled study of repetitive thoughts and behavior in adults with autisitc disorder and obsessive-compulsive disorder. *American Journal of Psychiatry, 152,* 772-777.

933. McNally, R. J., & Shin, L. M. (1995). Association of intelligence with severity of posttraumatic stress disorder symptoms in Vietnam combat veterans. *American Journal of Psychiatry, 152,* 936-938.

934. Mendelberg, H. E. (1995). Inpatient treatment of mood disorders. *Psychological Reports, 76,* 819–824.

935. Migliorelli, R., Petracca, G., Tesón, A., Sabe, L., Leiguarda, R., & Starkstein, S. E. (1995). Neuropsychiatric and neuropsychological correlates of delusions in Alzheimer's Disease. *Psychological Medicine, 25,* 505–513.

936. Millis, S. R., Putnam, S. H., Adams, K. M., & Ricker, J. H. (1995). The California Verbal Learning Test in the detection of incomplete effort in neuropsychological evaluation. *Psychological Assessment, 7,* 463–471.

937. Mitrushina, M., & Satz, P. (1995). Base rates of the WAIS-R intersubtest scatter and VIQ-PIQ discrepancy in normal elderly. *Journal of Clinical Psychology, 51,* 70-78.

938. Mitrushina, M., Uchiyama, C., & Satz, P. (1995). Heterogeneity of cognitive profiles in normal aging: Implications for early manifestations of Alzheimer's disease. *Journal of Clinical and Experimental Neuropsychology, 17,* 374-382.

939. Mittenberg, W., Theroux-Fichera, S., & Zielinski, R. E. (1995). Identification of malingered head injury on the Wechsler Adult Intelligence Scale—Revised. *Professional Psychology: Research and Practice, 26,* 491–498.

940. Moore, L. H., Brown, W. S., Markee, T. E., Theberge, D. C., & Zui, J. C. (1995). Bimanual coordination in dyslexic adults. *Neuropsychologia, 33,* 781–793.

941. Morgan, C. D., Nordin, S., & Murphy, C. (1995). Odor identification as an early marker for Alzheimer's Disease: Impact of lexical functioning and detection sensitivity. *Journal of Clinical and Experimental Neuropsychology, 17,* 793–803.

942. Morgan, S. F., & Wheelock, J. (1995). Comparability of WAIS-R digit symbol and the Symbol Digit Modalities Test. *Perceptual and Motor Skills, 80,* 631–634.

943. Morris, R. C., Abrahams, S., & Polkey, C. E. (1995). Recognition memory for words and faces following unilateral temporal lobectomy. *British Journal of Clinical Psychology, 34,* 571–576.

944. Motomura, N., Redbrake, A., Hartje, W., & Willmes, K. (1995). Sensorimotor learning in ideomotor apraxia. *Perceptual and Motor Skills, 81,* 1123–1129.

945. Mottron, L., & Belleville, S. (1995). Perspective production in a savant autistic draughtsman. *Psychological Medicine, 25,* 639–648.

946. Nagle, R. J., & Bell, N. L. (1995). Clinical utility of Kaufman's "amazingly" short forms of the WAIS-R with educable mentally retarded adolescents. *Journal of Clinical Psychology, 51,* 396-400.

947. Nezu, C., Nezu, A. M., Rothenberg, J. L., Dellicarpini, L., & Groag, I. (1995). Depression in adults with mild mental retardation: Are cognitive variables involved? *Cognitive Therapy and Research, 19,* 227–239.

948. O'Mahony, J. F., & Doherty, B. (1995). Comparability of correlates of original and revised Wechsler Adult Intelligence Scales in an alcoholic-abusing population. *Journal of Clinical Psychology, 51,* 123-128.

949. Orpwood, L., & Warrington, K. (1995). Word specific impairments in naming and spelling but not reading. *Cortex, 31,* 239-265.

950. Park, S., Holzman, P. S., & Lenzenweger, M. F. (1995). Individual differences in spatial working memory in relation to schizotypy. *Journal of Abnormal Psychology, 104,* 355-363.

951. Parker, E. S., Eaton, E. M., Whipple, S. C., Heseltine, P. W. R., & Bridge, T. P. (1995). University of California Repeatable Episodic Memory Test. *Journal of Clinical and Experimental Neuropsychology, 17,* 926–936.

952. Parker, K. C. H., & Atkinson, L. (1995). Computation of Wechsler Adult Intelligence Scale—Revised factor scores: Equal and differential weights. *Psychological Assessment, 7,* 456–462.

953. Patterson, M., Slate, J. R., Jones, C. H., & Steger, H. S. (1995). The effects of practice administrations in learning to administer and score the WAIS-R: A partial replication. *Educational and Psychological Measurement, 55,* 32-37.

954. Persinger, M. A., & Richards, P. M. (1995). Foot agility and toe gnosis/graphaesthesia as potential indicators of integrity of the medial cerebral surface: Normative data and comparison with clinical populations. *Perceptual and Motor Skills, 80,* 1011–1024.

955. Phillips, N. A., & McGlone, J. (1995). Grouped data do not tell the whole story: Individual analysis of cognitive change after temporal lobectomy. *Journal of Clinical and Experimental Neuropsychology, 17,* 713–724.

956. Piven, J., Arndt, S., Bailey, J., Havercamp, S., Andreasen, N. C., & Palmer, P. (1995). An MRI study of brain size in autism. *American Journal of Psychiatry, 152,* 1145–1149.

957. Plassman, B. L., Welsh, K. A., Helms, M., Brandt, J., Page, W. F., & Breitner, J. C. S. (1995). Intelligence and education as predictors of cognitive state in late life: A 50-year follow-up. *Neurology, 45,* 1446–1450.

958. Pollux, P. M. J., Wester, A., & DeHaon, E. H. F. (1995). Random generation deficit in alcoholic Korsakoff patients. *Neuropsychologia, 33,* 125–129.

959. Portin, R., Saarijarvi, S., Joukamaa, M., & Salokangas, R. K. R. (1995). Education, gender and cognitive performance in a 62-year-old normal population: Results from the Turva Project. *Psychological Medicine, 25,* 1295–1298.

960. Poynton, A. M., Kartsounis, L. D., & Bridges, P. K. (1995). A prospective clinical study of steretactic subcaudate tractotomy. *Psychological Medicine, 25,* 763–770.

961. Ramig, L. O., Countryman, S., Thompson, L. L., & Horii, Y. (1995). Comparison of two forms of intensive speech treatment for Parkinson's disease. *Journal of Speech and Hearing Research, 38,* 1232–1251.

962. Rasile, D. A., Burg, J. S., Burright, R. G., & Donovick, P. J. (1995). The relationship between performance on the Gordon Diagnostic System and other measures of attention. *International Journal of Psychology, 30,* 35–45.

963. Rasmusson, D. X., & Brandt, J. (1995). Instability of cognitive asymmetry in Alzheimer's disease. *Journal of Clinical and Experimental Neuropsychology, 17,* 449-458.

964. Resnick, S. M., Trotman, K. M., Kawas, C., & Zonderman, A. B. (1995). Age-associated changes in specific errors on the Benton Visual Retention Test. *Journal of Gerontology: Psychological Sciences, 50*B, 171-178.

965. Robertson, I. H., Tegner, R., Tham, K., Lo, A., & Nimmo-Smith, I. (1995). Sustained attention training for unilateral neglect: Theoretical and rehabilitation implications. *Journal of Clinical and Experimental Neuropsychology, 17,* 416-430.

966. Rosenfeld, B., & Turkheimer, E. (1995). Multidimensional representation of decision-making in chronic schizophrenics. *Multivariate Behavioral Research, 30,* 199–211.

967. Ryan, J. J., Lopez, S. J., & Sumerall, S. W. (1995). Base rate of "10 to 11" clocks among patients referred for neuropsychologtical evaluation. *Perceptual and Motor Skills, 81,* 1138.

968. Ryan, J. J., Paolo, A. M., & Dunn, G. E. (1995). Analysis of a WAIS-R old-age normative sample in terms of gender, years of education, and pre-retirement occupation. *Assessment, 2,* 225–231.

969. Saarnio, P. K. (1995). WAIS digit symbol and block design scores in abstinent alcoholics: A replication. *Perceptual and Motor Skills, 80,* 112-114.

970. Sahgal, A., McKeith, I. G., Galloway, P. H., Tasker, N., & Steckler, T. (1995). Do differences in visuospatial ability between senile dementias of the Alzheimer and Lewy body types reflect differences solely in mnemonic function? *Journal of Clinical and Experimental Neuropsychology, 17,* 35-43.

971. Salerno, J. A., Grady, C., Mentis, M., Gonzalez-Aviles, A., Wagner, E., Schapiro, M. B., & Rapaport, S. I. (1995). Brain metabolic function in older men with chronic essential hypertension. *Journal of Gerontology: Medical Sciences, 50*A, 147-154.

972. Salthouse, T. A. (1995). Differential age-related influences on memory for verbal-symbolic information and visual-spatial information? *Journal of Gerontology, 50,* 193–201.

973. Sands, J. R., & Harrow, M. (1995). Vulnerability to psychosis in unipolar major depression: Is premorbid functioning involved? *American Journal of Psychiatry, 152,* 1009-1015.

974. Sass, K. J., Buchanan, C. P., Kraemer, S., Westerveld, M., Kim, J. H., & Spencer, D. D. (1995). Verbal memory impairment resulting from hippocampal neuron loss among epileptic patients with structural lesions. *Neurology, 45,* 2154–2158.

975. Seki, K., Yajima, M., & Sugishita, M. (1995). The efficacy of kinesthetic reading treatment for pure alexia. *Neuropsychologia, 33,* 595–609.

976. Sharp, D., Hay, D. F., Paulby, S., Schniicker, G., Allen, H., & Kumar, R. (1995). The impact of postnatal depression on boys' intellectual development. *Journal of Child Psychology and Psychiatry, 36,* 1315–1336.

977. Shaw, C., & Aggleton, J. P. (1995). Evidence for the independence of recognition and recency memory in amnesic subjects. *Cortex, 31,* 57-71.

978. Sherman, E. M. S., Strauss, E. S., Spellacy, F., & Hunter, M. (1995). Construct validity of WAIS-R factors: Neuropsychological test correlates in adults referred for evaluation of possible head injury. *Psychological Assessment, 7,* 440–444.

979. Shuttleworth-Jordan, A. B., & Bode, S. G. (1995). Taking account of age-related differences on digit symbol and incidental recall for diagnostic purposes. *Journal of Clinical and Experimental Neuropsychology, 17,* 439-448.

980. Slaghuis, W. L., & Bakker, V. J. (1995). Forward and backward visual masking of contour by light in positive- and negative-symptom schizophrenia. *Journal of Abnormal Psychology, 104,* 41-54.

981. Slater, A. (1995). Individual differences in infancy and later IQ. *Journal of Child Psychology and Psychiatry and Allied Disciplines, 36,* 69-112.

982. Sloan, E. P., Fenton, G. W., Kennedy, N. S. J., & MacLennan, J. M. (1995). Electroencephalography and single photon emission computed tomography in dementia: A comparative study. *Psychological Medicine, 25,* 631–638.

983. Slomkowski, C., Klein, R. G., & Mannuzza, S. (1995). Is self-esteem an important outcome in hyperactive children? *Journal of Abnormal Child Psychology, 23,* 303-315.

984. Small, G. W., LaRue, A., Komo, S., Kaplan, A., & Mandelkern, M. A. (1995). Predictors of cognitive change in middle-aged and older adults with memory loss. *American Journal of Psychiatry, 152,* 1757–1764.

985. Smith, M. L., Leonard, G., Crane, J., & Milner, B. (1995). The effects of frontal- or temporal-lobe lesions on susceptibility to interference in spatial memory. *Neuropsychologia, 33,* 275–285.

986. Smith, R. L., Goode, K. T., La Marche, J. A., & Boll, T. J. (1995). Selective Reminding Test short form administration: A comparison of two through twelve trials. *Psychological Assessment, 7,* 177-182.

987. Smith, S. A., & Hudson, R. L. (1995). A quick screening test of competency to stand trial for defendents with mental retardation. *Psychological Reports, 76,* 91-97.

988. Solomon, P. R., Brett, M., Groccia-Ellison, M. E., Oyler, C., Tomsai, M., & Pendlebury, W. W. (1995). Classical conditioning in patients with Alzheimer's disease: A multiday study. *Psychology and Aging, 10,* 248-254.

989. Spafford, C. S., Grosser, G. S., Donatelle, J. R., Squillace, S. R., & Dana, J. P. (1995). Contrast sensitivity differences between proficient and disabled readers using colored lenses. *Journal of Learning Disabilities, 28,* 240–252.

990. Spencer, T., Wilens, T., Biederman, J., Faraone, S. V., Ablon, S., & Lapey, K. (1995). A double-blind, crossover comparison of methylphenidate and placebo in adults with childhood-onset attention deficit hyperactivity disorder. *Archives of General Psychiatry, 52,* 434–443.

991. Stough, C., Nettelbeck, T., Cooper, C., & Bates, T. (1995). Strategy use in Jensen's RT paradigm: Relationships to intelligence? *Australian Journal of Psychology, 47,* 61–65.

992. Strauss, E., Loring, D., Chelune, G., Hunter, M., Hermann, B., Perrine, K., Westerveld, M., Trenerry, M., & Barr, W. (1995). Predicting cognitive impairment in epilepsy: Findings from the Bozeman Epilepsy Consortium. *Journal of Clinical and Experimental Neuropsychology, 17,* 909–917.

993. Sullivan, T. E., & Hawkins, K. A. (1995). Support for abbreviation of the Wide Range Achievement Test—Revised spelling subtest in neuropsychological assessments. *Journal of Clinical Psychology, 51,* 552–554.

994. Sutker, P. B., & Allain, A. N. (1995). Psychological assessment of aviators captured in World War II. *Psychological Assessment, 7,* 66-68.

995. Sutker, P. B., Davis, J. M., Uddo, M., & Ditta, S. R. (1995). War zone stress, personal resources, and PTSD in Persian Gulf War returnees. *Journal of Abnormal Psychology, 104,* 444–452.

996. Swoboda, K. J., & Jenike, M. A. (1995). Frontal abnormalities in a patient with obsessive-compulsive disorder: The role of structural lesions in obsessive-compulsive behavior. *Neurology, 45,* 2130–2134.

997. Takahashi, N., Kawamura, M., Hirayama, K., Shiota, J., & Isono, O. (1995). Prosopagnosia: A clinical and anatomical study of four patients. *Cortex, 31,* 317-329.

998. Thompson, A. P. (1995). Test-retest evaluation of a four-subtests WAIS-R short form with young offenders. *Journal of Clinical Psychology, 51,* 410-414.

999. Thompson, L. A. (1995). Encoding and memory for visible speech and gestures: A comparison between young and older adults. *Psychology and Aging, 10,* 215-228.

1000. Tisdwell, P., Dias, P. S., Sagar, H. J., Mayes, A. R., & Battersby, R. D. E. (1995). Cognitive outcome after aneurysm rupture: Relationship to aneurysm site and perioperative complications. *Neurology, 45,* 875–882.

1001. Tordjman, S., Anderson, G. M., McBride, P. A., Hertzig, M. E., Snow, M. E., Hall, L. M., Ferrari, P., & Cohen, D. J. (1995). Plasma androgens in autism. *Journal of Autism and Developmental Disorders, 25,* 295–304.

1002. Trichard, C., Martinot, J. L, Alagille, M., Masure, M. C., Hardy, P., Ginestet, D., & Feline, A. (1995). Time course of prefrontal lobe dysfunction in severely depressed in-patients: A longitudinal neuropsychological study. *Psychological Medicine, 25,* 79-85.

1003. Tuokko, H., Kristjansson, E., & Miller, J. (1995). Neuropsychological detection of dementia: An overview of the neuropsychological component of the Canadian study of health and aging. *Journal of Clinical and Experimental Neuropsychology, 17,* 325-373.

1004. Turnbull, O. H., Laws, K. R., & McCarthy, R. A. (1995). Object recognition without knowledge of object orientation. *Cortex, 31,* 387-395.

1005. Umbricht, D., Degreef, G., Barr, W. B., Lieberman, J. A., Pollack, S., & Schaul, N. (1995). Postictal and chronic psychoses in patients with temporal lobe epilepsy. *American Journal of Psychiatry, 152,* 224-231.

1006. Upton, D., & Corcoran, R. (1995). The role of the right temporal lobe in card sorting: A case study. *Cortex, 31,* 405-409.

1007. van Spaendonck, K. P. M., Berger, H. J. C., Horstink, M. W. I. M., Borm, G. F., & Cools, A. R. (1995). Card sorting performance in Parkinson's Disease: A comparison between acquisition and shifting performance. *Journal of Clinical and Experimental Neuropsychology, 17,* 918–925.

1008. Ward, L. C., & Ryan, J. J. (1995). Validity and time savings in the selection of short forms of the Wechsler Adult Intelligence Scale—Revised. *Psychological Assessment, 8,* 69–72.

1009. Ward, M. J., & Carlson, E. A. (1995). Associations among adult attachment representations, maternal sensitivity, and infant-mother attachment in a sample of adolescent mothers. *Child Development, 66,* 69-79.

1010. Waterfall, M. L., & Crowe, S. F. (1995). Meta-analytic comparison of the components of visual cognition in Parkinson's Disease. *Journal of Clinical and Experimental Neuropsychology, 17,* 759–772.

1011. White, N., Green, A., & Steiner, R. (1995). An investigation of differences between three age groups in verbal and spatial task performance using the dual-task paradigm. *Brain and Cognition, 28,* 59–78.

1012. Wible, C. G., Shenton, M. E., Hokama, H., Kikinis, R., Jotesz, F. A., Metcalf, D., & McCarley, R. W. (1995). Prefrontal cortex and schizophrenia: A quantitative magnetic resonance imaging study. *Archives of General Psychiatry, 52,* 279–288.

1013. Wilson, B. A., Baddeley, A. D., & Kapor, N. (1995). Dense amnesia in a professional musician following herpes simplex virus encephalitis. *Journal of Clinical and Experimental Neuropsychology, 17,* 668–681.

1014. Wishart, H. A., Strauss, E., Hunter, M., & Moll, A. (1995). Interhemispheric transfer in multiple sclerosis. *Journal of Clinical and Experimental Neuropsychology, 17,* 937–940.

1015. Wisniewski, J. J., Andrews, T. J., & Mulick, J. A. (1995). Objective and subjective factors in the disproportionate referral of children for academic problems. *Journal of Consulting and Clinical Psychology, 63,* 1032–1076.

1016. Wong, C. T., Day, J. D., Maxwell, S. E., & Meara, N. M. (1995). A multitrait-multimethod study of academic and social intelligence in college students. *Journal of Educational Psychology, 87,* 117-133.

1017. Woodard, J. L., & Axelrod, B. N. (1995). Parsimonious prediction of Wechsler Memory Scale—Revised memory indices. *Psychological Assessment, 7,* 445-449.

1018. Woodworth, S. J., DeFries, J. C., Fulker, D. W., Olson, R. K., & Pennington, B. F. (1995). Reading performance and verbal short-term memory: A twin study of reciprocal causation. *Intelligence, 20,* 145–167.

1019. Yazgan, M. Y., Wexler, B. E., Kinsbourne, M., Peterson, B., & Leckman, J. F. (1995). Functional significance of individual variations in callosal area. *Neuropsychologia, 33,* 769–779.

1020. Yehuda, R., Keefe, R. S. E., Harvey, P. D., Levengood, R. A., Gerber, D. K., Geni, J., & Siever, L. J. (1995). Learning and memory in combat veterans with posttraumatic stress disorder. *American Journal of Psychiatry, 152,* 137-139.

1021. Young, H. F., & Bentall, R. P. (1995). Hypothesis testing in patients with persecutory delusions: Comparison with depressed and normal subjects. *British Journal of Clinical Psychology, 34,* 353–369.

1022. Youngjohn, J. R. (1995). Confirmed attorney coaching prior to neuropsychological evaluation. *Assessment, 2,* 279–283.

1023. Zaidel, D. W., Zaidel, E., Oxbury, S. M., & Oxbury, J. M. (1995). The interpretation of sentence ambiguity in patients with unilateral focal brain surgery. *Brain and Language, 51,* 458–468.

1024. Zeitlin, S. B., & Polivy, J. (1995). Coprophagia as a manifestation of obsessive-compulsive disorder: A case report. *Journal of Behavior Therapy and Experimental Psychiatry, 26,* 57–63.

1025. Zucco, G. M., Tessari, A., & Soresi, S. (1995). Remembering spatial locations: Effects of material and intelligence. *Perceptual and Motor Skills, 80,* 499–503.

1026. Zurrón, M., & Díaz, F. (1995). Auditory and visual evoked potentials in individuals with organic and cultural-familial mental retardation. *American Journal on Mental Retardation, 100,* 271–282.

1027. Aggleton, J. P., & Shaw, C. (1996). Amnesia and recognition memory: A re-analysis of psychometric data. *Neuropsychologia, 34,* 51–62.

1028. Ahola, K., Vilkki, J., & Servo, A. (1996). Frontal tests do not detect frontal infarctions after ruptured intracranial aneurysm. *Brain and Cognition, 31,* 1–16.

1029. Alexander, M. P., & Annett, M. (1996). Crossed aphasia and related anomalies of cerebral organization: Case reports and a genetic hypothesis. *Brain and Language, 55,* 213–239.

1030. Arceneaux, J. M., Cheramic, G. M., & Smith, C. W. (1996). Gender differences in WAIS-R age-corrected scaled scores. *Perceptual and Motor Skills, 83,* 1211–1215.

1031. Armon, C., Shin, C., Miller, P., Carwile, S., Brown, E., Edinger, J. D., & Paul, R. G. (1996). Reversible Parkinsonism and cognitive impairment with chronic valproate use. *Neurology, 47,* 626–635.

1032. Arnett, P. A., Rao, S. M., Hussain, M., Swanson, S. J., & Hammeke, T. A. (1996). Conduction aphasia in multiple sclerosis: A case report with MRI findings. *Neurology, 47,* 576–578.

1033. Axelrod, B. N., Woodard, J. L., Schretlen, D., & Benedict, R. H. B. (1996). Corrected estimates of WAIS-R Short Form reliability and standard error of measurement. *Psychological Assessment, 8,* 222–223.

1034. Bailey, A., Goode, S., Pickles, A., Robertson, S., Gottesman, I., & Rutter, M. (1996). A broader phenotype of autism: The clinical spectrum in twins. *Journal of Child Psychology and Psychiatry, 37,* 785–801.

1035. Barrett, D. H., Green, M. L., Morris, R., Giles, W. H., & Croft, J. B. (1996). Cognitive functioning and post-traumatic stress disorder. *American Journal of Psychiatry, 153,* 1492–1494.

1036. Beats, B. C., Sahakian, B. J., & Levy, R. (1996). Cognitive performance in tests sensitive to frontal lobe dysfunction in the elderly depressed. *Psychological Medicine, 26,* 591–603.

1037. Beatty, W. W., Hames, K. A., Blanco, C. R., Nixon, S. J., & Tivis, L. J. (1996). Visuospatial perception, construction and memory in alcoholism. *Journal of Studies on Alcohol, 57,* 136–143.

1038. Beatty, W. W., Wilbanks, S. L., Blanco, C. R., Hames, K. A., Tivis, R., & Paul, R. H. (1996). Memory disturbance in Multiple Sclerosis: Reconsideration of patterns of performance on the Selective Reminding Test. *Journal of Clinical and Experimental Neuropsychology, 18,* 56–62.

1039. Becker, D. F., Edell, W. S., Fujioka, T. A., Levy, K. N., & McGlashan, T. H. (1996). Attentional and intellectual deficits in unmedicated behavior-disordered adolescent in patients. *Journal of Youth and Adolescence, 25,* 127–135.

1040. Berent, S., Giordani, B., Gilman, S., Junck, L., Klurn, K. J., & Koeppe, R. A. (1996). Psychological factors and PET measured glucose matabolism in olivopontocerebellar atrophy. *Assessment, 3,* 339–349.

1041. Binder, J. R., Swanson, S. J., Hammeke, T. A., Morris, G. L., Mueller, W. M., Fischer, M., Benbadis, S., Frost, J. A., Rao, S. M., & Haughton, V. M. (1996). Determination of a language dominance using functional MRI: A comparison with the Wada test. *Neurology, 46,* 978–984.

1042. Bird, M., & Kinsella, G. (1996). Long-term cued recall of tasks in senile dementia. *Psychology and Aging, 11,* 45–46.

1043. Blaha, J., & Wallbrown, F. H. (1996). Hierarchical factor structure of the Wechsler Intelligence Scale for Children—III. *Psychological Assessment, 8,* 214–218.

1044. Block, J., & Kremen, A. M. (1996). IQ and ego-resiliency: Conceptual and empirical corrections and separateness. *Journal of Personality and Social Psychology, 70,* 349–361.

1045. Breslau, N., Brown, G. G., Del Dotto, J. E., Kumar, S., Ezhuthachan, S., Andreski, P., & Hufnagle, K. G. (1996). Psychiatric sequelae of low birth weight at 6 years of age. *Journal of Abnormal Child Psychology, 24,* 385–400.

1046. Brunfaut, E., & d'Ydewalle, G. (1996). A comparison of implicit memory tasks in Korsakoff and alcoholic patients. *Neuropsychologia, 34,* 1143–1150.

1047. Bryan, J., & Luszcz, M. A. (1996). Speed of information processing as a mediator between age and free-recall performance. *Psychology and Aging, 11,* 3–9.

1048. Budd, K. S., & Holdsworth, M. J. (1996). Issues in clinical assessment of minimal parenting competence. *Journal of Clinical Child Psychology, 25,* 1–14.

1049. Burgess, P. W., & Shallice, T. (1996). Bizarre responses, rule detection and frontal lobe lesions. *Cortex, 32,* 241–259.

1050. Burgess, P. W., & Shallice, T. (1996). Response suppression, initiation and strategy use following frontal lobe lesions. *Neuropsychologia, 34,* 263–273.

1051. Cammalleri, R., Gangitano, M., D'Amelio, M., Raieli, V., Raimondo, D., & Camarda, R. (1996). Transient topographical amnesia and cingulate cortex damage. *Neuropsychologia, 34,* 321–326.

1052. Carlesimo, G. A., Marfia, G. A., Loosses, A., & Caltagirone, C. (1996). Recency effect in anterograde amnesia: Evidence for distinct memory states underlying enhanced retrieval of terminal items in immediate and delayed recall paradigms. *Neuropsychologia, 34,* 177–184.

1053. Carvajal, H., Schrader, M. S., & Holmes, C. B. (1996). Retest reliability of the Wechsler Adult Intelligence Scale—Revised for 18 to 19-year-olds. *Psychological Reports, 78,* 211–214.

1054. Channon, S. (1996). Executive dysfunction in depression: The Wisconsin Card Sorting Test. *Journal of Affective Disorders, 39,* 107–114.

1055. Chari, G., Shaw, P. J., & Sahgal, A. (1996). Nonverbal visual attention, but not recognition memory or learning, processes are impaired in motor neurone disease. *Neuropsychologia, 34,* 377–385.

1056. Cipolotti, L., & Warrington, E. K. (1996). Does recognizing orally spelled words depend on reading? An investigation into a case of better written than oral spelling. *Neuropsychologia, 34,* 427–440.

1057. Cockburn, J. (1996). Failure of prospective memory after acquired brain damage: Preliminary investigation and suggestions for future directions. *Journal of Clinical and Experimental Neuropsychology, 18,* 304–309.

1058. Cohen, R. L., & Borsoi, D. (1996). The role of gestures in description-communication: A cross-sectional study of aging. *Journal of Nonverbal Behavior, 20,* 45–63.

1059. Cornelissen, P. L., Hansen, P. C., Bradley, L., & Stein, J. F. (1996). Analysis of perceptual confusions between nine sets of consonant-vowel sounds in normal and dyslexic adults. *Cognition, 59,* 275–306.

1060. Corrigan, P. W., Buican, B., & McCracken, S. (1996). Can severely mentally ill adults reliably report their needs? *Journal of Nervous and Mental Disease, 184,* 523–529.

1061. Craissati, J., & McClurg, G. (1996). The Challenge Project: Perpetrators of child sexual abuse in south east London. *Child Abuse & Neglect, 20,* 1067–1077.

1062. Crawford, J. R., & Allan, K. M. (1996). WAIS-R subtest scatter: Base-rate data from a healthy UK sample. *British Journal of Clinical Psychology, 35,* 235–247.

1063. Crawford, J. R., Mychalkin, B., Johnson, D. A., & Moore, J. W. (1996). WAIS-R short-forms: Criterion validity in healthy and clinical samples. *British Journal of Clinical Psychology, 35,* 638–640.

1064. Crouch, J. A., Greve, K. W., & Brooks, J. (1996). The California Card Sorting Test dissociate verbal and non-verbal concept formation abilities. *British Journal of Clinical Psychology, 35,* 431–434.

1065. della Rocchetta, A. I., Cipolotti, L., & Warrington, E. K. (1996). Topographical disorientation: Selective impairment of locomotor space? *Cortex, 32,* 727–735.

1066. Diamond, B. J., Mayes, A. R., & Meudell, P. R. (1996). Autonomic and recognition indices of memory in amnesic and healthy control subjects. *Cortex, 32,* 439–459.

1067. Dimitrov, M., Grafman, J., & Hollnagel, C. (1996). The effects of frontal lobe damage on everyday problem solving. *Cortex, 32,* 357–366.

1068. Docherty, N. M., Hawkins, K. A., Hoffman, R. E., Quinlan, D. M., Rakfeldt, J., & Sledge, W. H. (1996). Working memory, attention, and communication disturbances in schizophrenia. *Journal of Abnormal Psychology, 105,* 212–219.

1069. Downes, J. J., Davis, E. J., Davies, P. D. M., Perfect, T. J., Wilson, K., Mayes, A. R., & Sagar, H. J. (1996). Stem-completion priming in Alzheimer's disease: The importance of target word articulation. *Neuropsychologia, 34,* 63–75.

1070. Duchesneau, A. P. (1996). Alexithymia and visual perception. *Perceptual and Motor Skills, 83,* 291–298.

1071. Dukewich, T. L., Borkowski, J. G., & Whitman, T. L. (1996). Adolescent mothers and child abuse potential: An evaluation of risk factors. *Child Abuse & Neglect, 20,* 1031–1047.

1072. Dykens, E. (1996). The draw-a-person task in persons with mental retardation: What does it measure? *Research in Developmental Disabilities, 17,* 1–13.

1073. Eronen, M., Hakola, P., & Tiihonen, J. (1996). Mental disorders and homicidal behavior in Finland. *Archives of General Psychiatry, 53,* 497–501.

1074. Eronen, M., Tiihonen, J., & Hakola, P. (1996). Schizophrenia and homicidal behavior. *Schizophrenia Bulletin, 22,* 83–89.

1075. Fastenau, P. S., Denburg, N. L., & Abeles, N. (1996). Age differences in retrieval: Further support for the resource-reduction hypothesis. *Psychology and Aging, 11,* 140–146.

1076. Ferraro, F. R. (1996). Cognitive slowing in closed-head injury. *Brain and Cognition, 32,* 429–440.

1077. Ferraro, F. R., & Chelminski, I. (1996). Preliminary normative data on the Geriatric Depression Scale—Short Form (GDS-SF) in a young adult sample. *Journal of Clinical Psychology, 52,* 443–447.

1078. Ferraro, F. R., & Okerlund, M. (1996). Failure to inhibit irrelevant information in non-clinical schizotypal individuals. *Journal of Clinical Psychology, 52,* 389–394.

1079. Fisher, N. J., Rourke, B. P., Bieliauskas, L., Giordani, B., Berent, S., & Foster, N. L. (1996). Neuropsychological subgroups of patients with Alzheimer's disease. *Journal of Clinical and Experimental Neuropsychology, 18,* 349–370.

1080. Flashman, L. A., Flaum, M., Gupta, S., & Andreasen, N. C. (1996). Soft signs and neuropsychological performance in schizophrenia. *American Journal of Psychiatry, 153,* 526–532.

1081. Fujii, D. E. (1996). Kolb's learning styles and potential cognitive remediations of brain-injured individuals: An exploratory factor analysis study. *Professional Psychology: Research and Practice, 27,* 266–271.

1082. Gallassi, R., Morreale, A., Montagna, P., Cortelli, P., Avoni, P., Castellani, R., Gambetti, P., & Lugaresi, E. (1996). Fatal familial insomnia: Behavioral and cognitive features. *Neurology, 46,* 935–939.

1083. Gansler, D. A., Covall, S., McGrath, N., & Oscar-Berman, M. (1996). Measures of prefrontal dysfunction after closed head injury. *Brain and Cognition, 30,* 194–204.

1084. Glick, M., & Zigler, E. (1996). Premorbid competence, thought-action orientation, and outcome in psychiatric patients with mild mental retardation. *Development and Psychopathology, 8,* 585–595.

1085. Glover, D., Maltzman, I., & Williams, C. (1996). Food preferences among individuals with and without Prader-Willi Syndrome. *American Journal on Mental Retardation, 101,* 195–205.

1086. Glutting, J. J., Youngstrom, E. A., Oakland, T., & Watkins, M. W. (1996). Situational specificity and generality of test behaviors for samples of normal and referred children. *School Psychology Review, 25,* 94–107.

1087. Gottesman, R. L. Bennett, R. E., Nathan, R. G., & Kelly, M. S. (1996). Inner-city adults with severe reading difficulties: A closer look. *Journal of Learning Disabilities, 29,* 589–597.

1088. Greenbaum, B., Graham, S., & Scales, W. (1996). Adults with learning disabilities: Occupational and social status after college. *Journal of Learning Disabilities, 29,* 167–173.

1089. Hall, M., Whaley, R., Robertson, K., Hamby, S., Wilkins, J., & Hall, C. (1996). The correlation between neuropsychological and neuroanatomic changes over time in asymptomatic and symptomatic HIV-1-infected individuals. *Neurology, 46,* 1697–1702.

1090. Hall, S., Pinkston, S. L., Szalda-Petree, A. C., & Coronis, A. R. (1996). The performance of healthy older adults on the Continuous Visual memory Test and the Visual-Motor Integration Test: Preliminary findings. *Journal of Clinical Psychology, 52,* 449–454.

1091. Hanley, J. R., & Kay, J. (1996). Reading speed in pure alexia. *Neuropsychologia, 34,* 1165–1174.

1092. Heinze, M. C., & Grisso, T. (1996). Review of instruments assessing parenting competencies used in child custody evaluations. *Behavior Sciences and the Law, 14,* 293–313.

1093. Helmstaedter, C., Kemper, B., & Elger, C. E. (1996). Neuropsychological aspects of frontal lobe epilepsy. *Neuropsychologia, 34,* 399–406.

1094. Hermann, B. P., Seidenberg, M., Wyler, A., Davies, K., Christeson, J., Moran, M., & Stroup, E. (1996). The effects of human hippocampal resection on the serial position curve. *Cortex, 32,* 323–334.

1095. Hess, T. M., Pullen, S. M., & McGee, K. A. (1996). Acquisition of prototype-based information about social groups in adulthood. *Psychology and Aging, 11,* 179–190.

1096. Horner, M. D., Flashman, L. A., Freides, D., Epstein, C. M., & Bakay, R. A. E. (1996). Temporal lobe epilepsy and performance on the Wisconsin Card Sorting Test. *Journal of Clinical and Experimental Neuropsychology, 18,* 310–313.

1097. Hutner, N., & Oscar-Berman, M. (1996). Visual laterality patterns for the perception of emotional words in alcoholic and aging individuals. *Journal of Studies on Alcohol, 57,* 144–154.

1098. Ingles, J. L., Mate-Kole, C. C., & Connolly, J. F. (1996). Evidence for multiple routes of speech production in a case of fluent aphasia. *Cortex, 32,* 199–219.

1099. Isaacs, E., Christie, D., Vargha-Khadem, F., & Mishkin, M. (1996). Effects of hemispheric side of injury, age at injury, and presence of seizure disorder on functional ear and hand asymmetries in hemiplegic children. *Neuropsychologia, 34,* 127–137.

1100. Iverson, G. L., & Franzen, M. D. (1996). Using multiple objective memory procedures to detect simulated malingering. *Journal of Clinical and Experimental Neuropsychology, 18,* 38–51.

1101. Iverson, G. L., Myers, B., Bengtson, M. L., & Adams, R. L. (1996). Concurrent validity of a WAIS-R seven-subtest short form in patients with brain impairment. *Psychological Assessment, 8,* 319–323.

1102. Janowsky, J. S., Carper, R. A., & Kaye, J. A. (1996). Asymmetrical memory decline in normal aging and dementia. *Neuropsychologia, 34,* 527–535.

1103. Jenike, M. A., Breiter, H. C., Baer, L., Kennedy, D. N., Savage, C. R., Olivares, M. J., O'Sullivan, R. L., Shera, D. M., Rauch, S. L., Keuthen, N., Rosen, B. R., Caviness, V. S., & Filipek, P. A. (1996). Cerebral structure abnormalities in obsessive-compulsive disorder: A quantitative morphometric magnetic resonance imaging study. *Archives of General Psychiatry, 53,* 625–632.

1104. Jeste, D. V., Heaton, S. C., Paulsen, J. S., Ercoli, L., Harris, M. J., & Heaton, R. K. (1996). Clinical and neuropsychological comparison of psychotic depression with nonpsychotic depression and schizophrenia. *American Journal of Psychiatry, 153,* 490–496.

1105. Johannes, S., Kussmaul, C. L., Münte, T. F., & Mangun, G. R. (1996). Developmental dyslexia: Passive visual stimulation provides no evidence for a magnocellular processing defect. *Neuropsychologia, 34,* 1123–1127.

1106. John, S., & Ovsiew, F. (1996). Erotomania in a brain-damaged male. *Journal of Disability Research, 40,* 279–283.

1107. Johnson, S. K., DeLuca, J., Diamond, B. J., & Natelson, B. H. (1996). Selective impairment of auditory processing in chronic fatigue syndrome: A comparison with multiple sclerosis and healthy controls. *Perceptual and Motor Skills, 83,* 51–62.

1108. Kaplan, K. J., & Harrow, M. (1996). Positive and negative symptoms as risk factors for later suicidal activity in schizophrenics versus depressives. *Suicide and Life-Threatening Behavior, 26,* 105–121.

1109. Kapur, N., Thompson, S., Cook, P., Lang, D., & Brice, J. (1996). Anterograde but not retrograde memory loss following combined mammillary body and medical thalamic lesions. *Neuropsychologia, 34,* 1–8.

1110. Kartsounis, L. D., & Shallice, T. (1996). Modality specific semantic knowledge loss for unique items. *Cortex, 32,* 109–119.

1111. Keenan, P. A., Jacobson, M. W., Soleyami, R. M., Mayes, M. D., Stress, M. E., & Yaldoo, D. T. (1996). The effect on memory of chronic prednisone treatment in patients with systemic disease. *Nursing Research, 47,* 1396–1402.

1112. Keilp, J. G., Alexander, G. E., Stern, Y., & Prohovnik, I. (1996). Inferior parietal perfusion, lateralization, and neuropsychological dysfunction in Alzheimer's disease. *Brain and Cognition, 32,* 365–383.

1113. Koivisto, M., Portin, R., & Rinne, J. O. (1996). Perceptual priming in Alzheimer's and Parkinson's diseases. *Neuropsychologia, 34,* 449–457.

1114. Kosson, D. S. (1996). Psychopathy and dual-task performance under focusing conditions. *Journal of Abnormal Psychology, 105,* 391–400.

1115. Kurz, A., Egensperger, R., Haupt, M., Lautenschlager, N., Romero, B., Graeber, M. B., & Müller, V. (1996). Apolipoprotein E E4 allele, cognitive decline, and deterioration of everyday performance in Alzheimer's disease. *Neurology, 47,* 440–448.

1116. Lee, R. E. (1996). FIRO-B scores and success in a positive peer-culture residential treatment program. *Psychological Reports, 78,* 215–220.

1117. Lesser, I. M., Boone, K. B., Mehringer, C. M., Wohl, M. A., Miller, B. L., & Berman, N. G. (1996). Cognition and white matter hyperintensities in older depressed patients. *American Journal of Psychiatry, 153,* 1280–1287.

1118. Lewine, R. R. J., Walker, E. F., Shurett, R., Caudle, J., & Haden, C. (1996). Sex differences in neuropsychological functioning among schizophrenic patients. *American Journal of Psychiatry, 153,* 1178–1184.

1119. Liebson, E., White, R. F., & Albert, M. L. (1996). Cognitive inconsistencies in abnormal illness behavior and neurological disease. *Journal of Nervous and Mental Disease, 184,* 122–125.

1120. Lindsay, W. R., & Morrison, F. M. (1996). The effects of behavioural relaxation on cognitive performance in adults with severe intellectual disabilities. *Journal of Disability Research, 40,* 285–290.

1121. Little, A. J., Templer, D. I., Persel, C. S., & Ashley, M. J. (1996). Feasibility of the neuropsychological spectrum in prediction of outcome following head injury. *Journal of Clinical Psychology, 52,* 455–460.

1122. Lojek-Osiejuk, E. (1996). Knowledge of scripts reflected in discourse of aphasics and right-brain-damaged patients. *Brain and Language, 53,* 58–80.

1123. MacKenzie, I. R. A., McLachlan, R. S., Kubu, C. S., & Miller, L. A. (1996). Prospective neuropsychological assessment of nondemented patients with biopsy-proven senile plaques. *Neurology, 46,* 475–479.

1124. Maguire, E. A., Burke, T., Phillips, J., & Staunton, H. (1996). Topographical disorientation following unilateral temporal lobe lesions in humans. *Neuropsychologia, 34,* 993–1001.

1125. Manning, L., & Warrington, E. K. (1996). Two routes to naming: A case study. *Neuropsychologia, 34,* 809–817.

1126. Marson, D. C., Chatterjee, A., Ingram, K. K., & Harrell, L. E. (1996). Toward a neurologic model of competency: Cognitive predictors of capacity to consent in Alzheimer's disease using three different legal standards. *Neurology, 46,* 666–672.

1127. Martin, R. C., Hayes, J. S., & Gouvier, W. D. (1996). Differential vulnerability between postconcussion self-report and objective malingering tests in identifying simulated mild head injury. *Journal of Clinical and Experimental Neuropsychology, 18,* 265–275.

1128. Massman, P. J., & Doody, R. S. (1996). Hemispheric asymmetry in Alzheimer's Disease is apparent in motor functioning. *Journal of Clinical and Experimental Neuropsychology, 18,* 110–121.

1129. Massman, P. J., Kneiter, K. T., Jankovic, J., & Doody, R. S. (1996). Neuropsychological functioning in cortical-basal ganglionic degeneration: Differences from Alzheimer's disease. *Neurology, 46,* 720–726.

1130. Mattioli, F., Grassi, F., Perani, D., Cappo, S. F., Miozzo, A., & Fazio, F. (1996). Persistent post-traumatic retrograde amnesia: A neuropsychological and (18F) FDG PET study. *Cortex, 32,* 121–129.

1131. Maylor, E. A., & Wing, A. M. (1996). Age differences in postural stability are increased by additional cognitive demands. *Journal of Gerontology, 51,* 143–154.

1132. McGeorge, P., Crawford, J. R., & Kelly, S. W. (1996). The relationship between WAIS-R abilities and speed of processing in a word identification task. *Intelligence, 23,* 175–190.

1133. Mehta, Z., & Newcombe, F. (1996). Selective loss of verbal imagery. *Neuropsychologia, 34,* 441–447.

1134. Michiels, V., Cluydts, R., Fischler, B., Hoffmann, G., Le Bon, O., & De Meirleir, K. (1996). Cognitive functioning in patients with chronic fatigue syndrome. *Journal of Clinical and Experimental Neuropsychology, 18,* 666–677.

1135. Mockler, D., Riordan, J., & Sharma, T. (1996). A comparison of the NART (restandardized) and the NART-R (revised). *British Journal of Clinical Psychology, 35,* 567–572.

1136. Moen, I., & Sundet, K. (1996). Production and perception of word tones (pitch accents) in patients with left and right hemisphere damage. *Brain and Language, 53,* 267–281.

1137. Mohr, B., Müller, V., Mattes, R., Rosin, R., Federmann, B., Strehl, V., Pulvermüller, F., Müller, F., Lutzenberger, W., & Birbaumer, N. (1996). Behavioral treatment of Parkinson's disease leads to improvement of motor skills and to tremor reduction. *Behavior Therapy, 27,* 235–255.

1138. Moore, L. H., Brown, W. S., Markee, T. E., Theberge, D. C., & Zui, J. C. (1996). Callosal transfer of finger localization information in phonologically dyslexic adults. *Cortex, 32,* 311–322.

1139. Morice, R., & Delahunty, A. (1996). Frontal/executive impairments in schizophrenia. *Schizophrenia Bulletin, 22,* 125–137.

1140. Morton, N., Polkey, C. E., Cox, T., & Morris, R. G. (1996). Episodic memory dysfunction during sodium amytal testing of epileptic patients in relation to posterior cerebral artery perfusion. *Journal of Clinical and Experimental Neuropsychology, 18,* 24–37.

1141. Murphy, D. G. M., DeCarli, C., McIntosh, A. R., Daly, E., Mentis, M. J., Pietrini, P., Szczepanik, J., Schapiro, M. B., Grady, C. L., Horwitz, B., & Rapoport, S. I. (1996). Sex differences in human brain morphometry and metabolism: An in vivo quantitative magnetic resonance imaging and positron emission tomography study on the effect of aging. *Archives of General Psychiatry, 53,* 585–594.

1142. Murphy, K. R., & Barkley, R. A. (1996). Parents of children with attention-deficit/hyperactivity disorder: Psychological and attentional impairment. *American Journal of Orthopsychiatry, 66,* 93–102.

1143. Neelon, V. J., Champagne, M. T., Carlson, J. R., & Funk, S. G. (1996). The NEECHUM Confusion Scale: Construction, validation, and clinical testing. *Nursing Research, 45,* 324–330.

1144. Nettelbeck, T., Rabbitt, P. M. A., Wilson, C., & Batt, R. (1996). Uncoupling learning from initial recall: The relationship between speed and memory in old age. *British Journal of Psychology, 87,* 593–607.

1145. Niznikiewicz, M., & Squires, N. K. (1996). Phonological processing and the role of strategy in silent reading: Behavioral and electrophysiological evidence. *Brain and Language, 52,* 342–364.

1146. O'Donnell, B. F., Swearer, J. M., Smith, L. T., Nestor, P. G., Shenton, M. E., & McCarley, R. W. (1996). Selective deficits in visual perception and recognition in schizophrenia. *American Journal of Psychiatry, 153,* 687–692.

1147. O'Mahony, J. F., & Doherty, B. (1996). Intellectual impairment among recently abstinent alcohol abusers. *British Journal of Clinical Psychology, 35,* 77–83.

1148. Ogden, J. A. (1996). Phonological dyslexia and phonological dysgraphia following left and right hemispherectomy. *Neuropsychologia, 34,* 905–918.

1149. Ozonoff, S., & Miller, J. N. (1996). An exploration of right-hemisphere contributions to the pragmatic impairments of autism. *Brain and Language, 52,* 411–434.

1150. Palmer, B. W., Boone, K. B., Lesser, I. M., Wohl, M. A., Berman, N., & Miller, B. L. (1996). Neuropsychological deficits among older depressed patients with predominently psychological or vegatative symptoms. *Journal of Affective Disorders, 41,* 17–24.

1151. Paolo, A. M., Ryan, J. J., Tröster, A. I., & Hilmer, C. D. (1996). Utility of the Barona demographic equations to estimate premorbid intelligence: Information from the WAIS-R standardization sample. *Journal of Clinical Psychology, 52,* 335–343.

1152. Parker, R. S., & Rosenblum, A. (1996). IQ loss and emotional dysfunction after mild head injury incurred in a motor vehicle accident. *Journal of Clinical Psychology, 52,* 32–43.

1153. Partiot, A., Vérin, M., Pillion, B., Teixeira-Ferreira, C., Agid, Y., & Dubois, B. (1996). Delayed response tasks in basal ganglia lesions in man: Further evidence for a striatofrontal cooperation in behavioural adaptation. *Neuropsychologia, 34,* 709–721.

1154. Paul, S. T. (1996). Search for semantic inhibition failure during sentence comprehension by younger and older adults. *Psychology and Aging, 11,* 10–20.

1155. Pietrini, P., Furey, M. L., Graff-Radford, N., Freo, U., Alexander, G. E., Grady, C. L., Dani, A., Mentis, M. J., & Schapiro, M. B. (1996). Preferential metabolic involvement of visual cortial areas in a subtype of Alzheimer's Disease: Clinical implications. *American Journal of Psychiatry, 153,* 1261–1268.

1156. Powell, D. H., & Hiatt, M. D. (1996). Auditory and visual recall of forward and backward digit spans. *Perceptual and Motor Skills, 82,* 1099–1103.

1157. Raquet, M. L., Campbell, D. A., Berry, D. T., Schmitt, F. A., & Smith, G. T. (1996). Stability of intelligence and intellectual predictors in older persons. *Psychological Assessment, 8,* 154–160.

1158. Rasmusson, D. X., Carson, K. A., Brookmeyer, R., Kawas, C., & Brandt, J. (1996). Predicting rate of cognitive decline in probable Alzheimer's disease. *Brain and Cognition, 31,* 133–147.

1159. Report of the Therapeutics and Technology Assessment Subcommittee of the American Academy of Neurology. (1996). Assessment: Neuropsychological testing of adults: Considerations for neurologists. *Neurology, 47,* 592.

1160. Rich, J. B., Bylsma, F. W., & Brandt, J. (1996). Item priming and skill learning in amnesia. *Journal of Clinical and Experimental Neuropsychology, 18,* 148–158.

1161. Richer, F., & Lepage, M. (1996). Frontal lesions increase post-target interference in rapid stimulus streams. *Neuropsychologia, 34,* 509–514.

1162. Rosselli, M., & Ardila, A. (1996). Cognitive effects of cocaine and polydrug abuse. *Journal of Clinical and Experimental Neuropsychology, 18,* 122–135.

1163. Rossini, E. D., Schwartz, D. R., & Braun, B. G. (1996). Intellectual functioning of inpatients with dissociative identity disorder and dissociative disorder not otherwise specified: Cognitive and neuropsychological aspects. *Journal of Nervous and Mental Disease, 184,* 289–294.

1164. Rovert, J., & Alvarez, M. (1996). Thyroid hormone and attention in school-age children with congenital hypothyroidism. *Journal of Child Psychology and Psychiatry, 37,* 579–585.

1165. Ryan, J. J., Lopez, S. J., & Paolo, A. M. (1996). Digit span performance of persons 75–96 years of age: Base rates and associations with selected demographic variables. *Psychological Assessment, 8,* 324–327.

1166. Schacter, D. L., Curran, T., Galluccio, L., Milberg, W. P., & Bates, J. F. (1996). False recognition and the right frontal lobe: A case study. *Neuropsychologia, 34,* 793–808.

1167. Schuerholz, L. J., Baumgardner, T. L., Singer, H. S., Reiss, A. L., & Denckla, M. B. (1996). Neuropsychological status of children with Tourette's syndrome with and without attention deficit hyperactivity disorder. *Neurology, 46,* 958–964.

1168. Seddoh, S. A. K., Robin, D. A., Sim, H-S., Hageman, C., Moon, J. B., & Folkins, J. W. (1996). Speech thinking in apraxia of speech versus conduction aphasia. *Journal of Speech and Hearing Research, 39,* 590–603.

1169. Seki, K., Ishiai, S., Y., & Fujimoto, Y. (1996). Appearance and disappearance of unilateral spatial neglect for an object: influence of attention-attracting peripheral stimuli. *Neuropsychologia, 34,* 819–826.

1170. Shuren, J. E., Brott, T. G., Schefft, B. K., & Houston, W. (1996). Preserved color imagery in an achromatopsic. *Neuropsychologia, 34,* 485–489.

1171. Siegert, R. J., & Warrington, E. K. (1996). Spared retrograde memory with anterograde amnesia and widespread cognitive deficits. *Cortex, 32,* 177–185.

1172. Simon, E. W., Rosen, M., & Ponpipom, A. (1996). Age and IQ as predictors of emotion identification in adults with mental retardation. *Research in Developmental Disabilities, 17,* 383–389.

1173. Simpson, D. M., Dorfman, D., Olney, R. K., Mckinley, G., Dobkin, J., So, Y., Berger, J., Ferdon, M. B., Fiedman, B., & The Peptide Neuropathy Study Group. (1996). Peptide T in the treatment of painful distal neuropathy associated with AIDS: Results of a placebo-controlled trial. *Nursing Research, 47,* 1254–1259.

1174. Sirigu, A., & Grafman, J. (1996). Selective impairments within episodic memories. *Cortex, 32,* 83–95.

1175. Smith, M. L. (1996). Recall of frequency of occurrence of self-generated and examiner-provided words after frontal or temporal lobectomy. *Neuropsychologia, 34,* 553–563.

1176. Snyder, P. J., & Harris, L. J. (1996). Where in the world am I? Sex and handedness differences in knowledge of geography. *Perceptual and Motor Skills, 82,* 1379–1385.

1177. Spruill, J. (1996). Composite SAS of the Stanford-Binet Intelligence Scale, Fourth Edition: Is it determined by only one area of SAS? *Psychological Assessment, 8,* 328–330.

1178. Stablum, F., Mogentale, C., & Umilta, C. (1996). Executive functioning following mild closed head injury. *Cortex, 32,* 261–278.

1179 Staudinger, V. M., & Baltes, P. B. (1996). Interactive minds: A facilitative setting for wisdom-related performance. *Journal of Personality and Social Psychology, 71,* 746–762.

1180. Stern, Y., Liu, X., Albert, M., Brandt, J., Jacobs, D. M., Del Castillo-Castaneda, C., Marder, K., Bell, K., Sano, M., Bylsma, F., Lafleche, G., & Tsai, W-Y. (1996). Application of the growth curve approach to modeling the progression of Alzheimer's disease. *Journal of Gerontology, 51,* 179–184.

1181. Strong, M. J., Grace, G. M., Orange, J. B., & Leeper, H. A. (1996). Cognition, language, and speech in amyotrophic lateral sclerosis: A review. *Journal of Clinical and Experimental Neuropsychology, 18,* 291–303.

1182. Strough, C., Brebner, J., Nettelbeck, T., Cooper, C. J., Bates, T., & Mangan, G. L. (1996). The relationship between intelligence, personality and inspection time. *British Journal of Psychology, 87,* 255–268.

1183. Sulway, M. R., Broe, G. A., Creasey, H., Dent, O. F., Jorm, A. F., Kos, S. C., & Tennant, C. C. (1996). Are malnutrition and stress risk factors for accelerated cognitive decline? A prisoner of war study. *Neurology, 46,* 650–655.

1184. Tang, C. S-K., Lau, B. H-B., & Chang, S. S-Y. (1996). Factor structure of the Chinese version of the WAIS-R for Chinese adults in the lowest percentiles of IQ. *Journal of Clinical Psychology, 52,* 345–355.

1185. Taylor, E. A. (1996). Age-related impairment in an event-based prospective-memory task. *Psychology and Aging, 11,* 74–78.

1186. Thompson, L. L., Riggs, P. D., Mikulich, S. K., & Crowley, T. J. (1996). Contribution of ADHD symptoms to substance problems and delinquency in conduct-disordered adolescents. *Journal of Abnormal Child Psychology, 24,* 325–347.

1187. Tierney, M. C., Szalai, J. P., Snow, W. G., Fisher, R. H., Nores, A., Nadon, G., Dunn, E., & St. George-Hyslop, P. H. (1996). Prediction of probable Alzheimer's disease in mentally-impaired patients: A prospective longitudinal. *Neurology, 46,* 661–665.

1188. Tierney, M. C., Szalai, J. P., Snow, W. G., Fisher, R. H., Tsuda, T., Chi, H., McLachlan, D. R., & St. George-Hyslop, P. H. (1996). A prospective study of the clinical utility of Apo E genotype in the prediction of outcome in patients with memory impairment. *Neurology, 46,* 149–154.

1189. Troyer, A. K., Fisk, J. D., Archibald, C. J., Ritvo, P. G., & Murray, T. J. (1996). Conceptual reasoning as a mediator of verbal recall in patients with multiple sclerosis. *Journal of Clinical and Experimental Neuropsychology, 18,* 211–219.

1190. Tuokko, H., & Woodward, T. S. (1996). Development and validation of a demographic correction system for neuropsychological measures used in the Canadian study of health and aging. *Journal of Clinical and Experimental Neuropsychology, 18,* 479–616.

1191. Valencia-Flores, M., Bliwise, D. L., Guilleminault, C., Cilveti, R., & Clark, A. (1996). Cognitive function in patients with sleep apnea after acute nocturnal nasal continuous positive airway pressure (CPAP) treatment. *Journal of Clinical and Experimental Neuropsychology, 18,* 197–210.

1192. Van Horn, G., Arnett, F. C., & Dimachkie, M. M. (1996). Reversible dementia and chorea in a young woman with the lupus anticoagulant. *Neurology, 46,* 1599–1603.

1193. Van Spaendonck, K. P. M., Berger, H. J. C., Horstink, M. W. I. M., Borm, G. F., & Cools, A. R. (1996). Memory performance under varying cueing conditions in patients with Parkinson's disease. *Neuropsychologia, 34,* 1159–1164.

1194. Van Spaendonek, K. P. M., Berger, H. J. C., Horstink, M. W. I. M., Buytenhuijs, E. L., & Cools, A. R. (1996). Executive functions and disease characteristics in Parkinson's Disease. *Neuropsychologia, 34,* 617–626.

1195. Vanderrloeg, R. D., Schinka, J. A., & Axelrod, B. N. (1996). Estimation of WAIS-R premorbid intelligence: Current ability and demographic data used in a best-performance fashion. *Psychological Assessment, 8,* 404–411.

1196. Verhaeghen, P., & Marcoen, A. (1996). On the mechanisms of plasticity in young and older adults after instruction in the method of loci: Evidence for an amplification model. *Psychology and Aging, 11,* 165–178.

1197. Wachs, T. D., McCabe, G., Moussa, W., Yunis, F., Kirksey, A., Galal, O., Harrison, G., & Jerome, G. (1996). Cognitive performance of Egyptian adults as a function of nutritional intake and sociodemographic factors. *Intelligence, 22,* 129154.

1198. Wagner, E. E. (1996). Measured intelligence of problematic patients with chronic pain. *Perceptual and Motor Skills, 82,* 939–943.

1199. Waldstein, S. R., Malloy, P. F., Stout, R., & Longabaugh, R. (1996). Predictors of neuropsychological impairment in alcoholics: Antisocial versus nonantisocial subtypes. *Addictive Behaviors, 21,* 21–27.

1200. Waldstein, S. R., Polefrone, J. M., Fazzari, T. V., Manuck, S. B., Jennings, J. R., Ryan, C. M., Muldoon, M. F., & Shapiro, A. P. (1996). Hypertension and neuropsychological performance in men: Interactive effects of age. *Health Psychology, 15,* 102–109.

1201. Ween, J. E., Verfaellie, M., & Alexander, M. P. (1996). Verbal memory function in mild aphasia. *Neurology, 47,* 795–801.

1202. Weglage, J., Schmidt, E., Funders, B., Pietsch, M., & Ullrich, K. (1996). Sustained attention in untreated non-PKU-hyperphenyla laninemia. *Journal of Clinical and Experimental Neuropsychology, 18,* 343–348.

1203. Wilens, T. E., Biederman, J., Prince, J., Spencer, T. J., Faraone, S. V., Warburton, R., Schleifer, D., Harding, M., Linehan, C., & Geller, D. (1996). Six-week, double-blind, placebo-controlled study of desipramine for adult attention deficit hyperactivity disorder. *American Journal of Psychiatry, 153,* 1147–1153.

1204. Winocur, G., Moscovitch, M., & Bruni, J. (1996). Heightened interference on implicit, but not explicit, tests of negative transfer: Evidence from patients with unilteral temporal lobe lesions and normal old people. *Brain and Cognition, 30,* 44–58.

1205. Wolkin, A., Sanfilipo, M., Duncan, E., Ångrist, ı., Wolf, A. P., Cooper, T. B., Brodie, J. D., Laska, E., & Rotrosen, J. P. (1996). Blunted change in cerebral glucose utilization after haloperidol treatment in schizophrenic patients with prominent negative symptoms. *American Journal of Psychiatry, 153,* 346–354.

1206. Woodard, J. L., Benedict, R. H. B., Roberts, V. J., Goldstein, F. C., Kinner, K. M., Capruso, D. X., & Clark, A. N. (1996). Short-form alternatives to the judgment of line orientation test. *Journal of Clinical and Experimental Neuropsychology, 18,* 898–904.

1207. Yirmiya, N., Solomonica-Levi, D., & Shulman, C. (1996). The ability to manipulate behavior and to understand manipulation of beliefs: A comparison of individuals with autism, mental retardation, and normal development. *Developmental Psychology, 32,* 62–69.

1208. Yirmiya, N., Solomonica-Levi, D., Shulman, C., & Pilowsky, T. (1996). Theory of mind abilities in individuals with autism, Down syndrome, and mental retardation of unknown etiology: The role of age and intelligence. *Journal of Child Psychology and Psychiatry, 37,* 1003–1014.

1209. Young, A. W., Hellowell, D. J., Van De Wal, C., & Johnson, M. (1996). Facial expression processing after amygdalotomy. *Neuropsychologia, 34,* 31–39.

1210. Yurgelun-Todd, D. A., Waternaux, C. M., Cohen, B. M., Gruber, S. A., English, C. D., & Renshaw, P. F. (1996). Functional magnetic resonance imaging of schizophrenic patients and comparison subjects during word production. *American Journal of Psychiatry, 153,* 200–205.

1211. Zarb, J. (1996). Correlates of depression in cognitively impaired hospitalized elderly referred for neuropsychological assessment. *Journal of Clinical and Experimental Neuropsychology, 18,* 713–723.

1212. Zillmer, E. A., & Perry, W. (1996). Cognitive neuropsychological abilities and related psychological disturbance: A factor model of neuropsychological, Rorschach, and MMPI indices. *Assessment, 3,* 209–224.

1213. Abrahams, S., Pickering, A., Polkey, C. E., & Morris, R. G. (1997). Spatial memory deficits in patients with unilateral damage to the right hippocampal formation. *Neuropsychologia, 35,* 11–24.

1214. Åkefeldt, A. Åkefeldt, B., & Gillberg, C. (1997). Voice, speech and language characteristics of children with Prader-Willi syndrome. *Journal of Disability Research, 41,* 302–311.

1215. Alarcón, M., DeFries, J. C., Light, J. G., & Pennington, B. F. (1997). A twin study of mathematics disability. *Journal of Learning Disabilities, 30,* 617–623.

1216. Alexander, G. E., Furey, M. L., Grady, C. L., Pietrini, P., Brady, D. R., Mentis, M. J., & Schapiro, M. B. (1997). Association of premorbid intellectual function with cerebral metabolism in Alzheimer's Disease: Implications for the cognitive reserve hypothesis. *American Journal of Psychiatry, 154,* 165–172.

1217. Alexander, M. P. (1997). Specific semantic memory loss after hypoxic-ischemic injury. *Neurology, 48,* 165–172.

1218. Allen, P. A., Smith, A. F., Jerge, K. A., & Vires-Collins, H. (1997). Age differences in mental multiplication: Evidence for peripheral but not central decrements. *Journal of Gerontology, 52,* 81–90.

1219. Alster, E. H. (1997). The effects of extended time on algebra test scores for college students with and without learning disabilities. *Journal of Learning Disabilities, 30,* 222–227.

1220. Avants, S. K., Margolin, A., McMahon, T. J., & Kosten, T. R. (1997). Association between self-report of cognitive impairment, HIV status, and cocaine use in a sample of cocaine-dependent methadone-maintained patients. *Addictive Behaviors, 22,* 599–611.

1221. Bates, M. E. (1997). Stability of neuropsychological assessments early in alcoholism treatment. *Journal of Studies on Alcohol, 58,* 617–621.

1222. Baynes, K., Tramo, M. J., Reeves, A. G., & Gazzaniga, M. S. (1997). Isolation of a right hemisphere cognitive system in a patient with anarchic (alien) hand sign. *Neuropsychologia, 35,* 1159–1173.

1223. Berardi, A., Haxby, J. V., DeCarli, C., & Schapiro, M. B. (1997). Face and word memory differences are related to patterns of right and left lateral ventricle size in healthy aging. *Journal of Gerontology, 52,* 54–61.

1224. Berger, S. G., Chibnall, J. T., & Gfeller, J. D. (1997). Construct validity of the computerized version of the category test. *Journal of Clinical Psychology, 53,* 723–726.

1225. Bleecker, M. L., Lindgren, K. N., & Ford, D. P. (1997). Differential contribution of current and cumulative indices of lead dose to neuropsychological performance by age. *Neurology, 48,* 639–645.

1226. Boatman, D., Hall, C., Goldstein, M. H., Lesser, R., & Gordon, B. (1997). Neuroperceptual differences in consonant and vowel discrimination: As revealed by direct cortical electrical interference. *Cortex, 33,* 83–98.

1227. Bornstein, R. F., & O'Neill, R. M. (1997). Construct validity of the Rorschach oral dependency (ROD) scale: Relationship of ROD scores to WAIS-R scores in a psychiatric inpatient sample. *Journal of Clinical Psychology, 53,* 99–105.

1228. Bowden, S. C., Dodds, B., Whelan, G., Long, C., Dudgeon, P., Ritter, A., & Clifford, C. (1997). Confirmatory factor analysis of the Wechsler Memory Scale—Revised in a sample of clients with alcohol dependency. *Journal of Clinical and Experimental Neuropsychology, 19,* 755–762.

1229. Bowler, D. M., Matthews, N. J., & Gardner, J. M. (1997). Asperzer's syndrome and memory: Similarity to autism but not amnesia. *Neuropsychologia, 35,* 65–70.

1230. Breier, J. I., Brookshire, B. L., Fletcher, J. M., Thomas, A. B., Plenger, P. M., Wheless, J. W., Willmore, L. J., & Papanicolaou, A. (1997). Identification of side of seizure onset in temporal lobe epilepsy using memory tests in the context of reading deficits. *Journal of Clinical and Experimental Neuropsychology, 19,* 161–171.

1231. Breier, J. I., Mullani, N. A., thomas, A. B., Wheless, J. W., Plenger, P. M., Gould, K. L., Papanicolaou, A., & Willmore, L. J. (1997). Effects of duration of epilepsy on the uncoupling of metabolism and blood flow in complex partial seizures. *Neurology, 48,* 1047–1053.

1232. Brennan, M., Welsh, m. C., & Fisher, C. B. (1997). Aging and executive function skills: An examination of a community-dwelling older adult population. *Perceptual and Motor Skills, 84,* 1187–1197.

1233. Brooker, A. E. (1997). Performance on the Wechsler Memory Scale—Revised for patients with mild traumatic brain injury and mild dementia. *Perceptual and Motor Skills, 84,* 131–138.

1234. Bruggemans, E. F. Van de Vijver, F. J. R., & Huysmans, H. A. (1997). Assessment of cognitive deterioration in individual patients following cardiac surgery: Correcting for measurement error and practice effects. *Journal of Clinical and Experimental Neuropsychology, 19,* 543–559.

1235. Buschke, H., Sliwinski, M. J., Kuslansky, G., & Lipton, R. B. (1997). Diagnosis of early dementia by the Double Memory Test: Encoding specificity improves diagnostic sensitivity and specificity. *Nursing Research, 48,* 989–997.

1236. Carbonnel, S., Charnallet, A., David, D., & Pellat, J. (1997). One or several semantic systems (s)? Maybe none: Evidence from a case study of modality and category-specific "semantic" impairment. *Cortex, 33,* 391–417.

1237. Carlesimo, G. A., Marotta, L., & Vicari, S. (1997). Long-term memory in mental retardation: Evidence for a specific impairment in subjects with Down's syndrome. *Neuropsychologia, 35,* 71–79.

1238. Carswell, L. M., Graves, R. E., Snow, W. G., & Tierney, M. C. (1997). Postdicting verbal IQ of elderly individuals. *Journal of Clinical and Experimental Neuropsychology, 19,* 914–921.

1239. Cermak, L. S., Mather, M., & Hill, R. (1997). Unconscious influences on amnesics' word-stem completion. *Neuropsychologia, 35,* 605–610.

1240. Chapman, S. B., Rosenberg, R. N., Weiner, M. F., & Shore, A. (1997). Autosomal dominant progressive syndrome of motor-speech loss without dementia. *Neurology, 49,* 1298–1306.

1241. Ciesielski, K. T., Harris, R. J., Hart, B. L., & Pabst, H. F. (1997). Cerebellar hypoplasia and frontal lobe cognitive deficits in disorders of early childhood. *Neuropsychologia, 35,* 643–655.

1242. Clark, C. M., Jecova, C., Klonoff, H., Bremer, B., Hayden, M., & Paty, D. (1997). Pathological association and dissociation of functional systems in multiple sclerosis and Huntington's disease. *Journal of Clinical and Experimental Neuropsychology, 19,* 63–76.

1243. Codori, A-M., Slavney, P. R., Young, C., Miglioretti, D. L., & Brandt, J. (1997). Predictors of psychological adjustment to genetic testing for Huntington's Disease. *Health Psychology, 16,* 36–50.

1244. Corey-Bloom, J., Sabbagh, M. N., Bondi, M. W., Hansen, L., Alford, M. F., Masliah, E., & Thal, L. J. (1997) Hyziocampal sclerosis contributes to dementia in the elderly. *Neurology, 48,* 154–160.

1245. Craissati, J., & McClurg, G. (1997). The Challenge Project: a treatment program evaluation for perpetrators of child sexual abuse. *Child Abuse & Neglect, 21,* 637–648.

1246. Crawford, J. R., Allan, K. M., McGeorge, P., & Kelly, S. M. (1997). Base rate data on the abnormality of subtest scatter for WAIS-R short-forms. *British Journal of Clinical Psychology, 36,* 433–444.

1247. Crowe, S. F., Dingjan, P., & Helme, R. D. (1997). The neurocognitive basis of word-finding difficulty in Alzheimer's disease. *Australian Psychologist, 32,* 114–119.

1248. Dalla Barba, G., Mantovan, M. C., Ferruzza, E., & Denes, G. (1997). Remembering and knowing the past: A case study of isolated retrograde amnesia. *Cortex, 33,* 143–154.

1249. Dalla Barbara, G., Roisse, M-F., Bartolomeo, P., & Bachoud-Lévi, A-C. (1997). Confabulation following rupture of posterior communicating artery. *Cortex, 33,* 563–570.

1250. Day, R. H., Sparrow, W. A., Shinkfield, A., & Zerman, L. (1997). Impairment in the perception of 2D shape by adults with mild intellectual disability: An exploratory investigation. *Australian Journal of Psychology, 49,* 139–143.

1251. De Renzi, E., & Saetti, M. C. (1997). Associative agnosia and optic aphasia: Qualitative or quantitative difference? *Cortex, 33,* 115–130.

1252. Del Ser, T., González-Montalvo, J. I., Martínez-Espinosa, S., Delgado-Villapalos, C., & Bermejo, F. (1997). Estimation of premorbid intelligence in Spanish people with the Word Accentuation Test and its application to the dianosis of dementia. *Brain and Cognition, 33,* 343–356.

1253. Demeurisse, G., Hublet, C., Paternot, J., Colson, C., & Serniclaes, W. (1997). Pathogenesis of subcortical visuo-spatial neglect. A HMPAO SPECT study. *Neuropsychologia, 35,* 731–735.

1254. Demsky, Y. I., Gass, C. S., & Golden, C. J. (1997). Common short forms of the Spanish Wechsler Adult Intelligence Scale. *Perceptual and Motor Skills, 85,* 1121–1122.

1255. Dodrill, C. B., Arnett, J. L., Sommerville, K. W., & Shu, V. (1997). Cognitive and quality of life effects of differing dosages of tiagabine in epilepsy. *Neurology, 48,* 1025–1031.

1256. Doyon, J., Gaudreau, D., Laforce, R., Jr., Castonguay, M., Bédard, P. J., Bédard, F., & Bouchard, J-P. (1997). Role of the striatum, cerebellum, and frontal lobes in the learning of a visuomotor sequence. *Brain and Cognition, 34,* 218–245.

1257. Duckworth, M. P., Jezzi, A., Adams, H. E., & hale, D. (1997). Information processing in chronic pain disorder: A preliminary analysis. *Journal of Psychopathology and Behavioral Assessment, 19,* 239–255.

1258. Dukoff, R., & Sunderland, T. (1997). Durable power of attorney and informed consent with Alzheimer's Disease patients: A clinical study. *American Journal of Psychiatry, 154,* 1070–1075.

1259. Eisenstein, N., & Engelhart, C. I. (1997). Comparison of the K-BIT with short forms of the WAIS-R in a neuropsychological population. *Psychological Assessment, 9,* 57–62.

1260. Fabiani, M., & Friedman, D. (1997). Dissociations between memory for temporal order and recognition memory in aging. *Neuropsychologia, 35,* 129 141.

1261. Fahle, M., & Daum, I. (1997). Visual learning and memory as functions of age. *Neuropsychologia, 35,* 1583–1589.

1262. Feldman, M. A., & Walton-Allen, N. (1997). Effects of maternal mental retardation and poverty on intellectual, academic, and behavioral status of school-age children. *American Journal on Mental Retardation, 101,* 352–364.

1263. Ferri, B. A., Gregg, N., & Heggoy, S. J. (1997). Profiles of college students demonstrating learning disabilities with and without giftedness. *Journal of Learning Disabilities, 30,* 552–559.

1264. Fisher, N. J., Rourke, B. P., Bieliauskas, L. A., Giordani, B., Berent, S., & Foster, N. L. (1997). Unmasking the heterogeneity of Alzheimer's Disease: Care studies of individuals from distinct neuropsychological subgroups. *Journal of Clinical and Experimental Neuropsychology, 19,* 713–754.

1265. Flitman, S., O'Grady, J., Cooper, U., & Grafman, J. (1997). Pet imaging of maze processing. *Neuropsychologia, 35,* 409–420.

1266. Galski, T., Ehle, H. T., & Williams, J. B. (1997). Off-road driving evaluations for persons with cerebral injury: A factor analytic study of predriver and simulator testing. *American Journal of Occupational Therapy, 51,* 352–359.

1267. Gass, C. S., & Apple, C. (1997). Cognitive complaints in closed-head injury: Relationship to memory test performance and emotional disturbance. *Journal of Clinical and Experimental Neuropsychology, 19,* 290–299.

1268. Gimse, R., Björgen, I. A., Tjell, C., Tyssedal, J. S., & Bø, K. (1997). Reduced cognitive functions in a group of whiplash patients with demonstrated disturbances in the posture control system. *Journal of Clinical and Experimental Neuropsychology, 19,* 838–849.

1269. Gold, J. M., Carpenter, C., Randolph, C., Goldberg, T. E., & Weinberger, D. R. (1997). Auditory working memory and Wisconsin Card Sorting Test performance in schizophrenia. *Archives of General Psychiatry, 54,* 159–165.

1270. Gold, M., Nadeau, S. E., Jacobs, D. H., Adair, J. C., Rothi, L. J. G., & Heilman, K. M. (1997). Adynamic aphasia: A transcortical motor aphasia with defective semantic strategy formation. *Brain and Language, 57,* 374–393.

1271. Goldenberg, G., & Hagmann, S. (1997). The meaning of meaningless gestures: A study of visuo-imitative apraxia. *Neuropsychologia, 35,* 333–341.

1272. Grober, E., Merling, A., Heimlich, T., & Lipton, R. B. (1997). Free and cued selective reminding and selective reminding in the elderly. *Journal of Clinical and Experimental Neuropsychology, 19,* 643–654.

1273. Ham, H. P., & Parsons, O. A. (1997). Organization of psychological functions in alcoholics and nonalcoholics: A test of the compensatory hypothesis. *Journal of Studies on Alcohol, 58,* 67–74.

1274. Helmstaedter, C., Kurthen, M., Linke, D. B., & Elger, C. E. (1997). Patterns of language dominance in focal left and right hemisphere epilepsies: Relation to MRI findings, EEG, sex, and age at onset of epilepsy. *Brain and Cognition, 33,* 135–150.

1275. Hinton-Bayre, A. D., Geffen, G., & McFarland, K. (1997). Mild head injury and speed of information processing: A prospective study of professional rugby league players. *Journal of Clinical and Experimental Neuropsychology, 19,* 275–289.

1276. Hodgins, D. C., Leigh, G., Milne, R., & Gerrish, R. (1997). Drinking goal selection in behavioral self-management treatment of chronic alcoholics. *Addictive Behaviors, 22,* 247–255.

1277. Hopp, G. A., Dixon, R. A., Grut, M., & Bäckman, L. (1997). Longitudinal and psychometric profiles of two cognitive status tests in very old adults. *Journal of Clinical Psychology, 53,* 673–686.

1278. Horikoshi, T., Asari, Y., Watanabe, A., Nagaseki, Y., Nukui, H., Sasaki, H., & Komiya, K. (1997). Music alexia in a patient with mild pure alexia: Distrubed visual perception of nonverbal meaningful figures. *Cortex, 33,* 187–194.

1279. Hornak, J., Oxbury, S., Oxbury, J., Iversen, S. D., & Gaffan, D. (1997). Hemifeld-specific visual recognition memory impairments in patients with unilateral temporal lobe removals. *Neuropsychologia, 35,* 1311–1315.

1280. Hulette, C., Nochlin, D., McKeel, D., Morris, J. C., Mirra, S. S., Sumi, S. M., & Heyman, A. (1997). Clinical-neuropathologic findings in multi-infarct dementia: A report of autopsied cases. *Neurology, 48,* 668–672.

1281. Incalzi, R. A., Gemma, A., Landi, F., Pagano, F., Capparella, O., Snider, F., Manni, R., & Carbonin, P. V. (1997). Neuropsychologic effects of carotid endarterectomy. *Journal of Clinical and Experimental Neuropsychology, 19,* 785–794.

1282. Iverson, G. L., Myers, B., & Adams, R. L. (1997). Comparison of two computational formulas for a WAIS-R seven subtest short form. *Journal of Clinical Psychology, 53,* 465–470.

1283. Ivnik, R. J., Smith, G. E., Lucas, J. A., Tangalos, E. G., Kokmen, E., & Petersen, R. C. (1997). Free and cued selective reminding test: MOANS norms. *Journal of Clinical and Experimental Neuropsychology, 19,* 676–691.

1284. Jacobs, D. M., Sano, M., Albert, S., Schofield, P., Dooneief, G., & Stern, Y. (1997). Cross-cultural neuropsychological assessment: A comparison of randomly selected, demographically matched cohorts of English- and Spanish-speaking older adults. *Journal of Clinical and Experimental Neuropsychology, 19,* 331–339.

1285. Jäncke, L., Wunerlich, G., Schlaug, G., & Steinmetz, H. G, (1997). A case of collosal agenesis with strong anatomical and functional asymmetrics. *Neuropsychologia, 35,* 1389–1394.

1286. Jimerson, S., Carlson, E., Rotert, M., Egeland, B., & Sroufe, L. A. (1997). A prospective, longitudinal study of the correlates and consequences of early grade retention. *Journal of School Psychology, 35,* 3–25.

1287. Johnson-Greene, D., Adams, K. M., Gilman, S., Koeppe, R. A., Junck, L., Kluin, K. J., Martorello, S., & Heumann, M. (1997). Effects of abstisence and relapse upon neuropsychological function and cerebral glucose metabolism in severe chronic alcoholism. *Journal of Clinical and Experimental Neuropsychology, 19,* 378–385.

1288. Johnstone, B., Holland, D., & Hewett, J. E. (1997). The construct validity of the category test: Is it a measure of reasoning or intelligence? *Psychological Assessment, 9,* 28–33.

1289. Joseph, B., Overmier, J. B., & Thompson, T. (1997). Food- and nonfood-related differential outcomes in equivalence learning by adults with Pruder-Willi Syndrome. *American Journal on Mental Retardation, 101,* 374–386.

1290. Jurado, M. A., Junqué, C., Pujol, J., Oliver, B., & Vendrell, P. (1997). Impaired estimation of word occurrence frequency in frontal lobe patients *Neuropsychologia, 35,* 635–641.

1291. Karmiloff-Smith, A., Grant, J., Berthoud, I., Davies, M., Howlin, P., & Udivin, O. (1997). Language and Williams syndrome: How intact is "intact"? *Child Development, 68,* 246–262.

1292. Kemper, S. (1997). Metalinguistic judgments in normal aging and Alzheimer's disease. *Journal of Gerontology, 52,* 147–155.

1293. Kerns, K. A., Don, A., Mateer, C. A., & Streissguth, A. P. (1997). Cognitive deficits in nonretarded adults with Fetal Alcohol Syndrome. *Journal of Learning Disabilities, 30,* 685–693.

1294. Kessler, J., Markowitsch, H. J., Huber, M., Kalbe, E., Weber-Luxenburger, G., & Kock, P. (1997). Massive and persistent antugrade amnesia in the absence of detectable brain damage: Anterograde psychogenic amnesia or gross reduction in sustained effort? *Journal of Clinical and Experimental Neuropsychology, 19,* 604–614.

1295. Kluger, A., Gianutsos, J. G., Golomb, J., Ferris, S. H., George, A. E., Franssen, E., & Reisberg, B. (1997). Patterns of motor impairment in normal aging, mild cognitive decline, and early Alzheimer's disease. *Journal of Gerontology, 52,* 28–39.

1296. Kobari, M., Nogawa, S., Sugimoto, Y., & Fukuuchi, Y. (1997). Familial idiopathic brain calcification with autosomal dominant inheritance. *Neurology, 48,* 645–649.

1297. Kopelman, M. D., Stanhope, N., & Kingsley, D. (1997). Temporal and spatial context memory in patients with focal frontal, temporal lobe, and diencephalic lesions. *Neuropsychologia, 35,* 1533–1545.

1298. Kwon, L. M., Rourke, S. B., & Grant, I. (1997). Intermanual differences on motor and psychomotor tests in alcoholics: No evidence for selective right-hemisphere dysfunction. *Perceptual and Motor Skills, 84,* 403–414.

1299. Letore, F., Lassonde, M., Vellette, N., & Guillemot, J-P. (1997). Unilateral and bilateral temperature comparisons in acallosal and split-brain subjects. *Neuropsychologia, 35,* 1225–1231.

1300. Lieh-mak, F., & Lee, W. H. (1997). Cognitive deficit measures in schizophrenia: Factor structure and clinical correlates. *American Journal of Psychiatry, 154* (Supp), 39–46.

1301. Lovell, D. M., Williams, J. M. G., & Hill, A. B. (1997). Selective processing of shape-related words in women with eating disorders, and those who have recovered. *British Journal of Clinical Psychology, 36,* 421–432.

1302. Lovrich, D., Cheng, J. C., Velting, D. M., & Kazmerski, V. (1997). Auditory ERPs during rhyme and semantic processing: Effects of reading ability in college students. *Journal of Clinical and Experimental Neuropsychology, 19,* 313–330.

1303. Mackner, L. M., Starr, R. H., Jr., & Black, M. M. (1997). The cumulative effect of neglect and failure to thrive on cognitive functioning. *Child Abuse & Neglect, 21,* 691–700.

1304. Marcotte, T. D., van Gorp, W., Hinkin, C. H., & Osato, S. (1997). Concurrent validity of the Neurobehavioral Cognitive Status Exam subtests. *Journal of Clinical and Experimental Neuropsychology, 19,* 386–395.

1305. Mayes, A. R., Daum, I., Markowisch, H. J., & Sauter, B. (1997). The relationship between retrograde and anterograde amnesiz in patients with typical global amnesia. *Cortex, 33,* 197–217.

1306. McCormick, L., Nielsen, T., Ptito, M., Hassainta, F., Ptito, A., Villemure, J.-G., Vera, C., & Montplaisir, J. (1997). REM sleep dream mentation in right hemispherectomized patients. *Neuropsychologia, 35,* 695–701.

1307. McKinzey, R. K., & Russell, E. W. (1997). A partial cross-validation of a Halstead-Reitan Battery malingering formula. *Journal of Clinical and Experimental Neuropsychology, 19,* 484–488.

1308. Mendez, M. F., Cherrier, M. M., & Perryman, K. M. (1997). Differences between Alzheimer's disease and vascular dementia on information processing measures. *Brain and Cognition, 34,* 301–310.

1309. Mennemeier, M., Crosson, B., Williamson, D. J., Nadeau, S. E., Fennell, E., Valenstein, E., & Heilman, K. M. (1997). Tapping, talking and the thalamus: Possible influence of the intralaminar nuclei on basal ganglia function. *Neuropsychologia, 35,* 183–193.

1310. Michaels, C. A., Lazar, J. W., & Risucci, D. A. (1997). A neuropsychological approach to assessment of adults with learning disabilities in vocational rehabilitation. *Journal of Learning Disabilities, 30,* 544–551.

1311. Mizuno, M., Kato, M., Sartori, G., Okawaza, H., & Kashima, H. (1997). Performance characteristics of chronic schizophrenia on attention tests sensitive to unilateral brain damage. *Journal of Nervous and Mental Disease, 185,* 427–433.

1312. Moore, P. M., & Baker, G. A. (1997). Psychometric properties and factor structure of the Wechsler Memory Scale—Revised in a sample of persons with intractable epilepsy. *Journal of Clinical and Experimental Neuropsychology, 19,* 897–905.

1313. Morgan, A. W., Sullivan, S. A., Darden, C., & Gregg, N. (1997). Measuring the intelligence of college students with learning disabilities: A comparison of results obtained on the WAIS-R and the KAIT. *Journal of Learning Disabilities, 30,* 560–565.

1314. Mori, E., Hirono, N., Yamashita, H., Imamura, T., Ikejiri, Y., Ikeda, M., Kitagaki, H., Shimomura, T., & Yoneda, Y. (1997). Premorbid brain size as a determinant of reserve capacity against intellectual decline in Alzheimer's Disease. *American Journal of Psychiatry, 154,* 18–24.

1315. Morrow, D. G., Stine-Morrow, E. A. L., Leirer, V. O., Andrassy, J. M., & Kahn, J. (1997). The role of reader age and focus of attention in creating situation models from narratives. *Journal of Gerontology, 52,* 73–80.

1316. Moscovitch, M., & Melo, B. (1997). Strategic retrieval and the frontal lobes: Evidence from confabulation and amnesia. *Neuropsychologia, 35,* 1017–1034.

1317. Nakamura, H., Nakanishi, M., Hamanaka, T., Nakaaki, S., Furukawa, T., & Masui, T. (1997). Dissociations between reading responses and semantic priming effects in a dyslexic patient. *Cortex, 33,* 753–761.

1318. Natsopoulos, D., Katsaroo, Z., Alevriadou, A., Grouios, G., Bostantzopoulou, S., & Mentenopoulas, G. (1997). Deductive and inductive reasoning in Parkinson's disease patients and normal controls: Review and experimental evidence. *Cortex, 33,* 463–481.

1319. Nestor, P. G., Kimble, M. O., O'Donnell, B. F., Smith, L., Niznikiewicz, M., Shenton, M. E., & McCarley, R. (1997). Aberrant semantic activation in schizophrenia: A neurophysiological study. *American Journal of Psychiatry, 154,* 640–646.

1320. Nielsen-Bohlman, L., Ciranni, M., Shimamura, A. P., & Knight, R. T. (1997). Impaired word-stem priming in patients with temporal-occipital lesions. *Neuropsychologia, 35,* 1087–1092.

1321. North, K. N., Riccardi, V., Samango-Sprouse, C., Ferner, R., Moore, B., Legius, E., Ratner, N., & Denckla, m. B. (1997). Cognitive function and academic performance in neurofibromatosis 1: Concensus statement from NF1 Cognitive Disorders Task Force. *Neurology, 48,* 1121–1127.

1322. Ochipa, C., Rapcsak, S. Z., Maher, L. M., Rothi, L. J. G., Bowers, D., & Heilman, K. M. (1997). Selective deficit of praxis imagery in ideomotor apraxia. *Neurology, 49,* 474–480.

1323. Oxbury, S., Oxbury, J., Renowden, S., Squier, W., & Carpenter, K. (1997). Severe amnesia: An unusual late complication after temporal lobectomy. *Neuropsychologia, 35,* 975–988.

1324. Paolo, A. M., Ryan, J. J., & Tröster, A. I. (1997). Estimating premorbid WAIS-R intelligence in the elderly: An extension and cross validation of new regression equations. *Journal of Clinical Psychology, 53,* 647–656.

1325. Paolo, A. M., Tröster, A. I., & Ryan, J. J. (1997). California Verbal Learning Test: Normative data for the elderly. *Journal of Clinical and Experimental Neuropsychology, 19,* 220–234.

1326. Paolo, A. M., Tröster, A. I., Ryan, J. J., & Koller, W. C. (1997). Comparison of WART and Barona demographic equation premorbid IQ estimates in Alzheimer's Disease. *Journal of Clinical Psychology, 53,* 713–722.

1327. Paradiso, S., Lamberty, G. J., Garvey, M. J. & Robinson, R. G. (1997). Cognitive impairment in the euthymic phase of chronic unipolar depression. *Journal of Nervous and Mental Disease, 185,* 748–754.

1328. Pelazer, M. & Benke, T. (1997). Arithmetic facts without meaning. *Cortex, 33,* 697–710.

1329. Peper, M., & Irle, E. (1997). Categorical and dimensional decoding of emotional intonations in patients with focal brain lesions. *Brain and Language, 58,* 233–264.

1330. Peru, A., & Fabbro, F. (1997). Thalamic amnesia following venous infarction: Evidence from a single case study. *Brain and Cognition, 33,* 278–294.

1331. Petrides, M. (1997). Visuo-motor conditional associative learning after frontal and temporal lesions in the human brain. *Neuropsychologia, 35,* 989–997.

1332. Piven, J., Bailey, J., Ranson, B. J., & Arndt, S. (1997). An MRI study of the corpus callosum in autism. *American Journal of Psychiatry, 154,* 1051–1056.

1333. Piven, J., Palmer, P., Jacobi, D., Childress, D., & Arndt, S. (1997). Broader autism phenotype: Evidence from a family history study of multiple-incidence autism families. *American Journal of Psychiatry, 154,* 185–190.

1334. Pontius, A. A. (1997). No gender difference in spatial representation by school children in northwest Pakistan. *Journal of Cross-Cultural Psychology, 28,* 779–786.

1335. Porterfield, T., Cook, M., Deary, I. J., & Ebmeier, K. P. (1997). Neuropsychological function and diurnal variation in depression. *Journal of Clinical and Experimental Neuropsychology, 19,* 906–913.

1336. Rapport, L. J., Axelrod, B. N., Theisen, m. E., Brines, D. B., Kalechstein, A. D., & Ricker, J. H. (1997). Relationship of IQ to verbal learning and memory: Test and retest. *Journal of Clinical and Experimental Neuropsychology, 19,* 655–666.

1337. Rizzo, M., & Darling, W. (1997). Reading with cerebral tunnel vision. *Neuropsychologia, 35,* 53–63.

1338. Rizzo, T. A., Metzger, B. E., Dooley, S. L., & Cho, N. H. (1997). Early malnutrition and child neurobehavioral development: Insights from the study of children of diabetic mothers. *Child Development, 68,* 26–38.

1339. Roman, D. D., Kubo, S. H., Ormaza, S., Francis, G. S., Bank, A. J., & Shumway, S. J. (1997). Memory improvement following cardiac transplantation. *Journal of Clinical and Experimental Neuropsychology, 19,* 692–697.

1340. Ross, S. J. M., & Hodges, J. R. (1997). Preservation of famous person knowledge in a patient with severe post anoxic amnesia. *Cortex, 33,* 733–742.

1341. Rowe, E. W., & Shean, G. (1997). Card-sort performance and syndromes of schizophrenia. *Genetic Psychology Monographs, 123,* 197–209.

1342. Ruff, R. M., Light, R. H., Parker, S. B., & Levin, H. S. (1997). The psychological construct of word fluency. *Brain and Language, 57,* 394–405.

1343. Russell, A. J., Munro, J. C., Jones, P. B., Hemsley, D. R., & Murray, R. M. (1997). Schizophrenia and the myth of intellectual decline. *American Journal of Psychiatry, 154,* 635–639.

1344. Schafer, J., & Fals-Stewart, W. (1997). Spousal violence and cognitive functioning among men recovering from multiple substance abuse. *Addictive Behaviors, 22,* 127–130.

1345. Schagen, S., Schmand, B., de Sterke, S., & Lindeboom, J. (1997). Amsterdam Short-Term Memory Test: A new procedure for detection of feigned memory deficits. *Journal of Clinical and Experimental Neuropsychology, 19,* 43–51.

1346. Schofield, P. W., Marder, K., Dooneief, G., Jacobs, D. M., Sano, M., & Stern, Y. (1997). Association of subjective memory complaints with subsequent cognitive decline in community-dwelling elderly individuals with baseline cognitive impairment. *American Journal of Psychiatry, 154,* 609–615.

1347. Seger, C. A., Rabin, L. A., Zarella, M., & Gabrieli, J. D. E. (1997). Preserved verb generation priming in global amnesia. *Neuropsychologia, 35,* 1069–1074.

1348. Seidman, L. J., Caplan, B. B., Tolomiczenko, G. S., Turner, W. M., Penk, W. E., Schutt, R. K., & Goldfinger, S. M. (1997). Neuropsychological function in homeless mentally ill individuals. *Journal of Nervous and Mental Disease, 185,* 3–12.

1349. Sillanpaa, M. C., Agaza, L. M., Milner, I. B., Podany, E. C., Axelrod, B. N., & Brown, G. G. (1997). Gulf War veterans: A neuropsychological examination. *Journal of Clinical and Experimental Neuropsychology, 19,* 211–219.

1350. Silverstein, M. L., Harrow, M., Mavroleft-Eros, G. & Close, D. (1997). Neuropsychological dysfunction and clinical outcome in psychiatric disorders: A two-year follow-up study. *Journal of Nervous and Mental Disease, 185,* 722–729.

1351. Small, B. J., Viitanen, M., Winbald, B., & Bächman, L. (1997). Cognitive changes in very old persons with dementia: The influence of demographic, psychometric, and biological variables. *Journal of Clinical and Experimental Neuropsychology, 19,* 245–260.

1352. Snow, M., & Thurber, S. (1997). Cognitive imbalance and antisocial personality characteristics. *Journal of Clinical Psychology, 53,* 351–354.

1353. Stark, M. E., Grafman, J., & Fertig, E. (1997). A restricted "spotlight" of attention in visual object recognition. *Neuropsychologia, 35,* 1233–1249.

1354. Stuss, D. T., Peterkin, I., Guzman, D. A., Guzman, C., & Troyer, A. K. (1997). Chronic obstructive pulmonary disease: Effects of hypoxia on neurological and neuropsychological measures. *Journal of Clinical and Experimental Neuropsychology, 19,* 515–524.

1355. Suhr, J., Tranel, D., Wefel, J., & Barrash, J. (1997). Memory performance after head injury: Contributions of malingering, litigation status, psychological factors, and medication use. *Journal of Clinical and Experimental Neuropsychology, 19,* 500–514.

1356. Takahashi, N., Kawamura, M., Shiota, J., Kasahata, N., & Hirayama, K. (1997). Pure topographic disorientation due to right retrosplenial lesion. *Neurology, 49,* 464–469.

1357. Tanaka, Y., Miyazama, Y., Akaoka, F., & Yamada, T. (1997). Amnesia following damage to the mammillary bodies. *Neurology, 48,* 160–165.

1358. Tranel, D., Damasio, H., & Damasio, A. R. (1997). A neural basis for the retrieval of conceptual knowledge. *Neuropsychologia, 35,* 1319–1327.

1359. Tun, C. G., Tun, P. A., & Wingfield, A. (1997). Cognitive function following long-term spinal cord injury. *Rehabilitation Psychology, 42,* 163–182.

1360. Turntsull, O. H. (1997). A double dissociation between knowledge of object identity and object orientation. *Neuropsychologia, 35,* 567–570.

1361. Tyler, L. K., Karmiloff-Smith, A., Voice, J. K., Stevens, T., Grant, J., Udwin, O., Davies, M., & Howlin, P. (1997). Do individuals with Williams Syndrome have bizarre semantics? Evidence for lexical organization using an on-line task. *Cortex, 33,* 515–527.

1362. Vallar, G., Di Betta, A. M., & Silver, M. C. (1997). The phonological short-term store-rehearsed system: Patterns of impairment and neural correlates. *Neuropsychologia, 35,* 795–812.

1363. von Zerssen, D., Asukai, N., Tsuda, H., Ono, Y., Kizaki, Y., & Cho, Y. (1997). Personality traits of Japanese patients in remission from an episode of primary unipolar depression. *Journal of Affective Disorders, 44,* 145–152.

1364. Walker, N., Philbin, D. A., & Fisk, A. D. (1997). Age related differences in movement control: Adjusting submovement structure to optimize performance. *Journal of Gerontology, 52,* 40–52.

1365. Watt, S., Jokel, R., & Behrmann, M. (1997). Surface dyslexia in nonfluent progressive aphasia. *Brain and Language, 56,* 211–233.

1366. Welch, L. W., Nimmerrichter, A., Gilliland, R., King, D. E., & Martin, P. R. (1997). "Wineglass" confabulations among brain-damaged alcoholics on the Wechsler Memory Scale—Revised visual reproduction subtest. *Cortex, 33,* 543–551.

1367. Wiens, A. N., Fuller, K. H., & Crossen, J. R. (1997). Paced Auditory Serial Addition Test: Adult norms and moderator variables. *Journal of Clinical and Experimental Neuropsychology, 19,* 473–483.

1368. Wilson, B. A., Clare, L., Young, A. W., & Hodges, J. R. (1997). Knowing where and knowing what: A double dissociation. *Cortex, 33,* 529–541.

1369. Wishart, L. R., & Lee, T. D. (1997). Effects of aging and reduced relative frequency of knowledge of results on learning a motor skill. *Perceptual and Motor Skills, 84,* 1107–1122.

1370. Wood, P. K., Sher, K. J., Erickson, D. J., & DeBord, K. A. (1997). Predicting academic problems in college from freshman alcohol involvement. *Journal of Studies on Alcohol, 58,* 200–210.

1371. Yamashita, H., Hirano, N., Ikeda, M., Ikejiri, Y., Imamura, T., Shimomura, T., & Mori, E. (1997). Examining the diagnostic utility of the Fuld cholinergic deficit profile on the Japanese WAIS-R. *Journal of Clinical and Experimental Neuropsychology, 19,* 300–304.

1372. Yasuda, K., Watanabe, O., & Ono, Y. (1997). Dissociation between semantic and autobiographic memory: A case report. *Cortex, 33,* 623–638.

1373. Zlotnick, C., & Agnew, J. (1997). Neuropyshcological function and psychological status of alcohol rehabilitation program residents. *Addictive Behaviors, 22,* 183–194.

1374. Aylward, E. H., Anderson, N. B., Bylsma, F. W., Wagster, M. V., Barta, P. E., Sherr, M., Feeney, J., Davis, A., Rosenblatt, A., Pearlson, G. D., & Ross, C. A. (1998). Frontal lobe volume in patients with Huntington's disease. *Neurology, 50,* 252–258.

1375. Bartolomeo, P., Barba, G. D., Boisse, M.-F., Bachoud-Levi, Degos, J.-D., & Boller, F. (1998). Right-side neglect in Alzheimer's disease. *Neurology, 51,* 1207–1209.

1376. Baum, K. M., & Nowicki, S., Jr. (1998). Perception of emotion: Measuring decoding accuracy of adult prosodic cues varying in intensity. *Journal of Nonverbal Behavior, 22,* 89–107.

1377. Baynes, K., Kegl, J. A., Brentari, D., Kussmaul, C., & Poizner, H. (1998). Chronic auditory agnosia following Landau-Kleffner syndrome: A 23 year outcome study. *Brain and Language, 63,* 381–425.

1378. Berman, I., Merson, A., Viegner, B., Losonezy, M. F. Pappas, D., & Green, A. I. (1998). Obsessions and compulsions at a district cluster of symptoms in schizophrenia: A neuropsychological study. *Journal of Nervous and Mental Disease, 186,* 150–156.

1379. Broks, P., Young, A. W., Maratos, E. J., Coffey, P. J., Calder, A. J., Isaac, C. L., Mayes, A. R., Hodges, J. R., Montaldi, D., Cezayirli, E., Roberts, N., & Hadley, D. (1998). Face processing impairment after encephalitis: Amygdala damage and recognition of fear. *Neuropsychologia, 36,* 59–70.

1380. Burch, G., S. J., Steel, C., & Hemsley, d. R. (1998). Oxford-Liverpool Inventory of Feelings and Experiences: Reliability in an experimental population. *British Journal of Clinical Psychology, 37,* 107–108.

1381. Carlesimo, G. A., Mauri, M., Graceffa, A. M. S., Fadda, L., Loasses, A., Lorusso, S., & Caltagirone, C. (1998). Memory performance in young, elderly, and very old healthy individuals versus patients with Alzheimer's Disease: Evidence for discontinuity between normal and pathological aging. *Journal of Clinical and Experimental Neuropsychology, 20,* 14–29.

1382. Carmelli, D., Swan, G. E., Reed, T., Miller, B., Wolf, P. A., Jarvik, G. P., & Schellenberg, G. D. (1998). Midlife cardiovascular risk factors, ApoE, and cognitive decline in elderly male twins. *Neurology, 50,* 1580–1585.

1383. Cochrane, H. J., Baker, G. A., & Mendell, P. R. (1998). Simulating a memory impairment: Can amnesics implicitly outperform simulators? *British Journal of Clinical Psychology, 37,* 31–48.

1384. DeShon, R. P., Smith, M. R., Chan, D., & Schmitt, N. (1998). Can racial differences in cognitive test performance be reduced by presenting problems in a social context? *Journal of Applied Psychology, 83,* 438–451.

1385. Dobbins, I. G., Kroll, N. E. A., Tulving, E., Knight, R. T., & Gazzaniga, M. S. (1998). Unilateral medial temporal lobe memory impairment: Type deficit, function deficit, or both? *Neuropsychologia, 36,* 115–127.

1386. Enns, R. A., & Reddon, J. R. (1998). The factor structure of the Wechsler Adult Intelligence Scale—Revised: One or two but not three factors. *Journal of Clinical Psychology, 54,* 447–459.

1387. Ferraro, F. R., & Dukart, A. (1998). Cognitive inhibition in individuals prone to homophobia. *Journal of Clinical Psychology, 54,* 155–162.

1388. Fukatsu, R., Yamadori, A., & Fujii, T. (1998). Impaired recall and preserved encoding in prominent amnesic syndrome: A case of basal forebrain amnesia. *Neurology, 50,* 539–541.

1389. Ghaziuddin, M., Weidmer-Mikhail, E., & Ghaziuddin, N. (1998). Comorbidity of Asperger syndrome: A preliminary report. *Journal of Disability Research, 42,* 279–283.

1390. Giancola, P. R., Mezzich, A. C., & Tarter, R. E. (1998). Disruptive, delinquent and aggressive behavior in female adolescents with a psychoactive substance use disorder: Relation to executive cognitive functioning. *Journal of Studies on Alcohol, 59,* 560–567.

1391. Grimshaw, G. M., Adelstein, A., Bryden, M. P., & MacKinnon, G. E. (1998). First-language acquisition in adolescence: Evidence for a critical period for verbal language development. *Brain and Language, 63,* 237–255.

1392. Helmstaedter, C., Gleibner, O., Zentner, J., & Elger, C. E. (1998). Neuropsychological consequences of epilepsy surgery in frontal lobe epilepsy. *Neuropsychologia, 36,* 333–341.

1393. Hoaken, P. N. S., Assaad, J-M., & Pihl, R. O. (1998). Cognitive functioning and the inhibition of alcohol-induced aggression. *Journal of Studies on Alcohol, 59,* 599–607.

1394. Hodgson, C., & Ellis, A. W. (1998). Last in, first to go: Age of acquisition and naming in the elderly. *Brain and Language, 64,* 146–163.

1395. Howlin, P., Davies, M., & Udwin, O. (1998). Cognitive functioning in adults with Williams syndrome. *Journal of Child Psychology and Psychiatry, 39,* 183–189.

1396. Johnson, K. A., Jones, K., Holman, B. L., Becker, J. A., Spiers, P. A., Satlin, A., & Albert, M. S. (1998). Preclinical prediction of Alzheimer's disease using SPECT. *Neurology, 50,* 1563–1571.

1397. Kanne, S. M., Balota, D. A., Storandt, M., McKeel, D. W., & Morris, J. C. (1998). Relating anatomy to function in Alzheimer's disease: Neuropsychological profiles predict regional neuropathology 5 years later. *Neurology, 50,* 979–985.

1398. Karatekin, C., & Asarnow, R. F. (1998). Components of visual search in childhood-onset schizophrenia and attention-deficit/hyperactivity disorder. *Journal of Abnormal Child Psychology, 26,* 367–380.

1399. Laws, K. R., McKenna, P. J., & Kondel, T. K. (1998). On the distinction between access and store disorders in schizophrenia: A question of deficit severity? *Neuropsychologia, 36,* 313–321.

1400. Libon, D. J., Bogdanoff, B., Cloud, B. S., Skalina, S., Giovannetti, T., Gitlin, H. L., & Bonavita, J. (1998). Declarative and procedural leaving, quantitative measures of the hippocampus, and subcortical white alterations in Alzheimer's Disease and ischaemic vascular dementia. *Journal of Clinical and Experimental Neuropsychology, 20,* 30–41.

1401. Lindsay, W. R., Neilson, C. Q., Morrison, F., & Smith, A. H. W. (1998). The treatment of six men with a learning disability convicted of sex offenses with children. *British Journal of Clinical Psychology, 37,* 83–98.

1402. Louth, S. M., Hare, R. D., & Linden, W. (1998). Psychopathy and alexithymia in female offenders. *Canadian Journal of Behavioural Science, 30,* 91–98.

1403. Macklin, M. L., Metzger, L. J., Litz, B. T., McNally, R. J., Lasko, N. B., Orr, S. P., & Pitman, R. K. (1998). Lower precombat intelligence is a risk factor for posttraumatic stress disorder. *Journal of Consulting and Clinical Psychology, 66,* 323–326.

1404. Majumder, P. P., Moss, H. B., & Murrelle, L. (1998). Familial and nonfamilial factors in the prediction of disruptive behaviors in boys at risk for substance abuse. *Journal of Child Psychology and Psychiatry, 39,* 203–213.

1405. Manly, J. J., Jacobs, D. M., Sano, M., Bell, K., Merchant, C. A., Small, S. A., & Stern, Y. (1998). Cognitive test performance among nondemented elderly Africa Americans and Whites. *Neurology, 50,* 1238–1245.

1406. Marks, A. R., & Cermak, L. S., (1998). Intact temporal memory in amnesic patients. *Neuropsychologia, 36,* 935–943.

1407. McDonald, S., & Pearce, S. (1998). Requests that overcome listener reluctance: Impairment associated with executive dysfunction in brain injury. *Brain and Language, 61,* 88–104.

1408. Mega, M. S., Thompson, P. M., Cummings, J. L., Back, C. L., Xu, M. L., Zohoori, S., Goldkorn, A., Moussai, J., Fairbanks, L., Small, G. W., & Toga, A. W. (1998). Sulcal variability in the Alzheimer's brain: Correlations with cognition. *Neurology, 50,* 145–151.

1409. Mostofsky, S. H., Mazzocco, m. M. M., Aakalu, G., Warsofsky, I. S., Denckla, M. B., & Reiss, A. L. (1998). Decreased cerebellar posterior vermis size in fragile X syndrome: Correlation with neurocognitive performance. *Neurology, 50,* 121–130.

1410. Patel, A. D., Peretz, I., Tramo, M., & Labreque, R. (1998). Processing prosodic and musical patterns: A neuropsychological investigation. *Brain and Language, 61,* 123–144.

1411. Paulhus, D. L., Lysy, D. C., & Yik, M. S. M. (1998). Self-report measures of intelligence: Are they useful as proxy IQ tests? *Journal of Personality, 66,* 525–554.

1412. Putzke, J. D., Williams, M. A., & Boll, T. J. (1998). A defensive response set and the relation between cognitive and emotional functioning: A replication. *Perceptual and Motor Skills, 86,* 251–257.

1413. Rae, C., Karmiloff-Smith, A., Lee, M. A., Dixon, R. M., Grant, J., Blamire, A. M., Thompson, C. H., Styles, P., & Radda, G. K. (1998). Brain biochemistry in Williams syndrome: Evidence for a role of the cerebellum in cognition? *Neurology, 51,* 33–40.

1414. Rapcsak, S. Z., Kaszniak, A. W., Reminger, S. L., Glisky, M. L., Glisky, E. L., & Comer, J. F. (1998). Dissociation between verbal and autonomic measures of memory following frontal lobe damage. *Neurology, 50,* 1259–1265.

1415. Schweizer, K. (1998). Visual search, reaction time, and cognitive ability. *Perceptual and Motor Skills, 86,* 79–84.

1416. Seki, K., Ishiai, S., Koyama, Y., Sato, S., Hirabayashi, H., Inaki, K., & Nakayama, T. (1998). Effects of unilateral spatial neglect on spatial agraphia of Kana and Kanjc letters. *Brain and Language, 63,* 256–275.

1417. Shultz, J. M., Aman, M. G., & Rojahn, J. (1998). Psychometric evaluation of a measure of cognitive decline in elderly people with mental retardation. *Research in Developmental Disabilities, 19,* 63–71.

1418. Silberg, J. L. (1998). Dissociative symptomatology in children and adolescents as displayed on psychological testing. *Journal of Personality Assessment, 71,* 421–439.
1419. Tiberti, C., Sabe, L., Kuzis, G., Cuerva, A. G., Leiguarda, R., & Starkstein, S. E. (1998). Prevalence and correlates of the catastrophic reaction in Alzheimer's disease. *Neurology, 50,* 546–548.
1420. van Gorp, W, G., Altshuler, L., Theberge, D. C., Wilkins, J., & Dixon, W. (1998). Cognitive impairment in euthymic bipolar patients with and without prior alcohol dependence: A preliminary study. *Archives of General Psychiatry, 55,* 41–46.
1421. Witte, R. H., Phillips, L., & Kakela, M. (1998). Job satisfaction of college graduates with learning disabilities. *Journal of Learning Disabilities, 31,* 259–265.
1422. Young, D. A., Zakzanis, K. K., Bailey, C., Davila, R., Griese, J., Sartory, G., & Thom, A. (1998). Further parameters of insight and neuropsychological deficit in schizophrenia and other chronic mental disease. *Journal of Nervous and Mental Disease, 186,* 44–50.

[2861]

Wechsler Individual Achievement Test.

Purpose: For assessing educational achievement of children and adolescents.
Population: Ages 5–19.
Publication Date: 1992.
Acronym: WIAT.
Administration: Individual.
Comments: Standardized with Weschler Intelligence Scale for Children—III (2862).
Author: The Psychological Corporation.
Publisher: The Psychological Corporation.

a) WIAT SCREENER.

Scores, 4: Basic Reading, Mathematics Reading, Spelling, Screener Composite.
Price Data, 1999: $80 per complete WIAT Screener kit including 25 record forms, stimulus booklet 1, and screener manual; $27 per 25 record forms; $27 per screener manual; $59 per stimulus booklet 1.
Time: (10–18) minutes.

b) WIAT.

Scores, 13: Basic Reading, Reading Comprehension, Total Reading, Mathematics Reasoning, Numerical Operations, Total Mathematics, Listening Comprehension, Oral Expression, Total Language, Spelling, Written Expression, Total Writing, Total Composite.
Price Data: $273 per complete WIAT kit including 25 WIAT record forms, 5 screener record forms, 25 response booklets, stimulus booklet 1, stimulus booklet 2, and manual (387 pages); $34.50 per 25 record forms; $14.50 per 25 response booklets; $81.50 per stimulus booklet 1, $118 per stimulus booklet 2; $59 per manual.
Time: (30–75) minutes.

Cross References: For reviews by Terry Ackerman and Steven Ferrara, see 13:359 (17 references).

TEST REFERENCES

1. Bakken, J. P., Mastropieri, M. A., & Scruggs, T. E. (1997). Reading comprehension on expository science material and students with learning disability: A comparison of strategies. *The Journal of Special Education, 31,* 300–324.
2. Glutting, J. J., Robins, P. M., & de Lancey, E. (1997). Discriminant validity of test observations for children with attention deficit/hyperactivity. *Journal of School Psychology, 35,* 391–401.
3. Masten, A. S., Sesma, A., Jr., Si-Asar, R., Lawrence, C., Miliotis, D., & Dionne, J. A. (1997). Educational risks for children experiencing homelessness. *Journal of School Psychology, 35,* 27–46.
4. McDermott, P. A., & Glutitng, J. J. (1997). Informing stylistic learning behavior, disposition, and achievement through ability subtests—or, more illusions of meaning. *School Psychology Review, 26,* 163–175.

[2862]

Wechsler Intelligence Scale for Children—Third Edition.

Purpose: A "measure of a child's intellectual ability."
Population: Ages 6-0 to 16-11.
Publication Dates: 1971-1991.
Acronym: WISC-III.
Scores, 13 to 16: Verbal (Information, Similarities, Arithmetic, Vocabulary, Comprehension, Digit Span [optional], Total); Performance (Picture Completion, Coding, Picture Arrangement, Block Design, Object Assembly, Symbol Search [optional], Mazes [optional], Total), Total.
Administration: Individual.
Price Data, 1999: $625 per complete box kit; $682.50 per complete kit with attaché or soft-sided case; $73.50 per manual ('91, 294 pages); $90.50 per stimulus book; $37 per 25 mazes response booklets; $141 per 100 mazes response booklets; $37 per 25 symbol search response booklets; $$141 per 100 symbol search response booklets; $72 per 25 record forms; $276.50 per 100 record forms; $201.50 per 6 object assembly puzzles.
Time: Core subtests: 50–70 minutes; Supplemental: 10–15 minutes.
Author: David Wechsler.
Publisher: The Psychological Corporation.
Cross References: For reviews by Jeffrey P. Braden and Jonathan Sandoval, see 12:412 (409 references); see also T4:2939 (911 references); for reviews of an earlier edition by Morton Bortner, Douglas K. Detterman, and Joseph C. Witt and Frank Gresham, see 9:1351 (299 references); see also T3:2602 (645 references); for reviews by David Freides and Randolph H. Whitworth, and excerpted reviews by Carol Kehr Tittle and Joseph Petrosko, see 8:232 (548 references); see also T2:533 (230 references); for reviews by David Freides and R. T. Osborne of the original edition, see 7:431 (518 references); for a review by Alvin G. Burnstein, see 6:540 (155 references); for reviews by Elizabeth D. Fraser, Gerald R. Patterson, and Albert I. Rabin, see 5:416 (111 references); for reviews by James M. Anderson, Harold A. Delp, and Boyd R. McCandless, and an excerpted review by Laurance F. Shaffer, see 4:363 (22 references).

TEST REFERENCES

1. Brown, B., Haegerstrom-Portnoy, G., Adams, A. J., Yingling, C. D., Galin, D., Herron, J., & Marcus, M. (1983). Predictive eye movements do not discriminate between dyslexic and control children. *Neuropsychologia, 21,* 121–128.
2. Kraft, R. H. (1983). The effect of sex, laterality and familial handedness on intellectual abilities. *Neuropsychologia, 21,* 79–89.
3. Blackburn, D. W., Bonvillian, J. D., & Ashby, R. P. (1984). Manual communication as an alternative mode of language instruction for children with severe reading disabilities. *Language, Speech, and Hearing Services in Schools, 15,* 22–31.
4. Kee, D. W., Bathurst, K., & Hellige, J. B. (1984). Lateralized interference in finger tapping: Assessment of block design activities. *Neuropsychologia, 22,* 197–203.

5. Salend, S. J., & Andress, M. J. (1984). Decreasing stuttering in an elementary-level student. *Language, Speech, and Hearing Services in Schools, 15,* 16–21.

6. Santostefano, S., Rieder, C., & Berk, S. A. (1984). The structure of fantasied movement in suicidal children and adolescents. *Suicide and Life-Threatening Behavior, 14,* 3–16.

7. Siegel, L. S. (1984). A longitudinal study of a hyperlexic child: Hyperlexia as a language disorder. *Neuropsychologia, 22,* 577–585.

8. Temple, C. M. (1984). Surface dyslexia in a child with epilepsy. *Neuropsychologia, 22,* 569–576.

9. Wolff, P. H., Cohen, C., & Drake, C. (1984). Impaired motor timing control in specific reading retardation. *Neuropsychologia, 22,* 587–600.

10. Glass, M. R., Franks, J. R., & Potter, R. E. (1986). A comparison of two tests of auditory selective attention. *Language, Speech, and Hearing Services in Schools, 17,* 300–306.

11. Asbury, C. A., Adderly-Kelly, B., & Knuckle, E. P. (1987). Relationships among WISC-R performance categories and measured ethnic identity in Black adolescents. *Journal of Negro Education, 56,* 173–183.

12. Brown, S. W., & Yakimowski, M. E. (1987). Intelligence scores of gifted students on the WISC-R. *Gifted Child Quarterly, 31,* 130–134.

13. Colangelo, N., & Brower, P. (1987). Labeling gifted youngsters: Long-term impact on families. *Gifted Child Quarterly, 31,* 75–78.

14. Cornell, D. G., & Grossberg, I. W. (1987). Family environment and personality adjustment in gifted program children. *Gifted Child Quarterly, 31,* 59–64.

15. Gresham, F. M., & Reschly, D. J. (1987). Sociometric differences between mildly handicapped and nonhandicapped Black and White students. *Journal of Educational Psychology, 79,* 195–197.

16. Grigsby, J. P., Kemper, M. B., & Hagerman, R. J. (1987). Developmental Gerstmann Syndrome without aphasia in Fragile X Syndrome. *Neuropsychologia, 25,* 881–891.

17. Grubb, H. J. (1987). Intelligence at the low end of the curve: Where are the racial differences? *The Journal of Black Psychology, 14,* 25–34.

18. Hall, P. K., & Jordan, L. S. (1987). An assessment of a controlled association task to identify word-finding problems in children. *Language, Speech, and Hearing Services in Schools, 18,* 99–111.

19. Keane, K. J., & Kretschmer, R. E. (1987). Effect of mediated learning intervention on cognitive task performance with a deaf population. *Journal of Educational Psychology, 79,* 49–53.

20. Kraft, R. H., Hsia, T. C., Roberts, T., & Hallum, A. (1987). Reading comprehension performance and laterality: Evidence for concurrent validity of dichotic, dichhaptic and EEG laterality measures. *Neuropsychologia, 25,* 817–827.

21. Marcus, J., Hans, S. L., Nagler, S., Auerbach, J. G., Mirsky, A. F., & Aubrey, A. (1987). Review of the NIMH Israeli Kibbutz-City study and the Jerusalem infant development study. *Schizophrenia Bulletin, 13,* 425-438.

22. Moore, D. W., & Wilson, B. J. (1987). On the search for a characteristic WISC-R subtest profile of reading/learning disabled children. *Reading Research and Instruction, 26,* 133–140.

23. Moore, E. G. J. (1987). Ethic social milieu and Black children's intelligence test achievement. *Journal of Negro Education, 56,* 44–52.

24. Moore, L. C., & Sawyers, J. K. (1987). The stability of original thinking in young children. *Gifted Child Quarterly, 31,* 126–129.

25. Ostergaard, A. L. (1987). Episodic, semantic and procedural memory in a case of amnesia at an early age. *Neuropsychologia, 25,* 341–357.

26. Reid, M. K., & Borkowski, J. G. (1987). Causal attributions of hyperactive children: Implications for teaching strategies and self-control. *Journal of Educational Psychology, 79,* 296–307.

27. Richert, E. S. (1987). Rampant problems and promising practices in the identification of disadvantaged gifted students. *Gifted Child Quarterly, 31,* 149–154.

28. Scruggs, T. E., Mastropieri, M. A., McLoone, B. B., Levin, J. R., & Morrison, C. R. (1987). Mnemonic facilitation of learning disabled students' memory for expository prose. *Journal of Educational Psychology, 79,* 27–34.

29. Smith, K., & Griffiths, P. (1987). Defective lateralized attention for non-verbal sounds in developmental dyslexia. *Neuropsychologia, 25,* 259–268.

30. Aram, D., & Ekelman, B. L. (1988). Scholastic aptitude and achievement among children with unilateral brain lesions. *Neuropsychologia, 26,* 903–916.

31. Asarnow, J. R., & Carlson, G. (1988). Suicide attempts in preadolescent child psychiatry inpatients. *Suicide and Life-Threatening Behavior, 18,* 129–136.

32. Baum, S. (1988). An enrichment program for gifted learning disabled students. *Gifted Child Quarterly, 32,* 226–230.

33. Baum, S., & Owen, S. V. (1988). High ability/learning disabled students: How are they different? *Gifted Child Quarterly, 32,* 321–326.

34. Boliek, C. A., Obrzut, J. E., & Shaw, D. (1988). The effects of hemispatial and asymmetrically focused attention on dichotic listening with normal and learning-disabled children. *Neuropsychologia, 26,* 417–433.

35. Chapman, J. W. (1988). Cognitive-motivational characteristics and academic achievement of learning disabled children: A longitudinal study. *Journal of Educational Psychology, 80,* 357–365.

36. Chapman, J. W., & McAlpine, P. D. (1988). Students' perceptions of ability. *Gifted Child Quarterly, 32,* 222–225.

37. Corballis, M. C., & Sergent, J. (1988). Imagery in a commissurotomized patient. *Neuropsychologia, 26,* 13–26.

38. Dennis, M., Farrell, K., Hoffman, H. J., Hendrick, E. B., Becker, L. E., & Murphy, E. G. (1988). Recognition memory of item, associative and serial-order information after temporal lobectomy for seizure disorder. *Neuropsychologia, 26,* 53–65.

39. Gallucci, N. T. (1988). Emotional adjustment of gifted children. *Gifted Child Quarterly, 32,* 273–276.

40. Green, K., Fine, M. J., & Tollefson, N. (1988). Family systems characteristics and underachieving gifted adolescent males. *Gifted Child Quarterly, 32,* 267–272.

41. Jackson, N. E., Donaldson, G. W., & Cleland, L. N. (1988). The structure of precocious reading ability. *Journal of Educational Psychology, 80,* 234–243.

42. Jeeves, M. A., & Silver, P. H. (1988). The formation of finger grip during prehension in an acallosal patient. *Neuropsychologia, 26,* 153–159.

43. Jeeves, M. A., Silver, P. H., & Jacobson, I. (1988). Bimanual co-ordination in callosal agenesis and partial commissurotomy. *Neuropsychologia, 26,* 833–850.

44. Juel, C. (1988). Learning to read and write: A longitudinal study of 54 children from first through fourth grades. *Journal of Educational Psychology, 80,* 437–447.

45. Karnes, F. A., & D'Ilio, V. R. (1988). Comparison of gifted children and their parents' perception of the home environment. *Gifted Child Quarterly, 32,* 277–279.

46. Kiselica, M. S. (1988). Helping an aggressive adolescent through the "before, during, and after program." *The School Counselor, 35,* 299–306.

47. Kistner, J. A., Osborne, M., & LeVerrier, L. (1988). Causal attributions of learning-disabled children: Developmental patterns and relation to academic progress. *Journal of Educational Psychology, 80,* 82–89.

48. Lehrer, R., Guckenberg, T., & Lee, O. (1988). Comparative study of the cognitive consequences of inquiry-based logo instruction. *Journal of Educational Psychology, 80,* 543–553.

49. Levin, M. L. (1988). Sequelae to marital disruption in children. *Journal of Divorce, 12*(2/3), 25–80.

50. Mercer, J. R. (1988). Ethnic differences in IQ scores: What do they mean? (A response to Lloyd Dunn). *Hispanic Journal of Behavioral Sciences, 10,* 199–218.

51. Natsopoulos, D., & Xeromeritou, A. (1988). Understanding complement clauses by educable mentally retarded and nonretarded children and young adults. *International Journal of Psychology, 23,* 663–683.

52. Obrzut, J. E., Conrad, P. F., Bryden, M. P., & Boliek, C. A. (1988). Cued dichotic listening with right-handed, left-handed, bilingual and learning-disabled children. *Neuropsychologia, 26,* 119–131.

53. Ogden, J. A. (1988). Language and memory functions after long recovery periods in left-hemispherectomized subjects. *Neuropsychologia, 26,* 645–659.

54. Rimm, S., & Lowe, B. (1988). Family environments of underachieving gifted students. *Gifted Child Quarterly, 32,* 353–359.

55. Sharpley, C. F. (1988). Effects of implicit rewards on adults' motor skills responses. *Journal of Educational Psychology, 80,* 244–246.

56. Stiles-Davis, J., Janowsky, J., Engel, M., & Nass, R. (1988). Drawing ability in four young children with congenital unilateral brain lesions. *Neuropsychologia, 26,* 359–371.

57. Torgesen, J. K., Rashotte, C. A., & Greenstein, J. (1988). Language comprehension in learning disabled children who perform poorly on memory span tests. *Journal of Educational Psychology, 80,* 480–487.

58. Valencia, R. R. (1988). The McCarthy Scales and Hispanic children: A review of psychometric research. *Hispanic Journal of Behavioral Sciences, 10,* 81–104.

59. Whitworth, R. H. (1988). Comparison of Anglo and Mexican American male high school students classified as learning disabled. *Hispanic Journal of Behavioral Sciences, 10,* 127–137.

60. Zeidner, M., Klingman, A., & Papko, O. (1988). Enhancing students' test coping skills: Report of a psychological health education program. *Journal of Educational Psychology, 80,* 95–101.

61. Zhang, H. (1988). Psychological measurement in China. *International Journal of Psychology, 23,* 101–117.

62. Chi, M. T. H., Hutchinson, J. E., & Robin, A. F. (1989). How inferences about novel domain-related concepts can be constrained by structured knowledge. *Merrill-Palmer Quarterly, 35,* 27–62.

63. Ciesielski, K. T. (1989). Event-related potentials in children with specific visual cognitive disability. *Neuropsychologia, 27,* 303–313.

64. Cornell, D. G. (1989). Child adjustment and parent use of the term "gifted." *Gifted Child Quarterly, 33,* 59–64.

65. Curfs, L. M. G., Schreppers-Tijdink, G., Wiegers, A., Borghgraef, M., & Fryns, J. P. (1989). Intelligence and cognitive profile in the fra(X) syndrome: A longitudinal study in 18 fra(X) boys. *Journal of Medical Genetics, 26,* 443–446.

66. Duran, R. P. (1989). Assessment and instruction of at-risk Hispanic students. *Exceptional Children, 56,* 154–158.

67. Figueroa, R. A. (1989). Psychological testing of linguistic-minority students: Knowledge gaps and regulations. *Exceptional Children, 56,* 145–152.

68. Goldman, S. R., Mertz, D. L., & Pellegrino, J. W. (1989). Individual differences in extended practice functions and solution strategies for basic addition facts. *Journal of Educational Psychology, 81,* 481–496.

69. Goldsmiths-Phillips, J. (1989). Word and context in reading development: A test of the interactive-compensatory hypothesis. *Journal of Educational Psychology, 81,* 299–305.

70. Graham, S., & Harris, K. R. (1989). Components analysis of cognitive strategy instruction: Effects on learning disabled students' compositions and self-efficacy. *Journal of Educational Psychology, 81,* 353–361.

71. Graham, S., & Harris, K. R. (1989). Improving learning disabled students' skills at composing essays: Self-instructional strategy training. *Exceptional Children, 56,* 201–214.

72. Grosser, G. S., & Spafford, C. S. (1989). Perceptual evidence for an anomalous distribution of rods and cones in the retinas of dyslexics: A new hypothesis. *Perceptual and Motor Skills, 68,* 683–698.

73. Grossman, F. M., & Galvin, G. A. (1989). Referred children's cognitive patterns on the WISC-R. *Perceptual and Motor Skills, 68,* 1307–1311.

74. Hugdahl, K., & Marklund, E. (1989). Dichotic listening in children with serious language problems. *Perceptual and Motor Skills, 68,* 1291–1301.

75. Judd, T. P., & Bilsky, L. H. (1989). Comprehension and memory in the solution of verbal arithmetic problems by mentally retarded and nonretarded individuals. *Journal of Educational Psychology, 81,* 541–546.

76. Karnes, F. A., & D'Ilio, V. R. (1989). Leadership positions and sex role stereotyping among gifted children. *Gifted Child Quarterly, 33,* 76–78.

77. Kistner, J. A., & Gatlin, D. F. (1989). Sociometric differences between learning-disabled and nonhandicapped students: Effects of sex and race. *Journal of Educational Psychology, 81,* 118–120.

78. Krebs, P., Eickelberg, W., Krobath, H., & Baruch, I. (1989). Effects of physical exercise on peripheral vision and learning in children with spina bifida manifesta. *Perceptual and Motor Skills, 68,* 167–174.

79. Lasseter, J., Privette, G., Brown, C. C., & Duer, J. (1989). Dance as a treatment approach with a multidisabled child: Implications for school counseling. *The School Counselor, 36,* 310–315.

80. Levinson, H. N. (1989). Abnormal optokinetic and perceptual span parameters in cerebellar-vestibular dysfunction and learning disabilities or dyslexia. *Perceptual and Motor Skills, 68,* 35–54.

81. Moskowitz, D. S., & Schwartzman, A. E. (1989). Painting group portraits: Studying life outcomes for aggressive and withdrawn children. *Journal of Personality, 57,* 723–746.

82. Mundy-Castle, A. C., Wilson, D. J., Sibanda, P. S., & Sibanda, J. S. (1989). Cognitive effects of logo among black and white Zimbabwean girls and boys. *International Journal of Psychology, 24,* 539–546.

83. Neeman, R. L., Sawicki, J. S., & Neeman, M. (1989). Factor structure of perceptual-motor attributes in normal children: A cross-validation. *Perceptual and Motor Skills, 68,* 291–298.

84. Obrzut, J. E., Conrad, P. F., & Boliek, C. A. (1989). Verbal and nonverbal auditory processing among left- and right-handed good readers and reading-disabled children. *Neuropsychologia, 27,* 1357–1371.

85. Ortiz, V. Z., & Gonzalez, A. (1989). Validation of a short form of the WISC-R with accelerated and gifted Hispanic students. *Gifted Child Quarterly, 33,* 152–155.

86. Palisano, R. J., & Dichter, C. G. (1989). Comparison of two tests of visual-motor development used to assess children with learning disabilities. *Perceptual and Motor Skills, 68,* 1099–1103.

87. Renick, M. J., & Harter, S. (1989). Impact of social comparisons on the developing self-perceptions of learning disabled students. *Journal of Educational Psychology, 81,* 631–638.

88. Renken, B., Egeland, B., Marvinney, D., Mangelsdorf, S., & Sroufe, L. A. (1989). Early childhood antecedents of aggression and passive-withdrawal in early elementary school. *Journal of Personality, 57,* 257–281.

89. Roberts, T. A., & Kraft, R. H. (1989). Developmental differences in the relationship between reading comprehension and hemispheric alpha patterns: An EEG study. *Journal of Educational Psychology, 81,* 322–328.

90. Scarborough, H. S. (1989). Prediction of reading disability from familial and individual differences. *Journal of Educational Psychology, 81,* 101–108.

91. Segal, N. L. (1989). Origins and implications of handedness and relative birth weight for IQ in monozygotic twin pairs. *Neuropsychologia, 27,* 549–561.

92. Tegano, D. W., & Moran, J. D., III. (1989). Developmental study of the effect of dimensionality and presentation mode on original thinking of children. *Perceptual and Motor Skills, 68,* 1275–1281.

93. Watkins, C. E., Jr., Edinger, J. D., Shipley, R. H., Reinberg, J. A., Godin, K. W., Hunton-Shoup, J., McKay, B. L., Parra, R., Klaus, A., Polk, N., & Settle, K. (1989). WISC-R and WAIS-R odd- and even-item short forms: Criterion validity in three patient samples. *Rehabilitation Psychology, 34,* 175–183.

94. Banich, M. T., Levine, S. C., Kim, H., & Huttenlocher, P. (1990). The effects of developmental factors on IQ in hemiplegic children. *Neuropsychologia, 28,* 35–47.

95. Bishop, D. V. M. (1990). Handedness, clumsiness and developmental language disorders. *Neuropsychologia, 28,* 681–690.

96. Busch, K. G., Zagar, R., Hughes, J. R., Arbit, J., & Russell, R. E. (1990). Adolescents who kill. *Journal of Clinical Psychology, 46,* 472–485.

97. Callahan, C. M., Cornell, D. G., & Loyd, B. (1990). Perceived competence and parent-adolescent communication in high ability adolescent females. *Journal for the Education of the Gifted, 13,* 256–269.

98. Davidson, R. J., Leslie, S. C., & Saron, C. (1990). Reaction time measures of interhemispheric transfer time in reading disabled and normal children. *Neuropsychologia, 28,* 471–485.

99. Duffy, F. H., & McAnulty, K. (1990). Neurophysiological heterogeneity and the definition of dyslexia: Preliminary evidence for plasticity. *Neuropsychologia, 28,* 555–571.

100. Durrant, J. E., Voelker, S., & Cunningham, C. E. (1990). Academic, social, and general self-concepts of behavioral subgroups of learning disabled children. *Journal of Educational Psychology, 82,* 657–663.

101. Flor-Henry, P. (1990). Influence of gender in schizophrenia as related to other psychopathological syndromes. *Schizophrenia Bulletin, 16,* 211–227.

102. Gottfried, A. E. (1990). Academic intrinsic motivation in young elementary school children. *Journal of Educational Psychology, 82,* 525–538.

103. Gould, J. H., & Glencross, D. J. (1990). Do children with a specific reading disability have a general serial-ordering deficit? *Neuropsychologia, 28,* 271–278.

104. Graham, S. (1990). The role of production factors in learning disabled students' composition. *Journal of Educational Psychology, 82,* 781–791.

105. Hansen, L., Salmon, D., Galasko, D., Masliah, E., Katzman, R., DeTeresa, R., Thal, L., Pay, M. M., Hofstetter, R., Klauber, M., Rice, V., Butters, N., & Alford, M. (1990). The Lewy body variant of Alzheimer's disease: A clinical and pathologic entity. *Neurology, 40,* 1–8.

106. Kelly, K. R., & Colangelo, N. (1990). Effects of academic ability and gender on career development. *Journal for the Education of the Gifted 13,* 168–175.

107. Kershner, J. R., & Morton, L. L. (1990). Directed attention dichotic listening in reading disabled children: A test of four models of maladaptive lateralization. *Neuropsychologia, 28,* 181–198.

108. Kochanek, T. T., Kabacoff, R. I., & Lipsitt, L. P. (1990). Early identification of developmentally disabled and at-risk preschool children. *Exceptional Children, 56,* 528–538.

109. Kowall, M. A., Watson, G. M. W., & Madak, P. R. (1990). Concurrent validity of the Test of Nonverbal Intelligence with referred suburban and Canadian native children. *Journal of Clinical Psychology, 46,* 632–636.

110. Lovet, M. W., Warren-Chaplin, P. M., Ransby, M. J., & Borden, S. L. (1990). Training the word recognition skills of reading disabled children: Treatment and transfer effects. *Journal of Educational Psychology, 82,* 769–780.

111. Mann, V. A., Sasanuma, S., Sakuma, N., & Masaki, S. (1990). Sex differences in cognitive abilities: A cross-cultural perspective. *Neuropsychologia, 28,* 1063–1077.

112. Mattingly, J. C., & Bott, D. A. (1990). Teaching multiplication facts to students with learning problems. *Exceptional Children, 56,* 438–449.

113. Mills, J. R., & Jackson, N. E. (1990). Predictive significance of early giftedness: The case of precocious reading. *Journal of Educational Psychology, 82,* 410–419.

114. Silverstein, A. B. (1990). Notes on the reliability of Wechsler short forms. *Journal of Clinical Psychology, 46,* 194–196.

115. Strauss, E., Satz, P., & Wada, J. (1990). An examination of the crowding hypothesis in epileptic patients who have undergone the carotid amytal test. *Neuropsychologia, 28,* 1221–1227.

116. Ulicny, G. R., Adler, A. B., & Jones, M. L. (1990). Training effective interview skills to attendent service users. *Rehabilitation Psychology, 35,* 55–66.

117. Zentall, S. S. (1990). Fact-retrieval automatization and math problem solving by learning disabled, attention-disordered, and normal adolescents. *Journal of Educational Psychology, 82,* 856–865.

118. Ackerman, P. T., Dykman, R. A., Holloway, C., Paal, N. P., & Gocio, M. Y. (1991). A trial of piracetam in two subgroups of students with dyslexia enrolled in summer tutoring. *Journal of Learning Disabilities, 24,* 542–549.

119. Andrews, L. W., & Gutkin, T. B. (1991). The effects of human versus computer authorship on consumer's perceptions of psychological reports. *Computers in Human Behavior, 7,* 311–317.

120. Armstrong, T. P., Hansen, L. A., Salmon, D. P., Masliah, E., Pay, M., Kunin, J. M., & Katzman, R. (1991). Rapidly progressive dementia in a patient with the Lewy body variant of Alzheimer's disease. *Neurology, 41,* 1178–1180.

121. Blake, R., Field, B., Foster, C., Platt, F., & Wertz, P. (1991). Effect of FM auditory trainers on attending behaviors of learning-disabled children. *Language, Speech, and Hearing Services in Schools, 22,* 111–114.

122. Brown, R. T., Madan-Swain, A., & Baldwin, K. (1991). Gender differences in a clinic-referred sample of attention-deficit-disordered children. *Child Psychiatry and Human Development, 22,* 111–128.

123. Bullard, S. C., & Schirmer, B. R. (1991). Understanding questions: Hearing-impaired children with learning problems. *Volta Review, 93,* 235–245.

124. Cousens, P., Ungerer, J. A., Crawford, J. A., & Stevens, M. M. (1991). Cognitive effects of childhood leukemia therapy: A case for four specific deficits. *Journal of Pediatric Psychology, 16,* 475–488.

125. Dennis, M., Spiegler, B. J., Hoffman, H. J., Hendrick, E. B., Humphreys, R. P., & Becker, L. E. (1991). Brain tumors in children and adolescents—I: Effects on working, associative and serial-order memory of IQ, age of tumor onset and age of tumor. *Neuropsychologia, 29,* 813–827.

126. Dennis, M., Spiegler, C. R., Hoffman, H. J., Hendrick, E. B., Humphreys, R. P., & Chuang, S. (1991). Brain tumors in children and adolescents—II: The neuroanatomy of deficits in working, associative and serial-order memory. *Neuropsychologia, 29,* 829–847.

127. Eviator, Z., & Zaidel, E. (1991). The effects of word length and emotionality on hemispheric contribution to lexical decision. *Neuropsychologia, 29,* 415–428.

128. Feazell, D. M., Quay, H. C., & Murray, E. J. (1991). The validity and utility of Lanyon's Psychological Screening Inventory in a youth services agency sample. *Criminal Justice and Behavior, 18,* 166–179.

129. Friedrich, W. N., Lovejoy, M. C., Shaffer, J., Shurtleff, D. B., & Beilke, R. L. (1991). Cognitive abilities and achievement status of children with myelomeningocele: A contemporary sample. *Journal of Pediatric Psychology, 16,* 423–428.

130. Fujiki, M., & Brinton, B. (1991). The verbal noncommunicator: A case study. *Language, Speech, and Hearing Services in Schools, 22,* 322–333.

131. Kamphaus, R. W., Frick, P. J., & Lahey, B. B. (1991). Methodological issues and learning disabilities diagnosis in clinical populations. *Journal of Learning Disabilities, 24,* 613–618.

132. Kershner, J. R., & Stringer, R. W. (1991). Effects of reading and writing on cerebral laterality in good readers and children with dyslexia. *Journal of Learning Disabilities, 24,* 560–567.

133. Kochanska, G. (1991). Socialization and temperament in the development of guilt and conscience. *Child Development, 62,* 1379–1392.

134. Kolko, D. J., Watson, S., & Faust, J. (1991). Fire safety/prevention skills training to reduce involvement with fire in young psychiatric inpatients: Preliminary findings. *Behavior Therapy, 22,* 269–284.

135. Lassonde, M., Sauerwein, H., Chicoine, A. J., & Geoffroy, G. (1991). Absence of disconnexion syndrome in callosal agenesis and early callosotomy: Brain reorganization or lack of structural specificity during ontogeny? *Neuropsychologia, 29,* 481–495.

136. Morison, P., & Masten, A. S. (1991). Peer reputation in middle childhood as a predictor of adaptation in adolescence: A seven-year follow-up. *Child Development, 62,* 991–1007.

137. Pinto, A. C. (1991). Reading rates and digit span in bilinguals: The superiority of mother tongue. *International Journal of Psychology, 26,* 471–483.

138. Portes, P. R. (1991). Assessing children's cognitive environment through parent-child interactions. *Journal of Research and Development in Education, 24*(3), 30–37.

139. Rescoria, L., Parker, R., & Stolley, P. (1991). Ability, achievement, and adjustment in homeless children. *American Journal of Orthopsychiatry, 61,* 210–220.

140. Rubin, H., Patterson, P. A., & Kantor, M. (1991). Morphological development and writing ability in children and adults. *Language, Speech, and Hearing Services in Schools, 22,* 228–235.

141. Sabban, Y. P. (1991). The effect of heterogeneous groups on the interactions of working-class subjects in problem-solving discussions. *Journal of Research and Development in Education, 24*(4), 11–18.

142. Sakheim, G. A., Osborn, E., & Abrams, D. (1991). Toward a clearer differentiation of high-risk from low-risk fire-setters. *Child Welfare, 70,* 489–503.

143. Salyer, K. M., Holmstrom, R. W., & Noshpitz, J. D. (1991). Learning disabilities as a childhood manifestation of severe psychopathology. *American Journal of Orthopsychiatry, 61,* 230–240.

144. Shelton, B. S., Gast, D. L., Wolery, M., & Winterling, V. (1991). The role of small group interaction in facilitating observational and incidental learning. *Language, Speech, and Hearing Services in Schools, 22,* 123–133.

145. Stewart, S. M., Silver, C. H., Nici, J., Waller, D., Campbell, R., Uany, R., & Andrews, W. S. (1991). Neuropsychological function in young children who have undergone liver transplantation. *Journal of Pediatric Psychology, 16,* 569–583.

146. Tansey, M. A. (1991). Wechsler (WISC-R) changes following treatment of learning disabilities via EEG biofeedback training in a private practice setting. *Australian Journal of Psychology, 43,* 147–153.

147. Williams, J., Richman, L., & Yarbrough, D. (1991). A comparison of memory and attention in Turner syndrome and learning disability. *Journal of Pediatric Psychology, 16,* 585–593.

148. Wright, S. K., & Ashman, A. F. (1991). The relationship between meter recognition, rhythmic notation, and information processing competence. *Australian Journal of Psychology, 43,* 139–146.

149. Abkarian, G. G. (1992). Communication effects of prenatal alcohol exposure. *Journal of Communication Disorders, 25,* 221–240.

150. Andersson, B. E. (1992). Effects of day-care on cognitive and socioemotional competence of thirteen-year-old Swedish school children. *Child Development, 63,* 20–36.

151. Aram, D. M., Morris, R., & Hall, N. E. (1992). The validity of discrepancy criteria for identifying children with developmental language disorders. *Journal of Learning Disabilities, 25,* 549–554.

152. Barnes, M. A., & Dennis, M. (1992). Reading in children and adolescents after early onset hydrocephalus and in normally developing age peers: Phonological analysis, word recognition, word comprehension, and passage comprehension skill. *Journal of Pediatric Psychology, 17,* 445–465.

153. Barnett, A., & Henderson, S. E. (1992). Some observations on the figure drawings of clumsy children. *British Journal of Educational Psychology, 62,* 341–355.

154. Benson, M. J. (1992). Beyond the reaction range concept: A developmental, contextual, and situational model of the heredity-environment interplay. *Human Relations, 45,* 937–956.

155. Brandt, P., Magyary, D., Hammond, M., & Barnard, K. (1992). Learning and behavioral-emotional problems of children born preterm at second grade. *Journal of Pediatric Psychology, 17,* 291–311.

156. Burd, L., Kauffman, D. W., & Kerbeshian, J. (1992). Tourette syndrome and learning disabilities. *Journal of Learning Disabilities, 25,* 598–604.

157. Carvajal, H. H., Roth, L. A., Holmes, C. B., & Page, G. L. (1992). The effect of grade level on WISC-R IQs of 6-year-olds. *Bulletin of the Psychonomic Society, 30,* 317–318.

158. Cornwall, A. (1992). The relationship of phonological awareness, rapid naming, and verbal memory to severe reading and spelling disability. *Journal of Learning Disabilities, 25,* 532–538.

159. Deci, E. L., Hodges, R., Pierson, L., & Tomassone, J. (1992). Autonomy and competence as motivational factors in students with learning disabilities and emotional handicaps. *Journal of Learning Disabilities, 25,* 457–471.

160. Dykman, R. A., & Ackerman, P. T. (1992). Diagnosing dyslexia: IQ regression plus cut-points. *Journal of Learning Disabilities, 25,* 574–576.

161. Faigel, H. C., Doak, E., Howard, S. D., & Sigel, M. L. (1992). Emotional disorders in learning disabled adolescents. *Child Psychiatry and Human Development, 23,* 31–40.

162. Felton, R. H., & Wood, F. B. (1992). A reading level match study of nonword reading skills in poor readers with varying IQ. *Journal of Learning Disabilities, 25,* 318–326.

163. Gustafsson, J. (1992). The relevance of factor analysis for the study of group differences. *Multivariate Behavioral Research, 27,* 239–247.

164. Jirsa, R. E. (1992). The utility of the P3 AERP in children with auditory processing disorders. *Journal of Speech and Hearing Research, 35,* 903–912.

165. Kail, R., & Park, Y-S. (1992). Global developmental change in processing time. *Merrill-Palmer Quarterly, 38,* 525–541.

166. Kline, R. B., Snyder, J., Guilmette, S., & Castellanos, M. (1992). Relative usefulness of elevation, variability, and shape information from WISC-R, K-ABC, and Fourth Edition Stanford-Binet profiles in predicting agreement. *Psychological Assessment, 4,* 426–432.

167. Lamm, O., & Epstein, R. (1992). Specific reading impairments—Are they to be associated with emotional difficulties? *Journal of Learning Disabilities, 25,* 605–615.

168. Lewis, B. A., & Thompson, L. A. (1992). A study of developmental speech and language disorders in twins. *Journal of Speech and Hearing Research, 35,* 1086–1094.

169. Madison, C. L., & Wong, E. Y. F. (1992). Use of the Clark-Madison Test of Oral Language with the hearing-impaired: A content validity and comparative study. *Journal of Communication Disorders, 25,* 241–250.

170. Mandoki, M. W., Sumner, G. S., & Matthews-Ferrari, K. (1992). Evaluation and treatment of rage in children and adolescents. *Child Psychiatry and Human Development, 22,* 227–235.

171. Martlew, M. (1992). Handwriting and spelling: Dyslexic children's abilities compared with children of the same chronological age and younger children of the same spelling level. *British Journal of Educational Psychology, 62,* 375–390.

172. McElreath, L. H., & Roberts, M. C. (1992). Perceptions of Acquired Immune Deficiency Syndrome by children and their parents. *Journal of Pediatric Psychology, 17,* 477–490.

173. Milling, L. M., Campbell, N. B., Bush, E., & Laughlin, A. (1992). The relationship of suicidality and psychiatric diagnosis in hospitalized pre-adolescent children. *Child Psychiatry and Human Development, 23,* 41–49.

174. Morris-Friehe, M. J., & Sanger, D. D. (1992). Language samples using three story elicitation tasks and maturation effects. *Journal of Communication Disorders, 25,* 107–124.

175. Nass, R., Sadler, A. E., & Sidtis, J. J. (1992). Differential effects of congenital versus acquired unilateral brain injury on dichotic listening performance: Evidence for sparing and asymmetric crowding. *Neurology, 42,* 1960–1965.

176. Natsopoulos, D., Kiosseoglou, G., & Xeromeritou, A. (1992). Handedness and spatial ability in children: Further support for Geschwind's hypothesis of "pathology of superiority" and for Annett's theory of intelligence. *Genetic Psychology Monographs, 118,* 103–126.

177. Pennington, B. F., Gilger, J. W., Olson, R. K., & DeFries, J. C. (1992). The external validity of age- versus IQ-discrepancy definitions of reading disability: Lessons from a twin study. *Journal of Learning Disabilities, 25,* 562–573.

178. Prichard, S., & Epting, F. C. (1992). Children and death: New horizons in theory and measurement. *Omega, 24,* 271–274.

179. Rabiner, D. L., & Gordon, L. V. (1992). The coordination of conflicting social goals: Differences between rejected and nonrejected boys. *Child Development, 63,* 1344–1350.

180. Shaywitz, B. A., Fletcher, J. M., Holahan, J. M., & Shaywitz, S. E. (1992). Discrepancy compared to low achievement definitions of reading disability: Results from the Connecticut longitudinal study. *Journal of Learning Disabilities, 25,* 639–648.

181. Siegel, L. S. (1992). An evaluation of the discrepancy definition of dyslexia. *Journal of Learning Disabilities, 25,* 618–629.

182. Sinclair, E., & Alexson, J. (1992). Special education placements of language disordered children in a psychiatric population. *Child Psychiatry and Human Development, 23,* 131–143.

183. Soltys, S. M., Kashani, J. H., Dandoy, A. C., Vaidya, A. F., & Reid, J. C. (1992). Comorbidity for disruptive behavior disorders in psychiatrically hospitalized children. *Child Psychiatry and Human Development, 23,* 87-98.

184. Swanson, H. L., & Ramalgia, J. M. (1992). The relationship between phonological codes on memory and spelling tasks for students with and without learning disabilities. *Journal of Learning Disabilities, 25,* 396–407.

185. Taylor, H. G., & Schatschneider, C. (1992). Academic achievement following childhood brain disease: Implications for the concept of learning disabilities. *Journal of Learning Disabilities, 25,* 630–638.

186. Walsh, A. (1992). The P>V sign in corrections: Is it a useful diagnostic tool? *Criminal Justice and Behavior, 19,* 372–383.

187. Williams, D. L., Gridley, B. E., & Fitzhugh-Bell, K. (1992). Cluster analysis of children and adolescents with brain damage and learning disabilities using neuropsychological, psychoeducational, and sociobehavioral variables. *Journal of Learning Disabilities, 25,* 290–299.

188. Yirmiya, N., Sigman, M. D., Kasari, C., & Mundy, P. (1992). Empathy and cognition in high-functioning children with autism. *Child Development, 63,* 150–160.

189. Yoshinaga-Itano, C., & Ruberry, J. (1992). The Colorado Individual Performance profile for Hearing-Impaired Students: A data-driven approach to decision making. *Volta Review, 94,* 159–187.

190. Ackerman, P. T., & Dykman, R. A. (1993). Phonological processes, confrontational naming, and immediate memory in dsylexia. *Journal of Learning Disabilities, 26,* 597–609.

191. Aram, D. M., Morris, R., & Hall, N. E. (1993). Clinical and research congruence in identifying children with specific language impairment. *Journal of Speech and Hearing Research, 36,* 580–591.

192. Brown, R. T., Armstrong, F. D., & Eckman, J. R. (1993). Neurocognitive aspects of pediatric sickle cell disease. *Journal of Learning Disabilities, 26,* 33–45.

193. Carvajal, H., Hayes, J. E., Miller, H. R., Wiebe, D. A., & Weaver, K. A. (1993). Comparisons of the vocabulary scores and IQs on the Wechsler Intelligence Scale for Children—III and the Peabody Picture Vocabulary Test—Revised. *Perceptual and Motor Skills, 76,* 28–30.

194. Catts, H. W. (1993). The relationship between speech-language impairments and reading disabilities. *Journal of Speech and Hearing Research, 36,* 948–958.

195. Celano, M. P., & Geller, R. J. (1993). Learning, school, performance, and children with asthma: How much at risk? *Journal of Learning Disabilities, 26,* 23–32.

196. Dautrich, B. R. (1993). Visual perceptual differences in the dyslexic reader: Evidence of greater visual peripheral sensitivity to color and letter stimuli. *Perceptual and Motor Skills, 76,* 755–764.

197. de Jong, P. F. (1993). The relationship between students' behaviour at home and attention and achievement in elementary school. *British Journal of Educational Psychology, 63,* 201–213.

198. Delgado-Hachey, M., & Miller, S. A. (1993). Mothers' accuracy in predicting their children's IQs: Its relationship to antecedent variables, mothers' academic achievement demands, and children's achievement. *Journal of Experimental Education, 62,* 43–59.

199. Dennis, M., & Barnes, M. A. (1993). Oral discourse after early-onset hydrocephalus: Linguistic ambiguity, figurative language, speech acts, and script-based inferences. *Journal of Pediatric Psychology, 18,* 639–652.

200. Ducharme, J. M., & Popynick, M. (1993). Errorless compliance to parental requests: Treatment effects and generalization. *Behavior Therapy, 24,* 209–226.

201. Elliot, L. L., & Hammer, M. A. (1993). Fine-grained auditory discrimination: Factor structures. *Journal of Speech and Hearing Research, 36,* 396–409.

202. Graham, S., Schwartz, S. S., & MacArthur, C. A. (1993). Knowledge of writing and the composing process, attitude toward writing, and self-efficacy for students with and without learning disabilities. *Journal of Learning Disabilities, 26,* 237–249.

203. Hill, L. R., Klauber, M. R., Salmon, D. P., Yu, E. S. H., Liu, W.T., Zhang, M., & Katzman, R. (1993). Functional status,education, and the diagnosis of dementia in the Shanghai survey. *Neurology, 43,* 138–145.

204. Hsieh, S-L. J., & Tori, C. D. (1993). Neuropsychological and cognitive effects of Chinese language instruction. *Perceptual and Motor Skills, 77,* 1071–1081.

205. Humphries, T., & Bone, J. (1993). Use of IQ criteria for evaluating the uniqueness of the learning disability profile. *Journal of Learning Disabilities, 26,* 348–351.

206. Kamann, M. P., & Wong, B. Y. L. (1993). Inducing adaptive coping self-statements in children with learning disabilities through self-instruction training. *Journal of Learning Disabilities, 26,* 630–638.

207. Kaplan, B. J., Polatajko, H. J. Wilson, B. N., & Faris, P. D. (1993). Reexamination of sensory integration treatment: A combination of two efficacy studies. *Journal of Learning Disabilities, 26,* 342–347.

208. Katz, L. Goldstein, G., Rudisin, S., & Bailey, D. (1993). A neuropsychological approach to the Bannatyne recategorization of the Wechsler Intelligence Scales in adults with learning disabilities. *Journal of Learning Disabilities, 26,* 65–72.

209. Katzman, R. (1993). Education and the prevalence of dementia and Alzheimer's disease. *Neurology, 43,* 13–20.

210. Kearney, C. A., & Drabman, R. S. (1993). The write-say method for improving spelling accuracy in children with learning disabilities. *Journal of Learning Disabilities, 26,* 52–56.

211. Kline, R. B., Snyder, J., Guilmette, S., & Castellanos, M. (1993). External validity of the profile variability index for the K-ABC, Stanford-Binet, and WISC-R: Another cul-de-sac. *Journal of Learning Disabilities 26,* 557–567.

212. Koscinski, S. T., & Gast, D. L. (1993). Use of constant time delay in teaching multiplication facts to students with learning disabilities. *Journal of Learning Disabilities, 26,* 533–544.

213. Labbé, E. E., Delaney, D., Olson, K., & Hickman, H. (1993). Skim-temperature biofeedback training: Cognitive and developmental factors in a non-clinical child population. *Perceptual and Motor Skills, 76,* 955–962.

214. Lis, A., & Magro, T. (1993). Study of Longeot's test of formal operational thinking in a group of Italian adolescents. *Perceptual and Motor Skills, 76,* 739–752.

215. Little, S. S. (1993). Nonverbal learning disabilities and socioemotional functioning: A review of recent literature. *Journal of Learning Disabilities, 26,* 653–665.

216. MacMillan, D. L., Gresham, F. M., & Siperstein, G. N. (1993). Conceptual and psychometric concerns about the 1992 AAMR definition of mental retardation. *American Journal on Mental Retardation, 98,* 325–335.

217. Moore, L. W., Sweeney, J. J., & Butterfield, P. H. (1993). Differential effects of primary activity and computer reinforcement on decreasing the off-task behavior of three special education populations. *Journal of Instructional Psychology, 20,* 132–144.

218. Mulhern, R. K., Carpentieri, S., Slema, S., Stone, P., & Fairclough, D. (1993). Factors associated with social and behavioral problems among children recently diagnosed with brain tumor. *Journal of Pediatric Psychology, 18,* 339–350.

219. Newman, S., Fields, H., & Wright, S. (1993). A developmental study of specific spelling disability. *British Journal of Educational Psychology, 63,* 287–296.

220. Risser, M. G., & Bowers, T. G. (1993). Cognitive and neuropsychological characteristics of attention deficit hyperactivity disorder children receiving stimulant medications. *Perceptual and Motor Skills, 77,* 1023–1031.

221. Rourke, B. P. (1993). Arithmetic disabilities, specific and otherwise: A neuropsychological perspective. *Journal of Learning Disabilities, 26,* 214–226.

222. Rovet, J. F. (1993). The psychoeducational characteristics of children with Turner syndrome. *Journal of Learning Disabilities, 26,* 333–341.

223. Shalev, R. S., & Gross-Tsur, V. (1993). Developmental dyscalculia and medical assessment. *Journal of Learning Disabilities, 26,* 134–137.

224. Szajnberg, M. D., Krall, V. K., Davis, P., Treem, W., & Hyams, J. (1993). Psychopathology and relationship measures in children with inflammatory bowel disease and their parents. *Child Psychiatry and Human Development, 23,* 215–232.

225. Tirosh, E., & Canby, J. (1993). Autism with hyperlexia: A distinct syndrome? *American Journal on Mental Retardation, 98,* 84–92.

226. Vaughn, S., Schumm, J. S., & Gordon, J. (1993). Which motoric condition is most effective for teaching spelling to students with and without learning disabilities? *Journal of Learning Disabilities, 26,* 191–198.

227. Vaughn, S., Zaragoza, N., Hogan, A., & Walker, J. (1993). A four-year longitudinal investigation of the social skills and behavior problems of students with learning disabilities. *Journal of Learning Disabilities, 26,* 404–412.

228. Wadsworth, S. J., DeFries, J. C., & Fulker, D. W. (1993). Cognitive abilities of children at 7 and 12 years of age in the Colorado Adoption Project. *Journal of Learning Disabilities, 26,* 611–615.

229. Williams, J., Zolten, A. J., Rickert, V. I., Spence, G. T., & Ashcraft, E. W. (1993). Use of nonverbal tests to screen for writing dysfluency in school-age children. *Perceptual and Motor Skills, 76,* 803–809.

230. Zimet, S. G., & Farley, G. K. (1993). Academic achievement of children with emotional disorders treated in a day hospital program: An outcome study. *Child Psychiatry and Human Development, 23,* 183–202.

231. Ackerman, P. T., Dykman, R. A., Oglesby, D. M., & Newton, J. E. O. (1994). EEG power spectra of children with dyslexia, slow learners, and normally reading children with ADD during verbal processing. *Journal of Learning Disabilities, 27,* 619–630.

232. Aram, D. M., & Eisele, J. A. (1994). Intellectual stability in children with unilateral brain lesions. *Neuropsychologia, 32,* 85–95.

233. Asarnow, J. R., Tompson, M. C., & Goldstein, M. J. (1994). Childhood-onset schizophrenia: A follow-up study. *Schizophrenia Bulletin, 20,* 599–617.

234. Asarnow, R. F., Asamen, J., Granholm, E., Sherman, T., Watkins, J. M., & Williams, M. E. (1994). Cognitive/neuropsychological studies of children with a schizophrenic disorder. *Schizophrenia Bulletin, 20,* 647–669.

235. Bellaire, S., Plante, E., & Swisher, L. (1994). Bound-morpheme skills in the oral language of school-age, language-impaired children. *Journal of Communication Disorders, 27,* 265–279.

236. Blachman, B. A. (1994). What we have learned from longitudinal studies of phonological processing and reading, and some unanswered questions: A response to Torgesen, Wagner, and Rashotte. *Journal of Learning Disabilities, 27,* 287–291.

237. Borzone de Manrique, A., & Signorini, A. (1994). Phonological awareness, spelling and reading abilities in Spanish-speaking children. *British Journal of Educational Psychology, 64,* 429–439.

238. Brody, G. H., Stoneman, Z., Flor, D., McCrary, C., Hastings, L., & Conyers, O. (1994). Financial resources, parent psychological functioning, parent co-caregiving, and early adolescent competence in rural two-parent African-American families. *Child Development, 65,* 590–605.

239. Butler, R., & Marinor-Glassman, D. (1994). The effects of educational placement and grade level on the self-perceptions of low achievers and students with learning disabilities. *Journal of Learning Disabilities, 27,* 325–334.

240. Campbell, F. A., & Ramey, C. T. (1994). Effects of early intervention on intellectual and academic achievement: A follow-up study of children from low income families. *Child Development, 65,* 684–698.

241. Caplan, R. (1994). Communication deficits in childhood schizophrenia spectrum disorders. *Schizophrenia Bulletin, 20,* 671–683.

242. Chovan, W., & Benfield, J. R., Jr. (1994). Varied sign language stystems and their mediating effects on the WISC-R verbal subtests of profoundly deaf students: A replication. *Perceptual and Motor Skills, 78,* 61–62.

243. Cohen, M. J., Branch, W. B., & Hynd, G. W. (1994). Receptive prosody in children with left or right hemisphere dysfunction. *Brain and Language, 47,* 171–181.

244. Cole, K. N., Mills, P. E., & Kelley, D. (1994). Agreement of assessment profiles used in cognitive referencing. *Language, Speech, and Hearing Services in Schools, 25,* 25–31.

245. D'Amato, R. C., Lidiak, S. E., & Lassiter, K. S. (1994). Comparing verbal and nonverbal intellectual functioning with the TONI and WISC-R. *Perceptual and Motor Skills, 78,* 701–702.

246. Dagenais, P. A., Critz-Crosby, P., Fletcher, S. G., & McCutcheon, M. J. (1994). Comparing abilities of children with profound hearing impairments to learn consonants using electropalatography or traditional aural-oral techniques. *Journal of Speech and Hearing Research, 37,* 687–699.

247. Durlak, C. M., Rose, E., & Bursuck, W. D. (1994). Preparing high school students with learning disabilities for the transition to post-secondary education: Teaching the skills of self-determination. *Journal of Learning Disabilities, 27,* 51–59.

248. Eisele, J. A., & Aram, D. M. (1994). Comprehension and imitation of syntax following early hemisphere damage. *Brain and Language, 46,* 212–231.

249. Elfenbein, J. L., Hardin-Jones, M. A., & Davis, J. M. (1994). Oral communication skills of children who are hard of hearing. *Journal of Speech and Hearing Research, 37,* 216–226.

250. Erlenmeyer-Kimling, L., Cornblatt, B. A., Rock, D., Roberts, S., Bell, M., & West, A. (1994). The New York high-risk project: Anhedonia, attentional deviance, and psychopathology. *Schizophrenia Bulletin, 20,* 141–153.

251. Fawcett, A. J., & Nicolson, R. I. (1994). Naming speed in children with dyslexia. *Journal of Learning Disabilities, 27,* 641–646.

252. Felsenfeld, S., Broen, P. A., & McGue, M. (1994). A 28-year follow-up of adults with a history of moderate phonological disorder: Educational and occupational results. *Journal of Speech and Hearing, 37,* 1341–1353.

253. Fergusson, D. M., Horwood, L. J., & Lynskey, M. T. (1994). A longitudinal study of early childhood education and subsequent academic achievement. *Australian Psychologist, 29,* 110–115.

254. Flanagan, D. P., Alfonso, V. C., & Flanagan, R. (1994). A review of the Kaufman Adolescent and Adult Intelligence Test: An advancement in cognitive assessment? *School Psychology Review, 23,* 512–525.

255. Fletcher, J., & Martinez, G. (1994). An eye-movement analysis of the effects of scotopic sensitivity correction on parsing and comprehension. *Journal of Learning Disabilities, 27,* 67–70.
256. Fox, E. (1994). Grapheme-phoneme correspondence in dyslexic and matched control readers. *British Journal of Psychology, 85,* 41–53.
257. Frith U., & Happé, F. (1994). Autism: Beyond "theory of mind." *Cognition, 50,* 115–132.
258. García-Vázquez, E., & Ehly, S. W. (1994). Acculturation and intelligence: Effects of acculturation on problem-solving. *Perceptual and Motor Skills, 78,* 501–502.
259. Gaskins, I. W., Guthrie, J. T., Satlow, E., Ostertag, J., Six, L., Byrne, J., & Connor, B. (1994). Integrating instruction of science, reading, and writing: Goals, teacher development, and assessment. *Journal of Research in Science Teaching, 31,* 1039–1056.
260. Geers, A., & Moog, J. (1994). Description of the CID sensory aids study. *Volta Review, 96,* 1–11.
261. Ghaziuddin, M., Butler, E., Tsai, L., & Ghaziuddin, N. (1994). Is clumsiness a marker for Asperger syndrome? *Journal of Intellectual Disability Research, 38,* 519–527.
262. Glez, J. E. J., & Lopez, M. R. (1994). Is it true that the differences in reading performance between students with and without LD cannot be explained by IQ? *Journal of Learning Disabilities, 27,* 155–163.
263. Glutting, J. J., McDermott, P. A., Prifitera, A., & McGrath, E. A. (1994). Core profile types for the WISC-III and WIAT: Their development and application in identifying multivariate IQ-achievement discrepancies. *School Psychology Review, 23,* 619–639.
264. Gordon, M., Mettelmen, B. B., & Irwin, M. (1994). Sustained attention and grade retention. *Perceptual and Motor Skills, 78,* 555–560.
265. Grantham-McGregor, S., Powell, C., Walker, S., Chang, S., & Fletcher, P. (1994). The long-term follow-up of severely malnourished children who participated in an intervention program. *Child Development, 65,* 428–439.
266. Herrero, M. E., Hechtman, L., & Weiss, G. (1994). Antisocial disorders in hyperactive subjects from childhood to adulthood: Predictive factors and characterization of subgroups. *American Journal of Orthopsychiatry, 64,* 510–521.
267. Hoehn, T. P., & Baumeister, A. A. (1994). A critique of the application of sensory integration therapy to children with learning disabilities. *Journal of Learning Disabilities, 27,* 338–350.
268. Korkman, M., & Häkkinen-Rihu, P. (1994). A new classification of developmental language disorders (DLD). *Brain and Language, 47,* 96–116.
269. Korkman, M., & Pesonen, A. (1994). A comparison of neuropsychological test profiles of children with attention deficit-hyperactivity disorder and/or learning disorder. *Journal of Learning Disabilities, 27,* 383–392.
270. Lamm, O., & Epstein, R. (1994). Dichotic listening performance under high and low lexical work load in subtypes of developmental dyslexia. *Neuropsychologia, 32,* 757–785.
271. Lee, C. P., & Obrzut, J. E. (1994). Taxonomic clustering and frequency associations as features of semantic memory development in children with learning disabilities. *Journal of Learning Disabilities, 27,* 454–462.
272. Levy-Shiff, R., Einat, G., Mogilner, M. B., Lerman, M., & Krikler, R. (1994). Biological and environmental correlates of developmental outcome of prematurely born infants in early adolescence. *Journal of Pediatric Psychology, 19,* 63–78.
273. Lewandowski, L., & Arcangelo, K. C. (1994). The social adjustment and self-concept of adults with learning disabilities. *Journal of Learning Disabilities, 27,* 598–605.
274. Loveland, K. A., Stehbens, J., Constant, C., Bordeaux, J. D., Sirois, P., Bell, T. S., & Hill, S. (1994). Hemophilia growth and development study: Baseline neurodevelopmental findings. *Journal of Pediatric Psychology, 19,* 223–239.
275. Lyytinen, P., Rasku-Puttonen, H., Poikkeus, A., Laakso, M., & Ahonen, T. (1994). Mother-child teaching strategies and learning disabilities. *Journal of Learning Disabilities, 27,* 186–192.
276. Maag, J. W., Irvin, D. M., Reid, R., & Vasa, S. F. (1994). Prevalence and predictors of substance use: A comparison between adolescents with and without learning disabilities. *Journal of Learning Disabilities, 27,* 223–234.
277. Masutto, C., Bravar, L., & Fabbro, F. (1994). Neurolinguistic differentiation of children with subtypes of dyslexia. *Journal of Learning Disabilities, 27,* 520–526.
278. Minder, B., Das-Smaal, E. A., Brand, E. F. J. M., & Orlebeke, J. F. (1994). Exposure to lead and specific attentional problems in school children. *Journal of Learning Disabilities, 27,* 393–399.
279. Moss, H. A., Browers, P., Wolters, P. L., Wiener, L., Hersh, S., & Pizzo, P. A. (1994). The development of a Q-Sort behavioral rating procedure for pediatric HIV patients. *Journal of Pediatric Psychology, 19,* 27–46.
280. North, K., Joy, P., Yuille, D., Cocks, N., Mobb, E., Hutchins, P., McHugh, K., & deSilva, M. (1994). Specific learning disability in children with neurofibromatosis type 1: Significance of MRI abnormalities. *Neurology, 44,* 878–883.
281. Orbach, I., Weiner, M., Har-Even, D., & Eshel, Y. (1994). Children's perceptions of death and interpersonal closeness to the dead person. *Omega, 30,* 1–12.
282. Pintrich, P. R., Anderman, E. M., & Klobucar, C. (1994). Intraindividual differences in motivation and cognition in students with and without learning disabilities. *Journal of Learning Disabilities, 27,* 360–370.
283. Piven, J., Wzorek, M., Landa, R., Lainhart, J., Bolton, P., Chase, G. A., & Folstein, S. (1994). Personality characteristics of the parents of autistic individuals. *Psychological Medicine, 24,* 783–795.
284. Records, N. L., & Tomblin, J. B. (1994). Clinical decision making: Describing the decision rules of practicing speech-language pathologists. *Journal of Speech and Hearing Research, 37,* 144–156.
285. Reid, R., Maag, J. W., Vasa, S. F., & Wright, G. (1994). Who are the children with attention deficit-hyperactivity disorder? A school-based survey. *The Journal of Special Education, 28,* 117–137.
286. Roberts, J. E., Burchinal, M. R., & Campbell, F. (1994). Otitis media in early childhood and patterns of intellectual development and later academic performance. *Journal of Pediatric Psychology, 19,* 347–367.
287. Rochon, E., & Waters, G. S. (1994). Sentence comprehension in patients with Alzheimer's disease. *Brain and Language, 46,* 329–349.
288. Russell, A. T. (1994). The clinical presentation of childhood-onset schizophrenia. *Schizophrenia Bulletin, 20,* 631–646.
289. Sadeh, A., Hayden, R. M., McGuire, J. P. D., Sachs, H., & Civita, R. (1994). Somatic, cognitive and emotional characteristics of abused children in a psychiatric hospital. *Child Psychiatry and Human Development, 24,* 191–200.
290. Sampson, R. J., & Laub, J. H. (1994). Urban poverty and the family context of delinquency: A new look at structure and process in a classic study. *Child Development, 65,* 523–540.
291. Shapiro, E. G., Lockman, L. A., Knopman, D., & Krivit, W. (1994). Characteristics of the dementia in late-onset metachromatic leukodystrophy. *Neurology, 44,* 662–665.
292. Sikora, D. M., & Plapinger, D. S. (1994). Using standardized tests to identify learning disabilities in students with sensorineural hearing impairments. *Journal of Learning Disabilities, 27,* 352–359.
293. Spencer, E. K., & Campbell, M. (1994). Children with schizophrenia: Diagnosis, phenomenology, and pharmacotherapy. *Schizophrenia Bulletin, 20,* 713–725.
294. Trammel, D. L. Schloss, P. J., & Alper, S. (1994). Using self-recording, evaluation, and graphing to increase completion of homework assignments. *Journal of Learning Disabilities, 27,* 75–81.
295. Vaughn, S., & Hogan, A. (1994). The social competence of students with learning disabilities over time: A within-individual examination. *Journal of Learning Disabilities, 27,* 292–303.
296. Watkins, M. W., & Kush, J. C. (1994). Wechsler subtest analysis: The right way, the wrong way, or no way? *School Psychology Review, 23,* 640–651.
297. Wolters, P. L., Brouwers, P., Moss, H. A., & Pizzo, P. A. (1994). Adaptive behavior of children with symptomatic HIV infection before and after zidovudine therapy. *Journal of Pediatric Psychology, 19,* 47–61.
298. Yates, B. T., Hecht-Lewis, R., Fritsch, R. C., & Goodrich, W. (1994). Locus of control in severely disturbed adolescents: loci for peers, parents, achievement, relationships, and problems. *Journal of Youth and Adolescence, 23,* 289–314.
299. Young, D. W., & Childs, N. A. (1994). Family images of hospitalized adolescents: The failure to generate shared understandings. *Psychiatry, 57,* 258–267.
300. Abrahamsen, E. P., & Sprouse, P. T. (1995). Fable comprehension by children with learning disabilities. *Journal of Learning Disabilities, 28,* 302–308.
301. Ackerman, P. T., Dykman, R. A., Oglesby, D. M., & Newton, J. E. O. (1995). EEG power spectra of dysphonetic and nondysphonetic poor readers. *Brain and Language, 49,* 140–152.
302. Allen, S. R., & Thorndike, R. M. (1995). Stability of the WAIS-R and WISC-III factor structure using cross-validation of covariance structures. *Journal of Clinical Psychology, 51,* 648–657.
303. Arehole, S., Augustine, L. E., & Simhadri, R. (1995). Middle latency response in children with learning disabilities: Preliminary findings. *Journal of Communication Disorders, 28,* 21–38.
304. Baker, J. M. (1995). Inclusion in Minnesota: Educational experiences of students with learning disabilities in two elementary schools. *The Journal of Special Education, 29,* 133–143.
305. Baker, J. M. (1995). Inclusion in Virginia: Educational experiences of students with learning disabilities in one elementary school. *The Journal of Special Education, 29,* 116–123.
306. Baker, J. M. (1995). Inclusion in Washington: Educational experiences of students with learning disabilities in one elementary school. *The Journal of Special Education, 29,* 155–162.
307. Banerji, M., & Dailey, R. A. (1995). A study of the effects of an inclusion model on students with specific learning disabilities. *Journal of Learning Disabilities, 28,* 511–522.
308. Biederman, J., Milberger, S., Faraone, S. V., Kiely, K., Guite, J., Mick, E., Ablon, S., Warburton, R., & Reed, E. (1995). Family-environment risk factors for attention-deficit hyperactivity disorder: A test of Rotter's indicators of adversity. *Archives of General Psychiatry, 52,* 464–470.
309. Biederman, J., Milberger, S., Faraone, S. V., Lapey, K. A., Reed, E. D., & Seidman, L. J. (1995). No confirmation of Geschwind's hypothesis of associations between reading disability, immune disorders, and motor preference in ADHD. *Journal of Abnormal Child Psychology, 23,* 545–552.
310. Biederman, J., Santangelo, S. L., Faraone, S. V., Kiely, K., Guite, J., Mick, E., Reed, E. D., Kraus, I., Jellinek, M., & Perrin, J. (1995). Clinical correlates of enuresis in ADHD and non-ADHD children. *Journal of Child Psychology and Psychiatry and Allied Disciplines, 36,* 865–877.
311. Bird, J., Bishop, D. V. M., & Freeman, N. H. (1995). Phonological awareness and literacy development in children with expressive phonological impairments. *Journal of Speech and Hearing Research, 38,* 446–462.
312. Black, K. C., & Hynd, G. W. (1995). Epilepsy in the school aged child: Cognitive-behavioral characteristics and effects on academic performance. *School Psychology Quarterly, 10,* 345–358.
313. Bluechardt, M. H., & Shephard, R. J. (1995). Using an extracurricular physical activity program to enhance social skills. *Journal of Learning Disabilities, 28,* 160–169.
314. Bowey, J. A. (1995). Socioeconomic status differences in preschool phonological sensitivity and first-grade reading achievement. *Journal of Educational Psychology, 87,* 476–487.

315. Branch, W. B., Cohen, M. J., & Hynd, G. W. (1995). Academic achievement and attention-deficit/hyperactivity disorder in children with left- or right-hemisphere dysfunction. *Journal of Learning Disabilities, 28,* 35–43, 64.
316. Brigham, F. J., Scruggs, T. E., & Mastropieri, M. A. (1995). Elaborative maps for enhanced learning of historical information: Uniting spatial, verbal, and imaginal information. *The Journal of Special Education, 28,* 440–460.
317. Brookshire, B. L., Fletcher, J. M., Bohan, T. P., Landry, S. H., Davidson, K. C., & Francis, D. J. (1995). Verbal and nonverbal skill discrepancies in children with hydrocephalus: A five-year longitudinal follow-up. *Journal of Pediatric Psychology, 20,* 785–800.
318. Butler, D. L. (1995). Promoting strategic learning by postsecondary students with learning disabilities. *Journal of Learning Disabilities, 28,* 170–190.
319. Campbell, F. A., & Ramey, C. T. (1995). Cognitive and school outcomes for high-risk African-American students at middle adolescence: Positive effects of early intervention. *American Educational Research Journal, 32,* 743–772.
320. Chamrad, D. L., Robinson, N. M., & Junos, P. M. (1995). Consequences of having a gifted sibling: Myths and realities. *Gifted Child Quarterly, 39,* 135–145.
321. Charebois, P., LeBlanc, M., Tremblay, R. E., Gagnon, C., & Larivée, S. (1995). Teacher, mother, and peer support in the elementary school as protective factors against juvenile delinquency. *International Journal of Behavioral Development, 18,* 1–22.
322. Claude, D., & Firestone, P. (1995). The development of ADHD boys: A 12-year follow-up. *Canadian Journal of Behavioural Science, 27,* 226–249.
323. Cornoldi, C., Vecchia, R. D., & Tressoldi, P. E. (1995). Visuo-spatial working memory limitations in low visuo-spatial high verbal intelligence children. *Journal of Child Psychology and Psychiatry, 36,* 1053–1064.
324. Curfs, L. M. G., Hoondert, V., van Lieshout, C. F. M., & Fryns, J. P. (1995). Personality profiles of youngsters with Prader-Willis syndrome and youngsters attending regular schools. *Journal of Intellectual Disability Research, 39,* 241–248.
325. DeVos, K. J., Wyllie, E., Geckler, C., Kotagal, P., & Comair, Y. (1995). Language dominance in patients with early childhood tumors near left hemisphere language areas. *Neurology, 45,* 349–356.
326. Donders, J. (1995). Validity of the Kaufman Brief Intelligence Test (K-BIT) in children with traumatic brain injury. *Assessment, 2,* 219–224.
327. Duncan, R. D., Kennedy, W. A., & Patrick, C. J. (1995). Four-factor model of recidivism in male juvenile offenders. *Journal of Clinical Child Psychology, 24,* 250–257.
328. Dunlap, G., Clarke, S., Jackson, M., Wright, S., Ramos, E., & Brinson, S. (1995). Self-monitoring of classroom behaviors with students exhibiting emotional and behavioral challenges. *School Psychology Quarterly, 10,* 165–177.
329. Duvelleroy-Hommet, C., Gillet, P., Billard, C., Loisel, M. L., Barthez, M. A., Santini, J. J., & Autret, A. (1995). Study of unilateral hemisphere performance in children with developmental dysphasia. *Neuropsychologia, 33,* 823–834.
330. Eckert, T. L., Shapiro, E. S., & Lutz, J. G. (1995). Teachers' ratings of the acceptability of curriculum-based assessment methods. *School Psychology Review, 24,* 497–511.
331. Eden, G. F., Stein, J. F., Wood, H. M., & Wood, F. B. (1995). Temporal and spatial processing in reading disabled and normal children. *Cortex, 31,* 451–468.
332. Eden, G. F., Stein, J. F., Wood, M. H., & Wood, F. B. (1995). Verbal and visual problems in reading disability. *Journal of Learning Disabilities, 28,* 272–290.
333. Evans, J. H., Ferre, L., Ford, L. A., & Green, J. L. (1995). Decreasing Attention Deficit Hyperactivity Disorder symptoms utilizing an automated classroom reinforcement device. *Psychology in the Schools, 32,* 210–219.
334. Felsenfeld, S., McGue, M., & Broen, P. A. (1995). Familial aggregation of phonological disorders: Results from a 28-year follow-up. *Journal of Speech and Hearing Research, 38,* 1091–1107.
335. Flannery, K. A., & Liederman, J. (1995). Is there really a syndrome involving the co-occurrence of neurodevelopmental disorder, talent, non-right handedness and immune disorder among children? *Cortex, 31,* 503–515.
336. Fonseca, A. C., & Yule, W. (1995). Personality and antisocial behavior in children and adolescents: An enquiry into Eysenck's and Gray's theories. *Journal of Abnormal Child Psychology, 23,* 767–781.
337. Fuller, M., & McLeod, P. J. (1995). Judgments of control over a contingently responsive animation by students with and without learning disabilities. *Canadian Journal of Behavioural Science, 27,* 171–186.
338. Gadow, K. D., Sverd, J., Sprafkin, J., Nolan, E. E., & Ezor, S. N. (1995). Efficacy of methylphenidate for attention-deficit hyperactivity disorder in children with tic disorder. *Archives of General Psychiatry, 52,* 444–455.
339. Ghaziuddin, M., Leininger, L., & Tsai, L. (1995). Brief report: Thought disorder in Asperger syndrome: Comparison with high-functioning autism. *Journal of Autism and Developmental Disorders, 25,* 311–317.
340. Gibson, L., Glynn, S. M., Takahashi, T., & Britton, B. K. (1995). Imagery and the prose recall of mildly retarded children. *Contemporary Educational Psychology, 20,* 476–482.
341. Giddan, J. J., Wahl, J., & Brogan, M. (1995). Importance of communication training for psychiatric residents and mental health trainees. *Child Psychiatry and Human Development, 26,* 19–28.
342. Gillam, R. B., Cowan, N., & Day, L. S. (1995). Sequential memory in children with and without language impairment. *Journal of Speech and Hearing Research, 38,* 393–402.
343. Gjerde, P. F. (1995). Alternative pathways to chronic depressive symptoms in young adults: Gender differences in developmental trajectories. *Child Development, 66,* 1277–1300.
344. Goldfarb, L. P., Plante, T. G., Brentar, J. T., & DiGregorio, M. (1995). Administering the digit span subtest of the WISC–III: Should the examiner make eye contact or not? *Assessment, 2,* 313–318.
345. Greenbaum, B., Graha, S., & Scales, W. (1995). Adults with learning disabilities: Educational and social experiences during college. *Exceptional Children, 61,* 460–471.
346. Gross-Tsur, V., Shaleu, R. S., Manor, O., & Amir, N. (1995). Developmental right-hemisphere syndrome: Clinical spectrum of the nonverbal learning disability. *Journal of Learning Disabilities, 28,* 80–86.
347. Hannan, C. L., & Shore, B. M. (1995). Metacognition and high intellectual ability: Insights from the study of learning-disabled gifted students. *Gifted Child Quarterly, 39,* 95.
348. Hart, E. L., Lahey, B. B., Loeber, R., Applegate, B., & Frick, P. J. (1995). Developmental change in Attention-Deficit Hyperactivity Disorder in boys: A four-year longitudinal study. *Journal of Abnormal Child Psychology, 23,* 729–749.
349. Hishinuma, E. S. (1995). WISC-III accommodations: The need for practitioner guidelines. *Journal of Learning Disabilities, 28,* 130–135.
350. Hogg, J., & Moss, S. (1995). The applicability of the Kaufman Assessment Battery for Children with older adults (50+ years) with moderate, severe and profound intellectual impairment. *Journal of Intellectual Disability Research, 39,* 167–176.
351. Holmbeck, G. N., & Faier-Routman, J. (1995). Spinal lesion level, shunt status, family relationships, and psychosocial adjustment in children and adolescents with spina bifida myelomeningocele. *Journal of Pediatric Psychology, 20,* 817–832.
352. Holmes, C. S., O'Brien, B., & Greer, T. (1995). Cognitive functioning and academic achievement in children with insulin-dependent diabetes mellitus (IDDM). *School Psychology Quarterly, 10,* 329–345.
353. Holtz, B. A., & Lehman, E. B. (1995). Development of children's knowledge and use of strategies for self-control in a resistance-to-distraction task. *Merrill-Palmer Quarterly, 41,* 361–380.
354. Hugdahl, K., Helland, T., Faerevaag, M. K., Lyssand, E. T., & Asbjornsen, A. (1995). Absence of ear advantage on the consonant-vowel dichotic listening test in adolescent and adult dyslexics: Specific auditory-phonetic dysfunction. *Journal of Clinical and Experimental Neuropsychology, 17,* 833–840.
355. Karnes, F. A., & McGinnis, J. C. (1995). Self-actualization and locus of control of gifted children in fourth through eighth grades. *Psychological Reports, 76,* 1039–1042.
356. Katusic, S. K., Colligan, R. C., Beard, C. M., O'Fallon, W. M., Bergstralli, E. J., Jacobsen, S. J., & Kurland, L. T. (1995). Mental retardation in a birth cohort, 1976–1980, Rochester, Minnesota. *American Journal on Mental Retardation, 100,* 335–344.
357. Kershner, J. R., & Graham, N. A. (1995). Attentional control over language lateralization in dyslexic children: Deficit or delay? *Neuropsychologia, 33,* 39–51.
358. Kinsella, G., Prior, M., Sawyer, M., Murtagh, D., Eisenmajer, R., Anderson, J., Bryan, D., & Klug, G. (1995). Neuropsychological deficit and academic performance in children and adolescents following traumatic brain injury. *Journal of Pediatric Psychology, 20,* 753–767.
359. Kokubun, M., Haishi, K., Okuzumi, H., & Hosobuchi, T. (1995). Factors effecting age of walking by children with mental retardation. *Perceptual and Motor Skills, 80,* 547–552.
360. Komori, H., Matsuishi, T., Yamado, S., Yamashita, Y., Ohtaki, E., & Kato, H. (1995). Cerebrospinal fluid biopterin and biogenic amine metabolites during oral R-THBP therapy for infantile autism. *Journal of Autism and Developmental Disorders, 25,* 183–193.
361. Konstantareas, M. M., & Lampropoulou, V. (1995). Stress in Greek mothers with deaf children. *American Annals of the Deaf, 140,* 264–270.
362. Lernhart, L. A., & Rabiner, D. L. (1995). An integrative approach to the study of social competence in adolescence. *Development and Psychopathology, 7,* 543–561.
363. Light, J. G., & DeFries, J. C. (1995). Comorbidity of reading and mathematics disabilities: Genetic and environmental etiologies. *Journal of Learning Disabilities, 8,* 96–106.
364. Lincoln, A. J., Courchesne, E., Harms, L., & Allen, M. (1995). Sensory modulation of auditory stimuli in children with autism and developmental language disorder: Event-related brain potential evidence. *Journal of Autism and Developmental Disorders, 25,* 521–539.
365. Lyon, M. A. (1995). A comparison between WISC-III and WISC-R scores for learning disabilities reevaluations. *Journal of Learning Disabilities, 28,* 253–255.
366. MacArthur, C. A., & Haynes, J. B. (1995). Student assistant for learning from text: A hypermedia reading aid. *Journal of Learning Disabilities, 28,* 150–159.
367. Margalit, M., & Ben-Dov, I. (1995). Learning disabilities and social environments: Kibbutz versus city comparisons of loneliness and social competence. *International Journal of Behavioral Development, 18,* 519–536.
368. McBride, J. A., & Panksepp, J. (1995). An examination of the phenomenology and the reliability of ratings of compulsive behavior in autism. *Journal of Autism and Developmental Disorders, 25,* 381–396.
369. McClellan, J., Adams, J., Douglas, D., McCurry, C., & Storck, M. (1995). Clinical characteristics related to severity of sexual abuse: A study of seriously mentally ill youth. *Child Abuse & Neglect, 19,* 1245–1254.
370. Mirsky, A. F. (1995). Perils and pitfalls of the path to normal potential: The role of impaired attention. Homage to Herbert G. Birch. *Journal of Clinical and Experimental Neuropsychology, 17,* 481–498.
371. Morgan, C. D., Nordin, S., & Murphy, C. (1995). Odor identification as an early marker for Alzheimer's Disease: Impact of lexical functioning and detection sensitivity. *Journal of Clinical and Experimental Neuropsychology, 17,* 793–803.

372. Moss, H. B., Vanyukov, M., Majumder, P. P., Kirisci, L., & Tarter, R. E. (1995). Prepubertal sons of substance abusers: Influences of parental and familial substance abuse on behavioral disposition, IQ, and school achievement. *Addictive Behaviors, 20,* 345–358.

373. Nippold, M. A. (1995). School-age children and adolescents: Norms for word definition. *Language, Speech, and Hearing Services in Schools, 26,* 320–325.

374. Oetting, J. B., Rice, M. L., & Swank, L. K. (1995). Quick incidental learning (QUIL) of words by school-age children with and without SLI. *Journal of Speech and Hearing Research, 38,* 434–445.

375. Olenchak, F. R. (1995). Effects of enrichment on gifted/learning-disabled students. *Journal for the Education of the Gifted, 18,* 385–399.

376. Oram, G. D., Cornell, D. G., & Rutemiller, L. A. (1995). Relations between academic aptitude and psychosocial adjustment in gifted program students. *Gifted Child Quarterly, 39,* 236–244.

377. Overstreet, S., Goins, J., Chen, R. S., Holmes, C. S., Greer, T., Dunlap, W. P., & Frentz, J. (1995). Family environment and the interrelation of family structure, child behavior, and metabolic control for children with diabetes. *Journal of Pediatric Psychology, 20,* 435–447.

378. Paternite, C. E., Loney, J., & Roberts, M. A. (1995). External validation of oppositional disorder and attention deficit disorder with hyperactivity. *Journal of Abnormal Child Psychology, 23,* 453–471.

379. Pau, C. S. (1995). The deaf child and solving problems of arithmetic: The importance of comprehensive reading. *American Annals of the Deaf, 140,* 287–290.

380. Payette, K. A., Clarizio, H. F., Phillips, S. E., & Bennett, D. E. (1995). Effects of simple and regressed discrepancy models and cutoffs on severe discrepancy determination. *Psychology in the Schools, 32,* 93–102.

381. Piven, J., Arndt, S., Bailey, J., Havercamp, S., Andreasen, N. C., & Palmer, P. (1995). An MRI study of brain size in autism. *American Journal of Psychiatry, 152,* 1145–1149.

382. Plapinger, D. S., & Sikora, D. M. (1995). The use of standardized test batteries in assessing the skill development of children with mild-to-moderate sensorineural hearing loss. *Language, Speech, and Hearing Services in Schools, 26,* 39–44.

383. Pletan, M. D. Robinson, N. M., Berringer, V. W., & Abbott, R. D. (1995). Parents' observations of kindergartners who are advanced in mathematical reasoning. *Journal for the Education of the Gifted, 19,* 30–44.

384. Porretta, D. L., & Surburg, P. R. (1995). Imagery and physical practice in the acquisition of gross motor timing of coincidence by adolescents with mild mental retardation. *Perceptual and Motor Skills, 80,* 1171–1183.

385. Qouta, S., Punamäki, R., & Sarraj, E. E. (1995). The relations between traumatic experiences, activity, and cognitive and emotional responses among Palestinian children. *International Journal of Psychology, 30,* 289–304.

386. Rellinger, E., Borkowski, J. G., Turner, L. A., & Hale, C. A. (1995). Perceived task difficulty and intelligence: Determinants of strategy use and recall. *Intelligence, 20,* 125–143.

387. Richards, C. M., Symons, D. K., Greene, C. A., & Szuszkiewicz, T. A. (1995). The bidirectional relationship between achievement and externalizing behavior problems of students with learning disabilities. *Journal of Learning Disabilities, 28,* 8–17.

388. Roberts, J. E., Burchinal, M. R., & Clarke-Klein, S. M. (1995). Otitis media in early childhood and cognitive, academic, and behavior outcomes at 12 years of age. *Journal of Pediatric Psychology, 20,* 645–660.

389. Rose, S. A., & Feldman, J. F. (1995). Prediction of IQ and specific cognitive abilities at 11 years from infancy measures. *Developmental Psychology, 31,* 685–696.

390. Sanders-Phillips, K., Moisan, P. A., Wadlington, S., Morgan, S., & English, K. (1995). Ethnic differences in psychological functioning among Black and Latino sexually abused girls. *Child Abuse & Neglect, 19,* 691–706.

391. Schachar, R., Tannock, R., Marriott, M., & Logan, G. (1995). Deficient inhibitory control in Attention Deficit Hyperactivity Disorder. *Journal of Abnormal Child Psychology, 23,* 411–437.

392. Schloss, P. J., Alper, S., Young, H., Arnold-Reid, G., Aylward, M., & Dudenhoeffer, S. (1995). Acquisition of functional sight words in community-based recreation settings. *The Journal of Special Education, 29,* 84–96.

393. Schuerholz, L. J., Harris, E. L., Baumgardner, T. L., Reiss, A. L., Freund, L. S., Church, R. P., Mohr, J., & Denckla, M. B. (1995). An analysis of two discrepancy-based models and a processing-deficit approach in identifying learning disabilities. *Journal of Learning Disabilities, 28,* 18–29.

394. Seidman, L. J., Benedict, K. B., Biederman, J., Bernstein, J. H., Sewerd, K., Milberger, S., Norman, D., Mick, E., & Faraone, S. V. (1995). Performance of children with ADHD on the Rey-Osterrieth Complex Figure: A pilot neuropsychological study. *Journal of Child Psychology and Psychiatry, 36,* 1459–1473.

395. Shaler, R. S., Auerbach, J., & Gross-Tsur, V. (1995). Developmental dyscalculia behavioral and attentional aspects: A research note. *Journal of Child Psychology and Psychiatry, 36,* 1261–1268.

396. Shaywitz, B. A., Holford, T. R., Holahan, J. M., Fletcher, J. M., Stuebing, K. K., Francis, D. J., & Shaywitz, S. E. (1995). A Matthew effect for IQ but not for reading: Results from a longitudinal study. *Reading Research Quarterly, 30,* 894–906.

397. Shields, J. D., Green, R., Cooper, B. A. B., & Ditton, P. (1995). The impact of adults' communication clarity versus communication deviance on adolescents with learning disabilities. *Journal of Learning Disabilities, 28,* 372–384.

398. Siegel, J., Cook, R., & Gerard, J. (1995). Differential categorization of words by learning disabled, gifted, and nonexceptional students. *Perceptual and Motor Skills, 81,* 243–250.

399. Simon, E. W., Rappaport, D. A., Papka, M., & Woodruff-Pak, D. S. (1995). Fragile-X and Down's syndrome: Are there syndrome-specific cognitive profiles at low IQ levels. *Journal of Intellectual Disability Research, 39,* 326–330.

400. Slate, J. R. (1995). Discrepancies between IQ and index scores for a clinical sample of students: Useful diagnostic indicators? *Psychology in the Schools, 32,* 103–108.

401. Slate, J. R., & Fawcett, J. (1995). Validity of the WISC-III for deaf and hard of hearing persons. *American Annals of the Deaf, 140,* 250–254.

402. Slate, J. R., & Jones, C. H. (1995). Preliminary evidence of the validity of the WISC-III for African American students undergoing special education evaluation. *Educational and Psychological Measurement, 55,* 1039–1046.

403. Smith, D. S., & Nagle, R. J. (1995). Self-perceptions and social comparisons among children with LD. *Journal of Learning Disabilities, 28,* 364–371.

404. Spafford, C. S., Grosser, G. S., Donatelle, J. R., Squillace, S. R., & Dana, J. P. (1995). Contrast sensitivity differences between proficient and disabled readers using colored lenses. *Journal of Learning Disabilities, 28,* 240–252.

405. Stark, R. E., Bleile, K., Brandt, J., Freeman, J., & Vining, E. P. G. (1995). Speech-language outcomes of hemispherectomy in children and young adults. *Brain and Language, 51,* 406–421.

406. Stevens, L. J., & Bliss, L. S. (1995). Conflict resolution abilities of children with specific language impairment and children with normal language. *Journal of Speech and Hearing Research, 38,* 599–611.

407. Su, C., Chien, T., Chena, K., & Lin, Y. (1995). Performance of older adults with and without cerebrovascular accident on the Test of Visual-Perceptual Skills. *The American Journal of Occupational Therapy, 49,* 491–499.

408. Sullivan, G. S., Mastropieri, M. A., & Scruggs, T. E. (1995). Reasoning and remembering: Coaching students with learning disabilities to think. *The Journal of Special Education, 29,* 310–322.

409. Sverd, J., Sheth, R., Fuss, J., & Levine, J. (1995). Prevalence of pervasive developmental disorder in a sample of psychiatrically hospitalized children and adolescents. *Child Psychiatry and Human Development, 25,* 221–240.

410. Tardif, C., Plumet, M-H., Beaudichon, J., Waller, D., Bouvard, M., & Leboyer, M. (1995). Micro-analysis of social interactions between autistic children and normal adults in semi-structured play situations. *International Journal of Behavioral Development, 18,* 727–747.

411. Vance, B., & Fuller, G. B. (1995). Relation of scores on WISC-III and WRAT-III for a sample of referred children and youth. *Psychological Reports, 76,* 371–374.

412. VanStrien, J. W., Stolk, B. D., & Zuiker, S. (1995). Hemisphere-specific treatment of dyslexia subtypes: Better reading with anxiety-laden words? *Journal of Learning Disabilities, 28,* 30–34.

413. Vargo, F. E., Grosser, G. S., & Spafford, C. S. (1995). Digit span and other WISC-R scores in the diagnosis of dyslexia in children. *Perceptual and Motor Skills, 80,* 1219–1229.

414. Waber, D. P., & McCormick, M. C. (1995). Late neuropsychological outcomes in preterm infants of normal IQ: Selective vulnerability of the visual system. *Journal of Pediatric Psychology, 20,* 721–735.

415. Wachs, T. D., Bishry, Z., Moussa, W., Yunis, F., McCabe, G., Harrison, G., Sweifi, E., Kirksey, A., Galal, O., Jerome, N., & Shaheen, F. (1995). Nutritional intake and context as predictors of cognition and adaptive behaviour of Egyptian school-age children. *International Journal of Behavioral Development, 18,* 425–450.

416. Wallander, J. L., & Venters, T. L. (1995). Perceived role restriction and adjustment of mothers of children with chronic physical disability. *Journal of Pediatric Psychology, 20,* 619–632.

417. Watson, C., & Willows, D. M. (1995). Information-processing patterns in specific reading disability. *Journal of Learning Disabilities, 28,* 216–231.

418. White, N., Green, A., & Steiner, R. (1995). An investigation of differences between three age groups in verbal and spatial task performance using the dual-task paradigm. *Brain and Cognition, 28,* 59–78.

419. Wilson, B. N., Polatajko, H. J., Kaplan, B. J., & Faris, P. (1995). Use of Bruininks-Oseretsky Test of Motor Proficiency in occupational therapy. *The American Journal of Occupational Therapy, 49,* 8–17.

420. Wilson, K. G., Stelzer, J., Bergman, J. N., Kral, M. J., Inayatullah, M., & Elliott, C. A. (1995). Problem solving, stress, and coping in adolescent suicide attempts. *Suicide and Life-Threatening Behavior, 25,* 241–252.

421. Wisniewski, J. J., Andrews, T. J., & Mulick, J. A. (1995). Objective and subjective factors in the disproportionate referral of children for academic problems. *Journal of Consulting and Clinical Psychology, 63,* 1032–1076.

422. Wolff, S., & McGuire, R. J. (1995). Schizoid personality in girls: A follow-up study—What are the links with Asperger's Syndrome? *Journal of Child Psychology and Psychiatry and Allied Disciplines, 36,* 793–817.

423. Woodworth, S. J., DeFries, J. C., Fulker, D. W., Olson, R. K., & Pennington, B. F. (1995). Reading performance and verbal short-term memory: A twin study of reciprocal causation. *Intelligence, 20,* 145–167.

424. Yamada, J. (1995). Developmental deep dyslexia in Japanese: A case study. *Brain and Language, 51,* 444–457.

425. Yasutake, D., & Bryan, T. (1995). The influence of affect on the achievement and behavior of students with learning disabilities. *Journal of Learning Disabilities, 28,* 329–334.

426. Yeates, K. O., Enrile, B. G., Loss, N., & Blumenstein, E. (1995). Verbal learning and memory in children with myelomeningocele. *Journal of Pediatric Psychology, 20,* 801–815.

427. Young, R. L., & Nettelbeck, T. (1995). The abilities of a musical savant and his family. *Journal of Autism and Developmental Disorders, 25,* 231–248.

428. Zaidel, D. W., Zaidel, E., Oxbury, S. M., & Oxbury, J. M. (1995). The interpretation of sentence ambiguity in patients with unilateral focal brain surgery. *Brain and Language, 51,* 458–468.

429. Zigmond, N. (1995). Inclusion in Kansas educational experiences of students with learning disabilities in one elementary school. *The Journal of Special Education, 29,* 144–154.

430. Zurrón, M., & Díaz, F. (1995). Auditory and visual evoked potentials in individuals with organic and cultural-familial mental retardation. *American Journal on Mental Retardation, 100,* 271–282.

431. Abell, S. C., Von Brieson, P. D., & Watz, L. S. (1996). Intellectual evaluations of children using human figure drawings: An empirical investigation of two methods. *Journal of Clinical Psychology, 52,* 67–74.

432. Abikoff, H., Courtney, M. E., Szeibel, P. J., & Koplewiez, H. S. (1996). The effects of audiotry stimulation on the arithmatic performance of children with ADHD and nondisabled children. *Journal of Learning Disabilities, 29,* 238–246.

433. Ariel, R., & Sadeh, M. (1996). Congenital visual agnosia and prosopagnosia in a child: A case report. *Cortex, 32,* 221–240.

434. Badian, N. A. (1996). Dyslexia: A validation of the concept at two age levels. *Journal of Learning Disabilities, 29,* 102–112.

435. Banden, H., Dooley, J., Buckley, D., Camfield, P., Gordon, K., Riding, M., & Llewellyn, G. (1996). MRI and nonverbal cognitive deficits in children with neurofibromatosis 1. *Journal of Clinical and Experimental Neuropsychology, 18,* 784–792.

436. Barnett, K. P., Clarizio, H. F., & Payette, K. A. (1996). Grade retention among students with learning disabilities. *Psychology in the Schools, 33,* 285–293.

437. Baumgardner, T. L., Singer, H. S., Denckla, M. B., Rubin, M. A., Abrams, M. T., Colli, M. J., & Reiss, A. L. (1996). Corpus callosum morphology in children with Tourette syndrome and attention deficit hyperactivity disorder. *Neurology, 47,* 477–482.

438. Becker, D. F., Edell, W. S., Fujioka, T. A., Levy, K. N., & McGlashan, T. H. (1996). Attentional and intellectual deficits in unmedicated behavior-disordered adolescent in patients. *Journal of Youth and Adolescence, 25,* 127–135.

439. Beidel, D. C., Fink, C. M., & Turner, S. M. (1996). Stability of anxious symptomatology in children. *Journal of Abnormal Child Psychology, 24,* 257–269.

440. Bennetto, L., Pennington, B. F., & Rogers, S. J. (1996). Infant and impaired memory functions in autism. *Child Development, 67,* 1816–1835.

441. Bibby, P. A., Lamb, S. J., Leyden, G., & Wood, D. (1996). Season of birth and gender effects in children attending moderate learning difficulty schools. *British Journal of Educational Psychology, 66,* 159–168.

442. Bickett, L. R., Milich, R., & Brown, R. T. (1996). Attributional styles of aggressive boys and their mothers. *Journal of Abnormal Child Psychology, 24,* 457–472.

443. Blackson, T. C., Tarter, R. E., Loeber, R., Ammerman, R. T., & Windle, M. (1996). The influence of paternal substance abuse and difficult temperament in fathers and sons on son's disengagement from family to deviant peers. *Journal of Youth and Adolescence, 25,* 389–411.

444. Blaha, J., & Wallbrown, F. H. (1996). Hierarchical factor structure of the Wechsler Intelligence Scale for Children—III. *Psychological Assessment, 8,* 214–218.

445. Breslau, N., Brown, G. G., Del Dotto, J. E., Kumar, S., Ezhuthachan, S., Andreski, P., & Hufnagle, K. G. (1996). Psychiatric sequelae of low birth weight at 6 years of age. *Journal of Abnormal Child Psychology, 24,* 385–400.

446. Brody, G. H., Stoneman, Z., & Flor, D. (1996). Parental religiosity, family processes, and youth competence in rural, two-parent African American families. *Developmental Psychology, 32,* 696–706.

447. Burchinal, M. R., Follmer, A., & Bryant, D. M. (1996). The relations of maternal social support and family structure with maternal responsiveness and child outcomes among African American families. *Developmental Psychology, 32,* 1073–1083.

448. Capron, C., & Duyme, M. (1996). Effect of socioeconomic status of biological and adoptive parents on WISC-R subtest scores of their French adopted children. *Intelligence, 22,* 259–275.

449. Carte, E. T., Nigg, J. T., & Hinshaw, S. P. (1996). Neuropsychological functioning, motor speed, and language processing in boys with and without ADHD. *Journal of Abnormal Child Psychology, 24,* 481–498.

450. Castellanos, F. X., Giedd, J. N., Marsh, W. L., Hamburger, S. D., Vaituzis, A. C., Dickstein, D. P., Sarfatti, S. E., Vauss, Y. C., Snell, J. W., Lange, N., Kaysen, D., Krain, A. L., Ritchie, G. F., Rajapakse, J. C., & Rapoport, J. L. (1996). Quantitative brain magnetic resonance imaging in attention-deficit hyperactivity disorder. *Archives of General Psychiatry, 53,* 607–616.

451. Chan, D. W., & Lin, W. Y. (1996). The two- and three-dimensional models of the HK-WISC: A confirmatory factor analysis. *Measurement and Evaluation in Counseling and Development, 28,* 191–199.

452. Cohen, N. J., Barwick, M. A., Horodezky, N., & Isaacson, L. (1996). Comorbidity of language and social-emotional disorders: Comparison of psychiatric outpatients and their siblings. *Journal of Clinical Child Psychology, 25,* 192–200.

453. Colyer, S. P., & Collins, B. C. (1996). Using natural cues within prompt levels to teach the next dollar strategy to students with disabilities. *The Journal of Special Education, 30,* 305–318.

454. Courbois, Y. (1996). Evidence for visual imagery deficits in persons with mental retardation. *American Journal on Mental Retardation, 101,* 130–148.

455. Dahlgren, S. D., & Trillingsgaard, A. (1996). Theory of mind in non-retarded children with autism and Asperger's syndrome: A research note. *Journal of Child Psychology and Psychiatry, 37,* 759–763.

456. Das-Smaal, E. A., Klapwijk, M. J. G., & van der Leij, A. (1996). Training of perceptual unit processing in children with a reading disability. *Cognition and Instruction, 14,* 221–250.

457. della Rocchetta, A. I., Cipolotti, L., & Warrington, E. K. (1996). Topographical disorientation: Selective impairment of locomotor space? *Cortex, 32,* 727–735.

458. Demont, E., & Gombest, J. E. (1996). Phonological awareness as a predictor of recoding skills and syntactic awareness as a predictor of comprehension skills. *British Journal of Educational Psychology, 66,* 315–332.

459. Devenny, D. A., Silverman, W. P., Hill, A. L., Jenkins, E., Sersen, E. A., & Wisniewski, K. E. (1996). Normal aging in adults with Down's syndrome: A longitudinal study. *Journal of Disability Research, 40,* 208–221.

460. Dittrichová, J., Brichácek, V., Mandys, F., Paul, K., Sobotková, D., Tautermannová, M., Vondrácek, J., & Zezuláková, J. (1996). The relationship of early behaviour to later developmental outcome for preterm children. *International Journal of Behavioral Development, 19,* 517–532.

461. Donders, J. (1996). Cluster subtypes in the WISC-III standardization sample: Analysis of factor index scores. *Psychological Assessment, 8,* 312–318.

462. Dumont, R., Cruse, C. L., Price, L., & Whelley, P. (1996). The relationship between the Differential Ability Scales (DAS) and the Wechsler Intelligence Scale for Children—Third Edition (WISC-III) for students with learning disabilities. *Psychology in the Schools, 33,* 203–209.

463. Dykens, E. (1996). The draw-a-person task in persons with mental retardation: What does it measure? *Research in Developmental Disabilities, 17,* 1–13.

464. Edelman, S. (1996). A review of the Wechsler Intelligence Scale for Children-Third Edition (WISC-III). *Measurement and Evaluation in Counseling and Development, 28,* 219–224.

465. Eden, G. F., Stein, J. F., Wood, H. M., & Wood, F. B. (1996). Differences in visuospatial judgment in reading-disabled and normal children. *Perceptual and Motor Skills, 82,* 155–177.

466. Einfeld, S. L., & Tonge, B. J. (1996). Population prevalence of psychopathology in children and adolescents with intellectual disability: I. Rationale and methods. *Journal of Disability Research, 40,* 91–98.

467. Elwan, F. Z. (1996). Factor structure of the Kaufman Assessment Battery for Children with Egyptian schoolchildren. *Psychological Reports, 78,* 99–110.

468. Fergusson, D. M., & Lynskey, M. T. (1996). Adolescent resilency to family adversity. *Journal of Child Psychology and Psychiatry, 37,* 281–292.

469. Fergusson, D. M., Horwood, L. J., Caspi, A., Moffitt, T. E., & Silva, P. A. (1996). The (artefactual) remission of reading disability: Psychometric lessons in the study of stability and change in behavioral development. *Developmental Psychology, 32,* 132–140.

470. Fergusson, D. M., Lynskey, M. T., & Horwood, J. (1996). Factors associated with continuity and changes in disruptive behavior patterns between childhood and adolescence. *Journal of Abnormal Child Psychology, 24,* 533–553.

471. Ferro, J., Foster-Johnson, L., & Dunlap, G. (1996). Relation between curricular activities and problem behaviors of studentswith mental retardation. *American Journal on Mental Retardation, 101,* 184–194.

472. Fornham, A., & Weir, C. (1996). Lay theories of child development. *The Journal of Genetic Psychology, 157,* 211–226.

473. Francis, D. J., Fletcher, J. M., Shaywitz, B. A., Shaywitz, S. E., & Rourke, B. P. (1996). Defining learning and language disabilities: Conceptual and psychometric issues with the use of IQ tests. *Language, Speech, and Hearing Services in Schools, 27,* 132–143.

474. Francis, D. J., Shaywitz, S. E., Stuebing, K. K., Shaywitz, B. A., & Fletcher, J. M. (1996). Developmental lag versus deficit models of reading disability: A longitudinal, individual growth curves analysis. *Journal of Educational Psychology, 88,* 3–17.

475. Frazier, J. A., Giedd, J. N., Hamburger, S. D., Albus, K. E., Kaysen, D., Vaituzis, A. C., Rajapakse, J. C., Lenaine, M. C., McKenna, K., Jacobsen, L. K., Gordon, C. T., Brier, A., & Rapoport, J. L. (1996). Brain anatomic magnetic resonance imaging in childhood-onset schizophrenia. *Archives of General Psychiatry, 53,* 617–624.

476. Fujiki, M., Brinton, B., & Todd, C. M. (1996). Social skills of children with specific language impairment. *Language, Speech, and Hearing Services in Schools, 27,* 195–202.

477. Giancola, P. R., Martin, C. S., Tarter, R. E., Pelham, W. E., & Moss, H. B. (1996). Executive cognitive functioning and aggressive behavior in preadolescent boys at high risk for substance abuse/dependence. *Journal of Studies on Alcohol, 57,* 352–359.

478. Gillberg, C., Ovebrant, P., Carlsson, G., Hedström, A., & Silfvenilis, H. (1996). Autism and epilepsy (and tuberous sclerosis?) in two pre-adolescent boys: Neuropsychiatric aspects before and after epilepsy surgery. *Journal of Disability Research, 40,* 75–81.

479. Glutting, J. J., Youngstrom, E. A., Oakland, T., & Watkins, M. W. (1996). Situational specificity and generality of test behaviors for samples of normal and referred children. *School Psychology Review, 25,* 94–107.

480. Gomez, R., & Hazeldine, P. (1996). Social information processing in mild mentally retarded children. *Research in Developmental Disabilities, 17, 217–227.*

481. Gray, R. M., Livingston, R. B., Marshall, R. M., & Haak, R. A. (1996). Use of the long vs. short form of the Speech Sounds Perception Test in a school-age population. *Perceptual and Motor Skills, 82,* 475–480.

482. Greenbaum, B., Graham, S., & Scales, W. (1996). Adults with learning disabilities: Occupational and social status after college. *Journal of Learning Disabilities, 29,* 167–173.

483. Greene, C., Symons, S., & Richards, C. (1996). Elaborative interrogation effects for children with learning disabilities: Isolated facts versus connected prose. *Contemporary Educational Psychology, 21,* 19–42.

484. Gresham, F., M., MacMillan, D. L., & Bocian, K. M. (1996). Learning disabilities, low achievement, and mild mental retardation: More alike than different? *Journal of Learning Disabilities, 29,* 570–581.

485. Hagell, A., Rutter, M., & Yule, W. (1996). Reading problems and antisocial behviour: Developmental trends in comorbidity. *Journal of Child Psychology and Psychiatry, 37,* 405–418.

486. Hallmayer, J., Hebert, J. M., Spiker, D., Lotspeich, L., McMahon, W. M., Petersen, P. B., Nicholas, P., Ringree, C., Linn, A. A., Cavalli-Sforza, L. L., Risch, N., & Ciaranello, R. D. (1996). Autism and the X chromosome: Multipoint sib-pair analysis. *Archives of General Psychiatry, 53,* 985–989.

487. Happé, F. G. E. (1996). Studying weak central coherence at low levels: Children with autism do not succumb to visual illusions: A research note. *Journal of Child Psychology and Psychiatry, 37,* 873–877.

488. Heller, T. L., Baker, B. L., Henker, B., & Hinshaw, S. P. (1996). Externalizing behavior and cognitive functioning from preschool to first grade: Stability and predictors. *Journal of Clinical Child Psychology, 25,* 376–387.

489. Herrera-Graf, M., Dipert, Z. J., & Hinton, R. N. (1996). Exploring the effective use of the vocabulary/block design short form with a special school population. *Educational and Psychological Measurement, 56,* 522–528.

490. Howlin, P., & Jones, D. P. H. (1996). An assessment approach to abuse allegations made through facilitated communication. *Child Abuse & Neglect, 20,* 103–110.

491. Humphries, T., Krekewich, K., & Snider, L. (1996). Evidence of nonverbal learning disability among learning disabled boys with sensory integrative dysfunction. *Perceptual and Motor Skills, 82,* 979–987.

492. Isaacs, E., Christie, D., Vargha-Khadem, F., & Mishkin, M. (1996). Effects of hemispheric side of injury, age at injury, and presence of seizure disorder on functional ear and hand asymmetries in hemiplegic children. *Neuropsychologia, 34,* 127–137.

493. Jacobsen, L. K., Giedd, J. N., Vaituzis, A. C., Hamburger, S. D., Rajapakse, J. C., Frazier, J. A., Kaysen, D., Lenane, M. C., McKenna K., Gordon, C. T., & Rapoport, J. L. (1996). Temporal lobe morphology in childhood-onset schizophrenia. *American Journal of Psychiatry, 153,* 355–361.

494. Kabrich, M., & McCutchen, D. (1996). Phonemic support incomprehension: Comparisons between children with and without mild mental retardation. *American Journal on Mental Retardation, 100,* 510–527.

495. Kaufman, A. S., Kaufman, J. C., Balgopal, R., & McLean, J. E. (1996). Comparison of three WISC-III short forms: Weighing psychometric, clinical, and practical factors. *Journal of Clinical Child Psychology, 25,* 97–105.

496. Kelly, T. P., & Britton, P. G. (1996). Sex differences on an adaptation of the digit symbol subtest of the Wechsler Intelligence Scale for Children—III. *Perceptual and Motor Skills, 83,* 843–847.

497. Klaczynski, P. A., & Gordon, D. H. (1996). Everyday statistical reasoning during adolescence and young adulthood: Motivational, general ability, and developmental influences. *Child Development, 67,* 2873–2891.

498. Kokubun, M., Haishi, K., Okuzumi, H., Hosobuchi, T., & Koike, T. (1996). Predictive value of age of walking for later motor performance in children with mental retardation. *Journal of Disability Research, 40,* 529–534.

499. Korkman, M., Liikkanen, A., & Fellman, V. (1996). Neuropsychological consequences of very low birth weight and asphyxia at term: Follow-up until school-age. *Journal of Clinical and Experimental Neuropsychology, 18,* 220–233.

500. Krusch, D. A., Klorman, R., Brumaghim, J. T., Fitzpatrick, P. A., Borgstedt, A. D., & Strauss, J. (1996). Methylphenidate slows reactions of children with attention deficit disorder during and after an error. *Journal of Abnormal Child Psychology, 24,* 633–650.

501. Kumra, S., Frazier, J. A., Jacobsen, L. K., McKenna, K., Gordon, C. T., Lenane, M. C., Hamburger, S. C., Smith, A. K., Albus, K. E., Alaghband-Rad, J., & Rapoport, J. L. (1996). Childhood-onset schizophrenia: A double-blind clozapine-haloperidol comparison. *Archives of General Psychiatry, 53,* 1090–1097.

502. Lavin, C. (1996). The relationship between the Wechsler Intelligence Scale for Children—Third Edition and the Kaufman Test of Educational Achievement. *Psychology in the Schools, 33,* 119–123.

503. Law, J. G., Jr., & Faison, L. (1996). WISC-III and KAIT results in adolescent delinquent males. *Journal of Clinical Psychology, 52,* 699–703.

504. Lee, R. E. (1996). FIRO-B scores and success in a positive peer-culture residential treatment program. *Psychological Reports, 78,* 215–220.

505. Leffert, J. S., & Siperstein, G. N. (1996). Assessment of social-cognitive processes in children with mental retardation. *American Journal on Mental Retardation, 100,* 441–455.

506. Levin, H. S., Fletcher, J. M., Kusnerik, L., Kufera, J. A., Lilly, M. A., Duffy, F. F., Chapman, S., Mendelsohn, D., & Bruce, D. (1996). Semantic memory following pediatric head injury: Relationship to age, severity of injury, and MRI. *Cortex, 32,* 461–478.

507. Lorsbach, T. C., Wilson, S., & Reimer, J. F. (1996). Memory for relevant and irrelevant information: Evidence of deficient inhibitory processes in language/learning disabled children. *Contemporary Educational Psychology, 21,* 447–466.

508. Lovrich, D., Cheng, J. C., & Velting, D. M. (1996). Late cognitive brain potentials, phonological and semantic classification of spoken words, and reading ability in children. *Journal of Clinical and Experimental Neuropsychology, 18,* 161–177.

509. Lukens, J., & Hurrell, R. M. (1996). A comparison of the Stanford-Binet IV and the WISC-III with mildly retarded children. *Psychology in the Schools, 33,* 24–27.

510. MacArthur, C. A., Graham, S., Haynes, J. B., & DeLaPaz, S. (1996). Spelling checkers and students with learning disabilities: Performance comparisons and impact on spelling. *The Journal of Special Education, 30,* 35–57.

511. MacMillan, D. L., Gresham, F. M., Lopez, M. F., & Bocian, K. M. (1996). Comparison of students nominated for prereferral interventions by ethnicity and gender. *The Journal of Special Education, 30,* 133–151.

512. MacMillan, D. L., Gresham, F. M., Siperstein, G. N., & Bocian, K. M. (1996). The labyrinth of IDEA: School decisions on referred students with subaverage general intelligence. *American Journal on Mental Retardation, 101,* 161–174.

513. MacMillan, D. L., Siperstein, G. N., & Gresham, F. M. (1996). A challenge to the viability of mild mental retardation as a diagnostic category. *Exceptional Children, 62,* 356–371.

514. Manis, F. R., Seidenberg, M. S., Doi, L. M., McBride-Chang, C., & Petersen, A. (1996). On the bases of two subtypes of development dyslexia. *Cognition, 58,* 157–195.

515. Mayes, S. D., handford, H. A., Schaefer, J. H., Scogno, C. A., Neagley, S. R., Michael-Good, L., & Pelco, L. E. (1996). The relationship of HIV status, type of coagulation disorder, and school absenteeism to cognition, educational performance, mood, and behavior of boys with hemophilia. *The Journal of Genetic Psychology, 157,* 137–151.

516. McBride-Chang, C. (1996). Models of speech perception and phonological processing in reading. *Child Development, 67,* 1836–1856.

517. McFadden, T. V. (1996). Creating language impairments in typically achieving children: The pitfalls of "normal" normative sampling. *Language, Speech, and Hearing Services in Schools, 27,* 3–9.

518. Mellanby, J., Anderson, R., Campbell, B., & Westwood, E. (1996). Cognitive determinants of verbal underachievement at secondary school level. *British Journal of Educational Psychology, 66,* 483–500.

519. Melnick, S. M., & Hinshaw, S. P. (1996). What they want and what they get: The social goals of boys with ADHD and comparison boys. *Journal of Abnormal Child Psychology, 24,* 169–185.

520. Milberger, S., Biederman, J., Faraone, S. V., Chen, L., & Jones, J. (1996). Is maternal smoking during pregnancy a risk factor for attention deficit hyperactivity disorder in children? *American Journal of Psychiatry, 153,* 1138–1142.

521. Mitchell, T. V., & Quittner, A. L. (1996). Multimethod study of attention and behavior problems in hearing-impaired children. *Journal of Clinical Child Psychology, 25,* 83–96.

522. Moore, B. D., Slopis, J. M., Schomer, D., Jackson, E. F., & Levy, B. M. (1996). Neuropsycholgical significance of areas of high signal intensity on brain MRI's of children with neurofibromatosis. *Neurology, 46,* 1660–1668.

523. Moss, H. A., Wolters, P. L., Browers, P., Hendricks, M. L., & Pizzo, P. A. (1996). Impairment of expressive behavior in pediatric HIV-infected patients with evidence of CNS disease. *Journal of Pediatric Psychology, 21,* 379–400.

524. Moulden, J. A., & Persinger, M. A. (1996). Visuospatial/vocabulary differences in boys and girls and a potential age-dependent drift in vocabulary proficiency. *Perceptual and Motor Skills, 82,* 472–474.

525. Noll, R. B., Vannatta, K., Koontz, K., Kalinyak, K., Bukowski, W. M., & Davies, W. H. (1996). Peer relationships and emotional well-being of youngsters with sickle cell disease. *Child Development, 67,* 423–436.

526. North, K. N., Miller, G., Iannaccone, S. T., Clemens, P. R., Chad, D. A., Bella, I., Smith, T. W., Beggs, A. H., & Specht, L. A. (1996). Cognitive dysfunction as the major presenting feature of Becker's muscular dystrophy. *Neurology, 46,* 461–465.

527. North, T., & Donlan, C. (1996). Nonword repetition as a behavioral marker for inherited language impairment: Evidence from a twin study. *Journal of Child Psychology and Psychiatry, 37,* 391–403.

528. O'Brien, B. S., & Frick, P. J. (1996). Reward dominance: Associations with anxiety, conduct problems, and psychopathy in children. *Journal of Abnormal Child Psychology, 24,* 223–240.

529. Oosterlaan, J., & Sergeant, J. A. (1996). Inhibition in ADHD, aggressive, and anxious children: A biologically based model of child psychopathology. *Journal of Abnormal Child Psychology, 24,* 19–36.

530. Paquette, C., Tosoni, C., Lassonde, M., & Peretz, I. (1996). Atypical hemispheric specialization in intellectual deficiency. *Brain and Language, 52,* 474–483.

531. Paradis, C. M., Gironda, F., & Bennett, M. (1996). Cognitive impairment in Schwartz-Jampel syndrome: A case study. *Brain and Language, 56,* 301–305.

532. Phelps, L. (1996). Discriminative validity of the WRAML with ADHD and LD children. *Psychology in the Schools, 33,* 5–12.

533. Putnam, J., Markovchick, K., Johnson, D. W., & Johnson, R. T. (1996). Cooperative learning and peer acceptance of students with learning disabilities. *The Journal of Social Psychology, 136,* 741–752.

534. Reynolds, C. R., Sanchez, S., & Willson, V. L. (1996). Normative tables for calculating the WISC-III performance and full scale IQs when symbol search is substituted for coding. *Psychological Assessment, 8,* 378–382.

535. Riccio, C. A., Cohen, M. J., Hynd, G. W., & Keith, R. W. (1996). Validity of the Auditory Continuous Performance Test in differentiating central processing auditory disorders with and without ADHD. *Journal of Learning Disabilities, 29,* 561–566.

536. Robins, R. W., John, O. P., Caspi, A., Moffitt, T. E., & Stouthamer-Loeber, M. (1996). Resilient, overcontrolled, and undercontrolled boys: Three replicable personality types. *Journal of Personality and Social Psychology, 70,* 157–171.

537. Robinson, N. M., Abbott, R. D., Berninger, V. W., & Busse, J. (1996). The structure of abilities in math-precocious young children: Gender similarities and differences. *Journal of Educational Psychology, 88,* 341–352.

538. Rogers, S. J., Bennetto, L., McEvoy, R., & Pennington, B. F. (1996). Imitation and pantomime in high-functioning adolescents with autism spectrum disorders. *Child Development, 67,* 2060–2073.

539. Rose, S. A., & Feldman, J. F. (1996). Memory and processing speed in preterm children at eleven years: A comparison with full-terms. *Child Development, 67,* 2005–2021.

540. Ross, G., Lipper, E., & Auld, P. A. M. (1996). Cognitive abilities and early precursors of learning disabilities in very-low-birthweight children with normal intelligence and normal neurological status. *International Journal of Behavioral Development, 19,* 563–580.

541. Rovet, J., & Alvarez, M. (1996). Thyroid hormone and attention in school-age children with congenital hypothyroidism. *Journal of Child Psychology and Psychiatry, 37,* 579–585.

542. Rovet, J., Netley, C., Keenan, M., Bailey, J., & Stewart, D. (1996). The psychoeducational profile of boys with Klinefelter Syndrome. *Journal of Learning Disabilities, 29,* 189–196.

543. Rund, B. R., Oie, M., & Sundet, K. (1996). Backward-masking deficit in adolescents with schizophrenic disorders or attention deficit hyperactivity disorder. *American Journal of Psychiatry, 153,* 1154–1157.

544. Rutland, A. F., & Campbell, R. N. (1996). The relevance of Vygotsky's theory of the "zone of proximal development" to the assessment of children with intellectual disabilities. *Journal of Disability Research, 40,* 151–158.

545. Sabers, D. L. (1996). By their tests we will know them. *Language, Speech, and Hearing Services in Schools, 27,* 102–108.

546. Saigh, P. A., Yule, W., & Inamdar, S. C. (1996). Imaginal flooding of traumatized children and adolescents. *Journal of School Psychology, 34,* 163–183.

547. Sarphare, G., & Aman, M. G. (1996). Parent- and self-ratings of anxiety in children with mental retardation: Agreement levels and test-retest reliability. *Research in Developmental Disabilities, 17,* 27–39.

548. Schuerholz, L. J., Baumgardner, T. L., Singer, H. S., Reiss, A.L., & Denckla, M. B. (1996). Neuropsychological status of children with Tourette's syndrome with and without attention deficit hyperactivity disorder. *Neurology, 46,* 958–964.

549. Segal, N. L., Connelly, S. L., & Topoloski, T. D. (1996). Twin children with unfamiliar partners: Genotypic and gender influences on cooperation. *Journal of Child Psychology and Psychiatry, 37,* 731–735.

550. Sigelman, C., Derenowski, E., Woods, T., Mukai, T., Alfeld-Liron, C., Durazo, O., & Maddock, A. (1996). Mexican-American and Anglo-American children's responsiveness to a theory-centered AIDS education program. *Child Development, 67,* 253–266.

551. Silverthorn, P., Frick, P. J., Kuper, K., & Ott, J. (1996). Attention Deficit Hyperactivity disorder and sex: A test of two etiological models to explain the male predominance. *Journal of Clinical Child Psychology, 25,* 52–59.

552. Slaghuis, W. L., Twell, A. J., & Kingston, K. R. (1996). Visual and language processing disorders are concurrent in dyslexia and continue into adulthood. *Cortex, 32,* 413–438.

553. Slate, J. R., & Fawcett, J. (1996). Gender differences in Weschler performance scores of school-age children who are deaf or hard of hearing. *American Annals of the Deaf, 141,* 19–23.

554. Smart, D., Sanson, A., & Prior, M. (1996). Connections between reading disability and behavioral problems: Testing temporal and causal hypotheses. *Journal of Abnormal Child Psychology, 24,* 363–383.

555. Smyth, M. M., & Scholey, K. A. (1996). The relationship between articulation time and memory performance in verbal and visuospatial tasks. *British Journal of Psychology, 87,* 179–191.

556. Solís-Cámara, R., P. (1996). Random and cognitive responders on the Matching Familiar Figures Test: Alternatives for users. *Perceptual and Motor Skills, 83,* 543–562.

557. Sparks, R., Ganschow, L., & Thomas, A. (1996). Role of intelligence tests in speech/language referrals. *Perceptual and Motor Skills, 83,* 195–204.

558. Spruill, J. (1996). Composite SAS of the Stanford-Binet Intelligence Scale, Fourth Edition: Is it determined by only one area of SAS? *Psychological Assessment, 8,* 328–330.

559. Stanford, M. S., & Barratt, E. S. (1996). Verbal skills, fingertapping, and cognitive tempo define a second-order factor of temporal information processing. *Brain and Cognition, 31,* 35–45.

560. Stark, R. E., & Heinz, J. M. (1996). Perception of stop consonants in children with expressive and receptive-expressive language impairments. *Journal of Speech and Hearing Research, 39,* 676–686.

561. Swanson, H. L., & Trahan, M. (1996). Learning disabled and average readers' working memory and comprehension: Does metacognition play a role? *British Journal of Educational Psychology, 66,* 333–355.

562. Swanson, S., & Howell, C. (1996). Test anxiety in adolescents with learning disabilities and behavior disorders. *Exceptional Children, 62,* 389–397.

563. Temple, C. M., & Carney, R. (1996). Reading skills in children with Turner's Syndrome: An analysis of hyperlexia. *Cortex, 32,* 335–345.

564. Teo, A., Carlson, E., Mathieu, P. J., Egeland, B., & Sroufe, L. A. (1996). A prospective longitudinal study of psychosocial predictors of achievement. *Journal of School Psychology, 34,* 285–306.

565. Thompson, L. L., Riggs, P. D., Mikulich, S. K., & Crowley, T. J. (1996). Contribution of ADHD symptoms to substance problems and delinquency in conduct-disordered adolescents. *Journal of Abnormal Child Psychology, 24,* 325–347.

566. Tsemberis, S., & Miller, A. C. (1996). Expert judgments of computer-based and clinician-written reports. *Computers in Human Behavior, 12,* 167–175.

567. Uecker, A., & Nadel, L. (1996). Spatial locations gone awry: Object and spatial memory deficits in children with fetal alcohol syndrome. *Neuropsychologia, 34,* 209–223.

568. van der Lely, H. K. J., & Tollwerck, L. (1996). A grammatical specific lanaguage impairment in children: An autosomal dominant inheritance? *Brain and Language, 52,* 484–504.

569. Vance, H., Maddux, C. D., Fuller, G. B., & Awadh, A. M. (1996). A longitudinal comparison of WISC-III and WISC-R scores of special education students. *Psychology in the Schools, 33,* 113–118.

570. Vaughn, S., Elbaum, B. E., & Schumm, J. S. (1996). The effects of inclusion on the social functioning of students with learning disabilities. *Journal of Learning Disabilities, 29,* 598–608.

571. Vicari, S., Brizzolara, D., Carlesimo, G. A., Pezzini, G., & Volterra, V. (1996). Memory abilities in children with Williams Syndrome. *Cortex, 32,* 503–514.

572. Volterra, V., Capirci, O., Pezzini, G., Sabbadini, L., & Vicari, S. (1996). Linguistic abilities in Italian children with Williams Syndrome. *Cortex, 32,* 663–677.

573. Walz, N. C., & Benson, B. A. (1996). Labeling and discrimination of facial expressions by aggressive and nonaggressive men with mental retardation. *American Journal on Mental Retardation, 101,* 282–291.

574. Ward-Lonergan, J. M., Liles, B. Z., & Owen, S. V. (1996). Contextual strategy instruction: Socially/emotionally maladjusted adolescents with language impairments. *Journal of Communication Disorders, 29,* 107–124.

575. Waring, S., Margot, P., Sanson, A., & Smart, D. (1996). Predictors of "recovery" from reading disability. *Australian Journal of Psychology, 48,* 160–166.

576. Watkins, M. W. (1996). Diagnostic utility of the WISC-III developmental index as a predictor of learning disabilities. *Journal of Learning Disabilities, 29,* 305–312.

577. Webster, R. E., Hall, C. W., Brown, M. B., & Bolen, L. M. (1996). Memory modality differences in children with Attention Deficit Hyperactive Disorder with and without learning disabilities. *Psychology in the Schools, 33,* 193–201.

578. Weglage, J., Schmidt, E., Funders, B., Pietsch, M., & Ullrich, K. (1996). Sustained attention in untreated non-PKU-hyperphenyla laninemia. *Journal of Clinical and Experimental Neuropsychology, 18,* 343–348.

579. Wiig, E. H., Jones, S. S., & Wiig, E. D. (1996). Computer-based assessment of word knowledge in teens with learning disabilities. *Language, Speech, and Hearing Services in Schools, 27,* 21–28.

580. Wilson, M. S., & Reschly, D. J. (1996). Assessment in school psychology training and practice. *School Psychology Review, 25,* 9–23.

581. Yirmiya, N., & Shulman, C. (1996). Seriation, conservation, and theory of mind abilities in individuals with autism, individuals with mental retardation, and normally developing children. *Child Development, 67,* 2045–2059.

582. Yirmiya, N., Solomonica-Levi, D., & Shulman, C. (1996). The ability to manipulate behavior and to understand manipulation of beliefs: A comparison of individuals with autism, mental retardation, and normal development. *Developmental Psychology, 32,* 62–69.

583. Yirmiya, N., Solomonica-Levi, D., Shulman, C., & Pilowsky, T. (1996). Theory of mind abilities in individuals with autism, Down syndrome, and mental retardation of unknown etiology: The role of age and intelligence. *Journal of Child Psychology and Psychiatry, 37,* 1003–1014.

584. Yoshinaga-Itano, C. Snyder, L. S., & Mayberry, R. (1996). Can lexical/semantic skills differentiate deaf or hard-of-hearing readers and nonreaders? *Volta Review, 98* 39–61.

585. Yoshinaga-Itano, C., Snyder, L. S., & Mayberry, R. (1996). How deaf and normally hearing students convey meaning within and between written sentences. *Volta Review, 98,* 9–38.

586. Zimmerman, I. L., & Woo-Sam, J. M. (1996). Is retesting with the WISC-III a defensible procedure? *Perceptual and Motor Skills, 82,* 349–350.

587. Alarcón, M., DeFries, J. C., Light, J. G., & Pennington, B. F. (1997). A twin study of mathematics disability. *Journal of Learning Disabilities, 30,* 617–623.

588. Andrews, T. J., Wisniewski, J. J., & Mulick, J. A. (1997). Variables influencing teachers' decision to refer children for school psychological assessment. *Psychology in the Schools, 34,* 239–244.

589. Bakken, J. P., Mastropieri, M. A., & Scruggs, T. E. (1997). Reading comprehension on expository science material and students with learning disability: A comparison of strategies. *The Journal of Special Education, 31,* 300–324.

590. Ball, J. D., Tiernan, M., Janusz, J., & Furr, A. (1997). Sleep patterns among children with attention-deficit hyperactivity disorder: A reexamination of parent perceptions. *Journal of Pediatric Psychology, 22,* 389–398.

591. Benliman, H., & Morodes, S. (1997). Indicators of feminine gender identity in latency-aged boys in the Draw a Person and the Rorschach tests. *Journal of Clinical Psychology, 53,* 143–157.

592. Biederman, J., Faranoe, S. V., Hatch, M., Mennin, D., Taylor, A., & George, P. (1997). Conduct disorder with and without mania in a referred sample of ADHD children. *Journal of Affective Disorders, 44,* 177–188.

593. Bishop, D. V. M. (1997). Pre- and perinatal hazards and family bakcground in children with specific language impairments: A study of twins. *Brain and Language, 56,* 1–26.

594. Bowey, J. A. (1997). What does non-word repetition measure? A reply to Gatnercole and Baddeley. *Journal of Experimental Child Psychology, 67,* 295–301.

595. Bradley, S. J., Taylor, M. J., Rovet, J. F., Goldberg, E., Hood, J., Wachsmuth, R., Azcue, M. P., & Pencharz, P. B. (1997). Assessment of brain function in adolescent anorexia nervosa before and after weight gain. *Journal of Clinical and Experimental Neuropsychology, 19,* 20–33.

596. Brewer, V. R., Moore, B. D., III, & Hiscock, M. (1997). Learning disability subtypes in children with neurofibromatosis. *Journal of Learning Disabilities, 30,* 521–533.

597. Brinton, B., Fujiki, M., Spencer, J. C., & Robinson, L. A. (1997). The ability of children with specific language impairment to access and participate in an ongoing interaction. *Journal of Speech, Language, and Hearing Research, 40,* 1011–1025.

598. Burchinal, M. R., Campbell, F. A., Bryant, D. M., Wasik, H., & Ramey, C. T. (1997). Early intervention and mediating processes in cognitive performance of children of low-income African American families. *Child Development, 68,* 935–954.

599. Carroll, J. B. (1997). Commentary on Keith and Witta's hierarchial and cross-age confirmatory factor analysis of the WISC-III. *School Psychology Quarterly, 12,* 108–109.

600. Ciesielski, K. T., Harris, R. J., Hart, B. L., & Pabst, H. F. (1997). Cerebellar hypoplasia and frontal lobe cognitive deficits in disorders of early childhood. *Neuropsychologia, 35,* 643–655.

601. Corey-Bloom, J., Sabbagh, M. N., Bondi, M. W., Hansen, L., Alford, M. F., Masliah, E., & Thal, L. J. (1997) Hyziocampal sclerosis contributes to dementia in the elderly. *Neurology, 48,* 154–160.

602. Cruz, E. B., Brier, N. M., & Reznikoff, M. (1997). An examination of the relationship between form level ratings on the Rorschach and learning disability status. *The Journal of Psychology, 131,* 167–174.

603. Davis, J. T., Parr, G., & Lan, W. (1997). Differences between learning disability subtypes classified using the Revised Woodcock-Johnson Psycho-Educational Battery. *Journal of Learning Disabilities, 30,* 346–352.

604. Donders, J. (1997). A short form of the WISC-III for clinical use. *Psychological Assessment, 9,* 15–20.

605. Duncan, R. M., & Pratt, M. W. (1997). Microgenetic change in the quantity and quality of preschoolers' private speech. *International Journal of Behavioral Development, 20,* 367–383.

606. Elwan, F. Z. (1997). Achievement in school in relation to simulaneous and sequential cognitive processes among young Egyptian students. *Perceptual and Motor Skills, 84,* 1139–1148.

607. Faust, M., Dimitrovsky, L., & Davidi, S. (1997). Naming difficulties in language-disabled children: Preliminary findings with the application of the tip-of-the tongue paradigm. *Journal of Speech, Language, and Hearing Research, 40,* 1026–1036.

608. Feldman, M. A., & Walton-Allen, N. (1997). Effects of maternal mental retardation and poverty on intellectual, academic, and behavioral status of school-age children. *American Journal on Mental Retardation, 101,* 352–364.

609. Felsenfeld, S., & Plomin, R. (1997). Epidemiological and offspring analyses of developmental speech disorders using data from the Colorado Adoption Project. *Journal of Speech, Language, and Hearing Research, 40,* 778–791.

610. Ferri, B. A., Gregg, N., & Heggoy, S. J. (1997). Profiles of college students demonstrating learning disabilities with and without giftedness. *Journal of Learning Disabilities, 30,* 552–559.

611. Filipek, P. A., Semrud-Clikeman, M., Steingard, R. J., Renshaw, P. F., Kennedy, D. N., & Biederman, J. (1997). Volumetric MRI analysis comparing subjects having attention-deficit hyperactivity disorder with normal controls. *Neurology, 48,* 589–601.

612. Foxcroft, C. D. (1997). Note on reliability and validity of the school-entry group screening measure. *Perceptual and Motor Skills, 85,* 161–162.

613. Frank, E. G., Foley, G. M., & Kuchuk, A. (1997). Cognitive functioning in school-age children with human immunodeficiency virus. *Perceptual and Motor Skills, 85,* 267–272.

614. Fuller, G. B., Vance, H. B., & Awadh, A. M. (1997). Interscorers' agreement of the Human Figure Drawings with a referred group of children. *Perceptual and Motor Skills, 84,* 882.

615. Fury, G., Carlson, E. A., & Sroufe, L. A. (1997). Children's representations of attachment relationships in family drawings. *Child Development, 68,* 1154–1164.

616. Garnier, H. E., Stein, J. A., & Jacobs, J. K. (1997). The process of dropping out of high school: A 19-year perspective. *American Educational Research Journal, 34,* 395–419.

617. Gillberg, C., MeLander, H., von Knorring, A-L., Janols, L-O., Thernland, G., Hägglöf, B., Eidevall-Wallin, L., Gustafsson, P., & Kopp, S. (1997). Long-term stimulant treatment of children with attention-deficit hyperactivity disorder symptoms: A randomized, double-blind, placebo-controlled trial. *Archives of General Psychiatry, 54,* 857–864.

618. Glutting, J. J., McDermott, P. A., Watkins, M. M., Kush, J. C., & Konold, T. R. (1997). The base rate problem and its consequences for interpreting children's ability profiles. *School Psychology Review, 26,* 176–188.

619. Glutting, J. J., Robins, P. M., & de Lancey, E. (1997). Discriminant validity of test observations for children with attention deficit/hyperactivity. *Journal of School Psychology, 35,* 391–401.

620. Graf, M., & Hinton, R. N. (1997). Correlations for the Developmental Visual-Motor Integration Test and the Wechsler Intelligence Scale for Children—III. *Perceptual and Motor Skills, 84,* 699–702.

621. Gresham, F. M., & Witt, J. C. (1997). Utility of intelligence tests for treatment planning, classification, and placement decissions: Recent empirical findings and future directions. *School Psychology Quarterly, 12,* 249–267.

622. Gresham, F. M., MacMillan, D. L., & Bocian, K. M. (1997). Teachers as "tests": Differential validity of teacher judgements in identifying students at-risk for learning disabilities. *School Psychology Review, 26,* 47–60.

623. Griffiths, P., Tarrini, M., & Robinson, P. (1997). Executive functional psychosocial adjustment in children with early treated phenylketonuria: Correlation with historical and concurrent phenylalanine levels. *Journal of Disability Research, 41,* 317–323.

624. Handen, B. L., Janosky, J., & McAuliffe, S. (1997). Long-term follow-up of children with mental retardation/borderline intellectual functioning and ADHD. *Journal of Abnormal Child Psychology, 25,* 287–295.

625. Harden, A., & Sahl, R. (1997). Psychopathology in children and adolescents with developmental disorders. *Research in Developmental Disabilities, 18,* 369–382.

626. Hill, D. E., Ciesielski, K. T., Sethre-Hofstad, L., Duncan, M. H., & Lorenzi, M. (1997). Visual and verbal short-term memory deficits in childhood leukemia survivors after intrathecal chemotherapy. *Journal of Pediatric Psychology, 22,* 861–870.

627. Hinshaw, S. P., Zupan, B. A., Simmel, C., Nigg, J. T., & Melnick, S. (1997). Peer status in boys with and without attention-deficit hyperactivity disorder: Predictions from overt and covert antisocial behavior, social isolation, and authoritative parenting beliefs. *Child Development, 68,* 880–896.

628. Huter, V., Taylor, S., & Vargha-Khadem, F. (1997). A longitudinal study of early intellectual development in hemiplegic children. *Neuropsychologia, 35,* 289–298.

629. Jacobsen, L. K., Frazier, J. A., Malhotra, A. K., Karoum, F., McKenna, K., Gordon, C. T., Hamburger, S. D., Lenane, M. C., Pickar, D., Potter, W. Z., & Rapoport, J. L. (1997). Cerebrospinal fluid monamine metabolites in childhood-onset schizophrenia. *American Journal of Psychiatry, 154,* 69–74.

630. Jimerson, S., Carlson, E., Rotert, M., Egeland, B., & Sroufe, L. A. (1997). A prospective, longitudinal study of the correlates and consequences of early grade retention. *Journal of School Psychology, 35,* 3–25.

631. Johnson, L., Graham, S., & Harris, K. R. (1997). The effects of goal setting and self-instruction in learning a reading comprehension strategy: A study of students with learning disabilities. *Journal of Learning Disabilities, 30,* 80–91.

632. Joshi, P. K., & Rosenburg, L. A. (1997). Children's behavioral response to residential treatment. *Journal of Clinical Psychology, 53,* 567–573.

633. Kanazawa, T., Shimizu, S., Kamada, J., Tanabe, H., & Itoigawa, N. (1997). Intelligence and learning disabilities in 6- to 8-year-old children weighing under 1000 grams at birth. *International Journal of Behavioral Development, 20,* 179–188.

634. Kappers, E. J. (1997). Outpatient treatment of dyslexia through stimulation of the cerebral hemispheres. *Journal of Learning Disabilities, 30,* 100–125.

635. Karmiloff-Smith, A., Grant, J., Berthoud, I., Davies, M., Howlin, P., & Udivin, O. (1997). Language and Williams syndrome: How intact is "intact"? *Child Development, 68,* 246–262.

636. Keith, T. Z. (1997) What does the WISC-III measure? A reply to Carroll and Kranzler. *School Psychology Quarterly, 12,* 117–118.

637. Keith, T. Z., & Witta, E. L. (1997). Hierarchial and cross-age confirmatory factor analysis of the WISC-III: What does it measure? *School Psychology Quarterly, 12,* 89–107.

638. Kokubun, M., Shinmyo, T., Ogith, M., Morith, K., Furuta, M., Haishi, K., Okuzumi, H., & Kolke, T. (1997). Comparison of postural control of children with Down Syndrome and those with other forms of mental retardation. *Perceptual and Motor Skills, 84,* 499–504.

639. Krangler, J. H. (1997). What does the WISC-III measure? Comments on the relationship between intelligence, working memory capacity, and information processing speed and efficiency. *School Psychology Quarterly, 12,* 110–116.

640. Krassowski, E., & Plante, E. (1997). IQ variability in children with SLI: Implications for use of cognitive referencing in determining SLI. *Journal of Communication Disorders, 30,* 1–9.

641. Lamminmäki, T., Ahonen, T., deBarra, H. T., Tolvanen, A., Michelsson, K., & Lyytinen, H. (1997). Two-year group treatment for children with learning difficulties: Assessing effects of treatment duration and pretreatment characteristics. *Journal of Learning Disabilities, 30,* 354–364.

642. Levy-Shiff, R., Zoran, N., & Shulman, S. (1997). International and domestic adoption: Child, parents, and family adjustment. *International Journal of Behavioral Development, 20,* 109–129.

643. Macmann, G. M. & Barnett, D. W. (1997). A critical appraisal of intelligence testing with the WISC-III. Introduction to the series. *School Psychology Quarterly, 12,* 193–196.

644. Macmann, G. M., & Barnett, D. W. (1997). Reliability of interpretations for Kaufman's "Intelligence Testing" approach to the WISC-III. *School Psychology Quarterly, 12,* 197–234.

645. Maller, S. J. (1997). Deafness and WISC-III item difficulty: Invariance and fit. *Journal of School Psychology, 35,* 299–314.

646. Maller, S. J., & Ferron, J. (1997). WISC-III factor invariance across deaf and standardization samples. *Educational and Psychological Measurement, 57,* 987–994.

647. Marshall, R. M., Hynd, G. W., Handwerk, M. J., & Hall, J. (1997). Academic underachievement in ADHD subtypes. *Journal of Learning Disabilities, 30,* 635–642.

648. Mathijssen, J. J. P., Koot, H. M., Verhulst, F. C., De Bruyn, E. E. J., & Oud, J. H. L. (1997). Family functioning and child psychopathology: Individual versus composite family scores. *Family Relations, 46,* 247–255.

649. McClure, E., Rogeness, G. A., & Thompson, N. M. (1997). Characteristics of adolescent girls with depressive symptoms in a so-called 'normal' sample. *Journal of Affective Disorders, 42,* 187–197.

650. McDermott, P. A., & Glutitng, J. J. (1997). Informing stylistic learning behavior, disposition, and achievement through ability subtests—or, more illusions of meaning. *School Psychology Review, 26,* 163–175.

651. McGrath, N. M., Anderson, N. E., Hope, J. K. A., Croxson, M. C., & Powell, K. F. (1997). Anterior opercular syndrome, caused by herpes simplex encephalitis. *Neurology, 49,* 494–497.

652. McGrew, K. S., & Wrightson, N. (1997). The calculation of new and improved WISC-III subtest reliability, uniqueness, and general factor characteristic information through the use of data smoothing procedures. *Psychology in the Schools, 34,* 181–196.

653. McLaughlin, S. C., & Saccuzzo, D. P. (1997). Ethnic and gender differences in locus of control in children referred to gifted programs: The effects of vulnerability factors. *Journal for the Education of the Gifted, 20,* 268–283.

654. Milling, L., Giddan, J. J., Campbell, N. B., Bush, E., & Laughlin, A. (1997). Preadolescent suicidal behavior: The role of cognitive functioning. *Child Psychiatry and Human Development, 28,* 103–115.

655. Molfese, V. J., DiLalla, L. F., & Bunce, D. (1997). Prediction of the intelligence test scores of 3- to 8-year-old children by home environment, socioeconomic status, and biomedical risks. *Merrill-Palmer Quarterly, 43,* 219–234.

656. Närhi, V., Räsänen, P., Metsäpelto, R-L., & Ahonen, T. (1997). Trail making test in assessing children with reading disabilities: A test of executive functions or content information. *Perceptual and Motor Skills, 84,* 1355–1362.

657. Nigg, J. T., Swanson, J. M., & Hinshaw, S. P. (1997). Covert visual spatial attention in boys with attention deficit hyperactivity disorder: Lateral effects, methylphenidate response and results for parents. *Neuropsychologia, 35,* 165–176.

658. Palladino, P., Poli, P., Masi, G., & Marcheschi, M. (1997). Impulsive-reflective cognitive style, metacognition, and emotion in adolescence. *Perceptual and Motor Skills, 84,* 47–57.

659. Piek, J. P., & Edwards, K. (1997). The identification of children with developmental coordination disorder by class and physical education teachers. *British Journal of Educational Psychology, 67,* 55–67.

660. Piven, J., Bailey, J., Ranson, B. J., & Arndt, S. (1997). An MRI study of the corpus callosum in autism. *American Journal of Psychiatry, 154,* 1051–1056.

661. Piven, J., Palmer, P., Jacobi, D., Childress, D., & Arndt, S. (1997). Broader autism phenotype: Evidence from a family history study of multiple-incidence autism families. *American Journal of Psychiatry, 154,* 185–190.

662. Piven, J., Saliba, K., Bailey, J., & Arndt, S. (1997). An MRI study of autism: The cerebellum revisited. *Neurology, 49,* 546–551.

663. Pogson, D. (1997). Issues for consideration in dihydropteridine reductase (DHPR) deficiency: A variant form of hyperphenylalaninaemia. *Journal of Disability Research, 41,* 208–214.

664. Pontius, A. A. (1997). No gender difference in spatial representation by school children in northwest Pakistan. *Journal of Cross-Cultural Psychology, 28,* 779–786.

665. Purvis, K. L., & Tannock, R. (1997). Language abilities in children with Attention Deficit Hyperactivity disorder, reading disabilities, and normal controls. *Journal of Abnormal Child Psychology, 25,* 133–144.

666. Richman, L. C., & Millard, T. (1997). Brief report: Cleft lip and palate: Longitudinal behavior and relationships of cleft conditions to behavior and achievement. *Journal of Pediatric Psychology, 22,* 487–494.

667. Rizzo, T. A., Metzger, B. E., Dooley, S. L., & Cho, N. H. (1997). Early malnutrition and child neurobehavioral development: Insights from the study of children of diabetic mothers. *Child Development, 68,* 26–38.

668. Robertson, S. B., & Weismer, S. E. (1997). The influence of peer models on the play scripts of children with specific language impairment. *Journal of Speech, Language, and Hearing Research, 40,* 49–61.

669. Rose, S. A., & Feldman, J. F. (1997). Memory and speed: Their role in the relation of infant information processing to later IQ. *Child Development, 68,* 630–641.

670. Schinka, J. A., Vanderploeg, R. D., & Curtiss, G. (1997). WISC-III subtest scatter as a function of highest subtest scaled score. *Psychological Assessment, 9,* 83–88.

671. Schultz, M. K. (1997). WISC-III and WJ-R Tests of Achievement: Concurrent validity and learning disability identification. *The Journal of Special Education, 31,* 377–386.

672. Serna, R. W., Dube, W. V., & McIlvane, W. J. (1997). Assessing same/different judgments in individuals with severe intellectual disabilities: A status report. *Research in Developmental Disabilities, 18,* 343–368.

673. Shibagaki, M., & Furuya, T. (1997). Baseline respiratory sinus arrhythmia and heart-rate responses during auditory stimulation of children with attention-deficit hyperactivity disorder. *Perceptual and Motor Skills, 84,* 967–975.

674. Slate, J. R., Jones, C. H., & Saarnio, D. A. (1997). WISC-III IQ scores and special education diagnosis. *The Journal of Psychology, 131,* 119–120.

675. Sloutsky, V. M. (1997). Institutional care and developmental outcomes of 6- and 7-year-old children: A contextualist perspective. *International Journal of Behavioral Development, 20,* 131–151.

676. Smith, A. M., Gacono, C. B., & Kaufman, L. (1997). A Rorschach comparison of psychopathic and nonpsychopathic conduct disordered adolescents. *Journal of Clinical Psychology, 53,* 289–300.

677. Snyder, C. R., Hoza, B., Pelham, W. E., Rapoff, M., Ware, L., Danovsky, M., Highberger, L., Rubinstein, H., & Stahl, K. J. (1997). The development and validation of the Children's Hope Scale. *Journal of Pediatric Psychology, 22,* 399–421.

678. Snyder, M. C., & Bambara, L. M. (1997). Teaching secondary students with learning disabilities to self-manage classroom survival skills. *Journal of Learning Disabilities, 30,* 534–543.

679. Spitz, R. V., Tallal, P., Flax, J., & Benasich, A. A. (1997). Look who's talking: A prospective study of familial transmission of language impairments. *Journal of Speech, Language, and Hearing Research, 40,* 990–1001.

680. Stark, R. E., & McGregor, K. K. (1997). Follow-up study of a right- and a left-hemispherectomized child: Implications for localization and impairment of language in children. *Brain and Language, 60,* 222–242.

681. Stone, C. A. (1997). Correspondences among parent, teacher, and student perceptions of adolescents' learning disabilities. *Journal of Learning Disabilities, 30,* 660–669.

682. Swan, D., & Goswami, V. (1997). Picture naming deficits in developmental dyslexia: The phonological representations hypothesis. *Brain and Language, 56,* 334–353.

683. Tsatsanis, K. D., Fuerst, D. R., & Rourke, B. P. (1997). Psychosocial dimensions of learning disabilities: External validation and relationship with age and academic functioning. *Journal of Learning Disabilities, 30,* 490–502.

684. Tyler, L. K., Karmiloff-Smith, A., Voice, J. K., Stevens, T., Grant, J., Udwin, O., Davies, M., & Howlin, P. (1997). Do individuals with Williams Syndrome have bizarre semantics? Evidence for lexical organization using an on-line task. *Cortex, 33,* 515–527.

685. Valencia, R. R., & Rankin, R. J. (1997). WISC-R factor structures among white, Mexican American, and African American children: A research note. *Psychology in the Schools, 34,* 11–16.

686. Vallance, D. D., & Wintre, M. G. (1997). Discourse processes underlying social competence in children with language learning disabilities. *Development and Psychopathology, 9,* 95–108.

687. Vanderark, S. D., & Mostardi, R. A. (1997). Detail, pressure, and completion of Draw-A-Person produced during silence or rock music. *Perceptual and Motor Skills, 84,* 1354.

688. Walton, J. R., Nuttall, R. L., & Nuttal, E. V. (1997). The impact of war on the mental health of children: A Salvadoran study. *Child Abuse & Neglect, 21,* 737–749.

689. Watkins, M. W., Kush, J. C., & Glutting, J. J. (1997). Prevalence and diagnostic utility of the WISC-III SCAD profile among children with disabilities. *School Psychology Quarterly, 12,* 235–248.

690. Watkins, M. W., Kush, J. C., & Gluttring, J. J. (1997). Discriminant and predictive validity of the WISC-III ACID profile among children with learning disabilities. *Psychology in the Schools, 34,* 309–320.

691. Watson, T. S., & Ray, K. P. (1997). The effects of differential units of measurement on instructional decision making. *School Psychology Quarterly, 12,* 42–53.

692. Wodrich, D. L., & Tholl, L. M. (1997). Childhood Tourette's Syndrome and the Thematic Apperception Test: is there a recognizable pattern? *Perceptual and Motor Skills, 85,* 635–641.

693. Wolman, C., van den Broek, P., & Lorch, R. F., Jr. (1997). Effects of causal structure on immediate and delayed story recall by children with mild mental retardation, children with learning disabilities, and children without disabilities. *The Journal of Special Education, 30,* 439–455.

694. Yeates, K. O., & Taylor, H. G. (1997). Predicting premorbid neuropsychological functioning following pediatric traumatic brain injury. *Journal of Clinical and Experimental Neuropsychology, 19,* 825–837.

695. Zimmerman, I. L., & Woo-Sam, J. M. (1997). Review of the criterion-related validity of the WISC-III: The first five years. *Perceptual and Motor Skills, 85,* 531–546.

696. Ackerman, P. T., McPherson, W. B., Oglesby, D. M., & Dykman, R. A. (1998). EEG power spectra of adolescent poor readers. *Journal of Learning Disabilities, 31,* 83–90.

697. Anderson, L. E., & Walsh, J. A. (1998). Prediction of adult criminal status from juvenile psychological assessment. *Criminal Justice and Behavior, 25,* 226–239.

698. Antozzi, C., Granata, T., Aurisano, N., Zardini, G., Confalonieri, P., Airaghi, G., Mantegazza, R., & Spreafico, R. (1998). Long-term selective IgG immuno-absorption improves Rasmussen's encephalitis. *Neurology, 51,* 302–305.

699. Asbjornsen, A. E., & Bryden, M. P. (1998). Auditory attentional shifts in reading-disabled students: Quantification of attentional effectiveness by the Attentional Shift Index. *Neuropsychologia, 36,* 143–148.

700. Baum, K. M., & Nowicki, S., Jr. (1998). Perception of emotion: Measuring decoding accuracy of adult prosodic cues varying in intensity. *Journal of Nonverbal Behavior, 22,* 89–107.

701. Bear, G. G., Minke, K. M., Griffin, S. M., & Deemer, S. A. (1998). Achievement-related perceptions of children with learning disabilities and normal achievement: Group and developmental differences. *Journal of Learning Disabilities, 31,* 91–104.

702. Berquin, P. C., Giedd, J. N., Jacobsen, L. K., Hamburger, S. D., Krain, A. L., Rapoport, J. L., & Castellanos, F. X. (1998). Cerebellum in attention-deficit hyperactivity disorder: A morphometric MRI study. *Neurology, 50,* 1087–1093.

703. Bishop, D. V. M., & Bishop, S. J. (1998). "Twin language": A risk factor for language impairment? *Journal of Speech, Language, and Hearing Research, 41,* 150–160.

704. Bryant, P., Nunes, T., & Bindman, M. (1998). Awareness of language in children who have reading difficulties: Historical comaprisons in a longitudinal study. *Journal of Child Psychology and Psychiatry, 39,* 501–510.

705. Chapman, S. B., Levin, H. S., Wanke, A., Weyrauch, j., & Kufera, J. (1998). Discourse after closed head injury in young children. *Brain and Language, 61,* 420–449.

706. Chaziuddin, M., & Butler, E. (1998). Clumsiness in autism and Asperger syndrome: A further report. *Journal of Disability Research, 42,* 43–48.

707. Cochrane, H. J., Baker, G. A., & Mendell, P. R. (1998). Simulating a memory impairment: Can amnesics implicitly outperform simulators? *British Journal of Clinical Psychology, 37,* 31–48.

708. Dennis, M., Barnes, M. A., Wilkinson, M., & Humphreys, R. P. (1998). How children with head injury represent real and deceptive emotion in short narratives. *Brain and Language, 61,* 450–483.

709. Elbro, C., Borstrom, I., & Petersen, D. K. (1998). Predicting dyslexia from kindergarten: The importance of directness of phonological representations of lexical items. *Reading Research Quarterly, 33,* 36–60.

710. Ewing-Cobbs, L., Brookshire, B., Scott, M. A., & Fletcher, J. M. (1998). Children's narratives following traumatic brain injury: Linguistic structure, cohesion, and thematic recall. *Brain and Language, 61,* 395–419.

711. Farel, A. M., Hooper, S. R., Teplin, S. W., Henry, M. M., & Kraybill, E. N. (1998). Very-low-birthweight infants at seven years: An assessment of the health and neurodevelopmental risk conveyed by chronic lung disease. *Journal of Learning Disabilities, 31,* 118–126.

712. Gass, C. S., Demsky, Y. I., & Martin, P. C. (1998). Factor analysis of the WISC-R (Spanish version) at 11 age levels between 6 1/2 and 16 1/2 years. *Journal of Clinical Psychology, 54,* 109–113.

713. Giancola, P. R., Mezzich, A. C., & Tarter, R. E. (1998). Disruptive, delinquent and aggressive behavior in female adolescents with a psychoactive substance use disorder: Relation to executive cognitive functioning. *Journal of Studies on Alcohol, 59,* 560–567.

714. Goodman, R., Yude, C., Richards, H., & Taylor, E. (1998). Rating child psychiatric caseness from detailed case histories. *Journal of Child Psychology and Psychiatry, 37,* 369–379.

715. Grimshaw, G. M., Adelstein, A., Bryden, M. P., & MacKinnon, G. E. (1998). First-language acquisition in adolescence: Evidence for a critical period for verbal language development. *Brain and Language, 63,* 237–255.

716. Handwerk, M. L., & Marshall, R. M. (1998). Behavioral and emotional problems of students with learning disabilities, serious emotional disturbance, or both conditions. *Journal of Learning Disabilities, 31,* 327–338.

717. Howlin, P., Davies, M., & Udwin, O. (1998). Cognitive functioning in adults with Williams syndrome. *Journal of Child Psychology and Psychiatry, 39,* 183–189.

718. Hyman, I. A., Wojtowicz, A., Lee, K. D., Haffner, M. E., Fiorello, C. A., Storlazzi, J. J., & Rosenfeld, J. (1998). School-based methylphenidate placebo protocols: Methodological and practical issues. *Journal of Learning Disabilities, 31,* 581–594, 614.

719. Inoue, K., Nadakoka, T., Oiji, A., Morioka, Y., Totsuka, S., Kanbayashi, Y., & Hukui, T. (1998). Clinical evaluation of attention-deficit hyperactivity disorder by objective quantitative measures. *Child Psychiatry and Human Development, 28,* 179–188.

720. Jarrold, C., Baddeley, A. D., & Herres, A. K. (1998). Verbal and nonverbal abilities in the Williams syndrome phenotype: Evidence for diverging developmental erajectiories. *Journal of Child Psychology and Psychiatry, 39,* 511–523.

721. Karatekin, C., & Asarnow, R. F. (1998). Componants of visual search in childhood-onset schizophrenia and attention-deficit/hyperactivity disorder. *Journal of Abnormal Child Psychology, 26,* 367–380.

722. Kehle, J. J., Madaus, m. R., Baratta, V. S., & Bray, M. A. (1998). Augmented self-modeling as a treatment for children with selective mutism. *Journal of School Psychology, 36,* 247–260.

723. Macias, M., Saylor, C., Watson, M., & Spratt, E. (1998). Children with both developmental and behavioral needs: Profile of two clinic populations. *Child Psychiatry and Human Development, 28,* 135–148.

724. MacMillan, D. L., Gresham, F. M., & Bocian, K. M. (1998). Discrepancy between definitions of learning disabilities and school practices: An empirical investigation. *Journal of Learning Disabilities, 31,* 314–326.

725. Meyer, M. S., Wood, F. B., Hart, L. A., & Felton, R. H. (1998). Selective predictive value of rapid automatized naming in poor readers. *Journal of Learning Disabilities, 31,* 106–117.

726. Minder, B., Das-Smaal, E. A., & Orlebeke, J. F. (1998). Cognition in children does not suffer from very low lead exposure. *Journal of Learning Disabilities, 31,* 494–502.

727. Mostofsky, S. H., Mazzocco, m. M. M., Aakalu, G., Warsofsky, I. S., Denckla, M. B., & Reiss, A. L. (1998). Decreased cerebellar posterior vermis size in fragile X syndrome: Correlation with neurocognitive performance. *Neurology, 50,* 121–130.

728. Muter, V., & Snowling, M. (1998). Concurrent and logitudinal predictors of reading: The role of metalinguistic and short-term memory skills. *Reading Research Quarterly, 33,* 320–337.

729. Oakland, T., Black, J. L., Stanford, G., Nussbaum, N. L., & Balise, R. R. (1998). An evaluation of the dyslexia training program: A multisensory method for promoting reading in students with reading disabilities. *Journal of Learning Disabilities, 31,* 140–147.

730. Rae, C., Karmiloff-Smith, A., Lee, M. A., Dixon, R. M., Grant, J., Blamire, A. M., Thompson, C. H., Styles, P., & Radda, G. K. (1998). Brain biochemistry in Williams syndrome: Evidence for a role of the cerebellum in cognition? *Neurology, 51,* 33–40.

731. Rankhorn, B., England, G., Collins, S. M., Lockavitch, J. F. & Algozzine, B. (1998). Effects of the failure free reading program on students with severe reading disabilities. *Journal of Learning Disabilities, 31,* 307–312.

732. Roeyers, H., Keymeulen, H., & Buysse, A. (1998). Differentiating attention-deficit/hyperactivity disorder from pervasive developmental disorder not otherwise specified. *Journal of Learning Disabilities, 31,* 365–371.

733. Saklofske, D. H., Hildebrand, D. K., Reynolds, C. R., & Willson, V. L. (1998). Substituting symbol search for coding on the WISC-III: Canadian normative tables for performance and full scale IQ scores. *Canadian Journal of Behavioural Science, 30,* 57–68.

734. Silberg, J. L. (1998). Dissociative symptomatology in children and adolescents as displayed on psychological testing. *Journal of Personality Assessment, 71,* 421–439.

735. Slate, J. R. (1998). Sex differences in WISC-III IQs: Time for separate norms? *Journal of Psychology, 132,* 677–679.

736. Smithee, J. A. F., Klorman, R., Brumaghim, J. T., & Borgstedt, A. D. (1998). Methylphenidate does not modify the impact of response frequency or stimulus sequence on performance and event-related potentials of children with attention deficit hyperactivity disorder. *Journal of Abnormal Child Psychology, 26,* 233–245.

737. Sprouse, C. A., Hall, C. W., Webster, R. E., & Bolen, L. M. (1998). Social perception in students with learning disabilities and attention-deficit/hyperactivity disorder. *Journal of Nonverbal Behavior, 22,* 125–134.

738. Tomblin, J. B., & Buckwalter, P. R. (1998). Heritability of poor language achievement among twins. *Journal of Speech, Language, and Hearing Research, 41,* 188–199.

739. Vallance, D. D., Cummings, R. L., & Humphries, T. (1998). Mediators of the risk for problem behavior in children with language learning disabilities. *Journal of Learning Disabilities, 31,* 160–171.

740. Wiers, R. W., Gunning, W. B., & Sergeant, J. A. (1998). Is a mild deficit in executive functions in boys related to childhood ADHD or to parental multigenerational alcoholism? *Journal of Abnormal Child Psychology, 26,* 415–430.

[2863]

Weschler Memory Scale III.

Purpose: Designed to "provide a detailed assessment of clinically relevant aspects of memory functioning" using both auditory and visual stimulus.

Population: Ages 16–89 years.

Publication Dates: 1945–1997.

Acronym: WMS-III.

Scores, 22: Six primary subtests yielding 10 scores (Logical Memory I, Logical Memory II, Verbal Paired Associates I, Verbal Paired Associates II, Letter-Numbering Sequencing, Faces I, Faces II, Family Pictures I, Family Pictures II, Spatial Span); five Optional Subtests yielding 6 scores (Information and Orientation, Word Lists I, Word Lists II, Mental Control, Visual Reproduction I, Visual Reproduction II); Five Supplemental Scores (Recall Total, Recognition Total, Copy Total, Discrimination Total, Percent Retention).

Administration: Individual.

Price Data: Available from publisher.

Time: (30–35) minutes for primary subtests.

Comments: "When used in conjunction with the WAIS-III, it is possible to compute ability-memory difference scores"; WAIS-III/WMS-III Writer interpretive report software available for use with IBM or compatible PC with at least 486 processor.

Author: David Weschler.

Publisher: The Psychological Corporation.

Cross References: See T4:2940 (117 references); for reviews of an earlier edition by E. Scott Huebner and Robert C. Reinehr, see 11:465 (166 references); see also 9:1355 (49 references); T3:2607 (96 references); 8:250 (36 references); T2:592 (70 references), and 6:561 (9 references); for reviews of the original version by Ivan Norma Mensh and Joseph Newman, see 4:364 (6 references); for a review by Kate Levine Kogan, see 3:302 (3 references).

TEST REFERENCES

1. Butters, N., Albert, M. S., Sax, D. S., Miliotis, P., Nagode, J., & Sterste, A. (1983). The effect of verbal mediators on the pictorial memory of brain-damaged patients. *Neuropsychologia, 21,* 307–323.

2. Cermak, L. S., & O'Connor, M. (1983). The anterograde and retrograde retrieval ability of a patient with amnesia due to encephalitis. *Neuropsychologia, 21,* 213–234.

3. Haxby, J. V., Lundgren, S. L., & Morley, G. K. (1983). Short-term retention of verbal, visual shape and visuospatial location information in normal and amnesic subjects. *Neuropsychologia, 21,* 25–33.

4. Howes, J. L. (1983). Effects of experimenter- and self-generated imagery on the Korsakoff patient's memory performance. *Neuropsychologia, 21,* 341–349.

5. Zola-Morgan, S., Cohen, N. J., & Squire, L. R. (1983). Recall of remote episodic memory in amnesia. *Neuropsychologia, 21,* 487–500.

6. Bentin, S., Sahar, A., & Moscovitch, M. (1984). Intermanual information transfer in patients with lesions in the trunk of the corpus callosum. *Neuropsychologia, 22,* 601–611.

7. Hirst, W., & Volpe, B. T. (1984). Encoding of spatial relations with amnesia. *Neuropsychologia, 22,* 631–634.

8. Ogden, J. A. (1984). Dyslexia in a right-handed patient with a posterior lesion of the right cerebral hemisphere. *Neuropsychologia, 22,* 265–280.

9. Sandson, J., & Albert, M. L. (1984). Varieties of perseveration. *Neuropsychologia, 22,* 715–732.
10. Winocur, G., Oxbury, S., Roberts, R., Agnetti, V., & Davis, C. (1984). Amnesia in a patient with bilateral lesions to the thalamus. *Neuropsychologia, 22,* 123–143.
11. Glisky, E. L., & Schacter, D. L. (1987). Acquisition of domain-specific knowledge in organic amnesia: Training for computer-related work. *Neuropsychologia, 25,* 893–906.
12. Grady, C. L., Haxby, J. V., Horwitz, B., Berg, G., & Rapoport, S. I. (1987). Neuropsychological and cerebral metabolic function in early vs. late onset dementia of the Alzheimer type. *Neuropsychologia, 25,* 807–816.
13. Grigsby, J. P., Kemper, M. B., & Hagerman, R. J. (1987). Developmental Gerstmann Syndrome without aphasia in Fragile X Syndrome. *Neuropsychologia, 25,* 881–891.
14. Mayes, A. R., Pickering, A., & Fairbairn, A. (1987). Amnesic sensitivity to proactive interference: Its relationship to priming and the causes of amnesia. *Neuropsychologia, 25,* 211–220.
15. McAndrews, M. P., Glisky, E. L., & Schacter, D. L. (1987). When priming persists: Long-lasting implicit memory for a single episode in amnesic patients. *Neuropsychologia, 25,* 497–506.
16. Ostergaard, A. L. (1987). Episodic, semantic and procedural memory in a case of amnesia at an early age. *Neuropsychologia, 25,* 341–357.
17. Rybarczyk, B. D., Hart, R. P., & Harkins, S. W. (1987). Age and forgetting rate with pictorial stimuli. *Psychology and Aging, 2,* 404-406.
18. Squire, L. R., Shimamura, A. P., & Graf, P. (1987). Strength and duration of priming effects in normal subjects and amnesic patients. *Neuropsychologia, 25,* 195–210.
19. Aggleton, J. P., Nicol, R. M., Huston, A. E., & Fairbairn, A. F. (1988). The performance of amnesic subjects on tests of experimental amnesia in animals: Delayed matching-to-sample and concurrent learning. *Neuropsychologia, 26,* 903–916.
20. Glisky, E. L., & Schacter, D. L. (1988). Long-term retention of computer learning by patients with memory disorders. *Neuropsychologia, 26,* 173–178.
21. Gurd, J. M., Bessell, N. J., Bladon, R. A. W., & Bamford, J. M. (1988). A case of foreign accent syndrome, with follow-up clinical, neuropsychological and phonetic descriptions. *Neuropsychologia, 26,* 237–251.
22. Ogden, J. A. (1988). Language and memory functions after long recovery periods in left-hemispherectomized subjects. *Neuropsychologia, 26,* 645–659.
23. Blonder, L. X., Gur, R. E., Gur, R. C., Saykin, A. J., & Hurtig, H. I. (1989). Neuropsychological functioning in hemiparkinsonism. *Brain and Cognition, 9,* 244-257.
24. Dakof, G. A., & Mendelsohn, G. A. (1989). Patterns of adaptation to Parkinson's disease. *Health Psychology, 8,* 355–372.
25. Everett, J., Laplante, L., & Thomas, J. (1989). The selective attention deficit in schizophrenia: Limited resources or cognitive fatigue? *The Journal of Nervous and Mental Disease, 177,* 735-738.
26. Farah, M. J., Hammond, K. M., Mehta, Z., & Ratcliff, G. (1989). Category-specificity and modality-specificity in semantic memory. *Neuropsychologia, 27,* 193–200.
27. Faust, D., & Fogel, B. S. (1989). The development and initial validation of a sensitive bedside cognitive screening test. *The Journal of Nervous and Mental Disease, 177,* 25-31.
28. Glisky, E. L., & Schacter, D. L. (1989). Extending the limits of complex learning in organic amnesia: Computer training in a vocational domain. *Neuropsychologia, 27,* 107–120.
29. Hall, J. L., Gonder-Frederick, L. A., Chewning, W. W., Silveira, J., & Gold, P. E. (1989). Glucose enhancement of performance on memory tests in young and aged humans. *Neuropsychologia, 27,* 1129–1138.
30. Janowsky, J. S., Shimamura, A. P., & Squire, L. R. (1989). Source memory impairment in patients with frontal lobe lesions. *Neuropsychologia, 27,* 1043–1056.
31. Lang, C. J. G. (1989). Continuous figure recognition in dementia and unilateral cerebral damage. *Neuropsychologia, 27,* 619–628.
32. Malloy, P., Noel, N., Rodgers, S., Longabaugh, R., & Beattie, M. (1989). Risk factors for neuropsychological impairment in alcoholics: Antisocial personality, age, years of drinking and gender. *Journal of Studies on Alcohol, 50,* 422–426.
33. Mayes, A. R., & Gooding, P. (1989). Enhancement of word completion priming in amnesics by cueing with previously novel associates. *Neuropsychologia, 27,* 1057–1072.
34. Nissen, M. J., Willingham, D., & Hartman, M. (1989). Explicit and implicit remembering: When is learning preserved in amnesia? *Neuropsychologia, 27,* 341–352.
35. Ogden, J. A. (1989). Visuospatial and other "right-hemispheric" functions after long recovery periods in left-hemispherectomized subjects. *Neuropsychologia, 27,* 765–776.
36. Pickering, A. D., Mayes, A. R., & Fairbairn, A. F. (1989). Amnesia and memory for modality information. *Neuropsychologia, 27,* 1249–1259.
37. Rapesak, S. Z., Kaszniak, A. W., & Rubens, A. B. (1989). Anomia for facial expressions: Evidence for a category specific visual-verbal disconnection syndrome. *Neuropsychologia, 27,* 1031–1041.
38. Saykin, A. J., Gur, R. C., Sussman, N. M., O'Connor, M. J., & Gur, R. E. (1989). Memory deficits before and after temporal lobectomy: Effect of laterality and age of onset. *Brain and Cognition, 9,* 191-200.
39. Altepeter, T. S., Adams, R. L., Buchanan, W. L., & Buck, P. (1990). Luria memory Words Test and Wechsler Memory Scale: Comparison of utility in discriminating neurologically impaired from controls. *Journal of Clinical Psychology, 29,* 190–193.
40. Alterman, A. I., Kushner, H., & Holahan, J. M. (1990). Cognitive functioning and treatment outcome in alcoholics. *The Journal of Nervous and Mental Disease, 178,* 494-499.
41. Barr, W. B., Goldberg, E., Wasserstein, J., & Novelly, R. A. (1990). Retrograde amnesia following unilateral temporal lobectomy. *Neuropsychologia, 28,* 243–255.
42. Bolla, K. I., Lindgren, K. N., Bonaccorsy, C., & Bleecker, M. L. (1990). Predictors of verbal fluency (FAS) in the healthy elderly. *Journal of Clinical Psychology, 46,* 623–628.
43. Bottini, G., Cappa, S., Geminiani, G., & Sterzi, R. (1990). Topographic disorientation—A case report. *Neuropsychologia, 28,* 309–312.
44. Dubois, B., Pillon, B., Sternic, N., Lhermitte, F., & Agid, Y. (1990). Age-induced cognitive disturbances in Parkinson's disease. *Neurology, 40,* 38–41.
45. Eustache, F., Lechevalier, B., Viader, F., & Lambert, J. (1990). Identification and discrimination disorders in auditory perception: A report on two cases. *Neuropsychologia, 28,* 257–270.
46. Frisk, V., & Milner, B. (1990). The relationship of working memory to the immediate recall of stories following unilateral temporal or frontal lobectomy. *Neuropsychologia, 28,* 121–135.
47. Frisk, V., & Milner, B. (1990). The role of the left hippocampal region in the acquisition and retention of story content. *Neuropsychologia, 28,* 349–359.
48. Giordani, B., Boivin, M. J., Hall, A. L., Foster, N. L., Lehtihen, S. J., Bluemlein, L. A., & Berent, S. (1990). The utility and generality of Mini-Mental State Examination scores in Alzheimer's disease. *Neurology, 40,* 1894–1896.
49. Harper, R. G., Kotik-Harper, D., & Kirby, H. (1990). Psychometric assessment of depression in an elderly general medical population: Over- or underassessment? *The Journal of Nervous and Mental Disease, 178,* 113-119.
50. Heilman, K. M., Bowers, D., Watson, R. T., Day, A., Valenstein, E., Hammond, E., & Duara, R. (1990). Frontal hypermetabolism and thalamic hypometabolism in a patient with abnormal orienting and retrosplenial amnesia. *Neuropsychologia, 28,* 161–169.
51. Oscar-Berman, M., Pulaski, J. L., Hutner, N., Weber, D. A., & Freedman, M. (1990). Cross-modal functions in alcoholism and aging. *Neuropsychologia, 28,* 851–869.
52. Peterson, J. B., Rothfleisch, J., Zelazo, P. D., & Pihl, R. O. (1990). Acute alcohol intoxication and cognitive functioning. *Journal of Studies on Alcohol, 51,* 114–122.
53. Rausch, R., & Ary, C. M. (1990). Supraspan learning in patients with unilateral anterior temporal lobe resections. *Neuropsychologia, 28,* 111–120.
54. Robertson, I. H. (1990). Digit span and visual neglect: A puzzling relationship. *Neuropsychologia, 28,* 217–222.
55. Shaw, C., Kentridge, R. W., & Aggleton, J. P. (1990). Cross-modal matching by amnesic subjects. *Neuropsychologia, 28,* 665–671.
56. Shimamura, A. P., Janowsky, J. S., & Squire, L. R. (1990). Memory for the temporal order of events in patients with frontal lobe lesions and amnesic patients. *Neuropsychologia, 28,* 803–813.
57. Strauss, E., Satz, P., & Wada, J. (1990). An examination of the crowding hypothesis in epileptic patients who have undergone the carotid amytal test. *Neuropsychologia, 28,* 1221–1227.
58. Taylor, A. E., Saint-Cyr, J. A., & Lang, A. E. (1990). Memory and learning in early Parkinson's disease: Evidence for a "frontal lobe syndrome". *Brain and Cognition, 13,* 211-232.
59. Verfaellie, M., Cermak, L. S., Blackford, S. D., & Weiss, S. (1990). Strategic and automatic priming of semantic memory in alcoholic Korsakoff patients. *Brain and Cognition, 13,* 178-192.
60. Young, A. W., De Haan, E. H. F., Newcombe, F., & Hay, D. C. (1990). Facial neglect. *Neuropsychologia, 28,* 391–415.
61. Cermak, L. S., Verfaellie, M., Milberg, W., Letourneau, L., & Blackford, S. (1991). A further analysis of perceptual identification priming in alcoholic Korsakoff patients. *Neuropsychologia, 29,* 725–736.
62. Claus, J. J., Ludwig, C., Mohr, E., Gioffra, M., Blin, J., & Chase, T. N. (1991). Nootropic drugs in Alzheimer's disease: Symptomatic treatment with pramiracetam. *Neurology, 41,* 570–574.
63. Danion, J., Willard-Schroeder, D., Zimmerman, M., Grange, D., Schlienger, J., & Singer, L. (1991). Explicit memory and repetition priming in depression. *Archives of General Psychiatry, 48,* 707-711.
64. Farah, M. J., McMullen, P. A., & Meyer, M. M. (1991). Can recognition of living things be selectively impaired? *Neuropsychologia, 29,* 185–193.
65. Goldman, R. S., Avelrod, B. N., & Tandon, R. (1991). Analysis of executive functioning in schizophrenics using the Wisconsin Card Sorting Test. *The Journal of Nervous and Mental Disease, 179,* 507-508.
66. Hartman, M. (1991). The use of semantic knowledge in Alzheimer's disease: Evidence for impairment of attention. *Neuropsychologia, 29,* 213–228.
67. Hillis, A. E., & Caramazza, A. (1991). Deficit to stimulus-centered, letter shape represenations in a case of "unilateral neglect." *Neuropsychologia, 29,* 1223–1240.
68. Hyyppä, M. T., Kronholm, E., & Mattlar, C-E. (1991). Mental well-being of good sleepers in a random population sample. *British Journal of Medical Psychology, 64,* 25–34.
69. Joyce, E. M., & Robbins, T. W. (1991). Frontal lobe function in Korsakoff and non-Korsakoff alcoholics: Planning and spatial working memory. *Neuropsychologia, 29,* 709-723.
70. Klonoff, H., Clark, C., Oger, J., Paty, D., & Li, D. (1991). Neuropsychological performance in patients with mild multiple sclerosis. *The Journal of Nervous and Mental Disease, 179,* 127-131.

71. Knopmon, D., & Nissen, M. J. (1991). Procedural learning is impaired in Huntington's disease: Evidence from the serial reaction time task. *Neuropsychologia, 29,* 245–254.

72. Loewenstein, D. A., D'Elia, L., Guteman, A., Eisdorfer, C., Wilkie, F., LaRue, A., Mintzer, J., & Duara, R. (1991). The occurrence of different intrusive errors in patients with Alzheimer's disease, multiple cerebral infarctions, and major depression. *Brain and Cognition, 16,* 104-117.

73. Lucas, J. A., Telch, M. J., & Bigler, E. D. (1991). Memory functioning in panic disorder: A neuropsychological perspective. *Journal of Anxiety Disorders, 5,* 1-20.

74. Mahurin, R. K., DeBettignies, B. H., & Pirozzolo, F. J. (1991). Structured assessment of independent living skills: Preliminary report of a performance measure of functional abilities in dementia. *Journal of Gerontology, 46,* 58–66.

75. Mayes, A. R., Meudell, P. R., & MacDonald, C. (1991). Disproportionate intentional spatial-memory impairments in amnesia. *Neuropsychologia, 29,* 771–784.

76. Miller, B. L., Cummings, J. L., Villanueva-Meyer, J., Boone, K., Mehringer, C. M., Lesser, I. M., & Mena, I. (1991). Frontal lobe degeneration: Clinical, neuropsychological, and SPECCT characteristics. *Neurology, 41,* 1374–1382.

77. Nestor, P. G., Parasuraman, R., Haxby, J. V., & Grady, C. L. (1991). Divided attention and metabolic brain dysfunction in mild dementia of the Alzheimer's type. *Neuropsychologia, 29,* 379–387.

78. Paller, K. A., Mayes, A. R., McDermott, M., Pickering, A. D., & Meudell, P. R. (1991). Indirect measures of memory in a duration-judgment task are normal in amnesic patients. *Neuropsychologia, 29,* 1007–1018.

79. Rice, D. M., Buchsbaum, M. S., Hardy, D., & Burgwald, L. (1991). Focal left temporal slow EEG activity in related to a verbal recent memory deficit in a non-demented elderly population. *Journal of Gerontology, 46,* 144–151.

80. Rodriguez, R. (1991). Hand motor patterns after the correction of left-nondominant-hand mirror writing. *Neuropsychologia, 29,* 1191–1203.

81. Sagar, H. J., Sullivan, E. V., Cooper, J. A., & Jordan, N. (1991). Normal release from proactive interference in untreated patients with Parkinson's disease. *Neuropsychologia, 29,* 1033–1044.

82. Shoqeirat, M. A., & Mayes, A. R. (1991). Disproportionate incidental spatial-memory and recall deficits in amnesia. *Neuropsychologia, 29,* 749–769.

83. Teri, L., Reifler, B. V., Veith, R. C., Barnes, R., White, E., McLean, P., & Raskind, M. (1991). Imipramine in the treatment of depressed Alzheimer's patients: Impact on cognition. *Journal of Gerontology, 46,* 372–377.

84. Tramo, M. J., & Bharucha, J. J. (1991). Musical priming by the right hemisphere post-callosotomy. *Neuropsychologia, 29,* 313–325.

85. Verfaellie, M., Cermak, L. S., Letourneau, L., & Zuffante, P. (1991). Repetition effects in a lexical decision task: The role of episodic memory in the performance of alcoholic Korsakoff patients. *Neuropsychologia, 29,* 641–657.

86. Atkinson, L. (1992). The Wechsler Memory Scale—Revised: Abnormality of selected index differences. *Canadian Journal of Behavioural Science, 24,* 537-539.

87. Bachman, D. L., Wolf, P. A., Linn, R., Knoefel, J. E., Cobb, J., Belanger, A., D'Agostino, R. B., & White, L. R. (1992). Prevalence of dementia and probable senile dementia of the Alzheimer type in the Framingham study. *Neurology, 42,* 115–119.

88. Bromet, E. J., Schwartz, J. E., Fennig, S., Geller, L., Jandorf, L., Kovasznay, B., Lavelle, J., Miller, A., Pato, C., Ram, R., & Rich, C. (1992). The epidemiology of psychosis: The Suffolk County Mental Health Project. *Schizophrenia Bulletin, 18,* 243–255.

89. Cermak, L. S., Verfaellie, M., Sweeney, M., & Jacoby, L. L. (1992). Fluency versus conscious recollection in the word completion performance of amnesic patients. *Brain and Cognition, 20,* 367-377.

90. Dartigues, J. F., Gagnon, M., Mazaux, J. M., Baberger-Gateau, P., Commenges, D., Lettenneur, L., & Orgogozo, J. M. (1992). Occupation during life and memory performance in nondemented French elderly community residents. *Neurology, 42,* 1697–1701.

91. DeLuca, J. (1992). Cognitive dysfunction after aneurysm of the anterior communicating artery. *Journal of Clinical and Experimental Neuropsychology, 14,* 924-934.

92. Diamond, R., White, R. F., Myers, R. H., Mastromauro, C., Koroshetz, W. J., Butters, N., Rothstein, D. M., Moss, M. B., & Vasterling, J. (1992). Evidence of presymptomatic cognitive decline in Huntington's disease. *Journal of Clinical and Experimental Neuropsychology, 14,* 961-975.

93. Galski, T., Bruno, R. L., & Ehle, H. T. (1992). Driving after ceerbral damage: A model with implications for evaluation. *The American Journal of Occupational Therapy, 46,* 324-332.

94. Jack, C. R., Peterson, R. C., O'Brien, P. C., & Tangalos, E. G. (1992). MR-based hippocampal volumetry in the diagnosis of Alzheimer's disease. *Neurology, 42,* 183–188.

95. Kaplan, R. F., Meadows, M.-E., Vincent, L. C., Logigan, E. L., & Steere, A. C. (1992). Memory impairment and depression in patients with Lyme encephalopathy: Comparison with fibromyalgia and nonpsychotically depressed patients. *Neurology, 42,* 1263–1267.

96. Lichtenberg, P. A., & Christensen, B. (1992). Extended normative data for the logical memory subtests of the Wechsler Memory Scale—Revised: Responses from a sample of cognitively intact elderly medical patients. *Psychological Reports, 71,* 745-746.

97. MeKitrick, L. A. Camp, C. J., & Black, F. W. (1992). Prospective memory intervention in Alzheimer's Disease. *Journal of Gerontology, 47,* 337–343.

98. Meyers, C. A., & Abbruzzese, J. L. (1992). Cognitive functioning in cancer patients: Effect of previous treatment. *Neurology, 42,* 434–436.

99. Morrow, L. A., Robin, N., Hodgson, M. J., & Ramis, H. (1992). Assessment of attention and memory efficiency in persons with solvent neurotoxicity. *Neuropsychologia, 30,* 911-922.

100. Pappas, B. A., Sunderland, T., Weingartner, H. M., Vitiello, B., Martinson, H., & Putnam, K. (1992). Alzheimer's Disease and feeling-of-knowing for knowledge and episodic memory. *Journal of Gerontology, 47,* 159–164.

101. Peavy, G. M., Herzog, A. G., Rubin, N. P., & Mesulam, M.-M. (1992). Neuropsychological aspects of dementia of motor neuron disease: A report of two cases. *Neurology, 42,* 1004–1008.

102. Peterson, J. B., Finn, P. R., & Pihl, R. O. (1992). Cognitive dysfunction and the inherited predisposition to alcoholism. *Journal of Studies on Alcoholism, 53,* 154–160.

103. Peterson, R. C., Smith, G., Kokmen, E., Ivnik, R. J., & Tangalos, E. G. (1992). Memory function in normal aging. *Neurology, 42,* 396–401.

104. Samson, S., & Zatorre, R. J. (1992). Learning and retention of melodic and verbal information after unilateral temporal lobectomy. *Neuropsychologia, 30,* 815-826.

105. Scheffers, M. K., Johnson, R., Grafman, J., Dale, J. K., & Straus, S. E. (1992). Attention and short-term memory in chronic fatigue syndrome patients: An event-related potential analysis. *Neurology, 42,* 1667–1675.

106. Scherder, E. J. A., Bouma, A., & Steen, L. (1992). Influence of transcutaneous electrical nerve stimulation on memory in patients with dementia of the Alzheimer type. *Journal of Clinical and Experimental Neuropsychology, 14,* 951-960.

107. Smith, M. E., & Oscar-Berman, M. (1992). Resource-limited information processing in alcoholism. *Journal of Studies on Alcohol, 53,* 514–518.

108. Sweeney, J. A., Haas, G. L., & Li, S. (1992). Neuropsychological and eye movement abnormalities in first-episode and chronic schizophrenia. *Schizophrenia Bulletin, 18,* 283–293.

109. Swirsky-Sacchetti, T., Mitchell, D. R., Seward, J., Gonzales, C., Lublin, F., Knobler, R., & Field, H. L. (1992). Neuropsychological and structural brain lesions in multiple sclerosis: A regional analysis. *Neurology, 42,* 1291–1295.

110. Verfaellie, M., Milberg, W. D., Cermak, L. S., & Letourneau, L. L. (1992). Priming of spatial configurations in alcoholic Korsakoff's amnesia. *Brain and Cognition, 18,* 34-45.

111. Almkvist, O., Backman, L., Basun, H., & Wahlund, L. (1993). Patterns of neuropsychological performance in Alzheimer's desease and vascular dementia. *Cortex, 29,* 661-673.

112. Arbuckle, T. Y., & Gold, D. P. (1993). Aging, inhibition, and verbosity. *Journal of Gerontology, 48,* 225–232.

113. Bachman, D. L., Wolf, P. A., Linn, R. T., Knoefel, J. E., Cobb, J. L., Belanger, A. J., White, L. R., & D'Agostino, R. B. (1993). Incidence of dementia and probable Alzheimer's disease in a general population: The Framingham Study. *Neurology, 43,* 515–519.

114. Baker, G. A., Hanley, J. R., Jackson, H. F., Kimmance, S., & Slade, P. (1993). Detecting the faking of amnesia: Performance differences between simulators and patients with memory impairment. *Journal of Clinical and Experimental Neuropsychology, 15,* 668-684.

115. Barba, G. D. (1993). Different patterns of confabulation. *Cortex, 29,* 567-581.

116. Beeson, P. M., Bayles, K. A., Rubens, A. B., & Kaszniak, A. W. (1993). Memory impairment and executive control in individuals with stroke-induced aphasia. *Brain and Language, 45,* 253–275.

117. Benke, T. (1993). Two forms of apraxia in Alzheimer's disease. *Cortex, 29,* 715-725.

118. Chouinard, M. J., & Braun, C. M. J. (1993). A meta-analysis of the relative sensitivity of neuropsychological screening tests. *Journal of Clinical and Experimental Neuropsychology, 15,* 591-607.

119. Clausen, T., & Scott, R. (1993). Factor analysis of the WAIS-R and verbal memory and visual memory indices of the Wechsler Memory Scale—Revised, for a vocational rehabilitation sample. *Perceptual and Motor Skills, 76,* 907–911.

120. Cooper, J. A., & Sagar, H. J. (1993). Incidental and intentional recall in Parkinson's disease: An account based on diminished attentional resources. *Journal of Clinical and Experimental Neuropsychology, 15,* 713-731.

121. Cooper, J. A., Sagar, H. J., & Sullivan, E. V. (1993). Short-term memory and temporal ordering in early Parkinson's disease: Effects of disease chronicity and medication. *Neuropsychologia, 31,* 933-949.

122. DeLuca, J. (1993). Predicting neurobehavioral patterns following anterior communicating artery aneurysm. *Cortex, 29,* 639-647.

123. DeRenzi, E., & Lucchelli, F. (1993). Dense retrograde amnesia, intact learning capability and abnormal forgetting rate: A consolidation deficit? *Cortex, 29,* 449-466.

124. Deweer, B., Pillon, B., Michon, A., & Dubois, B. (1993). Mirror reading in Alzheimer's disease: Normal skill learning and acquisition of item-specific information. *Journal of Clinical and Experimental Neuropsychology, 15,* 789-804.

125. Dvara, R., Lopez-Alberola, R. F., Barker, W. W., Loewenstein, D. A., Zatinsky, M., Eisdorfer, C. E., & Weinberg, G. B. (1993). A comparison of familial and sporadic Alzheimer's disease. *Neurology, 43,* 1377–1384.

126. Egan, V. G., Chiswick, A., Brettle, R. P., & Goodwin, G. M. (1993). The Edinburgh cohort of HIV-positive drug users: The relationship between auditory P3 latency, cognitive function and self-rated mood. *Psychological Medicine, 23,* 613-622.

127. Garland, M. A., Parsons, O. A., & Nixon, S. J. (1993). Visual-spatial learning in nonalcoholic young adults with and those without a family history of alcoholism. *Journal of Studies on Alcohol, 54,* 219–224.

128. Goldberg, T. E., Torrey, E. F., Gold, J. M., Ragland, J. D., Bigelow, L. B., & Weinberger, D. R. (1993). Learning and memory in monozygotic twins discordant for schizophrenia. *Psychological Medicine, 23,* 71-85.

129. Gooding, P. A., van Eijk, R., Mayes, A. R., & Meudell, P. (1993). Preserved pattern completion priming for novel, abstract geometric shapes in amnesics of several aetiologies. *Neuropsychologia, 31,* 789-810.

130. Hestad, K., Aukrust, A., Ellersten, B., Klove, H., & Wilberg, K. (1993). Neuropsychological deficits in HIV-1 seropositive and seronegative intravenous drug users. *Journal of Clinical and Experimental Neuropsychology, 15,* 732-742.

131. Hill, R. D., Storandt, M., & Malley, M. (1993). The impact of long-term exercise training on psychological function in older adults. *Journal of Gerontology, 48,* 12–17.

132. Howieson, D. B., Holm, L. A., Kaye, J. A., Oken, B. S., & Howieson, J. (1993). Neurologic function in the optimally healthy oldest old: Neuropsychological evaluation. *Neurology, 43,* 1882–1886.

133. Krupp, L. B., Masur, D. M., & Kaufman, L. D. (1993). Neurocognitive dysfunction in the eosinophilia-myalgia syndrome. *Neurology, 43,* 931–936.

134. Larrabee, G. J., Youngjohn, J. R., Sudilovsky, A., & Crook, T. H. (1993). Accelerated forgetting in Alzheimer-type dementia. *Journal of Clinical and Experimental Neuropsychology, 15,* 701-712.

135. Loewenstein, D. A., Argûelles, T., Barker, W. W., & Duara, R. (1993). A comparative analysis of neuropsychological test performance of Spanish-speaking and English-speaking patients with Alzheimer's Disease. *Journal of Gerontology, 48,* 142–149.

136. Loring, D. W., Murro, A. M., Meador, K. J., Lee, G. P., Gratton, C. A., Nichols, M. E., Gallagher, B. B., King, D. W., & Smith, J. R. (1993). Wada memory testing and hippocampal volume measurements in the evaluation for temporal lobectomy. *Neurology, 43,* 1789–1793.

137. Malva, C. L. D., Stuss, D. T., D'Alton, J., & Willmer, J. (1993). Capture errors and sequencing after frontal brain lesions. *Neuropsychologia, 31,* 363-372.

138. Markowitsch, H. J., Calabrese, P., Haupts, M., Durwen, H. F., Liess, J., & Gehlen, W. (1993). Searching for the anatomical basis of retrograde amnesia. *Journal of Clinical and Experimental Neuropsychology, 15,* 947-967.

139. Markowitsch, H. J., von Cramon, D. Y., & Schuri, U. (1993). Mnestic performance profile of a bilateral diencephalic infarct patient with preserved intelligence and severe amnesic disturbances. *Journal of Clinical and Experimental Neuropsychology, 15,* 627-632.

140. Martin, R. C., Bolter, J. F., Todd, M. E., Gouvier, W. D., & Niccolls, R. (1993). Effects of sophistication and motivation on the detection of malingered memory performance using a computerized forced-choice task. *Journal of Clinical and Experimental Neuropsychology, 15,* 867-880.

141. Mayes, A. R., Downes, J. J., Shoqeirat, M., Hall, C., & Sagar, H. J. (1993). Encoding ability is preserved in amnesia: Evidence from a direct test of encoding. *Neuropsychologia, 31,* 745-759.

142. Mennemeier, M., Garner, R. D., & Heilman, K. M. (1993). Memory, mood, and measurement in hypothyroidism. *Journal of Clinical and Experimental Neuropsychology, 15,* 822-831.

143. Meyerhoff, P. J., Mackay, S., Bachman, L., Poole, N., Dillon, W. P., Weiner, M. W., & Fein, G. (1993). Reduced brain N-acetylaspartate suggests neuronal loss in cognitively impaired human immunodeficiency virus-seropositve individuals: In viro 1H magnetic resonance spectroscopic imaging. *Neurology, 43,* 509–515.

144. Nicholson, N. L., & Blanchard, E. B. (1993). A controlled evaluation of behavioral treatment of chronic headache in the elderly. *Behavior Therapy, 24,* 395–408.

145. O'Carroll, R. E., Moffoot, A., Ebmeier, K. P., Murray, C., & Goodwin, G. M. (1993). Korsakoff's syndrome, cognition and clonidine. *Psychological Medicine, 23,* 341-347.

146. Pierce, T. W., Madden, D. J., Siegel, W. C., & Blumenthal, J. A. (1993). Effects of aerobic exercise on cognitive and psychosocial functioning in patients with mild hypertension. *Health Psychology, 12,* 286–291.

147. Prigatano, G. P., & Amin, K. (1993). Digit Memory Test: Unequivocal cerebral dysfunction and suspected malingering. *Journal of Clinical and Experimental Neuropsychology, 15,* 537-546.

148. Rankin, E. J., Gilner, F. H., Gfeller, J. D., & Katz, B. M. (1993). Efficacy of progressive muscle relaxation for reducing state anxiety among elderly adults on memory tasks. *Perceptual and Motor Skills, 77,* 1395–1402.

149. Ryan, L., Clark, C. M., Klonoff, H., & Paty, D. (1993). Models of cognitive deficit and statistical hypotheses: Multiple sclerosis, an example. *Journal of Clinical and Experimental Neuropsychology, 15,* 563-577.

150. Saling, M. M., Berkovic, S. F., O'Shea, M. F., Kalnins, R. M., Darby, D. G., & Bladin, P. F. (1993). Lateralization of verbal memory and unilateral hippocampal sclerosis: Evidence of task-specific effects. *Journal of Clinical and Experimental Neuropsychology, 15,* 608-618.

151. Shuren, J., Geldmacher, D., & Heilman, K. M. (1993). Nonoptic aphasia: Aphasia with preserved confrontation naming in Alzheimer's disease. *Neurology, 43,* 1900–1907.

152. Trenerry, M. R., Jack, C. R., Ivnik, R. J., Sharbrough, F. W., Cascino, G. D., Hirschorn, K. A., Marsh, W. R., Kelly, P. J., & Meyer, F. B. (1993). MRI hippocampal volumes and memory function before and after temporal lobectomy. *Neurology, 43,* 1800–1805.

153. Tröster, A. I., Butters, N., Salmon, D. P., Cullum, C. M., Jacobs, D., Brandt, J., & White, R. F. (1993). The diagnostic utility of savings scores: Differentiating Alzheimer's and Huntington's diseases with the logical memory and visual reproduction tests. *Journal of Clinical and Experimental Neuropsychology, 15,* 773-788.

154. Trueblood, W., & Schmidt, M. (1993). Malingering and other validity considerations in the neuropsychological evaluation of mild head injury. *Journal of Clinical and Experimental Neuropsychology, 15,* 578-590.

155. von Cramon, D. Y., Markowitsch, H. J., & Schuri, U. (1993). The possible contribution of the septal region to memory. *Neuropsychologia, 31,* 1159-1180.

156. Wade, J. B., Hart, R. P., & Dougherty, L. M. (1993). Factors related to the severity of Tardive Dyskinesia. *Brain and Cognition, 23,* 71-80.

157. Watson, B. V., & Miller, T. K. (1993). Auditory perception, phonological processing, and reading ability/disability. *Journal of Speech and Hearing Research, 36,* 850–863.

158. Woodard, J. L. (1993). Confirmatory factor analysis of the Wechsler Memory Scale—Revised in a mixed clinical population. *Journal of Clinical and Experimental Neuropsychology, 15,* 968-973.

159. Zatorre, R. J., & Halpern, A. R. (1993). Effect of unilateral temporal-lobe excision on perception and imagery of songs. *Neuropsychologia, 31,* 221-232.

160. Zielinski, J. J. (1993). A comparison of the Wechsler Memory Scale—Revised and the Memory Assessment Scales: Administrative, clinical, and interpretive issues. *Professional Psychology: Research and Practice, 24,* 353–359.

161. Anderson, S. W., & Rizzo, M. (1994). Hallucinations following occipital lobe damage: A pathological activation of visual representations. *Journal of Clinical and Experimental Neuropsychology, 16,* 651-663.

162. Arbuckle, T. Y., Chaikelson, J. S., & Gold, D. P. (1994). Social drinking and cognitive functioning revisited: The role of intellectual endowment and psychological distress. *Journal of Studies on Alcohol, 55,* 352–361.

163. Beers, S. R., Goldstein, G., & Katz, L. J. (1994). Neuropsychological differences between college students with learning disabilities and those with mild head injury. *Journal of Learning Disabilities, 27,* 315–324.

164. Blanchard, J. J., Kring, A. M., & Neale, J. M. (1994). Flat affect in schizophrenia: A test of neuropsychological models. *Schizophrenia Bulletin, 20,* 311–325.

165. Blanchard, J. L., & Neale, J. M. (1994). The neuropsychological signature of schizophrenia: Generalized or differential deficit? *American Journal of Psychiatry, 151,* 40-48.

166. Brown, R. G., Scott, L. C., Bench, C. J., & Dolan, R. J. (1994). Cognitive function in depression: Its relationship to the presence and severity of intellectual decline. *Psychological Medicine, 24,* 829-847.

167. Brugge, K. L., Nichols, S. L., Salmon, D. P., Hill, L. R., Delis, D. C., Aaron, L., & Trainer, D. A. (1994). Cognitive impairment in adults with Down's Syndrome: Similarities to early cognitive changes in Alzheimer's disease. *Neurology, 44,* 232–238.

168. Burgess, A. P., Riccio, M., Jadresic, D., Pugh, K., Catalan, J., Hawkins, D. A., Baldeweg, T., Lovett, E., Gruzelier, J., & Thompson, C. (1994). A longitudinal study of the neuropsychiatric consequences of HIV-1 infection in gay men. I. Neuropsychological performance and neurological status at baseline and at 12-month follow-up. *Psychological Medicine, 24,* 885-895.

169. Busatto, G. F., Costa, D. C., Ell, P. J., Pilowsky, L. S., David, A. S., & Kerwin, R. W. (1994). Regional cerebral flow (rCBF) in schizophrenia during verbal memory activation: A 99mTC-HMPAO single photon emission tomography (SPET) study. *Psychological Medicine, 24,* 463-472.

170. Butter, C. M., & Trobe, J. D. (1994). Integrative agnosia following progressive multifocal leukoencephalopathy. *Cortex, 30,* 145-158.

171. Bylsma, F. W., Peyser, C. E., Folstein, S. E., Folstein, M. L., Ross, C., & Brandt, J. (1994). EEG power spectra in Huntington's disease: Clinical and neuropsychological correlates. *Neuropsychologia, 32,* 137–150.

172. Calabrese, P., Fink, G. R., Markowitsch, H. J., Kessler, J., Durwen, H. F., Liess, J., Haupts, M., & Gehlen, W. (1994). Left hemisphere neuronal heterotopia: A PET, MRI, EEG, and neuropsychological investigation of a university student. *Neurology, 44,* 302–305.

173. Carlesimo, G. A. (1994). Perceptual and conceptual priming in amnesic and alcoholic patients. *Neuropsychologia, 32,* 903–921.

174. Chertkow, H., Bub, D., Bergman, H., Bruemmer, A., Merling, A., & Rothfleisch, J. (1994). Increased semantic priming in patients with dementia of the Alzheimer's type. *Journal of Clinical and Experimental Neuropsychology, 16,* 608-622.

175. Christensen, H., Mackinnon, A., Jorm, A. F., Henderson, A. S., Scott, L. R., & Korten, A. E. (1994). Age differences and interindividual variation in cognition in community-dwelling elderly. *Psychology and Aging, 9,* 381-390.

176. Davous, P., & Boller, F. (1994). Trancortical alexia with agraphia following a right temporo-occipital hemotoma in a right-handed patient. *Neuropsychologia, 32,* 1263–1272.

177. DCCT Research Group (1994). A screening algorithm to identify clinically significant changes in neuropsychological functions in the diabetes control and complications trial. *Journal of Clinical and Experimental Neuropsychology, 16,* 303-316.

178. DeWeer, B., Ergis, A. M., Fossati, P., Pillon, B., Boller, F., Agid, Y., & Dubois, B. (1994). Explicit memory, procedural learning, and lexical priming in Alzheimer's disease. *Cortex, 30,* 113-126.

179. Diamond, B. J., Valentine, T., Mayes, A. R., & Sandel, M. E. (1994). Evidence of covert recognition in a prosopagnosic patient. *Cortex, 30,* 377-393.

180. Farlow, M., Murrell, J., Ghetti, B., Unverzagt, F., Zeldenrust, S., & Benson, M. (1994). Clinical characteristics in a kindred with early-onset Alzheimer's disease and their linkage to a G->T change at position 2149 of the amyloid percursor protein gene. *Neurology, 44,* 105–111.

181. Feinberg, T. E., Schindler, R. J., Ochoa, E., Kwan, P. C., & Farah, M. J. (1994). Associative visual agnosia and alexia without prosopagnosia. *Cortex, 30,* 395-412.

182. Gabrieli, J. D. E., Keane, M. M., Stanger, B. Z., Kjelgaard, M. M., Corkin, S., & Growdon, J. H. (1994). Dissociations among structural-perceptual, lexical-semantic, and event-fact memory systems in Alzheimer, amnesic, and normal subjects. *Cortex, 30,* 75-103.

183. Gfeller, J. D., & Katz, B. M. (1994). Anxiety states and sustained attention in a cognitively intact elderly sample: Preliminary results. *Psychological Reports, 75,* 1176-1178.
184. Gooding, P. A., Mayes, A. R., & Meudell, P. (1994). Long lasting indirect memory performance for abstract shapes in amnesics and matched controls. *Neuropsychologia, 32,* 1135–1143.
185. Greiffenstein, M. F., Baker, W. J., & Gola, T. (1994). Validation of malingered amnesia measures with a large clinical sample. *Psychological Assessment, 6,* 218-224.
186. Grunseit, A. C., Perdices, M., Dunbar, N., & Cooper, D. A. (1994). Neuropsychological function in asymptomatic HIV-1 infection: Methodological issues. *Journal of Clinical and Experimental Neuropsychology, 16,* 898-910.
187. Hittmair-Delazer, M., Denes, G., Semenza, C., & Mantovan, M. C. (1994). Anomia for people's names. *Neuropsychologia, 32,* 465–476.
188. Hom, J., Turner, M. B., Risser, R., Bonte, F. J., & Tintner, R. (1994). Cognitive deficits in asymptomatic first-degree relatives of Alzheimer's disease patients. *Journal of Clinical and Experimental Neuropsychology, 16,* 568-576.
189. Horton, A. M., Jr. (1994). Identification of neuropsychological deficit: Levels of assessment. *Perceptual and Motor Skills, 79,* 1251-1255.
190. Howell, R. A., Saling, M. M., Bradley, D. C., & Berkovic, S. F. (1994). Interictal language fluency in temporal lobe epilepsy. *Cortex, 30,* 469-478.
191. Humes, L. E., Watson, B. V., Christensen, L. A., Cokely, C. G., Halling, D. C., & Lee, L. (1994). Factors associated with individual differences in clinical measures of speech recognition among the elderly. *Journal of Speech and Hearing Research, 37,* 465–474.
192. Hunkin, N. M., Parkin, A. J., & Longmore, B. E. (1994). Aetiological variation in the amnesic syndrome: Comparisons using the list discrimination task. *Neuropsychologia, 32,* 819–825.
193. Kaplan, R. F., Meadows, M.-E., Verfaellie, M., Kwan, E., Ehrenberg, B. L., Bromfield, E. B., & Cohen, R. A. (1994). Lateralization of memory for the visual attributes of objects: Evidence from the posterior cerebral artery amobarbital test. *Neurology, 44,* 1069–1073.
194. Kapur, N., Ellison, D., Parkin, A. J., Hunkin, N. M., Burrows, E., Sampson, S. A., & Morrison, E. A. (1994). Bilateral temporal lobe pathology with sparing of medial temperal lobe structures: Lesion profile and pattern of memory disorder. *Neuropsychologia, 32,* 23–38.
195. Khan, A., Mirolo, M. H., Claypoole, K., Bhang, J., Cox, G., Horita, A., & Tucker, G. (1994). Effects of low-dose TRH on cognitive deficits in the ECT postictal state. *American Journal of Psychiatry, 151,* 1694-1696.
196. Kish, S. J., El-Awar, M., Stuss, D., Nobrega, J., Currier, R., Aita, J. F., Schut, L., Zoghbi, H. Y., & Freedman, M. (1994). Neuropsychological test performance in patients with dominantly inherited spinocerebellar ataxia: Relationahip to ataxis severity. *Neurology, 44,* 1738–1746.
197. Kopelman, M. D., Christensen, H., Puffett, A., & Stanhope, N. (1994). The great escape: A neuropsychological study of psychogenic amnesia. *Neuropsychologia, 32,* 675–691.
198. Kopelman, M. D., Green, R. E. A., Guinan, E. M., Lewis, P. D. R., & Stanhope, N. (1994). The case of the amnesic intelligence officer. *Psychological Medicine, 24,* 1037-1045.
199. Kremen, W. S., Seidman, L. J., Pepple, J. R., Lyons, M. J., Tsuang, M. T., & Faraone, S. V. (1994). Neuropsychological risk indicators for schizophrenia: A review of family studies. *Schizophrenia Bulletin, 20,* 103–119.
200. Lyness, S. A., Eaton, E. M., & Schneider, L. S. (1994). Cognitive performance in older and middle-aged depressed outpatients and controls. *Journal of Gerontology: Psychological Sciences, 49*(Pt.1), 129-136.
201. Marcos, T., Salamero, M., Gutiérrez, F., Catalán, R., Gasto, C., & Lázaro, L. (1994). Cognitive dysfunctions in recovered melancholic patients. *Journal of Affective Disorders, 32,* 133-137.
202. Mayes, A. R., Downes, J. J., Symons, V., & Shoqeirat, M. (1994). Do amnesics forget faces pathologically fast? *Cortex, 30,* 543-563.
203. Meadows, M.-E., Kaplan, R. F., & Bromfield, E. B. (1994). Cognitive recovery with vitamin B12 therapy: A longitudinal neuropsychological assessment. *Neurology, 44,* 1764–1765.
204. Mitrushina, M., Drebing, C., Uchiyama, C., Satz, P., Van Gorp, W., & Chervinsky, A. (1994). The pattern of deficit in different memory components in normal aging and dementia of Alzheimer's type. *Journal of Clinical Psychology, 50,* 591-596.
205. Murphy, D. G. M., Allen, G., Haxby, J. V., Largay, K. A., Daly, E., White, B. J., Powell, L. M., & Schapiro, M. B. (1994). The effects of sex steroids and the X chromosome on female brain function: A study of the neuropsychology of adult Turner syndrome. *Neuropsychologia, 32,* 1309–1323.
206. O'Carrol, R. E., & Badenoch, L. D. (1994). The inter-rater reliability of the Wechsler Memory Scale—Revised Visual Memory Test. *British Journal of Clinical Psychology, 33,* 208-210.
207. O'Carrol, R. E., Curran, S. M., Ross, M., Murray, C., Riddle, W., Moffoot, A. P. R., Ebmeier, K. P., & Goodwin, G. M. (1994). The differentiation of major depression from dementia of the Alzheimer type using within-subject neuropsychological discrepency analysis. *British Journal of Clinical Psychology, 33,* 23-32.
208. Odenheimer, G. L., Beaudet, M., Jette, A. M., Albert, M. S., Grande, L., & Minaker, K. L. (1994). Performance-based driving evaluation of the elderly driver: Safety, reliability, and validity. *Journal of Gerontology: Medical Sciences, 49*(Pt. 2), 153-159.
209. Ortiz, T., Loeches, M. M., Miguel, F., Abdad, E. V., & Puente, A. E. (1994). P300 latency and amplitude in the diagnosis of dementia. *Journal of Clinical Psychology, 50,* 381-388.
210. Palmer, B. W., Boone, K. B., Chang, L., Lee, A., & Black, S. (1994). Cognitive deficits and personality patterns in maternally versus paternally inherited myotonic dystrophy. *Journal of Clinical and Experimental Neuropsychology, 16,* 784-795.
211. Parkin, A. J., Rees, J. E., Hunkin, N. M., & Rose, P. E. (1994). Impairment of memory following discrete thalamic infarction. *Neuropsychologia, 32,* 39–51.
212. Parkin, A. J., Yeomans, J., & Bindschaedler, C. (1994). Further characterization of the executive memory impairment following frontal lobe lesions. *Brain and Cognition, 26,* 23–42.
213. Perrine, K., Devinsky, O., Vysal, S., Luciano, P. J., & Dogali, M. (1994). Left temporal neocortex mediation of verbal memory: Evidence from functional mapping with cortical stimulation. *Neurology, 44,* 1845–1850.
214. Peterson, R. C., Smith, G. E., Ivnik, R. J., Kokmen, E., & Tangalos, E. G. (1994). Memory function in very early Alzheimer's disease. *Neurology, 44,* 867–872.
215. Pillon, B., Deweer, B., Michon, A., Malapani, C., Agid, Y., & Dubois, B. (1994). Are explicit memory disorders of progressive supranuclear palsy related to damage to striatofrontal circuits? Comparison with Alzheimer's, Parkinson's, and Huntington's disease. *Neurology, 44,* 1264–1270.
216. Rankin, E. J., & Gore, P. A., Jr. (1994). Task equivalence and a failure to detect interference effects among the logical memory stories of the Wechsler Memory Scale—Revised. *Perceptual and Motor Skills, 78,* 291–294.
217. Robertson, I. H., & North, N. T. (1994). One hand is better than two: Motor extinction of left hand advantage in unilateral neglect. *Neuropsychologia, 32,* 1–11.
218. Rochon, E., & Waters, G. S. (1994). Sentence comprehension in patients with Alzheimer's disease. *Brain and Language, 46,* 329–349.
219. Rugg, M. D., Pearl, S., Walker, P., Roberts, R. C., & Holdstock, J. S. (1994). Word repetition effects on event-related potentials in healthy young and old subjects, and in patients with Alzheimer-type dementia. *Neuropsychologia, 32,* 381–398.
220. Shaw, C., & Aggleton, J. P. (1994). The ability of amnesic subjects to estimate time intervals. *Neuropsychologia, 32,* 857–873.
221. Siscoe, K. L., Segel, M. D., LaGrange, M. R., Templer, D. I., & Richardson, R. L. (1994). Exploration of the neuropsychological spectrum in clients of heterogeneous disabilities. *Perceptual and Motor Skills, 78,* 815-816.
222. Sunderland, T., Cohen, R. M., Molchan, S., Lawlor, B. A., Mellow, A. M., Newhouse, P. A., Tariot, D. N., Mueller, E. A., & Murphy, D. L. (1994). High-dose selegiline in treatment-resistant older depressive patients. *Archives of General Psychiatry, 51,* 607-615.
223. Tata, P. R., Rollings, J., Collins, M., Pickering, A., & Jacobson, R. R. (1994). Lack of cognitive recovery following withdrawal from long-term benzodiazepine use. *Psychological Medicine, 24,* 203-213.
224. Tomer, A., Larrabee, G. J., & Crook, T. H. (1994). Structure of everyday memory in adults with age-associated memory impairment. *Psychology and Aging, 9,* 606-615.
225. Trueblood, W. (1994). Qualitative and quantitative characteristics of malingered and other invalid WAIS-R and clinical memory data. *Journal of Clinical and Experimental Neuropsychology, 16,* 597-607.
226. Twum, M., & Parenté, R. (1994). Role of imagery and verbal labeling in the performance of paired associates tasks by persons with closed head injury. *Journal of Clinical and Experimental Neuropsychology, 16,* 630-639.
227. Verfaellie, M., & Cermak, L. S. (1994). Acquisition of generic memory in amnesia. *Cortex, 30,* 293-303.
228. Weddell, R. A. (1994). Effects of subcortical lesion site on human emotional behavior. *Brain and Cognition, 25,* 161-193.
229. Baltes, M. M., Kuhl, K. P., Gutzmann, H., & Sowarka, D. (1995). Potential of cognitive plasticity as a diagnostic instrument: A cross-validation and extension. *Psychology and Aging, 10,* 167-172.
230. Barba, G. D., Parlato, V., Iavarone, A., & Boller, F. (1995). Anosognosia, intrusions and "frontal" functions in Alzheimer's disease and depression. *Neuropsychologia, 33,* 247–259.
231. Bergin, P. S., Thompson, P. J., Fish, D. R., & Shorvon, S. D. (1995). The effect of seizures on memory for recently learned material. *Neurology, 45,* 236–240.
232. Bremner, J. D., Randall, P., Scott, T. M., Bronen, R. A., Seibyl, J. P., Southwick, S. M., Delaney, R. C., McCarthy, G., Charney, D. S., & Innis, R. B. (1995). MRI-based measurment of hippocampal volume in patients with combat-related posttraumatic stress disorder. *American Journal of Psychiatry, 152,* 973-981.
233. Britton, J. W., Vitti, R. J., Ahlskog, J. E., Robinson, R. G., Kremor, B., & Hayden, M. R. (1995). Hereditary late-onset chorea without significant dementia: Genetic evidence for substantial phenotypic variation in Huntington's disease. *Neurology, 45,* 443–447.
234. Bromley, S. M., & Doty, R. L. (1995). Odor recognition memory is better under bilateral than unilateral test conditions. *Cortex, 31,* 25-40.
235. Calabrese, P., Markowitsch, H. J., Harders, A. G., Scholz, M., & Gehlen, W. (1995). Fornix damage and memory: A case report. *Cortex, 31,* 555–564.
236. Campion, D., Brice, A., Hannequin, D., Tardieu, S., Dubois, B., Calenda, A., Brun, E., Penet, C., Tayot, J., Martinez, M., Bellis, M., Mallet, J., Agid, Y., & Clerget-Darpoux, F. (1995). A large pedigree with early-onset Alzheimer's disease: Clinical, neuropathologic, and genetic characterization. *Neurology, 45,* 80–85.
237. Caselli, R. J., Smith, B. E., & Osborne, D. (1995). Primary lateral sclerosis: A neuropsychological study. *Neurology, 45,* 2005–2009.
238. Christensen, H., Henderson, A. S., Jorm, A. F., MacKinnon, A. J., Scott, R., & Korten, A. G. (1995). ICD-10 mild cognitive disorder: Epidemiological evidence on its validity. *Psychological Medicine, 25,* 105-120.

239. Cockburn, J. (1995). Task interruption in prospective memory: A frontal lobe function? *Cortex, 31,* 87-97.

240. D'Esposito, M., Verfaellie, M., Alexander, M. P., & Katz, D. I. (1995). Amnesia following traumatic bilateral fornix transection. *Neurology, 45,* 1546–1550.

241. Daum, I., Schugens, M. M., Spieker, S., Poser, U., Schonle, P. W., & Birbaumer, N. (1995). Memory and skill acquisition in Parkinson's disease and frontal lobe dysfunction. *Cortex, 31,* 413–432.

242. DeCarli, C., Murphy, D. G. M., Trauh, M., Grady, C. L., Haxby, J. V., Gillette, J. A., Salerno, J. A., Conzales-Aviles, A., Horwitz, B., Rapoport, S. I., & Schapiro, M. B. (1995). The effect of white matter hyperintensity volume on brain structure, cognitive performance, and cerebral metabolism of glucose in 51 healthy adults. *Neurology, 45,* 2077–2084.

243. della Rocchetta, A. I., Gadian, D. G., Connelly, A., Polkey, C. E., Jackson, G. D., Watkins, K. E., Johnson, C. L., Mishkin, M., & Vargha-Khadem, F. (1995). Verbal memory impairment after right temporal lobe surgery: Role of contralateral damage as revealed by 1H magnetic resonance spectroscopy and T2 relaxometry. *Neurology, 45,* 797–802.

244. Dominey, P., Decety, J., Broussolle, E., Chazot, G., & Jeannerod, M. (1995). Motor imagery of a lateralized sequential task is asymmetrically slowed in hemi-Parkinson's patients. *Neuropsychologia, 33,* 727–741.

245. Dywan, C. A., McGlone, J., & Fox, A. (1995). Do intracarotid barbiturate injections offer a way to investigate hemispheric models of anosognosia? *Journal of Clinical and Experimental Neuropsychology, 17,* 431-438.

246. Eckhardt, M. J., Stapleton, J. M., Rawlings, R. R., Davis, E. Z., & Grodin, D. M. (1995). Neuropsychological functioning in detoxified alcoholics between 18 and 35 years of age. *American Journal of Psychiatry, 152,* 53-59.

247. Erblich, J., & Earleywine, M. (1995). Distraction does not impair memory during intoxication: Support for the attention-allocation model. *Journal of Studies on Alcohol, 56,* 444–448.

248. Eustache, F., Rioux, P., Desgranges, B., Marchal, G., Taboue, M. C. P., Dary, M., Lechevalier, B., & Baron, J.-C. (1995). Healthy aging, memory subsystemy and regional cerebral oxygen consumption. *Neuropsychologia, 33,* 867–887.

249. Farah, M. J., Levinson, K. L., & Klein, K. L. (1995). Face perception and within-category discrimination in prosopagnosia. *Neuropsychologia, 33,* 661–674.

250. Faraone, S. V., Seidman, L. J., Kremen, W. S., Pepple, J. R., Lyons, M. J., & Tsuang, M. T. (1995). Neuropsychological functioning among the nonpsychotic relatives of schizophrenic patients: A diagnostic efficiency analysis. *Journal of Abnormal Psychology, 104,* 286-304.

251. Fery, P., Vincent, E., & Bredart, S. (1995). Personal name anomia: A single case study. *Cortex, 31,* 191-198.

252. Finkel, D., Whitfield, K., & McGue, M. (1995). Genetic and environmental influences on functional age: A twin study. *Journal of Gerontology: Psychological Sciences, 50*B, 104-113.

253. Gershberg, F. B., & Shimamura, A. P. (1995). Impaired use of organizational strategies in free recall following frontal lobe damage. *Neuropsychologia, 33,* 1305–1333.

254. Gfeller, J. D., Meldrum, D. L., & Jacobi, K. A. (1995). The impact of constructional impairment on the WMS-R visual reproduction subtests. *Journal of Clinical Psychology, 51,* 58-63.

255. Goel, V., & Grofman, J. (1995). Are the frontal lobes implicated in "planning" functions? Interpreting data from the Tower of Hanoi. *Neuropsychologia, 33,* 623–642.

256. Gold, D. P., & Arbuckle, T. Y. (1995). A longitudinal study of off-target verbosity. *Journal of Gerontology, 50,* 307–315.

257. Goldenberg, G., Mullbacher, W., & Nowak, A. (1995). Imagery without perception: A case study of anosognosia for cortical blindness. *Neuropsychologia, 33,* 1373–1382.

258. Graf, P., Uttle, B., & Tuokko, H. (1995). Color- and Picture-Word Stroop Tests: Performance changes in old age. *Journal of Clinical and Experimental Neuropsychology, 17,* 390-415.

259. Grossman, M., MicKanin, J., Onishi, K., & Hughes, E. (1995). An aspect of sentence processing in Alzheimer's disease: Quantifier-nonagreement. *Neurology, 45,* 85–91.

260. Gupta, S. R., Mlcoch, A. G., Scolaro, C., & Moritz, T. (1995). Bromocriptine treatment of nonfluent aphasia. *Neurology, 45,* 2170–2173.

261. Habib, M., Daquin, G., Milandre, L., Royere, M. L., Rey, M., Lanteri, A., Salamon, G., & Khalil, R. (1995). Mutism and auditory agnosia due to bilateral insular damage—role of the insula in human communication. *Neuropsychologia, 33,* 327–339.

262. Harden, P. W., & Pihl, R. O. (1995). Cognitive function, cardiovascular reactivity, and behavior in boys at high risk for alcoholism. *Journal of Abnormal Psychology, 104,* 94-103.

263. Hinton, V. J., Halperin, J. M., Dobkin, C. S., Ding, X. H., Brown, W. T., & Miezejeski, C. M. (1995). Cognitive and molecular aspects of fragile X. *Journal of Clinical and Experimental Neuropsychology, 17,* 518–528.

264. Hodges, J. R., & Patterson, K. (1995). Is semantic memory consistently impaired early in the course of Alzheimer's disease? Neuroanatomical and diagnostic implications. *Neuropsychologia, 33,* 441–459.

265. Hokkanen, L., Launes, J., Vataja, R., Valanne, L., & Iivanainen, M. (1995). Isolated retrograde amnesia for autobiographical material associated with acute left temporal lobe encephalitis. *Psychological Medicine, 25,* 203-208.

266. Holamon, B., Morris, G., & Retzlaff, P. (1995). Event-related potentials during delayed recognition of Wechsler Memory Scale-R paired associate learning. *Journal of Clinical Psychology, 51,* 391-395.

267. Holdstock, J. S., Shaw, C., & Aggleton, J. P. (1995). The performance of amnesic subjects on tests of delayed matching-to-sample and delayed matching-to-position. *Neuropsychologia, 33,* 1583–1596.

268. Huang, H. S., & Hanley, J. R. (1995). Phonological awareness and visual skills in learning to read Chinese and English. *Cognition, 54,* 73–98.

269. Hunkin, N. M., & Parkin, A. J. (1995). The method of vanishing cues: An evaluation of its effectiveness in teaching memory-impaired individuals. *Neuropsychologia, 33,* 1255–1279.

270. Hunkin, N. M., Parkin, A. J., Bradley, V. A., Burrows, E. H., Aldrich, F. K., Jonsari, A., & Burdon-Cooper, C. (1995). Focal retrograde amnesia following closed head injury: A case study and theoretical account. *Neuropsychologia, 33,* 509–525.

271. Huron, C., Danion, J.-M., Giacomoni, F., Grange, D., Robert, P., & Rizzo, L. (1995). Impairment of recognition memory with, but not without, conscious recollection in schizophrenia. *American Journal of Psychiatry, 152,* 1737–1742.

272. Ivnik, R. J., Smith, G. E., Malec, J. F., Petersen, R. C., & Tangalos, E. G. (1995). Long-term stability and intercorrelations of cognitive abilities in older persons. *Psychological Assessment, 7,* 155-161.

273. Koivisto, K., Reinikainen, K. J., Hänninen, T., Vanhanen, M., Helkala, E.-L., Mykkänen, L., Laakso, M., Pyörälä, K., & Riekkinen, P. J. (1995). Prevalence of age-associated memory impairment in a randomly selected population from eastern Finland. *Neurology, 45,* 741–747.

274. Larrabee, G. J., & Curtiss, G. (1995). Construct validity of various verbal and visual memory tests. *Journal of Clinical and Experimental Neuropsychology, 17,* 536–547.

275. Lichtenberg, P. A., Ross, T., Millis, S. R., & Manning, C. A. (1995). The relationship between depression and cognition in older adults: A cross-validation study. *Journal of Gerontology, 50,* 25–32.

276. Mitrushina, M., Uchiyama, C., & Satz, P. (1995). Heterogeneity of cognitive profiles in normal aging: Implications for early manifestations of Alzheimer's disease. *Journal of Clinical and Experimental Neuropsychology, 17,* 374-382.

277. Morris, R. C., Abrahams, S., & Polkey, C. E. (1995). Recognition memory for words and faces following unilateral temporal lobectomy. *British Journal of Clinical Psychology, 34,* 571–576.

278. Mottron, L., & Belleville, S. (1995). Perspective production in a savant autistic draughtsman. *Psychological Medicine, 25,* 639–648.

279. O'Mahony, J. F., & Doherty, B. (1995). Comparability of correlates of original and revised Wechsler Adult Intelligence Scales in an alcoholic-abusing population. *Journal of Clinical Psychology, 51,* 123-128.

280. Parks, E. D., & Balon, R. (1995). Autobiographical memory for childhood events: Patterns of recall in psychiatric patients with a history of alleged trauma. *Psychiatry, 56,* 199–208.

281. Persinger, M. A., & Richards, P. M. (1995). Foot agility and toe gnosis/graphaesthesia as potential indicators of integrity of the medial cerebral surface: Normative data and comparison with clinical populations. *Perceptual and Motor Skills, 80,* 1011–1024.

282. Persinger, M. A., & Richards, P. M. (1995). Women reconstruct more details than men in a complex five-minute narrative: Implications for right-hemispheric factors in the serial memory effect. *Perceptual and Motor Skills, 80,* 403–410.

283. Phillips, N. A., & McGlone, J. (1995). Grouped data do not tell the whole story: Individual analysis of cognitive change after temporal lobectomy. *Journal of Clinical and Experimental Neuropsychology, 17,* 713–724.

284. Quayhagen, M. P., Quayhagen, M., Corbeil, R. R., Roth, P. A. & Rodgers, J. A. (1995). A dyadic remediation program for care recipients with dementia. *Nursing Research, 44,* 153–159.

285. Rasile, D. A., Burg, J. S., Burright, R. G., & Donovick, P. J. (1995). The relationship between performance on the Gordon Diagnostic System and other measures of attention. *International Journal of Psychology, 30,* 35–45.

286. Sass, K. J., Buchanan, C. P., Kraemer, S., Westerveld, M., Kim, J. H., & Spencer, D. D. (1995). Verbal memory impairment resulting from hippocampal neuron loss among epileptic patients with structural lesions. *Neurology, 45,* 2154–2158.

287. Schmitter-Edgecombe, M., Fahy, J. F., Whelan, J. P., & Long, C. J. (1995). Memory remediation after severe closed head injury: Notebook training versus supportive therapy. *Journal of Consulting and Clinical Psychology, 63,* 484-489.

288. Shaw, C., & Aggleton, J. P. (1995). Evidence for the independence of recognition and recency memory in amnesic subjects. *Cortex, 31,* 57-71.

289. Silver, H., Geraisy, N., & Schwartz, M. (1995). No difference in the effect of biperiden and amantadine on Parkinsonian- and Tardive Dyskinesia-type involuntary movements: A double-blind crossover, placebo-controlled study in medicated chronic schizophrenic patients. *Journal of Clinical Psychiatry, 56,* 167–170.

290. Sinnett, E. R., & Holen, M. C. (1995). Chance performance in the absence of norms for neuropsychological tests—a clinical note. *Journal of Clinical Psychology, 51,* 400-402.

291. Solomon, P. R., Brett, M., Groccia-Ellison, M. E., Oyler, C., Tomsai, M., & Pendlebury, W. W. (1995). Classical conditioning in patients with Alzheimer's disease: A multiday study. *Psychology and Aging, 10,* 248-254.

292. Stern, Y., Liu, X., Marder, K., Todak, G., Sano, M., Ehrhardt, A., & Gorman, J. (1995). Neuropsychological changes in a prospectively followed cohort of homosexual and bisexual men with and without HIV infection. *Neurology, 45,* 467–472.

293. Stout, J. C., Salmon, D. P., Butters, N., Taylor, M., Peavy, G., Heindel, W. C., Delis, D. C., Ryan, L., Atkinson, J. H., Chandler, J. L., Grant, I., & The HNRC Group (1995). Decline in working memory associated with HIV infection. *Psychological Medicine, 25,* 1221–1232.

294. Strauss, E., Loring, D., Chelune, G., Hunter, M., Hermann, B., Perrine, K., Westerveld, M., Trenerry, M., & Barr, W. (1995). Predieting cognitive impairment in epilepsy: Findings from the Bozeman Epilepsy Consortium. *Journal of Clinical and Experimental Neuropsychology, 17,* 909–917.

295. Swoboda, K. J., & Jenike, M. A. (1995). Frontal abnormalities in a patient with obsessive-compulsive disorder: The role of structural lesions in obsessive-compulsive behavior. *Neurology, 45,* 2130–2134.

296. Tisdwell, P., Dias, P. S., Sagar, H. J., Mayes, A. R., & Battersby, R. D. E. (1995). Cognitive outcome after aneurysm rupture: Relationship to aneurysm site and perioperative complications. *Neurology, 45,* 875–882.

297. Tison, F., Dartigues, J. F., Auriacombe, S., Letenneur, L., Boller, F., & Alperovitch, A. (1995). Dementia in Parkinson's disease: A population-based study in ambulatory and institutionalized individuals. *Neurology, 45,* 705–708.

298. Tuokko, H., Kristjansson, E., & Miller, J. (1995). Neuropsychological detection of dementia: An overview of the neuropsychological component of the Canadian study of health and aging. *Journal of Clinical and Experimental Neuropsychology, 17,* 325-373.

299. van der Hurk, P. R., & Hodges, J. R. (1995). Episodic and semantic memory in Alzheimer's disease and progressive supranuclear palsy: A comparative study. *Journal of Clinical and Experimental Neuropsychology, 17,* 459-471.

300. Waterfall, M. L., & Crowe, S. F. (1995). Meta-analytic comparison of the components of visual cognition in Parkinson's Disease. *Journal of Clinical and Experimental Neuropsychology, 17,* 759–772.

301. Wilson, B. A., Baddeley, A. D., & Kapor, N. (1995). Dense amnesia in a professional musician following herpes simplex virus encephalitis. *Journal of Clinical and Experimental Neuropsychology, 17,* 668–681.

302. Woodard, J. L., & Axelrod, B. N. (1995). Parsimonious prediction of Wechsler Memory Scale—Revised memory indices. *Psychological Assessment, 7,* 445–449.

303. Young, R. L., & Nettelbeck, T. (1995). The abilities of a musical savant and his family. *Journal of Autism and Developmental Disorders, 25,* 231–248.

304. Aggleton, J. P., & Shaw, C. (1996). Amnesia and recognition memory: A re-analysis of psychometric data. *Neuropsychologia, 34,* 51–62.

305. Alexander, M. P., & Annett, M. (1996). Crossed aphasia and related anomalies of cerebral organization: Case reports and a genetic hypothesis. *Brain and Language, 55,* 213–239.

306. Armon, C., Shin, C., Miller, P., Carwile, S., Brown, E., Edinger, J. D., & Paul, R. G. (1996). Reversible Parkinsonism and cognitive impairment with chronic valproate use. *Neurology, 47,* 626–635.

307. Axelrod, B. N., Putnam, S. H., Woodard, J. L., & Adams, K. M. (1996). Cross-validation of predicted Wechsler Memory Scale—Revised scores. *Psychological Assessment, 8,* 73–75.

308. Beatty, W. W., Hames, K. A., Blanco, C. R., Nixon, S. J., & Tivis, L. J. (1996). Visuospatial perception, construction and memory in alcoholism. *Journal of Studies on Alcohol, 57,* 136–143.

309. Cockburn, J. (1996). Failure of prospective memory after acquired brain damage: Preliminary investigation and suggestions for future directions. *Journal of Clinical and Experimental Neuropsychology, 18,* 304–309.

310. Croisile, B., Brabant, M-J., Carmoi, T., Lepage, Y., Aimard, G., & Trillet, M. (1996). Comparison between oral and written spelling in Alzheimer's disease. *Brain and Language, 54,* 361–387.

311. Crouch, J. A., Greve, K. W., & Brooks, J. (1996). The California Card Sorting Test dissociate verbal and non-verbal concept formation abilities. *British Journal of Clinical Psychology, 35,* 431–434.

312. Daniel, D. G., Goldberg, T. E., Weinberger, D. R., Kleinman, J. E., Pickar, D., Lubick, L. J., & Williams, T. S. (1996). Different side effect profiles of risperidone and clozapine in 20 outpatients with schizophrenia or schizoaffective disorder: A pilot study. *American Journal of Psychiatry, 153,* 417–419.

313. Diamond, B. J., Mayes, A. R., & Meudell, P. R. (1996). Autonomic and recognition indices of memory in amnesic and healthy control subjects. *Cortex, 32,* 439–459.

314. Fastenau, P. S., Denburg, N. L., & Abeles, N. (1996). Age differences in retrieval: Further support for the resource-reduction hypothesis. *Psychology and Aging, 11,* 140–146.

315. Fisher, N. J., Rourke, B. P., Bieliauskas, L., Giordani, B., Berent, S., & Foster, N. L. (1996). Neuropsychological subgroups of patients with Alzheimer's disease. *Journal of Clinical and Experimental Neuropsychology, 18,* 349–370.

316. Flashman, L. A., Flaum, M., Gupta, S., & Andreasen, N. C. (1996). Soft signs and neuropsychological performance in schizophrenia. *American Journal of Psychiatry, 153,* 526–532.

317. Galloway, S., Malloy, P., Kohn, R., Gillard, E., Duffy, J., Rogg, J., Tung, G., Richardson, E., Thomas, C., & Westlake, R. (1996). MRI and neuropsychological differences in early- and late-life-onset geriatric depression. *Neurology, 46,* 1567–1574.

318. Gass, C. S. (1996). MMPI-2 variables in attention and memory test performance. *Psychological Assessment, 8,* 135–138.

319. Gfeller, J. D., & Horn, G. J. (1996). The East Boston Memory Test: A clinical screening measure for memory impairment in the elderly. *Journal of Clinical Psychology, 52,* 191–196.

320. Glennerster, A., Palace, J., Warburton, D., Oxbury, S., & Newsum-Davis, J. (1996). Memory in myasthenia gravis: Neuropsychological tests of central cholinergic function before and after effective immunologic treatment. *Neurology, 46,* 1138–1142.

321. Greene, J. D. W., Baddeley, A. D., & Hodges, J. R. (1996). Analysis of the episodic memory deficit in early Alzheimer's disease: Evidence from the Doors and People Test. *Neuropsychologia, 34,* 537–551.

322. Hall, M., Whaley, R., Robertson, K., Hamby, S., Wilkins, J., & Hall, C. (1996). The correlation between neuropsychological and neuroanatomic changes over time in asymptomatic and symptomatic HIV-1-infected individuals. *Neurology, 46,* 1697–1702.

323. Hanley, J. R., & Kay, J. (1996). Reading speed in pure alexia. *Neuropsychologia, 34,* 1165–1174.

324. Hinkin, C. H., van Gorp, W. G., Satz, P., Marcotte, T., Durvasula, R. S., Wood, S., Campbell, L., & Baluda, M. R., (1996). Actual versus self-reported cognitive dysfunction in HIV-1 infection: Memory-meta memory dissociations. *Journal of Clinical and Experimental Neuropsychology, 18,* 431–443.

325. Hodges, J. R., Patterson, K., Graham, N., & Dawson, K. (1996). Naming and knowing in dementia of Alzheimer's type. *Brain and Language, 54,* 302–325.

326. Hutner, N., & Oscar-Berman, M. (1996). Visual laterality patterns for the perception of emotional words in alcoholic and aging individuals. *Journal of Studies on Alcohol, 57,* 144–154.

327. Ingles, J. L., Mate-Kole, C. C., & Connolly, J. F. (1996). Evidence for multiple routes of speech production in a case of fluent aphasia. *Cortex, 32,* 199–219.

328. Iverson, G. L., & Franzen, M. D. (1996). Using multiple objective memory procedures to detect simulated malingering. *Journal of Clinical and Experimental Neuropsychology, 18,* 38–51.

329. Janowsky, J. S., Carper, R. A., & Kaye, J. A. (1996). Asymmetrical memory decline in normal aging and dementia. *Neuropsychologia, 34,* 527–535.

330. Keenan, P. A., Jacobson, M. W., Soleyami, R. M., Mayes, M. D., Stress, M. E., & Yaldoo, D. T. (1996). The effect on memory of chornic prednisone treatment in patients with systemic disease. *Nursing Research, 47,* 1396–1402.

331. Lesser, I. M., Boone, K. B., Mehringer, C. M., Wohl, M. A., Miller, B. L., & Berman, N. G. (1996). Cognition and white matter hyperintensities in older depressed patients. *American Journal of Psychiatry, 153,* 1280–1287.

332. Liebson, E., White, R. F., & Albert, M. L. (1996). Cognitive inconsistencies in abnormal illness behavior and neurological disease. *Journal of Nervous and Mental Disease, 184,* 122–125.

333. Lucas, M. D., & Sonnenberg, B. R. (1996). Neuropsychological trends in the Parkinsonian-plus Syndrome: A pilot study. *Journal of Clinical and Experimental Neuropsychology, 18,* 88–97.

334. Marson, D. C., Chatterjee, A., Ingram, K. K., & Harrell, L. E. (1996). Toward a neurologic model of competency: Cognitive predictors of capacity to consent in Alzheimer's disease using three different legal standards. *Neurology, 46,* 666–672.

335. Massman, P. J., & Doody, R. S. (1996). Hemispheric asymmetry in Alzheimer's Disease is apparent in motor functioning. *Journal of Clinical and Experimental Neuropsychology, 18,* 110–121.

336. Massman, P. J., Kneiter, K. T., Jankovic, J., & Doody, R. S. (1996). Neuropsychological functioning in cortical-basal ganglionic degeneration: Differences from Alzheimer's disease. *Neurology, 46,* 720–726.

337. Moore, C. A., & Lichtenberg, P. A. (1996). Neuropsychological prediction of independent functioning in a geriatric sample: A double cross-validational study. *Rehabilitation Psychology, 41,* 115–130.

338. Morton, N., Polkey, C. E., Cox, T., & Morris, R. G. (1996). Episodic memory dysfunction during sodium amytal testing of epileptic patients in relation to posterior cerebral artery perfusion. *Journal of Clinical and Experimental Neuropsychology, 18,* 24–37.

339. O'Mahony, J. F., & Doherty, B. (1996). Intellectual impairment among recently abstinent alcohol abusers. *British Journal of Clinical Psychology, 35,* 77–83.

340. O'Shea, M. F., Saling, M. M., Bladin, P. F., & Berkovic, S. F. (1996). Does naming contribute to memory self-report in temporal lobe epilepsy? *Journal of Clinical and Experimental Neuropsychology, 18,* 98–109.

341. Palmer, B. W., Boone, K. B., Lesser, I. M., Wohl, M. A., Berman, N., & Miller, B. L. (1996). Neuropsychological deficits among older depressed patients with predominently psychological or vegatative symptoms. *Journal of Affective Disorders, 41,* 17–24.

342. Partiot, A., Vérin, M., Pillion, B., Teixeira-Ferreira, C., Agid, Y., & Dubois, B. (1996). Delayed response tasks in basal ganglia lesions in man: Further evidence for a striatofrontal cooperation in behavioural adaptation. *Neuropsychologia, 34,* 709–721.

343. Pliskin, N. H., Hamer, D. P., Goldstein, D. S., Towle, V. L., Reder, A. T., Noronha, A., & Arnason, B. G. W. (1996). Improved delayed visual production test performance in multiple sclerosis patients receiving interferon B-1b. *Neurology, 47,* 1463–1468.

344. Report of the Therapeutics and Technology Assessment Subcommittee of the American Academy of Neurology. (1996). Assessment: Neuropsychological testing of adults: Considerations for neurologists. *Neurology, 47,* 592.

345. Retzlaff, P. D., & Morris, G. L. (1996). Event-related potentials during the Continuous Visual Memory Test. *Journal of Clinical Psychology, 52,* 43–47.

346. Rich, J. B., Bylsma, F. W., & Brandt, J. (1996). Item priming and skill learning in amnesia. *Journal of Clinical and Experimental Neuropsychology, 18,* 148–158.

347. Rosselli, M., & Ardila, A. (1996). Cognitive effects of cocaine and polydrug abuse. *Journal of Clinical and Experimental Neuropsychology, 18,* 122–135.

348. Roth, R. M., & Baribeau, j. (1996). Performance of subclinical compulsive checkers on putative tests of frontal and temporal lobe memory functions. *Journal of Nervous and Mental Disease, 184,* 411–416.

349. Rouleau, N., & Belleville, S. (1996). Irrelevant speech effect in aging: An assessment of inhibitory processes in working memory. *Journal of Gerontology, 51,* 356–363.

350. Schmidtke, K., Handschu, R., & Vollmer, H. (1996). Cognitive procedural learning in amnesia. *Brain and Cognition, 32,* 441–467.

351. Seddoh, S. A. K., Robin, D. A., Sim, H-S., Hageman, C., Moon, J. B., & Folkins, J. W. (1996). Speech thinking in apraxia of speech versus conduction aphasia. *Journal of Speech and Hearing Research, 39,* 590–603.

352. Siegert, R. J., & Warrington, E. K. (1996). Spared retrograde memory with anterograde amnesia and widespread cognitive deficits. *Cortex, 32,* 177–185.

353. Simpson, D. M., Dorfman, D., Olney, R. K., Mckinley, G., Dobkin, J., So, Y., Berger, J., Ferdon, M. B., Fiedman, B., & The Peptide Neuropathy Study Group. (1996). Peptide T in the treatment of painful distal neuropathy associated with AIDS: Results of a placebo-controlled trial. *Nursing Research, 47,* 1254–1259.

354. Sirigu, A., & Grafman, J. (1996). Selective impairments within episodic memories. *Cortex, 32,* 83–95.

355. Sullivan, K. (1996). Estimates of interrater reliability for the logical memory subtest of the Wechsler Memory Scale—Revised. *Journal of Clinical and Experimental Neuropsychology, 18,* 707–712.

356. Sulway, M. R., Broe, G. A., Creasey, H., Dent, O. F., Jorm, A. F., Kos, S. C., & Tennant, C. C. (1996). Are malnutrition and stress risk factors for accelerated cognitive decline? A prisoner of war study. *Neurology, 46,* 650–655.

357. Tierney, M. C., Szalai, J. P., Snow, W. G., Fisher, R. H., Tsuda, T., Chi, H., McLachlan, D. R., & St. George-Hyslop, P. H. (1996). A prospective study of the clinical utility of Apo E genotype in the prediction of outcome in patients with memory impairment. *Neurology, 46,* 149–154.

358. Tierney, M. C., Szalai, J. P., Snow, W. G., Fisher, R. H., Nores, A., Nadon, G., Dunn, E., & St. George-Hyslop, P. H. (1996). Prediction of probable Alzheimer's disease in mentally-impaired patients: A prospective longitudinal. *Neurology, 46,* 661–665.

359. Tuokko, H., & Woodward, T. S. (1996). Development and validation of a demographic correction system for neuropsychological measures used in the Canadian study of health and aging. *Journal of Clinical and Experimental Neuropsychology, 18,* 479–616.

360. Waldstein, S. R., Polefrone, J. M., Fazzari, T. V., Manuck, S. B., Jennings, J. R., Ryan, C. M., Muldoon, M. F., & Shapiro, A. P. (1996). Hypertension and neuropsychological performance in men: Interactive effects of age. *Health Psychology, 15,* 102–109.

361. Zarb, J. (1996). Correlates of depression in cognitively impaired hospitalized elderly referred for neuropsychological assessment. *Journal of Clinical and Experimental Neuropsychology, 18,* 713–723.

362. Baynes, K., Tramo, M. J., Reeves, A. G., & Gazzaniga, M. S. (1997). Isolation of a right hemisphere cognitive system in a patient with anarchic (alien) hand sign. *Neuropsychologia, 35,* 1159–1173.

363. Beauregard, M., Chertkow, H., Gold, D., Karama, S., Benhamou, J., Babins, L., & Faucher, A. (1997). Word priming with brief multiple presentation technique: Preservation in amnesia. *Neuropsychologia, 35,* 611–621.

364. Berardi, A., Haxby, J. V., DeCarli, C., & Schapiro, M. B. (1997). Face and word memory differences are related to patterns of right and left lateral ventricle size in healthy aging. *Journal of Gerontology, 52,* 54–61.

365. Bieliauskas, L. A., Fastenau, P. S., Lacy, M. A., & Roper, B. L. (1997). Use of the odds ratio to translate neuropsychological test scores into real-world outcomes: From statistical significance to clinical significance. *Journal of Clinical and Experimental Neuropsychology, 19,* 889–896.

366. Bowden, S. C., Dodds, B., Whelan, G., Long, C., Dudgeon, P., Ritter, A., & Clifford, C. (1997). Confirmatory factor analysis of the Wechsler Memory Scale—Revised in a sample of clients with alcohol dependency. *Journal of Clinical and Experimental Neuropsychology, 19,* 755–762.

367. Brooker, A. E. (1997). Performance on the Wechsler Memory Scale—Revised for patients with mild traumatic brain injury and mild dementia. *Perceptual and Motor Skills, 84,* 131–138.

368. Bruggemans, E. F. Van de Vijver, F. J. R., & Huysmans, H. A. (1997). Assessment of cognitive deterioration in individual patients following cardiac surgery: Correcting for measurement error and practice effects. *Journal of Clinical and Experimental Neuropsychology, 19,* 543–559.

369. Buschke, H., Sliwinski, M. J., Kuslansky, G., & Lipton, R. B. (1997). Diagnosis of early dementia by the Double Memory Test: Encoding specificity improves diagnostic sensitivity and specificity. *Nursing Research, 48,* 989–997.

370. Carbonnel, S., Charnallet, A., David, D., & Pellat, J. (1997). One or several semantic systems (s)? Maybe none: Evidence from a case study of modality and category-specific "semantic" impairment. *Cortex, 33,* 391–417.

371. Cermak, L. S., Mather, M., & Hill, R. (1997). Unconscious influences on amnesics' word-stem completion. *Neuropsychologia, 35,* 605–610.

372. Chatterjee, A., Yapundich, R., Mennemeier, M., Mountz, J. M., Inampudi, C., Pan, J. W., & Mitchell, G. W. (1997). Thalamic thought disorder: On being "a bit addled." *Cortex, 33,* 419–440.

373. Chertkow, H., Bub, D., Deaudon, C., & Whitehead, V. (1997). On the status of object concepts in aphasia. *Brain and Language, 58,* 203–232.

374. Ciesielski, K. T., Harris, R. J., Hart, B. L., & Pabst, H. F. (1997). Cerebellar hypoplasia and frontal lobe cognitive deficits in disorders of early childhood. *Neuropsychologia, 35,* 643–655.

375. Cunningham, J. M., Pliskin, N. H., Cassisi, J. E., Tsang, B., & Rao, S. M. (1997). Relationship between confabulation and measures of memory and executive function. *Journal of Clinical and Experimental Neuropsychology, 19,* 867–877.

376. Dalla Barba, G., Mantovan, M. C., Ferruzza, E., & Denes, G. (1997). Remembering and knowing the past: A case study of isolated retrograde amnesia. *Cortex, 33,* 143–154.

377. Dalla Barbara, G., Roisse, M-F., Bartolomeo, P., & Bachoud-Lévi, A-C. (1997). Confabulation following rupture of posterior communicating artery. *Cortex, 33,* 563–570.

378. Dodrill, C. B., & Ojemann, G. A. (1997). An exploratory comparison of three methods of memory assessment with the intracarotid amobarbital procedure. *Brain and Cognition, 33,* 210–223.

379. Dukoff, R., & Sunderland, T. (1997). Durable power of attorney and informed consent with Alzheimer's Disease patients: A clinical study. *American Journal of Psychiatry, 154,* 1070–1075.

380. Fisher, N. J., Rourke, B. P., Bieliauskas, L. A., Giordani, B., Berent, S., & Foster, N. L. (1997). Unmasking the heterogeneity of Alzheimer's Disease: Care studies of individuals from distinct neuropsychological subgroups. *Journal of Clinical and Experimental Neuropsychology, 19,* 713–754.

381. Gass, C. S., & Apple, C. (1997). Cognitive complaints in closed-head injury: Relationship to memory test performance and emotional disturbance. *Journal of Clinical and Experimental Neuropsychology, 19,* 290–299.

382. Geffen, G. M. Geffen, L., Bishop, K., & Manning, L. (1997). Extended delayed recall of AVLT word lists: Effects of age and sex on adult performance. *Australian Journal of Psychology, 49,* 78–84.

383. Gilley, D. W., & Wilson, R. S. (1997). Criterion-related validity of the Geriatric Depression Scale in Alzheimer's Disease. *Journal of Clinical and Experimental Neuropsychology, 19,* 489–499.

384. Gold, J. M., Carpenter, C., Randolph, C., Goldberg, T. E., & Weinberger, D. R. (1997). Auditory working memory and Wisconsin Card Sorting Test performance in schizophrenia. *Archives of General Psychiatry, 54,* 159–165.

385. Hornak, J., Oxbury, S., Oxbury, J., Iversen, S. D., & Gaffan, D. (1997). Hemifeld-specific visual recognition memory impairments in patients with unilateral temporal lobe removals. *Neuropsychologia, 35,* 1311–1315.

386. Huang, H. S., & Hanley, J. R. (1997). A longitudinal study of phonological awareness, visual skills, and Chinese reading acquisition among first-graders in Taiwan. *International Journal of Behavioral Development, 20,* 249–268.

387. Ivnik, R. J., Smith, G. E., Lucas, J. A., Tangalos, E. G., Kokmen, E., & Petersen, R. C. (1997). Free and cued selective reminding test: MOANS norms. *Journal of Clinical and Experimental Neuropsychology, 19,* 676–691.

388. Johnson, M. K., O'Connor, M. O., & Cantor, J. (1997). Confabulation, memory deficits, and frontal dysfunction. *Brain and Cognition, 34,* 189–206.

389. Johnstone, B., Holland, D., & Hewett, J. E. (1997). The construct validity of the category test: Is it a measure of reasoning or intelligence? *Psychological Assessment, 9,* 28–33.

390. Jokeit, H., Ebner, A., Holthausen, H., Markowitsch, H. J., Moch, A., Rannek, H., Schutz, R., & Tuxhorn, I. (1997). Individual prediction of change in delayed recall of prose passages after left-sided anterior temporal lobectomy. *Neurology, 49,* 481–487.

391. Kopelman, M. D., Stanhope, N., & Kingsley, D. (1997). Temporal and spatial context memory in patients with focal frontal, temporal lobe, and diencephalic lesions. *Neuropsychologia, 35,* 1533–1545.

392. Krauss, G. L., Summerfield, M., Brandt, J., Breiter, S., & Rochkin, D. (1997). Mesial temporal spikes interfere with working memory. *Neurology, 49,* 975–980.

393. Leonard, C. L., Waters, G. S., & Caplan, D. (1997). The use of contextual information related to general word knowledge by right brain-damaged individuals in pronoun resolution. *Brain and Language, 57,* 343–359.

394. Marcotte, T. D., van Gorp, W., Hinkin, C. H., & Osato, S. (1997). Concurrent validity of the Neurobehavioral Cognitive Status Exam subtests. *Journal of Clinical and Experimental Neuropsychology, 19,* 386–395.

395. McGrath, N. M., Anderson, N. E., Hope, J. K. A., Croxson, M. C., & Powell, K. F. (1997). Anterior opercular syndrome, caused by herpes simplex encephalitis. *Neurology, 49,* 494–497.

396. Moore, P. M., & Baker, G. A. (1997). Psychometric properties and factor structure of the Wechsler Memory Scale—Revised in a sample of persons with intractable epilepsy. *Journal of Clinical and Experimental Neuropsychology, 19,* 897–905.

397. Nielsen-Bohlman, L., Ciranni, M., Shimamura, A. P., & Knight, R. T. (1997). Impaired word-stem priming in patients with temporal-occipital lesions. *Neuropsychologia, 35,* 1087–1092.

398. Oxbury, S., Oxbury, J., Renowden, S., Squier, W., & Carpenter, K. (1997). Severe amnesia: An unusual late complication after temporal lobectomy. *Neuropsychologia, 35,* 975–988.

399. Papagno, C., & Baddeley, A. (1997). Confabulation in a dysexecutive patient: Implication for models of retrieval. *Cortex, 33,* 743–752.

400. Rapport, L. J., Axelrod, B. N., Theisen, m. E., Brines, D. B., Kalechstein, A. D., & Ricker, J. H. (1997). Relationship of IQ to verbal learning and memory: Test and retest. *Journal of Clinical and Experimental Neuropsychology, 19,* 655–666.

401. Reinkemeier, M., Marowitsch, H. J., Rauch, M., & Kessler, J. (1997). Differential impairments in recalling people's names: A case study in search of neuroanatomical correlates. *Neuropsychologia, 35,* 677–684.

402. Ross, S. J. M., & Hodges, J. R. (1997). Preservation of famous person knowledge in a patient with severe post anoxic amnesia. *Cortex, 33,* 733–742.

403. Schagen, S., Schmand, B., de Sterke, S., & Lindeboom, J. (1997). Amsterdam Short-Term Memory Test: A new procedure for detection of feigned memory deficits. *Journal of Clinical and Experimental Neuropsychology, 19,* 43–51.

404. Schmidtke, K., & Vollmer, H. (1997). Retrograde amnesia: A study of its relation to anterograde amnesia and semantic memory deficits. *Neuropsychologia, 35,* 505–518.

405. Seger, C. A., Rabin, L. A., Zarella, M., & Gabrieli, J. D. E. (1997). Preserved verb generation priming in global amnesia. *Neuropsychologia, 35,* 1069–1074.

406. Seidman, L. J., Caplan, B. B., Tolomiczenko, G. S., Turner, W. M., Penk, W. E., Schutt, R. K., & Goldfinger, S. M. (1997). Neuropsychological function in homeless mentally ill individuals. *Journal of Nervous and Mental Disease, 185,* 3–12.

407. Stark, M. E., Grafman, J., & Fertig, E. (1997). A restricted "spotlight" of attention in visual object recognition. *Neuropsychologia, 35,* 1233–1249.

408. Stuss, D. T., Peterkin, I., Guzman, D. A., Guzman, C., & Troyer, A. K. (1997). Chronic obstructive pulmonary disease: Effects of hypoxia on neurological and neuropsychological measures. *Journal of Clinical and Experimental Neuropsychology, 19,* 515–524.

409. Tanaka, Y., Miyazama, Y., Akaoka, F., & Yamada, T. (1997). Amnesia following damage to the mammillary bodies. *Neurology, 48,* 160–165.
410. Tivis, L. J., & Parsons, O. A. (1997). Assessment of prose recall performance in chronic alcoholics: Recall of essential versus detail propositions. *Journal of Clinical Psychology, 53,* 233–242.
411. Troster, A. I., Fields, J. A., Wilkinson, S. B., Pahwa, R., Miyawaki, E., Lyons, K. E., & Koller, W. C. (1997). Unilateral pallidal stimulation for Parkinson's disease: Neurobehavioral functioning before and 3 months after electrode implantation. *Neurology, 49,* 1078–1083.
412. Welch, L. W., Nimmerrichter, A., Gilliland, R., King, D. E., & Martin, P. R. (1997). "Wineglass" confabulations among brain-damaged alcoholics on the Wechsler Memory Scale—Revised visual reproduction subtest. *Cortex, 33,* 543–551.
413. Baynes, K., Kegl, J. A., Brentari, D., Kussmaul, C., & Poizner, H. (1998). Chronic auditory agnosia following Landau-Kleffner syndrome: A 23 year outcome study. *Brain and Language, 63,* 381–425.
414. Broks, P., Young, A. W., Maratos, E. J., Coffey, P. J., Calder, A. J., Isaac, C. L., Mayes, A. R., Hodges, J. R., Montaldi, D., Cezayirli, E., Roberts, N., & Hadley, D. (1998). Face processing impairment after encephalitis: Amygdala damage and recognition of fear. *Neuropsychologia, 36,* 59–70.
415. Cochrane, H. J., Baker, G. A., & Mendell, P. R. (1998). Simulating a memory impairment: Can amnesics implicitly outperform simulators? *British Journal of Clinical Psychology, 37,* 31–48.
416. DeRonchi, D., Fratiglioni, L., Rucci, P., Paternico, A., Graziani, S., & Dalmonte, E. (1998). The effect of education on dementia occurrence in an Italian population with middle to high socioeconomic status. *Neurology, 50,* 1231–1238.
417. Dobbins, I. G., Kroll, N. E. A., Tulving, E., Knight, R. T., & Gazzaniga, M. S. (1998). Unilateral medial temporal lobe memory impairment: Type deficit, function deficit, or both? *Neuropsychologia, 36,* 115–127.
418. Flitman, S. S., Grafman, J., Wassermann, E. M., Cooper, V., O'Grady, J., Pascual-Leone, A., & Hallett, M. (1998). Linguistic processing during repetitive transcranial magnetic stimulation. *Neurology, 50,* 175–181.
419. Fukatsu, R., Yamadori, A., & Fujii, T. (1998). Impaired recall and preserved encoding in prominent amnesic syndrome: A case of basal forebrain amnesia. *Neurology, 50,* 539–541.
420. Hashimoto, R., Tanaka, Y., & Yoshida, M. (1998). Selective kana jaronagraphia following right hemispheric infarction. *Brain and Language, 63,* 50–63.
421. Johnson, K. A., Jones, K., Holman, B. L., Becker, J. A., Spiers, P. A., Satlin, A., & Albert, M. S. (1998). Preclinical prediction of Alzheimer's disease using SPECT. *Neurology, 50,* 1563–1571.
422. Kanne, S. M., Balota, D. A., Storandt, M., McKeel, D. W., & Morris, J. C. (1998). Relating anatomy to function in Alzheimer's disease: Neuropsychological profiles predict regional neuropathology 5 years later. *Neurology, 50,* 979–985.
423. Kohler, S., Black, S. E., Sinden, M., Szekely, C., Kidron, D., Parker, J. L., Foster, J. K., Moscovitch, M., Wincour, G., Szalai, J. P., & Bronskill, M. J. (1998). Memory impairments associated with hippocampal versus parahippocampal-gyrs atrophy: An MR volumetry study in Alzheimer's disease. *Neuropsychologia, 36,* 901–914.
424. Libon, D. J., Bogdanoff, B., Cloud, B. S., Skalina, S., Giovannetti, T., Gitlin, H. L., & Bonavita, J. (1998). Declarative and procedural leaving, quantitative measures of the hippocampus, and subcortical white alterations in Alzheimer's Disease and ischaemic vascular dementia. *Journal of Clinical and Experimental Neuropsychology, 20,* 30–41.
425. Marks, A. R., & Cermak, L. S., (1998). Intact temporal memory in amnesic patients. *Neuropsychologia, 36,* 935–943.
426. McDonald, S., & Pearce, S. (1998). Requests that overcome listener reluctance: Impairment associated with executive dysfunction in brain injury. *Brain and Language, 61,* 88–104.
427. Mega, M. S., Thompson, P. M., Cummings, J. L., Back, C. L., Xu, M. L., Zohoori, S., Goldkorn, A., Moussai, J., Fairbanks, L., Small, G. W., & Toga, A. W. (1998). Sulcal variability in the Alzheimer's brain: Correlations with cognition. *Neurology, 50,* 145–151.
428. Morel, K. R. (1998). Development and preliminary validation of a forced-choice test of response bias for posttraumatic stress disorder. *Journal of Personality Assessment, 70,* 299–314.
429. Patel, A. D., Peretz, I., Tramo, M., & Labreque, R. (1998). Processing prosodic and musical patterns: A neuropsychological investigation. *Brain and Language, 61,* 123–144.
430. Putzke, J. D., Williams, M. A., & Boll, T. J. (1998). A defensive response set and the relation between cognitive and emotional functioning: A replication. *Perceptual and Motor Skills, 86,* 251–257.
431. van Buchem, M. A., Grossman, R. I., Armstrong, C., Polansky, M., Miki, Y., Heyning, F. H., Boncoeur-Martel, M. P., Wei, L., Udupa, J. K., Grossman, M., Kolson, D. L., & McGowan, J. C. (1998). Correlation of volumetric magnetization transfer imaging with clinical data in MS. *Neurology, 50,* 1609–1617.

[2864]

Wechsler Preschool and Primary Scale of Intelligence—Revised.

Purpose: Developed "for assessing the intelligence of children."

Population: Ages 3–7.3 years.

Publication Dates: 1949-1989.

Acronym: WPPSI-R.

Scores, 13 to 15: Verbal (Information, Comprehension, Arithmetic, Vocabulary, Similarities, Sentences [optional], Total), Performance (Object Assembly, Geometric Design, Block Design, Mazes, Picture Completion, Animal Pegs [optional], Total), Total.

Administration: Individual.

Price Data, 1999: $44.50 per 25 maze test books; $15 per 50 geometric design sheets; $81 per set of 9 blocks; $44.50 per set of 28 animal house cylinders; $104 per animal house board; $46 per geometric design, block design, and picture completion stimulus booklet; $44.50 per 25 record forms; $70 per manual ('89, 239 pages).

Time: [75] minutes.

Author: David Wechsler.

Publisher: The Psychological Corporation.

Cross References: See T4:2941 (38 references); for reviews by Bruce A. Bracken and Jeffery P. Braden, see 11:466 (118 references); for a review by B. J. Freeman of an earlier edition, see 9:1356 (33 references); see also T3:2608 (280 references), 8:234 (84 references), and T2:538 (30 references); for reviews by Dorothy H. Eichorn and A. B. Silverstein, and excerpted reviews by C. H. Ammons and O. A. Oldridge (with E. E. Allison), see 7:434 (56 references).

TEST REFERENCES

1. Hall, P. K., & Jordan, L. S. (1987). An assessment of a controlled association task to identify word-finding problems in children. *Language, Speech, and Hearing Services in Schools, 18,* 99–111.
2. Moore, L. C., & Sawyers, J. K. (1987). The stability of original thinking in young children. *Gifted Child Quarterly, 31,* 126–129.
3. Sameroff, A., Seifer, R., Zax, M., & Barocas, R. (1987). Early indicators of developmental risk: Rochester longitudinal study. *Schizophrenia Bulletin, 13,* 383–394.
4. Aram, D., & Ekelman, B. L. (1988). Scholastic aptitude and achievement among children with unilateral brain lesions. *Neuropsychologia, 26,* 903–916.
5. Valencia, R. R. (1988). The McCarthy Scales and Hispanic children: A review of psychometric research. *Hispanic Journal of Behavioral Sciences, 10,* 81–104.
6. Ben-Yochanan, A., & Katz, Y. (1989). Validation of a school readiness battery for a referred sample of Israeli elementary school students. *Perceptual and Motor Skills, 68,* 651–654.
7. Chermak, G. D., & Fisher, J. M. (1989). Association between paired subtests of auditory sequential memory administered to preschool children. *Perceptual and Motor Skills, 68,* 255–258.
8. Curfs, L. M. G., Schreppers-Tijdink, G., Wiegers, A., Borghgraef, M., & Fryns, J. P. (1989). Intelligence and cognitive profile in the fra(X) syndrome: A longitudinal study in 18 fra(X) boys. *Journal of Medical Genetics, 26,* 443–446.
9. Geary, D. C., & Burlingham-Dubree, M. (1989). External validation of the strategy choice model for addition. *Journal of Experimental Child Psychology, 47,* 175-192.
10. Kirtley, C., Bryant, P., MacLean, M., & Bradley, L. (1989). Rhyme, rime, and the onset of reading. *Journal of Experimental Child Psychology, 48,* 224-245.
11. McEvoy, R. E., & Johnson, D. L. (1989). Comparison of an intelligence test and a screening battery as predictors of reading ability in low income, Mexican American children. *Hispanic Journal of Behavioral Sciences, 11,* 274–282.
12. Nass, R., Peterson, H. D., & Koch, D. (1989). Differential effects of congenital left and right brain injury on intelligence. *Brain and Cognition, 9,* 258-266.
13. Savicki, V. (1989). Computers in the child and youth care field. *Child Welfare, 68,* 505–516.
14. Segal, N. L. (1989). Origins and implications of handedness and relative birth weight for IQ in monozygotic twin pairs. *Neuropsychologia, 27,* 549–561.
15. Tegano, D. W., & Moran, J. D., III (1989). Developmental study of the effect of dimensionality and presentation mode on original thinking of children. *Perceptual and Motor Skills, 68,* 1275–1281.
16. Banich, M. T., Levine, S. C., Kim, H., & Huttenlocher, P. (1990). The effects of developmental factors on IQ in hemiplegic children. *Neuropsychologia, 28,* 35–47.
17. Crowe, S. F., & Hay, D. A. (1990). Neuropsychological dimensions of the Fragile X syndrome: Support for a non-dominant hemisphere dysfunction hypothesis. *Neuropsychologia, 28,* 9–16.

18. Nass, R., Baker, S., Sadler, A. E., & Sidtis, J. J. (1990). The effects of precocious adrenarche on cognition and hemispheric specialization. *Brain and Cognition, 14,* 59-69.
19. Schulte, A. C., Osborne, S. S., & McKinney, J. D. (1990). Academic outcomes for students with learning disabilities in consultation and resource programs. *Exceptional Children, 57,* 162-172.
20. Silverstein, A. B. (1990). Notes on the reliability of Wechsler short forms. *Journal of Clinical Psychology, 46,* 194–196.
21. Bhatia, M. S., Nigam, V. R., Bohra, N., & Malik, S. C. (1991). Attention deficit disorder with hyperactivity among paediatric outpatients. *Journal of Child Psychology and Psychiatry and Allied Disciplines, 32,* 297-306.
22. Jensen, A. M., & Harper, D. C. (1991). Correlates of concern in parents of high-risk infants at age five. *Journal of Pediatric Psychology, 16,* 429–445.
23. Leung, C. B. (1991). Effects of word-related variables on vocabulary growth through repeated read-aloud events. *Yearbook of National Reading Conference, 40,* 491-498.
24. Stewart, S. M., Silver, C. H., Nici, J., Waller, D., Campbell, R., Uany, R., & Andrews, W. S. (1991). Neuropsychological function in young children who have undergone liver transplantation. *Journal of Pediatric Psychology, 16,* 569–583.
25. Abkarian, G. G. (1992). Communication effects of prenatal alcohol exposure. *Journal of Communication Disorders, 25,* 221–240.
26. Aram, D. M., Morris, R., & Hall, N. E. (1992). The validity of discrepancy criteria for identifying children with developmental language disorders. *Journal of Learning Disabilities, 25,* 549–554.
27. Gerken, K. C., & Hodapp, A. F. (1992). Assessment of preschoolers at-risk with the WPPSI-R and the Stanford-Binet L-M. *Psychological Reports, 71,* 659-664.
28. Lewis, B. A. (1992). Pedigree analysis of children with phonology disorders. *Journal of Learning Disabilities, 25,* 586–597.
29. Lewis, B. A., & Freebairn, L. (1992). Residual effects of preschool phonology disorders in grade school, adolescence, and adulthood. *Journal of Speech and Hearing Research, 35,* 819–831.
30. Razavieh, A., & Shahim, S. (1992). A short form of the Wechsler Preschool and Primary Scale of Intelligence for use in Iran. *Psychological Reports, 71,* 863-866.
31. Rouet, J. F., Ehrlich, R. M., & Sorbara, D. L. (1992). Neurodevelopment in infants and preschool children with congenital hypothyroidism: Etiological and treatment factors affecting outcome. *Journal of Pediatric Psychology, 17,* 187–213.
32. Selzer, S. C., Lindgren, S. D., & Blackman, J. A. (1992). Long-term neuropsychological outcome of high risk infants with intracranial hemmorhage. *Journal of Pediatric Psychology, 17,* 407–422.
33. Thompson, A. P. (1992). Subtest scatter is not an indicator of inaccuracy for short-form estimates of I.Q. *Psychological Reports, 70,* 889-890.
34. Alpern, L., & Lyons-Ruth, K. (1993). Preschool children at social risk: Chronicity and timing of maternal depressive symptoms and child behavior problems at school and at home. *Development and Psychopathology, 5,* 371-387.
35. Aram, D. M., Morris, R., & Hall, N. E. (1993). Clinical and research congruence in identifying children with specific language impairment. *Journal of Speech and Hearing Research, 36,* 580–591.
36. Carvajal, H. H., Parks, C. S., Parks, J. P., Logan, R. A., & Page, G. L. (1993). A concurrent validity study of the Wechsler Preschool and Primary Scale of Intelligence—Revised and Columbia Mental Maturity Scale. *Bulletin of the Psychonomic Society, 31,* 33–34.
37. Catts, H. W. (1993). The relationship between speech-language impairments and reading disabilities. *Journal of Speech and Hearing Research, 36,* 948–958.
38. Cotugno, A. J. (1993). The diagnosis of Attention Deficit Hyperactivity Disorder (ADHD) in community mental health centers: Where and when. *Psychology in the Schools, 30,* 338-344.
39. Karr, S. K., Carvajal, H., Elser, D., Bays, K., Logan, R. A., & Page, G. L. (1993). Concurrent validity of the WPPSI-R and the McCarthy Scales of Children's Abilities. *Psychological Reports, 72,* 940-942.
40. MacMillan, D. L., Gresham, F. M., & Siperstein, G. N. (1993). Conceptual and psychometric concerns about the 1992 AAMR definition of mental retardation. *American Journal on Mental Retardation, 98,* 325–335.
41. Montgomery, J. W. (1993). Haptic recognition of children with specific language impairment: Effects of response modality. *Journal of Speech and Hearing Research, 36,* 98–104.
42. Reich, J. N., & Cleland, J. W. (1993). Children born at risk: What's happening in kindergarten? *Psychology in the Schools, 30,* 50-52.
43. Sameroff, A. J., Seifer, R., Baldwin, A., & Baldwin, C. (1993). Stability of intelligence from preschool to adolescence: The influence of social and family risk factors. *Child Development, 64,* 80-97.
44. Aram, D. M., & Eisele, J. A. (1994). Intellectual stability in children with unilateral brain lesions. *Neuropsychologia, 32,* 85–95.
45. Asendorpf, J. B., & van Aken, M. A. G. (1994). Traits and relationship status: Stranger versus peer group inhibition and test intelligence versus peer group competence as early predictors of later self-esteem. *Child Development, 65,* 1786-1798.
46. Bagnato, S. J., & Neisworth, J. T. (1994). A national study of the social and treatment "invalidity" of intelligence testing for early intervention. *School Psychology Quarterly, 9,* 81-102.
47. Cole, K. N., Mills, P. E., & Kelley, D. (1994). Agreement of assessment profiles used in cognitive referencing. *Language, Speech, and Hearing Services in Schools, 25,* 25–31.
48. Duncan, G. J., Brooks-Gunn, J., & Klebanov, P. K. (1994). Economic deprivation and early childhood development. *Child Development, 65,* 296–318.
49. Eaves, L. C., Ho, H. H., & Eaves, D. M. (1994). Subtypes of autism by cluster analyses. *Journal of Autism and Developmental Disorders, 24,* 3-22.
50. Eisele, J. A., & Aram, D. M. (1994). Comprehension and imitation of syntax following early hemisphere damage. *Brain and Language, 46,* 212–231.
51. Geers, A., & Moog, J. (1994). Description of the CID sensory aids study. *Volta Review, 96,* 1–11.
52. Gyurke, J. S. (1994). A reply to Bagnato and Neisworth: Intelligent versus intelligence testing of preschoolers. *School Psychology Quarterly, 9,* 109-112.
53. Hoehn, T. P., & Baumeister, A. A. (1994). A critique of the application of sensory integration therapy to children with learning disabilities. *Journal of Learning Disabilities, 27,* 338–350.
54. Kaiser, A. P., & Hester, P. P. (1994). Generalized effects of enhanced milieu teacher. *Journal of Speech and Hearing, 37,* 1320–1340.
55. Kaufman, A. S. (1994). A reply to Macmann and Barnett. Lessons from the blind men and the elephant. *School Psychology Quarterly, 9,* 199-207.
56. Keith, T. Z. (1994). Intelligence is important. Intelligence is complex. *School Psychology Quarterly, 9,* 209-221.
57. Kelly, D. J., & Rice, M. L. (1994). Preferences for verb interpretation in children with specific language impairment. *Journal of Speech and Hearing Research, 37,* 182–192.
58. Lewis, C. D., & Lorentz, S. (1994). Comparison of the Leiter International Performance Scale and the Wechsler Intelligence Scales. *Psychological Reports, 74,* 521-522.
59. Macmann, G. M., & Barnett, D. W. (1994). Some additional lessons from the Wechsler scales: A rejoinder to Kaufman and Keith. *School Psychology Quarterly, 9,* 223-236.
60. Macmann, G. M., & Barnett, D. W. (1994). Structural analysis of correlated factors: Lessons from the verbal-performance dichotomy of the Wechsler scales. *School Psychology Quarterly, 9,* 161-197.
61. McCrone, E. R., Egeland, B., Kalkoske, M., & Carlson, E. A. (1994). Relations between early maltreatment and mental representations of relationships assessed with projective storytelling in middle childhood. *Development and Psychopathology, 6,* 99-120.
62. Meyer, L. A., Stahl, S. A., & Wardrop, J. L. (1994). Effects of reading storybooks aloud to children. *The Journal of Educational Research, 88,* 69–85.
63. Muter, V., Snowling, M., & Taylor, S. (1994). Orthographic analogies and phonological awareness: Their role and significance in early reading development. *Journal of Child Psychology and Psychiatry and Allied Disciplines, 35,* 293-310.
64. Nellis, L., & Gridley, B. E. (1994). Review of the Bayley Scales of Infant Development—Second Edition. *Journal of School Psychology, 32,* 201-209.
65. Pianta, R. C., & Egeland, B. (1994). Predictors of instability in children's mental test performance at 24, 48, and 96 months. *Intelligence, 18,* 145-163.
66. Pine, D. S., Weese-Mayer, D. E., Silvestri, J. M., Davies, M., Whitaker, A. H., & Klein, D. F. (1994). Anxiety and congenital central hypoventilation syndrome. *American Journal of Psychiatry, 151,* 864-870.
67. Reid, R., Maag, J., Vasa, S. F., & Wright, G. (1994). Who are the children with attention deficit-hyperactivity disorder? A school-based survey. *The Journal of Special Education, 28,* 117–137.
68. Restall, G., & Magill-Evans, J. (1994). Play and preschool children with autism. *The American Journal of Occupational Therapy, 48,* 113-120.
69. Rice, M. L., Oetting, J. B., Marquis, J., Bode, J., & Pae, S. (1994). Frequency of input effects on word comprehension of children with specific language impairment. *Journal of Speech and Hearing Research, 37,* 106–122.
70. Roberts, J. E., Burchinal, M. R., & Campbell, F. (1994). Otitis media in early childhood and patterns of intellectual development and later academic performance. *Journal of Pediatric Psychology, 19,* 347–367.
71. Sadeh, A., Hayden, R. M., McGuire, J. P. D., Sachs, H., & Civita, R. (1994). Somatic, cognitive and emotional characteristics of abused children in a psychiatric hospital. *Child Psychiatry and Human Development, 24,* 191–200.
72. Spencer, E. K., & Campbell, M. (1994). Children with schizophrenia: Diagnosis, phenomenology, and pharmacotherapy. *Schizophrenia Bulletin, 20,* 713–725.
73. Steinhausen, H. C., Willms, J., & Spohr, H. L. (1994). Correlates of psychopathology and intelligence in children with fetal alcohol syndrome. *Journal of Child Psychology and Psychiatry and Allied Disciplines, 35,* 323-331.
74. Stewart, S. M., Kennard, B. D., Waller, D. A., & Fixler, D. (1994). Cognitive function in children who receive organ transplantation. *Health Psychology, 13,* 3-13.
75. Tsushima, W. T. (1994). Short form of the WPPSI and WPPSI-R. *Journal of Clinical Psychology, 50,* 877-880.
76. Bird, J., Bishop, D. V. M., & Freeman, N. H. (1995). Phonological awareness and literacy development in children with expressive phonological impairments. *Journal of Speech and Hearing Research, 38,* 446–462.
77. Bowey, J. A. (1995). Socioeconomic status differences in preschool phonological sensitivity and first-grade reading achievement. *Journal of Educational Psychology, 87,* 476–487.
78. Boyum, L. A., & Parke, R. D. (1995). The role of family emotional expressiveness in the development of children's social competence. *Journal of Marriage and the Family, 57,* 593–608.
79. Campbell, F. A., & Ramey, C. T. (1995). Cognitive and school outcomes for high-risk African-American students at middle adolescence: Positive effects of early intervention. *American Educational Research Journal, 32,* 743–772.
80. Carter, J. D., & Swanson, H. L. (1995). The relationship between intelligence and vigilance in children at risk. *Journal of Abnormal Child Psychology, 23,* 201-220.
81. Cunningham, C. E., Bremner, R., & Boyle, M. (1995). Large group community-based parenting programs for families of preschoolers at risk for disruptive behaviors disorders: Utilization, cost effectiveness, and outcome. *Journal of Child Psychology and Psychiatry, 36,* 1141–1159.

82. Curfs, L. M. G., Hoondert, V., van Lieshout, C. F. M., & Fryns, J. P. (1995). Personality profiles of youngsters with Prader-Willi syndrome and youngsters attending regular schools. *Journal of Intellectual Disability Research, 39,* 241–248.

83. Donahue, M. L., & Pearl, R. (1995). Conversational interactions of mothers and their preschool children who had been born preterm. *Journal of Speech and Hearing Research, 38,* 1117–1125.

84. Feagans, L. V., Fendt, K., & Farran, D. C. (1995). The effects of day care intervention on teachers' ratings of the elementary school discourse skills in disadvantaged children. *International Journal of Behavioral Development, 18,* 243–261.

85. Felsenfeld, S., McGue, M., & Broen, P. A. (1995). Familial aggregation of phonological disorders: Results from a 28-year follow-up. *Journal of Speech and Hearing Research, 38,* 1091–1107.

86. Flaks, D. K., Ficher, I., Masterpasqua, F., & Joseph, G. (1995). Lesbians choosing motherhood: A comparative study of lesbian and heterosexual parents and their children. *Developmental Psychology, 31,* 105-114.

87. Gjerde, P. F. (1995). Alternative pathways to chronic depressive symptoms in young adults: Gender differences in developmental trajectories. *Child Development, 66,* 1277–1300.

88. Gresham, K. M., MacMillan, D. L., & Siperstein, G. N. (1995). Critical analysis of the 1992 AAMR definition: Implications for school psychology. *School Psychology Quarterly, 10,* 1-19.

89. Gross-Tsur, V., Shaleu, R. S., Manor, O., & Amir, N. (1995). Developmental right-hemisphere syndrome: Clinical spectrum of the nonverbal learning disability. *Journal of Learning Disabilities, 28,* 80–86.

90. Guralnick, M. J., Connor, R. T., & Hammond, M. (1995). Parent perspective of peer relationships and friendships in integrated and specialized programs. *American Journal on Mental Retardation, 99,* 457–476.

91. Guralnick, M. J., Connor, R. T., Hammond, M., Gottman, J. M., & Kinnish, K. (1995). Immediate effects of mainstreamed settings on the social interactions and social integration of preschool children. *American Journal on Mental Retardation, 100,* 359–377.

92. Hodapp, R. M. (1995). Definitions in mental retardation: Effects on research, practice, and perceptions. *School Psychology Quarterly, 10,* 24-28.

93. Holmbeck, G. N., & Faier-Routman, J. (1995). Spinal lesion level, shunt status, family relationships, and psychosocial adjustment in children and adolescents with spina bifida myelomeningocele. *Journal of Pediatric Psychology, 20,* 817–832.

94. Janzen-Wilde, M. L., Duchan, J. F., & Higginbotham, D. J. (1995). Successful use of facilitated communication with an oral child. *Journal of Speech and Hearing Research, 38,* 658–676.

95. Katusic, S. K., Colligan, R. C., Beard, C. M., O'Fallon, W. M., Bergstralli, E. J., Jacobsen, S. J., & Kurland, L. T. (1995). Mental retardation in a birth cohort, 1976–1980, Rochester, Minnesota. *American Journal on Mental Retardation, 100,* 335–344.

96. Lassiter, K. S., & Bardos, A. (1995). The relationship between young children's academic achievement and measures of intelligence. *Psychology in the Schools, 32,* 170–177.

97. Lozoff, B., Park, A. M., Radan, A. E., & Wolf, A. W. (1995). Using the HOME Inventory with infants in Costa Rica. *International Journal of Behavioral Development, 18,* 277–295.

98. Marcell, M. M., Ridgeway, M. M., Sewell, D. H., & Whelan, M. L. (1995). Sentence imitation by adolescents and young adults with Down's syndrome and other intellectual disabilities. *Journal of Intellectual Disability Research, 39,* 215–232.

99. Matson, J. L. (1995). Comments on Gresham, MacMillan, and Siperstein's paper "Critical analysis of the 1992 AAMR definition: Implications for school psychology." *School Psychology Quarterly, 10,* 20-23.

100. Pearl, R., & Donahue, M. (1995). Brief report: Four years after a preterm birth: Children's development and their mother's beliefs and expectations. *Journal of Pediatric Psychology, 20,* 363–370.

101. Pletan, M. D., Robinson, N. M., Berringer, V. W., & Abbott, R. D. (1995). Parents' observations of kindergartners who are advanced in mathematical reasoning. *Journal for the Education of the Gifted, 19,* 30–44.

102. Schatz, J., & Hamdam-Allen, G. (1995). Effects of age and IQ on adaptive behavior domains for children with autism. *Journal of Autism and Developmental Disorders, 25,* 51-60.

103. Slater, A. (1995). Individual differences in infancy and later IQ. *Journal of Child Psychology and Psychiatry and Allied Disciplines, 36,* 69-112.

104. Stothard, S. E., & Holme, C. (1995). A comparison of phonological skills in children with reading comprehension difficulties and children with decoding difficulties. *Journal of Child Psychology and Psychiatry and Allied Disciplines, 36,* 399-408.

105. Williamson, D. A., & Bolton, P. (1995). Brief report: Atypical autism and tuberous sclerosis in a sibling pair. *Journal of Autism and Developmental Disorders, 25,* 435–442.

106. Yoder, P. J., Spruytenberg, H., Edwards, A., & Davies, B. (1995). Effect of verbal routine contexts and expansions on gains in the mean length of utterance in children with developmental delays. *Language, Speech, and Hearing Services in Schools, 26,* 21–32.

107. Zelkowitz, P., Papageorgiou, A., Zelazo, P. R., & Weiss, M. J. S. (1995). Behavioral adjustment in very low and normal birth weight children. *Journal of Clinical Child Psychology, 24,* 21-30.

108. Badian, N. A. (1996). Dyslexia: A validation of the concept at two age levels. *Journal of Learning Disabilities, 29,* 102–112.

109. Baumeister, A. A., & Baeharach, V. R. (1996). A critical analysis of the Infant Health and Development Program. *Intelligence, 23,* 79–104.

110. Beitchman, J. H., Brownlie, E. B., Inglis, A., Wild, J., Ferguson, B., Schachter, D., Lancee, W., Wilson, B., & Mathews, R. (1996). Seven-year follow-up of speech/language impaired and control children: Psychiatric outcome. *Journal of Child Psychology and Psychiatry, 37,* 961–970.

111. Blaha, J., & Wallbrown, F. H. (1996). Hierarchical factor structure of the Wechsler Intelligence Scale for Children—III. *Psychological Assessment, 8,* 214–218.

112. Brooks-Gunn, J., & Klebanov, P. K. (1996). Ethnic differences in children's intelligence test scores: Role of economic deprivation, home environment, and maternal characteristics. *Child Development, 67,* 396–408.

113. Burchinal, M. R., Follmer, A., Bryant, D. M. (1996). The relations of maternal social support and family structure with maternal responsiveness and child outcomes among African American families. *Developmental Psychology, 32,* 1073–1083.

114. Einfeld, S. L., & Tonge, B. J. (1996). Population prevalence of psychopathology in children and adolescents with intellectual disability: I. Rationale and methods. *Journal of Disability Research, 40,* 91–98.

115. Guralnick, M. J., Connor, R. T., Hammond, M. A., Gottman, J. M., & Kinnish, K. (1996). The peer relations of preschool children with communication disorders. *Child Development, 67,* 471–489.

116. Humphries, T., Krekewich, K., & Snider, L. (1996). Evidence of nonverbal learning disability among learning disabled boys with sensory integrative dysfunction. *Perceptual and Motor Skills, 82,* 979–987.

117. Isaacs, E., Christie, D., Vargha-Khadem, F., & Mishkin, M. (1996). Effects of hemispheric side of injury, age at injury, and presence of seizure disorder on functional ear and hand asymmetries in hemiplegic children. *Neuropsychologia, 34,* 127–137.

118. Kaplan, C. (1996). Predictive validity of the WPPSI-R: A four year follow-up study. *Psychology in the Schools, 33,* 211–220.

119. Livingston, J. A., & Gentile, J. R. (1996). Mastery learning and the decreasing variability hypothesis. *Journal of Educational Research, 90,* 67–86.

120. Marvin, C., & Kasal, K. R. (1996). A semantic analysis of signed communication in an activity-based classroom for preschool children who are deaf. *Language, Speech, and Hearing Services in Schools, 27,* 57–67.

121. Miller, L. T., & Vernon, P. A. (1996). Intelligence, reaction time, and working memory in 4- to 6-year old children. *Intelligence, 22,* 155–190.

122. Mottron, L., Décarie, J. C., Mineau, S., Aroichane, M., & Pépin, J. P. (1996). F-30. Overlapping between symptoms of autism and visual agnosia: A case study. *Brain and Cognition, 32,* 339–341.

123. Robinson, N. M., Abbott, R. D., Berninger, V. W., & Busse, J. (1996). The structure of abilities in math-precocious young children: Gender similarities and differences. *Journal of Educational Psychology, 88,* 341–352.

124. Teo, A., Carlson, E., Mathieu, P. J., Egeland, B., & Sroufe, L. A. (1996). A prospective longitudinal study of psychosocial predictors of achievement. *Journal of School Psychology, 34,* 285–306.

125. Tomblin, J. B., Records, N. L., & Zhang, X. (1996). A system for the diagnosis of specific language impairment in kindergarten children. *Journal of Speech and Hearing Research, 39,* 1284–1294.

126. Werts, M. G., Wolery, M., Venn, M. L., Deinblowski, D., & Doren, H. (1996). Effects of transition-based teaching with instructive feedback on skill acquisition by children with and without disabilities. *Journal of Educational Research, 90,* 75–86.

127. Yirmiya, N., Solomonica-Levi, D., & Shulman, C. (1996). The ability to manipulate behavior and to understand manipulation of beliefs: A comparison of individuals with autism, mental retardation, and normal development. *Developmental Psychology, 32,* 62–69.

128. Yirmiya, N., Solomonica-Levi, D., Shulman, C., & Pilowsky, T. (1996). Theory of mind abilities in individuals with autism, Down syndrome, and mental retardation of unknown etiology: The role of age and intelligence. *Journal of Child Psychology and Psychiatry, 37,* 1003–1014.

129. Bortolini, V., Caselli, M. C., & Leonard, L. B. (1997). Grammatical deficits in Italian-speaking children with specific language impairment. *Journal of Speech, Language, and Hearing Research, 40,* 809–820.

130. Bowey, J. A. (1997). What does non-word repetition measure? A reply to Gatnercole and Baddeley. *Journal of Experimental Child Psychology, 67,* 295–301.

131. Burchinal, M. R., Campbell, F. A., Bryant, D. M., Wasik, H., & Ramey, C. T. (1997). Early intervention and mediating processes in cognitive performance of children of low-income African American families. *Child Development, 68,* 935–954.

132. Campbell, T., Dollaghan, C., Needleman, H., & Janosky, J. (1997). Reducing bias in language assessment: Processing-dependent measures. *Journal of Speech, Language, and Hearing Research, 40,* 519–525.

133. Clauke, A. T., & Kurtz-Costes, B. (1997). Television viewing, educational quality of the home environment, and school readiness. *Journal of Educational Research, 90,* 279–285.

134. Glosser, G., Grugan, P., & Friedman, R. B. (1997). Semantic memory impairment does not impact on phonological and orthographic processing in a case of developmental hyperlexia. *Brain and Language, 56.* 2344–247.

135. Gottman, J. M., Guralnick, M. J., Wilson, B., Swanson, C. C., & Murray, J. D. (1997). What should be the focus of emotional regulation in children? A nonlinear dynamic mathematical model of children's peer interaction in groups. *Development and Psychopathology, 9,* 421–452.

136. Guralnick, M. J. (1997). Peer social networks of young boys with developmental delays. *American Journal on Mental Retardation, 101,* 595–612.

137. Katz, L. F., & Gottman, J. M. (1997). Buffering children from marital conflict and dissolution. *Journal of Clinical Child Psychology, 26,* 257–171.

138. Krassowski, E., & Plante, E. (1997). IQ variability in children with SLI: Implications for use of cognitive referencing in determining SLI. *Journal of Communication Disorders, 30,* 1–9.
139. Leonard, L. B., Eyer, J. A., Bedore, L. M., & Grela, B. G. (1997). Three accounts of the grammatical morpheme difficulties of English-speaking children with specific language impairment. *Journal of Speech, Language, and Hearing Research, 40,* 741–753.
140. Rhodes, R. L., Whitten, J. D., & Copeland, E. P. (1997). Early intervention with at-risk Hispanic students: Effectiveness of the Piacceleration Program in developing Piagetian intellectual processes. *Journal of Experimental Education, 65,* 318–328.
141. Tomblin, J. B., Smith, E., & Zhang, X. (1997). Epidemiology of specific language impairment: Prenatal and perinatal risk factors. *Journal of Communication Disorders, 30,* 325–344.
142. Badian, N. A. (1998). A validation of the role of preschool phonological and orthographic skills in the prediction of reading. *Journal of Learning Disabilities, 31,* 472–481.
143. Fagot, B. I., & Lee, L. D. (1998). Teacher ratings of externalizing behavior at school entry for boys and girls: Similar early prediction and different correlates. *Journal of Child Psychology and Psychiatry, 39,* 555–566.
144. Glass, P., Bulas, D. I., Wagner, A. E., Rajasingham, S. R., Civitello, L. A., & Coffman, C. E. (1998). Pattern of neuropsychological deficit at age five years following neonatal unilateral brain injury. *Brain and Language, 63,* 346–356.
145. Newman, J., Noel, A., Chen, R., & Matsopoulos, A. S. (1998). Temperament, selected moderating variables and early reading achievement. *Journal of School Psychology, 36,* 215–232.
146. Silberg, J. L. (1998). Dissociative symptomatology in children and adolescents as displayed on psychological testing. *Journal of Personality Assessment, 71,* 421–439.

[2865]

Weinberg Depression Scale for Children and Adolescents.

Purpose: Designed to detect depression in children and adolescents.
Population: Children and adolescents with at least a 4th grade reading level.
Publication Dates: 1987–1998.
Acronym: WDSCA.
Scores: Total score only.
Administration: Individual.
Price Data, 1999: $94 per complete kit; $39 per examiner's manual ('98, 40 pages); $29 per 50 summary sheets; $29 per 50 student response sheets.
Time: (5) minutes.
Comments: Normed on children diagnosed with major depression, ages 7 to 18; a self-report measure; WDSCA items based in part on the DSM-IV criteria.
Authors: Warren A. Weinberg, Caryn R. Harper, and Graham J. Emslie.
Publisher: PRO-ED.

[2866]

Weiss Comprehensive Articulation Test.

Purpose: "For making a thorough diagnosis of articulation and its associated parameters."
Population: All ages.
Publication Dates: 1978-1980.
Acronym: WCAT.
Scores, 5: Articulation, Articulation Age, Intelligibility, Stimulability, Number of Misarticulations.
Administration: Individual.
Forms, 2: Nonreading Subjects, Reading Subjects.
Price Data, 1999: $98 per complete kit including picture cards, sentence card, 50 picture response forms, 50 sentence response forms, and manual ('80, 32 pages); $34 per 100 picture response forms; $34 per 100 sentence response forms.
Time: [20] minutes.
Author: Curtis E. Weiss.
Publisher: PRO-ED.
Cross References: See T4:2942 (2 references); for a review by Richard J. Schissel, see 9:1357.

TEST REFERENCES

1. Garn-Nunn, P. G., & Martin, V. (1992). Using conventional articulation tests with highly unintelligible children: identification and programming concerns. *Language, Speech, and Hearing Services in Schools, 23,* 52–60.
2. Hodson, B. W. (1992). Clinical forum: Phonological assessment and treatment. Applied phonology: Constructs, contributions, and issues. *Language, Speech, and Hearing Services in Schools, 23,* 247–253.
3. Tyler, A. A., Figurski, G. R., & Langsdale, T. (1993). Relationships between acoustically determined knowledge of stop place and voicing contrasts and phonological treatment progress. *Journal of Speech and Hearing Research, 36,* 746–549.
4. Tyler, A. A., & Sandoval, K. T. (1994). Preschoolers with phonological and language disorders: Treating different linguistic domains. *Language, Speech, and Hearing Services in Schools, 25,* 215–234.
5. Arehole, S., Augustine, L. E., & Simhadri, R. (1995). Middle latency response in children with learning disabilities: Preliminary findings. *Journal of Communication Disorders, 28,* 21–38.

[2867]

WeldTest—Form A-C.

Purpose: "Measures knowledge and skills in welding areas."
Population: Welding job applicants.
Publication Dates: 1984–1998.
Scores: 7 areas: Print Reading, Welding/Cutting and Arc Air Cutting, Welder Maintenance and Operation, Tools/Machines/Material and Equipment, Mobile Equipment and Rigging, Production Welding Calculations, Total.
Administration: Group.
Price Data, 1998: $12 per consumable self-scoring booklet; $24.95 per manual ('98, 16 pages).
Time: (60) minutes.
Comments: Self-scoring instrument.
Author: Roland T. Ramsay.
Publisher: Ramsay Corporation.
Cross References: For reviews by John Peter Hudson, Jr. and David C. Roberts, see 13:360.

[2868]

Weller-Strawser Scales of Adaptive Behavior for the Learning Disabled.

Purpose: Designed "to assess the adaptive behavior of the learning disabled student."
Population: Learning disabled students ages 6-12, 13-18.
Publication Date: 1981.
Acronym: WSSAB.
Scores, 5: Social Coping, Relationships, Pragmatic Language, Production, Total.
Administration: Individual.
Levels, 2: Elementary, Secondary.

Price Data, 1999: $40 per test kit including manual (112 pages) and 50 test forms (specify level); $20 per 50 test forms (specify level); $17 per manual; $17 per specimen set.
Time: Administration time not reported.
Comments: Ratings by teachers.
Authors: Carol Weller and Sherri Strawser.
Publisher: Academic Therapy Publications.
Cross References: For a review by Thomas G. Haring, see 10:387 (1 reference); see also 9:1359 (1 reference).

TEST REFERENCES

1. Little, S. S. (1993). Nonverbal learning disabilities and socioemotional functioning: A review of recent literature. *Journal of Learning Disabilities, 26,* 653–665.
2. Cole, J. C., Muenz, T. A., Ouchi, B. Y., Kaufman, N., & Kaufman, A. S. (1997). The impact of pictorial stimulus on written expression output of adolescents and adults. *Psychology in the Schools, 34,* 1–9.

[2869]

Welsh Figure Preference Test.

Purpose: A nonverbal approach to personality measurement and research incorporating the Barron-Welsh Art Scale.
Population: Ages 6 and over.
Publication Dates: 1959-1980.
Acronym: WFPT.
Scores, 27: Don't Like Total, Repeat, Conformance, Barron-Welsh Art Scale, Revised Art Scale, Male-Female, Neuropsychiatric, Children, Movement, 5 Sex-Symbol Scores, and 13 Figure-Structure Preference Scores.
Administration: Group or individual.
Price Data: Available from publisher.
Time: (50) minutes.
Comments: For research use only; self-administering.
Author: George S. Welsh.
Publisher: Mind Garden.
Cross References: See T4:2945 (5 references); for a review by Julien Worland, see 9:1360 (1 reference); see also T3:2613 (4 references), T2:1437 (34 references), and P:287 (24 references); for a review by Harold Borko and an excerpted review by Gordon V. Anderson, see 6:197 (20 references); for information for Barron-Welsh Art Scale, see T3:243 (15 references).

TEST REFERENCE

1. Kaiser, A. P., & Hester, P. P. (1994). Generalized effects of enhanced milieu teacher. *Journal of Speech and Hearing, 37,* 1320–1340.

[2870]

Wepman's Auditory Discrimination Test, Second Edition.

Purpose: Measures children's ability to hear spoken English accurately, specifically to "discriminate between commonly used phonemes in the English language."
Population: Ages 4-0 to 8-11.
Publication Dates: 1958-1987.
Acronym: ADT.
Scores: Total score yielding Qualitative score, Standard score, Percentile rank.
Administration: Individual.
Forms, 2: 1A, 2A.
Price Data, 1999: $82 per complete kit including 200 tests (100 each of Forms 1A and 2A) and manual ('87, 58 pages); $29.95 per 100 tests (specify form); $34 per manual.
Time: (15-20) minutes.
Authors: Joseph M. Wepman (test) and William M. Reynolds (manual).
Publisher: Western Psychological Services.
Cross References: See T4:2946 (1 reference); for a review by Mary Pannbacker and Grace Middleton, see 11:467 (5 references); see also T3:226 (31 references), 8:932 (74 references), and T2:2028 (82 references); for a review by Louis M. DiCarlo of the original edition, see 6:940 (2 references).

TEST REFERENCES

1. Nelson, R., & Lignugaris/Kraft, B. (1989). Postsecondary education for students with learning disabilities. *Exceptional Children, 56,* 246–265.
2. Pillon, B., Dubois, B., Ploska, A., & Agid, Y. (1991). Severity and specificity of cognitive impairment in Alzheimer's, Huntington's, and Parkinson's diseases and progressive supranuclear palsy. *Neurology, 41,* 634–643.
3. Rouet, J. F., Ehrlich, R. M., & Sorbara, D. L. (1992). Neurodevelopment in infants and preschool children with congenital hypothyroidism: Etiological and treatment factors affecting outcome. *Journal of Pediatric Psychology, 17,* 187–213.
4. Cohen, M. J., Branch, W. B., & Hynd, G. W. (1994). Receptive prosody in children with left or right hemisphere dysfunction. *Brain and Language, 47,* 171–181.
5. Rovert, J. & Alvarez, M. (1996). Thyroid hormone and attention in school-age children with congenital hypothyroidism. *Journal of Child Psychology and Psychiatry, 37,* 579–585.

[2871]

Wesman Personnel Classification Test.

Purpose: Developed to measure verbal reasoning and numerical ability.
Population: Grades 10-12 and applicants and employees.
Publication Dates: 1946-1965.
Acronym: PCT.
Scores, 3: Verbal, Numerical, Total.
Administration: Group or individual.
Forms, 3: A, B, C.
Price Data, 1999: $63 per 25 test booklets including key (specify form) and manual ('65, 28 pages); $29.50 per examination kit including test booklet, record form, and manual; $231 per 100 test booklets including key and manual (specify form).
Time: 28 minutes.
Author: Alexander G. Wesman.
Publisher: The Psychological Corporation.
Cross References: See T4:2947 (5 references), T3:2614 (4 references), and T2:480 (2 references); for a review by Arthur C. MacKinney, and an excerpted review by Jack C. Merwin, see 7:400 (7 references); see also 5:399 (8 references); for reviews by John C. Flanagan

and Erwin K. Taylor, see 4:331 (3 references); for an excerpted review, see 3:253.

TEST REFERENCES

1. Arthur, W., Jr., & Olson, E. (1991). Computer attitudes, computer experience, and their correlates: An investigation of path linkages. *Teaching of Psychology, 18,* 51-54.

2. Havenstein, N. M. A., & Alexander, R. A. (1991). Rating ability in performance judgments: The joint influence of implicit theories and intelligence. *Organizational Behavior and Human Decision Processes, 50,* 300–323.

3. Cooksey, R. W., & Athanason, J. A. (1994). Assessing differences in accuracy of self-estimates of vocational interests: An idiographic analysis using profile decomposition. *Australian Journal of Psychology, 46,* 112–117.

4. Wong, C. T., Day, J. D., Maxwell, S. E., & Meara, N. M. (1995). A multitrait-multimethod study of academic and social intelligence in college students. *Journal of Educational Psychology, 87,* 117-133.

[2872]

The Wessex Revised Portage Language Checklist.

Purpose: Designed as a guide in the design of individualized teaching activities.
Population: Developmentally delayed and mentally handicapped children mental ages 0-1, 1-2, 2-3, 3-4.
Publication Date: 1983.
Scores: No scores.
Administration: Individual.
Levels, 4: 0-1, 1-2, 2-3, 3-4 in one booklet.
Manual: No manual.
Price Data: Available from publisher.
Authors: Mollie White and Kathy East.
Publisher: NFER-Nelson Publishing Co., Ltd. [England].
Cross References: For reviews by Kenneth L. Sheldon and Lawrence J. Turton, see 9:1361.

[2873]

Western Aphasia Battery.

Purpose: "To evaluate the main clinical aspects of language function" as well as nonverbal skills.
Population: Adolescents and adults with language disorders.
Publication Dates: 1980-1982.
Acronym: WAB.
Scores: 17 obtained subscores which form 7 major scores: Spontaneous Speech, Comprehension, Repetition, Naming, Reading and Writing, Praxis, Construction (optional), plus 2 derived scores: Aphasia Quotient, Cortical Quotient (optional).
Administration: Individual.
Price Data, 1999: $120.50 per complete kit including 25 test booklets, manual ('80, 3 pages), and stimulus cards; $24 per 25 test booklets; $87 per stimulus cards; $17 per manual; $1.50 each per Koh's blocks (each two-color block: four blocks are required for testing); $25.50 per 50 answer documents; $330.50 per Raven's test booklets.
Time: [60-70] minutes.
Comments: Other test materials (e.g., cup, comb, flower) must be supplied by examiner; a computerized record form (1993) is also available (hardware requirements—DOS-based PC/4.0 or higher, 640K RAM, one hard or floppy drive).
Author: Andrew Kertesz.
Publisher: The Psychological Corporation.
Cross References: See T4:2949 (33 references); for a review by Francis J. Pirozzolo, see 9:1362 (1 reference).

TEST REFERENCES

1. Butterworth, B., Howard, D., & Mcloughlin, P. (1984). The semantic deficit in aphasia: The relationship between semantic errors in auditory comprehension and picture naming. *Neuropsychologia, 22,* 409–426.

2. Hall, P. K., & Jordan, L. S. (1987). An assessment of a controlled association task to identify word-finding problems in children. *Language, Speech, and Hearing Services in Schools, 18,* 99–111.

3. Neils, J., Brennan, M. M., Cole, M., Boller, F., & Gerdeman, B. (1988). The use of phonemic cueing with Alzheimer's disease patients. *Neuropsychologia, 26,* 351–354.

4. Emery, O. B., & Breslau, L. D. (1989). Language deficits in depression: Comparisons with SDAT and normal aging. *Journal of Gerontology, 44,* 85–92.

5. Kirk, A., & Kertesz, A. (1989). Hemispheric contributions to drawing. *Neuropsychologia, 27,* 881–886.

6. Shuttleworth, E. C., & Huber, S. J. (1989). The picture absurdities test in the evaluation of dementia. *Brain and Cognition, 11,* 50-59.

7. Schacter, D. L., Rapscak, S. Z., Rubens, A. B., Thoran, M., & Laguna, J. (1990). Priming effects in a letter-by-letter reader depend upon access to the word form system. *Neuropsychologia, 28,* 1079–1094.

8. Raade, A. S., Rothi, L. J. G., & Heilman, K. M. (1991). The relationship between buccofacial and limb apraxia. *Brain and Cognition, 16,* 130-146.

9. Peach, R. K. (1992). Factors underlying neuropsychological test performance in chronic severe traumatic brain injury. *Journal of Speech and Hearing Research, 35,* 810–818.

10. Sakurai, Y., Kurisaki, H., Takeda, K., Iwata, M., Bandoh, M., Watanabe, T., & Momose, T. (1992). Japanese crossed Wernicke's aphasia. *Neurology, 42,* 144–148.

11. Suzuki, I., Shimuzu, H., Ishijima, B., Tani, K., Sugishita, M., & Adachi, N. (1992). Aphasic seizure caused by focal epilepsy in the left fusiform gyrus. *Neurology, 42,* 2207–2210.

12. Tompkins, C. A., Boada, R., & McGarry, K. (1992). The access and processing of familiar idioms by brain damaged and normally aging adults. *Journal of Speech and Hearing Research, 35,* 626–637.

13. Beeson, P. M., Bayles, K. A., Rubens, A. B., & Kaszniak, A. W. (1993). Memory impairment and executive control in individuals with stroke-induced aphasia. *Brain and Language, 45,* 253–275.

14. Bracy, C. B., & Drummond, S. S. (1993). Word retrieval in fluent and nonfluent dysphasia: Utilization of pictogram. *Journal of Communication Disorders, 26,* 113–128.

15. Goodglass, H., Christiansen, J. A., & Gallagher, R. (1993). Comparison of morphology and syntax in free narrative and structured tests: Fluent vs. nonfluent aphasics. *Cortex, 29,* 377-407.

16. Nicholas, L. E., & Brookshire, R. H. (1993). A system for quantifying the informativeness and efficiency of the connected speech of adults with aphasia. *Journal of Speech and Hearing Research, 36,* 338–350.

17. Shapiro, L. P., Gordon, B., Hack, N., & Killackey, J. (1993). Verb-argument structure processing in complex sentences in Broca's and Wernicke's aphasia. *Brain and Language, 45,* 423–447.

18. Shuren, J., Geldmacher, D., & Heilman, K. M. (1993). Nonoptic aphasia: Aphasia with preserved confrontation naming in Alzheimer's disease. *Neurology, 43,* 1900–1907.

19. Zurif, E., Swinney, D., Prather, P., Soloman, J., & Bushell, C. (1993). An on-line analysis of syntactic processing in Broca's and Wernicke's aphasia. *Brain and Language, 45,* 448–464.

20. Bell, B. D. (1994). Pantomine recognition impairment in aphasia: An analyses of error types. *Brain and Language, 47,* 269–278.

21. Code, C., Rowley, D., & Kertesz, A. (1994). Predicting recovery from aphasia with connectionist networks: Preliminary comparisons with multiple regression. *Cortex, 30,* 527-532.

22. Feinberg, T. E., Schindler, R. J., Ochoa, E., Kwan, P. C., & Farah, M. J. (1994). Associative visual agnosia and alexia without prosopagnosia. *Cortex, 30,* 395-412.

23. Maher, L. M., Rothi, L. J. G., & Heilman, K. M. (1994). Lack of error awareness in an aphasic patient with relatively preserved auditory comprehension. *Brain and Language, 46,* 402–418.

24. Mega, M. S., & Alexander, M. P. (1994). Subcortical aphasia: The core profile of capsulostriatal infarction. *Neurology, 44,* 1824–1829.

25. Miozzo, A., Soardi, M., & Cappa, S. F. (1994). Pure anomia with spared action naming due to a left temporal lesion. *Neuropsychologia, 32,* 1101–1109.

26. Polster, M. R., & Rapczak, S. Z. (1994). Hierarchical stimuli and hemispheric specialization: Two case studies. *Cortex, 30,* 487-497.

27. Tompkins, C. A., Bloise, C. G. R., Timko, M. L., & Baumgaertner, A. (1994). Working memory and inference revision in brain-damaged and normally aging adults. *Journal of Speech and Hearing, 37,* 896–912.

28. Best, W. (1995). A reverse length effect in dysphasic naming: When elephant is easier than ant. *Cortex, 31,* 637–652.

29. Christiansen, J. A. (1995). Cohesence violations and propositional usage in the narratives of fluent aphasics. *Brain and Language, 51,* 291–317.

30. D'Esposito, M., & Alexander, M. P. (1995). Subcortical aphasia: Distinct profiles following left putaminal hemorrhage. *Neurology, 45,* 38–41.

31. D'Esposito, M., Verfaellie, M., Alexander, M. P., & Katz, D. I. (1995). Amnesia following traumatic bilateral fornix transection. *Neurology, 45,* 1546–1550.

32. Foundas, A. L., Macauley, B. L., Raymer, A. M., Maher, L. M., Heilman, K. M., & Gonzalez, Rothi, L. J. (1995). Gesture laterality in aphasic and apraxic stroke patients. *Brain and Cognition, 29,* 204–213.

33. Freed, D. B., Marshall, R. C., & Nippold, M. A. (1995). Comparison of personalized cueing and provided cueing on the facilitation of verbal labeling by aphasic subjects. *Journal of Speech and Hearing Research, 38,* 1081–1090.

34. Gershberg, F. B., & Shimamura, A. P. (1995). Impaired use of organizational strategies in free recall following frontal lobe damage. *Neuropsychologia, 33,* 1305–1333.

35. Gold, M., Adair, J. C., Jacobs, D. H., & Heilman, K. M. (1995). Right-left confusion in Gerstmann's Syndrome: A model of body centered spatial orientation. *Cortex, 31,* 267-283.

36. Goren, A. R., Fine, J., Manaim, H., & Apter, A. (1995). Verbal and nonverbal expressions of central deficits in schizophrenia. *The Journal of Nervous and Mental Disease, 183,* 715–719.

37. Greehouse, J. B., Bromberg, J. A., & Fromm, D. (1995). An introduction to logistic regression with an application to the analysis of language recovery following a stroke. *Journal of Communication Disorders, 28,* 229–246.

38. Gupta, S. R., Mlcoch, A. G., Scolaro, C., & Moritz, T. (1995). Bromocriptine treatment of nonfluent aphasia. *Neurology, 45,* 2170–2173.

39. Maher, L. M., Chatterjeee, A., Rothi, L. J. G., & Heilman, K. M. (1995). A grammatic sentence production: The use of a temporal-spatial stragegy. *Brain and Language, 49,* 105–124.

40. Migliorelli, R., Petracca, G., Tesón, A., Sabe, L., Leiguarda, R., & Starkstein, S. E. (1995). Neuropsychiatric and neuropsychological correlates of delusions in Alzheimer's Disease. *Psychological Medicine, 25,* 505–513.

41. Migliorelli, R., Teson, A., Sabe, L., Petracchi, M., Leiguarda, R., & Starkstein, S. E. (1995). Prevalence and correlates of dysthymia and major depression among patients with Alzheimer's Disease. *American Journal of Psychiatry, 152,* 37-44.

42. Neils, J., Roeltgen, D. P., & Greer, A. (1995). Spelling and attention in early Alzheimer's disease: Evidence for impairment of the graphemic buffer. *Brain and Language, 49,* 241–262.

43. Nicholas, L. E., & Brookshire, R. H. (1995). Presence, completeness, and accuracy of main concepts in the connected speech of non-brain-damaged adults and adults with aphasia. *Journal of Speech and Hearing Research, 38,* 145–156.

44. Seki, K., Yajima, M., & Sugishita, M. (1995). The efficacy of kinesthetic reading treatment for pure alexia. *Neuropsychologia, 33,* 595–609.

45. Shuren, J. E., & Heilman, K. M. (1995). Reading comprehension in a transcortical motor aphasic. *Neurology, 45,* 1418.

46. Shuren, J. E., Hammond, C. S., Maher, L. M., Rothi, L. J. G., & Heilman, K. M. (1995). Attention and anosognosia: The case of a jargon aphasic patient with unawareness of language deficit. *Neurology, 45,* 376–378.

47. Takahashi, N., Kawamura, M., Hirayama, K., Shiota, J., & Isono, O. (1995). Prosopagnosia: A clinical and anatomical study of four patients. *Cortex, 31,* 317-329.

48. Thompson, C. K., & Shapiro, L. P. (1995). Training sentence production in a grammatism: Implications for normal and disordered language. *Brain and Language, 50,* 201–224.

49. Warren, R. M., & Gardner, D. A. (1995). Aphasics can distinguish permuted orders of phonemes—but only if presented rapidly. *Journal of Speech and Hearing, 38,* 473–476.

50. York, C. D., & Cermak, S. A. (1995). Visual perception and praxis in adults after stroke. *The American Journal of Occupational Therapy, 49,* 543–550.

51. Alexander, M. P., & Annett, M. (1996). Crossed aphasia and related anomalies of cerebral organization: Case reports and a genetic hypothesis. *Brain and Language, 55,* 213–239.

52. Belander, S. A., Duffy, R. J., & Coelho, C. A. (1996). The assessment of limb apraxia: An investigation of task effects and their cause. *Brain and Cognition, 32,* 384–404.

53. Hanlon, R. E., & Edmondson, J. A. (1996). Disconnected phonology: A linguistic analysis of phonemic jargon aphasia. *Brain and Language, 55,* 199–212.

54. Ingles, J. L., Mate-Kole, C. C., & Connolly, J. F. (1996). Evidence for multiple routes of speech production in a case of fluent aphasia. *Cortex, 32,* 199–219.

55. Kohn, S. E., Smith, K. L., & Alexander, M. P. (1996). Differential recovery from impairment to the phonological lexicon. *Brain and Language, 52,* 129–149.

56. Shuren, J. E., Greenwald, M., & Heilman, K. M. (1996). Spontaneous grammatical corrections in an anomic aphasic. *Neurology, 47,* 845–846.

57. Shuren, J. E., Maher, L. M. & Heilman, K. M. (1996). The role of visual imagery in spelling. *Brain and Language, 52,* 365–372.

58. Thompson, C. K., Shapire, L. P., Tait, M. E., Jacobs, B. J., & Schneider, S. L. (1996). Training *Wh*-question production in agrammatic aphasia: Analysis of argument and adjunct movement. *Brain and Language, 52,* 175–228.

59. Alexander, M. P. (1997). Specific semantic memory loss after hypoxic-ischemic injury. *Neurology, 48,* 165–172.

60. Berndt, R. S., Mitchum, C. C., & Wayland, S. (1997). Patterns of sentence comprehension in aphasia: A consideration of three hypotheses. *Brain and Language, 60,* 197–221.

61. Chertkow, H., Bub, D., Deaudon, C., & Whitehead, V. (1997). On the status of object concepts in aphasia. *Brain and Language, 58,* 203–232.

62. Crosson, B., Moberg, P. J., Boone, J. R., Rothi, L. J. G., & Raymer, A. (1997). Category-specific naming deficit for medical terms after dominant thalamic/capsular hemorrhage. *Brain and Language, 60,* 407–442.

63. Ehrlich, J. S., Obler, L. K., & Clark, L. (1997). Ideational and semantic contributions to narrative production in adults with dementia of the Alzheimer's type. *Journal of Communication Disorders, 30,* 79–99.

64. Gold, M., Nadeau, S. E., Jacobs, D. H., Adair, J. C., Rothi, L. J. G., & Heilman, K. M. (1997). Adynamic aphasia: A transcortical motor aphasia with defective semantic strategy formation. *Brain and Language, 57,* 374–393.

65. Heilman, K. M., Maher, L. M., Greenwald, M. L., & Rothi, L. J. G. (1997). Conceptual apraxia from lateralized lesions. *Neurology, 49,* 457–464.

66. Katz, R. C., & Wertz, R. T. (1997). The efficacy of computer-provided reading treatment for chronic aphasic adults. *Journal of Speech, Language, and Hearing Research, 40,* 493–507.

67. Marcotte, T. D., van Gorp, W., Hinkin, C. H., & Osato, S. (1997). Concurrent validity of the Neurobehavioral Cognitive Status Exam subtests. *Journal of Clinical and Experimental Neuropsychology, 19,* 386–395.

68. Mori, E., Hirono, N., Yamashita, H., Imamura, T., Ikejiri, Y., Ikeda, M., Kitagaki, H., Shimomura, T., & Yoneda, Y. (1997). Premorbid brain size as a determinant of reserve capacity against intellectual decline in Alzheimer's Disease. *American Journal of Psychiatry, 154,* 18–24.

69. Pashek, G. V. (1997). A case study of gesturally cued naming in aphasia: Dominant versus nondominant hand training. *Journal of Communication Disorders, 30,* 349–366.

70. Raymer, A. M., Maher, L. M., Foundas, A. L., Heilman, K. M., & Rothi, L. J. G. (1997). The significance of body part as tool errors in limb apraxia. *Brain and Cognition, 34,* 287–292.

71. Raymer, A. M., Moberg, P., Crosson, B., Nadeau, S., & Rothi, L. J. G. (1997). Lexical-semantic deficits in two patients with dominant thalamic infarction. *Neuropsychologia, 35,* 211–219.

72. Thompson, C. K., Shapiro, L. P., Ballard, K. J., Jacobs, B. J., Schneider, S. S., & Tait, M. E. (1997). Training and generalized production of wh- and NP-movement structures in a grammatic aphasia. *Journal of Speech, Language, and Hearing Research, 40,* 228–244.

73. Imamura, T., Takatsuki, Y., Fujimori, M., Hirono, N., Ikejiri, Y., Shimomura, T., Hashimoto, M., Yamashita, H., & Mori, E. (1998). Age at onset and language disturbances in Alzheimer's disease. *Neuropsychologia, 36,* 945–949.

74. Shillcock, R., & Hackett, K. (1998). Intact higher-level constraints on the pronunciation of new written words by nonfluent dysphasics. *Brain and Language, 63,* 143–156.

[2874]

The Western Personality Inventory.

Purpose: Identifies alcoholics and potential alcoholics and measures extent of alcohol addiction.

Population: Adults.

Publication Dates: 1963-1988.

Acronym: WPI.

Scores, 14: Anxiety, Depressive Fluctuations, Emotional Sensitivity, Resentfulness, Incompleteness, Aloneness, Interpersonal Relations, Total, Regularity of Drinking, Preference for Drinking over Other Activities, Lack of Controlled Drinking, Rationalization of Drinking, Excessive Emotionality, Total.

Administration: Individual or group.

Manual: No manual; use manuals for The Manson Evaluation and The Alcadd Test.

Price Data, 1999: $92 per complete kit including 5 AutoScore test forms, 2 prepaid mail-in answer sheets for computer scoring and interpretation, Manson Evaluation Manual, and Alcadd Manual; $29.50 per Manson Evaluation Manual or Alcadd Manual; $9.50 per mail-in answer sheet; $135 per IBM microcomputer disk (25 uses).

Time: Administration time not reported.

Comments: Combination of The Manson Evaluation (1577) and The Alcadd Test (132).

Author: Morse P. Manson.

Publisher: Western Psychological Services.

[2875]

Wharton Attitude Survey.

Purpose: A peer group evaluative tool to identify problems in the classroom.
Population: Grades 7-12.
Publication Date: 1978.
Scores: Ratings in 8 areas: Physical Surroundings, Materials, Subject, Teacher, Self, Other Students, Class Disrupters, Other Comments.
Administration: Group.
Price Data: Available from publisher.
Time: (10-15) minutes.
Author: Kenneth Wharton, Jr.
Publisher: Paul Amidon & Associates.

[2876]

What Do You Say?

Purpose: Designed as a self-assessment tool to identify communication style and relate it to two basic types of human interactions: parent-child (McGregor's Theory X) and adult-adult (Theory Y).
Population: Employees.
Publication Dates: 1986-1991.
Scores, 4: Empathic, Critical, Searching, Advising.
Administration: Group or individual.
Price Data, 1990: $80 per complete kit including 20 inventories, 20 answer sheets, and 20 interpretation booklets.
Time: [20] minutes administration; [10] minutes scoring; [30-60] minutes interpretation.
Comments: Self-administered, self-scored.
Authors: Training House, Inc.
Publisher: Training House, Inc.
Cross References: For reviews by William L. Deaton and Gerald L. Stone, see 12:413.

[2877]

Whisler Strategy Test.

Purpose: "To discover how effective the individual is in drawing on his abilities and knowledges to demonstrate his general competence."
Population: Business and industry.
Publication Dates: 1955-1961.
Scores, 6: 4 direct scores (Number Circled-Boldness, Number Attempted-Speed, Number Right-Accuracy, Net Strategy), and 2 derived scores (Caution, Hypercaution).
Administration: Group.
Price Data, 1985: $5 per 25 tests; $5 per specimen set including manual ('59, 3 pages).
Time: (25) minutes.
Comments: Measures "intelligence action" or strategic ability.
Author: Laurence Whisler.
Publisher: Psychometric Affiliates.
Cross References: See T2:2292 (1 reference); for reviews by Jean Maier Palormo and Paul F. Ross, see 6:1110 (1 reference).

TEST REFERENCE

1. Burch, J. W. (1995). Typicality range deficit in schizophrenics' recognition of emotion in faces. *Journal of Clinical Psychology, 51,* 140-152.

[2878]

Whitaker Index of Schizophrenic Thinking.

Purpose: Measures degrees of schizophrenic thinking.
Population: Mental patients.
Publication Dates: 1973-1980.
Acronym: WIST.
Scores, 4: Similarities, Word Pairs, New Inventions, Total.
Administration: Individual.
Forms, 2: A, B.
Price Data, 1999: $75 per complete kit; $16.50 or less per 25 tests (specify Form A or B); $10.50 per scoring key; $42.50 per manual ('80, 92 pages).
Time: (20) minutes.
Comments: Manual title is Objective Measurement of Schizophrenic Thinking: A Practical and Theoretical Guide to the Whitaker Index of Schizophrenic Thinking.
Author: Leighton C. Whitaker.
Publisher: Western Psychological Services.
Cross References: See T4:2955 (2 references); for a review by Stephen G. Flanagan, see 11:469 (12 references); see also T3:2620 (20 references); for reviews by Bertram D. Cohen and Robert W. Payne, see 8:710 (4 references).

TEST REFERENCE

1. Bolado, A. L. O., & Whitaker, L. C. (1990). Standardization of the Whitaker Index of Schizophrenic Thinking (WIST) in a Mexican population: A multivariate study. *Journal of Clinical Psychology, 46,* 140–147.

[2879]

Wide Range Achievement Test 3.

Purpose: To measure the skills needed to learn reading, spelling, and arithmetic.
Population: Ages 5-75.
Publication Dates: 1940-1993.
Acronym: WRAT3.
Scores: 3 subtests: Reading, Spelling, Arithmetic.
Administration: Individual in part.
Forms: 2 equivalent forms: Blue, Tan.
Price Data, 1999: $125 per starter set including 25 Blue test forms, 25 Tan test forms, 25 profile/analysis forms, set of 2 plastic cards for Reading/Spelling, and manual ('93, 188 pages) in attache case; $27 per 25 test forms (specify Blue or Tan); $20 per 25 profile/analysis forms; $14 per set of 2 plastic cards for Reading/Spelling; $40 per manual; $32 per attache case.

Time: (15-30) minutes.
Author: Gary S. Wilkinson.
Publisher: Wide Range, Inc.
Cross References: For reviews by Linda Mabry and Annie W. Ward, see 12:414 (111 references); see also T4:2956 (121 references); for reviews by Elaine Clark and Patti L. Harrison, see 10:389 (161 references); for reviews by Paula Matuszek of an earlier edition and Philip A. Saigh of an earlier edition, see 9:1364 (103 references); see also T3:2621 (249 references), 8:37 (117 references), and T2:50 (35 references); for reviews by Jack C. Merwin and Robert L. Thorndike of an earlier edition, see 7:36 (49 references); see also 6:27 (15 references); for reviews by Paul Douglas Courtney, Verner M. Sims, and Louis P. Thorpe of the 1946 edition, see 3:21.

TEST REFERENCES

1. Siegel, L. S. (1984). A longitudinal study of a hyperlexic child: Hyperlexia as a language disorder. *Neuropsychologia, 22,* 577–585.

2. Wolff, P. H., Cohen, C., & Drake, C. (1984). Impaired motor timing control in specific reading retardation. *Neuropsychologia, 22,* 587–600.

3. Catts, H. W., & Kamhi, A. G. (1986). The linguistic basis of reading disorders: Implications for the speech-language pathologist. *Language, Speech, and Hearing Services in Schools, 17,* 329–341.

4. Blanton, P. D., & Gouvier, W. D. (1987). Sex differences in visual information processing following right cerebrovascular accidents. *Neuropsychologia, 25,* 713–717.

5. Frick, R. W. (1987). A dissociation of conscious visual imagery and visual short-term memory. *Neuropsychologia, 25,* 707–712.

6. Grigsby, J. P., Kemper, M. B., & Hagerman, R. J. (1987). Developmental Gerstmann Syndrome without aphasia in Fragile X Syndrome. *Neuropsychologia, 25,* 881–891.

7. Vandergoot, D. (1987). Review of placement research literature: Implications for research and practice. *Rehabilitation Counseling Bulletin, 30,* 243–272.

8. Juel, C. (1988). Learning to read and write: A longitudinal study of 54 children from first through fourth grades. *Journal of Educational Psychology, 80,* 437–447.

9. Levin, M. L. (1988). Sequelae to marital disruption in children. *Journal of Divorce, 12*(2/3), 25–80.

10. Whitworth, R. H. (1988). Comparison of Anglo and Mexican American male high school students classified as learning disabled. *Hispanic Journal of Behavioral Sciences, 10,* 127–137.

11. de Bettencourt, L. U., Zigmond, N., & Thornton, H. (1989). Follow-up of postsecondary-age rural learning disabled graduates and dropouts. *Exceptional Children, 56,* 40–49.

12. Keyes, K. L. (1989). The counselor's role in helping students with limited English proficiency. *The School Counselor, 37,* 144–148.

13. Koenig, L. A., & Biel, C. D. (1989). A delivery system of comprehensive language services in a school district. *Language, Speech, and Hearing Services in Schools, 20,* 338–365.

14. Levinson, H. N. (1989). Abnormal optokinetic and perceptual span parameters in cerebellar-vestibular dysfunction and learning disabilities or dyslexia. *Perceptual and Motor Skills, 68,* 35–54.

15. Loring, D. W., Meador, K. J., & Lee, G. P. (1989). Differential-handed response to verbal and visual spatial stimuli: Evidence of specialized hemispheric processing following callosotomy. *Neuropsychologia, 27,* 811–827.

16. McCue, M. (1989). The role of assessment in the vocational rehabilitation of adults with specific learning disabilities. *Rehabilitation Counseling Bulletin, 33,* 18–37.

17. Nelson, R., & Lignugaris/Kraft, B. (1989). Postsecondary education for students with learning disabilities. *Exceptional Children, 56,* 246–265.

18. Newman, R. S., & Stevenson, H. W. (1989). Childrens' achievement and causal attributions in mathematics and reading. *Journal of Experimental Education, 58,* 197–212.

19. Roberts, T. A., & Kraft, R. H. (1989). Developmental differences in the relationship between reading comprehension and hemispheric alpha patterns: An EEG study. *Journal of Educational Psychology, 81,* 322–328.

20. Wade, S. E., & Trathen, W. (1989). Effect of self-selected study methods on learning. *Journal of Educational Psychology, 81,* 40–47.

21. Weinberg, W. A., McLean, A., Snider, R. L., Rintelmann, J. W., & Brumback, R. A. (1989). Comparison of reading and listening-reading techniques for administration of SAT reading comprehension subtest: Justification for the bypass approach. *Perceptual and Motor Skills, 68,* 1015–1018.

22. Zacker, J., Pepper, B., & Kirshner, M. C. (1989). Neuropsychological characteristics of young adult chronic psychiatric patients: Preliminary observations. *Perceptual and Motor Skills, 68,* 391–399.

23. Durrant, J. E., Voelker, S., & Cunningham, C. E. (1990). Academic, social, and general self-concepts of behavioral subgroups of learning disabled children. *Journal of Educational Psychology, 82,* 657–663.

24. Kochanek, T. T., Kabacoff, R. I., & Lipsitt, L. P. (1990). Early identification of developmentally disabled and at-risk preschool children. *Exceptional Children, 56,* 528–538.

25. Lovet, M. W., Warren-Chaplin, P. M., Ransby, M. J., & Borden, S. L. (1990). Training the word recognition skills of reading disabled children: Treatment and transfer effects. *Journal of Educational Psychology, 82,* 769–780.

26. Mann, V. A., Sasanuma, S., Sakuma, N., & Masaki, S. (1990). Sex differences in cognitive abilities: A cross-cultural perspective. *Neuropsychologia, 28,* 1063–1077.

27. O'Donnell, J. P., Romero, J. J., & Leicht, D. J. (1990). A comparison of language deficits in learning-disabled, head-injured, and nondisabled young adults: Results from an abbreviated aphasia screening test. *Journal of Clinical Psychology, 46,* 310–315.

28. Sabornie, E. J., Marshall, K. J., & Ellis, E. S. (1990). Restructuring of mainstream sociometry with learning disabled and nonhandicapped students. *Exceptional Children, 56,* 314–323.

29. Sapp, M. (1990). Psychoeducational correlates of junior high at-risk students. *The High School Journal, 73,* 232–234.

30. Tammany, J. M., Evans, R. G., & Barnett, R. W. (1990). Personality and intellectual characteristics of adult male felons as a function of offence category. *Journal of Clinical Psychology, 46,* 906–911.

31. Ackerman, P. T., Dykman, R. A., Holloway, C., Paal, N. P., & Gocio, M. Y. (1991). A trial of piracetam in two subgroups of students with dyslexia enrolled in summer tutoring. *Journal of Learning Disabilities, 24,* 542–549.

32. Brown, R. T., Madan-Swain, A., & Baldwin, K. (1991). Gender differences in a clinic-referred sample of attention-deficit-disordered children. *Child Psychiatry and Human Development, 22,* 111–128.

33. Friedrich, W. N., Lovejoy, M. C., Shaffer, J., Shurtleff, D. B., & Beilke, R. L. (1991). Cognitive abilities and achievement status of children with myelomeningocele: A contemporary sample. *Journal of Pediatric Psychology, 16,* 423–428.

34. Ganschow, L., Sparks, R. L., Javorsky, J., Pohlman, J., & Bishop-Marbury, A. (1991). Identifying native language difficulties among foreign language learners in college: A "foreign" language learning disability? *Journal of Learning Disabilities, 24,* 530–541.

35. Ollo, C., Johnson, R., & Grafman, J. (1991). Signs of cognitive change in HIV disease: An event-related brain potential study. *Neurology, 41,* 209–215.

36. Rescoria, L., Parker, R., & Stolley, P. (1991). Ability, achievement, and adjustment in homeless children. *American Journal of Orthopsychiatry, 61,* 210–220.

37. Salyer, K. M., Holmstrom, R. W., & Noshpitz, J. D. (1991). Learning disabilities as a childhood manifestation of severe psychopathology. *American Journal of Orthopsychiatry, 61,* 230–240.

38. Williams, K. S., Ochs, J., Williams, J. M., & Mulhern, R. K. (1991). Parental report of everyday cognitive abilities among children treated for acute lymphoblastic leukemia. *Journal of Pediatric Psychology, 16,* 13–26.

39. Bigler, E. D. (1992). The neurobiology and neuropsychology of adult learning disorders. *Journal of Learning Disabilities, 25,* 488–506.

40. Burd, L., Kauffman, D. W., & Kerbeshian, J. (1992). Tourette syndrome and learning disabilities. *Journal of Learning Disabilities, 25,* 598–604.

41. Cornwall, A. (1992). The relationship of phonological awareness, rapid naming, and verbal memory to severe reading and spelling disability. *Journal of Learning Disabilities, 25,* 532–538.

42. Dykman, R. A., & Ackerman, P. T. (1992). Diagnosing dyslexia: IQ regression plus cut-points. *Journal of Learning Disabilities, 25,* 574–576.

43. Fletcher, J. M., Francis, D. J., Rourke, B. P., Shaywitz, S. E., & Shaywitz, B. A. (1992). The validity of discrepancy-based definitions of reading disabilities. *Journal of Learning Disabilities, 25,* 555–561.

44. Karlinsky, H., Vanla, G., Haines, J. L., Ridgley, J., Bergeron, C., Mortilla, M., Tupler, R. G., Percy, M. E., Robitaille, Y., Noldy, N. E., Yip, T. C. K., Tanzi, R. E., Gusella, J. F., Becker, R., Berg, J. M., McLachlan, D. R. C., & St. George-Hyslop, P. H. (1992). Molecular and prospective phenotypic characterization of a pedigree with familial Alzheimer's disease and a missensemutuation in codon 717 of the B-amyloid precursor protein gene. *Neurology, 42,* 1445–1453.

45. Kline, R. B., Snyder, J., Guilmette, S., & Castellanos, M. (1992). Relative usefulness of elevation, variability, and shape information from WISC-R, K-ABC, and Fourth Edition Stanford-Binet profiles in predicting agreement. *Psychological Assessment, 4,* 426–432.

46. Lewis, B. A., & Thompson, L. A. (1992). A study of developmental speech and language disorders in twins. *Journal of Speech and Hearing Research, 35,* 1086–1094.

47. Light, J., & Lindsay, P. (1992). Message-encoding techniques for augmentative communication systems: The recall performances of adults with severe speech impairments. *Journal of Speech and Hearing Research, 35,* 853–864.

48. Siegel, L. S. (1992). An evaluation of the discrepancy definition of dyslexia. *Journal of Learning Disabilities, 25,* 618–629.

49. Sinclair, E., & Alexson, J. (1992). Special education placements of language disordered children in a psychiatric population. *Child Psychiatry and Human Development, 23,* 131–143.

50. Swanson, H. L., & Ramalgia, J. M. (1992). The relationship between phonological codes on memory and spelling tasks for students with and without learning disabilities. *Journal of Learning Disabilities, 25,* 396–407.

51. Taylor, H. G., & Schatschneider, C. (1992). Academic achievement following childhood brain disease: Implications for the concept of learning disabilities. *Journal of Learning Disabilities, 25,* 630–638.

52. Vogel, S. A., & Adelman, P. B. (1992). The success of college students with learning disabilities: Factors related to educational attainment. *Journal of Learning Disabilities, 25,* 430–441.
53. Williams, D. L., Gridley, B. E., & Fitzhugh-Bell, K. (1992). Cluster analysis of children and adolescents with brain damage and learning disabilities using neuropsychological, psychoeducational, and sociobehavioral variables. *Journal of Learning Disabilities, 25,* 290–299.
54. Ackerman, P. T., & Dykman, R. A. (1993). Phonological processes, confrontational naming, and immediate memory in dsylexia. *Journal of Learning Disabilities, 26,* 597–609.
55. Brown, R. T., Armstrong, F. D., & Eckman, J. R. (1993). Neurocognitive aspects of pediatric sickle cell disease. *Journal of Learning Disabilities, 26,* 33–45.
56. Goldberg, T. E., Hyde, T. M., Kleinman, J. E., & Weinberger, D. R. (1993). Course of schizophrenia: Neuropsychological evidence for a static encephalopathy. *Schizophrenia Bulletin, 19,* 797–804.
57. Humphries, T., & Bone, J. (1993). Use of IQ criteria for evaluating the uniqueness of the learning disability profile. *Journal of Learning Disabilities, 26,* 348–351.
58. Katz, L., Goldstein, G., Rudisin, S., & Bailey, D. (1993). A neuropsychological approach to the bannatyne recategorization of the Wechsler Intelligence Scales in adults with learning disabilities. *Journal of Learning Disabilities, 26,* 65–72.
59. Kline, R. B., Snyder, J., Guilmette, S., & Castellanos, M. (1993). External validity of the profile variability index for the K-ABC, Stanford-Binet, and WISC-R: Another cul-de-sac. *Journal of Learning Disabilities, 26,* 557–567.
60. Krupp, L. B., Masur, D. M., & Kaufman, L. D. (1993). Neurocognitive dysfunction in the eosinophilia-myalgia syndrome. *Neurology, 43,* 931–936.
61. Little, S. S. (1993). Nonverbal learning disabilities and socioemotional functioning: A review of recent literature. *Journal of Learning Disabilities, 26,* 653–665.
62. Naglieri, J. A., & Reardon, S. M. (1993). Traditional IQ is irrelevant to learning disabilities—intelligence is not. *Journal of Learning Disabilities, 26,* 127–133.
63. Newman, S., Fields, H., & Wright, S. (1993). A developmental study of specific spelling disability. *British Journal of Educational Psychology, 63,* 287–296.
64. Risser, M. G., & Bowers, T. G. (1993). Cognitive and neuropsychological characteristics of attention deficit hyperactivity disorder children receiving stimulant medications. *Perceptual and Motor Skills, 77,* 1023–1031.
65. Rourke, B. P. (1993). Arithmetic disabilities, specific and otherwise: A neuropsychological perspective. *Journal of Learning Disabilities, 26,* 214–226.
66. Rovert, J. F. (1993). The psychoeducational characteristics of children with Turner syndrome. *Journal of Learning Disabilities, 26,* 333–341.
67. Rovert, J. F., Ehrlich, R. M., Czuchta, D., & Akler, M. (1993). Psychoeducational characteristics of children and adolescents with insulin-dependent diabetes mellitus. *Journal of Learning Disabilities, 26,* 7–22.
68. Wood, D. A., Rosenberg, M. S., & Carran, D. T. (1993). The effects of tape-recorded self-instruction cues on the mathematics performance of students with learning disabilities. *Journal of Learning Disabilities, 26,* 250–258.
69. Zimet, S. G., & Farley, G. K. (1993). Academic achievement of children with emotional disorders treated in a day hospital program: An outcome study. *Child Psychiatry and Human Development, 23,* 183–202.
70. Ackerman, P. T., Dykman, R. A., Oglesby, D. M., & Newton, J. E. O. (1994). EEG power spectra of children with dyslexia, slow learners, and normally reading children with ADD during verbal processing. *Journal of Learning Disabilities, 27,* 619–630.
71. Beers, S. R., Goldstein, G., & Katz, L. J. (1994). Neuropsychological differences between college students with learning disabilities and those with mild head injury. *Journal of Learning Disabilities, 27,* 315–324.
72. Brier, N. (1994). Targeted treatment for adjudicated youth with learning disabilities: Effects on recidivism. *Journal of Learning Disabilities, 27,* 215–222.
73. Butler, R., & Marinor-Glassman, D. (1994). The effects of educational placement and grade level on the self-perceptions of low achievers and students with learning disabilities. *Journal of Learning Disabilities, 27,* 325–334.
74. Corrigan, P. W., Wallace, C. J., Schade, M. L., & Green, M. F. (1994). Learning medication self-management skills in schizophrenia: Relationships with cognitive deficits and psychiatric symptoms. *Behavior Therapy, 25,* 5–15.
75. D'Annunzio, A. (1994). College students as tutors for adults in a campus-based literacy program. *Journal of Reading, 37,* 472–479.
76. Durlak, C. M., Rose, E., & Bursuck, W. D. (1994). Preparing high school students with learning disabilities for the transition to post-secondary education: Teaching the skills of self-determination. *Journal of Learning Disabilities, 27,* 51–59.
77. Fletcher, J. & Martinez, G. (1994). An eye-movement analysis of the effects of scotopic sensitivity correction on parsing and comprehension. *Journal of Learning Disabilities, 27,* 67–70.
78. Grantham-McGregor, S., Powell, C., Walker, S., Chang, S., & Fletcher, P. (1994). The long-term follow-up of severely malnourished children who participated in an intervention program. *Child Development, 65,* 428–439.
79. Jason, L. A., Reyes, O., Danner, K. E., & De La Torre, G. (1994). Academic achievement as a buffer to peer rejection for transfer children. *Journal of Instructional Psychology, 21,* 352–352.
80. Korkman, M., & Pesonen, A. (1994). A comparison of neuropsychological test profiles of children with attention deficit-hyperactivity disorder and/or learning disorder. *Journal of Learning Disabilities, 27,* 383–392.
81. Kremen, W. S., Seidman, L. J., Pepple, J. R., Lyons, M. J., Tsuang, M. T., & Faraone, S. V. (1994). Neuropsychological risk indicators for schizophrenia: A review of family studies. *Schizophrenia Bulletin, 20,* 103–119.
82. Lapan, R., & Reynolds, R. E. (1994). The selective attention strategy as a time-dependent phenomenon. *Contemporary Educational Psychology, 19,* 379–398.
83. Lewandowski, L., & Arcangelo, K. C. (1994). The social adjustment and self-concept of adults with learning disabilities. *Journal of Learning Disabilities, 27,* 598–605.
84. Loveland, K. A., Stehbens, J., Constant, C., Bordeaux, J. D., Sirois, P., Bell, T. S., & Hill, S. (1994). Hemophilia growth and development study: Baseline neurodevelopmental findings. *Journal of Pediatric Psychology, 19,* 223–239.
85. Lovett, M. W., Barrow, R. W., Forbes, J. E., Cuksts, B., & Steinbach, K. A. (1994). Computer speech-based training of literacy skills in neurologically impaired children: A controlled evaluation. *Brain and Language, 47,* 117–154.
86. Meyer, L. A., Stahl, S. A., & Wardrop, J. L. (1994). Effects of reading storybooks aloud to children. *The Journal of Educational Research, 88,* 69–85.
87. Murphy, D. G. M., Allen, G., Haxby, J. V., Largay, K. A., Daly, E., White, B. J., Powell, L. M., & Schapiro, M. B. (1994). The effects of sex steroids and the X chromosome on female brain function: A study of the neuropsychology of adult Turner syndrome. *Neuropsychologia, 32,* 1309–1323.
88. Peterson, R. C., Smith, G. E., Ivnik, R. J. Kokmen, E., & Tangalos, E. G. (1994). Memory function in very early Alzheimer's disease. *Neurology, 44,* 867–872.
89. Prior, M., Kinsella, G., Sawyer, M., Bryan, D., & Anderson, V. (1994). Cognitive and psychosocial outcome after head injury in children. *Australian Psychologist, 29,* 116–123.
90. Reid, R., Maag, J., Vasa, S. F., & Wright, G. (1994). Who are the children with attention deficit-hyperactivity disorder? A school-based survey. *The Journal of Special Education, 28,* 117–137.
91. Shafrir, V., & Siegel, L. S. (1994). Preference for visual scanning strategies versus phonological rehearsal in university students with reading disabilities. *Journal of Learning Disabilities, 27,* 583–588.
92. Shafrir, V., & Siegel, L. S. (1994). Subtypes of learning disabilities in adolescents and adults. *Journal of Learning Disabilities, 27,* 123—134.
93. Stanford, L. D., & Hynd, G. W. (1994). Congruence of behavioral symptomatology in children with ADD/H, ADD/WO, and learning disabilities. *Journal of Learning Disabilities, 27,* 243–253.
94. Swanson, H. L. (1994). Short-term memory and working memory: Do both contribute to our understanding of academic achievement in children and adults with learning disabilities? *Journal of Learning Disabilities, 27,* 34–50.
95. Walker, D., Greenwood, C., Hart, B., & Carter, J. (1994). Prediction of school outcomes based on early language production and socioeconomic factors. *Child Development, 65,* 606–621.
96. Yates, B. T., Hecht-Lewis, R., Fritsch, R. C., & Goodrich, W. (1994). Locus of control in severely disturbed adolescents: loci for peers, parents, achievement, relationships, and problems. *Journal of Youth and Adolescence, 23,* 289–314.
97. Ackerman, P. T., Dykman, R. A., Oglesby, D. M., & Newton, J. E. O. (1995). EEG power spectra of dysphonetic and nondysphonetic poor readers. *Brain and Language, 49,* 140–152.
98. Apthorp, H. S. (1995). Phonetic coding and reading in college students with and without learning disabilities. *Journal of Learning Disabilities, 28,* 342–352.
99. August, G. J., Realmuto, G. M., Crosby, R. D., & MacDonald, A. W. (1995). Community-based multiple-gate screening of children at risk for conduct disorder. *Journal of Abnormal Child Psychology, 23,* 521–544.
100. Biederman, J., Milberger, S., Faraone, S. V., Kiely, K., Guite, J., Mick, E., Ablon, S., Warburton, R., & Reed, E. (1995). Family-environment risk factors for attention-deficit hyperactivity disorder: A test of Rotter's indicators of adversity. *Archives of General Psychiatry, 52,* 464–470.
101. Biederman, J., Milberger, S., Faraone, S. V., Lapey, K. A., Reed, E. D., & Seidman, L. J. (1995). No confirmation of Geschwind's hypothesis of associations between reading disability, immune disorders, and motor preference in ADHD. *Journal of Abnormal Child Psychology, 23,* 545–552.
102. Biederman, J., Santangelo, S. L., Faraone, S. V., Kiely, K., Guite, J., Mick, E., Reed, E. D., Kraus, I., Jellinek, M., & Perrin, J. (1995). Clinical correlates of enuresis in ADHD and non-ADHD children. *Journal of Child Psychology and Psychiatry and Allied Disciplines, 36,* 865–877.
103. Branch, W. B., Cohen, M. J., & Hynd, G. W. (1995). Academic achievement and attention-deficit/hyperactivity disorder in children with left- or right-hemisphere dysfunction. *Journal of Learning Disabilities, 28,* 35–43, 64.
104. Brigham, F. J., Scruggs, T. E., & Mastropieri, M. A. (1995). Elaborative maps for enhanced learning of historical information: Uniting spatial, verbal, and imaginal information. *The Journal of Special Education, 28,* 440–460.
105. Britton, J. W., Vitti, R. J., Ahlskog, J. E., Robinson, R. G., Kremor, B., & Hayden, M. R. (1995). Hereditary late-onset chorea without significant dementia: Genetic evidence for substantial phenotypic variation in Huntington's disease. *Neurology, 45,* 443–447.
106. Carlson-Greene, B., Morris, R. D., & Krawiecki, N. (1995). Family and illness predictors of outcome in pediatric brain tumors. *Journal of Pediatric Psychology, 20,* 769–784.
107. Chamrad, D. L., Robinson, N. M., & Junos, P. M. (1995). Consequences of having a gifted sibling: Myths and realities. *Gifted Child Quarterly, 39,* 135–145.
108. Clarke-Klein, S., & Hodson, B. W. (1995). A phonologically based analysis of misspellings by third graders with disordered phonology histories. *Journal of Speech and Hearing Research, 38,* 839–849.
109. Claude, D., & Firestone, P. (1995). The development of ADHD boys: A 12-year follow-up. *Canadian Journal of Behavioural Science, 27,* 226–249.
110. DeVos, K. J., Wyllie, E., Geckler, C., Kotagal, P., & Comair, Y. (1995). Language dominance in patients with early childhood tumors near left hemisphere language areas. *Neurology, 45,* 349–356.
111. Duncan, R. D., Kennedy, W. A., & Patrick, C. J. (1995). Four-factor model of recidivism in male juvenile offenders. *Journal of Clinical Child Psychology, 24,* 250–257.
112. Flannery, K. A., & Liederman, J. (1995). Is there really a syndrome involving the co-occurrence of neurodevelopmental disorder, talent, non-right handedness and immune disorder among children? *Cortex, 31,* 503–515.

113. Fleischer, S. J., Avelar, C., Latorre, S. E., Ramirez, J., Cubillos, S., Christiansen, H., & Blaufarb, H. (1995). Evaluation of a Judo/community organization program to treat predelinquent Hispanic immigrant early adolescents. *Hispanic Journal of Behavior Sciences, 17,* 237–248.

114. Fuller, M., & McLeod, P. J. (1995). Judgments of control over a contingently responsive animation by students with and without learning disabilities. *Canadian Journal of Behavioural Science, 27,* 171–186.

115. Ganschow, L., & Sparks, R. (1995). Effects of direct instruction in Spanish phonology on the native-language skills and foreign-language aptitude of at-risk foreign-language learners. *Journal of Learning Disabilities, 28,* 107–120.

116. Gaskins, R. W., Gaskins, I. W., Anderson, R. C., & Schommer, M. (1995). The reciprocal relationship between research and development: An example involving a decoding strand for poor readers. *Journal of Reading Behavior, 27,* 337–377.

117. Grant, G. M., Salcedo, V., Hynan, L. S., Frisch, M. B., & Poster, K. (1995). Effectiveness of quality of life therapy for depression. *Psychological Reports, 76,* 1203–1208.

118. Holmes, C. S., O'Brien, B., & Greer, T. (1995). Cognitive functioning and academic achievement in children with insulin-dependent diabetes mellitus (IDDM). *School Psychology Quarterly, 10,* 329–345.

119. Janzen-Wilde, M. L., Duchan, J. F., & Higginbotham, D. J. (1995). Successful use of facilitated communication with an oral child. *Journal of Speech and Hearing Research, 38,* 658–676.

120. Joshi, R. M. (1995). Assessing reading and spelling skills. *School Psychology Review, 24,* 361–375.

121. Kardash, C. M., & Scholes, R. J. (1995). Effects of preexisting beliefs and repeated readings on belief change, comprehension, and recall of persuasive text. *Contemporary Educational Psychology, 20,* 201–221.

122. Kershner, J. R., & Graham, N. A. (1995). Attentional control over language lateralization in dyslexic children: Deficit or delay? *Neuropsychologia, 33,* 39–51.

123. Kinsella, G., Prior, M., Sawyer, M., Murtagh, D., Eisenmajer, R., Anderson, J., Bryan, D., & Klug, G. (1995). Neuropsychological deficit and academic performance in children and adolescents following traumatic brain injury. *Journal of Pediatric Psychology, 20,* 753 767.

124. Light, J. G., & DeFries, J. C. (1995). Comorbidity of reading and mathematics disabilities: Genetic and environmental etiologies. *Journal of Learning Disabilities, 28,* 96–106.

125. Lincoln, A. J., Courchesne, E., Harms, L., & Allen, M. (1995). Sensory modulation of auditory stimuli in childeren with autism and developmental language disorder: Event-related brain potential evidence. *Journal of Autism and Developmental Disorders, 25,* 521–539.

126. MacDonald, G. W., & Cornwall, A. (1995). The relationship between phonological awareness and reading and spelling achievement eleven years later. *Journal of Learning Disabilities, 28,* 523–527.

127. Martino, G., & Winner, E. (1995). Talents and disorders: Relationships among handedness, sex, and college major. *Brain and Cognition, 29,* 66–84.

128. Maydak, M., Stromer, R., MacKay, H. A., & Stoddard, L. T. (1995). Stimulus classes in matching to sample and sequence production: The emergence of numeric relations. *Research in Developmental Disabilities, 16,* 179–204.

129. Morrison, F. J., Smith, L., & Dow-Ehrensberger, M. (1995). Education and cognitive development: A natural experiment. *Developmental Psychology, 31,* 789–799.

130. Nurss, J. R., Baker, D. W., Davis, T. C., Parker, R. M., & Williams, M. V. (1995). Difficulties in functional health literacy screening in Spanish-speaking adults. *Journal of Reading, 38,* 632–637.

131. Paternite, C. E., Loney, J., & Roberts, M. A. (1995). External validation of oppositional disorder and attention deficit disorder with hyperactivity. *Journal of Abnormal Child Psychology, 23,* 453–471.

132. Persinger, M. A., & Richards, P. M. (1995). Foot agility and toe gnosis/graphaesthesia as potential indicators of integrity of the medial cerebral surface: Normative data and comparison with clinical populations. *Perceptual and Motor Skills, 80,* 1011–1024.

133. Rellinger, E., Borkowski, J. G., Turner, L. A., & Hale, C. A. (1995). Perceived task difficulty and intelligence: Determinants of strategy use and recall. *Intelligence, 20,* 125–143.

134. Richards, C. M., Symons, D. K., Greene, C. A., & Szuszkiewicz, T. A. (1995). The bidirectional relationship between achievement and externalizing behavior problems of students with learning disabilities. *Journal of Learning Disabilities, 28,* 8–17.

135. Sapp, M., Farrell, W., & Durand, H. (1995). Cognitive-behavioral therapy: Applications for African-American middle school at-risk students. *Journal of Instructional Psychology, 22,* 169–177.

136. Schachar, R., Tannock, R., Marriott, M., & Logan, G. (1995). Deficient inhibitory control in Attention Deficit Hyperactivity Disorder. *Journal of Abnormal Child Psychology, 23,* 411–437.

137. Seidman, L. J., Benedict, K. B., Biederman, J., Bernstein, J. H., Sewerd, K., Milberger, S., Norman, D., Mick, E., & Faraone, S. V. (1995). Performance of children with ADHD on the Rey-Osterrieth Complex Figure: A pilot neuropsychological study. *Journal of Child Psychology and Psychiatry, 36,* 1459–1473.

138. Shany, M. T., & Biemiller, A. (1995). Assisted reading practice: Effects on performance for poor readers in grades 3 and 4. *Reading Research Quarterly, 30,* 382–395.

139. Slate, J. R., & Fawcett, J. (1995). Validity of the WISC-III for deaf and hard of hearing persons. *American Annals of the Deaf, 140,* 250–254.

140. Spafford, C. S., Grosser, G. S., Donatelle, J. R., Squillace, S. R., & Dana, J. P. (1995). Contrast sensitivity differences between proficient and disabled readers using colored lenses. *Journal of Learning Disabilities, 28,* 240–252.

141. Sparks, R. L., Ganschow, L., & Patton, J. (1995). Prediction of performance in first-year foreign language courses: Connections between native and foreign language learning. *Journal of Educational Psychology, 87,* 638–655.

142. Spencer, T., Wilens, T., Biederman, J., Faraone, S. V., Ablon, S., & Lapey, K. (1995). A double-blind, crossover comparison of methylphenidate and placebo in adults with childhood-onset attention deficit hyperactivity disorder. *Archives of General Psychiatry, 52,* 434–443.

143. Sullivan, G. S., Mastropieri, M. A., & Scruggs, T. E. (1995). Reasoning and remembering: Coaching students with learning disabilities to think. *The Journal of Special Education, 29,* 310–322.

144. Sullivan, T. E., & Hawkins, K. A. (1995). Support for abbreviation of the Wide Range Achievement Test—Revised spelling subtest in neuropsychological assessments. *Journal of Clinical Psychology, 51,* 552–554.

145. Tangel, D. M., & Blachman, B. A. (1995). Effect of phoneme awareness instruction on the invented spelling of first-grade children: A one-year follow-up. *Journal of Reading Behavior, 27,* 153–185.

146. Treiman, R., Zukowski, A., & Richmond-Welty, E. D. (1995). What happened to the "n" of sink? Children's spellings of final consonant clusters. *Cognition, 55,* 1–38.

147. Vance, B., & Fuller, G. B. (1995). Relation of scores on WISC-III and WRAT-III for a sample of referred children and youth. *Psychological Reports, 76,* 371–374.

148. Vrana, S. R., Roodman, A. & Beckham, J. C. (1995). Selective processing of trauma-relevant words in posttraumatic stress disorder. *Journal of Anxiety Disorders, 9,* 515–530.

149. Watson, C., & Willows, D. M. (1995). Information-processing patterns in specific reading disability. *Journal of Learning Disabilities, 28,* 216–231.

150. Zigmond, N. (1995). Inclusion in Pennsylvania: Educational experiences of students with learning disabilities in one elementary school. *The Journal of Special Education, 29,* 124–132.

151. Abikoff, H., Courtney, M. E., Szeibel, P. J., & Koplewiez, H. S. (1996). The effects of audiotry stimulation on the arithmatic performance of children with ADHD and nondisabled children. *Journal of Learning Disabilities, 29,* 238–246.

152. August, G. J., Realmuto, G. M., MacDonald, A. W., III, Nugent, S. M., & Crosby, R. (1996). Prevalence of ADHD and comorbid disorders among elementary school children screened for disruptive behavior. *Journal of Abnormal Child Psychology, 24,* 571–595.

153. Banden, H., Dooley, J., Buckley, D., Camfield, P., Gordon, K., Riding, M., & Llewellyn, G. (1996). MRI and nonverbal cognitive deficits in children with neurofibromatosis 1. *Journal of Clinical and Experimental Neuropsychology, 18,* 784–792.

154. Beckham, J. C., Lytle, B. L., Vrana, S. R., Hertzberg, M. A., Feldman, M. E., & Shipley, R. H. (1996). Smoking withdrawal symptoms in response to a trauma-related stressor among Vietnam combat veterans with posttraumatic stress disorder. *Addictive Behaviors, 21,* 93–101.

155. Bempechat, J., Nakkula, M. J., Wu, J. T., & Ginsberg, H. P. (1996). Attributions as predictors of mathematics achievement: A comparative study. *Journal of Research and Development in Education, 29,* 53–59.

156. Boetsch, E. A., Green, P. A., & Pennington, B. F. (1996). Psychosocial correlates of dyslexia across the life span. *Development and Psychopathology, 8,* 539–562.

157. Budd, K. S., & Holdsworth, M. J. (1996). Issues in clinical assessment of minimal parenting competence. *Journal of Clinical Child Psychology, 25,* 1–14.

158. Capaldi, D. M., Crosby, L., & Stoolmiller, M. (1996). Predicting the timing of first sexual intercourse for at-risk adolescent males. *Child Development, 67,* 344–359.

159. Contos, A. L., Gries, L. T., & Sliss, V. (1996). Correlates of therapy referral in foster children. *Child Abuse & Neglect, 20,* 921–931.

160. Francis, D. J., Fletcher, J. M., Shaywitz, B. A., Shaywitz, S. E., & Rourke, B. P. (1996). Defining learning and language disabilities: Conceptual and psychometric issues with the use of IQ tests. *Language, Speech, and Hearing Services in Schools, 27,* 132–143.

161. Gottesman, R. L. Bennett, R. E., Nathan, R. G., & Kelly, M. S. (1996). Inner-city adults with severe reading difficulties: A closer look. *Journal of Learning Disabilities, 29,* 589–597.

162. Greene, C., Symons, S., & Richards, C. (1996). Elaborative interrogation effects for children with learning disabilities: Isolated facts versus connected prose. *Contemporary Educational Psychology, 21,* 19–42.

163. Gresham, F., M., MacMillan, D. L., & Bocian, K. M. (1996). Learning disabilities, low achievement, and mild mental retardation: More alike than different? *Journal of Learning Disabilities, 29,* 570–581.

164. Heinze, M. C., & Grisso, T. (1996). Review of instruments assessing parenting competencies used in child custody evaluations. *Behavior Sciences and the Law, 14,* 293–313.

165. Humphries, T., Krekewich, K., & Snider, L. (1996). Evidence of nonverbal learning disability among learning disabled boys with sensory integrative dysfunction. *Perceptual and Motor Skills, 82,* 979–987.

166. Johannes, S., Kussmaul, C. L., Münte, T. F., & Mangun, G. R. (1996). Developmental dyslexia: Passive visual stimulation provides no evidence for a magnocellular processing defect. *Neuropsychologia, 34,* 1123–1127.

167. John, S., & Ovsiew, F. (1996). Erotomania in a brain-damaged male. *Journal of Disability Research, 40,* 279–283.

168. Juel, C. (1996). What makes literacy tutoring effective? *Reading Research Quarterly, 31,* 268–289.

169. Liebson, E., White, R. F., & Albert, M. L. (1996). Cognitive inconsistencies in abnormal illness behavior and neurological disease. *Journal of Nervous and Mental Disease, 184,* 122–125.

170. Lorsbach, T. C., Wilson, S., & Reimer, J. F. (1996). Memory for relevant and irrelevant information: Evidence of deficient inhibitory processes in language/learning disabled children. *Contemporary Educational Psychology, 21,* 447–466.

171. Lovett, M. W., Borden, S. L., Warren-Chapman, P. M., Lacerenza, L., DeLuca, T., & Giovinazzo, R. (1996). Text comprehension training for disabled readers: An evaluation of reciprocal teaching and text analysis training programs. *Brain and Language, 54,* 447–480.

172. Lovrich, D., Cheng, J. C., & Velting, D. M. (1996). Late cognitive brain potentials, phonological and semantic classification of spoken words, and reading ability in children. *Journal of Clinical and Experimental Neuropsychology, 18,* 161–177.

173. MacMillan, D. L., Gresham, F. M., Lopez, M. F., & Bocian, K. M. (1996). Comparison of students nominated for prereferral interventions by ethnicity and gender. *The Journal of Special Education, 30,* 133–151.

174. MacMillan, D. L., Gresham, F. M., Siperstein, G. N., & Bocian, K.M. (1996). The labyrinth of IDEA: School decisions on referred students with subaverage general intelligence. *American Journal on Mental Retardation, 101,* 161–174.

175. McDonald, C., Brown, G. G., & Gorell, J. M. (1996). Impaired set-shifting in Parkinson's Disease: New evidence from a lexical decision task. *Journal of Clinical and Experimental Neuropsychology, 18,* 793–809.

176. Moore, B. D., Slopis, J. M., Schomer, D., Jackson, E. F., & Levy, B. M. (1996). Neuropsycholgical significance of areas of high signal intensity on brain MRI's of children with neurofibromatosis. *Neurology, 46,* 1660–1668.

177. Niznikiewicz, M., & Squires, N. K. (1996). Phonological processing and the role of strategy in silent reading: Behavioral and electrophysiological evidence. *Brain and Language, 52,* 342–364.

178. Ross, G., Lipper, E., & Auld, P. A. M. (1996). Cognitive abilities and early precursors of learning disabilities in very-low-birthweight children with normal intelligence and normal neurological status. *International Journal of Behavioral Development, 19,* 563–580.

179. Rovert, J., & Alvarez, M. (1996). Thyroid hormone and attention in school-age children with congenital hypothyroidism. *Journal of Child Psychology and Psychiatry, 37,* 579–585.

180. Rovert, J., Netley, C., Keenan, M., Bailey, J., & Stewart, D. (1996). The psychoeducational profile of boys with Klinefelter Syndrome. *Journal of Learning Disabilities, 29,* 189–196.

181. Slate, J. R., & Fawcett, J. (1996). Gender differences in Weschler performance scores of school-age children who are deaf or hard of hearing. *American Annals of the Deaf, 141,* 19–23.

182. Sparks, R. L., & Ganschow, L. (1996). Teacher's perceptions of students' foreign language academic skills and affective characteristics. *Journal of Educational Research, 89,* 172–185.

183. Stanford, M. S., & Barratt, E. S (1996). Verbal skills, finger tapping, and cognitive tempo define a second-order factor of temporal information processing. *Brain and Cognition, 31,* 35–45.

184. Strong, M. J., Grace, G. M., Orange, J. B., & Leeper, H. A. (1996). Cognition, language, and speech in amyotrophic lateral sclerosis: A review. *Journal of Clinical and Experimental Neuropsychology, 18,* 291–303.

185. Timmons, P. L., Oehlet, M. E., Sumerall, S. W., Timmons, C. W., & Borgers, S. B. (1996). Stress inoculation training for maladaptive anger: Comparison of group counseling versus computer guidance. *Computers in Human Behavior, 12,* 51–64.

186. Waring, S., Margot, P., Sanson, A., & Smart, D. (1996). Predictors of "recovery" from reading disability. *Australian Journal of Psychology, 48,* 160–166.

187. Wilens, T. E., Biederman, J., Prince, J., Spencer, T. J., Faraone, S. V., Warburton, R., Schleifer, D., Harding, M., Linehan, C., & Geller, D. (1996). Six-week, double-blind, placebo-controlled study of desipramine for adult attention deficit hyperactivity disorder. *American Journal of Psychiatry, 153,* 1147–1153.

188. Wilson, M. S., & Reschly, D. J. (1996). Assessment in school psychology training and practice. *School Psychology Review, 25,* 9–23.

189. Alarcón, M., DeFries, J. C., Light, J. G., & Pennington, B. F. (1997). A twin study of mathematics disability. *Journal of Learning Disabilities, 30,* 617–623.

190. Alexander, G. E., Furey, M. L., Grady, C. L., Pietrini, P., Brady, D. R., Mentis, M. J., & Schapiro, M. B. (1997). Association of premorbid intellectual function with cerebral metabolism in Alzheimer's Disease: Implications for the cognitive reserve hypothesis. *American Journal of Psychiatry, 154,* 165–172.

191. Alster, E. H. (1997). The effects of extended time on algebra test scores for college students with and without learning disabilities. *Journal of Learning Disabilities, 30,* 222–227.

192. Bakken, J. P., Mastropieri, M. A., & Scruggs, T. E. (1997). Reading comprehension on expository science material and students with learning disability: A comparison of strategies. *The Journal of Special Education, 31,* 300–324.

193. Ball, J. D., Tiernan, M., Janusz, J., & Furr, A. (1997). Sleep patterns among children with attention-deficit hyperactivity disorder: A reexamination of parent perceptions. *Journal of Pediatric Psychology, 22,* 389–398.

194. Biederman, J., Faranoe, S. V., Hatch, M., Mennin, D., Taylor, A., & George, P. (1997). Conduct disorder with and without mania in a referred sample of ADHD children. *Journal of Affective Disorders, 44,* 177–188.

195. Blackmore, A. M., & Pratt, C. (1997). Grammatical awareness and reading in grade 1 children. *Merrill-Palmer Quarterly, 43,* 567–590.

196. Breier, J. I., Brookshire, B. L., Fletcher, J. M., Thomas, A. B., Plenger, P. M., Wheless, J. W., Willmore, L. J., & Papanicolaou, A. (1997). Identification of side of seizure onset in temporal lobe epilepsy using memory tests in the context of reading deficits. *Journal of Clinical and Experimental Neuropsychology, 19,* 161–171.

197. Brewer, V. R., Moore, B. D., III, & Hiscock, M. (1997). Learning disability subtypes in children with neurofibromatosis. *Journal of Learning Disabilities, 30,* 521–533.

198. Cantos, A. L., Gries, l. T., & Slis, V. (1997). Behavioral correlates of parental visiting during family foster care. *Child Welfare, 76,* 309–329.

199. Ciesielski, K. T., Harris, R. J., Hart, B. L., & Pabst, H. F. (1997). Cerebellar hypoplasia and frontal lobe cognitive deficits in disorders of early childhood. *Neuropsychologia, 35,* 643–655.

200. Cruz, E. B., Brier, N. M., & Reznikoff, M. (1997). An examination of the relationship between form level ratings on the Rorschach and learning disability status. *The Journal of Psychology, 131,* 167–174.

201. Feldman, M. A., & Walton-Allen, N. (1997). Effects of maternal mental retardation and poverty on intellectual, academic, and behavioral status of school-age children. *American Journal on Mental Retardation, 101,* 352–364.

202. Filipek, P. A., Semrud-Clikeman, M., Steingard, R. J., Renshaw, P. F., Kennedy, D. N., & Biederman, J. (1997). Volumetric MRI analysis comparing subjects having attention-deficit hyperactivity disorder with normal controls. *Neurology, 48,* 589–601.

203. Fisher, N. J., Rourke, B. P., Bieliauskas, L. A., Giordani, B., Berent, S., & Foster, N. L. (1997). Unmasking the heterogeneity of Alzheimer's Disease: Care studies of individuals from distinct neuropsychological subgroups. *Journal of Clinical and Experimental Neuropsychology, 19,* 713–754.

204. Galen, L. W., Henderson, M. J., & Whitman, R. D. (1997). The utility of novelity seeking, harm avoidance, and expectancy in the prediction of drinking. *Addictive Behaviors, 22,* 93–106.

205. Glosser, G., Grugan, P., & Friedman, R. B. (1997). Semantic memory impairment does not impact on phonological and orthographic processing in a case of developmental hyperlexia. *Brain and Language, 56.* 2344–247.

206. Gold, J. M., Carpenter, C., Randolph, C., Goldberg, T. E., & Weinberger, D. R. (1997). Auditory working memory and Wisconsin Card Sorting Test performance in schizophrenia. *Archives of General Psychiatry, 54,* 159–165.

207. Gresham, F. M., MacMillan, D. L., & Bocian, K. M. (1997). Teachers as "tests": Differential validity of teacher judgements in identifying students at-risk for learning disabilities. *School Psychology Review, 26,* 47–60.

208. Hart, T. M., Berninger, V. M., & Abbott, R. D. (1997). Comparison of teaching single or multiple orthographic-phonological connections for word recognition and spelling: Implications for instructional consultation. *School Psychology Review, 26,* 279–297.

209. Kerns, K. A., Don, A., Mateer, C. A., & Streissguth, A. P. (1997). Cognitive deficits in nonretarded adults with Fetal Alcohol Syndrome. *Journal of Learning Disabilities, 30,* 685–693.

210. Lovrich, D., Cheng, J. C., Velting, D. M., & Kazmerski, V. (1997). Auditory ERPs during rhyme and semantic processing: Effects of reading ability in college students. *Journal of Clinical and Experimental Neuropsychology, 19,* 313–330.

211. Marshall, R. M., Hynd, G. W., Handwerk, M. J., & Hall, J. (1997). Academic underachievement in ADHD subtypes. *Journal of Learning Disabilities, 30,* 635–642.

212. McBride, H. E. A., & Siegel, L. S. (1997). Learning disabilities and adolescent suicide. *Journal of Learning Disabilities, 30,* 652–659.

213. McClure, E., Rogeness, G. A., & Thompson, N. M. (1997). Characteristics of adolescent girls with depressive symptoms in a so-called 'normal' sample. *Journal of Affective Disorders, 42,* 187–197.

214. Purvis, K. L., & Tannock, R. (1997). Language abilities in children with Attention Deficit Hyperactivity disorder, reading disabilities, and normal controls. *Journal of Abnormal Child Psychology, 25,* 133–144.

215. Schwartz, T. H., Ojemann, G. A., & Dodrill, C. B. (1997). Reading errors following right hemisphere injection of sodium amobarbital. *Brain and Language, 58,* 70–91.

216. Seidman, L. J., Caplan, B. B., Tolomiczenko, G. S., Turner, W. M., Penk, W. E., Schutt, R. K., & Goldfinger, S. M. (1997). Neuropsychological function in homeless mentally ill individuals. *Journal of Nervous and Mental Disease, 185,* 3–12.

217. Siperstein, G. N., & Leffert, J. S. (1997). Comparison of socially accepted and rejected children with mental retardation. *American Journal on Mental Retardation, 101,* 339–351.

218. Snyder, M. C., & Bambara, L. M. (1997). Teaching secondary students with learning disabilities to self-manage classroom survival skills. *Journal of Learning Disabilities, 30,* 534–543.

219. Sparks, R. L., Ganschow, L., Artzer, M., & Patton, J. (1997). Foreign language proficiency of at-risk and not-at-risk learners over 2 years of foreign language instruction: A follow-up study. *Journal of Learning Disabilities, 30,* 92–98.

220. Tsatsanis, K. D., Fuerst, D. R., & Rourke, B. P. (1997). Psychosocial dimensions of learning disabilities: External validation and relationship with age and academic functioning. *Journal of Learning Disabilities, 30,* 490–502.

221. Velting, O. N., & Whitehurst, G. J. (1997). Inattention-hyperactivity and reading achievement in children from low-income families: A longitudinal model. *Journal of Abnormal Child Psychology, 25,* 321–331.

222. Ackerman, P. T., McPherson, W. B., Oglesby, D. M., & Dykman, R. A. (1998). EEG power spectra of adolescent poor readers. *Journal of Learning Disabilities, 31,* 83–90.

223. Baer, R. A., Ballenger, J., & Kroll, L. S. (1998). Detection of underreporting on the MMPI-A in clinical and community samples. *Journal of Personality Assessment, 71,* 98–113.

224. Baynes, K., Kegl, J. A., Brentari, D., Kussmaul, C., & Poizner, H. (1998). Chronic auditory agnosia following Landau-Kleffner syndrome: A 23 year outcome study. *Brain and Language, 63,* 381–425.

225. Bear, G. G., Minke, K. M., Griffin, S. M., & Deemer, S. A. (1998). Achievement-related perceptions of children with learning disabilities and normal achievement: Group and developmental differences. *Journal of Learning Disabilities, 31,* 91–104.

226. Berman, I., Merson, A., Viegner, B., Losonezy, M. F. Pappas, D., & Green, A. I. (1998). Obsessions and compulsions at a district cluster of symptoms in schizophrenia: A neuropsychological study. *Journal of Nervous and Mental Disease, 186,* 150–156.
227. Berquin, P. C., Giedd, J. N., Jacobsen, L. K., Hamburger, S. D., Krain, A. L., Rapoport, J. L., & Castellanos, F. X. (1998). Cerebellum in attention-deficit hyperactivity disorder: A morphometric MRI study. *Neurology, 50,* 1087–1093.
228. Carthy, L., & Archer, R. P. (1998). Factor structure of the MMPI-A content scales: Item-level and scale-level findings. *Journal of Personality Assessment, 71,* 84–97.
229. Cashel, M. L., Rogers, R., Sewell, K. W., & Holliman, N. B. (1998). Preliminary validation of the MMPI-A for a male delinquent sample: An investigation of clinical correlates and discriminant validity. *Journal of Personality Assessment, 71,* 49–69.
230. Louth, S. M., Hare, R. D., & Linden, W. (1998). Psychopathy and alexithymia in female offenders. *Canadian Journal of Behavioural Science, 30,* 91–98.
231. MacMillan, D. L., Gresham, F. M., & Bocian, K. M. (1998). Discrepancy between definitions of learning disabilities and school practices: An empirical investigation. *Journal of Learning Disabilities, 31,* 314–326.
232. Morel, K. R. (1998). Development and preliminary validation of a forced-choice test of response bias for posttraumatic stress disorder. *Journal of Personality Assessment, 70,* 299–314.
233. Oakland, T., Black, J. L., Stanford, G., Nussbaum, N. L., & Balise, R. R. (1998). An evaluation of the dyslexia training program: A multisensory method for promoting reading in students with reading disabilities. *Journal of Learning Disabilities, 31,* 140–147.
234. Smithee, J. A. F., Klorman, R., Brumaghim, J. T., & Borgstedt, A. D. (1998). Methylphenidate does not modify the impact of response frequency or stimulus sequence on performance and event-related potentials of children with attention deficit hyperactivity disorder. *Journal of Abnormal Child Psychology, 26,* 233–245.
235. Chiappe, P., & Siegel, L. S. (1999). Phonological awareness and reading acquisition in English- and Punjabi-Speaking Canadian children. *Journal of Educational Psychology, 91,* 20–28.
236. Comeau, L., Cormier, P., Grandmaison, E., & Lacroix, D. (1999). A longitudinal study of plumological processing skills in children learning to read in a second language. *Journal of Educational Psychology, 91,* 29–43.
237. Metsala, J. L. (1999). Young children's phonological awareness and nonword repetition as a function of vocabulary development. *Journal of Educational Psychology, 91,* 3–19.

[2880]

Wide Range Assessment of Memory and Learning.

Purpose: "Psychometric instrument which allows the user to evaluate a child's ability to actively learn and memorize a variety of information."
Population: Ages 5 through 17.
Publication Date: 1990.
Acronym: WRAML.
Scores, 4: Verbal Memory Index, Visual Memory Index, Learning Index, General Memory Index.
Administration: Individual.
Price Data, 1999: $345 per complete kit including 25 sets of forms, supplies, and manual (160 pages); $40 per 25 examiner forms; $42 per 25 response forms; $40 per manual.
Time: (45-60) minutes.
Comments: Screening section available on Examiner Form.
Authors: David Sheslow and Wayne Adams.
Publisher: Wide Range, Inc.
Cross References: For reviews by Richard M. Clark and Frederic J. Medway, see 11:470.

TEST REFERENCES

1. Sikora, D. M., & Plapinger, D. S. (1994). Using standardized tests to identify learning disabilities in students with sensorineural hearing impairments. *Journal of Learning Disabilities, 27,* 352–359.
2. Farmer, J. E., & Peterson, L. (1995). Pediatric traumatic brain injury: Promoting successful school reentry. *School Psychology Review, 24,* 230–243.
3. Plapinger, D. S., & Sikora, D. M. (1995). The use of standardized test batteries in assessing the skill development of children with mild-to-moderate sensorineural hearing loss. *Language, Speech, and Hearing Services in Schools, 26,* 39–44.
4. Paradis, C. M., Gironda, F., & Bennett, M. (1996). Cognitive impairment in Schwartz-Jampel syndrome: A case study. *Brain and Language, 56,* 301–305.
5. Phelps, L. (1996). Discriminative validity of the WRAML with ADHD and LD children. *Psychology in the Schools, 33,* 5–12.
6. Hill, D. E., Ciesielski, K. T., Sethre-Hofstad, L., Duncan, M. H., & Lorenzi, M. (1997). Visual and verbal short-term memory deficits in childhood leukemia survivors after intrathecal chemotherapy. *Journal of Pediatric Psychology, 22,* 861–870.
7. Sparks, R. L., Ganschow, L., Artzer, M., & Patton, J. (1997). Foreign language proficiency of at-risk and not-at-risk learners over 2 years of foreign language instruction: A follow-up study. *Journal of Learning Disabilities, 30,* 92–98.

[2881]

Wide Range Assessment of Visual Motor Abilities.

Purpose: A standardized assessment of visual-motor, visual-spatial, and fine motor skills.
Population: Ages 3–17 years.
Publication Date: 1995.
Acronym: WRAVMA.
Scores, 4: Fine Motor, Visual-Spatial, Visual-Motor, Visual-Motor Integration Composite.
Administration: Individual.
Price Data, 1999: $40 per manual (151 pages); $48 per 25 drawing or matching forms; $40 per 25 examiner record forms; $50 per pegboard with pegs; $12 per pencil and marker resupply pack; $38 per soft attache case.
Time: (15–30) minutes; (5–10) minutes per subtest.
Comments: Best results when "integrated with data from other standardized tests and clinical observations"; test should be interpreted by "those with graduate or equivalent professional training in cognitive assessment."
Authors: Wayne Adams and David Sheslow.
Publisher: Wide Range, Inc.

[2882]

Wide Range Interest-Opinion Test.

Purpose: Intended as "an inventory of work interests."
Population: Ages 5 and over.
Publication Dates: 1970-1979.
Acronym: WRIOT.
Scores, 26: 18 occupational interests (Art, Literature, Music, Drama, Sales, Management, Office Work, Personal Service, Protective Service, Social Service, Social Science, Biological Science, Physical Science, Number, Mechanics, Machine Operation, Outdoor, Athletics) and 8 vocational attitudes (Sedentariness, Risk, Ambition, Chosen Skill Level, Sex Stereotype, Agreement, Negative Bias, Positive Bias).
Administration: Group.
Price Data, 1999: $150 per complete kit; $30 per picture book; $30 per 50 answer sheets; $48 per scoring stencils; $30 per 50 profile report forms; $40 per manual ('79, 118 pages).
Time: (40-60) minutes.

Authors: Joseph F. Jastak and Sarah Jastak.
Publisher: Wide Range, Inc.
Cross References: See T4:2959 (1 reference); for reviews by Louis M. Hsu and Caroline A. Manuele, see 9:1366; for a review by Donald G. Zytowski, see 8:1029.

[2883]

Wide-Span Reading Test.

Purpose: To assess "a child's skill in decoding printed symbols into meaningful sounds of language, in fitting meanings to groups of sounds, and in construing the structural relationship of meanings in their total semantic and syntactical context."
Population: Ages 7-10 to 14-11.
Publication Dates: 1972-1984.
Scores: Total score only.
Administration: Group.
Forms, 2: A, B.
Price Data, 1989: £34.50 per complete kit; £10.65 per 25 pupil's booklets (specify Form A or B); £4.20 per 25 answer sheets; £6.90 per manual ('83, 36 pages); £7.90 per specimen set.
Time: 30(40) minutes.
Author: Alan Brimer.
Publisher: NFER-Nelson Publishing Co., Ltd. [England].
Cross References: For reviews by Mariam Jean Dreher and Priscilla A. Drum, see 10:390; see also T3:2625 (1 reference); for reviews by David J. Carroll and William Yule, see 8:747.

TEST REFERENCE

1. McManus, I. C. (1995). Familial sinistrality: The utility of calculating exact genotype probabilities for individuals. *Cortex, 31,* 3-24.

[2884]

The Wiesen Test of Mechanical Aptitude.

Purpose: Designed to measure mechanical aptitude for purpose of personnel selection.
Population: Applicants for jobs requiring mechanical aptitude.
Publication Dates: 1997–1998.
Acronym: WTMA.
Scores, 12: Total Score and 11 research scores: Basic Machines, Movement of Simple and Complex Objects, Center of Gravity and Gravity, Basic Electricity/Electronics, Transfer of Heat, Basic Physical Properties of Matter and Materials, Miscellaneous, Academic, Kitchen Objects, Non-Kitchen Objects, Other Everyday Objects.
Administration: Group.
Price Data, 1998: $25 per 25 answer sheets; $150 per 10 test booklets; $15 per main scoring stencil; $150 per set of 11 research subscore stencils; $75 per specimen set including 1 test, technical manual ('98, 73 pages), and answer sheet; $65 per technical manual; quantity discounts available on all items.
Time: Administration time not reported.
Comments: A 60-item multiple-choice objective test; computer scoring available.
Author: Joel P. Wiesen.
Publisher: Applied Personnel Research.

[2885]

Wife's or Husband's Marriage Questions.

Purpose: Designed as "a comprehensive marriage analysis system."
Population: Husbands, wives.
Publication Date: 1994.
Administration: Individual or group.
Forms, 2: Wife's Marriage Questions, Husband's Marriage Questions.
Manual: No manual.
Price Data, 1998: $10 per 20 forms (specify Husband or Wife).
Time: Administration time not reported.
Author: Allan Roe.
Publisher: Diagnostic Specialists, Inc.

[2886]

Wiig Criterion Referenced Inventory of Language.

Purpose: "Designed to assist speech-language pathologists and special and regular educators in the diagnosis of children with language disorders and language delays."
Population: Ages 4 through 13.
Publication Date: 1990.
Acronym: Wiig CRIL.
Scores: 4 modules: Semantics, Morphology, Syntax, Pragmatics.
Administration: Individual.
Price Data, 1999: $250 per complete kit including Professional's Guide (63 pages), all 4 stimulus manuals and 10 each of all four record forms; price information for the module package (specify Semantics, Morphology, Syntax, or Pragmatics) including stimulus manual and 10 record forms available from publisher; $37 per 20 record forms (specify Semantics, Morphology, Syntax, or Pragmatics).
Time: Untimed.
Author: Elisabeth H. Wiig.
Publisher: The Psychological Corporation.
Cross References: For reviews by Clinton W. Bennett and Judith R. Johnston, see 13:361.

[2887]

Williams Awareness Sentence Completion.

Purpose: To measure Black awareness and consciousness.
Population: Ages 15 and over.
Publication Dates: 1972-1976.
Acronym: WASC.

Scores: 6 response categories: Anglocentric, Dissemblance or Dissimulation, Afro-Centric, Socio-Centric, Anthro-Centric, Uncommitted.
Administration: Group.
Price Data, 1983: $12 per 20 tests, including manual ('76, 30 pages); $3.50 per manual.
Time: Administration time not reported.
Author: Robert L. Williams.
Publisher: Robert L. Williams & Associates, Inc. [No reply from publisher; status unknown].
Cross References: For a review by Clifford H. Swensen, see 9:1367.

[2888]

Williams Intelligence Test for Children with Defective Vision.

Purpose: "Should discriminate between ... degrees of mental ability."
Population: Ages 5-15 (blind and partially sighted).
Publication Date: 1956.
Scores: Total score only.
Administration: Individual.
Price Data, 1989: £126.50 per complete kit; £5.20 per 12 record forms; £10.95 per handbook (54 pages plus fold-out IQ conversion tables).
Time: [60] minutes.
Author: M. Williams.
Publisher: NFER-Nelson Publishing Co., Ltd. [England].
Cross References: See T2:540 (1 reference); for a review by T. Ernest Newland, see 6:541 (2 references).

TEST REFERENCE

1. Newton, T. J. (1989). Occupational stress and coping with stress: A critique. *Human Relations, 42,* 441–461.

[2889]

Wilson Driver Selection Test.

Purpose: Constructed to measure aptitudes related to safe driving.
Population: Prospective motor vehicle operators.
Publication Dates: 1961-1984.
Scores, 7: Visual Attention, Depth Visualization, Recognition of Simple Detail, Recognition of Complex
Detail, Eye-Hand Coordination, Steadiness, Total.
Administration: Group.
Price Data, 1999: $95.40 per test package; $3.75 per key; $54.60 per manual ('61, 28 pages) and manual supplement ('84, 17 pages); $41 per specimen set.
Time: 26(50) minutes.
Author: Clark L. Wilson.
Publisher: Martin M. Bruce, Ph.D.
Cross References: For reviews by Willard A. Kerr and D. H. Schuster, see 6:1200.

[2890]

The Wilson Teacher-Appraisal Scale.

Purpose: To evaluate instructor performance based on student perceptions.
Population: Grades 7-16.
Publication Dates: 1948-1957.
Scores: Ratings in 3 areas: Personal Appraisal, Course Appraisal, Teacher Rank.
Administration: Group.
Manual: No manual.
Price Data: Not available.
Time: [10-15] minutes.
Comments: Ratings of instructors by themselves and by students; rating forms for teachers taken from A Self Appraisal Scale for Teachers (2351).
Author: Howard Wilson.
Publisher: Administrative Research Associates [No reply from publisher; status unknown].
Cross References: For a review by James R. Hayden, see 6:711.

TEST REFERENCE

1. Follman, J. (1992). Secondary school students' ratings of teacher effectiveness. *The High School Journal, 75,* 168-178.

[2891]

Wisconsin Behavior Rating Scale.

Purpose: "A least biased adaptive behavior scale" to "provide adequate assessment, intervention, and evaluation" of severely and profoundly retarded individuals and of persons functioning below the developmental level of 3 years.
Population: Persons functioning below the developmental level of 3 years.
Publication Dates: 1979-1991.
Acronym: WBRS.
Scores, 12: Gross Motor, Fine Motor, Expressive Language, Receptive Language, Play Skills, Socialization, Domestic Activity, Eating, Toileting, Dressing, Grooming, Total.
Administration: Group.
Price Data, 1997: $12 per 25 scales; $40 per 100 scales ('91, 12 pages); $2.50 per specimen set including scale and manual ('83, 30 pages).
Time: (10-15) minutes.
Comments: "The assessment is performed by interviewing informants who are most familiar with the behavior of the person being evaluated."
Authors: Agnes Song, Stephen Jones, Janet Lippert, Karin Metzgen, Jacqueline Miller, and Christopher Borreca.
Publisher: Central Wisconsin Center for the Developmentally Disabled.
Cross References: For reviews by Pat Mirenda and Harvey N. Switzky, see 11:472 (1 reference).

[2892]

Wisconsin Card Sorting Test, Revised and Expanded.

Purpose: "Developed ... as a measure of abstract reasoning among normal adult populations" and "has increasingly been employed as a clinical neuropsychological instrument."

Population: Ages 6.5–89.

Publication Dates: 1981–1993.

Acronym: WCST.

Scores, 11: Number of Trials Administered, Total Number Correct, Total Number of Errors, Perseverative Responses, Perseverative Errors, Nonperseverative Errors, Conceptual Level Responses, Number of Categories Completed, Trials to Complete First Category, Failure to Maintain Set, Learning to Learn.

Administration: Individual.

Price Data: Price information available from publisher for complete kit including manual ('93, 234 pages), 2 decks of cards, and 25 record booklets; price information also available from publisher for computer version.

Time: (20–30) minutes.

Comments: Additional materials necessary for testing include a pen or pencil and a clipboard.

Authors: Robert K. Heaton, Gordon J. Chelune, Jack L. Talley, Gary G. Kay, and Glenn Curtiss.

Publisher: Psychological Assessment Resources, Inc.

Cross References: See T4:2967 (96 references); for reviews by Byron Egeland and Robert P. Markley of an earlier edition, see 9:1372 (11 references).

TEST REFERENCES

1. Stuss, D. T., Benson, D. F., Kaplan, E. F., Weir, W. S., Naeser, M. A., Lieberman, I., & Ferrill, D. (1983). The involvement of orbitofrontal cerebrum in cognitive tasks. *Neuropsychologia, 21,* 235–248.
2. Sandson, J., & Albert, M. L. (1984). Varieties of perseveration. *Neuropsychologia, 22,* 715–732.
3. Lee, G. P., Loring, D. W., Flanigin, H. F., Smith, J. R., & Meador, K. J. (1988). Electrical stimulation of the human hippocampus produces verbal intrusions during memory testing. *Neuropsychologia, 26,* 623–627.
4. Weddell, R. A., Trevarthen, C., & Miller, J. D. (1988). Reaction of patients with focal cerebral lesions to success or failure. *Neuropsychologia, 26,* 373–385.
5. Beatty, W. W., Goodkin, D. E., Beatty, P. A., & Monson, N. (1989). Frontal lobe dysfunction and memory impairment in patients with chronic progressive multiple sclerosis. *Brain and Cognition, 11,* 73-86.
6. Bellack, A. S., Morrison, R. L., & Mueser, K. T. (1989). Social problem solving in schizophrenia. *Schizophrenic Bulletin, 15,* 101–116.
7. Berger, H. J. C., Van Hoof, J. J. M., Van Spaendonck, K. P. M., Harstink, M. W. I., Van Den Bercken, J. H. L., Jaspers, R., & Cools, A. R. (1989). Haloperidol and cognitive shifting. *Neuropsychologia, 27,* 629–639.
8. Blonder, L. X., Gur, R. E., Gur, R. C., Saykin, A. J., & Hurtig, H. I. (1989). Neuropsychological functioning in hemiparkinsonism. *Brain and Cognition, 9,* 244-257.
9. Canavan, A. G. M., Passingham, R. E., Marsden, C. D., Quinn, N., Wyke, M., & Polkey, C. E. (1989). The performance on learning tasks of patients in the early stages of Parkinson's disease. *Neuropsychologia, 27,* 141–156.
10. Erickson, R. C. (1989). Applications of cognitive testing to group therapies with the chronically mentally ill. *International Journal of Group Psychotherapy, 39,* 223–235.
11. Janowsky, J. S., Shimamura, A. P., & Squire, L. R. (1989). Source memory impairment in patients with frontal lobe lesions. *Neuropsychologia, 27,* 1043–1056.
12. Kelly, M. S., Best, C. T., & Kirk, U. (1989). Cognitive processing deficits in reading disabilities: A prefrontal cortical hypothesis. *Brain and Cognition, 11,* 275-293.
13. Loring, D. W., Meador, K. J., & Lee, G. P. (1989). Differential-handed response to verbal and visual spatial stimuli: Evidence of specialized hemispheric processing following callosotomy. *Neuropsychologia, 27,* 811–827.
14. Mayes, A. R., & Gooding, P. (1989). Enhancement of word completion priming in amnesics by cueing with previously novel associates. *Neuropsychologia, 27,* 1057–1072.
15. Rapesak, S. Z., Kaszniak, A. W., & Rubens, A. B. (1989). Anomia for facial expressions: Evidence for a category specific visual-verbal disconnection syndrome. *Neuropsychologia, 27,* 1031–1041.
16. Robertson, I. (1989). Anomalies in the laterality of omissions in unilateral left visual neglect: Implications for an attentional theory of neglect. *Neuropsychologia, 27,* 157–165.
17. Szatmari, P., Bartolucci, G., Bremner, R., Bond, S., & Rich, S. (1989). A follow-up study of high-functioning autistic children. *Journal of Autism and Developmental Disorders, 19*(2), 213-225.
18. Weddell, R. A. (1989). Recognition memory for emotional facial expressions in patients with focal cerebral lesions. *Brain and Cognition, 11,* 1-17.
19. Bartfai, A., Winborg, I.-M., Nordstrom, P., & Asberg, M. (1990). Suicidal behavior and cognitive flexibility: Design and verbal fluency after attempted suicide. *Suicide and Life-Threatening Behavior, 20,* 254–266.
20. Dubois, B., Pillon, B., Sternic, N., Lhermitte, F., & Agid, Y. (1990). Age-induced cognitive disturbances in Parkinson's disease. *Neurology, 40,* 38–41.
21. Flor-Henry, P. (1990). Influence of gender in schizophrenia as related to other psychopathological syndromes. *Schizophrenia Bulletin, 16,* 211–227.
22. Gur, R. E., Gur, R. C., & Saykin, A. J. (1990). Neurobehavioral studies in schizophrenia: Implications for regional brain dysfunction. *Schizophrenia Bulletin, 16,* 445–451.
23. Lueger, R. J., & Gill, K. J. (1990). Frontal-lobe cognitive dysfunction in conduct disorder adolescents. *Journal of Clinical Psychology, 46,* 696–706.
24. Peterson, J. B., Rothfleisch, J., Zelazo, P. D., & Pihl, R. O. (1990). Acute alcohol intoxication and cognitive functioning. *Journal of Studies on Alcohol, 51,* 114–122.
25. Ricci, C., & Blundo, C. (1990). Perception of ambiguous figures after focal brain lesions. *Neuropsychologia, 28,* 1163–1173.
26. Robbins, T. W. (1990). The case for frontostriatal dysfunction in schizophrenia. *Schizophrenia Bulletin, 16,* 391–402.
27. Robertson, I. H. (1990). Digit span and visual neglect: A puzzling relationship. *Neuropsychologia, 28,* 217–222.
28. Rumsey, J. M., & Hamburger, S. D. (1990). Neuropsychological divergence of high-level autism and severe dyslexia. *Journal of Autism and Developmental Disorders, 20*(2), 155-168.
29. Shimamura, A. P., Janowsky, J. S., & Squire, L. R. (1990). Memory for the temporal order of events in patients with frontal lobe lesions and amnesic patients. *Neuropsychologia, 28,* 803–813.
30. Wetzig, D. L., & Hardin, S. I. (1990). Neurocognitive deficits of alcoholism: An intervention. *Journal of Clinical Psychology, 46,* 219–229.
31. Breier, A., Schreiber, J. L., Dyer, J., & Pickar, D. (1991). National Institute of Mental Health longitudinal study of chronic schizophrenia. *Archives of General Psychiatry, 48,* 239-246.
32. Cohen, R. M., Berg, P., Canavan, A. G. M., & Hopmann, G. (1991). Slow cortical potentials (SCPS) in schizophrenic patients during performance of the Wisconsin Card Sorting Test. *Neuropsychologia, 29,* 195–205.
33. Everett, J., Thomas, J., Cote, F., Levesque, J., & Michaud, D. (1991). Cognitive effects of psychostimulant medication in hyperactive children. *Child Psychiatry and Human Development, 22,* 79–87.
34. Goldman, R. S., Avelrod, B. N., & Tandon, R. (1991). Analysis of executive functioning in schizophrenics using the Wisconsin Card Sorting Test. *The Journal of Nervous and Mental Disease, 179,* 507-508.
35. Joyce, E. M., & Robbins, T. W. (1991). Frontal lobe function in Korsakoff and non-Korsakoff alcoholics: Planning and spatial working memory. *Neuropsychologia, 29,* 709-723.
36. Mayes, A. R., Meudell, P. R., & MacDonald, C. (1991). Disproportionate intentional spatial-memory impairments in amnesia. *Neuropsychologia, 29,* 771–784.
37. Miller, B. L., Cummings, J. L., Villanueva-Meyer, J., Boone, K., Mehringer, C. M., Lesser, I. M., & Mena, I. (1991). Frontal lobe degeneration: Clinical, neuropsychological, and SPECCT characteristics. *Neurology, 41,* 1374–1382.
38. Opler, L. A., Rosenkilde, C. E., & Fiszbein, A. (1991). Neurocognitive features of chronic schizophrenic inpatients. *The Journal of Nervous and Mental Disease, 179,* 638-640.
39. Pillon, B., Dubois, B., Ploska, A., & Agid, Y. (1991). Severity and specificity of cognitive impairment in Alzheimer's, Huntington's, and Parkinson's diseases and progressive supranuclear palsy. *Neurology, 41,* 634–643.
40. Plasky, P. (1991). Antidepressant usage in schizophrenia. *Schizophrenia Bulletin, 17,* 649–657.
41. Rao, S. M., Leo, G. J., Bernardin, L., & Unverzagt, F. (1991). Cognitive dysfunction in multiple sclerosis. I. Frequency, patterns, and prediction. *Neurology, 41,* 685–691.
42. Sauer, J. L., & Damasio, A. R. (1991). Preserved access and processing of social knowledge in a patient with acquired sociopathy due to ventromedial frontal damage. *Neuropsychologia, 29,* 1241–1249.
43. Shoqeirat, M. A., & Mayes, A. R. (1991). Disproportionate incidental spatial-memory and recall deficits in amnesia. *Neuropsychologia, 29,* 749–769.
44. Starkstein, S. E., & Robinson, R. G. (1991). Dementia of depression in Parkinson's disease and stroke. *The Journal of Nervous and Mental Disease, 179,* 593-601.
45. Akshoomoff, N. A., Courchesne, E., Press, G. A., & Iragui, V. (1992). Contribution of the cerebellum to neuropsychological functioning: Evidence from a case of cerebellar degenerative disorder. *Neuropsychologia, 30,* 315-328.

46. Cynn, V. E. H. (1992). Persistence and problem solving skills in young male alcoholics. *Journal of Studies on Alcohol, 53,* 57–62.

47. Delis, D. C., Squire, L. R., Bihrle, A., & Massman, P. (1992). Componential analysis of problem-solving ability: Performance of patients with frontal lobe damage and amnesic patients on a new sorting test. *Neuropsychologia, 30,* 683-697.

48. DeLuca, J. (1992). Cognitive dysfunction after aneurysm of the anterior communicating artery. *Journal of Clinical and Experimental Neuropsychology, 14,* 924-934.

49. Diamond, R., White, R. F., Myers, R. H., Mastromauro, C., Koroshetz, W. J., Butters, N., Rothstein, D. M., Moss, M. B., & Vasterling, J. (1992). Evidence of presymptomatic cognitive decline in Huntington's disease. *Journal of Clinical and Experimental Neuropsychology, 14,* 961-975.

50. Flint, J., & Goldstein, L. H. (1992). Familial calcification of the basal ganglia: A case report and review of the literature. *Psychological Medicine, 22,* 581-595.

51. Heinze, H., Münte, T. F., Gobiet, W., Niemann, H., & Ruff, R. M. (1992). Parallel and serial visual search after closed head injury: Electrophysiological evidence for perceptual dysfunctions. *Neuropsychologia, 30,* 495-514.

52. Hoff, A. L., Riordan, H., O'Donnell, D., Stritzke, P., Neale, C., Boccio, A., Anand, A. K., & DeLisi, L. E. (1992). Anomalous lateral sulcus asymmetry and cognitive function in first-episode schizophrenia. *Schizophrenia Bulletin, 18,* 257–273.

53. Huebner, R. A. (1992). Autistic disorder: A neuropsychological enigma. *The American Journal of Occupational Therapy, 46,* 487-501.

54. Karlinsky, H., Vanla, G., Haines, J. L., Ridgley, J., Bergeron, C., Mortilla, M., Tupler, R. G., Percy, M. E., Robitaille, Y., Noldy, N. E., Yip, T. C. K., Tanzi, R. E., Gusella, J. F., Becker, R., Berg, J. M., McLachlan, D. R. C., & St. George-Hyslop, P. H. (1992). Molecular and prospective phenotypic characterization of a pedigree with familial Alzheimer's disease and a missense mutuation in codon 717 of the B-amyloid precursor protein gene. *Neurology, 42,* 1445–1453.

55. Liberman, R. P., & Green, M. F. (1992). Whither cognitive-behavioral therapy for schizophrenia? *Schizophrenia Bulletin, 18,* 27–35.

56. Northam, E., Bowden, S., Anderson, V., & Court, J. (1992). Neuropsychological functioning in adolescents with diabetes. *Journal of Clinical and Experimental Neuropsychology, 14,* 881-900.

57. Peterson, J. B., Finn, P. R., & Pihl, R. O. (1992). Cognitive dysfunction and the inherited predisposition to alcoholism. *Journal of Studies on Alcoholism, 53,* 154–160.

58. Sweeney, J. A., Haas, G. L., & Li, S. (1992). Neuropsychological and eye movement abnormalities in first-episode and chronic schizophrenia. *Schizophrenia Bulletin, 18,* 283–293.

59. Swirsky-Sacchetti, T., Mitchell, D. R., Seward, J., Gonzales, C., Lublin, F., Knobler, R., & Field, H. L. (1992). Neuropsychological and structural brain lesions in multiple sclerosis: A regional analysis. *Neurology, 42,* 1291–1295.

60. Vilkki, J. (1992). Cognitive flexibility and mental programming after closed head injuries and anterior or posterior cerebral excisions. *Neuropsychologia, 30,* 807-814.

61. Wolkin, A., Sanfilipo, M., Wolf, A. D., Angrist, B., Brodie, J. D., & Rotrosen, J. (1992). Negative symptoms and hypofrontality in chronic schizophrenia. *Archives of General Psychiatry, 49,* 959-965.

62. Arbuckle, T. Y., & Gold, D. P. (1993). Aging, inhibition, and verbosity. *Journal of Gerontology, 48,* 225–232.

63. Barba, G. D. (1993). Different patterns of confabulation. *Cortex, 29,* 567-581.

64. Beatty, W. W. (1993). Age differences on the California Card Sorting Test: Implications for the assessment of problem solving by the elderly. *Bulletin of the Psychonomic Society, 31,* 511–514.

65. Beatty, W. W., Jocic, Z., Monson, N., & Staton, R. D. (1993). Memory and frontal lobe dysfunction in schizophrenia and schizoaffective disorder. *The Journal of Nervous and Mental Disease, 181,* 448-453.

66. Beatty, W. W., Katzung, V. M., Nixon, S. J., & Moreland, V. J. (1993). Problem-solving deficits in alcoholics: Evidence from California Card Sorting Test. *Journal of Studies on Alcohol, 54,* 687–692.

67. Cooper, J. A., & Sagar, H. J. (1993). Incidental and intentional recall in Parkinson's disease: An account based on diminished attentional resources. *Journal of Clinical and Experimental Neuropsychology, 15,* 713-731.

68. Cooper, J. A., Sagar, H. J., & Sullivan, E. V. (1993). Short-term memory and temporal ordering in early Parkinson's disease: Effects of disease chronicity and medication. *Neuropsychologia, 31,* 933-949.

69. Corcoran, R., & Thompson, P. (1993). Epilepsy and poor memory: Who complains and what do they mean? *British Journal of Clinical Psychology, 32,* 199-208.

70. Crockett, D. J. (1993). Cross-validation of WAIS-R prototypical patterns of intellectual functioning using neuropsychological test scores. *Journal of Clinical and Experimental Neuropsychology, 15,* 903-920.

71. DeLuca, J. (1993). Predicting neurobehavioral patterns following anterior communicating artery aneurysm. *Cortex, 29,* 639-647.

72. Deweer, B., Pillon, B., Michon, A., & Dubois, B. (1993). Mirror reading in Alzheimer's disease: Normal skill learning and acquisition of item-specific information. *Journal of Clinical and Experimental Neuropsychology, 15,* 789-804.

73. Eslinger, P. J., & Grattan, L. M. (1993). Frontal lobe and frontal-striatal substrates for different forms of human cognitive flexibility. *Neuropsychologia, 31,* 17-28.

74. Goldberg, T. E., Hyde, T. M., Kleinman, J. E., & Weinberger, D. R. (1993). Course of schizophrenia: Neuropsychological evidence for a static encephalopathy. *Schizophrenia Bulletin, 19,* 797–804.

75. Gooding, P. A., van Eijk, R., Mayes, A. R., & Meudell, P. (1993). Preserved pattern completion priming for novel, abstract geometric shapes in amnesics of several aetiologies. *Neuropsychologia, 31,* 789-810.

76. Harvey, P. D., Mohs, R. C., & Davidson, M. (1993). Leukotomy and aging in chronic schizophrenia: A followup study 40 years after psychosurgery. *Schizophrenia Bulletin, 19,* 723–732.

77. Lawson, A. E. (1993). Deductive reasoning, brain maturation, and science concept acquisition: Are they linked? *Journal of Research in Science Teaching, 30,* 1029-1051.

78. Markowitsch, H. J., Calabrese, P., Haupts, M., Durwen, H. F. Liess, J., & Gehlen, W. (1993). Searching for the anatomical basis of retrograde amnesia. *Journal of Clinical and Experimental Neuropsychology, 15,* 947-967.

79. Markowitsch, H. J., von Cramon, D. Y., & Schuri, U. (1993). Mnestic performance profile of a bilateral diencephalic infarct patient with preserved intelligence and severe amnesic disturbances. *Journal of Clinical and Experimental Neuropsychology, 15,* 627-632.

80. Mayes, A. R., Downes, J. J., Shoqeirat, M., Hall, C., & Sagar, H. J. (1993). Encoding ability is preserved in amnesia: Evidence from a direct test of encoding. *Neuropsychologia, 31,* 745-759.

81. McBurnett, K., Harris, S. M., Swanson, J. M., Pfiffner, L. J., Tamm, L., & Freeland, D. (1993). Neuropsychological and psychophysiological differentiation of inattention/overactivity and aggression/defiance symptom groups. *Journal of Clinical Child Psychology, 22,* 165-171.

82. Ozonoff, S., Rogers, S. J., Farnham, J. M., & Pennington, B. F. (1993). Can standard measures identify subclinical markers of autism? *Journal of Autism and Developmental Disorders, 23*(3), 429-441.

83. Penn, D. L., Van Der Does, A. J. W., Spaulding, W. D., Garbin, C. D., Linszen, D., & Dingemans, P. (1993). Information processing and social cognitive problem solving in schizophrenia. *The Journal of Nervous and Mental Disease, 181,* 13-20.

84. Perrine, K. (1993). Differential aspects of conceptual processing in the Category Test and Wisconsin Card Sorting Test. *Journal of Clinical and Experimental Neuropsychology, 15,* 461-473.

85. Rothlind, J. C., Bylsma, F. W., Peyser, C., Folstein, S. E., & Brandt, J. (1993). Cognitive and motor correlates of everyday functioning in early Huntington's disease. *The Journal of Nervous and Mental Disease, 181,* 194-199.

86. Roxborough, H., Muir, W. J., Blackwood, D. H. R., Walker, M. T., & Blackburn, I. M. (1993). Neuropsychological and P300 abnormalities in schizophrenics and their relatives. *Psychological Medicine, 23,* 305-314.

87. Rugle, L., & Melamed, L. (1993). Neuropsychological assessment of attention problems in pathological gamblers. *The Journal of Nervous and Mental Disease, 181,* 107-112.

88. Schmidt, R., Fazekas, F., Offenbacher, H., Dusek, T., Zach, E., Reinhart, B., Grieshofer, P., Freidl, W., Eber, B., Schumacher, M., Koch, M., & Lechner, H. (1993). Neuropsychologic correlates of MRI white matter hyperintensities: A study of 150 normal volunteers. *Neurology, 43,* 2490–2494.

89. Schwab, K., Grafman, J., Salazar, A. M., & Kraft, J. (1993). Residual impairments and work status 15 years after penetrating head injury: Report from the Vietnam Head Injury Study. *Neurology, 43,* 95–103.

90. Strauss, E., & Hunter, M. (1993). Wisconsin Card Sorting performance: Effects of age of onset of damage and laterality of dysfunction. *Journal of Clinical and Experimental Neuropsychology, 15,* 896-902.

91. Vallar, G., & Papagno, C. (1993). Preserved vocabulary acquisition in Down's syndrome: The role of phonological short-term memory. *Cortex, 29,* 467-483.

92. van den Broek, M. D., Bradshaw, C. M., & Szabadi, E. (1993). Utility of the modified Wisconsin Card Sorting Test in neuropsychological assessment. *British Journal of Clinical Psychology, 32,* 333-343.

93. van der Does, A. J. W., Dingemans, P. M. A. J., Linszen, D. H., Nugter, M. A., & Scholte, W. F. (1993). Symptom dimensions and cognitive and social functioning in recent-onset schizophrenia. *Psychological Medicine, 23,* 745-753.

94. Verin, M., Partiot, A., Pillon, B., Malapani, C., Agid, Y., & DuBois, B. (1993). Delayed response tasks and prefrontal lesions in main-evidence for self generated patterns of behaviour with poor environmental modulation. *Neuropsychologia, 31,* 1379-1396.

95. Weinrich, M., McCall, D., Shoosmith, L., Thomas, K., Katzenberger, K., & Weber, C. (1993). Locative prepositional phrases in severe aphasia. *Brain and Language, 45,* 21–45.

96. Arbuckle, T. Y., Chaikelson, J. S., & Gold, D. P. (1994). Social drinking and cognitive functioning revisited: The role of intellectual endowment and psychological distress. *Journal of Studies on Alcohol, 55,* 352–361.

97. Arnett, P. A., Rao, S. M., Bernardin, L., Grafman, J., Yetkin, F. Z., & Lobeck, L. (1994). Relationship between frontal lobe lesions and Wisconsin Card Sorting Test performance in patients with multiple sclerosis. *Neurology, 44,* 420–425.

98. Asarnow, R. F., Asamen, J., Granholm, E., Sherman, T., Watkins, J. M., & Williams, M. E. (1994). Cognitive/neuropsychological studies of children with a schizophrenic disorder. *Schizophrenia Bulletin, 20,* 647–669.

99. Baddeley, A., & Wilson, B. A. (1994). When implicit learning fails: Amnesia and the problem of error elimination. *Neuropsychologia, 32,* 53–68.

100. Beatty, W. W., & Monson, N. (1994). Picture and motor sequencing in multiple sclerosis. *Journal of Clinical and Experimental Neuropsychology, 16,* 165-172.

101. Bellack, A. S., & Mueser, K. T. (1994). Psychosocial treamtent for schizophrenia. *Schizophrenia Bulletin, 19,* 317–336.

102. Blanchard, J. J., Kring, A. M., & Neale, J. M. (1994). Flat affect in schizophrenia: A test of neuropsychological models. *Schizophrenia Bulletin, 20,* 311–325.

103. Blanchard, J. L., & Neale, J. M. (1994). The neuropsychological signature of schizophrenia: Generalized or differential deficit? *American Journal of Psychiatry, 151,* 40-48.

104. Braff, D. L. (1994). Information processing and attention dysfunctions in schizophrenia. *Schizophrenia Bulletin, 19,* 233–259.

105. Buchanan, R. W., Strauss, M. E., Kirkpatrick, B., Holstein, C., Breier, A., & Carpenter, W. T., Jr. (1994). Neuropsychological impairments in deficit vs. nondeficit forms of schizophrenia. *Archives of General Psychiatry, 51,* 804-811.

106. Burgess, A. P., Riccio, M., Jadresic, D., Pugh, K., Catalan, J., Hawkins, D. A., Baldeweg, T., Lovett, E., Gruzelier, J., & Thompson, C. (1994). A longitudinal study of the neuropsychiatric consequences of HIV-1 infection in gay men. I. Neuropsychological performance and neurological status at baseline and at 12-month follow-up. *Psychological Medicine, 24,* 885-895.

107. Calabrese, P., Fink, G. R., Markowitsch, H. J., Kessler, J., Durwen, H. F., Liess, J., Haupts, M., & Gehlen, W. (1994). Left hemisphere neuronal heterotopia: A PET, MRI, EEG, and neuropsychological investigation of a university student. *Neurology, 44,* 302–305.

108. Cohen, J. D., & Servan-Schreiber, D. (1994). Schizophrenic deficits: Neuroleptics and the prefrontal cortex-A reply. *Schizophrenia Bulletin, 20,* 417–421.

109. Convit, A., Volavka, J., Czobor, P., DeAsis, J., & Evangelista, C. (1994). Effect of subtle neurological dysfunction on response to haloperidol treatment in schizophrenia. *American Journal of Psychiatry, 151,* 49-56.

110. Corrigan, P. W., Wallace, C. J., Schade, M. L., & Green, M. F. (1994). Learning medication self-management skills in schizophrenia: Relationships with cognitive deficits and psychiatric symptoms. *Behavior Therapy, 25,* 5–15.

111. Cuesta, M. J., & Peralta, V. (1994). Lack of insight in schizophrenia. *Schizophrenia Bulletin, 20,* 359–366.

112. Damos, D. L., & Parker, E. S. (1994). High false alarm rates on a vigilance task may indicate recreational drug use. *Journal of Clinical and Experimental Neuropsychology, 16,* 713-722.

113. Daniele, A., Giustolisi, L., Silveri, M. C., Colosimo, L., & Gainotti, G. (1994). Evidence for a possible neuroanatomical basis for lexical processing of nouns and verbs. *Neuropsychologia, 32,* 1325–1341.

114. Dywan, J., Segalowitz, S. J., & Williamson, L. (1994). Source monitoring during name recognition in older adults: Psychometric and electrophysiological correlates. *Psychology and Aging, 9,* 568-577.

115. Farlow, M., Murrell, J., Ghetti, B., Unverzagt, F., Zeldenrust, S., & Benson, M. (1994). Clinical characteristics in a kindred with early-onset Alzheimer's disease and their linkage to a G->T change at position 2149 of the amyloid percursor protein gene. *Neurology, 44,* 105–111.

116. Gold, J. M., Hermann, B. P., Randolph, C., Wyler, A. R., Goldberg, T. E., & Weinberger, D. R. (1994). Schizophrenia and temporal lobe epilepsy: A neuropsychological analysis. *Archives of General Psychiatry, 51,* 265-272.

117. Gottschalk, L. A. (1994). The development, validation, and applications of a computerized measurement of cognitive impairment from the content analysis of verbal behavior. *Journal of Clinical Psychology, 50,* 349-361.

118. Grossi, D., Becker, J. T., & Trojano, L. (1994). Visuospatial imagery in Alzheimer disease. *Perceptual and Motor Skills, 78,* 867-874.

119. Gur, R. E., & Pearlson, G. D. (1994). Neuroimaging in schizophrenia research. *Schizophrenia Bulletin, 19,* 337–353.

120. Heaton, R., Paulsen, J. S., McAdams, L. A., Kuck, J., Zisook, S., Braff, D., Hams, J., & Jeste, D. V. (1994). Neuropsychological deficits in schizophrenics: Relationships to age, chronicity, and dementia. *Archives of General Psychiatry, 51,* 469-476.

121. Hunkin, N. M., Parkin, A. J., & Longmore, B. E. (1994). Aetiological variation in the amnesic syndrome: Comparisons using the list discrimination task. *Neuropsychologia, 32,* 819–825.

122. Hyde, T. M., Nawroz, S., Goldberg, T. E., Bigelow, L. B., Strong, D., Ostrem, J. L., Weinberger, D. R., & Kleinman, J. E. (1994). Is there cognitive decline in schizophrenia? A cross-sectional study. *British Journal of Psychiatry, 164,* 494-500.

123. Kish, S. J., El-Awar, M., Stuss, D., Nobrega, J., Currier, R., Aita, J. F., Schut, L., Zoghbi, H. Y., & Freedman, M. (1994). Neuropsychological test performance in patients with dominantly inherited spinocerebellar ataxia: Relationship to ataxis severity. *Neurology, 44,* 1738–1746.

124. Kramer, A. F., Humphrey, D. G., Larish, J. F., Logan, G. D., & Strayer, D. L. (1994). Aging and inhibition: Beyond a unitary view of inhibitory processing in attention. *Psychology and Aging, 9,* 491-512.

125. Kremen, W. S., Seidman, L. J., Pepple, J. R., Lyons, M. J., Tsuang, M. T., & Faraone, S. V. (1994). Neuropsychological risk indicators for schizophrenia: A review of family studies. *Schizophrenia Bulletin, 20,* 103–119.

126. Krystal, J. H., Karper, L. P., Seibyl, J. P., Freeman, G. K., Delaney, R., Bremner, J. D., Heninger, G. R., Bowers, M. B., Jr., & Charney, D. S. (1994). Subanesthetic effects of the noncompetitive NMDA antagonist, ketamine, in humans: Psychotomimetic, perceptual, cognitive, and neuroendocrine responses. *Archives of General Psychiatry, 51,* 199-214.

127. Lenzenweger, M. F., & Korfine, L. (1994). Perceptual aberrations, schizotypy, and the Wisconsin Card Sorting Test. *Schizophrenia Bulletin, 20,* 345–357.

128. Lysaker, P., & Bell, M. (1994). Insight and cognitive impairment in schizophrenia. *The Journal of Nervous and Mental Disease, 182,* 656–660.

129. Lysaker, P., Bell, M., Milstein, R., Bryson, G., & Beam-Goulet, J. (1994). Insight and psychosocial treatment compliance in schizophrenia. *Psychiatry, 57,* 307-315.

130. Malapani, C., Pillon, B., Dubois, B., & Agid, Y. (1994). Impaired simultaneous cognitive task performance in Parkinson's disease: A dopamine-related dysfunction. *Neurology, 44,* 319-326.

131. Mayes, A. R., Downes, J. J., Symons, V., & Shoqeirat, M. (1994). Do amnesics forget faces pathologically fast? *Cortex, 30,* 543-563.

132. Meadows, M.-E., Kaplan, R. F., & Bromfield, E. B. (1994). Cognitive recovery with vitamin B12 therapy: A longitudinal neuropsychological assessment. *Neurology, 44,* 1764–1765.

133. Mega, M. S., & Alexander, M. P. (1994). Subcortical aphasia: The core profile of capsulostriatal infarction. *Neurology, 44,* 1824–1829.

134. Metz, J. T., Johnson, M. D., Pliskin, N. H., & Luchins, D. J. (1994). Maintenance of training effects on the Wisconsin Card Sorting Test by patients with schizophrenia or affective disorders. *American Journal of Psychiatry, 151,* 120-122.

135. Meudell, P. R., Mayes, A. R., & MacDonald, C. (1994). Dual task performance in amnesic and normal people: Does resource depletion cause amnesia? *Cortex, 30,* 159-166.

136. O'Donnell, J. P., Macgregor, L. A., Dabrowski, J. J., Oestreicher, J. M., & Romero, J. J. (1994). Construct validity of neuropsychological tests of conceptual and attentional abilities. *Journal of Clinical Psychology, 50,* 596-600.

137. Ozonoff, S., & McEvoy, R. E. (1994). A longitudinal study of executive function and theory of mind development in autism. *Development and Psychopathology, 6,* 415-431.

138. Palmer, B. W., Boone, K. B., Chang, L., Lee, A., & Black, S. (1994). Cognitive deficits and personality patterns in maternally versus paternally inherited myotonic dystrophy. *Journal of Clinical and Experimental Neuropsychology, 16,* 784-795.

139. Parkin, A. J., & Lawrence, A. (1994). A dissociation in the relation between memory tasks and frontal lobe tests in the normal elderly. *Neuropsychologia, 32,* 1523–1532.

140. Parkin, A. J., Rees, J. E., Hunkin, N. M., & Rose, P. E. (1994). Impairment of memory following discrete thalamic infarction. *Neuropsychologia, 32,* 39–51.

141. Pettegrew, J. W., Keshavan, M. S., & Minshew, N. J. (1994). 31P nuclear magnetic resonance spectroscopy: Neurodevelopment and schizophrenia. *Schizophrenia Bulletin, 20,* 35–53.

142. Pillon, B., Deweer, B., Michon, A., Malapani, C., Agid, Y., & Dubois, B. (1994). Are explicit memory disorders of progressive supranuclear palsy related to damage to striatofrontal circuits? Comparison with Alzheimer's, Parkinson's, and Huntington's disease. *Neurology, 44,* 1264–1270.

143. Podraza, A. M., Bornstein, R. A., Whitacre, C. C., Para, M. F., Fass, R. J., Rice, R. R., & Nasrallah, H. A. (1994). Neuropsychological performance and CD4 levels in HIV-1 asymptomatic infection. *Journal of Clinical and Experimental Neuropsychology, 16,* 777-783.

144. Pogge, D. L., Stokes, J. M., & Harvey, P. D. (1994). Empirical evaluation of the factorial structure of attention in adolescent psychiatric patients. *Journal of Clinical and Experimental Neuropsychology, 16,* 344-353.

145. Rapczak, S. Z., Polster, M. R., Comer, J. F., & Rubens, A. B. (1994). False recognition and misidentification of faces following right hemisphere damage. *Cortex, 30,* 565-583.

146. Robertson, I. H., & North, N. T. (1994). One hand is better than two: Motor extinction of left hand advantage in unilateral neglect. *Neuropsychologia, 32,* 1–11.

147. Rochon, E., & Waters, G. S. (1994). Sentence comprehension in patients with Alzheimer's disease. *Brain and Language, 46,* 329–349.

148. Serper, M. R., & Harvey, P. D. (1994). The need to integrate neuropsychological and experimental schizophrenia research. *Schizophrenia Bulletin, 20,* 1–11.

149. Shaw, C., & Aggleton, J. P. (1994). The ability of amnesic subjects to estimate time intervals. *Neuropsychologia, 32,* 857–873.

150. Sobell, L. C., Toneatto, T., & Sobell, M. (1994). Behavioral assessment and treatment planning for alcohol, tobacco, and other drug problems: Current status with an emphasis on clinical applications. *Behavior Therapy, 25,* 533–580.

151. Spencer, W. D., & Raz, N. (1994). Memory for facts, source, and context: Can frontal lobe dysfunction explain age-related differences? *Psychology and Aging, 9,* 149-159.

152. Stratta, P., Mancini, F., Mattei, P., Casacchia, M., & Rossi, A. (1994). Information processing strategy to remediate Wisconsin Card Sorting Test performance in schizophrenia: A pilot study. *American Journal of Psychiatry, 151,* 915-918.

153. Strauss, M. E. (1994). Relations of symptoms to cognitive deficits in schizophrenia. *Schizophrenia Bulletin, 19,* 215- 231.

154. Strauss, M. E., & Summerfelt, A. (1994). Response to Serper and Harvey. *Schizophrenia Bulletin, 20,* 13–21.

155. VanderPloeg, R. D., Schinka, J. A., & Retzlaff, P. (1994). Relationships between measures of auditory verbal learning and executive functioning. *Journal of Clinical and Experimental Neuropsychology, 16,* 243-252.

156. Weddell, R. A. (1994). Effects of subcortical lesion site on human emotional behavior. *Brain and Cognition, 25,* 161-193.

157. Yeates, K. O., & Mortensen, M. E. (1994). Acute and chronic neuropsychological consequences of mercury vapor poisoning in two early adolescents. *Journal of Clinical and Experimental Neuropsychology, 16,* 209-222.

158. Zesiger, P., Pegna, A., & Rilliet, B. (1994). Unilateral dysgraphia of the dominant hand in a left-hander: A disruption of graphic motor pattern selection. *Cortex, 30,* 673-683.

159. Abbruzzese, M., Bellodi, L., Ferri, S., & Scarone, S. (1995). Frontal lobe dysfunction in schizophrenia and obsessive-compulsive disorder. A neuropsychlogical study. *Brain and Cognition, 27,* 202-212.

160. Anderson, C. V., Bigler, E. D., & Blatter, D. D. (1995). Frontal lobe lesions, diffuse damage, and neuropsychological functioning in traumatic brain injured patients. *Journal of Clinical and Experimental Neuropsychology, 17,* 900–908.

161. Beatty, W. W., Paul, R. H., Wilbanks, S. L., Hames, K. A., Blanco, C. R., & Goodkin, D. E. (1995). Identifying multiple sclerosis patients with mild or global cognitive impairment using the Screening Examination for Cognitive Impairment (SEFCI). *Neurology, 45,* 718–723.

162. Berman, K. F., Ostrem, J. L., Randolph, C., Gold, J., Goldberg, T. E., Copola, R., Carson, R. E., Herscovitch, P., & Weinberger, D. R. (1995). Physiological activation of a critical network during performance of the Wisconsin Card Sorting Test: A positron emission tomography study. *Neuropsychologia, 33,* 1027–1046.

163. Binetti, G., Magni, E., Padovani, A., Coppan, S. F., Bianchetti, A., & Trabucchi, M. (1995). Release from proactive interference in early Alzheimer's disease. *Neuropsychologia, 33,* 379–384.

164. Blake, P. Y., Pincus, J. H., & Buckner, C. (1995). Neurologic abnormalities in murderers. *Neurology, 45,* 1641–1647.

165. Brandt, J., Bylsma, F. W., Aylward, E. H., Rothlind, J., & Gow, C. A. (1995). Impaired source memory in Huntington's Disease and its relation to basil ganglia atrophy. *Journal of Clinical and Experimental Neuropsychology, 17,* 868–877.

166. Britton, J. W., Vitti, R. J., Ahlskog, J. E., Robinson, R. G., Kremor, B., & Hayden, M. R. (1995). Hereditary late-onset chorea without significant dementia: Genetic evidence for substantial phenotypic variation in Huntington's disease. *Neurology, 45,* 443–447.

167. Caselli, R. J., Smith, B. E., & Osborne, D. (1995). Primary lateral sclerosis: A neuropsychological study. *Neurology, 45,* 2005–2009.

168. Ciesielski, K. T., Waldorf, A. V., & Jung, R. E. (1995). Anterior brain deficits in chronic alcoholism: Cause and effect? *The Journal of Nervous and Mental Disease, 183,* 756–761.

169. Cockburn, J. (1995). Task interruption in prospective memory: A frontal lobe function? *Cortex, 31,* 87-97.

170. Crawford, T. J., Haeger, B., Kennard, C., Reveley, M. A., & Henderson, L. (1995). Saccadic abnormalities in psychotic patients. I. Neuroleptic-free psychotic patients. *Psychological Medicine, 25,* 461–471.

171. Crawford, T. J., Haegger, B., Kennard, C., Reveley, M. A., & Henderson, L. (1995). Saccadic abnormalities in psychotic patients. II. The role of neuroleptic treatment. *Psychological Medicine, 25,* 473–483.

172. Cuesta, M. J., Peralta, V., Caro, F., & de Leon, J. (1995). Is poor insight in psychotic disorders associated with poor performance on the Wisconsin Card Sorting Test? *American Journal of Psychiatry, 152,* 1380–1382.

173. DeRenzi, E., & di Pellegrino, G. (1995). Sparing of verbs and preserved, but ineffectual reading in a patient with impaired word production. *Cortex, 31,* 619–636.

174. Dominey, P., Decety, J., Broussolle, E., Chazot, G., & Jeannerod, M. (1995). Motor imagery of a lateralized sequential task is asymmetrically slowed in hemi-Parkinson's patients. *Neuropsychologia, 33,* 727–741.

175. Eckhardt, M. J., Stapleton, J. M., Rawlings, R. R., Davis, E. Z., & Grodin, D. M. (1995). Neuropsychological functioning in detoxified alcoholics between 18 and 35 years of age. *American Journal of Psychiatry, 152,* 53-59.

176. Faraone, S. V., Seidman, L. J., Kremen, W. S., Pepple, J. R., Lyons, M. J., & Tsuang, M. T. (1995). Neuropsychological functioning among the nonpsychotic relatives of schizophrenic patients: A diagnostic efficiency analysis. *Journal of Abnormal Psychology, 104,* 286-304.

177. Feldman, J., Kerr, B., & Streissguth, A. D. (1995). Correlational analyses of procedural and declarative learning performance. *Intelligence, 20,* 87-114.

178. Fischer, R. S., Alexander, M. P., D'esposito, M., & Otto, R. (1995). Neuropsychological and neuroanatomical correlates of confabulation. *Journal of Clinical and Experimental Neuropsychology, 17,* 20-28.

179. Gershberg, F. B., & Shimamura, A. P. (1995). Impaired use of organizational strategies in free recall following frontal lobe damage. *Neuropsychologia, 33,* 1305–1333.

180. Gershuny, B. S., & Sher, K. J. (1995). Compulsive checking and anxiety in a nonclinical sample: Differences in cognition, behavior, personality and affect. *Journal of Psychopathology and Behavioral Assessment, 17,* 19–38.

181. Gold, D. P., & Arbuckle, T. Y. (1995). A longitudinal study of off-target verbosity. *Journal of Gerontology, 50,* 307–315.

182. Gold, M., Adair, J. C., Jacobs, D. H., & Heilman, K. M. (1995). Right-left confusion in Gerstmann's Syndrome: A model of body centered spatial orientation. *Cortex, 31,* 267-283.

183. Habib, M., Daquin, G., Milandre, L., Rogere, M. L., Rey, M., Lanteri, A., Salamon, G., & Khalil, R. (1995). Mutism and auditory agnosia due to bilateral insular damage-role of the insula in human communication. *Neuropsychologia, 33,* 327–339.

184. Harden, P. W., & Pihl, R. O. (1995). Cognitive function, cardiovascular reactivity, and behavior in boys at high risk for alcoholism. *Journal of Abnormal Psychology,* 104, 94-103.

185. Hermann, B., & Seidenberg, M. (1995). Executive system dysfunction in temporal lobe epilepsy: Effects of nociferous cortex versus hippocampal pathology. *Journal of Clinical and Experimental Neuropsychology, 17,* 809–819.

186. Holdstock, J. S., Shaw, C., & Aggleton, J. P. (1995). The performance of amnesic subjects on tests of delayed matching-to-sample and delayed matching-to-position. *Neuropsychologia, 33,* 1583–1596.

187. Hopkins, R. O., Kesner, R. P., & Goldstein, M. (1995). Item and order recognition memory in subjects with hypoxic brain injury. *Brain and Cognition, 27,* 180-201.

188. Hunkin, N. M., & Parkin, A. J. (1995). The method of vanishing cues: An evaluation of its effectiveness in teaching memory-impaired individuals. *Neuropsychologia, 33,* 1255–1279.

189. Hunkin, N. M., Parkin, A. J., Bradley, V. A., Burrows, E. H., Aldrich, F. K., Jonsari, A., & Burdon-Cooper, C. (1995). Focal retrograde amnesia following closed head injury: A case study and theoretical account. *Neuropsychologia, 33,* 509–525.

190. Jeste, D. V., Harris, M. J., Krull, A., Kuck, J., McAdams, L. A., & Heaton, R. (1995). Clinical and neuropsychological characteristics of patients with late-onset schizophrenia. *American Journal of Psychiatry, 152,* 722-730.

191. Kosslyn, S. M., Hamilton, S. E., & Bernstein, J. H. (1995). The perception of curvature can be selectively disrupted by prosopagnosia. *Brain and Cognition, 27,* 36-58.

192. Lapierre, D., Braun, C. M. J., & Hodgins, S. (1995). Ventral frontal deficits in psychopathy: Neuropsychological test findings. *Neuropsychologia, 33,* 139–151.

193. Levine, B., Stuss, D. T., & Milberg, W. P. (1995). Concept generation: Validation of a test of executive functioning in a normal aging population. *Journal of Clinical and Experimental Neuropsychology, 17,* 740–758.

194. Lysaker, P., & Bell, M. (1995). Work rehabilitation and improvements in insight in schizophrenia. *The Journal of Nervous and Mental Disease, 183,* 103-106.

195. Lysaker, P. H., Bell, M. D., & Bioty, S. M. (1995). Cognitive deficits in schizophrenia: Prediction of symptom change for participators in work rehabilitation. *The Journal of Nervous and Mental Disease, 183,* 332–336.

196. Lysaker, P. H., Bell, M. D., Zito, W. S., & Bioty, S. M. (1995). Social skills at work: Deficits and predictors of improvement in schizophrenia. *The Journal of Nervous and Mental Disease, 183,* 688–697.

197. Migliorelli, R., Petracca, G., Tesón, A., Sabe, L., Leiguarda, R., & Starkstein, S. E. (1995). Neuropsychiatric and neuropsychological correlates of delusions in Alzheimer's Disease. *Psychological Medicine, 25,* 505–513.

198. Migliorelli, R., Tesón, A., Sabe, L., Petracchi, M., Leiguarda, R., & Starkstein, S. E. (1995). Prevalence and correlates of dysthymia and major depression among patients with Alzheimer's Disease. *American Journal of Psychiatry, 152,* 37-44.

199. Mirsky, A. F. (1995). Perils and pitfalls of the path to normal potential: The role of impaired attention. Homage to Herbert G. Birch. *Journal of Clinical and Experimental Neuropsychology, 17,* 481–498.

200. Papagno, C., & Marsile, C. (1995). Transient left-sided alien hand with callosal and unilateral fronto-mesial damage: A case study. *Neuropsychologia, 33,* 1703–1709.

201. Park, S., Holzman, P. S., & Lenzenweger, M. F. (1995). Individual differences in spatial working memory in relation to schizotypy. *Journal of Abnormal Psychology, 104,* 355-363.

202. Paulsen, J. S., Salmon, D. P., Monsch, A. U., Butters, N., Swenson, M. R., & Bondi, M. W. (1995). Discrimination of cortical from subcortical dementias on the basis of memory and problem-solving tests. *Journal of Clinical Psychology, 51,* 48-58.

203. Peyser, C. E., Folstein, M., Chase, G. A., Starkstein, S., Brandt, J., Cockrell, J. R., Bylsma, F., Coyle, J. T., McHugh, P. R., & Folstein, S. E. (1995). Trial of d-2-Tocopherol in Huntington's disease. *American Journal of Psychiatry, 152,* 1771–1775.

204. Ragland, J. D., Gur, R. C., Deutsch, G. K., Censits, D. M., & Gur, R. E. (1995). Reliability and construct validity of the Paired-Associate Recognition Test: A test of declarative memory using Wisconsin Card Sorting stimuli. *Psychological Assessment, 7,* 25-32.

205. Shaw, C., & Aggleton, J. P. (1995). Evidence for the independence of recognition and recency memory in amnesic subjects. *Cortex, 31,* 57-71.

206. Sherman, E. M. S., Strauss, E. S., Spellacy, F., & Hunter, M. (1995). Construct validity of WAIS-R factors: Neuropsychological test correlates in adults referred for evaluation of possible head injury. *Psychological Assessment, 7,* 440–444.

207. Sirigu, A., Zalla, T., Pillon, B., Grafman, J., Agid, Y., & Dubois, B. (1995). Selective impairments in managerial knowledge following pre-frontal cortex damage. *Cortex, 31,* 301-316.

208. Tarter, R. E., Switalz, J., Lu, S., & Van Thiel, D. (1995). Abstracting capacity in cirrhotic alcoholics: Negative findings. *Journal of Studies on Alcohol, 56,* 99–103.

209. Tisdwell, P., Dias, P. S., Sagar, H. J., Mayes, A. R., & Battersby, R. D. E. (1995). Cognitive outcome after aneurysm rupture: Relationship to aneurysm site and perioperative complications. *Neurology, 45,* 875–882.

210. Upton, D., & Corcoran, R. (1995). The role of the right temporal lobe in card sorting: A case study. *Cortex, 31,* 405-409.

211. van Spaendonck, K. P. M., Berger, H. J. C., Horstink, M. W. I. M., Borm, G. F., & Cools, A. R. (1995). Card sorting performance in Parkinson's Disease: A comparison between acquisition and shifting performance. *Journal of Clinical and Experimental Neuropsychology, 17,* 918–925.

212. Weyandt, L. L., Linterman, I., & Rice, J. A. (1995). Reported prevalence of attentional difficulties in a general sample of college students. *Journal of Psychopathology and Behavioral Assessment, 17,* 293–304.

213. Alexander, M. P., & Annett, M. (1996). Crossed aphasia and related anomalies of cerebral organization: Case reports and a genetic hypothesis. *Brain and Language, 55,* 213–239.

214. Arnett, P. A., Rao, S. M., Hussain, M., Swanson, S. J., & Hammeke, T. A. (1996). Conduction aphasia in multiple sclerosis: A case report with MRI findings. *Neurology, 47,* 576–578.

215. Axelrod, B. N., Goldman, R. S., Heaton, R. K., Curtiss, G., Thompson, L. L., Chelune, G. J., & Kay, G. G. (1996). Discriminability of the Wisconsin Card Sorting Test using the standardization sample. *Journal of Clinical and Experimental Neuropsychology, 18,* 338–342.

216. Barrett, D. H., Green, M. L., Morris, R., Giles, W. H., & Croft, J. B. (1996). Cognitive functioning and post-traumatic stress disorder. *American Journal of Psychiatry, 153,* 1492–1494.

217. Bennetto, L., Pennington, B. F., & Rogers, S. J. (1996). Infant and impaired memory functions in autism. *Child Development, 67,* 1816–1835.

218. Channon, S. (1996). Executive dysfunction in depression: The Wisconsin Card Sorting Test. *Journal of Affective Disorders, 39,* 107–114.

219. Cockburn, J. (1996). Failure of prospective memory after acquired brain damage: Preliminary investigation and suggestions for future directions. *Journal of Clinical and Experimental Neuropsychology, 18,* 304–309.

220. Crouch, J. A., Greve, K. W., & Brooks, J. (1996). The California Card Sorting Test dissociate verbal and non-verbal concept formation abilities. *British Journal of Clinical Psychology, 35,* 431–434.

221. Crowe, S. F. (1996). The performance of schizophrenic and depressed subjects on tests of fluency: Support for a compromise in dorsolateral prefrontal functioning. *Australian Psychologist, 31,* 204–209.

222. Daniel, D. G., Goldberg, T. E., Weinberger, D. R., Kleinman, J. E., Pickar, D., Lubick, L. J., & Williams, T. S. (1996). Different side effect profiles of risperidone and clozapine in 20 outpatients with schizophrenia or schizoaffective disorder: A pilot study. *American Journal of Psychiatry, 153,* 417–419.

223. Deckel, A. W., Hesselbrock, V., & Bauer, L. (1996). Antisocial personality disorder, childhood delinquency, and frontal brain functioning: EEG and neuropsychological findings. *Journal of Clinical Psychology, 52,* 639–650.

224. Dimitrov, M., Grafman, J., & Hollnagel, C. (1996). The effects of frontal lobe damage on everyday problem solving. *Cortex, 32,* 357–366.

225. Flashman, L. A., Flaum, M., Gupta, S., & Andreasen, N. C. (1996). Soft signs and neuropsychological performance in schizophrenia. *American Journal of Psychiatry, 153,* 526–532.

226. Gansler, D. A., Covall, S., McGrath, N., & Oscar-Berman, M. (1996). Measures of prefrontal dysfunction after closed head injury. *Brain and Cognition, 30,* 194–204.

227. Giovagnoli, A. R., & Avanzini, G. (1996). Forgetting rate and interference effects on a verbal memory distractor task in patients with temporal lobe epilepsy. *Journal of Clinical and Experimental Neuropsychology, 18,* 259–264.

228. Horner, M. D., Flashman, L. A., Freides, D., Epstein, C. M., & Bakay, R. A. E. (1996). Temporal lobe epilepsy and performance on the Wisconsin Card Sorting Test. *Journal of Clinical and Experimental Neuropsychology, 18,* 310–313.

229. John, S., & Ovsiew, F. (1996). Erotomania in a brain-damaged male. *Journal of Disability Research, 40,* 279–283.

230. Kirkby, B. S., Van Horn, J. D., Ostrem, J. L., Weinberger, D. R., & Berman, K. F. (1996). Cognitive activation during PET: A case study of monozygotic twins dicordent for closed head injury. *Neuropsychologia, 34,* 689–697.

231. Lesser, I. M., Boone, K. B., Mehringer, C. M., Wohl, M. A., Miller, B. L., & Berman, N. G. (1996). Cognition and white matter hyperintensities in older depressed patients. *American Journal of Psychiatry, 153,* 1280–1287.

232. Lewine, R. R. J., Walker, E. F., Shurett, R., Caudle, J., & Haden, C. (1996). Sex differences in neuropsychological functioning among schizophrenic patients. *American Journal of Psychiatry, 153,* 1178–1184.

233. Little, A. J., Templer, D. I., Persel, C. S., & Ashley, M. J. (1996). Feasibility of the neuropsychological spectrum in prediction of outcome following head injury. *Journal of Clinical Psychology, 52,* 455–460.

234. Lucas, M. D., & Sonnenberg, B. R. (1996). Neuropsychological trends in the Parkinsonian-plus Syndrome: A pilot study. *Journal of Clinical and Experimental Neuropsychology, 18,* 88–97.

235. Lysaker, P. H., Bell, M. D., Bioty, S., & Zito, W. S. (1996). Performance on the Wisconsin Card Sorting Test as a predictor of rehospitalization in schizophrenia. *Journal of Nervous and Mental Disease, 184,* 319–321.

236. Lysaker, P. H., Bell, M. D., Bioty, S. M., & Zito, W. S. (1996). Cognitive impairment and substance abuse history as predictors of the temporal stability of negative symptoms in schizophrenia. *Journal of Nervous and Mental Disease, 184,* 21–26.

237. McDonald, C., Brown, G. G., & Gorell, J. M. (1996). Impaired set-shifting in Parkinson's Disease: New evidence from a lexical decision task. *Journal of Clinical and Experimental Neuropsychology, 18,* 793–809.

238. McDonald, S., & Pearce, S. (1996). Clinical insights into pragmatic theory: Frontal lobe deficits and sarcasm. *Brain and Language, 53,* 81–104.

239. Mehta, Z., & Newcombe, F. (1996). Selective loss of verbal imagery. *Neuropsychologia, 34,* 441–447.

240. Miller, L. A., & Tippett, L. J. (1996). Effects of focal brain lesions on visual problem-solving. *Neuropsychologia, 34,* 387–398.

241. Morice, R., & Delahunty, A. (1996). Frontal/executive impairments in schizophrenia. *Schizophrenia Bulletin, 22,* 125–137.

242. Murphy, K. R., & Barkley, R. A. (1996). Parents of children with attention-deficit/hyperactivity disorder: Psychological and attentional impairment. *American Journal of Orthopsychiatry, 66,* 93–102.

243. Nichelli, P., Alway, D., & Grafman, J. (1996). Perceptual timing in cerebellar degeneration. *Neuropsychologia, 34,* 863–871.

244. Nisbet, H., Siegert, R., Hunt, M., & Fairley, N. (1996). Improving schizophrenic in-patients' Wisconsin card-sorting performance. *British Journal of Clinical Psychology, 35,* 631–633.

245. Osmon, D. C., Zigun, J. R., Suchy, Y., & Blint, A. (1996). W-12. Whole-brain MRI activation on Wisconsin-like card-sorting measures: Clues to test specificity. *Brain and Cognition, 30,* 308–310.

246. Palmer, B. W., Boone, K. B., Lesser, I. M., Wohl, M. A., Berman, N., & Miller, B. L. (1996). Neuropsychological deficits among older depressed patients with predominently psychological or vegatative symptoms. *Journal of Affective Disorders, 41,* 17–24.

247. Paolo, A. M., Axelrod, B. N., Troster, A. I., Blackwell, K. T., & Koller, W. C. (1996). Utility of a Wisconsin Card Sorting Test Short Form in persons with Alzheimer's and Parkinson's Disease. *Journal of Clinical and Experimental Neuropsychology, 18,* 892–897.

248. Pillon, B., Dubois, B., & Agid, Y. (1996). Testing cognition may contribute to the diagnosis of movement disorders. *Neurology, 46,* 329–334.

249. Pillon, B., Ertle, S., Deweer, B., Sarazin, M., Agid, Y., & Dubois, B. (1996). Memory for spatial location is affected in Parkinson's disease. *Neuropsychologia, 34,* 77–85.

250. Rosselli, M., & Ardila, A. (1996). Cognitive effects of cocaine and polydrug abuse. *Journal of Clinical and Experimental Neuropsychology, 18,* 122–135.

251. Rueckert, L., & Grafman, J. (1996). Sustained attention deficits in patients with right frontal lesions. *Neuropsychologia, 34,* 953–963.

252. Salthouse, T. A., Hancock, H. E., Meinz, E. J., & Hambrick, D. Z. (1996). Interrelations of age, visual acuity, and cognitive functioning. *Journal of Gerontology, 51,* 317–330.

253. Schuerholz, L. J., Baumgardner, T. L., Singer, H. S., Reiss, A. L., & Denckla, M. B. (1996). Neuropsychological status of children with Tourette's syndrome with and without attention deficit hyperactivity disorder. *Neurology, 46,* 958–964.

254. Siegert, R. J., & Warrington, E. K. (1996). Spared retrograde memory with anterograde amnesia and widespread cognitive deficits. *Cortex, 32,* 177–185.

255. Sirigu, A., Zalla, T., Pillon, B., Grafman, J., Agid, Y., & Dubois, B. (1996). Encoding of sequence and boundaries of scripts following prefrontal lesions. *Cortex, 32,* 297–310.

256. Strong, M. J., Grace, G. M., Orange, J. B., & Leeper, H. A. (1996). Cognition, language, and speech in amyotrophic lateral sclerosis: A review. *Journal of Clinical and Experimental Neuropsychology, 18,* 291–303.

257. Tien, A. Y., Ross, D. E., Pearlson, G., & Strauss, M. E. (1996). Eye movements and psychopathology in schizophrenia and bipolar disorder. *Journal of Nervous and Mental Disease, 184,* 331–338.

258. Troyer, A. K., Fisk, J. D., Archibald, C. J., Ritvo, P. G., & Murray, T. J. (1996). Conceptual reasoning as a mediator of verbal recall in patients with multiple sclerosis. *Journal of Clinical and Experimental Neuropsychology, 18,* 211–219.

259. Tung, G., Richardson, E., Thomas, C., & Westlake, R. (1996). MRI and neuropsychological differences in early- and late-life-onset geriatric depression. *Neurology, 46,* 1567–1574.

260. Van Spaendonek, K. P. M., Berger, H. J. C., Horstink, M. W. I. M., Buytenhuijs, E. L., & Cools, A. R. (1996). Executive functions and disease characteristics in Parkinson's Disease. *Neuropsychologia, 34,* 617–626.

261. Wolkin, A., Sanfilipo, M., Duncan, E., Angrist, G., Wolf, A. P., Cooper, T. B., Brodie, J. D. Laska, E., & Rotrosen, J. P. (1996). Blunted change in cerebral glucose utilization after haloperidol treatment in schizophrenic patients with prominent negative symptoms. *American Journal of Psychiatry, 153,* 346–354.

262. Abbruzzese, M., Ferri, S., & Scarone, S. (1997). The selective breakdown of frontal functions in patients with obsessive-compulsive disorder and in patients with schizophrenia: A double dissociation experimental finding. *Neuropsychologia, 35,* 907–912.

263. Barceló, F., Sanz, M., Molina, V., & Rubia, F. J. (1997). The Wisconsin Card Sorting Test and the assessment of frontal function: A validation study with event-related potentials. *Neuropsychologia, 35,* 399–408.

264. Bell, M. D., Greig, T. C., Kaplan, E., & Bryson, G. (1997). Wisconsin Card Sorting Test dimensions in schizophrenia: Factorial, predictive, and divergent validity. *Journal of Clinical and Experimental Neuropsychology, 19,* 933–941.

265. Ciesielski, K. T., Harris, R. J., Hart, B. L., & Pabst, H. F. (1997). Cerebellar hypoplasia and frontal lobe cognitive deficits in disorders of early childhood. *Neuropsychologia, 35,* 643–655.

266. Corey-Bloom, J., Sabbagh, M. N., Bondi, M. W., Hansen, L., Alford, M. F., Masliah, E., & Thal, L. J. (1997) Hyziocampal sclerosis contributes to dementia in the elderly. *Neurology, 48,* 154–160.

267. Cunningham, J. M., Pliskin, N. H., Cassisi, J. E., Tsang, B., & Rao, S. M. (1997). Relationship between confabulation and measures of memory and executive function. *Journal of Clinical and Experimental Neuropsychology, 19,* 867–877.

268. Curran, T., Schacter, D. L., Norman, K. A., & Galluccio, L. (1997). False recognition after right frontal lobe infarction: Memory for general and specific information. *Neuropsychologia, 35,* 1035–1049.

269. De Renzi, E., Lucchelli, F., Muggia, S., & Spinnler, H. (1997). Is memory loss without anatomical damage tantamount to a psychogenic deficit? The case of pure retrograde amnesia. *Neuropsychologia, 35,* 781–794.

270. Fabiani, M., & Friedman, D. (1997). Dissociations between memory for temporal order and recognition memory in aging. *Neuropsychologia, 35,* 129–141.

271. Ferraro, F. R., Wonderlich, S., & Jocic, Z. (1997). Performance variability as a new theoretical mechanism regarding eating disorders and cognitive processing. *Journal of Clinical Psychology, 53,* 117–121.

272. Gold, J. M., Carpenter, C., Randolph, C., Goldberg, T. E., & Weinberger, D. R. (1997). Auditory working memory and Wisconsin Card Sorting Test performance in schizophrenia. *Archives of General Psychiatry, 54,* 159–165.

273. Gold, M., Nadeau, S. E., Jacobs, D. H., Adair, J. C., Rothi, L. J. G., & Heilman, K. M. (1997). Adynamic aphasia: A transcortical motor aphasia with defective semantic strategy formation. *Brain and Language, 57,* 374–393.

274. Hänninen, T., Hallikainen, M., Koivisto, K., Partanen, K., Laakso, M. P., Riekkinen, P. J., Sr., & Soininen, H. (1997). Decline of frontal lobe functions in subjects with age-associated memory impairment. *Neurology, 48,* 148–153.

275. Heindel, W. C., Cahn, D. A., & Salmon, D. P. (1997). Non-associative lexical priming is impaired in Alzheimer's disease. *Neuropsychologia, 35,* 1365–1372.

276. Johnson, M. K., O'Connor, M. O., & Cantor, J. (1997). Confabulation, memory deficits, and frontal dysfunction. *Brain and Cognition, 34,* 189–206.

277. Lucey, J. V., Burness, C. E., Costa, D. C., Cacinovic, S., Pilowsky, L. S., Ell, P. J., Marks, I. M., & Kerwin, R. W. (1997). Wisconsin Card Sorting Test (WCST) errors and cerebral blood flow in obsessive-compulsive disorder (OCD). *British Journal of Medical Psychology, 70,* 403–411.

278. Mayes, A. R., Daum, I., Markowisch, H. J., & Sauter, B. (1997). The relationship between retrograde and anterograde amnesia in patients with typical global amnesia. *Cortex, 33,* 197–217.

279. McDowell, S., Whyte, J., & D'Esposito, M. (1997). Working memory impairments in traumatic brain injury: Evidence from a dual-task paradigm. *Neuropsychologia, 35,* 1341–1353.

280. McGrath, N. M., Anderson, N. E., Hope, J. K. A., Croxson, M. C., & Powell, K. F. (1997). Anterior opercular syndrome, caused by herpes simplex encephalitis. *Neurology, 49,* 494–497.

281. Moscovitch, M., & Melo, B. (1997). Strategic retrieval and the frontal lobes: Evidence from confabulation and amnesia. *Neuropsychologia, 35,* 1017–1034.

282. Nestor, P. G., Kimble, M. O., O'Donnell, B. F., Smith, L., Niznikiewicz, M., Shenton, M. E., & McCarley, R. (1997). Aberrant semantic activation in schizophrenia: A neurophysiological study. *American Journal of Psychiatry, 154,* 640–646.

283. Oxbury, S., Oxbury, J., Renowden, S., Squier, W., & Carpenter, K. (1997). Severe amnesia: An unusual late complication after temporal lobectomy. *Neuropsychologia, 35,* 975–988.

284. Papagno, C., & Baddeley, A. (1997). Confabulation in a dysexecutive patient: Implication for models of retrieval. *Cortex, 33,* 743–752.

285. Raymer, A. M., Moberg, P., Crosson, B., Nadeau, S., & Rothi, L. J. G. (1997). Lexical-semantic deficits in two patients with dominant thalamic infarction. *Neuropsychologia, 35,* 211–219.

286. Reinkemeier, M., Marowitsch, H. J., Rauch, M., & Kessler, J. (1997). Differential impairments in recalling people's names: A case study in search of neuroanatomical correlates. *Neuropsychologia, 35,* 677–684.

287. Robertson, I. H., Manly, T., Andrade, J., Baddeley, B. T., & Yiend, J. (1997). "Oops!": Performance correlates of everyday attentional failures in traumatic brain injured and normal subjects. *Neuropsychologia, 35,* 747–758.

288. Rowe, E. W., & Shean, G. (1997). Card-sort performance and syndromes of schizophrenia. *Genetic Psychology Monographs, 123,* 197–209.

289. Seidman, L. J., Caplan, B. B., Tolomiczenko, G. S., Turner, W. M., Penk, W. E., Schutt, R. K., & Goldfinger, S. M. (1997). Neuropsychological function in homeless mentally ill individuals. *Journal of Nervous and Mental Disease, 185,* 3–12.

290. Sillanpaa, M. C., Agaza, L. M., Milner, I. B., Podany, E. C., Axelrod, B. N., & Brown, G. G. (1997). Gulf War veterans: A neuropsychological examination. *Journal of Clinical and Experimental Neuropsychology, 19,* 211–219.

291. Stuss, D. T., Peterkin, I., Guzman, D. A., Guzman, C., & Troyer, A. K. (1997). Chronic obstructive pulmonary disease: Effects of hypoxia on neurological and neuropsychological measures. *Journal of Clinical and Experimental Neuropsychology, 19,* 515–524.

292. Tanaka, Y., Miyazama, Y., Akaoka, F., & Yamada, T. (1997). Amnesia following damage to the mammillary bodies. *Neurology, 48,* 160–165.

293. Troster, A. I., Fields, J. A., Wilkinson, S. B., Pahwa, R., Miyawaki, E., Lyons, K. E., & Koller, W. C. (1997). Unilateral pallidal stimulation for Parkinson's disease: Neurobehavioral functioning before and 3 months after electrode implantation. *Neurology, 49,* 1078–1083.

294. Aylward, E. H., Anderson, N. B., Bylsma, F. W., Wagster, M. V., Barta, P. E., Sherr, M., Feeney, J., Davis, A., Rosenblatt, A., Pearlson, G. D., & Ross, C. A. (1998). Frontal lobe volume in patients with Huntington's disease. *Neurology, 50,* 252–258.

295. Baynes, K., Kegl, J. A., Brentari, D., Kussmaul, C., & Poizner, H. (1998). Chronic auditory agnosia following Landau-Kleffner syndrome: A 23 year outcome study. *Brain and Language, 63,* 381–425.

296. Berman, I., Merson, A., Viegner, B., Losonezy, M. F. Pappas, D., & Green, A. I. (1998). Obsessions and compulsions at a district cluster of symptoms in schizophrenia: A neuropsychological study. *Journal of Nervous and Mental Disease, 186,* 150–156.

297. DeBaun, M. R., Schatz, J., Siegel, M. J., Koby, M., Craft, S., Resar, L., Chu, J.-Y., Launius, G., Dadash-Zadeh, M., Lee, R. B., & Noetzel, M. (1998). Cognitive screening examinations for silent cerebral infarcts in sickle cell disease. *Neurology, 50,* 1678–1682.

298. Fukatsu, R., Yamadori, A., & Fujii, T. (1998). Impaired recall and preserved encoding in prominent amnesic syndrome: A case of basal forebrain amnesia. *Neurology, 50,* 539–541.

299. Hale, J. B., Hoeppner, J. B., DeWitt, M. B., Coury, D. L., Ritacco, D. G., & Trommer, B. (1998). Evaluating medication response in ADHD: Cognitive, behavioral, and single-subject methodology. *Journal of Learning Disabilities, 31,* 595–607.

300. Handwerk, M. L., & Marshall, R. M. (1998). Behavioral and emotional problems of students with learning disabilities, serious emotional disturbance, or both conditions. *Journal of Learning Disabilities, 31,* 327–338.

301. McDonald, S., & Pearce, S. (1998). Requests that overcome listener reluctance: Impairment associated with executive dysfunction in brain injury. *Brain and Language, 61,* 88–104.

302. Miller, B. L., Cummings, J., Mishkin, F., Boone, K., Prince, F., Penton, M., & Cotman, C. (1998). Emergence of artistic talent in frontotemporal dementia. *Neurology, 51,* 978–982.

303. Mostofsky, S. H., Mazzocco, M. M. M., Aakalu, G., Warsofsky, I. S., Denckla, M. B., & Reiss, A. L. (1998). Decreased cerebellar posterior vermis size in fragile X syndrome: Correlation with neurocognitive performance. *Neurology, 50,* 121–130.

304. Nayak, M. B., & Milner, J. S. (1998). Neuropsychological functioning: Comparison of mothers at high- and low-risk for child physical abuse. *Child Abuse & Neglect, 22,* 687–703.

305. Rapcsak, S. Z., Kaszniak, A. W., Reminger, S. L., Glisky, M. L., Glisky, E. L., & Comer, J. F. (1998). Dissociation between verbal and autonomic measures of memory following frontal lobe damage. *Neurology, 50,* 1259–1265.

306. Tiberti, C., Sabe, L., Kuzis, G., Cuerva, A. G., Leiguarda, R., & Starkstein, S. E. (1998). Prevalence and correlates of the catastrophic reaction in Alzheimer's disease. *Neurology, 50,* 546–548.

307. van Buchem, M. A., Grossman, R. I., Armstrong, C., Polansky, M., Miki, Y., Heyning, F. H., Boncoeur-Martel, M. P., Wei, L., Udupa, J. K., Grossman, M., Kolson, D. L., & McGowan, J. C. (1998). Correlation of volumetric magnetization transfer imaging with clinical data in MS. *Neurology, 50,* 1609–1617.

308. van Gorp, W, G., Altshuler, L., Theberge, D. C., Wilkins, J., & Dixon, W. (1998). Cognitive impairment in euthymic bipolar patients with and without prior alcohol dependence: A preliminary study. *Archives of General Psychiatry, 55,* 41–46.

309. Young, D. A., Zakzanis, K. K., Bailey, C., Davila, R., Griese, J., Sartory, G., & Thom, A. (1998). Further parameters of insight and neuropsychological deficit in schizophrenia and other chronic mental disease. *Journal of Nervous and Mental Disease, 186,* 44–50.

[2893]

Wolf Expressive/Receptive Language & Speech Checklist.

Purpose: "To determine where the pupil's expressive and receptive language and speech fit into a developmental hierarchy of skills."

Population: Birth-10 years.

Publication Date: 1988.

Acronym: WERLS.

Scores: 2 ratings: Expressive, Receptive.

Administration: Individual.

Manual: No manual.

Price Data: Available from publisher.

Time: Administration time not reported.

Author: Enid G. Wolf-Schein.

Publisher: Psychometrics Canada Ltd. [Canada] [No reply from publisher; status unknown].

[2894]

Wolf Student Behavior Screening.

Purpose: Designed "to make a quick assessment of the student's behavior."

Population: Students.

Publication Date: 1988.

Scores, 5: Social Skills, Self Concept, Relations with Teachers/Peers, Classroom Behavior, Total.

Administration: Individual.

Manual: No manual.

Price Data: Available from publisher.

Time: Administration time not reported.

Comments: Observations made by teachers.

Author: Enid G. Wolf-Schein.

Publisher: Psychometrics Canada Ltd. [Canada] [No reply from publisher; status unknown].

[2895]

The Wolfe Computer Operator Aptitude Test.

Purpose: Used "to evaluate a candidate's potential for work as a computer operator."

Population: Applicants for computer training or employment.
Publication Dates: 1979-1982.
Acronym: WCOAT.
Scores: Total score only.
Administration: Group.
Price Data, 1999: $150 per candidate.
Foreign Language Edition: French edition available.
Time: (90) minutes.
Comments: Detailed report provided on each candidate.
Author: Jack M. Wolfe.
Publisher: Rose Wolfe.

[2896]

Wolfe Programming Language Test: COBOL.

Purpose: Used to assess candidate proficiency in programming in COBOL.
Population: Programmers and trainees.
Publication Date: [c1982].
Scores: Total score only.
Administration: Group.
Price Data, 1998: $125 per candidate.
Time: (120) minutes.
Comments: Test previously listed as Wolfe Programming Language Test: COBOL.
Author: Jack M. Wolfe.
Publisher: Rose Wolfe.

[2897]

Wolfe-Spence Programming Aptitude Test.

Purpose: Designed as a screening test to identify persons who should receive further consideration for hiring or training for programming.
Population: Applicants in computer programming.
Publication Date: 1970.
Scores: Total score and percentile.
Administration: Group.
Price Data, 1999: $70 per candidate.
Time: (120) minutes.
Authors: Jack M. Wolfe and Richard J. Spence.
Publisher: Rose Wolfe.

[2898]

Wonderlic Basic Skills Test.

Purpose: "A short form measure of adult language and math skills ... designed to measure the job-readiness of teenagers and adults."
Population: Teenagers and adults.
Publication Date: 1994–1998.
Acronym: WBST.
Scores, 9: Test of Verbal Skills (Word Knowledge, Sentence Construction, Information Retrieval, Total), Test of Quantitative Skills (Explicit, Applied, Interpretive, Total), Composite Score.
Subtests, 2: Test of Verbal Skills, Test of Quantitative Skills.
Administration: Group or individual.
Forms: 2 equivalent forms for each subtest: VS-1, VS-2 for Test of Verbal Skills; QS-1, QS-2 for Test of Quantitative Skills.
Price Data, 1998: $85 per 25 tests, manual ('98, 92 pages), and necessary software for either the Verbal or Quantitative subtests; $110 per composite set including 25 Verbal subtests, 25 Quantitative subtests, manual, and necessary software; $120 per User's Manual for Ability-to-Benefit Testing ('98, 86 pages).
Time: (20) minutes for each subtest.
Comments: The Verbal and Quantitative Skills subtests may be administered together or separately, and are available as separate booklets; scoring requires using IBM-compatible PC; the WBST has been approved by the U.S. Department of Education for use in qualifying postsecondary students for Title IV Federal financial assistance and schools using the WBST for this purpose must follow special procedures and guidelines published in the User's Manual for Ability-to-Benefit Testing.
Authors: Eliot R. Long, Victor S. Artese, and Winifred L. Clonts.
Publisher: Wonderlic Personnel Test, Inc.
Cross References: For reviews by Thomas F. Donlon and Gerald S. Hanna, see 13:362.

[2899]

Wonderlic Personnel Test and Scholastic Level Exam.

Purpose: Designed to be used by businesses and schools to measure general cognitive ability in order to determine "how easily individuals can be trained, how well they can adjust and solve problems on the job, and how well satisfied they are likely to be with the demands of the job."
Population: Ages 15 and up.
Publication Dates: 1939–1998.
Acronym: WPS and SLE.
Scores: Total score only.
Administration: Individual or group.
Forms: 6 alternate forms of the WPT, and 4 alternate forms of the SLE.
Price Data, 1998: $1.70 per test.
Foreign Language and Special Editions: Canadian, Swedish, French, Spanish, Tagalog, Vietnamese, German, Chinese, Portuguese, Japanese, Korean, Russian, large print, braille, and audio editions.
Time: 12 minutes.
Comments: Computer-administered version available; alternate forms exist to reduce risk of retesting with identical form.

Author: Charles Wonderlic.
Publisher: Wonderlic Personnel Test, Inc.
Cross References: See T4:2972 (11 references); for a review by Marcia J. Belcher of an earlier edition, see 11:475 (10 references); for reviews by Frank L. Schmidt and Lyle F. Schoenfeldt, see 9:1385 (8 references); see also T3:2638 (24 references), and T2:482 (10 references); for reviews by Robert C. Droege and John P. Foley, Jr., see 7:401 (28 references); for reviews by N. M. Downie and Marvin D. Dunnette, see 6:513 (17 references); see also 5:400 (59 references); for reviews by H. E. Brogden, Charles D. Flory, and Irving Lorge, see 3:269 (7 references); see also 2:1415 (2 references).

TEST REFERENCES

1. Elias, P. K., Elias, M. F., Robbins, M. A., & Gage, P. (1987). Acquisition of word-processing skills by younger, middle-age, and older adults. *Psychology and Aging, 2,* 340-348.
2. Aks, D. J., & Coren, S. (1990). Is susceptibility to distraction related to mental ability? *Journal of Educational Psychology, 82,* 388–390.
3. Johnson, D. S., & Kanfer, R. (1992). Goal-performance relations: The effects of initial task complexity and task practice. *Motivation and Emotion, 16,* 117–141.
4. McKelvie, S. J. (1992). Does memory contaminate test-retest reliability? *The Journal of General Psychology, 119,* 59-72.
5. Cornwell, J. M., & Manfredo, P. A. (1994). Kolb's learning style theory revisited. *Educational and Psychological Measurement, 54,* 299–316.
6. Lancaster, S. J., Colarelli, S. M., King, D. W., & Beehr, T. A. (1994). Job applicant similarity on cognitive ability, vocational interests, and personality characteristics: Do similar persons choose similar jobs? *Educational and Psychological Measurement, 54,* 299-316.
7. McKelvie, S. J. (1994). Validity and reliability findings for an experimental short form of the Wonderlic Personnel Test in an academic testing. *Psychological Reports, 75,* 907-910.
8. Mill, D., Gray, T., & Mandel, D. R. (1994). Influence of research methods and statistics courses on everyday reasoning, critical abilities, and belief in unsubstantiated phenomena. *Canadian Journal of Behavioural Science, 26,* 246-258.
9. Rosse, J. G., Miller, J. L., & Stecher, M. D. (1994). A field study of job applicants' reactions to personality and cognitive ability testing. *Journal of Applied Psychology, 79,* 987-992.
10. Sackett, P. R., & Ostgaard, D. J. (1994). Job-specific applicant pools and national norms for cognitive ability tests: Implications for range restriction corrections in validation research. *Journal of Applied Psychology, 79,* 680-684.
11. Crant, J. M. (1995). The proactive personality scale and objective job performance among real estate agents. *Journal of Applied Psychology, 80,* 532–537.
12. Overholser, J. C. (1996). The dependent personality and interpersonal problems. *Journal of Nervous and Mental Disease, 184,* 8–16.
13. Schuhmann, E. M., Foote, R. C., Eybert, S. M., Boggs, S. R., & Algina, J. (1996). Efficacy of parent-child interaction therapy: Interim report of a randomized trial with short-term maintenance. *Journal of Clinical Child Psychology, 27,* 34–45.
14. Chan, D. (1997). Racial subgroup differences in predictive validity perceptions on personality and cognitive ability tests. *Journal of Applied Psychology, 82,* 311–320.
15. Dodrill, C. B., Arnett, J. L., Sommerville, K. W., & Shu, V. (1997). Cognitive and quality of life effects of differing dosages of tiagabine in epilepsy. *Neurology, 48,* 1025–1031.
16. Martocchio, J. J., & Judge, T. A. (1997). Relationship between conscientiousness and learning in employee training: mediating influences of self-deception and self-efficacy. *Journal of Applied Psychology, 82,* 764–773.
17. Whitney, D. J., & Schmitt, N. (1997). Relationship between culture and responses to biodata employment items. *Journal of Applied Psychology, 82,* 113–129.
18. Barrick, M. R., Stewart, G. L., Neubert, M. J., & Mount, M. K. (1998). Relating member ability and personality to work-team processes and team effectiveness. *Journal of Applied Psychology, 83,* 377–391.
19. Paulhus, D. L., Lysy, D. C., & Yik, M. S. M. (1998). Self-report measures of intelligence: Are they useful as proxy IQ tests? *Journal of Personality, 66,* 525–554.
20. Witt, L. A. (1998). Enhancing organizational goal congruence: A solution to organizational politics. *Journal of Applied Psychology, 83,* 666–674.

[2900]

Woodcock Diagnostic Reading Battery.

Purpose: "Provides a diagnostic test that assesses reading achievement and important related abilities."
Population: Ages 4–95.
Publication Date: 1997.
Acronym: WDRB.
Scores, 17: Letter-Word Identification, Word Attack, Reading Vocabulary, Passive Comprehension, Incomplete Words, Sound Blending, Oral Vocabulary, Listening Comprehension, Memory for Sentences, Visual Matching, Total Reading, Broad Reading, Basic Reading Skills, Reading Comprehension, Phonological Awareness, Oral Comprehension, Reading Aptitude.
Administration: Individual.
Price Data, 1999: $273 per complete kit; $37 per 25 recording forms; $45 per examiner's manual (152 pages); $40 per norms manual (161 pages); $175 per scoring and interpretation program (Windows or Macintosh).
Time: (60) minutes; (20–25) minutes for four reading achievement tests only.
Comments: Battery comprises selected tests from the Woodcock-Johnson Psycho-Educational Battery—Revised; for educational, clinical, or research purposes; optional to use any combination of the subtests that are relevant to individual subjects.
Author: Richard W. Woodcock.
Publisher: The Riverside Publishing Company.

[2901]

Woodcock-Johnson Psycho-Educational Battery—Revised.

Purpose: Co-normed instruments designed to measure cognitive abilities, scholastic aptitudes, and achievement.
Population: Ages 2-90.
Publication Dates: 1977-1991.
Acronym: WJ-R.
Administration: Individual.
Parts, 2: Cognitive, Achievement.
Price Data, 1999: $498 per complete WJ-R kit (Cognitive and Form A Achievement); $49 per technical manual ('91, 367 pages); $220 per computer scoring system (select Apple or IBM).
Comments: Aptitude/Achievement discrepancies can be calculated using actual norms when the Cognitive and Achievement Sections have been administered; 1977 edition still available; the Early Development Scale for Preschool Children is composed of fewer tests.
Authors: Richard W. Woodcock (examiner's manuals and test books), M. Bonner Johnson (test books), Nancy Mather (examiner's manuals), Kevin S. McGrew (technical manual), and Judy K. Werder (technical manual).
Publisher: Riverside Publishing.

a) TESTS OF ACHIEVEMENT.
Scores: 9 Standard Battery test scores: Letter-Word Identification, Passage Comprehension, Calculation, Applied Problems, Dictation, Writing Samples, Science, Social Studies, Humanities

plus 5 Standard Battery cluster scores derived from combinations of the above test scores: Broad Reading, Broad Mathematics, Broad Written Language, Broad Knowledge, Skills and the Ability to Calculate Intra-Achievement Discrepancies, and 9 Supplemental Battery test scores: Word Attack, Reading Vocabulary, Quantitative Concepts, Proofing, Writing Fluency, Punctuation & Capitalization, Spelling, Usage, Handwriting plus 6 Supplemental Battery Cluster scores derived from combinations of scores from the Standard Battery and Supplemental Battery: Basic Reading Skills, Reading Comprehension, Basic Mathematics Skills, Mathematics Reasoning, Basic Writing Skills, Written Expression.

Forms, 2: A, B.

Price Data: $275 per complete kit including Standard and Supplemental test books, 25 test records, 25 subject response books, examiner's manual ('89, 230 pages), and norms tables ('89, 275 pages) (select Form A or B); $48 per set of 25 test records and 25 subject response books (select Form A or B).

Time: (50-60) minutes for the Standard Battery; additional administration time for the Supplemental Battery not reported.

Comments: Tests may be administered separately.

b) TESTS OF COGNITIVE ABILITY.

Scores: 7 Standard Battery test scores plus 1 cluster score: Memory for Names, Memory for Sentences, Visual Matching, Incomplete Words, Visual Closure, Picture Vocabulary, Analysis-Synthesis, Broad Cognitive Ability (Standard or Early Development) and 14 Supplemental Battery test scores: Visual-Auditory Learning, Memory for Words, Cross Out, Sound Blending, Picture Recognition, Oral Vocabulary, Concept Formation, Delayed Recall (Memory for Names, Visual-Auditory Learning), Numbers Reversed, Sound Patterns, Spatial Relations, Listening Comprehension, Verbal Analogies plus 14 Supplemental Battery cluster scores derived from combinations of scores from the Standard Battery and Supplemental Battery: Broad Cognitive Ability-Extended Scale, Cognitive Factor (Long-Term Retrieval, Short-Term Memory, Processing Speed, Auditory Processing, Visual Processing, Comprehension-Knowledge, Fluid Reasoning), Scholastic Aptitude (Reading, Mathematics, Written Language, Knowledge), Oral Language (Oral Language, Oral Language Aptitude), Ability to Calculate Intracognitive Discrepancies.

Price Data: $498 per complete kit including Standard and Supplemental test books, 25 test records, audiocassettes, examiner's manual ('89, 204 pages), and norms tables ('89, 297 pages); $308 per complete Standard kit; $275 per Supplemental expansion including test book, 25 test records, audiocassette, examiner's manual, and norms tables (to be used only in conjunction with the Standard Battery); $48 per 25 Standard and Supplemental test records; $36 per 25 Standard test records.

Time: (30-40) minutes for the Standard Battery; an additional 40 minutes required to administer the Supplemental Battery.

Cross References: For reviews by Jack A. Cummings and by Steven W. Lee and Elaine Flory Stefany, see 12:415 (56 references); see also T4:2973 (90 references); for reviews by Jack A. Cummings and Alan S. Kaufman of the 1977 edition, see 9:1387 (6 references); see also T3:2639 (3 references).

TEST REFERENCES

1. Burns, J. M., & Collins, M. D. (1987). Parents' perceptions of factors affecting the reading development of intellectually superior accelerated readers and intellectually superior nonreaders. *Reading Research and Instruction, 26,* 239–246.
2. Aram, D., & Ekelman, B. L. (1988). Scholastic aptitude and achievement among children with unilateral brain lesions. *Neuropsychologia, 26,* 903–916.
3. Obrzut, J. E., Conrad, P. F., Bryden, M. P., & Boliek, C. A. (1988). Cued dichotic listening with right-handed, left-handed, bilingual and learning-disabled children. *Neuropsychologia, 26,* 119–131.
4. Figueroa, R. A. (1989). Psychological testing of linguistic-minority students: Knowledge gaps and regulations. *Exceptional Children, 56,* 145–152.
5. Graham, S., & Harris, K. R. (1989). Improving learning disabled students' skills at composing essays: Self-instructional strategy training. *Exceptional Children, 56,* 201–214.
6. McCue, M. (1989). The role of assessment in the vocational rehabilitation of adults with specific learning disabilities. *Rehabilitation Counseling Bulletin, 33,* 18–37.
7. Nelson, R., & Lignugaris/Kraft, B. (1989). Postsecondary education for students with learning disabilities. *Exceptional Children, 56,* 246–265.
8. Obrzut, J. E., Conrad, P. F., & Boliek, C. A. (1989). Verbal and nonverbal auditory processing among left- and right-handed good readers and reading-disabled children. *Neuropsychologia, 27,* 1357–1371.
9. Scarborough, H. S. (1989). Prediction of reading disability from familial and individual differences. *Journal of Educational Psychology, 81,* 101–108.
10. Zacker, J., Pepper, B., & Kirshner, M. C. (1989). Neuropsychological characteristics of young adult chronic psychiatric patients: Preliminary observations. *Perceptual and Motor Skills, 68,* 391–399.
11. Gottfried, A. E. (1990). Academic intrinsic motivation in young elementary school children. *Journal of Educational Psychology, 82,* 525–538.
12. Graham, S. (1990). The role of production factors in learning disabled students' composition. *Journal of Educational Psychology, 82,* 781–791.
13. Sabornie, E. J., Marshall, K. J., & Ellis, E. S. (1990). Restructuring of mainstream sociometry with learning disabled and nonhandicapped students. *Exceptional Children, 56,* 314–323.
14. Andrews, L. W., & Gutkin, T. B. (1991). The effects of human versus computer authorship on consumer's perceptions of psychological reports. *Computers in Human Behavior, 7,* 311–317.
15. Bullard, S. C., & Schirmer, B. R. (1991). Understanding questions: Hearing-impaired children with learning problems. *Volta Review, 93,* 235–245.
16. Das, J. P., & Mishra, R. K. (1991). Relation between memory span, naming time, speech rate, and reading competence. *Journal of Experimental Education, 59,* 129–139.
17. Ganschow, L., Sparks, R. L., Javorsky, J., Pohlman, J., & Bishop-Marbury, A. (1991). Identifying native language difficulties among foreign language learners in college: A "foreign" language learning disability? *Journal of Learning Disabilities, 24,* 530–541.
18. Williams, K. S., Ochs, J., Williams, J. M., & Mulhern, R. K. (1991). Parental report of everyday cognitive abilities among children treated for acute lymphoblastic leukemia. *Journal of Pediatric Psychology, 16,* 13–26.
19. Felton, R. H., & Wood, F. B. (1992). A reading level match study of nonword reading skills in poor readers with varying IQ. *Journal of Learning Disabilities, 25,* 318–326.
20. Gregg, N., Hoy, C., King, M., Moreland, C., & Jagota, M. (1992). The MMPI-2 profile of adults with learning disabilities in university and rehabilitation settings. *Journal of Learning Disabilities, 25,* 386–395.
21. Shaywitz, B. A., Fletcher, J. M., Holahan, J. M., & Shaywitz, S. E. (1992). Discrepancy compared to low achievement definitions of reading disability: Results from the Connecticut longitudinal study. *Journal of Learning Disabilities, 25,* 639–648.
22. Vogel, S. A., & Adelman, P. B. (1992). The success of college students with learning disabilities: Factors related to educational attainment. *Journal of Learning Disabilities, 25,* 430–441.

23. Yoshinaga-Itano, C., & Ruberry, J. (1992). The Colorado Individual Performance profile for Hearing-Impaired Students: A data-driven approach to decision making. *Volta Review, 94,* 159–187.

24. Auchus, M., Kose, G., & Allen, R. (1993). Body-image distortion and mental imagery. *Perceptual and Motor Skills, 77,* 719–728.

25. Graham, S., Schwartz, S. S., & MacArthur, C. A. (1993). Knowledge of writing and the composing process, attitude toward writing, and self-efficacy for students with and without learning disabilities. *Journal of Learning Disabilities, 26,* 237–249.

26. Kaplan, B. J., Polatajko, H. J., Wilson, B. N., & Faris, P. D. (1993). Reexamination of sensory integration treatment: A combination of two efficacy studies. *Journal of Learning Disabilities, 26,* 342–347.

27. Kearney, C. A., & Drabman, R. S. (1993). The write-say method for improving spelling accuracy in children with learning disabilities. *Journal of Learning Disabilities, 26,* 52–56.

28. Little, S. S. (1993). Nonverbal learning disabilities and socioemotional functioning: A review of recent literature. *Journal of Learning Disabilities, 26,* 653–665.

29. Litzinger, M. J., Duvall, B., & Little, P. (1993). Movement of individuals with complex epilepsy from an institution into the community: Seizure control and functional outcomes. *American Journal on Mental Retardation, 98,* 52–57.

30. Masterson, J. J. (1993). The performance of children with language-learning disabilities on two types of cognitive tasks. *Journal of Speech and Hearing Research, 36,* 1026–1036.

31. McPhail, J. C. (1993). Adolescents with learning disabilities: A comparative life-stream interpretation. *Journal of Learning Disabilities, 26,* 617–629.

32. Morris, R. D., Krawiecki, N. S., Wright, J. A., & Walter, L. W. (1993). Neuropsychological, academic, and adaptive functioning in children who survive in-hospital cardiac arrest and resuscitation. *Journal of Learning Disabilities, 26,* 46–51.

33. Naglieri, J. A., & Reardon, S. M. (1993). Traditional IQ is irrelevant to learning disabilities—intelligence is not. *Journal of Learning Disabilities, 26,* 127–133.

34. Vaughn, S., Schumm, J. S., & Gordon, J. (1993). Which motoric condition is most effective for teaching spelling to students with and without learning disabilities? *Journal of Learning Disabilities, 26,* 191–198.

35. Vaughn, S., Schumm, J. S., & Kouzekanani, K. (1993). What do students with learning disabilities think when their general education teachers make adaptations? *Journal of Learning Disabilities, 26,* 545–555.

36. Watson, B. V., & Miller, T. K. (1993). Auditory perception, phonological processing, and reading ability/disability. *Journal of Speech and Hearing Research, 36,* 850–863.

37. Beers, S. R., Goldstein, G., & Katz, L. J. (1994). Neuropsychological differences between college students with learning disabilities and those with mild head injury. *Journal of Learning Disabilities, 27,* 315–324.

38. Bellaire, S., Plante, E., & Swisher, L. (1994). Bound-morpheme skills in the oral language of school-age, language-impaired children. *Journal of Communication Disorders, 27,* 265–279.

39. Campbell, F. A., & Ramey, C. T. (1994). Effects of early intervention on intellectual and academic achievement: A follow-up study of children from low income families. *Child Development, 65,* 684–698.

40. Durlak, C. M., Rose, E., & Bursuck, W. D. (1994). Preparing high school students with learning disabilities for the transition to post-secondary education: Teaching the skills of self-determination. *Journal of Learning Disabilities, 27,* 51–59.

41. Hoehn, T. P., & Baumeister, A. A. (1994). A critique of the application of sensory integration therapy to children with learning disabilities. *Journal of Learning Disabilities, 27,* 338–350.

42. Hughes, C. A., & Suritsky, S. K. (1994). Note-taking skills of university students with and without learning disabilities. *Journal of Learning Disabilities, 27,* 20–24.

43. Masterson, J. J., & Perrey, C. D. (1994). Research to practice: A program for training analogical reasoning skills in children with language disorders. *Language, Speech, and Hearing Services in Schools, 25,* 268–270.

44. Pearl, R., & Bryan, T. (1994). Getting caught in misconduct: Conceptions of adolescents with and without learning disabilities. *Journal of Learning Disabilities, 27,* 193–197.

45. Pintrich, P. R., Anderman, E. M., & Klobucar, C. (1994). Intraindividual differences in motivation and cognition in students with and without learning disabilities. *Journal of Learning Disabilities, 27,* 360–370.

46. Reid, R., Maag, J. W., Vasa, S. F., & Wright, G. (1994). Who are the children with attention deficit-hyperactivity disorder? A school-based survey. *The Journal of Special Education, 28,* 117–137.

47. Roberts, J. E., Burchinal, M. R., & Campbell, F. (1994). Otitis media in early childhood and patterns of intellectual development and later academic performance. *Journal of Pediatric Psychology, 19,* 347–367.

48. Trammel, D. L., Schloss, P. J., & Alper, S. (1994). Using self-recording, evaluation, and graphing to increase completion of homework assignments. *Journal of Learning Disabilities, 27,* 75–81.

49. August, G. J., Realmuto, G. M., Crosby, R. D., & MacDonald, A. W. (1995). Community-based multiple-gate screening of children at risk for conduct disorder. *Journal of Abnormal Child Psychology, 23,* 521–544.

50. Baker, J. M. (1995). Inclusion in Virginia: Educational experiences of students with learning disabilities in one elementary school. *The Journal of Special Education, 29,* 116–123.

51. Baker, J. M. (1995). Inclusion in Washington: Educational experiences of students with learning disabilities in one elementary school. *The Journal of Special Education, 29,* 155–162.

52. Bender, B. (1995). Are asthmatic children educationally handicapped? *School Psychology Quarterly, 10,* 274–291.

53. Bickley, P. G., Keith, T. Z., & Wolfle, L. M. (1995). The three-stratum theory of cognitive abilities: Test of structure of intelligence across the life span. *Intelligence, 20,* 309328.

54. Bluechardt, M. H., & Shephard, R. J. (1995). Using an extracurricular physical activity program to enhance social skills. *Journal of Learning Disabilities, 28,* 160–169.

55. Brigham, F. J., Scruggs, T. E., & Mastropieri, M. A. (1995). Elaborative maps for enhanced learning of historical information: Uniting spatial, verbal, and imaginal information. *The Journal of Special Education, 28,* 440–460.

56. Campbell, F. A., & Ramey, C. T. (1995). Cognitive and school outcomes for high-risk African-American students at middle adolescence: Positive effects of early intervention. *American Educational Research Journal, 32,* 743–772.

57. Daneman, M., Nemeth, S., Stanton, M., & Huelsman, K. (1995). Working memory as a predictor of reading achievement in orally educated hearing-impaired children. *Volta Review, 97,* 225–241.

58. Eden, G. F., Stein, J. F., Wood, H. M., & Wood, F. B. (1995). Temporal and spatial processing in reading disabled and normal children. *Cortex, 31,* 451–468.

59. Eden, G. F., Stein, J. F., Wood, M. H., & Wood, F. B. (1995). Verbal and visual problems in reading disability. *Journal of Learning Disabilities, 28,* 272–290.

60. Feagans, L. V., Fendt, K., & Farran, D. C. (1995). The effects of day care intervention on teachers' ratings of the elementary school discourse skills in disadvantaged children. *International Journal of Behavioral Development, 18,* 243–261.

61. Felton, R. H., & Pepper, P. P. (1995). Early identification and intervention of phonological deficits in kindergarten and early elementary children at risk for reading disability. *School Psychology Review, 24,* 405–414.

62. Ganschow, L., & Sparks, R. (1995). Effects of direct instruction in Spanish phonology on the native-language skills and foreign-language aptitude of at-risk foreign-language learners. *Journal of Learning Disabilities, 28,* 107–120.

63. Giddan, J. J., Wahl, J., & Brogan, M. (1995). Importance of communication training for psychiatric residents and mental health trainees. *Child Psychiatry and Human Development, 26,* 19–28.

64. Gillam, R. B., Cowan, N., & Day, L. S. (1995). Sequential memory in children with and without language impairment. *Journal of Speech and Hearing Research, 38,* 393–402.

65. Joshi, R. M. (1995). Assessing reading and spelling skills. *School Psychology Review, 24,* 361–375.

66. Luetke-Stahlman, B. (1995). Social interaction: Assessment and intervention with regard to students who are deaf. *American Annals of the Deaf, 140,* 295–303.

67. McGrew, K., & Murphy, S. (1995). Uniqueness and general factor characteristics of the Woodcock-Johnson Tests of Cognitive Ability—Revised. *Journal of School Psychology, 33,* 235–245.

68. Moore, L. H., Brown, W. S., Markee, T. E., Theberge, D. C., & Zui, J. C. (1995). Bimanual coordination in dyslexic adults. *Neuropsychologia, 33,* 781–793.

69. Payette, K. A., Clarizio, H. F., Phillips, S. E., & Bennett, D. E. (1995). Effects of simple and regressed discrepancy models and cutoffs on severe discrepancy determination. *Psychology in the Schools, 32,* 93–102.

70. Roberts, J. E., Burchinal, M. R., & Clarke-Klein, S. M. (1995). Otitis media in early childhood and cognitive, academic, and behavior outcomes at 12 years of age. *Journal of Pediatric Psychology, 20,* 645–660.

71. Schloss, P. J., Alper, S., Young, H., Arnold-Reid, G., Aylward, M., & Dudenhoeffer, S. (1995). Acquisition of functional sight words in community-based recreation settings. *The Journal of Special Education, 29,* 84–96.

72. Schuerholz, L. J., Harris, E. L., Baumgardner, T. L., Reiss, A. L., Freund, L. S., Church, R. P., Mohr, J., & Denckla, M. B. (1995). An analysis of two discrepancy-based models and a processing-deficit approach in identifying learning disabilities. *Journal of Learning Disabilities, 28,* 18–29.

73. Shaywitz, B. A., Holford, T. R., Holahan, J. M., Fletcher, J. M., Stuebing, K. K., Francis, D. J., & Shaywitz, S. E. (1995). A Matthew effect for IQ but not for reading: Results from a longitudinal study. *Reading Research Quarterly, 30,* 894–906.

74. Siegel, J., Cook, R., & Gerard, J. (1995). Differential categorization of words by learning disabled, gifted, and nonexceptional students. *Perceptual and Motor Skills, 81,* 243–250.

75. Sullivan, G. S., Mastropieri, M. A., & Scruggs, T. E. (1995). Reasoning and remembering: Coaching students with learning disabilities to think. *The Journal of Special Education, 29,* 310–322.

76. Waber, D. P., & McCormick, M. C. (1995). Late neuropsychological outcomes in preterm infants of normal IQ: Selective vulnerability of the visual system. *Journal of Pediatric Psychology, 20,* 721–735.

77. Walton, P. D. (1995). Rhyming ability, phoneme identity, letter-sound knowledge, and the use of orthographic analogy by prereaders. *Journal of Educational Psychology, 87,* 587–597.

78. Wilson, B. N., Polatajko, H. J., Kaplan, B. J., & Faris, P. (1995). Use of Bruininks-Oseretsky Test of Motor Proficiency in occupational therapy. *The American Journal of Occupational Therapy, 49,* 8–17.

79. Wisniewski, J. J., Andrews, T. J., & Mulick, J. A. (1995). Objective and subjective factors in the disproportionate referral of children for academic problems. *Journal of Consulting and Clinical Psychology, 63,* 1032–1076.

80. Yasutake, D., & Bryan, T. (1995). The influence of affect on the achievement and behavior of students with learning disabilities. *Journal of Learning Disabilities, 28,* 329334.

81. Zigmond, N. (1995). Inclusion in Kansas educational experiences of students with learning disabilities in one elementary school. *The Journal of Special Education, 29,* 144–154.

82. August, G. J., Realmuto, G. M., MacDonald, A. W., III, Nugent, S.M., & Crosby, R. (1996). Prevalence of ADHD and comorbid disorders among elementary school children screened for disruptive behavior. *Journal of Abnormal Child Psychology, 24,* 571–595.

83. Barnett, K. P., Clarizio, H. F., & Payette, K. A. (1996). Grade retention among students with learning disabilities. *Psychology in the Schools, 33,* 285–293.

84. Berninger, V., Whitaker, D., Feng, Y., Swanson, H. L., & Abbott, R. D. (1996). Assessment of planning, translating, and revising in junior high writers. *Journal of School Psychology, 34,* 23–52.

85. Carlisle, J. F., & Chang, V. (1996). Evaluation of academic capabilities in science by students with and without learning disabilities and their teachers. *The Journal of Special Education, 30,* 18–34.

86. Carte, E. T., Nigg, J. T., & Hinshaw, S. P. (1996). Neuropsychological functioning, motor speed, and language processing in boys with and without ADHD. *Journal of Abnormal Child Psychology, 24,* 481–498.

87. Eden, G. F., Stein, J. F., Wood, H. M., & Wood, F. B. (1996). Differences in visuospatial judgment in reading-disabled and normal children. *Perceptual and Motor Skills, 82,* 155–177.

88. Francis, D. J., Fletcher, J. M., Shaywitz, B. A., Shaywitz, S. E., & Rourke, B. P. (1996). Defining learning and language disabilities: Conceptual and psychometric issues with the use of IQ tests. *Language, Speech, and Hearing Services in Schools, 27,* 132–143.

89. Francis, D. J., Shaywitz, S. E., Stuebing, K. K., Shaywitz, B. A., & Fletcher, J. M. (1996). Developmental lag versus deficit models of reading disability: A longitudinal, individual growth curves analysis. *Journal of Educational Psychology, 88,* 3–17.

90. Gottesman, R. L. Bennett, R. E., Nathan, R. G., & Kelly, M. S. (1996). Inner-city adults with severe reading difficulties: A closer look. *Journal of Learning Disabilities, 29,* 589–597.

91. Hicks, P., & Bolen, L. M. (1996). Review of the Woodcock-Johnson Psycho-Educational Battery—Revised. *Journal of School Psychology, 34,* 93–102.

92. Javorsky, J. (1996). An examination of youth with attention-deficit/hyperactivity disorder and language learning disabilities: A clinical study. *Journal of Learning Disabilities, 29,* 247–258.

93. John, S., & Ovsiew, F. (1996). Erotomania in a brain-damaged male. *Journal of Disability Research, 40,* 279–283.

94. Lupart, J. L., & Pyryt, M. C. (1996). "Hidden gifted" students: Underachiever prevalence and profile. *Journal for the Education of the Gifted, 20,* 36–53.

95. McGrew, K. S., & Knopik, S. N. (1996). The relationship between intra-cognitive scatter on the Woodcock-Johnson Psycho-Educational Battery—Revised and school achievement. *Journal of School Psychology, 34,* 351–364.

96. McGrew, K. S., Bruininks, R. H., & Johnson, D. R. (1996). Confirmatory factor analytic investigation of Greenspan's model of personal competence. *American Journal on Mental Retardation, 100,* 533–545.

97. Moore, B. D., Slopis, J. M., Schomer, D., Jackson, E. F., & Levy, B. M. (1996). Neuropsychological significance of areas of high signal intensity on brain MRI's of children with neurofibromatosis. *Neurology, 46,* 1660–1668.

98. Moore, L. H., Brown, W. S., Markee, T. E., Theberge, D. C., & Zui, J. C. (1996). Callosal transfer of finger localization information in phonologically dyslexic adults. *Cortex, 32,* 311–322.

99. Rovet, J., Netley, C., Keenan, M., Bailey, J., & Stewart, D. (1996). The psychoeducational profile of boys with Klinefelter Syndrome. *Journal of Learning Disabilities, 29,* 189–196.

100. Schuerholz, L. J., Baumgardner, T. L., Singer, H. S., Reiss, A. L., & Denckla, M. B. (1996). Neuropsychological status of children with Tourette's syndrome with and without attention deficit hyperactivity disorder. *Neurology, 46,* 958–964.

101. Sparks, R. L., & Ganschow, L. (1996). Teacher's perceptions of students' foreign language academic skills and affective characteristics. *Journal of Educational Research, 89,* 172–185.

102. Teo, A., Carlson, E., Mathieu, P. J., Egeland, B., & Sroufe, L. A. (1996). A prospective longitudinal study of psychosocial predictors of achievement. *Journal of School Psychology, 34,* 285–306.

103. Vaughn, S., Elbaum, B. E., & Schumm, J. S. (1996). The effects of inclusion on the social functioning of students with learning disabilities. *Journal of Learning Disabilities, 29,* 598–608.

104. Wiig, E. H., Jones, S. S., & Wiig, E. D. (1996). Computer-based assessment of word knowledge in teens with learning disabilities. *Language, Speech, and Hearing Services in Schools, 27,* 21–28.

105. Wilson, M. S., & Reschly, D. J. (1996). Assessment in school psychology training and practice. *School Psychology Review, 25,* 9–23.

106. Yoshinaga-Itano, C., & Downey, D. M. (1996). The psychoeducational characteristics of school-aged students in Colorado with educationally significant hearing losses. *Volta Review, 98,* 65–96.

107. Yoshinaga-Itano, C. Snyder, L. S., & Mayberry, R. (1996). Can lexical/semantic skills differentiate deaf or hard-of-hearing readers and nonreaders? *Volta Review, 98* 39–61.

108. Alster, E. H. (1997). The effects of extended time on algebra test scores for college students with and without learning disabilities. *Journal of Learning Disabilities, 30,* 222–227.

109. Andrews, T. J., Wisniewski, J. J., & Mulick, J. A. (1997). Variables influencing teachers' decision to refer children for school psychological assessment. *Psychology in the Schools, 34,* 239–244.

110. Bakken, J. P., Mastropieri, M. A., & Scruggs, T. E. (1997). Reading comprehension on expository science material and students with learning disability: A comparison of strategies. *The Journal of Special Education, 31,* 300–324.

111. Bolen, L. M., Kimball, D. J., Hall, C. W., & Webster, R. E. (1997). A comparison of visual and auditory processing tests on the Woodcock-Johnson Tests of Cognitive Ability, Revised and the Learning Efficiency Test-II. *Psychology in the Schools, 34,* 321–328.

112. Burchinal, M. R., Campbell, F. A., Bryant, D. M., Wasik, B. H., & Ramey, C. T. (1997). Early intervention and medicating processes in cognitive performance of children of low-income African American families. *Child Development, 68,* 935–954.

113. Campbell, T., Dollaghan, C., Needleman, H., & Janosky, J. (1997). Reducing bias in language assessment: Processing-dependent measures. *Journal of Speech, Language, and Hearing Research, 40,* 519–525.

114. Chen, R. S., & Vellutino, F. R. (1997). Prediction of reading ability: A cross-validation study of the simple view of reading. *Journal of Literacy Research, 29,* 1–24.

115. Davis, J. T., Parr, G., & Lan, W. (1997). Differences between learning disability subtypes classified using the Revised Woodcock-Johnson Psycho-Educational Battery. *Journal of Learning Disabilities, 30,* 346–352.

116. Galper, A., Wigfield, A., & Seefeldt, C. (1997). Head Start parents' beliefs about children's abilities, task values, and performances on different activities. *Child Development, 68,* 897–907.

117. Hinshaw, S. P., Zupan, B. A., Simmel, C., Nigg, J. T., & Melnick, S. (1997). Peer status in boys with and without attention-deficit hyperactivity disorder: Predictions from overt and covert antisocial behavior, social isolation, and authoritative parenting beliefs. *Child Development, 68,* 880–896.

118. Isaka, E., & Plante, E. (1997). Short-term and working memory differences in language/learning disabled and normal adults. *Journal of Communication Disorders, 30,* 427–437.

119. Jiménez, R. T. (1997). The strategic reading abilities and potential of five low-literacy Latina/o readers in middle school. *Reading Research Quarterly, 32,* 224–243.

120. Jimerson, S., Carlson, E., Rotert, M., Egeland, B., & Sroufe, L. A. (1997). A prospective, longitudinal study of the correlates and consequences of early grade retention. *Journal of School Psychology, 35,* 3–25.

121. Johnson, L., Graham, S., & Harris, K. R. (1997). The effects of goal setting and self-instruction in learning a reading comprehension strategy: A study of students with learning disabilities. *Journal of Learning Disabilities, 30,* 80–91.

122. Lamminmäki, T., Ahonen, T., deBarra, H. T., Tolvanen, A., Michelsson, K., & Lyytinen, H. (1997). Two-year group treatment for children with learning difficulties: Assessing effects of treatment duration and pretreatment characteristics. *Journal of Learning Disabilities, 30,* 354–364.

123. Laurent, J. (1997). Characteristics of the standard and supplemental batteries of the Woodcock-Johnson Tests of Cognitive Ability—Revised with a college sample. *Journal of School Psychology, 35,* 403–416.

124. McGrew, K. S., Keith, T. Z., Flanagan, D. P., & Vanderwood, M. (1997). Beyond *g*: The impact of gf-gc specific cognitive abilities research on the future use and interpretation of intelligence tests in the schools. *School Psychology Review, 26,* 189–210.

125. Michaels, C. A., Lazar, J. W., & Risucci, D. A. (1997). A neuropsychological approach to assessment of adults with learning disabilities in vocational rehabilitation. *Journal of Learning Disabilities, 30,* 544–551.

126. Schultz, M. K. (1997). WISC-III and WJ-R Tests of Achievement: Concurrent validity and learning disability identification. *The Journal of Special Education, 31,* 377–386.

127. Snyder, M. C., & Bambara, L. M. (1997). Teaching secondary students with learning disabilities to self-manage classroom survival skills. *Journal of Learning Disabilities, 30,* 534–543.

128. Sparks, R. L., Ganschow, L., Artzer, M., & Patton, J. (1997). Foreign language proficiency of at-risk and not-at-risk learners over 2 years of foreign language instruction: A follow-up study. *Journal of Learning Disabilities, 30,* 92–98.

129. Stipek, D. J., & Ryan, R. H. (1997). Economically disadvantaged preschoolers: Ready to learn but further to go. *Developmental Psychology, 33,* 711–723.

130. Zimmerman, I. L., & Woo-Sam, J. M. (1997). Review of the criterion-related validity of the WISC-III: The first five years. *Perceptual and Motor Skills, 85,* 531–546.

131. Carthy, L., & Archer, R. P. (1998). Factor structure of the MMPI-A content scales: Item-level and scale-level findings. *Journal of Personality Assessment, 71,* 84–97.

132. Flanagan, D. P., & McGrew, K. S. (1998). Interpreting intelligence tests from contemporary Gf-Ge theory: Joint confirmatory factor analysis of the WJ-R and KAIT in a non-white sample. *Journal of School Psychology, 36,* 151–182.

133. Handwerk, M. L., & Marshall, R. M. (1998). Behavioral and emotional problems of students with learning disabilities, serious emotional disturbance, or both conditions. *Journal of Learning Disabilities, 31,* 327–338.

134. Meyer, M. S., Wood, F. B., Hart, L. A., & Felton, R. H. (1998). Selective predictive value of rapid automatized naming in poor readers. *Journal of Learning Disabilities, 31,* 106–117.

135. Shelton, T. L., Barkley, R. A., Crosswait, C., Moorehouse, M., Fletcher, K., Barrett, S., Jenkins, L., & Metevia, L. (1998). Psychiatric and psychological morbidity as a function of adaptive disability in preschool children with aggressive and hyperactive-impulsive-inattention behavior. *Journal of Abnormal Child Psychology, 26,* 475–494.

136. Ward-Lonergan, J. M., Liles, B. Z., & Anderson, A. M. (1998). Listening comprehension and recall abilities in adolescents with language-learning disabilities and without disabilities for social studies lectures. *Journal of Communication Disorders, 31,* 1–32.

137. Witte, R. H., Phillips, L., & Kakela, M. (1998). Job satisfaction of college graduates with learning disabilities. *Journal of Learning Disabilities, 31,* 259–265.

138. Jimerson, S., Egeland, B., & Teo, A. (1999). A longitudinal study of achievement projectories: Factors associated with change. *Journal of Educational Psychology, 91,* 116–126.

139. Justice, E. M., Lindsey, L. L., & Morrow, S. F. (1999). The relation of self-perceptions to achievement among African American preschoolers. *Journal of Black Psychology, 25,* 48–60.

140. Wigfield, A., Galper, A., Denton, K., & Seefeldt, C. (1999). Teacher's beliefs about former head start and non-head start first-grade children's motivation, performance, and future educational prospects. *Journal of Educational Psychology, 91,* 98–104.

[2902]

Woodcock Language Proficiency Battery—Revised.

Purpose: Intended to measure abilities and achievement in oral language, reading, and written language as well as English language competence.
Population: Ages 2-90+.
Publication Dates: 1980-1991.
Acronym: WLPB-R.
Scores, 25: Oral Language (Memory for Sentences, Picture Vocabulary, Oral Vocabulary, Listening Comprehension, Verbal Analogies), Reading (Letter-Word Identification, Passage Comprehension, Work Attack, Reading Vocabulary), Written Language (Dictation, Writing Samples, Proofing, Writing Fluency), Punctuation and Capitalization, Spelling, Usage, Handwriting, Oral Language, Broad Reading, Basic Reading Skills, Reading Comprehension, Broad Written Language, Basic Writing Skills, Written Expression, Broad English Ability.
Administration: Individual.
Price Data, 1999: $279 per complete test including test book, audio cassette, 25 response booklets, 25 test records, examiner's manual ('91, 219 pages), and norm tables (258 pages); $48 per 25 response booklets and 25 test records.
Foreign Language Edition: Spanish edition available.
Time: (20-60) minutes.
Comments: Battery is a subset of the tests included in the Woodcock-Johnson Psycho-Educational Battery—Revised (2901).
Author: Richard W. Woodcock.
Publisher: Riverside Publishing.
Cross References: For reviews by Irvin J. Lehmann and G. Michael Poteat, see 12:416 (3 references); see also T4:2974 (1 reference); for reviews by Ruth Noyce and Michelle Quinn, see 9:1388.

TEST REFERENCES

1. Aaron, P. G. (1995). Differential diagnosis of reading disabilities. *School Psychology Review, 24,* 345–360.
2. Joshi, R. M. (1995). Assessing reading and spelling skills. *School Psychology Review, 24,* 361–375.
3. Bond, C. L., Ross, S. M., Smith, L. J., & Nunnery, J. A. (1996). The effects of the sing, spell, read and write program on reading achievement of beginning readers. *Reading Research and Instruction, 35,* 122–141.
4. Zima, B. T., Wells, K. B., Benjamin, B., & Duan, N. (1996). Mental health problems among homeless mothers: Relationship to service use and child mental health problems. *Archives of General Psychiatry, 53,* 332–338.
5. Campbell, T., Dollaghan, C., Needleman, H., & Janosky, J. (1997). Reducing bias in language assessment: Processing-dependent measures. *Journal of Speech, Language, and Hearing Research, 40,* 519–525.

[2903]

Woodcock-McGrew-Werder Mini-Battery of Achievement.

Purpose: Constructed as a brief, wide-range test of basic skills and knowledge.
Population: Ages 4–90.
Publication Date: 1994.
Acronym: MBA.
Scores, 5: Basic Skills (Reading, Writing, Mathematics, Total), Factual Knowledge.
Administration: Individual.
Price Data, 1999: $170 per complete kit including test book including examiner's manual (37 pages), 25 test records with subject worksheets, and 5.25-inch and 3.5-inch computer disks; $26 per 25 test records and subject worksheets.
Time: (25–30) minutes.
Authors: Richard W. Woodcock, Kevin McGrew, and Judy Werder.
Publisher: Riverside Publishing.
Cross References: For reviews by William B. Michael and Eleanor E. Sanford, see 13:363.

TEST REFERENCES

1. Williams, J., Zolten, A. J., Rickert, V. I., Spence, G. T., & Ashcraft, E. W. (1993). Use of nonverbal tests to screen for writing dysfluency in school-age children. *Perceptual and Motor Skills, 76,* 803–809.
2. Hooper, S. R. (1995). Relationship between the Luria-Nebraska Neuropsychological Battery and Woodcock-Johnson Tests of Achievement—Revised in children with psychiatric impairment. *Perceptual and Motor Skills, 80,* 1353–1354.

[2904]

Woodcock-Muñoz Language Survey.

Purpose: "Designed for measuring cognitive-academic language proficiencies."
Population: Ages 4–adults.
Publication Date: 1993.
Acronym: LS-E; LS-S.
Scores, 7: Picture Vocabulary, Verbal Analogies, Letter-Word Identification, Dictation, Oral Language, Reading-Writing, Broad Ability.
Administration: Individual.
Editions, 2: LS-E (English language); LS-S (Spanish language).
Price Data, 1999: $200 per complete battery including manual (117 pages), scoring, and reporting software (3.5-inch disks), specify English or Spanish edition and IBM or Apple; $27 per 25 test forms.
Foreign Language Edition: Available in English and Spanish.
Time: (15–20) minutes.
Authors: Richard W. Woodcock and Ana F. Muñoz-Sandoval.
Publisher: Riverside Publishing.
Cross References: For reviews by Linda Crocker and Chi-Wen Kao, see 13:364.

[2905]

Woodcock Reading Mastery Tests—Revised [1998 Normative Update].

Purpose: To measure "several important aspects of reading ability."
Population: Kindergarten through adult.
Publication Dates: 1973–1998.
Scores, 11: Readiness Cluster (Visual-Auditory Learning, Letter Identification, Total), Basic Skills

Cluster (Word Identification, Word Attack, Total), Reading Comprehension Cluster (Word Comprehension, Passage Comprehension, Total), Total Reading—Full Scale, Total Reading—Short Scale, plus a Supplementary Letter Checklist.

Administration: Individual.

Forms, 2: G, H (includes Reading Achievement tests only).

Price Data, 1999: $314.95 per Form G and Form H combined kit including Form G and Form H test books, 25 each of test records, sample Form G & H summary record form, pronunciation guide cassette, sample report to parents, and examiner's manual ('98, 214 pages); $234.95 per Form G complete kit including materials in combined kit for Form G only; $229.95 per Form H complete kit including materials in combined kit for Form H only; $39.95 per 25 test records (specify Form G or Form H); $23.95 per 25 Form G and H summary record forms; $19.95 per 25 reports to parents; $199.95 per ASSIST scoring software (specify IBM PC/XT/AT, PS/2, and compatibles of Apple IIc, enhanced IIe, and IIGS).

Time: (40–45) minutes for entire battery; (15) minutes for Short Scale.

Comments: Test same as 1987 edition but with 1998 norms for grades K–12 and ages 5–22.

Author: Richard W. Woodcock.

Publisher: American Guidance Service, Inc.

Cross References: See T4:2976 (34 references); for reviews by Robert B. Cooter, Jr. and Richard M. Jaeger, see 10:391 (38 references); see also T3:2641 (17 references); for reviews by Carol Anne Dwyer and J. Jaap Tuinman, and excerpted reviews by Alex Bannatyne, Richard L. Allington, Cherry Houck (with Larry A. Harris), and Barton B. Proger of the 1973 edition, see 8:779 (7 references).

TEST REFERENCES

1. Catts, H. W., & Kamhi, A. G. (1986). The linguistic basis of reading disorders: Implications for the speech-language pathologist. *Language, Speech, and Hearing Services in Schools, 17,* 329–341.

2. Pratt, A. C., & Brady, S. (1988). Relation of phonological awareness to reading disability in children and adults. *Journal of Educational Psychology, 80,* 319–323.

3. Goldsmiths-Phillips, J. (1989). Word and context in reading development: A test of the interactive-compensatory hypothesis. *Journal of Educational Psychology, 81,* 299–305.

4. Koenig, L. A., & Biel, C. D. (1989). A delivery system of comprehensive language services in a school district. *Language, Speech, and Hearing Services in Schools, 20,* 338–365.

5. Levinson, H. N. (1989). Abnormal optokinetic and perceptual span parameters in cerebellar-vestibular dysfunction and learning disabilities or dyslexia. *Perceptual and Motor Skills, 68,* 35–54.

6. Lewandowski, L. J., & Martens, B. K. (1989). Selecting and evaluating standardized reading tests. *Journal of Reading, 33,* 384-388.

7. Torgesen, J. K., Wagner, R. K., Balthazar, M., Davis, C., Morgan, S., Simmons, K., Stage, S., & Zirps, F. (1989). Developmental and individual differences in performance on phonological synthesis tasks. *Journal of Experimental Child Psychology, 47,* 491-505.

8. Chase, C. H., & Tallal, P. (1990). A developmental, interactive activation model of the Word Superiority Effect. *Journal of Experimental Child Psychology, 49,* 448-487.

9. Cunningham, A. E., & Stanovich, K. E. (1990). Assessing print exposure and orthographic processing skill in children: A quick measure of reading experience. *Journal of Educational Psychology, 82,* 733–740.

10. Davidson, R. J., Leslie, S. C., & Saron, C. (1990). Reaction time measures of interhemispheric transfer time in reading disabled and normal children. *Neuropsychologia, 22,* 471–485.

11. Ball, E. W., & Blachman, B. A. (1991). Does phoneme awareness training in kindergarten make a difference in early word recognition and developmental spelling? *Reading Research Quarterly, 26,* 49-66.

12. Bowers, P. G., & Swanson, L. B. (1991). Naming speed deficits in reading disability: Multiple measures of a singular process. *Journal of Experimental Child Psychology, 51,* 195-219.

13. Gleason, M., Carnine, D., & Vala, N. (1991). Cumulative versus rapid introduction of new information. *Exceptional Children, 57,* 353-358.

14. Kim, W. J., Hahn, S. U., Kish, J., Rosenberg, L., & Harris, J. (1991). Separation reaction of psychiatrically hospitalized children: A pilot study. *Child Psychiatry and Human Development, 22,* 53-67.

15. Kinney, M. A., & Harry, A. L. (1991). An informal inventory for adolescents that assesses the reader, the text, and the task. *Journal of Reading, 34,* 643-647.

16. Parker, R. I., Tindal, G., & Hasbrouck, J. (1991). Progress monitoring with objective measures of writing performance for students with mild disabilities. *Exceptional Children, 58,* 61-73.

17. Shefelbine, J., & Calhoun, J. (1991). Variability in approaches to identifying polysyllabic words: A descriptive study of sixth graders with highly, moderately, and poorly developed syllabication strategies. *Yearbook of National Reading Conference, 40,* 169-177.

18. Wolery, M., Cybriwsky, C. A., Gast, D. L., & Boyle-Gast, K. (1991). Use of constant time delay and attentional responses with adolescents. *Exceptional Children, 57,* 462-474.

19. Barker, T. A., Torgesen, J. K., & Wagner, R. K. (1992). The role of orthographic processing skills on five different reading tasks. *Reading Research Quarterly, 27,* 335-345.

20. Barnes, M. A., & Dennis, M. (1992). Reading in children and adolescents after early onset hydrocephalus and in normally developing age peers: Phonological analysis, word recognition, word comprehension, and passage comprehension skill. *Journal of Pediatric Psychology, 17,* 445–465.

21. Cornwall, A. (1992). The relationship of phonological awareness, rapid naming, and verbal memory to severe reading and spelling disability. *Journal of Learning Disabilities, 25,* 532–538.

22. Fuchs, L. S., & Deno, S. L. (1992). Effects of curriculum within curriculum-based measurement. *Exceptional Children, 58,* 232-243.

23. Hansen, J., & Bowey, J. A. (1992). Orthographic rimes as functional units of reading in fourth-grade children. *Australian Journal of Psychology, 44,* 37–44.

24. Hoff, A. L., Riordan, H., O'Donnell, D., Stritzke, P., Neale, C., Boccio, A., Anand, A. K., & DeLisi, L. E. (1992). Anomalous lateral sulcus asymmetry and cognitive function in first-episode schizophrenia. *Schizophrenia Bulletin, 18,* 257–273.

25. Lewis, B. A., & Freebairn, L. (1992). Residual effects of preschool phonology disorders in grade school, adolescence, and adulthood. *Journal of Speech and Hearing Research, 35,* 819–831.

26. Mahony, D. L., & Mann, V. A. (1992). Using children's humor to clarify the relationship between linguistic awareness and early reading ability. *Cognition, 45,* 163–186.

27. Malone, L. D., & Mastropieri, M. A. (1992). Reading comprehension instruction: Summarization and self-monitoring training for students with learning disabilities. *Exceptional Children, 58,* 270-279.

28. Masterson, J. J., & Kamhi, A. G. (1992). Linguistic trade-offs in school-age children with and without language disorders. *Journal of Speech and Hearing Research, 35,* 1064–1075.

29. Siegel, L. S. (1992). An evaluation of the discrepancy definition of dyslexia. *Journal of Learning Disabilities, 25,* 618–629.

30. Tangel, D. M., & Blachman, B. A. (1992). Effect of phoneme awareness instruction on kindergarten children's invented spelling. *Journal of Reading Behavior, 24,* 233-261.

31. Abbott, R. D., & Berninger, V. W. (1993). Structural equation modelling of relationships among developmental skills and writing skills in primary- and intermediate-grade writers. *Journal of Educational Psychology, 85,* 478-508.

32. Ackerman, P. T., & Dykman, R. A. (1993). Phonological processes, confrontational naming, and immediate memory in dsylexia. *Journal of Learning Disabilities, 26,* 597–609.

33. Bowers, P. G. (1993). Text reading and rereading: Determinants of fluency beyond word recognition. *Journal of Reading Behavior, 25,* 133-153.

34. Catts, H. W. (1993). The relationship between speech-language impairments and reading disabilities. *Journal of Speech and Hearing Research, 36,* 948–958.

35. Danoff, B., Harris, K. R., & Graham, S. (1993). Incorporating strategy instruction within the writing process in the regular classroom: Effects on the writing of students with and without learning disabilities. *Journal of Reading Behavior, 25,* 295-322.

36. Felton, R. H. (1993). Effects of instruction on the decoding skills of children with phonological-process problems. *Journal of Learning Disabilities, 26,* 583–589.

37. Geva, E., Wade-Woolley, L., & Shany, M. (1993). The concurrent development of spelling and decoding in two different orthographies. *Journal of Reading Behavior, 25,* 383-406.

38. Graham, S., Schwartz, S. S., & MacArthur, C. A. (1993). Knowledge of writing and the composing process, attitude toward writing, and self-efficacy for students with and without learning disabilities. *Journal of Learning Disabilities, 26,* 237–249.

39. Hurford, D. P., Darrow, L. J., Edwards, T. L., Howerton, C. J., Mote, C. R., Schauf, J. D., & Coffey, P. (1993). An examination of phonemic processing abilities in children during their first-grade year. *Journal of Learning Disabilities, 26,* 167–177.

40. Jackson, N. E., Donaldson, G. W., & Mills, J. R. (1993). Components of reading skill in postkindergarten precocious readers and level-matched second graders. *Journal of Reading Behavior, 25,* 181-208.

41. Katz, L., & Goldstein, G. (1993). The Luria-Nebraska Neuropsychological Battery and the WAIS-R in assessment of adults with specific learning disabilities. *Rehabilitation Counselor Bulletin, 36,* 190–198.

42. Kenny, D. T., & Chekaluk, E. (1993). Early reading performance: A comparison of teacher-based and test-based assessments. *Journal of Learning Disabilities, 26,* 227–236.

43. Little, S. S. (1993). Nonverbal learning disabilities and socioemotional functioning: A review of recent literature. *Journal of Learning Disabilities, 26,* 653–665.

44. Manis, F. R., Custodio, R., & Szeszulski, P. A. (1993). Development of phonological and orthographic skill: A 2-year longitudinal study of dyslexic children. *Journal of Experimental Child Psychology, 56,* 64-86.

45. Mann, V. A. (1993). Phoneme awareness and future reading ability. *Journal of Learning Disabilities, 26,* 259–269.

46. Rovet, J. F. (1993). The psychoeducational characteristics of children with Turner syndrome. *Journal of Learning Disabilities, 26, 333–341.*

47. Uhry, J. K., & Shepherd, M. J. (1993). Segmentation/spelling instruction as part of a first-grade reading program: Effects on several measures of reading. *Reading Research Quarterly, 28,* 219-233.

48. Watson, B. V., & Miller, T. K. (1993). Auditory perception, phonological processing, and reading ability/disability. *Journal of Speech and Hearing Research, 36,* 850–863.

49. Ackerman, P. T., Dykman, R. A., Oglesby, D. M., & Newton, J. E. O. (1994). EEG power spectra of children with dyslexia, slow learners, and normally reading children with ADD during verbal processing. *Journal of Learning Disabilities, 27,* 619–630.

50. Colegrove, R. W., Jr., & Huntzinger, R. M. (1994). Academic, behavioral, and social adaptation of boys with hemophilia/HIV disease. *Journal of Pediatric Psychology, 19,* 457-473.

51. Das, J. P., Mishra, R. K., & Kirby, J. R. (1994). Cognitive patterns of children with dyslexia: A comparison between groups with high and average nonverbal intelligence. *Journal of Learning Disabilities, 27,* 235–242.

52. Das, J. P., Mok, M., & Mishra, R. K. (1994). The role of speech processes and memory in reading disability. *The Journal of General Psychology, 121,* 131–146.

53. Eaves, R. C., Williams, P., Winchester, K., & Darch, C. (1994). Using teacher judgement and IQ to estimate reading and mathematics achievement in a remedial-reading program. *Psychology in the Schools, 31,* 261-272.

54. Goldstein, G., Minshew, N. J., & Siegel, D. J. (1994). Age differences in academic achievement in high-functioning autistic individuals. *Journal of Clinical and Experimental Neuropsychology, 16,* 671-680.

55. Hansen, J., & Bowey, J. A. (1994). Phonological analysis skills, verbal working memory, and reading ability in second-grade children. *Child Development, 65,* 938-950.

56. Hurford, D. P., Johnston, M., Nepote, P., Hampton, S., Moore, S., Neal, J., Mueller, A., McGeorge, K., Huff, L., Awad, A., Tatro, C., Juliano, C., & Huffman, D. (1994). Early identification and remediation of phonological-processing deficits in first-grade children at risk for reading disabilities. *Journal of Learning Disabilities, 27,* 647–659.

57. Hurford, D. P., Schauf, J. D., Bunce, L., Blaich, T., & Moore, K. (1994). Early identification of children at risk for reading disabilities. *Journal of Learning Disabilities, 27,* 371–382.

58. Meyer, L. A., Stahl, S. A., & Wardrop, J. L. (1994). Effects of reading storybooks aloud to children. *The Journal of Educational Research, 88,* 69–85.

59. Minshew, N. J., Goldstein, G., Taylor, H. G., & Siegel, D. J. (1994). Academic achievement in high functioning autistic individuals. *Journal of Clinical and Experimental Neuropsychology, 16,* 261-270.

60. Morton, L. L. (1994). Interhemispheric balance patterns detected by selective phonemic dichotic laterality measures in four clinical subtypes of reading-disabled children. *Journal of Clinical and Experimental Neuropsychology, 16,* 556-567.

61. Pinell, G. S., Lyons, C. A., DeFord, D. E., Bryk, A. S., & Seltzer, M. (1994). Comparing instructional models for the literacy education of high-risk first graders. *Reading Research Quarterly, 29,* 9-40.

62. Ross, S. M., & Smith, L. J. (1994). Effects of the Success for All model on kindergarten through second grade reading achievement, techers' adjustment, and classroom-school climate at an inner-city school. *The Elementary School Journal, 95,* 121–138.

63. Scruggs, T. E., Mastropieri, M. A., & Sullivan, G. S. (1994). Promoting relational thinking: Elaborative interrogation for students with mild disabilities. *Exceptional Children, 60,* 450-457.

64. Shafrir, V., & Siegel, L. S. (1994). Subtypes of learning disabilities in adolescents and adults. *Journal of Learning Disabilities, 27,* 123–134.

65. Spear-Swerling, L., & Sternberg, R. J. (1994). The road not taken: An integrative theoretical model of reading disability. *Journal of Learning Disabilities, 27,* 91–103.

66. Stanford, L. D., & Hynd, G. W. (1994). Congruence of behavioral symptomatology in children with ADD/H, ADD/WO, and learning disabilities. *Journal of Learning Disabilities, 27,* 243–253.

67. van Ijzendoorn, M. H., & Bus, A. G. (1994). Meta-analytic confirmation of the nonword reading deficit in developmental dyslexia. *Reading Research Quarterly, 29,* 267-275.

68. VanWagenen, M. A., Williams, R. L., & McLaughlin, T. F. (1994). Use of assisted reading to improve reading rate, word accuracy, and comprehension with ESL Spanish-speaking students. *Perceptual and Motor Skills, 79,* 227-230.

69. Baker, J. M. (1995). Inclusion in Virginia: Educational experiences of students with learning disabilities in one elementary school. *The Journal of Special Education, 29,* 116–123.

70. Bowey, J. A. (1995). Socioeconomic status differences in preschool phonological sensitivity and first-grade reading achievement. *Journal of Educational Psychology, 87,* 476–487.

71. Das, J. P., Mishra, R. K., & Pool, J. E. (1995). An experiment on cognitive remediation of word-reading disability. *Journal of Learning Disabilities, 28,* 66–79.

72. Feldman, J., Kerr, B., & Streissguth, A. D. (1995). Correlational analyses of procedural and declarative learning performance. *Intelligence, 20,* 87-114.

73. Felton, R. H., & Pepper, P. P. (1995). Early identification and intervention of phonological deficits in kindergarten and early elementary children at risk for reading disability. *School Psychology Review, 24,* 405–414.

74. Ganschow, L., & Sparks, R. (1995). Effects of direct instruction in Spanish phonology on the native-language skills and foreign-language aptitude of at-risk foreign-language learners. *Journal of Learning Disabilities, 28,* 107–120.

75. Hoba, M. E., & Ramisetty-Mikler, S. (1995). The language skills and concepts of early and nonearly readers. *The Journal of Genetic Psychology, 156,* 313–331.

76. Joshi, R. M. (1995). Assessing reading and spelling skills. *School Psychology Review, 24,* 361–375.

77. Kershner, J. R., & Graham, N. A. (1995). Attentional control over language lateralization in dyslexic children: Deficit or delay? *Neuropsychologia, 33,* 39–51.

78. Kertoy, M. K., & Goetz, K. M. (1995). The relationship between listening performance on the sentence verification technique and other measures of listening comprehension. *Contemporary Educational Psychology, 20,* 320–339.

79. MacArthur, C. A., & Haynes, J. B. (1995). Student assistant for learning from text: A hypermedia reading aid. *Journal of Learning Disabilities, 28,* 150–159.

80. MacDonald, G. W., & Cornwall, A. (1995). The relationship between phonological awareness and reading and spelling achievement eleven years later. *Journal of Learning Disabilities, 28,* 523–527.

81. Majsterek, D. J., & Ellenwood, A. E. (1995). Phonological awareness and beginning reading: Evaluation of a school-based screening procedure. *Journal of Learning Disabilities, 28,* 449–456.

82. Mardell-Czudnowski, C. (1995). Performance of Asian and White children on the K-ABC: Understanding information processing differences. *Assessment, 2,* 19-29.

83. Martens, B. K., Steele, E. S., Massie, D. R., & Diskin, M. T. (1995). Curriculum bias in standardized tests of reading decoding. *Journal of School Psychology, 33,* 287–296.

84. McBride-Chang, C. (1995). What is phonological awareness? *Journal of Educational Psychology, 87,* 179-192.

85. McGuinness, D., McGuinness, C., & Donohue, J. (1995). Phonological training and the alphabet principle: Evidence for reciprocal causality. *Reading Research Quarterly, 30,* 830–852.

86. O'Connor, R. E., & Jenkins, J. R. (1995). Improving the generalization of sound/symbol knowledge: Teaching spelling to kindergarten children with disabilities. *The Journal of Special Education, 29,* 255–275.

87. Ross, S. M., Smith, L. J., Casey, J., & Slavin, R. E. (1995). Increasing the academic success of disadvantaged children: An examination of alternative early intervention program. *American Educational Research Journal, 32,* 773–800.

88. Shany, M. T., & Biemiller, A. (1995). Assisted reading practice: Effects on performance for poor readers in grades 3 and 4. *Reading Research Quarterly, 30,* 382–395.

89. Shapiro, S. K., & Simpson, R. G. (1995). Koppitz scoring system as a measure of Bender-Gestalt performance in behaviorally and emotionally disturbed adolescents. *Journal of Clinical Psychology, 51,* 108-112.

90. Sparks, R. L., Ganschow, L., & Patton, J. (1995). Prediction of performance in first-year foreign language courses: Connections between native and foreign language learning. *Journal of Educational Psychology, 87,* 638–655.

91. Sullivan, G. S., Mastropieri, M. A., & Scruggs, T. E. (1995). Reasoning and remembering: Coaching students with learning disabilities to think. *The Journal of Special Education, 29,* 310–322.

92. Sverd, J., Sheth, R., Fuss, J., & Levine, J. (1995). Prevalence of pervasive developmental disorder in a sample of psychiatrically hospitalized children and adolescents. *Child Psychiatry and Human Development, 25,* 221–240.

93. Vasey, M. W., Daleiden, E. L., Williams, L. L., & Brown, L. M. (1995). Biased attention in childhood anxiety disorders: A preliminary study. *Journal of Abnormal Child Psychology, 23,* 267-279.

94. Yates, C. M., Berninger, V. W., & Abbott, R. D. (1995). Specific writing disabilities in intellectually gifted children. *Journal for the Education of the Gifted, 18,* 131-155.

95. Badian, N. A. (1996). Dyslexia: A validation of the concept at two age levels. *Journal of Learning Disabilities, 29,* 102–112.

96. Baumann, J. F. (1996). "Coping with reading disability" —12 years later. *Journal of Adolescent & Adult Literacy, 39,* 532–535.

97. Castles, A., & Holmes, V. M. (1996). Subtypes of developmental dyslexia and lexical acquisition. *Australian Journal of Psychology, 48,* 130–135.

98. Lovett, M. W., Borden, S. L., Warren-Chapman, P. M., Lacerenza, L., DeLuca, T., & Giovinazzo, R. (1996). Text comprehension training for disabled readers: An evaluation of reciprocal teaching and text analysis training programs. *Brain and Language, 54,* 447–480.

99. Lovrich, D., Cheng, J. C., & Velting, D. M. (1996). Late cognitive brain potentials, phonological and semantic classification of spoken words, and reading ability in children. *Journal of Clinical and Experimental Neuropsychology, 18,* 161–177.

100. Manis, F. R., Seidenberg, M. S., Doi, L. M., McBride-Chang, C., & Petersen, A. (1996). On the bases of two subtypes of development dyslexia. *Cognition, 58,* 157–195.
101. Mauer, D. M., & Kamhi, A. G. (1996). Factors that influence phoneme-grapheme correspondence learning. *Journal of Learning Disabilities, 29,* 259–270.
102. McBride-Chang, C. (1996). Models of speech perception and phonological processing in reading. *Child Development, 67,* 1836–1856.
103. Pratt, C., Kemp, N., & Martin, F. (1996). Sentence context and word recognition in children with average reading ability and with a specific reading disability. *Australian Journal of Psychology, 48,* 155–159.
104. Rovert, J., & Alvarez, M. (1996). Thyroid hormone and attention in school-age children with congenital hypothyroidism. *Journal of Child Psychology and Psychiatry, 37,* 579–585.
105. Smith, L. J., Ross, S. M., & Casey, J. (1996). Multi-site comparison of the effects of success for all on reading achievement. *Journal of Literacy Research, 28,* 329–353.
106. Sparks, R., Ganschow, L., & Thomas, A. (1996). Role of intelligence tests in speech/language referrals. *Perceptual and Motor Skills, 83,* 195–204.
107. Sparks, R. L., & Ganschow, L. (1996). Teacher's perceptions of students' foreign language academic skills and affective characteristics. *Journal of Educational Research, 89,* 172–185.
108. Troia, G. A. Roth, F. P., & Yeni-Komshian, G. H. (1996). Word frequency and age effects in normally developing children's phonological processing. *Journal of Speech and Hearing Research, 39,* 1099–1108.
109. Filipek, P. A., Semrud-Clikeman, M., Steingard, R. J., Renshaw, P. F., Kennedy, D. N., & Biederman, J. (1997). Volumetric MRI analysis comparing subjects having attention-deficit hyperactivity disorder with normal controls. *Neurology, 48,* 589–601.
110. Gauger, L. M., Lombardino, L. J., & Leonard, C. M. (1997). Brain morphology in children with specific language impairment. *Journal of Speech, Language, and Hearing Research, 40,* 1272–1284.
111. Hart, T. M., Berninger, V. M., & Abbott, R. D. (1997). Comparison of teaching single or multiple orthographic-phonological connections for word recognition and spelling: Implications for instructional consultation. *School Psychology Review, 26,* 279–297.
112. Lance, D. M., Swanson, L. A., & Peterson, H. A. (1997). A validity study of an implicit phonological awareness paradigm. *Journal of Speech, Language, and Hearing Research, 40,* 1002–1010.
113. Lewis, B. A., & Freebairn, L. (1997). Subgrouping children with familial phonologic disorders. *Journal of Communication Disorders, 30,* 385–402.
114. Lovrich, D., Cheng, J. C., Velting, D. M., & Kazmerski, V. (1997). Auditory ERPs during rhyme and semantic processing: Effects of reading ability in college students. *Journal of Clinical and Experimental Neuropsychology, 19,* 313–330.
115. Marshall, R. M., Hynd, G. W., Handwerk, M. J., & Hall, J. (1997). Academic underachievement in ADHD subtypes. *Journal of Learning Disabilities, 30,* 635–642.
116. McBride, H. E. A., & Siegel, L. S. (1997). Learning disabilities and adolescent suicide. *Journal of Learning Disabilities, 30,* 652–659.
117. Velting, O. N., & Whitehurst, G. J. (1997). Inattention-hyperactivity and reading achievement in children from low-income families: A longitudinal model. *Journal of Abnormal Child Psychology, 25,* 321–331.
118. Ackerman, P. T., McPherson, W. B., Oglesby, D. M., & Dykman, R. A. (1998). EEG power spectra of adolescent poor readers. *Journal of Learning Disabilities, 31,* 83–90.
119. Burns, G. L., & Kondrick, P. A. (1998). Psychological behaviorisms reading therapy program: Parents as reading therapists for their children's reading disability. *Journal of Learning Disabilities, 31,* 278–285.
120. Hyman, I. A., Wojtowicz, A., Lee, K. D., Haffner, M. E., Fiorello, C. A., Storlazzi, J. J., & Rosenfeld, J. (1998). School-based methylphenidate placebo protocols: Methodological and practical issues. *Journal of Learning Disabilities, 31,* 581–594, 614.
121. Mathes, P. G., Howard, J. K., Allen, S. H., & Fuchs, D. (1998). Peer-assisted learning strategies for first-grade readers: Responding to the needs of diverse learners. *Reading Research Quarterly, 33,* 62–94.
122. Newman, J., Noel, A., Chen, R., & Matsopoulos, A. S. (1998). Temperament, selected moderating variables and early reading achievement. *Journal of School Psychology, 36,* 215–232.
123. Comeau, L., Cormier, P., Grandmaison, E., & Lacroix, D. (1999). A longitudinal study of plumological processing skills in children learning to read in a second language. *Journal of Educational Psychology, 91,* 29–43.

[2906]

Word Finding Referral Checklist.

Purpose: Designed as "a tool for observing oral language in the classroom for the presence of word-finding behaviors."
Population: Ages 5 to 90.
Publication Date: 1992.
Scores: Item scores only.
Administration: Group.
Manual: No manual.
Price Data, 1995: $25 per 25 checklists.
Time: Administration time not reported.
Comments: Ratings by teachers, parents, and other caregivers.
Authors: D. J. German and A. E. German.
Publisher: PRO-ED.

[2907]

Word Fluency.

Purpose: Measures ability to produce appropriate words rapidly for fluency in verbal expression.
Population: Positions requiring sharp verbal communication skills.
Publication Dates: 1959-1961.
Scores: Total score only.
Administration: Individual or group.
Price Data, 1998: $57 per start-up kit including 25 test booklets and interpretation and research manual ('59, 30 pages); $44 per 25 test booklets (quantity discounts available); $19.75 per interpretation and research manual.
Time: 10 minutes.
Author: Human Resource Center, The University of Chicago.
Publisher: NCS (Rosemont).
Cross References: See T4:2979 (6 references), T3:2645 (1 reference), and T2:594 (2 references); for a review by James E. Kennedy, see 6:562.

TEST REFERENCES

1. Baehr, M. E., & Orban, J. A. (1989). The role of intellectual abilities and personality characteristics in determining success in higher-level positions. *Journal of Vocational Behavior, 35,* 270-287.
2. Klonoff, H., Clark, C., Oger, J., Paty, D., & Li, D. (1991). Neuropsychological performance in patients with mild multiple sclerosis. *The Journal of Nervous and Mental Disease, 179,* 127-131.
3. Ryan, L., Clark, C. M., Klonoff, H., & Paty, D. (1993). Models of cognitive deficit and statistical hypotheses: Multiple sclerosis, an example. *Journal of Clinical and Experimental Neuropsychology, 15,* 563-577.
4. Taylor, H. G., Barry, C. T., & Schatschneider, C. (1993). School-age consequences of haemophilus influenzae Type b meningitis. *Journal of Clinical Child Psychology, 22,* 196-206.
5. Meadows, M. E., Kaplan, R. F., & Bromfield, E. B. (1994). Cognitive recovery with vitamin B12 therapy: A longitudinal neuropsychological assessment. *Neurology, 44,* 1764–1765.
6. Stracciari, A., Ghidoni, E., Guarino, M., Poletti, M., & Pazzaglia, P. (1994). Post-traumatic retrograde amnesia with selective impairment of autobiographical memory. *Cortex, 30,* 459-468.
7. Carlesimo, G. A., Fadda, L., Marfia, G. A., & Caltagirone, C. (1995). Explicit memory and repetition priming in dementia: Evidence for a common basic mechanism underlying conscious and unconscious retrieval deficits. *Journal of Clinical and Experimental Neuropsychology, 17,* 44-57.
8. Cooke, D. L., & Kausler, D. H. (1995). Content memory and temporal memory for actions in survivors of traumatic brain injury. *Journal of Clinical and Experimental Neuropsychology, 17,* 90-99.
9. Kindlon, D., Mezzacappa, E., & Earls, F. (1995). Psychometric properties of impulsivity measures: Temporal stability, validity and factor structure. *Journal of Child Psychology and Psychiatry and Allied Disciplines, 36,* 645-661.

[2908]

Word Identification Scale.

Purpose: Designed as "an informal reading survey that allows a teacher to quickly identify" a student's readability level in terms of "decoding and word recognition skills."
Population: Students.

Publication Dates: 1988–1999.
Acronym: WIS.
Scores: Total score only.
Administration: Individual.
Manual: No manual.
Price Data, 1999: $14 per complete set including plasticized word card with instructions and 50 recording forms.
Time: (5–10) minutes.
Author: John Arena.
Publisher: Academic Therapy Publications.

[2909]

The Word Memory Test.

Purpose: Designed for symptom validity testing—detecting malingering and feigning in comparison to cases of true brain injury and amnesia.
Population: Adults.
Publication Dates: 1995–1996.
Acronym: WMT.
Scores, 5: Immediate Recognition, Delayed Recognition, Multiple Choice, Paired Associates, Free Recall.
Administration: Individual.
Forms, 2: Oral, Computerized.
Price Data, 1996: $300 per complete test including copyable administration forms and unlimited administration/scoring disk; $25 per manual ('96, 132 pages).
Time: (15) minutes.
Comments: Computerized form (C-WMT) self-administered.
Authors: Paul Green, Kevin Astner, and Lyle M. Allen.
Publisher: CogniSyst, Inc.

[2910]

Word Recognition and Phonic Skills.

Purpose: "Designed to give the teacher two assessments of a child's word recognition ability."
Population: Ages 5.0 to 8.6.
Publication Date: 1994.
Acronym: WRaPS.
Scores: Word Recognition.
Administration: Group.
Price Data, 1999: £9.99 per 20 test booklets; £10.50 per diagnostic scoring template; £9.99 per manual (31 pages); £10.99 per specimen set including one copy of test form and manual.
Time: (30) minutes.
Authors: Clifford Carver and David Moseley.
Publisher: Hodder & Stoughton Educational [England].

TEST REFERENCE

1. Beech, John R., & Keys, A. (1997). Reading, vocabulary and language preference in 7- to 8-year-old bilingual Asian children. *British Journal of Educational Psychology, 67,* 405–414.

[2911]

The WORD Test.

Purpose: Designed to assess expressive vocabulary and semantics.
Population: Ages 7 and over.
Publication Date: 1981.
Scores, 7: Associations, Synonyms, Semantic Absurdities, Antonyms, Definitions, Multiple Definitions, Total.
Administration: Group.
Price Data: Available from publisher.
Time: (20-30) minutes.
Authors: Carol Jorgensen, Mark Barrett, Rosemary Huisingh, and Linda Zachman.
Publisher: LinguiSystems, Inc.
Cross References: See T4:2983 (2 references); for reviews by Mavis Donahue and Nambury S. Raju, see 9:1393.

TEST REFERENCES

1. Gillam, R. B., Cowan, N., & Day, L. S. (1995). Sequential memory in children with and without language impairment. *Journal of Speech and Hearing Research, 38,* 393–402.
2. Liles, B. Z., Duffy, R. J., Merritt, D. D., & Purcell, S. L. (1995). Measurement of narrative discourse ability in children with language disorders. *Journal of Speech and Hearing Research, 38,* 415–425.
3. Nippold, M. A. (1995). School-age children and adolescents: Norms for word definition. *Language, Speech, and Hearing Services in Schools, 26,* 320–325.
4. Stevens, L. J., & Bliss, L. S. (1995). Conflict resolution abilities of children with specific language impairment and children with normal language. *Journal of Speech and Hearing Research, 38,* 599–611.
5. Purvis, K. L., & Tannock, R. (1997). Language abilities in children with Attention Deficit Hyperactivity disorder, reading disabilities, and normal controls. *Journal of Abnormal Child Psychology, 25,* 133–144.
6. Ward-Lonergan, J. M., Liles, B. Z., & Anderson, A. M. (1998). Listening comprehension and recall abilities in adolescents with language-learning disabilities and without disabilities for social studies lectures. *Journal of Communication Disorders, 31,* 1–32.

[2912]

Work Adjustment Inventory.

Purpose: "Designed to evaluate adolescents' and young adults' temperament toward work activities, work environments, other employees, and other aspects of work."
Population: Adolescents and young adults.
Publication Date: 1994.
Acronym: WAI.
Scores, 7: Activity, Empathy, Sociability, Assertiveness, Adaptability, Emotionality, WAI Quotient.
Administration: Group or individual.
Price Data, 1999: $79 per complete kit.
Time: (15–20) minutes.
Author: James E. Gilliam.
Publisher: PRO-ED.
Cross References: For reviews by Mark J. Benson and Wayne J. Camara, see 13:365.

[2913]

The Work Adjustment Scale.

Purpose: "A measure of a student's behavioral readiness for employment."
Population: Junior and senior high school students.

Publication Date: 1991.
Acronym: WAS.
Scores, 4: Work Related Behavior, Interpersonal Relations, Social/Community Expectations, Total.
Administration: Individual.
Price Data, 1999: $59.50 per complete kit including technical manual (27 pages), 50 rating forms, and intervention manual (171 pages); $12.50 per technical manual; $31 per 50 rating forms; $16 per intervention manual.
Time: (12–15) minutes.
Comments: Ratings by teachers.
Author: Stephen B. McCarney.
Publisher: Hawthorne Educational Services, Inc.
Cross References: For reviews by Ric Brown and Chantale Jeanrie, see 13:366.

[2914]

Work Aptitude: Profile and Practice Set.

Purpose: "Designed specifically to sample the more common abilities needed for the range of jobs to which educational leavers with minimal qualifications can apply."
Population: Ages 15-17.
Publication Date: 1985.
Scores: 6 subtests: Using Words, Using Your Eyes, Working With Numbers, How Things Work, Being Accurate, Thinking Logically.
Administration: Group.
Price Data: Available from publisher.
Time: (5) minutes per test.
Author: Saville & Holdsworth, Ltd.
Publisher: Macmillan Education Ltd. [England] [No reply from publisher; status unknown].
Cross References: For a review by Kevin R. Murphy, see 10:394.

[2915]

Work Aspect Preference Scale.

Purpose: "Constructed to assess the qualities of work that individuals consider important to them."
Population: Grades 10-12 and college and adults.
Publication Date: 1983.
Acronym: WAPS.
Scores: 13 scales: Independence, Co-Workers, Self-Development, Creativity, Money, Life Style, Prestige, Altruism, Security, Management, Detachment, Physical Activity, Surroundings.
Administration: Group.
Price Data, 1994: A$9 per 10 question booklets; $4.10 per scoring key; $4.20 per 10 answer sheets; $1 per profile; $20 per manual (58 pages); $22.50 per specimen set excluding scoring key.
Time: (10-20) minutes.
Author: Robert Pryor.
Publisher: Australian Council for Educational Research Ltd. [Australia].
Cross References: See T4:2987 (1 reference).

TEST REFERENCES

1. Macnab, D., & Fitzsimmons, G. W. (1987). A multitrait-multimethod study of work-related needs, values, and preferences. *Journal of Vocational Behavior, 30,* 1-15.
2. Hesketh, B., Durant, C., & Pryor, R. (1990). Career compromise: A test of Gottfredson's (1981) theory using a policy-capturing procedure. *Journal of Vocational Behavior, 36,* 97-108.
3. Pryor, R. G. L. (1990). An investigation of factors affecting the stability of work aspect preferences. *Australian Psychologist, 25,* 189–209.
4. Vondracek, F. W., Shimizu, K., Schulenberg, J., Hostetler, M., & Sakayanagi, T. (1990). A comparison between American and Japanese students' work values. *Journal of Vocational Behavior, 36,* 274-286.
5. Schmidt, A-M., & Callan, V. J. (1992). Evaluating the effectiveness of a career intervention. *Australian Psychologist, 27,* 123–126.
6. Schulenberg, J., Vondracek, F. W., & Kim, J. R. (1993). Career certainty and short-term changes in work values during adolescence. *Career Development Quarterly, 41,* 268-284.
7. Dose, J. J. (1997). Work values: An integrative framework and illustrative application to organizational socialization. *Journal of Occupational and Organizational Psychology, 70,* 219–240.
8. Skorikov, V. B., & Vondracek, F. W. (1997). Longitudinal relationships between part-time work and career development in adolescents. *Career Development Quarterly, 45,* 221–235.

[2916]

Work Attitudes Questionnaire (Version for Research).

Purpose: "Designed to differentiate the 'workaholic' or the Type A personality from the highly committed worker."
Population: Managers.
Publication Dates: 1980-1981.
Acronym: WAQ.
Scores, 3: Work Commitment, Psychological Health, Total.
Administration: Group.
Price Data, 1994: $25 per complete kit including 25 questionnaires and manual ('80, 18 pages); $20 per 50 questionnaires.
Time: Administration time not reported.
Authors: Maxene S. Doty and Nancy E. Betz.
Publisher: Marathon Consulting and Press.
Cross References: For a review by Mary L. Tenopyr, see 9:1395.

[2917]

Work Environment Scale, Second Edition.

Purpose: Developed to "measure the social environments of different types of work settings."
Population: Employees and supervisors.
Publication Dates: 1974-1989.
Acronym: WES.
Scores, 10: Involvement, Peer Cohesion, Supervisor Support, Autonomy, Task Orientation, Work Pressure, Clarity, Control, Innovation, Physical Comfort.
Administration: Group.
Forms, 3: Real (R), Ideal (I), Expected (E).
Price Data, 1999: $27.75 per 25 test booklets (Form R); $38.75 per 25 test booklets (select Form I or

E); $10 per 50 answer sheets; $34.40 per 25 self-scorable answer sheets; $13.20 per set of scoring stencils; $8.50 per 25 profiles; $121.80 per 10 prepaid narrative report answer sheets; $29.25 per 25 interpretive report forms; $41.80 per manual (57 pages); $17.25 per preview kit.
Time: [15-20] minutes.
Comments: A part of the Social Climate Scales (2445).
Authors: Rudolf H. Moos and Paul N. Insel (tests).
Publisher: Consulting Psychologists Press, Inc.
Cross References: For reviews by Ralph O. Mueller and Eugene P. Sheehan, see 12:417 (6 references); see also T4:2989 (19 references); for a review by Rabindra N. Kanungo, see 9:1398 (1 reference); see also T3:2652 (2 references) and 8:713 (3 references). For a review of the Social Climate Scales, see 8:681.

TEST REFERENCES

1. Hipwell, A. E., Tyler, P. A., & Wilson, C. M. (1989). Sources of stress and dissatisfaction among nurses in four hospital environments. *British Journal of Medical Psychology, 62,* 71–79.
2. Finney, J. W., & Moos, R. H. (1991). The long-term course of treated alcoholism: I. Mortality, relapse and remission rates and comparisons with community controls. *Journal of Studies on Alcohol, 52,* 44–54.
3. Plante, A., & Bouchard, L. (1995). Occupational stress, burnout, and professional support in nurses working with dying patients. *Omega, 32,* 93–109.
4. Amabile, T., Conti, R., Coon, H., Lazenby, J., & Herron, M. (1996). Assessing the work environment for creativity. *Academy of Management Journal, 39,* 11154–1184.
5. Moos, R. H., & Moos, B. S. (1997). The staff workplace and the quality and outcome of substance abuse treatment. *Journal of Studies on Alcohol, 59,* 43–51.

[2918]

The Work Experience Survey.

Purpose: Designed as a "structured interview protocol for identifying barriers (and possible solutions) to career maintenance" for a disabled person.
Population: "Individuals with disabilities who are either employed or about to begin employment."
Publication Date: 1995.
Acronym: WES.
Scores: Not scored.
Administration: Individual.
Price Data, 1998: $7.50 per 50 surveys; $5 per manual (59 pages).
Time: (30–60) minutes.
Comments: Administered in a face-to-face or telephone interview.
Authors: Richard T. Roessler (survey and manual), Cheryl A. Reed (manual), and Phillip D. Rumrill (manual).
Publisher: The National Center on Employment & Disability.

[2919]

Work Information Inventory.

Purpose: Designed to assess employee morale by utilizing the direction of perception techniques.
Population: Employee groups in industry.
Publication Date: 1958.
Acronym: WII.
Scores: Total score only.
Administration: Group.
Price Data, 1985: $5 per 25 tests; $5 per specimen set.
Time: (15) minutes.
Author: Raymond E. Bernberg.
Publisher: Psychometric Affiliates.
Cross References: For additional information and a review by Albert K. Kurtz, see 8:1057.

[2920]

Work Keys Assessments.

Purpose: "For teaching and assessing employability skills."
Population: Grade 10 to adult.
Publication Dates: 1992–1994.
Administration: Group.
Price Data: Available from publisher.
Author: ACT, Inc.
Publisher: ACT, Inc.

a) READING FOR INFORMATION ASSESSMENT.
Purpose: "Measures the learner's skill in reading and understanding work-related instructions and policies."
Scores: Total score only.
Levels: 5 reading skill levels.
Time: (45) minutes.

b) APPLIED MATHEMATICS ASSESSMENT.
Purpose: "Measures the learner's skill in applying mathematical reasoning to work-related problems."
Scores: Total score only.
Levels: 5 mathematics skill levels.
Time: (45) minutes.

c) LISTENING ASSESSMENT.
Purpose: "Measures the learner's skill at listening to and understanding work-related messages."
Scores: Total score only.
Levels: 5 listening skill levels.
Time: [40] minutes.
Comments: Constructed-response; administered via audiotape; hand-scored by ACT.

d) WRITING ASSESSMENT.
Purpose: "Measures the learner's skill at writing work-related messages."
Scores: Total score only.
Levels: 5 writing skill levels.
Time: [40] minutes.
Comments: Constructed-response; administered via audiotape; hand-scored by ACT.

e) LOCATING INFORMATION ASSESSMENT.
Purpose: "Measures the learner's skill in using information taken from workplace graphics such

as diagrams, floor plans, tables, forms, graphs, charts, and instrument gauges."
Scores: Total score only.
Levels: 4 information skill levels.
Time: (45) minutes.
f) TEAMWORK ASSESSMENT.
Purpose: "Measures the learner's skill in choosing behaviors and/or actions that simultaneously support team interrelationships and lead toward the accomplishment of work tasks."
Parts: 2.
Scores: Total score only.
Levels: 4 teamwork skill levels.
Time: (80) minutes.
Comments: Administered via videotape.
g) APPLIED TECHNOLOGY ASSESSMENT.
Purpose: "Measures the learner's skill in solving problems of a technological nature."
Scores: Total score only.
Levels: 4 applied technology levels.
Time: (45) minutes.
h) OBSERVATION ASSESSMENT.
Purpose: "Measures the learner's skill in paying attention to instructions and demonstrations, and in noticing details."
Scores: Total score only.
Levels: 4 observation levels.
Time: (60) minutes.
Comments: Administered via videotape.

[2921]

[Work Motivation].

Purpose: Assesses assumptions and practices characterizing attempts to motivate employees, and evaluate employee motivational needs and values.
Population: Managers, employees.
Publication Dates: 1967-1973.
Scores, 5: Basic-Creature Comfort, Safety and Order, Belonging and Affiliation, Ego-Status, Actualization and Self-Expression.
Administration: Group.
Manual: No manual.
Price Data, 1992: $49.95 per 10-pack of test instruments.
Time: [15-30] minutes.
Comments: Self-administered inventory.
Authors: Jay Hall and Martha Williams.
Publisher: Teleometrics International.
a) MANAGEMENT OF MOTIVES INDEX.
Purpose: Assesses assumptions and practices characterizing attempts to motivate employees.
Acronym: MMI.
b) WORK MOTIVATION INVENTORY.
Purpose: Evaluate employee motivational needs and values.
Acronym: WMI.
Cross References: See T3:2655 (4 references) and 8:1189 (3 references).

[2922]

Work Motivation Inventory: A Test of Adult Work Motivation.

Purpose: Measures the importance people place on four major goals or values related to career development decisions.
Population: Ages 16-Adult.
Publication Dates: 1985-1987.
Acronym: WMI.
Scores, 5: Bias, Accomplishment, Recognition, Power, Affiliation.
Administration: Group or individual.
Price Data, 1998: $8.75 per manual ('87, 25 pages).
Time: (10-15) minutes.
Comments: Self-administered survey; mail-in to publisher for narrative report processing.
Authors: Larry A. Braskamp and Martin L. Maehr.
Publisher: MetriTech, Inc.
a) WMI NARRATIVE REPORTS.
Price Data: $34 per narrative report kit including manual, processing of 5 reports, and 5 pre-paid test booklets; $5,255-$8,255 per narrative report including processing and answer sheets.
Comments: Oriented to the test taker and features extensive interpretive information and guidelines for applying the test results to the test taker's career and life planning; based on parent program SPECTRUM.
b) WMI/PC MICROCOMPUTER VERSION.
Price Data: $105 per 10 administration disks; $237.50 per 25 administration disks; $400 per 50 administration disks; $14 per manual; $27 per 50 test booklets/answer sheets; $18 per 50 decision model worksheets.
Comments: Supports both on-line and off-line testing; IBM version only.
Cross References: For reviews by Cyril J. Sadowski and Terry A. Stinnett, see 12:366.

[2923]

Work Performance Assessment.

Purpose: Designed to assess "work-related social/interpersonal skills."
Population: Job trainees.
Publication Dates: 1987–1988.
Acronym: WPA.
Scores: 19 supervisory demands: Greet Each Trainee, Direct Trainee to Work Station and Explain Nature of Work, Provide Vague Instructions, Explain Supervisory Error, Provide Detailed Instructions, Observe Trainees Working, Stand Next to Trainee, Create a Distraction, Show New Way to Work, Introduce Time

Pressure, Criticize Trainee's Work, Compliment Trainee's Work, Ask Trainees to Switch Tasks, Ask Trainees to Socialize, Direct Trainees to Work Together, Ask Trainees to Criticize Each Other, Ask Trainees to Compliment Each Other, Observe Trainees Completing the Task Together, Socialize with Each Trainee, yielding a Total Score.
Administration: Group.
Price Data, 1993: $5 per manual ('87, 41 pages); $15 per 25 scripts and rating forms.
Time: (60–70) minutes.
Comments: Ratings by supervisor.
Authors: Richard Roessler, Suki Hinman, and Frank Lewis.
Publisher: The National Center on Employment & Disability.
Cross References: For reviews by Caroline Manuele-Adkins and Gerald R. Schneck, see 13:367.

[2924]
Work Personality Profile.

Purpose: Designed to "assess fundamental work role requirements that are essential to achievement and maintenance of suitable employment."
Population: Vocational rehabilitation clients.
Publication Date: 1986.
Acronym: WPP.
Scores, 16: Acceptance of Work Role, Ability to Profit from Instruction or Correction, Work Persistence, Work Tolerance, Amount of Supervision Required, Extent Trainee Seeks Assistance from Supervisor, Degree of Comfort or Anxiety with Supervisor, Appropriateness of Personal Relations with Supervisor, Teamwork, Ability to Socialize with Co-Workers, Social Communication Skills, Task Orientation, Social Skills, Work Motivation, Work Conformance, Personal Presentation.
Administration: Individual.
Price Data, 1994: $5 per manual (40 pages); $20 per floppy disk; $7.50 per 50 tests; $10 per 100 tests; $30 per complete set (including manual, diskette, and 50 tests).
Time: (5-10) minutes.
Comments: Observational ratings by vocational evaluators; to be administered after one week (20-30 hours) in evaluation setting; available on diskette.
Authors: Brian Bolton and Richard Roessler.
Publisher: National Center on Employment & Disability.
Cross References: See T4:2994 (1 reference); for a review by Ralph O. Mueller and Paula J. Dupuy, see 11:476.

TEST REFERENCES

1. Wilson, M. J., Engels, D., Hartz, J. D., & Foster, D. E. (1987). The Employability Inventory: An overview. *Journal of Employment Counseling, 24,* 62–68.
2. Lysaker, P., Bell, M., Milstein, R., Bryson, G., & Beam-Goulet, J. (1994). Insight and psychosocial treatment compliance in schizophrenia. *Psychiatry, 57,* 307–315.
3. Lysaker, P. H., Bell, M. D., Zito, W. S., & Bioty, S. M. (1995). Social skills at work: Deficits and predictors of improvement in schizophrenia. *The Journal of Nervous and Mental Disease, 183,* 688–697.
4. Bell, M. D., Greig, T. C., Kaplan, E., & Bryson, G. (1997). Wisconsin Card Sorting Test dimensions in schizophrenia: Factorial, predictive, and divergent validity. *Journal of Clinical and Experimental Neuropsychology, 19,* 933–941.

[2925]
Work Preference Questionnaire.

Purpose: To determine preferred job activities.
Population: Business and industry.
Publication Date: 1982.
Scores: Weighted combinations of 150 items into 16 dimensions of work: Making Decisions/Communicating and Having Responsibility, Operating Vehicles, Using Machines-Tools-Instruments, Performing Physical Activities, Operating Keyboard and Office Equipment, Monitoring and/or Controlling Equipment and/or Processes, Working Under Uncomfortable Conditions, Working With Art-Decor Entertainment, Performing Supervisory Duties, Performing Estimating Activities, Processing Written Information, Working With Buyers Customers-Salespersons, Working Under Hazardous Conditions, Performing Paced and/or Repetitive Activities, Working With Aerial and Aquatic Equipment, Catering/Serving/Smelling/Tasting.
Administration: Group.
Price Data: Available from publisher.
Time: Administration time not reported.
Comments: Also known as Work Activity Questionnaire.
Authors: Robert C. Mecham, Alma F. Harris (test), Ernest J. McCormick (test), and P. R. Jenneret (test).
Publisher: PAQ Services, Inc.

[2926]
Work Readiness Profile.

Purpose: "Developed as a tool for the initial descriptive assessment of individuals with disabilities."
Population: Older adolescents and adults with disabilities.
Publication Date: 1995.
Scores, 14: Physical Effectiveness (Health, Travel, Movement, Fine Motor Skills, Gross Motor Skills and Strength, Total Average), Personal Effectiveness (Social and Interpersonal, Work Adjustment, Communication Effectiveness, Abilities and Skills, Literacy and Numeracy, Total Average), Hearing, Vision.
Administration: Group.
Price Data, 1995: $75 per set including manual (64 pages), 10 answer books, 10 group record forms, and 10 individual record forms; $15 per 10 answer books; $6 per 10 group record forms; $6 per 10 individual record forms; $45 per manual.
Time: (10–15) minutes.

Comments: Self-administered or ratings by informant.
Author: Helga A. H. Rowe.
Publisher: Australian Council for Educational Research Ltd. [Australia].

[2927]

Work Skills Series Production.

Purpose: Designed to measure the ability to understand instructions, work with numbers, and accurately check machine settings visually.
Population: Manufacturing and production employees and prospective employees.
Publication Date: 1990.
Acronym: WSS.
Scores: Total score only for each of 3 tests: Understanding Instructions (VWP1), Working with Numbers (NWP2), Visual Checking (CWP3).
Administration: Individual or group.
Price Data: Available from publisher.
Time: 12 minutes for VWP1; 10 minutes for NWP2; 7 minutes for CWP3; 29(40) minutes for complete battery.
Author: Saville & Holdsworth Ltd.
Publisher: Saville & Holdsworth.
Cross References: For reviews by Brian Bolton and Wayne J. Camara, see 12:418.

[2928]

Work Temperament Inventory.

Purpose: Identifies "personal traits" of the worker that are then matched to suitable occupations.
Population: Workers.
Publication Date: 1993.
Acronym: WTI.
Scores: 12 scales: Directive, Repetitive, Influencing, Variety, Expressing, Judgments, Alone, Stress, Tolerances, Under, People, Measurable.
Administration: Group.
Price Data, 1993: $30 per complete set including manual (39 pages), software, and 50 forms; $5 per manual; $20 per software (5.25-inch disk); $7.50 per 50 forms.
Time: (15–20) minutes.
Authors: Brian Bolton and Jeffrey Brookings.
Publisher: The National Center on Employment & Disability.
Cross References: For reviews by Peter F. Merenda and Alan J. Raphael, see 13:368.

[2929]

Working—Assessing Skills, Habits, and Style.

Purpose: "Designed to assess personal habits, skills, and styles that are associated with a positive work ethic."
Population: High school and college students and potential employees.
Publication Date: 1996.
Scores: 9 competencies: Taking Responsibility, Working in Teams, Persisting, Having A Sense of Quality, Life-Long Learning, Adapting to Change, Problem Solving, Information Processing, Systems Thinking.
Administration: Group.
Price Data, 1996: $4 each for 1–49 instruments, $3.50 each for 50–499; $3 each for 500–1999; $2.50 each for 2000–4999; $2 each for 5000+; technical and applications manuals available upon request (price information available from publisher); user's manual free with each order.
Time: (30–35) minutes.
Comments: Inventory for self-rating; can be self-administered and self-scored.
Authors: Curtis Miles (test and user's manual), Phyllis Grummon (test, user's manual, and technical manual), and Karen M. Maduschke (technical manual).
Publisher: H & H Publishing Co., Inc.

[2930]

Workplace Skills Survey.

Purpose: Designed to provide "information regarding basic work ethics and employment skills."
Population: Job applicants and employees.
Publication Date: 1998.
Acronym: WSS.
Scores, 7: Communication, Adapting to Change, Problem Solving, Work Ethics, Technological Literacy, Teamwork, Composite.
Administration: Individual or group.
Price Data, 1998: $40 per introductory kit including 5 reusable test booklets, 20 answer/score sheets, and technical manual; $30 per 20 answer/score sheets; $18 per 10 reusable test booklets.
Time: 20 minutes.
Author: Industrial Psychology International, Ltd.
Publisher: Industrial Psychology International, Ltd.

[2931]

World Government Scale.

Purpose: Measures attitudes toward world government.
Population: Students.
Publication Date: 1985.
Scores: Total score only.
Administration: Group.
Manual: No manual.
Price Data, 1998: $1 per scale.
Time: [12] minutes.
Author: Panos D. Bardis.
Publisher: Donna Bardis.

[2932]

World History/Objective Tests.

Purpose: To assess students' general knowledge of world history.
Population: 1, 2 semesters high school.
Publication Dates: 1961-1970.
Scores: Total score only for each of 14 tests: The Earliest Civilizations, The Greeks, The Romans, The Middle Ages, The Bridge to Modern Times, First Semester Examination, The Era of Political Revolutions, The Age of Revolutions Continues, Imperialism/Nationalism/and World War I, Between the Two Great Wars, World War II, The Postwar World, Second Semester Examination, Final Examination.
Administration: Group.
Manual: No manual.
Price Data, 1994: $10.95 per test book including tests and response key.
Time: [50] minutes for unit tests; [60] minutes for other tests.
Comments: Formerly called Objective Tests in World History.
Author: Earl Bridgewater.
Publisher: Perfection Learning Corp.

[2933]

Writing Process Test.

Purpose: "Measures the quality of students' written products."
Population: Grades 2–12.
Publication Dates: 1991–92.
Acronym: WPT.
Scores, 14: Development [First Pass (Purpose/Focus, Audience, Vocabulary, Style/Tone, Total), Second Pass (Support/Development, Organization/Coherence, Total)], Fluency [Third Pass (Sentence Structure/Variety, Grammar/Usage, Capitalization/Punctuation, Spelling, Total)], Total.
Administration: Group.
Editions, 2: Individual, Classroom.
Price Data, 1999: $174 per complete kit including test manual ('92, 144 pages), technical manual ('92, 40 pages), 25 analytic scales, 25 Form A first draft booklets, and 25 revision booklets; $55 per test manual; $18 per 25 analytic record forms; $19 per 25 first draft booklets; $13 per 25 revision booklets; $35 per technical manual; $55 per scoring videotape.
Time: [45] minutes (+30 minutes for revision).
Authors: Robin Warden and Thomas A. Hutchinson.
Publisher: PRO-ED.
Cross References: For reviews by Ernest W. Kimmel and Sandra Ward, see 13:369 (1 reference).

[2934]

The Written Expression Test.

Purpose: To "measure written expression objectively."
Population: Grades 1 to 6.
Publication Dates: 1979-1982.
Acronym: WET.
Scores, 5: Productivity, Mechanics, Handwriting, Maturity, Composite.
Administration: Individual or group.
Price Data: Not available.
Time: (30) minutes.
Authors: Clark Johnson and Sharon Hubly.
Publisher: McClain [No reply from publisher; status unknown].
Cross References: For reviews by Noel Gregg and Lyn Haber, see 10:396.

TEST REFERENCE

1. Branch, W. B., Cohen, M. J., & Hynd, G. W. (1995). Academic achievement and attention-deficit/hyperactivity disorder in children with left- or right-hemisphere dysfunction. *Journal of Learning Disabilities, 28,* 35–43, 64.

[2935]

Written Language Assessment.

Purpose: Assesses writing ability.
Population: Grades 3-12.
Publication Date: 1989.
Acronym: WLA.
Scores, 5: General Writing Ability, Productivity, Word Complexity, Readability, Written Language Quotient.
Administration: Group.
Price Data, 1999: $65 per complete kit including 25 each of 3 writing record forms, 25 scoring/profile forms, manual ('89, 111 pages), and hand counter; $18 per 25 each of 3 writing record forms; $12 per 25 scoring/profile forms; $20 per manual; $12 per hand counter; $20 per specimen set.
Time: (45-60) minutes.
Authors: J. Jeffrey Grill and Margaret M. Kirwin.
Publisher: Academic Therapy Publications.
Cross References: For reviews by Stephen Jurs and Mary Ross Moran, see 11:477.

TEST REFERENCES

1. Spaulding, C. L. (1989). Written Language Assessment (WLA). *Journal of Reading, 33,* 68-69.
2. Resta, S. P., & Eliot, J. (1994). Written expression in boys with attention deficit disorder. *Perceptual and Motor Skills, 79,* 1131-1138.

[2936]

Written Language Syntax Test.

Purpose: Designed as a "screening instrument used to provide information on student performance in written language syntax."
Population: Ages 10-17 hearing-impaired.
Publication Date: 1981.
Acronym: WLST.

Scores: Total score only.
Administration: Group or individual.
Levels, 3: 1, 2, 3.
Price Data, 1988: $6 per 10 tests (specify Level 1, 2, or 3); $4 per 10 screening tests; $4 per 10 individual data folders; $10 per administrator's package including manual (33 pages) and one copy of each item.
Time: (10-20) minutes for screening test, (40-60) minutes per test.
Comments: Contains "Screening Test" to determine appropriate level for administration.
Author: Sharon R. Berry.
Publisher: Gallaudet University Press.
Cross References: For reviews by Michael W. Casby and Judith R. Johnston, see 9:1404.

[2937]

XYZ Inventory.

Purpose: Designed to identify underlying managerial assumptions about human nature.
Population: Managers and prospective managers.
Publication Dates: 1970-1981.
Scores: 3 scales: Theory X—Man is Beast, Theory Y—Man is Self-Actualizing, Theory Z—Man is Rational Being.
Administration: Group.
Price Data, 1998: $40 per complete kit including 10 test inventories, fact sheet, and administration guide.
Time: (10-20) minutes.
Authors: W. J. Reddin and J. Brian Sullivan.
Publisher: Organizational Tests Ltd. [Canada].
Cross References: For reviews by Paul R. Sackett and Neal Schmitt, see 9:1405.

[2938]

Yardsticks.

Purpose: "Criterion-referenced tests in mathematics."
Population: Ages 6, 7, 8, 9, 10, 11.
Publication Dates: 1973-1980.
Scores: Objectives-based scores only.
Administration: Group.
Levels, 6: Corresponding to ages.
Price Data: Available from publisher.
Time: Administration time not reported.
Author: NFER-Nelson Publishing Co., Ltd.
Publisher: NFER-Nelson Publishing Co., Ltd. [England].

[2939]

Young Adult Behavior Checklist and Young Adult Self-Report.

Purpose: "Designed to provide standardized descriptions of behavior, feelings, thoughts, and competencies."
Publication Date: 1997.
Scores, 11: Anxious/Depressed, Withdrawn, Somatic Complaints, Thought Problems, Attention Problems, Intrusive, Aggressive Behavior, Delinquent Behavior, Internalizing, Externalizing, Total.
Administration: Group.
Price Data, 1997: $10 per 25 test booklets (specify instrument); $10 per 25 profiles for hand scoring (specify instrument); $25 per manual (217 pages); $7 per template for hand scoring (specify instrument); $220 for computer program scoring.
Author: Thomas M. Achenbach.
Publisher: Child Behavior Checklist.

a) YOUNG ADULT BEHAVIOR CHECKLIST.
Population: Young adults.
Time: (10–15) minutes.
Comments: Ratings by parents.

b) YOUNG ADULT SELF-REPORT.
Population: Ages 18–30.
Time: (15–20) minutes.

MMY TEST REVIEWERS

Test descriptions in Tests in Print V *include cross references to reviews in previous* Mental Measurements Yearbooks *for tests still in print and those reviewers are also listed in the Names Index. This listing of* MMY *Test Reviewers lists all reviewers in the entire* MMY *series. The numbers after the names represent the* Mental Measurements Yearbooks *in which reviews appear.*

Harold H. Abelson, 3
Murray Aborn, 4
Phillip L. Ackerman, 11-13
Terry A. Ackerman, 12-13
Fred L. Adair, 8
Carol Adams, 9
Clifford R. Adams, 6
Elizabeth C. Adams, 4
Georgia S. Adams, 7-8
Gerald R. Adams, 9
Mary Friend Adams, 8
Russell L. Adams, 9-10
Susan F. Adams, 12
C. J. Adcock, 5-7
Dorothy C. Adkins, 3-7
Dan L. Adler, 5
Seymour Adler, 10
Janet G. Afflerbach, 5
Lois G. Afflerbach, 5
Frederick B. Agard, 3
J. Stanley Ahmann, 6-9
Lewis R. Aiken, 9, 12
Mary D. Ainsworth, 5
Peter W. Airasian, 8-10
Mark Albanese, 11-13
Lewis E. Albright, 6-8
Norma A. Albright, 2
Bruce K. Alcorn, 11-12
John Charles Alderson, 8
Lawrence M. Aleamoni, 8-9, 11-12
Charlene M. Alexander, 12
Ralph A. Alexander, 9
Bob Algozzine, 9
Henry A. Alker, 7-8
Doris V. Allen, 9-10
Lawrence Allen, 9
Mary J. Allen, 9
Nancy L. Allen, 11
Robert M. Allen, 8
Sarah J. Allen, 11-12
Richard L. Allington, 9-10
Julie A. Allison, 12-13
John C. Almack, 1-2
William D. Altus, 4
Jean D. Amberson, 4
Sueann Robinson Ambron, 8
Vera M. Amerson, 3
Anne Anastasi, 1-11
Nicholas Anastasiow, 7-8
Kenneth N. Anchor, 12
Charles V. Anderson, 8
David O. Anderson, 11-13
Howard R. Anderson, 1-7
Irving H. Anderson, 1, 3

James M. Anderson, 3-4, 6
John O. Anderson, 11-12
Kenneth E. Anderson, 4, 6
Robert P. Anderson, 8-9
Jerrilyn. V. Andrews, 11-13
Lawrence Andrus, 2
Harvey A. Andruss, 3
Charles J. Ansorge, 9
Edgar Anstey, 6
Paul A. Arbisi, 12-13
Francis X. Archambault, Jr., 9, 11-12
Robert P. Archer, 11
Joyce A. Arditti, 12
Edward N. Argulewicz, 9
James A. Armentrout, 8
Christian O. Arndt, 2
Dwight L. Arnold, 4-5
Gwen F. Arnold, 4
Edward Aronow, 12
Raoul A. Arreola, 12-13
Judith A. Arter, 9
F. Marion Asche, 12
Philip Ash, 11-13
Ronald A. Ash, 9, 12
E. Jack Asher, Jr., 11
Theodore A. Ashford, 3, 5
Lear Ashmore, 8-9
Alexander W. Astin, 6-7
Carolyn Peluso Atkins, 9
Samuel D. Atkins, 1-2
Deborah H. Atlas, 12
Jeffrey A. Atlas, 11-13
Kathryn Hu-Pei Au, 9
Mark W. Aulls, 9
James T. Austin, 9, 11-13
Mary C. Austin, 6
Stephen N. Axford, 11-13
Frederic L. Ayer, 3-4
George W. Ayer, 8
J. Douglas Ayers, 6-8, 11
Glen P. Aylward, 11-13
Kris L. Baack, 12
James C. Babcock, 2
Patricia A. Bachelor, 11-13
Lyle F. Bachman, 11-12
Philip Backlund, 13
Ellen H. Bacon, 10-11
Beth D. Bader, 12
Andrew R. Baggaley, 5-6
Stephen J. Bagnato, 9
Sherry K. Bain, 12
Leonard L. Baird, 7
Janet Baldwin, 12
Thomas S. Baldwin, 7-8, 10
Benjamin Balinsky, 4-5
Rachel S. Ball, 2
Warren R. Baller, 4-5
Irol W. Balsley, 6
Deborah L. Bandalos, 12
K. Denise Bane, 11
Charlotte E. K. Banks, 4-5
Nicholas W. Bankson, 8-11
Allan G. Barclay, 7
James R. Barclay, 9-10
Laura L. B. Barnes, 11-13
Walter Barnes, 1
David W. Barnett, 10-12
Rita M. Barnett, 12
W. Leslie Barnette, Jr., 8
Andrés Barona, 11, 13
A. S. Barr, 3
Rebecca C. Barr, 7-8
Richard S. Barrett, 6
Thomas C. Barrett, 6
Frank Barron, 5
William M. Bart, 11-12
Brendan John Bartlett, 9
W. L. Bashaw, 7
Alan R. Bass, 8
David J. Bateson, 12
Donald H. Baucom, 9
Ernest A. Bauer, 11-12
Robert H. Bauernfeind, 5-8
Ronald Baumanis, 9
Deborah N. Bauserman, 9
Brent Baxter, 3-5
Ernest Edward Bayles, 1
Nancy Bayley, 2-3, 5
Kenneth L. Bean, 5-6
Robert M. Bear, 3-4
Harold P. Bechtoldt, 4-7
Isabel L. Beck, 9
Michael D. Beck, 11-13
Roland L. Beck, 2-3
Samuel J. Beck, 2, 5
Wesley C. Becker, 6
Ralph C. Bedell, 3, 5
H. R. Beech, 6
Martha C. Beech, 9
Fred S. Beers, 1
Isaac I. Bejar, 8
Marcia J. Belcher, 11
John E. Bell, 4-6
Peter Della Bella, 13
Camilla Persson Benbow, 11
Kathryn M. Benes, 11-12
James K. Benish, 13
Albert A. Bennett, 2-3
Clinton W. Bennett, 12-13
George K. Bennett, 3-7
Jeri Benson, 11, 13
Mark J. Benson, 12-13
Nicholas Benson, 13
Philip G. Benson, 9-12

Marsha Bensoussan, 13
Peter M. Bentler, 6-7
Arthur L. Benton, 3-4, 7
Stephen L. Benton, 11-12
H. E. Benz, 2
Ralph F. Berdie, 3-7
Harry D. Berg, 3-8
Paul Conrad Berg, 7
Allen Berger, 7-9
Michael Berger, 8
Betty Bergstrom, 13
Ronald A. Berk, 9, 12-13
Hinsdale Bernard, 12-13
H. John Bernardin, 9-12
Rita Sloan Berndt, 9-10
Jean-Jacques Bernier, 11-12
Robert G. Bernreuter, 1-4
Frank M. Bernt, 12-13
Joan D. Berryman, 9
Frederick Bessai, 11-13
Emmett A. Betts, 6
William Betz, 1, 3
Charles L. Bickel, 2
John Biggs, 9
Marion A. Bills, 3
Walter V. Bingham, 1
William C. Bingham, 6, 8
L. B. Birch, 6-7
Herbert G. W. Bischoff, 9
Lisa G. Bischoff, 11-13
Bruce H. Biskin, 11-12
Reign H. Bittner, 3-4
Harold H. Bixler, 3-4
Ake Bjerstedt, 5-6
Donald B. Black, 6-7
Hillel Black, 6
John D. Black, 5-6, 8-9
J. M. Blackburn, 2
James H. Blackhurst, 1
E. G. Blackstone, 3
Martha Blackwell, 12
C. B. Blakemore, 6
Emery P. Bliesmer, 6
Lynn S. Bliss, 10-12
Sonya Blixt, 12
Jack Block, 8
Martin E. Block, 12
Paul J. Blommers, 3-6
Benjamin S. Bloom, 3-5, 7
Lisa A. Bloom, 12-13
Bruce M. Bloxom, 7-9
Milton L. Blum, 3-4
James A. Blumenthal, 9
Jack L. Bodden, 7-9
Ann E. Boehm, 9
Carol A. Boliek, 11
Joan Bollenbacher, 5
Nancy B. Bologna, 12
Brian F. Bolton, 8-9, 11-13
David L. Bolton, 12-13
Guy L. Bond, 2
Stephen J. Boney, 12
Gwyneth M. Boodoo, 9
Ivan A. Booker, 1-4
Daniel R. Boone, 7-8
Roger A. Boothroyd, 12-13
Edward S. Bordin, 3-5
Fred H. Borgen, 7-9
William Borgen, 9
Harold Borko, 6-7
Christopher Borman, 9-10
Walter C. Borman, 8-9
John R. Bormuth, 7
Robert A. Bornstein, 9-12
Morton Bortner, 6, 8-9
Michael D. Botwin, 12
Thomas J. Bouchard, Jr., 7-8
William R. Boulton, 9
Nicholas G. Bountress, 9
John E. Bowers, 6
Gregory J. Boyle, 11-13
J. David Boyle, 12
Bruce A. Bracken, 9-12
Jeffrey P. Braden, 11-12
E. J. G. Bradford, 3-4
John M. Bradley, 9
Robert H. Bradley, 9
Thomas B. Bradley, 9
Francis F. Bradshaw, 1
John C. Brantley, 11
Marla R. Brassard, 9
James Braswell, 7-8
John R. Braun, 7-9
Arthur H. Brayfield, 4-6
W. C. Brenke, 3
Ann Brewington, 3
Ann Brickner, 7
Robert G. Bridgham, 7
M. Alan Brimer, 5-7
Elizabeth L. Bringsjord, 13
Frank W. Broadbent, 9
Stanley L. Brodsky, 8
Linda E. Brody, 10, 12
Hubert E. Brogden, 3-4
Susan M. Brookhart, 12-13
Jeffrey B. Brookings, 13
Nelson Brooks, 1-6
M. Eustace Broom, 2
R. A. Brotemarkle, 3
W. Dale Brotherton, 13
Diane Browder, 10
Alfred S. Brown, 3
Andrew W. Brown, 2
Charles M. Brown, 6

Clara M. Brown, 1-2
Douglas T. Brown, 9-10
Frederick G. Brown, 7-9, 11
James Dean Brown, 11-13
Michael B. Brown, 13
Ric Brown, 9, 12-13
Robert D. Brown, 9-11, 13
Scott W. Brown, 11-12
Steven D. Brown, 9
Virginia L. Brown, 11
William A. Brownell, 1-5
Richard Brozovich, 11-12
Leo J. Brueckner, 1-4
Roger S. Bruning, 9-10
Jennifer A. Brush, 13
James E. Bryan, 5-8
Miriam M. Bryan, 4, 6-8
N. Dale Bryant, 5-8
Diane Nelson Bryen, 9
Aaron D. Buchanan, 8
Jayne E. Bucy, 13
Karen S. Budd, 11
William D. Buffington, 8
Albert M. Bugaj, 12-13
Alan C. Bugbee, Jr., 12-13
Norman A. Buktenica, 9
Michael B. Bunch, 11-13
Mary Anne Bunda, 11-13
Linda K. Bunker, 9-12
Robert L. Burch, 4
Kenneth E. Burchett, 8
Thomas C. Burgess, 6
Carolyn L. Burke, 7
Paul C. Burnett, 11, 13
R. Will Burnett, 4
Donald G. Burns, 4
Emily T. Burr, 3
Alvin G. Burstein, 6-7
Cyril Burt, 3, 5
Nancy W. Burton, 7
John Christian Busch, 12
Nancy A. Busch-Rossnagel, 9-10
Brenda R. Bush, 10-11
Ray R. Buss, 9
R. T. Busse, 11
Guy T. Buswell, 2
H. J. Butcher, 7
James N. Butcher, 8-9
Katharine G. Butler, 7-8, 10-12
John K. Butler, Jr., 9
Dorcas Susan Butt, 8-9
Margaret C. Byrne, 7-9
Leonard S. Cahen, 7-8
G. P. Cahoon, 3-4
James R. Caldwell, 7
Kathryn Hoover Calfee, 8
Robert C. Calfee, 8-10
Carolyn M. Callahan, 12-13
Leroy G. Callahan, 8
Wayne J. Camara, 12-13
Bonnie W. Camp, 9-10
Cameron J. Camp, 10-11, 13
David P. Campbell, 6-8
Donald T. Campbell, 4-6
Dugal Campbell, 6
Hank Campbell, 10
Iris Amos Campbell, 9
J. Arthur Campbell, 6, 8-9
Joel T. Campbell, 6-7
Thomas F. Campbell, 13
Vincent N. Campbell, 7
Anthony A. Cancelli, 9
Joyce L. Carbonell, 9
Karen T. Carey, 11-13
Cindy I. Carlson, 11
James E. Carlson, 12
Janet F. Carlson, 11-13
Joellen V. Carlson, 11-13
Kenneth A. Carlson, 8
Roger D. Carlson, 11
Thorsten R. Carlson, 7-8
James C. Carmer, 11-12
Arlene E. Carney, 12
Russell N. Carney, 12-13
C. Dale Carpenter, 9-13
W. L. Carr, 2
David J. Carroll, 8-9
John B. Carroll, 4-8
L. Ray Carry, 7
Harold D. Carter, 1-4
Launor F. Carter, 4
W. H. Cartwright, 3
J. Manuel Casas, 9-10
Michael W. Casby, 9
Thomas F. Cash, 9
Frank P. Cassaretto, 5
Burton M. Castner, 2
Robert S. Cathcart, 5
Psyche Cattell, 1, 3
Raymond B. Cattell, 2
Darrell N. Caulley, 12
Courtney B. Cazden, 7-8
Stella Center, 1
Edward J. Cervenka, 8
Robert W. Ceurvorst, 9
Hester Chadderdon, 1-2, 4
Robert C. Challman, 4, 6-7
E. G. Chambers, 3-5
Carolyn Chaney, 11
Laura H. Chapman, 8
Clinton I. Chase, 7-10
Henry Chauncey, 3, 6
Maurice Chazan, 7
Henry M. Cherrick, 9

Kathleen Barrows Chesterfield, 9
Brad S. Chissom, 7-8
Mary Mathai Chittooran, 13
James P. Choca, 13
Andrew Christensen, 9
Sandra L. Christenson, 11
Edmund P. Churchill, 3
Ruth D. Churchill, 3, 5
Joseph C. Ciechalski, 11-13
Gregory J. Cizek, 11-13
Charles D. Claiborn, 9, 12
Cherry Ann Clark, 5
D. F. Clark, 7
Elaine Clark, 10, 12-13
Gale W. Clark, 5
J. F. Clark, 5
John L. D. Clark, 7-8
John R. Clark, 2
Kenneth E. Clark, 4
Philip M. Clark, 8-9
Richard M. Clark, 9, 11
Willis W. Clark, 6
H. Harrison Clarke, 4
Glen U. Cleeton, 3
W. V. Clemans, 6
Dorothy M. Clendenen, 5-7
Jeanette N. Cleveland, 9
Victor B. Cline, 7
James R. Clopton, 8-10
Richard W. Coan, 6-8
Harriet C. Cobb, 9
Larry R. Cochran, 9-12
Charles N. Cofer, 3-5
William E. Coffman, 3, 5-9, 11
Andrew D. Cohen, 12
Annabel J. Cohen, 12-13
Bertram D. Cohen, 6, 8
Jacob Cohen, 6-8
John Cohen, 3
S. Alan Cohen, 7
Stephen L. Cohen, 8
Sanford J. Cohn, 9
Theodore Coladarci, 12
Nicholas Colangelo, 10
Debra E. Cole, 12
Nancy S. Cole, 7-9
Thomas R. Coleman, 9
Roberta R. Collard, 7
Carol J. Collins, 13
Deborah Collins, 12
Richard Colwell, 7-10
W. D. Commins, 1-4
Andrew L. Comrey, 5, 7-8
Judith C. Conger, 11-12
Collie W. Conoley, 11-13
Clinton C. Conrad, 2
Herbert S. Conrad, 1-4
Norman A. Constantine, 11-12
Alicia Skinner Cook, 9, 11
John Cook, 7-9
Walter W. Cook, 2-3, 5
Donna K. Cooke, 12
Norma Cooke, 9
William W. Cooley, 6
Clyde H. Coombs, 3
Colin Cooper, 13
M. Allan Cooperstein, 13
Robert B. Cooter, Jr., 10-11
Mary Kay Corbitt, 9
Stephen M. Corey, 1-2
Virginia E. Corgan, 10
Alice J. Corkill, 11-13
Ethel L. Cornell, 1
Merith Cosden, 11-13
Giuseppe Costantino, 9-10
William C. Cottle, 5
Stuart A. Courtis, 1, 4
Douglas Courtney, 3-4
John A. Courtright, 9-10
James R. Cox, 9
Marion Monroe Cox, 1, 3
Richard C. Cox, 8
John A. Cox, Jr., 5
Hazel M. Crain, 9
Rick Crandall, 8
A. Garr Cranney, 8
Charles J. Cranny, 8
Albert B. Crawford, 2
Douglas H. Crawford, 9
John Crawford, 13
William R. Crawford, 6-7
Kevin D. Crehan, 11-13
Michelle M. Creighton, 11
Diana Crespo, 13
William J. E. Crissy, 4
R. Lenox Criswell, 2
John O. Crites, 6-9
Linda M. Crocker, 9-11, 13
Lysle W. Croft, 3-4
Lee J. Cronbach, 3-10
Lawrence A. Crosby, 9
Lawrence H. Cross, 12-13
Susan L. Crowley, 12
Douglas P. Crowne, 6
William M. Cruickshank, 4
Thomas E. Culliton, Jr., 6
Jack A. Cummings, 9-10, 12
Oliver W. Cummings, 9
Bert P. Cundick, 9-10
Edward E. Cureton, 1-2, 4
Louise W. Cureton, 4
Thomas K. Cureton, 3
William L. Curlette, 11-12
William Curr, 5

Francis D. Curtis, 1-2
Mary E. Curtis, 9
Michael J. Curtis, 9
Stephanie L. Cutlan, 13
Peter A. Dahl, 8
W. Grant Dahlstrom, 4-6, 8
John T. Dailey, 4-5
Edgar Dale, 3
Reginald R. Dale, 5
Fred L. Damarin, 8-9
Rik Carl D'Amato, 11-12
Larry G. Daniel, 12
Mark H. Daniel, 12-13
John C. Daniels, 5
M. Harry Daniels, 9-10
John G. Darley, 1-2
Richard E. Darnell, 8-9
Ralph F. Darr, Jr., 11-13
J. P. Das, 9-10
Jane Dass, 8
John H. Daugherty, 3
James M. Daum, 9
Charles Davidshofer, 9
Brandon Davis, 11, 13
Charlotte Croon Davis, 3-6, 8
D. Russell Davis, 4-5
Edwin W. Davis, 3
Frederick B. Davis, 1-5, 7
Paul C. Davis, 6
Robert A. Davis, 3
Stanley E. Davis, 6
Steven F. Davis, 11-13
Parker Davis, Jr., 3
Mark L. Davison, 9
Helen C. Dawe, 3
Robyn M. Dawes, 8
Carolyn Dawson, 8
Linda S. Day, 11
Ayres G. D'Costa, 11-13
Gary J. Dean, 12-13
Raymond S. Dean, 9
Lester W. Dearborn, 6
William W. Deardorff, 12-13
William L. Deaton, 11-12
David A. Decoster, 10
James Deese, 5
Frank P. DeLay, 2
Connie Kubo Della-Piana, 13
Gabriel M. Della-Piana, 6, 11
Vincent J. Dell'Orto, 8
Dennis J. Deloria, 7-9
Harold A. Delp, 4
Robert H. Deluty, 9
Randy Demaline, 8
Robert G. Demaree, 4, 7-8
Gerald E. DeMauro, 11-13
Marilyn E. Demorest, 10
George D. Demos, 6
Jennifer Denicolis, 12
Joseph W. Denison, 9
Evelyn Deno, 7
Susan K. Deri, 3
Mayhew Derryberry, 3
Lawrence G. Derthick, 5
Harry R. DeSilva, 2
Lizanne Destefano, 11-12
Douglas K. Detterman, 9
M. Vere DeVault, 7
Edward F. deVillafranca, 8
Anthony J. DeVito, 9
Joseph C. Dewey, 1-2
Michael L. Dey, 9
Robert E. Deysach, 10
Denise M. DeZolt, 11-13
Esther E. Diamond, 8-9, 11-13
Louis M. DiCarlo, 6
Charles F. Dicken, 6
Gwendolen S. Dickson, 1, 3
Paul B. Diederich, 1-2, 7
Allan O. Diefendorf, 11-12
John S. Diekhoff, 3-5
Thomas E. Dinero, 12
Jonathan G. Dings, 12
Robert L. Dipboye, 8
Jean Dirks, 9
David N. Dixon, 9-11-13
Gregory H. Dobbins, 9-10, 12
Keith S. Dobson, 9
Richard F. Docter, 7
Leland K. Doebler, 9
Janice A. Dole, 9-10
Elizabeth J. Doll, 10, 12-13
Robert H. Dolliver, 7-9
George Domino, 7-10, 12-13
Mavis L. Donahue, 9-10
Hei-Ki Dong, 9
Thomas F. Donlon, 8, 13
Jerome E. Doppelt, 4-8
Dan Douglas, 11
Harl R. Douglass, 2-3
E. Thomas Dowd, 9, 11-13
N. M. Downie, 6
John Downing, 8
Kenneth O. Doyle, Jr., 8
Vincent R. D'Oyley, 7
Ronald S. Drabman, 9
Raleigh M. Drake, 2-5
Richard M. Drake, 2-3
Penelope W. Dralle, 12
Ralph Mason Dreger, 8
Arnold Dresden, 1
Paul L. Dressel, 3-8
James Drever, 2
Philip H. Dreyer, 8-9

Laura A. Driscoll, 8
Robert C. Droege, 7
Priscilla A. Drum, 8-10
Robert J. Drummond, 11-13
Cynthia Ann Druva-Roush, 11-12
Judy R. Dubno, 9, 13
Linda M. DuBois, 9
Philip H. DuBois, 3, 6-7
John H. Duckitt, 9
Curtis Dudley-Marling, 9
Gerald G. Duffy, 7
Lydia A. Duggins, 5
Stanley G. Dulsky, 2-3
Stephen B. Dunbar, 11
Harold B. Dunkel, 2-6
Jack W. Dunlap, 1-3
James A. Dunn, 7
S. S. Dunn, 5-6
Marvin D. Dunnette, 6
Carl J. Dunst, 9-10, 13
Daniel R. Dupecher, 8
Mary M. Dupuis, 9
Paula J. Dupuy, 11
Richard P. Duran, 9
Walter N. Durost, 4-8
David M. Dush, 9
Ralph D. Dutch, 6-8
August Dvorak, 2
Beatrice J. Dvorak, 3
Patricia L. Dwinell, 9
Carol Anne Dwyer, 8
Calvin O. Dyer, 9
Henry S. Dyer, 5-6
Robert Dykstra, 7-8
Norman Eagle, 5, 7-8
Douglas B. Eamon, 9
Maurice J. Eash, 8
Howard Easley, 2
Robert L. Ebel, 4-8
Bruce J. Eberhardt, 9-10
Del Eberhardt, 12
Tim Eck, 12
Allen Jack Edwards, 10, 12
Bateman Edwards, 2
Reginald Edwards, 5
Ron Edwards, 10-11
Byron R. Egeland, 8-9
Stewart Ehly, 10
Lee H. Ehman, 8
Linnea C. Ehri, 9
Jonathan Ehrlich, 11
William J. Eichman, 6-8
Dorothy H. Eichorn, 5-8
Philip Eisenberg, 3
Richard Elardo, 9
Bradley Elison, 12
John Elkins, 9
Arthur S. Ellen, 11
William Eller, 6
Warwick B. Elley, 8
Judy L. Elliott, 13
M. H. Elliott, 3
Stephen N. Elliott, 9-11
Steven D. Elliott, 9
Albert Ellis, 3-7
Theresa H. Elofson, 12
Susan Embretson (Whitely), 9
Lon L. Emerick, 8
W. G. Emmett, 3-4
Norman S. Endler, 8-9
George Engelhard, Jr., 11-13
Max D. Engelhart, 1-2, 4-6
John M. Enger, 11-13
Bertram Epstein, 4
Jayne H. Epstein, 9
William P. Erchul, 10-11
James B. Erdmann, 11-13
Gerald L. Ericksen, 6-7
Deborah B. Erickson, 9-13
Lawrence W. Erickson, 6-8
Richard C. Erickson, 8, 10
Emanuel E. Ericson, 2
Claire B. Ernhart, 12
Leonard D. Eron, 5-7
Joan Ershler, 11
Anna S. Espenschade, 4-5
Barbara F. Esser, 6-7
Alvin C. Eurich, 1-2
James R. Evans, 9
Beth L. Evard, 9
Alexander Even, 7
Lorraine D. Eyde, 8-9
Julian Fabry, 9, 11-12
Jennifer J. Fager, 12-13
Doreen Ward Fairbank, 12-13
Shauna Faltin, 12
Xitao Fan, 13
Frank H. Farley, 9
Richard F. Farmer, 13
Paul R. Farnsworth, 1-3, 5-6
Roger Farr, 7-8
Ray N. Faulkner, 1-2
Richard W. Faunce, 11-12
Harold P. Fawcett, 2-5
Jay W. Fay, 1
Karen Fay, 13
Ethel M. Feagley, 3
Howard F. Fehr, 4
Elizabeth Fehrer, 3
Henry Feinberg, 1
Candice Feiring, 9-10
Shirley C. Feldmann, 8
Leonard S. Feldt, 5-8
Susan Felsenfeld, 12

Ray Fenton, 12-13
George A. Ferguson, 3-6
Leonard W. Ferguson, 6
Ephrem Fernandez, 13
Steven Ferrara, 11, 13
Robert H. Ferrell, 5
Trenton R. Ferro, 12-13
C. E. Ficken, 2
James A. Field, Jr., 5
Gordon Fifer, 5
Nikola N. Filby, 8
Maynard D. Filter, 11
Amy Finch-Williams, 10
Diane Billings Findley, 11
Warren G. Findley, 2-8
Stefan R. Fink, 8
Louis J. Finkle, 9
Carmen J. Finley, 11-12
Martin A. Fischer, 13
Seymour Fisher, 6
Wayne D. Fisher, 6
Joshua A. Fishman, 5
John L. Fisk, 9
Donald W. Fiske, 5
James A. Fitzgerald, 5
Colleen Fitzmaurice, 10
Anne R. Fitzpatrick, 11
Robert Fitzpatrick, 7-13
Dawn P. Flanagan, 12
John C. Flanagan, 1, 3-4, 6
Stephen G. Flanagan, 11
John W. Fleenor, 11-13
Lisa Fleisher, 9
C. M. Fleming, 4
W. G. Fleming, 6
Charles D. Flory, 1, 3
Joseph J. Foley, 8
John P. Foley, Jr., 5-7
Mary O. Folsom, 7
Marie C. Fontana, 8
Thomas G. Foran, 1
Donna Ford, 12
Laurie Ford, 11-12
Rex L. Forehand, 9
Bertram R. Forer, 6
Frank J. Fornoff, 6, 8-9
Elaine Forsyth, 3
Robert A. Forsyth, 7-8
Tomlinson Fort, 2
Jim C. Fortune, 11-13
Judson W. Foust, 2
Hanford M. Fowler, 4-5
Raymond D. Fowler, Jr., 7-8
Charles Fox, 2
Glen Fox, 13
Hazel M. Fox, 10
Lynn H. Fox, 8-9
Robert A. Fox, 9
Austin C. Frank, 8
Thomas T. Frantz, 7-8
Michael D. Franzen, 9
Stephen L. Franzoi, 9
Robert B. Frary, 9, 12-13
Barry J. Fraser, 9
Elizabeth D. Fraser, 5-6
Wayne A. Frederick, 5
Norman Frederiksen, 3-8
Norman Fredman, 12
B. J. Freeman, 9
Frank S. Freeman, 4-5
David Freides, 7-8
J. Joseph Freilinger, 8
Patricia K. Freitag, 13
John W. French, 3-8
Joseph L. French, 7
Robert L. French, 6
Sidney J. French, 3
Bruce R. Fretz, 9
Benno G. Fricke, 5-6
Marilyn Friend, 10
David A. Frisbie, 8-9
Clifford P. Froehlich, 4-5
Gustav J. Froehlich, 3-6
Benjamin Fruchter, 5
Edward B. Fry, 6-8
Maurine A. Fry, 9
Douglas H. Fryer, 3
Verne C. Fryklund, 2
Douglas Fuchs, 10
Lynn S. Fuchs, 9-10
Mark H. Fugate, 12-13
Martin Fujiki, 9-10
Solomon M. Fulero, 12
Paul H. Furfey, 1
Michael Furlong, 12-13
Elaine Furniss, 12
Edward J. Furst, 6-8
Robert K. Gable, 9, 11-13
Lena R. Gaddis, 11-13
N. L. Gage, 4-5
Eugene L. Gaier, 5
Rosslyn Gaines, 7
John P. Galassi, 9
Peggy E. Gallaher, 13
Gloria A. Galvin, 10-11
Leann M. Gamache, 12
Bessie Lee Gambrill, 2
Ronald J. Ganellen, 12-13
H. C. Ganguli, 9
Calvin P. Garbin, 11
Eugene E. Garcia, 9-10
Eric F. Gardner, 4-10
Sol L. Garfield, 7
Alan Garfinkel, 8-9, 11, 13

Ruth Garner, 9
Edgar R. Garrett, 7
Henry E. Garrett, 1-5
Jack E. Gebart-Eaglemont, 13
Ann L. Gebhardt, 2
Karl W. Gehrkens, 2
Kurt F. Geisinger, 11-13
John Geisler, 13
Kenneth E. Gell, 2
Karen Geller, 13
Judy Lynn Genshaft, 9
J. Raymond Gerberich, 2-6
Kathryn Clark Gerken, 9-10
Joanne C. Gersten, 8
Maribeth Gettinger, 10
Esther Geva, 9
John J. Geyer, 7-8
Edwin E. Ghiselli, 3
Cecil A. Gibb, 5-7
H. H. Giles, 1-2
Ronald B. Gillam, 11-13
Jerry S. Gilmer, 12
John W. Gittinger, 5
Gene V Glass, 7-8
James R. Glennon, 6
Goldine C. Gleser, 6-9
John A. Glover, 11
Lewis R. Goldberg, 7-8
Charles J. Golden, 9
Stephen L. Golding, 8-9
Bert A. Goldman, 6-7, 11-13
Leo Goldman, 6
Ronald Goldman, 8
Steven H. Goldman, 9
Marcel L. Goldschmid, 7
Diane Goldsmith, 12
Keith Goltry, 2
Ronald H. Good, III, 11
Elizabeth J. Goodacre, 7
Florence L. Goodenough, 2-3
Joan F. Goodman, 9
Clarence J. Goodnight, 7
Leonard D. Goodstein, 6-8
William L. Goodwin, 8
Rodney K. Goodyear, 9
Betty N. Gordon, 9
Edwin Gordon, 7
Hans C. Gordon, 2-3
Leonard V. Gordon, 6-8
John B. Gormly, 9
Elliot L. Gory, 9, 11
Edward Earl Gotts, 9
Harrison G. Gough, 4-9, 11-12
Neil Gourlay, 5
C. Ray Graham, 8
Grace Graham, 1-2
John R. Graham, 11-12
Steve Graham, 9, 11-13
Susan L. Graham-Clay, 9
Larry B. Grantham, 12
Vicki, Gratopp, 12
M. Elizabeth Graue, 12
Carol A. Gray, 9
William S. Gray, 1, 3-4
Felice J. Green, 13
Kathy E. Green, 12-13
Russel F. Green, 6-7
Edward B. Greene, 3-5
Harry A. Greene, 2-3
Jeffrey H. Greenhaus, 9
Noel Gregg, 10
Frank M. Gresham, 9-13
Konrad Gries, 4-5
J. Jeffrey Grill, 8-13
Arnold B. Grobman, 7
Hulda Grobman, 7-8
Martin G. Groff, 9
Norman E. Gronlund, 8
Richard E. Gross, 5-8
Fred M. Grossman, 9-10
Foster E. Grossnickle, 1-4
William R. Grove, 3-4
Melissa M. Groves, 13
Wilson H. Guertin, 5-6
Richard E. Guest, 11
Walter S. Guiler, 4
J. P. Guilford, 1-5
Robert M. Guion, 8-10, 12-13
Sami Gulgoz, 11-12
Arlen R. Gullickson, 7-8, 12
R. Gulliford, 7
Harold Gulliksen, 1-2, 4
John Flagg Gummere, 2
Faith Gunning, 13
John W. Gustad, 5
Rhonda L. Gutenberg, 9-10
George M. Guthrie, 8-9
John T. Guthrie, 7-8
Barbara Lapp Gutkin, 10
Terry B. Gutkin, 9
Thomas W. Guyette, 9-10, 12
Natasha Gwartney, 12
Malcolm D. Gynther, 7-8
Lyn R. Haber, 9-10
Laura B. Hadley, 2
John H. Haefner, 5-6
Edward H. Haertel, 9, 13
Elizabeth Hagen, 5-7
Rosa A. Hagin, 9, 11, 13
Michio P. Hagiwara, 7-8
Amos L. Hahn, 9
Milton E. Hahn, 3-4, 6
A. Ralph Hakstian, 7-8
Thomas M. Haladyna, 11-13

Robert Leslie Hale, 9
Alfred E. Hall, 8
Bruce W. Hall, 11
Cathy W. Hall, 9-11
Penelope K. Hall, 11-12
W. E. Hall, 3
Wallace B. Hall, 6
Raphael M. Haller, 7-8
Harvey Halpern, 8
Ronald K. Hambleton, 8-9, 11-12
Wade L. Hamil, 11
Scott B. Hamilton, 9
Thomas A. Hammeke, 9
Nelson G. Hanawalt, 3-5
C. H. Handschin, 2
Karl R. Hanes, 13
Gerald S. Hanna, 8-9, 11-13
Lavone A. Hanna, 2-3
Paul R. Hanna, 4
Michael J. Hannafin, 9
Mary Elizabeth Hannah, 9
Jane Hansen, 9
Joe B. Hansen, 13
Jo-Ida C. Hansen, 8-9
Michael C. Hansen, 13
Gary R. Hanson, 7
Richard E. Harding, 10, 12-13
David S. Hargrove, 10
Thomas G. Haring, 10-11
Marilyn J. Haring-Hidore, 9
Lenore W. Harmon, 8-10
Delwyn L. Harnisch, 11-13
Dennis C. Harper, 9-10, 13
Robert A. Harper, 6-7
Thomas H. Harrell, 11
Thomas W. Harrell, 3
Philip L. Harriman, 4-6
Robert G. Harrington, 9-10, 13
Albert J. Harris, 3, 6-7
Chester W. Harris, 3-4
Dale B. Harris, 4-8
David P. Harris, 7-8
Jerry D. Harris, 9
Larry A. Harris, 7-8
Robert C. Harris, 7
Theodore L. Harris, 6
Jesse G. Harris, Jr., 6
Mary T. Harrison, 7
Patti L. Harrison, 9-11, 13
Charles M. Harsh, 3-4
Stuart N. Hart, 10, 12
Verna Hart, 9, 11
Ruth N. Hartley, 8
Bruce W. Hartman, 10
Hope J. Hartman, 11
George W. Hartmann, 1, 4
Rodney T. Hartnett, 8-9
Timothy S. Hartshorne, 10
Louis D. Hartson, 1
Maurice L. Hartung, 1, 3
Anne L. Harvey, 11
Leo M. Harvill, 11-13
Michael R. Harwell, 11-13
Glen Hass, 3
J. O. Hassler, 1-2
J. Thomas Hastings, 4-6, 8
Richard S. Hatch, 6
Starke R. Hathaway, 3
Clifford V. Hatt, 9
John T. Hatten, 8-9
John Hattie, 12-13
Keith Hattrup, 12-13
G. E. Hawkins, 2
David G. Hawkridge, 7-8
Mary R. Haworth, 5-6
Linda White Hawthorne, 9
Edward N. Hay, 3-5
James R. Hayden, 5-6
Steven C. Hayes, 11
Theodore L. Haycs, 13
Leslie M. Haynes, 4
Sandra D. Haynes, 13
William O. Haynes, 9-10, 12
E. Charles Healey, 10
Kenneth L. Heaton, 4
Martine Hébert, 11-13
Deborah Hecht, 11
Natalie L. Hedberg, 11-12
Earle R. Hedrick, 2
David K. Heenan, 5-6
Lloyd H. Heidgerd, 6
Louis J. Heifetz, 10
Edith S. Heil, 10
Louis M. Heil, 2
Alfred B. Heilbrun, Jr., 5-10
Nancy Heilman, 11
Alice W. Heim, 4-7
Harry Heller, 2
William H. Helme, 6
G. C. Helmstadter, 7, 9
John K. Hemphill, 6-7
Carlen Henington, 13
V. A. C. Henmon, 1
James J. Hennessy, 10
Mary Henning-Stout, 10-13
Edwin R. Henry, 4
Stephan A. Henry, 10
William E. Henry, 4-5
William Hered, 6
David O. Herman, 12-13
Patricia Herman, 9
Edward S. Herold, 9
Edwin L. Herr, 9-10
Virgil E. Herrick, 4-5

Allen K. Hess, 9-13
Kathryn D. Hess, 11-12
Robert M. Hess, 12
John R. Hester, 11
William L. Heward, 9
Julia A. Hickman, 10
Peggy A. Hicks, 13
Elfrieda H. Hiebert, 9
A. N. Hieronymus, 5-7
A. Dirk Hightower, 10
E. H. C. Hildebrandt, 3
Walker H. Hill, 5
John R. Hills, 6-9
Robert W. Hiltonsmith, 9, 11-13
Philip Himelstein, 7
Elmer D. Hinckley, 4
C. B. Hindley, 6
Laura Hines, 9
J. Scott Hinkle, 11
Michael D. Hiscox, 9
Marshall S. Hiskey, 6-7
Jean Hoard, 2
James R. Hobson, 2-5
Emil H. Hoch, 8
Elton Hocking, 3-4
James O. Hodges, 8
Barbara W. Hodson, 9
James V. Hoffman, 9
Robert Hogan, 7-10
Thomas P. Hogan, 8
Dorothy E. Holberg, 3
Raymond H. Holden, 7
Warren S. Holmes, 2
Robert R. Holt, 4
Wayne H. Holtzman, 5, 7
Charles Holzwarth, 2
Susan P. Homan, 9
L. Michael Honaker, 11
Charles H. Honzik, 4
Marjorie P. Honzik, 6-7
Albert B. Hood, 8
Joyce E. Hood, 8-9
Stephen B. Hood, 8
Stephen R. Hooper, 10-13
Kenneth D. Hopkins, 6-9, 11
John L. Horn, 7
Thomas D. Horn, 7-8
John E. Horrocks, 5-6
Clark W. Horton, 2-5
Daniel L. Householder, 8
Charles Houston, 12
Carl I. Hovland, 3-5
Robert W. Howard, 2
Edgar Howarth, 8
George W. Howe, 9
Kenneth W. Howell, 9-10
Robert J. Howell, 10
Duncan Howie, 5
Monica M. Hoye, 3
Cyril J. Hoyt, 4-7
Kenneth B. Hoyt, 6
Louis M. Hsu, 9
Te-Fang Hua, 13
Mary E. Huba, 11
Carl J. Huberty, 7-9
Anita M. Hubley, 13
Edith M. Huddleston, 4
John Peter Hudson, Jr., 13
E. Scott Huebner, 10-11, 13
Mildred H. Huebner, 7-8
Jan N. Hughes, 10-11
Selma Hughes, 11-12
Violet Hughes, 2
Doncaster G. Humm, 2
Lloyd G. Humphreys, 3-6, 9
Joel Hundert, 9
John D. Hundleby, 6
Stephen Hunka, 6
Albert L. Hunsicker, 4
E. Patricia Hunt, 2
Jane V. Hunt, 7-8
Thelma Hunt, 3
William A. Hunt, 3
George W. Hunter, 1-2
Archer W. Hurd, 1
David P. Hurford, 13
Sylvia M. Hutchinson, 10
Robert R. Hutzell, 9
George W. Hynd, 9
Ludwig Immergluck, 3
James C. Impara, 11
Henry A. Imus, 3
Mario Iona, 8
Carl Isenhart, 13
Steven Isonio, 13
Stephen H. Ivens, 12-13
Annette M. Iverson, 11-12
Margaret Ives, 3
Edward F. Iwanicki, 8-9
Douglas N. Jackson, 7-9
Joseph F. Jackson, 2-3
Robert W. B. Jackson, 5
Richard M. Jaeger, 8-10
Alice N. Jameson, 3
Colleen B. Jamison, 7
Patsy Arnett Jaynes, 11
Frank C. Jean, 1
Chantale Jeanrie, 13
Jeffrey A. Jenkins, 11-13
John R. Jennings, 5
Arthur R. Jensen, 5-7, 9
Joanne L. Jensen, 12
Patrick J. Jeske, 9
Carl F. Jesness, 7

Richard Jessor, 5
Frank B. Jex, 6
James E. Jirsa, 9
A. Pemberton Johnson, 5
Cecil D. Johnson, 5
Dale D. Johnson, 8
Jerry Johnson, 11
Laura B. Johnson, 2
Leland P. Johnson, 4
Marjorie S. Johnson, 8
Palmer O. Johnson, 1-5
Richard T. Johnson, 6-8
Richard W. Johnson, 8-10, 12-13
Robert Johnson, 13
Ronn Johnson, 10
Ruth Johnson, 12
Sylvia T. Johnson, 11
Wayde Johnson, 11
Sharon Johnson-Lewis, 11
Joseph A. Johnston, 7
Judith R. Johnston, 9, 13
Barry W. Jones, 9-10
Carleton C. Jones, 1-2
Clive Jones, 7
David Jones, 7
Dorothy L. Jones, 7
Edward S. Jones, 1-2
Elizabeth L. Jones, 12
H. Gwynne Jones, 6
Harold E. Jones, 1-4
James A. Jones, 12
Katherine S. Jones, 12
Kenneth J. Jones, 6
Kevin M. Jones, 12-13
Ll. Wynn Jones, 2
Randall L. Jones, 8
Randall M. Jones, 9
Robert A. Jones, 5
Worth R. Jones, 5-6
A. M. Jordan, 2
Richard H. Jordan, 3
Helen L. Jorstad, 8
Gerald A. Juhnke, 13
Lee N. June, 9
Ehud Jungwirth, 8
Samuel Juni, 9-13
James J. Jupp, 9
Clifford E. Jurgensen, 3-6
Stephen Jurs, 11-12
Joseph Justman, 5
Javaid Kaiser, 11-13
Paul E. Kambly, 4
Randy W. Kamphaus, 9-13
Michael Kane, 13
Rabindra N. Kanungo, 9-10
Chi-Wen Kao, 13
David E. Kapel, 11
Barbara J. Kaplan, 11-13
Robert M. Kaplan, 10
Stuart A. Karabenick, 9
Harry W. Karn, 4
M. Ray Karnes, 4
Mitchell Karno, 12
Lawrence M. Kasdon, 7-9
Walter Kass, 5
Edward S. Katkin, 8
Walter Katkovsky, 6, 11
Martin R. Katz, 5-8
Raymond A. Katzell, 3-8
James M. Kauffman, 9
Alan S. Kaufman, 8-10. 13
Nadeen L. Kaufman, 9, 13
Walter V. Kaulfers, 1-7
Kenneth A. Kavale, 10
Michael G. Kavan, 11-13
Michael J. Kavanagh, 8
T. J. Keating, 2
J. A. Keats, 5-6
John M. Keene, Jr., 9
J. Ward Keesling, 9
Thomas J. Kehle, 9-10
Jerard F. Kehoe, 11
Gertrude Keir, 4
Patricia B. Keith, 12-13
Timothy Z. Keith, 9-10, 12
Thomas Kellaghan, 8
Harold R. Keller, 10
Mary Lou Kelley, 9-13
Truman L. Kelley, 2
Theodore E. Kellogg, 4-5
E. Lowell Kelly, 3-7
William E. Kendall, 6
Katherine G. Keneally, 4
James E. Kennedy, 6-7
Patricia H. Kennedy, 9
Kathryn W. Kenney, 10, 12
Douglas T. Kenny, 5
Leonard Kenowitz, 9
Grace H. Kent, 2-3
Barbara K. Keogh, 8-9
Robert E. Keohane, 2
Newell C. Kephart, 7
Barbara A. Kerr, 9-10, 12
Nancy Kerr, 9
Willard A. Kerr, 3-4, 6-7
Anne R. Kessler, 13
Kathy S. Kessler, 11-12
Gilbert C. Kettelkamp, 6
Thomas E. Kieren, 8
Kenneth A. Kiewra, 11-13
Edward Kifer, 9
Jeremy Kilpatrick, 7-8
Ernest W. Kimmel, 11, 13
Elaine F. Kinder, 1

Glen D. King, 8
John D. King, 12
Joseph E. King, 3
Suzanne King, 12
Forrest A. Kingsbury, 2
G. Gage Kingsbury, 12
Albert J. Kingston, 6-8
Lucien B. Kinney, 2, 4
Richard T. Kinnier, 13
John R. Kinzer, 3
Wayne K. Kirchner, 6
Barbara A. Kirk, 7
Jean Powell Kirnan, 11-13
Karyll Kiser, 12
Philip M. Kitay, 6-7
Helen Kitchens, 13
Tom Kitwood, 8
Paul M. Kjeldergaard, 6
Seymour G. Klebanoff, 4
Benjamin Kleinmuntz, 6-10
Milton V. Kline, 6
Paul Kline, 7-8
William E. Kline, 7-8
Martin Kling, 7-8
Robert R. Knapp, 7
Samuel J. Knapp, 9
Thomas R. Knapp, 9, 13
Catharine C. Knight, 12
Howard M. Knoff, 9-13
John F. Knutson, 7
William R. Koch, 11-12
Stephen L. Koffler, 12-13
Kate L. Kogan, 3-4
William S. Kogan, 4
David Kopel, 1-2
Rebecca J. Kopriva, 12
Abraham K. Korman, 8
Stephen M. Koziol, Jr., 8
Ernest J. Kozma, 11
Jack J. Kramer, 9
John H. Kranzler, 12
David R. Krathwohl, 5
Thomas R. Kratochwill, 9
Charles J. Krauskopf, 7-8
Carole M. Krauthamer, 12
Roy A. Kress, 7-9
A. C. Krey, 1
Philip H. Kriedt, 6
S. David Kriska, 12
Russell P. Kropp, 5
Damon Krug, 13
Morris Krugman, 3-5
Sally Kuhlenschmidt, 13
John D. Krumboltz, 6
David J. Krus, 9
Dietmar Kuchemann, 9
Frederic Kuder, 2-3
Jay Kuder, 11
Phyllis Kuehn, 12
F. Kuhlmann, 2
Deborah King Kundert, 10-12
Antony John Kunnan, 13
Dana G. Kurfman, 7-8
Albert K. Kurtz, 4-6, 8
Koressa Kutsick, 10
W. C. Kvaraceus, 3-4
Kwong-Liem Karl Kwan, 13
Lou LaBrant, 2
Barbara Lachar, 11, 13
David Lachar, 11
Eleanor M. Ladd, 8
Robert Lado, 7
Linda A. Lagomarsino, 9
Matthew E. Lambert, 11, 13
Nadine M. Lambert, 9
Elaine L. La Monica, 8
W. Elmer Lancaster, 2
Daniel Landis, 7
Herbert A. Landry, 2
Edward Landy, 5
Frank J. Landy, 8
Suzanne Lane, 11
William Steve Lang, 11-13
Theos A. Langlie, 1
Aimée Langlois, 12
Charles R. Langmuir, 3-6
Gerald V. Lannholm, 3-5
Richard I. Lanyon, 7-9, 11-12
Luis M. Laosa, 8
Glenda Lappan, 8-9
Peter A. Lappan, Jr., 6-8
William S. Larson, 2-6
Julian J. Lasky, 7
Robert L. Lathrop, 7
Allan L. LaVoie, 8-9
Joseph G. Law, Jr., 11-13
J. S. Lawes, 6-7
Kimberly A. Lawless, 13
C. H. Lawshe, Jr., 3
Gary W. Lawson, 9
Martha E. Layman, 4
Wilbur L. Layton, 4-11
Robert A. Leark, 13
Steven B. Leder, 12
Herbert Lederer, 8
Richard Ledgerwood, 1
James Ledvinka, 9
Courtland C. Lee, 9
J. Murray Lee, 1, 5
S. G. Lee, 6-7
Steven W. Lee, 10-13
D. Welty Lefever, 1-6
Sue M. Legg, 12
Paul R. Lehman, 7-10

Irvin J. Lehmann, 6-13
Richard Lehrer, 11
Roger T. Lennon, 4-5
Theodore F. Lentz, 3
Francis E. Lentz, Jr., 9-10
J. Paul Leonard, 2-3
Frederick T. L. Leong, 11-13
Richard Lesh, 9
Donald A. Leton, 7-9
S. Alvin Leung, 11-13
Ralph G. Leverett, 13
Eugene E. Levitt, 6-8
Philip M. Levy, 6
Seymour Levy, 6
Mary A. Lewis, 11-13
Roy D. Lewis, 5
Lester M. Libo, 7-8
Peter D. Lifton, 9
John Liggett, 5-6
Glynn D. Ligon, 9
Paul M. Limbert, 1
David P. Lindeman, 9
E. F. Lindquist, 5
Mary Montgomery Lindquist, 8-9
Rick Lindskog, 11-13
C. Mauritz Lindvall, 7-8
W. Line, 2
James C. Lingoes, 6
James B. Lingwall, 8
Robert L. Linn, 8-10
Maria Prendes Lintel, 13
Gary E. Lintereur, 8, 10
Richard Lippa, 9
Robert W. Lissitz, 11
William M. Littell, 7
Orrel E. Little, 3
Wei-Ping Liu, 13
Alice K. Liveright, 2
John Wills Lloyd, 9
Steven G. LoBello, 11-13
Aileene S. Lockhart, 7
Jane Loevinger, 4, 8
R. Duane Logue, 8
Paul R. Lohnes, 6-8
Walter F. W. Lohnes, 7
Paul S. Lomax, 3
John W. Lombard, 7-8
Charles J. Long, 12-13
John A. Long, 3
Louis Long, 3
Steven H. Long, 11-13
Andrew Longacre, 2
Alfred P. Longo, 13
Frank M. Loos, 4
Emilia C. Lopez, 13
Peter G. Loret, 6
Irving Lorge, 2-3, 5
Margaret F. Lorimer, 6
Maurice Lorr, 5-8
C. M. Louttit, 1-4
Kenneth Lovell, 6-7
Benson P. Low, 9
Rodney L. Lowman, 9-10
Brenda H. Loyd, 9, 12
S. Ruben Lozano, 9
Ardie Lubin, 4
William H. Lucio, 6
William H. Lucow, 5
Leslie Eastman Lukin, 13
James Lumsden, 5, 8
Robert W. Lundin, 5-7
Clifford E. Lunneborg, 7-8
Patricia W. Lunneborg, 8-9
David T. Lykken, 6-8
Howard B. Lyman, 6-7
Joan I. Lynch, 9-10
Hugh Lytton, 8
Henry S. Maas, 3
Linda Mabry, 12
Gloria Maccow, 13
John MacDonald, 13
F. Charles Mace, 9-10
Gordon N. MacKenzie, 3-4
Arthur C. MacKinney, 6-8
Saunders MacLane, 6
David MacPhee, 11-13
George F. Madaus, 8-9
Faith Madden, 4
Cleborne D. Maddux, 10-13
Thomas W. Mahan, Jr., 6
Roderick K. Mahurin, 11-12
James Mainwaring, 5
Koressa Kutsick Malcolm, 11, 13
Julius B. Maller, 1-2
Susan J. Maller, 13
George G. Mallinson, 6-8
Jacqueline V. Mallinson, 6-8
Berenice Mallory, 2
Margaret E. Malone, 13
Dean R. Malsbary, 8
Milton M. Mandell, 4
Lester Mann, 7-9
M. Jacinta Mann, 5
John Manning, 5, 7
Winton H. Manning, 6
Herschel T. Manuel, 2-5
Caroline Manuele-Adkins, 9-10, 12-13
Gregory J. Marchant, 12-13
Gary L. Marco, 11-13
Carol Mardell-Czudnowski, 10
Suzanne Markel-Fox, 12
Robert P. Markley, 9-10
Howard J. Markman, 9
Melvin R. Marks, 6

Marc Marschark, 12
Herbert W. Marsh, 9
David Marshall, 10
Brian K. Martens, 10-11
Charles Wm. Martin, 11
Roy P. Martin, 9
William E. Martin, Jr., 13
Stanley S. Marzolf, 3
Bertram B. Masia, 6
Carolyn E. Massad, 8
Joseph D. Matarazzo, 9-10
Johnny L. Matson, 9
Ross W. Matteson, 4
Paula Matuszek, 9
Francis N. Maxfield, 1-2
James Maxwell, 3-5
Susanna Maxwell, 9
Samuel T. Mayo, 6-9
Arthur B. Mays, 2
James J. Mazza, 10
Charles C. McArthur, 7
John N. McCall, 7
Raymond J. McCall, 5
W. C. McCall, 2
William A. McCall, 2
James M. McCallister, 3
R. Steve McCallum, 9
Susan McCammon, 10
Boyd R. McCandless, 4, 6-7
James J. McCarthy, 7-9
Kevin J. McCarthy, 12
James Leslie McCary, 8
Robert L. McCaul, 2-3
Clara J. McCauley, 2
Rebecca J. McCauley, 11-13
Erin McClure, 12
Scott R. McConnell, 11
Robert R. McCrae, 9
R. W. McCulloch, 5
Constance M. McCullough, 2-3, 5, 7
S. P. McCutchen, 1-2
Hiram L. McDade, 9
Arthur S. McDonald, 6
D. W. McElwain, 4-5
William C. McGaghie, 8
Ellen McGinnis, 10
Kevin S. McGrew, 10
Christine H. McGuire, 5-8
David E. McIntosh, 12
Robert M. McIntyre, 9
Michael G. McKee, 7
William T. McKee, 10
Margaret G. McKim, 3-4
Joyce R. McLarty, 11
Kenneth F. McLaughlin, 6
John McLeish, 4, 7
Mary J. McLellan, 12-13
Jonathon C. McLendon, 6
John McLeod, 8
Robert J. McMahon, 9
Robert F. McMorris, 9-13
Douglas M. McNair, 7-8
Michael McNamara, 12
Sharon McNeely, 12
Malcolm R. McNeil, 10-13
Jeanette McPherrin, 2
John V. McQuitty, 3-4
Louis L. McQuitty, 4
Douglas J. McRae, 11-13
Leija V. McReynolds, 8
Paul McReynolds, 7-10
Damian McShane, 11
Richard A. Meade, 5
Arthur W. Meadows, 5
David J. Mealor, 9-11
I. G. Meddleton, 5
Albert E. Meder, Jr., 5
Maria Medina-Diaz, 13
Frederic J. Medway, 11, 13
Paul E. Meehl, 3
Edwin I. Megargee, 7-8
Howard D. Mehlinger, 7-8
William A. Mehrens, 7-9, 11-13
Sheila Mehta, 13
Manfred J. Meier, 7-9, 11
Norman C. Meier, 2
Scott T. Meier, 12-13
William B. Meldrum, 1, 3
P. L. Mellenbruch, 5
Gary B. Melton, 9-10, 12
Richard S. Melton, 6, 8
H. Meltzer, 3
David M. Memory, 9
Gerald A. Mendelsohn, 6
Kevin Menefee, 11-12
Robert J. Menges, 8
Ivan N. Mensh, 4
Gerald M. Meredith, 7
Peter F. Merenda, 11-13
Philip R. Merrifield, 6
Jack C. Merwin, 6-8
William R. Merz, Jr., 12-13
Bernadine Meyer, 5
Donald L. Meyer, 6
John H. Meyer, 3
C. Edward Meyers, 8
Marcee J. Meyers, 9
Joan J. Michael, 7
William B. Michael, 4-13
William J. Micheels, 4-5
Grace Middleton, 11
Christopher P. Migotsky, 12
T. R. Miles, 5-6, 8
John E. Milholland, 5-8

C. Dean Miller, 9
Gloria E. Miller, 10
John K. Miller, 9
Jon F. Miller, 9
Lovick C. Miller, 7-8
M. David Miller, 11-12
Robert J. Miller, 11-13
Sherri K. Miller, 11
Jason Millman, 6-9
Craig N. Mills, 9, 11-12
John A. Mills, 13
J. B. Miner, 2
J. H. Minnick, 2
Patricia L. Mirenda, 10-12
Lorenz Misbach, 3
Ronald W. Mitchell, 7
James V. Mitchell, Jr., 7-8
Arthur Mittman, 6-8
Glenn Moe, 9
Huberto Molina, 8
William G. Mollenkopf, 3-4, 8
Floyd V. Monaghan, 7
Eason Monroe, 3
Marion Monroe, 1, 3
Judith A. Monsaas, 12-13
Joseph E. Moore, 2-4, 6
Terence Moore, 6
Walter J. Moore, 7
Mary Ross Moran, 11-12
Kevin L. Moreland, 9-13
G. A. V. Morgan, 5-7
Alice E. Moriarty, 7
Claudia J. Morner, 12
Sherwyn Morreale, 12-13
John B. Morris, 5
Coleman Morrison, 6
Frances Crook Morrison, 5-6
Gale M. Morrison, 9, 12-13
Nathan Morrison, 3
Thomas F. Morrison, 2
Irving Morrissett, 8
H. T. Morse, 3
N. W. Morton, 1-2, 4
P. L. Morton, 2
Harold E. Moser, 5
Donald L. Mosher, 7-8
David Moshman, 10
Charles I. Mosier, 2-3
C. Scott Moss, 6
Pamela A. Moss, 9, 11
Kevin W. Mossholder, 9-10
Stephan J. Motowidlo, 8-9
Donald E. Mowrer, 10
Robert R. Mowrer, 10
Paul M. Muchinsky, 9, 12-13
Daniel J. Mueller, 10
Kate Hevner Mueller, 5
Ralph O. Mueller, 11-13
Ann M. Muench, 11
Ina V. S. Mullis, 8
Leo A. Munday, 7
Allyn M. Munger, 6
Carolyn Colvin Murphy, 10
Joseph A. Murphy, 7-8
Kevin R. Murphy, 9-12
Wilbur F. Murra, 1-2
Elsie Murray, 4
Mildred Murray-Ward, 13
James L. Mursell, 1-3
Bernard I. Murstein, 6-8
Charles T. Myers, 5, 8
Roberta S. Myers, 9
Sheldon S. Myers, 6-7
Dean H. Nafziger, 8, 11
Jack A. Naglieri, 9, 11
Philip Nagy, 12-13
Louis C. Nanassy, 5
Doris E. Nason, 8
Diana S. Natalicio, 8-9
Theodor F. Naumann, 6-7
Leo Nedelsky, 5-6
Charles O. Neidt, 5-6
Edward A. Nelsen, 9
Clarence H. Nelson, 3-8
Jack L. Nelson, 8
Myrna K. Ness, 9
Debra Neubert, 11-12
Charles Neuringer, 8
Andrew F. Newcomb, 9
Theodore Newcomb, 2
Phyllis L. Newcomer, 8-9
Gwendolyn Newkirk, 10
T. Ernest Newland, 6-7
Bernard H. Newman, 7
Dianna L. Newman, 10-13
E. Jean Newman, 13
Isadore Newman, 12
Joseph Newman, 4
Kenneth R. Newton, 5
Arthur M. Nezu, 10
William H. Nibbelink, 8
Lois Nichols, 12
David S. Nichols, 9, 11
Robert C. Nichols, 6, 8-9
John Nisbet, 5-7
Stanley D. Nisbet, 4-7
Michael Nissenbaum, 12
Anthony J. Nitko, 8-13
Victor H. Noll, 1-7
Patricia Noller, 9
Claude E. Norcross, 4
Warren T. Norman, 5-7
Janet A. Norris, 9-13
Raymond C. Norris, 5

Robert D. North, 5-7
Paul A. Northrop, 1-2
Christine Novak, 12
Ruth M. Noyce, 9-10
Edward S. Noyes, 2-3
Jum C. Nunnally, 7
Thomas Oakland, 8-9
C. A. Oakley, 2-3
C. O. Oakley, 3
Thomas C. O'Brien, 7-8
John E. Obrzut, 9, 11
Anna S. Ochoa, 8-9
Salvador Hector Ochoa, 12-13
Charles W. Odell, 1-3
Judy Oehler-Stinnett, 10-13
Lynn R. Offermann, 13
Betty T. Ogletree, 13
Kevin E. O'Grady, 9-10
Stephen Olejnik, 11-12
Donald W. Oliver, 6
Mary Ellen Oliverio, 5, 7-8
Esteban L. Olmedo, 9
D. Joe Olmi, 11-13
Carl J. Olson, 7
Albert C. Oosterhof, 12-13
Don B. Oppenheim, 9
Pedro T. Orata, 2
Michael D. Orlansky, 9
Jacob S. Orleans, 2-6
David B. Orr, 6-7
John C. Ory, 9
Timothy M. Osberg, 11
Agnes E. Osborne, 3
Alan Osborne, 7-8
R. T. Osborne, 7
Worth J. Osburn, 1-2, 4
Stuart Oskamp, 7-8
Alton O'Steen, 2
Steven J. Osterlind, 11-13
Nicki N. Ostrom, 9
Donald P. Oswald, 13
Jay L. Otis, 3-4
Terry Overton, 11-13
Steven V. Owen, 11-13
William A. Owens, 6, 8-9
Robert E. Owens, Jr., 9-10
C. Robert Pace, 3-8
Abbot Packard, 12
Albert G. Packard, 3
Ellis Batten Page, 6-9
Kathleen D. Paget, 9-10, 13
Ian C. Palmer, 12
Orville Palmer, 5
Osmond E. Palmer, 5-7
Jean M. Palormo, 6
Josephine B. Pane, 7
Mary Pannbacker, 11
Anthony W. Paolitto, 12-13
Gino Parisi, 7
Jayne A. Parker, 9
Anna Parsek, 2
Charles K. Parsons, 9-12
A. Harry Passow, 4, 8-9, 11-12
Donald G. Paterson, 2-4
Gerald R. Patterson, 5
Willard W. Patty, 4
Walter Pauk, 7
Jerome D. Pauker, 6-9
Sharon E. Paulson, 13
David A. Payne, 6-7
Douglas S. Payne, 9
Frank D. Payne, 9
Robert W. Payne, 6-9
William G. Peacher, 4
I. Carolyn Pearson, 13
Mary Ellen Pearson, 9-11
John Gray Peatman, 2
Elazar J. Pedhazur, 8-9
E. A. Peel, 4-5
Charles W. Pendleton, 8
Douglas A. Penfield, 12
John P. Penna, 8
L. S. Penrose, 3
William H. Perkins, 7
Carole Perlman, 13
Kathleen N. Perret, 5
Barbara Perry-Sheldon, 10
Charles C. Peters, 1
Jerry L. Peters, 10
Charles A. Peterson, 9-10, 12-13
Christopher Peterson, 9
Donald R. Peterson, 6
Gary W. Peterson, 9
Harold A. Peterson, 7-10
Norman G. Peterson, 9
Reece L. Peterson, 9
Rolf A. Peterson, 8, 10
Shailer Peterson, 3
Julia Pettiette-Doolin, 10
Steven I. Pfeiffer, 9-13
Susanna W. Pflaum, 9
LeAdelle Phelps, 10, 12-13
Roger P. Phelps, 7-8
Gary W. Phillips, 9
S. E. Phillips, 9-10
Theodore G. Phillips, 5-7
Nick J. Piazza, 10
Eugene (Geno) Pichette, 13
James Pickering, 9
Hale C. Pickett, 3
Douglas A. Pidgeon, 5-9
John Pierce-Jones, 5-6
Ellen V. Piers, 6
Wayne C. Piersel, 9-10, 13

Myrtle L. Pignatelli, 2
Len Pikaart, 7-8
A. E. G. Pilliner, 5-8
Paul Pimsleur, 6
James W. Pinkney, 9-10, 12-13
Rudolf Pintner, 1
Francis J. Pirozzolo, 9
David J. Pittenger, 13
Barbara S. Plake, 9
Gus P. Plessas, 6-9
Lynnette B. Plumlee, 3, 5-7
Joseph G. Ponterotto, 11
Marcel O. Ponton, 13
Robert C. Pooley, 2-7
Mark Pope, 11-12
Donald B. Pope-Davis, 12
Mary S. Poplin, 9
Lyman W. Porter, 6
James M. Porter, Jr., 3
William D. Porterfield, 11
Stanley D. Porteus, 2
C. Dale Posey, 10
Winifred L. Post, 4-5
G. Michael Poteat, 10-13
James A. Poteet, 9-10
Kenneth E. Poucher, 8
Thomas E. Powell, 11
Stephen Powers, 9
Elizabeth M. Prather, 9-11
Michael W. Pratt, 9
Sheila R. Pratt, 13
Norman T. Pratt, Jr., 1-2
Daniel A. Prescott, 1
Joan Preston, 7
Ralph C. Preston, 3-4
H. Vernon Price, 5
Jack Price, 7
Ray G. Price, 3, 6-7
Roy A. Price, 2-3
Erich P. Prien, 13
Hugh F. Priest, 7
George P. Prigatano, 9
M. L. Kellmer Pringle, 4-7
Barry M. Prizant, 11
Glen W. Probst, 7
Barton B. Proger, 8-9
H. Thompson Prout, 9
Richard C. Pugh, 12-13
Earl V. Pullias, 2
Alan C. Purves, 7-8
Joan E. Pynes, 10
Fred Pyrczak, 8
M. Y. Quereshi, 7-8
Michelle Quinn, 9
Albert I. Rabin, 4-5, 7
S. Rachman, 6
John A. Radcliffe, 5-6
Rudolf E. Radocy, 12-13
Jeffrey S. Rain, 12-13
Nambury S. Raju, 9, 11-13
Bikkar S. Randhawa, 11-13
John F. Randolph, 3
Earl F. Rankin, 7-8
Alan J. Raphael, 13
Evelyn Raskin, 4
Leslie T. Raskind, 10
Michael M. Ravitch, 9
Glen E. Ray, 12
Alton L. Raygor, 6, 8
S. A. Rayner, 5
Mark D. Reckase, 9
James C. Reed, 7-9, 12-13
Michael L. Reed, 9
Homer B. C. Reed, Jr., 8-9
Edwin H. Reeder, 3-4
Ronald E. Reeve, 9
William R. Reevy, 6
Barbara A. Reilly, 11-12
David H. Reilly, 9
Robert C. Reinehr, 11-13
Robert A. Reineke, 11-12
Richard J. Reisboard, 8
Ralph M. Reitan, 6-7
Willard E. Reitz, 7
H. H. Remmers, 1, 3, 5
K. Ann Renninger, 9
Joseph S. Renzulli, 9
Harvey Resnick, 9
Paul Retzlaff, 11-13
Cecil R. Reynolds, 9, 11-13
Maynard C. Reynolds, 5
Sharon B. Reynolds, 10
William M. Reynolds, 9
Marvin Reznikoff, 7
James A. Rice, 8
Gilbert J. Rich, 3
R. Lynn Richards, 10
Roger A. Richards, 5-9, 11, 13
T. W. Richards, 4
James M. Richards, Jr., 7-8
J. A. Richardson, 5
M. W. Richardson, 1-2
S. C. Richardson, 5
Bert O. Richmond, 9
James H. Ricks, Jr., 4-6, 8
T. Andrew Ridenour, 13
Paul R. Rider, 2
Stanley E. Ridley, 9
C. Alan Riedesel, 6-8
William Rieman, III, 3-4
Edward G. Rietz, 5
Henry L. Rietz, 1
Janet Morgan Riggs, 9
Seymour Rigrodsky, 7

Alice R. Rines, 8
Henry D. Rinsland, 1-4
Charlene Rivera, 11
Harry N. Rivlin, 4-5
James P. Rizzo, 6
A. Oscar H. Roberts, 7
David C. Roberts, 13
Holland Roberts, 2-6
Mark W. Roberts, 9, 11
Donald U. Robertson, 11
Gary J. Robertson, 9-10, 13
Elizabeth A. Robinson, 9
Eric Robinson, 12
G. Edith Robinson, 7
H. Alan Robinson, 6-8
Helen M. Robinson, 4-7
Richard D. Robinson, 8
Alec Rodger, 2-4
David A. Rodgers, 7
Ronald C. Rodgers, 9
Bruce G. Rogers, 9-13
Carl R. Rogers, 2
Cyril A. Rogers, 5
Frederick R. Rogers, 2
Margaret R. Rogers, 12
Virginia M. Rogers, 7
W. Todd Rogers, 7
Cynthia A. Rohrbeck, 11, 13
Samuel Roll, 10
Deborah D. Roman, 12-13
Thomas A. Romberg, 7-8
Leonard G. Rorer, 7
Carl L. Rosen, 7-9
Ephraim Rosen, 4
Gerald A. Rosen, 13
Marvin Rosen, 8
John H. Rosenbach, 7-9
Robert L. Rosenbaum, 8
Jennifer A. Rosenblatt, 13
Sylvia Rosenfield, 9-10
Arlene Coopersmith Rosenthal, 9-11
Nancy L. Roser, 8-9
Benjamin Rosner, 5-7
Jerome Rosner, 7
Alan O. Ross, 6
C. C. Ross, 2-3
Charles S. Ross, 4-5
Paul F. Ross, 6
Myron F. Rosskopf, 5
Michael J. Roszkowski, 9-10, 12-13
Rodney W. Roth, 11
Harold F. Rothe, 4
Robert D. Rothermel, 9
Barbara A. Rothlisberg, 11-13
John W. M. Rothney, 1, 3-7
Julian B. Rotter, 3
Pamela Carrington Rotto, 12
James B. Rounds, 9-10, 12
Byron P. Rourke, 9
Denise M. Rousseau, 9-10
Harold L. Royer, 6
Arthur B. Royse, 5-6
Thaddeus Rozecki, 13
Ronald H. Rozensky, 11
Donald L. Rubin, 11
Stanley I. Rubin, 6
Floyd L. Ruch, 3-4, 6
Giles M. Ruch, 2
Herbert C. Rudman, 9, 12-13
Lawrence M. Rudner, 11-12
Robert Rueda, 10
C. H. Ruedisili, 3
Mabel E. Rugen, 3
David L. Rule, 10
Edward A. Rundqust, 3
William H. Rupley, 9
David H. Russell, 2-4
Harry J. Russell, 2-3
Michael Lee Russell, 13
James O. Rust, 9-10
John Rust, 12
Leo P. Ruth, 8
Roger A. Ruth, 7-8
Joseph M. Ryan, 11
Michael Ryan, 9-10
David G. Ryans, 3-4, 6
Jane A. Rysberg, 9-10
Richard Rystrom, 7-8
Darrell L. Sabers, 8-13
Donna S. Sabers, 13
Everett B. Sackett, 1, 6
Paul R. Sackett, 9
Cyril J. Sadowski, 12-13
H. Bradley Sagen, 6-7
Philip A. Saigh, 9
Perry Sailor, 12
Kenneth Sakauye, 12
Rachel Salisbury, 2
John Salvia, 9
Vincent J. Samar, 11-12
David T. Sanchez, 9
Daryl Sander, 9
C. Sanders, 5
James R. Sanders, 9
Jonathan Sandoval, 9-10, 12-13
Claude A. Sandy, 12
Eleanor E. Sanford, 11-13
Dixie D. Sanger, 9
Toni E. Santmire, 9-10
Janice Santogrossi, 10
H. J. Sants, 6
Bert R. Sappenfield, 5-6
Irwin G. Sarason, 6
Theodore R. Sarbin, 4

Helen Sargent, 4
I. David Satlow, 5
George A. Satter, 3-4
Jerome M. Sattler, 8-10
Richard A. Saudargas, 10
Aulus W. Saunders, 2
David M. Saunders, 11
David R. Saunders, 5
William I. Sauser, Jr., 9-13
Jean-Guy Savard, 7
Diane J. Sawyer, 9-13
Gilbert Sax, 8
Peter Scales, 9
Dale P. Scannell, 9, 11-13
Douglas E. Scates, 1, 3, 5
William L. Schaaf, 4
Willis C. Schaefer, 4
William D. Schafer, 11-13
Joyce Parr Schaie, 8
K. Warner Schaie, 8-9
Susan J. Schenck, 9-10
Johann H. Schepers, 6
Alvin W. Schindler, 1-2, 4
Steven P. Schinke, 10, 12
Richard F. Schmid, 9
Frank L. Schmidt, 8-9, 13
John F. Schmitt, 9
Neal Schmitt, 9, 12-13
Gerald R. Schneck, 13
Arnold E. Schneider, 3
Leroy H. Schnell, 2-3
Lyle F. Schoenfeldt, 7-10
Patricia Schoenrade, 12-13
Wiliiam Schofield, 4-6
Fred J. Schonell, 2, 4-5
William B. Schrader, 4-6
H. E. Schrammel, 1
Fredrick A. Schrank, 9-10
Gregory Schraw, 12
Robert L. Schreiner, 8
Herbert Schueler, 3-6
Douglas G. Schultz, 4, 6-7
Geoffrey F. Schultz, 11
Harold A. Schultz, 4, 6
Dale H. Schunk, 9
Richard Schupbach, 8
Donald H. Schuster, 6-7
Richard E. Schutz, 6-9
Joseph J. Schwab, 3
Gene Schwarting, 9, 12-13
Neil H. Schwartz, 9-10
Mariette Schwarz, 6
Dean M. Schweickhard, 2
Gladys C. Schwesinger, 4
Craig S. Scott, 8
Louise B. Scott, 5
Owen Scott, III, 11
May V. Seagoe, 4
Carl E. Seashore, 2
Harold G. Seashore, 3-6
Virginia Seavey, 3
Don Sebolt, 12
Charles Secolsky, 9
William Seeman, 4
Stanley J. Segal, 6
David Segel, 1, 3-4
Esther F. Segner, 2
S. B. Sells, 5-7
R. B. Selover, 3
Gary B. Seltzer, 11
Boris Semenonoff, 6
Melvin I. Semmel, 7
Trevor E. Sewell, 9
Robert E. Shafer, 9
Laurance F. Shaffer, 3-6
Marcia B. Shaffer, 9-12
Timothy Shanahan, 9
Spencer Shank, 1
Gregory A. Shannon, 11
David A. Shapiro, 10-12
Edward S. Shapiro, 10-11
Stephen Sharp, 8
Marvin E. Shaw, 8
Steven R. Shaw, 12-13
Carleton B. Shay, 7-8
Marion F. Shaycoft, 5-6
Steward M. Shear, 11
Cynthia M. Sheehan, 9
Eugene P. Sheehan, 12-13
Eugene C. Sheeley, 7-9
Linda Jensen Sheffield, 9-10
Kenneth L. Sheldon, 9-10
William D. Sheldon, 4
Sylvia Shellenberger, 9
Ralph L. Shelton, 7-8
John W. Shepard, 10
Lorrie A. Shepard, 8-9
June Ellen Shepherd, 11
James W. Sherbon, 12
Susan M. Sheridan, 11
Bruce Shertzer, 9-10
John C. Sherwood, 6-9
Benjamin Shimberg, 3-4, 6-7, 9
Stanley L. Shinall, 8
Agnes E. Shine, 12
Richard E. Shine, 7
Kenneth G. Shipley, 9-11, 13
Walter C. Shipley, 3
Mariela C. Shirley, 13
Amy H. Shively, 11
Sidney W. Shnayer, 8
Edwin S. Shneidman, 5
Edward J. Shoben, Jr., 4
J. Harlan Shores, 4

Louis Shores, 4
Lawrence D. Shriberg, 8
Mark D. Shriver, 13
Evan D. Shull, 7
L. K. Shumaker, 2
Craig S. Shwery, 13
Sylvia Sibley, 10
Edward A. Silver, 9
Arthur B. Silverstein, 7-11
Joan Silverstein, 10
Wesley E. Sime, 13
Richard L. Simpson, 9
Esther Sinclair, 10
Jacob O. Sines, 8-9
Harry Singer, 7-8
Kusum Singh, 12-13
Edward R. Sipay, 7-8
Bertram C. Sippola, 11-12
Rodney W. Skager, 7
Edgar P. Slack, 3
Robert B. Slaney, 9-10
Patrick Slater, 3
Wayne H. Slater, 13
William Sloan, 4-5
Robert L. Slonaker, 9
Alfred L. Smith, Jr., 12
C. Ebblewhite Smith, 2
Corinne Roth Smith, 9-10
Donald E. P. Smith, 5-6
Douglas K. Smith, 10, 12-13
Fred M. Smith, 7
Gerald R. Smith, 9
Henry P. Smith, 4
I. Macfarlane Smith, 4-6
J. Philip Smith, 8
Jane E. Smith, 7
Janet V. Smith, 13
Jeffrey K. Smith, 9-10, 12-13
Kenneth J. Smith, 7-9
Lyman J. Smith, 7
Mary Lee Smith, 8
Michael D. Smith, 9
Nick L. Smith, 8
Nila Banton Smith, 4
Percival Smith, 2
Philip L. Smith, 9
Sharon L. Smith, 9
William L. Smith, 8
Alfred L. Smith, Jr., 11
Charles D. Smock, 7
Daniel W. Snader, 3
Jeffrey H. Snow, 11-12
Brooke Snyder, 12
William U. Snyder, 3
Gargi Roysircar Sodowsky, 11-12
David C. Solly, 11
Robert J. Solomon, 5-6
Ronald K. Sommers, 8-9, 11
Anita Miller Sostek, 8
Larry Sowder, 8
George D. Spache, 3-7
Steven D. Spaner, 12
Emma Spaney, 4-5
C. Spearman, 2
Donald Spearritt, 5
Janet E. Spector, 13
Robert K. Speer, 2
Daniel G. Spencer, 9
Douglas Spencer, 2-3
Peter L. Spencer, 2
Charles D. Spielberger, 8
Robert Spies, 13
Donna Spiker, 11-12
Susan K. Spille, 12
Herbert F. Spitzer, 3-4
Jaclyn B. Spitzer, 9, 11, 13
Gilbert M. Spivack, 9
Bernard Spolsky, 6
Michael J. Sporakowski, 12
Scott Spreat, 12
Otfried Spreen, 6
Barrie G. Stacey, 9
Michael J. Stahl, 9-10
Steven A. Stahl, 11
Robert F. Stahmann, 8
Gary J. Stainback, 11, 13
Jayne E. Stake, 9-13
Robert E. Stake, 6
John M. Stalnaker, 1-2, 4-6
Roy W. Stanhope, 5
Julian C. Stanley, 4-6
Charles W. Stansfield, 8-10
Joel Stark, 7-8
E. P. Starke, 4
Stanley Starkman, 9
Anna S. Starr, 1
Edward R. Starr, 13
Russell G. Stauffer, 5-6
John E. Stecklein, 6
Elaine Flory Stefany, 12
Leslie P. Steffe, 7-8
Harry L. Stein, 5-6
Jack M. Stein, 6-7
Margot B. Stein, 13
Stephanie Stein, 11-13
Wendy J. Steinberg, 10
William Stephenson, 4-6
F. E. Sterling, 9
Robert J. Sternberg, 9
Jay R. Stewart, 13
Krista J. Stewart, 9-10
Naomi Stewart, 4-6
Sheldon L. Stick, 9-10
Charles A. Stickland, 4

Harlan J. Stientjes, 11-12
Terry A. Stinnett, 10-13
William A. Stock, 11-12
Howard Stoker, 11
Joseph P. Stokes, 9-10
Clarence R. Stone, 2
Gerald L. Stone, 9-13
L. Joseph Stone, 4-5
Mark Stone, 9
Gary Stoner, 11
Janet M. Stoppard, 9
Phillip S. Strain, 9
David Strand, 10
Ruth M. Strang, 1-2, 5
Richard K. Stratton, 12
Christine F. Strauss, 12
Lois T. Strauss, 11
Lawrence J. Stricker, 6, 8
Ruth Strickland, 5
Douglas C. Strohmer, 9
Stanley R. Strong, 8-9
Charles R. Strother, 3-5
J. B. Stroud, 3
Hans H. Strupp, 7
Richard B. Stuart, 9-13
Dewey B. Stuit, 3-4
George W. Sturrock, 5
Gabrielle Stutman, 12-13
Frederick H. Stutz, 3, 5
Michael J. Subkoviak, 9, 11-13
Richard R. Sudweeks, 13
Hoi K. Suen, 11-13
Alan R. Suess, 7-8, 10
Richard M. Suinn, 7
Gail M. Sullivan, 11
Patricia M. Sullivan, 9
W. L. Sumner, 4
Norman D. Sundberg, 5-9, 11-13
Donna L. Sundre, 12-13
Yong H. Sung, 9
Donald E. Super, 3-6, 8
J. P. Sutcliffe, 5
John Sutherland, 5-6
Rosemary E. Sutton, 11-13
Marilyn N. Suydam, 7-9
John G. Svinicki, 10
Edward O. Swanson, 6
H. Lee Swanson, 9
Richard A. Swanson, 7-8
Robert M. Swanson, 8
Robert S. Swanson, 8
Jon D. Swartz, 8-9
Cabrini S. Swassing, 10
Mark E. Swerdlik, 9, 11-13
Harvey N. Switzky, 9, 11-12
Percival M. Symonds, 2-5
Hilda Taba, 1-2, 4
Harold Takooshian, 12
Abraham J. Tannenbaum, 6
Kikumi K. Tatsuoka, 9, 11
Maurice Tatsuoka, 11
Earl S. Taulbee, 8
Calvin W. Taylor, 5
Cie Taylor, 9
Erwin K. Taylor, 3-7
Howard R. Taylor, 3-4
Hugh Taylor, 7
John M. Taylor, 10
Ronald N. Taylor, 8
Wallace W. Taylor, 2-3
Florence M. Teagarden, 2-5
Lorene Teegarden, 2
Phyllis Anne Teeter, 9
Auke Tellegen, 8-9
Cathy Fultz Telzrow, 9-10, 12
Mildred C. Templin, 4
Edward A. Tenney, 2
W. Wesley Tennyson, 5
Mary L. Tenopyr, 9-10
James S. Terwilliger, 11-12
Anita S. Tesh, 12-13
E. W. Testut, 11
James B. Tharp, 2, 4
Paul W. Thayer, 6, 8-10
Herbert A. Thelen, 3
William N. Thetford, 6
C. L. Thiele, 2-3
Charles S. Thomas, 1-2
Cleveland A. Thomas, 5
Ruth G. Thomas, 9-10
Albert S. Thompson, 1-2, 4-6
Anton Thompson, 4
Donald Thompson, 12-13
John H. Thompson, 1
Nora M. Thompson, 11-13
Richard A. Thompson, 8
Edith I. M. Thomson, 3
Godfrey H. Thomson, 2
Robert L. Thorndike, 2-8
Robert M. Thorndike, 8
George C. Thornton III, 9-10, 12-13
Robert H. Thouless, 3
Pamela S. Tidwell, 12
David V. Tiedeman, 4-8
Ernest W. Tiegs, 1-3
Robert J. Tierney, 9-10
Joseph Tiffin, 1
James A. Till, 8
Murray H. Tillman, 8
Gerald Tindal, 11-13
Miles A. Tinker, 4
C. Alan Titchenal, 10
Carol Kehr Tittle, 7, 9, 11-12
Hazel M. Toliver, 3

Robert Tolsma, 9
Ruth E. Tomes, 11-12
Gail E. Tompkins, 9-10
Kathleen T. Toms, 11
Tony Toneatto, 11-12
Barry W. Tones, 10
Herbert A. Tonne, 1, 3, 5
Herbert A. Topps, 3
T. L. Torgerson, 3
Joseph Torgesen, 9
Michelle T. Toshima, 10
Esther Stavrou Toubanos, 12
Roger L. Towne, 11-12
Agatha Townsend, 3, 5-6
Marion R. Trabue, 1-2
Ross E. Traub, 12
Kenneth J. Travers, 7
Robert M. W. Travers, 3-5
Arthur E. Traxler, 1-7
Donald J Treffinger, 9
Michael S. Trevisan, 11-13
Carolyn Triay, 11
Frances O. Triggs, 3
Harold C. Trimble, 6-8
Marie E. Trost, 2
Maurice E. Troyer, 3
R. M. Tryon, 1-2
Robert C. Tryon, 2
Jalie A. Tucker, 11
Bruce W. Tuckman, 8
J. Jaap Tuinman, 8
Simon H. Tulchin, 2-3
June M. Tuma, 9
Timothy L. Turco, 10
Kerri Turk, 12
Mary E. Turnbull, 4-6
Clarence E. Turner, 2-6
Mervyn L. Turner, 5
Austin H. Turney, 1-2
Lawrence J. Turton, 7-10, 12
F. T. Tyler, 3
Leona E. Tyler, 4-7
Ralph W. Tyler, 2-3, 5
Thomas A. Tyler, 8
Aharon Tziner, 9
Judy A. Ungerer, 9
C. C. Upshall, 3
Susana Urbina, 12-13
Marguerite Uttley, 3
Nicholas A. Vacc, 9-13
Curtis C. Vail, 1
Rebecca W. Valcarce, 9
Paolo Valesio, 7
Robert E. Valett, 7
William J. Valmont, 8
Forrest L. Vance, 6-7
Henry Van Engen, 4
Wilfred G. Van Gorp, 11-13
James P. Van Haneghan, 12-13
Gerald R. Van Hecke, 8
Gabriele van Lingen, 13
Byron H. Van Roekel, 5-9
Neil J. Van Steenberg, 4-5
Wendy Van Wyhe, 12
Stanley F. Vasa, 9-10
Robert P. Vecchio, 9
Donald J. Veldman, 6-7
Frank R. Vellutino, 8
William M. Verdi, 13
Magdalen D. Vernon, 5-6
Philip E. Vernon, 2, 4-9
Dolores Kluppel Vetter, 11, 13
Verna L. Vickery, 5
Donald J. Viglione, Jr., 9
Peter Villanova, 11
Roland Vinette, 3
Chockalingam Viswesvaran, 13
Morris S. Viteles, 2-3
Daniel E. Vogler, 12
Alex Voogel, 11
David P. Wacker, 9-10
J. R. Jefferson Wadkins, 7-8
Edwin E. Wagner, 9
Guy W. Wagner, 1
John Wagner, 7
William W. Waite, 3-4
J. V. Waits, 3
John F. Wakefield, 11
William J. Waldron, 12-13
Helen M. Walker, 1
Robert Wall, 13
Shavaun M. Wall, 9
W. D. Wall, 4
S. Rains Wallace, 4-5
Wimburn L. Wallace, 5-8
Norman E. Wallen, 6
Niels G. Waller, 11-13
James A. Walsh, 7-8
W. Bruce Walsh, 7
Edwin Wandt, 4, 7
Morey J. Wantman, 4-6
Richard A. Wantz, 10, 12
F. W. Warburton, 4-5
Annie W. Ward, 11-13
Charles F. Ward, 7
Sandra Ward, 13
William C. Ward, 7-8
George Wardlow, 10
James L. Wardrop, 8-10
E. M. Waring, 9
David M. Wark, 7
Charles F. Warnath, 6, 8
Neil D. Warren, 3, 5
Willard G. Warrington, 5-7

Ruth W. Washburn, 3
Orest E. Wasyliw, 12
Alan T. Waterman, 2
Betsy Waterman, 13
Eugene A. Waters, 2
Everett Waters, 9
John G. Watkins, 6
Marley W. Watkins, 9
Ralph K. Watkins, 2
Richard W. Watkins, 7-8
Betty U. Watson, 9
Goodwin Watson, 1-3
Robert I. Watson, 3
T. Steuart Watson, 11-13
J. Fred Weaver, 5
Larry Weber, 12
Harold Webster, 5-6
William J. Webster, 7, 9
David Wechsler, 2-3
Thaddeus E. Weckowicz, 8
M. O'Neal Weeks, 9
Zona R. Weeks, 9
Walter L. Wehner, 8-9
Charles C. Weidemann, 1-2
David P. Weikart, 7
Sharon L. Weinberg, 9, 11-13
Annette B. Weinshank, 9
Sheldon A. Weintraub, 7-8
David L. Weis, 9
Susan Ellis Weismer, 11
David J. Weiss, 7-8
Ellen Weissinger, 12-13
Henry Weitz, 3-8
R. A. Weitzman, 9
Carolyn M. Welch, 3
Wayne W. Welch, 8
A. T. Welford, 4
Beth L. Wellman, 3
F. L. Wells, 1-3
J. Steven Welsh, 11, 13
Lesley A. Welsh, 13
Charles Wenar, 9
Tim L. Wentling, 8
Joseph M. Wepman, 7
Emmy E. Werner, 6-7
Paul D. Werner, 13
Edgar B. Wesley, 1-4
Alexander G. Wesman, 4-7
Leonard J. West, 7-9
Bert W. Westbrook, 7-9, 11-13
Carol E. Westby, 11-13
George Westby, 4-6
Stephanie Western, 12
Alida S. Westman, 8-9, 11-12
Frederick L. Westover, 4
Harry G. Wheat, 2
D. K. Wheeler, 5
Kenneth G. Wheeler, 9
Patricia H. Wheeler, 11-12
Edward M. White, 8
Howard R. White, 4
Karl R. White, 9
Kenneth V. White, 11
Shirley A. White, 9
Sue White, 9-10
Susan Embretson (Whitely), 9
Sally Anita Whiting, 9
Dean K. Whitla, 6
Carroll A. Whitmer, 2-3
Richard G. Whitten, 13
Randolph H. Whitworth, 8
Lillian A. Whyte, 9
Thomas A. Widiger, 9, 11
J. Lee Wiederholt, 8-9
Margaret Rogers Wiese, 11
Martin J. Wiese, 12
James D. Wiggins, 9
Jerry S. Wiggins, 6-7, 10
Linda F. Wightman, 11-12
Elisabeth H. Wiig, 9
Richard L. Wikoff, 9-10
Katherine W. Wilcox, 3
Terry M. Wildman, 12
William K. Wilkinson, 10-13
S. S. Wilks, 1-2
Haydn S. Williams, 5
J. Robert Williams, 6
Janice G. Williams, 11-13
Jean M. Williams, 12
John M. Williams, 11
Robert T. Williams, 9-13
David M. Williamson, 13
Edmund G. Williamson, 1-2
Warren W. Willingham, 6
Carl G. Willis, 7-8
Margaret Willis, 2
W. Grant Willis, 11-12
John M. Willits, 3, 5
Victor L. Willson, 8-10, 12
J. Richard Wilmeth, 6
David R. Wilson, 9
Guy M. Wilson, 1-3
James W. Wilson, 7
Robert M. Wilson, 9
Marlene Wadsworth Winell, 9
Herbert D. Wing, 4-6
Hilda Wing, 11-13
Harris Winitz, 8
William L. Winnett, 7
George P. Winship, Jr., 6-7
R. Winterbourn, 5
Robert D. Wirt, 6-7
Steven L. Wise, 9-10, 12
Emory E. Wiseman, 7

Stephen Wiseman, 3, 5
Ernest C. Witham, 2
E. Lea Witla, 13
Joseph C. Witt, 9-10, 12-13
L. Alan Witt, 11–12
J. Richard Wittenborn, 3-4
Donna Wittmer, 12
Paul A. Witty, 3
David L. Wodrich, 9
Kristen Wojcik, 13
Richard M. Wolf, 8-9, 11-13
Dael L. Wolfle, 1-2, 4
Leroy Wolins, 6
James A. Wollack, 12
Myra N. Womble, 13
E. F. Wonderlic, 3
Hugh B. Wood, 2
Michelle Wood, 13
Ray G. Wood, 3
Clifford Woody, 1, 3
D. A. Worcester, 2-4
Edward A. Workman, 9
Julien Worland, 9
Blaine R. Worthen, 7-9, 12-13
F. Lynwood Wren, 3
C. Gilbert Wrenn, 1-2, 5
Benjamin D. Wright, 9
Claudia R. Wright, 11-13
Dan Wright, 9-12
Logan Wright, 11-12
Robert L. Wright, 7
William J. Wright, 8
J. Wayne Wrightstone, 1-3, 5
Jack Wrigley, 5
Thomas A. Wrobel, 11
Michael K. Wynne, 12
Kaoru Yamamoto, 8
Alfred Yates, 5
Aubrey J. Yates, 7
Albert H. Yee, 7
Frank R. Yekovich, 9
Tamela Yelland, 12
Dale Yoder, 4
John W. Young, 12
James E. Ysseldyke, 8-12
William Yule, 8
Robert H. Zabel, 9
Peter Zachar, 13
Louis C. Zahner, 2-3, 5
Dan Zakay, 9
O. L. Zangwill, 3
John A. Zarske, 9-10
Sheldon Zedeck, 8-9, 11-13
Paul F. Zelhart, 10
Edwin Ziegfeld, 2-4
Wayne S. Zimmerman, 6-7
Fred Zimring, 9
Joseph E. Zins, 9
Leland C. Zlomke, 10-13
Steven Zucker, 13
Marvin Zuckerman, 9
Donald G. Zytowski, 7-9, 12

INDEX OF TITLES

This title index includes a comprehensive listing of tests currently in print and included in this volume as well as out-of-print (or status unknown) tests that were listed in Tests in Print IV, *and* The Twelfth *and* Thirteenth Mental Measurements Yearbooks. *Numbers without colons refer to in-print tests included in* Tests in Print V. *Numbers with colons refer to out-of-print tests not listed in this volume; readers interested in these tests are referred to the last volume listing the tests. For example, T4:1826 refers to test 1826 in* Tests in Print IV*; 12:399 refers to test 399 in* The 12th MMY. *Superseded titles are listed with a cross reference to the present title. All numbers refer to test entries, not to page numbers.*

AAMR Adaptive Behavior Scale—Residential and Community, Second Edition, 1
AAMD Adaptive Behavior Scale, see AAMR Adaptive Behavior Scale—School, Second Edition, 2
AAMD-Becker Reading-Free Vocational Interest Inventory, see Reading-Free Vocational Interest Inventory, Revised, 2177
AAMR Adaptive Behavior Scale—School, Second Edition, 2
AATG German Test, see National German Examination for High School Students, 1761
AATG National Standardized Testing Program, see National German Examination for High School Students, 1761
The ABC Inventory to Determine Kindergarten and School Readiness, 3
Aberrant Behavior Checklist, 4
Ability Explorer, 5
Abortion Scale, 6
Abuse Risk Inventory for Women, Experimental Edition, 7
Academic Advising Inventory, 8
Academic Aptitude Test: Non-Verbal Intelligence: Acorn National Aptitude Tests, 9
Academic Aptitude Test: Verbal Intelligence: Acorn National Aptitude Tests, 10
Academic Freedom Survey, 11
Academic Proficiency Battery, 12
Academic-Technical Aptitude Tests, T4:12
ACCESS—A Comprehensive Custody Evaluation Standard System, 13
Access Management Survey, 14
Accounting Aptitude Test, 15
Accounting Clerk Staff Selector, 16
Accounting Program Admission Test, 17
ACCUPLACER: Computerized Placement Tests, 18
ACDI-Corrections Version and Corrections Version II, 19
ACER Adult Form B, see ACER Word Knowledge Test, 34
ACER Advanced Test B40, 20
ACER Advanced Test BL-BQ, New Zealand Revision, 21
ACER Advanced Test B90: New Zealand Edition, 22
ACER Advanced Tests AL and AQ (Second Edition) and BL-BQ, 23
ACER Applied Reading Test, 24
ACER Higher Test PL-PQ, New Zealand Revision, 25
ACER Intermediate Test F, 26
ACER Intermediate Test G, 27
ACER Mechanical Comprehension Test, 28
ACER Mechanical Reasoning Test, 29
ACER Short Clerical Test, 30
ACER Speed and Accuracy Tests, 31

ACER Test of Learning Ability, 32
ACER Test of Reasoning Ability, 12:6
ACER Tests of Basic Skills—Blue Series, 12:7
ACER Tests of Basic Skills—Green Series, 33
ACER Word Knowledge Test, 34
Achievement Identification Measure, 35
Achievement Identification Measure—Teacher Observation, 36
Achievement Motivation Profile, 37
Achievement Test—Hebrew Language, T4:36
Achievement Test—Jewish Life and Observances, T4:37
Achievement Test for Accounting Graduates, 38
Achievement Test in Jewish History, T4:35
Achievement Test—The State of Israel, T4:38
Achievement Tests: Grades 1-8, 39
Achieving Behavioral Competencies, 40
Ackerman-Schoendorf Scales for Parent Evaluation of Custody, 41
ACS Cooperative Examination in General-Organic-Biological Chemistry, 42
ACS Cooperative Examination in Physical Chemistry, 43
ACS Examination in Analytical Chemistry, 44
ACS Examination in Analytical Chemistry, Graduate Level, T4:45
ACS Examination in Biochemistry, 45
ACS Examination in Brief Organic Chemistry, T4:47
ACS Examination in General Chemistry, 46
ACS Examination in General Chemistry (Brief Test), 47
ACS Examination in High School Chemistry [Advanced Level], 48
ACS Examination in High School Chemistry [Lower Level], 49
ACS Examination in Inorganic Chemistry, 50
ACS Examination in Instrumental Determinations, 51
ACS Examination in Organic Chemistry, 52
ACS Examination in Organic Chemistry, Graduate Level, T4:53
ACS Examination in Physical Chemistry for Life Sciences, 53
ACS Examination in Physical Chemistry, Graduate Level, T4:55
ACS Examination in Polymer Chemistry, 54
ACS-NSTA Examination in High School Chemistry [Advanced Level], see ACS Examination in High School Chemistry [Advanced Level], 48
ACS-NSTA Examination in High School Chemistry [Lower Level], see ACS Examination in High School Chemistry [Lower Level], 49
ACS Toledo Chemistry Placement Examination, 55
ACT Assessment, 56
ACT Assessment Program, see ACT Assessment, 56
ACT Career Planning Program, T4:60
The ACT Evaluation/Survey Service, 57
ACT Proficiency Examination in Abnormal Psychology, T4:62
ACT Proficiency Examination in Adult Nursing, T4:63
ACT Proficiency Examination in Anatomy and Physiology, T4:64
ACT Proficiency Examination in Fundamentals of Nursing, T4:65
ACT Proficiency Examination in Microbiology, T4:66
ACT Proficiency Examination in Occupational Strategy, Nursing, T4:67
ACT Proficiency Examination in Professional Strategies, Nursing, T4:68
ACT Proficiency Examination in Psychiatric/Mental Health Nursing, T4:69
ACT Proficiency Examination in Reading Instruction in the Elementary School, T4:70
ACT Proficiency Examination Program, T4:71
ACT Proficiency Examinations in Commonalities in Nursing Care, Areas A and B, T4:72
ACT Proficiency Examinations in Differences in Nursing Care, Areas A, B, C, T4:73
ACT Proficiency Examinations in Health Restoration, Areas I and II, T4:74
ACT Proficiency Examinations in Health Support, Areas I and II, T4:75
ACT Proficiency Examinations in Maternal and Child Nursing, T4:76
ACT Study Power Assessment and Inventory, 12:11
ACT Study Skills Assessment and Inventory (College Edition), 12:12
Action Research Skill Inventory, T4:79
Adaptability Test, 58
Adaptation of Study of Values: A Scale for Measuring the Dominant Interests in Personality, Third Edition, see Study of Values: British Edition, 1965, 2539
Adaptation of the McCarthy Scales of Children's Abilities, see McCarthy Screening Test, 1613
An Adaptation of the Wechsler Preschool and Primary Scale of Intelligence for Deaf Children, T4:81
Adapted Sequenced Inventory of Communication Development, 12:13
Adaptive Behavior Evaluation Scale, Revised, 59
Adaptive Behavior Inventory, 60
Adaptive Behavior Inventory for Children, 61
Adaptive Behavior: Street Survival Skills Questionnaire, 62
Adaptive Functioning Index, 63
Adaptive Style Inventory, 64
ADD-H Comprehensive Teacher's Rating Scale, see ADD-H: Comprehensive Teacher's Rating Scale, Second Edition [1998 Revision], 65
ADD-H: Comprehensive Teacher's Rating Scale, Second Edition [1998 Revision], 65
Addiction Research Center Inventory, 66
Additional Personality Factor Inventory—2, T4:91
Aden-Crosthwait Adolescent Psychology Achievement Test, T4:92
ADHD Rating Scale–IV, 67

The Adjective Check List, 68
The Adjustment Inventory, T4:94
Adjustment Scales for Children and Adolescents, 69
Adolescent and Adult Psychoeducational Profile: Volume IV, 70
Adolescent Apperception Cards, 71
Adolescent Coping Scale, 72
Adolescent Diagnostic Interview, 73
Adolescent Dissociative Experiences Scale, 74
Adolescent Drinking Index, 75
Adolescent Language Screening Test, 76
Adolescent Psychopathology Scale, 77
Adolescent Separation Anxiety Test, 78
Adolescent Symptom Inventory-4, 79
Adult Attention Deficit Disorder Behavior Rating Scale, 80
Adult Attention Deficit Disorders Evaluation Scale, 81
Adult Basic Learning Examination, Second Edition, 82
Adult Career Concerns Inventory, 83
Adult Language Assessment Scales, 84
Adult Neuropsychological Questionnaire, 85
Adult Personality Inventory [Revised], 86
Adult Rating of Oral English, 87
Adult Self Expression Scale, 88
Adult Suicidal Ideation Questionnaire, 89
Advanced Measures of Music Audiation, 90
Advanced Placement Examination in American History, see Advanced Placement Examination in United States History, 117
Advanced Placement Examination in Art History, 91
Advanced Placement Examination in Biology, 92
Advanced Placement Examination in Calculus, 93
Advanced Placement Examination in Chemistry, 94
Advanced Placement Examination in Comparative Government and Politics, 95
Advanced Placement Examination in Computer Science, 96
Advanced Placement Examination in English (Composition and Literature), see Advanced Placement Examination in English (Literature and Composition), 98
Advanced Placement Examination in English (Language and Composition), 97
Advanced Placement Examination in English (Literature and Composition), 98
Advanced Placement Examination in Environmental Science, 99
Advanced Placement Examination in European History, 100
Advanced Placement Examination in French Language, 101
Advanced Placement Examination in French Language, Level 3, see Advanced Placement Examination in French Language, 101
Advanced Placement Examination in French Literature, 102
Advanced Placement Examination in French Literature, Level 3, see Advanced Placement Examination in French Literature, 102
Advanced Placement Examination in German Language, 103
Advanced Placement Examination in German Language, Level 3, see Advanced Placement Examination in German Language, 103
Advanced Placement Examination in History of Art, see Advanced Placement Examination in Art History, 91
Advanced Placement Examination in International English Language, 104
Advanced Placement Examination in Latin Literature, 105
Advanced Placement Examination in Latin Literature, Level 3, see Advanced Placement Examination in Latin Literature, 105
Advanced Placement Examination in Latin (Vergil), 106
Advanced Placement Examination in Latin, Level 3 (Vergil), see Advanced Placement Examination in Latin (Vergil), 106
Advanced Placement Examination in Macroeconomics, 107
Advanced Placement Examination in Mathematics, see Advanced Placement Examination in Calculus, 93
Advanced Placement Examination in Microeconomics, 108
Advanced Placement Examination in Music Theory, 109
Advanced Placement Examination in Physics, 110
Advanced Placement Examination in Psychology, 111
Advanced Placement Examination in Spanish Language, 112
Advanced Placement Examination in Spanish Language, Level 3, see Advanced Placement Examination in Spanish Language, 112
Advanced Placement Examination in Spanish Literature, 113
Advanced Placement Examination in Spanish Literature, Level 3, see Advanced Placement Examination in Spanish Literature, 113
Advanced Placement Examination in Statistics, 114
Advanced Placement Examination in Studio Art, 115
Advanced Placement Examination in United States Government and Politics, 116
Advanced Placement Examination in United States History, 117
Advanced Placement Examinations, 118
Advanced Test Battery, 119
Affective Perception Inventory, 120
The Affective Perception Inventory/College Level, 121
Affective Sensitivity Scale, see Kagan Affective Sensitivity Scale, 1374
Affects Balance Scale, see Derogatis Affects Balance Scale [Revised], 791

Age Projection Test, 122
Ages and Stages Questionnaires, 123
AGS Early Screening Profiles, 124
Ahr's Individual Development Survey, T4:140
AH1 Forms X and Y, 125
AH2/AH3, 126
AH4: Group Test of General Intelligence, 127
AH5 Group Test of High Grade Intelligence, 128
AH6 Group Tests of High Level Intelligence, 129
A. I. Survey, 130
AICPA Accounting Program Admission Test, see Accounting Program Admission Test, 17
Alberta Essay Scales: Models, 131
The Alcadd Test, Revised Edition, 132
Alcohol Clinical Index, 133
Alcohol Dependence Scale, 134
Alcohol Use Disorders Identification Test, 135
Alcohol Use Inventory, 136
Algebra, Geometry and Trigonometry Test for Stds 9 and 10, T4:147
Algebra Test for Engineering and Science: National Achievement Tests, 137
Alleman Leadership Development Questionnaire, 138
Alleman Mentoring Scales Questionnaire, 139
Alleman Relationship Value Questionnaire, 140
Alienation Index Survey, see A. I. Survey, 130
Allied Health Professions Admission Test, 141
Alpha Biographical Inventory, see Biographical Inventory Form U, 311
Alphabet Mastery, T4:153
Alternate Uses, 142
The American Drug and Alcohol Survey, 143
American High School Mathematics Examination, 144
American History: Junior High—Objective, 145
American History: Senior High—Objective, 146
The American Home Scale, 147
American Invitational Mathematics Examination, 148
American Junior High School Mathematics Examination, 149
American Literacy Test, 150
American Numerical Test, 151
The American Occupational Therapy Association, Inc. Fieldwork: Evaluation for the Occupation Therapist, 152
Analysis of Readiness Skills: Reading and Mathematics, T4:165
Analytic Learning Disability Assessment, 153
Analytical Aptitude Skills Evaluation, 154
Analytical Thinking Test, 155
Analyzing the Communication Environment, 156
Ann Arbor Learning Inventory [1996 Edition], 157
The Anomalous Sentences Repetition Test, 12:29
The ANSER System-Aggregate Neurobehavioral Student Health and Educational Review, see ANSER System-Aggregate Neurobehavioral Student Health and Educational Review [Revised 1997], 158
The ANSER System-Aggregate Neurobehavioral Student Health and Educational Review [Revised 1997], 158
The Anxiety Scale for the Blind, T4:172
Anxiety Scales for Children and Adults, 12:30
AO Sight Screener, T4:174
Aphasia Diagnostic Profiles, 159
Applied Knowledge Test, 160
Appraisal Interview and Card Sort, 161
Appraise Your World, 162
Apraxia Battery for Adults, 163
The Apraxia Profile: A Descriptive Assessment Tool for Children, 164
Aprenda: La Prueba de Logros en Espanol, see Aprenda®: La prueba de logros en español—Segunda edición., 165
Aprenda®: La prueba de logros en español—Segunda edición., 165
The APT Inventory, 166
APT Manual Dexterity Test, T4:182
Aptitude Assessment Battery: Programming, 167
Aptitude for and Sensitivity to Music, T4:184
The Aptitude Index Battery: Career Profile System, see Career Profile System, Second Edition, 421
Aptitude Interest Inventory, 168
Aptitude Test Battery for Adults, T4:185
Aptitude Tests for School Beginners, 169
Aptitudes Associates Test of Sales Aptitude, see Sales Comprehension Test, 2269
Aptitudes Associates Test of Sales Aptitude: A Test for Measuring Knowledge of Basic Principles of Selling, Revised, 170
APU Occupational Interests Guide, see JIIG-CAL Occupational Interests Guide, 1342
Arithmetic Index, 171
Arithmetic Skills Assessment Test, 172
Arithmetic Test (Fundamentals and Reasoning): Municipal Tests: National Achievement Tests, 173
Arithmetic Reasoning Test, T4:188
Arithmetic Test: National Achievement Tests, 174
Arizona Articulation Proficiency Scale, Second Edition, 175
The Arizona Battery for Communication Disorders of Dementia, 176
Arlin-Hills Attitude Surveys, 177
Arlin Test of Formal Reasoning, 178
Armed Services—Civilian Vocational Interest Survey, 179
Armed Services Vocational Aptitude Battery [14th Edition], see Armed Services Vocational Aptitude Battery [Forms 18/19], 180
Armed Services Vocational Aptitude Battery [Forms 18/19], 180
Arousal Seeking Tendency Scale, 181
Arthur Point Scale of Performance Tests, 182
Ashland Interest Assessment, 183
ASIST: A Structured Addictions Assessment Interview for Selecting Treatment, 184

ASPIRE (A Sales Potential Inventory for Real Estate), 12:32
The Assertiveness Skills Inventory, 185
ASSESS Expert System Version 5.X, 186
Assessing and Teaching Phonological Knowledge, 187
Assessing Linguistic Behaviors: Assessing Prelinguistic and Early Linguistic Behaviors in Developmentally Young Children, T4:199
Assessing Motivation to Communicate, 188
Assessing Reading Difficulties: A Diagnostic and Remedial Approach, 189
Assessing Specific Competencies, 190
Assessing Your Team: Seven Measures of Team Success, 191
Assessment and Placement Services for Community Colleges, 192
Assessment for Persons Profoundly or Severely Impaired, 193
Assessment in Infancy: Ordinal Scales of Psychological Development, 194
Assessment in Mathematics, 195
Assessment in Nursery Education, 196
Assessment Inventory for Management, 197
Assessment of Adaptive Areas, 198
The Assessment of Aphasia and Related Disorders, Second Edition, 199
Assessment of Career Decision Making, 200
Assessment of Chemical Health Inventory, 201
Assessment of Children's Language Comprehension, 1983 Revision, 202
Assessment of Competencies for Instructor Development, 203
Assessment of Conceptual Organization (ACO): Improving, Writing, Thinking, and Reading Skills, 204
Assessment of Core Goals, 205
Assessment of Developmental Levels by Observation, 206
Assessment of Fluency in School-Age Children, 207
Assessment of Individual Learning Style: The Perceptual Memory Task, 208
Assessment of Intelligibility of Dysarthric Speech, 209
Assessment of Interpersonal Relations, 210
Assessment of Language-Related Functional Activities, 211
Assessment of Living Skills and Resources, 212
Assessment of Parenting Skills: Infant and Preschooler, 213
The Assessment of Phonological Processes—Revised, 214
Assessment of Qualitative and Structural Dimensions of Object Representations, Revised Edition, 215
Assessment of School Needs for Low-Achieving Students: Staff Survey, 216
A.S.S.E.T.S.: A Survey of Students' Educational Talents and Skills, 217
Association Adjustment Inventory, 218
Athletic Motivation Inventory, 219
Athlete's Affective Response Profile, see Sports Emotion Test, 2475
Attention Deficit Disorder Behavior Rating Scales, 220
Attention Deficit Disorders Evaluation Scale, Second Edition, 221
The Attention Deficit Disorders Evaluation Scale Secondary-Age Student, 222
Attention-Deficit/Hyperactivity Disorder Test, 223
Attention-Deficit Scales for Adults, 224
Attention Disorders in Children: School-Based Assessment, Diagnosis, and Treatment, 225
The Attentional and Interpersonal Style Inventory, 226
Attitudes Toward Mainstreaming Scale, 227
Attitudes Toward Working Mothers Scale, 228
Auditory Continuous Performance Test, 229
The Auditory Discrimination and Attention Test, T4:230
Auditory Memory Span Test, 230
Auditory Selective Attention Test, 231
Auditory Sequential Memory Test, 232
Australian Second Language Proficiency Ratings, 233
Autism Screening Instrument for Educational Planning, Second Edition, 234
The Autistic Continuum: An Assessment and Intervention Schedule, 235
Automated Office Battery, 236

Bader Reading and Language Inventory, 237
The Balanced Emotional Empathy Scale, 238
Ball Aptitude Battery, 239
The Bangs Receptive Vocabulary Checklist, T4:239
Bankson-Bernthal Test of Phonology, 240
Bankson Language Screening Test, see Bankson Language Test—2, 241
Bankson Language Test—2, 241
The Barclay Classroom Assessment System, T4:243
Bar-Ilan Picture Test for Children, 242
BarOn Emotional Quotient Inventory, 243
Barsch Learning Style Inventory, 244
BASC Monitor for ADHD, 245
Basic Achievement Skills Individual Screener, 246
Basic Economics Test, 247
Basic Educational Skills Test, 248
Basic English Literacy Skills Test, 249
Basic English Skills Test, 250
Basic Inventory of Natural Language, 251
Basic Language Concepts Test, T4:249
Basic Living Skills Scale, 252
Basic Mathematics Tests, 253
Basic Number Diagnostic Test [1996 Edition], 254
Basic Number Screening Test [1996 Edition], 255
Basic Personality Inventory, 256
Basic Reading Inventory, Seventh Edition, 257
Basic School Skills Inventory—Diagnostic, see Basic School Skills Inventory, Third Edition, 258
Basic School Skills Inventory—Screen, T4:257

Basic School Skills Inventory, Third Edition, 258
Basic Sight Word Test, T4:258
Basic Skills Inventory, T4:259
Basic Skills Locater Test, 259
Basic Tests Series, 260
Basic Visual-Motor Association Test, 261
BASIS-A Inventory [Basic Adlerian Scales for Interpersonal Success—Adult Form], 262
Bass Orientation Inventory, 263
Batería Woodcock-Muñoz—Revisada, 264
Bateria Woodcock Psico-Educativa en Español [Woodcock Spanish Psycho-Educational Battery], see Batería Woodcock-Muñoz—Revisada, 264
Battelle Developmental Inventory, 265
Battelle Developmental Inventory Screening Test, 266
Battle's Depression Inventories for Children and Adults, see North American Depression Inventories for Children and Adults, 1803
Battery for Health Improvement, 267
Bay Area Functional Performance Evaluation, Second Edition, 268
Bayley Infant Neurodevelopmental Screener, 269
Bayley Scales of Infant Development, Second Edition, 270
BCD Test, see Maryland/Baltimore County Design for Adult Basic Education, 1588
Beck Anxiety Inventory [1993 Edition], 271
Beck Depression Inventory—II, 272
Beck Hopelessness Scale [Revised], 273
Beck Scale for Suicide Ideation, 274
Becker Work Adjustment Profile, 275
Bedside Evaluation and Screening Test of Aphasia, see Bedside Evaluation Screening Test, Second Edition, 277
Bedside Evaluation of Dysphagia, 276
Bedside Evaluation Screening Test, Second Edition, 277
Beery Picture Vocabulary Test and Beery Picture Vocabulary Screening Series, 278
Behavior Analysis Forms for Clinical Intervention, 279
Behavior Assessment System for Children [Revised], 280
Behavior Change Inventory, T4:276
Behavior Dimensions Rating Scale, 281
Behavior Dimensions Scale, 282
Behavior Disorders Identification Scale, 283
Behavior Evaluation Scale—2, 284
Behavior Rating Instrument for Autistic and Other Atypical Children, 2nd Edition, 285
Behavior Rating Profile, Second Edition, 286
Behavior Rating Scale, 287
Behavior Status Inventory, 288
Behavioral Academic Self-Esteem, 289
Behavioral and Emotional Rating Scale: A Strength-Based Approach to Assessment, 290
Behavioral Assessment of Pain Questionnaire, 291
Behavioral Characteristics Progression, 292
Behavioral Characteristics Progression, see Help for Special Preschoolers ASSESSMENT CHECKLIST: Ages 3–6, 1194
Behavioral Objective Sequence, 293
Behaviour Problems: A System of Management, 294
Behavioural Assessment of the Dysexecutive Syndrome, 295
Belbin Team-Roles Self-Perception Inventory, 296
Bell Object Relations and Reality Testing Inventory, 297
Bem Sex-Role Inventory, 298
Bench Mark Measures, 299
BENCHMARKS, 300
[Bender-Gestalt Test], 301
Bennett Mechanical Comprehension Test, Second Edition, 302
Benton Visual Retention Test, Fifth Edition, 303
The Ber-Sil Spanish Test, 304
Bessell Measurement of Emotional Maturity Scales, T4:295
BEST Instruments, 305
Bilingual Home Inventory, 306
Bilingual Syntax Measure, 307
Bilingual Two Language Battery of Tests, 308
Bilingual Verbal Ability Tests, 309
Bingham Button Test, T4:300
Biofeedback Certification Examination, 310
Biographical Inventory Form U, 311
Biographical Inventory Form U, see Student Talent and Risk Profile, 2537
Bi/Polar Inventory of Core Strengths, 312
Birds of Different Feathers Work Style Assessment, 313
Birmingham Object Recognition Battery, 314
Birth to Three Assessment and Intervention System, 315
The BITCH Test (Black Intelligence Test of Cultural Homogeneity), 316
The Blacky Pictures: A Technique for the Exploration of Personality Dynamics, 317
The Blind Learning Aptitude Test, 318
The Block-Design Test, see Kohs Block-Design Test, 1410
The Block Survey and S.L.I.D.E., 319
Bloom Sentence Completion Survey, T4:309
Bloomer Learning Test, see Bloomer Learning Test—Neurologically Enhanced, 320
Bloomer Learning Test—Neurologically Enhanced, 320
Blox Test, 321
The Boder Test of Reading-Spelling Patterns, 322
Boehm Test of Basic Concepts—Preschool Version, 323
Boehm Test of Basic Concepts—Revised, 324
Book Review Tests, see Literature Tests/Objective and Essay, 1509
Booker Profiles in Mathematics: Numeration and Computation, 325

The Booklet Category Test, Second Edition, 326
Borromean Family Index, 327
Boston Assessment of Severe Aphasia, 328
The Boston Diagnostic Aphasia Examination, see Assessment of Aphasia and Related Disorders, Second Edition, 199
Boston Qualitative Scoring System for the Rey-Osterrieth Complex Figure, 329
Botel Reading Inventory, 330
Bracken Basic Concept Scale—Revised, 331
Braille Assessment Inventory, 332
The BrainMap, T4:320
Brazelton Neonatal Behavioral Assessment Scale-380, see Neonatal Behavioral Assessment Scale, 3rd Edition, 1770
The Bricklin/Elliot Child Custody Evaluation, 333
Bricklin Perceptual Scales, 334
Brief Derogatis Psychiatric Rating Scale, 335
Brief Hopkins Psychiatric Rating Scale, see Brief Derogatis Psychiatric Rating Scale, 335
Brief Neuropsychological Cognitive Examination, 336
Brief Symptom Inventory, 337
Brief Test of Head Injury, 338
BRIGANCE® Diagnostic Assessment of Basic Skills—Spanish Edition, 339
BRIGANCE® Diagnostic Comprehensive Inventory of Basic Skills, Revised, 340
BRIGANCE® Diagnostic Employability Skills Inventory, 341
BRIGANCE® Diagnostic Inventory of Basic Skills, 342
BRIGANCE® Diagnostic Inventory of Essential Skills, 343
Brigance Diagnostic Inventory of Early Development, see Revised BRIGANCE® Diagnostic Inventory of Early Development, 2213
BRIGANCE® Diagnostic Life Skills Inventory, 344
BRIGANCE® Early Preschool Screen for Two-Year-Old and Two-and-a-Half-Year-Old Children, 345
BRIGANCE K & 1 Screen for Kindergarten and First Grade, see BRIGANCE® K & 1 Screen for Kindergarten and First Grade Children [Revised], 346
BRIGANCE® K & 1 Screen for Kindergarten and First Grade Children [Revised], 346
BRIGANCE® Preschool Screen, 347
Bristol Achievement Tests, 348
Bristol Language Development Scales, 12:54
Bristol Social Adjustment Guides, T4:335
British Ability Scales: Second Edition, 349
British Picture Vocabulary Scales, 350
Brown Attention-Deficit Disorder Scales, 351
Bruce Vocabulary Inventory, 352
Bruininks-Oseretsky Test of Motor Proficiency, 353
Buffalo Reading Test for Speed and Comprehension, 354
Burks' Behavior Rating Scales, 355
Burns Brief Inventory of Communication and Cognition, 356
Burns/Roe Informal Reading Inventory: Preprimer to Twelfth Grade, Fifth Edition, 357
Burt Word Reading Test, New Zealand Revision, 358
Bury Infant Check, 359
Business Analyst Skills Evaluation, 360
Business Judgment Test, Revised, 361
Buswell-John Diagnostic Test for Fundamental Processes in Arithmetic, T4:348
Butcher Treatment Planning Inventory, 362
The Butler Life Science Concept Test, T4:349
The Bzoch-League Receptive-Expressive Emergent Language Scale: For the Measurement of Language Skills in Infancy, see Receptive-Expressive Emergent Language Test, Second Edition, 2189

C-R Opinionaire, 363
The CAHPER Fitness-Performance II Test, T4:350
CAI Study Skills Test, T4:351
California Achievement Tests, Fifth Edition, 364
California Achievement Tests, Forms E and F, see California Achievement Tests, Fifth Edition, 364
The California Child Q-Set, 365
California Computerized Assessment Package, 366
The California Critical Thinking Dispositions Inventory, 367
California Critical Thinking Skills Test, 368
California Critical Thinking Skills Test: College Level, see California Critical Thinking Skills Test, 368
California Diagnostic Mathematics Tests, 369
California Diagnostic Reading Tests, 370
The California Life Goals Evaluation Schedules, 371
California Preschool Social Competency Scale, T4:360
California Psychological Inventory, Third Edition, 372
The California Q-Set; California Q-Set Personality for Adults (Revised Edition), see California Q-Sort (Revised Adult Set), 373
California Q-Sort (Revised Adult Set), 373
California Test of Personality, 374
California Verbal Learning Test, Children's Version, 375
California Verbal Learning Test, Research Edition, Adult Version, 376
Callahan Anxiety Pictures, T4:365
The Callier-Azusa Scale: G Edition, 377
The Camden Memory Tests, 378
Campbell-Hallam Team Development Survey, 379
Campbell™ Interest and Skill Survey, 380
Campbell Leadership Index, 381
Campbell Organizational Survey, 382
Canadian Achievement Survey Tests for Adults, 383
Canadian Achievement Tests, Second Edition, 384
Canadian Cognitive Abilities Test, Form K, 385
Canadian Dental Aptitude Test, 386
Canadian Occupational Interest Inventory, 387
Canadian Test of Cognitive Skills, 388
Canadian Tests of Basic Skills, Forms 7 and 8, 389
The Candidate Profile Record, 390

Canfield Instructional Styles Inventory, 391
Canfield Learning Styles Inventory, 392
The Canfield Time Problems Inventory, see Time Problems Inventory, 2762
CAP Assessment of Writing, 12:63
Capitalization and Punctuation Tests, 393
Cardall Test of Practical Judgement, 394
Career Ability Placement Survey, 395
Career Anchors: Discovering Your Real Values, Revised Edition, 396
Career Assessment Inventories for the Learning Disabled, 397
Career Assessment Inventory™—The Enhanced Version, 398
Career Assessment Inventory™—Vocational Version, 399
Career Assessment Program, see Aptitude Interest Inventory, 168
Career Attitudes and Strategies Inventory: An Inventory for Understanding Adult Careers, 400
Career Beliefs Inventory, 401
Career Counseling Personal Data Form, 402
Career Decision-Making Self-Efficacy Scale, 403
Career Decision Scale, 404
Career Development Inventory [Consulting Psychologists Press, Inc.], 405
Career Directions Inventory, 406
The Career Exploration Inventory, 407
Career Exploration Series, 1992 Revision, 408
Career Factors Inventory, 409
Career Guidance Inventory, 410
Career Interest Inventory, 411
Career Interests Test, T4:397
Career IQ Test, 412
Career Maturity Inventory, 413
Career Occupational Preference System, Interest Inventory, Form R, 414
Career Occupational Preference System, Intermediate Inventory, 415
Career Occupational Preference System—Professional Level Interest Inventory, 416
Career Orientation Placement and Evaluation Survey, 417
Career Planning Survey, 418
Career Problem Check List, 419
Career Profile Inventory, 420
The Career Profile System, Second Edition, 421
Career Survey, T4:405
Career Thoughts Inventory, 422
Career Values Card Sort, 423
Caregiver-Teacher Report Form, 424
Caregiver's School Readiness Inventory, 12:65
Carey Temperament Scales, 425
Caring Relationship Inventory, 426
Carlson Psychological Survey, 427
Carolina Picture Vocabulary Test (for Deaf and Hearing Impaired), 428
Carroll Depression Scales, 429
Carrow Auditory-Visual Abilities Test, T4:411
Carrow Elicited Language Inventory, 430
CAT/5 Listening and Speaking Checklist, 431
The Category-Specific Names Test, 432
Cattell Infant Intelligence Scale, 433
CERAD (Consortium to Establish a Registry for Alzheimer's Disease) Assessment Battery, 434
Certified Picture Framer Examination, 435
CGP Self-Scoring Placement Tests in English and Mathematics (Drawn from the CGP), T4:416
Change Abilitator, 436
Change Agent Questionnaire, 437
Chapin Social Insight Test, 438
Character Assessment Scale, 439
Characteristics Scale, 440
Chart of Initiative and Independence, 441
Charteris Reading Test, 12:67
Chatterji's Non-Language Preference Record, T4:422
Checklist for Child Abuse Evaluation, 442
Checklist/Guide to Selecting a Small Computer, T4:425
Checklist of Adaptive Living Skills, 443
Chelsea Diagnostic Mathematics Tests, 444
The Chessington O.T. Neurological Assessment Battery, 445
Chicago Early Assessment and Remediation LaboratorY, 446
Child Abuse/Husband Abuse/Wife Abuse, 447
The Child Abuse Potential Inventory, Form VI, 448
Child and Adolescent Adjustment Profile [Revised], 449
Child Anxiety Scale, 450
The Child "At Risk" for Drug Abuse Rating Scale, 12:70
Child Behavior Checklist, 451
Child Care Inventory, 452
The CHILD Center Operational Assessment Tool, T4:435
Child Development Inventory, 453
Child Development Review, 454
Child Language Ability Measures, 455
Child Neuropsychological Questionnaire, 456
Child Personality Rating Scale, see Personality Rating Scale, 1964
Child Sexual Behavior Inventory, 457
Child Well-Being Scales and Rating Form, 458
The Childhood Autism Rating Scale, 459
The Childhood Psychosis Rating Scale, see Childhood Autism Rating Scale, 459
Childhood Trauma Questionnaire, 460
Children at Risk Screener: Kindergarten and Preschool, 461
Children of Alcoholics Screening Test, 462
Children's Abilities Scales, 463
Children's Academic Intrinsic Motivation Inventory, 464
Childrens Adaptive Behavior Scale, Revised, 465
Children's Apperception Test [1991 Revision], 466

Children's Apperceptive Story-Telling Test, 467
Children's Articulation Test, 468
Children's Attention and Adjustment Survey, 469
Children's Auditory Verbal Learning Test-2, 470
Children's Category Test, 471
Children's Depression Inventory, 472
Children's Depression Rating Scale, Revised, 473
Children's Depression Scale [Second Research Edition], 12:77
Children's Embedded Figures Test, 474
Children's Inventory of Self-Esteem, 475
Children's Manifest Anxiety Scale, see Revised Children's Manifest Anxiety Scale, 2214
Children's Memory Scale, 476
Children's Personality Questionnaire, 1985 Edition, 477
Children's Problems Checklist, 478
Children's Role Inventory, 479
Children's Version of The Family Environment Scale, 480
Chinese Proficiency Test, 481
Chinese Speaking Test, 482
Choosing a Career, see Rothwell Miller Values Blank, 2256
Christensen Dietary Distress Inventory, 483
Christensen-Guilford Fluency Tests, T4:461
Chronic Pain Battery, 484
Chronicle Career Quest, 485
CID Phonetic Inventory, 486
CID Picture SPINE, 487
CID Preschool Performance Scale, 488
The City University Colour Vision Test, Second Edition 1980, 489
Clark-Madison Test of Oral Language, T4:468
The Clark Wilson Group Multi-Level Feedback Instruments and Development Programs, 490
Clarke Sex History Questionnaire, 491
Class Achievement Test in Mathematics, 492
The Class Activities Questionnaire, 493
Classic PSB—Nursing School Aptitude Examination (R.N.), see Revised PSB—Nursing School Aptitude Examination (R. N.), 2222
Classroom Atmosphere Questionnaire, T4:472
The Classroom Communication Skills Inventory: Listening and Speaking Checklist, 494
Classroom Environment Index, T4:474
Classroom Environment Scale, Third Edition, 495
Classroom Reading Inventory, Seventh Edition, 496
CLEP General Examinations, 497
CLEP General Examinations: English Composition and English Composition Test with Essay, 498
CLEP General Examinations: Humanities, 499
CLEP General Examinations: Mathematics, 500
CLEP General Examinations: Natural Sciences, 501
CLEP General Examinations: Social Sciences and History, 502
CLEP Subject Examination in American Government, 503
CLEP Subject Examination in American History I: Early Colonizations to 1877, see CLEP Subject Examination in History of the United States: Early Colonizations to 1877, 517
CLEP Subject Examination in American History II: 1865 to the Present, see CLEP Subject Examination in History of the United States II: 1865 to the Present, 518
CLEP Subject Examination in American Literature, 504
CLEP Subject Examination in Analysis and Interpretation of Literature, see CLEP Subject Examination in Analyzing and Interpreting Literature, 505
CLEP Subject Examination in Analyzing and Interpreting Literature, 505
CLEP Subject Examination in Calculus with Elementary Functions, 506
CLEP Subject Examination in College Algebra, 507
CLEP Subject Examination in College Algebra-Trigonometry, 508
CLEP Subject Examination in College Composition, see CLEP Subject Examination in Freshman College Composition, 514
CLEP Subject Examination in College French, Levels 1 and 2, see CLEP Subject Examination in College-Level French Language, Levels 1 and 2, 509
CLEP Subject Examination in College-Level French Language, Levels 1 and 2, 509
CLEP Subject Examination in College Level German, Levels 1 and 2, see CLEP Subject Examination in College-Level German Language, Levels 1 and 2, 510
CLEP Subject Examination in College-Level German Language, Levels 1 and 2, 510
CLEP Subject Examination in College Spanish, Levels 1 and 2, see CLEP Subject Examination in College-Level Spanish Language, Levels 1 and 2, 511
CLEP Subject Examination in College-Level Spanish Language, Levels 1 and 2, 511
CLEP Subject Examination in Computers and Data Processing, see CLEP Subject Examination in Information Systems and Computer Applications, 520
CLEP Subject Examination in Educational Psychology, 512
CLEP Subject Examination in English Literature, 513
CLEP Subject Examination in Freshman English, see CLEP Subject Examination in Freshman College Composition, 514
CLEP Subject Examination in Freshman College Composition, 514
CLEP Subject Examination in General Biology, 515
CLEP Subject Examination in General Chemistry, 516
CLEP Subject Examination in General Psychology, see CLEP Subject Examination in Introductory Psychology, 522
CLEP Subject Examination in History of the United States: Early Colonizations to 1877, 517

CLEP Subject Examination in History of the United States II: 1865 to the Present, 518
CLEP Subject Examination in Human Growth and Development, 519
CLEP Subject Examination in Information Systems and Computer Applications, 520
CLEP Subject Examination in Introduction to Management, see CLEP Subject Examination in Principles of Management, 526
CLEP Subject Examination in Introductory Accounting, see CLEP Subject Examination in Principles of Accounting, 524
CLEP Subject Examination in Introductory Business Law, 521
CLEP Subject Examination in Introductory Macroeconomics, see CLEP Subject Examination in Principles of Macroeconomics, 525
CLEP Subject Examination in Introductory Marketing, see CLEP Subject Examination in Principles of Marketing, 527
CLEP Subject Examination in Introductory Microeconomics, see CLEP Subject Examination in Principles of Microeconomics, 528
CLEP Subject Examination in Introductory Psychology, 522
CLEP Subject Examination in Introductory Sociology, 523
CLEP Subject Examination in Principles of Accounting, 524
CLEP Subject Examination in Principles of Macroeconomics, 525
CLEP Subject Examination in Principles of Management, 526
CLEP Subject Examination in Principles of Marketing, 527
CLEP Subject Examination in Principles of Microeconomics, 528
CLEP Subject Examination in Trigonometry, 529
CLEP Subject Examination in Western Civilization I: Ancient Near East to 1648, 530
CLEP Subject Examination in Western Civilization II: 1648 to the Present, 531
Clerical Abilities Battery, 532
Clerical Aptitude Test: Acorn National Aptitude Tests, 533
Clerical Aptitudes, 534
Clerical Skills Series, 535
Clerical Staff Selector, see Senior Clerical Skills Test, 2374
Client/Server Skills Test, 536
Clifton Assessment Procedures for the Elderly, 537
Clinical Analysis Questionnaire, 538
Clinical Evaluation of Language Fundamentals—Preschool, 539
Clinical Evaluation of Language Fundamentals—Revised Screening Test, see Clinical Evaluation of Language Fundamentals—3 Screening Test, 542
Clinical Evaluation of Language Fundamentals, Third Edition, 540
Clinical Evaluation of Language Fundamentals, Third Edition—Observational Rating Scales, 541
Clinical Evaluation of Language Fundamentals—3 Screening Test, 542
Clinical Experience Record for Nursing Students, 543
Clinical Rating Scale, 544
Clinical Record Keeping System, T4:527
Clinical Support System Battery, 12:82
The Clock Test, 545
Closed Head Injury Screener, 546
Closed High School Placement Test, 547
Closure Flexibility (Concealed Figures), 548
Closure Speed (Gestalt Completion), 549
Cloze Reading Tests 1-3, Second Edition, 550
Clyde Mood Scale, 551
Clymer-Barrett Prereading Battery, see Clymer-Barrett Readiness Test, Revised Edition, 552
Clymer-Barrett Readiness Test, Revised Edition, 552
C.O.A.C.H.: Cayuga-Onondaga Assessment for Children with Handicaps, Version 7.0, 553
Coaching Effectiveness Survey, 554
Coaching Process Questionnaire, 555
Coaching Skills Inventory, 556
Coddington Life Events Scales, 557
Cognistat (The Neurobehavioral Cognitive Status Examination), 558
Cognitive Abilities Scale, 559
Cognitive Abilities Test, Form 5, 560
Cognitive Abilities Test, Second Edition [British Edition], 561
Cognitive Behavior Rating Scales, 562
Cognitive Control Battery, 563
Cognitive Diagnostic Battery, 564
Cognitive Observation Guide, 12:83
Cognitive Skills Assessment Battery, Second Edition, 565
Cognitive Symptom Checklists, 566
CogScreen Aeromedical Edition, 567
Coitometer, 568
College Adjustment Scales, 569
College Basic Academic Subjects Examination, 570
College Board Achievement Test in American History and Social Studies, see College Board SAT II: American History and Social Studies Subject Test, 593
College Board Achievement Test in Biology, see College Board SAT II: Biology Subject Test, 595
College Board Achievement Test in Chemistry, see College Board SAT II: Chemistry Subject Test, 596
College Board Achievement Test in European History and World Cultures, see College Board SAT II: World History Subject Test, 613
College Board Achievement Test in French Reading, see College Board SAT II: French Subject Test, 598

College Board Achievement Test in German Reading, see College Board SAT II: German Subject Test, 600
College Board Achievement Test in Latin, see College Board SAT II: Latin Subject Test, 603
College Board Achievement Test in Literature, see College Board SAT II: Literature Subject Test, 604
College Board Achievement Test in Mathematics, see College Board SAT II: Mathematics Level IC and SAT II: Mathematics Level IIC, 605
College Board Achievement Test in Physics see College Board SAT II: Physics Subject Test, 607
College Board Achievement Test in Spanish Reading, see College Board SAT II: Spanish Subject Test, 608
College Board Admissions Testing Program, see College Board SAT Program, 615
College Board Descriptive Tests System, 571
College Board English Composition Test with Essay, see College Board SAT II: Writing Subject Test, 614
College Board Institutional SAT II: American History and Social Studies Subject Test, 572
College Board Institutional SAT II: Biology E/M Subject Test, 573
College Board Institutional SAT II: Chemistry Subject Test, 574
College Board Institutional SAT II: Chinese with Listening Subject Test, 575
College Board Institutional SAT II: English Language Proficiency Test, 576
College Board Institutional SAT II: French Subject Test, 577
College Board Institutional SAT II: French with Listening Subject Tests, 578
College Board Institutional SAT II: German Subject Test, 579
College Board Institutional SAT II: German with Listening Subject Test, 580
College Board Institutional SAT II: Italian Subject Test, 581
College Board Institutional SAT II: Japanese with Listening Subject Test, 582
College Board Institutional SAT II: Latin Subject Test, 583
College Board Institutional SAT II: Literature Subject Test, 584
College Board Institutional SAT II: Mathematics Level IC Subject Tests, and SAT II: Mathematics Level II C Subject Tests, 585
College Board Institutional SAT II: Modern Hebrew Subject Test, 586
College Board Institutional SAT II: Physics Subject Test, 587
College Board Institutional SAT II: Spanish Subject Test, 588
College Board Institutional SAT II: Spanish with Listening Subject Test, 589
College Board Institutional SAT II: World History Subject Test, 590
College Board Institutional SAT II: Writing Subject Test, 591
College Board One-Hour Achievement Test in American History and Social Studies (Drawn from the SAT II: Subject Tests), see College Board Institutional SAT II: American History and Social Studies Subject Test, 572
College Board One-Hour Achievement Test in Biology (Drawn from the SAT II: Subject Tests), see College Board Institutional SAT II: Biology E/M Subject Test, 573
College Board One-Hour Achievement Test in Chemistry (Drawn from the SAT II: Subject Tests), see College Board Institutional SAT II: Chemistry Subject Test, 574
College Board One-Hour Achievement Test in French Reading (Drawn from the SAT II: Subject Tests), see College Board Institutional SAT II: French Subject Test, 577
College Board One-Hour Achievement Test in French with Listening (Drawn from the SAT II: Subject Tests), see College Board Institutional SAT II: French with Listening Subject Tests, 578
College Board One-Hour Achievement Test in German Reading (Drawn from the SAT II: Subject Tests), see College Board Institutional SAT II: German Subject Test, 579
College Board One-Hour Achievement Test in German with Listening (Drawn from the SAT II: Subject Tests), see College Board Institutional SAT II: German with Listening Subject Test, 580
College Board One-Hour Achievement Test in Italian Reading (Drawn from the SAT II: Subject Tests), see College Board Institutional SAT II: Italian Subject Test, 581
College Board One-Hour Achievement Test in Latin Reading (Drawn from the SAT II: Subject Tests), see College Board Institutional SAT II: Latin Subject Test, 583
College Board One-Hour Achievement Test in Modern Hebrew (Drawn from the SAT II: Subject Tests), see College Board Institutional SAT II: Modern Hebrew Subject Test, 586
College Board One-Hour Achievement Test in Physics (Drawn from the SAT II: Subject Tests), see College Board Institutional SAT II: Physics Subject Test, 587
College Board One-Hour Achievement Test in Spanish Reading (Drawn from the SAT II: Subject Tests), see College Board Institutional SAT II: Spanish Subject Test, 588
College Board One-Hour Achievement Test in Spanish with Listening (Drawn from SAT II: Subject Tests), see College Board Institutional SAT II: Spanish with Listening Subject Test, 589

College Board One-Hour Achievement Test in World History (Drawn from the SAT II: Subject Tests), see College Board Institutional SAT II: World History Subject Test, 590
College Board One-Hour Achievement Tests (Drawn from the SAT II: Subject Tests), see Institutional SAT Program (Institutional SAT I: Reasoning Test and SAT II: Subject Tests), 1274
College Board SAT I Reasoning Test, 592
College Board SAT II: American History and Social Studies Subject Test, 593
College Board SAT II: Biology E/M Subject Test, 594
College Board SAT II: Biology Subject Test, 595
College Board SAT II: Chemistry Subject Test, 596
College Board SAT II: English Language Proficiency Test, 597
College Board SAT II: French Subject Test, 598
College Board SAT II: French with Listening Subject Test, 599
College Board SAT II: German Subject Test, 600
College Board SAT II: German with Listening Subject Test, 601
College Board SAT II: Korean with Listening Subject Test, 602
College Board SAT II: Latin Subject Test, 603
College Board SAT II: Literature Subject Test, 604
College Board SAT II: Mathematics Level IC and SAT II: Mathematics Level IIC, 605
College Board SAT II: Modern Hebrew Subject Test, 606
College Board SAT II: Physics Subject Test, 607
College Board SAT II: Spanish Subject Test, 608
College Board SAT II: Spanish with Listening Subject Test, 609
College Board SAT II: Subject Test in American History and Social Studies, see College Board SAT II: American History and Social Studies Subject Test, 593
College Board SAT II: Subject Test in Biology, see College Board SAT II: Biology Subject Test, 595
College Board SAT II: Subject Test in Chemistry, see College Board SAT II: Chemistry Subject Test, 596
College Board SAT II: Subject Test in Chinese with Listening, 610
College Board SAT II: Subject Test in Italian, 611
College Board SAT II: Subject Test in Japanese with Listening, 612
College Board SAT II: Subject Test in Latin, see College Board SAT II: Latin Subject Test, 603
College Board SAT II: Subject Test in Literature, see College Board SAT II: Literature Subject Test, 604
College Board SAT II: Subject Test in Modern Hebrew, see College Board SAT II: Modern Hebrew Subject Test, 606
College Board SAT II: Subject Test in Physics, see College Board SAT II: Physics Subject Test, 607
College Board SAT II: Subject Test in World History, see College Board SAT II: World History Subject Test, 613
College Board SAT II: Subject Tests in French, see College Board SAT II: French Subject Test, 598
College Board SAT II: Subject Tests in German, see College Board SAT II: German Subject Test, 600
College Board SAT II: Subject Tests in Mathematics, see College Board SAT II: Mathematics Level IC and SAT II: Mathematics Level IIC, 605
College Board SAT II: Subject Tests in Spanish, see College Board SAT II: Spanish Subject Test, 608
College Board SAT II: World History Subject Test, 613
College Board SAT II: Writing Subject Test, 614
College Board SAT Program, 615
College Board Scholastic Aptitude Test and Test of Standard Written English, see College Board SAT I Reasoning Test, 592
College Characteristics Index, T4:582
College English Placement Test, T4:583
College English Test: National Achievement Tests, 616
College Level Examination Program, 617
College Major Interest Inventory, 618
College Outcome Measures Program, 619
College Placement Test in American History and Social Studies, see College Board Institutional SAT II: American History and Social Studies Subject Test, 572
College Placement Test in Biology, see College Board Institutional SAT II: Biology E/M Subject Test, 573
College Placement Test in Chemistry, see College Board Institutional SAT II: Chemistry Subject Test, 574
College Placement Test in European History and World Cultures, see College Board Institutional SAT II: World History Subject Test, 590
College Placement Test in French Listening-Reading, see College Board Institutional SAT II: French with Listening Subject Tests, 578
College Placement Test in French Reading, see College Board Institutional SAT II: French Subject Test, 577
College Placement Test in German Listening-Reading, see College Board Institutional SAT II: German with Listening Subject Test, 580
College Placement Test in German Reading, see College Board Institutional SAT II: German Subject Test, 579
College Placement Test in Hebrew Reading, see College Board Institutional SAT II: Modern Hebrew Subject Test, 586
College Placement Test in Italian Reading, see College Board Institutional SAT II: Italian Subject Test, 581

College Placement Test in Latin Reading, see College Board Institutional SAT II: Latin Subject Test, 583
College Placement Test in Literature, see College Board Institutional SAT II: Literature Subject Test, 584
College Placement Test in Physics, see College Board Institutional SAT II: Physics Subject Test, 587
College Placement Test in Spanish Listening-Reading, see College Board Institutional SAT II: Spanish with Listening Subject Test, 589
College Placement Test in Spanish Reading, see College Board Institutional SAT II: Spanish Subject Test, 588
College Placement Tests, see Institutional SAT Program (Institutional SAT I: Reasoning Test and SAT II: Subject Tests), 1274
College Placement Tests in English Composition; College Board One-Hour Achievement Test in Writing (Drawn From the SAT II: Subject Tests), see College Board Institutional SAT II: Writing Subject Test, 591
College Placement Tests in Mathematics; College Board One-Hour Achievement Test in Mathematics (Drawn From the SAT II: Subject Tests), see College Board Institutional SAT II: Mathematics Level IC Subject Tests, and SAT II: Mathematics Level II C Subject Tests, 585
College Student Experiences Questionnaire, 620
Collegiate Assessment of Academic Proficiency, 621
Collis-Romberg Mathematical Problem Solving Profiles, 622
Colorado Educational Interest Inventory, see College Major Interest Inventory, 618
Colored Overlay Assessment Kit, 623
Columbia Mental Maturity Scale, Third Edition, 624
The Columbus: Picture Analysis of Growth Towards Maturity, 625
Combined Cognitive Preference Inventory, 626
The Common-Metric Questionnaire, 627
Communication Abilities Diagnostic Test, 628
Communication Activities of Daily Living, Second Edition, 629
Communication and Symbolic Behavior Scales, 630
Communication Knowledge Inventory [Revised], 631
Communication Response Style: Assessment, 632
Communication Sensitivity Inventory, 633
Communication Skills Profile, 634
Communicative Abilities in Daily Living, see Communication Activities of Daily Living, Second Edition, 629
Communicative Evaluation Chart From Infancy to Five Years, T4:601
Community College Goals Inventory, T4:602
Community College Student Experiences Questionnaire, Second Edition, 635
Community Opinion Inventory, Revised Edition, 636
Community Oriented Programs Environment Scale, 637
Competency-Based Performance Improvement: Organizational Assessment Package, 638
The Competent Speaker Speech Evaluation Form, 639
A Complaint Is a Gift Profile, 640
Complex Figure Test, 641
Composite International Diagnostic Interview, 642
Comprehension of Oral Language, 643
Comprehensive Ability Battery, 644
Comprehensive Adult Student Assessment System, 645
Comprehensive Affair Worksheets, 646
Comprehensive Assessment of Reading Strategies, 647
Comprehensive Assessment of School Environments, 648
Comprehensive Assessment of School Environments Information Management System, 649
Comprehensive Assessment of Symptoms and History, 650
Comprehensive Behavior Rating Scale for Children, 651
Comprehensive Drinker Profile, 652
A Comprehensive English Language Test for Speakers of English as a Second Language, T4:615
Comprehensive Identification Process [Revised], 653
Comprehensive Personality Profile, 654
Comprehensive Receptive and Expressive Vocabulary Test, 655
Comprehensive Receptive and Expressive Vocabulary Test—Adult, 656
Comprehensive Scales of Student Abilities: Quantifying Academic Skills and School-Related Behavior Through the Use of Teacher Judgments, 657
Comprehensive Screening Test for Determining Optimal Communication Mode, 658
Comprehensive Sex History, 659
Comprehensive Spouse's Worksheets, 660
Comprehensive Test of Adaptive Behavior, 661
Comprehensive Test of Nonverbal Intelligence, 662
Comprehensive Test of Visual Functioning, 663
Comprehensive Testing Program III, 664
Comprehensive Tests of Basic Skills, Fourth Edition, 665
Computer-Based Test of English as a Foreign Language and Test of Written English, 666
The Computer Category Test, 667
Computer Literacy Skills Profile, 668
Computer Operator Aptitude Battery, 669
Computer Programmer Aptitude Battery, 670
[Computer Programmer Test Package], T4:627
Computerized Assessment of Response Bias: Revised Edition, 671
Comrey Personality Scales, 672
Comrey Personality Scales—Short Form, 673
Concept Assessment Kit—Conservation, 674
Concept Attainment Test, T4:631
Concepts Involved in Body Positions and Space, see Hill Performance Test of Selected Positional Concepts, 1206

Conceptual Systems Test, T4:632
Concise Word Reading Tests, T4:633
Conflict Management Appraisal, 675
Conflict Management Survey, 676
Conflict Style Inventory, 677
Conners' Adult ADHD Rating Scales, 678
Conners' Continuous Performance Test, 679
Conners-March Developmental Questionnaire, 680
Conners' Rating Scales—Revised, 681
Consequences, 682
Content Inventories: English, Social Studies, Science, 683
Content Mastery Examinations for Educators, 684
Contextual Memory Test, 685
Continuing Education Assessment Inventory, 686
Continuous Symbol Checking Test, T4:641
Continuous Visual Memory Test [Revised], 687
Controller/Accountant Staff Selector, 688
The Conversational Skills Rating Scale: An Instructional Assessment of Interpersonal Competence, 689
Coolidge Axis II Inventory, 690
Cooper Assessment for Stuttering Syndromes, 691
Cooper-Farran Behavioral Rating Scales, 12:94
The Cooper-McGuire Diagnostic Word-Analysis Test, T4:644
The Cooperative Institutional Research Program, 692
Cooperative Preschool Inventory, Revised Edition, 693
Coopersmith Self-Esteem Inventories, 694
Coping Inventory, 695
Coping Inventory, see Early Coping Inventory, 878
Coping Inventory for Stressful Situations, 696
Coping Resources Inventory, 697
Coping Responses Inventory—Adult and Youth, 699
Coping Resources Inventory for Stress, 698
Coping With Health Injuries and Problems, 700
Coping with Stress, 701
COPSystem Picture Inventory of Careers, 702
The Cornell Class-Reasoning Test, Form X, 703
The Cornell Conditional-Reasoning Test, 704
The Cornell Critical Thinking Tests, 705
The Cornell Inventory for Student Appraisal of Teaching and Courses, 706
The Cornell Learning and Study Skills Inventory, 707
Cornell Medical Index—Health Questionnaire, 708
Cornell Word Form 2, 709
Correctional Institutions Environment Scale, Second Edition, 710
Correctional Officers' Interest Blank, 711
Correctional Policy Inventory: A Survey of Correctional Philosophy and Characteristic Methods of Dealing with Offenders, 712
Corrective Reading Mastery Tests, T4:663
Cosmetology Student Admissions Evaluation, 713
Cotswold Junior Ability Tests, 714
Cotswold Personality Assessment P.A. 1, 715
Counselor and Client Verbal Response Category Systems, 716
Couple's Pre-Counseling Inventory, Revised Edition, 1987, 717
The Couples BrainMap, T4:669
Course Evaluation Questionnaire, T4:670
Course-Faculty Instrument, T4:672
Course Finder, 718
A Courtship Analysis, T4:673
CPF [Second Edition], 719
CPH Patient Attitude Scale, T4:675
Crane Oral Dominance Test: Spanish/English, 720
Crawford Psychological Adjustment Scale, 721
Crawford Small Parts Dexterity Test, 722
Creative Behavior Inventory, 723
Creative Styles Inventory, 13:86
Creativity Assessment Packet, 724
Creativity Attitude Survey, 725
Creativity Tests for Children, 726
The Creatrix Inventory, 727
Cree Questionnaire, 728
Crichton Vocabulary Scale, 729
Criterion Test of Basic Skills, 730
Criterion Validated Written Test for Emergency Medical Practitioner, 731
Criterion Validated Written Test for Fire Medic, 732
Criterion Validated Written Tests for Clerical Worker, T4:689
Criterion Validated Written Tests for Firefighter, 733
Criterion Validated Written Tests for Police Officer, 734
Critical Reasoning Test Battery, 735
Critical Reasoning Tests, 736
Croft Readiness Assessment in Comprehension Kit, T4:694
Cross-Cultural Adaptability Inventory, 737
Cross Reference Test, 738
Crown-Crisp Experiential Index, 739
CRS Placement/Diagnostic Test, 740
CTB Kindergarten–Grade 1 Assessment Activities, 741
CTB Performance Assessment, 742
CTB Portfolio Assessment System, 743
CTB Writing Assessment System, 744
Cultural Literacy Test, 12:99
Culture Fair Intelligence Test, 745
Culture Free Intelligence Test, see Culture Fair Intelligence Test, 745
Culture-Free Self-Esteem Inventories, Second Edition, 746
Culture-Free Self-Esteem Inventories for Children and Adults, see Culture-Free Self-Esteem Inventories, Second Edition, 746
Culture Shock Inventory [Revised], 747
Current and Past Psychopathology Scales, 748
Current News Test, 749
Curriculum Frameworks Assessment System, 750
Curtis Completion Form, 751
Curtis Interest Scale, 752
[Curtis Object Completion and Space Form Tests], 753

Curtis Verbal-Clerical Skills Tests, 754
The Custody Quotient, T4:708
Customer Reaction Survey, 755
Customer Service Representative, see Customer Service Skills Test, 756
Customer Service Skills Test, 756
Cutrona Child Study Profile of Psycho-Educational Abilities, 757
Cutrona Reading Inventory, 758

DABERON: A Screening Device for School Readiness, see DABERON-2: Screening for School Readiness, Second Edition, 759
DABERON-2: Screening for School Readiness, Second Edition, 759
Daily Stress Inventory, 760
The D.A.L.E. System: Developmental Assessment of Life Experiences, see Developmental Assessment of Life Experiences (1998 Edition), 805
Dallas Pre-School Screening Test, 761
DANTES Subject Standardized Tests, 762
Das-Naglieri Cognitive Assessment System, 763
Database Analyst Staff Selector, 764
Database Professional Staff Selector, see Database Analyst Staff Selector, 764
Dating Problems Checklist, T4:718
A Dating Scale, 765
Davidson Trauma Scale, 766
DCS—A Visual Learning and Memory Test for Neuropsychological Assessment, 767
DECAD (Departmental Evaluation of Chairpersons Activities for Development), see IDEA Feedback for Department Chairs, 1233
Decision Making Inventory, 768
Decoding Skills Test, 769
Deductive Reasoning Test, T4:722
Defense Mechanisms Inventory [Revised], 770
Defining Issues Test, 771
DeGangi-Berk Test of Sensory Integration, 772
Degrees of Reading Power [Revised], 773
Degrees of Word Meaning, 774
Delaware County Silent Reading Test, Second Edition, 775
Dementia Rating Scale, 776
The Demos D Scale: An Attitude Scale for the Identification of Dropouts, 777
The Demos Dropout Scale, see Demos D Scale: An Attitude Scale for the Identification of Dropouts, 777
The Dennis Test of Child Development, 778
Dennis Test of Scholastic Aptitude, 779
Dental Admission Test, 780
Dental Aptitude Testing Program, see Dental Admission Test, 780
Dental Assistant Test, 781
Dental Receptionist Test, 782
Denver Articulation Screening Exam, 783
Denver Audiometric Screening Test, 784
Denver Community Mental Health Questionnaire—Revised, T4:738
Denver Developmental Screening Test, see Denver II (Denver Developmental Screening Test), 788
Denver Eye Screening Test, 785
Denver Handwriting Analysis, 786
Denver Prescreening Developmental Questionnaire II, 787
Denver II (Denver Developmental Screening Test), 788
Departmental Evaluation of Chairperson Activities for Development, see IDEA Feedback for Department Chairs, 1233
Depression Adjective Check Lists, see State Trait-Depression Adjective Check Lists, 2499
Depression and Anxiety in Youth Scale, 789
Depressive Experiences Questionnaire, 790
Derogatis Affects Balance Scale [Revised], 791
Derogatis Psychiatric Rating Scale, 792
Derogatis Sexual Functioning Inventory, 793
Derogatis Stress Profile, 794
Description of Body Scale, 795
Descriptive Tests of Language Skills; Descriptive Tests of Mathematics Skills, see College Board Descriptive Tests System, 571
Detention Promotion Tests—Complete Service, 796
Determining Needs in Your Youth Ministry, 12:104
Detroit Tests of Learning Aptitude—Adult, 797
Detroit Tests of Learning Aptitude, Fourth Edition, 798
Detroit Tests of Learning Aptitude—Primary, Second Edition, 799
Developing Cognitive Abilities Test [Second Edition], T4:755
Developing Skills Checklist, 800
Developing The High-Performance Workplace, 801
Developing the Leader Within, 802
Developmental Activities Screening Inventory, Second Edition, 803
A Developmental Assessment for Students with Severe Disabilities, Second Edition, 804
A Developmental Assessment for the Severely Handicapped, see Developmental Assessment for Students with Severe Disabilities, Second Edition, 804
Developmental Assessment of Life Experiences (1998 Edition), 805
Developmental Assessment of Young Children, 806
Developmental Challenge Profile: Learning from Job Experiences, 807
Developmental History Checklist for Children, 808
Developmental Indicators for the Assessment of Learning, Third Edition, 809
Developmental Observation Checklist System, 810
Developmental Profile II, 811
Developmental Task Analysis, 812
Developmental Tasks for Kindergarten Readiness—II, 813

Developmental Teaching Objectives and Rating Form—Revised, 814
Developmental Test of Visual-Motor Integration, 4th Edition, Revised, 815
Developmental Test of Visual Perception, Second Edition, 816
Devereux Adolescent Behavior Scale, see Devereux Scales of Mental Disorders, 818
Devereux Behavior Rating Scale—School Form, 817
Devereux Child Behavior Rating Scale, see Devereux Scales of Mental Disorders, 818
Devereux Scales of Mental Disorders, 818
The Devine Inventory, 819
DF Opinion Survey, see Dynamic Factors Survey, 865
Diagnosing Organizational Culture, 820
Diagnosis and Remediation of Handwriting Problems, T4:773
Diagnostic Achievement Battery, Second Edition, 821
Diagnostic Achievement Test for Adolescents, Second Edition, 822
A Diagnostic Achievement Test in Spelling, T4:776
Diagnostic Assessments of Reading, 823
Diagnostic Guide to DSM III, T4:778
Diagnostic Interview for Borderline Patients, 824
Diagnostic Inventory for Screening Children, 13:99
Diagnostic Mathematics Profiles, 825
Diagnostic Reading Record, Second Edition, 826
Diagnostic Reading Scales, 827
Diagnostic Reading Tests, T4:783
The Diagnostic Screening Batteries, 828
Diagnostic Screening Test: Achievement, 829
Diagnostic Screening Test: Language, Second Edition, 830
Diagnostic Screening Test: Math, Third Edition, 831
Diagnostic Screening Test: Reading, Third Edition, 832
Diagnostic Screening Test: Spelling, Third Edition, 833
Diagnostic Spelling Potential Test, 834
Diagnostic Spelling Test, 835
Diagnostic Teacher-Rating Scale, 836
Diagnostic Test for Students of English as a Second Language, T4:793
Diagnostic Test of Arithmetic Strategies, T4:794
Diagnostic Test of Library Skills—Advanced Edition, 13:101
Diagnostic Tests for Minimal Math Competencies, T4:797
Diagnostic Tests in Mathematics, T4:798
Differential Ability Scales, 837
Differential Aptitude Tests—Computerized Adaptive Edition, 12:117
Differential Aptitude Tests, Fifth Edition, 838
Differential Aptitude Tests for Personnel and Career Assessment, 839
The Differential Diagnostic Technique, 840
Differential Test Battery, see Morrisby Profile, 1717
Differential Test of Conduct and Emotional Problems, 841
Digit Vigilance Test, 842
Digital Finger Tapping Test, 12:121
Dimensions of Excellence Scales [1991 Edition], 843
Dimensions of Self-Concept, 844
Diplomacy Test of Empathic Ability, see Diplomacy Test of Empathy, 845
Diplomacy Test of Empathy, 845
Discourse Comprehension Test, 13:102
Dissociative Experiences Scale, 846
Dissociative Features Profile, 847
Distar Mastery Tests, T4:810
Diversity Awareness Profile, 848
Dodd Test of Time Estimation, see Functional Time Estimation Questionnaire, 1068
Domestic Violence Inventory, 849
Dos Amigos Verbal Language Scales, 850
Draw-A-Person Quality Scale, 851
Draw A Person: Screening Procedure for Emotional Disturbance, 852
The Draw-A-Person, 853
Draw A Person: A Quantitative Scoring System, 854
Draw-a-Story: Screening for Depression and Age or Gender Differences [Revised], 855
Draw-a-Story: Screening for Depression and Emotional Needs, see Draw-a-Story: Screening for Depression and Age or Gender Differences [Revised], 855
Driver Risk Inventory—II, 856
[Driver Selection Forms and Tests], 857
Dropout Prediction & Prevention, 12:126
Drug-Taking Confidence Questionnaire, 858
Drug Use Questionnaire, 859
d2 Test of Attention, 860
Durrell Analysis of Reading Difficulty, Third Edition, 861
Dvorine Color Perception Testing Charts, see Dvorine Color Vision Test, 862
Dvorine Color Vision Test, 862
Dvorine Pseudo-Isochromatic Plates see Dvorine Color Vision Test, 862
Dyadic Adjustment Scale, 863
Dyadic Parent-Child Interaction Coding System: A Manual, 864
Dynamic Factors Survey, 865
Dysarthria Examination Battery, 866
Dyslexia Determination Test, Second Edition, 867
Dyslexia Schedule, T4:828
Dyslexia Screening Instrument, 868
The Dyslexia Screening Survey, 869
Dysphagia Evaluation Protocol, 870

E. S. Survey, 871
Early Child Development Inventory, 872
The Early Childhood Attention Deficit Disorders Evaluation Scale, 873

The Early Childhood Behavior Scale, 874
Early Childhood Environment Rating Scale—Revised, 875
Early Childhood Inventory–4, 876
Early Childhood Physical Environment Observation Schedules and Rating Scales, 877
Early Coping Inventory, 878
Early Intervention Developmental Profile, 879
Early Language Milestone Scale, Second Edition, 880
Early Language Skills Checklist, 881
Early Learning: Assessment and Development, 882
Early Mathematical Language, 883
Early Mathematics Diagnostic Kit, 884
Early Memories Procedure, 885
Early School Assessment, 886
Early School Inventory, 887
Early School Personality Questionnaire, 888
Early Screening Inventory—Revised, 889
Early Screening Profiles, see AGS Early Screening Profiles, 124
Early Screening Project, 890
Early Speech Perception Test, 891
Early Years Easy Screen, 892
Eating Disorder Inventory-2, 893
Eating Inventory, 894
Eby Gifted Behavior Index, 895
Eckstein Audiometers, 896
[Economics/Objective Tests], 897
Economics Tests, see [Economics/Objective Tests], 897
ECOScales, 898
Edinburgh Picture Test, 899
The Edinburgh Questionnaires (1982 Edition), 900
Edinburgh Reading Tests, 901
Educational Abilities Scales, 902
Educational Administrator Effectiveness Profile, 903
Educational Development Series (1992 Edition), 904
Educational Interest Inventory, 905
Educational Leadership Practices Inventory, 906
Educational Process Questionnaire, 907
Edwards Personal Preference Schedule, 908
The Effective School Battery, 909
Effective Study Test, T4:864
Effectiveness Motivation Scale, 910
The Egan Bus Puzzle Test, 911
Ego Function Assessment, 912
The Ego Strength Q-Sort Test, 913
Eidetic Parents Test, 914
Eight State Questionnaire, 915
Einstein Assessment of School-Related Skills, 916
E.I.T.S. Clerical Tests, see Office Skills Series, 1835
Ekwall/Shanker Reading Inventory—Third Edition, 917
El Circo, 918
Electrical and Electronics Test, 919
Electrical Maintenance Trainee—Form UKI-1C, 920
Electrical Sophistication Test, 921
Electromechanical Vocational Assessment Manuals, 922
Electron Test—Form H-C, 923
Electronic and Instrumentation Technician Test—Form 2, 924
Electronics Test—Form G2, see Electron Test—Form H-C, 923
Elias Family Opinion Survey, see Family Adjustment Test, 1005
Eliot-Pearson Screening Inventory, see Early Screening Inventory—Revised, 889
Eliot-Price Perspective Test, 925
Elizur Test of Psycho-Organicity: Children and Adults, T4:881
Embedded Figures Test, 926
Emo Questionnaire, 927
Emotional and Behavior Problem Scale, 928
Emotional Behavioral Checklist, 929
The Emotional Empathic Tendency Scale, see Balanced Emotional Empathy Scale, 238
Emotional or Behavior Disorder Scale, 930
Emotional Problems Scales, 931
Emotions Profile Index, 932
The Empathy Test, 933
Employability Development Plan, 934
The Employability Inventory, 935
Employability Maturity Interview, 936
Employee Aptitude Survey, Second Edition, 937
Employee Assistance Program Inventory, 938
Employee Effectiveness Profile, 939
Employee Involvement Status Survey, 940
Employee Involvement Survey, 941
Employee Performance Appraisal, 942
[Employee Rating and Development Forms], 943
Employee Reliability Inventory, 944
The Employment Barrier Identification Scale, T4:900
Employment Values Inventory, 945
Empowerment Inventory, 946
End-of-Course Tests, 947
Endeavor Instructional Rating System, 948
Endicott Work Productivity Scale, 949
[The Endler Anxiety Scales], see Endler Multidimensional Anxiety Scales, 950
Endler Multidimensional Anxiety Scales, 950
English as a Second Language Oral Assessment, Second Edition, 951
English Picture Vocabulary Test, 952
English Placement Test, 953
English Progress Test, 954
English Skills Assessment, 955
English Test: Municipal Tests: National Achievement Tests, 956
English Test: National Achievement Tests, 957
Enhanced ACT Assessment, see ACT Assessment, 56
Enneagram Personality Portraits Inventory and Profile, 958
Ennis-Weir Argumentation Test, Level X: An Essay Test of Rational Thinking Ability, see Ennis-Weir Critical Thinking Essay Test, 959

Ennis-Weir Critical Thinking Essay Test, 959
ENRIGHT Diagnostic Inventory of Basic Arithmetic Skills, T4:915
Entrance Examination for Schools of Nursing, see Entrance Examination for Schools of Nursing [RN Entrance Examination], 960
Entrance Examination for Schools of Nursing [RN Entrance Examination], 960
Entrance Examination for Schools of Practical/Vocational Nursing, 961
Entrepreneurial and Executive Quotient; Entrepreneurial Quotient, see EQ Questionnaire, 966
Entrepreneurial Style and Success Indicator, 962
Environmental Response Inventory, 963
Eosys Word Processing Aptitude Battery, 964
EPS Sentence Completion Technique, 965
EQ Questionnaire, 966
ERB Comprehensive Testing Program II, see Comprehensive Testing Program III, 664
ERB Writing Assessment, 967
Erhardt Developmental Prehension Assessment, 968
Erhardt Developmental Vision Assessment, 969
Erotometer: A Technique for the Measurement of Heterosexual Love, 970
ESL/Adult Literacy Scale, 971
ETS Tests of Applied Literacy Skills, 972
ETSA Tests, 973
Evaluating Acquired Skills in Communication, see Revised Evaluating Acquired Skills in Communication, 2215
Evaluating Courses for Inclusion of New Scholarship on Women, 974
Evaluating Diversity Training, 975
Evaluating Educational Programs for Intellectually Gifted Students, 976
Evaluating Movement and Posture Disorganization in Dyspraxic Children, 977
Evaluating the Participant's Employability Skills, 978
Evaluation Aptitude Test, 979
Evaluation Disposition Toward the Environment, 980
Evaluation Modality Test, 981
Evaluation of Basic Skills, 982
Evanston Early Identification Scale, Field Research Edition, T4:938
Everstine Trauma Response Index, 983
Everyday Life Activities: Photo Series, 984
Examination for the Certificate of Competency in English, 985
Examination for the Certificate of Proficiency in English, 986
Examining for Aphasia, Third Edition, 987
Executive Administrative Assistant Skills Test, 988
[Executive, Industrial, and Sales Personnel Forms], 989
Executive Profile Survey, 990
The Experiencing Scale, 991
EXPLORE, 992
Explore the World of Work, 993
Expressional Growth Through Handwriting Evaluation Scale, T4:945
Expressive One-Word Picture Vocabulary Test, Revised, 994
Expressive Vocabulary Test, 995
The Extended Merrill-Palmer Scale, 996
Eyberg Child Behavior Inventory, 997
Eysenck Personality Inventory, 998
Eysenck Personality Inventory, see Eysenck Personality Questionnaire [Revised], 999
Eysenck Personality Questionnaire [Revised], 999

FACES II & FACES III, 1000
Facial Action Coding System, 1001
The Facial Interpersonal Perception Inventory, 1002
Faculty Morale Scale for Institutional Improvement, 1003
A Familism Scale, 1004
Family Adaptability & Cohesion Evaluation Scales, see FACES II & FACES III, 1000
Family Adjustment Test, 1005
Family Apperception Test, 1006
Family Assessment Form: A Practice-Based Approach to Assessing Family Functioning, 1007
Family Assessment Measure Version III, 1008
Family Day Care Rating Scale, 1009
Family Environment Scale, Third Edition, 1010
Family Relations Test, 1011
Family Relations Test: Children's Version, 1012
Family Relationship Inventory, 1013
Family Risk Scales, 13:125
Family Satisfaction Scale, 1014
Family System Test, 1015
A Family Violence Scale, 1016
Famous Sayings, 1017
The Farnsworth-Munsell 100-Hue Test for the Examination of Color Discrimination, T4:969
Farnum Music Test, T4:970
The Farnum String Scale: A Performance Scale for All String Instruments, 1018
Fast Health Knowledge Test, 1986 Revision, 1019
Fast-Tyson Health Knowledge Test, 1975 Edition, see Fast Health Knowledge Test, 1986 Revision, 1019
F.A.T.S.A. Test (Flowers Auditory Test of Selective Attention), 1020
Fear Survey Schedule, 1021
Feedback Edition of the Strength Development Inventory, 1022
Feedback Portrait of Overdone Strengths, 1023
Feedback Portrait of Personal Strengths, 1024
Feelings, Attitudes, and Behaviors Scale for Children, 1025
Fels Parent Behavior Rating Scales, 1026
The Field Work Performance Report, see American Occupational Therapy Association, Inc. Fieldwork Evaluation for the Occupation Therapist, 152
50 Grammar Quizzes for Practice and Review, 1027

Figurative Language Interpretation Test, 1028
Figure Classification Test, 1029
The Filipino Work Values Scale, 1030
Fine Dexterity Test, 1031
Fire Promotion TestsComplete Service, 1032
Firefighter Learning Simulation, 1033
Firefighter Selection Test [Revised], 1034
Firestone Assessment of Self-Destructive Thoughts, 1035
The FIRO Awareness Scales, 1036
First Grade Readiness Checklist, T4:983
First Words and First Sentences Tests, 1037
First Year Algebra Test: National Achievement Tests, 1038
FirstSTEP: Screening Test for Evaluating Preschoolers, 1039
The Fisher-Logemann Test of Articulation Competence, 1040
The Five P's (Parent/Professional Preschool Performance Profile) [Revised], 1041
Flags: A Test of Space Thinking, see Space Thinking (Flags), 2460
Flanagan Aptitude Classification Tests, 1042
Flanagan Industrial Tests, 1043
Fleishman Job Analysis Survey, 1044
Flex Style Negotiating, 1045
Florida Cumulative Guidance Record, Revised, T4:991
Flowers-Costello Tests of Central Auditory Abilities, 1046
Fluharty Preschool Speech and Language Screening Test, 1047
Food Choice Inventory, T4:994
Food Protection Certification Test, 1048
The Forer Structured Sentence Completion Test, 1049
The Forer Vocational Survey, 1050
A Form Series Test, (Industrial Version), T4:998
Formal Reading Inventory, 1051
Forms for Behavior Analysis with Children, 1052
Four Picture Test, Third Revised Edition, 1053
The Fred Test, T4:1003
French Comprehension Tests, 1054
French Reading Diagnostic Tests for Early French Immersion Primary Classes, 1055
Frenchay Aphasia Screening Test, T4:1006
Frenchay Dysarthria Assessment, 1056
Friedman Well-Being Scale, 1057
Fuld Object-Memory Evaluation, 1058
Full-Range Picture Vocabulary Test, 1059
The Fullerton Language Test for Adolescents, Second Edition, 1060
Functional Communication Profile, 1061
Functional Fitness Assessment for Adults over 60 Years, Second Edition, 1062
Functional Grammar Test, 1063
Functional Linguistic Communication Inventory, 1064
Functional Needs Assessment, 1065
Functional Performance Record, 1066
Functional Skills Screening Inventory, 1067
Functional Time Estimation Questionnaire, 1068

GAINS: A Pre-test and Post-test for Measuring Career Development Competency Progress, 1069
GAP Reading Comprehension Test, Third Edition, T4:1019
GAPADOL, T4:1020
The Gardner Children's Projective Battery, 1070
Gates-MacGinitie Reading Tests, 2nd Canadian Edition, 1071
Gates-MacGinitie Reading Tests, Third Edition, 1072
Gates-McKillop-Horowitz Reading Diagnostic Test, Second Edition, 1073
The Geist Picture Interest Inventory, 1074
General Ability Measure for Adults, 1075
General Chemistry Test: National Achievement Tests, 1076
General Clerical Ability Test: ETSA Test 3A, 1077
General Clerical Test, 1078
General Health Questionnaire, 1079
General Management In-Basket, 1080
General Mental Ability Test: ETSA Test 1A, 1081
General Physics Test: National Achievement Tests, 1082
General Processing Inventory, 1083
General Science Test, T4:1032
General Science Test: National Achievement Tests, 1084
The Gesell Child Developmental Age Scale,T4:1034
The Gesell Developmental Observation, 1085
Gesell Developmental Schedules, see Gesell Preschool Test, 1086
The Gesell Developmental Tests, see Gesell Developmental Observation, 1085
Gesell Developmental Tests, see Gesell Preschool Test, 1086
Gesell Preschool Test, 1086
The Gesell School Readiness Test, see Gesell Developmental Observation, 1085
Gibson Spiral Maze, Second Edition, 1087
Gifted and Talented Scale, 1088
Gifted Evaluation Scale, Second Edition, 1089
The Gifted Program Evaluation Survey, 1090
Gilliam Autism Rating Scale, 1091
Gillingham-Childs Phonics Proficiency Scales, T4:1041
Gilmore Oral Reading Test, 1092
Global Assessment Scale, 1093
GOALS®: A Performance-Based Measure of Achievement, 1094
Goldman-Fristoe Test of Articulation, 1095
Goldman-Fristoe-Woodcock Test of Auditory Discrimination, 1096
The Golombok Rust Inventory of Marital State, T4:1047
The Golombok Rust Inventory of Sexual Satisfaction, T4:1048

Goodenough Draw-a-Man Test, see Goodenough-Harris Drawing Test, 1097
Goodenough-Eagle modification of the Embedded Figures Test, see Children's Embedded Figures Test, 474
Goodenough-Harris Drawing Test, 1097
The Goodman Lock Box, 1098
The Gordon Diagnostic System, 1099
Gordon Occupational Check List II, 1100
Gordon Personal Profile—Inventory, 1101
Gottschaldt Figures, see Closure Flexibility (Concealed Figures), 548
Gottschaldt Figures [NIPR], T4:1054
Goyer Organization of Ideas Test, Form S (Revised), 1102
Graded Arithmetic-Mathematics Test, 1103
Graded Naming Test, 1104
Graded Word Spelling Test, Second Edition, 1105
Graduate and Managerial Assessment, 1106
Graduate Management Admission Test, 1107
Graduate Program Self-Assessment Service, 1108
Graduate Record Examinations: Aptitude and Advanced, see Graduate Record Examinations: Subject Tests, 1124
The Graduate Record Examinations Biochemistry, Cell and Molecular Biology Test, 1109
The Graduate Record Examinations Biology Test, 1110
The Graduate Record Examinations (General) Biology Test, see The Graduate Record Examinations Biology Test, 1110
The Graduate Record Examinations Chemistry Test, 1111
The Graduate Record Examinations Computer Science Test, 1112
The Graduate Record Examinations Economics Test, 1113
The Graduate Record Examinations Education Test, T4:1063
The Graduate Record Examinations Engineering Test, 1114
The Graduate Record Examinations—General Test, 1115
The Graduate Record Examinations Geology Test, 1116
The Graduate Record Examinations History Test, 1117
The Graduate Record Examinations Literature in English Test, 1118
The Graduate Record Examinations Mathematics Test, 1119
The Graduate Record Examinations Music Test, 1120
The Graduate Record Examinations Physics Test, 1121
The Graduate Record Examinations Political Science Test, T4:1072
The Graduate Record Examinations Psychology Test, 1122
The Graduate Record Examinations Sociology Test, 1123
Graduate Record Examinations: Subject Tests, 1124
Grammar Test Packet, 1125
Grammatical Analysis of Elicited Language—Pre-Sentence Level, 1126
Grammatical Analysis of Elicited Language—Simple Sentence Level, Second Edition, 1127
Grandparent Strengths and Needs Inventory, 1128
Grassi Basic Cognitive Evaluation, T4:1081
The Grassi Block Substitution Test: For Measuring Organic Brain Pathology, T4:1082
Gravidometer, 1129
Gray Oral Reading Tests—Diagnostic, 1130
Gray Oral Reading Tests—Third Edition, see Gray Oral Reading Tests—Diagnostic, 1130
Gray Oral Reading Tests, Third Edition, 1131
Gregorc Style Delineator, 1132
Grid Test of Schizophrenic Thought Disorder, 1133
The Grief Experience Inventory, 12:168
Griffiths Mental Development Scales [Revised], 1134
Grooved Pegboard Test, 1135
Group Achievement Identification Measure, 1136
Group Cohesiveness: A Study of Group Morale, 1137
Group Diagnostic Reading Aptitude and Achievement Tests, 1138
Group Diagnostic Reading Aptitude and Achievement Tests, Intermediate Form, 1139
Group Embedded Figures Test, 1140
Group Environment Scale, Second Edition, 1141
Group Inventory for Finding Creative Talent, 1142
Group Inventory For Finding Interests, 1143
Group Literacy Assessment, 1144
Group Mathematics Test, Second Edition, 1145
The Group Personality Projective Test, 1146
Group Process Questionnaire, 1147
Group Reading Test, see SPAR Spelling and Reading Tests, Third Edition, 2467
Group Reading Test, Fourth Edition, 1148
Group Shorr Imagery Test, 1149
Group Styles Inventory, 1150
Group Test for Indian South Africans, T4:1106
Group Test 82, 1151
Group Tests 70 and 70B, 1152
Group Tests 90A and 90B, 1153
Group Tests of Musical Abilities, 1154
GROW—The Marriage Enrichment Program, T4:1110
Guidance Test Battery for Secondary Pupils (Standard 8), T4:1111
Guide to the Assessment of Test Session Behavior for the WISC-III and the WIAT, 1155
The Guilford-Martin Inventory of Factors, see Guilford-Zimmerman Temperament Survey, 1158
The Guilford-Martin Personnel Inventory, see Guilford-Zimmerman Temperament Survey, 1158
The Guilford-Zimmerman Aptitude Survey, 1156
The Guilford-Zimmerman Interest Inventory, 1157
The Guilford-Zimmerman Temperament Survey, 1158

Hahnemann Elementary School Behavior Rating Scale, 1161
Hahnemann High School Behavior Rating Scale, 1162
Hall Occupational Orientation Inventory, 1163
Halstead-Reitan Neuropsychological Test Battery, 1164
Halstead Russell Neuropsychological Evaluation System, 1165
Hamilton Depression Inventory, 1166
Hammill Multiability Achievement Test, 1167
Hammill Multiability Intelligence Test, 1168
The Hand Test [Revised], 1169
Hand-Tool Dexterity Test, 1170
Hannah-Gardner Test of Verbal and Nonverbal Language Functioning, 1171
Hanson Silver Management Style Inventory, see Management Style Inventory [Hanson Silver Strong & Associates], 1562
Happiness Measures, 1172
Harding Skyscraper, T4:1125
Harding Stress-Fair Compatibility Test, T4:1126
Hare P-Scan, 1173
Hare Psychopathy Checklist–Revised, 1174
Hare Psychopathy Checklist: Screening Version, 1175
Harmonic Improvisation Readiness Record and Rhythm Improvisation Readiness Record, 1176
The Harrington-O'Shea Career Decision-Making System Revised, 1177
The Harrison-Stroud Reading Readiness Profiles, T4:1129
The Hartman Value Profile, T4:1130
Harvard Group Scale of Hypnotic Susceptibility, T4:1131
Hassles and Uplifts Scales, Research Edition, 1178
Hausa Speaking Test, 1179
Hay Aptitude Test Battery [Revised], 1180
Health and Daily Living, Second Edition, 1181
Health and Safety Education Test: National Achievement Tests, 1182
Health Attribution Test, 1183
Health Education Test: Knowledge and Application: Acorn National Achievement Tests, Revised Edition, 1184
Health Knowledge Test for College Freshmen: National Achievement Tests, 1185
Health Problems Checklist, 1186
Health Status Questionnaire, 1187
Health Test: National Achievement Tests, 1188
Healy Pictorial Completion Tests, 1189
The Hearing Measurement Scale, 1190
Hebrew Speaking Test, 1191
HELP Checklist (Hawaii Early Learning Profile), 1192
Help Desk Support Staff Selector, 1193
Help for Special Preschoolers ASSESSMENT CHECKLIST: Ages 3–6, 1194
Henderson-Moriarty ESL/Literacy Placement Test, 1195
Henmon-Nelson Ability Test, Canadian Edition, 1196
The Henmon-Nelson Tests of Mental Ability, T4:1150
Herrmann Brain Dominance Instrument [Revised], 1197
Heterosocial Adequacy Test, T4:1152
High Level Battery: Test A/75, 1198
High Level Estimation Test, T4:1154
High Level Figure Classification Test, 1199
High School Career-Course Planner, 1200
High School Characteristics Index, T4:1157
High School Interest Questionnaire, T4:1158
High School Personality Questionnaire, 1201
High School Placement Test-Open Edition, 1202
High School Reading Test: National Achievement Tests, 1203
High-School Subject Tests, T4:1161
High/Scope Child Observation Record for Ages 2 1/2–6, 1204
Highlands Dependency Questionnaire, see Self-Administered Dependency Questionnaire, 2350
Hill Interaction Matrix, 1205
Hill Performance Test of Selected Positional Concepts, 1206
Hilson Adolescent Profile, 1207
Hilson Adolescent Profile—Version S, 1208
Hilson Career Satisfaction Index, 1209
Hilson Personnel Profile/Success Quotient, 1210
The Hoffer-Osmond Diagnostic Test, T4:1168
Hogan Development Survey, 1211
Hogan Personality Inventory [Revised], 1212
Holden Psychological Screening Inventory, 1213
Holtzman Inkblot Technique, 1214
Home Environment Questionnaire, HEQ-2R and HEQ-1R, 1215
Home Observation for Measurement of the Environment, 1216
Home Screening Questionnaire, 1217
The Hooper Visual Organization Test, 1218
Hopkins Psychiatric Rating Scale, see Derogatis Psychiatric Rating Scale, 792
House-Tree-Person and Draw-A-Person as Measures of Abuse in Children: A Quantitative Scoring System, 1219
How A Child Learns, T4:1175
How Am I Doing? A Self-Assessment for Child Caregivers, 1220
How-I-Feel-Questionnaire, see State-Trait Anxiety Inventory for Children, 2498
How Supervise?, 1221
How Well Do You Know Your Interests, 1222
How Well Do You Know Yourself?, 1223
Howarth Mood Adjective Check List, T4:1180
Howarth Personality Questionnaire, T4:1181
Howell Prekindergarten Screening Test, 1224
H.R.R. Pseudoisochromatic Plates for Detecting, Classifying and Estimating the Degree of Defective Color Vision, 1159
H-T-P: House-Tree-Person Projective Technique, 1160

Hudson Education Skills Inventory, T4:1184
Hughes Basic Gross Motor Assessment, 1225
Human Figure Drawing Test, 1226
Human Information Processing Survey, 1227
Human Loyalty Expressionaire, 1228
Human Relations Inventory, 1229
Humanics National Child Assessment Form [Revised], 1230
The Hundred Pictures Naming Test, 1231
Hunter-Grundin Literacy Profiles, 1232
Hutchins Behavior Inventory, 12:184

ICES: Instructor and Course Evaluation System, T4:1194
IDEA, see IDEA Student Ratings of Instruction, 1236
IDEA Feedback for Department Chairs, 1233
IDEA Oral Language Proficiency Test, 1234
IDEA Reading and Writing Proficiency Test, 1235
IDEA Student Ratings of Instruction, 1236
IDEAS: Interest Determination, Exploration and Assessment System™, 1237
The Identi-Form System for Gifted Programs, 1238
The IES Test, 1239
Illinois Course Evaluation Questionnaire, T4:1201
Illinois Test of Psycholinguistic Abilities, Revised Edition, 1240
Illness Behaviour Questionnaire, Third Edition, 1241
Imagery and Disease, 1242
Imagery of Cancer, see Imagery and Disease, 1242
Impact Message Inventory, Research Edition, 1243
Incentives Management Index, 1244
Independent Living Behavior Checklist, 1245
Independent Living Scales, 1246
Independent Mastery Testing System for Math Skills, 1247
Independent Mastery Testing System for Writing Skills, 1248
Independent School Entrance Examination, 1249
Index of Personality Characteristics, T4:1210
Indiana-Oregon Music Discrimination Test, T4:1212
Indiana Physical Fitness Test, T4:1211
Indiana Student Scale: A Measure of Self-Esteem, 1250
Individual Directions Inventory, 1251
Individual Scale for Indian South Africans, T4:1213
Individual Service Strategy Portfolio, 1252
Individual Style Survey, 1253
Individualised Classroom Environment Questionnaire, 1254
Individualized Criterion Referenced Testing 12011107
Indonesian Speaking Test, 1255
Industrial Reading Test, 1256
The Industrial Sentence Completion Form, T4:1220
Industrial Test Battery, 1257
The Infanib, 1258
Infant Development Inventory, 1259
Infant Index, 1260
Infant Mullen Scales of Early Learning, see Mullen Scales of Early Learning: AGS Edition, 1728
The Infant Reading Tests, 1261
Infant Screening, 1262
Infant-Toddler Developmental Assessment, 1263
Infant/Toddler Environment Rating Scale, 1264
Infant/Toddler Symptom Checklist, 1265
Inferred Self-Concept Scale, 1266
Influence Strategies Exercise, 1267
The Influence Styles Inventory, 1268
Informal Reading Comprehension Placement Test [Revised], 1269
Information System Skills, 1270
Information Test on Drugs and Drug Abuse, T4:1231
Information Test on Human Reproduction, T4:1232
Information Test on Smoking and Health, T4:1233
Informeter: An International Technique for the Measurement of Political Information, 1271
Initial Placement Inventory, 1272
Inquiry Mode Questionnaire: A Measure of How You Think and Make Decisions, 12:189
INSIGHT Inventory [Revised], 1273
Institutional Goals Inventory, T4:1238
Institutional SAT Program (Institutional SAT I: Reasoning Test and SAT II: Subject Tests), 1274
The Instructional Environment System—II, 1275
Instructional Leadership Evaluation and Development Program (ILEAD), 1276
Instructional Skills Assessment, 1277
Instructional Styles Inventory, see Canfield Instructional Styles Inventory, 391
Instrument for Disability Screening [Developmental Edition], 1278
Instrument Technician, 1279
Instrument Timbre Preference Test, 1280
Integrated Assessment System®, 1281
Integrated Literature and Language Arts Portfolio Program, 12:191
Integrated Visual and Auditory Continuous Performance Test, 1282
Integrated Writing Test, 1283
INteraction CHecklist for Augmentative Communication, Revised Edition, 1284
Interaction Index, 13:154
Interest Explorer, 1285
Intermediate Booklet Category Test, 1286
Intermediate Mathematics Test I, see Mathematics Attainment Test DE2, 1597
Intermediate Measures of Music Audiation, 1287
Intermediate Personality Questionnaire for Indian Pupils (Standards 6 to 8), T4:1250
Intermediate Visual and Auditory Continuous Performance Test, see Integrated Visual and Auditory Continuous Performance Test, 1282
Internalizing Symptoms Scale for Children, 1288
Interpersonal Adjective Scales, 1289

Interpersonal Behavior Survey, 1290
Interpersonal Check List, 1291
Interpersonal Communication Inventory, 1292
Interpersonal Conflict Scale, see Partner Relationship Inventory (Research Edition), 1895
Interpersonal Relations Questionnaire, 1293
Interpersonal Style Inventory, 1294
Interpersonal Style Questionnaire, 1295
Interpersonal Trust Surveys, 1296
Intra- and Interpersonal Relations Scale, 1297
Intrex Questionnaires, 1298
Intuitive Mechanics (Weights & Pulleys), 1299
Inventory for Client and Agency Planning, 1300
Inventory for Counseling & Development, T4:1261
Inventory No. II, 1301
Inventory of Anger Communication, 1302
An Inventory of Certain Feelings, 1303
Inventory of Drinking Situations, 1304
Inventory of Drug Taking Situations, 1305
Inventory of Factors STDCR, see The Guilford-Zimmerman Temperament Survey, 1158
Inventory of Interests, 1306
Inventory of Language Abilities, T4:1267
Inventory of Language Abilities, Level II, T4:1268
Inventory of Learning Processes–R, 1307
Inventory of Perceptual Skills, 1308
Inventory of Positive Thinking Traits, 1309
An Inventory of Religious Activities and Interests, 1310
Inventory of Suicide Orientation-30, 1311
Inventory of Vocational Interests: Acorn National Aptitude Tests, 1312
Inwald Personality Inventory [Revised], 1313
Inwald Survey 5, 1314
Iowa Algebra Aptitude Test, Fourth Edition, 1315
Iowa Parent Behavior Inventory, 1316
Iowa Social Competency Scales, 1317
Iowa Tests of Basic Skills, Forms K, L, and M, 1318
Iowa Tests of Educational Development, Forms K, L, and M, 1319
Iowa Tests of Music Literacy, Revised, 1320
Iowa's Severity Rating Scales for Speech and Language Impairments, 12:196
The IPAT Anxiety Scale, 1321
IPAT Depression Scale, 1322
IPI Job-Tests Program, 1323
IPMA Correctional Officer Test, 1324
IPMA Fire Service Tests, 1325
IPMA Police Service Tests, 1326
Irenometer, 1327
IS Manager/Consultant Skills Evaluation, 1328
IS Project Leader Skills Evaluation, 1329
IS Sales Assessment Battery, 1330
Is This Autism? A Checklist of Behaviours and Skills for Children Showing Autistic Features, see The Autistic Continuum: An Assessment and Intervention Schedule, 235
I-SPEAK Your Language™: A Survey of Personal Styles, 1331
It Scale for Children, 1332

Jackson Personality Inventory—Revised, 1333
Jackson Vocational Interest Survey [1995 Revision], 1334
Jacobsen-Kellogg Self Description Inventory II, T4:1298
Jail Inmate Inventory, 1335
Jansky Diagnostic Battery, 1336
Jansky Screening Index, 1337
Jenkins Activity Survey, 1338
Jenkins Non-Verbal Test, 1986 Revision, 1339
JEVS Work Sample Evaluation System, T4:1304
Jesness Behavior Checklist, 1340
The Jesness Inventory, 1341
JIIG-CAL Occupational Interests Guide, 1342
Job Activity Preference Questionnaire, 1343
[Job Application Forms], T4:1307
Job Attitude Analysis, 1344
Job Attitude Scale, 1345
Job Awareness Inventory, 1346
A Job Choice Decision-Making Exercise, 1347
The Job Descriptive Index, see Job Descriptive Index (1997 Revision) and The Job in General Scales, 1348
Job Descriptive Index (1997 Revision) and The Job in General Scales, 1348
Job Descriptive Index and Retirement Descriptive Index, see Job Descriptive Index (1997 Revision) and The Job in General Scales, 1348
Job Ideas and Information Generator-Computer Assisted Learning, see JIIG-CAL Occupational Interests Guide, 1342
Job Interactions Inventory, 1349
JOB-O, 1350
Job Search Inventory, 1351
Job Seeking Skills Assessment, 1352
Job Skills Tests, 1353
Job Stress Survey, 1354
Job Style Indicator, 1355
Job-Tests Program, see IPI Job-Tests Program, 1323
Job Training Assessment Program, T4:1318
Jobmatch, 1356
The John Test, T4:1320
Johnson-Kenney Screening Test, 1357
Johnson Temperament Analysis, see Taylor-Johnson Temperament Analysis [1992 Edition], 2618
Johnston Informal Reading Inventory, 1358
Joliet 3-Minute Preschool Speech and Language Screen, 1359
Joliet 3-Minute Speech and Language Screening, see Joliet 3-Minute Speech and Language Screen (Revised), 1360
Joliet 3-Minute Speech and Language Screen (Revised), 1360

The Jones-Mohr Listening Test, 1361
Jordan Left-Right Reversal Test (1990 Edition), 1362
Joseph Pre-School and Primary Self-Concept Screening Test, 1363
Journalism Test, 1364
Jr.-Sr. High School Personality Questionnaire, see High School Personality Questionnaire, 1201
Judgement of Occupational Behavior-Orientation, see JOB-O, 1350
Jung Personality Questionnaire, 1365
Jungian Type Survey: The Gray-Wheelwrights Test (16th Revision), 1366
Junior Aptitude Tests for Indian South Africans, T4:1330
Junior Eysenck Personality Inventory, 1367
Junior High School Mathematics Test: Acorn Achievement Tests, 1368
Junior High School Test of Economics, see Test of Economic Knowledge, 2685
Junior Personality Quiz, see High School Personality Questionnaire, 1201
Junior Rating Scale, 1369
Junior Scholastic Proficiency Battery, T4:1334
Junior South African Individual Scales, 1370
Just-in-Time Training Assessment Instrument, 1371
Juvenile Automated Substance Abuse Evaluation, 1372
Juvenile Justice Policy Inventory, 1373

Kagan Affective Sensitivity Scale, 1374
Kahn Intelligence Tests, see Kahn Intelligence Tests: Experimental Form, 1375
Kahn Intelligence Tests: Experimental Form, 1375
Kahn Stick Figure Personality Test, see The Group Personality Projective Test, 1146
Kahn Test of Symbol Arrangement, 1376
Kasanin-Hanfmann Concept Formation Test, see Modified Vygotsky Concept Formation Test, 1714
Katz Adjustment Scale, T4:1340
Katz-Zalk Opinion Questionnaire, 1377
Kaufman Adolescent and Adult Intelligence Test, 1378
Kaufman Assessment Battery for Children, 1379
Kaufman Brief Intelligence Test, 1380
Kaufman Developmental Scale, 1381
Kaufman Functional Academic Skills Test, 1382
Kaufman Infant and Preschool Scale, 1383
Kaufman Short Neuropsychological Assessment Procedure, 1384
Kaufman Survey of Early Academic and Language Skills, 1385
Kaufman Test of Educational Achievement [1998 Normative Update], 1386
Keegan Type Indicator, 1387
Keele Pre-School Assessment Guide, 1388
Kelvin Measurement of Ability in Infant Classes, 1389
Kendrick Assessment Scales of Cognitive Ageing, 1390
Kendrick Battery for the Detection of Dementia in the Elderly, see Kendrick Assessment of Cognitive Ageing, 1390
Kendrick Cognitive Tests for the Elderly, see Kendrick Assessment of Cognitive Ageing, 1390
Kent Infant Development Scale, see Kent Inventory of Developmental Skills [1996 Standardization], 1391
Kent Inventory of Developmental Skills [1996 Standardization], 1391
Kent-Rosanoff Word List, see Association Adjustment Inventory, 218
Keyboard Skills Test, T4:1354
KeyMath Revised: A Diagnostic Inventory of Essential Mathematics [1998 Normative Update], 1392
KEYS: Assessing the Climate for Creativity, 1393
Khan-Lewis Phonological Analysis, 1394
Khatena-Morse Multitalent Perception Inventory, 1395
Khatena Torrance Creative Perception Inventory, 1396
Kilander-Leach Health Knowledge Test, T4:1357
Kilmann-Saxton Culture-Gap Survey [Revised], 1397
Kilmanns Organizational Belief Survey, 1398
Kindergarten Language Screening Test, Second Edition, 1399
Kindergarten Readiness Test, 1400
Kindergarten Screening Inventory, T4:1361
Kinetic Drawing System for Family and School: A Handbook, 1401
Kipnis-Schmidt Profiles of Organizational Influence Strategies, 1402
The Kirkpatrick Management and Supervisory Skills Series, 1403
Kirton Adaption-Innovation Inventory [1998 Edition], 1404
Kit of Factor Referenced Cognitive Tests, 1405
Kit of Reference Tests for Cognitive Factors, see Kit of Factor Referenced Cognitive Tests, 1405
Knowledge of Occupations Test, 1406
Knox's Cube Test, 1407
Kohlberg's Moral Judgment Interview, 1408
The Kohlman Evaluation of Living Skills, 1409
Kohn Problem Checklist/Kohn Social Competence Scale, 13:171
The Kohs Block-Design Test, 1410
Kolbe Conative Index, 1411
Krantz Health Opinion Survey, 1412
Kuder General Interest Survey, Form E, 1413
Kuder Occupational Interest Survey, Revised (Form DD), 1985, T4:1375
Kuder Preference Record—Vocational, T4:1376
Kuhlmann-Anderson Tests, Eighth Edition, 1414
Kundu Introversion Extroversion Inventory, 1415
Kundu Neurotic Personality Inventory, 1416
Kwalwasser Music Talent Test, T4:1380

La Monica Empathy Profile, 1417
La Prueba de Realizacion, Segunda Edicion, 1418
The Lake St. Clair Incident, 1419

Language Arts Assessment Portfolio, 13:172
Language Assessment Battery, T4:1385
Language Assessment Scales, see Language Assessment Scales—Oral, 1420
Language Assessment Scales, see Language Assessment Scales, Reading and Writing, 1421
Language Assessment Scales—Oral, 1420
Language Assessment Scales, Reading and Writing, 1421
Language Facility Test, 1422
Language Imitation Test, 1423
Learning Preference Assessment, see Self-Directed Learning Readiness Scale, 2359
Language Processing Test, 1424
Language Proficiency Test, 1425
Language Proficiency Tests, T4:1392
Language Proficiency Test Series, 1426
Language Sampling, Analysis, and Training—Third Edition, 1427
Language Sampling and Analysis, T4:1394
Language-Structured Auditory Retention Span Test, T4:1395
The Laurita-Trembley Diagnostic Word Processing Test, 1428
Law Enforcement Assessment and Development Report, 1429
Law Enforcement Candidate Record, 1430
Law Enforcement Perception Questionnaire, T4:1399
The LAW-PSI Adult Life History Questionnaire, 1431
The LAW-PSI Child/Adolescent Life History Questionnaire, 1432
LAW-PSI Sexual History Questionnaire, 1433
Law School Admission Test, 1434
The Lawrence Psychological Forensic Examination, 1435
Leader Behavior Analysis II, 1436
Leader Behavior Description Questionnaire, Form 12, 1437
Leader Behavior Questionnaire, Revised, 1438
The Leadership Ability Evaluation, 1439
Leadership and Self-Development Scale, 1440
Leadership Appraisal Survey, 1441
Leadership Competency Inventory, 1442
Leadership Effectiveness Analysis, 1443
Leadership Opinion Questionnaire, 1444
Leadership Practices Inventory—Delta, 1445
Leadership Practices Inventory—Individual Contributor [Second Edition], 1446
Leadership Practices Inventory [Management Research Associates], 1447
Leadership Practices Inventory [Pfeiffer & Company International Publishers], 1448
The Leadership Q-Sort Test (A Test of Leadership Values), 1449
Leadership Skills Inventory, T4:1413
Leadership Skills Inventory [Consulting Resource Group], 1450
Leading Edge Portrait, 1451
Learned Behaviors Profile—Self/Other, 1452
Learning Ability Profile, 1453
Learning and Memory Battery, 1454
Learning and Study Strategies Inventory, 1455
Learning and Study Strategies Inventory—High School Version, 1456
Learning Behaviors Scale, Research Edition, 1457
The Learning Channel Preference Checklist, 1458
Learning Disabilities Diagnostic Inventory, 1459
Learning Disability Evaluation Scale (Renormed), 1460
Learning Disability Rating Procedure, 1461
Learning Efficiency Test-II (1992 Revision), 1462
Learning Environment Inventory, T4:1424
Learning Inventory of Kindergarten Experiences, 12:216
Learning Methods Test, T4:1426
Learning Organization Practices Profile, 1463
Learning Preference Inventory, 1464
Learning Preference Scales, 1465
Learning Process Questionnaire, 1466
Learning Skills Profile, 1467
Learning Style Identification Scale, 1468
Learning-Style Inventory [McBer and Company], 1469
Learning Style Inventory [Price Systems, Inc.], 1470
Learning-Style Inventory, Revised Scoring, 1471
Learning Style Profile, 1472
Learning Styles and Strategies, 1473
Learning Styles Inventory [Creative Learning Press, Inc.], 1474
Learning Styles Inventory [Educational Activities, Inc.], 1475
Learning Styles Inventory [Humanics Media], see Canfield Learning Styles Inventory, 392
Learning Styles Inventory [Piney Mountain Press, Inc.], 1476
Learning Through Listening, 1477
Learning/Working Styles Inventory, 1478
Leatherman Leadership Questionnaire [Revised], 1479
Leatherman Leadership Questionnaire: 360 degree Leadership Profile, 1480
Leeds Scales for the Self-Assessment of Anxiety and Depression, 1481
Leisure Activities Blank, T4:1441
The Leisure Diagnostic Battery, 12:220
Leisure Interest Inventory, 1482
Leisure Search Inventory, see Leisure/Work Search Inventory, 1483
Leisure/Work Search Inventory, 1483
The Leiter Adult Intelligence Scale, 1484
Leiter International Performance Scale—Revised, 1485
Leiter-Partington Adult Performance Scale, see The Leiter Adult Intelligence Scale, 1484
Let's Talk Inventory For Children, T4:1447
The Level of Service Inventory—Revised, 1486
Level of Service Inventory—Revised: Screening Version, 1487
Levine-Pilowsky [Depression] Questionnaire, 1488

Lewis Counseling Inventory, 1489
Lexington Developmental Scales, 1490
Library Skills, 1491
The Life Adjustment Inventory, 1492
Life Event Scales for Children and Adolescents, see Coddington Life Events Scales, 557
Life Experiences Checklist, 12:221
Life Roles Inventory, 1493
Life Skills, Forms 1 and 2, T4:1456
Life Space Analysis Profile, 1494
Life Stressors and Social Resources Inventory—Adult Form, 1495
Life Stressors and Social Resources Inventory—Youth Form, 1496
Life Style Questionnaire, 1497
Life Styles Inventory, 1498
Life Themes Inventory, T4:1460
Lifestyle Assessment Questionnaire, 1499
Light's Retention Scale [Revised Edition 1991], 1500
Ligondé Equivalence Test, 1501
The Lincoln-Oseretsky Motor Development Scale, 1502
Lindamood Auditory Conceptualization Test, Revised Edition, 1503
Linguistic Awareness in Reading Readiness, 1504
Listen Up: Skills Assessment, 1505
Listening Comprehension, T4:1467
Listening Comprehension Test, 1506
Listening Comprehension Test in English, T4:1469
The Listening for Meaning Test, 1507
Listening Styles Profile, 1508
Literature Tests/Objective, see Literature Tests/Objective and Essay, 1509
Literature Tests/Objective and Essay, 1509
Living in the Reader's World: Locator Test, 1510
Living Language, 1511
LOCO (Learning Opportunities Coordination): A Scale for the Assessment of Coordinated Learning Opportunities in Living Units for People with a Handicap, 1512
Loewenstein Occupational Therapy Cognitive Assessment, 1513
Logical Reasoning, 1514
The Lollipop Test: A Diagnostic Screening Test of School Readiness—Revised, 1515
London House Personnel Selection Inventory, see Personnel Selection Inventory, 1972
London Reading Test, 1516
Longitudinal Interval Follow-up Evaluation, 2nd Edition, 1517
Looking at MySELF, 1518
Lore Leadership Assessment, 1519
Lorimer Braille Recognition Test: A Test of Ability in Reading Braille Contractions, 1520
Lorr Outpatient Mood Scale, see Profile of Mood States, 2076
LOTE Reading and Listening Tests, 1521
Louisville Behavior Checklist, 1522
A Love Attitudes Inventory, T4:1485
Love Factor Inventory, see Personal Relationship Inventory, 1946
Lucas Grason-Stadler Audiometers, 1523
Luria-Nebraska Neuropsychological Battery: Children's Revision, 1524
Luria-Nebraska Neuropsychological Battery: Forms I and II, 1525

M-Scale: An Inventory of Attitudes Toward Black/White Relations in the United States, 1526
MAC Checklist for Evaluating, Preparing, and/or Improving Standardized Tests for Limited English Speaking Students, 1527
MacArthur Communicative Development Inventories, 1528
The Macmillan Diagnostic Reading Pack, 1529
Macmillan Graded Word Reading Test, 1530
Macmillan Group Reading Test, 1531
Macmillan Reader Placement Test, 1532
MacQuarrie Test for Mechanical Ability, 1533
Maculaitis Assessment Program, Commercial Edition, 1534
Maferr Inventory of Feminine Values, 1535
Maferr Inventory of Masculine Values, 1536
Maintaining Reading Efficiency Tests, see Reading Efficiency Tests, 2174
Maintest—Forms NC-1, B, C, 1537
Major Field Tests, 1538
The Major-Minor-Finder, 1986-1996 Edition, 1539
Make A Picture Story, 1540
Making a Terrific Career Happen, 1541
Making Work Teams Work, 1542
Malingering Probability Scale, 1543
Management and Graduate Item Bank, 1544
Management & Leadership Systems, 1545
Management Appraisal Survey, 1546
Management Change Inventory, 1547
Management Coaching Relations [Revised], 1548
Management Development Profile, see SkillScan for Management Development, 2424
Management Effectiveness Analysis, 1549
Management Effectiveness Profile System, 1550
Management Interest Inventory, 1551
Management Inventory on Leadership and Motivation, see Management Inventory on Leadership, Motivation and Decision-Making, 1552
Management Inventory on Leadership, Motivation and Decision-Making, 1552
Management Inventory on Managing Change, 1553
Management Inventory on Modern Management, 1554
Management Inventory on Performance Appraisal and Coaching, 1555
Management Inventory on Time Management, 1556
Management of Differences Inventory, 1557
Management Practices Audit, see Management Effectiveness Profile System, 1550

Management Practices Update, 1558
Management Relations Survey, 1559
Management Situation Checklist, 1560
Management Style Diagnosis Test, Third Edition, 1561
Management Style Inventory [Hanson Silver Strong & Associates], 1562
Management Style Inventory [Training House, Inc.], 1563
Management Styles Inventory, 1564
Management Transactions Audit, 1565
Manager Profile Record, 1566
Manager Style Appraisal, 1567
Manager/Supervisor Staff Selector, 1568
Managerial and Professional Job Functions Inventory, 1569
Managerial Assessment of Proficiency MAP™, 1570
Managerial Competence Index, 1571
Managerial Competence Review, 1572
Managerial Competency Questionnaire, 1573
Managerial Philosophies Scale, 1574
Managerial Style Questionnaire, 1575
Manchester Personality Questionnaire, 1576
The Manson Evaluation, Revised Edition, 1577
Manual Dexterity Test, 1578
MAPP: Motivational Appraisal of Personal Potential, 1579
Marianne Frostig Developmental Test of Visual Perception, Third Edition, see Developmental Test of Visual Perception, Second Edition, 816
Marital Check-Up Kit, 13:192
A Marital Communication Inventory, 1580
Marital Evaluation Checklist, 1581
Marital Satisfaction Inventory—Revised, 1582
A Marriage Adjustment Form, T4:1539
A Marriage Analysis, Experimental Edition, T4:1540
The Marriage and Family Attitude Survey, 1583
A Marriage Evaluation, T4:1542
The Marriage Expectation Inventories, T4:1543
Marriage Inventory, T4:1544
A Marriage Prediction Schedule, T4:1545
A Marriage Role Expectation Inventory, T4:1546
Marriage Scale (For Measuring Compatibility of Interests), 1584
Martin S-D Inventory, 1585
Martinek-Zaichkowsky Self-Concept Scale for Children, 1586
Maryland Addictions Questionnaire, 1587
Maryland/Baltimore County Design for Adult Basic Education, 1588
Maryland Parent Attitude Survey, 1589
Maryland Test Behavior Checklist, see Psychometric Behavior Checklist, 2116
Maslach Burnout Inventory, 1590
Matching Assistive Technology & Child, 1591
Matching Familiar Figures Test, 1592
Matching Person and Technology, 1593
MATE [Marital ATtitude Evaluation], 1594
Mathematical Olympiads, 1595
Mathematics Attainment Test C1, 1596
Mathematics Attainment Test DE2, 1597
Mathematics Attainment Test EF, 1598
Mathematics Attitude Inventory, 1599
Mathematics Competency Test, 1600
Mathematics 8–12, 1601
Mathematics Self-Efficacy Scale, 1602
Mathematics 7, 1603
A Mathematics Test for Grades Four, Five and Six, 1604
Mathematics Test for Seniors, T4:1563
Mathematics Test: McGraw-Hill Basic Skills System, T4:1564
Mathematics Topic Pre-Tests, 1605
Mather-Woodcock Group Writing Tests, 1606
Matrix Analogies Test, 1607
Maudsley Personality Inventory, see Eysenck Personality Inventory, 998
Maudsley Personality Inventory, T4:1567
The MbM Questionnaire: Managing by Motivation, Third Edition, 1608
McCall-Crabbs Standard Test Lessons in Reading, 1609
McCarron-Dial System, 1610
McCarthy Individualized Diagnostic Reading Inventory, Revised Edition, 1611
McCarthy Scales of Children's Abilities, 1612
McCarthy Screening Test, 1613
McCormick Job Performance Measurement "Rates-Scales", T4:1573
McDowell Vision Screening Kit, 1614
The McGill Pain Questionnaire, 1615
The McGuire-Bumpus Diagnostic Comprehension Test, T4:1574
The mCircle Instrument, T4:1575
McLeod Phonic Worksheets, T4:1576
MD5 Mental Ability Test, 1616
MDS Vocational Interest Exploration System, 1617
Meadow-Kendall Social-Emotional Assessment Inventory for Deaf and Hearing Students, 1618
Means-Ends Problem-Solving Procedure, 1619
Measure of Achieving Tendency, 1620
Measure of Arousal Seeking Tendency, see Arousal Seeking Tendency Scale, 181
Measure of Child Stimulus Screening and Arousability, 1621
Measure of Individual Differences in Dominance-Submissiveness, 1622
Measure of Questioning Skills, 1623
Measurement of Counselor Competencies: A Self-Assessment, 1624
The Measurement of Moral Judgment, 1625
Measurement of Self Concept in Kindergarten Children, T4:1587
Measures in Post Traumatic Stress Disorder: A Practitioner's Guide, 1626

Measures of Affiliative Tendency and Sensitivity to Rejection, 1627
Measures of Individual Differences in Temperament, 1628
Measures of Language Skills for Two- to Seven-Year-Old Children, see Child Language Ability Measures, 455
Measures of Musical Abilities, 1629
Measures of Pleasure-, Arousal-, and Dominance-Inducing Qualities of Parental Attitudes, 1630
Measures of Psychosocial Development, 1631
Mechanical Aptitude Test: Acorn National Aptitude Tests, 1632
Mechanical Aptitudes, 1633
Mechanical Comprehension Test, Second Edition, T4:1595
Mechanical Familiarity Test: ETSA Test 5A, 1634
Mechanical Knowledge Test: ETSA Test 6A, 1635
Mechanical Movements, 1636
MecTest (A Test for Maintenance Mechanics), 1637
Medical College Admission Test, 1638
Medical Ethics Inventory, 1639
Medical School Instructor Attitude Inventory, 1640
Meeker Behavioral Correlates, 1641
Melvin-Smith Receptive-Expressive Observation, 1642
Memory and Behavior Problems Checklist and The Burden Interview, 1643
Memory Assessment Scales, 1644
Memory-For-Designs Test, 1645
Menometer, 1646
Menstrual Distress Questionnaire, 1647
Mental Status Checklist for Adolescents, 1648
Mental Status Checklist for Adults, 1988 Revision, 1649
Mental Status Checklist for Children, 1650
Mentoring/Coaching Skills Assessment, see Mentoring Skills Assessment, 1651
Mentoring Skills Assessment, 1651
Mentoring Style Indicator, 1652
Merit Rating Series, T4:1613
Merrill-Palmer Scale of Mental Tests, 1653
The Meta Contrast Technique, 4th Edition, 1654
Meta-Motivation Inventory, 1655
Metaphon, 1656
Metropolitan Achievement Tests®, Seventh Edition, 1657
Metropolitan Performance Assessment: Integrated Performance Tasks, 1658
Metropolitan Readiness Tests, Sixth Edition, 1659
Meyer-Kendall Assessment Survey, 1660
Michigan Alcohol Screening Test, 1661
Michigan English Language Assessment Battery, 1662
Michigan Prescriptive Program in English, 1663
Michigan Test of Aural Comprehension, T4:1622
Michigan Test of English Language Proficiency, 1664
MicroCog: Assessment of Cognitive Functioning, 1665
Microcomputer User Aptitude Test, 1666
The MIDAS: Multiple Intelligence Developmental Assessment Scales, 1667
Middlesex Hospital Questionnaire, see Crown-Crisp Experiential Index, 739
Milani-Comparetti Motor Development Screening Test, 1668
MILCOM Patient Data Base System, 1669
Military Environment Inventory, 1670
Mill Hill Vocabulary Scale, 1671
Miller Analogies Test, 1672
Miller Assessment for Preschoolers, 1673
Miller Common Sense Scale, 1674
Miller Depression Scale, 1675
Miller Emotional Maturity Scale, 1676
Miller Getting Along With People Scale, 1677
Miller Happiness Scale, 1678
Miller Love Scale, 1679
Miller Marriage Satisfaction Scale, 1680
Miller Motivation Scale, 1681
Miller Psychological Independence Scale, 1682
Miller Self-Concept Scale, 1683
Miller Stress Scale, 1684
Millon Adolescent Clinical Inventory, 1685
Millon Adolescent Personality Inventory, see Millon Adolescent Clinical Inventory, 1685
Millon Behavioral Health Inventory, 1686
Millon Clinical Multiaxial Inventory—III [Second Edition], 1687
Millon Index of Personality Styles, 1688
MindMaker6, T4:1636
Miner Sentence Completion Scale, 1689
Mini Inventory of Right Brain Injury, 1690
Minneapolis Preschool Screening Instrument, 1691
Minnesota Child Development Inventory, see Child Development Inventory, 453
Minnesota Clerical Assessment Battery, 1692
Minnesota Clerical Test, 1693
Minnesota Computer Assessment, see Test of Variables of Attention (Version 7.03), 2720
Minnesota Importance Questionnaire, 1694
Minnesota Infant Development Inventory, see Infant Development Inventory, 1259
Minnesota Job Description Questionnaire, 1695
Minnesota Manual Dexterity Test, 1696
Minnesota Manual Dexterity Test, see Minnesota Rate of Manipulation Test, 1969 Edition, 1700
Minnesota Multiphasic Personality Inventory-2, 1697
Minnesota Multiphasic Personality Inventory-Adolescent, 1698
Minnesota Percepto-Diagnostic Test, Revised Edition, 1699
Minnesota PreKindergarten Inventory, see Preschool Development Inventory, 2040
Minnesota Preschool Inventory, see Preschool Development Inventory, 2040
Minnesota Rate of Manipulation Test, 1969 Edition, 1700

Minnesota Satisfaction Questionnaire, 1701
Minnesota Satisfactoriness Scales, 1702
Minnesota School Attitude Survey, T4:1651
Minnesota Spatial Relations Test, Revised Edition, 1703
Minnesota Test for Differential Diagnosis of Aphasia, 13:203
Mirror Edition of the Personal Values Inventory, 1704
Mirror-Couple Relationship Inventory, 1705
The Missouri Children's Picture Series, 1706
Missouri Kindergarten Inventory of Developmental Skills, Alternate Form, 1707
MKM Binocular Preschool Test, 1708
MKM Monocular and Binocular Reading Test, 1709
MKM Picture Arrangement Test, 1710
Mobile Vocational Evaluation, 1711
Modern Language Aptitude Test, T4:1661
Modern Occupational Skills Tests, 1712
Modern Photography Comprehension Test, 1713
The Modified Version of the Bender-Gestalt Test for Preschool and Primary School Children, T4:1664
Modified Vygotsky Concept Formation Test, 1714
Monitoring Basic Skills Progress—Second Edition, 1715
The Mooney Problem Check Lists, 1950 Revision, 1716
The Moreton Mathematics Tests, T4:1668
Morrisby Profile, 1717
Mossford Assessment Chart for the Physically Handicapped, 1718
The Mother-Child Relationship Evaluation, 1980 Edition, 12:242
Mother/Infant Communication Screening, 12:243
Motivated Skills Card Sort, 1719
Motivated Strategies for Learning Questionnaire, 1720
Motivation Analysis Test, 1721
Motivation Assessment Scale, 1722
Motivational Patterns Inventory, 1723
Motives, Values, Preferences Inventory, 1724
Motor-Free Visual Perception Test—Revised, 1725
Motor-Free Visual Perception Test—Vertical, 1726
Movement Assessment Battery for Children, 1727
Mullen Scales of Early Learning: AGS Edition, 1728
The Multidimensional Addictions and Personality Profile, 1729
Multidimensional Anxiety Scale for Children, 1730
Multidimensional Aptitude Battery, 1731
Multidimensional Assessment and Planning Form, 1732
Multidimensional Assessment of Philosophy of Education, T4:1680
Multidimensional Health Profile, 1733
The Multidimensional Maturity Scale, T4:1681
Multidimensional Self Concept Scale, 1734
The Multidimensional Self-Esteem Inventory, 1735
Multifactor Leadership Questionnaire, see Multifactor Leadership Questionnaire for Research, 1736
Multifactor Leadership Questionnaire for Research, 1736
Multifactor Leadership Questionnaire for Teams, 1737
Multilevel Academic Survey Test, 1738
Multilevel Informal Language Inventory, 1739
Multilingual Aphasia Examination, Third Edition, 1740
Multimedia Learning Styles, 1741
Multimodal Life History Questionnaire, 1742
Multiphasic Environmental Assessment Procedure, 1743
Multiphasic Sex Inventory, 1744
Multiple Affect Adjective Check List, Revised, 1745
Multiple Assessments, Programs, and Services (MAPS) of the College Board, 1746
The Multiple Purpose Self Trainer, 1747
Multiscore Depression Inventory, 1748
Multistate Professional Responsibility Examination, T4:1694
Multiscore Depression Inventory for Children, 1749
Murphy-Meisgeier Type Indicator for Children, 1750
Music Achievement Tests 1, 2, 3, and 4, 1751
Musical Aptitude Profile [1995 Revision], 1752
Musical Aptitude Test, 1753
Musical Talent Profile, see Musical Aptitude Profile [1995 Revision], 1752
Mutually Responsible Facilitation Inventory, T4:1699
My Class Inventory, T4:1700
My Vocational Situation, 1754
Myers-Briggs Type Indicator, Form M, 1755

Naglieri Nonverbal Ability Test, 1756
NASA Moon Survival Task, 1757
National Achievement Test [Second Edition], T4:1704
National Adult Reading Test, Second Edition, 1758
National Assessment of Educational Progress—-Released Exercises, 1759
National Educational Development Tests, 1760
National German Contest for High School Students, see National German Examination for High School Students, 1761
National German Examination for High School Students, 1761
National Institute for Personnel Research High Level Battery, see High Level Battery: Test A/75, 1198
National Institute for Personnel Research Normal Battery, 1762
National Police Officer Selection Test, 1763
National Proficiency Survey Series, T4:1711
National Spanish Examinations, 1764
[NCRI Achievement Tests in Hebrew], T4:1713
Neale Analysis of Reading Ability, Revised British Edition, 1765
NEEDS Survey, 1766
Nelson-Denny Reading Test, Forms G and H, 1767
The Nelson Reading Skills Test, Forms 3 and 4, 1768
NEO-4, 1769
The NEO Personality Inventory, see Revised NEO Personality Inventory, 2218
Neonatal Behavioral Assessment Scale, 3rd Edition, 1770

NEPSY: A Developmental Neuropsychological Assessment, 1771
Network Analyst Staff Selector, 1772
Network Technician Staff Selector, 1773
Neurobehavioral Assessment of the Preterm Infant, 13:207
Neurological Dysfunctions of Children, 1774
The Neuropsychological Impairment Scale, 1775
Neuropsychological Questionnaire, 1776
Neuropsychological Status Exam, 1777
Neuropsychology Behavior and Affect Profile, 1778
The Neuroticism Scale Questionnaire, 1779
New Jersey Test of Reasoning Skills—Form B, 1780
New Macmillan Reading Analysis, 1781
New South African Group Test, T4:1725
The New Sucher-Allred Reading Placement Inventory, T4:1726
New Technology Tests: Computer Commands, 1782
New Technology Tests: Computer Rules, 1783
NewGAP, 1784
Newsweek NewsQuiz, 1785
N.I.I.P. Engineering Apprentice Selection Test Battery, 1786
NIIP Engineering Arithmetic Test EA4, 1787
Nims Observation Checklist, 1788
19 Field Interest Inventory, 1789
1994 Strong Interest Inventory, 1790
The Nisonger Questionnaire for Parents, 1791
NOCTI Experienced Worker Assessments, 1792
NOCTI Industrial Assessments, 1793
NOCTI Job Ready Assessments, 1794
NOCTI SOCAT Tests, see NOCTI Job Ready Assessments, 1794
NOCTI TOCT Tests, see NOCTI Experienced Worker Assessments, 1792
Noncognitive Variables and Questionnaire, 1795
Non-Language Multi-Mental Test, 1796
Non-Language Test of Verbal Intelligence—Form 768, T4:1815
Non-Readers Intelligence Test, see Non-Reading Intelligence Tests, Levels 1-3, 1797
Non-Reading Intelligence Tests, Levels 1-3, 1797
Non-Verbal Ability Tests, 12:259
Nonverbal Form, 1798
Nonverbal Reasoning, 1799
Non-Verbal Reasoning Test, see Nonverbal Reasoning, 1799
Non-Verbal Tests, 1800
Normative Adaptive Behavior Checklist, 1801
Norris Educational Achievement Test, 1802
North American Depression Inventories for Children and Adults, 1803
Northwestern Syntax Screening Test, 1804
NPF [Second Edition], 1805
NTE Core Battery, T4:1824
NTE Core Battery, see The Praxis Series: Professional Assessments for Beginning Teachers, 2026
NTE Programs, T4:1825
NTE Specialty Area Tests: Agriculture, T4:1826
NTE Specialty Area Tests: Art Education, T4:1827
NTE Specialty Area Tests: Audiology, T4:1828
NTE Specialty Area Tests: Biology and General Science, T4:1829
NTE Specialty Area Tests: Business Education, T4:1830
NTE Specialty Area Tests: Chemistry, Physics, and General Science, T4:1831
NTE Specialty Area Tests: Early Childhood Education, T4:1832
NTE Specialty Area Tests: Education in the Elementary School, T4:1833
NTE Specialty Area Tests: Education of Mentally Retarded Students, T4:1834
NTE Specialty Area Tests: Educational Administration and Supervision, T4:1835
NTE Specialty Area Tests: English Language and Literature, T4:1836
NTE Specialty Area Tests: French, T4:1837
NTE Specialty Area Tests: German, T4:1838
NTE Specialty Area Tests: Home Economics Education, T4:1839
NTE Specialty Area Tests: Introduction to the Teaching of Reading, T4:1840
NTE Specialty Area Tests: Library Media Specialist, T4:1841
NTE Specialty Area Tests: Mathematics, T4:1842
NTE Specialty Area Tests: Music Education, T4:1843
NTE Specialty Area Tests: Physical Education, T4:1844
NTE Specialty Area Tests: Reading Specialist, T4:1845
NTE Specialty Area Tests: School Guidance and Counseling, T4:1846
NTE Specialty Area Tests: Social Studies, T4:1847
NTE Specialty Area Tests: Spanish, T4:1848
NTE Specialty Area Tests: Speech Communication, T4:1849
NTE Specialty Area Tests: Speech-Language Pathology, T4:1850
Number Test DE, 1806
Number Test 1, see Number Test DE, 1806
Nurse Aide Practice Test, 1807
Nutrition Information Test, T4:1854

OARS Multidimensional Functional Assessment Questionnaire, 1808
Oaster Stressors Scales, 1809
Object-Oriented Programmer Analyst, 1810
The Object Relations Technique, 1811
Objective-Analytic (O-A) Test Battery, T4:1858
Objective Tests in American History, see American History: Junior High—Objective, 145
Objective Tests in American History, see American History: Senior High—Objective, 146
Objective Tests in English, see Literature Tests/Objective and Essay, 1509

Objective Tests in World History, see World History/Objective Tests, 2932
O'Brien Vocabulary Placement Test, 1812
Observation Ability Test for the Police Service, 1813
Observation of Type Preference, 1814
Observational Emotional Inventory—Revised, 1815
Occupational Aptitude Survey see Occupational Aptitude Survey and Interest Schedule, Second Edition—Interest Schedule, 1817
Occupational Aptitude Survey and Interest Schedule, Second Edition—Aptitude Survey, 1816
Occupational Aptitude Survey and Interest Schedule, Second Edition—Interest Schedule, 1817
Occupational Interest Inventories, 1818
Occupational Interest Rating Scale, 1819
Occupational Interest Schedule, see Occupational Aptitude Survey and Interest Schedule, Second Edition—Aptitude Survey, 1816
Occupational Interests Card Sort, 1820
The Occupational Interests Explorer, 12:265
The Occupational Interests Surveyor, 12:266
Occupational Personality Assessment, 1821
Occupational Personality Questionnaire, 1822
Occupational Relationships Profile, 1823
Occupational Stress Indicator, 1824
Occupational Stress Inventory—Revised Edition, 1825
Occupational Test Series—Basic Skills Tests, 1826
Occupational Test Series: General Ability Tests, 1827
Occupational Type Profile, 1828
Occ-U-Sort, 1829
O'Connor Finger Dexterity Test, T4:1874
O'Connor Tweezer Dexterity Test, T4:1875
Oetting Michaels Anchored Ratings for Therapists, 1830
Oetting's Computer Anxiety Scale, 1831
Offer Self-Image Questionnaire for Adolescents, Revised, 1832
Office Arithmetic Test: ETSA Test 2A, 1833
Office Skills Achievement Test, 1834
Office Skills Series, 1835
Office Skills Tests, 1836
Office Systems Battery, 1837
Official GED Practice Test, 1838
Ohio Classification Test, see The Ohio Penal Classification Test, 1840
Ohio Functional Assessment Battery: Standardized Tests for Leisure and Living Skills, 1839
The Ohio Penal Classification Test, 1840
Ohio School Library/Media Test, T4:1886
The Ohio Tests of Articulation and Perception of Sounds, T4:1887
Ohio Vocational Interest Survey, Second Edition, 1841
Older Persons Counseling Needs Survey, 1842
Oliphant Auditory Discrimination Memory Test, T4:1890
Oliphant Auditory Synthesizing Test, T4:1891
Oliver Organization Description Questionnaire, 1843
Open System Assessment for Managers, T4:1893
Opinions About Deaf People Scale, 1844
Opinions Toward Adolescents, 1845
Optometry Admission Testing Program, 1846
Optometry College Admission Test, see Optometry Admission Testing Program, 1846
Oral and Written Language Scales: Listening Comprehension and Oral Expression, 1847
Oral and Written Language Scales: Written Expression, 1848
Oral English/Spanish Proficiency Placement Test, 1849
Oral Language Evaluation, Second Edition, 12:270
Oral Motor Assessment and Treatment: Improving Syllable Production, 1850
Oral-Motor/Feeding Rating Scale, 1851
Oral Speech Mechanism Screening Examination—Revised, 1852
Organic Dysfunction Survey Schedules, 1853
Organic Integrity Test, 1854
Organization Health Survey, 1855
Organizational Assessment Survey, 1856
Organizational Behavior Profile, 1857
Organizational Beliefs Questionnaire, 1858
Organizational Change-Readiness Scale, 1859
Organizational Climate Exercise II, 1860
Organizational Climate Index, T4:1905
Organizational Competence Index, 1861
Organizational Culture Inventory, 1862
Organizational Value Dimensions Questionnaire: Business Form, T4:1908
Orientation and Motivation Inventory, T4:1909
The Orientation Inventory, see Bass Orientation Inventory, 263
Orientation Test for Professional Accounting, 12:273
Original PSB-Aptitude for Practical Nursing Examination, see Revised PSB—Aptitude for Practical Nursing Examination, 2220
Orleans-Hanna Algebra Prognosis Test, Third Edition, 1863
The "Orton" Intelligence Test, No. 4, 1864
Oseretsky Tests of Motor Proficiency, see Bruininks-Oseretsky Test of Motor Proficiency, 353
Oseretsky Tests of Motor Proficiency, see The Lincoln-Oseretsky Motor Development Scale, 1502
OSOT Perceptual Evaluation, 1865
Otis-Lennon Mental Ability Test; Otis-Lennon School Ability Test, Sixth Edition, see Otis-Lennon School Ability Test, Seventh Edition, 1866
Otis-Lennon School Ability Test, Seventh Edition, 1866
Our Class and Its Work, 1867

PACE, 1868
PACS Pictures: Language Elicitation Materials, T4:1916
P-ACT+, see PLAN, 1997
Pain Apperception Test, 1869

Pain Assessment Battery, Research Edition, 1870
Pain Patient Profile, 1871
Pair Attraction Inventory, 1872
Paper and Pencil Games, 1873
P.A.R. Admissions Test, T4:1919
PAR: Proficiency Assessment Report, 1874
Parallel Spelling Tests, Second Edition, 1875
A Parent-Adolescent Communication Inventory, 1876
Parent-Adolescent Communication Scale, 1877
Parent As A Teacher Inventory [Revised], 1878
Parent Awareness Skills Survey, 1879
Parent Behavior Checklist, 1880
Parent Behavior Form, 1881
Parent-Child Communication Inventory, 1882
Parent-Child Relationship Inventory, 1883
Parent/Family Involvement Index, 1884
Parent Opinion Inventory, Revised Edition, 1885
Parent Perception of Child Profile, 1886
Parent Readiness Evaluation of Preschoolers, T4:1928
The Parenthood Questionnaire, 1887
Parenting Satisfaction Scale, 1888
Parenting Stress Index, Third Edition, 1889
Parents' Evaluation of Developmental Status, 1890
Parents' Observation of Study Behaviors Survey, 1891
Parker Team Player Survey, 1892
A Partial Index of Modernization: Measurement of Attitudes Toward Morality, 1893
Participative Management Survey, 1894
Partner Relationship Inventory (Research Edition), 1895
PathFinder—My Individual Career Plan, 1896
Pathways to Independence, Second Edition, 1897
Pattern Relations Test, T4:1941
The Patterned Elicitation Syntax Screening Test, see The Patterned Elicitation Syntax Test (Revised) with Morphonemic Analysis, 1898
The Patterned Elicitation Syntax Test (Revised) with Morphonemic Analysis, 1898
Paulhus Deception Scales: Balanced Inventory of Desirable Responding, 1899
PDI Employment Inventory and PDI Customer Service Inventory, 1900
Peabody Developmental Motor Scales and Activity Cards, 1901
Peabody Individual Achievement Test—Revised [1998 Normative Update], 1902
Peabody Picture Vocabulary Test-III, 1903
Peacock Profile, 1904
Pediatric Early Elementary Examination—II [Revised], 1905
Pediatric Evaluation of Disability Inventory, 1906
Pediatric Examination of Educational Readiness, 1907
Pediatric Examination of Educational Readiness at Middle Childhood [Revised], 1908
Pediatric Extended Examination at Three, 1909
PEEK—Perceptions, Expectations, Emotions, and Knowledge About College, 1910
Peg Board, 1911
Penguin Index, 1912
Pennsylvania Bi-Manual Worksample, T4:1951
People Performance Profile, 1913
The People Process, 1914
People Smarts: Behavioral Profiles, 1915
Perception of Ability Scale for Students, 1916
Perception-Of-Relationships-Test, 1917
Perceptions of Parental Role Scales, 1918
Perceptual Battery, see Blox Test, 321
The Perceptual Maze Test, T4:1956
Perceptual-Motor Assessment for Children & Emotional/Behavioral Screening Program, 1919
Per-Flu-Dex Tests, 1920
Performance Assessment of Syntax: Elicited and Spontaneous, T4:1959
Performance Levels of a School Program Survey, 1921
[Performance Review Forms], 1922
Performance Skills Leader, 1923
Persian Achievement Tests, T4:1962
Personal Achievement Formula, 1924
Personal Adjustability Test, see Personal Adjustment Index: ETSA Test 8A, 1926
Personal Adjustment and Role Skills Scale [Revised], 1925
Personal Adjustment Index: ETSA Test 8A, 1926
Personal Assessment of Intimacy in Relationships, 1927
Personal Audit, 1928
Personal Career Development Profile, see 16PF® Personal Career Development Profile, 2419
The Personal Communication Plan, 12:285
Personal Directions, 1929
Personal Distress Inventory and Scales, T4:1970
Personal Dynamics Profile, 1930
Personal Experience Inventory, 1931
Personal Experience Inventory for Adults, 1932
Personal Experience Screening Questionnaire, 1933
Personal History Checklist for Adults, 1934
A Personal Inventory, 1935
Personal Inventory of Needs, 1936
Personal Opinion Matrix, 1937
Personal Orientation Dimensions, 1938
Personal Orientation Inventory, 1939
The Personal Preference Scale, 1940
Personal Problems Checklist, see Personal Problems Checklist—Adult, 1941
Personal Problems Checklist—Adult, 1941
Personal Problems Checklist for Adolescents, 1942
Personal Profile System, T4:1982
Personal Questionnaire, 1943
Personal Questionnaire Rapid Scaling Technique, 1944
Personal Reaction Index, 1945
Personal Relations Inventory, T4:1986
Personal Relationship Inventory, 1946
Personal Resource Questionnaire, 1947
Personal Skills Map, 1948
Personal Stress Assessment Inventory, 1949
Personal Style Assessment, 1950

Personal Style Assessment, Jung-Parry Form, 1951
Personal Style Indicator, 1952
Personal Style Inventory, 1953
Personal Styles Inventory [PSI-120] [1999 Revision], 1954
Personal Success Profile, 1955
Personal Values Inventory, T4:1994
Personal Values Inventory [Personal Strengths Publishing], 1956
Personal Values Questionnaire, 1957
Personality Adjective Check List, 1958
Personality Assessment Inventory, 1959
Personality Assessment Screener, 1960
Personality Disorder Interview-IV: A Semistructured Interview for the Assessment of Personality Disorders, 1961
Personality Inventory for Children, Revised Format, 1962
Personality Inventory for Youth, 1963
Personality Rating Scale, 1964
Personality Research Form, 3rd Edition, 1965
PERSONALYSIS®, 1966
Personnel Assessment Selection System, 1967
[Personnel Interviewing Form], 1968
Personnel Performance Problems Inventory, 1969
Personnel Reaction Blank, 1970
Personnel Relations Survey [Revised], 1971
Personnel Selection Inventory, 1972
Personnel Test Battery, 1973
Personnel Tests for Industry, 1974
Pharmacy College Admission Test, 1975
Phase II Profile Integrity Status Inventory and ADdendum, 1976
Phelps Kindergarten Readiness Scale, 1977
Philadelphia Head Injury Questionnaire, 1978
Phonetic Reading Chain Oral Reading Diagnostic Decoding Test, 1979
Phonological Assessment Battery [Standardised Edition], 1980
Phonological Assessment of Child Speech, T4:2014
Phonological Process Analysis, 12:294
Phonological Processes Assessment and Intervention, T4:2015
Phonovisual Diagnostic Tests, [1975 Revision], 1981
Photo Articulation Test, Third Edition, 1982
PHSF Relations Questionnaire, 1983
Picha-Seron Career Analysis, 1984
Pictographic Self Rating Scale, 1985
Pictorial Interest Inventory, T4:2021
Pictorial Reasoning Test, 1986
The Pictorial Scale of Perceived Competence and Social Acceptance for Young Children, 1987
Pictorial Study of Values: Pictorial Allport-Vernon, T4:2023
Pictorial Test of Intelligence, T4:2024
Picture Articulation & Language Screening Test, T4:2025
Picture Identification Test, 1988
Picture Situation Test, T4:2027
Picture Test A, 1989
Picture Vocational Interest Questionnaire for Adults, 1990
Piers-Harris Children's Self-Concept Scale (The Way I Feel About Myself), 1991
A Pill Scale, 1992
The Pin Test, 1993
Pintner-Manikin Test, 1994
Pintner-Paterson Feature Profile Test, 1995
PIP Developmental Charts, Second Edition, 1996
PLAN, 1997
Plane Geometry: National Achievement Tests, 1998
Plane Trigonometry: National Achievement Tests, 1999
Planning Career Goals, 2000
Plant Worker Staff Selector, see Warehouse/Plant Worker Staff Selector, 2851
The Play Observation Scale, 2001
Police Promotion Tests—Complete Service, 2002
Police Selection Test, 2003
Politte Sentence Completion Test, 2004
Pollack-Branden Inventory, 2005
Polyfactorial Study of Personality, 2006
The Poppleton Allen Sales Aptitude Test, 2007
Porch Index of Communicative Ability, 2008
Porch Index of Communicative Ability in Children, T4:2048
Portable Tactual Performance Test, 2009
Porteous Problem Checklist, T4:2050
Porteus Mazes, 2010
Portland Digit Recognition Test, 2011
Portland Problem Behavior Checklist—Revised, 2012
Portrait of Overdone Strengths, 2013
Portrait of Personal Strengths, 2014
Portuguese Speaking Test, 2015
Position Analysis Questionnaire, 2016
Positive and Negative Syndrome Scale, 2017
Posttraumatic Stress Diagnostic Scale, 2018
Power and Performance Measures, 2019
Power Base Inventory, 2020
Power Management Inventory, 2021
Power Management Profile, 2022
Practical Maths Assessments, 2023
The Pragmatics Profile of Early Communication Skills, see Pragmatics Profile of Everyday Communication Skills in Children, 2025
Pragmatics Profile of Everyday Communication Skills in Adults, 2024
Pragmatics Profile of Everyday Communication Skills in Children, 2025
The Praxis Series: Professional Assessments for Beginning Teachers, 2026
Predictive Ability Test, Adult Edition, 2027
Predictive Screening Test of Articulation, 2028
PRE-LAS English, 2029
Preliminary Diagnostic Questionnaire, 2030

Preliminary SAT/National Merit Scholarship Qualifying Test, 2031
Preliminary Scholastic Aptitude Test, a shortened version of the College Board Scholastic Aptitude Test, see Preliminary SAT/National Merit Scholarship Qualifying Test, 2031
Preliminary Test of English as a Foreign Language, 2032
A Premarital Communication Inventory, 2033
The Premarital Counseling Kit, T4:2070
Premier PSB—Reading Comprehension Examination, see Revised PSB—Reading Comprehension Examination, 2223
PREPARE/ENRICH, 2034
Pre-Professional Skills Test, see The Praxis Series: Professional Assessments for Beginning Teachers, 2026
PreReading Expectancy Screening Scales, T4:2072
Pre-Referral Intervention Manual [Revised and Updated Second Edition], 2035
Preschool and Kindergarten Behavior Scales, 2036
Preschool and Kindergarten Interest Descriptor, 2037
Preschool and Kindergarten Performance Profile, T4:2075
Pre-School Behavior Checklist, 2038
The Preschool Behavior Questionnaire, 2039
Preschool Behavior Rating Scale, T4:2078
Preschool Development Inventory, 2040
Preschool Developmental Profile, 2041
Preschool Embedded Figures Test, 2042
The Preschool Evaluation Scale, 2043
Preschool Language Assessment Instrument, 2044
Preschool Language Scale–3, 2045
Preschool Performance Scale, see CID Preschool Performance Scale, 488
Preschool Screening Instrument, 2046
Preschool Screening System, 2047
Preschool Screening Test, see Preschool Skills Test, 2049
Preschool Self-Concept Picture Test, 2048
Preschool Skills Test, 2049
Prescriptive Reading Performance Test, T4:2089
Prescriptive Teaching Series, T4:2090
Present State Examination, 2050
The Press Test, 2051
The Preverbal Assessment-Intervention Profile, see Assessment for Persons Profoundly or Severely Impaired, 193
Pre-Verbal Communication Schedule, 2052
The Prevocational Assessment and Curriculum Guide, 2053
Prevocational Assessment Screen, 2054
Primary Academic Sentiment Scale, T4:2097
Primary Empathic Abilities, see Diplomacy Test of Empathy, 845
The Primary Language Screen, 2055
Primary Measures of Music Audiation, 2056
Primary Mechanical Ability Tests, 2057
Primary Reading Test, 2058
Primary Reading Test 1, see Reading Tests A and BD, 2185
Primary Reading Test 2, see Reading Tests A and BD, 2185
Primary Test of Cognitive Skills, 2059
Primary Test of Economic Understanding, 2060
Printing Performance School Readiness Test, 12:308
Prison Inmate Inventory, 2061
Problem Behavior Inventory [Adult & Adolescent Screening Forms], 2062
Problem Experiences Checklist, 2063
Problem-Solving Decision-Making Style Inventory, 2064
The Problem Solving Inventory, 2065
Process and Diagnostic Screening Test, see Structure of Intellect Learning Abilities Test, 2518
A Process for In-School Screening of Children with Emotional Handicaps, see Pupil Behavior Rating Scale, 2122
Process Skills Rating Scales, 12:310
Process Technician Test, 2066
Production and Maintenance Technician Test, 2067
Productive Practices Survey, 2068
Productivity Assessment Questionnaire, T4:2113
Productivity Environmental Preference Survey, 2069
Productivity Profile, 2070
Professional and Managerial Position Questionnaire, 2071
Professional Employment Test, 2072
Proficiency Battery in English and Mathematics for Indian South Africans, T4:2117
Profile of a School, 2073
Profile of Adaptation to Life, 2074
Profile of Adaptation to Life—Clinical Scale, see Profile of Adaptation to Life, 2074
Profile of Adaptation to Life—Holistic Scale, see Profile of Adaptation to Life, 2074
Profile of Aptitude for Leadership, 2075
Profile of Mood States, 2076
Profile of Mood States, Bi-Polar Form, 2077
Profile of Nonverbal Sensitivity, 2078
[Profiles from Rensis Likert Associates, Inc.], 2079
Profiles of Organizational Influence Strategies, see Kipnis-Schmidt Profiles of Organizational Influence Strategies, 1402
Profiles of Problem Solving, 2080
Program for Assessing Youth Employment Skills, 2081
Program for the Acquisition of Language with the Severely Impaired, 2082
Program Self-Assessment Service, 2083
Programmer Analyst Aptitude Test, see Programmer Analyst Aptitude Test Two-Hour Version, 2085
Programmer Analyst Aptitude Test One-Hour Version, 2084
Programmer Analyst Aptitude Test Two-Hour Version, 2085

Programmer Aptitude Battery, 2086
Programmer Aptitude/Competence Test System, T4:2132
Programmer Aptitude Series, 2087
Progress Assessment Chart of Social and Personal Development, 2088
Progress Assessment Chart of Social Development, see Progress Assessment Chart of Social and Personal Development, 2088
The Progress Evaluation Scales, T4:2135
Progress Tests in Maths, 2089
Progressive Achievement Test of Mathematics [Revised], 2090
Progressive Achievement Tests in Mathematics, 2091
Progressive Achievement Tests in Reading: Reading Comprehension and Reading Vocabulary Tests, 2092
Progressive Achievement Tests of Listening Comprehension [Revised], 2093
Progressive Achievement Tests of Reading [Revised], 2094
Progressive Achievement Tests of Study Skills, 2095
Progressive Matrices, see Raven Progressive Matrices, 2163
Project Implementation Profile, 2096
Project Management Competency Assessment, 2097
Project Management Knowledge & Skills Assessment, 2098
Projective Assessment of Aging Method, T4:2144
A Projective Index of Body Awareness, 2099
Proof-Reading Tests of Spelling, 2100
Prosody-Voice Screening Profile, 12:315
Prospector: Discovering the Ability to Learn and to Lead, 2101
Prout-Strohmer Personality Inventory, see Emotional Problems Scales, 931
Proverbs Test, 2102
PSB-Aptitude for Practical Nursing Examination, see Revised PSB—Aptitude for Practical Nursing Examination, 2220
PSB-Health Occupations Aptitude Examination, see Revised PSB—Health Occupations Aptitude Examination, 2221
PSB—Nursing School Aptitude Examination (R. N.), see Revised PSB—Nursing School Aptitude Examination (R. N.), 2222
PSB—Reading Comprehension Examination, see Revised PSB—Reading Comprehension Examination, 2223
PSC-Survey ADT, 2103
PSC Survey-SA, 2104
PSI Basic Skills Tests for Business, Industry, and Government, 2105
The Psychap Inventory, 2106
Psychiatric Diagnostic Interview—Revised, 2107
Psychiatric Evaluation Form, 2108
Psychiatric Outpatient Mood Scale, see Profile of Mood States, 2076
Psychotic Reaction Profile, see Psychotic Inpatient Profile, 2120
The Psychiatric Status Schedules: Subject Form, Second Edition, 2109
Psychodiagnostic Test Report Blank, 2110
Psychoeducational Profile Revised, 2111
Psycho-Epistemological Profile, 2112
Psycholinguistic Assessments of Language Processing in Aphasia, 2113
Psychologic and Neuropsychiatric Assessment Manual, 2114
Psychological Screening Inventory, 2115
Psychometric Behavior Checklist, 2116
Psychosocial Adjustment to Illness Scale, 2117
Psychosocial Pain Inventory [Revised], 2118
Psychotherapy Outcome Kit (Including Quality of Emotional Life Self-Report), 2119
Psychotic Inpatient Profile, 2120
PSYPERCEPT-170, 2121
Pupil Behavior Rating Scale, 2122
The Pupil Rating Scale Revised: Screening for Learning Disabilities, 2123
The Purdue High School English Test, T4:2166
Purdue Interest Questionnaire, 2124
Purdue Pegboard, 2125
The Purpose in Life Test, 2126
The Pyramid Scales, 2127

The Q-Tags Test of Personality, 2128
Quality Culture Assessment, 2129
Quality of Life Enjoyment and Satisfaction Questionnaire, 2130
Quality of Life Inventory, 2131
Quality of Life Questionnaire, 2132
The Quality of School Life Scale, T4:2173
Quality Potential Assessment, 2133
QUEST, 2134
A Questionnaire Measure of Individual Diffferences in Achieving Tendency, see Measure of Achieving Tendency, 1620
Questionnaire Measure of Stimulus Screening and Arousability, see Questionnaire Measure of Trait Arousability (Or Its Converse, Stimulus Screening), 2135
Questionnaire Measure of Trait Arousability (Or Its Converse, Stimulus Screening), 2135
Questionnaire On Resources and Stress, T4:2177
QUESTS: A Life-Choice Inventory, 2136
QUIC Tests, 2137
Quick Cognitive Inventory, 2138
Quick Informal Assessment, 2139
Quick Language Assessment Inventory, 2140
Quick Neurological Screening Test, 2nd Revised Edition, 2141
Quick Phonics Survey, 2142
Quick Programming Aptitude Test, T4:2185
Quick Quizzes for U.S. History Classes, 2143

Quick Score Achievement Test, T4:2187
Quick Screen of Phonology, 2144
Quick Screening Scale of Mental Development, T4:2189
Quick Spelling Inventory, 2145
The Quick Test, 2146
Quickview Social History, 2147

Racial Attitude Test, 2148
The RAD Scales, T4:2194
Rahim Organizational Conflict Inventories, 2149
Ramsay Corporation Job Skills—Health Care Reading Test, 2150
Ramsay Corporation Job Skills—Machinist Test, 2151
Ramsay Corporation Job Skills—Mechanic Evaluation Test, 2152
Ramsay Corporation Job Skills—Office Arithmetic Test, 2153
Ramsay Corporation Job Skills—Office Reading Test, 2154
Ramsay Corporation Job Skills—PrinTest—Forms A-C and B-C, 2155
Ramsay Corporation Job Skills—Reading Electrical Drawings & Schematics, 2156
Ramsay Corporation Job Skills—Reading Prints & Drawings, see Ramsay Corporation Job Skills—PrinTest—Forms A-C and B-C, 2155
Ramsay Corporation Job Skills—Supervisory Reading Test, 2157
RAND-36 Health Status Inventory, 2158
Randall's Island Performance Series, see CID Preschool Performance Scale, 488
Randt Memory Test, 2159
Rapid Personality Questionnaire, 2160
A Rating Inventory for Screening Kindergartners, 12:320
Rating of Behavior Scale, 2161
Rating Scale of Communication in Cognitive Decline, 2162
Raven Progressive Matrices, 2163
RBH Arithmetic Fundamentals Test, 2164
The RBH Arithmetic Reasoning Test, 2165
The RBH Non-Verbal Reasoning Test, see RBH Test of Non-Verbal Reasoning, 2169
RBH Shop Arithmetic Test, 2166
RBH Test of Chemical Comprehension, 2167
RBH Test of Language Skills, 2168
RBH Test of Learning Ability, see Test of Learning Ability, 2696
RBH Test of Non-Verbal Reasoning, 2169
RBH Test of Reading Comprehension, 2170
Reactions to Everyday Situations, T4:2216
Readiness for Kindergarten, T4:2217
Reading Ability Series, 2171
Reading Comprehension Battery for Aphasia, Second Edition, 2172
Reading Comprehension Test DE, 2173
Reading Efficiency Tests, 2174
Reading Evaluation Adult Diagnosis, Fifth Edition, 2175
Reading Evaluation and Diagnostic Screen, 2176
Reading/Everyday Activities in Life, T4:2225
Reading for Understanding Placement Test, T4:2227
Reading-Free Vocational Interest Inventory, Revised, 2177
Reading Index, 2178
Reading Progress Tests, 2179
Reading Skills Diagnostic Test III, Level 4, 2180
Reading Style Inventory, 2181
Reading Test AD, 2182
Reading Test (Comprehension and Speed): Municipal Tests: National Achievement Tests, 2183
Reading Test: McGraw-Hill Basic Skills System, T4:2232
Reading Test SR-A and SR-B, 2184
Reading Tests A and BD, 2185
Reading Tests EH 1-2, 2186
Reading Vocabulary Test, 2187
Reality Check Survey, 2188
Receptive-Expressive Emergent Language Test, Second Edition, 2189
Receptive-Expressive Observation, see Melvin-Smith Receptive-Expressive Observation, 1642
Receptive One-Word Picture Vocabulary Test, 2190
Receptive One-Word Picture Vocabulary Test: Upper Extension, 2191
Receptive Oral Language Inventory, 2192
Recognition Memory Test, 2193
Recovery Attitude and Treatment Evaluator, 2194
REHAB: Rehabilitation Evaluation Hall and Baker, 2195
Rehabilitation Checklist, 2196
Rehabilitation Client Rating Scale, T4:2242
Rehabilitation Compliance Scale, 2197
Reid Report, 2198
Reiss-Epstein-Gursky Anxiety Sensitivity Index, 2199
Relating to Each Other: A Questionnaire for Students, 13:260
Relating with Colleagues: A Questionnaire for Faculty Members, 13:261
A Religion Scale, 2200
A Religious Attitudes Inventory, T4:2248
The Renfrew Bus Story, 2201
Repeatable Battery for the Assessment of Neuropsychological Status, 2202
Research Personnel Review Form, 2203
Responsibility and Independence Scale for Adolescents, 2204
Retail Sales Skills Test, 2205
Retail Store Manager Staff Selector, 2206
Retirement Activities Card Sort Planning Kit, 2207
Retirement Activities Kit, see Retirement Activities Card Sort Planning Kit, 2207
Retirement Descriptive Index, 2208
Reversal Test, 2209

The Reversals Frequency Test, 2210
Revised Behavior Problem Checklist, 2211
Revised Beta Examination, Second Edition, 2212
Revised BRIGANCE® Diagnostic Inventory of Early Development, 2213
Revised Children's Manifest Anxiety Scale, 2214
Revised Denver Prescreening Developmental Questionnaire, see Denver Prescreening Developmental Questionnaire II, 787
Revised Developmental Screening Inventory—1980, T4:2259
Revised Edinburgh Functional Communication Profile, 12:328
Revised Evaluating Acquired Skills in Communication, 2215
Revised Hamilton Rating Scale for Depression, 2216
Revised Minnesota Paper Form Board Test, Second Edition, 2217
Revised NEO Personality Inventory, 2218
Revised Pre-Reading Screening Procedures, 2219
Revised PSB—Aptitude for Practical Nursing Examination, 2220
Revised PSB—Health Occupations Aptitude Examination, 2221
Revised PSB—Nursing School Aptitude Examination (R. N.), 2222
Revised PSB—Reading Comprehension Examination, 2223
The Revised Sheridan Gardiner Test of Visual Acuity, 2224
Revised Test of Understanding in College Economics, see Test of Understanding in College Economics, Third Edition, 2718
Revised Token Test, 2225
Rey Auditory Verbal Learning Test, 2226
Rey Complex Figure Test and Recognition Trial, 2227
Reynell Developmental Language Scales: Third Edition [British Edition], 2228
Reynell Developmental Language Scales [U.S. Edition], 2229
Reynell-Zinkin Scales: Developmental Scales for Young Visually Handicapped Children Part 1—Mental Development, T4:2273
Reynolds Adolescent Depression Scale, 2230
Reynolds Child Depression Scale, 2231
Reynolds Depression Screening Inventory, 2232
Rhode Island Test of Language Structure, 2233
Richmond Tests of Basic Skills: Edition 2, 2234
The Riley Articulation and Language Test, Revised, 2235
Riley Inventory of Basic Learning Skills, 2236
Riley Motor Problems Inventory, see Oral Motor Assessment and Treatment: Improving Syllable Production, 1850
Riley Preschool Developmental Screening Inventory, T4:2280
Ring and Peg Tests of Behavior Development, T4:2281
Risk-Taking-Attitude-Values Inventory, 2237
Risk Taking Inventory & Guide, 2238
The Rivermead Behavioural Memory Test [Second Edition], 2239
Rivermead Perceptual Assessment Battery, 2240
Riverside Curriculum Assessment System, 13:268
Riverside Performance Assessment Series, 2241
Roberts Apperception Test for Children [with new Interpretive Handbook], 2242
Rockford Infant Developmental Evaluation Scales, 2243
Roeder Manipulative Aptitude Test, 2244
Rogers Criminal Responsibility Assessment Scales, 2245
Rogers Personal Adjustment Inventory: Revised, T4:2289
Rokeach Value Survey, 2246
Rorschach, 2247
Rorshach Method, see Rorschach, 2247
Rorshach Psychodiagnostics, see Rorschach, 2247
Rorshach Test, see Rorschach, 2247
The Rosenzweig Picture-Frustration Study, 2248
Ross Information Processing Assessment—Geriatric, 2249
Ross Information Processing Assessment—Primary, 2250
Ross Information Processing Assessment, Second Edition, 2251
Ross Test of Higher Cognitive Processes, 2252
Roswell-Chall Auditory Blending Test, 2253
Roswell-Chall Diagnostic Reading Test of Word Analysis Skills, Revised and Extended, 2254
Rothwell-Miller Interest Blank, 2257
Rothwell Miller Interest Blank (Revised), 2255
Rothwell Miller Values Blank, 2256
Rotter Incomplete Sentences Blank, Second Edition, 2258
Roughness Discrimination Test, 2259
Rucker-Gable Educational Programming Scale, T4:2302
Rust Inventory of Schizotypal Cognitions, 2260
The Rutgers Drawing Test, 2261
Rutgers Social Attribute Inventory, T4:2305
The Ruth Fry Symbolic Profile, 2262

S-D Proneness Checklist, 2263
Safran Student's Interest Inventory, Third Edition, 2264
Sales Achievement Predictor, 2265
Sales Aptitude Test: ETSA Test 7A, 2266
Sales Attitude Check List, 2267
Sales Competency Inventory, 2268
Sales Comprehension Test, 2269
Sales Effectiveness Analysis, 2270
Sales Effectiveness Survey, 2271
Sales Motivation Inventory, Revised, 2272
Sales Motivation Survey, 2273

Sales Personality Questionnaire, 2274
Sales Relations Survey, 2275
The Sales Sentence Completion Blank, 2276
Sales Staff Selector, 2277
Sales Style Diagnosis Test, 2278
Sales Style Indicator, 2279
Sales Transaction Audit, 2280
Salford Sentence Reading Test, 2281
The Salience Inventory, 2282
Sand: Concepts About Print Test, 2283
Santostefano Tests of Cognitive Control, see Cognitive Control Battery, 563
SAQ-Adult Probation [Substance Abuse Questionnaire], 2284
SAQ-Adult Probation III, 2285
SAQS Chicago Q Sort, 2286
Scale for Assessing Emotional Disturbance, 2287
Scale for the Assessment of Negative Symptoms, 2288
Scale for the Assessment of Positive Symptoms, 2289
Scale for the Assessment of Thought, Language, and Communication, 2290
Scale of Feelings and Behavior of Love: Revised, 2291
Scale of Marriage Problems: Revised, 2292
Scaled Curriculum Achievement Levels Test, 2293
The Scales for Effective Teaching, 13:272
Scales for Predicting Successful Inclusion, 2294
Scales for Rating the Behavioral Characteristics of Superior Students, 2295
Scales of Adult Independence, Language and Recall, 2296
Scales of Cognitive Ability for Traumatic Brain Injury, 2297
Scales of Early Communication Skills for Hearing-Impaired Children, 2298
Scales of Independent Behavior—Revised, 2299
SCAN: A Screening Test for Auditory Processing Disorders, 2300
SCAN-A: A Test for Auditory Processing Disorders in Adolescents and Adults, 2301
SCC Clerical Skills Series, 2302
The Scenotest: A Practical Technique for Understanding Unconscious Problems and Personality Structure, 2303
Schaie-Thurstone Adult Mental Abilities Test, 2304
Schedule for Affective Disorders and Schizophrenia, Third Edition, 2305
Schedule for Nonadaptive and Adaptive Personality, 2306
A Schedule of Adaptive Mechanisms in CAT Responses, 2307
The Schedule of Growing Skills: Second Edition, 2308
The Schedule of Recent Experience, T4:2344
Scholastic Abilities Test for Adults, 2309
Scholastic Achievement Test for English Lower Standards 2 and 3, T4:2346
Scholastic Achievement Test for English Lower Standards 9 and 10, T4:2347
Scholastic Achievement Test in Arithmetic, T4:2348
Scholastic Achievement Test of English Second Language Standard I, T4:2349
Scholastic Achievement Tests for English First Language, T4:2350
Scholastic Aptitude Test Battery for Pupils in Standards 2 and 3, T4:2351
Scholastic Proficiency Battery, T4:2352
School-Age Care Environment Rating Scale, 2310
School Apperception Method, T4:2353
School Archival Records Search, 2311
School Assessment Survey, 2312
School Atmosphere Questionnaire, T4:2356
School Attitude Measure, Second Edition, 2313
School Behavior Checklist, T4:2358
School Effectiveness Questionnaire, 2314
School Environment Preference Survey, 2315
School Function Assessment, 2316
School Interest Inventory, T4:2361
School Leaders Licensure Assessment, 2317
The School Motivation Analysis Test, 2318
School Problem Screening Inventory, Fifth Edition, T4:2363
The School Readiness Checklist, T4:2364
School-Readiness Evaluation by Trained Teachers, 2319
School Readiness Survey, Second Edition, T4:2366
School Readiness Test, 2320
School Situation Survey, 2321
School Social Behavior Scales, 2322
School Social Skills Rating Scale, 2323
Schubert General Ability Battery, 2324
Scientific Knowledge and Aptitude Test, T4:2372
Scientific Orientation Test, 2325
SCL-90-Analogue, 2326
SCL-90-R, see Symptom Checklist-90-Revised, 2603
Scorable Self-Care Evaluation (Revised), 2327
SCREEN [Senf-Comrey Ratings of Extra Educational Need], T4:2375
Screening Assessment for Gifted Elementary Students, 2328
Screening Assessment for Gifted Elementary Students—Primary, 2329
Screening Children for Related Early Educational Needs, T4:2378
Screening Form for District Manager Selection, 2330
Screening Instrument for Targeting Educational Risk, T4:2380
Screening Kit of Language Development, 2331
Screening Speech Articulation Test, T4:2382
Screening Test for Developmental Apraxia of Speech, 2332
Screening Test for Educational Prerequisite Skills, 2333
Screening Test for the Luria-Nebraska Neuropsychological Battery: Adult and Children's Forms, 2334
Screening Test of Academic Readiness, T4:2386
Screening Test of Adolescent Language, T4:2387
Screening Test of Spanish Grammar, 2335

Screening Tests for Identifying Children with Specific Language Disability, see Slingerland Screening Tests for Identifying Children with Specific Language Disability, 2428
Search Institute Profiles of Student Life, see Search Institute Profiles of Student Life: Attitudes and Behaviors, 2336
Search Institute Profiles of Student Life: Attitudes and Behaviors, 2336
Second Language Oral Test of English, 2337
Secondary & College Reading Inventory, Second Edition, 2338
Secondary Level English Proficiency Test, 2339
Secondary-School Record, 2340
Secondary Screening Profiles, 2341
SEED Developmental Profiles, 2342
The Seeking of Noetic Goals Test, 2343
Seguin-Goddard Formboards, 2344
Selby MillSmith Adaptive Ability Tests, 2345
Selby MillSmith Values Indices, 2346
SELECT Associate Screening System, 2347
[Selection Interview Forms], 2348
SELF (Self-Concept Evaluation of Location Form), T4:2401
Self-Actualization Inventory, see Self-Actualization Test, 2349
Self-Actualization Test, 2349
Self-Administered Dependency Questionnaire, 2350
A Self Appraisal Scale for Teachers, 2351
Self-Assessment in Writing Skills, 2352
Self-Awareness Profile, 2353
Self-Concept Adjective Checklist, 2354
The Self-Concept and Motivation Inventory: What Face Would You Wear?, 2355
Self-Concept as a Learner Scale, 2356
Self Concept Scale, Secondary Level, 2357
Self-Description Inventory, T4:2411
Self-Description Questionnaire—I, II, III, 2358
Self-Directed Learning Readiness Scale, 2359
Self-Directed Search, 4th Edition [Forms R, E, and CP], 2360
Self-Esteem Index, 2361
The Self-Esteem Inventory, 2362
Self-Esteem Questionnaire, 2363
Self-Motivated Career Planning Guide, 2364
Self Observation Scales, 2365
Self-Perception Inventory: Nursing Forms, 2366
Self Perception Inventory [Psychologists and Educators, Inc.], 2367
Self-Perception Inventory [SOARES Associates], 2368
Self-Perception Profile for College Students, 2369
Self Profile Q-Sort, 2370
Self-Report Inventory, T4:2424
Self-Report Inventory, see The Multidimensional Self-Esteem Inventory, 1735
Self-Scoring Mathematics Placement Tests, T4:2425
Self-Scoring Reading Placement Test, T4:2426
Self-Scoring Written English Expression Placement Test, T4:2427
Self Worth Inventory, 2371
The Senior Apperception Technique [1985 Revision], 2372
Senior Aptitude Tests, 2373
Senior Clerical Skills Test, 2374
Senior South African Individual Scale—Revised, 2375
Sensory Evaluation Kit, 2376
Sensory Integration and Praxis Tests, 2377
Sensory Integration Inventory—Revised for Individuals with Developmental Disabilities, 2378
Sentence Completion Series, 2379
Sentence Completion Test, 2380
Sentence Completion Tests, 2381
Sentence Comprehension Test, Revised Edition, T4:2436
Sentence Imitation Screening Tests, T4:2437
Separation Anxiety Test, see Adolescent Separation Anxiety Test, 78
Sequenced Inventory of Communication Development, Revised Edition, 2382
Sequential Assessment of Mathematics Inventories: Standardized Inventory, 2383
Service Animal Adaptive Intervention Assessment, 2384
Service Excellence, 2385
ServiceFirst, 2386
Severe Cognitive Impairment Profile, 2387
The Severity and Acuity of Psychiatric Illness Scales—Adult Version, 2388
The Sex Attitudes Survey and Profile, Trial Edition, T4:2441
Sex Knowledge Inventory, T4:2442
Sex-Role Egalitarianism Scale, 2389
Sexometer, 2390
Sexual Abuse Screening Inventory, 2391
Sexual Adaptation and Functioning Test, 2392
Sexual Adjustment Inventory, 2393
The Sexual Compatibility Test, T4:2447
The Sexual Communication Inventory, 2394
The Sexual Concerns Checklist, Experimental Edition, T4:2448
Sexual Violence Risk-20, 2395
Sexuality Experience Scales, 2396
SF-36 Health Survey, 2397
Shapes Analysis Test, 2398
Shapiro Control Inventory, 2399
Sheltered Employment Work Experience Program, 2400
The Sheridan Gardiner Test of Visual Acuity, see The Revised Sheridan Gardiner Test of Visual Acuity, 2224
Ship Destination Test, 2401
Shipley-Hartford Retreat Scale for Measuring Intellectual Impairment, see Shipley Institute of Living Scale, 2402
Shipley Institute of Living Scale, 2402

Shipley-Institute of Living Scale for Measuring Intellectual Impairment, see Shipley Institute of Living Scale, 2402
Shoplifting Inventory, 2403
Shorr Imagery Test, 2404
Short Category Test, Booklet Format, 2405
Short Employment Tests, Second Edition, 2406
Short Form Test of Academic Attitude, see Test of Cognitive Skills, Second Edition, 2677
Short Imaginal Processes Inventory, 2407
Short Tests of Clerical Ability, 2408
Shortened Edinburgh Reading Test, 2409
Shutt Primary Language Indicator Test, T4:2460
Signals Listening Test, T4:2461
Silver Drawing Test of Cognition and Emotion [Third Edition Revised], 2410
Silver Drawing Test of Cognitive and Creative Skills, see Silver Drawing Test of Cognition and Emotion [Third Edition Revised], 2410
Silver Drawing Test of Cognitive Skills and Adjustment, see Silver Drawing Test of Cognition and Emotion [Third Edition Revised], 2410
The Singer-Loomis Inventory of Personality, Experimental Edition, see The Singer-Loomis Type Deployment Inventory, 2411
The Singer-Loomis Type Deployment Inventory, 2411
The Single and Double Simultaneous (Face-Hand) Stimulation Test, T4:2464
SIPOAS: Styles in Perception of Affect Scale, 2412
Situational Attitude Scale, 2413
Situational Confidence Questionnaire, 2414
Situational Leadership®, 2415
Situational Preference Inventory, 2416
Sixteen Personality Factor Questionnaire, Fifth Edition, 2417
16PF® Human Resource Development Report, 2418
16PF® Personal Career Development Profile, 2419
Skills and Attributes Inventory, 2420
Skills Assessment Module, 2421
Skills for Independent Living, 2422
Skills Inventory for Teachers, see Skills Inventory for Teams, 2423
Skills Inventory for Teams, 2423
SkillScan for Management Development, 2424
SKILLSCOPE for Managers, 2425
Sklar Aphasia Scale, Revised 1983, 2426
Slingerland College-Level Screening for the Identification of Language Learning Strengths and Weaknesses, 2427
Slingerland Screening Tests for Identifying Children with Specific Language Disability, 2428
Sloan Achromatopsia Test, T4:2479
Slosson Articulation Language Test with Phonology, 2429
Slosson Drawing Coordination Test, 2430
Slosson Drawing Coordination Test for Children and Adults, see Slosson Drawing Coordination Test, 2430
Slosson Full-Range Intelligence Test, 2431
Slosson Intelligence Test [1991 Edition], 2432
Slosson Oral Reading Test [Revised], 2433
Slosson Test of Reading Readiness, 2434
Small Business Assessment, 2435
Small College Goals Inventory, T4:2486
Smedley Hand Dynamometer, 2436
Smell Identification Test™ [Revised], 2437
Smit-Hand Articulation and Phonology Evaluation, 2438
Smith-Johnson Nonverbal Performance Scale, 2439
Smoker Complaint Scale, 2440
Snijders-Oomen Non-Verbal Intelligence Scale for Young Children; Non-Verbal Intelligence Scale S.O.N. 2 1/2–7, see Snijders-Oomen Non-Verbal Intelligence Test—Revised, 2441
Snijders-Oomen Non-Verbal Intelligence Test—Revised, 2441
Social Adjustment Scale—Self Report, 2442
Social and Prevocational Information Battery—Revised, 2443
Social Behavior Assessment, see Social Behavior Assessment Inventory, 2444
Social Behavior Assessment Inventory, 2444
Social Behaviour Assessment Schedule, Third Edition, T4:2494
The Social Climate Scales, 2445
Social Competence and Behavior Evaluation, Preschool Edition, 2446
Social-Emotional Dimension Scale, 2447
Social Intelligence Test: George Washington University Series [SPECIAL EDITION], T4:2497
Social Maturity Scale for Blind Preschool Children: A Guide to Its Use, T4:2498
Social Phobia and Anxiety Inventory, 2448
Social Reticence Scale, 2449
Social Skills for Adults with Severe Retardation—An Inventory and Training Program, 2450
Social Skills for Severely Retarded Adults—An Inventory and Training Program, see Social Skills for Adults with Severe Retardation—An Inventory and Training Program, 2450
Social Skills Inventory, Research Edition, 2451
Social Skills Rating System, 2452
Social Styles Analysis, 2453
Socio-Economic Status Scales, T4:2504
Socio-Sexual Knowledge & Attitudes Test, 2454
Softball Skills Test, 2455
Solid Geometry: National Achievement Tests, 2456
Somatic Inkblot Series, 2457
The South African Individual Scale for the Blind, T4:2509
South African Personality Questionnaire, T4:2510
The South African Picture Analysis Test, T4:2511

South African Wechsler Adult Individual Intelligence Scale, T4:2512
South African Written Language Test, 2458
The Southern California Ordinal Scales of Development, 2459
Southern California Postrotary Nystagmus Test, see Sensory Integration and Praxis Tests, 2377
Southern California Sensory Integrative Tests, see Sensory Integration and Praxis Tests, 2377
Space Thinking (Flags), 2460
Spadafore Attention Deficit Hyperactivity Disorder Rating Scale, 2461
Spadafore Diagnostic Reading Test, 2462
Spanish Assessment of Basic Education, Second Edition, 2463
A Spanish Computerized Adaptive Placement Exam, 2464
Spanish/English Reading Comprehension Test [Revised], 2465
Spanish Structured Photographic Expressive Language Test, 2466
SPAR Reading Test, see SPAR Spelling and Reading Tests, Third Edition, 2467
SPAR Spelling and Reading Tests, Third Edition, 2467
SPAR Spelling Test, see SPAR Spelling and Reading Tests, Third Edition, 2467
Spatial Orientation Memory Test, 2468
Spatial Relations Test, see Minnesota Spatial Relations Test, Revised Edition, 1703
Specific Language Disability Test, 2469
SPECTRUM-I: A Test of Adult Work Motivation, see Work Motivation Inventory: A Test of Adult Work Motivation, 2922
Speech and Language Evaluation Scale, 2470
Speech-Ease Screening Inventory (K—1), 2471
Speech Evaluation of the Patient with a Tracheostomy Tube, 2472
Spelling Test: McGraw-Hill Basic Skills System, T4:2526
Spelling Test: National Achievement Tests, 2473
Spellmaster, T4:2528
Spiritual Well-Being Scale, 2474
Sports Emotion Test, 2475
Spousal Assault Risk Assessment Guide, 2476
SRA Arithmetic Index, see Arithmetic Index, 171
SRA Attitude Survey, T4:2532
SRA Clerical Aptitudes, see Clerical Aptitudes, 534
SRA Mechanical Aptitudes, see Mechanical Aptitudes, 1633
SRA Nonverbal Form, see Nonverbal Form, 1798
SRA Pictorial Reasoning Test, see Pictorial Reasoning Test, 1986
SRA Placement and Counseling Program, T4:2537
SRA Reading Index, see Reading Index, 2178
SRA Sales Attitudes Check List, see Sales Attitude Check List, 2267
SRA Test of Mechanical Concepts, see Test of Mechanical Concepts, 2700
SRA Typing 5, see Typing 5, 2786
SRA Typing Skills, T4:2541
SRA Verbal Classification Form, see Verbal Form, 2807
SRA Verbal Form, see Verbal Form, 2807
St. Lucia Graded Word Reading Test, T4:2308
St. Lucia Reading Comprehension Test, T4:2309
Staff Burnout Scale for Health Professionals, T4:2543
Standard PSB-Health Occupations Aptitude Examination, see Revised PSB—Health Occupations Aptitude Examination, 2221
Standard Progressive Matrices [Australian Edition], 2477
Standard Progressive Matrices, New Zealand Standardization, 2478
The Standard Reading Tests, T4:2546
The Standard Timing Model, 2479
Standardized Bible Content Tests, 2480
Standardized Reading Inventory, Second Edition, 2481
Standardized Test of Computer Literacy and Computer Anxiety Index (Version AZ), Revised, 2482
Stanford Achievement Test—Abbreviated Version—8th Edition, 2483
Stanford Achievement Test, Ninth Edition, 2484
Stanford Hypnotic Susceptibility Scale, T4:2557
Speech-Ease Screening Inventory (K—1), 2485
Stanford Diagnostic Mathematics Test, Fourth Edition, 2486
Stanford Diagnostic Reading Test, Fourth Edition, 2487
Stanford Early School Achievement Test, Third Edition, 2488
Stanford Writing Assessment Program, Third Edition, 2489
The Stanton Inventory, T4:2559
The Stanton Profile, 2490
The Stanton Survey and the Stanton Survey Phase II, 2491
STAR Math™, 2492
STAR Reading™, 2493
STARS Test (Short Term Auditory Retrieval and Storage), 2494
START—Strategic Assessment of Readiness for Training, 2495
State-Trait Anger Expression Inventory [1996 Edition], 2496
State-Trait Anxiety Inventory, 2497
State-Trait Anxiety Inventory for Children, 2498
State Trait-Depression Adjective Check Lists, 2499
Statistically Validated Written Tests for Police Officer, see Criterion Validated Written Tests for Police Officer, 734
The Steenburgen Diagnostic-Prescriptive Math Program, 2500
Stenographic Skill-Dictation Test, 12:372

Stenographic Skills Test: ETSA Test 4A, 2501
Stephens Oral Language Screening Test, 2502
Stern Activities Index, T4:2569
The Stieglitz Informal Reading Inventory: Assessing Reading Behaviors from Emergent to Advanced Levels, 2503
STIM/CON: Prognostic Inventory for Misarticulating Kindergarten and First Grade Children, 2504
Stokes/Gordon Stress Scale, 2505
Strategic Decision Making Inventory, 2506
Strength Deployment Inventory, 2507
Strengthening Effectiveness of Board and Committee Members, T4:2573
Stress Analysis System, T4:2574
Stress Audit, 2508
Stress Impact Scale, 12:373
Stress in General Scale, 2509
Stress Index for Parents of Adolescents, 2510
Stress Indicator & Health Planner, 2511
Stress Management Questionnaire [Revised], 2512
Stress Resiliency Profile, 2513
Stress Response Scale, 2514
Strohmer-Prout Behavior Rating Scale, see Emotional Problems Scales, 931
Strohmer-Prout Sentence Completion Technique, see EPS Sentence Completion Technique, 965
Stromberg Dexterity Test, 2515
Strong Interest Inventory [Fourth Edition], see 1994 Strong Interest Inventory, 1790
Strong-Campbell Interest Inventory, see 1994 Strong Interest Inventory, 1790
Stroop Color and Word Test, 2516
Stroop Neuropsychological Screening Test, 2517
Structure of Intellect Learning Abilities Test, 2518
Structured Clinical Interview for DSM-IV Axis I Disorders: Clinician Version, 2519
Structured Clinical Interview for DSM-IV Axis II Personality Disorders, 2520
Structured Interview for Disorders of Extreme Stress & Traumatic Antecedents Questionnaire—Self Report, 2521
Structured Interview of Reported Symptoms, 2522
Structured Pediatric Psychosocial Interview, T4:2586
Structured Photographic Articulation Test Featuring Dudsberry, 2523
Structured Photographic Expressive Language Test, 2524
STS Educational Development Series: Scholastic Tests, see Educational Development Series (1992 Edition), 904
Student Adaptation to College Questionnaire, 2525
Student Adjustment Inventory, 2526
Student Developmental Task and Lifestyle Inventory, 2527
Student Developmental Task Inventory, Revised, Second Edition, see Student Developmental Task and Lifestyle Inventory, 2527
Student Educational Assessment Screening, 2528
Student Evaluation of Teacher Instrument II, T4:2594
Student Evaluation Scale, 2529
Student Goals Exploration, 2530
Student Instructional Report II, 2531
Student Opinion Inventory, Revised Edition, 2532
Student Referral Checklist, 2533
Student Rights Scales, 2534
Student Self-Concept Scale, 2535
Student Styles Questionnaire, 2536
Student Talent and Risk Profile, 2537
Study Attitudes and Methods Survey [Revised Short Form], 2538
Study Habits Evaluation and Instruction Kit, T4:2605
Study of Values: A Scale for Measuring the Dominant Interests in Personality, Third Edition, T4:2606
Study of Values: British Edition, 1965, 2539
Study Process Questionnaire, 2540
The Study Skills Counseling Evaluation, 2541
Study Skills Surveys, T4:2610
Study Skills Test: McGraw-Hill Basic Skills System, T4:2611
Stuttering Prediction Instrument for Young Children, 2542
Stuttering Severity Instrument for Children and Adults, Third Edition, 2543
Stycar Hearing Tests, T4:2614
Stycar Language Test, T4:2615
Stycar Vision Tests, 2544
Style of Learning and Thinking, 2545
Styles of Conflict Inventory, 2546
[Styles of Leadership and Management], see Leadership Appraisal Survey, 1441 and Management Appraisal Survey, 1546
Styles of Leadership Survey, 2547
Styles of Management Inventory, 2548
Styles of Teamwork Inventory, 2549
Substance Abuse Life Circumstance Evaluation, 2550
Substance Abuse Relapse Assessment, 2551
Substance Abuse Screening Test, 2552
Substance Abuse Subtle Screening Inventory, 2553
Substance Use Disorders Diagnosis Schedule, 2554
Subsumed Abilities Test, 2555
Subtest of Municipal Battery, see Arithmetic Test (Fundamentals and Reasoning): Municipal Tests: National Achievement Tests, 173
Suffolk Reading Scale, 2556
Suicidal Ideation Questionnaire, 2557
Suicide Intervention Response Inventory [Revised], 2558
Suicide Probability Scale, 2559
SUPERA, 2560
Supervisory Change Relations, 2561
Supervisory Coaching Relations, 2562
Supervisory Communication Relations, 2563
Supervisory Human Relations, 2564
Supervisory Inventory on Communication, 2565
Supervisory Inventory on Discipline, T4:2635

Supervisory Inventory on Grievances, T4:2636
Supervisory Inventory on Human Relations, 2566
Supervisory Inventory on Labor Relations, T4:2638
Supervisory Inventory on Safety, T4:2639
Supervisory Job Discipline, 2567
Supervisory Job Instruction, 2568
Supervisory Job Safety, 2569
Supervisory Potential Test, 2570
Supervisory Practices Inventory, 2571
Supervisory Practices Test, Revised, 2572
Supervisory Profile Record, 2573
Supervisory Simulator, 2574
Supervisory Skills Inventory, 2575
Supervisory Union Relations, 2576
SUP'R Star Profiles, 2577
Survey of Educational Leadership Practices (T3:2365), see Educational Leadership Practices Inventory, 906
Survey of Employee Access, 2578
Survey of Functional Adaptive Behaviors, 2579
Survey of Influence Effectiveness, 2580
Survey of Interpersonal Values, 2581
Survey of Management Perception, 2582
Survey of Management Practices, 2583
Survey of Organizational Climate, 2584
Survey of Organizational Culture, 2585
Survey of Organizational Stress, 2586
Survey of Organizations, 2587
Survey of Personal Values, 2588
Survey of Student Assessment of Study Behaviors, 2589
Survey of Student Opinion of Instruction, 2590
Survey of Study Habits and Attitudes, 2591
Survey of Work Styles, 2592
Survey of Work Values, Revised, Form U, 2593
Surveys of Problem-Solving and Educational Skills, T4:2666
Surveys of Research Administration and Environment, 2594
Sutter-Eyberg Student Behavior Inventory, 2595
Swanson-Cognitive Processing Test, 2596
Swassing-Barbe Modality Index, 2597
Sweet Technical Information Test, 2598
Symbol Digit Modalities Test, 2599
Symbol Elaboration Test, 2600
Symbolic Play Test, Second Edition, 2601
Symptom Assessment-45 Questionnaire, 2602
Symptom Checklist-90-Revised, 2603
Symptom Scale—77, 2604
System for Testing and Evaluation of Potential, 2605
System of Multicultural Pluralistic Assessment, 2606
System to Plan Early Childhood Services, 12:385
Systematic Screening for Behavior Disorders, 2607
Systems Analysis Aptitude Test, 2608
Systems Programming Aptitude Test, 2609

T. A. Survey, 2610
Tapping Students' Science Beliefs: A Resource for Teaching and Learning, 2611
The Tapping Test: A Predictor of Typing and Other Tapping Operations, 2612
TARC Assessment Inventory for Severely Handicapped Children, T4:2685
Target Mathematics Tests, 2613
Tasks of Emotional Development Test, 2614
TAT Analysis Sheet, 2615
TAV Selection System, 2616
The Taylor-Helmstadter Pair Comparison Scale of Aesthetic Judgment, 2617
Taylor-Johnson Temperament Analysis [1992 Edition], 2618
TD (Tardive Dyskinesia) Monitor, 2619
Teacher Assessment of Grammatical Structures, 2620
A Teacher Attitude Inventory: Identifying Teacher Positions in Relation to Educational Issues and Decisions, 2621
Teacher Evaluation Scale, 12:386
Teacher Observation Scales for Identifying Children with Special Abilities, 2622
Teacher Opinion Inventory, Revised Edition, 2623
Teacher Opinionaire on Democracy, 2624
Teacher Role Survey (Revised), 2625
Teacher Stress Inventory, T4:2697
Teacher Values Inventory, 2626
Teacher's Handbook of Diagnostic Inventories, Second Edition, 2627
Teacher's Handbook of Diagnostic Screening, Second Edition, 2628
Teacher's School Readiness Inventory, 12:387
Teaching Resource and Assessment of Critical Skills, 2629
Team Competency Assessment, 2630
Team-Development Inventory, 2631
Team Development Survey, 2632
The Team Effectiveness Analysis Form, T4:2704
Team Effectiveness and Meeting Strategy, 2633
Team Effectiveness Survey, 2634
The Team Leadership Practices Inventory, 2635
Team Process Diagnostic, 2636
Teamness Index, 2637
Teamwork Appraisal Survey, 2638
Technical Personnel Recruiting Inventory, 2639
Technical Support Staff Selector, 2640
Technical Test Battery, 2641
Technical Test Battery [British Edition], 2642
Technician Electrical Test—-Form A2, 2643
Technician Mechanical Test—Form A2, 2644
Technology and Internet Assessment, 2645
Telemarketing Staff Selector, 2646
TEMAS (Tell-Me-A-Story), 2647
Temperament and Values Inventory, T4:2717
Temperament Assessment Battery for Children, T4:2718
Temperament Comparator, 2648
Temperament Inventory, 2649
Temple University Short Syntax Inventory, 2650

Templin-Darley Tests of Articulation, Second Edition, 2651
Tennessee Self-Concept Scale, Second Edition, 2652
Tennis Skills Test Manual, 2653
TerraNova, 2654
Test Anxiety Inventory, see Test Attitude Inventory, 2656
Test Anxiety Profile, 2655
Test Attitude Inventory, 2656
Test for Auditory Comprehension of Language—Third Edition, 2657
Test for Auditory Figure-Ground Discrimination, T4:2728
Test for Colour-Blindness, 2658
Test for Creative Thinking—Drawing Production, 2659
Test for Examining Expressive Morphology, 2660
Test for Oral Language Production, 2661
Test for the Reception of Grammar, 2662
Test Lessons in Primary Reading, Second Enlarged and Revised Edition, 2663
Test Lessons in Reading Figurative Language, 2664
Test of Ability to Subordinate, T4:2734
Test of Abstract Reasoning, see Test of Perceptual Organization, 2707
Test of Academic Achievement Skills—Reading, Arithmetic, Spelling, and Listening Comprehension, 2665
Test of Academic Performance, 2666
Test of Adolescent/Adult Word Finding, 2667
Test of Adolescent and Adult Language, Third Edition, 2668
Test of Adolescent Language—2, see Test of Adolescent and Adult Language, Third Edition, 2668
Test of Articulation in Context, 2669
Test of Attitude Toward School, 2670
Test of Auditory Analysis Skills, 2671
Test of Auditory Comprehension, 2672
Test of Auditory-Perceptual Skills, 2673
Test of Awareness of Language Segments, 2674
Test of Basic Assumptions, 2675
Test of Children's Language: Assessing Aspects of Spoken Language, Reading, and Writing, 2676
Test of Cognitive Skills, Second Edition, 2677
Test of Cognitive Style in Mathematics, 2678
Test of Computational Processes, T4:2747
Test of Concept Utilization, T4:2748
Test of Creativity, 2679
Test of Early Language Development, Third Edition, 2680
Test of Early Mathematics Ability, Second Edition, 2681
Test of Early Reading Ability—2, 2682
Test of Early Reading Ability—Deaf or Hard of Hearing, 2683
Test of Early Socioemotional Development, T4:2753
Test of Early Written Language, Second Edition, 2684
Test of Economic Knowledge, 2685
Test of Economic Literacy, Second Edition, 2686
Test of Economic Understanding, see Test of Economic Literacy, Second Edition, 2686
Test of Elementary Economics, see Basic Economics Test, 247
Test of English as a Foreign Language, Revised, and Test of Written English, see Computer-Based Test of English as a Foreign Language and Test of Written English, 666
Test of English as a Foreign Language, see Computer-Based Test of English as a Foreign Language and Test of Written English, 666
Test of English for International Communication (TOEIC), 2687
Test of English Proficiency Level, 2688
A Test of English Usage, T4:2760
Test of Grammatically Correct Spanish/English, Written and Oral, T4:2761
Test of Gross Motor Development, 2689
Test of Inference Ability in Reading Comprehension, 2690
Test of Initial Literacy, 2691
A Test of Interests, see Scientific Orientation Test, 2325
Test of Kindergarten/First Grade Readiness Skills, 2692
Test of Language Competence—Expanded Edition, 2693
Test of Language Development—Intermediate, Third Edition, 2694
Test of Language Development—Primary, Third Edition, 2695
Test of Learning Ability, 2696
Test of Library/Study Skills, 2697
Test of Listening Accuracy in Children, T4:2771
Test of Mathematical Abilities for Gifted Students, 2698
Test of Mathematical Abilities, Second Edition, 2699
Test of Mechanical Concepts, 2700
Test of Memory and Learning, 2701
Test of Memory Malingering, 2702
Test of Minimal Articulation Competence, 2703
Test of Motor Impairment, Henderson Revision, see Movement Assessment Battery for Children, 1727
Test of Nonverbal Intelligence, Third Edition, 2704
Test of Oral and Limb Apraxia, 2705
Test of Oral Structures and Functions, 2706
Test of Orientation for Rehabilitation Patients, 13:332
Test of Perceptual Organization, 2707
Test of Phonological Awareness, 2708
Test of Pragmatic Language, 2709
Test of Pragmatic Skills, Revised Edition, T4:2782
Test of Problem Solving, 2710
Test of Reading and Number: Inter-American Series, 2711
Test of Reading Comprehension, Third Edition, 2712
Test of Relational Concepts, T4:2786
Test of Retail Sales Insight, 2713
Test of Sales Insight, see Test of Retail Sales Insight, 2713

Test of Scholastic Abilities, 2714
Test of Sensory Functions in Infants, 2715
Test of Social Insight, 2716
Test of Spoken English, 2717
Test of Syntactic Abilities, T4:2792
Test of Understanding in College Economics, Third Edition, 2718
Test of Understanding in Personal Economics, 2719
Test of Variables of Attention (Version 7.03), 2720
Test of Visual Analysis Skills, 2721
Test of Visual-Motor Integration, 2722
Test of Visual-Motor Skills, 2723
Test of Visual-Perceptual Skills (Non-Motor), 2724
Test of Word Finding, 2725
Test of Word Finding in Discourse, 2726
Test of Word Knowledge, 2727
Test of Work Competency and Stability, 2728
Test of Written English, 2729
Test of Written Expression, 2730
Test of Written Language—Third Edition, 2731
Test of Written Spelling, Fourth Edition, 2732
Test on Appraising Observations, 2733
Testing Academic Achievement; Multiple Assessment Programs and Services, see Multiple Assessments, Programs, and Services (MAPS) of the College Board, 1746
TestWell: Wellness Inventory, see TestWell: Wellness Inventory for Windows, 2746
TestWell: Wellness Inventory—College Version, see TestWell: Wellness Inventory for Windows—College Version, 2747
Tests for Everyday Living, 2734
Tests of Achievement and Proficiency, Forms K, L, and M, 2735
Tests of Achievement in Basic Skills: Mathematics, 2736
Tests of Adult Basic Education, Forms 7 & 8, 2737
Tests of Adult Basic Education Work-Related Foundation Skills, 2738
Tests of Adult Basic Education Work-Related Problem Solving, 2739
Tests of Basic Experiences 2, 2740
Tests of General Ability: Inter-American Series, 2741
Tests of General Educational Development [The GED Tests], 2742
Tests of Reading Comprehension, 2743
Tests of Reading: Inter-American Series, 2744
Test on the Fundamentals of Hebrew, T4:2807
Test on Understanding Science, T4:2808
Tests of Social Intelligence, T4:2819
TestWell: Health Risk Appraisal, 2745
TestWell: Wellness Inventory for Windows, 2746
TestWell: Wellness Inventory for Windows—College Version, 2747
Thanatometer, 2748
Thematic Apperception Test, 2749
Themes Concerning Blacks, 2750
Theological School Inventory, 2751
Therapy Attitude Inventory, 2752
Thinking About My School, 2753
Thinking Creatively in Action and Movement, 2754
Thinking Creatively With Sounds and Words, Research Edition, 2755
Third Edition; Oral Verbal Intelligence Test, see Non-Reading Intelligence Tests, Levels 1-3, 1797
Thomas-Kilmann Conflict Mode Instrument, 2756
The 3-R's Test, T4:2832
Thurstone Primary Mental Abilities Test, see Schaie-Thurstone Adult Mental Abilities Test, 2304
Thurstone Temperament Schedule, 2757
Thurstone Test of Mental Alertness, 2758
Tickmaster, T4:2835
Tiffany Control Scales, 2759
The Time of Your Life, 2760
Time Perception Inventory, 2761
Time Problems Inventory, 2762
Time Questionnaire: Assessing Suicide Potential, T4:2839
The Time-Sample Behavioral Checklist, 2763
Time Use Analyzer, 2764
Timed Typings for Holidays, 2765
TMJ Scale, 2766
T.M.R. Performance Profile for the Severely and Moderately Retarded, T4:2843
T.M.R. School Competency Scales, T4:2844
Toddler and Infant Motor Evaluation, 2767
The Token Test for Children, 2768
Tool Room Attendant, 2769
Tooze Braille Speed Test: A Test of Basic Ability in Reading Braille, 2770
Torrance Tests of Creative Thinking, 2771
Total Quality Management Readiness Index, 13:350
Tower of London: Research Version, 2772
The Toy World Test, T4:2851
TQ_Manager Inventory and Feedback From Others, 2773
Trade Aptitude Test Battery, 2774
Trainee Performance Sample, see PathFinder—My Individual Career Plan, 1896
Trainer's Assessment of Proficiency (TAP), 2775
Trait Evaluation Index, 2776
The Trait Pleasure-Displeasure Scale, 2777
Transdisciplinary Play-Based Assessment, Revised Edition, 2778
Transition Behavior Scale, 2779
Transition Planning Inventory, 2780
Transition-to-Work Inventory: A Job Placement System for Workers with Severe disAbilities, 2781
Trauma Symptom Inventory, 2782
Treatment Intervention Inventory, 2783
Triadal Equated Personality Inventory, 2784
Troubled Talk Test, 2785
Trustworthiness Attitude Survey, see T. A. Survey, 2610

Twitchell-Allen Three-Dimensional Personality Test, T4:2859
Typing 5, 2786
Typing Skill Test, T4:2860
Typing Test for Business, 2787

The Uncritical Inference Test, 2788
Understanding and Managing Stress, 2789
Understanding Communication, 2790
Uniform Child Custody Evaluation System, 2791
Universal Nonverbal Intelligence Test, 2792
University Residence Environment Scale [Revised], 2793
Useful Field of View, 2794
USES Basic Occupational Literacy Test, 2795
USES Clerical Skills Tests, 2796
USES General Aptitude Test Battery, 2797
USES General Aptitude Test Battery for the Deaf, 2798
USES Nonreading Aptitude Test Battery, 1982 Edition, 2799
Uses Test, 2800
Utah Test of Language Development—3, 2801
Utah Verbal Language Development Scale, see Utah Test of Language Development—3, 2801

Validity Indicator Profile, 2802
Values Inventory, 2803
Values Inventory for Children, T4:2874
Visual Perceptual Skills Inventory, T4:2888
Values Preference Indicator, 2804
The Values Scale, Second Edition, 2805
Vasectomy Scale: Attitudes, 2806
Verbal Form, 2807
Verbal Reasoning, 2808
VESPAR: A Verbal and Spatial Reasoning Test, 2809
Veterinary Aptitude Test, see Veterinary College Admission Test, 2810
Veterinary College Admission Test, 2810
Victoria Symptom Validity Test, 2811
Vincent Mechanical Diagrams Test, 1979 Revision, 2812
Vineland Adaptive Behavior Scales, 2813
Vineland Social-Emotional Early Childhood Scales, 2814
Vineland Social Maturity Scale, see Vineland Adaptive Behavior Scales, 2813
A Violence Scale, 2815
The Visual Aural Digit Span Test, 2816
Visual Discrimination Test, 2817
Visual Functioning Assessment Tool, 2818
Visual Memory Test, 2819
Visual Search and Attention Test, 2820
Visual Skills Appraisal, 2821
Visual-Verbal Test, 1981 Edition, T4:2891
VITAL Checklist and Curriculum Guide, T4:2892
Voc-Tech Quick Screener, 2822
Vocabulary Comprehension Scale, T4:2893
Vocabulary Test: McGraw-Hill Basic Skills System, T4:2894
Vocabulary Test: National Achievement Tests, 2823
Vocational Adaptation Rating Scales, 2824
The Vocational Apperception Test: Advanced Form, 2825
Vocational Assessment and Curriculum Guide, 2826
Vocational Behavior Checklist, 2827
Vocational Decision-Making Interview—Revised, 2828
Vocational Development Inventory, see Career Maturity Inventory, 413
Vocational Exploration and Insight Kit, T4:2900
Vocational Information Profile, T4:2901
Vocational Interest and Sophistication Assessment, 2829
Vocational Interest, Experience, and Skill Assessment, 2830
Vocational Interest, Experience and Skill Assessment (VIESA), 2nd Canadian Edition, 2831
Vocational Interest Inventory and Exploration Survey, 2832
Vocational Interest Inventory—Revised, 2833
Vocational Interest Questionnaire for Pupils in Standards 6-10, T4:2907
Vocational Learning Styles, see Learning/Working Styles Inventory, 1478
Vocational Opinion Index, 2834
Vocational Preference Inventory, 1985 Edition, 2835
Vocational Research Interest Inventory, 2836
A Voice Assessment Protocol For Children and Adults, 2837
Vulpe Assessment Battery—Revised, 2838
Vygotsky Test, see Modified Vygotsky Concept Formation Test, 1714

Wahler Physical Symptoms Inventory, 2839
WAIS-R NI, 2840
Waksman Social Skills Rating Scale, 2841
Walden CICS/VS Command Level Proficiency Test, 2842
Walden DOS JCL (VS, VSE) Proficiency Test, 2843
Walden OS/JCL Proficiency Test, 2844
Walden Programming Language Test: COBOL, see Wolfe Programming Language Test: COBOL, 2896
Walden Structured Analysis and Design Concepts Proficiency Test, 2845
Walden Structured COBOL Proficiency Test, 2846
Walden TSO/SPF Proficiency Test, 2847
Walker Problem Behavior Identification Checklist, 2848
W-APT Programming Aptitude Test, 2849
Ward Atmosphere Scale (Third Edition), 2850
Warehouse/Plant Worker Staff Selector, 2851
Washer Visual Acuity Screening Technique, 2852
The Washington Pre-College Test, T4:2927
The Watkins-Farnum Performance Scale: A Standardized Achievement Test for All Band Instruments, 2853
Watson-Barker Listening Test, 2854

Watson-Barker Listening Test—High School Version, 2855
Watson Diagnostic Mathematics Test: Computation, Fourth Edition, T4:2931
Watson English Usage and Appreciation Test, Fourth Edition, T4:2932
Watson-Glaser Critical Thinking Appraisal, 2856
Watson-Glaser Critical Thinking Appraisal, Form S, 2857
Watson Number-Readiness Test, Fifth Edition, T4:2934
Watson Reading-Readiness Test, T4:2935
Ways of Coping Questionnaire, Research Edition, 2858
Wechsler Abbreviated Scale of Intelligence, 2859
Wechsler Adult Intelligence Scale—Third Edition, 2860
Wechsler Individual Achievement Test, 2861
Wechsler Intelligence Scale for Children—Third Edition, 2862
Wechsler Memory Scale III, 2863
Wechsler Preschool and Primary Scale of Intelligence—Revised, 2864
Weights and Pulleys: A Test of Intuitive Mechanics, see Intuitive Mechanics (Weights & Pulleys), 1299
Weinberg Depression Scale for Children and Adolescents, 2865
Weiss Comprehensive Articulation Test, 2866
Weld Test—Form A-C, 2867
Welding Test, see Weld Test—Form A-C, 2867
Weller-Strawser Scales of Adaptive Behavior for the Learning Disabled, 2868
Welsh Figure Preference Test, 2869
Wepman's Auditory Discrimination Test, Second Edition, 2870
Wesman Personnel Classification Test, 2871
The Wessex Revised Portage Language Checklist, 2872
Western Aphasia Battery, 2873
The Western Personality Inventory, 2874
The Western Personnel Tests, T4:2951
Western Psychological Services, see Brief Neuropsychological Cognitive Examination, 336
Wharton Attitude Survey, 2875
What Do You Know About Photography?, see Modern Photography Comprehension Test, 1713
What Do You Say?, 2876
Whisler Strategy Test, 2877
Whitaker Index of Schizophrenic Thinking, 2878
Wide Range Achievement Test 3, 2879
Wide Range Assessment of Memory and Learning, 2880
Wide Range Assessment of Visual Motor Abilities, 2881
Wide Range Intelligence-Personality Test [1978 Edition], T4:2958
Wide Range Interest-Opinion Test, 2882
Wide-Span Reading Test, 2883
The Wiesen Test of Mechanical Aptitude, 2884
Wife's or Husband's Marriage Questions, 2885
Wiig Criterion Referenced Inventory of Language, 2886
Williams Awareness Sentence Completion, 2887
Williams Intelligence Test for Children with Defective Vision, 2888
The Wilson Battery of Multi-Level Management & Organization Surveys, see The Clark Wilson Group Multi-Level Feedback Instruments and Development Programs, 490
Wilson Driver Selection Test, 2889
The Wilson Teacher-Appraisal Scale, 2890
Wisconsin Behavior Rating Scale, 2891
Wisconsin Card Sorting Test, Revised and Expanded, 2892
Wolf Expressive/Receptive Language & Speech Checklist, 2893
Wolf Student Behavior Screening, 2894
The Wolfe Computer Operator Aptitude Test, 2895
Wolfe Microcomputer User Aptitude Test, see Microcomputer User Aptitude Test, 1666
Wolfe Programming Language Test: COBOL, 2896
Wolfe Systems Analysis Aptitude Test, see Systems Analysis Aptitude Test, 2608
Wolfe-Spence Programming Aptitude Test, 2897
Wolfe-Winrow CICS/VS Command Level Proficiency Test, see Walden CICS/VS Command Level Proficiency Test, 2842
Wolfe-Winrow DOS JCL (VS, VSE) Proficiency Test, see Walden DOS JCL (VS, VSE) Proficiency Test, 2843
Wolfe-Winrow OS JCL Proficiency Test, see Walden OS/JCL Proficiency Test, 2844
Wolfe-Winrow Structured Analysis and Design Concepts Proficiency Test, see Walden Structured Analysis and Design Concepts Proficiency Test, 2845
Wolfe-Winrow Structured COBOL Proficiency Test, see Walden Structured COBOL Proficiency Test, 2846
Wolfe-Winrow TSO/SPF Proficiency Test, see Walden TSO/SPF Proficiency Test, 2847
Wonderlic Basic Skills Test, 2898
Wonderlic Personnel Test and Scholastic Level Exam, 2899
Woodcock Diagnostic Reading Battery, 2900
Woodcock-Johnson Psycho-Educational Battery—Revised, 2901
Woodcock Language Proficiency Battery—Revised, 2902
Woodcock-McGrew-Werder Mini-Battery of Achievement, 2903
Woodcock-Muñoz Language Survey, 2904
Woodcock Reading Mastery Tests—Revised [1998 Normative Update], 2905
Word and Number Assessment Inventory, T4:2977
Word Discrimination Test, T4:2978
Word Finding Referral Checklist, 2906

Word Fluency, 2907
Word Identification Scale, 2908
Word Intelligibility by Picture Identification, T4:2980
The Word Memory Test, 2909
Word Processor Assessment Battery, T4:2981
Word Recognition and Phonic Skills, 2910
Word Recognition Test, T4:2982
The WORD Test, 2911
Work Adjustment Inventory, 2912
The Work Adjustment Scale, 2913
Work Aptitude: Profile and Practice Set, 2914
Work Aspect Preference Scale, 2915
Work Attitudes Questionnaire (Version for Research), 2916
Work Environment Scale, Second Edition, 2917
The Work Experience Survey, 2918
Work Information Inventory, 2919
Work Keys Assessments, 2920
[Work Motivation], 2921
Work Motivation Inventory: A Test of Adult Work Motivation, 2922
Work Performance Assessment, 2923
Work Personality Profile, 2924
Work Preference Questionnaire, 2925
Work Readiness Profile, 2926
Work Skills Series Production, 2927
Work Temperament Inventory, 2928
Work Values Inventory, T4:2998
Working—Assessing Skills, Habits, and Style, 2929
Workplace Skills Survey, 2930
World Government Scale, 2931
World History/Objective Tests, 2932
Writing Process Test, 2933
Writing Test: McGraw-Hill Basic Skills System, T4:3003
The Written Expression Test, 2934
Written Language Assessment, 2935
Written Language Syntax Test, 2936

XYZ Inventory, 2937

Yardsticks, 2938
Y.E.M.R. Performance Profile for the Young Moderately and Mildly Retarded, T4:3009
Young Adult Behavior Checklist and Young Adult Self-Report, 2939

INDEX OF RECENTLY OUT-OF-PRINT TESTS

The Index of Recently Out-of-Print Tests is a listing of tests that appeared in Tests in Print IV, The Twelfth Mental Measurements Yearbook, *and/or* The Thirteenth Mental Measurements Yearbook *but that do not appear in* Tests in Print V. *The publishers of most of these tests have advised that the tests are now out of print. For some others, status has been unknown for over 10 years and the last known publisher is no longer in business and the tests are not published by a different publisher. All the tests in this new index are also integrated into the Index of Titles. All numbers refer to test entries, not page numbers. For example, T4:233 refers to test 233 in* Tests in Print IV, *12:121 refers to test 121 in* The 12th MMY, *and 13:301 refers to test 301 in* The 13th MMY.

Academic-Technical Aptitude Tests, T4:12
ACER Test of Reasoning Ability, 12:6
ACER Tests of Basic Skills—Blue Series, 12:7
Achievement Test—Hebrew Language, T4:36
Achievement Test in Jewish History, T4:35
Achievement Test—Jewish Life and Observances, T4:37
Achievement Test—The State of Israel, T4:38
ACS Examination in Analytical Chemistry, Graduate Level, T4:45
ACS Examination in Brief Organic Chemistry, T4:47
ACS Examination in Organic Chemistry, Graduate Level, T4:53
ACS Examination in Physical Chemistry, Graduate Level, T4:55
ACT Career Planning Program, T4:60
ACT Proficiency Examination in Abnormal Psychology, T4:62
ACT Proficiency Examination in Adult Nursing, T4:63
ACT Proficiency Examination in Anatomy and Physiology, T4:64
ACT Proficiency Examination in Fundamentals of Nursing, T4:65
ACT Proficiency Examination in Microbiology, T4:66
ACT Proficiency Examination in Occupational Strategy, Nursing, T4:67
ACT Proficiency Examination in Professional Strategies, Nursing, T4:68
ACT Proficiency Examination in Psychiatric/Mental Health Nursing, T4:69
ACT Proficiency Examination in Reading Instruction in the Elementary School, T4:70
ACT Proficiency Examination Program, T4:71
ACT Proficiency Examinations in Commonalities in Nursing Care, Areas A and B, T4:72
ACT Proficiency Examinations in Differences in Nursing Care, Areas A, B, C, T4:73
ACT Proficiency Examinations in Health Restoration, Areas I and II, T4:74
ACT Proficiency Examinations in Health Support, Areas I and II, T4:75
ACT Proficiency Examinations in Maternal and Child Nursing, T4:76
ACT Study Power Assessment and Inventory, 12:11
ACT Study Skills Assessment and Inventory (College Edition), 12:12
Action Research Skill Inventory, T4:79
An Adaptation of the Wechsler Preschool and Primary Scale of Intelligence for Deaf Children, T4:81
Adapted Sequenced Inventory of Communication Development, 12:13
Additional Personality Factor Inventory—2, T4:91

Aden-Crosthwait Adolescent Psychology Achievement Test, T4:92
The Adjustment Inventory, T4:94
Ahr's Individual Development Survey, T4:140
Algebra, Geometry and Trigonometry Test for Stds 9 and 10, T4:147
Alphabet Mastery, T4:153
Analysis of Readiness Skills: Reading and Mathematics, T4:165
The Anomalous Sentences Repetition Test, 12:29
The Anxiety Scale for the Blind, T4:172
Anxiety Scales for Children and Adults, 12:30
AO Sight Screener, T4:174
APT Manual Dexterity Test, T4:182
Aptitude for and Sensitivity to Music, T4:184
Aptitude Test Battery for Adults, T4:185
Arithmetic Reasoning Test, T4:188
ASPIRE (A Sales Potential Inventory for Real Estate), 12:32
Assessing Linguistic Behaviors: Assessing Prelinguistic and Early Linguistic Behaviors in Developmentally Young Children, T4:199
The Auditory Discrimination and Attention Test, T4:230

The Bangs Receptive Vocabulary Checklist, T4:239
The Barclay Classroom Assessment System, T4:243
Basic Language Concepts Test, T4:249
Basic School Skills Inventory—Screen, T4:257
Basic Sight Word Test, T4:258
Basic Skills Inventory, T4:259
Behavior Change Inventory, T4:276
Bessell Measurement of Emotional Maturity Scales, T4:295
Bingham Button Test, T4:300
Bloom Sentence Completion Survey, T4:309
The BrainMap, T4:320
Bristol Language Development Scales,12:54
Bristol Social Adjustment Guides, T4:335
Buswell-John Diagnostic Test for Fundamental Processes in Arithmetic, T4:348
The Butler Life Science Concept Test, T4:349

The CAHPER Fitness-Performance II Test, T4:350
CAI Study Skills Test, T4:351
California Preschool Social Competency Scale, T4:360
Callahan Anxiety Pictures, T4:365
CAP Assessment of Writing, 12:63
Career Interests Test, T4:397
Career Survey, T4:405
Caregiver's School Readiness Inventory, 12:65
Carrow Auditory-Visual Abilities Test, T4:411
CGP Self-Scoring Placement Tests in English and Mathematics (Drawn from the CGP), T4:416
Charteris Reading Test, 12:67
Chatterji's Non-Language Preference Record, T4:422
Checklist/Guide to Selecting a Small Computer, T4:425
The Child "At Risk" for Drug Abuse Rating Scale, 12:70
The CHILD Center Operational Assessment Tool, T4:435
Children's Depression Scale [Second Research Edition], 12:77
Christensen-Guilford Fluency Tests, T4:461
Clark-Madison Test of Oral Language, T4:468
Classroom Atmosphere Questionnaire, T4:472
Classroom Environment Index, T4:474
Clinical Record Keeping System, T4:527
Clinical Support System Battery, 12:82
Cognitive Observation Guide, 12:83
College Characteristics Index, T4:582
College English Placement Test, T4:583
Communicative Evaluation Chart From Infancy to Five Years, T4:601
Community College Goals Inventory, T4:602
A Comprehensive English Language Test for Speakers of English as a Second Language, T4:615
[Computer Programmer Test Package], T4:627
Concept Attainment Test, T4:631
Conceptual Systems Test, T4:632
Concise Word Reading Tests, T4:633
Continuous Symbol Checking Test, T4:641
Cooper-Farran Behavioral Rating Scales, 12:94
The Cooper-McGuire Diagnostic Word-Analysis Test, T4:644
Corrective Reading Mastery Tests, T4:663
The Couples BrainMap, T4:669
Course Evaluation Questionnaire, T4:670
Course-Faculty Instrument, T4:672
A Courtship Analysis, T4:673
CPH Patient Attitude Scale, T4:675
Creative Styles Inventory, 13:86
Criterion Validated Written Tests for Clerical Worker, T4:689
Croft Readiness Assessment in Comprehension Kit, T4:694
Cultural Literacy Test, 12:99
The Custody Quotient, T4:708

Dating Problems Checklist, T4:718
Deductive Reasoning Test, T4:722
Denver Community Mental Health Questionnaire—Revised, T4:738
Determining Needs in Your Youth Ministry, 12:104
Developing Cognitive Abilities Test [Second Edition], T4:755
Diagnosis and Remediation of Handwriting Problems, T4:773
A Diagnostic Achievement Test in Spelling, T4:776
Diagnostic Guide to DSM III, T4:778
Diagnostic Inventory for Screening Children, 13:99
Diagnostic Reading Tests, T4:783
Diagnostic Test for Students of English as a Second Language, T4:793
Diagnostic Test of Arithmetic Strategies, T4:794

Diagnostic Test of Library Skills—Advanced Edition, 13:101
Diagnostic Tests for Minimal Math Competencies, T4:797
Diagnostic Tests in Mathematics, T4:798
Differential Aptitude Tests—Computerized Adaptive Edition, 12:117
Digital Finger Tapping Test, 12:121
Discourse Comprehension Test, 13:102
Distar Mastery Tests, T4:810
Dropout Prediction & Prevention, 12:126
Dyslexia Schedule, T4:828

Effective Study Test, T4:864
Elizur Test of Psycho-Organicity: Children and Adults, T4:881
The Employment Barrier Identification Scale, T4:900
ENRIGHT Diagnostic Inventory of Basic Arithmetic Skills, T4:915
Evanston Early Identification Scale, Field Research Edition, T4:938
Expressional Growth Through Handwriting Evaluation Scale, T4:945

Family Risk Scales, 13:125
The Farnsworth-Munsell 100-Hue Test for the Examination of Color Discrimination, T4:969
Farnum Music Test, T4:970
First Grade Readiness Checklist, T4:983
Florida Cumulative Guidance Record, Revised, T4:991
Food Choice Inventory, T4:994
A Form Series Test, (Industrial Version), T4:998
The Fred Test, T4:1003
Frenchay Aphasia Screening Test, T4:1006

GAP Reading Comprehension Test, Third Edition, T4:1019
GAPADOL, T4:1020
General Science Test, T4:1032
The Gesell Child Developmental Age Scale,T4:1034
Gillingham-Childs Phonics Proficiency Scales, T4:1041
The Golombok Rust Inventory of Marital State, T4:1047
The Golombok Rust Inventory of Sexual Satisfaction, T4:1048
Gottschaldt Figures [NIPR], T4:1054
The Graduate Record Examinations Education Test, T4:1063
The Graduate Record Examinations Political Science Test, T4:1072
Grassi Basic Cognitive Evaluation, T4:1081
The Grassi Block Substitution Test: For Measuring Organic Brain Pathology, T4:1082
The Grief Experience Inventory, 12:168
Group Test for Indian South Africans, T4:1106
GROW—The Marriage Enrichment Program, T4:1110
Guidance Test Battery for Secondary Pupils (Standard 8), T4:1111

Harding Skyscraper, T4:1125
Harding Stress-Fair Compatibility Test, T4:1126
The Harrison-Stroud Reading Readiness Profiles, T4:1129
The Hartman Value Profile, T4:1130
Harvard Group Scale of Hypnotic Susceptibility, T4:1131
The Henmon-Nelson Tests of Mental Ability, T4:1150
Heterosocial Adequacy Test, T4:1152
High Level Estimation Test, T4:1154
High School Characteristics Index, T4:1157
High School Interest Questionnaire, T4:1158
High-School Subject Tests, T4:1161
The Hoffer-Osmond Diagnostic Test, T4:1168
How A Child Learns, T4:1175
Howarth Mood Adjective Check List, T4:1180
Howarth Personality Questionnaire, T4:1181
Hudson Education Skills Inventory, T4:1184
Hutchins Behavior Inventory, 12:184

ICES: Instructor and Course Evaluation System, T4:1194
Illinois Course Evaluation Questionnaire, T4:1201
Index of Personality Characteristics, T4:1210
Indiana Physical Fitness Test, T4:1211
Indiana-Oregon Music Discrimination Test, T4:1212
Individual Scale for Indian South Africans, T4:1213
Individualized Criterion Referenced Testing, 12:187
The Industrial Sentence Completion Form, T4:1220
Information Test on Drugs and Drug Abuse, T4:1231
Information Test on Human Reproduction, T4:1232
Information Test on Smoking and Health, T4:1233
Inquiry Mode Questionnaire: A Measure of How You Think and Make Decisions, 12:189
Institutional Goals Inventory, T4:1238
Integrated Literature and Language Arts Portfolio Program, 12:191
Interaction Index, 13:154
Interest Questionnaire for Indian South Africans, T4:1248
Intermediate Personality Questionnaire for Indian Pupils (Standards 6 to 8), T4:1250
Inventory for Counseling & Development, T4:1261
Inventory of Language Abilities, T4:1267
Inventory of Language Abilities, Level II, T4:1268
Iowa's Severity Rating Scales for Speech and Language Impairments, 12:196

Jacobsen-Kellogg Self Description Inventory II, T4:1298
JEVS Work Sample Evaluation System, T4:1304
[Job Application Forms], T4:1307
Job Training Assessment Program, T4:1318
The John Test, T4:1320
Junior Aptitude Tests for Indian South Africans, T4:1330
Junior Scholastic Proficiency Battery, T4:1334

Katz Adjustment Scale, T4:1340
Keyboard Skills Test, T4:1354
Kilander-Leach Health Knowledge Test, T4:1357
Kindergarten Screening Inventory, T4:1361
Kohn Problem Checklist/Kohn Social Competence Scale, 13:171
Kuder Occupational Interest Survey, Revised (Form DD), 1985, T4:1375
Kuder Preference Record—Vocational, T4:1376
Kwalwasser Music Talent Test, T4:1380

Language Arts Assessment Portfolio, 13:172
Language Assessment Battery, T4:1385
Language Proficiency Tests, T4:1392
Language Sampling and Analysis, T4:1394
Language-Structured Auditory Retention Span Test, T4:1395
Law Enforcement Perception Questionnaire, T4:1399
Leadership Skills Inventory, T4:1413
Learning Environment Inventory, T4:1424
Learning Inventory of Kindergarten Experiences, 12:216
Learning Methods Test, T4:1426
Leisure Activities Blank, T4:1441
The Leisure Diagnostic Battery, 12:220
Let's Talk Inventory For Children, T4:1447
Life Experiences Checklist, 12:221
Life Skills, Forms 1 and 2, T4:1456
Life Themes Inventory, T4:1460
Listening Comprehension, T4:1467
Listening Comprehension Test in English, T4:1469
A Love Attitudes Inventory, T4:1485

Marital Check-Up Kit, 13:192
A Marriage Adjustment Form, T4:1539
A Marriage Analysis, Experimental Edition, T4:1540
A Marriage Evaluation, T4:1542
The Marriage Expectation Inventories, T4:1543
Marriage Inventory, T4:1544
A Marriage Prediction Schedule, T4:1545
A Marriage Role Expectation Inventory, T4:1546
Mathematics Test for Seniors, T4:1563
Mathematics Test: McGraw-Hill Basic Skills System, T4:1564
Maudsley Personality Inventory, T4:1567
McCormick Job Performance Measurement "Rates-Scales", T4:1573
The McGuire-Bumpus Diagnostic Comprehension Test, T4:1574
The mCircle Instrument, T4:1575
McLeod Phonic Worksheets, T4:1576
Measurement of Self Concept in Kindergarten Children, T4:1587
Mechanical Comprehension Test, Second Edition, T4:1595
Merit Rating Series, T4:1613
Michigan Test of Aural Comprehension, T4:1622
MindMaker6, T4:1636
Minnesota School Attitude Survey, T4:1651
Minnesota Test for Differential Diagnosis of Aphasia, 13:203
Modern Language Aptitude Test, T4:1661
The Modified Version of the Bender-Gestalt Test for Preschool and Primary School Children, T4:1664
The Moreton Mathematics Tests, T4:1668
The Mother-Child Relationship Evaluation, 1980 Edition, 12:242
Mother/Infant Communication Screening, 12:243
Multidimensional Assessment of Philosophy of Education, T4:1680
The Multidimensional Maturity Scale, T4:1681
Multistate Professional Responsibility Examination, T4:1694
Mutually Responsible Facilitation Inventory, T4:1699
My Class Inventory, T4:1700

National Achievement Test [Second Edition], T4:1704
National Proficiency Survey Series, T4:1711
[NCRI Achievement Tests in Hebrew], T4:1713
Neurobehavioral Assessment of the Preterm Infant, 13:207
New South African Group Test, T4:1725
The New Sucher-Allred Reading Placement Inventory, T4:1726
Non-Language Test of Verbal Intelligence—Form 768, T4:1815
Non-Verbal Ability Tests, 12:259
NTE Core Battery, T4:1824
NTE Programs, T4:1825
NTE Specialty Area Tests: Agriculture, T4:1826
NTE Specialty Area Tests: Art Education, T4:1827
NTE Specialty Area Tests: Audiology, T4:1828
NTE Specialty Area Tests: Biology and General Science, T4:1829
NTE Specialty Area Tests: Business Education, T4:1830
NTE Specialty Area Tests: Chemistry, Physics, and General Science, T4:1831
NTE Specialty Area Tests: Early Childhood Education, T4:1832
NTE Specialty Area Tests: Education in the Elementary School, T4:1833
NTE Specialty Area Tests: Education of Mentally Retarded Students, T4:1834
NTE Specialty Area Tests: Educational Administration and Supervision, T4:1835
NTE Specialty Area Tests: English Language and Literature, T4:1836
NTE Specialty Area Tests: French, T4:1837
NTE Specialty Area Tests: German, T4:1838
NTE Specialty Area Tests: Home Economics Education, T4:1839
NTE Specialty Area Tests: Introduction to the Teaching of Reading, T4:1840
NTE Specialty Area Tests: Library Media Specialist, T4:1841

NTE Specialty Area Tests: Mathematics, T4:1842
NTE Specialty Area Tests: Music Education, T4:1843
NTE Specialty Area Tests: Physical Education, T4:1844
NTE Specialty Area Tests: Reading Specialist, T4:1845
NTE Specialty Area Tests: School Guidance and Counseling, T4:1846
NTE Specialty Area Tests: Social Studies, T4:1847
NTE Specialty Area Tests: Spanish, T4:1848
NTE Specialty Area Tests: Speech Communication, T4:1849
NTE Specialty Area Tests: Speech-Language Pathology, T4:1850
Nutrition Information Test, T4:1854

Objective-Analytic (O-A) Test Battery, T4:1858
O'Connor Finger Dexterity Test, T4:1874
O'Connor Tweezer Dexterity Test, T4:1875
The Occupational Interests Explorer, 12:265
The Occupational Interests Surveyor, 12:266
Ohio School Library/Media Test, T4:1886
The Ohio Tests of Articulation and Perception of Sounds, T4:1887
Oliphant Auditory Discrimination Memory Test, T4:1890
Oliphant Auditory Synthesizing Test, T4:1891
Open System Assessment for Managers, T4:1893
Oral Language Evaluation, Second Edition, 12:270
Organizational Climate Index, T4:1905
Organizational Value Dimensions Questionnaire: Business Form, T4:1908
Orientation and Motivation Inventory, T4:1909
Orientation Test for Professional Accounting, 12:273

PACS Pictures: Language Elicitation Materials, T4:1916
P.A.R. Admissions Test, T4:1919
Parent Readiness Evaluation of Preschoolers, T4:1928
Pattern Relations Test, T4:1941
Pennsylvania Bi-Manual Worksample, T4:1951
The Perceptual Maze Test, T4:1956
Performance Assessment of Syntax: Elicited and Spontaneous, T4:1959
Persian Achievement Tests, T4:1962
The Personal Communication Plan, 12:285
Personal Distress Inventory and Scales, T4:1970
Personal Profile System, T4:1982
Personal Relations Inventory, T4:1986
Personal Values Inventory, T4:1994
Phonological Assessment of Child Speech, T4:2014
Phonological Process Analysis, 12:294
Phonological Processes Assessment and Intervention, T4:2015
Pictorial Interest Inventory, T4:2021
Pictorial Study of Values: Pictorial Allport-Vernon, T4:2023
Pictorial Test of Intelligence, T4:2024
Picture Articulation & Language Screening Test, T4:2025
Picture Situation Test, T4:2027
Porch Index of Communicative Ability in Children, T4:2048
Porteous Problem Checklist, T4:2050
The Premarital Counseling Kit, T4:2070
Pre-Professional Skills Test, T4:2071
PreReading Expectancy Screening Scales, T4:2072
Preschool and Kindergarten Performance Profile, T4:2075
Preschool Behavior Rating Scale, T4:2078
Prescriptive Reading Performance Test, T4:2089
Prescriptive Teaching Series, T4:2090
Primary Academic Sentiment Scale, T4:2097
Printing Performance School Readiness Test, 12:308
Process Skills Rating Scales, 12:310
Productivity Assessment Questionnaire, T4:2113
Proficiency Battery in English and Mathematics for Indian South Africans, T4:2117
Programmer Aptitude/Competence Test System, T4:2132
The Progress Evaluation Scales, T4:2135
Projective Assessment of Aging Method, T4:2144
Prosody-Voice Screening Profile, 12:315
The Purdue High School English Test, T4:2166

The Quality of School Life Scale, T4:2173
Questionnaire On Resources and Stress, T4:2177
Quick Programming Aptitude Test, T4:2185
Quick Score Achievement Test, T4:2187
Quick Screening Scale of Mental Development, T4:2189

The RAD Scales, T4:2194
A Rating Inventory for Screening Kindergartners, 12:320
Reactions to Everyday Situations, T4:2216
Readiness for Kindergarten, T4:2217
Reading for Understanding Placement Test, T4:2227
Reading Test: McGraw-Hill Basic Skills System, T4:2232
Reading/Everyday Activities in Life, T4:2225
Rehabilitation Client Rating Scale, T4:2242
Relating to Each Other: A Questionnaire for Students, 13:260
Relating with Colleagues: A Questionnaire for Faculty Members, 13:261
A Religious Attitudes Inventory, T4:2248
Revised Developmental Screening Inventory—1980, T4:2259
Revised Edinburgh Functional Communication Profile, 12:328
Reynell-Zinkin Scales: Developmental Scales for Young Visually Handicapped Children Part 1—Mental Development, T4:2273
Riley Preschool Developmental Screening Inventory, T4:2280
Ring and Peg Tests of Behavior Development, T4:2281
Riverside Curriculum Assessment System, 13:268

Rogers Personal Adjustment Inventory: Revised, T4:2289
Rucker-Gable Educational Programming Scale, T4:2302
Rutgers Social Attribute Inventory, T4:2305

The Scales for Effective Teaching, 13:272
The Schedule of Recent Experience, T4:2344
Scholastic Achievement Test for English Lower Standards 2 and 3, T4:2346
Scholastic Achievement Test for English Lower Standards 9 and 10, T4:2347
Scholastic Achievement Test in Arithmetic, T4:2348
Scholastic Achievement Test of English Second Language Standard I, T4:2349
Scholastic Achievement Tests for English First Language, T4:2350
Scholastic Aptitude Test Battery for Pupils in Standards 2 and 3, T4:2351
Scholastic Proficiency Battery, T4:2352
School Apperception Method, T4:2353
School Atmosphere Questionnaire, T4:2356
School Behavior Checklist, T4:2358
School Interest Inventory, T4:2361
School Problem Screening Inventory, Fifth Edition, T4:2363
The School Readiness Checklist, T4:2364
School Readiness Survey, Second Edition, T4:2366
Scientific Knowledge and Aptitude Test, T4:2372
SCREEN [Senf-Comrey Ratings of Extra Educational Need], T4:2375
Screening Children for Related Early Educational Needs, T4:2378
Screening Instrument for Targeting Educational Risk, T4:2380
Screening Speech Articulation Test, T4:2382
Screening Test of Academic Readiness, T4:2386
Screening Test of Adolescent Language, T4:2387
SELF (Self-Concept Evaluation of Location Form), T4:2401
Self-Description Inventory, T4:2411
Self-Report Inventory, T4:2424
Self-Scoring Mathematics Placement Tests, T4:2425
Self-Scoring Reading Placement Test, T4:2426
Self-Scoring Written English Expression Placement Test, T4:2427
Sentence Comprehension Test, Revised Edition, T4:2436
Sentence Imitation Screening Tests, T4:2437
The Sex Attitudes Survey and Profile, Trial Edition, T4:2441
Sex Knowledge Inventory, T4:2442
The Sexual Compatibility Test, T4:2447
The Sexual Concerns Checklist, Experimental Edition, T4:2448
Shutt Primary Language Indicator Test, T4:2460
Signals Listening Test, T4:2461
The Single and Double Simultaneous (Face-Hand) Stimulation Test, T4:2464
Sloan Achromatopsia Test, T4:2479
Small College Goals Inventory, T4:2486
Social Behaviour Assessment Schedule, Third Edition, T4:2494
Social Intelligence Test: George Washington University Series [SPECIAL EDITION], T4:2497
Social Maturity Scale for Blind Preschool Children: A Guide to Its Use, T4:2498
Socio-Economic Status Scales, T4:2504
The South African Individual Scale for the Blind, T4:2509
South African Personality Questionnaire, T4:2510
The South African Picture Analysis Test, T4:2511
South African Wechsler Adult Individual Intelligence Scale, T4:2512
Spelling Test: McGraw-Hill Basic Skills System, T4:2526
Spellmaster, T4:2528
SRA Attitude Survey, T4:2532
SRA Placement and Counseling Program, T4:2537
SRA Typing Skills, T4:2541
St. Lucia Graded Word Reading Test, T4:2308
St. Lucia Reading Comprehension Test, T4:2309
Staff Burnout Scale for Health Professionals, T4:2543
The Standard Reading Tests, T4:2546
Stanford Hypnotic Susceptibility Scale, T4:2557
The Stanton Inventory, T4:2559
Stenographic Skill-Dictation Test, 12:372
Stern Activities Index, T4:2569
Strengthening Effectiveness of Board and Committee Members, T4:2573
Stress Analysis System, T4:2574
Stress Impact Scale, 12:373
Structured Pediatric Psychosocial Interview, T4:2586
Student Evaluation of Teacher Instrument II, T4:2594
Study Habits Evaluation and Instruction Kit, T4:2605
Study of Values: A Scale for Measuring the Dominant Interests in Personality, Third Edition, T4:2606
Study Skills Surveys, T4:2610
Study Skills Test: McGraw-Hill Basic Skills System, T4:2611
Stycar Hearing Tests, T4:2614
Stycar Language Test, T4:2615
Supervisory Inventory on Discipline, T4:2635
Supervisory Inventory on Grievances, T4:2636
Supervisory Inventory on Labor Relations, T4:2638
Supervisory Inventory on Safety, T4:2639
Surveys of Problem-Solving and Educational Skills, T4:2666
System to Plan Early Childhood Services, 12:385

TARC Assessment Inventory for Severely Handicapped Children, T4:2685
Teacher Evaluation Scale, 12:386
Teacher Stress Inventory, T4:2697

Teacher's School Readiness Inventory, 12:387
The Team Effectiveness Analysis Form, T4:2704
Temperament and Values Inventory, T4:2717
Temperament Assessment Battery for Children, T4:2718
Test for Auditory Figure-Ground Discrimination, T4:2728
Test of Ability to Subordinate, T4:2734
Test of Computational Processes, T4:2747
Test of Concept Utilization, T4:2748
Test of Early Socioemotional Development, T4:2753
A Test of English Usage, T4:2760
Test of Grammatically Correct Spanish/English, Written and Oral, T4:2761
Test of Listening Accuracy in Children, T4:2771
Test of Orientation for Rehabilitation Patients, 13:332
Test of Pragmatic Skills, Revised Edition, T4:2782
Test of Relational Concepts, T4:2786
Test of Syntactic Abilities, T4:2792
Test on the Fundamentals of Hebrew, T4:2807
Test on Understanding Science, T4:2808
Tests of Social Intelligence, T4:2819
The 3-R's Test, T4:2832
Tickmaster, T4:2835
Time Questionnaire: Assessing Suicide Potential, T4:2839
T.M.R. Performance Profile for the Severely and Moderately Retarded, T4:2843
T.M.R. School Competency Scales, T4:2844
Total Quality Management Readiness Index, 13:350
The Toy World Test, T4:2851
Twitchell-Allen Three-Dimensional Personality Test, T4:2859
Typing Skill Test, T4:2860
Values Inventory for Children, T4:2874
Visual Perceptual Skills Inventory, T4:2888
Visual-Verbal Test, 1981 Edition, T4:2891
VITAL Checklist and Curriculum Guide, T4:2892
Vocabulary Comprehension Scale, T4:2893
Vocabulary Test: McGraw-Hill Basic Skills System, T4:2894
Vocational Exploration and Insight Kit, T4:2900
Vocational Information Profile, T4:2901
Vocational Interest Questionnaire for Pupils in Standards 6-10, T4:2907

The Washington Pre-College Test, T4:2927
Watson Diagnostic Mathematics Test: Computation, Fourth Edition, T4:2931
Watson English Usage and Appreciation Test, Fourth Edition, T4:2932
Watson Number-Readiness Test, Fifth Edition, T4:2934
Watson Reading-Readiness Test, T4:2935
The Western Personnel Tests, T4:2951
Wide Range Intelligence-Personality Test [1978 Edition], T4:2958
Word and Number Assessment Inventory, T4:2977
Word Discrimination Test, T4:2978
Word Intelligibility by Picture Identification, T4:2980
Word Processor Assessment Battery, T4:2981
Word Recognition Test, T4:2982
Work Values Inventory, T4:2998
Writing Test: McGraw-Hill Basic Skills System, T4:3003

Y.E.M.R. Performance Profile for the Young Moderately and Mildly Retarded, T4:3009

INDEX OF ACRONYMS

This Index of Acronyms refers the reader to the appropriate test in Tests in Print V. *In some cases tests are better known by their acronyms than by their full titles, and this index can be of substantial help to the person who knows the former but not the latter. Acronyms are only listed if the author or publisher has made substantial use of the acronym in referring to the test, or if the test is widely known by the acronym. A few acronyms are also registered trademarks (e.g., SAT); where this is known to us, only the test with the registered trademark is referenced. There is some danger in the overuse of acronyms, but this index, like all other indexes in this work, is provided to make the task of identifying a test as easy as possible. All numbers refer to test numbers, not page numbers.*

AAA: Assessment of Adaptive Areas, 198
AABP: Aptitude Assessment Battery: Programming, 167
AAC: Adolescent Apperception Cards, 71
AADDBRS: Adult Attention Deficit Disorder Behavior Rating Scale, 80
A-ADDES: Adult Attention Deficit Disorders Evaluation Scale, 81
AAI: Association Adjustment Inventory, 218
AAI: Academic Advising Inventory, 8
AALI: Ann Arbor Learning Inventory [1996 Edition], 157
AAPEP: Adolescent and Adult Psychoeducational Profile: Volume IV, 70
AAPS: Arizona Articulation Proficiency Scale, Second Edition, 175
AASE: Analytical Aptitude Skills Evaluation, 154
ABA: Apraxia Battery for Adults, 163
ABC: Aberrant Behavior Checklist, 4
ABC: Achieving Behavioral Competencies, 40
ABCD: The Arizona Battery for Communication Disorders of Dementia, 176
ABES: Adaptive Behavior Evaluation Scale, Revised, 59
ABI: Adaptive Behavior Inventory, 60
ABIC: Adaptive Behavior Inventory for Children, 61
ABLE: Adult Basic Learning Examination, Second Edition, 82
ABS-RC:2: AAMR Adaptive Behavior Scale—Residential and Community, Second Edition, 1
ABS-S:2: AAMR Adaptive Behavior Scale—School, Second Edition, 2
ACAT: The Computer Category Test, 667
ACCI: Adult Career Concerns Inventory, 83
ACDI: ACDI-Corrections Version and Corrections Version II, 19
ACDM: Assessment of Career Decision Making, 200
ACE: Analyzing the Communication Environment, 156
ACG: Assessment of Core Goals, 205
ACHI: Assessment of Chemical Health Inventory, 201
ACL: The Adjective Check List, 68
ACLC: Assessment of Children's Language Comprehension, 1983 Revision, 202
ACO: Assessment of Conceptual Organization (ACO): Improving, Writing, Thinking, and Reading Skills, 204
ACPT: Auditory Continuous Performance Test, 229
ACS: Adolescent Coping Scale, 72
ACTeRS: ADD-H: Comprehensive Teacher's Rating Scale, Second Edition [1998 Revision], 65
ADAT: Attention Disorders in Children: School-Based Assessment, Diagnosis, and Treatment, 225

ADDBRS: Attention Deficit Disorder Behavior Rating Scales, 220
ADDES: Attention Deficit Disorders Evaluation Scale, Second Edition, 221
ADDES-S: The Attention Deficit Disorders Evaluation Scale Secondary-Age Student, 222
A-DES: Adolescent Dissociative Experiences Scale, 74
ADHDT: Attention-Deficit/Hyperactivity Disorder Test, 223
ADI: Adolescent Drinking Index, 75
ADI: Adolescent Diagnostic Interview, 73
ADLO: Assessment of Developmental Levels by Observation, 206
ADP: Aphasia Diagnostic Profiles, 159
ADS: Alcohol Dependence Scale, 134
ADSA: Attention-Deficit Scales for Adults, 224
ADSS: Attention Disorders in Children: School-Based Assessment, Diagnosis, and Treatment, 225
ADT: Wepman's Auditory Discrimination Test, Second Edition, 2870
AFI: Adaptive Functioning Index, 63
AFSC: Assessment of Fluency in School-Age Children, 207
AHPAT: Allied Health Professions Admission Test, 141
AHSME: American High School Mathematics Examination, 144
AIA: Ashland Interest Assessment, 183
AIDS: Assessment of Intelligibility of Dysarthric Speech, 209
Aii: Aptitude Interest Inventory, 168
AIM: Achievement Identification Measure, 35
AIM: Assessment Inventory for Management, 197
AIM-TO: Achievement Identification Measure—Teacher Observation, 36
AIME: American Invitational Mathematics Examination, 148
AIR: Assessment of Interpersonal Relations, 210
AJHSME: American Junior High School Mathematics Examination, 149
AKT: Applied Knowledge Test, 160
AL-AQ (2nd Edition): ACER Advanced Tests AL and AQ (Second Edition) and BL-BQ, 23
A-LAS®: Adult Language Assessment Scales, 84
ALDA: Analytic Learning Disability Assessment, 153
ALDQ: Alleman Leadership Development Questionnaire, 138
ALFA: Assessment of Language-Related Functional Activities, 211
ALNAS: The ACT Evaluation/Survey Service, 57
ALSAR: Assessment of Living Skills and Resources, 212
ALST: Adolescent Language Screening Test, 76
AMI: Athletic Motivation Inventory, 219
AMP: Achievement Motivation Profile, 37
AMS: Access Management Survey, 14
AMSQ: Alleman Mentoring Scales Questionnaire, 139
AMTC: Assessing Motivation to Communicate, 188
ANE: Assessment in Nursery Education, 196
ANQ: Adult Neuropsychological Questionnaire, 85
ANSER System: The ANSER System-Aggregate Neurobehavioral Student Health and Educational Review [Revised 1997], 158
AOB: Automated Office Battery, 236
AOII: Occupational Interest Inventories, 1818
AOS: The ACT Evaluation/Survey Service, 57
AP®: Advanced Placement Examinations, 118
A-PAC1: Progress Assessment Chart of Social and Personal Development, 2088
APAT: Accounting Program Admission Test, 17
APB: Academic Proficiency Battery, 12
API: Adult Personality Inventory [Revised], 86
API: Affective Perception Inventory, 120
API: The Affective Perception Inventory/College Level, 121
APP-R: The Assessment of Phonological Processes—Revised, 214
APPSI: Assessment for Persons Profoundly or Severely Impaired, 193
Aprenda 2: Aprenda®: La prueba de logros en español—Segunda edición, 165
APS: Adolescent Psychopathology Scale, 77
APSIP: Assessment of Parenting Skills: Infant and Preschooler, 213
APT: Age Projection Test, 122
AQSDOR: Assessment of Qualitative and Structural Dimensions of Object Representations, Revised Edition, 215
ARCI: Addiction Research Center Inventory, 66
ARI: Abuse Risk Inventory for Women, Experimental Edition, 7
AROE: Adult Rating of Oral English, 87
ARVQ: Alleman Relationship Value Questionnaire, 140
AS: The ACT Evaluation/Survey Service, 57
ASAT: Auditory Selective Attention Test, 231
ASB: Aptitude Tests for School Beginners, 169
ASCA: Adjustment Scales for Children and Adolescents, 69
ASCVIS: Armed Services—Civilian Vocational Interest Survey, 179
ASES: Adult Self Expression Scale, 88
ASI: Adaptive Style Inventory, 64
ASI: The Assertiveness Skills Inventory, 185
ASI: Reiss-Epstein-Gursky Anxiety Sensitivity Index, 2199
ASI-4: Adolescent Symptom Inventory-4, 79
ASIEP-2: Autism Screening Instrument for Educational Planning, Second Edition, 234
ASIQ: Adult Suicidal Ideation Questionnaire, 89
ASIST: ASIST: A Structured Addictions Assessment Interview for Selecting Treatment, 184
ASLPR: Australian Second Language Proficiency Ratings, 233

ASNLAS: Assessment of School Needs for Low-Achieving Students: Staff Survey, 216
ASPECT: Ackerman-Schoendorf Scales for Parent Evaluation of Custody, 41
ASQ: The IPAT Anxiety Scale, 1321
ASQ: Ages and Stages Questionnaires, 123
ASSESS: ASSESS Expert System Version 5.X, 186
ASVAB: Armed Services Vocational Aptitude Battery [Forms 18/19], 180
ATAG: Achievement Test for Accounting Graduates, 38
ATB: Advanced Test Battery, 119
ATD PA: Matching Person and Technology, 1593
ATFR: Arlin Test of Formal Reasoning, 178
ATMS: Attitudes Toward Mainstreaming Scale, 227
AUDIT: Alcohol Use Disorders Identification Test, 135
AUI: Alcohol Use Inventory, 136
AWM: Attitudes Toward Working Mothers Scale, 228
AYW: Appraise Your World, 162

BAB: Ball Aptitude Battery, 239
BACON: Accounting Clerk Staff Selector, 16
BADS: Behavioural Assessment of the Dysexecutive Syndrome, 295
BAEDPMC: IS Manager/Consultant Skills Evaluation, 1328
BAEDPSA: IS Sales Assessment Battery, 1330
BaFPE: Bay Area Functional Performance Evaluation, Second Edition, 268
BAI: Beck Anxiety Inventory [1993 Edition], 271
BAI: Braille Assessment Inventory, 332
BALEADS: IS Project Leader Skills Evaluation, 1329
BAP: Behavioral Assessment of Pain Questionnaire, 291
BarOn EQ-i: BarOn Emotional Quotient Inventory, 243
BAS II: British Ability Scales: Second Edition, 349
BASA: Boston Assessment of Severe Aphasia, 328
BASC: Behavior Assessment System for Children [Revised], 280
BASC Monitor for ADHD: BASC Monitor for ADHD, 245
BASE: Behavioral Academic Self-Esteem, 289
BASIS: Basic Achievement Skills Individual Screener, 246
BASIS-A: BASIS-A Inventory [Basic Adlerian Scales for Interpersonal Success—Adult Form], 262
BASLCUS: Customer Service Skills Test, 756
Batería-RCOG: Batería Woodcock-Muñoz—Revisada, 264
BBCS-R.: Bracken Basic Concept Scale—Revised, 331
BBRS: Burks' Behavior Rating Scales, 355
BBTOP: Bankson-Bernthal Test of Phonology, 240
BCP: Behavioral Characteristics Progression, 292
BCT: The Booklet Category Test, Second Edition, 326
BDF: Birds of Different Feathers Work Style Assessment, 313
BDI: Battelle Developmental Inventory, 265
BDI Screening Test: Battelle Developmental Inventory Screening Test, 266
BDI-II: Beck Depression Inventory—II, 272
BDIS: Behavior Disorders Identification Scale, 283
BDP: Comprehensive Drinker Profile, 652
B-DPRS™: Brief Derogatis Psychiatric Rating Scale, 335
BDRS: Behavior Dimensions Rating Scale, 281
BDS: Behavior Dimensions Scale, 282
BED: Bedside Evaluation of Dysphagia, 276
BEES: The Balanced Emotional Empathy Scale, 238
BERS: Behavioral and Emotional Rating Scale: A Strength-Based Approach to Assessment, 290
BEST: Basic Educational Skills Test, 248
B.E.S.T: Basic English Skills Test, 250
BEST: BEST Instruments, 305
BEST-2: Bedside Evaluation Screening Test, Second Edition, 277
BES-2: Behavior Evaluation Scale—2, 284
BET: Basic Economics Test, 247
BETA-II: Revised Beta Examination, Second Edition, 2212
B40: ACER Advanced Test B40, 20
BGMA: Hughes Basic Gross Motor Assessment, 1225
BGT: [Bender-Gestalt Test], 301
BHI: Battery for Health Improvement, 267
BHI: Bilingual Home Inventory, 306
BI: Biographical Inventory Form U, 311
BIC: Bury Infant Check, 359
BINL: Basic Inventory of Natural Language, 251
BINS: Bayley Infant Neurodevelopmental Screener, 269
BITCH: The BITCH Test (Black Intelligence Test of Cultural Homogeneity), 316
BJT: Business Judgment Test, Revised, 361
BLAT: The Blind Learning Aptitude Test, 318
BL-BQ: ACER Advanced Tests AL and AQ (Second Edition) and BL-BQ, 23
BLSS: Basic Living Skills Scale, 252
BLT-NE: Bloomer Learning Test—Neurologically Enhanced, 320
BLT-2: Bankson Language Test—2, 241
BMCT: Bennett Mechanical Comprehension Test, Second Edition, 302
Boehm-R: Boehm Test of Basic Concepts—Revised, 324
BOLT: USES Basic Occupational Literacy Test, 2795
BORB: Birmingham Object Recognition Battery, 314
BORRTI: Bell Object Relations and Reality Testing Inventory, 297
BOS: Behavioral Objective Sequence, 293
BP: The Blacky Pictures: A Technique for the Exploration of Personality Dynamics, 317
BPI: Basic Personality Inventory, 256

BPICS: Bi/Polar Inventory of Core Strengths, 312
BPS: Bricklin Perceptual Scales, 334
BPS: BRIGANCE® Preschool Screen, 347
BPVS: British Picture Vocabulary Scales, 350
BQSS: Boston Qualitative Scoring System for the Rey-Osterrieth Complex Figure, 329
BRI: Botel Reading Inventory, 330
BRIAAC: Behavior Rating Instrument for Autistic and Other Atypical Children, 2nd Edition, 285
Brief CDS: Carroll Depression Scales, 429
Brown ADD Scales: Brown Attention-Deficit Disorder Scales, 351
BRP-2: Behavior Rating Profile, Second Edition, 286
BRS: Emotional Problems Scales, 931
BRS: McCarron-Dial System, 1610
BRSS: Devereux Behavior Rating Scale—School Form, 817
BSI: Behavior Status Inventory, 288
BSI®: Brief Symptom Inventory , 337
BSID-II: Bayley Scales of Infant Development, Second Edition, 270
BSM I: Bilingual Syntax Measure, 307
BSM II: Bilingual Syntax Measure, 307
BSRI: Bem Sex-Role Inventory, 298
BSS: Beck Scale for Suicide Ideation, 274
BSSI-3: Basic School Skills Inventory, Third Edition, 258
BST: PSI Basic Skills Tests for Business, Industry, and Government, 2105
BTHI: Brief Test of Head Injury, 338
BTPI: Butcher Treatment Planning Inventory, 362
Burns Inventory: Burns Brief Inventory of Communication and Cognition, 356
BVAT: Bilingual Verbal Ability Tests, 309
BVMAT: Basic Visual-Motor Association Test, 261
BVRT: Benton Visual Retention Test, Fifth Edition, 303
BWAP: Becker Work Adjustment Profile, 275

CAAP: Collegiate Assessment of Academic Proficiency, 621
CAARS: Conners' Adult ADHD Rating Scales, 678
CAAS: Children's Attention and Adjustment Survey, 469
CAB: Clerical Abilities Battery, 532
CAB: Comprehensive Ability Battery, 644
CABS: Childrens Adaptive Behavior Scale, Revised, 465
CADeT: Communication Abilities Diagnostic Test, 628
CADL-2: Communication Activities of Daily Living, Second Edition, 629
CAIMI: Children's Academic Intrinsic Motivation Inventory, 464
CAIN: Standardized Test of Computer Literacy and Computer Anxiety Index (Version AZ), Revised, 2482
CAK: Concept Assessment Kit—Conservation, 674
CalCAP: California Computerized Assessment Package, 366
CALS: Checklist of Adaptive Living Skills, 443
Canadian TCS: Canadian Test of Cognitive Skills, 388
C&RT: The Creatrix Inventory, 727
CAP: Creativity Assessment Packet, 724
CAP Inventory: The Child Abuse Potential Inventory, Form VI, 448
CAPE: Clifton Assessment Procedures for the Elderly, 537
CAPPS: Current and Past Psychopathology Scales, 748
CAPS: Career Ability Placement Survey, 395
CAPS: Measures in Post Traumatic Stress Disorder: A Practitioner's Guide, 1626
CAQ: Change Agent Questionnaire, 437
CAQ: The Class Activities Questionnaire, 493
CAQ: Clinical Analysis Questionnaire, 538
CAQ-90: California Q-Sort (Revised Adult Set), 373
CARB: Computerized Assessment of Response Bias: Revised Edition, 671
CARS: The Childhood Autism Rating Scale, 459
CARS: Children at Risk Screener: Kindergarten and Preschool, 461
CARS: Comprehensive Assessment of Reading Strategies, 647
CAS: Character Assessment Scale, 439
CAS: Child Anxiety Scale, 450
CAS: Children's Abilities Scales, 463
CAS: Cognitive Abilities Scale, 559
CAS: College Adjustment Scales, 569
CAS: Creativity Attitude Survey, 725
CAS: Das-Naglieri Cognitive Assessment System, 763
CASAS: Comprehensive Adult Student Assessment System, 645
CASE: Comprehensive Assessment of School Environments, 648
CASE-IMS: Comprehensive Assessment of School Environments Information Management System, 649
CASH: Comprehensive Assessment of Symptoms and History, 650
CASI: Career Attitudes and Strategies Inventory: An Inventory for Understanding Adult Careers, 400
CASS-A: Cooper Assessment for Stuttering Syndromes, 691
CASS-C: Cooper Assessment for Stuttering Syndromes, 691
CAST: Canadian Achievement Survey Tests for Adults, 383
CAST: Children of Alcoholics Screening Test, 462
CAST: Children's Apperceptive Story-Telling Test, 467
C.A.T.: Children's Apperception Test [1991 Revision], 466
CAT: Children's Articulation Test, 468

CAT: Cognitive Abilities Test, Second Edition [British Edition], 561
CAT: The Computer Category Test, 667
CAT/2: Canadian Achievement Tests, Second Edition, 384
CAT/5: California Achievement Tests, Fifth Edition, 364
CATI: Coolidge Axis II Inventory, 690
CATIM: Class Achievement Test in Mathematics, 492
CAVLT-2: Children's Auditory Verbal Learning Test-2, 470
CBCL: Child Behavior Checklist, 451
CBI: Career Beliefs Inventory, 401
CBI1: Creative Behavior Inventory, 723
CBI2: Creative Behavior Inventory, 723
CBRS: Cognitive Behavior Rating Scales, 562
CBRSC: Comprehensive Behavior Rating Scale for Children, 651
CBRT: Clymer-Barrett Readiness Test, Revised Edition, 552
CCAE: Checklist for Child Abuse Evaluation, 442
CCAI: Cross-Cultural Adaptability Inventory, 737
CCAT: Canadian Cognitive Abilities Test, Form K, 385
CCB: Cognitive Control Battery, 563
CCEI: Crown-Crisp Experiential Index, 739
CCF: Curtis Completion Form, 751
CCPI: Combined Cognitive Preference Inventory, 626
CCQ: The California Child Q-Set, 365
CCQ: Chronicle Career Quest, 485
CCSEQ-2: Community College Student Experiences Questionnaire, Second Edition, 635
CCSI: The Classroom Communication Skills Inventory: Listening and Speaking Checklist, 494
CCT: Children's Category Test, 471
CCTDI: The California Critical Thinking Dispositions Inventory, 367
CCTST: California Critical Thinking Skills Test, 368
CCTT: The Cornell Critical Thinking Tests, 705
CC-2: Automated Office Battery, 236
CDB: Cognitive Diagnostic Battery, 564
CDDI: Christensen Dietary Distress Inventory, 483
CDI: Career Development Inventory [Consulting Psychologists Press, Inc.], 405
CDI: Career Directions Inventory, 406
CDI: Child Development Inventory, 453
CDI: Children's Depression Inventory, 472
CDI: MacArthur Communicative Development Inventories, 1528
CDM-R: The Harrington-O'Shea Career Decision-Making System Revised, 1177
CDMSE: Career Decision-Making Self-Efficacy Scale, 403
CDMT: California Diagnostic Mathematics Tests, 369
CDP: Comprehensive Drinker Profile, 652
CDR: Child Development Review, 454
CDRS-R: Children's Depression Rating Scale, Revised, 473
CDRT: California Diagnostic Reading Tests, 370
CDS: Carroll Depression Scales, 429
CDS-R: Carroll Depression Scales, 429
CEAI: Continuing Education Assessment Inventory, 686
CEFT: Children's Embedded Figures Test, 474
CEI: The Career Exploration Inventory, 407
CELF-Preschool: Clinical Evaluation of Language Fundamentals—Preschool, 539
CELF—3: Clinical Evaluation of Language Fundamentals, Third Edition, 540
CELF-3: Clinical Evaluation of Language Fundamentals, Third Edition—Observational Rating Scales, 541
CELF-3 Screening Test: Clinical Evaluation of Language Fundamentals—3 Screening Test, 542
CELI: Carrow Elicited Language Inventory, 430
CERAD: CERAD (Consortium to Establish a Registry for Alzheimer's Disease) Assessment Battery, 434
CERNS: Clinical Experience Record for Nursing Students, 543
CES: Career Exploration Series, 1992 Revision, 408
CES: Classroom Environment Scale, Third Edition, 495
CF: Course Finder, 718
CFI: Career Factors Inventory, 409
CFIT: Culture Fair Intelligence Test, 745
CFP: Cognitive Diagnostic Battery, 564
CFR: Cognitive Diagnostic Battery, 564
CFSEI-2: Culture-Free Self-Esteem Inventories, Second Edition, 746
CFT: Complex Figure Test, 641
CGI: Career Guidance Inventory, 410
CGS: Kilmann-Saxton Culture-Gap Survey [Revised], 1397
Chicago EARLY: Chicago Early Assessment and Remediation LaboratorY, 446
CHIP: Coping With Health Injuries and Problems, 700
CHIS: Closed Head Injury Screener, 546
CI: Content Inventories: English, Social Studies, Science, 683
CI: The Kirkpatrick Management and Supervisory Skills Series, 1403
CIBS-R: BRIGANCE® Diagnostic Comprehensive Inventory of Basic Skills, Revised, 340
CIDI: Composite International Diagnostic Interview, 642
CIES: Correctional Institutions Environment Scale, Second Edition, 710
CIF: Comprehensive Drinker Profile, 652
CII: Chart of Initiative and Independence, 441
CIIS: Cattell Infant Intelligence Scale, 433
CILD: Career Assessment Inventories for the Learning Disabled, 397
CIP: Comprehensive Identification Process [Revised], 653

CIRP: The Cooperative Institutional Research Program, 692
CISE: Children's Inventory of Self-Esteem, 475
CISS™: Campbell™ Interest and Skill Survey, 380
CISS: Coping Inventory for Stressful Situations, 696
CLAM: Child Language Ability Measures, 455
CLASSIC: The Cornell Learning and Study Skills Inventory, 707
CLEP: College Level Examination Program, 617
CLES: Coddington Life Events Scales, 557
CLGES: The California Life Goals Evaluation Schedules, 371
CLI: Campbell Leadership Index, 381
CMA: Conflict Management Appraisal, 675
CMEE: Content Mastery Examinations for Educators, 684
CMI: Career Maturity Inventory, 413
CMII: College Major Interest Inventory, 618
CMMS: Columbia Mental Maturity Scale, Third Edition, 624
CMQ: The Common-Metric Questionnaire, 627
CMS: Conflict Management Survey, 676
CMS: Clyde Mood Scale, 551
CMS: Children's Memory Scale, 476
CMT: Contextual Memory Test, 685
CNQ: Child Neuropsychological Questionnaire, 456
COAB: Computer Operator Aptitude Battery, 669
COACH: C.O.A.C.H.: Cayuga-Onondaga Assessment for Children with Handicaps, Version 7.0, 553
COCON: Controller/Accountant Staff Selector, 688
CODT: Crane Oral Dominance Test: Spanish/English, 720
CogAT: Cognitive Abilities Test, Form 5, 560
Cognistat: Cognistat (The Neurobehavioral Cognitive Status Examination), 558
CogScreen-AE: CogScreen Aeromedical Edition, 567
COIB: Correctional Officers' Interest Blank, 711
COII: Canadian Occupational Interest Inventory, 387
College BASE: College Basic Academic Subjects Examination, 570
COMP: College Outcome Measures Program, 619
COMPAS: Oetting's Computer Anxiety Scale, 1831
COMPLIT: Computer Literacy Skills Profile, 668
COPES: Career Orientation Placement and Evaluation Survey, 417
COPES: Community Oriented Programs Environment Scale, 637
COPS-II: Career Occupational Preference System, Intermediate Inventory, 415
COPS-P: Career Occupational Preference System—Professional Level Interest Inventory, 416
COPS-PIC: COPSystem Picture Inventory of Careers, 702
COPS-R: Career Occupational Preference System, Interest Inventory, Form R, 414
COR: High/Scope Child Observation Record for Ages 2 1/2–6, 1204
COS: The ACT Evaluation/Survey Service, 57
COS: Campbell Organizational Survey, 382
COTNAB: The Chessington O.T. Neurological Assessment Battery, 445
CP3: Personnel Test Battery, 1973
CP4: Personnel Test Battery, 1973
CP7: Personnel Test Battery, 1973
CP7: Programmer Aptitude Series, 2087
CP8: Personnel Test Battery, 1973
CPAB: Computer Programmer Aptitude Battery, 670
CPAI: The Kirkpatrick Management and Supervisory Skills Series, 1403
CPAS: Crawford Psychological Adjustment Scale, 721
CPB: Chronic Pain Battery, 484
CPC: Children's Problems Checklist, 478
CPCI: Couple's Pre-Counseling Inventory, Revised Edition, 1987, 717
CPCL: Career Problem Check List, 419
CPF: Certified Picture Framer Examination, 435
CPF: CPF [Second Edition], 719
CPI: California Psychological Inventory, Third Edition, 372
CPI: Cooperative Preschool Inventory, Revised Edition, 693
CPP: Comprehensive Personality Profile, 654
CPQ: Children's Personality Questionnaire, 1985 Edition, 477
CPQ: Coaching Process Questionnaire, 555
CPS: Carlson Psychological Survey, 427
CPS Short Form: Comrey Personality Scales—Short Form, 673
CPT: Chinese Proficiency Test, 481
CPT: Conners' Continuous Performance Test, 679
CPTs: ACCUPLACER: Computerized Placement Tests, 18
CPVT: Carolina Picture Vocabulary Test (for Deaf and Hearing Impaired), 428
CQ: Cree Questionnaire, 728
CREVT: Comprehensive Receptive and Expressive Vocabulary Test, 655
CREVT-A: Comprehensive Receptive and Expressive Vocabulary Test—Adult, 656
CRI: Caring Relationship Inventory, 426
CRI: Classroom Reading Inventory, Seventh Edition, 496
CRI: Children's Role Inventory, 479
CRI: Coping Resources Inventory, 697
CRI: Coping Responses Inventory—Adult and Youth, 699
CRIS: Coping Resources Inventory for Stress, 698
CRS: Clinical Rating Scale, 544
CRS: Customer Reaction Survey, 755
CRS-R: Conners' Rating Scales—Revised, 681
CRT: Critical Reasoning Tests, 736
CRTB: Critical Reasoning Test Battery, 735
CSAB: Cognitive Skills Assessment Battery, Second Edition, 565

CSBI: Child Sexual Behavior Inventory, 457
CSBS: Communication and Symbolic Behavior Scales, 630
CSC: Cognitive Symptom Checklists, 566
CSEQ: College Student Experiences Questionnaire, 620
CSI: Coaching Skills Inventory, 556
CSI: Conflict Style Inventory, 677
CSI: Culture Shock Inventory [Revised], 747
CSIT: Chapin Social Insight Test, 438
CSNAS: The ACT Evaluation/Survey Service, 57
CSPDT: Crawford Small Parts Dexterity Test, 722
CSRS: The Conversational Skills Rating Scale: An Instructional Assessment of Interpersonal Competence, 689
CSSA: Comprehensive Scales of Student Abilities: Quantifying Academic Skills and School-Related Behavior Through the Use of Teacher Judgments, 657
CST: Chinese Speaking Test, 482
CST: Comprehensive Screening Test for Determining Optimal Communication Mode, 658
CTAB: Comprehensive Test of Adaptive Behavior, 661
CTBS: Canadian Tests of Basic Skills, Forms 7 and 8, 389
CTBS/4: Comprehensive Tests of Basic Skills, Fourth Edition, 665
CTI: Career Thoughts Inventory, 422
CTONI: Comprehensive Test of Nonverbal Intelligence, 662
CTP: California Test of Personality, 374
CTPIII: Comprehensive Testing Program III, 664
CTQ: Childhood Trauma Questionnaire, 460
C-TRF: Caregiver-Teacher Report Form, 424
CTS: Carey Temperament Scales, 425
CTVF: Comprehensive Test of Visual Functioning, 663
CV/FES: Children's Version of The Family Environment Scale, 480
CVCST: Curtis Verbal-Clerical Skills Tests, 754
CVLT: California Verbal Learning Test, Research Edition, Adult Version, 376
CVLT-C: California Verbal Learning Test, Children's Version, 375
CVMT: Continuous Visual Memory Test [Revised], 687

D.A.L.E. System: Developmental Assessment of Life Experiences (1998 Edition), 805
d2 Test: d2 Test of Attention, 860
DA5: Advanced Test Battery, 119
DA5: Programmer Aptitude Series, 2087
DAB-2: Diagnostic Achievement Battery, Second Edition, 821
DABERON-2: DABERON-2: Screening for School Readiness, Second Edition, 759
DABS: Derogatis Affects Balance Scale [Revised], 791
DANTES: DANTES Subject Standardized Tests, 762
DAP: Diversity Awareness Profile, 848
DAP: The Draw-A-Person, 853
DAP:SPED: Draw A Person: Screening Procedure for Emotional Disturbance, 852
DAR: Diagnostic Assessments of Reading, 823
DARD: Durrell Analysis of Reading Difficulty, Third Edition, 861
DAS: Draw-a-Story: Screening for Depression and Age or Gender Differences [Revised], 855
DAS: Differential Ability Scales, 837
DAS: Dyadic Adjustment Scale, 863
DASE: Denver Articulation Screening Exam, 783
DASH-2: A Developmental Assessment for Students with Severe Disabilities, Second Edition, 804
DASI-II: Developmental Activities Screening Inventory, Second Edition, 803
DAST: Denver Audiometric Screening Test, 784
DAST-20: Drug Use Questionnaire, 859
DAT: Dental Admission Test, 780
DAT: Differential Aptitude Tests, Fifth Edition, 838
DAT for PCA: Differential Aptitude Tests for Personnel and Career Assessment, 839
DATA-2: Diagnostic Achievement Test for Adolescents, Second Edition, 822
DAYC: Developmental Assessment of Young Children, 806
DAYS: Depression and Anxiety in Youth Scale, 789
DBPRDF: Database Analyst Staff Selector, 764
DC3: Critical Reasoning Test Battery, 735
DCD: The Dennis Test of Child Development, 778
DDS: The Demos D Scale: An Attitude Scale for the Identification of Dropouts , 777
DDT: The Differential Diagnostic Technique, 840
DDT: Dyslexia Determination Test, Second Edition, 867
DEP: Dysphagia Evaluation Protocol, 870
DEQ: Depressive Experiences Questionnaire, 790
DEQ-A: Depressive Experiences Questionnaire, 790
DES: Dissociative Experiences Scale, 846
DES-II: Measures in Post Traumatic Stress Disorder: A Practitioner's Guide, 1626
DEST: Denver Eye Screening Test, 785
DFOS: Dynamic Factors Survey, 865
DFP: Dissociative Features Profile, 847
DHA: Denver Handwriting Analysis, 786
DIAL-3: Developmental Indicators for the Assessment of Learning, Third Edition, 809
DISC: Sentence Completion Tests, 2381
DIT: Defining Issues Test, 771
DMI: Decision Making Inventory, 768
DMI: Defense Mechanisms Inventory [Revised], 770
DOBS: Description of Body Scale, 795
DOCS: Developmental Observation Checklist System, 810

DOES: Dimensions of Excellence Scales [1991 Edition], 843
DOF: Child Behavior Checklist, 451
DOSC: Dimensions of Self-Concept, 844
DP-II: Developmental Profile II, 811
DPICS: Dyadic Parent-Child Interaction Coding System: A Manual, 864
DPQS: Draw-A-Person Quality Scale, 851
DPRS: Derogatis Psychiatric Rating Scale, 792
Draw A Person: QSS: Draw A Person: A Quantitative Scoring System, 854
DRI-II: Driver Risk Inventory—II, 856
DRP: Degrees of Reading Power [Revised], 773
DRS: Dementia Rating Scale, 776
DRS-81: Diagnostic Reading Scales, 827
DSC: Developing Skills Checklist, 800
DSFI: Derogatis Sexual Functioning Inventory, 793
DSI: Daily Stress Inventory, 760
DSMD: Devereux Scales of Mental Disorders, 818
DSP: Derogatis Stress Profile, 794
DSPT: Diagnostic Spelling Potential Test, 834
DST: Decoding Skills Test, 769
DST: Diagnostic Spelling Test, 835
DSTA: Diagnostic Screening Test: Achievement, 829
DSTL: Diagnostic Screening Test: Language, Second Edition, 830
DSTM: Diagnostic Screening Test: Math, Third Edition, 831
DSTR: Diagnostic Screening Test: Reading, Third Edition, 832
DSTS: Diagnostic Screening Test: Spelling, Third Edition, 833
DT8: Advanced Test Battery, 119
DT8: Programmer Aptitude Series, 2087
DT8: Technical Test Battery [British Edition], 2642
DT/CEP: Differential Test of Conduct and Emotional Problems, 841
DTCQ.: Drug-Taking Confidence Questionnaire, 858
DTKR-II: Developmental Tasks for Kindergarten Readiness—II, 813
DTLA-A: Detroit Tests of Learning Aptitude—Adult, 797
DTLA-4: Detroit Tests of Learning Aptitude, Fourth Edition, 798
DTLA-P:2: Detroit Tests of Learning Aptitude—Primary, Second Edition, 799
DTORF-R: Developmental Teaching Objectives and Rating Form—Revised, 814
DTS: College Board Descriptive Tests System, 571
DTS: Davidson Trauma Scale, 766
DTSA: Dennis Test of Scholastic Aptitude, 779
DTVP-2: Developmental Test of Visual Perception, Second Edition, 816
DVI: Domestic Violence Inventory, 849
DVT: Digit Vigilance Test, 842
DWM: Degrees of Word Meaning, 774
EAEP: Educational Administrator Effectiveness Profile, 903
E&ITT: Electronic and Instrumentation Technician Test—Form 2, 924
EAPI: Employee Assistance Program Inventory, 938
EAS: Educational Abilities Scales, 902
EAS: Employee Aptitude Survey, Second Edition, 937
EASIC: Revised Evaluating Acquired Skills in Communication, 2215
EAT.: Evaluation Aptitude Test, 979
EBC: Emotional Behavioral Checklist, 929
EBC: McCarron-Dial System, 1610
EBDS: Emotional or Behavior Disorder Scale, 930
EBPS: Emotional and Behavior Problem Scale, 928
ECADDES: The Early Childhood Attention Deficit Disorders Evaluation Scale, 873
ECBI: Eyberg Child Behavior Inventory, 997
ECBS: The Early Childhood Behavior Scale, 874
ECCE: Examination for the Certificate of Competency in English, 985
ECDI: Early Child Development Inventory, 872
ECERS-R: Early Childhood Environment Rating Scale—Revised, 875
ECI-4: Early Childhood Inventory–4, 876
ECPE: Examination for the Certificate of Proficiency in English, 986
EDEN: Evaluation Disposition Toward the Environment, 980
EDI: Eating Disorder Inventory-2, 893
EDPA: Erhardt Developmental Prehension Assessment, 968
EDS: Educational Development Series (1992 Edition), 904
EDVA: Erhardt Developmental Vision Assessment, 969
EEPIGS: Evaluating Educational Programs for Intellectually Gifted Students, 976
EFA: Ego Function Assessment, 912
EFA-3: Examining for Aphasia, Third Edition, 987
EFT: Embedded Figures Test, 926
EI: Empowerment Inventory, 946
8SQ: Eight State Questionnaire, 915
EII: Educational Interest Inventory, 905
EIRS: Endeavor Instructional Rating System, 948
EIS: Employee Involvement Survey, 941
ELA: Everyday Life Activities: Photo Series, 984
ELM Scale-2: Early Language Milestone Scale, Second Edition, 880
ELPI: Educational Leadership Practices Inventory, 906
ELPT: College Board Institutional SAT II: English Language Proficiency Test, 576
ELPT: College Board SAT II: English Language Proficiency Test, 597
ELS: Early Language Skills Checklist, 881
EMAS: Endler Multidimensional Anxiety Scales, 950
EMDK: Early Mathematics Diagnostic Kit, 884

EMI: Employability Maturity Interview, 936
EMT: Evaluation Modality Test, 981
ENGLIT: Basic English Literacy Skills Test, 249
ENRICH: PREPARE/ENRICH, 2034
EOT: Cognitive Diagnostic Battery, 564
EOWPVT: Expressive One-Word Picture Vocabulary Test, Revised, 994
EPA: Employee Performance Appraisal, 942
EPI: Eysenck Personality Inventory , 998
EPI: Emotions Profile Index, 932
EPPS: Edwards Personal Preference Schedule, 908
EPQ: Educational Process Questionnaire, 907
EPQ-R: Eysenck Personality Questionnaire [Revised], 999
EPS: Emotional Problems Scales, 931
EPT: Eidetic Parents Test, 914
EPT: English Placement Test, 953
EQ Questionnaire: EQ Questionnaire, 966
ERI: Employee Reliability Inventory, 944
ERI: Environmental Response Inventory, 963
ESA: Early School Assessment, 886
ESA: English Skills Assessment, 955
ESB: The Effective School Battery, 909
ESI: Early School Inventory, 887
ESI-R: Early Screening Inventory—Revised, 889
ESLOA: English as a Second Language Oral Assessment, Second Edition, 951
ESP: Early Screening Project, 890
ESP: Early Speech Perception Test, 891
ESPQ: Early School Personality Questionnaire, 888
ESQST: The Ego Strength Q-Sort Test, 913
ESRI: Ekwall/Shanker Reading Inventory—Third Edition, 917
ESS: The ACT Evaluation/Survey Service, 57
ESSI: Entrepreneurial Style and Success Indicator, 962
ET3: Technical Test Battery [British Edition], 2642
ET PA: Matching Person and Technology, 1593
ETRI: Everstine Trauma Response Index, 983
EVT: Expressive Vocabulary Test, 995
E-WOW: Explore the World of Work, 993
EWPS: Endicott Work Productivity Scale, 949
EXEC: The Clark Wilson Group Multi-Level Feedback Instruments and Development Programs, 490
EXP: The Experiencing Scale, 991

FAB-C: Feelings, Attitudes, and Behaviors Scale for Children, 1025
FACES II: FACES II & FACES III, 1000
FACES III: FACES II & FACES III, 1000
FACS: Facial Action Coding System, 1001
FACT: Flanagan Aptitude Classification Tests, 1042
FAF: Family Assessment Form: A Practice-Based Approach to Assessing Family Functioning, 1007
FAM-III: Family Assessment Measure Version III, 1008
FASSS: The ACT Evaluation/Survey Service, 57
FAST: Family System Test, 1015
FAST: Firestone Assessment of Self-Destructive Thoughts, 1035
FAT: Family Adjustment Test, 1005
FAT: Family Apperception Test, 1006
FATSA: F.A.T.S.A. Test (Flowers Auditory Test of Selective Attention), 1020
FCP: Functional Communication Profile, 1061
FDCRS: Family Day Care Rating Scale, 1009
FDP: Comprehensive Drinker Profile, 652
FDT: Fine Dexterity Test, 1031
FES: Family Environment Scale, Third Edition, 1010
FGT: Functional Grammar Test, 1063
FIAT: Sentence Completion Tests, 2381
FIPI: The Facial Interpersonal Perception Inventory, 1002
FIRO-B: The FIRO Awareness Scales 1036
FIRO-BC: The FIRO Awareness Scales, 1036
FIRO-F: The FIRO Awareness Scales, 1036
FIST: Sentence Completion Tests, 2381
FIT: Flanagan Industrial Tests, 1043
F-JAS: Fleishman Job Analysis Survey, 1044
FLASC: Sentence Completion Tests, 2381
FLCI: Functional Linguistic Communication Inventory, 1064
FLIT: Figurative Language Interpretation Test, 1028
FLS: Firefighter Learning Simulation, 1033
F-LTOAC: The Fisher-Logemann Test of Articulation Competence, 1040
FNA: Functional Needs Assessment, 1065
FOME: Fuld Object-Memory Evaluation, 1058
FPBRS: Fels Parent Behavior Rating Scales, 1026
FPR: Functional Performance Record, 1066
FPT: Four Picture Test, Third Revised Edition, 1053
FRI: Family Relationship Inventory, 1013
FRI: Formal Reading Inventory, 1051
FRT: Family Relations Test, 1011
FSS: Fear Survey Schedule, 1021
FSSCT: The Forer Structured Sentence Completion Test, 1049
FSSI: Functional Skills Screening Inventory, 1067
FST: Firefighter Selection Test [Revised], 1034
FTEQ: Functional Time Estimation Questionnaire, 1068
FVS: The Forer Vocational Survey, 1050
FWBS: Friedman Well-Being Scale, 1057
FWVS: The Filipino Work Values Scale, 1030

GAEL-P: Grammatical Analysis of Elicited Language—Pre-Sentence Level, 1126
GAEL-S: Grammatical Analysis of Elicited Language—Simple Sentence Level, Second Edition, 1127
GAIM: Group Achievement Identification Measure, 1136
GAINS I: GAINS: A Pre-test and Post-test for Measuring Career Development Competency Progress, 1069
GAINS II: GAINS: A Pre-test and Post-test for Measuring Career Development Competency Progress, 1069

GAMA: General Ability Measure for Adults, 1075
GARS: Gilliam Autism Rating Scale, 1091
GAS: Global Assessment Scale, 1093
GATB: USES General Aptitude Test Battery, 2797
GATB for the Deaf: USES General Aptitude Test Battery for the Deaf, 2798
GATSB: Guide to the Assessment of Test Session Behavior for the WISC-III and the WIAT, 1155
GC: Group Cohesiveness: A Study of Group Morale, 1137
GCPB: The Gardner Children's Projective Battery, 1070
GCT: General Clerical Test, 1078
GDS: The Gordon Diagnostic System, 1099
GED Tests: Tests of General Educational Development [The GED Tests], 2742
GEFT: Group Embedded Figures Test, 1140
GES: Gifted Evaluation Scale, Second Edition, 1089
GES: Group Environment Scale, Second Edition, 1141
GFW: Goldman-Fristoe-Woodcock Test of Auditory Discrimination, 1096
GHQ: General Health Questionnaire, 1079
GHQ-28: Measures in Post Traumatic Stress Disorder: A Practitioner's Guide, 1626
GIFFI: Group Inventory For Finding Interests, 1143
GIFT: Group Inventory for Finding Creative Talent, 1142
GIST: Sentence Completion Tests, 2381
GLA: Group Literacy Assessment, 1144
GMA: Graduate and Managerial Assessment, 1106
GMAT: Graduate Management Admission Test, 1107
GMIB: General Management In-Basket, 1080
GMRT: Gates-MacGinitie Reading Tests, Third Edition, 1072
GOALS®: GOALS®: A Performance-Based Measure of Achievement, 1094
GOCL II: Gordon Occupational Check List II, 1100
GOII: Occupational Interest Inventories, 1818
GOIT: Goyer Organization of Ideas Test, Form S (Revised), 1102
GORT: Gilmore Oral Reading Test, 1092
GORT-D: Gray Oral Reading Tests—Diagnostic, 1130
GORT-3: Gray Oral Reading Tests, Third Edition, 1131
GPI: General Processing Inventory, 1083
GPII: The Geist Picture Interest Inventory, 1074
GPP-I: Gordon Personal Profile—Inventory, 1101
GPSA: Graduate Program Self-Assessment Service, 1108
GRE: The Graduate Record Examinations—General Test, 1115
GRE: Graduate Record Examinations: Subject Tests, 1124
GRE: The Graduate Record Examinations Biochemistry, Cell and Molecular Biology Test, 1109
GRE: The Graduate Record Examinations Biology Test, 1110
GRE: The Graduate Record Examinations Chemistry Test, 1111
GRE: The Graduate Record Examinations Computer Science Test, 1112
GRE: The Graduate Record Examinations Economics Test, 1113
GRE: The Graduate Record Examinations Engineering Test, 1114
GRE: The Graduate Record Examinations Geology Test, 1116
GRE: The Graduate Record Examinations History Test, 1117
GRE: The Graduate Record Examinations Literature in English Test, 1118
GRE: The Graduate Record Examinations Mathematics Test, 1119
GRE: The Graduate Record Examinations Music Test, 1120
GRE: The Graduate Record Examinations Physics Test, 1121
GRE: The Graduate Record Examinations Psychology Test, 1122
GRE: The Graduate Record Examinations Sociology Test, 1123
GRT: Group Reading Test, Fourth Edition, 1148
GSI: Group Styles Inventory, 1150
GSIT: Group Shorr Imagery Test, 1149
GSNI: Grandparent Strengths and Needs Inventory, 1128
GT 70: Group Tests 70 and 70B, 1152
GT 70B: Group Tests 70 and 70B, 1152
GTSTD: Grid Test of Schizophrenic Thought Disorder, 1133
GWL: Ekwall/Shanker Reading Inventory—Third Edition, 917
GWRT: Macmillan Graded Word Reading Test, 1530
GWT: Mather-Woodcock Group Writing Tests, 1606
GZAS: The Guilford-Zimmerman Aptitude Survey, 1156
GZII: The Guilford-Zimmerman Interest Inventory, 1157
GZTS: The Guilford-Zimmerman Temperament Survey, 1158

HADS: Measures in Post Traumatic Stress Disorder: A Practitioner's Guide, 1626
HAMAT: Hammill Multiability Achievement Test, 1167
HAMIT: Hammill Multiability Intelligence Test, 1168
HAP: Hilson Adolescent Profile, 1207
HAP-S: Hilson Adolescent Profile—Version S, 1208
HaST: Hausa Speaking Test, 1179
HAT: Health Attribution Test, 1183
HBDI: Herrmann Brain Dominance Instrument [Revised], 1197
HCSI: Hilson Career Satisfaction Index, 1209
HCT PA: Matching Person and Technology, 1593

HDI: Hamilton Depression Inventory, 1166
HDL: Health and Daily Living, Second Edition, 1181
HDS: Hogan Development Survey, 1211
HEDCO: Help Desk Support Staff Selector, 1193
HELP Checklist: HELP Checklist (Hawaii Early Learning Profile), 1192
HELP: Henderson-Moriarty ESL/Literacy Placement Test, 1195
HEQ: Home Environment Questionnaire, HEQ-2R and HEQ-1R, 1215
HESB: Hahnemann Elementary School Behavior Rating Scale, 1161
HFDT: Human Figure Drawing Test, 1226
HHSB: Hahnemann High School Behavior Rating Scale, 1162
HIM: Hill Interaction Matrix, 1205
HIP Survey: Human Information Processing Survey, 1227
HIT: Holtzman Inkblot Technique, 1214
HM: Happiness Measures, 1172
HMS: The Hearing Measurement Scale, 1190
HOME: Home Observation for Measurement of the Environment, 1216
HPI: Hogan Personality Inventory [Revised], 1212
HPNT: The Hundred Pictures Naming Test, 1231
HPP/SQ: Hilson Personnel Profile/Success Quotient, 1210
HPSI: Holden Psychological Screening Inventory, 1213
HRDR: 16PF® Human Resource Development Report, 2418
HRI: Human Relations Inventory, 1229
HRI: The Kirkpatrick Management and Supervisory Skills Series, 1403
HRNES: Halstead Russell Neuropsychological Evaluation System, 1165
HSCCP: High School Career-Course Planner, 1200
HSFS: The ACT Evaluation/Survey Service, 57
HSPQ: High School Personality Questionnaire, 1201
HSPT: Closed High School Placement Test, 547
HSPT: High School Placement Test-Open Edition, 1202
HSQ: Health Status Questionnaire, 1187
HSQ: Home Screening Questionnaire, 1217
HST: Hebrew Speaking Test, 1191
HSSOS: The ACT Evaluation/Survey Service, 57
HS-WBLT: Watson-Barker Listening Test—High School Version, 2855
HTDT: Hand-Tool Dexterity Test, 1170
H-T-P/D-A-P: House-Tree-Person and Draw-A-Person as Measures of Abuse in Children: A Quantitative Scoring System, 1219
H-T-P: H-T-P: House-Tree-Person Projective Technique, 1160
HVDT: McCarron-Dial System, 1610

IAAT: Iowa Algebra Aptitude Test, Fourth Edition, 1315
IAC: Inventory of Anger Communication, 1302
IAS®: Integrated Assessment System®, 1281
IAS: Interpersonal Adjective Scales, 1289
IBCT: Intermediate Booklet Category Test, 1286
IBQ: Illness Behaviour Questionnaire, Third Edition, 1241
IBS: BRIGANCE® Diagnostic Inventory of Basic Skills, 342
IBS: Interpersonal Behavior Survey, 1290
ICAP: Inventory for Client and Agency Planning, 1300
ICEQ: Individualised Classroom Environment Questionnaire, 1254
ICI: Interpersonal Communication Inventory, 1292
ICL: Interpersonal Check List, 1291
IDA: Infant-Toddler Developmental Assessment, 1263
IDEAS™: IDEAS: Interest Determination, Exploration and Assessment System™, 1237
IDI: Individual Directions Inventory, 1251
IDI: Infant Development Inventory, 1259
IDS: Instrument for Disability Screening [Developmental Edition], 1278
IDS: Inventory of Drinking Situations, 1304
IDTS: Inventory of Drug Taking Situations, 1305
IEQ: Rehabilitation Compliance Scale, 2197
IES: BRIGANCE® Diagnostic Inventory of Essential Skills, 343
IES: Measures in Post Traumatic Stress Disorder: A Practitioner's Guide, 1626
IIPS: Intra- and Interpersonal Relations Scale, 1297
ILBC: Independent Living Behavior Checklist, 1245
ILEAD: Instructional Leadership Evaluation and Development Program (ILEAD), 1276
ILP-R: Inventory of Learning Processes–R, 1307
ILS: Independent Living Scales, 1246
IMI: Impact Message Inventory, Research Edition, 1243
IMI: Incentives Management Index, 1244
IMMA: Intermediate Measures of Music Audiation, 1287
IMO: Mathematical Olympiads, 1595
IMTS: Independent Mastery Testing System for Math Skills, 1247
IMTS: Independent Mastery Testing System for Writing Skills, 1248
INCH: INteraction CHecklist for Augmentative Communication, Revised Edition, 1284
IPI: Inwald Personality Inventory [Revised], 1313
IPS: Inventory of Perceptual Skills, 1308
IPT: IDEA Oral Language Proficiency Test, 1234
IPT R & W: IDEA Reading and Writing Proficiency Test, 1235
IRAI: An Inventory of Religious Activities and Interests, 1310
IRI: Burns/Roe Informal Reading Inventory: Preprimer to Twelfth Grade, Fifth Edition, 357
IRQ: Interpersonal Relations Questionnaire, 1293

IRT: Industrial Reading Test, 1256
IS5: Inwald Survey 5, 1314
ISCS: Inferred Self-Concept Scale, 1266
ISCS: Iowa Social Competency Scales, 1317
ISE: Influence Strategies Exercise, 1267
ISEE: Independent School Entrance Examination, 1249
ISI: Canfield Instructional Styles Inventory, 391
ISI: Interpersonal Style Inventory, 1294
ISO-30: Inventory of Suicide Orientation-30, 1311
ISS: Individual Style Survey, 1253
ISS: Information System Skills, 1270
ISS: Measures in Post Traumatic Stress Disorder: A Practitioner's Guide, 1626
ISSC: Internalizing Symptoms Scale for Children, 1288
ISSP: Individual Service Strategy Portfolio, 1252
IST: Indonesian Speaking Test, 1255
ITB: Industrial Test Battery, 1257
ITBI: Iowa Parent Behavior Inventory, 1316
ITBS: Iowa Tests of Basic Skills, Forms K, L, and M, 1318
ITED: Iowa Tests of Educational Development, Forms K, L, and M, 1319
ITERS: Infant/Toddler Environment Rating Scale, 1264
ITPA: Illinois Test of Psycholinguistic Abilities, Revised Edition, 1240
ITPT: Instrument Timbre Preference Test, 1280
ITS: Interpersonal Trust Surveys, 1296
ITSC: It Scale for Children, 1332
ITS-O: Interpersonal Trust Surveys, 1296
IVA: Integrated Visual and Auditory Continuous Performance Test, 1282
IWT: Integrated Writing Test, 1283

JAA: Job Attitude Analysis, 1344
JAI: Job Awareness Inventory, 1346
JAPQ: Job Activity Preference Questionnaire, 1343
JAS: Jenkins Activity Survey, 1338
JAS: Job Attitude Scale, 1345
JASAE: Juvenile Automated Substance Abuse Evaluation, 1372
JCE: A Job Choice Decision-Making Exercise, 1347
JDI: Job Descriptive Index (1997 Revision) and The Job in General Scales, 1348
JEPI: Junior Eysenck Personality Inventory, 1367
JI: The Jesness Inventory, 1341
JIG: Job Descriptive Index (1997 Revision) and The Job in General Scales, 1348
JII: Jail Inmate Inventory, 1335
JII: Job Interactions Inventory, 1349
JIRI: Johnston Informal Reading Inventory, 1358
JITT: Just-in-Time Training Assessment Instrument, 1371
JKST: Johnson-Kenney Screening Test, 1357
JOB-O: JOB-O, 1350
JPI-R: Jackson Personality Inventory—Revised, 1333
JPQ: Jung Personality Questionnaire, 1365
JRS: Junior Rating Scale, 1369
JSAIS: Junior South African Individual Scales, 1370
JSI: Jansky Screening Index, 1337
JSI: Job Search Inventory, 1351
JSI: Job Style Indicator , 1355
JSS: Job Stress Survey, 1354
JSSA: Job Seeking Skills Assessment, 1352
JVIS: Jackson Vocational Interest Survey [1995 Revision], 1334

KA: Kuhlmann-Anderson Tests, Eighth Edition, 1414
K-ABC: Kaufman Assessment Battery for Children, 1379
KAI: Kirton Adaption-Innovation Inventory [1998 Edition], 1404
KAIT: Kaufman Adolescent and Adult Intelligence Test, 1378
KART: Kendrick Assessment of Cognitive Ageing, 1390
KASS: Kagan Affective Sensitivity Scale, 1374
K-BIT: Kaufman Brief Intelligence Test, 1380
KCI-A: Kolbe Conative Index, 1411
KCI-B: Kolbe Conative Index, 1411
KCI-C: Kolbe Conative Index, 1411
KCI-R: Kolbe Conative Index, 1411
KCI-Y: Kolbe Conative Index, 1411
KCI-Z: Kolbe Conative Index, 1411
KCT: Knox's Cube Test, 1407
KDCT: Kendrick Assessment of Cognitive Ageing, 1390
KDS: Kaufman Developmental Scale, 1381
KDS: Kinetic Drawing System for Family and School: A Handbook, 1401
KELS: The Kohlman Evaluation of Living Skills, 1409
KeyMath-R: KeyMath Revised: A Diagnostic Inventory of Essential Mathematics [1998 Normative Update], 1392
K-FAST: Kaufman Functional Academic Skills Test, 1382
KHOS: Krantz Health Opinion Survey, 1412
KIDS: Kent Inventory of Developmental Skills [1996 Standardization], 1391
KIDS: Missouri Kindergarten Inventory of Developmental Skills, Alternate Form, 1707
KIPS: Kaufman Infant and Preschool Scale, 1383
KIST: Sentence Completion Tests, 2381
KIT:EXP: Kahn Intelligence Tests: Experimental Form, 1375
KLPA: Khan-Lewis Phonological Analysis, 1394
KLST-2: Kindergarten Language Screening Test, Second Edition, 1399
KMMPI: Khatena-Morse Multitalent Perception Inventory, 1395
KNPI: Kundu Neurotic Personality Inventory, 1416
KOLT: Kendrick Assessment of Cognitive Ageing, 1390
KOT: Knowledge of Occupations Test, 1406

KPAG: Keele Pre-School Assessment Guide, 1388
KRT: Kindergarten Readiness Test, 1400
K-SEALS: Kaufman Survey of Early Academic and Language Skills, 1385
K-SNAP: Kaufman Short Neuropsychological Assessment Procedure, 1384
K-TEA: Kaufman Test of Educational Achievement [1998 Normative Update], 1386
KTI: Keegan Type Indicator, 1387
KTSA: Kahn Test of Symbol Arrangement, 1376

LAC: Lindamood Auditory Conceptualization Test, Revised Edition, 1503
LAIS: The Leiter Adult Intelligence Scale, 1484
LAMB: Learning and Memory Battery, 1454
LAP: Learning Ability Profile, 1453
LARR: Linguistic Awareness in Reading Readiness, 1504
LAS-O: Language Assessment Scales—Oral, 1420
LASSI: Learning and Study Strategies Inventory, 1455
LASSI-HS: Learning and Study Strategies Inventory—High School Version, 1456
LAW R/W: Language Assessment Scales, Reading and Writing, 1421
LAW-PSI: The Lawrence Psychological Forensic Examination, 1435
LBAII: Leader Behavior Analysis II, 1436
LBC: Louisville Behavior Checklist, 1522
LBDQ-12: Leader Behavior Description Questionnaire, Form 12, 1437
LBP: Learned Behaviors Profile—Self/Other, 1452
LBQ: Leader Behavior Questionnaire, Revised, 1438
LBS: Learning Behaviors Scale, Research Edition, 1457
LCI: Leadership Competency Inventory, 1442
LCPC: The Learning Channel Preference Checklist, 1458
LCT: Listening Comprehension Test, 1506
LDDI: Learning Disabilities Diagnostic Inventory, 1459
LDES: Learning Disability Evaluation Scale (Renormed), 1460
LDRP: Learning Disability Rating Procedure, 1461
LDS: Lexington Developmental Scales, 1490
LEA: Leadership Effectiveness Analysis, 1443
LEAD: Situational Leadership®, 2415
LEADR: Law Enforcement Assessment and Development Report, 1429
LECR: Law Enforcement Candidate Record, 1430
Leiter-R: Leiter International Performance Scale—Revised, 1485
LEP: La Monica Empathy Profile, 1417
LET: Ligondé Equivalence Test, 1501
LET-II: Learning Efficiency Test-II (1992 Revision), 1462
LFMT: The Listening for Meaning Test , 1507
LFT: Language Facility Test, 1422
LH-STEP: System for Testing and Evaluation of Potential, 2605
LIFE II: Longitudinal Interval Follow-up Evaluation, 2nd Edition, 1517
LII: Leisure Interest Inventory, 1482
LISRES-A: Life Stressors and Social Resources Inventory—Adult Form, 1495
LISRES-Y: Life Stressors and Social Resources Inventory—Youth Form, 1496
LIT: Language Imitation Test, 1423
LLQ: Leatherman Leadership Questionnaire [Revised], 1479
LLQ: Leatherman Leadership Questionnaire: 360 degree Leadership Profile, 1480
LMDMI: The Kirkpatrick Management and Supervisory Skills Series, 1403
LNNB-C: Luria-Nebraska Neuropsychological Battery: Children's Revision, 1524
LOCO: LOCO (Learning Opportunities Coordination): A Scale for the Assessment of Coordinated Learning Opportunities in Living Units for People with a Handicap, 1512
LOPP: Learning Organization Practices Profile, 1463
LOQ: Leadership Opinion Questionnaire, 1444
LOTCA: Loewenstein Occupational Therapy Cognitive Assessment, 1513
LPD: Levine-Pilowsky [Depression] Questionnaire, 1488
LPI: Leadership Practices Inventory [Pfeiffer & Company International Publishers], 1448
LPI: Learning Preference Inventory, 1464
LPI: The Team Leadership Practices Inventory, 2635
LPI-Delta: Leadership Practices Inventory—Delta, 1445
LPI-IC: Leadership Practices Inventory—Individual Contributor [Second Edition], 1446
LPQ: Learning Process Questionnaire, 1466
LPSP: Learning Preference Scales, 1465
LPSS: Learning Preference Scales, 1465
LPST: Learning Preference Scales, 1465
LPT: Language Processing Test, 1424
LPT: Language Proficiency Test, 1425
LPTS: Language Proficiency Test Series, 1426
LQST: The Leadership Q-Sort Test (A Test of Leadership Values), 1449
LRI: Life Roles Inventory, 1493
LRS: Light's Retention Scale [Revised Edition 1991], 1500
LRT: London Reading Test, 1516
LS: Situational Leadership®, 2415
LS-E: Woodcock-Muñoz Language Survey, 2904
LS-S: Woodcock-Muñoz Language Survey, 2904
LSAP: Life Space Analysis Profile, 1494
LSAT: Law School Admission Test, 1434
LSAT-3: Language Sampling, Analysis, and Training—Third Edition, 1427
LSC: The Lake St. Clair Incident, 1419
LSI: Canfield Learning Styles Inventory, 392
LSI: Learning-Style Inventory [McBer and Company], 1469

LSI: Learning Style Inventory [Price Systems, Inc.], 1470
LSI: Learning Styles Inventory [Creative Learning Press, Inc.], 1474
LSI: Learning Styles Inventory [Educational Activities, Inc.], 1475
LSI: Leisure/Work Search Inventory, 1483
LSI: Life Styles Inventory, 1498
LSI-IIa: Learning-Style Inventory, Revised Scoring, 1471
LSI-R: The Level of Service Inventory—Revised, 1486
LSI-R:SV: Level of Service Inventory—Revised: Screening Version, 1487
LSIS: Learning Style Identification Scale, 1468
LSP: Learning Skills Profile, 1467
LSP: Learning Style Profile, 1472
LSQ: Life Style Questionnaire, 1497

MAACL-R: Multiple Affect Adjective Check List, Revised, 1745
MAB: Multidimensional Aptitude Battery, 1731
MAC: Maculaitis Assessment Program, Commercial Edition, 1534
MACH: Measure of Achieving Tendency, 1620
MACI: Millon Adolescent Clinical Inventory, 1685
MACPH: Mossford Assessment Chart for the Physically Handicapped, 1718
MAE: Multilingual Aphasia Examination, Third Edition, 1740
MAI: Appraisal Interview and Card Sort, 161
MAI: Mathematics Attitude Inventory, 1599
MAND: McCarron-Dial System, 1610
MAP: Miller Assessment for Preschoolers, 1673
MAP: Multidimensional Assessment and Planning Form, 1732
MAPP: MAPP: Motivational Appraisal of Personal Potential, 1579
MAPP: The Multidimensional Addictions and Personality Profile, 1729
MAPS: Multiple Assessments, Programs, and Services (MAPS) of the College Board, 1746
MAPS: Make A Picture Story, 1540
MAQ: Maryland Addictions Questionnaire, 1587
MAS: Memory Assessment Scales, 1644
MASC: Multidimensional Anxiety Scale for Children, 1730
MASC-10: Multidimensional Anxiety Scale for Children, 1730
MAST: Arousal Seeking Tendency Scale, 181
MAST: Michigan Alcohol Screening Test, 1661
MAST: Multilevel Academic Survey Test, 1738
MAT: Motivation Analysis Test, 1721
MAT: Miller Analogies Test, 1672
MAT: Music Achievement Tests 1, 2, 3, and 4, 1751
MAT7™: Metropolitan Achievement Tests®, Seventh Edition, 1657
MATCH: Making a Terrific Career Happen, 1541
MATCH: Matching Assistive Technology & Child, 1591
MATE: MATE [Marital ATtitude Evaluation], 1594
MATE: PREPARE/ENRICH, 2034
MBA: Woodcock-McGrew-Werder Mini-Battery of Achievement, 2903
MBHI: Millon Behavioral Health Inventory, 1686
MBI: Maslach Burnout Inventory, 1590
MbM Questionnaire: The MbM Questionnaire: Managing by Motivation, Third Edition, 1608
MBPC: Memory and Behavior Problems Checklist and The Burden Interview, 1643
MBT: Myers-Briggs Type Indicator, Form M, 1755
MCAB: Minnesota Clerical Assessment Battery, 1692
MCAT: Medical College Admission Test, 1638
MCI: The Kirkpatrick Management and Supervisory Skills Series, 1403
MCI: Managerial Competence Index, 1571
MCI: A Marital Communication Inventory, 1580
MCMI-III: Millon Clinical Multiaxial Inventory—III [Second Edition], 1687
MCPS: The Missouri Children's Picture Series, 1706
MCQ: Managerial Competency Questionnaire, 1573
MCR: Management Coaching Relations [Revised], 1548
MCR: Managerial Competence Review, 1572
MCT: Minnesota Clerical Test, 1693
MCT: The Meta Contrast Technique, 4th Edition, 1654
MDI: Multiscore Depression Inventory, 1748
MDI-C: Multiscore Depression Inventory for Children, 1749
MDQ: Menstrual Distress Questionnaire, 1647
MDS: McCarron-Dial System, 1610
MDT: Manual Dexterity Test, 1578
MEA: Management Effectiveness Analysis, 1549
MEAP: Multiphasic Environmental Assessment Procedure, 1743
MEC: Marital Evaluation Checklist, 1581
MEI: Medical Ethics Inventory, 1639
MEI: Military Environment Inventory, 1670
MELAB: Michigan English Language Assessment Battery, 1662
MEPS: Management Effectiveness Profile System, 1550
MEPS: Means-Ends Problem-Solving Procedure, 1619
MFD: Memory-For-Designs Test, 1645
MFF: Matching Familiar Figures Test, 1592
MFT: Major Field Tests, 1538
MGIB: Management and Graduate Item Bank, 1544
MHP-H: Multidimensional Health Profile, 1733
MHP-P: Multidimensional Health Profile, 1733
MHV: Mill Hill Vocabulary Scale, 1671
MIDAS: The MIDAS: Multiple Intelligence Developmental Assessment Scales, 1667
MIFV: Maferr Inventory of Feminine Values, 1535
MILI: Multilevel Informal Language Inventory, 1739

MILMD: Management Inventory on Leadership, Motivation and Decision-Making, 1552
MIMC: Management Inventory on Managing Change, 1553
MIMM: Management Inventory on Modern Management, 1554
MIMV: Maferr Inventory of Masculine Values, 1536
MIPAC: Management Inventory on Performance Appraisal and Coaching, 1555
MIPS: Millon Index of Personality Styles, 1688
MIQ: Minnesota Importance Questionnaire, 1694
MIRBI: Mini Inventory of Right Brain Injury, 1690
MIST: Sentence Completion Tests, 2381
MITM: Management Inventory on Time Management, 1556
MJDQ: Minnesota Job Description Questionnaire, 1695
MKAS: Meyer-Kendall Assessment Survey, 1660
MLQ: Multifactor Leadership Questionnaire for Research, 1736
MLQT: Multifactor Leadership Questionnaire for Teams, 1737
MLS: Management & Leadership Systems, 1545
MMF: The Major-Minor-Finder, 1986-1996 Edition, 1539
MMI: Meta-Motivation Inventory, 1655
MMI: [Work Motivation], 2921
MMPI-A: Minnesota Multiphasic Personality Inventory-Adolescent, 1698
MMPI-2: Minnesota Multiphasic Personality Inventory-2, 1697
MMTIC: Murphy-Meisgeier Type Indicator for Children, 1750
MODI: Management of Differences Inventory, 1557
MOST: Modern Occupational Skills Tests, 1712
Movement ABC: Movement Assessment Battery for Children, 1727
MP: Morrisby Profile, 1717
MPA: Metropolitan Performance Assessment: Integrated Performance Tasks, 1658
M-PAC1: Progress Assessment Chart of Social and Personal Development, 2088
MPAS: Maryland Parent Attitude Survey, 1589
MPCL: The Mooney Problem Check Lists, 1950 Revision, 1716
MPD: Measures of Psychosocial Development, 1631
MPDT: Minnesota Percepto-Diagnostic Test, Revised Edition, 1699
MPJFI: Managerial and Professional Job Functions Inventory, 1569
MPQ: Manchester Personality Questionnaire, 1576
MPQ: The McGill Pain Questionnaire, 1615
MPR: Manager Profile Record, 1566
MPS: Individual Style Survey, 1253
MPS: Malingering Probability Scale, 1543
MPS: Managerial Philosophies Scale, 1574
MPSI: Minneapolis Preschool Screening Instrument, 1691
MPT: Matching Person and Technology, 1593
MPU: Management Practices Update, 1558
MRET: Reading Efficiency Tests, 2174
MRI: The Kirkpatrick Management and Supervisory Skills Series, 1403
MRMT: Minnesota Rate of Manipulation Test, 1969 Edition, 1700
MRS: Management Relations Survey, 1559
MRT®6: Metropolitan Readiness Tests, Sixth Edition, 1659
MS: M-Scale: An Inventory of Attitudes Toward Black/White Relations in the United States, 1526
MS: Situational Leadership®, 2415
MSA: Mentoring Skills Assessment, 1651
MSC: Management Situation Checklist, 1560
MSCA: McCarthy Scales of Children's Abilities, 1612
MSCS: Miner Sentence Completion Scale, 1689
MSCS: Multidimensional Self Concept Scale, 1734
MSDT: Management Style Diagnosis Test, Third Edition, 1561
MSEI: The Multidimensional Self-Esteem Inventory, 1735
MSES: Mathematics Self-Efficacy Scale, 1602
MSI: Management Style Inventory [Hanson Silver Strong & Associates], 1562
MSI: Mentoring Style Indicator, 1652
MSI: Multiphasic Sex Inventory, 1744
MSI-R: Marital Satisfaction Inventory—Revised, 1582
MSLQ: Motivated Strategies for Learning Questionnaire, 1720
MSQ: Managerial Style Questionnaire, 1575
MSQ: Minnesota Satisfaction Questionnaire, 1701
MSRT: Minnesota Spatial Relations Test, Revised Edition, 1703
MSS: Minnesota Satisfactoriness Scales, 1702
MST: McCarthy Screening Test, 1613
MT4: Technical Test Battery [British Edition], 2642
MTA: Management Transactions Audit, 1565
MTELP: Michigan Test of English Language Proficiency, 1664
MTM: The Clark Wilson Group Multi-Level Feedback Instruments and Development Programs, 490
MUSAT J: Musical Aptitude Test, 1753
MUSAT S: Musical Aptitude Test, 1753
MVE: Mobile Vocational Evaluation, 1711
MVPI: Motives, Values, Preferences Inventory, 1724
MVPT-R: Motor-Free Visual Perception Test—Revised, 1725
MVPT-V: Motor-Free Visual Perception Test—Vertical, 1726
MVS: My Vocational Situation, 1754
MZSCS: Martinek-Zaichkowsky Self-Concept Scale for Children, 1586

NA2: Advanced Test Battery, 119
NA2: Programmer Aptitude Series, 2087
NA4: Advanced Test Battery, 119

PAC-1: Progress Assessment Chart of Social and Personal Development, 2088
PAC-2: Progress Assessment Chart of Social and Personal Development, 2088
PACE: PACE, 1868
PACG: The Prevocational Assessment and Curriculum Guide, 2053
PACI: A Parent-Adolescent Communication Inventory, 1876
PACL: Personality Adjective Check List, 1958
PAF: Multiphasic Environmental Assessment Procedure, 1743
PAI: Pair Attraction Inventory, 1872
PAI: Personality Assessment Inventory, 1959
PAIR: Personal Assessment of Intimacy in Relationships, 1927
PAIS: Psychosocial Adjustment to Illness Scale, 2117
PAL: Profile of Aptitude for Leadership, 2075
PAL Scale: Profile of Adaptation to Life, 2074
PALPA: Psycholinguistic Assessments of Language Processing in Aphasia, 2113
PALS: Program for the Acquisition of Language with the Severely Impaired, 2082
PANSS: Positive and Negative Syndrome Scale, 2017
PAQ: Position Analysis Questionnaire, 2016
PAS: Personality Assessment Screener, 1960
PAS: Prevocational Assessment Screen, 2054
PAS: Programmer Aptitude Series, 2087
PASAT: The Poppleton Allen Sales Aptitude Test, 2007
PASS: Parent Awareness Skills Survey, 1879
PASS: Perception of Ability Scale for Students, 1916
PASS: Personnel Assessment Selection System, 1967
PAT: Listening Comprehension: Progressive Achievement Tests of Listening Comprehension [Revised], 2093
PAT: Pain Apperception Test, 1869
PAT: Predictive Ability Test, Adult Edition, 2027
PAT: Progressive Achievement Tests in Reading: Reading Comprehension and Reading Vocabulary Tests, 2092
PAT-3: Photo Articulation Test, Third Edition, 1982
PATM: Progressive Achievement Test of Mathematics [Revised], 2090
PATMATHS: Progressive Achievement Tests in Mathematics, 2091
PAYES: Program for Assessing Youth Employment Skills, 2081
P-BAP: Behavioral Assessment of Pain Questionnaire, 291
PBC: Psychometric Behavior Checklist, 2116
PBC: Parent Behavior Checklist, 1880
PBCL: Pre-School Behavior Checklist, 2038
PBF: Parent Behavior Form, 1881
P.B.I.: Pollack-Branden Inventory, 2005
PBI: Power Base Inventory, 2020
PBQ: The Preschool Behavior Questionnaire, 2039
PBRS: Pupil Behavior Rating Scale, 2122
PCAT: Pharmacy College Admission Test, 1975
PCCI: Parent-Child Communication Inventory, 1882
PCDP: 16PF® Personal Career Development Profile, 2419
PCG: Planning Career Goals, 2000
PCI: A Premarital Communication Inventory, 2033
PCL:CV: Hare Psychopathy Checklist: Screening Version, 1175
PCL-R: Hare Psychopathy Checklist–Revised, 1174
PCRI: Parent-Child Relationship Inventory, 1883
PCT: Wesman Personnel Classification Test, 2871
PDI: Preschool Development Inventory, 2040
PDI—IV: Personality Disorder Interview-IV: A Semistructured Interview for the Assessment of Personality Disorders, 1961
PDI-R: Psychiatric Diagnostic Interview—Revised, 2107
PDMS: Peabody Developmental Motor Scales and Activity Cards, 1901
PDP: Personal Dynamics Profile, 1930
PDQ: Preliminary Diagnostic Questionnaire, 2030
PDQII: Denver Prescreening Developmental Questionnaire II, 787
PDRT: Portland Digit Recognition Test, 2011
PDS: Posttraumatic Stress Diagnostic Scale, 2018
PDS:BIDR: Paulhus Deception Scales: Balanced Inventory of Desirable Responding, 1899
PEDI: Pediatric Evaluation of Disability Inventory, 1906
PEDS: Parents' Evaluation of Developmental Status, 1890
PEEK: PEEK—Perceptions, Expectations, Emotions, and Knowledge About College, 1910
PEER: Pediatric Examination of Educational Readiness, 1907
PEERAMID-2: Pediatric Examination of Educational Readiness at Middle Childhood [Revised], 1908
PEET: Pediatric Extended Examination at Three, 1909
PEEX-2: Pediatric Early Elementary Examination—II [Revised], 1905
PEF: Psychiatric Evaluation Form, 2108
PEFT: Preschool Embedded Figures Test, 2042
PEI: Personal Experience Inventory, 1931
PEI-A: Personal Experience Inventory for Adults, 1932
PEP: Psycho-Epistemological Profile, 2112
PEP-R: Psychoeducational Profile Revised, 2111
PEPS: Productivity Environmental Preference Survey, 2069
PES: The Preschool Evaluation Scale, 2043
PESQ: Personal Experience Screening Questionnaire, 1933
PEST: The Patterned Elicitation Syntax Test (Revised) with Morphonemic Analysis, 1898
PET: Professional Employment Test, 2072
PFDT: Cognitive Diagnostic Battery, 564

PHCSCS: Piers-Harris Children's Self-Concept Scale (The Way I Feel About Myself), 1991
PHI: The Psychap Inventory, 2106
PHIQ: Philadelphia Head Injury Questionnaire, 1978
PHSF: PHSF Relations Questionnaire, 1983
PI: Penguin Index, 1912
PI: A Personal Inventory, 1935
PIAT-R: Peabody Individual Achievement Test—Revised [1998 Normative Update], 1902
PIC: Personality Inventory for Children, Revised Format, 1962
PICA: Porch Index of Communicative Ability, 2008
PII: Prison Inmate Inventory, 2061
PIL: The Purpose in Life Test, 2126
PIP: Project Implementation Profile, 2096
PIP: Psychotic Inpatient Profile, 2120
PIT: Picture Identification Test, 1988
PIY: Personality Inventory for Youth, 1963
PKBS: Preschool and Kindergarten Behavior Scales, 2036
PKRS: Phelps Kindergarten Readiness Scale, 1977
PLAB: Phonological Assessment Battery [Standardised Edition], 1980
PLAI: Preschool Language Assessment Instrument, 2044
PLANT: Warehouse/Plant Worker Staff Selector, 2851
PLS-3: Preschool Language Scale–3, 2045
PLSPS: Performance Levels of a School Program Survey, 1921
P-MAC/ESP: Perceptual-Motor Assessment for Children & Emotional/Behavioral Screening Program, 1919
PMI: Power Management Inventory, 2021
PMMA: Primary Measures of Music Audiation, 2056
PMP: Power Management Profile, 2022
PMPQ: Professional and Managerial Position Questionnaire, 2071
PMS: Participative Management Survey, 1894
PMT: Assessment of Individual Learning Style: The Perceptual Memory Task, 208
PNAM: Psychologic and Neuropsychiatric Assessment Manual, 2114
PNEE: Entrance Examination for Schools of Practical/Vocational Nursing, 961
POD: Personal Orientation Dimensions, 1938
POI: Personal Orientation Inventory, 1939
POIS: Kipnis-Schmidt Profiles of Organizational Influence Strategies, 1402
POLIF: Multiphasic Environmental Assessment Procedure, 1743
POMS: Profile of Mood States, 2076
POMS-BI: Profile of Mood States, Bi-Polar Form, 2077
PONS: Profile of Nonverbal Sensitivity, 2078
POPS: Profiles of Problem Solving, 2080
PORT: Perception-Of-Relationships-Test, 1917
POS: The Play Observation Scale, 2001
POS: Profile of a School, 2073
POST: National Police Officer Selection Test, 1763
PP: Peacock Profile, 1904
PPA: Pragmatics Profile of Everyday Communication Skills in Adults, 2024
P-PAC: Progress Assessment Chart of Social and Personal Development, 2088
PPBC-R: Portland Problem Behavior Checklist—Revised, 2012
PPC: Personal Problems Checklist for Adolescents, 1942
PPC: Pragmatics Profile of Everyday Communication Skills in Children, 2025
PPCP: Parent Perception of Child Profile, 1886
PPG: Paper and Pencil Games, 1873
PPM: Power and Performance Measures, 2019
PPP: People Performance Profile, 1913
PPP: Situational Leadership®, 2415
PPPI: Personnel Performance Problems Inventory, 1969
PPRS: Perceptions of Parental Role Scales, 1918
PPS: The Personal Preference Scale, 1940
PPS: Productive Practices Survey, 2068
PPVT-III: Peabody Picture Vocabulary Test III, 1903
PQRST: Personal Questionnaire Rapid Scaling Technique, 1944
PRB: Personnel Reaction Blank, 1970
PRBUSAN: Business Analyst Skills Evaluation, 360
PRCLERIC: Senior Clerical Skills Test, 2374
PRE-LAS: PRE-LAS English, 2029
Pre-TOEFL®: Preliminary Test of English as a Foreign Language, 2032
PREPARE: PREPARE/ENRICH, 2034
PREPARE-MC: PREPARE/ENRICH, 2034
PRETOS: Proof-Reading Tests of Spelling, 2100
PRF: Personality Research Form, 3rd Edition, 1965
PRI: Partner Relationship Inventory (Research Edition), 1895
PRI: Personal Relationship Inventory, 1946
PRIDE: Preschool and Kindergarten Interest Descriptor, 2037
PRIM: Pre-Referral Intervention Manual [Revised and Updated Second Edition], 2035
PROGANI: Programmer Analyst Aptitude Test One-Hour Version, 2084
PRQ-85: Personal Resource Questionnaire, 1947
PRS: Personality Rating Scale, 1964
PRS: Personnel Relations Survey [Revised], 1971
PRSECTY: Executive Administrative Assistant Skills Test, 988
PRT: Pictorial Reasoning Test, 1986
PRT: Primary Reading Test, 2058
PS Leader: Performance Skills Leader, 1923
PS-CPT: Preschool Self-Concept Picture Test, 2048
PSAI: Personal Stress Assessment Inventory, 1949
PSAS: Program Self-Assessment Service, 2083
PSAT/NMSQT: Preliminary SAT/National Merit Scholarship Qualifying Test, 2031

PSCA: Picha-Seron Career Analysis, 1984
PSCT: Politte Sentence Completion Test, 2004
PSE: Present State Examination, 2050
PSI-120: Personal Styles Inventory [PSI-120] [1999 Revision], 1954
PSI: Parenting Stress Index, Third Edition, 1889
PSI: Personal Style Inventory, 1953
PSI: Personnel Selection Inventory, 1972
PSI: The Problem Solving Inventory, 2065
PSI: Psychological Screening Inventory, 2115
PSM: Personal Skills Map, 1948
PSP: Polyfactorial Study of Personality, 2006
PSPI: Psychosocial Pain Inventory [Revised], 2118
PSS: Parenting Satisfaction Scale, 1888
PSS: Preschool Screening System, 2047
PSSI: Preschool Screening Instrument, 2046
PSS-2: The Psychiatric Status Schedules: Subject Form, Second Edition, 2109
PST: Police Selection Test, 2003
PST: Portuguese Speaking Test, 2015
PSTA: Predictive Screening Test of Articulation, 2028
PSYPERCEPT-170: PSYPERCEPT-170, 2121
PTEU: Primary Test of Economic Understanding, 2060
PTI: Personnel Tests for Industry, 1974
PTM: Progress Tests in Maths, 2089
PTPS: Parker Team Player Survey, 1892
P-TPT: Portable Tactual Performance Test, 2009
PTT: Process Technician Test, 2066
PVCS: Pre-Verbal Communication Schedule, 2052
PVI: Picture Vocational Interest Questionnaire for Adults, 1990
PVI®: Personal Values Inventory [Personal Strengths Publishing], 1956
PVQ: Personal Values Questionnaire, 1957
PVS: Beery Picture Vocabulary Test and Beery Picture Vocabulary Screening Series, 278
PVT Beery Picture Vocabulary Test and Beery Picture Vocabulary Screening Series, 278

QCA: Quality Culture Assessment, 2129
QCI: Quick Cognitive Inventory, 2138
QELSR: Psychotherapy Outcome Kit (Including Quality of Emotional Life Self-Report), 2119
QIA: Quick Informal Assessment, 2139
Q-LES-Q: Quality of Life Enjoyment and Satisfaction Questionnaire, 2130
QLQ: Quality of Life Questionnaire, 2132
QNST-II: Quick Neurological Screening Test, 2nd Revised Edition, 2141
QOLI: Quality of Life Inventory, 2131
QPA: Quality Potential Assessment, 2133
QPS: Quick Phonics Survey, 2142
QSI: Quick Spelling Inventory, 2145
QSP: Quick Screen of Phonology, 2144
QT: The Quick Test, 2146
Q-TTP: The Q-Tags Test of Personality, 2128
QUESTS: QUESTS: A Life-Choice Inventory, 2136
QVIP: The Clark Wilson Group Multi-Level Feedback Instruments and Development Programs, 490

R-36 HSI: RAND-36 Health Status Inventory, 2158
RAATE–CE: Recovery Attitude and Treatment Evaluator, 2194
RAATE–Q: Recovery Attitude and Treatment Evaluator, 2194
RADS: Reynolds Adolescent Depression Scale, 2230
RALT: The Riley Articulation and Language Test, Revised, 2235
RATC: Roberts Apperception Test for Children [with new Interpretive Handbook], 2242
RAVLT: Rey Auditory Verbal Learning Test, 2226
RBANS: Repeatable Battery for the Assessment of Neuropsychological Status, 2202
RBMT: The Rivermead Behavioural Memory Test [Second Edition], 2239
RBPC: Revised Behavior Problem Checklist, 2211
RCBA-2: Reading Comprehension Battery for Aphasia, Second Edition, 2172
RCFT: Rey Complex Figure Test and Recognition Trial, 2227
RCJS-PrinTest: Ramsay Corporation Job Skills—PrinTest—Forms A-C and B-C, 2155
RCJS—Reading Electrical Drawings & Schematics: Ramsay Corporation Job Skills—Reading Electrical Drawings & Schematics, 2156
RCK: Communication Knowledge Inventory [Revised], 631
RCL: Rehabilitation Checklist, 2196
RCMAS: Revised Children's Manifest Anxiety Scale, 2214
R-CRAS: Rogers Criminal Responsibility Assessment Scales, 2245
RCS: Reality Check Survey, 2188
RCS: Rehabilitation Compliance Scale, 2197
RDI: Retirement Descriptive Index, 2208
RDLS: Reynell Developmental Language Scales [U.S. Edition], 2229
RDLS III: Reynell Developmental Language Scales: Third Edition [British Edition], 2228
RDSI: Reynolds Depression Screening Inventory, 2232
RDT: Roughness Discrimination Test, 2259
READ: Reading Evaluation Adult Diagnosis, Fifth Edition, 2175
READS: Reading Evaluation and Diagnostic Screen, 2176
REEL-2: Receptive-Expressive Emergent Language Test, Second Edition, 2189
REHAB: REHAB: Rehabilitation Evaluation Hall and Baker, 2195
REO: Melvin-Smith Receptive-Expressive Observation, 1642
RESIF: Multiphasic Environmental Assessment Procedure, 1743
RETSALES: Retail Sales Skills Test, 2205

RFSP: The Ruth Fry Symbolic Profile, 2262
R-FVII: Reading-Free Vocational Interest Inventory, Revised, 2177
RHRSD: Revised Hamilton Rating Scale for Depression, 2216
RI: Reading Index, 2178
RIBLS: Riley Inventory of Basic Learning Skills, 2236
RIDES: Rockford Infant Developmental Evaluation Scales, 2243
RIPA—2: Ross Information Processing Assessment, Second Edition, 2251
RIPA-G: Ross Information Processing Assessment—Geriatric, 2249
RIPA-P: Ross Information Processing Assessment—Primary, 2250
RISA: Responsibility and Independence Scale for Adolescents, 2204
RISB: Rotter Incomplete Sentences Blank, Second Edition, 2258
RISC: Rust Inventory of Schizotypal Cognitions, 2260
RIST: Sentence Completion Tests, 2381
RITLS: Rhode Island Test of Language Structure, 2233
RMIB: Rothwell-Miller Interest Blank, 2257
RMIB: Rothwell Miller Interest Blank (Revised), 2255
RMPFBT: Revised Minnesota Paper Form Board Test, Second Edition, 2217
RMT: Randt Memory Test, 2159
RMT: Recognition Memory Test, 2193
RMVB: Rothwell Miller Values Blank, 2256
RNEE: Entrance Examination for Schools of Nursing [RN Entrance Examination], 960
ROBS: Rating of Behavior Scale, 2161
ROC: Rahim Organizational Conflict Inventories, 2149
ROLI: Receptive Oral Language Inventory, 2192
ROWPVT: Receptive One-Word Picture Vocabulary Test, 2190
ROWPVT: Receptive One-Word Picture Vocabulary Test: Upper Extension, 2191
RPAB: Rivermead Perceptual Assessment Battery, 2240
R-PAS: Riverside Performance Assessment Series, 2241
RPM: Raven Progressive Matrices, 2163
RPQ: Rapid Personality Questionnaire, 2160
RPRF: Research Personnel Review Form, 2203
RPT: Reading Progress Tests, 2179
RS: Multiphasic Environmental Assessment Procedure, 1743
RSALES: Retail Store Manager Staff Selector, 2206
RSCCD: Rating Scale of Communication in Cognitive Decline, 2162
RSDT-III: Reading Skills Diagnostic Test III, Level 4, 2180
RSI: Reading Style Inventory, 2181
RSM: Situational Leadership®, 2415
RTAVI: Risk-Taking-Attitude-Values Inventory, 2237
RTBS: Edition 2: Richmond Tests of Basic Skills: Edition 2, 2234
RTT: Revised Token Test, 2225
S3 Rating Scale: School Social Skills Rating Scale, 2323
SA-45: Symptom Assessment-45 Questionnaire, 2602
SAA: The ACT Evaluation/Survey Service, 57
SAAIA: Service Animal Adaptive Intervention Assessment, 2384
SAAT: Systems Analysis Aptitude Test, 2608
SABE/2: Spanish Assessment of Basic Education, Second Edition, 2463
SACL: Sales Attitude Check List, 2267
SACQ: Student Adaptation to College Questionnaire, 2525
S-ADHD-RS: Spadafore Attention Deficit Hyperactivity Disorder Rating Scale, 2461
SADQ: Self-Administered Dependency Questionnaire, 2350
SADS: Schedule for Affective Disorders and Schizophrenia, Third Edition, 2305
SAED: Scale for Assessing Emotional Disturbance, 2287
SAFT: Sexual Adaptation and Functioning Test, 2392
SAGES: Screening Assessment for Gifted Elementary Students, 2328
SAGES-P: Screening Assessment for Gifted Elementary Students—Primary, 2329
SAI: Sexual Adjustment Inventory, 2393
SAI: Skills and Attributes Inventory, 2420
SAI: Student Adjustment Inventory, 2526
SAILR: Scales of Adult Independence, Language and Recall, 2296
SALCE: Substance Abuse Life Circumstance Evaluation, 2550
Sales AP: Sales Achievement Predictor, 2265
SALT-P: Slosson Articulation Language Test with Phonology, 2429
SAM: Khatena Torrance Creative Perception Inventory, 1396
SAM: School Attitude Measure, Second Edition, 2313
SAM: Skills Assessment Module, 2421
SAMI: Sequential Assessment of Mathematics Inventories: Standardized Inventory, 2383
SAMS: Study Attitudes and Methods Survey [Revised Short Form], 2538
SANS: Scale for the Assessment of Negative Symptoms, 2288
SAPS: Scale for the Assessment of Positive Symptoms, 2289
SAQ: SAQ-Adult Probation [Substance Abuse Questionnaire], 2284
SAQ: SAQ-Adult Probation III, 2285
SAQS: SAQS Chicago Q Sort, 2286
SARA: Spousal Assault Risk Assessment Guide, 2476
SARA: Substance Abuse Relapse Assessment, 2551
SARS: School Archival Records Search, 2311
SAS: School Assessment Survey, 2312
SAS: Situational Attitude Scale, 2413
SAS: Sklar Aphasia Scale, Revised 1983, 2426

SASI: Sexual Abuse Screening Inventory, 2391
SASSI: Substance Abuse Subtle Screening Inventory, 2553
SAS-SR: Social Adjustment Scale—Self Report, 2442
SAST: Sentence Completion Tests, 2381
SAST: Substance Abuse Screening Test, 2552
S.A.T.: The Senior Apperception Technique [1985 Revision], 2372
SAT: Senior Aptitude Tests, 2373
SAT: Shapes Analysis Test, 2398
SAT: Subsumed Abilities Test, 2555
SAT I: College Board SAT I Reasoning Test, 592
SAT Program: College Board SAT Program, 615
SATA: Scholastic Abilities Test for Adults, 2309
SAWLT: South African Written Language Test, 2458
S-B: Speech-Ease Screening Inventory (K—1), 2485
SBA: Small Business Assessment, 2435
SBAI.: Social Behavior Assessment Inventory, 2444
SBCT: Standardized Bible Content Tests, 2480
SCAC: Self-Concept Adjective Checklist, 2354
SCAL: Self-Concept as a Learner Scale, 2356
SCALE: Scaled Curriculum Achievement Levels Test, 2293
SCAMIN: The Self-Concept and Motivation Inventory: What Face Would You Wear?, 2355
SCAN: SCAN: A Screening Test for Auditory Processing Disorders, 2300
SCAN-A: SCAN-A: A Test for Auditory Processing Disorders in Adolescents and Adults, 2301
SCAP: The ACT Evaluation/Survey Service, 57
S-CAPE: A Spanish Computerized Adaptive Placement Exam, 2464
SCATBI: Scales of Cognitive Ability for Traumatic Brain Injury, 2297
SCBE: Social Competence and Behavior Evaluation, Preschool Edition, 2446
SCES: Multiphasic Environmental Assessment Procedure, 1743
SCI: The Sexual Communication Inventory, 2394
SCI: Shapiro Control Inventory, 2399
SCI: Styles of Conflict Inventory, 2546
SCICA: Child Behavior Checklist, 451
SCID-CV: Structured Clinical Interview for DSM-IV Axis I Disorders: Clinician Version, 2519
SCID-II: Structured Clinical Interview for DSM-IV Axis II Personality Disorders, 2520
SCIP: Severe Cognitive Impairment Profile, 2387
SCL-90-R: Symptom Checklist-90-Revised, 2603
SCOM: Supervisory Communication Relations, 2563
SCORE: Supervisory Coaching Relations, 2562
SCOSD: The Southern California Ordinal Scales of Development, 2459
SCP: The Clark Wilson Group Multi-Level Feedback Instruments and Development Programs, 490
S-CPT: Swanson-Cognitive Processing Test, 2596
SCS: Sentence Completion Series, 2379
SCS: Smoker Complaint Scale, 2440
SCT: Sales Comprehension Test, 2269
SCT: Sentence Completion Test, 2380
SCT: Short Category Test, Booklet Format, 2405
SDCT: Slosson Drawing Coordination Test, 2430
SDI®: Strength Deployment Inventory, 2507
SDI/PVI: Feedback Edition of the Strength Development Inventory, 1022
SDLRS: Self-Directed Learning Readiness Scale, 2359
SDMT: Stanford Diagnostic Mathematics Test, Fourth Edition, 2486
SDMT: Symbol Digit Modalities Test, 2599
SDQ: Self-Description Questionnaire—I, II, III, 2358
SDRT: Spadafore Diagnostic Reading Test, 2462
SDRT4: Stanford Diagnostic Reading Test, Fourth Edition, 2487
SDS: Self-Directed Search, 4th Edition [Forms R, E, and CP], 2360
SDT: Silver Drawing Test of Cognition and Emotion [Third Edition Revised], 2410
SDT: Stromberg Dexterity Test, 2515
SDTLI: Student Developmental Task and Lifestyle Inventory, 2527
SE: Coopersmith Self-Esteem Inventories, 694
SEA: Sales Effectiveness Analysis, 2270
SEA: Survey of Employee Access, 2578
SEAI: Meadow-Kendall Social-Emotional Assessment Inventory for Deaf and Hearing Students, 1618
SEAS: Student Educational Assessment Screening, 2528
SECERS: School-Age Care Environment Rating Scale, 2310
SECS: Scales of Early Communication Skills for Hearing-Impaired Children, 2298
SEDS: Social-Emotional Dimension Scale, 2447
SEEC: Vineland Social-Emotional Early Childhood Scales, 2814
SEI: Self-Esteem Index, 2361
SELECT: SELECT Associate Screening System, 2347
S/E PAC: Progress Assessment Chart of Social and Personal Development, 2088
SEPS: School Environment Preference Survey, 2315
SEQ: School Effectiveness Questionnaire, 2314
SEQ: Self-Esteem Questionnaire, 2363
SES: Sexuality Experience Scales, 2396
SES: Student Evaluation Scale, 2529
SESAT: Stanford Early School Achievement Test, Third Edition, 2488
SESBI: Sutter-Eyberg Student Behavior Inventory, 2595
SET: Short Employment Tests, Second Edition, 2406
SET: Sports Emotion Test, 2475
SET: Symbol Elaboration Test, 2600
SETT: School-Readiness Evaluation by Trained Teachers, 2319
SEWEP: Sheltered Employment Work Experience Program, 2400
SF-36: SF-36 Health Survey, 2397
SFA: School Function Assessment, 2316
SFAB: Survey of Functional Adaptive Behaviors, 2579

S-FRIT: Slosson Full-Range Intelligence Test, 2431
SGAB: Schubert General Ability Battery, 2324
SGE: Student Goals Exploration, 2530
SGS II: The Schedule of Growing Skills: Second Edition, 2308
SGSS: Stokes/Gordon Stress Scale, 2505
SHAPE: Smit-Hand Articulation and Phonology Evaluation, 2438
SHQ: Clarke Sex History Questionnaire, 491
SHR: Supervisory Human Relations, 2564
SI: The Salience Inventory, 2282
SI: Shoplifting Inventory, 2403
SIB-R: Scales of Independent Behavior—Revised, 2299
SIC: Supervisory Inventory on Communication, 2565
SICD-R: Sequenced Inventory of Communication Development, Revised Edition, 2382
SIDES: Structured Interview for Disorders of Extreme Stress & Traumatic Antecedents Questionnaire—Self Report, 2521
SIFT: Skills Inventory for Teams, 2423
SIG: Stress in General Scale, 2509
SIHP: Stress Indicator & Health Planner, 2511
SIHR: Supervisory Inventory on Human Relations, 2566
SIL: Skills for Independent Living, 2422
SILS: Shipley Institute of Living Scale, 2402
SIPI: Short Imaginal Processes Inventory, 2407
SIPOAS: SIPOAS: Styles in Perception of Affect Scale, 2412
SIPT: Sensory Integration and Praxis Tests, 2377
SIQ: Suicidal Ideation Questionnaire, 2557
SIRI: The Stieglitz Informal Reading Inventory: Assessing Reading Behaviors from Emergent to Advanced Levels, 2503
SIRI: Suicide Intervention Response Inventory [Revised], 2558
SIR II: Student Instructional Report II, 2531
SIRS: Structured Interview of Reported Symptoms, 2522
SIS: Bay Area Functional Performance Evaluation, Second Edition, 268
SIS: Sentence Completion Tests, 2381
SIS: Somatic Inkblot Series, 2457
SIT: Shorr Imagery Test, 2404
SIT: Smell Identification Test™ [Revised], 2437
SIT-R: Slosson Intelligence Test [1991 Edition], 2432
SIV: Survey of Interpersonal Values, 2581
16PF: Sixteen Personality Factor Questionnaire, Fifth Edition, 2417
SJD: Supervisory Job Discipline, 2567
SJI: Supervisory Job Instruction, 2568
SJS: Supervisory Job Safety, 2569
SKOLD: Screening Kit of Language Development, 2331
SL: Situational Leadership®, 2415
SLDT: Specific Language Disability Test, 2469
SLE: Wonderlic Personnel Test and Scholastic Level Exam, 2899
SLEP: Secondary Level English Proficiency Test, 2339
SLES: Speech and Language Evaluation Scale, 2470
SLOTE: Second Language Oral Test of English, 2337
SLP: The Clark Wilson Group Multi-Level Feedback Instruments and Development Programs, 490
SL-TDI: The Singer-Loomis Type Deployment Inventory, 2411
SMAT: The School Motivation Analysis Test, 2318
S-MCP: Self-Motivated Career Planning Guide, 2364
SMI: Sales Motivation Inventory, Revised, 2272
SMP: The Clark Wilson Group Multi-Level Feedback Instruments and Development Programs, 490
SMP: Survey of Management Perception, 2582
SMP: Survey of Management Practices, 2583
SMQ: Stress Management Questionnaire [Revised], 2512
SNAP: Schedule for Nonadaptive and Adaptive Personality, 2306
SNAQ: The ACT Evaluation/Survey Service, 57
SNST: Stroop Neuropsychological Screening Test, 2517
SOA: Cognitive Diagnostic Battery, 564
SOC: Survey of Organizational Culture, 2585
SOI-LA: Structure of Intellect Learning Abilities Test, 2518
SOLAT: Style of Learning and Thinking, 2545
SOLST: Stephens Oral Language Screening Test, 2502
SOMPA: System of Multicultural Pluralistic Assessment, 2606
SON-R 2 1/2–7: Snijders-Oomen Non-Verbal Intelligence Test—Revised, 2441
SON-R 5 1/2–17: Snijders-Oomen Non-Verbal Intelligence Test—Revised, 2441
SONG: The Seeking of Noetic Goals Test, 2343
SOO-2000: Survey of Organizations, 2587
S.OR.T.: Scientific Orientation Test, 2325
SORT-R: Slosson Oral Reading Test [Revised], 2433
SOS: The ACT Evaluation/Survey Service, 57
SOS: Self Observation Scales, 2365
SOS: Survey of Organizational Stress, 2586
SOTU: Matching Assistive Technology & Child, 1591
SOTU: Matching Person and Technology, 1593
SOV: Study of Values: British Edition, 1965, 2539
S-PAC1: Progress Assessment Chart of Social and Personal Development, 2088
S-PAC2: Progress Assessment Chart of Social and Personal Development, 2088
SPAI.: Social Phobia and Anxiety Inventory, 2448
SPAR: SPAR Spelling and Reading Tests, Third Edition, 2467
SPAT: Systems Programming Aptitude Test, 2609
SPAT-D: Structured Photographic Articulation Test Featuring Dudsberry, 2523
SPELT: Spanish Structured Photographic Expressive Language Test, 2466
SPELT-II: Spanish Structured Photographic Expressive Language Test, 2466

SPELT-II: Structured Photographic Expressive Language Test, 2524
SPELT II: Structured Photographic Expressive Language Test, 2524
SPELT-P: Spanish Structured Photographic Expressive Language Test, 2466
SPELT-P: Structured Photographic Expressive Language Test, 2524
SPI: Self-Perception Inventory: Nursing Forms, 2366
SPI: Self-Perception Inventory [SOARES Associates], 2368
SPI: Self Perception Inventory [Psychologists and Educators, Inc.], 2367
SPI: Situational Preference Inventory, 2416
SPI: Stuttering Prediction Instrument for Young Children, 2542
SPI: Supervisory Practices Inventory, 2571
SPIB-R: Social and Prevocational Information Battery—Revised, 2443
SPM: Standard Progressive Matrices, New Zealand Standardization, 2478
SPP: The ACT Evaluation/Survey Service, 57
SPQ: Sales Personality Questionnaire, 2274
SPQ: Study Process Questionnaire, 2540
SPQS: Self Profile Q-Sort, 2370
SPR: The Clark Wilson Group Multi-Level Feedback Instruments and Development Programs, 490
SPR: Supervisory Profile Record, 2573
SPS: Suicide Probability Scale, 2559
SPSI: Scales for Predicting Successful Inclusion, 2294
SPT: Supervisory Potential Test, 2570
SPT: Supervisory Practices Test, Revised, 2572
SPV: Survey of Personal Values, 2588
SR-A: Reading Test SR-A and SR-B, 2184
SR-B: Reading Test SR-A and SR-B, 2184
SRBCSS: Scales for Rating the Behavioral Characteristics of Superior Students, 2295
SRES: Sex-Role Egalitarianism Scale, 2389
SRI: Emotional Problems Scales, 931
SRI-2: Standardized Reading Inventory, Second Edition, 2481
SRP: Stress Resiliency Profile, 2513
SRS: Social Reticence Scale, 2449
SRS: Stress Response Scale, 2514
SRS: Student Rights Scales, 2534
SRT: School Readiness Test, 2320
SS-77: Symptom Scale—77, 2604
SSAIS-R: Senior South African Individual Scale—Revised, 2375
SSBD: Systematic Screening for Behavior Disorders, 2607
SSBS: School Social Behavior Scales, 2322
SSCB: The Sales Sentence Completion Blank, 2276
SSCE: Scorable Self-Care Evaluation (Revised), 2327
SSCS: Student Self-Concept Scale, 2535
SSHA: Survey of Study Habits and Attitudes, 2591
SSI: Sales Style Indicator, 2279
SSI: Social Skills Inventory, Research Edition, 2451
SSI: Supervisory Skills Inventory, 2575
SSI-3: Stuttering Severity Instrument for Children and Adults, Third Edition, 2543
SSKAT: Socio-Sexual Knowledge & Attitudes Test, 2454
SSMP: The Clark Wilson Group Multi-Level Feedback Instruments and Development Programs, 490
SSP: Secondary Screening Profiles, 2341
SSQ: Student Styles Questionnaire, 2536
SSR: The Clark Wilson Group Multi-Level Feedback Instruments and Development Programs, 490
SSR: Secondary-School Record, 2340
SSRS: Social Skills Rating System, 2452
SSRT: Salford Sentence Reading Test, 2281
SSS: School Situation Survey, 2321
SSSQ: Adaptive Behavior: Street Survival Skills Questionnaire, 62
ST7: Advanced Test Battery, 119
ST7: Programmer Aptitude Series, 2087
ST7: Technical Test Battery [British Edition], 2642
ST9: Programmer Aptitude Series, 2087
ST9: Technical Test Battery [British Edition], 2642
ST-DACL: State Trait-Depression Adjective Check Lists, 2499
ST-LNNB-A: Screening Test for the Luria-Nebraska Neuropsychological Battery: Adult and Children's Forms, 2334
ST-LNNB-C: Screening Test for the Luria-Nebraska Neuropsychological Battery: Adult and Children's Forms, 2334
STA: Sales Transaction Audit, 2280
STAI: State-Trait Anxiety Inventory, 2497
STAIC: State-Trait Anxiety Inventory for Children, 2498
STAMAT: Schaie-Thurstone Adult Mental Abilities Test, 2304
Stanford 9: Stanford Achievement Test, Ninth Edition, 2484
STAR Profile: Student Talent and Risk Profile, 2537
STARS: STARS Test (Short Term Auditory Retrieval and Storage), 2494
START: START—Strategic Assessment of Readiness for Training, 2495
STAXI: State-Trait Anger Expression Inventory [1996 Edition], 2496
STCA: Short Tests of Clerical Ability, 2408
STCL: Standardized Test of Computer Literacy and Computer Anxiety Index (Version AZ), Revised, 2482
STEPS: Screening Test for Educational Prerequisite Skills, 2333
STI: Styles of Teamwork Inventory, 2549
STIT: Sweet Technical Information Test, 2598
STRR: Slosson Test of Reading Readiness, 2434
STSG: Screening Test of Spanish Grammar, 2335
SUDDS: Substance Use Disorders Diagnosis Schedule, 2554

SupSim: Supervisory Simulator, 2574
SUR: Supervisory Union Relations, 2576
SVIB-SCII: 1994 Strong Interest Inventory, 1790
SVR-20: Sexual Violence Risk-20, 2395
SVT: Stycar Vision Tests, 2544
SWBS: Spiritual Well-Being Scale, 2474
SWI: Self Worth Inventory, 2371
SWS: Survey of Work Styles, 2592

TAAS: Test of Auditory Analysis Skills, 2671
TABE: Tests of Adult Basic Education, Forms 7 & 8, 2737
TABE-PS: Tests of Adult Basic Education Work-Related Problem Solving, 2739
TABE WF: Tests of Adult Basic Education Work-Related Foundation Skills, 2738
TABS: Measures in Post Traumatic Stress Disorder: A Practitioner's Guide, 1626
TABS-M: Tests of Achievement in Basic Skills: Mathematics, 2736
TAC: Test of Articulation in Context, 2669
TAC: Test of Auditory Comprehension, 2672
TACL-3: Test for Auditory Comprehension of Language—Third Edition, 2657
TAGS: Teacher Assessment of Grammatical Structures, 2620
TAI: A Teacher Attitude Inventory: Identifying Teacher Positions in Relation to Educational Issues and Decisions, 2621
TAI: Test Attitude Inventory, 2656
TAIS: The Attentional and Interpersonal Style Inventory, 226
TALS: Test of Awareness of Language Segments, 2674
TAMS: Thinking About My School, 2753
TAP: Test Anxiety Profile, 2655
TAP: Tests of Achievement and Proficiency, Forms K, L, and M, 2735
TAP: Trainer's Assessment of Proficiency (TAP), 2775
TAPS: Test of Auditory-Perceptual Skills, 2673
TAQ-S: Structured Interview for Disorders of Extreme Stress & Traumatic Antecedents Questionnaire—Self Report, 2521
TARC: The Tapping Test: A Predictor of Typing and Other Tapping Operations, 2612
TAS: Teamwork Appraisal Survey, 2638
TAS: Test of Attitude Toward School, 2670
TASC: Sentence Completion Tests, 2381
TAT: Thematic Apperception Test, 2749
TAV: TAV Selection System, 2616
TAWF: Test of Adolescent/Adult Word Finding, 2667
TBA: Test of Basic Assumptions, 2675
TBS: Transition Behavior Scale, 2779
TC: Temperament Comparator, 2648
TCAM: Thinking Creatively in Action and Movement, 2754
TCB: Themes Concerning Blacks, 2750
TCS: Tiffany Control Scales, 2759
TCS/2: Test of Cognitive Skills, Second Edition, 2677
TCSM: Test of Cognitive Style in Mathematics, 2678
TCSW: Thinking Creatively With Sounds and Words, Research Edition, 2755
TCT-DP: Test for Creative Thinking—Drawing Production, 2659
TD Monitor: TD (Tardive Dyskinesia) Monitor, 2619
TDI: Team-Development Inventory, 2631
TDS: Campbell-Hallam Team Development Survey, 379
TDS: Team Development Survey, 2632
TDTA: Templin-Darley Tests of Articulation, Second Edition, 2651
T.E.A.M.S: Team Effectiveness and Meeting Strategy, 2633
TED: Tasks of Emotional Development Test, 2614
TEEM: Test for Examining Expressive Morphology, 2660
TEI: Trait Evaluation Index, 2776
TEK: Test of Economic Knowledge, 2685
TEL: Test of Economic Literacy, Second Edition, 2686
TEL: Tests for Everyday Living, 2734
TELD-3: Test of Early Language Development, Third Edition, 2680
TEMA-2: Test of Early Mathematics Ability, Second Edition, 2681
TEMAS: TEMAS (Tell-Me-A-Story), 2647
TEP: Management & Leadership Systems, 1545
TEPI: Triadal Equated Personality Inventory, 2784
TEPL: Test of English Proficiency Level, 2688
TERA-D/HH: Test of Early Reading Ability—Deaf or Hard of Hearing, 2683
TERA-2: Test of Early Reading Ability—2, 2682
TES: Team Effectiveness Survey, 2634
TEWL—2: Test of Early Written Language, Second Edition, 2684
TGA: Tests of General Ability: Inter-American Series, 2741
TGMD: Test of Gross Motor Development, 2689
THOR: Sentence Completion Tests, 2381
TI: Temperament Inventory, 2649
TIA: Technology and Internet Assessment, 2645
TIES-II: The Instructional Environment System—II, 1275
TII: Treatment Intervention Inventory, 2783
TII-J: Treatment Intervention Inventory, 2783
TIME: Version 1.0: Toddler and Infant Motor Evaluation, 2767
TIS: Measures in Post Traumatic Stress Disorder: A Practitioner's Guide, 1626
T-JTA: Taylor-Johnson Temperament Analysis [1992 Edition], 2618
TKFGRS: Test of Kindergarten/First Grade Readiness Skills, 2692
TKI.: Thomas-Kilmann Conflict Mode Instrument, 2756

TLC: Scale for the Assessment of Thought, Language, and Communication, 2290
TLC-Expanded: Test of Language Competence—Expanded Edition, 2693
TMA: Thurstone Test of Mental Alertness, 2758
T-MAC: Test of Minimal Articulation Competence, 2703
TMI: The Kirkpatrick Management and Supervisory Skills Series, 1403
TOA: Bay Area Functional Performance Evaluation, Second Edition, 268
TOAL-3: Test of Adolescent and Adult Language, Third Edition, 2668
TOAP: Test of Academic Performance, 2666
TOBE/2: Tests of Basic Experiences 2, 2740
TOCL: Test of Children's Language: Assessing Aspects of Spoken Language, Reading, and Writing, 2676
TOEFL: Computer-Based Test of English as a Foreign Language and Test of Written English,
TOEIC: Test of English for International Communication (TOEIC), 2687
TOIL: Test of Initial Literacy, 2691
TOLA: ACER Test of Learning Ability, 32
TOLA: Test of Oral and Limb Apraxia, 2705
TOLD-I:3: Test of Language Development—Intermediate, Third Edition, 2694
TOLD-P:3: Test of Language Development—Primary, Third Edition, 2695
TOLP: Test for Oral Language Production, 2661
TOL:RV: Tower of London: Research Version, 2772
TOMA-2: Test of Mathematical Abilities, Second Edition, 2699
TOMAGS: Test of Mathematical Abilities for Gifted Students, 2698
TOMAL: Test of Memory and Learning, 2701
TOMM: Test of Memory Malingering, 2702
TONI-3: Test of Nonverbal Intelligence, Third Edition, 2704
TOPA.: Test of Phonological Awareness, 2708
TOPL: Test of Pragmatic Language, 2709
TOPS: Test of Problem Solving, 2710
TORCH: Tests of Reading Comprehension, 2743
TORC-3: Test of Reading Comprehension, Third Edition, 2712
TOSCA: Test of Scholastic Abilities, 2714
TOSF: Test of Oral Structures and Functions, 2706
TOVA: Test of Variables of Attention (Version 7.03), 2720
TOWE: Test of Written Expression, 2730
TOWK: Test of Word Knowledge, 2727
TOWL-3: Test of Written Language—Third Edition, 2731
TPBA: Transdisciplinary Play-Based Assessment, Revised Edition, 2778
TPI: Transition Planning Inventory, 2780
TPLS: The Primary Language Screen, 2055
TPO: Test of Perceptual Organization, 2707
TQMI: TQ Manager Inventory and Feedback From Others, 2773
TQMO: TQ Manager Inventory and Feedback From Others, 2773
TRACS: Teaching Resource and Assessment of Critical Skills, 2629
TRAT: Trade Aptitude Test Battery, 2774
TRF: Child Behavior Checklist, 451
TRN: Test of Reading and Number: Inter-American Series, 2711
TROG: Test for the Reception of Grammar, 2662
TRS: Teacher Role Survey (Revised), 2625
TRSI: Test of Retail Sales Insight, 2713
TSBC: The Time-Sample Behavioral Checklist, 2763
TSE: Test of Spoken English, 2717
TSFI: Test of Sensory Functions in Infants, 2715
TSI: DeGangi-Berk Test of Sensory Integration, 772
TSI: Test of Social Insight, 2716
TSI: Theological School Inventory, 2751
TSI: Trauma Symptom Inventory, 2782
TSSB: Tapping Students' Science Beliefs: A Resource for Teaching and Learning, 2611
TTB: Technical Test Battery, 2641
TTB: Technical Test Battery [British Edition], 2642
TTB: Typing Test for Business, 2787
TTCT: Torrance Tests of Creative Thinking, 2771
TTS: Thurstone Temperament Schedule, 2757
TUCE III: Test of Understanding in College Economics, Third Edition, 2718
TUPE: Test of Understanding in Personal Economics, 2719
TUSSI: Temple University Short Syntax Inventory, 2650
TVAS: Test of Visual Analysis Skills, 2721
TVI: Teacher Values Inventory, 2626
TVMI: Test of Visual-Motor Integration, 2722
TVMS: Test of Visual-Motor Skills, 2723
TVPS: Test of Visual-Perceptual Skills (Non-Motor), 2724
TWCS: Test of Work Competency and Stability, 2728
TWE: Computer-Based Test of English as a Foreign Language and Test of Written English, 666
TWE: Test of Written English, 2729
TWF: Test of Word Finding, 2725
TWFD: Test of Word Finding in Discourse, 2726
TWI™: Transition-to-Work Inventory: A Job Placement System for Workers with Severe disAbilities, 2781
TWS-4: Test of Written Spelling, Fourth Edition, 2732

UCCES: Uniform Child Custody Evaluation System, 2791
UFOV: Useful Field of View, 2794
UNIT: Universal Nonverbal Intelligence Test, 2792
UPSIT: Smell Identification Test™ [Revised], 2437

URES: University Residence Environment Scale [Revised], 2793
USAMO: Mathematical Olympiads, 1595
UTLD-3: Utah Test of Language Development—3, 2801

VA1: Advanced Test Battery, 119
VA1: Programmer Aptitude Series, 2087
VA3: Advanced Test Battery, 119
VA3: Programmer Aptitude Series, 2087
VAB-R: Vulpe Assessment Battery—Revised, 2838
VACG: Vocational Assessment and Curriculum Guide, 2826
VADS Test: The Visual Aural Digit Span Test, 2816
VARS: Vocational Adaptation Rating Scales, 2824
VAT:ADV: The Vocational Apperception Test: Advanced Form, 2825
VBC: Vocational Behavior Checklist, 2827
VCAT: Veterinary College Admission Test, 2810
VC1: Critical Reasoning Test Battery, 735
VDMI-R: Vocational Decision-Making Interview—Revised, 2828
VESPAR: VESPAR: A Verbal and Spatial Reasoning Test, 2809
VFAT: Visual Functioning Assessment Tool, 2818
VI: Values Inventory, 2803
VIE: MDS Vocational Interest Exploration System, 1617
VIESA: Vocational Interest, Experience, and Skill Assessment, 2830
VIESA, 2nd Canadian Edition: Vocational Interest, Experience and Skill Assessment (VIESA), 2nd Canadian Edition, 2831
VII-R: Vocational Interest Inventory—Revised, 2833
VIP: Validity Indicator Profile, 2802
VISA: Vocational Interest and Sophistication Assessment, 2829
VMD: Vincent Mechanical Diagrams Test, 1979 Revision, 2812
VMGT: [Bender-Gestalt Test], 301
VMI: Developmental Test of Visual-Motor Integration, 4th Edition, Revised, 815
VOI: Vocational Opinion Index, 2834
VOT: The Hooper Visual Organization Test, 1218
VP5: Personnel Test Battery, 1973
VPI: Personnel Test Battery, 1973
VPI: Values Preference Indicator , 2804
VPI: Vocational Preference Inventory, 1985 Edition, 2835
VRII: Vocational Research Interest Inventory, 2836
VS: The Values Scale, Second Edition, 2805
VSA: Visual Skills Appraisal, 2821
VSAT: Visual Search and Attention Test, 2820
VSVT: Victoria Symptom Validity Test, 2811
VT1: Technical Test Battery [British Edition], 2642
VT5: Technical Test Battery [British Edition], 2642
VTQS: Voc-Tech Quick Screener, 2822
WAB: Western Aphasia Battery, 2873
WAI: Work Adjustment Inventory, 2912
WAIS-III: Wechsler Adult Intelligence Scale—Third Edition, 2860
WAPS: Work Aspect Preference Scale, 2915
W-APT: W-APT Programming Aptitude Test, 2849
WAQ: Work Attitudes Questionnaire (Version for Research), 2916
WAS: Ward Atmosphere Scale (Third Edition), 2850
WAS: The Work Adjustment Scale, 2913
WASC: Williams Awareness Sentence Completion, 2887
WASI: Wechsler Abbreviated Scale of Intelligence, 2859
WBRS: Wisconsin Behavior Rating Scale, 2891
WBST: Wonderlic Basic Skills Test, 2898
WCAT: Weiss Comprehensive Articulation Test, 2866
WCOAT: The Wolfe Computer Operator Aptitude Test, 2895
WCST: Wisconsin Card Sorting Test, Revised and Expanded, 2892
WDRB: Woodcock Diagnostic Reading Battery, 2900
WDSCA: Weinberg Depression Scale for Children and Adolescents, 2865
WERLS: Wolf Expressive/Receptive Language & Speech Checklist, 2893
WES: Work Environment Scale, Second Edition, 2917
WES: The Work Experience Survey, 2918
WET: The Written Expression Test, 2934
WFPT: Welsh Figure Preference Test, 2869
WGCTA: Watson-Glaser Critical Thinking Appraisal, 2856
WGCTA-S: Watson-Glaser Critical Thinking Appraisal, Form S, 2857
WIAT: Wechsler Individual Achievement Test, 2861
WII: Work Information Inventory, 2919
Wiig CRIL: Wiig Criterion Referenced Inventory of Language, 2886
WIS: Word Identification Scale, 2908
WISC-III: Wechsler Intelligence Scale for Children—Third Edition, 2862
WIST: Whitaker Index of Schizophrenic Thinking, 2878
WJ-R: Woodcock-Johnson Psycho-Educational Battery—Revised, 2901
WKOPAY: Khatena Torrance Creative Perception Inventory, 1396
WLA: Written Language Assessment, 2935
WLPB-R: Woodcock Language Proficiency Battery—Revised, 2902
WLST: Written Language Syntax Test, 2936
WMI: [Work Motivation], 2921
WMI: Work Motivation Inventory: A Test of Adult Work Motivation, 2922
WMICRO: Microcomputer User Aptitude Test, 1666
WMS-III: Wechsler Memory Scale III, 2863
WMT: The Word Memory Test, 2909

WNSS: The ACT Evaluation/Survey Service, 57
WPA: Work Performance Assessment, 2923
WPAB: Eosys Word Processing Aptitude Battery, 964
WPBIC: Walker Problem Behavior Identification Checklist, 2848
WPI: The Western Personality Inventory, 2874
WPP: Work Personality Profile, 2924
WPPSI-R: Wechsler Preschool and Primary Scale of Intelligence—Revised, 2864
WPS: Wonderlic Personnel Test and Scholastic Level Exam, 2899
WPSI: Wahler Physical Symptoms Inventory, 2839
WPT: Writing Process Test, 2933
WRAML: Wide Range Assessment of Memory and Learning, 2880
WRaPS: Word Recognition and Phonic Skills, 2910
WRAT3: Wide Range Achievement Test 3, 2879
WRAVMA: Wide Range Assessment of Visual Motor Abilities, 2881
WRIOT: Wide Range Interest-Opinion Test, 2882
WSS: Work Skills Series Production, 2927
WSS: Workplace Skills Survey, 2930
WSSAB: Weller-Strawser Scales of Adaptive Behavior for the Learning Disabled, 2868
WSSRS: Waksman Social Skills Rating Scale, 2841
WTI: Work Temperament Inventory, 2928
WTMA: The Wiesen Test of Mechanical Aptitude, 2884
WT PA: Matching Person and Technology, 1593
WVAST: Washer Visual Acuity Screening Technique, 2852
WVST: Kendrick Assessment of Cognitive Ageing, 1390
WWO: The Clark Wilson Group Multi-Level Feedback Instruments and Development Programs, 490

XT: The Clark Wilson Group Multi-Level Feedback Instruments and Development Programs, 490

YSR: Child Behavior Checklist, 451

CLASSIFIED SUBJECT INDEX

The Classified Subject Index classifies all tests included in Tests in Print V *into 19 major categories: Achievement, Behavior Assessment, Developmental, Education, English and Language, Fine Arts, Foreign Language, Intelligence and General Aptitude, Mathematics, Miscellaneous, Multi-Aptitude Batteries, Neuropsychological, Personality, Reading, Science, Sensory-Motor, Social Studies, Speech and Hearing, and Vocations. Each category appears in alphabetical order and tests are ordered alphabetically within each category. Some tests may appear in more than one category. The Miscellaneous category has 16 subcategories with tests ordered alphabetically within the subcategories. Each test entry includes test title, population for which the test is intended, and the test entry number in* Tests in Print V. *All numbers refer to test entry numbers, not to page numbers. Brief suggestions for the use of this index are presented in the introduction. The classifications have been used in the previous editions of the* MMY *and* TIP. *Revised definitions of the categories are effective with the upcoming* Fourteenth Mental Measurements Yearbook. *Most tests in* TIP V *have been classified using the new definitions, which are provided at the beginning of this index.*

Achievement

Tests that measure acquired knowledge across school subject content areas. Included here are test batteries that measure multiple content areas and individual subject areas not having separate classification categories. (Note: Some batteries include both achievement and aptitude subtests. Such batteries may be classified under the categories of either Achievement or Intelligence and Aptitude depending upon the principal content area.)

See also Fine Arts, Intelligence and General Aptitude, Mathematics, Reading, Science, and Social Studies.

Behavior Assessment

Tests that measure general or specific behavior within educational, vocational, community, or home settings. Included here are checklists, rating scales, and surveys that measure observer's interpretations of behavior in relation to adaptive or social skills, functional skills, and appropriateness or dysfunction within settings/situations.

Developmental

Tests that are designed to assess skills or emerging skills (such as number concepts, conservation, memory, fine motor, gross motor, communication, letter recognition, social competence) of young children (0-7 years) or tests which are designed to assess such skills in severely or profoundly disabled school-aged individuals. Included here are early screeners, developmental surveys/profiles, kindergarten or school readiness tests, early learning profiles, infant development scales, tests of play behavior, social acceptance/social skills; and preschool psychoeducational batteries. Content specific screeners, such as those assessing readiness, are classified by content area (e.g., Reading).

See also Neuropsychological and Sensory-Motor.

Education

General education-related tests, including measures of instructional/school environment, effective schools/teaching, study skills and strategies, learning styles and strategies, school attitudes, educational programs/curriculae, interest inventories, and educational leadership.

Specific content area tests (i.e., science, mathematics, social studies, etc.) are listed by their content area.

English and Language

Tests that measure skills in using or understanding the English language in spoken or written form. Included here are tests of language proficiency, applied literacy, language comprehension/development/proficiency, English skills/proficiency, communication skills, listening comprehension, linguistics, and receptive/expressive vocabulary. (Tests designed to measure the mechanics of speaking or communicating are classified under the category Speech and Hearing.)

Fine Arts

Tests that measure knowledge, skills, abilities, attitudes, and interests within the various areas of fine and performing arts. Included here are tests of aptitude, achievement, creativity/talent/giftedness specific to the Fine Arts area, and tests of aesthetic judgment.

Foreign Languages

Tests that measure competencies and readiness in reading, comprehending, and speaking a language other than English.

Intelligence and General Aptitude

Tests that measure general acquired knowledge, aptitudes, or cognitive ability and those that assess specific aspects of these general categories. Included here are tests of critical thinking skills, nonverbal/verbal reasoning, cognitive abilities/processing, learning potential/aptitude/efficiency, logical reasoning, abstract thinking, creative thinking/creativity; entrance exams and academic admissions tests.

Mathematics

Tests that measure competencies and attitudes in any of the various areas of mathematics (e.g., algebra, geometry, calculus) and those related to general mathematics achievement/proficiency. (Note: Included here are tests that assess personality or affective variables related to mathematics.)

Miscellaneous

Tests that cannot be sorted into any of the current MMY categories as listed and defined here. Included here are tests of handwriting, ethics and morality, religion, driving and safety, health and physical education, environment (e.g., classroom environment, family environment), custody decisions, substance abuse, and addictions. (See also Personality.)

Multi-Aptitude Batteries

The Multi-Aptitude category, used in previous volumes of the *MMY* and *TIP* will be discontinued effective with The *14th MMY.* Tests listed under this category will typically be listed under Intelligence and General Aptitude. These include placement tests, adult assessment systems, cognitive inventories, and aptitude batteries.

Neuropsychological

Tests that measure neurological functioning or brain-behavior relationships either generally or in relation to specific areas of functioning. Included here are neuropsychological test batteries, questionnaires, and screening tests. Also included are tests that measure memory impairment, various disorders or decline associated with dementia, brain/head injury, visual attention, digit recognition, finger tapping, laterality, aphasia, and behavior (associated with organic brain dysfunction or brain injury).

See also Developmental, Intelligence and General Aptitude, Sensory-Motor, and Speech and Hearing.

Personality

Tests that measure individuals' ways of thinking, behaving, and functioning within family and society. Included here are projective and apperception tests, needs inventories, anxiety/depression scales; tests assessing substance use/abuse (or propensity for abuse), risk taking behavior, general mental health, emotional intelligence, self-image/-concept/-esteem, empathy, suicidal ideation, schizophrenia, depression/hopelessness, abuse, coping skills/stress, eating disorders, grief, decision-making, racial attitudes; general motivation, attributions, perceptions; adjustment, parenting styles, and marital issues/satisfaction.

For content-specific tests, see subject area categories (e.g., math efficacy instruments are located in Mathematics). Some areas, such as substance abuse, are cross-referenced with the Personality category.

Reading

Tests that measure competencies and attitudes within the broadly defined area of reading. Included here are reading inventories, tests of reading achievement and aptitude, reading readiness/early reading ability, reading comprehension, reading decoding, and oral reading. (Note: Included here are tests that assess personality or affective variables related to reading.)

Science

Tests that measure competencies and attitudes within any of the various areas of science (e.g., biology, chemistry, physics), and those related to general science achievement/proficiency. (Note: Included here are tests that assess personality or affective variables related to science.)

Sensory-Motor

Tests that are general or specific measures of any or all of the five senses and those that assess fine or gross motor skills. Included here are tests of manual dexterity, perceptual skills, visual-motor skills, perceptual-motor skills, movement and posture, laterality preference, sensory integration, motor development, color blindness/discrimination, visual perception/organization, and visual acuity. (Note: See also the categories Neuropsychological and Speech and Hearing.)

Social Studies

Tests that measure competencies and attitudes within the broadly defined area of social studies. Included here are tests related to economics, sociology, history, geography, and political science, and those related to general social studies achievement/proficiency. (Note: Also included here are tests that assess personality or affective variables related to social studies.)

Speech and Hearing

Tests that measure the mechanics of speaking or hearing the spoken word. Included here are tests of articulation, voice fluency, stuttering, speech sound perception/discrimination, auditory discrimination/comprehension, audiometry, deafness, and hearing loss/impairment. (Note: See Developmental, English and Language, Neuropsychological, and Sensory-Motor.)

Vocations

Tests that measure employee skills, behaviors, attitudes, values, and perceptions relative to jobs, employment, and the work place or organizational environment. Included here are tests of management skill/style/competence, leader behavior, careers (development, exploration, attitudes); job- or work-related selection/admission/entrance tests; tests of work adjustment, team or group processes/communication/effectiveness, employability, vocational/occupational interests, employee aptitudes/competencies, and organizational climate.

See also Intelligence and General Aptitude, and Personality and also specific content area categories (e.g., Mathematics, Reading).

ACHIEVEMENT

ACER Tests of Basic Skills—Green Series, Year 3 and Year 6 in Australian school system, see 33
Achievement Test for Accounting Graduates, Accounting job applicants or employees, see 38
Adult Basic Learning Examination, Second Edition, Adults with less than 12 years of formal schooling, see 82
Ann Arbor Learning Inventory [1996 Edition], Grades K–1, Grades 2–4, Grades 5–8, see 157
Aprenda®: La prueba de logros en español—Segunda edición, Grades K.5–12.9, see 165
Assessment and Placement Services for Community Colleges, Entering community college students, see 192
Basic Achievement Skills Individual Screener, Grades 1–12 and post high school, see 246
Basic Educational Skills Test, Grades 1.5–5, see 248
BRIGANCE® Diagnostic Comprehensive Inventory of Basic Skills, Revised, Ages 5–13, see 340
BRIGANCE® Diagnostic Inventory of Basic Skills, Grades K-6, see 342
BRIGANCE® Diagnostic Inventory of Essential Skills, Grade 6-adult, see 343
BRIGANCE® Diagnostic Life Skills Inventory, Grades 2–8, see 344
Bristol Achievement Tests, Ages 8-0 to 11-11, see 348
California Achievement Tests, Fifth Edition, Grades K.0–K.9, K.6–1.6, 1.6–2.2, 1.6–3.2, 2.6–4.2, 3.6–5.2, 4.6–6.2, 5.6–7.2, 6.6–8.2, 7.6–9.2, 8.6–10.2, 9.6–11.2, 10.6–12.9, see 364
Canadian Achievement Survey Tests for Adults, Adults, see 383
Canadian Achievement Tests, Second Edition, Grades 2.6–12.9, see 384
Canadian Tests of Basic Skills, Forms 7 and 8, Grades K–2, 3–8, and 9–12, see 389
Closed High School Placement Test, Eighth grade students, see 547
College Basic Academic Subjects Examination, College students having completed the general education component of a college curriculum, see 570
Collegiate Assessment of Academic Proficiency, Students in the first 2 years of college, see 621
Comprehensive Testing Program III, Grades 1–2, 2–3, 3–4, 4–6, 6–8, 8–12, see 664
Comprehensive Tests of Basic Skills, Fourth Edition, Grades K.0–12.9, see 665
Criterion Test of Basic Skills, Grades K-8., see 730
CTB Kindergarten–Grade 1 Assessment Activities, Grades K–1, see 741
CTB Performance Assessment, Grades 2–11, see 742
CTB Portfolio Assessment System, Grades 1 & 2, 3, 4, 5 & 6, 7 & 8, see 743
Curriculum Frameworks Assessment System, Students in grades 1–12 from the California public school districts, see 750
Developing Skills Checklist, Ages 4–6.8, see 800
Diagnostic Achievement Battery, Second Edition, Ages 6-0 to 14-0, see 821

Diagnostic Achievement Test for Adolescents, Second Edition, Ages 12–0 to 18–11, see 822
Diagnostic Screening Test: Achievement, Grades K-12, see 829
Differential Ability Scales, Ages 2-6 to 17-11, see 837
Early School Assessment, End of prekindergarten to middle of kindergarten, middle of kindergarten to beginning of grade 1, see 886
End-of-Course Tests, Secondary school students, see 947
English Test: Municipal Tests: National Achievement Tests, Grades 3-8, see 956
Evaluation of Basic Skills, Ages 3 to 18, see 982
EXPLORE, Grade 8, see 992
GOALS®: A Performance-Based Measure of Achievement, Grades 1–12, see 1094
Hammill Multiability Achievement Test, Ages 7-0 to 17-11, see 1167
High School Placement Test-Open Edition, Eighth grade students, see 1202
Integrated Assessment System®, Grades 1–9, see 1281
Iowa Tests of Basic Skills, Forms K, L, and M, Grades K–9, see 1318
Iowa Tests of Educational Development, Forms K, L, and M, Grades 9–12, see 1319
Kaufman Functional Academic Skills Test, Ages 15–85 and over, see 1382
Kaufman Survey of Early Academic and Language Skills, 3-0 to 6-11, see 1385
Kaufman Test of Educational Achievement [1998 Normative Update], Grades 1 through 12, ages 6–22, see 1386
Kuhlmann-Anderson Tests, Eighth Edition, Grades K, 1, 2-3, 3-4, 5-6, 7-9, 9-12, see 1414
La Prueba de Realizacion, Segunda Edicion, Kindergarten–grade 12, see 1418
Ligondé Equivalence Test, Adults who left elementary or secondary school 15 to 20 years ago, see 1501
Maculaitis Assessment Program, Commercial Edition, ESL students in grades K-3, K-1, 2-3, 4-5, 6-8, 9-12, see 1534
Metropolitan Achievement Tests®, Seventh Edition, Grades K.0–12, see 1657
Metropolitan Performance Assessment: Integrated Performance Tasks, Ages 4-4 to 6-3; ages 5-5 to 7-0, see 1658
Monitoring Basic Skills Progress—Second Edition, Grades 1–7, see 1715
Multilevel Academic Survey Test, K-8 and high school students with reading or mathematics skills deficits, see 1738
National Assessment of Educational Progress—-Released Exercises, Ages 9 and 13 and 17; Grades 4, 8, and 12, see 1759
National Educational Development Tests, Grades 9-10, see 1760
Norris Educational Achievement Test, Ages 4-0 to 6-11, Ages 6-0 to 17-11, see 1802
Official GED Practice Test, Candidates preparing for the full-length GED, see 1838
Peabody Individual Achievement Test—Revised [1998 Normative Update], Grades K–12, see 1902
PLAN, Grade 10, see 1997
Progressive Achievement Tests of Study Skills, Standards 3-4 and Forms I-V (ages 9-15), see 2095
QUEST, Ages 7-8, see 2134
QUIC Tests, Grades 2-12, see 2137
Richmond Tests of Basic Skills: Edition 2, Ages 8-0 to 13-11, see 2234
Riverside Performance Assessment Series, Grades 1–12, see 2241
Scaled Curriculum Achievement Levels Test, Grades 3-8, see 2293
Secondary Screening Profiles, Junior high students, ages 10–13 years, see 2341
Spanish Assessment of Basic Education, Second Edition, Grades 1.0–1.9, 1.6–2.9, 2.6–3.9, 3.6–4.9, 4.6–6.9, 6.6–8.9, see 2463
Standardized Bible Content Tests, Bible college students, see 2480
Stanford Achievement Test—Abbreviated Version—8th Edition, Grades 1.5–12.9, see 2483
Stanford Achievement Test, Ninth Edition, Grades K.0–13.0, see 2484
Stanford Early School Achievement Test, Third Edition, Grades K.0-K.5, K.5-1.5, see 2488
The Steenburgen Diagnostic-Prescriptive Math Program, Grades 1-3, 4-6, see 2500
SUPERA, Spanish-speaking students, grades 1–11, see 2560
Teacher's Handbook of Diagnostic Inventories, Second Edition, Grades K-8, see 2627
Technology and Internet Assessment, Middle school, high school, and college students, potential and existing employees, see 2645
TerraNova, Grades K–12, see 2654
Test of Academic Achievement Skills—Reading, Arithmetic, Spelling, and Listening Comprehension, Ages 4-0 to 12-0, see 2665
Test of Academic Performance, Grades K–12, see 2666
Test of Reading and Number: Inter-American Series, Grade 4 entrants, see 2711
Tests of Achievement and Proficiency, Forms K, L, and M, Grades 9–12, see 2735
Tests of Adult Basic Education, Forms 7 & 8, Adults in Adult Basic Education programs, vocational-technical centers, and correctional facilities, see 2737
Tests of Adult Basic Education Work-Related Foundation Skills, Adults in vocational/technical programs, students in adult basic education programs 2-year colleges, and secondary school ROP & JTPA programs, see 2738
Tests of General Educational Development [The GED Tests], Candidates for high school equivalency diplomas, see 2742

Wechsler Individual Achievement Test, Ages 5–19, see 2861
Wide Range Achievement Test 3, Ages 5-75, see 2879
Wonderlic Basic Skills Test, Teenagers and adults, see 2898
Woodcock-McGrew-Werder Mini-Battery of Achievement, Ages 4–90, see 2903

BEHAVIOR ASSESSMENT

AAMR Adaptive Behavior Scale—Residential and Community, Second Edition, Persons with disabilities in residential and community settings, see 1
AAMR Adaptive Behavior Scale—School, Second Edition, Ages 3–21, see 2
Aberrant Behavior Checklist, Mentally retarded adolescents and adults, see 4
Achieving Behavioral Competencies, "Students who are seriously emotionally disturbed, closed head injured, juvenile offenders, learning disabled, or at-risk for school drop-out" and "adults served by voc rehab programs," see 40
Adaptive Behavior Evaluation Scale, Revised, Ages 5-0 to 18-0, see 59
Adaptive Behavior Inventory, Mentally retarded students ages 6-0 through 18-11 years and normal students ages 5-0 through 18-11 years, see 60
Adaptive Behavior Inventory for Children, Ages 5-11, see 61
ADD-H: Comprehensive Teacher's Rating Scale, Second Edition [1998 Revision], Grades K–adult, see 65
ADHD Rating Scale–IV, Ages 5–18 years, see 67
Adjustment Scales for Children and Adolescents, Ages 5–17, see 69
Adult Attention Deficit Disorder Behavior Rating Scale, Ages 16 and above, see 80
Adult Attention Deficit Disorders Evaluation Scale, Adults, see 81
Assessment of Adaptive Areas, Ages 3–60+ years, see 198
Assessment of Language-Related Functional Activities, People with suspected language or cognitive compromise, aged 16 to 95, see 211
Attention Deficit Disorder Behavior Rating Scales, School personnel and psychologists, see 220
Attention Deficit Disorders Evaluation Scale, Second Edition, Ages 3–20 years, ages 4–19 years, see 221
The Attention Deficit Disorders Evaluation Scale Secondary-Age Student, Ages 11.5–19, see 222
Attention Disorders in Children: School-Based Assessment, Diagnosis, and Treatment, Children with Attention Disorders, see 225
Attention-Deficit Scales for Adults, Adults, see 224
Attention-Deficit/Hyperactivity Disorder Test, Ages 3–23, see 223
The Autistic Continuum: An Assessment and Intervention Schedule, Ages 2–8, see 235
BASC Monitor for ADHD, Ages 4–18, see 245
Basic Skills Locater Test, Ages 15 to adult who are functioning below a 12th grade level, see 259
Bay Area Functional Performance Evaluation, Second Edition, Psychiatric patients, see 268
Behavior Analysis Forms for Clinical Intervention, Behavior therapy clients, see 279
Behavior Assessment System for Children [Revised], Ages 2 1/2–18, see 280
Behavior Dimensions Rating Scale, Ages 5–Adult, see 281
Behavior Dimensions Scale, Ages 3–19, see 282
Behavior Disorders Identification Scale, Ages 4.5-21, see 283
Behavior Evaluation Scale—2, Grades K-12, see 284
Behavior Rating Instrument for Autistic and Other Atypical Children, 2nd Edition, Autistic children, see 285
Behavior Rating Profile, Second Edition, Ages 6-6 to 18-6, see 286
Behavior Status Inventory, Psychiatric inpatients, see 288
Behavioral and Emotional Rating Scale: A Strength-Based Approach to Assessment, Ages 5-0 to 18-11, see 290
Behavioral Objective Sequence, Students (preschool through high school) with emotional and behavioral disorders, see 293
Brown Attention-Deficit Disorder Scales, Ages 12 to 18, Ages 18 and over, see 351
Burks' Behavior Rating Scales, Preschool–grade 9, see 355
C.O.A.C.H.: Cayuga-Onondaga Assessment for Children with Handicaps, Version 7.0, Preschool and school-aged learners with moderate, severe, or profound handicap, see 553
Caregiver-Teacher Report Form, Ages 2–5, see 424
Checklist of Adaptive Living Skills, Infants to adults, see 443
Child Behavior Checklist, Ages 2–18, see 451
Child Sexual Behavior Inventory, Ages 2–12, see 457
Children's Attention and Adjustment Survey, Ages 5–13, see 469
Comprehensive Behavior Rating Scale for Children, Ages 6–14, see 651
Comprehensive Test of Adaptive Behavior, Birth-age 60, see 661

Conners' Adult ADHD Rating Scales, Ages 18 and over, see 678
Conners' Continuous Performance Test, Ages 6 to adult, see 679
Conners' Rating Scales—Revised, Ages 3–17; self-report scales can be completed by 12- to 17-year-olds, see 681
Continuing Education Assessment Inventory, Mentally retarded adolescents and adults, see 686
Developmental Teaching Objectives and Rating Form—Revised, Ages 0–16 years, see 814
Devereux Behavior Rating Scale—School Form, Ages 5–18, see 817
Differential Test of Conduct and Emotional Problems, Grades K–12, see 841
Dyadic Parent-Child Interaction Coding System: A Manual, Children ages 2-10 and their parents, see 864
The Early Childhood Attention Deficit Disorders Evaluation Scale, 24–84 months, see 873
The Early Childhood Behavior Scale, 36–72 months, see 874
Early Screening Project, Ages 3–6, see 890
Eby Gifted Behavior Index, Elementary and high school and college students, see 895
Emotional and Behavior Problem Scale, Ages 4.5–21, see 928
Emotional or Behavior Disorder Scale, Ages 4.5 to 21, see 930
Eyberg Child Behavior Inventory, Ages 2–16, see 997
Fels Parent Behavior Rating Scales, Parents, see 1026
Forms for Behavior Analysis with Children, Children, see 1052
Functional Needs Assessment, Chronic psychiatric patients, see 1065
Gilliam Autism Rating Scale, Ages 3–22, see 1091
The Gordon Diagnostic System, Children, adolescents, and adults, see 1099
Guide to the Assessment of Test Session Behavior for the WISC-III and the WIAT, Ages 6–16, see 1155
Hahnemann Elementary School Behavior Rating Scale, Elementary school students in both regular and open classrooms, see 1161
Hahnemann High School Behavior Rating Scale, Grades 7-12, see 1162
Independent Living Scales, Adults with cognitive impairments, see 1246
Instrument for Disability Screening [Developmental Edition], Primary grade children, see 1278
Integrated Visual and Auditory Continuous Performance Test, Age 5 to adult, see 1282
Interpersonal Trust Surveys, Adults, see 1296
Iowa Social Competency Scales, Ages 3-12, see 1317
Jesness Behavior Checklist, Delinquents ages 13-29, see 1340
Leadership Practices Inventory—Individual Contributor [Second Edition], Nonmanagerial leaders, see 1446
Leadership Practices Inventory [Pfeiffer & Company International Publishers], Managers, see 1448
Learned Behaviors Profile—Self/Other, Adults, see 1452
Learning Skills Profile, Junior high to adults, see 1467
Louisville Behavior Checklist, Ages 4-6, 7-12, 13-17, see 1522
Millon Behavioral Health Inventory, Ages 17 and over undergoing medical care or evaluation, see 1686
Mossford Assessment Chart for the Physically Handicapped, Ages 5-18, see 1718
Motivation Assessment Scale, People with mental disabilities, see 1722
Normative Adaptive Behavior Checklist, Birth-21 years, see 1801
Parent Behavior Checklist, Parents of children ages 1 to 4, see 1880
Parent Behavior Form, Parents; ratings by ages 8-12, 12-18 and adults, see 1881
Parents' Observation of Study Behaviors Survey, Grades 6–13, see 1891
Portland Problem Behavior Checklist—Revised, Grades K–12, see 2012
Pre-Referral Intervention Manual [Revised and Updated Second Edition], K–12 students, see 2035
Preschool and Kindergarten Behavior Scales, Ages 3–6, see 2036
The Preschool Behavior Questionnaire, Ages 3-6, see 2039
Problem Behavior Inventory [Adult & Adolescent Screening Forms], Adults and adolescents, see 2062
Psychometric Behavior Checklist, Adults, see 2116
Pupil Behavior Rating Scale, Grades K-3, 3-7, see 2122
The Pupil Rating Scale Revised: Screening for Learning Disabilities, Grades K-6, see 2123
The Pyramid Scales, Handicapped persons ages birth to 78, see 2127
REHAB: Rehabilitation Evaluation Hall and Baker, Psychiatric patients who live in residential care, see 2195
Responsibility and Independence Scale for Adolescents, Ages 12.0-19.11, see 2204
Revised Behavior Problem Checklist, Grades K-12, see 2211
Scales of Independent Behavior—Revised, Infants to adults, with or without developmental disabilities, see 2299
School Function Assessment, Grades K–6, see 2316
School Social Behavior Scales, Grades K–12, see 2322
Scorable Self-Care Evaluation (Revised), Adolescent and adult occupational therapy clients, see 2327
Service Excellence, Customer service personnel, see 2385
Social Behavior Assessment Inventory, Grades K-9, see 2444
Social Competence and Behavior Evaluation, Preschool Edition, Children aged 30 months to 76 months, see 2446

Social Skills for Adults with Severe Retardation—An Inventory and Training Program, Severely or profoundly handicapped adolescents and adults, see 2450
Social Skills Rating System, Ages 3-0 to 4-11, grades K-6, grades 7-12, see 2452
Spadafore Attention Deficit Hyperactivity Disorder Rating Scale, Ages 5–19, see 2461
Survey of Student Assessment of Study Behaviors, Grades 6–13, see 2589
Sutter-Eyberg Student Behavior Inventory, Ages 2-17, see 2595
Systematic Screening for Behavior Disorders, Grades K–6, see 2607
Teaching Resource and Assessment of Critical Skills, People with special needs, see 2629
Test of Variables of Attention (Version 7.03), Ages 4–80, see 2720
Transition Behavior Scale, Grades 11-12, see 2779
Transition Planning Inventory, High school students with disabilities who need future planning, see 2780
Wolf Student Behavior Screening, Students, see 2894
Work Readiness Profile, Older adolescents and adults with disabilities, see 2926
Young Adult Behavior Checklist and Young Adult Self-Report, Young adults, ages 18–30, see 2939

DEVELOPMENTAL

The ABC Inventory to Determine Kindergarten and School Readiness, Ages 3.5–6.5, see 3
Adolescent and Adult Psychoeducational Profile: Volume IV, Adolescents and adults with moderate to severe mental retardation or autism, see 70
Ages and Stages Questionnaires, Ages 4–48 months, see 123
AGS Early Screening Profiles, Ages 2-0 to 6-11, see 124
Assessment for Persons Profoundly or Severely Impaired, Infants through adults who are preverbal and functioning with a mental age between approximately 0 and 8 months, see 193
Assessment in Infancy: Ordinal Scales of Psychological Development, Birth to age 2, see 194
Assessment in Nursery Education, Ages 3-5, see 196
Assessment of Developmental Levels by Observation, Birth-8 years, see 206
A.S.S.E.T.S.: A Survey of Students' Educational Talents and Skills, Kindergarten–grade 3, grades 4–6, see 217
Autism Screening Instrument for Educational Planning, Second Edition, Autistic individuals ages 18 months to adult, see 234
Basic School Skills Inventory, Third Edition, Ages 4-0 to 8-11, see 258
Battelle Developmental Inventory, Birth to 8 years, see 265
Battelle Developmental Inventory Screening Test, Birth to age 8, see 266
Bayley Infant Neurodevelopmental Screener, Ages 3–24 months, see 269
Bayley Scales of Infant Development, Second Edition, Ages 1–42 months, see 270
Behavioral Characteristics Progression, Physically and mentally handicapped children and adults, see 292
Bilingual Home Inventory, Nonnative speakers of English, see 306
Birth to Three Assessment and Intervention System, Birth to 3 years, see 315
The Block Survey and S.L.I.D.E., Preschool and kindergarten, see 319
Bracken Basic Concept Scale—Revised, Ages 2 1/2 to 8, see 331
BRIGANCE® Diagnostic Assessment of Basic Skills—Spanish Edition, Grades kindergarten–6, see 339
BRIGANCE® Early Preschool Screen for Two-Year-Old and Two-and-a-Half-Year-Old Children, Ages 2 to 2 1/2 years, see 345
BRIGANCE® K & 1 Screen for Kindergarten and First Grade Children [Revised], Grades K, 1, see 346
BRIGANCE® Preschool Screen, Ages 3–4, see 347
Bury Infant Check, Children in second term of infant school, see 359
The Callier-Azusa Scale: G Edition, Deaf-blind and severely/profoundly handicapped children, see 377
Chicago Early Assessment and Remediation LaboratorY, Ages 3-6, see 446
Child Development Inventory, Ages 1–3 to 6–3, see 453
Child Development Review, 18 months to age 5, see 454
Child Language Ability Measures, Ages 2-8, see 455
Children at Risk Screener: Kindergarten and Preschool, Ages 24–83 months, see 461
Childrens Adaptive Behavior Scale, Revised, Ages 5-11, see 465
Cognitive Control Battery, Ages 4-12, see 563
The Columbus: Picture Analysis of Growth Towards Maturity, Ages 5-18, see 625
Comprehensive Identification Process [Revised], Ages 2–6.5, see 653
Conners-March Developmental Questionnaire, Children, see 680
Cooperative Preschool Inventory, Revised Edition, Ages 3-6, see 693

Cutrona Child Study Profile of Psycho-Educational Abilities, K-3, see 757
Dallas Pre-School Screening Test, Ages 3-6, see 761
The Dennis Test of Child Development, Kgn-grade 1, see 778
Denver II (Denver Developmental Screening Test), Birth to age 6, see 788
Denver Prescreening Developmental Questionnaire II, Ages 0-9 months, 9-24 months, 2-4 years, 4-6 years, see 787
Developmental Activities Screening Inventory, Second Edition, Ages birth to 60 months, see 803
Developmental Assessment for Students with Severe Disabilities, Second Edition (A), Individuals functioning within the 0-6 year developmental range, see 804
Developmental Assessment of Life Experiences (1998 Edition), Individuals with developmental disabilities, see 805
Developmental Assessment of Young Children, Birth to age 5-11, see 806
Developmental History Checklist for Children, Ages 5-12, see 808
Developmental Indicators for the Assessment of Learning, Third Edition, Ages 3-0 to 6-11, see 809
Developmental Observation Checklist System, Birth to age 6, see 810
Developmental Profile II, Birth to age 9.5, see 811
Developmental Task Analysis, Grades K-6, see 812
Developmental Tasks for Kindergarten Readiness—II, Pre-kindergarten children, see 813
Early Child Development Inventory, Ages 1-3 to 3-0, see 872
Early Intervention Developmental Profile, Children with handicaps who function at the 0–35 month age level, see 879
Early Learning: Assessment and Development, Ages 5-3 and 5-6 through the first year of school and older children with specific learning disabilities, see 882
Early School Inventory, Ages 5–7, see 887
Early Screening Inventory—Revised, Ages 3–6, see 889
Early Years Easy Screen, Ages 4–5, see 892
ECOScales, Delayed child-significant adult dyads, see 898
The Egan Bus Puzzle Test, 20 months to 4 years, see 911
Einstein Assessment of School-Related Skills, Grades K-5, see 916
Erhardt Developmental Prehension Assessment, Children with cerebral palsy (spastic, athetoid, or mixed) from birth to adolescence, see 968
FirstSTEP: Screening Test for Evaluating Preschoolers, Preschool children, see 1039
The Five P's (Parent/Professional Preschool Performance Profile) [Revised], Children with disabilities functioning between the ages of 6 and 60 months, see 1041
The Gesell Developmental Observation, Ages 4.5-9, see 1085
Gesell Preschool Test, Ages 2.5-6, see 1086
The Goodman Lock Box, Children suspected of a developmental delay or specific learning disability or behavioral problem with chronological or mental ages 2.5-5.5, see 1098
Griffiths Mental Development Scales [Revised], Ages 0–2 years, Ages 2–8 years, see 1134
HELP Checklist (Hawaii Early Learning Profile), Ages birth-3, see 1192
Help for Special Preschoolers ASSESSMENT CHECKLIST: Ages 3–6, Ages 2-6 to 6-0, see 1194
High/Scope Child Observation Record for Ages 2 1/2–6, Ages 2 1/2–6 years, see 1204
Howell Prekindergarten Screening Test, Prekindergarten students, see 1224
Humanics National Child Assessment Form [Revised], Ages 0–3, 3–6, 6–9, see 1230
Infant Development Inventory, Birth to 18 months, see 1259
Infant Index, Students entering infant school (ages approximately 4–5 years), see 1260
Infant Screening, Ages 5-6, see 1262
Infant-Toddler Developmental Assessment, Birth to 3 years, see 1263
Johnson-Kenney Screening Test, Ages 5.5-6.5, see 1357
Kaufman Developmental Scale, Birth to age 9 and mentally retarded of all ages, see 1381
Keele Pre-School Assessment Guide, Children in nursery school, see 1388
Kelvin Measurement of Ability in Infant Classes, Ages 8-12, see 1389
Kent Inventory of Developmental Skills [1996 Standardization], Infants up to 15 months of age or young children whose developmental age is less than 15 months, see 1391
Kindergarten Readiness Test, Ages 4-6, see 1400
Learning Behaviors Scale, Research Edition, Kindergarten, see 1457
Lexington Developmental Scales, Ages birth-6 years, see 1490
MacArthur Communicative Development Inventories, 8–30 months, see 1528
Metropolitan Readiness Tests, Sixth Edition, PreKindergarten through grade 1, see 1659
Milani-Comparetti Motor Development Screening Test, Ages 1-16 months, see 1668
Miller Assessment for Preschoolers, Ages 2-9 to 5-8, see 1673
Minneapolis Preschool Screening Instrument, Ages 3-7 to 5-4, see 1691
Missouri Kindergarten Inventory of Developmental Skills, Alternate Form, Ages 48-72 months, see 1707
Movement Assessment Battery for Children, Ages 4–12 years, see 1727
Mullen Scales of Early Learning: AGS Edition, Birth to 68 months, see 1728

Neonatal Behavioral Assessment Scale, 3rd Edition, Ages 3 days through 2 months, see 1770
Oral-Motor/Feeding Rating Scale, Ages 1 and over, see 1851
PACE, Ages 4-6, see 1868
Parents' Evaluation of Developmental Status, Birth–8 years, see 1890
Pediatric Early Elementary Examination—II [Revised], Ages 6–9, see 1905
Pediatric Evaluation of Disability Inventory, Ages 6 months to 7.5 years, see 1906
Pediatric Examination of Educational Readiness, Ages 4-6, see 1907
Pediatric Examination of Educational Readiness at Middle Childhood [Revised], Ages 9 to 14-11, see 1908
Pediatric Extended Examination at Three, Ages 3-4, see 1909
Phelps Kindergarten Readiness Scale, Pre-kindergarten and early kindergarten, see 1977
Pictorial Scale of Perceived Competence and Social Acceptance for The Young Children, Preschool through second grade, see 1987
The Play Observation Scale, Preschool children, see 2001
Pre-School Behavior Checklist, Ages 2-5, see 2038
Pre-Verbal Communication Schedule, Children and adolescents and adults, see 2052
Preschool Development Inventory, Ages 3–6, see 2040
Preschool Developmental Profile, Children with handicaps who function at the 3–6 year age level, see 2041
The Preschool Evaluation Scale, Birth–72 months, see 2043
Preschool Language Scale–3, Ages birth to 6–11, see 2045
Preschool Screening Instrument, Ages 3-0 to 5-3, see 2046
Preschool Screening System, Ages 2-6 to 5-9, see 2047
Preschool Skills Test, Age 2 through Grade 2 level children, see 2049
Program for the Acquisition of Language with the Severely Impaired, Severely impaired children and adults, see 2082
Progress Assessment Chart of Social and Personal Development, Mentally handicapped young children, adolescents and adults, and children with Down's Syndrome, Profoundly and severely handicapped persons, see 2088
Psychoeducational Profile Revised, Autistic or communication-handicapped children whose chronological age is less than 12 years, see 2111
Revised BRIGANCE® Diagnostic Inventory of Early Development, Birth to age 7, see 2213
Rockford Infant Developmental Evaluation Scales, Birth-4 years, see 2243
The Schedule of Growing Skills: Second Edition, Ages 0–5 years, see 2308
Screening Test for Educational Prerequisite Skills, Ages 4-0 to 5-11, see 2333
SEED Developmental Profiles, Birth to 72 months, see 2342
Sequenced Inventory of Communication Development, Revised Edition, Ages 4 months through 4 years, see 2382
The Southern California Ordinal Scales of Development, Multihandicapped, developmentally delayed, and learning disabled children, see 2459
Spatial Orientation Memory Test, Ages 5-10, see 2468
Speech-Ease Screening Inventory (K—1), Grades K-1, see 2471
Student Educational Assessment Screening, Pre-kindergarten-grade 9, see 2528
Symbolic Play Test, Second Edition, Ages 1-3, see 2601
Teacher's Handbook of Diagnostic Screening, Second Edition, Ages 4, 6, and over, see 2628
Test of Kindergarten/First Grade Readiness Skills, Ages 3–6 to 7–0, see 2692
Test of Sensory Functions in Infants, Infants ages 4-18 months with regulatory disorders or developmental delays, see 2715
Tests of Basic Experiences 2, PreK-beginning of grade 1, end of K-end of grade 1, see 2740
Toddler and Infant Motor Evaluation, Ages 4 months to 3.5 years, see 2767
Transdisciplinary Play-Based Assessment, Revised Edition, Children developmentally functioning between infancy and 6 years of age, see 2778
Vineland Social-Emotional Early Childhood Scales, Birth to age 5-11, see 2814
Vulpe Assessment Battery—Revised, Children functioning between full term birth to six years of age, see 2838
Wisconsin Behavior Rating Scale, Persons functioning below the developmental level of 3 years, see 2891

EDUCATION

Academic Advising Inventory, Undergraduate students, see 8
Academic Freedom Survey, College students and faculty, see 11
Academic Proficiency Battery, College entrants, see 12
Achievement Identification Measure—Teacher Observation, "Students in all grades," see 36
The ACT Evaluation/Survey Service, High school and college students, prospective adult learners/students, graduates, see 57
Adaptive Style Inventory, Junior high through adult, see 64
Analytic Learning Disability Assessment, Ages 8-14, see 153

Arlin-Hills Attitude Surveys, Grades K–3, 4–6, 7–12, see 177
Assessment of School Needs for Low-Achieving Students: Staff Survey, Teachers and administrators, see 216
Barsch Learning Style Inventory, Students, see 244
The Class Activities Questionnaire, Students and teachers grades 6-12, see 493
Classroom Environment Scale, Third Edition, Junior high and senior high teachers and students, see 495
CLEP Subject Examination in Educational Psychology, Persons entering college or already in college, see 512
College Board Descriptive Tests System, Entering and continuing college students and upper level high school students, see 571
College Major Interest Inventory, High school and college students, see 618
College Outcome Measures Program, College students, see 619
College Student Experiences Questionnaire, College students, see 620
Community College Student Experiences Questionnaire, Second Edition, Community college students, see 635
Community Opinion Inventory, Revised Edition, Adults who do not have children enrolled in school, see 636
Comprehensive Assessment of School Environments, Junior and senior high schools, see 648
Comprehensive Assessment of School Environments Information Management System, Secondary schools, see 649
Content Mastery Examinations for Educators, Teachers, school administrators, and other educational specialists, entrants to colleges of education, see 684
The Cooperative Institutional Research Program, First-time, full-time entering college freshmen, see 692
The Cornell Inventory for Student Appraisal of Teaching and Courses, College teachers, see 706
The Cornell Learning and Study Skills Inventory, Grades 7-13, 13-16, see 707
Course Finder, Students entering higher education, see 718
DABERON-2: Screening for School Readiness, Second Edition, Ages 3-0 to 7-11, see 759
The Demos D Scale: An Attitude Scale for the Identification of Dropouts, Grades 7-12, see 777
Dimensions of Excellence Scales [1991 Edition], Schools or districts, see 843
Early Childhood Environment Rating Scale—Revised, Early childhood programs or classrooms (excluding infant and toddler programs), see 875
Educational Administrator Effectiveness Profile, Public school administrators, see 903
Educational Interest Inventory, Prospective college students, see 905
Educational Leadership Practices Inventory, Teachers and administrators, see 906
Educational Process Questionnaire, Grades 4-12, see 907
The Effective School Battery, Grades 7-12, teachers, see 909
Endeavor Instructional Rating System, College, see 948
Evaluating Courses for Inclusion of New Scholarship on Women, Post-secondary students, see 974
Evaluating Educational Programs for Intellectually Gifted Students, Learning environments for grades K-12, see 976
Faculty Morale Scale for Institutional Improvement, College faculty, see 1003
The Gifted Program Evaluation Survey, Gifted and talented programs, see 1090
Graduate Program Self-Assessment Service, Faculty members, students majoring in the department, and recent graduates, see 1108
IDEA Feedback for Department Chairs, College and university department chairpersons, see 1233
IDEA Student Ratings of Instruction, College faculty, see 1236
Independent School Entrance Examination, Grades 5-7, 8-11, or candidates for grades 6-8 and 9-12, see 1249
Individualised Classroom Environment Questionnaire, Junior and senior high school students and teachers, see 1254
Institutional SAT Program (Institutional SAT I: Reasoning Test and SAT II: Subject Tests), Entering college freshmen, see 1274
The Instructional Environment System—II, Grades K–12, see 1275
Instructional Leadership Evaluation and Development Program (ILEAD), School climates and leadership, see 1276
Instructional Skills Assessment, Instructors, see 1277
Interpersonal Style Questionnaire, Educators at grades K–12, see 1295
Inventory of Learning Processes–R, College and university students, see 1307
Junior Rating Scale, Ages 8-11, see 1369
Learning and Study Strategies Inventory, College students, see 1455
Learning and Study Strategies Inventory—High School Version, Grades 9–12, see 1456
Learning Preference Scales, Grades 4–12, Elementary and secondary teachers, Parents of school students, see 1465
Learning Style Inventory [Price Systems, Inc.], Grades 3–12, see 1470
Learning Styles and Strategies, Teachers, see 1473
Learning Styles Inventory [Educational Activities, Inc.], Intermediate and secondary level students, see 1475
Learning Styles Inventory [Piney Mountain Press, Inc.], Grades 9–10, see 1476

Learning-Style Inventory, Revised Scoring, Adults, see 1471
Learning/Working Styles Inventory, Grades 7-12 and adults, see 1478
The Life Adjustment Inventory, Grades 9-12, see 1492
Light's Retention Scale [Revised Edition 1991], Grades K-12, see 1500
Major Field Tests, Undergraduate students completing an academic major program, see 1538
Measure of Questioning Skills, Grades 3–10, see 1623
Motivated Strategies for Learning Questionnaire, College students, see 1720
Multimedia Learning Styles, Students in 7th–9th grades, see 1741
The Multiple Purpose Self Trainer, High school and adults, see 1747
Noncognitive Variables and Questionnaire, Minority college student applicants, see 1795
Oetting Michaels Anchored Ratings for Therapists, Graduate students and interns in counseling and clinical training, see 1830
Our Class and Its Work, Grades 3-12, see 1867
Parent Opinion Inventory, Revised Edition, Parents of school children, see 1885
PEEK—Perceptions, Expectations, Emotions, and Knowledge About College, Prospective college students, see 1910
Performance Levels of a School Program Survey, School teachers and administrators, see 1921
The Praxis Series: Professional Assessments for Beginning Teachers, Beginning and experienced teachers, see 2026
Profile of a School, Students, parents, and school personnel, see 2073
Program Self-Assessment Service, Faculty members, students majoring in the department, and recent graduates, see 2083
Scales for Predicting Successful Inclusion, Ages 5–18, see 2294
School Archival Records Search, Grades 1–12, see 2311
School Assessment Survey, lementary through senior high school teachers and administrators, see 2312
School Effectiveness Questionnaire, Students, teachers, parents, see 2314
School Environment Preference Survey, Grades 4-12, see 2315
School Leaders Licensure Assessment, Prospective school principals, see 2317
School Situation Survey, Grades 4-12, see 2321
School Social Skills Rating Scale, Elementary school and junior high school and high school, see 2323
School-Age Care Environment Rating Scale, Child care programs, see 2310
School-Readiness Evaluation by Trained Teachers, South African school beginners, see 2319
Secondary-School Record, Grades 9-12, see 2340
A Self Appraisal Scale for Teachers, Teachers, see 2351
Student Evaluation Scale, Grades 1-12, see 2529
Student Goals Exploration, College, see 2530
Student Instructional Report II, College teachers, see 2531
Student Opinion Inventory, Revised Edition, Grades 5–12, see 2532
Student Rights Scales, Grades 7-12, see 2534
Study Attitudes and Methods Survey [Revised Short Form], Junior high, high school, college, see 2538
The Study Skills Counseling Evaluation, High school and college, see 2541
Survey of Student Opinion of Instruction, High school systems, see 2590
Teacher Opinion Inventory, Revised Edition, Elementary and secondary school teachers, see 2623
Teacher Opinionaire on Democracy, Teachers, see 2624
Teacher Role Survey (Revised), Elementary, secondary, or technical school teachers, see 2625
Teacher Values Inventory, Teachers, see 2626
Test of Attitude Toward School, Boys in grades 1, 3, 5, see 2670
Thinking About My School, Grades 4-6, see 2753
The Wilson Teacher-Appraisal Scale, Grades 7-1, see 2890

ENGLISH AND LANGUAGE

Adolescent Language Screening Test, Ages 11–17, see 76
Adult Language Assessment Scales, Adults, see 84
Adult Rating of Oral English, Adult and secondary students in vocational education and employment training programs, see 87
Advanced Placement Examination in English (Language and Composition), High school students desiring credit for college-level courses and admission to advanced courses, see 97
Advanced Placement Examination in English (Literature and Composition), High school students desiring credit for college-level courses and admission to advanced courses, see 98
Advanced Placement Examination in International English Language, High school students desiring credit for college-level courses and admission to advanced courses, see 104
Alberta Essay Scales: Models, Grade 12 English students, see 131

American Literacy Test, Adults, see 150
Analyzing the Communication Environment, Preschool to adolescent children with severe disabilities, see 156
Assessing Motivation to Communicate, Postsecondary students, see 188
Assessment of Children's Language Comprehension, 1983 Revision, Ages 3-0 to 6-5, see 202
Assessment of Conceptual Organization (ACO): Improving, Writing, Thinking, and Reading Skills, Grades 4-6, 7-12, 10-adult, see 204
Bankson Language Test—2, Ages 3-0 to 6-11, see 241
Basic English Literacy Skills Test, Candidates for any position requiring a basic knowledge of the English language, see 249
Basic English Skills Test, Limited-English-speaking adults, see 250
Basic Inventory of Natural Language, Grades K–12, see 251
Beery Picture Vocabulary Test and Beery Picture Vocabulary Screening Series, Ages 2-6 to 39-11, Grades 2-12, see 278
Bilingual Two Language Battery of Tests, Students and adults having any level of language proficiency, see 308
Botel Reading Inventory, Grades 1–4, 1–6, 1–12, see 330
Bruce Vocabulary Inventory, Business and industry, see 352
Capitalization and Punctuation Tests, Students of English, see 393
Carolina Picture Vocabulary Test (for Deaf and Hearing Impaired), Deaf and hearing-impaired children ages 4–11.5 years, see 428
CAT/5 Listening and Speaking Checklist, Grades K–12, see 431
The Classroom Communication Skills Inventory: Listening and Speaking Checklist, Students, see 494
CLEP General Examinations: English Composition and English Composition Test with Essay, Persons entering college or already in college, see 498
CLEP Subject Examination in American Literature, Persons entering college or already in college, see 504
CLEP Subject Examination in Analyzing and Interpreting Literature, Persons entering college or already in college, see 505
CLEP Subject Examination in English Literature, Persons entering college or already in college, see 513
CLEP Subject Examination in Freshman College Composition, Persons entering college or already in college, see 514
Clinical Evaluation of Language Fundamentals—3 Screening Test, Ages 6-0 to 21-11, see 542
Clinical Evaluation of Language Fundamentals, Third Edition—Observational Rating Scales, Ages 6–21, see 541
College Board Institutional SAT II: English Language Proficiency Test, Entering college freshmen, see 576
College Board Institutional SAT II: Literature Subject Test, Entering college freshmen, see 584
College Board Institutional SAT II: Writing Subject Test, Entering college freshmen, see 591
College Board SAT II: English Language Proficiency Test, Candidates for college entrance, see 597
College Board SAT II: Literature Subject Test, Candidates for college entrance, see 604
College Board SAT II: Writing Subject Test, Candidates for college entrance, see 614
College English Test: National Achievement Tests, High school and college freshmen, see 616
Communication Abilities Diagnostic Test, Ages 3-0 to 9-11, see 628
Communication Skills Profile, Individuals or teams within organizations, see 634
The Competent Speaker Speech Evaluation Form, Postsecondary students, see 639
Comprehension of Oral Language, Grades K-1, see 643
Comprehensive Receptive and Expressive Vocabulary Test, Ages 4-0 to 17-11, see 655
Comprehensive Receptive and Expressive Vocabulary Test—Adult, Ages 18-0 to 89-11, see 656
Computer-Based Test of English as a Foreign Language and Test of Written English, University and college applicants, see 666
Conversational Skills Rating Scale: An Instructional Assessment of The Interpersonal Competence, Secondary and post-secondary students, see 689
CTB Writing Assessment System, Grades 2.0–12.9, see 744
Diagnostic Screening Test: Language, Second Edition, Grades 1-12, see 830
Diagnostic Screening Test: Spelling, Third Edition, Grades 1-12, see 833
Diagnostic Spelling Potential Test, Ages 7 and over, see 834
Diagnostic Spelling Test, Ages 8-12, see 835
Dos Amigos Verbal Language Scales, Ages 5-0 to 13-5, see 850
Early Language Milestone Scale, Second Edition, Birth to 36 months, see 880
Early Language Skills Checklist, Ages 3–5, see 881
English as a Second Language Oral Assessment, Second Edition, Adult nonnative speakers of English, see 951
English Picture Vocabulary Test, Ages 3-0 and over, Ages 5-0 to 8-11, Ages 7-0 to 11-11, Ages 11-0 and over, see 952
English Placement Test, Entrants to courses in English as a second language, see 953
English Progress Test, Ages 7-3 to 15-6, see 954
English Skills Assessment, Grades 11-12 and first year of post-secondary education, see 955

English Test: National Achievement Tests, Grades 3-12, see 957
ERB Writing Assessment, Grades 3–6, 7–9, 10–12, see 967
ESL/Adult Literacy Scale, Adults, see 971
ETS Tests of Applied Literacy Skills, Adults, see 972
Everyday Life Activities: Photo Series, Children with delay in language development, autistic children, and adults with a language or speech impairment sequel to brain damage, see 984
Examination for the Certificate of Competency in English, Nonnative speakers of English, see 985
Examination for the Certificate of Proficiency in English, Adults who are advanced level English-as-a-Second-Language speakers and who wish documentation for academic or employment purposes, see 986
Expressive Vocabulary Test, Ages 2.5–90 years, see 995
50 Grammar Quizzes for Practice and Review, Students, see 1027
Figurative Language Interpretation Test, Grades 4–10, see 1028
First Words and First Sentences Tests, Ages 18–36 months, see 1037
The Fullerton Language Test for Adolescents, Second Edition, Ages 11-18, see 1060
Functional Grammar Test, High school and college, see 1063
Functional Skills Screening Inventory, Age 6 through adult, see 1067
Goyer Organization of Ideas Test, Form S (Revised), College and adults, see 1102
Graded Word Spelling Test, Second Edition, Ages 6-0 to adults, see 1105
The Graduate Record Examinations Literature in English Test, Graduate school candidates, see 1118
Grammar Test Packet, High school students, see 1125
Grammatical Analysis of Elicited Language—Simple Sentence Level, Second Edition, Hearing-impaired ages 5-9, see 1127
Group Literacy Assessment, End of junior school and beginning of secondary school, see 1144
Hannah-Gardner Test of Verbal and Nonverbal Language Functioning, Ages 3.5-5.5, see 1171
Henderson-Moriarty ESL/Literacy Placement Test, Adult learners of English as a Second Language, see 1195
Hunter-Grundin Literacy Profiles, Ages 6.5-8, 7.10-9.3, 9-10, 9.10-11.5, 10.10-12.7, see 1232
IDEA Oral Language Proficiency Test, Preschool–grade 12, see 1234
IDEA Reading and Writing Proficiency Test, Grades 2–12, see 1235
Independent Mastery Testing System for Writing Skills, Adult students, see 1248
Integrated Writing Test, Grades 2–12, see 1283
Kindergarten Language Screening Test, Second Edition, Ages 4-0 through 6-11, see 1399
Language Assessment Scales—Oral, Grades 1-6, 7-12, see 1420
Language Assessment Scales, Reading and Writing, Language-minority students in grades 2-3, 4-6, 7-11, see 1421
Language Facility Test, Ages 3 and over, see 1422
Language Imitation Test, Educationally subnormal children, see 1423
Language Processing Test, Ages 5-0 to 11-11, see 1424
Language Proficiency Test, Grades 9 and over, see 1425
Language Proficiency Test Series, Grades K–12, specifically LEP students, see 1426
Language Sampling, Analysis, and Training—Third Edition, Children with language delay, see 1427
Learning Through Listening, Ages 10-11, 13-14, 17-18, see 1477
Listen Up: Skills Assessment, Grades 7–12 and adults, see 1505
Listening Comprehension Test, Nonnative speakers of English who wish to pursue academic work at universities where English is the medium of instruction, see 1506
The Listening for Meaning Test, Ages 3-0 to 18-11, see 1507
Listening Styles Profile, Adults, see 1508
Literature Tests/Objective and Essay, Middle school and high school, see 1509
MAC Checklist for Evaluating, Preparing, and/or Improving Standardized Tests for Limited English Speaking Students, ESL test developers, reviewers, and users, see 1527
Mather-Woodcock Group Writing Tests, Grades 2.0–16.9, see 1606
Michigan English Language Assessment Battery, Adult non-native speakers of English, see 1662
Michigan Prescriptive Program in English, Persons striving to obtain 10th grade equivalency or pass the GED Test, see 1663
Michigan Test of English Language Proficiency, College applicants from non-English-language countries, see 1664
Multilevel Informal Language Inventory, Ages 4-12, see 1739
Oral and Written Language Scales: Listening Comprehension and Oral Expression, Ages 3–21, see 1847
Oral and Written Language Scales: Written Expression, Ages 5–21, see 1848
Parallel Spelling Tests, Second Edition, Ages 6 to 13 years, see 1875
Pragmatics Profile of Everyday Communication Skills in Adults, Adolescents and adults, see 2024
Pragmatics Profile of Everyday Communication Skills in Children, Ages 9 months to 10 years, see 2025
PRE-LAS English, Ages 4-6, see 2029

Preliminary Test of English as a Foreign Language, College and other institutional applicants, grade 11 and over, from non-English-language countries, see 2032
Preschool Language Assessment Instrument, Ages 2.9 through 5.8, see 2044
The Primary Language Screen, Ages 5-7, see 2055
Progressive Achievement Tests of Listening Comprehension [Revised], Standards 1–4 and Forms 1–4 (ages 7–14) in New Zealand school system, see 2093
Proof-Reading Tests of Spelling, Standards 2-4 and Forms 1-2 (ages 8-13) in New Zealand school system, see 2100
Quick Informal Assessment, Grades K–12, see 2139
Quick Phonics Survey, Grades 1-4, see 2142
Quick Spelling Inventory, Grades 1-6, see 2145
RBH Test of Language Skills, Business and industry, see 2168
Receptive Oral Language Inventory, Grade 1, see 2192
The Renfrew Bus Story, Ages 3.6–7.0, see 2201
Reynell Developmental Language Scales: Third Edition [British Edition], 15 months to 7 years, see 2228
Reynell Developmental Language Scales [U.S. Edition], Ages 1-0 to 6-11, see 2229
Rhode Island Test of Language Structure, Hearing-impaired children ages 3-20, hearing children ages 3-6, see 2233
Screening Kit of Language Development, Ages 2-5, see 2331
Second Language Oral Test of English, Child and adult nonnative English speakers, see 2337
Secondary Level English Proficiency Test, Grades 7-12, see 2339
Self-Assessment in Writing Skills, Clerical, managerial, and sales employees, see 2352
Slingerland College-Level Screening for the Identification of Language Learning Strengths and Weaknesses, College or college graduates, see 2427
Slingerland Screening Tests for Identifying Children with Specific Language Disability, Grades 1-2.5, 2.5-3.5, 3.5-4, 5-6, see 2428
South African Written Language Test, South African pupils in Grade ii to Standard 5, see 2458
Spanish Structured Photographic Expressive Language Test, Ages 3-0 to 5-11, 4-0 to 9-5, see 2466
Spelling Test: National Achievement Tests, Grades 3-4, 5-8, 7-9, 10-12, see 2473
Stanford Writing Assessment Program, Third Edition, Grades 3–12, see 2489
Structured Photographic Expressive Language Test, Ages 3-0 to 5-11, ages 4-0 to 9-5, see 2524
Teacher Assessment of Grammatical Structures, Ages 2-4, 5-9, 9 and over, see 2620
Test for Auditory Comprehension of Language—Third Edition, Ages 3-0 to 9-11, see 2657
Test for Oral Language Production, Ages 4-6 to 10-5, see 2661
Test for the Reception of Grammar, Ages 4–12 years and also dysphasic adults, see 2662
Test Lessons in Reading Figurative Language, High school and college and adult learners, see 2664
Test of Adolescent and Adult Language, Third Edition, Ages 12-0 to 24-11, see 2668
Test of Adolescent/Adult Word Finding, Ages 12-80, see 2667
Test of Children's Language: Assessing Aspects of Spoken Language, Reading, and Writing, Ages 5–0 to 8–11, see 2676
Test of Early Language Development, Third Edition, Ages 2-0 to 7-11, see 2680
Test of Early Written Language, Second Edition, Ages 3–0 to 10–11, see 2684
Test of English for International Communication (TOEIC), Adult nonnative speakers of English, see 2687
Test of English Proficiency Level, Limited English proficient students in secondary and adult programs, see 2688
Test of Language Competence—Expanded Edition, Ages 5 through 18, see 2693
Test of Language Development—Intermediate, Third Edition, Ages 8-0 to 12-11, see 2694
Test of Language Development—Primary, Third Edition, Ages 4-0 to 8-11, see 2695
Test of Spoken English, Nonnative speakers of English, see 2717
Test of Word Finding, Grades 1-6, see 2725
Test of Word Finding in Discourse, Ages 6-6 to 12-11, see 2726
Test of Word Knowledge, Ages 5–17, see 2727
Test of Written English, Grades 1-6, see 2729
Test of Written Expression, Ages 6-6 to 14-11, see 2730
Test of Written Language—Third Edition, Ages 7-6 to 17-11, see 2731
Test of Written Spelling, Fourth Edition, Ages 6-0 to 18-11, see 2732
Troubled Talk Test, Adults, see 2785
Utah Test of Language Development—3, Ages 3-0 to 9-11, see 2801
Vocabulary Test: National Achievement Tests, Grades 3-8, 7-12, see 2823
The Wessex Revised Portage Language Checklist, Developmentally delayed and mentally handicapped children mental ages 0-1, 1-2, 2-3, 3-4, see 2872
Western Aphasia Battery, Adolescents and adults with language disorders, see 2873
Woodcock Language Proficiency Battery—Revised, Ages 2-90+, see 2902
Woodcock-Muñoz Language Survey, Ages 4–adults, see 2904
Word Finding Referral Checklist, Ages 5 to 90, see 2906

The WORD Test, Ages 7 and over, see 2911
Writing Process Test, Grades 2–12, see 2933
The Written Expression Test, Grades 1 to 6, see 2934
Written Language Assessment, Grades 3-12, see 2935
Written Language Syntax Test, Ages 10-17 hearing-impaired, see 2936

FINE ARTS

Advanced Measures of Music Audiation, Junior high school through college, see 90
Advanced Placement Examination in Art History, High school students desiring credit for college-level courses and admission to advanced courses, see 91
Advanced Placement Examination in Music Theory, High school students desiring credit for college-level courses and admission to advanced courses, see 109
Advanced Placement Examination in Studio Art, High school students desiring credit for college-level courses and admission to advanced courses, see 115
The Farnum String Scale: A Performance Scale for All String Instruments, Grades 7-12, see 1018
The Graduate Record Examinations Music Test, Graduate school candidates, see 1120
Group Tests of Musical Abilities, Ages 7–14, see 1154
Harmonic Improvisation Readiness Record and Rhythm Improvisation Readiness Record, Grades 3 through music graduate school, see 1176
Instrument Timbre Preference Test, Grades 4-12, see 1280
Intermediate Measures of Music Audiation, Grades 1-4, see 1287
Iowa Tests of Music Literacy, Revised, Grades 4–12, see 1320
Measures of Musical Abilities, Ages 7-14, see 1629
Music Achievement Tests 1, 2, 3, and 4, Grades 3–12, see 1751
Musical Aptitude Profile [1995 Revision], Grades 5–12, see 1752
Musical Aptitude Test, "White people" in standards 1-10 in South African schools, see 1753
Primary Measures of Music Audiation, K-3, see 2056
The Taylor-Helmstadter Pair Comparison Scale of Aesthetic Judgment, Ages 4 and over, see 2617
Watkins-Farnum Performance Scale: A Standardized Achievement The Test for All Band Instruments, Music students, see 2853

FOREIGN LANGUAGES

Advanced Placement Examination in French Language, High school students desiring credit for college-level courses and admission to advanced courses, see 101
Advanced Placement Examination in French Literature, High school students desiring credit for college-level courses and admission to advanced courses, see 102
Advanced Placement Examination in German Language, High school students desiring credit for college-level courses and admission to advanced courses, see 103
Advanced Placement Examination in Latin Literature, High school students desiring credit for college-level courses and admission to advanced courses, see 105
Advanced Placement Examination in Latin (Vergil), High school students desiring credit for college-level courses and admission to advanced courses, see 106
Advanced Placement Examination in Spanish Language, High school students desiring credit for college-level courses and admission to advanced courses, see 112
Australian Second Language Proficiency Ratings, Adolescents and adults, see 233
The Ber-Sil Spanish Test, Ages 5–12, 13–17, see 304
Bilingual Syntax Measure, Grades PK–2, 3–12, see 307
Chinese Proficiency Test, Adults, see 481
Chinese Speaking Test, Adults, see 482
CLEP Subject Examination in College-Level French Language, Levels 1 and 2, Persons entering college or already in college, see 509
CLEP Subject Examination in College-Level German Language, Levels 1 and 2, Persons entering college or already in college, see 510
CLEP Subject Examination in College-Level Spanish Language, Levels 1 and 2, Persons entering college or already in college, see 511
College Board Institutional SAT II: Chinese with Listening Subject Test, Entering college freshmen, see 575
College Board Institutional SAT II: French Subject Test, Entering college freshmen, see 577
College Board Institutional SAT II: French with Listening Subject Tests, Entering college freshmen, see 578

College Board Institutional SAT II: German Subject Test, Entering college freshmen, see 579
College Board Institutional SAT II: German with Listening Subject Test, Entering college freshmen, see 580
College Board Institutional SAT II: Italian Subject Test, Entering college freshmen, see 581
College Board Institutional SAT II: Japanese with Listening Subject Test, Entering college freshmen, see 582
College Board Institutional SAT II: Latin Subject Test, Entering college freshmen, see 583
College Board Institutional SAT II: Modern Hebrew Subject Test, Entering college freshmen, see 586
College Board Institutional SAT II: Spanish Subject Test, Entering college freshmen, see 588
College Board Institutional SAT II: Spanish with Listening Subject Test, Entering college freshmen, see 589
College Board SAT II: French Subject Test, Candidates for college entrance with 3–4 years high school French, see 598
College Board SAT II: French with Listening Subject Test, Candidates for college entrance with 3–4 years high school French, see 599
College Board SAT II: German Subject Test, Candidates for college entrance with 2–4 years high school German, see 600
College Board SAT II: German with Listening Subject Test, Candidates for college entrance with 2–4 years in high school German, see 601
College Board SAT II: Korean with Listening Subject Test, Candidates for college entrance with 2–4 years high school Korean, see 602
College Board SAT II: Latin Subject Test, Candidates for college entrance with 2–4 years high school Latin, see 603
College Board SAT II: Modern Hebrew Subject Test, Candidates for college entrance with 2–4 years high school Hebrew, see 606
College Board SAT II: Spanish Subject Test, Candidates for college entrance with 3–4 years high school Spanish, see 608
College Board SAT II: Spanish with Listening Subject Test, Candidates for college entrance with 3–4 years high school Spanish, see 609
College Board SAT II: Subject Test in Chinese with Listening, Candidates for college entrance with 2–4 years high school Chinese (Mandarin), see 610
College Board SAT II: Subject Test in Italian, Candidates for college entrance with 2–4 years high school Italian, see 611
College Board SAT II: Subject Test in Japanese with Listening, Candidates for college entrance with 2–4 years high school Japanese, see 612
El Circo, Ages 3-11 to 7-7, see 918
French Comprehension Tests, Grades K-2, 1-5, see 1054
French Reading Diagnostic Tests for Early French Immersion Primary Classes, Grades 1-3 English-speaking pupils whose main language of instruction is French, see 1055
Hausa Speaking Test, Adults, see 1179
Hebrew Speaking Test, Adults, see 1191
Indonesian Speaking Test, Adults, see 1255
LOTE Reading and Listening Tests, Secondary school students in their second year of learning another language, see 1521
National German Examination for High School Students, 2, 3, or 4 years high school, see 1761
National Spanish Examinations, Second semester of 1, 2, 3, 4-6 year Spanish students, see 1764
Oral English/Spanish Proficiency Placement Test, Ages 4-20, see 1849
Portuguese Speaking Test, College students and adults, see 2015
Quick Language Assessment Inventory, Grades K-6, see 2140
Screening Test of Spanish Grammar, Spanish-speaking children ages 3-6, see 2335
A Spanish Computerized Adaptive Placement Exam, College students, see 2464
Spanish/English Reading Comprehension Test [Revised], Grades 1–6, see 2465

INTELLIGENCE AND GENERAL APTITUDE

Academic Aptitude Test: Non-Verbal Intelligence: Acorn National Aptitude Tests, Grades 7—16 and adults, see 9
Academic Aptitude Test: Verbal Intelligence: Acorn National Aptitude Tests, Grades 7–16 and adults, see 10
ACCUPLACER: Computerized Placement Tests, Entry level students in 2-year and 4-year institutions, see 18
ACER Advanced Test B40, Ages 13 and over, see 20
ACER Advanced Test B90: New Zealand Edition, College students and adults, see 22

ACER Advanced Test BL-BQ, New Zealand Revision, College and superior adults, see 21
ACER Advanced Tests AL and AQ (Second Edition) and BL-BQ, College and "superior adults", see 23
ACER Higher Test PL-PQ, New Zealand Revision, Grades 9 and over, see 25
ACER Intermediate Test F, Ages 10–15, see 26
ACER Intermediate Test G, Ages 10-15, see 27
ACER Test of Learning Ability, Grades 4, 6, see 32
ACER Word Knowledge Test, Australian years 9–11, see 34
AH1 Forms X and Y, Ages 7-11 for classroom purposes and 5-11 for research, see 125
AH2/AH3, Ages 9 and over, see 126
AH4: Group Test of General Intelligence, Ages 10 and over, see 127
AH5 Group Test of High Grade Intelligence, "Highly intelligent pupils" ages 13 and over, see 128
AH6 Group Tests of High Level Intelligence, "Highly intelligent" individuals age 16 through college and university, see 129
Alternate Uses, Grades 6-16 and adults, see 142
Analytical Thinking Test, Adults, see 155
Arlin Test of Formal Reasoning, Grades 6-12 and adults, see 178
Arthur Point Scale of Performance Tests, Ages 4.5 to "superior" adults, see 182
Assessment of Individual Learning Style: The Perceptual Memory Task, Ages 4 and over, see 208
Auditory Memory Span Test, Ages 5–8, see 230
Auditory Sequential Memory Test, Ages 5–8, see 232
Batería Woodcock-Muñoz—Revisada, Spanish speaking ages 2 and over, see 264
Bilingual Verbal Ability Tests, Ages 5 and over, see 309
The BITCH Test (Black Intelligence Test of Cultural Homogeneity), Adolescents and adults, see 316
Boehm Test of Basic Concepts—Preschool Version, Ages 3-0 to 5-0, see 323
Boehm Test of Basic Concepts—Revised, Grades K–2, see 324
British Ability Scales: Second Edition, Ages 2.6 to 17.11, see 349
British Picture Vocabulary Scales, Ages 2.5–18, see 350
The California Critical Thinking Dispositions Inventory, High school, college, and adult, see 367
California Critical Thinking Skills Test, College and adult, see 368
Canadian Cognitive Abilities Test, Form K, Grades K–2, 3–12, see 385
Canadian Test of Cognitive Skills, Grades 2–12, see 388
Cardall Test of Practical Judgement, Adults in business and industry, see 394
Cattell Infant Intelligence Scale, Ages 3-30 months, see 433
Children's Abilities Scales, Ages 11-0 to 12-6, see 463
Children's Category Test, Ages 5-0 to 16-11, see 471
CID Preschool Performance Scale, Hearing- and language-impaired and normal children ages 2 to 5-5, see 488
Closure Flexibility (Concealed Figures), Wide range of higher level occupations personnel, see 548
Closure Speed (Gestalt Completion), Employees in wide range of occupations, see 549
Cognitive Abilities Scale, Ages 2-0 to 3-11, see 559
Cognitive Abilities Test, Form 5, Grades K–3, 3–12, see 560
Cognitive Abilities Test, Second Edition [British Edition], Ages 7-15, see 561
Cognitive Diagnostic Battery, Psychiatric and retarded patients, see 564
College Board SAT I Reasoning Test, Candidates for college entrance, see 592
College Board SAT Program, Candidates for college entrance, see 615
Columbia Mental Maturity Scale, Third Edition, 3.5–10 years, see 624
Combined Cognitive Preference Inventory, Students, see 626
Complex Figure Test, Ages 16 and over, see 641
Comprehensive Adult Student Assessment System, Adults, see 645
Comprehensive Scales of Student Abilities: Quantifying Academic Skills and School-Related Behavior Through the Use of Teacher Judgments, Ages 6–0 to 17–0, see 657
Comprehensive Test of Nonverbal Intelligence, Ages 6-0 to 90-11, see 662
Concept Assessment Kit—Conservation, Ages 4-7, see 674
Consequences, Grades 9-16, see 682
Continuous Visual Memory Test [Revised], Ages 8–80+, see 687
The Cornell Class-Reasoning Test, Form X, Grades 4-12, see 703
The Cornell Conditional-Reasoning Test, Grades 4-12, see 704
The Cornell Critical Thinking Tests, Grades 4-14, Advanced and gifted high school students and college students and adults, see 705
Cotswold Junior Ability Tests, Ages 8.5-9.5, 9.5-10.5, see 714
Creativity Attitude Survey, Grades 4-6, see 725
Cree Questionnaire, Individuals in a variety of occupations; clients in vocational and career counseling, see 728
Crichton Vocabulary Scale, Ages 4.5-11, see 729
Critical Reasoning Test Battery, Students and employees ages 15 and over, see 735
Critical Reasoning Tests, Prospective managers, see 736
Culture Fair Intelligence Test, Ages 4-8 and educable mentally retarded adults, Ages 8-14 and average IQ adults, senior high, college, and high IQ adults, see 745

Das-Naglieri Cognitive Assessment System, Ages 5 to 17-11, see 763
Dennis Test of Scholastic Aptitude, Grades 4-8, 5-8, see 779
Detroit Tests of Learning Aptitude—Adult, Ages 16-0 and over, see 797
Detroit Tests of Learning Aptitude, Fourth Edition, Ages 6-0 to 17-11, see 798
Detroit Tests of Learning Aptitude—Primary, Second Edition, Ages 3–9, see 799
Edinburgh Picture Test, Ages 6-6 to 8-3, see 899
Eliot-Price Perspective Test, Grades 2 and over, see 925
Ennis-Weir Critical Thinking Essay Test, High school and college, see 959
Evaluation Aptitude Test, Candidates for college and graduate school entrance, see 979
Expressive One-Word Picture Vocabulary Test, Revised, Ages 2–12, 12–16, see 994
The Extended Merrill-Palmer Scale, Ages 3–5, see 996
Figure Classification Test, Applicants for industrial work with 7 to 9 years of schooling, see 1029
Fuld Object-Memory Evaluation, Ages 70-90 regardless of language and sensory handicaps, see 1058
Full-Range Picture Vocabulary Test, Ages 2 and over, see 1059
General Ability Measure for Adults, Ages 18–96, see 1075
General Processing Inventory, Ages 5–75 years, see 1083
Gifted and Talented Scale, Grades 4-6, see 1088
Gifted Evaluation Scale, Second Edition, Grades K–12, see 1089
Goodenough-Harris Drawing Test, Ages 3-15, see 1097
Graduate and Managerial Assessment, Undergraduate and graduate students, see 1106
Graduate Management Admission Test, Applicants to study in graduate management education, see 1107
The Graduate Record Examinations—General Test, Graduate school candidates, see 1115
Group Tests 70 and 70B, Ages 15 and over, see 1152
Group Tests 90A and 90B, Ages 15 and over, see 1153
The Guilford-Zimmerman Aptitude Survey, Grades 9-16 and adults, see 1156
Hammill Multiability Intelligence Test, Ages 6-0 to 17-0, see 1168
Healy Pictorial Completion Tests, Ages 5 and over, see 1189
Henmon-Nelson Ability Test, Canadian Edition, Grades 3–6, 6–9, 9–12, see 1196
High Level Battery: Test A/75, Adults with at least 12 years of education, see 1198
High Level Figure Classification Test, Grades 10-12, see 1199
Industrial Test Battery, Individuals with less than 7 years of formal schooling, see 1257
Inventory No. II, Ages 16 and over, see 1301
Jenkins Non-Verbal Test, 1986 Revision, Australian years 3–8, see 1339
Junior South African Individual Scales, South African children ages 3.0-7.11, see 1370
Kahn Intelligence Tests: Experimental Form, Ages 1 month and over (particularly the verbally or culturally handicapped), see 1375
Kaufman Adolescent and Adult Intelligence Test, Ages 11 to 85+, see 1378
Kaufman Assessment Battery for Children, Ages 2.5 to 12.5, see 1379
Kaufman Brief Intelligence Test, Ages 4-90, see 1380
Kaufman Infant and Preschool Scale, Ages 1 month-48 months and mentally retarded individuals whose preacademic functioning age does not exceed 48 months, see 1383
Kendrick Assessment Scales of Cognitive Ageing, Ages 40–92, see 1390
Khatena-Morse Multitalent Perception Inventory, Ages 6 to adult, see 1395
Kit of Factor Referenced Cognitive Tests, Various grades 6-college level, see 1405
Knox's Cube Test, Ages 3-8, 9 and over, see 1407
The Kohs Block-Design Test, Mental ages 5-20, see 1410
Learning Ability Profile, Grades 5-16 and adults, see 1453
Learning Disability Evaluation Scale (Renormed), Grades K–12, see 1460
Learning Disability Rating Procedure, Grades K-12, see 1461
Learning Efficiency Test-II (1992 Revision), Ages 5-75, see 1462
The Leiter Adult Intelligence Scale, Adults, see 1484
Leiter International Performance Scale—Revised, Ages 2.0–20.11, adults, see 1485
Logical Reasoning, Grades 9-16 and adults, see 1514
Matrix Analogies Test, Ages 5-0 to 17-11, see 1607
McCarthy Scales of Children's Abilities, Ages 2.6–8.6, see 1612
McCarthy Screening Test, Ages 4-6.5, see 1613
MD5 Mental Ability Test, Supervisors to managers, see 1616
Memory Assessment Scales, Ages 18 and over, see 1644
Merrill-Palmer Scale of Mental Tests, Ages 24-63 months, see 1653
The MIDAS: Multiple Intelligence Developmental Assessment Scales, Age 14 to adult, see 1667
Mill Hill Vocabulary Scale, Ages 6.5-16.5, Ages 18–adult, see 1671
Miller Analogies Test, Applicants for graduate schools, see 1672
Modified Vygotsky Concept Formation Test, Older children and adolescents and adults, see 1714
Morrisby Profile, Age 14–adults, see 1717

Multidimensional Aptitude Battery, High school and adults, see 1731
Naglieri Nonverbal Ability Test, Grades K–12, see 1756
New Jersey Test of Reasoning Skills—Form B, Reading level grade 5 and over, see 1780
Non-Language Multi-Mental Test, Grades 3-8 and adults, see 1796
Non-Reading Intelligence Tests, Levels 1-3, Ages 6-4 to 8-3, 7-4 to 9-3, 8-4 to 10-11, see 1797
Non-Verbal Tests, Ages 8-11, 10-15, see 1800
Nonverbal Form, Individuals in a wide variety of occupations and vocational counseling, see 1798
Nonverbal Reasoning, Individuals in a variety of occupations, see 1799
The Ohio Penal Classification Test, Penal institutions, see 1840
The "Orton" Intelligence Test, No. 4, Ages 9-14, see 1864
Otis-Lennon School Ability Test, Seventh Edition, Grades K–12, see 1866
Paper and Pencil Games, Pupils in their second, third and fourth years in South African school system, see 1873
Peabody Picture Vocabulary Test-III, Ages 2.5–90, see 1903
Pictorial Reasoning Test, Entry-level positions in a variety of occupations, see 1986
Picture Test A, Ages 6-9 to 8-3, see 1989
Pintner-Manikin Test, Ages 2 and over, see 1994
Pintner-Paterson Feature Profile Test, Ages 4 and over, see 1995
Porteus Mazes, Ages 3-adult, see 2010
Power and Performance Measures, Ages 16 and over, see 2019
Predictive Ability Test, Adult Edition, Ages 17 and over, see 2027
Preliminary SAT/National Merit Scholarship Qualifying Test, Grades 10-11, see 2031
Preschool and Kindergarten Interest Descriptor, Ages 3-6, see 2037
Primary Test of Cognitive Skills, Grades K-1, see 2059
Proverbs Test, Grades 5-12 and college and adults, see 2102
Psycho-Epistemological Profile, College and adults, see 2112
The Quick Test, Ages 2 and over, see 2146
Randt Memory Test, Ages 20-90, see 2159
Raven Progressive Matrices, Ages 6-65, see 2163
RBH Test of Non-Verbal Reasoning, Business and industry, see 2169
Receptive One-Word Picture Vocabulary Test, Ages 2-0 to 11-11, see 2190
Receptive One-Word Picture Vocabulary Test: Upper Extension, Ages 12-0 to 15-11, see 2191
Recognition Memory Test, Adult patients referred for neuropsychological assessment, see 2193
Revised Beta Examination, Second Edition, Ages 16-64, see 2212
Riley Inventory of Basic Learning Skills, Grades K-8, see 2236
Ross Test of Higher Cognitive Processes, Grades 4-6, see 2252
Schaie-Thurstone Adult Mental Abilities Test, Ages 22-84, see 2304
Scholastic Abilities Test for Adults, Ages 16 through 70, see 2309
Schubert General Ability Battery, Grades 12-16 and adults, see 2324
Screening Assessment for Gifted Elementary Students, Ages 7-0 to 12-11, see 2328
Screening Assessment for Gifted Elementary Students—Primary, Ages 5-0 to 8-11, see 2329
Selby MillSmith Adaptive Ability Tests, Junior school–adult, see 2345
Senior Aptitude Tests, Standards 8-10 in South African schools, college, and adults, see 2373
Senior South African Individual Scale—Revised, Ages 7-0 to 16-11, see 2375
Ship Destination Test, Grades 9 and over, see 2401
Shipley Institute of Living Scale, Ages 14 and over, see 2402
Silver Drawing Test of Cognition and Emotion [Third Edition Revised], Ages 5 and over, see 2410
Slosson Full-Range Intelligence Test, Ages 5–21, see 2431
Slosson Intelligence Test [1991 Edition], Ages 4-0 and over, see 2432
Smith-Johnson Nonverbal Performance Scale, Ages 2-4, see 2439
Snijders-Oomen Non-Verbal Intelligence Test—Revised, Dutch children ages 2-6 to 7-0, Dutch children ages 5-6 to 17-0, see 2441
Space Thinking (Flags), Industrial employees, see 2460
Speech-Ease Screening Inventory (K—1), Ages 2-adult, see 2485
Standard Progressive Matrices [Australian Edition], Students in years 3-11 (ages 8.3 to 17.2), see 2477
Standard Progressive Matrices, New Zealand Standardization, New Zealand children ages 8-15, see 2478
Structure of Intellect Learning Abilities Test, Preschool-adult, see 2518
Subsumed Abilities Test, Ages 9 and over, see 2555
Swanson-Cognitive Processing Test, Ages 5 to adult, see 2596
Teacher Observation Scales for Identifying Children with Special Abilities, Junior and middle primary school, see 2622
Technical Test Battery [British Edition], Apprentice and technical personnel, see 2642
Test of Cognitive Skills, Second Edition, Grades 2–3, 4–5, 6–7, 8–9, 10–11, 11–12, see 2677
Test of Creativity, Adolescents and adults, see 2679

Test of Learning Ability, Industrial and business applicants, see 2696
Test of Memory and Learning, Ages 5 to 19, see 2701
Test of Nonverbal Intelligence, Third Edition, Ages 6-0 through 89-11, see 2704
Test of Perceptual Organization, "Normals and psychiatric patients ages 12 and over," see 2707
Test of Problem Solving, Ages 6-12, see 2710
Test of Scholastic Abilities, Ages 9-0 to 14-11, see 2714
Test on Appraising Observations, Grade 10 to adult, see 2733
Tests of Adult Basic Education Work-Related Problem Solving, Students in secondary schools, vocational education programs, adult basic education programs, and junior colleges, and employees in industry, see 2739
Tests of General Ability: Inter-American Series, Grades Kgn-1.5, 2-3, 4-6, 7-9, 10-13.5, see 2741
Thinking Creatively in Action and Movement, Ages 3–8, see 2754
Thinking Creatively With Sounds and Words, Research Edition, Grades 3–12, adults, see 2755
Thurstone Test of Mental Alertness, Wide variety of occupations, see 2758
The Token Test for Children, Ages 3-12, see 2768
Torrance Tests of Creative Thinking, Grades K through graduate school, see 2771
The Uncritical Inference Test, Adolescents and adults, see 2788
Universal Nonverbal Intelligence Test, Ages 5–17, see 2792
USES General Aptitude Test Battery for the Deaf, Hearing impaired adults, see 2798
Verbal Form, Employees in a wide variety of occupations, see 2807
Verbal Reasoning, Wide variety of occupations and vocational counseling, see 2808
Visual Discrimination Test, Ages 5-8, see 2817
Visual Memory Test, Ages 5-8, see 2819
Watson-Glaser Critical Thinking Appraisal, Form S, Adults with at least a ninth grade education, see 2857
Wechsler Abbreviated Scale of Intelligence, Ages 6–89, see 2859
Wechsler Adult Intelligence Scale—Third Edition, Ages 16–89, see 2860
Wechsler Intelligence Scale for Children—Third Edition, Ages 6-0 to 16-11, see 2862
Wechsler Memory Scale III, Ages 16–89 years, see 2863
Wechsler Preschool and Primary Scale of Intelligence—Revised, Ages 3–7.3 years, see 2864
Wide Range Assessment of Memory and Learning, Ages 5 through 17, see 2880
The Wiesen Test of Mechanical Aptitude, Applicants for jobs requiring mechanical aptitude, see 2884
Williams Intelligence Test for Children with Defective Vision, Ages 5-15 (blind and partially sighted), see 2888
Wisconsin Card Sorting Test, Revised and Expanded, Ages 6.5–89, see 2892
Wonderlic Personnel Test and Scholastic Level Exam, Ages 15 and up, see 2899
Woodcock-Johnson Psycho-Educational Battery—Revised, Ages 2-90, see 2901

MATHEMATICS

Advanced Placement Examination in Calculus, High school students desiring credit for college-level courses and admission to advanced courses, see 93
Advanced Placement Examination in Statistics, High school students desiring credit for college-level courses and admission to advanced courses, see 114
Algebra Test for Engineering and Science: National Achievement Tests, College entrants, see 137
American High School Mathematics Examination, High school students competing for individual and school awards, see 144
American Invitational Mathematics Examination, American and Canadian high school students, see 148
American Junior High School Mathematics Examination, American and Canadian students in grade 8 or below, see 149
American Numerical Test, Adults in "vocations which emphasize shop and white collar skills," see 151
Arithmetic Index, Individuals in a variety of occupations and rehabilitation environments, see 171
Arithmetic Skills Assessment Test, High school and adults, see 172
Arithmetic Test (Fundamentals and Reasoning): Municipal Tests: National Achievement Tests, Grades 3–6, 6–8, see 173
Arithmetic Test: National Achievement Tests, Grades 3–8., see 174
Assessment in Mathematics, Primary and lower secondary school children, see 195
Basic Mathematics Tests, Ages 7-0 to 8-0, 8-0 to 9-0, 9-7 to 10-10, 10-0 to 12-6, 12-0 to 14-6, see 253
Basic Number Diagnostic Test [1996 Edition], Ages 5–7, see 254
Basic Number Screening Test [1996 Edition], Ages 7–12, see 255

Booker Profiles in Mathematics: Numeration and Computation, Ages 7–16, see 325
California Diagnostic Mathematics Tests, Grades 1.1-6.9, see 369
Chelsea Diagnostic Mathematics Tests, Ages 10-15, see 444
Class Achievement Test in Mathematics, Years 4-5, 6-7 in Australian schools, see 492
CLEP General Examinations: Mathematics, Persons entering college or already in college, see 500
CLEP Subject Examination in Calculus with Elementary Functions, Persons entering college or already in college, see 506
CLEP Subject Examination in College Algebra, Persons entering college or already in college, see 507
CLEP Subject Examination in College Algebra-Trigonometry, Persons entering college or already in college, see 508
CLEP Subject Examination in Principles of Accounting, Persons entering college or already in college, see 524
CLEP Subject Examination in Trigonometry, Persons entering college or already in college, see 529
College Board Institutional SAT II: Mathematics Level IC Subject Tests, and SAT II: Mathematics Level II C Subject Tests, Entering college freshmen, see 585
College Board SAT II: Mathematics Level IC and SAT II: Mathematics Level IIC, Candidates for college entrance, see 605
Collis-Romberg Mathematical Problem Solving Profiles, Ages 9–13, 13–17, see 622
Diagnostic Mathematics Profiles, Australian school years 3–6, see 825
Diagnostic Screening Test: Math, Third Edition, Grades 1-11, see 831
Early Mathematical Language, Children in their first year at school, see 883
Early Mathematics Diagnostic Kit, Ages 4-8, see 884
First Year Algebra Test: National Achievement Tests, One year high school, see 1038
Graded Arithmetic-Mathematics Test, Ages 5–12, see 1103
The Graduate Record Examinations Mathematics Test, Graduate school candidates, see 1119
Group Mathematics Test, Second Edition, Ages 6.5-8.10 and older underachieving students, see 1145
Independent Mastery Testing System for Math Skills, Adult students, see 1247
Iowa Algebra Aptitude Test, Fourth Edition, Grades 7–8, see 1315
Junior High School Mathematics Test: Acorn Achievement Tests, Grades 7-9, see 1368
KeyMath Revised: A Diagnostic Inventory of Essential Mathematics [1998 Normative Update], Grades K–9, ages 6–22, see 1392
Mathematical Olympiads, Secondary school, see 1595
Mathematics 7, Ages 6-10 to 7-9, see 1603
Mathematics 8–12, Ages 8-12, see 1601
Mathematics Attainment Test C1, Ages 9-12, see 1596
Mathematics Attainment Test DE2, Ages 10-12, see 1597
Mathematics Attainment Test EF, Ages 11-0 to 13-6, see 1598
Mathematics Attitude Inventory, Grades 7-12, see 1599
Mathematics Competency Test, Ages 11 to adult, see 1600
Mathematics Test for Grades Four, Five and Six (A), Grades 4-6, see 1604
Mathematics Topic Pre-Tests, Form 3 (junior secondary) students in New Zealand school system, see 1605
NIIP Engineering Arithmetic Test EA4, Age 15-adult, see 1787
Number Test DE, Ages 10-6 to 12-6, see 1806
Orleans-Hanna Algebra Prognosis Test, Third Edition, Grades 7 and over, see 1863
Plane Geometry: National Achievement Tests, High school, see 1998
Plane Trigonometry: National Achievement Tests, Grades 10-16, see 1999
Practical Maths Assessments, Age 9–13, see 2023
Profiles of Problem Solving, Grades 4–6, see 2080
Progress Tests in Maths, Ages 7-8, 8-9, 9-10, 10-11, 11-12, 12-13, see 2089
Progressive Achievement Test of Mathematics [Revised], Ages 8-0 to 14-11, see 2090
Progressive Achievement Tests in Mathematics, Australian students in years 3-8, see 2091
Ramsay Corporation Job Skills—Office Arithmetic Test, Adults, see 2153
RBH Arithmetic Fundamentals Test, Business and industry, see 2164
The RBH Arithmetic Reasoning Test, Business and industry, see 2165
RBH Shop Arithmetic Test, Industry, see 2166
Sequential Assessment of Mathematics Inventories: Standardized Inventory, Grades K-8, see 2383
Solid Geometry: National Achievement Tests, High school students, see 2456
Stanford Diagnostic Mathematics Test, Fourth Edition, Grades 1.5–13.0, see 2486
STAR Math™, Grades 3–12, see 2492
Target Mathematics Tests, Levels 2–5, 2–6, see 2613
Test of Cognitive Style in Mathematics, Ages 8-adult, see 2678
Test of Early Mathematics Ability, Second Edition, Ages 3-0 to 8-11, see 2681
Test of Mathematical Abilities for Gifted Students, Ages 6–12, see 2698
Test of Mathematical Abilities, Second Edition, Ages 8-0 to 18-11, see 2699
Tests of Achievement in Basic Skills: Mathematics, Preschool-kindergarten, grades 1, 2, 3-4, 4-6, 7-9, 10-adult., see 2736
Yardsticks, Ages 6, 7, 8, 9, 10, 11, see 2938

MISCELLANEOUS

Basic Tests Series, High school seniors and college entrants and job applicants, see 260
Cognitive Skills Assessment Battery, Second Edition, PreK-K, see 565
Community Oriented Programs Environment Scale, Patients and staff of community oriented psychiatric facilities, see 637
Creativity Assessment Packet, Ages 6 through 18, see 724
Facial Action Coding System, Adults., see 1001
Functional Time Estimation Questionnaire, Ages 7–11, see 1068
Gregorc Style Delineator, Adults, see 1132
Herrmann Brain Dominance Instrument [Revised], Adults, see 1197
Hill Interaction Matrix, Prospective members, members, and leaders of psychotherapy groups, see 1205
Illinois Test of Psycholinguistic Abilities, Revised Edition, Ages 2-10, see 1240
Jansky Diagnostic Battery, Kindergarten, see 1336
Level of Service Inventory—Revised: Screening Version, Ages 16 and older, see 1487
The Level of Service Inventory—Revised, Ages 16 and older, see 1486
Life Stressors and Social Resources Inventory—Adult Form, Healthy adults, psychiatric patients, and medical patients, see 1495
Life Stressors and Social Resources Inventory—Youth Form, Ages 12–18, see 1496
Lifestyle Assessment Questionnaire, Adults ages 18–60 with a minimum of 12th grade education, see 1499
Matching Person and Technology, Clients, students, or employees, see 1593
Mathematics Self-Efficacy Scale, College freshmen, see 1602
Menometer, Adolescents and adults, see 1646
Mental Status Checklist for Adults, 1988 Revision, Adults, see 1649
Mentoring Skills Assessment, Mentors, coaches, and mentees, see 1651
Mentoring Style Indicator, Mentors of youth and proteges, new hires, employees, new teachers, college students, and educational administrators, see 1652
MILCOM Patient Data Base System, Medical patients, see 1669
Military Environment Inventory, Military personnel, see 1670
Modern Photography Comprehension Test, Photography students, see 1713
Multiphasic Environmental Assessment Procedure, Nursing home residents, residential care facilities, congregate apartments, see 1743
Multiphasic Sex Inventory, Juvenile males, adult males, see 1744
Older Persons Counseling Needs Survey, Ages 60 and over, see 1842
Opinions About Deaf People Scale, Adults, see 1844
Pain Assessment Battery, Research Edition, Patients with chronic pain, see 1870
Partial Index of Modernization: Measurement of Attitudes Toward Morality (A), Children and adults, see 1893
Personal Experience Inventory for Adults, Age 19 and older, see 1932
Personal Experience Screening Questionnaire, Adolescents, see 1933
Personal Questionnaire, Adolescents and adults, see 1943
Productivity Environmental Preference Survey, Adults, see 2069
[Profiles from Rensis Likert Associates, Inc.], Group members, see 2079
Quality of Life Inventory, Ages 18 and over, see 2131
Quality Potential Assessment, Adults, see 2133
Recovery Attitude and Treatment Evaluator, Adults, see 2194
Retirement Activities Card Sort Planning Kit, Retired adults or adults who plan to retire, see 2207
Retirement Descriptive Index, Retirees, see 2208
Service Animal Adaptive Intervention Assessment, Occupational, physical, and recreational therapists, assistive technology professionals, and animal assisted therapy specialists, see 2384
Shoplifting Inventory, Shoplifting offenders, see 2403
Smell Identification Test™ [Revised], People 5 years and up with suspected olfactory dysfunction, see 2437
Smoker Complaint Scale, Persons quitting smoking, see 2440
The Social Climate Scales, Members of various groups, see 2445
Standardized Test of Computer Literacy and Computer Anxiety Index (Version AZ), Revised, Students in introductory computer literacy courses, see 2482
Survey of Organizational Stress, High school and college, government and private enterprise, see 2586
Swassing-Barbe Modality Index, Children and adults, see 2597
System of Multicultural Pluralistic Assessment, Ages 5–11, see 2606
Team Effectiveness and Meeting Strategy, Groups or teams, see 2633
Tests for Everyday Living, Junior and senior high school, see 2734
Thanatometer, Adults, see 2748
Time Use Analyzer, Adults, see 2764
The Time-Sample Behavioral Checklist, Adults in residential treatment settings, see 2763

Timed Typings for Holidays, Students in typing classes, see 2765
University Residence Environment Scale [Revised], University students and staff, see 2793
Vineland Adaptive Behavior Scales, Birth through age 18-11 and low-functioning adults, ages 3 through 12-11, see 2813
Ward Atmosphere Scale (Third Edition), Patients and staff members, see 2850

ADJUSTMENT/ADAPTIVE FUNCTIONING

Adaptive Behavior: Street Survival Skills Questionnaire, Ages 9.5 and over, see 62
Adaptive Functioning Index, Ages 14 and over in rehabilitation or special education settings, see 63
Assessment of Living Skills and Resources, Community-dwelling elders, see 212
Auditory Selective Attention Test, Adults, see 231
Functional Performance Record, Individuals of all ages with disabilities, see 1066
The Kohlman Evaluation of Living Skills, Occupational therapy clients with living skill deficits, see 1409
LOCO (Learning Opportunities Coordination): A Scale for the Assessment of Coordinated Learning Opportunities in Living Units for People with a Handicap, Residents of any type of living units where people with a handicap live with the assistance of care givers, see 1512
Matching Assistive Technology & Child, Children with disabilities, ages 0–5, see 1591
OARS Multidimensional Functional Assessment Questionnaire, Ages 65 and over, see 1808
The Prevocational Assessment and Curriculum Guide, Mentally retarded individuals, see 2053
Rating Scale of Communication in Cognitive Decline, Persons suffering from a prolonged illness, see 2162
Skills for Independent Living, Educable mentally retarded secondary students and low-achieving nonretarded secondary school students, see 2422
Social and Prevocational Information Battery—Revised, Mildly mentally retarded students in grades 7-12, see 2443
Specific Language Disability Test, "Average to high IQ" children in grades 6-8, see 2469
Survey of Functional Adaptive Behaviors, Ages 16 and over, see 2579

ALCOHOL AND SUBSTANCE USE

Addiction Research Center Inventory, Drug addicts, see 66
Adolescent Diagnostic Interview, Ages 12–18, see 73
Alcohol Clinical Index, Adults at-risk for alcohol problems, see 133
Alcohol Use Disorders Identification Test, Adults, see 135
The American Drug and Alcohol Survey, Schools and school districts, see 143
ASIST: A Structured Addictions Assessment Interview for Selecting Treatment, Adults, see 184
Assessment of Chemical Health Inventory, Adolescents, adults, see 201
Drug Use Questionnaire, Clients of addiction treatment, see 859
Drug-Taking Confidence Questionnaire, Clients of addiction treatment, see 858
Inventory of Drinking Situations, Ages 18 to 75, see 1304
Inventory of Drug Taking Situations, Drug or alcohol users, see 1305
Michigan Alcohol Screening Test, Adults, see 1661
QUESTS: A Life-Choice Inventory, Grades 9-12, see 2136
SAQ-Adult Probation [Substance Abuse Questionnaire], Adult probationers, see 2284
Situational Confidence Questionnaire, Adult alcoholics, see 2414
Substance Abuse Relapse Assessment, Adolescents and adults, see 2551
Substance Abuse Screening Test, Ages 13–adult, see 2552
Substance Use Disorders Diagnosis Schedule, Suspected alcohol or drug abusers, see 2554

BLIND

The Blind Learning Aptitude Test, Blind ages 6–20, see 318
Braille Assessment Inventory, Ages 6–18, see 332
Lorimer Braille Recognition Test: A Test of Ability in Reading Braille Contractions, Students (ages 7-13) in grade 2 Braille, see 1520
Tooze Braille Speed Test: A Test of Basic Ability in Reading Braille, Students (Ages 7-13) in Grades 1 or 2 Braille, see 2770

BUSINESS EDUCATION AND RELATIONSHIPS

Alleman Leadership Development Questionnaire, Mentors and proteges, see 138
Alleman Mentoring Scales Questionnaire, Mentors and proteges, see 139
Alleman Relationship Value Questionnaire, Mentors and proteges, see 140
Diagnosing Organizational Culture, Adults, see 820
Entrepreneurial Style and Success Indicator, Adults, see 962
Evaluating Diversity Training, Diversity-training managers, see 975
Group Environment Scale, Second Edition, Group members and leaders, see 1141
I-SPEAK Your Language™: A Survey of Personal Styles, Employees, see 1331

Influence Strategies Exercise, Managers and employees, see 1267
Inventory for Client and Agency Planning, Ages 3 months to adult, see 1300
Kilmann-Saxton Culture-Gap Survey [Revised], Work team members, employees, see 1397
Kipnis-Schmidt Profiles of Organizational Influence Strategies, Organizational members, see 1402
Management of Differences Inventory, Business managers, see 1557
Small Business Assessment, Small businesses, see 2435
Whisler Strategy Test, Business and industry, see 2877

CRIMINAL JUSTICE

Correctional Institutions Environment Scale, Second Edition, Residents and staff of correctional facilities, see 710
Correctional Policy Inventory: A Survey of Correctional Philosophy and Characteristic Methods of Dealing with Offenders, Correctional managers, see 712
Juvenile Justice Policy Inventory, Juvenile justice professionals, see 1373
The Lawrence Psychological Forensic Examination, Juvenile, criminal, and civil justice clients, see 1435
Prison Inmate Inventory, Prison inmates, see 2061
Rogers Criminal Responsibility Assessment Scales, Criminals, see 2245

DRIVING AND SAFETY

Driver Risk Inventory—II, Convicted DUI and DWI offenders, see 856
Wilson Driver Selection Test, Prospective motor vehicle operators, see 2889

FAMILY AND RELATIONSHIPS

ACCESS—A Comprehensive Custody Evaluation Standard System, Children, parents, and others involved in child custody evaluations, see 13
Ackerman-Schoendorf Scales for Parent Evaluation of Custody, Parents engaged in a dispute over custody of their children, see 41
Assessment of Interpersonal Relations, Ages 9–0 to 19–11, see 210
Assessment of Parenting Skills: Infant and Preschooler, Parents of children between birth and 5 years of age, see 213
Bricklin Perceptual Scales, Ages 6 and over, see 334
The Bricklin/Elliot Child Custody Evaluation, Families involved in child custody situations, see 333
Checklist for Child Abuse Evaluation, Children and adolescents., see 442
Child Abuse/Husband Abuse/Wife Abuse, Children, husbands, wives, see 447
Child Care Inventory, Child care programs, see 452
Child Well-Being Scales and Rating Form, Child welfare practitioners, see 458
Childhood Trauma Questionnaire, Ages 12 and up, see 460
Children's Version of The Family Environment Scale, Ages 5-12, see 480
Clarke Sex History Questionnaire, Sex offenders, see 491
Clinical Rating Scale, Couples and families, see 544
Comprehensive Affair Worksheets, Individuals who have had an affair, see 646
Comprehensive Spouse's Worksheets, Spouses of persons who had an affair, see 660
Early Childhood Physical Environment Observation Schedules and Rating Scales, Directors and staff of child care centers, early childhood teachers, see 877
Erotometer: A Technique for the Measurement of Heterosexual Love, Adults, see 970
FACES II & FACES III, Families, see 1000
A Familism Scale, Adolescents and adults, see 1004
Family Assessment Form: A Practice-Based Approach to Assessing Family Functioning, Families receiving home-based services, see 1007
Family Assessment Measure Version III, Families, see 1008
Family Day Care Rating Scale, Consumers of day care services, day care providers, agency supervisors, and researchers, see 1009
Family Environment Scale, Third Edition, Ages 11–adult, see 1010
Family Satisfaction Scale, Families, see 1014
Family System Test, Individuals and families, see 1015
A Family Violence Scale, Adolescents and adults, see 1016
Grandparent Strengths and Needs Inventory, Grandparents of children 6 and over, see 1128
Gravidometer, Adolescents and adults, see 1129
Home Environment Questionnaire, HEQ-2R and HEQ-1R, Grades 4-6, see 1215
Home Observation for Measurement of the Environment, Birth to age 3, early childhood, middle childhood, see 1216
Home Screening Questionnaire, Birth to age 3, ages 3-6, see 1217
How Am I Doing? A Self-Assessment for Child Caregivers, Caregivers of children with disabilities, see 1220
Infant/Toddler Environment Rating Scale, Infant/toddler day care centers, see 1264
The LAW-PSI Adult Life History Questionnaire, Adults, see 1431
The LAW-PSI Child/Adolescent Life History Questionnaire, Children/adolescents, see 1432
The LAW-PSI Sexual History Questionnaire, Adults, see 1433
Marital Evaluation Checklist, Married couples in counseling, see 1581
The Marriage and Family Attitude Survey, Adolescents and adults, see 1583

Marriage Scale (For Measuring Compatibility of Interests), Premarital and marital counselee, see 1584
MATE [Marital ATtitude Evaluation], Couples, see 1594
Miller Marriage Satisfaction Scale, Individuals who are dating, living together or who are married, see 1680
Mirror-Couple Relationship Inventory, Engaged and married couples, see 1705
Nims Observation Checklist, Parents and children, see 1788
The Nisonger Questionnaire for Parents, Handicapped children ages 2-8, see 1791
Pair Attraction Inventory, College and adults, see 1872
Parent Perception of Child Profile, Parents, see 1886
Parent-Adolescent Communication Scale, Adolescents and their parents, see 1877
Parent-Child Communication Inventory, Children and parents, see 1882
Parent/Family Involvement Index, Parents with children in special education programs, see 1884
The Parenthood Questionnaire, Youth who are prospective parents or who may work with children in the future, see 1887
Parenting Satisfaction Scale, Adults with dependent children, see 1888
Perceptions of Parental Role Scales, Parents, see 1918
Personal Assessment of Intimacy in Relationships, Couples, see 1927
Personal Relationship Inventory, Ages 15 and over, see 1946
A Pill Scale, Adults, see 1992
A Premarital Communication Inventory, Premarital couples, see 2033
PREPARE/ENRICH, Couples, see 2034
Sex-Role Egalitarianism Scale, High school to adult, see 2389
Sexometer, Adolescents and adults, see 2390
Sexual Abuse Screening Inventory, Preschool through adolescence, see 2391
Scale of Marriage Problems: Revised, Couples, see 2292
Spousal Assault Risk Assessment Guide, Individuals suspected of or being treated for spousal or family-related assault, see 2476
Styles of Conflict Inventory, Heterosexual couples, see 2546
Uniform Child Custody Evaluation System, Professionals involved in custody evaluation, see 2791
Vasectomy Scale: Attitudes, Adults, see 2806
Wife's or Husband's Marriage Questions, Husbands, wives, see 2885

HEALTH AND PHYSICAL EDUCATION

The ANSER System-Aggregate Neurobehavioral Student Health and Educational Review [Revised 1997], Children ages 3+, suspected of having learning difficulties, see 158
The Arizona Battery for Communication Disorders of Dementia, Alzheimer's patients, see 176
Behavioral Assessment of Pain Questionnaire, Subacute and chronic pain patients, see 291
Coitometer, Adults, see 568
Comprehensive Sex History, Adults, see 659
Cornell Medical Index—Health Questionnaire, Ages 14 and over, see 708
Eating Inventory, Ages 17 and older, see 894
Fast Health Knowledge Test, 1986 Revision, High school and college, see 1019
Functional Fitness Assessment for Adults over 60 Years, Second Edition, Adults over age 60, see 1062
Health and Daily Living, Second Edition, Students ages 12-18, Adults, see 1181
Health Problems Checklist, Adults, see 1186
Health Status Questionnaire, Ages 14 and older, see 1187
Krantz Health Opinion Survey, College, healthy adults, and chronic disease populations, see 1412
Medical Ethics Inventory, First year medical students, see 1639
Multidimensional Health Profile, Ages 18 and over, see 1733
Organic Dysfunction Survey Schedules, Adult clients, see 1853
Psychosocial Pain Inventory [Revised], Chronic pain patients, see 2118
RAND-36 Health Status Inventory, Adults, see 2158
Rehabilitation Checklist, Adults, see 2196
Rehabilitation Compliance Scale, Severely injured patients ages 17–85 years, see 2197
Sexual Adaptation and Functioning Test, White adults ages 16 and over, see 2392
Sexual Violence Risk-20, Individuals suspected to be at-risk for committing sexual violence, see 2395
SF-36 Health Survey, Ages 14 and older, see 2397
Softball Skills Test, Grades 5-12 and college, see 2455
Stress Indicator & Health Planner, Adults, see 2511
Tennis Skills Test Manual, High school and college, see 2653
Test of Auditory Analysis Skills, Children, see 2671
Test of Visual Analysis Skills, Children, see 2721
TestWell: Health Risk Appraisal, Adults ages 18–60 with a minimum of 10th grade education, see 2745
TestWell: Wellness Inventory for Windows, Adults with a minimum of 10th grade education, see 2746
TestWell: Wellness Inventory for Windows—College Version, College students, see 2747

HANDWRITING

Denver Handwriting Analysis, Grades 3–8, see 786

LEARNING DISABILITIES

Achievement Identification Measure, School age children, see 35

Career Assessment Inventories for the Learning Disabled, Ages 6-adult, see 397
Dyslexia Determination Test, Second Edition, Grades 2–12, see 867
Jordan Left-Right Reversal Test (1990 Edition), Ages 5-12, see 1362
Pathways to Independence, Second Edition, Disadvantaged school-aged children and mentally and otherwise handicapped teenagers and adults and rehabilitating brain-damaged and geriatric patients, see 1897
PIP Developmental Charts, Second Edition, Mentally handicapped children birth to age 5, see 1996
Pollack-Branden Inventory, Grades 1-12, see 2005
Weller-Strawser Scales of Adaptive Behavior for the Learning Disabled, Learning disabled students ages 6-12, 13-18, see 2868

PHILOSOPHY

C-R Opinionaire, Grades 11-16 and adults, see 363

PSYCHOLOGY

Counselor and Client Verbal Response Category Systems, Counselors in training, see 716
The Experiencing Scale, Counselors and counselor trainees, see 991

RECORD AND REPORT FORMS

Psychodiagnostic Test Report Blank, Psychologists, see 2110
Quickview Social History, Ages 16 and older, see 2147

SOCIO-ECONOMIC STATUS

The American Home Scale, Grades 8–16, see 147

STUDY SKILLS

Library Skills, High school, see 1491

TEST PROGRAMS

ACT Assessment, Grades 10–12, see 56
Advanced Placement Examinations, High school students desiring credit for college-level courses and admission to advanced courses, see 118
CLEP Subject Examination in Human Growth and Development, Persons entering college or already in college, see 519
CLEP Subject Examination in Introductory Psychology, Persons entering college or already in college, see 522
College Level Examination Program , 1-2 years of college or equivalent, see 617
DANTES Subject Standardized Tests, College students wishing to earn credit by examination, see 762
Educational Development Series (1992 Edition), Grades K-12, see 904
The Graduate Record Examinations Psychology Test, Graduate school candidates, see 1122
Graduate Record Examinations: Subject Tests, Graduate school candidates, see 1124
The Identi-Form System for Gifted Programs, Grades K-12, see 1238
Multiple Assessments, Programs, and Services (MAPS) of the College Board, Entering and continuing college students, see 1746

MULTI-APTITUDE BATTERIES

Aptitude Tests for School Beginners, Grade 1 entrants, see 169
Armed Services Vocational Aptitude Battery [Forms 18/19], High school, junior college, and young adult applicants to the Armed Forces, see 180
CLEP General Examinations, Persons entering college or already in college, see 497
Comprehensive Ability Battery, Ages 15 and over, see 644
Differential Aptitude Tests, Fifth Edition, Grades 7–9, grades 10–12 and adults, see 838
Differential Aptitude Tests for Personnel and Career Assessment, Adult, see 839
Educational Abilities Scales, Ages 13-15, see 902
Perceptual-Motor Assessment for Children & Emotional/Behavioral Screening Program, Ages 4-0-15-11, see 1919
Quick Cognitive Inventory, Grades 1-3, see 2138
Trade Aptitude Test Battery, First-year South African students in the technical fields, see 2774
USES General Aptitude Test Battery, Grades 1–12 and adults, see 2797
USES Nonreading Aptitude Test Battery, 1982 Edition, Disadvantaged grades 9–12 and adults, see 2799
The Visual Aural Digit Span Test, Ages 5-6 to 12, see 2816

NEUROPSYCHOLOGICAL

Adult Neuropsychological Questionnaire, Adults, see 85
Aphasia Diagnostic Profiles, Adults with acquired brain damage, see 159
Apraxia Battery for Adults, Adolescent and adult patients, see 163
Bedside Evaluation Screening Test, Second Edition, Patients with language deficits, see 277
Behavioural Assessment of the Dysexecutive Syndrome, Ages 16 and above, see 295
Birmingham Object Recognition Battery, Population not provided, see 314
Bloomer Learning Test—Neurologically Enhanced, Grades 1–11 and adults, see 320
The Booklet Category Test, Second Edition, Ages 15 and older, see 326
Boston Qualitative Scoring System for the Rey-Osterrieth Complex Figure, Ages 18–94, see 329
Brief Neuropsychological Cognitive Examination, Ages 18 and older, see 336
Brief Test of Head Injury, Acute and long-term head-injured adults, see 338
Burns Brief Inventory of Communication and Cognition, Adults with neurological impairment, see 356
California Computerized Assessment Package, Ages 21–58, see 366
California Verbal Learning Test, Children's Version, Ages 5–16, see 375
California Verbal Learning Test, Research Edition, Adult Version, 17–80 years, see 376
The Camden Memory Tests, Population not provided, see 378
The Category-Specific Names Test, Children and adults, see 432
CERAD (Consortium to Establish a Registry for Alzheimer's Disease) Assessment Battery, Patients with mild to moderate dementia, see 434
The Chessington O.T. Neurological Assessment Battery, Ages 16-65+, see 445
Child Neuropsychological Questionnaire, Children, see 456
Children's Auditory Verbal Learning Test-2, Ages 6-6 to 17-11, see 470
Children's Memory Scale, Ages 5–16, see 476
Clifton Assessment Procedures for the Elderly, Ages 60 and over, see 537
The Clock Test, Ages 65 and older, see 545
Closed Head Injury Screener, English-speaking adults, see 546
Cognistat (The Neurobehavioral Cognitive Status Examination), Adults, see 558
Cognitive Behavior Rating Scales, Patients with possible neurological impairment, see 562
Cognitive Symptom Checklists, Ages 16 and older, see 566
CogScreen Aeromedical Edition, Aviators ages 25–73 with 12 or more years of education, see 567
Comprehensive Test of Visual Functioning, Ages 8 and over, see 663
The Computer Category Test, Ages 9–14, adult, see 667
Computerized Assessment of Response Bias: Revised Edition, Severely impaired neurologic patients, mild traumatic brain injury patients, non-neurologic simulators, see 671
Contextual Memory Test, Adults, see 685
DCS—A Visual Learning and Memory Test for Neuropsychological Assessment, Ages 6–70, see 767
Dementia Rating Scale, Individuals suffering from brain dysfunction, see 776
Digit Vigilance Test, Ages 17–80, see 842
Functional Linguistic Communication Inventory, Adults diagnosed with Alzheimer's disease, see 1064
Graded Naming Test, Ages 20 and over, see 1104
Halstead Russell Neuropsychological Evaluation System, Neuropsychological patients, see 1165
Halstead-Reitan Neuropsychological Test Battery, Ages 5-8, 9-14, 15 and over, see 1164
The Human Information Processing Survey, Adults, see 1227
Infanib, Infants from birth to 18 months corrected gestational age, see 1258
Intermediate Booklet Category Test, Ages 9–14, see 1286
Kaufman Short Neuropsychological Assessment Procedure, Ages 11 to 85, see 1384
Learning and Memory Battery, Ages 20 to 80, see 1454
Learning Disabilities Diagnostic Inventory, Ages 8-0 to 17-11, see 1459
Loewenstein Occupational Therapy Cognitive Assessment, Ages 6 to 12 and brain-injured adults, see 1513
Luria-Nebraska Neuropsychological Battery: Children's Revision, Ages 8-12, see 1524
Luria-Nebraska Neuropsychological Battery: Forms I and II, Ages 15 and over, see 1525
McCarron-Dial System, Normal and handicapped individuals ages 3 to adult, see 1610
MicroCog: Assessment of Cognitive Functioning, Ages 18–89, see 1665
Mini Inventory of Right Brain Injury, Ages 20 and over, see 1690
National Adult Reading Test, Second Edition, Ages 20-70, see 1758
NEPSY: A Developmental Neuropsychological Assessment, Ages 3–12, see 1771

Neurological Dysfunctions of Children, Ages 3-10, see 1774
The Neuropsychological Impairment Scale, Ages 18 and older, see 1775
Neuropsychological Questionnaire, Children and adults, see 1776
Neuropsychological Status Exam, Neuropsychological patients, see 1777
Neuropsychology Behavior and Affect Profile, Brain-impaired individuals ages 15 and over, see 1778
Ohio Functional Assessment Battery: Standardized Tests for Leisure and Living Skills, Adults experiencing slight to profound impairment in cognitive ability, see 1839
Organic Integrity Test, Ages 5 and over, see 1854
Philadelphia Head Injury Questionnaire, Head trauma patients, see 1978
Portable Tactual Performance Test, Ages 5 to adult, see 2009
Portland Digit Recognition Test, Adults, see 2011
Psycholinguistic Assessments of Language Processing in Aphasia, Adults with aphasia, see 2113
Quick Neurological Screening Test, 2nd Revised Edition, Ages 5 and over, see 2141
Repeatable Battery for the Assessment of Neuropsychological Status, Ages 20–89, see 2202
Revised Token Test, Preliminary normative data based on the following standardization samples: non-brain-damaged, left hemisphere brain-damaged, right hemisphere brain-damaged, see 2225
Rey Auditory Verbal Learning Test, Ages 7–89, see 2226
Rey Complex Figure Test and Recognition Trial, Ages 18–89, see 2227
The Rivermead Behavioural Memory Test [Second Edition], Brain-damaged persons, ages 11 to elderly adult; brain-damaged children, ages 5–10, see 2239
Rivermead Perceptual Assessment Battery, Adult stroke and head injury patients, see 2240
Ross Information Processing Assessment—Geriatric, Geriatric patients, see 2249
Ross Information Processing Assessment—Primary, "Ages 5-0 through 12-11 who have acquired or developmental problems involving the brain," see 2250
Ross Information Processing Assessment, Second Edition, Ages 15–90, see 2251
Scales of Adult Independence, Language and Recall, Adults with dementia, see 2296
Scales of Cognitive Ability for Traumatic Brain Injury, Patients with acquired brain damage, see 2297
Screening Test for the Luria-Nebraska Neuropsychological Battery: Adult and Children's Forms, Ages 8-12, 13 and older, see 2334
Sensory Integration and Praxis Tests, Ages 4-8.11, see 2377
Severe Cognitive Impairment Profile, Severely demented patients, see 2387
Short Category Test, Booklet Format, Ages 15 and over, see 2405
Sklar Aphasia Scale, Revised 1983, Brain-damaged adults, see 2426
Stroop Color and Word Test, Ages 7 and over, see 2516
Stroop Neuropsychological Screening Test, Ages 18 and over, see 2517
Symbol Digit Modalities Test, Ages 8 and over, see 2599
TD (Tardive Dyskinesia) Monitor, Patients receiving chronic neuroleptic maintenance, see 2619
Test of Memory Malingering, Ages 16 to 84, see 2702
Test of Oral and Limb Apraxia, Ages 20–99, see 2705
Tower of London: Research Version, Children and adolescents and adults, see 2772
VESPAR: A Verbal and Spatial Reasoning Test, People "who have suffered physical or cognitive impairments as a result of neurological illness," see 2809
Visual Search and Attention Test, Ages 18 and over, see 2820
WAIS-R NI, Ages 16–74, see 2840
The Word Memory Test, Adults, see 2909

PERSONALITY

Abortion Scale, Older adolescents and adults, see 6
Abuse Risk Inventory for Women, Experimental Edition, Women seeking medical or mental health services, see 7
ACDI-Corrections Version and Corrections Version II, Troubled youth between the ages of 12 and 18 years in juvenile probation, parole, and corrections programs, see 19
Achievement Motivation Profile, Ages 14 and older in high school, junior college, and college, see 37
Adaptability Test, Job applicants, see 58
The Adjective Check List, High school and over, see 68
Adolescent Apperception Cards, Ages 12–19, see 71
Adolescent Coping Scale, Ages 12–18, see 72
Adolescent Dissociative Experiences Scale, Ages 11–17, see 74
Adolescent Drinking Index, Ages 12–17, see 75
Adolescent Psychopathology Scale, Ages 12–19, see 77
Adolescent Separation Anxiety Test, Ages 11-18, see 78
Adolescent Symptom Inventory-4, Ages 12–18, see 79

Adult Personality Inventory [Revised], Ages 16–adult, see 86
Adult Self Expression Scale, Adults, see 88
Adult Suicidal Ideation Questionnaire, Ages 18 and over, see 89
Affective Perception Inventory, Grades 1-3, 4-8, 9-12, see 120
The Affective Perception Inventory/College Level, Post-secondary school students, see 121
Age Projection Test, Adults, see 122
A. I. Survey, Job applicants, see 130
The Alcadd Test, Revised Edition, Adults, see 132
Alcohol Dependence Scale, Problem drinkers, see 134
Alcohol Use Inventory, Adults and adolescents suspected of problem drinking, see 136
Appraise Your World, Adults, see 162
The APT Inventory, Adults, see 166
Arousal Seeking Tendency Scale, Ages 15 and older, see 181
The Assertiveness Skills Inventory, Adults, see 185
Assessment of Core Goals, High school and over, see 205
Assessment of Qualitative and Structural Dimensions of Object Representations, Revised Edition, Adolescents and adults (patients and normals), see 215
Association Adjustment Inventory, Normal and institutionalized adults, see 218
Athletic Motivation Inventory, Male and female athletes ages 13 and older and coaches, see 219
The Attentional and Interpersonal Style Inventory, Adults and adolescents, see 226
Attitudes Toward Mainstreaming Scale, Teachers, see 227
Attitudes Toward Working Mothers Scale, Adults, see 228
The Balanced Emotional Empathy Scale, Ages 15 and older, see 238
Bar-Ilan Picture Test for Children, Ages 4–16, see 242
BarOn Emotional Quotient Inventory, Ages 16 and older, see 243
Basic Living Skills Scale, Grades 3–6, see 252
Basic Personality Inventory, Adult and adolescent, see 256
BASIS-A Inventory [Basic Adlerian Scales for Interpersonal Success—Adult Form], Adults, see 262
Battery for Health Improvement, Patients 18–65 who are being evaluated or treated for an injury, see 267
Beck Anxiety Inventory [1993 Edition], Adults and adolescents ages 17 and over, see 271
Beck Depression Inventory—II, Ages 13 and over, see 272
Beck Hopelessness Scale [Revised], Adolescents and adults ages 17 and over, see 273
Beck Scale for Suicide Ideation, Adults and adolescents ages 17 and over, see 274
Behavior Rating Scale, Grades K–8, see 287
Behavioral Academic Self-Esteem, Preschool–grade 8, see 289
Behaviour Problems: A System of Management, Problem behavior children in a classroom situation, see 294
Bell Object Relations and Reality Testing Inventory, Ages 18 and older, see 297
Bem Sex-Role Inventory, High school and college and adults, see 298
BEST Instruments, Adults, see 305
Bi/Polar Inventory of Core Strengths, Managers and adults in organizational settings, see 312
Biographical Inventory Form U, Grades 7–12, see 311
The Blacky Pictures: A Technique for the Exploration of Personality Dynamics, Ages 5 and over, see 317
Borromean Family Index, Adolescents and adults, see 327
Brief Derogatis Psychiatric Rating Scale, Psychiatric and medical patients, see 335
Brief Symptom Inventory , Adults and adolescents age 13 or older, see 337
Butcher Treatment Planning Inventory, Adults in therapy, see 362
The California Child Q-Set, Children, see 365
The California Life Goals Evaluation Schedules, Ages 15 and over, see 371
California Psychological Inventory, Third Edition, Ages 13 and over, see 372
California Q-Sort (Revised Adult Set), Adults, see 373
California Test of Personality, Grades K-3, 4-8, 7-10, 9-14, adults, see 374
Campbell Leadership Index, Leaders, see 381
Canfield Instructional Styles Inventory, Instructors, see 391
Canfield Learning Styles Inventory, Junior High School, High School, College, Adults in business settings, see 392
Career Beliefs Inventory, 13 years and above, see 401
Carey Temperament Scales, Ages 0-1 to 12-0, see 425
Caring Relationship Inventory, Premarital and marital counselees, see 426
Carlson Psychological Survey, Adult and adolescent offenders, see 427
Carroll Depression Scales, 17 years and over, see 429
Change Agent Questionnaire, Adults, see 437
Chapin Social Insight Test, Ages 13 and over, see 438
Character Assessment Scale, Adults, see 439
Characteristics Scale, Grades K-8, see 440
Chart of Initiative and Independence, Mentally handicapped adults, see 441
The Child Abuse Potential Inventory, Form VI, Male and female parents or primary caregivers who are suspected of physical child abuse, see 448
Child and Adolescent Adjustment Profile [Revised], Children and adolescents seen in mental health programs, outpatient and inpatient, health care programs, and schools, see 449

Child Anxiety Scale, Ages 5–12 years, see 450
The Childhood Autism Rating Scale, Ages 2 and over, see 459
Children of Alcoholics Screening Test, School-age children through adults, see 462
Children's Academic Intrinsic Motivation Inventory, Grades 4-8, see 464
Children's Apperception Test [1991 Revision], Ages 3–10, see 466
Children's Apperceptive Story-Telling Test, Ages 6–13, see 467
Children's Depression Inventory, Ages 8-17, see 472
Children's Depression Rating Scale, Revised, Ages 6–12, see 473
Children's Embedded Figures Test, Ages 5-12, see 474
Children's Inventory of Self-Esteem, Ages 5–12, see 475
Children's Personality Questionnaire, 1985 Edition, Ages 8–12, see 477
Children's Problems Checklist, Ages 5-12, see 478
Children's Role Inventory, Adult children of alcoholics, see 479
Christensen Dietary Distress Inventory, Ages 18 and above, see 483
Chronic Pain Battery, Patients ages 18 and over, see 484
Clinical Analysis Questionnaire, Ages 16 and over, see 538
Clyde Mood Scale, Normals and schizophrenics, see 551
Coddington Life Events Scales, Ages 5 and under, ages 6–11, ages 12–19, see 557
College Adjustment Scales, College and university students, see 569
Communication Response Style: Assessment, Adults, see 632
Composite International Diagnostic Interview, Adults, see 642
Comprehensive Assessment of Symptoms and History, Psychiatric patients, see 650
Comprehensive Drinker Profile, Problem drinkers and alcoholics, friends and family of the client, see 652
Comprehensive Personality Profile, Adults, see 654
Comrey Personality Scales, Ages 16 and over, see 672
Comrey Personality Scales—Short Form, High school, college, and adults, see 673
Conflict Management Appraisal, Adults, see 675
Conflict Management Survey, Adults, see 676
Conflict Style Inventory, Adults, see 677
Coolidge Axis II Inventory, Ages 15 and older, see 690
Coopersmith Self-Esteem Inventories, Ages 8-15, 16 and above, see 694
Coping Inventory, Ages 3-16, adults, see 695
Coping Inventory for Stressful Situations, Adults, Adolescents, see 696
Coping Resources Inventory, Middle school-age to adult, see 697
Coping Resources Inventory for Stress, Adults, see 698
Coping Responses Inventory—Adult and Youth, Ages 12–18, 18 and older, see 699
Coping With Health Injuries and Problems, Adults, see 700
Coping with Stress, Adults, see 701
Cornell Word Form 2, Adults, see 709
Cotswold Personality Assessment P.A. 1, Ages 11-16, see 715
Couple's Pre-Counseling Inventory, Revised Edition, 1987, Married or cohabiting couples beginning counseling, see 717
CPF [Second Edition], Ages 16–adult, see 719
Crawford Psychological Adjustment Scale, Psychiatric inpatient, see 721
Creative Behavior Inventory, Grades 1-6, 7-12, see 723
Creativity Tests for Children, Grades 4-6, see 726
The Creatrix Inventory, Members of organizations, see 727
Cross-Cultural Adaptability Inventory, Trainers and professionals who work with culturally diverse and cross-culturally oriented populations, see 737
Crown-Crisp Experiential Index, Normal and psychoneurotic adults, see 739
Culture Shock Inventory [Revised], Managers, see 747
Culture-Free Self-Esteem Inventories, Second Edition, Ages 5-0 through adult, see 746
Current and Past Psychopathology Scales, Ages 15-84, see 748
Curtis Completion Form, Grades 11-16 and adults, see 751
Customer Reaction Survey, Salespeople, see 755
Daily Stress Inventory, Ages 18 and over, see 760
A Dating Scale, Adolescents and adults, see 765
Davidson Trauma Scale, Adults who have been exposed to a serious trauma, see 766
Decision Making Inventory, High school and college, working adults, see 768
Defense Mechanisms Inventory [Revised], Adults and college students, see 770
Defining Issues Test, Grades 9-12 and college and adults, see 771
Depression and Anxiety in Youth Scale, Ages 6-0 to 19-0, see 789
Depressive Experiences Questionnaire, Adolescents and adults (patients and normals), see 790
Derogatis Affects Balance Scale [Revised], Adults, see 791
Derogatis Psychiatric Rating Scale, Adults and adolescents, see 792
Derogatis Sexual Functioning Inventory, Adults, see 793
Derogatis Stress Profile, Adults, see 794
Description of Body Scale, Adolescents and adults, see 795
Devereux Scales of Mental Disorders, Ages 5–12, 13–18, see 818

Diagnostic Interview for Borderline Patients, Patients, see 824
The Diagnostic Screening Batteries, Ages 2 to adults, see 828
Diagnostic Teacher-Rating Scale, Grades 4-12, see 836
The Differential Diagnostic Technique, Ages 6–12 years, ages 12 and over, see 840
Dimensions of Self-Concept, Grades 4-6, Grades 7–12, College, Adult workers, see 844
Diplomacy Test of Empathy, Business and industrial personnel, see 845
Dissociative Experiences Scale, Late adolescent–adult, see 846
Dissociative Features Profile, Children and adolescents, see 847
Diversity Awareness Profile, Employees or managers, see 848
Domestic Violence Inventory, Ages 12–18, adults, see 849
Draw A Person: Screening Procedure for Emotional Disturbance, Ages 6–17, see 852
Draw-A-Person Quality Scale, Ages 16-25, see 851
The Draw-A-Person, Ages 5 and over, see 853
Draw-a-Story: Screening for Depression and Age or Gender Differences [Revised], Ages 5 and over, see 855
Dyadic Adjustment Scale, People who have any committed couple relationship including unmarried cohabitation, see 863
Dynamic Factors Survey, Grades 12-16 and adults, see 865
E. S. Survey, Job applicants and employees, see 871
Early Childhood Inventory–4, Ages 3–6, see 876
Early Coping Inventory, Ages 4-36 months, see 878
Early Memories Procedure, Ages 10 and over with at least a fourth-grade reading level, see 885
Early School Personality Questionnaire, Ages 6-8, see 888
Eating Disorder Inventory-2, Ages 12 and over, see 893
The Edinburgh Questionnaires (1982 Edition), Adults, see 900
Edwards Personal Preference Schedule, College and adults, see 908
Effectiveness Motivation Scale, Ages 3-5, see 910
Ego Function Assessment, Adults, see 912
The Ego Strength Q-Sort Test, Grades 9-16 and adults, see 913
Eidetic Parents Test, Clinical patients and marriage and family counselees, see 914
Eight State Questionnaire, Ages 17 and over, see 915
Embedded Figures Test, Ages 10 and over, see 926
Emo Questionnaire, Clinical and research applications, see 927
Emotional Behavioral Checklist, Ages 16 and over, see 929
Emotional Problems Scales, Ages 14 and over, see 931
Emotions Profile Index, College and adults, see 932
The Empathy Test, Junior high school and over, see 933
Employee Assistance Program Inventory, Adults seeking vocational counseling, see 938
Employee Involvement Survey, Business and industry employees, see 941
Employee Reliability Inventory, Prospective employees, see 944
Endler Multidimensional Anxiety Scales, Ages 15 and over, see 950
Enneagram Personality Portraits Inventory and Profile, Work team members, see 958
Environmental Response Inventory, College and adults, see 963
EPS Sentence Completion Technique, Mildly mentally handicapped ages 14 and over, see 965
Evaluation Disposition Toward the Environment, High school and college, see 980
Evaluation Modality Test, Adults, see 981
Everstine Trauma Response Index, Adults, see 983
Executive Profile Survey, Prospective executives, see 990
Eysenck Personality Inventory, Adults, see 998
Eysenck Personality Questionnaire [Revised], College and general adults including those with lower education levels, Ages 7–15, 16 and over, see 999
The Facial Interpersonal Perception Inventory, Ages 5 and over, see 1002
Family Adjustment Test, Ages 12 and over, see 1005
Family Apperception Test, Ages 6 and over, see 1006
Family Relations Test, Ages 7–12, ages 13–17, adults, married couples, see 1011
Family Relations Test: Children's Version, Ages 3–15, see 1012
Family Relationship Inventory, Young children, adolescents, and adults, see 1013
Famous Sayings, Grades 9-16 and business and industry, see 1017
Fear Survey Schedule, College and adults, see 1021
Feelings, Attitudes, and Behaviors Scale for Children, Ages 6–13, see 1025
Firestone Assessment of Self-Destructive Thoughts, Ages 16–80, see 1035
The FIRO Awareness Scales, Age 13 and over, see 1036
The Forer Structured Sentence Completion Test, Ages 10-18 and adults, see 1049
The Forer Vocational Survey, Adolescents and adults, see 1050
Four Picture Test, Third Revised Edition, Ages 10 and over, see 1053
Friedman Well-Being Scale, Adults, see 1057
The Gardner Children's Projective Battery, Children who are able to respond verbally to questions about their thoughts and perceptions, see 1070
General Health Questionnaire, Adolescents to adults, see 1079

Global Assessment Scale, Psychiatric patients and possible psychiatric patients, see 1093
Gordon Personal Profile—Inventory, Grades 9–12 and college and adults, see 1101
Grid Test of Schizophrenic Thought Disorder, Adults, see 1133
Group Achievement Identification Measure, Grades 5-12, see 1136
Group Cohesiveness: A Study of Group Morale, Adults, see 1137
Group Embedded Figures Test, Older children, adolescents, adults, see 1140
Group Inventory for Finding Creative Talent, Grades K-2, 3-4, 5-6, see 1142
Group Inventory For Finding Interests, Grades 6-12, see 1143
The Group Personality Projective Test, Ages 12 and over, see 1146
Group Shorr Imagery Test, Adults, see 1149
Group Styles Inventory, Group members, see 1150
The Guilford-Zimmerman Temperament Survey, Ages 16 through adult, see 1158
H-T-P: House-Tree-Person Projective Technique, Ages 3 and over, see 1160
Hamilton Depression Inventory, Adults, see 1166
The Hand Test [Revised], Ages 5 and older, see 1169
Happiness Measures, Ages 16 and over, see 1172
Hare P-Scan, Ages 13 and older, see 1173
Hare Psychopathy Checklist–Revised, Prison inmates, see 1174
Hare Psychopathy Checklist: Screening Version, Adults age 18 and over, see 1175
Hassles and Uplifts Scales, Research Edition, Adults, see 1178
Health Attribution Test, High school and college and adult patients, see 1183
High School Personality Questionnaire, Ages 12-18, see 1201
Hilson Adolescent Profile, Ages 10 to 19, see 1207
Hilson Adolescent Profile—Version S, Ages 10–19, see 1208
Hogan Development Survey, Ages 16 and older, see 1211
Hogan Personality Inventory [Revised], College students and adults, see 1212
Holden Psychological Screening Inventory, Ages 14 and older, see 1213
Holtzman Inkblot Technique, Ages 5 and over, see 1214
House-Tree-Person and Draw-A-Person as Measures of Abuse in Children: A Quantitative Scoring System, Ages 7–12, see 1219
How Well Do You Know Your Interests, Grades 9-12, college, adults, see 1222
How Well Do You Know Yourself?, Grades 9-12, college, office and factory workers, see 1223
Human Figure Drawing Test, Clients in psychotherapy, see 1226
Human Loyalty Expressionaire, College and university students, see 1228
Human Relations Inventory, Grades 9-16 and adults, see 1229
The IES Test, Ages 10 and over and latency period girls, see 1239
Illness Behaviour Questionnaire, Third Edition, Pain clinic, psychiatric, and general practice patients, see 1241
Imagery and Disease, Cancer patients, Spinal pain patients, Diabetic patients, see 1242
Impact Message Inventory, Research Edition, College, see 1243
Independent Living Behavior Checklist, Behaviorally impaired adults, see 1245
Indiana Student Scale: A Measure of Self-Esteem, Middle school, high school, and university students, see 1250
Individual Directions Inventory, Adults, see 1251
Individual Style Survey, Ages 10–18, Adults, see 1253
Inferred Self-Concept Scale, Grades 1-6, see 1266
INSIGHT Inventory [Revised], Adults age 21 and over, students age 16–21, see 1273
Internalizing Symptoms Scale for Children, Ages 8–13, see 1288
Interpersonal Adjective Scales, Ages 18 and up, see 1289
Interpersonal Behavior Survey, Grades 9-16 and adults, see 1290
Interpersonal Check List, Adults, see 1291
Interpersonal Communication Inventory, Grade 9 to adult, see 1292
Interpersonal Relations Questionnaire, "White pupils" in Standards 5-7 in South African schools, see 1293
Interpersonal Style Inventory, Ages 14 and over, see 1294
Intra- and Interpersonal Relations Scale, Bantu pupils in Forms IV and V in South African schools, see 1297
Intrex Questionnaires, Psychiatric patients and normals, see 1298
Inventory of Anger Communication, High school and adults, see 1302
An Inventory of Certain Feelings, Applicants for employment, see 1303
Inventory of Positive Thinking Traits, Adults and adolescents, see 1309
Inventory of Suicide Orientation-30, Adolescents, see 1311
Inwald Personality Inventory [Revised], Public safety, security, and law enforcement applicants (post-conditional job offer only), see 1313
Iowa Parent Behavior Inventory, Parents, see 1316
IPAT Depression Scale, Adults, see 1322
It Scale for Children, Ages 5-6, see 1332
Jackson Personality Inventory—Revised, Adolescents and adults, see 1333

Jail Inmate Inventory, Jail inmates with a sixth grade or above reading level, see 1335
Jenkins Activity Survey, Employed adults ages 25-65, see 1338
The Jesness Inventory, Ages 8 and older, see 1341
Job Attitude Analysis, Production and clerical workers, see 1344
Job Attitude Scale, Adults, see 1345
Job Stress Survey, Adults ages 18 and older, see 1354
Joseph Pre-School and Primary Self-Concept Screening Test, Ages 3-6 to 9-11, see 1363
Jung Personality Questionnaire, Standards 7 and 8 and 10 in South African school system, see 1365
Jungian Type Survey: The Gray-Wheelwrights Test (16th Revision), Adults, see 1366
Junior Eysenck Personality Inventory, Ages 7-16, see 1367
Juvenile Automated Substance Abuse Evaluation, Adolescents, see 1372
Kagan Affective Sensitivity Scale, Persons in the helping professions, see 1374
Kahn Test of Symbol Arrangement, Ages 6 and over, see 1376
Katz-Zalk Opinion Questionnaire, Grades 1-6, see 1377
Keegan Type Indicator, Adults, see 1387
Khatena Torrance Creative Perception Inventory, Age 12–adult, see 1396
Kinetic Drawing System for Family and School: A Handbook, Ages 5-20, see 1401
Kirton Adaption-Innovation Inventory [1998 Edition], British and U.S. adults and teenagers over age 14, see 1404
Kohlberg's Moral Judgment Interview, Ages 10 and over, see 1408
Kolbe Conative Index, Adults, Job applicants, Supervisors, Youth (5th grade reading level), Students, see 1411
Kundu Introversion Extroversion Inventory, Adults, see 1415
Kundu Neurotic Personality Inventory, Adults, see 1416
La Monica Empathy Profile, Managers/helpers/teachers in industry, education, and health care, see 1417
The Lake St. Clair Incident, Adults, see 1419
The Leadership Ability Evaluation, Grades 9-16 and adults, see 1439
Leadership and Self-Development Scale, College, see 1440
Leadership Competency Inventory, Adults, see 1442
Leadership Effectiveness Analysis, Managers, supervisors, individual contributors at all levels, see 1443
Leadership Opinion Questionnaire, Supervisors and prospective supervisors, see 1444
Leadership Practices Inventory [Management Research Associates], Supervisors, see 1447
The Leadership Q-Sort Test (A Test of Leadership Values), Adults, see 1449
The Learning Channel Preference Checklist, Grades 5-13, see 1458
Learning Preference Inventory, Elementary through adult students, see 1464
Learning Process Questionnaire, Secondary students, see 1466
Learning Style Identification Scale, Grades 1-8, see 1468
Learning Style Profile, Grades 6-12, see 1472
Learning Styles Inventory [Creative Learning Press, Inc.], Grades 4-12 and teachers, see 1474
Learning-Style Inventory [McBer and Company], Grade 6 through adults, see 1469
Leeds Scales for the Self-Assessment of Anxiety and Depression, Psychiatric patients, see 1481
Leisure Interest Inventory, College students, see 1482
Levine-Pilowsky [Depression] Questionnaire, Adults, see 1488
Lewis Counseling Inventory, Adolescents in school, see 1489
Life Roles Inventory, Junior high students–adults, see 1493
Life Space Analysis Profile, Adults, see 1494
Life Styles Inventory, Adults, see 1498
Longitudinal Interval Follow-up Evaluation, 2nd Edition, Individuals who have received treatment for depression, see 1517
Looking at MySELF, Grades 3-6, Grades 7-12, see 1518
Maferr Inventory of Feminine Values, Junior and senior high school, college and adults, see 1535
Maferr Inventory of Masculine Values, Junior and senior high school, college and adults, see 1536
Make A Picture Story, Age 6 and over, see 1540
Malingering Probability Scale, Ages 17 and over, see 1543
Management Effectiveness Analysis, Managers and supervisors at all levels, see 1549
Management Style Inventory [Training House, Inc.], Industry, see 1563
Managerial Philosophies Scale, Managers, see 1574
Manchester Personality Questionnaire, Adults, see 1576
The Manson Evaluation, Revised Edition, Adults, see 1577
A Marital Communication Inventory, Married couples, see 1580
Marital Satisfaction Inventory—Revised, Couples who are married or living together, see 1582
Martin S-D Inventory, Clients and patients, see 1585
Martinek-Zaichkowsky Self-Concept Scale for Children, Grades 1-8, see 1586
Maryland Addictions Questionnaire, Ages 17 and older, see 1587
Maryland Parent Attitude Survey, Parents, see 1589
Maslach Burnout Inventory, Members of the helping professions, including educators and human service professionals, see 1590

Matching Familiar Figures Test, Ages 5-12, 13 and over, see 1592
Meadow-Kendall Social-Emotional Assessment Inventory for Deaf and Hearing Students, Ages 3-6, 7-21, see 1618
Means-Ends Problem-Solving Procedure, Adults, see 1619
Measure of Achieving Tendency, Ages 15 and older, see 1620
Measure of Child Stimulus Screening and Arousability, Ages 3 months to 7 years, see 1621
Measure of Individual Differences in Dominance-Submissiveness, Ages 15 and older, see 1622
The Measurement of Moral Judgment, Ages 10 and over, see 1625
Measures in Post Traumatic Stress Disorder: A Practitioner's Guide, Adults, see 1626
Measures of Affiliative Tendency and Sensitivity to Rejection, Ages 15 and older, see 1627
Measures of Individual Differences in Temperament, Ages 15 and older, see 1628
Measures of Pleasure-, Arousal-, and Dominance-Inducing Qualities of Parental Attitudes, Parents of children ages 3 months to 7 years, see 1630
Measures of Psychosocial Development, Ages 13 and over, see 1631
Meeker Behavioral Correlates, Industry, see 1641
Memory and Behavior Problems Checklist and The Burden Interview, Dementia patients and their families, Caregivers of elderly and disabled persons, see 1643
Memory-For-Designs Test, Ages 8.5 and over, see 1645
Menstrual Distress Questionnaire, Women who experience strong to severe premenstrual or menstrual distress, see 1647
Mental Status Checklist for Adolescents, Ages 13-17, see 1648
Mental Status Checklist for Children, Ages 5-12, see 1650
The Meta Contrast Technique, 4th Edition, Children and adults, see 1654
Meta-Motivation Inventory, Managers and persons in leadership positions, see 1655
Meyer-Kendall Assessment Survey, Business employees and job applicants, see 1660
Miller Common Sense Scale, Ages 15 to adult, see 1674
Miller Depression Scale, Ages 15 years and over, see 1675
Miller Emotional Maturity Scale, Adults with reading levels at 7th grade or above, see 1676
Miller Getting Along With People Scale, Ages 15 to adult, see 1677
Miller Happiness Scale, Grade 7 reading level or higher, see 1678
Miller Love Scale, Ages 16 to adult, see 1679
Miller Motivation Scale, Individuals who have a grade seven reading level or greater, see 1681
Miller Psychological Independence Scale, High school students and athletes, see 1682
Miller Self-Concept Scale, Individuals with a seventh-grade or higher reading level, see 1683
Miller Stress Scale, Individuals with reading level at or above the 7th grade, see 1684
Millon Adolescent Clinical Inventory, Ages 13-19, see 1685
Millon Clinical Multiaxial Inventory—III [Second Edition], "Adults [18+] who are seeking [or in] mental health treatment and who have eighth-grade reading skills," see 1687
Millon Index of Personality Styles, Adults, see 1688
Miner Sentence Completion Scale, Workers and prospective workers in management, professional, and entrepreneurial or task-oriented occupations, see 1689
Minnesota Multiphasic Personality Inventory-2, Ages 18 and over, see 1697
Minnesota Multiphasic Personality Inventory-Adolescent, Ages 14-18, see 1698
Minnesota Percepto-Diagnostic Test, Revised Edition, Ages 5-16 and adults, see 1699
The Missouri Children's Picture Series Ages 5-16, see 1706
The Mooney Problem Check Lists, 1950 Revision, Junior high–adults, see 1716
Motivation Analysis Test, High school seniors and adults, see 1721
Motivational Patterns Inventory, Organizational members, see 1723
Motives, Values, Preferences Inventory, Adults, see 1724
The Multidimensional Addictions and Personality Profile, Adolescents and adults experiencing substance abuse and mental health disorders, see 1729
Multidimensional Anxiety Scale for Children, Ages 8–19, see 1730
Multidimensional Assessment and Planning Form, Counselees, see 1732
Multidimensional Self Concept Scale, Grades 5-12, see 1734
The Multidimensional Self-Esteem Inventory, College students, see 1735
Multimodal Life History Questionnaire, Adult counseling clients, see 1742
Multiple Affect Adjective Check List, Revised, Ages 20-79, see 1745
Multiscore Depression Inventory, Ages 13 through adult, see 1748
Multiscore Depression Inventory for Children, Ages 8–17, see 1749
Murphy-Meisgeier Type Indicator for Children, Ages 7–12, see 1750
Myers-Briggs Type Indicator, Form M, Ages 14 and older, see 1755

NASA Moon Survival Task, Individuals who work, or anticipate working, in a group setting, see 1757
NEEDS Survey, Adults, see 1766
NEO-4, Ages 18 and older, see 1769
The Neuroticism Scale Questionnaire, Ages 13 and over, see 1779
North American Depression Inventories for Children and Adults, Grades 2-9, Ages 15 and over, see 1803
NPF [Second Edition], Ages 16-adult, see 1805
Oaster Stressors Scales, Adults, see 1809
The Object Relations Technique, Counselees ages 11 and over, see 1811
Observation of Type Preference, Adults, see 1814
Observational Emotional Inventory—Revised, Students and adults, see 1815
Occupational Personality Questionnaire, Business and industry, see 1822
Occupational Stress Indicator, Employees, see 1824
Occupational Stress Inventory—Revised Edition, Age 18 years and over, see 1825
Occupational Type Profile, Adults, see 1828
Oetting's Computer Anxiety Scale, Entering college freshmen, see 1831
Offer Self-Image Questionnaire for Adolescents, Revised, Ages 13-18, see 1832
Oliver Organization Description Questionnaire, Adults, see 1843
Opinions Toward Adolescents, College and adults, see 1845
Pain Apperception Test, Adults, see 1869
Pain Patient Profile, Pain patients aged 17–76, see 1871
Parent As A Teacher Inventory [Revised], Mothers and fathers of children ages 3–9, see 1878
Parent Awareness Skills Survey, Parents involved in custody decisions, see 1879
A Parent-Adolescent Communication Inventory, Parents and adolescents, see 1876
Parent-Child Relationship Inventory, Parents of 3–15-year-old children, see 1883
Parenting Stress Index, Third Edition, Parents of children 12 years old or younger, see 1889
Partner Relationship Inventory (Research Edition), Married couples, see 1895
Paulhus Deception Scales: Balanced Inventory of Desirable Responding, Agcs 16 and older, see 1899
The People Process, Adults, see 1914
Perception of Ability Scale for Students, Grades 3-6, see 1916
Perception-Of-Relationships-Test, Children age 3 and over, see 1917
Personal Adjustment and Role Skills Scale [Revised], Mental health patients and clinic clients, see 1925
Personal Audit, Individuals in a variety of professional occupations, see 1928
Personal Directions, Adults, see 1929
Personal Experience Inventory, Ages 12-18, see 1931
Personal History Checklist for Adults, Adult clients of mental health services, see 1934
A Personal Inventory, Ages 16 and over, see 1935
Personal Inventory of Needs, Employees, see 1936
Personal Orientation Dimensions, High school, college, and adults, see 1938
Personal Orientation Inventory, High school, college, and adults, see 1939
The Personal Preference Scale, Ages 15 and over, see 1940
Personal Problems Checklist—Adult, Adults, see 1941
Personal Problems Checklist for Adolescents, Adolescents, see 1942
Personal Questionnaire Rapid Scaling Technique, Psychiatric patients, see 1944
Personal Reaction Index, Employees, see 1945
Personal Resource Questionnaire, Ages 18-80, see 1947
Personal Skills Map, Ages 13–19, see 1948
Personal Stress Assessment Inventory, Adults, see 1949
Personal Style Assessment, Adults, see 1950
Personal Style Assessment, Jung-Parry Form, Adults, see 1951
Personal Style Indicator, Adults, see 1952
Personal Style Inventory, Adults, see 1953
Personal Styles Inventory [PSI-120] [1999 Revision], Adults, see 1954
Personal Values Inventory [Personal Strengths Publishing], Adolescents and adults with sixth grade or above reading levels, see 1956
Personal Values Questionnaire, Adults, see 1957
Personality Adjective Check List, Ages 16-adult, see 1958
Personality Assessment Inventory, Ages 18-adult, see 1959
Personality Assessment Screener, Ages 18 and older, see 1960
Personality Disorder Interview-IV: A Semistructured Interview for the Assessment of Personality Disorders, Ages 18 and older, see 1961
Personality Inventory for Children, Revised Format, Ages 3-16, see 1962
Personality Inventory for Youth, Ages 9–18, see 1963
Personality Rating Scale, Grades 4-12, see 1964
Personality Research Form, 3rd Edition, Grade 6-college, adults, see 1965
PERSONALYSIS®, Leaders, employees, families, individuals, see 1966
Personnel Selection Inventory, Job applicants, see 1972
Phase II Profile Integrity Status Inventory and ADdendum, Job applicants and employees in staff positions, see 1976
PHSF Relations Questionnaire, Standards 6-10 in South African school system, college, and adults, see 1983
Pictographic Self Rating Scale, High school and college, see 1985
Picture Identification Test, High school and college, see 1988

Piers-Harris Children's Self-Concept Scale (The Way I Feel About Myself), Grades 4-12, see 1991
Politte Sentence Completion Test, Grades 1-8, 7-12, and adults functioning at elementary school level, see 2004
Polyfactorial Study of Personality, Adults, see 2006
Portrait of Overdone Strengths, Adults, see 2013
Portrait of Personal Strengths, Adults, see 2014
Positive and Negative Syndrome Scale, Psychiatric patients, see 2017
Posttraumatic Stress Diagnostic Scale, Ages 18–65, see 2018
Preschool Embedded Figures Test, Ages 2 1/2 to 5 years, see 2042
Preschool Self-Concept Picture Test, Ages 4-5, see 2048
Present State Examination, Adult psychiatric patients, see 2050
Problem Experiences Checklist, Adolescents, adults, see 2063
The Problem Solving Inventory, Age 16 and above, see 2065
Problem-Solving Decision-Making Style Inventory, High school and college and adults in organizational settings, see 2064
Profile of Adaptation to Life, Adults seen in mental health and self-development programs, see 2074
Profile of Mood States, College and psychiatric outpatients, see 2076
Profile of Mood States, Bi-Polar Form, Ages 18–adult, see 2077
Profile of Nonverbal Sensitivity, Grades 3-16 and adults, see 2078
A Projective Index of Body Awareness, Mental patients, see 2099
The Psychap Inventory, Adolescents and adults, see 2106
Psychiatric Diagnostic Interview—Revised, Ages 18 and older, see 2107
Psychiatric Evaluation Form, Psychiatric patients and nonpatients, see 2108
The Psychiatric Status Schedules: Subject Form, Second Edition, Psychiatric patients and nonpatients, see 2109
Psychologic and Neuropsychiatric Assessment Manual, Children and adults, see 2114
Psychological Screening Inventory, Ages 16 and over, see 2115
Psychosocial Adjustment to Illness Scale, Medical patients or their immediate relatives, see 2117
Psychotherapy Outcome Kit (Including Quality of Emotional Life Self-Report), Age 15 and under, Age 16 and older, see 2119
Psychotic Inpatient Profile, Mental patients, see 2120
The Purpose in Life Test, Adults, see 2126
The Q-Tags Test of Personality, Ages 6 and over, see 2128
Quality of Life Enjoyment and Satisfaction Questionnaire, Adults with mental or medical disorders, see 2130
Quality of Life Questionnaire, Ages 18 and over, see 2132
Questionnaire Measure of Trait Arousability (Or Its Converse, Stimulus Screening), Ages 15 and older, see 2135
Racial Attitude Test, Adults, see 2148
Rapid Personality Questionnaire, Ages 16 years and over, see 2160
Rating of Behavior Scale, Children and adolescents and adults, see 2161
Reid Report, Job applicants, see 2198
Reiss-Epstein-Gursky Anxiety Sensitivity Index, Adults, see 2199
A Religion Scale, Adolescents and adults, see 2200
Revised Children's Manifest Anxiety Scale, Ages 6-19, see 2214
Revised Hamilton Rating Scale for Depression, Depressed individuals, see 2216
Revised NEO Personality Inventory, Ages 17 and older, see 2218
Reynolds Adolescent Depression Scale, Grades 7-12, see 2230
Reynolds Child Depression Scale, Grades 3-6, see 2231
Reynolds Depression Screening Inventory, Ages 18–89, see 2232
Risk Taking Inventory & Guide, Managers, see 2238
Risk-Taking-Attitude-Values Inventory, Ages 3 and over, see 2237
Roberts Apperception Test for Children [with new Interpretive Handbook], Ages 6–15, see 2242
Rokeach Value Survey, Ages 11 and over, see 2246
Rorschach, Ages 5 and over, see 2247
A Rosenzweig Picture-Frustration Study, Ages 4-13, 12-18, 18 and over, see 2248
Rotter Incomplete Sentences Blank, Second Edition, College students, adults, high-school students, see 2258
Rust Inventory of Schizotypal Cognitions, Age 18 and over, see 2260
The Ruth Fry Symbolic Profile, Ages 14 and over, see 2262
S-D Proneness Checklist, Depressed or suicidal clients, see 2263
Sales Personality Questionnaire, Sales applicants, see 2274
Sales Transaction Audit, Salespeople, see 2280
The Salience Inventory, Upper elementary through adult, see 2282
SAQ-Adult Probation III, Adult offenders, see 2285
SAQS Chicago Q Sort, College and adults, see 2286
Scale for Assessing Emotional Disturbance, Students ages 5-0 to 18-11, see 2287
Scale for the Assessment of Negative Symptoms, Psychiatric inpatients and outpatients of all ages, see 2288

Scale for the Assessment of Positive Symptoms, Psychiatric inpatients and outpatients of all ages, see 2289
Scale of Feelings and Behavior of Love: Revised, College and adults, see 2291
Scales for Rating the Behavioral Characteristics of Superior Students, Population unspecified, developed from research with students in grades 4-6, see 2295
Scenotest: A Practical Technique for Understanding Unconscious The Problems and Personality Structure, Children and adolescents, see 2303
Schedule for Affective Disorders and Schizophrenia, Third Edition, Adults, see 2305
Schedule for Nonadaptive and Adaptive Personality, Ages 18 and older, see 2306
A Schedule of Adaptive Mechanisms in CAT Responses, Children, see 2307
School Attitude Measure, Second Edition, Grades 1-2, 3-4, 5-6, 7-8, 9-12, see 2313
The School Motivation Analysis Test, Ages 12-17, see 2318
SCL-90-Analogue, Adults and adolescents, see 2326
Search Institute Profiles of Student Life: Attitudes and Behaviors, Grades 6–12, see 2336
The Seeking of Noetic Goals Test, Adolescents and adults, see 2343
Self Concept Scale, Secondary Level, Grades 7-12, see 2357
Self Observation Scales, Grades K-3, 4-6, 7-9, 10-12, see 2365
Self Perception Inventory [Psychologists and Educators, Inc.], Ages 12 and over, see 2367
Self Profile Q-Sort, Grades 2-8, see 2370
Self Worth Inventory, Adults, see 2371
Self-Actualization Test, Managers and students of administration, see 2349
Self-Administered Dependency Questionnaire, Ages 8-15, see 2350
Self-Awareness Profile, Industry, see 2353
Self-Concept Adjective Checklist, Grades K-8, see 2354
The Self-Concept and Motivation Inventory: What Face Would You Wear?, Age 4-kindergarten, grades 1-3, 3-6, 7-12, see 2355
Self-Concept as a Learner Scale, Grades 4-12, see 2356
Self-Description Questionnaire—I, II, III, Ages 5–12, 13–17, 16–Adult, see 2358
Self-Directed Learning Readiness Scale, Age 15 and over, see 2359
Self-Esteem Index, Ages 7-0 to 18-11, see 2361
The Self-Esteem Inventory, Adolescents and adults, see 2362
Self-Esteem Questionnaire, Ages 9 and over, see 2363
Self-Perception Inventory: Nursing Forms, Student nurses and professional staff, see 2366
Self-Perception Inventory [SOARES Associates], Grades 1–12, grades 9–12 and adults, student teachers, nurses, see 2368
Self-Perception Profile for College Students, College students, see 2369
The Senior Apperception Technique [1985 Revision], Ages 65 and over, see 2372
Sentence Completion Series, Adolescents and adults, see 2379
Sentence Completion Test, High school and college, see 2380
Sentence Completion Tests, Adults, adolescents, and children, see 2381
The Severity and Acuity of Psychiatric Illness Scales—Adult Version, Adults, see 2388
Sexual Adjustment Inventory, People accused or convicted of sexual offenses, see 2393
The Sexual Communication Inventory, Premarital and marital counselees, see 2394
Sexuality Experience Scales, Adults, see 2396
Shapiro Control Inventory, Ages 14–88, see 2399
Shorr Imagery Test, College students and adults, see 2404
Short Imaginal Processes Inventory, Adolescents and adults, see 2407
The Singer-Loomis Type Deployment Inventory, High school and college and adults, see 2411
SIPOAS: Styles in Perception of Affect Scale, Age 18 to adult, see 2412
Situational Attitude Scale, College and adults, see 2413
Situational Preference Inventory, Grades 9-16 and adults, see 2416
Sixteen Personality Factor Questionnaire, Fifth Edition, Ages 16 and over, see 2417
16PF® Human Resource Development Report, Managerial candidates, see 2418
Social Adjustment Scale—Self Report, Adults, see 2442
Social Phobia and Anxiety Inventory, Ages 14 and older, see 2448
Social Reticence Scale, High school and college and adults, see 2449
Social Skills Inventory, Research Edition, Ages 14 and over reading at or above the eighth grade level, see 2451
Social Styles Analysis, Adults, see 2453
Social-Emotional Dimension Scale, Ages 5.5-18.5, see 2447
Socio-Sexual Knowledge & Attitudes Test, Developmentally disabled ages 18-42 and non-retarded persons of all ages, see 2454
Somatic Inkblot Series, Ages 3 and over, see 2457
Spiritual Well-Being Scale, Adults, see 2474
Sports Emotion Test, High school through adult athletes, see 2475
The Stanton Survey and the Stanton Survey Phase II, Applicants for employment, see 2491
State Trait-Depression Adjective Check Lists, Ages 14 and older, see 2499
State-Trait Anger Expression Inventory [1996 Edition], Ages 13 and up, see 2496

State-Trait Anxiety Inventory, Grades 9-16 and adults, see 2497
State-Trait Anxiety Inventory for Children, Grades 4-6, see 2498
Stokes/Gordon Stress Scale, Healthy individuals over age 65, see 2505
Strength Deployment Inventory, Adults, see 2507
Stress Audit, Adults, see 2508
Stress Index for Parents of Adolescents, Parents of 11–19-year-olds, see 2510
Stress Management Questionnaire [Revised], Adults and adolescents, see 2512
Stress Resiliency Profile, Employees, see 2513
Stress Response Scale, Ages 5-14, see 2514
Structured Clinical Interview for DSM-IV Axis I Disorders: Clinician Version, Psychiatric or general medical patients ages 18 or older, see 2519
Structured Clinical Interview for DSM-IV Axis II Personality Disorders, Adults receiving psychiatric or general medical care, see 2520
Structured Interview for Disorders of Extreme Stress & Traumatic Antecedents Questionnaire—Self Report, Adults potentially affected with Post Traumatic Stress Disorder, see 2521
Structured Interview of Reported Symptoms, Ages 18 and over, see 2522
Student Adaptation to College Questionnaire, College freshmen, see 2525
Student Adjustment Inventory, Upper elementary, junior high, senior high, and beginning college students, see 2526
Student Developmental Task and Lifestyle Inventory, College students ages 17-24, see 2527
Student Referral Checklist, Grades K-6, 7-12, see 2533
Student Self-Concept Scale, Grades 3–12, see 2535
Student Styles Questionnaire, Ages 8–13, see 2536
Student Talent and Risk Profile, Grades 5-12, see 2537
Study of Values: British Edition, 1965, ollege and adults, see 2539
Study Process Questionnaire, College students, see 2540
Style of Learning and Thinking, Grades K-5, 6-12, see 2545
Substance Abuse Life Circumstance Evaluation, Adults, see 2550
Substance Abuse Subtle Screening Inventory, Ages 12-18, adults, see 2553
Suicidal Ideation Questionnaire, Grades 7-9, 10-12, see 2557
Suicide Intervention Response Inventory [Revised], Mental health paraprofessionals, see 2558
Suicide Probability Scale, Ages 14 and over, see 2559
SUP'R Star Profiles, Adults, see 2577
Supervisory Human Relations, Supervisors and potential supervisors, see 2564
Supervisory Union Relations, Supervisors and potential supervisors, see 2576
Survey of Interpersonal Values, Individuals in a variety of occupations and job levels, see 2581
Survey of Management Perception, Supervisors and executives, see 2582
Survey of Organizational Climate, Employees, see 2584
Survey of Organizational Culture, Employees of organizations, see 2585
Survey of Personal Values, Individuals in a variety of occupations, high school and college students, see 2588
Survey of Work Values, Revised, Form U, Employees, see 2593
Symbol Elaboration Test, Ages 6 and over, see 2600
Symptom Assessment-45 Questionnaire, Ages 13 and over, reading at the 6th grade level or higher, see 2602
Symptom Checklist-90-Revised, Adults and adolescents age 13 and older, see 2603
Symptom Scale—77, Adolescents and adults, see 2604
T. A. Survey, Employees, see 2610
Tasks of Emotional Development Test, Ages 6-11, 12-18, see 2614
TAT Analysis Sheet, Ages 4 and over, see 2615
TAV Selection System, Adults, see 2616
Taylor-Johnson Temperament Analysis [1992 Edition], Ages 13 and up, see 2618
A Teacher Attitude Inventory: Identifying Teacher Positions in Relation to Educational Issues and Decisions, Teachers, see 2621
Team Development Survey, Work team members, see 2632
Team-Development Inventory, Work-team members, see 2631
TEMAS (Tell-Me-A-Story), Ages 5-18, see 2647
Temperament Comparator, Managers, supervisors, salespeople, and other higher-level professionals., see 2648
Temperament Inventory, College and adults, see 2649
Tennessee Self-Concept Scale, Second Edition, Ages 7 to 90, see 2652
Test Anxiety Profile, Grades 9–12 and college, see 2655
Test Attitude Inventory, High school and college students, see 2656
Test for Creative Thinking—Drawing Production, Age 4–adult, see 2659
Test of Basic Assumptions, Adults, see 2675
Test of Social Insight, Grades 6-12, 13-16 and adults, see 2716
Test of Work Competency and Stability, Ages 21 and over, see 2728
Thematic Apperception Test, Ages 4 and over, see 2749
Themes Concerning Blacks, Blacks ages 4 and over, see 2750
Therapy Attitude Inventory, Parents, see 2752
Thomas-Kilmann Conflict Mode Instrument, Managers, see 2756

Thurstone Temperament Schedule, Variety of occupations from entry-level to management, see 2757
Tiffany Control Scales, Adolescents and adults, see 2759
Time Perception Inventory, Students in time management courses, see 2761
Time Problems Inventory, Management and administrative personnel, see 2762
TMJ Scale, TM [temporomandibular] dental patients ages 13 and over, see 2766
Trait Evaluation Index, College and adults, see 2776
The Trait Pleasure-Displeasure Scale, Ages 15 and older, see 2777
Trauma Symptom Inventory, Ages 18 and older, see 2782
Treatment Intervention Inventory, Ages 12–18; Adult counseling clients, see 2783
Triadal Equated Personality Inventory, Adult males, see 2784
Understanding and Managing Stress, Adults, see 2789
Uses Test, Ages 11-13, see 2800
Validity Indicator Profile, Ages 18–69, see 2802
Values Inventory, Managers and students of management, see 2803
Values Preference Indicator , Adults, see 2804
The Values Scale, Second Edition, Junior high school to adult, see 2805
Victoria Symptom Validity Test, Ages 18 and over, see 2811
A Violence Scale, Adolescents and adults, see 2815
The Vocational Apperception Test: Advanced Form, College, see 2825
Wahler Physical Symptoms Inventory, Adults, see 2839
Waksman Social Skills Rating Scale, Grades K-12, see 2841
Walker Problem Behavior Identification Checklist, Preschool to grade 6, see 2848
Ways of Coping Questionnaire, Research Edition, Adults, see 2858
Weinberg Depression Scale for Children and Adolescents, Children and adolescents with at least a 4th grade reading level, see 2865
Welsh Figure Preference Test, Ages 6 and over, see 2869
The Western Personality Inventory, Adults, see 2874
Wharton Attitude Survey, Grades 7-12, see 2875
What Do You Say?, Employees, see 2876
Whitaker Index of Schizophrenic Thinking, Mental patients, see 2878
Wide Range Interest-Opinion Test, Ages 5 and over, see 2882
Williams Awareness Sentence Completion, Ages 15 and over, see 2887
Work Information Inventory, Employee groups in industry, see 2919
Work Motivation Inventory: A Test of Adult Work Motivation, Ages 16-Adult, see 2922
Work Personality Profile, Vocational rehabilitation clients, see 2924

READING

ACER Applied Reading Test, Apprentices, trainees, technical and trade personnel, see 24
Achievement Tests: Grades 1-8, Grades 1–8, see 39
Assessing Reading Difficulties: A Diagnostic and Remedial Approach, Ages 5 and over, see 189
Bader Reading and Language Inventory, Children and adolescents and adults, see 237
Basic Reading Inventory, Seventh Edition, Pre-primer through grade 12, grades 3–12, see 257
Bench Mark Measures, Ungraded, see 299
The Boder Test of Reading-Spelling Patterns, Grades K–12 and adult, see 322
Buffalo Reading Test for Speed and Comprehension, Grades 9–16, see 354
Burns/Roe Informal Reading Inventory: Preprimer to Twelfth Grade, Fifth Edition, Beginning readers–grade 12, see 357
Burt Word Reading Test, New Zealand Revision, Ages 6-0 to 12-11 years, see 358
California Diagnostic Reading Tests, Grades 1.1-12, see 370
Classroom Reading Inventory, Seventh Edition, Grades 2-8, high school and adults, see 496
Cloze Reading Tests 1-3, Second Edition, Ages 8-0 to 10-6, 8-5 to 11-10, 9-5 to 12-6, see 550
Clymer-Barrett Readiness Test, Revised Edition, Grades K-1, see 552
Comprehensive Assessment of Reading Strategies, Grades 3–8, see 647
Content Inventories: English, Social Studies, Science, Grades 4-12, see 683
Crane Oral Dominance Test: Spanish/English, Ages 4-8, see 720
CRS Placement/Diagnostic Test, Grades Preprimer-2, see 740
Cutrona Reading Inventory, Grades K-6, 7-12, and adult, see 758
Decoding Skills Test, Grades 1.0-5.8+, see 769
Degrees of Reading Power [Revised], Grades 1–12, see 773
Degrees of Word Meaning, Grades 3–8+, see 774
Delaware County Silent Reading Test, Second Edition, Grades 1.5, 2, 2.5, 3, 3.5, 4, 5, 6, 7, 8, see 775

Diagnostic Assessments of Reading, Grades 1–12, see 823
Diagnostic Reading Record, Second Edition, Ages 4 to adult, see 826
Diagnostic Reading Scales, Grades 1-7 and poor readers in Grades 8-12, see 827
Diagnostic Screening Test: Reading, Third Edition, Grades 1-12, see 832
Durrell Analysis of Reading Difficulty, Third Edition, Grades 1-6, see 861
Dyslexia Screening Instrument, Grades 1–12, ages 6–21, see 868
The Dyslexia Screening Survey, Children in primary grades, see 869
Edinburgh Reading Tests, Ages 7-0 to 9-0, 8-6 to 10-6, 10-0 to 12-6, 12-0 to 16-0, see 901
Ekwall/Shanker Reading Inventory—Third Edition, Grades 1–9, see 917
Formal Reading Inventory, Grades 1-12, see 1051
Gates-MacGinitie Reading Tests, 2nd Canadian Edition, Grades K.7–12, see 1071
Gates-MacGinitie Reading Tests, Third Edition, Grades K.6-12, see 1072
Gates-McKillop-Horowitz Reading Diagnostic Test, Second Edition, Grades 1-6, see 1073
Gilmore Oral Reading Test, Grades 1-8, see 1092
Gray Oral Reading Tests—Diagnostic, Ages 5-6 to 12-11, see 1130
Gray Oral Reading Tests, Third Edition, Ages 7-0 to 18-11, see 1131
Group Diagnostic Reading Aptitude and Achievement Tests, Grades 3-9, see 1138
Group Diagnostic Reading Aptitude and Achievement Tests, Intermediate Form, Grades 3–9, see 1139
Group Reading Test, Fourth Edition, Ages 6:4 to 8:11 and less able children 8:0 to 11:11, see 1148
High School Reading Test: National Achievement Tests, Grades 7-12, see 1203
Industrial Reading Test, Grade 9 and over vocational students and applicants or trainees in technical or vocational training programs, see 1256
The Infant Reading Tests, Ages 4-7 to 7, see 1261
Informal Reading Comprehension Placement Test [Revised], Grades 1–8 for typical learners and grades 8–12 remedially; adult education students, see 1269
Initial Placement Inventory, Grades 1-8, see 1272
Jansky Screening Index, Kindergarten, see 1337
Johnston Informal Reading Inventory, Grades 7-12, see 1358
The Laurita-Trembley Diagnostic Word Processing Test, Grades 1.9-4.9, 5.0-college, see 1428
The Lincoln-Oseretsky Motor Development Scale, Ages 6-14, see 1502
Linguistic Awareness in Reading Readiness, Grades K-1, see 1504
Living in the Reader's World: Locator Test, Adults at reading grade levels 2.0-6.0, see 1510
The Lollipop Test: A Diagnostic Screening Test of School Readiness—Revised, First grade entrants, see 1515
London Reading Test, Ages 10-7 to 12-4, see 1516
The Macmillan Diagnostic Reading Pack, Reading ages 5-6, 6-7, 7-8, 8-9, see 1529
Macmillan Graded Word Reading Test, Ages 6-3 to 13-3, see 1530
Macmillan Group Reading Test, Ages 6-3 to 13-3, see 1531
Macmillan Reader Placement Test, Grades 1 and over, see 1532
Maryland/Baltimore County Design for Adult Basic Education, Adult nonreaders, see 1588
McCall-Crabbs Standard Test Lessons in Reading, Reading level grades 3-8, see 1609
McCarthy Individualized Diagnostic Reading Inventory, Revised Edition, Grades K-12, see 1611
MKM Monocular and Binocular Reading Test, Grades 1-2, 3 and over, see 1709
Neale Analysis of Reading Ability, Revised British Edition, Ages 6-13, see 1765
The Nelson Reading Skills Test, Forms 3 and 4, Grades 3–9, see 1768
Nelson-Denny Reading Test, Forms G and H, Grades 9–16 and adult, see 1767
New Macmillan Reading Analysis, Ages 6-11, see 1781
NewGAP, Grades 2-5, see 1784
O'Brien Vocabulary Placement Test, Grades 1–6, see 1812
Phonetic Reading Chain Oral Reading Diagnostic Decoding Test, Students having difficulties in phonics, see 1979
Phonovisual Diagnostic Tests, [1975 Revision], Grades 3-12, see 1981
Primary Reading Test, Ages 6-10, Ages 7-12, see 2058
Progressive Achievement Tests in Reading: Reading Comprehension and Reading Vocabulary Tests, Years 3-9 in Australian school system, see 2092
Progressive Achievement Tests of Reading [Revised], Standards 2-4, Forms 1-2, Forms 3-4 in New Zealand schools (Ages 8-14), see 2094
Ramsay Corporation Job Skills—Health Care Reading Test, Adults, see 2150
Ramsay Corporation Job Skills—Office Reading Test, Adults, see 2154
Ramsay Corporation Job Skills—Supervisory Reading Test, Adults, see 2157
RBH Test of Reading Comprehension, Business and industry, see 2170
Reading Ability Series, Ages 7-0 to 8-11, 8-0 to 9-11, 9-0 to 10-11, 10-0 to 11-11, 11-0 to 12-11, 12-0 to 13-11, see 2171

Reading Comprehension Battery for Aphasia, Second Edition, Pre-adolescent to geriatric aphasic people, see 2172
Reading Comprehension Test DE, Ages 10-0 to 12-10, see 2173
Reading Efficiency Tests, Grades 7-16 and adults, see 2174
Reading Evaluation Adult Diagnosis, Fifth Edition, Illiterate adult students, see 2175
Reading Evaluation and Diagnostic Screen, Ages 4-15, see 2176
Reading Index, Individuals in a variety of occupations and rehabilitation environments, see 2178
Reading Progress Tests, Ages 5-0 to 12-2, see 2179
Reading Skills Diagnostic Test III, Level 4, Grades 2.5-12, see 2180
Reading Style Inventory, Grades 1-12, see 2181
Reading Test AD, Ages 8-0 to 10-7, see 2182
Reading Test (Comprehension and Speed): Municipal Tests: National Achievement Tests, Grades 3-6, 6-8, see 2183
Reading Test SR-A and SR-B, Ages 7-6 to 11-11, see 2184
Reading Tests A and BD, 1, 2-4 years primary school, see 2185
Reading Tests EH 1-2, Ages 11-0 to 15-1, see 2186
Reading Vocabulary Test, Ages 7-12, see 2187
Reversal Test, Entrants to grade 1, see 2209
The Reversals Frequency Test, Ages 5-0 to 15-11, see 2210
Revised Pre-Reading Screening Procedures, First grade entrants, see 2219
Revised PSB—Reading Comprehension Examination, Secondary and postsecondary students applying or enrolled in terminal vocational or occupational programs, general population, see 2223
Roswell-Chall Diagnostic Reading Test of Word Analysis Skills, Revised and Extended, Reading levels grades 1–4, see 2254
Roughness Discrimination Test, Blind children in grades Kgn-1, see 2259
Salford Sentence Reading Test, Ages 6-0 to 10-6, see 2281
Sand: Concepts About Print Test, Ages 5-0 to 7-0, see 2283
School Readiness Test, End of Kindergarten through first 3 weeks of Grade 1, see 2320
Secondary & College Reading Inventory, Second Edition, Grades 7 through college, see 2338
Shortened Edinburgh Reading Test, Ages 10-0 to 11-6, see 2409
Slosson Oral Reading Test [Revised], Preschool-adult, see 2433
Slosson Test of Reading Readiness, Latter kindergarten-grade 1, see 2434
Spadafore Diagnostic Reading Test, Grades 1-12 and adults, see 2462
SPAR Spelling and Reading Tests, Third Edition, Ages 7-0 to 12-11 years, see 2467
Standardized Reading Inventory, Second Edition, Children with reading ability not exceeding eighth grade level, see 2481
Stanford Diagnostic Reading Test, Fourth Edition, Grades 1.5–12.9, see 2487
STAR Reading™, Grades 1–12, see 2493
The Stieglitz Informal Reading Inventory: Assessing Reading Behaviors from Emergent to Advanced Levels, Grades 1–9, see 2503
Suffolk Reading Scale, Ages 6-12, see 2556
Survey of Study Habits and Attitudes, Grades 7-12, 12-14, see 2591
Test Lessons in Primary Reading, Second Enlarged and Revised Edition, Children, see 2663
Test of Awareness of Language Segments, Ages 4-6 and over, see 2674
Test of Early Reading Ability—2, Ages 3-0 to 9-11, see 2682
Test of Early Reading Ability—Deaf or Hard of Hearing, Deaf and hard of hearing children ages 3-0 to 13-11, see 2683
Test of Inference Ability in Reading Comprehension, Grades 6–8, see 2690
Test of Initial Literacy, Ages 7-12, see 2691
Test of Library/Study Skills, Grades 2-5, 4-9, 8-12, see 2697
Test of Reading Comprehension, Third Edition, Ages 7-0 to 17-11, see 2712
Tests of Reading Comprehension, Grades 3-7, 6-10, see 2743
Tests of Reading: Inter-American Series, Grades 1-2, 2-3, 4-6, 7-9, 10-12, see 2744
Understanding Communication, Variety of occupations, see 2790
Watson-Glaser Critical Thinking Appraisal, Grades 9-12 and college and adults, see 2856
Wide-Span Reading Test, Ages 7-10 to 14-11, see 2883
Woodcock Diagnostic Reading Battery, Ages 4–95, see 2900
Woodcock Reading Mastery Tests—Revised [1998 Normative Update], Kindergarten through adult, see 2905
Word Identification Scale, Students, see 2908
Word Recognition and Phonic Skills, Ages 5.0 to 8.6, see 2910

SCIENCE

ACS Cooperative Examination in General-Organic-Biological Chemistry, Nursing and other paramedical and home economics students, see 42
ACS Cooperative Examination in Physical Chemistry, 1 year college, see 43
ACS Examination in Analytical Chemistry, 1 year college, see 44
ACS Examination in Biochemistry, 1 year college, see 45
ACS Examination in General Chemistry, 1 year college, see 46
ACS Examination in General Chemistry (Brief Test), 1 year college, see 47
ACS Examination in High School Chemistry [Advanced Level], Advanced high school chemistry students., see 48
ACS Examination in High School Chemistry [Lower Level], High school first year chemistry students, see 49
ACS Examination in Inorganic Chemistry, 1 year college, see 50
ACS Examination in Instrumental Determinations, 1 year college, see 51
ACS Examination in Organic Chemistry, 1 year college, see 52
ACS Examination in Physical Chemistry for Life Sciences, 1 year college, see 53
ACS Examination in Polymer Chemistry, 1 year college, see 54
ACS Toledo Chemistry Placement Examination, 1 year college, see 55
Advanced Placement Examination in Biology, High school students desiring credit for college-level courses and admission to advanced courses, see 92
Advanced Placement Examination in Chemistry, High school students desiring credit for college-level courses and admission to advanced courses, see 94
Advanced Placement Examination in Computer Science, High school students desiring credit for college-level courses and admission to advanced courses, see 96
Advanced Placement Examination in Environmental Science, High school students desiring credit for college-level courses and admission to advanced courses, see 99
Advanced Placement Examination in Physics, High school students desiring credit for college-level courses and admission to advanced courses, see 110
Advanced Placement Examination in Psychology, High school students desiring credit for college-level courses and admission to advanced courses, see 111
CLEP General Examinations: Natural Sciences, Persons entering college or already in college, see 501
CLEP Subject Examination in General Biology, Persons entering college or already in college, see 515
CLEP Subject Examination in General Chemistry, Persons entering college or already in college, see 516
College Board Institutional SAT II: Biology E/M Subject Test, Entering college freshmen, see 573
College Board Institutional SAT II: Chemistry Subject Test, Entering college freshmen, see 574
College Board Institutional SAT II: Physics Subject Test, Entering college freshmen, see 587
College Board SAT II: Biology E/M Subject Test, Candidates for college entrance with one-year courses in biology and algebra, see 594
College Board SAT II: Biology Subject Test, Candidates for college entrance with one-year courses in biology and algebra, see 595
College Board SAT II: Chemistry Subject Test, Candidates for college entrance with one-year course in introductory chemistry at the college-preparatory level, see 596
College Board SAT II: Physics Subject Test, Candidates for college entrance with one-year course in introductory physics at the college-preparatory level., see 607
General Chemistry Test: National Achievement Tests, Grades 10-16, see 1076
General Physics Test: National Achievement Tests, Grades 10-16, see 1082
General Science Test: National Achievement Tests, Grades 7-9, see 1084
Graduate Record Examinations Biochemistry, Cell and Molecular The Biology Test, Graduate school candidates, see 1109
The Graduate Record Examinations Biology Test, Graduate school candidates, see 1110
The Graduate Record Examinations Chemistry Test, Graduate school candidates, see 1111
The Graduate Record Examinations Geology Test, Graduate school candidates, see 1116
The Graduate Record Examinations Physics Test, Graduate school candidates, see 1121
Health Education Test: Knowledge and Application: Acorn National Achievement Tests, Revised Edition, Grades 7-13, see 1184
Health Knowledge Test for College Freshmen: National Achievement Tests, College freshmen, see 1185
Health Test: National Achievement Tests, Grades 3-8, see 1188
Scientific Orientation Test, Students in school years 5 to 12, see 2325
Surveys of Research Administration and Environment, Research and engineering and scientific firms, see 2594
Tapping Students' Science Beliefs: A Resource for Teaching and Learning, Primary grade level students, see 2611

SENSORY-MOTOR

Basic Visual-Motor Association Test, Grades 1–9, see 261
[Bender-Gestalt Test], Ages 4 and over, see 301
Benton Visual Retention Test, Fifth Edition, Age 8–adults, see 303
Bruininks-Oseretsky Test of Motor Proficiency, Ages 4-6 through 14-5, see 353
The City University Colour Vision Test, Second Edition 1980, Adults and children, see 489
Colored Overlay Assessment Kit, Individuals experiencing reading and writing problems due to suspected visual perception problems, see 623
d2 Test of Attention, Adults, see 860
DeGangi-Berk Test of Sensory Integration, Ages 3-5, see 772
Denver Eye Screening Test, Ages 6 months and over, see 785
Developmental Test of Visual Perception, Second Edition, Ages 4-0 to 10-11, see 816
Developmental Test of Visual-Motor Integration, 4th Edition, Revised, Ages 3-0 to 17-11, see 815
Dvorine Color Vision Test, Ages 3 and over, see 862
Dysphagia Evaluation Protocol, Adult patients, see 870
Erhardt Developmental Vision Assessment, All ages, see 969
Evaluating Movement and Posture Disorganization in Dyspraxic Children, Learning disabled children ages 5 and above, see 977
Gibson Spiral Maze, Second Edition, Children and adults, see 1087
Grooved Pegboard Test, Ages 5 to 8-12, 9 to 14-12, 15 to adult, see 1135
H.R.R. Pseudoisochromatic Plates for Detecting, Classifying and Estimating the Degree of Defective Color Vision, People who may have color vision deficiency, see 1159
Hill Performance Test of Selected Positional Concepts, Visually impaired children ages 6-10, see 1206
The Hooper Visual Organization Test, Ages 13 and over, see 1218
Hughes Basic Gross Motor Assessment, Ages 6-12 believed to have minor motor dysfunctions, see 1225
Infant/Toddler Symptom Checklist, 7–30 months, see 1265
Inventory of Perceptual Skills, Ages 5–10, see 1308
Manual Dexterity Test, Ages 16 and over, see 1578
McDowell Vision Screening Kit, Birth to age 21, see 1614
The McGill Pain Questionnaire, People in pain, see 1615
Melvin-Smith Receptive-Expressive Observation, Grades 1-12, see 1642
Minnesota Manual Dexterity Test, Ages 13–adult, see 1696
MKM Binocular Preschool Test, Preschool, see 1708
MKM Picture Arrangement Test, Grades K-6, see 1710
Motor-Free Visual Perception Test—Revised, Ages 4–11, adults, see 1725
Motor-Free Visual Perception Test—Vertical, People with brain injuries, see 1726
OSOT Perceptual Evaluation, Adults, see 1865
Peabody Developmental Motor Scales and Activity Cards, Birth to 83 months, In, 1901
The Pin Test, Ages 16 to 69 with normal or corrected vision, see 1993
The Revised Sheridan Gardiner Test of Visual Acuity, Age 5 and over, see 2224
The Rutgers Drawing Test, Ages 4-6, 6-9, see 2261
Seguin-Goddard Formboards, Age 4 to adult, see 2344
Sensory Evaluation Kit, Ages 2 to adult, see 2376
Sensory Integration Inventory—Revised for Individuals with Developmental Disabilities, Developmentally disabled occupational therapy clients school aged to adults, see 2378
Slosson Drawing Coordination Test, Ages 1-adult, see 2430
Smedley Hand Dynamometer, Ages 6-18, see 2436
Stycar Vision Tests, Normal and handicapped children 6 months and over, see 2544
The Tapping Test: A Predictor of Typing and Other Tapping Operations, High school., see 2612
Test for Colour-Blindness, Ages 4 and over, see 2658
Test of Gross Motor Development, Ages 3-10, see 2689
Test of Visual-Motor Integration, Ages 4–17, see 2722
Test of Visual-Motor Skills, Ages 2–13., see 2723
Test of Visual-Perceptual Skills (Non-Motor), Ages 4-12, see 2724
Useful Field of View, Adults, see 2794
Visual Functioning Assessment Tool, Visually impaired in grades preschool and over, see 2818
Visual Skills Appraisal, Grades K-4, see 2821
Washer Visual Acuity Screening Technique, Mental ages 2-6 and over, see 2852
Watson-Barker Listening Test, Adults in business, professions, and college, see 2854
Watson-Barker Listening Test—High School Version, Grades 7-12, see 2855

SOCIAL STUDIES

Advanced Placement Examination in Comparative Government and Politics, High school students desiring credit for college-level courses and admission to advanced courses, see 95
Advanced Placement Examination in European History, High school students desiring credit for college-level courses and admission to advanced courses, see 100
Advanced Placement Examination in Macroeconomics, High school students desiring credit for college-level courses and admission to advanced courses, see 107
Advanced Placement Examination in Microeconomics, High school students desiring credit for college-level courses and admission to advanced courses, see 108
Advanced Placement Examination in United States Government and Politics, High school students desiring credit for college-level courses and admission to advanced courses, see 116
Advanced Placement Examination in United States History, High school students desiring credit for college-level courses and admission to advanced courses, see 117
American History: Junior High—Objective, 1, 2 semesters Grades 7–9, see 145
American History: Senior High—Objective, 1, 2 semesters high school, see 146
Basic Economics Test, Grades 4–6, see 247
CLEP General Examinations: Humanities, Persons entering college or already in college, see 499
CLEP General Examinations: Social Sciences and History, Persons entering college or already in college, see 502
CLEP Subject Examination in American Government, Persons entering college or already in college, see 503
CLEP Subject Examination in History of the United States: Early Colonizations to 1877, Persons entering college or already in college, see 517
CLEP Subject Examination in History of the United States II: 1865 to the Present, Persons entering college or already in college, see 518
CLEP Subject Examination in Introductory Sociology, Persons entering college or already in college, see 523
CLEP Subject Examination in Principles of Macroeconomics, Persons entering college or already in college, see 525
CLEP Subject Examination in Principles of Microeconomics, Persons entering college or already in college, see 528
CLEP Subject Examination in Western Civilization I: Ancient Near East to 1648, Persons entering college or already in college, see 530
CLEP Subject Examination in Western Civilization II: 1648 to the Present, Persons entering college or already in college, see 531
College Board Institutional SAT II: American History and Social Studies Subject Test, Entering college freshmen, see 572
College Board Institutional SAT II: World History Subject Test, Entering college freshmen, see 590
College Board SAT II: American History and Social Studies Subject Test, Candidates for college entrance with one-year American history course at the college-preparatory level, see 593
College Board SAT II: World History Subject Test, Candidates for college entrance, see 613
Current News Test, Grades 9-12, see 749
[Economics/Objective Tests], 1 semester high school, see 897
The Graduate Record Examinations Economics Test, Graduate school candidates, see 1113
The Graduate Record Examinations History Test, Graduate school candidates, see 1117
The Graduate Record Examinations Sociology Test, Graduate school candidates, see 1123
Health and Safety Education Test: National Achievement Tests, Grades 3-6, see 1182
Informeter: An International Technique for the Measurement of Political Information, Adults, see 1271
Irenometer, Adults, see 1327
M-Scale: An Inventory of Attitudes Toward Black/White Relations in the United States, College and adults, In, 1526
Newsweek NewsQuiz, Grades 9-12, see 1785
Primary Test of Economic Understanding, Grades 2-3, see 2060
Quick Quizzes for U.S. History Classes, Grades 6-12, see 2143
Test of Economic Knowledge, Grades 8-9, see 2685
Test of Economic Literacy, Second Edition, Grades 11-12, see 2686
Test of Understanding in College Economics, Third Edition, Introductory economics students, see 2718
Test of Understanding in Personal Economics, High school, see 2719

SPEECH AND HEARING

The Apraxia Profile: A Descriptive Assessment Tool for Children, Ages 3–13, see 164
Arizona Articulation Proficiency Scale, Second Edition, Ages 1-6 to 13-11, see 175
Assessing and Teaching Phonological Knowledge, Young children, see 187
The Assessment of Aphasia and Related Disorders, Second Edition, Aphasic patients, ages 5.5–59, see 199
Assessment of Fluency in School-Age Children, Ages 5–18, see 207
Assessment of Intelligibility of Dysarthric Speech, Adult and adolescent dysarthric speakers, see 209
The Assessment of Phonological Processes—Revised, Ages 3-0 through 12-0, see 214
Auditory Continuous Performance Test, Ages 6 to 11, see 229
Bankson-Bernthal Test of Phonology, Ages 3-9, see 240
Bedside Evaluation of Dysphagia, Adults neurologically impaired, see 276
Boston Assessment of Severe Aphasia, Aphasic adults, see 328
Carrow Elicited Language Inventory, Ages 3-7, In, 430
Children's Articulation Test, Ages 3–11, see 468
CID Phonetic Inventory, Hearing-impaired children, IN, 486
CID Picture SPINE, Hearing-impaired children ages 6-13, see 487
Clinical Evaluation of Language Fundamentals—Preschool, Preschool and early elementary, see 539
Clinical Evaluation of Language Fundamentals, Third Edition, Ages 6.0–21.11, see 540
Communication Activities of Daily Living, Second Edition, Aphasic adults, see 629
Communication and Symbolic Behavior Scales, 6 months to 24 months, see 630
Comprehensive Screening Test for Determining Optimal Communication Mode, Low functioning nonspeaking persons, see 658
Cooper Assessment for Stuttering Syndromes, Ages 3–13 years, Adolescents and adults age 13 and over, see 691
Denver Articulation Screening Exam, Ages 2.5 to 7.0, see 783
Denver Audiometric Screening Test, Ages 3-6, see 784
Draw A Person: A Quantitative Scoring System, Ages 5-17, see 854
Dysarthria Examination Battery, Children and adults, see 866
Early Speech Perception Test, Ages 3–6, ages 6–15, see 891
Eckstein Audiometers, All ages, see 896
Examining for Aphasia, Third Edition, Adolescents and adults, see 987
F.A.T.S.A. Test (Flowers Auditory Test of Selective Attention), Grades 1-6, see 1020
The Fisher-Logemann Test of Articulation Competence, Preschool to adult, see 1040
Flowers-Costello Tests of Central Auditory Abilities, Grades K-6, see 1046
Fluharty Preschool Speech and Language Screening Test, Ages 2-6, see 1047
Frenchay Dysarthria Assessment, Ages 12 and over, see 1056
Functional Communication Profile, Aphasic adults, see 1061
Goldman-Fristoe Test of Articulation, Ages 2 and over, see 1095
Goldman-Fristoe-Woodcock Test of Auditory Discrimination, Ages 3-8 years and over, see 1096
Grammatical Analysis of Elicited Language—Pre-Sentence Level, Hearing-impaired children ages 3-6, see 1126
The Hearing Measurement Scale, Adults, see 1190
The Hundred Pictures Naming Test, Ages 4-6 to 11-11, see 1231
INteraction CHecklist for Augmentative Communication, Revised Edition, Augmentative system users, see 1284
Joliet 3-Minute Preschool Speech and Language Screen, 2.5–4.5 years, see 1359
Joliet 3-Minute Speech and Language Screen (Revised), Grades K, 2, 5, see 1360
The Jones-Mohr Listening Test, Persons in educational and training programs, see 1361
Khan-Lewis Phonological Analysis, Ages 2-0 to 5-11, see 1394
Lindamood Auditory Conceptualization Test, Revised Edition, All ages, see 1503
Living Language, Language-impaired children, IN, 1511
Lucas Grason-Stadler Audiometers, Ages 6 and over, see 1523
Metaphon, Ages 3.5-7, see 1656
Multilingual Aphasia Examination, Third Edition, Ages 6–69, see 1740
Northwestern Syntax Screening Test, Ages 3-8, see 1804
Oral Motor Assessment and Treatment: Improving Syllable Production, Ages 4-11, see 1850
Oral Speech Mechanism Screening Examination—Revised, Age 5 through adults, see 1852
The Patterned Elicitation Syntax Test (Revised) with Morphonemic Analysis, Ages 3–0 to 7–6, see 1898
Phonological Assessment Battery [Standardised Edition], Ages 5–15, see 1980

Photo Articulation Test, Third Edition, Ages 3–8, see 1982
Porch Index of Communicative Ability, Aphasic adults, see 2008
Predictive Screening Test of Articulation, Grade 1, see 2028
Quick Screen of Phonology, Ages 3-0 to 7-11, see 2144
Receptive-Expressive Emergent Language Test, Second Edition, Children from birth to 3 years of age, see 2189
Revised Evaluating Acquired Skills in Communication, Children 3 months to 8 years with severe language impairments, see 2215
The Riley Articulation and Language Test, Revised, Grades K-2, see 2235
Roswell-Chall Auditory Blending Test, Grades 1–4 and "older students with reading difficulties," see 2253
Scale for the Assessment of Thought, Language, and Communication, Manics, depressives, and schizophrenics, see 2290
Scales of Early Communication Skills for Hearing-Impaired Children, Ages 2-0 to 8-11, see 2298
SCAN: A Screening Test for Auditory Processing Disorders, Ages 3-11, see 2300
SCAN-A: A Test for Auditory Processing Disorders in Adolescents and Adults, Ages 12 to 50, see 2301
Screening Test for Developmental Apraxia of Speech, Ages 4-12, see 2332
Slosson Articulation Language Test with Phonology, Ages 3-0 to 5-11, see 2429
Smit-Hand Articulation and Phonology Evaluation, Ages 3–9, see 2438
Speech and Language Evaluation Scale, Ages 4.5-18, see 2470
Speech Evaluation of the Patient with a Tracheostomy Tube, Adults with artificial airways, see 2472
STARS Test (Short Term Auditory Retrieval and Storage), Grades 1-6, see 2494
Stephens Oral Language Screening Test, Prekindergarten-grade 1, see 2502
STIM/CON: Prognostic Inventory for Misarticulating Kindergarten and First Grade Children, Grades K-3, see 2504
Structured Photographic Articulation Test Featuring Dudsberry, Ages 3-9, see 2523
Stuttering Prediction Instrument for Young Children, Ages 3-8, see 2542
Stuttering Severity Instrument for Children and Adults, Third Edition, School-age children and adults, see 2543
Temple University Short Syntax Inventory, Ages 3-0 to 4-11, see 2650
Templin-Darley Tests of Articulation, Second Edition, Ages 3 and over, see 2651
Test for Examining Expressive Morphology, Ages 3-0 to 8-12, see 2660
Test of Articulation in Context, Preschool through elementary-school-aged children, see 2669
Test of Auditory Comprehension, Hearing impaired ages 4-17, see 2672
Test of Auditory-Perceptual Skills, Ages 4–12, see 2673
Test of Minimal Articulation Competence, Ages 3 to adult, see 2703
Test of Oral Structures and Functions, Ages 7-Adults, see 2706
Test of Phonological Awareness, Ages 5–8, see 2708
Test of Pragmatic Language, Ages 5-0 to 13-11, see 2709
Voice Assessment Protocol For Children and Adults (A), Children and adults, see 2837
Weiss Comprehensive Articulation Test, All ages, see 2866
Wepman's Auditory Discrimination Test, Second Edition, Ages 4-0 to 8-11, see 2870
Wiig Criterion Referenced Inventory of Language, Ages 4 through 13, see 2886
Wolf Expressive/Receptive Language & Speech Checklist, Birth-10 years, see 2893
Word Fluency, Positions requiring sharp verbal communication skills, see 2907

VOCATIONS

Ability Explorer, Middle school students through adults, see 5
Access Management Survey, Adults, see 14
Accounting Aptitude Test, First-year college students, see 15
Accounting Clerk Staff Selector, Candidates for the position of accounting clerk or bookkeeping clerk, see 16
Accounting Program Admission Test, College level elementary accounting students, see 17
ACER Mechanical Comprehension Test, Ages 13.5 and over, see 28
ACER Mechanical Reasoning Test, Ages 15 and over, see 29
ACER Short Clerical Test, Age 15 and over, see 30
ACER Speed and Accuracy Tests, Ages 13.5 and over, see 31
Adult Career Concerns Inventory, Ages 24 and over, see 83

Advanced Test Battery, Personnel at graduate level or in management positions, see 119
Allied Health Professions Admission Test, Applicants to 4-year allied health programs, see 141
The American Occupational Therapy Association, Inc. Fieldwork Evaluation for the Occupation Therapist, Occupational therapy students, see 152
Analytical Aptitude Skills Evaluation, Entry-level and experienced candidates for positions requiring the ability to analyze business problems, see 154
Applied Knowledge Test, Ages 14-18, see 160
Appraisal Interview and Card Sort, Professionals and managers, see 161
Aptitude Assessment Battery: Programming, Programmers and trainees, see 167
Aptitude Interest Inventory, High school to adult, see 168
Aptitudes Associates Test of Sales Aptitude: A Test for Measuring Knowledge of Basic Principles of Selling, Revised, Applicants for sales positions and general population, see 170
Armed Services—Civilian Vocational Interest Survey, Grades 11—12, see 179
Ashland Interest Assessment, Adults and adolescents, see 183
ASSESS Expert System Version 5.X, Potential employees and candidates for promotion in professional, managerial, and sales positions, see 186
Assessing Specific Competencies, Individuals seeking employment, see 190
Assessing Your Team: Seven Measures of Team Success, Teams, see 191
Assessment Inventory for Management, Managers, see 197
Assessment of Career Decision Making, Adolescents and adults, see 200
Assessment of Competencies for Instructor Development, Instructors in industrial settings, see 203
Automated Office Battery, Student and employed clerical staff, see 236
Ball Aptitude Battery, High school and adults, see 239
Bass Orientation Inventory, College and industry, see 263
Becker Work Adjustment Profile, Mentally retarded, physically disabled, emotionally disturbed, learning disabled, and economically disadvantaged, ages 13 and over, see 275
Belbin Team-Roles Self-Perception Inventory, Teams, see 296
BENCHMARKS, Managers and executives, see 300
Bennett Mechanical Comprehension Test, Second Edition, Industrial employees and high school and adult applicants for mechanical positions or engineering schools, see 302
Biofeedback Certification Examination, Entry-level biofeedback service providers, see 310
Birds of Different Feathers Work Style Assessment, Organization employees, see 313
Blox Test, Job applicants with at least 10 years of education, see 321
BRIGANCE® Diagnostic Employability Skills Inventory, Prospective job-applicants, see 341
Business Analyst Skills Evaluation, Candidates for business analyst positions, see 360
Business Judgment Test, Revised, Adults, see 361
Campbell™ Interest and Skill Survey, Ages 15 years to adult, see 380
Campbell Organizational Survey, Working adults, see 382
Campbell-Hallam Team Development Survey, Members of intact working teams, see 379
Canadian Dental Aptitude Test, Dental school applicants, see 386
Canadian Occupational Interest Inventory, High school or college students, see 387
The Candidate Profile Record, Applicants for clerical positions, see 390
Career Ability Placement Survey, Junior high, high school, college, and adults, see 395
Career Anchors: Discovering Your Real Values, Revised Edition, Adults, see 396
Career Assessment Inventory™—The Enhanced Version, Grade 9 through adult, see 398
Career Assessment Inventory™—Vocational Version, Grade 9 through adult, see 399
Career Attitudes and Strategies Inventory: An Inventory for Understanding Adult Careers, Adults seeking vocational counseling, see 400
Career Counseling Personal Data Form, Vocational counselees, see 402
Career Decision Scale, Grades 9-12 and college, see 404
Career Decision-Making Self-Efficacy Scale, College students, see 403
Career Development Inventory [Consulting Psychologists Press, Inc.], High school through adults, see 405
Career Directions Inventory, High school and college and adults, see 406
The Career Exploration Inventory, Adults, see 407
Career Exploration Series, 1992 Revision, Grades 7–12 and college and adults, see 408
Career Factors Inventory, Ages 13 and over, see 409
Career Guidance Inventory, Students and prospective students at trade, vocational, or technical school, or at community college, see 410
Career Interest Inventory, Grades 7–9, Grades 1–12 and adults, see 411
Career IQ Test, Ages 13–adults, see 412
Career Maturity Inventory, Grades 6-12, see 413
Career Occupational Preference System, Interest Inventory, Form R, Grade 6 through high school, see 414
Career Occupational Preference System, Intermediate Inventory, Elementary through high school with 4th grade reading level, see 415

Career Occupational Preference System—Professional Level Interest Inventory, College and adult professionals, college-bound senior high school students, see 416
Career Orientation Placement and Evaluation Survey, Grade 7 through high school, college, and adult, see 417
Career Planning Survey, Grades 8–10, see 418
Career Problem Check List, Ages 14-17, see 419
Career Profile Inventory, Adults, see 420
The Career Profile System, Second Edition, Insurance sales representatives and candidates for insurance, see 421
Career Thoughts Inventory, Adults, college students, and high school students, see 422
Career Values Card Sort, Adults, see 423
Certified Picture Framer Examination, Individuals actively involved in the business of picture framing for one year, see 435
Change Abilitator, Teams, see 436
Chronicle Career Quest, Grades 7–10, Grades 9–16 and adult, see 485
The Clark Wilson Group Multi-Level Feedback Instruments and Development Programs, Organizations, executives, managers, and employees, see 490
CLEP Subject Examination in Information Systems and Computer Applications, Persons entering college or already in college, see 520
CLEP Subject Examination in Introductory Business Law, Persons entering college or already in college, see 521
CLEP Subject Examination in Principles of Management, Persons entering college or already in college, see 526
CLEP Subject Examination in Principles of Marketing, Persons entering college or already in college, see 527
Clerical Abilities Battery, Clerical applicants and employees and business school students, see 532
Clerical Aptitude Test: Acorn National Aptitude Tests, Grades 7-12 and adult clerks, see 533
Clerical Aptitudes, Applicants for office personnel positions, see 534
Clerical Skills Series, Clerical worker, see 535
Client/Server Skills Test, Information technology professionals who possess some basic knowledge or experience in a client/server environment, see 536
Clinical Experience Record for Nursing Students, Nursing students and nurses, see 543
Coaching Effectiveness Survey, Managers, see 554
Coaching Process Questionnaire, Managers and employees, see 555
Coaching Skills Inventory, Adults, see 556
The Common-Metric Questionnaire, Job incumbents, supervisors, job analysts, see 627
Communication Knowledge Inventory [Revised], High school through adult, see 631
Communication Sensitivity Inventory, Managers, see 633
Competency-Based Performance Improvement: Organizational Assessment Package, Business managers, see 638
A Complaint Is a Gift Profile, Employees, supervisors, and managers, see 640
Computer Literacy Skills Profile, Candidates whose job responsibilities will include utilizing common software packages, see 668
Computer Operator Aptitude Battery, Experienced computer operators and trainees, see 669
Computer Programmer Aptitude Battery, Students, programmer trainees, entry-level and experienced, see 670
Controller/Accountant Staff Selector, Candidates for the position of controller/accountant, see 688
COPSystem Picture Inventory of Careers, Elementary through adult-non-verbal, see 702
Correctional Officers' Interest Blank, Applicants for jobs in penal institutions and correctional agencies, see 711
Cosmetology Student Admissions Evaluation, Cosmetology school applicants, see 713
Crawford Small Parts Dexterity Test, High school and adults, see 722
Criterion Validated Written Test for Emergency Medical Practitioner, Prospective paramedics, see 731
Criterion Validated Written Test for Fire Medic, Prospective firefighter/fire medic candidates, see 732
Criterion Validated Written Tests for Firefighter, Prospective firefighters, see 733
Criterion Validated Written Tests for Police Officer, Prospective police officers, see 734
Cross Reference Test, Clerical job applicants, see 738
Curtis Interest Scale, Grades 9-16 and adults, see 752
[Curtis Object Completion and Space Form Tests], Applicants for mechanical and technical jobs, see 753
Curtis Verbal-Clerical Skills Tests, Applicants for clerical positions, see 754
Customer Service Skills Test, Candidates for customer service position, see 756
Database Analyst Staff Selector, Candidates for database positions, see 764
Dental Admission Test, Dental school applicants, see 780
Dental Assistant Test, Dental assistant applicants, see 781
Dental Receptionist Test, Dental receptionist applicants, see 782
Detention Promotion Tests—Complete Service, Detention workers under consideration for promotion, see 796
Developing The High-Performance Workplace, Organizational employees, see 801
Developing the Leader Within, Management personnel, see 802

Developmental Challenge Profile: Learning from Job Experiences, Managers, see 807
The Devine Inventory, Employees and prospective employees, see 819
[Driver Selection Forms and Tests], Truck drivers, see 857
Electrical and Electronics Test, Students in electrical or electronics programs ages 15 and over, see 919
Electrical Maintenance Trainee—Form UKE-1C, Applicants for jobs requiring electrical knowledge and skills, see 920
Electrical Sophistication Test, Job applicants, see 921
Electromechanical Vocational Assessment Manuals, Blind or visually impaired adults, see 922
Electron Test—Form H-C, Electronics employees and applicants for electronics jobs, see 923
Electronic and Instrumentation Technician Test—Form 2, Applicants or incumbents for jobs where electronics and instrumentation knowledge is a necessary part of training or job activities, see 924
Employability Development Plan, Employees, see 934
The Employability Inventory, Prospective employees, see 935
Employability Maturity Interview, Rehabilitation clients, see 936
Employee Aptitude Survey, Second Edition, Ages 16 to adult, see 937
Employee Effectiveness Profile, Managers, see 939
Employee Involvement Status Survey, Employees, see 940
Employee Performance Appraisal, Business and industry, see 942
[Employee Rating and Development Forms], Executive, industrial, office, and sales personnel, see 943
Employment Values Inventory, Adults, see 945
Empowerment Inventory, Work team members/employees, see 946
Endicott Work Productivity Scale, Adults, see 949
Entrance Examination for Schools of Nursing [RN Entrance Examination], Applicants to schools of registered nursing, see 960
Entrance Examination for Schools of Practical/Vocational Nursing, Applicants to practical/vocational nursing schools, see 961
Eosys Word Processing Aptitude Battery, Job candidates for work processor operator positions, see 964
EQ Questionnaire, Adult, see 966
ETSA Tests, Employees and job applicants, see 973
Evaluating the Participant's Employability Skills, Individuals seeking employment, see 978
Executive Administrative Assistant Skills Test, Candidates with all levels of experience for the position of executive administrative assistant, see 988
[Executive, Industrial, and Sales Personnel Forms], Applicants for executive, industrial, office, and sales positions, see 989
Explore the World of Work, Elementary and special education, see 993
Feedback Edition of the Strength Development Inventory, Adults, see 1022
Feedback Portrait of Overdone Strengths, Adults, see 1023
Feedback Portrait of Personal Strengths, Adults, see 1024
The Filipino Work Values Scale, Filipino employees and students, see 1030
Fine Dexterity Test, Applicants for jobs involving fine motor dexterity, see 1031
Fire Promotion TestsComplete Service, Firefighters, see 1032
Firefighter Learning Simulation, Applicants for firefighter trainee positions, see 1033
Firefighter Selection Test [Revised], Applicants for firefighter trainee positions, see 1034
Flanagan Aptitude Classification Tests, Individuals in a variety of lower-level industrial or mechanical positions, see 1042
Flanagan Industrial Tests, Supervisory, technical, office, skilled labor, and other industrial positions, see 1043
Fleishman Job Analysis Survey, Adults, see 1044
Flex Style Negotiating, Employees and managers, see 1045
Food Protection Certification Test, Food industry personnel, see 1048
GAINS: A Pre-test and Post-test for Measuring Career Development Competency Progress, Grades 4–7, 8–11, see 1069
The Geist Picture Interest Inventory, Grades 8-16 and adults, see 1074
General Clerical Ability Test: ETSA Test 3A, Job applicants, see 1077
General Clerical Test, Clerical applicants and workers, see 1078
General Management In-Basket, Supervisors and managers, see 1080
General Mental Ability Test: ETSA Test 1A, Job applicants, see 1081
Gordon Occupational Check List II, Grades 8-12 and adults, see 1100
The Graduate Record Examinations Computer Science Test, Graduate school candidates, see 1112
The Graduate Record Examinations Engineering Test, Graduate school candidates, see 1114
Group Process Questionnaire, Adults, see 1147
Group Test 82, Ages 15 and over, see 1151
The Guilford-Zimmerman Interest Inventory, College and adults, see 1157
Hall Occupational Orientation Inventory, Grades 3–7, 8–16 and adults, low-literate adults, junior high students–adults, see 1163
Hand-Tool Dexterity Test, Adolescents and adults, see 1170
The Harrington-O'Shea Career Decision-Making System Revised, Grade 7 and over, see 1177

Hay Aptitude Test Battery [Revised], Applicants for clerical and plant positions, see 1180
Help Desk Support Staff Selector, Candidates for Help Desk positions, see 1193
High School Career-Course Planner, Grades 8 and 9, see 1200
Hilson Career Satisfaction Index, Public safety/security officers, see 1209
Hilson Personnel Profile/Success Quotient, High school through adult, see 1210
How Supervise?, Supervisors, see 1221
IDEAS: Interest Determination, Exploration and Assessment System™, Grades 7-12 and adults, see 1237
Incentives Management Index, Sales managers, see 1244
Individual Service Strategy Portfolio, Human service clients, see 1252
The Influence Styles Inventory, Managers, see 1268
Information System Skills, Information processing job applicants, see 1270
Instrument Technician, Applicants and incumbents for jobs requiring technical knowledge of instrumentation, see 1279
Interest Explorer, Adolescents and adults, see 1285
Intuitive Mechanics (Weights & Pulleys), Industrial positions, see 1299
Inventory of Interests, Adolescents and adults, see 1306
An Inventory of Religious Activities and Interests, High school and college, see 1310
Inventory of Vocational Interests: Acorn National Aptitude Tests, Grades 7-16 and adults, see 1312
Inwald Survey 5, All occupations including public safety/security, clerical, managerial, sales, and entry-level, see 1314
The IPAT Anxiety Scale, Ages 14 and over, see 1321
IPI Job-Tests Program, Job applicants and employees in industry, see 1323
IPMA Correctional Officer Test, Prospective correctional personnel, see 1324
IPMA Fire Service Tests, Prospective Fire Service personnel, see 1325
IPMA Police Service Tests, Prospective police service personnel, see 1326
IS Manager/Consultant Skills Evaluation, Candidates for IS Manager or IS Consultant positions, see 1328
IS Project Leader Skills Evaluation, Candidates for Project Leader position, see 1329
IS Sales Assessment Battery, Candidates for information services (IS) sales positions, see 1330
Jackson Vocational Interest Survey [1995 Revision], High school and above, see 1334
JIIG-CAL Occupational Interests Guide, Year 9/S2 in British/Scottish school systems, Years 10-11/S3-S4 in British/Scottish school systems, see 1342
Job Activity Preference Questionnaire, Adults, see 1343
Job Awareness Inventory, Average and special needs students in Grades 10-12, see 1346
Job Choice Decision-Making Exercise (A), High school and college and adults, see 1347
Job Descriptive Index (1997 Revision) and The Job in General Scales, Employees, see 1348
Job Interactions Inventory, Employees, training program participants, career planning and outplacement clients, see 1349
Job Search Inventory, Job applicants, see 1351
Job Seeking Skills Assessment, Vocational rehabilitation clients, see 1352
Job Skills Tests, Job applicants and industrial workers, see 1353
Job Style Indicator, Adults, see 1355
JOB-O, Grades 4–7, Junior high school through adult, Grades 10–12 and adult, see 1350
Jobmatch, Pupils geared toward nonacademic occupations, see 1356
Journalism Test, High school, see 1364
Just-in-Time Training Assessment Instrument, Adults, see 1371
KEYS: Assessing the Climate for Creativity, Employees, see 1393
Kilmanns Organizational Belief Survey, Employees, see 1398
The Kirkpatrick Management and Supervisory Skills Series, Supervisors and all levels of managers, see 1403
Knowledge of Occupations Test, High school, see 1406
Kuder General Interest Survey, Form E, Grades 6-12, see 1413
Law Enforcement Assessment and Development Report, Applicants for law enforcement positions, see 1429
Law Enforcement Candidate Record, Candidates for law enforcement positions, see 1430
Law School Admission Test, Law school entrants, see 1434
Leader Behavior Analysis II, Middle and upper level managers, see 1436
Leader Behavior Description Questionnaire, Form 12, Supervisors, see 1437
Leader Behavior Questionnaire, Revised, Managers and employees, see 1438
Leadership Appraisal Survey, Adults, see 1441
Leadership Practices Inventory—Delta, Managers and employees, see 1445
Leadership Skills Inventory [Consulting Resource Group], Adults, see 1450
Leading Edge Portrait, Age 13 and over, see 1451
Learning Organization Practices Profile, Organizations, see 1463
Leatherman Leadership Questionnaire: 360 degree Leadership Profile, Leaders, managers, supervisors, team leaders, potential leaders, supervisors, and executives, see 1480

Leatherman Leadership Questionnaire [Revised], Managers, supervisors, team leaders, and potential leaders, see 1479
Leisure/Work Search Inventory, Adults, see 1483
Life Style Questionnaire, Ages 14 and over, see 1497
Lore Leadership Assessment, Adults working in organizations, see 1519
MacQuarrie Test for Mechanical Ability, Grades 7 and over, see 1533
Maintest—Forms NC-1, B, C, Applicants and incumbents for jobs requiring practical mechanical and electrical knowledge, see 1537
The Major-Minor-Finder, 1986-1996 Edition, High school and college, see 1539
Making a Terrific Career Happen, High school graduates, college students, and adults, see 1541
Making Work Teams Work, Employees, see 1542
Management and Graduate Item Bank, Graduate level and senior management applicants, see 1544
Management Appraisal Survey, Employees, see 1546
Management Change Inventory, Managers and prospective managers, see 1547
Management Coaching Relations [Revised], Managers and potential managers, see 1548
Management Effectiveness Profile System, Managers and coworkers, see 1550
Management Interest Inventory, Managers, see 1551
Management Inventory on Leadership, Motivation and Decision-Making, Managers and manager trainees, see 1552
Management Inventory on Managing Change, Managers, see 1553
Management Inventory on Modern Management, Managers, see 1554
Management Inventory on Performance Appraisal and Coaching, Managers, see 1555
Management Inventory on Time Management, Managers, see 1556
Management & Leadership Systems, Management personnel, see 1545
Management Practices Update, Individuals involved in the management of others, see 1558
Management Relations Survey, Subordinates to managers, see 1559
Management Situation Checklist, Managers, see 1560
Management Style Diagnosis Test, Third Edition, Managers, see 1561
Management Style Inventory [Hanson Silver Strong & Associates], Administrators and leaders, see 1562
Management Styles Inventory, Adults, see 1564
Management Transactions Audit, Managers, see 1565
Manager Profile Record, Prospective managers, see 1566
Manager Style Appraisal, Adults, see 1567
Manager/Supervisor Staff Selector, Candidates for managerial and supervisory positions, see 1568
Managerial and Professional Job Functions Inventory, Middle and upper level managers and higher-level professionals, see 1569
Managerial Assessment of Proficiency MAP™, Managers, see 1570
Managerial Competence Index, Individuals who manage or are being assessed for their potential to manage others, see 1571
Managerial Competence Review, Subordinates to managers, see 1572
Managerial Competency Questionnaire, Managers, see 1573
Managerial Style Questionnaire, Persons in managerial situations, see 1575
MAPP: Motivational Appraisal of Personal Potential, Employees at all levels, see 1579
Matching Person and Technology, Clients, students, or employees, see 1593
The MbM Questionnaire: Managing by Motivation, Third Edition, Managers and supervisors, see 1608
MDS Vocational Interest Exploration System, High school–adults, see 1617
Measurement of Counselor Competencies: A Self-Assessment, School counselors, see 1624
Mechanical Aptitude Test: Acorn National Aptitude Tests, Grades 7-16 and adults, see 1632
Mechanical Aptitudes, Applicants for industrial positions, training programs, and vocational counseling, see 1633
Mechanical Familiarity Test: ETSA Test 5A, Job applicants, see 1634
Mechanical Knowledge Test: ETSA Test 6A, Job applicants, see 1635
Mechanical Movements, Employees and potential employees in industrial positions, see 1636
MecTest (A Test for Maintenance Mechanics), Applicants and incumbents for maintenance jobs, see 1637
Medical College Admission Test, Applicants for admission to member colleges of the Association of American Medical Colleges and to other participating institutions, see 1638
Medical School Instructor Attitude Inventory, Medical school faculty members,see 1640
Mentoring Skills Assessment, Mentors, coaches, and mentees, see 1651
Mentoring Style Indicator, Mentors of youth and proteges, new hires, employees, new teachers, college students, and educational administrators, see 1652
Microcomputer User Aptitude Test, Applicants for positions involving the use of microcomputers, see 1666
Minnesota Clerical Assessment Battery, Secretaries and other clerical workers, see 1692
Minnesota Clerical Test, Grades 8-12 and adults, see 1693
Minnesota Importance Questionnaire, Ages 16 and over, see 1694

Minnesota Job Description Questionnaire, Employees and supervisors, see 1695
Minnesota Rate of Manipulation Test, 1969 Edition, Grades 7 to adult, see 1700
Minnesota Satisfaction Questionnaire, Business and industry, see 1701
Minnesota Satisfactoriness Scales, Employees, see 1702
Minnesota Spatial Relations Test, Revised Edition, Ages 16 and over, see 1703
Mirror Edition of the Personal Values Inventory, Adolescents and adults reading at sixth grade level or above, see 1704
Mobile Vocational Evaluation, Adults, see 1711
Modern Occupational Skills Tests, Potential and current office employees, see 1712
Motivated Skills Card Sort, Adults, see 1719
Multifactor Leadership Questionnaire for Research, Management personnel, see 1736
Multifactor Leadership Questionnaire for Teams, Management personnel, see 1737
My Vocational Situation, High school and college and adult, see 1754
N.I.I.P. Engineering Apprentice Selection Test Battery, Engineering apprentices, see 1786
National Institute for Personnel Research Normal Battery, South African Standards 6-10 and job applicants with 8-11 years of education, see 1762
National Police Officer Selection Test, Police officer candidates, see 1763
Network Analyst Staff Selector, Candidates for technical network positions, see 1772
Network Technician Staff Selector, Candidates for the position of network technicia, see 1773
New Technology Tests: Computer Commands, Applicants for computer-related jobs, see 1782
New Technology Tests: Computer Rules, Applicants for computer-related jobs, see 1783
19 Field Interest Inventory, Standards 8-10 in South African school system and college and adults, see 1789
1994 Strong Interest Inventory, Ages 16 and over, see 1790
NOCTI Experienced Worker Assessments, Technical teachers and potential teachers and journey workers, see 1792
NOCTI Industrial Assessments, Industrial employees and potential employees, see 1793
NOCTI Job Ready Assessments, Students in vocational and technical programs, see 1794
Nurse Aide Practice Test, Nurse aides, see 1807
Object-Oriented Programmer Analyst, Candidates for the position of object-oriented programmer analyst, see 1810
Observation Ability Test for the Police Service, Candidates for police entry-level and promotional positions, see 1813
Occ-U-Sort, Grades 7 and over and adults, see 1829
Occupational Aptitude Survey and Interest Schedule, Second Edition—Aptitude Survey, Grades 8-12, see 1816
Occupational Aptitude Survey and Interest Schedule, Second Edition—Interest Schedule, Grades 8-12, see 1817
Occupational Interest Inventories, Adults, see 1818
Occupational Interest Rating Scale, Ages 14 and over, see 1819
Occupational Interests Card Sort, Adults, see 1820
Occupational Personality Assessment, Individuals seeking vocational counseling, see 1821
Occupational Relationships Profile, Adults, see 1823
Occupational Test Series—Basic Skills Tests, New trainees and employees, see 1826
Occupational Test Series: General Ability Tests, Employees and candidates for employment, see 1827
Office Arithmetic Test: ETSA Test 2A, Job applicants, see 1833
Office Skills Achievement Test, Office employees, see 1834
Office Skills Series, Applicants for clerical positions, see 1835
Office Skills Tests, Applicants for clerical positions, see 1836
Office Systems Battery, Applicants for clerical positions, see 1837
Ohio Vocational Interest Survey, Second Edition, Grades 7-college and adults, see 1841
Optometry Admission Testing Program, Optometry school applicants, see 1846
Organization Health Survey, Managers and administrators and supervisors in government and industry, see 1855
Organizational Assessment Survey, Adult, see 1856
Organizational Behavior Profile, Organizations, see 1857
Organizational Beliefs Questionnaire, Organizations, see 1858
Organizational Change-Readiness Scale, Employees, see 1859
Organizational Climate Exercise II, Work groups, see 1860
Organizational Competence Index, Individuals who, as part of a group or organization, share in the responsibilities of attaining a goal or objective, see 1861
Organizational Culture Inventory, Organizational members, see 1862
PAR: Proficiency Assessment Report, Supervisors and managers, see 1874
Parker Team Player Survey, Employees, see 1892
Participative Management Survey, Individuals involved in a leadership capacity with others, see 1894
PathFinder—My Individual Career Plan, Severely mentally retarded adolescents and adults, see 1896
PDI Employment Inventory and PDI Customer Service Inventory, Job applicants, see 1900
Peacock Profile, Employees, see 1904

Peg Board, Applicants for electrical and light engineering assembly jobs, see 1911
Penguin Index, Employees, see 1912
People Performance Profile, Organization members, see 1913
People Smarts: Behavioral Profiles, Adults, see 1915
Per-Flu-Dex Tests, High school and college and industry, see 1920
[Performance Review Forms], Employees, managers, see 1922
Performance Skills Leader, Employees in leadership positions, see 1923
Personal Achievement Formula, Managers, see 1924
Personal Adjustment Index: ETSA Test 8A, Job applicants, see 1926
Personal Dynamics Profile, Current personnel and potential employees, see 1930
Personal Opinion Matrix, Employees, see 1937
Personal Success Profile, Current personnel and potential employees, see 1955
Personnel Assessment Selection System, Retail and business applicants, and applicants for police/fire/security positions, see 1967
[Personnel Interviewing Form], Business and industry, see 1968
Personnel Performance Problems Inventory, Management and administrative personnel, see 1969
Personnel Reaction Blank, Ages 15 to adult, see 1970
Personnel Relations Survey [Revised], Managers, see 1971
Personnel Test Battery, Office and sales groups, see 1973
Personnel Tests for Industry, Trade school and adults, see 1974
Pharmacy College Admission Test, Pharmacy college applicants, see 1975
Picha-Seron Career Analysis, Middle school-adult, see 1984
Picture Vocational Interest Questionnaire for Adults, Long-term South African prisoners who have passed Standard 5, see 1990
Planning Career Goals, Grades 8-12, see 2000
Police Promotion Tests—Complete Service, Police officers, see 2002
Police Selection Test, Police officer applicants, see 2003
The Poppleton Allen Sales Aptitude Test, Adults, see 2007
Position Analysis Questionnaire, Business and industrial jobs, see 2016
Power Base Inventory, Work team members, leaders, managers, supervisors, see 2020
Power Management Inventory, Managers, see 2021
Power Management Profile, Managers, see 2022
Preliminary Diagnostic Questionnaire, Persons involved with vocational rehabilitation agencies or facilities and workers' compensation claimants, see 2030
The Press Test, Managers and high-level professionals, see 2051
Prevocational Assessment Screen, Grades 9-12, see 2054
Primary Mechanical Ability Tests, Applicants for positions requiring mechanical ability, see 2057
Process Technician Test, Applicants or incumbents for jobs where process knowledge is a necessary part of training or job activities, see 2066
Production and Maintenance Technician Test, Applicants or incumbents for jobs where production and maintenance knowledge is a necessary part of training or job activities, see 2067
Productive Practices Survey, Managers, see 2068
Productivity Profile, Employees, see 2070
Professional and Managerial Position Questionnaire, Professional and managerial jobs, see 2071
Professional Employment Test, Potential managerial, administrative, and professional employees, see 2072
Profile of Aptitude for Leadership, Adults, see 2075
Program for Assessing Youth Employment Skills, Adolescents and young adults with low verbal skills, see 2081
Programmer Analyst Aptitude Test One-Hour Version, Entry-level and experienced applicants for programmer analyst positions, see 2084
Programmer Analyst Aptitude Test Two-Hour Version, Applicants for programmer analyst positions, see 2085
Programmer Aptitude Battery, Adults naive to programming task, see 2086
Programmer Aptitude Series, Computer programming personnel, see 2087
Project Implementation Profile, Project managers and team members, see 2096
Project Management Competency Assessment, Project managers, see 2097
Project Management Knowledge & Skills Assessment, Project managers, see 2098
Prospector: Discovering the Ability to Learn and to Lead, Managers and executives, see 2101
PSC Survey-SA, Job applicants or current employees, see 2104
PSC-Survey ADT, Job applicants, see 2103
PSI Basic Skills Tests for Business, Industry, and Government, Prospective clerical, administrative, and customer service employees, see 2105
PSYPERCEPT-170, Managers, see 2121
Purdue Interest Questionnaire , Freshmen engineering students, see 2124
Purdue Pegboard, Assembly, general factory and various industrial positions and vocational rehabilitation, see 2125
Quality Culture Assessment, Managers and personnel, see 2129
Rahim Organizational Conflict Inventories, Managers, employees, supervisors, see 2149

Ramsay Corporation Job Skills—Machinist Test, Machinist job applicants, see 2151
Ramsay Corporation Job Skills—Mechanic Evaluation Test, Mechanic job applicants, see 2152
Ramsay Corporation Job Skills—PrinTest—Forms A-C and B-C, Adults, see 2155
Ramsay Corporation Job Skills—Reading Electrical Drawings & Schematics, Adults, see 2156
RBH Test of Chemical Comprehension, Employee applicants and applicants for nurses training, see 2167
Reading-Free Vocational Interest Inventory, Revised, Ages 13 and ove, see 2177
Reality Check Survey, Adults, see 2188
Research Personnel Review Form, Research and engineering and scientific firms, see 2203
Retail Sales Skills Test, Candidates for the position of retail salesperson, see 2205
Retail Store Manager Staff Selector, Candidates for the position of store manager or assistant manager, see 2206
Revised Minnesota Paper Form Board Test, Second Edition, Grade 9 and over, see 2217
Revised PSB—Aptitude for Practical Nursing Examination, Applicants for admission to practical/vocational nursing schools, see 2220
Revised PSB—Health Occupations Aptitude Examination, Candidates for admission to programs of study for the allied health occupations, see 2221
Revised PSB—Nursing School Aptitude Examination (R. N.), Prospective nursing students, see 2222
Roeder Manipulative Aptitude Test, Elementary school to adult, see 2244
Rothwell Miller Interest Blank (Revised), Ages 13 and over, see 2255
Rothwell Miller Values Blank, Ages 15 and older, see 2256
Rothwell-Miller Interest Blank, Ages 12 and over, see 2257
Safran Student's Interest Inventory, Third Edition, Grades 5-9, 9-12, see 2264
Sales Achievement Predictor, Adults, see 2265
Sales Aptitude Test: ETSA Test 7A, Job applicants, see 2266
Sales Attitude Check List, Applicants for sales positions, In, 2267
Sales Competency Inventory, Salespeople, see 2268
Sales Comprehension Test, Sales applicant, see 2269
Sales Effectiveness Analysis, Salespeople, see 2270
Sales Effectiveness Survey, Sales and business development professionals, see 2271
Sales Motivation Inventory, Revised, Prospective and employed salespeople, see 2272
Sales Motivation Survey, Salespeople, see 2273
Sales Relations Survey, Salespeople, see 2275
The Sales Sentence Completion Blank, Applicants for sales positions, see 2276
Sales Staff Selector, Candidates for sales representative positions, see 2277
Sales Style Diagnosis Test, Salespeople, see 2278
Sales Style Indicator , Sales personnel, see 2279
SCC Clerical Skills Series, Job applicants, see 2302
Screening Form for District Manager Selection, Applicants for newspaper district manager positions, see 2330
Selby MillSmith Values Indices, Adults, see 2346
SELECT Associate Screening System, Prospective employees, see 2347
[Selection Interview Forms], Business and industry, see 2348
Self-Directed Search, 4th Edition [Forms R, E, and CP], Ages 12 and above, see 2360
Self-Motivated Career Planning Guide, High school and college and adults, see 2364
Senior Clerical Skills Test, Candidates for clerical positions, see 2374
ServiceFirst, Employees in service-oriented positions, see 2386
Shapes Analysis Test, Ages 14 and over, see 2398
Sheltered Employment Work Experience Program, Mentally retarded teenagers and adults, see 2400
Short Employment Tests, Second Edition, Adults, see 2406
Short Tests of Clerical Ability, Applicants for office positions, see 2408
Situational Leadership®, Managers, leaders, administrators, supervisors, and staff, see 2415
16PF® Personal Career Development Profile, Ages 16 and over, see 2419
Skills and Attributes Inventory, Non-management positions, see 2420
Skills Assessment Module, Average, handicapped, and disadvantaged vocational training school students ages 14-18, see 2421
Skills Inventory for Teams, Early intervention practitioners, see 2423
SkillScan for Management Development, Sales managers, see 2424
SKILLSCOPE for Managers, Managers, see 2425
The Standard Timing Model, Mechanics, see 2479
The Stanton Profile, Employment applicants, see 2490
START—Strategic Assessment of Readiness for Training, Adults, see 2495
Stenographic Skills Test: ETSA Test 4A, Job applicants, see 2501
Strategic Decision Making Inventory, Business managers, see 2506
Stress in General Scale, Employees, see 2509
Stromberg Dexterity Test, Trade school and adults, see 2515
Styles of Leadership Survey, Adults, see 2547
Styles of Management Inventory, Adults, see 2548

Styles of Teamwork Inventory, Individuals whose work responsibilities require work-team cooperation, see 2549
Supervisory Change Relations, Supervisors and prospective supervisors, see 2561
Supervisory Coaching Relations, Supervisors and potential supervisors, see 2562
Supervisory Communication Relations, Supervisors and potential supervisors, see 2563
Supervisory Inventory on Communication, Supervisors and prospective supervisors, see 2565
Supervisory Inventory on Human Relations, Supervisors and prospective supervisors, see 2566
Supervisory Job Discipline, Supervisors and potential supervisors, see 2567
Supervisory Job Instruction, Supervisors and potential supervisors, see 2568
Supervisory Job Safety, "Blue-collar" supervisors and potential supervisors, see 2569
Supervisory Potential Test, Supervisors or potential supervisors, see 2570
Supervisory Practices Inventory, Managers or administrators, see 2571
Supervisory Practices Test, Revised, Supervisors, see 2572
Supervisory Profile Record, Prospective supervisors, see 2573
Supervisory Simulator, First-level supervisors and/or forepersons, see 2574
Supervisory Skills Inventory, First-line supervisors, see 2575
Survey of Employee Access, Adults, see 2578
Survey of Influence Effectiveness, Business and government professionals, see 2580
Survey of Management Practices, Subordinates of managers, see 2583
Survey of Organizations, Employees, see 2587
Survey of Work Styles, Adults, see 2592
Sweet Technical Information Test, Ages 14-17, see 2598
System for Testing and Evaluation of Potential, Managerial and professional personnel, see 2605
Systems Analysis Aptitude Test, Applicants for computer systems analyst position, see 2608
Systems Programming Aptitude Test, Systems programmers, see 2609
Team Competency Assessment, Team members, see 2630
Team Effectiveness Survey, Team members, see 2634
The Team Leadership Practices Inventory, Managers, see 2635
Team Process Diagnostic, Individuals whose work responsibilities require work-team cooperation, see 2636
Teamness Index, Individuals whose work responsibilities require work-team cooperation, see 2637
Teamwork Appraisal Survey, Individuals whose work responsibilities require work-team cooperation, see 2638
Technical Personnel Recruiting Inventory, Research, engineering, and scientific firms, see 2639
Technical Support Staff Selector, Candidates for the position of technical support, see 2640
Technical Test Battery, Technical job applicants and incumbents entry level to professional, see 2641
Technician Electrical Test—-Form A2, Electrical workers and applicants for electrical jobs, see 2643
Technician Mechanical Test—Form A2, Mechanical workers and applicants for mechanical jobs, see 2644
Telemarketing Staff Selector, Candidates for the position of telemarketing representative, see 2646
Test of Mechanical Concepts, Applicants for industrial positions, see 2700
Test of Retail Sales Insight, Retail clerks and student, see 2713
Theological School Inventory, Incoming seminary students, see 2751
The Time of Your Life, Employees, see 2760
Tool Room Attendant, Applicants for maintenance jobs, see 2769
TQ Manager Inventory and Feedback From Others, Business managers, see 2773
Trainer's Assessment of Proficiency (TAP), Trainers, see 2775
Transition-to-Work Inventory: A Job Placement System for Workers with Severe disAbilities, Individuals with severe disabilities, see 2781
Typing 5, Administrative assistants, secretaries, and any position requiring typing ability, see 2786
Typing Test for Business, Applicants for typing positions, see 2787
USES Basic Occupational Literacy Test, Educationally disadvantaged adults, see 2795
USES Clerical Skills Tests, Applicants for clerical positions, see 2796
Veterinary College Admission Test, Veterinary college applicants, see 2810
Vincent Mechanical Diagrams Test, 1979 Revision, Ages 15-adult, see 2812
Voc-Tech Quick Screener, Non-college bound high school students and adults, see 2822
Vocational Adaptation Rating Scales, Ages 13-50 (mentally retardcd individuals), see 2824
Vocational Assessment and Curriculum Guide, Mentally retarded employees, see 2826
Vocational Behavior Checklist, Vocational rehabilitation clients, see 2827
Vocational Decision-Making Interview—Revised, Disabled individuals who need to make vocational decisions, see 2828
Vocational Interest and Sophistication Assessment, Retarded adolescents and young adults, see 2829
Vocational Interest, Experience, and Skill Assessment, Grades 8-10, 11-adults, see 2830

Vocational Interest, Experience and Skill Assessment (VIESA), 2nd Canadian Edition, Grades 8-10, 11-adults, see 2831
Vocational Interest Inventory and Exploration Survey, Vocational education students, see 2832
Vocational Interest Inventory—Revised, High school juniors and seniors, see 2833
Vocational Opinion Index, Disadvantaged trainees in vocational skills programs, In, 2834
Vocational Preference Inventory, 1985 Edition, High school and college and adults, see 2835
Vocational Research Interest Inventory, High school and adults, see 2836
W-APT Programming Aptitude Test, Programmers and general population, see 2849
Walden CICS/VS Command Level Proficiency Test, Applicants for computer training or employment, see 2842
Walden DOS JCL (VS, VSE) Proficiency Test, Applicants for computer training or employment, see 2843
Walden OS/JCL Proficiency Test, Applicants for computer training or employment, see 2844
Walden Structured Analysis and Design Concepts Proficiency Test, Candidates for EDP systems analysts/designers, see 2845
Walden Structured COBOL Proficiency Test, Applicants for computer training or employment, see 2846
Walden TSO/SPF Proficiency Test, Applicants for computer training or employment, see 2847
Warehouse/Plant Worker Staff Selector, Applicants for plant work, see 2851
Weld Test—Form A-C, Welding job applicants, see 2867
Wesman Personnel Classification Test, Grades 10-12 and applicants and employees, see 2871
The Wolfe Computer Operator Aptitude Test, Applicants for computer training or employment, see 2895
Wolfe Programming Language Test: COBOL, Programmers and trainees, see 2896
Wolfe-Spence Programming Aptitude Test, Applicants in computer programming, see 2897
Work Adjustment Inventory, Adolescents and young adults, see 2912
The Work Adjustment Scale, Junior and senior high school students, see 2913
Work Aptitude: Profile and Practice Set, Ages 15-17, see 2914
Work Aspect Preference Scale, Grades 10-12 and college and adults, see 2915
Work Attitudes Questionnaire (Version for Research), Managers, see 2916
Work Environment Scale, Second Edition, Employees and supervisors, see 2917
The Work Experience Survey, "Individuals with disabilities who are either employed or about to begin employment," see 2918
Work Keys Assessments, Grade 10 to adult, see 2920
[Work Motivation], Managers, employees, see 2921
Work Performance Assessment, Job trainees, see 2923
Work Preference Questionnaire, Business and industry, see 2925
Work Skills Series Production, Manufacturing and production employees and prospective employees, see 2927
Work Temperament Inventory, Workers, see 2928
Working—Assessing Skills, Habits, and Style, High school and college students and potential employees, see 2929
Workplace Skills Survey, Job applicants and employees, see 2930
XYZ Inventory, Managers and prospective managers, see 2937

PUBLISHERS DIRECTORY AND INDEX

This directory and index gives the names and test entry numbers of all publishers represented in Tests in Print V. *Current addresses are listed for all publishers for which this is known. Those publishers for which a current address is not available are listed as "Address Unknown." As a new feature beginning in* Tests in Print V, *this directory and index also provides telephone and FAX numbers and email and Web page addresses for those publishers who responded to our request for this information. Please note that all test numbers refer to test entry numbers, not page numbers. Publishers are an important source of information about catalogs, specimen sets, price changes, test revisions, and many other matters.*

Ablin Press Distributors
700 John Ringling Blvd. #1603
Sarasota, FL 34236-1504
Telephone: 941-361-7521
FAX: 941-361-7521
Tests: 855, 2410

Academic Therapy Publications
20 Commercial Boulevard
Novato, CA 94949-6191
Telephone: 800-422-7249
FAX: 415-883-3720
E-mail: atp@aol.com
Web URL: www.atpub.com
Tests: 157, 244, 397, 730, 786, 834, 850, 971, 994, 1028, 1068, 1362, 1425, 1461, 1462, 1500, 1663, 1725, 1726, 1784, 2038, 2138, 2141, 2142, 2145, 2190, 2191, 2192, 2236, 2252, 2461, 2462, 2500, 2671, 2721, 2729, 2821, 2868, 2908, 2935

Accrediting Association of Bible Colleges
P.O. Box 780339
Orlando, FL 32878
Telephone: 407-207-0808
FAX: 407-207-0840
E-mail: exdir@aabc.org
Web URL: www.aabc.org
Tests: 2480

ACS DivCHED Examinations Institute
Clemson University
223 Brackett Hall
Box 341913
Clemson, SC 29634-1913
Telephone: 864-656-1249
FAX: 864-646-1250
E-mail: acsxm@clemson.edu
Web URL: www.tigerched.clemson.edu/
Tests: 42, 43, 44, 45, 46, 47, 48, 49, 50, 51, 52, 53, 54, 55

ACT, Inc.
2201 N. Dodge Street
P.O. Box 168
Iowa City, IA 52243-0168
Telephone: 319-337-1000
FAX: 319-339-3021
Web URL: www.act.org
Tests: 56, 57, 418, 619, 621, 992, 1997, 2313, 2830, 2920

Addiction Research Foundation
Marketing Services
33 Russell Street
Toronto, Ontario M5S 2S1
Canada
Tests: 133, 134, 184, 858, 859, 1304, 1305, 2414

ADE Incorporated
P.O. Box 660
Clarkston, MI 48347
Tests: 1372, 1766, 2550

Administrative Research Associates
[Address Unknown]
Tests: 2351, 2890

Adult Self Expression Scale
c/o John P. Galassi
CB#3500
Peabody Hall
University of North Carolina
Chapel Hill, NC 27599-3500
Telephone: 919-962-9196
FAX: 919-962-1533
E-mail: jgalassi@email.unc.edu
Tests: 88

Advantage Learning Systems, Inc.
P.O. Box 8036
Wisconsin Rapids, WI 54495-8036
Telephone: 800-338-4204
FAX: 715-424-4242
E-mail: answers@advlearn.com
Web URL: www.advlearn.com
Tests: 2492, 2493

Age and Cognitive Performance Research Centre
Department of Psychology
University of Manchester
Manchester M13 9PL
England
Tests: 2662

AJA Associates
c/o Marchman Psychology
720 South Dubuque
Iowa City, IA 52240
Tests: 1740

The Alemany Press
(Janus Book Publishers, Inc.)
Data Scan
P.O. Box 7604
West Trenton, NJ 08628
Tests: 1195, 2337, 2688

The Allington Corporation
P.O. Box 125
Remington, VA 22734
Tests: 1422

Allyn & Bacon
Department 894
160 Gould Street
Needham Heights, MA 02194-2310
Tests: 917, 2503, 2627, 2628

Alternatives for Contemporary Education, Inc.
1217 Ironwood Drive
Fairborn, OH 45324
Telephone: 937-754-3981
E-mail: drgeiman@worldnet.att.net
Tests: 1083

American Association for Active Lifestyles and Fitness
1900 Association Drive
Reston, VA 22091
Telephone: 800-213-7193
FAX: 703-476-9527
E-mail: AAALF@AAHPERD.ORG
Web URL: www.aahperd.org/aaalf/aaalf.htm
Tests: 1062, 2455, 2653

American Association of Teachers of German, Inc.
112 Haddontowne Court, #104
Cherry Hill, NJ 08034-3668
Tests: 1761

American Dental Association
211 East Chicago Avenue
Chicago, IL 60611-2678
Telephone: 312-440-2684
FAX: 312-487-4105
E-mail: kramerg@ada.org
Web URL: www.ada.org
Tests: 386, 780

American Guidance Service, Inc.
4201 Woodland Road
Circle Pines, MN 55014-1796
Telephone: 800-328-2560
FAX: 612-786-5603
E-mail: agsmail@agsnet
Web URL: www.agsnet.com
Tests: 124, 245, 280, 353, 469, 809, 995, 1095, 1096, 1177, 1378, 1379, 1380, 1382, 1384, 1385, 1386, 1392, 1394, 1700, 1703, 1728, 1847, 1848, 1902, 1903, 2452, 2535, 2813, 2814, 2905

The American Occupational Therapy Association, Inc.
4720 Montgomery Lane
Bethesda, MD 20814-3425
Tests: 152, 1409

American Printing House for the Blind, Inc.
1839 Frankfort Avenue
P.O. Box 6085
Louisville, KY 40206-0085
Tests: 324, 2259

American Psychiatric Press, Inc.
1400 K Street, NW Suite 1101
Washington, DC 20005
Tests: 642, 2519, 2520

Paul S. Amidon & Associates, Inc.
1966 Benson Avenue
St. Paul, MN 55116-3299
Tests: 2875

Dr. Nancy C. Andreasen
Department of Psychiatry
MHCRC, 2911 JPP
200 Hawkins Drive
Iowa City, IA 52242-1057
Telephone: 319-356-4720
FAX: 319-356-2587
E-mail: Katelyn-dasse@uiowa.edu
Tests: 650, 2288, 2289, 2290

Andrews University Press
Berrien Springs, MI 49104-1700
Tests: 2649

Applied Personnel Research
27 Judith Road
Newton, MA 02459-1715
Telephone: 617-244-8859
E-mail: wiesen@personnelselection.com
Web URL: www.personnelselection.com/apr.htm
Tests: 2884

Applied Symbolix
800 N. Wells Street, Suite 200
Chicago, IL 60610
Tests: 630

ARBOR, Inc.
ARBOR Corporate Center
One West Third Street
Media, PA 19063
Telephone: 610-566-8700
FAX: 610-566-9482
E-mail: carolleach@juno.com
Tests: 2834

The Assessment and Development Centre
6890 East Sunrise Drive, #120-382
Tucson, AZ 85750
Telephone: 520-299-5501
FAX: 520-299-5348
E-mail: sanqassess@aol.com
Web URL: www.stressmaster.com
Tests: 1887, 2512

Assessment Enterprises
925 Hayslope Drive
Knoxville, TN 37919
Tests: 1347

Assessment Resource Center
College of Education
University of Missouri-Columbia
2800 Maguire Blvd.
Columbia, MO 65211
Telephone: 800-366-8232
FAX: 573-882-8937
E-mail: collegebase!asc.missouri.edu
Web URL: www.coe.missouri.edu/~arcwww/
Tests: 570, 1707

Assessment Systems Corporation
2233 University Avenue, Suite 200
St. Paul, MN 55114-1629
Telephone: 651-647-9220
FAX: 651-647-0412
E-mail: info@assess.com
Web URL: www.assess.com
Tests: 1692

Assessment Systems International, Inc.
15350 W. National Avenue, Suite 205
New Berlin, WI 53151-5158
Tests: 1545

Associated Consultants in Education
P.O. Box 875
Suffern, NY 10901
Tests: 305, 2577

The Associated Examining Board
Stag Hill House
Guildford, Surrey GU2 5XJ
England
Telephone: +44 1483 506506
FAX: +44 1483 300152
E-mail: cjadhav@aeb.org.uk
Web URL: www.aeb.org.uk
Tests: 260

Association for the Education and Welfare of the Visually Handicapped
ATTN: Mrs. S. A. Clamp, Deputy Head
St. Vincent's School for the Blind
Yew Tree Lane
West Derby, Liverpool L12 9HN
England
Tests: 1520, 2770

Association of American Colleges and Universities
1818 R Street, NW
Washington, DC 20009
Telephone: 202-387-3760
FAX: 202-265-9532
E-mail: pubs_desk@aacu.nw.dc.us
Web URL: www.aacu-edu.org
Tests: 974

Association of American Medical Colleges
2501 M Street, NW Lbby 26
Washington, DC 20037-1300
Tests: 1638

Australian Council for Educational Research Ltd.
19 Prospect Hill Road
Private Bag 55
Camberwell, Victoria 3124
Australia
Tests: 20, 23, 24, 26, 27, 28, 29, 30, 31, 32, 33, 34, 72, 187, 325, 492, 622, 825, 955, 1231, 1254, 1339, 1465, 1466, 1521, 1600, 2080, 2091, 2092, 2477, 2485, 2540, 2598, 2611, 2743, 2915, 2926

Australian Department of Immigration and Multicultural Affairs
Benjamin Offices
Chan St, Belconnen
ACT 2617
Australia
Tests: 233

Aviat
101 North Main
Ann Arbor, MI 48104
Tests: 1147

Thomas F. Babor
Department of Community Medicine
University of Connecticut
Farmington, CT 06030-1910
FAX: 860-679-2374
E-mail: babor@nso.uchc.edu
Tests: 135

Ball Foundation
800 Roosevelt Road
Building C, Suite 120
Glen Ellyn, IL 60137-5850
Tests: 239

Ballard & Tighe Publishers
480 Atlas Street
Brea, CA 92821
Tests: 1234, 1235, 2139

The Barber Center Press, Inc.
136 East Avenue
Erie, PA 16507
Telephone: 814-453-7661
FAX: 814-455-1132
E-mail: gabcmain@drbarbercenter.org
Web URL: www.drbarbercenter.org
Tests: 686, 805, 2400

Donna Bardis
1533 Orkney Drive
Toledo, OH 43606
Telephone: 419-535-6146
E-mail: pbardis@pop3.utoledo.edu
Tests: 6, 327, 568, 765, 970, 1004, 1016, 1129, 1271, 1327, 1646, 1893, 1992, 2200, 2390, 2748, 2806, 2815, 2931

Barrett and Associates, Inc.
500 West Exchange St.
Akron, OH 44302-1428
Telephone: 330-762-2323
E-mail: ddoverspike@uakron.edu
Tests: 231

Bay State Psychological Associates, Inc.
225 Friend Street
Boston, MA 02114
Telephone: 800-438-2772
FAX: 617-367-5888
E-mail: jerry@eri.com
Web URL: www.eri.com
Tests: 944

James R. Beatty
College of Business Administration
San Diego State University
San Diego, CA 92182
Tests: 1278

Lenore Behar
1821 Woodburn Road
Durham, NC 27705
Telephone: 919-489-1888
FAX: 919-489-1832
E-mail: lbehar@psych.mc.duke.edu
Tests: 2039

Behavior Data Systems, Ltd.
P.O. Box 44256
Phoenix, AZ 85064-4256
Tests: 856, 2284, 2783

Behavior Science Systems, Inc.
P.O. Box 580274
Minneapolis, MN 55458
Telephone: 612-929-6220
FAX: 612-920-4925
Tests: 453, 454, 872, 1259, 1935, 2040

Behavioral-Developmental Initiatives
14636 North 55th Street
Scottsdale, AZ 85254
Telephone: 800-405-2313
FAX: 602-494-2688
E-mail: bdi@temperament.com
Web URL: www.b-di.com
Tests: 425

Behaviordata, Inc.
2166 The Alameda
San Jose, CA 95126-1144
Telephone: 408-998-8840
FAX: 408-985-2340
E-mail: BDI@phc.net
Tests: 983, 2399

The Ber-Sil Co.
3412 Seaglen Drive
Rancho Palos Verdes, CA 90275
Tests: 304

Ian Berg
[Address Unknown]
Tests: 2350

Berrent Publishing Company
1025 Northern Blvd.
Roslyn, NY 11576
Tests: 1534

Nancy E. Betz, Ph.D.
2758 Kensington Place West
Columbus, OH 43202
Tests: 403

Millard J. Bienvenu, Ph.D.
Northwest Publications
710 Watson Drive
Natchitoches, LA 7145
Telephone: (318) 352-5313
Tests: 185, 1292, 1302, 1309, 1580, 1876, 1882, 2033, 2362, 2394

Bigby, Havis, & Associates, Inc.
12750 Merit Drive, Suite 660
Dallas, TX 75251
Telephone: 972-233-6055
FAX: 972-233-3154
E-mail: kcapelle@bigby.com
Web URL: www.bigby.com
Tests: 186, 2347

Bilingual Educational Services, Inc.
2514 South Grand Avenue
Los Angeles, CA 90007-9979
Tests: 720, 740

Laurence M. Binder, Ph.D.
Providence Health Systems
11308 SW 68th Pkwy
Tigard, OR 97223-8679
Tests: 2011

Biobehavioral Associates
1330 Beacon Street
Brookline, MA 02146
Tests: 2508

Biofeedback Certification Institute of America
10200 W 44th Avenue, Suite 304
Wheat Ridge, CO 80033-2840
Tests: 310

Blanchard Training & Development, Inc.
125 State Place
Escondido, CA 92025-1398
Tests: 1436

Sidney J. Blatt
Yale University School of Medicine
Department of Psychiatry
25 Park Street
New Haven, CT 06519
Telephone: 203-785-2090
FAX: 203-785-7357
E-mail: sidney.blatt@yale.edu
Tests: 215, 790

Gerald S. Blum
127 Via Alicia
Santa Barbara, CA 93108
Tests: 317

Book-Lab
[Address Unknown]
Tests: 1224, 2005

Boston Massachusetts General Hospital
Department of Psychiatry
Bullfinch 3
55 Fruit
Boston, MA 02114
Tests: 1517

Bowling Green State University
Department of Psychology
Bowling Green, OH 43403
Telephone: 419-372-8247
FAX: 419-372-6013
E-mail: jdiebgnet.bgsu.edu
Web URL: www.bgsu.edu/departments/psych/JDI
Tests: 1348, 2208, 2509, 2593

Brador Publications, Inc.
P.O. Box 149
Scotland, CT 06264
Tests: 320, 2180

BrainTrain
727 Twin Ridge Lane
Richmond, VA 23235
Telephone: 804-320-0105
FAX: 804-320-0242
E-mail: ginger@braintrain-online.com
Tests: 1282

Branden Publishing, Co.
17 Station Street
Box 843
Brookline Village
Boston, MA 02147
Tests: 308

Brandon House, Inc.
P.O. Box 240
Bronx, NY 10471
Tests: 122, 914

Patricia Brandt, Ph.D.
Parent Child Nursing
School of Nursing
University of Washington
Seattle, WA 98195
Tests: 1947

Brigham Young University
Humanities Research Center
Foreign Language Testing
Provo, UT 84602
Tests: 2464

British Columbia Institute Against Family Violence
409 Granville Street, Suite 551
Vancouver, BC V6C 1T2
Canada
Tests: 2395

Brookes Publishing Co., Inc. (Paul H.)
P.O. Box 10624
Baltimore, MD 21285-0624
Tests: 123, 553, 2778

Brougham Press
P.O. Box 2702
Olathe, KS 66063-0702
Telephone: 800-360-6244
FAX: 913-782-1116
Tests: 475

Brown and Benchmark Publishers, a Division of Wm. C. Brown Communications
2460 Kerper Blvd.
Dubuque, IA 51001
Tests: 496

Martin M. Bruce, Ph.D.
22516 Caravelle Circle
Boca Raton, FL 33433
Telephone: 561-393-2428
FAX: 561-362-6185
E-mail: brucepubl@aol.com
Tests: 170, 218, 352, 361, 402, 535, 942, 1713, 1922, 1968, 2006, 2269, 2272, 2276, 2348, 2555, 2572, 2716, 2776, 2889

Arnold R. Bruhn and Associates
7910 Woodmont Avenue, Suite 1300
Bethesda, MD 20814
Tests: 885

Brunner/Mazel, Inc.
1900 Frost Road, Suite 101
Bristol, PA 19007-1598
Tests: 224

Business Research Support Services
Ohio State University
College of Business
1775 College Road
Columbus, OH 43210-1309
Tests: 1437

The California Academic Press
217 La Cruz Avenue
Millbrae, CA 94030
Telephone: 650-697-5628
FAX: 650-697-5628
E-mail: steveATCAP@aol.com
Web URL: www.calpress.com
Tests: 367, 368

California Counseling Centers
22797 Barton Rd., Suite 200
Grand Terrace, CA 92324
Tests: 1431, 1432, 1433, 1435

Callier Center for Communication Disorders
University of Texas at Dallas
1966 Inwood Road
Dallas, TX 75235
Tests: 377

Cambridge Center for Behavioral Studies
Publications Department
336 Baker Avenue
Concord, MA 01742
Tests: 279, 1853

The Cambridge Stratford Study Skills Institute
8560 Main Street
Williamsville, NY 14221
Tests: 1891, 2589

Cambridge University Press
110 Midland Avenue
Port Chester, NY 10573-4930
Telephone: 800-872-7423
FAX: 914-937-4712
Tests: 1408, 1625, 1770, 2050

Camelot Unlimited
c/o Michael Lavelli
5757 N. Sheridan Road, Suite 13B
Chicago, IL 60660
Telephone: 773-506-6285
FAX: 508-519-8187
E-mail: CamelotUnlimited@Yahoo.com
Tests: 462

Canadian Test Centre
Educational Assessment Services
85 Citizen Court, Suite 7 & 8
Markham, Ontario L6G 1A8
Canada
Tests: 383, 384, 388

Canyonlands Publishing, Inc.
141 S. Park Avenue
Tucson, AZ 85719
Tests: 176, 1064

Career Research and Testing, Inc.
P.O. Box 611930
San Jose, CA 95161-1930
Telephone: 408-441-9100
FAX: 408-441-9101
E-mail: tests @careertrainer.com
Web URL: www.careertrainer.com
Tests: 423, 1719, 1820, 2207

CASAS
8910 Clairemont Mesa Blvd.
San Diego, CA 92123-1104
Telephone: 619-292-2900
FAX: 619-292-2910
E-mail: bwalsh@casas.org
Web URL: www.casas.org
Tests: 645

Wilfred A. Cassell
[Address Unknown]
Tests: 2099, 2457

The CATI Corporation
10 East Costilla
Colorado Springs, CO 80903
Tests: 690

Center for Applied Linguistics
1118 - 22nd Street, NW
Washington, DC 20037
Tests: 250, 481, 482, 1179, 1191, 1255, 2015

Center for Architecture and Urban Planning Research
University of Wisconsin-Milwaukee
P.O. Box 413
Milwaukee, WI 53201-0413
Tests: 877

Center for Creative Leadership
One Leadership Place
P.O. Box 2630
Greensboro, NC 27438-6300
Tests: 300, 807, 1393, 2101, 2425

The Center for Management Effectiveness
P.O. Box 1202
Pacific Palisades, Ca 90272
Telephone: 310-459-6052
FAX: 310-459-9307
E-mail: kindlerCME@aol.com
Tests: 1557, 1949, 2238, 2506

Center for Rehabilitation Effectiveness
Boston University
635 Commonwealth Avenue
Boston, MA 02215
Telephone: 617-358-0175
FAX: 617-353-7500
E-mail: smhaley@bu.edu
Web URL:www.bu.edu/cre/
Tests: 1906

Center for the Study of Ethical Development
University of Minnesota
206-A Burton Hall
178 Pillsbury Drive, SE
Minneapolis, MN 55455
Tests: 771

Center for the Study of Higher Education
The University of Memphis
Memphis, TN 38152
Tests: 620, 635

Central Institute for the Deaf
818 South Euclid Avenue
St. Louis, MO 63110
Telephone: 314-977-0133
FAX: 314-977-0023
E-mail: dgushleff@cid.wustl.edu
Web URL: www.cid.wustl.edu
Tests: 486, 487, 891, 1126,1127, 2298, 2620

Central Wisconsin Center for the Developmentally Disabled
317 Knutson Drive
Madison, WI 53704
Tests: 2891

Centreville School
6201 Kennett Pike
Wilmington, DE 19807
Telephone: 302-571-0230
FAX: 302-571-0270
E-mail: language@del.net
Tests: 2201

CERAD Administrative CORE
Box 2203
Duke University Medical Center
Box 3203
Durham, NC 27710
Tests: 434, 1808

Vicentita M. Cervera, Ed.D.
13 Miller Street
San Francisco Del Monte
Quezon City 1105
Philippines
Telephone: 411-2673
FAX: 371-6490
E-mail: vcervera@skyinet.net
Tests: 1030

CFKR Career Materials
11860 Kemper Road, Unit 7
Auburn, CA 95603
Tests: 179, 408, 993, 1200, 1350, 1518, 1539, 2822

Jay L. Chambers
258 Mackeys Lane
Fairfield, VA 24435-2303
Telephone: 540-258-2661
E-mail: ibis@cfrw.com
Tests: 1988

Chapman, Brook & Kent
[Address Unknown]
Tests: 552

The Chauncey Group International
Educational Testing Service
P.O. Box 6604
Princeton, NJ 08541-6604
Tests: 2687

Checkmate Plus, Ltd.
P.O. Box 696
Stony Brook, NY 11790-0696
Telephone: 800-779-4292
FAX: 516-360-3432
E-mail: inpo@checkmateplus.com
Web URL: www.checkmateplus.com
Tests: 79, 876

CHECpoint Systems, Inc.
1520 N. Waterman Avenue
San Bernardino, CA 92404
Tests: 251

Child Behavior Checklist
University Medical Education Associates
1 South Prospect Street, Room 6434
Burlington, VT 05401-3456
Telephone: 802-656-8313
FAX: 802-656-2602
E-mail: checklist@uvm.edu
Web URL: checklist.uvm.edu
Tests: 424, 451, 2939

Child Development Centers of the Bluegrass, Inc.
465 Springhill Drive
Lexington, KY 40503
Tests: 1490

Child Development Resources
P.O. Box 280
Norge, VA 23127-0280
Tests: 1220, 2423

Child Welfare League of America, Inc.
Publications Department
440 First Street, NW Suite #310
Washington, DC 20001-2085
Telephone: 202-638-2952
FAX: 202-638-4004
E-mail: sgretchen@cwla.org
Web URL: www.cwla.org
Tests: 458, 1007

Larry Christensen, Ph.D.
Chair, Department of Psychology
University of South alabama
6641 Sugar Creek Drive
Mobile, AL 36695
Telephone: 334-460-6321
FAX: 334-460-6320
E-mail: LChriste@usamail.usouthal.edu
Tests: 483

Chronicle Guidance Publications, Inc.
Aurora Street
P.O. Box 1190
Moravia, NY 13118-1190
Tests: 413, 485, 1948

The Clark Wilson Group
1320 Fenwick Lane, Suite 708
Silver Springs, MD 20910
Tests: 490, 2097, 2098

Clinical Psychometric Research, Inc.
P.O. Box 619
Riderwood, MD 21139
Telephone: 800-245-0277
FAX: 410-321-6341
E-mail: mdero@aol.com
Web URL: derogatis-tests.com
Tests: 791, 793, 794, 2117

Clinician's View
6007 Osuna Road, NE
Albuquerque, NM 87109
Tests: 977

Clyde Computing Service
[Address Unknown]
Tests: 551

CogniSyst, Inc.
3937 Nottaway Road
Durham, NC 27707
Tests: 671, 1870, 2397, 2909

CogScreen LLC
5021 Seminary Road, Suite 110
Alexandria, VA 22311
Tests: 567

The College Board
45 Columbus Avenue
New York, NY 10023-6992
Tests: 18, 192, 571, 572, 573, 574, 575, 576, 577, 578, 579, 580, 581, 582, 583, 584, 585, 586, 587, 588, 590, 591, 593, 594, 595, 596, 597, 598, 599, 600, 601, 602, 603, 604, 605, 606, 607, 608, 609, 613, 614, 1274, 1746

Communication Skill Builders—A Division of The Psychological Corporation
555 Academic Court
San Antonio, TX 78204-9941
Telephone: 800-211-8378
FAX: 800-232-1223
E-mail: www.hbtpc.com
Tests: 156, 164, 866, 1359, 1360, 1898, 2215, 2660

John D. Cone
Department of Psychology & Family Studies
United States International University
10455 Pomerado Road
San Diego, CA 92131
Telephone: 619-635-4744
FAX: 619-635-4585
E-mail: jcone@usiu.edu
Web URL: www.usiu.edu/jcone
Tests: 1884, 2127

Consulting Psychologists Press, Inc.
3803 East Bayshore Road
P.O. Box 10096
Palo Alto, CA 94303
Telephone: 800-624-1765
FAX: 650-969-8608
Web URL: www.cpp-db.com
Tests: 68, 83, 289, 372, 401, 405, 409, 474, 495, 618, 694, 697, 711, 926, 963, 1010, 1036, 1140, 1141, 1156, 1157, 1158, 1451, 1590, 1750, 1754, 1755, 1790, 1895, 1970, 2042, 2065, 2149, 2246, 2282, 2445, 2451, 2546, 2805, 2917

Consulting Resource Group International, Inc.
#886 — 200 West Third Street
Sumas, WA 98295-8000
Tests: 962, 1355, 1450, 1952, 2279, 2371, 2511, 2804

CORE Corporation
Pleasant Hill Executive park
391 Taylor Blvd., Suite 110
Pleasant Hill, CA 94523-2275
Tests: 2386

C.P.S., Inc.
P.O. Box 83
Larchmont, NY 10538
Telephone: 914-833-1633
FAX: 914-833-1633
Tests: 466, 912, 2110, 2307, 2372

Virginia Crandall, Ph.D.
Division of Development Psychology
Wright State University
School of Medicine
800 Livermore Street
Yellow Spring, OH 45387
Tests: 1026

Paul L. Crawford
3046 Mt. Vernon Road
Hurricane, WV 25526
Telephone: 304-757-6221
Tests: 721

Creative Learning Press, Inc.
P.O. Box 320
Mansfield Center, CT 06250
Tests: 493, 723, 1474, 2295

Creative Therapeutics, Inc.
155 County Road
P.O. Box 522
Cresskill, NJ 07626-0522
Tests: 1070, 2210

Critical Thinking Books & Software
ATTN: John Baker
P.O. Box 448
Pacific Grove, CA 93950-0448
Telephone: 800-458-4849
FAX: 831-393-3277
E-mail: ct@criticalthinking.com
Web URL: www.criticalthinking.com
Tests: 705

CTB/McGraw-Hill
20 Ryan Ranch Road
Monterey, CA 93940-5703
Tests: 84, 364, 369, 370, 374, 431, 461, 665, 693, 741, 742, 743, 744, 750, 800, 827, 886, 918, 947, 1413, 1420, 1421, 1533, 1760, 2000, 2029, 2059, 2422, 2443, 2463, 2560, 2654, 2677, 2737, 2738, 2739, 2740

Curriculum Associates, Inc.
153 Rangeway Road
P.O. Box 2001
North Billerica, MA 01862-0901
Telephone: 800-225-0248
FAX: 800-366-1158
E-mail: cainfo@curriculumassociates.com
Web URL: www.curriculumassociates.com
Tests: 339, 340, 341, 342, 343, 344, 345, 346, 347, 647, 2213

Cutronics Educational Institute
[Address Unknown]
Tests: 757, 758

Cypress Lake Media
[Address Unknown]
Tests: 1172, 2106

Dallas Educational Services
P.O. Box 833114
Richardson, TX 75083-3114
Telephone: 972-234-6371
FAX: 972-437-5342
Tests: 252, 761, 1088, 1624, 2357

Dansk Psykologisk Forlag
Hans Knudsense Plads 1A
2100 Kobenhavn O
Copenhagen, Denmark
Tests: 242

Dartnell
4660 Ravenswood Avenue
Chicago, IL 60640
Tests: 857, 943, 989

DBM Publishing
275 Broad Hollow Road
Melville, NY 11747
Telephone: 516-753-2904
FAX: 516-756-2571
E-mail: maureen-sullivan@dbm.com
Web URL: dbm.com
Tests: 1331

Delaware County Intermediate Unit
Dr. Nicholas A. Spennato
Language Arts Specialist
6th and Olive Streets
Media, PA 19063
Telephone: 610-565-4880
FAX: 610-565-1315
E-mail: nspen@itrc.dciu.k12pa.us
Tests: 775

William H. Dennis
Trumbull County Reading Clinic
255 Bonnie Brae Avenue, NE
Warren, OH 44483
Tests: 778, 779

Denver Developmental Materials, Inc.
P.O. Box 6919
Denver, CO 80206-0919
Telephone: 800-419-4729
FAX: 303-355-5622
Tests: 783, 784, 785, 787, 788, 1217

Department of Research Assessment and Training
1051 Riverside Drive, Unit 123
New York, NY 10032
Telephone: 212-543-5536
FAX: 212-543-5386
Tests: 748, 949, 1093, 2108, 2109, 2130, 2305

Development Associates, Inc.
1730 North Lynn Street
Arlington, VA 22209-2023
Telephone: 703-276-0677
FAX: 703-276-0432
E-mail: tstephenson@devassocl.com
Web URL: www.devassocl.com
Tests: 87

Developmental Reading Distributors
5879 Wyldewood Lakes Ct.
Fort Myers, FL 33919
Tests: 2174

Developmental Therapy Institute, Inc.
P.O. Box 5153
Athens, GA 30604-5153
Telephone: 706-369-5689
FAX: 706-369-5690
E-mail: mmwood@arches.uga.edu
Web URL: www.uga.edu/dttp
Tests: 814

Donald W. Devine & Associates
9403 Kenwood Road, Suite D-104
Cincinnati, OH 45242
Tests: 819

Diagnostic Counseling Services, Inc.
P.O. Box 6178
Kokomo, IN 46904-6178
Tests: 1729

Diagnostic Specialists, Inc.
1170 North 660 West
Orem, UT 84057
Telephone: 801-225-7698
Tests: 447, 646, 659, 660, 2381, 2885

DocuTrac, Inc.
[Address Unknown]
Tests: 1187, 2604

Rodney L. Doran, Ph.D.
Professor of Science Education
State University of New York at Buffalo
Department of Learning and Instruction
593 Baldy Hall
Buffalo, NY 14260
Tests: 1639

Dragon Press
127 Sycamore Avenue
Mill Valley, CA 94941-2821
Tests: 468

Dr. Maurice J. Eash, Director
Institute of Learning and Teaching
Univ. of Massachusetts—Boston
Harbor Campus
Boston, MA 02125-3393
Tests: 1867

Eckstein Bros., Inc.
4807 W. 118th Place
Hawthorne, CA 90250
Telephone: 323-772-6113
FAX: 310-644-3869
E-mail: ebinc@jps.net
Tests: 896

Ed & Psych Associates
2071 South Atherton St., Suite 900
State College, PA 16801
Telephone: 814-235-9115
FAX: 814-235-9115
Tests: 69

EdITS/Educational and Industrial Testing Service
P.O. Box 7234
San Diego, CA 92167
Telephone: 800-416-1666
FAX: 619-226-1666
E-mail: edits@k-online.com
Web URL: www.edits.net
Tests: 395, 414, 415, 416, 417, 426, 672, 673, 674, 702, 844, 998, 999, 1021, 1367, 1541, 1745, 1872, 1938, 1939, 2076, 2077, 2315, 2538, 2736

Education Associates, Inc.
340 Crab Orchard Road
P.O. Box 4290
Frankfort, NY 40604
Telephone: 800-626-2950
FAX: 502-227-8608
E-mail: stw@e-a-i.com
Web URL: www.educationassociates.com
Tests: 190, 935, 978

Educational Activities, Inc.
ATTN: Rose Falco
1937 Grand Avenue
Baldwin, NY 11510
Telephone: 800-645-3739
FAX: 516-379-7429
E-mail: learn@edact.com
Web URL: www.edact.com
Tests: 172, 1269, 1475, 1812

Educational Assessment Service, Inc.
W6050 Apple Road
Watertown, WI 53098-3937
Telephone: 920-261-1118
FAX: 920-261-6622
E-mail: srimm@globaldialog.com
Web URL: www.SylviaRimm.com
Tests: 35, 36, 1136, 1142, 1143, 2037

Educational Evaluations
Awre Newnham
Gloucestershire GL14 1ET
England
Telephone: 01594 510503
FAX: 01594 510503
Tests: 160, 952, 1261, 1507, 1819, 2187

Educational & Industrial Test Services Ltd.
83 High Street
Hemel Hempstead
Hertfordshire HP1 3AH
England
Telephone: +44 (0) 1442 215521
FAX: +44 (0) 1442 240531
E-mail: post@morrisby.demon.co.uk
Web URL: www.morrisby.co.uk
Tests: 1031, 1270, 1578, 1911, 1943

Educational & Psychological Consultants, Inc.
1715 West Worley, Suite A
Columbia, MO 65203-2603
Telephone: 573-446-6232
E-mail: edcojk@showme.missouri.edu
Tests: 1954

Educational Publications
532 E. Blacklidge
Tucson, AZ 85705
Tests: 1358

Educational Records Bureau
220 East 42nd Street, Suite 100
New York, NY 10017-5006
Telephone: 212-672-9800
FAX: 212-370-4096
E-mail: info@erbtest.org
Web URL: www.erbtest.org
Tests: 664, 967, 1249

Educational Research Consultants, Inc.
[Address Unknown]
Tests: 1642

Educational Studies & Development
1942 Furhman
Muskegon, MI 49441
Tests: 3

Educational Teaching Aids
[Address Unknown]
Tests: 446

Educational Testing Service
Publication Order Services
P.O. Box 6736
Princeton, NJ 08541-6736
Telephone: 609-921-9000
FAX: 609-734-5410
Web URL: www.ets.org
Tests: 91, 92, 93, 94, 95, 96, 97, 98, 99, 100, 101, 102, 103, 104, 105, 106, 107, 108, 109, 110, 111, 112, 113, 114, 115, 116, 117, 118, 497, 498, 499, 500, 501, 502, 503, 504, 505, 506, 507, 508, 509, 510, 511, 512, 513, 514, 515, 516, 517, 518, 519, 520, 521, 522, 523, 524, 525, 526, 527, 528, 529, 530, 531, 571, 572, 573, 574, 575, 576, 577, 578, 579, 580, 581, 582, 583, 584, 585, 586, 587, 588, 589, 590, 591, 592, 593, 594, 595, 596, 597, 598, 599, 600, 601, 602, 603, 604, 605, 606, 607, 608, 609, 610, 611, 612, 613, 614, 615, 617, 666, 762, 1048, 1107, 1108, 1109, 1110, 1111, 1112, 1113, 1114, 1115, 1116, 1117, 1118, 1119, 1120, 1121, 1122, 1123, 1124, 1274, 1405, 1538, 1746, 1759, 2026, 2031, 2032, 2083, 2317, 2339, 2531, 2717

Educators Publishing Service, Inc.
31 Smith Place
Cambridge, MA 02138-1089
Telephone: 800-225-5750
FAX: 617-547-0412
E-mail: cps@epsbooks.com
Web URL: www.epsbooks.com
Tests: 158, 299, 1905, 1907, 1908, 1909, 2219, 2253, 2254, 2427, 2428, 2469

Educators'/Employers' Tests and Services Associates
P.O. Box 327
Saint Thomas, PA 17252
Telephone: 717-369-4222
FAX: 717-369-2344
E-mail: psb@epix.net
Web URL: eetsa.com
Tests: 836, 973, 1077, 1081, 1634, 1635, 1833, 1926, 1964, 2266, 2501

Carl N. Edwards, Ph.D.
P.O. Box 279
Dover, MA 02030
Tests: 2416

Dr. Paul Ekman
Human Interaction Library
University of California—San Francisco
401 Parnassus Avenue, Box HIL
San Francisco, CA 94143-0984
FAX: 415-476-7629
Tests: 1001

Elbern Publications
P.O. Box 09497
Columbus, OH 43209
Telephone: 614-235-2643
FAX: 614-237-2637
Tests: 275, 2177

Dr. John Eliot
Institute for Child Study
University of Maryland
College Park, MD 20742
Tests: 925

Ellsworth Krebs Associates
3615 130th Avenue, NE
Bellevue, WA 98005
Telephone: 425-883-4762
FAX: 425-883-4762
Tests: 449, 1925, 2074

Ellsworth & Vandermeer Press, Ltd.
4405 Scenic Drive
Nashville, TN 37204
Telephone: 615-386-0061
FAX: 615-386-0346
E-mail: evpress@edge.net
Web URL: edge.net/~evpress
Tests: 1890

Patricia B. Elmore, Ph.D.
College of Education, Dean's Office
Mail Code 4624
Southern Illinois University at Carbondale
Carbondale, IL 62901-4624
Telephone: 618-453-2415
FAX: 618-453-1646
E-mail: pbelmore@siu.edu
Web URL: www.siu.edu/~epse1/elmore/
Tests: 287, 440, 1440

Endeavor Information Systems, Inc.
1317 Livingston Street
Evanston, IL 60201
Tests: 948

Meryl E. Englander
Professor Emeritus of Counseling and Educational Psychology
3508 William Court
Bloomington, IN 47401
Tests: 1250

English Language Institute
University of Michigan
3021 N. University Building
1205 North University Avenue
Ann Arbor, MI 48109-1057
Telephone: 734-764-2416
FAX: 734-763-0369
E-mail: melabelium@umich.edu
Web URL: www.lsa.umich.edu/eli/testing.html
Tests: 953, 985, 986, 1506, 1662, 1664

Enhanced Performance Systems, Inc.
1010 University Avenue, Suite 265
San Diego, CA 92103
Telephone: 619-497—0156
FAX: 619-497-0820
E-mail: sagal@enhanced-performance.com
Web URL: www.enhanced-performance.com
Tests: 226

Robert H. Ennis, Ph.D.
495 East Lake Road
Sanibel Island, FL 33957
Telephone: 941-395-1435 (FL)
Telephone: 217-344-2038 (IL)
FAX: E-mail: rhennis@uiuc.edu
Tests: 959

ERISys
Box 1635
Pawtucket, RI 02862
Tests: 2047

Exceptional Education
P.O. Box 15308
Seattle, WA 98155

Telephone: 425-486-4510
FAX: 425-486-4510
Tests: 2053, 2826

Sheila M. Eyberg, Ph.D.
Department of Clinical & Health Psychology
Box J-165
Health Sciences Center
University of Florida
Gainesville, FL 32610
Tests: 864, 997, 2595, 2752

Faculty of Education
Memorial University of Newfoundland
St. John's, Newfoundland A1B 3XS
Canada
Tests: 2733

Dr. Charles G. Fast, Publisher
Route 1, Box 54A
Novinger, MO 63559
Tests: 1019

Fearon/Janus
[Address Unknown]
Tests: 812, 869

Grace Fivars
Psychometric Techniques Associates
5701 Centre Avenue, #511
Pittsburgh, PA 15206-3707
Telephone: 412-362-3022
Tests: 543, 2612

Foreworks
Box 82289
Portland, OR 97282
Telephone: (503) 653-2614
E-mail: inquiries@foreworks.com
Web URL: www.foreworks.com
Tests: 2459, 2672

Myles I. Friedman
College of Education
University of South Carolina
Columbia, SC 29208
Tests: 2027

Functional Resources
3905 Huntington Drive
Amarillo, TX 79019-4047
Telephone: 806-353-1114
FAX: 806-353-1114
Tests: 1067

Gallaudent University Press
800 Florida Avenue, NE
Washington, DC 20002-3695
Tests: 2936

General Educational Development Testing Service of the American Council on Education (GED)
One Dupont Circle, NW Suite 250
Washington, DC 20036-1163
Telephone: 202-939-9490
FAX: 202-775-8578
E-mail: ged@ace.nche.edu
Web URL: www.gedtest.org
Tests: 2742

Gerontology Center
College of Health and Human Development
The Pennsylvania State University
105 Henderson Building South
University Park, PA 16802-6500
Telephone: 814-865-1710
FAX: 814-863-9423
E-mail: GERO@psu.edu
Web URL: geron.psu.edu
Tests: 1643

G.I.A. Publications, Inc.
7404 South Mason Avenue
Chicago, IL 60638
Telephone: 708-496-3800
FAX: 708-496-3828
E-mail: custserv@giamusic.com
Web URL: www.giamusic.com
Tests: 90, 1176, 1280, 1287, 1320, 1752, 2056

Robert Gibson & Sons, Glasgow, Ltd.
17 Fitzroy Place
Glasgow, Scotland G3 7SF
United Kingdom
Tests: 714, 715, 1389, 1864

Golden Educational Center
857 Lake Blvd.
Redding, CA 96003
Tests: 1283

Gordon Systems, Inc.
P.O. Box 746
DeWitt, NY 13214
Tests: 1099

Robert S. Goyer
Department of Communication
Arizona State University
Tempe, AZ 85287
Tests: 1102

Graham-Field
400 Rabro Drive
Hauppauge, NY 11788
Tests: 2658

Gregorc Associates Inc.
15 Doubleday Road
P.O. Box 351
Columbia, CT 06237
Telephone: 860-228-0093
FAX: 860-228-0093
Tests: 1132

GRM Educational Consultancy
P.O. Box 154
Beecroft, NSW 2119
Australia
Telephone: 61-2-9484-1598
FAX: 61-2-9875-3638
Tests: 2325

Guglielmino & Associates
734 Marble Way
Boca Raton, FL 33432
Telephone: 561-392-0379
FAX: 561-392-0379
E-mail: lguglielmino@rocketmail.com
Web URL: sdlglobal.com
Tests: 2359

Guidance Testing Associates
St. Mary's University
One Camino Santa Maria
San Antonio, TX 78284
Tests: 643, 1306, 2711, 2741, 2744

Guilford Publications, Inc.
Department 5X
72 Spring Street
New York, NY 10012
Tests: 67

H & H Publishing Co., Inc.
1231 Kapp Drive
Clearwater, FL 33765
Telephone: 800-366-4079
FAX: 727-442-2195
E-mail: hhservice@hhpublishing.com
Web URL: www.hhpublishing.com
Tests: 1455, 1456, 1910, 2495, 2645, 2929

Hahnemann Medical College & Hospital
Department of Mental Health Sciences
230 North Broad Street
Philadelphia, PA 19102
Tests: 1161, 1162, 1619

Hanson Silver Strong & Associates, Inc.
[Address Unknown]
Tests: 1464, 1473, 1562

Harcourt Brace Educational Measurement
555 Academic Court
San Antonio, TX 78204-2498
Telephone: 800-211-8378
FAX: 800-232-1223
E-mail: customer_service2@hbtpc.com
Web URL: www.hbem.com
Tests: 165, 1094, 1756, 1866, 2484, 2486, 2487, 2489

Susan Harter, Ph.D.
University of Denver
Department of Psychology
2155 South Race Street
Denver, CO 80208-0204
Tests: 1987, 2369

Joseph Hartman Counsulting Psychology, Inc.
Bishop Square, Suite 100
5700 St. Augustine Road
Jacksonville, FL 32207-8042
Tests: 2121

Harvard University Press
79 Garden Street
Cambridge, MA 02138
Telephone: 800-448-2242
FAX: 800-962-4983
E-mail: hup@harvard.edu
Web URL: 222.hup.harvard.edu
Tests: 2749

Dr. Robert J. Harvey
1030 S. Jefferson Forest Lane
Blacksburg, VA 24060-8984
Tests: 627

Hawthorne Educational Services, Inc.
800 Gray Oak Drive
Columbia, MO 65201
Telephone: 800-542-1673
FAX: 800-442-9509
Tests: 59, 81, 221, 222, 282, 283, 284, 332, 873, 874, 928, 930, 1089, 1460, 2035, 2043, 2470, 2779, 2913

Hay/McBer
Training Resources Group
116 Huntington Avenue
Boston, MA 02116
Telephone: 800-729-8074
FAX: 617-927-5060
E-mail: TRG_McBer@haygroup.com
Web URL: trgmcber@haygroup.com
Tests: 64, 555, 1267, 1442, 1467, 1469, 1471, 1560, 1573, 1575, 1860, 1957, 2268

The Health Institute
New England Medical Center #345
750 Washington Street
Boston, MA 02111
Tests: 2397

Health Prisms, Inc.
130 Pleasant Pointe Way
Fayetteville, GA 30214
Telephone: 770-460-0808
FAX: 770-460-0808
E-mail: kmath44@aol.com
Tests: 698

Heinemann
88 Post Road West
P.O. Box 5007
Westport, CT 06881
Tests: 2283

Herrmann International
794 Buffalo Creek Road
Lake Lure, NC 28746
Tests: 1197

Hester Evaluation Systems, Inc.
2410 SW Granthurst Avenue
Topeka, KS 66611-1274
Telephone: 800-832-3825
FAX: 785-357-4041
E-mail: hester@inlandnet.net
Tests: 1711

High/Scope Educational Research Foundation
600 North River Street
Ypsilanti, MI 48198-2898
Telephone: 734-485-2000
FAX: 734-485-0704
E-mail: info@highscope.org
Web URL: www:highscope.org
Tests: 1204

Higher Education Research Institute
UCLA Graduate School of Education
405 Hilgard Avenue
3005 Moore Hall
Los Angeles, CA 90024-1521
Tests: 692

Hilson Research, Inc.
P.O. Box 150239
82-28 Abingdon Road
Kew Gardens, NY 11415-0239
Tests: 1207, 1208, 1209, 1210, 1313, 1314

Hodder & Stoughton Educational
Hodder Headline PLC
338 Euston Road
London NW1 3BH
England
Telephone: 0171 873 6000
FAX: 0171 873 6024
E-mail: chas.knight@hodder.co.uk
Tests: 254, 255, 537, 550, 739, 826, 881, 899, 901, 998, 999, 1037, 1087, 1103, 1105, 1144, 1145, 1148, 1260, 1342, 1600, 1797, 1875, 1897, 1996, 2179, 2281, 2341, 2409, 2467, 2613, 2910

Hogan Assessment Systems, Inc.
P.O. Box 521176
Tulsa, OK 74152
Telephone: 918-749-0632
FAX: 918-749-0635
E-mail: aferg@webzone.net
Web URL: www.hoganassessments.com
Tests: 1211, 1212, 1724

Hogrefe & Huber Publishers
P.O. Box 2487
Kirkland, WA 98083
Telephone: 800-228-3749
FAX: 425-823-8324
E-mail: hh@hhpub.com
Web URL: www.hhpub.com
Tests: 767, 860, 1015, 2247, 2303

Home Inventory LLC
c/o Lorraine Coulson
13 Sanony Circle
Little Rock, AR 72209
Tests: 1216

Houghton Mifflin Company
222 Berkeley Street
Boston, MA 02116-3764
Tests: 357

Howdah Press
c/o Priscilla S. Hill, Ph.D.
3530 Damien, #117
LaVerne, CA 91750
Tests: 1205

Edwina E. Hubert, Ph.D.
313 Wellesley, SE
Albuquerque, NM 87106
Tests: 1482

Nancy Hughes, Ph.D.
University of Kansas
Psychological Clinic
315 Fraser Hall
Lawrence, KS 66045
Tests: 1225

Human Resource Development Press
(HRD Press)
22 Amherst Road
Amherst, MA 01002-9709
Telephone: 800-822-2801
FAX: 413-253-3490
E-mail: marketing@hrdpress.com
Web URL: www.hrdpress.com
Tests: 436, 638, 677, 801, 1045, 1268, 1371, 1438, 1608, 1858, 1859, 1876, 1923, 2630

Human Sciences Research Council
Private Bag X41
Pretoria 0001
South Africa
Telephone: +(27) 12 - 302-2166
FAX: +(27) 12 - 302-2994
E-mail: DJFM@silwane.hsrc.ac.za
Tests: 12, 169, 321, 1029, 1198, 1199, 1257, 1293, 1297, 1365, 1370, 1753, 1762, 1789, 1873, 1983, 1990, 2086, 2257, 2319, 2373, 2375, 2392, 2458, 2661, 2774

Human Services Resource Group
College of Business Administration
University of Nebraska—Omaha
Omaha, NE 68182-0048
Tests: 2585

Human Synergistics, Inc.
39819 Plymouth Road, C-8020
Plymouth, MI 48170-8020
Tests: 903, 1150, 1498, 1550, 1862, 2575, 2633

Humanics Learning
P.O. Box 7400
Atlanta, GA 30357-0400
Telephone: 404-874-2176
FAX: 404-874-1976
E-mail: humanics@mindspring.com
Tests: 452, 465, 1230, 1515

I-MED Instructional Materials & Equipment Distributors
1520 Cotner Avenue
Los Angeles, CA 90025
Telephone: 310-473-5588
FAX: 310-312-1743
Tests: 867

IDEA Center
Kansas State University
1615 Anderson Avenue
Manhattan, KS 66502-4073
Telephone: 785-532-5970
FAX: 785-532-5637
E-mail: idea@ksu.edu
Web URL: www.idea.ksu.edu
Tests: 1233, 1236

IDS Publishing Inc.
P.O. Box 389
Worthington, OH 43085
Tests: 2199

Illinois Critical Thinking Project
Dept. of Educational Policy Studies
University of Illinois at Urbana-Champaign
360 Education Bldg.
1310 South Sixth Street
Champaign, IL 61820
Tests: 703, 704

Imaginart International, Inc.
307 Arizona Street
Bisbee, AZ 85603
Telephone: 520-432-5741
FAX: 520-432-5134
E-mail: imaginart@aol.com
Tests: 276, 1284, 2472, 2669

Industrial Psychology International, Ltd.
4106 Fieldstone Road
Champaign, IL 61821
Telephone: 800-747-1119
FAX: 217-398-5798
E-mail: ipi@metritech.com
Web URL: www.metritech.com
Tests: 719, 1323, 1805, 2930

Insight Institute, Inc.
7205 NW Waukomis Drive
Kansas City, MO 64151
Telephone: 800-861-4769
FAX: 816-587-7198
E-mail: handleyp@aol.com
Tests: 1273

Institute for Behavioral Research in Creativity
1570 South 1100th East
Salt Lake City, UT 84105
Tests: 311, 907, 2537

Institute for Character Development
[Address Unknown]
Tests: 439

The Institute for Matching Person & Technology, Inc.
486 Lake Road
Webster, NY 14580
Telephone: 716-671-3461
FAX: 716-671-3461
E-mail: impt97@aol.com
Web URL: members.aol.com/IMPT97/Mpt.html
Tests: 1591, 1593, 2384

Institute for Personality and Ability Testing, Inc.
P.O. Box 1188
Champaign, IL 61824-1188
Telephone: 217-352-4739
FAX: 217-352-9674
E-mail: custserv@ipat.cfom
Web URL: www.ipat.com
Tests: 450, 477, 538, 644, 745, 888, 915, 990, 1183, 1201, 1242, 1321, 1322, 1429, 1721, 1732, 1779, 2318, 2364, 2417, 2418, 2419

Institute for Psycho-Imagination Therapy
(IPIT-Shorr Clinic)
111 N. La Cienega Blvd., #108
Beverly Hills, CA 90211
Tests: 1149, 2404

Institute for Somat Awareness
Michael Bernet, Ph.D.
1270 North Avenue, Suite 1-P
New Rochelle, NY 10804
Telephone: 914-633-1789
FAX: 914-633-3152
E-mail: mBernet@aol.com
Tests: 2412

Institute for the Advancement of Philosophy for Children
Montclair State University
Upper Montclair, NJ 07043
Telephone: 973-655-4277
FAX: 973-655-7834
E-mail: matkowski@saturn.montclair.edu
Tests: 1780

Institute of Athletic Motivation
1503 Crystal Circle
Antioch, CA 94509
Telephone: 925-754-2828
FAX: 925-978-1503
E-mail: WinslowWRI@aol.com
Tests: 219

The Institute of Foundational Training and Development
P.O. box 160220
Austin, TX 78716-0220
Tests: 312

Institute of Psychological Research, Inc.
34 Fleury Street West
Montreal, Quebec H3L 1S9
Canada
Telephone: 514-382-3000
FAX: 514-382-3007
Tests: 394, 1501, 1796, 2128, 2261, 2670, 2728

Institute of Rehabilitation Medicine
New York University Medical Center
400 East 34th Street
New York, NY 10016
Tests: 1061

Interim Publishers
3900 Scobie Road
Peninsula, OH 44264
Tests: 2502

International Assessment Network
7600 France Avenue South, Suite #550
Minneapolis, MN 55435-5939
Tests: 1579

International Association for the Study of Pain
909 NE 43rd Street, Suite 306
Seattle, WA 98105-6020
FAX: 206-547-6409
E-mail: iasp@locke.hs.washington.edu
Web URL: www.halcyon.com/iasp
Tests: 1615

International Career Planning Services, Inc.
254 Republic Avenue
Joliet, IL 60435
Tests: 1984

International LearningWorks®
1130 Main Avenue
P.O. Box 1310
Durango, CO 81302
Telephone: 800-344-0451
FAX: 970-385-7804
E-mail: learning@lorenet.com
Web URL: intllearningworks.com
Tests: 554, 1519, 1814, 2271, 2580

International Personnel Management Association
1617 Duke Street
Alexandria, VA 22314
Tests: 1324, 1325, 1326, 2302

International Society for General Semantics
P.O. Box 728
Concord, CA 94522
Telephone: 925-798-0311
FAX: 925-798-0312
E-mail: isgs@a.crl.com
Web URL: generalsemantics.com
Tests: 2785, 2788

International Training Consultants, Inc.
P.O. Box 35613
Richmond, VA 23235-0613
Tests: 1479, 1480

Invest Learning
Worldwide Development Headquarters
4660 S Hagadorn Road, Suite 520
East Lansing, MI 48823-5353
Tests: 168

Iowa State University Research Foundation, Inc.
Child Development Department
101 Child Development Building
Research Laboratories
Ames, IA 50011
Tests: 1316, 1317, 2482

Irvington Publishers, Inc.
RR1, Box 85-1
Lower Mill Road
North Stratford, NH 03590
Tests: 2078

R. B. Ishmael & Associates
[Address Unknown]
Tests: 1976

Israel Science Teaching Center
Hebrew University
Jerusalem 91904
Israel
Tests: 626

ITP Nelson Canada
1120 Birchmount Road
Scarborough, Ontario M1K 5G4
Canada
Telephone: 416-752-9100
FAX: 416-752-9646
E-mail: inquire@nelson.com
Web URL: www.nelson.com
Tests: 385, 387, 389, 1071, 1196, 1865, 2264, 2831

J-K Screening Test
711 Fifth Street East
Sonoma, CA 95476
Telephone: 707-938-1056
Tests: 1357

Janelle Publications, Inc.
P.O. Box 811
1189 Twombley Road
DeKalb, IL 60115
Telephone: 815-756-2300
FAX: 815-756-4799
Web URL: www.janellepublications.com
Tests: 2466, 2523, 2524

Jeannette Jansky
120 East 89th Street
New York, NY 10128
Tests: 1336, 1337

JIST Works, Inc.
720 North Park Avenue
Indianapolis, IN 46202-3431
Telephone: 800-648-5478
FAX: 800-547-8329
E-mail: jistworks@aol.com
Web URL: www.jist.com
Tests: 407, 934, 1252, 1483, 1896, 2828

Jossey-Bass/Pfeiffer
350 Sansome, 5th Floor
San Francisco, CA 94104
Tests: 191, 296, 396, 556, 634, 727, 820, 848, 939, 958, 975, 1296, 1361, 1402, 1445, 1446, 1448, 1452, 1463, 1505, 1508, 1723, 1857, 1913, 1914, 1915, 2064, 2453, 2635, 2631, 2789, 2854

C. G. Jung Educational Center of Houston, Texas, Inc.
[Address Unknown]
Tests: 2262

C. G. Jung Institute of San Francisco
2040 Gough Street
San Francisco, CA 94109
Tests: 1366

Jerome Kagan
Harvard University
33 Kirkland Street
1510 William James Hall
Cambridge, MA 02138
Tests: 1592

S. Karger AG
P.O. Box CH-4009
Allschwilerstrasse 10
Basel
Switzerland
Tests: 625

Warren Keegan Associates Press
210 Stuyvesant Avenue
Rye, NY 10580
Telephone: 914-967-9421
FAX: 914-967-2991
E-mail: wka@paceu.org
Tests: 1387

Keeler Instruments, Inc.
456 Parkway
Broomall, PA 19008
Telephone: 610-353-4350
FAX: 610-353-7814
Web URL: www.keelerusa.com
Tests: 489, 2224

Kendall/Hunt Publishing Company
4050 Westmark Drive
P.O. Box 1840
Dubuque, IA 52004-1840
Telephone: 800-228-0810
FAX: 800-772-9165
E-mail: orders@kendallhunt.com
Web URL: www.kendallhunt.com
Tests: 257, 683, 2338

Kent Developmental Metrics, Inc.
[Address Unknown]
Tests: 1391

Keystone Publications
[Address Unknown]
Tests: 713

Dr. Donald L. Kirkpatrick
1920 Hawthorne Drive
Elm Grove, WI 53122
Telephone: 414-784-8348
FAX: 414-784-7994
Tests: 1403, 1552, 1553, 1554, 1555, 1556, 2565, 2566

Marjorie H. Klein, Ph.D.
Department of Psychiatry
6001 Research Park Blvd.
Madison, WI 53717
Telephone: 608-263-6066
FAX: 608-265-4008
E-mail: mhklein@falstaff.wisc.edu
Tests: 991

Kolbe Corp
3421 N 44th Street
Phoenix, AZ 85018
Telephone: 602-840-9770
FAX: 602-952-2706
E-mail: info@kolbe.com
Web URL: www.kolbe.com
Tests: 1411

David S. Krantz
Department of Medical Psychology
Uniformed Services
University of the Health Sciences
4301 Jones Bridge Road
Bethesda, MD 20814-4799
E-mail: krantz@bob.usufa.usuhs.mil
Tests: 1412

Krieger Publishing Company
P.O. Box 9542
Melbourne, FL 32902-9542
Tests: 78

Ramanath Kundu
Department of Psychology
University of Calcutta
92 Acharya Prafulla Chandra Road
Calcutta 700009
India
Testss: 1415, 1416

Lafayette Instrument
P.O. Box 5729
3700 Sagamore Parkway North
Lafayette, IN 47903
Tests: 1135, 1696, 2244

Rolfe LaForge
83 Homestead Blvd.
Mill Valley, CA 94941
Telephone: 415-388-8121
E-mail: rlaforge@sfsu.edu
Tests: 1291

Larlin Corporation
P.O. Box 1730
Marietta, GA 30061
Tests: 2697

Law School Admission Council/Law School Admission Service
Box 40
Newtown, PA 18940-0040
Telephone: 215-968-1101
FAX: 215-968-1169
Web URL: www.lsac.org
Tests: 1434

Leadership Development Consulting Co.
5819 South Shandle
Mento, OH 44060
Tests: 138, 139, 140

Leadership Studies, Inc.
230 West Third Avenue
Escondido, CA 92025
Telephone: 760-741-6595
FAX: 760-747-9384
E-mail: randy@situational.com
Web URL: www.situational.com
Tests: 2415

Learning Publications, Inc.
Box 1326
5352 Gulf Drive
Holmes Beach, FL 33509
Tests: 217

Lentz Peace Research Laboratory
c/o UM-St. Louis
8001 Natural Bridge Road
St. Louis, MO 63121
Tests: 363, 1228, 2624

Hal Leonard Publishing Corporation
7777 West Bluemound Road
P.O. Box 13819
Milwaukee, WI 53213
Tests: 1018, 2853

Leonardo Press
[Address Unknown]
Tests: 1428

Lienhard School of Nursing
Pace University
Pleasantville/Briarcliff Campus
Bedford Road
Pleasantville, NY 10570
Telephone: 914-773-3534
FAX: 914-241-9066
E-mail: sstokes@pace.edu
Tests: 2505

Life Advance, Inc.
81 Front Street
Nyack, NY 10960
Telephone: 914-358-2539
E-mail: ellisonc@alliancesem.edu
Tests: 2474

Life Innovations, Inc.
P.O. Box 190
Minneapolis, MN 55440-0190
Telephone: 651-635-0511
FAX: 651-635-0716
E-mail: dolson@lifeinnovation.com
Web URL: lifeinnovation.com
Tests: 544, 1000, 1014, 1877, 1927, 2034

Life Science Associates
One Fenimore Road
Bayport, NY 11705
Telephone: 516-472-2111
FAX: 516-472-8140
E-mail: lifesciassoc@pipeline.com
Web URL:lifesciassoc.home.pipeline.com
Tests: 2159

LIMRA International
P.O. Box 208
Hartford, CT 06141-0208
Tests: 197, 421, 2424

LinguiSystems, Inc.
3100 4th Avenue
P.O. Box 747
East Moline, IL 61244
Tests: 1424, 2710, 2911

Literacy Volunteers of America, Inc.
635 James Street
Syracuse, NY 13203
Telephone: 315-472-0001
FAX: 315-472-0002
E-mail: lvanat@aol.com
Web URL: www.literacyvolunteers.org
Tests: 951, 2175

Lucas Grason-Stadler, Inc.
[Address Unknown]
Tests: 1523

Pamela S. Ludolph, Ph.D.
[Address Unknown]
Tests: 824

James B. Maas
The Center for Improvement of Undergraduate Education
115 Rand Hall
Cornell University
Ithaca, NY 14850
Tests: 706

Macmillan Education Ltd.
Houndsmills
Basingstoke, Hampshire RG21 2XS
England
Tests: 189, 195, 882, 883, 1262, 1356, 1477, 1529, 1530, 1531, 1781, 2089, 2914

Macmillan Publishing Co.
[Address Unknown]
Tests: 39, 237, 1272, 1532

Jean D'Arcy Maculatis, Ph.D.
P.O. Box 3056
Sea Bright, NY 07760
Tests: 1527

Maddak, Inc.
6 Industrial Road
Pequannock, NJ 07440-1993
Tests: 268, 1513, 2376

Madison Geriatric Research, Education, and Clinical Center
VA Medical Center
2500 Overlook Terrace
Madison, WI 53705
Telephone: 608-280-7000
Tests: 212

Dr. Wayne R. Maes
University of New Mexico
College of Education
Dept. of Counseling & Family Studies
Education Office Building #110
Albuquerque, NM 87131
Tests: 2625

Maferr Foundation, Inc.
9 East 81 Street
New York, NY 10028
Tests: 1535, 1536

Magic Lantern Publications
[Address Unknown]
Tests: 2391

Management & Personnel Systems, Inc.
2717 North Main St., #2
Walnut Creek, CA 94596
Tests: 1080, 2574

Management Research Associates
[Address Unknown]
Tests: 161, 906, 1447, 1747, 2582, 2586

Management Research Group
14 York Street, #301
Portland, ME 04101-4556
Telephone: 207-775-2173

FAX: 207-775-6796
E-mail: info@mrg.com
Web URL: www.mrg.com
Tests: 162, 1251, 1443, 1549, 1929, 2270, 2385

Management Research Institute, Inc.
11304 Spur Wheel Lane
Potomac, MD 20854
Telephone: 301-299-9200
FAX: 301-299-9227
E-mail: mrieaf@aol.com
Tests: 1044

Manatech Management Technologies, Inc.
[Address Unknown]
Tests: 1966

Mann Consulting Group
17250 Sunset Blvd., #216
Pacific Palisades, CA 90272
Tests: 1946

Marathon Consulting and Press
797 South Ashburton Road
Columbus, OH 43227-1027
Tests: 716, 768, 1918, 2916

Mason Media, Inc.
[Address Unknown]
Tests: 1374

Massachusetts School of Professional Psychology
T.E.D. Associates
221 Rivermoor Street
Boston, MA 02132
Telephone: 617-327-6777
FAX: 617-327-4447
E-mail: dabby@mspp.edu
Tests: 2614

MAT
Boston University
School of Music
855 Commonwealth Ave.
Boston, MA 02215
Tests; 1751

Mathematical Association of America/American Mathematical Society
Walter E. Mientka, Ph.D., Executive Director
Univeristy of Nebraska—Lincoln
1740 Vine
Lincoln, NE 68588-0658
Tests: 144, 148, 149, 1595

McCann Associates, Inc.
603 Corporate Drive West
Langhorne, PA 19047
Telephone: 215-860-8637
FAX: 215-860-9184
E-mail: McCannAssc@aol.com
Tests: 731, 732, 733, 734, 796, 1032, 1813, 2002

McCarron-Dial Systems
P.O. Box 45628
Dallas, TX 75245
Telephone: 214-634-2863
FAX: 214-634-9970
E-mail: mds@mccarrondial.com
Web URL: mccarrondial.com
Tests: 40, 62, 208, 929, 1610, 1617, 1815, 1919, 2579

McClain
10 Blue Grouse Ridge Road
Littleton, CO 80127-5704
Tests: 2934

Measurement for Human Resources
83 Rougeau Avenue
Winnipeg, Manitoba R2C 3X5
Canada
Tests: 1821

Media Materials, Inc.
1821 Portal Street
Baltimore, MD 21224
Tests: 1346, 1979

Albert Mehrabian, Ph.D.
1130 Alta Mesa Road
Monterey, CA 93940
Telephone: 831-649-5710
E-mail: am@haaj.com
Web URL: www.haaj.com/psych/
Tests: 181, 238, 455, 1620, 1621, 1622, 1627, 1628, 1630, 2135, 2777

The Mentoring Institute, Inc.
[Address Unknown]
Tests: 1652

Meta Development LLC
4313 Garnet Street
Regina, Saskatchewan S4S 6J8
Canada
Tests; 1674, 1675, 1676, 1677, 1678, 1679, 1680, 1681, 1682, 1683, 1684

Meta-Visions
43000 12 Oaks Crescent Drive, Suite #4055
Novi, MI 48377-3428
Telephone: 248-374-0971
FAX: 248-374-0973
E-mail: JWalkerM1@aol.com
Tests: 1655

MetriTech, Inc.
4106 Fieldstone Road
Champaign, IL 61821
Telephone: 800-747-4868
FAX: 217-398-5798
E-mail: mtinfo@metritech.com
Web URL: www.metritech.com
Tests: 65, 86, 1276, 1426, 1856, 1868, 2526, 2922

The Mews Press
Box 2052
Amagansett, NY 11930
FAX: 212-475-2428
Tests: 2203, 2594, 2639

MILCOM Systems, A Division of Hollister, Inc.
2000 Hollister Drive
Libertyville, IL 60048
Tests: 1669

Miller & Tyler Limited
Psychological Assessment and Counselling
96 Greenway
London N20 8EJ
England
Telephone: 44-181-445-7463
FAX: 44-181-445-0143
Tests: 2255, 2256

Mind Garden, Inc.
1690 Woodside Road, Suite #202
Redwood City, CA 94061
Telephone: 650-261-3500
FAX: 650-261-3505
E-mail: info@mindgarden.com
Tests: 7, 142, 205, 263, 298, 365, 373, 438, 546, 637, 682, 710, 802, 865, 1057, 1178, 1181, 1243, 1514, 1594, 1602, 1651, 1670, 1736, 1737, 1778, 1842, 2114, 2119, 2197, 2321, 2401, 2449, 2497, 2498, 2656, 2793, 2850, 2858, 2869

Ministry Inventories
ATTN: Richard A. Hunt, Ph.D.
Fuller Graduate School of Psychology
180 N. Oakland Avenue
Pasadena, CA 91101
Telephone: 626-584-5553
FAX: 626-584-9630
E-mail: rahunt@fuller.edu
Tests: 1310, 1705, 2751

Minneapolis Public Schools
254 Upton Avenue, South
Minneapolis, MN 55405
Tests: 1691

MKM
401 3rd St., Ste. 1
Rapid City, SD 57701
Tests: 1708, 1709, 1710

Modern Curriculum Press
4350 Equity Drive
Columbus, OH 43216
Tests: 330, 815, 916

Modern Learning Press, Inc.
P.O. Box 167
Rosemont, NJ 08556
Telephone: 800-627-5867
FAX: 609-397-3467
Tests: 1085, 1086

Monaco & Associates
4125 Gage Center Drive, Suite 204
Topeka, KS 66604
Tests: 1722

Moreno Educational Co.
7050 Belle Glade Lane
San Diego, CA 92119
Telephone: 619-461-0565
FAX: 619-469-1073
E-mail: moreno@mail.sdsu.edu
Tests: 1849, 2140, 2465

The Morrisby Organisation
83 High Street
Hemel Hempstead
Hertfordshire HP1 3AH
England
Telephone: +44 (0) 1442 215521
FAX: +44 (0) 1442 240531
E-mail: post@morrisby.demon.com.uk
Web URL: www.morrisby.co.uk
Tests: 718, 1717, 1835

James H. Morrison
10932 Rosehill Road
Overland Park, KS 66210
Tests: 1526, 2675

Moving Boundaries
1375 SW Blaine Court
Gresham, OR 97080
Telephone: 888-661-4433
FAX: 503-661-5304
E-mail: info@movingboundaries.com
Tests: 2411

Multi-Health Systems, Inc.
908 Niagara Falls Blvd.
North Tonawanda, NY 14120-2060
Telephone: 416-424-1700
FAX: 416-424-1736
E-mail: customerservice@mhs.com
Web URL: www.mhs.com
Tests: 243, 429, 472, 491, 545, 557, 667, 678, 679, 680, 681, 696, 700, 766, 863, 1008, 1025, 1173, 1174, 1175, 1213, 1340, 1341, 1454, 1486, 1487, 1699, 1730, 1899, 2017, 2132, 2196, 2442, 2448, 2476, 2521, 2602, 2619, 2702, 2772

Multiple Intelligences Research and Consulting, Inc.
1316 South Lincoln Street
Kent, OH 44240
Telephone: 330-673-8024
FAX: 330-673-8810
E-mail: sbranton@kent.edu
Web URL: www.angelfire.com/oh/themidas
Tests: 1667

Munroe-Meyer Institute for Genetics & Rehabilitation
University of Nebraska Medical Center
985450 Nebraska Medical Center
Omaha, NE 68198-5450
Telephone: 402-559-7467
FAX: 402-559-5737 (FAX)
E-mail: mrimedia@unmcvm.unmc.edu
Web URL: www.unmc.edu/mrimedia/meyertes.html
Tests: 1668

National Association of Secondary School Principals
P.O. Box 3250
1904 Association Drive
Reston, VA 22091-1598
Telephone: 800-253-7746
FAX: 703-476-5432
E-mail: nassp@nassp.org
Web URL: www.nassp.org
Tests: 648, 649, 1472, 2340

National Center for Research to Improve Postsecondary Teaching and Learning
2400 School of Education Building
The University of Michigan
Ann Arbor, MI 48109-1259
Tests: 1720, 2530

The National Center on Employment & Disability
P.O. Box 1358
Hot Springs, AR 71902
Tests: 936, 1352, 2918, 2923, 2924, 2928

National Clearinghouse of Rehabilitation Training Materials
5202 N. Richmond Hill Drive
Oklahoma State University
Stillwater, OK 74078-4080
Tests: 1844

National Communication Association
5101 Backlick Road, Bldg. E
Annandale, VA 22003
Tests: 188, 639, 689

National Council on Crime & Delinquency
685 Market Street, Suite 620
San Francisco, CA 94105
Tests: 712, 1373

National Council on Economic Education
1140 Avenue of the Americas
New York, NY 10036
Tests: 247, 2060, 2685, 2686, 2718, 2719

National Occupational Competency Testing Institute
500 N. Bronson Avenue
Big Rapids, MI 49307-2737
Tests: 1792, 1793, 1794

National Psychological Corporation
4/230 Kacheri Ghat
Agra-4
India
Tests: 2626

National Reading Styles Institute, Inc.
P.O. Box 737
Syosset, NY 11791-0737
Tests: 623, 2181

National Spanish Exam
2051 Mt. Zion Drive
Golden, CO 80401-1737
Telephone: 303-278-1021
FAX: 303-278-6400
Web URL: www.aatsp.org
Tests: 1764

National Study of School Evaluation
1699 E. Woodfield Road, #406
Schaumburg, IL 60173
Telephone: 847-995-9080
FAX: 847-995-9088
Web URL: www.nsse.org
Tests: 636, 1885, 2532, 2623

National Wellness Institute, Inc.
1300 College Court
P.O. Box 827
Stevens Point, WI 54481-2962
Telephone: 715-342-2969
FAX: 715-342-2979
E-mail: hwi@wellnessnwi.org
Web URL: www.wellnessnwi.org
Tests: 1499, 2745, 2746, 2747

NCS [Iowa City]
P.O. Box 30
Iowa City, IA 52244
Tests: 684

NCS [Minnetonka]
Sales Department
5605 Green Circle Drive
Minnetonka, MN 55343
Tests: 136, 267, 335, 337, 379, 380, 381, 382, 398, 399, 737, 792, 1075, 1237, 1311, 1685, 1686, 1687, 1697, 1698, 1871, 2018, 2131, 2147, 2326, 2603, 2802

NCS [Rosemont]
9701 West Higgins Road
Rosemont, IL 60018-4720
Telephone: 800-221-8378
FAX: 847-292-3400
E-mail: assessment@ncs.com
Web URL: assessments.ncs.com
Tests: 58, 171, 534, 548, 549, 669, 670, 728, 927, 1042, 1043, 1299, 1444, 1569, 1633, 1636, 1798, 1799, 1836, 1928, 1972, 1986, 2051, 2125, 2178, 2267, 2408, 2420, 2460, 2581, 2588, 2605, 2648, 2700, 2757, 2758, 2786, 2790, 2807, 2808, 2907

Robert A. Neimeyer, Ph.D.
Department of Psychology
Memphis State University
Memphis, TN 38152
Telephone: 901-678-4680
FAX: 901-678-2579
E-mail: neimeyer@memphis.edu
Tests: 2558

C. H. Nevins Printing Co.
311 Bryn Mawr Island
Bayshore Gardens
Bradenton, FL 34207
Tests: 1138, 1139

New Standards, Inc.
8441 Wayzata Blvd., Suite 105
Minneapolis, MN 55426-1349
Telephone: 800-755-6299
FAX: 612-797-9993
E-mail: tjk@newstandards.com
Tests: 2194, 2554

New Zealand Council for Educational Research
Education House West
178-182 Willis St.
Box 3237
Wellington 6000
New Zealand
Tests: 21, 22, 25, 358, 1605, 2090, 2093, 2094, 2095, 2100, 2478, 2622, 2714

Newspaper Advertising Bureau, Inc.
[Address Unknown]
Tests: 2330

Newsweek Magazine, Inc.
Newsweek Educational Department
251 W. 57th Street
New York, NY 10019
Tests: 749, 1785

NFER-Nelson Publishing Co., Ltd.
Darville House
2 Oxford Road East
Windsor, Berkshire SL4 1DF
England
Tests: 125, 126, 127, 128, 129, 196, 235, 253, 294, 348, 349, 350, 359, 419, 441, 444, 463, 561, 736, 835, 884, 892, 900, 902, 910, 954, 1011, 1012, 1066, 1079, 1104, 1106, 1151, 1152, 1153, 1154, 1369, 1388, 1390, 1423, 1489, 1504, 1511, 1516, 1596, 1597, 1598, 1601, 1603, 1626, 1629, 1656, 1712, 1718, 1758, 1765, 1782, 1783, 1786, 1787, 1800, 1806, 1811, 1824, 1826, 1827, 1944, 1980, 1989, 2023, 2024, 2025, 2038, 2052, 2058, 2134, 2171, 2173, 2182, 2184, 2185, 2186, 2193, 2228, 2234, 2240, 2308, 2539, 2544, 2556, 2601, 2691, 2812, 2872, 2883, 2888, 2938

Nichols & Molinder Assessments
437 Bowes Drive
Tacoma, WA 98466-7047
Telephone: 253-565-4539
FAX: 253-565-0164
Tests: 1744

NIDA Addiction Research Center
ATTN: Charles A. Haertzen, Ph.D.
c/o Baltimore City Hospital, Bldg. D-5#
4940 Eastern Avenue
Baltimore, MD 21224
Tests: 66

Norland Software
P.O. Box 84499
Los Angeles, CA 90073-0499
Telephone: 310-202-1832
FAX: 310-202-9431
E-mail: emiller@ucla.edu
Web URL: www.calcaprt.com
Tests: 366

Northern California Neurobehavioral Group, Inc.
909 Hyde Street, Suite #620
San Francisco, CA 94109-4835
Telephone: 415-922-5858
FAX: 415-922-5849
Tests: 558

Northwestern University Press
625 Colfax Street
Evanston, IL 60208-4210
Tests: 1804, 2335

Nottingham Rehab. Ltd.
17 Ludlow Hill Road
West Bridgeford, Nottingham NG2 6HD
England
Tests: 445

Nova Media, Inc.
1724 N. State
Big Rapids, MI 49307
Telephone: 616-796-4637
E-mail: trund@nov.com
Web URL: www.nov.com
Tests: 2148

NTS Research Corporation
209 Markham Drive
Chapel Hill, NC 27514
Tests: 2365

Dr. Thomas R. Oaster
School of Education
Educational Research & Psychology
University of Missouri—Kansas City
5100 Rockhill Road
Kansas City, MO 64110-2499
Tests: 1809, 2534

Occupational Research Centre
"Highlands" Gravel Path
Berkhamsted, Hertfordshire HP4 2PQ
United Kingdom
Tests: 1404

E. R. Oetting, Ph.D.
Psychology Department
Colorado State University
Fort Collins, CO 80523
Telephone: 970-491-1615
FAX: 970-491-0527
E-mail: goetting@lamar.colostate.edu
Tests: 1830, 1831, 2475, 2655

Ohio State University
The Nisonger Center
434A McCampbell Hall
1581 Dodd Drive
Columbus, OH 43210-1205
Tests: 1791, 2829

OISE Press
252 Bloor Street West
Toronto, Ontario M5S 1V5
Canada
Tests: 1054, 1055

Optometry Admission Testing Program
211 East Chicago Avenue, Suite 1846
Chicago, IL 60611-2678
Telephone: 312-440-2684
FAX: 312-587-4105
E-mail: kramerg@ada.org
Tests: 1846

Organizational Measurement Systems Press
P.O. Box 70586
Eugene, OR 97401
Telephone: 541-484-2715
FAX: 541-465-1602
E-mail: bminer046@msn.com
Tests: 1689, 1843

Organizational Tests Ltd.
P.O. Box 324
Fredericton, New Brunswick E3B 4Y9
Canada
Telephone: 506-452-7194
FAX: 506-452-2931
Tests: 631, 633, 747, 1547, 1548, 1561, 1855, 2278, 2349, 2561, 2562, 2563, 2564, 2567, 2568, 2569, 2570, 2576, 2803, 2937

OUTREACH
Pre-College Programs
KDES PAS6
Gallaudet University
800 Florida Avenue, NE
Washington, DC 20002
Telephone: 202-651-5340
FAX: 202-651-5708
E-mail: pcnmpprod@gallua.gallaudet.edu
Web URL: www.gallaudet.edu/prec.pweb
Tests: 1618

Ned Owens, Inc.
629 W. Centerville Road, Suite 201
Garland, TX 75041
Telephone: 972-278-1387
FAX: 972-278-1387
E-mail: nedowens@fni.com
Web URL: www.fni.net/nedowens
Tests: 80, 220

Oxford Psychologists Press Ltd.
Lambourne House
311-321 Banbury Road
Oxford OX2 7JH
United Kingdom
Tests: 729, 1671, 2163

Pain Resource Center, Inc.
P.O. Box 2836
Durham, NC 27715
Tests: 484, 2766

PAQ Services, Inc.
Data Processing Division
1625 North 1000 East
Logan, UT 84321
Tests: 1343, 2016, 2071, 2925

P.D.P. Press, Inc.
12015 N. July Avenue
Hugo, MN 55038
Tests: 2378

Pendrake, Inc.
3370 Southampton Drive
Reno, NV 89509
Tests: 291

Perceptual Learning Systems
P.O. Box 81633
Las Vegas, NV 89180-1633
Tests: 1020, 1046, 2494

Perfection Learning Corp.
10520 New York Avenue
Des Moines, IA 50322
Tests: 145, 146, 897, 1509, 2932

Person-O-Metrics, Inc.
20504 Williamsburg Road
Dearborn Heights, MI 48127
Telephone: 313-271-4631
E-mail: nmilchus@gatecom.com
Tests: 980, 2136, 2355

Personal Strengths Publishing
P.O. Box 2605
Carlsbad, CA 92018-2605
Telephone: 800-624-7347
FAX: 760-730-7368
E-mail: mail@PersonalStrengths.com
Web URL: www.PersonalStrengths.com
Tests: 1022, 1023, 1024, 1349, 1704, 1956, 2013, 2014, 2507

Personnel Decisions, Inc.
2000 Plaza VII Tower
45 South Seventh Street
Minneapolis, MN 55402-1608
Tests: 1900

Dr. Linda Phillips, Director
Centre for Research on Literacy
Faculty of Educacion
University of Alberta
Edmonton, Alberta T6G 2G5
Canada
Telephone: 403-492-4250
FAX: 403-492-0113
E-mail: linda.phillips@ualberta.ca
Web URL: www.ualberta.ca/edu
Tests: 2690

Phonovisual Products, Inc.
18761 North Frederick Avenue
P.O. Box 1410
Gaithersburg, MD 20875
Telephone: 800-283-4888
Tests: 1981

Dr. I. Pilowsky
University of Adelaide
Department of Psychiatry
Royal Adelaide Hospital
Adelaide 0001
South Australia
Tests: 1241, 1488

Piney Mountain Press, Inc.
P.O. Box 333
Cleveland, GA 30528
Telephone: 800-255-3127
FAX: 800-905-3127
E-mail: cyberguy@stc.net
Web URL: www.careernetworks.com
Tests: 259, 1476, 1478, 1741, 2054, 2421, 2832

Pinkerton Services Group
6100 Fairview Road, Suite 900
Charlotte, NC 28210-3277
Telephone: 800-528-5745
FAX: 704-554-1806
Web URL: www.pinkertons.com
Tests: 2490, 2491

Predictive Surveys Corporation
5802 Howard Avenue
LaGrange, IL 60525
Tests: 130, 871, 1967, 2103, 2104, 2610

Preschool Skills Test
c/o Carol Lepera
P.O. Box 1246
Greenwood, IN 46142
Telephone: 317-881-7606
Tests: 2049

Price Systems, Inc.
Box 1818
Lawrence, KS 66044
Telephone: 785-843-7892
FAX: 785-843-0101
E-mail: gprice@ukans.edu
Web URL: www.learningstyle.com
Tests: 1470, 2069

PRO-ED
8700 Shoal Creek Blvd.
Austin, TX 78757-6897
Telephone: 800-897-3202
FAX: 512-451-8542
E-mail: proedrd2@aol.com
Web URL: www.proedinc.com
Tests: 1, 2, 60, 70, 76, 159, 163, 193, 198, 207, 209, 210, 211, 214, 223, 234, 240, 241, 258, 277, 286, 290, 315, 328, 338, 428, 430, 467, 559, 628, 629, 655, 656, 657, 662, 724, 746, 759, 789, 797, 798,

799, 803, 804, 806, 810, 813, 816, 821, 822, 852, 880, 898, 987, 1040, 1047, 1051, 1056, 1091, 1130, 1131, 1167, 1168, 1288, 1399, 1427, 1459, 1503,1690, 1715, 1734, 1816, 1817, 1850, 1852, 1880, 1901, 1982, 2008, 2036, 2111, 2144, 2172, 2189, 2225, 2233, 2249, 2250, 2251, 2287, 2294, 2296, 2297, 2309, 2322, 2328, 2329, 2332, 2361, 2447, 2471, 2481, 2542, 2543, 2596, 2657, 2667, 2668, 2674, 2676, 2680, 2681, 2682, 2683, 2684, 2689, 2694, 2695, 2698, 2699, 2701, 2704, 2705, 2708, 2709, 2712, 2722, 2725, 2726, 2730, 2731, 2732, 2768, 2780, 2801, 2837, 2865, 2866, 2906, 2912, 2933

Professional Picture Framers Association
4305 Sarellen Road
Richmond, VA 23231-4311
Tests: 435

Program Development Associates
P.O. Box 2038
Syracuse, NY 13220-2038
Telephone: 800-543-2119
FAX: 315-452-0710
E-mail: pdassoc@servtech.com
Web URL: www.PDAssoc.com
Tests: 2629

Psychodiagnostic Test, Co.
Box 859
East Lansing, MI 48823
Tests: 1854

Psychogenics, Inc.
490 Oxford Street East
London, Ontario N5Y 3H7
Canada
Telephone: 519-642-1505
FAX: 519-642-1513
E-mail: alvin@execulink.com
Tests: 2176

Psychological & Educational Publications, Inc.
[Address Unknown]
Tests: 2665, 2673, 2692, 2723

Psychological Assessment and Services, Inc.
P.O. Box 1031
Iowa City, IA 52244
Tests: 1215, 1706

Psychological Assessment Resources, Inc.
P.O. Box 998
Odessa, FL 33556-9908
Telephone: 800-331-8378
FAX: 800-727-9329
Web URL: www.parinc.com
Tests: 75, 77, 85, 89, 278, 326, 329, 400, 404, 422, 442, 456, 457, 464, 470, 478, 562, 564, 566, 569, 652, 687, 699, 760, 770, 776, 808, 842, 893, 909, 931, 938, 965, 1166, 1186, 1219, 1286, 1289, 1354, 1495, 1496, 1581, 1631, 1644, 1648, 1649, 1650, 1733, 1735, 1769, 1776, 1777, 1825, 1889, 1934, 1941, 1942, 1953, 1959, 1960, 1961, 1993, 2009, 2012, 2118, 2211, 2218, 2227, 2230, 2231, 2232, 2245, 2248, 2360, 2379, 2387, 2444, 2496, 2499, 2510, 2514, 2517, 2522, 2533, 2551, 2557, 2782, 2791, 2811, 2820, 2835, 2841, 2892

The Psychological Corporation
555 Academic Court
San Antonio, TX 78204-2498
Telephone: 800-211-8378
FAX: 800-232-1223
E-mail: customer_service@HBTPC.com
Web URL: www.HBEM.com
Tests: 15, 17, 38, 61, 82, 141, 229, 246, 269, 270, 271, 272, 273, 274, 302, 303, 307, 322, 323, 324, 331, 351, 356, 362, 375, 376, 411, 433, 460, 471, 476, 494, 532, 539, 540, 541, 542, 624, 651, 661, 691, 722, 817, 818, 837, 838, 839, 854, 861, 862, 868, 887, 894, 908, 960, 961, 1035, 1039, 1078, 1092, 1097, 1100, 1101, 1155, 1170, 1214, 1221, 1246, 1256, 1281, 1338, 1457, 1528, 1576, 1607, 1611, 1612, 1613, 1657, 1658, 1659, 1665, 1671, 1672, 1673, 1688, 1693, 1716, 1727, 1738, 1739, 1771, 1801, 1807, 1841, 1863, 1888, 1974, 1975, 2010, 2044, 2045, 2082, 2123, 2158, 2163, 2202, 2212, 2217, 2258, 2260, 2300, 2301, 2314, 2383, 2388, 2406, 2483, 2488, 2515, 2536, 2591, 2606, 2666, 2693, 2703, 2727, 2781, 2787, 2794, 2810, 2816, 2840, 2856, 2857, 2859, 2860, 2861, 2862, 2863, 2864, 2871, 2873, 2886

Psychological Corporation Limited
United Kingdom
[Address Unknown]
Tests: 1727

Psychological Foundations of Education
University of Minnesota
178 Pillsbury Drive, SE
315 Burton Hall
Minneapolis, MN 55455
Tests: 1599

Psychological Growth Associates, Inc.
Products Division
3813 Tiffany Drive
Lawrence, KS 66049
Telephone: 785-841-1141
FAX: 785-749-2190
E-mail: 73204.303@compuserve. com
Tests: 2759

Psychological Publications, Inc.
P.O. Box 3577
Thousand Oaks, CA 91359-0577
Telephone: 800-345-8378
FAX: 805-373-1753
E-mail: TJTA@aol.com
Web URL: www.TJTA.com
Tests: 1013, 2618

Psychological Services Bureau, Inc.
P.O. Box 327
St. Thomas, PA 17252-0327
Telephone: 717-369-4222
FAX: 717-369-2344
E-mail: psb@epix.net
Web URL: psbtests.com
Tests: 2220, 2221, 2222, 2223

Psychological Services, Inc.
100 West Broadway, Suite #1100
Glendale, CA 91210
Telephone: 818-244-0033
FAX: 818-247-7223
E-mail: testinfo@psionline.com
Web URL: www.psionline.com
Tests: 937, 1033, 1034, 2003, 2072, 2105

Psychological Test Publications
Scamp's House
107 Pilton Street
Barnstaple, Devon
England
Tests: 1133, 1481

Psychological Test Specialists
Box 9229
Missoula, MT 59807
Tests: 1017, 1059, 1146, 1239, 1332, 1375, 1376, 1645, 2102, 2146, 2800, 2825

Psychologists and Educators, Inc.
Sales Division
P.O. Box 513
Chesterfield, MO 63006
Telephone: 314-536-2366
FAX: 314-434-2331
Tests: 177, 288, 707, 725, 1222, 1223, 1406, 1583, 1584, 1585, 1586, 1845, 2004, 2263, 2367, 2370, 2354, 2380, 2529, 2615, 2707, 2713

Psychology Press
325 Chestnut Street, Suite 800
Philadelphia, PA 19106
Telephone: 215-625-8900
FAX: 215-625-2940
Web URL: www.ppsypress.com
Tests: 314, 378, 432, 984, 2113, 2809

Psychology Press Inc.
P.O. Box 328
Brandon, VT 05733-0328
Telephone: 802-247-8312
FAX: 802-247-8312
E-mail: info@great-ideas.org
Web URL: www.great-ideas.org
Tests: 1977

Psychometric Affiliates
P.O. Box 807
Murfreesboro, TN 37133
Telephone: 615-890-6296
FAX: 615-890-6296
E-mail: jheritage@a1.mtsu.edu
Tests: 9, 10, 11, 137, 147, 150, 151, 173, 174, 533, 616, 738, 752, 753, 754, 845, 913, 921, 933, 956, 957, 979, 981, 1003, 1005, 1038, 1063, 1076, 1082, 1084, 1137, 1182, 1184, 1185, 1188, 1203, 1229, 1312, 1344, 1368, 1449, 1492, 1604, 1632, 1834, 1840, 1920, 1985, 1998, 1999, 2112, 2126, 2183, 2286, 2343, 2456, 2473, 2784, 2823, 2877, 2919

Psychometrics Canada Ltd.
[Address Unknown]
Tests: 206, 1253, 1493, 2528, 2893, 2894

PsykologiFörlaget AB
Box 47054
100 74 Stockholm
Sweden
Tests: 1654, 2209

Psytec Inc.
P.O. Box 564
DeKalb, IL 60115
Tests: 448

Publishers Test Service
2500 Garden Road
Monterey, CA 93940-5379
Tests: 1468, 1774, 1829, 2122, 2734

Donald K. Pumroy, Ph.D.
University of Maryland
Division of Human & Community Resources
College of Education
College Park, MD 20742
Tests: 1589

Purdue Research Foundation
Attn: William K. Lebold
Educational Research & Info System
Engineering and Administration Bldg.
Purdue University
West Lafayette, IN 47907
Tests: 2124

Ramsay Corporation
Boyce Station Offices
1050 Boyce Road
Pittsburgh, PA 15241
Telephone: 412-257-0732
FAX: 412-257-9929
E-mail: ramtom@aol.com
Web URL: www.ramsaycorp.com
Tests: 920, 923, 924, 1279, 1353, 1537, 1637, 2066, 2067, 2150, 2151, 2152, 2153, 2154, 2155, 2156, 2157, 2643, 2644, 2769, 2867

Reason House
1402 York Road, #207
Lutherville, MD 21093-6024
Tests: 828

Rebus Inc.
P.O. Box 4479
Ann Arbor, MI 48106-4479
Telephone: 800-435-3085
FAX: 734-665-4728
E-mail: mail@rebusinc.com
Web URL: www.rebusinc.com
Tests: 889

Rehabilitation Research and Training Center on Blindness and Low Vision
Mississippi State University
P.O. Drawer 6189
Mississippi State, MS 39762
Tests: 922

Reid Psychological Systems
153 West Ohio Street
Chicago, IL 60610
Tests: 2198

Reitan Neuropsychology Laboratory/Press
P.O. Box 66080
Tucson, AZ 85728-6080
Telephone: 520-882-2022
FAX: 520-884-0040
E-mail: reitanlab@aol.com
Tests: 1164

Renovex Corporation
1421 Jersey Avenue, N
Minneapolis, MN 55427
Tests: 201

Rensis Likert Associates, Inc.
[Address Unknown]
Tests: 2073, 2079, 2435, 2587

Research for Better Schools, Inc.
444 North Third Street
Philadelphia, PA 19123-4107
Telephone: 215-574-9300
FAX: 215-574-0133
E-mail: maguire@rbs.org
Web URL: www.rbs.org
Tests: 204, 216, 843, 1458, 2312

Research Press
Dept. G
P.O. Box 9177
Champaign, IL 61826
Tests: 293, 717, 1052, 1742, 2450, 2763

Richardson, Bellows, Henry & Co., Inc.
[Address Unknown]
Tests: 390, 1430, 1566, 2164, 2165, 2166, 2167, 2168, 2169, 2170, 2573, 2696

Richmond International, Inc.
1021 S. Rogers Circle, Suite #6
Boca Raton, FL 33487-2894
Telephone: 561-994-2112
FAX: 561-994-2235
Tests: 1159

Risk & Needs Assessment, Inc.
P.O. Box 44828
Phoenix, AZ 85064-4828
Tests: 19, 849, 1335, 2061, 2285, 2393, 2403

Riverside Publishing
425 Spring Lake Drive
Itasca, IL 60143-2079
Telephone: 800-323-9540
FAX: 630-467-7192
Web URL: www.riverpub.com
Tests: 5, 202, 264, 265, 266, 281, 309, 443, 560, 763, 823, 1060, 1072, 1263, 1285, 1300, 1315, 1318, 1319, 1418, 1606, 1767, 1768, 2204, 2241, 2299, 2485, 2735, 2792, 2900, 2901, 2902, 2903, 2904

Rocky Mountain Behavioral Science Institute, Inc.
419 Canyon Avenue, Suite 316
Fort Collins, CO 80521
Telephone: 800-447-6354
FAX: 970-221-0595
Web URL: www.rmbsi.com
Tests: 143

Edwin F. Rosinski, Ed.D.
[Address Unknown]
Tests: 1640

Kenneth H. Rubin, Ph.D., Director
Center for Study of Families, Relationships & Child Development
Department of Human Development
3304 Benjamin Building
University of Maryland
College Park, MD 20742-1131
Tests: 2001

SAGE Publications
2455 Teller Road
Thousand Oaks, CA 09320
Tests: 1743

Dr. Shoukry D. Saleh, Chairman
Department of Management Sciences
University of Waterloo
Waterloo, Ontario N2L 3G1
Canada
Tests: 1345

San Jose State University
School of Education
One Washington Square
San Jose, CA 95192-0078
Tests: 306

The SASSI Institute
Route 2, Box 134
Springville, IN 47462
Telephone: 800-726-0526
FAX: 800-546-7995
E-mail: sassi@sassi.com
Web URL:www.sassi.com
Tests: 2553

Saville & Holdsworth
575 Boylston Street
Boston, MA 02116
Tests: 119, 236, 735, 964, 1544, 1551, 1818, 1822, 1973, 2087, 2274, 2641, 2642, 2927

Dr. K. Warner Schaie
Penn State Gerontology Center
105 Henderson
Penn State University
University Park, PA 16802
Telephone: 814-865-1710
FAX: 814-863-9423
E-mail: gero@psu.cdu
Web URL:geron.psu.edu
Tests: 2304

Ronald R. Schmeck, Professor
Department of Psychology
Southern Illinois University at Carbondale
Carbondale, IL 62901-6502
Tests: 1307

Nina G. Schneider, Ph.D.
Psychopharmacology Unit
VA Medical Center
Brentwood T350
Mail Code 691/B151D
Los Angeles, CA 90073
Tests: 2440

Scholastic Testing Service, Inc.
480 Meyer Road
Bensenville, IL 60106-1617
Tests: 547, 653, 695, 878, 904, 1128, 1163, 1202, 1227, 1395, 1396, 1414, 1623, 1878, 2137, 2243, 2320, 2545, 2754, 2755, 2771, 2852

Herman J. P. Schubert
500 Klein Road
Buffalo, NY 14221
Tests: 851

Scientific Management Techniques, Inc.
581 Boylston Street
Boston, MA 02116
Tests: 2479

SDQ Instruments, Publication Unit
Faculty of Education
Univ. of Western Sydney, MacArthur
P.O. Box 555
Campbell Town NSW 2560
Australia
Telephone: 612-9772-6428
FAX: 612-9772-6432
E-mail: k.johnson@uws.edu.au
Web URL: edweb.macarthur.uws.edu.au/self/
Tests: 2358

Search Institute
700 South 3rd Street, Suite 210
Minneapolis, MN 55415-1138
Telephone: 800-888-7828
FAX: 612-376-8956
Web URL: www.search-institute.org
Tests: 2336

SEFA (Publications) Ltd.
"The Globe"
4 Great William St.
Stratford-upon-Avon CV37-6RY
England
Tests: 1512, 2088

Selby MillSmith Ltd.
30 Circus Mews
Bath BA1 2PW
United Kingdom
Telephone: +44 1225-446655
FAX: +44 1225-446643
E-mail: Info@Selby MillSmith.com
Web URL: www.Selby MillSmith.com
Tests: 945, 1823, 1828, 2345, 2346

Melvin L. Selzer, MD.
6967 Paseo Laredo
La Jolla, CA 92037
Telephone: 619-459-1035
Tests: 1661

SenCom Associates
P.O. Box 36
Pacific Palisades, CA 90272
Tests: 1171

Sensonics, Inc.
P.O. Box 112
Haddon Heights, NJ 08035
Telephone: 609-547-7702
FAX: 609-547-5665
Web URL: www.smelltest.com
Tests: 2437

Sewall Early Education Developmental (SEED) Program
1360 Vine Street
Denver, CO 80206
Tests: 2342

The Sidran Foundation
2328 West Joppa Road, Suite 15
Lutherville, MD 21093
Telephone: 410-825-8888
FAX: 410-337-0747
E-mail: sidran@sidran.org
Web URL: www.sidran.org
Tests: 74, 846, 847

Sigma Assessment Systems, Inc.
511 Fort Street, Suite 435
P.O. Box 610984
Port Huron, MI 48061-0984
Telephone: 800-265-1285
FAX: 800-361-9411
E-mail: SIGMA@sigmaassessment systems.com
Web URL: www.sigmaassessmentsystems.com
Tests: 183, 256, 406, 427, 1333, 1334, 1731, 1965, 2115, 2389, 2407, 2592

Simon & Schuster Higher Education Group
200 Old Tappan Road
Tappan, NJ 07675
Tests: 972, 1247, 1248, 1510, 1588, 1838, 2081

Slosson Educational Publications, Inc.
P.O. Box 280
East Aurora, NY 14052-0280
Tests: 4, 153, 178, 480, 663, 829, 830, 831, 832, 833, 841, 1400, 2323, 2324, 2331, 2429, 2430, 2431, 2432, 2433, 2434, 2552, 2650, 2678, 2706, 2838

SOARES Associates
111 Teeter Rock Road
Trumbull, CT 06611
Tests: 120, 121, 2366, 2368

SOI Systems
45755 Goodpasture Road
P.O. Box D
Vida, OR 97488
Tests: 726, 781, 782, 1641

Sopris West
4093 Specialty Place
Longmont, CO 85040
Telephone: 800-547-6747
FAX: 303-776-5934
Web URL: www.sopriswest.com
Tests: 890, 1275, 1295, 2311, 2607

Special Child Publications
P.O. Box 33548
Seattle, WA 98133
Tests: 261, 1803, 2724

SPECTRA Incorporated, Publishers
P.O. Box 13591
New Orleans, LA 70185-3591
Telephone: 504-831-4440
FAX: 504-831-0631
E-mail: spectrainc@compuserve.com
Web URL: www.spectraweb.com
Tests: 2855

Stanard & Associates, Inc.
309 West Washington Street, Suite 1000
Chicago, IL 60606
Telephone: 312-553-0213
FAX: 312-553-0218
E-mail: sales@stanard.com
Web URL: www.stanard.com
Tests: 1763

Stevens, Thurow & Associates, Inc.
[Address Unknown]
Tests: 1301, 2057

Stoelting Co.
Oakwood Center
620 Wheat Lane
Wood Dale, IL 60191
Telephone: 630-860-9700
FAX: 630-860-9775
E-mail: psychtests@stoeltingco.com
Web URL: www.stoeltingco.com/tests
Tests: 182, 285, 488, 996, 1058, 1098, 1189, 1206, 1308, 1363, 1381, 1383, 1407, 1410, 1484, 1485, 1502, 1653, 1714, 1994, 1995, 2046, 2344, 2436, 2454, 2516, 2818

Stratton-Christian Press, Inc.
[Address Unknown]
Tests: 393, 1125, 1364, 1491

Student Development Associates, Inc.
110 Crestwood Drive
Athens, GA 30605
Tests: 8, 2527

Summa Information Systems, Inc.
Box 2172
Greenville, NC 27834
Tests: 2590

Clifford H. Swensen
Department of Psychological Sciences
Purdue University
1364 Psychological Sciences Building
West Lafayette, IN 47907-1364
Telephone: 765-496-6977
FAX: 765-496-2670
E-mail: cswensen@psych.purdue.edu
Tests: 2291, 2292

Swets Test Publishers
P.O. Box 820
2160 Sz Lisse
The Netherlands
Telephone: +31 252 435375
FAX: +31 252 435671
E-mail: stp@swets.nl
Web URL:www.swets.nl/
Tests: 641, 1053, 2396, 2441, 2659

Johanna Krout Tabin, Ph.D.
162 Park Avenue
Glencoe, IL 60022
Tests: 1303, 1940, 2600

TAV Selection System
12807 Arminta St.
North Hollywood, CA 91605
Telephone: 818-765-1884
Tests: 2616

Anne P. Taylor
9 Tumble Weed, NW
Albuquerque, NM 87120-1823
Telephone: 505-898-4678
FAX: 505-898-4689
E-mail: aetaylor@unm.com
Tests: 2617

Teachers College Press
Teachers College
Columbia University
525 W. 120th Street, Box 303
New York, NY 10027
Telephone: 212-678-3929
FAX: 212-678-4149
E-mail: puciatc@exchange.tc.columbia.edu
Web URL: www.tc.columbia.edu
Tests: 565, 875, 1009, 1073, 1264, 1609, 2310, 2663, 2664

Teleometrics International
1755 Woodstead Court
The Woodlands, TX 77380-0964
Tests: 14, 437, 675, 676, 755, 941, 1244, 1441, 1546, 1558, 1559, 1564, 1565, 1567, 1571, 1572, 1574, 1757, 1861, 1894, 1924, 1937, 1945, 1971, 2021, 2022, 2068, 2129, 2133, 2188, 2273, 2275, 2280, 2547, 2548, 2549, 2578, 2583, 2634, 2636, 2637, 2638, 2921

The Test Agency Ltd.
Cray House
Woodlands Road
Henley-on-Thames, Oxon RG9 4AE
England
Telephone: 01491 413413
FAX: 01491 572249
E-mail: testagency@aol.com
Web URL: www.testagency.com
Tests: 911, 919, 1134, 1232, 1497, 1576, 1616, 1837, 2007, 2019, 2160, 2398

Test Analysis & Development Corporation
2400 Park Lake Drive
Boulder, CO 80301
Telephone: 303-666-8651
FAX: 303-665-6045
Tests: 2363

Toby J. Tetenbaum
Fordham University
113 West 60 Street, Room 1119
New York, NY 10023
Telephone: 212-636-6439
FAX: 212-636-7875
E-mail: TobyJa@aol.com
Tests: 228

Thames Valley Test Company Ltd.
7-9 The Green
Flempton, Bury St.
Edmunds, Suffolk IP28 6EL
England
Telephone: +44 1284 728608
FAX: +44 1284 728166
E-mail: tvtc@msn.com
Tests: 295, 2239

Therapy Skill Builders—A Division of The Psychological Corporation
555 Academic Court
San Antonio, TX 78204-2498
Telephone: 800-211-8378
FAX: 800-232-1223
Web URL: www.hbtpc.com
Tests: 685, 870, 968, 969, 1065, 1258, 1265, 1839, 1851, 2316, 2327, 2767

Timao Foundation for Research and Development
[Address Unknown]
Tests: 795, 1002, 2161, 2237

Touchstone Applied Science Associates (TASA), Inc.
4 Hardscrabble Heights
P.O. Box 382
Brewster, NY 10509-0382
Web URL: www.tasa.com
Tests: 773, 774

Training House, Inc.
P.O. Box 3090
Princeton, NJ 08543-3090
Telephone: 609-452-1505
FAX: 609-452-2790
E-mail: training@traininghouse.com
Web URL: www.traininghouse.com
Tests: 155, 166, 203, 632, 701, 940, 1277, 1542, 1563, 1570, 1874, 1936, 1950, 1951, 2070, 2075, 2352, 2353, 2584, 2679, 2760, 2775, 2876

TRT Associates, Inc.
65 Eagle Ridge Drive
Highlands, NC 28741
Telephone: 828-526-9561
FAX: 828-526-9561 (press *)
E-mail: info@trt-basis.com
Web URL: www.mindspring.com/~trtbasis
Tests: 262

Trust Tutoring
912 Thayer Avenue, Suite #205
Silver Spring, MD 20910
Telephone: 301-589-0733
FAX: 301-589-0733 *51
E-mail: havis@erols.com
Web URL: www.wdn.com/trust
Tests: 982

21st Century Assessment
P.O. Box 608
South Pasadena, CA 91031
Telephone: 800-374-2100
FAX: 626-441-0614
Tests: 1958

U.S. Department of Labor
Employment and Training Administration
200 Constitution Avenue, NW
Washington, DC 20210
Tests: 1351, 2795, 2796, 2797, 2798, 2799

United States Military Entrance Processing Command
ATTN: Operations Directorate
2500 Green Bay Road
North Chicago, IL 60064-3094
Telephone: 800-323-0513
Web URL: www.dmdc.osd.mil/asvab
Tests: 180

United/DOK Publishers
[Address Unknown]
Tests: 248, 319, 658, 895, 976, 1090, 1238, 1921, 2055, 2162, 2504, 2621, 2753

Universal Attention Disorders, Inc.
4281 Katella Avenue, #215
Los Alamitos, CA 90720
Telephone: 800-729-2886
FAX: 714-229-8782
E-mail: info@tovatest.com
Web URL: www.tovatest.com
Tests: 2720

University of Alberta
6-102 Education North
Edmonton, Alberta T6G 2G5
Canada
Tests: 131

University of Georgia
College of Education
Division for the Education of Exceptional Children
Aderhold Hall
Athens, GA 30602
Tests: 227

University of Illinois Press
1325 South Oak Street
Champaign, IL 61820
Tests: 194, 318, 1240

The University of Iowa
Publications Order Service
2222 Old Hwy. 218 S.
Iowa City, IA 52242-1602
Telephone: 319-384-3808
FAX: 319-384-3806
Tests: 2651

University of Maryland
University Counseling Center
Shoemaker Hall
College Park, MD 20742
Tests: 1795, 2116, 2413

University of Michigan Press
839 Green Street
P.O. Box 1104
Ann Arbor, MI 48106-1104
Tests: 879, 2041

University of Minnesota Press
Test Division
Mill Place, Suite 290
111 Third Avenue, South
Minneapolis, MN 55401-2520
Telephone: 612-627-1963
FAX: 612-627-1980
Web URL: www.upress.umn.edu/tests
Tests: 879, 1697, 1698, 2041, 2306

University of New England
Publishing Unit
Armidale, New South Wales 2351
Australia
Tests: 1190

The University of Utah
Department of Psychology-SBS
390 South 1530 East
Salt Lake City, UT 84112-0251
Tests: 1298

Variety Pre-Schooler's Workshop
47 Humphrey Drive
Syosset, NY 11791-4098
Telephone: 516-921-7171 and 800-933-8779
FAX: 516-921-8130
E-mail: JFVPSW@aol.com
Tests: 1041

Village Publishing
73 Valle Drive
Furlong, PA 18925
Tests: 13, 213, 333, 334, 1788, 1879, 1886, 1917

Vine Publishing Ltd.
10 Elgin Rd.
Bournemouth BH49NL
UK
Telephone: 011-44-1202-761766
FAX: 011-44-1202-761766
Tests: 2195

Virtual Knowledge
200 Highland Avenue
Needham, MA 02194
Tests: 412

Vocational and Rehabilitation Research institute
3304—33rd Street, NW
Calgary, Alberta T2L 2A6
Canada
Tests: 63

Vocational Psychology Research
N657 Elliott Hall
University of Minnesota—Twin Cities
75 East River Road
Minneapolis, MN 55455-0344
Telephone: 612-625-1367
FAX: 612-626-0345
E-mail: vpr@tc.umn.edu
Tests; 1694, 1695, 1701, 1702

Vocational Research Institute
1528 Walnut Street, Suite 1502
Philadelphia, PA 19102
Tests: 2836

VORT Corporation
P.O. Box 60880
Palo Alto, CA 94306
Tests: 292, 1192, 1194

Dr. Walter B. Waetjen
8800 Walther Blvd., Apt. 3622
Baltimore, MD 21234-9016
Tests: 2356

Mazie Earle Wagner
[Address Unknown]
Tests: 354

J. Weston Walch, Publisher
P.O. Box 658
321 Valley Street
Portland, ME 04104-0658
Tests: 1027, 2143, 2765

Walden Personnel Performance, Inc.
4155 Sherbrooke, W #100
Montreal, Quebec H3Z 1K9
Canada
Telephone: 514-989-9555
FAX: 514-989-9934
E-mail: tests@waldentesting.com
Web URL: www.waldentesting.com
Tests: 16, 154, 249, 360, 536, 668, 688, 756, 764, 988, 1193, 1328, 1329, 1330, 1453, 1568, 1666, 1772, 1773, 1810, 2084, 2085, 2205, 2206, 2277, 2374, 2640, 2646, 2842, 2843, 2844, 2845, 2846, 2847, 2851

Arthur Weider
552 Laguardia Pl.
New York, NY 10012-1459
Tests: 708, 709

Otto Weininger
Ontario Institute for Studies in Education
The University of Toronto
252 Bloor Street West
Toronto, Ontario M5S 1V6
Canada
Telephone: 416-929-2348
FAX: 416-929-3440
Tests: 840

West Virginia Rehabilitation Research and Training Center
Barron Drive
P.O. Box 1004
Institute, WV 25112-1004
Tests: 1245, 2030, 2827

Western Michigan University
Division of Continuing Education
Office of Self-Instructional Programs
Ellsworth Hall, Room B102
Kalamazoo, MI 49008-5161
Tests: 2028

Western Psychological Services
12031 Wilshire Blvd.
Los Angeles, CA 90025-1251
Telephone: 310-478-2061
FAX: 310-478-7838
Tests: 37, 41, 71, 73, 132, 175, 200, 225, 230, 232, 297, 301, 336, 355, 371, 391, 392, 459, 473, 563, 751, 772, 777, 811, 853, 932, 950, 1006, 1049, 1050, 1074, 1160, 1165, 1169, 1218, 1226, 1266, 1290, 1294, 1401, 1419, 1439, 1522, 1524, 1525, 1540, 1543, 1577, 1582, 1587, 1614, 1647, 1660, 1748, 1749, 1775, 1802, 1832, 1869, 1883, 1916, 1931, 1932, 1933, 1962, 1963, 1969, 1978, 1991, 2062, 2063, 2107, 2120, 2214, 2216, 2226, 2229, 2235, 2242, 2265, 2293, 2333, 2334, 2377, 2382, 2402, 2405, 2426, 2438, 2439, 2446, 2468, 2518, 2525, 2541, 2559, 2571, 2599, 2647, 2652, 2715, 2761, 2762, 2764, 2817, 2819, 2824, 2833, 2839, 2848, 2870, 2874, 2878

Wide Range, Inc.
P.O. Box 3410
Wilmington, DE 19804-0250
Tests: 2879, 2880, 2881, 2882

Williams and Wilkins
351 West Camden Street
Baltimore, MD 21201-2436
Tests: 199

Dale E. Williams, Ph.D.
[Address Unknown]
Tests: 479

Robert L. Williams & Associates, Inc.
Educational & Psychological Services
6372-76 Delmar Blvd.
St. Louis, MO 63130
Tests: 316, 2750, 2887

Winslow Research Institute
1933 Windward Point
Discovery Bay, CA 94514
Telephone: 925-754-2828
FAX: 925-516-7015
E-mail: WinslowWRI@aol.com
Web URL: WinslowResearch.com
Tests: 1930, 1955

Wintergreen/Orchard House, Inc.
425 Spring Lake Drive
Itasca, IL 60143-2076
Tests: 410, 905, 1069

Rose Wolfe
c/o Walden Personnel Testing & Training, Inc.
4115 Sherbrooke, W #100
Montreal, Quebec H3Z 1K9
Canada
Tests: 167, 2608, 2609, 2895, 2896, 2897, 2849

Wonderlic Personnel Test, Inc.
1795 N. Butterfield Road
Libertyville, IL 60048-1238
Telephone: 800-323-3742
FAX: 847-680-9492
E-mail: testingservices@wonderlic.com
Web URL: www.wonderlic.com
Tests: 654, 966, 1180, 2898, 2899

Rosestelle B. Woolner
969 Ralph McGill Blvd., NE
Atlanta, GA 30306-4446
Tests: 2048

Judith Worell, Ph.D.
Educational & Counseling Psychology
245 Dickey Hall
University of Kentucky
Lexington, KY 40506-0017
Telephone: 606-257-7880
FAX: 606-257-5662
E-mail: jworell@pop.uky.edu
Tests: 1881

World Health Organization
[Switzerland]
[Address Unknown]
Tests: 135

XICOM
60 Woods Road
Tuxedo, NY 10987-3108
Tests: 313, 420, 640, 946, 1397, 1398, 1417, 1494, 1892, 1904, 1912, 2020, 2096, 2513, 2632, 2756, 2773

York Press, Inc.
[Address Unknown]
Tests: 769

Sue R. Zalk
Hunter College of the City University of New York
695 Park Avenue
New York, NY 10021
Tests: 1377

Zaner-Bloser Educational Publishers
2200 West Fifth Avenue
P.O. Box 16764
Columbus, OH 43216-6764
Web URL: www.zaner-bloser.com
Tests: 2597

INDEX OF NAMES

This analytical index indicates whether a citation refers to authorship of a test, a test review, or a reference for a specific test. Numbers refer to test entries, not to pages. The abbreviations and numbers following the names may be interpreted as follows: "test, 73" indicates authorship of test 73; "rev, 86" is based on information listed in the cross references for a test and indicates authorship of a previous review of test 86; "ref, 45(30)" indicates authorship of reference number 30 in the "Test References" section for test 45.

Aabye, S. M.: ref, 301 (46)
Aadland, R. L.: ref, 863 (8), 2603 (61)
Aakalu, G.: ref, 2860 (1409),2862 (727), 2892 (303)
Aalberg, V.: ref, 1079 (52)
Aalberg, V. A.: ref, 1079 (76), 1832 (17), 2603 (493)
Aaron, I. E.: rev, 330, 496, 1768, 2180, 2253, 2254
Aaron, L.: ref, 815 (14), 1164 (56), 1612 (46), 1903 (236), 2485 (117), 2860 (580), 2863 (167)
Aaron, P. G.: ref, 2902 (1)
Aarons, M.: test, 235
Aaronson, A. L.: ref, 1697 (467)
Aaronson, C.: ref, 2305 (34)
Aaronson, M.: test, 461
Aarsland, D.: ref, 2599 (33)
Abad-Gil, J.: ref, 538 (8), 1201 (6)
Abadee, P. S.: ref, 2860 (781)
Abasi, R.: ref, 1469 (11), 1590 (63)
Abbanto, K. R.: ref, 1338 (45), 2839 (6)
Abbar, M.: ref, 2305 (117)
Abbas, P. J.: ref, 1240 (39), 2657 (27), 2694 (19), 2695 (45), 2725 (6)
Abbate, M. F.: ref, 472 (105), 1000 (78)
Abbey, A.: ref, 2860 (234)
Abbey, K. J.: ref, 2558 (3)
Abbot-Shim, M.: ref, 1264 (6), 1889 (11), 1987 (22)
Abbott, J.: ref, 1079 (31)
Abbott, P.: ref, 1079 (31), 2239 (34)
Abbott, R. D.: test, 1379; ref, 1138 (1,2), 1379 (74,89), 1612 (29), 2485 (71), 2862 (383,537), 2864 (101,123), 2879 (208), 2901 (84), 2905 (31,94,111)
Abbott-Shim, M. S.: test, 452
Abbruzzese, J. L.: ref, 2860 (375), 2863 (98)
Abbruzzese, M.: ref, 2892 (159,262)
Abdad, E. V.: ref, 2863 (209)
Abdalla, I. A.: ref, 298 (100,135), 404 (31)
Abdel-Khalek, A. M.: ref, 272 (243), 998 (4), 999 (4,10), 1021 (2,20), 2497 (607)
Abedi, J.: ref, 2497 (579)
Abel, T.: ref, 2163 (101), 2485 (72)
Abeles, N.: ref, 2497 (552), 2603 (173), 2860 (1075), 2863 (314)
Abell, E. L.: rev, 364
Abell, S. C.: ref, 694 (112), 853 (14), 1097 (14), 1160 (3), 1832 (13), 2485 (188), 2652 (9), 2860 (552), 2862 (431)
Abelsohn, D.: ref, 1000 (11)
Abelson, J. L.: ref, 2497 (97)
Abidin, R. R.: test, 1889, 2520; ref, 372 (106), 694 (120)
Abikoff, H.: ref, 2862 (432), 2879 (151)
Abiodun, O. A.: ref, 2050 (53)
Abkarian, G. G.: ref, 175 (5), 1240 (8), 1903 (99), 2163 (80), 2382 (5), 2485 (43), 2694 (6), 2695 (11), 2860 (322), 2862 (149), 2864 (25)

Ablard, K. E.: ref, 615 (43)
Ablon, S.: ref, 1010 (69), 1092 (11), 2860 (801,990), 2862 (308,100,142)
Abney, O. L.: ref, 1135 (5), 2599 (7)
Abou-Saleh, M. T.: ref, 1166 (71,191)
Abouserie, R.: ref, 999 (55)
Aboyoun, D. C.: ref, 2417 (32)
Abraham, I. L.: ref, 273 (8), 1166 (37)
Abraham, J. A.: test, 1369
Abraham, L. M.: ref, 1701 (4)
Abraham, M.: test, 1166; ref, 1166 (106, 184)
Abraham, P. P.: ref, 2247 (49)
Abrahams, S.: ref, 641 (6), 1758 (48,82), 2193 (43), 2860 (943,1213), 2863 (277)
Abrahamsen, E. P.: ref, 2862 (300)
Abrami, P. C.: ref, 560 (2)
Abramis, D. J.: ref, 2603 (225)
Abramowitz, A. J.: ref, 681 (1)
Abrams, C. L.: ref, 1266 (1,2)
Abrams, D.: ref, 301 (19), 2247 (17), 2380 (4), 2749 (22), 2862 (142)
Abrams, D. B.: ref, 134 (6,8,14,15,20,27), 272 (90), 1661 (12,23,34), 2858 (41)
Abrams, E. Z.: ref, 270 (47), 2485 (238)
Abrams, J.: ref, 790 (2), 1021 (10), 2749 (10)
Abrams, M. R.: ref, 1010 (112), 2603 (504), 2858 (122), 2862 (437)
Abrams, R. C.: ref, 1093 (32)
Abramson, L.: ref, 270 (1), 2749 (18)
Abu-Freha, A.: ref, 2497 (75)
Abwender, D. A.: ref, 451 (80)
Academic Freedom Committee, Illinois Division, American Civil Liberties Union: test, 11
Accardo, C. M.: ref, 2417 (32)
Ace, M. E.: ref, 2531 (1)
Achard, S.: ref, 2813 (37)
Achenbach, T. M.: test, 424, 451, 2939; ref, 451 (135), 681 (70)
Acheson, S.: ref, 2485 (231)
Achilles, C. M.: ref, 2355 (3)
Achter, J. A.: ref, 302 (4), 1790 (9), 2539 (1)
Achterberg, J.: test, 1183, 1242
Acierno, R.: ref, 2497 (294)
Ackerman, D. L.: ref, 1093 (26)
Ackerman, M. J.: test, 41
Ackerman, P. L.: rev, 1279, 1385, 1595, 2488, 838 (21), 2218 (67)
Ackerman, P. T.: ref, 199 (11), 322 (6), 451 (47), 681 (28), 769 (2,4,5), 1130 (1), 1131 (10,11,17)f, 1164 (44), 1592 (13), 2862 (118,160,190,231,301,696), 2879 (31), 2879 (42,54,70,97,222), 2879 (222), 2905 (32,49,118)
Ackerman, T.: rev, 743, 2861; ref, 56 (16)
Ackerman, T. A.: rev, 799, 1784
Ackerman, V.: ref, 472 (195)
Ackley, G. B. E.: ref, 2860 (701)
Ackley, K. A.: ref, 451 (237)
Acklin, M. W.: ref, 2247 (50,79), 2749 (52)
Acosta, F. X.: ref, 337 (69)
ACS DivCHED Examinations Institute: test, 42, 43, 44, 45, 46, 47, 48, 53, 54, 55
ACT Career Planning Services: test, 2831
ACT, Inc.: test, 56, 57, 418, 621, 992, 1997, 2830
Action, G. J.: ref, 1079 (70), 1947 (7)
Adachi, N.: ref, 2860 (406), 2873 (11)
Adair, J. C.: ref, 376 (20), 1164 (150), 2227 (37), 2860 (870,1270), 2873 (35,64), 2892 (182,273)
Adair, N.: test, 3
Adam, B. S.: ref, 472 (21), 1991 (29), 2214 (12)
Adam, E. K.: ref, 1697 (506)
Adam, M.: ref, 1697 (15), 2860 (60)
Adaman, J. E.: ref, 2771 (34)
Adamczak, K.: ref, 2497 (225)
Adami, G. F.: ref, 893 (29)
Adami, H.: ref, 2305 (203)
Adamo, U. H.: ref, 2305 (220)
Adamo, V. H.: ref, 1697 (405), 2305 (131)
Adamovich, B.: test, 2297
Adams, A.: ref, 350 (22), 1612 (63)
Adams, A. J.: ref, 1072 (1), 1131 (1), 2862 (1)
Adams, C.: rev, 1535
Adams, C. D.: ref, 451 (48,164), 681 (82), 997 (14)
Adams, C. M.: ref, 1140 (40)
Adams, C. R.: test, 1928
Adams, D. M.: ref, 2258 (5)
Adams, D. R.: ref, 615 (18)
Adams, E.: test, 2034
Adams, E. V.: ref, 1612 (35)
Adams, G. L.: test, 661, 1801
Adams, G. R.: rev, 746; ref, 451 (267), 694 (133), 1010 (135)
Adams, H. E.: ref, 1697 (541), 2497 (548), 2860 (1257)
Adams, J.: ref, 337 (123), 2230 (1,12), 2230 (12), 2557 (7), 2862 (369)
Adams, J. D.: test, 2789
Adams, J. J.: ref, 1525 (6), 1697 (50,532)
Adams, K. M.: ref, 1164 (154), 2193 (42,49), 2860 (936,1287), 2863 (307)
Adams, M.: ref, 2230 (1,12), 2557 (7)
Adams, M. F.: rev, 247
Adams, M. S.: ref, 998 (47), 1697 (185)
Adams, N.: ref, 1758 (34), 2860 (806)
Adams, P.: ref, 2305 (140), 2599 (28)
Adams, R.: test, 2611; ref, 893 (14)
Adams, R. A.: ref, 1000 (28)
Adams, R. D.: ref, 1021 (34), 2076 (136)
Adams, R. L.: rev, 1525, 2141, 2193; ref, 853 (7), 1525 (7), 2860 (1101,1282), 2863 (39)
Adams, S. F.: rev, 978
Adams, S. G.: ref, 2519 (21), 2520 (22), 2860 (421)
Adams, S. G., Jr.: ref, 745 (13), 1697 (353)
Adams, S. H.: ref, 372 (59), 1697 (251)
Adams, S. M.: ref, 592 (8)
Adams, W.: test, 2666, 2880, 2881

Adams, W. F.: ref, 301 (5), 853 (1)
Adamson, L. B.: ref, 1903 (100)
Adan, A. M.: ref, 472 (24,123), 495 (11), 2214 (14,65)
Adcock, C. J.: rev, 1043, 1201, 1689, 2401, 2417, 2749
Adcock, D.: test, 647
Adderly-Kelly, B.: ref, 2599 (1)f, 2862 (11)
Addiction Research Foundation: test, 184
Addis, M. E.: ref, 272 (184)
ADE, Incorporated: test, 1372, 1766, 2550
Adegoke, A. R.: ref, 999 (42)
Adelman, P. B.: ref, 2879 (52), 2901 (22)
Adelman, S. A.: ref, 2603 (298)
Adelstein, A.: ref, 2704 (46), 2860 (1391)
Adelstein, A.: ref, 2862 (715)
Adelstein, T. B.: ref, 2860 (107,323)
Aderibigbe, Y. A.: ref, 2860 (882)
Adinoff, B.: ref, 999 (31), 1592 (9), 1697 (135), 2305 (27)
Adkins, D. C.: rev, 171, 937, 2178
Adkins, K. K.: ref, 2749 (65)
Adkinson, D. R.: test, 1290
Adler, A. B.: ref, 2860 (228), 2862 (116)
Adler, B.: ref, 999 (36), 1079 (13)
Adler, J.: ref, 1697 (48)
Adler, L. E.: ref, 2305 (4)
Adler, R.: ref, 451 (32,144), 1000 (100), 1079 (73), 2497 (98)
Adler, S.: rev, 1913
Adrian, M.: test, 1062
Advantage Learning Systems, Inc.: test, 2492, 2493
Affleck, G.: ref, 272 (15), 1661 (32)
Agami-Rozenblat, O.: ref, 298 (85), 538 (4)
Agarwal, A.: ref, 745 (2)
Agaza, L. M.: ref, 1135 (23), 1697 (572), 2226 (36), 2603 (554), 2860 (1349), 2892 (290)
Ager, J. W.: ref, 1216 (31), 1903 (181), 2860 (473)
Aggleton, J. P.: ref, 1758 (1,11,31,40,56), 2163 (18,28,32,39,46,48), 2860 (58,219,753, 896, 977, 1027), 2863 (19,55,220,267,288,304), 2892 (149, 186,205)
Agid, Y.: ref, 328 (1)f, 776 (33), 2163 (43,75,156, 183,295), 2227 (19), 2516 (44,82), 2517 (7), 2860 (168,298,605,720,818,1153), 2863 (44,178,215 ,236,342), 2870 (2), 2892 (20,39,94,130, 142,207, 248, 249,255)
Agius, R. M.: ref, 1079 (66), 1590 (59), 2218 (55)
Agle, D. P.: ref, 1010 (122), 1013 (2), 2076 (168)f, 2498 (62)
Agnetti, V.: ref, 2860 (18), 2863 (10)
Agnew, J.: ref, 2125 (29), 2860 (1373)
Agnew, R. M.: ref, 2603 (226)
Ago, Y.: ref, 2076 (174)
Agosti, V.: ref, 272 (244), 1166 (130,142,167), 2305 (211), 2603 (487)
Agostin, T. M.: ref, 853 (23), 1903 (514), 2452 (17), 2483 (1)
Agostinelli, G.: ref, 1757 (2)
Agras, W. S.: ref, 272 (144), 1010 (91), 2497 (535), 2603 (329)
Agrawal, S.: ref, 1661 (74)
Agresti, A. A.: ref, 1590 (28)
Agronick, G.: ref, 372 (89), 373 (29)
Aguirre-Deandreis, A. I.: ref, 2497 (100)
Ahava, G. W.: ref, 272 (337)
Ahern, G.: ref, 199 (18), 2860 (783)
Ahles, T. A.: ref, 1697 (200), 2199 (6), 2497 (3,128,17,346), 2519 (40), 2603 (172)
Ahlskog, J. E.: ref, 301 (47), 2516 (63), 2863 (233), 2879 (105), 2892 (166)
Ahluwalia, S. P.: test, 2626
Ahmad, A.: ref, 451 (85)
Ahmad, T.: ref, 2497 (345), 2516 (40)
Ahmann, J. S.: rev, 665, 2742
Ahmed, R. U.: ref, 999 (71)
Ahmed, S. M. S.: ref, 694 (124)
Aho, M.: test, 2219
Ahola, K.: ref, 2516 (58), 2860 (777,1028)
Ahola, V.: ref, 1166 (161)
Ahonen, T.: ref, 815 (45), 1903 (206,281), 2163 (129), 2247 (43), 2768 (18), 2862 (275,641,656), 2901 (122)
Ahrens, A. H.: ref, 893 (38)
Ahrens, J. A.: ref, 298 (150)
Ahrens, J. B.: test, 402
Ahrens, P. K.: ref, 2603 (267)
Ahsen, A.: test, 122, 914
Aida, Y.: ref, 863 (10)
Aiello, J. R.: ref, 2497 (483)
Aiken, L. R.: rev, 33, 56, 2329
Aikens, J. E.: ref, 272 (245), 2076 (162), 2858 (123)
Aikens, K. S.: ref, 2076 (162)
Aikman, K. G.: ref, 272 (121)
Aimard, G.: ref, 1166 (99), 2863 (310)
Ainley, M. D.: ref, 1466 (1)
Ainsworth, M. W.: ref, 462 (19)
Airaghi, G.: ref, 1903 (563), 2163 (347), 2227 (54), 2768 (42), 2862 (698)
Airasian, P. W.: rev, 364, 1318, 2182
Aita, J. F.: ref, 1218 (6), 1903 (275), 2163 (168), 2863 (196), 2892 (123)
Aiton, J. F.: ref, 2305 (13)
Aizenborg, D.: ref, 2305 (118)
Ajdukovic, M.: ref, 448 (19)
Akamatsu, T. J.: ref, 1965 (28)
Akamine, T. X.: ref, 2218 (64)
Akaoka, F.: ref, 2225 (18), 2226 (38), 2227 (51), 2860 (1357), 2863 (409), 2892 (292)
Âkefeldt, A.: ref, 2860 (1214)
Âkefeldt, B.: ref, 2860 (1214)
Akil, H.: ref, 2305 (50)
Akillas, E.: ref, 2497 (420)
Akiskal, H.: ref, 1093 (108), 2305 (125,160,172,210)
Akiskal, H. S.: ref, 1093 (107), 1697 (376), 2305 (97,119,135,211)

Akler, M.: ref, 2879 (67)
Akman, D.: ref, 337 (22), 1697 (119), 1991 (19)
Akram, S.: ref, 298 (92), 1697 (238)
Aks, D. J.: ref, 838 (9)f, 2146 (5), 2899 (2)
Akshoomoff, N.: ref, 1903 (30)
Akshoomoff, N. A.: ref, 1903 (101), 2860 (324), 2892 (45)
Al-Shabbout, M.: ref, 2305 (216)
Al-Shatti, A.: ref, 999 (71)
Alaghband-Rad, J.: ref, 2288 (71), 2289 (56), 2862 (501)
Alagille, M.: ref, 2516 (73), 2860 (1002)
Alamo, L.: ref, 2497 (4)
Alarcón, M.: ref, 1902 (93), 2860 (1215), 2862 (587), 2879 (189)
Alavi, A.: ref, 1672 (1), 2288 (48), 2289 (37)
Albaili, M. A.: ref, 2545 (3)
Albanese, M.: rev, 1975, 1978, 2162, 2220, 2715
Albano, A. M.: ref, 472 (220), 2214 (94,132), 2498 (48,59,60)
Albert, A.: ref, 793 (15)
Albert, H.: test, 434
Albert, J. H.: ref, 56 (5)
Albert, M.: ref, 2860 (1180)
Albert, M. L.: ref, 376 (9), 1164 (124), 2163 (5), 2860 (16,1119), 2863 (9,332), 2879 (169), 2892 (2)
Albert, M. S.: ref, 1164 (72), 1740 (1), 2227 (58), 2860 (2,471,1396), 2863 (1,208,421)
Albert, P.: ref, 1166 (50)
Albert, S.: ref, 303 (18), 776 (45), 1740 (21), 2860 (1284)
Alberti, E. T.: ref, 665 (57)
Albertini, G.: ref, 2163 (99)
Albertos, C.: ref, 2813 (123)
Alberts, J. L.: ref, 739 (8)
Alberts, N. F.: test, 12, 1789, 2373
Albertson, M. G.: ref, 2247 (97)
Albin, J. B.: test, 910
Albino, J. E. N.: ref, 1965 (22)
Alborzi, S.: ref, 301 (26), 1097 (8)
Albott, W. L.: ref, 1697 (453)
Albrecht, B.: ref, 1697 (306)
Albrecht, J. W.: ref, 1697 (176,220,252,359)
Albrecht, N. N.: ref, 1697 (252,359)
Albrecht, W.: ref, 1697 (307)
Albright, J. S.: ref, 998 (72)
Albright, L. E.: rev, 1694, 1701
Albritton, E.: ref, 1216 (32), 1903 (182)
Albus, K. E.: ref, 451 (116), 2288 (68,71), 2289 (52,56), 2305 (103), 2862 (475,501)
Albus, M.: ref, 1093 (82), 1517 (11)
Alcantara, P. R.: ref, 1485 (24), 1903 (219), 2813 (54)
Alcorn, B. K.: rev, 1500, 1792, 2067
Alcorn, J. D.: ref, 1745 (42), 2497 (351)
Alda, M.: ref, 2305 (212)
Alden, L. E.: ref, 272 (145), 790 (25)
Aldencamp, A. P.: ref, 1164 (36)
Aldenhoff, J. B.: ref, 1166 (27)
Alderdice, F. A.: ref, 999 (70), 2860 (553)
Alderfer, M. A.: ref, 2497 (417)
Alderman, N.: test, 295; ref, 337 (51)
Alderton, D. L.: ref, 180 (14), 1405 (20), 2163 (137)
Aldor, R.: ref, 372 (43), 908 (7), 2497 (29,59,328,329), 2498 (34)
Aldrich, F.: test, 2239
Aldrich, F. K.: ref, 1758 (42), 2193 (41), 2860 (900), 2863 (270), 2892 (189)
Aldrich, P. W.: ref, 694 (10)
Aldwin, C. M.: ref, 998 (27), 1697 (86,253,355), 2417 (9,30), 2603 (2,227,308), 2858 (111)
Aleamoni, L. A.: rev, 2636
Aleamoni, L. M.: rev, 497, 939, 1150, 1254
Alegria, M.: ref, 451 (14)
Alemi, B.: ref, 451 (183), 787 (3), 1379 (93)
Alessandra, T.: test, 1915
Alessandri, M.: ref, 1903 (81), 2485 (36)
Alessandri, S. M.: ref, 815 (34), 2039 (3), 2485 (32,44), 2657 (2)
Alessandroni, R.: ref, 2485 (214)
Alessi, N.: ref, 2710 (4)
Alessi, N. E.: ref, 2305 (24), 2813 (7)
Alevriadou, A.: ref, 272 (302), 272 (363)
Alevriadou, A.: ref, 2860 (1318)
Alexander, C. M.: rev, 1862
Alexander, G.: ref, 2485 (126)
Alexander, G. E.: ref, 2485 (234), 2860 (554,1112, 1155,1216), 2879 (190)
Alexander, J.: test, 2361; ref, 776 (20), 1607 (13), 1903 (348), 2485 (164), 2860 (834)
Alexander, J. E.: ref, 592 (22,66)
Alexander, J. M.: ref, 1903 (220)
Alexander, K. L.: ref, 364 (17)
Alexander, L. A.: ref, 893 (51)
Alexander, M. P.: ref, 1164 (91), 2163 (257), 2193 (59), 2860 (833,859,1029,1201,1217), 2863 (240,305), 2873 (24,30,31,51,55,59), 2892 (133, 178,213)
Alexander, P. A.: ref, 2163 (55)
Alexander, P. C.: ref, 272 (338), 1687 (37)
Alexander, R. A.: ref, 592 (4), 1965 (25), 2797 (1), 2871 (2)
Alexander, R. M.: rev, 1945
Alexander, R. W.: ref, 1697 (76)
Alexopoulos, G. S.: ref, 1166 (85), 2247 (38), 2603 (188), 2860 (469)
Alexson, J.: ref, 1049 (1), 1485 (13), 1902 (39), 2862 (182), 2879 (49)
Alfeld-Liron, C.: ref, 2862 (550)
Alfonso, V. C.: ref, 1378 (2), 2452 (11), 2485 (127), 2860 (618), 2862 (254)
Alford, B. A.: ref, 2417 (32), 2603 (32)
Alford, M.: ref, 2860 (184), 2862 (105)
Alford, M. F.: ref, 376 (15), 1164 (145), 2860 (1244), 2862 (601), 2892 (266)

Alger, J. R.: ref, 2860 (502)
Algina, J.: ref, 272 (376), 863 (93), 997 (30), 1889 (19), 1903 (580), 2752 (2), 2899 (13)
Algozzine, B.: test, 2431; rev, 2342; ref, 1300 (9), 2862 (731)
Ali, M. R.: ref, 999 (71)
Ali, S. M.: ref, 999 (71)
Aliminosa, D.: ref, 1392 (6), 1902 (25), 2860 (285)
Alison, V.: ref, 127 (1)
Aliver, J. M.: ref, 272 (94), 1010 (67), 1965 (62)
Alivisatos, B.: ref, 2860 (78)
Alker, H. A.: rev, 1697, 1721
Alkhadher, O.: ref, 838 (23)
Allain, A. N.: ref, 1697 (456), 2860 (994)
Allain, T.: ref, 1166 (72)
Allan, E. R.: ref, 335 (10)
Allan, K. M.: ref, 2860 (594,831,1062,1246)
Allan, P.: ref, 1689 (3)
Allan, S.: ref, 272 (175,246), 999 (84), 2603 (513)
Allan, T.: ref, 271 (10), 272 (268), 337 (171), 2497 (330,619)
Allan, W. D.: ref, 451 (165), 473 (4,8), 1000 (86), 2214 (129), 2603 (569)
Alleman, E.: test, 138, 139, 140
Allen, B. A.: ref, 2497 (667)
Allen, B. G.: ref, 2497 (218)
Allen, C.: ref, 298 (125)
Allen, D.: ref, 4 (4,19), 2382 (37), 2485 (218), 2680 (18), 2813 (131)
Allen, D. V.: test, 2331, 2382; rev, 2228, 2229, 2660, 2694
Allen, E.: test, 2007
Allen, G.: ref, 199 (16), 337 (94), 2010 (16), 2163 (179), 2516 (47), 2860 (703), 2863 (205), 2879 (87)
Allen, G. D.: ref, 2695 (12)
Allen, G. L.: ref, 615 (10), 644 (5), 1405 (32)
Allen, H.: ref, 451 (77), 1612 (80), 2860 (976)
Allen, H. N.: ref, 272 (162)
Allen, J.: ref, 2214 (54), 2305 (31), 2498 (40)
Allen, J. G.: ref, 337 (126), 846 (3,12), 1687 (38), 1697 (377,468)
Allen, J. L.: ref, 2497 (10)
Allen, J. P.: ref, 694 (65), 1661 (28), 1965 (33), 2603 (354,432,433)
Allen, L.: rev, 1325, 1429
Allen, L. A.: ref, 2305 (163)
Allen, L. M.: test, 2909
Allen, L. M., III: test, 671, 1870
Allen, M. : ref, 815 (27), 1903 (379), 2695 (41), 2862 (364), 2879 (125)
Allen, M. C.: ref, 1612 (16)
Allen, M. E.: ref, 1135 (5), 2599 (7)
Allen, M. H.: ref, 1379 (9), 2288 (54), 2289 (41)
Allen, M. J.: rev, 1686, 2488
Allen, N. B.: ref, 272 (247), 1903 (150), 1953 (1)
Allen, N. J.: ref, 1965 (52)
Allen, N. L.: rev, 391, 648
Allen, P. A.: ref, 2860 (19,325,422,555,556,1218)
Allen, R.: ref, 1697 (437), 2497 (553), 2901 (24)
Allen, S.: ref, 2487 (19)
Allen, S. F.: ref, 1000 (81)
Allen, S. G.: ref, 771 (15)
Allen, S. H.: ref, 2682 (13), 2905 (121)
Allen, S. J.: rev, 286, 1052, 1832
Allen, S. R.: ref, 2860 (791), 2862 (302)
Allen, T. W.: ref, 2497 (22)
Allgood, S. M.: ref, 1000 (12)
Alliger, G. M.: ref, 592 (4), 2797 (1)
Alliger, R.: ref, 1093 (39), 2288 (43), 2289 (33)
Allik, J.: ref, 2218 (111)
Allilaire, J. F.: ref, 2247 (83)
Allinder, R. M.: ref, 2484 (3)
Alling, C.: ref, 273 (28), 999 (181)
Allington, R. L.: rev, 1051, 2905
Allison, E. E.: rev, 2864
Allison, J.: ref, 1000 (33), 1939 (4)
Allison, J. A.: rev, 1010, 1889, 2546, 2593
Allman, C.: ref, 2603 (175)
Allman, T.: test, 1192
Allon, M.: ref, 2010 (13)
Allport, G. W.: test, 2539
Allred, K. D.: ref, 708 (3), 2497 (49)
Allsworth, J., ref, 2305 (239)
Allwood, V. E.: ref, 1755 (70), 2360 (8)
Almagor, M.: ref, 372 (81), 999 (110), 1582 (6), 1697 (384), 2417 (23)
Almeida, D. P.: ref, 1758 (32), 2193 (35)
Almeida, D. P.: ref, 2860 (792)
Almeida, O.: ref, 2050 (79)
Almkvist, O.: ref, 2860 (423), 2863 (111)
Almli, C. R.: ref, 2485 (236)
Almond, P. J.: test, 234
Almquist, F.: ref, 472 (227)
Alnaes, R.: ref, 1687 (24), 2519 (6), 2520 (6)
Alnot, S. D.: test, 1319
Aloia, M.: ref, 1903 (195), 2694 (10), 2695 (18), 2704 (12)
Alonqvist, F.: ref, 472 (231)
Alper, S.: ref, 342 (3), 2862 (294,392), 2901 (48,71)
Alper, T. M.: ref, 2031 (9)
Alper, V. S.: ref, 2603 (353)
Alpern, G.: test, 811
Alpern, L.: ref, 2039 (9), 2039 (10), 2864 (34)
Alperovitch, A.: ref, 2863 (297)
Alpert, A., ref, 272 (319), 1010 (128)
Alpert, C.: ref, 1095 (22), 1653 (11), 2382 (18), 2485 (107)
Alpert, J.: ref, 1166 (106)
Alpert, J. E.: ref, 1166 (41)
Alpert, M.: ref, 335 (10)f, 776 (8,12), 2288 (54,74), 2289 (41), 2860 (201,434,557)
Alpert-Gillis, L. J.: ref, 2498 (4)
Alpherts, W. C.: ref, 1164 (36)
Alphs, L. D.: ref, 2017 (8), 2050 (24), 2305 (83)

Alrus, M.: ref, 1166 (149)
Alster, E. H.: ref, 773 (5), 2860 (1219), 2879 (191), 2901 (108)
Alston, R. J.: ref, 404 (11), 404 (47), 1010 (57), 2117 (2)
Altabe, M.: ref, 893 (30), 1745 (63)
Altchiler, L.: ref, 2497 (295)
Altemus, M.: ref, 2603 (399)
Altepeter, T. S.: ref, 451 (7), 1525 (7), 2863 (39)
Alterman, A. I.: ref, 372 (27), 1661 (77), 1902 (15), 1903 (43), 2247 (21), 2305 (152), 2497 (574), 2603 (169,544,561), 2863 (40)
Althaus, M.: ref, 459 (26,37)
Althof, S. E.: ref, 863 (58), 2497 (421), 2603 (330)
Altieri, P.: ref, 2860 (700)
Altman, D. I.: ref, 2485 (236)
Altshuler, L.: ref, 376 (35), 1164 (187), 2227 (62), 2516 (122), 2860 (1420), 2892 (308)
Altshuler, L. L.: ref, 2305 (120)
Altus, W. D.: rev, 1059, 2010
Alva, S. A.: ref, 472 (109), 665 (42), 1991 (18,43), 2214 (58)
Alvarado, C. G.: test, 309
Alvarado, K. A.: ref, 1745 (15)
Alvarado, N.: ref, 2749 (36)
Alvarez, A.: ref, 2858 (44)
Alvarez, A. A.: ref, 745 (8), 2163 (143)
Alvarez, A. D.: ref, 2860 (734)
Álvarez, E.: ref, 1166 (168)
Alvarez, M.: ref, 430 (15), 451 (148), 672 (1), 681 (78), 694 (2), 815 (40), 1612 (89), 2860 (1164), 2862 (541), 2870 (5), 2879 (179), 2905 (104)
Alvarez, P.: ref, 1166 (209)
Alvir, J.: ref, 2288 (45), 2305 (123)
Alvir, J. M. J.: ref, 1093 (41), 2288 (64), 2305 (70,170)
Alvis, G. R.: ref, 838 (4)
Alway, D.: ref, 776 (32), 2892 (243)
Alzraki, A.: ref, 1093 (40)
Amabile, T.: ref, 1393 (1), 1404 (14), 2917 (4)
Amabile, T. M.: test, 1393; ref, 1755 (33)
Amadéo, S.: ref, 2305 (117)
Amador, J. A.: ref, 1140 (7)
Amador, X.: ref, 1166 (177), 2288 (56,88), 2289 (43,66)
Amador, X. F.: ref, 650 (10), 1093 (58), 2288 (85), 2289 (17,69), 2305 (77)
Amador-Campos, J. A.: ref, 474 (3,4,7), 538 (8), 1201 (6), 1612 (34)
Aman, M. G.: test, 4; ref, 4 (5,12,13,20,22), 459 (15), 681 (55,83), 811 (5), 1021 (41), 1216 (35), 1485 (32), 1612 (57), 1903 (61,295), 1962 (14), 2211 (18,50), 2485 (73,141,221), 2860 (1417), 2862 (547)
Amann, G.: test, 1919
Amato, P. P.: ref, 2484 (6)
Amato, P. R.: ref, 1010 (18)
Amatora, M.: test, 836
Amatora, S. M.: test, 1964
Ambrose, L. M.: ref, 2603 (570)
Ambrose, N. G.: ref, 214 (19), 1001 (12,17), 1485 (56)
Ambrose, P.: ref, 681 (45)f, 1903 (262)
Ambrosini, P. J.: ref, 272 (253), 2305 (214)
Ameli, R.: ref, 1093 (13), 2305 (35)
Amend, D.: ref, 2603 (239)
American Association of Teachers: test, 1761
American College Testing: test, 2920
American College Testing Program: test, 619
American Council on Education: test, 1838
American Guidance Service: test, 1703
American Institute of Certified Public Accountants: test, 17
American Institutes for Research: test, 1638, 2000
American Mathematical Association of Two Year Colleges: test, 144, 148, 149
American Occupational Therapy Association, Inc. (The): test, 152
American Statistical Association: test, 144, 148, 149
Amerikaner, M.: ref, 1000 (34)
Ames, D.: ref, 272 (247)
Ames, E. W.: ref, 787 (1)
Ames, L. B.: test, 1085, 1086
Ames, T.: test, 1529
Amess, J.: ref, 2050 (136), 2305 (157,158)
Amick, A. E.: ref, 793 (5), 2839 (2)
Amico, E.: ref, 1093 (64), 2519 (17), 2520 (18)
Amin, K.: ref, 681 (21), 1164 (51), 1903 (151), 2860 (424,508), 2863 (147)
Amin, Y.: ref, 1166 (191)
Amir, M.: ref, 1405 (8), 2163 (48), 2603 (434)
Amir, N.: ref, 681 (67), 1379 (68), 2050 (132), 2163 (244), 2497 (575), 2862 (346), 2864 (89)
Amireh, R.: ref, 1615 (1)
Amirkhan, J. H.: ref, 2218 (19)
Amisulpride Study Group: ref, 2603 (539)
Amm, C.: ref, 2497 (632)
Ammer, J. J.: test, 1167
Ammerman, R. T.: ref, 448 (20), 1889 (3), 2402 (53), 2603 (435) 2862 (443)
Ammons, C. H.: test, 2146; rev, 2, 625, 641, 1612, 2045, 2614, 2864
Ammons, H. S.: test, 1059
Ammons, R. B.: test, 1059, 2146, 2825; rev, 2, 625, 641, 1612, 2614
Amodeo, M.: ref, 1181 (25)
Amoore, J. E.: ref, 2437 (4)
Amori, B. A.: test, 1234, 1235
Amos, C. I.: ref, 2497 (662)
Amsel, R.: ref, 694 (11), 998 (92), 1927 (8)
Amsell, L.: ref, 4 (1)
Amsterdam, J. D.: ref, 1166 (86)
Amundson, N.: test, 1253
Amundson, N. E.: ref, 272 (153)
an der Heiden, W.: ref, 2050 (33)
Anagnopoulos, C.: ref, 776 (16), 2860 (291)
Anagnostopoulos, F.: ref, 1590 (37), 2858 (81)

Anand, A.: ref, 2305 (148), 2520 (36)
Anand, A. K.: ref, 326 (5), 2288 (21), 2289 (13), 2305 (66), 2892 (52), 2905 (24)
Anasagasti, J. I.: ref, 999 (5)
Anastasi, A.: rev, 58, 477, 560, 561, 798, 1097, 1156, 1196, 1379, 1866, 1965, 2005, 2485, 2758
Anastasio, G. D.: ref, 2497 (511)
Anastasiow, N.: rev, 1422, 2123
Anastopoulos, A. D.: test, 67; ref, 681 (12), 1903 (106), 2485 (45), 2603 (130,131)
Anchor, K. N.: rev, 1567, 2547
Ancy, J.: ref, 1166 (87)
Andelman, F.: ref, 199 (7)
Anderhalter, O.F.: test, 904, 2320
Anderman, E. M.: ref, 665 (58,67), 665 (67), 2862 (282), 2901 (45)
Andersen, B.: ref, 1093 (63)
Andersen, G. J.: ref, 1380 (14)
Andersen, S. M.: ref, 1745 (37,64), 2076 (137)
Anderson, A. J.: ref, 2559 (5)
Anderson, A. M.: ref, 540 (26), 798 (27), 994 (53), 1903 (585), 2667 (1), 2668 (7), 2693 (10), 2694 (27), 2710 (8), 2727 (1), 2731 (8), 2901 (136), 2911 (6)
Anderson, B.: ref, 136 (8), 272 (32), 1093 (99,113), 1697 (249), 2497 (79), 2603 (393)
Anderson, B. J.: ref, 372 (39), 998 (47), 1021 (14), 1697 (185)
Anderson, B. L.: ref, 793 (16)
Anderson, C.: ref, 337 (158), 451 (150)
Anderson, C. A.: ref, 2603 (228)
Anderson, C. J.: ref, 1903 (221)
Anderson, C. L.: ref, 272 (338), 1687 (37)
Anderson, C. V.: ref, 1164 (83), 2860 (793), 2892 (160)
Anderson, D.: ref, 451 (70), 771 (19), 1164 (147), 2214 (79)
Anderson, D. A.: ref, 272 (382), 893 (22), 999 (123)
Anderson, D. E.: test, 2625; ref, 1469 (1)
Anderson, D. H.: ref, 760 (1)
Anderson, D. J.: ref, 998 (56), 2603 (203)
Anderson, D. L.: ref, 681 (72)
Anderson, D. O.: rev, 1034, 1792, 2152, 2156, 2845
Anderson, E. A.: ref, 863 (11), 1216 (102)
Anderson, E. D.: ref, 760 (1)
Anderson, E. R.: ref, 472 (142)
Anderson, G.: ref, 271 (1), 272 (95), 846 (18)
Anderson, G. M.: ref, 2813 (109), 2860 (1001)
Anderson, G. V.: rev, 1222, 2869
Anderson, H. R.: rev, 572, 593
Anderson, I. H.: rev, 1659
Anderson, J.: ref, 1673 (1), 1901 (2), 2599 (29), 2862 (358), 2879 (123)
Anderson, J. C.: ref, 2050 (38,128,129)
Anderson, J. L.: ref, 2417 (37)
Anderson, J. M.: rev, 816, 2862; ref, 451 (169), 880 (1), 1216 (96)
Anderson, J. O.: rev, 385, 389, 470, 1196
Anderson, J. R.: ref, 1338 (34)
Anderson, K. E.: rev, 46, 55
Anderson, K. J.: ref, 998 (10,61), 999 (8)
Anderson, K. W.: ref, 271 (7)
Anderson, L. E.: ref, 1698 (19), 2247 (121), 2862 (697)
Anderson, M.: ref, 350 (33), 1779 (2), 2076 (104)
Anderson, M. Z.: ref, 298 (140)
Anderson, N.: ref, 272 (195), 838 (23), 2497 (568)
Anderson, N. B.: ref, 815 (49), 1164 (173), 1697 (117), 1740 (27), 2497 (15), 2516 (115), 2860 (1374), 2892 (294)
Anderson, N. E.: ref, 375 (5), 2227 (45), 2862 (651), 2863 (395), 2892 (280)
Anderson, N. J.: ref, 2497 (45)
Anderson, P.: ref, 451 (144), 1000 (100), 1079 (73)
Anderson, P. D.: test, 81, 1089
Anderson, P. E.: ref, 1755 (42,57), 2218 (34)
Anderson, P. E. D.: ref, 1697 (113)
Anderson, P. L.: test, 786
Anderson, R.: ref, 358 (12), 560 (3), 790 (14), 2862 (518)
Anderson, R. C.: ref, 1657 (15), 2487 (13), 2879 (116)
Anderson, R. G.: test, 1414
Anderson, R. J.: ref, 68 (21)
Anderson, R. L.: ref, 999 (147,168), 1166 (88,145), 1953 (2)
Anderson, R. P.: rev, 196, 653
Anderson, S. A.: ref, 301 (24), 2247 (28), 2614 (1)
Anderson, S. H.: ref, 2516 (7)
Anderson, S. W.: ref, 2860 (558), 2863 (161)
Anderson, T.: test, 2511
Anderson, T. D.: test, 962, 1355, 1450, 1652, 1952 2279
Anderson, V.: ref, 451 (44), 1079 (29), 1164 (38), 2879 (89), 2892 (56)
Anderson, V. R.: test, 2729
Anderson, W. B.: ref, 472 (23), 1340 (3)
Anderson, W. P.: ref, 694 (94)
Anderson, W. P., Jr.: ref, 83 (5), 1825 (2)
Anderson-Garlach, M.: ref, 1405 (22)
Anderson-Garlach, M. M.: ref, 2163 (212), 2860 (860)
Andersson, B. E.: ref, 2862 (150)
Andersson, L.: ref, 2497 (219)
Andia, A. M.: ref, 1164 (84), 2288 (42), 2289 (32)
Ando, H.: ref, 2288 (23), 2305 (69), 2860 (365), 2288 (23), 2305 (69), 2860 (365)
Andrade, A. R.: ref, 451 (244)
Andrade, J.: ref, 2516 (109), 2892 (287)
Andrade, N.: ref, 2497 (605)
Andrassy, J. M.: ref, 2860 (1315)
Andreasen, N. C.: test, 650, 2288, 2289, 2290; ref, 650 (1,3,4,8,11,13,14,16), 1093 (6,39,58,85), 1164 (35,121), 1485 (43), 1517 (3), 2017 (4), 2125 (22), 2288 (1,10,11,31,43,44,67), 2289 (1,7,8,23,33, 34,51), 2305 (51,52,89), 2516 (78), 2860 (150,349,946,1080)f, 2862 (381), 2863 (316), 2892 (225)
Andrellos, P. J.: test, 1906

Andres, D.: ref, 998 (2,95), 2163 (215)
Andreski, P.: ref, 999 (111,149), 2860 (1045), 2862 (445)
Andress, M. J.: ref, 2862 (5)
Andrew, B.: ref, 272 (241), 999 (46)
Andrew, C. L.: ref, 824 (4), 1093 (62)
Andrew, D. M.: test, 1693
Andrewes, D. G.: ref, 1758 (6), 2163 (33)
Andrews, B.: ref, 2050 (25,107,108,109,142)
Andrews, B. P.: ref, 372 (71)
Andrews, D.: test, 1487; ref, 1612 (96), 2695 (69)
Andrews, D. A.: test, 1486
Andrews, D. W.: ref, 451 (54)
Andrews, F. M.: ref, 2860 (234)
Andrews, G.: ref, 998 (18), 999 (47), 2603 (37)
Andrews, J.: ref, 272 (319), 1010 (128), 1466 (2), 2305 (40)
Andrews, J. A.: ref, 451 (166), 1010 (117), 2402 (14), 2497 (220)
Andrews, J. F.: ref, 340 (1)
Andrews, J. V.: rev, 257, 391, 822, 2611, 2691
Andrews, K.: ref, 1318 (2)
Andrews, L. W.: ref, 342 (1), 2862 (119), 2901 (14)
Andrews, N.: ref, 175 (1), 214 (1), 1040 (1), 1095 (1), 1485 (1), 1804 (1), 1982 (1), 2651 (1)
Andrews, S.: ref, 838 (17)
Andrews, T. J.: ref, 1379 (82,91), 2485 (185), 2860 (1015), 2862 (421,588), 2901 (79,109)
Andrews, V. H.: ref, 1745 (2)
Andrews, W. S.: ref, 2862 (145), 2864 (24)
Andrianopoulos, G. D.: ref, 2603 (201)
Andrykowski, M. A.: ref, 2076 (72,112,149)
Anelli, L. M.: ref, 1000 (49), 2034 (7)
Aneshensel, C. S.: test, 2407
Angelelli, J.: ref, 1000 (101), 1010 (113)
Angelini, C.: ref, 2860 (127)
Angelini, R.: ref, 2227 (52)
Angelis, P. J.: ref, 2717 (1)
Angell, A. G.: test, 2687
Angell, A. L.: ref, 875 (7,8), 1240 (31), 1903 (328)
Angell, K.: ref, 2076 (144)
Angelone, E. O.: ref, 1755 (10)
Angermeyer, M. C.: ref, 301 (57)
Angersbach, D.: ref, 1166 (214)
Angert, L.: ref, 2498 (9), 2603 (186)
Angleitner, A.: ref, 2218 (112)
Angold, A.: ref, 451 (107,108)
Angrilli, A.: ref, 1021 (43)
Angrist, B.: ref, 2860 (419), 2892 (61)
Angrist, G.: ref, 2892 (261)
Ångrist, I.: ref, 2860 (1205)
Angst, J.: ref, 2603 (33,284,285)
Anisman, H.: ref, 272 (213), 1166 (143)
Ankarb, G.: ref, 1790 (8), 2451 (4)
Anker, M.: ref, 2050 (84)
Ankuta, G. Y.: ref, 2603 (173)
Annecke, R.: ref, 1164 (158), 2227 (41)
Annett, M.: ref, 349 (29), 1596 (1), 2163 (34,257,258), 2234 (1), 2860 (1029), 2863 (305), 2873 (51), 2892 (213)
Annis, H. M.: test, 858, 1304, 1305, 2414; ref, 2414 (6), 2603 (555)
Anokhin, A.: ref, 2163 (259)
Anslander, W. F.: ref, 1010 (80)
Ansley, J.: ref, 1697 (289)
Ansley, T. N.: test, 1315, 1319; ref, 1318 (1), 1506 (1)
Ansorge, C. J.: rev, 560, 561
Anstadt, T.: ref, 1001 (2)
Anthenelli, R. M.: ref, 2305 (195)
Anthony, C. R.: ref, 337 (2)
Anthony, J.: test, 1011, 1012
Anthony, K.: ref, 1697 (285)
Anthony, S.: ref, 999 (35,108)
Antia, S. D.: ref, 2813 (55)
Antill, J. K.: ref, 298 (5,18), 372 (3,9), 672 (2,3), 863 (37), 1965 (3,10)
Anton, R. F.: ref, 1166 (44), 1661 (28)
Anton, W. D.: test, 569, 938
Antonak, R. F.: ref, 68 (21,43)
Antonarakis, S. E.: ref, 2050 (94)
Antoni, M. H.: ref, 2076 (177), 2603 (516)
Antonowicz, D.: ref, 694 (109), 1697 (462), 2497 (528), 2559 (11), 2704 (36)
Antonowicz, D. H.: ref, 372 (79)
Antozzi, C.: ref, 1903 (563), 2163 (347), 2227 (54), 2768 (42), 2862 (698)
Antrobus, J. S.: test, 2407
Aoki, T.: ref, 1166 (108), 2076 (150), 2076 (171)
Aoki, Y.: ref, 999 (72)
Aotaki-Phenice, L.: ref, 1370 (1)
Apedo, M. Y.: ref, 2603 (577)
Apfeldorf, W. J.: ref, 2199 (4)
Aplin, D. Y.: ref, 349 (4), 999 (48), 2860 (425)
Apodaca, J. X.: ref, 1697 (578)
Apperson, J. M.: ref, 2856 (7)
Apple, C.: ref, 1697 (546), 2860 (1267), 2863 (381)
Apple, R. F.: ref, 1582 (5)
Appleby, L.: ref, 650 (7), 2288 (17)
Applegate, B.: ref, 1582 (11), 2862 (348)
Appollonio, I. M.: ref, 1758 (21), 2860 (426)
Appollonio, J.: ref, 2860 (173)
Apter, A.: ref, 451 (178), 2163 (95), 2305 (218), 2603 (146), 2860 (875), 2873 (36)
Apter, J. T.: ref, 2305 (163)
Apter, S.: ref, 2305 (45)
Apter, S. H.: ref, 2288 (70), 2289 (55), 2305 (181)
Apthorp, H. S.: ref, 2860 (794), 2879 (98)
Arad, I.: ref, 1612 (88)
Arad, S.: ref, 2218 (103)
Aradom, T.: ref, 1164 (115), 1485 (48), 2163 (255), 2225 (10)
Aram, D.: ref, 994 (36), 1612 (5), 1903 (458), 1982 (13), 2485 (197), 2680 (14), 2813 (114), 2860 (59), 2862 (30), 2864 (4), 2901 (2)

Aram, D. M.: ref, 353 (1), 994 (6,8,11) 1096 (6), 1240 (12,15), 1612 (30), 1804 (7), 1903 (34,102, 152, 178,222), 1982 (5), 2225 (6), 2432 (6), 2485 (46, 74, 87), 2680 (5,6), 2768 (3,8,10,16), 2813 (30), 2860 (559,611), 2862 (151,191,232,248), 2864 (26,35,44,50)
Arató, M.: ref, 1166 (30)
Arbelle, S.: ref, 459 (27), 2228 (9), 2485 (108)
Arbisi, P.: ref, 2305 (31)
Arbisi, P. A.: rev, 1954, 2305, 2372; ref, 1697 (378,528)
Arbit, J.: ref, 301 (9), 1072 (14), 2484 (2), 2862 (96)
Arbona, C.: ref, 462 (2), 2498 (45)
Arbuckle, B.: ref, 472 (32)
Arbuckle, T.: ref, 998 (95), 2163 (215)
Arbuckle, T. Y.: ref, 998 (2,48,62,63,94), 1164 (40,55), 1661 (27), 2227 (14), 2860 (560), 2863 (112,162,256), 2892 (62,96,181)
Arcangelo, K. C.: ref, 2862 (273), 2879 (83)
Arce, R.: ref, 2497 (112)
Arceneaux, J. M.: ref, 2860 (1030)
Archambault, F. X., Jr.: rev, 571, 1734, 2652
Archbald, D.: ref, 1318 (5)
Archer, D.: test, 703, 2078
Archer, J.: ref, 298 (10,11), 2497 (221)
Archer, L.: ref, 1485 (36), 1612 (61), 2228 (15), 2813 (74)
Archer, P.: test, 788
Archer, R. P.: test, 1698; rev, 1697; ref, 1379 (99), 1697 (155,254,425,581), 1698 (9,21,26), 1902 (100), 2247 (20), 2860 (321), 2879 (228), 2901 (131)
Archibald, C. J.: ref, 376 (11), 2860 (1189) 2892 (258)
Arciniega, L. T.: ref, 135 (4), 272 (146)
Ard, W. R., Jr.: ref, 2299 (7)
Ardelean, V.: ref, 2163 (66), 2860 (259)
Ardila, A.: ref, 1164 (133), 2227 (31), 2860 (1162), 2863 (347), 2892 (250)
Arditti, J. A.: rev, 41, 298 (42), 1881 (1)
Ardo, K.: ref, 272 (374), 1745 (88)
Arehole, S.: ref, 301 (45), 798 (15), 1902 (63), 1903 (333), 2862 (303), 2866 (5)
Arena, J.: test, 834, 2908
Arena, J. G.: ref, 1178 (1), 2497 (16)
Arenberg, D.: ref, 2860 (42), 2860 (865)
Arend, R.: ref, 270 (29), 451 (86,181), 1612 (91), 1613 (2)
Arendt, J.: ref, 1166 (165)
Arensberg, K.: ref, 1040 (5)
Argentero, P.: ref, 2417 (5)
Argûelles, T.: ref, 2860 (484), 2863 (135)
Argulewicz, E. N.: rev, 918, 2295
Arias, I.: ref, 863 (61)
Arick, J. R.: test, 234
Arie, T.: ref, 537 (3)
Ariel, R.: ref, 1524 (2), 2862 (433)
Arkin, R. M.: ref, 838 (7,8)
Arkowitz, H.: ref, 2603 (390)
Arlin, M.: test, 177
Arlin, P. K.: test, 178
Armani, M.: ref, 2860 (127)
Armbruster, B. B.: ref, 1759 (7)
Armistead, L.: ref, 272 (379), 337 (172,186,196), 451 (188), 472 (217), 1661 (50), 2211 (12,29,44), 2839 (1)
Armitage, J. M.: ref, 2603 (248)
Armon, C.: ref, 2860 (1031), 2863 (306)
Armstrong, C.: ref, 231 (1), 303 (32), 2226 (9,42), 2227 (61), 2599 (43), 2863 (431), 2892 (307)
Armstrong, D.: ref, 561 (2)
Armstrong, F. D.: ref, 301 (28), 374 (1), 853 (8), 1379 (22), 1524 (1), 2862 (192), 2879 (55)
Armstrong, H. E.: ref, 1093 (48), 2497 (262)
Armstrong, J.: test, 74; ref, 1008 (2)
Armstrong, J. G.: ref, 2247 (6), 2380 (2)f, 2603 (34), 2749 (11), 2860 (151)
Armstrong, J. O.: ref, 1759 (7)
Armstrong, M. S.: ref, 2497 (410)
Armstrong, R. D.: ref, 180 (15)
Armstrong, S.: ref, 134 (28)
Armstrong, T. P.: ref, 1135 (4), 2862 (120)
Armstrong, V. H.: ref, 272 (377), 2497 (676)
Arnason, B. G. W.: ref, 272 (209), 1164 (131), 2125 (24), 2516 (83), 2863 (343)
Arndt, J.: ref, 272 (378)
Arndt, S.: ref, 650 (8,13,14), 1093 (6), 1164 (35), 1166 (137), 1485 (43,62,63), 1517 (3), 1653 (29), 2050 (37), 2288 (43,44), 2289 (33,34), 2860 (150,349,956,1332,1333), 2862 (381,660,661,662)
Arndt, S. V.: ref, 1093 (85)
Arnemann, C.: test, 667
Arnett, F. C.: ref, 2860 (1192)
Arnett, J. A.: ref, 1164 (85)
Arnett, J. L.: ref, 303 (15), 1135 (8,20), 1740 (18), 2076 (167), 2077 (5), 2226 (21), 2516 (22,96), 2599 (12), 2860 (450,1255), 2899 (15)
Arnett, P. A.: ref, 2860 (561,1032), 2892 (97,214)
Arnett, W. B.: ref, 1135 (1)
Arnkoff, D. B.: ref, 337 (14), 1925 (1), 2497 (114,468,469)
Arnold, D.: test, 2198
Arnold, D. H.: ref, 1240 (20), 1903 (223), 2228 (10)
Arnold, D. S.: ref, 875 (7)
Arnold, G. F.: rev, 1485
Arnold, H.: test, 826, 1781
Arnold, K. D.: test, 2444
Arnold, L. E.: ref, 459 (15), 2211 (18), 2485 (73)
Arnold, P. D.: test, 1986
Arnold, S. E.: ref, 2288 (48), 2289 (37)
Arnold-Reid, G.: ref, 342 (3), 2862 (392), 2901 (71)
Arnow, B.: ref, 2603 (329)
Arnow, B. A.: ref, 272 (144), 1010 (91), 2497 (535)
Arny, L.: ref, 1379 (48)
Aro, H. M.: ref, 272 (48,130)
Arocena, M.: ref, 1612 (35)
Aroichane, M.: ref, 2864 (122)
Aron, A.: ref, 1535 (1), 1755 (68)

Aron, E. N.: ref, 1755 (68)
Aronoff, D. N.: ref, 298 (25), 853 (3)
Aronoff, J.: ref, 2603 (455)
Aronow, E.: rev, 122, 467; ref, 2247 (80)
Aronson, E.: ref, 2497 (83,499)
Aronson, M. K.: ref, 1058 (2), 2860 (152)
Aronson, S. C.: ref, 2305 (148)
Aronsson, M.: ref, 1134 (3)
Arranz, B.: ref, 1166 (209)
Arreola, R.: rev, 1865
Arreola, R. A.: rev, 1652
Arreola, R. E.: rev, 1242
Arriaga, R. I.: ref, 324 (10), 331 (6), 1903 (456), 2768 (33)
Arrindell, W. A.: ref, 999 (5,176)
Arroyo, C. G.: ref, 2497 (422)
Arroyo, J. A.: ref, 135 (4), 272 (146)
Arruabarrena, I.: ref, 448 (3)
Arruabarrena, M. I.: ref, 448 (13)
Arruabarrena, M. J.: ref, 448 (4)
Arsenauelt, L.: ref, 1169 (6)
Arsenault, L.: ref, 1697 (455), 2247 (95)
Artese, V. S.: test, 2898
Arthier, K.: ref, 2559 (3)
Arthur, B. M.: ref, 1638 (3)
Arthur, C. R.: ref, 265 (8)
Arthur, G.: test, 182
Arthur, N.: ref, 271 (8,17), 272 (248,339)
Arthur, T. A. A.: ref, 1781 (1)
Arthur, W.: ref, 2163 (138)
Arthur, W., Jr.: test, 231; ref, 2163 (56), 2218 (42), 2871 (1)
Artzer, M.: ref, 1903 (555), 2879 (219), 2880 (7), 2901 (128)
Aruffo, J. F.: ref, 472 (49), 2214 (30)
Arvanitis, L. A.: ref, 2288 (82)
Arvey, R.: test, 1970
Arvey, R. D.: ref, 1701 (4)
Ary, C. M.: ref, 2860 (210), 2863 (53)
Aryee, S.: ref, 863 (22)
Asamen, J.: ref, 1903 (224), 2125 (10), 2862 (234), 2892 (98)
Asannow, J. R.: ref, 1962 (12)
Asare-Aboagye, Y.: ref, 2227 (22)
Asari, Y.: ref, 2860 (1278)
Asarnow, J. R.: ref, 451 (196), 1010 (3), 2862 (31,233)
Asarnow, R. F.: ref, 811 (3), 1379 (10), 1903 (224,573), 2125 (10), 2288 (32), 2289 (24), 2305 (91), 2813 (8), 2860 (534,1398), 2862 (234,721), 2892 (98)
Asberg, M.: ref, 2860 (154), 2892 (19)
Asbjornsen, A.: ref, 2860 (898), 2862 (354)
Asbjornsen, A. E.: ref, 2862 (699)
Asbury, C. A.: ref, 692 (1), 2599 (1), 2862 (11)
Asbury, R.: ref, 2497 (190)
Asche, F. M.: rev, 390, 1350
Ascione, F. R.: ref, 298 (79), 1000 (56)
Asendorpf, J. B.: ref, 365 (1), 373 (18), 624 (14), 1987 (9), 2864 (45)
Ash, P.: rev, 201, 236, 859, 893, 2526
Ash, R. A.: rev, 2016
Ashby, J. S.: ref, 1697 (300), 2603 (261)
Ashby, R. P.: ref, 1072 (2), 1240 (1) 2862 (3)
Ashcraft, E. W.: ref, 815 (13), 1135 (11), 2862 (229), 2903 (1)
Ashcroft, F.: ref, 1141 (5)
Asher, E. J., Jr.: rev, 410, 2525
Asher, J. W.: ref, 1991 (28), 2252 (2)
Asherson, P.: ref, 2050 (32,54)
Asheychik, R.: ref, 1697 (21)
Ashford, S. J.: ref, 2757 (1)
Ashford, T. A.: rev, 94
Ashforth, B. E.: ref, 1590 (24)
Ashley, E.: ref, 1592 (17)
Ashley, M. J.: ref, 326 (8), 1164 (125), 1525 (24), 2860 (1121), 2892 (233)
Ashley, N. D.: ref, 2076 (141)
Ashman, A.: ref, 2743 (3)
Ashman, A. F.: ref, 26 (2), 2862 (148)
Ashmore, L.: rev, 784, 1361
Ashmore, R. J.: ref, 2432 (23)
Ashria, I. H.: ref, 142 (7,8), 682 (4,5)
Ashtari, M.: ref, 1093 (41), 2305 (70)
Ashton, M. C.: ref, 372 (116), 672 (6), 1965 (85), 2417 (43)
Ashton, R.: ref, 1241 (3)
Ashton, T.: ref, 1697 (21)
Ashton, W. A.: ref, 298 (74)
Ashurst, D. I.: test, 2459
Ashworth, D. L.: ref, 1758 (59)
Asmundson, G.: ref, 950 (6)
Asmundson, G. J. G.: ref, 272 (91), 1166 (66), 2199 (5), 2497 (296,297,397), 2603 (128,157)
Asnis, G. M.: ref, 1166 (1,102), 1687 (20), 2305 (12), 2603 (105,331,451,510)
Aspell, D. D.: test, 958
Aspell, P. J.: test, 958
Aspinwall, L. G.: ref, 1697 (110)
Assaad, J-M.: ref, 2860 (1393)
Assenheimer, J. S.: ref, 2076 (132), 2603 (425)
Assessment Systems Corporation: test, 1692
Assh, S. D.: ref, 2076 (138)
Associated Examining Board (The): test, 260
Associates for Research in Behavior, Inc.: test, 2834
Assor, A.: ref, 372 (43), 908 (7)
Assouline, S. G.: ref, 615 (12), 1997 (1)
Asthana, H. S.: ref, 272 (340)
Astin, A. W.: test, 692; rev, 617, 1790
Astington, J. W.: ref, 2485 (204), 2680 (16)
Astner, K.: test, 2909
Åström, J.: ref, 1697 (201)
Asukai, N.: ref, 2860 (1363)
Atchinson, M.: ref, 2603 (532)
Athanason, J. A.: ref, 2871 (3)
Atkeson, B.: ref, 1745 (83)
Atkins, C. P.: rev, 1898

Atkinson, A.: ref, 272 (348), 2497 (666)
Atkinson, C.: ref, 2076 (57)
Atkinson, J. H.: ref, 272 (334), 376 (30), 776 (26), 1164 (77), 2858 (105), 2863 (293)
Atkinson, J. H., Jr., ref, 2076 (133)
Atkinson, L.: ref, 1086 (3), 2076 (105), 2813 (79), 2860 (326,327,952), 2863 (86)
Atkinson, M.: ref, 2858 (47)
Atkinson, R. M.: ref, 1697 (202)
Atlas, G.: ref, 1965 (47)
Atlas, J. A.: rev, 1231, 1253, 2358; ref, 846 (4), 1903 (225)
Attanasio, C. S.: ref, 1673 (8)
Attkisson, C.: ref, 2288 (15), 2289 (10), 2305 (62)
Attkisson, C. C.: ref, 1093 (53), 2076 (68), 2108 (3), 2305 (84), 2603 (210)
Atwater, L. E.: ref, 1736 (2), 1755 (22), 2417 (17)
Atwater, S. W.: ref, 353 (4), 1673 (5), 1901 (9)
Au, K. H.: rev, 683, 1758
Aube, J.: ref, 863 (59,60), 2246 (9)
Aubrey, A.: ref, 301 (1), 748 (1), 2305 (5), 2860 (39), 2862 (21)
AuBuchon, P. G.: ref, 998 (49), 1698 (6), 2497 (222)
Auchus, M.: ref, 2901 (24)
Auckland College of Education: test, 1605
Audet, J.: ref, 272 (326)
Audini, B.: ref, 1093 (59,70), 2050 (55,87)
Audiologic Services and Southwest School for the Hearing Impaired, Office of the Los Angeles County Superintendent of Schools: test, 2672
Auerbach, J.: ref, 451 (17,76), 1216 (19), 1903 (103), 2862 (395)
Auerbach, J. G.: ref, 301 (1,22), 451 (87), 748 (1,8), 1592 (11), 2010 (7), 2163 (87), 2305 (5,64), 2860 (39), 2862 (21)
Auerbach, S. M.: ref, 1243 (2), 1290 (2), 2120 (4), 2497 (298), 2603 (229)
August, G. J.: ref, 280 (2,3,4), 451 (18,184), 472 (154), 681 (57,71,72,84), 1010 (68), 1380 (3,9,10), 1991 (76), 2214 (88), 2452 (4), 2879 (99,152), 2901 (49,82)
Augustine, L. E.: ref, 301 (45)f, 798 (15), 1902 (63), 1903 (333), 2862 (303), 2866 (5)
Augustyn, G. T.: ref, 2288 (4), 2289 (2), 2305 (7), 2860 (63)
Aukes, D.: ref, 337 (64,109), 1697 (444), 2497 (273), 2603 (204)
Aukett, A.: test, 2308
Aukrust, A.: ref, 1164 (47), 1407 (2), 2860 (463), 2863 (130)
Auld, P. A. M.: ref, 816 (1), 2229 (15), 2485 (213), 2862 (540), 2879 (178)
Aulls, M. W.: rev, 358
Ault, M.: ref, 1770 (9)
Aumack, F. L.: test, 711
Aumiller, K.: ref, 681 (23)
Aureille, E.: ref, 2860 (340)
Auriacombe, S.: ref, 2863 (297)
Aurisano, N.: ref, 1903 (563), 2163 (347), 2227 (54), 2768 (42), 2862 (698)
Aust, C. F.: ref, 694 (111)
Austin, D. M.: ref, 56 (19)
Austin, E. J.: ref, 838 (18)
Austin, J. K.: ref, 1991 (44)
Austin, J. S.: ref, 1631 (1), 2315 (1), 2538 (1)
Austin, J. T.: rev, 152, 694, 1544, 1620, 1721, 1952; ref, 1697 (255)
Austin, M. C.: rev, 816
Austin, M. P.: ref, 2860 (328)
Austin, M-P.: ref, 272 (306)
Austin, W.: ref, 1653 (12)
Australian Council for Educational Research: test, 22, 30, 32, 955
Australian Council for Educational Research Ltd.: test, 20, 23, 28, 29 31, 2092
Autret, A.: ref, 2862 (329)
Auvenshine, A. A.: test, 1490
Avants, S. K.: ref, 1775 (3), 2860 (1220)
Avanzini, G.: ref, 2163 (270), 2892 (227)
Avelar, C.: ref, 2879 (113)
Avelrod, B. N.: ref, 2163 (65), 2860 (258), 2863 (65), 2892 (34)
Averbuch, S.: test, 1513
Averill, P. M.: ref, 1697 (501), 2497 (303,597), 2603 (235)
Avery, D. H.: ref, 1166 (13)
Avery, R. R.: ref, 1657 (3)
Avery-Smith, W.: test, 870
Avia, M. D.: ref, 2218 (118), 2656 (14)
Avila, C.: ref, 999 (109)
Avila, R.: ref, 451 (105), 472 (161)
Avins, A. L.: ref, 134 (35)
Avissar, S.: ref, 272 (249), 1166 (169)
Avolio, B. J.: test, 1736, 1737; ref, 2797 (2)
Avoni, P.: ref, 2768 (34), 2860 (1082)
Avraam, X.: ref, 272 (363)
Awad, A.: ref, 1903 (270), 2905 (56)
Awad, G. A.: ref, 2247 (19), 2749 (23)
Awadh, A. M.: ref, 1226 (3), 2862 (569,614)
Awaida, M.: ref, 349 (21), 350 (23)
Axelrod, B. N.: ref, 376 (26), 1135 (23), 1697 (572), 2193 (49), 2226 (36), 2603 (554), 2860 (1017,1033,1195,1336,1349), 2863 (302,307,400), 2892 (215,247,290)
Axford, S. N.: rev, 479, 759, 787, 1212
Axworthy, D.: ref, 2497 (642)
Aycock, D. W.: test, 698
Aydelott, S. T.: ref, 665 (18), 1072 (13)
Ayer, G. W.: rev, 112, 113
Ayers, D.: rev, 34
Ayers, J. D.: rev, 674, 1501, 2281, 2467
Ayers, T. S.: ref, 472 (6,145)
Ayllon, T.: ref, 1021 (24)
Aylor, S.: ref, 349 (16)

Aylward, E. H.: ref, 815 (19,49), 1164 (173), 1740 (27), 2289 (22), 2516 (62,115), 2860 (809,1374), 2892 (165,294)
Aylward, G. P.: test, 269; rev, 461, 662, 837, 1460
Aylward, M.: ref, 342 (3), 2862 (392), 2901 (71)
Ayoub, C.: ref, 2519 (38), 2520 (39)
Ayres, A. J.: test, 2377
Ayres, D.: test, 1504
Azari, N. P.: ref, 1240 (21)
Azcue, M. P.: ref, 272 (258), 893 (42), 1405 (39), 1903 (517), 2862 (595)
Azim, H. F. A.: ref, 2497 (134), 2603 (117,118,291)
Azouvi, P.: ref, 1164 (118), 2516 (77)
Azzoni, A.: ref, 1166 (185)

Baack, K. L.: rev, 2471
Baak, K.: ref, 1965 (26)
Baarda, B.: ref, 1697 (198)
Baba, V. V.: ref, 2531 (1)
Babasa, B.: ref, 1701 (43)
Babcock, R. L.: ref, 1405 (21), 2163 (139,194), 2860 (562)
Baberger-Gateau, P.: ref, 2863 (90)
Babich, A.: test, 1476
Babins, L.: ref, 2163 (310)
Babins, L.: ref, 2863 (363)
Babor, T.: ref, 2050 (10)
Babor, T. F.: test, 135; ref, 135 (1,2), 372 (83), 1661 (38), 1697 (157,183,389), 2497 (357), 2603 (149)
Baca, L.: ref, 472 (38)
Bacellar, H.: ref, 1135 (16), 2227 (21), 2599 (32)
Bachar, E.: ref, 337 (50,165,166,188), 2497 (223)
Bacharach, V. R.: ref, 1216 (110), 1903 (564), 2485 (239)
Bachelor, P. A.: rev, 443, 555, 650, 746, 1792, 1803
Bachiochi, P. D.: test, 1348
Bachman, D. L.: ref, 2860 (329), 2863 (87,113)
Bachman, L.: ref, 1058 (7), 2227 (12), 2860 (499,1351), 2863 (143)
Bachman, L. F.: rev, 2189; ref, 550 (2), 666 (8)
Bachoud-Levi: ref, 2860 (1375)
Bachoud-Lévi, A-C.: ref, 2860 (1249), 2863 (377)
Back, C. L.: ref, 1164 (181), 1740 (33), 2227 (59), 2860 (1408), 2863 (427)
Backenstaß, M.: ref, 1166 (202)
Backlund, P.: rev, 880
Backlund, P.: rev, 2093
Bäckman, L.: ref, 1525 (18), 2860 (423,563,888,1277), 2863 (111)
Bacon, E. H.: rev, 65, 1738
Bacon, G. M.: ref, 2008 (5)
Bacon, T. R.: test, 554, 1814, 2271, 2580
Baddeley, A.: ref, 1104 (1), 2163 (336), 2239 (6,17), 2863 (399), 2892 (99,284)
Baddeley, A. D.: ref, 349 (1,2), 350 (2,4,28,51), 776 (29), 837 (14), 1104 (12), 1758 (55,69), 2163 (47,64,105), 2227 (23), 2239 (3,7,27), 2860 (1013), 2862 (720), 2863 (301,321)
Baddeley, B. T.: ref, 2516 (109), 2892 (287)
Baddely, A: test, 2239
Baden, A. D.: ref, 997 (9)
Badenoch, L. D.: ref, 2863 (206)
Bader, B. D.: rev, 2142, 2323
Bader, L. A.: test, 237
Badian, N. A.: ref, 2484 (15), 2862 (434), 2864 (108,142), ref, 2905 (95)
Baeharach, V. R.: ref, 451 (92), 2485 (189), 2864 (109)
Baehr, G. O.: test, 927
Baehr, M. E.: test, 927, 1569, 2051, 2420, 2648, 352 (1), 548 (1); ref, 728 (1), 927 (1), 2648 (1), 2907 (1)
Baer, J. S.: ref, 337 (61), 652 (2)
Baer, L.: ref, 271 (5,16), 272 (223,335), 1697 (51), 2227 (26), 2402 (70), 2860 (1103)
Baer, P. E.: ref, 791 (3,10), 2117 (3)
Baer, R. A.: ref, 1697 (379,380,386), 1698 (20), 2879 (223)
Bagby, R. M.: test, 2522; ref, 790 (11,17), 1166 (89,90,170,171), 1697 (381,529), 2218 (43,44, 81,82), 2305 (164,213), 2603 (514)
Bagenholm, A.: ref, 234 (1)
Bagg, A.: ref, 1770 (4)
Baggaley, A. R.: rev, 865
Baghurst, P.: ref, 451 (281), ref, 1079 (110)
Bagley, C.: ref, 694 (42), 1832 (5), 2559 (1)
Bagley, C. A.: ref, 2065 (9)
Bagley, C. R.: ref, 694 (21)
Baglio, C. S.: ref, 4 (21)
Baglioni, A. J.: ref, 2497 (354)
Baglioni, A. J., Jr.: ref, 739 (3), 1338 (14), 2858 (14)
Bagnato, S. J.: rev, 2213; ref, 1612 (45), 2485 (109), 2864 (46)
Bagozzi, R. P.: ref, 1701 (16)
Bagwell, C. L.: ref, 337 (189)
Bagwell, W. W.: ref, 1166 (210)
Bahr, M. W.: ref, 2211 (3,4)
Bahri, T.: ref, 2516 (90)
Baider, L., : ref, 337 (167)
Baile, W. F.: ref, 2497 (662)
Bailey, A.: ref, 350 (13,24,36), 901 (1), 1653 (13,21,26), 2163 (145,195,260), 2228 (11,16,21), 2288 (72), 2289 (57), 2860 (427,571,795,1034)
Bailey, B.: ref, 377 (1), 2813 (11)
Bailey, C., ref, 2860 (1422), 2892 (309)
Bailey, D.: ref, 1525 (14), 2860 (476), 2862 (208), 2879 (58)
Bailey, D. B.: ref, 265 (6,11), 2382 (26)
Bailey, D. B., Jr.: ref, 265 (15)
Bailey, D. M.: ref, 353 (5)
Bailey, J.: ref, 1485 (43,63), 2860 (956,1332), 2862 (381,542,660,662), 2879 (180), 2901 (99)
Bailey, J. D.: ref, 2193 (11), 2860 (342)
Bailey, J. S.: ref, 2860 (701)
Bailey, P.: ref, 1166 (105)
Bailey, S.: ref, 2050 (91)
Bailey, S. M.: ref, 893 (23)

Bailey-Richardson, B.: rev, 78, 2343
Bain, A.: ref, 681 (41), 1765 (15)
Bain, B. A.: ref, 1612 (21), 1903 (62), 1903 (86), 2382 (4)
Bain, J. D.: ref, 1164 (78), 1240 (40), 1407 (4), 2092 (4), 2516 (53), 2599 (21), 2860 (754)
Bain, K. P.: ref, 1697 (5)
Bain, M. W.: ref, 557 (3), 2214 (7)
Bain, S. K.: rev, 2059
Baines, K. A.: test, 211
Bains, D. S.: ref, 1697 (228), 2402 (44)
Baird, L. L.: rev, 2771
Bakay, R. A. E.: ref, 2860 (1096), 2892 (228)
Bakeman, R.: ref, 1903 (306), 2485 (148)
Baker, A. G.: ref, 681 (63)
Baker, A. M.: ref, 694 (14)
Baker, B.: ref, 364 (7)
Baker, B. L.: ref, 451 (127), 451 (251), 1010 (133), 1379, 1991 (106), 2229 (10), 2862 (488)
Baker, C.: ref, 2252 (3), 2485 (62), 2606 (5)
Baker, D. A.: ref, 2497 (551)
Baker, D. B.: ref, 1099 (2), 2603 (332)
Baker, D. E.: ref, 462 (16), 2417 (22)
Baker, D. R.: ref, 1755 (13)
Baker, D. W.: ref, 2879 (130)
Baker, F.: ref, 2076 (159)
Baker, G.: ref, 2050 (74)
Baker, G. A.: ref, 1758 (92), 2860 (1312,1383), 2862 (707), 2863 (114,396,415)
Baker, H.: ref, 1697 (21)
Baker, H. F.: ref, 2239 (12)
Baker, J. A.: ref, 2230 (8), 2557 (3)
Baker, J. D.: ref, 893 (17), 2402 (36)
Baker, J. E.: ref, 2497 (235), 2860 (438)
Baker, J. M.: test, 1887; ref, 1386 (12), 2862 (304,305,306), 2901 (50,51), 2905 (69)
Baker, J. W., II: test, 1494
Baker, K. A.: ref, 2603 (571)
Baker, L. A.: ref, 301 (46)
Baker, M.: ref, 1745 (65)
Baker, N.: ref, 2305 (4)
Baker, R.: test, 2195
Baker, R. L.: ref, 2497 (576,577)
Baker, R. W.: test, 2525
Baker, S.: ref, 2864 (18)
Baker, S. B.: ref, 2497 (356)
Baker, S. R.: ref, 1040 (7), 1474 (1), 2771 (9)
Baker, T.: ref, 1040 (6), 2603 (86)
Baker, T. C.: ref, 1040 (7)
Baker, T. G.: ref, 2076 (134)
Baker, W. J.: ref, 2863 (185)
Baker-Pierce, L. A.: ref, 272 (147), 2603 (436), 2839 (7)
Baker-Ward, L.: ref, 1612 (31)
Bakermans-Kranenburg, M. J.: ref, 2163 (153)
Bakheit, M.: ref, 2497 (283)
Bakken, J. P.: ref, 246 (6), 1386 (24), 1902 (94), 2861 (1), 2862 (589), 2879 (192), 2901 (110)
Bakken, L.: ref, 1631 (3)
Bakker, V. J.: ref, 2860 (980)
Balach, L.: ref, 2603 (175)
Baldessarini, R. J.: ref, 2050 (77)
Baldeweg, T.: ref, 2050 (64,93), 2076 (97), 2239 (18), 2497 (384), 2860 (581), 2863 (168), 2892 (106)
Baldwin, A.: ref, 2146 (13), 2402 (22), 2864 (43)
Baldwin, A. L.: test, 1026; ref, 2146 (12), 2402 (15), 2603 (174)
Baldwin, C.: ref, 2146 (13), 2402 (22), 2864 (43)
Baldwin, C. D.: ref, 270 (26), 1903 (184), 2382 (35), 2402 (20), 2485 (90), 2813 (130)
Baldwin, C. P.: ref, 2146 (12), 2402 (15), 2603 (174)
Baldwin, D. A.: ref, 2228 (23)
Baldwin, J.: rev, 780
Baldwin, K.: ref, 246 (4), 799 (1), 815 (4), 1379 (11), 1379 (24), 1902 (22), 1903 (158), 2862 (122), 2879 (32)
Baldwin, L.: test, 2314
Baldwin, L. E.: ref, 2497 (303,597), 2603 (235)
Baldwin, M.: ref, 448 (8)
Baldwin, R. S.: ref, 615 (1), 666 (5), 2487 (3)
Baldwin, T. S.: rev, 318, 1792
Baldwin, T. T.: ref, 1107 (9), 1701 (12)
Baldy-Moulinier, M.: ref, 2305 (117)
Bales, D. W.: ref, 1903 (551)
Balgopal, R.: ref, 2862 (495)
Balinski, B.: rev, 2485
Balinsky, B.: test, 2348; rev, 1050, 2825
Balise, R. R.: ref, 769 (8), 2862 (729), 2879 (233)
Balistreri, E.: ref, 298 (12), 926 (3), 1140 (5)
Balistreri, T. M.: ref, 2289 (54)
Balke, G.: ref, 838 (13)
Ball, E. W.: ref, 1240 (13), 1503 (5), 1903 (63), 2253 (1), 2674 (4), 2905 (11)
Ball Foundation: test, 239
Ball, G.: ref, 1093 (36), 2497 (141), 2603 (119)
Ball, J. D.: ref, 1099 (4), 1697 (156), 1962 (22), 2862 (590), 2879 (193)
Ball, K. K.: test, 2794
Ball, N.: ref, 999 (121)
Ball, R. S.: test, 996; rev, 433
Ball, S.: ref, 272 (176,250), 372 (117), 846 (20,26), 2218 (135), 2433 (4), 2497 (608)
Balla, D. A.: test, 2813, 2814
Ballantyne, A. O.: ref, 815 (41), 1962 (21), 2485 (215)
Ballard, C. G.: ref, 1093 (60)
Ballard, E.: ref, 1380 (11), 2193 (50), 2603 (437)
Ballard, J. C.: ref, 2497 (536)
Ballard, K. J.: ref, 2873 (72)
Ballard, M. E.: ref, 272 (102), 462 (17)
Ballard, W. S.: test, 1234
Ballard-Reisch, D.: ref, 298 (57)
Ballenger, J.: ref, 1698 (20), 2879 (223)
Ballenger, J. C.: ref, 1166 (17,68), 2218 (96), 2603 (24,277,328)
Ballinger, B. B.: ref, 2858 (128)

Balogh, D. W.: ref, 1697 (93)
Balogun, J. A.: ref, 1590 (56)
Balon, R.: ref, 2863 (280)
Balota, D. A.: ref, 1164 (179), 2860 (1397), 2863 (422)
Balson, P. M.: ref, 2603 (160)
Baltaxe, C. A. M.: ref, 1903 (104)
Baltazar, P. L.: ref, 2603 (112)
Baltes, M. M.: ref, 2863 (229)
Baltes, P. B.: ref, 745 (1,3), 1405 (1), 2163 (7,19), 2163 (63), 2218 (74), 2860 (757), 2860 (1179)
Balthazar, M.: ref, 2905 (7)
Baltimore County Public Schools Office of Adult Education: test, 1588
Baltimore, D.: ref, 272 (227)
Baluch, B.: ref, 2497 (402)
Baluda, M. R.: ref, 272 (181), 376 (5), 1166 (113), 2863 (324)
Balzer, W. K.: test, 1348, 2509
Bam, S. K.: ref, 853 (23), 1903 (514), 2452 (17), 2483 (1)
Bambara, L. M.: ref, 1485 (37), 2382 (27), 2485 (153), 2862 (678), 2879 (218), 2901 (127)
Bamberg, E.: test, 2459
Bamburg, J. W.: ref, 4 (21), 2813 (148), 2860 (66), 2863 (21)
Bamford, K. A.: ref, 1903 (334), 2517 (2), 2860 (796)
Bamford, K. W.: ref, 1903 (64), 2163 (57)
Bamler, K.: ref, 271 (14), 2497 (656)
Banbury, M. M.: ref, 2295 (1)
Bancroft, J.: ref, 272 (83,96)
Bandalos, D. L.: rev, 204, 950; ref, 2656 (18)
Banden, H.: ref, 1135 (17), 1164 (119), 2862 (435), 2879 (153)
Bandera, L.: ref, 2163 (58)
Bandoh, M.: ref, 2860 (396), 2873 (10)
Bandura, A.: ref, 451 (88), 472 (155)
Bane, K. D.: rev, 771
Banerjee, S.: ref, 1390 (3)
Banerji, M.: ref, 1386 (13), 2862 (307)
Bangs, T. E.: test, 315
Banich, M. T.: ref, 2485 (20), 2860 (153), 2862 (94), 2864 (16)
Banjo, M. L.: ref, 2497 (455)
Bank, A. J.: ref, 1697 (567), 1740 (25)2226 (33), 2860 (1339)
Bank, L.: ref, 2860 (428)
Banks, C.: rev, 729, 2163, 2477, 2478
Banks, C. E. K.: rev, 1989
Banks, R.: ref, 2496 (3)
Banks, R. E.: ref, 2305 (13)
Banks, S. R.: ref, 1947 (8)
Bankson, N. W.: test, 240, 241, 2144; rev, 1047 ,2504, 2657
Bannatyne, A.: rev, 1096, 1362, 1392, 1902, 2189, 2335, 2905
Bannatyne, M.: rev, 1804
Bannister, D.: test, 1133
Bansal, S.: ref, 793 (7,15)
Banta, J.: ref, 1697 (10)
Banyard, V.: ref, 272 (86), 451 (124), 1697 (337), 2860 (710)
Banyard, V. L.: ref, 272 (251)
Bar, O.: ref, 1697 (87), 2652 (4)
Bar-Hamburger, R.: ref, 270 (23) 1612 (87)
Bar-Hillel, M.: ref, 56 (4), 592 (31), 1115 (8)
Bar-On, R.: test, 243
Baradaran, L. P.: ref, 472 (32)
Barak, Y.: ref, 681 (96), 2305 (247)
Barakat, L. P.: ref, 337 (35), 1000 (103), 1903 (105), 1987 (4), 2214 (115,117), 2497 (609,639), 2813 (15)
Baran, S. A.: ref, 2497 (423)
Baranek, G. T.: ref, 2813 (56,136)
Barasch, M.: ref, 451 (17), 1216 (19), 1903 (103)
Baratta, V. S.: ref, 2862 (722)
Barba, B. D. ref, 1770 (14)
Barba, G. D.: ref, 2768 (11), 2860 (429,797,1375), 2863 (115,230), 2892 (63)
Barba, R. H.: ref, 1866 (19)
Barbaranelli, C.: ref, 451 (88), 472 (155)
Barbarotto, R.: ref, 2163 (120), 2163 (261), 2225 (11)
Barbc, W. B.: test, 2597
Barbee, A. D.: ref, 998 (66)
Barber, B. K.: ref, 272 (138), 451 (75,89), 472 (156)
Barber Center Press, Inc.: test, 2400
Barber, G. A.: test, 686, 805
Barber, J. P.: ref, 272 (148)
Barber, M. A.: ref, 1903 (441)
Barbieri-Berger, S.: ref, 2860 (602)
Barbini, B.: ref, 2497 (505)
Barceló, F.: ref, 2892 (263)
Barch, D.: ref, 1903 (442), 2860 (564)
Barchas, J. D.: ref, 2288 (3)
Barcher, P. R.: test, 2824
Barclay, A. G.: rev, 817
Barclay, D. R.: ref, 451 (230), 2497 (659), 2603 (367)
Barclay, J. R.: test, 1868, 2526; rev, 909, 1867
Barclay, L. K.: test, 1868
Bardis, P. D.: test, 6, 327, 568, 765, 970, 1004, 1016, 1129, 1271, 1327, 1646, 1893, 1992, 2200, 2390, 2748, 2806, 2815, 2931
Bardos, A.: ref, 854 (2), 1379 (71), 1380 (8), 2864 (96)
Bardos, A. N.: test, 852, 1075; ref, 763 (1)
Barefoot, J. C.: ref, 272 (336), 1697 (117), 1697 (319), 2218 (116), 2497 (664)
Barenbaum, E.: test, 2676
Barenbaum, E. M.: test, 789
Barends, A.: ref, 2749 (28), 2860 (369)
Baribeau, j.: ref, 1745 (76), 2497 (591), 2863 (348)
Barik, H. C.: test, 1054
Baril, G. L.: ref, 2149 (2)
Baris, J. M.: ref, 1903 (397)
Barkan, J. H.: ref, 2163 (59)
Barker, C.: ref, 2603 (424)
Barker, J.: test, 785
Barker, L. L.: test, 1505, 1508, 2854, 2855

Barker, S. E.: ref, 893 (19)
Barker, T. A.: ref, 2163 (81), 2485 (47), 2905 (19)
Barker, W. W.: ref, 1058 (4), 2860 (451,484), 2863 (125,135)
Barkham, M.: ref, 272 (37,115,116,217,311,357), 2050 (56), 2497 (89), 2603 (63,226,230,259,301, 359,360,403,582)
Barki-Harrington, L.: ref, 272 (249), 1166 (169)
Barkley, C.: ref, 1517 (10)
Barkley, R. A.: ref, 451 (143,283), 681 (4,27,98), 1740 (5), 1889 (7), 1903 (65,106), 2402 (59), 2603 (131,482, 590), 2606 (4), 2860 (1142), 2892 (242), 2901 (135)
Barling, J.: ref, 1590 (12), 1736 (3), 2211 (10)
Barlow, D. H.: ref, 472 (219,220), 998 (40), 1021 (42), 1218 (2), 1697 (91), 2199 (9,10,13), 2214 (94,128,132), 2497 (17,26,60,74,109,153,449), 2498 (48,59,60)
Barlow, J.: test, 640
Barlow, S. H.: ref, 1697 (473), 2603 (443)
Barnard, E. L.: test, 1806, 2173
Barnard, K.: ref, 1010 (30), 1902 (29), 2862 (155)
Barnas, M. V.: ref, 694 (22), 2603 (79)
Barnes, C.: ref, 790 (29)
Barnes, G. E.: ref, 999 (24,184), 1140 (57), 1661 (31), 1697 (334,562), 2497 (649)
Barnes, G. M.: ref, 1000 (45)
Barnes, H.: test, 1877
Barnes, J.: test, 1465; ref, 998 (111)
Barnes, K.: ref, 1902 (48)
Barnes, L. L. B.: rev, 762, 1323, 1816, 1889, 2059, 2154
Barnes, M. A.: ref, 2693 (3), 2862 (152,199,708), 2905 (20)
Barnes, R.: ref, 2863 (83)
Barnes, T. D.: ref, 1991 (77)
Barnett, A.: ref, 1097 (5), 2862 (153)
Barnett, B.: ref, 2497 (99)
Barnett, D.: ref, 272 (253), 365 (5), 451 (90), 1903 (443), 1987 (17), 2305 (214)
Barnett, D. W.: rev, 124, 266, 809, 1090, 1485 (19), 1653 (9), 1903 (190), 2485 (95), 2813 (40), 2860 (487,679,680), 2862 (643,644), 2864 (59), 2864 (60)
Barnett, J.: ref, 2243 (1)
Barnett, J. E.: ref, 1318 (16)
Barnett, K. P.: ref, 2862 (436), 2901 (83)
Barnett, L. B.: ref, 615 (41)
Barnett, M. C.: ref, 1697 (256,258)
Barnett, R.: ref, 771 (22)
Barnett, R. C.: ref, 2497 (424), 2603 (80,132,133,231,232,333)
Barnett, R. M.: rev, 1090
Barnett, R. W.: ref, 1687 (13), 1697 (26,97), 1731 (1,2), 2417 (10), 2860 (226), 2879 (30)
Barnett, W. P.: ref, 1348 (1)
Barnett, W. S.: ref, 2299 (5)
Barnhart, J. E.: ref, 324 (1)
Barnhill, J.: ref, 1697 (184), 2305 (71)
Barnholtz, A.: ref, 298 (60)
Barnoski, E. J.: ref, 776 (59)
Barnum, R.: ref, 2519 (38), 2520 (39)
Barocas, R.: ref, 1178 (16), 1321 (1), 2864 (3)
Baron, H.: ref, 1822 (4,5), 2581 (2)
Baron, J.-C.: ref, 2516 (64), 2863 (248)
Baron, L. A.: ref, 451 (61)
Baron, P.: ref, 2230 (2)
Baron, R.: ref, 2497 (299), 2858 (73)
Baron, R. A.: ref, 1338 (5,24)
Baron, R. S.: ref, 2497 (154,224)
Baron, S.: ref, 1115 (4)
Baron-Cohen, S.: ref, 270 (10), 350 (11,14), 1485 (17), 1653 (5,15,23), 2163 (236), 2228 (23), 2662 (2), 2858 (59)
Barona, A.: rev, 306, 1397, 2499, 2554
Barone, C.: ref, 2497 (100)
Barone, D.: ref, 1072 (20)
Baroody, A. J.: test, 2681
Barr, H. M.: ref, 997 (24)
Barr, L. C.: ref, 2305 (148)
Barr, R.: ref, 1903 (338)
Barr, R. C.: rev, 827
Barr, W.: ref, 2860 (992), 2863 (294)
Barr, W. B.: ref, 1698 (16), 2163 (35), 2860 (1005), 2863 (41)
Barrash, J.: ref, 272 (324), 303 (23), 1697 (576), 2226 (37), 2860 (1355)
Barratt, E. S.: ref, 2862 (559), 2879 (183)
Barratt, M. S.: ref, 180 (8), 337 (21), 337 (127), 1216 (12,76), 1902 (21), 1903 (66)
Barrera, F. J.: ref, 4 (9)
Barrera, M.: ref, 451 (19)
Barrera, M. E.: ref, 256 (2)
Barrera, M., Jr.: ref, 998 (14)
Barrett, A. M.: ref, 1740 (28)
Barrett, D. E.: ref, 2758 (1), 2860 (737)
Barrett, D. H.: ref, 2860 (1035), 2892 (216)
Barrett, D. M.: ref, 451 (91), 472 (157), 2214 (89)
Barrett, E. B.: ref, 1701 (49)
Barrett, G. V.: test, 231
Barrett, J.: test, 145, 2459
Barrett, J. S.: test, 1497, 2019
Barrett, K.: ref, 1216 (37), 1216 (39) 2485 (112)
Barrett, K. C.: ref, 2497 (164)
Barrett, M.: test, 2710, 2911; ref, 350 (15), 615 (21), 1115 (6)
Barrett, P.: ref, 999 (119), 1822 (6)
Barrett, R. S.: rev, 263, 943
Barrett, S.: ref, 681 (98), 451 (283), 2603 (590), 2901 (135)
Barrett, T. C.: test, 552
Barrett, T. W.: ref, 2126 (4)
Barrick, M. R.: ref, 2899 (18)
Barrios, F. X.: ref, 271 (12,13), 272 (305), 337 (64,65,84,85,109,152,153,181), 1697 (231,338,444), 1698 (13), 2497 (273,648), 2559 (6,13), 2603 (204)

Barron, F.: rev, 908
Barron, S. I.: test, 1315
Barrow, R. W.: ref, 2879 (85)
Barrowclough, C.: ref, 2050 (57)
Barry, C. T.: ref, 433 (9), 1092 (9), 2768 (22), 2907 (4)
Barry, H.: ref, 2497 (32)
Barry, J.: test, 2471
Barry, N. S.: ref, 2076 (135)
Barry, W.: ref, 2749 (39)
Barsade, S. G.: ref, 1107 (1)
Barsch, J. R.: test, 244
Barsky, A. J.: ref, 1697 (52,256,697 (257,258), 2497 (300)
Bart, W. M.: rev, 235, 345, 1792
Barta, P. E.: ref, 815 (49), 1164 (173), 1740 (27), 2289 (22), 2516 (115), 2860 (1374), 2892 (294)
Bartell, S. S.: ref, 451 (49), 681 (58), 2247 (81)
Bartels, C. L.: ref, 472 (121)
Bartels, K. M.: ref, 2603 (357,459)
Bartels, S. J.: ref, 134 (12)
Bartelstone, J. H.: ref, 790 (18)
Bartfai, A.: ref, 2860 (154), 2892 (19)
Barth, J. M.: ref, 1903 (153)
Barth, J. T.: ref, 1164 (53), 1697 (237), 2860 (518)
Barth, R. P.: ref, 448 (2), 2497 (101)
Bartha, R.: ref, 2288 (78,79), 2289 (65)
Barthez, M. A.: ref, 2862 (329)
Bartholomew, J. B.: ref, 2497 (665)
Bartko, J. J.: ref, 863 (42), 2497 (114), 2860 (366)
Bartl, G.: ref, 2163 (160)
Bartlett, B. J.: rev, 1609, 2712
Bartlett, S. J.: ref, 1697 (469), 2076 (139)
Bartley, N.: ref, 665 (43)
Bartok, J.: ref, 681 (49), 1903 (276), 2010 (14)
Bartol, C. R.: ref, 1697 (118,158)
Bartol, K. M.: ref, 1755 (1), 2835 (1)
Bartolomeo, P.: ref, 2860 (1249,1375), 2863 (377)
Bartolucci, A. A.: ref, 1181 (1)
Bartolucci, G.: ref, 1903 (226), 2485 (19), 2768 (4), 2813 (4), 2860 (142), 2892 (17)
Barton, J.: ref, 998 (64), 2603 (81)
Barton, K. J.: ref, 1661 (52), 1697 (474)
Bartoov, B.: ref, 2603 (50)
Bartrop, R. W.: ref, 1166 (38), 2497 (155)
Bartusch, D. J.: ref, 373 (24), 2516 (59)
Baruch, G. K.: ref, 2603 (80)
Baruch, I.: ref, 2862 (78)
Baruch, P.: ref, 1166 (125,195), 2516 (103)
Baruth, L. G.: test, 1406
Barwick, M. A.: ref, 451 (104), 2862 (452)
Bascom, H. L.: test, 1013
Basford, J. R.: ref, 1697 (44)
Basford, P.: ref, 2497 (678)
Basham, R. B.: ref, 1698 (2)
Bashaw, W. L.: rev, 1315, 1863
Bashe, E.: ref, 298 (86)
Bashford, A.: test, 2111
Basili, L. A.: ref, 1379 (34), 1903 (210)
Basoglu, M.: ref, 272 (78), 1021 (29), 1166 (42), 2497 (301), 2497 (425), 2603 (233,234,288)
Basow, S. A.: ref, 298 (4,26,75)
Bass, B. A.: ref, 272 (149)
Bass, B. M.: test, 263, 1017, 1736, 1737; ref, 1736 (1)
Bass, C. M.: ref, 2603 (392)
Bass, J. D.: ref, 2813 (72)
Bass, L.: ref, 1903 (54)
Bassett, A.: ref, 2305 (49)
Bassett, A. S.: ref, 1697 (405), 2305 (131,220)
Bassett, D. L.: ref, 1697 (362)
Basso, A.: ref, 2163 (293), 2225 (15)
Basso, G.: ref, 2860 (843)
Bassuk, E. L.: ref, 1093 (12)
Basta, S. M.: ref, 538 (5), 1962 (8)
Bastiaanse, R.: ref, 2163 (196), 2768 (27)
Bastillo, J. R.: ref, 2288 (62)
Basu, D.: ref, 1697 (368)
Basu, J.: ref, 1367 (1), 2163 (60), 2248 (6)
Basun, H.: ref, 2860 (423), 2863 (111)
Bat-Chava, Y.: ref, 694 (43), 1991 (45)
Batchelder, S.: ref, 2603 (546)
Bate, M.: test, 196
Bate, S. M.: test, 2186
Bateman, D.: ref, 2239 (2)
Bates, B. C.: ref, 1697 (318), 2247 (65), 2749 (42)
Bates, E: test, 1528
Bates, G. W.: ref, 272 (33), 998 (55), 1687 (12), 1697 (96)
Bates, J. E.: ref, 451 (21,26,140,199), 1216 (23), 1903 (136)
Bates, J. F.: ref, 2227 (32), 2860 (1166)
Bates, L. W.: ref, 694 (44)
Bates, M. E.: ref, 326 (9), 376 (13), 1164 (31,81,140), 1661 (19), 2402 (10,35,61), 2516 (91), 2860 (330,768,1221)
Bates, T.: ref, 128 (2), 999 (173), 2163 (246,305), 2860 (991,1182)
Bates, T. C.: ref, 999 (49), 1732 (1)
Bateson, D. J.: rev, 1196, 2831
Bath, J. B.: test, 2678
Bathurst, K.: ref, 1379 (14), 2163 (140), 2860 (13), 2862 (4)
Bator, R. J.: ref, 1755 (68)
Batson, C. D.: ref, 2516 (8)
Batt, R.: ref, 1671 (6), 2860 (1144)
Battaglia, C.: test, 1238
Battersby, R. D. E.: ref, 1758 (54), 2860 (1000), 2863 (296), 2892 (209)
Battle, J.: test, 261, 746, 1803; ref, 1234 (1)
Baty, F. J.: ref, 1079 (28)
Baty, G.: ref, 2497 (618)
Baucom, D. H.: rev, 372; ref, 372 (54), 1582 (4)
Bauer, A. M.: test, 221, 1460
Bauer, E. A.: rev, 227, 931, 2336
Bauer, L.: ref, 1525 (21), 2010 (22), 2892 (223)

Bauer, M.: ref, 2497 (225)
Bauer, M. S.: ref, 2305 (28)
Bauer, R. H.: ref, 1866 (9,15)
Bauer, R. M.: ref, 199 (17), 2860 (10)
Bauer, S. C.: ref, 364 (27)
Bauermeister, J. J.: ref, 2656 (1)
Bauernfeind, R.H.: test, 904; rev, 1964
Baugher, M.: ref, 272 (259)
Baughman, W. A.: ref, 937 (3)
Baum, A.: test, 1412; ref, 1745 (27;37), 2076 (146), 2516 (50), 2603 (35,171,516), 2858 (89)
Baum, A. S.: ref, 2603 (338)
Baum, B. E.: ref, 2497 (156)
Baum, C. G.: ref, 337 (14), 1925 (1)
Baum, J. R.: ref, 1338 (43)
Baum, K. M.: ref, 451 (242), 1318 (22), 1740 (29), 1903 (565), 2860 (1376), 2862 (700)
Baum, S.: ref, 724 (1), 1142 (2), 1991 (2), 2771 (1), 2848 (1), 2862 (32,33)
Baum, S. F.: ref, 2076 (122)
Baum, S. M.: ref, 773 (4), 1657 (20), 1991 (89)
Baum, S. R.: ref, 163 (2)
Bauman, G. D.: ref, 1079 (32), 2858 (88)
Bauman, K. E.: ref, 1097 (4), 1903 (67), 2146 (8), 2163 (61)
Bauman, W.: ref, 2656 (10)
Baumanis, R.: rev, 2406, 2827
Baumann, A. T.: ref, 1755 (34)
Baumann, J. F.: ref, 1902 (81), 1903 (444), 2432 (29), 2905 (96)
Baumeister, A. A.: ref, 451 (92), 1216 (110), 1673 (7), 1903 (93,564), 2432 (17), 2485 (189,239), 2695 (27), 2862 (267), 2864 (53,109), 2901 (41)
Baumer, T.: ref, 376 (33), 2239 (35)
Baumgaertner, A.: ref, 2873 (27)
Baumgardner, A. H.: ref, 999 (28)
Baumgardner, T. L.: ref, 681 (66), 2860 (1167), 2862 (393,437,548), 2892 (253), 2901 (72,100)
Baumgartner, P.: ref, 433 (7), 459 (21), 2485 (92)
Baumler, B.: ref, 1790 (8), 2451 (4)
Baumstark, K. E.: ref, 771 (10), 2603 (38), 2858 (12)
Bauserman, D. N.: rev, 1489
Bauserman, R.: ref, 298 (93), 998 (59)
Bauserman, R. L.: ref, 998 (122)
Bauserman, S. A. K.: ref, 863 (61)
Bava, A.: ref, 2163 (269)
Bawtree, S.: test, 735, 964, 2087
Baxter, A.: ref, 837 (2)
Baxter, G. P.: ref, 665 (44)
Baxter, L. R., Jr.: ref, 1093 (40), 1166 (150)
Baxter, S.: ref, 448 (8)
Bay, R. C.: ref, 451 (20), 472 (26), 2214 (16)
Baydar, N.: ref, 1216 (26,93,94), 1903 (154)
Baydoun, R.: ref, 1836 (1)
Bayles, K. A.: test, 176, 1064; ref, 2863 (116), 2873 (13)
Bayley, N.: test, 270; rev, 1134, 2860
Baynes, K.: ref, 1164 (174), 1903 (566), 2163 (348) 2731 (7), 2860 (1222,1377), 2863 (362,413), 2879 (224), 2892 (295)
Bayog, R. D.: ref, 136 (7), 1661 (26)
Bays, K.: ref, 2864 (39), 1612 (36)
Bayse, D. J.: ref, 1000 (12)
Bazyk, S.: ref, 1668 (1)
Beach, S. R. H.: ref, 272 (62,155,280), 863 (6,7,19, 23,47), 2519 (12,19,20), 2520 (12,20,21)
Beail, N.: ref, 272 (281), 2603 (538)
Beal, D.: ref, 1697 (2)
Beale, I. L.: ref, 2485 (1)
Beales, J. N.: ref, 372 (12)
Beals, J.: ref, 462 (1), 472 (14,38)
Beam-Goulet, J.: ref, 2432 (19), 2892 (129), 2924 (2)
Beaman, J.: ref, 2326 (1), 2603 (213,214,305)
Beamish, P.: ref, 372 (16), 1338 (16)
Bean, G.: ref, 2050 (58), 2603 (238)
Beange, H.: ref, 1903 (445), 2163 (262), 2813 (112)
Bear, D. R.: ref, 1072 (20)
Bear, G. G.: ref, 665 (92), 694 (130), 1734 (5), 1991 (104), 2211 (2,17), 2358 (15), 2485 (240), 2862 (701), 2879 (225)
Beard, C. M.: ref, 1612 (73), 2485 (170), 2860 (910), 2862 (356), 2864 (95)
Beardsall, L.: ref, 2237 (1), 2239 (13)
Bearley, W. L.: test, 1859
Bearn, J.: ref, 1166 (72)
Beasley, M.: ref, 2181 (1)
Beasley, T. M.: ref, 1470 (4), 2069 (1)
Beaton, A. A.: ref, 2497 (102)
Beats, B. C.: ref, 1390 (7), 1758 (57), 2860 (1036)
Beattie, B. L.: test, 545
Beattie, M.: ref, 1164 (11), 2860 (117), 2863 (32)
Beattie, M. C.: ref, 134 (8)
Beatty, J. R.: test, 1278
Beatty, M.: ref, 451 (72)
Beatty, P. A.: ref, 272 (1), 2892 (5)
Beatty, W. W.: ref, 199 (12), 272 (1,63,150,151), 1093 (44), 2402 (16,28,37,54), 2497 (537), 2519 (22), 2520 (23), 2599 (3,26), 2860 (430,798,1037,1038), 2863 (308), 2892 (5,64,65,66,100,161)
Beauchamp, K. D. F.: ref, 289 (3)
Beauchemin, K. M.: ref, 2076 (140)
Beaudet, M.: ref, 1164 (72), 2863 (208)
Beaudett, M. S.: ref, 134 (4)
Beaudichon, J.: ref, 2111 (2), 2163 (247), 2862 (410)
Beaumont, J. G.: ref, 1671 (1), 2163 (45)
Beauregard, M.: ref, 2163 (310), 2863 (363)
Beauvais, F.: test, 143; ref, 143 (1)
Beavers, W. R.: ref, 1000 (97)
Bebbington, P.: ref, 537 (1,4), 1093 (80), 2050 (73), 2050 (98), 2050 (103)
Bebko, J. M.: ref, 1903 (446)
Bebout, R. R.: ref, 134 (36)
Bebruille, B.: ref, 2860 (130)
Bech, K.: ref, 451 (19)

Bech, P.: ref, 1166 (172)
Bechtel, R.: test, 2114
Bechtold, D. W.: ref, 2557 (8)
Bechtoldt, H.: rev, 838, 1156
Bechtoldt, H. P.: rev, 302, 1042, 1323, 2797
Beck, A. T.: test, 271, 272, 273, 274; ref, 271 (9), 272 (2,3,266), 273 (1,2,27), 1166 (183), 2519 (5,27), 2520 (5,28), 2603 (217409)
Beck, B. L.: ref, 592 (85)
Beck, H. P.: ref, 615 (20)
Beck, I. L.: rev, 1515, 2682; ref, 1657 (14)
Beck, J. G.: ref, 272 (226), 1166 (157), 2076 (22,106), 2305 (90), 2497 (302,303,596,597,610), 2519 (35), 2603 (3,235)
Beck, K. W.: ref, 999 (97)
Beck, L.: ref, 2031 (1)
Beck, M. D.: rev, 1392, 1400, 2682, 2737
Beck, S.: ref, 1405 (32)
Beck, S. J.: rev, 317, 373, 2247; ref, 472 (131), 557 (7)
Becker, A. H.: ref, 2369 (2)
Becker, B. J.: ref, 592 (10)
Becker, D. F.: ref, 2603 (426), 2860 (1039), 2862 (438)
Becker, E.: ref, 2497 (304,480)
Becker, H.: test, 1067
Becker, J.: ref, 272 (31), 790 (15)
Becker, J. A.: ref, 2227 (58), 2860 (1396), 2863 (421)
Becker, J. T.: ref, 1135 (2,13,16,26), 1164 (180), 1740 (8), 2227 (21), 2599 (4,25,32,40), 2860 (200,636,772,799), 2892 (118)
Becker, J. V.: ref, 853 (6), 1697 (203), 2247 (30), 2749 (31)
Becker, L. A.: ref, 2497 (533), 2603 (430)
Becker, L. E.: ref, 1096 (3), 2860 (64,246), 2862 (38,125)
Becker, R.: ref, 2227 (8), 2860 (364), 2879 (44), 2892 (54)
Becker, R. E.: ref, 2497 (68)
Becker, R. L.: test, 275, 2177
Becker, T. E.: ref, 1701 (22)
Becker, W. C.: rev, 1017
Becker-Lausen, E.: ref, 272 (97), 846 (10)
Beckett, J.: ref, 298 (105), 1036 (10)
Beckham, E.: ref, 1517 (4)
Beckham, J. C.: ref, 1178 (4), 1697 (530), 2497 (531), 2603 (46), 2879 (148,154)
Beckie, J. L.: ref, 389 (9), 900 (2), 1072 (34)
Becklund, J. D.: test, 2422
Beckman, H. T.: ref, 272 (252), 2603 (515)
Beckmann, J.: ref, 2860 (435)
Beckwith, J. B.: ref, 298 (101)
Beckwith, L.: ref, 1216 (17)
Bédard, F.: ref, 2125 (25), 2860 (1256)
Bedard, M. A.: ref, 776 (52)
Bedard, M.-A.: ref, 1164 (163), 1218 (18), 2226 (28), 2227 (46)
Bédard, P. J.: ref, 2125 (25) 2860 (1256)
Bedeian, A. G.: ref, 68 (34,44), 372 (15), 999 (100), 1701 (14)
Bedell, G.: ref, 1673 (1), 1901 (2)
Bedell, M. B.: ref, 1107 (9)
Bedell, R. C.: rev, 1716
Bederman, J.: ref, 1092 (5), 2860 (331)
Bedi, G.: ref, 451 (58)
Bedore, L. M.: ref, 1485 (60), 2864 (139)
Bedrick, J.: ref, 1661 (77)
Beech, H. R.: rev, 1811
Beech, J. R.: ref, 349 (21,35), 350 (23,42), 2163 (311), 2556 (2), 2910 (1)
Beech, M. C.: rev, 1232
Beeferman, D.: ref, 472 (209), 694 (126), 2305 (230)
Beeghly, M.: ref, 1903 (227)
Beehr, T. A.: ref, 1590 (6), 1965 (55), 2899 (6)
Beekman, A. T. F.: ref, 2163 (307)
Beer, J.: ref, 694 (27,28), 1697 (199), 2497 (46)
Beer, R.: ref, 1166 (31)
Beers, S. R.: ref, 2603 (236), 2860 (565), 2863 (163), 2879 (71), 2901 (37)
Beersma, D. G. M.: ref, 1166 (48,83,175)
Beery, K. E.: test, 278, 815, 1283
Beery, L. C.: ref, 1166 (173)
Beery, Q.: ref, 1040 (6)
Beery, S. H.: ref, 451 (80)
Beeson, P. M.: ref, 159 (1,2), 163 (3), 2863 (116), 2873 (13)
Beggs, A. H.: ref, 2862 (526)
Beggs, D. L.: test, 287
Begin, A.: ref, 793 (7)
Begin, L.: test, 387
Begley, A.: ref, 337 (156)
Beh, H. C.: ref, 908 (2)
Behan, P. O.: ref, 2497 (283)
Behar, L.: test, 2039
Behavior Data Systems: test, 2284, 856, 2783
Behen, J. M.: ref, 2497 (305), 2603 (237)
Behler, J. J.: ref, 286 (1)
Behrens, B. C.: ref, 863 (2)
Behrens, C.: ref, 2227 (42)
Behrens, Chr.: ref, 776 (49), 1164 (159), 1758 (91)
Behrens, D.: ref, 451 (195), 2497 (629)
Behrens, J.: ref, 1128 (4)
Behrmann, M.: ref, 1903 (559), 2227 (53), 2860 (1365)
Behrns, H.: test, 172
Beidel, D. C.: test, 2448; ref, 451 (93), 998 (107), 2497 (18), 2498 (13,28,33,49,57,58), 2519 (34), 2520 (35), 2862 (439)
Beiler, M. E.: ref, 794 (1), 893 (7), 2065 (3)
Beilke, R. L.: ref, 815 (5), 2862 (129), 2879 (33)
Beirne-Smith, M.: ref, 1300 (6)
Beisenherz, P.: ref, 1140 (18), 2856 (5)
Beiser, M.: ref, 2050 (58), 2603 (238)
Beishuizen, M.: ref, 2163 (102)
Beitchman, J. H.: test, 1025; ref, 241 (4), 337 (22), 451 (94), 815 (35), 1697 (119), 1903 (447), 1991 (19), 2695 (47), 2864 (110)
Beitman, B. D.: ref, 337 (7), 2519 (7), 2520 (7), 2603 (198)

Bejar, I. I.: rev, 307; ref, 1405 (14)
Belander, S. A.: ref, 2008 (12), 2873 (52)
Belanger, A.: ref, 2860 (329), 2863 (87)
Belanger, A. J.: ref, 2863 (113)
Bélanger, C.: ref, 2497 (641)
Belanger, S. A.: ref, 1379 (52,88), 2008 (13)
Belbin, M.: test, 296
Belcher, M. J.: rev, 57, 192, 2578, 2899
Belding, M. A.: ref, 1697 (582)
Belfer, P. L.: ref, 1021 (11), 2497 (157)
Belfiore, P. J.: ref, 2485 (158)
Belgrave, F. Z.: ref, 1947 (8)
Bell, B. D.: ref, 2873 (20)
Bell, I. R.: ref, 2603 (239,334)
Bell, J. E.: rev, 466, 1005, 1011, 1012, 1053
Bell, J. J.: ref, 1093 (1), 2603 (15)
Bell, K.: ref, 303 (29), 776 (61), 1740 (32), 2125 (7), 2516 (16), 2860 (310,512,11801405)
Bell, K. L.: ref, 694 (65), 2860 (907)
Bell, L. C.: ref, 592 (49)
Bell, L. M.: ref, 2358 (12)
Bell, M.: ref, 297 (1), 1697 (280), 2017 (10), 2305 (99), 2432 (18,19), 2862 (250), 2892 (128), 2892 (129), 2892 (194), 2924 (2)
Bell, M. D.: test, 297; ref, 2017 (14), 2017 (15), 2432 (25,30), 2892 (195,196,235,236,264), 2924 (3,4)
Bell, N. J.: ref, 1000 (10)
Bell, N. L.: ref, 2485 (102,176), 2860 (946)
Bell, R.: ref, 1093 (71), 2050 (90)
Bell, R. Q.: ref, 451 (282)
Bell, R. W.: ref, 2497 (360)
Bell, S. M.: ref, 2452 (5)
Bell, T. S.: ref, 1135 (12), 2813 (67), 2862 (274), 2879 (84)
Bell, W.: ref, 2497 (283)
Bell-Dolan, D.: ref, 2214 (59)
Bell-Dolan, D. J.: ref, 451 (50), 472 (43,110)
Bella, I.: ref, 2862 (526)
Bella, P. D.: rev, 2720
Bellack, A. S.: ref, 1093 (15), 1619 (2), 2305 (42,57), 2519 (11), 2520 (11), 2860 (569), 2892 (6,101)
Bellaire, S.: ref, 1804 (8), 2862 (235)
Bellaire, S.: ref, 2901 (38)
Bellak, L.: test, 466, 912, 2110, 2372; rev, 1811
Bellak, S. S.: test, 466
Bellanti, C. J.: ref, 2211 (48)
Bellavia, C. W.: ref, 2603 (419)
Bellerose, S. B.: ref, 793 (11), 2077 (4)
Belleville, R. E.: test, 66
Belleville, S.: ref, 2860 (945), 2863 (278,349)
Bellinger, D. C.: ref, 1216 (10)
Bellingrath, E.: test, 566
Bellini, J.: ref, 1790 (11), 1954 (1)
Bellis, M.: ref, 2227 (19), 2860 (818), 2863 (236)
Bellissimo, A.: ref, 1000 (88)
Belliveau, J. M.: ref, 538 (7)
Bellman, M.: test, 2308
Bello, J.: ref, 272 (309)
Bellodi, L.: ref, 2892 (159)
Bellugi, U. : ref, 815 (32), 1379 (80), 1725 (7)
Belmont, B.: ref, 1093 (51), 1093 (100), 2076 (67)
Belouad, F.: ref, 451 (46)
Belsky, J.: ref, 451 (95), 1010 (38), 1770 (2, 10), 1965 (12,30), 2218 (3,20,45,46,47,80)
Beltran, E.: ref, 337 (86)
Belyea-Caldwell, S.: ref, 998 (75,76), 2603 (282,283), 2858 (78,79)
Belza, B. L.: ref, 2076 (51)
Bem, D. J.: ref, 373 (4)
Bem, S. L.: test, 298
Bemak, F.: ref, 1079 (101), 2603 (572)
Beman, I.: ref, 335 (10)
Bempechat, J.: ref, 298 (8586) 538 (4), 2879 (155)
Ben, R.: ref, 1903 (163), 2485 (78)
Benabarre, A.: ref, 2305 (238)
Benasich, A. A.: ref, 270 (11,41), 451 (96), 1216 (77), 2485 (190), 2695 (70), 2862 (679)
Benavidez, D. A.: ref, 681 (44), 2231 (2), 2813 (104)
Benazon, N. R.: ref, 2603 (564)
Benbadis, S.: ref, 2860 (1041)
Benbenishty, R.: ref, 863 (32), 2603 (161)
Benbow, C. D.: ref, 592 (22)
Benbow, C. P.: rev, 144, 1603; ref, 68 (1,49), 302 (2,4), 592 (54,66,88), 615 (7,11,14), 771 (25), 1010 (86), 1156 (2), 1790 (9), 2163 (36,241), 2539 (1)
Bence, V. M.: ref, 1697 (385)
Bench, C. J.: ref, 2860 (579), 2863 (166)
Bendania, A.: ref, 2516 (90)
Bendell, D.: ref, 272 (170,196), 451 (115,136), 1962 (13), 2076 (73,148)
Bender, B.: ref, 1392 (12), 2432 (22), 2901 (52)
Bender, L.: test, 301
Bender, W. N.: ref, 1697 (219), 1916 (2), 2497 (253)
Bendersky, M.: ref, 2382 (19)
Ben-Dov, I.: ref, 2452 (9), 2862 (367)
Bene, E.: test, 1011, 1012
Benedict, K. B.: ref, 1092 (16), 2862 (394), 2879 (137)
Benedict, R. H. B.: ref, 776 (36), 2288 (32), 2289 (24), 2305 (91), 2860 (748,1033,1206)
Benedicto, J. A.: ref, 2525 (4)
Benes, K. M.: rev, 294, 1001, 1902, 2452
Benfield, J. R., Jr.: ref, 2862 (242)
Bengtson, M. L.: ref, 2860 (1101)
Benhamou, J.: ref, 2163 (310), 2863 (363)
Beniak, T. E.: ref, 687 (4)
Benight, C. C.: ref, 1338 (2), 2603 (516)
Benish, J. K.: rev, 269
Benitta, R.: ref, 301 (32), 2163 (127)
Benjamin, B.: ref, 451 (163), 1903 (513), 2902 (4)
Benjamin, G. A. H.: ref, 337 (1), 2603 (1)
Benjamin, J.: ref, 1092 (5), 1697 (22), 2603 (6), 2860 (331)
Benjamin, L. S.: test, 1298, 2520; ref, 1697 (226, 259,597)

Benjamin, M.: ref, 1000 (82)
Benke, T.: ref, 2163 (337), 2768 (12)f, 2860 (892,1328), 2863 (117)
Benkelfat, C.: ref, 2076 (74), 2497 (306,626), 2603 (240)
Benkert, O.: ref, 1166 (214)
Benliman, H.: ref, 853 (24)f, 2247 (111), 2862 (591)
Bennedetto, E.: ref, 1903 (512)
Bennet, C. W.: rev, 2523
Bennett, A.: ref, 289 (4), 385 (2)
Bennett, C. W.: rev, 1898, 2429, 2886
Bennett, D.: ref, 472 (185), 2214 (111), 2497 (585), 2668 (4), 2813 (128), 2858 (75)
Bennett, D. E.: ref, 2862 (380), 2901 (69)
Bennett, D. S.: ref, 272 (253), 451 (97), 2305 (214)
Bennett, G. K.: test, 302, 838, 839, 1170, 2406
Bennett, J. A.: ref, 1903 (21), 2163 (23), 2289 (58)
Bennett, K. M. B.: ref, 2860 (566,800)
Bennett, M.: ref, 1164 (130), 1903 (489), 2163 (294), 2227 (30), 2695 (58), 2768 (36), 2862 (531), 2880 (4)
Bennett, R. E.: ref, 301 (55), 1115 (3,15,23,26), 1405 (28), 2253 (2), 2771 (35), 2860 (1087), 2879 (161), 2901 (90)
Bennett, R. T.: ref, 337 (133)
Bennett, S.: ref, 694 (32), 1367 (3), 2498 (29)
Bennett, S. E.: ref, 337 (128)
Bennett, S. J.: ref, 2076 (141)
Bennett, T.: ref, 337 (174)
Bennetto, L.: ref, 375 (2), 2485 (191), 2862 (440,538), 2892 (217)
Bennetts, K.: ref, 272 (247)
Bennie, J.: ref, 2860 (699)
Benotsch, E. G.: ref, 1697 (531), 2858 (95)
Benowitz, L. I.: ref, 2860 (155)
Ben-Porath, J. S.: ref, 1697 (382)
Ben-Porath, Y.: ref, 2497 (349)
Ben-Porath, Y. S.: test, 1698; ref, 372 (81), 999 (110), 1697 (374), 1697 (383), 1697 (384,414, 528,544, 588), 2417 (23)
Ben-Porath, Y. W.: ref, 1697 (378)
Ben-Shakhar, G. B.: ref, 337 (118)
Benshoff, J. J.: ref, 2527 (1)
Bensing, J. M.: ref, 1079 (33)
Benson, A.: ref, 1014 (6)
Benson, B. A.: ref, 1903 (359,504), 2211 (40,49), 2862 (573)
Benson, D. F.: ref, 2860 (8), 2892 (1)
Benson, E.: ref, 2497 (369)
Benson, F. A.: test, 1791
Benson, H.: ref, 1991 (64), 2497 (255)
Benson, J.: rev, 1720, 2181, 2535
Benson, K. L.: ref, 1697 (128)
Benson, M.: ref, 2599 (16) 2860 (614), 2863 (180), 2892 (115)
Benson, M. J.: rev, 1006, 1880, 2526, 2912; ref, 2485 (48), 2497 (226), 2862 (154)
Benson, N.: rev, 2530
Benson, P.: rev, 819
Benson, P. G.: rev, 239, 1106, 1827, 2021, 2277, 2586
Bensoussan, M.: rev, 1191
Bentall, R. D.: ref, 1758 (33)
Bentall, R. P.: ref, 272 (4,13,53,143,279), 1758 (89), 1944 (1), 2050 (104,140), 2516 (1), 2860 (1021)
Bentin, S.: ref, 2163 (37), 2860 (11), 2863 (6)
Bentler, P. M.: test, 674; rev, 1291, 1657, 1991, 2652; ref, 790 (5)
Bentley, A.: test, 1629
Bentley, R. R.: rev, 1629
Benton, A. L.: test, 303, 1740; rev, 301, 1697, 2426, 2430, 2749
Benton, S. L.: rev, 392, 1132, 1243, 2731
Bentouim, A.: ref, 451 (59), 1011 (4), 1079 (41), 1987 (15)
Bentsen, H.: ref, 1079 (83)
Benvegnu, B.: ref, 2163 (226)
Ben-Yehuda, Y.: ref, 301 (16), 2860 (241)
Ben-Yochanan, A.: ref, 2864 (6)
Berardi, A.: ref, 2860 (1223), 2863 (364)
Berchick, R. J.: ref, 2519 (5), 2520 (5)
Berdie, R. F.: rev, 838, 1042
Berenbaum, H.: ref, 592 (30), 998 (86), 1903 (442), 2603 (300) 2860 (564)
Berenbaum, J.: ref, 2076 (37), 2497 (158)
Berenson, B. G.: test, 2116
Berent, G. P.: ref, 1664 (4,6)
Berent, S.: ref, 1166 (107), 1697 (542), 2227 (2), 2603 (438), 2860 (179,1040,1079,1264), 2863 (48,315,380), 2879 (203)
Berg, B. J.: ref, 2603 (82)
Berg, G.: ref, 2010 (1), 2163 (10), 2860 (34) 2863 (12)
Berg, G. E.: ref, 771 (19)
Berg, H. D.: rev, 117
Berg, I.: test, 2350; ref, 1481 (3)
Berg, I. J.: ref, 2193 (47)
Berg, J. M.: ref, 2227 (8), 2860 (364), 2879 (44), 2892 (54)
Berg, P.: ref, 2892 (32)
Berg-Larsen, R.: ref, 1079 (83)
Berge, P. S.: test, 648
Bergeman, C. S.: ref, 1010 (11), 2218 (7)
Bergen, A. E.: ref, 257 (2), 1903 (228)
Bergen, D. J.: ref, 68 (9)
Bergen, G. T.: ref, 1697 (158)
Berger, A.: rev, 707, 775, 1477, 2538, 2856, 2857
Berger, B. G.: ref, 999 (177), 2076 (62,163), 2358 (4)
Berger, H. J. C.: ref, 376 (12), 2226 (16), 2516 (35,75,87,88), 2860 (79,584,1007,1193,1194), 2892 (7), 2892 (211), 2892 (260)
Berger, J.: ref, 1135 (18), 2226 (14), 2516 (85), 2860 (1173), 2863 (353)
Berger, J. C.: ref, 298 (33)f, 853 (4), 1697 (84)
Berger, K.: ref, 472 (47), 2860 (467)
Berger, M.: rev, 2234; ref, 1166 (144), 1338 (6), 2497 (20), 2603 (7)
Berger, R. S.: ref, 2497 (590)

Berger, S. G.: ref, 1164 (141), 2860 (1224)
Berger, S. H.: ref, 1991 (5)
Bergering, A. J.: ref, 592 (27)
Bergeron, C.: ref, 2227 (8), 2860 (364), 2879 (44), 2892 (54)
Bergeron, M. G.: ref, 272 (375), 2498 (77)
Berggren, V.: ref, 2497 (129)
Berghout Austin, A. M.: ref, 1991 (77)
Bergin, D. A.: ref, 1455 (11)
Bergin, P. S.: ref, 2227 (18), 2863 (231)
Bergman, A. J.: ref, 353 (22), 451 (167)
Bergman, H.: ref, 1164 (57), 2860 (586), 2863 (174)
Bergman, J. N.: ref, 142 (6), 1619 (8), 2862 (420)
Bergman, K. S.: ref, 1093 (40)
Bergman, R. L.: ref, 2050 (17)
Bergmans, P. L. M.: ref, 335 (15)
Bergmans, R.: ref, 1166 (76), 1166 (78)
Bergstralli, E. J.: ref, 1612 (73), 2485 (170), 2860 (910), 2862 (356), 2864 (95)
Bergstrom, B.: rev, 2150, 2221
Bergwall, L.: ref, 298 (40), 615 (19), 665 (28), 1140 (15), 1866 (14), 2163 (52), 2485 (30), 2729 (2), 2771 (8)
Berhardt, B.: ref, 1903 (229), 2657 (10)
Beringer, M. L.: test, 304
Berk, L. A.: ref, 404 (12), 1334 (2), 2860 (156)
Berk, L. E.: ref, 681 (22)
Berk, M.: ref, 335 (14)
Berk, R. A.: test, 772; rev, 346, 1644, 2484
Berk, S. A.: ref, 2247 (2), 2862 (6)
Berkay, P. J.: test, 1844
Berkman, L. F.: ref, 2860 (471)
Berkovic, S. F.: ref, 1744 (8), 2860 (520), 2863 (150,190,340)
Berkowitz, M.: ref, 592 (34)
Berkowitz, R. I.: ref, 272 (144), 1010 (91), 2497 (535)
Berkson, G.: ref, 2813 (56,103,136)
Berlant, A. R.: ref, 2369 (10)
Berlin, L. J.: test, 2044
Berlin, S.: ref, 2858 (10)
Berman, A. L.: ref, 301 (15), 1697 (120), 2247 (11), 2860 (235)
Berman, I., : ref, 2860 (1378), 2879 (226), 2892 (296)
Berman, K. F.: ref, 376 (8), 2892 (162,230)
Berman, N.: ref, 1166 (136), 2227 (29), 2516 (81), 2603 (220), 2860 (1150), 2863 (341), 2892 (246)
Berman, N. G.: ref, 2860 (1117), 2863 (331), 2892 (231)
Berman, S. R.: ref, 472 (96), 1991 (70,71), 2498 (38,39)
Berman, W. H.: ref, 2497 (307)
Bermejo, F.: ref, 2163 (320), 2860 (1252)
Bermúdez, J.: ref, 272 (135), 999 (135)
Bernal, E. M.: ref, 2163 (59)
Bernal, G.: ref, 272 (341)
Bernard, H.: rev, 635, 1880, 2826
Bernard, L. C.: ref, 641 (1), 2226 (1), 2860 (157)
Bernard, M.: ref, 1965 (53)
Bernard-Paolucci, T. S.: ref, 1927 (6)
Bernardi, R. A.: ref, 771 (20), 1140 (37)
Bernardin, H. J.: rev, 1436, 1544, 1575, 1843, 2593
Bernardin, L.: ref, 272 (372), 326 (3), 1218 (4), 2076 (185), 2163 (76), 2497 (136), 2516 (14), 2860 (301,561), 2892 (41,97)
Bernardy, N.: ref, 337 (28), 2858 (30)
Bernazzani, O.: ref, 298 (165)
Bernberg, R. E.: test, 1229, 2919
Berndt, D. J.: test, 1748, 1749
Berndt, R. S.: rev, 199, 629, 1423; ref, 2873 (60)
Berndt, T. J.: ref, 495 (2)
Bernet, C. Z.: ref, 1697 (308), 1745 (41), 2519 (41), 2520 (41)
Bernet, M.: test, 2412
Bernhardt, E. B.: ref, 971 (1)
Bernheimer, L. P.: ref, 1010 (65), 1085 (4), 1216 (52), 2485 (228), 2813 (145)
Bernicri, F. J.: ref, 272 (98), 372 (82), 2218 (21)
Bernier, J. J.: rev, 389, 821
Bernieri, F.: ref, 298 (66)
Bernieri, F. J.: ref, 2078 (2), 2078 (7)
Berninger, V.: ref, 2901 (84)
Berninger, V. M.: ref, 2879 (208), 2905 (111), 1138 (1,2), 1379 (89), 1612 (29), 1903 (155), 2485 (71), 2862 (537), 2864 (123), 2905 (31,94)
Bernstein, B. L.: ref, 2858 (106)
Bernstein, D. P.: test, 460
Bernstein, G. A.: ref, 272 (100,101), 472 (22, 71,158,159), 2214 (13,35,90,91), 2498 (30), 2603 (439)
Bernstein, J.: ref, 2497 (103)
Bernstein, J. H.: ref, 1092 (16), 2516 (69), 2862 (394), 2879 (137), 2892 (191)
Bernstein, L.: ref, 2858 (2)
Bernstein, M. E.: ref, 1095 (7), 1618 (1), 1903 (107), 2672 (2), 2813 (16)
Bernstein, V. J.: ref, 2860 (567)
Bernstein-Hyman, R.: ref, 2017 (9)
Bernt, F. M.: rev, 434, 810, 1242
Bernthal, J.: ref, 2045 (3)
Bernthal, J. E.: test, 240, 2144
Berntson, B.: test, 201
Bernuth, C.: ref, 2369 (11)
Berquin, P. C.: ref, 451 (243), 2862 (702), 2879 (227)
Berrettini, W. H.: ref, 2305 (29)
Berrick, J. D.: ref, 1216 (95)
Berringer, V. W.: ref, 1379 (74), 2862 (383), 2864 (101)
Berry, C. C.: ref, 2497 (437), 2498 (50)
Berry, D. S.: ref, 2218 (48,83)
Berry, D. T.: ref, 2860 (1157)
Berry, D. T. R.: ref, 1697 (379,380,386,532)
Berry, G. L.: ref, 1755 (65), 2076 (152)
Berry, J. O.: ref, 1745 (52)
Berry, J. W.: ref, 272 (304), 708 (8), 999 (34), 1903 (21), 2163 (23)
Berry, L. A.: ref, 1697 (501)

Berry, P.: test, 1423
Berry, S. L.: ref, 1010 (54), 2498 (24)
Berry, S. R.: test, 2936
Berry, T. R.: ref, 2065 (35)
Berryman, C.: test, 227
Berryman, J. D.: test, 227; rev, 2466, 2524
Berryman-Miller, S.: ref, 620 (1)
Bers, S. A..: test, 790
Bersani, G.: ref, 1166 (33)
Bertani, A.: ref, 2497 (505)
Bertelsmann, F. W.: ref, 2599 (22)
Bertelson, A. D.: ref, 1697 (6)
Berthiaume, M.: ref, 298 (165)
Berthot, B. D.: ref, 1021 (40), 2497 (581)
Berthoud, I.: ref, 350 (44), 2662 (7), 2860 (1291), 2862 (635)
Berti, A.: ref, 2516 (33)
Bertman, L. J.: ref, 4 (3)
Bertolotti, G.: ref, 999 (16), 2497 (52)
Bertrand, N. P.: ref, 1755 (8), 2545 (1)
Bertuccelli, B.: ref, 2860 (442)
Berven, N. L.: ref, 2797 (4)
Berzonsky, M. D.: ref, 2858 (32)
Besag, F. M. C.: ref, 349 (9), 2239 (16)
Beschin, N.: ref, 2163 (263,312)
Besett, T.: ref, 337 (153), 1698 (13), 2559 (13)
Besett, T. M.: ref, 337 (110)
Bessai, F.: rev, 676, 1547, 1736, 2085, 2153
Bessant, K. C.: ref, 2540 (8)
Bessell, N. J.: ref, 2860 (66), 2863 (21)
Best, C. L.: ref, 1697 (496)
Best, C. T.: ref, 827 (4), 2210 (1), 2516 (4), 2892 (12)
Best, K. M.: ref, 2218 (58), 2603 (456)
Best, W.: ref, 2873 (28)
Bester, C.: ref, 999 (65)
Bestgen, Y.: ref, 1338 (13)
Betancourt, R.: ref, 1701 (43)
Betsworth, D. G.: ref, 1790 (13), 2360 (7)
Bettison, S.: ref, 1485 (49), 1903 (448)
Betts, A.: rev, 2254
Betts, D.: ref, 1745 (30)
Betz, N. E.: test, 403, 1602, 2916; ref, 404 (39,44), 694 (93), 1079 (34), 1754 (26), 1790 (10), 2497 (426)
Betz, P.: ref, 449 (3)
Betz, R. R.: ref, 1725 (6), 1908 (1)
Betz, W.: rev, 1368
Beukelman, D. R.: test, 209
Beukes, D. P. M.: test, 1198
Beutler, L.: ref, 272 (300)
Beutler, L. E.: ref, 2603 (274)
Beuzen, J. N.: ref, 1166 (57)
Beversdorf, D. Q.: ref, 1740 (28)
Beyer, F. S.: test, 216, 843
Beyerlein, M. M.: ref, 2258 (3)
Beyler, J.: ref, 1697 (190)
Bezouczko, N.: ref, 1318 (12)
Bhalla, S. K.: ref, 893 (31)
Bhang, J.: ref, 2860 (665), 2863 (195)
Bhardwaj, S.: ref, 999 (175), 1321 (10), 1697 (523), 2771 (44)
Bhartiya, V. R.: ref, 2603 (420)
Bharucha, J. J.: ref, 2860 (312), 2863 (84)
Bhatia, M. S.: ref, 681 (5), 2864 (21)
Bhattacharyua, A.: ref, 335 (13)
Biaggio, M. K.: ref, 1939 (1), 2126 (3)
Bialik, R. J.: ref, 1166 (64)
Bialystok, E.: ref, 1071 (2)
Bianchetti, A.: ref, 2516 (61), 2860 (804), 2892 (163)
Bianchi, M.: ref, 272 (253), 2305 (214)
Bibby, P. A.: ref, 2862 (441)
Bibich, A. M.: test, 1741
Biby, E. L.: ref, 2603 (573)
Bice, T. L.: ref, 2497 (110)
Bickel, W. K.: ref, 2076 (26)
Bickerton, W-L.: ref, 2214 (113), 2305 (205)
Bickett, L. R.: ref, 2862 (442)
Bickford-Wimer, P.: ref, 2305 (4)
Bickley, P. G.: ref, 2901 (53)
Bickman, L.: ref, 451 (244,269,270)
Bicknell, H.: ref, 2050 (119)
Biddle, S.: ref, 1367 (2)
Bieberich, A. A.: ref, 451 (230), 2497 (659)
Biedel, D. C.: ref, 2603 (36)
Biederman, J.: ref, 451 (168,187), 1010 (69,70,118), 1092 (11,12,13,14,16), 2305 (121,155,165,215, 221, 222,240), 2813 (140), 2860 (801,802,990,1203), 2862 (308,309,310,394,520,592,611), 2879 (100, 101,102,137,142,187,194,202), 2905 (109)
Biek, M.: ref, 999 (64)
Biel, C. D.: ref, 694 (13), 994 (2), 1060 (2), 1240 (3), 1421 (3), 1425 (1), 1902 (10), 2660 (1), 2694 (3), 2729 (1), 2879 (13), 2905 (4)
Bieliauskas, L.: ref, 1166 (107), 2860 (1079), 2863 (315)
Bieliauskas, L. A.: ref, 1697 (542), 2860 (1264), 2863 (365,380), 2879 (203)
Bieling, P. T.: ref, 272 (145), 790 (25)
Bieman-Copland, S.: ref, 2860 (568)
Biemer, C.: ref, 798 (1)
Biemiller, A.: ref, 389 (12), 861 (3), 2879 (138), 2905 (88)
Bienvenu, M.: test, 185
Bienvenu, M. J.: test, 1309, 1580, 1876, 1882, 2362, 2394
Bienvenu, M. J., Sr.: test, 1292, 1302, 2033
Bierer, B. A.: test, 1987
Bierhals, A. J.: ref, 1166 (173)
Bierman, K. L.: ref, 451 (261), 681 (23), 2211 (48)
Biernat, M.: ref, 908 (3), 2603 (73,241), 2749 (6)
Biersdorf, K. C.: test, 2116
Biesanz, J. C.: ref, 134 (23)
Bifulco, A.: ref, 2050 (59,18)
Bigby, Havis, & Associates, Inc.: test, 186, 2347
Bigelow, G. E.: ref, 2218 (85), 2603 (368), 2519 (23), 2520 (24)

Bigelow, L. B.: ref, 776 (15), 1093 (11,47), 1962 (17), 2193 (16), 2288 (40), 2813 (77), 2860 (460), 2863 (128) 2892 (122)
Biggar, H.: ref, 272 (354), 337 (190), 472 (222), 2211 (52)
Biggs, J.: test, 1466, 2540; rev, 244, 392; ref, 1466 (4), 2540 (1)
Bigler, E. D.: test, 2701; ref, 1164 (10,22,32,83), 1903 (36), 2497 (122), 2860 (245,278,332,540,793,803), 2863 (73), 2879 (39), 2892 (160)
Bigler, R. S.: ref, 1903 (108), 1991 (101)
Bigley, G. A.: ref, 1862 (2)
Bihrle, A.: ref, 2892 (47)
Bihun, J. T.: ref, 1903 (121)
Bijlsma, J. W. J.: ref, 2497 (620)
Bilder, R. M.: ref, 1093 (41), 2305 (70) 2860 (333)
Bilgic, R.: ref, 1701 (54)
Billard, C.: ref, 2862 (329)
Bille, H.: ref, 2497 (252)
Biller, E. F.: ref, 413 (11), 2282 (4)
Biller, J. A.: ref, 451 (195), 2497 (629)
Billing, L.: ref, 301 (36), 1097 (12), 1410 (2)
Billingham, R. E.: ref, 2759 (1)
Billings, S. W.: ref, 694 (45)
Billingslea, F. Y.: rev, 301
Bills, M. A.: rev, 10, 58, 533, 1312
Billups, A.: ref, 404 (32), 665 (59)
Bilsky, L. H.: ref, 2862 (75)
Binder, A.: ref, 270 (8), 1216 (66), 2189 (5)
Binder, J. C.: ref, 2682 (9)
Binder, J. R.: ref, 2860 (1041)
Binder, L. M.: test, 2011; ref, 1697 (260)
Binder, R. L.: ref, 2850 (2)
Bindman, M.: ref, 2862 (704)
Bindschaedler, C.: ref, 2226 (6), 2860 (714), 2863 (212)
Bindseil, K. D.: ref, 1166 (90), 2218 (44)
Binetti, G.: ref, 2516 (61), 2860 (804), 2892 (163)
Bingham, R. P.: ref, 2835 (2)
Binik, Y. M.: ref, 793 (11), 1697 (42), 2077 (4)
Binkoff, J. A.: ref, 134 (6,8,14), 1661 (12,23)
Binks, M.: ref, 272 (310)
Binney, V.: ref, 1011 (2)
Binns, H. J.: ref, 451 (86), 1613 (2)
Biofeedback Certification Institute of America: test, 310
Biondi, M.: ref, 1166 (217), 1697 (204)
Bioty, S.: ref, 2892 (235)
Bioty, S. M.: ref, 2017 (14,15), 2432 (25,30), 2892 (195,196,236), 2924 (3)
Birati, A.: ref, 302 (3), 1693 (2), 1697 (366), 2163 (192), 2217 (3)
Birbaumer, N.: ref, 2860 (684,835,1137), 2863 (241)
Birch, L. B.: rev, 389, 952, 2485
Birch, S. H.: ref, 1659 (11)
Birchler, G. R.: ref, 1661 (13,71)
Bird, A.: ref, 1758 (77), 2163 (298)
Bird, E.: test, 964
Bird, E. K.: ref, 1240 (22), 1379 (38), 1903 (230), 2485 (110), 2657 (11)
Bird, G. W.: ref, 2858 (23)
Bird, H.: ref, 451 (14)
Bird, H. R.: ref, 451 (98), 1903 (533)
Bird, J.: ref, 349 (22), 350 (25), 2862 (311), 2864 (76)
Bird, K.: ref, 1079 (39), 1241 (5)
Bird, K. D.: ref, 2860 (841)
Bird, M.: ref, 1058 (9), 2599 (11,34), 2860 (431,1042)
Birdseye, A. T.: ref, 565 (1)
Birdsong, B. D.: ref, 272 (346), 2603 (575)
Birenbaum, M.: ref, 538 (6), 644 (3)
Birk, T. J.: ref, 1338 (31), 1686 (3)
Birkinbine, J.: ref, 2813 (123)
Birmaher, B.: ref, 4 (11), 272 (259), 1166 (210), 2305 (216,245)
Birtchnell, J.: ref, 272 (5), 999 (25), 1079 (1), 1166 (2), 1291 (1), 1294 (1), 1697 (53)
Bisanz, J.: ref, 1902 (64), 2485 (159)
Bischof, G. P.: ref, 1000 (22), 1010 (71)
Bischoff, H. G. W.: rev, 844
Bischoff, L. G.: rev, 355, 452, 877, 1220, 1879
Biscoe, M.: test, 1516
Bish, A.: ref, 272 (106,152), 1011 (3), 1987 (14), 2497 (442,470,538,247)
Bishara, S. N.: ref, 199 (13), 1745 (35)
Bishop, D.: test, 2662; ref, 350 (12,16), 1240 (23), 2163 (141,152)
Bishop, D. R.: ref, 1164 (41), 1697 (205), 2402 (17)
Bishop, D. V. M.: ref, 349 (22), 350 (25), 540 (14,24), 2163 (349), 2862 (95,311,593,703), 2864 (76)
Bishop, K.: ref, 641 (8), 803 (1,2), 1653 (19,20), 1758 (87), 2163 (325), 2189 (3,4), 2226 (22), 2382 (29,30), 2485 (155,156), 2813 (82,83), 2863 (382)
Bishop, S. B.: ref, 2603 (26)
Bishop, S. J.: ref, 540 (24), 2163 (349), 2382 (24), 2862 (703)
Bishop, S. L.: ref, 2652 (10)
Bishop, S. R.: ref, 2497 (520)
Bishop-Clark, C.: ref, 998 (87), 1755 (51)
Bishop-Marbury, A.: ref, 2731 (1), 2860 (257), 2879 (34) 2901 (17)
Bishry, A.: ref, 999 (98), 2050 (92)
Bishry, Z.: ref, 2862 (415)
Biskin, B. H.: rev, 1157, 1464, 2496
Bisnaire, L. M. C.: ref, 1216 (5)
Bisno, A.: test, 2459
Bissette, G.: ref, 1697 (369), 2860 (778)
Bitner, B. L.: ref, 2856 (4)
Bittner, M. T.: ref, 695 (2), 2514 (1)
Bittner, R. H.: rev, 1180, 1632
Bivens, A.: ref, 1687 (39)
Biver, F.: ref, 1166 (181)
Bizot, E. B.: ref, 239 (1), 1701 (27), 1702 (2), 2797 (6), 2835 (12)
Bjerre, B. D.: ref, 337 (13)
Bjerstedt, A.: rev, 908, 2248
Bjorck, J. P.: ref, 2497 (611)
Bjorge, H.: ref, 1079 (83)

Björgen, I. A.: ref, 1164 (148), 2226 (23), 2860 (1268)
Björgvinsson, T.: ref, 256 (3)
Bjorklund, D. F.: ref, 1592 (3,17)
Bjorkman, S.: ref, 2039 (7)
Bjorn, J.: ref, 462 (18), 1661 (43)
Blacher, J.: ref, 2813 (137)
Blachman, B. A.: ref, 1903 (63,144,231,430), 2862 (236), 2879 (145), 2905 (11,30)
Black, A.: ref, 272 (265), 1166 (180)
Black, C. D.: ref, 1590 (32)
Black, D. D.: test, 2323
Black, F. W.: ref, 2860 (374), 2863 (97)
Black, J. D.: rev, 1439, 2581, 2716
Black, J. L.: ref, 769 (8), 2862 (729), 2879 (233)
Black, K. C.: ref, 2862 (312)
Black, K. J.: ref, 272 (254), 1166 (174)
Black, M.: ref, 1216 (27), 1770 (8)
Black, M. M.: ref, 270 (8,31), 337 (60,175), 448 (10), 1216 (36,66,103), 1770 (12), 2189 (5), 2860 (1303)
Black, S.: ref, 2516 (49), 2860 (712), 2863 (210), 2892 (138)
Black, S. A.: ref, 272 (70), 893 (12)
Black, S. E.: ref, 376 (31), 776 (47), 776 (60), 2863 (423)
Black-Olien, D.: ref, 791 (6)
Blackburn, D. W.: ref, 1072 (2), 1240 (1), 2862 (3)
Blackburn, I. M.: ref, 272 (6), 1166 (3), 2860 (515), 2892 (86)
Blackburn, I-M.: ref, 272 (54), 999 (95), 2497 (180,373)
Blacker, C. V. R.: ref, 2305 (217)
Blacker, J.: ref, 451 (251), 1010 (133), 1991 (106)
Blacker, K. H.: ref, 2603 (198)
Blackett, P.: ref, 337 (106), 472 (139), 2498 (54)
Blackford, S.: ref, 2860 (243), 2863 (61)
Blackford, S. D.: ref, 2860 (229), 2863 (59)
Blackman, D.: ref, 1590 (60)
Blackman, J. A.: test, 1909; ref, 342 (2), 815 (8), 1240 (10), 1612 (28), 2864 (32)
Blackman, M. C.: ref, 2218 (30)
Blackmon, R. C.: ref, 202 (1), 324 (3), 331 (1), 798 (6), 994 (3), 1424 (1), 1903 (97), 2190 (2), 2524 (1), 2660 (3), 2695 (10), 2710 (2), 2768 (7)
Blackmore, A. M.: ref, 1903 (515), 2879 (195)
Blackson, T. C.: ref, 451 (30), 1902 (65) 2010 (15), 2862 (443)
Blackwell, J.: ref, 2076 (105)
Blackwell, K. T.: ref, 2892 (247)
Blackwell, M.: rev, 1997, 2779
Blackwell, M. W.: rev, 281, 1455
Blackwood, A.: ref, 2248 (7)
Blackwood, D. H. R.: ref, 2163 (142), 2860 (515), 2892 (86)
Bladin, P. F.: ref, 1744 (8), 1758 (6), 2163 (33), 2860 (520), 2863 (150,340)
Bladon, R. A. W.: ref, 2860 (66), 2863 (21)
Blaha, J.: ref, 1866 (42), 2860 (1043), 2862 (444), 2864 (111)
Blaich, T.: ref, 1903 (271), 2905 (57)
Blain, M. D.: ref, 272 (140), 1694 (5), 1701 (26)
Blair, C.: ref, 1079 (35)
Blair, R. J. R.: ref, 350 (49)
Blair-Greiner, A.: ref, 2305 (138)
Blais, M. A.: ref, 1697 (387), 2247 (82), 2247 (122)
Blake, D. D.: ref, 2603 (369)
Blake, J.: ref, 1653 (12)
Blake, J. D.: ref, 1697 (479)
Blake, P. C.: ref, 694 (46)
Blake, P. Y.: ref, 1164 (86), 2892 (164)
Blake, R.: ref, 2862 (121)
Blake, S. E.: ref, 2247 (51)
Blakeley, R. W.: test, 2332
Blakely, W. A.: ref, 2860 (289)
Blakemore, C. B.: rev, 301
Blalock, J. A.: ref, 1697 (423)
Blamire, A. M.: ref, 350 (52), 1903 (577), 2163 (355), 2860 (1413), 2862 (730)
Blanc-Garin, J.: ref, 2860 (615)
Blanchard, E. B.: ref, 272 (131), 1338 (6), 1697 (23), 2497 (19,20,270,339,427,504), 2603 (7), 2863 (144)
Blanchard, J. J.: ref, 1000 (60), 2288 (33), 2305 (92), 2860 (569), 2863 (164), 2892 (102)
Blanchard, J. L.: ref, 2863 (165), 2892 (103)
Blanchard, K.: test, 1436
Blanchard-Fields, F.: ref, 298 (43), 2380 (1), 2858 (24), 2860 (236,570)
Blanco, C.: ref, 1697 (470)
Blanco, C. R.: ref, 272 (150,151), 2402 (37,54), 2497 (537), 2599 (26), 2860 (798,1037,1038), 2863 (308), 2892 (161)
Blanco, M. J.: ref, 745 (8), 2163 (143)
Blanco-Jerez, C.: ref, 1697 (470)
Bland, L. C.: ref, 2295 (3)
Bland, S. H.: ref, 2603 (517)
Blaney, N. T.: ref, 2076 (8)
Blaney, P. H.: ref, 1745 (48), 2771 (34)
Blank, L.: ref, 790 (29)
Blank, M.: test, 2044
Blank, M. K.: ref, 1959 (3)
Blankenship, V.: ref, 908 (5)
Blankestijn, P. J.: ref, 1697 (186), 2497 (189)
Blankstein, K. R.: ref, 790 (20)
Blanton, P. D.: ref, 2879 (4)
Blaske, D. M.: ref, 2211 (36), 2603 (337)
Blasutti, B.: ref, 694 (40), 1697 (193), 2497 (210), 2704 (8)
Blatt, J.: ref, 1903 (468), 2485 (203), 2813 (120)
Blatt, S. D.: ref, 451 (169), 880 (1), 1216 (96)
Blatt, S. J.: test, 215, 790; ref, 272 (342), 298 (136), 472 (55), 790 (7,19), 1093 (83), 2214 (32), 2247 (73) 2451 (1), 2603 (335,574), 2749 (48), 2860 (736)
Blattberg, K. J.: ref, 1582 (9)
Blatter, D. D.: ref, 1164 (83), 2860 (793,803), 2892 (160)
Blau, A. D.: ref, 1058 (8), 2125 (13), 2163 (174), 2860 (682)

Blau, B. I.: ref, 298 (113)
Blau, G.: ref, 1348 (7), 1701 (33,44), 1702 (3,4), 1866 (2)
Blaufarb, H.: ref, 2879 (113)
Blaylock, R. L.: ref, 994 (20), 2190 (4)
Blazer, J. A.: test, 2615
Blazina, C.: ref, 2497 (539), 2553 (3)
Bleau, R.: ref, 2497 (540)
Bleecker, M. L.: ref, 1164 (15), 1697 (37), 2226 (2,17), 2860 (110,158,1225), 2863 (42)
Bleeker, M. L.: ref, 272 (7), 1697 (24), 2860 (82)
Bleich, A.: ref, 863 (32), 2603 (146), 2603 (161)
Bleijenberg, G.: ref, 2497 (529)
Bleiker, E. M. A.: ref, 2497 (227)
Bleile, K.: ref, 994 (31), 1903 (427), 2768 (31), 2862 (405)
Bleile, K. M.: ref, 2045 (3)
Blenkin, H.: ref, 1079 (66), 1590 (59), 2218 (55)
Blennerhassett, L.: ref, 301 (37), 1379 (39), 2163 (144)
Blesch, G.: test, 3
Bless, E.: ref, 2519 (39), 2520 (40)
Blevins- Knabe, B.: ref, 1216 (61)
Blin, J.: ref, 2860 (244), 2863 (62)
Blinde, E. M.: ref, 1965 (39)
Blinkhorn, S.: test, 119, 1712, 2087
Blint, A.: ref, 2892 (245)
Blioner, E.: ref, 234 (1)
Bliss, L. B.: ref, 615 (42)
Bliss, L. S.: test, 2331, 2382; rev, 240, 2189, 2233, 2801; ref, 559 (1), 821 (2), 994 (32), 1903 (428), 2694 (18), 2704 (34), 2725 (5), 2768 (32), 2862 (406), 2911 (4)
Blissett, S. E.: ref, 1619 (9), 2771 (41)
Blitchington, W. P.: test, 2649
Bliwise, D. L.: ref, 303 (13) 1697 (388), 2218 (4), 2860 (1191)
Blixt, S.: rev, 886, 1472
Blizard, R.: ref, 1758 (77), 2163 (298)
Bloch, J. S.: test, 1041
Bloch, S.: ref, 335 (12), 1010 (100,101)
Block, J.: test, 365, 373; rev, 999; ref, 365 (2), 373 (14), 373 (26,32,34), 926 (19), 2042 (2), 2860 (1044)
Block, J. H.: ref, 365 (2)
Block, J. R.: ref, 2749 (30)
Block, M.: ref, 777 (1), 1991 (85)
Block, M. E.: rev, 805, 968
Block, M. R.: ref, 272 (221)
Block, P.: ref, 272 (17), 1166 (25), 2305 (25)
Block-Pedego, A.: test, 2311
Blockx, P.: ref, 1166 (77,127)
Bloem, G. M.: ref, 272 (79), 1166 (187)
Bloem, W. D.: ref, 1697 (68,228), 2050 (5), 2402 (44)
Bloise, C. G. R.: ref, 2873 (27)
Blondeau, R.: ref, 1216 (32), 1903 (182)
Blonder, L. X.: ref, 2860 (80), 2863 (23), 2892 (8)
Blondis, T. A.: ref, 2813 (107)
Blonk, R. W. B.: ref, 451 (99), 2603 (178)
Blood, D. J.: ref, 2497 (228)
Blood, G. W.: ref, 2498 (29)
Blood, I.: ref, 2382 (20)
Blood, I. M.: ref, 2498 (29)
Blood, L.: ref, 694 (66)
Bloom, B. L.: ref, 1000 (40), 2603 (527)
Bloom, B. S.: rev, 617
Bloom, F. A.: ref, 2860 (666)
Bloom, L.: rev, 817, 894
Bloom, L. A.: rev, 286, 895
Bloom, R. L.: ref, 2860 (432)
Bloomer, J.: test, 268
Bloomer, K.: ref, 1803 (1), 2497 (386)
Bloomer, R. A.: test, 320
Bloomer, R. H.: test, 2180
Bloomquist, M. J.: ref, 451 (18), 280 (2), 681 (72), 681 (84)
Bloomsma, D. I.: ref, 451 (206)
Blouin, D. C.: ref, 999 (170)
Blount, R. L.: ref, 451 (189), 1000 (105), 2497 (465)
Bloxam, B. M.: rev, 2417
Bloxham, G.: ref, 337 (51)
Bloxom, B.: rev, 1036, 1939
Bluechardt, M. H.: ref, 353 (15), 1386 (14), 2862 (313), 2901 (54)
Bluemlein, L. A.: ref, 2227 (2), 2860 (179), 2863 (48)
Blum, C. R.: ref, 404 (8), 2497 (12)
Blum, G. S.: test, 317
Blum, I. H.: ref, 2029 (2)
Blum, L. H.: test, 624
Blum, M.: test, 1551
Blum, M. L.: rev, 1703, 2797
Blumenfeld, P. C.: ref, 665 (8), 1657 (5)
Blumenstein, E.: ref, 2862 (426)
Blumenthal, J. A.: rev, 1338, 1412; ref, 272 (336), 303 (1,2), 791 (2), 1164 (23), 1338 (11), 1740 (3), 2218 (116), 2497 (21,104,275,436,664), 2516 (2,30), 2603 (8,83), 2860 (81,237,507), 2863 (146)
Blumenthal, R. S.: ref, 2496 (6)
Blumenthal, T. D.: ref, 2497 (230)
Blundo, C.: ref, 2860 (211), 2892 (25)
Blustein, D. L.: ref, 200 (1,3), 1965 (6)
Bø, K.: ref, 1164 (148), 2226 (23), 2860 (1268)
Boada, R.: ref, 2873 (12)
Boake, C.: ref, 376 (2,3), 2226 (7)
Board, B. J.: ref, 1274 (1)
Board of Education of the City of Chicago: test, 446
Boardman, A. F.: ref, 1697 (402)
Boardman, A. P.: ref, 2050 (68)
Boatman, D.: ref, 2860 (805,1226)
Boaz, T. L.: ref, 1697 (35)
Bobholz, J. H.: ref, 2860 (748)
Bobko, P.: ref, 2757 (1)
Boccellari, A.: ref, 2858 (65)
Boccio, A.: ref, 326 (5), 2288 (21), 2289 (13), 2305 (66), 2892 (52), 2905 (24)
Boccio-Smith, A.: ref, 1164 (60), 1697 (275), 2305 (98)
Boch, M.: ref, 777 (1), 1991 (85)

Bocherding, S.: ref, 1697 (172), 2497 (174)
Bochner, S.: ref, 1466 (8)
Bocian, K. M.: ref, 301 (56), 681 (74,75,94), 2163 (273), 2452 (14,15,19,24), 2607 (1), 2862 (484,511,512,622,724), 2879 (163,173,174,207,231)
Bodden, J. L.: rev, 398, 399, 1419
Bode, J.: ref, 265 (10), 624 (20), 1095 (27), 1379 (57), 1903 (301), 2485 (146), 2864 (69)
Bode, S. G.: ref, 2860 (979)
Bodenhamer, R.: ref, 2497 (497)
Boder, E.: test, 322
Bodfish, J. W.: ref, 4 (16)
Bodker, B. K.: ref, 66 (1), 2077 (3)
Bodkin, J. A.: ref, 1166 (91), 2076 (142)
Boehm, A. E.: test, 323, 324, 565; rev, 346
Boehnlein, J. K.: ref, 2305 (79)
Boekamp, J. R.: ref, 1758 (34), 2860 (806)
Boekman, L. F.: ref, 337 (114)
Boelens, H.: ref, 2813 (121)
Boenink, A. D.: ref, 1166 (175)
Boer, D. P.: test, 2395
Boer, F.: ref, 451 (31)
Boer, H.: ref, 4 (15)
Boergers, J.: ref, 472 (232)
Boeringa, J. A.: ref, 1697 (458)
Boersma, F. J.: test, 1916
Boes, J. L.: ref, 273 (31), 337 (88,89,113), 1093 (98), 1687 (30,31,32)
Boetsch, E. A.: ref, 337 (129), 1902 (82), 2163 (264), 2879 (156)
Bogaert, A. F.: ref, 999 (148), 1965 (72)
Bogart, C. J.: ref, 462 (15)
Bogdanoff, B.: ref, 376 (32), 2860 (1400), 2863 (424)
Boger, R.: ref, 1216 (33)
Bogerts, B.: ref, 1093 (41), 2305 (70)
Bogg, J.: ref, 1824 (4)
Boggiano, A. K.: ref, 615 (21), 1115 (6)
Boggio, R. M.: ref, 451 (138)
Boggs, K. R.: ref, 380 (1)
Boggs, S. R.: ref, 272 (376), 863 (93), 997 (30), 1889 (19), 1903 (580), 2230 (4), 2497 (200), 2752 (2), 2899 (13)
Bohac, D. L.: ref, 2860 (739)
Bohan, T. P.: ref, 815 (20), 1612 (65), 1612 (68), 2813 (88), 2862 (317)
Bohle, P.: ref, 998 (133), 1079 (102)
Bohlin, G.: ref, 2039 (11)
Bohn, M. J.: ref, 135 (2), 372 (83), 1661 (38), 1697 (389)
Bohnen, N. I.: ref, 2516 (20)
Bohon, L. M.: ref, 694 (47)
Bohra, N.: ref, 681 (5), 2864 (21)
Boican, B.: ref, 2860 (830)
Boisse, M.-F.: ref, 2860 (1375)
Boivin, M.: ref, 472 (70)
Boivin, M. J.: ref, 124 (1), 1164 (24), 2227 (2), 2860 (179), 2863 (48)
Bolado, A. L. O.: ref, 1697 (54), 2878 (1)
Bolden, S. H.: ref, 1755 (15)
Bolding, D. J.: ref, 1991 (20)
Bolduc, P. L.: ref, 2050 (9)
Bolen, L. M.: ref, 462 (9), 1386 (21), 1414 (3), 1462 (1,2,3), 2862 (577,737), 2901 (91,111)
Bolger, N.: ref, 791 (4), 998 (26,88), 2076 (107)
Bolgert, F.: ref, 2517 (1), 2860 (130,527)
Boliek, C. A.: rev, 301, 1690; ref, 1903 (15,18,40), 2860 (125), 2862 (34,52,84), 2901 (3,8)
Bolk, J. H.: ref, 2050 (49,134)
Bolk, R. J.: ref, 1991 (53)
Boll, T.: test, 471, 811
Boll, T. J.: test, 2405; ref, 1135 (27), 1164 (185), 1697 (592), 2247 (101), 2402 (46,71), 2517 (8), 2599 (41), 2860 (986,1412), 2863 (430)
Bolla, K. I.: ref, 1164 (15), 2226 (2), 2860 (158), 2863 (42)
Bolla-Wilson, K.: ref, 272 (7), 1697 (24,37), 2860 (82,110)
Boller, F.: ref, 2163 (156), 2225 (2),2860 (23,605,799,930,1375), 2863 (176,178,230,297), 2873 (3)
Bollinger, R.: test, 2162
Bollman, S. R.: ref, 1000 (62), 1580 (5)
Bolocofsky, D. N.: ref, 2230 (3)
Bologna, N. B.: rev, 687, 816
Bolser, C.: test, 647
Bolter, J. F.: ref, 2860 (493), 2863 (140)
Bolton, B.: test, 936, 2924, 2928; rev, 86, 152, 275, 372, 1313, 2107, 2927; ref, 404 (24), 1702 (1), 1790 (11), 1954 (1)
Bolton, B. F.: rev, 828, 1957, 2417
Bolton, D. L.: rev, 401, 1276, 1396, 2747
Bolton, P.: ref, 350 (13,24), 901 (1), 1485 (33), 1653 (13,1721), 2163 (145,195), 2228 (11,16), 2860 (334,427,571,721,795), 2862 (283), 2864 (105)
Bolton, S. O.: test, 1284
Bolwig, T.: ref, 272 (201)
Bolyard, B.: ref, 2710 (4)
Bomba, C.: ref, 994 (35)
Bombardier, C. H.: ref, 1661 (67), 1697 (206)
Bonaccorso, S.: ref, 1166 (217)
Bonaccorsy, C.: ref, 1164 (15), 2226 (2), 2860 (158), 2863 (42)
Bonanno, G. A.: ref, 2603 (336)
Bonavita, J.: ref, 376 (32), 2860 (1400), 2863 (424)
Boncoeur-Martel, M. P.: ref, 231 (1), 303 (32), 2226 (42), 2227 (61), 2599 (43), 2863 (431), 2892 (307)
Bond, A.: ref, 998 (93), 2050 (116), 2497 (451)
Bond, A. J.: ref, 2497 (229,428)
Bond, C. L.: ref, 861 (4), 2902 (3); rev, 861
Bond, L.: ref, 451 (32)
Bond, L. A.: ref, 337 (44), 2860 (192)
Bond, M. H.: ref, 2218 (66), 2756 (1)
Bond, N. A., Jr.: test, 865
Bond, S.: ref, 2485 (19), 2768 (4), 2813 (4), 2860 (142), 2892 (17)
Bondareff, W.: ref, 2860 (159)

Bonder, B. R.: ref, 1991 (46)
Bonderman, I. R.: ref, 214 (5)
Bondi, C. M.: ref, 272 (342), 2603 (574)
Bondi, M.: ref, 2860 (845)
Bondi, M. W.: ref, 376 (15), 776 (25), 1164 (145), 2860 (1244) 2862 (601), 2892 (202,266)
Bone, G. H. A.: ref, 2305 (27)
Bone, J.: ref, 2862 (205), 2879 (57)
Boni, R.: ref, 1216 (29)
Boninelli, I.: test, 2458
Bonjour, M.: ref, 1166 (101), 1661 (54)
Bonne, O.: ref, 337 (165,166), 1166 (92)
Bonneau, R. H.: ref, 337 (10), 2076 (57)
Bonner, M.: ref, 472 (13), 2498 (7)
Bonner, M. W.: ref, 117 (3)
Bonner, R. L.: ref, 1010 (1), 2065 (1)
Bonnet, A-M.: ref, 776 (54), 776 (63)
Bonnet, J-P.: ref, 2163 (181)
Bonneville, F.: ref, 298 (44)
Bonshek, A. J.: ref, 2065 (27), 2497 (461)
Bonta, J.: test, 1487
Bonta, J. L.: test, 1486
Bonte, F. J.: ref, 1164 (65),1697 (303), 2860 (648), 2863 (188)
Bontrager, A.: ref, 451 (218), 2452 (20), 2485 (233), 2813 (151)
Bonvillian, J. D.: ref, 1072 (2), 1240 (1), 2862 (3)
Boodoo, G. M.: rev, 835
Bookbinder, G. E.: test, 2281
Booke, C.: ref, 1740 (4)
Booker, B. L.: ref, 298 (37), 999 (20)
Booker, G.: test, 325
Booker, I. A.: rev, 1767
Bookman, J. R.: ref, 821 (1), 1386 (1), 1902 (4)
Bookstein, F. L.: ref, 997 (24)
Boomsma, F.: ref, 1697 (186), 2497 (189)
Boone, D.: ref, 272 (99), 273 (11), 1697 (390), 2559 (7)
Boone, D. E.: ref, 1697 (261), 2559 (4), 2860 (160,433,807)
Boone, D. R.: rev, 199, 2008, 2426
Boone, J. R.: ref, 2873 (62)
Boone, K.: ref, 1164 (182), 2227 (6), 2516 (13), 2516 (120), 2860 (286), 2863 (76), 2892 (37,302)
Boone, K. B.: ref, 1166 (136), 2227 (29), 2516 (49,81), 2860 (712,1117,1150), 2863 (210,331,341), 2892 (138,231,246)
Boone, M. L.: ref, 2516 (70)
Booth, B.: ref, 272 (314), 998 (131)
Booth, B. M.: ref, 272 (77)
Booth, J.A. G.: test, 387
Booth, J. R.: ref, 592 (50)
Booth, S. B.: test, 1230
Booth-Kewley, S.: ref, 2218 (14)
Boothby, J. L.: ref, 272 (384)
Boothroyd, R. A.: rev, 697, 1128, 1339, 1883
Borchardt, C. M.: ref, 272 (100,101), 472 (71,158,159), 2214 (35,90,91), 2498 (30), 2603 (439)
Bordeaux, J. D.: ref, 1135 (12), 2813 (67), 2862 (274), 2879 (84)
Borden, J. W.: ref, 998 (81), 2497 (308,309), 2603 (242,309)
Borden, M. C.: ref, 2813 (111)
Borden, S. L.: ref, 1092 (4,18), 1096 (2), 1902 (19), 2712 (1), 2862 (110), 2879 (25,171), 2905 (98)
Borden, W.: ref, 2858 (10)
Bordieri, J. E.: ref, 1444 (1), 2797 (4,5)
Bordin, E. S.: rev, 218, 908, 1223, 1312, 1790, 2716
Bordiun, C. M.: ref, 2211 (36), 2603 (337)
Bordnick, P. S.: ref, 1021 (35), 2603 (365)
Borduin, C. M.: ref, 771 (10)
Borenstein, B. D.: ref, 999 (18)
Borenstein, M.: ref, 1093 (35,75), 2288 (64), 2305 (70,170)
Borge, A. I. H.: ref, 1612 (64)
Borgeat, F.: ref, 298 (165)
Borgen, F. H.: test, 1695, 1790; rev, 352, 1243, 2527, 2793; ref, 1790 (10,12,15)
Borgen, W. A.: ref, 272 (153)
Borger, N.: ref, 681 (68)
Borgers, S. B.: ref, 1000 (50), 2497 (598), 2879 (185)
Borghgraef, M.: ref, 2862 (65), 2864 (8)
Borgquist, L.: ref, 2050 (26)
Borgstädt, S.: ref, 1166 (121)
Borgstedt, A. D.: ref, 681 (48), 1902 (55,88), 2862 (500,736), 2879 (234)
Borkenau, P.: ref, 2218 (22)
Borko, H.: rev, 2776, 2869
Borkovec, T. D.: ref, 1745 (2), 2497 (44,389)
Borkowski, J. G.: ref, 448 (22), 1592 (2), 1619 (4), 1903 (500), 2860 (1071), 2862 (26,386), 2879 (133)
Borland, J. H.: ref, 56 (2), 615 (15), 853 (15) 1337 (2), 1386 (6), 1903 (232), 2485 (111), 2681 (1), 2682 (6)
Borm, G. F.: ref, 376 (12), 2516 (35,75,87), 2860 (584,1007,1193), 2892 (211)
Borman, C.: rev, 311, 1817
Borman, W. C.: rev, 1559, 2267; ref, 180 (27)
Borman-Spurell, E.: ref, 2603 (433)
Bormann, C. A.: ref, 134 (25)
Bornholt, L. J.: ref, 26 (1)
Bornstein, M. H.: ref, 1333 (3), 1903 (449), 2229 (7)
Bornstein, R. A.: rev, 85, 456, 772, 776, 1690, 1774, 2040; ref, 681 (16), 1164 (73), 2860 (722), 2892 (143)
Bornstein, R. F.: ref, 1697 (503), 2247 (12,52,105, 112,123), 2603 (470), 2860 (238,1227)
Borochov, O.: ref, 298 (13)
Borod, J. C.: ref, 199 (7,9), 776 (8,11,12), 1740 (9), 2437 (2), 2860 (83,201,432,434)
Borofsky, G. L.: test, 944; ref, 944 (1)
Boronow, J. J.: ref, 1525 (11), 2860 (248)
Borreca, C.: test, 2891
Borrero, I. M. G.: ref, 2860 (734)
Bors, D. A.: ref, 2163 (103,197)

Borsoi, D.: ref, 2860 (1058)
Borson, A. J.: ref, 776 (48)
Borstelmann, L. J.: rev, 1085
Borstrom, I.: ref, 1903 (570), 2163 (351), 2862 (709)
Borthwick-Duffy, S. A.: ref, 2 (2), 451 (170), 2299 (3), 2813 (53,138)
Bortner, M.: rev, 2, 441, 729, 1671, 2163, 2477, 2478, 2817, 2862
Bortoli, L.: ref, 1021 (30)
Bortolini, V.: ref, 2864 (129)
Borzone de Manrique, A.: ref, 2862 (237)
Bos, H.: ref, 681 (42)
Boscarino, J. Å.: ref, 134 (35)
Boschini, C.: ref, 853 (2)
Bosley, F.: ref, 2497 (22)
Bosman, A. M. T.: ref, 2163 (198)
Bosmans, E.: ref, 1166 (76,78)
Boss, H. B.: ref, 1661 (4)
Bossé, R.: ref, 998 (27), 1697 (86), 2417 (9), 2603 (2,202)
Bostantjopoulou, S.: ref, 272 (363,302), 2860 (1318)
Boswell, D. L.: ref, 2247 (4,55), 2497 (331)
Botel, M.: test, 330
Bothwell, R.: ref, 272 (255), 1166 (176)
Botkin, J. R.: ref, 2497 (618)
Bott, D. A.: ref, 1392 (3), 2862 (112)
Bottge, B. A.: ref, 665 (45)
Botting, N.: ref, 1095 (43), 2163 (316)
Bottini, G.: ref, 2163 (38), 2863 (43)
Bottomley, P. A.: ref, 2860 (502)
Bottoms, B. L.: ref, 451 (194), 1010 (123)
Bottos, M.: ref, 1770 (14)
Botvin, G. J.: ref, 998 (132), 999 (118)
Botwin, M. D.: rev, 122 2218
Boubjerg, D. H.: ref, 2497 (256)
Bouchard, C.: ref, 472 (233), 2214 (138), 863 (84), 2858 (124)
Bouchard, J-P.: ref, 2125 (25), 2860 (1256)
Bouchard, L.: ref, 2917 (3)
Bouchard, S.: ref, 2497 (647)
Bouchard, T. J., Jr.: rev, 263, 838, 2417; ref, 372 (13), 1010 (19), 1701 (4), 1755 (74)
Boucher, B. H.: ref, 1903 (156)
Boucher, J.: ref, 350 (17,18,32)
Boudewyn, A. C.: ref, 272 (289), 2749 (77)
Boudewyns, P.: ref, 1697 (176,306,307)
Boudewyns, P. A.: ref, 1697 (55,78,220,252,359)
Boudigues, J-M.: ref, 2497 (461)
Boudreau, C. A.: ref, 56 (6), 592 (51)
Boudreau, J. W.: ref, 1178 (11)
Bouffard-Bouchard, T.: ref, 1866 (22)
Boughal, T.: ref, 2603 (563)
Bouhuys, A. L.: ref, 272 (79,256,271), 1079 (89), 1166 (48,175,187,190)
Bouhuys, N.: ref, 1166 (111)
Boukydis, C. F. Z.: ref, 1770 (16)
Boulard, N.: ref, 272 (320), 2497 (657), 2603 (553)
Boulet, J. R.: ref, 793 (8), 2860 (295)
Boulton-Lewis, G. M.: ref, 2540 (3)
Bouma, A.: ref, 1405 (31), 2240 (1), 2863 (106)
Bouma, J.: ref, 998 (129)
Bouman, T. K.: ref, 1745 (16)
Boundy, K.: ref, 4 (9)
Bountress, N. G.: rev, 1503
Bourchard, S.: ref, 650 (15), 1093 (97)
Bourg, S.: ref, 1697 (391), 2860 (808)
Bourgeois, A.: ref, 2076 (53), 2519 (24), 2520 (25), 2603 (176)
Bourgeois, M. J.: ref, 2076 (6), 2860 (141)
Bourke, S.: test, 2080
Bourque, T. A.: ref, 2516 (7)
Boutin, P.: ref, 650 (15), 1093 (97)
Boutros, N. N.: ref, 1697 (172), 2497 (174)
Boutselis, M.: ref, 337 (2)
Bouvard, M.: ref, 2111 (2), 2163 (247), 2862 (410)
Bovasso, M.: ref, 2860 (368)
Bovbjerg, D. H.: ref, 2076 (89)
Boveja, M. E.: ref, 1455 (13)
Boverie, P.: ref, 1469 (7)
Bovim, G.: ref, 1164 (87)
Bowden, C. L.: ref, 462 (18), 1661 (43), 2305 (95,166,202), 2603 (220)
Bowden, S.: ref, 1164 (38), 2892 (56)
Bowden, S. C.: ref, 2860 (1228), 2863 (366)
Bowen, D. J.: ref, 1745 (11)
Bowen, F.: ref, 472 (111)
Bowen, J. D.: ref, 776 (58)
Bowen, L.: ref, 2050 (52)
Bowen, R. C.: ref, 2497 (64)
Bowen, S.: ref, 1517 (12), 2305 (201)
Bowen-Jones, K.: ref, 272 (279), 1758 (33,89)
Bower, A.: ref, 2485 (160)
Bower, E. M.: test, 2122
Bower, T. A.: ref, 1661 (59)
Bowers, D.: ref, 2860 (186,1322), 2863 (50)
Bowers, J. E.: rev, 592
Bowers, L.: ref, 1011 (2)
Bowers, M. B., Jr.: ref, 2892 (126)
Bowers, P. G.: ref, 389 (5), 2905 (12,33)
Bowers, T. G.: ref, 301 (34), 303 (5), 2862 (220), 2879 (64)
Bowey, J. A.: ref, 1240 (26), 1903 (233,265,335,516), 2695 (26,34), 2862 (314,594), 2864 (77,130), 2905 (23,55,70)
Bowin, M. J.: ref, 1379 (23,63)
Bowker, A.: ref, 451 (245)
Bowland, J.: ref, 2603 (275), 2858 (71)
Bowlby, D.: ref, 451 (69), 472 (140)
Bowler, A. E.: ref, 1962 (17), 2288 (40), 2305 (87), 2813 (77), 2860 (536,572)
Bowler, D. M.: ref, 2860 (1229)
Bowler, K.: ref, 1093 (37)
Bowles, N. L.: ref, 2860 (573)
Bowling Green State University: test, 2593

Bowman, B. J.: ref, 272 (154), 1010 (119), 2497 (541), 2839 (8), 2858 (125)
Bowman, D.: ref, 1697 (471), 2497 (612), 2603 (440,518)
Bowman, E. S.: ref, 846 (13,18)
Bowman, M. L.: ref, 1582 (2)
Bowman, V.: ref, 1697 (471), 2603 (440)
Box, P.: ref, 1485 (59), 1903 (531), 2485 (227)
Boyatzis, R. E.: test, 64, 1467
Boyce, G. C.: ref, 265 (14), 1259 (1), 2299 (5)
Boyce, P.: ref, 998 (21), 999 (138,190), 1079 (103), 1166 (61)
Boyd, C. P.: ref, 2214 (116), 2230 (15)
Boyd, S.: ref, 1166 (114), 1697 (306), 2497 (561), 2603 (468)
Boyd, V. S.: ref, 1754 (18)
Boye, B.: ref, 1079 (83)
Boye, M. W.: ref, 1661 (80), 1687 (43), 1697 (585), 2553 (5)
Boyer, P.: ref, 272 (126,291), 2603 (539)
Boyer, R.: ref, 2050 (3)
Boyes, D. A.: ref, 694 (29), 2214 (17)
Boyes, M. C.: ref, 771 (15)
Boyette, S.: ref, 1697 (289)
Boyle, C. R.: ref, 694 (72)
Boyle, E. J.: ref, 1469 (4)
Boyle, G. J.: rev, 181, 631, 1345, 1404, 1498, 1959, 2258, 2260; ref, 326 (7), 1647 (2), 1697 (262), 1755 (52), 1959 (1), 2318 (1), 2860 (574)
Boyle, J.: test, 881, 1037
Boyle, J. D.: rev, 1154, 1751
Boyle, J. P.: ref, 952 (1), 1664 (2), 2187 (1)
Boyle, M.: ref, 272 (108), 451 (52), 2864 (81)
Boyle, M. H.: ref, 451 (60,171)
Boyle-Gast, K.: ref, 2905 (18)
Boylin, W. M.: ref, 301 (24), 2247 (28), 2614 (1)
Boys, M.: test, 1865
Boyum, L. A.: ref, 2864 (78)
Boze, M. M.: ref, 2076 (58)
Bozman, A. W.: ref, 2076 (22,106)
Braafladt, N.: ref, 472 (124)
Braaten, E. B.: ref, 272 (257), 2497 (613)
Braaten, S.: test, 293
Braaten, S. L.: ref, 495 (7)
Brabant, M-J.: ref, 1166 (99), 2863 (310)
Brabeck, M. M.: ref, 298 (138)
Bracalente, S.: ref, 2813 (96)
Bracey, G. W.: ref, 592 (77)
Bracha, H. S.: ref, 2288 (40), 2813 (77)
Bracha, S.: ref, 1962 (17)
Brachacki, G. W. Z.: ref, 349 (23)
Brack, C. J.: ref, 2402 (67), 2497 (643)
Brack, G.: ref, 2402 (67), 2497 (643)
Bracken, B. A.: test, 210, 331, 1734, 2792; rev, 488, 1530, 2112, 2252, 2864; ref, 331 (2), 451 (159), 681 (80), 694 (67), 694 (68), 746 (1), 1216 (28), 1734 (1,2,4,6), 1903 (157) 1991 (65,66), 2163 (104), 2361 (2), 2452 (16)
Bracken, J. S.: ref, 1689 (1)
Brackney, B. E.: ref, 1697 (392)
Bracy, C. B.: ref, 2873 (14)
Bradburg, T. N.: ref, 272 (155)
Bradbury, M.: ref, 2603 (279)
Bradbury, T. N.: ref, 272 (122), 999 (75,124)
Bradely, R. H.: ref, 1216 (37,38), 2485 (112,113)
Braden, C. J.: ref, 1412 (1)
Braden, J. P.: rev, 2240, 2862, 2864
Bradford, E. G.: rev, 1053
Bradford, E. J. G.: rev, 2402
Bradford, J. M. W.: ref, 793 (8), 2860 (295)
Bradley, B.: ref, 2076 (66)
Bradley, B. P.: ref, 2497 (372,429)
Bradley, B. S.: ref, 1903 (150)
Bradley, C. L.: ref, 2218 (119)
Bradley, D. C.: ref, 2863 (190)
Bradley, J. M.: rev, 1758, 2732
Bradley, L.: test, 189; ref, 350 (1), 2860 (764,1059), 2864 (10)
Bradley, R. H.: test, 1216; rev, 1085; ref, 451 (33), 1079 (80), 1216 (1,39,40,41,61,90,91), 1903 (234,506, 510), 2485 (114,115220)
Bradley, S. J.: ref, 272 (258), 451 (241), 853 (13), 893 (42), 1405 (39), 1903 (517), 2247 (48), 2862 (595)
Bradley, T. B.: rev, 391
Bradley, V. A.: ref, 1758 (42), 2193 (41), 2860 (900), 2863 (270) 2892 (189)
Bradley-Johnson, S.: test, 193, 559; ref, 344 (1), 662 (1), 665 (82)827 (11), 1657 (19), 1728 (2), 1903 (418)
Bradley-Klug, K. L.: ref, 681 (97)
Bradlye, R. H.: ref, 1216 (97), 2218 (84)
Bradshaw, C.: test, 1516; ref, 2603 (564)
Bradshaw, C. M.: ref, 2163 (193), 2860 (542,770), 2892 (92)
Bradshaw, J. L.: ref, 1164 (108), 1758 (23,88,101), 2860 (608)
Brady, B. A.: ref, 2813 (110)
Brady, D. R.: ref, 2860 (1216), 2879 (190)
Brady, F.: ref, 1140 (41)
Brady, G. F.: ref, 1348 (3)
Brady, K. T.: ref, 2519 (49), 2520 (49)
Brady, M. J.: ref, 2076 (72)
Brady, M. P.: ref, 1067 (1) 1903 (380), 2813 (97)
Brady, S.: ref, 1503 (2), 1903 (19) 2163 (21) 2905 (2)
Braet, C.: ref, 451 (172)
Braff, D.: ref, 2076 (123), 2247 (93,94), 2305 (151), 2860 (643), 2892 (120)
Braff, D. L.: ref, 1093 (13,24), 1164 (25,84), 2288 (30,42,73), 2289 (21,32,59), 2305 (35)
Braff, D. L.: ref, 2860 (239), 2892 (104)
Brage, D.: ref, 1876 (1)
Brailey, K.: ref, 2497 (401)
Braimen, S.: ref, 1093 (21)
Braio, A.: ref, 1470 (4), 2069 (1)
Braith, J. A.: ref, 998 (75,76), 2497 (11), 2603 (282,283), 2858 (17,78,79)

Braithwaite, V.: ref, 462 (7)
Brakefield, J. T.: ref, 1338 (12)
Braley, R. T.: ref, 1755 (69)
Brambilla, F.: ref, 1166 (69)
Bramsen, I.: ref, 1697 (304)
Branch, W. B.: ref, 798 (13,16), 815 (18), 1131 (12), 1379 (43,64), 1903 (244,336), 2724 (7,9), 2862 (243,315) 2870 (4), 2879 (103), 2934 (1)
Brancheu, M.: ref, 2519 (8), 2520 (8)
Brand, B.: ref, 272 (338), 1687 (37)
Brand, C. R.: ref, 838 (18)
Brand, E.: ref, 473 (6) 2230 (18), 2557 (10)
Brand, E. F.: ref, 2497 (430)
Brand, E. F. J. M.: ref, 815 (16), 2862 (278)
Brand, N.: ref, 2076 (164), 2516 (92)
Brand, S.: ref, 472 (24,123), 495 (11) 2214 (14,65)
Branden, A.: test, 2005
Brandl, L.: ref, 324 (4), 624 (6), 1903 (172)
Brandsma, J.: ref, 1697 (220)
Brandt, J.: ref, 815 (19,50), 994 (31), 1164 (175), 1740 (10), 1903 (427), 2226 (27), 2516 (18,32,62,72), 2768 (31), 2860 (514,809,957,963,1158, 1160,1180, 1243), 2862 (405), 2863 (153,171,346,392), 2892 (85,165,203)
Brandt, P.: test, 1947; ref, 1010 (30), 1902 (29), 2862 (155)
Branham, J. D.: ref, 1164 (64), 2212 (2), 2599 (19)
Brannan, A. M.: ref, 337 (130), 451 (269)
Brannick, M. T.: ref, 2497 (137)
Brannigan, G. G.: ref, 301 (27,46,60), 815 (46), 1866 (23), 2407 (4)
Brannock, J. C.: ref, 462 (12), 1405 (26)
Brannon, S. E.: ref, 1697 (40)
Brant, R.: ref, 2603 (192)
Brant- Zawadzki, M.: ref, 1407 (1), 2860 (172)
Brantley, P. J.: test, 760
Brar, J. S.: ref, 2305 (63,133)
Brashares, H. J.: ref, 1178 (10), 1181 (12)
Braskamp, L. A.: test, 1276, 1856, 2922
Brassard, M. R.: rev, 2122
Braswell, J.: rev, 2736; ref, 592 (78), 2031 (7)
Braswell, L.: ref, 681 (84), 1697 (306)
Brattson, A.: ref, 1096 (9), 2668 (1), 2694 (14), 2860 (912)
Braucht, G. N.: ref, 134 (25)
Brauer, H.: ref, 999 (53)
Brauer, S.: ref, 472 (17)
Brault, M.: ref, 1903 (584), 2485 (245)
Braumaghim, J. T.: ref, 1903 (548)
Braun, B. G.: ref, 846 (18), 2860 (1163)
Braun, C. L.: ref, 1404 (8)
Braun, C. M. J.: ref, 926 (10), 1174 (4), 2010 (9), 2010 (19), 2863 (118), 2892 (192)
Braun, J. R.: rev, 777, 2126, 2367
Braungart, J. M.: ref, 2382 (16)
Bravar, L.: ref, 322 (7), 2862 (277)
Braver, B. A.: ref, 1697 (207)
Braver, S. L.: ref, 451 (20), 472 (26,29,145), 1697 (539), 2214 (16,70) 2603 (9)
Braverman, B.: ref, 1697 (407)
Braverman, M.: ref, 1612 (8), 1903 (22), 2813 (1)
Bravo, M.: ref, 451 (14)
Braxton, L. E.: ref, 1697 (530)
Bray, J. H.: ref, 1991 (5)
Bray, M. A.: ref, 2862 (722)
Brayden, R. M.: ref, 2652 (6)
Brayfield, A. H.: rev, 845
Brazelton, T. B.: test, 1770
Brazzelli, M.: ref, 2163 (146), 2768 (24)
Breaux, A. M.: ref, 681 (46)
Brébion, G., : ref, 1166 (177), 2247 (83), 2288 (80), 2289 (66)
Brebner, J.: ref, 999 (173), 2163 (305)
Brebner, J.: ref, 2860 (1182)
Brecht, M.-L.: ref, 2076 (120)
Breckler, S. J.: ref, 2437 (1)
Breda, C.: ref, 451 (269)
Bredart, S.: ref, 2163 (211), 2860 (857) 2863 (251)
Bredenkamp, D.: ref, 2305 (224)
Breeden, S. A.: ref, 1694 (6), 1701 (28), 2797 (7)
Breedin, S. D.: ref, 1903 (567)
Breen, K.: ref, 1903 (235,337), 2163 (147), 2860 (575)
Breen, M. J.: ref, 451 (7)
Breen, M. P.: ref, 472 (112), 681 (59)
Breese, F. H.: test, 1026
Brehaut, J. C.: ref, 2516 (7)
Breier, A.: ref, 1093 (25), 2288 (62), 2516 (34), 2892 (31,105)
Breier, J. I.: ref, 2860 (1230,1231), 2879 (196)
Breisinger, G.: ref, 1697 (285)
Breiter, H. C.: ref, 2227 (26), 2860 (1103)
Breiter, H. J.: ref, 2402 (41)
Breiter, S.: ref, 2226 (27), 2863 (392)
Breitner, J. C. S.: ref, 2860 (957)
Brekke, J. S.: ref, 2305 (75)
Breland, H. M.: ref, 117 (3)
Brelsford, K. A.: ref, 459 (30,36), 1485 (30,42), 1612 (53,74), 1903 (279,382)
Bremer, B.: ref, 1164 (144), 2860 (1242)
Bremner, J. D.: ref, 2863 (232), 2892 (126)
Bremner, M.: ref, 2860 (444)
Bremner, R.: ref, 272 (108), 451 (52), 2485 (19), 2768 (4), 2813 (4), 2860 (142), 2864 (81), 2892 (17)
Brems, C.: ref, 272 (23), 298 (27,137), 448 (8), 770 (1), 853 (7), 1697 (56,472), 2247 (7), 2603 (471)
Brendel, G.: ref, 1166 (141)
Brender, W.: ref, 998 (92)
Brengelman, S.: ref, 665 (78)
Brennan, J.: ref, 998 (18), 2603 (37)
Brennan, M.: ref, 2497 (299), 2860 (1232)
Brennan, M. M.: ref, 2225 (2), 2873 (3)
Brennan, P.: ref, 2050 (78)
Brennan, P. J.: ref, 1181 (22)
Brennan, P. L. : ref, 699 (1), 1181 (21)

Brennan, R. T.: ref, 2497 (424), 2603 (333)
Brenneman, L. M.: ref, 1240 (39), 2657 (27), 2694 (19), 2695 (45), 2725 (6)
Brenner, C.: ref, 486 (3)
Brenner, H. D.: ref, 2288 (6), 2289 (4)
Brenner, K. J.: ref, 771 (7)
Brent, D.: ref, 665 (79), 2305 (245)
Brent, D. A.: ref, 272 (259), 2305 (167,216), 2603 (175)
Brentar, J. T.: ref, 2862 (344)
Brentari, D.: ref, 1164 (174), 1903 (566), 2163 (348), 2731 (7), 2860 (1377), 2863 (413), 2879 (224) 2892 (295)
Breslau, L. D.: ref, 1166 (7), 2305 (16), 2873 (4)
Breslau, N.: ref, 999 (111,149), 1010 (20), 1697 (57), 1903 (44), 2860 (1045), 2862 (445)
Breslin, C.: ref, 1697 (48)
Breslin, F. C.: ref, 272 (89), 1661 (33), 2858 (89)
Bresnick, B.: test, 788
Bressler, S.: ref, 1673 (2)
Brester, C.: ref, 1745 (15)
Breteles, R.: ref, 893 (47)
Breton, F.: ref, 2860 (130)
Brett, M.: ref, 2860 (988), 2863 (291)
Brettle, R. P.: ref, 2860 (453), 2863 (126)
Bretz, R. D., Jr.: ref, 1178 (11)
Bretzing, B. H.: rev, 261
Breuer, P.: ref, 2497 (458)
Brewer, B. W.: ref, 2076 (52)
Brewer, J. H.: test, 305, 2577
Brewer, V. R.: ref, 2862 (596), 2879 (197)
Brewin, C. R.: ref, 272 (55), 2858 (72)
Brewlin, F. C.: ref, 2603 (338)
Brewster, A. L.: ref, 448 (28)
Breyer, M.: ref, 1086 (1)
Breznitz, Z.: ref, 666 (12)
Brian, J. A.: ref, 1903 (450)
Briccetti, K. A.: ref, 1618 (2)
Brice, A.: ref, 2227 (19), 2860 (818), 2863 (236)
Brice, J.: ref, 1104 (13), 2193 (54), 2860 (1109)
Bricháček, V.: ref, 2485 (195), 2862 (460)
Brick, J.: ref, 1661 (19), 1697 (48)
Brickenkamp, R.: test, 860
Bricker, D.: test, 123; ref, 270 (42), 1612 (98)
Bricklin, B.: test, 13, 333, 334, 1879, 1886 1917; rev, 914
Brickman, E.: ref, 2603 (86)
Bridewell, W. B.: ref, 2603 (576)
Bridge, C. A.: ref, 665 (13)
Bridge, J.: ref, 4 (11), 2305 (167,245)
Bridge, T. P.: ref, 1758 (50), 2860 (951)
Bridgeman, B.: ref, 92 (1), 97 (1), 100 (1), 592 (52,78,105), 1115 (7), 2031 (7)
Bridges, A. F.: test, 1185
Bridges, K.: ref, 1079 (46), 2050 (124)
Bridges, M. R.: ref, 2247 (124)
Bridges, M. W.: ref, 1158 (2), 2497 (391)
Bridges, P. K.: ref, 1104 (10), 1758 (51), 2050 (126), 2163 (237), 2193 (45), 2225 (9), 2860 (960)
Bridgewater, E.: test, 146, 2932
Bridgman, L.: ref, 2247 (44)
Brief, A. P.: ref, 1348 (10), 1701 (15,17,45), 2858 (5)
Brier, A.: ref, 451 (116), 2288 (68), 2289 (52), 2862 (475)
Brier, N.: ref, 2860 (576), 2879 (72)
Brier, N. M.: ref, 2247 (115), 2749 (75), 2862 (602) 2879 (200)
Briere, J.: test, 2782; ref, 472 (129)
Brigance, A.: test, 342, 343
Brigance, A. H.: test, 339, 340, 341, 344, 345, 346, 347, 2213
Briggs, K. C.: test, 1755
Briggs, L.: ref, 2603 (519)
Briggs, S.: test, 2449; ref, 1697 (544)
Briggs, T.: ref, 540 (3), 2432 (26), 2704 (32)
Brigham, F. J.: ref, 1386 (15), 2862 (316), 2879 (104), 2901 (55)
Brighouse, A.: test, 1601
Brighton, C.: ref, 2599 (2)
Bril, T.: ref, 1166 (126)
Brilman, E.: ref, 2050 (41)
Brimer, A.: test, 348, 1261 2187, 2883
Brimer, M. A.: test, 160, 952, 954, 1507, 1819; rev, 1765
Brinch, K.: ref, 337 (13)
Brines, D. B.: ref, 376 (26), 2860 (1336), 2863 (400)
Bringle, R. G.: ref, 1115 (2)
Bringsjord, E. L.: rev, 364, 1434
Brink, M.: test, 2458
Brink, W.: ref, 2050 (41)
Brinker, R. P.: ref, 837 (2), 2813 (57)
Brinkerink-Carlier, M.: ref, 2163 (53)
Brinkman, A. G.: ref, 451 (99)
Brinkman, D.: ref, 1903 (257)
Brinkman, D. C.: ref, 472 (72), 473 (2), 1697 (263,445), 2247 (53)
Brinkman-Sull, D. C.: ref, 1697 (484)
Brinson, S.: ref, 2862 (328)
Brinton, B.: ref, 430 (2), 540 (15), 1060 (1), 1240 (43), 1424 (3), 1607 (15), 1903 (11,79,464), 2452 (12), 2657 (1), 2694 (2), 2695 (7,52), 2704 (39), 2768 (2), 2801 (1), 2860 (458,577), 2862 (130,476,597)
Brinton, C.: ref, 450 (1), 1321 (2), 2497 (34)
Briones, M.: ref, 1266 (2)
Brisebois, F.: ref, 650 (15), 1093 (97)
Brisswalter, J.: ref, 298 (108), 2497 (326)
Bristone, S.: ref, 1698 (5)
Britt, T. W.: ref, 2497 (230)
Britt, T. W., Jr.: ref, 301 (39)
Britton, B. K.: ref, 1866 (38), 2862 (340)
Britton, J. W.: ref, 301 (47), 2516 (63), 2863 (233), 2879 (105), 2892 (166)
Britton, P.: ref, 1590 (4)
Britton, P. G.: ref, 272 (16), 2862 (496)
Brizzolara, D.: ref, 1485 (55), 1903 (501), 2227 (34), 2862 (571)
Broadbent, F.: rev, 195

Broberg, A. G.: ref, 365 (8), 1216 (71)
Brocaar, M. P.: ref, 1485 (9), 1903 (113), 2860 (346)
Brock, D. M.: ref, 1010 (92)
Brock, K. J.: ref, 272 (260), 2497 (614)
Brock, S.: ref, 335 (14), 1072 (40)
Brodaty, H.: ref, 998 (21), 1166 (61)
Broderick, C. P.: ref, 272 (310)
Broderick, P.: ref, 2485 (13)
Brodginski, S. E.: ref, 2860 (443)
Brodie, J. D.: ref, 2860 (419,1205), 2892 (61,261)
Brodman, K.: test, 708
Brodnick, R. J.: ref, 592 (79)
Brodsgaard, I.: ref, 2497 (129)
Brodsky, B.: ref, 846 (14), 2603 (449)
Brodsky, B. S.: ref, 824 (4), 846 (5), 1093 (62)
Brodsky, S. L.: rev, 2198
Brody, E.: ref, 1698 (14)
Brody, G.: ref, 1661 (50), 2211 (44)
Brody, G. H.: ref, 272 (20), 337 (172), 451 (188), 472 (73), 863 (24), 1010 (14,31), 2211 (26), 2862 (238,446)
Brody, L. E.: rev, 976, 1088, 2090; ref, 68 (1), 93 (1), 615 (8,12,36)
Brody, N.: ref, 745 (10)
Brodzinsky, A. B.: ref, 1161 (1)
Brodzinsky, D. M.: ref, 1161 (1)
Broe, G. A.: ref, 1164 (136), 1758 (79), 2497 (667), 2860 (1183), 2863 (356)
Broen, P. A.: ref, 214 (6), 998 (42), 1059 (2), 1072 (43), 1240 (33), 1903 (115,255,356),, 2225 (4),, 2651 (3,4,14), 2657 (23), 2860 (348,616), 2862 (252,334), 2864 (85)
Broen, W. E., Jr.: test, 1962
Brogan, D.: ref, 373 (17), 1987 (8)
Brogan, M.: ref, 994 (23), 1903 (362), 2695 (35), 2862 (341), 2901 (63)
Brogan, R.: ref, 474 (5)
Brogden, H. E.: rev, 2899
Broida, J. P.: ref, 462 (4), 1010 (29)
Broks, P.: ref, 1758 (99), 2860 (1379), 2863 (414)
Brombach, A. M.: ref, 681 (72)
Bromberg, J. A.: ref, 2873 (37)
Bromberger, J. T.: ref, 1621 (1)
Brome, D. R.: ref, 1010 (127), 2603 (548)
Bromet, E.: ref, 2288 (56), 2289 (43)
Bromet, E. J.: ref, 2102 (1), 2288 (16,24), 2289 (11), 2305 (74), 2603 (139), 2860 (335), 2863 (88)
Bromfield, E. B.: ref, 1218 (8), 2227 (16), 2860 (658,93), 2863 (193,203), 2892 (132), 2907 (5)
Bromley, J.: ref, 1722 (2)
Bromley, S. M.: ref, 2437 (3), 2860 (810), 2863 (234)
Bronen, R. A.: ref, 2863 (232)
Bronnan, R. T.: ref, 2603 (232)
Bronskill, M. J.: ref, 376 (31), 776 (47,60), 2863 (423)
Bronstein, P.: ref, 1266 (1,2)
Bronzo, M.: ref, 2497 (97)
Brook, A.: ref, 2603 (10)
Brook, D. W.: ref, 2603 (10)
Brook, J. A.: ref, 2603 (339)
Brook, J. S.: ref, 2603 (10)
Brook, R. J.: ref, 2603 (339)
Brooke, R.: ref, 1367 (2)
Brooke, S. L.: ref, 2361 (3)
Brooker, A. E.: ref, 776 (39), 2860 (1233), 2863 (367)
Brookhart, S. M.: rev, 684, 1318, 2246
Brooking, J.: ref, 2497 (338)
Brookings, J.: test, 2928
Brookings, J. B.: rev, 2577, 2635; ref, 1702 (1)
Brookman, C. S.: ref, 472 (11)
Brookmeyer, R.: ref, 2860 (1158)
Brooks, B. B.: ref, 2860 (194)
Brooks, C. I.: ref, 1735 (1,4), 2497 (278), 2656 (9)
Brooks, G. C., Jr.: test, 2413
Brooks, J.: ref, 2860 (1064), 2863 (311), 2892 (220)
Brooks, J. H., II: ref, 56 (8), 337 (93), 2065 (14), 2369 (6), 2525 (9)
Brooks, J. O., III: ref, 2860 (765)
Brooks, L.: ref, 404 (37)
Brooks, P.: test, 2198
Brooks, W. B.: ref, 1697 (206)
Brooks-Gunn, J.: ref, 270 (11), 451 (34,96), 1010 (52),1079 (24,27,58), 1181 (13,14), 1216 (26, 45,50,77,78,79,93,94), 1832 (7), 1903 (154,242,278), 2485 (75,135,190,192), 2864 (48,112)
Brookshire, B.: ref, 1612 (99), 1903 (571), 2862 (710)
Brookshire, B. L.: ref, 815 (20), 1612 (65,68), 2813 (88), 2860 (1230), 2862 (317), 2879 (196)
Brookshire, R. H.: ref, 2008 (6,7,11), 2873 (16,43)
Brooner, R. K.: ref, 793 (22), 1697 (58), 2218 (85), 2519 (23,43), 2520 (24,43)
Brooten, D.: ref, 1216 (21)
Brooten, D. A.: ref, 1745 (71)
Brophy, A. L.: ref, 1697 (159,208,393)
Brophy, J. J.: ref, 1166 (43)
Brossard, C.: ref, 451 (173)
Brotherton, W. D.: rev, 1494
Brotman, A. W.: ref, 2519 (17), 2520 (18)
Brott, T. G.: ref, 2658 (2), 2860 (1170)
Broucek, W. G.: ref, 999 (191), 1755 (75), 2218 (120), 2417 (39)
Brough, P.: ref, 999 (180)
Broussolle, E.: ref, 2860 (844), 2863 (244), 2892 (174)
Broussolle, E. D. M.: ref, 1697 (88), 2402 (6)
Brouwers, P.: ref, 1612 (62), 2813 (81), 2862 (297)
Brow, N. W.: ref, 68 (52)
Browder, D.: rev, 1067
Brower, P.: ref, 2862 (13)
Browers, P.: ref, 1612 (55,85), 1903 (483), 2163 (288), 2862 (279,523)
Brown, A. C.: ref, 1010 (21)
Brown, A. S.: rev, 43; ref, 2860 (811)
Brown, A. W.: rev, 182
Brown, B.: ref, 1072 (1), 1131 (1), 2862 (1)

Brown, B. R.: ref, 2246 (14), 2076 (20)
Brown, B. S.: ref, 2603 (77)
Brown, B. W.: ref, 2860 (420)
Brown, B. W., Jr.: ref, 1770 (3)
Brown, C.: ref, 776 (62), 1166 (93), 2227 (60)
Brown, C. C.: ref, 2862 (79)
Brown, C. H.: ref, 2050 (23)
Brown, C. M.: rev, 330, 1981
Brown, D.: ref, 404 (2), 2497 (9), 2749 (18)
Brown, D. G.: test, 1332
Brown, D. T.: rev, 1334, 1685; ref, 1379 (40), 2485 (116), 2860 (578)
Brown, E.: ref, 2860 (1031), 2863 (306)
Brown, E. D.: ref, 1661 (25)
Brown, E. J.: ref, 2199 (13), 2497 (431)
Brown, E. R.: test, 2159
Brown, F.: rev, 2360
Brown, F. G.: rev, 348, 665, 2484
Brown, G. A.: ref, 2603 (3)
Brown, G. G.: ref, 1135 (23), 1697 (572), 1740 (12), 1903 (315), 2226 (36), 2402 (33), 2603 (554), 2860 (1045,1349), 2862 (445), 2879 (175), 2892 (237,290)
Brown, G. K.: test, 272
Brown, G. L.: ref, 1661 (55), 2305 (176)
Brown, G. M.: ref, 272 (288), 1166 (197)
Brown, G. P.: ref, 592 (80)
Brown, G. R.: ref, 793 (18), 2218 (49)
Brown, G. W.: ref, 2050 (18,25,27,59,60,61,62,108,110)
Brown, J.: ref, 272 (346), 1824 (6), 2603 (575)
Brown, J. A.: ref, 893 (39)
Brown, J. D.: rev, 482, 951, 1235, 1506, 2726
Brown, J. E.: test, 2633, 1475
Brown, J. H.: ref, 451 (23)
Brown, J. I.: test, 1767
Brown, J. M.: ref, 451 (174)
Brown, J. R.: ref, 2672 (1)
Brown, K.: ref, 272 (77), 999 (70), 2860 (553)
Brown, K. A.: ref, 665 (44)
Brown, K. W.: ref, 2218 (121)
Brown, L.: test, 60, 286, 2361, 2704; ref, 1216 (21), 2497 (574)
Brown, L. G.: ref, 2603 (384)
Brown, L. H.: test, 2379
Brown, L. J.: test, 2323
Brown, L. M.: ref, 472 (152), 999 (93), 2214 (86), 2498 (56), 2905 (93)
Brown, L. P.: ref, 1745 (78)
Brown, M.: test, 444
Brown, M. B.: rev, 400, 1499; ref, 1462 (2), 2862 (577)
Brown, M. C.: ref, 1218 (3), 2860 (276)
Brown, M. L.: ref, 331 (5), 837 (7)
Brown, M. T.: ref, 298 (20)
Brown, N.: ref, 2305 (188)
Brown, N. W.: ref, 68 (10,28,32), 697 (4), 1010 (120), 1140 (29), 1514 (1), 2401 (1)
Brown, N. Y.: ref, 337 (107)
Brown, P. M.: ref, 364 (5), 2045 (4)
Brown, R.: test, 911; rev, 821, 1102, 2652, 2913; ref, 1755 (17), 2125 (11), 2516 (39), 2599 (17), 2603 (112)
Brown, R. A.: ref, 256 (2)
Brown, R. D.: rev, 8, 619, 620, 1466, 2369, 2475, 2530, 2540
Brown, R. E.: ref, 265 (5), 1391 (1), 1612 (24), 1903 (114) 2382 (7,8)
Brown, R. F.: ref, 1072 (32)
Brown, R. G.: ref, 2860 (579), 2863 (166)
Brown, R. P.: ref, 2305 (45)
Brown, R. S.: ref, 1697 (294)
Brown, R. T.: ref, 246 (4), 301 (28), 374 (1), 451 (189), 799 (1), 815 (4), 853 (8), 1379 (11,24), 1524 (1), 1902 (22), 1903 (158),2862 (122,192,442), 2879 (32,55)
Brown, S. A.: ref, 134 (39), 1166 (70), 2305 (46), 2414 (3), 2497 (105), 2858 (90,116)
Brown, S. D.: rev, 2527, 2655; ref, 1754 (25)
Brown, S. L.: test, 879, 2041; ref, 1181 (1), 1697 (196), 2858 (60)
Brown, S. W.: rev, 563, 996, 1460, 2405; ref, 2862 (12)
Brown, T. A.: ref, 998 (40), 2199 (2,9,10,13), 2497 (53,109,153,159,449)
Brown, T. E.: test, 351
Brown, T. L.: ref, 2516 (116)
Brown, V. L.: test, 2668, 2699, 2712; rev, 1583, 2545
Brown, W.: test, 730
Brown, W. A.: ref, 2076 (108), 2288 (27), 2289 (18)
Brown, W. F.: test, 2591
Brown, W. S.: ref, 209 (5), 1740 (7), 2076 (23), 2599 (6), 2860 (240,534,940,1138), 2901 (68,98)
Brown, W. T.: ref, 303 (6), 1218 (10),2860 (891), 2863 (263)
Browne, B. A.: ref, 999 (73), 1000 (41)
Browne, M.: ref, 1166 (119)
Brownell, M. D.: ref, 2146 (10)
Brownell, R.: test, 2191
Brownell, W. A.: rev, 174
Brownlee-Deffeck, M.: ref, 2603 (4)
Brownlie, E. B.: ref, 241 (4), 451 (94), 815 (35), 1903 (447), 2695 (47), 2864 (110)
Broyles, S. J.: ref, 272 (282), 2218 (100)
Broyles, S. L.: ref, 2771 (42)
Brozgold, A.: ref, 776 (12), 2860 (434)
Brozovich, R.: rev, 841, 931
Brubaker, P. H.: ref, 1745 (22)
Brubeck, D.: ref, 694 (28)
Bruce, D.: ref, 375 (3), 2862 (506)
Bruce, M. M.: test, 170, 218, 352, 361, 535, 942, 1713, 2006, 2269, 2272, 2572
Bruce, M. S.: ref, 2497 (428)
Bruce, R. A.: ref, 1404 (11)
Bruch, M. A.: ref, 1745 (53)
Bruchon-Schweitzer, M.: ref, 2497 (432), 2858 (112)
Bruck, M.: ref, 1903 (338)
Bruckel, S.: ref, 2485 (83), 2599 (13), 2860 (457)
Bruckert, R.: ref, 2860 (100)

Bruder-Mattson, S. F.: ref, 272 (24), 2858 (11)
Bruemmer, A.: ref, 1164 (57), 2860 (586), 2863 (174)
Bruening, P.: ref, 337 (160)
Brugge, K. L.: ref, 815 (14), 1164 (56), 1612 (46), 1903 (236), 2485 (117), 2860 (580), 2863 (167)
Bruggeman, E. L.: ref, 771 (26)
Bruggemans, E. F.: ref, 1164 (142), 1740 (16), 2226 (18), 2516 (93), 2599 (37), 2860 (1234), 2863 (368)
Brugger, P.: ref, 776 (28), 1755 (34)
Brugha, T.: ref, 2050 (10)
Brugha, T. S.: ref, 2050 (39)
Bruhn, A. R.: test, 885
Bruijn, J. A.: ref, 1166 (164), 2305 (204)
Bruininks, R. H.: test, 124, 353, 443, 1300, 2299; ref, 443 (1), 1300 (1,2,3,5,6,10), 2901 (96)
Brumaghim, J. T.: ref, 681 (48), 1902 (55,88), 2862 (500,736), 2879 (234)
Brumback, R. A.: ref, 798 (4), 1092 (3), 1131 (5), 1240 (4), 1392 (2), 1902 (14), 1903 (42), 2432 (8), 2484 (1), 2879 (21)
Brumbelow, S.: ref, 1697 (99)
Brumfield, B. D.: ref, 266 (4), 451 (246)
Brun, E.: ref, 2227 (19), 2860 (818), 2863 (236)
Brunet, P.: ref, 2517 (1), 2860 (527)
Brunetti, D. G.: ref, 1697 (191), 1697 (583)
Brunetti, G.: ref, 1697 (204)
Brunfaut, E.: ref, 2239 (28), 2860 (1046)
Brungardt, J. B.: ref, 56 (9), 592 (81)
Brungardt, T. M.: ref, 2860 (214)
Bruni, J.: ref, 2860 (1204)
Bruning, R.: rev, 773, 1781; ref, 56 (11), 2010 (13)
Bruning, R. H.: rev, 357; ref, 773 (1)
Brunkhorst, B. J.: ref, 1759 (2)
Brunner, N. A.: ref, 301 (27), 1866 (23)
Bruno, R. L.: ref, 2860 (352), 2863 (93)
Bruns, D.: test, 267
Bruns, J.: ref, 2603 (112)
Brush, J. A.: rev, 1064
Brutten, S. R.: ref, 2717 (1)
Bruyer, R.: ref, 776 (18)
Bryan, D.: rcf, 451 (44), 1079 (29), 2599 (29), 2862 (358), 2879 (89,123)
Bryan, J.: ref, 1758 (58), 2860 (1047)
Bryan, J. E.: test, 2450; rev, 1185
Bryan, M. M.: rev, 364, 2484
Bryan, T.: ref, 1318 (23), 2862 (425), 2901 (44,80)
Bryan, Y. E.: ref, 272 (207), 2497 (582)
Bryant, B. R.: test, 198, 789, 797, 799, 822, 1130, 1131, 1168, 1459, 2309, 2708, 2730
Bryant, D.: ref, 180 (17), 451 (197), 1079 (16) 1216 (25,48)
Bryant, D. M.: ref, 270 (12,28), 630 (1), 875 (1), 1215 (4), 1216 (80,98), 1264 (4), 1612 (90), 2382 (33), 2485 (193,222), 2862 (447,598), 2864 (113,131), 2901 (112)
Bryant, F. B.: ref, 1338 (44), 2749 (4)
Bryant, J. T.: ref, 1903 (93)
Bryant, K. J.: ref, 68 (11), 372 (28), 963 (1), 2305 (76)
Bryant, N. D.: rev, 827, 1073
Bryant, P.: ref, 350 (1), 2163 (343), 2862 (704), 2864 (10)
Bryant, R. A.: ref, 1079 (36), 2497 (433,434), 2860 (812)
Bryant, T.: ref, 349 (9), 2239 (16)
Bryden, M. P.: ref, 1903 (18), 2704 (46), 2860 (1391), 2862 (52,699,715), 2901 (3)
Bryen, D. N.: rev, 2228, 2229
Bryk, A. S.: ref, 1072 (46), 2905 (61)
Bryne, D. G.: ref, 1965 (7)
Brynjoffsson, J.: ref, 2305 (180,141,199)
Bryson, G.: ref, 2432 (19), 2892 (129,264), 2924 (2,4)
Bryson, M.: ref, 389 (8)
Bryson, S.: ref, 1903 (446)
Bryson, S. E.: ref, 389 (1), 1071 (1), 1653 (14), 1657 (1), 1903 (237,450), 2860 (171)
Brzustowicz, L.: ref, 2305 (49)
Bub, D.: ref, 1164 (57), 2163 (314), 2860 (586), 2863 (174,373,61)
Bubenzer, D. L.: ref, 1927 (4,5)
Buch, J. L.: ref, 1095 (13)
Buchanan, C. P.: ref, 2860 (974), 2863 (286)
Buchanan, I.: ref, 246 (4), 1379 (24), 1903 (158), 1697 (356)
Buchanan, J. J.: ref, 1592 (3)
Buchanan, L. M.: ref, 2497 (231)
Buchanan, M.: test, 397
Buchanan, R.: ref, 2050 (24)
Buchanan, R. W.: ref, 2288 (62), 2516 (34), 2892 (105)
Buchanan, W. L.: ref, 1525 (7), 2863 (39)
Buchanun, K.: ref, 1470 (4), 2069 (1)
Buchholz, D.: ref, 1697 (386)
Buchkoski, J.: ref, 846 (22), 1697 (551)
Buchman, J. P.: ref, 2603 (520)
Bucholz, K. K.: ref, 999 (172), 2305 (195)
Buchsbaum, M. S.: ref, 301 (18), 2860 (302,883), 2863 (79)
Bucik, V.: ref, 2163 (290)
Buck, B.: ref, 776 (47)
Buck, D.: test, 2423
Buck, J. N.: test, 200, 1160
Buck, P.: ref, 1525 (7), 2863 (39)
Buck, R.: ref, 926 (1)
Buckelew, S. P.: ref, 337 (77), 2603 (4), 2603 (38,534), 2858 (12)
Buckhalt, J. A.: ref, 349 (26), 837 (9)
Buckingham, S. L.: ref, 1135 (13), 2599 (25), 2860 (772)
Buckland, N.: ref, 2497 (448)
Buckle, S.: ref, 1697 (66,67), 2076 (9,10)
Buckley, D.: ref, 1135 (17), 1164 (119), 2862 (435), 2879 (153)
Buckley, P.: ref, 1093 (61), 2050 (63)
Buckley, S.: ref, 4 (23)
Buckly, R.: test, 2072
Buckner, C.: ref, 1164 (86), 2892 (164)
Buckner, J. C.: ref, 451 (146), 2603 (486), 2813 (126)

Bucks, R. S.: ref, 1758 (59)
Buckwalter, P.: ref, 1096 (13), 1903 (558), 2695 (71)
Buckwalter, P. R.: ref, 1240 (51), 1379 (103), 1740 (36), 1903 (583), 2657 (37), 2668 (5), 2694 (25), 2695 (72), 2862 (738)
Bucy, J. E.: rev, 2487, 2731
Budd, K. S.: rev, 863, 1178
Budd, K. S.: ref, 997 (10), 1216 (20), 2127 (1), 2603 (134), 2860 (1048), 2879 (157)
Budesov, D.: ref, 56 (4), 592 (31), 1115 (8)
Budge, G. W. K.: test, 1481
Budgell, G. R.: ref, 1866 (35)
Budin, W. C.: ref, 794 (2)
Budman, S.: ref, 2603 (67)
Budman, S. H.: ref, 2603 (11,441)
Budney, A. J.: ref, 2603 (18)
Buehler, C.: ref, 449 (1,2,3), 451 (89)
Buehler, J. A.: test, 1366
Buell, M. J.: ref, 2682 (9)
Buesching, D. P.: ref, 2603 (253,552)
Buethe, E.: test, 663
Bugaj, A. M.: rev, 168, 1719, 2264, 2822
Bugbee, A. C.: rev, 2152
Bugbee, A. C., Jr.: rev, 141, 1279, 1846
Buhr, J.: ref, 1903 (139)
Buhrow, M.: ref, 708 (7)
Buican, B.: ref, 2860 (1060)
Buis, T.: ref, 1697 (381,529)
Buitelaar, J.: ref, 2813 (5)
Buitelaar, J. K.: ref, 451 (100), 681 (40),73)
Buki, V. M. V.: ref, 2050 (117), 2305 (136)
Bukowski, A. L.: ref, 472 (224)
Bukowski, W.: ref, 451 (245)
Bukowski, W. M.: ref, 337 (189), 472 (60,182), 2242 (7), 2862 (525)
Buktenica, N. A.: test, 815; rev, 1278
Bulas, D. I.: ref, 2125 (30), 2768 (43), 2864 (144)
Bulbena, A.: ref, 998 (35)
Bulcroft, R. A.: ref, 863 (17)
Bulik, C. M.: ref, 1166 (45), 2603 (36,39)
Bull, B. A.: ref, 1903 (68)
Bull, M. J.: ref, 2858 (91)
Bullard, S. C.: ref, 2862 (123), 2901 (15)
Bullion, C. M.: ref, 4 (2), 681 (50)
Bullock, L. M.: test, 281
Bullock, P.: ref, 1758 (73)
Bullock, W. B.: test, 157
Bulow, C. A.: ref, 2860 (767)
Buman, S.: ref, 2497 (430)
Bunce, D.: ref, 272 (261), 1079 (84), 1216 (105), 1590 (62), 2326 (3), 2485 (232), 2497 (615), 2862 (655)
Bunce, D. M.: ref, 592 (14)
Bunce, L.: ref, 1903 (271), 2905 (57)
Bunce, S. C.: ref, 999 (112)
Bunch, M. B.: rev, 369, 396, 410, 1807, 1820, 1967, 1984, 1249, 1331, 1825, 1860, 2071, 2427
Bundrick, C. M.: ref, 1938 (1), 1939 (7)
Bundy, A. C.: ref, 353 (3), 1903 (85)
Bunker, L. K.: rev, 805, 968, 1019, 1668, 2689
Buntaine, R. L.: ref, 1085 (3), 2484 (12)
Buongiorno, G.: ref, 2076 (101)
Burack, J. A.: ref, 1379 (15), 1607 (4), 1903 (512), 2485 (49), 2813 (17)
Burant, C.: ref, 863 (54)
Burbach, D. J.: ref, 1010 (55), 2603 (223), 2858 (58)
Burch, E. A., Jr.: ref, 1166 (44)
Burch, G. S. J.: ref, 1671 (8), 1758 (100), 2860 (1380)
Burch, H.: ref, 2544 (1)
Burch, J. W.: ref, 2877 (1)
Burchimal, M. R.: ref, 270 (12), 2382 (33)
Burchinal, M. R.: ref, 171 (2), 265 (6,11,15), 270 (28), 630 (1), 1215 (4), 1216 (58,73,80,98), 1264 (4), 1612 (58,90), 1903 (547), 2382 (26), 2485 (147,193,222),, 2700 (1), 2860 (732), 2862 (286, 388,447,598), 2864 (70), 2864 (113), 2864 (131), 2901 (47,70,112)
Burd, L.: test, 1068
Burd, L.: ref, 1902 (30), 2485 (50), 2862 (156), 2879 (40)
Burden, R. L.: ref, 1254 (1)
Burdett, A. D.: test, 2829
Burdon-Cooper, C.: ref, 1758 (42), 2193 (41), 2860 (900), 2863 (270), 2892 (189)
Bureau of Business and Economic Research, University of Iowa: test, 2060
Bureau of Business Research, Ohio State University: test, 1437
Bureau, Y. R. J.: ref, 1697 (341), 2860 (717)
Burg, J. S.: ref, 2860 (962), 2863 (285)
Burgard, P.: ref, 2860 (747)
Burge, D.: ref, 472 (213), 681 (56), 1010 (121), 2214 (124)
Burge, S.: ref, 1000 (25)
Burger, G. K.: ref, 1697 (59)
Burger, J. M.: ref, 999 (113), 2497 (435)
Burgess, A. P.: ref, 2050 (64,93), 2076 (97), 2239 (18), 2497 (384), 2860 (581), 2863 (168), 2892 (106)
Burgess, E.: ref, 1166 (94), 2076 (143), 2603 (442)
Burgess, E. D.: ref, 1697 (66,67), 2076 (9,10)
Burgess, I.: ref, 1021 (31), 1181 (19)
Burgess, P.: ref, 2860 (846)
Burgess, P. W.: test, 295; ref, 1758 (60,61), 2860 (1049,1050)
Burgess, T. C.: rev, 1716
Burghen, G. A.: ref, 1000 (3), 1010 (36)
Burgio, F.: ref, 2225 (15)
Burgomeister, B. B.: test, 624
Burgress, M. F.: ref, 999 (139), 2603 (407)
Burgwald, L.: ref, 301 (18), 2860 (302), 2863 (79)
Burhans, K. K.: ref, 1115 (16)
Buriel, R.: ref, 1010 (13)
Burish, T. G.: ref, 1745 (17)
Burk, J. P.: ref, 2603 (4)
Burke, A.: test, 2459

Burke, C.: ref, 451 (69), 472 (140)
Burke, C. L.: rev, 1072
Burke, C. M.: ref, 1755 (50), 2856 (9)
Burke, E. F.: ref, 1078 (1)
Burke, J.: ref, 1166 (114), 2050 (10), 2497 (561), 2603 (468)
Burke, K.: ref, 1612 (48)
Burke, M.: ref, 272 (20), 1010 (14)
Burke, P. M.: ref, 2305 (93,94)
Burke, R. J.: ref, 298 (102), 1590 (13,19,29,41)
Burke, R. V.: ref, 451 (149), 997 (13), 2065 (8)
Burke, T.: ref, 1140 (50), 2860 (1124)
Burker, E. J.: ref, 2076 (35), 2402 (21), 2497 (436), 2603 (121,340)
Burket, C. R.: ref, 364 (28)
Burkhead, E. J.: ref, 404 (11)
Burkholder, R.: test, 1887
Burks, H. F.: test, 355
Burleson, B.: ref, 1927 (7)
Burleson, B. R.: ref, 863 (63,85)
Burley, K.: ref, 298 (88), 2835 (15)
Burley-Allen, M.: test, 632
Burling, J. W.: ref, 2497 (232)
Burlingame, G. M.: ref, 1697 (339,473), 2603 (443)
Burlingham-Dubree, M.: ref, 2864 (9)
Burn, Y. R.: ref, 1612 (41,42)
Burnam, M. A.: ref, 2050 (3)
Burnand, B.: ref, 1166 (101), 1661 (54)
Burness, C. E.: ref, 2892 (277)
Burnett, J. W.: ref, 694 (94)
Burnett, K. F.: ref, 2076 (75)
Burnett, P.: ref, 998 (127), 1079 (96), 2497 (644)
Burnett, P. C.: rev, 2092, 2216; ref, 1079 (85)
Burnett, P. L.: ref, 2603 (243)
Burnett, R.: ref, 2497 (436)
Burnette, M. M.: ref, 760 (4), 2497 (106), 2603 (84,408)
Burnham, B. L.: ref, 790 (9,21)
Burnham, L.: test, 1930, 1955
Burnley, G. D.: ref, 681 (24)
Burns, A.: ref, 1779 (3), 1832 (9)
Burns, B.: ref, 2247 (98), 2402 (55)
Burns, B. J.: ref, 451 (107,108)
Burns, C. W.: rev, 1362
Burns, D. D.: ref, 2603 (207)
Burns, D. E.: ref, 665 (19)
Burns, G. L.: ref, 1131 (18), 2485 (241), 2595 (1), 2603 (70), 2905 (119)
Burns, J. M.: ref, 2485 (4,14,21), 2682 (1), 2901 (1)
Burns, J. W.: ref, 272 (343)
Burns, K. A.: ref, 272 (262), 2433 (2)
Burns, K. A.: ref, 2603 (521)
Burns, K. L.: ref, 2163 (231)
Burns, M. S.: test, 356
Burns, P. C.: test, 357
Burns, R. A.: ref, 1166 (71)
Burns, W. J.: ref, 272 (262), 690 (3), 1687 (34), 2433 (2), 2603 (521)
Burnside, R. M.: test, 1393
Burnstein, A. G.: rev, 2862
Burr, E. T.: rev, 2758
Burr, G.: ref, 2860 (779)
Burr, R.: ref, 2497 (231)
Burrell, L.: ref, 2858 (89)
Burright, R. G.: ref, 2860 (165,962), 2863 (285)
Burrow, W. H.: ref, 4 (5)
Burrows, E.: ref, 1104 (4), 2193 (23), 2239 (21), 2860 (659), 2863 (194)
Burrows, E. H.: ref, 1758 (42), 2193 (41), 2860 (900), 2863 (270), 2892 (189)
Burrows, G.: ref, 1166 (224)
Burrows, G. D.: ref, 1166 (17), 2076 (157), 2603 (24)
Burrows, R.: ref, 1294 (2), 1697 (61), 2519 (9), 2520 (9), 2603 (41)
Burrus-Mehl, F.: ref, 1166 (56)
Bursik, K.: ref, 298 (58), 2076 (24)
Burson, S. L., Jr.: rev, 46
Burstein, A. G.: rev, 2247, 2860
Bursuck, W. D.: ref, 1991 (68), 2860 (609), 2862 (247), 2879 (76), 2901 (40)
Burt, C.: rev, 2485
Burt, D. B.: ref, 815 (21), 1135 (14), 1485 (38), 1612 (66), 1903 (339), 2485 (161), 2813 (84)
Burt, M. K.: test, 307
Burti, L.: ref, 1093 (28)
Burton, D. B.: ref, 1380 (4), 2860 (582,813)
Burton, J.: ref, 2603 (93)
Burton, N. W.: ref, 592 (45,72,107)
Burton, S. D.: test, 810
Burzette, R. G.: ref, 337 (161)
Bus, A. G.: ref, 1092 (10), 1903 (109,325), 2905 (67)
Busatto, G. F.: ref, 2050 (65), 2863 (169)
Busby, K.: ref, 2603 (319)
Busby, R.: ref, 1697 (333), 2402 (31), 2860 (702)
Busby, R. M.: ref, 1687 (45), 2402 (44)
Busch, J. C.: rev, 1790, 2333
Busch, K. G.: ref, 301 (9), 1072 (14), 2484 (2), 2862 (96)
Busch-Rossnagel, N. A.: rev, 480, 1010, 2724; ref, 298 (12), 926 (3), 1140 (5), 2497 (212), 2531 (3)
Buschke, H.: ref, 2860 (1235), 2863 (369)
Busconi, A.: ref, 337 (195), 1010 (137), 2496 (5), 2497 (675)
Busenbark, D.: ref, 2860 (635)
Bush, A.: ref, 1408 (3)
Bush, B. R.: rev, 355, 1896
Bush, E.: ref, 451 (142), 472 (181), 694 (118), 1010 (43), 2862 (173,654)
Bush, J. P.: ref, 272 (71), 1000 (36), 2497 (11)
Bush, L. K.: ref, 2860 (790)
Bush, M.: ref, 272 (304)
Bush, N. F.: ref, 998 (115)
Bush, P. W.: ref, 134 (12)
Bush, S. L.: ref, 272 (102), 462 (17)
Bush, T.: ref, 2218 (16), 2603 (474)

Bushell, C.: ref, 2873 (19)
Bushell, C. M.: ref, 776 (40)
Bushman, B. J.: ref, 1745 (54)
Bushnell, J. A.: ref, 1166 (159)
Busquets, X.: ref, 1166 (109)
Buss, D. M.: ref, 999 (26,178), 1289 (1)
Buss, R. R.: rev, 827
Busse, J.: ref, 1379 (89), 2862 (537), 2864 (123)
Busse, R. T.: rev, 451; ref, 2444 (1), 2452 (6), 2841 (1)
Bussel, B.: ref, 1164 (118), 2516 (77)
Bussell, D. A.: ref, 472 (113,142)
Busto, U.: ref, 1093 (102), 2497 (512), 2603 (396)
Butcher, A. H.: ref, 1348 (10), 1701 (45)
Butcher, J. N.: test, 362, 1697, 1698; rev, 2417; ref, 1697 (86,209,264,578,584), 1698 (7,8)
Butki, B. D.: ref, 999 (177), 2076 (163)
Butkovsky, L.: ref, 430 (14), 1485 (52), 1903 (484), 2695 (57)
Butler, A.: ref, 1481 (3)
Butler, D. L.: ref, 2668 (3), 2860 (814), 2862 (318)
Butler, E.: ref, 353 (12), 1166 (95), 2813 (61), 2862 (261,706)
Butler, J. K., Jr.: rev, 1655, 1967, 2610
Butler, K. G.: rev, 209, 2228, 2229, 2470, 2801
Butler, L.: ref, 2860 (427)
Butler, L. S.: ref, 837 (2)
Butler, M. N.: test, 2825
Butler, R.: ref, 258 (1), 353 (11), 815 (15), 1072 (42), 1240 (24), 1379 (41), 1902 (52), 1987 (10), 2305 (180), 2377 (1), 2724 (6), 2862 (239), 2879 (73)
Butler, R. W.: ref, 1962 (19)
Butler, V. L.: ref, 1093 (5)
Butow, P. N.: ref, 1079 (86), 2076 (169)
Butt, D. S.: rev, 1340, 1341
Butter, C. M.: ref, 2860 (583), 2863 (170)
Butter, E. M.: ref, 2498 (76)
Butterfield, P. H.: ref, 2862 (217)
Butters, J.: ref, 272 (263)
Butters, N.: ref, 199 (10), 272 (334), 376 (30), 776 (7,21,25,26,28,34,41), 1164 (33), 2305 (32,130), 2603 (140), 2860 (2,184,344,845), 2862 (105), 2863 (1,92,153,293), 2892 (49,202)
Butterworth, B.: ref, 1104 (3,7), 2193 (19), 2860 (588,827), 2873 (1)
Buttolph, M. L.: ref, 1697 (51)
Button, E. J.: ref, 2603 (570)
Button, K.: ref, 1697 (217)
Buttrill, J.: ref, 798 (1)
Butyniec-Thomas, J.: ref, 389 (14)
Butzer, J. F.: ref, 1380 (11), 2193 (50), 2603 (437)
Buunk, B.: ref, 999 (195)
Buunk, B. P.: ref, 998 (129), 1079 (82), 1590 (61,68), 1697 (110),1745 (77)
Bux, D. A.: ref, 272 (182), 273 (21)
Buxbaum, L. J.: ref, 1903 (238)
Buyck, D.: ref, 337 (158), 451 (150)
Buydens-Branchey, L.: ref, 2519 (8), 2520 (8)
Buysse, A.: ref, 1612 (101), 2862 (732)
Buysse, D. J.: ref, 272 (307), 337 (72), 1166 (104,182,204), 2305 (173)
Buytenhuijs, E. L.: ref, 2226 (16), 2516 (35,88), 2860 (584,1194),2892 (260)
Buzwell, S.: ref, 2603 (275), 2858 (71)
Buzzanga, V. L.: ref, 2369 (2)
Bwibu, N.: ref, 2163 (78)
Bye, R. A.: test, 1315
Byers, E. S.: ref, 2076 (138)
Byers, S.: ref, 2749 (28), 2860 (369)
Bylsma, F.: ref, 2516 (72), 2860 (1180), 2892 (203)
Bylsma, F. W.: ref, 815 (19,49), 1164 (173), 1740 (10,27),2516 (32,62,115),, 2860 (514,809,1160, 1374),, 2863 (171,346), 2892 (85,165,294)
Byram, V.: ref, 472 (167)
Byravan, A.: ref, 2218 (23), 2417 (24)
Byrd, B.: ref, 372 (44), 1000 (42)
Byrd, D.: ref, 335 (9), 2288 (61), 2289 (47)
Byrd, M.: ref, 2860 (30)
Byrd, P. B.: test, 1286
Byrd, R. E.: test, 727, 1723
Byrne, A. E.: ref, 999 (50), 1333 (2), 1991 (47)
Byrne, B.: ref, 1903 (23)
Byrne, B. M.: ref, 385 (1), 1197 (1), 1590 (10,20,30,31), 1738 (1), 2358 (3)
Byrne, D. G.: ref, 999 (50), 1333 (2), 1338 (7,8),1991 (47)
Byrne, J.: ref, 2862 (259)
Byrne, J. M.: ref, 1902 (66), 1903 (340,346), 2860 (815)
Byrne, M. C.: rev, 1060, 1095, 1427, 2008
Byrne, N. M.: ref, 893 (43)
Byrnes, D. A.: ref, 311 (1), 1866 (13)
Byrnes, J. D.: ref, 592 (53), 2031 (6)
Bystritsky, A.: ref, 1021 (7), 1093 (26), 1705 (1), 2497 (54)
Bzdawka, A.: ref, 644 (2), 682 (1)
Bzoch, K. R.: test, 2189

Caballero, J. A.: test, 1230
Caballo, V. E.: ref, 999 (176)
Cacciola, J. S.: ref, 372 (27), 1661 (77), 2305 (152), 2603 (544)
Cacinovic, S.: ref, 2892 (277)
Cacioppo, J. T.: ref, 863 (56)
Cadavid, V.: ref, 1590 (15)
Caddell, J. M.: ref, 1697 (36), 2497 (36)
Cadieux, A.: ref, 1987 (18,19)
Cado, S.: ref, 337 (17,42)
Cado, S.: ref, 793 (4)
Cadoret, R. J.: ref, 2603 (458)
Caer, Y.: ref, 2305 (117)
Caffarra, P.: ref, 2860 (774)
Cafferty, T. P.: ref, 1140 (16)
Caggiula, A. R.: ref, 2516 (12)
Cahalane, J. F.: ref, 1093 (38), 2305 (61)

Cahan, S.: ref, 745 (16), 2163 (199)
Cahen, L. S.: rev, 547
Cahil, C. A.: ref, 272 (344)
Cahill, C.: ref, 2239 (12)
Cahill-Solis, T. L.: ref, 364 (12)
Cahn, D. A.: ref, 376 (21), 776 (44), 1164 (153), 2892 (275)
Cahn, W.: ref, 2603 (105)
Cahoon, B. J.: ref, 1697 (290)
Cain-Caston, M.: ref, 364 (8,18)
Caine, E. D.: ref, 1903 (334), 2517 (2), 2860 (796)
Caiola, M. A.: ref, 2402 (26)
Cairo, P. C.: ref, 83 (3)
Caison, W.: ref, 459 (2)
Caknevalla, N.: ref, 999 (88)
Calabrese, J. R.: ref, 1093 (110), 2305 (166,168,202)
Calabrese, P.: ref, 2163 (200), 2227 (15), 2239 (14), 2860 (492,816), 2863 (138,172,235), 2892 (78,107)
Calahan, C. A.: ref, 1755 (53)
Calamari, J. E.: ref, 2485 (11), 2497 (310)
Caldarella, P.: ref, 2452 (18)
Calder, A. J.: ref, 1758 (99), 2860 (1379), 2863 (414)
Calder, P.: ref, 1079 (6)
Caldwell, B. M.: test, 693, 1216; ref, 451 (33), 1216 (1,37,40,97), 2218 (84), 2485 (112,114)
Caldwell, D. F.: ref, 68 (15), 1348 (1)
Caldwell, D. S.: ref, 1178 (4)
Caldwell, K.: ref, 4 (9)
Calenda, A.: ref, 2227 (19), 2860 (818), 2863 (236)
Calev, A.: ref, 301 (16,48), 2860 (241,922)
Calfas, K. J.: ref, 272 (373), 1166 (223)
Calfee, K. H.: rev, 565
Calfee, R.: rev, 1072
Calfee, R. C.: rev, 1781, 2184
Calhoun, J.: ref, 2905 (17)
Calhoun, K. S.: ref, 793 (5), 998 (107), 2839 (2)
Calhoun, L. G.: ref, 337 (154), 893 (34), 2497 (218)
Caliandro, G.: ref, 794 (2)
Calise, C.: ref, 2163 (114)
Caliso, J. A.: ref, 448 (5)
Callahan, A. M.: ref, 272 (294), 1166 (199)
Callahan, C.: ref, 1379 (12), 2860 (242)
Callahan, C. M.: test, 2295; rev, 367, 1089, 1395, 2596; ref, 372 (30), 615 (22), 724 (6), 1140 (40), 1142 (5), 1143 (2), 1318 (11), 1877 (1), 2031 (3), 2295 (5,7), 2358 (14), 2771 (38), 2862 (97)
Callahan, E. C.: test, 2687
Callahan, L. G.: rev, 2740
Callahan, T.: ref, 142 (2)
Callahan, W. J.: ref, 1697 (162)
Callan, V. J.: ref, 272 (8), 1754 (13), 1755 (21), 2497 (24), 2915 (5)
Callanan, G. A.: ref, 2497 (55,160)
Callander, L.: ref, 2557 (9)
Callies, A.: ref, 1093 (20), 2603 (31,78)
Callisto, T. A.: test, 319
Calne, D. B.: ref, 335 (1),2125 (27), 2289 (6)
Calne, S.: ref, 335 (1), 2289 (6)
Calsyn, D. A.: ref, 1687 (1)
Calsyn, R. J.: ref, 337 (8,94,168)
Calsyn, R. J.: ref, 1181 (2)
Caltabiano, M. L.: ref, 1590 (21)
Caltagirone, C.: ref, 2163 (99,148,201,202,265), 2226 (19), 2227 (55), 2860 (820,1052,1381), 2907 (7)
Calvert, B.: test, 1800
Calvert, S. L.: ref, 298 (90)
Calvo, M. G.: ref, 999 (176), 2497 (4,233), 2656 (6)
Camara, K. A.: ref, 451 (1)
Camara, W. J.: rev, 2274, 2279, 2912, 2927
Camarata, M.: ref, 430 (14), 1485 (52), 1903 (484), 2695 (57)
Camarata, M. N.: ref, 2657 (12), 2695 (24)
Camarata, S. M.: ref, 430 (14), 1485 (52), 1903 (264,484), 2657 (12), 2695 (24,25,57)
Camarda, R.: ref, 2860 (1051)
Camasso, M. J.: ref, 875 (2)
The Cambridge Stratford Study Skills Institute: test, 1891, 2589
Cambridge, The Adult Education Company: test, 1247, 1248,1510
Cameron, C.: test, 2781
Cameron, C. M.: ref, 272 (211), 1671 (7), 2497 (451,584)
Cameron, L. C.: ref, 1379 (92)
Cameron, O. G.: ref, 2497 (97)
Camfield, P.: ref, 1135 (17), 1164 (119), 2862 (435), 2879 (153)
Camilli, G.: ref, 665 (46)
Cammalleri, R.: ref, 2860 (1051)
Cammen, T. J. M. V. D.: ref, 2497 (259)
Cammisa, K. M.: ref, 665 (60), 1919 (1)
Camp, B. W.: rev, 252, 315, 1259, 2299
Camp, C. C.: ref, 398 (2), 399 (1), 404 (23), 2282 (5)
Camp, C. J.: rev, 212, 1064, 2065, 2459; ref, 791 (13), 1903 (409), 2858 (110), 2860 (374), 2863 (97)
Camp, L.: test, 1818; ref, 1612 (51)
Campbel, S. B.: ref, 863 (48), 2485 (118)
Campbell, A.: test, 972
Campbell, B.: ref, 358 (12), 560 (3), 2862 (518)
Campbell, B. A.: test, 1986
Campbell, C. A.: ref, 2432 (23)
Campbell, D.: test, 379, 380, 381, 382; rev, 132, 1577; ref, 1991 (60), 2813 (51)
Campbell, D. A.: ref, 2860 (1157)
Campbell, D. P.: test, 1790; rev, 1141, 1713, 1790; ref, 379 (1)
Campbell, D. T.: ref, 1240 (49), 1659 (10), 2484 (10)
Campbell, E. M.: ref, 1300 (11)
Campbell, F.: ref, 1216 (58), 1612 (58), 2485 (147), 2860 (732), 2862 (286), 2864 (70), 2901 (47)
Campbell, F. A.: ref, 270 (28), 1216 (98), 1612 (67,90), 1902 (67), 2485 (162,222), 2860 (817), 2862 (240,319,598), 2864 (79,131), 2901 (39,56,112)

Campbell, I. A.: rev, 2813
Campbell, I. C.: ref, 2305 (188)
Campbell, I. M.: ref, 2498 (12)
Campbell, J.: ref, 1939 (3)
Campbell, J. A.: rev, 46, 94, 516, 1076
Campbell, J. C.: ref, 2603 (12), 2652 (1)
Campbell, J. D.: ref, 2218 (17,50)
Campbell, J. F.: ref, 1201 (2)
Campbell, J. P.: ref, 180 (20)
Campbell, J. R.: ref, 592 (15)
Campbell, J. T.: rev, 1221, 1449
Campbell, L.: ref, 272 (181), 376 (5), 1166 (113), 1687 (8), 2863 (324)
Campbell, L. A.: ref, 2497 (437), 2498 (50)
Campbell, M.: ref, 2862 (293), 2864 (72)
Campbell, M. A.: ref, 472 (74), 1021 (21), 2214 (36),2498 (31)
Campbell, N. B.: ref, 451 (142), 472 (181), 542 (1), 694 (118), 994 (37), 1010 (43), 1903 (466), 2862 (173,654)
Campbell, R.: ref, 1765 (7), 2193 (5), 2860 (161), 2862 (145), 2864 (24)
Campbell, R. A.: test, 475
Campbell, R. N.: ref, 2862 (544)
Campbell, S. B.: ref, 272 (11), 863 (12), 1903 (341), 2305 (19)
Campbell, S. E.: ref, 1592 (18), 2485 (119)
Campbell, T.: ref, 298 (157), 2225 (16), 2864 (132), 2901 (113),, 2902 (5)
Campbell, T. F.: rev, 1360; ref, 1240 (25), 1903 (342)
Campbell, T. L.: ref, 2230 (2)
Campbell, V. L.: ref, 2525 (1), 2860 (416)
Campion, D.: ref, 2227 (19), 2860 (818), 2863 (236)
Campion, J. E.: ref, 171 (1), 937 (2), 1043 (1), 1974 (1), 2105 (1)
Campion, M. A.: ref, 171 (1), 937 (2), 1043 (1), 1974 (1), 2105 (1)
Campling, G. M.: ref, 2076 (103)
Campos, A.: ref, 1396 (1), 2771 (2)
Campos, J.: ref, 2382 (6,16)
Campos, L. P.: ref, 1697 (25)
Campostano, A.: ref, 893 (29)
Canada, R.: ref, 364 (15), 2652 (7)
Canadian Test Centre: test, 383
Canadian Test Centre, Educational Assessment Services: test, 384, 388
Canaran, G.: ref, 2288 (78,79), 2289 (65)
Canavan, A. G. M.: ref, 2860 (84,85,99,162,435), 2892 (9,32)
Canby, J.: ref, 322 (5), 827 (8), 2862 (225)
Cancelli, A. A.: rev, 2211
Cancelmo, J. A.: ref, 1697 (160)
Cancienne, J.: ref, 846 (14), 2497 (317), 2519 (36), 2520 (37), 2603 (449)
Candela, K.: ref, 2749 (73)
Candell, G. L.: ref, 180 (4)
Candido, C. L.: ref, 694 (15), 1166 (35), 1697 (60)
Candler Lotvin, A. C.: ref, 1455 (10), 1866 (32)
Canetti, L.: ref, 337 (165,166,188), 2497 (593)
Canetto, S. S.: ref, 1580 (2), 2603 (13)
Canfield, A. A.: test, 391, 392, 1419, 1969, 2571, 2761, 2762, 2764
Canfield, D.: ref, 1619 (11)
Canfield, J. S.: test, 391, 2571
Canino, G.: ref, 451 (14), 1903 (533)
Cann, A.: ref, 337 (154), 893 (34), 2497 (218)
Cannava, P.: ref, 298 (137)
Canney, G.: ref, 1866 (6)
Canning, R. D.: ref, 337 (131)
Cannito, M. P.: ref, 209 (4)
Cannon, D. S.: ref, 1174 (5), 2218 (86)
Cannon, J. T.: ref, 2417 (32)
Cannon, M.: ref, 1653 (12)
Cannon, S. E.: ref, 1166 (91), 2076 (142)
Cannon, T.: ref, 2017 (6), 2288 (25), 2289 (14)
Cannon, T. D.: ref, 748 (6,10), 2050 (4,42,66,78,133), 2288 (75), 2289 (62)
Cannon, W. G.: ref, 1697 (457)
Caño, J. E.: ref, 1140 (42)
Canovas, C. P.: ref, 2247 (72)
Cantor, J.: ref, 2863 (388), 2892 (276)
Cantos, A. L.: ref, 451 (175), 1181 (26), 2879 (198)
Cantrell, P. J.: ref, 298 (89)
Cantwell, D. P.: ref, 1697 (170), 2452 (7)
Cantwell, R. H.: ref, 1466 (3)
Canul, G. D.: ref, 1697 (265)
Capalbo, C.: ref, 2218 (99), 2305 (226)
Capaldi, D. M.: ref, 451 (101, 1697 (121), 2879 (158)
Capasso, R.: ref, 2163 (176,226,333)
Capdevila, A.: ref, 272 (309)
Capirci, O.: ref, 540 (13), 1903 (502), 2862 (572)
Capitani, E.: ref, 2163 (120)
Caplan, B.: ref, 1592 (6), 2159 (1), 2163 (2), 2603 (511)
Caplan, B. B.: ref, 1697 (570), 2010 (23), 2860 (1348), 2863 (406), 2879 (216), 2892 (289)
Caplan, D.: ref, 2863 (393)
Caplan, L. J.: ref, 2860 (819)
Caplan, R.: ref, 674 (4), 2862 (241)
Caplan, R. D.: ref, 2497 (454)
Capleton, R. A.: ref, 1758 (62), 2288 (63), 2289 (48)
Capner, M.: ref, 1590 (21)
Capodieci, S.: ref, 298 (68), 2247 (25), 2603 (148)
Cappa, S.: ref, 2163 (38), 2863 (43)
Cappa, S. F.: ref, 1903 (45), 2163 (8,177), 2860 (163), 2873 (25)
Capparella, O.: ref, 2163 (328) 2860 (1281)
Cappelli, M.: ref, 451 (2)
Cappo, S. F.: ref, 2163 (284), 2860 (1130)
Capps, L.: ref, 433 (10), 2214 (92), 2228 (12), 2603 (444), 2813 (85)
Caprara, G. V.: ref, 451 (88), 472 (155)
Capri, S.: ref, 2288 (14), 2289 (9)
Capron, C.: ref, 2862 (448)

Capruso, D. X.: ref, 776 (36), 2860 (1206)
Capuzzo, N.: ref, 272 (164), 1079 (63), 2065 (24), 2497 (547)
Caracelli, V. J.: ref, 373 (3)
Caramazza, A.: ref, 2163 (67,176,226,333), 2863 (67)
Carames, R.: ref, 2497 (112)
Carbo, M.: test, 623, 2181
Carbonari, J. P.: ref, 136 (9)
Carbonell, J. L.: rev, 2565
Carbonin, P. V.: ref, 2163 (328), 2860 (1281)
Carbonneau, R.: ref, 1661 (78), 2039 (23)
Carbonnel, S.: ref, 2860 (1236), 2863 (370)
Cardall, A. J.: test, 394
Carden, A. I.: ref, 372 (29), 999 (27)
Cardinale, S.: ref, 1040 (6,7)
Cardoza, D.: ref, 615 (23)
Care, E.: ref, 399 (4)
Carey, J.: ref, 1939 (14)
Carey, K. B.: ref, 1304 (1), 1661 (39), 1745 (55), 2402 (4) 2603 (85)
Carey, K. T.: rev, 1, 193, 489, 1052
Carey, M. D.: ref, 2603 (85)
Carcy, M. P.: ref, 472 (92), 793 (6), 2214 (37,52), 2230 (16), 2402 (4), 2497 (311), 2498 (32)
Carey, N. B.: ref, 180 (37)
Carey, R. J.: ref, 1697 (4)
Carey, T. C.: ref, 2214 (37,93), 2230 (16), 2231 (5) 2497 (311), 2498 (32)
Carey, W. B.: test, 425
Cargo, A. P.: ref, 997 (11)
Cariglia-Bull, T.: ref, 1071 (4)
Carledge, G.: ref, 2452 (10)
Carlesimo, G.: ref, 1485 (55)
Carlesimo, G. A.: ref, 1903 (501), 2163 (148, 185,201,202,265), 2226 (19), 2227 (34,55), 2860 (585,820,1052,1237,1381), 2862 (571), 2863 (173), 2907 (7)
Carless, S. A.: ref, 1755 (70), 2360 (8)
Carlier, I. V. E.: ref, 2858 (126)
Carlin, A. S.: ref, 1705 (2)
Carlisle, J. F.: ref, 2901 (85)
Carlozzi, A. F.: ref, 1745 (47), 2497 (382)
Carlson, B. E.: ref, 1000 (13)
Carlson, C. F.: ref, 272 (264), 1697 (533), 2247 (113)
Carlson, C. I.: rev, 1012, 1918
Carlson, C. L.: ref, 681 (6)
Carlson, C. R.: ref, 2497 (5,56,176)
Carlson, D.: rev, 693
Carlson, E.: test, 74; ref, 373 (10), 451 (203), 1902 (91,95), 2860 (1286), 2862 (564,630), 2864 (124), 2901 (102,120)
Carlson, E. A.: ref, 451 (190), 1321 (9), 1965 (63), 2614 (2), 2749 (44), 2860 (1009), 2862 (615), 2864 (61)
Carlson, E. B.: test, 846; ref, 846 (18)
Carlson, G.: ref, 1010 (3), 2862 (31)
Carlson, G. A.: ref, 748 (9), 1093 (45), 1592 (10), 1697 (210)
Carlson, G. S.: ref, 2008 (3)
Carlson, J.: rev, 15, 17, 38; ref, 2444 (1), 2452 (6), 2841 (1)
Carlson, J. E.: rev, 1846
Carlson, J. F.: rev, 272, 843, 1758, 1917, 2231, 2499
Carlson, J. R.: ref, 2860 (1143)
Carlson, J. V.: rev, 1792, 1881
Carlson, K. A.: test, 427; rev, 710
Carlson, M. A.: ref, 1745 (46)
Carlson, M. C.: ref, 815 (50), 1164 (175)
Carlson, R.: ref, 272 (303), 2497 (646)
Carlson, R. D.: rev, 2038
Carlson, S. M.: ref, 1903 (557)
Carlson, T. R.: rev, 2170, 2320
Carlson-Greene, B.: ref, 1010 (72), 2485 (163), 2813 (86), 2879 (106)
Carlsson, G.: ref, 303 (8), 2862 (478)
Carlsson, S.: ref, 2497 (129)
Carlton-Ford, S.: ref, 1010 (52)
Carmel, S.: ref, 2497 (103,234)
Carmelli, D.: ref, 303 (26,30), 2599 (42), 2860 (919,1382)
Carmer, J. C.: rev, 1631, 1721, 2305, 2557
Carmichael, C. M.: ref, 998 (65)
Carmichael, M. S.: ref, 1697 (266)
Carmin, C. N.: ref, 1687 (13), 1697 (26,97), 1731 (1)
Carmody, T.: ref, 473 (5), 1166 (160)
Carmoi, T.: ref, 1166 (99), 2863 (310)
Carney, A. E.: rev, 891; ref, 214 (17), 240 (3), 1095 (26), 1982 (8), 2233 (2)
Carney, C. G.: test, 404
Carney, E. : ref, 214 (17), 240 (3), 1095 (26), 1982 (8), 2233 (2)
Carney, I.: test, 1220
Carney, R.: ref, 1765 (32), 2862 (563)
Carney, R. E.: test, 795, 1002, 2161, 2237
Carney, R. N.: rev, 1397, 1652, 2293
Carnine, D.: ref, 2905 (13)
Carnrike, C. L. M., Jr.: ref, 2117 (4)
Caro, F.: ref, 2892 (172)
Caro-Martinez, L. M.: ref, 459 (6), 811 (2), 1485 (6), 1653 (1)
Caropreso, E. J.: ref, 1379 (42), 1903 (239), 2163 (149)
Carpendale, J. I.: ref, 1408 (3)
Carpenter, B.: ref, 1903 (550), 2226 (32), 2710 (7)
Carpenter, C.: ref, 1164 (149), 2860 (1269), 2863 (384), 2879 (206), 2892 (272)
Carpenter, C. D.: rev, 209, 1094, 1421, 2213, 2453, 2488, 2665
Carpenter, C. J.: ref, 2860 (510)
Carpenter, K.: ref, 303 (19)f, 2227 (48), 2860 (1323), 2863 (398), 2892 (283)
Carpenter, K. M.: ref, 1745 (73), 2603 (341)
Carpenter, L. L.: ref, 1166 (15), 2603 (39)
Carpenter, P. K.: ref, 2485 (120)
Carpenter, S.: ref, 298 (103)

Carpenter, W. T.: ref, 650 (11), 2050 (11,24), 2288 (31), 2289 (23), 2305 (89)
Carpenter, W. T., Jr.: ref, 2516 (34), 2892 (105)
Carpentieri, S.: ref, 1612 (40), 2862 (218)
Carpentieri, S. C.: ref, 2813 (58)
Carper, R. A.: ref, 2860 (1102), 2863 (329)
Carpiniello, B.: ref, 272 (103)
Carr, C. R.: ref, 1740 (7), 2076 (23), 2599 (6), 2860 (240)
Carr, D. E.: ref, 451 (97)
Carr, J.: ref, 1903 (240), 2485 (121)
Carr, J. G.: ref, 272 (156)
Carr, K. F.: ref, 2858 (17)
Carr, M.: ref, 1380 (19)
Carr, R.: ref, 846 (22), 1697 (551)
Carr, R. E.: ref, 1697 (394)
Carr, S.: ref, 1321 (4)
Carr, S. H.: ref, 265 (1), 1725 (1), 2724 (1)
Carr, S. J.: ref, 2603 (93)
Carr, T. J.: ref, 2288 (55,78,79), 2289 (42,65)
Carr, V. J.: ref, 998 (119), 1079 (37,57,74), 2497 (578), 2603 (484)
Carr-Nangle, R. E.: ref, 2603 (367)
Carran, D. T.: ref, 2860 (547), 2879 (68)
Carreiras, M.: ref, 2497 (233), 2656 (6)
Carretta, T. R.: ref, 180 (23,32)
Carriger, M. S.: ref, 1903 (197), 2485 (97)
Carrillo, J.: ref, 2218 (118)
Carro, M. G.: ref, 863 (35)
Carrol, A.: ref, 681 (41), 1765 (15)
Carroll, A.: ref, 1661 (64)
Carroll, B.: test, 429
Carroll, D. J.: test, 901 rev, 299, 2883
Carroll, J. B.: rev, 644, 838, 1042, 1156, 1240, 1664, 2797; ref, 2862 (599)
Carroll, J. L.: ref, 708 (7)
Carroll, K. M.: ref, 2305 (76)
Carroll, S.: ref, 2860 (699)
Carroll, W. M.: ref, 2735 (1)
Carrow-Woolfolk, E.: test, 430, 1847, 1848, 2657
Carruth, A. K.: ref, 1000 (104), 1745 (79)
Carson, D. K.: ref, 451 (176), 811 (13), 1259 (2)
Carson, J. E.: ref, 2729 (3)
Carson, K. A.: ref, 815 (50), 1164 (175), 2860 (1158)
Carson, K. D.: ref, 592 (4), 2797 (1)
Carson, K. P.: ref, 1689 (2)
Carson, R.: ref, 2497 (438)
Carson, R. E.: ref, 2892 (162)
Carson, W. H.: ref, 1166 (44)
Carssow, K. L.: ref, 298 (137)
Carstensen, L. L.: ref, 2839 (3)
Carswell, L. M.: ref, 1758 (83), 2860 (1238)
Carta, M. G.: ref, 272 (103)
Carte, E. T.: ref, 665 (14), 1379 (6), 2010 (21), 2488 (2), 2862 (449), 2901 (86)
Carter, A. S.: ref, 472 (114), 2214 (60)
Carter, C.: ref, 1201 (4), 1903 (397)
Carter, C. S.: ref, 2603 (198,342)
Carter, D. B.: ref, 298 (93,117), 998 (59)
Carter, F. A.: ref, 1166 (45)
Carter, G. L.: ref, 1079 (37)
Carter, H. D.: rev, 1312, 1790
Carter, J.: ref, 665 (71), 1657 (13), 1866 (34), 1903 (326), 2485 (152), 2694 (11), 2695 (32, 2879 (95)
Carter, J. A.: test, 716
Carter, J. D.: ref, 2864 (80)
Carter, K. R.: ref, 665 (39), 2295 (2), 2359 (1)
Carter, L. E.: ref, 2516 (70)
Carter, M.: ref, 2239 (34)
Carter, M. J.: ref, 1697 (68), 2050 (5)
Carter, M. M.: ref, 2497 (438)
Carter, R. T.: ref, 2497 (161)
Carter, S.: test, 2579
Carthy, L.: ref, 1379 (99), 1698 (21), 1902 (100), 2879 (228), 2901 (131)
Carton, E.: ref, 472 (207)
Cartwright, C.: ref, 771 (28), 2497 (497)
Cartwright, L. K.: ref, 372 (60)
Cartwright, L. R.: ref, 1394 (5), 1852 (1), 1903 (208)
Cartwright, R. M.: ref, 298 (40), 615 (19), 665 (28), 1140 (15), 1866 (14), 2163 (52), 2485 (30), 2729 (2), 2771 (8)
Cartwright, S.: ref, 739 (4), 1824 (1,3)
Caruso, D. R.: ref, 2860 (343)
Caruso, L.: ref, 2497 (190)
Carvajal, H.: ref, 1612 (36), 1903 (24,159), 2485 (22), 2860 (86,821,1053), 2862 (193), 2864 (39)
Carvajal, H. H.: ref, 624 (4), 2485 (76), 2862 (157), 2864 (36)
Carver, C.: test, 2910
Carver, C. S.: ref, 272 (345), 372 (61), 1158 (2), 1697 (27,267), 2218 (87), 2497 (30,391)
Carver, R. P.: ref, 773 (2), 1903 (110), 2163 (82), 2860 (336)
Carwile, S.: ref, 1697 (278), 2860 (1031), 2863 (306)
Caryl, P. G.: ref, 128 (1,3), 2163 (203)
Casacchia, M.: ref, 1525 (10), 2892 (152)
Casanova, G. M.: ref, 448 (6)
CASAS: test, 645
Casas, J. M.: rev, 304, 918, 1534, 2628
Casby, M. W.: rev, 2936
Cascella, N. G.: ref, 1697 (88), 2402 (6)
Cascino, G. D.: ref, 2860 (537), 2863 (152)
Case, G.: ref, 998 (23), 1697 (106)
Case-Smith, J.: ref, 1901 (7,17), 2377 (2)
Casella, D. F.: ref, 998 (6)
Caselli, M. C.: ref, 2864 (129)
Caselli, R. J.: ref, 641 (2), 2517 (3), 2860 (822), 2863 (237), 2892 (167)
Casey, B.: ref, 1140 (55,56)
Casey, B. J.: ref, 2860 (436)
Casey, J.: ref, 861 (2,5), 1903 (413,495), 2695 (61), 2905 (87,105)
Casey, J. E.: ref, 1164 (26), 1903 (69)
Casey, M. B.: ref, 298 (28,138)

Casey, P.: ref, 1166 (95)
Casey, P. H.: ref, 451 (33), 1216 (37,38,39,40,41), 1903 (234), 2485 (112,113,114,115)
Casey, R.: ref, 1000 (103), 2214 (115), 2497 (609)
Casey, R. J.: ref, 451 (35), 1903 (376)
Casey, T. A.: ref, 1697 (273), 2860 (597)
Cash, T. F.: rev, 2349;ref, 2497 (53)
Cashel, M. L.: ref, 1698 (22), 1959 (2), 2553 (4), 2879 (229)
Cashew, V.M.: test, 904
Cashin, W. E.: test, 1236
Caso, A.: test, 308
Casper, R. C.: ref, 2305 (95)
Caspi, A.: ref, 358 (8), 365 (2,10), 373 (4,21,24), 451 (133), 1010 (38,98), 1612 (38), 2211 (22,37), 2516 (59), 2862 (469,536)
Cassady, S.: ref, 2305 (203)
Cassano, G. B.: ref, 1166 (205), 2603 (135,211)
Cassar, R.: ref, 694 (129)
Cassaretto, F. P.: rev, 46
Cassel, R.: test, 707, 2716
Cassel, R. N.: test, 913, 1146, 1439, 1449, 2713
Cassel, W. S.: ref, 1592 (17)
Cassell, W. A.: test, 2099, 2457
Cassens, H. L.: ref, 2497 (3)
Casserly, C.: test, 1493
Cassidy, J.: ref, 1903 (536), 2497 (475)
Cassidy, T.: ref, 273 (16), 1745 (66)
Cassisi, J. E.: ref, 376 (16), 1164 (146), 1740 (17), 1959 (5), 2516 (95), 2863 (375), 2892 (267)
Castanedo, S. H.: ref, 2050 (135), 2288 (59), 2289 (45)
Casteel, C. A.: ref, 665 (61), 705 (2)
Castellani, B.: ref, 697 (5), 2603 (522)
Castellani, M. E.: ref, 451 (158)
Castellani, R.: ref, 2768 (34), 2860 (1082)
Castellanos, F. X.: ref, 451 (102,243), 2305 (169), 2862 (450,702), 2879 (227)
Castellanos, M.: ref, 1379 (18,29), 2485 (57,94), 2860 (478), 2862 (166,211), 2879 (45,59)
Castelloe, P.: ref, 459 (16,35), 1485 (40), 1903 (350), 2813 (31), 2860 (437)
Castelnau, D.: ref, 2305 (117)
Castiello, U.: ref, 2860 (566,800)
Castillo, A.: ref, 1991 (21), 2498 (6), 2647 (1)
Castillo, C. S.: ref, 2050 (28,111), 2305 (228), 2813 (149)
Castillo-Canez, I.: ref, 1697 (578)
Castle, J. M.: ref, 358 (7), 1903 (241)
Castlebury, F. D.: ref, 1697 (534)
Castles, A.: ref, 2905 (97)
Castonguay, L. G.: ref, 272 (157,180), 991 (2), 2305 (122)
Castonguay, M.: ref, 2125 (25), 2860 (1256)
Castro, J.: ref, 999 (176)
Casualty Actuarial Society: test, 144, 148, 149
Casullo, M. M.: ref, 1991 (21), 2498 (6),2647 (1)
Catalan, J.: ref, 2050 (64,93), 2076 (97), 2239 (18), 2497 (384), 2860 (581), 2863 (168), 2892 (106)
Catalán, R.: ref, 998 (35), 1164 (70), 2860 (681), 2863 (201)
Catalano, J. F.: ref, 998 (114)
Catalano, M.: ref, 1166 (75)
Catania, J. A.: ref, 337 (12)
Catano, V.: ref, 272 (329)
Catanzaro, S.: ref, 451 (51)
Catanzaro, S. J.: ref, 472 (174), 1178 (10), 1181 (12), 2214 (106), 2258 (2), 2497 (542)
Cate, I. M. P-T.: ref, 270 (36)
Catell, P.: ref, 1939 (6)
Caterino, L. C.: ref, 2417 (18)
Caterson, I. D.: ref, 1166 (11)
Cathers, T.: ref, 1294 (3), 2533 (1)
Catlin, R.: test, 1665
Caton, H. R.: test, 324
Catron, T.: ref, 2498 (47)
Cattarin, J.: ref, 893 (27)
Cattell, A. K. S.: test, 745, 2417
Cattell, H. E. P.: test, 2417; ref, 2417 (25)
Cattell, M. D.: test, 1201
Cattell, P.: test, 433; rev, 1414
Cattell, R. B.: test, 477, 538, 644, 745, 888, 915, 1201 1321, 1721, 1779, 2318, 2417; rev, 374; ref, 2417 (25)
Catterson, J. H.: test, 861
Catts, H. W.: ref, 994 (7), 1095 (14), 1131 (9), 1503 (1,4,6), 1902 (1), 1903 (160,318), 2524 (4), 2674 (2,5), 2694 (1), 2695 (1,16), 2704 (21), 2768 (1,13), 2862 (194), 2864 (37), 2879 (3), 2905 (1,34)
Catts, S. V.: ref, 1903 (198)
Cauce, A. M.: ref, 2498 (16)
Caudle, J.: ref, 2125 (23), 2860 (1118), 2892 (232)
Caughy, M. O.: ref, 1216 (42), 1902 (53,83)
Caulley, D. N.: rev, 773
Cautela, J.: test, 1052
Cautela, J. R.: test, 279, 1052, 1853
Cavalli-Sforza, L. L.: ref, 2305 (22), 2862 (486)
Cavallo, G.: ref, 1021 (1)
Cavallotti, G.: ref, 2163 (8)
Cavanaugh, J. L.: ref, 1697 (72)
Cavanaugh, J. L., Jr.: ref, 1697 (488)
Cavazzoni, P.: ref, 2305 (212)
Cavell, T. A.: ref, 615 (48,49)
Cavenar, J. O., Jr.: ref, 998 (19), 2305 (30)
Caviness, V. S.: ref, 2227 (26), 2860 (1103)
Cazdan, C. B.: rev, 2740, 430, 2488
Cazzani, M.: ref, 2163 (263)
Ceballo, R.: ref, 272 (86), 1697 (337), 2860 (710)
Ceballos-Capitaine, A.: ref, 2076 (8)
Cebollero, A. M.: ref, 790 (29)
Ceccoli, S.: ref, 1525 (10)
Cecero, J. J.: ref, 1661 (68), 2218 (88)
Ceci, S. J.: ref, 1903 (338)
Cehen, Y-F.: test, 1236

Celano, M.: ref, 1093 (92)
Celano, M. P.: ref, 353 (6), 1164 (42), 2862 (195)
Celeste, B. L.: ref, 1697 (395), 1790 (6)
Celiberti, D. A.: ref, 2485 (77)
Cella, D. F.: ref, 1000 (35), 1164 (4), 1166 (8), 2076 (153), 2860 (94)
Cellar, D. F.: ref, 2218 (51)
Cellucci, T.: ref, 1697 (177)
Cenacchi, T.: ref, 1166 (69)
Censits, D. M.: ref, 2892 (204)
Center for Applied Linguistics: test, 250, 481, 1191, 1255
Center for Faculty Evaluation and Development: test, 1233
Center for Occupational and Professional Assessment: test, 1048
Center for Studies in Education and Human Development: test, 1618
Center for the Study of Aging and Human Development: test, 1808
Central Institute for the Deaf: test, 488
Centre for Research on Learning and Instruction, University of Edinburgh: test, 2341
Cerella, J.: ref, 2163 (9), 2860 (28)
Cerezo, M. A.: ref, 448 (26), 451 (103)
Cermak, L. S.: ref, 2860 (3,229,243,314,337, 412, 775, 1239,1406), 2863 (2,59,61,85,89,110,227, 371,425), 1218 (13), 1725 (8),1903 (1), 2724 (5), 2873 (50)
Cernovsky, Z. Z.: ref, 1697 (535), 2163 (313)
Cerny, J. A.: ref, 2497 (17)
Certification Board of the Professional Picture Framers Association: test, 435
Cerullo, F. M.: test, 916
Cervantes, E. A.: ref, 652 (4)
Cervantes, R. C.: ref, 1697 (7), 2603 (40)
Cervenka, E. J.: rev, 1664
Cervera, N.: ref, 1000 (13,61)
Cervera, V. M.: test, 1030
Cescato, M.: ref, 2603 (532)
Cezayirli, E.: ref, 1758 (99), 2860 (1379), 2863 (414)
CFKR Career Materials, Inc.: test, 993, 1200, 1518
Chabriat, H.: ref, 376 (33), 2239 (35)
Chacko, R. C.: ref, 1686 (7), 2288 (50)
Chad, D. A.: ref, 2862 (526)
Chadbourn, R. A.: rev, 1315
Chadbourne, J. W.: test, 162, 1929
Chadwick, P. D. J.: ref, 2050 (7)
Chaffer, D.: ref, 2497 (404)
Chaffin, M.: ref, 451 (177), 1380 (17), 1697 (161),2432 (33), 2860 (338)
Chahal, R.: ref, 2050 (23)
Chaikelson, J.: ref, 998 (95), 2163 (215)
Chaikelson, J. S.: ref, 998 (62), 1164 (55), 1661 (27), 2227 (14), 2863 (162), 2892 (96)
Chaiken, S. R.: ref, 180 (16), 745 (9)
Chakos, M.: ref, 2288 (45), 2305 (70,123)
Chakos, M. H.: ref, 2288 (64), 2305 (170)
Chakraborty, P. K.: ref, 2603 (95)
Chalder, T.: ref, 1079 (59)
Chalgujian, H.: ref, 1745 (10)
Chall, J. S.: test, 823, 2253, 2254
Challis, G. B.: ref, 2497 (162)
Challman, R. C.: rev, 2248
Chalmers, D. K.: ref, 136 (4)
Chamberlain, F.: ref, 1758 (24), 2050 (71), 2860 (624)
Chamberlain, K.: ref, 1178 (2,12), 2126 (10)
Chamberlain, L.: ref, 4 (14), 2052 (1)
Chambers, B.: ref, 560 (2)
Chambers, D. C.: test, 2459
Chambers, J. L.: test, 1988
Chambers, J. W., Jr.: ref, 272 (346), 2603 (575)
Chambers, L.: ref, 760 (3), 1697 (223)
Chambers, M. J.: ref, 298 (76)
Chambless, D. L.: ref, 2497 (86,163,168,462),2519 (53), 2520 (14,52), 2603 (352)
Chambliss, C.: ref, 2125 (20,21)
Champagne, J.: ref, 2603 (501)
Champagne, M. T.: ref, 2860 (1143)
Champion, H. R.: ref, 337 (14), 1925 (1)
Champlin, C. A.: ref, 799 (2)
Champney, H.: test, 1026
Chamrad, D. L.: ref, 2214 (61) 2862 (320), 2879 (107)
Chan, A. S.: ref, 776 (41)
Chan, D.: ref, 999 (150), 1106 (1), 1404 (15), 2163 (209,266), 2218 (89,122), 2860 (1384), 2899 (14)
Chan, D. W.: ref, 272 (104), 472 (75), 694 (48), 1079 (17), 1590 (42,43), 1825 (3), 1965 (77), 2218 (71), 2858 (61,92,93,94), 2862 (451)
Chan, L. K. S.: ref, 32 (1), 2092 (2), 2163 (20), 2487 (14), 2743 (2)
Chan, T.: ref, 1382 (1), 1384 (2), 2860 (637)
Chan-Yip, A.: ref, 451 (145)
Chance, B.: ref, 1745 (30)
Chandler, J. L.: ref, 776 (26), 1164 (77), 2858 (105), 2863 (293)
Chandler, L. A.: test, 2514
Chandler, S. K.: test, 2828
Chandler, T. A.: ref, 142 (1),682 (2)
Chandler-Holtz, D.: ref, 2603 (507)
Chandra, R.: ref, 2305 (93,94)
Chaney, C.: rev, 2674
Chaney, J. M.: ref, 337 (106), 472 (139), 2498 (54), 2603 (523,545)
Chang, A. S.: ref, 2858 (7)
Chang, E.: ref, 540 (4)
Chang, E. C.: ref, 2603 (576)
Chang, I.: ref, 1661 (52), 1697 (474)
Chang, L.: ref, 2516 (49), 2860 (712), 2863 (210), 2892 (138)
Chang, L-W.: ref, 1000 (62), 1580 (5)
Chang, S.: ref, 1134 (4), 1903 (263), 2485 (130),2862 (265), 2879 (78)
Chang, S. M.: ref, 1134 (6), 1216 (64), 1903 (361)
Chang, S. S-Y.: ref, 2860 (1184)
Chang, S-H.: ref, 908 (12), 1101 (2), 2417 (41)

Chang, V.: ref, 2901 (85)
Channell, R. W.: ref, 241 (1), 994 (1), 1240 (5), 1379 (4), 1903 (25,70), 2190 (1), 2695 (3,6)
Channon, S.: ref, 272 (158), 2193 (14), 2497 (235,236), 2860 (438,1054), 2892 (218)
Chansky, T. E.: ref, 2214 (8), 2498 (10)
Chantler, L.: ref, 1522 (1)
Chao, C.: test, 1987
Chao, G. T.: ref, 1701 (34)
Chao, L.: ref, 1140 (45)
Chao, W.: ref, 2326 (1), 2603 (213)
Chapelle, C.: ref, 666 (2,3), 1140 (2,3,21), 1592 (1)
Chapin, F. S.: test, 438
Chapin, K.: ref, 1697 (343)
Chapin, K. J.: ref, 1697 (475)
Chaplin, W.: ref, 1697 (451)
Chaplin, W. F.: ref, 1965 (41)
Chapman, J. P.: ref, 2305 (1)
Chapman, J. W.: test, 1916; ref, 358 (13), 1765 (34), 1903 (518), 1916 (1), 2091 (1), 2092 (1), 2714 (1,2,3), 2862 (35,36)
Chapman, L.: ref, 1959 (3)
Chapman, L. J.: ref, 2305 (1)
Chapman, R. C.: ref, 2858 (17)
Chapman, R. S.: ref, 1240 (22), 1379 (38), 1903 (230), 2485 (110), 2657 (11)
Chapman, S.: ref, 375 (3), 2862 (506)
Chapman, S. B.: ref, 375 (7), 994 (45), 2860 (1240), 2862 (705)
Chapman, T.: ref, 2218 (96)
Chapman, T. F.: ref, 2305 (132,147)
Chard, S. R.: ref, 451 (69), 472 (140)
Chari, G.: ref, 1758 (63), 2860 (1055)
Charlebois, P.: ref, 1340 (2), 1661 (69), 2039 (12), 2516 (43), 2862 (321)
Charles, D.: test, 716
Charles, G. A.: ref, 1166 (4), 2305 (14)
Charlton, P. F. C.: ref, 999 (143,151), 1079 (55), 2603 (418,445), 2858 (108,113)
Charlton, T.: ref, 2038 (3)
Charman, A. B. D.: ref, 2603 (583)
Charman, T.: ref, 350 (14), 472 (160), 1653 (15), 2662 (2)
Charnallet, A.: ref, 2860 (1236), 2863 (370)
Charness, N.: ref, 2860 (568)
Charney, D.: ref, 337 (144)
Charney, D. S.: ref, 372 (69), 1166 (123), 2863 (232), 2892 (126)
Chartier, G. M.: ref, 472 (76)
Chartier, M.: ref, 272 (91), 1166 (66), 2497 (397)
Chartrand, J. M.: test, 409; ref, 398 (2), 399 (1), 404 (13,23), 717 (1), 863 (75), 2282 (5)
Chase, C. H.: ref, 2485 (23), 2905 (8)
Chase, C. I.: rev, 666, 1240, 2032, 2410, 2484, 2771
Chase, G. A.: ref, 1485 (33), 1653 (4,17), 2050 (125), 2289 (22), 2516 (72), 2860 (299,721),2862 (283), 2892 (203)
Chase, K. A.: ref, 451 (247)
Chase, N. D.: ref, 592 (18)
Chase, T.: ref, 2860 (511)
Chase, T. N.: ref, 2050 (24), 2860 (244), 2863 (62)
Chase-Lansdale, P. L.: ref, 1902 (84), 1903 (242,451)
Chassin, L.: ref, 372 (24), 451 (19,27,39,43,262), 1661 (8), 1697 (101), 1757 (2)
Chastain, G.: ref, 272 (105)
Chastain, R. L.: ref, 2860 (29)
Chatman, J.: ref, 68 (15)
Chatman, J. A.: ref, 68 (12,39), 1107 (4)
Chatterjee, A.: ref, 209 (1), 376 (14), 1903 (343), 2288 (45), 2305 (123), 2768 (35), 2860 (1126), 2863 (334,372)
Chatterjeee, A.: ref, 209 (2), 1903 (384), 2873 (39)
Chauncey, H.: rev, 1319
Chavira, D.: ref, 1697 (578)
Chavira, V.: ref, 694 (62)
Chay, Y. W.: ref, 999 (51)
Chayer, D. E.: ref, 1300 (6)
Chazan, M.: rev, 1367
Chazan, R.: ref, 1903 (168)
Chazan, S.: ref, 301 (16), 2860 (241)
Chaziuddin, M.: ref, 2862 (706)
Chaziuddin, N.: ref, 473 (6), 2230 (18), 2557 (10)
Chazot, G.: ref, 2860 (844), 2863 (244), 2892 (174)
Check, J. M.: ref, 373 (35)
Checkley, S.: ref, 999 (162)
Checkley, S. A.: ref, 999 (41), 2305 (188)
Chekaluk, E.: ref, 349 (5), 1503 (8), 1903 (185),2123 (1), 2485 (93), 2905 (42)
Chelminski, I.: ref, 2860 (1077)
Chelune, G.: test, 2892; ref, 2860 (992), 2863 (294)
Chelune, G. J.: ref, 1698 (16), 2892 (215)
Chemtob, C. M.: ref, 1592 (19), 1697 (268), 2497 (312), 2516 (36)
Chen, C. L.: ref, 1093 (29), 2108 (4)
Chen, G. P.: ref, 1405 (35)
Chen, G-P.: ref, 2163 (324)
Chen, J.: ref, 2125 (7), 2516 (16), 2860 (310)
Chen, J-Y.: ref, 2516 (94)
Chen, K.: ref, 1216 (60)
Chen, L.: ref, 2305 (165), 2862 (520)
Chen, R.: ref, 459 (30,36), 1485 (30,42), 1612 (53,74), 1903 (279,382), 2497 (573), 2864 (145), 2905 (122)
Chen, R. S.: ref, 1010 (84), 2211 (42), 2862 (377), 2901 (114)
Chen, T.: ref, 1300 (3)
Chen, T. H.: ref, 1300 (1), 1378 (5)
Chen, W. J.: ref, 1092 (14)
Chen, X.: ref, 472 (115)
Chen, Y. W.: ref, 2813 (84)
Chen, Y-W.: ref, 451 (71), 815 (21), 1135 (14), 1485 (38), 1612 (66), 1903 (339), 2485 (161)
Chena, K.: ref, 301 (52), 815 (30), 2862 (407)
Cheng, C.: ref, 1010 (132), 2497 (616)
Cheng, D.: ref, 337 (52)

Cheng, J. C.: ref, 540 (9), 2485 (207), 2860 (1302), 2862 (508), 2879 (172,210), 2905 (99,114)
Cheng, P.: ref, 1592 (12)
Cheng, P. E.: ref, 1759 (18)
Chengappa, K. N. R.: ref, 2305 (133)
Chennault, S. A.: ref, 2813 (110)
Cheramic, G. M.: ref, 2860 (1030)
Cherbuliez, T.: ref, 1697 (13)
Cherian, V. I.: ref, 169 (1)
Cherkes-Julkowski, M.: ref, 2485 (242)
Cherlin, A. J.: ref, 1216 (69), 1903 (395)
Chermak, G. D.: ref, 1612 (9), 2864 (7)
Cherny, S. S.: ref, 270 (48), 2485 (244)
Cherpitel, C. J.: ref, 135 (3,6), 1661 (40,79)
Cherrick, H. M.: rev, 780, 1498
Cherrier, M. M.: ref, 2860 (1308)
Cherry, L.: ref, 815 (21),1135 (14),1485 (38), 1612 (66), 1903 (339), 2485 (161),2813 (84)
Chertkow, H.: ref, 1164 (57), 2163 (310,314), 2860 (586), 2863 (174,363,373), 2873 (61)
Chervinsky, A.: ref, 2860 (697,698), 2863 (204)
Cheseldine, S.: test, 1897
Chesney, M.: ref, 2858 (48)
Chesney, M. A.: ref, 2858 (36,65)
Chessor, D.: ref, 2091 (5)
Chester, B.: ref, 2305 (234)
Chesterfield, K. B.: rev, 664
Chethik, L.: ref, 272 (262), 2433 (2), 2603 (521)
Cheung, C.: ref, 771 (27)
Cheung, E.: ref, 272 (68), 1164 (50), 2516 (29), 2860 (498)
Cheung, E. C.: ref, 2603 (446)
Cheung, F. M.: ref, 372 (97), 1697 (476)
Cheung, H.: ref, 2860 (291)
Cheung, L. P.: ref, 272 (287), 1079 (94)
Cheung, M.: ref, 1093 (116)
Cheung, P. C.: ref, 999 (161)
Cheung, S.: ref, 495 (10), 2358 (7)
Cheung, S. M.: ref, 998 (8)
Chevron, E. S.: test, 215
Chew, A. L.: test, 1515
Chewning, W. W.: ref, 2863 (29)
Chi, H.: ref, 2768 (39)2860 (1188), 2863 (357)
Chi, M. T. H.: ref, 1903 (26), 2163 (24), 2862 (62)
Chi-Ching, Y.: ref, 1469 (5)
Chiappe, P.: ref, 2879 (235)
Chiara, G.: ref, 2858 (111)
Chiaunza, G. A.: ref, 2813 (32)
Chibnall, J. T.: ref, 1164 (141), 2497 (23), 2860 (1224)
Chicoine, A. J.: ref, 2125 (6), 2860 (272), 2862 (135)
Chien, T.: ref, 301 (52), 815 (30), 2862 (407)
Chilamkurti, C.: ref, 448 (9)
Chilcoat, H. D.: ref, 999 (149)
Child Health and Education Study, University of Bristol: test, 901
Childers, J. S.: ref, 1903 (243)
Childers, L. M.: ref, 1697 (557)
Children's Bureau of Southern California: test, 1007
Childress, D.: ref, 1485 (62), 1653 (29), 2860 (1333), 2862 (661)
Childs, G.: ref, 1457 (1,2)
Childs, N. A.: ref, 2860 (788), 2862 (299)
Childs, R.: test, 463, 1837
Chiles, C.: ref, 2516 (19)
Chin, K.: ref, 1697 (34)
Ching, J. W. J.: ref, 2749 (53)
Chinn, S. J.: test, 2678
Chinsky, J. M.: ref, 272 (97)
Chiodo, J.: ref, 2076 (6), 2860 (141)
Chiodo, L. M.: ref, 999 (26), 1289 (1)
Chipuer, H. M.: ref, 2218 (7)
Chirillo, T. K. B.: ref, 2651 (8)
Chiroz, C. E.: ref, 271 (12), 272 (305)
Chisholm, D. C.: ref, 1021 (22)
Chisholm, G.: ref, 1965 (26)
Chisholm, K.: ref, 787 (1)
Chisholm, V.: ref, 2076 (105)
Chisin, R.: ref, 1166 (92)
Chissom, B. S.: rev, 815, 816, 1850, 2599
Chiswick, A.: ref, 2860 (453), 2863 (126)
Chittooran, M. M.: rev, 642, 2043; ref, 1164 (43), 1903 (161)
Chiu, E.: ref, 1164 (108), 1758 (88)
Chiu, R. K.: ref, 2756 (2)
Chizmar, J. F.: test, 247
Chlumsky, M. L.: ref, 1697 (18)
Chmielewski, D.: ref, 1000 (107)
Cho, M. J.: ref, 272 (347), 1166 (218)
Cho, N. H.: ref, 1386 (25), 2860 (1338), 2862 (667)
Cho, Y.: ref, 2860 (1363)
Chobot, K.: ref, 1697 (543)
Choca, J.: test, 667
Choca, J. P.: rev, 262, 1688
Chochinou, H. M.: ref, 2305 (124)
Choi, H. S.: ref, 1991 (73)
Choler, B. J.: ref, 2603 (208)
Chon, C.: ref, 1010 (97)
Choquette, K. A.: ref, 134 (40), 1661 (13,25,71,84)
Chorpita, B. F.: ref, 472 (219), 2214 (94,28), 2498 (59,60)
Chouinard, M. J.: ref, 926 (10), 2010 (9), 2863 (118)
Chovan, W.: ref, 2857 (1), 2862 (242)
Chovaz, C. J.: ref, 1010 (44)
Chrisler, J. C.: ref, 272 (113), 298 (72,95), 1647 (4)
Christensen, A.: ref, 863 (66,78)
Christensen, A. J.: ref, 272 (80), 1412 (2), 1697 (531), 2497 (617), 2858 (95)
Christensen, A. P.: ref, 272 (8), 1274 (1), 2497 (24,439,440)
Christensen, B.: ref, 776 (10), 2863 (96)
Christensen, C. C.: ref, 1657 (9)
Christensen, D. H.: ref, 2034 (5)
Christensen, H.: ref, 999 (56,89,90,114), 1390 (4), 1697 (311), 1758 (26), 2193 (24), 2239 (19,22), 2599 (15), 2860 (587,667,823), 2863 (175,197,238)

Christensen, L.: test, 483; ref, 1294 (2), 1697 (61), 2076 (53,109), 2497 (107), 2519 (9,24), 2520 (9,25), 2603 (41,176)
Christensen, L. A.: ref, 2860 (652), 2863 (191)
Christensen, P. R.: test, 142, 682, 726, 865, 2401
Christensen, S. A.: ref, 694 (100), 1010 (76)
Christensen, S. H.: ref, 1758 (44)
Christensen, S. L.: ref, 246 (1)
Christenson, A. J.: ref, 2218 (52)
Christenson, C.: ref, 2305 (104)
Christenson, G. A.: ref, 2497 (313)
Christenson, S. : test, 1275
Christenson, S. L.: rev, 451
Christeson, J.: ref, 2860 (1094)
Christian, G.: test, 393, 1125
Christiansen, H.: ref, 2879 (113)
Christiansen, J.: ref, 998 (56), 1093 (16), 2603 (203)
Christiansen, J. A.: ref, 2873 (15,29)
Christianson, S. A.: ref, 2860 (439)
Christie, D.: ref, 2860 (1099), 2862 (492), 2864 (117)
Christison, G. W.: ref, 564 (4), 2120 (2), 2288 (12)
Christman, N. J.: ref, 273 (4), 1412 (3), 2117 (1)
Christo, G.: ref, 2497 (314)
Christodorescu, D.: ref, 2163 (66), 2860 (259)
Christodoulou, G. N.: ref, 1093 (69)
Christoffel, K. K.: ref, 451 (86,238), 1010 (131), 1613 (2)
Christophe, A.: ref, 272 (198)
Christopher, J. C.: ref, 272 (290)
Christopher, J. S.: ref, 451 (50)
Christopher, J. S.: ref, 472 (110)
Christophers, U.: test, 1765
Chronicle Guidance Publications, Inc.: test, 485
Chrousos, G.: ref, 1166 (94), 2076 (143), 2603 (442)
Chruch, A. T.: ref, 2218 (97)
Chu, J. A.: ref, 846 (18)
Chu, J.-Y.: ref, 375 (8), 2720 (1), 2892 (297)
Chu, P. C.: ref, 1755 (14)
Chua, J. W.: ref, 335 (13)
Chuang, A.: ref, 815 (21), 1135 (14),1485 (38), 1612 (66), 1903 (339), 2485 (161), 2813 (84)
Chuang, S.: ref, 1096 (4), 2860 (247), 2862 (126)
Chubon, R. A.: ref, 838 (2), 2417 (3)
Chuch, D.: ref, 2860 (883)
Chung, H-H.: ref, 495 (16), 1181 (27), 1991 (105)
Chung, M. C.: ref, 4 (14,15), 999 (107), 2052 (1), 2603 (320)
Chung, R. C-Y.: ref, 1079 (101), 2603 (572)
Chung, T. K. H.: ref, 272 (287), 793 (23), 1079 (94)
Chung, Y. B.: ref, 298 (104)
Church, A. H.: ref, 1755 (76)
Church, A. T.: ref, 2218 (64,90), 2835 (19)
Church, C. C.: ref, 451 (169), 880 (1), 1216 (96)
Church, R. P.: ref, 681 (66), 2862 (393), 2901 (72)
Churchill, E. R.: test, 2143
Churchill, L. R.: test, 2143
Chusmir, L. H.: ref, 68 (22)
Chwalisz, K.: ref, 337 (95,132), 1079 (12), 2603 (447)
Ciancio, C.: ref, 1697 (62)
Ciani, N.: ref, 272 (224), 1166 (33,156)
Ciaranello, R. D.: ref, 2862 (486)
Ciccaglione, S.: ref, 353 (7)
Cicchetti, C.: ref, 1613 (2)
Cicchetti, D.: ref, 365 (3,5,6), 373 (12,15), 472 (41,44,169,192), 694 (49), 1697 (356), 1903 (147,162,227,499,548)
Cicchetti, D. V.: test, 124, 2813, 2814
Cicerone, K. D.: ref, 2860 (4)
Ciechalski, J. C.: rev, 532, 1712, 2223, 2360, 2718
Ciesielski, K. T.: ref, 303 (14), 1164 (1,88,143), 1765 (6), 2163 (315), 2226 (20), 2227 (35), 2860 (824,825,1241), 2862 (63,600,626), 2863 (374), 2879 (199), 2880 (6), 2892 (168,265)
Ciesla, S. G.: test, 921
Cilli, G.: ref, 1169 (5)
Cilveti, R.: ref, 303 (13), 2860 (1191)
CIM Test Publishers: test, 1576
Cimbolic, P.: ref, 2497 (114)
Cinciripini, P. M.: ref, 2076 (110), 2603 (343)
Cincirpini, L. G.: ref, 2603 (448)
Cincirpini, P. M.: ref, 2603 (448)
Cipielewski, J.: ref, 2487 (10)
Cipolotti, L.: ref, 1104 (3,6,7), 1903 (344,452), 2193 (19,36), 2860 (588,826,827,1056,1065),, 2862 (457)
Cipponeri-Hoerchler, S.: test, 2470
Ciranni, M.: ref, 2860 (1320), 2863 (397)
Ciraulo, D.: ref, 1093 (64)
Cisler, R. A.: ref, 2557 (1)
Citrome, L.: ref, 335 (10)
Civelek, A. C.: ref, 2496 (6)
Civita, R.: ref, 2862 (289), 2864 (71)
Civitello, L. A.: ref, 2125 (30), 2768 (43), 2864 (144)
Cizadlo, T.: ref, 650 (13)
Cizek, G. J.: rev, 994, 1835, 2072, 2632
Claassen, N. C. W.: test, 1873
Claiborn, C. D.: rev, 1002, 1698, 1805; ref, 1965 (80), 2835 (26)
Clancy, J.: ref, 998 (56), 2603 (203)
Clancy, K.: ref, 1612 (96), 2695 (69)
Clancy, S. M.: ref, 2860 (589)
Clancy, T.: ref, 1093 (18)
Clancy-Colecchi, K.: ref, 272 (202), 1166 (133,184)
Clanton, L. D.: ref, 1590 (14)
Clapham, M. M.: ref, 2518 (3,4)
Clapp, R. G.: ref, 1404 (3)
Clar, W.: ref, 272 (356), 2603 (581)
Clardige, G.: ref, 999 (179)
Clare, A. W.: ref, 2050 (136), 2305 (157.158)
Clare, I. C. H.: ref, 2497 (474), 2860 (440,590,881)
Clare, L.: ref, 2163 (105), 2860 (1368)
Clarici, A.: ref, 2163 (269)
Claridge, G.: ref, 999 (74)
Clarihew, A.: ref, 358 (3)
Clarizio, H. F.: ref, 2862 (380,436), 2901 (69),83)
Clark, A.: ref, 303 (13), 1079 (60), 2860 (557,1191)

Clark, A. J.: ref, 1049 (2)
Clark, A. N.: ref, 776 (36), 2860 (1206)
Clark, B.: test, 1062
Clark, C.: ref, 364 (9), 1664 (5), 2860 (270), 2863 (70), 2907 (2)
Clark, C. A.: rev, 1376
Clark, C. D.: ref, 337 (79)
Clark, C. H.: ref, 1093 (94)
Clark, C. L.: ref, 2218 (73)
Clark, C. M.: ref, 1164 (144), 1697 (15), 2860 (60,517,1242), 2863 (149), 2907 (3)
Clark, C. R.: ref, 2603 (243)
Clark, D. A.: ref, 2603 (217,310)
Clark, D. B.: ref, 998 (53), 2498 (33)
Clark, D. C.: ref, 272 (64), 2305 (82)
Clark, D. F.: rev, 739
Clark, D. M.: ref, 863 (33), 1991 (40), 2519 (56), 2520 (55)
Clark, E.: rev, 800, 1513, 2735, 2879
Clark, E. N.: test, 2327
Clark, E. O.: ref, 1058 (1), 2860 (21)
Clark, E. S.: ref, 592 (8)
Clark, G.: ref, 474 (1)
Clark, G. M.: test, 2780
Clark, J.: test, 962, 1355, 1952
Clark, J.: ref, 2485 (33)
Clark, J. E.: ref, 2497 (249)
Clark, J. L.: ref, 1755 (26)
Clark, J. L. D.: rev, 953
Clark, K.: ref, 614 (1), 999 (179), 1697 (269), 2497 (315)
Clark, K. A.: ref, 1093 (7)
Clark, L.: ref, 2873 (63)
Clark, L. A.: test, 2306; ref, 272 (283), 372 (112), 1174 (5), 2076 (132), 2218 (6,86), 2497 (640), 2603 (425)
Clark, M.: ref, 538 (3)
Clark, M. E.: ref, 1697 (270,477), 2497 (316,543)
Clark, M. G.: ref, 1485 (50),1903 (453), 2382 (34), 2695 (48)
Clark, M. K.: test, 1532
Clark, M. L.: rev, 2092, 2094; ref, 298 (105), 1036 (10)
Clark, M. M.: ref, 798 (24), 1740 (13), 1903 (491), 1903 (568)
Clark, P.: ref, 846 (18)
Clark, P. M.: rev, 1453, 2704, 2755
Clark, R.: ref, 272 (262), 1093 (12), 1889 (8), 2433 (2), 2497 (482), 2603 (521)
Clark, R. E.: ref, 134 (12)
Clark, R. M.: rev, 723, 2880
Clark, R. T.: ref, 1079 (51), 1758 (52)
Clark, S.: test, 962, 1355, 1952
Clark, S. A.: ref, 1697 (162)
Clark, S. C.: ref, 1093 (58)
Clark, S. E.: ref, 2603 (565)
Clark, S. G.: test, 1316, 1317
Clark, W. C.: ref, 650 (10), 2289 (17), 2305 (77)
Clark, W. W.: test, 374; ref, 134 (35)
Clarke, D.: ref, 537 (3), 998 (111), 2525 (8)
Clarke, D. D.: ref, 838 (23)
Clarke, D. J.: ref, 4 (15)
Clarke, G. N.: ref, 1903 (163), 2305 (40), 2485 (78)
Clarke, P.: ref, 337 (169)
Clarke, S.: test, 1516; ref, 2862 (328)
Clarke, S. G.: ref, 1079 (20)
Clarke-Klein, S.: ref, 540 (1), 994 (21), 1503 (10), 2190 (5), 2879 (108)
Clarke-Klein, S. M.: ref, 1216 (73), 2862 (388), 2901 (70)
Clarkin, J. F.: ref, 1093 (8,29), 2108 (1,4), 2247 (38), 2603 (188,189), 2860 (469)
Clarkson-Smith, L.: ref, 2163 (39), 2860 (164)
Clary, C.: ref, 2603 (296)
Clasen, D. R.: ref, 2771 (28)
Claser, D.: ref, 2076 (187)
Classen, C.: ref, 272 (348), 2076 (144), 2497 (666)
Claude, D.: ref, 1902 (68), 1903 (345), 2862 (322), 2879 (109)
Clauke, A. T.: ref, 1659 (12), 2864 (133)
Claus, J. J.: ref, 2860 (244), 2863 (62)
Clausen, J. A.: ref, 373 (8)
Clausen, T.: ref, 2860 (441), 2863 (119)
Clauser, B.: ref, 1107 (2)
Clauser, B. E.: ref, 592 (90)
Clauson, J.: ref, 1266 (1,2)
Claussen, A. H.: ref, 472 (78), 1000 (66), 2211 (27)
Clavelle, P. R.: ref, 1698 (3)
Clawson, A.: test, 301
Claxton, R. P.: ref, 1755 (35,36)
Clay, D. L.: ref, 2603 (344)
Clay, M.: test, 2283
Claydon, J.: test, 835
Claypoole, K.: ref, 2860 (665), 2863 (195)
Clayton, P.: ref, 1697 (376), 2305 (119)
Cleanthous, C. C.: ref, 2126 (14)
Cleare, A. J.: ref, 1166 (72)
Cleary, P. D.: ref, 1697 (256,257,258,300)
Cleave, P. L.: ref, 214 (14,16), 624 (23,29), 1485 (16,27), 1903 (173,256,410),519,521), 2657 (6,15,32)
Cleeton, G. U.: rev, 394
Clegg, J. A.: ref, 270 (13), 2308 (1)
Clegg, M. R.: ref, 385 (1), 1197 (1)
Cleland, D. L.: rev, 496
Cleland, J. W.: ref, 2864 (42)
Cleland, L. N.: ref, 1902 (5), 2862 (41)
Clemens, P. R.: ref, 2862 (526)
Clement, L.: ref, 2603 (103)
Clément, R.: ref, 272 (163,204)
Clement, R. W.: ref, 1697 (536)
Clement-Heist, K.: ref, 301 (20)
Clements, A.: ref, 2050 (32,54)
Clements, D. H.: ref, 2771 (10)
Clements, J.: ref, 350 (30), 994 (25), 2163 (219)
Clements, K. M.: ref, 272 (321)
Clements, N.: ref, 615 (1), 666 (5)

Clements, R.: ref, 999 (182), 1079 (97)
Clements, W.: ref, 350 (15)
Clementz, B. A.: ref, 1697 (271)
Cleminshaw, H. K.: test, 1888
Clendenen, D. M.: rev, 836, 1790
Clercq, L. D.: ref, 2497 (127)
Clerehugh, J.: test, 892
Clerget-Darpoux, F.: ref, 2227 (19), 2860 (818), 2863 (236)
Cleveland, H. H.: ref, 1902 (90)
Cleveland, J. N.: rev, 871, 2762
Cliche, D.: ref, 650 (15), 1093 (97)
Cliffe, M.: ref, 1943 (1)
Clifford, C.: ref, 2860 (1228), 2863 (366)
Clifford, P. A.: ref, 1686 (1), 2497 (108)
Clifford, R. M.: test, 875, 1009, 1264; ref, 875 (1)
Clinch, J. J.: ref, 2305 (124)
Clingempeel, W. G.: ref, 451 (216)
Clipp, E. C.: ref, 373 (5), 2485 (223)
Cloitre, M.: ref, 846 (5,14), 1093 (112), 2199 (8), 2497 (317), 2498 (43), 2519 (36), 2520 (37), 2603 (191,302,449)
Cloninger, C. J.: test, 553; ref, 553 (1)
Cloninger, C. R.: ref, 999 (86,91), 1166 (55,79,200),1697 (196), 2077 (2), 2603 (271)
Clonts, W. L.: test, 2898
Clopton, J. R.: rev, 1872, 2033, 2854, 2855
Clopton, P.: ref, 2858 (19)
Close, D.: ref, 1164 (170), 2305 (235), 2860 (1350)
Closs, S. J.: test, 1342; ref, 1342 (1)
Cloud, B. S.: ref, 376 (32), 2860 (1400), 2863 (424)
Cloutier, P. F.: ref, 863 (34)
Clubb, P. A.: ref, 1612 (31)
Cluff, R. B.: ref, 1000 (63,64)
Clum, G. A.: ref, 1021 (32), 1619 (11), 2065 (2,10), 2199 (3)
Cluydts, R.: ref, 272 (200), 303 (24), 1164 (129), 1166 (131), 1697 (500), 2125 (28), 2163 (286,345), 2516 (114), 2603 (480), 2860 (1134)
Clyde, D. J.: test, 551
Clymer, T.: test, 552
Cnaan, R. A.: ref, 2603 (567)
Coallier, J-C.: ref, 404 (17)
Coan, R. N.: rev, 1214
Coan, R. W.: test, 888; rev, 1699, 1755, 1939
Coates, S. W.: test, 2042
Coates, T.: ref, 2858 (48)
Coates, T. J.: ref, 337 (12)
Coatsworth, J. D.: ref, 1902 (74)
Cobb, F. R.: ref, 303 (2), 1164 (23), 2497 (104), 2603 (83), 2860 (237)
Cobb, H. C.: rev, 20, 21, 22, 23
Cobb, J.: ref, 2860 (329), 2863 (87)
Cobb, J. L.: ref, 2863 (113)
Coblis, C. R.: ref, 694 (71)
Cobo-Lewis, A. B.: ref, 891 (1)
Coccar, E. F.: ref, 1166 (178)
Coccaro, E. F.: ref, 1166 (96)
Cocchi, S.: ref, 2497 (505)
Cocchini, G.: ref, 2163 (261,312), 2225 (11)
Cocco, K.: ref, 1697 (48)
Cochran, K. F.: ref, 838 (5)
Cochran, L.: rev, 697, 1825, 1913, 2007, 2364, 2832
Cochran, L. R.: rev, 1829
Cochrane, H. J.: ref, 2860 (1383), 2862 (707), 2863 (415)
Cockburn, J.: test, 2239, 2240
Cockburn, J.: ref, 1758 (12,22,64), 2163 (62,106,150,204), 2193 (37), 2239 (6,9,20,23,29), 2860 (828,1057), 2863 (239,309), 2892 (169,219)
Cockburn, J. M.: ref, 2239 (7)
Cockrell, J. R.: ref, 2516 (72), 2892 (203)
Cockroft, R.: ref, 2076 (53), 2519 (24), 2520 (25), 2603 (176)
Cocks, N.: ref, 837 (3), 1765 (19), 1903 (292), 2862 (280)
Codding, K. G.: test, 2692
Coddington, R. D.: test, 557
Code, C.: ref, 2873 (21)
Codina, V.: ref, 1338 (37)
Codori, A-M.: ref, 2860 (1243)
Coe, D.: ref, 2813 (104)
Coe, D. A.: ref, 459 (11), 2813 (14)
Coelho, C. A.: ref, 1379 (52,88), 2008 (12,13), 2873 (52)
Coetzee, T. M.: test, 169
Cofer, C. N.: rev, 1049, 1050, 2258
Coffey, P.: ref, 337 (133,174), 1903 (180), 2905 (39)
Coffey, P. J.: ref, 1758 (99), 2860 (1379), 2863 (414)
Coffman, C. E.: ref, 2125 (30), 2768 (43), 2864 (144)
Coffman, D. D.: ref, 2656 (15)
Coffman, W. E.: rev, 570, 1379, 2518
Cogan, R.: ref, 2749 (85)
Cogar, J. C.: ref, 893 (31)
Cogburn, H. E.: ref, 2218 (114)
Cohan, C. L.: ref, 272 (122), 791 (7,14), 999 (75,124)
Cohen, A. D.: rev, 2015
Cohen, A. J.: rev, 1154, 1752, 2673
Cohen, B.: ref, 1592 (7)
Cohen, B. A.: ref, 1135 (2), 2599 (4), 2860 (200)
Cohen, B. D.: rev, 927, 2006, 2878
Cohen, B. M.: ref, 1166 (91), 2076 (142), 2860 (1210)
Cohen, C.: ref, 280 (2), 1131 (2), 1903 (5), 1987 (1), 2862 (9), 2879 (2)
Cohen, D.: ref, 815 (52), 1340 (5), 2724 (13)
Cohen, D. J.: ref, 451 (137), 1093 (31), 2603 (475), 2813 (10,109), 2860 (932,1001)
Cohen, D. S.: ref, 1000 (65)
Cohen, E.: ref, 2603 (567)
Cohen, F.: ref, 2497 (569)
Cohen, G.: test, 2108; ref, 1093 (39), 2860 (591)
Cohen, G. M.: test, 2109
Cohen, H.: test, 2614
Cohen, I.: ref, 2813 (116)

Cohen, I. L.: ref, 459 (17), 2813 (33)
Cohen, J.: rev, 1321, 2246, 2318, 2776, 2784
Cohen, J. A.: ref, 472 (96), 1991 (70,71), 2498 (38,39)
Cohen, J. D.: ref, 2305 (196), 2892 (108)
Cohen, L.: ref, 199 (4), 2247 (114), 2516 (50)
Cohen, L. H.: ref, 999 (174), 2497 (611), 2498 (1)
Cohen, L. L.: ref, 1000 (105), 1115 (17)
Cohen, M.: ref, 1866 (20)
Cohen, M. J.: test, 476; ref, 229 (1), 462 (26), 798 (13,16), 815 (18), 1131 (12), 1379 (43,64), 1661 (49), 1903 (244,336), 2724 (7,9), 2862 (243,315,535), 2870 (4), 2879 (103), 2934 (1)
Cohen, N. J.: ref, 451 (104), 863 (36), 2860 (9), 2862 (452), 2863 (5)
Cohen, O.: ref, 298 (139)
Cohen, R.: ref, 2485 (122)
Cohen, R. A.: ref, 2860 (592,658), 2863 (193)
Cohen, R. L.: ref, 2860 (1058)
Cohen, R. M.: ref, 681 (39), 2076 (100), 2860 (550), 2863 (222), 2892 (32)
Cohen, S.: ref, 1166 (13), 2485 (61,122), 2695 (13)
Cohen, S. A.: rev, 2469, 2737
Cohen, S. L.: rev, 2280
Cohen, S. P.: test, 2046
Cohen, Y.: ref, 451 (105,178), 472 (161), 2305 (218)
Cohen-Kettenis, P. T.: ref, 2247 (114)
Cohler, B. J.: ref, 2603 (137)
Cohn, D.: ref, 337 (37)
Cohn, D. S.: ref, 1903 (71)
Cohn, J. F.: ref, 451 (282)
Cohn, S.: ref, 1135 (22), 1164 (169), 2226 (35), 2227 (50)
Cohn, S. J.: rev, 592, 1115
Cohon, A. W.: ref, 1745 (30)
Coiro, V.: ref, 1166 (21)
Cokely, C. G.: ref, 2860 (652), 2863 (191)
Coker, C. C.: ref, 1444 (1)
Coker, R. R.: ref, 1698 (1)
Coladarci, T.: rev, 2321
Colangelo, N.: rev, 976, 1088; ref, 413 (7), 1036 (5), 1997 (1), 2862 (13,106)
Colarelli, S. M.: ref, 1965 (55), 2899 (6)
Colarusso, R.: test, 1726
Colarusso, R. P.: test, 1725
Colbert, K. K.: ref, 337 (21,127), 1216 (12)
Colbry, S. L.: ref, 694 (95), 1010 (73), 1947 (4)
Colby, A.: test, 1408, 1625
Colby, S. M.: ref, 134 (15,19,20,27), 272 (90), 1661 (34)
Colder, C. R.: ref, 451 (27,179), 472 (193)
Cole, B.: ref, 376 (19), 776 (42)
Cole, C. M.: ref, 1697 (537)
Cole, C. W.: test, 2475, 2655
Cole, D. A.: ref, 472 (106,116,162), 2214 (62)
Cole, D. E.: rev, 89, 1879
Cole, E.: ref, 472 (38)
Cole, E. J.: ref, 1437 (4)
Cole, J. C.: ref, 2868 (2)
Cole, J. O.: ref, 1166 (91), 1903 (192), 2076 (142), 2860 (491)
Cole, K. N.: ref, 624 (15), 1379 (44), 1485 (25), 1612 (14,15,22,32,43,47,75), 1902 (46,75), 1903 (72,75,111,164,245,391), 2044 (3,5), 2485 (173),2657 (13), 2680 (2,8), 2682 (2,4,5,8), 2704 (16), 2862 (244), 2864 (47)
Cole, M.: ref, 2225 (2), 2873 (3)
Cole, N. S.: test, 1418; rev, 1638
Cole, P. M.: ref, 451 (46,162), 462 (5), 997 (11,25), 2497 (164)
Cole, R. E.: ref, 2860 (57)
Cole, S. W.: ref, 2076 (165)
Cole, V.: ref, 1997 (1)
Cole-Detke, H.: ref, 272 (159), 893 (32)
Colegrove, R., Jr.: ref, 451 (157), 472 (68,151), 1010 (115), 2498 (25)
Colegrove, R. W., Jr.: ref, 2905 (50)
Coleman, C. A.: test, 1490
Coleman, C. C.: ref, 1659 (8,13)
Coleman, D. F.: ref, 1701 (53)
Coleman, D. J.: ref, 286 (2)
Coleman, F. L.: ref, 1697 (272)
Coleman, J. C.: ref, 2858 (83)
Coleman, J. H.: test, 1222, 1223
Coleman, M. J.: ref, 2497 (544)
Coleman, R. E.: ref, 303 (1,2), 791 (2), 1164 (23), 1740 (3), 2497 (21,104), 2516 (2), 2603 (8,83), 2860 (81,237)
Coleton, M. I.: ref, 708 (9)
Colfer, M. V.: ref, 2305 (24)
Coll, C. G.: ref, 681 (87)
Coll, C. T. G.: ref, 1321 (4)
Collacott, R. A.: ref, 2382 (31)
Collard, R. R.: rev, 270
College Board and National Merit Scholarship Corporation: test, 2031
The College Board: test, 18, 571, 592, 593, 594, 595, 596, 597, 598, 599, 600, 601, 602, 603, 604, 605, 606, 607, 608, 609, 610, 611, 612, 613, 614
College Entrance Examination Board: test, 192, 666, 2032
Collette, L.: ref, 2858 (65)
Colletti, A. B.: test, 713
Colletti, G.: ref, 1697 (142)
Colletti, P. M.: ref, 2860 (159)
Colli, M. J.: ref, 2862 (437)
Collier, D.: ref, 2050 (32)
Collier, P.: ref, 2497 (175)
Colligan, R. C.: ref, 1612 (73), 1697 (324,430,499,587), 1698 (12), 2485 (170), 2860 (910), 2862 (356), 2864 (95)
Colligan, S. C.: ref, 2247 (101)
Collings, S. J.: ref, 337 (96)
Collins, A. R.: ref, 1140 (22)
Collins, B. C.: ref, 265 (7),811 (4), 2862 (453)
Collins, C.: rev, 2389, 2577

Collins, D.: rev, 221, 1068
Collins, F. L.: ref, 2497 (56)
Collins, J. F.: ref, 1517 (4)
Collins, J. M.: ref, 372 (109), 2218 (123)
Collins, J. W.: ref, 615 (35)
Collins, K. F.: test, 622
Collins, M.: ref, 2858 (84), 2863 (223)
Collins, M. A.: ref, 2603 (505)
Collins, M. D.: ref, 2485 (4), 2901 (1)
Collins, R. L.: ref, 66 (2), 272 (81), 2076 (76)
Collins, R. P.: ref, 708 (9)
Collins, S.: ref, 1040 (7)
Collins, S. M.: ref, 2862 (731)
Collins-Eaglin, J.: ref, 1720 (5)
Collinsworth, P.: ref, 1128 (3), 1866 (31)
Collison, B. B.: rev, 665
Colom, F.: ref, 2305 (238)
Colombo, G.: ref, 1169 (5), 2860 (127)
Colombo, N.: ref, 2163 (146), 2768 (24)
Colonese, K. L.: ref, 2603 (16)
Colosimo, L.: ref, 2163 (151), 2892 (113)
Colpin, H.: ref, 2497 (441)
Colquitt, J. A.: ref, 2218 (124)
Colson, C.: ref, 2163 (321), 2860 (1253)
Coltheart, M.: test, 2113
Colvin, C. R.: ref, 365 (4), 373 (16,26,38)
Colvin, R. J.: test, 2175
Colwell, J. B.: ref, 557 (1), 2749 (14)
Colwell, R.: test, 1751; rev, 1280, 1629
Colwill, S. J.: ref, 2234 (2)
Colyer, S. P.: ref, 2862 (453)
Comair, Y.: ref, 1902 (69), 2768 (28), 2862 (325), 2879 (110)
Comeau, L.: ref, 2704 (47), 2879 (236), 2905 (123)
Comer, D.: ref, 1939 (12)
Comer, J. F.: ref, 376 (34), 1740 (34), 2193 (30), 2860 (728,1414), 2892 (145,305)
Comer, R.: ref, 1177 (1)
Commander, N. E.: ref, 592 (82), 1755 (54), 1767 (7)
Commenges, D.: ref, 2860 (930), 2863 (90)
Commerford, M. C.: ref, 272 (160)
Commeyras, M.: ref, 665 (38)
Commins, N. L.: ref, 665 (11)
Commins, W. D.: rev, 1693, 1798, 2807
Commission on Professional Development of the Accrediting Association of Bible Colleges: test, 2480
Committee on the American Mathematics Competitions: test, 1595
Compas, B. E.: ref, 337 (70,73,104,134), 472 (77,163), 863 (35), 1661 (30), 2214 (38,95), 2603 (42,76,183,257)
Comptom, W. C.: ref, 2497 (517,680)
Compton, D. M.: ref, 1697 (557)
Compton, W. C.: ref, 272 (332), 1697 (360), 2218 (53)
Comrey, A. L.: test, 672, 673; rev, 219, 1721, 1920, 2797; ref, 672 (4),5)
Comunian, A. L.: ref, 2497 (318), 2656 (7,11)
Concari, S.: ref, 1169 (5)
Concha, M.: ref, 2227 (10), 2599 (9), 2860 (401)
Conder, R. L., Jr.: test, 671
The Conduct Problems Prevention Research Group: ref, 451 (63)
Cone, A.: ref, 2771 (12)
Cone, E. J.: ref, 2076 (20), 2603 (77)
Cone, J. D.: test, 1884, 2127
Cone, L. T.: ref, 2211 (36), 2603 (337)
Cones, J. H.: ref, 2858 (17)
Coney, J.: ref, 2755 (2)
Coney, R., III: test, 2314
Confalonieri, P.: ref, 1903 (563), 2163 (347), 2227 (54), 2768 (42), 2862 (698)
Confessore, G.: ref, 2359 (2)
Confon, J. T.: ref, 863 (86), 2076 (166)
Conger, J.: rev, 1917
Conger, J. C.: rev, 2451, 2858
Conger, K. J.: ref, 2603 (136)
Conger, R. D.: ref, 451 (121), 2218 (15,58,59), 2326 (1), 2603 (136,213,214,244,256,304,305,345,355, 456,457,458,531)
Connard, P.: test, 193
Connell, C. M.: ref, 1965 (13)
Connell, D. R.: test, 319
Connell, P. J.: ref, 430 (4,6,8), 624 (2,11,16,26), 2657 (14), 2695 (51)
Connell, S. K.: ref, 1697 (577)
Connell, T. J.: ref, 2771 (28)
Connelly, A.: ref, 2860 (838), 2863 (243)
Connelly, S. L.: ref, 1405 (23), 2862 (549)
Conners, C. K.: test, 678, 679, 680, 681; ref, 681 (89,90)
Conners, F. A.: ref, 2860 (343)
Connolly, A. J.: test, 1392
Connolly, J.: ref, 1093 (59,70), 2050 (55,87), 2305 (167)
Connolly, J. F.: ref, 1902 (66), 1903 (340,346,469), 2193 (53), 2860 (815,1098), 2863 (327), 2873 (54)
Connolly, K. J.: ref, 681 (51)
Connolly, P. M.: test, 490
Connor, B.: ref, 2862 (259)
Connor, E. J.: ref, 1697 (391), 2860 (808)
Connor, R. T.: ref, 451 (126), 2045 (2), 2657 (25,26,29), 2813 (92,93,119), 2864 (90,91,115)
Connor, S. L.: ref, 2603 (563)
Connors, G. J.: ref, 1661 (20,28)
Conoley, C. W.: rev, 272, 1267, 1411, 2557; ref, 1754 (11)
Conrad, H. S.: rev, 2742
Conrad, M.: ref, 1991 (48)
Conrad, P. F.: ref, 1903 (18,40), 2860 (125), 2862 (52,84), 2901 (3,8)
Console, D. A.: ref, 337 (126), 846 (12), 1697 (468)
Consortium to Establish a Registry for Alzheimer's Disease: test, 434
Constant, C.: ref, 1135 (12), 2813 (67), 2862 (274), 2879 (84)

Constantine, N. A.: rev, 446, 1750; ref, 1079 (16), 1216 (25)
Constantino, L.: test, 993
Constantinou, J.: ref, 1770 (3)
Conte, H. R.: ref, 1697 (122)
Conti, R.: ref, 1393 (1), 1404 (14), 2917 (4)
Conti-Ramsden, G.: ref, 350 (21,26,43), 1095 (43), 1485 (34,39,57), 2045 (1), 2163 (316)
Contos, A. L.: ref, 448 (21), 853 (20), 1226 (2), 2879 (159)
Contreras, J. M.: ref, 2603 (295)
Contreras, R.: ref, 863 (76)
Conture, E. G.: ref, 214 (15), 1095 (21), 1804 (6), 2543 (2)
Convit, A.: ref, 1164 (58), 2892 (109)
Conway, M.: ref, 298 (44,151), 2076 (2)
Conway, M. A.: ref, 2860 (591)
Conway, N.: test, 2472
Conway, V. J.: ref, 272 (49), 2858 (33)
Conyers, O.: ref, 472 (73), 2211 (26), 2862 (238)
Conzales-Aviles, A.: ref, 2860 (837), 2863 (242)
Cook, A.: ref, 272 (96), 1379 (48)
Cook, A. S.: rev, 537
Cook, B.: ref, 1040 (7), 2305 (17)
Cook, B. L.: ref, 2076 (157)
Cook, D.: ref, 1790 (11), 1954 (1)
Cook, D. B.: test, 840
Cook, E. T.: ref, 301 (31), 472 (53), 1164 (49), 1612 (37), 2516 (27), 2816 (1)
Cook, F.: ref, 350 (35), 1060 (7), 2725 (4)
Cook, G.: ref, 1140 (60), 1592 (28)
Cook, G. L.: ref, 926 (18), 1592 (22)
Cook, H.: ref, 2288 (84), 2749 (83)
Cook, J.: rev, 1145, 1596; ref, 2288 (15), 2289 (10), 2305 (62)
Cook, J. A.: ref, 2603 (137,208)
Cook, J. R.: test, 1068
Cook, M.: ref, 696 (2), 999 (185), 1740 (24), 2516 (108), 2860 (1335)
Cook, P.: ref, 1104 (13), 2193 (54), 2860 (1109)
Cook, R.: ref, 272 (106), 1011 (3), 1987 (14), 2497 (442,470), 2862 (398), 2901 (74)
Cook, R. S.: test, 1076, 1082
Cook, S. C.: ref, 2498 (41)
Cook, T. G.: ref, 1661 (77)
Cook, W. W.: rev, 2484
Cooke, A.: ref, 771 (23)
Cooke, A.: ref, 1697 (412)
Cooke, D. K.: rev, 1436, 2593; ref, 2497 (443)
Cooke, D. L.: ref, 2860 (829), 2907 (8)
Cooke, M.: ref, 2858 (65)
Cooke, N.: rev, 163
Cooke, R. A.: test, 1150, 1862
Cooke, R. G.: ref, 1093 (111), 1166 (90,97), 2218 (44), 2305 (171)
Cooksey, R. W.: ref, 2871 (3)
Cooley, E.: ref, 1590 (57), 1701 (50)
Cooley, E. L.: ref, 1010 (78)
Cooley, M. L.: ref, 1216 (13), 1902 (23), 1903 (73)
Cooley, M. R.: ref, 292 (1)
Cooley, V. C.: test, 1490
Coolidge, F. L.: test, 690
Coolidge, F. L.: ref, 690 (1)
Cools, A. R.: ref, 376 (12), 2226 (16), 2516 (35,75,87,88),2860 (79,584,1007,1193,1194), 2892 (7,211,260)
Coon, H.: ref, 1393 (1), 1404 (14), 2917 (4)
Coon, K. B.: test, 868
Cooney, G.: ref, 451 (79), 472 (147), 999 (141), 1012 (1), 1079 (54), 1991 (87)
Cooney, G. H.: ref, 26 (1)
Cooney, J.: ref, 1965 (21)
Cooney, J. B.: ref, 1072 (40)
Cooney, M.: ref, 1093 (71), 2050 (90)
Cooney, N.: ref, 372 (69)
Cooney, N. L.: ref, 134 (14), 372 (14), 1174 (1), 1661 (23,28), 1697 (63,183), 2603 (149)
Cooney, R.: ref, 998 (63), 2860 (560)
Cooney, T. M.: ref, 1010 (58,74,79)
Coons, A. E.: test, 1437
Coons, C. E.: test, 1217
Coons, J.: ref, 1745 (58), 2497 (486)
Coons, P.: ref, 846 (18)
Coons, P. M.: ref, 1697 (211)
Cooper, B. A. B.: ref, 1164 (111), 2862 (397)
Cooper, B. P.: ref, 2163 (212), 2860 (860)
Cooper, C.: rev, 718, 2345; ref, 915 (1), 1021 (19), 1824 (4,6), 2163 (246), 2497 (272), 2525 (3), 2860 (991)
Cooper, C. J.: ref, 999 (173), 2163 (305), 2860 (1182)
Cooper, C. L.: test, 1824; ref, 739 (2,3,4,5),1338 (14),1701 (53), 1824 (1,2,3,5), 2858 (14,75)
Cooper, C. R.: ref, 1405 (2)
Cooper, C. S.: test, 691
Cooper, D.: ref, 1697 (70)
Cooper, D. A.: ref, 2497 (340), 2863 (186)
Cooper, D. H.: ref, 2044 (2)
Cooper, D. L.: ref, 2527 (2)
Cooper, E.: ref, 724 (2, 2518 (2), 2754 (2), 2755 (1), 2771 (11)
Cooper, E. B.: test, 691
Cooper, H.: ref, 999 (28,115), 2078 (3)
Cooper, J. A.: ref, 1758 (19), 2863 (81,120,121), 2892 (67,68)
Cooper, J. E.: test, 2050; ref, 2050 (8,10)
Cooper, M. L.: ref, 1181 (18), 2603 (268)
Cooper, P.: ref, 270 (21,22), 1216 (86), 1612 (86)
Cooper, P. V.: ref, 1903 (46)
Cooper, R. M.: test, 1475
Cooper, S.: ref, 2247 (5), 2749 (7), 2860 (124)
Cooper, S. A.: ref, 2382 (31)
Cooper, S. D.: ref, 2603 (311)
Cooper, T.: ref, 1166 (179)
Cooper, T. B.: ref, 451 (220), 1166 (1), 1216 (108), 2305 (12), 2860 (297,924,1205), 2892 (261)
Cooper, U.: ref, 272 (270), 2860 (1265)

Cooper, V.: ref, 1135 (25), 2863 (418)
Cooper, Z.: ref, 2050 (127)
Coopersmith, S.: test, 289, 694
Cooperstein, M. A.: rev, 1495, 2207
Cooter, R. B., Jr.: rev, 2556, 2743, 2905; ref, 1072 (6)
Coots, J.: ref, 2813 (118)
Coovert, M. D.: ref, 999 (88)
Cope, C. S.: test, 1954
Cope, H.: ref, 2050 (88)
Cope, J. G.: ref, 448 (1)
Cope, W. E.: test, 2132
Copeland, D.: ref, 1000 (65), 2704 (10)
Copeland, E. J.: ref, 2065 (9)
Copeland, E. P.: ref, 809 (2), 1903 (549), 2864 (140)
Copeland, K. G.: ref, 863 (38),2497 (238)
Copes, W. S.: ref, 337 (14), 1925 (1)
Coplan, J.: test, 880
Coplan, J. D.: ref, 451 (220), 1166 (179), 1216 (108)
Copola, R.: ref, 2892 (162)
Copolov, D. L.: ref, 650 (2), 2305 (41), 2520 (36)
Coppan, S. F.: ref, 2516 (61), 2860 (804), 2892 (163)
Copping, W.: ref, 472 (90), 2211 (30), 2214 (50)
Copur, H.: ref, 1348 (4)
Corballis, M. C.: ref, 2860 (61,62,87,593), 2862 (37)
Corbeil, R. R.: ref, 2863 (284)
Corbera, X.: ref, 900 (1)
Corbitt, E. M.: test, 1961; ref, 272 (161), 273 (17), 1093 (96), 1166 (98)
Corbitt, M. K.: rev, 248, 1145
Corcoran, K. J.: ref, 1745 (81)
Corcoran, R.: ref, 2010 (10), 2050 (138), 2146 (19), 2163 (107), 2193 (15), 2860 (1006), 2892 (69,210)
Cordon, L. A.: ref, 1072 (51)
CORE Corporation: test, 2386
Coren, S.: ref, 838 (9), 2146 (5), 2899 (2)
Corey, E. R.: ref, 615 (24)
Corey, L. A.: ref, 999 (186)
Corey, S. M.: rev, 798
Corey-Bloom, J.: ref, 376 (15), 1164 (145), 2860 (1244), 2862 (601), 2892 (266)
Corgiat, M.: ref, 1021 (38),2497 (526)
Cori, L.: ref, 2703 (1)
Corin, E.: ref, 451 (147)
Corkill, A. J.: rev, 1155, 1462, 1878, 2181, 2236
Corkin, S.: ref, 1135 (21), 2860 (595,623), 2863 (182)
Corkindale, C.: ref, 863 (86), 2076 (166)
Corkum, P. V.: ref, 681 (25)
Corley, R.: ref, 1965 (67),2382 (6,16)
Corley, T. J.: ref, 2497 (381)
Corlis, M. E.: ref, 472 (208), 2214 (120)
Corman, C. L.: test, 2720
Cormier, H. J.: ref, 2519 (37), 2520 (38)
Cormier, P.: ref, 2704 (47), 2879 (236), 2905 (123)
Corn, A. L.: test, 2328, 2329
Cornblatt, B.: ref, 2305 (2,49)
Cornblatt, B. A.: ref, 1697 (280,405), 2305 (78,96,99,131,220), 2860 (452), 2862 (250)
Cornel, M.: ref, 1661 (29)
Cornelissen, P. L.: ref, 2860 (1059)
Cornelius, A.: ref, 404 (37), 2527 (8)
Cornelius, J.: ref, 450 (1), 824 (5), 1093 (56,76), 1321 (2), 2497 (34),2603 (215,307), 2860 (532)
Cornelius, J. R.: ref, 272 (265), 1166 (180)
Cornelius, M. D.: ref, 272 (265), 1166 (180)
Cornell, C. E.: ref, 2858 (54)
Cornell, D. G.: test, 824; ref, 289 (1,2,5), 292 (1), 372 (30,92,96), 615 (54), 665 (1), 694 (3), 902 (2), 1010 (2), 1657 (2), 1866 (39,41), 1877 (1), 1962 (1), 2214 (1,2,4,78),2295 (3), 2432 (3), 2485 (5,15), 2862 (14,64,97,376)
Cornes, C.: ref, 337 (156)
Cornille, M.: ref, 2163 (134)
Cornish, G.: test, 492
Cornish, K. A.: ref, 2218 (53)
Cornish, K. M.: ref, 350 (47), 2228 (24)
Cornoldi, C.: ref, 2860 (442), 2862 (323)
Corns, E.: ref, 451 (106)
Corns, K. M.: ref, 337 (149,162), 863 (62,82)
Cornwall, A.: ref, 694 (66), 1131 (8), 1903 (383), 2862 (158), 2879 (41,126), 2905 (21,80)
Cornwell, J. M.: ref, 2899 (5)
Cornwell, K.: ref, 790 (29), 1455 (7)
Coronis, A. R.: ref, 687 (2), 2860 (1090)
Corr, P. J.: ref, 999 (152), 2163 (281,350), 2497 (545)
Corrada, M.: ref, 1164 (171), 1758 (97)
Corran, T. M.: ref, 1322 (1)
Correll, J. A.: ref, 2497 (194)
Correll, R. E.: ref, 2860 (443)
Correra, G.: ref, 2163 (114)
Corrigan, A.: test, 953, 1664
Corrigan, P. W.: ref, 1590 (44,58), 1697 (64), 2050 (12,67), 2497 (444), 2519 (16), 2520 (17), 2860 (830,1060), 2879 (74), 2892 (110)
Corsi, P.: ref, 1903 (84), 2860 (288)
Corsini, R.: test, 2286
Corsini, R. J.: test, 1799, 2051, 2808
Corss, L.: rev, 773
Cortelli, P.: ref, 2768 (34), 2860 (1082)
Corter, C.: ref, 1745 (18)
Cortes, D. E.: ref, 2497 (390,571)
Cortese, L.: ref, 271 (3), 272 (205), 2288 (78,79,65)
Corty, E.: ref, 2519 (30,44), 2520 (31,44)
Corty, E. W.: ref, 863 (58), 2497 (421), 2603 (330)
Corwin, J.: ref, 2860 (297)
Coryell, W.: ref, 1093 (9,10,107,108), 1517 (1,2,5), 1697 (376,517), 2305 (97,119,125,160,161, 172, 179,200,219)
Coryell, W. A.: ref, 1093 (16)
Coryell, W. H.: ref, 2519 (15), 2520 (16)
Coscarelli, W. C.: test, 768
Cosden, M.: rev, 852, 854, 1006, 1304, 2414; ref, 307 (2)
Cosier, R. A.: ref, 1755 (12)
Coslett, H. B.: ref, 1903 (238)
Cossa, F. M.: ref, 2163 (25)

Costa, A. D.: ref, 2246 (6)
Costa, D. C.: ref, 1093 (50),1390 (3), 2050 (65), 2863 (169), 2892 (277)
Costa, D. T.: ref, 998 (38), 1158 (1), 1697 (152)
Costa, P. T.: test, 1769; ref, 793 (18), 999 (116), 2218 (24,49,66), 2519 (23), 2520 (24), 2860 (865)
Costa, P. T., Jr.: test, 2218; ref, 372 (49), 373 (2), 998 (3), 1697 (460), 1755 (6), 2218 (1,2,7,8, 37, 41, 129,130), 2860 (42)
Costantino, G.: test, 2647; rev, 304, 385, 2140; ref, 1991 (21), 2498 (6), 2603 (245), 2647 (1)
Costanza, D. P.: test, 1044; ref, 937 (3)
Costello, A.: ref, 199 (3), 1903 (60)
Costello, A. de-L.: ref, 1104 (6), 1903 (344), 2193 (36), 2860 (826)
Costello, A. J.: test, 2601
Costello, D.: ref, 540 (4)
Costello, E. J.: ref, 451 (107,108)
Costello, K. B.: test, 2818
Costello, M. R.: test, 1046
Costello, R. M.: ref, 1697 (212)
Costenbader, V. K.: ref, 1085 (3), 2484 (12)
Coster, W.: test, 2316
Coster, W. J.: test, 1906; ref, 1673 (11), 2377 (4)
Costin, F.: rev, 2531
Costin, S. E.: ref, 298 (144)
Cosyns, P.: ref, 272 (198), 1166 (5,20,58,77,127), 2497 (25)
Cote, A.: ref, 472 (90), 2211 (30), 2214 (50)
Cote, F.: ref, 2516 (11), 2892 (33)
Côté, G.: ref, 2519 (37),2520 (38)
Cote, L. J.: ref, 2860 (906)
Cotelingam, G. M.: ref, 2305 (137)
Cotman, C.: ref, 1164 (182), 2516 (120), 2892 (302)
Cottle, W. C.: rev, 547
Cotton, D. H. G.: ref, 256 (1)
Cotton, G. L.: ref, 1115 (4)
Cotton, L.: ref, 694 (83)
Cotton, M. M.: ref, 999 (17), 1765 (8),1991 (6)
Cotton, S.: ref, 863 (37), 1079 (67)
Cotugno, A. J.: ref, 301 (29), 469 (1), 563 (1), 681 (26,60), 853 (9), 1725 (3), 1991 (49), 2231 (3), 2242 (2), 2247 (31,84), 2864 (38)
Couchman, T.: test, 441
Coughlan, A. K.: ref, 2860 (785)
Coughlan, G. M.: ref, 272 (107), 2497 (445)
Coughlin, C.: ref, 1903 (454)
Coulehan, J. L.: ref, 272 (221)
Coulson, L. A.: ref, 1000 (62), 1580 (5)
Coulter, M. L.: ref, 451 (3)
Coulter, R. G.: ref, 337 (146)
Coulton, G. F.: ref, 372 (84), 1697 (396)
Countryman, S.: ref, 272 (133), 1164 (109), 2860 (961)
Counts, R. M.: ref, 1697 (123)
Coupet, S.: ref, 451 (124)
Coupland, N.: ref, 999 (121)
Courbois, Y.: ref, 2862 (454)
Courchesne, E.: ref, 815 (27), 1093 (13), 1903 (30,101,379), 2305 (35), 2695 (41), 2860 (324), 2862 (364), 2879 (125), 2892 (45)
Courlet, P.: ref, 2305 (117)
Courneya, K. S.: ref, 1745 (45), 2076 (90), 2497 (370)
Courneya, R. S.: ref, 1141 (3)
Cournos, F.: ref, 2017 (16)
Cournoyer, M.: ref, 1134 (8)
Cournoyer, R. J.: ref, 694 (96), 2497 (446)
Court, J.: ref, 1164 (38), 2892 (56)
Court, J. H.: test, 1671, 2163, 2478
Courtis, S. A.: rev, 1414
Courtney, M. E.: ref, 2862 (432), 2879 (151)
Courtney, P. D.: rev, 2879
Coury, D. L.: ref, 451 (258), 681 (92), 1099 (5), 1164 (177), 1379 (101), 1740 (31), 2516 (118), 2892 (299)
Cousens, P.: ref, 474 (2),1592 (8), 2862 (124)
Cousins, N.: ref, 2076 (13)
Cousson, F.: ref, 2497 (432),2858 (112)
Couture, G.: ref, 458 (2)
Couvillion, L. M.: ref, 1394 (13), 1903 (560), 2657 (36)
Covall, S.: ref, 2860 (1083), 2892 (226)
Coverstone, k. L.: ref, 1698 (1)
Covey, L.: ref, 2076 (113), 2497 (450)
Covington, C.: ref, 1770 (1)
Cowan, C. P.: ref, 1902 (36)
Cowan, M.: ref, 853 (21), 1697 (512), 2497 (231)
Cowan, N.: ref, 798 (17), 1903 (364), 2693 (4), 2704 (24), 2862 (342), 2901 (64), 2911 (1)
Cowan, P. A.: ref, 68 (4), 1902 (36)
Coward, D. D.: ref, 2076 (145)
Cowell, C.: ref, 2193 (11), 2860 (342)
Cowell, P. E.: ref, 2288 (57,65), 2289 (44,49)
Cowell, V.: ref, 199 (3), 1903 (60)
Cowen, E. L.: ref, 472 (69), 681 (34), 2498 (4,27)
Cowen, P. J.: ref, 272 (9), 1166 (6), 2076 (103,121)
Cowey, A.: ref, 2193 (5), 2860 (161)
Cowger, E. L., Jr.: ref, 2360 (12)
Cowley, D.: ref, 272 (142), 1687 (18), 2497 (527)
Cowley, D. S.: ref, 1705 (2), 2497 (244)
Cowley, J.: test, 2201
Cox, A. R.: test, 299
Cox, B. E.: ref, 2680 (19)
Cox, B. J.: ref, 950 (4), 2199 (7), 2305 (112), 2519 (25), 2520 (26), 2603 (371)
Cox, C.: ref, 1903 (334), 2517 (2), 2603 (586), 2860 (796)
Cox, C. L.: ref, 1010 (46)
Cox, D.: ref, 433 (8), 1085 (2), 2603 (144)
Cox, D. N.: test, 1175
Cox, D. R.: test, 671
Cox, G.: ref, 2860 (665), 2863 (195)
Cox, J. R.: rev, 1503, 2672
Cox, M. K.: ref, 1590 (17)
Cox, P. D.: ref, 665 (4)
Cox, R. C.: rev, 560, 561
Cox, S.: ref, 1903 (28,87)

Cox, T.: ref, 303 (9), 2227 (28), 2860 (1140), 2863 (338)
Cox, W. J.: ref, 2497 (237)
Coyle, J. T.: ref, 1093 (90), 1653 (4), 2516 (72), 2860 (299), 2892 (203)
Coyle, N.: ref, 372 (99)
Coyle, S.: ref, 272 (88)
Coyne, A. C.: ref, 2860 (19)
Coyne, J.: ref, 863 (36)
Coyne, L.: ref, 337 (126), 846 (3,12), 1687 (38), 1697 (377,468)
Cozolino, L.: ref, 846 (9), 2519 (55), 2520 (54)
Cozzarelli, C.: ref, 2603 (246)
Cracchiolo-Caraway, A.: ref, 273 (14), 337 (108)
Craddock, A. E.: ref, 2034 (3)
Cradock, M. M.: ref, 1164 (176)
Craft, L. L.: test, 654
Craft, S.: ref, 375 (8), 681 (45), 776 (58), 1903 (262), 2720 (1), 2892 (297)
Crafter, B.: ref, 462 (30)
Craggs, M.: ref, 270 (46)
Crago, M.: ref, 1010 (26), 1965 (73)
Craig, A.: ref, 540 (4), 1166 (38), 2497 (155,319)
Craig, A. R.: ref, 2497 (447)
Craig, B.: ref, 1437 (3)
Craig, C. H.: ref, 2651 (8)
Craig, H. K.: ref, 175 (6), 202 (2),1903 (165,166,246,347), 1982 (4), 2651 (6)
Craig, J.: ref, 790 (24), 1745 (62)
Craig, J. A.: ref, 863 (60)
Craig, J. R.: test, 1729
Craig, M. J.: ref, 337 (14), 1925 (1)
Craig, P.: test, 1729
Craig, R. J.: ref, 68 (23), 1687 (2,26,39), 1697 (163,213,494)
Craig, S. S.: ref, 372 (44), 1000 (42)
Craig, T. K. J.: ref, 2050 (68)
Craig-Shea, M. E.: ref, 1744 (4)
Craighead, L. W.: ref, 272 (162)
Craighead, W. E.: ref, 272 (162),472 (117), 863 (3,61), 2214 (63), 2603 (346)
Craik, F. I. M.: ref, 1903 (317), 2485 (151), 2860 (30)
Craik, R.: ref, 998 (22)
Crain, R. M.: ref, 331 (2), 694 (68), 1216 (28), 1734 (2), 1903 (157), 1991 (66), 2163 (104)
Crais, E. R.: ref, 265 (2)
Craissati, J.: ref, 1744 (7), 2860 (1061,1245)
Cramb, G.: ref, 2305 (13)
Cramer, D.: ref, 272 (362), 998 (28), 999 (52), 1079 (21,61), 2497 (448)
Cramer, P.: ref, 298 (163), 1987 (5), 2749 (2,5,19,74,82)
Cramer, R. E.: ref, 298 (45)
Cramer, S. H.: ref, 404 (36), 1754 (22), 1866 (5)
Cramond, B.: ref, 615 (13)
Cramp, L.: test, 1551
Crane, B. J.: test, 720, 740
Crane, J.: ref, 1216 (81), 2860 (985)
Cranny, C. J.: rev, 2786
Crano, W. D.: ref, 838 (11), 1072 (21)
Crant, J. M.: ref, 2218 (25), 2899 (11)
Crary, M. A.: ref, 1804 (3), 2651 (9)
Crase, S. J.: test, 1316, 1317
Craske, M. G.: ref, 592 (80), 2199 (10), 2497 (17,26,57,109,449), 2603 (524)
Craven, R.: ref, 2091 (5)
Crawford, C. B.: ref, 298 (106)
Crawford, D. H.: rev, 1145
Crawford, D. M.: test, 722
Crawford, J.: rev, 2311; ref, 364 (1)
Crawford, J. A.: ref, 474 (2), 1592 (8), 2862 (124)
Crawford, J. E.: test, 722
Crawford, J. R.: ref, 2860 (444,594,831,1062,1063, 1132,1246)
Crawford, P. L.: test, 721
Crawford, S. G.: ref, 389 (10)
Crawford, T. J.: ref, 1758 (35,36), 2163 (205,206), 2288 (46,47), 2289 (35,36), 2305 (126,127), 2892 (170,171)
Crawford, W. R.: rev, 49, 55
Crawley, B.: ref, 31 (1), 1036 (2), 1444 (3), 1755 (9), 1822 (1), 2163 (40)
Creamer, D. G.: ref, 8 (1)
Creamer, M.: ref, 2603 (254)
Creasey, G.: ref, 451 (51)
Creasey, G. L.: ref, 1010 (8)
Creasey, H.: ref, 1164 (136), 1758 (79), 2497 (667), 2860 (1183), 2863 (356)
Creed, P. A.: ref, 272 (349), 1079 (104)
Crehan, K. D.: rev, 770, 823, 1476, 1496, 2145, 2410
Creighton, C.: ref, 2599 (27)
Creighton, M. M.: rev, 2308
Crespo, D.: rev, 453
Crethar, H. C.: ref, 298 (129), 716 (2), 1755 (48), 2497 (398), 2603 (315)
Creti, L.: ref, 998 (92)
Crewe, N.: ref, 2860 (853)
Crews, T. M.: ref, 337 (119), 999 (137)
Crews, W. D., Jr.: ref, 2497 (320,321)
Crick, N. R.: ref, 472 (118)
Crimmins, D. B.: test, 1722
Crino, M. D.: ref, 298 (49)
Cripe, L. I.: ref, 1697 (397)
Cripe, L. J.: ref, 1164 (6), 2860 (109)
Crisp, A. H.: test, 739
Crisp, J.: ref, 1903 (455)
Critchlow, D. D.: test, 850
Critelli, J. W.: ref, 1697 (344), 1745 (9), 1965 (37), 2603 (289), 2749 (45)
Crites, J. O.: test, 413; rev, 372, 937, 1100, 1196, 1239, 1348, 1767, 1779, 1790, 1829, 1965, 2276, 2360, 2616, 2652, 2856, 2857, 413 (27)
Crits-Christoph, P.: ref, 272 (148)
Crittenden, P. M.: ref, 472 (78), 557 (2), 1000 (66), 1216 (9), 1612 (23), 2211 (6,27)
Critz-Crosby, P.: ref, 487 (1), 2862 (246)

Crnic, K.: ref, 451 (95), 2218 (20,46,47,80)
Croce, R.: ref, 777 (1), 1991 (85)
Crockenberg, S.: ref, 451 (109)
Crocker, A. D.: ref, 472 (194)
Crocker, B.: ref, 2603 (112)
Crocker, J.: ref, 694 (33,50), 1745 (29)
Crocker, L.: rev, 76, 494, 540, 2426, 2695, 2904
Crocker, L. M.: rev, 542
Crockett, D. J.: ref, 326 (6), 2497 (146), 2516 (21), 2860 (445), 2892 (70)
Crockett, L.: ref, 364 (19), 472 (48,172), 2214 (49,66,102,103)
Crocq, M-A.: ref, 1166 (105)
Croft, C.: test, 21, 22, 25, 358, 2100, 2714
Croft, J. B.: ref, 2860 (1035), 2892 (216)
Crofton, A.: ref, 272 (185), 273 (22)
Croisile, B.: ref, 1166 (99), 2863 (310)
Crombie, G.: ref, 385 (1), 1197 (1)
Cromwell, R. L.: ref, 1697 (398), 1745 (56), 2076 (111)
Cronan, S.: ref, 472 (105), 1000 (78)
Cronan, T. A.: ref, 324 (10), 331 (6), 1903 (456), 2768 (33)
Cronbach, L. J.: rev, 316, 372, 592, 1223, 2485, 2581, 2795
Crone, D. A.: ref, 875 (8), 1240 (31), 1903 (328)
Cronenwett, L.: ref, 1770 (1)
Cronin, M. E.: test, 1167, 2699
Cronin-Golomb, A.: ref, 2860 (595)
Cronkite, R. C.: test, 1181
Cronshan, S. F.: ref, 592 (4), 2797 (1)
Crook, T. H.: ref, 2860 (480,549), 2863 (134,224)
Croon, C. W.: rev, 2742
Croot, K.: ref, 350 (48), 1903 (569)
Cropanzano, R.: ref, 1590 (69), 1697 (99)
Crorsich, N.: ref, 272 (123), 746 (3)
Crosbie-Burnett, M.: ref, 2214 (39), 2231 (1)
Crosby, B.: test, 1913
Crosby, G.: test, 1913
Crosby, L.: ref, 451 (101), 2879 (158)
Crosby, L. A.: rev, 1107
Crosby, R.: ref, 472 (154), 1380 (10), 2214 (88), 2879 (152), 2901 (82)
Crosby, R. D.: ref, 272 (101), 280 (3), 451 (184), 472 (71,159), 681 (57,84), 1010 (68), 1380 (3), 1991 (76), 2214 (35,91), 2452 (4), 2497 (313), 2498 (30), 2879 (99), 2901 (49)
Cross, D. R.: ref, 496 (2), 827 (2), 1072 (4)
Cross, D. T.: ref, 2860 (408)
Cross, E. J.: ref, 68 (28), 1140 (29)
Cross, E. J., Jr.: ref, 68 (10,52), 697 (4), 1010 (120)
Cross, H. J.: ref, 1697 (265)
Cross, J. D.: ref, 1338 (46)
Cross, L. A.: ref, 1673 (11), 2377 (4)
Cross, L. H.: rev, 1318, 1350
Cross, P.: ref, 350 (11), 2858 (59), 2860 (590)
Cross, P. A.: ref, 1697 (244)
Cross, S. E.: ref, 1115 (10)
Crossen, J. R.: ref, 2860 (596,1367)
Crossley, S. A.: ref, 1903 (457)
Crossman, L. L.: ref, 1697 (273), 2860 (597)
Crosson, B.: test, 2517, 2820; ref, 199 (1,17), 1164 (167), 1740 (23), 2860 (1309), 2873 (62,71), 2892 (285)
Crosswait, C.: ref, 451 (283), 681 (98), 2603 (590),2901 (135)
Crothers, M.: ref, 1661 (53)
Crouch, J. A.: ref, 2860 (1064), 2863 (311), 2892 (220)
Croudace, T.: ref, 2050 (139)
Croughan, J.: ref, 2603 (220)
Croughwell, N.: ref, 2497 (436)
Crouse, J.: ref, 592 (35)
Crouter, A. C.: ref, 2214 (74)
Crow, L. A.: ref, 272 (40),451 (11)
Crow, L. D.: test, 1076, 1082, 1084, 1182
Crow, S. J.: ref, 2497 (313)
Crow, S. M.: ref, 771 (9)
Crow, T. J.: ref, 1164 (60), 1697 (275), 2305 (98), 2860 (190)
Crowe, E.: ref, 926 (21)
Crowe, H. P.: ref, 448 (7)
Crowe, S. F.: ref, 1097 (2), 1164 (114), 1166 (100), 1218 (12), 1410 (4), 1485 (4), 1758 (65,84),1903 (47), 2125 (3), 2288 (66), 2289 (50), 2860 (1010,1247), 2863 (300), 2864 (17), 2892 (221)
Crowe, T. K.: ref, 353 (4), 1673 (5), 1901 (6,9), 2724 (4)
Crowell, J. A.: ref, 472 (12),681 (7),2214 (6)
Crowhurst, M.: ref, 1072 (22)
Crowley, A. D.: test, 419
Crowley, S. L.: rev, 2763; ref, 472 (79,164), 1288 (2), 2214 (96), 2231 (6), 2498 (61), 2860 (1186), 2862 (565)
Crown, S.: test, 739
Crowne, D. P.: rev, 1239
Crowson, J. J.: ref, 1697 (398), 1745 (56), 2076 (111)
Crowson, M.: ref, 350 (11,13), 901 (1), 1653 (13), 2163 (145), 2228 (11,23), 2858 (59), 2860 (571)
Croxson, M. C.: ref, 375 (5), 2227 (45), 2862 (651), 2863 (395), 2892 (280)
Croyle, R. T.: ref, 2497 (618)
Crozier, K.: ref, 1901 (16), 2485 (124)
Crozier, L. C.: ref, 2860 (325)
Crozier, W. R.: ref, 694 (97)
Cruchian, G. P.: ref, 1740 (28)
Cruickshank, W. M.: rev, 1059, 2813
Cruise, R. J.: test, 2649
Crumbaugh, J. C.: test, 2126, 2343
Crumpler, M.: test, 2179
Cruse, C. L.: ref, 837 (10), 2862 (462)
Crutcher, K. A.: ref, 2860 (107)
Crutchley, A.: ref, 1095 (43), 2163 (316)
Cruz, E. B.: ref, 2247 (115), 2749 (75), 2862 (602), 2879 (200)
Cruz, S. G.: ref, 324 (10), 331 (6), 1903 (456), 2768 (33)
Cryer, D.: test, 875, 1264

Crystal, H.: ref, 1058 (2), 2860 (152)
Crystal, H. A.: ref, 1058 (8), 2125 (13), 2163 (174), 2860 (682)
Csapó, B.: ref, 2163 (317)
Csernansky, J. G.: ref, 1166 (96), 1697 (128), 2860 (598)
Csikszentmihalyi, M.: ref, 1965 (32,43,69), 2031 (5,10)
CTB Macmillan/McGraw-Hill: test, 431, 742, 743, 744, 750, 800, 886, 2463, 2738, 2739
CTB/McGraw-Hill: test, 364, 369, 370, 665, 947, 2560, 2654, 2677, 2737
Cubelli, R.: ref, 2163 (263,318), 2860 (774)
Cubic, B. A.: ref, 893 (11)
Cubillos, S.: ref, 2879 (113)
Cuddihy, S.: ref, 1178 (3)
Cudeck, R.: ref, 180 (20)
Cuerva, A. G.: ref, 303 (31), 1166 (229), 1740 (35), 2163 (356), 2860 (1419), 2892 (306)
Cuesta, M. J.: ref, 2288 (34,53), 2289 (16,25), 2860 (599), 2892 (111,172)
Cuesta, U.: ref, 998 (11)
Cuisinier, M. C. J.: ref, 2603 (469,535)
Cuksts, B.: ref, 2879 (85)
Cull, A.: ref, 1079 (35)
Cull, J. G.: test, 2559
Cullari, S.: ref, 893 (1), 1991 (50), 2652 (2)
Cullbertson, W. C.: test, 2772
Cullen, J. S.: ref, 1758 (44)
Cullen, P. C.: ref, 1093 (60)
Culley, D. C.: ref, 1697 (514)
Cullinan, D.: test, 2287
Cullom, M.: ref, 1093 (24), 1164 (25), 2860 (239)
Cullum, C. M.: ref, 2860 (245), 2863 (153)
Culp, A. M.: ref, 451 (130), 1216 (3)
Cumes-Rayner, D. P.: ref, 999 (36), 1079 (13)
Cummings, A.: ref, 68 (58), 1010 (44)
Cummings, A. L.: ref, 1140 (6), 1619 (3)
Cummings, E. M.: ref, 451 (248), 694 (22), 2214 (131), 2603 (79)
Cummings, J.: ref, 1164 (182), 2516 (120), 2892 (302)
Cummings, J. A.: rev, 264, 385, 994, 2518, 2901
Cummings, J. L.: ref, 1164 (181), 1740 (33),2227 (6,59), 2516 (13), 2860 (286,1408),2863 (76,427), 2892 (37)
Cummings, K. C.: ref, 1687 (9), 2076 (17)
Cummings, L. L.: ref, 1701 (5)
Cummings, R. L.: ref, 451 (288), 2693 (9), 2694 (26), 2862 (739)
Cummings, W. H., III: ref, 1755 (55)
Cummins, J.: test, 309
Cummins, R. A.: ref, 1021 (39), 2214 (99,100), 2497 (556), 2498 (63)
Cundick, B. C.: rev, 337
Cundick, B. P.: rev, 1214, 1401
Cundick, K. E.: ref, 272 (80)
Cuneo, P.: ref, 1517 (6)
Cunningham, A. E.: ref, 1503 (3), 1866 (10), 2163 (41), 2905 (9)
Cunningham, C. C.: ref, 2858 (37)
Cunningham, C. E.: ref, 272 (108), 451 (52), 681 (8), 997 (7), 1903 (74), 2862 (100), 2864 (81), 2879 (23)
Cunningham, J. D.: ref, 298 (5,18), 372 (3,9), 672 (2,3), 790 (6), 863 (37), 1965 (3,10)
Cunningham, J. M.: ref, 376 (16), 1164 (146), 1740 (17), 2516 (95), 2863 (375),, 2892 (267)
Cunningham, J. W.: ref, 1051 (2), 2694 (13)
Cunningham, M. R.: ref, 998 (66)
Cunningham, W. R.: ref, 1156 (4)
Cunnington, B. F.: test, 2755
Cunnington, R.: ref, 1758 (101)
Cupp, R. G.: ref, 298 (45)
Curbow, B.: ref, 2076 (159)
Cureton, E. E.: rev, 1180
Curfs, L. M. G.: ref, 373 (27,43), 451 (289), 2860 (832), 2862 (65,324), 2864 (8,82)
Curlette, W. L.: test, 262, 698
Curlette, W. L.: rev, 132, 675, 907
Curnow, K. W.: ref, 2771 (16)
Curran, H. V.: ref, 2497 (428)
Curran, J. G.: ref, 2305 (120)
Curran, J. P.: test, 915
Curran, P. J.: ref, 451 (43,262)
Curran, S. L.: ref, 2076 (112)
Curran, S. M.: ref, 2863 (207)
Curran, T.: ref, 376 (17), 2227 (32), 2860 (1166), 2892 (268)
Currie, J.: ref, 2497 (369)
Currie, L. J.: ref, 273 (8), 1166 (37)
Currier, R.: ref, 1218 (6), 1903 (275), 2163 (168), 2863 (196), 2892 (123)
Curry, C.: ref, 298 (107), 2029 (2)
Curry, J. F.: ref, 472 (23,117), 1340 (3), 2214 (63), 2603 (346)
Curry, L. A.: ref, 2369 (11)
Curry, L. M.: test, 1978
Curtis, A.: test, 882
Curtis, D.: test, 821; ref, 2305 (141), 2305 (180,199)
Curtis, F. D.: rev, 1084
Curtis, G. C.: ref, 2497 (97)
Curtis, J. W.: test, 738, 751, 752, 753, 754
Curtis, M. J.: rev, 1141
Curtis, P. A.: ref, 2211 (19)
Curtiss, G.: test, 2892; ref, 687 (1), 1164 (103), 2860 (746,917), 2862 (670), 2863 (274), 2892 (215)
Curtiss, S.: ref, 175 (8), 430 (5), 1485 (3,18), 1804 (4), 2382 (14), 2768 (17)
Cush, D. T.: ref, 2402 (21)
Cushing, G.: ref, 451 (208), 472 (203)
Cushway, D.: ref, 1079 (62)
Cusick, A.: ref, 1901 (14)
Cusick, G. M.: ref, 1697 (549)
Cuskelly, M.: ref, 863 (25), 2211 (13,20)
Custodio, R.: ref, 2905 (44)
Cuter, H. S. G.: ref, 134 (40), 1661 (84)
Cuthbert, B. N.: ref, 372 (74), 1021 (25)

Cutlan, S. L.: rev, 1665
Cutler, A.: test, 408, 1350, 1539
Cutler, S. E.: ref, 1991 (22)
Cutrona, C.: ref, 1997 (1)
Cutrona, M. P.: test, 757, 758
Cutter, H. S. G.: ref, 136 (7), 1661 (25,26,71)
Cutting, J.: ref, 2305 (15)
Cutting, W. A. M.: ref, 1379 (63)
Cutts, C. C.: rev, 2360
Cwnyn, J. P.: ref, 1338 (36)
Cybriwsky, C. A.: ref, 2905 (18)
Cynn, V. E. H.: ref, 272 (50), 2402 (11), 2892 (46)
Cyr, M.: ref, 451 (291), 472 (235), 2050 (69,102)
Cyr-Provost, M.: ref, 1697 (172), 2497 (174)
Cyranowski, J. M.: ref, 793 (16)
Czajka, J. A.: ref, 1697 (99)
Czajkowski, S. M.: ref, 2497 (58)
Czerlinsky, T.: test, 2828
Cziko, G. A.: ref, 550 (2), 666 (1,8)
Czobor, P.: ref, 1164 (58), 2892 (109)
Czuchta, D.: ref, 2879 (67)
Czyewski, D. I.: ref, 863 (38,77), 2497 (238,546)
Czyzewski, M. J.: ref, 2860 (38)

Daamen, J.: ref, 1590 (40)
Dabrowski, J. J.: ref, 1164 (71), 2860 (709), 2892 (136)
Dabul, B. L.: test, 163
Dacey, C. M.: ref, 272 (269), 846 (21), 1697 (295), 2497 (623)
Da Costa, G. A.: ref, 337 (22), 1697 (119), 1991 (19)
Dadash-Zadeh, M.: ref, 375 (8), 2720 (1), 2892 (297)
Dadds, M.: ref, 863 (25), 1991 (23), 2211 (9,13)
Dadds, M. R.: ref, 337 (87), 451 (91), 472 (157), 997 (20,28), 1925 (2), 1925 (3), 2214 (89,130)
Daems, C.: ref, 2163 (214), 2860 (868)
Daeppen, J-B.: ref, 1166 (101), 1661 (54)
Daeschler, C. V.: ref, 2603 (419)
Dagan, A.: ref, 337 (100)
Dagenais, P. A.: ref, 487 (1), 2862 (246)
Dager, S.: ref, 1166 (13)
D'Agostino, R. B.: ref, 2860 (329), 2863 (87,113)
Dahan, M.: ref, 302 (3), 1693 (2), 1697 (366), 2163 (192), 2217 (3)
Dahl, P. A.: rev, 48
Dahl, R.: ref, 2305 (245)
Dahl, R. E.: ref, 2305 (216)
Dahl, T. A.: rev, 324
Dahlgren, S. D.: ref, 2862 (455)
Dahlgren, S. O.: ref, 234 (1)
Dahlmeier, J.: ref, 451 (165), 473 (4)
Dahlmeier, J. M.: ref, 1000 (86)
Dahlquist, L. M.: ref, 863 (38,77), 2497 (238,546)
Dahlsgaard, K.: ref, 270 (37), 994 (49), 1528 (7), 2229 (16), 2657 (35), 2813 (152)
Dahlstrom, L. E.: ref, 1697 (5)
Dahlstrom, W. G.: test, 1697; rev, 218, 927, 1845; ref, 771 (23), 1697 (5,117,164,412,419)
Dahm, F.: ref, 273 (10), 2402 (32)
Dahm, J. W.: test, 1624
Dahms, W. T.: ref, 1316 (1)
Dai, X.: ref, 2860 (395,486)
Dai, Y.: ref, 272 (127)
Daie, N.: ref, 301 (21), 2247 (22), 2749 (24),2860 (339)
Daiger, D.: test, 1754
Dail, P. W.: ref, 1832 (1)
Dailey, J. T.: test, 1422; rev, 592, 1115, 1672
Dailey, R. A.: ref, 1386 (13), 2862 (307)
Daines, D.: ref, 550 (1)
Daisy, F.: ref, 1687 (1)
Dake, L.: ref, 68 (13)
Dakof, G. A.: ref, 68 (47), 2603 (14), 2860 (88), 2863 (24)
Dalack, G. W.: ref, 2076 (113), 2497 (450)
Dalakas, M. C.: ref, 1697 (269), 2497 (315)
Dale, A.: ref, 1338 (46)
Dale, G. A.: ref, 1698 (15)
Dale, J.: ref, 2402 (66)
Dale, J. A.: rev, 2680; ref, 1745 (80), 2860 (400), 2863 (105)
Dale, P.: test, 1528
Dale, P. S.: ref, 1612 (2,14,15,22,32,75), 1902 (75), 1903 (9,72,75,111,164,391), 2044 (3,5), 2485 (173), 2680 (1,2), 2682 (2,4,8)
Daleiden, E. L.: ref, 472 (152), 2214 (86), 2498 (56), 2905 (93)
Daley, A. J.: ref, 2077 (9)
Daley, K. E.: ref, 1903 (581), 2488 (10)
Daley, S. E.: ref, 1010 (121)
Dalgleish, T.: ref, 272 (211,278), 1079 (92), 1671 (7), 2497 (451,584,636)
Dalla Barba, G.: ref, 2247 (116), 2860 (1248), 2863 (376)
Dalla Barbara, G.: ref, 2860 (1249), 2863 (377)
Dalla, R. L.: ref, 451 (192)
Dallal, G. E.: ref, 893 (23)
Dallas Educational Services: test, 1088
Dalley, M. B.: ref, 2230 (3)
Dalmonte, E.: ref, 2863 (416)
Dalton, E. F.: test, 1234, 1235
D'Alton, J.: ref, 1903 (191), 2863 (137)
Dalton, J. G.: ref, 1697 (274), 2402 (25)
Dalton, M.: test, 300, 2425
Daltroy, L. H.: ref, 2076 (38)
Daly, D. L.: ref, 997 (13), 2065 (8)
Daly, E.: ref, 199 (16), 2010 (16), 2163 (179),2516 (47), 2860 (703,1141), 2863 (205), 2879 (87)
Daly, M.: ref, 2076 (128,151)
Daly, R. J.: ref, 1619 (1)
Dam, H.: ref, 272 (201)
Damarin, F.: rev, 270, 433, 724
Damasio, A. R.: ref, 326 (4), 1625 (1), 2146 (9), 2227 (3), 2860 (181,1358), 2892 (42)
Damasio, H.: ref, 2163 (15),2227 (3), 2860 (43,181,1358)

D'Amato, R. C.: rev, 86, 1197; ref, 1164 (43), 1321 (11), 1903 (161), 2313 (1), 2704 (17), 2862 (245)
Dame, S.: ref, 999 (62), 2497 (276)
D'Amelio, M.: ref, 2860 (1051)
Dameron, J. D.: test, 1624
Damhaut, P.: ref, 1166 (181)
D'Amico, C.: ref, 1405 (7)
Damin, P. B.: ref, 298 (79)
Damji, T.: ref, 272 (163)
Damos, D. L.: ref, 1164 (59), 2076 (77),2516 (37), 2860 (600), 2892 (112)
Dana, C.: ref, 1072 (7)
Dana, E. R., Jr.: ref, 462 (12), 1405 (26)
Dana, J. P.: ref, 2860 (989), 2862 (404), 2879 (140)
Dana, R. H.: rev, 2247, 2248, 2600, 2749; ref, 1697 (400)
Danber, S. L.: ref, 364 (17)
Dancer, J.: ref, 540 (16), 655 (1), 1047 (7), 1095 (44,45), 1902 (98), 2045 (5), 2668 (4)
Dancer, J. E.: ref, 2860 (786)
Dancer, L. S.: ref, 863 (39), 2559 (5)
Dancu, C. V.: test, 2448; ref, 2497 (18)
Dancyger, I. F.: ref, 893 (18)
Dander, D.: rev, 838
Dandoy, A. C.: ref, 1962 (4), 1991 (39), 2214 (26), 2862 (183)
Daneman, M.: ref, 2901 (57)
D'Angiola, N.: ref, 1903 (104)
d'Anglejan, A.: rev, 1054; ref, 1140 (1), 2163 (6)
Dangour, W.: ref, 2163 (91), 2860 (376)
Dani, A.: ref, 2485 (234), 2860 (1155)
Daniel, D. G.: ref, 2863 (312), 2892 (222)
Daniel, L. G.: rev, 485, 1723; ref, 2361 (4)
Daniel, M. H.: rev, 24, 1660, 2063, 2222
Daniele, A.: ref, 2163 (151), 2892 (113)
Daniele, R. J.: ref, 337 (43), 2858 (38)
Daniels, D.: ref, 875 (10), 1902 (77)
Daniels, K.: ref, 999 (180), 1079 (22)
Daniels, L. E.: ref, 1673 (2)
Daniels, M. H.: test, 200; rev, 1616, 2360, 2443
Daniels, R.: ref, 68 (33), 1599 (2)
Daniluk, J.: ref, 298 (162)
Danion, J.: ref, 2863 (63)
Danion, J. M.: ref, 1166 (56,139), 2288 (49), 2289 (38), 2860 (902), 2863 (271)
Danko, G.: ref, 2497 (605)
Dannals, R. F.: ref, 1697 (88), 2050 (125), 2402 (6), 2516 (18)
Danner, C. C.: ref, 272 (121)
Danner, K. E.: ref, 2879 (79)
D'Annunzio, A.: ref, 251 (1), 827 (5,9), 2879 (75)
Danoff, B.: ref, 2905 (35)
Danoff, N. L.: ref, 1216 (43)
Danos, D. O.: ref, 117 (3)
Danovsky, M.: ref, 472 (215), 1318 (20), 2214 (125), 2862 (677)
Dansereau, D. F.: ref, 1140 (24), 1755 (23)
Dansky, H.: test, 2836
Dantonio, M.: ref, 2497 (595)
Danzer, V. A.: test, 759
Dao, M.: test, 306
Daood, C. J.: ref, 1962 (11)
Daoust, P. M.: ref, 1485 (28)
D'Apollonia, S.: ref, 560 (2)
Daquin, G.: ref, 2863 (261), 2892 (183)
Darby, D. G.: ref, 2860 (520), 2863 (150)
Darch, C.: ref, 1392 (11), 2905 (53)
Darden, C.: ref, 1378 (9), 1903 (543), 2860 (1313)
Dark, V. J.: ref, 592 (54)
Darke, S.: ref, 2860 (282)
Darley, F. L.: test, 2651
Darley, J. G.: rev, 1790
Darling, W.: ref, 2860 (1337)
Darnell, R. E.: rev, 816
Darr, R. F., Jr.: rev, 1547, 1564, 1878, 2085, 2596, 2760
Darriet, D.: ref, 2860 (930)
Darrow, L. J.: ref, 1903 (180), 2905 (39)
Darsereau, D. F.: ref, 372 (4), 998 (7), 1140 (4)
Dartigues, J. F.: ref, 2860 (930), 2863 (90), 2863 (297)
Darwish, T. A.: ref, 999 (98), 2050 (92)
Dary, M.: ref, 2516 (64), 2863 (248)
Das Eiden, R.: ref, 863 (62), 1770 (15)
Das, J.: ref, 2603 (182)
Das, J. P.: test, 763; rev, 1227; ref, 763 (2,3,4), 776 (20), 1379 (65), 1607 (5,6,13), 1645 (4), 1903 (348), 2485 (164), 2860 (834), 2901 (16), 2905 (51,52,71)
Das, L.: ref, 337 (103),372 (94), 1706 (3), 2858 (102) (278,456,726)
Dasberg, H.: ref, 337 (118), 2288 (27), 2289 (18)
Dashiell, S. E.: test, 1284
Da Silva, H. G.: test, 306
Da Silva, M. A.: test, 306
Dass, P.: ref, 372 (106), 694 (120)
Das-Smaal, E. A.: ref, 815 (16), 1164 (89,183), 2163 (354), 2862
Date, A. L.: ref, 2749 (61)
Dattilo, J.: ref, 624 (3), 1903 (127)
Dauber, S. L.: ref, 615 (14)
D'Augelli, A. R.: ref, 337 (53),1965 (13)
Daugherty, E. H.: test, 808, 1650
Daugherty, M.: ref, 2754 (5), 2771 (36)
Daugherty, T. K.: ref, 999 (153), 2497 (506)
Daum, I.: ref, 303 (16), 2227 (43), 2860 (684,835,1261,1305), 2863 (241), 2892 (278)
Daum, J. M.: rev, 2750
Dautrich, B. R.: ref, 2860 (446), 2862 (196)
Davalos, M.: ref, 272 (277)
Davenport, L.: ref, 1407 (1), 2860 (172)
Davey, G. C. L.: ref, 272 (164,276), 1021 (31), 1079 (63), 1181 (19), 2065 (24), 2497 (322,547,635)
Davey, J.: ref, 1735 (3)
David, A.: ref, 1758 (45)

David, A. S.: ref, 650 (7), 1758 (32,96), 2050 (29,30,65,70), 2193 (20,35), 2288 (17), 2858 (62), 2860 (792), 2863 (169)
David, D.: ref, 2603 (347,380), 2860 (1236), 2863 (370)
David, H.: ref, 298 (165)
David, J. P.: ref, 2218 (91)
Davidi, S.: ref, 2862 (607)
Davidoff, J.: ref, 349 (8), 1104 (2)
Davidoff, J. B.: ref, 358 (1)
Davidshofer, C.: rev, 1334, 1346
Davidson, C. E.: ref, 1903 (168)
Davidson, D. A.: ref, 1673 (9)
Davidson, J.: test, 766; ref, 998 (19), 1036 (9), 1166 (162), 2305 (30), 2603 (503)
Davidson, J. A.: ref, 322 (4), 1765 (14), 2163 (132), 2768 (19)
Davidson, J. M.: ref, 1697 (266)
Davidson, K. C.: ref, 815 (20), 1612 (65,68), 2813 (88), 2862 (317)
Davidson, K. W.: ref, 2516 (38)
Davidson, L.: ref, 2603 (498)
Davidson, M.: ref, 1903 (247), 2017 (7), 2163 (115), 2288 (70), 2289 (55), 2305 (181), 2892 (76)
Davidson, R. A.: ref, 1687 (19),2860 (340)
Davidson, R. J.: ref, 998 (79), 1072 (15), 1131 (6), 2497 (403), 2862 (98), 2905 (10)
Davidson, W. B.: ref, 372 (45)
Davies, A.: ref, 451 (106)
Davies, A. D. M.: ref, 1758 (13), 2193 (6)
Davies, A. G.: ref, 1379 (63)
Davies, B.: ref, 803 (1,2), 1166 (32), 1653 (19,20,25), 2189 (3,4,6), 2382 (29,30), 2485 (155,156), 2497 (51), 2813 (82,83), 2864 (106)
Davies, B. A.: ref, 1079 (87)
Davies, F.: ref, 271 (3),272 (205)
Davies, K.: ref, 2860 (1094)
Davies, M.: ref, 350 (44,50), 451 (220), 994 (51), 1093 (21), 1216 (108), 1903 (296), 2163 (344), 2662 (7), 2813 (155), 2860 (1291,1361,1395), 2862 (635,684,717), 2864 (66)
Davies, M. F.: ref, 926 (14), 999 (192), 1140 (30), 1899 (1)
Davies, P. D. M.: ref, 1758 (66), 2193 (51), 2860 (1069)
Davies, P. L.: ref, 1901 (15), 2813 (59)
Davies, P. T.: ref, 451 (248), 2214 (131)
Davies, R.: ref, 1697 (6)
Davies, R. A.: ref, 2305 (188)
Davies, S.: ref, 349 (32), 350 (16), 1079 (72), 1765 (29),2163 (152)
Davies, S. L.: ref, 1166 (12)
Davies, W. H.: ref, 451 (195), 472 (60,182), 2242 (7), 2497 (629), 2862 (525)
Davies-Farmer, R. M.: ref, 1697 (64)
Davila, J.: ref, 272 (122), 999 (124), 1010 (121)
Davila, R.: ref, 2860 (1422), 2892 (309)
Davillier, M.: ref, 337 (160)
Davis, A.: ref, 815 (49), 1164 (173), 1740 (27), 2516 (115), 2860 (1374), 2892 (294)
Davis, B.: rev, 269, 887, 2223; ref, 272 (319), 337 (67), 1010 (128), 1535 (1), 1697 (65)
Davis, B. I.: ref, 2485 (7)
Davis, C.: ref, 998 (50,89), 999 (53,154,179,183), 2860 (18), 2863 (10), 2905 (7)
Davis, C. C.: rev, 514, 591, 614
Davis, C. E.: ref, 1072 (12)
Davis, C. G.: ref, 791 (12), 2603 (348)
Davis, C. L.: ref, 1021 (14)
Davis, C. S.: test, 1304
Davis, D.: ref, 1216 (104), 2288 (41), 2289 (31), 2305 (116)
Davis, D. R.: rev, 987
Davis, E. E.: rev, 1612
Davis, E. J.: ref, 1758 (66), 2193 (51), 2860 (1069)
Davis, E. Z.: ref, 1164 (90), 1592 (21), 2225 (7), 2497 (456), 2860 (848), 2863 (246), 2892 (175)
Davis, F. B.: rev, 591, 592, 614, 1414
Davis, G. A.: test, 1143; ref, 2771 (3)
Davis, G. C.: ref, 999 (111)
Davis, G. L.: ref, 372 (91)
Davis, G. Y.: ref, 2486 (3)
Davis, H.: ref, 451 (249), 1079 (105), 1216 (111), 1697 (176,307), 1889 (17)
Davis, H. L.: ref, 1903 (349)
Davis, J.: test, 2824
Davis, J. A.: ref, 2050 (137)
Davis, J. D.: ref, 376 (19), 776 (42)
Davis, J. M.: ref, 337 (121), 624 (5), 1010 (88), 1040 (8), 1379 (26), 2163 (110), 2305 (95,166,202), 2402 (47,48), 2497 (521,548), 2603 (414,415), 2651 (10), 2858 (107), 2860 (995), 2862 (249)
Davis, J. T.: ref, 2862 (603), 2901 (115)
Davis, K. L.: ref, 2288 (70), 2289 (55), 2305 (181,225)
Davis, M. C.: ref, 2516 (12)
Davis, M. S.: ref, 2603 (11)
Davis, P.: ref, 540 (16), 655 (1), 1095 (44,45), 1226 (1), 1612 (35), 1902 (98), 2045 (5), 2247 (45,90), 2380 (9), 2749 (34), 2862 (224)
Davis, P. C.: rev, 1484
Davis, P. J.: ref, 2076 (136)
Davis, P. K.: ref, 2132 (2)
Davis, R.: test, 1685, 1687; ref, 1093 (60)
Davis, R. C.: ref, 2603 (86)
Davis, R. L.: ref, 1072 (12)
Davis, S. E.: rev, 1985, 2541; ref, 337 (170); 1687 (27)
Davis, S. F.: rev, 203, 687, 962, 1562, 1874, 2369; ref, 1338 (36,39), 2369 (2)
Davis, T. C.: ref, 1902 (45), 2879 (130)
Davis, T. L.: ref, 2860 (811)
Davis, V.: ref, 472 (93), 1745 (43), 2076 (87)
Davis, W. E.: ref, 1687 (3,4)
Davis, Z. T.: ref, 665 (62)
Davis-Jacobson, C.: test, 741

Davison, G. C.: ref, 2497 (110)
Davison, M.: test, 771
Davison, M. L.: rev, 2484, 2699
Davous, P.: ref, 2863 (176)
Davy, J. A.: ref, 1701 (13)
Daw, J. L.: ref, 1386 (16)
Dawes, A.: ref, 2248 (4)
Dawes, R. M.: rev, 1141; ref, 372 (98)
Dawis, R. V.: test, 1694, 1695, 1701, 1702; ref, 1694 (3), 1701 (3)
Dawson, B. L.: ref, 2813 (65)
Dawson, C.: rev, 960
Dawson, D. V.: ref, 2227 (22)
Dawson, G.: ref, 459 (16,35), 1485 (31,40), 1653 (16), 1903 (350), 2382 (10), 2485 (140), 2498 (17), 2813 (18,31), 2860 (437)
Dawson, K.: ref, 776 (30), 2193 (52), 2863 (325)
Dawson, K. S.: ref, 1697 (218), 2402 (18), 2519 (26), 2520 (27)
Dawson, M. E.: ref, 1697 (188), 2305 (73), 2860 (384)
Dawson-Threat, J.: ref, 298 (152), 2527 (15)
Dax, E. M.: ref, 2076 (20), 2603 (77)
Day, A.: ref, 998 (71,93), 2050 (76,116), 2860 (186), 2863 (50)
Day, D. A.: ref, 1140 (56)
Day, D. V.: ref, 68 (34), 372 (15), 1338 (27), 1701 (14), 2163 (138)
Day, D. Y.: ref, 68 (44)
Day, H. D.: ref, 863 (27), 2211 (15)
Day, J. D.: ref, 1072 (51), 2860 (1016), 2871 (4)
Day, J. F.: ref, 694 (119)
Day, L. S.: rev, 2466; ref, 798 (17), 1903 (364), 2693 (4), 2704 (24), 2862 (342), 2901 (64), 2911 (1)
Day, R.: ref, 2749 (69)
Day, R. H.: ref, 2860 (1250)
DCCT Research Group.: ref, 926 (15), 2860 (601), 2863 (177)
D'Costa, A.: rev, 2474; ref, 1745 (49)
D'Costa, A. G.: rev, 65, 421, 2533
Deagle, D. A.: ref, 2497 (597)
Deagle, E. A.: ref, 2199 (2), 2497 (159)
Deagle, E. A., III: ref, 2497 (303), 2603 (235)
Deahl, M.: ref, 272 (5), 999 (25), 1079 (1), 1166 (2)
Deakins, S. A.: ref, 2288 (52)
Deal, J. E.: ref, 863 (26), 1000 (23), 2603 (138)
Deal, M.: ref, 1745 (27), 2603 (171)
Deal, S. N.: ref, 451 (53), 472 (119)
Dean, C.: ref, 1079 (65), 1093 (60)
Dean, E.: test, 1656
Dean, G. J.: rev, 205, 1892, 1936, 1957
Dean, N. G.: ref, 298 (23)
Dean, P.: ref, 2076 (74), 2497 (306), 2603 (240)
Dean, R. S.: rev, 326, 1164, 1407; ref, 1164 (43), 1697 (65,565), 1903 (161), 2417 (37)
DeAnda, J. R.: ref, 1697 (522)
Deane, F. P.: ref, 335 (4), 2497 (165), 2603 (557)
Deaner, S. L.: ref, 998 (51)
DeAquino Villar, I.: ref, 844 (3)
Deardorff, W. W.: rev, 231, 1978, 2746, 2766
Deary, I. J.: ref, 127 (3), 644 (4), 696 (2), 739 (1), 838 (18), 999 (9,155,185), 1079 (66), 1164 (160), 1590 (59), 1740 (24), 1758 (38), 2163 (154,207), 2218 (54,55), 2417 (33), 2516 (108), 2860 (1335)
DeAsis, J.: ref, 1164 (58), 2892 (109)
Deater-Deckard, K.: ref, 451 (252), 472 (221), 875 (11), 1264 (5), 1889 (4)
Deathe, A. B.: ref, 2592 (1)
Deaton, W. L.: rev, 819, 1458, 2402, 2876
Deaudon, C.: ref, 2163 (314), 2863 (373), 2873 (61)
DeAvila, E. A.: test, 84, 1420, 1421, 2029
Deb, S.: ref, 459 (39), 1903 (248)
Debachy, B.: ref, 2163 (214), 2860 (868)
deBarra, H. T.: ref, 815 (45), 2862 (641), 2901 (122)
DeBaryshe, B. D.: ref, 2682 (9)
Debats, D. L.: ref, 2603 (450)
DeBaun, M. R.: ref, 375 (8), 2720 (1), 2892 (297)
deBears, E.: ref, 2603 (178)
de Benis, M.: ref, 272 (350)
de Bettencourt, L. U.: ref, 2879 (11)
deBernard, A.: ref, 1612 (4), 1903 (13), 2044 (1)
DeBettignies, B. H.: ref, 1164 (29), 2860 (281), 2863 (74)
De Beurs, E.: ref, 1021 (17), 2603 (177,247,349,508)
DeBleser, R.: ref, 2225 (12)
DeBoe, J.: test, 2517, 2820
de Boeck, P.: ref, 745 (20), 1697 (124), 2163 (278), 2603 (87)
DeBoeck, P.: ref,
DeBoer, A.: test, 1295
DeBoer, M.: ref, 2497 (323,655)
deBoer, M. C.: ref, 2497 (239)
de Bonis, M.: ref, 1697 (124), 2603 (87)
DeBono, K. G.: ref, 2497 (324)
DeBord, K. A.: ref, 1661 (76), 2603 (357), 2860 (1370)
DeBroe, M. E.: ref, 1166 (58)
De Broeck, K.: ref, 2497 (292)
De Bruyn, E. E. J.: ref, 451 (276), 2862 (648)
DeBusk, R. F.: ref, 2076 (4)
Décarie, J. C.: ref, 2864 (122)
DeCarli, C.: ref, 303 (30), 2010 (18), 2599 (42), 2860 (502,837,1141,1223), 2863 (242,364)
DeCato, C. M.: ref, 301 (2), 2247 (21,54)
Decazy, A.: ref, 776 (52), 1164 (163), 1218 (18), 2226 (28), 2227 (46)
Decety, J.: ref, 2860 (844), 2863 (244), 2892 (174)
Dech, H.: ref, 1166 (202)
Deci, E. L.: ref, 2862 (159)
DeCiantis, S. M.: ref, 1470 (3)
Decina, P.: ref, 1166 (24)
Deckel, A. W.: ref, 1525 (21), 2010 (22), 2892 (223)
Decker, B. C.: ref, 1902 (45)
Deckner, C. W.: ref, 1903 (93)
DeClerck, L.: ref, 1166 (217)
DeClerck, L. S.: ref, 1166 (5), 2497 (25)
Decoster, D. A.: rev, 620

de Cubas, M. M.: ref, 451 (28), 1379 (25), 2242 (3), 2485 (79)
Dedrick, R. F.: ref, 451 (180)
Dee, C. C.: ref, 681 (79), 1380 (16)
Deeg, D. J. H.: ref, 999 (159), 2163 (307)
Deelman, B. G.: ref, 1164 (134), 2193 (47), 2226 (15), 2516 (86)
Deemer, S. A.: ref, 665 (92), 694 (130), 1734 (5), 1991 (104), 2358 (15), 2485 (240), 2862 (701), 2879 (225)
Deen, C. C.: test, 1490
Deeney, T.: test, 2316
Dees, S. M.: ref, 1140 (24), 1755 (23)
Deese, J.: rev, 2591
Defense Activity for Non-Traditional Education Support: test, 762
DeFerri, A.: ref, 1166 (21)
Deffenbach, K.: ref, 1903 (100)
Deffenbacher, J. L.: test, 2655; ref, 1021 (4)m 2497 (27,325,452,550,551)
DeFilippis, N. A.: test, 326
DeFilippo, C. L.: ref, 1407 (5)
DeFord, D. E.: ref, 1072 (46), 2905 (61)
DeForge, B. R.: ref, 1638 (1)
DeFries, J.: ref, 2382 (6)
DeFries, J. C.: ref, 798 (9,21), 1392 (10),1902 (33,35,49,50,73,80,93), 2382 (16), 2860 (391,533,1018,1215), 2862 (177,228,363,423,587), 2879 (124,189)
DeFuria, G. L.: test, 1296
DeGangi, G. A.: test, 772, 1265, 2715; ref, 772 (1), 1612 (33), 1901 (11), 2813 (34)
DeGarmo, D.: ref, 337 (135)
DeGenova, M. K.: ref, 2858 (63)
DeGood, D.: ref, 2603 (4)
DeGood, D. E.: ref, 2603 (65,125)
Degos, J.-D.: ref, 2860 (1375)
deGraauw, K. P. H. M.: ref, 2603 (469,535)
DeGrauw, A. J. C.: ref, 2076 (64), 2497 (274)
Degreef, G.: ref, 1093 (41),2305 (70), 2860 (1005)
DeGroen, J. H. M.: ref, 2497 (350)
de Groot, A. M. B.: ref, 2163 (198)
De Groot, C. M.: ref, 2603 (377)
De Groote, D.: ref, 1166 (194)
De Guire, M. J.: ref, 1010 (36)
De Haan, E. H. F.: ref, 2010 (3), 2163 (29), 2860 (233), 2863 (60)
de Haas, M. A.: ref, 2163 (153)
Dehaene, S.: ref, 199 (4)
DeHaon, E. H. F.: ref, 2860 (958)
de Hirsch, K.: test, 1337
Dehne, P.: test, 1668
Dei, T. P. S.: ref, 2497 (258)
Deinblowski, D.: ref, 994 (44), 1903 (509), 2485 (219), 2695 (64), 2813 (132), 2864 (126)
Deisinger, J. A.: ref, 1959 (5)
Deitrich-MacLean, G.: ref, 2652 (6)
Deitsch, S. E.: ref, 1697 (525)
Deitz, D.: ref, 1338 (30), 2497 (182)
Deitz, J. C.: ref, 270 (33), 353 (4), 1673 (5), 1901 (9,19), 2715 (1), 2724 (4)
Deitz, J. L.: ref, 1901 (6)
DeJong, A.: ref, 1266 (3)
de Jong, G. M.: ref, 1079 (64), 2497 (549)
de Jong, K. T.: ref, 2076 (64), 2497 (274)
de Jong, P. F.: ref, 1164 (89), 2862 (197)
de Jonge, J.: ref, 1590 (64)
de Keijser, J.: ref, 1079 (98)
Dekel, R.: ref, 2603 (589)
de Keuser, J.: ref, 1079 (77)
Dekker, M. J. A.: ref, 1164 (36)
Dekker, P. H.: ref, 2076 (64), 2497 (274)
Deklyen, M.: ref, 337 (136), 451 (110), 451 (228), 1903 (424)
DeKoninck, J.: ref, 1965 (36), 2497 (185)
Dekovic, M.: ref, 694 (75), 1079 (95)
DeLabry, L.: ref, 1697 (86)
deLacey, P. R.: ref, 999 (3)
DeLaCruz, A.: ref, 1697 (437)
de la Fuente, J. R.: test, 135
Delahanty, D. L.: ref, 2076 (146)
Delahunty, A.: ref, 1758 (75), 2860 (1139), 2892 (241)
de la Mare, M.: test, 1781, 2179
Delamatre, J. E.: ref, 1697 (165)
de Lancey, E.: ref, 2861 (2), 2862 (619)
Delaney, D.: ref, 472 (54), 2498 (22), 2862 (213)
Delaney, E. A.: test, 2485
Delaney, H. D.: ref, 1164 (37), 2076 (49), 2860 (377)
Delaney, R.: ref, 2603 (30), 2892 (126)
Delaney, R. C.: ref, 2863 (232)
Delaney,S.: ref, 1000 (76)
Delaney, S. M.: ref, 2497 (254)
DeLaPaz, S.: ref, 2731 (2), 2732 (1), 2862 (510)
De La Torre, G.: ref, 2879 (79)
DeLaVarga, M.: ref, 2050 (135), 2288 (59), 2289 (45)
DeLawyer, D. D.: test, 1884
Delazer, M.: ref, 2163 (271)
DelBoca, F. K.: ref, 1697 (157,183,491), 2603 (149)
del Carmen, R.: ref, 272 (207), 2497 (582)
Del Castillo-Castaneda, C.: ref, 2860 (1180)
Delcourt, M. A. B.: ref, 2295 (3)
Del Dotto, J. E.: ref, 2860 (1045), 2862 (445)
deLemos, M. M.: test, 26, 27, 34, 1339, 2477
DeLeo, D.: ref, 337 (54)
DeLeo, M.: ref, 2305 (133)
DeLeon, B.: ref, 298 (77)
deLeon, J.: ref, 2289 (16)
de Leon, J.: ref, 2892 (172)
DeLessio, J.: ref, 180 (10), 2163 (214)
Delgado, P. L.: ref, 1166 (123)
Delgado-Hachey, M.: ref, 2862 (198)
Delgado-Villapalos, C.: ref, 2163 (320), 2860 (1252)
Delgudri, J. C.: ref, 1657 (7), 1866 (7)
D'Elia, G.: ref, 1697 (201)
D'Elia, L.: test, 1993; ref, 1058 (3), 1758 (47), 1993 (1), 2860 (277), 2863 (72)

D'Elia, L. F.: test, 1778; ref, 1058 (1), 1135 (26), 1164 (180), 2599 (40), 2860 (21)
Delignieres, D.: ref, 298 (108), 2497 (326)
Delin, C. R.: ref, 999 (76)
Delin, P. S.: ref, 999 (76), 1697 (362)
Delis, D.: ref, 2305 (32)
Delis, D. C.: test, 375, 376, 2840; ref, 776 (21,26), 815 (14), 1164 (56), 1485 (12), 1612 (46), 1903 (236), 2225 (1), 2485 (117), 2860 (580), 2863 (167,293),2892 (47)
DeLisi, L. E.: ref, 326 (5), 1164 (60), 1697 (275), 2288 (21), 2289 (13), 2305 (20,66,98), 2892 (52), 2905 (24)
DeLisi, R.: ref, 592 (56)
Deliyannides, D.: ref, 1166 (142), 2603 (487)
Dell'aira, A. L.: ref, 1903 (397)
Della-Piana, C. K.: rev, 197, 1792
Della-Piana, G. M.: rev, 197, 1028, 1073, 1281, 2352
della Rocchetta, A. I.: ref, 2860 (838,1065), 2862 (457,243)
Dellarosa, D. M.: test, 870
Della Sala, S.: ref, 2163 (108,146,263,312), 2768 (24)
Delle Chiaie, R.: ref, 272 (234), 2497 (599)
Dellicarpini, L.: ref, 2860 (947)
Delliquadri, E.: ref, 451 (264)
Dellmann-Jenkins, M.: ref, 1927 (6)
Delmastio, M.: ref, 2497 (621)
del Medico, V.: ref, 4 (20), 681 (83), 2211 (50), 2485 (221)
DeLongis, A.: ref, 2218 (69), 2858 (117)
Deloria, D.: rev, 882
Deloria, D. J.: rev, 1673
deLorimier, S.: ref, 790 (3)
de Lorimier, S.: ref, 1903 (351)
Delp, H. A.: rev, 1484, 2862
del Philor, A. H.: ref, 2218 (129)
del Pilar González Fontao, M.: ref, 1396 (5)
Del Ser, T.: ref, 2163 (320), 2860 (1252)
Deltito, J. A.: ref, 1093 (27), 1166 (63), 2603 (88)
DeLuca, J.: ref, 272 (186,187), 2860 (165,341,447,602,1107), 2863 (91,122), 2892 (48, 2892 (71)
DeLuca, R. V.: ref, 694 (29), 2214 (17)
DeLuca, T.: ref, 1092 (18), 2712 (1), 2879 (171), 2905 (98)
Deluga, R. J.: ref, 1402 (1)
Deluty, R.: rev, 2074
Deluty, R. H.: rev, 449, 1622, 1925
delValle, C.: ref, 270 (16), 272 (169)
Delvenne, V.: ref, 1166 (181)
Delys, S. M.: ref, 1697 (126)
Demadura, T.: ref, 776 (21)
De Maertalaer, V.: ref, 1166 (181)
DeMaio-Esteves, M.: ref, 2858 (13)
Demakis, G. J.: ref, 2076 (78)
de Man, A. F.: ref, 2497 (268)
de Man, K. J.: ref, 1166 (164), 2305 (204)
DeMane, N.: ref, 1093 (8), 2108 (1)
Demaray, M. K.: ref, 2444 (1), 2452 (6), 2841 (1)
DeMarco, A.: ref, 666 (12)
DeMarco, S.: ref, 624 (1)
Demaree, R. G.: rev, 672, 1021, 2616
Demarest, J.: ref, 298 (59)
DeMarie-Dreblow, D.: ref, 1010 (83), 1866 (12)
DeMars, P. A.: ref, 1469 (2)
DeMauro, G. E.: rev, 291, 822, 1404, 1605, 2366
Demb, J. M.: ref, 1653 (3), 2485 (34)
Dembo, M. H.: ref, 298 (15), 665 (65)
Dembo, Y.: ref, 2163 (95)
Dembroski, T. M.: ref, 2497 (58)
Demby, A.: ref, 2603 (11,67,441)
Demedts, P.: ref, 1166 (126)
De Meirleir, K.: ref, 272 (200), 1164 (129), 1166 (131), 1697 (500), 2163 (286), 2603 (480), 2860 (1134)
Demertzis, A.: ref, 1991 (107)
Demetoe, J. D.: ref, 1727 (1), 1987 (20)
Demeurisse, G.: ref, 2163 (321), 2860 (1253)
de Meyer, R. E.: ref, 373 (43), 451 (289)
Deming, M. P.: ref, 615 (50), 1455 (6)
Demis, C. A.: ref, 1903 (283)
Demo, D. H.: ref, 2497 (226)
Demont, E.: ref, 2163 (267), 2862 (458)
Demorest, M. E.: rev, 658, 1618
Demos, G. D.: test, 777, 2541
Demsky, Y. I.: ref, 2860 (1254), 2862 (712)
DeMulder, E.: ref, 1093 (100)
DeMyer, M. K.: ref, 2288 (4), 2289 (2), 2305 (7), 2860 (63)
DeMyer, W. E.: ref, 2288 (4), 2289 (2), 2305 (7), 2860 (63)
Demyttenaese, K.: ref, 2497 (441)
Denahan, A.: ref, 2603 (342)
Den Boer, J. A.: ref, 1166 (154),2603 (497)
Denburg, N. L.: ref, 2497 (552,622), 2860 (1075), 2863 (314)
Dencker, S. J.: ref, 2288 (6), 2289 (4)
Denckla, M. B.: ref, 681 (66), 2860 (1167,1321,1409), 2862 (393,437,548,727), 2892 (253,303), 2901 (72,100)
Den Dulk, A.: ref, 1166 (194)
Denes, G.: ref, 199 (14), 2193 (22), 2247 (116), 2860 (647,1248), 2863 (187,376)
Denham, S. A.: ref, 1316 (2), 2039 (6)
Den Hartog, D. N.: ref, 1736 (5)
den Heijer, M.: ref, 2050 (134)
Denia, M.: ref, 999 (5)
Denicoff, K.: ref, 2305 (120)
DeNicolis, J.: rev, 1792
Denieli, R.: ref, 78 (1)
DeNisi, A. S.: ref, 1140 (16)
Denison, J. W.: rev, 2724
Deniston, W. M.: ref, 372 (46)
Denman, N.: ref, 472 (94), 2076 (88)
Denmark, R. M.: test, 713

Dennebaum, J. M.: ref, 1866 (28)
Dennerstein, L.: ref, 2497 (130)
Denney, C.: ref, 1903 (408)
Dennis, K. E.: ref, 1412 (4), 2076 (147)
Dennis, M.: ref, 1096 (3,4), 2193 (11), 2693 (3), 2860 (64,246,247,342), 2862 (38,125,126,152,199,708), 2905 (20)
Dennis, R. E.: ref, 553 (1)
Dennis, W.: test, 2800
Dennis, W. H.: test, 778, 779
Deno, E.: rev, 2428
Deno, S.: ref, 1987 (1)
Deno, S. L.: ref, 2905 (22)
Denollet, J.: ref, 2076 (54), 2497 (240)
Denollt, J.: ref, 1686 (2), 2497 (166)
De-Nour, A. K.: ref, 337 (165,166,167)
Denson, S. E.: ref, 270 (26,35), 1612 (95), 2382 (35), 2813 (130),146)
Dent, C. W.: ref, 472 (186)
Dent, O. B.: ref, 1697 (467)
Dent, O. F.: ref, 1164 (136), 1758 (79), 2497 (667), 2860 (1183), 2863 (356)
Denton, K.: ref, 1745 (67), 1902 (103), 2901 (140)
Denton, K. L.: ref, 1408 (3)
Denton, W. H.: ref, 863 (63,85)
Den Velde, W. O.: ref, 2497 (350)
Denzler, P.: ref, 2163 (184)
DePadova, A.: ref, 2516 (6)
DePaepe, J. L.: ref, 353 (7)
Department of Testing Services: test, 386, 780
DePaúl, J.: ref, 448 (3,4,13,14)
DePaulo, B. M.: ref, 2078 (1)
DePaulo, R.: ref, 2050 (125)
DePauw, K. W.: ref, 2193 (13)
De Pavia, S.: ref, 1897 (1)
De Potter, B.: ref, 1686 (2), 2497 (166)
DePriest, M.: ref, 1093 (93), 2289 (39)
Depue, R. A.: ref, 2305 (31)
DeQuattro, V. L.: ref, 2497 (110)
Derby, J. F.: ref, 2076 (45,46,86)
Derecho, C. N.: ref, 1166 (102), 1687 (20), 2603 (451)
Derenowski, E.: ref, 2862 (550)
DeRenzi, E.: ref, 2163 (109,155,208,210,319), 2860 (448,603,836,839,842,1251), 2863 (123),2892 (173,269)
DeReuck, J.: ref, 2163 (214), 2860 (868)
Derevensky, J.: ref, 289 (4), 385 (2)
de Rijk, A. E.: ref, 1590 (64)
DeRisio, C.: ref, 1166 (21)
Derlin, R. L.: ref, 2559 (5)
Derlyen, M.: ref, 681 (11), 1903 (80), 2603 (99)
Dermen, D.: test, 1405
Dermout, K. M. T.: ref, 1079 (42)
DeRoeck, J.: ref, 303 (24), 2125 (28), 2163 (345), 2516 (114)
Derogatis, L. R.: test, 335, 337, 791, 792, 793, 794, 2117, 2326, 2603
DeRonchi, D.: ref, 2863 (416)
DeRosa, A. P.: ref, 372 (44), 1000 (42), 1991 (42)
DeRosa, R.: ref, 272 (162)
Derrick, A. M.: ref, 451 (152), 472 (187), 473 (3)
Derry, P.: ref, 1745 (27)
Derry, P. A.: ref, 1010 (44), 1697 (538)
Derryberry, D.: ref, 999 (77,134), 2497 (327,508)
DeRubeis, R. J.: ref, 998 (41), 1093 (42),1697 (167,173), 1705 (3), 2305 (122)
de Ruiter, C.: ref, 2247 (114)
de Saint Martin, A.: ref, 350 (39)
Desaulty, A.: ref, 2163 (214), 2860 (868)
Desforges, D. M.: ref, 1965 (58)
Desforges, M.: test, 1260
Desgranges, B.: ref, 2516 (64), 2863 (248)
DeShon, R. P.: ref, 2163 (209), 2218 (122), 2860 (1384)
Deshpande, S. A.: ref, 376 (4)
deSilva, M.: ref, 837 (3), 1765 (19), 1903 (292), 2862 (280)
Desmarais, L. B.: ref, 180 (33)
Desmond, D. W.: ref, 2860 (407,408,604)
Desmond, J. E.: ref, 2163 (339)
deSnyder, N. S.: ref, 2603 (40)
Desnyder, R.: ref, 272 (198),1166 (76,77,78,127,128)
de Sonneville, L.: ref, 2860 (747)
de Sonneville, L. M. J.: ref, 681 (9,42)
DeSoto, C. B.: test, 1587, 1775; ref, 1775 (1,2)
DeSoto, J. L.: test, 1587, 1775; ref, 1775 (1,2)
DeSousa, D. J.: ref, 620 (5)
DeSouza, E.: ref, 1745 (21,24)
D'Esposito, M.: ref, 1164 (91,161), 1740 (22), 2226 (9), 2516 (104), 2860 (833,859), 2863 (240), 2873 (30,31), 2892 (178,279)
DeSrabo, W.: ref, 771 (18)
Desrosiers, G.: ref, 63 (1), 1903 (10),2860 (31)
Desselle, D. D.: ref, 694 (69)
de St. Aubin, E.: ref, 2246 (8), 2749 (78)
D'Este, A.: ref, 1770 (14)
DeStefano, L.: rev, 770, 1457, 1963
Detera-Wadleigh, S.: ref, 2305 (29)
DeTeresa, R.: ref, 2860 (184), 2862 (105)
de Sterke, S.: ref, 1164 (168), 2226 (34), 2239 (32), 2516 (110), 2860 (1345), 2863 (403)
Detre, T.: ref, 2288 (3)
Detterman, D. K.: rev, 2441, 2862; ref, 2860 (343)
Detzer, M. J.: ref, 793 (13), 2603 (329)
D'Eugenio, D. B.: test, 879, 2041
Deus, J.: ref, 272 (309)
Deuschl, G.: ref, 2163 (54), 2603 (495)
Deutsch, A.: ref, 2163 (37)
Deutsch, F. M.: ref, 298 (7)
Deutsch, G. K.: ref, 2892 (204)
Deutsch, S. I.: ref, 1903 (92)
Dev, P. C.: ref, 464 (5), 2313 (2)
Devanand, D. P.: ref, 272 (203), 1166 (24,103,148), 2305 (45)

DeVane, C. L.: ref, 272 (165)
DeVaney, S.: ref, 1338 (41), 2076 (79)
The Developmental Therapy Institute, Inc.: test, 814
Devenis, L. E.: ref, 200 (3), 1965 (6)
Devenny, D. A.: ref, 2862 (459)
de V. Heyns, I.: ref, 1991 (26)
DeVillafranca, E. F.: rev, 49
Devine, C.: ref, 68 (53), 462 (7)
Devine, D.: ref, 337 (71), 472 (80), 2211 (29,46)
Devine, D. W.: test, 819
Devine, J.: ref, 272 (343)
Devins, G. M.: ref, 1697 (66,67), 2076 (9,10)
Devinsky, O.: ref, 2227 (17), 2863 (213)
Devito, A. J.: rev, 739, 1755
Devlin, A. S.: ref, 298 (72,95)
Devlin, M. J.: ref, 2603 (562)
Devlin, P.: ref, 2076 (15)
DeVos, K. J.: ref, 1902 (69), 2768 (28), 2862 (325), 2879 (110)
DeVreese, L. P.: ref, 2658 (1)
DeVries, H.: ref, 451 (65,66), 681 (40)
de Vries, J.: ref, 1745 (16)
de Vries, L.: ref, 349 (31), 451 (131)
DeVries, R.: rev, 674
Dew, M. A.: ref, 337 (72,156), 1166 (104,182), 2305 (173), 2603 (43,139,248)
Dewart, H.: test, 2024, 2025
Deweer, B.: ref, 776 (33,54,63); ref, 2163 (156,183), 2516 (82), 2860 (449,605,720), 2863 (124,178,215), 2892 (72,142,249)
Dewey, D.: ref, 353 (16), 815 (22), 1903 (167)
Dewey, M. E.: ref, 272 (279), 997 (23), 1079 (50), 1758 (89), 2050 (104)
Dewey, T.: ref, 2076 (61)
Dewhurst, J.: ref, 298 (167), 998 (135)
Dewick, H. C.: ref, 1758 (13), 2193 (6)
de Wied, D.: ref, 2813 (5)
DeWire, H.: test, 2751
DeWit, H.: ref, 66 (1), 2077 (3)
DeWitt, M. B.: ref, 451 (258), 681 (92), 1099 (5), 1164 (177), 1379 (101), 1740 (31), 2516 (118), 2892 (299)
Dewolfe, A.: ref, 999 (15)
DeWolfe, D.: ref, 2603 (75), 2858 (22)
Dewson, M.: test, 2670
Dey, A. N.: ref, 134 (27)
Dey, M. L.: rev, 1855
Deysach, R. E.: rev, 134, 824
DeZolt, D. M.: rev, 442, 889, 1905, 2001, 2211
deZwaan, M.: ref, 2497 (313)
D'Haese, P. C.: ref, 1166 (58)
D'Hondt, P.: ref, 1166 (58)
Diakidoy, I. N.: ref, 2487 (13)
Dial, J. G.: test, 929, 1610, 1815, 1919, 2579
Diamond, B. J.: ref, 272 (187), 2860 (606,1066,1107), 2863 (179,313)
Diamond, D. L.: ref, 1661 (42)
Diamond, E. E.: rev, 423, 565, 904, 1797, 1947, 2177, 2360, 2740, 2829
Diamond, I. D.: ref, 2239 (10)
Diamond, R.: ref, 1164 (33), 2603 (140), 2860 (344), 2863 (92), 2892 (49)
Diamons, A.: ref, 2749 (78)
Dias, P. S.: ref, 1758 (54), 2860 (1000), 2863 (296), 2892 (209)
Diascro, M. N.: ref, 745 (10)
Díaz, F.: ref, 2860 (1026), 2862 (430)
Diaz, L.: ref, 2813 (137)
Diaz, R.: ref, 1745 (48)
Diaz, T.: ref, 999 (118)
DiBartolo, P. M.: ref, 472 (220), 2214 (132)
Dibenedetto, B.: test, 769
Di Betta, A. M.: ref, 2225 (19), 2860 (1362)
DiBiase, R.: ref, 1987 (13)
DiCarlo, L. M.: rev, 987, 2870
DiCerbo, P. A.: test, 87
DiCesare, F.: ref, 2159 (3)
Dichter, C. G.: ref, 2862 (86)
Dick, E. L.: ref, 1166 (210)
Dick, H.: ref, 2860 (699)
Dick, M. B.: ref, 2860 (89)
Dick, R. W.: ref, 2557 (8)
Dicken, C. F.: rev, 1101
Dickens, S.: ref, 2076 (105)
Dickens, S. E.: test, 2522; ref, 1166 (90,170,171), 2218 (44,81,82), 2305 (213), 2603 (514)
Dickerson, F. B.: ref, 1525 (11), 2860 (248)
Dickey, S. E.: test, 1982
Dickinson, D.: ref, 2195 (1)
Dickinson, D. K.: ref, 1903 (249)
Dickinson, L. G.: ref, 2497 (359)
Dickson, G. S.: rev, 1790
Dickson, K.: ref, 1697 (244)
Dickson, S.: ref, 2288 (54), 2289 (41)
Dickstein, D. P.: ref, 451 (102), 2862 (450)
Dickstein, S.: ref, 790 (4), 999 (19), 1166 (152), 1216 (88), 2603 (496)
DiClemente, C. C.: ref, 136 (9), 1661 (28)
Di Dio, L.: ref, 2246 (9)
Die, A. H.: ref, 1745 (1), 2402 (2)
Diedrich, G. K.: ref, 2603 (141)
Diefendorf, A. O.: rev, 214, 1656, 2504, 2671
Diehl, M.: ref, 372 (99)
Diekhoff, J. S.: rev, 98
Diekstra, R. F. W.: ref, 1021 (44), 2603 (559)
Diener, E.: ref, 337 (66),1172 (1), 2218 (9,76)
Diener, M. L.: ref, 272 (109), 2497 (453)
Dienske, H.: ref, 459 (26)
Dienstbier, R. A.: ref, 2163 (275,276)
Diep, T-S.: ref, 1166 (105)
Dierendonck, D.: ref, 1590 (53)
Dierks, C.: ref, 776 (49), 2227 (42)
Dierks, Ch.: ref, 1164 (158,159), 1758 (91), 2227 (41)
Dies, R. R.: ref, 2603 (323)

Diessner, R.: ref, 771 (17), 1408 (9)
Dietrich, M.: ref, 4 (18)
Dietrich, M. S.: ref, 2652 (6)
Dietz, K. R.: ref, 270 (29), 451 (181), 1612 (91)
Di Fazio, R.: ref, 298 (44)
Difillipo, E.: ref, 2749 (39)
DiGirolamo, A. M.: ref, 472 (195), 863 (30), 2603 (154)
Digiusto, E.: ref, 2860 (841)
DiGregorio, M.: ref, 2862 (344)
DiIorio, C.: ref, 1947 (6)
Dijken, W. A.: ref, 1166 (52,53), 2603 (265)
Dikmen, S.: ref, 1164 (62)
DiLalla, D. L.: ref, 459 (28), 1697 (401), 2218 (57), 2246 (11), 1216 (85,105), 2485 (232), 2862 (655)
DiLavore, P. C.: ref, 837 (4), 1653 (22), 1903 (352)
Dilks, S. L. E.: ref, 2195 (2)
Dill, D. L.: ref, 846 (18), 2380 (3),2603 (113)
Diller, L.: ref, 337 (43), 1745 (13), 2858 (38)
D'Ilio, V. R.: ref, 1010 (4,10), 2485 (9,16), 2862 (45,76)
Dillon, D. R.: ref, 246 (5), 301 (49), 2485 (174)
Dillon, W.: ref, 1407 (1), 2860 (172)
Dillon, W. P.: ref, 1058 (7), 2227 (12), 2860 (499), 2863 (143)
Dilsaver, S. C.: ref, 2305 (202)
Dimachkie, M. M.: ref, 2860 (1192)
Dimatteo, C.: ref, 2497 (621)
DiMatteo, R.: test, 703, 2078
Dimiceli, S.: ref, 1770 (3)
DiMichele, V.: ref, 1525 (10)
Dimitrov, M.: ref, 2860 (1067), 2892 (224)
Dimitrovsky, L.: ref, 303 (27),863 (49), 2226 (39), 2862 (607)
Dinan, T. G.: ref, 1166 (59), 1481 (1), 2305 (175)
Dinero, T. E.: rev, 797, 1816
Ding, X. H.: ref, 303 (6), 1218 (10), 2860 (891),2863 (263)
Dingemans, D. M.: ref, 2050 (48)
Dingemans, P.: ref, 1619 (5), 2050 (43), 2603 (206), 2892 (83)
Dingemans, P. M.: ref, 1697 (478)
Dingemans, P. M. A. J.: ref, 2050 (47), 2892 (93)
Dingjan, P.: ref, 1758 (84), 2860 (1247)
Dings, J. G.: rev, 848
Dini, M. L.: ref, 56 (7)
Dinning, W. D.: ref, 1338 (29)
Dinsmore, S.: ref, 1697 (269), 2497 (315)
Dinur, B.: ref, 1991 (83), 2358 (6)
Dinur, C.: ref, 2497 (494)
Dinwiddle, S. H.: ref, 999 (172)
Dion, C.: ref, 650 (15), 1093 (97)
Dion, M. R.: ref, 1697 (539)
Dionne, J. A.: ref, 2861 (3)
Dionne, M.: ref, 998 (89), 999 (154)
Dipboye, R. L.: rev, 1437; ref, 592 (40), 1755 (63)
di Pellegrino, G.: ref, 2163 (208), 2860 (839,840, 842,843), 2892 (173)
Dipert, Z. J.: ref, 2862 (489)
DiPietro, J. A.: ref, 1216 (42), 1612 (16), 1902 (53)
Direnfeld, D. M.: ref, 2305 (112), 2603 (371)
Dirks, D. D.: ref, 1903 (354)
Dirks, J.: rev, 1245
Dirkzwager, A.: ref, 838 (19)
Dishion, T. J.: ref, 451 (54)
Dishith, P.: ref, 271 (9), 272 (266), 273 (27),1166 (183)
DiSimoni, F.: test, 2768
Diskin, M. T.: ref, 2905 (83)
Disorbio, J. C.: test, 267
Disorbio, J. M.: test, 267
Dissanayake, C.: ref, 270 (14), 539 (1), 540 (5), 1903 (457), 2228 (22), 2485 (194)
Disselkamp-Tietze, J.: ref, 2497 (121)
Ditta, S. R.: ref, 337 (121), 1010 (88), 2402 (47,48), 2497 (521), 2603 (414,415), 2858 (107), 2860 (995)
Dittes, J. E.: test, 2751
Dittmann-Kohli, F.: ref, 745 (1,3), 1405 (1), 2163 (7,19,63)
Ditto, B.: ref, 998 (12), 1338 (9), 2497 (28)
Ditto, P. H.: ref, 1697 (402)
Ditton, P.: ref, 1164 (111), 2862 (397)
Dittrichová, J.: ref, 2485 (195), 2862 (460)
Divgi, D. R.: ref, 180 (2)
Divine, G. W.: ref, 1697 (206)
Divis, B.: ref, 776 (20), 1607 (13), 1903 (348), 2485 (164), 2860 (834)
Division of Testing and Certification: test, 1664
Dix, T.: ref, 2076 (11)
Dixen, J.: ref, 1697 (266)
Dixon, D. C.: ref, 2497 (241)
Dixon, D. N.: rev, 675, 717, 1582, 1748, 2064, 2147, 2522; ref, 592 (89)
Dixon, D. R.: ref, 2603 (520)
Dixon, L.: ref, 2076 (12)
Dixon, M. J.: ref, 1000 (98)
Dixon, P.: ref, 272 (346), 2603 (575)
Dixon, R. A.: ref, 2860 (1277)
Dixon, R. M.: ref, 350 (52), 1903 (577), 2163 (355), 2860 (1413), 2862 (730)
Dixon, W.: ref, 272 (219), 273 (25), 376 (35), 1135 (13), 1164 (187), 2065 (29), 2227 (62), 2516 (122), 2599 (25), 2860 (772,1420), 2892 (308)
Dixon, W. A.: ref, 694 (105), 2497 (515)
Doak, E.: ref, 2860 (347), 2862 (161)
Doakes, S. S.: ref, 270 (45),1687 (35)
Doane, J. A.: ref, 2749 (3)
Dobbins, C.: ref, 2860 (166)
Dobbins, D. A.: ref, 2163 (157)
Dobbins, G. H.: rev, 1660, 1937, 2071, 2571, 2634
Dobbins, I. G.: ref, 2860 (1385), 2863 (417)
Dobkin, C. S.: ref, 303 (6), 1218 (10), 2860 (891), 2863 (263)
Dobkin, J.: ref, 1135 (18), 2226 (14), 2516 (85), 2860 (1173), 2863 (353)

Dobkin, P.: ref, 2497 (190)
Dobkin, P. L.: ref, 1661 (69,78), 2039 (14,16,23)
Dobranski, T.: ref, 1755 (65), 2076 (152)
Dobson, B.: test, 953, 1664
Dobson, K. S.: rev, 1808; ref, 272 (184,355,374), 1745 (88), 2305 (128),2603 (350)
Dobson, S. H.: ref, 1405 (32)
Doby, V. J.: ref, 2497 (454)
Docherty, N. M.: ref, 2017 (12), 2288 (7), 2289 (5), 2305 (37,174), 2860 (1068)
Dockrell, J.: ref, 2 (1),2813 (90)
Dócon, A.: ref, 451 (103)
Docter, R. F.: rev, 2010
DocuTrac, Inc.: test, 1187
Dodd, B.: ref, 1503 (13), 1765 (21), 1903 (365),2704 (25)
Dodd, J. M.: test, 1068
Doddi, S.: ref, 1093 (35,75)
Dodds, B.: ref, 2860 (1228), 2863 (366)
Dodds, J.: test, 788
Dodge, C. S.: ref, 2497 (68)
Dodge, K. A.: ref, 451 (26,140,199), 472 (36)
Dodge, K. L.: ref, 863 (70)
Dodrill, C. B.: ref, 303 (15), 1135 (8,20), 1697 (125), 1740 (18), 2076 (167), 2077 (5),2226 (21), 2516 (10,22,96), 2599 (12), 2860 (167,450,1255), 2863 (378), 2879 (215), 2899 (15)
Dodson, D. L.: ref, 838 (4)
Dodson, S.: test, 315
Dodson, S. L.: ref, 1866 (42)
Doebler, L. K.: rev, 21, 23
Doelling, J. L.: ref, 1010 (22)
Doepke, K.: ref, 246 (4), 1379 (24), 1903 (158)
Doering, M.: ref, 1694 (2), 1695 (1)
Doering, M. M.: ref, 1694 (8), 1695 (2)
Doernberger, C. H.: ref, 472 (56)
Doershuk, C. F.: ref, 1316 (1)
Doescher, S. M.: ref, 1903 (112),156)
Dogali, M.: ref, 2227 (17), 2863 (213)
Dohan, F. C., Jr.: ref, 376 (10)
Doherty, B.: ref, 2860 (948,1147), 2863 (279,339)
Doherty, S.: ref, 815 (32), 1379 (80),1725 (7)
Doherty, V. W.: test, 2293
Doherty, W. J.: ref, 1000 (7), 1036 (5)
Doi, L. M.: ref, 2862 (514), 2905 (100)
Doig, B.: test, 33, 825, 2080, 2611
Dolan, B.: ref, 1991 (78)
Dolan, C. A.: ref, 2858 (34)
Dolan, E. M.: ref, 1000 (72)
Dolan, I.: ref, 694 (38)
Dolan, L.: ref, 2695 (5)
Dolan, L. J.: test, 2313
Dolan, R. J.: ref, 2860 (579), 2863 (166)
Dolan, R. T.: ref, 1517 (4)
Dolan, S.: test, 1832
Dole, J. A.: rev, 830, 2190, 2191, 2660; ref, 1866 (16)
Dolente, A.: test, 2551
Dolgin, M.: ref, 451 (157), 472 (68), 472 (151), 1010 (115), 2498 (25)
Dolhert, N.: ref, 2860 (765)
Dolinsky, A.: ref, 1093 (21)
Dolinsky, Z. S.: ref, 1697 (157)
Doll, B.: rev, 451, 912; ref, 694 (51), 1386 (3), 2214 (27), 2230 (13), 2485 (80)
Doll, E. J.: rev, 1386
Doll, H. A.: ref, 337 (99,137,141), 1079 (87), 2050 (113), 2603 (453)
Doll, L.: ref, 337 (161)
Doll, R. C.: test, 1492
Dollaghan, C.: ref, 2225 (16), 2864 (132), 2901 (113), 2902 (5)
Dollaghan, C. A.: ref, 1903 (62,342)
Dollinger, S. J.: ref, 2218 (56,57), 2246 (10,11), 2860 (897)
Dollinger, S. M. C.: ref, 2218 (26)
Dolliver, R. H.: rev, 1163, 1790, 2360, 2364
Dolz, L.: ref, 451 (103)
Domanic, J.: ref, 448 (6)
Dombalis, A. O.: ref, 2603 (361)
Dombrose, L. A.: test, 1239
Dombrowski, L. B.: test, 1065
Domenci, L.: ref, 2360 (1)
Domenech, E.: ref, 472 (61)
Dominey, P.: ref, 2860 (844), 2863 (244), 2892 (174)
Domino, G.: rev, 381, 666, 768, 1311, 1356, 1841, 2032, 2126, 2177, 2198, 2260, 2829; ref, 68 (36), 272 (166), 273 (18), 372 (101), 2126 (15)
Domitrovic, L. A.: ref, 2497 (622)
Domken, M.: ref, 999 (78), 1166 (46)
Dompierre, S.: ref, 708 (4)
Don, A.: ref, 376 (22), 2860 (1293), 2879 (209)
Doná, G.: ref, 708 (8)
Donaghy, T.: ref, 451 (176), 811 (13), 1259 (2)
Donahoe, C. P.: ref, 1697 (68), 2050 (5), 2288 (8)
Donahue, K.: ref, 1697 (580)
Donahue, M.: rev, 2725, 2911; ref, 430 (13), 798 (19), 1040 (11), 1240 (37), 1804 (13), 1903 (402), 2694 (16), 2864 (100)
Donahue, M. L.: ref, 430 (11), 540 (2), 1240 (32), 1804 (11), 1903 (353), 2864 (83)
Donaldson, D.: ref, 451 (105), 472 (161)
Donaldson, G. W.: ref, 1592 (14), 1902 (5,43), 2862 (41), 2905 (40)
Donatelle, J. R.: ref, 2860 (989), 2862 (404), 2879 (140)
Donders, J.: ref, 1380 (5,11), 2193 (50), 2603 (437), 2862 (326,461,604)
Done, D. J.: ref, 358 (1), 2860 (190)
Donelson, E.: ref, 790 (29)
Donenberg, G. R.: ref, 451 (182)
Doneshka, P.: ref, 2146 (18)
Dong, H.: rev, 160
Dong, Q.: ref, 472 (81,153), 2214 (40,87)
Donison, D.: ref, 2497 (149)

Donlan, C.: ref, 540 (10), 2163 (292), 2662 (6), 2862 (527)
Donlon, T. F.: rev, 38, 75, 1001, 2737, 2898
Donnay, D. A. C.: ref, 1790 (12,14)
Donnellan, A. M.: ref, 1903 (8)
Donnelly, M.: ref, 472 (120)
Donnelly, M. H.: ref, 413 (10)
Donoghue, J. R.: ref, 118 (1), 1759 (10,11)
Donohue, J.: ref, 1903 (389), 2125 (16), 2768 (30), 2905 (85)
Donohue, M. V.: ref, 372 (85)
Donovan, C. M.: test, 879
Donovan, D. M.: ref, 134 (2), 272 (14), 1661 (15), 2860 (108)
Donovan, J. E.: ref, 2498 (33)
Donovan, J. M.: ref, 2497 (242)
Donovan, M.: ref, 451 (238), 1010 (131)
Donovan, S. J.: ref, 1166 (142), 2603 (487)
Donovick, P. J.: ref, 2860 (165,962), 2863 (285)
Doody, R.: ref, 2288 (50)
Doody, R. S.: ref, 1164 (127), 2860 (1128,1129), 2863 (335,336)
Doolabh, A.: ref, 1965 (21)
Dooley, J.: ref, 1135 (17), 1164 (119), 2862 (435), 2879 (153)
Dooley, S. L.: ref, 1386 (25), 2860 (1338), 2862 (667)
Dooneief, G.: ref, 303 (18), 776 (45), 1740 (21), 2125 (7), 2516 (16), 2860 (310,512,907,1284,1346)
Dopkins, S.: ref, 2860 (607)
Doppelt, J. B.: test, 2787, 1974; rev, 361, 1107, 1222, 1444, 1702, 2031
Dorais, S.: ref, 256 (4), 1697 (508)
Doran, R. L.: test, 1639
Doren, H.: ref, 994 (44), 1903 (509), 2485 (219), 2695 (64), 2813 (132), 2864 (126)
Dorfman, D.: ref, 1135 (18), 2226 (14), 2516 (85), 2860 (1173), 2863 (353)
Dorfman, W. I.: ref, 1697 (495)
Dorfman-Etrog, P.: ref, 2305 (118)
Dorhofer, D.: ref, 272 (320), 2497 (657), 2603 (553)
Dorland, S.: ref, 2076 (39)
Dorn, F. J.: ref, 404 (5)
Dorn, L. D.: ref, 1166 (94), 2076 (143), 2603 (442)
Dornic, S.: ref, 998 (13)
Dorosh, M.: ref, 1008 (2)
Dorris, G.: ref, 273 (14), 337 (108), 1697 (285)
Dorsey, D. W.: ref, 180 (27)
Dor-Shav, N. K.: ref, 2163 (42), 2248 (5)
Dose, J. J.: ref, 1694 (10), 2915 (7)
Dose, M.: ref, 2603 (287)
Dossetor, D. R.: ref, 1079 (23)
Doster, R. J.: test, 1230
Doty, M. S.: test, 2916
Doty, R. L.: test, 2437; ref, 2437 (3,4), 2860 (810), 2863 (234)
Douban, J.: ref, 472 (219), 2214 (128)
Double, D. B.: ref, 2050 (31)
Douce, L. A.: ref, 298 (29)
Dougall, A. L.: ref, 2076 (146)
Dougall, N.: ref, 1166 (65)
Dougher, M. J.: ref, 2077 (1)
Dougherty, E. H.: test, 1648
Dougherty, L. M.: ref, 2860 (544), 2863 (156)
Dougherty, R. W.: ref, 272 (208)
Douglas, C. J.: ref, 272 (360), 273 (34)
Douglas, D.: rev, 306, 2687; ref, 2862 (369)
Douglas, G.: ref, 72 (1), 1379 (96)
Douglas, J.: ref, 1434 (2)
Douglas, J. A.: ref, 1434 (1), 1759 (16)
Douglas, M. S.: ref, 2305 (57)
Douglas, P.: ref, 451 (125), 472 (168)
Douglas, S. M.: ref, 472 (34)
Douglas, V. I.: ref, 681 (21,63), 1903 (151,488), 2860 (424)
Douglass, F. M., IV: ref, 1697 (276), 1755 (24,37)
Douglass, R.: ref, 1697 (276), 1755 (24,37)
Douse, N. A.: ref, 298 (78), 999 (54)
Doussard-Roosevelt, J.: ref, 451 (111), 787 (2), 1379 (83), 1889 (5)
Doussard-Roosevelt, J. A.: ref, 451 (183), 787 (3),1379 (93)
Dover, A.: ref, 389 (6,11)
Doverspike, D.: test, 231
Doverspike, D. D.: ref, 2218 (51)
Dow, M. G.: ref, 2603 (26)
Dowall, R. L.: test, 490
Dowd, C. T.: ref, 372 (62), 1965 (48)
Dowd, E. T.: rev, 271, 273, 1219, 2652
Dowd, R.: ref, 2497 (509)
Dowdall, D.: ref, 2497 (168)
Dowdney, L.: ref, 350 (53), 863 (94), 1079 (112), 1612 (78), 1745 (61)
Dowe, D. L.: ref, 335 (12), 1010 (100,101)
Dow-Ehrensberger, M.: ref, 2485 (175), 2879 (129)
Downe, A. G.: ref, 1036 (11)
Downes, J. J.: ref, 1390 (2), 1758 (2,7,10,66), 2193 (17,26,51), 2860 (90,206,215,495,685,1069), 2863 (141,202), 2892 (80,131)
Downey, D. M.: ref, 2813 (134), 2901 (106)
Downey, G.: ref, 999 (156), 2603 (73,452)
Downey, J.: ref, 337 (36), 1093 (1), 2603 (15)
Downey, K. K.: ref, 272 (267), 376 (18), 1697 (182,540), 2402 (62), 2405 (1), 2516 (97)
Downie, N. M.: rev, 2899
Downing, J.: test, 1504
Downing, R.: ref, 998 (58)
Downs, J. C.: test, 2323
Downs, M.: test, 784
Downs, W. R.: ref, 271 (12), 272 (305), 1661 (2,22)
Dowse, J.: ref, 272 (167)
Dowton, S. B.: ref, 681 (45), 1903 (262)
Doyle, A.: ref, 280 (2,3), 451 (184)
Doyle, A. B.: ref, 863 (50)
Doyle, A. E.: ref, 1745 (50)

Doyle, A-B.: ref, 1903 (351)
Doyle, C.: ref, 999 (56)
Doyle, K. O., Jr.: rev, 948
Doyle, S. S.: ref, 1379 (62), 1903 (330), 2651 (16), 2657 (21), 2695 (33)
Doyle, T.: ref, 4 (19)
Doyon, J.: ref, 2125 (25), 2860 (249,250,1256)
Doyon, M.: ref, 472 (233), 2214 (138)
Dozier, A.: ref, 326 (2)
Dozier, M.: ref, 337 (97), 2603 (89)
Dozois, D. J. A.: ref, 1687 (41), 2603 (350)
Drabman, R. S.: rev, 2444; ref, 2862 (210), 2901 (27)
Dracup, K. A.: ref, 2076 (187)
Dragna, M.: ref, 298 (45)
Draine, J.: ref, 1093 (77,103)
Drake, A. I.: ref, 2860 (845)
Drake Beam Morin, Inc.: test, 1331
Drake, C.: ref, 1131 (2), 1903 (5), 2862 (9), 2879 (2)
Drake, H.: ref, 2050 (68)
Drake, M. E.: ref, 1164 (30), 1697 (141), 2860 (293)
Drake, R. E.: ref, 134 (4,12,23,36)
Drake, R. M.: rev, 745, 1315, 2212, 2741
Dralle, P. W.: rev, 75
Drapeau, A.: ref, 451 (147)
Dras, S. R.: ref, 1697 (47)
Drasgow, F.: ref, 56 (10), 180 (3,4,9,28)
Drasin, R. E.: ref, 272 (117)
Drebing, C.: ref, 2305 (4), 2860 (697,698), 2863 (204)
Dreger, R. M.: rev, 2413, 2497
Dreher, M. J.: rev, 1071, 2184, 2883; ref, 1072 (32), 1759 (8)
Dreman, S.: ref, 451 (185), 1000 (106), 2497 (29,59, 328,329), 2498 (34)
Dresden, J.: ref, 1903 (87)
Dresden, J. H.: ref, 2805 (2)
Dressel, J. H.: ref, 1072 (16)
Dressel, P. L.: rev, 93, 118, 617
Dressler, W. W.: ref, 1338 (10)
Drew, C.: ref, 2299 (2), 2485 (98)
Drews, J. E.: test, 2041
Drexler, H.: ref, 301 (48),2860 (922)
Dreyer, P. H.: rev, 88, 1010
Dreyfus, D.: test, 250
Dreyfuss, D.: ref, 1093 (64)
Drinka, T. J. K.: test, 212
Driscoll, J. M.: ref, 1701 (51), 1825 (7)
Driver, J. E.: ref, 1047 (1), 1240 (7), 2660 (2), 2695 (9)
Droege, R. C.: rev, 1043, 2899
Drolet, J-L.: ref, 2126 (5)
Droney, J. M.: ref, 1735 (4)
Drop, M. J.: ref, 1661 (29)
Droppleman, L. F.: test, 2076
Drose, G. S.: ref, 644 (5)
Drost, D. J.: ref, 2288 (55,78,79), 2289 (42,65)
Drotar, D.: ref, 1010 (122), 1013 (2), 1903 (68,396), 2076 (168), 2485 (178), 2497 (589), 2498 (62), 1316 (1)
Druckman, J.: ref, 1010 (21)
Druckman, J. M.: test, 2034
Drudge, O.: ref, 2117 (4)
Drum, P. A.: rev, 1073, 2725, 2883
Drumheller, A.: ref, 2497 (268)
Drumheller, P. M.: ref, 2858 (55)
Drumheller, P. M., Jr.: ref, 2858 (83)
Drummond, J. E.: ref, 2485 (66)
Drummond, P. D.: ref, 999 (79)
Drummond, R. J.: rev, 136, 1637, 1792
Drummond, S. P. A.: ref, 272 (132), 1166 (80)
Drummond, S. S.: test, 866; ref, 2873 (14)
Drumwright, A. F.: test, 783
Druss, B.: ref, 2603 (498)
Druva-Roush, C. A.: rev, 797, 1034, 2763, 2845
Dryden, M.: ref, 1903 (424)
Duan, N.: ref, 451 (163), 1903 (513), 2902 (4)
Duara, R.: ref, 1058 (3), 2860 (186,277,484), 2863 (50,72,135)
Duarte, M. E.: ref, 83 (1), 2282 (10), 2805 (1)
Dubas, J. S.: ref, 372 (40), 2860 (382)
Dube, A.: ref, 451 (42), 1000 (71)
Dube, W. V.: ref, 1903 (552), 2862 (672)
Dubno, J. R.: rev, 231, 1190
Dubois, B.: ref, 328 (1), 776 (33,54,63), 2163 (43,75,156,183,295), 2227 (19), 2516 (44,82),2517 (7), 2860 (168,298,449,605,720,818,1153), 2863 (44,124,178,215,236,342), 2870 (2), 2892 (20,39,72,94,130,142,207,248,249,255)
Dubois, D. D.: test, 638, 801
DuBois, D. L.: ref, 56 (8), 337 (39,93), 472 (24,82, 121,123), 495 (11), 1010 (59), 2065 (14), 2214 (14, 41 ,65), 2369 (6), 2525 (9)
DuBois, L. M.: rev, 780, 1498
Dubois, P. H.: rev, 592, 1638
DuBose, P. B.: ref, 592 (95)
DuBoulay, G.: ref, 2050 (34)
Dubow, E.: ref, 1216 (22), 1903 (128)
Dubow, E. F.: ref, 1216 (6,44), 1902 (16,54), 1903 (48), 2497 (142)
Dubowitz, H.: ref, 270 (8,31), 337 (175), 1216 (66), 2189 (5)
Dubowitz, L. M. S.: ref, 349 (31), 451 (131)
DuBreuil, S. C.: ref, 999 (139), 1697 (244), 2603 (407)
Duchan, J. F.: ref, 175 (12), 815 (25), 994 (27), 1379 (70), 1725 (5), 1903 (373), 2813 (95), 2864 (94), 2879 (119)
Ducharme, J. M.: ref, 1901 (16), 2485 (81,123,124,196), 2813 (113),2862 (200)
Duchen, L. W.: ref, 2163 (100), 2860 (415)
Duchesneau, A. P.: ref, 1218 (15), 2860 (1070)
Duck, J. M.: ref, 1991 (7)
Duckett, E.: ref, 472 (100), 1010 (104)
Duckitt, J.: rev, 1294, 1481; ref, 1965 (49)
Duckworth, M. P.: ref, 1697 (541), 2860 (1257)
Dudek, S. Z.: ref, 2771 (22)
Dudenhoeffer, S.: ref, 342 (3), 2862 (392), 2901 (71)

Dudgeon, B.: ref, 1590 (54)
Dudgeon, P.: ref, 2860 (1228),2863 (366)
Dudley, J.: ref, 2497 (64)
Dudley, P.: test, 1477
Dudley, R. E. J.: ref, 1758 (85,86)
Due-Madsen, J.: ref, 2497 (252)
Duen-mun Lai, F.: ref, 793 (23)
Duer, J.: ref, 2862 (79)
Duffy, A.: ref, 2305 (212)
Duffy, F. F.: ref, 375 (3), 2862 (506)
Duffy, F. H.: ref, 1903 (49), 2485 (24), 2862 (99)
Duffy, J.: ref, 1218 (16), 2599 (35), 2863 (317)
Duffy, J. C.: ref, 2305 (26)
Duffy, J. F.: ref, 1697 (71)
Duffy, J. R.: ref, 2008 (2)
Duffy, L.: ref, 2159 (4), 2858 (64)
Duffy, R. J.: ref, 430 (12), 798 (18), 1060 (5), 1240 (35), 1379 (52,88), 1903 (378), 2008 (2,12,13), 2694 (15), 2873 (52), 2911 (2)
Dufour, M.: ref, 337 (143), 2402 (58)
Dufresne, J.: ref, 681 (21), 1903 (151), 2860 (424)
Dugan, E. P.: ref, 1485 (28)
Dugas, M. J.: ref, 2065 (16)
Dugbartey, A. T.: ref, 2603 (577)
Dugbartey, M. T.: ref, 2603 (577)
Duggan, C.: ref, 272 (110), 998 (90), 2305 (129)
Duggan, C. F.: ref, 998 (29), 2050 (13)
Duggins, L. A.: rev, 1092
Dugoni, B.: ref, 998 (72)
Duilt, R. A.: ref, 846 (5)
Duiven-voorden, H.: ref, 1166 (53), 2603 (265)
Dukarm, C. P.: ref, 893 (37)
Dukart, A.: ref, 1767 (9), 2860 (1387)
Duke, L. M.: test, 329
Duke, M. P.: ref, 665 (41,66)
Duker, P. C.: ref, 1903 (205)
Dukerich, J. M.: ref, 771 (6)
Dukewich, T. L.: ref, 448 (22), 2860 (1071)
Dukoff, R.: ref, 2860 (1258), 2863 (379)
Dukowitz, L.: ref, 1727 (1), 1987 (20)
Dulaney, C. L.: ref, 1903 (250)
Dulay, H. C.: test, 307
Dulit, R.: ref, 846 (14), 2603 (449)
Dulit, R. A.: ref, 824 (4), 1093 (62)
Dumas, J. E.: test, 2446; ref, 451 (112), 997 (21,26)
Dumenci, L.: ref, 1000 (109), 2218 (27)
Dumka, L.: ref, 472 (63)
Dumka, L. E.: ref, 451 (186), 863 (64), 1661 (41)
Dumont, F.: ref, 853 (19)
Dumont, R.: ref, 837 (10), 2862 (462)
Dunahoo, C. L.: ref, 2497 (349)
Dunbar, N.: ref, 2497 (340), 2863 (186)
Dunbar, S. B.: test, 1318; rev, 571, 2221; ref, 592 (75), 1086 (1)
Duncan, E.: ref, 2860 (1205), 2892 (261)
Duncan, G. J.: ref, 1079 (24,27,58), 1181 (13,14), 1216 (45,50,79), 2485 (192), 2864 (48)
Duncan, J.: ref, 1140 (59), 1671 (4), 1767 (3)
Duncan, J.: ref, 2860 (846)
Duncan, K.: ref, 2076 (109)
Duncan, M.: ref, 2485 (122)
Duncan, M. H.: ref, 2862 (626), 2880 (6)
Duncan, N.: ref, 68 (54)
Duncan, R. C.: ref, 2497 (179)
Duncan, R. D.: ref, 1697 (403), 2862 (327), 2879 (111)
Duncan, R. M.: ref, 2862 (605)
Duncan, S.: ref, 1903 (284)
Duncan, S. C.: ref, 451 (166,250), 1010 (60,117)
Duncan, S. E.: test, 84, 1420, 1421, 2029
Duncan, S. F.: ref, 863 (40)
Duncan, T. E.: ref, 451 (250), 1010 (60)
Duncombe, M. E.: ref, 1758 (23), 2860 (608)
Dundas, I.: ref, 1000 (43)
Dundas, R.: ref, 2497 (642)
Dungee-Anderson, D.: ref, 298 (105),1036 (10)
Dunham, R. B.: ref, 1701 (5)
Dunkel, H. B.: rev, 579, 600, 603
Dunkel-Schetter, C.: ref, 791 (7,9,14), 2076 (40), 2497 (62,184), 2858 (35)
Dunkley, D. M.: ref, 790 (20)
Dunlap, D.: test, 2291,2292
Dunlap, G.: ref, 2485 (199), 2813 (117), 2862 (328,471)
Dunlap, J. W.: rev, 1657
Dunlap, K.: rev, 862
Dunlap, W. P.: ref, 827 (3), 1010 (84), 2211 (42), 2862 (377)
Dunlop, R.: ref, 1779 (3), 1832 (9)
Dunn, A.: ref, 2373 (1)
Dunn, C.: test, 2309; ref, 4 (19), 2309 (1), 2485 (165), 2813 (110), 2860 (852)
Dunn, D. S.: ref, 615 (25)
Dunn, E.: ref, 2768 (38), 2860 (1187),2863 (358)
Dunn, G.: ref, 739 (8), 1758 (24), 2050 (71,135), 2234 (2), 2288 (59), 2289 (45), 2860 (624)
Dunn, G. E.: ref, 2860 (968)
Dunn, J. A.: rev, 1097
Dunn, J. T.: ref, 1697 (404)
Dunn, K.: test, 1470, 2069
Dunn, L. M.: test, 350, 952,1903
Dunn, M.: ref, 994 (36), 1902 (64), 1903 (458), 1965 (61), 1982 (13), 2382 (37), 2485 (159,197,218), 2680 (14,18), 2813 (114),131)
Dunn, M. A.: ref, 1096 (9), 2668 (1), 2694 (14), 2860 (912)
Dunn, M. B.: ref, 1755 (8), 2545 (1)
Dunn, N. J.: ref, 1181 (20), 2305 (85), 2414 (4)
Dunn, R.: test, 1470, 1472, 2069; ref, 1470 (4,5), 2069 (1,2), 2181 (1), 2497 (364)
Dunn, S. E.: ref, 1716 (2)
Dunn, S. M.: ref, 1079 (86), 2076 (169)
Dunne, E. J.: ref, 2288 (52)
Dunne, F.: ref, 2305 (15)
Dunne, M.: ref, 999 (36), 1079 (13)
Dunne, M. P.: ref, 999 (172)

Dunner, D. L.: ref, 272 (142), 1166 (13), 1687 (18), 2497 (244,527)
Dunnette, M. D.: rev, 973, 1077, 1081,1634, 1635, 1833, 1926, 2266, 2501, 2899
Dunson, R. M.: ref, 681 (43)
Dunst, C. J.: rev, 3, 270, 1224, 1261, 1905
Dunstan, L. V.: ref, 1991 (67)
Dunton, S.: ref, 430 (2), 1060 (1), 1903 (11), 2657 (1), 2694 (2), 2768 (2)
DuPaul, G. J.: test, 67; ref, 681 (12,27,97), 1592 (20), 2485 (45),2603 (130)
DuPont, R. L.: ref, 1166 (17), 2603 (24)
Dupont, R. M.: ref, 2305 (32,130)
DuPre, R. L.: ref, 2305 (225)
Dupuis, M. M.: rev, 1588
Dupuy, P. J.: rev, 2361, 2924
Dura, J.: ref, 2813 (139)
Dura, J. R.: ref, 2076 (55)
Duran, G.: ref, 2497 (632)
Duran, R.: ref, 788 (2), 1010 (53)
Duran, R. P.: ref, 2862 (66)
Duran, R. R.: rev, 643
Durand, E. J.: ref, 2858 (87)
Durand, H.: ref, 694 (104), 2879 (135)
Durand, V. M.: test, 1722; ref, 863 (43)
Durant, C.: ref, 2835 (8), 2915 (2)
Durazo, O.: ref, 2862 (550)
Durden, W. G.: ref, 615 (41)
Durel, L. A.: ref, 1697 (27),2497 (30)
Durgunoglu, A. Y.: ref, 2029 (1)
Durham, C. C.: ref, 1348 (15)
Durham, R. C.: ref, 271 (10), 272 (268), 337 (171), 2497 (330,619)
Durham, T. W.: ref, 272 (384), 1697 (534), 1903 (243)
Durking, M. W.: ref, 641 (5), 2076 (118), 2227 (20), 2517 (4), 2599 (30)
Durlak, C. M.: ref, 1991 (68), 2860 (609), 2862 (247), 2879 (76), 2901 (40)
Durodoye, B. A.: ref, 1582 (12)
Durost, W. N.: rev, 2741
Durrant, J. D.: ref, 998 (53),2497 (562)
Durrant, J. E.: ref, 2862 (100), 2879 (23)
Durrell, D. D.: test, 861
Durrheim, K.: ref, 1754 (20)
Durso, F. T.: ref, 1140 (14), 1697 (126)
Durvasula, R. S.: ref, 272 (181), 376 (5), 1166 (113), 2863 (324)
Durwen, H. F.: ref, 2227 (15), 2239 (14), 2860 (492), 2863 (138,172), 2892 (78,107)
Dusek, T.: ref, 2860 (525), 2892 (88)
Dusewicz, R. A.: test, 843
Dush, D. M.: rev, 1214; ref, 1697 (335)
Dushay, R.: ref, 2288 (52)
Dustman, R. E.: ref, 303 (4), 1164 (34), 2076 (41), 2516 (17), 2860 (345)
Dustman, T. J.: ref, 303 (4), 1164 (34), 2076 (41), 2516 (17), 2860 (345)
Dutch, R. D.: rev, 348, 715, 1148
Duthie, B.: ref, 1697 (8,69), 1698 (1)
Duthie, L. A.: ref, 1661 (14)
Dutka, S.: ref, 665 (93)
duToit, L. B. H.: test, 1365
Dutra, R. L.: ref, 2860 (729)
Duunk, B. P.: ref, 1079 (56)
Duval, F.: ref, 1166 (105), 2305 (33)
Duvall, B.: ref, 2901 (29)
Duvall, J.: ref, 863 (36)
Duvdevani, I.: ref, 1010 (107)
Duvelleroy-Hommet, C.: ref, 2862 (329)
Duyckaerts, C.: ref, 2517 (1), 2860 (527)
Duyme, M.: ref, 2862 (448)
Duyvesteyn, M. G. C.: ref, 1216 (75)
Dvara, R.: ref, 1058 (4), 2860 (451), 2863 (125)
Dvir, T.: ref, 2497 (455)
Dvorak, A.: rev, 1196
Dvorine, I.: test, 862
Dweck, C. S.: ref, 1115 (16)
Dwinell, P. L.: rev, 1142
Dworkin, R. H.: ref, 650 (5,10,12), 2017 (5), 2288 (18), 2289 (17), 2305 (77,78), 2860 (452)
Dworkin, S. F.: ref, 2603 (44)
Dwyer, C. A.: rev, 2905
Dwyer, F. M.: ref, 1140 (39)
Dwyer, M.: ref, 793 (9), 1697 (178), 1744 (3)
Dwyer, T. J.: ref, 2018 (1), 2782 (2)
Dyce, J. A.: ref, 273 (19)
Dyck, J. L.: ref, 1405 (33)
Dyck, M. J.: ref, 272 (189), 999 (29), 2603 (90,270,473)
d'Ydewalle, G.: ref, 2239 (28), 2860 (1046)
Dye, D. A.: test, 2105
Dyer, C. O.: rev, 1797, 1866
Dyer, E. D.: ref, 372 (86), 1790 (7)
Dyer, H. S.: rev, 1222, 1657
Dyer, J.: ref, 1093 (25), 2892 (31)
Dyer, K.: ref, 1903 (76), 2432 (13), 2485 (35), 2813 (9)
Dyk, P. H.: ref, 1216 (16)
Dykeman, C.: ref, 2218 (28)
Dykeman, J. J.: ref, 2218 (28)
Dykens, E.: ref, 451 (113), 815 (36), 1380 (12), 2247 (13), 2813 (115,116), 2860 (251,1072), 2862 (463)
Dykens, E. M.: ref, 4 (6), 1378 (3), 1379 (13,17,66), 1380 (6), 2813 (60,87)
Dykes, M. K.: test, 804
Dykman, R.: ref, 451 (177), 1380 (17),2432 (33)
Dykman, R. A.: ref, 199 (11), 322 (6), 451 (47), 472 (85), 681 (28), 769 (2,4,5), 1130 (1), 1131 (10,11,17), 1164 (44), 1592 (13), 2862 (118,160,190, 231, 301,696), 2879 (31,42,54,70,97,222), 2905 (32,49,118)
Dykstra, R.: rev, 1659
Dykstra, T. A.: ref, 538 (5), 1962 (8)
Dymock, S.: ref, 358 (6)
Dyne, A. M.: ref, 2540 (3)
Dyrnes, S.: ref, 900 (5)

Dyson, L. L.: ref, 1010 (45,93), 1991 (90)
Dywan, C. A.: ref, 1902 (66), 1903 (340,346),2860 (815,847), 2863 (245)
Dywan, J.: ref, 2860 (610), 2892 (114)
Dzindolet, M. T.: ref, 998 (77)
Dziobek, J. F.: ref, 1093 (12)
D'Zurilla, T. J.: ref, 908 (10), 999 (117), 1619 (7), 1697 (399), 2065 (15)

Eagan, A. E.: ref, 695 (3), 2858 (96)
Eagger, S.: ref, 1390 (2), 1758 (10), 2860 (215)
Eagle, M.: ref, 1706 (2)
Eagle, M. N.: ref, 1697 (192), 1706 (1), 2247 (29)
Eagle, N.: rev, 1840
Eagles, J. M.: ref, 459 (39)
Eaker, D.: ref, 298 (113)
Ealy, M.: test, 2645
Earl, W. L.: ref, 337 (37)
Earle-Boyer, E. A.: ref, 2288 (5), 2289 (3), 2305 (8)
Earles, J. A.: ref, 180 (24)
Earleywine, M.: ref, 372 (35), 1697 (89,166,277), 2010 (15), 2863 (247)
Earls, F.: ref, 1164 (102), 2516 (68)f, 2907 (9)
Early, J.: ref, 298 (92), 1697 (238)
Earn, B. M.: ref, 1000 (76)
Eash, M. J.: test, 1867; rev, 495
Easley, H. P.: rev, 1196
Easley, M. J.: ref, 2603 (91), 2858 (25)
Eason, A.: ref, 472 (232)
Eason, S.: ref, 2497 (595)
East, K.: test, 2872
Easterbrooks, M. A.: ref, 1903 (168)
Eastin, D.: test, 2471
Eastman, L.: ref, 372 (110)
Eastman, N.: ref, 2076 (61)
Easton, C.: ref, 1166 (34)
Easton, D. L.: ref, 214 (16), 1485 (27), 1903 (256), 2657 (15)
Eaton, E. M.: ref, 337 (82), 1164 (69), 1758 (50), 2520 (45), 2599 (20), 2860 (676,951), 2863 (200)
Eaton, H. M.: ref, 2076 (38)
Eaton, W. W.: ref, 2050 (112), 2288 (24), 2305 (74)
Eaves, D.: test, 2476
Eaves, D. M.: ref, 1485 (26), 1903 (251), 2485 (125), 2864 (49)
Eaves, J.: ref, 2433 (1)
Eaves, L. C.: ref, 1485 (26), 1903 (251), 2485 (125), 2864 (49)
Eaves, L. J.: ref, 999 (58, 160), 2603 (273)
Eaves, R. C.: test, 2431, 1392 (11), 2905 (53)
Ebbit, B.: ref, 2860 (379)
Ebel, R. L.: rev, 1638, 2484, 2686
Eber, B.: ref, 2860 (525), 2892 (88)
Eberenz, K. P.: ref, 893 (19), 2603 (356)
Eberhardt, B. J.: rev, 200, 1350, 2415
Eberhardt, D.: rev, 2822
Eberhart-Wright, A.: ref, 451 (130)
Eberlin, M.: ref, 459 (18), 2485 (82), 2813 (35)
Eberly, R. E.: ref, 1697 (127,140,479)
Ebert, L.: ref, 2603 (155,209)
Ebmeier, H.: ref, 615 (2), 1657 (6)
Ebmeier, K. P.: ref, 696 (2), 999 (185), 1166 (65), 1740 (24), 2240 (2), 2516 (108)
Ebmeier, K. P.: ref, 2860 (328,385,699,1335), 2863 (145,207)
Ebner, A.: ref, 2863 (390)
Ebner, D.: ref, 372 (68), 2247 (64)
Ebner, D. L.: ref, 2247 (70)
Eby, J. W.: test, 895
Echols, L. D.: ref, 1902 (85), 1903 (459)
Eck, T.: rev, 1308
Eckardt, M. J.: ref, 1661 (55), 2305 (27,176), 2497 (626)
Eckblad, G. F.: ref, 1000 (44,59)
Eckert, E.: ref, 272 (229), 1697 (520)
Eckert, E. D.: ref, 893 (5), 2497 (313)
Eckert, T. L.: ref, 301 (44), 1592 (20), 1902 (59,70), 2862 (330)
Eckhardt, C. I.: ref, 2497 (638)
Eckhardt, M. J.: ref, 1164 (90), 1592 (21), 2225 (7), 2497 (456), 2860 (848), 2863 (246), 2892 (175)
Ecki, C. L.: ref, 1010 (122), 1013 (2), 2076 (168)
Eckl, L.: ref, 2498 (62)
Eckman, J. R.: ref, 246 (4), 301 (28), 374 (1), 853 (8), 1379 (24), 1524 (1), 1903 (158), 2862 (192), 2879 (55)
Eckstein Bros., Inc.: test, 896
Eddy, J. M.: ref, 863 (13)
Edeburn, C.: test, 1436
Edelberg, R.: ref, 2497 (93)
Edelbrock, C.: ref, 681 (4), 1903 (65), 2606 (4)
Edelbrock, C. S.: ref, 1740 (5)
Edell, W. S.: ref, 1093 (46), 2860 (1039), 2862 (438)
Edelman, N.: test, 788
Edelman, S.: ref, 2862 (464)
Edelsohn, G.: ref, 364 (19), 472 (48), 472 (172), 2214 (49,66,102,103)
Edelsohn, G. A.: ref, 451 (3)
Edelstein, B. A.: ref, 1697 (250), 2050 (52)
Eden, D.: ref, 1590 (65), 2497 (380,455)
Eden, G. F.: ref, 1503 (11), 2862 (331,332,465), 2901 (58,59,87)
Edens, J. F.: ref, 2018 (1), 2782 (2)
Edfeldt, A. W.: test, 2209
Ediger, E.: ref, 272 (358)
Ediger, J. M.: ref, 2603 (128,157)
Edinger, J. D.: ref, 1697 (278), 2860 (145,1031), 2862 (93), 2863 (306)
Edison, M.: ref, 621 (1,2)
Edland, S. D.: ref, 776 (27,58)
Edmonds, S.: ref, 2126 (8)
Edmondson, J. A.: ref, 2873 (53)
Edmonson, B.: test, 2454
Edson, A.: test, 1269

Education Associates: test, 190,978
Educational & Industrial Test Services Ltd.: test, 1031, 1270, 1578, 1911, 1943
The Educational Institute of Scotland: test, 901
Educational Records Bureau: test, 664, 967
Educational Records Bureau, Inc.: test, 1249
Educational Technologies, Inc.: test, 168
Educational Testing Service: test, 91, 92, 93, 94, 95, 96, 97, 98, 99, 100, 101, 102, 103, 104, 105, 106, 107, 108, 109, 110, 111, 112, 113, 114, 115, 116, 117, 118, 192, 497, 498, 400, 500, 501, 502, 503, 504, 505, 506, 507, 508, 509, 510, 511, 512, 513, 514, 515, 516, 517, 518, 519, 520, 521, 522, 523, 524, 525, 526, 527, 528, 529, 530, 531, 572, 573, 574, 575, 576, 577, 578, 579, 580, 581, 582, 583, 584, 585, 586, 587, 588, 589, 590, 591, 592, 593, 594, 595, 596, 597, 598, 599, 600, 601, 602, 603, 604, 605, 606, 607, 608, 609, 610, 611, 612, 613, 614, 615, 617, 666, 918, 972, 1108, 1109, 1110, 1111, 1112, 1113, 1114, 1115, 1116, 1117, 1118, 1119, 1120, 1121, 1122, 1123, 1125, 1274, 1538, 1746, 2026, 2031, 2032, 2083, 2317, 2339, 2531, 2687
Edwards, A.: ref, 1653 (25), 2189 (6), 2864 (106)
Edwards, A. J.: rev, 455, 898, 1877, 2668
Edwards, A. L.: test, 908; rev, 373, 913
Edwards, C.D.: test, 2498
Edwards, C. N.: test, 2416
Edwards, D. L.: ref, 2218 (52)
Edwards, D. R. L.: ref, 1166 (71)
Edwards, D. W.: ref, 1697 (437)
Edwards, J.: ref, 272 (33), 540 (6,8), 1131 (16), 1240 (34,47), 1380 (7,13,15), 1687 (12,15), 1697 (96), 1804 (12,14), 1903 (169,377,460,472), 2695 (40,49,54)
Edwards, J.: ref, 2704 (29,37,40), 2725 (3,7)
Edwards, J. E.: ref, 180 (10)
Edwards, J. M.: test, 950
Edwards, J. R.: ref, 739 (3), 1338 (14), 1694 (9), 2858 (14)
Edwards, K.: ref, 1727 (2), 2862 (659)
Edwards, K. J.: ref, 2247 (44)
Edwards, M. C.: ref, 472 (13), 2498 (7)
Edwards, M. L.: ref, 214 (7,26), 1095 (21), 1394 (1), 1804 (6)
Edwards, R.: test, 143; rev, 562, 2482, 2689; ref, 272 (351)
Edwards, R. H. T.: ref, 2050 (104)
Edwards, R. L.: ref, 788 (1)
Edwards, R. W.: ref, 143 (1)
Edwards, S.: test, 2228
Edwards, T. L.: ref, 1903 (180), 2905 (39)
Eells, G. T.: ref, 2247 (55), 2497 (331)
Eells, T. D.: ref, 2603 (249)
Efran, J. S.: ref, 2497 (420)
Efron, C.: test, 1987
Egan, D. F.: test, 911
Egan, I.: ref, 838 (18)
Egan, M.: ref, 1010 (25)
Egan, V.: ref, 999 (80), 2163 (158)
Egan, V. G.: ref, 2860 (453), 2863 (126)
Egasso, H.: ref, 1164 (115), 1485 (48), 2163 (255), 2225 (10)
Egeland, B.: rev, 2892; ref, 373 (7), 373 (10), 451 (203,292), 846 (15), 1216 (7,56,113), 1321 (8), 1697 (506), 1902 (17,41,91,95,101), 2039 (1), 2076 (95), 2614 (2), 2749 (44), 2860 (169,1286), 2862 (88,564,630), 2864 (61,65,124), 2901 (102,120,138)
Egeland, B. R.: rev, 258, 624
Egelko, S.: ref, 1745 (13)
Egensperger, R.: ref, 1525 (23), 2860 (1115)
Eger, D. L.: test, 2055
Eggebeen, D. J.: ref, 1612 (19)
Egler, L.: ref, 451 (124)
Eglinton, E.: ref, 349 (29), 2163 (258)
Egolf, B. P.: ref, 1612 (72)
Ehde, D.: ref, 1661 (67)
Ehle, H. T.: ref, 2163 (323), 2227 (36), 2860 (352,1266), 2863 (93)
Ehler, J. G.: ref, 272 (265), 1166 (180)
Ehlers, A.: ref, 2497 (457,458,481)
Ehlers, S.: ref, 234 (1), 459 (19), 1903 (170), 2228 (7), 2768 (14)
Ehly, S. W.: ref, 2862 (258)
Ehrenberg, B. L.: ref, 2860 (658), 2863 (193)
Ehrenreich, J. H.: ref, 2749 (12), 2860 (170)
Ehrensing, R. H.: ref, 1166 (47)
Ehrhardt, A.: ref, 2125 (7,18), 2516 (16), 2860 (310), 2863 (292)
Ehrhardt, A. A.: ref, 337 (34), 1093 (1), 2163 (124), 2516 (28), 2603 (15), 2860 (496)
Ehrhardt, J. C.: ref, 650 (16)
Ehri, L. C.: rev, 1428; ref, 1903 (302)
Ehrlich, J.: rev, 2251; ref, 790 (26), 2076 (173)
Ehrlich, J. S.: ref, 2873 (63)
Ehrlich, R. M.: ref, 1097 (7), 1134 (1), 1612 (27) 2193 (11), 2228 (6), 2860 (342,394), 2864 (31), 2870 (3), 2879 (67)
Ehrlichman, H.: ref, 2437 (2)
Ehrmann, L.: ref, 1697 (358)
Ehrmann, L. C.: ref, 1697 (245)
Eichenberger, S.: ref, 451 (23)
Eichinger, J.: ref, 298 (46), 433 (2), 1590 (11), 1759 (3), 2432 (9), 2485 (25), 2813 (6)
Eichman, W. J.: rev, 1925, 2076
Eichorn, D. H.: rev, 1381, 2864
Eickelberg, W.: ref, 2862 (78)
Eidevall-Wallin, L.: ref, 2862 (617)
Eidson, T. A.: ref, 2369 (12)
Eigen, H.: ref, 863 (30), 2603 (154)
Eilers, R. E.: ref, 891 (1)
Eimer, B. N.: test, 1870
Einarsson-Backes, L. M.: ref, 265 (3), 1901 (8)

Einat, G.: ref, 472 (91), 681 (52), 863 (53), 1010 (63), 2498 (37), 2862 (272)
Einfeld, S. L.: ref, 270 (15), 1134 (7), 1903 (461), 2485 (198), 2862 (466), 2864 (114)
Einhorn, A.: ref, 1166 (85)
Einstein, D.: ref, 2218 (125)
Eisdorfer, C.: ref, 1058 (3), 2076 (8), 2860 (277), 2863 (72)
Eisdorfer, C. E.: ref, 1058 (4), 2860 (451), 2863 (125)
Eisele, J. A.: ref, 994 (11), 1804 (7), 1903 (222), 2225 (6), 2860 (559,611), 2862 (232,248), 2864 (44,50)
Eisemann, M.: ref, 999 (5)
Eisen, A. R.: ref, 1991 (24), 2497 (60,111)
Eisen, J. L.: ref, 2519 (1), 2520 (1)
Eisenberg, J. M.: test, 828
Eisenberg, L.: ref, 451 (251), 1010 (133), 1991 (106), 1903 (354)
Eisenberg, M.: ref, 1264 (6), 1889 (11), 1987 (22)
Eisenberg, N.: ref, 365 (9), 1001 (5)
Eisenmajer, R.: ref, 2599 (29), 2862 (358), 2879 (123)
Eisenson, J.: test, 987
Eisenstadt, T. H.: ref, 864 (3), 997 (12), 1987 (7), 2752 (1)
Eisenstein, N.: ref, 1380 (18), 2860 (1259)
Eiser, C.: ref, 449 (4)
Eiser, J. R.: ref, 449 (4)
Eiserman, W. D.: ref, 265 (4,13), 1000 (24)
Eiserman, W. D.: ref, 1096 (8), 2524 (2,7), 2657 (4,22)
Eisner, H.: test, 1368
Eison, A. R.: ref, 472 (127), 1991 (79), 2214 (68)
Eissner, D.: ref, 1166 (27)
Eitel, S. K.: ref, 1010 (59)
Ekdahl, M. M.: ref, 2813 (75)
Eke, M.: ref, 2076 (155)
Ekelman, B. L.: ref, 1612 (5), 2860 (59), 2862 (30), 2864 (4), 2901 (2)
Ekerdt, D. J.: ref, 2603 (2)
Ekern, M. D.: ref, 2497 (313)
Eklund, K.: ref, 1164 (60), 1697 (275), 2305 (98)
Ekman, P.: test, 1001; ref, 1001 (4,15)
Ekstrom, R. B.: test, 1405
Ekwall, E. E.: test, 917
el Saor, W.: ref, 2603 (279)
El-Awar, M.: ref, 1218 (6), 1903 (275), 2163 (168), 2863 (196), 2892 (123)
El-Guebaly, N.: ref, 62 (20), 134 (28), 337 (143), 402 (58)
El-Korasky, A.: ref, 1866 (36)
El-Zahhar, N. E.: ref, 2656 (3)
Elaad, I.: ref, 404 (27)
Elardo, R.: rev, 875
Elashoff, R.: ref, 2076 (13, 56)
Elazar, B.: test, 1513
Elbaum, B. E.: ref, 1991 (108), 2484 (9), 2862 (570), 2901 (103)
Elbert, M.: ref, 214 (8), 1095 (40), 1852 (6), 1903 (480), 2680 (17)
Elbro, C.: ref, 1903 (570), 2163 (351), 2862 (709)
Elcholtz, G. E.: ref, 202 (1), 324 (3), 331 (1), 798 (6), 994 (3), 1424 (1), 1903 (97), 2190 (2), 2524 (1), 2660 (3), 2695 (10), 2710 (2), 2768 (7)
Elder, G. H.: ref, 2603 (566)
Elder, G. H., Jr.: ref, 373 (4,5), 451 (121), 2218 (15,59), 2485 (223), 2603 (136,244,256,355,457)
Eldredge, J. L. : ref, 592 (67)
Eldredge, K.: ref, 2603 (329)
Eldredge, K. L.: ref, 893 (15)
Eldredge, L.: ref, 1072 (23)
Eldredge, N.: ref, 2813 (55)
Eldridge, J. L.: ref, 1318 (7)
Eldridge, N. S.: ref, 1927 (1)
Eley, T. C.: ref, 451 (252), 472 (221)
Elfenbein, J. L.: ref, 624 (5), 1040 (8), 1379 (26), 2163 (110), 2651 (10), 2862 (249)
Elger, C. E.: ref, 2226 (29), 2860 (1093,1274,1392)
Elia, J.: ref, 681 (29)
Elias, G.: test, 1005
Elias, J. W.: ref, 2497 (360)
Elias, M.: ref, 495 (16), 1181 (27), 1991 (105)
Elias, M. F.: ref, 1164 (2,16,45,120), 2497 (61), 2860 (454,506), 2899 (1)
Elias, P. K.: ref, 1164 (2,120), 2899 (1)
Eliason, M. J.: ref, 265 (8)
Eliot, J.: test, 925; ref, 301 (43), 2373 (1), 2935 (2)
Elison, B.: rev, 1895, 1946
Elizur, A.: ref, 681 (96), 2305 (247)
Elizur, Y.: ref, 2603 (69)
Elkin, I.: ref, 272 (111,194), 1517 (4)
Elkins, D. E.: ref, 1698 (26)
Elkins, J.: rev, 358, 2092, 2094; ref, 1240 (40), 1765 (16), 2092 (4)
Ell, P. J.: ref, 1093 (50), 1390 (3), 2050 (65), 2863 (169), 2892 (277)
Ellard, J. H.: ref, 2603 (101)
Ellason, J. W.: ref, 2017 (13)
Ellen, A. S.: rev, 1230, 1780
Ellenbogen, M. A.: ref, 2076 (74), 2497 (306), 2603 (240)
Ellenwood, A. E.: ref, 1240 (36), 1386 (19), 1903 (385), 2905 (81)
Ellerman, D. A.: ref, 2246 (3)
Ellersten, B.: ref, 1164 (47), 1407 (2), 2860 (463), 2863 (130)
Elley, W. B.: test, 2093, 2094, 2095
Elling, K. A.: ref, 272 (121)
Ellingson, J. E.: ref, 372 (118)
Ellington, L.: ref, 2497 (136)
Elliot, A. J.: ref, 1965 (50)
Elliot, D. J.: ref, 472 (4), 1903 (50), 1991 (8)
Elliot, G.: test, 13, 213, 333, 1886
Elliot, L. L.: ref, 1903 (171), 2651 (11), 2768 (15), 2862 (201)
Elliot, R.: ref, 1758 (37), 2860 (849)
Elliot, S. N.: rev, 2
Elliot, T. R.: ref, 337 (98), 998 (67), 2065 (11,17)
Elliott, C.: test, 349

Elliott, C. A.: ref, 142 (6), 1619 (8), 2862 (420)
Elliott, C. D.: test, 837
Elliott, C. E.: ref, 997 (23), 1079 (50)
Elliott, D.: ref, 1903 (51), 2163 (44), 2432 (10)
Elliott, J. L.: rev, 2020, 2546
Elliott, M. R.: ref, 200 (2)
Elliott, R.: ref, 72 (3), 1079 (51,90), 1758 (52), 2358 (11)
Elliott, R. O., Jr.: ref, 1903 (77)
Elliott, S. N.: test, 2452, 2535; rev, 266, 451, 463, 769, 1098, 2483, 2484, 2452 (13,21)
Elliott, T.: ref, 372 (17)
Elliott, T. R.: ref, 998 (68), 1014 (7), 1745 (4,5), 2065 (12,25)
Ellis, A.: rev, 317, 426, 1005, 1160, 2618; ref, 349 (13)
Ellis, A. L.: ref, 1337 (1)
Ellis, A. W.: ref, 349 (11), 1758 (102) 1765 (17), 2163 (163), 2478 (2), 2860 (1394)
Ellis, B. B.: ref, 395 (1)
Ellis, C. G.: test, 1961
Ellis, E.: ref, 2076 (136)
Ellis, E. S.: ref, 355 (1), 2879 (28), 2901 (13)
Ellis, J. B.: ref, 298 (109), 2076 (42)
Ellis, L.: ref, 324 (7)
Ellis, M. C.: ref, 1140 (48)
Ellis, M. V.: ref, 200 (3), 1965 (6)
Ellis, N. R.: ref, 1903 (250)
Ellis, R. J.: ref, 1437 (1)
Ellis, T. E.: ref, 272 (168), 273 (20), 1687 (21), 2065 (26), 2402 (56), 2559 (12)
Ellis-MacLeod, E.: ref, 451 (120)
Ellison, C. W.: test, 2474
Ellison, D.: ref, 1104 (4), 2193 (23), 2239 (21), 2860 (659), 2863 (194)
Ellison, P. H.: test, 1258
Elloy, D. F.: ref, 1590 (45)
Ells, J. G.: ref, 1903 (289)
Ellsworth, R. B.: test, 449, 1925, 2074
Ellsworth, S. L.: test, 449, 1925
Ellwood, M. S.: ref, 2603 (92)
Elm, D. R.: ref, 771 (6)
Elmacian, S.: ref, 2497 (379)
Elmer, E.: ref, 2076 (48)
Elmore, P. B.: test, 287, 440, 1440
Elmslie, H.: test, 295
Elofson, T. H.: rev, 1977, 2055
Elphick, R.: ref, 2163 (268)
Elsenga, S.: ref, 2603 (45)
Elsenrathe, D.: test, 1499
Elser, D.: ref, 1612 (36), 2864 (39)
Elsworth-Cox, L.: ref, 2497 (551)
Elton, M.: ref, 298 (57)
Elwan, F. Z.: ref, 1379 (84,94), 2860 (850), 2862 (467,606)
Ely, C. M.: ref, 999 (1)
Emanuele, S.: ref, 1745 (80)
Embretson, S. E.: ref, 180 (29), 592 (83), 1405 (34)
Embretson (Whitely), S.: rev, 349, 565
Emde, R.: ref, 2039 (22), 2382 (6), 270 (48), 337 (180), 451 (217), 994 (48), 2485 (244)
Emerson, E.: ref, 1722 (2)
Emerson, E. N.: ref, 472 (164), 2214 (96), 2231 (6), 2498 (61)
Emery, C. F.: ref, 303 (1,2), 791 (2), 1164 (23), 1740 (3), 2497 (21,104), 2516 (2), 2603 (8,83), 2860 (81,237)
Emery, O. B.: ref, 1166 (7), 2305 (16), 2873 (4)
Emmelkamp, E. M. G.: ref, 2603 (45)
Emmelkamp, P. M.: ref, 2497 (336)
Emmelkamp, P. M. G.: ref, 1079 (64), 2497 (549), 2603 (182), 2603 (250)
Emmen, H. H.: ref, 2599 (22)
Emmerson, R. Y.: ref, 303 (4), 1164 (34), 2076 (41), 2516 (17), 2860 (345)
Emmett, W. G.: rev, 1414
Emmons, C.: ref, 2603 (73)
Emmons, R. A.: ref, 337 (23), 999 (30), 1965 (23)
Emmons, R. D.: ref, 694 (70)
Emoe, R. N.: ref, 2382 (16)
Emory, L. E.: ref, 1697 (537)
Emslie, G.: ref, 472 (65), 1991 (61)
Emslie, G. J.: test, 2865; ref, 473 (5), 2305 (192)
Emslie, H.: ref, 1671 (4), 1767 (3), 2860 (846)
Enderby, P. M.: test, 1056
Endicott, J.: test, 748, 949, 1093, 2108, 2109, 2130, 2305; ref, 1093 (10,107,108), 1517 (1,3,6), 1697 (376,617), 2288 (3), 2305 (18,97,119,125, 160,161,172,179,200,220,236)
Endicott, N. A.: ref, 1697 (28)
Endler, N. S.: test, 696, 700, 950; rev, 181, 2498; ref, 272 (25), 950 (1,4), 950 (4), 1079 (66), 1590 (59), 2218 (55)
Endresen, I. M.: ref, 2497 (271)
Endriga, M. C.: ref, 270 (30), 681 (11), 1903 (80), 2603 (99)
Endrign, M. C.: ref, 270 (40), 863 (90), 1010 (129)
Engdahl, B. E.: ref, 1697 (127,140,479)
Engebretson, K. M.: ref, 1991 (33)
Engel, J. M.: ref, 270 (33), 1901 (19), 2715 (1)
Engel, K. L.: test, 2763
Engel, M.: ref, 815 (2), 2862 (56)
Engel, N. A.: ref, 2214 (42), 2497 (332), 2498 (35)
Engelhard, G., Jr.: rev, 372, 744, 961, 1966, 2106, 2487
Engelhart, C. I.: ref, 1380 (18), 2860 (1259)
Engelhart, M. D.: rev, 56, 574, 596, 1111
Engelmann, H. O.: test, 981
Engels, D.: ref, 935 (1), 2924 (1)
Engels, M.: ref, 1697 (279)
Engels, M-L.: ref, 2603 (251)
Engen, E.: test, 2233
Engen, T.: test, 2233
Enger, J. M.: rev, 149, 825, 884, 2587; ref, 694 (71)
Engineer, P.: ref, 2300 (1), 2768 (5)
England, G.: ref, 2862 (731)

England, G. W.: test, 1701
Englander, M. E.: test, 1250
Engle, A.: ref, 1745 (73)
Engle, P. L.: ref, 2497 (62)
Engle-Friedman, M.: ref, 793 (7)
Engler, L. B.: ref, 2603 (367)
Englesson, I. L.: ref, 853 (5)
Englesson, J. L.: ref, 2247 (74)
Engley, E.: ref, 2497 (116), 2656 (4)
English and Romanian Adoptees (ERA) Study Team (The): ref, 787 (4), 1612 (100)
English, C. D.: ref, 2860 (1210)
English, J.: ref, 624 (3), 1166 (165), 1903 (127)
English, K.: ref, 301 (50), 472 (144), 788 (3), 1612 (94), 1991 (86), 2657 (5), 2862 (390)
English, L. D.: ref, 2163 (251)
English Language Institute of the University of Michigan: test, 986
English Language Institute of the University of Michigan, Testing and Certification Division (The): test, 985
English Language Institute Testing and Certification Division (The): test, 1662
Engstrom, C. M.: ref, 2413 (1)
Engström, G.: ref, 273 (28), 999 (181)
Engstrom, I.: ref, 472 (25), 2163 (83), 2214 (15)
Ennis, R. H.: test, 704, 705, 959
Enns, M.: ref, 2305 (124)
Enns, M. W.: ref, 2497 (284)
Enns, R. A.: ref, 2860 (1386)
Eno, L.: ref, 1515 (1)
Enos, M. M.: test, 2313
Enright, A.: ref, 893 (2), 1010 (9), 2603 (20)
Enright, M.: ref, 1115 (26)
Enright, M. S.: ref, 401 (2), 404 (40,41), 1754 (27)
Enrile, B. G.: ref, 2862 (426)
Ensom, R.: ref, 337 (148), 863 (80), 1000 (99), 1903 (473), 1991 (92)
Entwisle, D. R.: ref, 364 (17)
Epkins, C. C.: ref, 472 (45,83,122,165,166), 2214 (28,43,64,97,98)
Epperson, D. L.: ref, 298 (50,154), 495 (13), 1290 (4), 1602 (1), 2497 (565)
Epperson, M. J.: ref, 1010 (8)
Epping-Jordan, J. E.: ref, 337 (70,73,104), 472 (77), 2214 (38)
Epstein, A. M.: ref, 301 (54)
Epstein, C. M.: ref, 2860 (1096), 2892 (228)
Epstein, D.: ref, 1338 (1)
Epstein, E. E.: ref, 134 (24,34), 863 (65), 1405 (8), 1661 (61), 2163 (48)
Epstein, J. A.: ref, 999 (118), 1965 (34), 2078 (1)
Epstein, J. H.: rev, 1991
Epstein, J. N.: ref, 681 (89,90), 875 (7,8), 1240 (20,31), 1903 (223,328), 2228 (10)
Epstein, L. H.: ref, 2498 (13)
Epstein, M. H.: test, 290, 2287
Epstein, N.: ref, 2603 (91), 2858 (25)
Epstein, R.: ref, 2860 (367), 2862 (167), 2862 (270)
Epstein, S.: test, 1735
Epstein, W. V.: ref, 2076 (51)
Epstein-Kaye, T.: ref, 1517 (6)
Epting, F. C.: ref, 1903 (137), 2862 (178)
Erb, L.: test, 2666; ref, 999 (127)
Erber, J. T.: ref, 2402 (26)
Erblich, J.: ref, 2863 (247)
Erchul, W. P.: rev, 36, 843, 2588
Ercoli, L.: ref, 2288 (69), 2289 (53), 2860 (1104)
Erdmann, A. J., Jr.: test, 708
Erdmann, J. B.: rev, 192, 1434, 2810
Erdos, G.: ref, 142 (7,8), 682 (4,6)
Erez, M.: ref, 298 (13)
Erford, B. T.: ref, 403 (1), 404 (45), 681 (85), 768 (2)
Ergis, A. M.: ref, 2163 (156), 2860 (605), 2863 (178)
Erhardt, D.: test, 678
Erhardt, J. C.: ref, 1093 (85)
Erhardt, R. P.: test, 968, 969
Erickan, K.: ref, 364 (22), 665 (88)
Erickson, D.: rev, 969, 1696, 2468, 2723; ref, 2050 (58), 2603 (238)
Erickson, D. B.: rev, 1530, 2732
Erickson, D. J.: ref, 1661 (76), 2860 (1370)
Erickson, G. C.: ref, 1903 (257)
Erickson, J. G.: test, 653
Erickson, L. W.: rev, 2786
Erickson, M. F.: ref, 1216 (7), 1902 (17), 2039 (1), 2860 (169)
Erickson, M. T.: ref, 2433 (1)
Erickson, R. C.: rev, 1792, 2066; ref, 2227 (1), 2402 (3), 2860 (91), 2892 (10)
Erickson, R. L.: test, 2028
Erickson, S.: ref, 699 (4)
Ericson, G. D.: ref, 413 (16), 2813 (36)
Erikson, J.: test, 1263
Eriksson, M.: ref, 301 (36), 1097 (12), 1410 (2)
Erin, J. N.: test, 804
Erkanli, A.: ref, 451 (107,108)
Erlenmeyer-Kimling, L.: ref, 1697 (280,405), 2305 (2,49,78,99,131,220), 2860 (452), 2862 (250)
Erlich, H. S.: ref, 2652 (3)
Ermani, M.: ref, 2860 (127)
Ernhart, C. B.: rev, 469, 800
Ernst, J.: ref, 326 (1)
Eron, L. D.: rev, 2247, 2749; ref, 451 (57)
Eronen, M.: ref, 1697 (406,480,481), 2247 (85,99,100), 2860 (851,1073,1074)
Errera, P.: ref, 2497 (401)
Errico, A. L.: ref, 272 (65), 2497 (243)
Ershler, J.: rev, 266
Ertle, S.: ref, 776 (33,54), 2516 (82), 2892 (249)
Ertmer, P. A.: ref, 1720 (1)
Ervin, K. S.: ref, 298 (64)
Erwin, E.: ref, 2749 (25)

Erwin, R. J.: ref, 199 (8), 2288 (75), 2289 (62), 2497 (173)
Eschbach, L.: ref, 2527 (3)
Escobar, J. I.: ref, 1093 (72), 2050 (3,95)
Escobar, M. D.: ref, 200 (2)
Escribá, P. V.:ref, 1166 (109)
Esdaile, S. A.: ref, 1878 (1), 1889 (6)
Eshel, Y.: ref, 2862 (281)
Eskay, R.: ref, 2305 (27)
Eskenazi, J.: ref, 694 (81)
Eskes, G. A.: ref, 2860 (171)
Eskin, M.: ref, 2559 (8)
Eslinger, P. J.: ref, 2860 (612), 2892 (73)
Esmaili, S.: ref, 1166 (206)
Esonis, S.: test, 1052
Espenschade, A.: rev, 353, 1502
Espey, L.: test, 1544
Espin, C.: ref, 1987 (1)
Espin, C. A.: ref, 1072 (52)
Espinosa, M.: ref, 270 (45), 1687 (35)
Espinosa, M. P.: ref, 2163 (175)
Esposito, D.: ref, 1135 (22), 1164 (169), 2226 (35), 2227 (50)
Esposito, S. A.: ref, 1000 (83)
Esquilin, S. C.: ref, 457 (1)
Essan, C. A.: ref, 2858 (114)
Esselman, P. C.: ref, 2603 (351)
Esser, G.: ref, 624 (19), 1240 (27)
Essex, M. J.: ref, 1889 (8), 2496 (4), 2497 (482,661), 2603 (483)
Essig, M.: ref, 1166 (202)
Esterling, B. A.: ref, 2076 (57)
Estes, R. E.: ref, 1164 (7)
Estroff, D. B.: ref, 270 (16), 272 (169), 1612 (48)
Estroff, S. D.: ref, 1291 (3)
Etezadi, J.: ref, 998 (95), 2163 (215)
Eth, S.: ref, 1093 (72), 2050 (95), 2288 (19)
Éthier, L. S., : ref, 458 (2)
Ethington, C. A.: test, 635
Etienne, M. A.: ref, 2497 (478)
Etnier, J. L.: ref, 2076 (127)
Etscheidt, M. A.: ref, 1697 (407)
Etzion, D.: ref, 1590 (65)
Euhardy, R.: test, 212
Eunson, K. M.: ref, 272 (6), 1166 (3)
Eustache, F.: ref, 2516 (64), 2863 (45), 2863 (248)
Evangelista, C.: ref, 1164 (58), 2892 (109)
Evans, A. S.: test, 2220, 2222
Evans, B. K.: ref, 1590 (22)
Evans, C.: ref, 272 (5), 1079 (1), 1166 (2), 2603 (400)
Evans, C. R.: ref, 2860 (786)
Evans, D. E.: ref, 1166 (196)
Evans, D. L.: ref, 2076 (94), 2076 (122)
Evans, D. M.: ref, 1181 (20), 2414 (4)
Evans, D. R.: test, 2132; ref, 2603 (526)
Evans, D. W.: ref, 2813 (60)
Evans, E. G.: ref, 472 (24,123), 495 (11), 2214 (14,65)
Evans, G.: ref, 694 (20), 2835 (10)
Evans, G. T.: ref, 495 (9), 2445 (1)
Evans, J.: test, 730
Evans, J. H.: ref, 2862 (333)
Evans, J. J.: test, 295
Evans, J. L.: ref, 540 (7,17), 1391 (1), 1903 (165,462,520), 2382 (7)
Evans, J. R.: rev, 2516
Evans, K. M.: ref, 999 (17), 1765 (8), 1991 (6)
Evans, L.: ref, 1021 (1,8), 2497 (82)
Evans, L. H.: ref, 1903 (195), 2694 (10), 2695 (18), 2704 (12)
Evans, M. D.: ref, 777 (1), 998 (41), 1093 (42), 1697 (167,173), 1991 (85)
Evans, N. J.: ref, 1755 (72)
Evans, P. D.: ref, 1338 (15)
Evans, R.: ref, 2199 (7)
Evans, R. G.: ref, 1731 (2), 2417 (10), 2860 (226), 2879 (30)
Evans, S.: ref, 1093 (112)
Evans, S. L.: ref, 270 (19)
Evans-Fernandez, S. E.: test, 2535
Evard, B. L.: rev, 2140
Evenden, J. L.: ref, 1758 (2,10)
Evenden, J. L.: ref, 2860 (90,215)
Evenhuis, H. M.: ref, 1485 (9), 1903 (113), 2860 (346)
Evens, J.: ref, 771 (22)
Everett, B. L.: ref, 472 (21), 1991 (29), 2214 (12)
Everett, J.: ref, 1166 (125,195), 2516 (3,11,103), 2863 (25), 2892 (33)
Everett, J. E.: ref, 1590 (45)
Everhart, K.: ref, 280 (2)
Everill, J.: ref, 846 (6)
Everingston, C.: ref, 2485 (165), 2860 (852)
Evers, A. W. M.: ref, 2497 (620)
Everson, M. D.: ref, 451 (3)
Everson, S. A.: ref, 2497 (459)
Everstine, L.: test, 983
Eviator, Z.: ref, 2860 (252), 2862 (127)
Ewell, K. K.: ref, 451 (80)
Ewert, M.: ref, 2603 (187,266)
Ewigman, B.: ref, 997 (18)
Ewing, A.: ref, 1128 (2)
Ewing, L. J. : ref, 863 (12), 1592 (18), 2485 (119)
Ewing-Cobbs, L.: ref, 1612 (99), 1903 (571), 2862 (710)
Exner, C. E.: ref, 353 (8), 772 (2), 1673 (6), 1901 (12)
Exner, J. E., Jr.: rev, 373; ref, 2247 (101)
Ey, S.: ref, 337 (134), 472 (163), 2214 (95)
Eyberg, S.: test, 2752; ref, 864 (3), 997 (12), 1987 (7), 2752 (1)
Eyberg, S. M.: test, 864, 997, 2595; ref, 265 (14), 2595 (2)
Eybert, S. M.: ref, 272 (376), 863 (93), 997 (30), 1889 (19), 1903 (580), 2752 (2), 2899 (13)

Eyde, L. D.: rev, 2302, 2408, 2700
Eyer, J. A.: ref, 1485 (60), 2864 (139)
Eysenbach, K.: ref, 1166 (202)
Eysenck, H. J.: test, 998, 999; rev, 372, 739, 1214, 1481, 1697, 2247, 2757, 372 (87), 999 (49), 999 (119), 1732 (1), 1822 (6)
Eysenck, S. B. G.: test, 998, 999, 1367; ref, 999 (10), 999 (119)
Ezhuthachan, S.: ref, 2860 (1045), 2862 (445)
Ezor, S. N.: ref, 2862 (338)

Fabbri, C.: ref, 2497 (621)
Fabbro, F.: ref, 322 (7), 2163 (269,338), 2860 (1330), 2862 (277)
Faber, R. J.: ref, 2497 (313)
Faber, S. D.: ref, 2497 (310)
Fabes, R. A.: ref, 365 (9), 1001 (5)
Fabiani, M.: ref, 1740 (19), 2860 (1260), 2892 (270)
Fabiano, R. J.: ref, 2860 (853)
Fabrega, H.: ref, 2050 (2)
Fabrega, H., Jr.: ref, 451 (114)
Fabry, J.: rev, 85, 1648, 1743, 1853
Facione, N. C.: test, 367
Facione, P. A.: test, 367, 368
Factor, A.: ref, 1300 (4)
Factor, D. C.: ref, 811 (1), 2813 (3), 2813 (20)
Fad, K. M.: test, 40
Fadda, L.: ref, 2163 (148,201,202), 2226 (19), 2227 (55), 2860 (820,1381), 2907 (7)
Faden, V.: ref, 1965 (33)
Faerevaag, M. K.: ref, 2860 (898), 2862 (354)
Fagan, D. J.: ref, 998 (38), 1158 (1), 1697 (152)
Fagan, J.: ref, 1333 (8)
Fagan, J. F., III.: ref, 2485 (178)
Fagan, P.: ref, 793 (22)
Fagan, P. J.: ref, 793 (18), 2218 (49,130)
Fagan, W. T.: ref, 2432 (2)
Fager, J. J.: rev, 657, 1647, 2686, 2718
Fagerlin, A.: ref, 1720 (4)
Fagerstrom, R.: ref, 1697 (168,281)
Fagg, J.: ref, 272 (241), 999 (46)
Fagin, H. T.: test, 1222, 1223
Fagley, N. S.: ref, 1140 (9)
Faglia, L.: ref, 1697 (222)
Fagot, B. I.: ref, 451 (253), 863 (41), 2864 (143)
Fahey, J. L.: ref, 2076 (13,56,85), 2860 (664)
Fahle, M.: ref, 303 (16), 2860 (1261)
Fahy, J. F.: ref, 2603 (401), 2863 (287)
Fahy, T. A.: ref, 1093 (80), 2050 (88,103)
Faier-Routman, J.: ref, 1903 (372), 2485 (169), 2862 (351), 2864 (93)
Faigel, H. C.: ref, 2860 (347), 2862 (161)
Faillace, L. A.: ref, 1661 (20)
Fairbairn, A.: ref, 2860 (40), 2863 (14)
Fairbairn, A. F.: ref, 1758 (1,4), 2163 (18), 2193 (3), 2860 (58), 2860 (128), 2863 (19), 2863 (36)
Fairbank, D. W.: rev, 235, 283, 285, 2041
Fairbank, J. A.: ref, 1697 (36,325), 2497 (36)
Fairbanks, L.: ref, 1164 (181), 1740 (33), 2227 (59), 2860 (1408), 2863 (427)
Fairburn, C. G.: ref, 337 (99,137,141), 1079 (87), 2050 (113), 2076 (121), 2603 (93,179,311,453)
Fairclough, D.: ref, 1612 (40,2862)
Fairclough, D. L.: ref, 472 (34)
Fairley, J. J.: ref, 2497 (667)
Fairley, N.: ref, 2892 (244)
Faison, L.: ref, 1378 (7), 2862 (503)
Faith, M. S.: ref, 337 (55), 793 (12), 2396 (1)
Fakouri, M. E.: ref, 298 (96)
Falbo, T.: ref, 863 (10)
Falcioni, J.: ref, 2519 (29), 2520 (30)
Falconer, C. W.: ref, 298 (30) 1014 (3), 1965 (14)
Falconer, J.: ref, 298 (30), 1014 (3), 1965 (14)
Falender, C. A.: test, 1621, 1630
Falger, P. R. J.: ref, 2497 (350)
Falgout, J. C.: ref, 838 (1,3), 2860 (36)
Falk, B.: ref, 1697 (282)
Falk, R. F.: ref, 592 (64), 1115 (13)
Falke, R. L.: ref, 2076 (40), 2858 (35)
Falkenberg, B. A.: ref, 381 (1), 895 (1), 1089 (1), 1439 (1), 1444 (4), 2295 (8) 2547 (1)
Falkowski, J.: ref, 999 (25)
Fallon, B. A.: ref, 1697 (283)
Fallon, S.: ref, 2519 (50), 2520 (50)
Fallon, T.: ref, 1903 (252)
Fals-Stewart, W.: ref, 1959 (6), 2497 (654), 2860 (613,1344)
Faltin, S.: rev, 2244
Faltus, F.: ref, 1166 (67)
Falus, A.: ref, 1166 (30)
Famularo, R.: ref, 2519 (38), 2520 (39)
Fan, L.: ref, 1405 (35)
Fan, R. M.: ref, 372 (97), 1697 (476)
Fan, X.: rev, 657
Fanchiang, S.: ref, 1533 (1)
Fandal, A. W.: test, 1217
Fang, Z.: ref, 2680 (19)
Fann, J. R.: ref, 2603 (351)
Fann, K. D.: ref, 448 (15)
Fanshawe, J. P.: ref, 1079 (85)
Fantie, B. D.: ref, 2402 (66)
Fantuzzo, J. W.: ref, 2486 (2,3), 2860 (289)
Farace, E.: ref, 2860 (410,540)
Farah, M. J.: ref, 2163 (159), 2860 (92,253,854), 2863 (26,64,181,249), 2873 (22)
Faraone, F. V.: ref, 2305 (221)
Faraone, S.: ref, 2305 (165)
Faraone, S. V.: ref, 451 (168), 1010 (69,70,118), 1092 (5,11,12,13, 14,16), 1093 (84), 1164 (68), 1218 (7), 1645 (3), 1697 (408, 2305 (121,240), 1965 (66), 2305 (215), 2516 (42,65), 2860 (331,671,801,802, 855, 990,1203), 2862 (308,309,310,394,520,592), 2863 (199,250), 2879 (81,100,101,102,137, 142, 187,194), 2892 (125,176)

Faravelli, C.: ref, 2497 (621)
Farber, B.: ref, 1300 (7)
Farber, B. A.: ref, 337 (185)
Färber, D.: ref, 1166 (121)
Farberow, N. L.: ref, 272 (51), 337 (38), 1697 (1), 2417 (1,15)
Farbisz, R.: ref, 997 (10), 1216 (20), 2127 (1), 2603 (134)
Fardig, D.: test, 2314
Farel, A. M.: ref, 815 (51), 1740 (30), 1889 (18), 2724 (12), 2862 (711)
Farhney, M. R.: ref, 1386 (8), 1607 (9), 2485 (143)
Faries, D. E.: ref, 1166 (51)
Fariña, F.: ref, 2497 (112)
Farinaro, E.: ref, 2603 (517)
Faris, P.: ref, 353 (20), 2432 (28), 2862 (419), 2901 (78)
Faris, P. D.: ref, 353 (10), 2432 (16), 2862 (207), 2901 (26)
Farish, S.: test, 2091
Farley, F. H.: rev, 2484
Farley, G. K.: ref, 2862 (230), 2879 (69)
Farley, M.: ref, 846 (16)
Farley, R. C.: ref, 404 (4,6,24), 936 (1), 1754 (4)
Farlow, M.: ref, 2599 (16), 2860 (614), 2863 (180), 2892 (115)
Farmer, A.: ref, 2050 (14)
Farmer, A. E.: ref, 2050 (19)
Farmer, H. S.: ref, 298 (140)
Farmer, J. E.: ref, 375 (1), 2880 (2)
Farmer, L.: ref, 2749 (39)
Farmer, R. F.: rev, 483, 817; ref, 272 (352), 998 (91), 2497 (460)
Farnham, J. M.: ref, 459 (24), 2892 (82)
Farnill, D.: ref, 337 (9)
Farnsworth, P. R.: rev, 1629
Farnum, S. E.: test, 1018, 2853
Farr, B.: test, 1281
Farr, J. M.: test, 1252
Farr, M.: test, 934
Farr, R.: test, 1281; rev, 552
Farrah, G. A.: test, 2355
Farran, D. C.: ref, 1902 (71), 2864 (84), 2901 (60)
Farrand, L. L.: ref, 1010 (46)
Farrell, A. D.: ref, 272 (71)
Farrell, E.: ref, 2497 (130)
Farrell, K.: ref, 2860 (64), 2862 (38)
Farrell, M.: ref, 560 (2), 1765 (16)
Farrell, M. P.: ref, 1000 (45)
Farrell, W.: ref, 694 (104), 2879 (135)
Farrell, W. C.: ref, 272 (316), 1697 (568), 2497 (653)
Farrell, W. J.: ref, 353 (9), 1901 (13), 2724 (3)
Farrell-Holtan, J.: test, 212
Farren, C. K.: ref, 2305 (175)
Farris, M.: ref, 4 (18)
Farver, J. A. M.: ref, 1903 (355)
Fasiceka, A. L.: ref, 1093 (79)
Fasiczka, A.: ref, 1166 (173)
Fasiczka, A. L.: ref, 793 (14), 1093 (78)
Fasiska, E. J.: test, 966
Fass, R. J.: ref, 1164 (73), 2860 (722), 2892 (143)
Fassinger, R. E.: ref, 298 (31), 404 (14), 1701 (51), 1825 (7)
Fast, C. G.: test, 1019
Fastenau, P. S.: ref, 2227 (24), 2497 (552,622), 2860 (1075), 2863 (314,365)
Fathman, A. K.: test, 2337
Fatkenheuer, B.: ref, 2050 (33)
Fauber, R.: ref, 2839 (1)
Faucett, J.: ref, 2603 (342)
Faucett, J. M.: ref, 791 (13), 2858 (110)
Faucher, A.: ref, 2163 (310), 2863 (363)
Faude, J.: ref, 790 (2), 2749 (10)
Faulkner, G.: test, 2511
Faull, K. F.: ref, 1697 (128)
Faulstick, M. E.: ref, 2214 (37), 2497 (311), 2498 (32)
Faunce, R. W.: rev, 1544, 2548, 2760
Faure, S.: ref, 2860 (615)
Faust, C. J.: ref, 1093 (110), 2305 (168)
Faust, D.: ref, 301 (3), 1164 (3), 1525 (1), 2860 (93), 2863 (27)
Faust, J.: ref, 2214 (44), 2839 (4), 2862 (134)
Faust, M.: ref, 2862 (607)
Faustman, W. O.: ref, 1697 (128)
Faux, S. F.: ref, 2305 (150) 2860 (497)
Fava, J. L.: ref, 68 (38)
Fava, M.: ref, 272 (176,202)
Fava, M.: ref, 1166 (41,86,106,133,141,162,184), 2199 (11), 2519 (39), 2520 (40), 2603 (503)
Favaro, A., : ref, 893 (52), 2603 (578)
Faw, G. D.: ref, 2132 (2)
Fawcett, A. J.: ref, 349 (23), 2862 (251)
Fawcett, H. P.: rev, 2856, 2857
Fawcett, J.: ref, 1093 (23) 2305 (82,210), 2862 (401,553), 2879 (139,181)
Fawcett, J. A.: ref, 1093 (22)
Fawcett, S.: ref, 272 (152), 2497 (538)
Fawson, P.: ref, 1072 (26)
Fawzy, F. I.: ref, 2076 (13,56)
Fawzy, N. W.: ref, 2076 (13,56)
Fay, K.: rev, 1220
Fazekas, F.: ref, 2860 (525), 2892 (88)
Fazio, B. B.: ref, 324 (4), 624 (6,17,25,26,30), 809 (1), 811 (12), 1903 (172,253), 2695 (50,51,65)
Fazio, F.: ref, 2163 (185,284), 2860 (1130)
Fazzari, T. V.: ref, 1135 (19), 2497 (603), 2516 (89), 2860 (1200), 2863 (360)
Feaganes, J. R.: ref, 2218 (40)
Feagans, L. V.: ref, 1902 (71), 2382 (20), 2864 (84), 2901 (60)
Fear, F.: ref, 791 (16)
Feasby, T. E.: ref, 1615 (1)
Feather, N. T.: ref, 1079 (2), 2246 (1,2)

Feazell, D. M.: ref, 2115 (1) 2862 (128)
Febbraro, G.: ref, 1619 (11)
Febbraro, G. A.: ref, 1021 (32)
Febbraro, G. A. R.: ref, 2065 (10)
Fechway, T.: ref, 270 (24), 2229 (13)
Feder, M.: ref, 1166 (85)
Federman, B.: ref, 2050 (112)
Federmann, B.: ref, 2860 (1137)
Fedio, P.: ref, 1687 (19), 2860 (340)
Fedoroff, J. P.: ref, 2050 (28)
Fedorovich, S. E.: ref, 694 (72)
Fee, M.: ref, 2860 (674)
Fee, V. E.: ref, 459 (11), 681 (44), 2813 (14)
Feehan, C.: ref, 2214 (113), 2305 (205)
Feehan, M.: ref, 358 (5), 1097 (6), 1853 (1), 1903 (131), 2211 (16), 2228 (4), 2485 (63), 2497 (31)
Feeley, J. T.: ref, 2487 (4)
Feeley, N.: ref, 1580 (1), 2858 (6)
Feeney, J.: ref, 815 (49), 1164 (173), 1740 (27), 2516 (115), 2860 (1374), 2892 (294)
Fegley, S.: ref, 1408 (8)
Feicht, R.: ref, 372 (29), 999 (27)
Feigenbaum, J. D.: ref, 1758 (67)
Feil, E. G.: test, 890
Feild, H. S.: ref, 372 (84), 1697 (396)
Feiler, R.: ref, 875 (10), 1902 (77)
Fein, D.: test, 2840; ref, 1612 (8,11,12), 1903 (22, 52,53,369), 2382 (37), 2485 (168,218), 2680 (18), 2813 (1,94,131)
Fein, G.: ref, 1058 (7), 1407 (1), 2227 (12), 2860 (172,499), 2863 (143)
Fein, G. G.: ref, 1216 (29)
Fein, S.: ref, 1965 (58)
Feinberg, T. E.: ref, 2163 (159), 2863 (181), 2873 (22)
Feinburg, H.: rev, 798
Feingold, A.: ref, 2860 (455)
Feinstein, A.: ref, 2125 (11), 2516 (39), 2599 (17)
Feinstein, C.: ref, 472 (47), 1903 (369), 2382 (37), 2485 (168,218), 2680 (18), 2813 (94,131), 2860 (467)
Feinstein, E.: ref, 2603 (287)
Feinstein, L. G.: ref, 2076 (40), 2858 (35)
Feinstein, S. B.: ref, 272 (185), 273 (22)
Feiring, C.: rev, 1224, 1391; ref, 1010 (47), 1612 (92)
Feist, G. J.: ref, 68 (35), 373 (19)
Feitler, F. C.: ref, 1072 (33)
Feixas, G.: ref, 2305 (43)
Fekken, G. C.: ref, 256 (1), 404 (12), 1334 (2), 1965 (1,42,51), 2860 (156)
Felce, D.: ref, 4 (8), 1590 (60), 1897 (1)
Feldhirsen, J. F.: ref, 1991 (28), 2252 (2)
Feldhusen, J. F.: ref, 493 (1), 592 (32,84), 838 (10), 1991 (9)
Feldman, H.: ref, 681 (46)
Feldman, H. M.: ref, 265 (5), 1391 (1), 1612 (24,49,52), 1903 (114,254), 2382 (7,8,21)
Feldman, J.: ref, 2860 (856), 2892 (177), 2905 (72)
Feldman, J. F.: ref, 451 (236), 681 (19), 2813 (154), 2862 (389,539,669)
Feldman, J. J.: ref, 2010 (6), 2860 (317)
Feldman, L.: ref, 2247 (51)
Feldman, L. A.: ref, 2076 (114)
Feldman, L. B.: ref, 1580 (2), 2603 (13)
Feldman, M.: ref, 2497 (436)
Feldman, M. A.: ref, 1216 (99), 2813 (142), 2860 (1262), 2862 (608), 2879 (201)
Feldman, M. E.: ref, 1697 (530), 2879 (154)
Feldman, S. I.: ref, 999 (156), 2603 (452)
Feldman, S. S.: ref, 472 (15), 699 (4), 1010 (27,40)
Feldman-Koffler, F.: ref, 272 (136) 1166 (81)
Feldstein, M.: ref, 2603 (11), 2603 (67)
Feldt, L. S.: test, 1319; rev, 514; ref, 1318 (8)
Feldt, R. C.: ref, 1767 (1,2), 1767 (2), 2856 (2)
Féline, A.: ref, 272 (350), 2516 (73), 2860 (1002)
Fell, R.: ref, 2288 (72), 2289 (57)
Fellman, V.: ref, 2862 (499)
Fellowes, D.: ref, 2050 (119)
Fellows, B.: ref, 4 (23)
Felner, R. D.: ref, 472 (24,82,121,123), 495 (11,1010), 2214 (14,41,65)
Felron, D. C.: ref, 1685 (2)
Felsen, I.: ref, 2652 (3)
Felsenfeld, S.: rev, 2144, 2523; ref, 540 (18), 998 (42), 1059 (2), 1072 (43), 1216 (100), 1240 (33), 1903 (115,255,356), 2225 (4), 2651 (4,14), 2657 (23), 2860, 2862 (252,334,609), 2864 (85)
Felson, R. B.: ref, 615 (26)
Feltham, D. W.: test, 2264
Felton, B. J.: ref, 2858 (1)
Felton, R. H.: ref, 769 (1,3,7), 1072 (55), 1503 (7,16), 1903 (116,576), 2163 (353), 2671 (1), 2862 (162,725), 2901 (19,61,134), 2905 (36,73)
Fendt, K.: ref, 1902 (71), 2864 (84), 2901 (60)
Feng, H.: ref, 2452 (10)
Feng, Y.: ref, 2901 (84)
Fennell, E.: ref, 1740 (23), 2860 (620,1309)
Fennig, S.: ref, 2102 (1), 2288 (16,56), 2289 (11,43), 2860 (335), 2863 (88)
Fennis, J. F. M.: ref, 2497 (529)
Fenson, L.: test, 1528
Fensta, H. N.: ref, 2497 (193)
Fentiman, J.: test, 2459
Fenton, G. W.: ref, 537 (2), 1390 (6), 1758 (53), 2497 (330), 2860 (982)
Fenton, R.: rev, 376, 2223
Fenton, T.: ref, 2519 (38), 2520 (39)
Fenton, W. S.: ref, 2288 (36), 2289 (27), 2860 (617)
Fenwick, J. W.: ref, 2076 (26)
Fenwick, T. L.: ref, 2860 (456)
Ferarnow, M. D.: ref, 1010 (102)
Fercho, M. C.: ref, 1697 (347), 2603 (297)
Ferdinand, R. F.: ref, 451 (232)
Ferdon, M. B.: ref, 1135 (18), 2226 (14), 2516 (85), 2860 (1173), 2863 (353)

Fergus, K. D.: ref, 2519 (25), 2520 (26)
Ferguson, B.: ref, 241 (4), 451 (94), 815 (35), 1903 (447), 2695 (47), 2864 (110)
Ferguson, D. M.: ref, 2091 (2)
Ferguson, G. A.: rev, 127
Ferguson, K. S.: ref, 272 (269), 846 (21), 2497 (623)
Ferguson, L. W.: rev, 2406
Ferguson, S. A.: ref, 2860 (642)
Ferguson, S. J.: ref, 1079 (67)
Fergusson, D. M.: ref, 358 (4,11), 681 (10,30,31), 694 (113,114), 1216 (46,62), 2091 (3,4), 2094 (1,3), 2211 (28,38,39,47), 2714 (4,5,6), 2862 (253,468, 469,470)
Fergusson, L. C.: ref, 1140 (31), 2065 (27), 2497 (461)
Ferketich, S. L.: ref, 2497 (76,266,333)
Fernandez, E.: rev, 273, 1166
Fernández, H.: ref, 853 (2)
Fernández, M. C.: ref, 1903 (117)
Ferner, R.: ref, 2860 (1321)
Ferng, H.: ref, 1093 (40)
Ferns, W.: ref, 2305 (194)
Fernstrom, P.: ref, 2211 (4,14)
Ferrando, P. J.: ref, 998 (69)
Ferrara, K.: ref, 1697 (99)
Ferrara, S.: rev, 208, 260, 2861; ref, 1657 (12)
Ferrarese, C.: ref, 2860 (173)
Ferrari, J. R.: ref, 592 (85)
Ferrari, P.: ref, 2813 (109), 2860 (1001)
Ferraro, F. R.: ref, 272 (105), 1767 (4,9), 2599 (38), 2860 (1076,1077,1078,1387), 2892 (271)
Ferraro, J. M.: test, 828
Ferraro, R.: ref, 1697 (21)
Ferre, L.: ref, 2862 (333)
Ferrell, K. A.: ref, 265 (15)
Ferrell, R. H.: rev, 1117
Ferrer, K.: ref, 451 (105), 472 (161)
Ferri, B. A.: ref, 2860 (1263), 2862 (610)
Ferri, S.: ref, 2892 (159,262)
Ferrier, I. N.: ref, 1166 (16,151)
Ferrill, D.: ref, 2860 (8), 2892 (1)
Ferrini-Mundy, J.: ref, 615 (32)
Ferris, S. H.: ref, 1164 (156), 2125 (26), 2860 (1295)
Ferriss, S. J.: ref, 2497 (228)
Ferro, J.: ref, 2485 (199), 2813 (117), 2862 (471)
Ferro, T. R.: rev, 1132, 1465, 1936
Ferron, J.: ref, 180 (17,18)
Ferron, J.: ref, 1216 (47,48,49,63), 1903 (357), 2862 (646)
Ferruzza, E.: ref, 2247 (116), 2860 (1248), 2863 (376)
Ferry, F.: test, 408, 1350, 1539; ref, 2860 (1353), 2863 (407)
Fery, P.: ref, 2163 (211), 2860 (857), 2863 (251)
Feske, U.: ref, 337 (75), 2497 (462), 2603 (352)
Festa, J.: ref, 272 (310)
Festinger, D. S.: ref, 271 (11), 272 (296), 1687 (44)
Fetler, M. F.: ref, 592 (16)
Fetrow, R. A.: ref, 2860 (428)
Fettig, D. M.: ref, 2163 (252), 2497 (532)
Fewell, R. R.: test, 803, 1901; ref, 433 (13), 803 (3), 804 (1), 1653 (27), 1901 (18), 2189 (7)
Fey, M. E.: ref, 175 (1), 214 (1,9,14,16), 1040 (1), 1095 (1), 1485 (1,16,27), 1804 (1), 1903 (173,256,521), 1982 (1), 2651 (1), 2657 (6,15,32) 2704 (2)
Feyh, J. M.: ref, 853 (16)
Fiatarone, M. A.: ref, 272 (321)
Fibel, B.: ref, 1697 (13)
Ficher, I.: ref, 2864 (86)
Fichman, L.: ref, 790 (12)
Fichten, C. S.: ref, 694 (11), 998 (92)
Fichter, M. M.: ref, 2603 (252,489)
Fichter, M. S.: ref, 2603 (525)
Ficzere, S. A.: ref, 2668 (3)
Fidler, M.: test, 348
Fiedler, L. J.: ref, 298 (6)
Fiedman, B.: ref, 1135 (18), 2226 (14), 2516 (85), 2860 (1173), 2863 (353)
Field, B.: ref, 2862 (121)
Field, C. D.: ref, 1164 (147)
Field, D. T.: ref, 2230 (17), 2231 (7)
Field, H. L.: ref, 1218 (5), 2599 (10), 2863 (109), 2892 (59)
Field, J.: ref, 1832 (10)
Field, J. A., Jr.: rev, 117
Field, N. P.: ref, 272 (272,348), 2218 (94), 2497 (630,666)
Field, T.: ref, 270 (16), 272 (169,170,196,277), 451 (28,115,136), 615 (27), 1379 (25), 1770 (17), 1962 (13), 1991 (25), 2076 (73,148), 2242 (3), 2485 (79), 2497 (507), 2498 (67)
Field, T. M.: ref, 272 (210)
Fielding, B.: ref, 373 (17), 1987 (8)
Fielding-Barnsley, R.: ref, 1903 (23)
Fields, D. L.: ref, 1448 (1)
Fields, H.: ref, 2862 (219), 2879 (63)
Fields, J. A.: ref, 271 (15), 272 (330), 376 (28), 776 (56), 1135 (24), 1218 (19), 1378 (10), 1740 (26), 2076 (181), 2516 (112), 2863 (411), 2892 (293)
Fields, J. H.: ref, 2485 (126)
Fields, R. B.: ref, 1697 (475)
Fielo, J.: ref, 2858 (17)
Fiere, R. R.: ref, 2860 (297)
Fierman, E. J.: ref, 2305 (135)
Fiese, B. H.: ref, 1216 (57), 1735 (2), 2485 (142)
Fifer, S. K.: ref, 2603 (253,552)
Figueredo, A. J.: ref, 337 (105), 372 (101), 2126 (15)
Figueroa, M.: ref, 2860 (407)
Figueroa, R. A.: ref, 1379 (5), 1903 (27), 2606 (2), 2862 (67), 2901 (4)
Figueroa, R. E.: ref, 2227 (4)
Figurski, G. R.: ref, 1095 (20), 2866 (3)
File, Q. W.: test, 1221
Filion, D. L.: ref, 2288 (30), 2289 (21), 2402 (42)

Filipek, P. A.: ref, 451 (187), 2227 (26), 2305 (222), 2813 (140), 2860 (1103), 2862 (611), 2879 (202), 2905 (109)
Filipenko, V. V.: ref, 1079 (68)
Filippelli, L. A.: ref, 1991 (30)
Filoteo, J. V.: ref, 376 (19), 776 (21,42)
Fils-Aime, M-L.: ref, 1661 (55), 2305 (176)
Filter, M. D.: rev, 2837
Fimm, B.: ref, 2163 (160)
Finaly-Neumann, E.: ref, 592 (11)
Finch, A. J., Jr.: ref, 472 (92), 2214 (52)
Finch, J. F.: ref, 998 (14,39)
Finch, M. D.: ref, 2860 (379)
Finch-Williams, A.: rev, 76
Fincham, F. D.: ref, 272 (155), 472 (28), 863 (19), 2214 (18), 2519 (19), 2520 (20)
Findlay, J. M.: ref, 2860 (316)
Findley, D. B.: rev, 1452
Findley, J. C.: ref, 272 (353)
Findley, L. J.: ref, 350 (19), 2860 (661)
Findley, W. G.: rev, 56, 118, 364, 617, 665, 1657, 2742
Fine, J.: ref, 2860 (875) 2873 (36)
Fine, M.: ref, 2749 (29)
Fine, M. A.: ref, 1181 (6,16), 2603 (58)
Fine, M. J.: ref, 1000 (1), 1014 (1), 1612 (6), 2862 (40)
Fine, P. R.: ref, 1014 (7)
Fine, S.: ref, 472 (46), 681 (32)
Finegan, J. E.: ref, 1965 (52)
Finger, W. W.: ref, 771 (10)
Fingeret, A. L.: ref, 134 (14), 1661 (23)
Fink, B.: ref, 875 (9), 1264 (3)
Fink, C. M.: ref, 495 (7), 909 (1), 2498 (57), 2862 (439)
Fink, G. R.: ref, 2227 (15), 2863 (172), 2892 (107)
Fink, J. J.: test, 1957
Fink, L.: test, 460
Fink, S. R.: rev, 510
Fink, S. V.: ref, 1947 (5)
Finkel, D.: ref, 2860 (858), 2863 (252)
Finkelberg, S.: ref, 2247 (49)
Finkelhor, D.: ref, 2417 (31)
Finkelstein, F. O.: ref, 272 (227)
Finkelstein, S. H.: ref, 272 (227)
Finkle, L. J.: rev, 1245
Finlayson, L.: test, 1201
Finlayson, S. B.: ref, 2141 (1)
Finley, C. J.: rev, 1392, 1657, 2234
Finley, V. S.: ref, 2295 (9)
Finn, J. D.: ref, 665 (75), 2355 (3)
Finn, P. R.: ref, 372 (35,113), 999 (194), 1164 (166), 1661 (16,72,85), 1697 (89,166,564,596), 2010 (8), 2227 (9,49), 2497 (677) 2860 (392,750), 2863 (102), 2892 (57)
Finn, R. F.: ref, 1169 (2), 2247 (78)
Finney, J. W.: test, 1181;ref, 134 (30), 337 (194), 472 (13), 997 (15,17), 1010 (28,32), 1181 (5,7,23,28), 1495 (1), 2414 (5), 2498 (7), 2917 (2)
Finnigan, J. P.: test, 2773
Finucane, B.: ref, 2813 (116)
Fioravanti, M.: ref, 2159 (3)
Fiore, M. C.: ref, 2076 (134)
Fiorello, C. A.: ref, 451 (263), 681 (93), 1392 (15), 2862 (718), 2905 (120)
Fiori-Cowley, A.: ref, 270 (21)
Fireman, M. J.: ref, 1697 (103), 2305 (44)
Firestone, G.: test, 1290
Firestone, L. A.: test, 1035
Firestone, P.: ref, 337 (148), 451 (22), 863 (80), 1000 (99), 1216 (5), 1902 (68), 1903 (345), 1903 (473), 1991 (92), 2862 (322), 2879 (109)
Firestone, R. W.: test, 1035
Firestone, W. A.: test, 2312
First, M. B.: test, 2519, 2520
Firth, H.: ref, 1590 (4)
Firth-Cozens, J.: ref, 2497 (167), 2603 (142)
Fischel, J. E.: ref, 875 (7)
Fischer, A. R.: ref, 1754 (25)
Fischer, C. T.: ref, 2247 (56)
Fischer, D. G.: ref, 1590 (22)
Fischer, J. S.: ref, 272 (245), 2858 (123)
Fischer, K.: ref, 2603 (155,209)
Fischer, K. W.: ref, 2860 (672)
Fischer, M.: ref, 451 (254), 681 (4), 1903 (65), 2606 (4) 2860 (1041)
Fischer, M. A.: rev, 18, 1360
Fischer, R.: ref, 1095 (22), 1653 (11), 2382 (18), 2485 (107)
Fischer, R. S.: ref, 1164 (91), 2860 (859), 2892 (178)
Fischer, S.: ref, 998 (30), 1947 (2)
Fischler, B.: ref, 272 (200), 1164 (129), 1166 (131), 1697 (500), 2163 (286), 2603 (480), 2860 (1134)
Fischler, J. L.: ref, 1755 (38)
Fisek, G. O.: ref, 1401 (1)
Fiset, L.: ref, 135 (5), 2497 (624)
Fish, B.: ref, 2305 (3)
Fish, D. R.: ref, 2227 (18), 2863 (231)
Fish, M.: ref, 1770 (2), 2218 (3)
Fishbein, D. H.: ref, 372 (63,100), 999 (81), 1697 (284,482)
Fishbein, H. D.: ref, 1657 (23)
Fishco, V. V.: test, 1767
Fishel, P. T.: ref, 459 (22), 1653 (8), 1903 (188)
Fisher, A. G.: ref, 353 (3), 1903 (85)
Fisher, B. J.: ref, 1939 (5), 2497 (553)
Fisher, C. B.: ref, 2860 (1232)
Fisher, D.: ref, 1058 (2), 2860 (152)
Fisher, D. G.: ref, 2603 (471)
Fisher, D. J.: test, 1147
Fisher, E.: ref, 893 (27)
Fisher, E. B.: ref, 1010 (80)
Fisher, G.: ref, 1093 (7)
Fisher, G. L.: ref, 2553 (1)
Fisher, H. B.: test, 1040
Fisher, J.: test, 2134

Fisher, J. E.: ref, 875 (8), 1240 (31), 1903 (328)
Fisher, J. M.: ref, 1612 (9), 2864 (7)
Fisher, J. P.: test, 1231
Fisher, K. A.: test, 1147
Fisher, L.: ref, 350 (49), 1000 (25)
Fisher, M.: ref, 451 (55), 681 (61), 1099 (3), 1740 (5)
Fisher, N.: ref, 998 (43)
Fisher, N. J.: ref, 1166 (107), 1697 (542), 2860 (1079,1264)
Fisher, N. J.: ref, 2863 (315,380), 2879 (203)
Fisher, P.: test, 1865; ref, 451 (151), 2305 (197)
Fisher, P. A.: ref, 270 (40), 863 (90), 1010 (129)
Fisher, R. H.: ref, 2768 (38,39), 2860 (1187,1188), 2863 (358)
Fisher, S. G.: ref, 1036 (12), 2417 (40)
Fisherman, S.: ref, 2163 (70)
Fishman, B.: ref, 337 (30,48), 2497 (192), 2860 (54)
Fishman, J. A.: rev, 2758
Fisk, A. D.: ref, 1405 (22), 2163 (212), 2860 (860,1364)
Fisk, J. D.: ref, 376 (11), 2860 (1189), 2892 (258)
Fisk, J. L.: rev, 564
Fiske, D. W.: rev, 908
Fisman, S.: ref, 1485 (36), 1612 (61), 2228 (15), 2813 (74)
Fiszbein, A.: test, 2017; ref, 564 (5), 2017 (1), 2146 (2), 2892 (38)
Fiszdon, J.: ref, 272 (195), 2497 (568)
Fitts, W. H.: test, 2652
Fitz, A. G.: ref, 2860 (688)
Fitzgerald, G. A.: ref, 681 (39), 2860 (550)
Fitzgerald, H. E.: ref, 272 (128), 1178 (13), 1661 (51), 2485 (83), 2599 (13), 2860 (457)
Fitzgerald, J.: ref, 257 (4), 364 (4,26)
Fitzgerald, J. A.: rev, 2473
Fitzgerald, L. F.: ref, 2603 (357,459)
Fitzgerald, T. E.: ref, 926 (6), 2603 (94), 2860 (254)
Fitzgerald, W.: ref, 791 (16)
Fitzgibbon, M. L.: ref, 1164 (4), 1166 (8), 2603 (180,463), 2860 (94)
Fitzhugh-Bell, K.: ref, 2860 (417), 2862 (187), 2879 (53)
Fitzmaurice, C.: rev, 324
Fitzpatrick, A. R.: rev, 82, 260
Fitzpatrick, M.: ref, 1093 (36), 2497 (141), 2603 (119)
Fitzpatrick, P. A.: ref, 681 (48), 1902 (55,88), 2862 (500)
Fitzpatrick, P. M.: ref, 2860 (83)
Fitzpatrick, R.: rev, 190, 352, 535, 1666, 2311, 2314, 2578, 2587
Fitzsimmons, C.: ref, 2860 (700)
Fitzsimmons, G. W.: test, 1493; ref, 1694 (1) 2915 (1)
Fitzsimmons, L. M.: ref, 272 (203)
Fivars, G.: test, 543, 2612
Fixler, D.: ref, 433 (12), 1086 (2), 1164 (80), 1240 (30), 1612 (60), 1902 (60), 2485 (150), 2860 (760), 2864 (74)
Flaherty, J. A.: ref, 1661 (7,17) 2076 (50), 2603 (60, 156)
Flaherty, L. T.: ref, 451 (82), 1000 (94)
Flaherty, M. A.: ref, 724 (4), 1991 (31), 2771 (17)
Flahrerty, L. T.: ref, 451 (83), 1000 (95), 2230 (11)
Flaks, D. K.: ref, 2864 (86)
Flamini, R.: ref, 335 (7)
Flanagan, D. P.: rev, 1378, 2142, 2229; ref, 837 (12), 1378 (2,8) 1379 (100), 2452 (11), 2485 (127), 2485 (230) 2860 (618), 2862 (254), 2901 (124,132)
Flanagan, J. C.: test, 543, 1042, 1043, 2612; rev, 2871
Flanagan, J. L.: ref, 2163 (322) 2172 (1), 2225 (17)
Flanagan, R.: ref, 1378 (2), 1379 (67), 2485 (127) 2860 (618), 2862 (254)
Flanagan, S. G.: rev, 1748, 2878
Flanigan, H. F.: ref, 2227 (4)
Flanigin, H. F.: ref, 2860 (68), 2892 (3)
Flannery, D. J.: ref, 451 (36)
Flannery, G. J.: ref, 272 (26)
Flannery, K. A.: ref, 2651 (15,17), 2862 (335), 2879 (112)
Flannery, R. B., Jr.: ref, 272 (26)
Flannery-Schroeder, E.: ref, 472 (150)
Flannery-Schroeder, E. C.: ref, 1021 (45), 2214 (85,133), 2498 (55,75)
Flasher, A.: ref, 1991 (97)
Flashman, L. A.: ref, 1164 (121), 2125 (22), 2288 (67), 2289 (51), 2516 (78), 2860 (1080,1096), 2863 (316), 2892 (225,228)
Flatter, C.: ref, 1000 (73)
Flaum, M.: ref, 650 (4,14,16), 1093 (6,39,58,85), 1164 (121), 2017 (4), 2125 (22), 2288 (11,43,44,67), 2289 (8,33,34,51), 2305 (52), 2516 (78), 2860 (150,1080), 2863 (316), 2892 (225)
Flaum, M. A.: ref, 650 (8), 1164 (35), 1517 (3), 2860 (349)
Flax, J.: ref, 270 (41), 994 (36), 1903 (458), 1982 (13), 2485 (197), 2680 (14), 2695 (70), 2813 (114), 2862 (679)
Flay, B. R.: ref, 472 (186)
Flccnor, J.: ref, 413 (5), 1755 (78)
Fleenor, J. W.: rev, 622, 820, 1315, 2383, 2587; ref, 372 (64), 372 (110), 1404 (10), 1754 (16)
Flegenheimer, W.: ref, 2603 (129)
Fleischer, C. A.: ref, 1965 (73)
Fleischer, S. J.: ref, 2879 (113)
Fleisher, L.: rev, 248
Fleishman, E.: test, 1444
Fleishman, E. A.: test, 1044, 937 (3)
Fleiss, J.: ref, 2603 (562)
Fleming, A. S.: ref, 1745 (18)
Fleming, C. M.: test, 714, 715, 1389
Fleming, G. M.: ref, 272 (132), 1166 (80)
Fleming, J. S.: ref, 464 (3)
Fleming, K.: ref, 2050 (114)
Fleming, W. G.: rev, 2541
Fletcher, B.: ref, 739 (9)

Fletcher, B. C.: ref, 739 (6)
Fletcher, C.: ref, 998 (20)
Fletcher, C. M.: ref, 34 (1), 2226 (3)
Fletcher, J.: test, 2781; ref, 2860 (619), 2862 (255), 2879 (77)
Fletcher, J. D.: ref, 389 (2)
Fletcher, J. M.: ref, 375 (3), 815 (20), 1051 (1), 1612 (65,68,99), 1903 (571), 2813 (88), 2860 (1230), 2862 (180,317,396,473,474,506,710), 2879 (43,160,196), 2901 (21,73,88,89)
Fletcher, K.: ref, 451 (283), 681 (98), 2603 (590), 2901 (135)
Fletcher, K. E.: ref, 1903 (106), 2603 (131,298)
Fletcher, M. A.: ref, 2603 (516)
Fletcher, P.: test, 2228, 1134 (4), 1903 (263), 2485 (130), 2862 (265), 2879 (78)
Fletcher, R.: test, 489
Fletcher, S. G.: ref, 487 (1), 2862 (246)
Fletcher-Flinn, C. M.: ref, 350 (45)
Flett, G. L.: ref, 272 (358), 790 (20), 2557 (9)
Fleury, M.: ref, 1140 (38)
Flewelling, R. L.: ref, 1097 (4), 1903 (67), 2146 (8), 2163 (61)
Flexer, C.: ref, 1240 (14), 1903 (174), 1903 (175)
Flicek, M.: ref, 681 (13)
Flick, S. N.: ref, 2497 (244)
Flink, C.: ref, 1115 (6)
Flint, A. J.: ref, 1166 (73)
Flint, J.: ref, 2860 (350), 2892 (50)
Flipsen, P.: ref, 994 (22), 1095 (31), 1903 (358), 2190 (6), 2657 (24)
Flitman, S.: ref, 272 (270), 2860 (1265)
Flitman, S. S.: ref, 1135 (25), 2863 (418)
Floden, R. E.: rev, 246
Flood, K.: ref, 2076 (83)
Flor, D.: ref, 472 (73), 2211 (26), 2862 (238), 2862 (446)
Flor-Henry, P.: ref, 2862 (101), 2892 (21)
Flores, H.: ref, 2038 (3)
Florian, V.: ref, 298 (9), 337 (25), 863 (32), 1590 (3), 1697 (214), 2603 (161), 2749 (16)
Florine, I.: ref, 271 (16), 272 (335), 2402 (70)
Flory, C. D.: rev, 1974, 2899
Flory, M.: ref, 451 (151), 2305 (197)
Flowers, A.: test, 1020, 1046, 2494
Flowers, D. L.: ref, 322 (3), 2497 (95)
Floyd, F. J.: ref, 863 (14), 1010 (33), 1903 (78,118,176), 2485 (84), 2603 (181)
Floyd, M.: ref, 2497 (612), 2603 (518)
Fluharty, N. B.: test, 1047
Flynn, C. A.: ref, 272 (358)
Flynn, J. R.: ref, 2485 (85)
Flynn, K.: ref, 2288 (29), 2289 (20)
Flynn, L.: ref, 273 (29)
Flynn, W. R.: ref, 1590 (45)
Flynt, S. W.: ref, 364 (7)
Foa, E.: ref, 272 (195), 2497 (568)
Foa, E. B.: test, 2018; ref, 272 (112,359), 846 (25), 1001 (13), 2497 (348,463,464,671), 2519 (54), 2520 (53)
Focsoneanu, M.: ref, 1166 (186)
Fodor, E. M.: ref, 2749 (54)
Foegen, A.: ref, 1072 (52)
Fogarty, G. J.: ref, 838 (14), 1825 (5), 1825 (6), 2360 (3)
Fogarty, L. A.: ref, 2076 (159)
Fogas, B.: ref, 472 (17)
Fogas, B. S.: ref, 272 (76), 451 (20), 472 (26), 1010 (56), 2214 (16), 2603 (224)
Fogel, B. S.: ref, 301 (3), 1164 (3), 1525 (1), 2860 (93), 2863 (27)
Fogel, T.: ref, 1758 (47), 1993 (1)
Fogg, L.: ref, 1525 (12), 2050 (16), 2305 (60), 2860 (307)
Fogg, L. F.: ref, 1093 (22), 2305 (210)
Fogle, E. E.: ref, 68 (45), 2218 (29)
Fogle, P. T.: test, 2249
Fok, L. Y.: ref, 771 (9)
Folds, J. D.: ref, 1166 (196)
Foley, B.: ref, 472 (185), 2214 (111), 2497 (585), 2813 (128)
Foley, G. M.: ref, 815 (43), 2862 (613)
Foley, J.: ref, 2497 (81)
Foley, J. P., Jr.: rev, 989, 1701, 2267, 2899
Folger, T.: ref, 1405 (38)
Foliart, R.: ref, 2603 (205)
Folio, M. R.: test, 1901
Folk, L.: ref, 1991 (50)
Folkard, S.: ref, 2603 (81)
Folkers, E.: ref, 1215 (1)
Folkins, J. W.: ref, 303 (10), 641 (7), 1740 (14), 2226 (13), 2860 (1168), 2863 (351)
Folkman, S.: test, 1178, 2858; ref, 863 (88), 2858 (2,3,36,48,65,)
Follick, M. J.: ref, 2858 (41)
Follman, J.: ref, 836 (1), 2531 (2), 2890 (1)
Follmer, A.: ref, 1215 (4), 2485 (193), 2862 (447), 2864 (113)
Folstein, M.: ref, 2516 (72), 2892 (203)
Folstein, M. F.: ref, 2050 (23)
Folstein, M. L.: ref, 2863 (171)
Folstein, S.: ref, 1485 (33), 1653 (17), 2860 (721), 2862 (283)
Folstein, S. E: ref, 1653 (4), 1740 (10), 2516 (18,32,72), 2860 (299,514,), 2863 (171), 2892 (85,203)
Foltz, L.: ref, 1000 (107)
Fombonne, E.: ref, 2813 (37)
Fomborne, E.: ref, 451 (252), 472 (221)
Fonagy, P.: ref, 272 (171), 999 (157), 2497 (554), 2603 (454)
Fonseca, A. C.: ref, 999 (120), 2862 (336)
Fontaine, J.: ref, 1697 (581)
Fontana, A.: ref, 337 (144)
Fontana, A. F.: ref, 2603 (16,30)
Fontana, D.: ref, 999 (55)
Fontana, M. C.: rev, 1040, 1804

Fontao, M. P. G.: ref, 1396 (3)
Foody, R.: ref, 448 (12)
Foon, A. E.: ref, 1697 (29)
Foose, S. M.: ref, 270 (34), 1216 (101), 1903 (530), 2382 (38)
Fooshee, S. G.: ref, 1337 (1)
Foote, R. : ref, 2595 (2)
Foote, R. C.: ref, 272 (376), 863 (93), 997 (30), 1889 (19), 1903 (580), 2752 (2), 2899 (13)
Forbes, D.: ref, 2603 (254)
Forbes, G. B.: ref, 301 (61), 451 (255), 1903 (572), 2720 (2)
Forbes, J. E.: ref, 2879 (85)
Forceville, E. J. M.: ref, 1164 (36)
Ford, C. T.: ref, 241 (1), 1240 (5), 1903 (70), 2695 (6)
Ford, D.: rev, 73
Ford, D. P.: ref, 2226 (17), 2860 (1225)
Ford, E.: ref, 776 (21)
Ford, G. R.: ref, 708 (9)
Ford, J. G.: ref, 337 (56), 2497 (245)
Ford, J. S.: test, 937
Ford, L.: rev, 1385, 2082, 2191
Ford, L. A.: ref, 2862 (333)
Ford, R. Q.: ref, 2247 (73), 2749 (48), 2860 (736)
Ford-Richards, J. M.: ref, 1378 (14), 1790 (17)
Fordyce, M. W.: test, 1172, 2106
Fore, S.: ref, 998 (82)
Forehand, R.: ref, 272 (72,354,379), 337 (71,172,186, 190, 196), 451 (188,227), 472 (58,80,217,218, 222), 863 (24), 1010 (31), 1661 (50), 2211 (1,12, 24, 29,44,45,46,52), 2214 (44,127), 2839 (1,4)
Forer, B. R.: test, 1049, 1050; rev, 218, 1214
Foreyt, J. P.: ref, 998 (52)
Forgacs, A.: ref, 893 (25), 1079 (48)
Forgas, J. P.: ref, 998 (1)
Forgatch, M. S.: ref, 2860 (95,428)
Forgays, D. G.: ref, 1338 (25)
Forgays, D. K.: ref, 1338 (25)
Forlun, B.: ref, 2163 (197)
Forman, D.: test, 2278
Forms-Santacana, M.: ref, 1612 (83)
Formyduval, D. L.: ref, 68 (45,51), 2218 (29)
Forness, S. R.: ref, 2452 (24)
Forney, D. A.: ref, 1755 (72)
Forney, D. S.: ref, 1469 (6)
Forney, J.: ref, 679 (1), 681 (35)
Fornham, A.: ref, 2485 (200), 2862 (472)
Fornoff, F. J.: rev, 46, 48, 49, 50, 55
Forns, M.: ref, 1140 (7)
Forns-Santacana, M.: ref, 474 (4), 538 (8), 624 (7), 1201 (6), 1612 (34)
Forrest, A.: test, 619
Forrest, G. C.: ref, 863 (33), 1991 (40)
Forrest, K.: ref, 1056 (1)
Forrester, A. W.: ref, 2050 (118)
Forrin, B.: ref, 2163 (103)
Forsman, A.: ref, 1164 (60), 1697 (275), 2305 (98)
Forster, M.: test, 33
Forsterling, F.: ref, 1965 (77), 2218 (71)
Forsyth, D. M.: ref, 1000 (55)
Forsyth, R. A.: test, 1319; rev, 1767
Forte, J. A.: ref, 1000 (14,15)
Forth, A.: ref, 472 (46)
Forth, A. E.: ref, 2402 (65)
Fortone, J.: ref, 1300 (8)
Fortune, B.: ref, 1300 (11)
Fortune, J.: rev, 905; ref, 1300 (11)
Fortune, J. C.: rev, 1430, 1763, 1792, 1807, 1673 (4)
Fos, L.: ref, 1991 (97)
Foss, D. H.: ref, 1140 (32)
Foss-Goodman, D.: ref, 998 (5), 1338 (3)
Fossati, P.: ref, 2163 (156), 2860 (605), 2863 (178)
Foster, A.: ref, 337 (158), 451 (150), 745 (4)
Foster, C.: ref, 2862 (121)
Foster, D. E. : ref, 935 (1), 2924 (1)
Foster, D. F.: ref, 1903 (257)
Foster, F. M.: test, 136
Foster, G. D.: ref, 272 (382)
Foster, H. G.: ref, 2704 (19), 2860 (646)
Foster, H., Jr.: ref, 538 (1)
Foster, J. K.: ref, 376 (31), 776 (60), 2863 (423)
Foster, K. C.: ref, 1903 (257)
Foster, L. G.: ref, 2813 (136)
Foster, N. L.: ref, 1166 (107), 1697 (542), 2227 (2), 2860 (179,1079,1264), 2863 (48,315,380), 2879 (203)
Foster, R.: test, 202
Foster, S.: ref, 1386 (26)
Foster, S. L.: ref, 451 (50), 472 (110)
Foster, V.: ref, 771 (11), 1408 (4)
Foster, Y. A.: ref, 2497 (625)
Foster-Johnson, L.: ref, 2485 (199), 2813 (117), 2862 (471)
Foti, R. J.: ref, 1405 (17)
Fotos, S. S.: ref, 550 (3)
Fouad, N. A.: ref, 413 (4,14), 694 (98), 1790 (13,15), 2360 (7)
Fouche, F. A.: test, 12, 1789, 1983, 2373
Fouly, K. A.: ref, 550 (2), 666 (1,8)
Foundas, A. L.: ref, 2860 (620), 2873 (32.70)
Fournet, G. P.: ref, 1164 (7)
Fournet, L.: ref, 1128 (4)
Fournet, L. M.: ref, 2369 (4)
Fournier, D. G.: test, 2034
Fournier, J.-P.: ref, 650 (15), 1093 (97)
Fourqueran, J. M.: ref, 1470 (1), 1750 (1)
Fouts, J. T.: ref, 495 (6)
Fow, N.: ref, 1697 (285)
Fow, N. R.: ref, 1697 (483)
Fowers, B. J.: ref, 863 (4), 1580 (3), 1582 (3,11), 1927 (2), 2034 (1,4)
Fowler, A. E.: ref, 1051 (1)
Fowler, B.: ref, 893 (27)

Fowler, C.: ref, 2247 (96)
Fowler, D.: ref, 1758 (24), 2050 (71), 2860 (624)
Fowler, H. M.: rev, 1196
Fowler, J. C.: ref, 1697 (550), 2247 (118,122)
Fowler, J. L.: ref, 2858 (41)
Fowler, J. S.: ref, 2860 (779)
Fowler, M. E.: ref, 1115 (28)
Fowler, P. C.: ref, 2860 (174)
Fowler, W.: ref, 641 (1), 2226 (1), 2860 (157)
Fowler-Kerry, S.: ref, 2497 (113), 2498 (8)
Fowles, M. E.: ref, 1115 (25)
Fox, A.: ref, 1903 (198), 2860 (847), 2863 (245)
Fox, D.: ref, 615 (51)
Fox, D. D.: ref, 1697 (409)
Fox, D. J.: test, 1535, 1536
Fox, E.: ref, 349 (10), 1745 (11), 2497 (32), 2862 (256)
Fox, G.: test, 718; rev, 2345
Fox, I.: ref, 2603 (296)
Fox, J.: ref, 998 (50,89)
Fox, L. H.: rev, 2677, 2755
Fox, N. A.: ref, 997 (25), 2497 (475)
Fox, R.: ref, 1135 (3), 2599 (5), 2860 (217)
Fox, R. A.: test, 1880; rev, 2039; ref, 1880 (1)
Foxall, G. R.: ref, 1404 (1,2)
Foxcroft, C. D.: ref, 301 (59), 404 (30), 1612 (93), 2862 (612)
Foxman, D.: test, 2023
Foxx, R. M.: ref, 2132 (2), 2860 (96)
Foy, D. W.: ref, 846 (9), 2519 (47,55), 2520 (48,54)
Foyster, J.: test, 492
Fraboni, M.: ref, 1697 (62,70,104)
Fragapane, L.: ref, 1095 (29) 1903 (313), 2657 (18)
Frager, A. M.: ref, 82 (1), 217 (1), 496 (3)
Frame, C.: ref, 2211 (12)
France, A-C. I.: ref, 2603 (353)
France, C.: ref, 998 (12), 1338 (9), 2497 (28)
France, C. R.: ref, 2497 (525)
France, N.: test, 561, 2058, 2234
Frances, A.: ref, 337 (30), 1093 (36), 2076 (12), 2497 (141), 2603 (119)
Frances, A. J.: ref, 824 (4), 1093 (62), 1166 (14), 2417 (6)
Franchini, L.: ref, 2603 (255)
Francis, A.: ref, 337 (48), 2497 (192)
Francis, C. R.: ref, 1697 (169), 2402 (12)
Francis, D. J.: ref, 815 (20), 1051 (1), 1294 (4), 1612 (65,68), 2417 (21), 2813 (88), 2862 (317,396,473,474), 2879 (43,160), 2901 (73,88,89)
Francis, G.: ref, 272 (225)
Francis, G. S.: ref, 1697 (567), 1740 (25), 2226 (33), 2860 (1339)
Francis, J.: test, 1955
Francis, J. L.: test, 1930
Francis, J. M.: test, 1457
Francis, L. J.: ref, 694 (99,115,125), 999 (37,38,82,125), 1367 (6)
Francis, M.: ref, 1140 (34)
Francis, S. K.: ref, 1000 (41)
Franco, F.: ref, 2229 (4), 2813 (89)
Francoeur, E.: ref, 1903 (338)
Frank, A.: test, 2423; ref, 2603 (326)
Frank, A. C.: rev, 1163
Frank, A. F.: ref, 2109 (1), 2247 (8), 2603 (19), 2749 (13) 2860 (175)
Frank, D. I.: ref, 694 (84)
Frank, E.: ref, 272 (32), 337 (156), 793 (14), 1093 (63,78,79,99,224), 1166 (15,182,215), 2497 (79), 2603 (39,393)
Frank, E. G.: ref, 815 (43), 2862 (613)
Frank, E. L.: ref, 2295 (9)
Frank, E. M.: ref, 1240 (42), 1903 (463)
Frank, G.: ref, 776 (49), 1164 (159), 1758 (91), 2227 (42), 2247 (32,33,34,35,36,37,57,58,59,60,61)
Frank, N.: ref, 272 (225)
Frank, N. C.: ref, 451 (189), 2497 (465)
Frank, R. G.: ref, 1745 (4), 2603 (4,38,344,523), 2858 (12), 2860 (262)
Frank, R. W.: test, 1979
Frank, S.: ref, 1010 (94)
Frank, S. E. R.: ref, 462 (26), 1661 (49)
Frank, S. J.: ref, 1612 (25), 1698 (23), 2230 (17), 2231 (7)
Frankel, F.: ref, 1697 (170), 2452 (7)
Frankenburg, W. K.: test, 783, 784, 785, 787, 788, 1217
Frankiewicz, R. G.: ref, 1000 (34), 1294 (4), 1755 (58), 2417 (21)
Frankle, A. H.: ref, 2115 (4), 2860 (861)
Franklin, A.: ref, 265 (12)
Franklin, C.: ref, 694 (26), 1000 (20), 1207 (1)
Franklin, J.: ref, 1481 (3)
Franklin, J. A.: ref, 1010 (134)
Franklin, K. W.: ref, 2065 (25)
Frankowski, J. J.: ref, 1903 (121)
Franks, J. R.: ref, 1096 (1), 1612 (1), 2485 (3), 2862 (10)
Franks, R.: ref, 2305 (4)
Fransella, F.: test, 1133
Franssen, E.: ref, 1164 (156), 2125 (26), 2860 (1295)
Frantz, T. T.: rev, 1841, 2264
Franz, C. E.: ref, 68 (25), 1414 (1)
Franzen, M. D.: rev, 2225; ref, 1525 (22), 1697 (386,422), 2860 (1100), 2863 (328)
Franzoi, S. L.: rev, 1290
Frary, R. B.: rev, 264, 1102, 1672, 2207
Fraser, B. J.: test, 1254; rev, 2714; ref, 1254 (1)
Fraser, E. D.: rev, 2485, 2862
Fraser, K. P.: ref, 2065 (30), 2813 (110)
Frassinetti, F.: ref, 2516 (33), 2860 (843)
Frasure-Smith, N.: ref, 2497 (466)
Fratiglioni, L.: ref, 1525 (18), 2860 (563,888), 2863 (416)
Frattali, C.: test, 629
Frattola, L.: ref, 2860 (173)
Frazer, N.: ref, 2497 (353)
Frazier, J.: ref, 2305 (134)

Frazier, J. A.: ref, 451 (116), 2288 (68,71), 2289 (52,56), 2305 (103,242), 2862 (475,493,501,629)
Frazier, P. A.: ref, 337 (74,117,198), 1590 (52)
Frazier, P. H.: ref, 998 (5), 1338 (3)
Frazier, R.: ref, 472 (11)
Frazier, S. E.: ref, 694 (74), 2076 (3)
Frederick, C.: ref, 1735 (11), 2076 (178), 2218 (113)
Frederick, C. M.: ref, 893 (33,53) 1735 (8)
Frederick, R. I.: test, 2802
Frederickson, N.: test, 1980
Frederiksen, N.: rev, 838, 1042
Fredman, G.: ref, 1765 (11)
Fredman, N.: rev, 618
Free, M. L.: ref, 1697 (442)
Freeark, K.: ref, 1612 (25)
Freebairn, L.: ref, 540 (21), 1095 (11,46), 1394 (12), 2680 (4), 2695 (67), 2704 (5), 2706 (2), 2732 (2), 2864 (29), 2905 (25,113)
Freeberg, A. L.: ref, 1010 (95)
Freeberg, N. E.: test, 972
Freed, D. B.: ref, 2008 (9), 2873 (33)
Freed, J.: ref, 4 (11)
Freedenfeld, R. N.: ref, 2603 (289), 2749 (45,55)
Freedman, A. H.: ref, 451 (82,83), 1000 (94,95), 2230 (11)
Freedman, M.: ref, 776 (2,6,13), 1218 (6), 1903 (275), 2163 (168), 2305 (100), 2860 (205), 2863 (51,196), 2892 (123)
Freedman, R.: ref, 2305 (4)
Freedom, D. S.: ref, 451 (20), 472 (26), 2214 (16)
Freeland, D.: ref, 2892 (81)
Freeman, A.: ref, 1687 (6)
Freeman, B. J.: rev, 451, 2864; ref, 234 (2), 2813 (64)
Freeman, C.: ref, 1079 (35)
Freeman, C. M.: ref, 451 (80)
Freeman, C. P.: ref, 2050 (91)
Freeman, F. S.: rev, 324
Freeman, G. K.: ref, 2892 (126)
Freeman, H. R.: ref, 298 (110)
Freeman, J.: ref, 994 (31), 1903 (427), 2163 (161), 2485 (128), 2768 (31), 2862 (405)
Freeman, L. N.: ref, 451 (117)
Freeman, N.: ref, 811 (1)
Freeman, N. H.: ref, 349 (22), 350 (25), 2862 (311), 2864 (76)
Freeman, R.: ref, 1517 (12), 2305 (201)
Freeman, V. S.: ref, 592 (33)
Freer, C.: ref, 1671 (4), 1767 (3)
Freese, P. R.: ref, 798 (10), 1903 (146), 2725 (1), 2860 (409)
Freeston, M. H.: ref, 2065 (16)
Freides, D.: rev, 2485, 2862; ref, 2860 (1096), 2892 (228)
Freidl, W.: ref, 2860 (525), 2892 (88)
Freigang, B.: ref, 451 (256)
Freiheit, S. R.: ref, 1697 (484)
Freilinger, J. J.: rev, 230, 232
Freitag, P. K.: rev, 645
Fremaux, D.: ref, 272 (126,291)
Fremouw, W.: ref, 142 (2), 272 (102), 462 (17)
French, C. C.: ref, 272 (172), 999 (192), 1671 (1), 1899 (1), 2163 (45), 2497 (63,509,555,588)
French, J. L.: test, 1196; rev, 693
French, J. W.: test, 1405; rev, 726, 865, 1312, 1920
French, L. A.: ref, 853 (10), 2749 (32)
French, R. L.: rev, 1115, 2835
French, S. J.: rev, 46
Frenkel, E.: ref, 2305 (80)
Frenken, J.: test, 2396
Frentz, J.: ref, 451 (260), 1010 (84), 2211 (42), 2862 (377)
Freo, U.: ref, 2485 (234), 2860 (1155)
Frescka, E.: ref, 2288 (70), 2289 (55), 2305 (181)
Frese, B. H.: ref, 462 (8)
Fressola, D. R.: test, 2470
Fretz, B. R.: rev, 408, 1808
Freudenthaler, H. H.: ref, 2163 (180,230)
Freukel, M.: ref, 2603 (410)
Freund, J. H.: test, 693
Freund, J. S.: ref, 1405 (3)
Freund, L.: ref, 2813 (116)
Freund, L. S.: ref, 681 (66), 2860 (351), 2862 (393), 2901 (72)
Frey, J.: ref, 1000 (54)
Frey, P. D.: ref, 815 (37), 2704 (38)
Frey, P. W.: test, 948
Frick, P. J. : test, 651; ref, 246 (2), 451 (153), 651 (1,2), 1380 (1), 1592 (25), 1697 (272), 2211 (33), 2214 (45), 2862 (131, 348,528,551)
Frick, R. W.: ref, 1156 (1), 2879 (5)
Frick, U.: ref, 2603 (525)
Fricke, B. G.: rev, 615, 1101, 1188
Fridhandler, B.: ref, 2603 (187,266)
Fridjhon, P.: ref, 1991 (16), 2163 (51), 2860 (223)
Fridlund, A. J.: test, 375
Fridrich, A.: ref, 451 (36)
Fried, B.: ref, 863 (32), 2603 (161)
Fried, H. S.: ref, 2437 (1)
Fried, J.: test, 741
Fried, J. E.: ref, 451 (220), 1216 (108)
Fried, J. H.: ref, 2527 (1)
Friedberg, L.: ref, 298 (32), 893 (4)
Friedel, L. A.: ref, 1212 (1)
Friedhoff, A. J.: ref, 790 (26), 2076 (173)
Friedland, J. G.: test, 37, 2265
Friedlander, Y.: ref, 1010 (136), 1661 (83)
Friedler, Y.: ref, 2163 (46)
Friedlinger, M.: ref, 1166 (202)
Friedman, A.: ref, 2749 (26,27,37)
Friedman, B.: ref, 2758 (1), 2860 (737)
Friedman, C. B.: ref, 592 (3)
Friedman, D.: ref, 1740 (19), 2146 (14)f, 2860 (621,884,1260), 2892 (270)
Friedman, E. S.: ref, 1166 (207), 2305 (233), 272 (73), 371 (1), 998 (6), 999 (66), 2218 (11), 2496 (2), 2497 (291)

Friedman, I. A.: ref, 1590 (46)
Friedman, J. L.: test, 1041
Friedman, J. M. H.: ref, 1166 (1), 2305 (12)
Friedman, J. M. K.: ref, 2603 (105)
Friedman, K. E.: ref, 891 (1)
Friedman, L.: test, 2781, 1697 (388), 2050 (115), 2218 (4), 2305 (225)
Friedman, L. C.: ref, 791 (3,10), 2117 (3)
Friedman, L. S.: ref, 863 (17)
Friedman, M. A.: ref, 2076 (170)
Friedman, M. I.: test, 546, 2027
Friedman, P. H.: test, 1057
Friedman, R.: ref, 1338 (30), 1991 (64), 2497 (182,255)
Friedman, R. A.: ref, 1093 (86,87), 1166 (120,129)
Friedman, R. B.: ref, 1903 (525), 2864 (134), 2879 (205)
Friedman, R. J.: ref, 451 (46,162,180)
Friedman, R. S.: ref, 1093 (5)
Friedman, S.: ref, 1140 (60), 1592 (28)
Friedman, S. J.: ref, 926 (18), 1318 (1), 1506 (1), 1592 (22)
Friedmann, M. S.: ref, 68 (29)
Friedmann, R.: ref, 2305 (78), 2860 (452)
Friedrich, F. J.: ref, 776 (31)
Friedrich, S.: ref, 68 (53)
Friedrich, V.: ref, 1164 (60), 1697 (275), 2305 (98)
Friedrich, W.: ref, 853 (18), 997 (19), 1903 (298), 2039 (13)
Friedrich, W. N.: test, 457; ref, 451 (291), 472 (235), 815 (5), 1000 (65), 1522 (2), 2862 (129), 2879 (33)
Friedt, L. R.: ref, 301 (4)
Friel, J. P.: ref, 1213 (1), 1333 (5)
Friend, M.: rev, 1884
Friend, R.: ref, 998 (75,76), 2497 (140,473), 2603 (282,283), 2858 (78,79)
Frier, B. M.: ref, 127 (3), 1164 (160), 1758 (38)
Fries-Dias, C.: ref, 2599 (28)
Friesen, W. V.: test, 1001
Frigo, M.: ref, 2860 (173)
Friman, P.: ref, 997 (15)
Frisbie, D. A.: test, 1318; rev, 118, 617; ref, 1318 (2)
Frisby, C.: ref, 2813 (110)
Frisby, C. L.: ref, 705 (4)
Frisch, G. R.: ref, 2603 (292)
Frisch, M. B.: test, 2131; ref, 2879 (117)
Frisell, W. R.: rev, 45
Frishman, W. H.: ref, 1058 (2), 2860 (152)
Frisk, V.: ref, 2662 (1), 2860 (176,177,255), 2863 (46,47)
Frisman, L.: ref, 337 (184)
Frisoni, G. B.: ref, 337 (54)
Frist, W. H.: ref, 2076 (117)
Fristad, M.: ref, 2107 (1)
Fristad, M. A.: ref, 681 (14)
Fristoe, M.: test, 1095, 1096; ref, 1903 (407)
Frith, C. D.: ref, 2050 (72,89,138), 2146 (19,20), 2239 (12), 2860 (190)
Frith, U.: test, 1980; ref, 350 (7), 926 (16), 1485 (21), 2858 (70), 2860 (528), 2862 (257)
Frith, V.: ref, 349 (36)
Fritsch, R. C.: ref, 1902 (62)
Fritsch, R. C.: ref, 2860 (787), 2862 (298), 2879 (96)
Fritz, G. K.: ref, 2214 (46)
Fritz, J.: ref, 1883 (1)
Fritze, J.: ref, 1166 (50)
Fritzsche, B. A.: test, 2360
Froehlich, C. P.: rev, 2797
Froehlich, G. J.: rev, 2742
Froelich, G. J.: rev, 1319
Fromm, D.: test, 629; ref, 2873 (37)
Fromme, K.: ref, 2076 (84,149)
Frone, M. R.: ref, 1181 (18), 2603 (17,579)
Frost, A. G.: ref, 998 (100), 1036 (13)
Frost, A. K.: ref, 451 (8), 472 (5)
Frost, C. J.: ref, 272 (75)
Frost, F.: ref, 2603 (205)
Frost, J. A.: ref, 2860 (1041)
Frost, R.: ref, 272 (199)
Frueh, B. C.: ref, 846 (19), 1697 (410,516,543), 2247 (86)
Fry, E. B.: rev, 82
Fry, M. A.: rev, 2219
Fry, P. S.: ref, 1590 (47)
Fry, R. T.: test, 2262
Frydenberg, E.: test, 72; ref, 25 (1), 72 (2), 2858 (66)
Frye, B. J.: ref, 1072 (19)
Frye, D.: ref, 1903 (512)
Frye, L. H.: ref, 2603 (277)
Fryns, J. P.: ref, 373 (27,43), 451 9289), 2860 (832), 2862 (65,324), 2864 (8,82)
Fucci, B. R.: ref, 2211 (36), 2603 (337)
Fuchs, C.: ref, 451 (226), 472 (216), 1903 (359), 2211 (40), 2214 (126)
Fuchs, D.: test, 1715; rev, 560, 561, 1101, 665 (76,93), 2211 (3,4,14), 2484 (3), 2487 (19), 2682 (13), 2905 (121)
Fuchs, L. S.: test, 1715; rev, 207; ref, 665 (76,93), 2211 (3,4,14), 2484 (3), 2487 (19), 2905 (22)
Fuchs-Beauchamp, K. D.: ref, 2485 (86), 2754 (4)
Fudala, J. B.: test, 175
Fudala, P. J.: ref, 2703 (1)
Fudge, H.: ref, 2305 (36,224)
Fudge, R.: ref, 2288 (74)
Fuehrer, A.: ref, 298 (74)
Fuentes, F.: ref, 459 (8), 1903 (81), 2485 (36,37)
Fuerst, D.: ref, 376 (4)
Fuerst, D. R.: ref, 2862 (683), 2879 (220)
Fuertes, J. N.: ref, 592 (55)
Fugate, M. H.: rev, 270, 1476, 2001
Fuggle, P.: ref, 349 (32), 1079 (72), 1765 (29)
Fuh, J.: ref, 301 (38), 2860 (622)
Fuhrer, M. J.: ref, 2417 (16)
Fuhrman, R. W.: ref, 372 (88)
Fuhrman, T.: ref, 1000 (84)
Fujihara, S.: ref, 999 (72)

Fujii, D. E.: ref, 1469 (8), 2860 (1081)
Fujii, T.: ref, 303 (28), 2163 (352), 2226 (40), 2227 (56), 2860 (1388), 2863 (419), 2892 (298)
Fujiki, M.: rev, 2428; ref, 430 (2), 540 (15), 1240 (43), 1424 (3), 1607 (15), 1903 (11,79,464), 2452 (12), 2657 (1), 2694 (2), 2695 (7,52), 2704 (39), 2768 (2), 2801 (1), 2860 (458,577), 2862 (130,476,597), 1060 (1)
Fujimori, M.: ref, 2873 (73)
Fujimoto, Y.: ref, 2860 (1169)
Fujino, D. C.: ref, 1093 (116)
Fujioka, T. A.: ref, 2860 (1039), 2862 (438)
Fujita, F.: ref, 2218 (76)
Fujito, K.: ref, 1010 (34)
Fukatsu, R.: ref, 303 (28), 2163 (352), 2226 (40), 2227 (56), 2860 (1388), 2863 (419), 2892 (298)
Fukui, T.: ref, 2076 (174)
Fukumoto, A.: ref, 1903 (376)
Fukunaga, C.: ref, 2749 (53)
Fukunishi, I.: ref, 1010 (34,48), 1166 (108), 1219 (1), 1697 (286), 2076 (150,171)
Fukuuchi, Y.: ref, 2860 (1296)
Fukuyama, M. A.: ref, 404 (7)
Fuld, P. A.: test, 1058
Fulero, S. M.: rev, 1174
Fulia, R.: ref, 2132 (2)
Fulker, D.: ref, 2039 (22)
Fulker, D. W.: ref, 270 (48), 451 (73,118,252), 472 (221), 798 (21), 1392 (10), 1902 (50,80), 2382 (6,16), 2485 (244), 2860 (1018), 2862 (228,2862)
Fulkerson, J. A.: ref, 451 (42), 1000 (71), 1832 (16)
Fullard, W.: test, 425
Fuller, B.: ref, 1216 (82)
Fuller, B. E.: ref, 1755 (61)
Fuller, D.: ref, 2860 (146)
Fuller, G. B.: test, 1699; ref, 301 (30), 665 (77), 1226 (3), 1699 (1,2), 2704 (9), 2862 (411,569,614), 2879 (147)
Fuller, J. B.: ref, 1736 (4)
Fuller, K. H.: ref, 2497 (334), 2860 (1367)
Fuller, M.: ref, 2862 (337), 2879 (114)
Fuller, M. G.: ref, 1661 (42)
Fuller, M. L.: ref, 2484 (13)
Fuller, T.: ref, 472 (27)
Fullerton, C. S.: ref, 337 (150), 1093 (5), 2603 (200,378,420)
Fultz, J.: ref, 448 (17)
Funari, D. J.: ref, 1697 (233)
Funder, D. C.: ref, 372 (88), 373 (26,38), 2218 (30)
Funderburk, B.: ref, 864 (3), 997 (12), 1987 (7), 2752 (1)
Funders, B.: ref, 2860 (1202), 2862 (578)
Fung, A. S. M.: ref, 694 (117), 2497 (570)
Funk, S. G.: ref, 175 (9), 430 (7), 1047 (3), 2651 (13), 2695 (21), 2860 (1143)
Funkenstein, H.: test, 1665
Fuqua, D. R.: ref, 404 (1,8,29), 413 (3,8), 1140 (11), 1754 (1,9), 2497 (6,23,80)
Furac, C. J.: ref, 372 (79), 694 (64), 1321 (7), 1697 (248)
Furby, A.: ref, 2163 (214), 2860 (868)
Furey, M. L.: ref, 2485 (234), 2860 (1155,1216), 2879 (190)
Furfey, P. H.: rev, 2813
Furlong, M.: rev, 1832, 2452
Furlong, M. J.: rev, 451, 1275
Furman, J. M.: ref, 998 (53), 2497 (562)
Furnham, A.: ref, 272 (55), 372 (47), 999 (11,87), 1755 (25), 2160 (1)
Furniss, E.: rev, 773
Furr, A.: ref, 1099 (4), 1962 (22), 2862 (590), 2879 (193)
Furst, D. W.: ref, 2559 (3)
Furst, E. J.: rev, 1790, 2686
Furstenberg, F. F.: ref, 1216 (26), 1903 (154)
Furukawa, T.: ref, 1079 (25,88), 2163 (335), 2226 (30), 2227 (47), 2860 (1317)
Furukawo, M.: ref, 1903 (293)
Furuno, S.: test, 1192
Furuta, M.: ref, 2862 (638)
Furuya, T.: ref, 2862 (673)
Fury, G.: ref, 451 (190), 2862 (615)
Fusco, J.: ref, 2813 (137)
Fuss, J.: ref, 2862 (409), 2905 (92)
Futcher, W. G. A.: test, 2649
Futihara, S.: ref, 273 (26)
Fydrich, T.: ref, 2497 (168)
Fyer, A. J.: ref, 1592 (7), 2218 (96), 2305 (34,132,147)
Fyer, M. R.: ref, 824 (4), 1093 (62)

Gaa, J. P.: ref, 1000 (34)
Gaa, R.: ref, 1755 (58)
Gabardi, L.: ref, 2115 (2)
Gabbard, C.: ref, 353 (17)
Gabel, D. L.: ref, 592 (14)
Gabel, S.: ref, 451 (118), 462 (18), 1661 (43), 1697 (30)
Gable, R. K.: test, 2321; rev, 1136, 1631, 1720, 2293, 2358
Gabler, E. R.: rev, 374
Gabrieli, D. E.: ref, 2163 (339)
Gabrieli, J. D. E.: ref, 2860 (623,1347), 2863 (182,405)
Gabrielli, W. F.: ref, 2076 (25)
Gabriels, T.: ref, 998 (111)
Gacono, C. B.: ref, 2247 (14,67,119,124), 2402 (7), 2860 (256), 2862 (676)
Gaddis, L. R.: rev, 4, 70, 2040, 2043
Gade, A.: ref, 2860 (178)
Gadian, D. G.: ref, 2860 (838), 2863 (243)
Gadish, O.: ref, 644 (1), 999 (23)
Gadow, K. D.: test, 79, 876; ref, 681 (53,54), 2862 (338)
Gadzella, B. M.: ref, 2856 (11)
Gaeddert, W.: ref, 298 (19)
Gaffan, D.: ref, 2227 (38), 2860 (1279), 2863 (385)
Gaffan, E. A.: ref, 1066 (1)
Gage, M. G.: ref, 2034 (5)

Gage, N. L.: rev, 2484
Gage, P.: ref, 2899 (1)
Gagliese, L.: ref, 1697 (349), 2497 (392)
Gagné, F.: ref, 1866 (29), 2485 (129)
Gagne, M.: ref, 68 (8)
Gagnon, C.: ref, 1340 (2), 1866 (33), 2039 (17), 2862 (321)
Gagnon, M.: ref, 2860 (930), 2863 (90)
Gaier, D. J.: ref, 1645 (1), 2860 (101)
Gaier, E. L.: rev, 2102; ref, 666 (13)
Gaines, R.: ref, 811 (9), 1086 (4)
Gaines, R. W.: ref, 1181 (26)
Gainotti, G.: ref, 1166 (185), 2163 (151), 2892 (113)
Gaitens, T.: ref, 451 (256)
Gajria, M.: ref, 1072 (29)
Galai, N.: ref, 1135 (16,22), 1164 (169), 2226 (35), 2227 (21,50), 2599 (32)
Galal, O.: ref, 2163 (308), 2860 (1197), 2862 (415)
Galambos, N. L.: ref, 2497 (198)
Galanter, M.: ref, 1697 (122)
Galasko, D.: ref, 776 (34), 2860 (184), 2862 (105)
Galassi, J. P.: test, 88; rev, 2655, 2656; ref, 337 (68)
Galbraith, G. C.: ref, 2163 (111)
Galda, L.: ref, 1903 (28,87,404)
Galderisi, S.: ref, 1525 (10)
Galen, L. W.: ref, 2879 (204)
Galilee-Weisstub, E.: ref, 337 (188)
Galin, D.: ref, 1072 (1), 1131 (1), 2862 (1)
Gall, N. G.: ref, 182 (1), 2008 (4), 2860 (311)
Gall, T. L.: ref, 2603 (526)
Gallacher, F.: ref, 298 (141), 1021 (33), 2017 (6), 2288 (25,48,75), 2289 (14,37,62)
Gallacher, J. E. J.: ref, 2497 (205)
Gallagher, A. M.: ref, 592 (56)
Gallagher, B. B.: ref, 641 (4,5), 2076 (19,118), 2227 (11,20), 2517 (4), 2599 (30), 2860 (198), 2863 (136)
Gallagher, D.: ref, 1903 (290)
Gallagher, R.: ref, 2873 (15)
Gallagher, R. W.: ref, 1697 (544)
Gallagher, S. A.: ref, 615 (33,34), 705 (5), 1755 (3), 2163 (84)
Gallagher, T. M.: ref, 1903 (212), 2695 (22), 2704 (14)
Gallagher-Thompson, D.: ref, 272 (51), 337 (38), 2417 (15)
Gallaher, P. E.: rev, 262, 1309
Gallant, S. J.: ref, 2603 (95)
Gallassi, R.: ref, 2768 (34), 2860 (1082)
Galletly, C.: ref, 1164 (147)
Galletly, C. A.: ref, 2603 (243)
Galli, I.: ref, 298 (67)
Gallimore, R.: ref, 2813 (118)
Gallo, P.: ref, 2227 (52)
Gallo, S. : ref, 615 (21)
Gallops, M. S.: ref, 2305 (34)
Galloway, D.: ref, 561 (2)
Galloway, P. H.: ref, 1390 (5), 2860 (970)
Galloway, S.: ref, 1218 (16), 2599 (35), 2863 (317)
Gallucci, N. T.: ref, 1697 (215,287), 2485 (8), 2862 (39)
Galluccio, L.: ref, 376 (17), 2227 (32), 2860 (1166), 2892 (268)
Gallup, P.: ref, 337 (184)
Galotti, K. M.: ref, 2484 (7)
Galper, A.: ref, 1902 (103), 1903 (522), 2901 (116,140)
Galski, T.: ref, 2163 (323), 2227 (36) 2860 (352,1266), 2863 (93)
Galvin, G. A.: rev, 916, 1269, 2037, 2862 (73)
Galvin, M. R.: ref, 451 (191)
Galvin, P. P.: test, 294
Galynker, I.: ref, 1166 (186)
Gamache, L. M.: rev, 2312
Gambetti, P.: ref, 2768 (34), 2860 (1082)
Gamble, W. C.: ref, 451 (192), 2497 (335)
Gandard, M.: ref, 615 (32)
Gandolfo, P.: ref, 893 (29)
Gandolfo, R.: ref, 1021 (38), 1697 (485), 2497 (526)
Gandour, J.: ref, 1490 (1)
Ganellen, R. J.: rev, 291, 828, 2522; ref, 1697 (288), 2247 (62)
Gangadhar, B. N.: ref, 1166 (87)
Gange, S. J.: ref, 1745 (30)
Gangestad, S. W.: ref, 999 (45,64)
Gangitano, M.: ref, 2860 (1051)
Gangoli, R.: ref, 2305 (133)
Ganguli, H. C.: rev, 427, 2491
Ganguli, R.: ref, 2305 (63)
Gannaway, T. W.: test, 2836
Gannon, L.: ref, 2076 (80)
Ganor, Y.: ref, 745 (16), 2163 (199)
Ganschow, L.: ref, 541 (1), 547 (1), 1503 (12,15), 1767 (6), 1903 (360,422,496,497,555), 2668 (2), 2693 (7), 2694 (22), 2695 (62), 2731 (1,3), 2860 (257), 2862 (557), 2879 (34,115,141,182,219), 2880 (7), 2901 (17,62,101,128), 2905 (74,90,106,107)
Gansler, D. A.: ref, 1218 (2), 1697 (91), 2497 (74), 2860 (1083), 2892 (226)
Ganster, D. C.: ref, 998 (80)
Gantoos, P.: ref, 451 (145)
Ganz, P. A.: ref, 863 (8), 2603 (61)
Ganzach, Y.: ref, 592 (17), 1697 (545)
Ganzell, S.: ref, 1645 (1), 2860 (101)
Gara, M. A.: ref, 270 (17), 272 (173), 2305 (163)
Garamoni, G.: ref, 1093 (78)
Garamoni, G. G.: ref, 1093 (79)
Garamoni, G. L.: ref, 793 (14)
Garbarino, J.: ref, 451 (119)
Garber, J.: ref, 472 (35,36,124,143,223), 2603 (327,580)
Garber, N.: ref, 175 (2), 1040 (2), 1095 (2), 1982 (2)
Garbin, C. D.: ref, 1619 (5), 2050 (43), 2603 (206), 2892 (83)
Garbin, C. P.: rev, 1610, 2009; ref, 1697 (47)
Garbutt, J. C.: ref, 2305 (53)

Garcia, B. F.: ref, 2603 (591)
Garcia, C. I.: ref, 2656 (1)
Garcia, E. E.: rev, 307, 1527, 1534
Garcia, J. M.: ref, 209 (4)
Garcia, M. C. M.: ref, 2247 (72)
Garcia, T.: test, 1720; ref, 1720 (2)
Garcia-Sevilla, J. A.: ref, 1166 (109)
García-Vázquez, E.: ref, 2862 (258)
Gard, F.: ref, 1104 (8)\, 1758 (39)
Gard, T. L.: ref, 2858 (106)
Garden, A. M.: ref, 1755 (4)
Gardener, J. E.: test, 1844
Gardiner, P. A.: test, 2224
Gardiner, W. L.: test, 704
Gardner, D. A.: ref, 2873 (49)
Gardner, D. G.: ref, 1701 (5)
Gardner, E.: rev, 1319
Gardner, E. F.: test, 82, 2484, 2487; rev, 25, 1058, 1119, 1137, 1196, 1568, 1659, 2304
Gardner, J.: ref, 1697 (451)
Gardner, J. M.: ref, 2860 (1229)
Gardner, J. M. M.: ref, 1134 (6), 1216 (64), 1903 (361)
Gardner, J. O.: test, 1171
Gardner, M. F.: test, 994, 2190, 2665, 2673, 2723, 2724
Gardner, P. D.: ref, 1701 (34)
Gardner, R. A.: test, 1070, 2210
Gardner, R. C.: ref, 950 (2,3), 1321 (3), 2497 (42,125,126)
Gardner, S.: test, 726
Garely, L.: ref, 944 (1)
Garety, P. A.: ref, 1758 (24), 2050 (71), 2860 (624)
Garfinkel, A.: rev, 250, 1235, 2139, 2688
Garfinkel, B. D.: ref, 472 (22), 2214 (13)
Garfinkel, P. E.: ref, 893 (18)
Garfinkle, J. R.: ref, 272 (272), 2218 (94), 2497 (630)
Gariboldi, A.: ref, 1216 (29)
Garis, J. W.: ref, 404 (15)
Garland, A. F.: ref, 451 (120), 472 (84)
Garland, C.: test, 2423
Garland, D.: test, 2007
Garland, M. A.: ref, 2863 (127)
Garlinski, J. H.: ref, 2603 (354)
Garman, M.: test, 2228
Garmezy, N.: ref, 1902 (74)
Garmon, L. C.: ref, 771 (24)
Garn-Nunn, P. G.: ref, 175 (3), 214 (2,10), 1040 (3), 1095 (3,8), 1394 (2), 1982 (3), 2651 (5), 2866 (1)
Garneau, Y.: ref, 650 (15), 1093 (97)
Garner, D. M.: test, 893
Garner, E. H.: ref, 1698 (24)
Garner, P. W.: ref, 1001 (16), 1010 (61), 2704 (10)
Garner, R.: rev, 189
Garner, R. D.: ref, 2497 (265), 2863 (142)
Garnet, K. E.: ref, 1093 (46)
Garnier, H.: ref, 2813 (118)
Garnier, H. E.: ref, 2862 (616)
Garretson, H. B.: ref, 1612 (12), 1903 (53)
Garrett, H. E.: rev, 1414
Garrett, K. K.: ref, 214 (11)
Garrett, P.: ref, 180 (17,28), 1216 (47,48,49,63), 1903 (357)
Garrod, A.: ref, 998 (93), 2050 (116)
Garrod, A. C.: ref, 1408 (5)
Garron, D. C.: ref, 272 (372), 2076 (185)
Garside, D.: test, 667
Garske, J. P.: ref, 1697 (4)
Garthoeffner, J. L.: ref, 1000 (91), 1297 (1), 2497 (510)
Gartland, H. J.: ref, 863 (27), 2211 (15)
Gartner, A. F.: ref, 1093 (32)
Gartner, J. D.: ref, 1093 (32)
Garton, A. F.: ref, 451 (128)
Garver, D. L.: ref, 2305 (153)
Garvey, J. J.: ref, 272 (174), 1166 (110)
Garvey, M.: ref, 2305 (17)
Garvey, M. J.: ref, 998 (41), 1093 (42), 1166 (203), 1697 (167,173), 1705 (3), 2076 (157), 2516 (107), 2860 (1327)
Garvill, J.: ref, 2860 (439)
Garvin, V.: ref, 337 (57,58), 451 (12), 1000 (46,47), 1178 (7), 2603 (502)
Gaskell, G.: ref, 2 (1), 2813 (90)
Gaskin, V. T.: ref, 2813 (110)
Gaskins, I. W.: ref, 1657 (15), 2862 (259), 2879 (116)
Gaskins, R. W.: ref, 1657 (15), 2879 (116)
Gasparini, F.: ref, 1166 (185)
Gasperini, M.: ref, 2497 (505), 2603 (255)
Gass, C. S.: ref, 1697 (289,386,486,487,546), 2860 (1254,1267), 2862 (712), 2863 (318,381)
Gass, K. A.: ref, 2858 (7)
Gast, D. L.: ref, 265 (7), 811 (4), 1902 (27), 2694 (5), 2862 (144,212), 2905 (18)
Gasto, C.: ref, 998 (35), 1164 (70), 2860 (681), 2863 (201), 2305 (238)
Gatchel, R. J.: ref, 1697 (411)
Gates, A. I.: test, 1073
Gates, E. E.: rev, 2614
Gath, D.: ref, 998 (71,93), 2050 (35,76,116)
Gathercole, S. E.: ref, 349 (1,2), 350 (2,4,22,27,28), 1612 (63,69), 2163 (47,64,213)
Gatherum, A.: ref, 1000 (101), 1010 (113)
Gatlin, D. F.: ref, 1902 (9), 2485 (17), 2862 (77)
Gatto, N.: ref, 272 (300)
Gatz, M.: ref, 337 (33)
Gaudin, J. M., Jr.: ref, 458 (1)
Gaudino, E. A.: ref, 1164 (92)
Gaudreau, D.: ref, 2125 (25), 2860 (1256)
Gauger, L. M.: ref, 540 (19), 994 (46), 2695 (66), 2704 (45), 2905 (110)
Gaughan, E.: ref, 1000 (85)
Gaul, R.: ref, 2749 (5)
Gaulin, C. A.: ref, 1240 (25)

Gaultney, J. F.: ref, 1866 (37)
Gaumer, H. R.: ref, 2603 (160)
Gaus, V.: ref, 1735 (6)
Gaustad, M. G.: ref, 1000 (69)
Gauthier, J. G.: ref, 272 (375), 2498 (77)
Gauthier, L.: ref, 2010 (5), 2603 (455)
Gauthier, S.: ref, 776 (52), 1164 (163), 1218 (18), 2010 (5), 2226 (28), 2227 (46)
Gauthier, S. V.: test, 1399
Gauthrer, J. G.: ref, 2519 (37), 2520 (38)
Gavazzi, S. M.: ref, 1000 (77), 2603 (379)
Gavin, D. A. W.: ref, 1738 (1)
Gavin, D. R.: ref, 134 (5,29), 272 (35), 1661 (9)
Gavin, M. B.: ref, 1079 (100)
Gavin, W. J.: ref, 1901 (15), 1903 (465), 2229 (8), 2813 (59)
Gay, E. C.: test, 1217
Gay, G.: ref, 665 (22)
Gay, M. L.: test, 88
Gay, N.: ref, 681 (49), 1903 (276), 2010 (14)
Gayant, C.: ref, 272 (126)
Gaydon, V.: ref, 1991 (16), 2163 (51), 2860 (223)
Gaydos, G. R.: ref, 997 (14)
Gaylord-Ross, R.: ref, 301 (20)
Gayton, W. F.: ref, 272 (230)
Gazadag, G. E.: ref, 2485 (153)
Gazaway, P.: ref, 793 (22)
Gazdag, G. E.: ref, 1485 (37), 2189 (2), 2382 (27)
Gazis, J.: ref, 1687 (15)
Gazzaniga, M. S.: ref, 2860 (1222,1385), 2863 (362,417)
Ge, X.: ref, 451 (121), 2218 (15,58,59), 2603 (244,256,345,355,456,457,458)
Gearhart, L. P.: ref, 771 (19)
Geary, D. C.: ref, 1405 (6,35), 2163 (324), 2864 (9)
Gebart-Eaglemont, J. E.: rev, 1576, 2075
Geckler, C.: ref, 1902 (69), 2768 (28), 2862 (325), 2879 (110)
Geddes, J.: ref, 2050 (72)
Geddes, J. R.: ref, 2050 (91)
Geenan, R.: ref, 2497 (620)
Geer, F. A.: ref, 462 (15)
Geers, A.: ref, 486 (1,2,3), 994 (12), 1126 (1,2), 1127 (1,2), 1903 (258), 2233 (1), 2298 (1,2), 2860 (97), 2862 (260), 2864 (51)
Geers, A. E.: test, 487, 488, 891, 1126, 1127, 2298; ref, 1903 (545), 2813 (150), 2860 (353)
Geerts, E.: ref, 272 (256), 1166 (111,187)
Geffen, G.: ref, 2599 (39), 2860 (1275)
Geffen, G. M.: ref, 641 (8), 1758 (87), 2163 (325), 2226 (22), 2863 (382)
Geffen, L.: ref, 641 (8), 1758 (87), 2163 (325), 2226 (22), 2863 (382)
Geffken, G. R.: ref, 2214 (42), 2497 (332), 2498 (35,46), 2813 (13,47)
Geffner, D.: ref, 1096 (12)
Gehlen, W.: ref, 2163 (200), 2227 (15), 2239 (14), 2860 (492,816), 2863 (138,172,235), 2892 (78,107)
Gehring, T.: test, 1015
Gehrlein, T. M.: ref, 592 (40)
Geiger, M. A.: ref, 1469 (4)
Geisinger, K. F.: rev, 1571, 1763, 1792, 2222, 2738, 2857; ref, 592 (57), 1115 (11)
Geisler, J.: rev, 922, 2643
Geisler, M. W.: ref, 1164 (92)
Geisler, S.: ref, 2288 (45,64), 2305 (123,170)
Geisler, S. H.: ref, 2305 (70), 2860 (333)
Geisler-Bernstein, E.: test, 1307
Geisser, M. E.: ref, 2497 (169)
Geissler, L. J.: ref, 134 (25)
Geissler, T.: ref, 999 (83)
Geist, C. R.: ref, 68 (5)
Geist, H.: test, 1074
Geist, R.: ref, 337 (52)
Geisthardt, C.: ref, 699 (3)
Gejman, P. V.: ref, 2305 (29)
Gekoski, N.: test, 2276
Gekoski, W. L.: ref, 1965 (70), 2525 (11)
Gelade, G.: ref, 142 (5), 682 (3), 1404 (12)
Gelade, G. A.: ref, 2218 (92)
Gelb, F. S.: test, 2500
Gelder, B. C.: ref, 2417 (37)
Gelder, M.: ref, 2519 (56), 2520 (55)
Geldmacher, D.: ref, 2227 (13), 2860 (530), 2863 (151), 2873 (18)
Gelernter, C. S.: ref, 272 (92), 2305 (114), 2497 (114,405)
Gelernter, J.: ref, 2305 (29)
Gelfand, A. N.: ref, 846 (11)
Gelfand, D. M.: ref, 270 (18), 1216 (18)
Gelfand, M. D.: ref, 846 (11)
Gelfin, Y.: ref, 1166 (92)
Gelink, M.: test, 2406
Gelkopf, M.: ref, 1745 (28)
Gellatly, I. R.: ref, 1965 (74)
Geller, B.: ref, 2305 (134)
Geller, D.: ref, 2860 (1203), 2879 (187)
Geller, K.: rev, 1384, 2701
Geller, L.: ref, 2102 (1), 2288 (16), 2289 (11), 2860 (335), 2863 (88)
Geller, R. J.: ref, 353 (6), 1164 (42), 2862 (195)
Gelling, P. D.: ref, 1745 (20), 2860 (361)
Gellman, E. S.: ref, 592 (34)
Geminiani, G.: ref, 2163 (38), 2863 (43)
Gemma, A.: ref, 2163 (328), 2860 (1281)
Gemmill, W. D.: ref, 2214 (93), 2231 (5)
Gençöz, F.: ref, 1903 (523)
Gendlin, E. T.: test, 991
Gendreau, P.: ref, 999 (14), 2603 (25)
General Educational Development Testing Service of the American Council on Education: test, 2742
Genest, M.: ref, 2497 (64,341)
Geni, J.: ref, 2860 (1020)
Genn, M. M.: rev, 317, 466
Gennaro, S.: ref, 270 (2,20), 1745 (12)

Gensheimer, L. K.: ref, 472 (6,39,145)
Gentile, C.: ref, 472 (3), 2214 (3), 2498 (3)
Gentile, J. R.: ref, 994 (40), 2485 (206), 2695 (55), 2864 (119)
Gentilini, M.: ref, 2517 (1), 2860 (527)
Gentry, B.: ref, 1047 (7), 1095 (45), 1902 (98), 2045 (5)
Gentry, N.: ref, 1386 (16)
Gentry, V.: ref, 353 (17)
Genung, L. T.: ref, 2132 (3)
Geoffroy, G.: ref, 2125 (6), 2860 (272), 2862 (135)
George, A.: ref, 2603 (215), 2860 (532)
George, A. A.: ref, 134 (32), 1661 (56)
George, A. E.: ref, 1164 (156), 2125 (26), 2860 (1295)
George, A., Nathan, S.: ref, 1093 (56)
George, B. L.: ref, 2749 (38)
George, C.: ref, 1266 (3)
George, C. E.: ref, 2497 (170)
George, C. J.: ref, 1093 (74,99), 2603 (393)
George, D. T.: ref, 1661 (55), 2305 (27.176), 2497 (626)
George, E. L.: ref, 2603 (527)
George, J. M.: ref, 1701 (15,17,52), 2246 (12)
George, L. K.: ref, 303 (1,2), 791 (2), 1010 (66), 1164 (23), 1740 (3), 2497 (21,104), 2516 (2), 2603 (8,83,321,322), 2858 (86), 2860 (81,237)
George, M. S.: ref, 272 (294), 1166 (199)
George, P.: ref, 451 (168), 1010 (118), 2305 (215), 2862 (592), 2879 (194)
Georgi, J. M.: ref, 1661 (46)
Georgiou, N.: ref, 1758 (88)
Georgotas, A.: ref, 1166 (9)
Geraisy, N.: ref, 335 (8), 2863 (289)
Gerard, A. B.: test, 1883
Gerard, J.: test, 1425; ref, 2862 (398), 2901 (74)
Gerardi, M. A.: ref, 1338 (6), 2497 (20), 2603 (7)
Gerardi, R.: ref, 1338 (6), 2497 (20), 2603 (7)
Gerardi, R. J.: ref, 1697 (290)
Gerber, A.: test, 2650
Gerber, D. K.: ref, 2860 (1020)
Gerber, G. L.: ref, 298 (47)
Gerber, J.: ref, 1903 (24), 2860 (86)
Gerber, K. E.: ref, 1697 (1), 2417 (1)
Gerber, M. F.: test, 759
Gerber, M. M.: ref, 1991 (102)
Gerber, P. J.: ref, 1701 (23)
Gerbing, D. W.: ref, 2417 (12)
Gerdeman, B.: ref, 2225 (2), 2873 (3)
Gerew, A. B.: ref, 1021 (5)
Gergelis, R. E.: ref, 1687 (10)
Gerhard, C.: test, 204
Gerhardt, G. A.: ref, 2305 (4)
Gericke, J. S.: test, 1990
Gerig, T. M.: ref, 364 (13)
Gerken, K. C.: rev, 1363, 2590; ref, 265 (8), 2485 (51), 2864 (27)
Gerken, M. A.: test, 1468
Gerler, E. R.: ref, 771 (1,8)
Gerlsma, C.: ref, 2497 (336), 2603 (182,250)
German, A. E.: test, 2906
German, D. J.: test, 2667, 2725, 2726, 2906
Gerrards-Hesse, A.: ref, 1745 (38)
Gerrish, R.: ref, 2860 (1276)
Gershberg, F. B.: ref, 2860 (862), 2863 (253), 2873 (34), 2892 (179)
Gershkoff-Stowe, L.: ref, 1528 (4)
Gershman, L.: ref, 1021 (9)
Gershon, A.: test, 726
Gershon, E.: ref, 815 (52), 2724 (13)
Gershon, E. S.: ref, 2305 (29)
Gershuny, B. S.: ref, 1661 (73), 2497 (463,467), 2892 (180)
Gerson, A.: ref, 1697 (409)
Gersons, B. P. R.: ref, 2858 (126)
Gerstan, M.: ref, 200 (5)
Gersten, J. C.: ref, 472 (14,38)
Gersten, R.: ref, 364 (3), 665 (78)
Gersten, R. M.: test, 1896
Gerstman, L. J.: ref, 2860 (432)
Gerter, A.: ref, 272 (171), 999 (157), 2497 (554), 2603 (454)
Gerther, B. L.: ref, 1095 (23), 1379 (45), 1903 (259), 2229 (3)
Gerwood, J. B.: ref, 2126 (16)
Gest, S.: ref, 1902 (74)
Gest, S. D.: ref, 557 (4), 2076 (172), 2603 (528)
Getman, G. N.: test, 2821
Getson, P.: test, 1618
Getto, C. J.: test, 2118
Geva, E.: rev, 550; ref, 1903 (177), 2905 (37)
Gewirtz, J. C.: ref, 298 (86)
Geyer, M.: ref, 893 (25), 1079 (48)
Geyer, M. A.: ref, 1093 (13), 2288 (73), 2289 (59), 2305 (35)
Gfeller, J. D.: ref, 1164 (93,141,176), 2498 (23,36), 2860 (863,1224), 2863 (148,183,254,319)
Ghaemi, S. N.: ref, 272 (202), 1166 (133)
Ghalichebuf, M.: ref, 2651 (18)
Ghatala, E. S.: ref, 592 (12), 1903 (41), 2031 (2)
Ghavnani, G.: test, 2240
Ghaziuddin, M.: ref, 353 (12), 2247 (87), 2305 (243), 2710 (4), 2813 (61), 2860 (864,1389), 2862 (261,339)
Ghaziuddin, N.: ref, 353 (12), 2230 (10), 2230 (14), 2305 (243), 2557 (5), 2813 (61), 2860 (1389), 2862 (261)
Ghetti, B.: ref, 2599 (16), 2860 (614), 2863 (180), 2892 (115)
Ghidoni, E.: ref, 2163 (188), 2516 (54), 2768 (26), 2819 (1), 2907 (6)
Ghiselli, E. E.: rev, 1700, 2125
Ghiselli, W.: ref, 1745 (24)
Ghiz, L.: ref, 272 (113)
Ghormley, M. R.: ref, 2402 (67), 2497 (643)
Ghubash, R.: ref, 2050 (73)

Giacometti, K. R.: ref, 1240 (21), 2860 (502)
Giacomoni, F.: ref, 2288 (49), 2289 (38), 2860 (902), 2863 (271)
Giaconia, R. M.: ref, 472 (190)
Giambra, L. M.: ref, 2407 (3), 2860 (865)
Gianakos, I.: ref, 298 (2,8,142)
Giancola, P. R.: ref, 451 (122), 1661 (44), 2010 (24), 2305 (177,244), 2516 (117), 2860 (625,626), 2860 (1390), 2862 (477,713)
Giangreco, M. F.: test, 553; ref, 553 (1)
Giannetti, R. A.: test, 2147
Giannini, A. J.: ref, 2218 (31)
Gianoulakis, C.: ref, 1661 (57)
Gianutsos, J. G.: ref, 1164 (156), 2125 (26), 2860 (1295)
Gibb, C. A.: rev, 1137, 1439, 1444, 1449
Gibbins, S.: ref, 999 (108)
Gibbon, M.: test, 1093, 2519, 2520
Gibbons, B.: ref, 844 (5)
Gibbons, R. D.: ref, 272 (64,111)
Gibbs, D.: ref, 694 (115)
Gibbs, J.: test, 1625
Gibbs, J. C.: ref, 2860 (308)
Gibbs, J. J.: ref, 2603 (96)
Gibbs, N. A.: ref, 2306 (1)
Gibertini, M.: ref, 1687 (14)
Gibson, D. L.: test, 1702
Gibson, H. B.: test, 1087; rev, 2010
Gibson, L.: ref, 1866 (38), 2862 (340)
Gibson, M.: test, 2134
Gibson, R. J.: ref, 694 (111)
Gibson (Robert) & Sons, Glasgow, Ltd.: test, 1864
Gibson, S. J.: ref, 1322 (1)
Gick, M.: ref, 2603 (529)
Giddan, J. J.: test, 202; ref, 542 (1); ref, 994 (23,37), 1903 (362,466), 2695 (35), 2862 (341,654), 2901 (63)
Gidron, Y.: ref, 696 (1)
Gidycz, C. A.: ref, 793 (20), 846 (17), 1697 (493), 2603 (476)
Giedd, J.: ref, 2305 (103,232)
Giedd, J. N.: ref, 451 (102,116,243), 2288 (68), 2289 (52), 2862 (450,475,493,702), 2879 (227)
Giegl, M. L.: ref, 2656 (20)
Giel, R.: ref, 2050 (10)
Gierut, J. A.: ref, 1095 (38), 1485 (51), 2680 (15), 2695 (53)
Giesler, J.: ref, 472 (71), 2214 (35), 2498 (30)
Gift, A. G.: ref, 337 (24), 2497 (115,171)
Gil, K. M.: ref, 1010 (55,66,112), 2603 (46,97,223,321,322,504), 2858 (58,86,122)
Gil-Ad, I.: ref, 2497 (414)
Gilat, I.: ref, 1991 (97)
Gilbar, O.: ref, 337 (25,100)
Gilbert, D. C.: ref, 2497 (175)
Gilbert, D. G.: ref, 1338 (18), 2076 (18)
Gilbert, K.: ref, 1338 (39)
Gilbert, L. A.: test, 1918; ref, 863 (39), 1927 (1)
Gilbert, M.: ref, 472 (46)
Gilbert, M. J.: ref, 1697 (7)
Gilbert, P.: ref, 272 (175,246), 999 (84), 2603 (513)
Gilbert, P. L.: ref, 1135 (9), 1164 (48), 2288 (28), 2289 (19), 2860 (474)
Gilberts, R.: test, 289
Gilbertson, M.: ref, 175 (11), 994 (24), 1903 (363), 2524 (8), 2695 (36), 2704 (23)
Gilbertson, M. W.: ref, 2288 (58)
Gilbreath, C.: test, 2832
Giles, D. E.: ref, 272 (132,136,307), 1166 (80,81,204)
Giles, L.: ref, 1903 (465), 2229 (8)
Giles, W. H.: ref, 2860 (1035), 2892 (216)
Giles-Sims, J.: ref, 1216 (65), 2214 (39)
Gilewski, M.: ref, 272 (51), 337 (38), 2417 (15)
Gilgen, A. R.: ref, 298 (60)
Gilger, J. W.: ref, 798 (9), 1405 (6), 1902 (31,33,35,49), 2163 (85), 2860 (391,533), 2862 (177)
Gilhooly, M. L. M.: ref, 1808 (2)
Gilhooly, M. M. L.: ref, 2858 (128)
Gilinsky, A. S.: ref, 2860 (627)
Gilison, G. J.: ref, 838 (18)
Gill, D. D.: ref, 2860 (500)
Gill, H. S.: ref, 592 (66)
Gill, K. J.: ref, 1164 (20), 1379 (7), 2226 (4), 2892 (23)
Gill, M.: ref, 2050 (32,54)
Gill, N. T.: ref, 694 (12)
Gill, S.: ref, 1318 (4)
Gill, S. J.: ref, 1288 (1)
Gill, W. S.: test, 2559
Gillam, R. B.: rev, 241, 540, 2466, 2543, 2667, 2706; ref, 798 (7,17,23), 799 (2), 1485 (64), 1902 (32,89), 1903 (364), 2682 (12), 2693 (4), 2704 (3,24,43), 2862 (342), 2901 (64), 2911 (1)
Gillard, C. J.: test, 537
Gillard, E.: ref, 1218 (16), 2599 (35), 2863 (317)
Gillaspy, J. A., Jr.: ref, 298 (157)
Gillberg, C.: ref, 234 (1), 303 (8), 459 (19), 1136 (1), 1903 (170), 2163 (218), 2228 (7,18), 2768 (14), 2860 (1214), 2862 (478,617)
Gilleland, K.: ref, 413 (5)
Giller, E. L.: ref, 790 (22), 2497 (119), 2519 (14), 2520 (15)
Gillespie, C.: test, 1085, 1086, 1072 (17)
Gillet, P.: ref, 2862 (329)
Gillette, G. M.: ref, 2305 (53)
Gillette, J. A.: ref, 2010 (18), 2860 (837), 2863 (242)
Gillette, Y.: test, 898
Gilley, D. W.: ref, 776 (43), 1166 (188), 1405 (16), 1740 (20), 2125 (8), 2863 (383)
Gillham, B.: test, 254, 255, 1037
Gilliam, J. E.: test, 223, 1091, 2294 2912
Gilliam, T. C.: ref, 2305 (20) 2305 (49)
Gilliard, D. J.: ref, 1689 (2)
Gillies, R.: ref, 2498 (41)
Gillies, R. M.: ref, 26 (2)
Gilliland, R.: ref, 272 (333), 2860 (1366), 2863 (412)
Gillin, J. C.: ref, 2076 (125), 2305 (32,2305)

Gillis, C. L.: ref, 2076 (51)
Gillis, J. J.: ref, 1902 (49) 2860 (533)
Gillis, J. S.: test, 450; ref, 272 (98), 372 (82), 2078 (7), 2218 (21), 2497 (246)
Gillis, M. K.: ref, 257 (1), 496 (1)
Gillis, R.: ref, 2603 (398)
Gillman, I.: ref, 998 (30), 1947 (2)
Gillon, G.: ref, 1503 (13), 1765 (21), 1903 (365), 2704 (25)
Gillund, B.: ref, 1767 (4)
Gilman, S.: ref, 1164 (154), 2603 (438), 2860 (1040), 2860 (1287)
Gilmartin, B. G.: ref, 999 (2)
Gilmer, J. S.: rev, 780
Gilmor, R. L.: ref, 2288 (4), 2289 (2), 2305 (7), 2860 (63)
Gilmore, A.: test, 21, 25 358, 2100, 2714
Gilmore, E. C.: test, 1092
Gilmore, G.: rev, 1706
Gilmore, J. V.: test, 1092
Gilmore, R.: ref, 2860 (620)
Gilner, F. H.: ref, 337 (59), 2498 (23), 2603 (185), 2863 (148)
Gilpin, M.: ref, 1294 (3), 2533 (1)
Gilroy, F. D.: ref, 272 (156)
Gilsbach, J. M.: ref, 2860 (903)
Gilvarry, K.: ref, 1093 (80), 2050 (98,103)
Gimenez, M. M.: ref, 908 (11)
Gimse, R.: ref, 1164 (148), 2226 (23), 2860 (1268)
Ginanneschi, A.: ref, 2497 (621)
Ginestet, D.: ref, 2516 (73), 2860 (1002)
Gingas, J.: ref, 2497 (647)
Gingras, J.: ref, 272 (326)
Gingrich, D.: ref, 1661 (35,75), 2603 (317,556)
Ginsberg, H. J.: ref, 1612 (35)
Ginsberg, H. P.: ref, 2879 (155)
Ginsberg, J.: ref, 1697 (4)
Ginsberg, R.: ref, 1701 (23)
Ginsburg, G. S.: ref, 2214 (139), 2498 (78)
Ginsburg, H. P.: test, 2681
Ginsburg, M. D.: ref, 2486 (3)
Ginter, D. W.: ref, 2856 (11)
Ginter, E. J.: ref, 2214 (47)
Gioffra, M.: ref, 2860 (244), 2863 (62)
Giordane, B.: ref, 1379 (23)
Giordani, B.: ref, 124 (1), 272 (267), 376 (18), 1166 (107), 1379 (63), 1697 (540,542), 2227 (2), 2402 (62), 2405 (1), 2516 (97), 2603 (438), 2860 (179,1040,1079,1264), 2863 (48,315,380), 2879 (203)
Giordano, P.: ref, 1338 (36,39)
Giordano-Beech, M.: ref, 1735 (6)
Giovagnoli, A. R.: ref, 2163 (270), 2892 (227)
Giovanelli, G.: ref, 2485 (214)
Giovannelli, J.: ref, 451 (264)
Giovannetti, T.: ref, 376 (32), 2860 (1400), 2863 (424)
Giovinazzo, R.: ref, 1092 (18), 2712 (1), 2879 (171), 2905 (98)
Gipson, M.: ref, 2497 (14)
Gipson, M. T.: ref, 2599 (28)
Girard, R.: ref, 1612 (25)
Girdler, S. S.: ref, 760 (2), 2516 (23), 2858 (49)
Girelli, L.: ref, 2163 (271,340)
Girodo, M.: ref, 2603 (98)
Girolametto, L.: ref, 811 (14), 1134 (2), 1240 (44), 1528 (2), 2190 (7), 2382 (13,22), 2485 (224), 2601 (3)
Giron, A.: ref, 2603 (347)
Giron, M.: ref, 1093 (88)
Gironda, F.: ref, 1164 (130), 1903 (489), 2163 (294), 2227 (30), 2695 (58), 2768 (36), 2862 (531), 2880 (4)
Gist, D.: ref, 337 (59), 2603 (185)
Gist, L.: ref, 2497 (612), 2603 (518)
Gist, M. E.: ref, 1107 (7)
Gitelson, I. B.: ref, 1881 (3)
Gitlin, H. L.: ref, 376 (32), 2860 (1400), 2863 (424)
Gitlin, M.: ref, 999 (142), 1697 (188), 2305 (73), 2860 (384)
Gitlin, M. J.: ref, 1093 (89)
Gittens, T.: test, 235
Giuffra, L. A.: ref, 2305 (22)
Giuliano, T. A.: ref, 998 (108)
Giunta, C. T.: ref, 1661 (30), 2603 (183,257)
Giustolisi, L.: ref, 2892 (113), 2163 (151)
Givens, G. D.: ref, 624 (1)
Gjerde, P. F.: ref, 365 (7), 373 (6,28), 2860 (866), 2862 (343), 2864 (87)
Gjerris, A.: ref, 1166 (172)
Gjesme, T.: ref, 2497 (476)
Gjone, H.: ref, 451 (56,193)
Gladis, M. M.: ref, 2305 (101)
Gladsjo, J. A.: ref, 1661 (36)
Gladstone, T. R. G.: ref, 272 (82)
Glaluis, M. F.: ref, 2163 (142)
Glanville, D.: ref, 1991 (107)
Glanz, L. M.: ref, 273 (12)
Glaros, A.: ref, 1697 (35)
Glascoe, F. P.: test, 340, 1890
Glaser, E. M.: test, 2856, 2857
Glaser, R.: ref, 337 (10), 1698 (10), 2076 (57,119)
Glasgow, A.: ref, 451 (235)
Glasgow, C.: test, 2201
Glasgow, R. E.: ref, 776 (14)
Glass, C. R.: ref, 1021 (11), 2497 (157,468,469)
Glass, D. C.: ref, 1590 (50)
Glass, D. R.: ref, 1517 (4)
Glass, M. R.: ref, 1096 (1), 1612 (1), 2485 (3), 2862 (10)
Glass, P.: ref, 2125 (30), 2768 (43), 2864 (144)
Glass, R. M.: ref, 1166 (34)
Glassco, J. D.: ref, 272 (226), 1166 (157), 2497 (596)
Glassman, A. H.: ref, 2076 (113), 2497 (450)
Glaubman, H.: ref, 1903 (524)
Glaubman, R.: ref, 1903 (524)
Glauser, A.: ref, 2214 (47)
Glazebrook, C.: ref, 2050 (139)
Glazer, W. M.: test, 2619

Gleason, J. B.: ref, 2813 (76)
Gleason, M.: ref, 2905 (13)
Gleason, R.: ref, 2076 (34), 2440 (1)
Gleaves, D. H.: ref, 893 (19), 2218 (123), 2603 (356)
Gleibner, O.: ref, 2860 (1392)
Gleiter, C. H.: ref, 1166 (216)
Glenberg, A. M.: ref, 2603 (316)
Glencross, D. J.: ref, 1765 (9), 2860 (180), 2862 (103)
Glenister, J. M.: test, 1231
Glenn, S. W.: ref, 272 (10,52), 1661 (58), 2497 (172)
Glennerster, A.: ref, 1758 (68), 2863 (320)
Glenwick, D. S.: ref, 2531 (3), 2860 (604)
Glenwright, J.: ref, 2497 (372)
Gleser, G. C.: test, 770; rev, 88, 682, 1169, 1535, 2108, 2120, 2108 (2), 2603 (47)
Glez, J. E. J.: ref, 2862 (262)
Glick, I. D.: ref, 1093 (8,28,29), 2108 (1,4)
Glick, M.: ref, 1093 (46), 2247 (13), 2813 (91), 2860 (251,867,1084)
Glick, M. P.: ref, 433 (13), 803 (3), 804 (1), 1653 (27), 1901 (18), 2189 (7)
Glick, S. M.: ref, 2497 (234)
Glidden-Tracey, CE.: ref, 2360 (4)
Glinos, F.: ref, 298 (59)
Glisky, E. L.: ref, 376 (34), 1740 (34), 2860 (32,41,65,98,1414), 2863 (11,15,20,28), 2892 (305)
Glisky, M. L.: ref, 376 (34), 1740 (34), 2860 (1414), 2892 (305)
Glisson, C.: ref, 451 (257)
Glitz, D.: ref, 2497 (97)
Glock, M. D.: rev, 151
Glomb, T. M.: ref, 1348 (14)
Glosser, G.: ref, 776 (59), 1903 (525), 2864 (134), 2879 (205)
Glover, A.: ref, 2038 (5)
Glover, D.: ref, 2485 (201), 2860 (1085)
Glover, G. H.: ref, 2163 (339)
Glover, H.: ref, 1697 (291), 2603 (258)
Glover, J. A.: test, 648; rev, 2223
Glover, R.: ref, 2288 (3)
Glover, R. J.: ref, 771 (21), 1011 (1), 1991 (3)
Glovinsky-Fahsholtz, D.: ref, 1991 (32)
Glue, P.: ref, 999 (121)
Glutting, J.: test, 2536
Glutting, J. J.: test, 1155; ref, 837 (11), 1155 (1), 1457 (3), 2860 (1086), 2861 (2,4), 2862 (263,479,618, 619,650,689,690)
Glynn, S. M.: ref, 1093 (72), 1866 (38), 2050 (95), 2288 (19), 2862 (340)
Glyshaw, K.: ref, 2498 (1)
Gnagey, P. A.: test, 153, 829, 830, 832
Gnagey, T. D.: test, 153, 829, 830, 831, 832, 833
Gnagy, E. M.: ref, 1745 (83)
Gniwesch, L.: ref, 1093 (112), 1166 (120)
Gnocchini, F.: ref, 2813 (122)
Gnys, M. A.: ref, 998 (73)
Gobiet, W.: ref, 2860 (356), 2892 (51)
Gocio, M. Y.: ref, 2862 (118), 2879 (31)
Godber, D.: test, 1601
Goddard, H. H.: test, 2344
Goddard, H. W.: ref, 863 (40)
Godefroy, O.: ref, 1164 (122), 2163 (214), 2860 (868)
Godfrey, H. P. D.: ref, 199 (13), 1745 (35), 2497 (247)
Godfrey Thomson Unit, University of Edinburgh: test, 899, 901, 2409
Godin, K. W.: ref, 2860 (145), 2862 (93)
Godlewski, M. C.: ref, 2860 (781)
Godman, B. A.: rev, 560
Godovy, J. F.: ref, 2076 (102), 2497 (411)
Godsall, R. E.: ref, 776 (37)
Goduka, I. N.: ref, 1370 (1)
Godwin, D. D.: ref, 298 (42), 1881 (1)
Goebel, G.: ref, 2603 (264)
Goebel, H. H.: ref, 376 (33), 2239 (35)
Goehl, H.: test, 2650
Goel, V.: ref, 2860 (869), 2863 (255)
Goelman, H.: ref, 1216 (8)
Goering, P.: ref, 2050 (141)
Goeters, S.: ref, 2516 (52)
Goetsch, V. L.: ref, 2497 (416)
Goetz, C. G.: ref, 1405 (16), 2125 (8)
Goetz, E. T.: ref, 665 (63) 2487 (7)
Goetz, K. M.: ref, 2704 (28), 2905 (78)
Goetz, R.: ref, 337 (31,91), 2603 (279,299)
Goetz, R. R.: ref, 273 (23), 337 (145), 1166 (115), 2603 (366,549)
Goevremont, D. C.: ref, 681 (12), 1903 (106), 2485 (45), 2603 (130,131)
Goff, D. C.: ref, 335 (11), 1093 (64,90), 2519 (17), 2520 (18)
Goffin, B.: ref, 451 (22)
Goffin, R. D.: ref, 1965 (75)
Goffman, L.: ref, 994 (28), 1095 (34), 1485 (41), 1852 (4), 1903 (375), 2543 (1)
Goh, D. S.: ref, 817 (1), 1902 (34), 2486 (1), 2860 (354)
Gohara, A. F.: ref, 1338 (31), 1686 (3)
Goins, J.: ref, 1010 (84), 2211 (42), 2862 (377)
Goisman, R.: ref, 1093 (73), 1517 (9), 2519 (46), 2520 (47)
Goisman, R. M.: ref, 1517 (6), 2305 (135,178)
Goka, R.: ref, 2076 (16)
Goktepe, J. R.: ref, 298 (14)
Gola, T.: ref, 2863 (185)
Gold, A.: ref, 1485 (58), 1653 (28), 2813 (144)
Gold, A. E.: ref, 127 (3), 1758 (38)
Gold, D.: ref, 998 (2), 2163 (310), 2863 (363)
Gold, D. P.: ref, 998 (48,62,94,95), 1164 (40,55), 1661 (27), 2163 (215), 2227 (14), 2863 (112,162,256), 2892 (62,96,181)
Gold, J.: ref, 2892 (162)
Gold, J. M.: ref, 1093 (11,47), 1164 (94,149), 1927 (4,5), 2115 (3), 2193 (16), 2603 (184), 2860 (460, 510,628,871,1269), 2863 (128,384), 2879 (206), 2892 (116,272)

Gold, M.: ref, 376 (20), 1164 (150), 2227 (37), 2860 (870,1270), 2873 (35,64), 2892 (182,273)
Gold, M. V.: ref, 2545 (5)
Gold, P. E.: ref, 2863 (29)
Gold, P. W.: ref, 2305 (27)
Gold, R.: ref, 2497 (410)
Goldberg, A. P.: ref, 2076 (147)
Goldberg, B.: ref, 4 (9)
Goldberg, D.: test, 1079; rev, 2050; ref, 1079 (46), 2050 (124)
Goldberg, D. S.: test, 809
Goldberg, E.: ref, 272 (258), 893 (42), 1405 (39), 1903 (517), 2163 (35), 2862 (595), 2863 (41)
Goldberg, E. H.: ref, 472 (1), 1097 (1)
Goldberg, J.: ref, 1697 (488)
Goldberg, J. F.: ref, 2050 (6)
Goldberg, J. O.: ref, 1697 (435)
Goldberg, J. P.: ref, 893 (23)
Goldberg, L. R.: rev, 372, 1333
Goldberg, M. D.: ref, 2295 (3)
Goldberg, M. E.: ref, 1661 (59)
Goldberg, R.: ref, 2050 (94)
Goldberg, S.: ref, 270 (32), 1086 (3), 1485 (58), 1653 (28), 2076 (105), 2813 (79), 2813 (144)
Goldberg, S. J.: ref, 1178 (1), 2497 (16)
Goldberg, T. E.: ref, 776 (15), 1093 (11,47), 1164 (46,94,149), 2163 (112), 2193 (16), 2516 (24), 2860 (459,460,510,628,871,1269), 2863 (128, 312,384), 2879 (56,206), 2892 (74,116,122,162, 222,272)
Goldberg, W. A.: ref, 863 (5), 1612 (82), 2497 (33)
Goldblatt, V.: ref, 2050 (119)
Golden, C. J.: test, 1524, 1525, 2334, 2516; rev, 1774, 2225; ref, 2860 (1254)
Golden, J.: ref, 745 (4)
Golden, N.: ref, 364 (3)
Golden, R. N.: ref, 4 (16), 1166 (196), 2076 (94,122)
Goldenberg, G.: ref, 2860 (872,873,1271), 2863 (257)
Goldenberg, I.: ref, 1093 (73), 1517 (9), 2305 (135), 2519 (46), 2520 (47)
Goldenberg, I. M.: ref, 2305 (178)
Goldenberg, J. M.: ref, 2305 (189)
Goldfarb, L. P.: ref, 2862 (344)
Goldfarb, S. M.: ref, 451 (191)
Goldfinger, S. M.: ref, 1697 (569,570), 2010 (23), 2860 (1348), 2863 (406), 2879 (216), 2892 (289)
Goldfried, M. R.: ref, 272 (157,180), 991 (2), 2305 (122)
Goldin, L.: ref, 665 (25)
Goldin, L. R.: ref, 2305 (29)
Golding, G.: ref, 1408 (1)
Golding, J. M.: ref, 2050 (3), 2076 (7)
Golding, S. H.: test, 248
Golding, S. J. J.: ref, 128 (3), 2163 (203)
Golding, S. L.: rev, 2115, 2559
Goldkorn, A.: ref, 1164 (181), 1740 (33), 2227 (59), 2860 (1408), 2863 (427)
Goldman, B.: test, 1137
Goldman, B. A.: rev, 284, 407, 1150, 1473, 2212, 2670
Goldman, B. D.: ref, 2485 (52)
Goldman, D.: ref, 999 (31), 1166 (130), 1592 (9), 1697 (135), 2305 (234)
Goldman, H. H.: ref, 2108 (3)
Goldman, M. S.: ref, 272 (283), 372 (112), 999 (88), 2497 (640)
Goldman, R.: test, 1095, 1096; ref, 1386 (26)
Goldman, R. S.: ref, 2163 (65), 2860 (258), 2863 (65), 2892 (34,215)
Goldman, S.: rev, 160; ref, 1166 (181)
Goldman, S. H.: ref, 239 (1), 1701 (27), 1702 (2), 2797 (6), 2835 (12)
Goldman, S. L.: ref, 2497 (337), 2603 (502)
Goldman, S. R.: ref, 665 (12), 1485 (2), 2862 (68)
Goldman, V. J.: ref, 771 (23), 1697 (412)
Goldman, W. P.: ref, 2860 (629)
Goldman-Hall, B. J.: ref, 1000 (38)
Goldmeier, E.: ref, 2860 (607)
Goldney, R. D.: ref, 273 (6), 1079 (10)
Goldschmid, M. L.: test, 674; rev, 560, 561
Goldsmiths-Phillips, J.: ref, 2862 (69), 2905 (3)
Goldstein, A.: ref, 2497 (163)
Goldstein, A. D.: test, 785
Goldstein, A. J.: ref, 337 (75), 2497 (86), 2520 (14)
Goldstein, B. C.: ref, 251 (2), 1234 (3), 1420 (2), 1902 (42)
Goldstein, D.: ref, 472 (30), 615 (31,52), 1274 (2), 2214 (21)
Goldstein, D. J.: ref, 301 (39)
Goldstein, D. L.: ref, 2603 (523)
Goldstein, D. S.: ref, 272 (209), 1164 (131), 2125 (24), 2516 (83), 2863 (343)
Goldstein, F. C.: ref, 776 (36), 1740 (4), 2860 (629,1206)
Goldstein, G.: ref, 798 (11), 1072 (37), 1164 (27), 1379 (46), 1386 (7), 1525 (9,13,14), 2603 (236), 2860 (475,476,565,630,696), 2862 (208), 2863 (163), 2879 (58,71), 2901 (37), 2905 (41,54,59)
Goldstein, H.: ref, 788 (3), 1612 (94)
Goldstein, J. M.: ref, 1093 (12)
Goldstein, L. H.: ref, 272 (109), 2497 (453), 2858 (68), 2860 (99,350), 2892 (50)
Goldstein, M.: ref, 2892 (187)
Goldstein, M. H.: ref, 2860 (1226)
Goldstein, M. J.: ref, 68 (29), 1697 (188), 2050 (17,122,130,137), 2288 (6), 2289 (4), 2305 (73), 2860 (33,384), 2862 (233)
Goldstein, R. B.: ref, 2305 (110,140,223)
Goldstein, S.: ref, 2125 (7), 2516 (16), 2860 (310)
Goldsworthy, C.: test, 1739
Goldwater, L.: ref, 1697 (71)
Golin, A. K.: ref, 2252 (3), 2485 (62), 2606 (5)
Golinkoff, M.: ref, 1166 (10), 1903 (29)
Gollan, J. K.: ref, 272 (184,355), 1093 (68), 1517 (6), 2519 (42), 2520 (42)
Gollnisch, G.: ref, 2218 (93)
Golomb, A.: ref, 451 (137), 2603 (475)

Golomb, J.: ref, 1164 (156), 2125 (26), 2860 (1295)
Golombok, S.: ref, 272 (106,139,152), 1011 (3), 1987 (14), 2497 (442,470,522,538)
Golshan, S.: ref, 2076 (125)
Gomberg, E. S. L.: ref, 1697 (216)
Gombest, J. E.: ref, 2163 (267), 2862 (458)
Gómez, J. C.: ref, 270 (10) 1653 (23)
Gomez, R.: ref, 1903 (467), 2862 (480)
Gomez-Beneyto, M.: ref, 1093 (88)
Gomez-Benito, J.: ref, 624 (7), 1612 (83)
Gomille, J.: ref, 1166 (144)
Gonder-Frederick, L.: ref, 2603 (144)
Gonder-Frederick, L. A.: ref, 2863 (29)
Gondoli, D. M.: ref, 1661 (2)
Gono, S.: ref, 2860 (472)
Gonon, M. A. H.: ref, 2860 (100)
Gonzales, C.: ref, 1218 (5), 2599 (10), 2863 (109), 2892 (59)
Gonzales, M.: ref, 1697 (578)
Gonzales-Aviles, A.: ref, 2010 (18)
Gonzalez, A.: ref, 2862 (85)
Gonzalez, C.: ref, 2553 (4)
González, G.: ref, 2519 (45)
González, M. A.: ref, 1396 (1)
Gonzalez, N.: ref, 2603 (9)
González, P.: ref, 272 (313)
Gonzalez, Rothi, L. J.: ref, 2873 (32)
Gonzalez, V.: ref, 1234 (4), 2704 (18)
Gonzalez-Aviles, A.: ref, 1164 (110), 1740 (11), 2010 (20), 2860 (971)
González-Montalvo, J. I.: ref, 2163 (320), 2860 (1252)
Good, E. S.: ref, 337 (79)
Good, G. E.: ref, 272 (260), 1697 (300), 1754 (25), 2065 (19), 2497 (614), 2603 (261,357,459)
Good, J. L.: ref, 771 (28)
Good, M.: ref, 2497 (471)
Good, R.: ref, 48 (1), 49 (1)
Good, R. H., III: rev, 973; ref, 1612 (84), 1659 (6)
Good-Ellis, M.: ref, 1093 (8), 2108 (1)
Goodday, R.: ref, 696 (1)
Goode, K. T.: ref, 2402 (46), 2860 (986)
Goode, S.: ref, 350 (13,36,), 459 (1), 901 (1), 1653 (13,26), 2163 (145,260), 2228 (11,21), 2860 (114,571,1034)
Goodenough, F. L.: test, 1097
Goodglass, H.: test, 199; ref, 2860 (83), 2873 (15)
Goodhart, W.: ref, 2860 (146)
Goodin, M.: ref, 772 (1), 1612 (33), 1901 (11), 2813 (34)
Gooding, P.: ref, 2193 (2), 2860 (119), 2863 (33), 2892 (14)
Gooding, P. A.: ref, 2193 (21), 2860 (461,631), 2863 (129,184), 2892 (75)
Goodjoin, R.: ref, 615 (24)
Goodkin, D. E.: ref, 272 (1,300), 2402 (37), 2599 (26), 2860 (798), 2892 (5,161)
Goodlin-Jones, B. L.: ref, 1582 (15)
Goodman, A. B.: ref, 2305 (102)
Goodman, G. S.: ref, 451 (194), 1010 (123), 1612 (17)
Goodman, J. F.: test, 1098; rev, 1996; ref, 270 (47), 2485 (238)
Goodman, J. T.: ref, 451 (22)
Goodman, R.: ref, 2860 (874), 2862 (714)
Goodman, S. H.: ref, 373 (17), 472 (125), 1216 (2), 1903 (533), 1987 (8)
Goodman, W. K.: ref, 2305 (148), 2860 (932)
Goodnick, P.: ref, 1697 (291), 2305 (166), 2603 (258)
Goodnick, P. J.: ref, 2050 (117), 2305 (136)
Goodnough, G.: ref, 83 (5)
Goodnow, J. J.: ref, 26 (1), 1903 (455)
Goodrich, G. A.: ref, 298 (79)
Goodrich, W.: ref, 1093 (5), 1902 (62), 2860 (787), 2862 (298), 2879 (96)
Goodstein, J.: test, 1857
Goodstein, L. D.: rev, 1140, 1536, 2499, 2581
Goodwin, D. A. J.: ref, 2230 (4)
Goodwin, F.: ref, 1697 (376), 2305 (119)
Goodwin, G. M.: ref, 272 (83), 1166 (65), 2240 (2), 2860 (328,385,453,699), 2863 (126,145,207)
Goodwin, W. L.: rev, 453
Goodyer, I. M.: ref, 1079 (111), 2305 (248)
Goolkasian, P.: ref, 272 (366)
Goonan, B.: ref, 246 (4), 1379 (24), 1903 (158)
Goossens, M.: ref, 270 (4), 2229 (1)
Gopfert, M.: ref, 2050 (104)
Gorassni, D. R.: ref, 2771 (4)
Gordijn, M. C. M.: ref, 1166 (48)
Gordon, A. L.: ref, 2305 (189)
Gordon, A. S.: ref, 2603 (10)
Gordon, B.: ref, 1135 (3), 2227 (10), 2599 (5,9), 2860 (217,401,805,1226), 2873 (17)
Gordon, B. N.: rev, 1522, 2088; ref, 1612 (18,31), 1903 (260)
Gordon, C. J.: ref, 1071 (3), 1866 (1,11), 2487 (6)
Gordon, C. T.: ref, 451 (116), 2288 (68,71), 2289 (52,56), 2305 (103,137,242), 2860 (436), 2862 (475,493,501,629)
Gordon, D. H.: ref, 2862 (497)
Gordon, D. S.: ref, 2858 (128)
Gordon, E.: ref, 272 (88) 790 (2), 1166 (160), 2749 (10)
Gordon, E. E.: test, 90, 1176, 1280, 1287, 1320, 1752, 2056
Gordon, H. C.: rev, 1767
Gordon, J.: ref, 2488 (6), 2862 (226), 2901 (34)
Gordon, K.: ref, 1135 (17), 1164 (119), 2862 (435), 2879 (153)
Gordon, L. V.: test, 1100, 1101, 1716, 2315, 2581, 2588; rev, 777; ref, 2862 (179)
Gordon, M.: test, 1099; ref, 451 (37,55), 681 (61), 1099 (1,3), 1903 (261), 2862 (264)
Gordon, R.: ref, 459 (8), 1697 (254), 1903 (54), 2485 (37)
Gordon, R. A.: ref, 1902 (84), 1903 (451), 337 (43), 2858 (38)
Gordon, S. E.: test, 2505

Gordon, W. A.: ref, 1061 (1), 1745 (13), 2860 (357,404)
Gordy, C. C.: ref, 1755 (31)
Gore, C. L.: ref, 2516 (116)
Gore, P. A., Jr.: ref, 2863 (216)
Goreczny, A. J.: ref, 1697 (441), 2603 (150,387)
Gorelick, D. A.: ref, 2703 (1)
Gorell, J. M.: ref, 1740 (12), 1903 (315), 2402 (33), 2879 (175), 2892 (237)
Goren, A. R.: ref, 2860 (875), 2873 (36)
Gorey-Ferguson, L.: ref, 863 (87), 1888 (1), 1889 (9), 2603 (533)
Gorfine, M.: ref, 1166 (92)
Gorfinkle, K.: ref, 2497 (69)
Gorham, D. R.: test, 1214, 2102
Gorham, M. M.: ref, 209 (5)
Gorman, B. S.: ref, 2181 (1), 2603 (386)
Gorman, J.: ref, 2125 (7,18), 2516 (16), 2860 (310), 2863 (292)
Gorman, J. M.: ref, 273 (23), 337 (31,34,91,145), 650 (10), 1093 (58), 1166 (115,177,179), 1592 (7), 2163 (124), 2288 (80, 85), 2289 (17,66,69), 2305 (34,77), 2516 (28), 2603 (279,299,549), 2860 (496)
Gorman, K. S.: ref, 2163 (272)
Gorman, S.: ref, 2835 (7)
Gorman, T.: test, 2171, 2691
Gormly, J. B.: rev, 1628
Gorp, W. V.: ref, 2860 (697)
Gorsuch, R.L.: test, 2497; ref, 1686 (1), 2497 (108), 2860 (289)
Gortman, M.: ref, 337 (164)
Gortman, M. B.: ref, 1697 (447), 2218 (38)
Gortner, E.: ref, 272 (184)
Gortner, E. T.: ref, 272 (355)
Gorton, T.: ref, 2050 (119)
Gory, E. L.: rev, 275, 2213
Gorzalka, B. B.: ref, 337 (46), 793 (10,21,24)
Goss, J. D.: ref, 2076 (81)
Goss, R. L.: ref, 298 (7)
Gosselin, C.: ref, 1903 (482)
Gosselin, M.: ref, 272 (326)
Gossette, R. L.: ref, 694 (52), 844 (2), 2497 (248), 2656 (8)
Gossop, M.: ref, 999 (62), 2497 (276)
Goswami, U.: ref, 350 (3,5,6,9,46)
Goswami, V.: ref, 2467 (1), 2862 (682)
Gotham, H. J.: ref, 337 (138,159), 1661 (60,65), 2218 (60), 2603 (460)
Gotlib, I. H.: ref, 272 (67), 863 (35), 998 (130), 1010 (50), 1243 (1), 2305 (193), 2497 (366,492), 2858 (74,97)
Gott, P. S.: ref, 372 (1), 1697 (3), 1790 (1), 1903 (2), 2163 (3), 2247 (1), 2417 (2), 2860 (12)
Gottermeier, L.: ref, 1407 (5)
Gottesman, I.: ref, 350 (24,36), 1653 (21,26), 2163 (195,260), 2228 (16,21), 2860 (795,1034)
Gottesman, I. I.: ref, 1697 (401,405), 1962 (17), 2288 (40), 2305 (131,220), 2813 (77)
Gottesman, N.: ref, 1216 (7), 1902 (17), 2039 (1), 2860 (169)
Gottesman, R. L.: test, 916; ref, 301 (55), 2253 (2), 2860 (1087), 2879 (161), 2901 (90)
Gottfredson, D. C.: ref, 565 (1), 909 (1)
Gottfredson, G. D.: test, 400; ref, 565 (1)
Gottfredson, G. G.: test, 909
Gottfried, A.: ref, 1379 (14)
Gottfried, A. E.: test, 464; ref, 464 (1,3,4), 665 (20), 2862 (102), 2901 (11)
Gottfried, A. W.: ref, 464 (3,4)
Gottheil, E.: ref, 998 (101), 2402 (40), 2603 (313,375)
Gottlieb, B. W.: ref, 1275 (1), 1657 (17)
Gottlieb, J.: ref, 681 (99), 1275 (1), 1657 (17)
Gottlieb, L. N.: ref, 1580 (1), 1927 (8), 2858 (6)
Gottlieb, R.: ref, 790 (23)
Gottman, J. M.: ref, 451 (126,205), 2045 (2), 2657 (26,29,33), 2813 (93,119,141), 2864 (91,115,135, 137)
Gotto, A. M.: ref, 998 (52)
Gotto, J.: ref, 1686 (7)
Gotts, E. E.: rev, 320
Gottschack, L. A.: ref, 1697 (547), 2399 (1), 2402 (63), 2603 (530)
Gottschalk, L. A.: test, 2114; ref, 1164 (61), 2402 (27), 2860 (632), 2892 (117)
Goud, M.: ref, 451 (65)
Gough, H. G.: test, 68,372,438,711, 1970; rev, 477, 727, 913, 926, 1223, 1732, 2199, 2634; ref, 372 (65)
Gould, J.: ref, 1093 (92)
Gould, J. H.: ref, 1765 (9), 2860 (180), 2862 (103)
Gould, K. L.: ref, 2860 (1231)
Gould, M. S.: ref, 451 (151), 2305 (197)
Gould, R. A.: ref, 272 (176), 2199 (3)
Gould, S. J.: ref, 298 (48)
Goulet, P.: ref, 2860 (633)
Gourlay, N.: rev, 954
Gournay, K.: ref, 2497 (338)
Gourovitch, M. L.: ref, 681 (45), 1903 (262)
Gouvier, W. D.: ref, 301 (4), 2860 (493,1127), 2863 (140), 2879 (4)
Gouze, K. R.: ref, 337 (149)
Govi, A.: ref, 1166 (21)
Gow, C. A.: ref, 815 (19), 2516 (62), 2860 (809), 2892 (165)
Gow, L.: ref, 2540 (2)
Gowen, J. W.: ref, 2485 (52)
Gowen, T. L.: test, 1978
Gowers, S. G.: ref, 472 (167)
Goyer, R. S.: test, 1102
Grabowski, J.: ref, 2603 (551)
Grace, G. M.: ref, 1164 (135), 2227 (33), 2860 (1181), 2879 (184), 2892 (256)
Grace, J.: ref, 1096 (10)
Grace, M. C.: ref, 2108 (2,5), 2603 (47)
Graceffa, A. M. S.: ref, 2227 (55), 2860 (1381)
Graceley, E. J.: ref, 2497 (163)

Gracia, E.: ref, 1010 (75), 2603 (358)
Grad, O. T.: ref, 272 (177), 999 (158)
Graduate Management Admission Council: test, 1107
Graduate Record Examination Board: test, 666, 1538, 2032
Grady, C.: ref, 1164 (110), 1740 (11), 2010 (20), 2860 (971)
Grady, C. L.: ref, 1240 (21), 2010 (1,18), 2163 (10), 2485 (234), 2860 (34,290,502,837,1141,1155,1216), 2863 (12,77,242), 2879 (190)
Grady, D. A.: ref, 2603 (18)
Graeber, M. B.: ref, 1525 (23), 2860 (1115)
Graf, M.: ref, 815 (44), 2862 (620)
Graf, P.: ref, 2516 (66,113), 2860 (50,876), 2863 (18,258)
Graff-Radford, N.: ref, 2860 (1155)
Graff-Radford, N. R.: ref, 2227 (3), 2860 (181)
Grafman, J.: ref, 272 (270), 335 (6), 776 (32), 999 (63), 1135 (7,25), 1697 (269), 1758 (21), 2193 (57), 2402 (66), 2497 (132,315), 2860 (264,292,400,426, 561,1067,1174,1265,1353), 2863 (105,354,407,418), 2879 (35), 2892 (89,97,207,224,243,251,255)
Grafton, F. C.: ref, 180 (35)
Graha, S.: ref, 615 (53), 2860 (877), 2862 (345)
Graham, C. R.: rev, 307
Graham, D. P.: ref, 1166 (221)
Graham, F. K.: test, 1645
Graham, J. M.: test, 1304, 2414
Graham, J. R.: test, 1697, 1698; rev, 1065, 1452 1697 (264,320,364,588), 1698 (27)
Graham, K. S.: ref, 2163 (162)
Graham, L.: ref, 1071 (5)
Graham, N.: ref, 776 (30), 909 (1), 2193 (52), 2863 (325)
Graham, N. A.: ref, 2862 (357), 2879 (122), 2905 (77)
Graham, S.: rev, 131, 2030, 2665, 2666; ref, 1902 (8,18), 2432 (4,5,11,15), 2485 (166), 2731 (2), 2732 (1), 2860 (1088), 2862 (70,71,104,202,482,510,631), 2901 (5,12,25,121), 2905 (35,38)
Graham, S. Schafer, W. D.: rev, 349
Graham-Bermann, S. A.: ref, 451 (123,124)
Graham-Pole, J.: ref, 2230 (4), 2497 (200), 2498 (46)
Gramling, S. E.: ref, 1697 (352)
Grana, A. S.: ref, 690 (1)
Granata, T.: ref, 1903 (563), 2163 (347), 2227 (54), 2768 (42), 2862 (698)
Granby, C. D.: ref, 771 (17)
Grande, G. E.: ref, 998 (112), 1745 (69)
Grande, L.: ref, 1164 (72), 2863 (208)
Grandmaison, E.: ref, 2704 (47), 2879 (236), 2905 (123)
Graner, D.: ref, 1040 (7)
Grangé, D.: ref, 1166 (56,139), 2288 (49), 2289 (38), 2860 (902), 2863 (63,271)
Granger, D. A.: ref, 451 (38,125), 472 (168), 681 (33), 2214 (48)
Granholm, E.: ref, 1903 (224), 2125 (10), 2862 (234), 2892 (98)
Grannemann, B. D.: ref, 1745 (6)
Grant, A.: rev, 1768
Grant, D. B.: ref, 1613 (1)
Grant, G. M.: ref, 2879 (117)
Grant, I.: ref, 272 (334), 337 (16,19,47), 376 (30), 776 (26), 1093 (24), 1164 (25,77,157), 1166 (70), 2076 (133), 2414 (3), 2603 (66), 2858 (18,19,20,90,105), 2860 (239,1298), 2863 (293)
Grant, J.: ref, 350 (44,52), 1903 (577), 2163 (344,355), 2662 (7), 2860 (1291,1361,1413), 2862 (635), 2862 (684,730)
Grant, K. A.: ref, 134 (26)
Grant, K. E.: ref, 337 (70), 472 (77), 863 (35), 2214 (38)
Grant, M.: test, 135; ref, 2076 (29)
Grant, R. P. J.: ref, 1697 (222)
Grant, V. J.: ref, 2417 (7,20)
Grantham, L. B.: rev, 994
Grantham-McGregor, S.: ref, 1134 (4), 1903 (263), 2485 (130), 2862 (265), 2879 (78)
Grantham-McGregor, S. M.: ref, 1134 (6), 1216 (64), 1903 (361)
Grassi, F.: ref, 2163 (284), 2860 (1130)
Grassi, L.: ref, 1166 (189)
Grattan, E.: ref, 2214 (113), 2305 (205)
Grattan, L. M.: ref, 2860 (612), 2892 (73)
Gratton, C. A.: ref, 2227 (11), 2863 (136)
Grau, C.: ref, 900 (1)
Grau, J.: ref, 272 (242)
Graue, M. E.: rev, 2333
Gravel, J. S.: ref, 2382 (9), 2485 (53)
Graves, R. E.: ref, 1758 (83), 2860 (1238)
Gravitt, G. W.: ref, 472 (125)
Graw, P.: ref, 1166 (165,219)
Gray, A.: ref, 337 (195), 1010 (137), 1455 (10), 1866 (32), 2496 (5), 2497 (675)
Gray, A. M.: test, 2592
Gray, C. A.: rev, 813
Gray, C. D.: ref, 2860 (831)
Gray, H.: test, 1366
Gray, J.: ref, 784 (1), 999 (62), 1612 (70), 1903 (366), 2076 (66), 2497 (276)
Gray, J. A.: ref, 999 (152), 2497 (545)
Gray, J. J.: ref, 2497 (156)
Gray, M. M.: test, 1652
Gray, M. W.: ref, 571 (4), 615 (40)
Gray, N.: ref, 1965 (73)
Gray, R. M.: ref, 1164 (123,126), 2862 (481)
Gray, S.: ref, 240 (4), 539 (2), 994 (52), 1379 (102), 1903 (51,574), 2163 (44), 2190 (9), 2382 (40), 2432 (10), 2524 (13)
Gray, T.: ref, 2899 (8)
Gray, W. A.: test, 1652
Graybill, D.: ref, 1010 (81), 1697 (429), 2248 (7)
Grayston, A. D.: ref, 694 (29), 2214 (17)
Graziani, S.: ref, 2863 (416)
Graziano, W. G.: ref, 998 (44), 2218 (42)

Grebstein, L.: ref, 272 (337), 337 (123)
Greco, C. M.: ref, 272 (235)
Greco, E.: ref, 1687 (16)
Greco, P.: ref, 1010 (80)
Greden, J. F.: ref, 1093 (17)
Gredler, M. E.: ref, 1115 (29), 1672 (5)
Greehouse, J. B.: ref, 2873 (37)
Greek, A.: ref, 1216 (93)
Greeley, J. D.: ref, 2414 (1)
Green, A.: ref, 2163 (254), 2860 (634,790,1011), 2862 (418)
Green, A. I.: ref, 2860 (1378), 2879 (226), 2892 (296)
Green, A. J.: ref, 448 (27), 1889 (13), 2497 (651)
Green, B. L.: ref, 2108 (2,5), 2603 (47)
Green, C. J.: test, 1686
Green, E.: ref, 1697 (214)
Green, F. J.: rev, 2223, 2712
Green, J.: ref, 2860 (182)
Green, J. L.: ref, 2862 (333)
Green, J. P.: ref, 1115 (12)
Green, K.: ref, 1000 (1), 1014 (1), 1612 (6), 2862 (40)
Green, K. E.: rev, 475, 1218, 2805; ref, 2163 (86,326)
Green, L.: ref, 1991 (26)
Green, L. F.: test, 1457
Green, M.: ref, 271 (1), 272 (95)
Green, M. F.: ref, 1645 (1), 2050 (12,67,114), 2305 (104), 2519 (16), 2520 (17), 2860 (101), 2879 (74), 2892 (55,110)
Green, M. L.: ref, 2860 (1035), 2892 (216)
Green, M. W.: ref, 2497 (472)
Green, P.: ref, 1140 (21), 1902 (31), 2163 (85)
Green, P. A.: ref, 337 (129), 1902 (82), 2163 (264), 2879 (156)
Green, P. J.: ref, 2218 (91)
Green, R.: ref, 1164 (111), 2862 (397)
Green, R. C.: ref, 776 (37), 2860 (629)
Green, R. E. A.: ref, 2193 (25), 2860 (668), 2863 (198)
Green, R. F.: rev, 2741
Green, R. G.: ref, 863 (15), 1000 (14,15)
Green, R-J.: ref, 1000 (96), 1010 (21,96)
Green, S. D. R.: ref, 1379 (63)
Green, V. A.: ref, 1036 (8)
Green, W. P.: test, 2909
Greenbaum, B.: ref, 615 (53), 2860 (877,1088), 2862 (345,482)
Greenbaum, P. E.: ref, 451 (180)
Greenberg, D.: ref, 2288 (27), 2289 (18)
Greenberg, G.: ref, 681 (47)
Greenberg, J.: ref, 272 (378) 298 (158), 838 (22), 1672 (1)
Greenberg, L. M.: test, 2720
Greenberg, L. S.: ref, 2603 (389)
Greenberg, M. A.: ref, 2076 (43), 2603 (461)
Greenberg, M. T.: ref, 301 (31), 451 (228), 472 (53), 557 (6), 681 (11), 1164 (49), 1612 (37), 1903 (80,424), 2516 (27), 2603 (99), 2816 (1)
Greenberg, R. L.: ref, 2519 (5), 2520 (5)
Greenberg, R. P.: ref, 1697 (46), 2247 (12), 2248 (3), 2749 (9), 2860 (238)
Greenberger, E.: ref, 1010 (97), 1612 (82), 2497 (33,65,376)
Greenblatt, D. J.: ref, 998 (23), 1697 (106)
Greenblatt, R. L.: ref, 1687 (3,4)
Greene, A. F.: ref, 1697 (292), 2497 (249)
Greene, A. L.: ref, 2860 (393)
Greene, B.: ref, 2497 (339)
Greene, B.W.: ref, 1661 (64)
Greene, C.: ref, 2862 (483), 2879 (162)
Greene, C. A.: ref, 469 (2), 2862 (387), 2879 (134)
Greene, D.: ref, 2527 (16)
Greene, E. B.: rev, 361, 2797
Greene, H. A.: test, 1315; rev, 957
Greene, J. D. W.: ref, 776 (29), 1758 (69), 2863 (321)
Greene, J. W.: ref, 472 (18,19), 2498 (14,15), 2603 (327)
Greene, K. L.: ref, 298 (51)
Greene, R.: ref, 1697 (380)
Greene, R. L.: ref, 1697 (532,595,598)
Greenfield, E.: ref, 404 (37)
Greenfield, S.: ref, 2497 (627)
Greenglass, E.: ref, 1590 (19,41)
Greenglass, E. R.: ref, 1338 (35), 1590 (13), 2497 (250)
Greenhaus, J. H.: rev, 1969; ref, 2497 (1,55,160)
Greenhill, L.: ref, 4 (11), 451 (220), 1216 (108)
Greenhouse, J. B.: ref, 1093 (30), 1166 (215)
Greenier, K. D.: ref, 2749 (54)
Greeno, C.: ref, 893 (26)
Greenslade, K. E.: ref, 1745 (83)
Greenspan, R.: ref, 999 (7)
Greenspan, S. I.: test, 2715
Greenspoon, A.: ref, 2603 (146)
Greenstein, J.: ref, 665 (9), 2485 (12), 2862 (57)
Greenwald, A. G.: ref, 694 (81)
Greenwald, C.: test, 716
Greenwald, D. F.: ref, 1093 (65), 1697 (293,548), 1745 (68)
Greenwald, E.: ref, 337 (42), 793 (1,3)
Greenwald, M.: ref, 2873 (56)
Greenwald, M. L.: ref, 2873 (65)
Greenway, A. P.: ref, 1697 (490), 2247 (103)
Greenway, P.: ref, 1697 (560), 2603 (547)
Greenwood, C.: ref, 665 (71), 1657 (13), 1866 (34), 1903 (326), 2485 (152), 2694 (11), 2695 (32), 2879 (95)
Greenwood, C. R.: ref, 665 (47), 1657 (7,11), 1866 (7,17,24,30)
Greenwood, K. M.: ref, 791 (5), 2497 (197)
Greenwood, L.: ref, 999 (24)
Greer, A.: ref, 2873 (42)
Greer, E. A.: ref, 1866 (16)
Greer, R. A.: ref, 298 (113)
Greer, T.: ref, 451 (260), 1010 (84), 1131 (13), 2211 (42), 2862 (352,377), 2879 (118)
Greger, L. M.: ref, 272 (149)
Gregg, C. H.: ref, 2076 (16)

Gregg, G. R.: ref, 1697 (413)
Gregg, N.: rev, 1469, 1471, 2934; ref, 1378 (9), 1697 (171), 1903 (543), 2860 (355,1263,1313), 2862 (610), 2901 (20)
Gregorc, A. F.: test, 1132
Gregory, M. C.: ref, 1412 (2)
Greiffenstein, M. F.: ref, 2863 (185)
Greig, M. E.: test, 904
Greig, T. C.: ref, 2892 (264), 2924 (4)
Greiner, A. R.: ref, 1745 (83)
Greiner, N.: ref, 2247 (63)
Greis, A. B.: test, 1490
Grela, B. G.: ref, 1485 (60), 2864 (139)
Grelling, B. Z.: ref, 272 (338), 1687 (37)
Gremy, I. M.: ref, 337 (63), 451 (29), 472 (59)
Grenyer, B. F. S.: ref, 2603 (462)
Gresham, F.: rev, 856, 1411, 2862
Gresham, F. M.: test, 2452 2535; rev, 805, 855, 1889, 2210, 2214, 61 (2), 301 (56), 681 (74,75,94), 1902 (2), 2163 (273), 2299 (1), 2452 (1,13,14,15,19,24), 2607 (1), 2813 (41,124), 2860 (488), 2862 (15,216,484,511,512,513,621,622,724), 2864 (40), 2879 (163,173,174,207,231)
Gresham, K. M.: ref, 2860 (878), 2864 (88)
Greve, K. W.: ref, 2860 (1064), 2863 (311), 2892 (220)
Grewal, A.: ref, 1166 (123)
Grey, N.: ref, 272 (124), 273 (13), 2076 (115), 2497 (488)
Gribble, P. A.: ref, 681 (34)
Gribbons, B.: ref, 844 (3,6)
Gribbons, B. C.: ref, 844 (4)
Gridley, B. E.: ref, 298 (97), 837 (1), 1612 (56), 2860 (417), 2862 (187), 2864 (64), 2879 (53)
Grier, P. E.: ref, 538 (3)
Gries, K.: rev, 583, 603
Gries, L. T.: ref, 448 (21), 451 (175), 853 (20), 1226 (2), 2879 (159,198)
Griese, J.: ref, 2860 (1422), 2892 (309)
Grieshofer, P.: ref, 2860 (525), 2892 (88)
Grievink, E. H.: ref, 2163 (113,182), 2229 (2)
Griez, E.: ref, 2497 (530)
Griez, E. J.: ref, 2497 (583)
Griffen, B. W.: ref, 926 (20), 1318 (9)
Griffen, E.: ref, 1164 (4), 1166 (8), 2860 (94)
Griffen, M. M.: ref, 926 (20), 1318 (9)
Griffin, J. R.: test, 867
Griffin, K. W.: ref, 2497 (473)
Griffin, M.: ref, 1181 (25)
Griffin, P. E.: ref, 233 (1), 2743 (1)
Griffin, R. W.: ref, 1701 (18)
Griffin, S. M.: ref, 665 (92), 694 (130), 1734 (5) 1991 (104), 2358 (15), 2485 (240), 2862 (701), 2879 (225)
Griffin, T. M.: ref, 1612 (51)
Griffith, B. P.: ref, 2603 (248)
Griffith, C. L.: test, 755, 1565, 2280
Griffith, F.: rev, 1659
Griffith, P. L.: ref, 665 (32), 1072 (24), 1697 (549)
Griffith, R. C.: ref, 2305 (13)
Griffith, R. W.: ref, 298 (49)
Griffith, W. I.: ref, 298 (63), 372 (36)
Griffiths, D.: ref, 2813 (142)
Griffiths, H.: ref, 2050 (19)
Griffiths, H. W.: ref, 1166 (16)
Griffiths, J.: ref, 272 (213), 1166 (143)
Griffiths, M. D.: ref, 1991 (10)
Griffiths, P.: ref, 303 (17), 818 (1), 1105 (1), 1592 (23), 1765 (4), 2125 (14), 2226 (24), 2516 (98), 2862 (29,623)
Griffiths, R.: test, 1134
Griffiths, R. F.: ref, 1079 (100)
Griger, M. L.: ref, 335 (2) 1697 (143), 2603 (116)
Griggs, L. G.: test, 1955
Griggs, R. A.: ref, 615 (3)
Griggs, S. A.: ref, 2181 (1)
Grigorenko, E. L.: ref, 472 (114), 2214 (60)
Grigoroiu-Serbanescu, M.: ref, 2163 (66), 2860 (259)
Grigsby, J.: ref, 1164 (95), 2860 (879)
Grigsby, J. P.: ref, 1903 (12), 2860 (35), 2862 (16), 2863 (13), 2879 (6)
Grill, J. J.: test, 2935; rev, 3, 4, 70, 284, 809, 928, 1905, 2045, 2376
Grillo, J.: ref, 1697 (294)
Grillon, C.: ref, 1093 (13,30), 2305 (35)
Grilo, C. M.: ref, 1685 (2)
Grima, A.: ref, 118 (1), 1115 (27), 1759 (10)
Grimes, M.: ref, 1745 (82)
Grimes, S. K.: ref, 1455 (12), 1746 (1)
Grimm, D. W.: ref, 298 (83), 298 (115), 1582 (7)
Grimm, S. D.: ref, 2218 (90)
Grimmell, D.: ref, 298 (61), 1745 (19)
Grimshaw, G. M.: ref, 2704 (46), 2860 (1391), 2862 (715)
Grimsley, G.: test, 937
Gripshover, D. L.: ref, 1697 (295)
Grisby, J.: ref, 2860 (635)
Grishenko-Roze, N.: ref, 1965 (77), 2218 (71)
Grisich, C. F.: ref, 791 (8), 2497 (280)
Grispini, A.: ref, 1166 (33)
Grissett, N. I.: ref, 2603 (463)
Grisso, T.: ref, 41 (1), 1697 (489), 1802 (1), 2247 (102), 2749 (66), 2860 (1092), 2879 (164)
Griswold, D.: ref, 1128 (4)
Grittmann, L.: ref, 337 (110)
Gritz, E. R.: ref, 2497 (662)
Grizenko, N.: ref, 451 (145)
Groag, I.: ref, 2860 (947)
Grobbelaar, P. E.: test, 1983
Grober, E.: ref, 2860 (1272)
Grober, S.: ref, 1061 (1), 2860 (357)
Grobman, H.: rev, 2719
Groccia-Ellison, M. E.: ref, 2860 (988), 2863 (291)
Grochocinski, V.: ref, 1166 (215)
Grochowski, S.: ref, 2017 (9), 2146 (18), 2485 (126)
Grodin, D. M.: ref, 1164 (90), 1592 (21), 2225 (7), 2497 (456), 2860 (848), 2863 (246), 2892 (175)

Grodsky, A.: ref, 2407 (3)
Groeger, J. A.: ref, 998 (112), 1745 (69)
Groenman, N.: ref, 1697 (498)
Grof, E.: ref, 2305 (212)
Grof, P.: ref, 1166 (49), 2305 (212)
Groff, M. G.: rev, 1776
Groff, P.: rev, 1148
Grofman, J.: ref, 2860 (869), 2863 (255)
Grognet, A.: test, 250
Grolnick, W. S.: ref, 1657 (8)
Gromly, J. B.: rev, 1158
Grond, M.: ref, 2497 (120)
Gronlund, N. E.: rev, 1657, 2737
Groothues, C.: ref, 2305 (224)
Gropen, T. I.: ref, 2860 (408)
Groppenbacher, N.: ref, 472 (63)
Gropperbacher, N.: ref, 472 (39)
Grosch, J. W.: ref, 1716 (4)
Gross, A. B.: test, 1236
Gross, A. M.: ref, 472 (137)
Gross, H.: test, 348, 2187
Gross, M. U. M.: ref, 694 (30), 2485 (54)
Gross, R. E.: rev, 502
Gross, W. C.: ref, 2759 (1)
Gross-Tsur, V.: ref, 301 (35), 451 (76), 681 (38,67,68), 1379 (68), 2163 (244), 2862 (223,346,395), 2864 (89)
Grossberg, I. W.: ref, 289 (1), 665 (1), 694 (3), 1010 (2), 1657 (2), 1962 (1), 2214 (1), 2485 (5), 2862 (14)
Grosser, G. S.: ref, 2860 (102,989), 2862 (72,404,413), 2879 (140)
Grossi, D.: ref, 2163 (114), 2227 (52), 2860 (636), 2892 (118)
Grossman, D.: ref, 1378 (1) 1384 (1)
Grossman, E.: ref, 2813 (105)
Grossman, F.: ref, 2545 (5)
Grossman, F. M.: rev, 867, 869, 1935; ref, 2695 (2), 2862 (73)
Grossman, H.: test, 306
Grossman, I.: ref, 1382 (1), 1384 (2), 2860 (637)
Grossman, J.: ref, 1378 (1), 1384 (1)
Grossman, L. S.: ref, 793 (19), 1697 (72,298,299,370)
Grossman, L. S.: ref, 1744 (5), 2050 (6)
Grossman, M.: ref, 231 (1), 303 (32), 815 (23), 2226 (5,9,42), 2227 (61), 2599 (43), 2863 (259,431), 2892 (307)
Grossman, R. I.: ref, 231 (1), 303 (32), 2226 (42), 2227 (61), 2288 (57), 2289 (44), 2599 (43), 2863 (431), 2892 (307)
Grossnickle, F. E.: rev, 173
Grossnickle, W. F.: ref, 448 (1)
Grosz, D.: ref, 2485 (126), 2603 (105)
Grote, C. L.: ref, 2860 (880)
Grote, G. F.: ref, 1965 (24)
Grote, K.: test, 848
Grotelueschen, A.: rev, 1866
Grotevant, H. D.: ref, 1405 (2)
Groth, S.: ref, 1745 (39)
Groth-Marnat, G.: ref, 694 (131), 1226 (4), 2652 (11)
Grotpeter, J. K.: ref, 472 (118)
Grouios, G.: ref, 272 (302), 2860 (1318)
Grout, L.: ref, 2039 (6)
Grout, L. A.: ref, 2860 (368)
Grove, J.: ref, 350 (26), 1485 (39), 2045 (1)
Grove, J. R.: ref, 999 (177), 2076 (163), 2358 (2)
Grove, T. R.: ref, 2497 (269)
Grove, W. M.: ref, 998 (41), 1093 (42), 1697 (167,173)
Grove, W. R.: rev, 182
Grover, G. N.: ref, 2497 (279)
Grover, S. A.: ref, 2050 (136), 2305 (157), 2305 (158)
Grover, S. L.: ref, 771 (16)
Groves, M. M.: rev, 1263
Groves, S.: test, 2080
Grow, C. R.: ref, 997 (13), 2065 (8)
Grow, V. M.: ref, 893 (33), 1735 (8)
Growdon, J. H.: ref, 1135 (21), 2860 (595), 2860 (623), 2863 (182)
Groze, V.: ref, 1000 (16)
Groze, V. K.: ref, 1000 (75)
Grubaugh, S. J.: ref, 550 (4)
Grubb, H. J.: ref, 326 (2), 694 (53), 2862 (17)
Gruber, C.: test, 1543
Gruber, C. P.: test, 1802, 1963, 2229
Gruber, E. J.: ref, 2771 (12)
Gruber, F. A.: ref, 1903 (311), 1982 (11)
Gruber, S. A.: ref, 2860 (1210)
Gruber-Baldini, A. L.: ref, 2304 (4)
Grubin, D.: ref, 998 (70)
Gruden, D.: ref, 2247 (9)
Gruder, F. A.: ref, 1095 (28), 1394 (8), 1982 (10)
Gruen, R.: ref, 1093 (1), 2603 (15)
Gruen, R. J.: ref, 790 (26), 2076 (173)
Gruenberg, E. M.: ref, 2050 (23)
Gruenewald, A.: ref, 1000 (16)
Grugan, P.: ref, 1903 (525), 2864 (134), 2879 (205)
Grummon, K.: ref, 2858 (67)
Grummon, P.: test, 2929
Grundin, H. U.: test, 1232
Grunhaus, L.: ref, 2305 (50)
Grunhaus, L. J.: ref, 1093 (17)
Grunseit, A. C.: ref, 2497 (340), 2863 (186)
Grur, R. C.: ref, 2860 (54)
Grut, M.: ref, 2860 (1277)
Gruys, M. L.: ref, 372 (118)
Gruzelier, J.: ref, 2050 (64,93), 2076 (97), 2193 (29), 2239 (18), 2497 (384), 2860 (581), 2863 (168), 2892 (106)
Grych, J. H.: ref, 472 (28), 2214 (18)
Gryskiewicz, S. S.: test, 1393
Guariglia, C.: ref, 2163 (306)
Guarino, M.: ref, 2163 (188), 2516 (54), 2768 (26), 2819 (1), 2907 (6)
Guarnaccia, C. A.: ref, 998 (39)
Guastello, D. D.: ref, 644 (2), 682 (1)

Guastello, S. J.: ref, 644 (2), 682 (1), 694 (45)
Guckenberg, T.: ref, 2862 (48)
Gude, T.: ref, 2497 (252)
Gudjonsson, G. H.: ref, 2497 (474), 2860 (440,529, 590,881)
Guerra, N. G.: ref, 451 (57)
Guertin, T. L.: ref, 2163 (186)
Guertin, W. H.: rev, 981, 2860
Guess, D.: ref, 1770 (9,11)
Guevara, l. F.: ref, 1687 (40), 1688 (1), 1958 (1)
Guger, S.: ref, 1901 (16), 2485 (124)
Guglielmino, L. M.: test, 2359
Guidance Testing Associates: test, 643, 1306
Guido, J. R.: ref, 2017 (16)
Guidotti, A.: ref, 1697 (369), 2860 (778)
Guidubaldi, J.: test, 265, 266, 1888
Guilford, A. M.: test, 76
Guilford, J. P.: test, 142, 682, 726, 865, 1156, 1157, 1158, 1514, 2401; rev, 1115, 11196, 1321, 1672
Guilleminault, C.: ref, 303 (13) 2860 (1191)
Guillemot, J-P.: ref, 2860 (1299)
Guilmette, S.: ref, 1379 (18,29), 2485 (57,94), 2860 (478), 2862 (166,211), 2879 (45,59)
Guimón, J.: ref, 1166 (109)
Guinan, E. M.: ref, 2193 (25), 2860 (668), 2863 (198)
Guion, R. M.: rev, 401, 944, 1101, 1494, 1701, 2272
Guisinger, S.: ref, 68 (4,17)
Guite, J.: ref, 1010 (69,70)f, 1092 (11,13), 2305 (121,155,165), 2860 (801), 2862 (308,310), 2879 (100,102)
Guiton, G.: ref, 665 (81)
Gulati, A.: test, 1347
Guldner, G. T.: ref, 337 (139)
Gulgoz, S.: rev, 2300, 2479, 2641
Gullette, I.: test, 2697
Gullickson, A. R.: rev, 825, 2740
Gulliken, H.: rev, 1315
Gulliksen, H.: rev, 1863
Gullion, C. M.: ref, 2305 (192)
Gulliver, S. B.: ref, 134 (19,20,27), 272 (90), 1661 (34), 2076 (26)
Gullone, E.: ref, 893 (54), 1021 (36,39), 2214 (19,99,100,116,136), 2230 (15,19), 2497 (178,556), 2498 (63)
Gullotta, C. S.: ref, 681 (29)
Gully, S. M.: ref, 1965 (83)
Gum, S.: ref, 998 (106), 2603 (405)
Gummow, L. J.: ref, 2076 (16)
Gump, B. B.: ref, 2497 (628)
Gumpel, T.: ref, 681 (91)
Güncer, B.: ref, 2771 (23)
Gunderson, J. G.: test, 824; ref, 2109 (1), 2247 (8), 2603 (19), 2749 (13), 2860 (175)
Gundry, L. K.: ref, 1862 (1)
Gunn, P.: ref, 2211 (20)
Gunnar, M.: ref, 472 (169)
Gunning, F.: rev, 2297
Gunning, W. B.: ref, 451 (290), 2862 (740)
Gunzburg, A. L.: test, 1512
Gunzburg, H. C.: test, 1512, 2088
Gupchup, G. V.: ref, 1590 (32)
Gupman, A.: ref, 793 (22)
Guppy, A.: ref, 999 (180), 1079 (22)
Gupta, B.: ref, 1093 (104)
Gupta, B. S.: ref, 998 (128), 2417 (38), 2497 (645)
Gupta, S.: ref, 1164 (121), 2125 (22), 2288 (67), 2289 (51), 2516 (78), 2860 (1080), 2863 (316), 2892 (225)
Gupta, S. R.: ref, 2163 (216), 2863 (260), 2873 (38)
Guptill, A. M.: ref, 1338 (29)
Gur, R. C.: ref, 199 (8), 592 (58), 1164 (17), 1525 (8), 1672 (1), 1752 (1), 2017 (6), 2288 (25,48,57,65), 2289 (14,37,44,49), 2497 (173), 2860 (76,80,137, 269,744), 2863 (23,38), 2892 (8,22,204)
Gur, R. E.: ref, 199 (8), 592 (58), 1164 (17), 1525 (8), 1672 (1), 2017 (6), 2288 (25,48,57,65,75), 2289 (14,37,44,49,62) 2497 (173), 2860 (54,80,137,744), 2863 (23,38), 2892 (8,22,119,204)
Guralnick, M. J.: ref, 451 (126), 2045 (2), 2657 (25,26,29,33,34), 2813 (92,93,119,141,143), 2864 (90,91,115,135,136)
Gurd, J. M.: ref, 1768 (1), 2860 (66), 2863 (21)
Gureje, O.: ref, 2860 (882)
Gurevich, M.: ref, 998 (89)
Gurklis, J. A.: ref, 2288 (58)
Gurland, B. J.: ref, 1166 (103)
Gurley, D. N.: ref, 2039 (4)
Gurling, H.: ref, 2305 (199)
Gurling, H. M. D.: ref, 2305 (141,180)
Gurman, E. B.: ref, 298 (62,111)
Gurvit, M.: test, 2212
Gusella, J. F.: ref, 2227 (8), 2860 (364), 2879 (44), 2892 (54)
Gussekloo, J.: ref, 1079 (42)
Gustad, J. W.: rev, 908
Gustafson, K. E.: ref, 472 (136), 1010 (41,66), 2214 (76), 2603 (166,167,321,322), 2858 (46,86)
Gustafson, R.: ref, 998 (96), 1101 (1)
Gustafson, S. B.: ref, 1701 (46)
Gustafsson, J.: ref, 838 (13), 2862 (163)
Gustafsson, P.: ref, 2862 (617)
Gustafsson, P. A.: ref, 2038 (2)
Gustavson, A. R.: ref, 272 (70), 893 (12)
Gustavson, C. R.: ref, 272 (70), 893 (12)
Gustavson, J. C.: ref, 272 (70), 893 (12)
Gustavsson, P.: ref, 273 (28), 999 (181)
Guteman, A.: ref, 1058 (3), 2860 (277), 2863 (72)
Gutenberg, R. L.: rev, 1106, 2022
Guthrie, D.: ref, 1085 (4), 2076 (56), 2485 (228), 2813 (118,145), 2856 (11), 2860 (534)
Guthrie, G.: rev, 538
Guthrie, G. M.: rev, 1586; ref, 1965 (1)
Guthrie, I. K.: ref, 365 (9)
Guthrie, J. T.: ref, 2862 (259)
Guthrie, M. R.: ref, 1590 (54)

Guthrie, P. C.: ref, 1697 (296)
Gutiérrez, F.: ref, 999 (103), 2860 (681), 2863 (201), 1164 (70)
Gutierrez, G.: ref, 2860 (402)
Gutierrez, L.: ref, 624 (3), 1903 (127)
Gutierrez, M.: ref, 307 (2)
Gutierrez, M. A.: ref, 2230 (14)
Gutierrez, P. M.: ref, 271 (12), 272 (305)
Gutierrez-Clellen, V. F.: ref, 307 (1), 1234 (5), 2335 (1)
Gutierrez-Esteinou, r.: ref, 1166 (160)
Gutkin, T. B.: rev, 2752; ref, 342 (1), 2010 (13), 2862 (119), 2901 (14)
Gutterman, D. F.: ref, 2076 (1)
Guttman, L.: ref, 1405 (8), 2163 (48)
Guttman, R.: ref, 1405 (8), 2163 (48)
Gutzmann, H.: ref, 2863 (229)
Guy, B.: ref, 1770 (9)
Guydish, J.: ref, 272 (356), 2603 (581)
Guyette, T. W.: rev, 251, 1421, 1424, 2427
Guze, B. H.: ref, 1093 (40)
Guzick, D. S.: ref, 2497 (459)
Guzman, A. M.: ref, 2497 (99)
Guzman, C.: ref, 303 (22), 376 (27), 776 (55), 1164 (172), 2860 (1354), 2863 (408), 2892 (291)
Guzman, D. A.: ref, 303 (22), 376 (27), 776 (55), 1164 (172), 2860 (1354), 2863 (408), 2892 (291)
Guzzetta, J.: Morrow, R.: test, 704
Gwartney, N.: rev, 1308
Gynther, M. D.: rev, 372, 1697
Gysbers, N. C.: ref, 1754 (7)
Gyurke, J. S.: ref, 1612 (50) 2485 (131), 2864 (52)
Gyynn, S. M.: ref, 2603 (525)

Haaga, D. A. F.: ref, 271 (6), 272 (232), 1166 (94), 1697 (326), 2076 (143), 2603 (442)
Haager, D.: ref, 2452 (8)
Haak, R. A.: ref, 1164 (123,126), 2862 (481)
Haaland, K. Y.: ref, 199 (5), 1164 (62), 2860 (260,638)
Haan, N.: ref, 373 (1)
Haas, B.: ref, 1216 (4)
Haas, G.: ref, 2076 (12), 2288 (84), 2749 (83)
Haas, G. L.: ref, 272 (161), 273 (12,17), 1093 (8,29,95), 1166 (98), 2108 (1,4), 2146 (11), 2288 (20,26), 2289 (12,15), 2863 (108), 2892 (58)
Haase, J. L.: ref, 998 (82)
Haavisto, T.: ref, 745 (18)
Habenicht, D.: ref, 1401 (3)
Haber, L.: rev, 1420, 1424, 2029, 2934
Habershaim, N.: ref, 2603 (68), 2858 (21)
Habib, M.: ref, 2163 (274), 2863 (261), 2892 (183)
Habif, V. L.: ref, 793 (5), 2839 (2)
Habing, B.: ref, 1434 (2)
Habke, A. M.: ref, 950 (6), 1687 (29)
Haby, J. V.: ref, 1240 (21)
Hack, M.: ref, 353 (19), 815 (31), 994 (33), 1379 (78), 1982 (12), 2125 (19), 2813 (108)
Hack, N.: ref, 2873 (17)
Hackeloer, H. J.: ref, 376 (33), 2239 (35)
Hackett, C. A.: ref, 271 (10), 272 (268), 337 (171), 2497 (619)
Hackett, G.: test, 1602
Hackett, K.: ref, 2873 (74)
Hackman, R.: ref, 1939 (9)
Hackmann, A.: ref, 2519 (56), 2520 (55)
Haddad, C.: ref, 433 (4), 2813 (12)
Haddock, G.: ref, 1944 (1)
Haden, C.: ref, 2125 (23), 2860 (1118), 2892 (232)
Hadfield, C.: test, 445
Hadfield, O. D.: ref, 1140 (32), 1755 (39)
Hadi, F.: ref, 472 (202)
Hadjez, J.: ref, 681 (96), 2305 (247)
Hadjistavropoulos, T.: test, 545; ref, 2497 (341)
Hadler, J. R.: ref, 2214 (51)
Hadley, D.: ref, 1758 (99), 2860 (1379), 2863 (414)
Hadley, P. A.: ref, 1095 (23), 1379 (45), 1903 (259), 2229 (3)
Hadley, S. T.: test, 973, 1634, 1635
Hadley, S. W.: ref, 2288 (3)
Hadzi-Pavlovic, A.: ref, 999 (138)
Hadzi-Pavlovic, D.: ref, 272 (306), 998 (21), 999 (190), 1079 (39,103), 1166 (61), 1241 (5)
Haeger, B.: ref, 1758 (35), 2163 (205), 2288 (46), 2289 (35), 2305 (126), 2892 (170)
Haegerstrom-Portnoy, G.: ref, 1072 (1), 1131 (1), 2862 (1)
Haegger, B.: ref, 1758 (36), 2163 (206), 2288 (47), 2289 (36), 2305 (127), 2892 (171)
Haemmerlie, F. M.: ref, 372 (16), 1338 (16), 2525 (2,4)
Haenen, M-A.: ref, 272 (193), 2497 (566)
Haertel, E. H.: rev, 1657
Haertel, G. D.: rev, 555, 1792
Haertzen, C.: ref, 2703 (1)
Haertzen, C. A.: test, 66; ref, 1697 (73), 2076 (20), 2402 (5), 2603 (48,77)
Haeske-Dewick, H. C.: ref, 1758 (70)
Hafer, A. A.: ref, 404 (16)
Haffmans, P. M. J.: ref, 1166 (52,53), 2603 (265)
Haffner, J.: ref, 745 (24)
Haffner, M. E.: ref, 451 (263), 681 (93),1392 (15), 2862 (718), 2905 (120)
Hafner, A.: ref, 1058 (2), 2860 (152)
Hafner, H.: ref, 2050 (33)
Hafner, R. J.: ref, 337 (140,169,192)
Hagan, J. S.: test, 2470
Hagans, C.: ref, 298 (20)
Hagberg, B. S.: ref, 1134 (3)
Hagedorn, L. S.: ref, 621 (1,2)
Hagekull, B.: ref, 2039 (11)
Hagell, A.: ref, 1765 (26), 2862 (485)
Hageman, C.: ref, 303 (10), 641 (7), 1740 (14), 2226 (13), 2860 (1168), 2863 (351)
Hagemann, M.: ref, 1318 (12)
Hagen, E.: test, 560, 561; rev, 573, 595, 2488
Hagen, E. P.: test, 385, 2485

Hagen, J. W.: ref, 2603 (100)
Hagen, K.: ref, 2163 (221)
Hagen, N.: ref, 1615 (1)
Hagerman, R.: ref, 2813 (116), 2860 (351)
Hagerman, R. J.: ref, 1903 (12), 2860 (35), 2862 (16), 2863 (13), 2879 (6)
Hägglöf, B.: ref, 2862 (617)
Hagglund, K. J.: ref, 2603 (344)
Hagin, R. A.: rev, 120, 121, 334, 374, 477, 2282, 2720
Hagiwara, M. P.: rev, 101, 102, 509
Hagley, F.: test, 2556
Hagmann, S.: ref, 2860 (1271)
Hagopian, L. P.: ref, 2211 (5), 2214 (5,29), 2497 (131), 2498 (5)
Hagues, N.: test, 2023
Hahlweg, K.: ref, 2603 (287)
Hahn, A.: ref, 1615 (1)
Hahn, A. L.: rev, 1516
Hahn, M. B.: ref, 2603 (490)
Hahn, M. E.: test, 371; rev, 170, 1074
Hahn, R.: ref, 672 (4)
Hahn, S. U.: ref, 301 (17), 1392 (5), 1902 (24),2247 (15), 2749 (20), 2905 (14)
Hahn-Barma, V.: ref, 776 (63)
Haidar, S. A.: ref, 2603 (377)
Haier, R. J.: ref, 2163 (221), 2860 (883)
Haines, C. J.: ref, 272 (287), 1079 (94)
Haines, J.: test, 1085, 1086
Haines, J.: ref, 697 (6)
Haines, J. L.: ref, 2227 (8), 2860 (364), 2879 (44), 2892 (54)
Haines, K. B.: ref, 1394 (5), 1852 (1),1903 (142,208), 2694 (8), 2704 (7)
Haines, L. D.: ref, 2674 (3)
Haines, M. E.: ref, 272 (178), 2402 (57)
Hains, A. A.: ref, 451 (195), 694 (73), 2230 (5), 2497 (342,513,629)
Hainsworth, M. L.: test, 2047
Hainsworth, P. K.: test, 2047
Haishi, K.: ref, 2862 (359,498,638)
Haislett, J.: ref, 404 (16)
Hajek, P.: ref, 999 (122)
Hakami, M.: ref, 1405 (3)
Hakeren, G.: ref, 666 (12)
Hakim-Larson, J.: ref, 472 (194), 1735 (10), 2858 (4)
Häkkinen-Rihu, P.: ref, 2768 (25), 2862 (268)
Hakola, P.: ref, 1697 (480,481), 2247 (99,100), 2860 (1073,1074)
Hakstian, A. R.: test, 644; rev, 2707
Haladyna, T. M.: rev, 14, 1687, 1822, 2484
Halamish, R.: ref, 337 (50), 2497 (223)
Halaris, A.: ref, 1093 (34)
Halberstadt, A. G.: ref, 2078 (6), 2497 (475)
Halbreich, U.: ref, 1166 (1), 2305 (12)
Halbreich, V.: ref, 1166 (162), 2603 (503)
Halderson, C.: test, 648
Hale, A. S.: ref, 1166 (12)
Hale, C. A.: ref, 1903 (500), 2862 (386), 2879 (133)
Hale, D.: ref, 1697 (541), 2860 (1257)
Hale, J. B.: ref, 451 (258), 681 (92), 1099 (5), 1164 (177), 1379 (101), 1740 (31), 2516 (118), 2892 (299)
Hale, V. E.: ref, 2497 (66)
Hale, W. W., III: ref, 272 (271), 1079 (89), 1166 (190)
Haley, G.: ref, 472 (46)
Haley, K. L.: ref, 1903 (264), 2695 (25)
Haley, S.: test, 2316
Haley, S. M.: test, 1906
Haley, W. E.: ref, 708 (9), 1181 (1)
Halford, W. K.: ref, 863 (2), 1093 (91), 1178 (3)
Halinski, R. S.: test, 247
Hall, A.: ref, 272 (41)
Hall, A. E.: rev, 522, 1140
Hall, A. L.: ref, 2227 (2), 2860 (179), 2863 (48)
Hall, B.: ref, 472 (8)
Hall, B. A.: test, 2257
Hall, B. J. D.: ref, 128 (3), 2163 (203)
Hall, B. W.: rev, 1782, 1783
Hall, C.: ref, 1469 (11), 1590 (63), 2193 (17), 2227 (25), 2516 (79), 2860 (495,1089,1226), 2863 (141,322), 2892 (80)
Hall, C. D.: ref, 2076 (135)
Hall, C. W.: rev, 1388, 1466, 1908, 1950, 2540, 2618; ref, 462 (9), 1414 (3), 1462 (1,2,3), 2862 (577,737), 2901 (111)
Hall, E.: ref, 1469 (11),1590 (63)
Hall, F. J.: ref, 1755 (61)
Hall, G.: ref, 2603 (75),2858 (22)
Hall, G. C. N.: ref, 1340 (4), 2402 (38)
Hall, J.: test, 14, 437, 675, 676, 703, 755, 941, 1244, 1441, 1546, 1558, 1559, 1564, 1565, 1567, 1571, 1572, 1712, 1757, 1861, 1894, 1924, 1937, 1945, 1971, 2021, 2022, 2068, 2078, 2133, 2188, 2273, 2275, 2280, 2547, 2548, 2549, 2578, 2583, 2634, 2636, 2637, 2638, 2921; ref, 246 (7), 280 (5), 451 (231), 2862 (647), 2879 (211), 2905 (115)
Hall, J. A.: ref, 1000 (32), 2078 (6)
Hall, J. A. Y.: ref, 2125 (15)
Hall, J. E., III: ref, 1697 (217)
Hall, J. L.: ref, 2863 (29)
Hall, J. N.: test, 2195
Hall, J. W.: rev, 82
Hall, K.: ref, 1903 (77)
Hall, L. A.: ref, 448 (29), 2039 (4)
Hall, L. G.: test, 1163
Hall, L. M.: ref, 2813 (109), 2860 (1001)
Hall, M.: ref, 337 (156), 349 (20,33), 1166 (182), 2227 (25), 2516 (79), 2860 (1089), 2863 (322)
Hall, M. H.: ref, 2516 (50)
Hall, N. E.: ref, 994 (6,8), 1096 (6), 1240 (12,15), 1612 (30), 1903 (102,152,178), 1982 (5),2485 (46,74,87), 2680 (5,6), 2768 (8,10,16), 2813 (30), 2862 (151,191), 2864 (26,35)
Hall, P. K.: rev, 175, 2470; ref, 199 (2), 798 (2), 1612 (3), 2008 (1), 2485 (6), 2862 (18), 2864 (1), 2873 (2)

Hall, R. E.: ref, 202 (1), 324 (3), 331 (1), 798 (6), 994 (3), 1424 (1), 1903 (97), 2190 (2), 2524 (1), 2660 (3), 2695 (10), 2710 (2), 2768 (7)
Hall, R. H.: ref, 372 (4), 998 (7), 1140 (4), 2656 (12)
Hall, R. J.: ref, 298 (164)
Hall, R. V.: ref, 1657 (7), 1866 (7)
Hall, S.: ref, 451 (58), 687 (2),2860 (1090)
Hall, V. C.: rev, 674; ref, 1592 (5)
Hall, W. B.: rev, 933
Hall, W. E.: rev, 2742
Hall, W. S.: ref, 592 (50)
Hallam, G.: test, 379
Halle, T. G.: ref, 272 (117)
Haller, D. L.: ref, 1697 (218), 2402 (18), 2519 (26), 2520 (27)
Haller, E.: ref, 2850 (2)
Haller, P.: ref, 376 (33), 2239 (35)
Haller, R. M.: rev, 175, 1061, 2235, 2651
Haller-Peck, S. M.: ref, 451 (169), 880 (1), 1216 (96)
Hallet, M.: ref, 1758 (21), 2860 (426)
Hallett, M.: ref, 1135 (25), 2863 (418)
Halliday, M. S.: ref, 1781 (1)
Hallikaincn, M.: ref, 1164 (152), 2516 (99), 2892 (274)
Halling, D. C.: ref, 2860 (652), 2863 (191)
Halliwell, M.: test, 1516
Hallman, W.: ref, 2603 (168)
Hallmayer, J.: ref, 2862 (486)
Hallstrom, C.: ref, 272 (152), 2497 (538)
Hallum, A.: ref, 2862 (20)
Halman, L. J.: ref, 2860 (234)
Halmi, K. A.: ref, 272 (229), 1697 (520)
Halperin, J. M.: ref, 303 (6), 451 (58), 1218 (10), 2860 (891), 2863 (263)
Halpern, A. R.: ref, 2860 (551), 2863 (159)
Halpern, A. S.: test, 2422, 2443, 2734
Halpern, H.: rev, 1061
Halpern-Felsher, B. L.: ref, 811 (9),1086 (4)
Halsey, H., Jr.: ref, 838 (3), 2860 (36)
Halsey, J. H., Jr.: ref, 838 (1)
Halsey, L. B.: ref, 448 (17)
Halstead, M. E.: test, 2257
Haltiner, A.: ref, 2050 (97)
Haltiwanger, J.: test, 2316
Haltiwanger, J. T.: test, 1906
Halton, A.: ref, 272 (58), 1000 (37)
Halvari, H.: ref, 2497 (476)
Halverson, C. F., Jr.: ref, 863 (26), 1000 (23), 2603 (138)
Ham, H. P.: ref, 326 (10), 1164 (151), 2402 (64), 2485 (83), 2599 (13), 2860 (457,1273)
Ham, S.: ref, 1201 (3)
Hamada, R. S.: ref, 1592 (19), 1697 (268), 2497 (312), 2516 (36)
Hamanaka, T.: ref, 2163 (335), 2226 (30), 2227 (47), 2860 (1317)
Hamann, M. S.: ref, 2603 (377)
Hamberger, M. J.: ref, 2860 (884)
Hambleton, R.: test, 1436
Hambleton, R. K.: rev, 302, 838, 1657, 2500; ref, 1107 (2,3)
Hambrick, D. Z.: ref, 2892 (252)
Hamburger, S.: ref, 2305 (232)
Hamburger, S. C.: ref, 2288 (71), 2289 (56), 2862 (501)
Hamburger, S. D.: ref, 451 (102,116,243), 863 (42), 1010 (49), 2288 (68), 2289 (52), 2305 (137), 2860 (213,366), 2862 (450,475,493,629,702), 2879 (227), 2892 (28)
Hamby, S.: ref, 2227 (25), 2516 (79), 2860 (1089), 2863 (322)
Hamby, S. L.: ref, 2076 (135)
Hamdam-Allen, G.: ref, 1485 (44), 1653 (24), 2813 (102), 2864 (102)
Hamdi, E.: ref, 1166 (191), 2050 (73)
Hamer, D. P.: ref, 272 (209), 1164 (131), 2125 (24), 2516 (83), 2863 (343)
Hames, K. A.: ref, 272 (150,151), 2402 (37,54), 2497 (537), 2599 (26), 2860 (798,1037,1038), 2863 (308), 2892 (161)
Hamil, W. L.: rev, 878
Hamill, S.: ref, 2497 (33)
Hamilton, A.: ref, 1697 (2)
Hamilton, C. E.: ref, 373 (20), 875 (4,5)
Hamilton, C. J.: ref, 298 (143), 1140 (43)
Hamilton, E. B.: ref, 451 (196)
Hamilton, J. A.: ref, 2603 (95)
Hamilton, L.: ref, 1485 (64), 2682 (12)
Hamilton, L. B.: ref, 665 (40)
Hamilton, M.: test, 1481
Hamilton Region Mathematics Writing Group: test, 1605
Hamilton, S. B.: ref, 2497 (7)
Hamilton, S. E.: ref, 2516 (69), 2892 (191)
Hamlett, C.: test, 1715; ref, 665 (93)
Hamlett, C. L.: ref, 665 (76),2484 (3)
Hamlett, K. W.: ref, 1010 (35,41), 2603 (166,167), 2858 (46)
Hamlin, C. L.: ref, 1697 (291), 2603 (258)
Hammeke, T.: rev, 2225
Hammeke, T. A.: test, 1525; rev, 326; ref, 2860 (1032,1041), 2892 (214)
Hammen, C.: ref, 472 (213), 681 (56), 999 (142), 1010 (121), 1093 (89), 1991 (48), 2076 (33), 2214 (124)
Hammen, C. J.: ref, 592 (80)
Hammer, A. L.: test, 697, 1755, 1790; ref, 697 (1), 2497 (216)
Hammer, D.: ref, 4 (13),472 (89)
Hammer, E.: test, 1067
Hammer, E. F.: test, 1160
Hammer, K.: ref, 451 (197)
Hammer, L. B.: ref, 272 (179), 1745 (70)
Hammer, L. D.: ref, 2305 (138)
Hammer, M.: ref, 1405 (18)
Hammer, M. A.: ref, 1903 (171), 2651 (11), 2768 (15), 2862 (201)

Hammer, R. E.: ref, 1140 (44)
Hammerlie, F. M.: ref, 2525 (5)
Hammett, E.: ref, 998 (19), 2305 (30)
Hammill, D.: test, 1726
Hammill, D. D.: test, 258, 286, 655, 656, 657, 662, 797, 798, 799, 816, 1167, 1168, 1459, 1725, 2668, 2680, 2682, 2683, 2694, 2695, 2712, 2722, 2731, 2732; ref, 1240 (16)
Hammock, R. G.: ref, 4 (7)
Hammon, S.: ref, 2497 (190)
Hammond, C. S.: ref, 1096 (11), 1903 (419), 2873 (46)
Hammond, D. C.: test, 1732
Hammond, E.: ref, 2860 (186), 2863 (50)
Hammond, G. D.: ref, 451 (215), 1962 (23)
Hammond, J. A.: ref, 1697 (422)
Hammond, K. M.: ref, 2860 (92), 2863 (26)
Hammond, M.: ref, 864 (1), 997 (6), 1010 (30), 1902 (29), 2039 (2), 2657 (25,26), 2813 (92,93), 2862 (155), 2864 (90),91)
Hammond, M. A.: ref, 451 (126), 2045 (2), 2657 (29), 2813 (119), 2864 (115)
Hammond, W. A.: ref, 272 (114)
Hammond-Laurence, K.: ref, 2214 (139), 2498 (78)
Hammond-Lawrence, K.: ref, 451 (93), 2498 (58)
Hamp-Lyons, L.: ref, 666 (9)
Hampes, W. P.: ref, 1631 (2), 2218 (115)
Hampson, E.: ref, 1405 (9), 2125 (4), 2860 (183)
Hampson, R. B.: ref, 1000 (97)
Hampson, S. E.: ref, 776 (14)
Hampton, C.: ref, 998 (75,76), 2603 (282,283), 2858 (78,79)
Hampton, S.: ref, 1903 (270), 2905 (56)
Hamrick, H. M.: ref, 1216 (1)
Hams, J.: ref, 2860 (643),2892 (120)
Hams, T. O.: ref, 2050 (61)
Hamsher, deS.: test, 1740
Hamson, C. O.: ref, 2163 (324)
Han, Y. S.: ref, 272 (360), 273 (34)
Hanawalt, N. G.: rev, 303
Hanburg, H. G.: test, 78
Hancin-Bhatt, B.: ref, 2029 (1)
Hancock, D. R.: ref, 592 (59)
Hancock, G. R.: ref, 665 (72)
Hancock, H.: ref, 540 (4)
Hancock, H. E.: ref, 2892 (252)
Hancock, K.: ref, 1166 (38), 2497 (155)
Hancock, M. R.: ref, 1318 (3)
Hand, L.: test, 2438; ref, 1040 (10), 1095 (25), 1394 (7), 1903 (285)
Handal, P.: ref, 337 (62)
Handal, P. J.: ref, 337 (59,107), 2525 (10), 2603 (185)
Handelsman, M. M.: ref, 272 (257), 2497 (613)
Handen, B.: ref, 4 (12)
Handen, B. L.: ref, 681 (46,86), 2485 (225),2862 (624)
Handerson, H.: ref, 1903 (92)
Handford, H. A.: ref, 451 (139), 472 (178), 2485 (209), 2862 (515)
Handleman, J. S.: ref, 459 (8), 1903 (54,81), 2485 (36,37)
Handler, L.: ref, 1401 (3), 1697 (418,455,550), 2247 (89,95,118,125)
Handley, P.: test, 1273
Handley-Derry, M.: ref, 1485 (58), 1653 (28), 2813 (144)
Handlin, D.: ref, 68 (46), 998 (97), 2497 (477)
Handmaker, S. D.: ref, 2860 (824)
Handschu, R.: ref, 2863 (350)
Handwerger, B. A.: ref, 1962 (19)
Handwerk, M. J.: ref, 246 (7), 2862 (647), 2879 (211), 2905 (115)
Handwerk, M. L.: ref, 451 (259), 1160 (4), 1164 (178), 1378 (12), 2242 (8), 2516 (119), 2722 (1), 2862 (716), 2892 (300), 2901 (133)
Hanes, K. R.: rev, 274, 885
Haney, W. V.: test, 2788
Hanfmann, E.: test, 1714
Hanin, I.: ref, 2305 (95)
Hank, G.: ref, 2603 (287)
Hanks, D. L.: ref, 1517 (7)
Hanley, J. R.: ref, 350 (31), 1104 (8), 1758 (13,39), 1903 (527), 2163 (327), 2193 (6), 2860 (1091), 2863 (114,268,323,386)
Hanlon, R. E.: ref, 2873 (53)
Hann, D. M.: ref, 451 (130)
Hanna, G.: test, 1768
Hanna, G. L.: ref, 451 (198), 472 (196), 1697 (170)
Hanna, G. S.: test, 1767, 1863; rev, 431, 773, 838, 1428, 2111, 2434, 2898
Hanna, L. A.: rev, 1319
Hanna, P. R.: rev, 2484
Hanna, S. E.: ref, 337 (120)
Hannafin, M. J.: rev, 1500
Hannah, E. P.: test, 1171
Hannah, M. E.: rev, 227; ref, 1965 (67)
Hannah, M. T.: ref, 68 (36), 372 (101), 2126 (15), 2603 (390)
Hannah, W.: ref, 68 (36)
Hannan, C. L.: ref, 2485 (167), 2862 (347)
Hannan, J.: ref, 337 (172), 451 (188)
Hannan, K.: ref, 1216 (33), 2498 (16)
Hannay, H. J.: ref, 838 (1,3), 2860 (36,683)
Hannequin, D.: ref, 2227 (19), 2860 (818), 2863 (236)
Hanner, M. A.: test, 1424
Hänninen, T.: ref, 1164 (152), 2516 (99), 2860 (913), 2863 (273), 2892 (274)
Hannon, R.: ref, 2599 (28)
Hans, S. L.: ref, 301 (1,22), 748 (1,8), 1592 (11), 2010 (7), 2163 (87), 2305 (5,64), 2860 (39,567), 2862 (21)
Hansbarger, A.: ref, 1866 (42)
Hanschu, B.: test, 2378
Hansell, J.: ref, 337 (57,58), 1000 (46,47), 1178 (7)
Hansell, P. S.: ref, 794 (2)
Hansen, C. E.: ref, 1965 (11)
Hansen, C. P.: ref, 1697 (31)

Hansen, G. G. R.: ref, 1095 (13)
Hansen, J.: rev, 1529; ref, 1240 (26), 1903 (265), 2417 (19), 2695 (26), 2905 (23,55)
Hansen, J. B.: rev, 744, 2731
Hansen, J. B.: ref, 493 (1)
Hansen, J. C.: test, 1790; rev, 1342
Hansen, J. S.: ref, 2218 (48)
Hansen, J. T.: ref, 2850 (3)
Hansen, J-I. C.: ref, 298 (29)
Hansen, L.: ref, 376 (15), 1164 (145), 2860 (184,1244), 2862 (105,601), 2892 (266)
Hansen, L. A.: ref, 776 (34), 1135 (4), 2862 (120)
Hansen, M. C.: rev, 2406
Hansen, P. C.: ref, 2860 (1059)
Hansen, P. M.: ref, 2485 (11)
Hansen, S.: ref, 451 (33), 1216 (40), 2485 (114)
Hansen, T. L.: test, 1900
Hansen, V.: ref, 1079 (43)
Hanser, S. B.: ref, 272 (84), 337 (76), 2076 (82)
Hansford, B.: ref, 495 (1)
Hanson, A. R.: ref, 665 (4)
Hanson, C. L.: ref, 1000 (3), 1010 (36)
Hanson, E.: ref, 2856 (7)
Hanson, G. R.: test, 1910, 1918; rev, 1107
Hanson, J. R.: test, 1464, 1473, 1562
Hanson, K. M.: ref, 2065 (31)
Hanson, R.: ref, 68 (36)
Hanson, R. N.: rev, 2360
Hanson, W. E.: ref, 1965 (80), 2835 (26)
Hansson, K.: ref, 2228 (17)
Hansson, L.: ref, 2050 (26)
Hanusa, B. H.: ref, 1621 (1), 2305 (208)
Happ, L. K.: ref, 2860 (368)
Happé, F.: ref, 926 (16), 2858 (70), 2860 (639), 2862 (257)
Happe, F. G. E.: ref, 350 (29,37), 1903 (367), 2860 (640), 2862 (487)
Happel, R. L.: ref, 337 (179), 1697 (561), 2218 (109)
Haque, W.: ref, 2603 (448)
Har-Even, D.: ref, 450 (2), 472 (91), 681 (52), 1697 (87), 2498 (37), 2652 (4), 2862 (281)
Harackiewicz, J. M.: ref, 1965 (34,50)
Haraldsson, E.: ref, 1903 (368), 2163 (217)
Harasym, P. H.: ref, 1132 (1), 1755 (62)
Harbers, H. M.: ref, 624 (24), 1485 (47), 1903 (438)
Harbin, G.: ref, 180 (17), 1216 (48)
Harbour, A.: ref, 624 (1)
Harby, M. L.: test, 2663
Harcourt Brace Educational Measurement: test, 2484, 2486, 2489
Harcovitch, S.: ref, 1485 (58), 1653 (28), 2813 (144)
Harden, A.: ref, 2485 (226), 2862 (625)
Harden, L.: test, 71
Harden, M.: ref, 2076 (6), 2860 (141)
Harden, P. W.: ref, 681 (62), 1367 (4), 2807 (1), 2863 (262), 2892 (184)
Harden, T.: ref, 1093 (37)
Harder, D. W.: ref, 1093 (65), 1687 (5), 1697 (293,548), 1745 (68)
Harders, A. G.: ref, 2163 (200), 2860 (816), 2863 (235)
Hardesty, V. A.: ref, 451 (219)
Hardgrave, B. C.: ref, 1107 (8)
Hardiman, C. J.: test, 2162
Hardin, M. T.: ref, 1093 (31), 2813 (10)
Hardin, S. I.: ref, 2860 (232), 2892 (30)
Hardin-Jones, M. A.: ref, 1040 (8), 2862 (249)
Harding, K.: ref, 790 (4), 999 (19), 2305 (155), 2860 (1203), 2879 (187)
Harding, R. E.: rev, 1068, 2255, 2667, 2747, 2756
Harding, S.: ref, 540 (4)
Hardman, M. L.: ref, 2299 (2), 2485 (98)
Hardy, C.: ref, 863 (50)
Hardy, C. J.: ref, 2860 (502)
Hardy, D.: ref, 301 (18), 2860 (302), 2863 (79)
Hardy, D. F.: ref, 1000 (48)
Hardy, D. W.: ref, 793 (19)
Hardy, E.: test, 276
Hardy, G.: ref, 2603 (403)
Hardy, G. E.: ref, 272 (37,115,116,217,311,357), 2050 (56), 2497 (89,167), 2603 (63,142,230,259,301, 359, 360,582)
Hardy, L.: ref, 2497 (263,557)
Hardy, L. H.: test, 1159
Hardy, P.: ref, 2516 (73), 2860 (1002)
Hare, B. R.: ref, 694 (1)
Hare, J.: ref, 2034 (6)
Hare, R. D.: test, 1173, 1174, 1175; ref, 272 (364), 694 (72), 2860 (1402), 2879 (230)
Harel, S.: ref, 270 (23), 1612 (87)
Harford, T. C.: ref, 2402 (8)
Harger, G. J.: ref, 2497 (343)
Hargrave, G. E.: ref, 372 (67), 1697 (301)
Hargrove, D. S.: rev, 1429, 1590
Hargrove, P. M.: ref, 175 (4), 430 (3), 1903 (31), 2332 (1), 2695 (4)
Haring, B.: ref, 2497 (225)
Haring, T. G.: rev, 62, 1738, 2030, 2868
Harkins, S. W.: ref, 337 (98), 998 (67), 2065 (11,17), 2860 (45), 2863 (17)
Harkness, A. R.: ref, 1612 (38), 1697 (414), 2211 (22)
Harkness, K. L.: ref, 1166 (89), 2218 (43), 2305 (164)
Harlan, C.: ref, 708 (1), 2497 (8)
Harlen, W.: test, 348
Harlow, L.: ref, 337 (123)
Harlow, L. L.: ref, 2132 (1)
Harm, O. J.: ref, 372 (45)
Harman, H. H.: test, 1405
Harman, L. W.: ref, 298 (104)
Harman, M. J.: ref, 462 (2,19)
Harmon, L. W.: test, 1790; rev, 360, 404, 1535, 1554, 2420; ref, 1790 (10,15)
Harmon, R. J.: ref, 784 (1), 1612 (70), 1903 (366)
Harms, L.: ref, 815 (27), 1903 (379),2695 (41), 2862 (364), 2879 (125)

Harms, T.: test, 875, 1009, 1264,2310
Harnadek, M. C. S.: ref, 1697 (538)
Harnett-Sheehan, K.: ref, 2603 (64)
Harnisch, D. L.: rev, 33, 570, 1066, 1948, 2137,2699
Harnish, M. J.: ref, 2402 (28)
Harold, G. T.: ref, 2603 (531)
Harpaz, I.: ref, 2771 (6)
Harper, C. R.: test, 2865
Harper, D. C.: rev, 803, 811, 855, 2243, 2511; ref, 815 (6), 1216 (14), 2225 (3), 2864 (22)
Harper, G. W.: ref, 681 (15)
Harper, H.: ref, 2050 (131),2603 (226,412)
Harper, R.: ref, 399 (5), 2433 (3)
Harper, R. G.: ref, 337 (11), 1164 (18), 1686 (7), 1697 (74), 2288 (50), 2860 (185), 2863 (49)
Harrell, A. V.: test, 75
Harrell, E. H.: ref, 2860 (790)
Harrell, L. E.: ref, 2768 (35), 2860 (1126),2863 (334)
Harrell, M.: test, 566
Harrell, S. P.: ref, 592 (43)
Harrell, T. H.: ref, 1698 (4)
Harrell, T. W.: rev, 2125
Harrigan, J. A.: ref, 999 (85), 2497 (123,344,558)
Harrigan, K. M.: ref, 2497 (558)
Harriman, P. L.: rev, 851, 1160, 1332
Harrington, C. M.: ref, 462 (32), 1582 (13)
Harrington, D.: ref, 270 (8), 448 (10), 1216 (36,66), 2189 (5)
Harrington, D. E.: ref, 1525 (15), 2163 (187)
Harrington, D. L.: ref, 199 (5), 2860 (260,638)
Harrington, J.: ref, 272 (318), 273 (32), 1166 (151)
Harrington, J. C.: test, 5
Harrington, M. E.: ref, 748 (5)
Harrington, R.: ref, 1093 (109), 2214 (114), 2305 (36,224), 2860 (334)
Harrington, R. G.: rev, 2, 158, 1099, 1462; ref, 2860 (395)
Harrington, S.: ref, 2599 (28)
Harrington, S. A.: rev, 2591
Harrington, T. F.: test, 5, 1177
Harris, A. C.: ref, 298 (112)
Harris, A. E.: ref, 2288 (32), 2289 (24), 2305 (91)
Harris, A. F.: test, 1343, 2925
Harris, A. J.: test, 1532; rev, 1092
Harris, B.: ref, 1166 (31)
Harris, C.: ref, 2252 (4), 2295 (4)
Harris, D.: ref, 1755 (17)
Harris, D. B.: test, 1097, 1991; rev, 853, 1011, 1012, 1026, 1706, 1964
Harris, D. M.: ref, 2240 (3), 2860 (885)
Harris, D. P.: rev, 614
Harris, E.: ref, 1093 (8), 2108 (1)
Harris, E. L.: ref, 681 (66), 2862 (393), 2901 (72)
Harris, E. S.: ref, 337 (131)
Harris, G. J.: ref, 2289 (22)
Harris, G. T.: ref, 1174 (2)
Harris, J.: ref, 301 (17), 1392 (5), 1902 (24), 2247 (15), 2749 (20), 2905 (14)
Harris, J. A.: test, 2836; ref, 495 (15), 963 (2), 1010 (130), 1965 (84)
Harris, J. L.: ref, 1903 (119), 2115 (5)
Harris, K.: ref, 1697 (472)
Harris, K. C.: ref, 251 (2), 1234 (3), 1420 (2), 1902 (42)
Harris, K. R.: ref, 1379 (33), 1902 (8), 2432 (4,5), 2485 (104), 2862 (70,71,631), 2901 (5,121), 2905 (35)
Harris, L. A.: rev, 1318, 2183, 2905
Harris, L. J.: ref, 2860 (1176)
Harris, L. M.: ref, 1021 (34)
Harris, M.: ref, 134 (36), 999 (138,190), 1079 (103,106)
Harris, M. A.: ref, 1000 (3)
Harris, M. J.: ref, 466 (1), 1164 (100),1757 (1), 1965 (15), 2242 (6), 2288 (30,69,72), 2289 (21,53,57), 2749 (70), 2860 (908,1104), 2892 (190)
Harris, N. G. S.: test, 329
Harris, O. J.: ref, 298 (49)
Harris, P.: ref, 350 (18)
Harris, P. L.: ref, 1903 (94), 2662 (8)
Harris, P. T.: ref, 1216 (1)
Harris, R.: ref, 1697 (279)
Harris, R. J.: ref, 303 (14), 1164 (143), 2163 (315), 2226 (20), 2227 (35), 2860 (824,1241), 2862 (600), 2863 (374), 2879 (199), 2892 (265)
Harris, R. N.: ref, 1000 (14)
Harris, R. N., Jr.: ref, 1000 (15)
Harris, S.: ref, 433 (14), 2229 (9), 2485 (202)
Harris, S. L.: ref, 459 (8), 1903 (54,81), 2485 (36,37,77)
Harris, S. M.: ref, 893 (20), 2527 (9), 2892 (81)
Harris, T.: ref, 2050 (18)
Harris, T. O.: ref, 2050 (27,59,62),110)
Harris, W.: ref, 2076 (93)
Harris, W. G.: test, 2490; rev, 2491
Harrison, D. A.: ref, 1166 (71)
Harrison, D. K.: ref, 1592 (4), 2860 (138)
Harrison, D. W.: ref, 2497 (320,321)
Harrison, G.: ref, 2050 (139), 2163 (308), 2860 (1197), 2862 (415)
Harrison, G. N.: ref, 2050 (8)
Harrison, M. M.: ref, 2860 (500)
Harrison, M. T.: rev, 2787
Harrison, P.: ref, 1379 (92)
Harrison, P. A.: test, 2554
Harrison, P. L.: test, 124, 2813; rev, 1, 930, 1500, 1760, 2879
Harrison, R.: test, 820
Harrison, R. H.: ref, 1697 (297)
Harrison, S. A.: ref, 268 (1)
Harrison, W.: ref, 337 (90), 1166 (162), 2076 (108), 2603 (503)
Harrist, A. W.: ref, 451 (199)
Harrop, R.: ref, 1697 (15), 2860 (60)
Harrow, M.: ref, 1164 (170), 1525 (12), 2050 (6,16), 2305 (105,142,235), 2860 (318,743,973,1108,1350)
Harry, A. L.: ref, 357 (1), 496 (4), 2905 (15)
Harsey, P.: test, 2415
Harsh, C. M.: rev, 302, 2417, 2757

Harshbarger, J.: ref, 694 (93), 1079 (34),2497 (426)
Harskamp, F. V.: ref, 2497 (259)
Harstink, M. W. I.: ref, 2860 (79), 2892 (7)
Hart, B.: ref, 665 (71), 1657 (13), 1697 (160), 1866 (34), 1903 (326), 2485 (152), 2694 (11), 2695 (32), 2879 (95)
Hart, B. L.: ref, 303 (14), 1164 (143), 2163 (315), 2226 (20), 2227 (35), 2860 (1241, 2862 (600), 2863 (374), 2879 (199), 2892 (265)
Hart, D.: ref, 272 (272), 1408 (8), 2218 (94), 2497 (630)
Hart, E. L.: ref, 2862 (348)
Hart, J.: ref, 472 (169)
Hart, J. B.: ref, 1866 (42)
Hart, K.: test, 444, 892
Hart, K. E.: ref, 1647 (3)
Hart, K. J.: ref, 771 (26), 1697 (347), 2603 (297)
Hart, L.: ref, 1991 (84)
Hart, L. A.: ref, 769 (7), 1072 (55), 1503 (16), 1903 (576), 2163 (353), 2862 (725), 2901 (134)
Hart, L. R.: ref, 301 (40), 2247 (117), 2860 (462)
Hart, M. N.: ref, 2227 (3), 2860 (181)
Hart, R. P.: ref, 2010 (17), 2402 (34), 2860 (45,544,761), 2863 (17,156)
Hart, S.: ref, 270 (16), 272 (169), 353 (17)
Hart, S. D.: test, 1175, 2395, 2476
Hart, S. N.: rev, 448, 462, 544, 1933
Hart, S. S.: ref, 665 (40)
Hart, T. M.: ref, 2879 (208), 2905 (111)
Hart, V.: rev, 1316, 1728,2005
Harter, S.: test, 1987, 2369; ref, 2862 (87)
Hartje, W.: ref, 2860 (944)
Hartka, E.: ref, 373 (1)
Hartleben, J.: test, 661
Hartley, A. A.: ref, 2163 (39), 2860 (164)
Hartley, D.: ref, 2603 (266)
Hartley, J.: ref, 350 (12), 1240 (23), 2163 (141)
Hartley, J. T.: ref, 2402 (1)
Hartley, L.: ref, 2497 (67)
Hartley, R. E.: ref, 2558 (2)
Hartman, A. D.: test, 2787
Hartman, A. H.: ref, 451 (74), 889 (1)
Hartman, B.: ref, 794 (2)
Hartman, B. W.: rev, 179; ref, 404 (8,25), 2497 (12)
Hartman, D. K.: ref, 665 (38), 2031 (4,8)
Hartman, H. J.: rev, 563, 2405
Hartman, J.: test, 2121
Hartman, J. M.: ref, 2484 (13)
Hartman, J. S.: ref, 999 (85), 2497 (344)
Hartman, K.: ref, 2858 (5)
Hartman, M.: ref, 2860 (123,261), 2863 (34,66)
Hartman, R. K.: test, 2295
Hartman, S.: ref, 1755 (71)
Hartman, S. J.: ref, 298 (49), 771 (9)
Hartman, V. L.: ref, 337 (106), 451 (69), 472 (139,140), 2498 (54), 2603 (545)
Hartmann, D. J.: ref, 1939 (5)
Hartmann, G. W.: rev, 363, 2624
Hartnett, R. T.: rev, 57, 686; ref, 592 (1)
Hartshorne, T. S.: rev, 769, 1620
Hartsough, C.: test, 469
Hartsough, C. S.: test, 2122; rev, 78; ref, 469 (3)
Hartung, G. H.: ref, 998 (52)
Hartung, J. P.: test, 1528
Hartung, P. J.: ref, 83 (4), 2282 (12), 2805 (3)
Hartz, J.: ref, 624 (3), 1903 (127)
Hartz, J. D.: test, 935; ref, 935 (1), 2924 (1)
Harvey, A.: ref, 592 (78), 2031 (7)
Harvey, A. G.: ref, 1079 (36), 2497 (433,434), 2860 (812)
Harvey, A. L.: rev, 971, 1792
Harvey, I.: ref, 2050 (14,34,74,80), 2860 (656)
Harvey, J. B.: test, 1546, 1564, 1567, 2547, 2548
Harvey, M.: ref, 2860 (641,886)
Harvey, P. D.: ref, 1164 (74), 2017 (7), 2163 (115), 2288 (5,7), 2289 (3,5), 2290 (2), 2305 (8,11,37,225), 2860 (723,1020), 2892 (76,144,148)
Harvey, R. J.: test, 627; ref, 1755 (40,56)
Harvie, A.: ref, 1592 (23), 2125 (14)
Harvill, L.: ref, 1697 (455), 2247 (95)
Harvill, L. M.: rev, 1478, 1483, 1975, 2272
Harville, D. L.: ref, 180 (34)
Harwell, M.: rev, 2314
Harwell, M. R.: rev, 719, 1916, 2366, 2855
Harwood, M. K.: ref, 134 (1)
Hasbrouck, J.: ref, 2905 (16)
Hasbrouck, L.: ref, 893 (40)
Haselager, G. J. T.: ref, 1832 (15)
Hasher, L.: ref, 1405 (23)
Hashimoto, M.: ref, 2873 (73)
Hashimoto, R.: ref, 2227 (57), 2863 (420)
Hashtroudi, S.: ref, 1903 (92), 2860 (642)
Hashway, R. M.: ref, 56 (19)
Hasin, D. S.: ref, 2305 (179)
Haskell, W. L.: ref, 2076 (4)
Haskett, M. E.: ref, 448 (11,15), 2039 (5), 2485 (38), 2603 (361)
Haskett, R. F.: ref, 1093 (17), 2305 (50)
Haskin, B. S.: test, 2041
Haslam, N.: ref, 748 (10), 2050 (133), 2519 (27), 2520 (28), 2749 (84)
Haslett, T.: ref, 2497 (668)
Haspiel, G. S.: test, 468
Hassainta, F.: ref, 2860 (1306)
Hassan, F. A. A.: ref, 2603 (290)
Hassanein, R. S.: ref, 926 (9), 1140 (26)
Hasse-Sander, I.: ref, 2226 (29)
Hasselbring, T. S.: ref, 665 (45)
Hassler, M.: ref, 1405 (10)
Hassmen, H.: ref, 998 (58)
Hassmen, P.: ref, 592 (60)
Hastings, B.: ref, 2603 (224)
Hastings, J. T.: rev, 979, 2031, 2484
Hastings, L.: ref, 472 (73), 2211 (26), 2862 (238)
Hastings, T.: ref, 1010 (77)

Hastings, T. L.: ref, 451 (200)
Hastrup, J. L.: ref, 1000 (26)
Hasvold, T.: ref, 1079 (43)
Hatch, J. P.: ref, 1697 (172), 2497 (174)
Hatch, M.: ref, 451 (168), 1010 (118), 2305 (215), 2862 (592), 2879 (194)
Hatch, R. S.: rev, 845
Hatcher, C.: ref, 1010 (6)
Hatcher, G.: test, 2653
Hatcher, J.: ref, 2076 (37), 2497 (158)
Hatcher, J. W.: ref, 2497 (251)
Hatcher, P. J.: ref, 349 (11), 1765 (17), 2163 (163)
Hateley, B.: test, 313, 640, 1904, 1912
Hatfield, E.: ref, 450 (1), 1321 (2), 1927 (7), 2497 (34)
Hatfield, F.: test, 2697
Hatsukami, D.: ref, 893 (5)
Hatt, C. V.: rev, 466, 2407
Hatten, J. T.: rev, 2657
Hattie, J.: rev, 384, 385, 1521, 2652; ref, 495 (1), 1759 (4), 2076 (39)
Hattie, J. A.: ref, 1466 (7)
Hatton, C.: ref, 2858 (98)
Hatton, D. D.: ref, 265 (15)
Hattrup, K.: rev, 838, 923, 2643
Hatzichriston, C.: ref, 2122 (1,2), 2358 (5,8), 2120 (3)
Hatzitaskos, P. K.: ref, 1166 (192), 2497 (631)
Hau, K.: ref, 771 (3)
Hauck, M.: ref, 1903 (369), 2485 (168), 2813 (94)
Haude, R. H.: ref, 2497 (286)
Hauenstein, N. M. A.: ref, 1405 (17)
Hauff, E.: ref, 1093 (66), 2050 (75), 2603 (260)
Haug, H-J.: ref, 1166 (219)
Haugh, O. M.: test, 2735
Haughton, V. M.: ref, 2860 (1041)
Haupt, D.: ref, 337 (152)
Haupt, M.: ref, 1525 (23), 2860 (1115)
Haupts, M.: ref, 2227 (15), 2239 (14), 2860 (492), 2863 (138,172), 2892 (78,107)
Hauser, D. L.: ref, 2860 (159)
Hauser, P.: ref, 2305 (120)
Hauser, S. T.: ref, 694 (65), 2603 (354,432,433)
Hauser, W. A.: ref, 2860 (407)
Haut, J. S.: ref, 2860 (262)
Haut, M. W.: ref, 2860 (262)
Hauxn, J. J.: ref, 2517 (1), 2860 (527)
Hauzer, R. C.: ref, 2497 (583)
Havenaar, J. M.: ref, 1079 (68,69)
Havenstein, N. M. A.: ref, 1965 (25), 2871 (2)
Havercamp, S.: ref, 1485 (43), 2860 (956), 2862 (381)
Havercamp, S. M.: ref, 2199 (14)
Havermans, T.: ref, 449 (4)
Haviland, M. G.: ref, 272 (64)
Havis, L.: test, 982
Haw, C. E.: ref, 1079 (38)
Hawken, L.: ref, 2076 (146)
Hawker, J.: test, 2021, 2022
Hawkey, D.: test, 119, 735, 964, 2087, 2642
Hawkins, A. J.: ref, 1612 (19)
Hawkins, D.: ref, 997 (10), 1216 (20), 2127 (1), 2603 (134)
Hawkins, D. A.: ref, 2050 (64,93), 2076 (97), 2239 (18), 2497 (384), 2860 (581), 2863 (168), 2892 (106)
Hawkins, J. M.: ref, 1093 (93), 2289 (39)
Hawkins, K. A.: ref, 2305 (174), 2860 (993), 2860 (1068), 2879 (144)
Hawkins, S.: ref, 337 (160)
Hawks, B. K.: ref, 404 (20)
Hawley, D. E.: ref, 389 (2)
Hawley, G. A.: test, 1631
Hawley, T. L.: ref, 272 (117)
Haworth, J. T.: ref, 1079 (20)
Haworth, M.: test, 2307
Haworth, M. R.: rev, 1160, 2485
Hawryluk, G. A.: ref, 2860 (500)
Hawton, K.: ref, 272 (241), 998 (71), 999 (46), 2050 (76)
Haxby, J. V.: ref, 199 (16), 2010 (1,16,18), 2163 (10,179), 2485 (234), 2516 (47), 2860 (5,34,290,703, 837,1223), 2863 (3,12,77,205,242,364), 2879 (87)
Hay, D. A.: ref, 1097 (2), 1485 (4), 1903 (47), 2125 (3), 2864 (17)
Hay, D. C.: ref, 2010 (3), 2860 (233), 2863 (60)
Hay, D. F.: ref, 451 (77), 1612 (71), 1612 (80), 2860 (976)
Hay, E. N.: test, 1180; rev, 534
Hay, I.: ref, 1916 (3), 2358 (10), 2743 (3)
Hay, P.: ref, 998 (105)
Hay, P. J.: ref, 337 (141)
Hay-McBer Training Resources Group: test, 1560
Hay/McBer: test, 2268
Hayamizu, T.: ref, 2380 (5)
Hayashida, M.: ref, 2603 (169)
Haycock, L. A.: ref, 2497 (669)
Hayden, J. R.: rev, 547, 2890
Hayden, L. C.: ref, 1166 (152), 1216 (88), 2603 (496)
Hayden, M.: ref, 1164 (144), 1300 (3), 2860 (1242)
Hayden, M. R.: ref, 301 (47), 2516 (63), 2863 (233), 2879 (105), 2892 (166)
Hayden, R. M.: ref, 2862 (289), 2864 (71)
Hayes, A.: ref, 2485 (160)
Hayes, A. M.: ref, 272 (157,180), 991 (2), 2305 (122)
Hayes, B.: test, 2509; ref, 1040 (10), 1095 (25), 1394 (7), 1903 (285)
Hayes, B. K.: ref, 1021 (34), 2485 (88)
Hayes, B. T.: ref, 1095 (45), 2045 (5)
Hayes, C. G.: ref, 592 (9)
Hayes, D. P.: ref, 592 (106)
Hayes, H.: ref, 1481 (3)
Hayes, J. A.: ref, 337 (173)
Hayes, J. E.: ref, 1903 (159), 2485 (76), 2862 (193)
Hayes, J. S.: ref, 2860 (1127)
Hayes, L. J.: ref, 2382 (15)
Hayes, M.: ref, 2497 (98)

Hayes, R. L.: ref, 1093 (91)
Hayes, S. C.: rev, 760, 1455; ref, 2382 (15)
Hayes, S. G.: ref, 1093 (2)
Hayes, T. L.: rev, 1671, 2746
Hayes, Z. L.: ref, 745 (11), 1072 (44)
Hayford, J. R.: ref, 1010 (54), 1613 (2), 2498 (24)
Hayhurst, H.: ref, 2050 (127)
Haynes, J. B.: ref, 2731 (2), 2732 (1), 2862 (366), 2862 (510), 2905 (79)
Haynes, L. T.: ref, 2076 (47)
Haynes, O. M.: ref, 1333 (3), 1903 (449), 1965 (26), 2229 (7)
Haynes, S. D.: rev, 483, 894
Haynes, W. O.: rev, 628, 2044, 2215, 2657; ref, 1095 (5)
Hays, B. J.: ref, 2214 (110), 2498 (65)
Hays, C. E.: ref, 2498 (69)
Hays, G. M.: ref, 405 (2), 2360 (2)
Hays, J. R.: ref, 1164 (96), 2402 (39), 2860 (887)
Hays, L. W.: ref, 337 (170), 1687 (27)
Hays, P.: ref, 2076 (140)
Hays, P. A.: ref, 2603 (362)
Hays, R. B.: ref, 337 (12)
Hays, R. D.: test, 2158
Hayslip, B.: ref, 2258 (1,3)
Hayslip, B., Jr.: ref, 745 (17)
Haythronthwaite, J.: ref, 2497 (119)
Hayward, C.: ref, 2305 (138)
Hayward, L.: ref, 271 (8), 272 (248)
Hayward, M.: ref, 2603 (338)
Hayward, P.: ref, 2497 (345), 2516 (40)
Haywood, T. W.: ref, 793 (19), 1697 (298,299,370,488), 1744 (5)
Hazeldine, P.: ref, 1903 (467),2862 (480)
Hazelhurst, J. H.: test, 2057
Hazell, P. L.: ref, 1079 (37)
Hazelrigg, P. J.: ref, 2078 (3)
Hazlewood, R.: ref, 272 (218)
Hazzard, A.: ref, 1093 (92), 2498 (9), 2603 (186)
Head, L. Q.: ref, 2497 (116), 2656 (4)
Healey, E. C.: rev, 207
Healy, C. C.: ref, 2282 (11)
Healy, J. M.: ref, 451 (9)
Healy, M. A.: ref, 2527 (2)
Healy, W.: test, 1189
Heap, I.: ref, 2860 (674)
Heard, H. L.: ref, 1093 (48), 2497 (262)
Hearn, M. D.: ref, 1697 (32)
Hearn, S.: ref, 798 (1)
Hearne, D.: ref, 1142 (4), 2771 (37)
Hearst, J.: test, 2342
Hearst-Ikeda, D.: ref, 272 (112)
Heath, A. C.: ref, 999 (58,86,160,172), 2603 (273)
Heather, N.: ref, 1661 (21), 2414 (1)
Heatherton, T. F.: ref, 893 (21)
Heaton, A. W.: ref, 998 (31)
Heaton, R.: ref, 1093 (24), 1164 (25,100), 2860 (239,643,908), 2892 (120,190)
Heaton, R. K.: test, 2118, 2892; ref, 272 (334), 376 (30), 1164 (77,84), 2288 (42,69), 2289 (32,53), 2860 (1104), 2892 (215)
Heaton, S. C.: ref, 2288 (69), 2289 (53), 2860 (1104)
Heaven, P. C. L.: ref, 999 (12,65,87), 1338 (8), 1965 (7)
Heavey, C. L.: ref, 863 (66,78)
Heavey, L.: ref, 1903 (267), 2163 (164)
Hebding, J.: ref, 2603 (380)
Heberlein, W.: ref, 776 (16)
Hebert, J. M.: ref, 2862 (486)
Hebert, M.: rev, 388, 389, 821,1384
Hebert, R.: test, 1726
Hecht, B. F.: ref, 2813 (38)
Hecht, D.: rev, 2855
Hecht, D. B.: ref, 472 (224)
Hecht-Lewis, R.: ref, 1902 (62), 2860 (787), 2862 (298), 2879 (96)
Hechtman, L.: ref, 2603 (262), 2862 (266)
Hectors, A.: ref, 451 (65)
Hedberg, N. L.: rev, 1420
Hedges, S. M.: ref, 2497 (468,469)
Hedgespeth, J.: ref, 1008 (3), 2553 (2)
Hedin, B. A.: ref, 2856 (3)
Hedlund, J.: ref, 2218 (102)
Hedlund, S.: ref, 1745 (57), 2305 (139)
Hedrick, D. K.: ref, 1841 (1)
Hedrick, D. L.: test, 2382
Hedrick, W. B.: ref, 1051 (2), 2694 (13)
Hedström, A.: ref, 303 (8), 2862 (478)
Heefner, A. S.: ref, 1289 (2)
Heemsbergen, J.: ref, 459 (1), 2860 (114)
Heenan, D. K.: rev, 590, 613
Heeren, T.: ref, 272 (19,58), 273 (3), 1000 (5,37)
Heeren, T. J.: ref, 1079 (42)
Heeringa, H. M.: test, 211
Heermann, J. A.: ref, 1770 (6)
Heersink, N.: ref, 1290 (3), 1697 (415), 1744 (6), 2603 (363)
Heesink, J. A. M.: ref, 1079 (82), 1745 (77)
Heffer, R. W.: ref, 2358 (16), 2704 (33)
Heflinger, C. A.: ref, 337 (130), 451 (269)
Hegarty, J. D.: ref, 2050 (77)
Hegarty, M.: ref, 592 (86)
Hegel, M. T.: ref, 2199 (6), 2497 (346), 2519 (40)
Hegeman, I. M.: ref, 2497 (195)
Heger, A.: ref, 472 (52)
Heggoy, S. J.: ref, 2860 (1263), 2862 (610)
Hegstrom, J. L.: ref, 298 (63), 372 (36)
Hegvik, R. L.: test, 425
Heiberger, A. M.: ref, 853 (14), 1160 (3), 2860 (552)
Heidemann, W.: ref, 451 (65)
Heidrich, A.: ref, 1166 (50)
Heifetz, L. J.: rev, 252, 2299; ref, 298 (46), 1590 (11)
Heil, E. S.: rev, 347, 2176
Heilbrun, A. B.: ref, 893 (4)
Heilbrun, A. B., Jr.: test, 68; rev, 288, 365, 751, 844, 908, 1101, 2102; ref, 298 (32), 745 (4)

Heiligenstein, J. H.: ref, 1166 (51)
Heilman, K. M.: ref, 209 (1,2), 376 (20), 1096 (11),1164 (150), 1740 (23,28), 1903 (343,384, 419), 2227 (13,37), 2497 (265), 2860 (186,530, 620,870,1270, 1309,1322), 2863 (50,142,151), 2873 (8,18,23,32, 35,39,45,46,56,57,64,65,70), 2892 (182,273)
Heilman, N.: rev, 863, 1178; ref, 997 (10), 1216 (20), 2127 (1), 2603 (134)
Heim, A. W.: test, 125,126, 127, 128, 129, 2398; rev, 998, 2255
Heiman, M. L.: ref, 457 (1)
Heimann, M.: ref, 2163 (218), 2228 (18)
Heimberg, C.: ref, 2017 (6), 2288 (25), 2289 (14)
Heimberg, R. G.: ref, 472 (220), 2065 (5),2199 (13), 2214 (132), 2497 (68,378,431), 2498 (48),2516 (48), 2305 (65)
Heimlich, T.: ref, 2860 (1272)
Heindel, W.: ref, 2305 (32,130)
Heindel, W. C.: ref, 376 (21), 776 (7,26,44), 1164 (153), 2863 (293), 2892 (275)
Heine, S. J.: ref, 2218 (50)
Heinemann, A. W.: ref, 2603 (571)
Heinlein, K. B.: ref, 1300 (8,11), 337 (77,142)
Heinrich, R. L.: ref, 863 (8), 2603 (61)
Heinssen, R. K.: ref, 1093 (5)
Heinz, J. M.: ref, 540 (11,12), 2862 (560)
Heinze, H.: ref, 2860 (356), 2892 (51)
Heinze, M. C.: ref, 41 (1), 1697 (489), 1802 (1), 2247 (102), 2749 (66), 2860 (1092), 2879 (164)
Heiser, M. A.: ref, 1040 (6,7)
Heiskanen, O.: ref, 2516 (58) 2860 (777)
Heiss, G. E.: ref, 2497 (307)
Heiss, W.: ref, 472 (37) 1181 (8)
Heiss, W. D.: ref, 2497 (120)
Heitkemper, M.: ref, 2603 (583)
Hekmat, H.: ref, 538 (2) 1745 (39)
Helgeson, V. S.: ref, 337 (78)
Helkala, E.-L.: ref, 776 (3), 2860 (103,913), 2863 (273)
Helland, T.: ref, 2860 (898), 2862 (354)
Hellawell, D. J.: ref, 2193 (13)
Helle, J.: ref, 1164 (87)
Helleday, J.: ref, 1164 (63)
Hellekson, L. E.: ref, 1072 (33)
Heller, H. S.: ref, 1740 (1)
Heller, J. H.: ref, 175 (9), 430 (7), 1047 (3), 2651 (13), 2695 (21), 2486 (2)
Heller, S. S.: ref, 791 (13), 2432 (21),2858 (110)
Heller, T.: ref, 999 (142), 1300 (4,7)
Heller, T. L.: ref, 451 (127), 1093 (89), 1379 (85), 2229 (10), 2862 (488)
Heller, W.: ref, 2497 (478)
Hellerstein, D. J.: ref, 337 (177), 2305 (229)
Hellige, J.: ref, 2860 (118)
Hellige, J. B.: ref, 2860 (13), 2862 (4)
Hellowell, D. J.: ref, 1758 (81), 2860 (1209)
Hellström, A.: ref, 272 (273)
Hellström, K.: ref, 1021 (12), 2497 (133)
Helm, W. H.: rev, 2051
Helm-Estabrooks, N.: test, 159, 328, 338, 2705; ref, 2860 (83)
Helme, R. D.: ref, 1322 (1), 1758 (84), 2860 (1247)
Helme, W. H.: rev, 1323
Helmes, E.: ref, 2592 (1)
Helms, B. J.: test, 2321
Helms, J. E.: ref, 2497 (161)
Helms, M.: ref, 2860 (957)
Helms, M. J.: ref, 272 (336), 2218 (116), 2497 (664)
Helmstadter, G. C.: rev, 2856, 2857
Helmstaedter, C.: ref, 2226 (29), 2860 (1093, 1274, 1392)
Helson, R.: ref, 68 (24,62), 372 (17,37,66,89,90,115), 373 (29,30,42),1697 (566), 2380 (11)
Helwig, S.: ref, 1612 (54), 1903 (288), 2485 (138)
Helzer, J. R.: ref, 799 (2)
Hemenover, S. H.: ref, 2163 (275,276)
Hemingway, T.: ref, 2163 (249)
Hemmelgarn, A.: ref, 451 (257)
Hemmer, V. H.: ref, 1095 (24), 1903 (266), 1982 (6)
Hemphill, J. K.: test, 1437; rev, 2581
Hemphill, L.: ref, 68 (6), 1612 (51), 1903 (55)
Hemphill, L. L.: ref, 1697 (18)
Hemsley, D. R.: ref, 1671 (8), 1758 (100), 2860 (1343,1380)
Henage, D.: test, 1089
Henchman, J.: test, 954
Henderson, A.: test, 2134
Henderson, A. S.: ref, 999 (56,89,90,114),1758 (44), 2239 (19,22), 2599 (15), 2860 (587,823), 2863 (175,238)
Henderson, C.: test, 1195
Henderson, D. C.: ref, 335 (11)
Henderson, J.: test, 2297; ref, 272 (144), 1010 (91), 2497 (535), 2603 (329)
Henderson, J. L.: ref, 1528 (3)
Henderson, L.: ref, 1758 (35,36), 2163 (205,206), 2288 (46,47), 2289 (35,36), 2305 (126,127), 2892 (170,171)
Henderson, L. W.: test, 889
Henderson, M. C.: ref, 793 (9), 998 (72), 1697 (132,178), 1744 (2,3)
Henderson, M. J.: ref, 999 (88), 2879 (204)
Henderson, P. A.: ref, 694 (4), 1991 (33)
Henderson, S.: ref, 349 (31), 451 (131), 1079 (61)
Henderson, S. E.: test, 1727; ref, 1097 (5), 1727 (1), 1987 (20), 2862 (153)
Henderson, S. H.: ref, 472 (142)
Henderson, S. N.: ref, 790 (6)
Henderson, V. L.: ref, 1612 (2), 1903 (9), 2680 (1)
Henderson, V. W.: ref, 776 (5), 2860 (147)
Hendler, M.: ref, 674 (2)
Hendrick, C.: ref, 863 (76)
Hendrick, E. B.: ref, 1096 (3,4), 2193 (11), 2860 (64,246,247,342), 2862 (38,125,126)

Hendrick, M.: ref, 2211 (1)
Hendrick, S. S.: ref, 863 (76)
Hendricks, F.: ref, 1754 (23), 2065 (18)
Hendricks, M. L.: ref, 1612 (85), 1903 (483), 2163 (288), 2862 (523)
Hendrickson, R.: ref, 372 (101), 2126 (15)
Hendrie, H. C.: ref, 2288 (4), 2289 (2), 2305 (7), 2860 (63)
Hendrix, C. C.: ref, 1000 (49), 2034 (7)
Hendrix, W. H.: ref, 1701 (21)
Hendrix-Frye, H.: test, 259, 1478
Hendry, E.: test, 954
Hendryx, M. S.: ref, 272 (64)
Hengeveld, M. W.: ref, 2050 (49)
Henggeler, S.: ref, 1000 (32)
Henggeler, S. W.: ref, 1000 (3), 1010 (36), 2211 (36), 2603 (337)
Heninger, G. R.: ref, 2892 (126)
Henke, C. J.: ref, 2076 (51)
Henker, B.: ref, 451 (38,127), 681 (33), 1379 (85), 2214 (92), 2229 (10), 2603 (444), 2862 (488)
Henly, G. A.: test, 73, 1694, 1931; ref, 73 (1), 1931 (1)
Hennessey, B. A.: ref, 1755 (33)
Hennessy, J. J.: rev, 770
Hennessy, M.: ref, 1947 (6)
Henning, G.: ref, 666 (9)
Henning, K.: ref, 337 (133,174)
Henning, K. R.: ref, 1697 (543)
Henning, M. M.: test, 1453
Henning-Stout, M.: rev, 1013, 1200, 1450, 1707, 1954, 1997, 2527, 2621
Henrichs, T. F.: ref, 1697 (75)
Henrichsen, L. E.: ref, 1664 (1)
Henriksson, W.: ref, 592 (61)
Henriques, G. R.: ref, 893 (34)
Henry, A.: ref, 1612 (59)
Henry, B.: ref, 358 (8), 1010 (98), 2211 (37)
Henry, C. S.: ref, 1000 (67,91), 1297 (1), 2497 (510)
Henry, J. H.: ref, 2050 (117), 2305 (136)
Henry, L. A.: ref, 350 (20,38), 1765 (18)
Henry, M. M.: ref, 815 (51), 1740 (30), 1889 (18), 2724 (12), 2862 (711)
Henry, P.: ref, 1754 (15)
Henry, S. A.: rev, 359, 463; test, 1006
Henry, W. E.: rev, 2825
Hensley, L.: test, 2653
Henson, L.: ref, 301 (22), 748 (8), 1592 (11), 2010 (7), 2163 (87), 2305 (64)
Henttonen, I.: ref, 472 (227)
Hepperlin, C. M.: ref, 472 (7)
Heppner, M. J.: ref, 1754 (17,23), 2065 (18)
Heppner, P. P.: test, 2065; ref, 694 (94,105), 1697 (300), 2065 (19,34,35), 2497 (515),2603 (261)
Hepps, D.: ref, 1612 (17)
Heptinstall, E.: ref, 1612 (78), 1745 (61)
Hepworth, C.: ref, 2050 (61,62,110)
Hepworth, J. T.: ref, 2497 (569)
Herberman, R. B.: ref, 2076 (47)
Herbert, C. H.: test, 251
Herbert, D. L.: ref, 1697 (40)
Herbert, J.: ref, 1079 (111), 2305 (248)
Herbert, J. D.: ref, 1638 (2), 1697 (40)
Herbert, M.: ref, 2603 (494)
Herbert, T. B.: ref, 2603 (101)
Herbison, G. P.: ref, 2050 (38,44,45,128)
Herbst, J. H.: ref, 793 (18), 2218 (49), 2519 (23), 2520 (24)
Herd, D.: ref, 134 (18,37)
Hered, W.: rev, 46, 48, 49, 574, 596
Heresco-Levy, V.: ref, 2288 (27), 2289 (18)
Herholz, K.: ref, 2497 (120)
Herkov, M. J.: ref, 298 (113), 1698 (11), 2603 (241)
Herlache, L.: ref, 697 (2), 2497 (493)
Herlitz, A.: ref, 1525 (18), 2860 (563,888)
Herman, C. P.: ref, 2497 (383)
Herman, D. O.: rev, 404, 1043, 1342, 1406, 1467, 1670, 1792, 2007, 2779, 2833
Herman, H.: rev, 466
Herman, J. L.: ref, 1697 (160)
Herman, P.: rev, 1073
Herman, R.: ref, 2017 (16)
Herman, S. J.: ref, 665 (44)
Herman-Stahl, M.: ref, 472 (170)
Herman-Stahl, M. A.: ref, 272 (118)
Hermann, B.: ref, 2860 (889,992), 2863 (294), 2892 (185)
Hermann, B. B.: ref, 2050 (97)
Hermann, B. P.: ref, 376 (10), 1698 (16),1740 (2), 2860 (628,1094), 2892 (116)
Hermelin, B.: ref, 1097 (10), 1765 (20), 1903 (267), 2163 (128,164)
Hermsen, J. M.: ref, 337 (150)
Hernandez, A. E.: ref, 1379 (16)
Hernandez Ch., E.: test, 307
Hernandez, O. C.: ref, 794 (2)
Hernandez-Reif, M.: ref, 2498 (67)
Herndon, J. B.: ref, 8 (1)
Herning, R.: ref, 1697 (88), 2402 (6)
Herod, L. A.: ref, 349 (26), 837 (9)
Herold, D. M.: ref, 1448 (1)
Herold, E. S.: rev, 793, 2454
Herr, E. L.: rev, 2400; ref, 404 (42), 413 (6)
Herrenkohl, E. C.: ref, 1612 (72)
Herrenkohl, R. C.: ref, 1612 (72)
Herrera-Graf, M.: ref, 2862 (489)
Herrero, M. E.: ref, 2603 (262), 2862 (266)
Herres, A. K.: ref, 350 (51), 837 (14), 2862 (720)
Herrick, S. M.: ref, 998 (67), 2065 (11)
Herrick, V. E.: rev, 1318, 2484
Herring, E. L.: ref, 1697 (466)
Herring, L. K.: ref, 448 (25)
Herring, R. I.: ref, 2076 (20), 2603 (77)
Herriot, P.: ref, 31 (1), 1036 (2), 1444 (3), 1755 (9), 1822 (1), 2163 (40)
Herrmann, N.: test, 1197

Herrmann, P.: ref, 1164 (158), 2227 (41)
Herrmann, S. M.: ref, 68 (5)
Herron, J.: ref, 1072 (1), 1131 (1), 2862 (1)
Herron, M.: ref, 1393 (1), 1404 (14),2917 (4)
Herron, S. R.: test, 2684
Herron, W. G.: ref, 272 (322)
Hersch, P. D.: ref, 1697 (76)
Herschbach, P.: ref, 2497 (632)
Herscovitch, P.: ref, 681 (39), 2860 (550), 2892 (162)
Hersen, M.: ref, 1697 (282)
Hersey, P.: test, 2064
Hersh, S.: ref, 1612 (55), 2862 (279)
Hershberger, P. J.: ref, 2126 (6)
Hershberger, S. L.: ref, 337 (53), 998 (98), 2218 (32)
Hershey, C. F.: test, 2612
Hertel, P. T.: ref, 2497 (347)
Herth, T.: ref, 1166 (29)
Herting, R. L.: ref, 1903 (92)
Hertz, M. R.: ref, 2247 (23)
Hertzberg, M. A.: ref, 2879 (154)
Hertzig, M. E.: ref, 2813 (109), 2860 (1001)
Hertzka, A. F.: test, 1514
Hertzman, M.: ref, 2603 (342)
Hertzog, C.: ref, 1405 (5,22), 2163 (212), 2860 (860)
Herzberg, D.: ref, 1010 (121)
Herzig, J.: ref, 1093 (32)
Herzig, S. A.: test, 2825
Herzog, A. G.: ref, 2860 (390), 2863 (101)
Herzog, D. B.: ref, 2247 (82)
Herzog, E. P.: ref, 270 (17), 272 (173)
Herzog, J. E.: ref, 275 (1), 1902 (58), 1991 (75), 2860 (735)
Hesbegrave, R. J.: ref, 1903 (381), 2305 (144)
Heseltine, P. W. R.: ref, 1758 (50), 2860 (951)
Hesketh, B.: ref, 2835 (8), 2915 (2)
Hesketh, L. J.: ref, 624 (13,28), 1903 (217,508), 2657 (31), 2695 (23), 2768 (40)
Hess, A.: ref, 2603 (399)
Hess, A. K.: rev, 719, 1101, 1207,1687, 1958, 2218
Hess, J. M.: ref, 2703 (1)
Hess, K. A.: rev, 1714, 2444
Hess, K. D.: rev, 2858
Hess, R. S.: ref, 2313 (1)
Hess, T. M.: ref, 298 (114), 2163 (11), 2860 (20,37,644,1095)
Hess, W. D.: ref, 2527 (10)
Hesse, F. W.: ref, 1745 (38)
Hesse, K.: test, 255
Hesselbrock, V.: ref, 272 (15), 1525 (21), 1697 (157), 2010 (22), 2892 (223)
Hesselbrock, V. M.: ref, 1661 (32,47), 2305 (195)
Hesselink, J.: ref, 1164 (84), 2288 (42), 2289 (32), 2305 (130)
Hesselink, J. R.: ref, 1164 (77), 2305 (32)
Hessels, M. G. P.: ref, 2163 (296)
Hestad, K.: ref, 1164 (47), 1407 (2), 2860 (463), 2863 (130)
Hester, E. J.: test, 1711
Hester, J. R.: rev, 121, 571
Hester, K.: ref, 1736 (4)
Hester, P. P.: ref, 994 (14), 2382 (23), 2864 (54), 2869 (1)
Hetherington, E. M.: ref, 372 (104), 451 (216), 472 (62,184,229), 2860 (690)
Hetherington, M.: ref, 472 (113,142)
Hettler, B.: test, 1499
Heubner, A. M.: ref, 1408 (5)
Heuer, R.: test, 2650
Heumann, M.: ref, 1164 (154), 2860 (1287)
Heun, R.: ref, 2305 (108,145)
Heuser, J.: ref, 2603 (489)
Heuvel, F.: ref, 1079 (107), 2497 (670), 2603 (584)
Heverly, M. A.: ref, 451 (24), 815 (7), 1216 (24), 1379 (21)
Hevern, V. W.: ref, 1697 (374)
Hewes, P.: ref, 1903 (24), 2860 (86)
Hewes, R. L.: ref, 462 (33)
Hewett, J. B.: ref, 1386 (21)
Hewett, J. E.: ref, 2603 (38,534), 2858 (12), 2860 (1288), 2863 (389)
Hewitt, J. K.: ref, 270 (48), 2433 (1), 2485 (244)
Hewitt, P. L.: ref, 272 (358), 950 (6), 1687 (29), 2557 (9)
Hewitt, S. K.: ref, 1697 (129)
Hewlig, S. E.: ref, 991 (1)
Heyman, A.: ref, 2860 (1280)
Heyman, R. E.: ref, 863 (13)
Heyning, F. H.: ref, 231 (1), 303 (32), 2226 (42), 2227 (61), 2599 (43), 2863 (431), 2892 (307)
Heysteck, D.: ref, 2076 (131), 2603 (423)
Heywood, C. A.: ref, 2193 (5), 2860 (161)
Hiam, A. W.: test, 1045
Hiatt, D.: ref, 372 (67)
Hiatt, D.: ref, 1697 (301)
Hiatt, M. D.: ref, 2860 (1156)
Hibbard, J. K.: ref, 1697 (416),2247 (88), 2749 (56), 2860 (890)
Hibbard, M. R.: ref, 1061 (1), 1745 (13), 2860 (357,404)
Hibbard, S.: ref, 1697 (416), 2247 (88), 2749 (39,56,85), 2860 (890)
Hibbett, C.: ref, 301 (37), 1379 (39), 2163 (144)
Hibbs, E. D.: ref, 1010 (49), 2214 (104), 2860 (366)
Hibbs, N.: ref, 1965 (64)
Hibpshman, T.: test, 2432, 2552
Hichwa, R. D.: ref, 650 (13)
Hickey, J. E.: ref, 1697 (73), 2402 (5), 2603 (48)
Hickie, I.: ref, 998 (21,45)
Hickie, I.: ref, 1079 (39), 1166 (61,112), 1241 (5)
Hickling, E. J.: ref, 2497 (427)
Hickman, H.: ref, 472 (54), 2498 (22), 2862 (213)
Hickman, J. A.: rev, 1131
Hickman, L. A.: test, 164
Hicks, D.: ref, 2603 (195)
Hicks, J. S.: test, 1041
Hicks, M. W.: ref, 1000 (63,64)

Hicks, P.: ref, 2901 (91)
Hicks, P. A.: rev, 2592, 2705
Hicks, R.: ref, 272 (69), 273 (9), 694 (59), 1079 (18), 2076 (63)
Hicks, R. A.: ref, 2858 (103)
Hicks, R. E.: ref, 272 (349), 1079 (104), 2305 (53)
Hiebert-Murphy, D.: ref, 337 (191), 699 (5)
Hien, D.: ref, 2288 (84), 2749 (83)
Hieronymous, A. N.: test, 1318
Hieronymus, A. N.: test, 389, 2234; rev, 82, 2737
Higa, J.: ref, 1740 (7), 2076 (23), 2599 (6), 2860 (240, 534)
Higginbotham, D. J. : ref, 175 (12), 815 (25), 994 (27), 1379 (70), 1725 (5), 1903 (373), 2813 (95), 2864 (94), 2879 (119)
Higginbotham, M. B.: ref, 303 (2), 1164 (23), 2497 (104), 2603 (83), 2860 (237)
Higgins, B.: ref, 2603 (532)
Higgins, C. A.: ref, 1965 (16)
Higgins, D.: ref, 2452 (11)
Higgins, D. J.: ref, 2782 (1)
Higgins, E. S.: ref, 1962 (17), 2288 (40), 2813 (77)
Higgins, E. T.: ref, 790 (1),2603 (5)
Higgins, M. J.: rev, 2591
Higgins, N. C.: ref, 1590 (1)
Higgins, S. T.: ref, 2076 (26)
Higgins, T.: ref, 926 (21)
Higgs, M. L.: ref, 2603 (532)
High, R.: ref, 615 (35)
High/Scope Educational Research Foundation: test, 1204
Highberger, L.: ref, 472 (215), 1318 (20), 2214 (125), 2862 (677)
Hight, T. L.: ref, 717 (2), 863 (92)
Hightower, A. D.: rev, 559, 811
Hightower, E.: ref, 372 (111)
Hightower, J.: ref, 2299 (2), 2485 (98)
Hiks, L.: ref, 495 (14)
Hildebrand, D. K.: ref, 2862 (733)
Hildebrandt, G.: ref, 272 (370), 2497 (673)
Hiley-Young, B.: ref, 2603 (369)
Hilgert, L. D.: ref, 301 (5), 853 (1)
Hilhorst, R. C.: ref, 681 (9)
Hill, A.: test, 1656
Hill, A. B.: ref, 272 (292), 893 (44), 2860 (1301)
Hill, A. J.: ref, 1010 (134)
Hill, A. L.: ref, 404 (38), 1647 (3), 2603 (364), 2862 (459)
Hill, B. K.: test, 1300, 2299
Hill, C. A.: ref, 2218 (95), 2497 (559)
Hill, C. E.: test, 716; ref, 2497 (663)
Hill, C. R.: ref, 2603 (263)
Hill, D.: ref, 2498 (17)
Hill, D. E.: ref, 2862 (626), 2880 (6)
Hill, E.: ref, 473 (6), 1697 (397), 2230 (18), 2557 (10)
Hill, E. L.: ref, 2247 (52)
Hill, E. W.: test, 1206
Hill, G.: ref, 1866 (26)
Hill, H. E.: test, 66
Hill, J.: ref, 2305 (36)
Hill, J. W.: ref, 997 (23), 1079 (50)
Hill, K.: ref, 1000 (104), 1745 (79)
Hill, K. G.: ref, 1755 (33)
Hill, L. R.: ref, 815 (14), 1058 (5), 1164 (56), 1612 (46), 1903 (236), 2485 (117), 2860 (464,580), 2862 (203), 2863 (167)
Hill, M.: ref, 791 (16)
Hill, O. W.: ref, 1755 (26), 2163 (277), 2856 (3)
Hill, P.: test, 2743
Hill, R.: test, 1147; ref, 2860 (1239), 2863 (371)
Hill, R. D.: ref, 1525 (18), 2860 (465,563,888), 2863 (131)
Hill, S.: ref, 1135 (12), 2813 (67), 2862 (274), 2879 (84)
Hill, S. Y.: ref, 2305 (86,237)
Hill, T.: ref, 272 (44)
Hill, W. F.: test, 1205
Hill, W. H.: rev, 979, 2856, 2857
Hillbrand, M.: ref, 538 (1), 1697 (302), 2599 (18), 2704 (19), 2860 (645,646)
Hiller, W.: ref, 2603 (264)
Hillhouse, J.: ref, 337 (10)
Hillis, A. E.: ref, 2163 (67),2863 (67)
Hillman, L.: ref, 2247 (101)
Hillman, N.: ref, 997 (14)
Hillman, S. B.: ref, 694 (110,123), 1991 (100)
Hills, A. P.: ref, 893 (43)
Hills, H. A.: ref, 1590 (25),1697 (417)
Hills, H. I.: ref, 1697 (300), 2603 (261)
Hills, J. R.: rev, 56, 1222, 1274, 2500
Hilmer, C. D.: ref, 2860 (1151)
Hilsabeck, R.: ref, 1697 (294)
Hilsenroth, M.: ref, 1169 (6), 1697 (455), 2247 (95)
Hilsenroth, M. J.: ref, 1697 (416,418,454,550), 2247 (88,89,118,122,126), 2749 (56), 2860 (890)
Hilsman, R.: ref, 472 (143)
Hilton, B. A.: ref, 2126 (2), 2858 (8)
Hiltonsmith, R. W.: rev, 493, 872, 1823, 1886, 2435, 2682
Him, C.: ref, 1903 (163), 2485 (78)
Himelein, M. J.: ref, 2603 (464)
Himelstein, P.: rev, 2432
Himes, J. H.: ref, 1134 (6), 1216 (64), 1903 (361)
Himle, J. A: ref, 1021 (35)
Himsl, R.: test, 1623
Hinchman, K. A.: test, 2175
Hinckley, E. D.: rev, 1790
Hindelang, R. D.: ref, 2497 (58)
Hindley, C. B.: rev, 1134
Hines, A. R.: ref, 2417 (37)
Hines, C. V.: ref, 550 (5), 665 (49), 1532 (1)
Hines, L.: rev, 2407
Hines, M.: test, 1622
Hinkin, C. H.: ref, 272 (181,295), 376 (5,23), 1135 (13), 1166 (113), 1697 (330), 2599 (25), 2860 (772,1304), 2863 (324,394),2873 (67)

Hinkin, T. R.: ref, 1701 (6,20),35)
Hinkle, J. S.: rev, 1347; ref, 1716 (5), 1942 (1)
Hinman, S.: test, 1352,2923
Hinojosa, J.: ref, 1673 (1), 1901 (2)
Hinrichsen, G.: ref, 2305 (70)
Hinshaw, S. D.: ref, 665 (14), 1379 (6), 2488 (2)
Hinshaw, S. P.: ref, 451 (127,201),214),277), 472 (197), 1379 (85), 2010 (21), 2218 (132), 2229 (10), 2603 (228), 2862 (449,488,519,627,657), 2901 (86,117)
Hinson, D.: ref, 666 (10)
Hinton, M.: ref, 2860 (926)
Hinton, R. N.: ref, 815 (44), 2862 (489),2862 (620)
Hinton, V. J.: ref, 303 (6), 1218 (10), 2860 (891), 2863 (263)
Hinton-Bayre, A. D.: ref, 2599 (39), 2860 (1275)
Hiorns, R.: test, 2239; ref, 2239 (6)
Hipwell, A.: ref, 270 (22), 1216 (86), 1612 (86)
Hipwell, A. E.: ref, 2917 (1)
Hirabayashi, H.: ref, 2860 (1416)
Hirano, N.: ref, 2860 (1371)
Hirayama, K.: ref, 2860 (997,1356), 2873 (47)
Hirono, N.: ref, 2163 (334), 2860 (1314), 2873 (68,73)
Hirsch, B. E.: ref, 998 (53)
Hirsch, B. J.: ref, 337 (39)
Hirsch, E.: ref, 350 (39)
Hirsch, G. L.: ref, 1697 (68), 2050 (5)
Hirsch, L. S.: ref, 134 (34), 1661 (61)
Hirschfeld, R. M. A.: ref, 2305 (18)
Hirschhorn, D. B.: ref, 585 (1), 665 (48), 1866 (25)
Hirschman, J. E.: ref, 1612 (17)
Hirschman, R.: ref, 2402 (38)
Hirschorn, K. A.: ref, 2860 (537), 2863 (152)
Hirschowitz, J.: ref, 2288 (70), 2289 (55), 2305 (153,181)
Hirsh, S. R.: ref, 2288 (82)
Hirst, J. F.: ref, 2603 (400)
Hirst, W.: ref, 2863 (7)
Hirt, M.: ref, 301 (10), 538 (1), 1164 (19), 2860 (187)
Hiruma, N.: ref, 451 (162)
Hiscock, C. K.: ref, 1164 (64), 2212 (2), 2599 (19)
Hiscock, M.: ref, 389 (9), 900 (2), 1072 (34), 1164 (64), 2212 (2), 2599 (19), 2862 (596), 2879 (197)
Hiscox, M. D.: rev, 1414, 2095
Hishinuma, E. S.: ref, 1903 (370), 2862 (349)
Hiskey, M. S.: rev, 624
Hiss, H.: ref, 2497 (348)
Hitch, G. J.: ref, 1145 (1,2), 1781 (1), 2163 (68,170)
Hitchins, W. E.: ref, 413 (30)
Hite, T. L.: ref, 998 (106), 2603 (405)
Hitsman, B. L.: ref, 2497 (310)
Hittmair-Delazer, M.: ref, 199 (14), 2193 (22), 2860 (647,892), 2863 (187)
Hittner, J. B.: ref, 2497 (633), 2603 (341)
Hitz, L.: ref, 1697 (169), 2402 (12)
Hitzemann, R.: ref, 2860 (779)
HIV Neurobehavioral Research Center Group.: ref, 2858 (105)
Hix, M.: ref, 372 (68), 2247 (64)
Hixon, J. E.: ref, 1318 (16)
Hjelle, L. A.: ref, 1965 (53)
Hjelmquist, E.: ref, 1136 (1)
Hlavaty, J. H.: test, 1038, 1998, 1999, 2456
HNRC Group.: ref, 272 (334), 376 (30), 776 (26), 2076 (133), 2863 (293)
Ho, A. K.: ref, 1758 (101)
Ho, H.: ref, 745 (19)
Ho, H. H.: ref, 1485 (26), 1903 (251), 2485 (125), 2864 (49)
Hoaken, P. N. S.: ref, 2860 (1393)
Hoard, M. K.: ref, 2163 (324)
Hoare, P.: ref, 1079 (106)
Hoba, M. E.: ref, 2432 (24), 2682 (7), 2905 (75)
Hobart, C. J.: ref, 2858 (4)
Hobbs, S. H.: ref, 1178 (1), 2497 (16)
Hobfoll, S. E.: ref, 2497 (349)
Hobson, R. P.: ref, 350 (33)
Hocevar, D.: ref, 2497 (576,577), 2656 (3)
Hoch, C. C.: ref, 337 (72), 1166 (104), 2305 (173)
Hoch, E. H.: rev, 1792
Hochron, S. M.: ref, 1697 (394)
Hochstadt, N. J.: ref, 997 (10), 1216 (20), 2127 (1), 2603 (134)
Hockenberry, M.: ref, 2860 (738)
Hockney, R. A.: ref, 2076 (103)
Hocutt, A. M.: ref, 681 (37), 2211 (21)
Hodapp, A. F.: ref, 1903 (179), 2485 (51,89), 2864 (27)
Hodapp, R. M.: ref, 1379 (13,17), 2813 (60), 2860 (893), 2864 (92)
Hodgduin, C. A. L.: ref, 1166 (52)
Hodge, C. N.: ref, 298 (64)
Hodge, G. M.: ref, 72 (3), 1079 (26,90),1590 (33), 2358 (11)
Hodges, J. O.: rev, 247, 2060
Hodges, J. R.: ref, 350 (48), 641 (3), 776 (22,29,30), 1758 (69,94,99), 1903 (569), 2163 (162), 2193 (38,52), 2860 (1340,1368,1379), 2863 (264,299,321, 325,402,414)
Hodges, P.: ref, 893 (9), 1991 (35)
Hodges, R.: ref, 2862 (159)
Hodges, S.: ref, 998 (93), 2050 (116)
Hodges, W. F.: ref, 557 (1), 2749 (14)
Hodgins, C.: ref, 2860 (766)
Hodgins, D. C.: ref, 134 (28), 337 (143), 462 (20), 2402 (58), 2860 (1276)
Hodgins, H. S.: ref, 68 (54), 2078 (4)
Hodgins, S.: ref, 1174 (4), 2010 (19), 2892 (192)
Hodgkinson, P.: ref, 272 (278), 1079 (92), 2497 (636)
Hodgson, C.: ref, 1758 (102), 2478 (2), 2860 (1394)
Hodgson, M. J.: ref, 1697 (138), 2863 (99)
Hodiamont, P. O. G.: ref, 1079 (46), 2050 (124)
Hodson, B. W.: test, 214; rev, 2382, 2703; ref, 214 (12), 540 (1), 994 (21), 1095 (9), 1394 (3), 1503 (10), 2190 (5), 2866 (2), 2879 (108)
Hodtke, K. H.: ref, 2497 (513)

Hoeberlein-Miller, T. M.: ref, 1590 (56)
Hoeger, W.: test, 1062
Hoehn, T. P.: ref, 1673 (7), 2432 (17), 2695 (27), 2862 (267), 2864 (53), 2901 (41)
Hoehn-Saric, R.: ref, 272 (370), 2497 (673)
Hoekstra, R. R.: test, 2450
Hoekstra-Weebers, J. E. H. M.: ref, 1079 (107), 2497 (670), 2603 (584)
Hoeltje, C. O.: ref, 451 (128)
Hoeltke, G. M.: test, 1468
Hoencamp, E.: ref, 1166 (52,53), 2603 (265)
Hoepfner, R.: rev, 1612, 2771
Hoeppner, J. B.: ref, 451 (258), 681 (92), 1099 (5), 1164 (177), 1379 (101), 1740 (31), 2516 (118), 2892 (299)
Hoff, A. L.: ref, 326 (5), 2288 (21), 2289 (13), 2305 (66), 2892 (52), 2905 (24)
Hoffart, A.: ref, 272 (66,274), 2497 (252,479,634), 2858 (50)
Hoffenberg, S.: ref, 1991 (16), 2163 (51), 2860 (223)
Hoffer, N.: ref, 1140 (44)
Hoffman, B. J.: ref, 2749 (69)
Hoffman, H. J.: ref, 1096 (3,4), 2193 (11), 2860 (64,246,247,342), 2862 (38,125,126)
Hoffman, J.: ref, 1698 (25)
Hoffman, J. D.: ref, 1414 (3), 1462 (1)
Hoffman, J. V.: rev, 1529
Hoffman, K. D.: ref, 694 (111)
Hoffman, M. A.: ref, 451 (129), 557 (5), 998 (113), 2497 (663)
Hoffman, P. R.: ref, 214 (13)
Hoffman, R. E.: ref, 2305 (174), 2860 (1068)
Hoffman, R. G.: ref, 372 (91)
Hoffman, V.: test, 1440
Hoffman, W.: ref, 1485 (5)
Hoffmann, G.: ref, 272 (200), 1164 (129), 1166 (131,194), 1697 (500), 2163 (286, 2603 (480), 2860 (1134)
Hoffmann, N. G.: test, 2194, 2554
Hoffmeister, J. K.: test, 2363
Hoffschmidt, S.: ref, 2603 (137)
Hofmann, E.: ref, 2239 (8)
Hofmann, M.: ref, 1697 (157)
Hofmann, S. G.: ref, 2497 (375,480,481), 2520 (46)
Hofstede, G.: ref, 298 (153), 2581 (3)
Hofstetter, R.: ref, 307 (1), 1234 (5), 2335 (1), 2860 (184), 2862 (105)
Hoftman-Chemi, A.: ref, 372 (81), 999 (110), 1697 (384), 2417 (23)
Hogan, A.: ref, 1987 (2,12), 2211 (8,25), 2452 (2,3), 2488 (4,7), 2862 (227,295)
Hogan, D. B.: test, 1860
Hogan, J.: test, 1211, 1212, 1724; ref, 180 (5), 372 (6), 1697 (33)
Hogan, J. D.: ref, 1582 (9)
Hogan, R.: test, 1211, 1212, 1724; rev, 1201, 1832, 1965, 2218; ref, 68 (16), 180 (5), 372 (6), 373 (9), 1291 (2), 1697 (33,144)
Hogan, T. P.: rev, 144
Hogben, D.: ref, 34 (6)
Hoge, S. K.: ref, 2603 (298)
Hogervorst, E.: ref, 2516 (80)
Hogg, J.: ref, 1379 (69), 2860 (894), 2862 (350)
Hogg, K. E.: ref, 2858 (68)
Hogg, L. I.: ref, 2050 (20)
Hoglend, P.: ref, 2603 (585)
Hogue, A.: ref, 2496 (3)
Hoh, A.: ref, 2497 (121)
Hohagen, F.: ref, 1166 (144)
Hohmann, A. A.: ref, 2288 (15), 2289 (10), 2305 (62)
Hoien, T.: ref, 2599 (33)
Hoitt, J.: ref, 1903 (225)
Hojat, M.: ref, 999 (18)
Hokama, H.: ref, 2288 (60), 2289 (46), 2305 (159), 2860 (1012)
Hoke, L.: ref, 2247 (5), 2749 (7), 2860 (124)
Hokkanen, L.: ref, 2860 (895), 2863 (265)
Holaday, M.: ref, 2247 (127)
Holahan, C. J.: ref, 699 (1,2), 1181 (21), 1496 (1), 2497 (406), 2498 (51)
Holahan, C. K.: ref, 699 (1), 1181 (21)
Holahan, J. M.: ref, 1902 (15), 1903 (43), 2862 (180,396), 2863 (40), 2901 (21,73)
Holamon, B.: ref, 2863 (266)
Holbrey, A.: ref, 893 (16)
Holcomb, L.: ref, 1612 (54), 1903 (288), 2485 (138)
Holden, E. W.: ref, 1000 (107)
Holden, G. W.: ref, 2065 (6)
Holden, R. H.: rev, 270
Holden, R. R.: test, 1213; ref, 256 (1), 272 (275), 273 (30),1965 (1,42,51,64)
Holder, D.: ref, 272 (259)
Holderness, C.: ref, 451 (34), 1832 (7)
Holdgrafer, G.: ref, 994 (13), 1095 (32), 1903 (371)
Holdgrapher, G.: ref, 1095 (33)
Holdstock, J. S.: ref, 1758 (30,40), 2193 (39), 2860 (896), 2863 (219,267), 2892 (186)
Holdsworth, M. J.: ref, 2860 (1048),2879 (157)
Holdsworth, R.: test, 119, 735, 735, 1551, 1551, 1818, 1973, 2087
Holdt, P. A.: ref, 2407 (2)
Holen, A.: ref, 2603 (336)
Holen, M. C.: ref, 1164 (112), 1697 (453), 2863 (290)
Holford, T. R.: ref, 2862 (396), 2901 (73)
Holi, M. J.: ref, 1079 (76), 2603 (493)
Holiday-Goodman, M.: ref, 1590 (32)
Holland, A.: ref, 2860 (23)
Holland, A. D.: ref, 1697 (51)
Holland, A. J.: ref, 2239 (33)
Holland, A. L.: test, 629; ref, 159 (1,2), 163 (3), 199 (3), 265 (5), 540 (25), 1612 (24), 1903 (60,114), 2382 (8), 2596 (1), 2668 (6)
Holland, A. M.: ref, 837 (6)
Holland, C. J.: ref, 1755 (42,57), 2218 (34), 2860 (897)

Holland, D.: ref, 2860 (1288), 2863 (389)
Holland, D. C.: ref, 2860 (897)
Holland, J. C.: ref, 2497 (58)
Holland, J. L.: test, 400, 1754, 2360, 2835; rev, 2771
Holland, M. L.: ref, 2036 (1)
Holland, P. J.: ref, 1590 (34)
Hollander, E.: ref, 1592 (7), 2603 (410)
Hollands, R.: test, 2089
Hollandsworth, J. G., Jr.: test, 88
Hollenbeck, A. R.: ref, 1178 (16)
Hollenbeck, J. R.: ref, 1965 (8,78), 2218 (102)
Hollengsworth, P. M.: ref, 665 (35), 1072 (27)
Hollenshead, J. D.: ref, 1689 (4)
Hollerbach, A. D.: ref, 1770 (5)
Holliday, G. A.: ref, 2417 (34)
Hollien, H.: rev, 2651
Hollifield, M.: ref, 2218 (96)
Holliman, N. B.: ref, 1698 (22), 2879 (229)
Holliman, W. B.: ref, 694 (103)
Hollin, C. R.: ref, 337 (51)
Hollings, A. E.: ref, 1000 (82)
Hollings, R.: ref, 1903 (260)
Hollingsworth, D. K.: ref, 1525 (17)
Hollingsworth, M.: ref, 1466 (2)
Hollingsworth, P. M.: ref, 592 (67), 1318 (7)
Hollis, W: ref, 624 (24), 1485 (47), 1903 (438)
Hollister, J. M.: ref, 2050 (78)
Hollister, P.: test, 1914
Hollnagel, C.: ref, 2860 (1067), 2892 (224)
Hollon, S. D.: ref, 998 (41), 1093 (42), 1697 (167,173), 1705 (3), 2497 (438)
Holloway, A.: test, 669
Holloway, C.: ref, 2862 (118), 2879 (31)
Holloway, S. D.: ref, 693 (3), 1216 (82), 1987 (3), 2603 (102), 2858 (26)
Hollowood, T. M.: ref, 2813 (62)
Hollrah, J. L.: ref, 1697 (583)
Hollwey, S.: ref, 999 (130,131)
Holm, L. A.: ref, 2860 (468), 2863 (132)
Holman, B. L.: ref, 2227 (58), 2860 (1396), 2863 (421)
Holman, J. M., Jr.: ref, 1412 (2)
Holmbeck, G.: ref, 1010 (104)
Holmbeck, G. N.: ref, 863 (87), 1000 (84), 1888 (1), 1889 (9), 1903 (372), 2485 (169), 2603 (533), 2862 (351), 2864 (93)
Holme, C.: ref, 1765 (23), 2864 (104)
Holme, G.: ref, 337 (140,169)
Holmes, B. C.: ref, 2178 (1)
Holmes, C. B.: ref, 853 (16), 2860 (456,1053), 2862 (157)
Holmes, C. S.: ref, 451 (260), 1010 (84), 1131 (13), 2211 (42), 2862 (352,377), 2879 (118)
Holmes, D. L.: ref, 994 (35)
Holmes, D. T.: ref, 2603 (586)
Holmes, D. W.: test, 428
Holmes, E. P.: ref, 1590 (44), 2497 (444)
Holmes, F. J.: test, 1920
Holmes, I. W. M.: ref, 1991 (13)
Holmes, J. A.: ref, 2603 (49)
Holmes, J. G.: ref, 337 (120)
Holmes, V. M.: ref, 2905 (97)
Holmes-Eber, P.: ref, 2305 (38)
Holmgren, R.: ref, 365 (9)
Holmgren, S.: ref, 1093 (3), 2603 (28)
Holmlund, U.: ref, 1697 (201)
Holmlund, V.: ref, 2603 (143)
Holmstrom, R. W.: ref, 451 (15), 2242 (1), 2247 (18), 2402 (19), 2485 (41), 2862 (143), 2879 (37)
Holobow, N. E.: ref, 1903 (6)
Holroyd, S.: ref, 1485 (17)
Holsboer, F.: ref, 1166 (29)
Holst, P.: ref, 2516 (58), 2860 (144,776,777)
Holst, P. M.: ref, 592 (97), 2656 (19)
Holstein, C.: ref, 2516 (34), 2892 (105)
Holston, S. G.: ref, 1697 (330)
Holstrom, R. W.: ref, 1661 (68), 2218 (88)
Holt, C. S.: ref, 337 (179), 998 (56), 1697 (561), 2218 (109), 2305 (65), 2498 (48), 2603 (203)
Holt, K. D.: ref, 365 (3), 373 (15), 472 (44), 694 (49), 1903 (162)
Holt, R.: ref, 1657 (22), 1866 (43), 2488 (9)
Holt, R. R.: rev, 466
Holt, S.: test, 133
Holte, A.: ref, 1093 (57), 2050 (51), 2247 (47)
Holthausen, H.: ref, 2863 (390)
Holtz, B. A.: ref, 2862 (353)
Holtzman, W. H.: test, 1214, 2591
Holzberg, C.: test, 1865
Holzer, C. P.: ref, 1093 (112)
Holzman, P. S.: ref, 592 (93), 1965 (68), 2497 (503,544), 2860 (387,950), 2892 (201)
Hom, J.: ref, 1164 (65), 1697 (303), 2860 (648), 2863 (188)
Homan, S. P.: ref, 550 (5), 665 (49), 1532 (1)
Homatidis, S.: ref, 1485 (10)
Hommer, D.: ref, 2305 (103)
Hommerding, K. D.: ref, 1965 (61)
Hon, J.: ref, 2239 (33)
Honaker, M.: ref, 1698 (4)
Honda, M.: ref, 1010 (48)
Honeycutt, J. M.: ref, 694 (54)
Hong, B. A.: ref, 1697 (65)
Hong, E.: ref, 1470 (2)
Hong, W.: ref, 2305 (103)
Hons, B.: ref, 1079 (57)
Hons, R. B.: ref, 1697 (66,67), 2076 (9,10)
Honzik, C. H.: rev, 132, 1577
Honzik, M. P.: rev, 1097, 1375
Hood, A. B.: rev, 692
Hood, J.: rev, 1611, 2712; ref, 272 (258), 893 (42), 1405 (39), 1903 (517), 2862 (595)
Hood, J. E.: ref, 337 (22), 1697 (119), 1991 (19)
Hood, S. B.: rev, 1020
Hoodguin, K. A. L.: ref, 2603 (469)

Hoodin, R. B.: ref, 175 (4),430 (3), 1903 (31), 2332 (1), 2695 (4)
Hoogduin, K. A. L.: ref, 2603 (535)
Hook, G.: test, 2653
Hook, J. D.: test, 1290
Hook, M.: ref, 337 (56), 2497 (245)
Hook, P.: test, 2653
Hooker, K.: ref, 2076 (129), 2126 (8)
Hooker, S.: ref, 1701 (43)
Hooks, K.: ref, 1903 (268)
Hoondert, V.: ref, 373 (27), 2860 (832), 2862 (324), 2864 (82)
Hooper, F. E.: rev, 46
Hooper, H. E.: test, 1218
Hooper, R.: ref, 270 (21,22), 1216 (86), 1612 (86)
Hooper, S.: ref, 2860 (649)
Hooper, S. R.: rev, 663, 1513, 1524, 2322, 2820; ref, 815 (51), 1525 (19), 1740 (30), 1889 (18), 1903 (155), 2724 (12), 2862 (711), 2903 (2)
Hooshyar, N.: ref, 2813 (76)
Hoover, D. W.: ref, 997 (16)
Hoover, H. D.: test, 389, 1315, 1318; ref, 592 (75)
Hoover, S. M.: ref, 838 (10)
Hoover, S. W.: ref, 1093 (5)
Hope, D. A.: ref, 472 (126), 2214 (67), 2305 (65), 2497 (68)
Hope, J. K. A.: ref, 375 (5), 2227 (45), 2862 (651), 2863 (395), 2892 (280)
Hope, R. A.: ref, 2603 (93,179)
Hope, T. L.: ref, 451 (261)
Hope, V.: ref, 1697 (278)
Hopf, D.: ref, 2122 (1), 2358 (5)
Hopkins, H. R.: ref, 2369 (3)
Hopkins, J.: ref, 272 (11), 2305 (19)
Hopkins, K. D.: rev, 560, 561, 665
Hopkins, R. O.: ref, 2892 (187)
Hopkins, T. F.: test, 2485
Hopmann, G.: ref, 2892 (32)
Hopp, G.: test, 2811; ref, 1697 (515)
Hopp, G. A.: ref, 2860 (1277)
Hoppe, S.: ref, 2497 (224)
Hops, H.: ref, 272 (319), 451 (250), 863 (17), 1010 (60,128), 2305 (40), 2402 (14), 2497 (220,366), 2858 (74)
Hopt, D.: ref, 2122 (2), 2358 (8)
Hopwood, M.: ref, 1166 (224)
Hoque-Nizamie, S.: ref, 272 (340)
Horan, J. J.: ref, 1991 (91)
Horan, M.: ref, 270 (3), 1000 (21)
Horen, B.: ref, 2288 (52)
Horiguchi, E.: ref, 2076 (174)
Horii, Y.: ref, 272 (133), 1164 (109), 2860 (961)
Horikoshi, T.: ref, 2860 (1278)
Horita, A.: ref, 2860 (665), 2863 (195)
Horn, A.: ref, 1405 (13), 2860 (230)
Horn, C.: ref, 56 (11)
Horn, C. J., Jr.: ref, 1697 (196)
Horn, E. E.: ref, 413 (11), 2282 (4), 1166 (119)
Horn, G. J.: ref, 2863 (319)
Horn, J. L.: test, 134, 136, 1721; rev, 1043, 1986, 2010
Horn, J. M.: ref, 2212 (3), 2485 (136), 2860 (675)
Horn, R.: ref, 2226 (29)
Horn, W. F.: ref, 681 (47)
Hornak, J.: ref, 2227 (38), 2860 (1279), 2863 (385)
Horne, D. J. de L.: ref, 1953 (1)
Horne, M.: ref, 1755 (65), 2076 (152)
Horner, J.: test, 2172
Horner, M. D.: ref, 2860 (1096), 2892 (228)
Horner, R. H.: ref, 2299 (7)
Hornig-Rohan, M.: ref, 1166 (86)
Horodezky, N.: ref, 451 (104), 2862 (452)
Horohov, J. E.: ref, 624 (31), 1095 (48), 1903 (546), 2695 (68)
Horowitz, E. C.: test, 1073
Horowitz, H. A.: ref, 2603 (491)
Horowitz, L. A.: ref, 451 (202), 472 (198), 1010 (124)
Horowitz, M.: ref, 2218 (61), 2603 (187,465)
Horowitz, M. J.: ref, 2603 (219,266,336,413)
Horrobin, D.: ref, 272 (351)
Horstink, M. W. I. M.: ref, 376 (12), 2226 (16), 2516 (35,75,87,88), 2860 (584,1007,1193,1194), 2892 (211,260)
Horton, A.: test, 545
Horton, A. M., Jr.: ref, 1164 (66,67,97,98,99), 2402 (29), 2860 (466,650), 2863 (189)
Horton, C.: test, 2536
Horton, C. W.: rev, 92, 573, 595, 1110
Horton, R. W.: ref, 1166 (12)
Horton, S. V.: ref, 1657 (9)
Horvat, M. A.: ref, 777 (1), 1991 (85)
Horvath, M.: ref, 413 (30)
Horvath, P.: ref, 1661 (6), 1697 (77)
Horwath, E.: ref, 2305 (140,223)
Horwitz, A. V.: ref, 2603 (466,587)
Horwitz, B.: ref, 1240 (21), 2010 (1,18), 2163 (10), 2485 (234), 2860 (34,502,837,1141),2863 (12,242)
Horwitz, S. J.: ref, 353 (1), 1903 (34), 2432 (6), 2768 (3)
Horwitz, W.: ref, 1987 (11)
Horwood, J.: ref, 358 (11), 694 (114), 2094 (3), 2211 (47), 2862 (470)
Horwood, L. J.: ref, 358 (4), 681 (10,30,31), 1216 (46,62), 2091 (2,3,4), 2094 (1), 2211 (28,38,39), 2714 (4,5,6), 2862 (253,469)
Hosaka, C. M.: test, 1192
Hosaka, T.: ref, 2076 (171)
Hoskins, C. N.: test, 1895
Hosman, C.: ref, 1010 (114), 2603 (509)
Hosobuchi, T.: ref, 2862 (359,498)
Hosokawa, T.: ref, 999 (57)
Hossain, Z.: ref, 2497 (507)
Hossair, Z.: ref, 272 (210)
Hosseini, A. A.: ref, 301 (26), 1097 (8)
Hostetler, M.: ref, 404 (9,10), 2915 (4)
Hostsand, S. D.: ref, 271 (11), 272 (296)

Hotopf, M. H.: ref, 2858 (69)
Hotovy, L. A.: ref, 272 (320), 2497 (657), 2603 (553)
Hotte, J. P.: ref, 1987 (6), 1991 (34)
Hotz, G.: test, 338
Houchens, P.: ref, 337 (195), 1010 (137), 2496 (5), 2497 (675)
Houck, C.: rev, 2905; ref, 1687 (6)
Houck, J. W.: ref, 838 (16)
Houck, P.: ref, 1166 (182)
Houck, P. R.: ref, 272 (221), 337 (156), 1093 (99), 1166 (104), 2305 (173), 2603 (393)
Hough, R. L.: ref, 451 (120), 1697 (325), 2050 (3)
Houghton, S.: ref, 72 (1), 681 (41), 1379 (96), 1765 (15)
Houghton, T. G.: ref, 878 (1)
Houlberg, K.: ref, 349 (20)
Houle, L.: ref, 2603 (218)
Houndoulesi, V.: ref, 2318 (1)
Hourtané, M.: ref, 272 (350)
House, E. R.: ref, 1903 (269)
House, J. D.: ref, 1115 (5), 1122 (2), 1672 (3,4)
House, J. S.: ref, 2603 (126)
House, L. I.: test, 658
House, R.: ref, 272 (318), 273 (32), 1166 (151)
House, W. J.: ref, 372 (45)
Houseal, M.: ref, 1166 (135)
Householder, D. L.: rev, 1792
Housman, D.: ref, 272 (19,58), 273 (3), 1000 (5,37), 2050 (94)
Houston, B. K.: ref, 1697 (130), 1881 (2), 2218 (72)
Houston, C.: rev, 381, 635
Houston, D. M.: ref, 1745 (40)
Houston, L. N.: ref, 1647 (1)
Houston, R. L.: test, 216
Houston, W.: ref, 2658 (2), 2860 (1170)
Houts, R.: ref, 462 (6)
Houx, P. J.: ref, 2516 (102)
Hovander, D.: ref, 1036 (5)
Hovanitz, C. A.: ref, 272 (24), 1186 (1), 1697 (34), 2858 (11)
Hovens, J. E.: ref, 1697 (304), 2497 (350)
Hovland, C. I.: rev, 1115, 1672, 2856, 2857
Howard, B. L.: ref, 472 (171), 2214 (101), 2498 (64)
Howard, D.: ref, 163 (1), 349 (7,24), 350 (10), 1097 (11), 1240 (19), 2228 (8), 2873 (1)
Howard, D. V.: ref, 2860 (705)
Howard, J.: ref, 270 (45), 1216 (17), 1687 (35), 2603 (526)
Howard, J. B.: ref, 270 (31), 337 (175)
Howard, J. H.: ref, 2860 (705)
Howard, J. K.: ref, 2682 (13), 2905 (121)
Howard, K. I.: test, 1832; ref, 1832 (14), 2603 (274)
Howard, P.: test, 445
Howard, R.: ref, 2050 (70,79), 2193 (20), 2858 (62)
Howard, R. J.: ref, 1758 (32), 2193 (35), 2860 (792)
Howard, R. W.: rev, 616
Howard, S. D.: ref, 2860 (347), 2862 (161)
Howard-Rose, D.: ref, 1379 (47), 1612 (52), 2163 (116)
Howe, B. L.: ref, 226 (1)
Howe, G. W.: ref, 472 (47,142), 997 (9), 2860 (467)
Howe, J. T.: ref, 2519 (21), 2520 (22), 2860 (421)
Howe, M. L.: ref, 1072 (54)
Howell, A.: ref, 2076 (2)
Howell, C.: ref, 1991 (98), 2591 (4), 2656 (22), 2862 (562)
Howell, D. C.: ref, 337 (70,73,104,134), 472 (77,163), 2214 (38,95), 2860 (192)
Howell, J.: test, 1656
Howell, J. M.: ref, 1965 (16)
Howell, K. K.: ref, 331 (2), 1216 (28), 1903 (157), 2163 (104)
Howell, K. W.: test, 1738; rev, 158, 301, 1275, 2481
Howell, R. A.: ref, 2863 (190)
Howell, R. J.: rev, 711, 2245
Howell, S. C.: ref, 451 (23)
Howell Township Public Schools: test, 1224
Howell-White, S.: ref, 2603 (466)
Howells, L.: ref, 2860 (481)
Howerton, C. J.: ref, 1903 (180), 2905 (39)
Howerton, D. L.: ref, 694 (71)
Howes, C.: ref, 373 (20), 875 (3,4,5,6), 1264 (1,2), 1903 (526)
Howes, J. L.: ref, 2860 (6), 2863 (4)
Howie, D.: rev, 21, 23, 1514
Howie, P. M.: ref, 1485 (45), 1903 (423)
Howie, V. M.: ref, 1903 (184), 2402 (20), 2485 (90)
Howieson, D. B.: ref, 2860 (468), 2863 (132)
Howieson, J.: ref, 2860 (468), 2863 (132)
Howland, C. A.: ref, 2417 (16)
Howland, R. H.: ref, 1166 (207), 2305 (233)
Howlin, P.: ref, 350 (30,44,50), 994 (25,38,51), 1765 (27), 2163 (219,344), 2662 (7), 2813 (155), 2860 (1291,1361,1395), 2862 (490,635,684,717)
Howson, A.: ref, 272 (88)
Hoy, C.: ref, 1697 (171), 2860 (355), 2901 (20)
Hoy, F.: ref, 1965 (38)
Hoyer, G.: ref, 1079 (43)
Hoyer, W. J.: ref, 2860 (25,589)
Hoyle, R. H.: ref, 665 (8), 1657 (5)
Hoyt, C. J.: rev, 1315, 1863
Hoyt, D. D.: test, 1233
Hoyt, D. P.: test, 1236
Hoyt, D. R.: ref, 451 (237)
Hoyt, K. B.: rev, 1100, 1157
Hoza, B.: ref, 472 (215), 1318 (20), 1903 (203), 2211 (23), 2214 (125), 2862 (677)
Hraba, J.: ref, 2603 (467)
Hresko, W. P.: test, 657, 810, 1167, 2680, 2682, 2683, 2684
Hsia, T. C.: ref, 2862 (20)
Hsieh, S-L. J., : ref, 1379 (27), 2163 (117), 2862 (204)
Hsu, H.: ref, 1903 (200)
Hsu, L. K. G.: ref, 2603 (103)
Hsu, L. M.: rev, 2212, 2882; ref, 1697 (174,05)
Hsuing, H.: ref, 2076 (101)
Hu, T.: ref, 337 (26)

Hua, T.: rev, 482
Huang, C. D.: ref, 2218 (97)
Huang, C-Y.: ref, 908 (12), 1101 (2), 2417 (41)
Huang, H. S.: ref, 350 (31), 1903 (527), 2163 (327), 2863 (268,386)
Huang, J.: ref, 1140 (45)
Huang, S. L.: ref, 1318 (15)
Huang, S-Y. L.: ref, 495 (12)
Huba, G. J.: test, 132, 1577, 2407
Huba, M. E.: rev, 2175, 2674; ref, 298 (152), 2527 (15)
Hubbard, B.: ref, 2218 (78)
Hubbard, J. J.: ref, 557 (4)
Hubbard, J. W.: ref, 2288 (6), 2289 (4)
Hubbs-Tait, L.: ref, 451 (130), 771 (24)
Hubchen, K.: test, 1860
Huber, M.: ref, 2227 (40), 2516 (101), 2860 (1294)
Huber, S. J.: ref, 1525 (4), 2873 (6)
Huber, T. J.: ref, 1093 (93), 2289 (39)
Hubert, E. E.: test, 1482
Huberty, T. J.: ref, 1991 (44)
Hublet, C.: ref, 2163 (321), 2860 (1253)
Hubley, A. M.: rev, 212, 303; ref, 999 (189), 1405 (36)
Hubly, S.: test, 2934
Huchingson, J.: ref, 2295 (6)
Huchingson, R.: ref, 2295 (6)
Huckaby, W. J.: ref, 1698 (24)
Huckel, L. H.: ref, 1965 (11)
Hudak, M. A.: ref, 298 (80), 1469 (1)
Huddleston, E. N.: ref, 1697 (425), 1698 (9)
Hudes, E. S.: ref, 134 (35)
Hudiburg, R. A.: ref, 2603 (267)
Hudson, A.: ref, 1093 (71), 2050 (90)
Hudson, J. D., Jr.: ref, 171 (1), 937 (2), 1043 (1),1974 (1), 2105 (1)
Hudson, J. I.: ref, 893 (24), 1166 (23,160)
Hudson, J. P., Jr.: rev, 2151, 2867
Hudson, L. M.: ref, 771 (13)
Hudson, R. L.: ref, 2813 (106), 2860 (987)
Hudson, T.: ref, 863 (87), 1888 (1), 1889 (9), 2603 (533)
Huebner, E. S.: rev, 166, 811, 1620, 2328, 2361, 2863; ref, 1590 (66), 1991 (69), 2218 (131)
Huebner, M. H.: rev, 2817
Huebner, R. A.: ref, 1612 (26), 1903 (120), 2860 (358), 2892 (53)
Huelsman, K.: ref, 2901 (57)
Huergo, M.: ref, 2656 (1)
Huesmann, L. R.: ref, 451 (57)
Hufano, L.: rev, 1612
Huff, F. J.: ref, 776 (38)
Huff, L.: ref, 1903 (270), 2905 (56)
Huff, M. E.: ref, 2497 (452)
Huffman, D.: ref, 1903 (270), 2905 (56)
Huffman, L. C.: ref, 272 (207), 2497 (582)
Huffman, L. E. : ref, 592 (44)
Huffman, S.: ref, 1469 (7)
Hufnagle, K. G.: ref, 2860 (1045), 2862 (445)
Hugdahl, K.: ref, 1164 (5,63), 1240 (2), 2860 (898), 2862 (74,354)
Hughes, A.: test, 2228
Hughes, B.: test, 2471
Hughes, C.: ref, 349 (12,30), 614 (1), 1903 (468), 2485 (203), 2662 (3,5), 2813 (120)
Hughes, C. A.: ref, 2860 (651), 2901 (42)
Hughes, C. B.: ref, 794 (2)
Hughes, C. W.: ref, 199 (1), 472 (65), 473 (5), 1991 (61), 2305 (192)
Hughes, D.: ref, 2603 (350)
Hughes, D. C.: test, 2091
Hughes, D. L.: ref, 214 (14), 846 (8), 1485 (16), 1903 (173), 2657 (6)
Hughes, E.: ref, 815 (23), 2299 (6), 2863 (259)
Hughes, E. C.: ref, 372 (1), 1697 (3), 1790 (1), 1903 (2), 2163 (3), 2247 (1), 2417 (2), 2860 (12)
Hughes, G. M.: ref, 1657 (4)
Hughes, H. M.: ref, 337 (62,128), 1697 (169), 2402 (12)
Hughes, J.: ref, 472 (8)
Hughes, J. E.: test, 1225
Hughes, J. N.: rev, 705, 903, 1470, 1908; ref, 681 (43)
Hughes, J. R.: ref, 301 (9), 1072 (14), 2076 (26), 2484 (2), 2862 (96)
Hughes, K. P.: ref, 451 (130)
Hughes, M. T.: ref, 1095 (38), 1485 (51), 1991 (108), 2680 (15), 2695 (53)
Hughes, P.: test, 306
Hughes, R., Jr.: ref, 337 (79)
Hughes, S.: rev, 759, 788
Hughes, S. O.: ref, 136 (9)
Hughey, A. W.: ref, 666 (10), 1338 (41), 2076 (79)
Hughson, E. A.: test, 63
Hugler, H.: ref, 2050 (36)
Hugo, K.: ref, 1903 (468), 2485 (203), 2813 (120)
Huh, K.: ref, 2076 (19), 2860 (198)
Hui, C.: ref, 1701 (56)
Hui, E. K. P.: ref, 1590 (43), 2858 (94)
Huijnen, M. A. H.: test, 2441
Huisingh, R.: test, 2710, 2911
Huitema, B. E.: ref, 1115 (9)
Hukui, T.: ref, 1592 (27), 2862 (719)
Hulette, C.: ref, 2860 (1280)
Hulin, C. L.: test, 1348, 2208; ref, 1348 (14)
Hulittam, D.: ref, 2603 (529)
Hull, J.: ref, 2218 (99), 2305 (226)
Hull, J. G.: ref, 1166 (201)
Hull, J. W.: ref, 2247 (38), 2603 (188,189), 2860 (469)
Hulme, C.: ref, 349 (11,13,18,19,37), 1765 (17), 2163 (163)
Hulse, J. A.: ref, 1613 (1)
Hulsey, T.: ref, 2247 (39)
Hulsey, T. C.: ref, 451 (4)
Hulsing, M. M.: ref, 331 (4), 994 (26), 2233 (4), 2695 (37)
Hulstijn, W.: ref, 1166 (147,211)
Hultsch, D. F.: ref, 1405 (18,30,36)

Hum, A.: ref, 373 (33)
Human Resource Center, The University of Chicago: test, 2605, 2907
Human Sciences Research Council: test, 2375
Human Synergistics: test, 1550, 2575
Human Synergistics, Inc.: test, 903, 1923, 2630
Humberside Education Authority: test, 1262
Hume, W. G.: ref, 624 (1)
Humes, C. W.: ref, 1755 (18)
Humes, L. E.: ref, 2860 (652), 2863 (191)
Humfleet, G.: ref, 1164 (4), 1166 (8), 2860 (94)
Humphrey, D. G.: ref, 2860 (670), 2892 (124)
Humphrey, D. H.: ref, 1697 (419)
Humphrey, L. L.: ref, 2247 (51)
Humphreys, G. W.: test, 314
Humphreys, K.: ref, 337 (101), 1495 (1)
Humphreys, L. G.: rev, 303, 838, 1672, 2606, 2797
Humphreys, R. P.: ref, 1096 (3,4), 2193 (11), 2860 (246,247,342), 2862 (125,126,708)
Humphries, T.: ref, 353 (21),451 (288), 815 (38), 1240 (45), 1379 (86), 2693 (9), 2694 (26), 2862 (205,491, 739), 2864 (116), 2879 (57,165)
Humphry, R.: ref, 815 (24)
Hundert, J.: rev, 2088, 2450
Hundley, P. L.: ref, 1697 (175)
Hunkin, N. M.: ref, 1104 (4,9), 1758 (25,28,41,42), 2193 (23,40,41), 2239 (21), 2516 (67, 2860 (653,659, 713,899,900), 2863 (192,194,211,269, 270), 2892 (121, 140,188,189)
Hunsaker, S. L.: ref, 724 (6), 1142 (5), 1143 (2), 2295 (5,7,9), 2771 (38)
Hunsberger, B.: ref, 1408 (9)
Hunsicker, A. L.: rev, 132, 1577
Hunsley, J.: ref, 863 (67)
Hunt, A. E.: ref, 998 (114)
Hunt, A. T.: ref, 1093 (19)
Hunt, B.: ref, 403 (1), 404 (45), 768 (2)
Hunt, B. A.: test, 1569
Hunt, D.: ref, 999 (3)
Hunt, D. D.: ref, 1697 (90), 2858 (16)
Hunt, D. P.: ref, 592 (60)
Hunt, E.: ref, 180 (26)
Hunt, G. E.: ref, 1166 (11)
Hunt, J.: ref, 2076 (149)
Hunt, J. A.: test, 1705
Hunt, J. M.: test, 194
Hunt, J. V.: rev, 811, 1612, 2432
Hunt, M.: ref, 2892 (244)
Hunt, M. F.: ref, 1517 (6)
Hunt, P. F.: ref, 1754 (18)
Hunt, P. K.: ref, 1754 (21)
Hunt, R. A.: test, 1310, 1705
Hunt, R. G.: ref, 1755 (5)
Hunt, S.: ref, 2076 (162), 2527 (4)
Hunt, S. M.: ref, 1754 (18)
Hunt, T.: rev, 1693
Hunt, W.: ref, 2603 (505)
Hunt, W. A.: rev, 2402
Hunt, W. K.: ref, 2076 (26)
Hunter, C.: rev, 1097
Hunter, G. A.: ref, 2497 (278), 2656 (9)
Hunter, G. W.: rev, 1084
Hunter, J.: ref, 298 (107)
Hunter, J. A.: ref, 2358 (12)
Hunter, J. E.: ref, 451 (68)
Hunter, M. : ref, 1218 (11), 2860 (535,762, 978, 992,1014), 2863 (294), 2892 (90,206)
Hunter, T. A.: ref, 2417 (40)
Hunter, W.: ref, 1408 (1)
Hunter, W. F.: ref, 2247 (44)
Hunter, W. M.: ref, 451 (3)
Hunter-Grundin, E.: test, 1232
Huntington, D. D.: ref, 1697 (219), 1916 (2), 2497 (253)
The Huntington Study Group: ref, 272 (380), 1164 (186)
Huntley, M.: test, 1134
Huntley, R. A.: ref, 209 (5)
Huntley-Johnston, L.: ref, 592 (44)
Hunton-Shoup, J.: ref, 2860 (145), 2862 (93)
Huntoon, J.: ref, 1687 (38)
Huntzinger, R. M.: ref, 2497 (131), 2905 (50)
Huppert, F. A.: ref, 998 (99),1079 (40), 2237 (1), 2239 (13,33)
Hur, Y-M.: ref, 1755 (74)
Hurford, D. D.: ref, 2860 (901)
Hurford, D. P.: rev, 774, 2684; ref, 665 (21), 665 (50), 1903 (180,270,271), 2905 (39,56,57)
Hurlburt, R. T.: ref, 2407 (1), 2858 (70)
Hurlbut, S. C.: ref, 134 (4)
Hurley, J. D.: ref, 1021 (22)
Hurley, J. R.: ref, 1036 (3), 2218 (62,126,127)
Hurley, K.: ref, 1166 (215)
Huron, C.: ref, 2288 (49), 2289 (38), 2860 (902), 2863 (271)
Hurrell, R. M.: ref, 2485 (208), 2862 (509)
Hurst, S. R.: ref, 893 (50)
Hurt, D. J.: ref, 1292 (1)
Hurt, J.: ref, 763 (5)
Hurtig, A. L.: ref, 1881 (3)
Hurtig, H. I.: ref, 2860 (80), 2863 (23), 2892 (8)
Hurwitz, T. A.: ref, 335 (1), 2289 (6)
Hurwitz, T. D.: ref, 1697 (446), 2703 (2)
Husband, S. D.: ref, 272 (182), 273 (21), 1697 (420,582)
Husby, R.: ref, 1093 (57), 2050 (51), 2247 (47)
Husek, T. R.: rev, 1413
Huselid, R. F.: ref, 1673 (8),2603 (268)
Husic, F. T.: ref, 2163 (26)
Huska, J. A.: ref, 272 (206), 1697 (505), 2497 (580)
Huss, M. T.: ref, 1338 (36)
Hussain, M.: ref, 2860 (1032), 2892 (214)
Hussey, B.: ref, 2485 (52)
Hussong, A. M.: ref, 451 (39,262)
Huston, A. E.: ref, 1758 (1), 2163 (18), 2860 (58), 2863 (19)
Huston, R. E.: ref, 2835 (6)

Huszti, H. C.: ref, 337 (28), 2858 (30)
Hutcheson, G. D.: ref, 350 (26), 1485 (39), 2045 (1)
Hutcheson, J. J.: ref, 270 (31), 337 (60,175)
Hutcheson, K. G.: ref, 413 (28),2360 (9)
Hutchings, E. M. J.: test, 901
Hutchings, M. J.: test, 901
Hutchins, P.: ref, 837 (3), 1765 (19), 1903 (292), 2862 (280)
Hutchinson, E.: test, 300
Hutchinson, J.: ref, 1115 (24)
Hutchinson, J. E.: ref, 1903 (26), 2163 (24), 2862 (62)
Hutchinson, M. K.: ref, 1010 (74)
Hutchinson, S. M.: rev, 496
Hutchinson, T. A.: test, 898, 2383, 2933
Huteau, M.: ref, 2163 (181)
Huter, V.: ref, 2862 (628)
Hutner, N.: ref, 2860 (205,1097), 2863 (51,326)
Hutri, M.: ref, 272 (183), 2497 (560)
Huttenlocher, J.: test, 2059; ref, 2695 (38),2704 (26)
Huttenlocher, P.: ref, 2485 (20), 2860 (153), 2862 (94), 2864 (16)
Hütter, B. O.: ref, 2860 (903)
Hutton, H. E.: ref, 1697 (421)
Hutton, J. B.: test, 2447
Hutton, K.: ref, 2497 (106), 2603 (84)
Hutzell, R. R.: rev, 1290
Huxley, P.: ref, 270 (5), 1216 (30)
Huynh, H.: ref, 1657 (12)
Huyser, B.: ref, 2603 (534)
Huysmans, H. A.: ref, 1164 (142), 1740 (16), 2226 (18), 2516 (93), 2599 (37), 2860 (1234), 2863 (368)
Huzel, L. L.: ref, 2497 (254)
Hwang, C.: ref, 462 (19)
Hwang, C. P.: ref, 365 (8), 1216 (71)
Hwang, Y. R.: ref, 1379 (92)
Hyams, J.: ref, 2247 (45), 2380 (9), 2749 (34), 2862 (224)
Hyams, J. S.: ref, 1226 (1), 2247 (90)
Hyde, C.: ref, 451 (59), 1011 (4), 1079 (41), 1987 (15)
Hyde, J. S.: ref, 1889 (8), 2496 (4), 2497 (482,661)
Hyde, T. M.: ref, 776 (15), 1164 (46), 2163 (112), 2516 (24), 2860 (459), 2879 (56), 2892 (74,122)
Hyer, L.: ref, 1166 (114), 1697 (55,78,176,306,307), 2497 (561), 2603 (468)
Hyer, L. A.: ref, 1697 (220,252,359)
Hyle, P.: ref, 1216 (94)
Hylton, J.: ref, 1755 (71)
Hyman, B. T.: ref, 2227 (3), 2860 (181)
Hyman, I. A.: ref, 451 (263), 681 (93), 1392 (15), 2862 (718), 2905 (120)
Hyman, L.: ref, 2603 (426)
Hyman, R. B.: ref, 2485 (126), 2603 (510)
Hymel, S.: ref, 2358 (17)
Hynan, L. S.: ref, 2247 (70), 2879 (117)
Hynd, C. R.: ref, 592 (18)
Hynd, G. W.: rev, 2516; ref, 229 (1), 246 (7), 280 (5), 451 (231), 798 (13,16), 815 (18), 1131 (12), 1379 (43,64), 1903 (244,336), 2724 (7,9), 2813 (46), 2862 (243,312,315,535,647), 2870 (4), 2879 (93,103,211), 2905 (66,115), 2934 (1)
Hynes, G. J.: ref, 2858 (121)
Hyun, C. S.: ref, 2076 (56)
Hyyppä, M. T.: ref, 272 (45), 303 (3), 998 (32), 2860 (263), 2863 (68)

Iaboni, F.: ref, 681 (63)
Iacono, W. G.: ref, 1093 (67), 2050 (58,81), 2305 (31), 2603 (238)
Ialongo, N.: ref, 364 (19), 472 (48,86,172) 2214 (49,66,102,103)
Ialongo, N. S.: ref, 681 (47)
Iannaccone, S. T.: ref, 2862 (526)
Iannone, C.: ref, 272 (337)
Iansek, R.: ref, 1164 (108), 1758 (23,101), 2860 (608)
Iavarone, A.: ref, 2863 (230)
Ibel, S.: ref, 459 (18), 2485 (82), 2813 (35)
Ichimura, S.: ref, 2497 (399,400)
Iddon, J. L.: ref, 1758 (94)
Idleman, L. S.: ref, 615 (50), 1455 (6)
Idrikawa, T.: ref, 2860 (472)
Iedema, J.: ref, 1079 (95)
Ieronimo, C.: ref, 1166 (186)
Ievers, C. E.: ref, 1316 (1)
Iezzi, A.: ref, 1079 (91)
Ignchi, M. Y.: ref, 272 (182), 273 (21), 1697 (420,582)
Ihilevich, D.: test, 770
Iivanainen, M.: ref, 2860 (895), 2863 (265)
Ikata, N.: ref, 824 (3)
Ikeda, M.: ref, 2163 (334), 2860 (1314,1371), 2873 (68)
Ikeda, S. C.: ref, 451 (125), 472 (168)
Ikejiri, Y.: ref, 2163 (334), 2860 (1314,1371), 2873 (68,73)
Ilardi, S. S.: ref, 472 (117), 2214 (63), 2603 (346)
Iles, S.: ref, 2050 (35)
Ilg, F. L.: test, 1085
Ilgen, D. R.: ref, 1965 (78), 2218 (102)
Iliff, A.: test, 119
Iliffe, A.: test, 2087
Illback, R. J.: rev, 1141, 1453, 1461
Ilmer, S.: test, 124
Ilsley, J. E.: ref, 272 (119), 1166 (74), 1758 (43), 2239 (24), 2860 (904)
Imamura, T.: ref, 2163 (334), 2860 (1314,1371), 2873 (68,73)
Imber, S. D.: ref, 272 (221), 1517 (4)
Impara, J. C.: rev, 2090, 2091, 2222, 570 (1)
Inaki, K.: ref, 2860 (1416)
Inamdar, S. C.: ref, 2498 (66), 2862 (546)
Inampudi, C.: ref, 376 (14), 2863 (372)
Inatsuka, T. T.: test, 1192
Inayatullah, M.: ref, 142 (6), 1619 (8), 2862 (420)
Incalzi, R. A.: ref, 2163 (328), 2860 (1281)
Incesu, C.: ref, 2497 (301)

Incisa della Rocchetta, A.: ref, 2860 (470)
Inderbitzen, H. M.: ref, 472 (126,224), 2214 (67)
Industrial Psychology, Inc.: test, 1323
Industrial Psychology International, Ltd.: test, 2930
Industrial Training Research Unit: test, 1356
Ingersoll, K. S.: ref, 372 (92), 615 (54), 1866 (39)
Ingersoll-Dayton, B.: ref, 1014 (5)
Ingham, J.: ref, 2497 (364)
Ingles, J. L.: ref, 1903 (469), 2193 (53), 2860 (1098), 2863 (327), 2873 (54)
Inglis, A.: ref, 241 (4), 451 (94), 815 (35), 1903 (447), 2695 (47), 2864 (110)
Ingraham, C.: ref, 298 (46), 1590 (11)
Ingram, C.: ref, 2252 (4), 2295 (4)
Ingram, D.: ref, 1982 (7)
Ingram, D. E.: test, 233
Ingram, K. K.: ref, 2768 (35), 2860 (1126), 2863 (334)
Ingram, R. E.: ref, 1697 (308), 1745 (41,74), 2519 (41), 2520 (41)
Ingram-LeBlanc, C.: test, 2670
Inlow, F. H.: ref, 2857 (1)
Inman, M.: ref, 2497 (299)
Inman, M. L.: ref, 2497 (154)
Innis, R. B.: ref, 2863 (232)
Innocenti, M. S.: ref, 1259 (1)
Inoue, K.: ref, 1592 (27), 2862 (719)
Inouye, S. K.: ref, 2860 (471)
Insel, E.: test, 1269
Insel, P. N.: test, 2917
The Institute for Behavioral Research in Creativity: test, 311, 907, 2537
Integrated Teaching Team: test, 1283
International Assessment Network: test, 1579
International LearningWorks: test, 554, 1519, 1814
International Personnel Management Association: test, 1324, 1325, 1326
International Testing and Training Programs, Educational Testing Service: test, 2717
Intrieri, R. C.: ref, 337 (80), 1745 (42), 2497 (351)
Inwald, R.: test, 1208, 1209, 1313, 1314
Inwald, R. E.: test, 1207, 1210; ref, 1313 (1), 1697 (145)
Inzitari, D.: ref, 2497 (621)
Ioannidis, G.: ref, 272 (316), 1697 (568), 2497 (653)
Iona, M.: rev, 110
IOX Assessment Associates: test, 684
IPAT Staff: test, 1429, 2418
Ippolito, M. F.: ref, 1216 (44), 1902 (54)
Iqbal, N.: ref, 1166 (1), 2305 (12), 2603 (105)
Iragui, V.: ref, 1903 (101), 2860 (324), 2892 (45)
Ireland, M.: ref, 1903 (528), 2647 (2)
Ireton, H.: test, 454, 872, 1259, 1935, 2040
Ireton, H. R.: test, 453
Irish, D.: ref, 2288 (62)
Irle, E.: ref, 303 (20), 1164 (164), 2860 (1329)
Irons, T. R.: ref, 1455 (10), 1866 (32)
Ironsmith, M.: ref, 2039 (7)
Ironson, G.: ref, 2603 (516)
Ironson, G. H.: test, 2509
Irvin, B. L.: ref, 1079 (70), 1947 (7)
Irvin, D. M.: ref, 75 (1), 694 (76), 2211 (31), 2862 (276)
Irvin, L. K.: test, 1896, 2422, 2443, 2734, 2380
Irvine, A. A.: ref, 2603 (144)
Irving, L. M.: ref, 1000 (53)
Irving, P. G.: ref, 1701 (53)
Irwin, C. E. Jr.: ref, 1000 (58)
Irwin, H. J.: ref, 462 (10,21), 846 (24)
Irwin, J. L.: test, 1348
Irwin, J. V.: test, 1490
Irwin, M.: ref, 451 (37), 1099 (1), 1661 (14), 1903 (261), 2305 (46), 2497 (105), 2860 (845), 2862 (264)
Isaac, A. R.: ref, 353 (13)
Isaac, C. L.: ref, 1758 (99), 2860 (1379), 2863 (414)
Isaacs, E.: ref, 2860 (1099), 2862 (492), 2864 (117)
Isaacson, L.: ref, 451 (104), 2862 (452)
Isaka, E.: ref, 1903 (529), 2901 (118)
Isaksen, S. G.: ref, 1404 (5,9)
Isenberg, D. P.: test, 2119
Isenhart, C.: rev, 1166, 1576
Ishiai, S.: ref, 2860 (472,1416)
Ishiai, S., Y.: ref, 2860 (1169)
Ishihara, S.: test, 2658
Ishijima, B.: ref, 2860 (406), 2873 (11)
Ishikawa, T.: ref, 2076 (174)
Islam, M. N.: ref, 2603 (410)
Ismail, M.: ref, 1466 (5)
Isobe, T. L.: ref, 708 (9)
Isonio, S.: rev, 2358
Isono, O.: ref, 2860 (997), 2873 (47)
Ito, H.: ref, 1010 (48)
Itoigawa, N.: ref, 2862 (633)
Itskowitz, R.: test, 242, 242 (1); ref, 863 (49)
Ittenbach, R. F.: ref, 1300 (5,6), 1379 (92)
Itzkovich, M.: test, 1513
Ivani-Chalian, R.: test, 2239; ref, 349 (9), 2239 (16)
Ivans-Chalian, R.: ref, 2239 (26)
Ivella, A.: ref, 2163 (333)
Ivens, S. H.: rev, 560, 1090, 1672, 2857
Ivers, H.: ref, 272 (375), 2498 (77)
Iversen, S. D.: ref, 2227 (38), 2860 (1279), 2863 (385)
Iverson, A.: ref, 1582 (4)
Iverson, A. M.: rev, 452, 1009, 1993
Iverson, G. L.: ref, 1525 (22), 1697 (422), 2860 (1100,1101,1282), 2863 (328)
Iverson, V. S.: test, 553
Ives, M.: rev, 2402
Ivins, R. G.: test, 1978
Ivnik, R. J.: ref, 2226 (25), 2860 (537,718,905,1283), 2863 (103,152,214,272,387), 2879 (88)
Ivon Cramon, D. Y.: ref, 2163 (118)
Iwanicki, E. F.: rev, 829, 831, 832, 833, 830
Iwata, M.: ref, 2860 (396), 2873 (10)

Iyengar, S.: ref, 272 (259)
Izaks, G. J.: ref, 1079 (42)
Izard, C. E.: ref, 1965 (26)
Izard, J.: test, 492
Izard, J. F.: test, 1600
Izzo, C. V.: ref, 66 (2), 272 (81), 2076 (76)

Jabalpurwala, S.: ref, 2603 (501)
Jablenski, A.: ref, 2050 (10)
Jablensky, A.: ref, 2050 (36,84)
Jabri, M. M.: ref, 1348 (6)
Jaccuzzo, D. P.: ref, 1866 (3)
Jack, C. R.: ref, 2860 (359,537), 2863 (94,152)
Jack, L. M.: ref, 303 (30), 2076 (160), 2599 (42)
Jackman, L. P.: ref, 893 (22), 999 (123)
Jacks, S. D.: ref, 2603 (551)
Jackson, A. E.: ref, 459 (37)
Jackson, A. S.: ref, 998 (52)
Jackson, B. B.: ref, 2603 (123)
Jackson, C.: ref, 2860 (803)
Jackson, C. Y.: ref, 1000 (110), 1021 (48), 2214 (140), 2230 (21), 2656 (25)
Jackson, D. L.: ref, 681 (90)
Jackson, D. N.: test, 183, 256, 406, 1333, 1334, 1731, 1965, 2592; rev, 932, 1201, 1622, 1630; ref, 1333 (4), 1334 (1,3), 1732 (2), 1790 (2), 1965 (1,2,4,19,20), 2218 (70)
Jackson, D. N., III: ref, 1732 (2)
Jackson, E.: ref, 265 (12)
Jackson, E. F.: ref, 815 (39), 1903 (481), 2671 (3), 2862 (522), 2879 (176), 2901 (97)
Jackson, E. W.: ref, 451 (234), 1638 (3)
Jackson, G. C.: ref, 2282 (11)
Jackson, G. D.: ref, 2860 (838), 2863 (243)
Jackson, H. F.: ref, 2863 (114)
Jackson, H. J.: ref, 272 (33), 1687 (12,15,96), 2520 (36)
Jackson, J.: ref, 540 (16), 655 (1), 1095 (44), 1902 (98)
Jackson, J. D.: ref, 908 (11)
Jackson, J. L.: ref, 793 (5), 2839 (2)
Jackson, K. M.: ref, 451 (186)
Jackson, L. A.: ref, 298 (64)
Jackson, L. D.: ref, 1734 (6)
Jackson, L. M.: ref, 2771 (4)
Jackson, M.: ref, 2862 (328)
Jackson, M. H.: ref, 364 (15), 2652 (7)
Jackson, M. T.: test, 81, 284
Jackson, N. E.: ref, 1592 (14), 1902 (5,20,43), 2862 (41,113), 2905 (40)
Jackson, P.: test, 2100, 2714
Jackson, P.: ref, 1079 (106)
Jackson, R. H.: ref, 1902 (45)
Jackson, R. K.: ref, 2288 (4), 2289 (2), 2305 (7), 2860 (63)
Jackson, S.: ref, 1010 (94), 2038 (1)
Jackson, S. E.: test, 1590
Jackson, S. L.: ref, 1755 (63)
Jackson, S. T.: ref, 2163 (322), 2172 (1), 2225 (17)
Jackson, T.: ref, 1079 (91), 1338 (45), 1697 (21), 2839 (6)
Jackson, T. W.: ref, 681 (43)
Jackson-Walker, S.: ref, 1698 (23)
Jackson-Wilson, A. G.: ref, 1000 (50)
Jacob, M. C.: ref, 2497 (119)
Jacob, R. G.: ref, 998 (53), 2497 (562), 2498 (33)
Jacob, T.: ref, 272 (12), 1661 (1), 2305 (85)
Jacobi, D.: ref, 1485 (62), 1653 (29), 2860 (1333), 2862 (661)
Jacobi, K. A.: ref, 1164 (93), 2860 (863), 2863 (254)
Jacobowitz, T.: ref, 592 (5)
Jacobs, B. J.: ref, 2873 (58,72)
Jacobs, D.: ref, 2863 (153)
Jacobs, D. H.: ref, 376 (20), 1164 (150), 2227 (37), 2860 (870,1270), 2873 (35,64), 2892 (182,273)
Jacobs, D. M.: ref, 303 (18,29), 776 (45,61), 1740 (21,32), 2860 (906,907,1180,1284,1346,1405)
Jacobs, E. V.: test, 2310
Jacobs, G.A.: test, 2497
Jacobs, G. D.: ref, 2497 (255)
Jacobs, J. E.: ref, 272 (285)
Jacobs, J. K.: ref, 2862 (616)
Jacobs, K. W.: ref, 2076 (58)
Jacobs, L.: ref, 1697 (114), 2860 (231)
Jacobs, L. C.: ref, 592 (3)
Jacobs, M.: ref, 2497 (195)
Jacobsberg, L.: ref, 337 (30,48), 2497 (192)
Jacobsen, A.: ref, 2247 (26)
Jacobsen, B.: ref, 2050 (42)
Jacobsen, B. K.: ref, 1079 (43)
Jacobsen, B. S.: ref, 1745 (71,78)
Jacobsen, L.: ref, 2305 (232)
Jacobsen, L. K.: ref, 451 (116,243), 2288 (68,71), 2289 (52,56), 2305 (242), 2862 (475,493,501,629,702), 2879 (227)
Jacobsen, P. B.: ref, 2076 (89), 2497 (69,256)
Jacobsen, S. J.: ref, 1612 (73), 2485 (170), 2860 (910), 2862 (356), 2864 (95)
Jacobson, A. M.: ref, 1021 (14)
Jacobson, B.: test, 717
Jacobson, B. J.: ref, 451 (224,225)
Jacobson, C. M.: ref, 1404 (4), 1755 (27)
Jacobson, I.: ref, 2862 (43)
Jacobson, J. L.: ref, 1216 (31), 1903 (121,181), 2860 (473)
Jacobson, J. W.: ref, 1903 (213)
Jacobson, L.: ref, 1740 (8)
Jacobson, M. G.: ref, 1072 (12)
Jacobson, M. W.: ref, 376 (7), 776 (19), 1166 (116), 1218 (9), 2193 (31), 2860 (731,1111), 2863 (330)
Jacobson, N. S.: ref, 272 (184,355)
Jacobson, R. R.: ref, 2858 (84)f, 2863 (223)
Jacobson, S. W.: ref, 1216 (31), 1903 (121,181), 2860 (473)
Jacobvitz, D.: ref, 1321 (9), 1965 (63)
Jacobvitz, D. B.: ref, 998 (115)
Jacoby, J.: test, 1574; ref, 1697 (122)
Jacoby, L. L.: ref, 2860 (337), 2863 (89)

Jacoby, R.: ref, 998 (43)
Jacques, N.: ref, 694 (132)
Jadresic, D.: ref, 2050 (64,93), 2076 (97), 2239 (18), 2497 (384), 2860 (581), 2863 (168), 2892 (106)
Jaedicke, S.: ref, 459 (29), 1000 (48), 2860 (654)
Jaeger, M. E.: ref, 592 (69)
Jaeger, R. M.: rev, 1115, 1247, 2905
Jaffe, J. H.: ref, 1697 (73,88), 2402 (5,6), 2603 (48)
Jagger, L.: ref, 399 (2), 401 (1), 1701 (24), 1790 (4)
Jaggi, J.: ref, 592 (58)
Jagota, M.: ref, 1697 (171), 2860 (355), 2901 (20)
Jain, R.: ref, 998 (128), 2417 (38), 2497 (645)
Jain, V. K.: ref, 694 (116)
Jakobsson, G.: ref, 234 (1)
Jakubowyc, N.: ref, 1631 (4), 2076 (186)
Jamelka, R.: ref, 1697 (148), 2559 (2)
James, J. B.: ref, 272 (289), 2749 (57),77)
James, K.: ref, 298 (81,158), 838 (22), 2451 (2)
James, L. A.: ref, 1701 (7)
James, L. D.: ref, 2497 (257), 2603 (190)
James, L. R.: ref, 1701 (7), 1965 (24)
James, S. P.: ref, 272 (132), 1166 (80)
James, T.: ref, 401 (3)
James-Myers, L.: ref, 2603 (58)
James-Tanner, S.: ref, 863 (67)
Jameson, P. B.: ref, 270 (18)
Jamieson, J.: ref, 666 (3), 1140 (3), 1592 (1), 2076 (83)
Jamison, C.: ref, 272 (120)
Jamison, C. B.: rev, 2219
Jampole, E. S.: ref, 724 (3,5)
Janakira-Maiah, N.: ref, 1166 (87)
Janca, H.: ref, 1166 (217)
Jäncke, L.: ref, 2860 (1285)
Janczur, B.: ref, 1590 (39)
Jandorf, L.: ref, 2102 (1), 2288 (16,56), 2289 (11,43), 2860 (335), 2863 (88)
Janelle, S.: ref, 2485 (55)
Jang, K. L.: ref, 495 (15), 963 (2), 1010 (130), 1965 (84), 2218 (63)
Jani, N.: ref, 1241 (4)
Jani, S.: ref, 1241 (4)
Janicak, P. G.: ref, 2305 (166)
Janikowski, T. P.: ref, 462 (33), 2797 (4,5)
Janisse, M. P.: ref, 1745 (44)
Jankovic, J.: ref, 2860 (1129), 2863 (336)
Jankowski, M. K.: ref, 337 (174)
Janniro, F.: ref, 2813 (63)
Janols, L-O.: ref, 2862 (617)
Janos, P. M.: ref, 372 (7), 771 (4)
Janosky, J.: ref, 681 (46,86), 2225 (16), 2485 (225), 2862 (624), 2864 (132), 2901 (113), 2902 (5)
Janosky, J. E.: ref, 1612 (49), 1903 (254), 2382 (21)
Janowiak, J. J.: ref, 1939 (9)
Janowski, C. L.: ref, 298 (70)
Janowsky, J.: ref, 815 (2), 2862 (56)
Janowsky, J. S.: ref, 776 (4,9), 2860 (104,220,1102), 2863 (30,56,329), 2892 (11,29)
Jansen, E. N. H.: ref, 335 (15)
Jansen, J. H. C.: ref, 272 (79,271), 1079 (89), 1166 (190)
Jansen, M. A.: ref, 708 (1), 2497 (8)
Jansing, C.: rev, 49
Jansky, J.: test, 1336, 1337
Janssen, H. J. E. M.: ref, 2603 (469,535)
Janssen, R.: ref, 745 (20), 2163 (278)
Janus, M.: ref, 270 (32)
Janusz, J.: ref, 1099 (4), 1962 (22), 2862 (590), 2879 (193)
Janzen, H.: ref, 763 (3)
Janzen-Wilde, M. L.: ref, 175 (12), 815 (25), 994 (27), 1379 (70), 1725 (5), 1903 (373), 2813 (95), 2864 (94), 2879 (119)
Jaquess, D. L.: ref, 997 (17)
Jaquet, G.: ref, 1166 (109)
Jarama, S. L.: ref, 1947 (8)
Jaranson, J. M.: ref, 2305 (234)
Jaremko, M. E.: ref, 2603 (32)
Jarrell, R. H.: ref, 56 (2), 615 (15)
Jarrett, D. B.: ref, 2305 (39)
Jarrett, L.: ref, 2497 (417)
Jarrett, M. E.: ref, 2603 (583)
Jarrett, P. J.: ref, 272 (265), 1166 (180)
Jarrico, S.: test, 322
Jarrold, C.: ref, 350 (17,18,51), 837 (14), 2862 (720)
Jarvik, G. P.: ref, 303 (26), 2860 (1382)
Jarvik, L. F.: ref, 1058 (1), 2860 (21,918)
Jarvis, A. H.: ref, 1086 (1)
Jarvis, P. A.: ref, 301 (23), 2356 (1), 2860 (360)
Jarwan, F.: ref, 592 (84)
Jason, L.: ref, 1166 (82)
Jason, L. A.: ref, 1991 (30), 2879 (79)
Jaspers, J. P. C.: ref, 1079 (107), 2497 (670), 2603 (584)
Jaspers, R.: ref, 2860 (79), 2892 (7)
Jastak, J. T.: test, 2882
Jastak, S.: test, 2882
Jautz, M.: ref, 1166 (105)
Javian, S.: ref, 1348 (3)
Javitt, D. C.: ref, 2146 (18)
Javorsky, D. J.: test, 329
Javorsky, J.: ref, 2731 (1), 2860 (257), 2879 (34), 2901 (17,92), 1000 (65)
Jayaram, G.: ref, 268 (1)
Jaycox, L. H.: ref, 272 (359), 846 (25), 2497 (671)
Jaynes, P. A.: rev, 250, 2029
Jean-Gilles, M.: ref, 557 (2), 1216 (9), 2211 (6)
Jeanjean, M.: ref, 1338 (13)
Jeanneret, P. R.: test, 1343, 2016, 2925
Jeannerod, M.: ref, 2860 (844), 2863 (244), 2892 (174)
Jeanrie, C.: rev, 2103, 2913
Jecova, C.: ref, 1164 (144), 2860 (1242)
Jedryoek, E.: ref, 2485 (217)
Jeeves, M. A.: ref, 2862 (42,43)
Jefferson, J. W.: ref, 2484 (8), 2603 (198)

Jefferson, T. W.: ref, 1697 (35)
Jeffery, P.: test, 492
Jeffery, R.: ref, 2497 (128)
Jeffree, D. M.: test, 1897, 1996
Jeffrey, A. C.: ref, 2076 (126)
Jeffrey, T. E.: test, 548, 549, 1299, 1636, 2460
Jeffs, M.: ref, 273 (14), 337 (108)
Jekelis, A.: ref, 2076 (98)
Jelinek, J.: ref, 2218 (33), 2858 (99)
Jellen, H. G.: test, 2659
Jellinek, M.: ref, 1010 (70), 1092 (13), 2305 (121), 2862 (310), 2879 (102)
Jellinek, M. S.: ref, 1092 (5), 2860 (331)
Jelm, J. M.: test, 1851
Jenike, M. A.: ref, 271 (5), 272 (223), 1164 (113), 1525 (20), 1697 (51), 2227 (26), 2517 (5), 2860 (996,1103), 2863 (295)
Jenkins, C. D.: test, 1338
Jenkins, E.: ref, 2862 (459)
Jenkins, F. J.: ref, 2076 (146)
Jenkins, J.: rev, 143, 935, 1136, 1464, 2050 (50)
Jenkins, J. A.: rev, 2618, 2738
Jenkins, J. M.: test, 1472; ref, 2485 (204), 2680 (16)
Jenkins, J. R.: ref, 451 (40), 1072 (35,45), 1503 (14), 1612 (14,32,43,44,75,76), 1902 (46,75), 1903 (72,164,247,391,398,399), 2044 (5), 2485 (173), 2671 (2), 2682 (2,4,5,8), 2905 (86)
Jenkins, L.: ref, 451 (283), 681 (98), 2603 (590), 2901 (135)
Jenkins, L. M.: ref, 1072 (45)
Jenkins, M.: ref, 2076 (123), 2247 (94)
Jenkins, M. M.: ref, 1095 (6), 2837 (1)
Jenkins, R. A.: ref, 1745 (17)
Jenkins, T. N.: test, 1222, 1223
Jenneke, W.: ref, 2497 (410)
Jenner, J. A.: ref, 272 (271), 1079 (89), 1166 (190)
Jenner, L.: ref, 4 (14), 2052 (1)
Jennings, J. R.: rev, 28, 29
Jennings, J. R.: ref, 337 (72), 1093 (78), 1135 (19), 2497 (603), 2516 (41,89), 2860 (1200), 2863 (360)
Jennings, R.: ref, 793 (14), 1093 (79)
Jens, K. G.: ref, 1612 (18), 1903 (260)
Jensen, A. M.: ref, 815 (6), 1216 (14), 2225 (3), 2864 (22)
Jensen, A. R.: rev, 1011, 1012, 1540, 1703, 2027, 2247, 2749; ref, 180 (19), 592 (62), 1866 (3), 2163 (130,165,166,169), 2485 (132)
Jensen, B.: ref, 694 (108), 1697 (461), 2704 (35)
Jensen, J.: rev, 1750; ref, 451 (70), 2214 (79)
Jensen, J. E.: ref, 2603 (483)
Jensen, J. L.: rev, 2312
Jensen, M. P.: ref, 863 (17)
Jensen, P.: ref, 337 (13)
Jensen, P. S.: ref, 557 (3), 2214 (7,33,104)
Jensen, S. B.: ref, 337 (13)
Jensterle, J.: ref, 2050 (89)
Jerge, K. A.: ref, 2860 (1218)
Jerger, S.: ref, 1216 (32), 1903 (182)
Jernigan, T.: ref, 1164 (84), 2288 (42), 2289 (32)
Jernigan, T. L.: ref, 2305 (32,130)
Jerome, G.: ref, 2163 (308), 2860 (1197)
Jerome, N.: ref, 2862 (415)
Jerrell, J.: ref, 337 (26)
Jerrell, J. M.: ref, 1000 (38)
Jesberger, J. A.: ref, 2050 (115)
Jeske, P. J.: rev, 1991
Jesness, C. F.: test, 1340, 1341; rev, 817; ref, 1340 (1)
Jesperen, B.: ref, 337 (13)
Jessor, R.: rev, 1376
Jeste, D. V.: ref, 335 (9), 1135 (9), 1164 (48,77,100), 2288 (28,61,69,72), 2289 (19,47,53,57), 2860 (474,643,908,1104), 2892 (120,190)
Jette, A. M.: ref, 1164 (72), 2863 (208)
Jeukendrop, A.: ref, 2516 (80)
Jewell, K.: ref, 815 (24)
Jewell, M.: ref, 1072 (35,45)
Jex, F. B.: rev, 1484
Jeziorowski, J.: ref, 1668 (1)
Jezzi, A.: ref, 1697 (541), 2860 (1257)
Jilton, R.: ref, 2603 (546)
Jiménez, R. T.: ref, 1657 (25), 2901 (119)
Jimerson, S.: ref, 451 (203,292), 1216 (113), 1902 (95,101), 2860 (1286), 2862 (630), 2901 (120,138)
Jipescu, I.: ref, 2163 (66), 2860 (259)
Jirele, T. J.: ref, 592 (72)
Jirikowie, T. L.: ref, 270 (33), 1901 (19), 2715 (1)
Jirsa, J. E.: rev, 61, 2122
Jirsa, R. E.: ref, 1096 (5), 2862 (164)
Jitendra, A. K.: ref, 994 (39)
Jo, H. I.: ref, 791 (16)
Jocic, Z.: ref, 199 (12), 1093 (44), 2599 (38), 2860 (430), 2892 (65,271)
Jody, D. N.: ref, 1093 (41)
Joe, G. W.: ref, 2860 (29)
Joffe, R.: ref, 1166 (171), 2218 (82), 2305 (213)
Joffe, R. T.: ref, 272 (288), 790 (11), 1093 (111), 1166 (89,90,97,197), 2218 (43,44), 2305 (164,171, 185)
Johann-Murphy, M.: ref, 270 (36)
Johannes, S.: ref, 2860 (1105), 2879 (166)
Johannet, C. M.: ref, 272 (360), 273 (34)
Johansen, J.: ref, 2553 (4)
Johansson, C. B.: test, 398, 399, 1237
Johansson, N.: ref, 2497 (117)
John, C. H.: ref, 1758 (85,86)
John, L. H.: ref, 451 (60)
John, O. P.: ref, 365 (10), 373 (21,35), 2862 (536)
John, R.: ref, 1166 (31)
John, S.: ref, 376 (6), 1218 (17), 1902 (86), 2860 (1106), 2879 (167), 2892 (229), 2901 (93)
Johndrow, D. A.: ref, 472 (136), 1178 (9), 2214 (76), 2603 (222)
Johns, D.: ref, 272 (275), 273 (30)
Johns, E.: test, 1201

Johns, G.: ref, 1590 (55)
Johns, J. L.: test, 257, 2338; ref, 1318 (17)
Johnsen, S. K.: test, 2328, 2329, 2698, 2704
Johnson, A.: ref, 2771 (20)
Johnson, A. K.: ref, 788 (1)
Johnson, B. A.: ref, 272 (259), 2305 (167)
Johnson, B. D.: ref, 2497 (569)
Johnson, B. J.: ref, 272 (343)
Johnson, B. K.: ref, 337 (27), 2603 (104), 2858 (27)
Johnson, C.: test, 1712, 2934
Johnson, C.: ref, 893 (2), 1010 (9), 2603 (20,214, 304)
Johnson, C. A.: ref, 448 (11), 2839 (9)
Johnson, C. C.: test, 1360
Johnson, C. D.: ref, 180 (25), 838 (11), 1072 (21)
Johnson, C. J.: ref, 214 (17), 240 (3), 1095 (26), 1903 (122), 1982 (8), 2233 (2), 2693 (5), 2710 (5)
Johnson, C. L.: ref, 2860 (838), 2863 (243)
Johnson, C. N.: ref, 2076 (84)
Johnson, D.: test, 250; ref, 2497 (107)
Johnson, D. A.: ref, 2860 (1063)
Johnson, D. J.: ref, 1240 (17), 1903 (183)
Johnson, D. L.: rev, 2189; ref, 776 (46), 815 (3), 1903 (37,184), 2402 (20), 2485 (90), 2864 (11)
Johnson, D. P.: ref, 2497 (563)
Johnson, D. R.: ref, 337 (144), 443 (1), 1300 (10), 2901 (96)
Johnson, D. S.: ref, 2899 (3)
Johnson, D. W.: ref, 286 (3), 2862 (533)
Johnson, E.: ref, 1341 (1), 1697 (518), 1902 (3)
Johnson, E. G.: ref, 1759 (18)
Johnson, E. H.: ref, 1697 (292), 2497 (175)
Johnson, E. S.: ref, 615 (33), 2163 (84)
Johnson, F. W.: ref, 2485 (132)
Johnson, G. F. S.: ref, 1166 (11)
Johnson, J.: test, 768; rev, 369, 2681; ref, 1040 (6), 1093 (21), 1866 (8)
Johnson, J. A.: ref, 372 (2), 2835 (3)
Johnson, J. C.: ref, 2603 (344,534)
Johnson, J. E.: ref, 272 (121,332), 853 (14), 1160 (3), 2860 (552)
Johnson, J. G.: ref, 272 (185,360), 273 (22,23,34), 337 (145), 1166 (115), 1903 (533), 2603 (366,470)
Johnson, J. H.: ref, 272 (316), 1010 (22), 1697 (568), 2497 (201,394,653)
Johnson, J. J.: ref, 1115 (5), 1122 (2)
Johnson, J. L.: test, 2604; ref, 1107 (9)
Johnson, J. M.: ref, 270 (34), 1216 (101), 1903 (530), 2382 (38)
Johnson, J. R.: ref, 298 (92), 1697 (238)
Johnson, J. T.: ref, 1965 (45)
Johnson, K. A.: ref, 2227 (58), 2860 (1396), 2863 (421)
Johnson, K. E.: ref, 1903 (272)
Johnson, L.: ref, 134 (10), 2862 (631), 2901 (121)
Johnson, L. J.: ref, 902 (1), 1379 (1), 2355 (1), 2485 (39,86), 2754 (1,4)
Johnson, L. S.: ref, 2527 (11)
Johnson, M.: ref, 1745 (31), 1758 (81), 2603 (199), 2860 (1209)
Johnson, M. B.: test, 2901
Johnson, M. D.: ref, 272 (122), 999 (124), 2892 (134)
Johnson, M. E.: ref, 272 (23), 298 (82), 1697 (56), 2247 (7), 2474 (1), 2603 (471), 2860 (642), 2863 (388), 2892 (276)
Johnson, M. M. S.: ref, 2860 (188)
Johnson, M. S.: rev, 496
Johnson, N. E.: ref, 2163 (186,240)
Johnson, N. W.: test, 873
Johnson, P.: test, 2854
Johnson, P. D.: ref, 451 (268), 472 (226), 2214 (135)
Johnson, P. O.: rev, 46, 607
Johnson, R.: test, 768; rev, 922, 1300, 1784, 2423, 2756; ref, 1135 (7), 1671 (4), 1767 (3), 2497 (132,605), 2860 (264,292,400), 2863 (105), 2879 (35)
Johnson, R. C.: test, 1357
Johnson, R. E.: test, 2439; ref, 2703 (1)
Johnson, R. H.: test, 2618
Johnson, R. S.: ref, 1697 (177)
Johnson, R. T.: rev, 151, 670; ref, 286 (3), 2862 (533)
Johnson, R. W.: rev, 83, 238, 387, 1493, 1790, 1933, 2277
Johnson, S.: test, 686; ref, 272 (12), 1661 (1)
Johnson, S. C.: ref, 2860 (803)
Johnson, S. D.: ref, 592 (103)
Johnson, S. K.: ref, 272 (186,187), 2860 (602,1107)
Johnson, S. L.: ref, 1166 (54), 2305 (106)
Johnson, S. M.: ref, 863 (34)
Johnson, S. T.: rev, 1515, 2383
Johnson, T.: ref, 665 (40)
Johnson, V.: ref, 1965 (9), 2603 (21)
Johnson, W. B.: ref, 694 (116)
Johnson, W. G.: ref, 2603 (367), 2860 (189)
Johnson-Greene, D.: ref, 1164 (154), 2860 (1287)
Johnson-Lewis, S.: rev, 844, 2336
Johnson-Martin, N.: ref, 2485 (52)
Johnsrude, I.: ref, 2860 (655)
Johnston, A. V.: test, 628
Johnston, C.: ref, 681 (32), 2603 (472), 2813 (25)
Johnston, C. S.: ref, 2246 (7)
Johnston, E. B.: test, 628
Johnston, I. C.: test, 2093, 2095
Johnston, J. A.: rev, 2835; ref, 1754 (17)
Johnston, J. R.: rev, 2886, 2936; ref, 175 (8), 324 (4), 430 (5), 451 (5), 624 (6), 798 (7), 1093 (4), 1485 (18,59), 1804 (4), 1902 (32), 1903 (172,531), 2382 (14), 2485 (227), 2704 (3), 2768 (17)
Johnston, M.: ref, 1903 (270), 2050 (57), 2905 (56)
Johnston, M. C.: test, 1358
Johnston, N. G.: ref, 1965 (75)
Johnston, R. S.: ref, 358 (2)
Johnston, W. M.: ref, 272 (276), 2497 (635)
Johnston-Cronk, K.: ref, 2050 (85)
Johnstone, B.: ref, 2860 (1288), 2863 (389)
Johnstone, E. C.: ref, 2050 (72), 2146 (20), 2860 (190)
Johnstone, M.: ref, 2050 (83)

Joiner, G. W.: ref, 893 (35)
Joiner, T.: ref, 272 (219), 273 (25), 2065 (29)
Joiner, T. E.: ref, 472 (173), 1697 (309), 2214 (105), 2242 (5), 2243 (1)
Joiner, T. E., Jr.: ref, 271 (2), 272 (188), 472 (174,191), 1697 (423), 2065 (22), 2214 (106,112), 2559 (10)
Joines, R. C.: test, 1080, 2574
Joint Council on Economic Education: test, 2719
Jokeit, H.: ref, 2863 (390)
Jokel, R.: ref, 1903 (559), 2227 (53), 2860 (1365)
Jokic, C.: ref, 1164 (118), 2516 (77)
Jolesz, F. A.: ref, 2305 (150), 2860 (497)
Jolles, I.: test, 1160
Jolles, J.: ref, 2516 (20,80,102)
Jolly, J. B.: ref, 272 (189), 472 (49,85), 2214 (30), 2603 (269,270,473)
Jones, B.: ref, 1379 (48)
Jones, B. W.: rev, 241, 2215
Jones, C.: rev, 2255
Jones, C. H.: ref, 2860 (309,953), 2862 (402,674)
Jones, C. J.: ref, 372 (93), 373 (31,36), 1697 (292)
Jones, C. L.: ref, 863 (38,77), 2497 (238,546)
Jones, D.: rev, 1133; ref, 1000 (110), 1021 (48), 2214 (140), 2230 (21), 2656 (25)
Jones, D. C.: ref, 298 (144), 462 (6), 1010 (61)
Jones, D. H.: ref, 180 (15)
Jones, D. L.: rev, 1998
Jones, D. N.: ref, 793 (2), 2603 (22)
Jones, D. P. H.: ref, 448 (16), 994 (38), 1765 (27), 2862 (490)
Jones, D. R.: ref, 717 (2), 863 (92)
Jones, E. E.: ref, 771 (7)
Jones, E. L.: rev, 805
Jones, E. M.: ref, 2860 (811)
Jones, F.: ref, 739 (6,9)
Jones, G.: ref, 270 (13), 2308 (1), 2497 (557)
Jones, G. E.: ref, 1745 (42), 2497 (351)
Jones, G. N.: test, 760
Jones, G. P.: ref, 298 (15)
Jones, G. R.: ref, 1701 (52), 2246 (12)
Jones, H. A.: ref, 1485 (37), 2189 (2), 2382 (27), 2485 (153)
Jones, H. E.: rev, 1716
Jones, I.: ref, 1903 (470)
Jones, J.: ref, 2862 (520)
Jones, J. A.: rev, 1472
Jones, J. E.: test, 1361, 1859, 2631
Jones, J. H.: ref, 1755 (47)
Jones, J. P.: ref, 694 (74)
Jones, J. W.: test, 462; ref, 1972 (1)
Jones, K.: ref, 2227 (58), 2860 (1396), 2863 (421)
Jones, K. M.: rev, 280, 1715
Jones, L.: ref, 2860 (69,70,105)
Jones, L. C.: ref, 1770 (6), 1991 (101)
Jones, L. K.: test, 1829; ref, 1177 (2), 2835 (7,13)
Jones, M.: ref, 350 (43), 679 (1), 681 (35), 1485 (57), 2193 (14), 2497 (236)
Jones, M. C.: ref, 392 (2)
Jones, M. G.: ref, 364 (13), 592 (63), 665 (86), 1657 (21)
Jones, M. L.: ref, 2860 (38,228), 2862 (116)
Jones, N. A.: ref, 272 (277)
Jones, P.: ref, 1093 (80), 2050 (98,103)
Jones, P. B.: ref, 2050 (80), 2860 (656,1343)
Jones, R.: ref, 265 (7), 537 (3), 811 (4), 2603 (93,179)
Jones, R. A.: rev, 547
Jones, R. J.: ref, 615 (10)
Jones, R. L.: rev, 600
Jones, R. M.: rev, 1935
Jones, R. N.: ref, 1903 (123)
Jones, R. W.: ref, 1107 (3)
Jones, S.: test, 33, 2891; ref, 272 (215), 337 (83), 1697 (510), 2497 (374,587), 2858 (118)
Jones, S. S.: ref, 681 (81), 2693 (8), 2694 (23), 2704 (44), 2862 (579), 2901 (104)
Jones, T. D.: ref, 999 (127)
Jones, T. M.: ref, 2603 (267)
Jones, W.: ref, 2603 (342)
Jones, W. H.: test, 2449
Jones, W. P.: ref, 1755 (28)
Jones-Gotman, M.: ref, 2226 (12), 2860 (67)
Jongbloed, L.: ref, 2599 (2), 2860 (265)
Jongmans, M.: ref, 349 (31), 451 (131), 1727 (1), 1987 (20)
Joniak, A. J.: ref, 1404 (7,13)
Jonker, C.: ref, 2163 (342)
Jonsari, A.: ref, 1758 (42), 2193 (41), 2860 (900), 2863 (270), 2892 (189)
Jonsdottir-Baldursson, T.: ref, 1661 (6), 1697 (77)
Jonsson, B.: ref, 301 (36), 1097 (12)
Jonsson, B.: ref, 1410 (2)
Jooc, Z.: ref, 2519 (22), 2520 (23)
Joram, E.: ref, 389 (8)
Jordaan, J. P.: test, 405
Jordan, A. C.: test, 616
Jordan, B. K.: ref, 1697 (325)
Jordan, B. T.: test, 1362; ref, 301 (11)
Jordan, C.: ref, 1659 (14)
Jordan, D. S.: ref, 2603 (266)
Jordan, H.: ref, 459 (1), 2860 (114)
Jordan, J. A.: ref, 337 (40), 1000 (27)
Jordan, L. S.: ref, 199 (2), 798 (2), 1612 (3), 2008 (1), 2485 (6), 2862 (18), 2864 (1), 2873 (2)
Jordan, M. L.: ref, 1661 (42)
Jordan, N.: ref, 1758 (19), 2863 (81)
Jordan, N. C.: ref, 2484 (14), 2695 (38), 2704 (26)
Jordan, S. G.: ref, 301 (11)
Jordon, A. E.: ref, 472 (116), 2214 (62)
Jordon, J. S.: ref, 1697 (206)
Jorge, R. E.: ref, 2050 (37)
Jorgensen, C.: test, 2710, 2911, 2342
Jorgensen, R. S.: ref, 1697 (519), 1745 (20), 2860 (361)
Jorgenson, S.: ref, 1216 (32), 1903 (182)
Jorm, A. F.: ref, 999 (56,89,90,114), 1164 (136), 1758 (44,79), 2239 (19,22), 2497 (667), 2599 (15), 2860 (587,823,1183), 2863 (175,238,356)

Jorstad, H. L.: rev, 598
Joscelyne, T.: ref, 1072 (5), 1765 (5)
Joseph, B.: ref, 1903 (532), 2860 (1289)
Joseph, G.: ref, 2864 (86)
Joseph, J.: test, 1363; ref, 337 (86)
Joseph, J. M.: ref, 1697 (332,559), 2516 (46,106)
Joseph, R.: ref, 404 (37)
Joseph, S.: ref, 272 (190,278,361), 1079 (92), 1367 (7), 2497 (352,636)
Josephson, S.: ref, 1093 (36), 2497 (141), 2603 (119)
Joshi, P. K.: ref, 451 (204), 2862 (632)
Joshi, R. M.: ref, 827 (10), 861 (1), 1072 (48), 1073 (2), 1092 (15), 1131 (14), 1657 (16), 1902 (72), 2879 (120), 2901 (65), 2902 (2), 2905 (76)
Josman, Z. E.: ref, 681 (36)
Jospeho, S.: ref, 2858 (19)
Jossa, F.: ref, 2603 (517)
Jotesz, F. A.: ref, 2288 (60), 2289 (46), 2305 (159), 2860 (1012)
Joubert, C. E.: ref, 694 (44,55)
Joubert, M.: test, 1293, 2319
Joukamaa, M.: ref, 1079 (47), 2860 (959)
Jouriles, E. N.: ref, 451 (138,209), 1582 (14), 2230 (9), 2557 (4)
Joy, D. S.: ref, 1972 (1)
Joy, K. L.: ref, 1697 (565)
Joy, P.: ref, 837 (3), 1765 (19), 1903 (292), 2862 (280)
Joyce, A. A.: ref, 2603 (290)
Joyce, A. S.: ref, 272 (191), 2497 (134,564), 2603 (117,118,291)
Joyce, E. M.: ref, 1758 (14), 2860 (266), 2863 (69)f, 2892 (35)
Joyce, P. R.: ref, 999 (91,96,163), 1166 (45,55,132, 146,159), 2519 (52), 2520 (51), 2603 (271,318, 481,492,519)
Joyner, D. J.: ref, 298 (53)
Joyner, S. E.: ref, 433 (1), 1903 (14), 2189 (1)
Ju, E. S. Y.: ref, 2603 (103)
Juang, L.: ref, 1216 (84)
Juárez, M. J.: ref, 1171 (1)
Juba, M.: ref, 771 (19), 1697 (113)
Judd, B. B.: ref, 1348 (3), 2860 (627)
Judd, D.: ref, 694 (11)
Judd, F. K.: ref, 2076 (157)
Judd, L. L.: ref, 1166 (225), 2076 (125), 2305 (198), 2603 (568)
Judd, T. P.: ref, 2862 (75)
Judd-Safian Asssociates: test, 1968
Judge, A. B.: ref, 2497 (663)
Judge, T. A.: ref, 1178 (11), 1348 (15), 2218 (98,105), 2899 (16)
Juejati, M.: ref, 1166 (82)
Juel, C.: ref, 827 (12), 1659 (2,5), 1767 (5), 2862 (44), 2879 (8,168)
Juergensen, P.: ref, 272 (227)
Juffer, F.: ref, 1216 (75)
Juhnke, G. A.: rev, 184
Julian, A., III: test, 1006
Julian, T. W.: ref, 2603 (379)
Juliano, C.: ref, 1903 (270), 2905 (56)
Jun, S.-P.: ref, 2860 (379)
Junck, L.: ref, 1164 (154), 2603 (438), 2860 (1040,1287)
June, L. N.: rev, 717
Jung, H. Y.: ref, 1166 (122)
Jung, J.: ref, 2603 (536), 2858 (51)
Jung, R. E.: ref, 1164 (88), 2860 (825), 2892 (168)
Jungeblut, A.: test, 972
Juni, S.: rev, 792, 846, 912, 1313, 2218, 2364, 2406, 2609, 2827; ref, 298 (83,115), 1582 (7), 2860 (657)
Junos, P. M.: ref, 2214 (61), 2862 (320), 2879 (107)
Junquê, C.: ref, 1164 (155), 2226 (26), 2516 (100), 2860 (1290)
Jupp, J. J.: rev, 795, 2135; ref, 998 (15), 1079 (26), 1590 (33), 1991 (10)
Jurado, M. A.: ref, 1164 (155), 2226 (26), 2516 (100), 2860 (1290)
Juran Institute: test, 2129
Jurden, F. H.: ref, 2860 (362,909)
Jurgensen, C. E.: rev, 2217, 2572, 2790
Jurich, A. P.: ref, 1000 (62), 1580 (5)
Jurich, J. A.: ref, 1000 (28), 2858 (63)
Jurkovic, G. L.: ref, 2557 (6)
Jurs, S.: rev, 1231, 2352, 2935
Juschka, B. B.: ref, 1132 (1), 1755 (62)
Jussim, L.: ref, 2497 (483)
Juster, H. R.: ref, 2199 (13), 2497 (431)
Justice, E. M.: ref, 289 (6), 301 (23), 1363 (2), 2356 (1), 2860 (360), 2901 (139)

Kabacoff, R.: ref, 472 (209), 694 (126), 2305 (230)
Kabacoff, R. I.: test, 162, 1251, 1443, 1929; ref, 301 (12), 1097 (3), 2485 (27), 2862 (108), 2879 (24)
Kabanoff, B.: ref, 2149 (1)
Kabrich, M.: ref, 1902 (87), 2862 (494)
Kaczala, C. M.: ref, 298 (39)
Kaczmarek, L.: ref, 788 (3), 1612 (94)
Kadden, R. M.: ref, 134 (14), 135 (1), 372 (14), 1174 (1), 1661 (23), 1697 (63,183), 2497 (357), 2603 (149)
Kaden, B.: ref, 2163 (184)
Kadish, R.: test, 2459
Kaemmer, B.: test, 1697, 1698
Kagan, H.: ref, 1374 (1), 1590 (48), 1825 (4)
Kagan, J: test, 1592; ref, 2382 (6), 2382 (16)
Kagan, (K). H.: ref, 2497 (484)
Kagan, N.: test, 1374
Kagan, N. I.: ref, 1374 (1), 1590 (48), 1825 (4), 2497 (484)
Kagan, S.: ref, 1657 (18), 2860 (915)
Kager, V. A.: ref, 1000 (107)
Kagitcibasi, C.: ref, 2258 (4)
Kahler, C. W.: ref, 134 (24), 863 (65)
Kahn, H.: test, 2829
Kahn, H. D.: ref, 117 (3)
Kahn, H. J.: ref, 2860 (267,633)

Kahn, J.: ref, 2860 (1315)
Kahn, J. H.: ref, 337 (146), 2065 (32), 2835 (27)
Kahn, J. V.: ref, 194 (1)
Kahn, R.: ref, 2603 (105)
Kahn, S. E.: ref, 298 (22)
Kahn, T. C.: test, 1146, 1375, 1376
Kahn, W. J.: ref, 1205 (1), 1716 (3)
Kail, R.: ref, 2163 (88), 2862 (165)
Kaiser, A. P.: ref, 994 (14), 1095 (22), 1653 (11), 2382 (18,23), 2485 (107), 2864 (54), 2869 (1)
Kaiser, C. F.: test, 1749
Kaiser, J.: rev, 905, 1252, 2069, 2680; ref, 8 (1)
Kaiser, N.: ref, 1166 (28)
Kakela, M.: ref, 2860 (1421), 2901 (137)
Kakuma, T.: ref, 1166 (85), 2305 (246), 2603 (189)
Kalangis, K.: ref, 451 (238), 1010 (131)
Kalbe, E.: ref, 2227 (40), 2516 (101), 2860 (1294)
Kalechstein, A. D.: ref, 376 (26), 2860 (1336), 2863 (400)
Kaleith, T. A.: ref, 451 (215), 1962 (23)
Kaler, S. R.: ref, 2813 (64)
Kalfers, W. V.: rev, 1764
Kalhorn, J.: test, 1026
Kalichman, S. C.: ref, 298 (92), 793 (9), 998 (72), 1697 (79,131,132,178,238), 1744 (1,2,3), 2497 (70,118,485), 2839 (5)
Kaliher, C.: ref, 2485 (11)
Kalikow, K.: ref, 1093 (21)
Kalimo, R.: ref, 2163 (69)
Kalinov, K.: ref, 2050 (36)
Kalinyak, K.: ref, 472 (182), 2242 (7), 2862 (525)
Kalkoske, M.: ref, 1216 (7), 1902 (17), 2039 (1), 2614 (2), 2749 (44), 2860 (169), 2864 (61)
Kallgren, C.: ref, 472 (38)
Kallgren, C. A.: ref, 472 (14)
Kallio, E.: ref, 1697 (369), 2860 (778)
Kalliopuska, M.: ref, 2163 (89)
Kalmár, M.: ref, 1010 (99), 1216 (83)
Kalnins, R. M.: ref, 2860 (520), 2863 (150)
Kalodner, C. R.: ref, 472 (86)
Kalogeras, K.: ref, 1697 (369), 2860 (778)
Kalsi, G.: ref, 2305 (141), 2305 (180), 2305 (199)
Kalter, N.: ref, 337 (3,57,58), 451 (6,12), 472 (2), 1000 (46,47), 1178 (7), 2497 (35)
Kalthoff, R. A.: ref, 1902 (40)
Kalucy, R. S.: ref, 2497 (135)
Kalus, O.: ref, 2603 (105)
Kamada, J.: ref, 2862 (633)
Kamann, M. P.: ref, 1072 (36), 1392 (8), 2862 (206)
Kamarck, T. W.: ref, 2516 (41)
Kamble, A.: ref, 1166 (166), 2305 (209)
Kambon, K.: ref, 272 (346), 2603 (575)
Kamel, F. N.: ref, 451 (87)
Kamhi, A. G.: ref, 175 (11), 994 (24), 1095 (10), 1394 (4), 1503 (1), 1902 (1), 1903 (363,374), 2524 (8,9), 2694 (1), 2695 (1,14,36,39), 2704 (6,23,27,41), 2768 (1,29), 2879 (3), 2905 (1,28,101)
Kaminer, H.: ref, 913 (1), 1697 (133), 2603 (106)
Kaminski, K.: ref, 2230 (10), 2557 (5)
Kaminski, R. A.: ref, 1612 (84), 1659 (6)
Kamiyama, Y.: ref, 1010 (48)
Kamphaus, R. W.: test, 245, 280; rev, 144, 822, 977, 1294, 2432, 2677, 2799; ref, 246 (2), 2862 (131)
Kamps, D. M.: ref, 1485 (28)
Kamps, W. A.: ref, 1079 (107), 2497 (670), 2603 (584)
Kamptner, N. L.: ref, 790 (29)
Kanazawa, T.: ref, 2862 (633)
Kanbayashi, Y.: ref, 1592 (27), 2862 (719)
Kandel, D.: ref, 451 (222)
Kandel, D. B.: ref, 1903 (533)
Kane, J. M.: ref, 2163 (111), 2288 (45,64), 2305 (70,123,170)
Kane, M.: rev, 1605, 2733
Kane, M. J.: ref, 1405 (23)
Kane, M. T.: ref, 2498 (2)
Kane, R. L.: ref, 2603 (298), 2860 (7)
Kanekar, S.: ref, 908 (9)
Kanevsky, L.: ref, 2432 (12), 2485 (26)
Kaney, S.: ref, 272 (4,13,53,279), 1758 (33,89), 2516 (1)
Kanfer, R.: ref, 2218 (67), 2899 (3)
Kang, G.: ref, 1000 (26)
Kangro, H. O.: ref, 2050 (136), 2305 (157,158)
Kaniasty, K.: ref, 337 (41,45)
Kaniel, S.: ref, 2163 (70,95)
Kanjee, A.: ref, 592 (90)
Kanne, S. M.: ref, 1164 (179), 2860 (1397), 2863 (422)
Kanner, A. D.: ref, 472 (15)
Kantner, A.: ref, 1661 (35), 2603 (317)
Kantor, M.: ref, 1903 (90), 2695 (8), 2768 (6), 2862 (140)
Kanungo, R. N.: rev, 2917
Kao, C.: rev, 481
Kao, C. F.: ref, 2497 (154)
Kao, C. W.: rev, 2904
Kao, T. C.: ref, 2603 (420)
Kapa, E.: ref, 2163 (285), 2771 (43)
Kapadia, P.: ref, 2107 (1)
Kapçi, E. G.: ref, 272 (362)
Kapel, D. E.: rev, 553, 905
Kapes, J. T.: ref, 1790 (5), 2805 (2)
Kaphael, B.: ref, 999 (36), 1079 (13)
Kaplan, A.: ref, 665 (89), 2860 (984)
Kaplan, A. S.: ref, 272 (288), 1166 (197)
Kaplan, B.: test, 2425
Kaplan, B. J.: rev, 650, 1735, 2017, 2216, 2618; ref, 353 (10,20), 389 (10), 451 (256), 2432 (16,28), 2862 (207,419), 2901 (26,78)
Kaplan, C.: ref, 2864 (118)
Kaplan, D. M.: ref, 404 (2), 1745 (58), 2497 (9,486)
Kaplan, E.: test, 199, 329, 375, 376, 1665, 2840; ref, 2892 (264), 2924 (4)
Kaplan, E. F.: ref, 2860 (8), 2892 (1)
Kaplan, H. L.: ref, 1093 (102), 2497 (512), 2603 (396)
Kaplan, K. J.: ref, 2860 (1108)

Kaplan, M. S.: rev, 1097; ref, 286 (2), 337 (176), 2858 (127)
Kaplan, M. T.: ref, 1673 (1), 1901 (2)
Kaplan, R. E.: test, 2425
Kaplan, R. F.: ref, 1218 (8), 1697 (179), 2227 (7,16), 2860 (363,592,658,693), 2863 (95), 2863 (193), 2863 (203), 2892 (132), 2907 (5)
Kaplan, R. M.: rev, 1186
Kaplan, S. P.: ref, 2417 (8)
Kaplan, Z.: ref, 2603 (434)
Kaplan-DeNour, A.: ref, 337 (188)
Kaplansky, L. M.: ref, 2305 (78), 2860 (452)
Kapor, N.: ref, 1104 (12), 1758 (55), 2227 (23), 2239 (27), 2860 (1013), 2863 (301), 2862 (634)
Kaprio, J.: ref, 998 (84)
Kapur, N.: ref, 1104 (4,13), 2193 (23,54), 2239 (2,21,34), 2860 (659), 2860 (1109), 2863 (194)
Karabenick, S. A.: rev, 1294, 1536, 1697 (392), 1720 (5)
Karacostas, D. D.: ref, 2553 (1)
Karajgi, B.: ref, 1093 (35,75)
Karama, S.: ref, 2163 (310), 2863 (363)
Karapetsas, A. B.: ref, 2227 (39)
Karatekin, C.: ref, 1903 (573), 2860 (1398), 2862 (721)
Karayiorgou, M.: ref, 2050 (94)
Karchmer, M. A.: test, 1618
Kardash, C. M.: ref, 2879 (121)
Kareken, D. A.: ref, 2860 (660)
Karger, H.: ref, 1166 (92)
Karl, M. A.: ref, 1164 (76)
Karlin, N. J.: ref, 2230 (3)
Karlinsky, H.: ref, 2227 (8), 2860 (364), 2879 (44), 2892 (54)
Karlsen, B.: test, 82, 2484, 2487
Karlson, K. W.: test, 2791
Karmiloff-Smith, A.: ref, 350 (44,52), 1903 (577), 2163 (344,355), 2662 (7), 2860 (1291,1361,1413), 2862 (635,684,730)
Karmos, J.: ref, 2581 (1)
Karn, H. W.: rev, 943
Karnath, H. O.: ref, 2163 (54)
Karnes, F. A.: ref, 1010 (4,10), 1607 (7), 1991 (80), 2163 (101,167), 2485 (9,16,72), 2862 (45,76,355)
Karnes, M. B.: ref, 902 (1), 1379 (1), 2355 (1), 2485 (39,86), 2754 (1,4)
Karney, B. R.: ref, 272 (122), 999 (124)
Karno, M.: rev, 1832, 2452; ref, 2050 (3,50), 2288 (15), 2289 (10), 2305 (62)
Karns, K.: ref, 665 (76,93)
Karol, D.: test, 2417
Karoly, P.: test, 1733; ref, 1697 (221)
Karonen, S.: ref, 1697 (369), 2860 (778)
Karoum, F.: ref, 2862 (629)
Karp, J. F.: ref, 1093 (113)
Karp, J. S.: ref, 2288 (48), 2289 (37)
Karp, S. A.: test, 474, 926, 1140; ref, 2402 (19)
Karper, L. P.: ref, 2892 (126)
Karr, S. K.: ref, 1612 (36), 2864 (39)
Karraker, K. H.: ref, 270 (19)
Karsh, K. G.: ref, 2485 (56)
Kartsounis, L. D.: ref, 350 (19), 1104 (10,14), 1758 (51), 2050 (126), 2163 (237), 2193 (7,45,55), 2225 (9), 2860 (268,661,960,1110)
Karver, M.: ref, 451 (244)
Kasahata, N.: ref, 2860 (1356)
Kasal, K. R.: ref, 324 (11), 994 (41), 1903 (475), 2229 (12), 2864 (120)
Kasanin, J.: test, 1714
Kasari, C.: ref, 270 (14), 433 (3,6,7,11,14), 459 (20,21,27,32), 539 (1), 540 (5), 674 (3), 2228 (3,9, 13,22), 2229 (5,9), 2402 (13), 2485 (91,92,108,139, 194,202), 2862 (188)
Kasdon, L. M.: rev, 258, 2487
Kashani, J. H.: ref, 451 (165), 473 (4,8), 1962 (4), 1991 (39), 2214 (26,129), 2603 (523,569), 2862 (183)
Kashden, J.: ref, 142 (2)
Kashima, H.: ref, 2288 (81), 2289 (67), 2860 (1311)
Kashini, J. H.: ref, 1000 (86)
Kashiwagi, A.: ref, 2860 (106)
Kashiwagi, T.: ref, 2860 (106)
Kashubeck, S.: ref, 337 (81), 462 (11,24), 694 (100), 893 (35,36), 1010 (76)
Kashy, D. A.: ref, 272 (178), 2402 (57)
Kasimatis, M.: ref, 998 (33), 1338 (26)
Kasius, M. C.: ref, 451 (232)
Kaskie, B.: ref, 451 (21), 1216 (23), 1903 (136)
Kaskowitz, G.: ref, 1467 (1)
Kasl, S. V.: ref, 1093 (99), 2603 (393)
Kaslow, N. J.: ref, 451 (287), 472 (105,125), 1000 (78), 1903 (582)
Kasnetz, M. D.: ref, 2858 (17)
Kaspi, S. P.: ref, 272 (176)
Kaspin, J.: ref, 1694 (2), 1695 (1)
Kass, R. E.: ref, 540 (17), 1903 (520)
Kassel, J. D.: ref, 998 (73), 1745 (75), 2497 (637)
Kasser, T.: ref, 1735 (3), 2146 (12), 2402 (15), 2603 (174)
Kassinove, H.: ref, 2497 (638)
Kasten, L.: ref, 272 (58), 1000 (37)
Kastin, A. J.: ref, 1166 (47)
Kastner, J.: ref, 1275 (1), 1657 (17)
Kastner, S.: ref, 1275 (1), 1657 (17)
Kasyanenko, A. P.: ref, 1079 (68,69)
Kaszniak, A. W.: ref, 376 (34), 1740 (34), 2193 (4), 2516 (5), 2603 (239), 2860 (129,745,1414), 2863 (37,116), 2873 (13), 2892 (15,305)
Katerndahl, D. A.: ref, 2603 (537)
Kathol, R. G.: ref, 337 (179), 1318 (22), 1697 (561), 1740 (29), 2218 (109)
Katholi, C. R.: ref, 838 (1,3)
Katholi, C. R.: ref, 2860 (36)
Katigbak, M. S.: ref, 2218 (64,90),97)
Katkin, E. S.: rev, 2497
Katkovsky, W.: rev, 855, 1239, 1479
Katlama, C.: ref, 2517 (1), 2860 (527)

Kato, H.: ref, 2862 (360)
Kato, M.: ref, 2288 (81), 2289 (67), 2860 (1311)
Katoff, L.: test, 1391
Katon, W.: ref, 2218 (16,96), 2603 (75,170,474), 2858 (22)
Katon, W. J.: ref, 846 (11), 2603 (351)
Katona, C. L. E.: ref, 1166 (12,71)
Katsanis, J.: ref, 451 (2), 1093 (67), 2050 (81)
Katsaroo, Z.: ref, 272 (302), 2860 (1318)
Katsarou, Z.: ref, 272 (363)
Katuma, T.: ref, 272 (322)
Katusic, S. K.: ref, 1612 (73), 2485 (170), 2860 (910), 2862 (356), 2864 (95)
Katz, A.: ref, 2246 (13)
Katz, A. N: ref, 2146 (1)
Katz, B.: ref, 337 (62)
Katz, B. M.: ref, 2498 (23,36), 2863 (148,183)
Katz, D. I.: ref, 2860 (833), 2863 (240), 2873 (31)
Katz, E. R.: ref, 451 (157), 472 (68,151), 1010 (115), 2498 (25)
Katz, I. M.: ref, 2218 (17,50)
Katz, I. R.: ref, 2076 (31)
Katz, J.: ref, 272 (280)
Katz, J. S.: ref, 1590 (56)
Katz, K. S.: ref, 349 (31), 451 (131), 1010 (35)
Katz, L.: ref, 798 (11), 1051 (1), 1072 (37), 1525 (13,14), 2860 (475,476), 2862 (208), 2879 (58), 2905 (41)
Katz, L. F.: ref, 451 (205), 2864 (137)
Katz, L. J.: ref, 2603 (236), 2860 (565), 2863 (163), 2879 (71), 2901 (37)
Katz, M.: ref, 2485 (58)
Katz, M. M.: ref, 2305 (95), 2603 (191,220)
Katz, M. R.: rev, 413, 1790
Katz, N.: test, 1513; ref, 1673 (10)
Katz, P.: test, 1377
Katz, R. C.: ref, 2008 (15), 2497 (14,353), 2873 (66)
Katz, S. H.: ref, 473 (6), 2230 (18), 2557 (10)
Katz, W. F.: ref, 163 (2)
Katz, Y.: ref, 2864 (6)
Katz, Y. J.: ref, 999 (125)
Katzaroff, M.: ref, 665 (93)
Katzell, R. A.: rev, 973, 1077, 1081, 1634, 1635, 1833, 1926, 1986, 2217, 2266, 2269, 2501
Katzenberger, K.: ref, 2163 (135), 2892 (95)
Katzenmeyer, W. G.: test, 2365
Katzman, D. K.: ref, 272 (284)
Katzman, G. P.: ref, 1166 (148)
Katzman, R.: ref, 776 (34), 1058 (2,5,6), 1135 (4), 2860 (152,184,464,477), 2862 (105,120,203,209)
Katzung, V. M.: ref, 272 (63), 2402 (16), 2892 (66)
Kauffman, D. W.: ref, 1902 (30), 2485 (50), 2862 (156), 2879 (40)
Kauffman, G. B.: rev, 50
Kaufman, A. S.: test, 124, 1378, 1379, 1380, 1382, 1383, 1384, 1385, 1386; rev, 229, 264, 624, 655, 2901; ref, 1378 (1,4,5,6,13,14), 1379 (9,28), 1384 (1), 1755 (29,64), 1790 (16,17), 2860 (662), 2862 (495), 2864 (55), 2868 (2)
Kaufman, C. C.: test, 1930, 1955
Kaufman, E. R.: ref, 2497 (195)
Kaufman, H.: test, 1381
Kaufman, J.: ref, 1379 (48), 2305 (216,245)
Kaufman, J. C.: ref, 1378 (4,5), 2862 (495)
Kaufman, L.: ref, 2247 (119), 2862 (676)
Kaufman, L. D.: ref, 2163 (119), 2516 (26), 2599 (14), 2860 (479), 2863 (133), 2879 (60)
Kaufman, M.: test, 1230
Kaufman, N.: test, 1378; ref, 451 (152), 472 (187), 473 (3), 2868 (2)
Kaufman, N. L.: test, 124, 1379, 1380, 1382, 1383, 1384, 1385, 1386; rev, 229, 655, 1086, 1613; ref, 1378 (5), 1755 (29)
Kaufmann, C. A.: ref, 650 (10), 2289 (17), 2305 (20,77)
Kauk, B.: test, 993
Kauk, R.: test, 179, 408, 1350, 1539, 2822
Kaulfers, W. V.: rev, 598
Kauneckis, D.: ref, 2214 (48)
Kausler, D. H.: ref, 1405 (3), 2860 (829), 2907 (8)
Kauth, M. R.: ref, 272 (27)
Kavale, K. A.: rev, 465
Kavan, M. G.: rev, 472, 746, 1803, 1959, 2372, 2551
Kavanagh, K.: ref, 863 (41)
Kåver, A.: ref, 1021 (12)
Kavoussi, R. J.: ref, 1166 (96,178)
Kavussanu, M.: ref, 2497 (487)
Kawamura, M.: ref, 2860 (997,1356), 2873 (47)
Kawamura, N.: ref, 2076 (174)
Kawas, C.: ref, 1164 (171), 1758 (97), 2860 (865, 964,1158)
Kawas, C. H.: ref, 815 (50), 1164 (175)
Kawasaki, T.: ref, 1166 (213)
Kay, G. G.: test, 567, 2892; ref, 349 (31), 451 (131), 2892 (215)
Kay, J.: test, 2113; ref, 337 (102), 2240 (3), 2603 (370), 2858 (100), 2860 (885,1091), 2863 (323)
Kay, J. A.: ref, 2497 (176)
Kay, S. R.: test, 564, 2017; ref, 564 (1,2,3), 1645 (2), 2017 (1,2,3), 2146 (2,7), 2485 (126), 2860 (218)
Kaye, A. L.: ref, 998 (75,76), 2603 (282,283), 2858 (78,79)
Kaye, G. L.: ref, 1755 (73)
Kaye, J. A.: ref, 2860 (468,1102), 2863 (132,329)
Kaye, K.: ref, 1164 (95)
Kaye, K.: ref, 2860 (635,879)
Kaye, W. H.: ref, 893 (26), 2497 (423)
Kaysen, D.: ref, 451 (102,116), 2288 (68), 2289 (52), 2305 (103), 2862 (450,475,493)
Kazak, A. E.: ref, 472 (185), 1000 (103), 2214 (111,115,117), 2497 (585,609,639), 2813 (128)
Kazarian, S. S.: ref, 2402 (41)
Kazdan, S.: ref, 2487 (19)
Kazdin, A. E.: ref, 2603 (193,272)
Kazes, M.: ref, 1166 (56)

Kazim, A.: ref, 1517 (6)
Kazmerski, V.: ref, 2860 (1302), 2879 (210), 2905 (114)
Kean, M.: ref, 2860 (89)
Keane, E. M.: ref, 2557 (8)
Keane, K. J.: ref, 2163 (12), 2862 (19)
Keane, M. M.: ref, 2860 (623), 2863 (182)
Keane, T. M.: ref, 272 (206), 1697 (36,290,505), 2497 (36,580)
Keaney, J. C.: ref, 846 (16)
Kearney, C. A.: ref, 472 (50,127), 1021 (18), 1991 (11,51,79), 2214 (68), 2497 (71), 2498 (21), 2862 (210), 2901 (27)
Kearns, M.: ref, 2497 (447)
Keathley, E. A.: ref, 451 (158)
Keating, D. P.: ref, 337 (149)
Keating, T. J.: rev, 2163, 2477, 2478
Keaton, P. H.: test, 749, 1785
Keats, J. A.: rev, 838
Keck, P. E.: ref, 2289 (54,58)
Keck, P. E., Jr.: ref, 1093 (93), 1166 (158), 2289 (39,60,61)
Keddie, A. M.: ref, 694 (31)
Kedem, D.: ref, 2603 (50)
Kee, D. W.: ref, 1379 (14), 2163 (140), 2860 (13), 2862 (4)
Kee, K.: ref, 2305 (42)
Keefe, C. K.: ref, 1174 (5), 2218 (86)
Keefe, F. J.: ref, 272 (28), 1178 (4), 2603 (46,51)
Keefe, J. W.: test, 648, 1472
Keefe, N.: ref, 681 (87), 1264 (6), 1889 (11), 1987 (22)
Keefe, R. S. E.: ref, 2288 (70), 2289 (55), 2305 (181, 225), 2860 (1020)
Keegan, D.: ref, 2497 (64)
Keegan, D. L.: ref, 2288 (6), 2289 (4)
Keegan, W. J.: test, 1387
Keel, P.: ref, 893 (21)
Keel, P. K.: ref, 1832 (16)
Keeley, E. J.: ref, 1672 (3,4)
Keeley, T. J.: ref, 413 (14)
Keenan, J. T.: ref, 837 (6)
Keenan, K.: ref, 451 (264), 1092 (5), 1965 (61,79), 2860 (331)
Keenan, M.: ref, 2862 (542), 2879 (180), 2901 (99)
Keenan, P. A.: ref, 376 (7), 776 (19), 1166 (116), 1218 (9), 2193 (31), 2860 (731,1111), 2863 (330)
Keene, J. M., Jr.: rev, 1425, 2735
Keeny, D. T.: rev, 466
Keesling, J. W.: rev, 2797, 2799
Kegel-Flom, P.: rev, 1846
Kegl, J. A.: ref, 1164 (174), 1903 (566), 2163 (348), 2731 (7), 2860 (1377), 2863 (413), 2879 (224), 2892 (295)
Kehle, J. J.: ref, 2862 (722)
Kehle, T. J.: rev, 129, 2112
Kehoe, J. F.: rev, 399, 1570
Kehoe, M.: ref, 1528 (5)
Kehoe, P. T.: test, 1855
Kehren, R.: ref, 540 (4)
Keifer-O'Donnel, R.: ref, 2299 (2), 2485 (98)
Keilin, W. G.: ref, 2497 (7)
Keilp, J. G.: ref, 2305 (96), 2860 (1112)
Keilty, J. W.: test, 2415
Keim, M.: ref, 2581 (1)
Keinonen, M.: ref, 1965 (19,77), 2218 (71)
Keir, G. H.: rev, 1367
Keith, B. R.: ref, 472 (136), 1010 (55,66), 1178 (9), 2214 (76), 2603 (222,223,321,322), 2858 (58,86)
Keith, P. B.: rev, 210, 227, 877, 1792
Keith, R. W.: test, 229, 2300, 2301; ref, 229 (1), 2300 (1), 2768 (5), 2862 (535)
Keith, S. J.: ref, 2288 (13)
Keith, T. Z.: rev, 736, 1378, 1921, 2441, 2677; ref, 837 (12), 1378 (8), 2485 (230), 2860 (663), 2862 (636,637), 2864 (56), 2901 (53,124)
Keitner, G.: ref, 1166 (84,152), 1216 (88), 2603 (496)
Keitner, G. I.: ref, 1093 (112), 1166 (193), 2603 (26)
Kelbey, T. J.: ref, 1991 (33)
Kelderman, H.: ref, 2163 (279)
Kellaghan, T.: rev, 2234; ref, 838 (18)
Kellam, S.: ref, 364 (19), 472 (48,172), 2214 (49,66,102,103)
Kellam, S. G.: ref, 472 (86)
Kelleher, K. J.: ref, 337 (131), 1079 (80), 1216 (38,41,90), 1903 (234,506), 2485 (113,115)
Kelleher, M.: ref, 2369 (8)
Kelleher, W. E.: ref, 1140 (52)
Kelleher, W. J.: ref, 2497 (241)
Keller, D.: ref, 592 (35)
Keller, D. S.: ref, 2749 (40)
Keller, H. R.: rev, 1941, 2841
Keller, J. M.: test, 975
Keller, J. W.: ref, 301 (33), 853 (12), 1160 (2), 2247 (40,41), 2380 (7), 2749 (33)
Keller, M.: ref, 1093 (10,73,108), 1517 (1,2,9), 1697 (376), 2305 (119,160,161,172,179), 2519 (46), 2520 (47)
Keller, M. B.: test, 1517; ref, 998 (109), 1092 (5), 1093 (68,106,107), 1158 (3), 1166 (63), 1517 (5,6,7), 1697 (513,517), 2305 (18,97,135,178, 189,200, 206,239), 2519 (42), 2520 (42), 2860 (331)
Keller, R. T.: ref, 1437 (2), 1701 (8)
Kellerman, H.: test, 932
Kellett, S.: ref, 272 (281), 2603 (538)
Kelley, B. C.: ref, 1590 (35)
Kelley, C.: test, 737
Kelley, D.: ref, 624 (15), 1379 (44), 1485 (25), 1612 (47), 1903 (245), 2657 (13), 2680 (8), 2704 (16), 2862 (244), 2864 (47)
Kelley, E. A.: test, 648
Kelley, F. A.: ref, 1701 (51), 1825 (7)
Kelley, J. E.: ref, 2076 (175)
Kelley, M. A.: ref, 1661 (48)
Kelley, M. E.: ref, 2288 (58)

Kelley, M. L.: rev, 279, 451, 1886, 2514, 2552, 2607; ref, 451 (41,48,164,200), 681 (82), 997 (3), 1000 (68), 2230 (7,16)
Kelley, S. J.: ref, 451 (10), 2603 (52,192)
Kellin, J.: ref, 2860 (489)
Kellman, E.: test, 953, 1664
Kelln, B. R. C.: ref, 1687 (41)
Kellner, R.: ref, 2603 (163,194,216)
Kellogg, C. E.: test, 2212
Kelloway, E. K.: ref, 1590 (12), 1736 (3)
Kelly, A. B.: ref, 1759 (5)
Kelly, A. E.: ref, 337 (146), 538 (6), 644 (3)
Kelly, D.: ref, 679 (1), 681 (35)
Kelly, D. B.: ref, 1697 (360)
Kelly, D. J.: ref, 624 (18,24), 1485 (47), 1903 (7,273,438), 2382 (1), 2485 (133), 2864 (57)
Kelly, E. J.: test, 841
Kelly, E. L.: rev, 372, 1321, 1745, 1779, 1965
Kelly, E. M.: ref, 994 (15,28), 1095 (34), 1485 (41), 1852 (2,4), 1903 (274,375), 2543 (1)
Kelly, I. W.: ref, 999 (83)
Kelly, J. S.: ref, 1166 (12)
Kelly, K. L.: ref, 1592 (10)
Kelly, K. R.: ref, 413 (7), 2862 (106)
Kelly, L. P.: ref, 773 (3)
Kelly, M.: ref, 358 (9), 739 (5), 2092 (3)
Kelly, M. D.: ref, 1164 (101)
Kelly, M. P.: ref, 2860 (14)
Kelly, M. S.: ref, 301 (55), 827 (4), 2210 (1), 2253 (2), 2516 (4), 2860 (1087), 2879 (161), 2892 (12), 2901 (90)
Kelly, P.: ref, 999 (78), 1166 (46)
Kelly, P. J.: ref, 2860 (537), 2863 (152)
Kelly, S. J.: ref, 1903 (534), 2163 (329)
Kelly, S. M.: ref, 2860 (1246,1132)
Kelly, T.: ref, 824 (5), 1093 (76), 1590 (49), 2603 (307)
Kelly, T. P.: ref, 2862 (496)
Kelly, V. A.: ref, 462 (29), 2858 (115)
Kelner, S.: ref, 2076 (183), 2749 (18)
Kelner, S. P.: test, 1442, 1573
Kelner, S. P., Jr.: test, 1860
Kelsey, R. M.: ref, 2603 (289), 2749 (45,55)
Kelsoe, J. R.: ref, 2076 (125)
Keltner, B.: ref, 1217 (1)
Keltner, D.: ref, 2603 (336)
Kember, D.: ref, 2540 (2)
Kemeny, M. E.: ref, 791 (11), 2076 (13,33,85,165), 2858 (82), 2860 (664)
Kemewy, A.: ref, 372 (41), 838 (12), 999 (44), 1140 (25)
Kemmann, E.: ref, 2497 (93)
Kemmerer, B. E.: ref, 998 (80)
Kemp, J.: ref, 2519 (10), 2520 (10), 2603 (53)
Kemp, N.: ref, 1758 (76), 1903 (492), 2163 (297), 2905 (103)
Kemp, R.: ref, 1758 (45)
Kemp, S.: test, 1771
Kemp, S. G.: ref, 705 (3)
Kempe, R. S.: ref, 784 (1), 1612 (70), 1903 (366)
Kempen, G. I. J. M.: ref, 999 (159)
Kemper, B.: ref, 2860 (1093)
Kemper, C. C.: ref, 2497 (550)
Kemper, K. J.: ref, 1216 (43)
Kemper, M. B.: ref, 1903 (12), 2860 (35), 2862 (16), 2863 (13), 2879 (6)
Kemper, S.: ref, 776 (16), 2860 (291,383,1292)
Kemper, T. R.: ref, 298 (69)
Kempton, T.: ref, 337 (71), 472 (80)
Kempton, T. L.: ref, 2214 (93), 2231 (5)
Kenardy, J.: ref, 2497 (237,258)
Kenardy, J. A.: ref, 1079 (37)
Kendall, A.: ref, 1803 (1), 2497 (386)
Kendall, B. S.: test, 1645
Kendall, E. L.: test, 1660
Kendall, J. C.: ref, 2603 (368)
Kendall, L. M.: test, 1348, 2208
Kendall, P. C.: ref, 451 (154), 472 (101,150,171,212), 473 (1,7), 1021 (45), 1166 (208), 1697 (180), 2214 (8,55,85,101,123,133), 2498 (2,10,42,55,64,73,75)
Kendall, W. E.: rev, 2276
Kendler, K. S.: ref, 999 (58,126,145,160,186), 2305 (21), 2603 (273)
Kendrick, D. C.: test, 1390; rev, 2010
Kendziora, K. T.: ref, 451 (265)
Kenkel, M. B.: ref, 337 (27), 2603 (104), 2858 (27)
Kenkel, S.: ref, 776 (49), 1164 (159), 1758 (91), 2227 (42)
Kennard, B. D.: ref, 433 (12), 1086 (2), 1164 (80), 1240 (30), 1612 (60), 1902 (60), 2485 (150), 2860 (760), 2864 (74)
Kennard, C.: ref, 1758 (35,36), 2163 (205,206), 2288 (46,47), 2289 (35,36), 2305 (126,127), 2892 (170,171)
Kennedy, A.: ref, 999 (67,68), 2076 (71), 2077 (7)
Kennedy, B. L.: ref, 1166 (220)
Kennedy, C.: ref, 199 (10)
Kennedy, D. N.: ref, 451 (187), 2227 (26), 2305 (222), 2813 (140), 2860 (1103) 2862 (611), 2879 (202), 2905 (109)
Kennedy, G. E.: ref, 1014 (2)
Kennedy, J. E.: rev, 1799, 2808, 2907
Kennedy, J. H.: ref, 694 (78)
Kennedy, J. J.: ref, 1755 (73)
Kennedy, J. L.: ref, 2305 (22)
Kennedy, N. S. J.: ref, 537 (2), 1390 (6), 1758 (53), 2860 (982)
Kennedy, P.: ref, 272 (123,124), 273 (13), 746 (3), 2076 (115), 2239 (2), 2497 (488)
Kennedy, P. H.: rev, 1232
Kennedy, R.: ref, 272 (171), 999 (157), 2497 (554), 2603 (454)
Kennedy, S.: ref, 337 (10)
Kennedy, S. H.: ref, 272 (284), 999 (183) 1166 (170,171), 2218 (81,82), 2305 (213), 2603 (514)

Kennedy, W. A.: ref, 1697 (403), 1991 (88), 2862 (327), 2879 (111)
Kennedy-Moore, E.: ref, 2076 (43)
Kennel, R.: ref, 337 (67)
Kenner, A. N.: ref, 2516 (25)
Kenney, K. W.: rev, 214, 468
Kenney, R. K.: test, 1357
Kenny, D.: ref, 893 (14)
Kenny, D. T.: ref, 349 (5), 1503 (8), 1903 (185), 2123 (1), 2485 (93), 2905 (42)
Kenny, M. E.: ref, 2525 (12)
Kenowitz, L.: rev, 284
Kent, G. H.: rev, 2485
Kent, M.: ref, 1216 (32), 1903 (182)
Kent, R. L.: ref, 298 (116)
Kentish, J.: ref, 2497 (372)
Kentle, R. L.: ref, 998 (74)
Kentridge, R. W.: ref, 1758 (11), 2860 (219), 2863 (55)
Kentros, M.: ref, 2218 (99), 2305 (226)
Kenyon, D.: test, 250, 2015
Kenyon-Jump, R.: ref, 2497 (106), 2603 (84)
Keogh, B. K.: rev, 565, 1362; ref, 1085 (4), 2485 (228), 2813 (145)
Keogh, D.: ref, 1619 (4)
Keogh, E.: ref, 999 (192), 1899 (1)
Keogh, M.: ref, 459 (17), 2813 (33)
Keogh, N. J.: ref, 1697 (241)
Kephart, N. C.: rev, 816
Ker, C.: test, 1217
Kerbeshian, J.: ref, 1902 (30), 2485 (50), 2862 (156), 2879 (40)
Kerby, D. S.: ref, 2813 (65)
Kerig, P. K.: ref, 451 (266), 472 (225), 1902 (36), 2214 (134)
Kerley, J. H.: ref, 472 (69), 2498 (27)
Kerley, S.: ref, 1079 (106)
Kermeen, P.: ref, 863 (68)
Kern, J. M.: ref, 1010 (77)
Kern, R. A.: ref, 4 (20), 459 (15), 681 (83), 2211 (18,50), 2485 (73,221)
Kern, R. M.: test, 262
Kernan, K. T.: ref, 1240 (46), 1379 (87), 2163 (280)
Kernberg, P.: ref, 1697 (13)
Kernis, M. H.: ref, 1745 (6)
Kerns, K. A.: ref, 376 (22), 2860 (1293) 2879 (209)
Kerns, R.: ref, 272 (353)
Kerns, R. D.: ref, 2497 (119), 2603 (16,30)
Kero, P.: ref, 1903 (186)
Kerr, B.: rev, 2537, 2553; ref, 1166 (24), 1965 (80), 2835 (26), 2860 (856), 2892 (177), 2905 (72)
Kerr, B. A.: rev, 768 1348, 2597
Kerr, J. A.: ref, 372 (68), 2247 (64)
Kerr, M.: ref, 472 (111,199)
Kerr, S. L.: ref, 1000 (52)
Kerr, W. A.: test, 147, 845, 933; rev, 2170, 2889
Kerry, R.: ref, 999 (143), 1079 (55), 2603 (418), 2858 (108)
Kerry, S. M.: ref, 1166 (12)
Kershaw, D.: ref, 2076 (35), 2603 (121)
Kershner, J.: ref, 815 (26), 1131 (15), 2860 (911)
Kershner, J. R.: ref, 2862 (107,132,357), 2879 (122), 2905 (77)
Kerslake, D.: test, 444
Kerssens, J. J.: ref, 1079 (33)
Kertesz, A.: test, 2873; ref, 2163 (27), 2873 (5,21)
Kertesz, S.: ref, 2860 (191)
Kertoy, M. K.: ref, 2704 (28), 2905 (78)
Kertzner, R.: ref, 337 (31,91), 2603 (299)
Kerwin, R. W.: ref, 1093 (50), 2050 (65), 2863 (169), 2892 (277)
Keshavan, M. S.: ref, 650 (9), 1166 (210), 2288 (22), 2305 (67,109), 2892 (141)
Keskitalo, P.: ref, 2247 (120)
Kesner, R. D.: ref, 2860 (107)
Kesner, R. P.: ref, 776 (46), 2860 (323), 2892 (187)
Kessler, A. R.: rev, 2673
Kessler, J.: ref, 2226 (31), 2227 (15,40), 2497 (120), 2516 (101), 2860 (1294), 2863 (172,401), 2892 (107,286)
Kessler, K.: rev, 214, 1656; ref, 2076 (34), 2440 (1)
Kessler, K. S.: rev, 2504, 2671
Kessler, R. C.: ref, 999 (58,160), 2603 (126)
Kestenbaum, C. J.: ref, 1697 (405), 2305 (131)
Kestenbaum, R.: ref, 2603 (129)
Kester, D. B.: ref, 1752 (1), 2860 (269,744)
Kestly, J.: ref, 1000 (55)
Ketler, T. A.: ref, 335 (7)
Ketsetzis, M.: ref, 451 (267), 694 (133), 1010 (135)
Kettelkamp, G. C.: rev, 579, 600, 1761
Ketter, T. A.: ref, 272 (294), 1166 (199)
Ketterson, T. U.: ref, 1697 (235,243)
Keunning, T. S.: ref, 1000 (55)
Keuthen, N.: ref, 2227 (26), 2860 (1103)
Kewman, D. G.: ref, 337 (20), 1902 (3), 2603 (72)
Key, C. C.: ref, 1590 (17)
Key, M. P.: ref, 451 (152), 472 (187), 473 (3)
Keyes, K. L.: ref, 2879 (12)
Keymeulen, H.: ref, 1612 (101), 2862 (732)
Keys, A.: ref, 349 (35), 350 (42), 2163 (311), 2556 (2), 2910 (1)
Keyser, C. S.: ref, 2860 (366)
Khaleefa, O. H.: ref, 142 (7,8), 682 (4,5)
Khaleque, A.: ref, 999 (71)
Khalil, A. H.: ref, 999 (98), 2050 (92)
Khalil, R.: ref, 2863 (261), 2892 (183)
Khalpey, M.: ref, 1965 (21)
Khan, A.: ref, 790 (15), 1166 (13), 2860 (665), 2863 (195)
Khan, L. M. L.: test, 1394
Khanna, R. K.: ref, 592 (38), 1140 (35)
Kharabi, F.: ref, 1645 (1), 2860 (101)
Khatena, J.: test, 1395, 1396, 2755
Khawaja, N. G.: ref, 2497 (177,354)
Khoo, G.: ref, 2451 (2)

Khoo, S.: ref, 2603 (416)
Khoshaba, D. M.: ref, 1697 (323)
Khouri, S.: ref, 1697 (490), 2247 (103)
Khurana, H.: ref, 272 (340)
Kibby, M. W.: ref, 665 (51), 827 (7), 1072 (8,38), 1903 (32)
Kibe, N.: ref, 2305 (241)
Kibria, N.: ref, 2603 (80)
Kicklighter, K. A.: test, 465
Kidd, G.: ref, 23 (1), 398 (1)
Kidd, J. R.: ref, 2305 (22)
Kidd, K. K.: ref, 2305 (22)
Kido, D. K.: ref, 1903 (334), 2517 (2), 2860 (796)
Kido, Y.: ref, 298 (126)
Kidorf, M.: ref, 1745 (7), 2218 (85), 2519 (43), 2520 (43)
Kidron, D.: ref, 376 (31), 776 (47,60), 2863 (423)
Kids 'N' Cars Research Team.: ref, 451 (238), 1010 (131)
Kiecolt-Glaser, J. K.: ref, 337 (10), 863 (56), 1698 (10), 2076 (57,119)
Kiely, K.: ref, 1010 (69,70), 1092 (11,13), 2305 (121), 2860 (801), 2862 (308,310), 2879 (100,102)
Kiely, M. C.: ref, 2603 (402)
Kiely, S. L.: ref, 2813 (148)
Kienapple, K.: ref, 270 (6), 2485 (96)
Kienholz, E.: ref, 2497 (395)
Kiernam, B.: ref, 240 (4), 539 (2), 994 (52), 1379 (102), 1903 (574), 2382 (40)
Kiernan, B.: ref, 540 (20), 994 (47), 1379 (95), 1903 (535), 2045 (6), 2190 (8,9), 2382 (39), 2524 (12,13)
Kiernan, C.: test, 2052
Kiernan, R. J.: test, 558
Kieschnick, E.: ref, 272 (86), 1697 (337), 2860 (710)
Kiesler, D. J.: test, 991, 1243; ref, 1243 (2,4), 1290 (2), 2120 (4), 2497 (298), 2603 (229)
Kiewra, K. A.: rev, 1456, 2545
Kifer, E.: rev, 56, 1319
Kihlstrom, J. F.: ref, 2860 (745)
Kihm, J. A.: test, 1348
Kikinis, R.: ref, 2288 (60), 2289 (46), 2305 (150,159), 2860 (497,1012)
Kikuchi, M.: ref, 1219 (1)
Kilborn, L. C.: ref, 1026 (1), 2497 (72)
Kilbourn, K.: ref, 2603 (516)
Kilgore, J.: ref, 1697 (21)
Kilic, C.: ref, 2603 (233)
Killackey, J.: ref, 2873 (17)
Killen, J. D.: ref, 2305 (138)
Kilmann, I.: test, 1398
Kilmann, R. H.: test, 1397, 1398, 2756
Kilmer, J.: ref, 1661 (67)
Kilpatrick, A. C.: ref, 458 (1)
Kilpatrick, D. G.: ref, 1697 (496)
Kilpatrick, J.: rev, 605
Kilpatrick, K. L.: ref, 1079 (108)
Kim, B. W.: ref, 2651 (8)
Kim, H.: ref, 900 (4), 2485 (20), 2860 (153,191), 2862 (94), 2864 (16)
Kim, H. R.: ref, 1434 (2)
Kim, J.: ref, 2545 (6), 2771 (39)
Kim, J. A.: ref, 163 (2)
Kim, J. H.: ref, 2860 (216,974), 2863 (286)
Kim, J. R.: ref, 404 (29), 2915 (6)
Kim, K.: ref, 2189 (2)
Kim, K. H.: ref, 272 (347), 1166 (218)
Kim, L. S.: ref, 472 (200), 2214 (118)
Kim, M. K.: ref, 272 (203)
Kim, S.: ref, 472 (146), 1590 (34), 2214 (82)
Kim, W. J.: ref, 301 (17), 1392 (5), 1902 (24), 2247 (15), 2749 (20), 2905 (14)
Kim, Y. K.: ref, 1903 (355)
Kim (Yoon), Y. H.: ref, 665 (63)
Kim-Goh, M.: ref, 2603 (369)
Kimball, D. J.: ref, 1462 (3), 2901 (111)
Kimbell, J.: ref, 2497 (678)
Kimble, M. O.: ref, 2305 (150), 2860 (1319), 2892 (282)
Kimmance, S.: ref, 2863 (114)
Kimmel, E. W.: rev, 947, 2933
Kimmel, S. E.: ref, 1093 (110), 2305 (168)
Kimura, D.: ref, 1405 (7), 2125 (15)
Kinder, A.: ref, 1822 (3)
Kinder, B. N.: ref, 1697 (410,586), 1959 (8), 2247 (86)
Kinder, E. F.: rev, 2813
Kinderman, P.: ref, 272 (53), 2050 (82,140)
Kinderman, T. A.: ref, 1391 (2)
Kindler, H. S.: test, 1557, 1949, 2238, 2506
Kindler, S.: ref, 301 (48), 1166 (28), 2860 (922)
Kindlon, D.: ref, 1164 (102), 2516 (68), 2519 (17), 2520 (18), 2907 (9)
Kindschi, C. L.: test, 2720
King, A. C.: ref, 134 (9), 272 (65), 681 (39), 2076 (4), 2497 (243), 2860 (550)
King, A. R.: ref, 1687 (42)
King, C. A.: ref, 2230 (9,10,14), 2557 (4,5)
King, C-A.: ref, 473 (6), 2230 (18), 2557 (10)
King, C. M.: test, 671
King, D. A.: ref, 2361 (4)
King, D. E.: ref, 272 (333), 2860 (1366), 2863 (412)
King, D. W.: test, 2389; ref, 298 (117), 641 (4,5), 1135 (5), 1590 (6), 1965 (55), 2076 (19,118), 2227 (11,20), 2517 (4), 2599 (7,30), 2860 (198), 2863 (136), 2899 (6)
King, E. A.: ref, 2305 (191)
King, E. F.: ref, 2305 (185)
King, E. H.: ref, 811 (5), 1216 (35)
King, G. A.: ref, 1107 (5), 1294 (3), 1965 (60), 2533 (1)
King, G. D.: rev, 1697
King, J. D.: test, 1311; rev, 1131, 2289
King, J. E.: test, 1798; ref, 1010 (78)
King, J. R.: ref, 665 (16)
King, J. W.: test, 1708, 1709, 1710
King, K.: ref, 337 (152)
King, K. B.: ref, 2077 (6)

King, L. A.: test, 2389; ref, 272 (282), 298 (117), 1590 (6), 2218 (100), 2749 (58), 2771 (42)
King, M.: ref, 1697 (171), 2860 (355), 2901 (20)
King, M. O.: ref, 1404 (6)
King, N. J.: ref, 472 (128), 1021 (39), 2214 (19,69,99,100), 2497 (178,556), 2498 (52,63)
King, P. M.: ref, 1755 (41)
King, P. R.: ref, 950 (5)
King, R.: test, 2733; ref, 824 (1), 2288 (3), 2305 (23)
King, R. E.: ref, 645 (1)
King, R. J.: ref, 1697 (128)
King, S.: rev, 2288, 2289; ref, 1000 (6,98)
King, V. L.: ref, 2218 (85)
King, W. L.: ref, 1140 (44)
King-Shaw, E.: test, 389
Kingree, J. B.: ref, 451 (287), 1903 (582)
Kingsbury, G. G.: rev, 2134, 2464
Kingsbury, N. A.: test, 1690
Kingsley, D.: ref, 1758 (90), 2860 (1297), 2863 (391)
Kingston, K.: ref, 272 (247)
Kingston, K. R.: ref, 2862 (552)
Kinicki, A. J.: ref, 1338 (2), 1701 (13)
Kinlaw, D. C.: test, 556
Kinner, K. M.: ref, 776 (36), 2860 (1206)
Kinney, D. K.: ref, 2519 (28), 2520 (29)
Kinney, M. A.: ref, 357 (1), 496 (4), 2905 (15)
Kinney, R. K.: ref, 1697 (411)
Kinney, T. R.: ref, 1010 (55,66), 2603 (97,223,321,322), 2858 (58,86)
Kinnier, R. T.: rev, 400, 423
Kinnish, K.: ref, 451 (126), 2045 (2), 2657 (26,29), 2813 (93,119), 2864 (91,115)
Kinsbourne, M.: ref, 389 (10), 1164 (116), 2860 (1019)
Kinscherff, R.: ref, 2519 (38), 2520 (39)
Kinsella, G.: ref, 451 (44), 1058 (9), 1079 (29), 2599 (29,34), 2860 (1042), 2862 (358), 2879 (89,123)
Kinzer, J. R.: rev, 1533, 1700
Kinzie, J. D.: ref, 2305 (79)
Kinzler, M. C.: test, 1359, 1360
Kinzler, P.: ref, 2239 (8)
Kiosseoglou, G.: ref, 272 (363), 2163 (92), 2862 (176)
Kiplinger, V. L.: ref, 592 (87), 1759 (15)
Kipnis, D.: test, 1402
Kipp, E.: ref, 2382 (20)
Kipper, D. A.: ref, 998 (116)
Kirasic, K. C.: ref, 1405 (32)
Kirby, H.: ref, 337 (11), 1164 (18), 1697 (74), 2860 (185), 2863 (49)
Kirby, J. R.: ref, 1072 (31), 1607 (5), 2905 (51)
Kirby, K. C.: ref, 271 (11), 272 (182,296), 273 (21), 1687 (44)
Kirby, M.: ref, 2603 (288)
Kirby, N.: ref, 270 (44), 2485 (237)
Kirby, P. C.: ref, 364 (6)
Kirby, R. S.: ref, 451 (33), 1079 (80), 1216 (40,90), 1903 (506), 2485 (114)
Kirch, D. G.: ref, 564 (4), 2120 (2), 2288 (12)
Kirchner, P.: ref, 1093 (39)
Kirchner, T.: ref, 1140 (7)
Kirchner, W. K.: rev, 1444
Kirchner-Nebot, T.: ref, 474 (3,7)
Kirischi, L.: ref, 2498 (33)
Kirisci, L.: ref, 1902 (76), 2862 (372)
Kirk, A.: ref, 2163 (27), 2873 (5)
Kirk, B. A.: rev, 1413, 1790
Kirk, J. J.: ref, 1701 (9)
Kirk, S. A.: test, 1240; ref, 1181 (11), 1181 (15), 1590 (23,36)
Kirk, U.: test, 1771; ref, 827 (4), 2210 (1), 2516 (4), 2892 (12)
Kirk, W. D.: test, 1240
Kirkby, B. S.: ref, 376 (8), 2892 (230)
Kirkby, R. J.: ref, 2077 (8), 2497 (355), 2858 (101)
Kirkcaldy, B.: ref, 372 (47), 1824 (5,6)
Kirkcaldy, B. D.: ref, 1824 (2)
Kirkhart, E.: test, 2411
Kirkhart, K. J.: ref, 2402 (65)
Kirkhart, L.: test, 2411
Kirkorian, R.: ref, 337 (102), 2603 (370), 2858 (100)
Kirkpatrick, B.: ref, 2050 (24), 2516 (34), 2892 (105)
Kirkpatrick, D. L.: test, 1403, 1552, 1553, 1554, 1555, 1556, 2565, 2566
Kirkpatrick, S. E.: ref, 2497 (437), 2498 (50)
Kirkpatrick, T.: ref, 815 (26), 1131 (15), 2860 (911)
Kirksey, A.: ref, 2163 (308), 2860 (1197), 2862 (415)
Kirkwood, J.: ref, 2076 (47)
Kirmayer, L. J.: ref, 1241 (1,6), 2603 (107)
Kirnan, J. P.: rev, 453, 807, 1736, 1792, 2244, 2421, 2447
Kirsch, E.: ref, 2497 (47)
Kirsch, I. J.: test, 972
Kirschenbaum, D. S.: ref, 2603 (180)
Kirschenbaum, R. J.: test, 723
Kirsh, S. J.: ref, 1903 (536)
Kirshner, H. S.: ref, 2860 (14)
Kirshner, M. C.: ref, 1164 (14), 2860 (148), 2879 (22), 2901 (10)
Kirtley, C.: ref, 350 (1), 2864 (10)
Kirton, M.: test, 1404
Kirton, M. J.: ref, 1470 (3)
Kirwin, M. M.: test, 2935
Kiselica, M. S.: ref, 2497 (356), 2862 (46)
Kiser, K.: rev, 73
Kish, J.: ref, 301 (17), 1392 (5), 1902 (24), 2247 (15), 2749 (20), 2905 (14)
Kish, S. J.: ref, 1218 (6), 1903 (275), 2163 (168), 2863 (196), 2892 (123)
Kishi, Y.: ref, 1166 (117,118), 2050 (118)
Kishton, J. M.: ref, 1965 (54)
Kisker, E.: ref, 875 (6), 1264 (2)
Kisler, V.: ref, 337 (95) 846 (7)
Kisler, V. A.: ref, 1745 (81)
Kispal, A.: test, 2171, 2691
Kissane, D. W.: ref, 335 (12), 1010 (100,101)

Kistner, J. A.: ref, 665 (6), 815 (1), 1902 (6,9), 2039 (5), 2485 (10,17,38), 2862 (47,77)
Kitagaki, H.: ref, 2163 (334), 2860 (1314), 2873 (68)
Kitamura, T.: ref, 273 (26), 999 (59,72)
Kitaoka, S. K.: ref, 746 (4)
Kitay, P. M.: rev, 301, 853
Kitchens, H.: rev, 987
Kitchens, K.: ref, 2076 (110), 2603 (343)
Kitson, G. C.: ref, 337 (135)
Kitson, M. E.: ref, 1903 (307)
Kitson, W. J. H.: ref, 1903 (477)
Kitwood, T.: rev, 2246
Kivlahan, D. R.: ref, 134 (2), 272 (14), 2860 (108)
Kivlighan, D. M.: ref, 1697 (300), 2603 (261)
Kizaki, Y.: ref, 2860 (1363)
Kizer, D. L.: ref, 2289 (54)
Kjelgaard, M. M.: ref, 2860 (623), 2863 (182)
Klaarenbeek, M. T. A.: ref, 1697 (304)
Klaczynski, P. A.: ref, 2862 (497)
Klapwijk, M. J. G.: ref, 2862 (456)
Klar, Y.: ref, 272 (192)
Klasko, J. S.: ref, 2497 (17)
Klassen, J.: ref, 1697 (66), 2076 (9)
Klauber, M.: ref, 2860 (184), 2862 (105)
Klauber, M. R.: ref, 1058 (5), 2860 (464), 2862 (203)
Klauminzer, G. W.: ref, 1697 (290)
Klaus, A.: ref, 2860 (145), 2862 (93)
Klausmeier, K.: ref, 1379 (2)
Klawsky, J. D.: ref, 2218 (51)
Kleban, M. H.: ref, 2076 (44)
Klebanov, P. K.: ref, 1079 (24,27,58), 1181 (13,14), 1216 (45,50,78,79), 2485 (75,192), 2864 (48,112)
Kleczewska, M. K.: ref, 2008 (3)
Kledaras, J. B.: ref, 1903 (132)
Klee, S.: rev, 477, 1621
Klee, T.: ref, 451 (176), 811 (13), 1259 (2)
Kleemeier, C.: ref, 2498 (9)
Kleijn, W. C.: ref, 2497 (227)
Kleiman, J.: ref, 2497 (404)
Kleiman, M. E.: ref, 2076 (75)
Klein, B. S.: test, 2376
Klein, D. F.: ref, 1166 (142,179), 1903 (296), 2305 (34,132), 2603 (487), 2864 (66)
Klein, D. N.: ref, 273 (24), 790 (4), 790 (14), 999 (19,147,166,168), 1166 (88,124,145), 1953 (2,3), 2305 (182,227)
Klein, E.: ref, 1745 (18)
Klein, H.: ref, 694 (7), 1582 (1), 1701 (2)
Klein, H. A.: ref, 2369 (3,7)
Klein, H. J.: ref, 1701 (34), 1965 (8)
Klein, J.: ref, 999 (105), 1697 (351), 2497 (393)
Klein, J. L.: ref, 2305 (154)
Klein, K.: ref, 694 (93), 1079 (34), 2497 (426)
Klein, K. L.: ref, 404 (39), 1754 (26), 2860 (854), 2863 (249)
Klein, M.: ref, 2516 (102)
Klein, M. D.: ref, 251 (2), 1234 (3), 1420 (2), 1902 (42)
Klein, M. H.: test, 991; ref, 1889 (8), 2497 (482), 2603 (483)
Klein, N.: ref, 353 (19) 815 (31), 994 (33), 1379 (78), 1982 (12), 2125 (19), 2813 (108)
Klein, R. G.: ref, 2860 (983)
Klein, R. L.: ref, 1862 (2)
Klein, S. K.: ref, 1096 (9), 2668 (1), 2694 (14), 2860 (912)
Klein, T. P.: ref, 451 (74), 889 (1)
Kleiner, K. A.: ref, 705 (6)
Kleinhauz, M.: ref, 2603 (499)
Kleinke, C. L.: ref, 1697 (310), 1745 (36)
Kleinknecht, R. A.: ref, 2603 (374,478)
Kleinman, A. M.: ref, 2305 (9)
Kleinman, J. E.: ref, 776 (15), 1164 (46), 2163 (112), 2516 (24), 2860 (459), 2863 (312), 2879 (56), 2892 (74,122,222)
Kleinman, M.: ref, 451 (151), 2305 (197)
Kleinman, P. H.: ref, 2519 (10), 2520 (10), 2603 (53)
Kleinmuntz, B.: rev, 915, 1831, 1976
Klemchuk, H. P.: ref, 2860 (192)
Klerman, G. L.: ref, 1093 (23), 1697 (52)
Klesius, J. P.: ref, 665 (32), 1072 (24)
Kleyboecker, K.: ref, 136 (10), 1661 (45), 1697 (426)
Kliegal, R.: ref, 745 (1), 1405 (1), 2163 (7)
Klieger, D. M.: ref, 298 (141), 1021 (23,33)
Kliegl, R.: ref, 745 (3), 2163 (19,63)
Klien, D. F.: ref, 2305 (147)
Klier, D.: ref, 472 (72), 1697 (263), 2247 (53)
Kliewer, W.: ref, 451 (268), 472 (51,177,226), 1010 (102), 2214 (20,108,135)
Kliger, A. S.: ref, 272 (227)
Klin, A.: ref, 1485 (7)
Kline, C. D.: ref, 1697 (467)
Kline, D. W.: ref, 2860 (49)
Kline, J.: ref, 1135 (9), 1164 (48), 2288 (28), 2289 (19), 2860 (474)
Kline, M.: ref, 451 (5)
Kline, N.: ref, 1135 (9), 1164 (48), 2288 (28), 2289 (19), 2860 (474)
Kline, P.: rev, 999; ref, 644 (7), 1822 (6)
Kline, R. B.: ref, 136 (2), 1379 (18,29), 1697 (80), 2485 (57,94), 2860 (478), 2862 (166,211), 2879 (45,59)
Kline, T. J. B.: ref, 1115 (18)
Kline, W. E.: rev, 499, 500
Klinedinst, J. K.: test, 1962
Kliner, L.: ref, 1745 (20), 2860 (361)
Klinetob, N. A.: ref, 863 (79)
Kling, F.: test, 2751
Kling, K. C.: ref, 2076 (158)
Klingenspor, B.: ref, 298 (118)
Klinger, J. K.: ref, 1072 (53)
Klinger, L. G.: ref, 459 (35), 1485 (40), 1903 (350), 2498 (17)
Klingman, A.: ref, 2656 (2), 2862 (60)
Klinkenberg, W. D.: ref, 337 (168)
Klions, H. L.: ref, 1745 (80)
Klip, E. C.: ref, 1079 (107), 2497 (670), 2603 (584)

Klobucar, C.: ref, 665 (67), 2862 (282), 2901 (45)
Klohnen, E. C.: ref, 68 (55), 372 (102), 373 (35,37)
Kloner, A.: ref, 337 (3), 451 (6), 472 (2), 2497 (35)
Klonman, R.: ref, 1902 (55)
Klonoff, E. A.: ref, 298 (65), 708 (5)
Klonoff, H.: ref, 1164 (144), 1697 (15), 2860 (60,270,517,1242), 2863 (70,149), 2907 (2,3)
Klopp, B.: ref, 365 (2)
Klorman, R.: ref, 681 (48), 1902 (88), 1903 (548), 2862 (500,736), 2879 (234)
Klos, T.: ref, 2163 (243)
Klosko, J.: ref, 1093 (36), 2497 (141), 2603 (119)
Klove, H.: ref, 1164 (47), 1407 (2), 2860 (463), 2863 (130)
Kluever, R. C.: ref, 2163 (86,326)
Klug, G.: ref, 2599 (29), 2862 (358), 2879 (123)
Kluger, A.: ref, 1164 (156), 2125 (26), 2860 (1295)
Kluger, A. N.: ref, 1348 (15)
Kluin, K. J.: ref, 1164 (154), 2860 (1287)
Klump, C. S.: test, 2491
Klurn, K. J.: ref, 2603 (438), 2860 (1040)
Klusman, L. E.: ref, 1164 (6), 2860 (109)
Kluwin, T. N.: ref, 1000 (69), 1759 (5,9,12)
Klysner, R.: ref, 337 (13)
Knackstedt, G.: ref, 298 (82)
Knapp, L. F.: test, 395, 414, 415, 416, 417
Knapp, L. G.: ref, 2813 (111)
Knapp, R. R.: test, 395, 414, 415, 416, 417, 2736
Knapp, T. R.: rev, 64, 1470, 2656
Knapp-Lee, L.: test, 416, 702, 1541
Knee, C. R.: ref, 1745 (72)
Knegtering, H.: ref, 1166 (53), 2603 (265)
Kneiter, K. T.: ref, 2860 (1129), 2863 (336)
Knesevich, M. A.: ref, 1697 (196)
Knibbe, R. A.: ref, 1661 (29)
Knight, B. G.: ref, 2603 (281)
Knight, C. B.: ref, 2497 (116), 2656 (4)
Knight, C. C.: rev, 1400
Knight, F. H.: ref, 451 (135)
Knight, G. P.: ref, 472 (87,88), 1000 (29,70), 1877 (2)
Knight, H. V.: ref, 1991 (80)
Knight, J. E.: ref, 2860 (824)
Knight, J. G.: ref, 771 (7)
Knight, P. A.: ref, 1701 (42)
Knight, R. D.: ref, 1661 (11), 2497 (96)
Knight, R. G.: ref, 199 (13), 1745 (35), 2497 (247)
Knight, R. T.: ref, 2225 (1), 2860 (1320,1385), 2863 (397,417)
Knight, W.: test, 392
Knippers, J. A.: ref, 298 (88), 2835 (15)
Knisely, J. S.: ref, 1697 (218), 2402 (18), 2519 (26), 2520 (27)
Knize, K.: ref, 1021 (15), 2603 (164)
Knobler, R.: ref, 1218 (5), 2599 (10), 2863 (109), 2892 (59)
Knobloch, O.: ref, 376 (33), 2239 (35)
Knoche, M.: ref, 1166 (50)
Knoefel, J. E.: ref, 2860 (329), 2863 (87,113)
Knoff, H. M.: test, 1401; rev, 35, 466, 472, 477, 1219, 1760, 1805, 1958, 1962; ref, 451 (180), 1962 (3)
Knoop, R.: ref, 1348 (11)
Knopik, S. N.: ref, 2901 (95)
Knopman, D.: ref, 2010 (4), 2860 (271,752), 2862 (291), 2863 (71)
Knopp, M. V.: ref, 1166 (202)
Knoras, K. M.: ref, 1697 (158)
Knorr, K.: ref, 2076 (135)
Knott, K.: ref, 998 (22)
Knott, V. J.: ref, 1166 (119)
Know, T. A.: ref, 2497 (7)
Knowdell, R. L.: test, 423, 1719, 1820, 2207
Knowles, A. D.: ref, 1903 (33,56)
Knowles, E. E.: ref, 1697 (81,82)
Knowles, E. S.: ref, 1333 (7)
Knox, A.: rev, 2651
Knox, D. E.: test, 2678
Knuckle, E. P.: ref, 2599 (1), 2862 (11)
Knudson, R. E.: ref, 1659 (4)
Knussen, C.: ref, 2858 (37,98)
Knutson, J. F.: rev, 2247
Koba, H.: test, 1506
Kobak, K. A.: test, 1166, 2232; ref, 89 (1)
Kobak, R.: ref, 272 (159), 893 (32)
Kobal, A.: test, 9, 533, 1312
Kobari, M.: ref, 2860 (1296)
Kobayashi, K.: ref, 2497 (139)
Kobe, F. H.: ref, 472 (89), 2485 (134), 2813 (66)
Kobel, A.: test, 10, 1632
Koberg, C. S.: ref, 68 (22)
Koblinsky, S. A.: ref, 1216 (102)
Kobrynowicz, D.: ref, 298 (75)
Kobus, D. A.: ref, 2516 (45), 2860 (666,694)
Koby, M.: ref, 375 (8), 2720 (1), 2892 (297)
Koch, C. C.: rev, 862
Koch, D.: ref, 2864 (12)
Koch, M.: ref, 2860 (525), 2892 (88)
Koch, W.: ref, 1096 (12), 2497 (208)
Koch, W. J.: ref, 271 (7), 2497 (146)
Koch, W. R.: rev, 17, 936, 1595
Kochanek, T. T.: ref, 301 (12), 1097 (3), 2485 (27), 2862 (108), 2879 (24)
Kochanska, A.: ref, 451 (132)
Kochanska, G.: ref, 272 (283), 372 (112), 1903 (376), 2076 (27), 2305 (54,55,68), 2497 (640), 2862 (133)
Kochenderfer, B. J.: ref, 1659 (8,13,7)
Kock, P.: ref, 2227 (40), 2516 (101), 2860 (1294)
Kock, W. J.: ref, 271 (18), 272 (368)
Kocoshis, S.: ref, 2305 (93,94)
Kocsis, J. H.: ref, 1093 (86,87,112), 1166 (14,120,129,162), 2417 (6), 2603 (503)
Koehn, K. A.: ref, 2497 (106), 2603 (84)
Koek, R.: ref, 2603 (112)
Koele, P.: ref, 1021 (17), 2603 (177,178,247,349,508)
Koenders, M. E. F.: ref, 2497 (259)
Koenig, A. L.: ref, 451 (132)

Koenig, L.: ref, 1832 (14)
Koenig, L. A.: ref, 694 (13), 994 (2), 1060 (2), 1240 (3), 1421 (3), 1425 (1), 1902 (10), 2660 (1), 2694 (3), 2729 (1), 2879 (13), 2905 (4)
Koenig, L. J.: ref, 272 (82), 681 (16), 2305 (142)
Koepke, L.: ref, 2034 (6)
Koeppe, R. A.: ref, 1164 (154), 2603 (438), 2860 (1040,1287)
Koeppl, D. M.: ref, 1697 (37), 2860 (110)
Koerner, K.: ref, 272 (184)
Koeske, G. F.: ref, 1181 (11,15), 1590 (23,36,49), 2603 (54)
Koeske, R. D.: ref, 1181 (11,15), 1590 (23,36), 2603 (54)
Koester, L. S.: ref, 811 (8)
Koestner, R.: ref, 68 (54,56), 298 (66), 373 (33), 790 (12,24), 863 (59,60), 1414 (2), 1745 (62), 1965 (27), 2078 (4), 2218 (65), 2246 (9), 2749 (21)
Koeter, M. W. J.: ref, 1079 (68), 2050 (15,21,22), 2603 (145)
Koff, E.: ref, 893 (23), 2380 (8)
Koffler, S. L.: rev, 469, 2054, 2769
Kofoed, L.: ref, 846 (22), 1697 (551)
Kogan, H.: ref, 2497 (231)
Kogan, K. L.: rev, 1714, 2863
Kogan, W. S.: rev, 1714
Kohanski, R.: ref, 2218 (35)
Kohl, R.: ref, 745 (17)
Kohlberg, K.: rev, 674
Kohlberg, L.: test, 1408, 1625
Kohler, M.: ref, 1698 (24)
Kohler, M. P.: ref, 2813 (63)
Kohler, S.: ref, 376 (31), 776 (60), 2863 (423)
Kohn, R.: ref, 1218 (16), 2599 (35), 2863 (317)
Kohn, S. E.: ref, 2873 (55)
Kohs, S. C.: test, 1410
Koike, T.: ref, 2862 (498)
Koivisto, A.: ref, 472 (231)
Koivisto, K.: ref, 1164 (152), 2516 (99), 2860 (913), 2863 (273), 2892 (274)
Koivisto, M.: ref, 2860 (1113)
Kojima, T.: ref, 2288 (23), 2305 (69), 2860 (365)
Kokkevi, A.: ref, 999 (5)
Kokmen, E.: ref, 2226 (25), 2860 (718,1283), 2863 (103,214,387), 2879 (88)
Kokubun, M.: ref, 2862 (359,498,638)
Kolar, D. C.: ref, 2218 (30)
Kolar, D. W.: ref, 373 (38)
Kolassa, J.: ref, 2247 (120)
Kolb, D. A.: test, 64, 1467, 1469, 1471
Kolb, L. C.: ref, 1697 (23), 2497 (19)
Kolbe, K.: test, 1411
Kolbe, R. H.: ref, 298 (84)
Kolen, M. J.: ref, 56 (15)
Kolitch, E. R.: ref, 93 (1), 615 (36)
Kolke, T.: ref, 2862 (638)
Kolko, D.: ref, 272 (259)
Kolko, D. J.: ref, 448 (23), 1010 (103), 2603 (193), 2862 (134)
Koller, H.: ref, 2485 (58)
Koller, J. R.: ref, 2417 (34)
Koller, M.: ref, 389 (11)
Koller, W. C.: ref, 271 (15), 272 (330), 376 (28), 776 (53,56), 1135 (24), 1218 (19), 1378 (10), 1740 (26), 1758 (95), 2076 (181), 2516 (112), 2860 (1326), 2863 (411), 2892 (247,293)
Kolloff, P. B.: ref, 1991 (9)
Kolodny, R.: ref, 1092 (5), 2860 (331)
Kolson, D. L.: ref, 231 (1), 303 (32), 2226 (42), 2227 (61), 2599 (43), 2863 (431), 2892 (307)
Kolt, G. S.: ref, 2077 (8), 2858 (101)
Kolvin, I.: ref, 1367 (5)
Kombos, N. A.: ref, 1164 (7)
Kominowski, R.: test, 201
Komiya, K.: ref, 2860 (1278)
Kommana, S.: ref, 1590 (58)
Kommerell, G.: ref, 2603 (495)
Komo, S.: ref, 2860 (984)
Komori, H.: ref, 2862 (360)
Komproe, I. H.: ref, 2603 (153)
Komulainen, E. J.: ref, 1079 (76), 2603 (493)
Kondel, T. K.: ref, 1758 (103), 2860 (1399)
Kondrick, P. A.: ref, 1131 (18), 2485 (241), 2905 (119)
Konefal, J.: ref, 2497 (179)
König, A.: ref, 1166 (144)
Konold, T. R.: test, 2510; ref, 2862 (618)
Konopak, B. C.: ref, 724 (5)
Konstadt, N.: test, 474
Konstantareas, M. M.: ref, 694 (101), 1485 (10), 1903 (575), 2862 (361)
Kontos, S.: ref, 665 (7), 693 (1), 1659 (3)
Kooiman, C. G.: ref, 2603 (500)
Koontz, K.: ref, 472 (60,182), 2242 (7), 2862 (525)
Koopman, C.: ref, 2076 (144), 2603 (397)
Koopman, P. L.: ref, 1736 (5)
Koopmans, I. H.: ref, 1745 (16)
Koopmans, M.: ref, 1000 (30)
Koot, H. M.: ref, 373 (43), 451 (206,276,289), 2862 (648)
Kopelman, M. D.: ref, 1390 (1,4), 1697 (311), 1758 (3,15,26,90), 2193 (1,24,25), 2239 (3), 2860 (111,667,668,1297), 2863 (197,198,391)
Koplewiez, H. S.: ref, 2862 (432), 2879 (151)
Kopp, S.: ref, 2862 (617)
Kopper, B. A.: ref, 271 (12,13), 272 (305), 298 (50,154), 337 (153,181), 1290 (4), 1698 (13,25), 2497 (565, 648), 2559 (13)
Koppitz, E. M.: test, 2816
Kopriva, R. J.: rev, 2726
Kopta, S. M.: ref, 451 (191), 2603 (274)
Korabik, K.: ref, 298 (122), 2149 (2)
Koran, L.: ref, 1166 (162), 2603 (503)
Koran, L. J.: ref, 389 (3)
Koreen, A.: ref, 2288 (45,64), 2305 (70,123,170)

Koreen, A. R.: ref, 2288 (35), 2289 (26), 2305 (107)
Koretzky, M. B.: ref, 1697 (83)
Korfine, L.: ref, 298 (145), 1697 (317), 1965 (56,65), 2497 (365), 2892 (127)
Korhonen, T. T.: ref, 1903 (186), 2860 (914)
Koritnik, D. R.: ref, 68 (8)
Korkman, M.: test, 1771; ref, 1725 (4), 2768 (25), 2862 (268,269,499), 2879 (80)
Korman, A. K.: rev, 1441, 1546, 1561, 2547, 2548
Korman, R.: ref, 2749 (39)
Korn, W. S.: test, 692
Korner, A. F.: ref, 1770 (3)
Kornfield, A. D.: ref, 1313 (2), 1697 (424)
Kornhaber, A.: ref, 1991 (64)
Kornhaber, C.: ref, 1991 (64)
Kornreich, C.: ref, 1166 (194)
Korol, M.: ref, 2108 (2), 2603 (47)
Koroshetz, W. J.: ref, 1164 (33), 2603 (140), 2860 (344), 2863 (92), 2892 (49)
Korten, A.: ref, 2050 (84)
Korten, A. E.: ref, 999 (56,89),90), 1758 (44), 2239 (19), 2599 (15), 2860 (587), 2863 (175)
Korten, A. G.: ref, 999 (114), 2239 (22), 2860 (823), 2863 (238)
Kos, S. C.: ref, 1164 (136), 1758 (79), 2860 (1183), 2863 (356)
Koschier, M.: test, 404
Koscinski, S. T.: ref, 2862 (212)
Kose, G.: ref, 2497 (553), 2901 (24)
Kosier, J. T.: ref, 1166 (117,118)
Kosier, T.: ref, 2305 (18)
Kosinski, F. A., Jr.: ref, 2756 (2)
Koskenvuo, M.: ref, 998 (84)
Koski, L. R.: ref, 2218 (73)
Koskinen, P.: ref, 1234 (2)
Koskinen, P. S.: ref, 2029 (2)
Kosloski, K.: ref, 1808 (3)
Koslow, S. H.: ref, 2305 (95), 2603 (220)
Koslowsky, M.: ref, 2603 (146)
Kosmo, S.: test, 935
Kosmoski, G. J.: ref, 665 (22)
Koss, M. P.: ref, 337 (105)
Kossak-Fuller, J.: ref, 451 (19)
Kosslyn, S. M.: ref, 2516 (69), 2892 (191)
Kosson, D. S.: ref, 2402 (65), 2860 (1114)
Kostanski, M.: ref, 893 (54), 2214 (136), 2230 (19)
Kostelny, K.: ref, 451 (119)
Kosten, T. R.: ref, 1775 (3), 2519 (29), 2520 (30), 2860 (1220)
Kostianovsky, D. J.: ref, 2288 (65), 2289 (49)
Kostis, J. B.: ref, 2076 (98)
Kotagal, P.: ref, 1902 (69), 2768 (28), 2862 (325), 2879 (110)
Kotchick, B. A.: ref, 272 (354), 337 (190), 451 (227), 472 (218,222), 2211 (52), 2214 (127)
Kotik-Harper, D.: ref, 337 (11), 1164 (18), 1697 (74), 2860 (185), 2863 (49)
Kotler, M.: ref, 2603 (434)
Kotler, T.: ref, 2603 (275), 2858 (71)
Koton, J.: ref, 2305 (50)
Kotrla, K. J.: ref, 2288 (50)
Kotsopoulos, S.: ref, 472 (90), 2211 (30), 2214 (50)
Kotzé, H. F.: ref, 1321 (5)
Kouros, C.: ref, 560 (2)
Koussos, L.: ref, 56 (17), 615 (55)
Kouzekanani, K.: ref, 1987 (2), 2211 (8), 2488 (4), 2901 (35)
Kouzes, J. M.: test, 1445, 1446, 1448, 2635; ref, 1447 (1)
Kouzetsova, L.: ref, 1965 (77), 2218 (71)
Kovacs, M: test, 472; ref, 2860 (669)
Kovaleski, M. E.: ref, 2860 (165)
Kovasznay, B.: ref, 2102 (1), 2288 (16), 2289 (11), 2860 (335), 2863 (88)
Kovenock, J.: ref, 1903 (433), 2163 (248)
Koverola, C.: ref, 472 (52)
Kovner, R.: ref, 2860 (607)
Kowalchuk, B.: test, 1311
Kowall, M. A.: ref, 2704 (1), 2862 (109)
Kowalski, R.: ref, 448 (24)
Kowalski, R. M.: ref, 68 (7)
Kowatch, R. A.: ref, 473 (5), 2076 (5), 2305 (192), 2497 (43)
Kowner, R.: ref, 2417 (26)
Koyama, T.: ref, 1166 (60)
Koyama, Y.: ref, 2860 (1416)
Kozachuk, W.: ref, 1241 (4)
Kozak, M. J.: ref, 2497 (348)
Kozak, V. J.: test, 1126, 2620, 2623
Kozarevich, M.: ref, 241 (3), 430 (10), 994 (19), 1095 (30), 1903 (314), 2190 (3), 2695 (30)
Kozberg, S. F.: ref, 2484 (7)
Koziol, S. M., Jr.: rev, 2740
Kozma, E. J.: rev, 906, 1563
Kozuch, P.: ref, 1010 (79)
Kraaimaat, F. W.: ref, 2497 (620)
Kraemer, B. D.: ref, 1341 (3)
Kraemer, H. C.: ref, 1079 (16), 1216 (25)
Kraemer, S.: ref, 2860 (974)f, 2863 (286)
Kraft, D.: ref, 863 (46)
Kraft, J.: ref, 335 (6), 999 (63), 2892 (89)
Kraft, R. H.: ref, 2862 (2,20,89), 2879 (19)
Kragh-Sørensen, P.: ref, 1166 (172)
Krahé, B.: ref, 298 (16)
Krain, A. L.: ref, 451 (102,243), 2862 (450,702), 2879 (227)
Kraiuhin, C.: ref, 272 (88)
Kraker, M. J.: ref, 1902 (44), 1903 (187)
Krakow, B.: ref, 2603 (194)
Kral, M. J.: ref, 142 (6), 1619 (8), 2858 (40), 2862 (420)
Krall, V.: ref, 1226 (1), 2247 (90)
Krall, V. K.: ref, 2247 (45), 2380 (9), 2749 (34), 2862 (224)
Kramarski, B.: ref, 2010 (11), 2163 (330), 2771 (24)

Kramer, A. F.: ref, 1380 (14), 2860 (670), 2860 (763), 2892 (124)
Kramer, B. J.: ref, 1643 (1,2)
Kramer, D.: ref, 1079 (93)
Kramer, J. H.: test, 375, 376
Kramer, J. J.: ref, 2497 (336)
Kramer, K.: ref, 1405 (2)
Kramer, L.: ref, 451 (61)
Kramer, S. I.: ref, 846 (8)
Kramer, T. A.: ref, 272 (189), 2603 (269,270,473)
Kramer, T. L.: ref, 2108 (5)
Krampen, G.: ref, 298 (67)
Krane, A.: ref, 1619 (6)
Krangler, J. H.: ref, 2862 (639)
Krantz, D. H.: ref, 592 (17)
Krantz, D. S.: test, 1412
Krantz, P. J.: ref, 1903 (307)
Kranzler, H. R.: ref, 135 (1,2), 372 (69,83,117), 846 (26), 1661 (38), 1697 (389,491), 2218 (135), 2433 (4), 2497 (357)
Kranzler, J.: ref, 2163 (232)
Kranzler, J. H.: rev, 2144, 2215; ref, 592 (62), 2163 (169)
Krasney, N.: ref, 372 (23), 571 (2), 615 (17), 2591 (2)
Krasney, N. S.: ref, 372 (10), 571 (1), 604 (1), 615 (5)
Krassowski, E.: ref, 2862 (640), 2864 (138)
Krasucki, C.: ref, 1758 (45)
Kraswegor, J.: ref, 2498 (67)
Kratochwill, T. R.: rev, 286, 465
Krau, E.: ref, 2282 (2)
Kräuchi, K.: ref, 1166 (165)
Kraus, I.: ref, 1010 (70), 1092 (5,13), 2305 (121,165), 2860 (331), 2862 (310), 2879 (102)
Krause, J. S.: ref, 2218 (128)
Krause, R.: ref, 1001 (2,3,7)
Krauskopf, C. J.: rev, 316, 1790, 2830, 2831
Krauss, G. L.: ref, 2226 (27), 2863 (392)
Krauss, M. W.: ref, 1000 (51)
Krauss, S.: ref, 2305 (31)
Krausz, Y.: ref, 1166 (92)
Krauthamer, C. M.: rev, 899, 1797
Kravitz, H. M.: ref, 793 (19), 1697 (299,488), 1744 (5)
Krawchick, F. B.: test, 2787
Krawiecki, N.: ref, 1010 (72), 2485 (163), 2813 (86), 2879 (106)
Krawiecki, N. S.: ref, 815 (11), 1379 (31), 1612 (39), 1903 (201), 2125 (9), 2485 (101), 2813 (43), 2901 (32)
Kraybill, E. N.: ref, 815 (51), 1740 (30), 1889 (18), 2724 (12), 2862 (711)
Krebs, D. L.: ref, 1408 (3)
Krebs, P.: ref, 2862 (78)
Kreeger, J. L.: ref, 1096 (10)
Kreimeyer, K. H.: ref, 2813 (55)
Kreiner, D. S.: ref, 1767 (8)
Kreipe, R. E.: ref, 893 (37), 1745 (50)
Kreitler, H.: ref, 1657 (18), 2860 (915)
Kreitler, S.: ref, 1657 (18), 1745 (28), 2860 (915)
Krekewich, K.: ref, 353 (21), 815 (38), 1240 (45), 1379 (86), 1485 (58), 1653 (28), 2813 (144), 2862 (491), 2864 (116), 2879 (165)
Kremen, A. M.: ref, 373 (34,39), 2860 (1044)
Kremen, W. S.: ref, 1093 (84), 1164 (68), 1218 (7), 1645 (3), 1697 (408), 1965 (66), 2516 (42,65), 2860 (671,855), 2863 (199,250), 2879 (81), 2892 (125,176)
Kremer, J. F.: ref, 1115 (2)
Kremor, B.: ref, 301 (47), 2516 (63), 2863 (233), 2879 (105), 2892 (166)
Krentzel, C. P.: ref, 1216 (10)
Kresanov, K.: ref, 472 (227)
Kresch, L. E.: ref, 2860 (932)
Kresheck, J. D.: test, 2466, 2523, 2524
Kress, R. A.: rev, 348, 1383, 2219
Kretschmer, R. E.: ref, 2163 (12), 2862 (19)
Kretz, L.: ref, 272 (338), 1687 (37)
Kreutzer, J. S.: ref, 1697 (552)
Kreuzer, J. A.: ref, 1096 (9), 2668 (1), 2694 (14), 2860 (912)
Krichev, A.: rev, 1362, 1612, 1725
Kriedt, P. H.: rev, 738, 2408
Kriege, G.: ref, 472 (38)
Krieger, J.: ref, 372 (38), 926 (8), 1697 (181), 2247 (24)
Krier, M.: ref, 472 (82), 2214 (41)
Krieshok, T. S.: ref, 1825 (1)
Krifcher, B.: ref, 1092 (5), 2860 (331)
Krikler, R.: ref, 472 (91), 681 (52), 863 (53), 1010 (63), 2498 (37), 2862 (272)
Krikorian, R.: ref, 681 (49), 1903 (276,471), 2010 (14)
Kring, A. M.: ref, 1000 (52,60), 2288 (33), 2305 (92,183), 2863 (164), 2892 (102)
Krishnamurthy, R.: ref, 1697 (425), 1698 (9)
Krishnan, B.: ref, 1661 (57)
Krishnan, K. R. R.: ref, 2603 (198)
Kriska, S. D.: rev, 990, 1080
Kristjansson, E.: ref, 2860 (1003), 2863 (298)
Kristoff, B.: ref, 459 (8), 1903 (54,81), 2485 (36,37)
Kritis, K. J.: ref, 83 (3)
Krivit, W.: ref, 2860 (752), 2862 (291)
Krobath, H.: ref, 2862 (78)
Kroc, R.: ref, 615 (16), 1455 (2)
Kroeger, D. W.: ref, 694 (102)
Kroeze, S.: ref, 272 (193), 2497 (566)
Kroger, J.: ref, 893 (10), 1685 (1)
Krogh, V.: ref, 2603 (517)
Krogh, Y.: ref, 2247 (26)
Kroll, J. F.: ref, 298 (7)
Kroll, L.: ref, 1093 (109)
Kroll, L. S.: ref, 1698 (20), 2879 (223)
Kroll, N. E. A.: ref, 2860 (1385), 2863 (417)
Kromrey, J. D.: ref, 56 (6), 550 (5), 592 (51), 665 (49), 1532 (1)
Kronenberger, W. G.: ref, 863 (28), 1010 (37), 2603 (147)
Kronholm, E.: ref, 272 (45), 303 (3), 998 (32), 2860 (263), 2863 (68)

Kropp, P. R.: test, 2395, 2476
Krotz, D.: test, 201
Krout, M. H.: test, 1940
Krueger, J.: ref, 1697 (536)
Krueger, M. T.: ref, 2497 (57)
Krueger, R. F.: ref, 451 (133)
Kruesi, M. J. P.: ref, 1010 (49), 2860 (366)
Krug, D.: rev, 269, 887; ref, 1697 (65)
Krug, D. A.: test, 234
Krug, S.: test, 538, 990
Krug, S. E.: test, 86, 719, 1321, 1322, 1323, 1805, 2318
Kruger, G.: ref, 2288 (6), 2289 (4)
Kruglanski, A. W.: ref, 998 (31), 2146 (17)
Krugman, M.: rev, 1160, 1716, 2247, 2485
Krulighan, D. M., Jr.: ref, 337 (183)
Krull, A.: ref, 1164 (100), 2860 (908), 2892 (190)
Krumboltz, J. D.: test, 401; rev, 1985; ref, 399 (3)
Krupnick, J. L.: ref, 272 (194)
Krupp, A.: ref, 2603 (395)
Krupp, L. B.: ref, 2163 (119), 2516 (26), 2599 (14), 2860 (479), 2863 (133), 2879 (60)
Kruppa, E.: ref, 2195 (1)
Krusch, D. A.: ref, 1902 (88), 2862 (500)
Kruskemper, G. M.: ref, 1697 (312), 2497 (358), 2603 (276)
Krutsch, A. J.: ref, 1903 (390)
Kryger, M. H.: ref, 2497 (284,518)
Kryscio, R. J.: ref, 2039 (4)
Krystal, J. H.: ref, 372 (69), 1166 (123), 2704 (19), 2860 (646), 2892 (126)
Krzanowski, W. J.: ref, 644 (7)
Krzystofiak, F. J.: ref, 1755 (5)
Kubeck, J.: test, 2785
Kubinski, J. A.: ref, 272 (235)
Kubitz, K. A.: ref, 2497 (260)
Kubo, S. H.: ref, 1697 (567), 1740 (25), 2226 (33), 2860 (1339)
Kubota, M. Y.: ref, 117 (3)
Kubu, C. S.: ref, 2860 (1123)
Kucera, E.: ref, 337 (162), 863 (82)
Kucera, G. D.: ref, 998 (53)
Kuch, K.: ref, 272 (78), 1166 (42), 2199 (7), 2603 (233,234,288,371)
Kuchemann, D.: test, 444; rev, 1863
Kucherlapati, R.: ref, 2050 (94)
Kuchuk, A.: ref, 815 (43), 2862 (613)
Kuck, J.: ref, 335 (9), 1093 (24), 1164 (25,84,100), 2288 (42,61), 2289 (32,47), 2860 (239,643,908), 2892 (120,190)
Kuczkowski, R.: ref, 1735 (5)
Kuczynski, L.: ref, 2076 (27), 2305 (55)
Kuder, J.: rev, 553
Kudler, H.: ref, 998 (19), 2305 (30)
Kudler, H. S.: ref, 1697 (530)
Kuehn, P.: rev, 1506, 1826
Kuehn, P. A.: ref, 2729 (3)
Kufeldt, K.: ref, 1008 (2)
Kufera, J.: ref, 375 (7), 2862 (705)
Kufera, J. A.: ref, 375 (3), 2862 (506)
Kugelmass, S.: ref, 301 (16), 2860 (241)
Kugelmass, S. C.: ref, 2305 (80)
Kugler, J.: ref, 1697 (312), 2497 (358), 2603 (276)
Kuh, G. D.: ref, 620 (2,5,6)
Kuhl, K. P.: ref, 2863 (229)
Kuhlenschmidt, S.: rev, 40, 2096
Kuhn, C.: ref, 2498 (67)
Kuhn, M. R.: ref, 2181 (2)
Kühner, C.: ref, 301 (57)
Kuhns, J. W.: test, 1774
Kuhs, H.: ref, 1166 (121)
Kuiken, D.: ref, 999 (146) 2126 (1)
Kuiper, M.: ref, 451 (100), 681 (73)
Kuiper, N. A.: ref, 2858 (52)
Kuipers, L.: ref, 1758 (24), 2050 (71), 2860 (624)
Kukull, W. A.: ref, 776 (27,58)
Kula, M. L.: ref, 272 (264), 1697 (533), 2247 (113)
Kulberg, J. M.: ref, 1866 (28)
Kulhanek, F.: ref, 2288 (6), 2289 (4)
Kulhavy, R. W.: ref, 2417 (18)
Kulick-Bell, R.: ref, 2603 (380)
Kulieke, M. J.: ref, 372 (10,23), 571 (1,2), 604 (1), 615 (5,17), 2369 (1), 2591 (2)
Kulig, B. M.: ref, 2599 (22)
Kulik, J. A.: ref, 1590 (51), 2497 (37,628)
Kulikowich, J. M.: ref, 2163 (55)
Kulka, R. A.: ref, 1697 (325)
Kulkarni, R.: ref, 472 (60)
Kuller, L. H.: ref, 2497 (459)
Kumagai, K.: ref, 1166 (212)
Kumar, C.: ref, 999 (162)
Kumar, G.: ref, 2603 (409)
Kumar, M.: ref, 2076 (177)
Kumar, M. A.: ref, 2603 (516)
Kumar, R.: ref, 451 (77), 999 (41), 1612 (71,80), 2305 (188,241), 2860 (976)
Kumar, R. C.: ref, 270 (46)
Kumar, S.: ref, 2860 (1045), 2862 (445)
Kumari, N.: ref, 272 (54), 2497 (180)
Kumari, V.: ref, 998 (117), 2163 (281,350), 2497 (567)
Kummer, A. W.: ref, 2651 (19)
Kumpulainew, K.: ref, 472 (227)
Kumpulsinen, K.: ref, 472 (231)
Kumra, S.: ref, 2288 (71), 2289 (56), 2305 (232), 2862 (501)
Kunce, J. T.: test, 1954; ref, 1755 (10), 2076 (170), 2417 (34)
Kundert, D. K.: rev, 869, 1131, 1139; ref, 324 (5), 665 (52,79), 1085 (1), 1903 (196), 2488 (5)
Kundu, R.: test, 1415, 1416
Kunik, M. E.: ref, 1166 (221)
Kunin, J. M.: ref, 1135 (4), 2862 (120)
Kunnan, A. J.: rev, 481, 482
Kunze, K. R.: test, 9, 10, 533, 1312, 1632
Kuper, K.: ref, 451 (153), 651 (2), 2862 (551)

Kuperis, S.: ref, 2668 (3)
Kupersmidt, J. B.: ref, 171 (2), 2700 (1)
Kupfer, D.: ref, 337 (156)
Kupfer, D. J.: ref, 272 (307), 337 (72), 793 (14), 824 (1), 1093 (30,63,78,79,99,113), 1166 (15,104,182,204,215), 2305 (23,39,173), 2603 (39,393)
Kupperbusch, C.: ref, 2246 (14)
Kupst, M. J.: ref, 337 (103), 372 (94), 1706 (3), 2858 (102)
Kurdek, L. A.: ref, 1010 (5), 1181 (6,16), 1582 (10), 2603 (23,55,56)
Kurian, M.: ref, 2417 (18)
Kurisaki, H.: ref, 2860 (396), 2873 (10)
Kurit, D. M.: ref, 863 (58), 2497 (421), 2603 (330)
Kurland, L. T.: ref, 1612 (73), 2485 (170), 2860 (910), 2862 (356), 2864 (95)
Kurthen, M.: ref, 2860 (1274)
Kurtines, W. M.: ref, 1010 (15), 1991 (4)
Kurtz, A. K.: rev, 2919
Kurtz, L.: ref, 695 (1), 1010 (62)
Kurtz-Costes, B.: ref, 1659 (12), 2864 (133)
Kurtzberg, D.: ref, 1096 (9), 2668 (1), 2694 (14), 2860 (912)
Kurusu, T. A.: ref, 717 (2), 863 (92)
Kurweit, N. L.: ref, 2695 (5)
Kurz, A.: ref, 301 (13), 1525 (23), 2860 (193,1115)
Kusché, C. A.: ref, 301 (31), 472 (53), 1164 (49), 1612 (37), 2516 (27), 2816 (1)
Kush, J. C.: ref, 474 (6), 2163 (282), 2862 (296,618,689,690)
Kushner, H.: ref, 1902 (15), 1903 (43), 2863 (40)
Kushner, M.: ref, 337 (7), 2519 (7), 2520 (7)
Kushner, M. G.: ref, 272 (195), 2497 (568)
Kuslansky, G.: ref, 2860 (1235), 2863 (369)
Kusnerik, L.: ref, 375 (3), 2862 (506)
Kussmaul, C.: ref, 1164 (174), 1903 (566), 2163 (348), 2731 (7), 2860 (1377), 2863 (413), 2879 (224), 2892 (295)
Kussmaul, C. L.: ref, 2860 (1105), 2879 (166)
Kutcher, G.: ref, 1745 (48)
Kutner, S. J.: ref, 2516 (9)
Kutsick, K.: rev, 1531, 1884
Kuttschreuter, M.: ref, 1697 (198)
Kuyken, W.: ref, 272 (55), 2858 (72)
Kuzak, E.: test, 784
Kuzis, G.: ref, 303 (31), 1166 (229), 1740 (35), 2163 (356), 2860 (1419), 2892 (306)
Kuznetsov, O.: ref, 2076 (101)
Kwan, E.: ref, 2860 (658), 2863 (193)
Kwan, P. C.: ref, 2163 (159), 2863 (181), 2873 (22)
Kwapil, T. R.: ref, 1093 (114), 2305 (184)
Kwiatkowski, C. F.: ref, 134 (25)
Kwiatkowski, J.: ref, 1095 (28), 1394 (8), 1903 (310,311), 1982 (9,10,11)
Kwok, D. C.: ref, 451 (134)
Kwon, J. S.: ref, 1166 (122)
Kwon, L. M.: ref, 1164 (157), 2860 (1298)
Kwon, Y-H.: ref, 298 (159)
Kyllo, L. B.: ref, 2076 (127)
Kyllonen, P. C.: ref, 180 (12), 1156 (3)
Kynette, D.: ref, 2860 (291,383)
Kypri, K.: ref, 2358 (12)

Laá, V.: ref, 270 (10), 1653 (23)
Laakso, M.: ref, 1903 (281), 2860 (913), 2862 (275), 2863 (273)
Laakso, M. L.: ref, 1903 (206), 2163 (129), 2247 (43), 2768 (18)
Laakso, M. P.: ref, 1164 (152), 2516 (99), 2892 (274)
Laaksonen, T.: ref, 998 (13)
Laasi, N.: ref, 1697 (68), 2050 (5)
Laatsch, L.: test, 667
Labbé, E. E.: ref, 472 (54), 2498 (22), 2862 (213)
Labbé, F. E.: ref, 1026 (1), 2497 (72)
Label, R.: test, 1666
Laberg, J. C.: ref, 652 (1)
Laberge, B.: ref, 272 (375), 2498 (77), 2519 (37), 2520 (38)
Labouvie-Vief, G.: ref, 372 (99), 2858 (4)
Labovitz, S. S.: ref, 1164 (85)
Labrecque, M. S.: ref, 272 (56), 2497 (181)
Labreque, M. S.: ref, 337 (6)
Labreque, R.: ref, 2225 (20), 2860 (1410), 2863 (429)
LaCasse, L.: ref, 2163 (221), 2860 (868)
Lacefield, P.: ref, 2603 (249)
Lacerenza, L.: ref, 1092 (18), 2712 (1), 2879 (171), 2905 (98)
Lachar, B.: rev, 1694, 2637
Lachar, B. L.: rev, 2511, 2745
Lachar, D.: test, 1962, 1963; rev, 855, 1650; ref, 1697 (465), 1962 (15,18), 2813 (71)
Lacharité, C.: ref, 458 (2)
Lachiewicz, A.: ref, 2813 (116)
Lachiewicz, A. M.: ref, 4 (2), 681 (50)
Lachman, M.: ref, 2749 (57)
Lachman, M. E.: ref, 1405 (4), 2163 (63)
Lackey, J. E.: test, 1063
Lackey, K. L.: ref, 2485 (76)
Lackovic-Grgin: ref, 694 (75)
Lacks, P.: ref, 1697 (6,38)
Lacro, J. P.: ref, 1135 (9), 1164 (48), 2288 (28), 2289 (19), 2860 (474)
Lacroix, D.: ref, 2704 (47), 2879 (236), 2905 (123)
Lacy, M. A.: ref, 2863 (365)
Ladd, G. W.: ref, 1659 (7,8,11,13), 1903 (200)
Ladd, J.: ref, 1745 (48)
Ladd, J. S.: ref, 1697 (313,492)
Laden, B.: ref, 180 (26)
Laden, J.: ref, 2282 (9), 2527 (5)
Ladish, C.: ref, 2860 (112)
Ladouceur, R.: ref, 2065 (16)
Laegreid, L.: ref, 1134 (3)
Laesch, K. B.: ref, 1421 (1)

Lafayette Instrument: test, 1696
Lafferty, J. C.: test, 1150, 1498, 1862, 2633
Laflamme, J. G.: ref, 2031 (11)
Lafleche, G.: ref, 2860 (1180)
Laforce, R., Jr.: ref, 2125 (25), 2860 (1256)
La Forge, R.: test, 1291
Lafreniere, K.: ref, 1079 (91)
LaFreniere, P. J.: test, 2446
Lafuse, W. P.: ref, 337 (10)
LaGasse, L.: ref, 1770 (16)
Lagos, C. J.: test, 301
LaGrange, L.: ref, 999 (127)
LaGrange, M. R.: ref, 2860 (755), 2863 (221)
LaGreca, A. M.: ref, 1010 (80), 2214 (80)
Laguna, J.: ref, 2873 (7)
Lah, M. I.: test, 2258
Lahey, B. B.: test, 651; ref, 246 (2), 1903 (533), 2862 (131,348)
Lahey, M.: ref, 540 (6,8), 1131 (16), 1240 (34,47), 1380 (7,13,15), 1804 (12,14), 1903 (169,377,460, 472), 2695 (40,49,54), 2704 (29,37,40), 2725 (3, 7)
Lahey, R.: test, 1090
Lahmeyer, H. W.: ref, 824 (1), 2305 (23)
Lahti, I.: ref, 2247 (120), 2288 (2), 2860 (53)
Lai, J.: ref, 2497 (261)
Lai, P.: ref, 1466 (4)
Laiacona, M.: ref, 2163 (58,108,120,261), 2225 (11)
Laikin, M.: ref, 2326 (2)
Lainhart, J.: ref, 1485 (33), 1653 (17), 2860 (721), 2862 (283)
Laird, E.: ref, 1300 (11)
Laird, J. T.: test, 1699
Lakein, D. A.: ref, 2402 (66)
Lakey, B.: ref, 790 (13), 2497 (38), 2497 (359,430)
Lakin, K. C.: ref, 1300 (1,3)
Läksy, K.: ref, 2247 (120)
Lall, R.: ref, 694 (116)
Lally, T.: ref, 2497 (117)
LaLone, L.: ref, 1697 (595)
LaLuz, E. J.: ref, 451 (84), 863 (73)
Lam, C. S.: ref, 1701 (1)
Lam, R. W.: ref, 1166 (123)
Lam, S. S. K.: ref, 1469 (12)
Lamacz, M.: ref, 2050 (94)
Lamal, P. A.: ref, 998 (16)
La Marche, J. A.: ref, 2402 (46), 2860 (986)
Lamb, D. G.: ref, 1697 (386)
Lamb, J.: ref, 1599 (2)
Lamb, M. E.: ref, 365 (8), 472 (32), 1216 (71)
Lamb, M. M.: rev, 374
Lamb, R. J.: ref, 272 (182), 273 (21)
Lamb, S. J.: ref, 2862 (441)
Lambe, E. K.: ref, 272 (284)
Lambert, E. W.: ref, 451 (244,269)
Lambert, J.: ref, 2863 (45)
Lambert, L.: ref, 2603 (194)
Lambert, L. D.: ref, 1140 (38)
Lambert, M. C.: ref, 451 (135)
Lambert, M. E.: rev, 1062
Lambert, M. J.: ref, 1697 (339), 1939 (14), 2497 (362), 2603 (388)
Lambert, M. T.: ref, 2860 (190)
Lambert, N.: test, 1, 2, 469
Lambert, N. M.: test, 2122; rev, 63, 1010; ref, 469 (3)
Lambert, W.: ref, 451 (270)
Lambert, W. E.: ref, 1903 (6)
Lamberti, G.: test, 767
Lamberti, J. J.: ref, 2497 (437), 2498 (50)
Lamberti, J. W.: ref, 337 (7), 2519 (7), 2520 (7)
Lamberts, R. D.: ref, 2858 (126)
Lamberty, G. J.: ref, 1166 (203), 2516 (107), 2860 (1327)
Lambiotte, J. G.: ref, 372 (4), 998 (7), 1140 (4)
Lamborn, S. D.: ref, 2860 (672)
Lamdin, D. J.: ref, 364 (20)
Lamke, T. A.: test, 1196
Lamm, O.: ref, 2860 (367), 2862 (167,270)
Lamminmäki, T.: ref, 815 (45), 2862 (641), 2901 (122)
Lamnin, A.: ref, 1687 (8)
Lamon, M.: ref, 2749 (8)
LaMonica, E. L.: test, 1417
LaMontagne, L. L.: ref, 2497 (569)
Lamparelli, M.: ref, 1612 (59)
Lamparski, D.: ref, 999 (31), 1592 (9), 1697 (135)
Lampman, L.: ref, 273 (14), 337 (108)
Lampropoulou, V.: ref, 694 (101), 2862 (361)
Lan, W.: ref, 2862 (603), 2901 (115)
Lan, W. Y.: ref, 1318 (6)
Lancaster, C.: ref, 1338 (45), 2839 (6)
Lancaster, S. J.: ref, 1965 (55), 2899 (6)
Lance, C. E.: ref, 1701 (10)
Lance, D. M.: ref, 1903 (537), 2905 (112)
Lancee, W.: ref, 241 (4), 451 (94), 815 (35), 1903 (447), 2695 (47), 2864 (110)
Lancioni, G. E.: ref, 2813 (96,121,122)
Land, V. C.: test, 954
Landa, R.: ref, 1485 (33), 1653 (17), 2860 (721), 2862 (283)
Landau, S.: ref, 681 (22)
Lande, B.: ref, 2497 (252)
Lander, J.: ref, 2497 (113), 2498 (8)
Lander, S.: ref, 2305 (124), 2858 (40)
Landerl, K.: ref, 349 (36)
Landers, A.: ref, 540 (16), 655 (1), 1095 (44)
Landers, D. M.: ref, 2076 (127), 2497 (260)
Landi, F.: ref, 2163 (328), 2860 (1281)
Landis, D.: ref, 1093 (7)
Landis, E. E.: ref, 1697 (391), 2860 (808)
Landis, R.: ref, 1661 (35,75), 2603 (317,556)
Landis, T.: ref, 2193 (5), 2860 (161)
Landman, J.: test, 1370
Landman, J. T.: test, 2734
Landon-Jimenez, D.: ref, 459 (17), 2813 (33)

Landre, N. A.: ref, 2008 (10), 2163 (220), 2288 (51), 2289 (40), 2305 (143)
Landreth, G. L.: ref, 1363 (1), 1889 (10)
Landrine, H.: ref, 298 (65), 708 (5)
Landro, N. I.: ref, 1093 (54), 2519 (32), 2520 (33)
Landrum, R. E.: ref, 998 (46), 1755 (19)
Landrus, R.: test, 70
Landry, J. C.: ref, 2218 (83)
Landry, R.: ref, 1653 (14), 1903 (237)
Landry, S. H.: ref, 270 (26,35), 815 (20), 1612 (65,68,95), 2382 (2,35), 2704 (10), 2813 (88,130,146), 2862 (317)
Landsbergis, P. A.: ref, 1338 (30), 2497 (182)
Landsman, I. S.: ref, 337 (14), 1925 (1)
Landsverk, J.: ref, 451 (280), 2813 (156)
Landsverk, J. L.: ref, 451 (120)
Landy, F. J.: rev, 676
Landy, S.: ref, 451 (271), 1012 (2)
Lane, B.: test, 686
Lane, H. S.: test, 488
Lane, I. M.: ref, 1348 (5), 1701 (19)
Lane, J. O.: ref, 2497 (15)
Lane, K. L.: ref, 2 (2), 451 (170), 2813 (138)
Lane, M.: ref, 791 (3,10), 2117 (3)
Lane, P. S., Jr.: ref, 1140 (11)
Lane, R. C.: ref, 301 (54)
Lane, S.: rev, 1318, 2090, 2244
Lane, S. J.: ref, 1673 (8)
Lane, T. J.: ref, 272 (15)
Lanezik, M.: ref, 1166 (50)
Lang, A.: ref, 1927 (8)
Lang, A. E.: ref, 2125 (5), 2860 (227,519), 2863 (58)
Lang, A. R.: ref, 681 (17), 1745 (7,83)
Lang, C.: ref, 272 (170,196), 451 (115,136), 1962 (13), 2076 (73,148)
Lang, C. J. G.: ref, 2863 (31)
Lang, D.: ref, 1104 (13), 2193 (54), 2860 (1109)
Lang, E.: ref, 2603 (73)
Lang, H.: ref, 272 (273)
Lang, M.: ref, 472 (40)
Lang, P. J.: test, 1021; ref, 372 (71), 1021 (25)
Lang, V.: test, 990
Lang, W. S.: rev, 1192, 1395, 1396, 2647
Lang-Takac, E.: ref, 472 (40), 1927 (3), 1965 (35)
Langan, M. K.: ref, 272 (300)
Langdon, D. W.: test, 2809
Lange, A.: ref, 1021 (17), 2603 (177,178,247,349,508)
Lange, G.: ref, 1216 (87), 1903 (204)
Lange, N.: ref, 451 (102), 2862 (450)
Langefeld, C. D.: ref, 298 (84)
Langevald, M. J.: test, 625
Langevin, R.: test, 491
Langhinrichsen-Rohling, J.: ref, 272 (285), 863 (51)
Langis, J.: ref, 298 (119), 863 (52)
Langley, J.: ref, 358 (8)
Langley, J. C.: test, 1871
Langley, M.: ref, 2603 (571)
Langley, M. B.: test, 803
Langmeyer, L.: ref, 1755 (46)
Langmuir, C. R.: test, 1974; rev, 1514
Langsdale, T.: ref, 1095 (20), 2866 (3)
Langston, C. A.: ref, 2218 (101)
Langston, J. W.: test, 558; ref, 2516 (9)
Languis, M.: test, 1472
Lanham, K.: ref, 1903 (163), 2485 (78)
Lankau, M. J.: ref, 2389 (1)
Lankford, J. S.: ref, 2497 (170,360)
Lanktree, C. B.: ref, 472 (129)
Lanning, K.: ref, 372 (8,70,103), 373 (22,40), 2218 (125)
Lannon, R. A.: ref, 2603 (197)
Lanphere, T.: test, 2669
Lansing, M. D.: test, 2111
Lanteri, A.: ref, 2863 (261), 2892 (183)
Lanton, W. J.: ref, 2218 (52)
Lanyon, R. I.: test, 1733, 2115; rev, 438, 637, 998, 1201, 1321, 1686, 1698, 1732, 2148
Lanzi, R. G.: ref, 1903 (578)
Lanzillotta, M.: ref, 1166 (185)
Laor, N.: ref, 451 (137), 2497 (414), 2603 (475)
Lapan, R.: ref, 2879 (82)
Lapan, S.: ref, 1903 (269)
Lapenz, S. K.: ref, 272 (286)
Lapey, K.: ref, 2860 (990) 2879 (142)
Lapey, K. A.: ref, 1092 (12), 2860 (802), 2862 (309), 2879 (101)
Lapham, S. C.: ref, 136 (10), 1661 (45,52), 1697 (426,474,553)
Lapidot, Y.: ref, 1590 (65)
Lapidus, L. B.: ref, 1140 (10)
Lapierre, D.: ref, 1174 (4), 2010 (19), 2892 (192)
Lapierre, Y. D.: ref, 1166 (64,119)
Lapitsky, L.: ref, 2076 (110), 2603 (343)
Laplante, B.: ref, 404 (17)
Laplante, L.: ref, 1166 (125), 2516 (3), 2863 (25)
LaPointe, L. L.: test, 2172
Lapp, W. M.: ref, 66 (2), 272 (81), 2076 (76)
Lappan, G.: rev, 2486
Lappan, P. A., Jr.: rev, 137, 508, 605
LaPrelle, J.: ref, 1097 (4), 1903 (67), 2146 (8), 2163 (61)
Lara-Cantú, M. A.: ref, 298 (3)
Laraia, M. T.: ref, 2603 (277)
Largay, K. A.: ref, 199 (16), 2010 (16), 2163 (179), 2516 (47), 2860 (703), 2863 (205), 2879 (87)
Larigneur, S.: ref, 2603 (372), 2860 (916)
Larimer, M. E.: ref, 337 (61), 652 (2)
Larish, J. F.: ref, 1380 (14), 2860 (670), 2892 (124)
Larivèe, S.: ref, 1866 (22), 2862 (321)
Larkin, K. T.: ref, 2497 (282)
Laron, Z.: ref, 2497 (414)
Laros, J. A.: test, 2441
Larrabee, G. J.: test, 687; ref, 687 (1), 1164 (103), 2860 (7,480,917), 2863 (134,224,274)
Larrick, R. D.: ref, 592 (36)
Larrivee, B.: ref, 1991 (102)

Larrivee, S.: ref, 1340 (2)
Larsen, A. E.: ref, 272 (285)
Larsen, D.: ref, 2115 (5)
Larsen, D. K.: ref, 2497 (518), 2603 (128,157)
Larsen, E.: test, 1857
Larsen, J.: ref, 1001 (14)
Larsen, J. D.: ref, 926 (4)
Larsen, J. K.: ref, 1166 (172)
Larsen, J. P.: ref, 2599 (33)
Larsen, R. J.: ref, 998 (33), 999 (112,187,193), 1338 (26), 1697 (571), 1697 (594)
Larsen, S. C.: test, 2668, 2730, 2731, 2732
Larsh, S. L.: ref, 1689 (4)
Larson, B. M.: ref, 863 (78)
Larson, D. K.: ref, 695 (2), 2514 (1)
Larson, E. B.: ref, 776 (27,58)
Larson, G. E.: ref, 180 (14,30), 1405 (20), 1866 (3), 2163 (137,221)
Larson, J.: ref, 2497 (226)
Larson, J. W.: test, 2464
Larson, L. M.: ref, 2065 (20)
Larson, M. G.: ref, 2076 (38)
Larson, R.: ref, 472 (175)
Larson, R. W.: ref, 1010 (104)
Larson, S.: test, 2552
Larson, S. L.: test, 663, 1400
Larsson, I.: ref, 2038 (2)
La Rue, A.: ref, 1058 (1,3), 2860 (21,277,918),919,984), 2863 (72)
LaRus, D. M.: ref, 1612 (31)
Larzelere, R.: ref, 997 (15)
Lascelles, M.: ref, 451 (2)
Laska, E.: ref, 2860 (1205), 2892 (261)
Lasko, N. B.: ref, 2497 (500), 2860 (1403)
Lassen, M. K.: ref, 472 (76)
Lasseter, J.: ref, 2862 (79)
Lassiter, K. S.: ref, 854 (2), 1164 (43), 1379 (71), 1380 (8), 1903 (161), 2704 (17), 2862 (245), 2864 (96)
Lassonde, M.: ref, 1218 (1), 2125 (2,6), 2163 (16), 2860 (44,272,1299), 2862 (135,530)
Last, C.: ref, 2497 (294)
Last, C. G.: ref, 472 (64), 1021 (13), 2214 (9,25,121), 2305 (231), 2498 (11,18,72)
Laszlo, J. I.: ref, 2485 (13)
Latham, C. J.: ref, 739 (8)
Latham, M.: ref, 666 (4)
Latimer, B. C.: ref, 2163 (231)
Latorre, S. E.: ref, 2879 (113)
Latz, T. T.: ref, 846 (8)
Lau, B. H-B.: ref, 2860 (1184)
Lau, M. A.: ref, 2860 (920)
Lau, S.: ref, 495 (5), 998 (8)
Laub, D.: ref, 2603 (426)
Laub, J. H.: ref, 2860 (741), 2862 (290)
Laucht, M.: ref, 624 (19), 1240 (27)
Lauer, K. J.: ref, 1404 (5)
Laughlin, A.: ref, 451 (142), 472 (181), 694 (118), 1010 (43), 2862 (173,654)
Laughlin, J. E.: test, 1322
Laughlin, P. R.: ref, 272 (314), 998 (131)
Laughrea, K.: ref, 2497 (641)
Lauibach, C. M.: ref, 2485 (212)
Laulumaa, V.: ref, 776 (3), 2860 (103)
Launes, J.: ref, 2860 (895), 2863 (265)
Launius, G.: ref, 375 (8), 2720 (1), 2892 (297)
Laurent, J.: ref, 472 (174), 2214 (51,106), 2901 (123)
Laurie, C. A.: ref, 1338 (32)
Laurita, R. E.: test, 1428
Laury, G.: ref, 335 (10)
Lautenschlager, G. J.: ref, 1701 (10)
Lautenschlager, N.: ref, 1525 (23), 2860 (1115)
Lauter, H.: ref, 301 (13), 2860 (193)
Lauver, D.: ref, 2076 (116,176), 2497 (183)
Lavach, J. F.: ref, 1164 (28), 1227 (1), 2860 (273)
Lavallee, L.: test, 387; ref, 2749 (76)
Lavallee, L. F.: ref, 2218 (50)
LaVallée, M.: ref, 708 (4)
Lave, J.: ref, 272 (221)
Lavee, Y.: test, 1000; ref, 1000 (17)
Lavelle, J.: ref, 2102 (1), 2288 (16), 2289 (11), 2860 (335), 2863 (88)
Lavelle, S.: ref, 1965 (31)
Lavergne, G.: ref, 1903 (584), 2485 (245)
Lavie, P.: ref, 913 (1), 1697 (133), 2603 (106)
Lavigne, J. V.: ref, 270 (29), 337 (103), 372 (94), 451 (86,181,238), 1010 (54,131), 1612 (91), 1613 (2), 1706 (3), 2498 (24), 2858 (102)
Lavigueur, S.: ref, 2039 (18)
Lavin, C.: ref, 1386 (22), 2862 (502)
Lavine, J. R.: ref, 337 (149)
Laviola, M.: ref, 1000 (31)
Lavoie, A. L.: rev, 927, 1322, 2581, 2649
Lavoie, M.: ref, 1745 (10)
Lavoie, M. E.: ref, 2039 (12), 2516 (43)
Lavoie, N.: ref, 2076 (83)
Lavori, P.: ref, 1093 (10), 1517 (1)
Lavori, P. W.: ref, 1093 (68), 1517 (5), 2305 (18), 2519 (42), 2520 (42)
Law, A.: ref, 2858 (73)
Law, J. G., Jr.: rev, 229, 1210, 2833, 2836; ref, 1378 (7), 2862 (503)
Law, K. S.: ref, 1701 (56)
Law School Admission Council: test, 1434
Law, T.: ref, 472 (142)
Law, W. A.: ref, 2497 (361)
Lawes, J. S.: rev, 2441
Lawless, K. A.: rev, 1331, 2096
Lawlis, G. F.: test, 1183, 1242
Lawlor, B. A.: ref, 2076 (100), 2863 (222)
Lawlor, G.: rev, 324
Lawrence, A.: ref, 142 (4), 1758 (27), 2892 (139)
Lawrence, B.: ref, 694 (32), 1367 (3)
Lawrence, C.: ref, 2861 (3)

Lawrence, C. W.: ref, 1903 (124)
Lawrence, J. W.: ref, 999 (153)
Lawrence, K. J.: ref, 846 (9), 2519 (55), 2520 (54)
Lawrence, R. E.: ref, 1093 (59,70), 2050 (55,87)
Lawrence, S.: ref, 1697 (318), 2247 (65), 2749 (42)
Lawrence, S. B.: test, 1431, 1432, 1433, 1435
Lawrence, S. D.: ref, 1965 (22)
Lawry, S.: ref, 1093 (92)
Laws, K. R.: ref, 1104 (11), 1758 (103), 2860 (1004,1399)
Lawshe, C. H.: test, 58
Lawshe, C. H., Jr.: rev, 1170, 1533
Lawson, A. E.: ref, 2892 (77)
Lawson, J.: ref, 337 (56), 2497 (245)
Lawson, L.: ref, 372 (48), 1694 (7)
Lawson, M. J.: ref, 34 (6)
Lawton, C. A.: ref, 1140 (33)
Lawton, M. P.: ref, 2076 (31,44)
Lawton, W. J.: ref, 2497 (617), 2858 (95)
Layman, M. J.: ref, 793 (20), 846 (17), 1697 (493), 2603 (476)
Layne, B. H.: ref, 1755 (60)
Layton, K.: ref, 540 (3), 2432 (26), 2704 (32)
Layton, T.: ref, 272 (247)
Layton, T. L.: test, 428; ref, 175 (9), 430 (7), 1047 (3), 2651 (13), 2695 (21)
Layton, W. L.: rev, 239, 477, 1694, 1790, 2421
Lazar, A.: ref, 1903 (82)
Lazar, J. W.: ref, 376 (24), 1687 (28), 1903 (541), 2860 (1310), 2901 (125)
Lazar, R. M.: ref, 2860 (4)
Lázaro, L.: ref, 1164 (70), 2860 (681), 2863 (201)
Lazaroff, L. B.: ref, 2107 (1)
Lazarte, A.: ref, 1021 (37)
Lazarus, A. A.: test, 1742
Lazarus, L.: ref, 999 (154)
Lazarus, R. S.: test, 1178, 2858; ref, 2858 (2,3)
Lazenby, J.: ref, 1393 (1), 1404 (14), 2917 (4)
Lazowski, L. E.: ref, 1661 (80), 1687 (43), 1697 (585), 2553 (5)
Lazrove, S.: ref, 2603 (426)
Le Blanc, P. M.: ref, 1590 (64)
Le Bon, O.: ref, 272 (200), 1164 (129), 1166 (131,194), 1697 (500), 2163 (286), 2603 (480), 2860 (1134)
Le Chanu, M. N.: ref, 1991 (64)
Leadbeater, B. J.: ref, 2382 (24)
Leader, J. B.: ref, 1166 (124)
Leafgren, F.: test, 1499
League, R.: test, 2189
Leahy, L. F.: ref, 199 (3), 1903 (60)
Leake, A.: ref, 1166 (16)
Leal, L.: ref, 665 (40)
Leark, R. A.: rev, 40, 2135
Learning Publications, Inc.: test, 217
Leary, M. R.: ref, 68 (7), 893 (8)
Lease, C. A.: ref, 1021 (19), 2497 (272), 2525 (3)
Lease, S. H.: ref, 462 (22)
Leathem, J.: ref, 335 (4), 2497 (165)
Leather, C. V.: ref, 350 (20), 1765 (18)
Leather, D. M.: ref, 1010 (74)
Leatherland, J.: ref, 1770 (4)
Leatherman, D.: ref, 2076 (93)
Leatherman, R. W.: test, 1479, 1480
Leavitt, F.: ref, 298 (33), 846 (23), 853 (4), 1697 (84,314,554)
Leavitt, L. A.: ref, 1216 (76)
Leavitt, R.: ref, 1903 (175)
LeBaron, D.: ref, 1903 (479)
Lebeaux, M. O.: ref, 1697 (124), 2603 (87)
Lebell, M.: ref, 2050 (85)
Leber, D.: ref, 451 (12), 472 (214)
Leber, W. R.: test, 2517, 2820
Lebert, F.: ref, 776 (35)
Leblanc, A. G.: test, 2728
LeBlanc, M.: ref, 1340 (2), 2126 (16), 2862 (321)
Lebmann, P.: ref, 272 (370), 2497 (673)
LeBoeuf, A.: ref, 1021 (5)
LeBold: test, 2124
Lebovits, A. H.: ref, 748 (7), 1093 (14), 2497 (67)
Leboyer, M.: ref, 2111 (2), 2163 (247), 2862 (410)
LeBuffe, P. A.: test, 817, 818
Lecci, L.: ref, 1697 (221), 2218 (5)
Lechevalier, B.: ref, 2516 (64), 2863 (45), 2863 (248)
Lechner, H.: ref, 2860 (525), 2892 (88)
Leckman, A. L.: ref, 1164 (37), 2076 (49), 2860 (377)
Leckman, J. F.: ref, 1093 (31), 1164 (116), 1379 (13,17), 2813 (10), 2860 (1019)
Leconte, P.: ref, 776 (35)
LeCouteur, A.: ref, 350 (24), 1653 (21), 2163 (195), 2228 (16), 2860 (427,795)
Lecrubier, Y.: ref, 2603 (539)
Leda, C.: ref, 337 (184)
Ledbetter, E.: test, 2624
Leddy, M. H.: ref, 2497 (362)
Leder, S. B.: rev, 328, 1056
Lederer, H.: rev, 510
Ledgerwood, R.: rev, 1657
Ledingham, J. E.: ref, 385 (1), 1197 (1)
Ledvinka, J.: rev, 1107
Lee, A.: ref, 272 (110), 998 (90), 2305 (129), 2516 (49), 2860 (712), 2863 (210), 2892 (138)
Lee, A. S.: ref, 998 (29), 2050 (13)
Lee, C.: ref, 292 (1), 1000 (87), 2076 (180), 2757 (1)
Lee, C. C.: rev, 311, 397
Lee, C. K.: test, 1618
Lee, C. P.: ref, 1607 (8), 2862 (271)
Lee, C. S.: ref, 2125 (27)
Lee, D.: test, 1626; ref, 999 (143), 1079 (55), 2603 (418), 2858 (108)
Lee, D. T. S.: ref, 272 (287), 1079 (94)
Lee, G.: ref, 2603 (467)
Lee, G. D.: ref, 2860 (194)
Lee, G. P.: ref, 641 (4), 1164 (9), 1903 (35), 2227 (4,11), 2860 (68,115), 2863 (136), 2879 (15), 2892 (3,13)
Lee, H. B.: ref, 2497 (363)

Lee, H. C. B.: ref, 694 (48), 1079 (17)
Lee, J.: ref, 2076 (47)
Lee, J. M.: rev, 1319
Lee, K. D.: ref, 451 (263), 681 (93), 1392 (15), 2862 (718), 2905 (120)
Lee, L.: ref, 2651 (19), 2860 (652), 2863 (191)
Lee, L. D.: ref, 451 (253), 2864 (143)
Lee, L. L.: test, 1804
Lee, M.: ref, 472 (175)
Lee, M. A.: ref, 350 (52), 1903 (577), 2163 (355), 2497 (97), 2860 (1413), 2862 (730)
Lee, M. D.: ref, 1405 (22), 2163 (212), 2860 (860)
Lee, O.: ref, 2862 (48)
Lee, P.: ref, 2305 (232)
Lee, P. W. H.: ref, 694 (117), 2497 (570)
Lee, R. B.: ref, 375 (8), 2720 (1), 2892 (297)
Lee, R. E.: ref, 2247 (104), 2860 (1116), 2862 (504)
Lee, R. T.: ref, 1590 (24)
Lee, R. Y. P.: ref, 999 (161)
Lee, S.: ref, 1697 (315), 2487 (7), 2603 (278)
Lee, S. G.: rev, 1053
Lee, S. W.: rev, 264, 544, 930, 2534, 2579, 2901; ref, 337 (97), 2603 (89)
Lee, T. D.: ref, 2860 (1369)
Lee, W. H.: ref, 2860 (1300)
Lee, Y.: ref, 1903 (355)
Lee, Y. B.: ref, 665 (74)
Lee, Y. S.: ref, 2497 (611)
Leedham, B.: ref, 2076 (117)
Leekam, S. R.: ref, 1903 (277)
Leeper, H. A.: ref, 1164 (135), 2227 (33), 2860 (1181), 2879 (184), 2892 (256)
Lees-Haley, P. R.: ref, 1697 (294,404,409,555)
Leevers, H.: ref, 2467 (1)
Leevers, H. J.: ref, 2662 (8)
Lefcourt, H. M.: ref, 2516 (38)
Lefebure, C.: ref, 776 (18)
Lefebure, V.: ref, 776 (18)
Lefebvre, D.: ref, 459 (5), 1612 (13)
Lefebvre, M.: ref, 863 (67)
Lefever, D. W.: rev, 364, 1196, 1221, 1323
LeFevre, J-A.: ref, 1903 (581), 2488 (10)
Leffert, J. S.: ref, 2485 (205), 2657 (30), 2862 (505), 2879 (217)
Lefkowitz, D. M.: ref, 2652 (8)
Lefkowitz, J.: ref, 1348 (8)
Lefley, H. P.: ref, 2603 (195)
Legan, L.: ref, 1697 (494)
Legg, B. H.: ref, 449 (2,3)
Legg, S. M.: rev, 1180, 2696
Leggio, M. G.: ref, 2163 (304)
Legius, E.: ref, 2860 (1321)
Legree, P. J.: ref, 180 (31,35), 2860 (343)
LeGrice, B.: ref, 863 (44)
Lehman, A.: ref, 2288 (15), 2289 (10), 2305 (62)
Lehman, A. F.: ref, 2519 (30,44), 2520 (31,44)
Lehman, D. R.: ref, 791 (12), 2218 (50), 2603 (348)
Lehman, E. B.: ref, 2860 (368), 2862 (353)
Lehman, P. R.: rev, 1280, 1320, 2056
Lehman, P. W.: test, 635
Lehman, R. A. W.: test, 2118
Lehmann, I. J.: rev, 48, 49, 247, 547, 2484, 2486, 2902
Lehmicke, N.: ref, 2858 (103)
Lehner, T.: ref, 2305 (20,49)
Lehnert, K. L.: ref, 473 (2), 1697 (445), 2258 (5)
Lehnung, M.: ref, 776 (49), 1164 (159), 1758 (91), 2227 (42)
Lehofer, M.: ref, 272 (370), 2497 (673)
Lehr, C.: test, 2653
Lehrer, P. M.: ref, 1697 (394)
Lehrer, R.: rev, 2092, 2556; ref, 1612 (4), 1903 (13), 2044 (1), 2862 (48)
Lehtihen, S. J.: ref, 2227 (2), 2860 (179), 2863 (48)
Lehto, H.: ref, 1166 (161)
Leibenluft, E.: ref, 1093 (94)
Leiblum, S.: ref, 457 (1)
Leicester, N.: ref, 1072 (45), 1612 (44)
Leicht, D. J.: ref, 2860 (204), 2879 (27)
Leichtman, M.: ref, 2247 (128)
Leiderman, L. J.: ref, 1697 (559), 2516 (106)
Leidy, N. K.: ref, 1166 (222)
Leigh, G.: ref, 2860 (1276)
Leigh, J.: ref, 372 (17), 2749 (28), 2860 (369)
Leigh, J. E.: test, 60, 258, 284
Leigh, N. M.: ref, 837 (6)
Leigh, P. N.: ref, 2858 (68)
Leigh, T.: ref, 272 (171), 999 (157), 2497 (554), 2603 (454)
Leighton, R. F.: ref, 1338 (31), 1686 (3)
Leiguarda, R.: ref, 303 (31), 1166 (82,229), 1740 (35), 2050 (120,121), 2163 (227,228,356), 2860 (935,1419), 2873 (40,41), 2892 (197,198,306)
Leikin, L. J.: ref, 1338 (17)
Leinhardt, G.: ref, 117 (2)
Leininger, L.: ref, 2247 (87), 2860 (864), 2862 (339)
Leirer, V.: ref, 2860 (700)
Leirer, V. O.: ref, 2860 (1315)
Leisen, J. C-C.: ref, 2076 (175)
Leitenberg, H.: ref, 337 (42,133,174), 793 (1,3,4,13)
Leiter, M.: test, 1590
Leiter, M. P.: ref, 1590 (7)
Leiter, R. G.: test, 1484
LeJeune, S. J.: test, 1604
Leland, H.: test, 1, 2
Leli, D. A.: ref, 838 (1,3), 2860 (36)
Lemanek, K. L.: ref, 459 (7,22), 1653 (2,8), 1903 (188), 1987 (11)
LeMay, C. S.: ref, 2078 (1)
Lemelin, S.: ref, 1166 (125,195), 2516 (103)
Lemerond, J.: ref, 2557 (1)
Lemkau, J. P.: ref, 372 (20), 1590 (2)
Lemke, S.: test, 1743; ref, 637 (1), 1743 (1)
Lemmon, C. R.: ref, 1697 (252,359)
Lemus, C. Z.: ref, 1166 (1), 2305 (12)

Lenaine, M. C.: ref, 451 (116), 2288 (68), 2289 (52), 2862 (475)
Lenane, M.: ref, 1010 (49)
Lenane, M. C.: ref, 863 (42), 2288 (71), 2289 (56), 2862 (493,501,629)
Lenart, E. B.: ref, 893 (23)
Lencz, T.: ref, 2860 (216)
Lenehan, M. C.: ref, 2497 (364)
Leng, N. R. C.: ref, 2239 (1)
Leng-Shiff, R.: ref, 557 (5)
Lengnick-Hall, C. A.: ref, 1469 (13)
Lengua, L. J.: ref, 451 (272), 472 (176,228), 2214 (70,107)
Lennings, C. J.: ref, 413 (19), 1779 (1), 2076 (59)
Lennon, R. T.: test, 1866
Lennon, S.: ref, 4 (11)
Lennon, T. J.: ref, 1697 (262), 1959 (1)
Lenski, S. D.: ref, 1318 (17)
Lentz, F. E., Jr.: rev, 279, 1522; ref, 2860 (305)
Lentz, M. J.: ref, 2603 (583)
Lentz, T. F.: test, 363, 2624; rev, 1716
Lentz, T. J.: test, 1228
Lenz, J.: ref, 2360 (6)
Lenz, J. G.: test, 422
Lenz, J. W.: ref, 760 (3), 1697 (223)
Lenzenweger, M. F.: ref, 298 (145), 592 (93), 650 (5), 1093 (32), 1697 (316,317), 1965 (56,65,68), 2497 (365,503,544), 2749 (41), 2860 (950), 2892 (127,201)
Leo, D. D.: ref, 298 (68), 2247 (25), 2603 (148)
Leo, E. L.: ref, 561 (2)
Leo, G. I.: ref, 134 (10), 2414 (2)
Leo, G. J.: ref, 326 (3), 1218 (4), 2163 (76), 2497 (136), 2516 (14), 2860 (301), 2892 (41)
Leon, A.: ref, 1166 (63), 2305 (31,125,161,172)
Leon, A. C.: ref, 1158 (3), 1166 (120), 1697 (513,517), 2199 (4,8), 2305 (200), 2498 (43), 2603 (302)
Leon, G. R.: ref, 451 (42), 1000 (71), 1832 (16)
Leòn-Carriòn, J.: ref, 1164 (8)
Leonard, A. C.: ref, 2108 (2,5), 2603 (47)
Leonard, B.: ref, 1405 (40)
Leonard, B. E.: ref, 1166 (59)
Leonard, B. R.: ref, 1485 (28)
Leonard, C. E.: ref, 2603 (488)
Leonard, C. L.: ref, 2863 (393)
Leonard, C. M.: ref, 540 (19), 994 (46), 2695 (66), 2704 (45), 2860 (620), 2905 (110)
Leonard, G.: ref, 1903 (84), 2860 (69,70,274, 275, 288,921,985)
Leonard, H. L.: ref, 863 (42)
Leonard, K. E.: ref, 134 (1,13,33,41), 136 (6), 272 (12), 1008 (1), 1661 (1,64), 2496 (1)
Leonard, L. B.: ref, 265 (9), 1485 (50,60), 1490 (1,2), 1852 (3), 1903 (453), 2382 (34), 2680 (9,12), 2695 (12,48), 2864 (129,139)
Leonard, M.: ref, 2603 (112)
Leonard, S. T.: ref, 1697 (495)
Leone, P. E.: ref, 495 (7)
Leong, E. J.: ref, 1132 (1), 1755 (62)
Leong, F. T. L.: rev, 72, 648, 1445, 1446, 1448, 1689, 2535, 2637; ref, 337 (52), 413 (12), 1754 (10), 2218 (56), 2246 (10), 2835 (11)
Leong, G. B.: ref, 1093 (72), 2050 (95), 2288 (19)
Leong, P.: ref, 1612 (92)
Leonhardt, G.: ref, 1166 (219)
Leoni, E. L.: ref, 462 (23), 1000 (89)
Leopold, N. A.: ref, 776 (48)
Lepage, M.: ref, 2860 (1161)
Lepage, Y.: ref, 1166 (99), 2863 (310)
LePen, C.: ref, 1166 (57)
Lepera, C.: test, 2049
LePine, J. A.: ref, 2218 (102)
Lepisto, B. L.: ref, 2247 (49)
Lepley, W. M.: test, 1928
Leplow, B.: ref, 776 (49), 1164 (158,159), 1758 (91), 2227 (41,42), 1218 (1), 2125 (2), 2163 (16), 2860 (44)
Lepore, S.: ref, 451 (268), 472 (226), 2214 (135)
Lepore, S. J.: ref, 2603 (477)
Lepoutre, L.: ref, 2497 (127)
Lepper, M. R.: ref, 1965 (58)
Lerer, B.: ref, 301 (16,48), 1166 (28,92), 2288 (27), 2289 (18), 2860 (241,922)
LeResche, L.: ref, 2603 (44)
Lerman, C.: ref, 2076 (128)
Lerman, M.: ref, 472 (91), 681 (52), 863 (53), 1010 (63), 2498 (37), 2862 (272)
Lermon, C.: ref, 2076 (151)
Lerner, M. S.: ref, 2065 (2)
Lerner, P. M.: ref, 2247 (91,129)
Lerner, Y.: ref, 451 (17), 1216 (19), 1903 (103)
Lernhart, L. A.: ref, 2860 (923), 2862 (362)
LeRoux, B.: ref, 135 (5), 2497 (624)
Leroux, M. D.: ref, 372 (18), 1697 (85), 2076 (14), 2603 (57)
Lersbruggen, A. B.: ref, 1079 (83)
Lesage, A.: ref, 2050 (39), 2603 (402)
Lesage, A. D.: ref, 2050 (69,102)
LeSage, M.: ref, 4 (10)
Lesch, K. P.: ref, 2497 (121)
Lesch, K-P.: ref, 1166 (26)
Leserman, J.: ref, 1166 (196), 2076 (122)
Lesiak, J. L.: test, 813
Lesiak, W. J.: test, 813
Lesko, L. M.: ref, 1000 (35)
Leslie, J.: test, 2425
Leslie, L. A.: ref, 863 (11)
Leslie, S. C.: ref, 1072 (15), 1131 (6), 2862 (98), 2905 (10)
Lespérance, F.: ref, 2497 (466)
Lesser, I. M.: ref, 1166 (17,136), 2227 (6,29), 2516 (13,81), 2603 (24,108), 2860 (286,1117,1150), 2863 (76,331,341), 2892 (37,231,246)
Lesser, R.: test, 2113; ref, 2860 (1226)
Lesser, R. P.: ref, 2860 (805)
Lestelle, V.: ref, 1093 (8), 2108 (1)

Lester, B. M.: ref, 1770 (16)
Lester, D.: ref, 272 (286), 998 (54,118,125)
Letarte, H.: ref, 2065 (16)
Letenneur, L.: ref, 2860 (930), 2863 (297)
Leton, D. A.: rev, 815, 1374, 2518
Letore, F.: ref, 2860 (1299)
Letourneau, E. J.: ref, 1697 (496)
Letourneau, L.: ref, 2860 (243,314), 2863 (61,85)
Letourneau, L. A.: ref, 298 (7)
Letourneau, L. L.: ref, 2860 (412), 2863 (110)
Letourneau, P. K.: ref, 1697 (66,67), 2076 (9,10)
Lettenneur, L.: ref, 2863 (90)
Letteri, C. A.: test, 1472
Letts, C.: test, 2228
Leu, P. W.: ref, 1321 (11)
Leudar, I.: ref, 2050 (83)
Leuder, D. C.: ref, 1755 (8), 2545 (1)
Leung, C. B.: ref, 2864 (23)
Leung, F.: ref, 2603 (218)
Leung, H. C. M.: ref, 272 (287), 1079 (94)
Leung, K.: ref, 372 (97), 495 (5), 1697 (476), 2756 (1)
Leung, M. C.: ref, 495 (4), 694 (23), 999 (32), 1010 (23), 2163 (72)
Leung, P. K.: ref, 2305 (79)
Leung, P. W. L.: ref, 451 (273), 681 (51), 694 (117), 2497 (570)
Leung, S. A.: rev, 931, 1493, 1874, 2188, 2418, 1754 (11)
Leung, S. W.: ref, 592 (94)
Leung, W. C.: ref, 694 (117), 2497 (570)
Levanon, I.: ref, 694 (8)
Levant, R. F.: ref, 1000 (18)
Levendosky, A. A.: ref, 472 (98), 1216 (53), 1903 (294)
Levendowsky, A. A.: ref, 451 (62), 472 (130)
Levengood, R. A.: ref, 2860 (1020)
Levenson, M. R.: ref, 998 (27), 1697 (86,253), 2417 (9), 2603 (2,227)
Leventhal, A.: ref, 2444 (1), 2452 (6), 2841 (1)
Leverett, J. P.: ref, 1697 (410), 2247 (86)
Leverett, R. G.: rev, 2798
Leverich, G. S.: ref, 272 (294), 1166 (199)
LeVerrier, L.: ref, 665 (6), 815 (1), 1902 (6), 2485 (10), 2862 (47)
Levesque, J.: ref, 2516 (11), 2892 (33)
Levi-Keren, M.: ref, 538 (6), 644 (3)
Levin, B. E.: ref, 1218 (3), 2860 (276)
Levin, H. S.: ref, 375 (3,7), 1740 (4), 2860 (1342), 2862 (506,705)
Levin, I.: ref, 1115 (1)
Levin, J. R.: ref, 2862 (28)
Levin, M.: ref, 2603 (524), 2860 (673)
Levin, M. L.: ref, 2862 (49), 2879 (9)
Levin, R.: ref, 68 (46), 272 (125), 998 (97,121), 2497 (477,489)
Levin, R. A.: ref, 2218 (134)
Levin, S.: ref, 2305 (75), 2603 (71)
Levine, A. C.: ref, 2076 (179)
Levine, B.: ref, 776 (23), 1758 (46), 2892 (193)
Levine, D. N.: ref, 2860 (155)
Levine, E. G.: ref, 1181 (1)
Levine, H. G.: ref, 2813 (38)
Levine, J.: ref, 2017 (8), 2305 (83), 2603 (30), 2862 (409), 2905 (92)
Levine, M. D.: test, 158, 1905, 1907, 1908, 1909
Levine, M. V.: ref, 56 (10), 180 (4,9,28)
Levine, S. B.: ref, 863 (58), 2497 (421), 2603 (330)
Levine, S. C.: test, 2059; ref, 2485 (20), 2695 (38), 2704 (26), 2860 (153,191), 2862 (94), 2864 (16)
Levine, W. R.: ref, 4 (7)
Levinson, D. F.: ref, 650 (6), 2305 (42,56,101), 2860 (924)
Levinson, E. M.: ref, 405 (2), 2360 (2)
Levinson, H. N.: ref, 1072 (9), 1092 (2), 1131 (3), 1902 (11), 2860 (113), 2862 (80), 2879 (14), 2905 (5)
Levinson, J. C.: ref, 2288 (5), 2289 (3), 2305 (8)
Levinson, K. L.: ref, 2860 (854), 2863 (249)
Levit, M.: test, 2675
Levitan, R. D.: ref, 272 (288), 1166 (197)
Levitt, A.: ref, 790 (11), 1166 (171), 2218 (82), 2305 (213)
Levitt, A. J.: ref, 272 (288), 1166 (89,90,197), 2218 (43,44), 2305 (164,185)
Levitt, E. E.: rev, 708, 1699
Levitt, M.: ref, 2305 (124)
Levitt, S. R.: test, 484, 2766
Levy, B. M.: ref, 815 (39), 1903 (481), 2671 (3), 2862 (522), 2879 (176), 2901 (97)
Levy, D. L.: ref, 2305 (70), 2497 (544)
Levy, E.: ref, 1166 (57)
Levy, G.: ref, 863 (32), 2603 (161)
Levy, K. N.: ref, 2860 (1039), 2862 (438)
Levy, L. H.: ref, 2076 (45,46,86)
Levy, P. M.: rev, 952
Levy, R.: ref, 1390 (2,7), 1758 (10,32,57), 2050 (79), 2193 (35), 2860 (215,792,1036)
Levy, S.: test, 1922; rev, 2566
Levy, S. M.: ref, 2076 (47)
Levy, S. R.: ref, 2557 (6)
Levy-Shiff, R.: ref, 303 (27), 451 (129), 472 (91,201), 681 (52), 863 (53), 998 (113), 1000 (108), 1010 (63), 1697 (87), 2226 (39), 1965 (57), 2498 (37,68), 2603 (540), 2652 (4,272,642)
Lew, W. J. F.: ref, 771 (3)
Lewandowski, L.: ref, 1386 (5,11,17,23), 1503 (9), 1903 (327), 2862 (273), 2879 (83)
Lewandowski, L. J.: ref, 2487 (1), 2516 (45), 2860 (694), 2905 (6)
Lewandowski, M. J.: test, 291
Lewicki, P.: ref, 272 (44)
Lewin, J.: ref, 1040 (7)
Lewin, M.: ref, 1697 (134)
Lewin, M. R.: ref, 2516 (70)
Lewin, T.: ref, 999 (36), 1079 (13), 2497 (98)
Lewin, T. J.: ref, 998 (119), 1079 (37,57,74), 2497 (578), 2603 (484)

Lewine, R. R. J.: ref, 2125 (23), 2860 (1118), 2892 (232)
Lewinsohn, P.: ref, 2305 (40)
Lewinsohn, P. M.: ref, 2305 (182,193,227), 2402 (14), 2497 (220,366), 2858 (74,97)
Lewis, A. B.: ref, 1093 (8), 2108 (1)
Lewis, B. A.: ref, 353 (1), 540 (21), 1095 (11,46), 1394 (12), 1903 (34,125), 2432 (6), 2680 (3,4), 2695 (67), 2704 (4,5), 2706 (1,2), 2732 (2), 2768 (3), 2862 (168), 2864 (28,29), 2879 (46), 2905 (25,113)
Lewis, C.: ref, 92 (1), 97 (1), 100 (1), 592 (52,105), 1145 (2), 2163 (170)
Lewis, C. A.: ref, 272 (190,361), 2358 (12)
Lewis, C. D.: ref, 1485 (29), 2864 (58)
Lewis, C. P.: ref, 2603 (64,198)
Lewis, D. A.: ref, 863 (16)
Lewis, D. C.: test, 1489
Lewis, D. M.: ref, 83 (4)
Lewis, F.: test, 2923; ref, 1697 (458)
Lewis, G.: ref, 999 (39), 1758 (77), 2163 (298)
Lewis, G. J.: ref, 2848 (2)
Lewis, H. A.: ref, 472 (177), 2214 (108)
Lewis, J. A.: ref, 2305 (78), 2860 (452)
Lewis, J. D.: ref, 1991 (80), 2163 (121)
Lewis, J. F.: test, 61, 2606
Lewis, J. L.: ref, 1010 (17)
Lewis, J. R.: ref, 1697 (318), 2247 (65), 2749 (42)
Lewis, K. D.: ref, 134 (24), 863 (65)
Lewis, K. R.: ref, 679 (1), 681 (77), 815 (21), 1135 (14), 1485 (38), 1612 (66), 1903 (339,490), 2485 (161,211), 2813 (84)
Lewis, M.: ref, 592 (37), 815 (34), 1612 (92), 2382 (19), 2485 (59)
Lewis, M. A.: rev, 14, 305, 1323, 1445, 1446, 1448, 1562, 2418
Lewis, M. C.: ref, 1010 (47)
Lewis, M. G.: ref, 2247 (49)
Lewis, M. H.: ref, 4 (16)
Lewis, N. D. C.: rev, 987
Lewis, N. P.: test, 1394
Lewis, P. D. R.: ref, 2193 (25), 2860 (668), 2863 (198)
Lewis, R.: test, 72; ref, 811 (3), 1379 (10), 2813 (8), 2858 (66)
Lewis, R. D.: rev, 2591
Lewis, R. F.: test, 842; ref, 1697 (182)
Lewis, S.: ref, 134 (24), 863 (65), 1093 (80), 2050 (98,103), 2858 (75)
Lewis, S. J.: ref, 1687 (5)
Lewis, S. W.: ref, 2050 (34,80), 2860 (656)
Lewis, T. B.: ref, 2603 (197)
Lewis, V.: ref, 350 (32)
Lewkowicz, C.: ref, 2749 (57)
Lewy, A.: ref, 459 (35), 1485 (40), 1903 (350)
Lewy, A. J.: ref, 1697 (103), 2305 (44), 2382 (10), 2813 (18)
Lex, B. W.: ref, 1661 (59)
Leyden, G.: ref, 2862 (441)
Leys, D.: ref, 2163 (214), 2860 (868)
Leyva, C.: ref, 1099 (2), 2603 (332)
LHE, Inc.: test, 436
Lhermitte, F.: ref, 2163 (43), 2860 (168), 2863 (44), 2892 (20)
L'Herrou, T. A.: ref, 272 (294), 1166 (199)
Li, B.: ref, 472 (115)
Li, D.: ref, 2860 (270), 2863 (70), 2907 (2)
Li, E.: ref, 56 (7)
Li, E. C.: ref, 199 (6), 2008 (8)
Li, P. P.: ref, 1166 (166), 2305 (209)
Li, S.: ref, 2050 (106), 2146 (11), 2288 (26), 2289 (15), 2863 (108), 2892 (58)
Li, S-J.: ref, 1128 (1)
Li, T-K.: ref, 1010 (136), 1661 (83)
Li, Y.: ref, 372 (58)
Liang, K.: ref, 2050 (112)
Liang, M. H.: ref, 2076 (38)
Liang, W. M.: ref, 337 (102), 2603 (370), 2858 (100)
Liang, X.: ref, 1216 (82)
Liao, D.: ref, 2076 (122)
Liao, H-Y.: ref, 908 (12), 1101 (2), 2417 (41)
Liao, K.: ref, 301 (38), 2860 (622)
Liaw, F.: ref, 1903 (278), 2485 (75), 2485 (135)
Libb, J. W.: ref, 1687 (6)
Libbrecht, I.: ref, 1166 (217)
Liben, L. S.: ref, 1903 (108)
Liberini, P.: ref, 1697 (222)
Liberman, D.: ref, 1000 (34), 1294 (4), 2417 (21)
Liberman, I. Y.: ref, 1051 (1), 2163 (37)
Liberman, R. P.: ref, 1093 (72), 2050 (52,85,95), 2288 (6,8), 2289 (4), 2603 (525), 2892 (55)
Libhaber, J.: ref, 2749 (57)
Libman, E.: ref, 998 (92)
Libo, L. M.: rev, 739
Libon, D. J.: ref, 376 (32), 2860 (1400), 2863 (424)
Licht, M. H.: test, 2763
Lichtenberg, P. A.: ref, 776 (10,17,24,50), 2863 (96,275,337)
Lichtenstein, R.: test, 1691
Lichtenstein, T.: ref, 1010 (105)
Lichtermann, D.: ref, 2305 (108,145)
Lichty, W.: ref, 1405 (3)
Lida-Pulik, H.: ref, 272 (350)
Liddle, B.: ref, 472 (10)
Lidiak, S. E.: ref, 2704 (17), 2862 (245)
Lidsky, D.: ref, 301 (48), 2860 (922)
Lie, A.: ref, 1240 (6)
Lie, N.: ref, 1169 (3)
Liebenaver, L. L.: ref, 681 (39), 2860 (550)
Lieberman, A.: ref, 1745 (13)
Lieberman, I.: ref, 2860 (8), 2892 (1)
Lieberman, J. A.: ref, 1093 (41), 2288 (35,45,64), 2289 (26), 2305 (21,70,107,123,170), 2860 (333,1005)
Lieberman, L.: ref, 301 (41)
Lieberman, M.: test, 1625
Liebler, A.: ref, 2218 (22)

Liebowitz, M.: ref, 2603 (342)
Liebowitz, M. R.: ref, 1592 (7), 2305 (34,65,147), 2603 (198)
Liebson, E.: ref, 376 (9), 1164 (124), 2860 (1119), 2863 (332), 2879 (169)
Liederman, J.: ref, 2651 (15,17), 2862 (335), 2879 (112)
Lieh-mak, F.: ref, 2860 (1300)
Liem, J. H.: ref, 272 (289), 2749 (77)
Liepman, M. R.: ref, 134 (6,14), 793 (7), 1661 (12,23)
Liese, L. H.: ref, 372 (26,80)
Liess, J.: ref, 2227 (15,14), 2860 (492), 2863 (138,172), 2892 (78,107)
Life Insurance Marketing and Research Association, Inc.: test, 421
Lifton, P. D.: rev, 1036, 1627
Lifton, W. M.: test, 904
Ligezinska, M.: ref, 337 (148), 863 (80), 1000 (99), 1903 (473), 1991 (92)
Liggett, J.: rev, 127, 1153
Light, H. W.: test, 1500
Light, J.: ref, 624 (3), 1903 (126,127), 2477 (1), 2879 (47)
Light, J. G.: ref, 1902 (73,93), 2860 (1215), 2862 (363,587), 2879 (124,189)
Light, K. C.: ref, 760 (2), 2516 (23), 2858 (34,49)
Light, R.: ref, 811 (3), 1379 (10), 2813 (8)
Light, R. H.: ref, 2860 (1342)
Lighter, J.: test, 228
Lightsey, R. O., Jr.: ref, 272 (290)
Lightstone, R.: ref, 1697 (64)
Lignugaris/Kraft, B.: ref, 56 (1), 615 (4), 798 (3), 1392 (1), 1902 (13), 1903 (39), 2432 (7), 2860 (22,122), 2870 (1), 2879 (17), 2901 (7)
Ligthart, G. J.: ref, 1079 (42)
Liikkanen, A.: ref, 2862 (499)
Likert, J. G.: test, 2073, 2079
Likert, R.: test, 2073, 2079, 2217
Likosky, W.: ref, 272 (300)
Liles, B. Z.: ref, 430 (12), 540 (26), 798 (18,25,27), 994 (43,53), 1060 (5), 1240 (35), 1903 (189,378,505,585), 2667 (1), 2668 (7), 2693 (10), 2694 (15,27), 2710 (8), 2727 (1), 2731 (8), 2862 (574), 2901 (136), 2911 (2,6)
Lilienfeld, S. O.: ref, 372 (71), 998 (36,53), 1697 (149,497), 2497 (378), 2516 (48)
Liljequist, L.: ref, 1697 (586), 1959 (8)
Lilley, J.: ref, 537 (3)
Lillian, L. B.: ref, 272 (310)
Lilly, J.: ref, 2497 (299)
Lilly, M. A.: ref, 375 (3), 2862 (506)
Lim, J.: ref, 1697 (584)
Lim, K. O.: ref, 1758 (8), 2860 (420)
Lim, T. K.: ref, 127 (2), 178 (1), 2163 (171)
Limacher, M. C.: ref, 2858 (54)
LIMRA International: test, 197, 2424
Limson, R.: ref, 999 (31), 1592 (9), 1697 (135)
Lin, A-H.: ref, 1166 (217)
Lin, E.: ref, 2218 (16), 2603 (474)
Lin, E. H. B.: ref, 2603 (170)
Lin, K.: ref, 301 (38), 2305 (9), 2519 (18), 2520 (19), 2860 (622)
Lin, L.: ref, 472 (153), 2214 (87)
Lin, W. Y.: ref, 2862 (451)
Lin, Y.: ref, 301 (52), 815 (30), 2862 (407)
Lin, Y. G.: ref, 1455 (1)
Lincoln, A.: ref, 1378 (6), 1755 (64)
Lincoln, A. J.: ref, 815 (27), 1379 (9), 1903 (379), 2695 (41), 2862 (364), 2879 (125)
Lincoln, N.: test, 2240
Lincoln, N. B.: ref, 2239 (4)
Lindamood, C. A.: rev, 1939
Lindamood, C. H.: test, 1503
Lindamood, P. C.: test, 1503
Lindan, C. P.: ref, 134 (35)
Lindberg, N.: ref, 1010 (121)
Lindblad, F.: ref, 2038 (2)
Lindblom, R.: ref, 234 (1)
Lindeboom, J.: ref, 1164 (168), 2226 (34), 2239 (32), 2516 (15,110), 2860 (1345), 2863 (403)
Lindecamp, D. P.: ref, 1755 (7)
Lindelow, G.: ref, 2050 (26)
Lindeman, D. P.: rev, 2681
Lindeman, M.: ref, 298 (94)
Lindeman, R. H.: test, 83, 405
Linden, M. V. D.: ref, 776 (18)
Linden, W.: ref, 272 (364), 760 (3), 1697 (223), 2497 (261), 2860 (1402), 2879 (230)
Lindenmayer, J.: ref, 2017 (9), 2485 (126)
Linder, D. E.: ref, 2497 (665)
Linder, J.: rev, 998
Linder, T. W.: test, 2778
Lindgren, K. N.: ref, 1164 (15), 2226 (2,17), 2860 (158,1225), 2863 (42)
Lindgren, M.: ref, 2603 (541)
Lindgren, S. D.: ref, 342 (2), 815 (8), 1240 (10), 1612 (28), 2305 (228), 2813 (149), 2864 (32)
Lindholm, B. W.: ref, 372 (95)
Lindholm, K. J.: ref, 665 (33), 672 (1), 694 (2)
Lindly, J. D.: ref, 2108 (5)
Lindner, H.: ref, 2858 (101)
Lindner, P.: ref, 1166 (27)
Lindner, R. M.: test, 2212
Lindquist, E. F.: test, 389, 2234
Lindquist, M. M.: rev, 254, 255
Lindsay, G. A.: test, 1369
Lindsay, K. A.: ref, 298 (146), 1697 (427), 2603 (373)
Lindsay, N.: test, 1069
Lindsay, P.: ref, 1903 (126), 2477 (1), 2879 (47)
Lindsay, P. H.: ref, 389 (8)
Lindsay, R.: ref, 2497 (417)
Lindsay, W. R.: ref, 1079 (28), 2860 (481,674,1120,1401)
Lindsey, J.: test, 33
Lindsey, L. L.: ref, 289 (6), 1363 (2), 2901 (139)
Lindskog, R.: rev, 618, 2671, 2727

Lindstrom, R.: ref, 1716 (2)
Lindstrõm, T. C.: ref, 2497 (490)
Lindvall, C. M.: rev, 1319
Lindy, J. D.: ref, 2108 (2), 2603 (47)
Lindzey, G.: test, 2539
Linehan, C.: ref, 2860 (1203), 2879 (187)
Linehan, M. M.: ref, 337 (153), 824 (2), 1093 (48), 1298 (1), 1698 (13), 2497 (262), 2559 (13)
Linehan, S. L.: ref, 1067 (1), 1903 (380), 2813 (97)
Lingam, S.: test, 2308
Lingjserde, O.: ref, 1079 (83)
Lingoes, J. C.: rev, 998
Lingondé, P.: test, 1501
Link, B.: ref, 2288 (52)
Link, C. G. G.: ref, 2288 (82)
Linke, D. B.: ref, 2860 (1274)
Linkenhoker, D.: test, 62
Links, J. M.: ref, 1697 (88), 2050 (125), 2402 (6)
Links, P. S.: ref, 1903 (381), 2305 (144)
Linn, A. A.: ref, 2862 (486)
Linn, L. S.: ref, 1021 (7), 1705 (1), 2497 (54)
Linn, M. C.: ref, 2163 (26,46)
Linn, R.: ref, 2860 (329), 2863 (87)
Linn, R. L.: rev, 324, 665, 780, 838, 1318, 1657; ref, 592 (87), 1759 (15)
Linn, R. T.: ref, 2863 (113)
Linna, S-L.: ref, 472 (227)
Linney, J. A.: ref, 337 (35), 1903 (105), 1987 (4), 2813 (15)
Linnoila, M.: ref, 999 (31), 1592 (9), 1661 (55), 1697 (135,369), 2288 (9), 2305 (27,48,88,176), 2497 (626), 2860 (778)
Linnville, S. E.: ref, 2860 (925)
Linssen, A. C. G.: ref, 2603 (221)
Linszen, D.: ref, 1619 (5), 2050 (43), 2603 (206), 2892 (83)
Linszen, D. H.: ref, 2050 (47,48), 2892 (93)
Lintel, M. P.: rev, 264, 2463
Lintereur, G. E.: rev, 1792
Linterman, I.: ref, 337 (124), 2163 (253), 2517 (6), 2820 (1), 2892 (212)
Linz, D.: ref, 1745 (60), 2603 (385)
Liotus, L.: ref, 2603 (175)
Liou, M.: ref, 1759 (18)
Lipetsker, B.: ref, 335 (13)
Lipke, H. J.: ref, 2497 (575)
Lipkens, R.: ref, 2382 (15)
Lipkus, I. M.: ref, 1697 (319,428)
Lipman, P. D.: ref, 2860 (819)
Lippa, R.: rev, 298; ref, 298 (1,160), 2218 (103)
Lipper, E.: ref, 816 (1), 2229 (15), 2485 (213), 2862 (540), 2879 (178)
Lipper, S.: ref, 998 (19), 2305 (30)
Lippert, J.: test, 2891
Lippke, B. A.: test, 1982
Lippke, L.: ref, 134 (39)
Lipschitz, D. S.: ref, 846 (4)
Lipschutz, L.: ref, 2860 (333)
Lipschutz, R. C.: ref, 2603 (552)
Lipsitt, L. P.: ref, 301 (12), 1097 (3), 2485 (27), 2862 (108), 2879 (24)
Lipsitz, J. D.: ref, 273 (23), 337 (145), 650 (10), 1166 (115), 2289 (17), 2305 (77), 2603 (279)
Lipson, J. G.: ref, 708 (6)
Lipson, K. J.: ref, 1010 (81), 1697 (429)
Liptak, J. J.: test, 407, 1483
Lipton, D. S.: ref, 2519 (10), 2520 (10), 2603 (53)
Lipton, R. B.: ref, 1058 (8), 2125 (13), 2163 (174), 2860 (682,1235,1272), 2863 (369)
Lirgg, C. D.: ref, 495 (8)
Lirón, F.: ref, 1166 (209)
Lis, A.: ref, 2163 (122), 2247 (109), 2860 (482), 2862 (214)
Lisak, D.: ref, 372 (19), 2749 (15)
Lish, J. D.: ref, 1166 (96), 2305 (140)
Lishman, W. A.: ref, 2858 (69)
Lisicia, K.: test, 566
Liskow, B.: ref, 136 (3), 1697 (136), 2603 (109)
Liss, J. A.: ref, 824 (5), 1093 (76), 2603 (307)
Lissitz, R. W.: rev, 148, 2737
Lister, S. C.: ref, 2497 (309)
Lisus, A.: ref, 1653 (12)
Litinsky, A. M.: ref, 2749 (84)
Litt, M. D.: ref, 372 (14), 1174 (1), 1697 (63,183), 2603 (149)
Little, A. J.: ref, 326 (8), 1164 (125), 1525 (24), 2860 (1121), 2892 (233)
Little, B. R.: ref, 2218 (5)
Little, J. M.: ref, 2497 (511)
Little, K. Y.: ref, 2305 (53)
Little, L. M.: ref, 997 (3)
Little, P.: ref, 2901 (29)
Little, S. G.: ref, 854 (1), 1097 (9)
Little, S. S.: ref, 1697 (224), 1962 (5), 1991 (52), 2078 (5), 2813 (39), 2848 (3), 2860 (483), 2862 (215), 2868 (1), 2879 (61), 2901 (28), 2905 (43)
Little, T.: ref, 2498 (41)
Littleford, C. D.: ref, 270 (43), 459 (40), 1528 (8)
Littlepage, G. E.: ref, 998 (100), 1036 (13)
Litty, C. G.: ref, 448 (24)
Litvan, I.: ref, 776 (51)
Litvan, J.: ref, 2860 (264)
Litz, B. T.: ref, 272 (206), 1697 (505), 2497 (580), 2860 (1403)
Litzinger, M. J.: ref, 2901 (29)
Liu, F.: ref, 2163 (324)
Liu, H. T.: ref, 2402 (67), 2497 (643)
Liu, L.: ref, 2010 (5)
Liu, S.: ref, 2214 (104)
Liu, S-H.: ref, 413 (23), 1701 (47)
Liu, W.: rev, 364
Liu, W. H.: ref, 1140 (49)
Liu, W. P.: rev, 1434
Liu, W. T.: ref, 1058 (5), 2860 (464), 2862 (203)

Liu, X.: ref, 2125 (18), 2860 (1180), 2863 (292)
Lively, B. T.: ref, 1590 (32)
Livermon, B. J.: ref, 2695 (5)
Livesley, W. J.: ref, 2218 (63)
Livingston, J. A.: ref, 994 (40), 2485 (206), 2695 (55), 2864 (119)
Livingston, R.: ref, 307 (3), 472 (49), 1379 (79), 2214 (30)
Livingston, R. B.: ref, 1164 (123),126), 2862 (481)
Livneh, H.: ref, 68 (43), 372 (5), 1697 (16), 2417 (4), 2497 (13), 2827 (1)
Livson, N.: ref, 372 (93), 373 (31)
Lizardi, H.: ref, 790 (14), 999 (147,168), 1166 (88,145), 1953 (2)
Llabre, M.: ref, 2603 (195)
Llabre, M. M.: ref, 472 (202), 1218 (3), 1697 (27), 2497 (30), 2860 (276)
Llewellyn, D.: ref, 2050 (32)
Llewellyn, G.: ref, 1135 (17), 1164 (119), 2862 (435), 2879 (153)
Llorens, L. A.: ref, 1991 (20)
Llorente, A. M.: ref, 1135 (26), 1164 (180), 2599 (40)
Lloyd, A.: ref, 1079 (39), 1241 (5)
Lloyd, E.: ref, 2228 (2)
Lloyd, J. W.: rev, 1768, 2254
Lloyd, L. L.: ref, 1903 (209)
Lloyd, M.: ref, 681 (10)
Lloyd, M. C.: test, 1981
Lo, A.: ref, 2860 (965)
Lo, E. S.: ref, 1166 (1), 2305 (12), 2860 (924)
Loadman, W. E.: test, 1791
Loas, G.: ref, 272 (126,291)
Loasses, A.: ref, 2227 (55), 2860 (1381)
Lobaugh, A. F.: ref, 1363 (1), 1889 (10)
Lobeck, L.: ref, 2860 (561), 2892 (97)
Lobel, M.: ref, 1779 (2), 2076 (104), 2497 (184)
Lobel, T. E.: ref, 298 (85,86), 538 (4), 694 (8)
LoBello, S. G.: rev, 1079, 1212, 1243, 2065, 2148, 2745
Löberg, T.: ref, 652 (1)
Loblines, D. B.: ref, 1991 (101)
A Local Chapter Committee, American Association of University Professors: test, 1003
Locascio, J. J.: ref, 1135 (21)
Lochman, J. E.: ref, 451 (63,179), 472 (193)
Lock, T.: ref, 1166 (71)
Lockavitch, J. F.: ref, 2862 (731)
Locke, A.: test, 1511
Locke, E. A.: ref, 1348 (15)
Locke, J.: ref, 2305 (237)
Lockhart, W. E.: test, 1663
Lockman, L. A.: ref, 2860 (752), 2862 (291)
Locraft, C.: ref, 2749 (67)
Loeb, D. F.: ref, 331 (4), 994 (26), 2233 (4), 2695 (37)
Loeb, K. L.: ref, 2603 (562)
Loeb, P. A.: test, 1246
Loebel, A.: ref, 2305 (70)
Loeber, R.: ref, 451 (114), 2862 (348,443)
Loeches, M. M.: ref, 2863 (209)
Loeffler, C. B.: ref, 1533 (1)
Loehlin, J. C.: ref, 2212 (3), 2485 (136), 2860 (675)
Loevinger, J.: rev, 1965
Loewenstein, D. A.: ref, 1058 (3,4), 2860 (277,451,484), 2863 (72,125,135)
Loewenstein, R. J.: ref, 846 (18), 2247 (6), 2380 (2), 2603 (34), 2749 (11), 2860 (151)
Loewenstein Rehabilitation Hospital: test, 1513
Loewenthal, K.: ref, 2050 (119)
Lof, G. L.: ref, 1095 (39), 1903 (474), 1982 (14), 2229 (11)
Loffler, W.: ref, 2050 (33)
Lofquist, L. H.: test, 1694, 1695, 1701, 1702; ref, 1694 (3), 1701 (3)
Logan, G.: ref, 2862 (391), 2879 (136)
Logan, G. D.: ref, 2860 (670), 2892 (124)
Logan, H.: ref, 2497 (154,224,299), 2858 (73)
Logan, K. J.: ref, 2543 (2)
Logan, R.: ref, 1408 (2)
Logan, R. A.: ref, 624 (4), 1612 (36), 2864 (36,39)
Logemann, J. A.: test, 1040; ref, 1040 (6,7)
Logie, R. H.: ref, 2163 (312)
Logigan, E. L.: ref, 1697 (179), 2227 (7), 2860 (363), 2863 (95)
Logsdon, D. A.: ref, 811 (5), 1216 (35)
Logue, R. D.: rev, 1804
Loher, B.: test, 648
Lohnes, P. R.: rev, 398, 399, 1413, 2835
Lohr, J. B.: ref, 2288 (29), 2289 (20)
Lohr, J. M.: ref, 2603 (374,478)
Lohr, N. E.: test, 824; ref, 1697 (22), 2603 (6)
Lohr-Flanders, M.: ref, 2695 (20)
Loisel, M. L.: ref, 2862 (329)
Loiselle, L.: ref, 1216 (32), 1903 (182)
Lojek-Osiejuk, E.: ref, 2860 (1122)
Lokan, J.: test, 33
Lokken, K. J.: ref, 1095 (6), 2837 (1)
Lombard, J. W.: rev, 2164, 2165, 2166, 2538
Lombardino, L. J.: ref, 540 (19), 994 (46), 2695 (66), 2704 (45), 2905 (110)
Lombardo, J. P.: ref, 298 (69), 998 (114)
Lombardo, M. M.: test, 300
Lon, C. J.: rev, 1665
Lonardi, L.: ref, 1661 (35), 2603 (317)
London, A.: ref, 1140 (8)
London, E. D.: ref, 1697 (88), 2402 (6)
London House: test, 1972
London, J.: ref, 557 (1), 2749 (14)
London, P.: ref, 472 (107)
Lonergan, W. G.: test, 1569
Loney, J.: ref, 451 (207), 681 (65), 1010 (85), 1592 (24), 2862 (378), 2879 (131)
Long, A.: ref, 2603 (350)
Long, B. C.: ref, 298 (17,124), 2149 (3), 2497 (39), 2603 (196), 2858 (53)
Long, B. E.: ref, 1754 (24), 2527 (12)

Long, C.: ref, 273 (16), 1745 (66), 2860 (1228), 2863 (366)
Long, C. G.: ref, 337 (51)
Long, C. J.: rev, 176, 2011, 2297; ref, 2603 (401), 2863 (287)
Long, E. R.: test, 2898
Long, G.: ref, 364 (5)
Long, K.: ref, 298 (62,111)
Long, K. A.: ref, 1697 (320), 1991 (53)
Long, N.: ref, 2211 (1), 2839 (1)
Long, P. J.: ref, 2519 (34), 2520 (35)
Long, R. G.: ref, 1405 (32)
Long, S. A.: ref, 665 (13)
Long, S. H.: rev, 630, 2650, 2708; ref, 214 (14,16), 1485 (16,27), 1903 (173,256,521), 2657 (6,15,32)
Long, S. W.: ref, 1902 (45)
Long, V. O.: ref, 298 (120), 1939 (10)
Longabaugh, R.: ref, 134 (8), 1164 (11,138), 2860 (117,1199), 2863 (32)
Longmore, B. E.: ref, 1758 (25), 2860 (653), 2863 (192), 2892 (121)
Longnecker, J.: ref, 337 (84), 1697 (338)
Longo, A. P.: rev, 2139, 2732
Longstaff, H. P.: test, 1693
Lonigan, C. J.: ref, 472 (92), 1240 (20), 1903 (223), 2214 (52), 2228 (10)
Lönnqvist, J.: ref, 1166 (138)
Lonski, A. B.: test, 137
Loo, R.: ref, 999 (128), 1469 (9)
Loo, S.: ref, 1903 (408)
Loo, S. K.: ref, 451 (274)
Look, C.: ref, 592 (89)
Loomis, M.: test, 2411
Loop, K.: ref, 1698 (23)
Loos, W.: ref, 2497 (427)
Loosberg, R.: ref, 1697 (498)
Loosen, P. T.: ref, 2497 (367)
Loosses, A.: ref, 2163 (265), 2860 (1052)
Lopes, C. E.: ref, 1965 (22)
Lopex, O. L.: ref, 2860 (799)
Lopez, E. C.: rev, 2463
Lopez, F. G.: ref, 1754 (6), 2497 (40), 2525 (1)
Lopez, M.: ref, 681 (47), 1612 (25)
Lopez, M. A.: ref, 2358 (16)
Lopez, M. F.: ref, 681 (75), 2452 (14), 2607 (1), 2862 (511), 2879 (173)
Lopez, M. R.: ref, 2862 (262)
Lopez, S.: ref, 2813 (137)
Lopez, S. J.: ref, 2860 (967,1165)
López, S. R.: ref, 1010 (116), 2050 (50)
Lopez-Alberola, R. F.: ref, 1058 (4), 2860 (451), 2863 (125)
López-Rupérez, F.: ref, 1140 (17)
LoPiccolo, J.: ref, 2603 (141)
Loranger, A. W.: ref, 1093 (32)
Loranger, M.: ref, 2217 (2)
Lorch, E. P.: ref, 1903 (268)
Lorch, R. F., Jr.: ref, 2862 (693)
Lord, C.: ref, 459 (1,9,12,29), 837 (4), 1485 (15), 1653 (7,22), 1903 (96,148,352), 2163 (71,98,125), 2813 (28), 2860 (114,315,411,654)
Lord, C. G.: ref, 373 (23), 1965 (58)
Lord, R. G.: ref, 1338 (27)
Lord, T.: ref, 1405 (40)
Lorentz, S.: ref, 1485 (29), 2864 (58)
Lorenz, F. O.: ref, 2218 (15), 2603 (136,244,256, 355,467)
Lorenzi, M.: ref, 2862 (626), 2880 (6)
Lorenzi-Cioldi, F.: ref, 298 (87)
Lorge, I.: test, 624, 1796; rev, 1974, 2899
Lories, G.: ref, 2163 (134)
Lorimer, J.: test, 1520
Loring, D.: ref, 2860 (992), 2863 (294)
Loring, D. W.: ref, 641 (4,5), 1135 (5), 1164 (9), 1698 (16), 1903 (35) 2076 (19,118), 2227 (4,11,20), 2517 (4), 2599 (7,30), 2860 (68,115,194,198), 2863 (136), 2879 (15), 2892 (3,13)
Lorr, J. A.: ref, 2076 (15)
Lorr, M.: test, 1294, 2076, 2077, 2120; rev, 2417; ref, 1687 (7,8), 2076 (15)
Lorrain, D.: ref, 2516 (56), 2860 (771)
Lorsbach, T. C.: ref, 2862 (507), 2879 (170)
Lorscheider, F. L.: ref, 1132 (1), 1755 (62)
Lortie-Lussier, M.: ref, 1965 (36), 2497 (185)
Lorusso, S.: ref, 2227 (55), 2860 (1381)
Losler, G. F.: ref, 68 (56), 2218 (65)
Losonezy, M. F.: ref, 2860 (1378), 2879 (226), 2892 (296)
Loss, N.: ref, 472 (131), 557 (7), 2862 (426)
Lotas, M.: ref, 1216 (21)
Loth, J.: test, 2305
Lotspeich, L.: ref, 2862 (486)
Lotstra, F.: ref, 1166 (181)
Lott, I.: ref, 2860 (883)
Loughead, T. A.: ref, 413 (23), 1701 (47)
Louie, A. K.: ref, 2603 (197)
Louis, B.: ref, 1612 (92), 2485 (59)
Lourie, A.: ref, 451 (109)
Lousig-Nont, G. M.: test, 1976
Louth, S. M.: ref, 272 (364), 2860 (1402), 2879 (230)
Louttit, C. M.: rev, 433, 2010, 2813
Lovaas, O. I.: ref, 459 (25), 1903 (199), 1962 (6,9), 2813 (42,50)
Lovallee, J.-C.: ref, 650 (15), 1093 (97)
Lovallo, W. R.: ref, 272 (65), 2497 (243)
Lovance, K. J.: ref, 1902 (37)
Lovato, C.: ref, 2451 (2)
Love, C. C.: ref, 694 (111)
Love, S. R.: ref, 2813 (104)
Lovegrove, W.: ref, 1765 (1,12,13), 2163 (4,73,123)
Lovegrove, W. J.: ref, 322 (4), 1765 (14), 2163 (132), 2768 (19)
Lovejoy, M. C.: ref, 815 (5), 2498 (69), 2862 (129), 2879 (33)
Lovelace, L.: ref, 1216 (85)

Loveland, K. A.: ref, 459 (30,36), 679 (1), 681 (77), 815 (21), 1135 (12,14), 1485 (8,30,38,42), 1612 (20,53,66,74), 1903 (83,279,339,382,403,490), 2382 (2), 2485 (161,211), 2813 (67,84), 2862 (274), 2879 (84)
Loveland-Cherry, C.: ref, 1770 (1)
Loveland-Cherry, C. J.: ref, 270 (3), 1000 (21)
Lovell, D. M.: ref, 272 (292), 893 (44), 2860 (1301)
Lovell, K.: rev, 348, 952
Lovemore, T.: ref, 2038 (3)
Lovet, M. W.: ref, 1092 (4), 1096 (2), 1902 (19), 2862 (110), 2879 (25)
Lovett, E.: ref, 2050 (64,93), 2076 (97), 2239 (18), 2497 (384), 2860 (581), 2863 (168), 2892 (106)
Lovett, M. W.: ref, 1092 (18), 2712 (1), 2879 (85), 2879 (171), 2905 (98)
Lovette, G. J.: ref, 790 (23)
Lovitt, T. C.: ref, 1657 (9)
Lovrich, D.: ref, 540 (9), 2485 (207), 2860 (1302), 2862 (508), 2879 (172,210), 2905 (99,114)
Low, B. P.: rev, 61, 1474
Low, C. A.: ref, 2525 (10)
Low, L. C. K.: ref, 694 (117), 2497 (570)
Low, N.: ref, 1079 (51), 1758 (52)
Lowe, B.: ref, 35 (1), 1142 (3), 1143 (1), 1902 (7), 2862 (54)
Lowe, C. B.: ref, 451 (74), 889 (1)
Lowe, C. F.: ref, 2050 (7)
Lowe, G.: ref, 2771 (29)
Lowe, K.: ref, 4 (4,8), 694 (106), 1590 (60), 1897 (1)
Lowe, M.: test, 2601
Lowe, R.: ref, 272 (124), 273 (13), 2076 (115), 2497 (488)
Lowe, R. C.: ref, 2749 (43)
Lowe, R. J.: ref, 214 (3), 1095 (4), 2651 (2)
Lowell, S.: ref, 266 (3), 1047 (6), 1379 (60,77), 1485 (35), 1607 (10), 2524 (10), 2680 (13)
Lowman, R. L.: rev, 1539, 2588; ref, 302 (1), 1693 (1), 2163 (13), 2856 (1)
Lown, J. M.: ref, 1000 (72)
Lowry, C. B.: ref, 853 (13), 2247 (48)
Lowry, J. L.: ref, 2603 (274)
Lowry, M. J.: ref, 1903 (132)
Lowther, M. A.: test, 2530
Loyd, B.: ref, 1877 (1), 2862 (97)
Loyd, B. H.: test, 2735; rev, 666, 1010, 2032, 2339, 2831, 372 (30)
Loza, W.: ref, 1174 (3)
Lozoff, B.: ref, 1216 (67), 2864 (97)
Lu, C.: ref, 1140 (46)
Lu, L.: ref, 999 (92), 1178 (5), 2603 (280), 2858 (28)
Lu, S.: ref, 2402 (49), 2892 (208)
Lubeck, D. P.: ref, 2603 (253,552)
Luber, B.: ref, 1166 (148)
Lubick, L. J.: ref, 2863 (312), 2892 (222)
Lubin, A.: rev, 2417
Lubin, B.: test, 1745, 2499; ref, 472 (93,94), 1745 (21,43,59,82,86,89), 2076 (87,88), 2107 (2), 2603 (394)
Lubin, H.: ref, 337 (144)
Lubinski, D.: ref, 68 (49), 302 (4), 592 (88), 771 (25), 1010 (86), 1790 (9), 2163 (241), 2539 (1)
Lubitsch, G.: ref, 2050 (119)
Lublin, F.: ref, 1218 (5), 2599 (10), 2863 (109), 2892 (59)
Luborsky, L.: ref, 272 (148), 2305 (162), 2402 (52), 2603 (431,462)
Lubow, R. E.: ref, 681 (36)
Luby, J.: ref, 2305 (134)
Lucas, B. A.: ref, 1697 (225), 2212 (1)
Lucas, C.: ref, 1481 (3)
Lucas Grason-Stadler Co., Inc.: test, 1523
Lucas, H.: ref, 1901 (16), 2485 (123,124)
Lucas, J. A.: ref, 1164 (10), 1903 (36), 2199 (1), 2226 (25), 2497 (122), 2860 (278,1283), 2863 (73,387)
Lucas, M. D.: ref, 2163 (283), 2226 (10), 2227 (27), 2863 (333), 2892 (234)
Lucas, P. R.: ref, 448 (28)
Lucca, A.: ref, 1166 (75)
Lucchelli, F.: ref, 2163 (109,155,319), 2860 (448,603,836), 2863 (123), 2892 (269)
Lucci, D.: ref, 1612 (8,11), 1903 (22,52), 2813 (1)
Luce, S. C.: ref, 1903 (76), 2432 (13), 2485 (35), 2813 (9)
Lucente, S.: ref, 2860 (613)
Lucey, J. V.: ref, 2892 (277)
Luchetta, T.: ref, 272 (372), 2076 (185)
Luchins, D.: ref, 1590 (44), 2497 (444)
Luchins, D. J.: ref, 2892 (134)
Luchman, A.: ref, 665 (23), 694 (16), 705 (1), 2252 (1), 2771 (7)
Luciani, J. J.: test, 1002
Luciano, G.: ref, 1705 (2)
Luciano, P. J.: ref, 2227 (17), 2863 (213)
Lucic, K. S.: ref, 2497 (123)
Lucier, G. E.: ref, 1132 (1), 1755 (62)
Lucini, V.: ref, 1166 (75)
Lucio, E.: ref, 1697 (321)
Lucke, J. C.: ref, 999 (36), 1079 (13)
Lucker, J. R.: ref, 1096 (12)
Lucking, C. H.: ref, 2163 (54)
Ludbrook, C.: ref, 337 (192)
Ludden, L.: test, 934
Ludden, L. L.: test, 1252
Ludgate, J.: ref, 2519 (56), 2520 (55)
Ludlow, C. L.: ref, 2305 (137)
Ludlow, L. H.: test, 1906
Ludman, E.: ref, 2603 (474)
Ludolph, P. S.: test, 824
Ludwig, A. M.: ref, 2858 (76)
Ludwig, C.: ref, 2860 (244), 2863 (62)
Luecken, L.: ref, 272 (336), 2218 (116), 2497 (664)
Lueger, R. J.: ref, 272 (252,365), 1164 (20), 1379 (7), 2226 (4), 2603 (515,588), 2892 (23)
Luepker, R. V.: ref, 1697 (32)
Luetke-Stahlman, B.: ref, 331 (4), 811 (10), 994 (26), 1618 (3), 2233 (4), 2695 (37), 2813 (98), 2901 (66)
Lufi, D.: ref, 2214 (31,71)

Lugaresi, E.: ref, 2768 (34), 2860 (1082)
Luhr, D. D.: ref, 2258 (3)
Luhtanen, R.: ref, 694 (33)
Lukashov, I.: ref, 270 (23), 1612 (87)
Lukens, E.: ref, 2288 (52)
Lukens, J.: ref, 2485 (208), 2862 (509)
Lukhele, R.: ref, 94 (1), 117 (4), 666 (15)
Lukin, L. E.: rev, 384, 946
Lukman, B.: ref, 2247 (26)
Lulun, B.: ref, 2499 (1)
Lum, C. U.: ref, 272 (34)
Lumb, D.: test, 884
Lumb, M.: test, 884
Lumley, M. A.: ref, 472 (208), 2076 (175), 2214 (120)
Lumpkin, J.: ref, 2858 (45)
Lumsden, J.: rev, 1240
Luna, M.: ref, 401 (3)
Lundberg, A. C.: ref, 2295 (5)
Lundeen, T. F.: test, 2766
Lundell, K.: test, 730
Lundgren, S. L.: ref, 2860 (5), 2863 (3)
Lundin, B.: ref, 2038 (2)
Lundin, R. W.: rev, 371, 1752
Lundy, A.: ref, 998 (101), 2402 (40), 2603 (200,375)
Lunenburg, F. C.: ref, 1590 (15)
Lunn, S.: ref, 2603 (110), 2860 (279)
Lunneborg, C. E.: ref, 372 (7), 771 (4)
Lunneborg, P. W.: test, 2833; rev, 1790
Luo, D.: ref, 2858 (91)
Lupart, J. L.: ref, 385 (3), 1991 (93), 2753 (1), 2901 (94)
Lupei, R. L.: ref, 1580 (2), 2603 (13)
Lupkowski, A. E.: ref, 615 (37), 694 (34)
Lushene, R.: test, 2497
Lushene, R.E.: test, 2498
Lusk, R.: ref, 1169 (1), 1401 (2), 1522 (3), 1902 (51), 1962 (10), 1991 (63), 2242 (4), 2247 (46), 2361 (1), 2380 (10), 2485 (105), 2498 (26), 2749 (35)
Lussier, Y.: ref, 298 (119), 451 (291), 472 (235), 863 (52,84), 2858 (124)
Luster, T.: ref, 1216 (4,6,22,33,51,84), 1902 (16,56), 1903 (48,128,280)
Lustig, J. L.: ref, 472 (29)
Luszcz, M.: ref, 2599 (11), 2860 (431,926)
Luszcz, M. A.: ref, 1758 (58), 2860 (485,1047)
Luthar, S. S.: ref, 451 (208), 472 (30,55,56,95,132,203), 790 (7,8), 1274 (2), 1379 (72), 1386 (18), 2163 (90), 2214 (21,32,53,72), 2380 (6), 2451 (1), 2478 (1), 2813 (99)
Lutherer, L.: ref, 2076 (6), 2860 (141)
Luttman, D.: ref, 1903 (184), 2402 (20), 2485 (90)
Luty, D. T.: ref, 1697 (385)
Lutz, J. G.: ref, 1612 (72), 1902 (70), 2862 (330)
Lutz, W. C.: test, 1468
Lutzenberger, W.: ref, 2860 (1137)
Lutzky, S. M.: ref, 2603 (281)
Luzzatti, C.: ref, 2163 (58), 2225 (12)
Luzzo, D. A.: ref, 401 (3), 404 (28), 405 (1), 413 (15,17,18,24,25,26,28,29,30), 2282 (8), 2360 (9), 2835 (14)
Lydiard, R. B.: ref, 1166 (68), 2603 (277,328)
Lydon, J.: ref, 791 (7,9,14,15)
Lykken, D. T.: rev, 551, 708, 1322, 1333; ref, 372 (107) 998 (36), 1697 (149)
Lykouras, L.: ref, 1093 (69)
Lyman, B. J.: ref, 2860 (49)
Lyman, H. B.: rev, 1902, 1903, 2860
Lyman, R. D.: ref, 1380 (1), 2211 (33)
Lynam, D.: ref, 365 (2)
Lynch, D. J.: ref, 1338 (31), 1686 (3)
Lynch, D. L.: ref, 451 (79,278), 472 (147,230), 694 (134), 999 (141), 1012 (1), 1079 (54,109), 1991 (87)
Lynch, E. W.: test, 879, 2041
Lynch, G. V.: ref, 1166 (220)
Lynch, I.: ref, 337 (14), 1925 (1)
Lynch, J. I.: rev, 2233, 2382, 2801
Lynch, M.: ref, 365 (3), 373 (15), 472 (44), 694 (49), 1903 (162)
Lynch, M. E.: ref, 373 (17), 1987 (8)
Lynch, M. J.: ref, 998 (10,8)
Lynch, P. M.: ref, 998 (17), 2497 (41,662)
Lynch, R. S.: ref, 2497 (550,551)
Lynch, S. J.: ref, 573 (1), 574 (1), 587 (1), 615 (38)
Lynch, V. J.: ref, 2603 (19)
Lynd-Stevenson, R. M.: ref, 272 (197,293)
Lyness, S. A.: ref, 337 (82), 1164 (69), 2520 (45), 2599 (20), 2860 (676), 2863 (200)
Lynn, D.: ref, 998 (24)
Lynn, R.: ref, 998 (124), 2038 (1), 2163 (172,173), 2304 (3), 2485 (137), 2860 (370,486,677)
Lynn, S. J.: ref, 793 (20), 846 (17), 1697 (12,454,493), 2247 (3), 2603 (476)
Lynn, T. F.: ref, 2695 (20)
Lynskey, M.: ref, 1216 (46), 2211 (39)
Lynskey, M. T.: ref, 358 (11), 681 (31), 694 (113,114), 2091 (2,3), 2094 (1,3), 2211 (28,38,47), 2714 (4,5), 2862 (253,468,470)
Lyon, J. M.: ref, 1000 (32)
Lyon, L. P.: test, 219, 1930, 1955
Lyon, M. A.: ref, 2813 (123), 2862 (365)
Lyons, A.: ref, 1178 (12)
Lyons, C. A.: ref, 1072 (46), 2905 (61)
Lyons, J. A.: ref, 1697 (322)
Lyons, J. S.: test, 2388
Lyons, K.: ref, 776 (16)
Lyons, K. E.: ref, 271 (15), 272 (330), 376 (28), 776 (56), 1135 (24), 1218 (19), 1378 (10), 1740 (26), 2076 (181), 2516 (112), 2863 (411), 2892 (293)
Lyons, L.: ref, 2603 (498)
Lyons, M. J.: ref, 791 (1), 1093 (84), 1164 (68), 1218 (7), 1645 (3), 1697 (408), 1965 (66), 2516 (42,65), 2860 (671,855), 2863 (199,250), 2879 (81), 2892 (125,176)
Lyons, T. M.: test, 759

Lyons-Ruth, K.: ref, 2039 (9,10), 2860 (280), 2864 (34)
Lysaker, P.: ref, 297 (1), 2017 (10), 2432 (18,19), 2892 (128,129,194), 2924 (2)
Lysaker, P. H.: ref, 2017 (14,15), 2432 (25,30), 2892 (195,196,235,236), 2924 (3)
Lyssand, E. T.: ref, 2860 (898), 2862 (354)
Lysy, D. C.: ref, 2860 (1411), 2899 (19)
Lysynchuk, L. M.: ref, 389 (4), 1072 (18)
Lytle, B. L.: ref, 1697 (530), 2879 (154)
Lytle, C.: ref, 472 (52)
Lytle, L. J.: ref, 1631 (3)
Lytton, H.: ref, 451 (134)
Lyytinen, H.: ref, 815 (45), 2862 (641), 2901 (122)
Lyytinen, P.: ref, 1903 (206,281), 2163 (129), 2247 (43), 2768 (18), 2862 (275)

Ma, H. K.: ref, 495 (4), 694 (23), 771 (12,27), 999 (32,161), 1010 (23), 2163 (72)
Maag, J.: ref, 1386 (9), 2485 (144), 2864 (67), 2879 (90)
Maag, J. W.: ref, 75 (1), 694 (76), 1379 (56), 2211 (31,34), 2432 (20), 2485 (145), 2862 (276,285), 2901 (46)
Maas, H. S.: rev, 147
Maas, J. B.: test, 706
Mabe, P. A.: ref, 472 (31), 1215 (2), 2214 (22)
Mabey, B.: test, 236
Mabry, L.: rev, 2879
Macaluso, J. M.: ref, 2288 (70), 2289 (55), 2305 (181)
Macan, T. H.: ref, 1338 (42)
MacAndrew, C.: ref, 1697 (39)
MacArthur, C.: ref, 2485 (166)
MacArthur, C. A.: ref, 2432 (15), 2731 (2), 2732 (1), 2862 (202,366,510), 2901 (25), 2905 (38,79)
Macaruso, P.: ref, 1392 (6), 1902 (25), 1903 (534), 2163 (329), 2860 (285)
Macauley, B. L.: ref, 2873 (32)
MacCann, R. G.: ref, 592 (6)
Macciocchi, S. N.: ref, 1164 (21), 1740 (6), 2860 (174,195)
MacCleod, A. K.: ref, 272 (46), 2497 (124)
Maccow, G.: rev, 789
MacDermid, S. M.: ref, 2858 (63)
MacDonald, A.: ref, 1140 (34)
MacDonald, A. W.: ref, 681 (57,71), 1010 (68), 1380 (3,9), 1991 (76), 2452 (4), 2879 (99), 2901 (49)
MacDonald, A. W. III: ref, 472 (154), 1380 (10), 2214 (88), 2879 (152), 2901 (82)
MacDonald, C.: ref, 1758 (16), 2193 (8), 2860 (283,695), 2863 (75), 2892 (36,135)
MacDonald, D. A.: ref, 1755 (42,57), 2218 (34), 2860 (897)
MacDonald, G. W.: ref, 1903 (383), 2879 (126), 2905 (80)
MacDonald, H.: ref, 350 (13), 901 (1), 1653 (13), 2163 (145), 2228 (11), 2860 (334,571)
Macdonald, I.: test, 441
MacDonald, J.: rev, 540, 2668
MacDonald, J. D.: test, 898
MacDonald, N. E.: ref, 451 (2)
MacDonold, V.: ref, 389 (1), 1071 (1), 1657 (1)
MacDougall, M.: ref, 1720 (1)
Mace, F. C.: rev, 1867, 2848
Mace, L. D.: ref, 2603 (523)
MacEwen, K. E.: ref, 2211 (10)
MacGinitie, R. K.: test, 1071, 1072
MacGinitie, W. H.: test, 1071, 1072
MacGregor, D.: ref, 1086 (3), 2813 (79)
Macgregor, L. A.: ref, 1164 (71), 2860 (709), 2892 (136)
Machado, A. M.: ref, 1135 (2), 1740 (8), 2599 (4), 2860 (200)
Macher, J.: ref, 2305 (33)
Macher, J-P.: ref, 1166 (105)
Machida, S.: ref, 693 (3), 1987 (3), 2603 (102), 2858 (26)
Machin, M. A.: ref, 272 (349), 1079 (104)
Macias, M.: ref, 451 (275), 2485 (243), 2862 (723)
Maciejewski, P. K.: ref, 1166 (173)
MacInnes, W. D.: ref, 1697 (386)
MacIntyre, P. D.: ref, 950 (2,3), 1321 (3), 2497 (42,125,126)
Mack, A. E.: ref, 798 (8), 994 (4), 1040 (4), 1903 (129), 2693 (2), 2694 (7), 2768 (9)
Mack, C.: ref, 272 (334), 376 (30)
Mack, W.: ref, 182 (1), 776 (5), 2008 (4), 2860 (147,311)
MacKay, D. G.: ref, 2860 (678)
Mackay, H. A.: ref, 1903 (283,387), 2879 (128)
Mackay, P. W.: ref, 1661 (15)
Mackay, S.: ref, 1058 (7), 2227 (12), 2860 (499), 2863 (143)
Mackenzie, B.: ref, 1765 (12,13), 2163 (73,123)
MacKenzie, E. P.: ref, 863 (81)
MacKenzie, I. R. A.: ref, 2860 (1123)
Mackenzie, R.: test, 901
Mackenzie, S. B.: ref, 1701 (39)
Mackenzie, T. B.: ref, 272 (195), 2497 (313), 2497 (568)
Mackie, B.: ref, 665 (34)
MacKinney, A. C.: rev, 1043, 2871
Mackinnon, A.: ref, 999 (56), 2239 (19,22), 2599 (15), 2860 (587), 2863 (175)
MacKinnon, A. J.: ref, 999 (89,90,114), 1758 (44), 2860 (823), 2863 (238)
MacKinnon, G. E.: ref, 2704 (46), 2860 (1391), 2862 (715)
MacKinnon-Lewis, C.: ref, 472 (32)
Macklin, E. D.: ref, 863 (21)
Macklin, M. L.: ref, 2860 (1403)
Mackner, L. M.: ref, 1216 (103), 2860 (1303)
MacLean, A. P.: ref, 863 (69)
MacLean, M.: ref, 350 (1), 2864 (10)
Maclean, P. R.: test, 1342
MacLean, W. E.: ref, 451 (53), 472 (119)
MacLean, W. E., Jr.: ref, 451 (215), 1962 (23)
MacLennan, J. M.: ref, 537 (2), 1390 (6), 1758 (53) 2860 (982)

MacLeod, A. K.: ref, 2497 (368)
MacLeod, C. M.: ref, 2163 (103)
MacLeod, K. M.: ref, 127 (3), 1758 (38)
Macmann, G. M.: ref, 1485 (19), 1653 (9), 1903 (190), 2485 (95), 2813 (40), 2860 (487,679,680), 2862 (643,644), 2864 (59,60)
MacMillan, D.: ref, 2860 (883)
MacMillan, D. L.: ref, 61 (2), 301 (56), 681 (74,75,94), 2163 (273), 2299 (1), 2452 (14,15,19,24), 2607 (1), 2813 (41,124), 2860 (488,878), 2862 (216,484,511,512,513,622,724), 2864 (40,88), 2879 (163,173,174,207,231)
MacMillan, D. R.: ref, 451 (152), 472 (187), 473 (3)
MacMillan, F.: ref, 2050 (72)
Macmillan, H.: ref, 2497 (491)
Macmillan Test Unit: test, 1530, 1531
Macnab, D.: test, 1493; ref, 1694 (1), 2915 (1)
MacNair, R. R.: ref, 998 (67), 2065 (11)
Macnamara, S. E.: ref, 2076 (16)
Macnee, C. L.: ref, 1697 (137), 2603 (111)
MacPhee, D.: rev, 1230, 2025, 2036, 2041, 2444; ref, 1883 (1)
MacQuarrie, T. W.: test, 1533
Macrosson, W. D. K.: ref, 1036 (12), 2417 (40)
Maculaitis, J. D.: test, 1527, 1534
Madak, P. R.: ref, 2704 (1), 2862 (109)
Madan-Swain, A.: ref, 799 (1), 815 (4), 1379 (11), 1902 (22), 2862 (122), 2879 (32)
Madaus, M. R.: ref, 2862 (722)
Madden, D. J.: ref, 303 (1,2), 791 (2), 1164 (23), 1338 (11), 1740 (3), 2497 (21,104,275), 2516 (2,30), 2603 (8,83), 2860 (81,237,507,556), 2863 (146)
Madden, N. A.: ref, 2695 (5)
Madden, P. A. F.: ref, 999 (172)
Madden, S. E.: ref, 1657 (22), 1866 (43), 2488 (9)
Maddever, H. M.: ref, 793 (5), 2839 (2)
Maddi, S. R.: ref, 1697 (323)
Maddock, A.: ref, 2862 (550)
Maddock, R. J.: ref, 2603 (198,342)
Maddocks, A.: ref, 1166 (41)
Maddox, M. A.: ref, 1047 (1), 1240 (7), 2660 (2), 2695 (9)
Maddox, T.: test, 258, 806
Maddux, C. D.: rev, 619, 1765, 2171, 2467, 2481, 2666, 2691; ref, 2862 (569)
Madge, E. M.: test, 1321, 1370
Madherc, S.: ref, 694 (24,56,77)
Madigan, E. A.: ref, 1216 (112), 1889 (20)
Madigan, M. F., Jr.: ref, 1338 (46)
Madigan, N. K.: ref, 2437 (2)
Madison, C. L.: test, 1399; ref, 270 (34), 1216 (101), 1903 (530), 2382 (38), 2860 (371), 2862 (169)
Madison, G.: ref, 2126 (1)
Madonia, M. J.: ref, 272 (221), 1166 (93)
Madonna, S.: ref, 694 (103)
Madonna, S., Jr.: ref, 1745 (33)
Madsen, C. H.: ref, 1000 (64)
Madsen, C. H., Jr.: ref, 2558 (3)
Maduschke, K. M.: test, 2929
Maehr, M. L.: test, 1276, 1856, 2922
Maercker, A.: ref, 2218 (61), 2603 (465)
Maes, L.: ref, 1166 (20)
Maes, M.: ref, 272 (198), 1166 (5,18,19,20,58,76, 77,78,126,127,128,198,217,230), 2497 (25,127)
Maes, S.: ref, 2497 (409)
Maes, W. R.: test, 2625
Maestri, A.: ref, 1166 (189)
Magaletta, P. R.: ref, 372 (22), 1965 (18)
Magana-Amato, A.: ref, 272 (74), 1166 (40)
Magee, R.: ref, 175 (10), 1040 (9), 1240 (28), 1804 (9) 1903 (282)
Maggioni, M.: ref, 1166 (69)
Magids, D. M.: ref, 2417 (42)
Magill-Evans, J.: ref, 1653 (18), 2813 (73), 2864 (68)
Magliano, L.: ref, 2305 (146,186)
Magner, N. R.: ref, 2149 (4)
Magni, E.: ref, 2516 (61), 2860 (804), 2892 (163)
Magnussen, S.: ref, 900 (5), 2860 (116)
Magoon, T. M.: test, 2116; ref, 1754 (18)
Magro, T.: ref, 2163 (122), 2860 (482), 2862 (214)
Magrun, W. M.: test, 977
Maguire, E. A.: ref, 1140 (50), 2860 (1124)
Maguire, K.: ref, 1166 (32), 2497 (51)
Maguire, R. W.: ref, 1903 (283)
Magura, S.: test, 458
Magureanu, S.: ref, 2163 (66), 2860 (259)
Magyar, I.: ref, 1166 (67)
Magyary, D.: ref, 1010 (30), 1902 (29), 2862 (155)
Mahabeer, M.: ref, 694 (57)
Mahalik, J. R.: ref, 694 (96), 2497 (446), 2603 (479)
Mahamed, F.: ref, 893 (21)
Maher, L. M.: ref, 209 (1,2), 1096 (11), 1903 (343, 384,419), 2860 (1322), 2873 (23,32,3946, 57, 65,70)
Mahler, H. I. M.: ref, 1661 (14), 2497 (37)
Maholick, L. T.: test, 2126
Mahon, M. E.: ref, 1947 (3)
Mahoney, A.: ref, 451 (138,209), 1582 (14)
Mahoney, F. C.: test, 2385
Mahoney, J. J.: test, 2101
Mahoney, J. T.: test, 162, 1251, 1443, 1549, 1929, 2270, 2385
Mahoney, N.: ref, 272 (343)
Mahony, D. L.: ref, 1903 (130), 2905 (26)
Mahorney, S. L.: ref, 998 (19), 2305 (30)
Mahowald, M. W.: ref, 1697 (446), 2703 (2)
Mahr, J. M.: ref, 2485 (100)
Mahurin, R. K.: rev, 670, 1135, 1165, 1993; ref, 1164 (29), 2860 (281), 2863 (74)
Maier, J. M.: ref, 561 (1)
Maier, N. R. F.: test, 2633
Maier, R.: ref, 999 (15)
Maier, W.: ref, 2305 (108,145)
Main, R.: ref, 1770 (4)
Maio, G. R.: ref, 2246 (13)

Maiphurs, J.: ref, 270 (16), 272 (169)
Maislin, G.: ref, 1166 (86)
Maisto, A. A.: ref, 2299 (6)
Maisto, S. A.: ref, 136 (11), 1661 (81), 2414 (7)
Maitlen, B.: test, 934
Maitlen, B. R.: test, 1252
Maiuro, R. D.: ref, 2603 (29,75), 2858 (9,22)
Maj, M.: ref, 1525 (10), 2305 (146,186)
Majeres, R. L.: ref, 1693 (3)
Major, B.: ref, 1745 (29), 2603 (246)
Majsterek, D. J.: ref, 1240 (36), 1386 (19), 1903 (385), 2905 (81)
Majumdar, S. K.: ref, 739 (8)
Majumder, P. P.: ref, 1902 (76), 2860 (1404), 2862 (372)
Mak, E.: ref, 335 (1), 2289 (6)
Makarem, K.: ref, 1380 (2)
Makaremi, A.: ref, 999 (40)
Maker, C. J.: ref, 1379 (2)
Makini, G.: ref, 2497 (605)
Makino, K.: ref, 1128 (3)
Makowski, T.: test, 1346
Maksymchuk, L. L.: ref, 694 (109), 1697 (462), 2497 (528), 2559 (11) 2704 (36)
Maky, M. M.: ref, 124 (1), 1379 (23)
Malabonger, V. A.: ref, 1657 (22), 1866 (43), 2488 (9)
Malacarne, P.: ref, 1166 (189)
Malafosse, A.: ref, 2305 (117)
Malamuth, N. M.: ref, 863 (66), 999 (13,93)
Malapani, C.: ref, 2163 (183), 2516 (44), 2860 (720), 2863 (215), 2892 (94,130,142)
Malarkey, W. B.: ref, 1698 (10), 2076 (119)
Malcarne, V. L.: ref, 337 (70,104), 472 (77), 2214 (38)
Malcolm, A. T.: ref, 1745 (44)
Malcolm, K. K.: rev, 705, 917, 1192, 2503
Malcom, P. J.: test, 1468
Malcomesius, N.: test, 2469
Maldonado, M.: ref, 694 (5)
Malearne, V. L.: ref, 1745 (74)
Malec, J. F.: ref, 1687 (9), 2076 (17), 2860 (905), 2863 (272)
Malgady, R. G.: test, 2647, 2824; ref, 1991 (21) 2497 (390,571), 2498 (6), 2603 (245), 2647 (1)
Malhotra, A.: ref, 1697 (368)
Malhotra, A. K.: ref, 2862 (629)
Malik, F.: ref, 999 (140)
Malik, S. C.: ref, 681 (5), 2864 (21)
Malinchoc, M.: ref, 1697 (324,430),499,587), 1698 (12)
Malinski, D.: ref, 451 (129), 998 (113)
Malla, A.: ref, 2288 (55,78,79), 2289 (42,65)
Malla, A. K.: ref, 271 (3), 272 (205)
Maller, R. G.: ref, 2497 (186)
Maller, S. J.: rev, 388, 2701; ref, 2862 (645,646)
Mallet, C. A.: ref, 2710 (1)
Mallet, J.: ref, 2227 (19), 2305 (117), 2860 (818), 2863 (236)
Malley, J. E.: ref, 451 (9)
Malley, M.: ref, 2860 (465), 2863 (131)
Malliaras, D.: ref, 1093 (69)
Mallinckrodt, B.: ref, 337 (147), 2656 (5)
Mallinson, G.: test, 904
Mallinson, G. G.: rev, 501
Mallinson, J.: test, 904
Mallory, R.: ref, 451 (22)
Malloy, P.: ref, 1164 (11), 1218 (16), 2599 (35), 2860 (117), 2863 (32,317)
Malloy, P. F.: ref, 1164 (138), 2860 (1199)
Malloy, T. E.: ref, 298 (70)
Malloy-Miller, T.: ref, 353 (18)
Malm, V.: ref, 2288 (6), 2289 (4)
Malone, K. M.: ref, 272 (161), 273 (17), 1093 (95,96), 1166 (98)
Malone, L. D.: ref, 1392 (7), 2485 (60), 2905 (27)
Malone, M. E.: rev, 1191, 1255
Malone, V.: ref, 2497 (369)
Maloney, S. E.: test, 1956
Maloni, J. A.: ref, 1745 (30)
Malow, B. A.: ref, 335 (7)
Maloy, R. M.: ref, 745 (17)
Malsbary, D. R.: rev, 2408
Malt, V. F.: ref, 1079 (83)
Maltzman, I.: ref, 372 (41), 838 (12), 999 (44), 1140 (25), 2485 (201), 2860 (1085)
Malva, C. L. D.: ref, 1903 (191), 2863 (137)
Mamberg, M. H.: ref, 997 (2)
Mampunza, S.: ref, 1166 (194)
Man in't Veld, A. J.: ref, 1166 (164), 1697 (186), 2305 (204), 2497 (189)
Management Research Associates: test, 161
Management Research Group Staff: test, 1549, 2270
Manaim, H.: ref, 2860 (875), 2873 (36)
Mancini, C.: ref, 272 (93,236), 2497 (149,293, 408, 491,572,600)
Mancini, F.: ref, 2892 (152)
Mancini, T.: ref, 1697 (352)
Mandal, M. K.: ref, 272 (340)
Mandel, D. R.: ref, 2899 (8)
Mandel, H. P.: test, 37, 2265
Mandeli, J.: ref, 863 (71), 2076 (179)
Mandelkern, M. A.: ref, 2860 (984)
Mandell, A. J.: ref, 1697 (431)
Mandell, M. M.: rev, 1221
Mandes, E.: ref, 2860 (489)
Mandin, H.: ref, 1697 (66,67), 2076 (9,10)
Mandoki, M. W.: ref, 2862 (170)
Mandys, F.: ref, 2485 (195), 2862 (460)
Manemmani, I.: ref, 1093 (27), 2603 (88)
Manfredo, P. A.: ref, 2899 (5)
Manfro, G. G.: ref, 2305 (187)
Mangan, G.: ref, 128 (2)
Mangan, G. L.: ref, 999 (173), 2163 (305), 2860 (1182)
Mangano, E. L.: ref, 2557 (2)
Mangelsdorf, S.: ref, 373 (7), 2862 (88)
Mangelsdorf, S. C.: ref, 272 (109), 2497 (453), 2603 (295)
Mangine, S.: test, 1961

Mangot, D.: ref, 2485 (234)
Mangun, G. R.: ref, 2860 (1105), 2879 (166)
Mangweth, B.: ref, 893 (24)
Mani, S.: ref, 1903 (538), 2163 (331)
Manicavasagar, V.: ref, 999 (138)
Manifold, V.: ref, 1697 (113)
Manimala, M. R.: ref, 2497 (465)
Manion, I. G.: ref, 337 (148), 863 (34,80), 1000 (99), 1903 (473), 1991 (92)
Manis, F. R.: ref, 2862 (514), 2905 (44,100)
Mankoo, B. S.: ref, 2305 (141,180)
Manley, C. M.: ref, 337 (107), 1010 (64), 1697 (235)
Manlove, E. E.: ref, 2382 (36)
Manly, J. J.: ref, 303 (29), 776 (61), 1740 (32), 2860 (1405)
Manly, J. T.: ref, 365 (5), 373 (12), 472 (41), 1903 (147)
Manly, T.: ref, 2516 (109), 2892 (287)
Mann, A.: ref, 1758 (77), 2163 (298)
Mann, B. J.: ref, 863 (81), 1697 (432), 2211 (36), 2497 (573), 2603 (337,376)
Mann, E.: ref, 2749 (53)
Mann, J.: ref, 1697 (67), 2076 (10)
Mann, J. J.: ref, 272 (161), 273 (17), 1093 (74,95,96), 1166 (14,98), 2417 (6)
Mann, L.: test, 2431; rev, 284, 816; ref, 2497 (135)
Mann, L. S.: ref, 1241 (4), 2218 (35)
Mann, M. F.: ref, 1697 (18)
Mann, P. H.: test, 2627, 2628
Mann, R. L.: test, 1946
Mann, R. L. E.: ref, 998 (102)
Mann, V. A.: ref, 815 (9), 1657 (10), 1903 (130), 2860 (196,490), 2862 (111), 2879 (26), 2905 (26,45)
Mannarino, A. P.: ref, 472 (96), 1991 (70,71), 2498 (38,39)
Manne, S. L.: ref, 2076 (89), 2497 (69), 2858 (15)
Mannheim, B.: ref, 298 (13)
Mannheim, G. B.: ref, 2860 (436)
Manni, R.: ref, 2163 (328), 2860 (1281)
Manning, B. H.: ref, 2754 (5), 2771 (36)
Manning, C. A.: ref, 776 (24), 2863 (275)
Manning, L.: ref, 641 (8), 1758 (71,87), 2163 (325), 2226 (22), 2860 (1125), 2863 (382)
Manning, M.: ref, 1596 (1), 2163 (34), 2234 (1)
Mannino, J. P.: test, 805
Mannuzza, S.: ref, 2218 (96), 2305 (34,132,147), 2860 (983)
Manoach, D. S.: ref, 1093 (90), 2125 (12), 2247 (66)
Manolis, M. B.: ref, 1745 (65)
Manor, O.: ref, 681 (67), 1379 (68), 2163 (244), 2862 (346), 2864 (89)
Manor-Bullock, R.: ref, 592 (89)
Mansfield, E.: ref, 2749 (78)
Mansfield, E. D.: ref, 2749 (68,69)
Mansfield, R.: test, 1957
Manson, M. P.: test, 132, 1577, 2874
Manson, S. M.: ref, 2557 (8)
Manstead, A. S. R.: ref, 350 (16), 2163 (152)
Mant, R.: ref, 2050 (32)
Mantegazza, R.: ref, 1903 (563), 2163 (347), 2227 (54), 2768 (42), 2862 (698)
Manteuffel, B.: ref, 1947 (6)
Manton, K. G.: ref, 2050 (84)
Mantovan, M. C.: ref, 199 (14), 2193 (22), 2247 (116), 2860 (647,1248), 2863 (187,376)
Mantzicopoulos, D.: ref, 665 (14), 1379 (6), 2488 (2)
Mantzicopoulos, P.: ref, 1379 (19)
Mantzicopoulos, P. Y.: ref, 364 (14), 665 (64), 1379 (49), 2211 (32,51) 2484 (5), 2488 (8)
Manu, P.: ref, 272 (15)
Manual, A.: ref, 1965 (31)
Manuck, S. B.: ref, 1135 (19), 2497 (603), 2516 (41,89), 2860 (1200), 2863 (360)
Manuel, G. M.: ref, 2603 (391)
Manuel, H.: rev, 1484
Manuel, H. T.: test, 2711, 2741, 2744
Manuele, C. A.: rev, 2882
Manuele-Adkins, C.: rev, 83, 1177, 2264, 2360, 2406, 2923
Manzeki, K. M.: ref, 124 (1), 1379 (23)
Manzella, L. M.: ref, 1745 (64), 2076 (137)
Manzoni, G. C.: ref, 1166 (21)
Mapou, R. L.: ref, 2497 (361)
Mar, D. K.: test, 2053, 2826
Marangell, L. B.: ref, 272 (294), 1166 (199)
Maratos, E. J.: ref, 1758 (99), 2860 (1379), 2863 (414)
Maravita, A.: ref, 2163 (222), 2860 (927)
Marcel, B. B.: ref, 1903 (192), 2860 (491)
Marcell, M. M.: ref, 1423 (1), 2485 (61,171), 2695 (13,42), 2860 (928), 2864 (98)
Marcellini, A.: ref, 298 (108), 2497 (326)
March, C. L.: ref, 863 (12), 1592 (18), 2485 (119)
March, J.: test, 1730
March, J. S.: test, 680; ref, 681 (90)
Marchal, G.: ref, 2516 (64), 2863 (248)
Marchand-Martella, N. E.: ref, 2860 (96)
Marchant, G. J.: rev, 990, 1883, 1963
Marcheschi, M.: ref, 472 (210), 2862 (658)
Marchese, A. C.: test, 543
Marchesi, C.: ref, 1166 (21)
Marchette, L.: ref, 1770 (4)
Marchetti, C.: ref, 2163 (77)
Marchioro, C. A.: ref, 298 (164)
Marcia, J. E.: ref, 2218 (119)
Marcic, D.: ref, 1404 (8)
Marciniak, E. M.: ref, 565 (1)
Marco, C. A.: ref, 998 (25), 1338 (22)
Marco, G. L.: rev, 1157, 2479, 2795
Marcoen, A.: ref, 1405 (37), 2599 (36), 2860 (1196)
Marcos, T.: ref, 999 (103), 1164 (70), 2860 (681), 2863 (201)
Marcotte, D.: ref, 2603 (391)
Marcotte, T.: ref, 272 (181), 376 (5), 1166 (113), 2863 (324)

Marcotte, T. D.: ref, 272 (295), 376 (23), 1135 (13), 2599 (25), 2860 (772,1304), 2863 (394), 2873 (67)
Marcovitch, S.: ref, 1086 (3), 2813 (79)
Marcus, D. S.: ref, 665 (2)
Marcus, J.: ref, 301 (1,22), 748 (1,8), 1592 (11), 2010 (7), 2163 (87), 2305 (5,64), 2860 (39), 2862 (21)
Marcus, L. M.: test, 2111; ref, 70 (1), 459 (14), 1653 (6), 2813 (27)
Marcus, M.: ref, 272 (11), 1072 (1), 1131 (1), 2305 (19), 2862 (1)
Marcus, M. D.: ref, 893 (15)
Marcus, R. F.: ref, 1000 (73)
Marcus, S. I.: test, 37, 2265
Marcus-Bernstein, C.: ref, 1808 (1)
Mardell-Czudnowski, C.: test, 809; rev, 2382; ref, 1379 (73), 1392 (13), 2905 (82)
Marder, K.: ref, 2125 (7,18), 2163 (124), 2516 (16,28), 2860 (310,496,512,906,907,1180,1346), 2863 (292)
Marder, S. R.: ref, 2050 (85), 2288 (8), 2603 (74)
Marengo, J.: ref, 1517 (8), 2305 (105)
Marengo, J. T.: ref, 2305 (60), 2860 (307,318)
Mareschaux, C.: ref, 350 (39)
Marfia, G. A.: ref, 2163 (201,265), 2860 (1052), 2907 (7)
Margalit, M.: ref, 2452 (9), 2862 (367)
Margolin, A.: ref, 1775 (3), 2860 (1220)
Margolin, D. I.: ref, 776 (31)
Margolis, H.: ref, 665 (34)
Margolis, R. L.: ref, 268 (1)
Margolius, F. R.: ref, 1770 (5)
Margot, P.: ref, 34 (5), 1765 (33), 2862 (575), 2879 (186)
Margraf, J.: ref, 2497 (304)
Mari, J. D.: ref, 2050 (86)
Maria, B. L.: ref, 2193 (11), 2860 (342)
Marin, D.: ref, 1166 (14), 2417 (6)
Marin, P. A.: ref, 200 (4), 404 (22)
Marin, P. B.: ref, 2860 (734)
Marinescu, E.: ref, 2163 (66), 2860 (259)
Marini, I.: ref, 746 (2)
Marinoni, M.: ref, 2497 (621)
Marinor-Glassman, D.: ref, 258 (1), 353 (11), 815 (15), 1072 (42), 1240 (24), 1379 (41), 1902 (52), 1987 (10), 2377 (1), 2724 (6), 2862 (239), 2879 (73)
Marion, M. J.: ref, 1095 (15), 1804 (5), 1903 (193), 2332 (2), 2651 (12), 2657 (7), 2801 (2)
Mariotto, M. J.: test, 2763; ref, 2120 (1)
Marjoribanks, K.: ref, 2163 (14,223),332)
Mark, K. I.: ref, 1010 (81), 1697 (429)
Mark, M.: ref, 301 (21), 2247 (22), 2749 (24), 2860 (339)
Markee, T. E.: ref, 2860 (940,1138), 2901 (68,98)
Markel-Fox, S.: rev, 701
Markham, K. M.: ref, 592 (63)
Markham, P.: ref, 666 (4)
Markham, R.: ref, 2860 (282)
Markham, S. E.: ref, 1755 (40)
Markiewicz, D.: ref, 863 (50)
Markland, D.: ref, 2497 (263)
Markland, O. N.: ref, 846 (13)
Markley, R. P.: rev, 2475, 2892
Marklund, E.: ref, 1164 (5), 1240 (2), 2862 (74)
Markoff, A. M.: test, 2138, 2192
Markos, J. R.: test, 1027
Markoulis, D.: ref, 771 (5)
Markovchick, K.: ref, 286 (3), 2862 (533)
Markow, T.: ref, 2288 (32), 2289 (24), 2305 (91)
Markowisch, H. J.: ref, 2227 (43), 2860 (1305), 2892 (278)
Markowitsch, H. J.: ref, 2163 (118,200), 2227 (15,40), 2239 (8,14,15), 2516 (101), 2860 (492,816,1294), 2863 (138,139,155,172,235,390), 2892 (78,79,107)
Markowitz, C.: ref, 994 (35)
Markowitz, J. C.: ref, 1093 (86), 1166 (120,129)
Markowitz, M.: test, 1909
Marks, A. R.: ref, 2860 (1406), 2863 (425)
Marks, D. F.: ref, 353 (13)
Marks, G.: ref, 337 (176), 2858 (127)
Marks, I.: ref, 999 (62), 2497 (276), 2497 (301)
Marks, I. M.: ref, 272 (78), 1021 (29), 1093 (59,70), 1166 (42), 2050 (55,87), 2603 (233,234,288), 2892 (277)
Marks, M.: ref, 999 (162), 1021 (29), 1698 (23)
Marks, M. N.: ref, 999 (41), 2305 (188,241)
Markt, C.: ref, 1745 (31), 2603 (199)
Markus, H. R.: ref, 1115 (10)
Markwardt, F. C., Jr.: test, 1902
Markwardt, R.: ref, 1300 (7)
Markway, K.: ref, 337 (64,65), 1697 (189,231), 2497 (273), 2603 (152,204)
Marlatt, G. A.: test, 652; ref, 337 (61), 652 (2)
Marleau, J. D.: ref, 298 (165)
Marler, M. R.: ref, 1093 (34), 1697 (98)
Marlett, N. J.: test, 63
Marlier, N.: ref, 1164 (118), 2516 (77)
Marlowe, D. B.: ref, 271 (11), 272 (182,296), 273 (21), 1687 (44), 1697 (372)
Marmar, C. R.: ref, 846 (2), 1697 (325), 2603 (427)
Marmarosh, C.: ref, 337 (98), 998 (68), 2065 (17)
Marmarosh, C. L.: ref, 2065 (12)
Marmurek, H. H. C.: ref, 2487 (11)
Marnell, M.: ref, 272 (144), 1010 (91), 2497 (535), 2603 (329)
Marotta, L.: ref, 2860 (1237)
Maroukakis, E.: ref, 2076 (60)
Marowitsch, H. J.: ref, 2226 (31), 2863 (401), 2892 (286)
Marquardt, T. P.: ref, 1095 (15), 1804 (5), 1903 (193), 2332 (2), 2651 (12), 2657 (7), 2801 (2)
Márquez, S.: ref, 1140 (42)
Marquis, J.: ref, 265 (10), 624 (20), 1095 (27), 1379 (57), 1657 (11), 1866 (30), 1903 (301), 2485 (146), 2864 (69)
Marr, M. B.: rev, 917
Marra, C.: ref, 1166 (185)
Marriott, M.: ref, 2862 (391), 2879 (136)
Marriott, P.: ref, 2076 (157)
Marrogenes, N. A.: ref, 1318 (12)

Marrs, A.: ref, 2305 (165)
Marschark, M.: rev, 2298
Marsden, C. D.: ref, 2860 (84,85,162), 2892 (9)
Marsden, D. B.: test, 889
Marsh, H. W.: test, 2358; rev, 289; ref, 298 (5,18), 372 (3,9), 672 (2,3), 1965 (3,10), 1991 (12,13), 2091 (5), 2146 (3,6), 2358 (1,3,13)
Marsh, J. T.: ref, 1740 (7), 2076 (23), 2599 (6), 2860 (240,534)
Marsh, N.: ref, 272 (123), 746 (3), 1853 (1), 2497 (31)
Marsh, W. L.: ref, 451 (102), 2305 (169), 2862 (450)
Marsh, W. R.: ref, 2860 (537), 2863 (152)
Marshall, C. W.: test, 183
Marshall, D.: rev, 2609
Marshall, K. J.: ref, 355 (1), 2879 (28), 2901 (13)
Marshall, M.: ref, 175 (10), 1040 (9), 1240 (28), 1804 (9), 1903 (282), 2050 (20)
Marshall, N. L.: ref, 681 (87), 2497 (424), 2603 (132,133,232,333)
Marshall, R. C.: ref, 2008 (9), 2873 (33)
Marshall, R. M.: ref, 246 (7), 451 (259), 1160 (4), 1164 (123,178), 1378 (12), 2242 (8), 2516 (119), 2722 (1), 2862 (481,647,716), 2879 (211), 2892 (300), 2901 (133), 2905 (115)
Marshall, T.: ref, 739 (1), 999 (9)
Marshburn, E.: ref, 811 (5), 1216 (35)
Marsico, D. S.: ref, 301 (14), 2860 (197)
Marsile, C.: ref, 2163 (233), 2225 (8), 2892 (200)
Marso, R. N.: ref, 665 (91)
Marson, D. C.: ref, 2768 (35), 2860 (1126), 2863 (334)
Marson, R. N.: ref, 665 (90)
Marston, N. C.: test, 69
Marteau, T. M.: ref, 2497 (642)
Martella, R. C.: ref, 2860 (96)
Marten, P. A.: ref, 2498 (48)
Marten-Mittage, B.: ref, 2497 (632)
Martens, B. K.: rev, 681, 1457, 1942; ref, 2487 (1), 2905 (6,83)
Marti-Vilalta, J. L.: ref, 272 (309)
Martier, S. S.: ref, 1216 (31), 1903 (181), 2860 (473)
Martin, A.: ref, 776 (40,57), 2497 (361), 2860 (340,784)
Martin, A. W.: test, 211
Martin, C. C.: ref, 776 (12), 2860 (434)
Martin, C. E.: ref, 615 (13)
Martin, C. L.: ref, 592 (7)
Martin, C. S.: ref, 451 (30,122), 1697 (89), 2010 (15), 2305 (177), 2862 (477)
Martin, C. W.: rev, 175, 1852
Martin, D.: ref, 2603 (114)
Martin, D. C.: ref, 1755 (1), 2835 (1)
Martin, D. G.: rev, 1214
Martin, D. V.: test, 1583
Martin, E. D.: ref, 2218 (18)
Martin, F.: ref, 404 (17), 694 (20), 999 (14), 1661 (62), 1758 (76), 1765 (1,12,13), 1903 (492), 2163 (4,73,123,297), 2603 (25), 2835 (10), 2905 (103)
Martin, J.: ref, 592 (27), 853 (21), 1140 (6), 1619 (3), 1697 (512), 2485 (134), 2813 (66)
Martin, J. A.: ref, 2076 (48)
Martin, J. B.: ref, 2497 (128)
Martin, J. E.: ref, 272 (373), 1166 (223)
Martin, J. K.: ref, 2497 (465)
Martin, J. L.: ref, 2050 (38,128,129)
Martin, J. M.: ref, 472 (162)
Martin, J. P.: ref, 2239 (10)
Martin, J. W.: ref, 1657 (22), 1866 (43), 2488 (9)
Martin, K.: ref, 1115 (26)
Martin, K. M.: ref, 1166 (150)
Martin, L.: ref, 337 (157), 460 (1,2)
Martin, L. Y.: ref, 1093 (27), 2305 (34,132), 2603 (88)
Martin, M.: test, 1583; ref, 1166 (77,127)
Martin, M. R.: ref, 2328 (1)
Martin, N. A.: test, 2141
Martin, N. G.: ref, 999 (86,172),2603 (273)
Martin, N. K.: ref, 1631 (1), 2315 (1), 2538 (1)
Martin, N. T.: ref, 1066 (1)
Martin, P. C.: ref, 2862 (712)
Martin, P. R.: ref, 272 (333), 2305 (27), 2860 (1366), 2863 (412)
Martin, R.: ref, 2218 (91,104), 2305 (212)
Martin, R. A.: ref, 1755 (65), 2076 (152), 2402 (41), 2858 (52)
Martin, R. B.: ref, 998 (134), 2076 (184)
Martin, R. C.: ref, 2227 (4), 2860 (493,1127), 2863 (140)
Martin, R. M.: test, 1083
Martin, R. P.: rev, 1832
Martin, S.: test, 2529; ref, 2228 (2)
Martin, S. L.: ref, 1972 (1)
Martin, T.: ref, 998 (124)
Martin, V.: ref, 214 (10), 1040 (3), 1095 (8), 1394 (2), 2651 (5), 2866 (1)
Martin, W.: ref, 1697 (15), 2860 (60)
Martin, W. E., Jr.: rev, 569, 1499
Martin, W. R. W.: ref, 2516 (9)
Martin, W. T.: test, 288, 1585, 1845, 2263, 2367, 2529, 2707
Martin-Cannici, C.: ref, 1959 (2)
Martin-Emerson, R.: ref, 1380 (14)
Martindale, C. J.: ref, 337 (37)
Martinek, N.: ref, 998 (127), 1079 (96), 2497 (644)
Martinek, T. J.: test, 1586
Martinez, A.: ref, 272 (170,196), 451 (115,136), 1962 (13), 2076 (73,148)
Martinez, A. J.: ref, 776 (38)
Martinez, E. A.: ref, 298 (120), 1939 (10)
Martinez, G.: ref, 2860 (619), 2862 (255), 2879 (77)
Martinez, J.: ref, 1166 (179)
Martinez, J. C.: ref, 1697 (436), 1866 (40)
Martinez, J. G. R.: ref, 56 (3)
Martinez, M.: ref, 650 (15), 1093 (97), 2227 (19), 2860 (818), 2863 (236)
Martinez, N. C.: ref, 56 (3)
Martinez, P.: ref, 1093 (100)
Martinez-Diaz, J. A.: ref, 2050 (52)
Martínez-Espinosa, S.: ref, 2163 (320), 2860 (1252)

Marting, M. S.: test, 697
Martinkowski, K. S.: ref, 2076 (46,86)
Martino, G.: ref, 2879 (127)
Martino, S.: ref, 1685 (2)
Martinot, J. L: ref, 2516 (73), 2860 (1002)
Martinsen, E. W.: ref, 272 (66), 2858 (50)
Martinson, H.: ref, 2863 (100)
Martlew, M.: ref, 2862 (171)
Martocchio, J. J.: ref, 1701 (36), 2218 (98,105), 2899 (16)
Marton, P.: ref, 1903 (479)
Martorell-Balanzo, B.: ref, 538 (8), 1201 (6)
Martorello, S.: ref, 1164 (154), 2860 (1287)
Maruff, P.: ref, 2497 (369)
Marullo, D. S.: ref, 2813 (153)
Maruyama, G.: ref, 1987 (1), 2858 (91)
Maruyama, G. M.: ref, 1072 (19)
Marvin, C.: ref, 324 (11), 994 (41), 1903 (475), 2229 (12), 2864 (120)
Marvin, R. S.: ref, 863 (89,91), 1889 (15,16)
Marvinney, D.: ref, 373 (7), 2862 (88)
Marwit, S. J.: ref, 472 (57)
Marx, F.: ref, 681 (87)
Maryolf, S. S.: rev, 1414
Marziali, E.: ref, 2603 (542)
Mas, C. A.: ref, 451 (23)
Masaki, S.: ref, 2860 (196), 2862 (111), 2879 (26)
Maschka, P.: test, 788
Masciuch, S.: ref, 270 (6), 2485 (96)
Masel, C.: ref, 540 (4)
Maser, J.: ref, 2305 (210)
Maser, J. D.: ref, 1093 (108), 1697 (376), 1697 (517), 2305 (97,119,160,200)
Masi, G.: ref, 472 (210), 2862 (658)
Maslach, C.: test, 1590; ref, 373 (25), 1590 (3)
Masliah, E.: ref, 376 (15), 776 (34), 1135 (4), 1164 (145), 2860 (184,1244), 2862 (105,120,601), 2892 (266)
Masling, J.: ref, 272 (125), 2497 (489)
Masny, A.: ref, 2076 (128), 2485 (21), 2682 (1)
Mason, B. J.: ref, 1166 (14), 2417 (6)
Mason, C.: ref, 1166 (112)
Mason, C. A.: ref, 270 (40), 863 (90), 1010 (129)
Mason, G. A.: ref, 2305 (53)
Mason, J. D.: ref, 2076 (6), 2860 (141)
Mason, J. M.: ref, 340 (1), 389 (13), 1659 (9)
Mason, J. W.: ref, 2519 (14), 2520 (15)
Mason, L. W.: ref, 272 (366)
Mason, P.: ref, 2050 (139)
Mass, R.: ref, 1965 (81)
Massaquoi, S.: ref, 1758 (21), 2860 (426)
Massel, H. K.: ref, 2050 (52)
Massey, T.: test, 929, 1919, 2579
Massie, D. R.: ref, 2905 (83)
Massingale, T. W.: ref, 270 (7), 2813 (45,72)
Massion, A. O.: ref, 998 (109), 1093 (68,106), 2305 (239), 2519 (42), 2520 (42)
Massle, E. D.: ref, 1001 (13), 2497 (464), 2519 (54), 2520 (53)
Massman, P.: ref, 2892 (47)
Massman, P. J.: ref, 1164 (127), 2860 (1128,1129), 2863 (335,336)
Masson, C. L.: ref, 1338 (18), 2076 (18)
Masson, H.: ref, 776 (52), 1164 (163), 1218 (18), 2226 (28), 2227 (46)
Masson, L. I.: test, 2128
Masson, M. E. J.: ref, 1405 (30)
Masten, A. S.: ref, 557 (4), 1902 (74), 2861 (3), 2862 (136)
Masten, W. G.: ref, 2497 (267), 2771 (25), 2856 (11)
Mastergeorge, A. B.: ref, 2813 (38)
Masterpasqua, F.: ref, 2864 (86)
Masters, G.: test, 2743
Masters, N.: ref, 272 (5), 1079 (1), 1166 (2)
Masters, R. S. W.: ref, 2497 (187)
Masterson, B. J.: ref, 272 (77)
Masterson, J.: ref, 349 (3), 350 (8)
Masterson, J. J.: ref, 624 (8), 1379 (50), 1485 (20), 1903 (194,195), 2694 (9,10), 2695 (14),17,18), 2704 (6,11,12), 2901 (30,43,28)
Mastromauro, C.: ref, 1164 (33), 2603 (140), 2860 (344), 2863 (92), 2892 (49)
Mastropieri, M. A.: ref, 246 (3,6)f, 665 (69,84), 1386 (10,15,20,24), 1392 (7), 1902 (94), 2485 (60,183), 2861 (1), 2862 (28,316,408,589), 2879 (104,143,192), 2901 (55,75,110) 2905 (27,63,91)
Masui, T.: ref, 2163 (335), 2226 (30), 2227 (47), 2860 (1317)
Masur, D.: ref, 1058 (2) 2860 (152)
Masur, D. M.: ref, 1058 (8), 2125 (13), 2163 (119,174), 2516 (26), 2599 (14), 2860 (479,682), 2863 (133), 2879 (60)
Masure, M. C.: ref, 2516 (73), 2860 (1002)
Masutto, C.: ref, 322 (7), 2862 (277)
Maswer, J. D.: ref, 1093 (107)
Maszk, P.: ref, 365 (9)
Matarazzo, J. D.: rev, 1390, 1639, 2159
Matchett, G.: ref, 2497 (322)
Mate-Kole, C. C.: ref, 1903 (469), 2193 (53), 2860 (1098), 2863 (327), 2873 (54)
Mateer, C. A.: ref, 376 (22), 2860 (1293), 2879 (209)
Maten, K. I.: ref, 337 (15)
Mates, T. E.: ref, 459 (3), 1991 (14)
Matese, M.: ref, 459 (31), 2813 (68)
Matese, M. J.: ref, 2813 (104)
Matheis, P. J.: ref, 2305 (228), 2813 (149)
Mathematical Association of America: test, 144, 148, 149
Matheny, K. B.: test, 698; ref, 698 (1)
Mather, M.: ref, 2860 (1239), 2863 (371)
Mather, N.: test, 1606, 2901
Matherne, J. L., III: ref, 2432 (21)
Mathes, P. G.: ref, 2682 (13), 2905 (121)
Matheson, C. C.: ref, 373 (20), 875 (4,5)
Mathew, J.: ref, 451 (145)
Mathew, R. J.: ref, 1661 (46)

Mathew, S. T.: ref, 1089 (2)
Mathew, V. G.: ref, 1661 (46)
Mathews, A.: ref, 2305 (207)
Mathews, F. N.: ref, 724 (5), 2485 (21), 2682 (1)
Mathews, R.: ref, 241 (4), 451 (94), 815 (35), 1903 (447), 2695 (47), 2864 (110)
Mathias, J. L.: ref, 451 (64), 1765 (22), 2214 (73), 2813 (100)
Mathias, S. D.: ref, 2603 (253)
Mathiesen, L.: ref, 2603 (110), 2860 (279)
Mathiesen, T.: ref, 2860 (116)
Mathieu, M.: ref, 298 (119), 863 (52)
Mathieu, P. J.: ref, 1902 (91), 2862 (564), 2864 (124), 2901 (102)
Mathieu, P. L.: test, 991
Mathijssen, J. J. P.: ref, 2862 (648)
Mathur, S.: ref, 1318 (23)
Mathyssen, J. J. P.: ref, 451 (276)
Maticka-Tyndale, E.: ref, 462 (20)
Matier, K.: ref, 451 (58)
Matlack, M. E.: ref, 1000 (73)
Matocha, H. R.: ref, 2163 (231)
Maton, K. I.: ref, 337 (149), 1141 (1), 1965 (40)
Maton, K. J.: ref, 337 (125)
Matsey, K. C.: ref, 472 (113)
Matson, J. L.: rev, 2342; ref, 4 (21), 459 (11,31), 681 (44), 2231 (2), 2485 (229), 2813 (14,68,104,147,148), 2860 (929), 2864 (99)
Matsopoulos, A. S.: ref, 2864 (145), 2905 (122)
Matsui, T.: ref, 298 (34,71,121)
Matsuishi, T.: ref, 2862 (360)
Matsumoto, D.: ref, 1001 (4,6,10), 2246 (14)
Matsushima, E.: ref, 2288 (23), 2305 (69), 2860 (365)
Matsuyama, S. S.: ref, 2860 (918)
Mattei, P.: ref, 2892 (152)
Mattes, J. A.: ref, 4 (1)
Mattes, R.: ref, 2860 (1137)
Matteson, R.: ref, 2860 (118)
Matthew, J. L.: ref, 2252 (3), 2485 (62), 2606 (5)
Matthews, D. A.: ref, 272 (15)
Matthews, D. B.: ref, 392 (1,2), 1590 (8), 2497 (73)
Matthews, G.: ref, 998 (102)
Matthews, J.: ref, 1166 (184)
Matthews, K. A.: ref, 1010 (16), 1697 (49), 2497 (459), 2516 (12)
Matthews, M. W.: ref, 1318 (18), 1903 (539)
Matthews, N. J.: ref, 2860 (1229)
Matthews, S. M.: ref, 2288 (13)
Matthews-Ferrari, K.: ref, 2862 (170)
Matthys, W.: ref, 451 (65,66)
Mattick, R. P.: ref, 1661 (21)
Mattingly, D.: ref, 2603 (340)
Mattingly, J. C.: ref, 1392 (3), 2862 (112)
Mattioli, F.: ref, 2163 (284), 2860 (1130)
Mattis, J.: ref, 451 (124)
Mattis, P. J.: ref, 2860 (683)
Mattis, S.: test, 776
Mattis, S. G.: ref, 472 (204)
Mattlar, C-E.: ref, 272 (45), 303 (3), 998 (32), 2860 (263), 2863 (68)
Mattoo, S. K.: ref, 1697 (368)
Mattoon, A.: ref, 272 (171), 999 (157), 2497 (554), 2603 (454)
Mattox, R. J.: ref, 1292 (1)
Mattson, R.: ref, 2603 (30)
Matula, K.: ref, 270 (27)
Matuszek, P.: rev, 343, 2879
Matuzas, W.: ref, 1166 (34)
Mauch, T. G.: ref, 337 (193)
Mauer, D. M.: ref, 2704 (41), 2905 (101)
Mauer, E. B.: ref, 1754 (7)
Mauger, P. A.: test, 1290
Maunder, R. G.: ref, 2305 (185)
Maurer, K.: ref, 2050 (33)
Maurer, M.: test, 2482
Mauri, A.: ref, 2860 (684)
Mauri, M.: ref, 2227 (55), 2860 (1381)
Maurice, J.: ref, 760 (3), 1697 (223)
Mauritz, K. H.: ref, 2163 (184)
Mavissakalian, M. R.: ref, 2603 (377)
Mavroleft-Eros, G.: ref, 1164 (170), 2305 (235), 2860 (1350)
Mawhood, L.: ref, 459 (1), 2860 (114)
Max, J. E.: ref, 2305 (228), 2813 (149)
Maxey, J.: ref, 2603 (249)
Maxey, J. E.: ref, 1997 (1)
Maxfield, F. N.: rev, 1196
Maxfield, F. W.: rev, 2485
Maxim, N.: ref, 893 (6)
Maxim, P. E.: ref, 1697 (90), 2858 (16)
Maxwell, J.: rev, 861, 2485
Maxwell, J. K.: ref, 1697 (397)
Maxwell, M. J.: test, 2116
Maxwell, S.: rev, 450, 462
Maxwell, S. E.: ref, 1619 (4), 1697 (345), 2016 (1), 2860 (1016), 2871 (4)
May, D. C.: ref, 324 (5), 665 (52,79), 1085 (1), 1903 (196), 2488 (5)
May, J.: ref, 2860 (74)
May, J. G.: ref, 827 (3)
May, K.: ref, 1216 (59), 1338 (40), 1902 (57), 1903 (304), 2860 (422)
Mayberg, H. S.: ref, 2516 (18)
Mayberry, P. W.: ref, 180 (37)
Mayberry, R.: ref, 2484 (11), 2731 (5), 2813 (135), 2862 (584,585), 2901 (107)
Mayberry, R. I.: ref, 2860 (494)
Mayberry, W.: ref, 1991 (15)
Maybery, M.: ref, 1903 (386), 2163 (224)
Maydak, M.: ref, 1903 (387), 2879 (128)
Maydeu-Olivares, A.: ref, 908 (10), 999 (117), 1619 (7), 1697 (399), 2065 (15)
Mayer, J. D.: ref, 997 (2), 2858 (77), 2860 (343)
Mayer, L. S.: ref, 472 (86)

Mayer, R. E.: ref, 592 (86), 1405 (24)
Mayerhoff, D.: ref, 2288 (64), 2305 (170)
Mayerhoff, D. I.: ref, 2305 (70), 2860 (333)
Mayerson, S. E.: ref, 2497 (58)
Mayes, A. R.: ref, 1758 (4,16,18,20,54,66,99), 2193 (2,3,8,9,10,17,21,26,51), 2227 (43), 2860 (40,119,128,283,294,306,386,461,495,606,631,685,695, 711,1000,1066,1069,1305,1379), 2863 (14,33,36, 75,78, 82,129,141,179,184,202,296,313,414), 2892 (14,36,43,75,80,131,135,209,278)
Mayes, L. C.: ref, 451 (137), 2603 (475)
Mayes, M. D.: ref, 376 (7), 1166 (116), 2860 (1111), 2863 (330)
Mayes, S. D.: ref, 451 (139), 472 (178), 2485 (209), 2862 (515)
Mayeux, R.: ref, 1166 (103), 2125 (7), 2163 (124), 2516 (16,28), 2860 (310,407,496,512,554,906)
Mayfield, J. W.: ref, 280 (6)
Mayleben, M. A.: ref, 2369 (2)
Maylor, E. A.: ref, 272 (29), 745 (12,21), 1671 (2,3,5), 2860 (591,686,1131)
Maynard, F.: ref, 337 (20), 2603 (72)
Maynard, I. W.: ref, 226 (1)
Mayo, A.: ref, 1093 (113)
Mayo, C. C.: test, 312
Mayo, J. P., Jr.: ref, 2305 (53)
Mayo, S. T.: rev, 904, 2704
Mayo, V. D.: ref, 1619 (10), 2065 (28)
Mayocchi, L.: ref, 2858 (121)
Mayr, S.: ref, 1036 (4)
Mayseless, O.: ref, 78 (1)
Mayti, C.: ref, 1697 (278)
Mayton, D. M. III: ref, 771 (17)
Mazaux, J. M.: ref, 2860 (930), 2863 (90)
Mazen, A. M.: ref, 372 (20)
Mazer, G. E.: rev, 1721
Maziade, M.: ref, 650 (15), 1093 (97)
Mazonson, P. D.: ref, 2603 (253)
Mazor, K. M.: ref, 592 (90), 1107 (2)
Mazumdar, S.: ref, 337 (156)
Mazur, E.: ref, 908 (4), 2214 (23)
Mazurick, J. L.: ref, 2603 (272)
Mazza, J. J.: ref, 1166 (227), 2230 (20)
Mazziotta, J. C.: ref, 1093 (40)
Mazzocco, M. M. M.: ref, 2860 (1409), 2862 (727), 2892 (303)
Mazzucchi, A.: ref, 2163 (222), 2860 (927)
Mboya, M. M.: ref, 364 (10)
McAdams, D. P.: ref, 999 (30), 1965 (23), 2076 (78), 2749 (4,68,69,78), 1164 (100), 2288 (72), 2289 (57), 2860 (643,908), 2892 (120,190)
McAdoo, H. P.: ref, 1216 (51), 1902 (56), 1903 (280)
McAdoo, W. G.: ref, 134 (7), 136 (5), 1697 (146), 2402 (9)
McAleavy, A.: ref, 2050 (91)
McAlister, L.: ref, 372 (76)
McAllister, C. G.: ref, 2603 (171)
McAlpine, D.: test, 2622
McAlpine, P. D.: ref, 1916 (1), 2714 (2), 2862 (36)
McAndrews, M. P.: ref, 2860 (41,284), 2863 (15)
McAninch, C. B.: ref, 466 (1), 2242 (6), 2749 (70)
McAnulty, H.: ref, 2163 (238)
McAnulty, K.: ref, 1903 (49), 2485 (24), 2862 (99)
McArdle, E. T.: ref, 2305 (187)
McArdle, J. J.: ref, 2860 (687)
McArdle, P.: ref, 1367 (5)
McArthur, C. C.: rev, 2247
McArthur, D. S.: test, 2242
McArthur, J.: ref, 1135 (3), 2599 (5), 2860 (217)
McArthur, J. C.: ref, 1135 (2,16,22), 1164 (169), 1740 (8), 2226 (35), 2227 (10,21,50), 2599 (4,9,32), 2860 (200,401)
McArthur, R.: test, 1226
McArthur-Jackson, C.: ref, 2497 (369)
McAuley, E.: ref, 1141 (3), 1145 (1), 1745 (45), 2076 (90), 2163 (68), 2497 (370,487)
McAuliffe, G.: ref, 399 (2), 401 (1), 1701 (24), 1790 (4)
McAuliffe, S.: ref, 681 (46,86), 2485 (225), 2862 (624)
McAuliffe, T. J.: ref, 665 (65)
McBer and Company: test, 555, 1267, 1575
McBride, H. E. A.: ref, 2731 (6), 2879 (212), 2905 (116)
McBride, J. A.: ref, 1903 (388), 2485 (172), 2860 (931), 2862 (368)
McBride, P. A.: ref, 2813 (109), 2860 (1001)
McBride-Chang, C.: ref, 1903 (323), 2862 (514,516), 2905 (84,100),102)
McBurnett, K.: ref, 2214 (45), 2892 (81)
McCabe, G.: ref, 2163 (308), 2860 (1197), 2862 (415)
McCabe, M.: ref, 472 (57), 998 (15)
McCabe, M. P.: ref, 2771 (13), 2782 (1)
McCabe, P. M.: ref, 2076 (177)
McCabe, P. P.: ref, 665 (34)
McCabe, S. B.: ref, 272 (67), 1010 (50), 1243 (1), 2497 (492)
McCaffery, L. K.: ref, 1386 (4), 2485 (103)
McCaffrey, R. J.: ref, 1218 (2), 1697 (91), 2065 (5), 2497 (74)
McCain, G. A.: ref, 272 (366)
McCain, N. L.: ref, 2076 (153)
McCall, D.: ref, 2163 (135), 2892 (95)
McCall, D. L.: ref, 863 (15)
McCall, J. N.: rev, 1100, 1413
McCall, M. W.: test, 2101
McCall, R. B.: ref, 1903 (197), 2485 (97)
McCall, R. J.: rev, 1214, 2247
McCall, W. A.: test, 1609, 1796, 2663, 2664
McCallum, M.: ref, 2497 (134), 2603 (117,118,543)
McCallum, R. S.: test, 2792; rev, 1903; ref, 2452 (5)
McCammon, S.: rev, 620, 1417
McCampbell, E.: test, 326
McCan, M.: ref, 265 (13), 1096 (8), 2524 (7), 2657 (22)
McCandless, B. R.: rev, 324, 1332, 2146, 2485, 2862
McCann Associates, Inc.: test, 731, 732, 733, 734, 796, 1032, 1813, 2002

McCann, D.: ref, 272 (317)
McCann, J. T.: ref, 1687 (10), 1939 (1), 2126 (3), 2247 (130)
McCann, K.: ref, 1093 (100)
McCann, S. J. H.: ref, 2656 (13)
McCanne, T. R.: ref, 448 (6,28), 2782 (3)
McCardle, P.: ref, 815 (10), 853 (11), 1379 (30), 1653 (10)
McCarley, R.: ref, 2860 (1319), 2892 (282)
McCarley, R. W.: ref, 2288 (60), 2289 (46), 2305 (150,159,190), 2860 (497,1012,1146)
McCarney, S.: test, 221
McCarney, S. B.: test, 59, 81, 222, 282, 284, 873, 874, 930, 1089, 1460, 2035, 2043, 2470, 2779, 2913
McCarrol, J. E.: ref, 337 (150)
McCarroll, J. E.: ref, 2603 (200,378)
McCarron, L.: test, 62, 208, 1919
McCarron, L. T.: test, 40, 929, 1610, 1617, 1815, 2579
McCarron, M. B.: test, 40
McCarthy, C. J.: ref, 2402 (67), 2497 (643)
McCarthy, D.: test, 1612, 1613
McCarthy, G.: ref, 2863 (232)
McCarthy, J.: rev, 552
McCarthy, J. J.: test, 1240; rev, 809
McCarthy, J. M.: ref, 495 (15), 963 (2), 1010 (130), 1965 (84)
McCarthy, K. A.: ref, 1227 (2)
McCarthy, K. J.: rev, 75
McCarthy, M.: ref, 451 (48,164), 681 (82)
McCarthy, P.: ref, 2497 (669)
McCarthy, R. A.: ref, 1104 (11), 2193 (12,33), 2860 (372,780,1004)
McCarthy, W. G.: test, 1611
McCartney, K.: ref, 681 (87), 1264 (6), 1889 (11), 1987 (22)
McCarton, C.: ref, 681 (19)
McCarty, J. J.: test, 150, 151
McCaul, A.: ref, 540 (4)
McCaul, E.: ref, 1902 (48)
McCaul, R. L.: rev, 1203
McCauley, C. D.: test, 300, 807
McCauley, R.: rev, 2543, 2694, 2708
McCauley, R. J.: rev, 2229, 2650: ref, 769 (6), 1056 (2), 1394 (11), 1852 (5)
McCaulley, M. H.: test, 1755
McClachlan, R. S.: ref, 1010 (44)
McClain, T. M.: ref, 999 (106)
McClannahan, L. E.: ref, 1903 (307)
McClearn, G. E.: ref, 1010 (11), 1405 (25), 2218 (7), 2860 (715)
McCleary, L.: ref, 2603 (542)
McClellan, J.: ref, 2862 (369)
McClellan, R. A.: test, 1900
McClelland, D.: ref, 2076 (183)
McClelland, D. C.: ref, 68 (25), 1414 (1), 1965 (27), 2749 (18,21)
McClelland, R.: ref, 389 (7)
McClendon, R. C.: ref, 1720 (3)
McClennen, S. E.: test, 2450
McClenny, B. D.: ref, 451 (111), 787 (2), 1379 (83), 1889 (5)
McClinton, B. K.: ref, 1698 (27)
McCloskey, L. A.: ref, 337 (105)
McCloskey, M.: ref, 1392 (6), 1902 (25), 2860 (285)
McCloy, R. A.: ref, 180 (20)
McClung, R. M.: test, 2627, 2628
McClure, E.: rev, 1135; ref, 375 (4), 451 (210), 542 (2), 2214 (119), 2227 (44), 2862 (649), 2879 (213)
McClure, J.: ref, 272 (167,263)
McClure, K.: ref, 199 (18), 2860 (783)
McClurg, G.: ref, 1744 (7), 2860 (1061,1245)
McCluskey-Fawcett, K.: ref, 1000 (53)
McCollum, K. L.: ref, 472 (93,94), 1745 (43), 2076 (87,88)
McCombs, A.: ref, 2839 (1)
McCombs, K. F.: test, 2454
McConaghy, N.: ref, 298 (147), 1903 (198)
McConatha, J. T.: ref, 998 (51)
McConaughy, E. K.: ref, 2860 (22)
McConaughy, S. H.: ref, 681 (70)
McConkey, R.: test, 1996
McConnachie, G.: ref, 459 (18), 2485 (82),2813 (35)
McConnel, F. M. S.: ref, 1040 (6,7)
McConnell, K. S.: test, 2294
McConnell, S. R.: rev, 2308
McConville, C.: ref, 915 (1)
McCormack, D. J.: ref, 1901 (3)
McCormick, C. B.: ref, 694 (78)
McCormick, C. E.: ref, 1903 (284)
McCormick, E. J.: test, 1343, 2016, 2071, 2925
McCormick, J.: ref, 72 (3), 1079 (90), 2358 (11)
McCormick, J. A.: ref, 2288 (32), 2289 (24), 2305 (91)
McCormick, L.: ref, 2860 (1306)
McCormick, M. C.: ref, 2862 (414), 2901 (76)
McCormick, M. E.: ref, 681 (79), 1380 (16)
McCormick, N. B.: ref, 298 (19,25), 853 (3)
McCormick, R. A.: ref, 2076 (132), 2218 (36), 2603 (425)
McCormick, S.: ref, 665 (15), 1072 (11)
McCormick, T. A.: ref, 2860 (171)
McCormick, W. C.: ref, 776 (58)
McCoun, M.: ref, 265 (4), 1000 (24), 2524 (2), 2657 (4)
McCourt, W. F.: ref, 1661 (25)
McCowan, C. J.: ref, 404 (47), 1010 (57), 2117 (2)
McCown, W.: test, 2604
McCown, W. G.: ref, 999 (15)
McCoy, D. L.: test, 2391
McCoy, G. C.: ref, 1338 (6), 2497 (20), 2603 (7)
McCoy, K.: ref, 863 (24), 1010 (31)
McCoy, K. J. M.: ref, 2557 (11)
McCoy, M. L.: ref, 1021 (23)
McCoy, W. J.: test, 2585
McCracken, J. T.: ref, 451 (125), 472 (168)
McCracken, L. M.: ref, 272 (297)

McCracken, R. S.: ref, 2065 (33)
McCracken, S.: ref, 2860 (1060)
McCracken, S. G.: ref, 1590 (58)
McCrady, B. S.: ref, 134 (24,34), 863 (65), 1661 (61)
McCrae, R. R.: test, 1769, 2218; rev, 771, 1440; ref, 372 (49), 373 (2), 998 (3), 999 (116), 1697 (460,581), 1755 (6), 2218 (1,2,7,8,24,37,41,66,129,130), 2860 (42)
McCranie, E. W.: ref, 1697 (78)
McCrary, C.: ref, 472 (73), 2211 (26), 2862 (238)
McCready, C.: ref, 540 (4), 2497 (32)
McCreary, D. R.: ref, 298 (35,122), 1745 (73)
McCreary, R. A.: ref, 592 (19)
McCrimmon, R. J.: ref, 1164 (160)
McCrone, E. R.: ref, 2614 (2), 2749 (44), 2864 (61)
McCrosky, J.: ref, 1007 (1)
McCue, M.: ref, 322 (1), 1072 (10), 1131 (4), 1164 (12), 1525 (2,9), 1902 (12), 2879 (16), 2901 (6)
McCue, R. E.: ref, 1166 (9)
McCulloch, B. J.: ref, 2858 (87)
McCulloch, K.: test, 349
McCulloch, P. B.: ref, 1697 (153), 2860 (320)
McCulloch, T. L.: rev, 433
McCullough, C. M.: rev, 616, 1768
McCullough, J. D.: ref, 998 (75,76), 2603 (282,283), 2858 (78,79)
McCullough, J. P.: ref, 2497 (11), 2858 (17)
McCullough, L.: ref, 2326 (2), 2603 (129)
McCullough, M. E.: ref, 717 (1), 863 (75)
McCune, K. J.: ref, 998 (75,76), 2603 (282,283), 2858 (78,79)
McCurry, C.: ref, 2862 (369)
McCurry, S. M.: ref, 776 (27), 2860 (688)
McCusker, J.: ref, 272 (199)
McCusker, P. J.: ref, 2860 (689)
McCutchan, J. A.: ref, 2076 (133), 2858 (105)
McCutchen, D.: ref, 1902 (87), 2862 (494)
McCutcheon, J. W.: ref, 68 (40), 1755 (15)
McCutcheon, L. E.: ref, 2856 (7)
McCutcheon, M. J.: ref, 487 (1), 2862 (246)
McDade, H. L.: ref, 1240 (42), 1903 (463)
McDaniel, D. M.: ref, 272 (30)
McDaniel, E. L.: test, 1266
McDaniel, M.: ref, 540 (3), 2432 (26), 2704 (32)
McDaniel, M. A.: ref, 1866 (4)
McDaniel, W. F.: ref, 1697 (556,557)
McDaniels, C.: ref, 1841 (1)
McDannold, S. B.: test, 2470
McDermott, J. B.: ref, 2497 (324)
McDermott, J. F.: ref, 2497 (605), 2749 (53)
McDermott, M.: ref, 1758 (18), 2193 (9), 2860 (294), 2863 (78)
McDermott, P. A.: test, 69, 1457; ref, 69 (1), 837 (5,6,11), 1155 (1), 1457 (3), 2497 (574), 2861 (4), 2862 (263,618,650)
McDermott, S.: ref, 1903 (538), 2163 (331)
McDermut, W.: ref, 1697 (326)
McDevitt, S. C.: test, 425
McDonald, C.: ref, 1740 (12), 2879 (175), 2892 (237)
McDonald, K.: ref, 337 (83), 2497 (374)
McDonald, L.: ref, 4 (19)
McDonald, M. A.: ref, 2163 (78,175)
McDonald, R.: ref, 1079 (57)
McDonald, R. M.: ref, 694 (58), 1991 (54)
McDonald, R. P.: ref, 372 (107)
McDonald, S.: ref, 1164 (128), 2226 (11,41), 2860 (1407), 2863 (426), 2892 (238,301)
McDonald-Miszczak, L.: ref, 1405 (36)
McDonald-Scott, P.: test, 2305
McDonnell, J.: ref, 2299 (2), 2485 (98)
McDonough, L.: ref, 1902 (96)
McDougall, A.: ref, 1941 (1), 2076 (123), 2247 (92,94), 2397 (1)
McDougall, D.: ref, 1036 (11)
McDougall, P.: ref, 2358 (17)
McDougall, S.: ref, 349 (13)
McDougle, C. J.: ref, 2305 (148), 2860 (932)
McDowd, J. M.: ref, 2288 (30), 2289 (21), 2402 (42)
McDowell, J. A.: ref, 1386 (2)
McDowell, J. E.: ref, 1697 (271)
McDowell, P. M.: test, 1614
McDowell, R. L.: test, 1614
McDowell, S.: ref, 1164 (161), 1740 (22), 2516 (104), 2892 (279)
McDuff, J. W.: ref, 2497 (641)
McDuff, P.: ref, 1340 (2)
McEachin, J. J.: ref, 459 (25), 1903 (199), 1962 (6,9), 2813 (42,50)
McEachran, A.: ref, 1093 (104)
McElheron, D.: ref, 1902 (34), 2486 (1), 2860 (354)
McElrath, J. A. V.: ref, 2603 (464)
McElreath, L. H.: ref, 2862 (172)
McElroy, J. C.: ref, 404 (18), 414 (1), 1754 (8), 1755 (11)
McElroy, S. L.: ref, 1093 (93), 1166 (158), 2289 (39,54,58,60,61), 2519 (31), 2520 (32)
McElwain, D.: test, 1791
McElwain, D. W.: rev, 28, 31, 2217
McEntire, E.: test, 2699
McEvoy, R.: ref, 2862 (538)
McEvoy, R. E.: ref, 459 (23,33), 815 (3), 1903 (37), 2485 (99), 2864 (11), 2892 (137)
McEvoy-Shields, K.: ref, 451 (24), 815 (7), 1216 (24), 1379 (21)
McEwen, M. K.: ref, 2413 (1)
McFadden, T. V.: ref, 798 (22,23), 994 (42), 1424 (4), 1902 (89), 1903 (476), 2432 (31), 2485 (210), 2695 (56), 2704 (42,43), 2710 (6), 2862 (517)
McFadyen, R. G.: ref, 1903 (477)
McFadyen-Ketchum, S. A.: ref, 451 (140)
McFall, M. E.: ref, 1661 (15)
McFall, S. A.: ref, 2724 (4)
McFarland, H.: ref, 1288 (1)
McFarland, K.: ref, 1164 (78), 1407 (4), 2516 (53), 2599 (21,39), 2860 (754,1275)
McFarland, P. H.: ref, 2214 (10)

McFarland, T.: ref, 1288 (1)
McFarlane, A. H.: ref, 1000 (88)
McFarlane, T.: ref, 2497 (383)
McFarlane, W. R.: ref, 2288 (52)
McFarlin, D. B.: ref, 2603 (17)
McFeeley, S.: ref, 2076 (47)
McFetridge, J. A.: ref, 2516 (105)
McGaghie, W. C.: rev, 2531
McGaha, J. E.: ref, 462 (23), 1000 (89)
McGain, B.: ref, 997 (22), 2211 (41)
McGarry, K.: ref, 2873 (12)
McGarva, A.: ref, 2407 (4)
McGauvran, M. E.: test, 887, 1659
McGeary, J.: ref, 1093 (38,79), 2305 (61)
McGee, K. A.: ref, 2860 (1095)
McGee, R.: ref, 358 (5,10), 1097 (6), 1903 (131), 2211 (7,11,16,35), 2228 (4), 2485 (63)
McGee, R. A.: ref, 1902 (97)
McGee, R. O.: ref, 2211 (37)
McGeorge, K.: ref, 1903 (270), 2905 (56)
McGeorge, P.: ref, 2860 (1132,1246)
McGhee, D. E.: ref, 459 (15), 2211 (18), 2485 (73)
McGhee, R.: test, 2730; ref, 301 (41)
McGiboney, G. W.: ref, 1201 (4)
McGinn, L. K.: ref, 1166 (102), 1687 (20), 2603 (331,451)
McGinnis, E.: rev, 2841
McGinnis, J. C.: ref, 1607 (7), 2862 (355)
McGinns, J. C.: ref, 2163 (167)
McGlashan, T. H.: ref, 2288 (15,36), 2289 (10,27), 2305 (62), 2603 (426), 2860 (617,1039), 2862 (438)
McGlone, J.: ref, 2860 (847,955), 2863 (245,283)
McGlynn, F. D.: ref, 1021 (37)
McGlynn, T.: ref, 2516 (6)
McGoldrick, J. A.: ref, 592 (27)
McGonigle, M. A.: ref, 1697 (597)
McGonigle, M. M.: ref, 1697 (226)
McGory, P. D.: ref, 650 (2), 2305 (41)
McGovern, L.: ref, 473 (6), 2230 (18), 2557 (10)
McGovern, M. A.: ref, 694 (17)
McGowan, J. C.: ref, 231 (1), 303 (32), 2226 (42), 2227 (61), 2599 (43), 2863 (431), 2892 (307)
McGowan, J. S.: ref, 2045 (3)
McGowan, R. W.: ref, 2076 (61,154)
McGowen, R. W.: ref, 226 (2)
McGrath, C.: ref, 1485 (64), 2682 (12)
McGrath, E. A.: ref, 2862 (263)
McGrath, N.: ref, 2860 (1083), 2892 (226)
McGrath, N. M.: ref, 375 (5), 2227 (45), 2862 (651), 2863 (395), 2892 (280)
McGrath, P.: ref, 451 (22)
McGrath, P. J.: ref, 451 (2), 696 (1), 1166 (130,142), 2603 (487)
McGrath, R. E.: ref, 272 (310), 1619 (9), 2771 (41)
McGraw, T. E.: ref, 997 (10), 1216 (20), 2127 (1), 2603 (134)
McGreevy, M. S. M., Jr.: ref, 1000 (73)
McGregor, A.: ref, 1166 (72)
McGregor, K. K.: ref, 265 (9), 994 (16,50) 1095 (12), 1096 (7), 1485 (61), 1852 (3), 1903 (478,540,556), 2680 (9), 2695 (12,15), 2725 (8,9,10), 2768 (41), 2862 (680)
McGregor, L. N.: ref, 2369 (2)
McGrew, J.: ref, 592 (30), 1697 (358,521)
McGrew, K.: test, 2903; ref, 2901 (67)
McGrew, K. S.: test, 332, 2901; ref, 443 (1), 837 (12), 1300 (1,2,5,9,10), 1378 (8), 1379 (92,100), 2485 (230), 2862 (652), 2901 (95,96,124,132)
McGue, M.: ref, 372 (13), 644 (6), 998 (42,65), 1010 (19), 1059 (2), 1072 (43), 1240 (33), 1903 (115,255,356), 2225 (4), 2651 (4,14), 2657 (23), 2860 (348,616,858), 2862 (252,334), 2863 (252), 2864 (85)
McGuffin, P.: ref, 2050 (14,32,54), 2214 (83)
McGuinness, C.: ref, 999 (70), 1903 (389), 2125 (16), 2768 (30), 2860 (553), 2905 (85)
McGuinness, D.: ref, 1903 (389), 2125 (16), 2768 (30),2905 (85)
McGuire, C.: rev, 117
McGuire, C. H.: rev, 780, 960, 2686, 2718
McGuire, J.: test, 2038
McGuire, J. M.: ref, 298 (113)
McGuire, J. P. D.: ref, 2862 (289), 2864 (71)
McGuire, K.: ref, 199 (10)
McGuire, M.: ref, 2305 (82)
McGuire, P.: ref, 1613 (2)
McGuire, P. K.: ref, 2050 (88)
McGuire, R. J.: ref, 2862 (422)
McGuire, S.: ref, 2860 (690)
McGuire, S. A.: ref, 2214 (74)
McHale, J. P.: ref, 1010 (125)
McHale, S. M.: ref, 298 (155), 472 (33,183), 2214 (24,74)
McHenry, M. A.: ref, 2860 (691)
McHugh, K.: ref, 272 (367), 837 (3), 1745 (87), 1765 (19), 1903 (292), 2862 (280)
McHugh, P. R.: ref, 2050 (23), 2516 (72), 2892 (203)
McHugh, T. A.: ref, 863 (18)
McHugo, G. J.: ref, 134 (23,36), 2247 (73), 2749 (48), 2860 (736)
McIlvane, W. J.: ref, 1903 (132,552), 2862 (672)
McInerney, C. A.: ref, 2485 (64), 2860 (373)
McInerney, M.: ref, 2485 (64), 2860 (373)
McInman, A. D.: ref, 2076 (62), 2358 (2), 2358 (4)
McIntire, R. M.: rev, 2571
McIntosh, A. R.: ref, 2860 (1141)
McIntosh, D. E.: rev, 2059; ref, 331 (5), 837 (1,7)
McIntosh, J. W.: ref, 1697 (19)
McIntosh-Michaelis, S. A.: ref, 2239 (10)
McIntyre, J.: ref, 337 (148), 863 (80), 1000 (99), 1903 (473), 1991 (92)
McIntyre, R. M.: rev, 2827
McIntyre, R. P.: ref, 1755 (35,36,43)
McIvor, D. L.: ref, 1697 (8,69)

McIvor, R. J.: ref, 2305 (188)
McKay, B. L.: ref, 2860 (145), 2862 (93)
McKay, J. R.: ref, 136 (11), 1661 (77,81), 2414 (7), 2497 (574), 2603 (544)
McKay, K. A.: ref, 620 (2)
McKay, M.: ref, 1457 (2), 1765 (28)
McKeachie, W. J.: test, 1720; rev, 706; ref, 1455 (1)
McKechnie, G. E.: test, 963
McKee, D. C.: ref, 303 (1,2), 791 (2), 1164 (23), 1740 (3), 2497 (21,104), 2516 (2), 2603 (8,83), 2860 (81,237)
McKee, G. R.: ref, 1697 (514)
McKee, K. J.: ref, 2858 (128)
McKee, M.: ref, 2218 (99), 2305 (226)
McKee, M. G.: rev, 908
McKee, W. T.: rev, 1275
McKeel, D.: ref, 2860 (1280)
McKeel, D. W.: ref, 1164 (179), 2860 (182,1397), 2863 (422)
McKeever, W. F.: ref, 1903 (390), 2217 (1)
McKeith, I. G.: ref, 1390 (5), 2860 (970)
McKellar, J. D.: ref, 1745 (74)
McKelvey, L.: ref, 1697 (531)
McKelvie, S. J.: ref, 2899 (4,7)
McKenna, K.: ref, 451 (116), 2288 (68,71), 2289 (52,56), 2305 (103,242), 2862 (475,493,501,629)
McKenna, P.: test, 432, 1104
McKenna, P. A.: ref, 2603 (557)
McKenna, P. J.: ref, 1758 (37,103), 2163 (105), 2860 (849,1399)
McKenry, P. C.: ref, 1000 (77), 2603 (379)
McKenzie, D. P.: ref, 335 (12), 1010 (100,101)
McKenzie, I. E.: ref, 1687 (41)
McKenzie, J.: ref, 2050 (85)
McKenzie, N.: ref, 694 (85)
McKenzie, S. J.: ref, 893 (11)
McKenzie-Mohr, D.: ref, 298 (36)
McKeon, R. T.: ref, 1010 (26)
McKeown, M. G.: ref, 1657 (14)
McKillip, R. H.: test, 2072
McKillop, A. S.: test, 1073
Mckinley, G.: ref, 1135 (18), 2226 (14), 2516 (85), 2860 (1173), 2863 (353)
McKinney, C. H.: ref, 2076 (177)
McKinney, J. D.: ref, 681 (37), 1379 (8), 2211 (21), 2485 (29), 2864 (19)
McKinney, M.: ref, 337 (36), 1216 (84)
McKinney, M. W.: test, 2766
McKinnon, K.: ref, 2017 (16)
McKinzey, R. K.: ref, 997 (22), 1164 (162), 2211 (41), 2860 (1307)
McKirnan, D. J.: ref, 337 (161)
McKnab, P.: ref, 1903 (24), 2485 (22), 2860 (86)
McKnight, D. L.: ref, 1697 (184), 2305 (71)
McKnight, J. D.: ref, 1590 (50)
McKusick, L.: ref, 337 (12)
McLachlan, D. R.: ref, 2768 (39), 2860 (1188), 2863 (357)
McLachlan, D. R. C.: ref, 2227 (8), 2860 (364), 2879 (44), 2892 (54)
McLachlan, R. S.: ref, 1697 (538), 2860 (1123)
McLaren, D.: ref, 815 (26), 1131 (15), 2860 (911)
McLarty, J. R.: rev, 1249, 2681
McLaughlin, D. E.: ref, 2030 (1)
McLaughlin, M.: ref, 998 (125)
McLaughlin, M. E.: ref, 180 (4,9)
McLaughlin, S. C.: ref, 1745 (41), 2519 (41), 2520 (41), 2862 (653)
McLaughlin, T. F.: ref, 389 (3), 2905 (68)
McLean, A.: ref, 798 (4), 1092 (3), 1131 (5), 1240 (4), 1392 (2), 1902 (14), 1903 (42), 2432 (8), 2484 (1), 2879 (21)
McLean, J. E.: ref, 1378 (4,6,13,14), 1755 (29,64), 1790 (16,17), 2862 (495)
McLean, P.: ref, 2863 (83)
McLean, P. D.: ref, 271 (7,18), 272 (368)
McLean, T.: test, 951
McLeavey, B. C.: ref, 1619 (1)
McLeish, J.: rev, 1629, 1752
McLellan, A. T.: ref, 2305 (162), 2402 (52), 2603 (431,544)
McLellan, D. L.: ref, 2239 (10)
McLellan, E.: test, 881
McLellan, M. J.: rev, 655, 2080, 2258, 2417
McLennan, J.: ref, 998 (55)
McLennan, J. D.: ref, 2163 (125)
McLeod, C.: ref, 2603 (529)
McLeod, D. B.: ref, 1599 (3)
McLeod, D. R.: ref, 272 (370), 2497 (673)
McLeod, J.: test, 1784
McLeod, P. J.: ref, 2862 (337), 2879 (114)
McLeod, R.: test, 1784
McLeod, S.: ref, 272 (214,215), 1040 (10), 1095 (25), 1394 (7,9), 1697 (509,510), 1903 (285), 2497 (586,587), 2858 (118), 2860 (280)
McLoone, B. B.: ref, 2862 (28)
Mcloughlin, P.: ref, 2873 (1)
McMahan, G. C.: ref, 592 (104)
McMahon, R. C.: ref, 1687 (22)
McMahon, R. J.: rev, 864
McMahon, T. J.: ref, 1775 (3), 2860 (1220)
McMahon, W. M.: ref, 2862 (486)
McManus, C.: ref, 349 (32), 1079 (72), 1765 (29)
McManus, I. C.: ref, 298 (37,78), 999 (20,54), 2163 (225), 2883 (1)
McManus, S. M.: ref, 2444 (1), 2452 (6), 2841 (1)
McMenamy, C. J.: ref, 2497 (14)
McMichael, H.: ref, 2125 (20)
McMillan, T. M.: ref, 2234 (2)
McMillen, D. L.: ref, 372 (39), 998 (47), 1697 (185)
McMorris, R. F.: rev, 364, 368, 1388, 1434, 1607
McMorris, T.: ref, 1140 (34,53)
McMullen, P. A.: ref, 2860 (253), 2863 (64)
McMurrain, T. T.: test, 1230
McMurray, M. A.: ref, 1140 (18), 2856 (5)

McMurray, N. E.: ref, 2498 (12)
McMurry, R. N.: test, 857, 943, 989, 1798, 1986
McNair, D.: rev, 538
McNair, D. M.: test, 2076, 2077; rev, 2499
McNally, R. J.: ref, 271 (5,16), 272 (223,335), 472 (179), 681 (76), 2076 (155), 2214 (109), 2402 (43,70), 2485 (11), 2497 (208,575), 2860 (933,1403)
McNamara, C. L.: ref, 893 (13), 2519 (33), 2520 (34)
McNamara, J. R.: ref, 1115 (12)
McNamara, M.: rev, 773
McNamee, G.: ref, 1093 (70), 2050 (87)
McNaughton, D.: ref, 614 (1)
McNaughton, M. E.: ref, 337 (16), 2858 (18)
McNear, D.: test, 332
McNeely, S.: rev, 136, 1436
McNeil, C. B.: ref, 864 (3), 997 (12), 1987 (7), 2752 (1)
McNeil, D. W.: ref, 1021 (46), 2497 (85,672), 2516 (70)
McNeil, J. E.: ref, 1104 (5), 2860 (692)
McNeil, K.: ref, 1755 (39)
McNeil, M. R.: test, 2225; rev, 199, 277, 1056, 1360, 1852; ref, 2008 (14), 2225 (5), 2768 (37)
McNeil, P.: ref, 999 (115)
McNeil, T. F.: ref, 1962 (17), 2288 (40), 2813 (77)
McNeill, B. W.: ref, 298 (129),716 (2), 1755 (48), 2497 (398), 2603 (315)
McNeish, T. J.: test, 852
McNell, K.: ref, 1687 (11), 1697 (92)
McNicol, D.: ref, 1765 (12,13), 2163 (73,123), 1010 (6, 2850 (2)
McNinch, G. W.: ref, 2771 (12)
McNoe, B.: ref, 2050 (44,45)
McNulty, J. L.: ref, 1697 (414,588)
McNulty, S. A.: ref, 999 (139), 2603 (407)
McPhail, J. C.: ref, 2901 (31)
McPherson, R. H.: ref, 372 (18), 1697 (85), 1755 (58), 2076 (14), 2603 (57)
McPherson, W. B.: ref, 1131 (17), 2862 (696), 2879 (222), 2905 (118)
McQuary, J. P.: rev, 1042
McQueeney, D. A.: ref, 272 (298)
McRae, D. J.: rev, 407, 663, 676, 1617, 2761
McReynolds, P.: rev, 927, 1321, 2064, 2318, 2618, 2649
McShane, D.: rev, 2545
McVicar, D.: ref, 472 (58)
McWhirter, B. T.: ref, 697 (2), 2497 (493)
McWhirter, E. H.: ref, 2360 (9)
McWilliam, R. A.: ref, 265 (6)
McWilliams, L.: test, 683
Mead, A. D.: ref, 56 (10), 180 (28)
Mead, F.: ref, 350 (6)
Mead, R. J.: test, 1224
Meador, K. J.: ref, 641 (4,5), 1135 (5), 1164 (9), 1903 (35), 2076 (19,118), 2227 (4,11,20), 2517 (4), 2599 (7,30), 2860 (68,115,194,198), 2863 (136), 2879 (15), 2892 (3,13)
Meador, K. S.: ref, 916 (1), 1379 (51), 1586 (2), 1903 (133,286),2044 (4), 2754 (3), 2771 (18,30)
Meadow, K. P.: test, 1618
Meadow-Orlans, K.: ref, 811 (8)
Meadow-Orlans, K. P.: ref, 811 (11), 1889 (1)
Meadows, A. T.: ref, 1000 (103), 2214 (115), 2497 (609)
Meadows, A. W.: rev, 865
Meadows, E. A.: ref, 2497 (449)
Meadows, G. A.: ref, 2199 (10)
Meadows, M.-E.: ref, 1218 (8), 1697 (179), 2227 (7,16), 2860 (363,592,658,693), 2863 (95,193,203), 2892 (132)
Meadows, M. E.: ref, 2907 (5)
Meagher, D.: ref, 1166 (95)
Meagher, R. B.: test, 1686
Mealey, D. L.: ref, 592 (20), 615 (16), 1455 (2)
Mealor, D. J.: rev, 63, 562, 1616, 2210, 2410
Means, B.: test, 1352
Meara, N. M.: ref, 2860 (1016),2871 (4)
Meares, H.: ref, 472 (82), 2214 (41)
Meares, R.: ref, 272 (88)
Mearns, J.: ref, 337 (193)
Mebane, A. H.: ref, 1166 (47)
Mecham, M. J.: test, 2801
Mecham, R. C.: test, 1343, 2016, 2925
Medina-Diaz, M.: rev, 165, 2080
Medley, I.: ref, 2050 (8,139)
Mednick, B. R.: ref, 2497 (576,577)
Mednick, S. A.: ref, 748 (2,5,6,10), 2050 (4,42,66,78,133)
Medoff-Cooper, B.: test, 425; ref, 270 (20),1216 (21)
Medoro, L.: ref, 2497 (385)
Medvedev, A.: ref, 1164 (137)
Medway, F. J.: rev, 210, 1220, 1500, 2880
Mee-Lee, D.: test, 2194
Meece, J. L.: ref, 364 (23), 665 (8,86), 1657 (5,21)
Meehl, P. E.: ref, 1697 (327)
Meeker, F.: ref, 615 (51)
Meeker, M.: test, 781, 782, 1641, 2518
Meeker, R.: test, 781, 782, 2518
Meenan, J. P.: ref, 199 (15)
Meerwaldt, J. D.: ref, 2163 (1)
Meeske, K.: ref, 1000 (103), 2214 (115), 2497 (609)
Meesters, Y.: ref, 272 (79), 1166 (175)
Meeus, W.: ref, 1079 (71,95)
Mefford, I.: ref, 1661 (55), 2305 (176)
Mega, M. S.: ref, 1164 (181), 1740 (33), 2227 (59), 2860 (1408), 2863 (427), 2873 (24), 2892 (133)
Megargee, E. I.: rev, 1146, 1340, 1745; ref, 1697 (9,328,558), 1698 (14)
Megel, M. E.: ref, 2214 (110), 2498 (65)
Meginnis, K. L.: ref, 297 (2), 451 (233)
Meguid, V.: ref, 451 (169), 880 (1), 1216 (96)
Mehdorn, M.: ref, 776 (49), 1164 (159),1758 (91), 2227 (42)
Mehler, B. L.: test, 2508
Mehlinger, H. D.: rev, 503

Mehr, D. G.: ref, 68 (57), 1396 (4)
Mehrabian, A.: test, 181, 238, 455, 1620, 1621, 1622, 1627, 1628, 1630, 2135, 2777; ref, 272 (299), 998 (126)
Mehrens, W. A.: rev, 762, 798, 904, 1319, 2488, 2685, 2734
Mehringer, C. M.: ref, 2227 (6), 2516 (13), 2860 (286,1117), 2863 (76,331), 2892 (37,231)
Mehryar, A. H.: ref, 301 (26), 1097 (8)
Mehta, M.: ref, 1079 (51), 1758 (52)
Mehta, M. D.: ref, 2497 (371)
Mehta, S.: rev, 1627
Mehta, Z.: ref, 1758 (72), 2860 (92,1133), 2863 (26), 2892 (239)
Meier, E.: ref, 1469 (7)
Meier, M. J.: rev, 1164, 2426, 2517
Meier, S. T.: rev, 1298, 1627
Meigs, C. B.: ref, 592 (19)
Meijden, W. V. D.: ref, 2497 (285)
Meijer, J.: ref, 2497 (530)
Meijer, J. A.: ref, 2497 (583)
Meijler-Iljina, L. I.: ref, 1079 (69)
Meiklejohn, L.: test, 2629
Meilijson, I.: ref, 2290 (1)
Meilijson, S.: ref, 2290 (1)
Meindl, J. R.: ref, 1444 (2), 1755 (5)
Meininger, J. C.: ref, 1338 (34)
Meins, W.: ref, 472 (133,134,180)
Meinz, E. J.: ref, 2892 (252)
Meir, E. I.: ref, 302 (3), 1693 (2), 1697 (366), 2163 (192), 2217 (3), 2497 (75,494), 2835 (28)
Meisels, S. J.: test, 889
Meisgeier, C.: test, 1750; ref, 1470 (1), 1750 (1)
Meisler, A. W.: ref, 793 (6), 2402 (4), 2603 (85)
MeKitrick, L. A.: ref, 2860 (374), 2863 (97)
Melamed, B. G.: ref, 2497 (200)
Melamed, L.: ref, 926 (12), 1407 (3), 1592 (15), 2010 (12), 2892 (87)
Melamed, L. E.: ref, 1135 (1)
Melamed, S.: ref, 2497 (75,494)
Melamed, T.: ref, 2417 (27,35), 2856 (10)
Melancon, S. M.: ref, 2407 (1)
MeLander, H.: ref, 2862 (617)
Melchior, A.: ref, 998 (63), 2860 (560)
Melchior, L. A.: test, 132
Meldrum, D.: ref, 301 (2)
Meldrum, D. L.: ref, 1164 (93), 2860 (863), 2863 (254)
Meldrum, W. B.: rev, 44
Meleis, A. I.: ref, 708 (6)
Melendez, F.: test, 85, 456, 1776
Melhuish, E. C.: ref, 1612 (64),2228 (2)
Melinat, E.: ref, 1755 (68)
Meline, T.: ref, 1095 (47)
Melinger, J.: test, 728
Mellanby, J.: ref, 358 (12), 560 (3), 2862 (518)
Mellenbergh, G. J.: ref, 68 (37)
Mellenbruch, P. L.: test, 1344, 1834, 2406
Mellerup, E.: ref, 272 (201)
Mellies, J. K.: ref, 376 (33), 2239 (35)
Mellman, T. A.: ref, 2603 (347,380)
Mello, N. K.: ref, 1661 (59)
Melloh, T.: ref, 337 (158), 451 (150)
Mellow, A. M.: ref, 2076 (100), 2863 (222)
Mellwraith, R. D.: ref, 2858 (40)
Melnick, S.: ref, 451 (201), 472 (197), 2862 (627), 2901 (117)
Melnick, S. M.: ref, 2862 (519)
Melnyk, B. M.: ref, 2497 (264,495)
Melnyk, W. T.: ref, 2656 (10)
Melo, B.: ref, 1758 (93), 2860 (1316), 2892 (281)
Melowski, F.: ref, 1697 (2)
Meloy, J. R.: ref, 1525 (6), 1697 (50), 2247 (14,67), 2402 (7), 2860 (256)
Melson, G. F.: ref, 1903 (200)
Melton, B.: ref, 2050 (112)
Melton, G. B.: rev, 448, 1434, 1639
Melton, G. R.: rev, 41
Melton, R. S.: rev, 753
Meltzer, H.: rev, 2618; ref, 272 (198)
Meltzer, H. Y.: ref, 335 (3), 1093 (61,10), 1166 (76), 2050 (6,3,115), 2288 (3,15), 2289 (10), 2305 (62,72,168)
Meltzer, L.: ref, 2369 (5)
Melzack, R.: test, 1615; ref, 1697 (240), 2497 (281)
Memory, D. M.: rev, 1516
Mena, F. J.: ref, 694 (5)
Mena, I.: ref, 2227 (6), 2516 (13), 2860 (286),2863 (76), 2892 (37)
Menaghan, E. G.: ref, 180 (7), 1216 (15,34,68), 1903 (57)
Menchon, J. M.: ref, 998 (35), 1166 (209)
Mendel, M. J.: ref, 2749 (28), 2860 (369)
Mendelberg, H. E.: ref, 1697 (433), 2860 (934)
Mendell, N. R.: ref, 2603 (563)
Mendell, P. R.: ref, 2860 (1383), 2862 (707), 2863 (415)
Mendels, J.: ref, 2603 (191)
Mendelsohn, D.: ref, 375 (3), 2862 (506)
Mendelsohn, G. A.: rev, 1755; ref, 68 (47), 2603 (14), 2860 (88), 2863 (24)
Mendelsohn, M.: ref, 1079 (78)
Mendelson, J. H.: ref, 1661 (59)
Mendelson, M. J.: ref, 681 (21), 1903 (151), 2860 (424)
Mendez, J.: ref, 1405 (26)
Mendez, M. F.: ref, 2860 (1308)
Mendez, R.: ref, 1612 (35)
Mendham, C. A.: ref, 739 (7), 999 (99)
Mendola, R.: ref, 272 (15)
Menduke, H.: ref, 2247 (97)
Menees, M. M.: ref, 462 (31), 1661 (63)
Meneese, W. B.: ref, 1010 (24)
Menefee, K.: rev, 889, 1603
Meneilly, G. S.: ref, 272 (68), 1164 (50), 2516 (29), 2860 (498)

Menendez, A. V.: ref, 2603 (391)
Mennemeier, M.: ref, 376 (14), 1740 (23), 2497 (265), 2860 (1309), 2863 (142,372)
Mennen, F. E.: ref, 472 (97,135), 2214 (75)
Mennin, D.: ref, 451 (168), 1010 (118), 2305 (165,215), 2862 (592), 2879 (194)
Menscer, D.: ref, 2497 (511)
Mensh, I. N.: rev, 303, 2863
Mensink, D.: ref, 763 (3)
Mentenopoulas, G.: ref, 272 (302), 2860 (1318), 272 (363)
Mentis, M.: ref, 1164 (110), 1740 (11), 2010 (20), 2860 (971)
Mentis, M. J.: ref, 2485 (234), 2860 (502,1141,1155, 1216), 2879 (190)
Menzies, R. G.: ref, 1021 (34)
Merali, Z.: ref, 272 (213)
Merali, Z.: ref, 1166 (143)
Merarech, Z. R.: ref, 2163 (285), 2771 (43)
Merbler, J. B.: test, 293
Mercer, G.: ref, 2050 (72)
Mercer, J.: ref, 2010 (17), 2402 (34),2860 (761)
Mercer, J. R.: test, 61, 2606; ref, 1903 (16)m 2862 (50)
Mercer, R. T.: ref, 2497 (76,66,333)
Merchant, A.: ref, 2050 (23)
Merchant, C. A.: ref, 303 (29), 776 (61), 1740 (32), 2860 (1405)
Mercier, L.: test, 1726
Mercincavage, J. E.: ref, 1735 (1)
Merckelbach, H.: ref, 998 (9), 999 (164)
Meredith, W.: ref, 373 (36), 1876 (1), 2860 (135,398)
Meredith, W. H.: ref, 1987 (21)
Meregalli, S.: ref, 2860 (173)
Merenda, P. E.: ref, 372 (50), 1697 (227)
Merenda, P. F.: rev, 931, 1065, 1821, 2107, 2146, 2484, 2928; ref, 68 (38), 280 (1), 372 (72), 1697 (329)
Merette, C.: ref, 650 (15), 1093 (97)
Mergendoller, J. R.: ref, 2682 (10)
Meric, H. J.: ref, 1755 (43)
Merikangas, K.: ref, 2603 (33,284)
Merikangas, K. R.: ref, 2603 (285)
Merling, A.: ref, 1164 (57), 2860 (586,1272), 2863 (174)
Merluzzi, T. V.: ref, 2117 (5)
Merralls, L.: ref, 1991 (84)
Merrell, K. W.: test, 1288, 2036, 2322; ref, 1288 (1,2), 2036 (1), 2299 (4), 2452 (18)
Merriam, A. E.: ref, 564 (3), 2146 (7)
Merrifield, P.: test, 996
Merrifield, P. R.: test, 142, 682, 726
Merril, E. C.: ref, 2485 (65)
Merrill, L. L.: ref, 448 (25), 853 (17), 2516 (45), 2860 (694)
Merriman, W. E.: ref, 1528 (6)
Merritt, D. D.: ref, 430 (12), 798 (18), 1060 (5), 1240 (35), 1903 (378), 2694 (15), 2911 (2)
Merritt, D. E.: ref, 2016 (2)
Merritt, K. A.: ref, 472 (136), 1178 (9), 2214 (76), 2603 (222)
Merritt, R. D.: ref, 1697 (93)
Merry, J.: ref, 2603 (441)
Mersch, P. P. A.: ref, 272 (256)
Merson, A.: ref, 2860 (1378), 2879 (226), 2892 (296)
Mertens, S. B.: ref, 337 (176), 2858 (127)
Mertesdorf, F. L.: ref, 999 (94)
Mertin, P.: ref, 451 (64), 1522 (1), 1765 (22), 2214 (73), 2813 (100)
Mertz, D. L.: ref, 665 (12), 1485 (2), 2862 (68)
Mervielde, I.: ref, 451 (172)
Mervis, C. B.: ref, 1903 (272)
Merwin, G.: ref, 413 (5)
Merwin, J.: test, 2484
Merwin, J. C.: rev, 364, 838, 2871, 2879
Merwin, M. M.: ref, 690 (1)
Mery, M.: rev, 674
Merydith, S. P.: ref, 1201 (5)
Merz, W. A., Sr.: rev, 2513
Merz, W. R.: rev, 2467
Merz, W. R., Sr.: rev, 34, 1130, 1148, 2301
Mesibov, G.: test, 70
Mesibov, G. B.: ref, 459 (2,4,10), 2860 (199)
Mesnikoff, A.: test, 2108
Messé, L.: ref, 2603 (455)
Messer, S. C.: ref, 472 (137)
Messer, W. S.: ref, 615 (3)
Messick, S.: test, 894
Messing, E. M.: ref, 1687 (9), 2076 (17)
Meston, C. M.: ref, 793 (21,24)
Mesulam, M.-M.: ref, 2860 (390), 2863 (101)
Metalsky, G. I.: ref, 1697 (309)
Metcalf, D.: ref, 2288 (60), 2289 (46), 2305 (159), 2860 (1012)
Metcalf, K.: test, 2471
Metcalf, K. K.: ref, 1755 (44)
Metevia, L.: ref, 451 (283), 681 (98), 2603 (590), 2901 (135)
Methorst, G. J.: ref, 2603 (120)
MetriTech, Inc.: test, 1276, 1426
Metsala, J. L.: ref, 1902 (102), 2879 (237)
Metsäpelto, R-L.: ref, 2862 (656)
Mettelmen, B. B.: ref, 451 (37), 1099 (1), 1903 (261), 2862 (264)
Metter, E. J.: ref, 1164 (171), 1758 (97)
Metter, J.: ref, 303 (21)
Metts, S.: ref, 1927 (7)
Metz, C.: ref, 272 (253), 2305 (214)
Metz, J. T.: ref, 2892 (134)
Metz, M. E.: test, 2546
Metz-Lutz, M. N.: ref, 350 (39)
Metzgen, K.: test, 2891
Metzger, B. E.: ref, 1386 (25), 2860 (1338), 2862 (667)
Metzger, L. J.: ref, 2860 (1403)
Metzke, C. W.: ref, 451 (285)
Metzler, A.: ref, 298 (20)

Metzler, A. E.: ref, 404 (7), 462 (32), 1582 (13)
Metzler, T.: ref, 846 (2)
Metzler, T. J.: ref, 2603 (427)
Metzner, R.: ref, 1939 (6)
Meudell, P.: ref, 2193 (21), 2860 (461,631), 2863 (129,184), 2892 (75)
Meudell, P. R.: ref, 1758 (16,18), 2193 (8,9), 2860 (283,294,386,695,1066), 2863 (75,78,313), 2892 (36,135)
Meulemans, T.: ref, 2516 (56), 2860 (771)
Meurgey, F.: ref, 1166 (57)
Mevarech, Z. R.: ref, 2010 (11), 2163 (330), 2771 (24)
Meyer, D. F.: ref, 893 (45,46)
Meyer, D. L.: rev, 1038; ref, 1338 (40)
Meyer, F. B.: ref, 2860 (537), 2863 (152)
Meyer, G. J.: ref, 1697 (589), 2247 (131)
Meyer, G. R.: test, 2325
Meyer, H. D.: test, 1660
Meyer, J.: test, 2470; ref, 2433 (1)
Meyer, J. A.: ref, 1745 (52)
Meyer, J. H.: ref, 571 (6)
Meyer, L. A.: ref, 2864 (62), 2879 (86), 2905 (58)
Meyer, M. M.: ref, 2860 (253), 2863 (64)
Meyer, M. S.: ref, 769 (7), 1072 (55), 1503 (16), 1903 (576), 2163 (353), 2862 (725), 2901 (134)
Meyer, R. E.: ref, 1697 (157)
Meyer, R. G.: ref, 1687 (11), 1697 (92)
Meyer, S. L.: ref, 540 (22)
Meyer, W. J. III.: ref, 1697 (537)
Meyerhoff, J. L.: ref, 2497 (468)
Meyerhoff, P. J.: ref, 1058 (7), 2227 (12), 2860 (499),2863 (143)
Meyerhoff, T. L.: ref, 2497 (469)
Meyerowitz, B. E.: ref, 2076 (117)
Meyers, A. B.: ref, 2603 (209,381)
Meyers, B. S.: ref, 1166 (85)
Meyers, C. A.: ref, 2860 (375), 2863 (98)
Meyers, C. E.: rev, 2443
Meyers, J.: test, 737
Meyers, J. E.: test, 2227
Meyers, K.: ref, 2603 (567)
Meyers, K. R.: test, 2227
Meyers, M. J.: rev, 834
Mezger, C.: test, 929, 1919, 2579
Mezzacappa, E.: ref, 1164 (102), 2516 (68), 2907 (9)
Mezzich, A. C.: ref, 2010 (24), 2305 (244), 2516 (117), 2860 (1390), 2862 (713)
Mhjdan, A.: ref, 2226 (12)
Mian, M.: ref, 1903 (479)
Miccio, A. W.: ref, 1095 (40), 1852 (6), 1903 (480), 2680 (17)
Miceli, G.: ref, 2163 (176,226,333)
Miceli, L.: ref, 2163 (340)
Michael, J. J.: test, 844, 2538
Michael, L. D.: test, 1708, 1709, 1710
Michael, N.: ref, 2134 (1)
Michael, R.: ref, 787 (4), 1612 (100)
Michael, S. T.: ref, 1697 (151), 2076 (36)
Michael, W. B.: test, 844, 2538; rev, 368, 787, 803, 882, 1042, 1414, 1673, 1909, 1987, 2222, 2903; ref, 844 (3,4,5,6), 1590 (34), 1755 (49), 2545 (6), 2771 (39)
Michael-Good, L.: ref, 451 (139), 472 (178), 2485 (209), 2862 (515)
Michaels, A.: ref, 2603 (71)
Michaels, C.: ref, 241 (3), 430 (10), 994 (19), 1095 (30), 1903 (314), 2190 (3), 2695 (30)
Michaels, C. A.: ref, 376 (24), 1687 (28), 1903 (541), 2860 (1310), 2901 (125)
Michaels, L.: test, 1830
Michaels, M.: ref, 472 (63)
Michaelson, B. S.: ref, 2076 (20), 2603 (77)
Michaelson, R. B.: test, 1013
Michailevskaya, V.: ref, 270 (23), 1612 (87)
Michaud, D.: ref, 2516 (11),2892 (33)
Michel, F.: ref, 2860 (100)
Michel, M.: ref, 863 (30), 2603 (154)
Michel, M. K.: ref, 451 (46)
Michell, G. F.: ref, 1166 (47)
Michels, J. D.: ref, 2218 (52)
Michels, J. L.: ref, 1735 (6)
Michels, K. A.: ref, 665 (23), 694 (16), 705 (1), 2252 (1), 2771 (7)
Michelson, D. J.: ref, 2497 (290)
Michelsson, K.: ref, 815 (45), 2862 (641), 2901 (122)
Michie, A.: ref, 2860 (674)
Michie, A. M.: ref, 1079 (28)
Michie, P. T.: ref, 1903 (198)
Michielin, P.: ref, 999 (16), 2497 (52)
Michiels, V.: ref, 272 (200), 1164 (129), 1166 (131), 1697 (500), 2163 (286), 2603 (480), 2860 (1134)
Michon, A.: ref, 694 (124), 2163 (183), 2860 (449,720), 2863 (124,215), 2892 (72,142)
Mick, E.: ref, 1010 (69,70), 1092 (11,13,16), 2305 (121,165,221,240), 2860 (801), 2862 (308,310,394), 2879 (100,102,137)
MicKanin, J.: ref, 815 (23),2226 (5), 2863 (259)
Middleton, E. B.: ref, 413 (23), 1701 (47)
Middleton, G.: rev, 2870
Middleton, H. C.: ref, 2497 (77,78)
Middleton, J. A.: ref, 2771 (28)
Middleton, W.: ref, 998 (127), 1079 (96), 2497 (644)
Midence, K.: ref, 349 (32), 1079 (72), 1765 (29)
Midgley, C.: ref, 472 (211), 665 (89)
Midha, K. K.: ref, 2288 (6), 2289 (4)
Midlarsky, E.: ref, 1965 (67)
Miedaner, J.: test, 1668
Mietz, A.: ref, 472 (128), 2214 (69), 2498 (52)
Miewald, J. M.: ref, 2305 (39)
Miezejeski, C. M.: ref, 303 (6), 1218 (10), 2860 (891), 2863 (263)
Migliorelli, R.: ref, 2050 (120,121), 2163 (227,228), 2860 (935), 2873 (40,41), 2892 (197,198)
Miglioretti, D. L.: ref, 2860 (1243)

Migotsky, C. P.: rev, 2789; ref, 2112 (1)
Miguel, F.: ref, 2863 (209)
Miguel, S. A.: test, 810
Mihalko, D.: ref, 1166 (68), 2603 (328)
Mihura, J. L.: ref, 1697 (191)
Mijares-Colmenares, B. E.: ref, 2497 (267), 2771 (25)
Mikail, S.: ref, 272 (325)
Mikami, N.: ref, 1219 (1)
Miki, Y.: ref, 231 (1), 303 (32), 2226 (42), 2227 (61), 2599 (43), 2863 (431), 2892 (307)
Miklowitz, D. J.: ref, 2050 (122)
Mikulecky, L.: ref, 592 (8)
Mikulich, S. K.: ref, 2860 (1186), 2862 (565)
Mikulincer, M.: ref, 863 (32), 2163 (42), 2248 (5), 2497 (377), 2603 (50,68,161), 2858 (21)
Mikulineer, M.: ref, 1697 (214), 2163 (28)
Mikulis, D. J.: ref, 272 (284)
Mikulka, P.: ref, 1697 (156)
Milan, S.: ref, 2497 (347)
Milandre, L.: ref, 2863 (261), 2892 (183)
Milberg, W.: ref, 1740 (1), 2163 (9), 2860 (28,243), 2863 (61)
Milberg, W. D.: ref, 2860 (412), 2863 (110)
Milberg, W. P.: ref, 776 (23), 1758 (46), 2227 (32), 2860 (1166), 2892 (193)
Milberger, S.: ref, 1010 (69), 1092 (11,12,14,16), 2305 (165), 2860 (801,802), 2862 (308,309,394,520), 2879 (100,101,137)
Milbrath, C.: ref, 2603 (187,266),413)
Milburn, S.: ref, 875 (10), 1902 (77)
Milchus, N. J.: test, 980, 2136, 2355
MILCOM Systems, A Division of Hollister, Inc.: test, 1669
Milenkovic, P.: ref, 2225 (5)
Miler, C. D.: rev, 391
Miles, C.: test, 2929
Miles, J.: ref, 1903 (287)
Miles, T. R.: rev, 1800
Milet, T.: ref, 863 (83), 2603 (512)
Milgram, N. A.: ref, 2163 (91),2860 (376)
Milgram, R. M.: ref, 1470 (2)
Milholland, J. E.: rev, 497, 745, 1319, 1866, 1986
Milianti, F.: ref, 1040 (7)
Milich, R.: ref, 466 (1), 997 (16), 1745 (65), 1903 (268,441), 2242 (6), 2749 (70), 2862 (442)
Miliotis, D.: ref, 2861 (3)
Miliotis, P.: ref, 2860 (2), 2863 (1)
Milkent, M. M.: ref, 1140 (20)
Mill, D.: ref, 2899 (8)
Millar, J.: ref, 2239 (34)
Millar, K.: ref, 2497 (283)
Millar, N.: ref, 2497 (429)
Millar, T. W.: ref, 2497 (518)
Millard, T.: ref, 2862 (666)
Millard, Y.: ref, 1466 (3)
Miller, A.: ref, 2102 (1), 2288 (16), 2289 (11), 2860 (335), 2863 (88)
Miller, A. B.: ref, 2519 (10), 2520 (10), 2603 (53)
Miller, A. C.: ref, 270 (36), 337 (43), 2858 (38), 2862 (566)
Miller, A. D.: ref, 2860 (886)
Miller, A. H.: ref, 1166 (1), 2305 (12)
Miller, A. R.: ref, 1697 (565)
Miller, B.: ref, 303 (26), 2860 (1382)
Miller, B. A.: ref, 1661 (2,5,18,22)
Miller, B. C.: ref, 1216 (16)
Miller, B. G.: ref, 2288 (82)
Miller, B. L.: ref, 303 (30), 1164 (182), 1166 (136), 2227 (6,29), 2516 (13,81,120), 2599 (42), 2860 (286,1117,1150), 2863 (76,331,341), 2892 (37,231, 246,302)
Miller, C.: ref, 2545 (5)
Miller, C. D.: rev, 392
Miller, C. S.: ref, 2603 (239)
Miller, D.: ref, 650 (14), 1166 (129), 2288 (43,44), 2289 (33,34), 2358 (13)
Miller, D. A. F.: ref, 1000 (53)
Miller, D. J.: ref, 272 (323), 1697 (575), 2498 (74), 2603 (150)
Miller, E.: ref, 1135 (3), 2599 (5), 2860 (217)
Miller, E. N.: test, 366; ref, 1135 (2,6,13,16,26), 1164 (180), 1740 (8), 2227 (21), 2599 (4,8,25,32,40), 2860 (200,287,772)
Miller, F.: test, 1364
Miller, F. G.: ref, 1661 (80), 1687 (43), 1697 (585), 2553 (5)
Miller, G.: test, 1623; ref, 2862 (526)
Miller, G. A.: test, 2553; ref, 1661 (80), 1687 (43), 1697 (585), 2497 (419,478), 2553 (5), 2704 (33)
Miller, G. E.: rev, 1317; ref, 1903 (38), 2603 (293)
Miller, H. B.: ref, 1697 (434)
Miller, H. J.: test, 1674, 1675, 1676, 1677, 1678, 1679, 1680, 1681, 1682, 1683, 1684
Miller, H. R.: ref, 1697 (435,457), 1903 (159), 2862 (193)
Miller, H. S.: ref, 1745 (22)
Miller, I.: ref, 1166 (152), 1216 (88), 2603 (496)
Miller, I. W.: ref, 1166 (84,193), 2603 (26)
Miller, J.: test, 2891; ref, 2497 (107), 2860 (1003), 2863 (298)
Miller, J. A.: test, 545
Miller, J. D.: ref, 1001 (1,8), 2860 (77), 2892 (4)
Miller, J. E.: ref, 1216 (104)
Miller, J. F.: rev, 542; ref, 175 (8), 270 (9), ,430 (5), 1485 (18), 1528 (1), 1804 (4), 2382 (14,17,28), 2485 (106,154), 2601 (1,2), 2768 (17), 2813 (80)
Miller, J. J.: ref, 1181 (10), 1991 (41)
Miller, J. K.: rev, 620
Miller, J. L.: ref, 937 (4), 2218 (134), 2899 (9)
Miller, J. N.: ref, 2860 (1149)
Miller, J. W.: ref, 448 (11), 2860 (182)
Miller, K.: ref, 2603 (326)
Miller, K. E.: ref, 451 (141), 495 (2)
Miller, K. M.: test, 1103, 1600, 2255, 2256
Miller, L.: ref, 2674 (1)

Miller, L. A.: ref, 199 (15), 1525 (25), 1903 (134), 2860 (1123), 2892 (240)
Miller, L. C.: test, 1522; rev, 2, 888,1706
Miller, L. H.: test, 2508
Miller, L. J.: test, 1039, 1485, 1673, 2767; ref, 1673 (10)
Miller, L. L.: test, 2174
Miller, L. S.: ref, 451 (220), 1216 (108)
Miller, L. T.: ref, 2864 (121)
Miller, M. D.: rev, 665, 1180, 1380; ref, 337 (156), 2860 (678)
Miller, M. H.: ref, 2519 (18), 2520 (19)
Miller, M. J.: ref, 298 (88), 908 (1), 1755 (2,20), 1790 (3), 2360 (10,12), 2835 (5,15)
Miller, M. L.: ref, 2218 (51), 2813 (75)
Miller, M. P.: ref, 1697 (18)
Miller, N. B.: ref, 592 (64), 1115 (13)
Miller, N. L.: ref, 1166 (120)
Miller, P.: ref, 1697 (278), 2860 (1031), 2863 (306)
Miller, P. A.: ref, 1010 (102)
Miller, P. H.: ref, 1866 (12)
Miller, P. M.: ref, 1140 (9)
Miller, R. J.: rev, 65, 80, 1237, 1465, 1817
Miller, R. S.: ref, 2451 (3)
Miller, S.: ref, 998 (12), 1079 (28), 1338 (9), 2417 (19), 2497 (28,188,412)
Miller, S. A.: ref, 2862 (198)
Miller, S. D.: ref, 364 (23)
Miller, S. M.: ref, 1166 (22), 2076 (128), 2076 (151)
Miller, T.: ref, 2497 (372)
Miller, T. K.: test, 2527; ref, 745 (7), 2860 (545), 2863 (157), 2901 (36), 2905 (48)
Miller, T. W.: ref, 451 (67), 472 (138), 1991 (81),2305 (149), 2498 (53)
Miller, V. I.: ref, 1697 (522)
Miller, W. B.: ref, 1965 (59)
Miller, W. P.: test, 652
Miller, W. R.: ref, 134 (26), 135 (4), 272 (146), 652 (4), 1141 (2,5), 1164 (37), 2076 (49), 2860 (377)
Miller, W. S.: test, 1672
Miller, Y.: ref, 472 (23), 1340 (3)
Miller-Heyl, J.: ref, 1883 (1)
Miller-Tutzaver, C.: ref, 1000 (39)
Millin, J.: ref, 1903 (175)
Milling, L.: ref, 451 (142), 472 (181), 542 (1), 694 (118), 994 (37), 1010 (43), 1903 (466), 2862 (654)
Milling, L. M.: ref, 2862 (173)
Millis, S. R.: ref, 376 (4), 776 (24), 2193 (42), 2860 (936), 2863 (275)
Millman, J.: test, 705
Millman, R. B.: ref, 2519 (10), 2520 (10), 2603 (53)
Millon, C.: test, 1685, 1687; ref, 2076 (8)
Millon, T.: test, 1685, 1686, 1687, 1688
Mills, B. C.: ref, 694 (67), 746 (1), 1734 (1), 1991 (65), 2361 (2)
Mills, B. S. L.: ref, 2039 (24)
Mills, C. J.: ref, 615 (43), 694 (10), 2163 (229)
Mills, C. N.: rev, 340, 713, 1478, 2069
Mills, D. E.: ref, 2516 (38)
Mills, E. A.: ref, 1903 (374), 2524 (9), 2695 (39), 2704 (27), 2768 (29)
Mills, J.: test, 1154
Mills, J. A.: rev, 931, 2513
Mills, J. K.: ref, 2603 (201,382)
Mills, J. R.: ref, 1592 (14), 1902 (20,43), 2862 (113), 2905 (40)
Mills, K.: ref, 2050 (68)
Mills, L. B.: ref, 1590 (66), 2218 (131)
Mills, P. E.: ref, 624 (15), 1379 (44), 1485 (25), 1612 (14,22,32,43,47,75), 1902 (46,75), 1903 (72,111, 164,245,391), 2044 (5), 2485 (173), 2657 (13), 2680 (8), 2682 (2,4,5,8), 2704 (16), 2862 (244), 2864 (47)
Mills, S. R.: ref, 2193 (27)
Mills, T. Y.: ref, 1140 (47,54)
Millsap, R.: ref, 373 (1)
Millson, W. A.: ref, 2163 (252), 2497 (532)
Millstein, S. G.: ref, 1000 (58)
Milne, J.: ref, 998 (63), 2860 (560)
Milne, R.: ref, 2860 (1276)
Milner, A. D.: ref, 2860 (641)
Milner, B.: ref, 1903 (84), 2662 (1), 2860 (17,69,70, 73,78,140,176,177,249, 250,255,274,275, 284,288, 470,655,719,726,727,921,985), 2863 (46,47)
Milner, I. B.: ref, 1135 (23), 1697 (572), 2226 (36), 2603 (554), 2860 (1349), 2892 (290)
Milner, J. S.: test, 448; ref, 272 (371), 448 (3,5,6,9, 12,14,17,18,25,28,30), 1010 (82), 1164 (184), 1380 (21), 2497 (674), 2516 (121), 2892 (304)
Milstein, R.: ref, 2432 (19), 2892 (129), 2924 (2)
Mims, A. A.: ref, 777 (1), 1991 (85)
Minakawa, K.: ref, 824 (3)
Minaker, K. L.: ref, 1164 (72), 2863 (208)
Minarck, M. L.: ref, 893 (38)
Minassian, A.: ref, 2076 (123), 2247 (94)
Mindell, J. A.: ref, 863 (43)
Minder, B.: ref, 815 (16), 1164 (183), 2163 (354), 2862 (278,726)
Minderaa, R. B.: ref, 459 (26,37)
Mindes, E. J.: ref, 717 (1), 863 (75)
Mindry, D.: ref, 2125 (7), 2516 (16), 2860 (310)
Mineau, S.: ref, 2864 (122)
Miner, C. R.: ref, 337 (177), 2305 (229)
Miner, J. B.: test, 1689; ref, 1689 (1)
Miner, J. L.: ref, 1010 (61)
Miner, M. E.: ref, 1612 (68), 2813 (88)
Miner, M. H.: ref, 1697 (421)
Minery, B.: ref, 2487 (4)
Minger, C.: ref, 404 (19), 413 (8), 1754 (9), 2497 (80)
Minges, J.: ref, 2305 (108,145)
Minichiello, W. E.: ref, 1697 (51)
Minifie, C. E.: ref, 1166 (170,171), 2218 (81,82), 2305 (213), 2603 (514)

Ministry of Education: test, 1605
Miniutti, A. M.: ref, 284 (1), 1902 (26), 2694 (4)
Minke, K. M.: ref, 665 (92), 694 (130), 1000 (93), 1734 (5), 1991 (104), 2358 (15), 2485 (240), 2862 (701), 2879 (225)
Minkonas, D. V.: ref, 681 (39), 2860 (550)
Minnaar, C. L. J.: test, 12
Minnaar, G. G.: test, 1297
Minne, C.: ref, 272 (110), 998 (90), 2305 (129)
Minner, B.: ref, 1166 (18)
Minnesota Employment Stabilization Research Institute: test, 1700
Minor, L. L.: ref, 302 (2), 615 (11), 1156 (2), 2163 (36)
Minor, S.: ref, 448 (24)
Minshew, N. J.: ref, 1379 (46), 1386 (7), 2305 (109), 2860 (630,696), 2892 (141), 2905 (54,59)
Minton, J. T.: ref, 2860 (691)
Mintz, J.: ref, 790 (15), 1697 (188), 2050 (85,130), 2288 (8), 2305 (73,120), 2603 (74), 2749 (3), 2860 (384)
Mintz, L. B.: ref, 272 (260), 462 (24), 893 (36,41), 2065 (31), 2497 (614)
Mintzer, J.: ref, 1058 (3), 2860 (277), 2863 (72)
Mintzes, J. J.: ref, 592 (63)
Miolo, G.: ref, 270 (9),1528 (1)
Miotti, M.: ref, 2860 (127)
Miotto, E. C.: ref, 1758 (73)
Miozzo, A.: ref, 2163 (177,284), 2860 (1130), 2873 (25)
Miramontes, O. B.: ref, 665 (11,24)
Mirand, A. L.: ref, 1181 (24)
Miranda, A. B.: ref, 1612 (51)
Miranda, J.: ref, 2603 (207)
Miranti, S. V.: ref, 2603 (571)
Mireault, G.: ref, 337 (70), 472 (77), 2214 (38)
Mireault, G. C.: ref, 337 (44), 2076 (26)
Mirenda, P.: rev, 788, 2111, 2891; ref, 1903 (91), 2657 (3)
Mirenda, P. L.: ref, 1903 (8)
Mirolo, M. H.: ref, 2860 (665), 2863 (195)
Mirra, S. S.: ref, 2860 (1280)
Mirsky, A. F.: ref, 301 (1,22), 748 (1,8), 1164 (104), 1592 (11), 1903 (392), 2010 (7, 2163 (87), 2305 (5,64), 2516 (71), 2860 (39), 2862 (21,370), 2892 (199)
Mirsky, J.: ref, 337 (178)
Mirza, M. A.: ref, 2860 (1)
Mishel, M. H.: ref, 2076 (28,29), 2858 (29)
Mishkin, F.: ref, 1164 (182), 2516 (120), 2892 (302)
Mishkin, M.: ref, 2860 (838,1099), 2862 (492), 2863 (243), 2864 (117)
Mishra, R. K.: ref, 763 (4), 1607 (5,6), 2901 (16), 2905 (51,52,71)
Mishra, S. P.: ref, 1379 (2)
Miskiel, L. W.: ref, 214 (17), 240 (3), 1095 (26), 1982 (8), 2233 (2)
Mislevy, R. J.: test, 972; ref, 666 (6)
Misra, A.: ref, 2860 (378)
Missouri Department of Elementary and Secondary Education: test, 1707
Mitchell, C. M.: ref, 2603 (340)
Mitchell, D. B.: ref, 2860 (24)
Mitchell, D. R.: ref, 1218 (5), 2599 (10), 2863 (109), 2892 (59)
Mitchell, E. S.: ref, 2603 (29), 2858 (9)
Mitchell, G. W.: ref, 376 (14), 2863 (372)
Mitchell, J.: test, 1226; ref, 1093 (87)
Mitchell, J. E.: ref, 893 (5), 2497 (313)
Mitchell, J. L.: test, 2071
Mitchell, J. V., Jr.: rev, 2793
Mitchell, L.: ref, 739 (1), 999 (9)
Mitchell, M. K.: test, 1195, 2459
Mitchell, P.: ref, 272 (306), 998 (21), 1166 (61)
Mitchell, S.: ref, 739 (2)
Mitchell, T. R.: ref, 1107 (7)
Mitchell, T. V.: ref, 2862 (521)
Mitchell, W. E.: ref, 1697 (102)
Mitchum, C. C.: ref, 2873 (60)
Mitchum, N. T.: ref, 694 (25)
Mithaug, D. E.: test, 2053, 2826
Mitrushina, M.: ref, 1135 (13), 1164 (105), 1758 (47), 1993 (1), 2599 (25), 2860 (697,698,772,937,938), 2863 (204,276), 2860 (582,939)
Mitterer, J.: ref, 1071 (2)
Mittleman, B.: test, 709
Mittler, P.: test, 1423
Mittman, A.: rev, 1604
Mitton, J. E.: ref, 1903 (381), 2305 (144)
Mitts, N.: ref, 451 (51)
Miyake, K.: ref, 2218 (13)
Miyake, Y.: ref, 824 (3)
Miyawaki, E.: ref, 271 (15), 272 (330), 376 (28), 776 (56), 1135 (24),, 1218 (19), 1378 (10), 1740 (26), 2076 (181), 2516 (112), 2863 (411), 2892 (293)
Miyazama, Y.: ref, 2225 (18), 2226 (38), 2227 (51), 2860 (1357), 2863 (409), 2892 (292)
Mize, J.: ref, 1903 (542)
Mizes, J. S.: ref, 88 (1)
Mizokawa, D. T.: ref, 1903 (64), 2163 (57)
Mizuno, M.: ref, 2288 (81), 2289 (67), 2860 (1311)
Mizuta, I.: ref, 451 (162)
Mlakar, J.: ref, 2050 (89)
Mlcoch, A. G.: ref, 2163 (216), 2863 (260), 2873 (38)
Moats, L. C.: test, 2732
Mobarek, N.: ref, 1166 (139)
Mobayed, M.: ref, 1481 (1)
Mobb, E.: ref, 837 (3), 1765 (19), 1903 (292), 2862 (280)
Moberg, P.: ref, 1164 (167), 2873 (71), 2892 (285)
Moberg, P. J.: ref, 2873 (62)
Mobley, B. D.: ref, 1697 (296)
Mobley, M.: ref, 2835 (20)
Mocellin, J. S. P.: ref, 2497 (496)
Moch, A.: ref, 2863 (390)
Mock, V.: ref, 2652 (5)
Mockler, D.: ref, 1758 (74), 2860 (1135)
Modestin, J.: ref, 2247 (9)

Moeller, J. R.: ref, 1166 (148), 2305 (45)
Moely, B. E.: ref, 665 (40)
Moen, I.: ref, 2163 (287), 2225 (13), 2860 (1136)
Moersch, M. S.: test, 879, 2041
Moeschberger, M. L.: ref, 811 (5), 1216 (35)
Moffett, B. S.: ref, 1000 (104), 1745 (79)
Moffit, T. E.: ref, 1010 (38)
Moffitt, K. H.: ref, 1745 (46)
Moffitt, T. E.: ref, 358 (8), 365 (2,10), 373 (21,24), 451 (133), 1010 (98), 1612 (38),2211 (22,37), 2516 (59), 2862 (469,536)
Moffoot, A.: ref, 2240 (2), 2860 (385), 2863 (145)
Moffoot, A. P. R.: ref, 272 (119), 1166 (74), 1758 (43), 2239 (24), 2860 (699,904), 2863 (207)
Mogentale, C.: ref, 2860 (1178)
Mogg, K.: ref, 2497 (372,429)
Mogilner, M.: ref, 472 (91), 681 (52), 2498 (37)
Mogilner, M. B.: ref, 863 (53), 1010 (63), 2862 (272)
Mogilner, S.: ref, 472 (91), 681 (52), 2498 (37)
Mohamad, K.: ref, 451 (85)
Mohan, R. N.: ref, 1093 (60)
Mohay, H. A.: ref, 1612 (41,42)
Mohr, B.: ref, 2860 (1137)
Mohr, D. C.: ref, 272 (300)
Mohr, E.: ref, 2860 (244,511), 2863 (62)
Mohr, J.: ref, 681 (66), 2862 (393), 2901 (72)
Mohr, J. P.: ref, 2860 (407,408)
Mohr, L.: test, 1361
Mohr, P. H.: ref, 771 (1)
Mohs, R.: ref, 2050 (115), 2860 (471)
Mohs, R. C.: ref, 2017 (7), 2163 (115), 2305 (225), 2892 (76)
Moilanen, I.: ref, 472 (227,231)
Moinat, S. M.: test, 2105
Moisan, D.: ref, 1697 (279), 2603 (251)
Moisan, P. A.: ref, 301 (50), 472 (144,205), 1991 (86), 2498 (70), 2862 (390)
Moisan, P. M.: ref, 472 (205), 2498 (70)
Moiser, C. I.: rev, 1221
Moises, H. W.: ref, 2305 (22)
Mok, M.: ref, 1607 (6), 2905 (52)
Mokerji, V.: ref, 2519 (7), 2520 (7)
Mokili, J. K. L.: ref, 1379 (63)
Mokkink, H. G. A.: ref, 2497 (529)
Mokrani, M.: ref, 2305 (33)
Mokrani, M-C.: ref, 1166 (105)
Mokros, H. B.: test, 473
Molchan, S.: ref, 2076 (100), 2863 (222)
Moleman, P.: ref, 1697 (186), 2497 (189)
Molfese, V. J.: ref, 1216 (85,105), 1612 (54), 1903 (288), 2485 (138,231,232), 2862 (655)
Molin, J.: ref, 272 (201)
Molina, B. S. G.: ref, 451 (43)
Molina, H.: rev, 2335, 2657
Molina, V.: ref, 2892 (263)
Molinari, V. A.: ref, 1166 (221)
Molinder, I.: test, 1744
Moline, M.: ref, 1093 (27), 2603 (88)
Molinet-Molina, M.: ref, 1903 (117)
Moll, A.: ref, 2860 (1014)
Moll, S. H.: ref, 1697 (98)
Mollard, S. J.: ref, 1338 (38)
Mollenkopf, W. G.: rev, 2634
Möller, A. T.: ref, 1321 (5), 2065 (23)
Moller, C.: test, 640
Möller, H.-J.: ref, 1166 (67),216)
Mollerstrom, W. W.: ref, 448 (18), 1010 (82)
Molloy, E.: ref, 1765 (12), 2163 (73)
Molloy, R.: ref, 998 (60)
Molnar, J.: ref, 451 (74), 889 (1)
Molock, S.: ref, 472 (47), 2860 (467)
Moloney, E.: ref, 2305 (199)
Moltó, J.: ref, 999 (109)
Momose, T.: ref, 2860 (396), 2873 (10)
Monaco, C.: ref, 2125 (20)
Monahan, C. J.: ref, 1754 (2), 2835 (4)
Monahan, D.: ref, 214 (4)
Monahan, P.: ref, 2076 (32)
Monck, E.: ref, 451 (59), 1011 (4), 1079 (41), 1987 (15)
Mondin, G.: ref, 1790 (8), 2451 (4)
Mondini, S.: ref, 2163 (245)
Moneta, G.: ref, 1010 (104)
Monford, P.: ref, 1093 (40)
Monforton, M.: ref, 2592 (1)
Mongrain, M.: ref, 298 (136), 790 (19,28)
Monk, A.: ref, 349 (13)
Monk, C. A.: ref, 592 (86)
Monk, J. S.: test, 1472
Monk, T. H.: ref, 337 (72), 1166 (104), 2305 (173)
Monker, J.: ref, 1612 (79), 1903 (416)
Monmer, J.: ref, 2497 (349)
Monopolis, S.: ref, 1697 (58)
Monos, D.: ref, 1590 (37), 2858 (81)
Monroe, M.: test, 1138, 1139
Monroe, M.: rev, 861
Monroe, S.: ref, 1166 (54), 2305 (106)
Monroe-Blum, H.: ref, 2603 (542)
Monsaas, J. A.: rev, 622, 774, 1315, 2157; ref, 1318 (18), 1903 (539)
Monsch, A. U.: ref, 776 (25,28), 2892 (202)
Monsen, R.: test, 487
Monson, N.: ref, 199 (12), 272 (1), 1093 (44), 2519 (22), 2520 (23), 2860 (430), 2892 (5,65,100)
Montag, M.: test, 2482
Montagna, D.: ref, 665 (47), 1866 (24)
Montagna, P.: ref, 2768 (34), 2860 (1082)
Montague, J.: ref, 540 (16), 655 (1),1095 (44)
Montague, J. C., Jr.: ref, 2860 (786)
Montague, L.: ref, 2050 (46)
Montague, M.: ref, 681 (37), 2211 (21)
Montaldi, D.: ref, 1758 (99), 2860 (1379), 2863 (414)
Montali, J.: ref, 1386 (23)
Montani, T. O.: ref, 2484 (14)
Montano, C. B.: ref, 272 (85)

Monteiro, M. G.: ref, 1661 (14)
Montepare, J. M.: ref, 68 (14)
Montgomery, D.: ref, 2497 (294)
Montgomery, D. E.: ref, 2603 (58)
Montgomery, E.: ref, 2247 (26)
Montgomery, H. A.: ref, 1141 (2)
Montgomery, J. K.: ref, 214 (5)
Montgomery, J. W.: ref, 1095 (35), 1903 (393), 2662 (4), 2695 (19), 2704 (30), 2864 (41)
Montgomery, M. S.: ref, 694 (79), 1734 (3), 1991 (72)
Montgomery, R. J. V.: ref, 1808 (3)
Montgomery, R. L.: ref, 2525 (2,5)
Montgomery, R. P. G.: ref, 136 (9)
Montgomery, R. W.: ref, 1021 (24)
Montgomery, S. A.: ref, 1166 (205)
Montgrain, N.: ref, 650 (15), 1093 (97)
Monti, P. M.: ref, 134 (6,8,14,15,19,20,27), 272 (90), 1661 (12,23,34)
Montoya, I. D.: ref, 2703 (1)
Montplaisir, J.: ref, 776 (52), 1164 (163), 1218 (18), 2226 (28), 2227 (46), 2860 (1306)
Montrose, D. M.: ref, 1166 (210)
Montuori, J.: test, 2498
Moody, D. S.: ref, 2603 (490)
Moog, J.: ref, 486 (1,2), 994 (12), 1126 (1,2), 1127 (1,2), 1903 (258), 2233 (1), 2298 (1,2), 2860 (97), 2862 (260), 2864 (51)
Moog, J. S.: test, 486, 487, 891, 1126, 1127, 2298, 2620, 2623; ref, 2860 (353)
Mook, J.: ref, 2497 (227)
Moon, G. W.: ref, 2860 (289)
Moon, J. B.: ref, 303 (10), 641 (7), 1740 (14), 2226 (13), 2860 (1168), 2863 (351)
Moon, S. M.: ref, 246 (5), 301 (49), 2485 (174)
Mooney, A.: ref, 2228 (2)
Mooney, R. L.: test, 1716
Moore, A.: ref, 1093 (109), 2214 (114)
Moore, A. D.: ref, 2860 (500)
Moore, B.: ref, 2860 (1321)
Moore, B. D.: ref, 815 (39), 1903 (481), 2671 (3),2862 (522), 2879 (176), 2901 (97)
Moore, B. D., III: ref, 2862 (596), 2879 (197)
Moore, C.: ref, 1092 (5), 2860 (331)
Moore, C. A.: ref, 2863 (337)
Moore, D.: ref, 2247 (93), 2305 (151), 2487 (2,5)
Moore, D. G.: ref, 350 (33)
Moore, D. M.: ref, 1140 (39)
Moore, D. W.: ref, 358 (9), 1765 (24), 2092 (3), 2094 (2), 2862 (22)
Moore, E. E.: ref, 641 (5), 1135 (5), 2076 (118), 2227 (20), 2517 (4), 2599 (7,30)
Moore, E. G. J.: ref, 2862 (23)
Moore, G. T.: test, 877
Moore, J. D.: ref, 1021 (40), 2497 (581)
Moore, J. E.: rev, 857
Moore, J. W.: ref, 2860 (1063)
Moore, K.: ref, 1903 (271), 2905 (57)
Moore, K. S.: ref, 1300 (11)
Moore, L. A.: ref, 2230 (7)
Moore, L. C.: ref, 2862 (24), 2864 (2)
Moore, L. H.: ref, 1697 (330), 2860 (940,1138), 2901 (68,98)
Moore, L. W.: ref, 2862 (217)
Moore, M.: ref, 1000 (3)
Moore, M. W.: ref, 2252 (3), 2485 (62), 2606 (5)
Moore, P.: ref, 2095 (1), 2305 (165)
Moore, P. J.: ref, 1697 (172), 2497 (174)
Moore, P. M.: ref, 1758 (92), 2860 (1312), 2863 (396)
Moore, R.: ref, 2497 (129)
Moore, R. G.: ref, 999 (95), 2497 (373)
Moore, R. H.: ref, 372 (73), 2402 (30)
Moore, S.: ref, 1903 (270), 2905 (56)
Moore, S. M.: ref, 1021 (36)
Moore, T.: ref, 2497 (171)
Moore-Hirschl, S.: test, 2509
Moorehouse, M.: ref, 451 (283), 681 (98), 2603 (590), 2901 (135)
Moorhead, A.: test, 1708, 1709
Moorman, R. H.: ref, 1701 (25,29)
Moos, B. S.: test, 1010, 1495, 1496; ref, 134 (30), 637 (2), 1181 (23), 2414 (5), 2917 (5)
Moos, R. H.: test, 495, 637, 699, 710, 1010, 1141, 1181, 1495, 1496, 1647, 1670, 1743, 2793, 2850, 2917; ref, 134 (30), 337 (194), 637 (1,2,3), 699 (1,2), 1010 (28,32,42), 1181 (3,5,7,9,10,21, 22, 23,28), 1495 (1), 1496 (1), 1743 (1,2), 1991 (41), 2414 (5), 2497 (290,406), 2498 (51), 2917 (2,5)
Moos (Rudolf) and Associates: test, 2445
Moosa, F.: ref, 1079 (78)
Moose, D.: ref, 301 (60), 815 (46)
Moossy, J.: ref, 776 (38)
Moran, J. D., III: ref, 2862 (92),2864 (15)
Moran, M.: ref, 2305 (203), 2860 (1094)
Moran, M. E.: ref, 1166 (129)
Moran, M. J.: ref, 214 (11), 1095 (5)
Moran, M. R.: rev, 59, 2935
Moran, P.: ref, 2050 (60)
Moran, P. B.: ref, 2034 (6)
Moran, P. J.: ref, 2497 (617)
Morano, C. D.: ref, 2557 (1)
Moranville, J.: ref, 1093 (24), 1164 (25), 1164 (84), 2288 (42), 2289 (32), 2860 (239)
Moravian College: test, 1247, 1248
Moray House Institute of Education: test, 901
Moreau, D.: ref, 451 (151), 2305 (197)
Morehead, M. K.: test, 1738
Morel, K. R.: ref, 1697 (590), 2863 (428), 2879 (232)
Moreland, C.: ref, 1697 (171), 2860 (355), 2901 (20)
Moreland, K. L.: rev, 771, 1304, 1976, 2343, 2482, 2483, 2484; ref, 1697 (331), 2247 (80)
Moreland, V. J.: ref, 272 (63), 2402 (16), 2892 (66)
Morell, M. A.: ref, 1338 (23), 1581 (1), 1582 (5)
Morency, A.: test, 230, 232, 2817, 2819
Moreno, C. R.: ref, 776 (8), 2860 (201)

Moreno, S.: test, 1849, 2140, 2465
Moretti, M. M.: ref, 272 (369)
Moretti, R. J.: ref, 2749 (80)
Morey, L. C.: test, 1959, 1960
Morf, M. E.: ref, 2218 (33), 2858 (99)
Morgan, A.: test, 328; ref, 999 (138,190), 1079 (103)
Morgan, A. W.: ref, 1378 (9), 1903 (543), 2860 (1313)
Morgan, B. B.: ref, 615 (10)
Morgan, C. D.: ref, 376 (1), 2860 (941), 2862 (371)
Morgan, D.: test, 1516; ref, 2860 (265)
Morgan, D. L.: test, 76; ref, 2856 (12)
Morgan, G. A. V.: rev, 348, 715, 1318
Morgan, J. C.: ref, 681 (79), 1380 (16)
Morgan, J. N.: ref, 592 (36)
Morgan, K.: ref, 537 (3)
Morgan, K. M.: ref, 337 (127), 1216 (102)
Morgan, L.: ref, 68 (26), 2247 (27)
Morgan, O. J.: ref, 2527 (3)
Morgan, R. K.: ref, 2856 (12)
Morgan, R. O.: ref, 2076 (8)
Morgan, S.: ref, 301 (50), 472 (144), 1991 (86), 2862 (390), 2905 (7)
Morgan, S. B.: ref, 68 (53), 472 (188), 1902 (40), 2813 (13,47,58)
Morgan, S. F.: ref, 2599 (31), 2860 (942)
Morgan, S. K.: ref, 665 (82), 827 (11), 1657 (19), 1903 (418)
Morgan, T. J.: ref, 846 (22), 1697 (551)
Morgenstern, H.: ref, 1058 (2), 2860 (152)
Mori, E.: ref, 2163 (334), 2860 (1314,1371), 2873 (68,73)
Mori, L.: ref, 681 (64), 1903 (394)
Moriarty, D.: ref, 893 (6)
Moriarty, J.: ref, 2193 (18), 2860 (501)
Moriarty, J. B.: test, 2030; ref, 2030 (1)
Moriarty, P.: test, 1195
Morice, R.: ref, 1758 (75), 2860 (1139), 2892 (241)
Moriconi, D. M.: ref, 1697 (436), 1866 (40)
Morier, D.: ref, 1965 (47)
Morin, C. M.: ref, 337 (83), 2010 (17), 2076 (5), 2402 (34), 2497 (43,374), 2860 (761)
Moring, J.: ref, 2247 (120), 2288 (2), 2860 (53)
Morioka, Y.: ref, 1592 (27), 2862 (719)
Morishima, A.: ref, 1093 (1), 2603 (15)
Morison, P.: ref, 2862 (136)
Morison, S. J.: ref, 787 (1), 2163 (252),2497 (532)
Morita, Y.: ref, 2076 (174)
Morith, K.: ref, 2862 (638)
Moritz, G.: ref, 2603 (175)
Moritz, M. S.: ref, 1525 (6), 1697 (50)
Moritz, S.: ref, 1965 (81)
Moritz, T.: ref, 2163 (216), 2863 (260), 2873 (38)
Moriya, H.: ref, 2288 (23), 2305 (69), 2860 (365)
Moriya, N.: ref, 824 (3)
Morley, G. K.: ref, 2860 (5), 2863 (3)
Morley, S.: ref, 272 (53)
Morman, R. R.: test, 2616
Morner, C. J.: rev, 57, 1567
Morodes, S.: ref, 853 (24), 2247 (111), 2862 (591)
Morokoff, P. J.: ref, 2603 (95)
Morra, S.: ref, 2163 (178)
Morral, A. R.: ref, 272 (359), 846 (25), 1697 (582), 2497 (671)
Morreale, A.: ref, 2768 (34), 2860 (1082)
Morreale, S.: rev, 470, 880, 2025, 2093
Morreau, L. E.: test, 443
Morrell, R. W.: ref, 2860 (202)
Morris, C.: ref, 615 (1), 666 (5)
Morris, C. D.: ref, 2485 (100)
Morris, D.: ref, 827 (6), 2305 (202)
Morris, D. D.: ref, 2305 (166)
Morris, D. W.: ref, 824 (6)
Morris, G.: ref, 2863 (266)
Morris, G. J.: test, 2633
Morris, G. L.: ref, 687 (3), 2860 (1041), 2863 (345)
Morris, J. C.: ref, 1164 (179), 2860 (182,1280,1397), 2863 (422)
Morris, J. E.: test, 2259
Morris, L. A.: test, 1887
Morris, L. W.: ref, 272 (16)
Morris, M. A.: ref, 1010 (126), 1991 (103)
Morris, N. M.: ref, 1903 (433), 2163 (248)
Morris, R.: test, 2840; ref, 994 (6), 1096 (6), 1240 (12), 1612 (30),1903 (102,152),1982 (5),2382 (37), 2485 (46,74,218), 2680 (5,18), 2768 (8,10), 2813 (30,131), 2860 (1035), 2862 (151,191), 2864 (26,35), 2892 (216)
Morris, R. C.: ref, 641 (6), 1758 (48), 2193 (43), 2860 (943), 2863 (277)
Morris, R. D.: ref, 815 (11), 1010 (72),1379 (31), 1533 (2), 1612 (39), 1903 (201), 2125 (9), 2485 (101,163), 2599 (24), 2813 (43,86), 2879 (106), 2901 (32)
Morris, R. G.: ref, 272 (16), 303 (9), 1758 (2,32,67,73,82,104), 2193 (35), 2227 (28), 2860 (90,792,1140,1213), 2863 (338)
Morris, R. J.: ref, 209 (5)
Morris, S. A.: ref, 2402 (21)
Morris, S. J.: ref, 272 (301)
Morris, T. L.: ref, 2498 (49)
Morris, Y.: ref, 272 (144), 1010 (91), 2497 (535)
Morris-Friehe, M. J.: ref, 1424 (2), 2862 (174)
Morris-Yates, A.: ref, 998 (18), 2603 (37)
Morrisby, M.: test, 718
The Morrisby Organisation: test, 1717, 1835
Morrisette, M. L.: ref, 1095 (38), 1485 (51), 2680 (15), 2695 (53)
Morrison, C. D.: ref, 353 (3), 1903 (85)
Morrison, C. R.: ref, 2862 (28)
Morrison, C. S.: ref, 893 (53)
Morrison, D.: ref, 364 (14), 665 (64), 1379 (19,49), 2211 (32), 2484 (5), 2488 (8)
Morrison, D. C.: ref, 665 (14), 1379 (6), 2488 (2)
Morrison, D. L.: ref, 999 (182), 1079 (97)
Morrison, D. R.: ref, 1216 (69), 1903 (395)

Morrison, E. A.: ref, 1104 (4), 2193 (23), 2239 (21), 2860 (659), 2863 (194)
Morrison, F.: ref, 2860 (1401)
Morrison, F. J.: ref, 1902 (64), 2485 (159), 2485 (175), 2879 (129)
Morrison, F. M.: ref, 2860 (1120)
Morrison, G. M.: rev, 852, 2739
Morrison, J. H.: test, 1526, 2675
Morrison, L. A.: ref, 272 (37), 2050 (131), 2497 (89), 2603 (63,412)
Morrison, L. P.: test, 2618
Morrison, M.: ref, 1115 (19), 2497 (268)
Morrison, M. E.: ref, 1095 (7), 1618 (1), 1903 (107), 2672 (2), 2813 (16)
Morrison, R. L.: ref, 1093 (15), 1619 (2), 2305 (42,57), 2519 (11), 2520 (11), 2892 (6)
Morrison, T.: ref, 1115 (19)
Morrison, T. L.: ref, 1582 (15), 1697 (437)
Morrison, W. L.: test, 1013, 2618
Morriss, R.: test, 225
Morrissett, I.: rev, 1113
Morrissey, E.: ref, 272 (31)
Morrow, B.: ref, 2050 (94)
Morrow, D.: ref, 2860 (700)
Morrow, D. G.: ref, 2860 (765,1315)
Morrow, G. R.: ref, 2497 (190)
Morrow, K. A.: ref, 2603 (383), 2858 (104)
Morrow, L. A.: ref, 1697 (138), 2863 (99)
Morrow, P. C.: ref, 404 (18), 414 (1), 1754 (8), 1755 (11)
Morrow, S. F.: ref, 289 (6), 1363 (2), 2901 (139)
Morse, C. A.: ref, 2497 (130)
Morse, D. T.: test, 1395
Morse, E. V.: ref, 2603 (160)
Morse, G.: ref, 337 (8), 1181 (2)
Morse, G. A.: ref, 337 (94,168)
Morse, R. M.: ref, 1697 (324)
Morss, J.: ref, 592 (33)
Mortati, S. G.: ref, 1697 (13)
Mortensen, E. L.: ref, 2860 (178)
Mortensen, M. E.: ref, 1903 (332), 2892 (157)
Mortilla, M.: ref, 2227 (8), 2860 (364),2879 (44), 2892 (54)
Mortimer, A. M.: ref, 2163 (105)
Mortimer, J. A.: ref, 2860 (379)
Mortimer, R. H.: ref, 1178 (3)
Morton, D.: ref, 2076 (13)
Morton, D. L.: ref, 2076 (56)
Morton, L. L.: ref, 2487 (16), 2862 (107), 2905 (60)
Morton, N.: ref, 303 (9), 2227 (28), 2860 (1140),2863 (338)
Morton, N. W.: test, 2212; rev, 302m 1790
Morton, R. L.: rev, 174
Morton, T. L.: ref, 451 (211)
Morton, W. A.: ref, 2519 (49), 2520 (49)
Morvant, M.: ref, 665 (78)
Mos, L. P.: test, 2112
Mos, P. A.: rev, 131
Moscarelli, M.: ref, 2288 (14), 2289 (9)
Mosco, C.: ref, 272 (234),2497 (599)
Moscovitch, M.: ref, 376 (31), 776 (60), 1758 (93), 2860 (11,1204,1316), 2863 (6,423), 2892 (281)
Moseley, D.: test, 2910
Moseley, L. G.: ref, 2497 (102)
Moseley, T. H., Jr.: ref, 2839 (9)
Moser, M.: ref, 272 (370), 2497 (673)
Moses, B. S.: test, 458
Moses, J. A., Jr.: ref, 1697 (128)
Moses, J. D.: ref, 2860 (666)
Mosher, D. L.: rev, 426, 2618
Moshman, D.: rev, 2534
Mosier, K.: ref, 2516 (19)
Moskowitz, D. S.: ref, 2218 (121), 2860 (120), 2862 (81)
Mosley, J. A.: ref, 998 (106), 2603 (405)
Mosley, J. L.: ref, 257 (2),694 (122), 1903 (119,228, 289,503)
Moss, E.: ref, 1903 (482), 2485 (28)
Moss, H. A.: ref, 1612 (55,62,85), 1903 (483), 2163 (288), 2813 (81), 2862 (279,297,523)
Moss, H. B.: ref, 451 (30,122), 1902 (76), 2010 (15), 2305 (27,177), 2860 (1404), 2862 (372,477)
Moss, M.: ref, 272 (32), 2497 (79)
Moss, M. B.: ref, 1164 (33), 2603 (140), 2860 (344), 2863 (92), 2892 (49)
Moss, M. H.: test, 2740
Moss, P. A.: rev, 1248
Moss, S.: ref, 1379 (69), 2860 (894), 2862 (350)
Moss, S. E.: ref, 298 (116)
Mossenson, L.: test, 2743
Mossey, J. M.: ref, 998 (22)
Mossholder, K. M.: rev, 2419, 2364
Mössner, J.: ref, 1166 (26)
Mostardi, R. A.: ref, 853 (25), 2862 (687)
Mostofsky, S. H.: ref, 2860 (1409), 2862 (727), 2892 (303)
Mostue, P.: test, 1860
Moszynski, S. Y.: ref, 1965 (28)
Mote, C. R.: ref, 1903 (180), 2905 (39)
Motiuk, L. L.: ref, 1697 (10)
Motl, J.: ref, 2497 (395)
Motomura, N.: ref, 2860 (944)
Motowidlo, S. J.: rev, 1565, 2267, 2272, 2587; ref, 180 (21)
Mott, P.: ref, 1619 (6)
Motta, R.: ref, 2497 (295)
Motta, R. W.: ref, 854 (1), 1097 (9), 1697 (332,559), 2516 (46,106)
Mottron, L.: ref, 2860 (945), 2863 (278), 2864 (122)
Mouanoutouna, V. L.: ref, 2603 (384)
Moulden, J. A.: ref, 2862 (524)
Moulin, D. E.: ref, 1615 (1)
Mount, L.: ref, 298 (151)
Mount, M. K.: ref, 2899 (18)
Mountz, J. M.: ref, 376 (14), 2863 (372)

Moussa, W.: ref, 2163 (308), 2860 (1197), 2862 (415)
Moussai, J.: ref, 1164 (181), 1740 (33), 2227 (59), 2860 (1408), 2863 (427)
Moussong-Kovács, E.: ref, 1166 (30)
Mouw, J. T.: ref, 592 (38), 1140 (35)
Mowchun, N.: ref, 2305 (124)
Mowrer, D. E.: rev, 1095, 1394
Mowrer, R. R.: rev, 652
Mowry, B. J.: ref, 650 (6), 2305 (56), 2305 (101)
Moxley, R.: test, 300, 2425
Moxness, K.: ref, 998 (24)
Moya, K. L.: ref, 2860 (155)
Moyes, I. C. A.: rev, 2050
Moyes, J.: ref, 272 (194)
Moyle, R. J.: ref, 2603 (243)
Moynihan, C.: test, 455
Mozingo, D.: ref, 2860 (701)
Mozley, D.: ref, 2288 (48), 2289 (37)
Mozley, L. H.: ref, 2288 (48), 2289 (37), 2860 (744)
Mpofu, E.: ref, 349 (14,15,25), 1466 (6)
Mrazek, D. A.: ref, 451 (73)
Mroczek, D. K.: ref, 2417 (30), 2603 (202)
Mrosek, S.: ref, 1166 (121)
Mruk, C.: ref, 1735 (10)
Mshelia, A. Y.: ref, 1140 (10)
Mu Alpha Theta: test, 144, 148, 149
Muamba, K.: ref, 1379 (23)
Muchinsky, P. M.: rev, 935, 1267, 1352, 2648, 2803
Mudar, P.: ref, 1181 (18)
Mudford, D. C.: ref, 4 (9)
Mudre, L. H.: ref, 1072 (11)
Muehlenhard, C. L.: ref, 694 (128)
Mueller, A.: ref, 1903 (270), 2905 (56)
Mueller, E. A.: ref, 2076 (100), 2863 (222)
Mueller, G. P.: ref, 2305 (65)
Mueller, J.: test, 558
Mueller, J. H.: ref, 272 (18), 2497 (269)
Mueller, N.: ref, 2038 (4)
Mueller, R. J.: ref, 615 (42)
Mueller, R. O.: rev, 382, 645, 1351, 2361, 2917, 2924
Mueller, T.: ref, 1093 (107),2305 (125)
Mueller, T. I.: ref, 1158 (3), 1517 (5), 1697 (513,517), 2305 (179,189,200)
Mueller, W. M.: ref, 2860 (1041)
Muench, A. M.: rev, 216
Muenchen, R. A.: ref, 1832 (12)
Muenz, L.: ref, 592 (58)
Muenz, L. R.: ref, 337 (177), 2305 (229)
Muenz, T. A.: ref, 2868 (2)
Mueser, K. T.: ref, 271 (9), 272 (266), 273 (27), 1093 (15), 1166 (183), 1619 (2), 2305 (42,57), 2519 (11),2520 (11), 2860 (569),2892 (6,101)
Mufson, L.: ref, 694 (35), 1903 (135)
Muggia, S.: ref, 2163 (319), 2860 (836), 2892 (269)
Múgica, P.: ref, 448 (14)
Muijen, M.: ref, 1093 (70,71),2050 (87,90)
Muik, E. A.: ref, 353 (9), 1901 (13), 2724 (3)
Muir, H. M.: ref, 2163 (142)
Muir, R.: ref, 2305 (31)
Muir, W. J.: ref, 2860 (515), 2892 (86)
Muirhead, J.: ref, 2076 (117)
Mukai, T.: ref, 2862 (550)
Mukerji, V.: ref, 337 (7)
Mukherjee, S.: ref, 2305 (45)
Mulcahey, M. J.: ref, 1725 (6), 1908 (1)
Mulcahy, R.: ref, 389 (7)
Mulder, A.: ref, 2603 (120)
Mulder, R. T.: ref, 999 (91,96,163), 1166 (55,132,146,159), 2288 (83), 2289 (68), 2519 (52), 2520 (51), 2603 (271,318,481,492)
Muldoon, M. F.: ref, 1135 (19), 2497 (603), 2516 (89), 2860 (1200), 2863 (360)
Mulford, M.: ref, 372 (98)
Mulhall, D.: ref, 1943 (1)
Mulhall, D. J.: test, 1066, 1944
Mulhall, P. F.: ref, 472 (123), 495 (11), 2214 (65)
Mulhern, R. K.: ref, 451 (230), 472 (34), 1612 (40), 2497 (659), 2860 (319), 2862 (218), 2879 (38), 2901 (18)
Mulick, J. A.: ref, 1379 (82,91), 2485 (134,185), 2813 (66), 2860 (1015), 2862 (421,588), 2901 (79,109)
Mullani, N. A.: ref, 2860 (1231)
Mullbacher, W.: ref, 2860 (873), 2863 (257)
Mullen, E. J.: ref, 404 (18), 414 (1), 1754 (8), 1755 (11)
Mullen, E. M.: test, 1728
Mullen, P. E.: ref, 2050 (38,44,45,128,129)
Mullen, R.: ref, 2497 (557)
Müller, F.: ref, 2860 (1137)
Müller, H.: ref, 2226 (29)
Muller, J.: ref, 272 (57,69), 273 (9), 694 (36,59), 1079 (14,18), 2076 (63)
Muller, J. A.: ref, 376 (33), 2239 (35)
Muller, R. T.: ref, 451 (68), 1178 (13)
Muller, S.: ref, 2305 (207)
Müller, V.: ref, 1525 (23), 2603 (287), 2860 (1115,1137)
Mulligan, M.: ref, 1056 (2)
Mulligan, R.: ref, 1758 (44)
Mulligan, S.: ref, 2377 (3)
Mullin, C. R.: ref, 1745 (60), 2603 (385)
Mullins, L. L.: ref, 337 (28,106), 451 (69), 472 (139,140), 2498 (54), 2603 (523,545, 2858 (30)
Mullis, A. K.: ref, 694 (37,60)
Mullis, R. L.: ref, 694 (37,60)
Mulloy, C.: ref, 459 (9), 2163 (71)
Mulrooney, L. L.: ref, 1901 (1)
Mulsant, B.: ref, 337 (156)
Mulsant, B. H.: ref, 1093 (104)
Multicenter AIDS Cohort Study.: ref, 1135 (3), 2599 (5), 2860 (217)
Multon, K. D.: ref, 337 (183)
Multon, K-D.: ref, 1754 (17)
Mulvihill, B. A.: ref, 1216 (54), 1379 (53), 2813 (70)
Mumford, M. D.: ref, 937 (3), 1701 (46)
Munday, L. A.: rev, 1434
Munday, R.: ref, 571 (3), 1599 (1), 1755 (59), 2497 (497)

Mundform, D. J.: ref, 1216 (37,39), 2485 (112)
Mundfrom, D. J.: ref, 451 (33), 1216 (38,40,41,61), 1903 (234), 2485 (113,114,115)
Mundy, P.: ref, 433 (3,10,11), 459 (32), 674 (3), 1962 (7), 2228 (3,12,13,5), 2485 (139), 2813 (44), 2862 (188)
Mundy-Castle, A.: ref, 999 (7)
Mundy-Castle, A. C.: ref, 2862 (82)
Munet-Vilaró, F.: ref, 1010 (25)
Munger, A. M.: rev, 728, 2051
Munick, M. L.: ref, 68 (51)
Munir, F.: ref, 350 (47), 2228 (24)
Munjack, D. J.: ref, 2603 (112)
Munkres, A. W.: test, 2443
Munkrold, O. G.: ref, 1079 (83)
Munley, P. H.: ref, 1687 (45), 1697 (94,228,333), 2402 (31,44), 2860 (702)
Munne, R.: ref, 1093 (75)
Muñoz, A.: ref, 1135 (3), 2599 (5),2860 (217)
Muñoz, R. F.: ref, 2519 (45)
Muñoz-Sandoval, A. F.: test, 264, 309, 2904
Munro, B. H.: ref, 1745 (71)
Munro, J.: test, 187
Munro, J. C.: ref, 2860 (1343)
Munro, S.: ref, 451 (271), 1012 (2)
Munroe, S. M.: ref, 134 (6,14), 1661 (12,23)
Munsch, J.: ref, 699 (3)
Munsell, L.: ref, 1455 (7)
Munsinger, H. L.: test, 2791
Munson, L.: ref, 803 (2), 1653 (20), 2189 (4), 2382 (30), 2485 (156), 2813 (83)
Munson, W. W.: ref, 1754 (12), 2282 (6,7)
Münte, T. F.: ref, 2860 (356),1105), 2879 (166), 2892 (51)
Munton, A. G.: ref, 1000 (90), 1079 (44), 2050 (123)
Mupier, R.: ref, 462 (30)
Muraki, E.: ref, 592 (72)
Muram, D.: ref, 999 (97)
Muran, C.: ref, 2326 (2)
Muran, J. C.: ref, 2603 (286,386,546)
Muransky, J. M.: ref, 1010 (83)
Muraoka, M. Y.: ref, 1592 (19),1697 (268), 2497 (312), 2516 (36)
Murdock, M. C.: ref, 1404 (5)
Mureau, M. A. M.: ref, 451 (212)
Murfin, P.: ref, 615 (1), 666 (5)
Muris, P.: ref, 999 (164)
Murphy, B. C.: ref, 365 (9)
Murphy, C.: ref, 376 (1), 2076 (94), 2860 (941), 2862 (371)
Murphy, C. C.: rev, 357, 1781; ref, 773 (1)
Murphy, C. M.: ref, 134 (38), 1661 (70)
Murphy, D. A.: ref, 681 (17), 1745 (83)
Murphy, D. G. M.: ref, 199 (16), 2010 (16,18), 2163 (179), 2516 (47), 2860 (502,703,837,1141), 2863 (205,242),2879 (87)
Murphy, D. L.: ref, 2076 (100), 2497 (626), 2863 (222)
Murphy, E.: test, 1750
Murphy, E. G.: ref, 2860 (64), 2862 (38)
Murphy, G. H.: ref, 1613 (1)
Murphy, H. D.: rev, 1042
Murphy, H. J.: ref, 1140 (55), 1140 (56)
Murphy, J. A.: rev, 102
Murphy, J. R.: ref, 1166 (194)
Murphy, K. K.: rev, 2704
Murphy, K. R.: test, 224; rev, 382, 1552, 2198, 2832, 2914; ref, 451 (143), 1889 (7), 2402 (59), 2603 (482), 2860 (1142), 2892 (242)
Murphy, L. B.: ref, 472 (136), 1178 (9), 2214 (76), 2603 (222)
Murphy, L. M. B.: ref, 1010 (126), 1991 (103)
Murphy, M.: ref, 2860 (427)
Murphy, M. A.: ref, 1686 (6), 1697 (438), 2402 (45)
Murphy, P.: ref, 2305 (141,180,199)
Murphy, P. H.: ref, 1140 (36)
Murphy, P. W.: ref, 1902 (45)
Murphy, S.: ref, 2901 (67)
Murphy, T.: ref, 272 (374), 1745 (88), 2497 (330)
Murphy, T. B.: ref, 997 (10), 1216 (20), 2127 (1), 2603 (134)
Murphy, W. D.: ref, 1697 (187)
Murphy-Weinberg, V.: ref, 2305 (50)
Murray, A.: ref, 4 (9), 451 (64), 1765 (22), 2214 (73), 2813 (100)
Murray, C.: test, 2427; ref, 272 (106), 1011 (3), 1612 (96), 1987 (14), 2240 (2), 2497 (442,470),2695 (69), 2860 (328), 2863 (145,207)
Murray, C. L.: ref, 272 (83)
Murray, C. M.: ref, 1619 (1)
Murray, D.: ref, 791 (16)
Murray, D. L.: ref, 2603 (399)
Murray, D. M.: ref, 1697 (32)
Murray, E.: rev, 862
Murray, E. J.: ref, 2115 (1), 2862 (128)
Murray, F. T.: ref, 1697 (35)
Murray, H. A.: test, 2749
Murray, H. G.: ref, 999 (21), 1140 (6), 1619 (3), 1965 (17)
Murray, J. B.: ref, 1093 (33), 1697 (139,229,439), 2076 (30), 2247 (16), 2497 (364)
Murray, J. D.: ref, 2657 (33), 2813 (141), 2864 (135)
Murray, J. F.: ref, 2247 (68)
Murray, K. T.: ref, 1215 (5)
Murray, L.: ref, 270 (21,22), 1216 (86), 1612 (86), 2228 (5)
Murray, L. H.: ref, 1402 (3)
Murray, L. L.: ref, 159 (1,2), 163 (3)
Murray, M.: ref, 1166 (222)
Murray, R.: ref, 272 (110), 998 (90), 1093 (80), 2050 (32,98,103), 2305 (129)
Murray, R. A.: ref, 2860 (309)
Murray, R. M.: ref, 998 (29), 1093 (50), 1166 (72), 2050 (13,34,74,80), 2860 (656,1343)
Murray, R. P.: ref, 999 (184), 1140 (57), 1661 (31), 1697 (334,562), 2497 (649)
Murray, T. D.: ref, 998 (52)
Murray, T. J.: ref, 376 (11), 2860 (1189), 2892 (258)

Murray, W. D.: ref, 1755 (40)
Murray-Branch, J.: ref, 377 (1), 2382 (17,28),2485 (106,154),2601 (1,2), 2813 (11,80)
Murray-Harvey, R.: ref, 2540 (4)
Murray-Ward, M.: rev, 1767, 2730
Murrell, J.: ref, 2599 (16), 2860 (614), 2863 (180), 2892 (115)
Murrelle, L.: ref, 2860 (1404)
Murrin, M. R.: ref, 1590 (25)
Murro, A. M.: ref, 641 (4), 2227 (11), 2863 (136)
Murry, W. D.: ref, 1755 (56)
Murstein, B. L.: rev, 466
Murtagh, D.: ref, 2599 (29), 2862 (358), 2879 (123)
Murtagh, M.: ref, 2258 (6)
Murtha, T. C.: ref, 2218 (67)
Musetti, L.: ref, 2603 (135)
Musgrave, J.: ref, 2797 (5)
Muskina, G.: ref, 451 (176), 811 (13),1259 (2)
Musonda, D.: ref, 592 (21)
Mussell, M. P.: ref, 2497 (313)
Musso, A.: ref, 1338 (6), 2497 (20), 2603 (7)
Mutch, W. J.: ref, 2858 (128)
Muter, V.: ref, 349 (16,39), 1240 (50), 1765 (36), 2862 (728), 2864 (63)
Mutter, S. A.: ref, 2247 (69), 2860 (704,705)
Mutti, M.: test, 2141
Mwamwenda, T. S.: ref, 998 (103), 999 (60)
Myatt, R.: ref, 2452 (7)
Mychalkin, B.: ref, 2860 (1063)
Myerholtz, L.: ref, 1661 (82), 1697 (591), 2553 (6)
Myers, B.: ref, 2860 (1101,1282)
Myers, B. J.: ref, 1010 (8)
Myers, C. D.: ref, 2519 (30,44), 2520 (31,44)
Myers, C. T.: rev, 2398
Myers, F. S.: ref, 1093 (94)
Myers, H. F.: ref, 592 (43)
Myers, I. B.: test, 1755
Myers, J. E.: test, 1842; ref, 462 (29), 2858 (115)
Myers, L. W.: ref, 2603 (361)
Myers, M. G.: ref, 134 (39), 272 (373), 1166 (223), 2858 (116)
Myers, P.: ref, 1991 (64)
Myers, R. A.: test, 405
Myers, R. E., III: ref, 495 (6)
Myers, R. H.: ref, 1164 (33), 2603 (140), 2860 (344), 2863 (92), 2892 (49)
Myers, R. M.: ref, 83 (3)
Myers, R. S.: rev, 2597
Myers, R. W.: ref, 1697 (549)
Myers, S. S.: rev, 2456
Myers, W. C.: ref, 1698 (11)
Mykkänen, L.: ref, 2860 (913), 2863 (273)
Myklebust, H. R.: test, 2123
Myles, B. S.: ref, 2111 (1)
Mynard, H.: ref, 1367 (7)
Myors, B.: ref, 2860 (121)
Myslobodsky, M. S.: ref, 1745 (32)
Naar, S.: ref, 1000 (40)
Naarala, M.: ref, 2247 (120), 2288 (2), 2860 (53)
Nabholz, S.: ref, 2076 (176)
Nablieri, J. A.: test, 1756
Nabors, L. A.: ref, 270 (12), 630 (1), 1216 (80), 1264 (4), 2382 (33)
Nachmias, R.: ref, 2163 (46)
Nadakoka, T.: ref, 1592 (27), 2862 (719)
Nadeau, S.: ref, 1164 (167), 2873 (71), 2892 (285)
Nadeau, S. E.: ref, 376 (20), 1164 (150), 1740 (23), 2227 (37), 2860 (1270,1309), 2873 (64), 2892 (273)
Nadel, L.: ref, 815 (42), 1379 (90), 2862 (567)
Nadler, A.: ref, 694 (38)
Nadon, G.: ref, 2768 (38), 2860 (1187), 2863 (358)
Naeser, M. A.: ref, 2860 (8), 2892 (1)
Naess, P.: ref, 1164 (87)
Naftolowitz, D.: ref, 2076 (94)
Nafziger, D.: rev, 2312
Nafziger, D. H.: rev, 216, 1406, 2000, 2795
Nagamoto, H.: ref, 2305 (4)
Nagao, D. H.: ref, 592 (7)
Nagaseki, Y.: ref, 2860 (1278)
Nagata, D. K.: ref, 1745 (3)
Nagel, D. E.: ref, 472 (206), 1903 (544), 2498 (71)
Nagel, S. K.: ref, 1612 (82)
Nagle, L. C.: ref, 272 (308)
Nagle, R. J.: ref, 1903 (309), 2485 (102,176), 2860 (503,946), 2862 (403)
Nagler, S.: ref, 301 (1), 748 (1), 2305 (5), 2860 (39), 2862 (21)
Naglieri, J. A.: test, 763, 817, 818, 852, 854, 1075, 1607; rev, 301, 1086, 1613, 1653; ref, 763 (1,5), 776 (20), 1379 (32), 1607 (2,3,13), 1903 (348), 2485 (164), 2860 (504,834), 2879 (62), 2901 (33)
Nagode, J.: ref, 2860 (2), 2863 (1)
Nagoshi, C. T.: ref, 2076 (25)
Nagy, M. C.: ref, 1590 (16)
Nagy, P.: rev, 1472, 2486, 2489
Nagy, R.: ref, 2603 (112)
Nagy, S.: ref, 1590 (16), 2076 (3)
Nagy, W. E.: ref, 2029 (1), 2487 (13)
Nah, K. O.: ref, 1140 (11)
Nahinsky, I. D.: ref, 451 (152), 472 (187), 473 (3)
Nahulu, L.: ref, 2497 (605)
Naibi, J.: ref, 2813 (123)
Nair, N. P. V.: ref, 1166 (172)
Nair, P.: ref, 448 (10), 1216 (27,36), 1770 (8)
Nairac, B.: ref, 1166 (71)
Nakaaki, S.: ref, 2163 (335), 2226 (30), 2227 (47), 2860 (1317)
Nakagawa, A.: ref, 2163 (289)
Nakamura, H.: ref, 2163 (335), 2226 (30), 2227 (47), 2860 (1317)
Nakamura, M.: ref, 175 (7)
Nakane, Y.: ref, 2497 (135)
Nakanishi, M.: ref, 2163 (335), 2226 (30), 2227 (47), 2860 (1317)

Nakano, K.: ref, 1178 (17), 1338 (19,20), 2858 (39), 1338 (21)
Nakayama, T.: ref, 2860 (1416)
Nakkula, M. J.: ref, 472 (107), 2879 (155)
Nameta, K.: ref, 1166 (213)
Namey, M.: ref, 272 (245), 2858 (123)
Namy, L. L.: ref, 1528 (4)
Nance-Sproson, T.: ref, 2227 (10), 2599 (9), 2860 (401)
Nandakomar, R.: ref, 592 (39), 180 (22), 1759 (13)
Náñez, J. E., Jr.: ref, 2163 (126)
Nanko, S.: ref, 2050 (32)
Nanna, M.: ref, 776 (17)
Nanni, C.: ref, 2497 (94)
Naoi, M.: ref, 926 (5)
Narayan, R.: ref, 998 (128), 2417 (38), 2497 (645)
Naremore, R. C.: ref, 624 (26), 2695 (51)
Närhi, V.: ref, 2862 (656)
Narsavage, G. L.: ref, 1745 (26,85), 2858 (80)
Nasby, W.: ref, 1965 (82), 2218 (106), 2749 (79)
Nash, H. C.: ref, 1647 (4)
Nash, J.: ref, 2497 (618)
Nash, L.: test, 1013
Nash, L. B.: ref, 1965 (22)
Nash, M. R.: ref, 1697 (416), 2247 (39), 2247 (88), 2749 (56), 2860 (890)
Nasrallah, H. A.: ref, 1164 (73), 2860 (722), 2892 (143)
Nass, R.: ref, 815 (2), 2860 (380), 2862 (56,175), 2864 (12,18)
Nassar, C. M.: ref, 893 (9), 1991 (35)
Nassau, J. H.: ref, 1903 (396)
Natalicio, D. S.: rev, 2335
Natelson, B. H.: ref, 272 (186,187), 2860 (1107)
Natemeyer, W. E.: test, 2064
Nathan, K. T.: ref, 1333 (7)
Nathan, M.: ref, 2305 (80)
Nathan, R. G.: ref, 301 (55), 2253 (2), 2860 (1087), 2879 (161), 2901 (90)
Nathan, S.: ref, 2603 (215), 2860 (532)
Nathanson, Y. E.: ref, 2603 (50)
Nation, K.: ref, 349 (37), 1765 (35), 2556 (3)
Nation, P. C.: ref, 1697 (335)
National Assessment of Educational Progress: test, 1759
National Association of Secondary School Principals: test, 2340
National Association of Secondary School Principals Task Force on Effective School Environments: test, 649
National Center for Education Statistics: test, 1759
National Council of State Boards of Nursing, Inc. (The): test, 1807
National Council of Teachers of Mathematics: test, 144, 148, 149
National Foundation for Educational Research: test, 253, 1596
National Foundation for Educational Research in England and Wales: test, 1597, 2173, 2182, 2184, 2185
National Institute for Personnel Research of Human Sciences Research Council: test, 321
National Institute of Industrial Psychology: test, 1151, 1152, 1153, 1786, 1787, 2812
National Occupational Competency Testing Institute: test, 1792, 1793, 1794
National Study of School Evaluation: test, 636, 1885, 2532
National Wellness Institute, Inc.: test, 2745, 2746, 2747
Natsopoulos, D.: ref, 272 (302), 1903 (17), 2163 (92), 2860 (1318), 2862 (51,176)
Natta, M. B.: ref, 337 (103), 372 (94), 1706 (3), 2858 (102)
Naugle, R. I.: ref, 1380 (4), 2860 (813)
Naumann, T. F.: rev, 728, 1761
Nauta, M. M.: ref, 495 (13), 1602 (1), 2065 (32)
Navarro, M. A.: ref, 1166 (209)
Navarro-Arias, R.: ref, 298 (3)
Naveh-Benjamin, M.: ref, 1455 (1)
Navertz, T.: ref, 2497 (136)
Navon, R.: ref, 242 (1)
Navran, L.: test, 1581
Nawroz, S.: ref, 776 (15), 2892 (122)
Nay, W. R.: ref, 451 (70), 2214 (79)
Nayak, M. B.: ref, 272 (371), 448 (30), 1164 (184), 1380 (21), 2497 (674), 2516 (121), 2892 (304)
Naylor, F.: ref, 23 (1), 398 (1)
Naylor, F. D.: ref, 399 (3)
Naylor, G. J.: ref, 1166 (22), 2305 (13)
Naylor, J.: ref, 298 (37), 999 (20)
Naylor, K.: ref, 2417 (28)
Naylor, M. W.: ref, 2230 (9,10), 2557 (4,5)
Naylor, S. T.: ref, 2860 (932)
Nazzaro, P.: ref, 2497 (175)
Ndanga, K.: ref, 124 (1), 1379 (23)
Neagley, S. R.: ref, 451 (139), 472 (178), 2485 (209), 2862 (515)
Neal, J.: ref, 1903 (270), 2905 (56)
Neal, M. B.: ref, 1014 (5)
Neal, W. R., Jr.: test, 227
Neale, C.: ref, 326 (5)
Neale, C.: ref, 2288 (21), 2289 (13), 2305 (66), 2892 (52), 2905 (24)
Neale, J. M.: ref, 1000 (52,60), 1181 (26), 2288 (33), 2305 (92,183), 2305 (183), 2863 (164,165), 2892 (102,103)
Neale, M.: test, 1765
Neale, M. C.: ref, 999 (58,160,186), 2603 (273)
Neale, M. D.: rev, 2485
Neath, J.: ref, 1790 (11), 1954 (1)
Nebelsick-Gullet, L. J.: ref, 2497 (418)
Nebes, R. D.: ref, 2860 (23)
Nechamkin, Y.: ref, 272 (249), 1166 (169)
Nedelsky, L.: rev, 110, 1121
Nee, J. C.: ref, 2305 (236)
Needham-Bennett, H.: ref, 1390 (3)

Needle, R. H.: ref, 1000 (7)
Needleman, H.: ref, 2225 (16), 2864 (132), 2901 (113), 2902 (5)
Needles, D. J.: ref, 373 (24), 2516 (59)
Neeley, L.: test, 2459
Neeley, R.: ref, 540 (3), 2432 (26), 2704 (32)
Neelon, F. A.: ref, 1697 (206)
Neelon, V. J.: ref, 2860 (1143)
Neels, H.: ref, 1166 (126)
Neely, D. L.: ref, 2656 (13)
Neeman, M.: ref, 2862 (83)
Neeman, R. L.: ref, 2862 (83)
Neemann, J.: test, 2369; ref, 557 (4)
Neemanne, J.: ref, 1902 (74)
Neeper, R.: test, 651
Negrin, N. S.: ref, 2485 (157)
Negy, C.: ref, 272 (303), 2497 (646)
Nehemkis, A. M.: ref, 1697 (1), 2417 (1)
Neher, W. R.: test, 1723
Nehme, E.: ref, 1653 (4), 2860 (299)
Neider, J.: ref, 1093 (20), 2603 (31,78)
Neiderhiser, J. M.: ref, 372 (104), 472 (229), 2603 (458), 2860 (690)
Neidhardt, J.: ref, 2603 (194)
Neidt, C. O.: rev, 364
Neighbors, B.: ref, 337 (172), 451 (188), 472 (58), 2211 (29,45)
Neigut, D.: ref, 2305 (93,94)
Neil, D.: ref, 791 (16)
Neils, J.: ref, 1903 (397), 2225 (2), 2873 (3), 2873 (42)
Neils-Strunjas, J.: ref, 776 (62), 2227 (60)
Neilson, C. Q.: ref, 2860 (1401)
Neilson, M.: ref, 999 (47)
Neiman, M. R.: ref, 1379 (52,88), 2008 (13)
Neimeyer, G. J.: ref, 298 (20), 404 (7), 2558 (1)
Neimeyer, R. A.: test, 2558; ref, 2305 (10,43), 2558 (1,2)
Neistadt, M. E.: ref, 301 (42), 1703 (1), 2860 (203,381,706,707,708)
Neiswanger, K.: ref, 1166 (15)
Neisworth, J. T.: test, 2204; ref, 1612 (45), 2485 (109), 2864 (46)
Neisz, J. R.: ref, 451 (125), 472 (168)
Neitzert, C. S., : ref, 999 (183)
Nekich, J. C.: ref, 1697 (388)
Nellen, E. H.: ref, 1689 (3)
Nelligan, D. W.: ref, 1745 (46)
Nellis, L.: ref, 1612 (56), 2864 (64)
Nelson, A. R.: test, 2776
Nelson, B.: ref, 2305 (216)
Nelson, C.: ref, 694 (61), 1697 (230), 2704 (13)
Nelson, C. C.: ref, 1000 (107), 2214 (54), 2498 (40)
Nelson, C. H.: rev, 92, 515, 1182
Nelson, C. W.: test, 906, 1447, 1747, 2582, 2586
Nelson, D. L.: ref, 1181 (4), 2603 (59)
Nelson, D. V.: ref, 791 (3,10), 1697 (440,501), 2117 (3), 2497 (498)
Nelson, E.: ref, 1000 (33), 1166 (200), 1939 (4)
Nelson, E. C.: ref, 1166 (79)
Nelson, G. M.: ref, 272 (155), 863 (6), 2519 (12), 2520 (12)
Nelson, H. E.: test, 1758
Nelson, J.: ref, 1007 (1), 2305 (232)
Nelson, J. P.: ref, 448 (28)
Nelson, K. E.: ref, 430 (14), 1485 (52), 1903 (264,484), 2163 (218), 2228 (18), 2657 (12), 2695 (24,25,57)
Nelson, L.: test, 1778; ref, 827 (6)
Nelson, L. D.: ref, 1697 (502)
Nelson, L. J.: ref, 538 (2)
Nelson, L. S.: ref, 1755 (30)
Nelson, M. J.: test, 1196
Nelson, M. K.: test, 2291, 2292
Nelson, P.: ref, 331 (4), 994 (26), 1745 (73), 2199 (1), 2233 (4), 2695 (37)
Nelson, P. B.: ref, 2065 (6)
Nelson, R.: ref, 56 (1), 615 (4), 798 (3), 1392 (1), 1902 (13), 1903 (39), 2432 (7), 2860 (122), 2870 (1), 2879 (17), 2901 (7)
Nelson, R. A.: ref, 2497 (44)
Nelson, W. L.: ref, 337 (62), 592 (65)
Nelson, W. M.: ref, 286 (1)
Nelson, W. M., III: ref, 1697 (347), 2603 (297)
Nelson, W. P.: ref, 1000 (18)
Nelson-Gardell, D.: ref, 451 (213)
Nelson-Gray, R.: ref, 998 (78), 1705 (4), 2497 (387)
Nelson-Gray, R. O.: rev, 281, 292; ref, 998 (91), 1697 (40,184), 2305 (71), 2497 (460)
Nemechek, S.: ref, 2218 (68)
Nemeroff, C.: ref, 1697 (369), 2860 (778)
Németh, A.: ref, 1166 (30)
Nemeth, C.: ref, 2516 (19)
Nemeth, S.: ref, 2901 (57)
Nennessy, J. J.: rev, 1212
Nepote, P.: ref, 1903 (270), 2905 (56)
Neri, L.: ref, 2288 (14), 2289 (9)
Neria, Y.: ref, 2603 (589)
Ness, M. K.: rev, 2750
Nesselroade, J. R.: ref, 1010 (11), 2076 (44), 2218 (7)
Nestadt, G.: ref, 2050 (23,94)
Nestor, P. G.: ref, 2305 (150,190), 2860 (290,497,1146,1319), 2863 (77), 2892 (282)
Netemeyer, R.: ref, 999 (144)
Netemeyer, R. G.: ref, 893 (22), 999 (123)
Netley, C.: ref, 2862 (542), 2879 (180), 2901 (99)
Nettelbeck, T.: ref, 270 (44), 301 (53), 349 (28), 999 (173), 1218 (14), 1240 (41), 1671 (6), 1765 (25), 2163 (246,256,305), 2485 (186,237) 2695 (46), 2771 (40), 2860 (991,1144,1182), 2862 (427), 2863 (303)
Nettelbladt, P.: ref, 2050 (26)
Nettelbladt, V.: ref, 2228 (17)
Netzer, D.: ref, 1612 (88)
Neubauer, A.: ref, 2163 (230)
Neubauer, A. C.: ref, 2163 (180,290)
Neubauer, R. M.: ref, 272 (44)
Neubert, D.: rev, 978, 1177, 2030

Neubert, M. J.: ref, 2899 (18)
Neuchterlein, K. H.: ref, 2050 (137)
Neufeld, R. W. J.: ref, 2288 (78,79), 2289 (65)
Neuhaus, S. M.: ref, 1340 (4)
Neukrug, E.: ref, 399 (2), 401 (1), 1701 (24), 1790 (4)
Neuman, G.: ref, 1836 (1)
Neuman, S. B.: ref, 1234 (2), 1903 (290), 2682 (3)
Neumann, C.: ref, 2163 (78)
Neumann, C. G.: ref, 2163 (175)
Neumann, E.: ref, 811 (3), 1379 (10), 2813 (8)
Neumann, Y.: ref, 592 (11)
Neumark, Y. D.: ref, 1010 (136), 1661 (83)
Neundorfer, M. M.: ref, 273 (8), 337 (29), 1166 (37), 2858 (31)
Neuringer, C.: rev, 2263
Nevill, D.: ref, 2282 (1)
Nevill, D. D.: test, 2282, 2805; ref, 404 (7)
Neville, H. A.: ref, 2065 (34)
Nevo, B.: ref, 301 (32), 771 (2), 2163 (127)
New York State Employment Service: test, 1351
New Zealand Council for Educational Research: test, 21,251605, 2478
Newberger, C. M.: ref, 337 (63), 451 (29), 472 (59)
Newberger, E. H.: ref, 337 (63), 451 (29), 472 (59)
Newborg, J.: test, 265, 266
Newburg, J. E.: test, 775
Newby, D.: ref, 2050 (46)
Newby, R. F.: ref, 451 (55,254), 681 (61), 1099 (3)
Newby, R. W.: ref, 2076 (91,99)
Newby, T. J.: ref, 1720 (1)
Newcomb, A. F.: ref, 337 (189)
Newcomb, K.: ref, 864 (3), 997 (12), 1987 (7), 2752 (1)
Newcomb, M. D.: ref, 462 (25), 790 (5), 863 (55), 2132 (1), 2603 (505)
Newcombe, F.: ref, 1758 (72), 2010 (3), 2163 (15,29), 2860 (43,233,1133), 2863 (60), 2892 (239)
Newcombe, N.: ref, 372 (40), 2860 (382)
Newcomer, J. W.: ref, 2860 (598)
Newcomer, L.: ref, 2231 (1)
Newcomer, P.: test, 2676
Newcomer, P. L.: test, 789, 821, 822, 2481, 2694, 2695; rev, 196, 653
Newcorn, J. H.: ref, 451 (58)
Newhouse, P. A.: ref, 2076 (100,156), 2863 (222)
Newland, G. A.: ref, 926 (2)
Newland, T. E.: test, 318, 624; rev, 2888
Newman, D. L.: rev, 217, 971, 1078, 1128, 1183, 2518; ref, 451 (34), 1832 (7)
Newman, D. R.: ref, 1866 (15)
Newman, E. J.: rev, 220, 1263
Newman, I.: rev, 89, 303, 2863; ref, 2163 (231), 2864 (145), 2905 (122)
Newman, J. L.: ref, 404 (1,19), 413 (3,8), 1754 (1,9), 2497 (6,80)
Newman, M.: ref, 2497 (436)
Newman, M. G.: ref, 2076 (43), 2497 (375,480,481), 2520 (46)
Newman, M. L.: ref, 1697 (560), 2603 (547)
Newman, R.: ref, 999 (106)
Newman, R. A.: ref, 1338 (40)
Newman, R. C., II: test, 2161
Newman, R. M.: ref, 1093 (93), 2289 (39)
Newman, R. S.: ref, 665 (25,53,80), 2879 (18)
Newman, S.: ref, 2862 (219), 2879 (63)
Newmann, J. P.: ref, 2603 (483)
Newmark, C. S.: ref, 1697 (225), 2212 (1)
Newmark, M.: ref, 2288 (52)
Newsholme, E. A.: ref, 272 (9), 1166 (6)
Newsom, J. T.: ref, 1166 (173)
Newspaper Advertising Bureau, Inc.: test, 2330
Newstead, S. E.: ref, 1469 (3)
Newsum-Davis, J.: ref, 1758 (68), 2863 (320)
Newton, J.: ref, 2557 (9)
Newton, J. E. O.: ref, 322 (6), 451 (47), 769 (5), 1131 (10,11), 2862 (231), 2862 (301), 2879 (70,97), 2905 (49)
Newton, J. R.: ref, 2050 (91)
Newton, J. S.: ref, 2299 (7)
Newton, K. R.: rev, 317
Newton, R. M.: test, 1954
Newton, T. J.: ref, 1079 (3), 2888 (1)
Newton, T. L.: ref, 1698 (10), 2076 (119)
Neyhart, A. E.: test, 857
Neyhart, H. L.: test, 857
Neylan, T.: ref, 2288 (9), 2305 (48)
Nezami, E.: ref, 1697 (584), 2497 (110)
Nezu, A. M.: rev, 1141, 1181; ref, 2860 (947)
Nezu, C.: ref, 2860 (947)
NFER-Nelson Publishing Co., Ltd.: test, 1598, 1782, 1783, 2938
Ng'andu, N.: ref, 180 (17,18), 1216 (47), 1216 (48,49,63), 1903 (357)
Ngunu, N.: ref, 124 (1), 1379 (23)
Nguyen, D.: ref, 451 (145)
Nguyen, K-L.: test, 306
Nguyen, L. H.: ref, 337 (69)
Niaura, R.: ref, 134 (20), 272 (90), 1661 (34), 2858 (109)
Niaura, R. S.: ref, 134 (8,15,27)
Niaz, M.: ref, 926 (7), 1140 (19), 2163 (74), 2771 (14)
Nibbelink, W. H.: rev, 1604
Nicassio, P. M.: ref, 1010 (51)
Niccolls, R.: ref, 2860 (493), 2863 (140)
NICHD Early Child Care Research Network: ref, 1216 (106,107), 2218 (107,108)
Nichelli, P.: ref, 776 (32), 2892 (243)
Nicholas, J. G.: ref, 1126 (3), 1903 (291,545), 2298 (3), 2813 (69,150)
Nicholas, L.: ref, 1754 (19)
Nicholas, L. E.: ref, 2008 (6,7,11), 2873 (16,43)
Nicholas, L. J.: ref, 1754 (20)
Nicholas, M.: test, 328
Nicholas, P.: ref, 2862 (486)
Nicholls, J.: ref, 1010 (89)

Nichols, C. W.: test, 205
Nichols, D. S.: rev, 1697; ref, 1697 (380)
Nichols, H. R.: test, 1744
Nichols, J. D.: ref, 1318 (10)
Nichols, J. M.: ref, 1661 (62)
Nichols, L.: rev, 1090
Nichols, M. E.: ref, 641 (4,5), 2076 (118), 2227 (11,20), 2517 (4), 2599 (30), 2863 (136)
Nichols, M. L.: ref, 771 (6)
Nichols, P.: ref, 893 (21)
Nichols, R. C.: rev, 560, 561, 644, 2707
Nichols, S. L.: ref, 815 (14), 1164 (56), 1612 (46), 1903 (236), 2485 (117)f, 2860 (580), 2863 (167)
Nicholson, C. L.: test, 2432, 2433
Nicholson, I. R.: ref, 271 (3), 272 (205)
Nicholson, N. L.: ref, 2497 (270), 2863 (144)
Nicholson, R.: ref, 1697 (529)
Nicholson, R. A.: ref, 1697 (381), 2860 (189)
Nicholson, T.: ref, 358 (7), 1903 (241)
Nici, J.: ref, 2862 (145), 2864 (24)
Nickel, E.: ref, 136 (3), 1697 (136), 2603 (109)
Nickel, O.: ref, 1166 (27)
Nickels, L.: ref, 163 (1)
Nico, D.: ref, 2163 (306)
Nicol, A. R.: ref, 1079 (23)
Nicol, R. M.: ref, 1758 (1), 2163 (18), 2860 (58), 2863 (19)
Nicole, L.: ref, 650 (15), 1093 (97)
Nicolson, R. I.: ref, 349 (23), 2862 (251)
Nideffer, R. M.: test, 226
Niedemann, G.: ref, 2603 (287)
Niederbuhl, J. M.: ref, 2485 (100)
Niederche, G.: ref, 301 (6), 1164 (13)
Niedermeier, C. L.: ref, 337 (107)
Nields, J. A.: ref, 1697 (283)
Nielsen, B. A.: ref, 1338 (45), 2839 (6)
Nielsen, H.: ref, 337 (13)
Nielsen, M. E.: ref, 1991 (9)
Nielsen, T.: ref, 2860 (1306)
Nielsen-Bohlman, L.: ref, 2860 (1320), 2863 (397)
Nielson, A. D.: ref, 1687 (29)
Niemann, H.: ref, 2860 (356), 2892 (51)
Niemi, H.: ref, 1166 (161)
Nierenberg, A. A.: ref, 272 (202), 1166 (106,133, 141)
Niermann, R.: ref, 1001 (12)
Nieto, D. S.: ref, 372 (21)
Nieto, E.: ref, 2305 (238)
Nieuwoudt, J.: ref, 1991 (67)
Nigal, D.: ref, 301 (16), 2860 (241)
Nigam, V. R.: ref, 681 (5), 2864 (21)
Nigg, J.: ref, 472 (197)
Nigg, J. T.: ref, 451 (201,214,277), 2010 (21), 2218 (132), 2862 (449,627,657), 2901 (86,117)
Nigro, G.: ref, 298 (67)
Nigrosh, E. E.: ref, 2525 (13)
Nihira, K.: test, 1, 2; ref, 1010 (65), 1216 (52)
Niizawa, J.: ref, 798 (1)
Niles, S.: ref, 413 (6)
Niles, S. G.: ref, 83 (2,4,5), 403 (1), 404 (15,45), 768 (2), 1754 (24), 1825 (2), 2282 (9), 2527 (5,12)
Nilsenroth, M. J.: ref, 2247 (96)
Nilsson, J. E.: ref, 1107 (6), 1115 (20)
Nimmerrichter, A.: ref, 272 (333), 2860 (1366), 2863 (412)
Nimmo-Smith, I.: ref, 2860 (965)
Nimorwicz, P.: ref, 2603 (43)
Nims, J. P.: test, 1788
Nippold, M. A.: ref, 1060 (3,4,6), 2008 (9), 2485 (177), 2693 (1), 2695 (43), 2862 (373), 2873 (33), 2911 (3)
Nirenberg, T. D.: ref, 134 (6,14), 793 (7), 1661 (12,23)
Nisbet, H.: ref, 2892 (244)
Nisbet, J.: rev, 127, 1800
Nisbet, S.: rev, 1103
Nisbett, R. E.: ref, 592 (36)
Nishikawa, T.: ref, 2860 (106)
Nishio, N.: ref, 1128 (3)
Nishizono-Maher, A.: ref, 824 (3)
Nisket, S.: rev, 954
Nissen, M. J.: ref, 2010 (4), 2860 (123,271), 2863 (34,71)
Nissenson, A. R.: ref, 1740 (7), 2076 (23), 2599 (6), 2860 (240)
Nist, S. L.: ref, 571 (5), 592 (20,29,91), 615 (16), 1455 (2,3,4)
Nitko, A. J.: rev, 364, 665, 1284, 1318, 1657, 2023, 2182, 2685; ref, 2163 (97), 2813 (26)
Nittrouer, S.: ref, 1903 (485), 2163 (291)
Nitz, A. J.: ref, 2497 (56)
Niver, J. M.: ref, 2704 (20)
Nivison, M. E.: ref, 2497 (271)
Nixon, G. W. H.: ref, 2497 (134), 2603 (118)
Nixon, M. C.: ref, 1903 (33,56)
Nixon, S. J.: ref, 272 (63,150), 451 (174), 1661 (58), 2402 (16,18,54), 2497 (537), 2860 (1037), 2863 (127,308), 2892 (66)
Niznikiewicz, M.: ref, 1903 (486), 2860 (1145,1319), 2879 (177), 2892 (282)
Njiokiktjien, C.: ref, 681 (9,42)
Nkaya, H. N.: ref, 2163 (181)
Noam, G. G.: ref, 2380 (3), 2603 (113)
Noble, E.: ref, 2499 (1)
Noble, E. P.: ref, 998 (37), 1201 (1), 1697 (150), 1962 (2), 2417 (13)
Noble, K. D.: ref, 2485 (66)
Noble, W. G.: test, 1190
Nobler, M. S.: ref, 272 (203), 1166 (148)
Nobrega, J.: ref, 1218 (6), 1903 (275), 2163 (168), 2863 (196), 2892 (123)
Nochajski, T. H.: ref, 1661 (18)
Nochlin, D.: ref, 2860 (1280)
Noda, A.: ref, 1405 (19)
Noder, M.: ref, 1166 (26)

Noel, A.: ref, 2864 (145), 2905 (122)
Noel, N.: ref, 1164 (11), 2860 (117), 2863 (32)
Noel, N. E.: ref, 134 (8)
Noeland, T. H.: ref, 1079 (83)
Noell, G. H.: ref, 2452 (13)
Noels, K. A.: ref, 272 (163,204)
Noetzel, M.: ref, 375 (8)
Noetzel, M.: ref, 2720 (1), 2892 (297)
Nofzinger, E.: ref, 1093 (78)
Nofzinger, E. A.: ref, 793 (14), 1697 (95)
Nogawa, S.: ref, 2860 (1296)
Noguchi, T.: ref, 1093 (49)
Noguchi, Y.: ref, 1010 (108)
Noguera, R.: ref, 1166 (168)
Noh, S.: ref, 2497 (204)
Noi, L. S.: ref, 1469 (5)
Nolan, B.: ref, 2603 (380)
Nolan, C. Y.: test, 2259
Nolan, E. E.: ref, 681 (53,54), 2862 (338)
Nolan, M.: ref, 2497 (98)
Nolan, P.: ref, 1079 (62)
Nolan, R. F.: ref, 272 (127)
Nolan, T.: ref, 451 (32)
Nolan, T. E.: ref, 1072 (25), 2487 (8)
Noland, J. R.: test, 1966
Noldy, N. E.: ref, 2227 (8), 2860 (364), 2879 (44), 2892 (54)
Nolen, W. A.: ref, 1166 (52)
Nolen-Hoeksema, S.: ref, 1991 (22)
Nolfe, G.: ref, 2163 (114)
Noll, J. G.: ref, 451 (202), 472 (198,206), 1010 (124), 1903 (544), 2498 (71)
Noll, R. B.: ref, 451 (215), 472 (60,182), 1962 (23), 2242 (7), 2485 (83), 2599 (13), 2860 (457), 2862 (525)
Noll, V. H.: rev, 150, 324, 1203
Noller, P.: ref, 863 (18), 1832 (2,8)
Nolte, C. A.: ref, 349 (31), 451 (131)
Nomora, N.: ref, 1010 (108)
Noojin, A. B.: ref, 337 (151)
Noonen, A.: ref, 272 (326)
Noor, N. M.: ref, 999 (129,165), 1079 (45)
Noordsy, D. L.: ref, 134 (4,12)
Nopoulos, P.: ref, 650 (14,16), 2288 (44), 2289 (34)
Nora, A.: ref, 620 (4), 621 (1,2)
Norbeck, J. S.: ref, 2497 (45)
Norbury, C. G.: ref, 2050 (99)
Norcliffe, H.: ref, 863 (60)
Norcross, C. E.: rev, 2484
Norcross, J. C.: ref, 372 (22), 1965 (18), 2858 (41)
Nord, D.: ref, 1754 (25)
Nordick, H.: ref, 1755 (66), 2360 (5), 2835 (21)
Nordin, S.: ref, 376 (1), 2860 (941), 2862 (371)
Nordloh, S. J.: ref, 1903 (397)
Nordstrom, G.: ref, 2050 (26)
Nordstrom, P.: ref, 2860 (154), 2892 (19)
Nordvik, H.: ref, 396 (1), 2835 (9)
Nores, A.: ref, 2768 (38), 2860 (1187), 2863 (358)
Noriega-Dimitric, R.: ref, 2603 (524)
Norlander, T.: ref, 998 (96), 1101 (1)
Norman, A. D.: ref, 2211 (17)
Norman, D.: ref, 1092 (5,16), 2305 (165), 2860 (331), 2862 (394), 2879 (137)
Norman, D. K.: ref, 2247 (82)
Norman, G. R.: ref, 1000 (88)
Norman, K. A.: ref, 376 (17), 2892 (268)
Norman, M. G.: ref, 271 (3), 272 (205)
Norman, P. A.: ref, 337 (99,137), 2050 (113), 2603 (453)
Norman, S.: ref, 2860 (291,383)
Norman, T.: ref, 350 (38), 1166 (224)
Norman, T. R., : ref, 2076 (157)
Norman, W. H.: ref, 2603 (26)
Norman, W. T.: rev, 752
Normandin, D.: ref, 694 (37)
Normandin, L.: ref, 2305 (246)
Noronha, A.: ref, 272 (209), 1164 (131), 2125 (24), 2516 (83), 2863 (343)
Norring, C.: ref, 1093 (3), 2603 (28)
Norris, F. H.: ref, 337 (41,45,163), 2497 (48)
Norris, J.: rev, 632, 2055
Norris, J. A.: rev, 496, 539, 1515, 2045, 2682
Norris, M. K.: ref, 1171 (1)
Norris, M. P.: ref, 272 (178), 2402 (57)
Norris, R. C.: rev, 1229
Norris, S. L. W.: ref, 998 (75,76), 2603 (282,283), 2858 (78,79)
Norris, S. P.: test, 2733; ref, 389 (13), 1659 (9)
Norsen, L. H. : ref, 2077 (6)
Norsworthy, N.: test, 2344
North, C. D.: ref, 472 (167)
North, K.: ref, 837 (3), 1765 (19), 1903 (292), 2862 (280)
North, K. N.: ref, 2860 (1321), 2862 (526)
North, N. T.: ref, 1758 (29), 2860 (733), 2863 (217), 2892 (146)
North, R. D.: rev, 364, 904, 2758
North, T.: ref, 540 (10), 2163 (292), 2662 (6), 2862 (527)
Northam, E.: ref, 451 (144), 1000 (100), 1079 (73), 1164 (38), 2892 (56)
Northoff, G.: ref, 1093 (115)
Northouse, L. L.: ref, 273 (14), 337 (108)
Northup, J.: ref, 451 (173)
Norton, A. M.: ref, 1903 (403)
Norton, G. R.: ref, 272 (358), 846 (1), 950 (4,6)
Norton, H. J.: ref, 2497 (511)
Norvell, N.: ref, 2603 (114)
Norvell, N. K.: ref, 1590 (25), 2858 (54)
Nosek, M. A.: ref, 2417 (16)
Noshirvani, H.: ref, 272 (78), 1166 (42), 2603 (233,234,288)
Noshpitz, J. D.: ref, 451 (15), 2242 (1), 2247 (18), 2485 (41), 2862 (143), 2879 (37)
Notoya, M.: ref, 1903 (293)
Nottelmann, E.: ref, 1093 (51), 2076 (67)

Noumair, D.: ref, 2519 (8), 2520 (8)
Nouri, S.: ref, 2497 (46)
Nouwen, A.: ref, 2497 (647)
Novacek, J.: ref, 68 (16), 373 (9), 1291 (2), 1697 (144), 2858 (3)
Novak, C.: rev, 319, 2134
Novak, J. D.: ref, 592 (21)
Novak, R. M.: ref, 2076 (153)
Novelly, R. A.: ref, 2163 (35), 2860 (216), 2863 (41)
Novik, T. S.: ref, 451 (56)
Novotny, M. F.: ref, 846 (1)
Novy, D. M.: ref, 1000 (34), 1294 (4), 1697 (440,501), 2417 (21), 2497 (498), 2498 (45)
Nowack, K. M.: test, 420
Nowak, A.: ref, 2860 (873), 2863 (257)
Nowicki, S., Jr.: ref, 451 (242), 472 (207), 665 (41,66), 1291 (3), 1318 (22), 1740 (29), 1903 (565), 1991 (107), 2603 (558), 2860 (1376), 2862 (700)
Noyce, R.: rev, 834, 2902
Noyce, R. M.: rev, 880, 2732
Noyes, C. R.: ref, 1318 (13)
Noyes, R.: ref, 998 (56), 1166 (17), 2076 (157), 2603 (24,203)
Noyes, R., Jr.: ref, 337 (179), 1093 (16), 1166 (68), 1241 (2), 1697 (561), 2218 (109), 2305 (17), 2519 (2), 2520 (2), 2603 (328)
Nuccio, I.: ref, 2519 (18), 2520 (19)
Nuechterlein, K. H.: ref, 1697 (188), 2050 (122,130), 2288 (32), 2289 (24), 2305 (73,91), 2860 (384)
Nugent, B.: ref, 771 (19)
Nugent, D. F.: ref, 1166 (59)
Nugent, J. K.: test, 1770
Nugent, S.: ref, 2603 (428)
Nugent, S. M.: ref, 472 (154), 1380 (10), 2214 (88), 2879 (152), 2901 (82)
Nugter, M. A.: ref, 2050 (47,48), 2892 (93)
Nuissier, J.: ref, 2497 (432), 2858 (112)
Nukui, H.: ref, 2860 (1278)
Numey, O. D.: test, 2136
Nunes, E.: ref, 1166 (142), 2603 (487)
Nunes, E. V.: ref, 1166 (130)
Nunes, T.: ref, 2862 (704)
Nunez, M. J. C.: ref, 2050 (135), 2288 (59), 2289 (45)
Nunn, G. D.: ref, 1991 (36)
Nunn, J. A.: ref, 1758 (104)
Nunn, K. P.: ref, 998 (119), 1079 (74), 2497 (578), 2603 (484)
Nunn, T.: test, 1516
Nunnery, J. A.: ref, 861 (4), 2902 (3)
Nunno, V. J.: ref, 2247 (63,106)
Nurmi, J.: ref, 745 (18)
Nurmi, J-E.: ref, 272 (220)
Nurnberger, J. I.: ref, 2305 (195)
Nurss, J. R.: test, 887, 1658, 1659; ref, 2879 (130)
Nussbaum, G.: ref, 2519 (14), 2520 (15)
Nussbaum, N. L.: ref, 769 (8), 2862 (729), 2879 (233)
Nussbaum, P. D.: ref, 1697 (441), 2603 (387)
Nutt, D. : ref, 999 (121)
Nutt, D. J.: ref, 2497 (626)
Nuttal, E. V.: ref, 2862 (688)
Nuttall, R. L.: ref, 298 (28,138), 2862 (688)
Nuyten, D.: ref, 1166 (230)
Nyamathi, A.: ref, 2076 (120)
Nyberg, A. M.: test, 131
Nyberg, V. R.: test, 131
Nydén, A.: ref, 1136 (1)
Nye, C. L.: ref, 272 (128)
Nyenhuis, D. L.: ref, 272 (372), 2076 (185)
Nyfield, G.: test, 119, 735, 964, 1973, 2087, 2642
Nyquist, L.: ref, 2860 (207)
Nyström, M., : ref, 1661 (24)
Nystul, M. S.: ref, 694 (70)

Oakes, J.: ref, 665 (81)
Oakland, C.: ref, 381 (1), 895 (1), 1089 (1), 1439 (1), 1444 (4), 2295 (8), 2547 (1)
Oakland, T.: test, 1155, 2536, 1866, 2432; ref, 381 (1), 769 (8), 895 (1), 1089 (1), 1439 (1), 1444 (4), 2295 (8), 2547 (1), 2860 (1086), 2862 (479,729), 2879 (233)
Oakley-Browne, M. A.: ref, 999 (163), 1166 (132), 1166 (159), 2603 (481)
Oaster, T. R.: test, 1809, 2534
Oates, R. K.: ref, 451 (79,278), 472 (147,230), 694 (134), 999 (141), 1012 (1), 1079 (54,109), 1991 (87)
Obeidallah, D. A.: ref, 298 (155), 472 (183)
Ober, B. A.: test, 375, 376;ref, 776 (1)
Oberklaid, F.: ref, 34 (2), 863 (29), 1079 (15), 2039 (8), 2485 (68), 2813 (21,48)
Oberzan, R. E.: ref, 641 (5), 2076 (118), 2227 (20), 2517 (4), 2599 (30)
Obiakor, F. E.: ref, 1991 (37)
Obikoya, O.: ref, 2860 (882)
Obler, L. K.: ref, 199 (7), 2860 (432), 2873 (63)
Oblowitz, N.: ref, 1991 (26)
Obonsaruin, M. C.: ref, 2193 (11), 2860 (342)
O'Bonsawin, M. C.: ref, 2860 (444)
O'Boyle, C.: ref, 2497 (32)
O'Boyle, M.: ref, 1697 (537)
O'Boyle, M. W.: ref, 592 (22,66)
O'Brien, B.: ref, 1131 (13), 2862 (352), 2879 (118)
O'Brien, B. S.: ref, 1380 (1), 1592 (25), 2211 (33), 2214 (45), 2862 (528)
O'Brien, C.: ref, 451 (24), 815 (7), 1216 (24), 1379 (21)
O'Brien, C. P. : ref, 2305 (162), 2402 (52), 2603 (169,431,561)
O'Brien, E. J.: test, 1735
O'Brien, G.: ref, 1367 (5)
O'Brien, J.: test, 1812
O'Brien, J. P.: ref, 2497 (278), 2656 (9)
O'Brien, K.: ref, 337 (67), 2603 (151)
O'Brien, K. M.: ref, 298 (150)
O'Brien, L.: test, 1458
O'Brien, M.: ref, 997 (27), 1096 (13), 1903 (558), 2695 (71)

O'Brien, M. A.: ref, 1902 (41)
O'Brien, M. J.: test, 1463
O'Brien, P. C.: ref, 2860 (359), 2863 (94)
O'Brien, R. M.: ref, 694 (52), 844 (2), 2497 (248), 2656 (8)
O'Brien, S. K.: ref, 1903 (487), 2813 (125)
O'Brien, S. P.: ref, 2218 (57), 2246 (11)
O'Brien, T. B.: ref, 2218 (69), 2858 (117)
O'Brien, T. D.: ref, 1140 (22)
O'Brien, T. P.: ref, 1140 (23)
O'Brien-Malone, A.: ref, 1903 (386), 2163 (224)
Obrosky, D. S.: ref, 2860 (669)
Obrzut, J. E.: rev, 301, 1690, 1776; ref, 1607 (8), 1903 (15,18,40), 2141 (1), 2860 (125), 2862 (34,52, 84, 271), 2901 (3,8)
O'Callaghan, M. J.: ref, 1612 (41,42)
O'Callaghan, T.: ref, 272 (33), 1687 (12,96)
Ocampo, K. A.: ref, 472 (88)
O'Carrol, R. E.: ref, 2863 (206,207)
O'Carroll, R.: ref, 2159 (4), 2858 (64)
O'Carroll, R. E.: ref, 272 (119), 1166 (65,74), 1758 (43), 2239 (24), 2240 (2), 2860 (328,385,699,904), 2863 (145)
Ocepek-Welikson, K.: ref, 272 (244), 1166 (130,142,167), 2305 (211), 2603 (487)
Ochipa, C.: ref, 2860 (1322)
Ochoa, A. S.: rev, 2060, 2686
Ochoa, E.: ref, 2163 (159), 2863 (181), 2873 (22)
Ochoa, S. H.: rev, 165, 367, 2709
Ochoa-Shargey, B.: ref, 2805 (2)
Ochs, J.: ref, 2860 (319), 2879 (38), 2901 (18)
O'Connell, A. N.: ref, 298 (21)
O'Connell, B. J.: ref, 2497 (396)
O'Connell, M.: ref, 2247 (5), 2749 (7), 2860 (124)
O'Connor, B. P.: ref, 1965 (76)
O'Connor, E.: ref, 472 (12), 681 (7), 2214 (6)
O'Connor, L. C.: ref, 433 (5), 994 (5), 1903 (140), 2459 (1), 2813 (22)
O'Connor, L. E.: ref, 272 (304)
O'Connor, M.: ref, 2288 (15), 2289 (10), 2305 (62), 2603 (179), 2860 (3), 2863 (2)
O'Connor, M. E.: ref, 337 (99,137), 1079 (87), 2050 (113), 2603 (93,453)
O'Connor, M. J.: ref, 1752 (1), 2402 (13), 2860 (137,269), 2863 (38)
O'Connor, M. O.: ref, 2863 (388), 2892 (276)
O'Connor, N.: ref, 1765 (20), 2497 (410)
O'Connor, R.: ref, 2813 (116)
O'Connor, R. E.: ref, 1072 (45), 1503 (14), 1612 (43,44,76), 1902 (46), 1903 (398,399), 2671 (2), 2682 (5), 2905 (86)
O'Connor, T. G.: ref, 451 (216), 472 (229), 694 (65)
O'Connor, T. J.: ref, 472 (142)
Odagaki, Y.: ref, 1166 (60)
Odell, C. W.: rev, 1657
O'Dell, D. R.: test, 1308
O'Dell, F. L.: ref, 298 (39)
Odendahl, B.: test, 1352
Odenheimer, G. L.: ref, 1164 (72)f, 2863 (208)
Odgers, P.: ref, 72 (1)
O'Donell, A. M.: ref, 372 (4), 998 (7), 1140 (4)
O'Donell, L.: ref, 994 (35)
O'Donnell, A. M.: ref, 592 (97), 2656 (19)
O'Donnell, B. F.: ref, 2305 (150,190), 2860 (497,1146,1319), 2892 (282)
O'Donnell, D.: ref, 326 (5), 2288 (21), 2289 (13), 2305 (66), 2892 (52), 2905 (24)
O'Donnell, J. P.: ref, 1164 (71), 2860 (204,709), 2879 (27), 2892 (136)
O'Donnell, W. E.: test, 1587, 1775; ref, 1775 (1,2)
Oehler-Stinnett, J.: rev, 65, 265, 323, 681
Oehler-Stinnett, J. J.: rev, 72, 1099, 1889
Oehlet, M. E.: ref, 2497 (598), 2879 (185)
Oei, T. P.: ref, 1021 (1)
Oei, T. P. S.: ref, 272 (8), 652 (3), 1021 (8)f, 1274 (1), 1661 (11), 1697 (442), 1698 (5), 2417 (19), 2497 (24,81,82,96,177,354,363,439)
Oejmal, A. E.: ref, 214 (16), 1485 (27), 1903 (256), 2657 (15)
Oepen, G.: ref, 2050 (77)
Oescher, J.: ref, 364 (6)
Oestreicher, J. M.: ref, 1164 (71), 2860 (709), 2892 (136)
Oetting, E. R.: test, 143, 1830, 1831, 2475, 2655; ref, 143 (1), 2497 (325,452,550,551)
Oetting, J. B.: ref, 265 (10), 324 (8), 624 (9,10,20,22,31), 1095 (16,17,27,48), 1379 (57), 1903 (139,202, 207,301,400,546), 2485 (146), 2695 (44,68), 2704 (31), 2862 (374), 2864 (69)
O'Fallon, A.: ref, 2402 (66)
O'Fallon, W. M.: ref, 1612 (73), 2485 (170), 2860 (910), 2862 (356), 2864 (95)
O'Farrell, M. K.: test, 716
O'Farrell, T. J.: ref, 134 (38,40), 136 (7,11), 1661 (13,25,26,70,71,81,84), 2414 (7)
Offenbacher, H.: ref, 2860 (525), 2892 (88)
Offer, D.: test, 1832; ref, 1832 (14)
Offermann, L. R.: rev, 2632
Office of Educational Research and Improvement: test, 1759
The Office of the Santa Cruz Superintendent of Schools: test, 292
Offord, D. R.: ref, 451 (60), 681 (8), 997 (7), 1903 (74)
Offord, K. P.: ref, 1697 (324,430,499,587), 1698 (12)
Ofir, L.: ref, 1903 (524)
Oftedal, M.: ref, 2599 (33)
Ogata, S.: ref, 1697 (443)
Ogawa, N.: ref, 2497 (501)
Ogawa, T.: ref, 301 (33), 853 (12), 1160 (2), 2247 (41), 2380 (7), 2417 (26), 2749 (33)
Ogden, J.: ref, 2076 (92)
Ogden, J. A.: ref, 838 (6), 1525 (3), 2225 (14), 2860 (15,61,71,126,1148), 2862 (53), 2863 (8,22,35)
Ogden, S.: ref, 342 (4), 815 (29), 837 (8), 1903 (414)

Ogden, W.: ref, 1755 (69)
Oger, J.: ref, 2860 (270), 2863 (70), 2907 (2)
Ogesby, D. M.: ref, 769 (4)
Ogilvie, B. C.: test, 1930, 1955
Ogiso, Y.: ref, 824 (3)
Ogith, M.: ref, 2862 (638)
Ogles, B. M.: ref, 2497 (362), 2603 (388)
Oglesby, D. M.: ref, 322 (6), 451 (47), 769 (5), 1131 (10,11,17), 2862 (231,301,696), 2879 (70,97,222), 2905 (49,118)
Ogletree, B. T.: rev, 375, 542; ref, 194 (2), 459 (13), 2382 (11), 2813 (19)
Ogletree, S. M.: ref, 298 (99)
Oglive, B. C.: test, 219
O'Grady, J.: ref, 272 (270), 1135 (25), 2860 (1265), 2863 (418)
Ohaeri, J. U.: ref, 2050 (40)
Ohandler, J. L.: ref, 272 (334), 376 (30)
Ohannessian, C. M.: ref, 1661 (32,47)
O'Hara, C.: test, 566
O'Hara, M. T.: ref, 451 (169), 880 (1), 1216 (96)
O'Hara, M. W.: ref, 863 (16)
O'Hara, P.: ref, 2050 (39)
O'Hara, R.: ref, 2860 (918)
O'Hare, D.: test, 490
O'Hearn, K. M.: ref, 1166 (210)
Ohene-Frempong, K.: ref, 1987 (11)
Ohira, H.: ref, 272 (129)
Ohlde, C.: ref, 1697 (291), 2603 (258)
Ohler, D. L.: ref, 405 (2), 2360 (2)
Ohlott, P.: test, 2425
Ohlott, P. J.: test, 807
Öhman, J.: ref, 2516 (58), 2860 (777)
Ohsawa, T.: ref, 298 (34)
Ohta, K.: ref, 2288 (23), 2305 (69), 2860 (365)
Ohta, Y.: ref, 2497 (135)
Ohtaki, E.: ref, 2862 (360)
Ohyama, M.: ref, 999 (57)
Oie, M.: ref, 2862 (543)
Oiji, A.: ref, 1592 (27), 2862 (719)
Oja, H.: ref, 2247 (120)
Ojemann, G. A.: ref, 2863 (378), 2879 (215)
Ojile, E.: ref, 1379 (65), 1645 (4)
O'Jile, J.: ref, 2860 (629)
Okada, F.: ref, 1166 (134)
Okamura, L.: ref, 999 (115)
Okamura-Birchard, F.: ref, 1072 (3)
Okasha, A.: ref, 999 (98), 2050 (92)
Okawaza, H.: ref, 2288 (81), 2289 (67), 2860 (1311)
O'Keane, V.: ref, 1166 (72)
O'Keeffe, J. L.: ref, 708 (3), 2497 (49)
O'Keeffe, M. K.: ref, 2858 (89)
O'Kelly, J.: ref, 2603 (543)
Oken, B. S.: ref, 2860 (468), 2863 (132)
Okerlund, M.: ref, 2860 (1078)
Okey, J.: ref, 697 (2), 2497 (493)
Okla, K.: ref, 337 (3), 451 (6), 472 (2), 2497 (35)
Okuda, J.: ref, 2860 (106)
Okun, A.: ref, 451 (62), 472 (98,130), 1216 (53), 1903 (294)
Okun, M. A.: ref, 998 (14), 2369 (4)
Okuzumi, H.: ref, 2862 (359,498,638)
O'Laughlin, S.: ref, 1697 (336)
Oldehinkel, A. J.: ref, 1079 (46), 2050 (124)
Oldehinkel, T.: ref, 2050 (41)
Oldfield, D.: ref, 2214 (110), 2498 (65)
Oldfield, K.: ref, 1115 (14), 1115 (24)
Oldham, G. R.: ref, 68 (58)
Oldman, A.: ref, 2076 (121)
Oldridge, O. A.: rev, 2864
O'Leary, D. S.: ref, 650 (13), 1093 (39,85)
O'Leary, E. S.: ref, 2603 (517)
O'Leary, K. D.: ref, 272 (62), 451 (247), 863 (7,19,23,47), 1181 (26), 2519 (19,20), 2520 (20,21)
O'Leary, S. G.: ref, 451 (265), 681 (1,3)
O'Leary, V.: test, 712, 1373
O'Leary-Kelly, A. M.: ref, 1701 (34)
Olejnik, S.: rev, 221, 1183, 1881, 1895; ref, 592 (20,91), 1455 (3)
Olenchak, F. R.: ref, 177 (1,2), 1991 (82), 2312 (1), 2862 (375)
Olenick, N. L.: ref, 136 (4)
Oleshansky, M. A.: ref, 2497 (468,469)
Oli, T. P. S.: ref, 2497 (440)
Olinger, L. J.: ref, 2858 (52)
Oliphant, G.: ref, 2860 (121)
Oliva, D.: ref, 2813 (96,122)
Olivardia, R.: ref, 893 (24)
Olivares, M. J.: ref, 2227 (26), 2860 (1103)
Olivárez, A., Jr.: ref, 1455 (8,10), 1866 (32), 2487 (7)
Oliveira, R. M.: ref, 1768 (1)
Oliver, B.: ref, 1164 (155), 2226 (26), 2516 (100), 2860 (1290)
Oliver, C. E.: ref, 353 (2), 1673 (3), 1725 (2), 1901 (4)
Oliver, J. E.: test, 410, 905
Oliver, J. E., Jr.: test, 1843
Oliver, L. L.: ref, 1340 (4), 2402 (38)
Oliver, N. M.: test, 169
Oliver, T. L.: ref, 1095 (13)
Oliverio, M. E.: rev, 2572
Olivier, L.: test, 2392
Ollendick, T.: ref, 893 (9), 1991 (35)
Ollendick, T. H.: ref, 472 (16,81,128,141,153,204), 1021 (19), 2211 (5), 2214 (5,11,19,40,69,77,87), 2497 (131,178,272), 2498 (5,52), 2525 (3), 2813 (2)
Oller, D. K.: ref, 891 (1), 1903 (117)
Oller, J. W., Jr.: rev, 307
Ollier, K.: ref, 472 (16), 2214 (11)
Ollo, C.: ref, 1135 (7), 2497 (132), 2860 (292), 2879 (35)
Olmedo, E. L.: rev, 2465
Olmi, D. J.: rev, 234, 284, 2204, 2692
Olmi, J.: rev, 193, 2082

Olmsted, C.: ref, 1612 (25)
Olney, R. K.: ref, 1135 (18), 2226 (14), 2516 (85), 2860 (1173), 2863 (353)
Olsen, C.: ref, 272 (190)
Olsen, D.: ref, 1657 (18), 2860 (915)
Olson, A. E.: ref, 2444 (1), 2452 (6), 2841 (1)
Olson, D.: ref, 2299 (7)
Olson, D. H.: test, 544, 1000, 1014, 1877, 1927, 2034; ref, 1000 (17,19,74)
Olson, E.: ref, 2163 (56), 2871 (1)
Olson, J.: ref, 2181 (1)
Olson, K.: ref, 472 (54), 1698 (23), 2076 (61), 2498 (22), 2862 (213)
Olson, K. R.: ref, 2218 (68)
Olson, M. S.: ref, 893 (39)
Olson, M. W.: ref, 257 (1), 496 (1)
Olson, R.: ref, 68 (23), 1687 (26,163)
Olson, R. A.: ref, 337 (28,106), 472 (139), 2498 (54), 2858 (30)
Olson, R. E.: ref, 1687 (2)
Olson, R. K.: ref, 798 (9,21), 1092 (6), 1902 (35,80), 2860 (391,1018), 2862 (177,423)
Olson, S. L.: ref, 272 (86), 451 (21), 1216 (23), 1697 (337), 1903 (136,203), 2211 (23), 2860 (710)
Olsson, R. H., Jr.: test, 1839
Olswang, L. B.: ref, 1612 (21), 1903 (86), 2382 (4)
Olszewski-Kubilins, P.: ref, 372 (23), 2591 (2), 571 (2), 592 (92), 615 (17)
Olszewski-Kubilius, P. M.: ref, 372 (10), 571 (1), 604 (1), 615 (5)
Oltman, P. K.: test, 474, 926, 1140
Oltmanns, T. F.: ref, 2306 (1)
O'Mahony, J.: ref, 999 (130)
O'Mahony, J. F.: ref, 999 (131), 2860 (948,1147), 2863 (279,339)
Omizo, M. M.: ref, 694 (9), 746 (4), 844 (1)
Omizo, S. A.: ref, 694 (9), 746 (4), 844 (1)
Onatsu, T.: ref, 745 (18)
Ondersma, S. J.: ref, 472 (208), 2214 (120)
O'Neal, E.: ref, 472 (21), 1991 (29), 2214 (12)
O'Neil, H. F.: ref, 2497 (579)
O'Neil, J. M.: ref, 2603 (357)
O'Neil, R.: ref, 2497 (33,65,376)
O'Neill, J.: ref, 2305 (199)
O'Neill, J. M.: ref, 1903 (121)
O'Neill, M. E.: ref, 1903 (488)
O'Neill, R. M.: ref, 1697 (503), 2247 (105,112), 2860 (1227)
Ones, D. S.: ref, 68 (59), 189 (1), 372 (105), 998 (120), 1697 (504), 2417 (36)
Onghena, P.: ref, 335 (12), 1010 (100,101)
Onglatco, M. L.: ref, 298 (71)
Onglatco, M. L. U.: ref, 298 (34)
Onishi, K.: ref, 815 (23), 2226 (9), 2863 (259)
Ono, Y.: ref, 4 (17), 273 (26), 303 (25), 2860 (1363,1372)
Onufrak, B.: ref, 265 (14)
Onwuegbuzie, A. J.: ref, 2069 (3)
Ooi, W. L.: ref, 1058 (2), 2860 (152)
Oosterhof, A. C.: rev, 488, 996, 1252, 1496, 1515, 2138
Oosterhof, L.: ref, 999 (176)
Oosterlaan, J.: ref, 451 (279), 681 (95), 1021 (47), 2862 (529)
Oosterveld, P.: ref, 838 (20)
Oosthuizen, S.: ref, 1659 (14)
Opacic, G.: ref, 694 (75)
Opalic, P.: ref, 1697 (41)
Opler, L. A.: test, 2017; ref, 564 (2,3,5), 650 (10), 2017 (1), 2146 (2,7), 2289 (17), 2305 (77), 2860 (218), 2892 (38)
Oppenheim, D.: ref, 337 (180), 451 (217), 994 (48)
Oppenheim, D. B.: rev, 27, 2026
Oppenheim, G. S.: test, 2821
Oppenheimer, B.: ref, 2603 (69)
Oppenheimer, K.: ref, 1000 (54)
Optometry Admission Testing Program: test, 1846
Oral, G.: ref, 2771 (23)
Oram, G. D.: ref, 289 (5), 372 (96), 902 (2), 1866 (41), 2214 (78), 2862 (376)
Orange, J. B.: ref, 1164 (135), 2227 (33), 2860 (1181), 2879 (184), 2892 (256)
Orbach, I.: ref, 450 (2), 2497 (377), 2862 (281)
Ørbæk, P.: ref, 2603 (541)
Orban, J. A.: ref, 352 (1), 548 (1), 728 (1), 927 (1), 2648 (1), 2907 (1)
Orbeck, A. L.: ref, 1093 (54), 2519 (32), 2520 (33)
Orcutt, H.: ref, 451 (194), 1010 (123)
Ordman, V. L.: ref, 694 (111)
Oreck, B. A.: ref, 773 (4), 1657 (20), 1991 (89)
O'Regan, S.: ref, 791 (15)
O'Reilly, A. W.: ref, 1333 (3), 1903 (449), 2229 (7)
O'Reilly, C. A., III: ref, 68 (15,39), 1107 (4), 1348 (1)
O'Reilly, K. A.: test, 1192
O'Reily, R. L.: ref, 1697 (535), 2163 (313)
Oreland, L.: ref, 273 (28), 999 (181)
Orengo, C. A.: ref, 1166 (221)
Orensanz-Munoz, L.: ref, 1697 (470)
Orenstein, D.: ref, 2305 (93)
Orenstein, S. H.: ref, 771 (18)
Orford, J.: ref, 1243 (3), 1291 (5)
Organista, K. C.: ref, 2519 (45)
Orgogozo, J. M.: ref, 2863 (90)
O'Riordan, J.: ref, 1619 (1)
Orlansky, M. D.: rev, 227
Orleans, J. B.: test, 1863
Orleans, J. S.: rev, 1188
Orlebeke, J. F.: ref, 815 (16), 1164 (183), 2076 (64), 2163 (354), 2497 (274), 2862 (278,726)
Orman, D. T.: ref, 272 (219), 273 (25), 2065 (29)
Ormaza, S.: ref, 1697 (567), 1740 (25), 2226 (33), 2860 (1339)
Orme, C. M.: ref, 1697 (42)

Ormel, J.: ref, 999 (159), 1079 (46,79), 2050 (15,41,124), 2603 (170,506)
Ormrod, J. A.: ref, 2603 (570)
Orndorff, R. M.: ref, 404 (42)
Ornduff, S. R.: ref, 2603 (289), 2749 (45,47,55)
Ornitz, E.: ref, 1697 (170)
Ornoy, A.: ref, 270 (23), 1612 (87)
Ornstein, P. A.: ref, 1612 (31)
Orosan, P.: ref, 337 (115,116)
Orpwood, L.: ref, 350 (34), 1903 (401), 2193 (44), 2860 (949)
Orr, D.: ref, 2858 (67)
Orr, D. B.: rev, 438, 1767, 1876
Orr, E.: ref, 1991 (83), 2358 (6), 2497 (29,59,83,499)
Orr, R. R.: ref, 1903 (20)
Orr, S. P.: ref, 2497 (199,500), 2860 (1403)
Orrell, M.: ref, 537 (1,4)
Orsillo, S. M.: ref, 272 (206), 1697 (505), 2497 (378,580), 2516 (48)
Orsulak, P.: ref, 2305 (166)
Orsulak, P. J.: ref, 272 (136), 1166 (81)
Ort, S.: ref, 2813 (116)
Ort, S. I.: ref, 1093 (31), 1379 (13,17), 2813 (10)
Ortegon, J.: ref, 459 (30,36), 1485 (30,42), 1612 (53,74), 1903 (279,382)
Ortiz, P.: ref, 2247 (72)
Ortiz, T.: ref, 2863 (209)
Ortiz, V. Z.: ref, 2862 (85)
Ortiz-Franco, L.: ref, 1405 (11)
Ortiz-Stanley, E.: test, 306
Orton, K. D.: rev, 361
Orvaschel, H.: ref, 472 (209), 694 (126), 2305 (230)
Ory, J. C.: rev, 1236, 2484
Osato, E.: ref, 2497 (501)
Osato, S.: ref, 272 (295), 376 (23), 2860 (1304), 2863 (394), 2873 (67)
Osbarsson, K. H.: ref, 1079 (83)
Osberg, T. M.: rev, 2353
Osborn, E.: ref, 301 (19), 2247 (17), 2380 (4), 2749 (22), 2862 (142)
Osborne, C.: ref, 2497 (668)
Osborne, D.: ref, 641 (2), 2517 (3), 2860 (822), 2863 (237), 2892 (167)
Osborne, J. K.: ref, 311 (1), 1866 (13)
Osborne, M.: ref, 665 (6), 815 (1), 1902 (6), 2485 (10), 2862 (47)
Osborne, P.: ref, 4 (12,20), 681 (83), 2211 (50), 2485 (221)
Osborne, R. T.: rev, 2862
Osborne, S. S.: ref, 1379 (8), 2485 (29), 2864 (19)
Osborne, W. L.: ref, 1338 (41), 2076 (79)
Osbrg, T. M.: rev, 2282
Osburn, W. J.: rev, 174, 1659, 2473
Oscar-Berman, M.: ref, 272 (60), 776 (2), 2860 (205,403,1083,1097), 2863 (51,107,326), 2892 (226)
O'Shea, A. J.: test, 1177
O'Shea, M. F.: ref, 1744 (8), 2860 (520), 2863 (150,340), 2050 (129)
Osher, F. C.: ref, 134 (4)
Osier, T. J.: ref, 2749 (73)
Osipow, S. H.: test, 404, 1825; ref, 404 (43), 2835 (28)
Oskamp, S.: rev, 1146, 2237
Oskin, D.: ref, 451 (268), 472 (226), 2214 (135)
Osman, A.: ref, 271 (12,13), 272 (305), 337 (64,65,84,85,109,110,152,153,181), 1697 (189,231, 338,444), 1698 (13,25), 2497 (273,648), 2559 (6,13), 2603 (152,204)
Osman, J. R.: ref, 271 (13), 337 (64,65,84,85, 109, 110,152,153,181), 1697 (189,231,338,444), 1698 (13, 25), 2497 (273,648), 2559 (6,13), 2603 (152, 204)
Osmon, D. C.: ref, 2892 (245)
Osness, W. H.: test, 1062
Osofsky, H. J.: ref, 2603 (160)
Osofsky, J. D.: ref, 451 (130), 1216 (3)
Osowiecki, D.: ref, 2860 (745)
Osseiran-Waines, N.: ref, 2497 (379)
Öst, L. G.: ref, 1021 (12), 2497 (133)
Ostander, R.: ref, 280 (3), 451 (18,184)
Ostbye, T.: ref, 303 (7), 2226 (8)
österberg, K.: ref, 2603 (541)
Ostergaard, A. L.: ref, 1765 (3), 2862 (25), 2863 (16)
Osterhaus, S. O. L.: ref, 2076 (64), 2497 (274)
Osterheider, M.: ref, 2497 (121)
Osterlind, S. J.: test, 570; rev, 664, 713, 2154, 2737
Osterling, J.: ref, 1485 (31), 1653 (16), 2485 (140)
Ostertag, J.: ref, 2862 (259)
Osterweil, Z.: ref, 1927 (3), 1965 (35)
Ostgaard, D. J.: ref, 2899 (10)
Ostrander, R.: ref, 451 (70), 2214 (79)
Ostrem, J. L.: ref, 376 (8), 776 (15), 2892 (122,162,230)
Ostroff, J. S.: ref, 1000 (35)
Ostrov, E.: test, 1832
Ostrove, J.: ref, 372 (90), 373 (30)
Ostrow, D. G.: ref, 337 (86)
O'Sullivan, G.: ref, 272 (78), 1166 (42), 2497 (428), 2603 (233,234)
O'Sullivan, G. H.: ref, 2603 (288)
O'Sullivan, J. T.: ref, 1072 (54)
O'Sullivan, P. J.: ref, 246 (1)
O'Sullivan, R. L.: ref, 271 (5), 272 (223), 2227 (26), 2860 (1103)
Oswald, A.: ref, 1079 (60)
Oswald, D. P.: rev, 234, 1091; ref, 2813 (2)
Oswald, L. M.: ref, 2603 (551)
Otero, A.: ref, 2305 (238)
Otero, R. F.: ref, 2656 (1)
Othmer, E.: test, 2107
Othmer, S. C.: test, 2107
Otis, A. S.: test, 1866
O'Toole, B. I.: ref, 451 (79), 472 (147), 999 (141), 1012 (1), 1079 (54), 1991 (87)
O'Toole, B. L.: ref, 451 (278), 472 (230), 694 (134), 1079 (109)

O'Toole, J. G.: ref, 272 (289), 2749 (77)
Otsuki, T.: ref, 2603 (591)
Ott, J.: ref, 451 (153), 651 (2), 2305 (49), 2862 (551)
Ottenbacher, K. J.: ref, 1901 (5,14)
Ottinger, D. R.: ref, 681 (15)
Otto, B. W.: ref, 2680 (19)
Otto, M. W.: ref, 272 (176), 1166 (63), 2077 (1), 2199 (11), 2305 (187), 2519 (39), 2520 (40)
Otto, R.: ref, 1164 (91), 2860 (859), 2892 (178)
Otto, R. K.: ref, 2018 (1)f, 2782 (2)
Otto, W.: ref, 592 (23)
O'Tuel, F. S.: ref, 694 (80), 705 (8), 2518 (1)
Ouchi, B. Y.: ref, 2868 (2)
Oud, J. H. L.: ref, 451 (276), 2862 (648)
Ouimette, P. C.: ref, 273 (24), 337 (194), 790 (14), 999 (147,166,168), 1166 (88,145), 1181 (28), 1953 (2,3)
Ousley, O. Y.: ref, 270 (43), 459 (10,40), 1528 (8)
Ovebrant, P.: ref, 303 (8), 2862 (478)
Over, D. E.: ref, 1758 (85,86)
Overall, J. E.: ref, 1294 (4), 2417 (21), 2860 (779)
Overaltó, J. M.: ref, 1166 (168)
Overcash, W. S.: ref, 337 (154)
Overholser, J. C.: ref, 472 (72), 473 (2), 1697 (263,445,484), 2247 (53), 2258 (5), 2603 (205), 2899 (12)
Overholster, J.: ref, 272 (225)
Overmier, J. B.: ref, 1903 (532), 2860 (1289)
Overstreet, S.: ref, 1010 (84), 2211 (42), 2862 (377)
Overton, T.: rev, 294, 1039, 2443, 2778
Oving, A.: ref, 2076 (164), 2516 (92)
Ovsiew, F.: ref, 376 (6), 1218 (17), 1902 (86), 2860 (1106), 2879 (167), 2892 (229), 2901 (93)
Owen, A. M.: ref, 1758 (7,17,49,94), 2860 (206)
Owen, C. L.: ref, 2858 (55,83)
Owen, J. P.: ref, 136 (10), 1661 (45), 1697 (426)
Owen, M.: ref, 1903 (184), 2050 (32,54), 2402 (20), 2485 (90)
Owen, M. T.: ref, 1216 (54), 1379 (53), 2497 (337), 2813 (70)
Owen, S. M.: ref, 2595 (1)
Owen, S. V.: rev, 18, 273, 621, 1201; ref, 724 (1), 773 (4), 798 (25), 994 (43), 1142 (2), 1657 (20), 1903 (505), 1991 (2,89), 2771 (1), 2848 (1), 2862 (33,574)
Owen, T. R.: test, 706
Owens, B. J.: ref, 2603 (419)
Owens, B. W.: test, 80, 220
Owens, D. G. C.: ref, 2050 (72), 2860 (190)
Owens, E. B.: ref, 451 (282), 1965 (79)
Owens, J. F.: ref, 2516 (12)
Owens, L.: test, 1465
Owens, M. D.: ref, 1010 (127), 2603 (548)
Owens, N.: test, 80, 220
Owens, R. E.: test, 1236
Owens, R. E., Jr.: test, 2082; rev, 1360, 2215
Owens, W. A.: rev, 1299, 1636, 2021
Ownby, R. L.: ref, 1687 (13), 1697 (26,97), 1731 (1)
Oxbury, J.: ref, 303 (19), 2227 (38,48), 2860 (1279,1323), 2863 (385,398), 2892 (283)
Oxbury, J. M.: ref, 2860 (1023), 2862 (428)
Oxbury, S.: ref, 303 (19), 1758 (68), 2227 (38,48), 2860 (18,1279,1323), 2863 (10,320,385,398), 2892 (283)
Oxbury, S. M.: ref, 2860 (1023), 2862 (428)
Oxman, T. E.: ref, 1166 (201), 2247 (73), 2749 (48), 2860 (736)
Oyefeso, A. O.: ref, 999 (42)
Oyler, C.: ref, 2860 (988), 2863 (291)
Oz, S.: ref, 2497 (380), 2749 (29)
Ozawa, M. N.: ref, 615 (44)
Ozer, D. J.: ref, 372 (51), 373 (6), 2603 (202)
Ozmen, E.: ref, 2497 (301)
Ozonoff, S.: ref, 459 (24,33), 2860 (1149), 2892 (82,137)

Paajanen, G. E.: test, 1900
Paal, N. P.: ref, 2862 (118), 2879 (31)
Pabis, R.: ref, 2860 (1)
Pabst, H. F.: ref, 303 (14), 1164 (143), 2163 (315), 2226 (20), 2227 (35), 2860 (1241), 2862 (600), 2863 (374), 2879 (199), 2892 (265)
Pace, C. R.: test, 620; rev, 495, 2624, 2742
Pace, T. M.: ref, 2603 (545)
Pachen, V.: ref, 451 (66)
Pachman, L. M.: ref, 1010 (54), 2498 (24)
Packard, A. G.: rev, 1763, 1807, 2125
Packard, P.: ref, 1697 (291), 2603 (258)
Packer, G.: ref, 790 (16), 998 (85)
Packman, V. S.: rev, 1951
Paclawskyj, T. R.: ref, 4 (21)
Padavich, D. L.: ref, 451 (132)
Padawer, J. R.: ref, 1697 (418,550), 2247 (118)
Paddison, P. L.: ref, 2497 (67)
Paden, E. P.: ref, 214 (19), 1001 (17), 1485 (56)
Padgett, M. Y.: ref, 1701 (12)
Padgett, R. J.: ref, 1903 (121)
Padilla, A. M.: ref, 672 (1), 694 (2,5), 2603 (40)
Padilla, E.: ref, 1612 (35)
Padilla, G.: ref, 2076 (29)
Padilla, R. V.: ref, 2163 (126)
Padilla-Cotto, L.: ref, 272 (341)
Padovani, A.: ref, 2516 (61), 2860 (804), 2892 (163)
Pae, S.: ref, 265 (10), 624 (20), 1095 (27), 1379 (57), 1903 (301), 2485 (146), 2864 (69)
Paez, D.: ref, 1962 (3)
Pagani, L.: ref, 472 (199)
Pagano, F.: ref, 2163 (328), 2860 (1281)
Page, A. C.: ref, 999 (47)
Page, E. B.: rev, 97, 98, 1319
Page, G. L.: ref, 624 (4), 1612 (36), 2862 (157), 2864 (36,39)
Page, R.: test, 2642
Page, W. F.: ref, 1697 (140), 2860 (957)
Pageau, D.: ref, 1216 (55)
Paget, K. D.: rev, 265, 479, 874, 1098, 1612
Pahwa, R.: ref, 271 (15), 272 (330), 376 (28), 776 (56), 1135 (24), 1218 (19), 1378 (10), 1740 (26), 2076 (181), 2516 (112), 2863 (411), 2892 (293)

Paik, M.: ref, 2860 (407)
Paikoff, R. L.: ref, 1010 (52)
Painter, K. M.: ref, 1333 (3), 1903 (449), 2229 (7)
Paisley, R.: ref, 771 (8)
Paitche, D.: test, 491
Paivio, S. C.: ref, 2603 (389)
Pajares, F.: ref, 2163 (232), 2358 (13)
Pakalnis, A.: ref, 1164 (30), 1697 (141), 2860 (293)
Pakenham, K. I.: ref, 337 (87)
Paker, M.: ref, 2497 (301)
Paker, O.: ref, 2497 (301)
Pakiz, B.: ref, 451 (8), 472 (5)
Pakstis, A. J.: ref, 2305 (22)
Palace, E. M.: ref, 337 (46,111), 793 (10,17), 2497 (502)
Palace, J.: ref, 1758 (68), 2863 (320)
Palacio-Quintin, E.: ref, 1216 (55)
Palacios, C.: ref, 1140 (17)
Palaniappan, A. K.: ref, 626 (1), 1396 (2), 1939 (11), 2771 (26,31,45)
Palenzuela, D. L.: ref, 999 (176)
Paley, B.: ref, 1010 (121)
Palinkas, L. A., : ref, 1166 (135)
Palisano, R. J.: ref, 2862 (86)
Pallack, L.: ref, 2858 (36)
Palladino, P.: ref, 2862 (658)
Pallandino, P.: ref, 472 (210)
Paller, K. A.: ref, 1758 (18), 2193 (9), 2860 (294,386,711), 2863 (78)
Pallett, W. H.: test, 1236
Pallier, G.: ref, 2163 (302)
Pallitto, L. M.: ref, 457 (1)
Pallmeyer, T. P.: ref, 1338 (6), 2497 (20), 2603 (7)
Pallon, S.: test, 2342
Palmer, A.: test, 1664
Palmer, B. C.: test, 1028, 2664
Palmer, B. W.: ref, 1166 (136), 2227 (29), 2516 (49,81), 2860 (712,1150), 2863 (210,341), 2892 (138,246)
Palmer, C.: ref, 1166 (222)
Palmer, D. J.: ref, 1991 (58)
Palmer, D. R.: test, 1456, 1910, 2495
Palmer, I. C.: rev, 1521; ref, 1107 (10)
Palmer, O. E.: rev, 616
Palmer, P.: ref, 1485 (43,62), 1653 (29), 2860 (956,1333), 2862 (381,661)
Palmer, S.: ref, 1697 (530)
Palmer, S. C.: ref, 2497 (417)
Palmer, S. E.: ref, 256 (2)
Palmeri, S.: test, 1263
Palmero, F.: ref, 1338 (37)
Palmour, R. M.: ref, 2076 (74), 2497 (306), 2603 (240)
Palomba, D.: ref, 1021 (43)
Palombarb, M. M.: ref, 2813 (62)
Palormo, J. M.: rev, 942, 2877
Palosaari, U. K.: ref, 272 (48,130)
Paloutzian, R. E.: test, 2474
Palti, H.: ref, 451 (17), 1216 (19), 1903 (103)
Pam, A.: ref, 2749 (59)
Pan, B. A.: ref, 350 (21), 1485 (34)
Pan, D.: ref, 2603 (591)
Pan, J. W.: ref, 376 (14), 2863 (372)
Panagiotides, H.: ref, 459 (35), 1485 (40), 1903 (350), 2498 (17)
Panak, W. F.: ref, 337 (85), 472 (35,36), 2559 (6)
Pancer, M.: ref, 449 (4)
Pancer, S. M.: ref, 1408 (9)
Pancheri, P.: ref, 1697 (204)
Pande, A. C.: ref, 1093 (17)
Pandina, R. J.: ref, 1164 (31), 2402 (10), 2860 (330)
Pando, F. Q.: ref, 2050 (135), 2288 (59), 2289 (45)
Pandya, K.: ref, 2497 (190)
Panerai, A. R.: ref, 1166 (69)
Paneth, N.: ref, 451 (236), 2813 (154)
Pang, M.: ref, 136 (8), 1697 (249)
Pang, M. G.: ref, 372 (39), 998 (47), 1697 (185)
Pang, V. O.: ref, 1991 (27)
Pangburn, L.: ref, 1338 (6), 2497 (20), 2603 (7)
Paniak, C. E.: ref, 1697 (434)
Panisset, M.: ref, 776 (52), 1164 (163), 1218 (18), 2226 (28), 2227 (46)
Panksepp, J.: ref, 1903 (388), 2485 (172), 2860 (931), 2862 (368)
Pannbacker, M.: rev, 2870
Pannonen, S. V.: ref, 1333 (4), 2218 (70)
Pannozzo, G. M.: ref, 665 (75)
Panopoulos, G.: ref, 1000 (105)
Pantel, J.: ref, 1166 (202)
Panter, A. T.: ref, 1965 (41)
Pantle, M.: ref, 372 (68), 2247 (64,70)
Panton, J. H.: ref, 1697 (5)
Panyard-Davis, J. L.: ref, 1962 (21)
Panzer, M.: ref, 1166 (4), 2305 (14)
Paoletti-Schelp, M.: test, 1067
Paolitto, A. W.: rev, 2035, 2601
Paolo, A. M.: ref, 376 (25), 776 (53), 1758 (95), 2860 (214, 395,582,968,1151,1165,1324,1325,1326), 2892 (247)
Papadatou, D.: ref, 1590 (37), 2858 (81)
Papageorgiou, A.: ref, 681 (69), 1987 (16), 2864 (107)
Papagno, C.: ref, 1903 (45), 2163 (54,133,233,293,336), 2225 (8), 2768 (23), 2860 (163,541), 2863 (399), 2892 (91,200,284)
Papalia, D.: ref, 2218 (73)
Papanicolaou, A.: ref, 2860 (1230,1231), 2879 (196)
Pape, K. E.: ref, 1901 (10)
Pape, S.: ref, 2305 (220)
Papenfuss, J. F.: test, 904
Papka, M.: ref, 1379 (76), 2432 (27), 2862 (399)
Papko, O.: ref, 2656 (2), 2862 (60)
Papouchis, N.: ref, 564 (3), 2146 (7)
Papp, L.: ref, 1592 (7)
Papp, L. A.: ref, 1166 (179), 2603 (342)
Pappas, B. A.: ref, 2863 (100)
Pappas, D.: ref, 2860 (1378), 2879 (226), 2892 (296)
Pappas, S.: ref, 180 (6)

Pappas, T.: ref, 272 (70), 893 (12)
Paquette, C.: ref, 2862 (530)
Para, M. F.: ref, 1164 (73), 2860 (722), 2892 (143)
Parachio, J. J.: test, 1898
Paradis, C. M., : ref, 1164 (130), 1903 (489), 2163 (294), 2227 (30), 2695 (58), 2768 (36), 2862 (531), 2880 (4)
Paradise, L. V.: ref, 364 (6)
Paradiso, S.: ref, 1166 (137,203), 2516 (107), 2860 (1327)
Parameswaran, G.: ref, 298 (148)
Páramo, M. F.: ref, 745 (25), 926 (22), 1140 (58)
Paraskevopoulos, J. N.: test, 1240
Parasuraman, R.: ref, 998 (60), 2860 (290), 2863 (77)
Parcel, T. B.: ref, 1216 (34)
Parcel, T. L.: ref, 180 (7), 1216 (15), 1216 (68), 1903 (57)
Parent, S.: ref, 1866 (22), 1903 (482)
Parente, A.: ref, 1382 (1), 1384 (2), 2860 (637)
Parenté, R.: ref, 2863 (226)
Parfitt, E.: ref, 2050 (32)
Pargament, K. I.: ref, 2498 (76)
Pariante, C. M.: ref, 272 (103)
Parides, M.: ref, 1093 (86), 1166 (120)
Parikh, S. V.: ref, 2050 (141)
Paris, S. G.: ref, 496 (2), 827 (2), 1072 (4)
Parise, P.: ref, 1697 (204)
Parish, T. B.: ref, 1991 (36)
Parish-Plass, J.: ref, 2214 (71)
Park, A. M.: ref, 1216 (67), 2864 (97)
Park, C. L.: ref, 863 (88)
Park, D. C.: ref, 2860 (202)
Park, H-S.: ref, 364 (27)
Park, S.: ref, 592 (93), 1965 (68), 2497 (503), 2860 (387,950), 2892 (201)
Park, Y. D.: ref, 641 (4)
Park, Y-S.: ref, 2163 (88), 2862 (165)
Parke, R. D.: ref, 1903 (153), 2497 (475), 2864 (78)
Parker, C. P.: ref, 1755 (63)
Parker, D. A.: ref, 2402 (8)
Parker, D. E.: ref, 4 (16)
Parker, E. M.: ref, 2029 (2)
Parker, E. S.: ref, 1164 (59), 1758 (50), 2076 (77), 2402 (8), 2516 (37), 2860 (600,951), 2892 (112)
Parker, G.: ref, 272 (306), 298 (167), 998 (21,45,135), 1079 (39), 1166 (61,112), 1166 (112), 1241 (5)
Parker, G. B.: ref, 2497 (99)
Parker, G. M.: test, 1892, 2632
Parker, J.: ref, 472 (98), 776 (47), 1216 (53), 1903 (294)
Parker, J. A.: rev, 244, 287
Parker, J. D. A.: test, 696, 700; ref, 272 (25), 681 (89), 790 (11), 950 (1)
Parker, J. G.: ref, 451 (62), 472 (130)
Parker, J. L.: ref, 376 (31), 776 (60), 2863 (423)
Parker, K. C. H.: ref, 2860 (952)
Parker, M.: ref, 2497 (425)
Parker, P. A.: ref, 1590 (51)
Parker, P. E.: ref, 68 (8)
Parker, R.: ref, 451 (13), 1903 (88), 2485 (40), 2862 (139), 2879 (36)
Parker, R. I.: ref, 2905 (16)
Parker, R. M.: test, 1816, 1817; ref, 1697 (339), 2879 (130)
Parker, R. S.: ref, 2860 (1152)
Parker, S. B.: ref, 1135 (10), 1164 (52), 2860 (1342)
Parker, W.: ref, 2749 (65)
Parker, W. D.: ref, 68 (61), 337 (182), 2218 (110,129, 133), 2603 (485)
Parker-Fisher, S.: ref, 679 (1), 681 (35)
Parkerson, S.: test, 1352; ref, 404 (24)
Parkes, K. R.: ref, 739 (7), 999 (43,99), 142 (4), 1104 (4,9), 1758 (25,27,28,41,42), 2193 (23,40,41), 2226 (6), 2239 (1,21), 2516 (67), 2860 (653,659,713, 714,899,900,192,194,211,212,269,270), 2892 (121,139,140,188,189)
Parkinson, J. A.: ref, 2193 (28)
Parkinson, M.: test, 718
Parks, C. S.: ref, 624 (4), 2864 (36)
Parks, C. W., Jr.: ref, 2860 (24)
Parks, E. B.: ref, 2497 (58)
Parks, E. D.: ref, 1697 (413), 2863 (280)
Parks, J. P.: ref, 624 (4), 2864 (36)
Parks, S. H.: ref, 2603 (115)
Parlato, V.: ref, 2863 (230)
Parloff, M. B.: ref, 1517 (4)
Parma, M.: ref, 2163 (222), 2860 (927)
Parmelee, P.: ref, 2076 (44)
Parmelee, P. A.: ref, 2076 (31)
Parnas, J.: ref, 748 (2,4,6), 748 (6,10), 2050 (1,4,42,66,133), 2603 (110), 2860 (279)
Parnell, T.: ref, 1698 (4)
Parnicky, J. J.: test, 2829
Parr, G.: ref, 2862 (603), 2901 (115)
Parra, E. B.: ref, 2603 (390)
Parra, L. F.: test, 1348, 2509
Parra, R.: ref, 2860 (145), 2862 (93)
Parraga, M. I.: ref, 2360 (4)
Parrila, R. K.: ref, 776 (20), 1607 (13), 1903 (348), 2485 (164), 2860 (834)
Parry, S. B.: test, 1542, 1570, 1951, 2353, 2775
Parry-Billings, M.: ref, 272 (9), 1166 (6)
Parsons, A.: ref, 25 (1)f, 72 (2)
Parsons, B.: ref, 451 (220), 1216 (108)
Parsons, C. K.: rev, 1348, 1563, 1564, 1855, 2208, 2584
Parsons, G. M.: ref, 1338 (38)
Parsons, O. A.: ref, 272 (10,52,65,328), 326 (10), 1164 (151), 2402 (28,50,64,69), 2497 (172,243,524), 2860 (1273), 2863 (127,410)
Partanen, K.: ref, 1164 (152), 2516 (99), 2892 (274)
Partiot, A.: ref, 2163 (295), 2860 (1153), 2863 (342), 2892 (94)
Partitt, G.: ref, 2077 (9)
Partonen, T.: ref, 1166 (62,138)
Partridge, A. J.: ref, 2076 (38)
Partridge, F. M.: ref, 2497 (247)

Partridge, S.: ref, 1697 (308)
Parush, S.: ref, 815 (52), 1673 (10), 2724 (13)
Parzer, P.: ref, 745 (24)
Pascal, G. R.: test, 301
Pascarella, E.: ref, 621 (1)
Pascarella, E. T.: ref, 620 (4), 621 (2)
Pascoe, J. M.: ref, 681 (47)
Pascual-Leone, A.: ref, 1135 (25), 2863 (418)
Pascual-Leone, J.: ref, 1140 (27), 1866 (8), 2163 (49)
Pashek, G. V.: ref, 2873 (69)
Pasini, A.: ref, 272 (224,234), 1166 (33,156), 2497 (599)
Paskewitz, D. A.: ref, 451 (82,83), 1000 (94,95,110), 1021 (48), 2214 (140), 2230 (11,21), 2656 (25)
Pasley, K.: ref, 1014 (6)
Pasnak, R.: ref, 1657 (22), 1866 (42,43), 2488 (9)
Pasnau, R. O.: ref, 1093 (26)
Pasquier, F.: ref, 776 (18,35)
Passchier, J.: ref, 2076 (64,131), 2497 (191,259,274,285), 2603 (423)
Passero, J. M.: ref, 2603 (419)
Passik, S. D.: ref, 790 (2), 2749 (10)
Passingham, R. E.: ref, 2860 (84,85,162), 2892 (9)
Passino, A. W.: ref, 1619 (4)
Passow, A. H.: rev, 56, 247, 1802, 2090, 2091, 2484, 2742
Pasternak, R. E.: ref, 1093 (104)
Pastonelli, C.: ref, 451 (88), 472 (155)
Pataki, C. S.: ref, 1592 (10)
Patchner, M. A.: ref, 448 (18), 1010 (82)
Pate, B.: ref, 1697 (15), 2860 (60)
Pate, D. S.: ref, 776 (31)
Pate, D. W.: ref, 2076 (96)
Patel, A. D.: ref, 2225 (20), 2860 (1410), 2863 (429)
Patel, R. K.: ref, 863 (44)
Patenaude, W.: ref, 1939 (14)
Paternico, A.: ref, 2863 (416)
Paternite, C. E.: ref, 451 (207), 681 (65), 1010 (85), 1592 (24), 2862 (378), 2879 (131)
Paternot, J.: ref, 2163 (321), 2860 (1253)
Paterson, D. G.: test, 1693, 1995; rev, 170, 533
Paterson, L.: ref, 1592 (23), 2125 (14)
Paterson, M. M.: ref, 2045 (4)
Pathak, D.: ref, 2603 (163,194,216)
Patilla, P.: test, 1601
Pato, C.: ref, 2102 (1), 2288 (16,24), 2289 (11), 2305 (74), 2860 (335), 2863 (88)
Patrick, C. J.: ref, 372 (74), 1021 (25,40), 1697 (403), 2497 (581), 2862 (327), 2879 (111)
Patrick, D. L.: ref, 2603 (253)
Patrick, J.: ref, 1903 (381), 2305 (144)
Patten, C. A.: ref, 272 (373), 1166 (223), 2076 (93)
Patterson, C. C.: test, 2690
Patterson, C. E. P.: ref, 1736 (4)
Patterson, C. J.: ref, 171 (2), 2700 (1)
Patterson, D. J.: ref, 68 (45), 2218 (29)
Patterson, G. R.: rev, 2862; ref, 2603 (345), 2860 (428)
Patterson, J.: ref, 1832 (10)
Patterson, K.: ref, 350 (48), 641 (3), 776 (22,30), 1903 (569), 2163 (162), 2193 (38,52), 2863 (264,325)
Patterson, M.: ref, 2860 (953)
Patterson, M. B.: ref, 2860 (555)
Patterson, P. A.: ref, 1903 (90), 2695 (8), 2768 (6), 2862 (140)
Patterson, S. M.: ref, 2516 (50)
Patterson, T. L.: ref, 337 (16,19,47), 1166 (70), 2414 (3), 2603 (66), 2858 (18,19,20,90,105)
Patterson, W. M.: ref, 2603 (342)
Pattie, A. H.: test, 537
Patton, D.: ref, 999 (184), 1140 (57), 1661 (31), 1697 (334,562), 2497 (649)
Patton, D. M.: ref, 2858 (63)
Patton, E.: ref, 2497 (612), 2603 (518)
Patton, J.: ref, 372 (68), 1503 (15), 1903 (422,555), 2247 (64), 2879 (141,219), 2880 (7), 2901 (128), 2905 (90)
Patton, J. M.: ref, 1379 (20), 1607 (1), 2163 (93), 2771 (19)
Patton, J. R.: test, 2309, 2780
Patton, M. J.: ref, 337 (183)
Patton, W.: ref, 1832 (2,8)
Paty, D.: ref, 1164 (144), 2860 (270,517,1242), 2863 (70,149), 2907 (2,3)
Paty, J.: ref, 998 (73)
Patz, R. J.: ref, 448 (20), 1889 (3), 2402 (53), 2603 (435)
Pau, C. S.: ref, 2862 (379)
Pauk, W.: test, 707
Pauker, J. D.: test, 1706, 1727, 1779, 2603, 2728
Paul, B. D.: ref, 1687 (45)
Paul, E. L.: ref, 1631 (4), 2076 (186), 2369 (8)
Paul, G. L.: test, 2763; ref, 2120 (1)
Paul, K.: ref, 2862 (460)
Paul, K. B.: test, 2509
Paul, K.: ref, 2485 (195)
Paul, L. C.: ref, 1697 (67), 2076 (10)
Paul, R.: ref, 1612 (96), 2695 (20,69)
Paul, R. G.: ref, 2860 (1031), 2863 (306)
Paul, R. H.: ref, 117 (1), 272 (151), 2402 (37), 2599 (26), 2860 (798,1038), 2892 (161)
Paul, S.: ref, 2485 (67), 2860 (388)
Paul, S. M.: ref, 708 (6)
Paul, S. T.: ref, 2860 (1154)
Paulby, S.: ref, 451 (77), 1612 (80), 2860 (976)
Paulhan, I.: ref, 2497 (432)
Paulhus, D. L: test, 1899; ref, 2860 (1411), 2899 (19)
Paulker, J. D.: rev, 2108
Paull, J. C.: ref, 272 (94), 1010 (67), 1965 (62)
Pauloski, B. R.: ref, 1040 (6,7)
Pauls, D. L.: ref, 472 (114), 2214 (60)
Pauls, K. K.: ref, 2860 (821)
Paulsen, J.: ref, 776 (21)
Paulsen, J. S.: ref, 776 (25), 2288 (69), 2289 (53), 2860 (643,1104), 2892 (120,202)
Paulus, D.: test, 704
Paulus, M.: ref, 2603 (568)

Paulus, M. P.: ref, 2288 (73), 2289 (59)
Paunonen, S. V.: ref, 372 (116), 672 (6), 999 (21), 1107 (5), 1965 (4,5,17,19,60,77,85), 2218 (66,71), 2417 (43)
Pava, J. A.: ref, 1166 (106,184), 2519 (39)
Pava, J. A.: ref, 2520 (40)
Paveza, G. J.: ref, 335 (5), 2305 (81)
Pavlou, S. N.: ref, 2497 (367)
Pavnonen, S. V.: ref, 1334 (1), 1790 (2), 1965 (2)
Pawl, R.: ref, 272 (343)
Pawlak, A. E.: ref, 793 (8), 2860 (295)
Pawletko, T. M.: ref, 472 (33), 2214 (24)
Pawliuk, N.: ref, 451 (145)
Pawluk, L. K.: ref, 1697 (446), 2703 (2)
Pay, C.: ref, 999 (140)
Pay, M.: ref, 1135 (4), 2862 (120)
Pay, M. M.: ref, 2860 (184), 2862 (105)
Payette, K. A.: ref, 2862 (380,436), 2901 (69,83)
Paykel, E. S.: ref, 1166 (12), 2050 (127), 2239 (25)
Payne, A.: ref, 272 (131), 2497 (504)
Payne, A. C.: ref, 875 (8), 1240 (31), 1903 (328)
Payne, A. F.: ref, 1404 (1,2)
Payne, C. K.: ref, 2497 (33)
Payne, D. M.: ref, 771 (9)
Payne, D. S.: rev, 739
Payne, F. D.: rev, 1536
Payne, R. B.: ref, 2497 (381)
Payne, R. W.: rev, 1133, 1645, 2603, 2878
Payne, T. J.: ref, 1697 (142), 2839 (9)
Paz, D.: ref, 1135 (13), 2599 (25), 2860 (772)
Paz, G. G.: ref, 1093 (72), 2050 (95), 2288 (19)
Pazzaglia, P.: ref, 2163 (188), 2516 (54), 2768 (26), 2819 (1), 2907 (6)
Pazzaglia, P. J.: ref, 272 (294), 1166 (199)
Peach, R. K.: ref, 1164 (39), 2860 (389), 2873 (9)
Peach, W. J.: ref, 821 (1), 1386 (1), 1902 (4)
Peak, P. K.: test, 2684
Peak, T.: ref, 272 (56), 2497 (181)
Pearce, P. S.: ref, 811 (14), 1240 (44), 1528 (2), 2190 (7), 2485 (224), 2601 (3)
Pearce, S.: ref, 1164 (128), 2226 (11,41), 2860 (1407), 2863 (426), 2892 (238,301)
Pearl, J. H.: ref, 1745 (47), 2497 (382)
Pearl, L.: ref, 1745 (53)
Pearl, R.: ref, 430 (11,13), 540 (2), 798 (19), 1040 (11), 1240 (32,37), 1804 (11,13), 1903 (353,402), 2694 (16), 2864 (83,100), 2901 (44)
Pearl, S.: ref, 1758 (30), 2863 (219)
Pearlson, G.: ref, 2288 (76), 2289 (63), 2402 (60), 2892 (257)
Pearlson, G. D.: ref, 815 (49), 1164 (173), 1740 (27), 2050 (125), 2289 (22), 2516 (115), 2860 (1374), 2892 (119,294)
Pearlson, G. D.: ref, 2892 (294)
Pearn, M.: test, 964
Pearsall, T.: ref, 1758 (59)
Pearson, B. Z.: ref, 1903 (117)
Pearson, D. A.: ref, 459 (30,36), 679 (1), 681 (55,77), 1485 (30,32,42), 1612 (53,57,74), 1903 (279), 1903 (295,382,403,490), 1962 (14,15), 2485 (141,211, 2813 (71)
Pearson, F.: ref, 2527 (14)
Pearson, G. R.: ref, 2076 (57)
Pearson, H. M.: ref, 298 (22)
Pearson, J. L.: ref, 790 (29)
Pearson, L.: test, 359
Pearson, L. C.: rev, 1442, 2104
Pearson, M. E.: rev, 202, 1804, 2382
Pearson, N. A.: test, 258, 662, 816, 1168, 2722
Pearson, P.: ref, 999 (140)
Pearson, P. D.: rev, 832, 1073, 665 (38)
Pearson, Q. M.: ref, 1348 (16)
Pearson, T.: ref, 2516 (116)
Pease, D.: test, 1316, 1317
Peavy, G.: ref, 272 (334), 376 (30), 776 (26), 2863 (293)
Peavy, G. M.: test, 2387; ref, 2860 (390);, 2863 (101)
Pechacová, Z.: ref, 2603 (467)
Peck, A. H.: ref, 1697 (83)
Peck, C. S.: test, 1545
Pecknold, J. C.: ref, 1166 (17), 2603 (24)
Pecnik, N.: ref, 448 (19)
Pécoud, A.: ref, 1166 (101), 1661 (54)
Pedersen, C.: ref, 2603 (110), 2860 (279)
Pedersen, C. A.: ref, 760 (2), 2516 (23), 2858 (49)
Pedersen, D. M.: ref, 372 (75)
Pedersen, F. A.: ref, 272 (207), 2497 (582)
Pedersen, J.: ref, 1991 (50)
Pedersen, N. L.: ref, 998 (98), 1010 (11), 1405 (25), 2218 (7,32), 2860 (715)
Pedlow, R.: ref, 863 (29), 1079 (15), 2039 (8), 2485 (68), 2813 (21)
Pedoto, J. P.: ref, 404 (25)
Pedrabissi, L.: ref, 1590 (26)
Pedraza, M.: ref, 134 (8,14), 1661 (23)
Pedro-Carroll, J. L.: ref, 2498 (4)
Peek, C. W.: ref, 1000 (10)
Peek, M. S.: ref, 994 (1), 1379 (4), 1903 (25), 2190 (1), 2695 (3)
Peeke, P. A.: ref, 1755 (77)
Peel, E. A.: rev, 1717, 1800
Peet, M.: ref, 272 (351)
Pegna, A.: ref, 2516 (60), 2860 (789), 2892 (158)
Pei-Hui, R. A.: ref, 298 (123)
Peindl, K. S.: ref, 2305 (208)
Peisner, E. S.: ref, 875 (1)
Peisner-Feinberg, E. S.: ref, 1903 (547)
Pejeau, C.: ref, 4 (12)
Pekarik, A.: ref, 337 (155)
Pelaez-Nogueras, M.: ref, 2497 (507)
Pélandeau, N.: ref, 472 (233), 2214 (138)
Pelazer, M.: ref, 2163 (337), 2860 (1328)
Pelc, I.: ref, 1166 (194)
Pelchat, R.: ref, 2017 (8), 2305 (83)

Pelco, L.: ref, 1522 (1)
Pelco, L. E.: ref, 451 (139), 472 (178), 2485 (209), 2862 (515)
Pelham, W. E.: ref, 451 (122), 472 (215), 681 (6,17), 1318 (20), 1745 (7,83), 2214 (125), 2305 (177), 2862 (477,677)
Pellat, J.: ref, 2860 (1236), 2863 (370)
Pellegrin, K. L.: ref, 1697 (543)
Pellegrini, A.: ref, 2860 (127)
Pellegrini, A. D.: ref, 1903 (28,87,404,470)
Pellegrini, D. S.: ref, 1010 (35)
Pellegrini, S. M.: test, 306
Pellegrino, J. W.: ref, 665 (12), 1485 (2), 2862 (68)
Peller-Porth, V.: ref, 1866 (9)
Pelletier, D.: ref, 472 (111), 1866 (33), 2039 (17)
Pellett, O.: ref, 128 (2)
Pellgrin, A.: ref, 472 (20)
Pelton, G. H.: ref, 2305 (148)
Pena, C. M.: ref, 180 (13), 745 (6)
Peña, L. M.: ref, 1698 (14)
Pence, A. R.: ref, 1216 (8)
Pencharz, P. B.: ref, 272 (258), 893 (42), 1405 (39), 1903 (517), 2862 (595)
Pendergrass, T.: ref, 1000 (65)
Pendlebury, W. W.: ref, 2860 (988), 2863 (291)
Pendleton, C. W.: rev, 1792
Pendleton, L.: ref, 1697 (98)
Pendleton, M.: ref, 2497 (47)
Pendziszewski, S.: ref, 2402 (44)
Penet, C.: ref, 2227 (19), 2860 (818), 2863 (236)
Penfield, D. A.: rev, 2213
Pengilly, J. W.: ref, 142 (1), 682 (2)
Penick, E. C.: test, 2107; ref, 2107 (2), 2603 (394)
Penick, J. M.: ref, 1318 (18), 1903 (539)
Peniston, E. G.: ref, 272 (137), 1687 (17)
Penk, W. E.: ref, 1697 (569,570), 2010 (23), 2860 (1348), 2863 (406), 2879 (216), 2892 (289)
Penkower, L.: ref, 2603 (139)
Penn, D. L.: ref, 1619 (5), 2050 (43), 2603 (206), 2892 (83)
Penna, J. P.: rev, 48
Pennebaker, J. W.: ref, 1338 (1), 1697 (99)
Penney, L. L.: ref, 2603 (383), 2858 (104)
Pennings, A.: ref, 2042 (1)
Pennings, A. H.: ref, 2163 (296)
Pennington, B. F.: ref, 337 (129), 375 (2), 459 (23,24), 798 (9,21), 1902 (31,35,49,80,82,93), 2163 (85,264), 2485 (99,191), 2860 (391,533,1018,1215), 2862 (177,423,440,538,587), 2879 (156,189), 2892 (82,217)
Pennington, M.: ref, 337 (143), 1697 (535), 2163 (313), 2402 (58)
Penrose, L. S.: rev, 1697
Penticoff, J.: ref, 1216 (21)
Pentland, B.: ref, 2193 (13)
Penton, M.: ref, 1164 (182), 2516 (120), 2892 (302)
Penzien, D. B.: ref, 2839 (9)
People Builders International, Inc.: test, 1948
Peoples, C. E.: ref, 2485 (178)
Peper, M.: ref, 303 (20), 1164 (164), 2860 (1329)
Pépin, J. P.: ref, 2864 (122)
Pépin, M.: ref, 2217 (2)
Peplin, C. M.: ref, 926 (4)
Peppard, F. R.: ref, 335 (1), 2289 (6)
Peppas, G. J.: ref, 2591 (1)
Pepper, B.: ref, 1164 (14), 2860 (148), 2879 (22), 2901 (10)
Pepper, C. M.: ref, 273 (24), 999 (166), 1953 (3)
Pepper, P. P.: ref, 2671 (1), 2901 (61), 2905 (73)
Pepple, J. R.: ref, 1093 (84), 1164 (68), 1218 (7), 1645 (3), 1697 (408), 2516 (42,65) 2860 (671,855), 2863 (199,250), 2879 (81), 2892 (125,176)
Pepplinkhuizen, L.: ref, 1166 (164), 2305 (204), 2497 (191)
The Peptide Neuropathy Study Group: ref, 1135 (18), 2226 (14), 2516 (85), 2860 (1173), 2863 (353)
Peralta, V.: ref, 2288 (34,53), 2289 (16,25), 2860 (599), 2892 (111,172)
Perani, D.: ref, 2163 (185,284), 2860 (1130)
Peräsalo, J.: ref, 1661 (24)
Percival, B.: test, 252, 2357
Percival, R. R.: test, 761, 1624
Perconte, S. T.: ref, 335 (2), 1697 (143), 2603 (116,150)
Percy, M. E.: ref, 2227 (8), 2860 (364), 2879 (44), 2892 (54)
Perdices, M.: ref, 2497 (340), 2863 (186)
Peredery, O. P.: ref, 1697 (341), 2860 (717)
Perel, J.: ref, 272 (221)
Perel, J. M.: ref, 272 (265), 337 (156), 1093 (56), 1166 (180), 2305 (216), 2603 (215), 2860 (532)
Perenyi, A.: ref, 1166 (224)
Peretti, C. S.: ref, 1166 (139)
Peretz, I.: ref, 2225 (20), 2860 (1410), 2862 (530), 2863 (429)
Perez, B.: ref, 1421 (4)
Perez, C. M.: ref, 2146 (15)
Perez, E.: ref, 540 (3), 2432 (26), 2704 (32)
Perez, F. I.: ref, 2603 (3)
Pérez, M. J.: ref, 2771 (2)
Pérez-Prado, E. M.: ref, 272 (341)
Pérez-solá, V.: ref, 1166 (168)
Perez-Strumolo, L.: ref, 272 (310)
Perez-Vidal, A.: ref, 1010 (15), 1991 (4)
Perfect, T. J.: ref, 1758 (66), 2193 (51), 2860 (1069)
Perfection Learning Corp.: test, 897, 1509
Perfetti, C. A.: ref, 592 (49)
Peri, T.: ref, 337 (50), 2497 (199,223,593)
Perini, G. I.: ref, 2860 (127)
Perkins, D. O.: ref, 1166 (196), 2076 (94,122)
Perkins, K.: ref, 2717 (1)
Perkins, M. N.: ref, 1171 (1)
Perkins, P.: ref, 2860 (57)
Perkins, P. G.: ref, 1470 (2)
Perkins, R. J. M.: ref, 68 (30)

Perkins, W. H.: rev, 2801
Perling, M. L.: test, 1230
Perlis, M. L.: ref, 272 (132,307), 1166 (80,204)
Perlman, C.: rev, 2712, 2730
Perlmuter, L. C.: ref, 2860 (296)
Perlmutter, M.: ref, 666 (7), 2860 (24,207)
Perloff, J. M.: ref, 2603 (207)
Perloff, J. N.: ref, 451 (146) 2603 (486), 2813 (126)
Perlstadt, H.: ref, 1216 (84)
Perman, S.: test, 2491
Perna, G.: ref, 2497 (505)
Perney, J.: test, 2320
Pernice, R.: ref, 1079 (75)
Perper, J. A.: ref, 2603 (175)
Perrey, C. D.: ref, 1379 (50), 2901 (43)
Perrin, J.: ref, 1010 (70), 1092 (5,13), 2305 (121,165), 2860 (331), 2862 (310), 2879 (102)
Perrin, S.: ref, 1021 (13), 2214 (25,121,130), 2305 (231), 2498 (18,72)
Perrine, A.: ref, 376 (10)
Perrine, K.: ref, 1698 (16), 2227 (17), 2860 (992), 2863 (213,294), 2892 (84)
Perrine, R. M.: ref, 462 (13), 1661 (37), 2076 (65)
Perris, C.: ref, 999 (5)
Perris, H.: ref, 999 (5)
Perron, A.: ref, 451 (291), 472 (235)
Perrone, K. M.: ref, 717 (2), 863 (92)
Perrova, I.: ref, 472 (160)
Perry, A.: ref, 433 (4), 811 (1), 1903 (446), 2813 (3,12,20)
Perry, A. R.: ref, 1338 (32)
Perry, C.: ref, 2247 (5), 2749 (7), 2860 (124)
Perry, C. K.: ref, 451 (176), 811 (13), 1259 (2)
Perry, C. L.: ref, 451 (42), 1000 (71)
Perry, J. C.: ref, 2603 (585)
Perry, K. J.: ref, 272 (112)
Perry, L. A.: test, 2434
Perry, M. S.: ref, 1687 (47), 1697 (600)
Perry, O. E., III: ref, 2497 (506)
Perry, P. J.: ref, 1166 (140)
Perry, R. P.: ref, 1338 (4)
Perry, S.: ref, 337 (30,48), 2497 (192)
Perry, S. M.: ref, 2417 (11)
Perry, S. W.: ref, 846 (14), 2603 (449)
Perry, W.: ref, 1164 (139), 1698 (17), 1941 (1), 2076 (123), 2247 (92,93,94,110), 2305 (151), 2397 (1), 2860 (1212)
Perry-Sheldon, B.: rev, 1041
Perryman, K. M.: ref, 2860 (1308)
Persaud, R.: ref, 2050 (74)
Persel, C. S.: ref, 326 (8), 1164 (125), 1525 (24), 2860 (1121), 2892 (233)
Persily, C. A.: ref, 1745 (78)
Persinger, M. A.: ref, 272 (147), 1135 (15), 1164 (106,107,165), 1697 (232,340,341,563), 1903 (405), 2516 (51), 2603 (436), 2839 (7), 2860 (505,716,717,954), 2862 (524), 2863 (281,282), 2879 (132)
Personal Strengths Publishing: test, 1023, 1024, 2013, 2014
Persons, J. B.: ref, 2603 (207)
Peru, A.: ref, 2163 (338), 2860 (1330)
Perugi, G.: ref, 2603 (135,211)
Perwien, A. R.: ref, 472 (159), 2214 (91)
Perz, C. A.: ref, 2497 (662)
Peselow, E. D.: ref, 272 (17), 1166 (25), 2305 (25), 2860 (297)
Peskin, H.: ref, 372 (93), 373 (31)
Pesonen, A.: ref, 1725 (4), 2862 (269), 2879 (80)
Pessoa-Brandao, L.: ref, 280 (4)
Pete-McGadney, J.: ref, 1832 (11)
Peterkin, I.: ref, 303 (22), 376 (27), 776 (55), 1164 (172), 2860 (1354), 2863 (408), 2892 (291)
Peters, D. K.: ref, 298 (89)
Peters, J.: ref, 2288 (9), 2305 (48)
Peters, J. E.: ref, 2247 (106)
Peters, J. L.: ref, 2288 (58)
Peters, J. M.: ref, 1697 (187)
Peters, L. C.: ref, 2860 (500)
Peters, M.: test, 2327
Peters, N. D.: ref, 863 (54)
Peters, R.: test, 2551
Peters, R. D.: ref, 863 (69)
Peters, S. A.: ref, 2163 (182)
Peters, S. A. F.: ref, 2163 (113), 2229 (2)
Peters-Bean, K. M.: ref, 999 (180)
Petersen, A.: ref, 2862 (514), 2905 (100)
Petersen, A. C.: ref, 272 (118), 472 (170), 1881 (3)
Petersen, D. K.: ref, 1903 (570), 2163 (351), 2862 (709)
Petersen, J. C.: test, 2512
Petersen, J. D.: ref, 1903 (511)
Petersen, P. B.: ref, 2862 (486)
Petersen, R. C.: ref, 2226 (25), 2860 (905,1283), 2863 (272,387)
Peterson, A. V.: ref, 2591 (1)
Peterson, B.: ref, 1164 (116), 2860 (1019)
Peterson, B. E.: ref, 2749 (71)
Peterson, B. L.: ref, 1697 (117)
Peterson, C.: rev, 694; ref, 999 (112), 1093 (55), 1178 (8), 2749 (46)
Peterson, C. A.: rev, 337, 824, 965; ref, 2247 (71,132), 1097 (13), 2163 (234)
Peterson, D. R.: test, 2211; rev, 2006
Peterson, G. W.: test, 422; ref, 404 (32), 665 (59)
Peterson, H. A.: rev, 783, 1047; ref, 1903 (537), 2905 (112), 2864 (12)
Peterson, J.: test, 1664
Peterson, J. B.: ref, 372 (35), 1661 (16), 1697 (166), 2010 (2,8), 2199 (12), 2227 (5,9) 2860 (208,392,920), 2863 (52,102), 2892 (24,57)
Peterson, J. C.: test, 1887
Peterson, J. M.: ref, 2603 (239,334)
Peterson, L.: ref, 375 (1), 472 (43), 681 (64), 997 (18),1661 (73), 1903 (394), 2498 (41), 2603 (523), 2880 (2)

Peterson, L. G.: ref, 998 (109), 1093 (106), 1517 (6)
Peterson, L. M.: test, 1618
Peterson, M. E.: ref, 2674 (3)
Peterson, M. S.: ref, 1379 (61), 2305 (115), 2813 (78)
Peterson, N. G.: rev, 1343
Peterson, R. A.: test, 2199; rev, 1212, 1214, 2247, 2508; ref, 2214 (33)
Peterson, R. C.: ref, 2860 (359,718), 2863 (94,103,214), 2879 (88)
Peterson, R. F.: ref, 538 (5), 1962 (8)
Peterson, R. L.: rev, 2422
Peterson, R. W.: ref, 2559 (3)
Peterson, S.: rev, 52
Peterson, S. K.: ref, 2497 (662)
Pethick, S.: test, 1528
Petit, D.: ref, 776 (52), 1164 (163), 1218 (18), 2226 (28), 2227 (46)
Petit, H.: ref, 776 (18,35)
Petitto, J. M.: ref, 1166 (196)
Petkova, E.: ref, 1166 (142), 2603 (487)
Petracca, G.: ref, 2050 (120), 2163 (227), 2860 (935), 2873 (40), 2892 (197)
Petracchi, M.: ref, 2050 (121), 2163 (228), 2873 (41), 2892 (198)
Petrides, M.: ref, 2860 (209,1331)
Petrie, K. J.: ref, 1991 (96)
Petrill, S. A.: ref, 270 (48) 1903 (411), 2485 (244)
Petriquin, S.: ref, 474 (5)
Petrolini, N.: ref, 1166 (21)
Petros, T. V.: ref, 2860 (262)
Petrosko, J.: rev, 2862
Petrosko, J. M.: rev, 624
Petrovich, D. V.: test, 1869
Petry, M. C.: ref, 199 (17)
Pett, M. A.: ref, 1178 (14)
Pettegrew, J. W.: ref, 2305 (109), 2892 (141)
Petti, A. R.: ref, 893 (29)
Pettice, Y. J.: ref, 2497 (511)
Pettiette-Doolin, J.: rev, 1215
Pettigrew, A. C.: ref, 1404 (6)
Pettigrew, K. D.: ref, 1240 (21)
Pettit, G. S.: ref, 451 (26,140,199), 1903 (542)
Pettus, W. C.: ref, 2856 (3)
Petty, F.: ref, 2305 (202)
Petty, J.: test, 442
Petty, R. E.: ref, 2749 (63)
Petursson, H.: ref, 2305 (141,180,199)
Petzel, T. P.: ref, 2497 (84)
Peveler, R. C.: ref, 337 (99), 2050 (113), 2603 (93),179)
Pewey, K. L.: ref, 1140 (24)
Peyrefitte, J.: ref, 2497 (443)
Peyrot, M.: ref, 1401 (4)
Peyser, C.: ref, 1740 (10), 2516 (32), 2860 (514), 2892 (85)
Peyser, C. E.: ref, 2516 (18,72), 2863 (171), 2892 (203)
Peyser, J.: ref, 1093 (8), 2108 (1)
Pezzarossa, B.: ref, 1687 (16)
Pezzini, G.: ref, 540 (13), 1485 (55), 1903 (501,502), 2227 (34), 2862 (571,572)
Pfeffer, C. R.: ref, 2305 (246)
Pfefferbaum, A.: ref, 1758 (8), 2860 (420)
Pfeiffer, J. A.: test, 1452
Pfeiffer, J. W.: test, 939, 1452
Pfeiffer, S. I.: test, 817, 818; rev, 133, 1012, 1215, 1797, 1877, 2554, 2579
Pfeiffer, S. J.: rev, 1278
Pfiffner, L. J.: ref, 2892 (81)
Pflaum, S. W.: rev, 1071
Pflug, B.: ref, 1093 (115)
Pfohl, B.: ref, 1093 (16,105)
Pfost, K. S.: ref, 272 (34)
Pfueller, U.: ref, 745 (24)
Pfurtscheller, G.: ref, 2163 (230)
Pham, D.: ref, 1697 (502)
Phares, V.: ref, 337 (112), 2369 (9)
Phelps, L.: test, 1977; rev, 375, 885, 1417, 2321; ref, 433 (8), 451 (218), 1085 (2), 1697 (342), 2452 (20), 2485 (233), 2813 (151), 2862 (532), 2880 (5)
Phelps, L. H.: ref, 1701 (37,38)
Phelps, M. E.: ref, 1093 (40), 1166 (150)
Phelps, R. E.: ref, 694 (119)
Phelps-Gunn, T.: test, 2709
Phelps-Terasaki, D.: test, 2709
Phifer, J. F.: ref, 2497 (48)
Phil, D.: ref, 2211 (43)
Philbin, D. A.: ref, 2860 (1364)
Philbin, M.: ref, 1469 (7), 1166 (214)
Philips, D.: test, 21, 25
Philips, H. C.: ref, 2497 (193)
Philliber, W. W.: ref, 645 (1)
Phillippe, K. A.: ref, 1903 (176), 2485 (84), 2603 (181)
Phillips, A. S.: ref, 999 (100)
Phillips, B.: ref, 1164 (30), 1697 (141), 2860 (293)
Phillips, C. P.: ref, 692 (1)
Phillips, D.: ref, 1264 (6), 1889 (11), 1987 (22), 2497 (86), 2520 (14)
Phillips, D. A.: ref, 875 (3,6), 1264 (1,2)
Phillips, E.: ref, 1166 (186)
Phillips, G.: ref, 1010 (112), 2603 (504), 2858 (122)
Phillips, J.: ref, 1140 (50), 2860 (1124)
Phillips, J. G.: ref, 1164 (108), 1758 (23,88,101), 2860 (608)
Phillips, J. M.: ref, 1965 (78,83)
Phillips, K. A.: ref, 271 (5), 272 (223), 1166 (141), 2519 (31), 2520 (32)
Phillips, L.: ref, 926 (11), 2516 (31), 2858 (36), 2860 (1421), 2901 (137)
Phillips, L. H.: ref, 127 (4), 999 (132), 2163 (235)
Phillips, L. M.: test, 2690; ref, 389 (13), 1659 (9)
Phillips, L. W.: ref, 1701 (16)
Phillips, M.: ref, 364 (24)
Phillips, M. J.: ref, 2497 (626)
Phillips, M. L.: ref, 1758 (96)
Phillips, M. M.: ref, 1903 (578)

Phillips, N. A.: ref, 2860 (955), 2863 (283)
Phillips, N. B.: ref, 665 (76)
Phillips, P. C.: ref, 472 (185), 2214 (111), 2497 (585), 2813 (128)
Phillips, S. E.: rev, 1319, 2753, 2862 (380), 2901 (69)
Phillips, S. M.: ref, 1000 (26)
Phillips, T. G.: rev, 607, 1082, 1121
Phillips, W.: ref, 270 (10), 926 (6), 1653 (5),23), 2163 (236), 2603 (94), 2860 (254)
Phillips, W. M.: ref, 2603 (212)
Phillips-Jones, L.: test, 802, 1651
Phillipson, H.: test, 1811
Philp, I.: ref, 2858 (128)
Philpot, M. P.: ref, 1390 (2,3), 1758 (10), 2860 (215)
Philpot, V. D.: ref, 694 (103), 1745 (33)
Phinney, J. S.: ref, 694 (62)
Pianta, R.: ref, 1902 (41)
Pianta, R. C.: ref, 863 (89,91), 1047 (5), 1216 (56), 1321 (8), 1612 (77), 1697 (506), 1889 (15,16), 2076 (95), 2864 (65)
Piasecki, J. M.: ref, 998 (41), 1697 (167)
Piasecki, M.: ref, 2516 (6)
Piatt, A. L.: rcf, 1697 (243)
Piazza, N.: ref, 2126 (16)
Piazza, N. J.: rev, 134, 652
Piburn, M.: ref, 1755 (13)
Picard, E. M.: ref, 1164 (26), 1903 (69)
Picard, S.: ref, 1697 (122)
Picco, R. D.: ref, 998 (77)
Pichette, E.: rev, 923
Pichot, P.: ref, 1697 (124), 2603 (87)
Pickar, D.: ref, 1093 (25), 2862 (629), 2863 (312), 2892 (31,222)
Pickelman, H.: ref, 998 (68), 2065 (25)
Pickens, J.: ref, 272 (170,196,210,277), 451 (115,136), 1962 (13), 2076 (73,148), 2497 (507)
Pickering, A.: ref, 1758 (82), 2858 (84)f, 2860 (40,1213), 2863 (14,223)
Pickering, A. D.: ref, 1758 (4,18), 2193 (3,9), 2860 (128,294), 2863 (36), 2863 (78)
Pickering, J.: rev, 419, 2835
Pickering, J. W.: ref, 413 (1)
Pickering, T.: ref, 1338 (30), 2497 (182)
Pickett, S.: ref, 2603 (137)
Pickett, S. A.: ref, 2603 (208)
Pickles, A.: ref, 350 (13,36), 901 (1), 1612 (78), 1653 (13,26), 1745 (61), 2163 (145,260), 2228 (11,21), 2305 (36,224), 2860 (334,571,756,1034)
Pickles, A. R.: ref, 451 (171)
Pickren, W. E.: ref, 2497 (169)
Pidgeon, D. A.: test, 1800; rev, 901, 1148, 1414, 2092, 2094
Piedmont, R. L.: ref, 68 (48), 372 (49), 2218 (8)
Piek, J. P.: ref, 1727 (2), 2862 (659)
Piekarski, A. M.: ref, 1697 (233)
Piele, P. K.: ref, 389 (2)
Pieper, C.: ref, 2603 (563)
Pieper, C. F.: ref, 272 (336), 2218 (116), 2497 (664)
Pieper, N.: ref, 1164 (158), 2227 (41)
Pierce, E. F.: ref, 2076 (61,96)
Pierce, E. W.: ref, 863 (12), 1592 (18), 2485 (119)
Pierce, G.: ref, 413 (29)
Pierce, G. R.: ref, 272 (308), 1010 (92)
Pierce, J. D., Jr.: ref, 2437 (4)
Pierce, J. L.: ref, 451 (219), 1701 (5)
Pierce, J. W.: ref, 1991 (55,94)
Pierce, L. G.: ref, 615 (20)
Pierce, S.: ref, 1903 (204)
Pierce, S. H.: ref, 1216 (87)
Pierce, T.: ref, 791 (14,15)
Pierce, T. W.: ref, 1164 (16), 2497 (61), 2497 (275), 2516 (30), 2860 (506,507), 2863 (146)
Pierce-Jones, J.: rev, 2716
Piercy, F. P.: ref, 1000 (8)
Pierre-Louis, S. J. C.: ref, 2860 (880)
Pierri, J. M.: ref, 1166 (210)
Piers, E. V.: test, 1991; rev, 1903, 2146
Piersel, W. C.: rev, 441, 478, 651
Piersma, H. L.: ref, 273 (31), 337 (88,89,113), 1093 (98), 1687 (30,31,32)
Pierson, E.: test, 2751
Pierson, L.: ref, 2862 (159)
Pietrini, P.: ref, 2485 (234), 2860 (1141,1155,1216), 2879 (190)
Pietsch, A.: ref, 2163 (249)
Pietsch, M.: ref, 2860 (1202), 2862 (578)
Pietz, J.: ref, 2860 (747)
Pigge, F. L.: ref, 665 (90,91)
Pigott, S.: ref, 2860 (719)
Pigott, T.: test, 2471
Pigott, T. A.: ref, 2603 (399)
Piha, J.: ref, 472 (227,231)
Pihl, R. O.: ref, 372 (35), 681 (62), 1021 (15), 1367 (4), 1661 (16,78), 1697 (166), 2010 (2,8), 2039 (14,23), 2199 (12), 2227 (5,9), 2603 (164), 2807 (1), 2860 (208,392,920,1393), 2863 (52,102,262), 2892 (24,57,184)
Pike, A.: ref, 472 (184)
Pike, K. M.: ref, 2603 (562)
Pike, R.: test, 1987
Pilar, J. D.: ref, 694 (39), 2497 (207)
Piletz, J. E.: ref, 1093 (34)
Pilisuk, M.: ref, 2603 (115)
Pilkonis, P.: ref, 1093 (43)
Pilkonis, P. A.: ref, 272 (111,194,342), 1093 (83), 1166 (215), 1517 (4), 2199 (8), 2498 (43), 2603 (302,335,574)
Pillard, R. C.: ref, 298 (128), 372 (32,77), 1697 (147), 2860 (313)
Pilliner, A. E. G.: rev, 1797
Pillion, B.: ref, 2163 (295), 2860 (1153), 2863 (342)
Pillner, A. E. F.: rev, 348
Pillon, B.: ref, 328 (1), 776 (33,54), 2163 (43,75,156,183), 2516 (44,82)f, 2517 (7), 2860

(168,298,449,605,720), 2863 (44,124,178,215), 2870 (2), 2892 (20,39,72,94,130,142,207,248,249,255)
Pillon, B. B.: ref, 776 (63)
Pillow, D. R.: ref, 272 (208), 462 (1), 472 (38)
Pilowsky, I.: test, 1241, 1488
Pilowsky, L. S.: ref, 1093 (50), 2050 (65), 2863 (169), 2892 (277)
Pilowsky, T.: ref, 2860 (1208), 2862 (583), 2864 (128)
Pimental, P. A.: test, 1690
Pimley, A.: ref, 2858 (3)
Pincus, A. L.: ref, 337 (114), 1697 (447), 2218 (38)
Pincus, J. H.: ref, 1164 (86), 2892 (164)
Pinder, R.: ref, 31 (1), 1036 (2), 1444 (3), 1755 (9), 1822 (1), 2163 (40)
Pindzola, R. H.: test, 2837; ref, 1095 (6), 2837 (1)
Pine, D.: ref, 1166 (179)
Pine, D. S.: ref, 451 (220), 1216 (108), 1903 (296), 2864 (66)
Pinell, G. S.: ref, 1072 (46), 2905 (61)
Pines, A. M.: ref, 2749 (26)
Piney Mountain Press, Inc.: test, 1741
Pini, S.: ref, 1166 (205), 2305 (110)
Pinkerton, R.: ref, 875 (11), 1264 (5), 1889 (4)
Pinkney, J. W.: rev, 405, 871, 961, 1200, 1350, 1539, 2151, 2155
Pinkney, P.: test, 2818
Pinkston, S. L.: ref, 687 (2), 2860 (1090)
Pino, C. J.: test, 480
Pinsent, C.: ref, 863 (67)
Pinsoneault, T. B.: ref, 1341 (2), 1697 (507), 1698 (18)
Pintado, J. I. C.: ref, 1903 (551)
Pintillie, D.: test, 350
Pintner, R.: test, 1994, 1995
Pinto, A.: ref, 1215 (1), 2557 (11)
Pinto, A. C.: ref, 2862 (137)
Pinto, J. K.: test, 2096; ref, 1469 (4)
Pinto-Martin, J. A.: ref, 451 (236), 2813 (154)
Pintrich, P. R.: test, 1720; ref, 665 (67), 1720 (2,4), 2862 (282), 2901 (45)
Piolti, R.: ref, 2860 (173)
Piotrowski, C.: ref, 301 (33), 853 (12), 1160 (2), 1687 (33), 2247 (40,41,107), 2380 (7), 2749 (33)
Pipe, M.-E.: ref, 2485 (1)
Piper, M. E.: ref, 180 (35), 272 (191), 2497 (134,564), 2603 (117,118,290,291,543)
Pipp, S.: ref, 2860 (672)
Pires, A.: ref, 650 (15), 1093 (97)
Pires, M.: ref, 999 (139), 2603 (407)
Pirie, J. : ref, 592 (12), 2031 (2)
Pirozzi, R.: ref, 2305 (146,186)
Pirozzolo, F. J.: rev, 2873; ref, 1164 (29), 2860 (281), 2863 (74)
Pirrello, V. E.: ref, 2603 (361)
Pisani, V. D.: ref, 2305 (82)
Pisterman, S.: ref, 451 (22)
Pistole, D. R.: ref, 2749 (47)
Pistole, M. C.: ref, 2076 (124)
Pitcaithly, D.: ref, 998 (102), 2860 (481)
Pither, R.: test, 892
Pithers, R. T.: ref, 1825 (5,6), 2360 (3)
Pithers, W.: ref, 301 (10), 1164 (19), 2860 (187)
Pithers, W. D.: ref, 337 (195), 1010 (137), 2496 (5), 2497 (675)
Pitman, R. K.: ref, 2497 (199,500), 2860 (1403)
Pitre, V.: ref, 1140 (24)
Pittenger, D. J.: rev, 1333, 2496; ref, 1755 (45)
Pittinsky, T.: ref, 1379 (48)
Piven, J.: ref, 1485 (33,43,62,63), 1653 (4,17,29), 2860 (299,721,956,1332,1333), 2862 (283,381,660,661, 662)
Pivik, J.: ref, 2497 (520)
Pizzamiglio, M. T.: ref, 298 (151)
Pizzo, P. A.: ref, 1612 (55,62,85), 1903 (483), 2163 (288), 2813 (81), 2862 (279,297,523)
Plake, B. S.: ref, 570 (1), 2497 (418,652), 2656 (24)
Plamondon, J.: ref, 2519 (37), 2520 (38)
Plant, E. A.: ref, 2496 (4), 2497 (661)
Plante, A.: ref, 2917 (3)
Plante, A. S.: ref, 1394 (13), 1903 (560), 2657 (36)
Plante, E.: ref, 241 (2), 266 (1), 266 (3), 324 (6), 331 (3), 430 (9), 624 (12), 628 (1), 798 (24), 994 (17), 1047 (2,6), 1240 (9,18), 1379 (35,54,60,77), 1485 (11,22,35), 1607 (10), 1740 (13), 1804 (8,10), 1903 (138,297,491,529,68) 2044 (6), 2233 (3) 2382 (12,25), 2524 (5,6,10) 2657 (16), 2660 (4), 2680 (7,10,13), 2695 (28), 2704 (15), 2801 (3), 2862 (235,640), 2864 (138), 2901 (38,118)
Plante, T. G.: ref, 2603 (391), 2860 (38), 2862 (344)
Planty, E.: test, 2566
Plapinger, D. S.: ref, 353 (14), 815 (17,28), 994 (18,29), 1903 (312,406), 2724 (8,10), 2862 (292,382), 2880 (1,3)
Plasky, P.: ref, 2305 (58), 2892 (40)
Plassman, B. L.: ref, 2860 (957)
Platon, M. J.: ref, 2358 (12)
Platt, F.: ref, 2862 (121)
Platt, J. J.: test, 1619; ref, 271 (11), 272 (182,296), 273 (21), 1687 (44)
Platz, T.: ref, 2163 (184)
Platzek, D.: test, 2498
Plaud, J. J.: ref, 2839 (9)
Playfer, J.: ref, 1758 (13), 2193 (6)
Pleck, J. H.: ref, 2497 (424), 2603 (80,133),333)
Plenger, P. M.: ref, 2860 (683,1230,1231), 2879 (196)
Pless, I. B.: ref, 2076 (38)
Plessas, G.: rev, 257
Pletan, M. D.: ref, 1379 (74), 2862 (383), 2864 (101)
Pliske, R. M.: ref, 2247 (69), 2860 (704)
Pliskin, N. H.: ref, 272 (209), 376 (16), 1164 (131,146), 1740 (17), 2125 (24), 2516 (83,95), 2863 (343,375), 2892 (134),267)
Plomin, R.: ref, 270 (39,48), 451 (252), 472 (62,142,184,221,229), 540 (18), 998 (98), 1010 (11) 1216 (70,100,109), 1405 (25), 2218 (7,32), 2382 (6,16), 2485 (244), 2860 (690,715), 2862 (609)

Ploska, A.: ref, 2163 (75), 2860 (298), 2870 (2), 2892 (39)
Plotnicov, K. H.: ref, 893 (26)
Plottner, G.: ref, 893 (25), 1079 (48)
Ployhart, R. E.: ref, 1212 (1)
Plucker, J. A.: ref, 1318 (11), 2358 (14)
Plude, D. J.: ref, 2163 (9), 2860 (25,28)
Plumet, M-H.: ref, 2111 (2), 2163 (247), 2862 (410)
Plummer, B.: ref, 451 (105), 472 (161)
Plutchik, R.: test, 932; ref, 1697 (122)
Pochyly, J. M.: ref, 1687 (4)
Pocius, K. E.: ref, 1755 (16)
Podany, E. C.: ref, 1135 (23), 1697 (572), 2226 (36), 2603 (554), 2860 (1349), 2892 (290)
Podraza, A. M.: ref, 1164 (73), 2860 (722), 2892 (143)
Podsakoff, P. M.: ref, 1701 (25,39)
Poehlmann, J. A.: ref, 1216 (57), 2485 (142)
Poelijoe, N. W.: ref, 1079 (68,69)
Pogash, R.: ref, 1661 (35,75), 2516 (6), 2603 (317,556)
Pogge, D. L.: ref, 1164 (74), 2860 (723), 2892 (144)
Pogson, D.: ref, 2862 (663)
Pogue-Geile, M.: ref, 2516 (41)
Pogue-Geile, M. F.: ref, 1164 (27)
Pohjola, J.: ref, 2288 (2), 2860 (53)
Pohl, J.: ref, 2498 (9)
Pohlman, J.: ref, 2731 (1), 2860 (257), 2879 (34), 2901 (17)
Poikkeus, A.: ref, 1903 (281), 2862 (275)
Poisson, S.: test, 1265
Poizner, H.: ref, 1164 (174), 1903 (566), 2163 (348), 2731 (7), 2860 (1377), 2863 (413), 2879 (224), 2892 (295)
Poláez-Nogueras, M.: ref, 272 (210)
Polaino-Lorente, A.: ref, 472 (61)
Poland, R. E.: ref, 1697 (369), 2519 (18), 2520 (19), 2860 (778)
Polansky, M.: ref, 231 (1), 303 (32), 2226 (42), 2227 (61), 2599 (43), 2863 (431), 2892 (307)
Polansky, N.: ref, 458 (1)
Polatajko, H. J.: ref, 353 (10,20), 2432 (16,28), 2862 (207,419), 2901 (26,78)
Polatin, P. B.: ref, 1697 (411)
Polefrone, J. M.: ref, 1135 (19), 2497 (603), 2516 (89), 2860 (1200), 2863 (360)
Poletti, M.: ref, 2163 (188), 2516 (54), 2768 (26), 2819 (1), 2907 (6)
Poli, P.: ref, 472 (210), 2862 (658)
Polich, J.: ref, 2860 (112)
Poling, A.: ref, 4 (10)
Poling, J.: ref, 372 (117), 846 (26), 2218 (135), 2433 (4)
Politano, P. M.: ref, 2497 (194)
Politte, A. J.: test, 2004, 2354, 2370
Polivy, J.: ref, 2497 (383,534), 2860 (1024)
Polizzi, T. B.: test, 635
Polk, M. J.: test, 868
Polk, N.: ref, 2860 (145), 2862 (93)
Polkey, C. E.: ref, 303 (9), 641 (6), 1758 (7,48,49,67,73,82,104), 2193 (43), 2227 (28), 2860 (84,85,99,162,206,838,943,1140,1213), 2863 (243,277,338), 2892 (9)
Polkey, L. E.: ref, 1758 (17)
Pollack, C.: test, 2005
Pollack, J.: ref, 2326 (2), 2603 (129), 2858 (48)
Pollack, M. H.: ref, 272 (176), 1166 (63), 2199 (11), 2305 (187)
Pollack, S.: ref, 2603 (494), 2860 (1005)
Pollak, C.: ref, 1093 (27), 2603 (88)
Pollak, S. D.: ref, 1903 (548)
Polland, R.: ref, 2558 (3)
Pollina, L.: ref, 694 (22), 2603 (79)
Pollina, L. K.: ref, 2860 (393)
Pollitt, E.: ref, 2163 (272)
Pollock, C.: ref, 998 (18), 2603 (37)
Pollock, J. I.: ref, 349 (17), 901 (2)
Pollock, L.: ref, 2860 (683)
Pollock, P. H.: ref, 1687 (23)
Pollock, S.: ref, 2858 (69)
Polloway, E. A.: rev, 786, 2731
Pollux, P. M. J.: ref, 2860 (958)
Polman, C. H.: ref, 2599 (22)
Polonsky, W. H.: ref, 1021 (14)
Polovin, L. B.: ref, 694 (119)
Pols, H.: ref, 2497 (530)
Pols, H. J.: ref, 2497 (583)
Polster, M. R.: ref, 2193 (30), 2860 (728), 2873 (26), 2892 (145)
Poltiel, L.: ref, 1822 (6)
Polz, L.: ref, 448 (26)
Pomerleau, C. S.: ref, 2516 (52)
Pomerleau, O. F.: ref, 272 (267), 376 (18), 1697 (540), 2402 (62), 2405 (1), 2516 (52,97)
Pomeroy, C.: ref, 893 (5)
Pond, R. E.: test, 2045
Ponds, R. W. H. M.: ref, 2516 (102)
Ponpipom, A.: ref, 2432 (32), 2813 (129), 2860 (1172)
Ponterotto, J. G.: rev, 1735, 1815
Pontes, E.: ref, 1901 (16), 2485 (123,124,196), 2813 (113)
Ponticas, Y.: ref, 998 (38), 1158 (1), 1697 (152)
Pontius, A. A.: ref, 1410 (1,3), 2860 (1334), 2862 (664)
Ponto, L. L. B.: ref, 650 (13)
Ponton, A.-M.: ref, 650 (15), 1093 (97)
Ponton, M. O.: rev, 542
Pool, J. E.: ref, 2905 (71)
Poole, A.: ref, 1631 (4), 2076 (186)
Poole, C.: ref, 25 (1), 72 (2)
Poole, D. A.: ref, 1370 (1)
Poole, J. L.: ref, 2860 (724)
Poole, N.: ref, 1058 (7), 2227 (12), 2860 (499), 2863 (143)
Pooley, R. C.: rev, 97, 98, 591, 614, 1118
Poon, L. W.: ref, 2860 (27), 2860 (202), 2860 (765)
Poorman, M. O.: ref, 2230 (17), 2231 (7)
Pop, V. J.: ref, 2603 (153)
Popa, S.: ref, 2163 (66), 2860 (259)
Pope, A. W.: ref, 451 (221)

Pope, G. A.: ref, 256 (4), 999 (189), 1213 (1), 1333 (5), 1697 (508)
Pope, H. G.: ref, 893 (24)
Pope, H. G., Jr.: ref, 1166 (23,160)
Pope, J. T.: ref, 694 (111)
Pope, K. S.: ref, 1697 (209), 1698 (7)
Pope, M.: rev, 408, 1413, 1824, 1826
Pope, R.: ref, 1697 (43), 2603 (27)
Pope, S. K.: ref, 1216 (38,41,91), 1903 (234,510), 2485 (113,115,220)
Pope-Davis, D. B.: rev, 848
Popiel, D. A.: ref, 2603 (95)
Popinga, M. R.: ref, 2299 (4)
Poplin, M. S.: rev, 1362
Popma, J.: ref, 404 (21)
Popp, D.: ref, 1166 (202)
Poppe, C. J.: ref, 2497 (310)
Poppleton, S.: test, 2007
Popynick, M.: ref, 1901 (16), 2485 (81,124,196), 2813 (113), 2862 (200)
Porcerelli, J. H.: ref, 2749 (60,85)
Porch, B. E.: test, 2008
Poreh, A.: ref, 1697 (234)
Poreh, A. M.: ref, 1405 (15), 1697 (343), 2771 (15), 2860 (725)
Porges, S. W.: ref, 451 (111,183), 787 (2,3), 1379 (83,93), 1889 (5)
Porkkeus, A. M.: ref, 1903 (206), 2163 (129), 2247 (43), 2768 (18)
Porrata, J. L.: ref, 999 (61,133)
Porretta, D. L.: ref, 2485 (179), 2862 (384)
Porritt, D. W.: ref, 1166 (38), 2497 (155)
Portello, J. Y.: ref, 298 (124), 2149 (3)
Porter, B.: test, 2471
Porter, E. H.: test, 1022, 1349, 1704, 1956, 2507
Porter, J.: ref, 2603 (292)
Porter, J. E.: ref, 2126 (12)
Porter, J. F.: ref, 1697 (344),1965 (37)
Porter, J. M., Jr.: rev, 1632
Porter, J. S.: ref, 1991 (84)
Porter, K.: ref, 2076 (7)
Porter, L. A.: ref, 2077 (6)
Porter, R. B.: test, 477
Portera, L.: ref, 2199 (4)
Porterfield, T.: ref, 696 (2), 999 (185), 1740 (24), 2516 (108), 2860 (1335)
Porterfield, W. D.: rev, 1479, 2527
Portes, P. R.: ref, 451 (23), 2862 (138)
Porteus, S. D.: test, 2010; rev, 2212
Portin, R.: ref, 272 (273), 1079 (47), 2860 (959,1113)
Portis, S. C.: ref, 1140 (28)
Portner, J.: test, 1000
Poser, U.: ref, 2860 (835), 2863 (241)
Posey, C. D.: rev, 464
Posner, B. K.: test, 1445
Posner, B. Z.: test, 1446, 1448, 2635; ref, 1447 (1)
Posner, C. M.: ref, 2858 (40)
Possamai, A.: ref, 1943 (1)
Post, R.: ref, 2305 (120)
Post, R. M.: ref, 272 (294), 335 (7), 1166 (199)
Post, W. L.: rev, 957
Post, Y. V.: ref, 2860 (691)
Poster, K.: ref, 2879 (117)
Postle, B. R.: ref, 1135 (21)
Poteat, G. M.: rev, 809, 884, 967, 1067, 1765, 2486, 2902; ref, 448 (1), 2039 (7)
Poteat, M.: rev, 798
Poteet, J. A.: rev, 959, 2712, 2729
Potenza, M. T.: ref, 570 (1), 2065 (20)
Pothast, H. L.: ref, 298 (125)
Potorti, P. F.: ref, 298 (24)
Pott, M.: ref, 451 (72)
Potter, A. E.: test, 479; ref, 462 (3), 462 (14), 479 (1)
Potter, C. G.: ref, 694 (119)
Potter, L.: test, 123; ref, 270 (42), 1612 (98)
Potter, R. E.: ref, 1096 (1), 1612 (1), 2008 (5), 2485 (3), 2862 (10)
Potter, W. Z.: ref, 2862 (629)
Potts, H.: ref, 2497 (372)
Potts, S. G.: ref, 2603 (392)
Potvin, A.: ref, 650 (15), 1093 (97)
Poublon, R. M. L.: ref, 2076 (131), 2603 (423)
Poucher, K. E.: rev, 1792
Pouget, E. R.: ref, 2860 (557)
Poulin, F.: ref, 472 (70)
Poulsen, C.: ref, 560 (2)
Poulson, C. L.: ref, 1903 (307)
Pound, J.: ref, 472 (52)
Pounder, D. G.: ref, 1701 (30)
Povall, L.: ref, 2452 (11)
Povick, E.: ref, 136 (3), 1697 (136), 2603 (109)
Powch, I. G.: ref, 2218 (72)
Powell, A. B.: test, 2360; ref, 2218 (39)
Powell, B. J.: test, 2107; ref, 136 (3), 1697 (136), 2603 (109)
Powell, C.: ref, 1134 (4), 1903 (263), 2485 (130), 2862 (265), 2879 (78)
Powell, C. A.: ref, 1134 (6), 1216 (64), 1903 (361)
Powell, D.: test, 1665
Powell, D. H.: ref, 2860 (1156)
Powell, F. C.: ref, 908 (6,8), 2218 (115)
Powell, G. N.: ref, 298 (126)
Powell, J.: ref, 999 (62), 2050 (32), 2076 (66), 2497 (276)
Powell, K. F.: ref, 375 (5), 2227 (45), 2862 (651), 2863 (395) 2892 (280)
Powell, L.: ref, 1379 (96)
Powell, L. M.: ref, 199 (16), 2010 (16), 2163 (179), 2516 (47), 2860 (703), 2863 (205), 2879 (87)
Powell, S. B.: ref, 4 (16)
Powell, T. E.: rev, 760
Powell, T. W.: ref, 324 (12), 1095 (41), 1485 (53), 2710 (3), 2813 (127)
Powell, W. R.: rev, 1072

Power, C. T.: test, 2763
Power, K. G.: ref, 1824 (7)
Power, M. J.: ref, 272 (55,211), 1079 (59), 1671 (7), 2497 (451,584)
Power, P. G.: test, 1754
Power, S. D.: ref, 1338 (38)
Power, T. G.: ref, 462 (5), 1000 (48), 1001 (16)
Power, T. J.: test, 67; ref, 451 (97), 681 (18), 2485 (18)
Powers, B.: ref, 472 (162)
Powers, D. E.: ref, 592 (94), 1115 (25), 1115 (28)
Powers, L. L.: ref, 2497 (251)
Powers, M.: ref, 472 (93,94), 1745 (43), 2076 (87,88)
Powers, R. E.: ref, 2289 (22)
Powers, S.: rev, 1849; ref, 788 (2), 1010 (53)
Powers, S. V.: ref, 1404 (9)
Powers, S. W.: ref, 997 (5)
Powers, T. A.: ref, 1414 (2)
Powers, W. J.: ref, 2485 (236)
Powlishta, K.: ref, 1697 (38)
Poxon, S. C.: test, 761
Poynton, A. M.: ref, 1104 (10), 1758 (51), 2050 (126), 2163 (237), 2193 (45), 2225 (9), 2860 (960)
Poznanski, E. O.: test, 473
Pozniak, A. L.: ref, 1079 (51), 1758 (52)
Prabhakaran, V.: ref, 2163 (339)
Pradignac, A.: ref, 1166 (56)
Praestholm, J.: ref, 2050 (66)
Prall, C., in 135 (5), 2497 (624)
Prange, A. J.: ref, 2305 (53)
Prapavessis, H.: ref, 999 (177), 2076 (163)
Prasad, K. B. G.: ref, 459 (39), 1903 (248)
Pratarelli, M. E.: ref, 540 (22)
Prater, K.: ref, 1790 (8), 2451 (4)
Prather, E. M.: test, 2382; rev, 1739, 2620, 2680
Prather, P.: ref, 2873 (19)
Pratkanis, A. R.: ref, 694 (81), 1348 (9), 1701 (40)
Pratowski, E.: ref, 2813 (105)
Pratt, A.: ref, 1408 (9)
Pratt, A. C.: ref, 1503 (2), 1903 (19), 2163 (21), 2905 (2)
Pratt, A. L.: ref, 1697 (235)
Pratt, C.: ref, 1758 (76), 1903 (349), 1903 (492,515), 2163 (297), 2879 (195), 2905 (103)
Pratt, L. A.: ref, 998 (109), 1093 (68,106), 2519 (42), 2520 (42)
Pratt, M. W.: rev, 1468; ref, 1408 (1,9), 1902 (36), 2862 (605)
Pratt, S. R.: rev, 1898
Preda, C.: ref, 815 (47)
Prediger, D. J.: ref, 180 (1)
Preisser, J.: ref, 2603 (340)
Prentice, N. M.: ref, 1903 (221)
Prescott, C. A.: ref, 999 (186), 2076 (1)
Prescott, J.: ref, 2414 (1)
Prescott, S. J.: ref, 2045 (4)
Prescott, T. E.: test, 2225
Preskorn, S. H.: ref, 2107 (1)
Press, G. A.: ref, 1903 (101), 2860 (324), 2892 (45)
Pressley, M.: ref, 389 (4), 592 (12,46), 1071 (4), 1072 (18), 1903 (38,41), 2031 (2)
Presson, C. C.: ref, 1757 (2)
Presson, P. K.: ref, 462 (12), 1405 (26)
Preston, J.: rev, 2128
Preston, K.: ref, 2246 (14)
Preston, L. A.: ref, 2218 (57), 2246 (11)
Preston, M. A.: ref, 462 (19)
Preston, R. C.: rev, 2484
Preszler, B.: ref, 399 (5), 2433 (3)
Pretorius, T.: ref, 1754 (19)
Pretorius, T. B.: ref, 1590 (38), 2065 (4,7), 2497 (277)
Prettyman, R.: ref, 537 (3)
Prewett, P. N.: ref, 1386 (4,8), 1607 (9,14), 2485 (103,143)
Prewett, R. N.: ref, 763 (1)
Prezant, D. W.: ref, 2305 (10)
Preziosi, T. J.: ref, 2050 (9)
Price, A. W.: ref, 451 (287), 1903 (582)
Price, C.: ref, 999 (140)
Price, D. E.: ref, 1755 (60)
Price, G. E.: test, 1470, 2069
Price, J. M.: ref, 451 (280), 2813 (156)
Price, J. R.: ref, 1697 (294)
Price, L.: test, 925; ref, 837 (10), 2862 (462)
Price, L. H.: ref, 2305 (148), 2860 (932)
Price, R. G.: rev, 2612
Price, S. J.: ref, 863 (1), 1000 (4)
Price, T. R.: ref, 2050 (28)
Prichard, S.: ref, 1903 (137), 2862 (178)
Priday, K.: ref, 1140 (34)
Priddy, J. M.: test, 1930, 1955
Priebe, S.: ref, 1166 (206), 2497 (225)
Prien, E. P.: rev, 64, 1860
Prien, R. F.: ref, 1093 (30)
Priest, B. L.: ref, 1096 (10)
Prifitera, A.: ref, 2862 (263)
Prigatano, G. P.: ref, 1164 (51), 2860 (508), 2863 (147)
Prigerson, H. G.: ref, 1093 (99), 1166 (173), 2603 (393)
Prigitano, G. N.: rev, 1853
Prikhojan, A.: ref, 1166 (186)
Prill, K. A.: ref, 2304 (2), 2860 (48)
Primac, D. W.: ref, 2247 (42)
Primavera, L. H.: ref, 272 (322), 2452 (11)
Prince, A. T.: ref, 665 (2)
Prince, F.: ref, 1164 (182), 2516 (120), 2892 (302)
Prince, J.: ref, 2860 (1203), 2879 (187)
Prince, J. P.: ref, 1790 (18)
Prince, J. S.: test, 2527
Prince, M.: ref, 1758 (77), 2163 (298)
Prince, R. J.: ref, 2860 (824)
Prince, S. E.: ref, 272 (184)
Pring, L.: ref, 1097 (10), 1903 (267), 2163 (128,164)
Pringele, M. L. K.: rev, 1097
Pringle, C. D.: ref, 592 (95)
Pringle, M. L. K.: rev, 1989

Prino, C. T.: ref, 1401 (4)
Prins, P. J. M.: ref, 451 (99)
Prinz, R. J.: ref, 2603 (293)
Prior, M.: ref, 34 (2,3,4), 451 (44), 863 (29), 1079 (15,29), 1485 (5), 1765 (30,31), 1903 (277), 2039 (8), 2485 (68), 2599 (29), 2813 (21,48), 2862 (358,554), 2879 (89,123)
Prior, M. R.: ref, 34 (1), 2226 (3)
Pritchard, B.: test, 2184
Privette, G.: ref, 1938 (1), 1939 (7), 2862 (79)
Prizant, B. M.: test, 630, 459
Prkachin, K. M.: ref, 2516 (38)
Probe, L.: ref, 272 (70), 893 (12)
Probert, B. S.: ref, 404 (7)
Prochaska, J. O.: ref, 2858 (41)
Procidano, M.: ref, 2858 (67)
Procter, E.: ref, 999 (11)
Proctor, T. B.: ref, 1991 (73)
Prodromidis, M.: ref, 365 (8), 1216 (71), 2497 (507)
Proescher, E. J.: ref, 451 (82), 1000 (94)
Proescher, E. L.: ref, 451 (83), 1000 (95), 2230 (11)
Proger, B. B.: rev, 175, 324, 552, 1096, 1902, 2045, 2123, 2189, 2428, 2707, 2736, 2740, 2905
Prohaska, M. L.: ref, 272 (21)
Prohovnik, I.: ref, 2305 (45), 2860 (408,554,1112)
PROJECT RHISE, Children's Development Center: test, 2243
Propper, R. E.: ref, 2860 (555)
Prosser, M.: ref, 1469 (10)
Prout, H. T.: test, 931, 965, 1401, 2291
Provence: test, 1263
Pruchno, R.: ref, 863 (54)
Prudic, J.: ref, 1166 (24,148), 2305 (45)
Prue, D. M.: ref, 134 (9)
Pryor, J.: ref, 1832 (10)
Pryor, R.: test, 2915; ref, 2835 (8), 2915 (2)
Pryor, R. G. L.: ref, 2915 (3)
Pryor, T. D.: test, 300
Przybeck, T. R.: ref, 2077 (2)
Psenicka, C.: ref, 2149 (5)
Psychological Assessment Resources, Inc.: test, 2009
The Psychological Corporation: test, 15, 38, 141, 165, 246, 411, 494, 532, 627, 960, 961, 1078, 1094, 1256, 1657, 1975, 2483, 2488, 2810, 2859, 2861
Psychological Services Bureau: test, 1077, 1634, 1635, 1833, 1926, 2266, 2501
Psychological Services Bureau, Inc.: test, 1081, 2220, 2223
Psychological Services Bureau Staff: test, 2221
Psychological Services, Inc.: test, 1033, 1034, 2003
Psychometric Research Unit, The Hatfield Polytechnic: test, 1106
Ptacek, J. T.: ref, 863 (70)
Ptito, A.: ref, 1218 (1), 2125 (2), 2163 (16), 2860 (44,72,1306)
Ptito, M.: ref, 1218 (1), 2125 (2), 2163 (16), 2860 (1306)
Puccio, G. J.: ref, 1404 (7,13)
Puce, A.: ref, 1758 (6), 2163 (33)
Puckering, C.: ref, 1612 (78), 1745 (61)
Puckett, J. M.: ref, 2860 (393)
Puente, A. E.: ref, 2863 (209)
Puffer, S. M.: ref, 1338 (12)
Puffett, A.: ref, 1390 (4), 1697 (311), 1758 (26), 2193 (24), 2860 (667), 2863 (197)
Pugh, J. L.: test, 698
Pugh, K.: ref, 2050 (64,93), 2076 (97), 2239 (18), 2497 (384), 2860 (581), 2863 (168), 2892 (106)
Pugh, M. A.: ref, 373 (23), 1965 (58)
Pugh, R. C.: rev, 141, 325, 380, 2678
Pugh, S.: ref, 893 (39)
Pujol, J.: ref, 272 (309), 1164 (155), 2226 (26) 2516 (100), 2860 (1290)
Pulakos, J.: ref, 1010 (106)
Pulaski, J. L.: ref, 2860 (205), 2863 (51)
Pulkkinen, L.: ref, 999 (167)
Pullan, M. D.: ref, 256 (4), 1697 (508)
Pullen, S. M.: ref, 298 (114), 2860 (644,1095)
Pullias, E. V.: rev, 1657
Pulos, S.: ref, 272 (212), 2402 (68)
Pulver, A. E.: ref, 2050 (94)
Pulvermüller, F.: ref, 2860 (1137)
Pumariega, A. J.: ref, 272 (70), 893 (12)
Pumfrey, P. D.: test, 1489
Pumroy, D. K.: test, 1589, 2116
Punamäki, R.: ref, 998 (104), 2248 (2)
Punamäki, R.: ref, 2862 (385)
Pungello, E. P.: ref, 171 (2), 2700 (1)
Puntennay, P. J.: ref, 2076 (141)
Pupo, F. A.: ref, 2402 (26)
Purcell, S. L.: ref, 430 (12), 798 (18), 1060 (5), 1240 (35), 1903 (378), 2694 (15), 2911 (2)
Purdie, N. M.: ref, 1466 (7)
Purdon, S. E.: ref, 2497 (367)
Purdue Research Foundation: test, 2125
Purdy, R. R.: ref, 1590 (2)
Purifoy, F. E.: ref, 2407 (3)
Purisch, A. D.: test, 1525
Purser, K. C. D.: ref, 2497 (402)
Purvis, K. L.: ref, 1424 (5), 2862 (665), 2879 (214), 2911 (5)
Pusch, D.: ref, 272 (374), 1745 (88), 2305 (128)
Putallaz, M.: ref, 1716 (2)
Putnam, F.: test, 74
Putnam, F. W.: test, 846; ref, 451 (202), 472 (198,206), 846 (18), 1010 (124), 1903 (323,544), 2498 (71)
Putnam, J.: ref, 286 (3), 2862 (533)
Putnam, K.: ref, 2863 (100)
Putnam, S. H.: ref, 2193 (42,49), 2860 (936), 2863 (307)
Putzke, J. D.: ref, 1135 (27), 1164 (185), 1697 (592) 2402 (71), 2517 (8), 2599 (41), 2860 (1412), 2863 (430)
Puukko, L-R.: ref, 1832 (17)

Puura, K.: ref, 472 (227,231)
Puwak, H.: ref, 788 (1)
Pykäläinen, L.: ref, 2247 (120)
Pyle, R. L.: ref, 893 (5)
Pynes, J. E.: rev, 1575
Pyörälä, K.: ref, 2860 (913), 2863 (273)
Pyrczak, F.: rev, 1318
Pyryt, M. C.: ref, 385 (3), 1991 (93), 2753 (1), 2901 (94)
Pyskoty, C.: ref, 1661 (17), 2076 (50), 2603 (156)
Pyszczynski, T.: ref, 272 (378)

Qin, J.: ref, 451 (194), 1010 (123)
Qouta, S.: ref, 998 (104), 2862 (385)
Quackenbush, D.: ref, 68 (42)
Quadflieg, N.: ref, 2603 (252)
Qualls, A. L.: ref, 1318 (8)
Qualls, D. L.: ref, 2218 (53)
Quamma, J. P.: ref, 557 (6)
Quartetti, D. A.: ref, 1866 (35)
Quas, J. A.: ref, 451 (194), 1010 (123)
Quasha, W. H.: test, 2217
Quay, H. C.: test, 2211; ref, 2115 (1), 2862 (128)
Quay, S.: ref, 2497 (144)
Quayhagen, M.: ref, 2863 (284)
Quayhagen, M. P.: ref, 2863 (284)
Quellette, C.: ref, 2305 (165)
Quellmalz, E. S.: rev, 142, 2026
Quenk, N. L.: test, 1755
Quereshi, M. Y.: rev, 672, 838, 1156
Quiggle, N. L.: ref, 472 (36)
Quigley, H.: test, 1516
Quigley, L. A.: ref, 337 (61); ref, 652 (2)
Quinby, S. S.: test, 1167
Quinlan, D. M.: test, 215, 790; ref, 790 (8), 1093 (83), 2305 (174), 2603 (335), 2860 (1068)
Quinlin, D. M.: ref, 298 (136), 790 (19)
Quinn, J.: test, 359; ref, 1437 (3)
Quinn, M.: rev, 2801, 2902
Quinn, N.: ref, 2860 (84,85,162), 2892 (9)
Quinn, P.: ref, 1470 (4), 2069 (1)
Quinn, P. O.: ref, 1962 (17), 2288 (40), 2813 (77)
Quinsey, V. L.: ref, 853 (6), 1174 (2), 1697 (203), 2247 (30), 2749 (31)
Quintana, H.: ref, 4 (11)
Quintana, S. M.: ref, 1697 (345), 2016 (1)
Quintar, B.: ref, 2247 (82)
Quintard, B.: ref, 2497 (432), 2858 (112)
Quitkin, F. M.: ref, 1166 (130,142), 2603 (487)
Quittner, A. L.: ref, 472 (195), 863 (30), 2603 (154), 2862 (521)

Ra, J. B.: ref, 615 (6)
Raab, J.: ref, 2193 (29)
Raade, A. S.: ref, 2873 (8)
Raban, B.: test, 1261, 1530
Rabb, D.: test, 1062
Rabb, K.: ref, 1466 (2)
Rabbit, J.: test, 1230
Rabbit, P.: ref, 127 (1)
Rabbitt, P. M. A.: ref, 127 (4), 745 (12), 999 (132), 1671 (6), 2163 (235), 2860 (686,1144)
Rabenau, C. V.: ref, 739 (7), 999 (99)
Rabian, B.: ref, 2214 (33)
Rabin, A.: rev, 1540
Rabin, A. I.: rev, 466, 2247, 2862
Rabin, B. S.: ref, 2305 (133)
Rabin, L. A.: ref, 2860 (1347), 2863 (405)
Rabiner, D. L.: ref, 2860 (923), 2862 (179,362)
Rabinovich, H.: ref, 272 (253), 2305 (214)
Rabinovitz, D.: ref, 2497 (209)
Rabinovitz, Y.: ref, 2497 (209)
Rabinowitz, S.: ref, 301 (21), 2247 (22), 2749 (24), 2860 (339)
Rabins, P. V.: ref, 2289 (22)
Rabkin, J. G.: ref, 273 (23), 337 (31,34,90,91,145), 1166 (115,228), 2603 (279,299,366,549)
Rabkin, R.: ref, 337 (90)
Rabold, D. E.: ref, 1903 (412), 2163 (239)
Rachman, S. J.: ref, 1021 (16,28), 2497 (145)
Racicot, B. M.: ref, 1338 (27)
Racine, Y. A.: ref, 451 (60)
Rack, J.: ref, 349 (18)
Rack, J. P.: ref, 1092 (6)
Radan, A. E.: ref, 1216 (67), 2864 (97)
Radcliffe, J.: ref, 472 (185), 2214 (111), 2485 (18), 2497 (585), 2813 (128)
Radcliffe, J. A.: rev, 908, 1101, 1229
Radda, G. K.: ref, 350 (52), 1903 (577), 2163 (355), 2860 (1413), 2862 (730)
Radecki-Bush, C.: ref, 272 (71)
Rademaker, A. W.: ref, 1040 (6)
Radford, M. H. B.: ref, 2497 (135)
Radke-Yarrow, M.: ref, 1093 (51,100), 2076 (67), 2305 (68)
Radnitz, C. L.: ref, 272 (310)
Rado, E. D.: ref, 2497 (84)
Radocy, R. E.: rev, 90, 1320, 1751
Radojevic, V.: ref, 1010 (51), 1716 (5), 1942 (1)
Radpour, L.: ref, 2230 (9,10), 2557 (4,5)
Radziszewska, B.: ref, 472 (186)
Rae, C.: ref, 350 (52), 1903 (577), 2163 (355), 2860 (1413), 2862 (730)
Rae, G.: ref, 2163 (238)
Raffaelli, M.: ref, 1010 (39)
Rafferty, J. E.: test, 2258
Rafferty, J. P.: ref, 1590 (2)
Rafilson, F.: ref, 1763 (1)
Rafman, S.: ref, 1987 (6), 1991 (34)
Raggio, D. J.: ref, 270 (7), 1375 (1), 2813 (45,72), 2860 (509)
Raghavendra, P.: ref, 1903 (407)
Ragin, A. B.: ref, 2305 (142)
Ragins, B. R.: ref, 1701 (41)

Ragland, D.: ref, 1093 (11)
Ragland, J. D.: ref, 592 (58), 1093 (47), 2193 (16), 2860 (460), 2863 (128), 2892 (204)
Raglin, J. S.: ref, 2497 (343)
Ragni, M. V.: ref, 2603 (43)
Rahe, R. H.: ref, 2076 (174)
Raheja, S. K.: ref, 2305 (191)
Rahim, M. A.: test, 2149; ref, 2149 (4), 2149 (5)
Rahman, A.: ref, 999 (71)
Rahmani, L.: test, 1513
Raieli, V.: ref, 2860 (1051)
Raimes, A.: ref, 1664 (3)
Raimondo, D.: ref, 2860 (1051)
Rain, J. S.: rev, 859, 1479, 2551; ref, 1348 (5), 1701 (19)
Raine, A.: ref, 999 (33), 2050 (8), 2211 (43), 2305 (59), 2860 (300)
Rainer, K. L.: ref, 472 (9)
Rainforth, B.: ref, 2813 (62)
Rains, G. D.: ref, 2860 (726,727)
Rainwater, A. J., III: ref, 1021 (46), 2497 (85,672)
Rait, D. S.: ref, 1000 (35)
Raj, A. B.: ref, 2603 (64)
Rajab, M. H.: ref, 272 (134,168), 273 (10,15,20), 1687 (21), 2065 (21,22,26), 2402 (32,56), 2559 (9,10,12)
Rajapakse, J. C.: ref, 451 (102,116), 2288 (68), 2289 (52), 2862 (450,475,493)
Rajasingham, S. R.: ref, 2125 (30), 2768 (43), 2864 (144)
Rajeski, W. J.: ref, 1745 (22)
Rajkhowa, S. J.: ref, 1079 (23)
Rajorb, M. H.: ref, 272 (219), 273 (25), 2065 (29)
Raju, N. S.: rev, 1318, 1537, 2155, 2309, 2911; ref, 180 (6,10), 1866 (35)
Rakes, T. A.: test, 683
Rakfeldt, J.: ref, 1697 (356), 2305 (174), 2603 (498), 2860 (1068)
Ralph, A.: ref, 1991 (84)
Ram, R.: ref, 2102 (1), 2288 (16,24), 2289 (11), 2305 (74), 2860 (335), 2863 (88)
Ramalgia, J. M.: ref, 322 (2), 2432 (14), 2862 (184), 2879 (50)
Ramana, R.: ref, 2050 (127)
Ramanaiah, N. V.: ref, 372 (46), 2218 (23), 2417 (24)
Ramelli, E.: ref, 1166 (189)
Ramey, C. T.: ref, 270 (28), 1216 (98), 1612 (67,90), 1902 (67), 1903 (578), 2485 (162,222), 2860 (817), 2862 (240,319,598), 2864 (79,131), 2901 (39,56,112), 1903 (578)
Ramig, L. O.: ref, 272 (133), 1164 (109), 2860 (961)
Ramirez, J.: ref, 2879 (113)
Ramirez, L. F.: ref, 335 (3)
Ramirez, R.: ref, 472 (38)
Ramis, H.: ref, 2863 (99)
Ramisetty-Mikler, S.: ref, 2432 (24), 2682 (7), 2905 (75)
Ramos, E.: ref, 2862 (328)
Ramsay, A.: ref, 615 (37), 694 (34)
Ramsay, D. S.: ref, 135 (5), 2497 (624)
Ramsay, R.: ref, 2559 (1)
Ramsay, R. T.: test, 920, 923, 924, 1279, 1353, 1537, 1637, 2066, 2067, 2150, 2151, 2152, 2153, 2154, 2155, 2156, 2157, 2643, 2644, 2769, 2867
Ramsberger, G.: test, 328
Ramsey, M.: ref, 2230 (6), 2231 (4)
Ramsey, S. E.: ref, 372 (113), 1164 (166), 1661 (72), 1697 (564), 2227 (49)
Ramsey, S. L.: ref, 373 (23)
Ran, M.: ref, 2050 (106)
Ranchor, A. V.: ref, 998 (129), 999 (104), 1079 (30)
Rand, G.: test, 1159
Rand, T. M.: test, 2385
Randahl, G.: ref, 1164 (62)
Randahl, G. J.: ref, 2797 (3)
Randall, F.: ref, 2497 (588)
Randall, P.: ref, 2863 (232)
Randall, Y.: ref, 272 (214), 1697 (509), 2497 (586)
Randell, G.: ref, 999 (191), 1755 (75), 2218 (120), 2417 (39)
Randey, J.: ref, 462 (12)
Randhawa, B. S.: rev, 15, 532, 947, 1028, 1281, 1712; ref, 999 (3), 1599 (4)
Randol, P.: test, 1741
Randolph, C.: test, 2202; ref, 1164 (149), 2860 (510,511,628,1269), 2863 (384), 2879 (206), 2892 (116,162,272)
Randolph, D. L.: ref, 2835 (17)
Randolph, E. T.: ref, 1093 (72), 2050 (95), 2288 (19)
Randt, C. T.: test, 2159
Rane, P. J.: ref, 272 (157), 991 (2)
Range, L. M.: ref, 1745 (25), 2076 (42)
Ranieri, W. F.: ref, 2603 (217,310,409)
Ranjan, R.: ref, 1166 (76,78,127)
Rankhorn, B.: ref, 2862 (731)
Rankin, E. F.: rev, 901
Rankin, E. J.: ref, 2498 (23), 2863 (148), 2863 (216)
Rankin, J. L.: ref, 2497 (589)
Rankin, R. J.: ref, 307 (3), 1379 (79), 2862 (685)
Rankin, S. R.: ref, 2076 (32)
Rannek, H.: ref, 2863 (390)
Ransby, M. J.: ref, 1092 (4), 1096 (2), 1902 (19), 2862 (110), 2879 (25)
Ransom, D. C.: ref, 1000 (25)
Ranson, B. J.: ref, 2860 (1332), 2862 (660)
Rao, A.: ref, 1402 (3)
Rao, K.: ref, 4 (2), 681 (50)
Rao, N.: ref, 665 (40)
Rao, R.: ref, 893 (26)
Rao, S. M.: ref, 272 (372), 326 (3), 376 (16), 1164 (146), 1218 (4), 1740 (17)f, 2076 (185), 2163 (76), 2497 (136), 2516 (14,95), 2860 (301,561,1032, 1041), 2863 (375), 2892 (41,97,214,267)
Rao, U.: ref, 472 (12), 681 (7), 2214 (6), 2305 (216)
Raoof, A.: ref, 681 (34)
Raote, R. G.: ref, 1697 (395), 1790 (6)
Rapaport, M. H.: ref, 1166 (225), 2076 (125)
Rapaport, S. I.: ref, 2860 (971)

Rapcsak, S. Z.: ref, 376 (34), 1740 (34), 2860 (1322,1414), 2892 (305), 2193 (30), 2860 (728), 2873 (26)f, 2892 (145)
Rape, R. N.: ref, 1000 (36)
Rapee, R. M.: ref, 451 (91), 472 (74,157), 998 (40), 1021 (21), 1218 (2), 1697 (91), 2214 (36,89), 2497 (60,74,153,385), 2498 (31)
Rapesak, S. Z.: ref, 2193 (4), 2516 (5), 2860 (129), 2863 (37), 2892 (15)
Raphael, A. J.: rev, 2496, 2928
Raphael, B.: ref, 998 (127), 1079 (96), 2497 (98,644)
Rapin, I.: ref, 1096 (9), 2382 (37), 2485 (218), 2668 (1), 2680 (18), 2694 (14), 2813 (131), 2860 (912)
Rapkin, B.: ref, 2497 (69)
Rapoff, M.: ref, 472 (215), 1318 (20), 2214 (125),2862 (677)
Rapoport, J. L.: ref, 451 (102,116,243), 681 (29), 863 (42), 1093 (21), 2288 (68,71), 2289 (52,56), 2305 (103,137,169,232,242), 2860 (366), 2862 (450,475,493,501,629,702), 2879 (227)
Rapoport, S. I.: ref, 1164 (110), 1740 (11), 2010 (1,18,20), 2163 (10), 2860 (34,502,837,1141), 2863 (12,242)
Rapp, N.: ref, 459 (5), 1612 (13)
Rapp, S. R.: ref, 134 (9), 337 (80), 1166 (173)
Rappaport, D. A.: ref, 1379 (76), 2432 (27), 2862 (399)
Rappaport, L. R.: ref, 472 (42), 2498 (20)
Rappaport, M.: ref, 2108 (3)
Rapport, D. J.: ref, 1093 (110), 2305 (168)
Rapport, L. J.: ref, 376 (26), 2860 (729)
Rapport, L. J.: ref, 2860 (781,1336), 2863 (400)
Rapport, M. D.: ref, 451 (274), 1592 (10), 1903 (408)
Rapscak, S. Z.: ref, 2873 (7)
Raquet, M. L.: ref, 2860 (1157)
Räsänen, E.: ref, 472 (227,231)
Räsänen, P.: ref, 2862 (656)
Rascle, N.: ref, 2858 (112)
Rash, T. A.: ref, 2485 (134), 2813 (66)
Rashbaum, W. K.: ref, 1697 (160)
Rashes, R.: ref, 1021 (31), 1181 (19)
Rashotte, C. A.: ref, 665 (9), 2485 (12), 2862 (57)
Rasile, D. A.: ref, 2860 (962), 2863 (285)
Rasing, E. J.: ref, 1903 (205)
Raskin, A.: ref, 2017 (8), 2305 (83)
Raskin, E.: test, 474, 926, 1140; rev, 574, 596
Raskin, G.: ref, 1661 (73)
Raskin, R.: ref, 68 (16), 373 (9), 999 (6), 1291 (2), 1697 (144)
Raskin, S. A.: ref, 199 (9), 776 (11), 1740 (9)
Raskind, L. T.: rev, 903, 1921
Raskind, M.: ref, 2863 (83)
Rasku-Puttonen, H.: ref, 1903 (206,281), 2163 (129), 2247 (43), 2768 (18), 2862 (275)
Rasmussen, C. H.: ref, 2474 (1)
Rasmussen, D. E.: ref, 2127 (2)
Rasmussen, J. K.: ref, 2305 (234)
Rasmussen, M.: ref, 2288 (7), 2289 (5), 2305 (37)
Rasmussen, P. R.: ref, 2076 (126)
Rasmussen, S.: ref, 1166 (152), 1216 (88), 2603 (496)
Rasmussen, S. A.: ref, 2519 (1), 2520 (1)
Rasmusson, D. X.: ref, 2860 (963,1158)
Rasulis, R., Jr.: ref, 2258 (6)
Ratakonda, S.: ref, 2288 (85), 2289 (69)
Ratcliff, G.: ref, 199 (3), 1903 (60), 2163 (15), 2860 (43,92), 2863 (26)
Ratey, J. J.: ref, 2010 (6), 2860 (317)
Rathbone, E. A.: ref, 1386 (17)
Rathge, R. W.: ref, 694 (60)
Rathke, M. L.: ref, 2485 (76)
Rathmell, G.: test, 2688
Rathner, G.: ref, 893 (25), 1079 (48)
Rathunde, K.: ref, 1965 (43)
Rathus, J. H.: ref, 2603 (510)
Ratliff-Crain, J.: ref, 2858 (89)
Ratner, H. H.: ref, 2487 (12)
Ratner, N.: ref, 2860 (1321)
Ratner, N. B.: ref, 270 (25), 540 (23), 1095 (24), 1903 (266,554), 1982 (6), 2163 (341), 2229 (14), 2543 (3)
Ratusny, D.: ref, 999 (53)
Rauch, M.: ref, 2226 (31), 2863 (401), 2892 (286)
Rauch, S. L.: ref, 2227 (26), 2860 (1103)
Rauch-Elnekave, H.: ref, 1991 (74)
Raudenbush, S. W.: ref, 2497 (424), 2603 (232,333)
Raulin, M. L.: ref, 1096 (10)
Rausch, R.: ref, 2860 (210), 2863 (53)
Rausford, S. N.: ref, 4 (2), 681 (50)
Rauter, V. K.: ref, 2603 (488)
Ravaglia, R.: ref, 2031 (9)
Raval, J.: ref, 2860 (159)
Ravaris, C. L.: ref, 2199 (6), 2497 (346), 2519 (40)
Raven, J.: test, 900, 1671, 2163, 2478
Raven, J. C.: test, 729, 1671, 2163, 2477, 2478
Raven, L. M.: ref, 694 (88), 1697 (367), 2497 (407), 2704 (22)
Raven-Brook, L.: ref, 694 (108), 1697 (461), 2704 (35)
Ravera, G.: ref, 893 (29)
Ravest, H. T.: ref, 2050 (125)
Ravida, A. I.: ref, 214 (16), 1485 (27), 1903 (256), 2657 (15)
Ravily, V.: ref, 1166 (57)
Ravindran, A. V.: ref, 272 (213), 1166 (64,143)
Ravindran, L.: ref, 2305 (212)
Ravitch, M. M.: rev, 1659
Ravitz, B.: ref, 999 (31), 1592 (9), 1697 (135)
Raviv, A.: ref, 495 (3), 2163 (91), 2860 (376)
Raviv, D.: ref, 798 (5), 1832 (3)
Rawlings, R.: ref, 1697 (369), 1965 (33), 2305 (87), 2860 (536,778)
Rawlings, R. R.: ref, 1164 (90), 1592 (21), 1962 (17), 2225 (7), 2288 (40), 2497 (456,626), 2813 (77), 2860 (848), 2863 (246), 2892 (175)

Rawson, H. E.: ref, 464 (2), 1803 (1), 2497 (386)
Rawson, M. D.: ref, 272 (218)
Ray, C.: ref, 926 (11), 2516 (31)
Ray, G. E.: rev, 1851
Ray, J. J.: ref, 363 (1)
Ray, K. P.: ref, 2862 (691)
Ray, M.: ref, 1767 (2)
Raychaudhuri, M.: rev, 914
Rayens, M. K.: ref, 448 (29)
Rayfield, A.: ref, 2595 (2)
Raygor, A. L.: rev, 2174
Rayki, O.: ref, 2603 (495)
Raykov, T.: ref, 1405 (29)
Rayman, J. R.: ref, 2360 (13)
Raymer, A.: ref, 2873 (62)
Raymer, A. M.: ref, 1164 (167), 2873 (32), 2873 (70,71), 2892 (285)
Raymond, C. L.: ref, 615 (7)
Raymond, N. C.: ref, 2497 (313)
Rayne, F. D.: rev, 298
Raynor, A. L.: rev, 1767
Raz, N.: ref, 745 (14), 1405 (27), 2860 (759), 2892 (151)
Razavich, A.: ref, 301 (26), 1097 (8), 2864 (30)
Razzano, C.: ref, 1166 (185)
Rea, M. R.: ref, 1745 (59)
Read, M. R.: test, 2107
Read, N. O.: ref, 200 (2)
Read, N. W.: ref, 1965 (82), 2218 (106), 2749 (79)
Read, T.: ref, 2305 (141,180)
Reagle, D. Y.: ref, 1444 (1)
Realini, J. P.: ref, 2603 (537)
Realmuto, G. M.: ref, 280 (4), 472 (154), 681 (84,57,71), 1010 (68), 1380 (3,9,10), 1991 (76), 2214 (88), 2452 (4), 2879 (99,152), 2901 (49,82)
Realo, A.: ref, 2218 (111)
Reams, R.: ref, 853 (18), 997 (19), 1903 (298), 2039 (13)
Reardon, R.: ref, 1697 (126), 2360 (6)
Reardon, R. C.: test, 422
Reardon, S. M.: ref, 1379 (32), 1607 (2), 2860 (504), 2879 (62), 2901 (33)
Reason, R.: test, 1980
Reasoner, J.: ref, 303 (1), 791 (2), 1740 (3), 2497 (21), 2516 (2), 2603 (8), 2860 (81)
Reaume, W. M.: ref, 337 (88,89)
Reaven, N. M.: ref, 472 (43)
Rebeta, J. L.: ref, 2497 (278), 2656 (9)
Rebok, G. W.: ref, 472 (86)
Reboy, L. M.: ref, 2856 (6)
Rebull, E. : ref, 999 (103)
Rech, J. F.: ref, 364 (21), 1140 (51), 1599 (5,6), 1991 (95)
Reckase, M. D.: rev, 2212
Records, N. L.: ref, 798 (10), 1096 (13) 1240 (29,39), 1379 (55), 1903 (146,299,558), 2524 (11), 2657 (17,27), 2694 (19), 2695 (29,45,63), 2725 (1,6), 2860 (409,730), 2862 (284) 2864 (125)
Rector, N.: ref, 1697 (529)
Rector, N. A.: ref, 2050 (58), 2603 (238)
Redbrake, A.: ref, 2860 (944)
Redd, W. H.: ref, 2076 (89), 2497 (69,256)
Reddin, W. J.: test, 631, 633, 747, 1547, 1548, 1561, 1855, 2278, 2349, 2561, 2562, 2563, 2564, 2568, 2570, 2576, 2803, 2937
Reddon, J. R.: ref, 256 (4), 1213 (1), 1333 (5), 1697 (508), 2860 (1386)
Reddy, M.: ref, 337 (91), 2603 (299)
Reder, A. T.: ref, 272 (209), 1164 (131), 2125 (24), 2516 (83), 2863 (343)
Redford, J. L.: ref, 1755 (58)
Redick, E.: ref, 1770 (4)
Redington, D.: ref, 2603 (187)
Redington, D. J.: ref, 2603 (266)
Redwine, L.: ref, 2603 (516)
Ree, M. J.: ref, 180 (23,24,32), 592 (79)
Reed, C. A.: test, 2918
Reed, D.: ref, 272 (314), 998 (131)
Reed, D. A.: ref, 272 (77)
Reed, D. L.: ref, 2497 (137)
Reed, E.: ref, 1010 (69), 1092 (11), 2860 (801), 2862 (308), 2879 (100)
Reed, E. D.: ref, 1010 (70), 1092 (12), 1092 (13), 2305 (121), 2860 (802), 2862 (309,310), 2879 (101,102)
Reed, G. M.: ref, 791 (11), 2858 (82)
Reed, H. B. C., Jr.: test, 2491; rev, 1206, 1901, 2377
Reed, J. C.: rev, 80, 456, 2430, 2599
Reed, J. R.: test, 569, 938
Reed, K. G.: test, 716
Reed, M. A.: ref, 999 (77,134), 2497 (327,508)
Reed, M. K.: ref, 272 (214,215), 472 (99), 694 (82), 1697 (346,509,510), 1962 (16), 2497 (586,587), 2858 (118)
Reed, M. L.: rev, 997
Reed, T.: ref, 303 (26,30), 459 (34), 1380 (2), 1903 (300), 2599 (42), 2860 (1382)
Reed, T. E.: ref, 2163 (130)
Reed, T. L.: ref, 1697 (70)
Reeder, K. P.: ref, 376 (4)
Reedy, S.: ref, 2497 (356)
Reeman, I. M.: ref, 272 (229), 1697 (520)
Rees, A.: ref, 272 (115,116,217,311), 2603 (301,359,360,403)
Rees, J. E.: ref, 1758 (28), 2860 (713), 2863 (211), 2892 (140)
Reese, H. W.: ref, 2860 (362)
Reeve, J.: ref, 1001 (11)
Reeves, A. G.: ref, 2860 (1222), 2863 (362)
Regard, M.: ref, 2193 (5), 2860 (161)
Regier, D.: ref, 2050 (10)
Regier, D. A.: ref, 1903 (533)
Regimbal, C.: ref, 324 (7)
Regis, H. A.: ref, 708 (2)
Reglin, G. L.: ref, 615 (18)
Regmi, M.: ref, 2540 (6)

Rehabilitation Research and Training Center on Blindness and Low Vision: test, 922
Rehm, M.: ref, 2369 (11)
Rehman, H.: ref, 2 (1), 2813 (90)
Reich, J.: ref, 1093 (16,68,73,101), 1517 (9), 2305 (178), 2519 (2,13,42,46), 2520 (2,13,42,47)
Reich, J. H.: ref, 337 (4), 998 (57), 1093 (52), 1517 (6), 1697 (236), 2076 (157), 2519 (3,4), 2520 (3,4)
Reich, J. N.: ref, 2864 (42)
Reich, J. W.: ref, 998 (14,39)
Reich, T.: ref, 2305 (13)
Reichard, C. C.: ref, 1903 (409)
Reichardt, C. S.: ref, 134 (25)
Reichel, A.: ref, 592 (11)
Reichler, R. J.: test, 459, 2111
Reid, B.: test, 2052
Reid, D. K.: test, 2680, 2682, 2683, 2369 (5)
Reid, H.: ref, 2603 (397,398)
Reid, J. C.: ref, 451 (165), 473 (4,8), 1000 (86), 1962 (4), 1991 (39), 2214 (26,129), 2603 (569), 2862 (183)
Reid, M. K.: ref, 1592 (2), 2862 (26)
Reid, N.: test, 21, 22, 25, 358, 2100, 2622, 2714
Reid, N. A.: test, 2090, 2091, 2093, 2094, 2095
Reid, P. T.: ref, 615 (39)
Reid Psychological Systems: test, 2198
Reid, R.: test, 67, 75 (1), 694 (76), 1379 (33,56), 1386 (9), 2211 (31,34), 2432 (20), 2485 (104,144,145), 2862 (276,285), 2864 (67), 2879 (90), 2901 (46)
Reidbord, S. P.: ref, 2603 (266)
Reiff, H. B.: ref, 1701 (23)
Reifler, B. V.: ref, 2863 (83)
Reifman, A.: ref, 1770 (15)
Reilley, R. R.: ref, 1697 (273), 2860 (597)
Reilly, B. A.: rev, 1178, 1723
Reilly, J. S.: test, 1528; ref, 1001 (14)
Reilly, K.: ref, 540 (4)
Reilly, M. E.: test, 1044
Reilly, S.: ref, 2860 (756)
Reimer, J. F.: ref, 2862 (507), 2879 (170)
Rein, A. S.: ref, 272 (369)
Rein, W.: ref, 2603 (539)
Reinarz, D.: ref, 272 (70), 893 (12)
Reinberg, J. A.: ref, 2860 (145), 2862 (93)
Reinehr, R. C.: rev, 190, 466, 837, 928, 965, 2863, 2429
Reinhart, B.: ref, 2860 (525), 2892 (88)
Reinhart, M. A.: ref, 790 (29)
Reinhart, M. I.: ref, 999 (50), 1333 (2,7,8), 1965 (7), 1991 (47)
Reinherz, H. Z.: ref, 472 (190)
Reinhold, D. P.: ref, 2076 (11)
Reinikainen, K. J.: ref, 2860 (913), 2863 (273)
Reinink, E.: ref, 1166 (48)
Reinkemeier, M.: ref, 2226 (31), 2863 (401), 2892 (286)
Reis, D. J.: ref, 1166 (109)
Reis, H. T.: ref, 1735 (9), 2077 (6)
Reis, S. M.: ref, 1474 (2), 2487 (17)
Reisberg, B.: ref, 1164 (156), 2125 (26), 2860 (1295)
Reisboard, R. J.: rev, 1362
Reise, S. P.: ref, 2218 (117)
Reisel, E.: ref, 495 (3)
Reisman, F. K.: test, 2383
Reisman, J. E.: test, 2378
Reisman, S.: ref, 1218 (3), 2860 (276)
Reiss, A.: ref, 1166 (28), 2813 (116)
Reiss, A. D.: ref, 68 (59), 189 (1), 372 (105), 998 (120), 1697 (504), 2417 (36)
Reiss, A. L.: ref, 681 (66), 2860 (351,1167,1409), 2862 (393,437,548,727), 2892 (253,303), 2901 (72,100)
Reiss, D.: ref, 372 (104), 472 (47,62,113,142,184,229), 1216 (72), 2860 (467,690)
Reiss, S.: test, 2199; ref, 2199 (14), 2497 (186)
Reitan, R. M.: test, 1164; rev, 1218, 1854
Reiter, G.: ref, 2860 (333)
Reiter, J.: ref, 337 (115,116)
Reitsma, P.: ref, 2441 (1)
Reitz, W.: test, 2355
Reivich, M.: ref, 2288 (48), 2289 (37)
Rejeski, W. J.: ref, 68 (8)
Rellinger, E.: ref, 1619 (4), 2862 (386), 2879 (133)
Remick, R.: ref, 335 (1), 2289 (6)
Remien, R. H.: ref, 273 (23), 337 (31,34,145), 1166 (115), 2603 (279,366,549), 2860 (407)
Remillard, G.: ref, 776 (52), 1164 (163), 1218 (18), 2226 (28), 2227 (46)
Reminger, S. L.: ref, 376 (34), 1740 (34), 2860 (1414), 2892 (305)
Remmers, H. H.: test, 1221; rev, 363, 1184, 1318
Remsberg, S.: ref, 2010 (17), 2402 (34), 2860 (761)
Renaud, C.: ref, 1140 (1), 2163 (6)
Renault, B.: ref, 2860 (130)
Renck, R.: test, 2808; ref, 2305 (224)
Rende, R. D.: ref, 472 (62)
Renfrey, G.: ref, 1021 (26); ref, 2603 (294)
Renick, M. J.: ref, 2862 (87)
Renken, B.: ref, 373 (7), 2862 (88)
Renn, J. A.: ref, 298 (90)
Renneberg, B.: ref, 2497 (86,163), 2520 (14)
Renner, B. R.: test, 459
Rennie, B. J.: ref, 1071 (3), 1866 (1)
Renninger, K. A.: rev, 1468
Renowden, S.: ref, 303 (19), 2227 (48), 2860 (1323), 2863 (398), 2892 (283)
Renshaw, P. D.: ref, 2540 (5)
Renshaw, P. F.: ref, 451 (187), 2305 (222), 2813 (140), 2860 (1210), 2862 (611), 2879 (202), 2905 (109)
Rensis Likert Associates, Inc.: test, 2435, 2587
Rentsch, J. R.: ref, 1348 (13), 1701 (48)
Rentz, A. L.: ref, 2527 (4)
Renzi, E. D.: ref, 2163 (185)
Renzulli, J. S.: test, 1474, 2295; rev, 2754, 1474 (2), 2487 (17)
Repacholi, B.: ref, 2039 (10), 2860 (280)
Repka, F. J.: ref, 1338 (31, 1686 (3)

Repman, J.: ref, 1318 (6)
Repp, A. C.: ref, 2485 (56)
Rerecich, R.: ref, 2115 (5)
Resar, L.: ref, 375 (8), 2720 (1), 2892 (297)
Resch, F.: ref, 745 (24)
Reschly, D. J.: ref, 301 (58), 853 (22), 1348 (12), 1902 (2), 2749 (72), 2862 (15,580), 2879 (188)f, 2901 (105)
Rescoria, L.: ref, 451 (13), 1903 (88), 2485 (40), 2862 (139), 2879 (36)
Rescorla, L.: ref, 270 (4,24,25), 270 (37), 994 (49), 1528 (7), 2229 (1,13,14,16), 2657 (35), 2813 (152)
Research Staff, United Consultants: test, 2784
Reske, J. R.: ref, 1580 (4), 2034 (2)
Resnick, G.: ref, 451 (1)
Resnick, H.: rev, 692, 1599
Resnick, H. S.: ref, 1697 (496)
Resnick, S. M.: ref, 303 (21), 592 (58), 2288 (48), 2289 (37), 2860 (964)
Resnikoff, M.: rev, 1146, 2247
Respess, D.: ref, 451 (260)
Rest, J.: ref, 771 (22)
Rest, J. R.: test, 771
Resta, S. P.: ref, 301 (43), 2935 (2)
Restall, G.: ref, 1653 (18), 2813 (73), 2864 (68)
Restrepo, M. A.: ref, 266 (1,3), 1047 (2,6), 1240 (9), 1379 (77), 1485 (11), 1903 (138), 2382 (12), 2524 (10), 2680 (13)
Retish, P.: ref, 413 (30)
Rettew, D. C.: ref, 863 (42)
Retzlaff, P.: rev, 132, 792, 1165, 1685, 1687, 2496; ref, 2860 (773), 2863 (266), 2892 (155)
Retzlaff, P. D.: ref, 687 (3), 1687 (14), 2863 (345)
Reubin, R.: ref, 1010 (6)
Reuland, M.: ref, 372 (63), 999 (81), 1697 (284)
Reuter, J.: test, 1391
Reuterman, N. A.: ref, 1697 (235)
Reutzel, D. R.: ref, 592 (67), 665 (35), 1072 (26,27), 1318 (7)
Reveley, M. A.: ref, 1758 (35,36), 2163 (205,206), 2288 (46,47), 2289 (35,36), 2305 (126,127), 2892 (170,171)
Revelle, W.: ref, 998 (10,61), 999 (8)
Revenson, T. A.: ref, 2858 (1)
Reves, J. G.: ref, 2497 (436)
Revich, M.: ref, 1672 (1)
Revicki, D. A.: ref, 1166 (222,226)
Rexnikoff, M.: ref, 2247 (80)
Rey, J. M.: ref, 472 (7)
Rey, M.: ref, 2863 (261), 2892 (183)
Reyes, C.: ref, 307 (2)
Reyes, E.: ref, 999 (127)
Reyes, J. A. S.: ref, 2218 (90)
Reyes, O.: ref, 2879 (79)
Reyes, P.: ref, 1701 (30)
Reyes, S.: ref, 337 (28,106), 472 (139), 2498 (54), 2858 (30)
Reyes-Lagunes, I.: ref, 1697 (321)
Reynell, J. K.: test, 2229
Reynolds, A.: ref, 788 (2), 1010 (53)
Reynolds, A. J.: ref, 1318 (4,12,24), 1759 (6)
Reynolds, C. A.: ref, 2433 (1)
Reynolds, C. F.: ref, 1093 (74,78,79,99,113), 2603 (393)
Reynolds, C. F., III: ref, 272 (233), 337 (72,156), 793 (14), 824 (1), 1093 (63), 1166 (104,163,173, 182, 215), 2305 (23,173)
Reynolds, C. K.: rev, 1687
Reynolds, C. M.: ref, 2159 (2), 2860 (131)
Reynolds, C. R.: test, 245, 280, 2214, 2701, 1062, 1079, 1962, 2017, 2414, 2517, 2606; ref, 280 (6), 2214 (122,137), 2862 (534,733)
Reynolds, D. M.: test, 1775
Reynolds, G. D.: ref, 2050 (8)
Reynolds, J.: ref, 200 (5), 1455 (5)
Reynolds, K. D.: ref, 472 (38)
Reynolds, M.: ref, 271 (4), 272 (216)
Reynolds, M. C.: rev, 1092
Reynolds, R. E.: ref, 2879 (82)
Reynolds, R. M.: ref, 1697 (457)
Reynolds, S.: ref, 272 (115,116,217), 1000 (90), 1079 (44), 2050 (123), 2603 (301,359,360,403)
Reynolds, S. B.: rev, 35, 1731
Reynolds, W. M.: test, 77, 89, 175, 1166, 2230, 2231, 2232, 2557, 2870, 2432, 2768; ref, 89 (1), 1166 (227), 2230 (20)
Reyome, N. D.: ref, 1161 (2)
Rezai, K.: ref, 650 (13), 1093 (39), 2227 (3), 2860 (181)
Rezek, P. J.: ref, 893 (8)
Reznick, J. S.: test, 1528; ref, 2382 (6,16), 2497 (195)
Reznik, I.: ref, 1745 (64), 2076 (137)
Reznikoff, M.: ref, 272 (160), 372 (38), 793 (2), 926 (8), 1697 (181), 1716 (1), 2247 (24,115), 2603 (22), 2749 (75), 2858 (67), 2862 (602), 2879 (200)
Rezvani, M.: ref, 1000 (86)
Rhea, S. A.: ref, 2076 (25)
Rheaume, J.: ref, 2065 (16)
Rheiner, N. W.: test, 2197
Rhines, J. S.: ref, 2603 (561)
Rhines, K. C.: ref, 2603 (561)
Rhoades, H. M.: ref, 2603 (551) 2860 (132)
Rhoades, K.: ref, 1216 (4)
Rhodes, B.: ref, 893 (10), 1685 (1)
Rhodes, C.: ref, 298 (11)
Rhodes, G. S.: rev, 2825
Rhodes, J. E.: ref, 2603 (155,209,295,381)
Rhodes, K.: ref, 2076 (80)
Rhodes, R. L.: ref, 809 (2), 1903 (549), 2864 (140)
Rhodes, S. R.: ref, 1694 (2,8), 1695 (1,2)
Rhodes, V.: ref, 2497 (221)
Rhue, J. W.: ref, 1697 (12), 2247 (3)
Rhyner, P. M. P.: ref, 2651 (8)
Riach, J.: ref, 358 (7), 1903 (241)
Ricard, R. J.: ref, 2704 (33)
Riccardi, V.: ref, 2860 (1321)
Ricci, C.: ref, 2860 (211), 2892 (25)

Ricciardi, A. M.: ref, 473 (2), 1697 (445)
Ricciardi, J. N., II: ref, 1697 (51)
Ricciardi, P. W.: ref, 1379 (81), 1902 (79), 1903 (440), 2228 (20), 2657 (28)
Riccio, C. A.: ref, 229 (1), 280 (5), 451 (231), 2813 (46), 2862 (535)
Riccio, L.: ref, 1697 (204), 2050 (64,93), 2076 (97), 2239 (18), 2497 (384), 2860 (581), 2863 (168), 2892 (106)
Riccomini, A. R.: test, 686
Rice, D. M.: ref, 301 (18), 2860 (302), 2863 (79)
Rice, G. H., Jr.: ref, 1755 (7)
Rice, J. A.: rev, 815; ref, 337 (124), 2163 (253), 2517 (6), 2820 (1), 2892 (212), 2305 (111)
Rice, K. G.: ref, 2525 (6)
Rice, M.: test, 2629
Rice, M. E.: ref, 1174 (2)
Rice, M. L.: ref, 265 (10), 324 (8), 624 (9,10, 18,20, 22,23,27,29), 1095 (16,17,23,27,36,42), 1379 (45,57, 75), 1903 (7,139,202,207,259,273,301, 400,410,415, 493, 519), 2229 (3,6), 2382 (1), 2485 (133, 146), 2695 (44,59), 2704 (31), 2862 (374), 2864 (57,69)
Rice, R. R.: ref, 1164 (73), 2860 (722), 2892 (143)
Rice, V.: ref, 2860 (184), 2862 (105)
Rich, A. R.: ref, 1010 (1), 2065 (1)
Rich, B. S.: test, 1315
Rich, C.: ref, 2102 (1), 2288 (16), 2289 (11), 2860 (335), 2863 (88)
Rich, D. A.: ref, 2217 (1)
Rich, J. B.: ref, 2860 (1160), 2863 (346)
Rich, L.: ref, 451 (69)f, 472 (140)
Rich, S.: ref, 2485 (19), 2768 (4), 2813 (4), 2860 (142), 2892 (17)
Richard, G. J.: test, 1424; ref, 1825 (1)
Richard, K.: ref, 2497 (330)
Richards, A.: ref, 272 (172), 2497 (63,509,555,588)
Richards, B. C.: ref, 1697 (99)
Richards, C.: ref, 2862 (483), 2879 (162)
Richards, C. M.: ref, 469 (2), 2862 (387), 2879 (134)
Richards, C. S.: ref, 272 (30)
Richards, D.: test, 191; ref, 999 (62), 2497 (276)
Richards, F. W.: ref, 2045 (4)
Richards, G. E.: ref, 2358 (1)
Richards, H.: ref, 2862 (714)
Richards, H. C.: ref, 2211 (17)
Richards, J. M., Jr.: rev, 963, 1638, 2445
Richards, J. S.: ref, 1014 (7)
Richards, L.: ref, 372 (76)
Richards, L. A.: ref, 893 (39)
Richards, M.: ref, 2125 (7), 2163 (124), 2516 (16,28), 2860 (310,496,512)
Richards, M. H.: ref, 472 (100), 694 (112), 1010 (104), 1832 (13), 1881 (3), 2652 (9)
Richards, P. M.: ref, 1135 (15), 1164 (107), 1697 (341) 1903 (405), 2860 (717,954), 2863 (281,282), 2879 (132)
Richards, R. A.: rev, 972, 2032, 2093, 2668, 2687
Richards, R. G.: test, 2821
Richards, R. L.: rev, 711, 2245
Richards, S. K.: ref, 1687 (22)
Richardson, Bellows, Henry & Co., Inc.: test, 390, 534, 1430, 1566, 1633, 2164, 2165, 2166, 2167, 2168, 2169, 2170, 2573, 2696
Richardson, C. C.: ref, 337 (103), 372 (94), 1706 (3), 2858 (102)
Richardson, D.: ref, 2288 (15), 2289 (10), 2305 (62)
Richardson, D. T.: ref, 451 (46), 1093 (100)
Richardson, E.: test, 769; ref, 1218 (16), 2599 (35), 2863 (317), 2892 (259)
Richardson, F. J., Jr.: ref, 2497 (650)
Richardson, J. L.: ref, 472 (186)
Richardson, J. T. E.: ref, 592 (96)
Richardson, K.: ref, 127 (5), 2163 (299)
Richardson, M. W.: rev, 1315
Richardson, N. A.: ref, 2288 (54), 2289 (41)
Richardson, P. K.: ref, 353 (4), 1673 (5), 1901 (9)
Richardson, R. L.: ref, 2860 (755), 2863 (221)
Richardson, S.: test, 2539
Richardson, S. A.: ref, 2485 (58)
Richardson, V.: ref, 2749 (1)
Richer, C.: ref, 863 (84), 2858 (124)
Richer, F.: ref, 2860 (1161)
Richert, E. S.: ref, 665 (3), 1142 (1), 2163 (17), 2355 (2), 2606 (1), 2862 (27)
Richeson, C.: ref, 2065 (25)
Richey, E. T.: ref, 1740 (2)
Richey, M. H.: test, 2116
Richgels, D. J.: ref, 324 (9), 2485 (14)
Richman, C. L.: ref, 1991 (57)
Richman, H.: ref, 998 (78), 1705 (4), 2497 (387)
Richman, J. A.: ref, 1661 (7,17,48), 2076 (50), 2603 (60,156)
Richman, L.: ref, 2862 (147)
Richman, L. C.: ref, 301 (25), 2862 (666)
Richman, N.: test, 2038
Richmond, B. O.: test, 465, 2214; rev, 1162, 2214 (47,122)
Richmond International, Inc.: test, 1159
Richmond, T. S.: ref, 1745 (85)
Richmond-Welty, E. D.: ref, 2879 (146)
Richter, M. A.: ref, 2305 (112)
Richters, J.: ref, 2214 (33)
Richters, J. E.: ref, 2214 (104)
Richtsmeier, A. J.: ref, 2497 (251)
Rickabaugh, C. A.: ref, 2603 (591)
Rickards, S.: ref, 462 (25)
Ricke, M. L.: ref, 644 (2), 682 (1)
Rickels, K.: ref, 998 (23,58), 1697 (106), 2603 (296)
Ricker, J. H.: ref, 376 (4,26), 776 (19), 1218 (9), 2193 (31,42), 2860 (731,936,1336), 2863 (400)
Rickert, V. I.: ref, 815 (13), 1135 (11), 2862 (229), 2903 (1)
Rickler, K.: ref, 1962 (17), 2288 (40), 2813 (77)
Rickman, M. D.: ref, 998 (79)

Rickwood, D. J.: ref, 1079 (49)
Riddel, J.: ref, 1056 (2)
Riddle, M. A.: ref, 1093 (31), 1379 (72), 1386 (18), 2813 (10,99)
Riddle, M. W.: ref, 303 (1), 791 (2), 1740 (3), 2497 (21), 2516 (2), 2603 (8), 2860 (81)
Riddle, W.: ref, 1166 (65), 2863 (207)
Riddoch, M. J.: test, 314
Ridenour, T. A.: rev, 1963; ref, 1697 (565)
Rideout, B. E.: ref, 2485 (212,235)
Rider, D. D.: ref, 665 (61)
Rider, K.: test, 892
Ridgeway, M. M.: ref, 1423 (1), 2485 (171), 2695 (42), 2860 (928), 2864 (98)
Ridgley, J.: ref, 2227 (8), 2860 (364), 2879 (44), 2892 (54)
Riding, M.: ref, 1135 (17), 1164 (119), 2862 (435), 2879 (153)
Ridley, C. A.: ref, 1036 (6)
Ridley, R. M.: ref, 2239 (12)
Ridley, S. E.: rev, 2370
Ridout, K. L.: ref, 272 (107), 2497 (445)
Riecher-Rossler, A.: ref, 2050 (33)
Rieck, M.: ref, 1612 (88)
Riedel, R. G., II.: ref, 298 (91)
Riedel, W.: ref, 2516 (80)
Rieder, C.: ref, 2247 (2), 2862 (6)
Riedesel, C. A.: rev, 2736
Rief, W.: ref, 2603 (252,264,489)
Riegel, B. J.: ref, 2076 (187)
Rieke, M. L.: ref, 694 (45)
Riekkinen, P.: ref, 776 (3), 2860 (103)
Riekkinen, P. J.: ref, 2860 (913), 2863 (273)
Riekkinen, P. J., Sr.: ref, 1164 (152), 2516 (99), 2892 (274)
Riemann, D.: ref, 1166 (144)
Riemann, R.: ref, 2218 (112)
Rierdan, J.: ref, 2380 (8)
Ries, B. J.: ref, 2516 (70)
Ries, R.: ref, 272 (142), 1687 (18), 2497 (527)
Riesch, G.: ref, 2860 (684)
Riesch, S. K.: ref, 1000 (55)
Riesenmy, K. R.: ref, 2107 (2), 2603 (394)
Rietz, E. G.: rev, 49
Rifai, A. H.: ref, 1093 (74,104)
Rifat, S. L.: ref, 1166 (73)
Rifkin, A.: ref, 1093 (35,75), 1166 (17), 2603 (24)
Rifkin, L.: ref, 2305 (199)
Rigby, E. D.: ref, 2858 (67)
Rigby, H.: ref, 1965 (76)
Riger, S.: ref, 2305 (38)
Riggio, R. E.: test, 2451; ref, 998 (6);, 1437 (4)
Riggs, D. S.: ref, 1001 (13), 2497 (463,464), 2519 (54), 2520 (53)
Riggs, E. R.: test, 692
Riggs, J. M.: rev, 746, 2366, 2368
Riggs, M. L.: ref, 1701 (42,43)
Riggs, P. D.: ref, 2860 (1186), 2862 (565)
Riguls, J.: ref, 1517 (12), 2305 (201)
Rijpma, S. E.: ref, 2497 (285)
Riklan, M.: ref, 2159 (2), 2860 (131)
Rikli, R. E.: test, 2455
Riley, A. M.: test, 2215
Riley, D.: ref, 337 (18)
Riley, E.: ref, 1745 (13)
Riley, G. D.: test, 1850, 2235, 2542, 2543
Riley, J.: test, 1850
Riley, L. R.: ref, 1866 (44)
Riley, M.: test, 975
Riley, N. J.: ref, 1866 (44)
Riley, S.: test, 2236
Riley, W. T.: ref, 472 (31), 1215 (2), 2214 (22)
Rilliet, B.: ref, 2516 (60), 2860 (789), 2892 (158)
Rilling, L. M.: ref, 376 (19), 776 (42)
Rime, B.: ref, 1338 (13)
Rimer, B. K.: ref, 2076 (151), 2218 (40)
Rimm, S.: ref, 35 (1), 1142 (3), 1143 (1), 1902 (7), 2862 (54)
Rimm, S. B.: test, 35, 36, 1136, 1142, 1143, 2037; ref, 1902 (37)
Rimmerman, A.: ref, 1010 (107), 1590 (5)
Rinaldi, A.: ref, 2305 (78), 2860 (452)
Rinard, K. D.: ref, 270 (34), 1216 (101), 1903 (530), 2382 (38)
Rinck, M.: ref, 2497 (304)
Rind, B. : ref, 592 (69)
Rinehart, S. D.: ref, 1072 (30,39)
Rinfret, N.: ref, 1965 (36), 2497 (185)
Ring, A.: ref, 681 (96), 2305 (247)
Ring, H. A.: ref, 2193 (18), 2860 (501)
Ring, N.: ref, 2050 (46)
Ringel, L.: test, 704
Ringel, N. B.: ref, 1525 (11), 2860 (248)
Ringelberg, H.: ref, 2247 (114)
Ringree, C.: ref, 2862 (486)
Ringrose, J.: ref, 451 (99)
Rinn, R. C.: ref, 2247 (76)
Rinne, J.: ref, 272 (273)
Rinne, J. O.: ref, 2860 (1113)
Rintelmann, J.: ref, 473 (5)
Rintelmann, J. W.: ref, 798 (4), 1092 (3), 1131 (5), 1240 (4), 1392 (2), 1902 (14), 1903 (42), 2305 (192), 2432 (8), 2484 (1), 2879 (21)
Rio, A.: ref, 1010 (15), 1991 (4)
Riordan, C.: ref, 592 (68)
Riordan, H.: ref, 326 (5), 2288 (21), 2289 (13), 2305 (66), 2892 (52), 2905 (24)
Riordan, J.: ref, 1758 (74), 2860 (1135)
Riordan, R. J.: ref, 413 (16), 2813 (36)
Rios, P.: ref, 350 (13), 901 (1), 1653 (13), 2163 (145), 2228 (11), 2860 (571)
Rioux, P.: ref, 2516 (64), 2863 (248)
Ripich, D. N.: ref, 1903 (411,550), 2226 (32), 2710 (7)
Ripley, J. S.: ref, 717 (2), 863 (92)
Rippetoe, L. R.: ref, 1697 (88), 2402 (6)

Ripple, C. H.: ref, 472 (95), 2214 (53), 2478 (1)
Risberg, J.: ref, 2497 (415)
Risch, N.: ref, 2862 (486)
Risch, S. C.: ref, (2305)
Risen, C. B.: ref, 863 (58), 2497 (421), 2603 (330)
Risinger, C. F.: test, 2735
Risinger, R.: ref, 298 (140)
Risinger, R. T.: ref, 2218 (19)
Risk & Needs Assessment, Inc.: test, 19, 849, 1335, 2061, 2285, 2393, 2403
Riso, L. P.: ref, 790 (14), 863 (7), 999 (147,168), 1166 (88,145,207), 1953 (2), 2305 (233)
Risser, M. G.: ref, 301 (34), 303 (5), 2862 (220), 2879 (64)
Risser, R.: ref, 1164 (65), 1697 (303), 2860 (648), 2863 (188)
Ristow, R. S.: ref, 413 (30)
Risucci, D. A.: ref, 376 (24), 1687 (28), 1903 (541), 2860 (1310), 2901 (125)
Ritacco, D. G.: ref, 451 (258), 681 (92), 1099 (5), 1164 (177), 1379 (101), 1740 (31), 2516 (118), 2892 (299)
Ritchie, D.: ref, 665 (68)
Ritchie, G. F.: ref, 451 (102), 2305 (169), 2862 (450)
Ritchie, K. L.: ref, 2065 (6)
Ritenour, A.: ref, 1093 (63,113)
Ritter, A.: ref, 2860 (1228), 2863 (366)
Ritter, W.: ref, 2146 (14,18), 2860 (621,884)
Ritterman, S. I.: ref, 2008 (8)
Rittler, M. C.: test, 1159
Ritvo, P. G.: ref, 376 (11), 2860 (1189), 2892 (258)
Ritzen, E. M.: ref, 1164 (63)
Ritzler, B.: ref, 1140 (59), 1697 (593), 2247 (133)
Riva, D.: ref, 1903 (579), 2225 (21)
Rivas-Chacon, R.: ref, 2498 (67)
Rivelli, S.: ref, 2076 (113), 2497 (450)
Rivera, C.: rev, 951, 2032
Rivera, D. M.: test, 2730
Rivera, D. P.: test, 198
Rivera, J.: ref, 2749 (59)
Rivera-Stein, M. A.: ref, 1592 (7)
Rivero, V. V.: ref, 1697 (304)
Riverside Publishing: test, 1285, 2241
Rivier, J.: ref, 2305 (50)
Rivière, A.: ref, 270 (10), 1653 (23)
Rizzardi, M.: ref, 2485 (214)
Rizzi, D. A.: ref, 337 (13)
Rizzi, L. P.: ref, 1962 (19)
Rizzo, L.: ref, 2288 (49), 2289 (38), 2860 (902), 2863 (271)
Rizzo, M.: ref, 2860 (558,1337), 2863 (161)
Rizzo, T. A.: ref, 1386 (25), 2860 (1338), 2862 (667)
Roach, M. A.: ref, 337 (21,127), 1216 (12,76)
Roache, J.: ref, 1661 (35,75), 2603 (317,556)
Roark, A. E.: rev, 2591
Robazza, C.: ref, 1021 (30)
Robb, J.: ref, 1166 (222)
Robb, J. C.: ref, 1093 (111), 1166 (97), 2305 (171)
Robbins, C.: ref, 1903 (302)
Robbins, D. R.: ref, 2305 (24)
Robbins, J. M.: ref, 1241 (1,6), 2603 (107)
Robbins, M. A.: ref, 1164 (2,16,45,120), 2497 (61), 2860 (454), 2899 (1)
Robbins, P. R.: ref, 272 (312)
Robbins, R. A.: ref, 2497 (138), 2603 (490)
Robbins, S.: test, 771
Robbins, S. B.: test, 409; ref, 404 (3,13)
Robbins, T. W.: ref, 349 (12), 1390 (2), 1758 (2,7,10, 14,17,37,49,94), 2662 (3), 2860 (90,206,215,266, 849), 2863 (69), 2892 (26,35)
Robbins-Brinson, L.: ref, 272 (346), 2603 (575)
Roberge, L. D.: ref, 1755 (30)
Roberson, L.: ref, 1348 (10), 1701 (45)
Roberson, T. A.: ref, 182 (1), 2008 (4), 2860 (311)
Robert, P.: ref, 2288 (49), 2289 (38), 2860 (902), 2863 (271)
Roberto, K. A.: ref, 2527 (1)
Roberts, A.: ref, 694 (83)
Roberts, A. C.: ref, 1390 (2), 1758 (2,10,17) 2860 (90,215)
Roberts, A. O. H.: rev, 302
Roberts, B.: ref, 68 (24), 372 (89), 373 (29)
Roberts, B. W.: ref, 68 (62), 372 (66,114,115), 373 (42), 1697 (566), 2380 (11)
Roberts, C.: test, 2854; ref, 349 (6), 666 (2), 1140 (2), 1902 (47), 2252 (4), 2295 (4)
Roberts, C. V.: test, 2855
Roberts, D. C.: rev, 920, 2867
Roberts, G. E.: test, 2242
Roberts, H.: rev, 354, 591, 614, 1203
Roberts, J.: ref, 270 (37), 994 (49), 1528 (7), 2229 (16), 2657 (35), 2813 (152), 2860 (386)
Roberts, J. E.: ref, 265 (2,11), 270 (12), 998 (130), 1216 (58,73), 1612 (58), 1745 (75), 2382 (26,33), 2485 (147), 2860 (732), 2862 (286,388), 2864 (70), 2901 (47,70)
Roberts, J. G.: ref, 630 (1), 1216 (80), 1264 (4)
Roberts, J. M. A.: ref, 2382 (3)
Roberts, J. W.: ref, 376 (19), 776 (42)
Roberts, K. H.: ref, 1862 (2)
Roberts, L.: ref, 694 (131), 1226 (4), 2652 (11)
Roberts, L. J.: ref, 134 (41)
Roberts, M. A.: ref, 451 (207), 681 (65), 1010 (85), 1592 (24), 2862 (378), 2879 (131)
Roberts, M. C.: ref, 2862 (172)
Roberts, M. H.: ref, 2239 (10)
Roberts, M. J.: ref, 2163 (300,301)
Roberts, M. W.: rev, 228, 1583, 1876, 1918, 2775; ref, 266 (4), 451 (246), 997 (5), 1903 (123)
Roberts, N.: ref, 1758 (99), 2860 (1379), 2863 (414)
Roberts, N. M.: ref, 2487 (7)
Roberts, R.: ref, 2860 (18), 2863 (10)
Roberts, R. C.: ref, 1758 (30), 2860 (641,886), 2863 (219)
Roberts, R. D.: ref, 2163 (302)
Roberts, R. E.: ref, 451 (71), 2402 (14), 2497 (220,366), 2858 (74), 2860 (132)

Roberts, R. J.: ref, 1697 (577), 2860 (880)
Roberts, R. L.: ref, 399 (5), 2433 (3)
Roberts, S.: ref, 1697 (280), 1770 (9), 2305 (99), 2862 (250)
Roberts, S. A.: ref, 1697 (405), 2305 (131), 2305 (220)
Roberts, S. L.: ref, 1338 (36)
Roberts, T.: ref, 2862 (20)
Roberts, T. A.: ref, 2862 (89), 2879 (19)
Roberts, T. G.: test, 2447
Roberts, T. W.: ref, 863 (1), 1000 (4)
Roberts, V. J.: ref, 776 (36), 2860 (1206)
Roberts, W. C.: ref, 998 (75,76), 2603 (282,283), 2858 (17,78,79)
Robertson, A.: test, 2134
Robertson, C.: ref, 272 (218), 451 (32)
Robertson, D. U.: rev, 1583, 2545
Robertson, G. J.: rev, 396, 559, 1719
Robertson, I.: ref, 1758 (5), 2860 (133), 2892 (16)
Robertson, I. H.: ref, 1758 (9,29), 1765 (10), 2193 (13), 2516 (109), 2860 (212,733,965), 2863 (54,217), 2892 (27,146,287)
Robertson, I. T.: ref, 1822 (3)
Robertson, J. F.: ref, 1010 (12)
Robertson, J. M.: ref, 2603 (357,459)
Robertson, K.: ref, 2227 (25), 2516 (79), 2860 (1089), 2863 (322)
Robertson, K. R.: ref, 2076 (135)
Robertson, M.: ref, 350 (11), 2858 (59)
Robertson, M. F.: ref, 337 (9)
Robertson, M. M.: ref, 1166 (71), 2193 (18), 2497 (235), 2860 (438,501)
Robertson, S.: ref, 350 (36), 1653 (26), 2163 (260), 2228 (21), 2860 (1034)
Robertson, S. B.: ref, 2862 (668)
Robichon, F.: ref, 2163 (274)
Robie, C.: test, 1348
Robillard, K.: ref, 694 (11)
Robin, A. F.: ref, 1903 (26), 2163 (24), 2862 (62)
Robin, D. A.: ref, 303 (10), 641 (7), 1740 (14), 2226 (13), 2305 (228), 2813 (149), 2860 (1168), 2863 (351)
Robin, N.: ref, 1697 (138), 2863 (99)
Robin, R. W.: ref, 2305 (234)
Robiner, W. N.: ref, 1745 (8), 2497 (87)
Robinett, R.: test, 408, 1350, 1539, 2822
Robins, C. J.: ref, 272 (17), 1166 (25), 1745 (48), 2305 (25)
Robins, E.: ref, 2603 (191)
Robins, P. M.: ref, 2861 (2), 2862 (619)
Robins, R. W.: ref, 365 (10), 373 (14,21), 2862 (536)
Robinson, A.: ref, 272 (250), 846 (20), 1991 (23), 2211 (9), 2497 (608)
Robinson, B.: ref, 1903 (306), 2485 (148)
Robinson, D. S.: test, 2687
Robinson, D. T.: ref, 1745 (23)
Robinson, E.: test, 2371, 2804; ref, 1166 (1), 2305 (12)
Robinson, E. A.: test, 864; rev, 1878
Robinson, E. T.: test, 1355, 1952
Robinson, H. J.: ref, 268 (1)
Robinson, H. M.: rev, 861
Robinson, J.: ref, 4 (18), 2039 (22), 2382 (6,16)
Robinson, J. R.: ref, 2497 (589)
Robinson, K.: ref, 2226 (9)
Robinson, L.: test, 33
Robinson, L. A.: ref, 540 (15), 2862 (597)
Robinson, L. C.: ref, 1000 (91), 1297 (1), 2497 (510)
Robinson, L. J.: ref, 1752 (1), 2860 (269)
Robinson, M.: test, 1370; ref, 1000 (14,15)
Robinson, M. D.: ref, 2497 (511)
Robinson, M. E.: ref, 2497 (169)
Robinson, N. M.: ref, 372 (7), 771 (4), 1379 (74,89), 2214 (61), 2862 (320,383,537), 2864 (101,123), 2879 (107)
Robinson, N. S.: ref, 472 (143)
Robinson, P.: ref, 303 (17), 818 (1), 2218 (16), 2226 (24), 2516 (98), 2603 (474), 2862 (623)
Robinson, P. J.: ref, 2497 (139)
Robinson, R.: ref, 2050 (62)
Robinson, R. B.: ref, 694 (84)
Robinson, R. D.: rev, 707
Robinson, R. G.: ref, 301 (47), 1166 (117,118,137,203), 2050 (9,28,37,111,118), 2516 (63,107), 2860 (1327), 2863 (233), 2879 (105), 2892 (44,166)
Robinson, R. K.: ref, 1939 (8)
Robinson, S. S.: ref, 2704 (10)
Robinson, T. O.: ref, 999 (169)
Robinson-Whelen, S.: ref, 298 (43), 2858 (24), 2860 (236)
Robitaille, Y.: ref, 2227 (8), 2860 (364), 2879 (44), 2892 (54)
Robson, A. L.: ref, 270 (38), 1612 (97), 1889 (12)
Rocchi, P.: ref, 2860 (442)
Rocha-Singh, I. A.: ref, 2497 (388)
Roche, L.: ref, 2091 (5)
Roche, L. A.: ref, 2358 (13)
Roche, S. E.: ref, 875 (2)
Rocheleau, A.: ref, 1264 (6), 1889 (11), 1987 (22)
Rochey, H. E.: ref, 2527 (13)
Rochkin, D.: ref, 2226 (27), 2863 (392)
Rochon, E.: ref, 1164 (75), 1903 (303), 2862 (287), 2863 (218), 2892 (147)
Rock, D.: ref, 1697 (280,405), 2305 (99,131,220), 2862 (250)
Rock, D. A.: test, 972; ref, 592 (45,72,107), 1115 (3,7,15,21), 1405 (28), 2771 (35)
Rock, S. L.: ref, 1216 (1)
Rocklin, T. R.: ref, 372 (4), 592 (97), 998 (7), 1140 (4), 2656 (16,19)
Roddy, M.: test, 971
Roderich, M. A.: ref, 1697 (448)
Rodger, A.: rev, 1533, 1632, 1633, 2217
Rodgers, B.: ref, 2050 (96)
Rodgers, D. A.: rev, 1697
Rodgers, J.: ref, 1079 (6)
Rodgers, J. A.: ref, 2863 (284)

Rodgers, J. L.: ref, 1216 (59), 1902 (57), 1903 (304)
Rodgers, R. C.: rev, 1414, 2095
Rodgers, S.: ref, 1164 (11), 2860 (117), 2863 (32)
Rodgers, W. L.: ref, 1216 (112), 1889 (20)
Rodin, J.: ref, 2603 (502)
Rodney, H. E.: ref, 462 (30)
Rodning, C.: ref, 1216 (17)
Rodrigue, J. R.: ref, 2214 (42), 2497 (305,332), 2498 (35,46), 2603 (237), 2813 (13,47)
Rodriguez, C. M.: ref, 448 (27), 1889 (13), 2497 (651)
Rodriguez, E.: ref, 272 (221)
Rodriguez, G.: ref, 2839 (9)
Rodriguez, M.: ref, 2860 (513)
Rodriguez, N.: ref, 2519 (47), 2520 (48)
Rodriguez, R.: ref, 2863 (80)
Rodriguez-Charbonier, S.: ref, 760 (4)
Rodriguez-Sutil, C.: ref, 2247 (72)
Rodriquez, A. L. T.: ref, 2860 (734)
Rodwell, D. N.: test, 2136
Roe, A.: test, 447, 646, 659, 660, 2381, 2885
Roe, B. D.: test, 357
Roeden, J. M.: ref, 2441 (2), 2813 (101)
Rocdcr, W. S.: tcst, 2244
Roehlke, H. J.: ref, 1697 (300), 2603 (261)
Roehrich, L.: ref, 2305 (27)
Roeltgen, D.: ref, 776 (62), 2227 (60)
Roeltgen, D. P.: ref, 2873 (42)
Roemer, L.: ref, 2497 (389)
Roenker, D. L.: test, 2794
Roese, N. J.: ref, 2246 (13)
Roeser, R. W.: ref, 472 (211)
Roesler, T. A.: ref, 694 (85)
Roessler, R.: test, 936, 2923, 2924
Roessler, R. T.: test, 2918; ref, 404 (4), 404 (6), 936 (1), 1754 (4)
Roetzel, K.: ref, 175 (4), 430 (3), 1903 (31), 2332 (1), 2695 (4)
Roeyers, H.: ref, 1612 (101), 2862 (732)
Roffeld, P.: ref, 298 (99)
Roffman, A. J.: ref, 275 (1), 1902 (58), 1991 (75), 2860 (735)
Roffwarg, H. P.: ref, 272 (136), 1166 (81)
Rogeness, G. A.: ref, 375 (4), 451 (210), 542 (2), 2214 (119), 2227 (44), 2862 (649), 2879 (213)
Rogere, M. L.: ref, 2892 (183)
Rogers, B. G.: rev, 278, 364, 743, 899, 1657, 1902, 2486, 2737, 2742
Rogers, B. J.: ref, 1697 (235)
Rogers, C.: ref, 561 (2)
Rogers, C. A.: rev, 1800
Rogers, D.: ref, 1745 (39)
Rogers, J.: ref, 1697 (15), 2860 (60)
Rogers, J. C.: ref, 1525 (9)
Rogers, J. H.: ref, 2603 (186,395)
Rogers, J. L.: ref, 2497 (56)
Rogers, L.: ref, 746 (2)
Rogers, M. D.: ref, 1517 (6)
Rogers, M. P.: ref, 2076 (38), 2305 (135)
Rogers, M. R.: rev, 1139, 1358
Rogers, P.: test, 703, 2078
Rogers, P. A.: ref, 1697 (440), 2497 (498)
Rogers, P. J.: ref, 2497 (472)
Rogers, R.: test, 2245, 2522; ref, 1697 (100,449,529), 1698 (22), 1959 (2), 2553 (4), 2879 (229)
Rogers, R. W.: ref, 372 (25)
Rogers, S. J.: test, 879, 2041; ref, 375 (2), 459 (23,24,28), 2485 (99,191), 2862 (440,538), 2892 (82,217)
Rogers, W. A.: ref, 1405 (22)
Rogers, W. T.: ref, 2656 (20)
Rogers, Y.: ref, 1612 (41,42)
Rogerson, B. S.: test, 658
Rogg, J.: ref, 1218 (16), 2599 (35), 2863 (317)
Rogler, L. H.: test, 2647; ref, 2497 (390,571), 2603 (245)
Rogosch, F.: ref, 372 (24), 472 (38), 1661 (8), 1697 (101)
Rogosch, F. A.: ref, 365 (3), 373 (15), 472 (44), 694 (49), 1903 (162)
Rohan, K. J.: ref, 272 (320), 2497 (657), 2603 (553)
Rohde, P.: ref, 2497 (366), 2858 (74)
Rohe, D. E.: ref, 1697 (44), 2218 (128)
Rohena-Diaz, E.: ref, 994 (39)
Rohling, M. L.: ref, 1166 (39)
Rohr, M.: ref, 1962 (20)
Rohrbeck, C. A.: rev, 7, 303, 1665, 2231
Rohsenow, D. J.: ref, 134 (8,14,15,19,20,27), 272 (90), 1661 (23,34)
Roid, G. H.: test, 1485, 2293, 2518, 2767
Roig, M.: ref, 2545 (4)
Roig-López, F.: ref, 474 (4), 1612 (34)
Roisse, M-F.: ref, 2860 (1249), 2863 (377)
Roitblat, H. L.: ref, 1592 (19), 1697 (268), 2497 (312), 2516 (36)
Roitman, G.: ref, 272 (249), 1166 (169)
Roitman, S. E. L.: ref, 2305 (225)
Roizen, N. J.: ref, 2813 (107)
Rojahn, J.: ref, 4 (12,13,20,22), 681 (83), 811 (5), 1216 (35), 1903 (412), 2163 (239), 2211 (50), 2485 (221), 2860 (1417)
Rojder, R.: ref, 1697 (347), 2603 (297)
Rojewski, J. W.: ref, 404 (33), 413 (20)
Rojo, N.: ref, 2218 (118)
Rokeach, M.: test, 2246
Rokosz, S. F.: ref, 2860 (443)
Rolfhus, E. L.: ref, 838 (21)
Roll, S.: rev, 711, 1435
Rolland, J.: ref, 2218 (129)
Rolland, J. P.: ref, 1590 (26), 2218 (133)
Roller, T. L.: ref, 2497 (361)
Rollings, J.: ref, 2858 (84), 2863 (223)
Rollins, K. B.: ref, 1047 (5), 1612 (77)
Rollins, P. R.: ref, 350 (21), 1485 (34)
Romach, M.: ref, 1093 (102), 2497 (512), 2603 (396)
Roman, D. D.: rev, 268, 338, 1066, 2297; ref, 687 (4), 1697 (102,567), 1740 (25), 2226 (33), 2860 (1339)
Roman, M. J.: ref, 776 (21)

Romanczyk, R. G.: ref, 2813 (75)
Romano, J.: ref, 272 (74), 1166 (40)
Romano, J. M.: ref, 863 (17)
Romanoski, A. J.: ref, 2050 (23)
Romans, S. E.: ref, 2050 (38,44,45,128,129)
Romberg, T. A.: test, 622
Romeo, Y.: ref, 2603 (275), 2858 (71)
Romer, N.: ref, 298 (38)
Romero, B.: ref, 301 (13), 1525 (23), 2860 (193,1115)
Romero, J. J.: ref, 1164 (71), 2860 (204,709), 2879 (27), 2892 (136)
Romero-Nieva, F. D.: ref, 2860 (734)
Romig, C.: ref, 1631 (3)
Romney, D. M.: ref, 272 (114), 694 (15,86), 1021 (5), 1166 (35), 1697 (60)
Romoser, R. C.: test, 2618
Romp, S. A.: ref, 2497 (514), 2749 (62)
Romsaas, E. P.: ref, 1687 (9), 2076 (17)
Romski, M. A.: ref, 202 (3)f, 433 (1), 1903 (14,100,305,306,329), 2189 (1), 2485 (148), 2657 (19)
Ron, M.: ref, 2125 (11), 2516 (39), 2599 (17)
Ron, M. A.: ref, 2050 (34,74)
Ronan, G. F.: ref, 2749 (61)
Ronan, K. R.: ref, 472 (101,212), 473 (1,7), 1166 (208), 2214 (55,123), 2498 (42,73)
Rondepierre, P.: ref, 2163 (214), 2860 (868)
Ronen-Eliav, H.: ref, 451 (185), 1000 (106)
Ronfeldt, H. M.: ref, 2603 (427)
Ronk, J.: ref, 451 (40)
Ronningstam, E. F.: ref, 2603 (19)
Roodman, A.: ref, 2497 (531), 2879 (148)
Roodman, A. A.: ref, 1178 (4)
Rooijmans, H. G. M.: ref, 2050 (49)
Roos, L. L.: ref, 2497 (418,652), 2656 (24)
Roosa, M.: ref, 472 (87,88), 1000 (29,70), 1877 (2)
Roosa, M. W.: ref, 451 (186), 462 (1), 472 (6,39,63,145), 863 (64), 1661 (41)
Roose, S. P.: ref, 272 (203), 2603 (562)
Root, J. H.: test, 2175
Roper, B. L.: ref, 2863 (365)
Roper, M.: ref, 2214 (104)
Rorer, L. G.: rev, 68, 2417
Rorrer-Woody, S.: ref, 615 (20)
Rorshach, H.: test, 2247
Rosa, M.: ref, 1040 (5)
Rosario, M.: ref, 2603 (397,398)
Roschmann, R.: ref, 900 (3)
Rose, C.: ref, 1379 (47), 1612 (52)
Rose, E.: ref, 1991 (68), 2860 (609), 2862 (247), 2879 (76), 2901 (40)
Rose, G. M.: ref, 2305 (4)
Rose, M. P.: ref, 1021 (37), 1697 (73)
Rose, M. R.: ref, 2402 (5), 2603 (48)
Rose, N.: ref, 998 (93), 2050 (116)
Rose, P. E.: ref, 1758 (28), 2860 (713), 2863 (211), 2892 (140)
Rose, R. D.: ref, 1697 (559), 2516 (106)
Rose, R. J.: ref, 998 (84)
Rose, S. A.: test, 2044; ref, 681 (19), 2862 (389,539,669)
Rose, S. L.: ref, 681 (19)
Rosel, J.: ref, 1338 (37)
Rosel, P.: ref, 1166 (209)
Rosen, A. B.: test, 870
Rosen, A. D.: ref, 1672 (1)
Rosen, B. R.: ref, 2227 (26), 2860 (1103)
Rosen, C. L.: rev, 724, 1725
Rosen, E.: rev, 317, 1053, 1160
Rosen, G. A.: rev, 627, 2279
Rosen, G. M.: ref, 1697 (450)
Rosén, I.: ref, 2603 (541)
Rosen, J.: ref, 2860 (884)
Rosen, J. C.: ref, 337 (17,115,116), 893 (3)
Rosen, K. S.: ref, 451 (72)
Rosén, L. A.: ref, 2115 (2)
Rosen, L. N.: ref, 337 (157), 460 (1,2)
Rosen, M.: ref, 2432 (32), 2813 (105,129), 2860 (1172)
Rosen, M. D.: ref, 1697 (343)
Rosen, R. C.: ref, 2076 (98)
Rosen, W.: ref, 1592 (7)
Rosenbach, J. H.: ref, 2163 (231)
Rosenbaum, A.: ref, 2603 (298)
Rosenbaum, D.: ref, 270 (29), 451 (86,181), 1612 (91), 1613 (2)
Rosenbaum, E.: ref, 1216 (60)
Rosenbaum, G.: ref, 1697 (475)
Rosenbaum, J.: ref, 1166 (86), 1166 (162), 2603 (503)
Rosenbaum, J. F.: ref, 272 (202), 1166 (41,63,106,133,184), 2199 (11), 2305 (187), 2519 (39), 2520 (40)
Rosenbaum, J. L.: ref, 2485 (236)
Rosenbaum, M.: ref, 2305 (193)
Rosenbaum, P.: ref, 1991 (60), 2813 (51)
Rosenbaum, T.: ref, 2498 (12)
Rosenberg, D. R.: ref, 1166 (210)
Rosenberg, E. L.: ref, 1001 (15)
Rosenberg, H.: ref, 1661 (82), 1697 (591), 2553 (6)
Rosenberg, J. M.: ref, 2860 (502)
Rosenberg, L.: ref, 301 (17), 1392 (5), 1902 (24), 2247 (15), 2749 (20), 2905 (14)
Rosenberg, L. R.: test, 2382
Rosenberg, M. S.: ref, 863 (31), 2498 (19), 2860 (547), 2879 (68)
Rosenberg, R.: ref, 272 (353), 2497 (119)
Rosenberg, R. L.: ref, 2603 (16)
Rosenberg, R. N.: ref, 994 (45), 2860 (1240)
Rosenberg, S.: ref, 270 (17), 272 (173)
Rosenberg, S. D.: ref, 2247 (73)f, 2749 (48), 2860 (736)
Rosenberger, R. L.: ref, 815 (24)
Rosenblatt, A.: ref, 815 (49), 1093 (53), 1164 (173), 1740 (27), 2076 (68), 2288 (15), 2289 (10), 2305 (62,84), 2516 (115), 2603 (210), 2860 (1374), 2892 (294)
Rosenblatt, J. A.: rev, 1275
Rosenbloom, M.: ref, 1758 (8)

Rosenbloom, P. C.: rev, 1119
Rosenblum, A.: ref, 2860 (1152)
Rosenblum, G. D.: ref, 272 (89), 1661 (33)
Rosenblum, L. A.: ref, 1166 (179)
Rosenburg, L. A.: ref, 451 (204), 2862 (632)
Rosendahl, E.: ref, 1166 (85)
Rosenfarb, I. S.: ref, 790 (15), 2050 (130), 2402 (21)
Rosenfeld, B.: ref, 2860 (966)
Rosenfeld, J.: ref, 451 (263), 681 (93), 1392 (15), 2862 (718), 2905 (120)
Rosenfeld, R. B.: ref, 1404 (8)
Rosenfield, S.: rev, 2073, 2621, 2753
Rosenheck, R.: ref, 337 (101,144,184)
Rosenkilde, C. E.: ref, 564 (5), 2892 (38)
Rosenlund, P.: test, 1472
Rosenman, R. H.: test, 1338
Rosenstein, D. S.: ref, 2603 (491)
Rosenstein, L. D.: ref, 1164 (10), 1903 (36)
Rosenstein, P.: ref, 1889 (2)
Rosenthal, A. C.: rev, 194, 208, 1387, 2334, 2459
Rosenthal, D. A.: ref, 1010 (27,40)
Rosenthal, G. T.: ref, 694 (121)
Rosenthal, H.: ref, 615 (34), 705 (5)
Rosenthal, J. A.: ref, 1000 (75)
Rosenthal, J. B.: ref, 1040 (10), 1095 (25), 1394 (7), 1903 (285)
Rosenthal, N. E.: ref, 1166 (135)
Rosenthal, R.: test, 703, 2078; ref, 1166 (186), 2497 (558)
Rosenthal, R. N.: ref, 337 (177), 2305 (229)
Rosenthal, S.: ref, 1264 (6), 1889 (11), 1987 (22), 2497 (190)
Rosenthal, T. L.: ref, 999 (97)
Rosenwasser, S. M.: ref, 298 (23)
Rosenzweig, S.: test, 2248
Roser, N. L.: rev, 827, 861, 901
Rosie, J. S.: ref, 2603 (290,291)
Rosin, R.: ref, 2860 (1137)
Rosinek, M.: test, 2054, 2421, 2426
Rosinski, E. F.: test, 1640
Roskos, K.: ref, 1903 (89), 2682 (3)
Rosmark, B.: ref, 1093 (3), 2603 (28)
Rosner, J.: test, 2671, 2721
Rosnow, R. L.: ref, 592 (69)
Rospenda, K. M.: ref, 1661 (48)
Ross, A. O.: rev, 2122
Ross, C.: ref, 2863 (171)
Ross, C. A.: ref, 815 (49), 846 (1,18), 1164 (173), 1740 (27), 2017 (13), 2050 (125), 2516 (115), 2860 (1374)f, 2892 (294)
Ross, C. K.: ref, 1010 (54), 2498 (24)
Ross, C. M.: test, 2252
Ross, C. S.: rev, 173
Ross, D. E.: ref, 2288 (76), 2289 (63), 2305 (203), 2402 (60)f, 2892 (257)
Ross, E. D.: ref, 1745 (13)
Ross, F. L.: ref, 2724 (2)
Ross, G.: ref, 615 (1), 666 (5), 816 (1), 2229 (15), 2485 (213), 2862 (540), 2879 (178)
Ross, H. E.: ref, 134 (5), 272 (35), 1661 (9)
Ross, J.: ref, 2163 (29)
Ross, J. A.: ref, 1140 (12)
Ross, J. D.: test, 2252
Ross, J. M.: ref, 301 (7), 2860 (134)
Ross, K. K.: ref, 1903 (498)
Ross, M.: ref, 1166 (65), 2860 (328), 2863 (207)
Ross, M. J.: ref, 272 (18), 2497 (590)
Ross, M. W.: ref, 1079 (7)
Ross, P. F.: rev, 937, 2877
Ross, R.: ref, 1485 (3)
Ross, S.: ref, 2402 (66)
Ross, S. J. M.: ref, 2860 (1340), 2863 (402)
Ross, S. L.: ref, 331 (5), 837 (7)
Ross, S. M.: ref, 861 (2,4,5), 1903 (413,495), 2695 (61), 2902 (3), 2905 (62,87,105)
Ross, T.: ref, 776 (24), 2860 (725), 2863 (275)
Ross, T. J.: ref, 1754 (5), 2163 (22)
Ross Thomson, L.: ref, 790 (13)
Ross-Swain, D.: test, 277, 2249, 2250, 2251
Rosse, J. G.: ref, 937 (4), 2218 (134)f, 2899 (9)
Rosselli, M.: ref, 1164 (133), 2227 (31), 2860 (1162), 2863 (347), 2892 (250)
Rossem, R. V.: ref, 451 (236), 2603 (398), 2813 (154)
Rosser, R.: ref, 999 (107), 2603 (320)
Rossi, A.: ref, 1525 (10), 2892 (152)
Rossini, E. D.: ref, 1164 (76), 2749 (80)f, 2758 (1), 2860 (737,1163)
Rossiter, C. M.: ref, 337 (6)
Rosskopf, M. F.: rev, 1368
Rossman, B. B. R.: ref, 863 (31), 1991 (38), 2498 (19)
Rossner, S. C.: ref, 2247 (52)
Rostain, A. L.: ref, 451 (97)
Rostami, A.: ref, 2226 (9)
Roswal, G. M.: ref, 777 (1), 1991 (85)
Roswell, F. G.: test, 823, 2253, 2254
Roszkowski, M. J.: rev, 270, 380, 1430, 2274
Rotert, M.: ref, 451 (203), 1902 (95), 2860 (1286), 2862 (630), 2901 (120)
Roth, C.: ref, 272 (259),2603 (175)
Roth, D. L.: ref, 708 (9)
Roth, F. P.: ref, 1902 (92), 2905 (108)
Roth, L.: ref, 690 (3), 1687 (34)
Roth, L. A.: ref, 2862 (157)
Roth, L. H.: ref, 2603 (248)
Roth, M.: ref, 1902 (48)
Roth, P. A.: ref, 2863 (284)
Roth, R. M.: ref, 1745 (76), 2497 (591), 2863 (348)
Roth, S.: ref, 372 (19), 697 (2), 2497 (493), 2749 (15)
Roth, W.: ref, 1140 (13,20)
Roth, W. T.: ref, 2497 (375,480,481), 2520 (46)
Rothbaum, F.: ref, 451 (72)
Rothbaum, P. A.: ref, 472 (37), 1181 (8)
Rothblum, E. D.: ref, 893 (31)
Rothen, M.: ref, 135 (5), 2497 (624)

Rothenberg, J. L.: ref, 2860 (947)
Rotheram-Borus, M. J.: ref, 1991 (96), 2305 (194), 2603 (397,398)
Rothermel, R. D., Jr.: rev, 1774
Rothfleisch, J.: ref, 1164 (57), 2010 (2), 2227 (5), 2860 (208,586), 2863 (52,174), 2892 (24)
Rothi, L. J. G.: ref, 199 (17), 209 (1,2), 376 (20), 1096 (11), 1164 (150,167), 1903 (343,384,419), 2227 (37), 2860 (1270,1322), 2873 (8,23,39,46,62,64, 65,70,71), 2892 (273,285)
Rothlind, J.: ref, 815 (19), 2516 (62), 2860 (809), 2892 (165)
Rothlind, J. C.: ref, 1740 (10), 2516 (32), 2860 (514), 2892 (85)
Rothlisberg, B.: rev, 977
Rothlisberg, B. A.: rev, 879, 1919, 2683
Rothney, J. W. M.: rev, 1492, 1790, 1841, 2485, 2813
Rothstein, D. M.: ref, 1164 (33), 2603 (140), 2860 (344), 2863 (92), 2892 (49)
Rothstein, M. G.: ref, 1107 (5), 1334 (1), 1790 (2), 1965 (2,60,75)
Rothwell, J. W.: test, 2255, 2256
Rothwell, W. J.: test, 801, 1371
Rotrosen, J.: ref, 2860 (297,419), 2892 (61)
Rotrosen, J. P.: ref, 2860 (1205), 2892 (261)
Rotter, J.: rev, 2749
Rotter, J. B.: test, 2258, 1697
Rotter, S. C.: ref, 2860 (590)
Rotto, P. C.: rev, 2417
Rouet, J. F.: ref, 1097 (7), 1134 (1), 1612 (27), 2228 (6), 2860 (394), 2864 (31), 2870 (3)
Rouleau, I.: ref, 199 (10)
Rouleau, N.: ref, 2863 (349)
Roumm, P. G.: test, 2220, 2222
Rounds, J.: ref, 337 (164), 398 (3), 406 (1), 414 (2), 415 (1), 416 (1), 1334 (4,5), 2835 (16,18,22,24,25)
Rounds, J. B.: rev, 398, 2054, 2835; ref, 1694 (3,4), 1701 (3)
Rounds, J. B., Jr.: test, 1694; rev, 410
Rounsaville, B.: ref, 1697 (157,356)
Rounsaville, B. J.: ref, 135 (1), 372 (117), 846 (26), 1697 (491), 2218 (135), 2305 (76), 2433 (4), 2497 (357)
Rourke, B. P.: rev, 2377; ref, 1164 (26), 1166 (107), 1697 (542), 1903 (69), 2860 (1079,1264), 2862 (221,473,683), 2863 (315,380), 2879 (43,65,160,203,220), 2901 (88)
Rourke, S. B.: ref, 815 (32), 1164 (157), 1379 (80), 1725 (7), 2860 (1298)
Rouse, M. J.: rev, 1097
Rouse, R. E.: ref, 1000 (73)
Rousseau, C.: ref, 451 (147)
Rousseau, D.: ref, 1903 (482)
Rousseau, D. M.: rev, 1655, 1967, 2610, 2805; ref, 1862 (1)
Rousseau, M. K.: ref, 1903 (307)
Rousseaux, M.: ref, 1164 (122)
Rousselle, C.: ref, 1131 (7) 2860 (303)
Roussos, J.: ref, 272 (306)
Roussos, L.: ref, 1434 (2)
Roussos, L. A.: ref, 180 (36), 1434 (1), 1759 (16)
Routh, C. P.: ref, 997 (23), 1079 (50)
Routh, D.: ref, 272 (196), 451 (136)
Rovert, J.: ref, 430 (15), 451 (148), 681 (78), 815 (40), 1612 (89), 2860 (1164), 2870 (5), 2879 (179,180), 2905 (104), 2879 (66,67)
Rovet, J.: ref, 2860 (738), 2862 (541,542), 2901 (99)
Rovet, J. F.: ref, 272 (258), 815 (12), 893 (42), 1392 (9), 1405 (39), 1903 (517), 1991 (56), 2862 (222,595), 2905 (46)
Rovine, M.: ref, 1965 (12)
Rowan, A. B.: ref, 2519 (47), 2520 (48)
Rowe, D. C.: ref, 451 (222), 1216 (59), 1902 (57,90), 1903 (304), 2860 (1341), 2892 (288)
Rowe, H. A. H.: test, 2926
Rowe, J. B.: ref, 1166 (146), 2603 (492)
Rowe, M.: ref, 472 (101), 473 (1), 2214 (55), 2498 (42), 2603 (524)
Rowe, S.: ref, 2050 (46)
Rowell, K.: test, 631, 747, 2349, 2803
Rowell, K. J.: test, 2563
Rowell, K. R.: test, 633
Rowilla, J.: ref, 272 (341)
Rowitz, L.: ref, 1300 (7)
Rowland, C.: test, 156
Rowland, P. B.: ref, 2813 (111)
Rowland, S.: ref, 1095 (38), 1485 (51), 2680 (15), 2695 (53)
Rowley, A. J.: ref, 2076 (127)
Rowley, D.: ref, 2873 (21)
Rowzee, R. D.: ref, 1697 (440), 2497 (498)
Roxborough, H.: ref, 2860 (515), 2892 (86)
Roxborough, M. R.: ref, 2163 (142)
Roy, A.: ref, 999 (31), 1592 (9), 1697 (135), 2076 (69)
Roy, M.-A.: ref, 650 (15), 999 (126), 1093 (97)
Roy-Burne, P. P.: ref, 272 (142), 1687 (18), 2497 (527)
Roy-Byrne, P.: ref, 1705 (2)
Roy-Byrne, P. P.: ref, 2497 (244)
Royal, W.: ref, 2227 (10), 2599 (9), 2860 (401)
Royal, W., III: ref, 1135 (22), 1164 (169), 2226 (35), 2227 (50)
Royalty, J.: ref, 705 (9,10)
Royce, J. R.: test, 2112
Royeen, C. B.: ref, 1673 (4)
Royere, M. L.: ref, 2863 (261)
Rozeboom, W. W.: ref, 2860 (304)
Rozecki, T.: rev, 2069, 2777
Rozell, E. J.: ref, 1939 (8)
Rozensky, R. H.: ref, 298 (76)
Rozin, P.: ref, 2860 (76)
Roznowski, M. J.: rev, 1490
Rozzini, R.: ref, 337 (54)
Ruback, R. B.: ref, 337 (163)
Rubba, P. A.: ref, 1866 (19)
Rubens, A. B.: ref, 2193 (4,30), 2516 (5), 2860 (129,728), 2863 (37,116), 2873 (7,13), 2892 (15,145)

Rubenstein, C. S.: ref, 2603 (399)
Rubenstein, D. F.: ref, 1687 (44)
Rubenstein, J. L.: ref, 272 (19,58), 273 (3), 1000 (5,37)
Ruberry, J.: ref, 2862 (189), 2901 (23)
Rubert, M. P.: ref, 272 (31)
Rubia, F. J.: ref, 2892 (263)
Rubin, A.: ref, 2835 (28)
Rubin, C.: ref, 272 (19,58), 273 (3), 1000 (5,37)
Rubin, D. L.: ref, 298 (51)
Rubin, H.: ref, 1903 (90), 2695 (8), 2768 (6), 2862 (140)
Rubin, K. H.: test, 2001; ref, 472 (115), 2039 (19,24)
Rubin, M. A.: ref, 2862 (437)
Rubin, N. P.: ref, 2860 (390), 2863 (101)
Rubin, R. T.: ref, 1166 (17), 2603 (24,108)
Rubin, S. I.: rev, 1323
Rubin, S. S.: ref, 2497 (196)
Rubino, I. A.: ref, 1687 (16)
Rubinow, D. R.: ref, 2497 (279)
Rubinson, E.: ref, 2603 (105)
Rubinstein, H.: ref, 472 (215), 1318 (20), 2214 (125), 2862 (677)
Rubio-Stipec, M.: ref, 451 (14)
Ruble, T. L.: ref, 1755 (12)
Rubonis, A. V.: ref, 134 (15,19)
Rucci, P.: ref, 2863 (416)
Ruch, F. L.: test, 937; rev, 943, 989
Ruch, W. W.: test, 2072, 2105
Rudas, N.: ref, 272 (103)
Rudd, B. H.: test, 2765
Rudd, M. D.: ref, 272 (134,168,219), 273 (10,15,20,25), 1687 (21), 2065 (21,22,26,29), 2402 (32,56), 2559 (9,10,12)
Rudd, N. M.: ref, 1000 (77)
Rudd, R.: ref, 1687 (15)
Rudd, R. P.: ref, 272 (33), 1687 (12,96)
Ruddell, M. R. H.: ref, 665 (36)
Ruddock, A.: ref, 2516 (76)
Ruddock, G.: test, 444, 2023
Ruddock, J. A.: ref, 1755 (77)
Rude, G. G.: ref, 451 (40)
Rude, S. S.: ref, 790 (9,21), 1590 (14), 1745 (57), 2305 (139)
Ruderman, M. N.: test, 807
Rudick, R. A.: ref, 272 (245), 2858 (123)
Rudisill, J. R.: ref, 1590 (2)
Rudisin, S.: ref, 1525 (14), 2860 (476), 2862 (208), 2879 (58)
Rudman, H. C.: test, 2484, 408, 886, 972, 2094
Rudner, L.: test, 1618
Rudner, L. M.: rev, 944, 1479, 2221
Rudolph, K. D.: ref, 472 (213), 681 (56), 2214 (124)
Rudy, L.: ref, 1612 (17)
Rudy, T. E.: ref, 272 (235)
Rudzinski, M.: ref, 1060 (4)
Rueckert, L.: ref, 2892 (251)
Rueda, R.: rev, 643, 1739, 1850; ref, 61 (1), 2606 (3)
Ruedisili, C. H.: rev, 1221
Ruef, M. L.: test, 309
Ruehlman, L. S.: test, 1733
Rues, J.: ref, 1770 (9)
Rueschenberg, E.: ref, 1010 (13)
Ruff, R. M.: ref, 272 (87), 1135 (10), 1164 (52), 2860 (356,1342), 2892 (51)
Ruffalo, P.: ref, 1824 (5)
Ruffalo, S. L.: ref, 2444 (1), 2452 (6,21), 2841 (1)
Ruffin, C. L.: ref, 1079 (19)
Rugen, M. E.: rev, 1184
Rugg, M. D.: ref, 1758 (30), 2863 (219)
Ruggiero, K. M.: ref, 2163 (309)
Rugle, L.: ref, 697 (5), 926 (12), 1407 (3), 1592 (15), 2010 (12), 2603 (522), 2892 (87)
Ruh, J.: ref, 681 (87), 1264 (6), 1889 (11), 1987 (22)
Ruiz-Caballero, J. A.: ref, 272 (135,313), 999 (135)
Rule, D. L.: rev, 1607
Ruma, P. R.: ref, 451 (149), 997 (13), 2065 (8)
Rumpold, G.: ref, 893 (25), 1079 (48)
Rumrill, P. D.: test, 2918
Rumsey, D. J.: ref, 2218 (77)
Rumsey, J. M.: ref, 2860 (213,436), 2892 (28)
Runco, M. A.: ref, 1227 (2), 2771 (22,27)
Rund, B. R.: ref, 1093 (54), 2519 (32), 2520 (33), 2862 (543)
Rundell, J. R.: ref, 2497 (361)
Rundquist, T. J.: test, 2148
Runtz, M. G.: ref, 694 (127), 2603 (550)
Runyon, D. K.: ref, 451 (3)
Rupert, L. J.: ref, 1612 (72)
Rupley, W. H.: rev, 1072, 1379 (37); ref, 1379 (97)
Rupp, A.: ref, 2860 (747)
Rupprecht, C.: ref, 1166 (26)
Rupprecht, M.: ref, 1166 (26)
Rupprecht, R.: ref, 1166 (26)
Ruscello, D. M.: test, 1852; ref, 1394 (5), 1852 (1), 1903 (142,208), 2651 (18), 2694 (8), 2704 (7)
Rusch, F. R.: test, 2826; ref, 474 (5)
Ruscitto, M. A.: ref, 2163 (114)
Rush, A. J.: ref, 272 (136), 473 (5), 1166 (4,81), 2305 (14,192)
Rush, J. C.: ref, 1107 (5), 1965 (60)
Rushing, B.: ref, 1927 (6)
Rushton, J. P.: ref, 999 (21), 1965 (17)
Rushton, R.: ref, 1036 (1)
Rusk, J.: test, 2160
Ruskin, E.: ref, 2229 (5)
Ruskin, E. M.: ref, 2228 (13)
Ruskin, J. N.: ref, 1697 (257), 2497 (300)
Russ, M. O.: ref, 2125 (17)
Russell, A.: ref, 1093 (80), 2050 (98,103)
Russell, A. J.: ref, 2860 (1343)
Russell, A. T.: ref, 2288 (37), 2289 (28), 2862 (288)
Russell, D. W.: ref, 272 (314), 998 (131)
Russell, E. W.: test, 1165; ref, 1164 (162), 2860 (166,1307)
Russell, G. L.: ref, 1093 (116)

Russell, J.: ref, 349 (12), 2662 (3)
Russell, J. A.: ref, 372 (52), 1001 (9), 1965 (44)
Russell, M.: test, 2417; ref, 1181 (18)
Russell, M. L.: rev, 338, 2705
Russell, R. E.: ref, 301 (9), 1072 (14), 2484 (2), 2862 (96)
Russell, R. J. H.: ref, 998 (110), 999 (101)
Russell, R. K.: ref, 893 (46)
Russell, T.: ref, 272 (360), 273 (34)
Russell, V.: ref, 2603 (319)
Russo, A.: ref, 1166 (205)
Russo, F.: ref, 272 (234), 2497 (599)
Russo, J.: ref, 272 (74), 1166 (40), 1697 (348), 2603 (29,75), 2858 (9,22,109)
Russo, J. R.: ref, 1010 (64)
Russo, M. A.: ref, 272 (234), 2497 (599)
Russo, P.: ref, 794 (2)
Rust, J.: test, 2260; rev, 22
Rust, J. O.: rev, 217, 1238, 2295, 2754; ref, 364 (11), 2484 (4)
Rustin, L.: ref, 350 (35), 1060 (7), 2725 (4)
Rustin, T.: ref, 2603 (551)
Rusting, C. L.: ref, 999 (193), 1697 (594)
Rutemiller, L. A.: ref, 289 (5), 372 (96), 902 (2), 1866 (41), 2214 (78), 2862 (376)
Ruth, L. P.: rev, 504, 614
Ruth, T.: ref, 1697 (15), 2860 (60)
Ruth, W. J.: ref, 2485 (149)
Ruther, N. M.: ref, 1991 (57)
Rutherford, M. J.: ref, 1661 (77), 2305 (152)
Rutigliano, P.: ref, 793 (22)
Rutland, A. F.: ref, 2862 (544)
Ruttenberg, B. A.: test, 285
Rutter, M.: ref, 350 (13,24,36), 459 (1), 837 (4), 901 (1), 1653 (5,13,21,22,26), 1903 (352), 2163 (145,195,236, 260), 2228 (11,16,21), 2305 (36,224), 2433 (1), 2860 (114,334,427,571,795,1034), 2862 (485)
Rutter, S. C.: ref, 2497 (474), 2860 (881)
Ruymann, F. B.: ref, 451 (215) 1962 (23)
Rvachew, S.: ref, 2228 (14)
Ryan, A. M.: ref, 1212 (1), 2218 (10,39)
Ryan, B. A.: ref, 451 (267), 694 (133, 1010 (135)
Ryan, C.: ref, 2860 (669)
Ryan, C. E.: ref, 1166 (84,193), 1166 (193)
Ryan, C. M.: ref, 449 (3), 926 (13), 1135 (19), 1697 (138), 2497 (603), 2516 (89), 2860 (516,1200), 2863 (360)
Ryan, G. T.: ref, 301 (46)
Ryan, J.: ref, 592 (88)
Ryan, J. J.: ref, 376 (25), 776 (53), 1758 (95), 2860 (214,395,582,739,967,968,1008,1151,1165,1324,1325,1326)
Ryan, J. M.: rev, 345, 2731; ref, 2835 (22)
Ryan, J. P.: test, 1224
Ryan, L.: ref, 272 (334), 376 (30), 776 (26), 2860 (517), 2863 (149,293), 2907 (3)
Ryan, L. C.: test, 1182
Ryan, M.: rev, 1693, 2824
Ryan, N. D.: ref, 2305 (216,245)
Ryan, R.: ref, 1735 (9), 2545 (4)
Ryan, R. H.: ref, 1902 (99), 2901 (129)
Ryan, R. M.: ref, 365 (6), 1657 (3,8), 1735 (3,5,11), 2076 (178), 2218 (113)
Ryan, S.: ref, 2519 (47), 2520 (48)
Ryan, T. V.: ref, 1164 (53), 1697 (237), 2860 (518)
Ryan-Wenger, N. M.: ref, 694 (18)
Ryans, D. G.: rev, 1799, 2757, 2808
Rybakowski, J. K.: ref, 1166 (155)
Rybarczyk, B. D.: ref, 2860 (45), 2863 (17)
Rychtarik, R. G.: ref, 134 (9)
Rycroft, P.: ref, 2603 (254)
Rydell, P. J.: ref, 1903 (91), 2657 (3)
Ryden, E. R.: test, 1985
Ryder, R. J.: ref, 1759 (14)
Ryff, C. D.: ref, 1333 (1), 1965 (29), 2126 (7)
Rylet, J.: ref, 2288 (78), 2289 (65)
Rylett, J.: ref, 2288 (55,79,42)
Rynard, D.: ref, 1216 (5)
Rynders, J.: test, 124
Rysavy, S. D.: ref, 2860 (649)
Rysberg, J. A.: rev, 270, 453
Ryser, G. R.: test, 2698

Saab, P. G.: ref, 1697 (27), 2497 (30)
Saah, A. J.: ref, 1135 (3), 2599 (5), 2860 (217)
Saam, R. H.: ref, 2497 (513)
Saarijarvi, S.: ref, 1079 (47), 1166 (161), 2860 (959)
Saarnio, D. A.: ref, 2862 (674)
Saarnio, P. K.: ref, 2860 (740,969)
Saayman, G. S.: ref, 1000 (11)
Sabatelli, R. M.: ref, 926 (1)
Sabatino, D. A.: rev, 353, 816
Sabbadini, L.: ref, 540 (13), 1903 (502), 2862 (572)
Sabbadini, M.: ref, 2163 (148,202), 2226 (19), 2860 (820)
Sabbagh, M. N.: ref, 376 (15), 1164 (145), 2860 (1244), 2862 (601), 2892 (266)
Sabban, Y. P.: ref, 2862 (141)
Sabbe, B.: ref, 1166 (147,211)
Sabbioni, M.: ref, 2076 (89)
Sabe, L.: ref, 303 (31), 1166 (82,229), 1740 (35), 2050 (120,121), 2163 (227,228,356), 2860 (935,1419), 2873 (40,41), 2892 (197,198,306)
Sabers, D. L.: rev, 406, 664, 809, 815, 1094, 1256, 2083, 1315; rev, 149, 906; ref, 298 (156), 1222 (1), 2651 (20), 2693 (6), 2694 (20), 2695 (60), 2835 (23), 2862 (545)
Sable, P.: ref, 337 (5,32)
Sabornie, E. J.: ref, 355 (1), 2879 (28), 2901 (13)
Sabourin, C.: ref, 1697 (385)
Sabourin, S.: ref, 298 (119), 404 (17), 451 (291), 472 (235), 863 (52,84), 999 (14), 2603 (25), 2858 (124)
Sabsay, S.: ref, 1240 (46) 1379 (87), 2163 (280)
Saccente, S.: ref, 1902 (98)
Sacco, J. M.: ref, 2218 (122)
Sacco, W. P.: ref, 2497 (137)
Saccuzzo, D. D.: ref, 2163 (186)
Saccuzzo, D. P.: ref, 2163 (240), 2862 (653)

Sacerdote, P.: ref, 1166 (69)
Sachdev, P.: ref, 998 (105)
Sachs, B.: ref, 448 (29), 2039 (4)
Sachs, G. S.: ref, 1166 (63)
Sachs, H.: ref, 2862 (289), 2864 (71)
Sachs, R.: ref, 298 (72)
Sack, R. L.: ref, 1697 (103), 2305 (44)
Sack, W. H.: ref, 1903 (163), 2485 (78)
Sackeim, H.: ref, 2288 (3)
Sackeim, H. A.: ref, 272 (203), 1166 (24,148), 2305 (45)
Sackett, P. R.: rev, 1343, 2937; ref, 180 (33), 372 (118), 2899 (10)
Sacks, A.: ref, 1697 (123)
Sacks, C. H.: ref, 2682 (10)
Sacks, M.: ref, 1093 (28)
Sadeh, A.: ref, 2862 (289), 2864 (71)
Sadeh, M.: ref, 1524 (2), 2862 (433)
Sadh, D.: ref, 298 (131)
Sadler, A. E.: ref, 2860 (380), 2862 (175), 2864 (18)
Sadoski, M.: ref, 705 (3), 2487 (7)
Sadowski, C.: ref, 2230 (7)
Sadowski, C. J.: rev, 197, 1792, 2922; ref, 2218 (114)
Saetti, M. C.: ref, 2860 (1251)
Saffran, E. M.: ref, 1903 (567)
Safran, C.: test, 2264
Safran, J. D.: ref, 2603 (263,386)
Safter, H. T.: ref, 2771 (5)
Safyer, A. W.: ref, 2603 (354)
Sagar, H. J.: ref, 1758 (19,54,66), 2193 (17,51), 2860 (495,1000,1069), 2863 (81,120,121,141,296), 2892 (67,68,80,209)
Sagen, H. B.: rev, 263, 2835
Sagrestano, L. M.: ref, 373 (25)
Sahakian, B. J.: ref, 1079 (51), 1390 (2,7), 1758 (2,7,10,17,32,37,49,52,57), 2193 (35), 2860 (90,206,215,792,849,1036)
Sahar, A.: ref, 2860 (11), 2863 (6)
Sahgal, A.: ref, 1390 (5), 1758 (63), 2860 (970,1055)
Sahin, D.: ref, 2497 (301)
Sahin, N.: ref, 272 (59)
Sahin, N. H.: ref, 272 (59)
Sahl, R.: ref, 2485 (226), 2862 (625)
Sahs, J. A.: ref, 337 (91), 2603 (299)
Saigal, J.: ref, 1991 (60), 2813 (51)
Saigh, P. A.: rev, 343, 2879, 2498 (66), 2862 (546)
Sailer, U.: ref, 2860 (892)
Sailor, P.: rev, 1790
Sailor, P. J.: ref, 2065 (20)
Sainato, D. M.: ref, 459 (5), 1612 (13)
Saini, S.: ref, 451 (178), 2305 (218)
Saint, D. J.: ref, 999 (102)
Saint-Cyr, J. A.: ref, 2125 (5), 2860 (227,519), 2863 (58)
Saisa, J.: ref, 2860 (439)
Saito, S.: ref, 1010 (34,108)
Saitzyk, A. R.: ref, 1010 (33), 1903 (118)
Saiz, J. L.: ref, 68 (51)
Saiz-Ruiz, J.: ref, 1697 (470)
Sajatovic, M.: ref, 335 (3)
Sakado, K.: ref, 1166 (212)
Sakado, M.: ref, 1166 (212)
Sakamoto, S.: ref, 273 (26), 1166 (213)
Sakauye, K.: rev, 176, 1743
Sakayanagi, T.: ref, 2915 (4)
Sakheim, G. A.: ref, 301 (19), 2247 (10,17), 2380 (4), 2749 (17,22), 2862 (142)
Sakin, J. W.: ref, 337 (162), 863 (82)
Sakkas, P. N.: ref, 1166 (192), 2497 (631)
Saklofske, D. H.: ref, 2862 (733)
Sakuma, N.: ref, 2860 (196), 2862 (111), 2879 (26)
Sakurada, M.: ref, 2288 (23), 2305 (69), 2860 (365)
Sakurai, Y.: ref, 2860 (396), 2873 (10)
Sala, S. D.: ref, 2163 (25,58,77)
Salamero, M.: ref, 999 (103), 1164 (70), 2860 (681), 2863 (201)
Salamon, A.: ref, 2603 (114)
Salamon, G.: ref, 2863 (261), 2892 (183)
Salas, M.: ref, 472 (37), 1181 (8)
Salaspuro, M.: ref, 1661 (24)
Salazar, A. M.: ref, 335 (6), 999 (63), 2497 (361), 2892 (89)
Salcedo, V.: ref, 2879 (117)
Sale, B. A.: ref, 2497 (558)
Saleh, S. D.: test, 1345
Salem, D. A.: ref, 337 (125)
Salend, S. J.: ref, 2862 (5)
Salerno, J. A.: ref, 1164 (110), 1740 (11), 2010 (18,20), 2860 (502,837,971), 2863 (242)
Sales, G.: ref, 2860 (649)
Saletsky, R. D.: ref, 451 (169), 880 (1), 1216 (96)
Salgado, J. F.: ref, 1822 (7)
Saliba, K.: ref, 1485 (63), 2862 (662)
Saling, C.: ref, 2525 (5)
Saling, M. M.: ref, 1744 (8), 2860 (520), 2863 (150,190,340)
Salinsky, M. C.: ref, 1697 (260)
Salisbury, C. L.: ref, 2813 (62)
Salisbury, D. F.: ref, 2305 (150)
Salisbury, S. B.: ref, 1341 (3)
Salkind, N. J.: test, 1592
Salkovskis, P.: ref, 2076 (121), 2519 (56), 2520 (55)
Salkovskis, P. M.: ref, 272 (327), 2497 (133,658)
Sallee, F. R.: ref, 272 (165)
Salloum, I. M.: ref, 272 (265), 1166 (180)
Salmela-Aro, K.: ref, 272 (220)
Salminen, S.: ref, 298 (127), 694 (87)
Salmon, D.: ref, 2860 (184), 2862 (105)
Salmon, D. D.: ref, 199 (10)
Salmon, D. P.: ref, 272 (334), 376 (21,30), 776 (7,21,25,26,28,34,41,44), 815 (14), 1058 (5), 1135 (4), 1164 (56,153), 1612 (46), 1903 (236), 2485 (117), 2860 (464,580), 2862 (120,203), 2863 (153,167,293), 2892 (202,275)
Salmon, J. D., Jr.: test, 2196
Salokangas, R. K. R.: ref, 1079 (47), 1166 (161), 2860 (959)

Salom, S. R.: ref, 2218 (4)
Salomon, M. S.: ref, 1166 (91), 2076 (142)
Salstone, R.: ref, 1697 (104)
Salter, D. W.: ref, 1755 (72)
Salthouse, T. A.: ref, 776 (37), 1405 (35), 2163 (131,324), 2304 (2), 2516 (84), 2860 (46,47,48,297, 521,522,523,972), 2892 (252)
Saltstone, R.: ref, 1697 (62,70)
Saltzberg, E.: ref, 893 (3)
Salus, D.: ref, 2115 (5)
Salvi, F.: ref, 1697 (222)
Salvia, J.: test, 2204; rev, 2768; ref, 1072 (29)
Salyer, K. M.: ref, 451 (15), 2242 (1), 2247 (18), 2485 (41), 2862 (143), 2879 (37)
Salzberg, A. D.: ref, 2214 (104)
Salzberg, C. L.: ref, 2860 (22)
Salzer, M. S.: ref, 451 (270), 2603 (300)
Samango-Sprouse, C.: ref, 2860 (1321)
Samar, V. J.: rev, 486, 487, 2298
Sameroff, A.: ref, 1321 (1), 2146 (12), 2402 (15), 2603 (174), 2864 (3)
Sameroff, A. J.: ref, 1166 (152), 1216 (88), 2146 (13), 2402 (22), 2603 (496), 2813 (57), 2864 (43)
Sammallahti, P.: ref, 1079 (52)
Sammallahti, P. R.: ref, 1079 (76), 1832 (17), 2603 (493)
Sampson, H.: ref, 272 (304)
Sampson, J. P.: ref, 1716 (5), 1942 (1)
Sampson, J. P., Jr.: test, 422
Sampson, P. D.: ref, 997 (24)
Sampson, R.: ref, 1408 (1)
Sampson, R. J.: ref, 2860 (741), 2862 (290)
Sampson, S. A.: ref, 1104 (4), 2193 (23), 2239 (21), 2860 (659), 2863 (194)
Samson, D.: ref, 2497 (193)
Samson, J.: ref, 1903 (192), 2860 (491)
Samson, S.: ref, 2860 (742), 2863 (104)
Samstag, L. W.: ref, 2326 (2), 2603 (286,386,546)
Samuel, J. V.: ref, 592 (14)
Samuels, C. A.: ref, 373 (32), 926 (19), 2042 (2)
The San Diego HIV Neurobehavioral Research Center Group: ref, 1164 (77)
Sanacore, J.: ref, 592 (28)
Sanavio, E.: ref, 999 (16), 2497 (52)
Sanchez, D. T.: rev, 2465
Sanchez, J.: ref, 1140 (17)
Sanchez, M. A. M.: ref, 2117 (5)
Sanchez, P.: rev, 720
Sanchez, S.: ref, 2862 (534)
Sánchez-Bernardos, M. L.: ref, 2218 (118)
Sanchez-Ramos, J.: ref, 1218 (3), 2860 (276)
Sand, L.: ref, 1166 (165)
Sand, S.: ref, 998 (121)
Sand, T.: ref, 1164 (87)
Sandage, S. J.: ref, 717 (1), 863 (75)
Sandberg, A. D.: ref, 1136 (1)
Sandel, M. E.: ref, 2860 (606), 2863 (179)
Sander, A. M.: ref, 1697 (552)
Sander, D.: rev, 1539
Sanderman, R.: ref, 998 (129), 999 (104,176,195), 1079 (30,56)
Sanders, B.: ref, 272 (97), 846 (10)
Sanders, C.: rev, 20, 22, 25; ref, 1902 (98)
Sanders, C. E.: ref, 68 (49), 771 (25), 1010 (86), 2163 (241)
Sanders, D.: ref, 372 (62)f, 1965 (48)
Sanders, G. O.: ref, 1697 (579)
Sanders, J. R.: test, 2555; rev, 2462
Sanders, M. J.: ref, 1010 (87)
Sanders, M. M.: ref, 1469 (13)
Sanders, M. R.: ref, 272 (315), 451 (223), 863 (2,44)
Sanders, R. E.: ref, 665 (21), 2860 (901)
Sanders, R. F.: ref, 1755 (71)
Sanders-Phillips, K.: ref, 301 (50), 472 (144,205), 1991 (86), 2498 (70), 2862 (390)
Sanderson, W. C.: ref, 1166 (102), 1687 (20), 1697 (372), 2603 (331,451)
Sandford, J. A.: test, 1282
Sandler, A. D.: test, 1905
Sandler, B. A.: ref, 2749 (60)
Sandler, I.: ref, 472 (17,189)
Sandler, I. N.: ref, 451 (272), 462 (1), 472 (38,51, 102,145,176,200,228,234), 1697 (539), 2214 (20,23, 107,118), 2603 (9)
Sandler, L. S.: ref, 2603 (128,157)
Sandman, C.: ref, 2860 (868)
Sandman, R. S.: test, 1599
Sandor, J. A.: test, 8
Sandoval, J.: test, 469; rev, 280, 874, 1590, 2606, 2862; ref, 372 (53) 1590 (27)
Sandoval, K. T.: ref, 214 (18), 1394 (10), 1903 (324), 2695 (31), 2866 (4)
Sands, C.: ref, 2076 (151)
Sands, D.: ref, 2860 (89)
Sands, E. S.: test, 277
Sands, J. R.: ref, 2305 (105), 2860 (743,973)
Sands, L. P.: ref, 2860 (135,398)
Sands, R.: ref, 2749 (1)
Sandson, J.: ref, 2163 (5), 2860 (16,182), 2863 (9), 2892 (2)
Sandvik, E.: ref, 337 (66), 1172 (1), 2218 (9)
Sandy, C. A.: rev, 319, 2653
Saneslow, C. A.,III: ref, 272 (342), 2603 (574)
Sanfilipo, M.: ref, 2860 (419,1205), 2892 (61,261)
Sanfilipo, M. P.: ref, 790 (10)
Sanford, E.: ref, 413 (5)
Sanford, E. E.: rev, 1155, 2246, 2471, 2903; ref, 413 (10,13)
Sang, J.: ref, 2218 (118)
Sanger, D. D.: rev, 540; ref, 1424 (2), 2862 (174)
Sänger-Alt, C.: ref, 1001 (3)
Sanikhani, M.: ref, 451 (241)
Sanna, L. J.: ref, 2497 (592)
Sannibale, C.: ref, 134 (3), 136 (1), 1079 (4), 1661 (3)

Sano, M.: ref, 303 (18,29), 776 (45,61), 1166 (103), 1697 (88), 1740 (21,32), 2125 (7,18), 2163 (124), 2402 (6), 2516 (16,28), 2860 (310,407,496,512, 906,907,1180,1284,1346,1405), 2863 (292)
Sansavini, A.: ref, 2485 (214)
Sanson, A.: ref, 34 (2,3,4,5), 863 (29), 1079 (15), 1765 (30,31,33), 2039 (8), 2485 (68), 2813 (21,48), 2862 (554,575), 2879 (186)
Sansone, L. A.: ref, 824 (6),1687 (46)
Sansone, R. A.: ref, 824 (6), 1687 (46)
The Santa Cruz County Office of Education: test, 1194
Santa-Barbara, J.: test, 1008
Santangelo, S. L.: ref, 1010 (70), 1092 (13), 2305 (121), 2862 (310), 2879 (102)
Santhouse, R.: ref, 2603 (103)
Santiago, J. V.: ref, 1010 (80)
Santiago-Rivera, A. L.: ref, 2858 (106)
Santilli, N. R.: ref, 771 (13)
Santinello, M.: ref, 1590 (26)
Santini, J. J.: ref, 2862 (329)
Santisteban, D.: ref, 1010 (15), 1991 (4)
Santmire, T. E.: rev, 178, 1942
Santogrossi, J.: rev, 2190, 2191
Santonastaso, P.: ref, 893 (52), 2603 (578)
Santor, D. A.: ref, 790 (27)
Santos de Barona, M.: ref, 615 (39)
Santos, S. J.: ref, 694 (47)
Santostefano, S.: test, 563; ref, 2247 (2), 2862 (6)
Santucci, L. M.: ref, 1166 (173)
Santulli, K. A.: ref, 665 (40)
Sanz, J.: ref, 2656 (14)
Sanz, M.: ref, 2892 (263)
Saper, Z.: ref, 1959 (3)
Sapp, G. L.: ref, 1386 (16,26), 2813 (63)
Sapp, M.: ref, 272 (316), 694 (19,104), 1697 (568), 2497 (653), 2656 (21), 2879 (29,135)
Sappenfield, B. R.: rev, 317, 2248
Sappington, J.: ref, 853 (21), 1697 (512)
Sara, G.: ref, 272 (88)
Saracco, M.: ref, 272 (224), 1166 (156)
Saracho, O. N.: ref, 1903 (308), 2682 (11)
Saragovi, C.: ref, 2246 (9)
Saran, A.: ref, 1093 (34)
Sarason, B. R.: ref, 272 (308), 1010 (92)
Sarason, I. G.: rev, 751; ref, 272 (308), 1010 (92)
Saravay, S. M.: ref, 2603 (494)
Sarazin, M.: ref, 776 (33), 2516 (82), 2892 (249)
Sarfatti, S. E.: ref, 451 (102), 2862 (450)
Sargeant, M.: ref, 2050 (32,54), 2498 (16)
Sargent, H.: rev, 2247
Sarimski, K.: ref, 1889 (14), 2052 (2)
Sarimurat, N.: ref, 2497 (301)
Sarkin, A. J.: ref, 324 (10), 331 (6), 1903 (456), 2768 (33)
Sarlo, M.: ref, 1021 (43)
Sarlo-McGarvey, N.: ref, 433 (4), 2813 (12,20)
Sarma, P. S. B.: ref, 364 (2)
Sarmany-Schuller, I.: ref, 2218 (115)
Sarmousakis, G.: rev, 914
Sarnie, M. K.: ref, 1697 (257), 2497 (300)
Sarno, M. T.: test, 1061
Saron, C.: ref, 1072 (15), 1131 (6), 2862 (98), 2905 (10)
Sarphare, G.: ref, 1021 (41), 2862 (547)
Sarrafzadeh, A.: ref, 1166 (165)
Sarraj, E. E.: ref, 998 (104), 2862 (385)
Sarros, A. M.: ref, 1590 (9)
Sarros, J. C.: ref, 1590 (9)
Sartori, G.: ref, 2288 (81), 2289 (67), 2860 (684,1311)
Sartorius, N.: test, 2050; ref, 2050 (10)
Sartory, G.: ref, 2860 (1422), 2892 (309)
Sarwer, D. B.: ref, 298 (92), 1697 (238)
Sas, L.: ref, 472 (108), 1903 (331), 2214 (57)
Sasaki, H.: ref, 2860 (1278)
Sasaki, S.: ref, 1128 (3)
Sasaki, Y.: ref, 1128 (3)
Sasanuma, S.: ref, 2860 (196), 2862 (111), 2879 (26)
Sashkin, M.: test, 677, 1268, 1438, 1608, 1858
Sass, K. J.: ref, 2860 (216,974), 2863 (286)
Sastre, M.: ref, 1166 (109)
Sastry, N.: ref, 776 (51)
Satake, E.: ref, 2484 (6)
Satish, V.: ref, 1661 (75), 2603 (556)
Satlin, A.: ref, 2227 (58), 2860 (1396), 2863 (421)
Satlow, E.: ref, 2862 (259)
Sato, S.: ref, 1128 (3), 1166 (212), 2860 (1416)
Sato, T.: ref, 272 (317), 1166 (212)
Sato, Y.: ref, 2305 (228), 2813 (149)
Satter, G. A.: rev, 302, 534
Satterfield, A. T.: ref, 694 (128)
Sattler, D. N.: ref, 1748 (1)
Sattler, J. M.: test, 2485; rev, 301, 1059, 1386, 1407, 1612, 2813
Satz, P.: test, 1778, 1993; ref, 272 (181), 376 (5), 811 (3), 1135 (2,6,13,26), 1164 (105,180), 1166 (113), 1379 (10), 1645 (1), 1697 (330), 1758 (47), 1993 (1), 2305 (104), 2599 (4,8,15,40), 2813 (8), 2860 (101,200,224,287,697,698,772,937,938), 2862 (115), 2863 (57,204,276,324)
Saucier, J.: ref, 2039 (18)
Saucier, J-F.: ref, 298 (165), 1661 (78), 2039 (23)
Saud-de-Numez, G.: ref, 926 (7), 2771 (14)
Saudargas, R. A.: rev, 495, 2590
Saudino, K. J.: ref, 270 (39), 1216 (109)
Sauer, J.: ref, 2305 (93)
Sauer, J. L.: ref, 326 (4), 1625 (1), 2146 (9), 2892 (42)
Sauerwein, H.: ref, 2125 (6), 2860 (272), 2862 (135)
Sauier, J.: ref, 2603 (372), 2860 (916)
Saul, D. L.: ref, 1178 (1), 2497 (16)
Saunders, B. E.: ref, 1697 (496), 2417 (29)
Saunders, D. E.: test, 422
Saunders, D. M.: rev, 1551, 2586
Saunders, D. R.: rev, 1158
Saunders, E. B.: ref, 2247 (19), 2749 (23)
Saunders, J.: test, 135

Saunders, P.: test, 2718
Saunders, W. B.: ref, 998 (19), 2305 (30)
Saundino, K.: ref, 270 (48), 2485 (244)
Sauser, W. I.: rev, 1253, 1972
Sauser, W. I., Jr.: rev, 133, 408, 990, 1352, 1566, 2071
Sauter, B.: ref, 2227 (43), 2860 (1305), 2892 (278)
Sautter, F. J.: ref, 2305 (153)
Savackas, M. L.: ref, 413 (9)
Savage, A. W.: test, 2346
Savage, C. R.: ref, 2227 (26), 2860 (1103)
Savage, H.: ref, 1240 (14), 1903 (174)
Savard, J.: ref, 272 (375), 2498 (77)
Saver, J.: ref, 2305 (94)
Savickas, M. L.: ref, 413 (27)
Savicki, V.: ref, 301 (8), 372 (11), 1160 (1), 1697 (45), 2860 (136), 2864 (13)
Saville & Holdsworth Ltd.: test, 1544, 1822, 2274, 2641, 2914, 2927
Saville, P.: test, 119, 735, 1201, 1973, 2087, 2642; ref, 1822 (2)
Savino, M.: ref, 1166 (205), 2603 (135,211)
Savoie, T.: ref, 2288 (41), 2289 (31), 2305 (116)
Savournin, R.: ref, 2603 (400)
Sawicki, J. S.: ref, 2862 (83)
Sawilowsky, S. S.: ref, 694 (110,123), 1991 (100)
Sawyer, D. I.: rev, 1269
Sawyer, D. J.: test, 2674; rev, 1060, 1148, 2040, 2175, 2176, 2434, 2743
Sawyer, J. D.: ref, 2603 (388)
Sawyer, M.: ref, 451 (44), 1079 (29), 2599 (29), 2862 (358), 2879 (89,123)
Sawyer, M. G.: ref, 451 (281), 1079 (110)
Sawyer, R.: ref, 56 (18)
Sawyers, J. K.: ref, 2862 (24), 2864 (2)
Sax, D. S.: ref, 1903 (1), 2860 (2), 2863 (1)
Saxley, E.: ref, 272 (137), 1687 (17)
Saxon, A. J.: ref, 1687 (1)
Saxton, M. J.: test, 1397
Saxton, T.: ref, 349 (33)
Saxty, M.: ref, 2050 (127)
Sayegh, L.: ref, 1903 (6)
Sayer, N.: ref, 2247 (132)
Sayers, S. L.: ref, 372 (54)
Sayette, M. A.: ref, 134 (20), 272 (89,90), 1661 (33,34)
Saykin, A. J.: ref, 1164 (17), 1525 (8), 1752 (1), 2860 (80,137,269,744), 2863 (23,38), 2892 (8,22)
Sayler, M. F.: ref, 1991 (9)
Sayles-Folks, S. L.: ref, 1592 (4), 2860 (138)
Saylor, C.: ref, 451 (275), 2485 (243), 2862 (723)
Saylor, C. F.: ref, 265 (14)
Sbrana, B.: ref, 2860 (442)
Scafidi, F.: ref, 1770 (17)
Scales, W.: ref, 615 (53), 2860 (877), 2860 (1088), 2862 (345,482)
Scandora, T. A.: ref, 1701 (41), 2389 (1)
Scanlon, C. R.: ref, 2115 (3), 2603 (184)
Scanlon, D. M.: ref, 1092 (17), 1903 (435)
Scanlon, J. W.: ref, 451 (183), 787 (3), 1379 (93)
Scanlon, K. B.: ref, 451 (183), 787 (3), 1379 (93)
Scanlon, M.: ref, 1166 (31)
Scanlon, M. B.: ref, 298 (56)
Scannell, D. P.: test, 389, 2735; rev, 204, 614, 1792, 2145
Scanzoni, J.: ref, 298 (42), 1881 (1)
Scarborough, H. S.: ref, 1612 (10), 1804 (2), 2488 (3), 2860 (139), 2862, 2901 (9)
Scarone, S. : ref, 2892 (159,262)
Scarr, S.: ref, 875 (11), 1264 (5,6), 1866 (21), 1889 (4,11), 1987 (22), 2163 (94), 2485 (69), 2860 (399, 524)
Scarvie, K. M.: ref, 815 (41), 2485 (215)
Scavone, J.: ref, 451 (209), 1582 (14)
Schaaf, K. K.: ref, 2782 (3)
Schaaf, R. C.: ref, 1901 (1)
Schaafsma, M. F.: ref, 2497 (99)
Schaap, C.: ref, 1010 (114), 2603 (509)
Schaberg, L.: ref, 2603 (428)
Schachar, R.: ref, 2862 (391), 2879 (136)
Schachter, D.: ref, 241 (4),451 (94), 815 (35), 1903 (447), 2695 (47), 2864 (110)
Schacter, D. L.: ref, 376 (17), 2227 (32), 2860 (32,41, 65,98,745,1166), 2863 (11,15,20,28), 2873 (7), 2892 (268)
Schacter, H.: rev, 1492
Schad, L. R.: ref, 1166 (202)
Schade, M. L.: ref, 2050 (67), 2879 (74), 2892 (110)
Schaefer, B.: test, 1504
Schaefer, C. E.: test, 725
Schaefer, J. H.: ref, 451 (139), 472 (178), 2485 (209), 2862 (515)
Schaefer, M. T.: test, 1927
Schaefer, W. C.: rev, 2807
Schaefer-Herman, P.: ref, 337 (79)
Schaefers, K. G.: ref, 495 (13), 1602 (1)
Schaeffer, C. M.: ref, 272 (338), 1687 (37)
Schaeffer, D.: test, 1821
Schaeffer, J.: test, 1821
Schafer, D. S.: test, 879
Schafer, J.: ref, 2497 (654), 2860 (1344)
Schafer, R. E.: rev, 833
Schafer, S.: ref, 2603 (112)
Schafer, W. D.: rev, 411, 645, 670
Schaffer, B.: test, 70
Schaffer, C. E.: test, 215, 790
Schaffer, W. D.: rev, 2191
Schag, C. A. C.: ref, 863 (8), 2603 (61)
Schagen, I. P.: ref, 2556 (1)
Schagen, S.: ref, 1164 (168), 2226 (34), 2239 (32), 2516 (110), 2860 (1345), 2863 (403), 2076 (123), 2247 (94)
Schaie, K. W.: test, 2304, 537, 1390, 2372, 372 (31), 1405 (5), 2304 (1,4)
Schall, M.: ref, 372 (41), 838 (12), 999 (44), 1140 (25)
Schaller, J. A.: ref, 2407 (4)
Schallow, J. R.: ref, 694 (127), 2603 (550)

Schalock, R. L.: ref, 2132 (3)
Schanberg, S.: ref, 2498 (67)
Schandler, S. L.: ref, 462 (12,26), 1405 (26), 1661 (49)
Schanfeli, W.: test, 1590
Schaper, M. W.: ref, 2441 (1)
Schapira-Beck, E.: ref, 863 (49)
Schapiro, M. B.: ref, 199 (16), 1164 (110), 1240 (21), 1740 (11), 2010 (16,18,20), 2163 (179), 2485 (234), 2516 (47), 2860 (502,703,837,971,1141, 1155,1216, 1223), 2863 (205,242,364), 2879 (87,190)
Schappe, S. P.: ref, 1701 (55)
Schare, M. L.: ref, 337 (55), 793 (12), 2396 (1)
Scharpé, S.: ref, 1166 (58,77,127,217), 2497 (127)
Schatschneider, C.: ref, 353 (19), 433 (9), 745 (5), 815 (31), 994 (33), 1092 (8,9), 1215 (3), 1379 (78), 1982 (12), 2125 (19), 2768 (22), 2813 (24,108), 2862 (185), 2879 (51), 2907 (4)
Schatschneider, C. W.: ref, 1379 (34), 1903 (210)
Schatz, E. L.: ref, 694 (90)
Schatz, J.: ref, 375 (8), 1485 (44), 1653 (24), 2720 (1), 2813 (102), 2864 (102), 2892 (297)
Schatzberg, A. F.: ref, 1903 (192), 2860 (491)
Schaub, M.: ref, 175 (10), 1040 (9), 1240 (28), 1804 (9), 1903 (282)
Schauben, L. J.: ref, 337 (74,117), 1590 (52)
Schaubroeck, J.: ref, 998 (80), 2016 (2)
Schauer, C. A.: ref, 199 (17)
Schauf, J. D.: ref, 1903 (180,271), 2905 (39,57)
Schaufeli, W. B.: ref, 1590 (39,40,53,61,64,68), 2603 (158)
Schaul, N.: ref, 2860 (1005)
Schaumann, H.: ref, 234 (1)
Scheck, C. L.: ref, 1701 (13)
Scheel, M. J.: ref, 1754 (11)
Scheffers, M. K.: ref, 2860 (400), 2863 (105)
Scheffers, W.: test, 2818
Schefft, B. K.: ref, 2658 (2), 2860 (1170)
Scheftner, W.: ref, 2305 (210)
Scheftner, W. A.: ref, 1093 (22,23)
Scheibe, G.: ref, 1093 (82), 1166 (149), 1517 (11)
Scheidegger, P.: ref, 2603 (33)
Scheidt, C. E.: ref, 2603 (495)
Scheier, I. H.: test, 1321, 1779
Scheier, L. M.: ref, 998 (132)
Scheier, M. F.: ref, 1158 (2), 2497 (391)
Scheike, T.: ref, 272 (201)
Schein, E. H.: test, 396
Scheiner, N.: ref, 772 (1), 1612 (33), 1901 (11), 2813 (34)
Schell, L. M.: test, 1768
Schellenbach, C. J.: ref, 1619 (4)
Schellenberg, G.: ref, 776 (58)
Schellenberg, G. D.: ref, 303 (26), 2860 (1382)
Scheltens, P.: ref, 2516 (15)
Schelvis, A. J.: ref, 1164 (36)
Schenck, S. J.: rev, 2625
Schenneman, J. D.: ref, 1115 (27)
Schepers, J. M.: rev, 1053
Scher, M. S.: ref, 1612 (49)f, 1903 (254), 2382 (21)
Scherder, E. J. A.: ref, 2240 (1), 2863 (106)
Scherer, D. G.: ref, 337 (158), 451 (150)
Scherer, J.: test, 1913; ref, 1093 (82), 1517 (11)
Scherer, M. J.: test, 1591, 1593
Scherer, R. F.: ref, 1590 (17), 2858 (55,83)
Schery, T. K.: ref, 433 (5), 994 (5), 1903 (140), 2459 (1), 2704 (20), 2813 (22)
Schexnayder, L. W.: ref, 2305 (153)
Schiavi, R. C.: ref, 863 (71), 2076 (179)
Schick, B.: ref, 2498 (41)
Schiefele, U.: ref, 1965 (69), 2031 (10), 2309 (2)
Schiff, B. B.: ref, 1697 (349), 2497 (392,514), 2749 (8,62)
Schiffman, E.: ref, 1592 (7)
Schiitz, A.: ref, 1333 (6)
Schilder, A. G. M.: ref, 2163 (113,182), 2229 (2)
Schill, T.: ref, 68 (31), 846 (7), 1697 (190,336)
Schilling, E. A.: ref, 791 (4), 998 (26)
Schincaglia, M.: ref, 1021 (43)
Schindler, A. W.: rev, 364
Schindler, R. J.: ref, 2163 (159), 2863 (181), 2873 (22)
Schinka, J. A.: test, 478, 808, 1186, 1648, 1649, 1650, 1777, 1934, 1941, 1942, 2533; ref, 1697 (586,595), 1698 (26), 1959 (4,8), 2860 (746,773,1195), 2862 (670), 2892 (155)
Schinke, S.: rev, 143, 893
Schinke, S. P.: rev, 462, 1181; ref, 999 (118)
Schinkel, A. M.: ref, 1010 (36)
Schippers, G. M.: ref, 2497 (239,323,655)
Schirling, J.: ref, 272 (337)
Schirmer, B. R.: ref, 2862 (123), 2901 (15)
Schissel, R. J.: rev, 2866
Schittecatte, M.: ref, 1166 (4), 2305 (14)
Schladale, J.: ref, 2858 (23)
Schlaudecker, C.: ref, 324 (7)
Schlaug, G.: ref, 2860 (1285)
Schlebusch, D.: test, 1293
Schlechte, J. A.: ref, 863 (16)
Schlegel, S.: ref, 1166 (27)
Schleifer, D.: ref, 2860 (1203), 2879 (187)
Schlein, I. S.: ref, 272 (310)
Schlenger, W. E.: ref, 1697 (325)
Schlenz, K. C.: ref, 1590 (54)
Schleyer, M.: ref, 1166 (50)
Schlienger, J.: ref, 2863 (63)
Schlienger, J. L.: ref, 1166 (56)
Schloss, P. J.: ref, 342 (3), 2862 (294,392), 2901 (48,71)
Schlosser, R. W.: ref, 1903 (209)
Schlosser, S.: ref, 451 (35)
Schlottmann, R. S.: ref, 1697 (191,583)
Schlundt, D. G.: ref, 893 (28), 2603 (367)
Schluter, J. L.: ref, 1697 (446), 2703 (2)
Schmand, B.: ref, 1164 (168), 2226 (34), 2239 (32), 2516 (110), 2860 (1345), 2863 (403)
Schmeck, R. R.: test, 1307
Schmeidler, J.: ref, 2305 (225)
Schmeiser, C.: test, 1491

Schmid, R. F.: rev, 1599
Schmidt, A.: ref, 272 (193), 1697 (498), 2497 (566)
Schmidt, A-M.: ref, 1754 (13), 1755 (21), 2915 (5)
Schmidt, C.: ref, 1697 (58)
Schmidt, C. P.: ref, 68 (40), 1755 (15)
Schmidt, C. W.: ref, 793 (18), 998 (38), 1158 (1), 1697 (152), 2218 (49,85), 2519 (23), 2520 (24)
Schmidt, E.: ref, 2860 (747,1202), 2862 (578)
Schmidt, F.: rev, 305
Schmidt, F. L.: rev, 1575, 2899; ref, 372 (109)
Schmidt, G. W.: ref, 998 (100), 1036 (13)
Schmidt, H. S.: ref, 1697 (95)
Schmidt, J. A.: ref, 1243 (2,4), 1290 (2), 1754 (18,21), 2120 (4), 2497 (298), 2603 (229)
Schmidt, J. P.: test, 1454
Schmidt, K. L.: ref, 472 (191), 1697 (309), 2214 (112), 2211 (19)
Schmidt, M.: test, 2226; ref, 1164 (54), 1697 (246), 2860 (538), 2863 (154)
Schmidt, M. F.: ref, 2603 (571)
Schmidt, M. H.: ref, 624 (19), 1240 (27)
Schmidt, M. W.: test, 2204
Schmidt, P. F.: test, 439
Schmidt, P. J.: ref, 2497 (279)
Schmidt, R.: ref, 2860 (525), 2892 (88)
Schmidt, S. M.: test, 1402; ref, 1402 (2,3)
Schmidt, W. H.: test, 313, 1904, 1912, 2773
Schmidt-Traub, S.: ref, 271 (14), 2497 (656)
Schmidtke, K.: ref, 2863 (350,404)
Schmit, M. J.: ref, 2218 (10,39)
Schmitt, F. A.: ref, 2860 (1157)
Schmitt, J. F.: rev, 1361
Schmitt, N.: test, 648, 838, 1355, 2075, 2937; ref, 2218 (122), 2860 (1384), 2899 (17)
Schmitter-Edgecombe, M.: ref, 2603 (401), 2863 (287)
Schmitz, C. D.: ref, 1697 (197)
Schmitz, J. B.: ref, 2076 (146)
Schmitz, J. M.: ref, 2603 (551)
Schmitz, P.: ref, 2076 (131), 2603 (423)
Schmitz, S.: ref, 451 (73,118), 2039 (22)
Schmock, K.: ref, 1095 (29), 1903 (313), 2657 (18)
Schmuckler, J.: rev, 49
Schmulbach, S.: ref, 615 (2), 1657 (6)
Schnall, P. L.: ref, 1338 (30), 2497 (182)
Schnayer, R.: ref, 1903 (20)
Schneck, C. M.: ref, 2860 (724)
Schneck, G. R.: rev, 2826, 2923
Schneider, A. M.: ref, 2485 (83), 2599 (13), 2860 (457)
Schneider, B.: ref, 1755 (78)
Schneider, B. H.: ref, 385 (1), 1197 (1)
Schneider, E.: ref, 1590 (56), 1673 (10)
Schneider, E. A.: test, 1907
Schneider, F.: ref, 1903 (412), 2163 (239)
Schneider, H. G.: ref, 2497 (88)
Schneider, K.: ref, 495 (16), 1181 (27, 1991 (105)
Schneider, L. S.: ref, 337 (82), 1164 (69), 2520 (45), 2599 (20), 2860 (676), 2863 (200)
Schneider, M. F.: test, 467
Schneider, M. S.: ref, 2497 (140)
Schneider, N. G.: test, 2440
Schneider, P.: ref, 1903 (494), 2694 (21)
Schneider, S.: ref, 2076 (85), 2860 (664)
Schneider, S. E.: ref, 2603 (212)
Schneider, S. G.: ref, 2076 (33)
Schneider, S. L.: ref, 1697 (212), 2873 (58)
Schneider, S. S.: ref, 2873 (72)
Schneider, W.: ref, 1592 (17)
Schneiderman, E.: ref, 2163 (242), 2620 (1)
Schneiderman, N.: ref, 1697 (27), 2497 (30)
Schneidmann, N. V.: rev, 433
Schneier, C. E.: ref, 298 (14)
Schneier, F. R.: ref, 2305 (147)
Schnell, L. H.: rev, 174
Schnell, R.: ref, 2497 (436)
Schnetderman, N.: ref, 2603 (516)
Schniebolk, S.: ref, 303 (2), 1164 (23), 2497 (104), 2603 (83), 2860 (237)
Schniicker, G.: ref, 451 (77), 1612 (80), 2860 (976)
Schnoll, S.: ref, 2519 (26), 2520 (27)
Schnoll, S. H.: ref, 1697 (218), 2402 (18)
Schnurr, P. P.: ref, 1697 (355), 2603 (308)
Schnyder, C.: ref, 1166 (101), 1661 (54)
Schoemaker, C.: ref, 893 (47)
Schoen, H. L.: test, 1315
Schoen, M. J.: ref, 1903 (309)
Schoen, S. F.: ref, 342 (4), 815 (29), 837 (8), 1903 (414)
Schoendorf, K.: test, 41
Schoenfeld, J.: ref, 376 (10)
Schoenfeld, L. S.: ref, 1697 (212)
Schoenfeldt, L. F.: rev, 1700, 2633, 2700, 2762, 2899
Schoenherr, S.: ref, 246 (4), 1379 (24), 1903 (158)
Schoenrade, P.: rev, 946, 1498, 2474, 2805
Schofer, J. L.: ref, 451 (238), 1010 (131)
Schoff, L. A.: ref, 592 (85)
Schofield, P.: ref, 303 (18), 776 (45), 1740 (21), 2860 (1284)
Schofield, P. W.: ref, 2860 (1346)
Schofield, W.: rev, 303, 2258
Scholarios, D. M.: ref, 180 (25)
Scholastic Testing Service, Inc.: test, 547, 1202, 2137
Scholes, R. J.: ref, 2879 (121)
Scholey, K. A.: ref, 2862 (555)
Scholfield, E. J.: ref, 272 (172), 2497 (555)
Scholing, A.: ref, 2497 (336)
Scholler, D. R.: ref, 790 (17)
Scholsinger, C.: ref, 2497 (576)
Scholte, W. F.: ref, 2050 (47,48), 2892 (93)
Scholz, M.: ref, 2163 (200), 2860 (816), 2863 (235)
Schomer, D.: ref, 815 (39), 1903 (481), 2671 (3), 2862 (522), 2879 (176), 2901 (97)
Schommer, M.: ref, 1405 (12), 1657 (15), 2879 (116)
Schonfeld, I. S.: ref, 451 (236), 2813 (154)
Schonfeld, L.: test, 2551
Schonfeld, W. H.: ref, 2603 (552)

Schonholtz, J.: ref, 1582 (8)
Schonle, P. W.: ref, 2860 (835), 2863 (241)
Schooler, C.: ref, 926 (5)
Schooler, N. R.: ref, 650 (9), 2288 (22,38), 2289 (29), 2305 (67)
Schopflocher, D.: ref, 999 (146)
Schopler, E.: test, 70, 459, 2111; ref, 70 (1), 459 (1,9,14), 1485 (15), 1653 (6,7), 1903 (148), 2163 (71,98,125), 2813 (27,28), 2860 (114,411)
Schorr, O.: ref, 2497 (69)
Schorr, S.: ref, 1697 (66,67), 2076 (9,10)
Schotte, C.: ref, 1166 (5,20,198), 2497 (25)
Schottenfeld, R.: ref, 2519 (29), 2520 (30)
Schrader, D.: ref, 1408 (2)
Schrader, M. S.: ref, 2860 (1053)
Schrader, W. B.: rev, 9, 10, 1672, 2324, 2401
Schraeder, B. D.: ref, 451 (24), 815 (7), 1216 (11,24), 1379 (21), 1728 (1)
Schrag, J. A.: ref, 451 (40)
Schram, M.: test, 212
Schrank, F. A.: rev, 179, 322, 406
Schraw, G.: rev, 1163, 1462, 1714; ref, 56 (11)
Schredl, M.: ref, 1697 (350)
Schreiber, E. H.: ref, 592 (98)
Schreiber, G.: ref, 272 (249), 1166 (169)
Schreiber, J. L.: ref, 1093 (25), 2892 (31)
Schreiber, K. N.: ref, 592 (98)
Schreiber, S.: ref, 2497 (199,593)
Schreibman, L.: ref, 994 (34), 1902 (96), 1903 (432), 2485 (184)
Schreier, S.: ref, 337 (3), 451 (6), 472 (2), 2497 (35)
Schreiner, R.: test, 1768
Schreiner, R. L.: rev, 827
Schreppers-Tijdink, G.: ref, 2862 (65), 2864 (8)
Schretlen, D.: ref, 1697 (105), 2860 (748,1033)
Schreuder, J. N.: ref, 1697 (304)
Schriesheim, C. A.: ref, 1701 (6,20,35)
Schriner, K. F.: ref, 404 (4,6), 936 (1), 1754 (4)
Schröder, J.: ref, 1166 (202)
Schroeder, C. G.: ref, 2835 (7)
Schroeder, D. A.: ref, 1697 (81,82), 2497 (10)
Schroeder, L. C.: test, 1609
Schroeder, S. R.: ref, 4 (7), 811 (5), 1216 (35)
Schteingart, J. S.: ref, 451 (74), 889 (1)
Schubert, D. S. P.: test, 354, 2324; ref, 2603 (205)
Schubert, H. J. P.: test, 851, 2324
Schuckit, M. A.: ref, 999 (105), 1166 (70), 1661 (14), 1697 (351), 2305 (46,154,195), 2414 (3), 2497 (105,393), 2858 (90), 2860 (845)
Schudel, W. J.: ref, 2497 (259)
Schudovizky, A.: ref, 2497 (414)
Schuele, C. M.: ref, 1095 (36), 1379 (75), 1903 (415), 2229 (6)
Schueler, H.: rev, 579
Schuerger, J. M.: ref, 1697 (165)
Schuerholz, L. J.: ref, 681 (66), 2860 (1167), 2862 (393,548), 2892 (253), 2901 (72,100)
Schugens, M. M.: ref, 2860 (835), 2863 (241)
Schuhmann, E. M.: ref, 272 (376), 863 (93), 997 (30), 1889 (19), 1903 (580), 2752 (2), 2899 (13)
Schulberg, H. C.: ref, 272 (221), 1166 (93), 2603 (248)
Schuldberg, D.: ref, 68 (4,17), 142 (3), 1140 (8), 1697 (239), 2258 (6), 2402 (23,51), 2858 (56), 2860 (526)
Schulenberg, J.: ref, 404 (29), 2915 (4,6)
Schulenberg, J. E.: ref, 404 (9,10), 1000 (28), 1405 (5)
Schuler, M.: ref, 1216 (27), 1770 (8), 1770 (12)
Schuller, B.: ref, 2603 (495)
Schuller, D. R.: ref, 790 (11), 1166 (89,90,170,171), 2218 (43,44,81,82), 2305 (164,213), 2603 (514)
Schulman, J. L.: ref, 337 (103), 372 (94), 1706 (3), 2858 (102)
Schulsinger, C.: ref, 2497 (577)
Schulsinger, F.: ref, 748 (2,10), 2050 (42,66,133)
Schulsinger, H.: ref, 748 (10), 2050 (42,133), 2603 (110), 2860 (279)
Schulte, A. C.: ref, 1379 (8), 2485 (29), 2864 (19)
Schulte, H. M.: ref, 2497 (121)
Schulte, L. E.: ref, 2860 (405)
Schultz, C. L.: ref, 791 (5,8), 2497 (197,280)
Schultz, D. G.: rev, 1633, 1834
Schultz, D. M.: ref, 1698 (1)
Schultz, G.: ref, 1697 (240), 2497 (281)
Schultz, G. F.: rev, 36
Schultz, L.: ref, 2247 (49)
Schultz, L. H.: ref, 451 (16), 1903 (98)
Schultz, M. K.: ref, 2862 (671), 2901 (126)
Schultz, N. C.: ref, 791 (5,8), 2497 (197,280), 1164 (16), 2497 (61)
Schultz, N. R., Jr.: ref, 1164 (2,45), 2860 (454)
Schultz, R.: ref, 272 (36), 2603 (62)
Schultz, S. K.: ref, 2050 (111)
Schultz, T. M.: ref, 2813 (103)
Schultz, W.: ref, 1036 (7)
Schulzer, M.: ref, 2125 (27)
Schumacher, J.: ref, 1697 (451)
Schumacher, M.: ref, 2860 (525), 2892 (88)
Schumm, J. S.: ref, 1386 (2), 1991 (108), 2484 (9), 2487 (3), 2488 (6), 2862 (226,570), 2901 (34,35,103)
Schumm, W. R.: ref, 1000 (62), 1580 (5)
Schunk, D. H.: rev, 289; ref, 665 (4)
Schur, S.: test, 1067
Schuri, U.: ref, 2163 (118), 2239 (15), 2863 (139,155), 2892 (79)
Schurr, K. T.: ref, 1686 (5)
Schuster, D. H.: rev, 2889; ref, 2518 (3)
Schuster, J. M.: ref, 1380 (4), 2860 (813)
Schuster, S. P.: ref, 2860 (678)
Schut, H. A. W.: ref, 1079 (77,98)
Schut, L.: ref, 1218 (6), 2163 (168), 2863 (196), 2892 (123)
Schutt, R. K.: ref, 1697 (569,570), 2010 (23), 2860 (1348), 2863 (406), 2879 (216), 2892 (289)
Schutte, C.: ref, 2497 (127)
Schutte, K. K.: ref, 1181 (22)

Schuttenberg, E. M.: ref, 298 (39)
Schutz, R.: ref, 2863 (390)
Schutz, R. E.: rev, 246, 838, 2741
Schutz, R. P.: test, 2826
Schutz, W.: test, 1036, 1594
Schwab, J. J.: ref, 1166 (220)
Schwab, K.: ref, 335 (6), 999 (63), 2892 (89)
Schwab, R.: test, 1590
Schwab-Stone, M.: ref, 1903 (252,533)
Schwager, M. T.: ref, 665 (53,80)
Schwanenflugal, P. J.: ref, 1903 (220), 1318 (13), 1380 (19)
Schwankovsky, L.: ref, 2497 (94)
Schwarting, G.: rev, 810, 823, 2046
Schwartz, B. L.: ref, 1903 (92)
Schwartz, D. R.: ref, 2860 (1163)
Schwartz, G.: ref, 2417 (28)
Schwartz, G. E.: ref, 1290 (1), 1697 (115), 1939 (2), 2603 (30,239,334)
Schwartz, J.: ref, 1697 (127)
Schwartz, J. E.: ref, 301 (48), 451 (207), 999 (147), 1166 (88), 1953 (2), 2102 (1), 2288 (16,24), 2289 (11), 2305 (74), 2860 (335,922), 2863 (88)
Schwartz, J. M.: ref, 1093 (40), 1166 (150)
Schwartz, L. S.: ref, 1115 (29), 1672 (5)
Schwartz, M.: ref, 335 (8), 2863 (289)
Schwartz, M. D.: ref, 2076 (128,151)
Schwartz, M. F.: ref, 1903 (567)
Schwartz, N. H.: rev, 1905; ref, 694 (129), 1903 (511)
Schwartz, R. G.: ref, 1095 (12), 2382 (32), 2695 (15)
Schwartz, S.: ref, 2485 (166), 2756 (1)
Schwartz, S. M.: ref, 1697 (352), 2432 (15), 2862 (202), 2901 (25), 2905 (38)
Schwartz, T. H.: ref, 2879 (215)
Schwartz, V.: ref, 1758 (21), 2860 (426)
Schwartzman, A.: ref, 998 (95), 2163 (215)
Schwartzman, A. E.: ref, 2860 (120), 2862 (81)
Schwarz, B.: ref, 1166 (144)
Schwarz, I.: ref, 323 (1), 324 (2)
Schwarz, J. C.: ref, 68 (60), 272 (240), 1687 (25), 2115 (6)
Schweers, J.: ref, 2603 (175)
Schweigert, P.: test, 156
Schweinberger, S. R.: ref, 2163 (243)
Schweitzer, I.: ref, 1166 (32), 2497 (51)
Schweitzer, J. B.: ref, 2485 (180)
Schweitzer, J. W.: ref, 790 (26), 2076 (173)
Schweitzer, L.: ref, 784 (1), 1612 (70), 1903 (366)
Schweizer, E.: ref, 998 (23,58), 1697 (106), 2603 (296)
Schweizer, K.: ref, 2163 (303), 2860 (1415)
Schwesinger, G. C.: rev, 745, 2010
Sciacchitano, A. M.: ref, 1745 (29)
Scialfa, C. T.: ref, 2860 (49,749)
Sciara, A. D.: ref, 1164 (53), 1697 (237), 2860 (518)
Science Research Associates: test, 171, 670, 1413, 1836, 2178, 2408, 2700, 2786
Science Research Associates, Inc.: test, 1760
Scientific Management Techniques, Inc.: test, 2479
Scogin, F.: ref, 272 (120), 1166 (39), 1697 (451,471), 2497 (612), 2603 (440,518)
Scogno, C. A.: ref, 451 (139), 472 (178), 2485 (209), 2862 (515)
Scokt, L. R.: ref, 2239 (19)
Scolaro, C.: ref, 2163 (216), 2863 (260), 2873 (38)
Scolley, R. W.: test, 1840
Scoloveno, M. A.: ref, 1947 (3)
Scopinaro, N.: ref, 893 (29)
Scott, A. B.: ref, 1697 (191,583), 2498 (76)
Scott, A. I. F.: ref, 1166 (65)
Scott, B.: ref, 2076 (105)
Scott, C. M.: ref, 2694 (17)
Scott, C. P.: ref, 272 (221)
Scott, C. R.: test, 2765
Scott, C. S.: ref, 2603 (195)
Scott, D.: ref, 999 (136)
Scott, J.: ref, 272 (255,318), 273 (32), 999 (78), 1166 (46,151,176)
Scott, K.: ref, 2076 (176)
Scott, L. C.: ref, 2860 (579), 2863 (166)
Scott, L. R.: ref, 999 (56), 2599 (15), 2860 (587), 2863 (175)
Scott, M. A.: ref, 1612 (99), 1903 (571), 2862 (710)
Scott, M. I.: ref, 1758 (59)
Scott, N. A.: ref, 2835 (27)
Scott, N. L.: test, 2832
Scott, O.: ref, 2497 (334)
Scott, O., III: rev, 2449
Scott, R.: ref, 999 (89,90,114), 1079 (61), 2239 (22), 2247 (72), 2860 (441,823), 2863 (119,238), 2860 (427)
Scott, S. G.: ref, 1404 (11)
Scott, S. K.: ref, 2603 (3)
Scott, S. S.: ref, 448 (15)
Scott, T. B.: ref, 2126 (4)
Scott, T. M.: ref, 2863 (232)
Scott, W.: ref, 1697 (308)
Scott, W. K.: ref, 1240 (42) 1903 (463)
Scott-Jones, D.: ref, 1659 (1)
Scotti, J. R.: ref, 1697 (322)
Scottish Education Department (The): test, 901
Scrimshaw, S. C. M.: ref, 2497 (62,184)
Scruggs, T. E.: ref, 246 (3,6), 665 (69,84), 1386 (10,15,20,24), 1902 (94), 2485 (183), 2861 (1), 2862 (28,316,408,589), 2879 (104,143,192), 2901 (55,75,110), 2905 (63,91)
Scudder, R. R.: ref, 994 (20), 2190 (4)
Scurfield, R.: ref, 1166 (114), 2497 (561), 2603 (468)
Sczrpratt, D. R.: ref, 838 (17)
Search Institute: test, 2336
Searight, H. R.: ref, 337 (59,62,107), 1010 (64), 1697 (235,243), 2603 (185)
Searles, J. S.: ref, 1661 (77)
Sears, H. A.: ref, 272 (377), 2497 (198,676)
Sears, L. L.: ref, 2860 (750)
Sears, S. F., Jr.: ref, 2497 (249)
Sears, S. J.: ref, 1755 (73)

Seashore, H.: rev, 1122, 1124
Seashore, H. G.: test, 838, 839
Seat, P. D.: test, 1962
Seaworth, T. B.: ref, 404 (1), 413 (3), 1754 (1), 2497 (6)
Seay, S.: ref, 2076 (110), 2603 (343)
Sebastian, S. B.: ref, 893 (19), 999 (170)
Sebolt, D.: rev, 2455
Sebrechts, M. M.: ref, 1115 (3,23,26)
Secada, W. G.: ref, 1420 (1)
Secolsky, C.: rev, 248, 1863
Secord, W.: test, 539, 540, 1739, 2693, 2703, 2727
Secord, W. A.: test, 541, 542
Secunda, S.: ref, 2603 (191)
Secunda, S. K.: ref, 2603 (220)
Seddoh, S. A. K.: ref, 303 (10), 641 (7), 1740 (14), 2226 (13), 2860 (1168), 2863 (351)
Sedey, A. L.: ref, 270 (9), 1528 (1)
Sedlacek, W. E.: test, 1795, 2413; ref, 592 (55), 2413 (1)
Seefeldt, C.: ref, 1902 (103), 1903 (522), 2901 (116,140)
Seefeldt, T.: ref, 863 (87), 1888 (1), 1889 (9), 2603 (533)
Seelbach, A.: ref, 1115 (6)
Seelbach, H.: ref, 1697 (312), 2497 (358), 2603 (276)
Seelbach, W. C.: ref, 1745 (1), 2402 (2)
Seeley, J. R.: ref, 2305 (182,227), 2497 (366), 2858 (74,97)
Seelig, W. R.: ref, 1000 (38)
Seeman, M. V.: ref, 1697 (529)
Seeman, W.: rev, 1928
Sefarbi, R.: ref, 1000 (9)
Segal, D. L.: ref, 690 (3), 1687 (34)
Segal, H.: ref, 2230 (10), 2557 (5)
Segal, H. G.: ref, 2230 (9), 2557 (4)
Segal, N. L.: ref, 1701 (4), 2862 (91,549), 2864 (14)
Segal, P. S.: ref, 2497 (134), 2603 (118)
Segal, S.: ref, 1000 (57), 2497 (288)
Segal, Z.: ref, 790 (17)
Segal, Z. V.: ref, 2603 (286)
Segal-Andrews, A. M.: ref, 451 (45)
Segalowitz, S. J.: ref, 2860 (610), 2892 (114)
Segarra, P.: ref, 999 (109)
Segel, D.: rev, 1315, 1414
Segel, M. D.: ref, 2860 (755), 2863 (221)
Segel, R. C.: test, 248
Seger, C. A.: ref, 2860 (1347), 2863 (405)
Seger, L.: ref, 2125 (17)
Segrin, C.: ref, 462 (31), 1661 (63)
Seguin, E.: test, 2344
Sei, H.: ref, 2076 (174)
Seibert, P. S.: ref, 272 (105)
Seibyl, J. P.: ref, 2863 (232), 2892 (126)
Seid, M.: ref, 472 (28), 2214 (18)
Seidel, J.: ref, 615 (1) 666 (5)
Seidel, J. F.: ref, 1379 (22)
Seidenberg, M.: ref, 376 (10), 2050 (97), 2860 (889,1094), 2892 (185)
Seidenberg, M. S.: ref, 2862 (514), 2905 (100)
Seidl, M.: test, 2817, 2819
Seidlitz, L.: ref, 337 (66), 1172 (1), 2218 (9)
Seidman, L. J.: ref, 199 (18), 1092 (12,16), , 1093 (84), 1164 (68), 1218 (7), 1645 (3), 1697 (408,570), 2010 (6,23), 2516 (42,65), 2860 (317,671,783,802, 855,1348), 2862 (309,394), 2863 (199,250,406), 2879 (81,101,137,216), 2892 (125,176,289)
Seidman, S. N.: ref, 1166 (228)
Seifer, R.: ref, 451 (105), 472 (161), 1086 (3), 1166 (152), 1216 (88), 1321 (1), 2146 (12,13), 2402 (15,22), 2603 (174,496), 2813 (57,79), 2864 (3,43)
Seifert, H.: ref, 323 (1), 324 (2)
Seifert, K. H.: ref, 404 (34), 413 (21)
Seigler, P. D.: ref, 694 (111)
Seikel, J. A.: ref, 270 (34), 1216 (101), 1903 (530), 2008 (5), 2382 (38)
Seilhamer, R. A.: ref, 2305 (85)
Seilhean, D.: ref, 2517 (1), 2860 (527)
Seillier-Moiseiwitsch, F.: ref, 2076 (135)
Seim, N. J.: test, 1244, 2273
Seiner, S. A.: ref, 270 (18)
Seisters, J.: ref, 1638 (3)
Seitamaa, M.: ref, 2247 (120)
Seitz, K. S.: ref, 1903 (390)
Sekaran, U.: ref, 1348 (2)
Seki, K.: ref, 2860 (975,1169,1416), 2873 (44)
Sekirnjak, G. C.: ref, 1697 (532)
Seklemian, P.: test, 2423
Selby, E. C.: ref, 1404 (9)
Selby MillSmith Ltd.: test, 945, 1823, 1828, 2345
Selection Consultation Center: test, 2302
Seleshi, E.: ref, 1697 (172), 2497 (174)
Self, C. A.: ref, 372 (25)
Self, E.: ref, 2417 (28)
Seligman, C.: ref, 2246 (13)
Seligman, R.: rev, 2360
Seligman, S.: ref, 2498 (67)
Selin, C. E.: ref, 1093 (40)
Sell, D. E.: test, 979, 1840
Seller, P.: ref, 365 (11)
Sellers, E.: ref, 1093 (102), 2497 (512), 2603 (396)
Sellers, M. I.: ref, 694 (53)
Sellman, J. D.: ref, 2288 (83), 2289 (68)
Sells, S. B.: rev, 709
Selman, A.: ref, 2497 (414)
Selman, R. L.: ref, 451 (16), 1903 (98)
Selmar, J. W.: test, 1982
Selnes, O.: ref, 1135 (13), 2599 (25), 2860 (772)
Selnes, O. A.: ref, 1135 (2,3,16,22,26), 1164 (169,180), 1740 (8), 2226 (35), 2227 (21,50), 2599 (4,5,32,40), 2860 (200,217)
Selover, R. B.: rev, 1693
Selrees, O. A.: ref, 2227 (10), 2599 (9), 2860 (401)
Seltzer, G. B.: rev, 2132
Seltzer, M.: ref, 1072 (46), 2905 (61)
Seltzer, M. H.: ref, 2603 (416)

Selz, K. A.: ref, 1697 (431)
Selzer, M. A.: ref, 1697 (13)
Selzer, M. L.: test, 1661
Selzer, S. C.: ref, 342 (2), 815 (8), 1240 (10), 1612 (28), 2864 (32)
Semb, G. B.: ref, 2856 (6)
Semel, E.: test, 539, 540, 541, 542
Semenchuk, E. M.: ref, 2497 (282)
Semenza, C.: ref, 199 (14), 2163 (245,340), 2193 (22), 2860 (647), 2863 (187)
Semeonoff, B.: rev, 1011, 1367, 2146
Semmel, M. I.: rev, 2, 2261; ref, 1991 (102)
Semple, J.: ref, 1758 (49)
Semple, S. J.: ref, 2858 (105)
Semple, W. E.: ref, 2603 (507)
Semrud-Clikeman, M.: ref, 451 (187), 2305 (222), 2813 (140), 2862 (611), 2879 (202), 2905 (109)
Sena, R.: ref, 2214 (92), 2603 (444)
Senchak, M.: ref, 134 (13,33), 136 (6), 1008 (1), 1661 (64), 2496 (1)
Seneca, J. J.: ref, 592 (2)
Sénéchal, M.: ref, 1612 (79), 1903 (416,581), 2488 (10)
Sengoz, A.: ref, 1166 (61)
Sengun, S.: ref, 1021 (29)
Senra, C.: ref, 1166 (153)
Seoman, J.: ref, 1216 (10)
Sequin, M.: ref, 2603 (402)
Sera, M. D.: ref, 1903 (551)
Serena, A.: ref, 2497 (621)
Sergeant, J. A.: ref, 451 (99,279,290), 681 (95), 1021 (47), 2862 (529,740)
Sergent, J.: ref, 2860 (62,87), 2862 (37)
Sergerstrom, B.: ref, 1965 (73)
Serio, C. D.: ref, 1243 (2), 1290 (2), 2120 (4), 2497 (298), 2603 (229)
Serling, D.: ref, 694 (93), 1079 (34), 2497 (426)
Serna, P.: ref, 2755 (2)
Serna, R. W.: ref, 1903 (552), 2862 (672)
Serniclaes, W.: ref, 2163 (321), 2860 (1253)
Seron, M. S.: test, 1984
Seroquel Study Group: ref, 2288 (82)
Serota, R. D.: ref, 998 (101), 2402 (40), 2603 (375)
Serper, M. R.: ref, 2288 (7,54), 2289 (5,41), 2290 (2), 2305 (37), 2892 (148)
Serra, M.: ref, 459 (37)
Sersen, E. A.: ref, 2862 (459)
Servan-Schreiber, D.: ref, 2305 (196), 2892 (108)
Service, N. M.: ref, 2860 (189)
Servin, J.: ref, 459 (31), 2813 (68)
Servo, A.: ref, 2516 (58), 2860 (777,1028)
Sesma, A., Jr.: ref, 2861 (3)
Seta, C. E.: ref, 1178 (6)
Seta, J. J.: ref, 1178 (6)
Seth, H.: ref, 459 (39)
Sethre-Hofstad, L.: ref, 2862 (626), 2880 (6)
Setoguchi, Y.: ref, 272 (237), 472 (42), 2497 (601), 2498 (20)
Setrakian, W.: ref, 1379 (19)
Settle, K.: ref, 2860 (145), 2862 (93)
Sevcik, R. A.: ref, 202 (3), 433 (1), 1903 (14,100,305, 306,329), 2189 (1), 2485 (148), 2657 (19)
Severs, W.: ref, 1661 (35,75), 2603 (317,556)
Severson, H. H.: test, 890, 2311, 2607
Seville, J. L.: ref, 2839 (9)
Sevin, B. M.: ref, 459 (11), 2813 (14)
Sevin, J. A.: ref, 459 (11), 2813 (14,104)
Sevy, S.: ref, 564 (2), 2017 (3), 2860 (218)
Seward, J.: ref, 1218 (5), 2599 (10), 2863 (109), 2892 (59)
Sewell, D.: test, 492
Sewell, D. D.: ref, 1164 (77), 1423 (1), 2485 (171), 2695 (42), 2860 (928), 2864 (98)
Sewell, K.: ref, 1959 (2)
Sewell, K. W.: ref, 1697 (449), 1698 (22), 2553 (4), 2879 (229)
Sewell, T. E.: rev, 694
Sewerd, K.: ref, 1092 (16), 2862 (394), 2879 (137)
Seymour, A. B.: ref, 1166 (210)
Seymour, R. J.: ref, 1697 (51)
Shachner, S. E.: ref, 337 (185)
Shack, J.: ref, 999 (15)
Shackelford, T. K.: ref, 999 (178,187), 1697 (571)
Shackleton, D.: ref, 2076 (131), 2603 (423)
Shackley, B.: ref, 1903 (404)
Shaddock, A. J.: ref, 1612 (18)
Shafer, K.: ref, 788 (3), 1612 (94), 2305 (130)
Shafer, R. E.: rev, 2729
Shaffer, C. E., Jr.: ref, 745 (13), 1697 (353)
Shaffer, D.: ref, 451 (117,151,220,236), 1093 (21), 1216 (108), 2305 (197), 2813 (154)
Shaffer, J.: ref, 815 (5), 2862 (129), 2879 (33)
Shaffer, J. C.: test, 951
Shaffer, L. F.: rev, 317, 372, 374, 466, 751, 862, 908, 987, 1101, 1158, 1196, 1321, 1323, 1376, 1484, 1485, 1964, 2010, 2247 2757, 2862
Shaffer, M. B.: rev, 153, 334, 466, 1169, 1177, 1650
Shafii, M.: ref, 451 (152), 472 (187), 473 (3)
Shafir, S.: ref, 790 (11)
Shafrir, U.: ref, 2163 (49)
Shafrir, V.: ref, 2860 (751), 2879 (91,92), 2905 (64)
Shagle, S. C.: ref, 272 (138), 451 (75)
Shah, A.: ref, 1485 (21), 2860 (528)
Shah, F.: ref, 472 (188)
Shahani, C.: ref, 592 (40)
Shaheen, F.: ref, 2862 (415)
Shahidi, S.: ref, 1338 (33)
Shahim, S.: ref, 301 (26), 1097 (8), 2864 (30)
Shaikh, S.: ref, 2050 (32)
Shaikh, T.: ref, 908 (9)
Shaler, R. S.: ref, 451 (76), 2862 (395)
Shaleu, R. S.: ref, 1379 (68), 2862 (346), 2864 (89)
Shalev, A.: ref, 2497 (593)
Shalev, A. Y.: ref, 337 (50,165,188), 2497 (199,223,500)
Shalev, R.: ref, 681 (68,91)
Shalev, R. S.: ref, 301 (35), 681 (38,67), 2163 (244), 2862 (223)

Shaley, A. Y.: ref, 337 (166)
Shallice, T.: ref, 1104 (14), 1758 (60,61), 2193 (55), 2860 (1049,1050,1110)
Sham, P.: ref, 272 (110), 998 (90), 1093 (80), 2050 (103), 2305 (129)
Sham, P. C.: ref, 2050 (98)
Shaman, A.: ref, 1916 (3), 2358 (10)
Shammi, P.: ref, 666 (12)
Shams, G. K.: ref, 998 (128), 2417 (38), 2497 (645)
Shanahan, M.: ref, 2603 (355)
Shanahan, M. J.: ref, 2485 (223)
Shanahan, T.: rev, 322
Shaner, A. L.: ref, 1093 (72), 2050 (95), 2288 (19)
Shanfield, S. B.: ref, 337 (1), 2603 (1)
Shank, M. D.: ref, 1755 (46)
Shanker, J. L.: test, 917
Shanklin, C. W.: ref, 1701 (49)
Shankweiler, D. P.: ref, 1051 (1)
Shannon, D. M.: ref, 2603 (313)
Shannon, G. A.: rev, 2138
Shany, M.: ref, 1903 (177), 2905 (37)
Shany, M. T.: ref, 389 (12), 861 (3), 2879 (138), 2905 (88)
Shapera, W.: ref, 863 (87), 1888 (1), 1889 (9), 2603 (533)
Shapira, B.: ref, 301 (16,48), 1166 (28,92), 2860 (241,922)
Shapire, L. P.: ref, 2873 (58)
Shapiro, A. H.: test, 2176
Shapiro, A. P.: ref, 1135 (19), 2497 (603), 2516 (89), 2860 (1200), 2863 (360)
Shapiro, C.: ref, 451 (194), 1010 (123)
Shapiro, D.: ref, 2199 (3)
Shapiro, D. A.: rev, 540, 628, 2668, 2680; ref, 272 (37, 115,116,217), 2050 (100,131), 2497 (89), 2603 (63, 226, 301,314,359,360, 403,411, 412)
Shapiro, D. E.: ref, 2497 (200)
Shapiro, D. H.: ref, 1697 (547), 2399 (1), 2402 (63), 2603 (530)
Shapiro, D. H., Jr.: test, 2399
Shapiro, E.: ref, 1216 (8)
Shapiro, E. G.: ref, 2860 (752), 2862 (291)
Shapiro, E. S.: rev, 357, 1391, 2211; ref, 301 (44), 681 (97), 1902 (59,70), 2860 (305), 2862 (330)
Shapiro, H.: test, 788
Shapiro, J.: ref, 2813 (137)
Shapiro, J. P.: ref, 451 (224,225)
Shapiro, L. P.: ref, 2873 (17,48,72)
Shapiro, R. W.: test, 1517
Shapiro, S.: ref, 349 (26), 837 (9), 1987 (2), 2211 (8), 2488 (4)
Shapiro, S. K.: ref, 301 (51), 1392 (14), 1697 (452), 1903 (417), 2905 (89)
Shapiro, W. R.: ref, 2860 (4)
Shappel, D. L.: test, 1163
Shapurian, R.: ref, 999 (18)
Sharabany, R.: ref, 78 (1)
Sharbrough, F. W.: ref, 2860 (537), 2863 (152)
Sharkansky, E. J.: ref, 999 (194), 1661 (85), 1697 (596), 2497 (677)
Sharma, A.: ref, 1697 (368)
Sharma, J. M.: test, 290
Sharma, T.: ref, 1758 (74), 2305 (141), 2860 (1135)
Sharma, W.: ref, 451 (58)
Sharp, A.: ref, 337 (120)
Sharp, D.: ref, 451 (77), 1612 (80), 2860 (976)
Sharp, D. S.: ref, 2497 (205)
Sharp, J. D.: test, 910
Sharpe, K. S.: ref, 2704 (19), 2860 (646)
Sharpe, M. H.: ref, 1758 (78), 1903 (1)
Sharpe, M. J.: ref, 694 (105), 2497 (515)
Sharpe, M. N.: test, 332
Sharpe, P. A.: ref, 1901 (5)
Sharpley, A. L.: ref, 2076 (103)
Sharpley, C. F.: ref, 1338 (38), 2862 (55)
Sharrock, R.: ref, 2860 (529)
Shattock, L.: ref, 2195 (2)
Shaughnessy, M. F.: ref, 1201 (3), 1380 (2), 2417 (28)
Shavelson, R. J.: ref, 665 (44)
Shaver, A. V.: ref, 665 (94)
Shaver, J.: ref, 2603 (583)
Shaver, P. R.: ref, 68 (57), 451 (194), 1010 (123), 1396 (4), 2218 (73)
Shaw, B.: ref, 372 (23), 571 (2), 615 (17), 2591 (2)
Shaw, C.: ref, 1758 (11,31,40,56), 2193 (32,39,46,48), 2860 (219,753,896,977,1027), 2863 (55,220,267, 288,304), 2892 (149,186,205)
Shaw, D.: ref, 451 (264), 1903 (15), 2288 (9), 2305 (48), 2862 (34)
Shaw, D. S.: ref, 451 (282), 1216 (74), 1965 (61,79)
Shaw, E. L.: ref, 615 (13)
Shaw, G. K.: ref, 739 (8)
Shaw, J. H.: test, 1184
Shaw, K. M.: test, 2530
Shaw, M. E.: rev, 1526, 2413
Shaw, P. J.: ref, 1758 (63), 2860 (1055)
Shaw, R.: ref, 999 (6)
Shaw, R. J.: ref, 272 (381), 893 (48), 1010 (138), 1735 (12)
Shaw, S. R.: rev, 1382, 1875, 2433, 2530
Shay, C. B.: rev, 2591
Shay, J.: ref, 272 (351)
Shaycoft, M. F.: rev, 547
Shaywitz, B. A.: ref, 1051 (1), 2862 (180,396,473,474), 2879 (43,160), 2901 (21,73,88,89)
Shaywitz, S. E.: ref, 1051 (1), 2862 (180,396,473,474), 2879 (43,160), 2901 (73,88,89)
Shea, M. E. C.: ref, 1697 (514)
Shea, M. T.: ref, 272 (111), 1093 (83), 1158 (3), 1517 (4), 1697 (513,517), 2305 (200,239), 2603 (335)
Shea, S. J.: ref, 1697 (514)
Shea, T.: ref, 2305 (125)
Shealy, L. S.: ref, 793 (9), 1697 (178), 1744 (3)
Shean, G.: ref, 2860 (1341), 2892 (288)
Shean, G. D.: ref, 1289 (2)
Shear, M. K.: ref, 337 (156), 1093 (36), 1166 (63), 2199 (4,8), 2497 (141,317), 2498 (43), 2519 (36), 2520 (37), 2603 (119,302)

Shear, P. K.: ref, 1485 (12), 2860 (845)
Shear, S. M.: rev, 2211
Sheard, C.: ref, 2050 (8)
Shearer, C. B.: test, 1667
Shearer, D. E.: ref, 303 (4), 1164 (34), 2076 (41), 2516 (17), 2860 (345)
Shearer, M.: test, 811
Shearer, S. L.: ref, 2519 (48)
Shearin, E. N.: ref, 1298 (1)
Shearun, E. N.: ref, 824 (2)
Shechter, J.: ref, 1592 (6)
Shechtman, Z.: ref, 1991 (97)
Shedd, D.: ref, 1040 (6,7)
Shedelbower, A.: ref, 665 (50)
Sheebar, L. B.: ref, 2497 (394)
Sheeber, L.: ref, 272 (319), 1010 (128)
Sheeber, L. B.: ref, 2497 (201)
Sheehan, C. M.: rev, 551
Sheehan, D. Y.: ref, 2603 (64)
Sheehan, E. P.: rev, 807, 1552, 1835, 2917
Sheehan, K. R.: ref, 571 (4), 615 (40)
Sheehan, O. T. O.: ref, 2527 (14)
Sheeley, E. C.: rev, 1020, 1096
Sheeran, T.: ref, 863 (89), 1889 (15)
Sheets, V.: ref, 472 (189)
Shefelbine, J.: ref, 2905 (17)
Shefelbine, J. L.: ref, 665 (26), 1903 (58), 2163 (50)
Sheffey, M. A.: ref, 2835 (2)
Sheffield, L. J.: rev, 195
Sheffield, M.: ref, 1939 (14)
Shefler, G.: ref, 337 (118)
Sheitman, B.: ref, 2288 (45), 2305 (123)
Shek, D. T. L.: ref, 272 (38), 273 (33), 999 (161), 1079 (8,53), 1481 (2,4), 2126 (9,13), 2497 (90,202,516)
Shekhar, A.: ref, 272 (176,250), 451 (191), 846 (20), 2497 (608)
Shekim, W.: ref, 1697 (170)
Sheldon, K. L.: rev, 658, 1618, 2872
Sheldon, K. M.: ref, 999 (171), 1735 (9), 1965 (45), 2603 (303)
Sheldon, W. D.: rev, 1768
Sheline, Y. I.: ref, 272 (254), 1166 (96,174)
Shell, D. F.: ref, 773 (1)
Shell, K. D.: test, 2124
Shell, R.: ref, 1000 (29), 1877 (2)
Shell, R. M.: ref, 472 (39)
Shellenberger, S.: rev, 307
Shelley, A.: ref, 1903 (198)
Shelton, B. S.: ref, 1902 (27), 2694 (5), 2862 (144)
Shelton, D. M.: ref, 2656 (5)
Shelton, K. K.: ref, 651 (1)
Shelton, R. C.: ref, 2497 (438)
Shelton, R. L.: rev, 1095, 1096, 2028, 2235
Shelton, T. L.: ref, 451 (283), 681 (12,98), 2485 (45), 2603 (130,590), 2901 (135)
Shen, D.: ref, 272 (166), 273 (18)
Shen, H.: ref, 672 (5)
Shen, Y-L.: ref, 1128 (1)
Shenaut, G. K.: ref, 776 (1)
Shenhar, S.: ref, 1000 (57), 2497 (288)
Shenkman, K.: ref, 798 (24), 1740 (13), 1903 (491)
Shenman, G. D.: ref, 2402 (2)
Shenson, H. L.: test, 962
Shenton, M. E.: ref, 2288 (60), 2289 (46), 2305 (150,159,190), 2860 (497,1012,1146,1319), 2892 (282)
Shepard, J. M.: ref, 1021 (4), 2497 (27)
Shepard, J. W.: rev, 219, 1334, 2537, 2835
Shepard, L.: rev, 2355, 2366, 2368
Shepard, L. A.: rev, 665, 2486
Shepard, M.: ref, 681 (20)
Shephard, R. J.: ref, 353 (15), 1386 (14), 2862 (313), 2901 (54)
Shepherd, J. E.: rev, 157, 1127
Shepherd, M. J.: ref, 1072 (41), 1130 (2), 2905 (47)
Shepherd, R. W.: ref, 863 (44)
Shepley, A.: ref, 540 (4)
Sheppard, B. H.: ref, 1716 (2)
Shepperd, J. A.: ref, 592 (41), 838 (7,8)
Shepperdson, B.: ref, 2088 (1), 2228 (19)
Sher, K. J.: ref, 134 (2), 272 (14), 337 (92,119,138,159), 372 (24), 999 (137), 1661 (8,60,65,66,73,76), 1697 (101), 2218 (18,60), 2497 (467), 2603 (460), 2860 (108,1370), 2892 (180)
Shera, D. M.: ref, 2227 (26), 2860 (1103)
Sheras, P. L.: test, 2510
Sherbenou, R. J.: test, 810, 2704
Sherbon, J. W.: rev, 90, 1752
Sherbourne, C. D.: ref, 2305 (198)
Sherer, M.: ref, 376 (2,3), 2226 (7)
Sheridan, K.: ref, 1135 (2,3), 1164 (4), 1166 (8), 2599 (4,5), 2860 (94,200,217)
Sheridan, M. D.: test, 2224, 2544
Sheridan, M. J.: ref, 462 (27,28), 1000 (92)
Sheridan, S. M.: rev, 1987, 2451; ref, 681 (79), 1380 (16), 1903 (431), 2452 (22)
Sherman, D.: rev, 1095
Sherman, E. E.: test, 1138, 1139
Sherman, E. M. S.: ref, 1218 (11), 2860 (978), 2892 (206)
Sherman, G. D.: ref, 1745 (1)
Sherman, M. D.: ref, 2497 (594)
Sherman, M. F.: ref, 272 (156), 694 (92), 2603 (368,470)
Sherman, R. G.: ref, 1755 (47)
Sherman, S. J.: ref, 1757 (2)
Sherman, T.: ref, 1903 (224), 2125 (10), 2862 (234), 2892 (98)
Shermis, M. D.: test, 2514
Sherr, M.: ref, 815 (49), 1164 (173), 1740 (27), 2516 (115), 2860 (1374), 2892 (294)
Sherrington, R.: ref, 2305 (180,199)
Sherrod, K. B.: ref, 2652 (6)
Sherry, B.: ref, 1216 (43)
Shertzer, B.: rev, 900
Sherwin, E.: ref, 337 (98), 2065 (17)

Sherwood, A.: ref, 2858 (34)
Sherwood, J. C.: rev, 505, 591, 614, 955
Sherwood, R.: ref, 1697 (233)
Sheslow, D.: test, 2666, 2880, 2881
Sheth, R.: ref, 2862 (409), 2905 (92)
Shewchuk, R.: ref, 2065 (25)
Shewchuk, R. M.: ref, 1014 (7)
Shibagaki, M.: ref, 2862 (673)
Shibayama, T.: ref, 1079 (25)
Shick, J.: test, 2653
Shields, A.: ref, 1115 (6)
Shields, A. M.: ref, 365 (6)
Shields, J. D.: ref, 1164 (111), 2862 (397)
Shiffman, S.: ref, 998 (73), 2497 (637)
Shifren, K.: ref, 298 (93), 998 (59,122), 2076 (129)
Shilkret, R.: ref, 2525 (13)
Shillcock, R.: ref, 2873 (74)
Shilliday, C.: ref, 2305 (78), 2860 (452)
Shima, S.: ref, 999 (59)
Shimamura, A. P.: ref, 776 (4,9), 2860 (50,104,220,862, 1320), 2863 (18,30,56,253,397), 2873 (34), 2892 (29, 179)
Shimazono, Y.: ref, 2288 (23), 2305 (69), 2860 (365)
Shimberg, B.: rev, 1074, 1836
Shimizu, A.: ref, 1166 (213)
Shimizu, K.: ref, 404 (9,10), 2915 (4)
Shimizu, S.: ref, 2862 (633)
Shimoda, K.: ref, 1093 (49)
Shimomura, T.: ref, 2163 (334), 2860 (1314,1371), 2873 (68,73)
Shimuzu, H.: ref, 2860 (406), 2873 (11)
Shin, C.: ref, 2860 (1031), 2863 (306)
Shin, L. M.: ref, 2402 (43), 2860 (933)
Shindledecker, R.: ref, 462 (18), 1661 (43)
Shine, P.: ref, 2497 (428)
Shinkfield, A.: ref, 2860 (1250)
Shinmyo, T.: ref, 2862 (638)
Shinotoh, H.: ref, 2125 (27)
Shiota, J.: ref, 2860 (997,1356), 2873 (47)
Shipley, K. G.: test, 2660; rev, 1284, 2044, 2620, 2694; ref, 1047 (1), 1240 (7), 2660 (2), 2695 (9)
Shipley, R. H.: ref, 2860 (145), 2862 (93), 2879 (154)
Shipley, W. C.: test, 2402; rev, 2163, 2212, 2477, 2478
Shipman, V.: test, 1780
Shipper, F.: ref, 2583 (1,2)
Shiraki, H.: ref, 2497 (400)
Shirk, S. R.: ref, 472 (214,232)
Shirley, M. C.: rev, 794, 2552
Shisslak, C. M.: ref, 1010 (26)
Shively, A. H.: rev, 2795
Shivy, V. A.: ref, 372 (78)
Shiwach, R. S.: ref, 2050 (99)
Shneidman, E. S.: test, 1540
Shoalson, I.: ref, 1903 (334), 2517 (2), 2860 (796)
Shoben, E. J., Jr.: rev, 1376
Shoemaker, D. M.: rev, 2677
Shoemaker, O. S.: ref, 2858 (17)
Shohdy, A.: ref, 999 (98), 2050 (92)
Shoken-Topaz, T.: ref, 298 (86)
Sholle-Martin, S.: ref, 2813 (7)
Shondrick, D. D.: ref, 1697 (382)
Shonk, S. M.: ref, 451 (90), 1903 (443), 1987 (17)
Shonn, G.: ref, 2305 (133)
Shook, C.: ref, 298 (137)
Shoosmith, L.: ref, 2163 (135), 2892 (95)
Shopen-Kofman, R.: ref, 2497 (377)
Shoqeirat, M.: ref, 2193 (17,26), 2860 (495,685), 2863 (141,202), 2892 (80,131)
Shoqeirat, M. A.: ref, 1758 (20), 2193 (10), 2860 (306), 2863 (82), 2892 (43)
Shore, A.: ref, 994 (45); ref, 2860 (1240)
Shore, B. M.: ref, 389 (6,11), 2485 (167), 2862 (347)
Shore, J. H.: ref, 2305 (79)
Shore, R.: ref, 893 (6)
Shore, W. J.: ref, 1140 (14), 1697 (126)
Shores, J. H.: rev, 364
Shores, M. M.: ref, 2497 (244)
Shorkey, C. T.: ref, 1321 (6)
Shorr, J. E.: test, 1149, 2404
Short, E.: ref, 272 (124) 273 (13), 2076 (115), 2497 (488)
Short, E. J.: ref, 1379 (34), 1903 (210)
Short, J. L.: ref, 472 (145)
Shortz, J. L.: ref, 717 (1), 863 (75)
Shorvon, S. D.: ref, 2227 (18), 2863 (231)
Shostrom, E. L.: test, 426, 1872, 1938, 1939
Shouldice, A.: ref, 863 (72), 1903 (141,429)
Shoultz, R.: test, 2175
Showers, C. J.: ref, 2076 (158)
Shprintzen, R. J.: ref, 2050 (94)
Shriberg, L. D.: rev, 1982, 2235; ref, 1095 (28), 1394 (6,8), 1903 (310,311), 1982 (9,10,11)
Shriver, M. D.: rev, 471, 1932
Shtasel, D. L.: ref, 2017 (6), 2288 (25,48,57), 2289 (14,37,44), 2860 (744)
Shu, V.: ref, 303 (15), 1135 (20), 1740 (18), 2076 (167), 2226 (21), 2516 (96), 2860 (1255), 2899 (15)
Shub, A. N.: test, 2105
Shuchter, S. R.: ref, 2603 (568)
Shuck, R. L.: ref, 998 (106), 2603 (405)
Shueler, H.: rev, 600
Shugar, G. J.: ref, 2497 (88)
Shuken, J.: ref, 776 (62), 2227 (60)
Shull-Senn, S.: ref, 665 (82), 1657 (19), 1903 (418)
Shulman, C.: ref, 234 (3), 459 (38), 674 (5), 2860 (1207,1208), 2862 (581,582,583), 2864 (127,128)
Shulman, S.: ref, 472 (201), 1000 (108), 2498 (68), 2603 (540), 2862 (642)
Shults, C. W.: ref, 776 (21)
Shultz, I. Z.: ref, 1294 (3), 2533 (1)
Shultz, J. M.: ref, 4 (22), 2860 (1417)
Shum, D. H. K.: ref, 1164 (78), 1407 (4), 2516 (53), 2599 (21), 2860 (754)
Shumway, S. J.: ref, 1697 (567), 1740 (25), 2226 (33), 2860 (1339)

Shuren, J.: ref, 2227 (13), 2860 (530), 2863 (151), 2873 (18)
Shuren, J. E.: ref, 1096 (11), 1903 (419), 2658 (2), 2860 (1170), 2873 (45,46,56,57)
Shurett, R.: ref, 2125 (23), 2860 (1118), 2892 (232)
Shurtleff, D. B.: ref, 815 (5), 2862 (129), 2879 (33)
Shusman, E. J.: ref, 1313 (1), 1697 (145)
Shuster, L. I.: ref, 1394 (5), 1852 (1), 1903 (142,208), 2694 (8), 2704 (7)
Shuttleworth, E. C.: ref, 1525 (4), 2873 (6)
Shuttleworth-Jordan, A. B.: ref, 2860 (979)
Shutty, M. S.: ref, 2603 (125)
Shutty, M. S., Jr.: ref, 2603 (65)
Shwery, C. S.: rev, 1470, 2150
Shybunko, D. E.: ref, 1010 (7), 1013 (1)
Si-Asar, R.: ref, 2861 (3)
Sibanda, J. S.: ref, 2862 (82)
Sibanda, P. S.: ref, 2862 (82)
Siber, D. E.: ref, 2402 (19)
Siblerud, R. L.: ref, 2497 (203,395), 2603 (159)
Sibley, A. M.: test, 452
Sichel, A. F.: ref, 837 (6)
Sick, C.: ref, 2239 (8)
Sickel, R. Z.: test, 1265
Siddall, J. W.: ref, 1697 (241)
Siddiqui, S.: ref, 1965 (21)
Sidio-Hall, M. A.: ref, 2656 (12)
Sidtis, J. J.: ref, 2860 (380), 2862 (175), 2864 (18)
Sieberhagen, K. J.: ref, 1321 (5)
Sief el Dawla, A.: ref, 999 (98), 2050 (92)
Siegal, L. S.: ref, 1134 (2), 2382 (13)
Siegal, M.: ref, 1097 (13), 1903 (553), 2163 (234), 2681 (2)
Siegel, D. J.: ref, 1379 (46), 1386 (7), 2860 (630,696), 2905 (54,59)
Siegel, G. M.: ref, 1379 (62), 1903 (330), 2651 (16), 2657 (21), 2695 (33)
Siegel, J.: ref, 2862 (398), 2901 (74)
Siegel, L.: rev, 1050, 1101, 1223, 1318, 1755, 2581
Siegel, L. S.: ref, 681 (8,25), 827 (1), 997 (1,7), 1073 (1), 1092 (1,7), 1240 (11), 1902 (38), 1903 (3,74,143,316), 2228 (1), 2485 (2), 2487 (18), 2731 (6), 2860 (751), 2862 (7,181), 2879 (1,48,91,92, 212,235), 2905 (29,64,116)
Siegel, M. J.: ref, 375 (8), 2720 (1), 2892 (297)
Siegel, S.: ref, 301 (20)
Siegel, W. C.: ref, 2497 (275), 2516 (30), 2860 (507), 2863 (146)
Siegel-Causey, E.: ref, 1770 (9,11)
Siegert, R.: ref, 272 (263), 2892 (244)
Siegert, R. J.: ref, 2193 (56), 2860 (1171), 2863 (352), 2892 (254)
Siegler, I. C.: ref, 272 (336), 1697 (117,319,428), 2218 (40,116), 2497 (664)
Siegman, A. W.: ref, 2496 (6)
Siegrist, M.: ref, 2516 (111)
Sieler, J. D.: ref, 280 (4)
Siemen, J. R.: ref, 2557 (2)
Siever, L. J.: ref, 2050 (115), 2305 (225), 2860 (1020)
Sievers, G.: ref, 1166 (68), 2603 (328)
Sigal, J. J.: ref, 68 (2), 2248 (1)
Sigal, M.: ref, 1745 (28)
Siganga, W. W.: ref, 1590 (32)
Sigel, M. L.: ref, 2860 (347), 2862 (161)
Sigelman, C.: ref, 2862 (550)
Sigman, M.: ref, 234 (2), 270 (14), 433 (3,6,10,11), 459 (20,32), 539 (1), 540 (5), 2163 (78,175), 2214 (92), 2228 (3,12,13,22), 2229 (5), 2402 (13), 2485 (91,139,194), 2603 (444), 2813 (85)
Sigman, M. D.: ref, 433 (7,14), 459 (21,27), 674 (3), 2228 (9), 2229 (9), 2485 (92,108,202), 2862 (188)
Sigmon, J. L., Jr.: ref, 2497 (511)
Sigmon, S.: ref, 272 (298)
Sigmon, S. T.: ref, 272 (320), 1697 (40), 2497 (657), 2603 (404,553)
Sigmundsson, T.: ref, 2305 (180)
Signer, B.: ref, 2497 (364)
Signorella, M. L.: ref, 298 (73)
Signoret, J. L.: ref, 2860 (130)
Signorini, A.: ref, 2862 (237)
Siimes, M. A.: ref, 1832 (17)
Sijde, P. C. V. D.: ref, 926 (17)
Sikkema, K. J.: ref, 2497 (485), 2839 (5)
Sikora, D. M.: ref, 353 (14), 815 (17,28), 994 (18,29), 1903 (312,406), 2724 (8,10), 2862 (292,382), 2880 (1,3)
Sikula, A., Sr.: ref, 2246 (6)
Silbereben, R. K.: ref, 298 (155), 472 (183)
Silberg, J. L.: test, 847; ref, 2433 (1), 2749 (86), 2860 (1418), 2862 (734), 2864 (146)
Silberg, N. T.: ref, 298 (4), 337 (17)
Silberman, C. S.: ref, 690 (3), 1687 (34)
Silburn, S. R.: ref, 451 (128)
Silfvenilis, H.: ref, 303 (8), 2862 (478), 2860 (439)
Silk, K. R.: test, 824; ref, 1697 (22), 2603 (6)
Sillanpää, M.: ref, 1903 (186)
Sillanpaa, M. C.: ref, 1135 (23), 1697 (572), 2226 (36), 2603 (554), 2860 (1349), 2892 (290)
Silove, D.: ref, 999 (138,190),1079 (103)
Silva, E.: ref, 2860 (280)
Silva, P. A.: ref, 358 (8), 1010 (38,98), 1612 (38), 2211 (22,37), 2862 (469)
Silva, R.: ref, 790 (26), 2076 (173)
Silvaroli, N. J.: test, 496
Silveira, J.: ref, 2863 (29)
Silver, C. H.: ref, 2862 (145), 2864 (24)
Silver, E. J.: ref, 997 (20,28), 1925 (2,3)
Silver, H.: ref, 335 (8), 2863 (289)
Silver, H. F.: test, 1464, 1473, 1562
Silver, M. C.: ref, 2225 (19), 2860 (1362)
Silver, P. H.: ref, 2862 (42,43)
Silver, R.: test, 2410
Silver, R. A.: test, 855

Silver, R. C.: ref, 791 (12), 2603 (101,348,477)
Silver, S.: test, 764; ref, 1697 (291), 2603 (258)
Silver, W. S.: ref, 1107 (7)
Silverberg, D. S.: ref, 451 (137), 2603 (475)
Silverglade, L.: ref, 1745 (49)
Silveri, M. C.: ref, 2163 (151,185,304), 2892 (113)
Silverira, J. C.: ref, 2497 (229)
Silverman, A. B.: ref, 472 (190)
Silverman, I. W.: ref, 2497 (142)
Silverman, J. M.: ref, 2305 (225)
Silverman, L. K.: ref, 592 (64), 1115 (13)
Silverman, M. M.: ref, 472 (121)
Silverman, P. R.: ref, 451 (25)
Silverman, R. J.: ref, 1093 (55), 1178 (8)
Silverman, S. W.: ref, 540 (23), 1903 (554), 2163 (341), 2543 (3)
Silverman, W. K.: ref, 451 (93), 472 (50,127), 1021 (18), 1991 (11,24,51,79), 2214 (68,80,139), 2497 (71,111), 2498 (21,58,78)
Silverman, W. P.: ref, 2862 (459)
Silvern, L.: ref, 615 (21), 694 (91)
Silvers, V. L.: ref, 1767 (8)
Silverstein, A. B.: rev, 564, 798, 1612, 1731, 2864; ref, 2860 (221,222), 2862 (114), 2864 (20)
Silverstein, J.: rev, 798, 2315
Silverstein, M. L.: ref, 1164 (170), 1525 (12), 2050 (16), 2305 (60,235), 2860 (307,1350)
Silverthorn, N. A.: ref, 1965 (70), 2525 (11)
Silverthorn, P.: ref, 451 (153), 651 (2), 2862 (551)
Silverton, L.: test, 71, 1543, 2062, 2063; ref, 748 (5)
Silvestri, J. M.: ref, 1903 (296), 2864 (66)
Silvestri, L.: ref, 2497 (595)
Silvestri, S.: ref, 1291 (4)
Sim, H-S.: ref, 303 (10), 641 (7), 1740 (14), 2226 (13), 2860 (1168), 2863 (351)
Sime, W. E.: rev, 184, 2399
Simeon, D.: ref, 2603 (410)
Simhadri, R.: ref, 301 (45), 798 (15), 1902 (63), 1903 (333), 2862 (303), 2866 (5)
Simith, M. L.: ref, 2860 (140)
Simmel, C.: ref, 451 (201), 472 (197), 2603 (228), 2862 (627), 2901 (117)
Simmens, S.: ref, 272 (194)
Simmens, S. J.: ref, 472 (142)
Simmering, M. J.: ref, 2218 (124)
Simmond, V.: test, 127
Simmonds, V.: test, 125, 126, 129, 2398
Simmons, A. D.: ref, 1093 (79)
Simmons, K.: ref, 2905 (7)
Simmons, R. G.: ref, 2603 (248)
Simon, Ch.: ref, 1166 (56)
Simon, D.: ref, 1745 (13)
Simon, E. W.: ref, 1379 (76), 1485 (54), 2432 (27,32), 2485 (234), 2813 (105,129), 2860 (1172), 2862 (399)
Simon, G.: ref, 2218 (16), 2603 (474)
Simon, G. E.: ref, 1079 (79), 2603 (506)
Simon, L.: ref, 272 (378)
Simon, M.: ref, 1697 (124), 2603 (87)
Simón, M. A.: ref, 999 (176)
Simon, M. J.: ref, 2146 (16)
Simon, P. M.: ref, 2603 (160)
Simon & Schuster Higher Education Group: test, 2081
Simoncini, L.: ref, 2163 (318)
Simond, S.: ref, 1965 (36), 2497 (185)
Simonian, S. J.: ref, 2860 (308)
Simonini, E.: ref, 1166 (205), 2603 (211)
Simonoff, E.: ref, 350 (24), 1653 (21), 2163 (195), 2228 (16), 2433 (1), 2860 (795,874)
Simons, A.: ref, 1166 (54), 2305 (106)
Simons, A. D.: ref, 272 (233), 1093 (38,43), 1166 (163,207), 2305 (61,233)
Simons, N.: test, 480
Simons, R. L.: ref, 1010 (12), 2218 (15,58), 2326 (1), 2603 (136,213,214,244,256,304,305,456)
Simonson, M.: test, 2482
Simonson, T. A.: ref, 1987 (23)
Simonton, D. K.: ref, 68 (3)
Simourd, D. J.: ref, 1174 (3), 1697 (573)
Simpson, D. M.: ref, 1135 (18), 2226 (14), 2516 (85), 2860 (1173), 2863 (353)
Simpson, F. M.: ref, 1140 (28)
Simpson, G.: ref, 136 (10), 1661 (45), 1697 (426), 2225 (1)
Simpson, G. L.: ref, 1697 (553)
Simpson, G. M.: ref, 2860 (924)
Simpson, H. B.: ref, 2305 (236)
Simpson, J.: ref, 2527 (2)
Simpson, J. A.: ref, 999 (45,64)
Simpson, K. C.: ref, 2498 (29)
Simpson, M. L.: ref, 571 (5), 592 (9,20,29), 615 (16), 1455 (2,4)
Simpson, R. G.: ref, 301 (51), 1392 (14), 1697 (452), 1903 (417), 2905 (89)
Simpson, R. J.: ref, 1824 (7), 2111 (1)
Simpson, S.: ref, 2076 (91,99)
Simpson-Housley, P.: ref, 2497 (371)
Sims, C. A.: rev, 2050
Sims, D. G.: ref, 1407 (5)
Sims, K.: ref, 1216 (84)
Sims, R.: ref, 1481 (3)
Sims, R. L.: ref, 2497 (443)
Sims, V. K.: ref, 1405 (24)
Sims, V. M.: rev, 147, 374, 2879
Sinacore, J.: ref, 1613 (2)
Sinacore, J. M.: ref, 1010 (54), 2498 (24)
Sinar, E.: ref, 2603 (591)
Sinar, E. F.: test, 1348
Sinclair, E.: rev, 465; ref, 1049 (1), 1485 (13), 1902 (39), 2862 (182), 2879 (49)
Sinclair, R. J.: ref, 1010 (5)
Sinclair, V.: ref, 4 (18)
Sinden, M.: ref, 376 (31), 776 (60), 2863 (423)

Sindsay, G.: test, 1260
Sines, J. O.: test, 1215, 1706; rev, 888, 2242; ref, 1215 (1,5)
Sines, L. K.: test, 1706
Singer, B.: test, 1814
Singer, C.: ref, 1218 (3), 2860 (276)
Singer, C. M.: ref, 1697 (103), 2305 (44)
Singer, E. A.: test, 329
Singer, H.: rev, 1073, 1659
Singer, H. S.: ref, 2860 (1167), 2862 (437,548,253), 2901 (100)
Singer, J.: test, 2411
Singer, J. A.: ref, 1745 (46)
Singer, J. L.: test, 2407; ref, 272 (272), 2218 (94), 2497 (630)
Singer, L.: ref, 1166 (56), 2863 (63)
Singer, L. T.: ref, 337 (160), 1216 (112), 1889 (20)
Singer, M.: ref, 1697 (593), 2247 (133)
Singer, R. D.: ref, 694 (47)
Singer, T. M.: ref, 272 (203)
Singer, V. A.: ref, 1379 (61), 2305 (115), 2813 (78)
Singh, B.: ref, 999 (36), 1079 (13)
Singh, B. S.: ref, 650 (2), 2305 (41)
Singh, G.: ref, 2038 (1)
Singh, H.: ref, 2305 (42), 2860 (924)
Singh, H. L.: test, 2626
Singh, I. L.: ref, 998 (60)
Singh, K.: rev, 1307, 1952
Singh, N. A.: ref, 272 (321)
Singh, N. N.: test, 4
Singh, S.: ref, 999 (175), 1321 (10), 1697 (523), 2771 (44)
Singleton, E. G.: ref, 1698 (15)
Singleton, R. M.: test, 294
Sinha, B. K.: ref, 690 (2), 1213 (1), 1333 (5)
Sinha, R. R.: ref, 1697 (536)
Sink, C. A.: ref, 1525 (15), 2163 (187), 2545 (2)
Sinka, I.: test, 2228
Sinkavich, F. J.: ref, 1455 (9)
Sinn, J. S.: ref, 298 (161)
Sinnett, E. R.: ref, 1164 (112), 1697 (242,354,453), 2863 (290)
Sinnott, J. D.: ref, 2860 (26)
Sinson, J.: test, 2088
Sipay, E. R.: test, 1532; rev, 2180
Sipe, J. W.: test, 201
Siperstein, G. N.: ref, 61 (2), 68 (6), 1903 (55), 2299 (1), 2452 (15), 2485 (205), 2657 (30), 2813 (41,124), 2860 (488,878), 2862 (216,505,512,513), 2864 (40,88), 2879 (174,217)
Sippola, B. C.: rev, 1984, 2069, 2585
Siqueland, L.: ref, 451 (154)
Siren, K. A.: ref, 1095 (37)
Sirigu, A.: ref, 2193 (57), 2860 (1174), 2863 (354), 2892 (207,255)
Sirois, P.: ref, 1135 (12), 2813 (67), 2862 (274), 2879 (84)
Sirota, A. D.: ref, 134 (15,19,20), 272 (90), 1661 (34)
Sirridge, S. T.: ref, 462 (15)
Siryk, B.: test, 2525
Siscoe, K. L.: ref, 2860 (755), 2863 (221)
Sison, C. E.: ref, 335 (10), 2288 (74)
Sison, R.: ref, 1763 (1)
Sitarenios, G.: ref, 681 (89)
Sittig, M.: ref, 1697 (285)
Siu, K. P.: ref, 1166 (166), 2305 (209)
Sivan, A. B.: test, 1740
Sivec, H. J.: ref, 1697 (454)
Siwers, B.: ref, 1164 (63)
Six, L.: ref, 2862 (259)
Sixbury, G. R.: test, 1236
Sjögren, B.: ref, 2305 (22)
Sjostrom, K.: ref, 1962 (17), 2288 (40), 2813 (77)
Ska, B.: ref, 2860 (633)
Skaff, M.: ref, 68 (47)
Skaggs, L. P.: ref, 372 (4), 998 (7), 1140 (4), 1140 (24)
Skalina, S.: ref, 376 (32), 2860 (1400), 2863 (424)
Skarakis-Doyle, E.: ref, 2710 (1)
Skare, S.: ref, 280 (3), 451 (184)
Skare, S. S.: ref, 681 (71,72,84), 1380 (9)
Skay, C. L.: ref, 2497 (669)
Skidd, J. E.: ref, 1987 (5)
Skillman, G. D.: ref, 853 (7)
Skinner, H. A.: test, 133, 134, 859, 1008; ref, 134 (5), 272 (35), 1661 (9)
Skinner, J. R.: ref, 472 (65), 1991 (61)
Skipper, B.: ref, 2218 (96)
Skipper, B. J.: ref, 136 (10), 1661 (45), 1697 (426,553)
Skitka, L. J.: ref, 1010 (64), 1697 (235,243)
Sklar, S. M.: test, 858, 1305; ref, 2414 (6), 2603 (555)
Skleder, A. A.: ref, 592 (69)
Skolnick, B. E.: ref, 592 (58)
Skorikov, V. B.: ref, 404 (46), 2915 (8)
Skorupa, J.: ref, 1590 (28)
Skuse, D.: ref, 1612 (78), 1745 (61), 2860 (756)
Skuy, M.: ref, 1991 (16), 2163 (51,95), 2860 (223)
Skydsbjerg, M.: ref, 2603 (110), 2860 (279)
Slaap, B. R.: ref, 1166 (154), 2603 (497)
Slack, A. K.: ref, 1701 (32)
Slade, E.: ref, 2305 (75)
Slade, P.: ref, 2863 (114)
Slade, P. D.: ref, 1944 (1)
Sladeczek, I. E.: ref, 1036 (6)
Slaghuis, W. L.: ref, 322 (4), 1765 (14), 2163 (132), 2768 (19), 2860 (980), 2862 (552)
Slaney, R. B.: rev, 408, 1497, 2805; ref, 200 (2), 2497 (563), 2835 (20)
Slap-Shelton, L.: ref, 2247 (21)
Slate, J. R.: ref, 540 (3), 694 (46), 746 (2), 1903 (420), 2432 (26), 2704 (32), 2860 (309,953), 2862 (400,401,402,553,674,735), 2879 (139,181)
Slater, A.: ref, 349 (27), 1240 (38), 1903 (421), 2485 (181), 2860 (981), 2864 (103)
Slater, B. R.: test, 565
Slater, J. J.: ref, 592 (42)
Slater, P.: rev, 1312

Slater, W. H.: rev, 967, 2489
Slaughter, S. J.: ref, 2860 (20)
Slaven, L.: ref, 2076 (180)
Slavens, S.: ref, 337 (152)
Slavich, R.: ref, 694 (119)
Slavin, L. A.: ref, 472 (9), 1000 (36)
Slavin, R. E.: ref, 364 (16), 665 (37), 861 (2), 1903 (413), 2695 (5), 2905 (87)
Slavkin, S. L.: ref, 2065 (5)
Slavney, P. R.: ref, 2860 (1243)
Slavotinek, A.: ref, 2603 (532)
Slawinowski, M. J.: test, 480
Slawson, C. D.: ref, 592 (24)
Sleator, E. K.: test, 65
Sledge, W. H.: ref, 2305 (174), 2603 (498), 2860 (1068)
Slee, P. T.: ref, 1010 (109)
Slema, S.: ref, 1612 (40), 2862 (218)
Slevin, C.: ref, 2850 (3)
Slevin, D. P.: test, 2096
Slick, D.: test, 2811
Slick, D. J.: ref, 1697 (515)
Slicker, E. K.: ref, 1991 (58)
Slifer, K. J.: ref, 2214 (29)
Slijper, F. M. E.: ref, 451 (212)
Slingerland, B. H.: test, 2219, 2428
Slis, V.: ref, 451 (175), 2879 (198)
Sliss, V.: ref, 448 (21), 853 (20), 1226 (2), 2879 (159)
Slivnick, P.: test, 11
Sliwinski, M.: ref, 199 (9), 776 (11), 994 (36), 1058 (8), 1061 (1), 1740 (9), 1903 (458, 1982 (13), 2125 (13), 2163 (174), 2485 (197), 2680 (14) 2813 (114), 2860 (357,682)
Sliwinski, M. J.: ref, 2860 (404,1235), 2863 (369)
Sloan, C. E.: ref, 1701 (10)
Sloan, E. P.: ref, 537 (2), 1390 (6), 1758 (53), 2860 (982)
Sloan, P.: ref, 1169 (6), 1697 (455), 2247 (95), 2749 (39)
Sloan, S. J.: test, 1824
Sloan, W.: test, 1502
Sloane, H. N.: ref, 1903 (123)
Sloane, K. D.: ref, 2163 (26)
Sloane, P. D.: ref, 2603 (340)
Slob, A. K.: ref, 451 (212)
Slobin, M. S.: test, 1239
Slocum, T. A.: ref, 1503 (14), 1612 (44), 1903 (399), 2671 (2)
Slomka, L.: ref, 1000 (26)
Slomkowski, C.: ref, 2860 (983)
Slonaker, R. L.: rev, 1996
Sloper, P.: ref, 998 (123), 1010 (110), 2858 (37), 2858 (98,119)
Slopes, P.: ref, 451 (155), 1010 (111)
Slopis, J. M.: ref, 815 (39), 1903 (481), 2671 (3), 2862 (522), 2879 (176), 2901 (97)
Slosson, R. L.: test, 2430, 2432, 2433
Slosson, S. W.: test, 2431
Sloutsky, V. M.: ref, 2862 (675)
Sluman, S. M.: ref, 2193 (58), 2239 (30,31)
Slutske, W. S.: ref, 999 (172)
Sluzewska, A.: ref, 1166 (155)
Small, A. M.: ref, 624 (5), 1379 (26), 2163 (110), 2651 (10)
Small, B. J.: ref, 1405 (18,30), 2860 (1351)
Small, G. W.: ref, 1164 (181), 1740 (33), 2227 (59), 2860 (984,1408), 2863 (427)
Small, J.: ref, 2305 (202)
Small, J. G.: ref, (2305), 2288 (82)
Small, S. A.: ref, 303 (29), 337 (18), 776 (61), 1740 (32), 2860 (1405)
Small, V.: test, 1046
Smalley, S. L.: ref, 2860 (402)
Smallish, L.: ref, 681 (4), 1740 (5), 1903 (65), 2606 (4)
Smart, D.: ref, 34 (2,3,4,5), 863 (29), 1079 (15), 1765 (30,31,33)f, 2039 (8), 2485 (68), 2813 (21,48), 2862 (554,575), 2879 (186)
Smart, D. L.: ref, 592 (104)
Smart, R. M.: ref, 2540 (7)
Smedley, B. D.: ref, 592 (43)
Smedley, F.: test, 2436
Smeraldi, E.: ref, 1166 (75), 2603 (255)
Smiroldo, B. B.: ref, 2485 (229), 2813 (147)
Smit, A. B.: test, 2438; ref, 240 (1,2), 1059 (1)
Smit, J. H.: ref, 2163 (342)
Smith, A.: test, 2599; ref, 349 (19), 994 (28), 1095 (34), 1485 (41), 1852 (4), 1903 (375), 2305 (232), 2543 (1)
Smith, A. D.: test, 2508
Smith, A. E.: rev, 1866
Smith, A. F.: ref, 2860 (1218)
Smith, A. H. W.: ref, 1079 (28), 2860 (1401)
Smith, A. J.: test, 2439; ref, 2497 (465)
Smith, A. K.: ref, 2288 (71), 2289 (56), 2862 (501)
Smith, A. L., Jr.: rev, 1078, 1670, 2106
Smith, A. M.: ref, 2247 (119), 2862 (676)
Smith, A. P.: ref, 2497 (283)
Smith, B.: ref, 270 (46), 472 (34), 777 (1), 1755 (59), 1991 (85)
Smith, B. D.: ref, 592 (82), 1687 (19), 1755 (54), 2545 (5), 2860 (340)
Smith, B. E.: ref, 641 (2), 2517 (3), 2860 (822), 2863 (237), 2892 (167)
Smith, B. F.: ref, 451 (230), 2497 (659)
Smith, B. L.: ref, 2247 (134)
Smith, B. T.: ref, 1725 (6), 1908 (1)
Smith, C.: ref, 1939 (12)
Smith, C. J.: ref, 2305 (225)
Smith, C. R.: rev, 60, 342, 465, 495
Smith, C. S.: ref, 1259 (1), 1701 (31)
Smith, C. W.: ref, 2860 (1030)
Smith, D.: ref, 853 (19), 1166 (114), 2497 (561), 2603 (468)
Smith, D. A.: ref, 863 (79), 1000 (52)
Smith, D. A. F.: test, 1720
Smith, D. B.: ref, 1755 (78)
Smith, D. E.: ref, 893 (15), 1832 (4,6,12)

Smith, D. E. P.: rev, 2790
Smith, D. G.: ref, 592 (13)
Smith, D. K.: rev, 1767, 2173, 2309, 2690
Smith, D. L.: ref, 1110 (1), 1118 (1), 1122 (1)
Smith, D. S.: ref, 2862 (403)
Smith, D. W.: ref, 846 (19), 1697 (516), 2417 (29)
Smith, E.: ref, 853 (21), 1096 (13), 1697 (512), 1903 (558), 2695 (71), 2864 (141)
Smith, E. B.: test, 1981
Smith, E. F.: ref, 844 (6)
Smith, E. H.: test, 2664
Smith, F.: test, 2333
Smith, F. E.: ref, 791 (3,10), 2117 (3)
Smith, G.: test, 1654; ref, 2863 (103)
Smith, G. D.: ref, 451 (158)
Smith, G. E.: ref, 2226 (25), 2860 (718,905,1283), 2863 (214,272,387), 2879 (88)
Smith, G. R.: rev, 120, 121
Smith, G. T.: ref, 1697 (532), 2860 (1157)
Smith, H.: ref, 451 (117)
Smith, H. R.: ref, 2497 (468,469)
Smith, I.: ref, 1613 (1)
Smith, I. M.: rev, 745, 753, 2460; ref, 1653 (14), 1903 (237)
Smith, J.: ref, 1903 (553), 2681 (2), 2860 (757)
Smith, J. A. L.: ref, 2163 (339)
Smith, J. E.: ref, 893 (13), 2519 (33), 2520 (34)
Smith, J. J.: test, 828
Smith, J. K.: rev, 621, 895, 2333, 2733
Smith, J. M.: test, 1642
Smith, J. O.: ref, 301 (7), 2860 (134)
Smith, J. P.: rev, 506, 507
Smith, J. R.: ref, 641 (4), 2227 (4,11), 2860 (68), 2863 (136), 2892 (3)
Smith, J. V.: rev, 789
Smith, K.: ref, 1000 (35), 1105 (1), 1765 (4), 2862 (29)
Smith, K. D.: ref, 462 (5)
Smith, K. E.: ref, 270 (26), 2382 (35), 2813 (130)
Smith, K. G.: ref, 1697 (440), 2497 (498)
Smith, K. J.: rev, 348, 552, 1092
Smith, K. L.: test, 2464; ref, 2873 (55)
Smith, K. R.: ref, 2497 (618)
Smith, L.: ref, 2485 (175), 2860 (1319), 2879 (129), 2892 (282)
Smith, L. B.: ref, 1485 (59), 1528 (4), 1903 (531), 2485 (227)
Smith, L. C.: ref, 1638 (3)
Smith, L. H.: test, 1474, 2295
Smith, L. J.: ref, 861 (2,4,5), 1903 (413,495), 2695 (61), 2902 (3), 2905 (62,87,105)
Smith, L. T.: ref, 2305 (190), 2860 (1146)
Smith, L. W.: ref, 337 (16,19,47), 2603 (66), 2858 (18,19,20)
Smith, M.: test, 196; ref, 272 (222), 451 (78), 875 (7), 1991 (23), 2211 (9), 2218 (36), 2860 (402)
Smith, M. B.: test, 2194
Smith, M. C.: ref, 1216 (89), 2860 (880)
Smith, M. E.: ref, 272 (60), 2860 (403), 2863 (107)
Smith, M. J.: ref, 1166 (177), 2247 (83), 2288 (80), 2289 (66)
Smith, M. L.: rev, 2755; ref, 2218 (53), 2860 (17,73,985,1175)
Smith, M. R.: ref, 2860 (1384)
Smith, M. W.: ref, 1903 (249)
Smith, N.: test, 1037
Smith, N. L.: rev, 670
Smith, N. R.: ref, 1689 (1)
Smith, P.: test, 349, 736, 1826, 1827; ref, 350 (18), 1903 (24), 2163 (150), 2860 (86)
Smith, P. C.: test, 1348, 2208, 2509
Smith, P. K.: ref, 350 (17), 1011 (2)
Smith, P. L.: test, 1844; rev, 835; ref, 1965 (38)
Smith, P. T.: test, 2239; ref, 1758 (12,22), 2163 (62,106), 2239 (9,20)
Smith, R.: ref, 272 (198), 337 (94)f, 998 (19), 2305 (30)
Smith, R. A.: test, 844
Smith, R. C.: ref, 335 (13)
Smith, R. L.: ref, 2402 (46), 2497 (436), 2860 (986)
Smith, R. P.: test, 1481
Smith, S.: test, 173, 174, 956, 957, 1084, 1188, 1203, 2183, 2473, 2823
Smith, S. A.: ref, 2813 (49,106), 2860 (531,987)
Smith, S. D.: ref, 1902 (31), 2163 (85)
Smith, S. L.: rev, 1588
Smith, S. M.: ref, 1902 (31), 2163 (85), 2749 (63)
Smith, S. P.: ref, 1697 (260)
Smith, S. R.: ref, 2247 (126)
Smith, T.: ref, 459 (25), 999 (105), 1697 (351), 1745 (58) 1903 (199), 1962 (6,9), 2497 (393,486), 2813 (42,50)
Smith, T. B.: ref, 1259 (1), 1745 (34)
Smith, T. E.: ref, 665 (27,54,83), 2218 (99), 2305 (226)
Smith, T. L.: ref, 337 (47), 1586 (1), 2860 (845)
Smith, T. W.: ref, 272 (80), 708 (3), 1412 (2), 1697 (226,597) 2497 (49,214), 2862 (526)
Smith, W. L., Jr.: ref, 2305 (228), 2813 (149)
Smith, W. P.: ref, 2497 (517)
Smith, Y. N.: ref, 665 (74)
Smith-Lovin, L.: ref, 1745 (23)
Smithee, J. A. F.: ref, 2862 (736), 2879 (234)
Smither, J. A.: ref, 1405 (33)
Smither, R. D.: ref, 372 (55)
Smits, C. H. M.: ref, 2163 (307,342)
Smits, R. C. F.: ref, 2599 (22)
Smits, S. J.: ref, 1965 (38)
Smock, C. D.: rev, 324, 674
Smoot, D. L.: ref, 681 (23)
Smutzler, N.: ref, 863 (51)
Smyrnios, K. X.: ref, 791 (8), 2497 (280,668)
Smyth, C.: ref, 2305 (199)
Smyth, K.: ref, 2858 (120)
Smyth, K. A.: ref, 2858 (42)
Smyth, M. M.: ref, 2862 (555)
Smyth, S.: test, 191
Smythe, P.: ref, 349 (29), 2163 (258)

Snarey, J.: ref, 1408 (2)
Snart, F.: ref, 763 (2)
Snedden, D.: rev, 182
Sneed, N. V.: ref, 1770 (5)
Snel, F. W. J. J.: ref, 926 (17)
Snell, J. W.: ref, 451 (102), 2862 (450)
Snell, K.: ref, 364 (9)
Snell, K.: ref, 1664 (5)
Snell, W. E., Jr.: ref, 998 (106), 2603 (405)
Snider, E. C.: ref, 2305 (152), 2497 (574)
Snider, F.: ref, 2163 (328), 2860 (1281)
Snider, L.: ref, 353 (21), 815 (38), 1240 (45), 1379 (86), 2862 (491), 2864 (116), 2879 (165)
Snider, P. R.: ref, 2076 (70), 2858 (57)
Snider, R. L.: ref, 798 (4), 1092 (3), 1131 (5), 1240 (4), 1392 (2), 1902 (14), 1903 (42), 2432 (8), 2484 (1), 2879 (21)
Snider, V. E.: ref, 364 (25), 1318 (19)
Snijders, J. T.: test, 2441
Snijders-Oomen, N.: test, 2441
Snitz, B. E.: ref, 687 (4)
Snodgrass, J. G.: ref, 2146 (14), 2860 (621)
Snow, C. E.: ref, 350 (21), 1485 (34)
Snow, C. W.: ref, 2039 (7)
Snow, D.: ref, 266 (2), 540 (20), 994 (47), 1047 (4), 1379 (59,95), 1903 (535), 2045 (6), 2190 (8), 2382 (39), 2524 (12), 2680 (11)
Snow, J. H.: rev, 1362, 1525
Snow, M.: ref, 1697 (574), 2860 (1352)
Snow, M. E.: ref, 2813 (109), 2860 (1001)
Snow, W. G.: ref, 1758 (83), 2768 (38,39), 2860 (1187,1188,1238), 2863 (357,358)
Snow-Turek, A. L.: ref, 1166 (221)
Snowden, L. R.: ref, 1093 (18,116)
Snowling, M.: ref, 349 (16,18,39), 1240 (50), 1765 (35,36), 2556 (3), 2862 (728), 2864 (63)
Snowling, M. J.: ref, 349 (19), 1092 (6)
Snyder, B.: rev, 1736
Snyder, C.: ref, 1533 (1)
Snyder, C. R.: ref, 472 (215), 1318 (20), 2214 (125), 2603 (404), 2862 (677)
Snyder, D.: ref, 1612 (48)
Snyder, D. K.: test, 1582
Snyder, F. R.: ref, 1697 (88), 2402 (6)
Snyder, I.: ref, 27 (1)
Snyder, J.: ref, 1379 (18,29), 1745 (14), 2485 (57,94), 2860 (478), 2862 (166,211), 2879 (45,59)
Snyder, K. S.: ref, 1697 (188)f, 2305 (73), 2860 (384)
Snyder, L. S.: ref, 2484 (11), 2731 (5), 2813 (135), 2862 (584), 2862 (585), 2901 (107)
Snyder, M. C.: ref, 2862 (678), 2879 (218), 2901 (127)
Snyder, P. J.: ref, 298 (128), 372 (77, 2860 (1176)
Snyder, R.: ref, 893 (40)
Snyder, R. D.: ref, 335 (12), 1010 (100,101)
Snyder, V.: ref, 1638 (3)
So, Y.: ref, 1135 (18), 2226 (14), 2516 (85), 2860 (1173), 2863 (353)
So-Kum Tang, C.: ref, 793 (23)
Soardi, M.: ref, 2163 (177), 2873 (25)
Soares, A. T.: test, 120, 121, 2366, 2368, 120, 121, 2366, 2368
Sobal, J.: ref, 1638 (1)
Sobel, E.: ref, 2305 (75)
Sobel, S.: ref, 2288 (64), 2305 (170)
Sobell, L. C.: ref, 134 (10,21,29), 1164 (79), 1525 (16), 1661 (74), 2414 (2), 2599 (23), 2603 (306), 2860 (758), 2892 (150)
Sobell, M.: ref, 134 (21), 1164 (79), 1525 (16), 2599 (23), 2603 (306), 2860 (758), 2892 (150)
Sobell, M. B.: ref, 134 (10,29), 1661 (74), 2414 (2)
Sobelman, S. A.: ref, 1164 (67)
Sobieska, M.: ref, 1166 (155)
Sobin, C.: ref, 2305 (140)
Sobol, M. P.: ref, 1000 (76)
Sobotková, D.: ref, 2485 (195), 2862 (460)
Sobral, J.: ref, 2497 (112)
Sobsey, D.: ref, 2127 (2)
Society of Actuaries: test, 144, 148, 149
Sodian, B.: ref, 350 (7)
Sodor, A. L.: test, 1982
Sodowsky, G. R.: rev, 632, 848, 1397, 1862
Soeken, K.: ref, 2497 (171)
Sofa-Dedeh, A.: ref, 893 (31)
Sohlberg, S.: ref, 1093 (3), 2603 (28)
Soininen, H.: ref, 776 (3), 1164 (152), 2516 (99), 2860 (103), 2892 (274)
Sokol, L.: ref, 2519 (5), 2520 (5)
Sokol, R.: ref, 1687 (6)
Sokol, R. J.: ref, 1216 (31), 1903 (181), 2860 (473)
Sokol, S. M.: ref, 1903 (534), 2163 (329)
Sokolov, J. L.: ref, 2813 (23)
Solanto, M. V.: ref, 451 (49), 681 (2,58), 1903 (59)f, 2247 (81)
Solberg, V. S.: ref, 337 (67), 1754 (25), 2525 (7)
Soldatos, C. R.: ref, 1166 (192), 2497 (631)
Soldz, S.: ref, 2603 (11,67,441)
Soleyami, R. M.: ref, 376 (7), 1166 (116), 2860 (1111), 2863 (330)
Soliday, J.: ref, 1590 (18), 2497 (211)
Solie, L. J.: ref, 298 (6)
Solís-Cámara, P.: ref, 1880 (1)
Solís-Cámara, R. P.: ref, 303 (11), 1592 (26), 2862 (556), 272 (308)
Sollner, W.: ref, 893 (25), 1079 (48)
Solly, D. C.: rev, 1610
Soloff, P. H.: ref, 824 (5), 1093 (56), 1093 (76), 2603 (215,307,532)
Soloman, J.: ref, 2873 (19)
Soloman, Z.: ref, 2603 (68), 2858 (21)
Solomon, C. R.: ref, 1134 (8)
Solomon, D.: ref, 2305 (125,172)
Solomon, D. A.: ref, 1158 (3), 1697 (513,517), 2305 (200)
Solomon, J.: ref, 1266 (3)
Solomon, L.: ref, 2227 (10), 2599 (9), 2860 (401)

Solomon, P.: ref, 1093 (77,103)
Solomon, P. R.: ref, 2860 (988), 2863 (291)
Solomon, R. A.: ref, 2603 (93)
Solomon, R. J.: rev, 2742
Solomon, S.: ref, 272 (378)
Solomon, Z.: ref, 863 (32), 2603 (69), 2603 (146,161,406,499,589)
Solomonica-Levi, D.: ref, 459 (38), 2860 (1207,1208), 2862 (582,583), 2864 (127,128)
Solovitz, B. L.: ref, 451 (71)
Soltys, S. M.: ref, 1962 (4), 1991 (39), 2214 (26), 2862 (183)
Somer, G.: ref, 1093 (102), 2497 (512), 2603 (396)
Somerfield, M. R.: ref, 2076 (159)
Somers, M. D.: ref, 768 (1)
Somerset Local Education Authority: test, 195
Somerville, J. A.: test, 329
Somerwill, H.: test, 883
Somlai, A.: ref, 2497 (485), 2839 (5)
Sommer, R.: ref, 999 (24)
Sommer, W.: ref, 2163 (243)
Sommers, R. K.: test, 2504; rev, 175, 2332; ref, 241 (3), 430 (10), 994 (19), 1095 (29,30), 1903 (313,314), 2190 (3), 2657 (18), 2695 (30)
Sommers-Flanagan, J.: ref, 1697 (46), 2248 (3), 2749 (9)
Sommerville, K. W.: ref, 303 (15), 1135 (8,20), 1740 (18), 2076 (167), 2077 (5), 2226 (21), 2516 (22,96), 2599 (12), 2860 (450,1255), 2899 (15)
Son, J.: ref, 1338 (45), 2839 (6)
Son, L.: ref, 615 (30)
Song, A.: test, 2891
Song, W.: ref, 372 (97), 1697 (476)
Sonies, B. C.: test, 2296; ref, 776 (51)
Sonne, S. C.: ref, 2519 (49), 2520 (49)
Sonneborn, D.: ref, 2218 (61), 2603 (465)
Sonnenberg, B. R.: ref, 2163 (283), 2226 (10), 2227 (27), 2863 (333), 2892 (234)
Sonnenberg, R. T.: ref, 1754 (11)
Sonnichsen, S. E.: ref, 337 (130)
Sontrop, J.: ref, 1697 (538)
Sonuga-Barke, E. J. S.: ref, 349 (20,33), 1612 (59)
Sood, R.: ref, 2017 (8), 2305 (83)
Soper, B.: ref, 694 (121)
Soper, H. V.: ref, 1903 (77)
Soper, J. C.: test, 2685, 2686
Soraci, S. A., Jr.: ref, 1903 (93)
Sorbara, D. L.: ref, 1097 (7), 1134 (1), 1612 (27), 2228 (6), 2860 (394), 2864 (31), 2870 (3)
Sorell, G.: ref, 1000 (10)
Sorensen, D. J.: ref, 2120 (1)
Sorensen, J. E.: ref, 2108 (3)
Sorensen, J. L.: ref, 272 (356), 2603 (581)
Sorensen, P. S.: ref, 337 (13)
Sorenson, A. S.: ref, 337 (13)
Sorenson, C.: test, 648
Sorenson, D. H.: ref, 2076 (28), 2858 (29)
Sorenson, D. S.: ref, 2076 (29)
Sorenson, E.: ref, 1341 (1), 1697 (518)
Sorenson, G.: rev, 413
Soresi, S.: ref, 2860 (1025)
Soriani, A.: ref, 2603 (211)
Soriano, J. L.: ref, 271 (5), 272 (223)
Sorkin, J. D.: ref, 2496 (6)
Sorrell, S.: ref, 2603 (279)
Sorrentino, R. M.: ref, 337 (120)
Sorri, A.: ref, 2247 (120), 2288 (2), 2860 (53)
Sosa, E.: ref, 2860 (883)
Sossen, P. L.: test, 2530
Sostek, A. M.: rev, 1770
Sotile, M. O.: test, 1006
Sotile, W. M.: test, 1006
Soto, S.: ref, 2603 (64)
Sotsby, S. M.: ref, 272 (194)
Sotsky, S. M.: ref, 272 (111), 1517 (4)
Souder, L.: rev, 2486
Soukup, V. M.: ref, 794 (1), 893 (7), 2065 (3)
Souliez, L.: ref, 776 (35)
Sourander, A.: ref, 451 (284)
Sousou, S. D.: ref, 1745 (84)
Southern, W. T.: ref, 2485 (7)
Southwick, S.: ref, 337 (144), 2497 (119)
Southwick, S. M.: ref, 790 (22), 2519 (14), 2520 (15), 2863 (232)
Souza, J.: ref, 1402 (1)
Sowa, C. J.: ref, 1754 (24), 2282 (9), 2527 (5,12)
Sowarka, D.: ref, 2863 (229)
Sowden, A.: ref, 2050 (119)
Sowell, E. J.: ref, 298 (40), 615 (19,45), 665 (28), 1140 (15), 1866 (14), 2163 (52), 2485 (30), 2729 (2), 2771 (8)
Spaan, M.: test, 953, 1506
Spaan, M.: test, 1664
Spaccarelli, S.: ref, 451 (226), 472 (146,216), 2214 (81,82,126)
Spache, G. D.: test, 827; rev, 861, 1073, 1981
Spackman, A. J.: ref, 2239 (10)
Spadafore, G. J.: test, 1461, 2461, 2462
Spadafore, S. J.: test, 1461, 2461
Spadoni, M.: ref, 2163 (222), 2860 (927)
Spafford, C. S.: ref, 2860 (102,989), 2862 (72,404,413), 2879 (140)
Spalding, N. V.: test, 2141
Spalletta, G.: ref, 272 (224), 1166 (156)
Spaner, S. D.: rev, 950
Spaney, E.: rev, 1315
Spanier, G. B.: test, 863
Spanos, N. P.: ref, 999 (139), 1697 (244), 2603 (407)
Spany, E.: rev, 1863
Spar, J. E.: ref, 1058 (1), 2860 (21)
Sparks, R.: ref, 541 (1), 1503 (12), 1903 (360,496), 2668 (2), 2693 (7), 2694 (22), 2695 (62), 2731 (3), 2862 (557), 2879 (115), 2901 (62), 2905 (74,106)
Sparks, R. L.: ref, 547 (1), 1503 (15), 1767 (6), 1903 (422,497,555), 2731 (1), 2860 (257), 2879 (34,141,182,219), 2880 (7), 2901 (17,101,128), 2905 (90,107)

Sparrevohn, R.: ref, 1485 (45), 1903 (423)
Sparrow, E.: test, 678
Sparrow, S. S.: test, 124, 2813, 2814; ref, 1379 (17,36,72), 1386 (18), 1485 (23), 2813 (52,99), 2860 (543)
Sparrow, W. A.: ref, 2860 (1250)
Sparta, S.: ref, 681 (45), 1903 (262)
Spataro, R.: ref, 1697 (483)
Spates, C. R.: ref, 1021 (26), 2603 (294,408)
Spaulding, C. L.: ref, 2935 (1)
Spaulding, S. C.: ref, 705 (6)
Spaulding, W.: ref, 1697 (47)
Spaulding, W. D.: ref, 1619 (5), 2050 (43), 2603 (206), 2892 (83)
Speaker, R. B., Jr.: ref, 550 (4)
Spear-Swerling, L.: ref, 2905 (65)
Spearing, D.: ref, 1092 (17), 1903 (435)
Specht, J. A.: ref, 592 (73)
Specht, L. A.: ref, 2862 (526)
Specker, S. M.: ref, 2497 (313)
Spector, H.: ref, 303 (27), 2226 (39)
Spector, J. E.: rev, 2723
Spector, P. E.: ref, 2497 (396)
Spedding, S.: ref, 2092 (2), 2487 (14)
Speece, D. L.: ref, 2044 (2)
Speech Communication Association: test, 188, 639
Speechley, K. N.: ref, 2497 (204)
Speed, N.: ref, 1697 (127)
Speer, R. F.: test, 1203
Speer, R. K.: test, 173, 174, 956, 957, 1084, 2183, 2473, 2823
Speer, R. V.: test, 1188
Speicher, B.: ref, 1408 (7)
Speicher, C.: ref, 337 (10)
Speight, S. L.: ref, 1939 (15)
Spellacy, F.: ref, 1218 (11), 2860 (978), 2892 (206)
Spellacy, F. J.: ref, 1697 (515)
Spellane, M. M.: ref, 1903 (498)
Speltz, M. L.: ref, 270 (30,40), 451 (228), 681 (11), 863 (90), 1010 (129), 1903 (80,424), 2603 (99)
Spence, G. T.: ref, 815 (13), 1135 (11), 2862 (229), 2903 (1)
Spence, J. T.: ref, 298 (52)
Spence, R. J.: test, 2897
Spence, S. E.: ref, 199 (13), 1745 (35)
Spence, S. H.: ref, 272 (39), 472 (10), 999 (22), 2497 (91)
Spencer, D.: rev, 374
Spencer, D. D.: ref, 2860 (216,974), 2863 (286)
Spencer, D. G.: rev, 1945
Spencer, E. K.: ref, 2862 (293), 2864 (72)
Spencer, F.: ref, 763 (2), 1754 (5), 2163 (22)
Spencer, J. C.: ref, 540 (15), 2862 (597)
Spencer, J. H.: ref, 1093 (8), 2108 (1)
Spencer, J. H., Jr.: ref, 1093 (29), 2108 (4)
Spencer, L.: ref, 487 (2)
Spencer, L. M.: test, 1860
Spencer, P.: ref, 811 (8)
Spencer, P. E.: ref, 811 (6,7)
Spencer, T.: ref, 1092 (5), 2305 (155), 2305 (165,240), 2860 (331,990), 2879 (142)
Spencer, T. J.: ref, 2860 (1203), 2879 (187)
Spencer, W. D.: ref, 745 (14), 1405 (27), 2860 (759), 2892 (151)
Spennato, N. A.: test, 775
Spense, S. H.: ref, 472 (103), 1021 (27), 2214 (56)
Sperling, M. B.: ref, 2497 (307)
Sperling, M. R.: ref, 1752 (1), 2860 (269)
Speroff, B. J.: test, 933
Speth, C.: test, 648
Spetter, D.: ref, 1010 (80)
Spevack, M.: ref, 1697 (35)
Speyer, H.: rev, 433
Spicer, J.: ref, 335 (4), 2497 (165)
Spicer, K. B.: ref, 1903 (315), 2402 (33)
Spicker, H. H.: ref, 2485 (7)
Spiegel, A. N.: ref, 1300 (9)
Spiegel, D.: ref, 272 (348), 2076 (144), 2497 (666)
Spiegel, D. L.: ref, 364 (4)
Spiegler, B. J.: ref, 1096 (3), 2193 (11), 2860 (246,342,125)
Spiegler, C. R.: ref, 1096 (4), 2860 (247), 2862 (126)
Spieker, S.: ref, 2498 (17), 2860 (835), 2863 (241)
Spielberger, C. D.: test, 1354, 2496, 2497, 2498, 2656; rev, 1021, 1869
Spielman, C. R.: ref, 1341 (3)
Spielman, L. A.: ref, 1166 (129)
Spielmann, D.: ref, 2247 (9)
Spiers, P.: ref, 2497 (47)
Spiers, P. A.: ref, 2227 (58), 2860 (1396), 2863 (421)
Spies, K.: ref, 1745 (38)
Spies, R.: rev, 2607
Spigelman, A.: ref, 853 (5), 2247 (74)
Spigelman, G.: ref, 853 (5), 2247 (74)
Spiker, D.: rev, 315, 1308, 1851, 2308; ref, 1079 (16), 1216 (25), 2485 (75), 2862 (486)
Spikman, J. M.: ref, 1164 (134), 2193 (47), 2226 (15) 2516 (86)
Spillman, R. E.: ref, 645 (1)
Spinazzola, L.: ref, 2163 (263)
Spingler, H.: ref, 1166 (50)
Spinhoven, P.: ref, 1021 (44), 2497 (660), 2603 (120,221,500,559)
Spink, K. S.: ref, 1141 (4)
Spinnler, H.: ref, 2163 (25,58,77,108,146,319), 2768 (24), 2860 (836), 2892 (269)
Spires, E. E.: ref, 1755 (14)
Spires, H. A.: ref, 592 (44), 615 (46), 2487 (15)
Spires, H. P.: test, 1617
Spiridigliozzi, G.: ref, 2813 (116)
Spiridigliozzi, G. A.: ref, 4 (2), 681 (50)
Spirito, A.: ref, 272 (225), 451 (105,178), 472 (161), 2305 (218), 2557 (6)
Spirits, A.: ref, 2214 (46)
Spiro, A.: ref, 1697 (253,355), 2417 (30), 2603 (227,308)

Spiro, A., III: ref, 2417 (9), 2603 (202), 2858 (111)
Spirrison, C. L.: ref, 1755 (31)
Spiti, R.: ref, 2497 (621)
Spitz, R. V.: ref, 270 (41), 2695 (70), 2862 (679)
Spitzberg, B. H.: test, 689
Spitzer, A.: ref, 863 (20), 2497 (150)
Spitzer, J. B.: rev, 304, 2301, 2673
Spitzer, R. L.: test, 748, 1093, 2108, 2109, 2305, 2519, 2520
Spitzer, S. B.: ref, 1697 (27), 2497 (30)
Spivack, G.: test, 1161, 1162, 1619
Spivack, G. M.: rev, 994
Spivey, N. N.: ref, 665 (16)
Splete, H.: ref, 200 (4), 404 (22)
Spock, A.: ref, 1010 (41,66), 2603 (166167,321), 2858 (46,86)
Spodek, B.: ref, 1903 (308)
Spohr, H. L.: ref, 624 (21), 2864 (73)
Spokane, A. R.: ref, 404 (20,38), 2603 (364)
Spooncer, F. A.: test, 1144
Sporakowski, M. J.: rev, 2063
Sprafkin, J.: test, 79, 876; ref, 472 (12), 681 (7), 2214 (6), 2862 (338)
Sprague, R. L.: test, 65
Spratt, E.: ref, 451 (275), 2485 (243), 2862 (723)
Spreafico, R.: ref, 1903 (563), 2163 (347), 2227 (54), 2768 (42), 2862 (698)
Spreat, S.: rev, 809, 1868
Sprecher, S.: ref, 1927 (7)
Spreen, O.: rev, 1218, 1645; ref, 287 (1)
Spreitzer, G. M.: test, 2101
Sprenkle, D. H.: ref, 863 (63), 1000 (8)
Sprich-Buckminster, S.: ref, 1092 (5), 2860 (331)
Spring, B.: ref, 1745 (11), 2076 (6,34), 2440 (1), 2860 (141)
Springer, J. A.: ref, 1697 (577)
Springer, L.: ref, 620 (4)
Springer, T.: ref, 2603 (11)
Springer, T. P.: ref, 2835 (5)
Springston, F. J.: ref, 2656 (13), 1408 (4)
Sprock, J.: ref, 2076 (123), 2247 (94)
Sprouse, C. A.: ref, 2862 (737)
Sprouse, P. T.: ref, 2862 (300)
Spruill, J.: ref, 2485 (216), 2860 (74,1177), 2862 (558)
Spruytenberg, H.: ref, 1653 (25), 2189 (6), 2864 (106)
Spurr, P.: ref, 451 (249), 1079 (105), 1216 (111), 1889 (17)
Squier, R. W.: ref, 2850 (1)
Squier, W.: ref, 303 (19), 2227 (48), 2860 (1323), 2863 (398), 2892 (283)
Squillace, S. R.: ref, 2860 (989), 2862 (404), 2879 (140)
Squire, L. R.: ref, 776 (4,9), 2860 (9,50,104,220), 2863 (5,18,30,56), 2892 (11,29,47)
Squires, J.: test, 123; ref, 270 (42), 1612 (98)
Squires, N. K.: ref, 1164 (92), 1903 (486), 2860 (1145), 2879 (177)
Squires, W. G.: ref, 998 (52)
Squires-Wheeler, E.: ref, 1697 (405), 2305 (49,131,220)
Srebnik, D.: ref, 337 (17), 793 (13), 893 (3)
Srinivasagam, N. M.: ref, 893 (26)
Sroufe, L. A.: ref, 373 (7,10), 451 (190,203), 1321 (9), 1902 (91,95), 1965 (63), 2860 (1286), 2862 (88,564,615,630), 2864 (124), 2901 (102,120)
Srsic, C. S.: ref, 271 (9), 272 (266), 273 (27), 1166 (183)
St. George-Hyslop, P. H.: ref, 2227 (8), 2768 (38,39), 2860 (364,1187,1188), 2863 (357,358), 2879 (44), 2892 (54)
St. James-Roberts, I.: ref, 2038 (1)
St. Laurent, C. M.: ref, 272 (264), 1697 (533), 2247 (113)
St. Lawrence, J. S.: ref, 298 (53)
St. Louis, K. O.: test, 1852; ref, 1095 (13)
St-Laurent, D.: ref, 1903 (482)
Staal, M. A.: ref, 1697 (598)
Stabenau, J. R.: ref, 1661 (10)
Stablum, F.: ref, 2860 (1178)
Stacey, B. G.: rev, 462
Stacey, C. A.: ref, 337 (33)
Stacey, K.: test, 2080
Stacey, S.: ref, 2599 (2)
Stack, J. A.: ref, 1093 (74)
Stacy, A. W.: ref, 2299 (3), 2813 (53)
Stadler, J.: ref, 462 (18), 1661 (43)
Stadler, J. G.: ref, 2497 (597)
Staff of the Division of Foreign Language Education: test, 1179, 482
Stafford, J.: rev, 827, 1092
Stafford, K. P.: ref, 1697 (382)
Stafford, L.: ref, 1580 (4), 2034 (2)
Stafiniak, P.: ref, 2860 (744)
Stage, K. B.: ref, 1166 (172)
Stage, S.: ref, 2905 (7)
Stager, S.: ref, 2305 (137)
Stagg, V.: ref, 265 (12)
Stahl, K. J.: ref, 472 (215), 1318 (20), 2214 (125), 2862 (677)
Stahl, M. J.: test, 1347; rev, 2105
Stahl, N. A.: ref, 592 (9)
Stahl, S.: ref, 1903 (404)
Stahl, S. A.: rev, 1130; ref, 1072 (12), 2181 (2), 2864 (62), 2879 (86), 2905 (58)
Stahmann, R. F.: rev, 426, 1413, 2618
Stahmer, A.: ref, 1902 (96)
Stahmer, A. C.: ref, 994 (30,34), 1485 (46), 1903 (425,432), 2485 (182,184)
Stainback, G. J.: rev, 492, 879, 2778
Stake, J. E.: rev, 166, 1620, 2072, 2371, 2512
Stake, R. E.: rev, 2484
Stalling, R. B.: ref, 2497 (3)
Stallings, G.: ref, 376 (2), 2226 (7)
Stallman, A. C.: ref, 665 (38)
Stallman, D.: ref, 2497 (617)
Stam, H. J.: ref, 2497 (162)
Stambrook, M.: ref, 2860 (500)
Stamoulis, D. T.: ref, 1755 (56)

Stamper, L.: test, 1618
Stanard & Associates, Inc.: test, 1763
Stanchev, P.: ref, 776 (47)
Stancik, E. J.: test, 1439
Stancliffe, R. J.: ref, 1903 (426), 2132 (4)
Standen, P. J.: ref, 270 (13), 2308 (1)
Standing, L.: ref, 998 (24)
Standley, P. D.: ref, 272 (127)
Staner, L.: ref, 1166 (194)
Stanfeld, S. A.: ref, 2497 (205)
Stanfield, K.: test, 1732
Stanford, G.: ref, 769 (8), 2862 (729), 2879 (233)
Stanford, L. D.: ref, 2879 (93), 2905 (66)
Stanford, M.: ref, 372 (68), 2247 (64)
Stanford, M. S.: ref, 2862 (559), 2879 (183)
Stangalino, C.: ref, 2163 (245)
Stanger, B. Z.: ref, 2860 (623), 2863 (182)
Stangl, D.: ref, 1093 (30)
Stangl, D. K.: ref, 451 (107,108)
Stanhope, N.: ref, 1390 (4), 1697 (311), 1758 (26,90), 2193 (24,25), 2860 (667,668,1297), 2863 (197,198, 391)
Stanik, P.: ref, 2498 (76)
Stankov, L.: ref, 838 (14), 2163 (302), 2860 (121,225)
Stankovic, S.: ref, 1687 (6)
Stanley, J. A.: ref, 2288 (55), 2289 (42)
Stanley, J. C.: rev, 2485, 2515; ref, 615 (8,12,28,29), 2485 (42)
Stanley, M. A.: ref, 272 (226), 998 (81), 1166 (157), 2497 (18,303,596,597,610), 2603 (235,309)
Stanovich, K. E.: ref, 705 (7), 1902 (85), 1903 (316,459), 2163 (41), 2487 (10), 2856 (8), 2905 (9)
Stansbury, K.: ref, 451 (38)
Stansfield, C.: rev, 1422
Stansfield, C. W.: test, 250, 2015; rev, 1195, 1527
Stanton, A. L.: ref, 272 (298), 2076 (35,70), 2214 (10), 2603 (121,162,404), 2858 (43,57)
Stanton, H.: ref, 472 (8)
Stanton, M.: ref, 2901 (57)
Stanton, S.: ref, 472 (8)
Stanton, S. P.: ref, 2289 (58)
Stanton, W.: ref, 2211 (7)
Stanwyck, D. J.: ref, 1767 (7)
Stapells, D. R.: ref, 1096 (9), 2668 (1), 2694 (14), 2860 (912)
Stapleton, J. M.: ref, 1164 (90), 1592 (21), 2225 (7), 2497 (456), 2860 (848), 2863 (246), 2892 (175)
Stapleton, L. A.: ref, 2497 (194)
Starcevic, V.: ref, 2519 (50), 2520 (50), 2603 (163,216)
Stark, C.: ref, 2497 (106), 2603 (84)
Stark, J.: test, 202, 984; rev, 2045, 2228, 2229
Stark, J. S.: test, 2530
Stark, K. D.: ref, 472 (11,191), 2214 (51,112)
Stark, M. E.: ref, 2860 (1353), 2863 (407)
Stark, R. E.: ref, 540 (11,12), 994 (31,50), 1903 (427,556), 2725 (10), 2768 (31,41), 2862 (405,560,680)
Stark, R. H.: test, 2006
Stark, R. S.: ref, 2497 (551)
Starkey, R. I.: test, 1165
Starkstein, S.: ref, 2516 (72), 2892 (203)
Starkstein, S. E.: ref, 303 (31), 1166 (82,229), 1740 (35), 2050 (9,28,120,121), 2163 (227,228,356), 2516 (18), 2860 (935,1419), 2873 (40,41), 2892 (44,197, 198,306)
Starr, A. S.: test, 2261, 2813
Starr, E. R.: rev, 569, 2147
Starr, R. H., Jr.: ref, 270 (31), 337 (60,175), 1216 (103), 1770 (12), 2860 (1303)
Starr, R. P.: test, 1609
Startup, M.: ref, 272 (357), 2050 (56), 2603 (230,301,403,582)
Statham, D. J.: ref, 999 (172)
Staton, R. D.: ref, 199 (12), 272 (1), 1093 (44), 2519 (22), 2520 (23), 2599 (3), 2860 (430), 2892 (65)
Stauber, H. Y.: ref, 472 (107)
Staudinger, U. M.: ref, 2860 (757)
Staudinger, V. M.: ref, 2218 (74), 2860 (1179)
Staunton, H.: ref, 1140 (50), 2860 (1124)
Stavrakaki, C.: ref, 472 (90), 2211 (30), 2214 (50)
Staw, B. M.: ref, 1107 (1)
Stead, G. B.: ref, 404 (30,35)
Stecher, M. D.: ref, 68 (22), 937 (4), 2218 (134), 2899 (9)
Stechler, G.: ref, 272 (19,58), 273 (3), 1000 (5,37)
Steck, G. M.: ref, 301 (24), 2247 (28), 2614 (1)
Stecker, P. M.: ref, 2211 (4)
Steckler, T.: ref, 1390 (5), 2860 (970)
Steckler, V.: rev, 2799
Stedge, D.: ref, 4 (11)
Stedman, L.: ref, 592 (70)
Steel, C.: ref, 1671 (8), 1758 (100), 2860 (1380)
Steel, D.: test, 935
Steel, K.: ref, 1294 (3), 2533 (1)
Steel, R. P.: ref, 1348 (13), 1701 (48)
Steele, C.: ref, 1011 (1), 1991 (3)
Steele, E. S.: ref, 2905 (83)
Steele, H.: ref, 272 (171), 997 (23), 999 (157), 1079 (50), 2497 (554), 2603 (454)
Steele, J. M.: test, 493, 619
Steele, M.: ref, 272 (171), 999 (157), 2497 (554), 2603 (454)
Steele, R. D.: ref, 2008 (3)
Steele, R. G.: ref, 337 (186), 451 (227), 472 (217,218), 1661 (50), 2211 (44), 2214 (127)
Steele, S.: ref, 2485 (196), 2813 (113)
Steele, T. E.: ref, 272 (227)
Steen, L.: ref, 2240 (1), 2863 (106)
Steen, S. C.: ref, 2525 (4)
Steenhuis, R. E.: ref, 303 (7), 2226 (8)
Steenman, H.: ref, 1740 (2)
Steer, R. A.: test, 271, 272, 273, 274; ref, 272 (2,3), 273 (1,2), 2603 (217,310,409)
Steere, A. C.: ref, 1697 (179), 2227 (7), 2860 (363), 2863 (95)
Stefanis, C.: ref, 1093 (69)
Stefanis, C. N.: ref, 1166 (192), 2497 (631)

Stefanovich, M.: ref, 2305 (49)
Stefans, V.: ref, 1902 (3)
Stefany, E. F.: rev, 264, 2901
Steffen, J. J.: ref, 2497 (123)
Stegagno, L.: ref, 1021 (43)
Steger, H. G.: ref, 1697 (407)
Steger, H. S.: ref, 2860 (953)
Stegner, B. L.: ref, 2108 (3)
Stehbens, J.: ref, 1135 (12), 2813 (67), 2862 (274), 2879 (84)
Stehbens, J. A.: ref, 451 (215), 1962 (23)
Steiger, A.: ref, 1166 (29)
Steiger, H.: ref, 2603 (218,501)
Steil, J. M.: ref, 68 (18)
Steimer, E.: ref, 1001 (3)
Steimer-Krause, E.: ref, 1001 (7)
Stein, A.: ref, 270 (22), 863 (33), 1216 (86), 1612 (86), 1991 (40), 2603 (311)
Stein, B. L.: ref, 1072 (31)
Stein, C. H.: ref, 1010 (95)
Stein, C. R.: ref, 1115 (9)
Stein, D.: ref, 681 (96), 1040 (6), 2305 (247)
Stein, D. J.: ref, 2603 (410)
Stein, J. A.: ref, 790 (5), 863 (55), 2076 (120), 2862 (616)
Stein, J. F.: ref, 1503 (11), 2860 (1059), 2862 (331,332, 465), 2901 (58,59,87)
Stein, J. L.: ref, 1697 (160)
Stein, K. F.: ref, 592 (71)
Stein, L. A. R.: ref, 1698 (27)
Stein, M. A.: ref, 2813 (107)
Stein, M. B.: rev, 2720; ref, 272 (91), 1166 (66), 2199 (5), 2497 (143,206,254,284,296,297,397,518)
Stein, M. I.: test, 2203, 2594, 2639
Stein, M. K.: ref, 1697 (547), 2399 (1)f, 2402 (63), 2603 (530)
Stein, P. N.: ref, 1061 (1) 2860 (357,404)
Stein, R. E. K.: ref, 997 (20,28), 1925 (2,3)
Stein, S.: rev, 323, 453, 2503
Stein, Z.: ref, 2163 (124), 2516 (28), 2860 (496)
Steinbach, K. A.: ref, 2879 (85)
Steinberg, B. E.: ref, 893 (48), 1735 (12)
Steinberg, H. R.: ref, 272 (206), 1697 (505), 2497 (580)
Steinberg, L.: ref, 1697 (519)
Steinberg, M.: ref, 1697 (356)
Steinberg, M. D.: ref, 2603 (494)
Steinberg, M. S.: ref, 1047 (5), 1612 (77)
Steinberg, W. J.: rev, 1607
Steinberger, L. G.: ref, 2603 (70)
Steinbrenner, B.: ref, 272 (370), 2497 (673)
Steindl, S. R.: ref, 326 (7), 2860 (574)
Steiner, D. D.: ref, 1348 (5), 1701 (11,19)
Steiner, H.: ref, 272 (381), 699 (4)f, 1010 (138), 1698 (24)
Steiner, R.: ref, 2163 (254), 2860 (634,1011), 2862 (418)
Steiner, V. G.: test, 2045
Steingard, R.: ref, 1092 (5), 2860 (331)
Steingard, R. J.: ref, 451 (187), 2305 (222), 2813 (140), 2862 (611), 2879 (202), 2905 (109)
Steingard, S.: ref, 2305 (196)
Steinhauer, J. C.: rev, 1790
Steinhauer, P. D.: test, 1008
Steinhauer, S. R.: ref, 2305 (86,237)
Steinhaus, L. A.: ref, 303 (4), 1164 (34), 2076 (41), 2516 (17), 2860 (345)
Steinhaus, S. D.: ref, 180 (10)
Steinhausen, H. C.: ref, 451 (285), 624 (21), 2864 (73)
Steinmann, A. G.: test, 1535, 1536
Steinmetz, H. G: ref, 2860 (1285)
Steinmetz, J. E.: ref, 2860 (750)
Steketee, G.: ref, 1697 (357), 2497 (92,144), 2519 (51), 2603 (312)
Steketee, G. S.: ref, 2305 (135)
Stellar, S.: ref, 2159 (2), 2860 (131)
Stelmack, R. M.: ref, 1903 (287)
Stelson, F. W.: ref, 272 (267), 376 (18), 1697 (540), 2402 (62), 2405 (1), 2516 (97)
Stelzer, J.: ref, 142 (6), 1619 (8), 2862 (420)
Stemberger, R. T.: ref, 998 (107)
Stemmler, M.: ref, 272 (118)
Stenberg, L.: ref, 451 (154)
Steneroth, G.: ref, 301 (36), 1097 (12), 1410 (2)
Stenner, A. J.: test, 2365
Stenquist, P. K.: ref, 1135 (13), 2599 (25), 2860 (772)
Stensel, H.: test, 2471
Stepanski, K.: ref, 298 (117)
Stephan, C. W.: ref, 68 (19)
Stephan, W. G.: ref, 68 (19)
Stephanos, M. J.: ref, 2860 (924)
Stephens, J.: ref, 459 (4), 2860 (199)
Stephens, M. I.: test, 2502
Stephens, T. M.: test, 2444
Stephenson, L. A.: ref, 462 (16), 2417 (22)
Stephenson, S.: ref, 2193 (14), 2497 (236)
Stephenson, W.: rev, 1158, 1449, 2286
Stephey, M.: test, 935
Stepien, W. J.: ref, 615 (34), 705 (5)
Steptoe, A.: ref, 999 (140), 2497 (678)
Sterling, C.: ref, 451 (105), 472 (161)
Sterling, F. E.: rev, 450
Sterling, H. M.: test, 2141
Sterling, R. C.: ref, 998 (101), 2402 (40), 2603 (313,375)
Stern, A. E.: ref, 451 (79), 472 (147), 999 (141), 1012 (1), 1079 (54), 1991 (87)
Stern, E. B.: ref, 863 (58), 926 (9), 1140 (26), 2497 (421), 2603 (330)
Stern, G. S.: ref, 298 (61), 1745 (19)
Stern, M.: ref, 1079 (32), 2858 (44,88)
Stern, M. I.: ref, 272 (322)
Stern, R. A.: test, 329; ref, 760 (2), 2076 (94,122), 2516 (23), 2858 (49)
Stern, R. C.: ref, 1316 (1)
Stern, R. M.: ref, 2288 (74)
Stern, Y.: ref, 303 (18,29), 776 (45,61), 1166 (103), 1740 (21,32), 2125 (7,18), 2163 (124), 2516 (16,18), 2860 (310,407, 408,496,512, 554,604,906,907,1112, 1180, 1284, 1346,1405), 2863 (292)

Sternberg, K. J.: ref, 365 (8), 1216 (71)
Sternberg, R. J.: rev, 2677; ref, 592 (25), 2905 (65)
Sternic, N.: ref, 2163 (43), 2860 (168), 2863 (44), 2892 (20)
Sterste, A.: ref, 2860 (2), 2863 (1)
Sterzi, R.: ref, 2163 (38), 2863 (43)
Stetner, F.: ref, 2076 (113), 2497 (450)
Stevens, A. A.: ref, 2858 (77)
Stevens, D. J.: ref, 364 (21), 1140 (51), 1599 (6), 1991 (95)
Stevens, D. T.: ref, 2247 (44)
Stevens, J.: ref, 472 (195), 2076 (80)
Stevens, L. J.: ref, 559 (1), 821 (2), 994 (32), 1903 (428), 2694 (18), 2704 (34), 2725 (5), 2768 (32), 2862 (406), 2911 (4)
Stevens, M.: ref, 2603 (357,459)
Stevens, M. J.: ref, 272 (34), 1010 (81), 1697 (429)
Stevens, M. M.: ref, 474 (2), 1592 (8), 2862 (124)
Stevens, N.: ref, 2497 (219)
Stevens, R. J.: ref, 364 (16), 665 (37)
Stevens, T.: ref, 2163 (344), 2860 (1361), 2862 (684)
Stevens, T. P. M.: ref, 1380 (19)
Stevens, Thurow & Associates, Inc.: test, 1301
Stevens, W.: ref, 2497 (127)
Stevens, W. J.: ref, 1166 (5), 2497 (25)
Stevenson, A. L.: ref, 2603 (89)
Stevenson, C. A. Z.: ref, 2603 (49)
Stevenson, C. M.: ref, 1528 (6)
Stevenson, H.: test, 236
Stevenson, H. W.: ref, 2879 (18)
Stevenson, J.: ref, 451 (193), 1093 (31), 1612 (59), 1765 (11), 1902 (49), 2813 (10), 2860 (533,874)
Stevenson, J. C.: ref, 495 (9), 2445 (1)
Stevenson, J. M.: ref, 1470 (5), 2069 (2)
Stevenson, M. R.: ref, 298 (54)
Stevenson, N. J.: ref, 2163 (301)
Stevenson-Hinde, J.: ref, 863 (72), 1903 (141,429), 2038 (5)
Steverink, N.: ref, 999 (159)
Steverwald, B. L.: ref, 2402 (65)
Steward, R. J.: ref, 791 (16), 908 (11), 1755 (77)
Stewart, A.: ref, 1241 (3)
Stewart, A. J.: ref, 372 (90), 373 (30), 451 (9), 2749 (64,71)
Stewart, A. L.: ref, 2211 (17)
Stewart, D.: ref, 2862 (542), 2879 (180), 2901 (99)
Stewart, D. A.: ref, 863 (33), 1991 (40)
Stewart, D. G.: ref, 134 (39)
Stewart, E. K.: test, 1547, 1548, 2561, 2562, 2563, 2564, 2567, 2568, 2569, 2576
Stewart, E. R.: ref, 1000 (77)
Stewart, F. M.: ref, 2193 (58) 2239 (30,31)
Stewart, G. L.: ref, 2218 (75), 2899 (18)
Stewart, G. W.: ref, 472 (7)
Stewart, J. E.: test, 2053, 2826
Stewart, J. R.: rev, 274
Stewart, J. W.: ref, 1166 (130,142), 2603 (487)
Stewart, K. B.: ref, 265 (3), 1901 (8)
Stewart, K. J.: rev, 237
Stewart, L.: ref, 1140 (27)
Stewart, M. A.: ref, 2603 (458)
Stewart, N.: rev, 1097, 2555
Stewart, P.: ref, 298 (45)
Stewart, S. H.: ref, 1021 (15), 2199 (12), 2497 (519), 2603 (164)
Stewart, S. L.: ref, 2039 (19)
Stewart, S. M.: ref, 433 (12), 472 (65), 1086 (2), 1164 (80), 1240 (30), 1612 (60), 1902 (60), 1991 (61), 2485 (150), 2860 (760), 2862 (145), 2864 (24,74)
Stewart, W. F.: ref, 1164 (171), 1758 (97)
Stewart-Bussey, D.: ref, 2258 (1)
Stice, C. F.: ref, 1755 (8), 2545 (1)
Stick, S. L.: rev, 214, 911, 1804, 1850
Stickney, F. A.: ref, 1590 (17)
Stieglitz, E. L.: test, 2503
Stiensmeier-Pelster, J.: ref, 2163 (30)
Stientjes, H. J.: rev, 283, 878, 1194
Stierwalt, J. A. G.: ref, 2305 (228), 2813 (149)
Stierwalt, S. L.: ref, 2218 (39)
Stifter, C. A.: ref, 1770 (2), 2218 (3), 2497 (475)
Stiles, J.: ref, 1001 (14)
Stiles, T. C.: ref, 2603 (416)
Stiles, W.: ref, 272 (217)
Stiles, W. B.: ref, 272 (116,357), 2050 (100,131), 2603 (314,360,411,412,582)
Stiles-Davis, J.: ref, 815 (2), 2862 (56)
Stilley, C. S.: ref, 272 (323), 1697 (575), 2498 (74)
Stillinger, C.: ref, 2031 (9)
Stillman, A.: test, 902
Stillman, R.: test, 377
Stilwell, B. M.: ref, 451 (191)
Stimmel, B. B.: ref, 863 (71)
Stinchfield, R. D.: ref, 73 (1), 1931 (1)
Stine, E. A. L.: ref, 2860 (418)
Stine, E. L.: ref, 2146 (4), 2860 (27,51)
Stine-Morrow, E. A. L.: ref, 2860 (1315)
Stinnett, T. A.: rev, 2, 477, 2012, 2443, 2810, 2922
Stinson, C.: ref, 2603 (187)
Stinson, C. H.: ref, 2603 (219,266,413)
Stipek, D.: ref, 875 (10), 1902 (77)
Stipek, D. J.: ref, 433 (7), 459 (21), 1902 (99), 2485 (92), 2901 (129)
Stirling, J.: ref, 2050 (46)
Stischer, B.: ref, 2247 (101)
Stith, L. E.: ref, 1657 (23)
Stith, S. M.: ref, 1000 (22), 1010 (71), 2858 (23)
Stitzer, M. L.: ref, 2519 (43), 2520 (43)
Stock, J. R.: test, 265t, 266
Stock, P. A.: ref, 2686 (2)
Stock, W.: ref, 2603 (141)
Stock, W. A.: rev, 929, 1172, 2653
Stocker, C. M.: ref, 472 (104)
Stocking, M. L.: ref, 666 (6)
Stocking, V. B.: ref, 615 (52)

Stoddard, A.: ref, 272 (199)
Stoddard, L. T.: ref, 1903 (132,387), 2879 (128)
Stoel-Gammon, C.: ref, 1528 (5), 1903 (229), 2657 (10)
Stoessel, P. W.: ref, 1166 (150)
Stogdill, R. M.: test, 1437
Stoiber, K. C.: ref, 878 (1)
Stoker, H.: rev, 2484
Stokes, A.: ref, 674 (1), 1392 (4), 2599 (1)
Stokes, H.: test, 820
Stokes, J. M.: ref, 1164 (74), 2860 (723), 2892 (144)
Stokes, J. P.: rev, 1580, 2855; ref, 337 (161), 1115 (1)
Stokes, N. A.: ref, 1901 (6)
Stokes, P. E.: ref, 2603 (220)
Stokes, S. A.: test, 2505
Stokes, S. L.: ref, 2694 (17)
Stolberg, A. L.: ref, 2603 (92)
Stolk, B. D.: ref, 2862 (412)
Stoll, M. F.: ref, 1266 (1)
Stoll, M. S.: ref, 1266 (2)
Stollack, G.: ref, 2603 (455)
Stollak, G.: ref, 451 (68)
Stoller, C. L.: ref, 1832 (14)
Stolley, M. R.: ref, 1697 (64), 2603 (180)
Stolley, P.: ref, 451 (13), 1903 (88), 2485 (40), 2862 (139), 2879 (36)
Stollwerck, L.: ref, 349 (38)
Stolman, C. J.: test, 1639
Stoltenberg, C. D.: ref, 298 (129), 716 (2), 1000 (81), 1755 (48), 2497 (398), 2603 (315)
Stoltzfus, E. R.: ref, 1405 (23)
Stolz, E.: ref, 2497 (285)
Stone, A.: ref, 798 (5), 1832 (3)
Stone, A. A.: ref, 2076 (43), 2603 (461)
Stone, C. A.: ref, 430 (4,6,8), 624 (2,11,16), 2657 (14), 2862 (681)
Stone, D.: ref, 372 (71)
Stone, D. N.: ref, 592 (99)
Stone, E.: ref, 1379 (19)
Stone, G. L.: rev, 717, 1174, 1294, 1307, 1489, 1950, 2876, 2407 (2)
Stone, I. R.: rev, 1169
Stone, J.: ref, 337 (83), 2010 (17), 2402 (34), 2497 (374), 2860 (761)
Stone, L. J.: rev, 466
Stone, M. H.: test, 1407; rev, 349
Stone, P.: ref, 1612 (40), 2862 (218)
Stone, S.: ref, 1142 (4), 2771 (37)
Stone, S. V.: ref, 2218 (130)
Stone, T. A.: test, 2660
Stone, W. L.: ref, 270 (43), 459 (6,7,22,40), 811 (2), 1485 (6), 1528 (8), 1653 (1,2,8), 1903 (188)
Stone-Romero, E. F.: ref, 272 (179), 372 (71), 1745 (70)
Stoneman, Z.: ref, 272 (20), 472 (73), 863 (24), 1010 (14,31), 2211 (26), 2862 (238,446)
Stoner, G.: rev, 2038
Stoner, S. B.: ref, 538 (3), 1903 (284)
Stones, C. R.: ref, 999 (65)
Stoney, C. M.: ref, 2516 (12)
Stoolmiller, M.: ref, 451 (101), 2879 (158)
Stoppard, J. M.: rev, 728, 2161; ref, 272 (231), 538 (7), 1243 (5)
Storandt, M.: ref, 1164 (179), 1697 (6), 2860 (465,1397), 2863 (131,422)
Storck, M.: ref, 2862 (369)
Stores, G.: ref, 4 (23)
Stores, R.: ref, 4 (23)
Storey, A. G.: test, 2128
Storlazzi, J. J.: ref, 451 (263), 681 (93), 1392 (15), 2862 (718), 2905 (120)
Stormey, P.: ref, 4 (3)
Stormont-Spurgin, M.: ref, 2039 (20)
Stormshak, E. A.: ref, 451 (228), 2211 (48)
Storoschuk, S.: ref, 459 (29), 2860 (654)
Stothard, S. E.: ref, 1765 (23), 2864 (104)
Stotland, E.: ref, 2497 (47)
Stotland, S.: ref, 790 (24), 1745 (62)
Stott, D. H.: test, 69, 910, 1457
Stott, L. H.: test, 996
Stouffer, G. A. W.: test, 973
Stouffer, G. A. W., Jr.: test, 1634, 1635, 2220, 2222
Stough, C.: ref, 128 (2), 2163 (246), 2860 (991)
Stout, G.: ref, 1216 (32), 1903 (182)
Stout, J. C.: ref, 776 (26), 2863 (293)
Stout, M. L.: ref, 893 (41)
Stout, R.: ref, 1164 (138), 2860 (1199)
Stout, W.: ref, 56 (17), 615 (55), 1434 (1,2), 1759 (16)
Stout, W. F.: ref, 180 (36)
Stouthamer-Loeber, M.: ref, 365 (2,10), 373 (21,24), 451 (133), 2516 (59), 2862 (536)
Stovel, K. W.: ref, 1010 (42), 1181 (9,10), 1991 (41)
Stowitschek, C.: ref, 451 (40)
Stowitschek, J. J.: ref, 2860 (22)
Stoynoff, S.: ref, 666 (14)
Stracciari, A.: ref, 2163 (188), 2516 (54), 2768 (26), 2819 (1), 2907 (6)
Strachan, A.: ref, 1093 (72), 2050 (95)
Strachoski, D.: ref, 2305 (138)
Strack, S.: test, 1958; ref, 68 (41), 1687 (7,8,40), 1688 (1), 1958 (1)
Strain, J. J.: ref, 748 (7), 1093 (14), 2497 (67)
Strain, P. S.: rev, 864; ref, 459 (5), 1612 (13)
Straits-Tröster, K.: ref, 2858 (105)
Straker, G.: ref, 1079 (78)
Strakowski, S. M.: ref, 1093 (93), 1166 (158), 2289 (39,54,58,60,61)
Strand, A. L.: test, 130, 871, 1967, 2103, 2104, 2610
Strand, D.: rev, 304, 1534
Strand, E. A.: ref, 2008 (14), 2768 (37)
Strand, M. L.: test, 2103, 2104
Strand, P. S.: ref, 272 (228), 451 (156)
Strandburg, R. J.: ref, 2860 (534)
Strang, J.: ref, 999 (62), 2497 (276)
Strang, R.: rev, 1790
Strange, C.: ref, 620 (3), 2527 (6)

Strassberg, D. S.: ref, 694 (106), 1290 (3), 1697 (415), 1698 (5), 1744 (6), 2497 (66), 2603 (363), 2860 (323)
Strassberg, Z.: ref, 451 (26,229,247)
Strategic Advantage, Inc.: test, 2602
Strathdee, G.: ref, 1093 (71), 2050 (90)
Strathman, A.: ref, 999 (28), 1661 (66)
Strathman, A. J.: ref, 2078 (3)
Stratta, L.: test, 1477
Stratta, P.: ref, 1525 (10), 2892 (152)
Stratton, K.: test, 393, 1125, 1364
Stratton, R. K.: rev, 1135
Straub, M.: ref, 2029 (2)
Strauman, T. J.: ref, 790 (1), 2603 (5,165,316)
Straus, L. T.: rev, 905
Straus, S. E.: ref, 2402 (66), 2860 (400), 2863 (105)
Strausberger, S.: ref, 2360 (6)
Strauss, C. C.: ref, 472 (64)
Strauss, C. F.: rev, 886; ref, 2282 (7)
Strauss, D. H.: ref, 1093 (58)
Strauss, E.: test, 2811; ref, 1697 (515), 1698 (16), 2860 (224,535,762,992,1014), 2862 (115), 2863 (57,294), 2892 (90)
Strauss, E. S.: ref, 1218 (11), 2860 (978), 2892 (206)
Strauss, H.: test, 242; ref, 242 (1)
Strauss, J.: ref, 681 (48), 1745 (50), 1902 (55,88), 2862 (500)
Strauss, J. S.: ref, 2050 (11), 2288 (3)
Strauss, M. A.: ref, 1216 (65)
Strauss, M. E.: ref, 1758 (34), 2017 (11), 2076 (1,132), 2288 (39,76), 2289 (30,63), 2305 (113), 2402 (60), 2516 (34,55), 2603 (425), 2860 (806), 2892 (105,153,154,257)
Strawser, S.: test, 2868
Strayer, D. L.: ref, 2860 (670,763), 2892 (124)
Strayer, J.: ref, 1340 (5)
Streeter, C. L.: ref, 694 (26), 1000 (20), 1207 (1)
Strehl, V.: ref, 2860 (1137)
Strehlow, U.: ref, 745 (24)
Strein, W.: ref, 694 (63), 1987 (23), 1991 (59)
Streiner, D.: ref, 272 (93), 2497 (408)
Streiner, D. L.: ref, 451 (281), 1079 (110), 1485 (36), 1612 (61), 1697 (435,457), 2050 (86), 2228 (15), 2497 (293), 2813 (74)
Streissguth, A. D.: ref, 2860 (856), 2892 (177), 2905 (72)
Streissguth, A. P.: ref, 376 (22), 997 (24), 2860 (1293), 2879 (209)
Strelau, J.: ref, 2218 (112)
Strentz, T.: ref, 1243 (2), 1290 (2), 2120 (4), 2497 (298), 2603 (229)
Stress, M. E.: ref, 376 (7), 1166 (116), 2860 (1111), 2863 (330)
Stretch, D. D.: ref, 1079 (23)
Streufert, S.: ref, 1661 (35,75), 2516 (6), 2603 (317,556)
Stricker, L. J.: rev, 908, 963, 999, 2648; ref, 592 (45,72, 107), 1115 (21)
Striegel, P.: ref, 1000 (79)
Striegel-Moore, R. H.: ref, 2603 (502)
Stringer, D. Y.: ref, 1736 (4)
Stringer, M.: ref, 270 (2), 1745 (12)
Stringer, R. W.: ref, 2862 (132)
Stringfellow, K.: ref, 1394 (9)
Stringfield, P.: ref, 1755 (25)
Stringfield, S.: test, 2039
Stritzke, P.: ref, 326 (5), 2288 (21), 2289 (13), 2305 (66), 2892 (52), 2905 (24)
Strobel, M. G.: ref, 2771 (22)
Strober, M.: ref, 1517 (12), 2305 (201)
Strobino, D. M.: ref, 1216 (42), 1902 (53)
Stroebe, M. S.: ref, 1079 (77,98)
Strohmeier, S. J.: ref, 301 (37), 1379 (39), 2163 (144)
Strohmer, D. C.: test, 931, 965; ref, 372 (78)
Strom, P.: ref, 1866 (31), 2771 (20), 1128 (1,2,3,4), 1866 (31), 2771 (20)
Strom, R. D.: test, 1128, 1878
Strom, S.: ref, 1128 (1,2,3,4), 1866 (31), 2771 (20)
Strom, S. K.: test, 1128
Stromberg, E. L.: test, 2515
Stromer, R.: ref, 1903 (283,387), 2879 (128)
Strommen, E. A.: ref, 790 (29)
Strong, D.: ref, 776 (15), 2892 (122)
Strong, E. K., Jr.: test, 1790
Strong, J.: ref, 1241 (3)
Strong, M. J.: ref, 1164 (135), 2227 (33), 2860 (1181), 2879 (184), 2892 (256)
Strong, R. W.: test, 195
Strong, S. R.: rev, 1243, 1895
Stronks, D. L.: ref, 2497 (285)
Strother, C. R.: rev, 987, 1540
Strough, C.: ref, 999 (173), 2163 (305), 2860 (1182)
Stroup, E.: ref, 2860 (1094)
Strowe, L.: test, 953, 1506, 1664
Strub, R. L.: ref, 1903 (409)
Strupp, H. H.: rev, 2109
Strutton, D.: ref, 2858 (45)
Stryker, S.: ref, 2525 (12)
Stuart, G. L.: ref, 272 (383)
Stuart, G. W.: ref, 2603 (277)
Stuart, J. E.: test, 1989
Stuart, M.: ref, 349 (3), 350 (8)
Stuart, R. B.: test, 717; rev, 863, 1495, 1581, 1685, 1892, 2132, 2394, 2411
Stuart, S.: ref, 1093 (43)
Stuber, M. L.: ref, 1000 (103), 2214 (115), 2497 (609)
Stuberg, W.: test, 1668
Studts, J. L.: ref, 2076 (112)
Stuebing, K. K.: ref, 1051 (1), 2862 (396,474), 2901 (73,89)
Stuebing, R. C.: ref, 2497 (123)
Stuit, D. B.: rev, 2217
Stull, S.: ref, 2305 (216)
Stulman, D. A.: ref, 272 (219), 273 (25), 2065 (29)

Stumpf, H.: ref, 1965 (46), 2218 (133)
Stumpf, S. A.: ref, 2858 (5)
Stunkard, A. J.: test, 894
Sturgill, S.: ref, 298 (137)
Sturgis, E. T.: ref, 2497 (5,56)
Sturmey, P.: ref, 4 (15)
Sturner, R. A.: ref, 175 (9), 430 (7), 1047 (3), 2651 (13), 2695 (21)
Sturney, P.: ref, 1722 (1)
Stuss, D.: ref, 1218 (6), 1903 (275), 2163 (168), 2863 (196), 2892 (123)
Stuss, D. T.: ref, 303 (22), 376 (27), 776 (23,55), 1164 (172), 1758 (46), 1903 (191), 2860 (8,1354), 2863 (137,408), 2892 (1,193,291)
Stutman, G.: rev, 434, 1269
Stutsman, R.: test, 1653
Stutts, M. L.: ref, 1697 (156)
Styan, G.: ref, 2497 (149)
Styles, P.: ref, 350 (52), 1903 (577), 2163 (355), 2860 (1413), 2862 (730)
Su, C.: ref, 301 (52), 815 (30), 2862 (407)
Su, S. S.: ref, 1000 (7)
Su-Neo, A. T.: ref, 1991 (84)
Suarez, E. C.: ref, 272 (336), 2218 (116), 2497 (664)
Suarez, I.: ref, 999 (85), 2497 (344)
Subich, L. M.: ref, 298 (2,8), 1790 (19)
Subkoviak, M. J.: rev, 121, 746, 1093, 1319, 1916, 2339, 2484, 2717
Suchday, S.: ref, 2497 (416)
Suchs, L. S.: rev, 917
Suchy, Y.: ref, 2892 (245)
Suczek, R.: test, 1291
Suddendorf, T.: ref, 350 (45)
Suddick, D. E.: ref, 571 (6)
Sudhalter, V.: ref, 459 (17), 2813 (33)
Sudilovsky, A.: ref, 2860 (480), 2863 (134)
Sudweeks, R. R.: rev, 917
Sue, M. B.: test, 2660
Sue, S.: ref, 1093 (81,116)
Suedfeld, P.: ref, 2749 (76)
Suelzer, M.: ref, 998 (56), 1093 (16), 2603 (203)
Suen, H. K.: rev, 929, 1750, 1909, 2338, 2732, 1140 (46)
Suess, A. R.: rev, 924, 1792
Sugahara, C.: ref, 2218 (61), 2603 (465)
Sugalski, T. D.: ref, 2497 (1)
Sugarman, D. B.: ref, 472 (78), 1000 (66), 1216 (65), 2211 (27)
Sugawara, A. I.: ref, 1903 (112,156)
Sugawara, M.: ref, 999 (59)
Sugden, D. A.: test, 1727
Sugden, R.: ref, 2017 (16)
Sugimoto, Y.: ref, 2860 (1296)
Sugishita, M.: ref, 2860 (52,406,472,975), 2873 (11,44)
Sugiyama, Y.: ref, 2497 (399,400)
Suh, C.: ref, 2603 (369)
Suh, E.: ref, 2218 (76)
Suh, K.: ref, 365 (9)
Suhr, J.: ref, 272 (324), 303 (23), 1697 (576), 2226 (37), 2860 (1355)
Suinn, R. M.: rev, 2652
Suis, J.: ref, 998 (25), 1338 (22)
Suiter, P. A.: test, 2627, 2628
Suk-Han, H. C.: ref, 2163 (343)
Sukhodolsky, D. G.: ref, 2497 (638)
Sullaway, M. E.: ref, 1338 (23), 1581 (1)
Sullivan, E. V.: ref, 1758 (19), 2860 (420), 2863 (81,121), 2892 (68)
Sullivan, G.: ref, 2288 (8)
Sullivan, G. S.: ref, 665 (69,84), 1386 (10,20), 2485 (183), 2862 (408), 2879 (143), 2901 (75), 2905 (63,91)
Sullivan, J. B.: test, 2570, 2937
Sullivan, K.: ref, 1903 (320,321), 2863 (355)
Sullivan, K. T.: ref, 272 (122), 999 (124)
Sullivan, L.: ref, 2860 (225)
Sullivan, L. A.: ref, 1178 (13), 2485 (83), 2599 (13), 2860 (457)
Sullivan, L. M.: ref, 364 (27)
Sullivan, M. A.: ref, 681 (3)
Sullivan, M. J. L.: ref, 272 (325,329), 2497 (520)
Sullivan, P. F.: ref, 999 (163), 1166 (132,146,159), 2519 (52), 2520 (51), 2603 (318,481,492)
Sullivan, P. M.: rev, 2439; ref, 2860 (405)
Sullivan, S. A.: ref, 1378 (9), 1903 (543), 2860 (1313)
Sullivan, T. E.: ref, 2860 (993), 2879 (144)
Sullivan-Burstein, K.: ref, 1318 (23)
Suls, J.: ref, 2218 (91)
Sulsky, L.: ref, 298 (43), 2858 (24), 2860 (236)
Sulsky, L. M.: ref, 1115 (18)
Sulway, M. R.: ref, 1164 (136), 1758 (79), 2860 (1183), 2863 (356)
Sulway, M-R.: ref, 2497 (667)
Sulzer-Azaroff, B.: ref, 2485 (180)
Sumerall, S. W.: ref, 2497 (598), 2860 (967), 2879 (185)
Sumerlin, J. R.: ref, 1938 (1), 1939 (7)
Sumi, S. M.: ref, 2860 (1280)
Summa Information Systems, Inc.: test, 2590
Summerfelt, A.: ref, 2516 (55), 2892 (154)
Summerfield, M.: ref, 2226 (27), 2863 (392)
Summers, B. A.: ref, 1758 (94)
Summers, C. R.: ref, 1000 (56)
Summers, J. A.: ref, 1903 (317), 2485 (151)
Summers, M.: ref, 1000 (56), 2417 (37)
Summers, P.: ref, 272 (379), 337 (196), 451 (227), 472 (218), 2214 (127)
Summers, S.: test, 2024, 2025
Summers, T. P.: ref, 1701 (21)
Summerville, M. B.: ref, 472 (105), 1000 (78)
Sumner, G. S.: ref, 2862 (170)
Sun, H. L.: ref, 1128 (1)
Sun, K.: ref, 2305 (134), 2860 (471)
Sunday, S. R.: ref, 272 (229), 1697 (520)
Sundberg, M. D.: ref, 56 (7)

Sundberg, N.: rev, 2547
Sundberg, N. D.: rev, 272, 1266, 1348, 1397, 1755, 2208, 2371, 2485
Sunde, B.: ref, 900 (5)
Sunderland, A.: ref, 2193 (58), 2239 (30,31), 2860 (764)
Sunderland, T.: ref, 776 (38,57), 2076 (100), 2860 (1258), 2863 (100,222,379)
Sundet, K.: ref, 2163 (287), 2225 (13), 2860 (1136), 2862 (543)
Sundre, D.: ref, 1000 (33), 1939 (4)
Sundre, D. L.: rev, 405, 1276, 1647, 1970
Sundvik, L.: ref, 298 (94)
Sung, Y. H.: rev, 160
Sunshine, W.: ref, 2498 (67)
Suomi, J.: ref, 2689 (1)
Suomi, R.: ref, 2689 (1)
Suozzi, J. M.: ref, 1697 (332,559), 2516 (46,106)
Super, D. E.: test, 83, 405, 2282, 2805; rev, 1693, 1717, 2000; ref, 2282 (1)
Super, J. T.: ref, 2749 (30)
Suppes, P.: ref, 2031 (9)
Suppes, T.: ref, 1166 (160)
Surburg, P. R.: ref, 2485 (179), 2689 (2), 2862 (384)
Surface, C. R.: ref, 298 (117)
Suritsky, S. K.: ref, 2860 (651), 2901 (42)
Surrey, J.: ref, 2603 (71)
Surtees, P. G.: ref, 1517 (10), 2050 (127), 2305 (26)
Susman, E. J.: ref, 2498 (29)
Susman, V. L.: ref, 1093 (32)
Susman-Stillman, A.: ref, 846 (15)
Susser, E.: ref, 2050 (101), 2288 (56), 2289 (43)
Süsser, K.: ref, 451 (234)
Sussman, H. M.: ref, 1095 (15), 1804 (5), 1903 (193), 2332 (2), 2651 (12), 2657 (7), 2801 (2)
Sussman, J. E.: ref, 994 (9,10), 1095 (18,19), 1903 (211), 2657 (8,9), 2768 (20,21)
Sussman, N. M.: ref, 1135 (8), 2077 (5), 2516 (22), 2599 (12), 2860 (54,137,450), 2863 (38)
Sutherland, L. F.: ref, 1825 (6), 2360 (3)
Sutherland, S. W.: ref, 2163 (32)
Sutker, P. B.: ref, 337 (121), 1010 (88), 1697 (456), 2402 (47,48), 2497 (401,521,548), 2603 (414,415), 2858 (107), 2860 (994,995)
Suttell, B. J.: test, 301
Sutter, J.: test, 2595
Sutton, A. E.: ref, 1903 (212), 2695 (22), 2704 (14)
Sutton, C.: ref, 1181 (4), 2603 (59)
Sutton, K. J.: ref, 2858 (111)
Sutton, R.: rev, 2699
Sutton, R. E.: rev, 635, 771, 1400, 1780
Sutton, S.: ref, 2497 (314)
Suy, E.: ref, 1166 (18,19)
Suydam, M. N.: rev, 255
Suzuki, I.: ref, 2860 (406), 2873 (11)
Suzuki, K.: ref, 1093 (28)
Suzuki, L. A.: ref, 844 (1)
Suzuki, S.: ref, 1903 (293)
Svanum, S.: ref, 134 (7), 136 (5), 1697 (146,245, 358, 521), 2402 (9)
Svartberg, M.: ref, 2603 (416)
Svenson, E.: ref, 1227 (2)
Sverd, J.: ref, 681 (54), 2862 (338,409), 2905 (92)
Sverko, B.: ref, 2282 (3)
Svikis, D. S.: ref, 793 (22), 1697 (58)
Svinicki, J.: test, 265, 266
Svinicki, J. G.: rev, 2012, 2127
Svrakic, D. M.: ref, 2077 (2)
Swaab-Barnereld, H.: ref, 451 (100), 681 (73)
Swaim, K. F.: ref, 1734 (4)
Swain, B. J.: ref, 337 (1), 2603 (1)
Swales, T. P.: ref, 1379 (22)
Swan, D.: ref, 350 (46), 2862 (682)
Swan, G. E.: ref, 303 (26,30), 2076 (160), 2599 (42), 2860 (919,1382)
Swank, L. K.: ref, 324 (8), 624 (22), 1903 (318,400), 2695 (44), 2704 (21,31), 2862 (374)
Swank, P.: ref, 1470 (1), 1750 (1), 1939 (3)
Swank, P. E.: ref, 270 (35), 1612 (95), 2813 (146)
Swank, P. R.: ref, 270 (26), 2382 (35), 2813 (130)
Swann, A.: ref, 2603 (191)
Swann, A. C.: ref, 2305 (156,166,202), 2603 (220)
Swann, W. B., Jr.: ref, 2358 (9)
Swanson, C. C.: ref, 2657 (33), 2813 (141), 2864 (135)
Swanson, D.: test, 771
Swanson, H. L.: test, 2596; rev, 261, 2816; ref, 322 (2), 560 (4), 665 (29,55,87), 798 (14,20), 1072 (40), 1379 (58), 1768 (2), 1866 (26), 1902 (61,78), 1903 (319), 2163 (189), 2432 (14), 2862 (184,561), 2864 (80), 2879 (50,94), 2901 (84)
Swanson, J. M.: ref, 451 (214), 681 (6), 2860 (30), 2862 (657), 2892 (81)
Swanson, L. A.: ref, 1490 (1,2), 1903 (537), 2905 (112)
Swanson, L. B.: ref, 389 (5), 2905 (12)
Swanson, S.: ref, 1991 (98), 2591 (4), 2656 (22), 2862 (562)
Swanson, S. C.: ref, 1697 (457)
Swanson, S. J.: ref, 2860 (1032,1041), 2892 (214)
Swanson, V.: ref, 1824 (7)
Swanston, H.: ref, 451 (278), 472 (230), 694 (134), 1079 (109)
Swart, D. J.: test, 169
Swartz, A. R.: ref, 1093 (68), 2519 (42), 2520 (42)
Swartz, J. D.: rev, 181, 1313, 2749
Swartzman, L. C.: ref, 2497 (93)
Swassing, C. S.: rev, 893, 2117
Swassing, R. H.: test, 2597
Swayze, V. W.: ref, 1093 (6,85,39), 2860 (150)
Swearer, J. M.: ref, 2305 (190), 2860 (1146)
Swedo, S. E.: ref, 863 (42)
Sweeney, J.: ref, 1166 (14), 2076 (12), 2417 (6)
Sweeney, J. A.: ref, 273 (12), 1093 (95), 1166 (10), 1903 (29), 2146 (11), 2288 (20,26), 2289 (12,15), 2863 (108), 2892 (58)
Sweeney, J. J.: ref, 2862 (217)

Sweeney, M.: ref, 2860 (337), 2863 (89)
Sweet, R.: test, 2598
Sweet, R. A.: ref, 1093 (104)
Sweetman, E.: ref, 790 (24), 1745 (62)
Swegart, L. A.: ref, 1216 (112), 1889 (20)
Sweifi, E.: ref, 2862 (415)
Swendsen, J.: ref, 999 (142), 1093 (89)
Sweney, A. B.: test, 1721, 2318
Swensen, C. H.: test, 2291, 2292; rev, 215, 2887
Swenson, C. C.: ref, 1991 (88)
Swenson, C. H., Jr.: rev, 2286
Swenson, M.: ref, 776 (21)
Swenson, M. R.: ref, 776 (25), 2892 (202)
Swerdlik, M. E.: rev, 340, 1072, 1866, 1875, 2487, 2731
Swerdlow, D.: ref, 776 (21)
Swett, C.: ref, 2603 (71,326)
Swett, C. P.: ref, 2603 (488)
Swettenham, J.: ref, 350 (40)
Swiatek, M. A.: ref, 56 (12), 68 (50), 592 (100)
Swickert, R. J.: ref, 2218 (19)
Swift, C.: ref, 430 (1), 2432 (1)
Swift, E. E.: ref, 272 (230)
Swift, M.: test, 1161, 1162
Swift, R. M.: ref, 2076 (101)
Swift, W.: ref, 2414 (1)
Swim, J. K.: ref, 1115 (17)
Swimson, R. P.: ref, 2603 (342)
Swinkels, A.: ref, 998 (108)
Swinkels, S. H. N.: ref, 681 (40)
Swinney, D.: ref, 2873 (19)
Swinson, R.: ref, 2603 (288)
Swinson, R. P.: ref, 272 (78), 1166 (17,42), 2519 (25), 2520 (26), 2603 (24,233,234)
Swirsky-Sacchetti, T.: ref, 1218 (5), 2599 (10), 2863 (109), 2892 (59)
Swisher, L.: ref, 266 (1,2,3), 540 (20), 624 (12), 994 (47), 1047 (2,4,6), 1240 (9,18), 1379 (35,59,60, 77, 95), 1485 (11,22,35), 1607 (10), 1804 (8), 1903 (138, 535), 2045 (6), 2190 (8), 2382 (12,39), 2524 (5,10,12), 2680 (7,11,13), 2704 (15), 2862 (235), 2901 (38)
Switalz, J.: ref, 2402 (49), 2892 (208)
Switzer, J.: test, 1802
Switzer, P.: ref, 1687 (6)
Switzky, H. N.: rev, 59, 292, 804, 2601, 2891
Swoboda, K. J.: ref, 1164 (113), 1525 (20), 2517 (5), 2860 (996), 2863 (295)
Sykes, W. E.: ref, 2218 (101)
Sykken, D. T.: rev, 373
Syloe, C.: ref, 893 (17), 2402 (36)
Sylvester, C. E.: ref, 2497 (573)
Symonds, P. M.: rev, 374, 1049, 1928, 2248
Symons, D. K.: ref, 451 (286), 469 (2), 1965 (86), 2497 (679), 2862 (387), 2879 (134)
Symons, S.: ref, 592 (27,46,73), 2862 (483), 2879 (162)
Symons, V.: ref, 2193 (26), 2860 (685), 2863 (202), 2892 (131)
Syvâlahti, E.: ref, 1166 (161)
Szabadi, E.: ref, 2860 (542), 2892 (92)
Szabo, P.: ref, 893 (25)f, 1079 (48)
Szádóczky, E.: ref, 1166 (30)
Szajnberg, M. D.: ref, 2247 (45), 2380 (9), 2749 (34), 2862 (224)
Szajnberg, N. M.: ref, 1226 (1), 2247 (90)
Szalai, J. P.: ref, 376 (31), 776 (47,60), 1697 (192), 1706 (1,2), 2247 (29), 2768 (38,39), 2860 (1187,1188), 2863 (357,358,423)
Szalda-Petree, A. C.: ref, 687 (2), 2860 (1090)
Szanto, K.: ref, 1093 (96)
Szapocznik, J.: ref, 1010 (15), 1991 (4), 2076 (8)
Szatmari, P.: ref, 1379 (36), 1485 (23,36), 1612 (61), 1991 (60), 2228 (15), 2485 (19), 2768 (4), 2813 (4,51,52,74), 2860 (142,543), 2892 (17)
Szczepanik, J.: ref, 2860 (1141)
Szczepanski, M.: test, 878
Szegedi, A.: ref, 1166 (214)
Szeibel, P. J.: ref, 2862 (432), 2879 (151)
Szekely, C.: ref, 376 (31), 776 (47,60), 2860 (738), 2863 (423)
Szempruch, J.: ref, 1903 (213)
Szeszulski, P. A.: ref, 2905 (44)
Sziklas, V.: ref, 2226 (12)
Szor, H.: ref, 2290 (1)
Szuba, M. P.: ref, 1093 (40)
Szumowski, E.: ref, 2813 (107)
Szumowski, E. K.: ref, 1592 (18), 2485 (119)
Szuszkiewicz, T. A.: ref, 469 (2), 2862 (387), 2879 (134)
Szymanski, L. A.: ref, 298 (95)
Szymanski, S.: ref, 2305 (70)
Szymanski, S. R.: ref, 2288 (75), 2289 (62)

Taal, M.: ref, 2163 (190)
Tabin, J. K.: test, 1303, 1940, 2600
Tabossi, P.: ref, 2163 (306)
Taboue, M. C. P.: ref, 2516 (64), 2863 (248)
Tacker, S.: ref, 2497 (551)
Tade, W. J.: test, 2429
Tafarodi, R. W.: ref, 2358 (9)
Tager-Flusberg, H.: ref, 1485 (14), 1903 (215,320,321)
Taggart, B.: test, 1227
Taggart, W.: test, 1227, 1953
Taggart-Hausladen, B.: test, 1953
Taghizadeh, P.: ref, 451 (165), 473 (4)
Taguchi, F.: ref, 2497 (15)
Taheri, C. M.: test, 278
Taiminen, T.: ref, 1166 (161)
Tait, M.: ref, 1701 (12)
Tait, M. E.: ref, 2873 (58,72)
Tait, R. C.: ref, 2497 (23)
Tak, Y.: ref, 2076 (116,176)
Takahashi, C.: ref, 798 (1)
Takahashi, G. S.: ref, 1093 (49)
Takahashi, N.: ref, 1166 (134), 2860 (997), 2860 (1356), 2873 (47)
Takahashi, T.: ref, 1866 (38), 2862 (340)

Takahashi, Y.: ref, 2860 (75)
Takahira, S.: ref, 592 (53), 2031 (6)
Takano, Y.: ref, 1405 (19)
Takaoka, N.: ref, 2497 (501)
Takatsuki, Y.: ref, 2873 (73)
Takazawa, N.: ref, 2050 (32)
Takeda, K.: ref, 2860 (396), 2873 (10)
Takeuchi, D. T.: ref, 1093 (81)
Takooshian, H.: rev, 736
Takushi, R.: ref, 1740 (7), 2076 (23), 2599 (6), 2860 (240)
Talajic, M.: ref, 2497 (466)
Talbert, F. S.: ref, 1697 (252,359)
Talbert, S.: ref, 1697 (306)
Talbot, D.: ref, 472 (42), 2498 (20)
Talbot, F.: ref, 272 (326), 2217 (2), 2497 (647)
Talbot, K. F.: ref, 2497 (286)
Talbot, R. J.: ref, 1404 (7,13)
Talcott, G. W.: ref, 2497 (241)
Taljaard, J. J.: test, 1990, 2774
Talken, T. R.: ref, 1697 (522)
Tallal, P.: ref, 175 (8), 270 (41), 430 (5), 1485 (3,12,18), 1804 (4), 2382 (14)f, 2485 (23), 2695 (70), 2768 (17), 2862 (679), 2905 (8)
Tallent-Runnells, M. K.: ref, 2328 (1)
Tallent-Runnels, M. K.: ref, 1455 (8,10), 1866 (32), 2771 (21)
Talley, J. L.: test, 470, 2892
Talley, M.: ref, 270 (31), 337 (175)
Tallis, F.: ref, 272 (164) 1079 (63), 2065 (24), 2497 (547)
Tallman, V. L.: ref, 1804 (3), 2651 (9)
Taloney, L.: ref, 1745 (24)
Talton, B. J.: ref, 226 (2), 2076 (154)
Tam, F.: ref, 2076 (105)
Tam, S-F.: ref, 2652 (12)
Tambs, K.: ref, 2603 (122)
Tamir, P.: test, 626
Tamm, L.: ref, 2892 (81)
Tamma, F.: ref, 2860 (173)
Tammany, J. M.: ref, 1731 (2), 2417 (10), 2860 (226), 2879 (30)
Tammienen, T.: ref, 472 (231)
Tamminen, T.: ref, 472 (227)
Tamminga, C. A.: ref, 2050 (24)
Tamny, T. R.: ref, 1687 (19)
Tamplin, A.: ref, 1079 (111), 2305 (248)
Tan, C.: ref, 1000 (35)
Tan, J.: ref, 1903 (94)
Tan, J. C. H.: ref, 272 (231), 1243 (5)
Tan, S. Y.: ref, 1686 (1), 2497 (108)
Tanabe, H.: ref, 2862 (633)
Tanaka, E.: ref, 273 (26)
Tanaka, Y.: ref, 2225 (18), 2226 (38), 2227 (51,57), 2860 (1357), 2863 (409,420), 2892 (292)
Tanaka-Matsumi, J.: ref, 1619 (10), 2065 (28)
Tancer, M. E.: ref, 272 (92), 2305 (114), 2497 (114,206,405)
Tanck, R. H.: ref, 272 (312)
Tandan, R. : ref, 1056 (2), 2163 (65), 2860 (258), 2863 (65), 2892 (34)
Tang, C. S.: ref, 1745 (9)
Tang, C. S. K.: ref, 1965 (37)
Tang, C. S-K.: ref, 1590 (67), 2860 (1184)
Tang, M.-X.: ref, 2163 (124), 2516 (28), 2860 (496), 1166 (103)
Tangalos, E. G.: ref, 2226 (25), 2860 (359,718,905,1283), 2863 (94,103,214,272,387), 2879 (88)
Tangel, D. M.: ref, 1903 (144,430), 2879 (145), 2905 (30)
Tanguay, P. E.: ref, 2860 (402)
Tanguy, M.: ref, 298 (20)
Tani, K.: ref, 2860 (406), 2873 (11)
Tankersley, M. J.: ref, 1697 (549)
Tannenbaum, A.: ref, 1770 (7), 1903 (145), 2163 (96), 2485 (70)
Tannenbaum, A. J.: rev, 745
Tannenbaum, L.: ref, 272 (379), 337 (196)
Tanner, B. A.: ref, 1697 (107,108,109)
Tanner, C. M.: ref, 1405 (16), 2125 (8)
Tanner, D. E.: ref, 615 (47)
Tannock, R.: ref, 1134 (2), 1424 (5), 2382 (13,22), 2862 (391,665), 2879 (136,214), 2911 (5)
Tansey, M. A.: ref, 2862 (146)
Tanskley, C. K.: ref, 1903 (214)
Tantam, D.: ref, 350 (16), 2050 (46), 2163 (152)
Tantamjarik, P.: ref, 2603 (591)
Tanz, R. R.: ref, 451 (238), 1010 (131)
Tanzi, R. E.: ref, 2227 (8), 2860 (364), 2879 (44), 2892 (54)
Tapert, S. F.: ref, 134 (39)
Taphoorn, M. J. B.: ref, 2516 (15)
Taplin, J. E.: ref, 1903 (445), 2163 (262), 2485 (88), 2813 (112)
Taradash, G.: ref, 665 (70), 1607 (11), 2163 (191), 2771 (32)
Tarbox, A. R.: ref, 1661 (20)
Tarbuck, A. F.: ref, 2239 (25), 2497 (368)
Tardieu, S.: ref, 2227 (19), 2860 (818), 2863 (236)
Tardif, C.: ref, 2111 (2), 2163 (247), 2862 (410)
Target, M.: ref, 272 (171), 999 (157), 2497 (554), 2603 (454)
Tari, A.: ref, 2749 (29)
Tariot, D. N.: ref, 2076 (100), 2863 (222)
Tariot, P. N.: ref, 2603 (586)
Tarlow, E. M.: ref, 271 (6), 272 (232)
Tarnowski, K. J.: ref, 472 (4), 1903 (50), 1991 (8), 2860 (308)
Tarran, M. J.: ref, 793 (3)
Tarrier, N.: ref, 271 (4), 272 (216), 2050 (57), 2497 (410)
Tarrier, R. B.: test, 1163
Tarrini, M.: ref, 303 (17), 818 (1), 2226 (24), 2516 (98), 2862 (623)
Tarter, R. E.: ref, 272 (323), 451 (30), 451 (122), 1697 (575), 1902 (76), 2010 (15,24), 2305 (177,244), 2402 (49), 2498 (74), 2516 (117), 2860 (1390), 2862 (372,443,477,713), 2892 (208)
Tasbihsazan, R.: ref, 270 (44), 2485 (237)

Tasca, G. A.: ref, 2603 (319)
Tashiro, N.: ref, 2305 (241)
Taska, L. S.: ref, 2076 (98)
Tasker, F.: ref, 272 (139), 2497 (522)
Tasker, N.: ref, 1390 (5), 2860 (970)
Tassé, M. J.: ref, 4 (13)
Tata, P. R.: ref, 2858 (84), 2863 (223)
Tate, A.: test, 2691
Tate, D. G.: ref, 337 (20,77,142), 2603 (72)
Tate, J. D.: ref, 694 (62)
Tate, U. S.: ref, 1000 (104), 1745 (79)
Tatemichi, M.: ref, 2076 (174)
Tatemichi, T. K.: ref, 2860 (407,408)
Tatenichi, T. K.: ref, 2860 (604)
Tateyama-Sniezek, K. M.: ref, 665 (30)
Tatro, C.: ref, 1903 (270), 2905 (56)
Tatsuoka, K.: rev, 2029
Tatsuoka, K. K.: rev, 666, 2032, 2717
Tatsuoka, M.: rev, 2688
Tattersall, P.: test, 2523
Taub, D. E.: ref, 1965 (39)
Taub, D. J.: ref, 2527 (17)
Taub, E.: ref, 863 (38), 2497 (238)
Taub, K.: ref, 1697 (66,67), 2076 (9,10)
Taulbee, E. S.: rev, 2850
Taussig, M. K.: ref, 592 (2)
Tautermannová, M.: ref, 2485 (195), 2862 (460)
Taverne, A.: ref, 1903 (431)
Taylor, A.: ref, 451 (168), 1010 (118), 2305 (215), 2862 (592), 2879 (194)
Taylor, A. E.: ref, 1697 (23), 2125 (5), 2497 (19,427), 2860 (227,519), 2863 (58), 1079 (26), 1590 (33)
Taylor, A. P.: test, 2617
Taylor, B. M.: ref, 1072 (19)
Taylor, B. P.: ref, 1166 (142), 2603 (487)
Taylor, C.: rev, 2714; ref, 1590 (14), 2050 (32,54)
Taylor, C. B.: ref, 2076 (4), 2305 (138), 2497 (375,480), 2520 (46)
Taylor, C. J.: ref, 1099 (2), 2603 (332)
Taylor, C. L.: ref, 1060 (6)
Taylor, D. L.: ref, 56 (13), 592 (101)
Taylor, D. M.: ref, 2163 (309)
Taylor, D. N.: ref, 694 (39,107), 2076 (130), 2497 (207,523)
Taylor, E.: ref, 350 (53), 863 (94), 1079 (112), 2862 (714)
Taylor, E. A.: ref, 745 (22), 2860 (1185)
Taylor, E. B.: ref, 790 (4), 999 (19)
Taylor, E. H.: ref, 1962 (17), 2288 (40), 2813 (77)
Taylor, E. K.: test, 2267; rev, 937, 1693, 1974, 2169, 2696, 2871
Taylor, E. M.: rev, 1085
Taylor, H. F.: test, 698
Taylor, H. G.: ref, 353 (19), 375 (6), 433 (9), 451 (239), 745 (5), 815 (31,48), 994 (33), 1092 (8,9), 1215 (3), 1379 (78), 1982 (12), 2125 (19), 2768 (22), 2813 (24,108), 2860 (696), 2862 (185,694), 2879 (51), 2905 (59), 2907 (4)
Taylor, H. R.: rev, 394, 2797
Taylor, J.: test, 348; ref, 265 (12), 1010 (8), 2485 (235), 2603 (123)
Taylor, J. C.: ref, 2813 (75)
Taylor, J. L.: ref, 2860 (765)
Taylor, J. M.: rev, 1896
Taylor, J. W., V: ref, 2358 (14)
Taylor, K.: ref, 1735 (6)
Taylor, K. A.: ref, 2497 (402)
Taylor, K. L.: ref, 2076 (89)
Taylor, K. M.: test, 403; ref, 404 (21,39), 1754 (26)
Taylor, L. J.: ref, 2516 (70)
Taylor, L. R.: ref, 1379 (92)
Taylor, M.: ref, 776 (26), 1619 (1), 1903 (386,557), 1903 (557), 2163 (224), 2863 (293)
Taylor, M. A.: ref, 2008 (10), 2050 (97,132), 2163 (220), 2288 (51), 2289 (40), 2305 (143)
Taylor, M. J.: ref, 265 (14), 272 (258,334)f, 376 (30), 893 (42), 1405 (39), 1903 (517), 2862 (595)
Taylor, P. A.: rev, 665
Taylor, P. G.: ref, 2540 (3)
Taylor, R.: ref, 451 (135), 2860 (343)
Taylor, R. A.: test, 1490
Taylor, R. G.: test, 618
Taylor, R. L.: test, 198
Taylor, R. M.: test, 1013t, 2618
Taylor, R. N.: rev, 1565, 2406
Taylor, S.: ref, 271 (7,18), 272 (368), 372 (64), 1021 (16,28), 1021 (28), 1166 (103), 1404 (10), 1754 (16), 1755 (78), 2132 (2), 2497 (145,146,208,287), 2603 (417), 2862 (628), 2864 (63)
Taylor, S. E.: ref, 791 (11), 1697 (110), 2076 (33,40,85,165), 2858 (35,82), 2860 (664)
Taylor, S. V.: ref, 999 (69), 1755 (32)
Taylor, T. R.: test, 1029, 1199, 1257, 2086, 2257
Tayot, J.: ref, 2227 (19), 2860 (818), 2863 (236)
Tazeau, Y. N.: ref, 298 (76)
Te'eni, D. R.: ref, 2247 (135)
Teachout, M. S.: ref, 180 (24)
Teaf, D.: ref, 136 (10), 1661 (45), 1697 (426)
Teagarden, F. M.: rev, 433, 2813
Teague, G. B.: ref, 134 (4,12)
Teague, J. E.: ref, 1755 (49)
Teague, R. B.: ref, 2603 (3)
Teal, P.: ref, 335 (1), 2289 (6)
Teare, J. F.: ref, 2559 (3)
Tearnan, B. H.: test, 291
Tebbutt, J.: ref, 451 (278), 472 (230), 694 (134), 1079 (109)
Tebbutt, J. S.: ref, 1661 (21)
Tebes, J.: ref, 2603 (498)
Tedeschi, R. G.: ref, 337 (154), 2497 (218)
Tedesco, L. A.: ref, 1965 (22)
Teegarden, L.: rev, 1700, 1703
Teegarden, L. A.: ref, 2603 (224)
Teeter, P. A.: rev, 68, 1383
Tegano, D. W.: ref, 1832 (4), 2862 (92), 2864 (15)

Teglasi, H.: ref, 2749 (67)
Tegner, R.: ref, 2860 (965)
Teichberg, D.: ref, 2860 (502)
Teicher, A.: ref, 681 (96), 2305 (247)
Teichman, Y.: ref, 1000 (57), 2497 (209,288)
Tein, J.: ref, 472 (63,102)
Tein, J. Y.: ref, 472 (38,145,200), 1000 (29), 1877 (2), 2214 (118)
Teixeira-Ferreira, C.: ref, 2163 (295), 2860 (1153), 2863 (342)
Tejeda, M. J.: ref, 2389 (1)
Telch, C. F.: ref, 272 (144), 1010 (91), 2497 (535), 2603 (329)
Telch, M. J.: ref, 2199 (1), 2497 (122), 2860 (278), 2863 (73)
Teleometrics International: test, 2129
Telford, R.: ref, 1079 (81)
Tellegen, A.: test, 1697, 1698, 998, 999, 1944; ref, 372 (81,107), 557 (4), 998 (36), 999 (110,149,383,384), 1902 (74), 2417 (23)
Tellegen, P.J.: test, 2441
Telner, J. I.: ref, 1166 (119)
Telzrow, C.: rev, 124, 898, 799, 875, 1262, 1363
Temkin, N.: ref, 1164 (62)
Temoshock, L. R.: ref, 2858 (105)
Temoshok, L. R.: ref, 2497 (361)
Tempelhoff, B.: ref, 337 (94)
Temple, C. M.: ref, 1765 (2,32), 1903 (4), 2862 (8,563)
Temple, J. A.: ref, 1318 (24)
Temple, R.: ref, 2835 (28)
Templer, D.: ref, 1697 (58)
Templer, D. I.: ref, 326 (8), 1021 (38), 1164 (125), 1525 (24), 1697 (457), 1745 (10,15), 2497 (526), 2860 (755,1121), 2863 (221), 2892 (233)
Templin, M. C.: test, 2651
Tems, C. L.: ref, 472 (65), 1991 (61)
Tench, E.: ref, 272 (153)
Tenenbaum, G.: ref, 2214 (31)
Tenenbaum, R.: ref, 298 (9)
Tennant, C.: ref, 2497 (667)
Tennant, C. C.: ref, 1164 (136), 1758 (79), 2860 (1183), 2863 (356)
Tennant, N.: ref, 2029 (2)
Tennen, H.: ref, 272 (15), 372 (117), 846 (26), 1661 (32), 2218 (135), 2433 (4)
Tenopyr, M. L.: rev, 2916
Teo, A.: ref, 451 (292), 1216 (113), 1902 (91,101), 2862 (564), 2864 (124), 2901 (102,138)
Teplin, S. W.: ref, 815 (51), 1740 (30), 1889 (18), 2724 (12), 2862 (711)
Teply, I.: ref, 776 (38)
Terborg, J. R.: test, 1574
Terenzini, P.: ref, 621 (1)
Terenzini, P. T.: ref, 620 (4), 621 (2)
Teri, L.: ref, 776 (27,58), 2860 (688), 2863 (83)
Terkelsen, K.: ref, 2218 (99), 2305 (226)
Terkuile, M. M.: ref, 2603 (221)
Terman, E. L.: test, 1796
Ternes, L. A.: ref, 2599 (3)
Terpstra, D. E.: ref, 1939 (8)
Terranova, M.: ref, 615 (10)
Terrazas, A.: ref, 2305 (87), 2860 (536)
Terre, L.: ref, 1745 (21,24)
Terrell, F.: ref, 794 (1), 893 (7), 2065 (3)
Terrell, S. L.: ref, 1040 (5)
Terrien, A.: ref, 272 (372), 2076 (185)
Terrio, L.: ref, 175 (10), 1040 (9), 1240 (28), 1804 (9), 1903 (282)
Terry, B.: ref, 665 (47), 1657 (11), 1866 (24,30)
Terry, D. J.: ref, 272 (49), 337 (87), 863 (18), 1079 (5), 2497 (50,147), 2858 (33,85,121)
Terry, H. E.: ref, 1000 (25)
Terry, P. C.: ref, 2076 (161)
Terry, W. S.: ref, 998 (82)
Terwilliger, J. S.: rev, 56
Tesfai, B.: ref, 1164 (115), 1485 (48), 2163 (255), 2225 (10)
Tesh, A.: rev, 2153, 2220, 960
Tesón, A.: ref, 2050 (120,121), 2163 (227,228), 2860 (935), 2873 (40,41), 2892 (197,198)
Tessari, A.: ref, 2860 (1025)
Tessier, D.: ref, 272 (68), 1164 (50), 2516 (29), 2860 (498)
Tessier, O.: ref, 1903 (351)
The Test Agency: test, 919, 1616
Test Development Committees, American Association of Teachers of Spanish and Portuguese: test, 1764
Test Development Unit of the Foundation for Educational Research in England and Wales: test, 1603
Testa, M.: ref, 1661 (22)
Testerman, M.: ref, 2581 (1)
Testut, E. W.: rev, 1919, 2052, 2298
Teszéri, G.: ref, 1166 (30)
Tetenbaum, T. J.: test, 228
Teti, D. M.: ref, 270 (18), 337 (149,162), 863 (62,82), 1216 (18)
Tetrault, L. A.: ref, 1701 (20)
Tetrud, J. W.: ref, 2516 (9)
Tett, R. P.: ref, 1965 (20)
Teuns, G.: ref, 2497 (259)
Teuscher, F.: ref, 2516 (52)
Tezuka, I.: ref, 1010 (108)
Tfedter, L. J.: ref, 615 (25)
Thackrey, M.: ref, 1697 (385)
Thackston-Williams, L.: ref, 1697 (360)
Thaker, G. K.: ref, 2050 (24), 2305 (203)
Thal, D.: test, 1528
Thal, D. J.: ref, 1528 (4)
Thal, L.: ref, 1164 (77), 2860 (184), 2862 (105)
Thal, L. J.: ref, 376 (15), 776 (34), 1164 (145), 2860 (1244), 2862 (601), 2892 (266)
Thalbourne, M. A.: ref, 1697 (361,362)
Tham, K.: ref, 2860 (965)
Thapar, A.: ref, 2214 (83)

Thara, R.: ref, 2050 (112)
Tharpe, B.: ref, 1697 (532)
Thase, M. E.: ref, 272 (233,265), 793 (14), 1093 (37,38,43,78,79), 1166 (54,162,163,180,207,215), 2305 (61,106,233), 2603 (503)
Thavundayil, J.: ref, 1661 (57)
Thayer, P. W.: rev, 1834, 1836, 2217, 2406, 2408
Thayer, R. E.: ref, 999 (106)
Theberge, D. C.: ref, 376 (35), 1164 (187), 2227 (62), 2516 (122), 2860 (940,1138,1420), 2892 (308), 2901 (68,98)
Thein, R. D.: ref, 2497 (499)
Theisen, M. E.: ref, 376 (26), 2860 (1336), 2863 (400)
Thelen, M.: ref, 2497 (627)
Thelen, M. H.: ref, 337 (187), 2497 (594)
Theodore, W. H.: ref, 335 (7)
Theodorou, A. E.: ref, 1166 (12)
Therapeutics and Technology Assessment Subcommittee of the American Academy of Neurology: ref, 1164 (132), 1697 (511), 2860 (1159), 2863 (344)
Theriault, C.: ref, 451 (291), 472 (235)
Thériault, J.: ref, 1927 (9)
Thernland, G.: ref, 2862 (617)
Theroux-Fichera, S.: ref, 2860 (939)
Thetford, W. N.: rev, 1214
Thibaudeau, G.: test, 2670
Thibaudeau, J.: ref, 2603 (218)
Thienemann, M.: ref, 272 (381), 1010 (138)
Thiesfeldt, R. M.: ref, 1903 (507)
Thissen, D.: ref, 94 (1,2,3), 117 (4)
Thoits, P. A.: ref, 337 (49), 2074 (1)
Tholl, L. M.: ref, 2749 (81), 2862 (692)
Thom, A.: ref, 2860 (1422), 2892 (309)
Thom, V. A.: ref, 1770 (3)
Thoma, S.: test, 771
Thomas, A.: ref, 541 (1), 1903 (496), 2668 (2), 2693 (7), 2694 (22), 2695 (62), 2731 (3), 2862 (557), 2905 (106)
Thomas, A. B.: ref, 2860 (1230,1231), 2879 (196)
Thomas, A. J.: ref, 1939 (15)
Thomas, A. M.: ref, 272 (72), 2211 (24,45)
Thomas, C.: ref, 1218 (16), 2599 (35), 2603 (591), 2863 (317), 2892 (259)
Thomas, D. M.: ref, 2603 (419), 2860 (749)
Thomas, E.: ref, 1612 (79), 1903 (416)
Thomas, E. M.: ref, 1903 (581), 2488 (10)
Thomas, G. F.: test, 2020
Thomas, G. V.: test, 1961
Thomas, J.: ref, 349 (19), 2516 (3,11), 2863 (25), 2892 (33)
Thomas, J. A.: ref, 1739 (1)
Thomas, J. M.: ref, 2050 (136), 2305 (157,158)
Thomas, J. W.: test, 312
Thomas, K.: ref, 2163 (135), 2892 (95)
Thomas, K. F.: ref, 1072 (39)
Thomas, K. W.: test, 946, 2020, 2513, 2756
Thomas, M.: test, 306
Thomas, N. G.: ref, 272 (117)
Thomas, P.: ref, 1000 (2), 2050 (46,83)
Thomas, R.: test, 2314; ref, 1166 (31)
Thomas, R. G.: rev, 1334, 1693, 1817, 2374
Thomas, R. N.: ref, 2497 (356)
Thomas, S.: ref, 2749 (85)
Thomas, S. P.: ref, 2497 (148)
Thomas, T. H.: ref, 999 (38)
Thomas, T. J.: test, 312
Thomas, T. M.: ref, 2305 (217)
Thomas, V.: ref, 1000 (79)
Thomas-Dobson, S.: ref, 1697 (457), 1745 (10,15)
Thomasgard, M.: ref, 337 (197)
Thomasson, H. R.: ref, 1010 (136), 1661 (83)
Thombs, D. L.: ref, 56 (14), 592 (102), 1735 (7)
Thompson, A.: ref, 1745 (22), 1927 (7), 2860 (766)
Thompson, A. P.: ref, 256 (3), 2860 (767,998), 2864 (33)
Thompson, A. S.: test, 83, 405
Thompson, B.: ref, 136 (10), 270 (27), 298 (157), 472 (79), 1140 (18), 1661 (45), 1697 (426,599), 1770 (9), 2603 (593), 2856 (5)
Thompson, B. S.: ref, 270 (31), 337 (175)
Thompson, C.: ref, 2050 (64,93), 2076 (97), 2239 (18), 2305 (191,217), 2497 (384), 2860 (581), 2863 (168), 2892 (106)
Thompson, C. H.: ref, 350 (52), 1903 (577), 2163 (355), 2860 (1413), 2862 (730)
Thompson, C. K.: ref, 2873 (48,58,72)
Thompson, D.: rev, 168, 485, 1413, 1820
Thompson, D. N.: ref, 560 (1), 2163 (31)
Thompson, E. C.: ref, 1991 (1)
Thompson, E. H., Jr.: ref, 298 (55)
Thompson, G. B.: test, 2811; ref, 358 (2)
Thompson, H.: ref, 2226 (9)
Thompson, I.: ref, 998 (34)
Thompson, J.: test, 207; ref, 999 (107), 2519 (44), 2520 (44), 2603 (320)
Thompson, J. A.: test, 329; ref, 999 (143,151), 1079 (55), 2603 (418,445), 2858 (108,113)
Thompson, J. K.: ref, 893 (27,30), 1745 (63), 2497 (137)
Thompson, J. M.: ref, 272 (140), 1694 (5), 1701 (26)
Thompson, J. P.: ref, 1697 (458)
Thompson, J. W.: ref, 2519 (30), 2520 (31)
Thompson, K. E.: ref, 1745 (25)
Thompson, K. M.: ref, 2860 (386)
Thompson, L.: ref, 272 (51), 337 (38), 2417 (15)
Thompson, L. A.: ref, 1903 (125), 2860 (999), 2862 (168), 2879 (46)
Thompson, L. L.: ref, 272 (133), 1164 (109), 2860 (961,1186), 2862 (565), 2892 (215)
Thompson, L. W.: ref, 272 (84), 337 (76), 2076 (82)
Thompson, M.: ref, 1612 (59), 2076 (154)
Thompson, M. C.: ref, 451 (196)
Thompson, M. E.: ref, 1533 (1), 2603 (248)
Thompson, M. P.: ref, 337 (163), 451 (287), 1903 (582)
Thompson, N. J.: ref, 1533 (2), 2599 (24)

Thompson, N. M.: rev, 539, 2468; ref, 375 (4), 451 (210), 542 (2), 1612 (68), 2214 (119), 2227 (44), 2813 (88), 2862 (649), 2879 (213)
Thompson, P.: ref, 1093 (61), 2010 (10), 2050 (63,115), 2163 (107), 2193 (15), 2892 (69)
Thompson, P. A.: ref, 1010 (122), 1013 (2), 1093 (110), 2076 (168), 2305 (168), 2498 (62)
Thompson, P. J.: ref, 2227 (18), 2863 (231)
Thompson, P. M.: ref, 1164 (181), 1740 (33), 2076 (125), 2227 (59), 2860 (1408), 2863 (427)
Thompson, R.: ref, 1697 (99)
Thompson, R. J.: ref, 1178 (9), 2603 (222)
Thompson, R. J., Jr.: ref, 472 (136), 863 (28), 1010 (37,41,55,66,112,126), 1991 (103), 2214 (76), 2603 (97,147,166,167,223,321,322,504), 2858 (46,58,86,122)
Thompson, R. W.: ref, 451 (149), 997 (13), 2065 (8)
Thompson, S.: ref, 1104 (13), 2193 (54), 2860 (1109)
Thompson, S. C.: ref, 791 (12), 2497 (94), 2603 (348,505,591)
Thompson, S. J.: ref, 1902 (96)
Thompson, S. K.: test, 2729
Thompson, T.: ref, 4 (18), 1903 (532), 2288 (55), 2289 (42), 2497 (289), 2860 (1289)
Thompson, T. M.: ref, 298 (79)
Thompson, W. B.: ref, 2497 (269)
Thompson, W. O.: ref, 641 (5), 2076 (118), 2227 (20), 2517 (4), 2599 (30)
Thomson, L. K.: test, 1409
Thomson, W. A.: ref, 2805 (2)
Thoran, M.: ref, 2873 (7)
Thorell, L-H.: ref, 1697 (201)
Thoreson, C. J.: ref, 2218 (98)
Thoreson, R. W.: ref, 2603 (383), 2858 (104)
Thorkildsen, R.: ref, 665 (68)
Thorn, B. E.: ref, 2497 (257), 2603 (190)
Thornby, J.: ref, 1697 (458)
Thorndike, R. L.: test, 385, 560, 561, 2485; rev, 372, 572, 593, 845, 888, 933, 1017, 2484, 2648, 2771, 2879
Thorndike, R. M.: rev, 644; ref, 2860 (791), 2862 (302)
Thorndike-Christ, T.: ref, 56 (11), 2656 (18)
Thorne, T.: test, 2459
Thornton, G.: rev, 2071
Thornton, G. C., III: rev, 390, 1792, 2149; ref, 1689 (4)
Thornton, H.: ref, 2879 (11)
Thornton, L. H.: ref, 694 (12)
Thornton, P. H.: ref, 2108 (3)
Thorp, D. M.: ref, 994 (34), 1903 (432), 2485 (184)
Thorpe, J.: ref, 2813 (29)
Thorpe, L. P.: test, 374; rev, 2879
Thorpe, S. J.: ref, 272 (327), 2497 (658)
Thorson, J. A.: ref, 908 (6,8), 2218 (115)
Thorstad, G.: ref, 1800 (1)
Thorum, A. R.: test, 1060
Thouless, R. H.: rev, 2856, 2857
Thrasher, S.: ref, 272 (278), 1079 (92), 2497 (636)
Threlfall, K. V.: ref, 937 (3)
Throneburg, R. N.: ref, 214 (19), 1001 (17), 1485 (56)
Thumin, F. J.: ref, 937 (1), 1697 (363)
Thummel, H.: ref, 472 (93,94), 1745 (43), 2076 (87,88)
Thurber, C.: ref, 1903 (215)
Thurber, C. A.: ref, 472 (148), 2214 (84)
Thurber, J. A.: ref, 272 (40), 451 (11)
Thurber, S.: rev, 2740; ref, 272 (40), 451 (11), 1525 (17), 1697 (574), 2860 (1352)
Thurlow, M. L.: ref, 246 (1), 1300 (2,5,6,9), 1300 (9)
Thurston, C. A.: ref, 1000 (55)
Thurstone, L. L.: test, 548, 549, 1299, 1636, 2460, 2757, 2758, 2807
Thurstone, T. G.: test, 728, 2758, 2790, 2807
Thvedt, J. E.: test, 1245
Thwaites, G. A.: ref, 2497 (325,452,551)
Thwing, E. J.: test, 453
Thyer, B. A.: ref, 1021 (35), 2603 (365,520)
Thyssen, T.: ref, 1697 (99)
Tibbles, P. N.: ref, 272 (61)
Tiberti, C.: ref, 303 (31), 1166 (229), 1740 (35), 2163 (356), 2860 (1419), 2892 (306)
Tidwell, M. C.: ref, 2218 (73)
Tidwell, P. S.: rev, 1420
Tiedeman, D. V.: rev, 56, 1074
Tiedemann, G. L.: ref, 2813 (25)
Tiedje, L. B.: ref, 2603 (73)
Tiegs, E. W.: test, 374
Tiemens, B. G.: ref, 1079 (79), 2603 (506)
Tien, A. Y.: ref, 2288 (76), 2289 (22,63), 2402 (60), 2892 (257)
Tien, H. C.: test, 1854
Tienari, P.: ref, 2247 (120), 2288 (2), 2860 (53)
Tiernan, M.: ref, 1099 (4), 1962 (22), 2862 (590), 2879 (193)
Tierney, A. M.: ref, 372 (54)
Tierney, M. C.: ref, 1758 (83), 2768 (38,39), 2860 (1187,1188,1238), 2863 (357,358)
Tierney, R. J.: rev, 1131, 1767, 2487, 2712
Tietzel, K.: ref, 2540 (5)
Tiffany, D. W.: test, 2759
Tiffany, P. G.: test, 2759; ref, 2759 (1)
Tiffin, J.: test, 58
Tiggeman, M.: ref, 273 (6), 1079 (10)
Tiggemann, M.: ref, 273 (5,7), 1079 (9,11)
Tighe, E. M.: ref, 1755 (33)
Tighe, P. L.: test, 1234, 1235
Tiihonen, J.: ref, 1697 (480,481), 2247 (99,100), 2860 (1073,1074)
Til, R.: ref, 459 (37)
Tilden, V. P.: ref, 1947 (1), 2076 (21)
Till, J. A.: rev, 202
Tiller, J.: ref, 1166 (32), 2497 (51)
Tilleskjor, C.: ref, 1697 (114), 2860 (231)
Tilley, A. J.: ref, 998 (133), 1079 (102)
Tilley, D.: ref, 1698 (5)
Tillman, M. H.: rev, 318
Timberlake, T.: ref, 2496 (3)

Timbrook, R. E.: ref, 1697 (320,364
Timken, D.: ref, 136 (8), 1697 (249)
Timko, C.: ref, 134 (30), 637 (3), 1010 (42), 1181 (9,10,23), 1743 (2), 1991 (41), 2414 (5), 2497 (290)
Timko, M. L.: ref, 2873 (27)
Timmerman, I. G. H.: ref, 1079 (64), 2497 (549)
Timmerman, L.: ref, 2497 (191)
Timmons, C. W.: ref, 2497 (598), 2879 (185)
Timmons, P. L.: ref, 2497 (598), 2879 (185)
Timmons-Mitchell, J.: ref, 2603 (507)
Tims, F. C.: ref, 2076 (177)
Tinajero, C.: ref, 745 (25), 926 (22), 1140 (58)
Tincoff, R.: ref, 2467 (1)
Tindal, G.: rev, 816, 968, 1194, 2111, 2905 (16)
Tindal, J.: rev, 1275, 2739
Tingle, J. B.: ref, 48 (1)f, 49 (1)
Tingley, E. C.: ref, 2813 (76)
Tinkcom, M.: ref, 1164 (37), 2076 (49), 2860 (377)
Tinker, M. A.: rev, 861, 862
Tinker, R. H.: ref, 2497 (533), 2603 (430)
Tinney, L.: ref, 472 (128), 2214 (69)
Tinney, L.: ref, 2498 (52)
Tinsley, H. E. A.: test, 1695; ref, 991 (1)
Tinson, D.: ref, 2860 (764)
Tinson, D. J.: ref, 2239 (4)
Tintner, R.: ref, 1164 (65), 1697 (303), 2860 (648), 2863 (188)
Tipp, J. E.: ref, 2305 (195)
Tipper, S. P.: ref, 2516 (7)
Tippett, L. J.: ref, 1525 (25), 2892 (240)
Tirch, D. D.: ref, 272 (310)
Tirosh, E.: ref, 322 (5), 827 (8), 2862 (225)
Tirre, W. C.: ref, 180 (11,13), 745 (6)
Tisak, J.: ref, 1701 (31)
Tisdale, M. J.: ref, 1697 (98)
Tisdwell, P.: ref, 1758 (54), 2860 (1000), 2863 (296), 2892 (209)
Tisher, M.: ref, 472 (40,149)
Tison, F.: ref, 2863 (297)
Tissot, S. L.: ref, 2163 (229)
Tittle, C. K.: rev, 205, 560, 561, 2443, 2855, 2862
Titus, M. N. D.: ref, 182 (1), 2008 (4), 2860 (311)
Titus, P.: test, 2471
Tivis, L. J.: ref, 272 (150,328), 2402 (50,54,69), 2497 (524,537), 2860 (1037), 2863 (308,410)
Tivis, R.: ref, 272 (151), 2860 (1038)
Tiwari, S.: ref, 745 (2)
Tix, A. P.: ref, 337 (198)
Tjaden, K.: ref, 209 (3)
Tjell, C.: ref, 1164 (148), 2226 (23), 2860 (1268)
Tjuius, T.: ref, 234 (1)
Tjus, T.: ref, 2163 (218), 2228 (18)
Tloczynski, J.: ref, 1939 (13)
Tobacyk, J. J.: ref, 226 (2), 298 (88), 2835 (15)
Tobey, E.: ref, 486 (3)
Tobey, G. Y.: ref, 1216 (11)
Tobey, P. E.: ref, 844 (4)
Tobin, A. R.: test, 2382
Tobin, D.: ref, 893 (2), 1010 (9), 2603 (20)
Tobin, J. W.: ref, 1697 (177)
Tobin, M. I.: ref, 854 (1), 1097 (9)
Toda, M. A.: ref, 999 (59)
Todak, G.: ref, 2125 (18), 2163 (124), 2516 (28), 2603 (549), 2860 (496), 2863 (292)
Todd, C. M.: ref, 1240 (43), 1424 (3), 1607 (15), 1903 (464), 2452 (12), 2695 (52), 2704 (39), 2862 (476)
Todd, D. M.: ref, 2603 (557)
Todd, J.: ref, 2749 (27,37)
Todd, M. E.: ref, 2860 (493), 2863 (140)
Todd, T.: ref, 2519 (10), 2520 (10), 2603 (53)
Todis, B.: test, 2311
Todorov, A. A.: ref, 2305 (111)
Toga, A. W.: ref, 1164 (181), 1740 (33), 2227 (59), 2860 (1408), 2863 (427)
Toglia, J. P.: test, 685
Tohen, M.: ref, 1093 (19), 2050 (77)
Tojek, T. M.: ref, 472 (208), 2214 (120)
Tokar, D. M.: ref, 991 (1)
Tokola, R.: ref, 1697 (369), 2860 (778)
Tokumitsu, Y.: ref, 1166 (134)
Tolan, P.: ref, 1000 (2)
Tolan, P. H.: ref, 451 (57)
Toland, A. M.: ref, 1661 (4)
Tolbert, H. A.: ref, 2017 (17)
Tolia, V.: ref, 472 (208), 2214 (120)
Tolin, D. F.: ref, 2603 (374,478)
Toll, D. M.: ref, 1485 (54)
Tölle, R.: ref, 1166 (121)
Tollefson, G. D.: ref, 1166 (51)
Tollefson, N.: ref, 1000 (1), 1014 (1), 1612 (6), 2485 (33), 2862 (40)
Tollison, C. D.: test, 1871
Tollwerck, L.: ref, 349 (34), 350 (41), 1240 (48), 2862 (568)
Tolomiczenko, G. S.: ref, 1697 (570), 2010 (23), 2860 (1348), 2863 (406), 2879 (216), 2892 (289)
Tolson, R. L.: ref, 1697 (202)
Tolvanen, A.: ref, 815 (45), 2862 (641), 2901 (122)
Toman, K. M.: ref, 1697 (418)
Tomarken, A. J.: ref, 2497 (403)
Tomassone, J.: ref, 2862 (159)
Tombaugh, T. N.: test, 1454, 2702
Tomblin, J. B.: ref, 798 (10), 1096 (13), 1240 (29,39,51), 1379 (55,103), 1740 (36), 1903 (146,299,558,583), 2524 (11), 2657 (17,27,37), 2668 (5), 2694 (19,15), 2695 (29,45,63,71,72), 2725 (1,6), 2860 (409), 2862 (284,738), 2864 (125,141)
Tombokan-Runtukohu, J.: ref, 2163 (97), 2813 (26)
Tomchin, E. M.: ref, 1318 (11), 2358 (14)
Tomer, A.: ref, 1156 (4), 2863 (224)
Tomes, R. E.: rev, 157, 1668, 2049
Tomko, T. N.: test, 705
Tomlin-Albanese, J. M.: ref, 1517 (6)
Tomlinson-Clarke, S.: ref, 2525 (8)

Tomoeda, C. K.: test, 176, 1064
Tompkins, C. A.: ref, 199 (3), 1903 (60), 2873 (12,27)
Tompkins, G. E.: rev, 959, 1144, 1531, 1663
Tompson, M. C.: ref, 2862 (233)
Toms, K. T.: rev, 971
Tomsai, M.: ref, 2860 (988), 2863 (291)
Tone, L. E.: ref, 2050 (125)
Toneatto, T.: rev, 73, 1577, 1931, 2284; ref, 134 (10,21), 1164 (79), 1525 (16), 2414 (2), 2599 (23), 2603 (306), 2860 (758), 2892 (150)
Tong, J.: ref, 1991 (99)
Tonge, B. J.: ref, 270 (15), 1134 (7), 1903 (461), 2485 (198), 2862 (466), 2864 (114)
Tonigan, J. S.: ref, 134 (26), 135 (4), 272 (146), 1141 (2,5), 1661 (28)
Tonkonogy, J.: test, 336
Toomey, R.: ref, 1965 (66), 2402 (51)
Toone, B.: ref, 1093 (80), 2050 (98,103)
Toone, B. K.: ref, 2050 (80), 2860 (656)
Toong, T. J. K.: ref, 1697 (88), 2402 (6)
Tooze, F.H.G.: test, 2770
Topol, P.: ref, 1716 (1)
Topoloski, T. D.: ref, 2862 (549)
Topolosky, S.: ref, 681 (14)
Toran, J.: ref, 2288 (52)
Tordjman, S.: ref, 2813 (109), 2860 (1001)
Torem, M.: ref, 846 (18)
Torgersen, S.: ref, 1687 (24), 2497 (252), 2519 (6), 2520 (6)
Torgerson, T. L.: rev, 1073
Torgesen, J.: rev, 1362
Torgesen, J. K.: test, 2708; ref, 665 (9), 1903 (257), 2163 (81), 2485 (12,47), 2862 (57), 2905 (7,19)
Tori, C. D.: ref, 1379 (27), 2163 (117), 2862 (204)
Torki, M. A.: ref, 998 (83)
Torney-Purta, J.: ref, 1903 (82)
Toro, M.: test, 1535, 1536
Toro, P. A.: ref, 716 (1), 2603 (124,419)
Toro-Zambrana, W.: ref, 2485 (158)
Toronto, A. S.: test, 2335
Torquati, J.: ref, 451 (36)
Torrance, E. P.: test, 1227, 1396, 2545, 2754, 2755, 2771; ref, 2771 (5)
Torre, C.: ref, 451 (236), 2813 (154)
Torres, B.: ref, 999 (176)
Torres, I.: ref, 650 (16)
Torrey, E. F.: ref, 1093 (47), 1164 (94), 1962 (17), 2193 (16), 2288 (40), 2305 (87), 2813 (77), 2860 (460,536,871), 2863 (128)
Torrey, F.: ref, 1093 (11)
Torrubia, R.: ref, 999 (109), 1166 (168)
Tosca, E.: test, 634
Toseland, R. W.: ref, 272 (56), 337 (6), 2497 (181)
Toshima, M. T.: rev, 1186
Tosi, C. B.: ref, 1000 (55)
Tosi, D. J.: rev, 1939; ref, 1686 (6), 1697 (438), 1745 (49), 2402 (45)
Tosoni, C.: ref, 2862 (530)
Toth, L. S.: ref, 1474 (1), 2771 (9)
Toth, S. L.: ref, 373 (12), 472 (41,192), 1903 (147,499)
Totoescu, A.: ref, 2163 (66), 2860 (259)
Totsuka, S.: ref, 1592 (27), 2862 (719)
Totten, G. L.: ref, 2497 (525)
Toubanos, E. S.: rev, 2320, 2683
Touchet, B.: ref, 1687 (46)
Touchette, P.: ref, 2860 (883)
Touchstone Applied Science Associates (TASA), Inc.: test, 773, 774
Tough, S.: ref, 2813 (142)
Touliatos, J.: ref, 372 (95)
Toupin, E. S. W. A.: ref, 615 (30)
Toupin, J.: ref, 2050 (69,102)
Tourigny, M.: ref, 472 (233), 2214 (138)
Tournier-Lasserve, E.: ref, 376 (33), 2239 (35)
Tourond, M.: test, 1055
Touzé, J.: ref, 1697 (252)
Touzé, J. H.: ref, 1697 (359)
Tovey, S. L.: ref, 272 (76), 1010 (56)
Towberman, D. B.: ref, 694 (58), 1991 (54)
Towbes, L. C.: ref, 999 (174), 2498 (1)
Towle, D.: ref, 2239 (5)
Towle, V. L.: ref, 272 (209), 1164 (131), 2125 (24), 2516 (83), 2863 (343)
Towne, R. L.: rev, 241, 328, 2706
Towner, G.: test, 2824
Towns-Miranda, L.: ref, 2247 (10), 2749 (17)
Townsend, A.: rev, 1767
Townsend, M.: ref, 694 (132)
Townsend, M. A. R.: ref, 358 (3), 495 (14)
Townsend, S. T.: ref, 2496 (6)
Townsend, T. G.: ref, 1947 (8)
Townshend, R.: ref, 2163 (142)
Townsley, R. M.: ref, 863 (19), 2519 (19,34), 2520 (20,35)
Toyer, E. A.: ref, 1698 (28)
Tozman, S.: ref, 2860 (1)
Trabert, W.: ref, 2497 (375), 2520 (46)
Trabucchi, M.: ref, 337 (54), 2516 (61), 2860 (804), 2892 (163)
Tracey, J. G.: ref, 2835 (22)
Tracey, S. A.: ref, 472 (219), 2214 (128)
Tracey, T. J.: ref, 398 (3), 406 (1), 414 (2), 415 (1), 416 (1), 716 (1), 1334 (4), 2749 (49), 2835 (16)
Tracey, T. J. G.: ref, 337 (164), 1334 (5), 2835 (18,24,25)
Trachtenberg, S.: ref, 1903 (322)
Tracy, D. M.: ref, 298 (41)
Tracy, J.: ref, 2125 (20,21)
Tracy, J. I.: ref, 1164 (81), 2402 (35), 2860 (768)
Tracy, L. S.: ref, 462 (24)
Trahan, D. E.: test, 687
Trahan, M.: ref, 560 (4), 665 (87), 1768 (2), 2862 (561)
Trainer, D. A.: ref, 815 (14), 1164 (56), 1612 (46), 1903 (236), 2485 (117), 2860 (580), 2863 (167)
Training House, Inc.: test, 155, 166, 203, 701, 940, 1277, 1563, 1874, 1936, 1950, 2075, 2352, 2584, 2679, 2760, 2876

Trakowski, J. H.: ref, 2076 (146)
Trammel, D. L.: ref, 2862 (294), 2901 (48)
Tramo, M.: ref, 2225 (20), 2860 (1410), 2863 (429)
Tramo, M. J.: ref, 2860 (312,1222), 2863 (84,362)
Tranel, D.: ref, 272 (324), 303 (23), 1697 (576), 2226 (37), 2227 (3), 2860 (181,1355,1358)
Tranh, M.: ref, 2010 (18)
Trapnell, P. D.: ref, 793 (21,24), 2218 (50)
Trask, P. C.: ref, 272 (320), 2497 (657), 2603 (553)
Träskman-Bendz, L.: ref, 273 (28), 999 (181)
Trathen, W.: ref, 1672 (2), 2879 (20)
Traub, R. E.: rev, 1089
Trauh, M.: ref, 2860 (837), 2863 (242)
Trauner, D.: ref, 1001 (14)
Trauner, D. A.: ref, 815 (41), 1962 (21), 2485 (215)
Trautman, P.: ref, 451 (151), 2305 (197)
Travers, R. M. W.: rev, 1084
Travis, M.: test, 228
Traw, R.: ref, 1318 (14), 1657 (24)
Traynor, C.: test, 209
Treadwell, K. R. H.: ref, 472 (150), 2214 (85), 2498 (55)
Treasure, J. L.: ref, 893 (16)
Treat, T. A.: ref, 272 (383)
Treboux, D.: ref, 451 (247)
Tredoux, C. G.: ref, 1754 (20)
Tredoux, M.: test, 169
Treem, W.: ref, 2247 (45), 2380 (9), 2749 (34), 2862 (224)
Treem, W. P.: ref, 1226 (1), 2247 (90)
Treffinger, D. J.: rev, 2771; ref, 1404 (9)
Tregaskes, M. R.: ref, 550 (1)
Trehub, S. E.: ref, 1528 (3)
Treiber, F. A.: ref, 472 (31), 1215 (2), 2214 (22)
Treiman, R.: ref, 2467 (1), 2879 (146)
Treliving, L. R.: ref, 2497 (330)
Tremblay, P. F.: ref, 950 (5)
Tremblay, R. E.: ref, 1340 (2), 1661 (69,78), 1866 (33), 2039 (14,15,16,17,18,23), 2603 (372), 2860 (916), 2862 (321)
Tremblay, R. M.: ref, 472 (199)
Trembley, P. W.: test, 1428
Tremont, G.: ref, 1697 (151), 2076 (36), 2497 (294)
Trenerry, M.: ref, 2860 (992), 2863 (294)
Trenerry, M. R.: test, 2517, 2820; ref, 1698 (16), 2860 (537), 2863 (152)
Trenholm, P.: ref, 2497 (680)
Trent, A. P.: ref, 1021 (38), 2497 (526)
Trent, D.: ref, 272 (175)
Trent, E. R.: test, 1418
Trent, J.: ref, 2497 (680)
Trent, L. K.: ref, 136 (12), 2603 (592)
Trent, N. H., III: ref, 1021 (38), 2497 (526)
Trent, R.: test, 1226
Tressoldi, P. E.: ref, 2862 (323)
Trevarthen, C.: ref, 1001 (1,8), 2860 (77), 2892 (4)
Trevisan, M.: ref, 2603 (517)
Trevisan, M. S.: rev, 24, 421, 1802, 1827, 2023, 2684, 2742; ref, 852 (1)
Trew, K.: ref, 298 (107)
Trexler, L. D.: ref, 272 (3), 273 (2)
Trichard, C.: ref, 2516 (73), 2860 (1002)
Trickett, E. J.: test, 495; ref, 495 (7), 2497 (100)
Trickett, P. K.: ref, 451 (202), 472 (198,206), 1010 (124), 1903 (323,544), 2498 (71)
Trief, P. M.: ref, 2117 (4)
Trierweiler, S. J.: ref, 1745 (3)
Triffleman, E.: ref, 372 (117), 846 (26) 2218 (135), 2433 (4)
Trigg, C. L.: ref, 474 (5)
Trillet, M.: ref, 1166 (99), 2863 (310)
Trillingsgaard, A.: ref, 2862 (455)
Trimble, H. C.: rev, 2090, 2091
Trinder, J.: ref, 1953 (1), 2497 (404)
Trinidad, A.: ref, 2218 (35)
Trinidad-Carrillo, M.: ref, 1790 (8), 2451 (4)
Triolo, S. J.: test, 224
Tripathi, H. L.: ref, 2076 (61)
Tripp, D. A.: ref, 272 (329)
Tripp, G.: ref, 451 (227), 472 (218), 2214 (127)
Trites, R.: test, 1135
Trivelli, C.: ref, 2163 (108)
Trobe, J. D.: ref, 2860 (583), 2863 (170)
Troia, G. A.: ref, 1902 (92), 2905 (108)
Troisi, A.: ref, 272 (224,234), 1166 (33,156), 2497 (599)
Trojano, L.: ref, 2227 (52), 2860 (636), 2892 (118)
Trommer, B.: ref, 451 (258), 681 (92), 1099 (5), 1164 (177), 1379 (101), 1740 (31), 2516 (118), 2892 (299)
Trommsdorff, A.: ref, 2858 (114)
Tronick, E. Z.: ref, 1770 (14)
Troop, N. A.: ref, 893 (16)
Trope, I.: ref, 2860 (54,76)
Troster, A. I.: ref, 271 (15), 272 (330), 376 (25,28), 776 (53,56), 1135 (24), 1218 (19), 1378 (10), 1740 (26), 1758 (95), 2076 (181), 2516 (112), 2860 (1151,1324, 1325,1326), 2863 (153,411), 2892 (247,293)
Trotman, K. M.: ref, 2860 (964)
Trotter, B. B.: ref, 449 (1,3)
Troughton, E.: ref, 2603 (458)
Troupin, A. S.: ref, 1697 (125), 2516 (10)
Troutman, J. A.: ref, 337 (110)
Troutner, N. M.: ref, 1072 (45)
Trowler, R.: ref, 893 (16)
Troyer, A. K.: ref, 303 (22), 376 (11,27), 776 (55), 1164 (172), 2860 (1189,1354), 2863 (408), 2892 (258,291)
Troyer, M. E.: test, 1184
Truax, P. A.: ref, 272 (184)
Trubilla, R. S.: ref, 893 (1), 2652 (2)
Trudeau, L.: ref, 615 (26)
Trudel, M.: ref, 1134 (8)
Trueblood, W.: ref, 1164 (54,82), 1697 (246,365), 2860 (538,769), 2863 (154,225)
Truett, K. R.: ref, 2603 (273)
Truglio, R.: ref, 472 (162)
Trujillo, M.: ref, 2603 (129)

Trull, T. J.: ref, 337 (92,122), 790 (18), 1697 (459,460), 1697 (460), 2218 (41)
Trump, D. L.: ref, 1687 (9), 2076 (17)
Trupin, E.: ref, 1697 (148), 2559 (2)
Truscott, D.: ref, 1697 (247), 2860 (539)
Trusheim, D.: ref, 592 (35)
Trusty, M. L.: ref, 337 (168)
Trute, B.: ref, 272 (141), 863 (9)
Truxillo, D. M.: ref, 1701 (11)
Tryebinski, J.: ref, 1965 (77), 2218 (71)
Tryon, W. W.: ref, 2516 (74)
Tsagarakis, C. I.: ref, 1755 (42,57), 2218 (34)
Tsai, G.: ref, 1093 (90), 1653 (4), 2860 (299)
Tsai, L.: ref, 353 (12), 2247 (87), 2813 (61), 2860 (864), 2862 (261,339)
Tsai, R.: ref, 1987 (21)
Tsai, W-Y.: ref, 2305 (179), 2860 (1180)
Tsang, B.: ref, 376 (16), 1164 (146), 1740 (17), 2516 (95), 2863 (375), 2892 (267)
Tsang, M. C.: ref, 694 (117), 2497 (570)
Tsatsanis, K. D.: ref, 2862 (683), 2879 (220)
Tschann, J. M.: ref, 451 (5), 1000 (58), 1093 (4)
Tschuschke, V.: ref, 2603 (323)
Tse, S.: ref, 353 (5)
Tsemberis, S.: ref, 2862 (566)
Tseng, C-H.: ref, 2225 (5)
Tseng, M. H.: ref, 2724 (5)
Tsien, S.: ref, 56 (10), 180 (28)
Tsuang, D.: ref, 272 (142), 1687 (18), 2497 (527)
Tsuang, M. T.: ref, 136 (7), 1092 (5,14), 1093 (19,84), 1164 (68), 1218 (7), 1645 (3), 1661 (26), 1697 (408), 1965 (66), 2305 (47), 2516 (42,65), 2860 (331,671,855), 2863 (199,250), 2879 (81), 2892 (125,176)
Tsuda, H.: ref, 2860 (1363)
Tsuda, T.: ref, 2768 (39), 2860 (1188), 2863 (357)
Tsui, J.: ref, 2125 (27)
Tsushima, W. T.: ref, 2864 (75)
Tsytsarev, S. V.: ref, 2497 (638)
Tttle, D. H.: ref, 2603 (125)
Tu, X.: ref, 272 (307), 1166 (204)
Tu, X. M.: ref, 1093 (113), 1166 (207), 2305 (233)
Tuason, V. B.: ref, 1093 (42), 1697 (173)
Tubi, N.: ref, 301 (16,48), 2860 (241,922)
Tubman, J. G.: ref, 134 (16,17), 472 (66,67), 2214 (34)
Tuck, B. F.: ref, 358 (9), 2092 (3)
Tucker, C. M.: ref, 2065 (30), 2813 (110)
Tucker, D. D.: ref, 893 (28)
Tucker, G.: ref, 2860 (665), 2863 (195)
Tucker, J. A.: rev, 1577, 1931; ref, 134 (32), 1661 (36,56)
Tucker, J. S.: ref, 272 (73), 371 (1), 999 (66), 2218 (11), 2496 (2), 2497 (291)
Tucker, R. W.: test, 2585
Tuckman, B. W.: rev, 2795, 2799
Tudehope, D. I.: ref, 1612 (41,42)
Tudin, P.: ref, 1079 (78)
Tugral, K. C.: ref, 2289 (58)
Tugson, V. B.: ref, 998 (41), 1697 (167)
Tuinman, J. J.: rev, 2905
Tulen, J. H. M.: ref, 1166 (164), 1697 (186), 2305 (204), 2497 (189,191)
Tuley, M. R.: ref, 1697 (102), 2417 (12)
Tully, L. A.: ref, 272 (315), 451 (223)
Tulving, E.: ref, 2860 (1385), 2863 (417)
Tuma, J. M.: rev, 1962
Tumuluru, R.: ref, 4 (20), 681 (83), 2211 (50), 2485 (221)
Tun, C. G.: ref, 2860 (1359)
Tun, P. A.: ref, 2860 (1359)
Tunali, B.: ref, 1485 (8), 1612 (20), 1903 (83)
Tunali-Kotoski, B.: ref, 459 (30,36), 1485 (30,42), 1612 (53,74), 1903 (279,382)
Tune, L. E.: ref, 2076 (1), 2289 (22)
Tung, G.: ref, 1218 (16), 2599 (35), 2863 (317), 2892 (259)
Tunick, R. H.: ref, 2860 (393)
Tunna, K.: ref, 1338 (4)
Tunnell, J.: ref, 571 (3), 1599 (1)
Tuokko, H.: test, 545; ref, 272 (68), 303 (12), 1164 (50), 1740 (15), 2516 (29,66), 2860 (498,876,1003, 1190), 2863 (258,298,359)
Tupler, L. A.: ref, 2227 (22)
Tupler, R. G.: ref, 2227 (8), 2860 (364), 2879 (44), 2892 (54)
Turaids, D.: test, 2468
Turbott, S. H.: ref, 1903 (61)
Turco, T. L.: rev, 331, 347
Turetsky, B.: ref, 1407 (1), 2288 (57), 2289 (44), 2860 (172)
Turetsky, B. I.: ref, 2288 (65), 2289 (49)
Turjanski, S.: ref, 2603 (539)
Turk, C. L.: ref, 2516 (70)
Turk, D. C.: ref, 272 (235)
Turk, K.: rev, 1385
Turk-Charles, S.: ref, 2839 (3)
Turkheimer, E.: ref, 1164 (22), 2860 (410,540,966)
Turkstra, L. S.: ref, 540 (25), 2596 (1), 2668 (6)
Turnbull, C.: ref, 1758 (13), 2193 (6)
Turnbull, O. H.: ref, 1104 (11), 2860 (1004)
Turnbull, W. W.: rev, 354, 1974
Turner, A.: test, 1282
Turner, C.: ref, 2498 (46)
Turner, C. W.: ref, 272 (80), 1412 (2), 1697 (226)
Turner, E. T.: ref, 2771 (16)
Turner, G. S.: ref, 209 (3)
Turner, G. Y.: ref, 2591 (3)
Turner, I.: ref, 298 (107)
Turner, J. A.: ref, 863 (17), 1036 (4), 1697 (202)
Turner, J. B.: ref, 2603 (126)
Turner, J. E.: ref, 472 (106)
Turner, K.: test, 892
Turner, K. M. T.: ref, 272 (315), 451 (223)
Turner, K. N.: ref, 2498 (28)
Turner, L. A.: ref, 1903 (500), 2432 (21), 2862 (386), 2879 (133)

Turner, M. B.: ref, 1164 (65), 1697 (303), 2860 (648), 2863 (188)
Turner, M. E.: ref, 1348 (9), 1701 (40)
Turner, M. W.: ref, 2498 (28), 2519 (34), 2520 (35)
Turner, N. E.: test, 858, 1305, 2414 (6), 2603 (555)
Turner, P. J.: ref, 1903 (95)
Turner, P. R.: ref, 1697 (522)
Turner, R. A.: ref, 1000 (58)
Turner, R. L.: ref, 298 (96)
Turner, S.: test, 1626; ref, 265 (12), 998 (123) 1010 (110), 2858 (37,98,119)
Turner, S. M.: test, 2448; ref, 998 (107), 2497 (18,562), 2498 (13,33,49,57), 2519 (34), 2520 (35), 2862 (439)
Turner, S. W.: ref, 999 (143), 1079 (55), 2603 (418), 2858 (108)
Turner, T.: ref, 337 (133), 863 (87), 1888 (1),1889 (9), 2603 (533)
Turner, W. E.: ref, 358 (13), 1765 (34), 1903 (518)
Turner, W. L.: ref, 1010 (57), 2117 (2)
Turner, W. M.: ref, 136 (7), 1661 (26), 1697 (570), 2010 (23), 2305 (47), 2860 (1348), 2863 (406), 2879 (216), 2892 (289)
Turney, A. H.: rev, 1414
Turntsull, O. H.: ref, 2860 (1360)
Turovsky, J.: ref, 2199 (13)
Turret, N.: ref, 272 (203)
Turton, L. J.: rev, 234, 240, 468, 1040, 2426, 2872
Tury, F.: ref, 893 (25), 1079 (48)
Tuska, S. A.: test, 543, 2612
Tuss, P.: ref, 745 (19)
Tutko, T. A.: test, 219, 1930, 1955
Tuttle, G. E.: ref, 372 (32), 1697 (147), 2860 (313)
Tuxhorn, I.: ref, 2863 (390)
Tuynman-Qua, H. G.: ref, 335 (15)
Tvason, V. B.: ref, 272 (174), 1166 (110)
Tweed, D. L.: ref, 451 (107,108)
Tweed, S. H.: ref, 1333 (1), 1965 (29), 2126 (7)
Tweedy, J. R.: ref, 199 (7)
Twell, A. J.: ref, 2862 (552)
Twijnstra, A.: ref, 2516 (20)
Twining, L.: ref, 2603 (386)
Twitchell, G.: ref, 999 (105), 1697 (351), 2497 (393)
Twitchell, G. R.: ref, 2305 (154)
Twum, M.: ref, 2863 (226)
Tyack, D.: test, 1427
Tyano, S.: ref, 2163 (95)
Tyc, V. L.: ref, 451 (230), 2497 (659)
Tye-Murray, N.: ref, 487 (2)
Tyerman, A.: test, 445
Tyerman, R.: test, 445
Tyhurst, J. S.: ref, 1697 (15), 2860 (60)
Tyler, A. A.: ref, 214 (18), 1095 (20), 1394 (10), 1903 (324), 2695 (31), 2866 (3,4)
Tyler, B.: test, 2255, 2256
Tyler, L. E.: rev, 548, 549, 752, 926, 1124, 1196
Tyler, L. K.: ref, 2163 (344), 2860 (1361), 2862 (684)
Tyler, P. A.: ref, 1079 (62), 2917 (1)
Tyler, R.: ref, 270 (45), 1687 (35)
Tyler, R. W.: rev, 572, 593
Tyler, S.: test, 1388
Tyma, S.: test, 953, 1664
Tymon, W. G.: test, 946
Tymon, W. G., Jr.: test, 2513
Tyrka, A. R.: ref, 748 (10), 2050 (133)
Tyrrell, G.: ref, 1093 (6), 2860 (150)
Tyson, K.: ref, 2125 (20,21)
Tyssedal, J. S.: ref, 1164 (148), 2226 (23), 2860 (1268)
Tziner, A.: rev, 2648, 2803; ref, 302 (3), 1693 (2), 1697 (366), 2163 (192), 2217 (3)
Tzukerman, Y.: ref, 2749 (27)
Tzuriel, D.: ref, 2163 (95)

U.S. Department of Labor: test, 2795, 2798
U.S. Department of Labor, Employment and Training Administration: test, 2796
U.S. Dept. of Education: test, 1759
U.S. Military Entrance Processing Command: test, 180
Uany, R.: ref, 2862 (145), 2864 (24)
Uccello, R.: ref, 2199 (11)
Uchino, B. N.: ref, 863 (56)
Uchiyama, C.: ref, 1164 (105), 1697 (502), 1758 (47), 1993 (1), 2860 (697,698,938,204,276)
Ucros, C. G.: ref, 1338 (13)
Udavari-Solner, A.: ref, 377 (1), 2813 (11)
Uddo, M.: ref, 337 (121), 1010 (88), 2402 (47,48), 2497 (401,521,548), 2603 (414,415), 2858 (107), 2860 (995)
Udivin, O.: ref, 350 (44), 2662 (7), 2860 (1291), 2862 (635)
Udry, E.: ref, 2076 (182)
Udry, E. M.: ref, 1590 (18), 2497 (211)
Udry, J. R.: ref, 1903 (433), 2163 (248)
Udupa, J. K.: ref, 231 (1), 303 (32), 2226 (42), 2227 (61), 2599 (43), 2863 (431), 2892 (307)
Udwin, O.: ref, 350 (50), 994 (51), 2163 (344), 2239 (11), 2813 (155), 2860 (1361,1395), 2862 (684,717)
Uecker, A.: ref, 815 (42), 1379 (90), 2862 (567)
Uehara, T.: ref, 1166 (212)
Ugaglia, K.: ref, 1092 (5), 2860 (331)
Uhde, T. W.: ref, 272 (92), 2305 (114), 2497 (114,143,206,405)
Uhlenhuth, E. H.: ref, 1166 (34), 2519 (50), 2520 (50), 2603 (163,216)
Uhler, J.: ref, 863 (87), 1888 (1), 1889 (9), 2603 (533)
Uhlman, F.: test, 1414
Uhry, J. K.: ref, 1072 (41), 1130 (2), 2905 (47)
Uitti, R. J.: ref, 2125 (27)
Ukeje, I.: ref, 1612 (92)
Uleman, J. S.: ref, 1115 (22)
Ulicni, S. K.: ref, 2218 (56), 2246 (10)
Ulicny, G. R.: ref, 2860 (38,228), 2862 (116)
Ullevig, C.: ref, 1697 (446), 2703 (2)
Ullmann, R. K.: test, 65

Ullrich, K.: ref, 2860 (1202), 2862 (578)
Ulm, G.: ref, 1164 (158), 2227 (41)
Ulrey, L. M.: ref, 2749 (46)
Ulrich, D. A.: test, 2689
Ulrich, R.: ref, 451 (114), 824 (5), 1093 (76), 2603 (307)
Ulrich, R. F.: ref, 1093 (56), 2603 (215), 2860 (532)
Ulstein, I.: ref, 1079 (83)
Ulug, B.: ref, 272 (331), 999 (188)
Ulusahin, A.: ref, 272 (331), 999 (188)
Umbel, V. M.: ref, 1903 (117)
Umbricht, D.: ref, 2860 (1005)
Umilta, C.: ref, 2516 (33), 2860 (1178)
Umlauf, R.: ref, 1745 (5)
Underwood, C.: ref, 265 (12)
Underwood, J. R.: ref, 2497 (267) 2771 (25)
Ungar, L.: ref, 2749 (16)
Unger, D. G.: ref, 1216 (13), 1902 (23), 1903 (73), 2603 (168)
Unger, M. A.: test, 2379
Ungerer, J. A.: ref, 474 (2), 1592 (8), 1903 (455), 2862 (124)
Ungerleider, S.: ref, 2076 (7)
United Cerebral Palsy of the Bluegrass: test, 1490
United States Employment Service: test, 2797, 2799
Unrau, N. J.: ref, 959 (2)
Unterbrink, C.: ref, 1697 (373)
Unverzagt, F.: ref, 326 (3), 1218 (4), 2163 (76), 2497 (136), 2516 (14), 2599 (16), 2860 (301,614), 2863 (180), 2892 (41,115)
Unwin, S. M.: test, 954
Uomoto, J. M.: ref, 2603 (351)
Upcraft, M. L.: ref, 2527 (7)
Updegraff, K. A.: ref, 2214 (74)
Updike, M. L.: ref, 2227 (10), 2599 (9), 2860 (401)
Upmanyu, S.: ref, 298 (130)
Upmanyu, V. V.: ref, 298 (130), 999 (175), 1321 (10), 1697 (523), 2771 (44)
Upperman, P. J.: ref, 2835 (19)
Upshur, J.: test, 1506, 1664
Upton, D.: ref, 2860 (1006), 2892 (210)
Urban, J.: ref, 373 (10)
Urban, K. K.: test, 2659
Urban, W. H.: test, 853
Urbanski, P. A.: ref, 2076 (153)
Urbina, S.: rev, 238, 256, 1273, 2329
Uren, G.: ref, 1079 (83)
Urquiza, A. J.: ref, 1379 (61), 1582 (15), 2305 (115), 2813 (78)
Ursano, R. J.: ref, 337 (150), 2603 (200,378,420)
Useda, J. D.: ref, 1697 (460), 2218 (41)
Usher, B. A.: ref, 997 (11)
Usher, C.: test, 300
Ushpiz, V.: ref, 557 (5)
Usmiani, S.: ref, 298 (162)
Ustad, K. L.: ref, 1697 (449)
Utley, C. A.: ref, 665 (47), 1866 (24)
Uttle, B.: ref, 2516 (66,113), 2860 (876), 2863 (258)
Utz, S. W.: ref, 2498 (44)
Uzgiris, I. C.: test, 194

Vacc, N. A.: rev, 184, 200, 399, 41, 471, 475, 1347, 2553, 2835
Vacha-Haase, T.: ref, 298 (166), 1687 (45), 2805 (2)
Vache, K.: ref, 2305 (207)
Vacher, C.: ref, 1166 (194)
Vachinich, S.: ref, 1000 (101), 1010 (113)
Vadi, M.: ref, 2218 (111)
Vagg, P. R.: test, 1354, 2497
Vaglum, P.: ref, 1093 (66), 2050 (75), 2603 (260)
Vähä-Eskeli, E.: ref, 1903 (186)
Vaidya, A. F.: ref, 1962 (4), 1991 (39), 2214 (26), 2862 (183)
Vaidya, S. R.: ref, 2383 (1)
Vail, N.: test, 904
Vaillant, C. O.: ref, 2485 (31)
Vaillant, G. E.: ref, 2485 (31)
Vaituzis, A. C.: ref, 451 (102,116), 2288 (68), 2289 (52), 2862 (450,475,493)
Vakil, E.: ref, 303 (27), 2226 (39)
Vala, N.: ref, 2905 (13)
Valadez, J. R.: ref, 665 (44)
Valanne, L.: ref, 2860 (895), 2863 (265)
Valdez, J.: ref, 2525 (7)
Valdiserri, M.: ref, 2860 (745)
Vale, W.: ref, 2305 (50)
Valencia, R. R.: ref, 307 (3), 665 (10), 693 (2), 1379 (3,79), 1421 (2), 1612 (7), 2488 (1), 2862 (58,685), 2864 (5)
Valencia, S. W.: ref, 665 (38), 1866 (16)
Valencia-Flores, M.: ref, 303 (13), 2860 (1191)
Valenstein, E.: ref, 1740 (23), 2860 (186,1309), 2863 (50)
Valenti, J. J.: test, 906
Valentine, E. R.: ref, 2050 (109)
Valentine, J. D.: ref, 2050 (109)
Valentine, L. D., Jr.: rev, 1965
Valentine, T.: ref, 2860 (606), 2863 (179)
Valentiner, D. P.: ref, 272 (195), 699 (2), 1496 (1), 2497 (406,568), 2498 (51)
Valeri-Gold, M.: ref, 615 (50), 1455 (6)
Valesio, P.: rev, 581
Valett, R. E.: test, 812, 869; rev, 2469
Valiquette, C. A. M.: ref, 2050 (69)
Valk, P.: ref, 1407 (1), 2860 (172)
Vallada, H.: ref, 2050 (32)
Vallance, D. D.: ref, 451 (288), 2452 (23), 2693 (9), 2694 (24,26), 2862 (686,739)
Vallar, G.: ref, 1903 (45), 2163 (133,306), 2225 (19), 2768 (23), 2860 (163,541,1362), 2892 (91)
Vallejo, J.: ref, 998 (35), 1166 (209), 2305 (238)
Vallerand, R. J.: ref, 1991 (17)
Valliant, P. M.: ref, 372 (79), 694 (40,61,64,88,108,109), 1321 (7), 1697 (193,230,248,367,461,462), 2497 (210,407,528), 2559 (11), 2704 (8,13,22,35,36)

Vallieres, E. F.: ref, 1991 (17)
Vallone, R. D.: ref, 1755 (68)
Valtierra, M.: ref, 1697 (522)
Valtolina, G.: ref, 1697 (524)
Valtorta, M.: ref, 1903 (538), 2163 (331)
Van Aarde, J. A.: ref, 413 (2)
Van Acker, R.: ref, 451 (57)
van Aken, M. A. G.: ref, 365 (1), 373 (18), 624 (14), 1832 (15), 1987 (9), 2864 (45)
Van Ameringen, M.: ref, 272 (93,236), 2497 (149,408, 491,572,600)
Van Ammers, E. C.: ref, 2288 (83), 2289 (68)
Van Arsdel, M.: ref, 1619 (11)
van Balkom, A. J. L. M.: ref, 2603 (178,247,349,508)
Van Bemmel, A. L.: ref, 1166 (83)
van Bon, W. H. J.: ref, 2163 (113,182), 2229 (2)
Van Bourgondien, M. E.: ref, 70 (1), 459 (14), 1653 (6), 2813 (27)
van Buchem, M. A.: ref, 231 (1), 303 (32), 2226 (42), 2227 (61), 2599 (43), 2863 (431), 2892 (307)
Van Buren, A.: ref, 2603 (558)
Van de Vijver, F. J. R.: ref, 1164 (142), 1740 (16), 2226 (18), 2516 (93), 2599 (37), 2860 (1234), 2863 (368)
Van de Vliert, E.: ref, 2149 (1)
Van de Vyvere, J.: ref, 1166 (126)
Van De Wal, C.: ref, 1758 (81), 2860 (1209)
van de Willige, G.: ref, 2050 (15)
Van De Woestijne, K. P.: ref, 2497 (292)
van dem Brink, W.: ref, 2050 (22)
Van Den Bercken, J. H. L.: ref, 2860 (79), 2892 (7)
van den Berg, B. J.: ref, 1903 (433), 2163 (248)
van den Berg, J. M.: test, 24
Van Den Bergh, O.: ref, 2497 (292)
van den Boom, D. C.: ref, 1612 (81), 1770 (13)
van den Bout, J.: ref, 1079 (68), 1079 (69,77,98)
van den Brink, W.: ref, 1079 (69), 2050 (15)
van den Broek, M. D.: ref, 2860 (542), 2892 (92)
van den Broek, P.: ref, 2862 (693)
van den Broek, Y.: ref, 2497 (409)
Van den Broucke, S.: ref, 2603 (324,421,422)
van den Heuvel, N.: ref, 2163 (307)
van den Heuvel, W. J. A.: ref, 998 (129)
van den Heuver, N.: ref, 2163 (342)
Van den Hoof-Dakker, R. H.: ref, 1166 (48)
van den Hoofdakker, R. H.: ref, 272 (271), 1079 (89), 1166 (83,111,190)
van den Hout, M.: ref, 272 (193), 2497 (566)
Van den Hout, M. A.: ref, 998 (9)
Van Den Ooord, E. J. C. G.: ref, 451 (206)
van der Broek, M. D.: ref, 2163 (193), 2860 (770)
Van Der Does, A. J. W.: ref, 1619 (5), 2050 (43,47,48), 2497 (660), 2603 (206), 2892 (83,93)
van der Ende, J.: ref, 451 (232), 999 (176)
van der Gaag, R. J.: ref, 451 (100, 681 (40,73)
van der Helm-Hylkema, H.: ref, 2076 (64), 2497 (274)
van der Hurk, P. R.: ref, 2863 (299)
van der Kolk, B. A.: test, 2521
van der Leij, A.: ref, 2862 (456)
van der Lely, H. K. J.: ref, 349 (7,34,38), 350 (10,41), 1097 (11), 1240 (19,48), 2228 (8), 2862 (568)
Van der Linden, M.: ref, 1164 (118), 2163 (134), 2516 (56,77), 2860 (771)
Van Der Mache, F.: ref, 2076 (131), 2603 (423)
van der Meere, J.: ref, 681 (68)
Van der Molen, G. M.: ref, 998 (9)
van der Pasch, M.: ref, 1079 (33)
Van Der Ploeg, H. M.: ref, 1697 (304), 2497 (227)
Van der Staak, C.: ref, 893 (47), 1010 (114), 2603 (509)
van der Staak, C. P. F.: ref, 2497 (239,323,655)
Van der Stoop, S. W.: ref, 1720 (4)
van der Velden, E.: ref, 1166 (164), 2305 (204)
Van Der Velden, H. G. M.: ref, 2497 (529)
Van der Zee, K.: ref, 999 (195)
Van Deusen, J.: ref, 1525 (5)
van Dierendonck, D.: ref, 1590 (61,68)
Van Dulmen, A. M.: ref, 2497 (529)
Van Dyck, R.: ref, 1021 (17,44), 1166 (52), 2497 (602,660), 2603 (177,178,247,349,508,559)
Van Dyke, C.: ref, 1407 (1), 2860 (172)
Van Egeren, L. A.: ref, 1698 (23), 2230 (17), 2231 (7)
van Eijk, R.: ref, 2860 (461), 2863 (129), 2892 (75)
van Elderen-van Kemenade, T.: ref, 2497 (409)
Van Engeland, H.: ref, 451 (65,66), 2813 (5)
Van Gastel, A.: ref, 1166 (77,127)
van Geert, P. L. C.: ref, 459 (37)
van Gent, E. M.: ref, 2603 (127)
Van Gerwen, L. J.: ref, 1021 (44), 2603 (559)
van Gorp, W.: ref, 272 (295), 376 (23), 1135 (16), 2599 (32), 2860 (698,1304), 2863 (204,394), 2873 (67)
van Gorp, W. G.: rev, 159, 1064, 1218, 1525, 2820; ref, 272 (181), 376 (5,35), 1135 (2,13), 1164 (187), 1166 (113), 1697 (330), 2227 (62), 2516 (122), 2599 (4,25), 2860 (200,772,1420), 2863 (324), 2892 (308)
van Grieken, N.: ref, 2603 (120)
van Haaster, I.: ref, 2050 (102)
Van Haneghan, J. P.: rev, 325, 443, 2204, 2611
Van Hasselt, V. B.: ref, 1697 (282)
Van Hecke, G. R.: rev, 43
van Hemert, A. M.: ref, 2050 (49,134)
Van Hoesen, G. W.: ref, 2227 (3), 2860 (181)
van Hoof, J.: ref, 1166 (147,211)
Van Hoof, J. J. M.: ref, 2860 (79), 2892 (7)
van Hooff, J.: ref, 681 (40)
Van Hooff, J. A. R. A. M.: ref, 451 (65)
Van Horn, G.: ref, 2860 (1192)
Van Horn, J. D.: ref, 376 (8), 2892 (230)
Van Horn, M.: ref, 472 (232)
Van Hort, W.: ref, 1093 (72), 2050 (95)
Van Hunsel, F.: ref, 1166 (217)
van Hunzel, F.: ref, 1166 (230)
Van Hutton, V.: test, 1219
van Ijzendoorn, M. H.: ref, 1092 (10), 1216 (75), 1903 (325), 2163 (153), 2905 (67)

van Kammen, D. P.: ref, 2288 (9,58), 2305 (48)
van Kammen, W. B.: ref, 2288 (9), 2305 (48)
van Kleeck, A.: ref, 1485 (64), 2682 (12)
van Knippenberg, F. C. E.: ref, 2076 (131), 2603 (423)
Van Kraayenoord, C. E.: ref, 1916 (3), 2358 (10), 2743 (3)
van Lennep, D. J.: test, 1053
van Lieshout, C. F. M.: ref, 373 (27,43), 451 (289), 1832 (15), 2860 (832), 2862 (324), 2864 (82)
van Lingen, G.: rev, 662, 2035
Van Loo, P.: ref, 451 (66)
van Mierlo, H.: ref, 1590 (40)
Van Muijen, J. J.: ref, 1736 (5)
van Os, J.: ref, 1093 (80), 2050 (80,103), 2860 (656)
van Praag, H.: ref, 2603 (105)
Van Praag, H. M.: ref, 564 (2), 2860 (218)
Van Putten, T.: ref, 2050 (85)
van Ree, J. M.: ref, 2813 (5)
Van Rensburg, E.: ref, 1659 (14)
Van Riper, C.: test, 2028
Van Roekel, B. H.: rev, 861, 901, 1072, 2254, 2487
Van Scotter, J. R.: ref, 180 (21)
Van Slyke, D. A.: ref, 472 (223), 2603 (580)
van Son, M. J.: ref, 2603 (153)
Van Spaendonck, K. P. M.: ref, 376 (12), 2516 (35), 2516 (75,87), 2860 (79,584,1007,1193), 2892 (7,211), 2226 (16), 2516 (88), 2860 (1194), 2892 (260)
Van Steenberg, N.: rev, 1158
Van Steenberg, N. J.: rev, 2757
Van Strien, J. W.: ref, 1405 (31)
Van Strien, T.: ref, 893 (49), 2603 (560)
Van Tassel-Baska, J.: ref, 2369 (1)
Van Thiel, D.: ref, 2402 (49), 2892 (208)
van Vliet, I. M.: ref, 1166 (154), 2603 (497)
Van Vunakis, H.: ref, 2603 (448)
Van Whitlock, R.: ref, 472 (93,94), 1745 (43,59, 82,86,89), 2076 (87,88), 2107 (2), 2603 (394)
van Widenfelt, B.: ref, 1010 (114), 2603 (509)
Van Wyk, P. H.: ref, 1000 (12)
Van Yperen, N. W.: ref, 2603 (158)
van Zanten, G. A.: ref, 1485 (9), 1903 (113), 2860 (346)
van Zijderveld, G.: ref, 2497 (602)
van Zomeren, A. H.: ref, 1164 (134), 2226 (15), 2516 (86)
van Zutphen, W. M.: ref, 1661 (29)
van-der Keshet, Y.: ref, 2247 (91)
VanAmeringen, M.: ref, 2497 (293)
Vance, B.: ref, 301 (30), 1699 (1), 2704 (9), 2862 (411), 2879 (147)
Vance, F. L.: rev, 68
Vance, H.: ref, 2862 (569)
Vance, H. B.: ref, 665 (77), 1226 (3), 1699 (2), 2862 (614)
Vance, H. R.: test, 2431
Vance, R.: ref, 241 (2), 266 (1), 324 (6), 331 (3), 430 (9), 540 (20), 628 (1), 994 (17,47), 1047 (2), 1240 (9), 1379 (54,95), 1485 (11), 1804 (10), 1903 (138,297,535), 2044 (6), 2045 (6), 2190 (8), 2233 (3), 2382 (12,25,39), 2524 (6,12), 2657 (16), 2660 (4), 2680 (10), 2695 (28), 2801 (3)
vanDam, G.: ref, 2163 (53)
Vandell, D. L.: ref, 2496 (4), 2497 (661)
Vandemeulebroecke, L.: ref, 2497 (441)
vandenBerg, A. R.: test, 1370
Vandenberg, B.: ref, 1903 (216)
Vandenberg, S. G.: rev, 625
Vandenbroucke, J. P.: ref, 2050 (49)
Vandenriessche, F.: ref, 2497 (292)
Vander Steene, G.: ref, 745 (20), 2163 (278)
Vanderark, S. D.: ref, 853 (25), 2862 (687)
VanDerEnde, J.: ref, 999 (5)
Vandereycken, W.: ref, 451 (172), 2603 (324,421,422)
Vandergoot, D.: ref, 1697 (14), 2860 (55), 2879 (7)
Vanderploeg, R. D.: ref, 2860 (746,773,1195), 2862 (670), 2892 (155)
Vanderwal, J. S.: ref, 337 (187)
Vanderwood, M.: ref, 837 (12), 1378 (8), 2485 (230), 2901 (124)
VanderZee, K. I.: ref, 1079 (56)
Vandevelde, R.: ref, 1166 (19)
Vandewoude, M.: ref, 1166 (5), 1166 (20), 2497 (25,127)
Vandiver, P. A.: ref, 337 (119), 999 (137)
Vandiver, R.: ref, 1697 (103), 2305 (44)
Vandiver, T.: ref, 997 (18)
Vandoolaeghe, E.: ref, 1166 (76,78,126,128,230)
Vandvik, I. H.: ref, 1000 (59)
VanEys, P. L.: ref, 1903 (390)
Vanhanen, M.: ref, 2860 (913), 2863 (273)
VanHooff, J. A. R. A. M.: ref, 451 (66)
VanHorn, M.: ref, 472 (214)
vanIJzendoorn, M. H.: ref, 1903 (109)
VanKeimpema, A. R. J.: ref, 2516 (15)
vanKleeck, A.: ref, 1421 (1)
Vanla, G.: ref, 2227 (8), 2860 (364), 2879 (44), 2892 (54)
vanLoenen, A. C.: ref, 2599 (22)
Vannatta, K.: ref, 472 (182), 2242 (7), 2862 (525)
vanPraag, H. M.: ref, 1166 (1), 2305 (12)
VanPutten, T.: ref, 2603 (74)
VanReekum, R.: ref, 1903 (381), 2305 (144)
Vansickle, T. R.: ref, 1790 (5)
VanStrien, J. W.: ref, 2862 (412)
VanTassel-Baska, J.: ref, 615 (9)
VanVelsor, E.: test, 2425
VanVoorhis, P.: ref, 1697 (17)
VanWagenen, M. A.: ref, 2905 (68)
VanWort, W.: ref, 2288 (19)
Vanyukov, M.: ref, 2862 (372)
Vanyukov, M. M.: ref, 2010 (15)
VanYyukov, M.: ref, 1902 (76)
Varca, P. E.: ref, 1701 (10)
Vargha-Khadem, F.: ref, 2860 (838,1099), 2862 (492,628), 2863 (243), 2864 (117)
Varghese, F. T.: ref, 1093 (91)
Varghese, T.: ref, 2305 (192)
Vargo, F. E.: ref, 2862 (413)

Varia, R.: ref, 372 (106), 694 (120)
Varma, V. K.: ref, 1697 (368)
Varnado, P. J.: ref, 999 (144)
Varnavides, R.: ref, 2497 (130)
Varney, N. R.: ref, 1697 (577), 2860 (880)
Varni, J. W.: ref, 272 (237), 451 (157), 472 (42,68,151), 1010 (115), 2497 (601), 2498 (20,25)
Vasa, S.: ref, 1903 (498)
Vasa, S. F.: rev, 799, 831, 1262; ref, 75 (1), 694 (76), 1379 (56), 1386 (9), 2211 (31,34), 2432 (20), 2485 (144,145), 2862 (276,285), 2864 (67), 2879 (90), 2901 (46)
Vasey, M. W.: ref, 472 (152), 2214 (86), 2498 (56), 2905 (93)
Vasile, R.: ref, 1093 (73), 1517 (9), 2519 (46), 2520 (47)
Vasile, R. G.: ref, 998 (57), 1093 (52), 1697 (236), 2305 (135)
Vasquez, A. M.: ref, 2603 (390)
Vasterling, J.: ref, 1164 (33), 2603 (140), 2860 (344), 2863 (92), 2892 (49)
Vasterling, J. J.: ref, 2497 (401,548)
Vataja, R.: ref, 2860 (895), 2863 (265)
Vater, S.: test, 1263
Vaughan, A.: ref, 1653 (12)
Vaughan, J. K.: ref, 863 (38), 2497 (238)
Vaughan, K.: ref, 2497 (410)
Vaughan-Cole, B.: ref, 1178 (14)
Vaughn, B. E.: ref, 1086 (3), 2813 (79)
Vaughn, H. G., Jr.: ref, 1096 (9), 2668 (1), 2694 (14), 2860 (912)
Vaughn, M. L.: ref, 280 (5)
Vaughn, M. L.: ref, 451 (231)
Vaughn, S.: ref, 1072 (53), 1386 (2), 1987 (2,12), 1991 (108), 2211 (8,25), 2452 (2,3,8), 2484 (9), 2488 (4,6,7), 2862 (226,227,295,570), 2901 (34,35,103)
Vaughn, V. L.: ref, 1991 (28), 2252 (2)
Vaughter, R. M.: ref, 298 (131)
Vauss, Y. C.: ref, 451 (102), 2862 (450)
Vavak, C. R.: ref, 1697 (130), 1881 (2)
Vazeux, R.: ref, 2517 (1), 2860 (527)
Vazquez, C. A.: ref, 1903 (434)
Vazquez-Barquero, J. L.: ref, 2050 (135), 2288 (59), 2289 (45)
Vazsonyi, A. T.: ref, 451 (36)
Vealey, R. S.: ref, 1590 (18), 2497 (211)
Vebanac, P.: ref, 335 (3)
Vecchia, R. D.: ref, 2862 (323)
Vecchio, R. P.: rev, 1180, 2051
Vecchione, V.: ref, 2163 (114)
Veeninga, A. T.: ref, 2603 (325)
Veerbeck, M.: ref, 451 (65)
Vehara, N.: ref, 272 (332)
Veiel, H. O. F.: ref, 301 (57), 376 (29)
Veith, R. C.: ref, 2863 (83)
Velasquez, J.: ref, 2065 (6)
Velasquez, R. J.: ref, 1697 (162,194,578)
Veldman, D. J.: rev, 670
Velicer, W. F.: ref, 1334 (3), 1965 (11)
Vellette, N.: ref, 2860 (1299)
Velligan, D. I.: ref, 2603 (89)
Vellutino, F. F.: ref, 1092 (17), 1903 (435)
Vellutino, F. R.: rev, 1357; ref, 2901 (114)
Velozo, C. A.: ref, 398 (4), 2797 (8)
Velting, D. M.: ref, 540 (9), 2485 (207), 2860 (1302), 2862 (508), 2879 (172,210)
Velting, D. M.: ref, 2905 (99,114)
Velting, O. N.: ref, 681 (88), 2879 (221), 2905 (117)
Veltkamp, L. J.: ref, 451 (67), 472 (138), 1991 (81), 2305 (149), 2498 (53)
Veltman, D. J.: ref, 2497 (602)
Venable, G. P.: test, 1427
Venable, W. M.: ref, 1697 (599), 2603 (593)
Venables, P. H.: ref, 2211 (43)
Vendrell, P.: ref, 1164 (155), 2226 (26), 2516 (100), 2860 (1290)
Venn, M. L.: ref, 994 (44), 1903 (509), 2485 (219), 2695 (64), 2813 (132), 2864 (126)
Venneri, A.: ref, 2860 (774)
Vennix, P.: test, 2396
Venter, A.: ref, 1485 (15), 1653 (7), 1903 (148), 2163 (98), 2813 (28), 2860 (411)
Venters, T. L.: ref, 1010 (90), 1903 (436), 2862 (416)
Ventrella, M. A.: ref, 2497 (5)
Ventura, J.: ref, 1697 (188), 2305 (73), 2860 (384)
Venturi, P.: ref, 1697 (204)
Vera, C.: ref, 2860 (1306)
Vera, M. N.: ref, 2076 (102), 2497 (411)
Verbanck, P.: ref, 1166 (194)
Verble, J. S.: ref, 1755 (60)
Verboncoeur, C. J.: ref, 2603 (552)
Verbraak, M.: ref, 893 (47)
Verbraecken, J.: ref, 303 (24), 2125 (28), 2163 (345), 2516 (114)
Verburg, K.: ref, 2497 (530,583)
Verda, M. R.: ref, 2498 (69)
Verdi, W. M.: rev, 2644
Verfaellie, M.: ref, 2193 (59), 2860 (229,243,314,337, 412,658,775,833,1201), 2863 (59,61,85,89,110,193, 27,240), 2873 (31)
Vergara, A. I.: ref, 999 (176)
Vergara, K. C.: ref, 891 (1)
Verhaeghen, P.: ref, 1405 (37), 2599 (36), 2860 (1196)
Verhage, F.: ref, 2497 (285)
Verheij, R.: ref, 2497 (191)
Verhoeff, N. P. L. G.: ref, 1093 (50)
Verhoeve, M.: test, 1334
Verhoeven, L. T.: ref, 2163 (79)
Verhulst, F. C.: ref, 451 (31,81,206,212,232,276), 2862 (648)
Vérin, M.: ref, 2163 (295), 2860 (1153), 2863 (342), 2892 (94)
Verkerk, R.: ref, 1166 (217)
Verkuyten, M.: ref, 1991 (62)
Vermeulen, S. C.: ref, 1408 (3)
Vernberg, E. M.: ref, 451 (80)
Verney, S. P.: ref, 2305 (207)

Vernon, L. N.: test, 1840
Vernon, M. D.: rev, 1765
Vernon, P. A.: ref, 495 (15), 963 (2), 1010 (130), 1731 (3), 1732 (2), 1965 (84)f, 2218 (63), 2864 (121)
Vernon, P. E.: test, 1103, 1105, 1600, 2539; rev, 374, 1156, 1201, 1396, 1717
Vernon, P. V.: rev, 725
Vernon, S. W.: ref, 2497 (662), 2860 (132)
Vernon-Feagans, L.: ref, 2382 (36)
Vernoy, M. W.: ref, 2516 (57)
Versluis-den Bieman, H. J. M.: ref, 451 (31,81)
Verspui, L.: ref, 2076 (164), 2516 (92)
Verstraeton, E.: ref, 303 (24), 2125 (28), 2163 (345), 2516 (114)
Vertommen, H.: ref, 2603 (324), 2603 (421), 2603 (422)
Vestergaard, A.: ref, 2050 (66)
Vestre, N. D.: test, 2120
Vetter, D. K.: rev, 494, 630, 2693
Viader, F.: ref, 2863 (45)
Vicari, S.: ref, 540 (13), 1485 (55), 1903 (501,502), 2163 (99), 2227 (34), 2860 (1237), 2862 (571,572)
Vickers, D.: ref, 1164 (137), 2163 (249)
Vickers, H.: ref, 1000 (80)
Vickers, H. S.: ref, 1000 (93)
Vickers, R. R., Jr.: ref, 2218 (14)
Vidailhet, M.: ref, 776 (54,63)
Vidotto, G.: ref, 999 (16), 2497 (52)
Viegner, B.: ref, 2860 (1378), 2879 (226), 2892 (296)
Vieira-Baker, C. C.: ref, 337 (149)
Viele, K.: ref, 540 (17), 1903 (520)
Vieta, E.: ref, 2305 (238)
Vig, S.: ref, 2485 (217)
Viggedal, G.: ref, 1134 (3)
Vigliardi, M. V.: ref, 2163 (114)
Viglione, D.: ref, 1941 (1), 2247 (92), 2397 (1)
Viglione, D. J.: ref, 790 (23)
Viglione, D. J., Jr.: rev, 2248; ref, 68 (26), 2247 (27,98), 2402 (55)
Vigneau, F.: ref, 1903 (584), 2485 (245)
Vignolo, L. A.: ref, 2163 (8)
ViHone, B. H.: ref, 2497 (114)
Viitanen, M.: ref, 2860 (1351)
Vik, P. W.: ref, 134 (39), 1166 (70), 2414 (3), 2858 (90)
Viken, R. J.: ref, 998 (84), 1903 (322)
Vila, J.: ref, 2076 (102), 2497 (411)
Vilkki, J.: ref, 2125 (1), 2516 (58), 2860 (56,143,144, 413,776,777,1028), 2892 (60)
Villa, A.: ref, 298 (68), 2247 (25), 2603 (148)
Villanova, P.: rev, 1843
Villanueva, M. R.: ref, 1697 (102)
Villanueva-Meyer, J.: ref, 2227 (6), 2516 (13), 2860 (286), 2863 (76), 2892 (37)
Villarreal, P.: ref, 337 (67), 2525 (7)
Villemure, J.-G.: ref, 2860 (1306)
Villongco, M. L.: test, 306
Vincent, A., ref, 1166 (195), 2516 (103)
Vincent, D.: test, 835, 1781, 2179
Vincent, E.: ref, 2163 (211), 2860 (857), 2863 (251)
Vincent, K.: ref, 1939 (3)
Vincent, K. R.: ref, 372 (18), 462 (19), 1294 (4), 1697 (85,111), 2076 (14), 2417 (21), 2603 (57)
Vincent, L. C.: ref, 1697 (179), 2227 (7), 2860 (363), 2863 (95)
Vincent, N.: ref, 1164 (137)
Vincent, P.: ref, 1166 (125,195), 2516 (103)
Vinent, K. R.: ref, 1698 (1)
Vines, C.: ref, 746 (2)
Vingerhoets, F. J. G.: ref, 2125 (27)
Vining, E. P. G.: ref, 994 (31), 1903 (427), 2768 (31), 2862 (405)
Vinkler, E.: ref, 450 (2)
Vinogradov, S.: ref, 2860 (351)
Violanti, J. M.: ref, 2603 (517)
Violato, C.: ref, 1466 (2), 2858 (47)
Virdin, L.: ref, 472 (38)
Virdin, L. M.: ref, 472 (87), 472 (88), 1000 (70)
Virella, B.: ref, 2498 (45)
Vires-Collins, H.: ref, 2860 (1218)
Virkkunen, M.: ref, 1697 (369), 2305 (88), 2860 (778)
Virtual Knowledge: test, 412
Virtue, C.: ref, 2603 (510)
Visintainer, P.: ref, 272 (36), 2603 (62)
Vispoel, W. D.: ref, 2656 (15)
Vispoel, W. P.: ref, 2656 (16)
Visscher, B.: ref, 1135 (2,6), 1740 (8), 2076 (85), 2599 (4,8), 2860 (200,287,664)
Visscher, B. R.: ref, 791 (11), 2858 (82)
Visscher, F.: ref, 2516 (15)
Visser, R. S. H.: test, 641
Viswanathan, M.: ref, 2163 (346)
Viswesvaran, C.: rev, 2777; ref, 68 (59), 189 (1), 372 (105), 998 (120), 1697 (504), 2417 (36)
Vitale, B. M.: test, 157
Vitali, G. J.: test, 663, 1400, 2434, 2706
Vitaliano, P. D.: ref, 2603 (29), 2858 (9)
Vitaliano, P. P.: ref, 272 (74), 1166 (40), 2603 (75), 2858 (22,109)
Vitaro, F.: ref, 472 (70,11,199), 1661 (78), 1866 (33), 2039 (14,15,16,17,23)
Viteles, M. S.: rev, 1700
Vitelli, R.: test, 950
Vitiello, B.: ref, 2863 (100)
Vito, D.: ref, 863 (67)
Vitti, R. J.: ref, 301 (47), 2516 (63), 2863 (233), 2879 (105), 2892 (166)
Vittone, B. J.: ref, 272 (92), 2305 (114), 2497 (405)
Vivian, D.: ref, 863 (51)
Viyse, S. A.: ref, 298 (95)
Vlachos, F. M.: ref, 2227 (39)
Vlahor, D.: ref, 2227 (10), 2599 (9), 2860 (401)
Vlahov, D.: ref, 1135 (22), 1164 (169), 2226 (35), 2227 (50)
V-Mar, I. D.: ref, 844 (5)

Vnek, N.: ref, 2860 (642)
Vockell, E. L.: ref, 665 (22)
Vodde-Hamilton, M.: ref, 1745 (83)
Voderholzer, V.: ref, 1166 (144)
Voelker, S.: ref, 1379 (81), 1902 (79), 1903 (440), 2228 (20), 2657 (28), 2862 (100), 2879 (23)
Voelkl, K. E.: ref, 665 (75)
Vogel, F.: ref, 2163 (259)
Vogel, S. A.: ref, 2879 (52), 2901 (22)
Vogler, D. E.: rev, 939, 2775
Vogt, E. R.: ref, 2163 (231)
Vogt, R. A.: ref, 272 (382), 1697 (469), 2076 (139)
Voica, M.: ref, 272 (370), 2497 (673)
Voice, J. K.: ref, 2163 (344), 2860 (1361), 2862 (684)
Voigts, A. L.: ref, 2497 (617)
Vojvoda, D.: ref, 2603 (426)
Volanth, A. J.: ref, 997 (2)
Volavka, J.: ref, 1164 (58), 2892 (109)
Volckens, J. S.: ref, 1697 (158)
Volden, J.: ref, 459 (12), 1903 (96), 2860 (315)
Volet, S. E.: ref, 2540 (5)
Volk, R. J.: ref, 337 (28), 2858 (30)
Volkmar, F.: ref, 2247 (13), 2860 (251)
Volkmar, F. R.: ref, 1379 (15,36), 1485 (23), 2485 (49), 2813 (17,52), 2860 (543,932,779)
Volling, B. L.: ref, 472 (32), 1770 (10), 1965 (30), 2382 (36)
Vollmer, H.: ref, 2863 (350,404)
Vollrath, D. A.: ref, 771 (6)
Vollrath, M.: ref, 1687 (24)
Volpe, A. D.: ref, 2008 (8)
Volpe, B. T.: ref, 2863 (7)
Volpe, L.: ref, 459 (18), 2485 (82), 2813 (35)
Volpe, M.: ref, 462 (26), 1661 (49)
Volpicelli, J. R.: ref, 2603 (169,561)
Volpicelli, L. A.: ref, 2603 (561)
Volterra, V.: ref, 540 (13), 1903 (501,502), 2227 (34), 2862 (571,572)
Volz, H-P.: ref, 1166 (67,216)
von Bardeleben, U.: ref, 1166 (29)
Von Bergen, C. W.: ref, 694 (121)
Von Brieson, P. D.: ref, 1097 (14), 2485 (188), 2862 (431)
von Cramon, D. Y.: ref, 2239 (8,15), 2863 (139,155), 2892 (79)
von Cranach, M.: ref, 2050 (36)
von Knorring, A-L.: ref, 2862 (617)
Von Korff, M.: ref, 2218 (16), 2603 (44,170)
von Mollendorf, J. W.: test, 2774
Von Roekel, B. H.: rev, 2253
Von Staabs, G.: test, 2303
von Zerssen, D.: ref, 2860 (1363)
VonCleve, E.: ref, 1697 (148), 2559 (2)
Vondra, J. I.: ref, 451 (90,282), 1216 (74), 1903 (443), 1965 (61,79), 1987 (17)
Vondracek, F. W.: ref, 404 (9,10,29,46), 1754 (14), 2915 (4,6,8)
Vondrácek, J.: ref, 2485 (195), 2862 (460)
VonKorff, M.: ref, 2603 (474)
Voogel, A.: rev, 2337
Voran, M.: ref, 875 (6), 1264 (2)
Voress, J. K.: test, 759, 806, 816, 2722
Vorst, H. C. M.: ref, 838 (20)
Vorstenbosch, M.: ref, 2050 (134)
Vorster, J.: test, 2458, 2661
Vostanis, P.: ref, 1010 (89), 2214 (113), 2305 (205)
Vouri, J.: ref, 2163 (69)
Voyten, K. K.: ref, 404 (44)
Vozzola, E.: ref, 298 (131)
Vrana, S. R.: ref, 2497 (531), 2879 (148,154)
Vraniak, D. A.: ref, 2603 (208)
Vuchinich, R.: ref, 863 (45,57)
Vuchinich, R. E.: ref, 1661 (36)
Vuchinich, S.: ref, 863 (45,57), 1903 (454)
Vullo, K.: ref, 1000 (26)
Vulpe, S. G.: test, 2838
Vunakis, H. V.: ref, 2076 (110), 2603 (343)
Vye, N. J.: ref, 389 (4), 1072 (18)
Vygotsky, L.: test, 1714
Vysal, S.: ref, 2227 (17), 2863 (213)
Vyse, S. A.: ref, 1745 (46)

Waadts, S.: ref, 2497 (632)
Waber, D. P.: ref, 2862 (414), 2901 (76)
Wachs, T. D.: ref, 2163 (308), 2860 (1197), 2862 (415)
Wachsmuth, R.: ref, 272 (258), 893 (42), 1405 (39), 1903 (517), 2862 (595)
Wachspress, M.: ref, 1093 (35)
Wachtel, J.: ref, 2498 (46)
Wachter, S.: ref, 2603 (19)
Wacker, D. P.: rev, 804, 2400
Waclawski, J.: ref, 1755 (76)
Wada, J.: ref, 2860 (224,762), 2862 (115), 2863 (57)
Waddell, S.: ref, 1987 (13)
Wadden, T. A.: ref, 272 (382), 1697 (469), 2076 (139)
Waddington, S. R.: ref, 2497 (212)
Wade, J. B.: ref, 2076 (5), 2497 (43), 2860 (544), 2863 (156)
Wade, S. E.: ref, 1672 (2), 2879 (20)
Wade, T.: ref, 271 (13), 337 (181), 2497 (648), 2603 (532)
Wade, W. A.: ref, 272 (383)
Wade-Woolley, L.: ref, 1903 (177), 2905 (37)
Wadell, D. C.: test, 1418
Wadhwa, N. K.: ref, 2497 (140,473)
Wadlington, S.: ref, 301 (50), 472 (144), 1991 (86), 2862 (390)
Wadsworth, S. J.: ref, 1392 (10), 1902 (50), 2862 (228)
Wadsworth, T.: ref, 1380 (2)
Waehler, C. A.: ref, 298 (134), 2749 (38)
Waetjen, W. B.: test, 2356
Waggener, N. M.: ref, 337 (68)
Wagner, A. E.: ref, 1612 (25), 2125 (30), 2768 (43), 2864 (144)
Wagner, B.: ref, 2603 (146)

Wagner, B. M.: ref, 2603 (76)
Wagner, C. C.: ref, 1243 (4)
Wagner, C. F.: ref, 2247 (96)
Wagner, C. R.: ref, 2247 (10), 2749 (17)
Wagner, D.: ref, 1140 (60), 1592 (28)
Wagner, E.: ref, 1164 (110), 1740 (11), 2010 (20), 2860 (971)
Wagner, E. E.: test, 1169; rev, 2248; ref, 301 (14), 1169 (2,3,4), 1959 (7), 2247 (75,76,78,96,136), 2860 (197,1198)
Wagner, G.: ref, 337 (90), 1001 (3,7)
Wagner, H. N., Jr.: ref, 1697 (88), 2050 (125), 2402 (6)
Wagner, J. K.: ref, 462 (13), 1661 (37)
Wagner, J. L.: ref, 681 (6)
Wagner, M. E.: test, 354, 851
Wagner, R. K.: ref, 2163 (81), 2485 (47), 2905 (7,19)
Wagner, R. M.: ref, 1436 (1)
Wagner, W.: ref, 472 (20)
Wagster, M. V.: ref, 815 (49), 1164 (173), 1740 (27), 2516 (115), 2860 (1374), 2892 (294)
Waguespack, M. M.: test, 868
Wahby, V.: ref, 2519 (14), 2520 (15)
Wahl, J.: ref, 994 (23), 1903 (362), 2695 (35), 2862 (341), 2901 (63)
Wahl, P.: ref, 2288 (3)
Wahlberg, K.: ref, 2288 (2), 2860 (53)
Wahlberg, K-E.: ref, 2247 (120)
Wahler, H. J.: test, 2839
Wahler, R. G.: ref, 272 (228), 297 (2), 451 (156,158,233)
Wahlsten, V. S.: ref, 1134 (5)
Wahlstrom, J.: ref, 1164 (60), 1697 (275), 2305 (98)
Wahlund, L.: ref, 2860 (423), 2863 (111)
Wainer, H.: ref, 94 (1,2,3), 117 (4), 666 (15), 1759 (17)
Waisberg, J. L.: ref, 2126 (12)
Waite, B. M.: ref, 1697 (302), 2599 (18), 2860 (645)
Waite, J.: ref, 537 (3)
Waites, M.: ref, 2519 (17), 2520 (18)
Waitley, D.: test, 1930, 1955
Waizman, A.: ref, 2305 (118)
Wakano, H.: ref, 2305 (241)
Wakefield, D.: ref, 1079 (39), 1241 (5)
Wakefield, J. F.: rev, 727
Waksman, S. A.: test, 2012, 2841
Walberg, H. J.: ref, 1759 (6)
Walbone, D.: ref, 2218 (73)
Walcott, D.: ref, 1740 (7)
Walczak, S.: ref, 272 (310)
Walczyk, J. J.: ref, 1592 (5)
Walden Personnel Performance, Inc.: test, 16, 249, 688, 756, 988, 1330, 2205, 2206, 2277, 2374, 2646, 2851
Walden Personnel Testing: test, 1568
Waldie, K.: ref, 287 (1)
Waldie, K. E.: ref, 694 (122), 1903 (503)
Waldinger, R. J.: ref, 2603 (326)
Waldkoetter, R. O.: ref, 1697 (579)
Waldman, D. A.: ref, 2797 (2)
Waldman, I. D.: ref, 745 (23), 2860 (524)
Waldo, M.: ref, 2305 (4)
Waldorf, A. V.: ref, 1164 (88), 2860 (825), 2892 (168)
Waldorf, V. A.: ref, 893 (13), 2519 (33), 2520 (34)
Waldren, T.: ref, 1000 (10)
Waldron, C.: ref, 2497 (231)
Waldron, J.: ref, 2497 (605)
Waldron, J. A.: ref, 2749 (53)
Waldron, W. J.: rev, 1080, 1537, 2635, 2789
Waldrop, D. G.: ref, 2835 (17)
Waldstein, S. R.: ref, 1135 (19), 1164 (138) 2497 (603), 2516 (89), 2860 (1199,1200), 2863 (360)
Wales, M. L.: ref, 233 (2) 971 (2)
Wales, R. J.: ref, 2520 (36)
Waligroski, K.: ref, 694 (53)
Walker, A. M.: ref, 373 (33)
Walker, B.: ref, 272 (215), 1697 (510), 2497 (587): ref, 2858 (118)
Walker, B. A.: ref, 2652 (10)
Walker, C. A.: ref, 1036 (12)
Walker, D.: ref, 665 (47,71), 681 (79), 1380 (16), 1657 (11,13), 1866 (24,30,34), 1903 (326), 2485 (152), 2694 (11), 2695 (32), 2879 (95)
Walker, E.: ref, 2218 (16), 2603 (474)
Walker, E. A.: ref, 846 (11)
Walker, E. F.: ref, 353 (22), 451 (167), 2125 (23), 2288 (41), 2289 (31), 2305 (116), 2860 (1118), 2892 (232)
Walker, E. M.: ref, 665 (5)
Walker, H. M.: test, 890, 2311, 2607, 2848
Walker, J.: ref, 2211 (25), 2452 (2), 2488 (7), 2862 (227)
Walker, J. A.: test, 1655
Walker, J. G.: ref, 863 (34)
Walker, J. U.: ref, 2305 (194)
Walker, K. C.: ref, 451 (159), 681 (80), 2452 (16)
Walker, L. M.: ref, 2771 (42)
Walker, L. S.: ref, 472 (18,19,223), 2498 (14,15), 2603 (327,580)
Walker, M.: ref, 1685 (2)
Walker, M. R.: ref, 2163 (142)
Walker, M. T.: ref, 2860 (515), 2892 (86)
Walker, M. V.: test, 1342
Walker, N.: ref, 2860 (1364)
Walker, N. L.: ref, 2076 (141)
Walker, P.: ref, 1145 (2), 1164 (147), 1758 (30), 2163 (170), 2863 (219)
Walker, R.: ref, 1758 (80), 2860 (316)
Walker, S.: ref, 472 (90), 1134 (4), 1903 (263), 2211 (30), 2214 (50), 2485 (130), 2862 (265), 2879 (78)
Walkey, F.: ref, 272 (41)
Wall, C. R.: ref, 272 (315), 451 (223)
Wall, D. D.: ref, 2603 (124,419)
Wall, R.: rev, 2157, 2690
Wall, S. M.: rev, 2123
Wall, W. D.: rev, 729, 2163, 2477, 2478
Wallace, A.: ref, 472 (131), 557 (7)

Wallace, C. J.: ref, 1697 (68), 2050 (5,67), 2879 (74), 2892 (110)
Wallace, C. S.: ref, 1010 (100)
Wallace, D. S.: ref, 373 (23)
Wallace, G. : test, 655, 656
Wallace, I. F.: ref, 681 (19), 2382 (9), 2485 (53)
Wallace, J.: ref, 1093 (105)
Wallace, K. A.: ref, 364 (11), 2484 (4)
Wallace, M.: test, 2364
Wallace, N. V.: ref, 451 (218), 2452 (20), 2485 (233), 2813 (151)
Wallace, S. R.: rev, 937, 2272, 857
Wallace, T. L.: ref, 2497 (325)
Wallace, W. L.: rev, 56, 592, 617
Wallach, M. A.: rev, 2771
Wallander, J. L.: ref, 337 (151), 1010 (90), 1903 (436), 2076 (162), 2813 (153), 2862 (416)
Wallbrown, F.: ref, 372 (62), 1965 (48)
Wallbrown, F. H.: ref, 1201 (5), 1687 (13), 1697 (26,97), 1731 (1), 2860 (1043), 2862 (444), 2864 (111)
Wallen, N. E.: rev, 1196
Waller, B.: ref, 272 (214), 1697 (509), 2497 (586)
Waller, D.: ref, 2111 (2), 2163 (247), 2862 (145,410), 2864 (24)
Waller, D. A.: ref, 433 (12), 1086 (2), 1164 (80), 1240 (30), 1612 (60), 1902 (60), 2485 (150), 2860 (760), 2864 (74)
Waller, G.: ref, 846 (6), 2516 (76)
Waller, M. I.: ref, 665 (17)
Waller, N. G.: rev, 271, 272, 846, 1313, 2288, 2563, 2564; ref, 372 (107), 998 (36), 1697 (149)
Waller, S.: ref, 739 (8)
Waller, T. G.: ref, 745 (11), 1072 (44)
Wallerstein, J. S.: ref, 1093 (4)
Wallesch, C.: ref, 1405 (13), 2163 (160), 2860 (230)
Wallesch, C.-W.: ref, 2163 (54)
Wallfisch, A.: ref, 2076 (110), 2603 (343,448)
Walling, D. P.: ref, 2652 (10)
Walls, R. T.: test, 1245, 2827; ref, 665 (94), 2030 (1)
Wallsten, S. M.: ref, 2163 (11), 2860 (37)
Wally, S.: ref, 1338 (43)
Walsh, A.: ref, 2076 (121), 2860 (414), 2862 (186)
Walsh, B.: ref, 451 (264)
Walsh, B. D.: ref, 2805 (2)
Walsh, B. T.: ref, 1093 (21), 2603 (562)
Walsh, C.: ref, 2050 (54)
Walsh, D.: ref, 2305 (21)
Walsh, J. A.: rev, 372, 770, 2417; ref, 1698 (19), 2247 (121), 2595 (1), 2862 (697)
Walsh, K.: ref, 272 (250), 846 (20), 2497 (608)
Walsh, M. E.: ref, 1338 (31), 1686 (3)
Walsh, S. K.: ref, 1455 (10), 1866 (32)
Walsh, W. B.: rev, 2835; ref, 695 (3), 1697 (395), 1790 (6), 2126 (6), 2835 (2,6), 2858 (96)
Walsh-Riddle, M.: ref, 303 (2), 1164 (23), 2497 (104), 2603 (83), 2860 (237)
Walstad, W. B.: test, 2685, 2686; ref, 2686 (1)
Walter, C.: ref, 1169 (6)
Walter, L. J.: ref, 1164 (45), 2860 (454)
Walter, L. W.: ref, 815 (11), 1379 (31), 1612 (39), 1903 (201), 2125 (9), 2485 (101), 2813 (43), 2901 (32)
Walter, V.: test, 2364, 2419
Walters, A.: test, 127
Walters, A. S.: test, 1288; ref, 1288 (2), 2813 (111)
Walters, D. A.: ref, 1404 (2)
Walters, E. E.: ref, 999 (145,160), 2603 (273)
Walters, G. D.: ref, 1697 (11,18)
Walters, M. C.: ref, 1661 (42)
Walther, D. J.: ref, 2065 (19)
Waltman, K. K.: ref, 1318 (21)
Walton, H. N.: test, 867
Walton, J. M.: ref, 998 (119), 1079 (74), 2497 (578), 2603 (484)
Walton, J. R.: ref, 2862 (688)
Walton, P. D.: ref, 1903 (437), 2901 (77)
Walton, S. A.: ref, 335 (14)
Walton, V. A.: ref, 2050 (44,45)
Walton-Allen, N.: ref, 1216 (99), 2860 (1262), 2862 (608), 2879 (201)
Walz, N. C.: ref, 1903 (504), 2211 (49), 2862 (573)
Walzer, C.: ref, 1166 (109)
Wampler, K. S.: ref, 863 (26), 1000 (23), 2603 (138)
Wampler, R. S.: ref, 1755 (38)
Wampold, B. E.: ref, 1178 (14)
Wanberg, C. R.: ref, 1079 (99,100), 2218 (77), 2858 (129)
Wanberg, K. W.: test, 136
Wander, M. R.: ref, 1186 (1)
Wanderling, J.: ref, 2050 (101)
Wandersman, A.: ref, 2603 (168)
Wang, A.: ref, 1987 (21)
Wang, C-M.: ref, 1128 (4)
Wang, D. F.: ref, 2050 (125)
Wang, G. J.: ref, 2860 (779)
Wang, H-Y. J.: ref, 791 (11), 2858 (82)
Wang, J.: ref, 666 (11)
Wang, J-J.: test, 1903
Wang, L.: ref, 2065 (34,35)
Wang, M. A.: ref, 1178 (6)
Wang, P. L.: test, 1714
Wang, P. P.: ref, 815 (32), 1379 (80), 1725 (7)
Wang, S.: ref, 301 (38), 2860 (622)
Wang, T.: ref, 2656 (16)
Wang, X.: ref, 94 (2,3)
Wang, Z.: ref, 180 (15)
Wangensteen, D.: ref, 272 (195), 2497 (568)
Wanigaratne, S.: ref, 2603 (424)
Wanke, A.: ref, 375 (7), 2862 (705)
Wanlass, R. L.: ref, 1697 (448)
Wannon, M.: ref, 681 (34)
Wanstall, K.: ref, 1021 (8), 2497 (82)
Wantabe, H. K.: ref, 2214 (104)
Wantman, M. J.: rev, 1638
Wantz, R. A.: rev, 1624, 1889, 2053

Warach, S.: ref, 1672 (1)
Warburton, D.: ref, 1758 (68), 2863 (320)
Warburton, R.: ref, 1010 (69), 1092 (11,14), 2860 (801,1203), 2862 (308), 2879 (100,187)
Warburton, V. L.: ref, 1697 (266)
Ward, A. W.: rev, 461, 1041, 2410, 2879
Ward, C.: ref, 298 (123), 999 (67,68), 2076 (71), 2077 (7)
Ward, C. F.: rev, 921
Ward, D.: ref, 998 (44)
Ward, G.: test, 492, 2091
Ward, J.: ref, 326 (7), 451 (221), 2860 (574)
Ward, J. P.: ref, 838 (4)
Ward, K. D.: ref, 2417 (30)
Ward, L. C.: ref, 1697 (47,112,463,471,600), 2603 (440), 2860 (1008)
Ward, M. F.: ref, 1903 (374), 2524 (9), 2695 (39), 2704 (27), 2768 (29)
Ward, M. J.: ref, 2860 (1009)
Ward, M. M.: ref, 2076 (160)
Ward, M. N.: test, 1490
Ward, P. B.: ref, 1903 (198)
Ward, S.: rev, 2338, 2933
Ward, S. L.: ref, 2452 (24)
Ward, T.: ref, 272 (263), 1758 (98)
Ward-Lonergan, J. M.: ref, 540 (26), 798 (25,27), 994 (43,53), 1903 (505,585), 2667 (1), 2668 (7), 2693 (10), 2694 (27)f, 2710 (8), 2727 (1), 2731 (8), 2862 (574), 2901 (136), 2911 (6)
Warden, R.: test, 2933
Wardle, J.: ref, 1991 (55,94), 2497 (345), 2516 (40)
Wardrop, J. L.: rev, 364, 1319, 2735; ref, 298 (140), 1866 (16), 2864 (62), 2879 (86), 2905 (58)
Ware, J. E.: ref, 1021 (7), 1705 (1), 2497 (54)
Ware, J. E., Jr.: test, 2397
Ware, L.: ref, 472 (215), 1318 (20), 2214 (125), 2862 (677)
Ware, L. M.: ref, 451 (130), 1216 (3)
Wareham, N. L. : ref, 1391 (1), 1612 (49), 1903 (254), 2382 (7,1)
Wares, B. R.: test, 2279
Waring, E. M.: rev, 1582
Waring, S.: ref, 34 (5), 1765 (33), 2862 (575), 2879 (186)
Warka, J.: ref, 1701 (43)
Warm, J. S.: ref, 1697 (34)
Warnath, C.: rev, 914
Warnath, C. F.: rev, 765
Warne, G.: ref, 451 (144), 1000 (100), 1079 (73)
Warner, B. S.: ref, 451 (160)
Warner, J.: test, 2291, 2292
Warner, R.: ref, 270 (5), 1216 (30)
Warner, V.: ref, 694 (35), 1903 (135)
Warnken, W. J.: ref, 2603 (298)
Warr, P.: ref, 1079 (60)
Warr-Leeper, G. A.: ref, 798 (8), 994 (4), 1040 (4), 1903 (129), 2693 (2), 2694 (7), 2768 (9)
Warren, L.: ref, 257 (4), 364 (26)
Warren, L. W.: ref, 1661 (53)
Warren, M. P.: ref, 451 (34), 1832 (7)
Warren, N. D.: test, 937, 1170, 2125
Warren, R. M.: ref, 2873 (49)
Warren, S.: ref, 337 (180), 451 (217), 994 (48)
Warren, S. F.: ref, 1485 (37), 2189 (2), 2382 (27), 2485 (153)
Warren, W. L.: test, 1160, 2216, 2652
Warren-Chaplin, P. M.: ref, 1092 (4), 1096 (2), 1902 (19), 2862 (110), 2879 (25)
Warren-Chapman, P. M.: ref, 1092 (18), 2712 (1), 2879 (171), 2905 (98)
Warrenburg, S.: ref, 2603 (30)
Warrick, P. D.: ref, 1607 (3)
Warrington, C. A.: ref, 2557 (2)
Warrington, E.: test, 378
Warrington, E. K.: test, 1104, 2193, 2809; ref, 1104 (3,5,7), 1758 (71), 1903 (235,337,452), 2163 (100,147), 2193 (7,12,19,33,56), 2860 (268,372,415, 575,588, 692,780,827,1056, 1065,1125,1171), 2862 (457), 2863 (352), 2892 (254)
Warrington, K.: ref, 350 (34), 1903 (401), 2193 (44), 2860 (949)
Warrington, W. G.: rev, 49
Warsh, J. J.: ref, 1166 (166), 2305 (209)
Warshaw, M.: ref, 1093 (108), 1697 (376), 2305 (119,160)
Warshaw, M. G.: ref, 998 (109), 1093 (68,106), 1158 (3), 1517 (6), 1697 (513), 2305 (135,178,189,206, 239), 2519 (42), 2520 (42)
Warsofsky, I. S.: ref, 2860 (1409), 2862 (727), 2892 (303)
Warzak, W. J.: ref, 1902 (3)
Wasek, P.: test, 2305
Washer, R. W.: test, 2852
Washington, J.: ref, 1485 (58), 1653 (28), 2813 (144)
Washington, J. A.: ref, 175 (6), 202 (2), 1903 (166,246,347), 1982 (4), 2651 (6)
Wasik, B. H.: ref, 1216 (98), 2901 (112)
Wasik, H.: ref, 270 (28), 1612 (90), 2485 (222), 2862 (598), 2864 (131)
Waskel, S. A.: ref, 1701 (37,38)
Waskerwitz, M. J.: ref, 451 (215), 1962 (23)
Wasserman, G. A.: ref, 451 (220), 1216 (108)
Wasserman, J. D.: ref, 270 (27)
Wassermann, E. M.: ref, 1135 (25), 2863 (418)
Wasserstein, J.: ref, 2163 (35), 2863 (41)
Wasserstein, S.: ref, 2214 (80)
Wasson, C.: ref, 1485 (58), 1653 (28), 2813 (144)
Wasylenki, D.: ref, 2050 (141)
Wasyliw, O. E.: rev, 268, 2011; ref, 793 (19), 1697 (299,370,488), 1744 (5)
Watabiki, S.: ref, 2860 (472)
Watanabe, A.: ref, 2860 (1278)
Watanabe, O.: ref, 303 (25), 2860 (1372)
Watanabe, T.: ref, 2860 (396), 2873 (10)
Watehouse, I. K.: ref, 272 (47), 1338 (28)

Waterfall, M. L.: ref, 1164 (114), 1218 (12), 1410 (4), 2860 (1010), 2863 (300)
Waterhouse, L.: ref, 1612 (8,11,12), 1903 (22,52,53,369), 2382 (37), 2485 (168,218), 2680 (18), 2813 (1,94,131)
Waterhouse, S. M. A.: test, 1762
Waterman, B.: rev, 201, 880, 2499; ref, 1386 (5), 1503 (9)
Waterman, B. B.: ref, 1386 (11,17), 1903 (327)
Waterman, G. S.: ref, 2305 (216)
Waterman, J.: ref, 1169 (1), 1401 (2), 1522 (3), 1902 (51,10), 1991 (63), 2242 (4), 2247 (46), 2361 (1), 2380 (10), 2485 (105), 2498 (26), 2603 (192), 2749 (35)
Waternaux, C.: ref, 2050 (77), 2603 (562)
Waternaux, C. M.: ref, 337 (63), 451 (29), 472 (59), 1093 (19), 2860 (1210)
Waters, D.: test, 1656
Waters, E.: rev, 1085
Waters, G. S.: ref, 1164 (75), 1903 (303), 2862 (287), 2863 (218,393), 2892 (147)
Waters, W. F.: ref, 745 (13), 1697 (353), 2497 (334)
Watkins, C. E., Jr.: ref, 2497 (539), 2525 (1), 2553 (3), 2860 (145,416), 2862 (93)
Watkins, D.: ref, 349 (15), 1466 (5,6,9), 2358 (7), 2540 (6)
Watkins, J.: ref, 272 (194)
Watkins, J. G.: test, 2853
Watkins, J. M.: ref, 1903 (224), 2125 (10), 2862 (234), 2892 (98)
Watkins, J. T.: ref, 272 (111), 1517 (4)
Watkins, K. E.: ref, 2860 (838), 2863 (243)
Watkins, L.: ref, 650 (13)
Watkins, M. M.: ref, 2862 (618)
Watkins, M. W.: ref, 837 (6), 2860 (1086), 2862 (296,479,576,689,690)
Watkins, P. C.: ref, 2305 (207)
Watkins, R. V.: ref, 624 (24), 1485 (47), 1903 (438,494), 2694 (21)
Watkinson, B.: ref, 2218 (5)
Watson, B. C.: ref, 2497 (188,412)
Watson, B. V.: ref, 745 (7), 2860 (545,652), 2863 (157,191), 2901 (36), 2905 (48)
Watson, C.: ref, 815 (33), 1072 (49), 1073 (3), 1903 (439), 2149 (2), 2163 (250), 2724 (11), 2862 (417), 2879 (149)
Watson, C. G.: ref, 771 (19), 1697 (113,114), 2860 (231)
Watson, D.: ref, 1701 (32), 2076 (132), 2218 (6,78,104), 2603 (425)
Watson, D. C.: ref, 690 (2)
Watson, G.: test, 2856; rev, 363
Watson, G. B.: test, 2857
Watson, G. M. W.: ref, 2704 (1), 2862 (109)
Watson, J. C.: ref, 272 (238), 991 (3), 2497 (604)
Watson, J. E.: ref, 999 (189), 1079 (80), 1216 (90), 1903 (506), 2603 (400)
Watson, K. B.: test, 1508
Watson, K. W.: test, 1505, 2854, 2855
Watson, L. W.: ref, 620 (6)
Watson, M.: ref, 451 (275), 2485 (243), 2862 (723)
Watson, M. B.: ref, 404 (30,35), 413 (2), 1374 (1), 1590 (48)
Watson, M. G.: ref, 1825 (4), 2497 (484)
Watson, P.: ref, 2239 (33)
Watson, R. J.: ref, 2540 (7)
Watson, R. T.: ref, 2860 (186), 2863 (50)
Watson, S.: ref, 2862 (134)
Watson, S. J.: ref, 2305 (50)
Watson, T. E.: ref, 1612 (18), 1903 (260)
Watson, T. S.: rev, 346, 370, 2036, 2432, 2595, 2704; ref, 2862 (691)
Watt, J. D.: ref, 2218 (77)
Watt, S.: ref, 1903 (559), 2227 (53), 2860 (1365)
Watters, J. J.: ref, 2163 (251)
Watts, A. F.: test, 954, 2182
Watts, G.: test, 1390
Watts, K. P.: test, 125, 126, 127, 129, 2398
Watts, R. H., Jr.: ref, 403 (1), 404 (45), 768 (2)
Watts, V.: ref, 1093 (59), 2050 (55)
Watz, L. S.: ref, 1097 (14), 2485 (188), 2862 (431)
Waugh, F. E.: ref, 1638 (2)
Waugh, L. M.: ref, 272 (315), 451 (223)
Waugh, R. P.: rev, 1240
Waugh, S.: ref, 472 (23), 1340 (3)
Wauters, A.: ref, 1166 (126)
Waxman, H. C.: test, 1867; ref, 495 (12), 1318 (15)
Way, L.: ref, 1093 (61), 2050 (63)
Way, N.: ref, 472 (107)
Wayland, S.: ref, 2873 (60)
Wayland, S. C.: ref, 2860 (418)
Wayment, H. A.: ref, 2603 (477)
Waysman, M.: ref, 863 (32), 2603 (69), 2603 (161)
Wcyoc, L. V.: ref, 2686 (1)
Weary, G.: ref, 1115 (22)
Weatherly, M.: ref, 665 (82), 1657 (19), 1903 (418)
Weatherman, K. E.: ref, 698 (1)
Weatherman, R. F.: test, 1300, 2299
Weathers, F. W.: ref, 272 (206), 1697 (505), 2497 (580)
Weatherstone, L.: ref, 999 (180)
Weaver, A. B.: ref, 472 (167)
Weaver, G. M.: ref, 1697 (195)
Weaver, J. B.: ref, 999 (169)
Weaver, K. A.: ref, 1903 (159), 2485 (76), 2862 (193)
Weaver, M. A.: ref, 2603 (490)
Weaver, M. T.: ref, 1338 (31), 1686 (3)
Weaver, T. E.: ref, 1745 (26,85), 2858 (80)
Webb, A.: ref, 1166 (160)
Webb, C.: ref, 1093 (92), 2498 (9)
Webb, C. T.: ref, 1638 (2)
Webb, E.: ref, 372 (69)
Webb, N. B.: ref, 2247 (10), 2749 (17)
Webb, R.: test, 1038, 1998, 1999, 2456
Webb, S. C.: test, 1310
Webb, T.: ref, 4 (15), 2860 (427)
Webb, W. G.: ref, 2860 (14)
Webber, E. M.: ref, 694 (89)
Webber, T.: test, 903, 1147
Webber, Y.: ref, 1991 (23), 2211 (9)
Weber, C.: ref, 265 (4,13), 1000 (24), 1096 (8), 2163 (135), 2524 (2,7), 2657 (4,22), 2892 (95)

Weber, D. A.: ref, 2860 (205), 2863 (51)
Weber, E. M.: ref, 837 (6)
Weber, J.: ref, 1408 (6), 2246 (5)
Weber, K.: ref, 2076 (132), 2603 (425)
Weber, L.: rev, 960, 2320
Weber, M.: ref, 2860 (725)
Weber, P.: test, 1238
Weber, R. C.: ref, 2813 (29)
Weber, T.: ref, 1736 (3)
Weber, T. A.: ref, 2860 (422,556)
Weber-Luxenburger, G.: ref, 2227 (40), 2516 (101), 2860 (1294)
Webster, A.: ref, 2497 (213)
Webster, C. D.: test, 2395, 2476
Webster, D. M.: ref, 2146 (17)
Webster, D. S.: ref, 127 (5)
Webster, I.: ref, 451 (22)
Webster, J.: ref, 1701 (17)
Webster, J. D.: ref, 2218 (12)
Webster, J. S.: ref, 2860 (729,781)
Webster, P. E.: ref, 1394 (13), 1903 (560), 2657 (36)
Webster, R. A.: ref, 1079 (37,57)
Webster, R. E.: test, 1462; ref, 462 (9), 1414 (3), 1462 (1,2,3), 2862 (577,737), 2901 (111)
Webster, W. J.: rev, 258, 821
Webster-Stratton, C.: ref, 272 (239), 451 (161), 863 (20), 864 (1,2), 997 (4,6,8), 2039 (2,21), 2497 (150,151)
Wechsler, D.: test, 709, 2860, 2862, 2863, 2864; rev, 1671, 2163, 2212, 2477, 2478
Weckowicz, T. E.: rev, 2076, 2120
Weddell, R. A.: ref, 1001 (1,8), 2193 (34), 2860 (77,782), 2863 (228), 2892 (4,18,156)
Weddington, W. W.: ref, 2076 (20), 2603 (77)
Wedgeworth, R.: ref, 697 (5), 2603 (522)
Wedman, J.: ref, 1405 (38)
Weed, N. C.: ref, 1698 (8,28)
Weekes, B. S.: ref, 272 (47), 372 (56), 1338 (28)
Weekes, J. R.: ref, 2163 (252), 2497 (532)
Weeks, D. E.: ref, 2305 (49)
Weeks, D. J.: ref, 1903 (51), 2163 (44), 2432 (10)
Weeks, M. O.: rev, 1143, 1237
Weeks, Z. R.: rev, 1490
Weems, C. F.: ref, 2214 (139), 2498 (78)
Ween, J. E.: ref, 2193 (59), 2860 (1201)
Weese-Mayer, D. E.: ref, 1903 (296), 2864 (66)
Wefel, J.: ref, 272 (324), 303 (23), 1697 (576), 2226 (37), 2860 (1355)
Wege, J. W.: ref, 2065 (23)
Wegelin, A.W.: test, 1753
Weglage, J.: ref, 2860 (747,1202), 2862 (578)
Wegner, D. M.: ref, 2497 (413)
Wegner, J.: ref, 331 (4), 994 (26), 2233 (4), 2695 (37)
Wehner, W. L.: rev, 1018, 2056
Wehrly, T. E.: ref, 272 (168), 273 (20), 1687 (21) 2065 (26), 2402 (56), 2559 (12)
Wei, L.: ref, 231 (1), 303 (32), 2226 (42), 2227 (61), 2599 (43), 2863 (431), 2892 (307)
Weible, A. L.: ref, 298 (7)
Weiden, P.: ref, 2076 (12)
Weider, A.: test, 709
Weidlich, S.: test, 767
Weidmer-Mikhail, E.: ref, 2305 (243), 2860 (1389)
Weidner, G.: ref, 2603 (563)
Weigel, D. J.: ref, 1014 (4)
Weigel, R. R.: ref, 1014 (4)
Weikart, D. P.: rev, 3
Weil, C. E.: ref, 298 (48)
Weil, G. R.: test, 2614
Weiler, E.: ref, 1903 (397)
Wein, S.: test, 215
Weinberg, G. B.: ref, 1058 (4), 2860 (451), 2863 (125)
Weinberg, L. D.: ref, 272 (353)
Weinberg, R. A.: rev, 1401; ref, 2860 (524)
Weinberg, S.: ref, 681 (99)
Weinberg, S. L.: rev, 25, 698, 2505, 2725, 771 (18)
Weinberg, W. A.: test, 2865; ref, 473 (5), 798 (4), 1092 (3), 1131 (5), 1240 (4), 1392 (2), 1902 (14), 1903 (42), 2432 (8), 2484 (1), 2879 (21)
Weinberger, D. A.: ref, 472 (112), 681 (59), 1290 (1), 1697 (115), 1939 (2)
Weinberger, D. R.: ref, 376 (8), 776 (15), 1093 (11), 1093 (47), 1164 (46,94,149), 2163 (112), 2193 (16), 2516 (24), 2860 (459,460,510,628,871,1269), 2863 (128,312,384), 2879 (56,206), 2892 (74,116,122,162, 222,230,272)
Weinberger, J.: ref, 1965 (27), 2076 (183), 2749 (21)
Weine, S. M.: ref, 2603 (426)
Weiner, I. B.: ref, 2247 (77,108)
Weiner, J.: ref, 337 (123)
Weiner, M.: ref, 2862 (281)
Weiner, M. F.: ref, 994 (45), 2860 (1240)
Weiner, M. W.: ref, 1058 (7), 2227 (12), 2860 (499), 2863 (143)
Weiner, R. U.: ref, 564 (3), 2146 (7)
Weiner, S.: ref, 257 (3), 1072 (47)
Weiner, W. J.: ref, 1218 (3), 2860 (276)
Weinert, C.: test, 1947; ref, 1947 (1), 2076 (21)
Weinfeld, M.: ref, 68 (2), 2248 (1)
Weinfurt, K. P.: ref, 2497 (650)
Weing, M.: ref, 665 (46)
Weingartner, H. M.: ref, 2863 (100)
Weininger, O.: test, 840
Weinrich, J. D.: ref, 298 (128), 372 (77), 2076 (133)
Weinrich, M.: ref, 2008 (3), 2163 (135), 2892 (95)
Weinschel, B.: ref, 2603 (494)
Weinshenker, B.: ref, 272 (325)
Weinstein, C. E.: test, 1455, 1456, 1910, 2495
Weinstein, C. S.: ref, 199 (18), 2010 (6), 2860 (317,783)
Weinstein, L.: ref, 2126 (14)
Weinstein, M. A.: test, 39, 1272
Weinstein, N.: ref, 998 (92)
Weinstein, S. P.: ref, 998 (101), 2402 (40), 2603 (313,375)
Weinstock, G.: test, 1425
Weintraub, J. K.: ref, 1697 (27), 2497 (30)

Weintraub, S.: test, 199, 1665; ref, 748 (3,9), 1093 (45), 1697 (210), 2305 (6)
Weintraub, S. A.: rev, 474, 1341
Weir, C.: ref, 2485 (200), 2862 (472)
Weir, E.: test, 959
Weir, F.: ref, 350 (12), 1240 (23), 2163 (141)
Weir, W. R. C.: ref, 926 (11), 2516 (31)
Weir, W. S.: ref, 272 (1), 2860 (8), 2892 (1)
Weis, D. L.: rev, 793
Weisberg, P.: ref, 674 (2), 1903 (507)
Weisbrod, M.: ref, 2749 (61)
Weise, C.: ref, 2603 (296)
Weise, C. C.: ref, 2603 (342)
Weishenker, N. J.: ref, 2305 (135)
Weisiger, B.: ref, 1903 (397)
Weisman, A.: ref, 2050 (50)
Weisman, A. G.: ref, 1010 (116)
Weisman, J. D.: ref, 1135 (13), 1697 (330), 2599 (25), 2860 (772)
Weismer, G.: ref, 209 (3), 1056 (1)
Weismer, S. E.: rev, 2052, 2725; ref, 624 (13,28), 1903 (217,508), 2382 (17,28), 2485 (106,154), 2601 (1,2), 2657 (31), 2695 (23), 2768 (40), 2813 (80), 2862 (668)
Weisner, T.: ref, 2813 (118)
Weisner, T. S.: ref, 1010 (65), 1216 (52)
Weiss, A. A.: ref, 1725 (6), 1908 (1)
Weiss, A. L.: ref, 175 (7), 1903 (149), 2524 (3), 2651 (7), 2725 (2)
Weiss, B.: ref, 451 (234), 472 (124), 2498 (47)
Weiss, C. E.: test, 2866
Weiss, D. J.: test, 1694, 1695, 1701, 1702; rev, 180, 2797
Weiss, D. S.: ref, 846 (2), 1697 (325), 2603 (427)
Weiss, G.: ref, 2603 (262), 2862 (266)
Weiss, J.: ref, 272 (304), 1338 (39)
Weiss, K. L.: ref, 863 (91), 1889 (16)
Weiss, L. H.: ref, 68 (60), 272 (240), 1687 (25), 2115 (6)
Weiss, M. J. S.: ref, 681 (69), 1987 (16), 2864 (107)
Weiss, M. R.: ref, 2369 (10)
Weiss, R. L.: ref, 863 (13)
Weiss, R. V.: ref, 69 (1)
Weiss, S.: ref, 2860 (229), 2863 (59)
Weissbein, D. A.: ref, 2163 (209)
Weissberg-Benchell, J.: ref, 451 (235)
Weissenburger, J. E.: ref, 272 (136), 1166 (81)
Weissinger, E.: rev, 1483, 2376
Weissler, K.: ref, 1657 (18), 2860 (915)
Weissman, H. N.: ref, 1697 (437)
Weissman, M.: ref, 2305 (224)
Weissman, M. D.: ref, 2246 (14)
Weissman, M. M.: ref, 694 (35), 1903 (135), 2305 (110,140,223)
Weissmann, M.: test, 2442
Weist, M. D.: ref, 451 (82,83,160), 1000 (94,95,110), 1021 (48), 2211 (5), 2214 (5,140), 2230 (11,21), 2498 (5), 2656 (25)
Weisz, J. R.: ref, 451 (182), 2214 (48)
Weitz, H.: rev, 533, 2612
Weitzman, E.: ref, 811 (14), 1240 (44), 1528 (2), 2190 (7), 2485 (224), 2601 (3)
Weitzman, L. M.: ref, 2065 (33)
Weitzman, R. A.: rev, 180
Weizman, A.: ref, 681 (96), 2305 (247)
Weizman, R.: ref, 451 (137), 2497 (414), 2603 (475)
Wekerle, C.: ref, 472 (108), 997 (21), 1903 (331), 2214 (57)
Wekking, E. M.: ref, 1697 (478)
Welch, G.: ref, 272 (41)
Welch, G. W.: ref, 1079 (86), 2076 (169)
Welch, J.: ref, 2860 (316)
Welch, L. W.: ref, 272 (333), 2860 (1366), 2863 (412)
Welch, R. R.: ref, 2076 (170)
Welch, S. L.: ref, 337 (99,137), 1079 (87), 2050 (113), 2603 (453)
Welker, C. J.: ref, 451 (224,225)
Welker, W. A.: ref, 1072 (30)
Welkowitz, J.: ref, 199 (7), 776 (8,12), 1745 (48), 2860 (201,434)
Weller, A.: ref, 298 (9)
Weller, C.: test, 397, 2868
Weller, E. B.: ref, 681 (14), 2107 (1)
Weller, R. A.: ref, 681 (14), 2107 (1)
Wellington, B.: ref, 2295 (1)
Wellmann, B. L.: rev, 433
Wells, A.: ref, 2519 (56), 2520 (55)
Wells, C.: ref, 2749 (39)
Wells, D.: ref, 2835 (5)
Wells, F. L.: rev, 798, 2485
Wells, G.: ref, 337 (148), 863 (80), 1000 (99), 1903 (473), 1991 (92)
Wells, J. E.: ref, 1166 (159)
Wells, K.: ref, 2288 (15), 2289 (10), 2305 (62)
Wells, K. B.: ref, 451 (163), 1903 (513), 2305 (198), 2902 (4)
Wells, K. C.: ref, 451 (179), 472 (193)
Wells, K. M.: ref, 2050 (3)
Wells, M.: ref, 298 (105), 1036 (10)
Wells, P. A.: ref, 998 (110), 999 (101)
Wells, S.: test, 1451
Wells-Parker, E.: ref, 136 (8), 372 (39), 998 (47), 1697 (185,249)
Welsh, G. S.: test, 2869
Welsh, J.: ref, 430 (14), 1485 (52), 1903 (484), 2695 (57)
Welsh, J. D.: ref, 997 (25), 1093 (51), 2076 (67)
Welsh, J. S.: rev, 459, 2692
Welsh, K. A.: ref, 2227 (22), 2860 (957)
Welsh, L. A.: rev, 2322
Welsh, M. C.: ref, 2860 (1232)
Welsh, P. A.: ref, 681 (29)
Welsh, R.: ref, 1903 (441)
Welsh, S.: rev, 1091
Welsh, W. M.: ref, 2749 (64)

Welte, J. W.: ref, 134 (22), 1181 (17,24)
Welte, P. O.: ref, 798 (12)
Weltman, K.: ref, 68 (18)
Weltzin, T. E.: ref, 893 (26), 2497 (423)
Wenar, C.: test, 285; rev, 228, 1630
Wenck, S.: test, 1160
Wendelboe, M.: ref, 459 (9), 2163 (71)
Wendt, P. E.: ref, 2497 (415)
Wendt, S.: ref, 337 (17)
Weng, L.: ref, 180 (19), 2163 (165)
Wenke, J.: ref, 1093 (115)
Wennstedt, L. W.: ref, 2065 (20)
Wentling, T. L.: rev, 1792
Wents, D.: test, 2459
Wentzel, K. R.: ref, 1866 (18)
Wenzlaff, R. M.: ref, 272 (21)
Wepman, J. M.: test, 230, 232, 2468, 2817, 2819, 2870; rev, 1854, 2428
Wepner, S. B.: ref, 2487 (4)
Werbeloff, M.: test, 1199
Werdegas, D.: ref, 272 (356), 2603 (581)
Werder, J.: test, 2903
Werder, J. K.: test, 2901
Werle, M.: ref, 997 (10), 1216 (20), 2127 (1), 2603 (134)
Werner, A.: ref, 2288 (54), 2289 (41)
Werner, E. E.: rev, 1485
Werner, E. O.: test, 2466, 2524
Werner, H.: ref, 2076 (85), 2860 (664)
Werner, L. J.: ref, 462 (4), 1010 (29)
Werner, P. D.: rev, 698, 794; ref, 1000 (96), 1010 (96)
Werner, P. H.: ref, 959 (1)
Werner, S. C.: ref, 1455 (5)
Werner, T. J.: test, 2827
Wershba-Gershon, P. M.: ref, 275 (1), 1902 (58), 1991 (75), 2860 (735)
Werthamer-Larson, L.: ref, 364 (19), 472 (172), 2214 (102)
Werthamer-Larsson, L.: ref, 472 (48), 2214 (49,66,103)
Werther, G.: ref, 451 (144), 1000 (100), 1079 (73)
Wertman-Elad, R.: ref, 681 (67), 2163 (244)
Werts, M. G.: ref, 994 (44), 1903 (509), 2485 (219), 2695 (64), 2813 (132), 2864 (126)
Wertz, P.: ref, 2862 (121)
Wertz, R. T.: ref, 2008 (3,15), 2873 (66)
Wesch, J.: ref, 1135 (13,16,26), 1164 (180), 1740 (8), 2227 (21), 2599 (25,32,40), 2860 (772)
Wesley, J. C.: ref, 592 (74,85)
Wesman, A. G.: test, 838, 839, 1974, 2871; rev, 118, 1319, 1434, 1638
Wesner, R. B.: ref, 1241 (2)
Wessely, S.: ref, 1079 (59), 1166 (72)
Wessler, R.: rev, 1965
Wesson, C. L.: ref, 2487 (9)
Wesson, V. A.: ref, 2305 (185)
West, A.: ref, 1697 (280), 2305 (99), 2862 (250)
West, C. A. C.: ref, 708 (9)
West, J. D.: ref, 1927 (4,5)
West, J. F.: test, 277
West, L. J.: rev, 2406, 2787
West, M.: ref, 462 (20), 1036 (1)
West, R.: ref, 999 (122)
West, R. F.: ref, 1902 (85), 1903 (459)
West, R. W.: ref, 694 (90)
West, S. A.: ref, 472 (189), 1093 (93), 1166 (158), 2289 (39,54,60,61)
West, S. G.: ref, 451 (272), 472 (38,102,228)
West, W. B.: ref, 2497 (517)
Westbrook, B. W.: rev, 410, 701, 760, 771, 1100, 1754, 1790, 2406; ref, 413 (5,10,13,22)
Westbrook, D.: ref, 999 (46)
Westby, C.: rev, 887, 1528
Westby, C. E.: rev, 1105, 2433, 2693, 2695
Westby, G.: rev, 1152, 1811, 2163, 2477, 2478
Westen, D.: ref, 1697 (22), 2218 (79), 2603 (6), 2749 (28), 2860 (369)
Westenberg, H. G. M.: ref, 1166 (154), 2603 (497)
Wester, A.: ref, 2860 (958)
Westera, J.: ref, 1765 (24), 2094 (2)
Westerman, M. A.: ref, 451 (84), 863 (73), 1582 (8)
Westermeyer, J.: ref, 1093 (20), 2603 (31,78,428)
Westermeyer, J. F.: ref, 2860 (318)
Western, S.: rev, 2011
Westerveld, M. : ref, 1698 (16), 2860 (216,974,992), 2863 (286,294)
Westlake, R.: ref, 1218 (16), 2599 (35), 2863 (317), 2892 (259)
Westling, D. L.: ref, 194 (2), 459 (13), 2382 (11), 2813 (19)
Westman, A. S.: rev, 841, 1470, 1696, 2377; ref, 372 (57)
Westman, M. J.: ref, 214 (6), 2651 (3)
Weston, A. D.: ref, 1903 (561), 1982 (15)
Weston, C. A.: ref, 863 (21)
Westreich, A. H.: ref, 1140 (59)
Westwood, E.: ref, 358 (12), 560 (3), 2862 (518)
Wetherby, A. M.: test, 630; ref, 194 (2), 459 (13), 2382 (11), 2813 (19)
Wetherington, C. M.: ref, 451 (180)
Wethington, E.: ref, 272 (222), 650 (5)
Wetter, D. W.: ref, 2076 (134)
Wetter, M. W.: ref, 1697 (379,380,386,525)
Wetterberg, L.: ref, 2305 (22)
Wetzel, H.: ref, 1166 (214)
Wetzel, L.: test, 2405
Wetzel, R. D.: ref, 1697 (196,371)
Wetzig, D. L.: ref, 2860 (232), 2892 (30)
Wetzig, L.: ref, 376 (33), 2239 (35)
Wetzler, S.: ref, 1166 (102), 1687 (20), 1697 (372), 2603 (165,191,451,510)
Wexler, B. E.: ref, 1164 (116), 2860 (1019)
Wexler, K.: ref, 624 (23,27), 1095 (42), 1903 (410,493), 2695 (59)
Weyandt, L. L.: ref, 337 (124), 2163 (253), 2517 (6), 2820 (1), 2892 (212)
Weybrew, B. B.: ref, 1697 (526)

Weyer, M.: ref, 472 (234)
Weyerer, S.: ref, 2603 (525)
Weyrauch, J.: ref, 375 (7), 2862 (705)
Whalen, C. K.: ref, 681 (33)
Whaley, R.: ref, 2227 (25), 2516 (79), 2860 (1089), 2863 (322)
Whaley, T. J.: ref, 2525 (6)
Whang, P. A.: ref, 592 (62), 665 (72), 2163 (166,169)
Wharton, K., Jr.: test, 2875
Whatley, S.: ref, 2050 (32)
Wheat, J.: ref, 571 (3), 1599 (1)
Wheatley, G. H.: ref, 838 (5)
Wheeler, I.: ref, 2126 (11)
Wheeler, J.: ref, 1697 (197)
Wheeler, K. G.: rev, 2491
Wheeler, M. S.: test, 262
Wheeler, P.: rev, 2684
Wheeler, P. H.: rev, 684
Wheeles, V. E.: ref, 298 (24)
Wheelock, J.: ref, 2599 (31), 2860 (942)
Wheelwright, J. B.: test, 1366
Wheelwright, J. H.: test, 1366
Whelan, G.: ref, 2860 (1228), 2863 (366)
Whelan, J. P.: ref, 2603 (401), 2863 (287)
Whelan, M. L.: ref, 1423 (1), 2485 (171), 2695 (42), 2860 (928), 2864 (98)
Wheless, J. W.: ref, 2860 (1230,1231), 2879 (196)
Whelihan, W.: ref, 2076 (101)
Whelley, P.: ref, 837 (10), 2862 (462)
Wherry, J. N.: ref, 272 (189), 451 (177), 472 (49), 1380 (17), 2214 (30), 2432 (33), 2603 (270,473)
Whetstone, R. D.: test, 618
Whetton, C.: test, 350, 463, 736, 902, 1765, 1826, 1827, 2171, 2691
Whetzel, D. L.: ref, 1866 (4)
Whiffen, V. E.: ref, 272 (140), 2603 (564,565)
While, D.: ref, 451 (155), 1010 (111)
Whipple, E. E.: ref, 272 (242), 864 (2), 997 (8), 1661 (51), 2497 (151)
Whipple, K.: ref, 372 (1), 1697 (3), 1790 (1), 1903 (2), 2163 (3), 2247 (1), 2417 (2), 2860 (12)
Whipple, M.: ref, 998 (118)
Whipple, S. C.: ref, 998 (37), 1201 (1), 1697 (150), 1758 (50), 1962 (2), 2417 (13), 2860 (951)
Whisler, E. W.: ref, 998 (100), 1036 (13)
Whisler, L.: test, 2877
Whisman, M. A.: ref, 863 (47), 2557 (11)
Whitacre, C. C.: ref, 1164 (73), 2860 (722), 2892 (143)
Whitaker, A.: ref, 1093 (21)
Whitaker, A. H.: ref, 451 (236), 1903 (296), 2813 (154), 2864 (66)
Whitaker, D.: ref, 2901 (84)
Whitaker, D. J.: ref, 298 (132), 2065 (13)
Whitaker, H. A.: ref, 2860 (267)
Whitaker, L. C.: test, 2878; ref, 1697 (54), 2878 (1)
Whitaker, P.: ref, 2497 (140)
Whitaker, S. L.: ref, 1959 (5)
Whitbeck, L. B.: ref, 451 (237), 2603 (136,305)
Whitbook, M.: ref, 875 (3) 1264 (1)
White, A. J.: test, 2295
White, A. P.: ref, 1079 (65)
White, B. J.: ref, 199 (16), 1140 (22), 2010 (16), 2163 (179), 2516 (47), 2860 (703), 2863 (205), 2879 (87)
White, C. S.: ref, 88 (2), 1379 (42), 1903 (239), 2163 (149), 2754 (5), 2771 (36)
White, D.: ref, 863 (71), 2076 (179)
White, D. A.: ref, 272 (334), 376 (30)
White, D. M.: ref, 1697 (103), 2305 (44)
White, D. R.: test, 2310
White, E.: ref, 2863 (83)
White, E. M.: rev, 513, 1118
White, H. R.: rev, 301; ref, 1661 (19), 1965 (9), 2603 (21,466,587)
White, J.: ref, 451 (133), 2497 (429)
White, J. G.: test, 1584
White, J. L.: ref, 373 (24), 2516 (59)
White, K.: ref, 1093 (68), 2305 (178), 2497 (144), 2519 (42), 2520 (42)
White, K. R.: rev, 644
White, L. A.: ref, 180 (27)
White, L. R.: ref, 2860 (329), 2863 (87,113)
White, M.: test, 2872
White, M. A.: ref, 1901 (10)
White, N.: ref, 2163 (254), 2860 (634,1011), 2862 (418)
White, P.: test, 1668
White, P. D.: ref, 2050 (136), 2305 (157,158)
White, R.: ref, 451 (4)
White, R. F.: ref, 376 (9), 1164 (33,124), 2603 (140), 2860 (344,1119), 2863 (92,153,332), 2879 (169), 2892 (49)
White, S.: rev, 811, 813, 2037
White, S. A.: rev, 2081
White, S. R.: ref, 335 (7), 650 (10), 2289 (17), 2305 (77)
White, T. L.: ref, 372 (61), 1697 (267)
White, W.: ref, 2497 (436)
White, W. F.: ref, 1755 (50), 2856 (9)
Whitebook, M.: ref, 875 (6), 1264 (2)
Whitehair, P. M.: ref, 1485 (54)
Whitehead, V.: ref, 2163 (314), 2863 (373), 2873 (61)
Whitehead, W. E.: ref, 1178 (15)
Whitehorst, G. J.: ref, 1240 (20), 1903 (223), 2228 (10)
Whitehouse, J.: test, 1718
Whitehouse, P. J.: ref, 1903 (411)
Whitehurst, G. J.: ref, 681 (88), 875 (7,8), 1240 (31), 1903 (328), 2879 (221), 2905 (117)
Whiteley, J. H.: ref, 2146 (10)
Whitely, B. E., Jr.: ref, 1755 (67)
Whiteman, J.: test, 1391
Whiteman, V. L.: ref, 1321 (6)
Whiteside, L.: ref, 451 (33), 1216 (37,38,39,40,41,61), 1903 (234), 2485 (112,113,114,115)
Whiteside-Mansell, L.: ref, 1216 (91), 1903 (510), 2485 (220)
Whitfield, K.: ref, 644 (6), 2860 (858), 2863 (252)
Whiting, S: test, 2240

Whiting, S. A.: rev, 2100
Whitla, D.: test, 1665
Whitla, D. K.: rev, 615
Whitley, B. E., Jr.: ref, 298 (97), 615 (51), 1697 (151), 2076 (36)
Whitlock, R. V.: ref, 2499 (1)
Whitman, D.: ref, 1697 (234)
Whitman, R. D.: ref, 1405 (15), 2771 (15), 2860 (725), 2879 (204)
Whitman, T. L.: ref, 448 (22), 1619 (4), 2860 (1071)
Whitmarsh, G. A.: ref, 1697 (43), 2603 (27)
Whitmer, C. A.: rev, 182, 1796
Whitmore, J. R.: test, 976, 2621, 2753
Whitmore, M.: ref, 615 (37), 694 (34)
Whitney, D. J.: ref, 2899 (17)
Whitney, K.: ref, 373 (25)
Whitney, M. L.: ref, 1010 (71)
Whitt, E. J.: ref, 621 (2)
Whitt, J. K.: ref, 451 (215), 1962 (23)
Whittal, M. L.: ref, 2497 (416)
Whittemore, P. B.: ref, 272 (42), 1166 (36)
Whitten, J. D.: ref, 809 (2), 1903 (549), 2864 (140)
Whitten, R. G.: rev, 159
Whittick, J. E.: ref, 1808 (2), 2858 (128)
Whittington, J. E.: ref, 998 (99), 1079 (40)
Whitworth, R. H.: rev, 2862; ref, 1697 (373), 2417 (11), 2862 (59), 2879 (10)
Whordley, D.: test, 1230
Whybrow, P. C.: ref, 2305 (28)
Whyte, J.: ref, 1164 (161), 1740 (22), 2516 (104), 2892 (279)
Whyte, L. A.: rev, 384
Wiart, L.: ref, 2860 (930)
Wible, C. G.: ref, 2288 (60), 2289 (46), 2305 (159), 2860 (1012)
Wichstrom, L.: ref, 298 (149), 1093 (57), 2050 (51), 2247 (47), 2603 (429)
Wickens, D. D.: ref, 2860 (19)
Wickens, T. D. : ref, 592 (80)
Wickett, J. C.: ref, 1731 (3)
Wicki, W.: ref, 2603 (33,285)
Wickrama, K. A. S.: ref, 2603 (566)
Wickramarante, P.: ref, 2305 (140,224)
Wickramaratne, P. J.: ref, 2305 (110,223)
Wicks, D.: ref, 2050 (34)
Widaman, K. F.: ref, 2 (2), 451 (170), 1965 (54), 2299 (3), 2813 (53,138)
Wideman, M. J.: test, 1412
Widiger, T. A.: test, 1961; rev, 1685, 1687, 1934, 2218; ref, 298 (146), 1697 (427, 2603 (373,395)
Widom, C. S.: ref, 1902 (28), 2146 (15)
Wiebe, D. A.: ref, 1903 (159), 2485 (76), 2862 (193)
Wiebe, D. J.: ref, 68 (42), 2497 (214,417)
Wiebe, J. S.: ref, 2218 (52), 2858 (95)
Wiebe, V. J.: ref, 272 (369)
Wieck, A.: ref, 999 (41,162), 2305 (188)
Wieczorek, C.: ref, 665 (74)
Wieczorek, W. F.: ref, 1661 (18)
Wiederholt, J. L.: test, 662, 1051, 1130, 1131, 2668; rev, 1240
Wiederholt, S. L.: test, 2712
Wiederman, M. W.: ref, 893 (50), 1687 (46)
Wiegand, W.: ref, 2050 (52)
Wiegers, A.: ref, 2862 (65), 2864 (8)
Wiegman, O.: ref, 1697 (198)
Wieizzbicki, M.: ref, 272 (367), 1745 (87)
Wieland, G.: ref, 1697 (532)
Wielgus, M. S.: ref, 2305 (11)
Wielkiewicz, R. M.: ref, 1962 (11)
Wiemer, M. J.: ref, 1093 (42), 1697 (173)
Wienberg, H.: ref, 2749 (27)
Wiener, A. S.: test, 1265
Wiener, L.: ref, 1612 (55), 2862 (279)
Wiener, W.: ref, 1745 (73)
Wiens, A. N.: ref, 2860 (596,1367)
Wiers, R. W.: ref, 451 (290), 2862 (740)
Wierson, M.: ref, 337 (172) 451 (188), 2211 (12), 2839 (1)
Wierzbicki, M.: ref, 1687 (36)
Wiese, M. J.: rev, 467, 892, 2111, 446
Wieseman, R. A.: ref, 1140 (28)
Wiesen, J. P.: test, 2884
Wiesmann, M.: ref, 2497 (121)
Wietlisbach, S.: ref, 772 (1), 1612 (33), 1901 (11), 2813 (34)
Wigfield, A.: ref, 1902 (103), 1903 (522), 2901 (116,140)
Wiggins, J. D.: rev, 1306; ref, 694 (6,20,90), 1754 (3), 2835 (10)
Wiggins, J. S.: test, 1289; rev, 1755, 1965
Wiggs, C. L.: ref, 776 (57), 2860 (784)
Wightman, J.: ref, 349 (18)
Wightman, L. F.: rev, 1689, 2425, 2548
Wightman, L. H.: ref, 1697 (475)
Wignall, M.: test, 882
Wiig, E.: test, 2693
Wiig, E. D.: ref, 681 (81), 2693 (8), 2694 (23), 2704 (44), 2862 (579), 2901 (104)
Wiig, E. H.: test, 539, 540, 541, 542, 2727, 2886; rev, 1903, 2428; ref, 681 (81), 1607 (12), 2693 (8), 2694 (12,23), 2704 (44), 2862 (579), 2901 (104)
Wikler, D.: ref, 1166 (181)
Wikoff, R. L.: rev, 234, 1300, 1316
Wiktorowicz, K.: ref, 1166 (155)
Wilbanks, S. L.: ref, 272 (151), 2402 (37), 2599 (26), 2860 (798,1038), 2892 (161)
Wilberg, K. : ref, 1164 (47), 1407 (2), 2860 (463), 2863 (130)
Wilbur, R.: ref, 2860 (146)
Wilcox, C.: ref, 694 (99), 999 (82)
Wilcox, H. E.: rev, 44
Wilcox, K. A.: ref, 1095 (36,37), 1379 (75), 1903 (415), 2229 (6)
Wilcox, K. N.: rev, 1160
Wilczenski, F. L.: ref, 592 (47)
Wilczynski, M.: ref, 2749 (43)

Wild, C. L.: ref, 1697 (134)
Wild, J.: ref, 241 (4), 451 (94), 815 (35), 853 (13), 1903 (447), 2247 (48), 2695 (47), 2864 (110)
Wild, T. C.: ref, 999 (146)
Wilde, M. C.: ref, 376 (3)
Wilder, D.: ref, 1166 (103)
Wildermuth, N. L.: ref, 1036 (8)
Wildin, S.: ref, 270 (26), 2382 (35), 2813 (130)
Wildman, T. M.: rev, 2236
Wildstein, A. B.: ref, 560 (1), 2163 (31)
Wilens, T.: ref, 2305 (155,165), 2860 (990), 2879 (142)
Wilens, T. E.: ref, 2305 (240), 2860 (1203), 2879 (187)
Wilensky, A. J.: ref, 2860 (167)
Wiley, C.: ref, 1164 (77)
Wiley, J.: ref, 615 (31)
Wiley, M. J.: ref, 776 (59)
Wilfley, D. E.: ref, 272 (144), 1010 (91), 2076 (170), 2497 (535)
Wilhelm, K.: ref, 272 (306), 298 (167), 790 (16), 998 (21,85,135), 999 (138,190), 1079 (103), 1166 (61)
Wilhelm, S.: ref, 271 (16), 272 (335), 2402 (70)
Wilk, S. L.: ref, 180 (33)
Wilkie, F.: ref, 1058 (3), 2860 (277), 2863 (72)
Wilkins, J.: ref, 376 (35), 1164 (187), 2227 (25,62), 2516 (79,122), 2860 (1089,1420), 2863 (322), 2892 (308)
Wilkins, J. W.: ref, 2076 (135)
Wilkins, S.: ref, 1093 (80), 2050 (103)
Wilkinson, A.: test, 1477
Wilkinson, A. D.: ref, 1436 (1)
Wilkinson, G. S.: test, 2879
Wilkinson, H.: ref, 2860 (592)
Wilkinson, H. J.: ref, 2497 (2)
Wilkinson, I. A. G.: ref, 1240 (40), 2092 (4)
Wilkinson, J. W.: ref, 2497 (2)
Wilkinson, K. M.: ref, 202 (3), 1903 (305,329), 2657 (19)
Wilkinson, L. J.: ref, 2360 (11)
Wilkinson, M.: ref, 2862 (708)
Wilkinson, N. C.: ref, 1140 (23)
Wilkinson, P.: ref, 272 (241)
Wilkinson, S. B.: ref, 271 (15), 272 (330), 376 (28), 776 (56), 1135 (24), 1218 (19), 1378 (10), 1740 (26), 2076 (181), 2516 (112), 2863 (411), 2892 (293)
Wilkinson, S. C.: ref, 1866 (27), 2163 (136)
Wilkinson, S. M.: ref, 2239 (10)
Wilkinson, W. K.: rev, 1671, 1946, 2255, 2323, 2449, 2514, 2709, 2789; ref, 2112 (1)
Wilks, S. S.: rev, 1863
Will, R. J.: test, 805
Willard, J.: ref, 272 (310)
Willard-Holt, C.: ref, 592 (32)
Willard-Schroeder, D.: ref, 2863 (63)
Willcox, M.: ref, 1748 (1)
Willcoxson, L.: ref, 1469 (10)
Willemsen, T. M.: ref, 298 (98)
Willerman, L.: ref, 2212 (3), 2485 (136), 2860 (675)
Williams, A. C. de C.: ref, 272 (107), 2497 (445)
Williams, B.: ref, 56 (10), 180 (4,28)
Williams, B. J.: ref, 376 (19), 776 (42)
Williams, B. W.: ref, 776 (5), 2860 (147)
Williams, C.: ref, 2485 (201), 2860 (1085)
Williams, C. D.: ref, 272 (373), 1166 (223)
Williams, C. J.: ref, 2860 (785)
Williams, C. L.: test, 1698; ref, 697 (6), 1697 (374), 1698 (8)
Williams, C. O.: test, 1234, 2139
Williams, C. P.: ref, 180 (6)
Williams, C. R.: ref, 1965 (8)
Williams, D.: ref, 68 (31), 2288 (3)
Williams, D. A.: ref, 272 (28), 2497 (257), 2603 (46,51,97),190)
Williams, D. E.: test, 479; ref, 462 (3,14), 479 (1)
Williams, D. L.: ref, 2860 (417), 2862 (187), 2879 (53)
Williams, E.: ref, 349 (33)
Williams, E. N.: ref, 2497 (663)
Williams, F.: test, 724, 1921
Williams, G.: ref, 272 (215), 1697 (510), 2497 (587), 2858 (118)
Williams, G. P.: ref, 1745 (36)
Williams, H. L.: test, 910
Williams, H. S.: rev, 28, 29
Williams, J.: ref, 815 (13), 1135 (11), 1697 (1), 1902 (40), 2050 (32,54), 2125 (7), 2288 (15), 2289 (10), 2305 (62), 2417 (1), 2516 (16), 2860 (310), 2862 (147,229), 2903 (1)
Williams, J. B.: ref, 2163 (323), 2227 (36), 2860 (1266)
Williams, J. B. W.: test, 2519, 2520; ref, 273 (23), 337 (31,34,91,145), 1166 (115), 2603 (279,299,366,549), 2860 (407)
Williams, J. E.: ref, 68 (9,51), 2218 (29), 2656 (17)
Williams, J. G.: rev, 7, 442, 642; ref, 1697 (217)
Williams, J. H.: test, 212
Williams, J. K.: ref, 301 (25)
Williams, J. M.: test, 562, 1644, 2053; ref, 1379 (81), 1902 (79), 1903 (440), 2228 (20), 2657 (28), 2860 (319,660), 2879 (38), 2901 (18)
Williams, J. M. G.: ref, 272 (46,292), 893 (44), 2497 (124), 2860 (1301)
Williams, J. R.: rev, 2122
Williams, K.: ref, 451 (287), 1903 (582)
Williams, K. C.: ref, 2813 (133)
Williams, K. E.: ref, 2519 (53), 2520 (52)
Williams, K. J.: ref, 1140 (16)
Williams, K. S.: ref, 2860 (319), 2879 (38), 2901 (18)
Williams, K. T.: test, 995, 1903
Williams, L.: ref, 540 (16), 655 (1), 1095 (44), 1903 (76), 2432 (13), 2485 (35), 2813 (9)
Williams, L. L.: ref, 472 (152), 2214 (86), 2498 (56), 2905 (93)
Williams, L. M.: ref, 863 (74), 1079 (108), 2288 (77), 2289 (64), 2417 (31)
Williams, M.: test, 883, 2888, 2921; ref, 998 (86), 2050 (80), 2211 (43), 2305 (134), 2860 (656)
Williams, M. A.: ref, 1135 (27), 1164 (185), 1697 (592), 2402 (71), 2517 (8), 2599 (41), 2860 (1412), 2863 (430)

Williams, M. C.: ref, 827 (3)
Williams, M. E.: ref, 1903 (224), 2125 (10), 2497 (110), 2862 (234), 2892 (98)
Williams, M. S.: test, 437, 1546, 1564, 1567, 1971, 2547, 2548
Williams, M. V.: ref, 2879 (130)
Williams, P.: test, 1079; ref, 1392 (11), 1671 (4), 1767 (3), 2905 (53)
Williams, P. G.: ref, 68 (42), 2497 (214)
Williams, R.: ref, 272 (278)
Williams, R.: ref, 1079 (92), 2497 (636)
Williams, R. A.: ref, 2211 (36), 2603 (42,337)
Williams, R. B.: ref, 272 (336), 1697 (319), 2218 (116), 2497 (664)
Williams, R. B., Jr.: ref, 1697 (117), 2497 (15)
Williams, R. E.: ref, 302 (1), 1693 (1), 2163 (13), 2856 (1)
Williams, R. L.: test, 316, 2750, 2887; ref, 1755 (60), 2497 (148), 2905 (68)
Williams, R. S.: ref, 303 (1), 791 (2), 1740 (3), 2497 (21), 2516 (2), 2603 (8), 2860 (81)
Williams, R. T.: rev, 76, 82, 257, 799, 1382, 1456, 2668, 2731
Williams, S.: test, 1824; ref, 358 (5,10), 1097 (6), 1903 (131), 2211 (16,35), 2228 (4), 2485 (63)
Williams, S. E.: ref, 199 (6), 2008 (8)
Williams, S. L.: test, 268
Williams, S. W.: ref, 298 (99)
Williams, T.: ref, 1066 (1)
Williams, T. M.: ref, 926 (13), 2860 (516)
Williams, T. S.: ref, 2863 (312), 2892 (222)
Williams, W.: ref, 372 (18), 553 (1), 1697 (85), 2076 (14), 2603 (57)
Williamson, D. A.: ref, 893 (11,17,19,22), 999 (123,144,170), 2402 (36), 2864 (105)
Williamson, D. E.: ref, 2305 (216)
Williamson, D. J.: ref, 1740 (23), 2860 (1309)
Williamson, D. M.: rev, 1355
Williamson, G. G.: test, 878
Williamson, G. M.: ref, 272 (36), 2603 (62)
Williamson, L.: ref, 2860 (610), 2892 (114)
Williamson, P. C.: ref, 2288 (55,78,79), 2289 (42), 2289 (65)
Williford, H. N.: ref, 893 (39)
Willingham, D.: ref, 2860 (123), 2863 (34)
Willingham, W. W.: rev, 1115, 1672
Willis, C.: ref, 349 (2), 350 (4), 2163 (64)
Willis, C. G.: rev, 508, 1177
Willis, E. L.: ref, 838 (3), 2860 (36)
Willis, G. B.: ref, 372 (10,23), 571 (1,2), 604 (1), 615 (5,17), 2591 (2)
Willis, S. L.: ref, 372 (31), 1405 (5), 2304 (1,4)
Willis, W. G.: rev, 854, 1339, 1734, 2334
Willison, J.: test, 1758
Willits, J. M.: rev, 58
Willmer, J.: ref, 1903 (191), 2863 (137)
Willmes, K.: ref, 2860 (944)
Willmore, L. J.: ref, 2860 (1230,1231), 2879 (196)
Willmoth, T.: ref, 998 (110)
Willms, J.: ref, 624 (21), 2864 (73)
Willows, D. M.: ref, 815 (33), 1072 (49), 1073 (3), 1903 (439), 2163 (250), 2724 (11), 2862 (417), 2879 (149)
Wills, K. E.: ref, 451 (238), 1010 (131)
Willson, E.: ref, 1822 (2)
Willson, V. L.: rev, 364, 839, 1318, 2696; ref, 1379 (37,97), 2862 (534,733)
Wilmeth, J. R.: rev, 1123
Wilmink, F. W.: ref, 1079 (46), 2050 (124)
Wilmotte, J.: ref, 1166 (4), 2305 (14)
Wilsher, C. R.: ref, 2239 (5)
Wilson, A.: ref, 790 (2), 2749 (10,40)
Wilson, A. A.: ref, 2050 (125)
Wilson, B.: test, 2239; ref, 241 (4), 451 (94), 815 (10,35), 853 (11), 1379 (30), 1653 (10), 1903 (447), 2239 (6), 2657 (33), 2695 (47), 2813 (141) 2864 (110,135)
Wilson, B. A.: test, 295; ref, 349 (8,9), 1104 (1,2,12), 1758 (55), 2227 (23), 2239 (3,7,16,17,26,27), 2860 (1013,1368), 2863 (301), 2892 (99)
Wilson, B. J.: ref, 2862 (22)
Wilson, B. L.: test, 2312
Wilson, B. N.: ref, 353 (10,20), 2432 (16,28), 2862 (207,419), 2901 (26,78)
Wilson, C.: ref, 272 (236), 1671 (6), 2497 (600), 2603 (292), 2860 (1144)
Wilson, C. C.: ref, 1607 (12), 2497 (152), 2694 (12)
Wilson, C. L.: test, 490, 2097, 2098, 2889
Wilson, C. M.: ref, 2917 (1)
Wilson, D.: ref, 999 (7), 1965 (21,31)
Wilson, D. J.: ref, 2862 (82)
Wilson, D. M.: ref, 2305 (138)
Wilson, D. R.: rev, 449, 1586, 1925
Wilson, G. L.: ref, 1697 (154)
Wilson, G. T.: ref, 272 (89), 1661 (33), 1697 (48), 2603 (562)
Wilson, H.: test, 2351, 2890
Wilson, J.: ref, 999 (122)
Wilson, J. A.: ref, 739 (1), 999 (9)
Wilson, J. F.: ref, 2603 (82)
Wilson, J. R.: ref, 2076 (25)
Wilson, J. S.: ref, 615 (52), 2247 (124)
Wilson, K.: ref, 1758 (66), 2193 (51)
Wilson, K.: ref, 2860 (1069)
Wilson, K. G.: ref, 142 (6), 298 (30), 1014 (3), 1619 (8), 1965 (14), 2305 (124), 2603 (128,157), 2858 (40), 2862 (420)
Wilson, K. L.: ref, 2540 (7)
Wilson, K. S.: ref, 202 (1), 324 (3), 331 (1), 798 (6), 994 (3), 1424 (1), 1903 (97), 2190 (2), 2524 (1), 2660 (3), 2695 (10), 2710 (2), 2768 (7)
Wilson, L.: ref, 2497 (353)
Wilson Learning Corporation: test, 2453
Wilson, M.: test, 1014; ref, 681 (91)
Wilson, M. A.: ref, 1755 (44)
Wilson, M. J.: test, 281; ref, 935 (1), 2924 (1)

Wilson, M. S.: ref, 301 (58), 853 (22), 1348 (12), 2749 (72), 2862 (580), 2879 (188), 2901 (105)
Wilson, R. C.: test, 142, 726
Wilson, R. J.: ref, 134 (11), 2246 (4)
Wilson, R. L.: ref, 1107 (8), 2860 (691)
Wilson, R. M.: rev, 1611
Wilson, R. S.: ref, 776 (43), 1166 (188), 1405 (16), 1740 (20), 2125 (8), 2863 (383)
Wilson, S.: ref, 999 (121), 1903 (243), 2862 (507), 2879 (170)
Wilson, S. A.: ref, 2497 (533), 2603 (430)
Wilson, S. E.: ref, 2497 (170)
Wilson, S. K.: ref, 1902 (97)
Wilson, S. M.: ref, 1000 (22), 2497 (226)
Wilson, S. R.: ref, 272 (242)
Wilson, T.: ref, 2305 (130)
Wilson, T. D.: ref, 863 (46)
Wilson, V.: ref, 1379 (16)
Wilson, W. H.: ref, 1661 (46)
Wilson-O'Conner, D.: ref, 1697 (483)
Wilton, K.: ref, 694 (132)
Wiltshire, S.: test, 2683
Wimmer, H.: ref, 349 (36)
Win, Z.: ref, 999 (140)
Winbald, B.: ref, 2860 (563,1351)
Winborg, I.-M.: ref, 2860 (154), 2892 (19)
Winchester, K.: ref, 1392 (11), 2905 (53)
Wincour, G.: ref, 376 (31), 776 (60), 2863 (423)
Wincze, J. P.: ref, 793 (7,15)
Wind, T. W.: ref, 694 (91)
Windham, R.: ref, 1755 (59), 2497 (497)
Windle, M.: ref, 1000 (39,102,109), 1661 (5), 1697 (375,464), 2862 (443)
Windle, R. C.: ref, 1697 (464)
Windsor, J.: ref, 1379 (62), 1903 (330,478), 2651 (16), 2657 (20,21), 2695 (33), 2725 (8)
Wineburg, S. S.: ref, 592 (26), 1072 (28), 1759 (1)
Winefield, A. H.: ref, 273 (5,6,7), 1079 (9,10,11)
Winefield, H. R.: ref, 273 (5,6,7), 1079 (9,10,11)
Winefordner, D. W.: test, 1841
Winell, M. W.: rev, 717
Wineman, N. M.: ref, 272 (43), 2858 (87)
Winer, J.: test, 404
Winer, J. L.: ref, 404 (26,43)
Wines, R.: test, 492
Winfield, L. F.: ref, 665 (56)
Wing, A. M.: ref, 745 (21), 1671 (5), 2860 (1131)
Wing, H.: rev, 302, 839, 973, 1163, 2221
Wing, H. D.: rev, 2853
Wing, J.: ref, 2050 (39)
Wing, J. K.: test, 2050; ref, 2050 (10)
Wing, L. : ref, 2382 (37), 2485 (218), 2680 (18), 2813 (131)
Wing, R. R.: ref, 2497 (459)
Wingard, J. A.: rev, 1657
Wingard, J. R.: ref, 2076 (159)
Winger-Bearskin, M.: ref, 1404 (8)
Winget, C.: ref, 2108 (2), 2603 (47)
Wingfield, A.: ref, 2146 (4), 2860 (27,51,418,1359)
Wink, P.: ref, 68 (20,27), 372 (33,42,60,108), 373 (11,13,41), 1697 (580)
Winkworth, A. L.: ref, 2076 (136)
Winn, W. D.: ref, 2163 (32)
Winne, P. H.: ref, 2163 (116)
Winner, E.: ref, 2879 (127)
Winning, C. D.: ref, 2065 (5)
Winocur, G.: ref, 2860 (18), 2860 (1204), 2863 (10)
Winoeur, S.: ref, 272 (69), 273 (9), 694 (59), 1079 (18), 2076 (63)
Winograd, E.: ref, 2860 (629)
Winograd, P. N.: ref, 665 (13)
Winokur, A.: ref, 2305 (28)
Winokur, G.: ref, 1093 (107,108), 2305 (97,125,160, 161,172)
Winrow, B.: test, 2085
Winrow, B. A.: test, 154, 360, 536, 668, 1193, 1328, 1329, 1772, 1773, 1810, 2084, 2640, 2842, 2843, 2844, 2845, 2846, 2847
Winslow, E. B.: ref, 451 (282), 1965 (79)
Winston, A.: ref, 2326 (2), 2603 (129,386,546)
Winston, R. B.: test, 8
Winston, R. B., Jr.: test, 2527; ref, 2527 (10)
Winter, D. G.: ref, 2749 (87)
Winterling, V.: ref, 1902 (27), 2694 (5), 2862 (144)
Winters, K. C.: test, 73, 1931, 1932, 1933; ref, 73 (1), 1931 (1)
Wintre, M. G.: ref, 2452 (23), 2694 (24), 2862 (686)
Winward, E. J.: ref, 372 (86), 1790 (7)
Winwood, E.: ref, 776 (38)
Wires, J. W.: ref, 1178 (16)
Wirshing, W. C.: ref, 2050 (85)
Wirt, R. D.: test, 1962; rev, 466, 477, 1367
Wirtz, P. W.: test, 75; ref, 2603 (544)
Wirtz, S. J.: ref, 1379 (61), 2305 (115), 2813 (78)
Wirz-Justice, A.: ref, 1166 (165), 1166 (219)
Wise, E. A.: ref, 1686 (4), 1697 (527)
Wise, G. W.: ref, 1939 (5)
Wise, P. S.: ref, 1745 (49), 1866 (5)
Wise, S.: rev, 827
Wise, S. L.: rev, 1831, 2464; ref, 2497 (418,652), 2656 (24)
Wise, T. N.: ref, 793 (18), 998 (38), 1158 (1), 1241 (4), 1697 (152), 2218 (35,49)
Wisecarver, S. J.: ref, 272 (75)
Wiseman, S.: rev, 1319
Wiser, S.: ref, 272 (157), 991 (2)
Wish, J. R.: test, 2454
Wishart, H. A.: ref, 2860 (1014)
Wishart, J. G.: ref, 2229 (4), 2813 (89)
Wishart, L. R.: ref, 2860 (1369)
Wiske, M. S.: test, 889
Wisner, K. L.: ref, 1621 (1), 2305 (208)
Wisniewski, J. J.: ref, 1379 (82,91), 2485 (185), 2860 (1015), 2862 (421,588), 2901 (79,109)

Wisniewski, K. E.: ref, 2862 (459)
Wiswell, R.: test, 1062
Witelson, S. F.: ref, 1697 (153), 2860 (320)
Witherspoon, K. M.: ref, 1939 (15)
Witkin, H. A.: test, 474, 926, 1140
Witryol, S. L.: ref, 364 (12), 665 (57)
Witt, E. A.: ref, 592 (75)
Witt, J. C.: rev, 280, 286, 324, 342, 855, 1275, 1715, 2862; ref, 2862 (621)
Witt, L. A.: rev, 1569, 1824, 1966, 2856 (13), 2899 (20)
Witta, E. L.: rev, 2104, 2423, 2862 (637)
Witte, R. H.: ref, 2860 (1421), 2901 (137)
Wittenborn, J. R.: rev, 2247, 2417, 2749
Wittig, A. F.: ref, 1686 (5)
Wittling, W.: ref, 900 (3)
Wittmer, D.: rev, 1868
Wittrock, D. A.: ref, 1697 (23), 2497 (19), 2839 (9)
Witty, P. A.: rev, 364
Witztum, E.: ref, 301 (21), 2247 (22), 2749 (24), 2860 (339)
Wixted, J. T.: ref, 1093 (15), 2519 (11), 2520 (11)
Wnek, L.: test, 265, 266
Wodrich, D. L.: rev, 1612; ref, 2749 (81), 2862 (692)
Woehlke, P.: ref, 1515 (1)
Woehr, D. J.: ref, 615 (48,49)
Woermke, C.: ref, 1965 (42)
Woerner, M.: ref, 2288 (45), 2305 (70), 2305 (123)
Woerner, M. G.: ref, 2288 (64), 2305 (170)
Woessner, R.: ref, 2603 (511)
Woff, I. R.: test, 24
Woffington, L. M.: ref, 272 (40), 451 (11)
Wohl, M. A.: ref, 1166 (136), 2227 (29), 2516 (81), 2860 (1117,1150), 2863 (331,341), 2892 (231, 246)
Wohlegmuth, E.: ref, 694 (93), 1079 (34), 2497 (426)
Wohlfarth, T.: ref, 1079 (69)
Woike, B. A.: ref, 1745 (51), 1965 (71), 2749 (50,51,73)
Wojcik, K.: rev, 807
Wojtowicz, A.: ref, 451 (263), 681 (93), 1392 (15), 2862 (718), 2905 (120)
Wolchik, S.: ref, 472 (17)
Wolchik, S. A.: ref, 451 (20), 472 (26,29), 1697 (539), 2214 (16,23), 2603 (9)
Wolcott, D.: ref, 2076 (23), 2599 (6) 2860 (240)
Wold, D. C.: ref, 2860 (786)
Wolery, M.: ref, 265 (7), 811 (4), 994 (44), 1902 (27), 1903 (509), 2485 (219), 2694 (5), 2695 (64), 2813 (132), 2862 (144), 2864 (126), 2905 (18)
Wolf, A. D.: ref, 2860 (419), 2892 (61)
Wolf, A. P.: ref, 2860 (779,1205), 2892 (261)
Wolf, A. W.: ref, 1216 (67), 2864 (97)
Wolf, D. P.: ref, 1612 (51)
Wolf, P.: ref, 557 (3), 2214 (7)
Wolf, P. A.: ref, 303 (26,30), 2599 (42), 2860 (329,1382), 2863 (87,113)
Wolf, P. J.: ref, 2603 (19)
Wolf, R. M.: rev, 431, 492, 1657, 1927, 2424; ref, 838 (15)
Wolf, S.: ref, 1701 (34)
Wolf, T. M.: ref, 791 (13), 2858 (110)
Wolf-Schein, E. G.: test, 206, 285, 2528, 2893, 2894
Wolfe, D. A.: ref, 472 (3,108), 1902 (97), 1903 (331), 2214 (3,57), 2498 (3)
Wolfe, J. H.: ref, 180 (30)
Wolfe, J. M.: test, 167, 2608, 2849, 2897
Wolfe, J. N.: ref, 694 (129), 1903 (511)
Wolfe, J. W.: test, 2609, 2895, 2896
Wolfe, M. F.: ref, 592 (106)
Wolfe, R. N.: ref, 592 (85,103), 1716 (4)
Wolfe, S.: test, 2342
Wolfe, V. V.: test, 1884; ref, 472 (3), 2214 (3), 2498 (3)
Wolfer, L. T.: ref, 592 (106)
Wolff, C. B.: ref, 337 (155)
Wolff, H. A.: ref, 1697 (196)
Wolff, H. G.: test, 708, 709
Wolff, P. H.: ref, 1131 (2,7), 1164 (115), 1485 (48), 1903 (5), 2163 (255), 2225 (10), 2860 (303), 2862 (9), 2879 (2)
Wolff, S.: ref, 2163 (142), 2862 (422)
Wolfle, L. M.: ref, 2901 (53)
Wolford, P. L.: ref, 4 (5)
Wolfson, M. A.: ref, 353 (22), 451 (167), 846 (4)
Wolk, L.: ref, 214 (15), 1095 (21), 1804 (6)
Wolk, S.: ref, 1321 (4)
Wolk, S. I.: ref, 2305 (140)
Wolke, D.: ref, 2860 (756)
Wolkin, A.: ref, 2860 (419,1205), 2892 (61,261)
Wolkind, S.: rev, 1770
Wolkon, G. H.: ref, 2305 (75)
Wollack, J. A.: rev, 2483, 2484
Wollersheim, J. P.: ref, 1697 (154)
Wollman, K.: ref, 2516 (50)
Wollmers, G.: ref, 472 (12), 681 (7), 2214 (6)
Wolman, C.: ref, 2862 (693)
Wolmarans, J. J.: test, 1753
Wolmer, L.: ref, 451 (137), 2497 (414), 2603 (475)
Woloshyn, V.: ref, 592 (12), 2031 (2)
Woloshyn, V. E.: ref, 389 (14)
Wolpe, J.: test, 1021; ref, 1021 (3,6,10)
Wolpin, J.: ref, 1590 (13)
Wolters, E. C.: ref, 335 (1,15), 2289 (6), 2516 (15)
Wolters, P. L.: ref, 1612 (55,62,85), 1903 (483), 2163 (288), 2813 (81), 2862 (279,297,523)
Woltmann, A. G.: rev, 466, 1097, 2258
Wolyniec, P. S.: ref, 2050 (94)
Womble, M. N.: rev, 1617, 1792
Women's Studies Program, Duke University: test, 974
Womer, F.: rev, 364
Wompold, B. E.: ref, 1790 (8), 2451 (4)
Wonck, L. S.: ref, 1321 (11)
Wonderlic, C.: test, 2899
Wonderlic, E. F.: rev, 533, 1693
Wonderlic Personnel Test, Inc.: test, 654, 966
Wonderlich, S.: ref, 2599 (38), 2892 (271)
Wonderlich, S. A.: ref, 1697 (259), 2599 (3)

Wong, B. Y. L.: ref, 1071 (5), 1072 (36), 1392 (8), 2668 (3), 2862 (206)
Wong, C.: ref, 2860 (797)
Wong, C. K.: ref, 272 (287), 1079 (94), 2860 (1016), 2871 (4)
Wong, C-S.: ref, 1701 (56)
Wong, D. F.: ref, 1697 (88), 2289 (22), 2402 (6)
Wong, D. T.: ref, 998 (66)
Wong, E. Y. F.: ref, 2860 (371), 2862 (169)
Wong, F. Y.: ref, 1745 (73)
Wong, H.: ref, 2603 (340)
Wong, J.: ref, 2050 (141)
Wong, J. L.: ref, 298 (132), 2065 (13), 2402 (24), 2860 (546)
Wong, M.: ref, 2603 (350)
Wong, M. M.: ref, 1965 (32)f, 2031 (5)
Wong, M. M. T.: ref, 451 (273)
Wong, S. E.: ref, 2050 (52)
Woo, B.: ref, 2860 (159)
Woo-Sam, J. M.: ref, 798 (26), 837 (13), 1378 (11), 1379 (98), 1380 (20), 1866 (45), 1903 (562), 2862 (586,695), 2901 (130)
Wood, A.: ref, 1093 (109), 2214 (114)
Wood, B.: ref, 863 (45,57)
Wood, C.: ref, 1036 (9)
Wood, D.: ref, 2862 (441)
Wood, D. A.: ref, 2860 (547), 2879 (68)
Wood, F. B.: ref, 769 (1,7), 1072 (55), 1503 (11,16), 1903 (116, 576), 2163 (353), 2497 (95), 2862 (162,331, 332, 465, 725), 2901 (19,58,59,87,134)
Wood, G. C.: ref, 2050 (104)
Wood, H.: ref, 2497 (468,469)
Wood, H. B.: rev, 1657
Wood, H. M.: ref, 2862 (331,465), 2901 (58,87)
Wood, J. I.: ref, 2848 (2)
Wood, J. V.: ref, 1735 (6)
Wood, M.: test, 1036; rev, 451; ref, 1166 (226)
Wood, M. D.: ref, 337 (119), 999 (137) 1661 (66)
Wood, M. H.: ref, 1503 (11), 2862 (332), 2901 (59)
Wood, M. M.: test, 814
Wood, P. C.: ref, 694 (110,123), 1991 (100)
Wood, P. K.: ref, 337 (159), 1010 (64), 1661 (65,76), 2603 (344), 2860 (1370)
Wood, P. S.: ref, 1697 (577)
Wood, R.: test, 1712; ref, 1079 (66), 1590 (59), 2218 (55)
Wood, S.: ref, 272 (181), 376 (5), 1166 (113), 1413 (1), 2497 (369), 2863 (324)
Wood, T.: ref, 365 (11)
Wood, T. A.: ref, 364 (7)
Woodall, K. L.: ref, 1010 (16), 1697 (49)
Woodard, E. A.: ref, 615 (10)
Woodard, J. L.: ref, 776 (36,37), 2193 (49), 2860 (548,1017,1033),1206), 2863 (158,302),307)
Woodard, P. G.: ref, 571 (6)
Woodard, R. J.: ref, 2689 (2)
Woodburn, S. S.: ref, 853 (2)
Woodburn, W.: ref, 298 (99)
Woodbury, M. A.: ref, 2050 (84)
Woodcock, R. W.: test, 264, 1096, 1300, 1606, 2299, 2900, 2901, 2902, 2903, 2904, 2905
Woodford, P. E.: rev, 720
Woodman, C.: ref, 998 (56), 2603 (203)
Woodman, C. L.: ref, 1166 (68) 2603 (328)
Woodruff, E.: ref, 389 (8)
Woodruff-Pak, D. S.: ref, 1379 (76), 2432 (27), 2862 (399)
Woods, B. T.: ref, 2519 (28), 2520 (29)
Woods, D. J.: ref, 272 (303), 2497 (646)
Woods, G.: ref, 1697 (176,307)
Woods, M. G.: ref, 1697 (78,220)
Woods, S. W.: ref, 2497 (195)
Woods, T.: ref, 2862 (550)
Woods, W. J.: ref, 134 (35)
Woodward, J.: ref, 364 (3)
Woodward, L.: ref, 350 (53), 863 (94), 1079 (112)
Woodward, T. S.: ref, 303 (12), 1740 (15), 2860 (1190), 2863 (359)
Woodworth, G. G.: ref, 487 (2)
Woodworth, S.: ref, 451 (95), 2218 (20,46,47,80)
Woodworth, S. J.: ref, 798 (21), 1902 (80), 2860 (1018), 2862 (423)
Woody, C.: rev, 2823
Woody, G. E.: ref, 2305 (162), 2402 (52), 2519 (10), 2520 (10), 2603 (53,431)
Woody, S.: ref, 271 (7,18), 272 (368)
Woody, S. R.: ref, 998 (53)
Wool, C.: ref, 1697 (258)
Woolfolk, R. L.: ref, 2305 (163), 2603 (18)
Woolger, C.: ref, 462 (5)
Woolley, H.: ref, 2603 (311)
Woolner, R. B.: test, 2048
Woolston, J. L.: ref, 1379 (72), 1386 (18), 2813 (99)
Wootton, E.: ref, 697 (5), 2603 (522)
Wootton, J.: ref, 651 (1)
Wootton, J. M.: ref, 2214 (45)
Wootton, R. R.: ref, 1697 (195)
Worcester, D. A.: rev, 798
Worchel, F.: ref, 472 (8,79)
Worden, J. W.: ref, 451 (25)
Worell, J.: test, 1881
Worell, L.: test, 1881
Work, W. C.: ref, 472 (69), 681 (34), 2498 (27)
Workman, E.: rev, 285
Workman, J. W.: ref, 298 (164)
Workman, M.: ref, 1697 (199)
Workman, R. H.: ref, 1166 (221)
Workman-Daniels, K.: ref, 998 (27), 1697 (86)
Worland, J.: rev, 2869
World Health Organization: test, 642
Worley, K.: ref, 2860 (572)
Worobec, T. G.: ref, 136 (7), 1661 (26)
Worobow, A. L.: ref, 298 (32)
Worsham, N. L.: ref, 337 (70,134), 472 (77,163), 2214 (38.95)
Worthen, B. R.: rev, 657, 917, 1790, 2462, 2763

Worthington, E. L., Jr.: ref, 717 (1,2), 863 (75,92)
Worthington, J. J., III: ref, 2305 (187)
Worthley, J. S.: ref, 771 (14)
Worthman, C. M.: ref, 451 (108)
Worthy, J.: ref, 1657 (14)
Wortman, C. B.: ref, 791 (12), 2603 (73,348, 461,477)
Woyshville, M. J.: ref, 1093 (110), 2305 (168)
Wozencraft, T.: ref, 472 (20)
Wozniak, J.: test, 1391
Woznica, J. G.: ref, 1697 (116)
Wray, D.: ref, 1903 (175)
Wrenn, C. G.: rev, 2591
Wright, A. F.: ref, 2305 (13)
Wright, B.: test, 2142, 2145
Wright, B. D.: test, 1407; rev, 349
Wright, C. R.: rev, 148, 1269, 1358, 1875, 1932, 2399; ref, 838 (16)
Wright, D.: rev, 237, 346, 1142, 1473, 2313, 2678, 2686
Wright, E. J.: ref, 863 (16)
Wright, E. N.: test, 385, 2264
Wright, F.: test, 283, 928
Wright, F. D.: ref, 2519 (5), 2520 (5)
Wright, G.: ref, 1379 (56), 1386 (9), 2211 (34), 2432 (20), 2485 (144,145), 2862 (285), 2864 (67), 2879 (90), 2901 (46)
Wright, H.: ref, 1765 (7)
Wright, J.: ref, 451 (291), 472 (235), 863 (84), 1619 (11), 2858 (124)
Wright, J. A.: ref, 815 (11), 1379 (31), 1612 (39), 1903 (201), 2125 (9), 2485 (101), 2813 (43), 2901 (32)
Wright, J. C.: ref, 1079 (81)
Wright, L.: rev, 73, 878, 1308; ref, 853 (15), 1337 (2), 1338 (40,45), 1386 (6), 1903 (232), 2485 (111), 2681 (1), 2682 (6), 2839 (6)
Wright, L. S.: ref, 272 (75)
Wright, P. H.: ref, 298 (56)
Wright, P. M.: ref, 592 (104)
Wright, R.: ref, 1021 (3)
Wright, R. E.: ref, 1107 (10)
Wright, S.: ref, 2862 (219,328), 2879 (63)
Wright, S. C.: ref, 2163 (309)
Wright, S. K.: ref, 2862 (148)
Wright, T. A.: ref, 1590 (69)
Wright, T. M.: ref, 2218 (117)
Wrightson, N.: ref, 2862 (652)
Wrightstone, J. W.: test, 9, 10, 533, 1312, 1492, 1632
Wrobel, N. H.: ref, 1697 (19,465), 1962 (18)
Wrobel, T. A.: ref, 1697 (19)
Wu, J. T.: ref, 2879 (155)
Wu, P.: ref, 1240 (49), 1659 (10), 2484 (10)
Wulfeck, B. B.: ref, 1903 (218)
Wunderlich, K. C.: test, 283
Wunerlich, G.: ref, 2860 (1285)
Wurrlow, G. F.: ref, 1166 (47)
Wurtman, J.: ref, 2076 (34), 2440 (1)
Wurtman, R.: ref, 2076 (34), 2440 (1)
Wyatt, R. J.: ref, 564 (4), 2120 (2), 2288 (12), 2860 (617)
Wydra, D.: ref, 298 (32)
Wygonik, E. J.: ref, 2758 (1), 2860 (737)
Wyke, M.: ref, 2860 (84,85,162), 2892 (9)
Wykes, T.: ref, 2050 (105)
Wyler, A.: ref, 2050 (97), 2860 (1094)
Wyler, A. R.: ref, 376 (10), 1740 (2), 2860 (628), 2892 (116)
Wylie, E.: test, 233
Wyllie, E.: ref, 1902 (69), 2768 (28), 2862 (325), 2879 (110)
Wyman, P. A.: ref, 472 (69), 681 (34), 2498 (27)
Wynes, B. J.: ref, 1072 (50)
Wynn, V.: ref, 2856 (7)
Wynne, D.: ref, 2497 (626)
Wynne, D. C.: ref, 413 (22), 448 (1), 1093 (57), 2050 (51), 2247 (47,120), 2288 (2), 2860 (53,57)
Wynne, M. K.: rev, 214, 1656; ref, 994 (20), 2190 (4)
Wyshak, G.: ref, 1697 (52)
Wzorek, M.: ref, 1485 (33), 1653 (17), 2860 (721), 2862 (283)
Xenakis, S. N.: ref, 557 (3), 2214 (7)
Xenikou, A.: ref, 2160 (1)
Xeromeritou, A.: ref, 1903 (17), 2163 (92), 2862 (51,176)
Xia, Y.: ref, 472 (153), 2214 (87)
Xiang, M., : ref, 2050 (106)
Xie, J. L.: ref, 1590 (55)
Xie, X.: ref, 2126 (14)
Xu, M. L.: ref, 1164 (181), 1740 (33), 2227 (59), 2860 (1408), 2863 (427)
Yacczower, M.: ref, 1001 (13), 2497 (464)
Yachimowicz, D. J.: ref, 2545 (2)
Yacker, N. L.: ref, 771 (18)
Yadalam, K.: ref, 2860 (924)
Yadalam, K. G.: ref, 2305 (42)
Yaffee, L. S.: ref, 679 (1), 681 (77), 1903 (403,490), 2485 (211)
Yager, J.: ref, 337 (47), 2858 (19)
Yagla, S. J.: ref, 337 (179), 1697 (561), 2218 (109)
Yairi, E.: ref, 214 (19), 1001 (12,17), 1485 (56)
Yajima, M.: ref, 2860 (975), 2873 (44)
Yakimowski, M. E.: ref, 2862 (12)
Yakura, C.: ref, 272 (68), 1164 (50), 2516 (29), 2860 (498)
Yaldoo, D. T.: ref, 376 (7), 1166 (116), 2860 (1111), 2863 (330)
Yale, S. A.: ref, 2288 (85), 2289 (69)
Yama, M. F.: ref, 272 (76), 1010 (56), 2603 (224)
Yamada, E. M.: ref, 681 (39), 2860 (550)
Yamada, J.: ref, 2862 (424)
Yamada, T.: ref, 2225 (18), 2226 (38), 2227 (51), 2860 (1357), 2863 (409), 2892 (292)
Yamado, S.: ref, 2862 (360)
Yamadori, A.: ref, 303 (28), 2163 (352), 2226 (40), 2227 (56), 2860 (1388), 2863 (419), 2892 (298)
Yamaguchi, M.: ref, 2519 (18), 2520 (19)
Yamamoto, C.: ref, 272 (372), 2076 (185)
Yamamoto, J.: ref, 337 (69)

Yamamoto, K.: test, 972; rev, 725, 726
Yamasaki, Y.: ref, 2076 (174)
Yamashita, H.: ref, 2163 (334), 2860 (1314,1371), 2873 (68,73)
Yamashita, I.: ref, 1166 (60)
Yamashita, K.: ref, 1166 (213)
Yamashita, T. S.: ref, 337 (160), 994 (8), 1240 (15), 1903 (178), 2485 (87), 2680 (6), 2768 (16)
Yamashita, Y.: ref, 2862 (360)
Yamauchi, H.: ref, 372 (58)
Yamilo, R.: ref, 272 (196), 451 (136)
Yammarino, F. J.: ref, 1736 (1,2), 1755 (22), 2417 (17)
Yan, W.: ref, 666 (13)
Yanagida, E.: ref, 2749 (53)
Yandell, L.: ref, 1338 (36)
Yando, R.: ref, 270 (16), 272 (169,170), 451 (115), 1612 (48), 1962 (13), 2076 (73,148)
Yanero, D.: ref, 2651 (18)
Yang, B.: ref, 472 (81,153), 1619 (11), 2214 (40),87)
Yang, Z. W.: ref, 2305 (133)
Yanico, B.: test, 404
Yanico, B. J.: ref, 462 (22)
Yanovski, A.: ref, 2247 (97)
Yao, J.: ref, 2288 (9), 2305 (48)
Yao, J. K.: ref, 2288 (58)
Yapundich, R.: ref, 376 (14), 2863 (372)
Yarandi, H. N.: ref, 2516 (105), 2858 (42,120)
Yarbrough, D.: ref, 2862 (147)
Yarbrough, D. B.: ref, 301 (25)
Yarbrough, D. W.: ref, 2771 (21)
Yarcheski, A.: ref, 1947 (3)
Yarczower, M.: ref, 2519 (54), 2520 (53)
Yarger, C. C.: ref, 2731 (4)
Yarnell, J. W. G.: ref, 2497 (205)
Yarnold, P. R.: ref, 298 (133), 1338 (44), 2305 (42)
Yarosz, D. R.: test, 2070
Yasuda, K.: ref, 303 (25), 2860 (1372)
Yasumoto, J.: ref, 592 (92)
Yasutake, D.: ref, 2862 (425), 2901 (80)
Yates, A.: ref, 1965 (73)
Yates, A. J.: rev, 2402
Yates, B. T.: ref, 1093 (5), 1902 (62), 2860 (787), 2862 (298), 2879 (96)
Yates, C. M.: ref, 1138 (2), 2905 (94)
Yates, K.: ref, 2656 (18)
Yates, M.: ref, 272 (318), 273 (32)
Yates, W.: ref, 2519 (2), 2520 (2), 2603 (458)
Yates, W. R.: ref, 272 (77)
Yazgan, M. Y.: ref, 1164 (116), 2860 (1019)
Ybema, J. F.: ref, 1079 (82), 1745 (77)
Yeates, K. O.: ref, 375 (6), 451 (16,239), 815 (48), 1903 (98,332), 2862 (426,694), 2892 (157)
Yeatman, F. F.: ref, 462 (15)
Yee, C. M.: ref, 1697 (188), 2305 (73), 2497 (419), 2860 (384)
Yee, D. L.: ref, 180 (26)
Yee, J.: ref, 1697 (483)
Yegidis, B. L.: test, 7
Yeh, L. S.: ref, 1008 (3), 2553 (2)
Yeh, M.: ref, 1093 (81)
Yeh, R. S.: ref, 1402 (2)
Yeh, S. S.: ref, 665 (95)
Yehuda, R.: ref, 790 (22), 2519 (14), 2520 (15), 2860 (1020)
Yekovich, F. R.: rev, 125
Yelin, E. H.: ref, 2076 (51)
Yelland, T.: rev, 256
Yen, H.: ref, 2497 (483)
Yen, W. M.: ref, 364 (28), 665 (73)
Yeni-Komshian, G. H.: ref, 1902 (92), 2905 (108)
Yeo, R. A.: ref, 1164 (22), 2077 (1), 2860 (540)
Yeomans, J.: ref, 2226 (6), 2860 (714), 2863 (212)
Yeomans, J. D. I.: ref, 2860 (785)
Yerachmiel, B.: ref, 2497 (414)
Yersin, B.: ref, 1166 (101), 1661 (54)
Yerxa, E. J.: ref, 182 (1), 2008 (4), 2860 (311)
Yesavage, J. A.: ref, 1697 (388), 2218 (4), 2860 (765)
Yesenosky, M.: ref, 372 (62), 1965 (48)
Yetkin, F. Z.: ref, 2860 (561), 2892 (97)
Yeung, A.: ref, 2214 (46), 1965 (66)
Yewchuk, C.: ref, 389 (7), 1991 (99)
Yi, Y.: ref, 1701 (16)
Yiend, J.: ref, 2516 (109), 2892 (287)
Yik, M. S. M.: ref, 2860 (1411), 2899 (19)
Ying, Y. W.: ref, 372 (26)
Ying, Y-W.: ref, 372 (34,80)
Yingling, C. D.: ref, 1072 (1), 1131 (1), 2862 (1)
Yip, T. C. K.: ref, 2227 (8), 2860 (364), 2879 (44), 2892 (54)
Yirmiya, N.: ref, 234 (2,3), 433 (3,6), 451 (87), 459 (20,38), 674 (3,5), 2485 (91), 2813 (85), 2860 (1207,1208), 2862 (188,581,582,583), 2864 (127,128)
Yochman, A.: ref, 815 (52), 2724 (13)
Yocom, P.: ref, 1405 (14)
Yoder, B.: ref, 1745 (5)
Yoder, C.: ref, 301 (6), 1164 (13)
Yoder, L. H.: ref, 139 (1)
Yoder, P. J.: ref, 803 (1,2), 1095 (22), 1653 (11,19,20,25), 2189 (2,3,4,6), 2382 (18,29,30), 2485 (107,155,156), 2813 (82,83), 2864 (106)
Yomamoto, K.: ref, 665 (46)
Yoman, J.: ref, 1697 (250)
Yonan, C. A.: ref, 2305 (105)
Yonce, L. J.: ref, 1697 (327)
Yoneda, Y.: ref, 2163 (334), 2860 (1314), 2873 (68)
Yong, L. M. S.: ref, 745 (15), 2771 (33)
Yonkers, K.: ref, 2305 (178)
Yonkers, K. A.: ref, 1093 (68), 2519 (42), 2520 (42)
York, C. D.: ref, 1218 (13), 1725 (8), 2873 (50)
York, J. L.: ref, 134 (22,31), 1181 (17)
York, R.: ref, 1745 (78)
York, S.: ref, 615 (24)
Yorkston, K. M.: test, 209
Yoshida, K.: ref, 270 (46), 2305 (241)

Yoshida, M.: ref, 2227 (57), 2863 (420)
Yoshinaga-Itano, C.: ref, 2484 (11), 2731 (5), 2813 (134,135), 2862 (189,584,585), 2901 (23,106,107)
Yoshioka, M.: ref, 2860 (52)
Youll, L. K.: ref, 337 (106), 472 (139), 2498 (54)
Youn, T.: ref, 1166 (122)
Young, A.: test, 975; ref, 2239 (2)
Young, A. H.: ref, 2076 (103)
Young, A. J.: ref, 665 (58)
Young, A. W.: ref, 1758 (80,81,85,86,99), 2010 (3), 2163 (29), 2193 (13), 2860 (233,316,386,1209, 1368,1379), 2863 (60,414)
Young, C.: ref, 2860 (1243)
Young, D.: test, 550, 1145, 1148, 1797, 1875, 2467, 2613
Young, D. A.: ref, 2860 (1422), 2892 (309)
Young, D. W.: ref, 2860 (788), 2862 (299)
Young, E. A.: ref, 2305 (50)
Young, E. C.: test, 1898
Young, G. A.: ref, 694 (60)
Young, G. C.: ref, 2050 (91)
Young, G. R.: ref, 1169 (2), 2247 (78)
Young, H.: ref, 342 (3), 2862 (392), 2901 (71)
Young, H. F.: ref, 272 (143), 2860 (1021)
Young, H. M.: ref, 272 (74), 1166 (40)
Young, J.: ref, 337 (30), 1686 (7)
Young, J. C.: test, 2736
Young, J. D.: ref, 1140 (55,56)
Young, J. W.: rev, 1380, 1644; ref, 592 (76)
Young, L. T.: ref, 1093 (111), 1166 (90,97,166), 2218 (44), 2305 (171,209)
Young, M.: ref, 777 (1), 1991 (85)
Young, M. A.: ref, 1093 (22,23), 2305 (210)
Young, M. D.: ref, 372 (4), 998 (7), 1140 (4)
Young, R. C.: ref, 1093 (32), 1166 (85)
Young, R. D.: ref, 1697 (89)
Young, R. L.: ref, 301 (53), 349 (28), 1218 (14), 1240 (41), 1765 (25), 2163 (256), 2485 (186), 2695 (46), 2771 (40), 2862 (427), 2863 (303)
Young, R. M.: ref, 652 (3), 2497 (96)
Young, R. M. D.: ref, 1661 (11), 2497 (81)
Young, S. N.: ref, 2076 (74), 2497 (306), 2603 (240)
Young, T. B.: ref, 2076 (134)
Youngblut, J. M.: ref, 270 (3), 1000 (21), 1216 (112), 1889 (20)
Younger, J.: ref, 1903 (226)
Youngjohn, J. R.: ref, 1164 (117), 1697 (386), 2860 (480,549,1022), 2863 (134)
Youngs, E. L.: ref, 2076 (161)
Youngstrom, E. A.: ref, 2860 (1086), 2862 (479)
Youniss, R. P.: test, 1294
Yousefi, F.: ref, 301 (26), 1097 (8)
Yousry, A. M.: ref, 1755 (5)
Youssef, I.: ref, 1697 (343)
Yovanoff, P.: ref, 1590 (57), 1701 (50)
Yovetich, N. A.: ref, 134 (36)
Ysseldyke, J.: test, 1275
Ysseldyke, J. E.: rev, 331, 761, 815, 822, 1707, 1767, 2377, 2487; ref, 246 (1), 1300 (9)
Yu, E. S. H.: ref, 1058 (5), 2860 (464), 2862 (203)
Yude, C.: ref, 2862 (714)
Yuen, N.: ref, 2497 (605)
Yuh, W. T. C.: ref, 650 (16), 1093 (85)
Yuill, N.: ref, 1072 (5), 1765 (5)
Yuille, D.: ref, 837 (3), 1765 (19), 1903 (292), 2862 (280)
Yule, S. A.: ref, 1093 (58)
Yule, W.: rev, 2883; ref, 272 (278), 472 (16)f, 999 (120), 1079 (92), 1765 (26), 2214 (11,130), 2239 (11), 2497 (636), 2498 (66), 2862 (336,485,546)
Yunis, F.: ref, 2163 (308), 2860 (1197), 2862 (415)
Yunot, K. D.: ref, 2485 (236)
Yurgelun-Todd, D.: ref, 1166 (23)
Yurgelun-Todd, D. A.: ref, 2519 (28), 2520 (29), 2860 (1210)
Yutrzenka, B. A.: ref, 1010 (24)
Yutzy, S.: ref, 1697 (371)
Yuzda, E.: ref, 350 (24), 1653 (21), 2163 (195), 2228 (16), 2860 (795)

Zaback, T. P.: ref, 298 (134)
Zaballero, A.: ref, 2497 (574)
Zabel, R. H.: rev, 2816
Zabrucky, K.: ref, 2487 (2,5,12)
Zaccaro, S. J.: ref, 1437 (3)
Zach, E.: ref, 2860 (525), 2892 (88)
Zachar, P.: rev, 1333, 1688
Zachary, R. A.: test, 2402
Zachman, L.: test, 2710, 2911
Zacker, J.: ref, 1164 (14), 2860 (148), 2879 (22), 2901 (10)
Zacks, R. T.: ref, 1405 (23)
Zadik, H.: ref, 998 (116)
Zaeny, J. P.: ref, 66 (1), 2077 (3)
Zagar, R.: ref, 301 (9), 1072 (14), 2484 (2), 2862 (96)
Zager, L. D.: ref, 1697 (20)
Zagora, M. A.: ref, 404 (36), 1754 (22)
Zahn, T.: ref, 2305 (103)
Zahn, T. P.: ref, 2305 (242), 2860 (366)
Zahn-Waxler, C.: ref, 451 (46,162), 997 (25), 2039 (22), 2382 (6,16), 2497 (164)
Zahr, L. K.: ref, 997 (29), 1216 (92)
Zaia, A. F.: ref, 451 (199)
Zaichowsky, L. D.: test, 1586
Zaidel, D. W.: ref, 2860 (1023), 2862 (428)
Zaidel, E.: ref, 2860 (252,1023), 2862 (127,428)
Zaitra, A. J.: ref, 2858 (15)
Zakaluk, B. L.: ref, 1072 (50)
Zakay, D.: rev, 2081
Zaki, H. S.: ref, 272 (235)
Zakoroski, S. G.: ref, 2516 (50)
Zakowski, S. G.: ref, 2603 (171)
Zakzanis, K. K.: ref, 2860 (1422), 2892 (309)
Zaldívar, F.: ref, 999 (176)
Zalewski, C.: ref, 1697 (155), 2247 (20), 2860 (321)
Zalewski, L. J.: ref, 2545 (2)

Zalk, S. R.: test, 1377
Zalla, T.: ref, 2892 (207,255)
Zambarano, R. J.: ref, 2076 (11)
Zambelli, G. C.: ref, 1991 (42)
Zamble, E.: ref, 694 (41), 998 (17), 2497 (41,215)
Zambrana, R. E.: ref, 2497 (62)
Zametkin, A.: ref, 2305 (103)
Zametkin, A. J.: ref, 681 (39), 2860 (550)
Zamir, R.: ref, 298 (147), 1661 (21)
Zammit, G. K.: ref, 1093 (32)
Zammit, S.: test, 33
Zammit, S. A.: test, 1521
Zamrini, E. Y.: ref, 1135 (5), 2599 (7)
Zamsky, E. S.: ref, 1903 (242)
Zanakos, S.: ref, 2497 (413)
Zane, T.: test, 1245, 2827
Zangwill, O. L.: rev, 1714
Zanis, D. A.: ref, 2603 (567)
Zanna, M. P.: ref, 298 (36)
Zanna, V.: ref, 1687 (16)
Zapf, S. A.: test, 2384
Zapotoczky, H-G.: ref, 272 (370), 2497 (673)
Zaragoza, N.: ref, 2211 (25), 2452 (2), 2488 (7), 2862 (227)
Zarantonello, M. M.: ref, 1697 (94)
Zarb, J.: ref, 2860 (1211), 2863 (361)
Zarbatany, L.: ref, 1745 (67)
Zarcone, V. P.: ref, 1697 (128)
Zardini, G.: ref, 1903 (563), 2163 (347), 2227 (54), 2768 (42), 2862 (698)
Zarella, M.: ref, 2860 (1347), 2863 (405)
Zargarpoor, S.: ref, 451 (245)
Zarit, J. M.: test, 1643
Zarit, S. H.: test, 1643; ref, 337 (2)
Zarske, J. A.: rev, 68, 1745
Zastowny, T. R.: ref, 1010 (17)
Zatinsky, M.: ref, 1058 (4), 2860 (451), 2863 (125)
Zatorre, R. J.: ref, 2860 (67,72,149,551,742), 2863 (104,159)
Zatz, L.: ref, 1407 (1), 2860 (172)
Zatzick, D. F.: ref, 846 (2)
Zautra, A. J.: ref, 998 (14,39)
Zavasnik, A.: ref, 272 (177), 999 (158)
Zax, M.: ref, 1321 (1), 2146 (12), 2402 (15), 2603 (174), 2864 (3)
Zea, M. C.: ref, 1947 (8)
Zealley, H.: ref, 1079 (66), 1590 (59), 2218 (55)
Zeanah, C. H.: ref, 1321 (4)
Zebb, B. J.: ref, 2305 (90), 2497 (302), 2519 (35)
Zebrawski, P. M.: ref, 1903 (149), 2524 (3), 2542 (1,2), 2651 (7), 2725 (2)
Zedeck, S.: rev, 300, 411, 1351, 1569, 1694, 1695, 2105, 2188, 2415, 2573
Zehler, A. M.: test, 87
Zehr, K. S.: ref, 1902 (85), 1903 (459)
Zehrbach, R. R.: test, 653
Zeichner, A.: ref, 1661 (44), 2860 (625,626)
Zeidner, J.: ref, 180 (25)
Zeidner, M.: ref, 697 (1,3), 771 (2), 2497 (216,606), 2656 (2,23), 2862 (60)
Zeigler, A. J.: ref, 298 (40), 615 (19), 665 (28), 1140 (15), 1866 (14), 2163 (52), 2485 (30), 2729 (2), 2771 (8)
Zeisloft-Falbey, B.: test, 1192
Zeiss, A. M.: ref, 776 (14)
Zeitlin, S.: test, 695, 878
Zeitlin, S. B.: ref, 2497 (317,519,534), 2519 (36), 2520 (37), 2860 (1024)
Zelazo, P. D.: ref, 1903 (512), 2010 (2), 2227 (5), 2860 (208), 2863 (52), 2892 (24)
Zelazo, P. R.: ref, 681 (69), 1987 (16), 2864 (107)
Zeldenrust, S.: ref, 2599 (16), 2860 (614), 2863 (180), 2892 (115)
Zelhart, P.: rev, 129
Zelickman, I.: test, 1516
Zelinsky, D. G.: ref, 1379 (13,17)
Zelkowitz, P.: ref, 681 (69), 863 (83), 1987 (16), 2603 (512), 2864 (107)
Zeller, J. M.: ref, 2076 (153)
Zeller, P. J.: ref, 1697 (376), 2305 (119)
Zemel, B.: ref, 372 (12)
Zemishlany, Z.: ref, 2305 (118)
Zeng, L.: ref, 56 (15)
Zennaro, A.: ref, 2247 (109)
Zentall, S. S.: ref, 665 (31,74), 1592 (16), 2039 (20), 2862 (117)
Zentner, J.: ref, 2860 (1392)
Zerahn-Hartung, C.: ref, 745 (24)
Zerman, L.: ref, 2860 (1250)
Zernitsky-Shurka, E.: ref, 2749 (16)
Zerowin, J.: ref, 2498 (76)
Zervas, L. J.: ref, 694 (92)
Zervas, Y.: ref, 2076 (60)
Zesiger, P.: ref, 2516 (60), 2860 (789), 2892 (158)
Zeskind, P. S.: ref, 448 (7)
Zetterström, R.: ref, 301 (36),1097 (12), 1410 (2)
Zettle, R. D.: ref, 272 (27), 1697 (466)
Zettler, A.: ref, 2497 (632)
Zettler-Segal, M.: ref, 998 (73)
Zezuláková, J.: ref, 2485 (195)f, 2862 (460)
Zhan, G.: ref, 272 (222)
Zhang, C.: ref, 1745 (30)
Zhang, H.: ref, 2417 (14), 2862 (61)
Zhang, J.: ref, 372 (97), 1434 (2), 1697 (476), 2050 (58), 2603 (238)
Zhang, M.: ref, 1058 (5), 2860 (464), 2862 (203)
Zhang, X.: ref, 1096 (13), 1903 (558), 2524 (11), 2695 (63,71), 2864 (125,141)
Zhang, Y.: ref, 2417 (14)
Zheng, X.: ref, 999 (34)
Zhu, C.: ref, 135 (5), 2497 (624)
Ziebart, D. A.: ref, 592 (99)
Ziedonis, D.: ref, 2519 (29), 2520 (30)
Zielinski, J. J.: ref, 1644 (1), 2863 (160)
Zielinski, R. E.: ref, 2860 (939)

Zielonka, P.: ref, 665 (32), 1072 (24)
Zigarmi, D.: test, 1436
Zigler, E.: ref, 472 (30,56), 1274 (2), 1657 (18), 2163 (90), 2214 (21), 2380 (6), 2497 (422), 2813 (91), 2860 (867,915,1084)
Zigler, E. F.: ref, 472 (84)
Zigmond, N.: ref, 342 (5), 665 (85), 2485 (187), 2862 (429), 2879 (11,150), 2901 (81)
Zigun, J. R.: ref, 2892 (245)
Zika, S.: ref, 1178 (2), 2126 (10)
Zillmann, D.: ref, 694 (111), 999 (169)
Zillmer, E.: test, 860; ref, 2860 (174)
Zillmer, E. A.: test, 2772; ref, 1164 (139), 1698 (17), 2247 (110), 2860 (1212)
Zima, B. T.: ref, 451 (163), 1903 (513), 2902 (4)
Zimering, R. T.: ref, 1697 (36), 2497 (36)
Zimerman, B.: ref, 2305 (134)
Zimet, S. G.: ref, 2862 (230), 2879 (69)
Zimmer, J.: ref, 307 (2), 745 (19)
Zimmerman, I. L.: test, 2045; ref, 798 (26), 837 (13), 1378 (11), 1379 (98), 1380 (20) 1866 (45), 1903 (562), 2862 (586,695), 2901 (130)
Zimmerman, J.: ref, 2603 (510)
Zimmerman, L. D.: ref, 1379 (72), 1386 (18), 2813 (99)
Zimmerman, M.: ref, 2519 (15), 2520 (16), 2863 (63)
Zimmerman, M. A.: ref, 337 (125), 1965 (40)
Zimmerman, P.: ref, 2163 (54,160)
Zimmerman, R.: ref, 893 (5)
Zimmerman, V.: ref, 1590 (18), 2497 (211)
Zimmerman, W. S.: test, 1156, 1157, 1158, 2538; rev, 592, 2031
Zimring, F.: rev, 1002
Zinbarg, R. E.: ref, 1021 (42)
Zinnbauer, B. J.: ref, 2498 (76)
Zinner, E. S.: ref, 1697 (156)
Zinni, V. R.: ref, 451 (240)
Ziol, E.: ref, 1903 (550), 2226 (32), 2710 (7)
Ziol, E. W.: ref, 1903 (411)
Zipursky, R. B.: ref, 272 (284), 1758 (8), 2860 (420)
Zirps, F.: ref, 2905 (7)
Zis, H. P.: ref, 1166 (123)
Zisook, S.: ref, 335 (9), 1093 (24), 1164 (25), 1697 (271), 2288 (61), 2289 (47), 2603 (568), 2860 (239,643), 2892 (120)
Zissok, S.: ref, 1164 (84), 2288 (42), 2289 (32)
Zitman, F.: ref, 1166 (147,211)
Zitman, F. G.: ref, 2441 (2), 2813 (101)
Zito, W. S.: ref, 2017 (15), 2432 (25,30), 2892 (196,235,236), 2924 (3)
Ziv, A.: ref, 644 (1), 999 (23)
Zivney, O. A.: ref, 2247 (39)
Zizolfi, S.: ref, 1169 (5)
Zlomke, L. C.: rev, 355, 978, 1896, 2607
Zlotnick, C.: ref, 1166 (84,193), 2125 (29), 2860 (1373)
Zmich, D. E.: ref, 863 (14), 1903 (78)
Zobel-Lachiusa, J.: ref, 1533 (1)
Zoghbi, H. Y.: ref, 1218 (6), 1903 (275), 2163 (168,196), 2892 (123)
Zohar, A. H.: ref, 298 (136), 790 (19)
Zohoori, S.: ref, 1164 (181), 1740 (33), 2227 (59), 2860 (1408), 2863 (427)
Zola-Morgan, S.: ref, 2860 (9), 2863 (5)
Zollman, D.: ref, 56 (9), 592 (81)
Zolten, A. J.: ref, 815 (13), 1135 (11), 2860 (790), 2862 (229), 2903 (1)
Zonderman, A. B.: ref, 303 (21), 2218 (66), 2860 (865,964)
Zook, K. B.: ref, 561 (1)
Zoran, N.: ref, 1472 (201), 2000 (108), 2498 (68), 2603 (540), 2862 (642)
Zorn, M.: ref, 272 (199)
Zornberg, G. L.: ref, 1166 (91), 2076 (142)
Zoss, S. K.: test, 1290
Zotti, A. M.: ref, 999 (16), 2497 (52)
Zouari, J.: ref, 2603 (362)
Zubenko, G. S.: ref, 776 (38), 1093 (99,104), 2603 (393)
Zubin, J.: ref, 1164 (27)
Zubrick, S.: ref, 349 (6), 1902 (47)
Zubrick, S. R.: ref, 451 (128)
Zucco, G. M.: ref, 2485 (157), 2860 (1025)
Zucker, K. J.: ref, 337 (22), 451 (241), 853 (13), 1697 (119), 1991 (19), 2247 (48)
Zucker, R. A.: ref, 272 (128), 1178 (13), 1661 (51), 2485 (83), 2599 (13), 2860 (457)
Zucker, S.: rev, 1041, 2791
Zucker, S. H.: test, 1738
Zuckerman, A.: ref, 998 (88), 2076 (107)
Zuckerman, M.: test, 1745; rev, 2417; ref, 298 (66) 1745 (72), 2218 (13)
Zuffante, P.: ref, 2860 (314), 2863 (85)
Zui, J. C.: ref, 2860 (940,1138), 2901 (68,98)
Zuiker, S.: ref, 2862 (412)
Zukowski, A.: ref, 2879 (146)
Zumbo, B. D.: ref, 999 (69,189), 1755 (32)
Zumtobel, D. C.: ref, 863 (78)
Zupan, B. A.: ref, 451 (201), 472 (197), 2862 (627), 2901 (117)
Zur-Szpiro, S.: ref, 1612 (78), 1745 (61)
Zuravin, S. J.: ref, 272 (22)
Zurif, E.: ref, 2873 (19)
Zuroff, D. C.: ref, 272 (342), 298 (136), 790 (3,12, 19,24,27), 1414 (2), 1745 (62), 2603 (574)
Zurrón, M.: ref, 2860 (1026), 2862 (430)
Zusman, J.: rev, 2050
Zuttermeister, P. C.: ref, 1991 (64)
Zwart, F. M.: ref, 2603 (127)
Zweigenhaft, R. L.: ref, 592 (48)
Zwick, R.: ref, 118 (1), 1759 (10)
Zwick, W. R.: ref, 134 (6,14), 1661 (12,23)
Zytowski, D. G.: rev, 413, 1100, 1163, 1310, 1817, 2882
Zywiak, W. H.: ref, 66 (2)
Zyzanski, S. J.: test, 1338

SCORE INDEX

This Score Index lists all the scores, in alphabetical order, for all the tests included in Tests in Print V. *Because test scores can be regarded as operational definitions of the variable measured, sometimes the scores provide better leads to what a test actually measures than the test title or other available information. The Score Index is very detailed, and the reader should keep in mind that a given variable (or concept) of interest may be defined in several different ways. Thus the reader should look up these several possible alternative definitions before drawing final conclusions about whether tests measuring a particular variable of interest can be located in* TIP V. *If the kind of score sought is located in a particular test or tests, the reader should then read the test descriptive information carefully to determine whether the test(s) in which the score is found is (are) consistent with reader purpose. Used wisely, the Score Index can be another useful resource in locating the right score in the right test. As usual, all numbers in the index are test numbers, not page numbers.*

A (antiestablishment): 771
A-expectation: 392
Abasement: 68, 908, 1965, 1988
Abasive: 1243
Abdomen: 133
Abilities: 1177
Abilities and Skills: 2926
Ability: 397, 445, 664
Ability Measures: 2000
Ability Scores: 1874
Ability to Abstract: 268
Ability to Analyze Course of Therapy: 1830
Ability to Benefit from Reminding: 1058
Ability to Calculate Intracognitive Discrepancies: 2901
Ability to Do Quantitative Thinking Advanced Skills: 1319
Ability to Exercise Judgment and Common Sense: 734
Ability to Exercise Judgment-Dealing With People: 734
Ability to Exercise Judgment-Map Reading: 734
Ability to Explain: 836
Ability to Follow Instructions: 63, 445
Ability to Form Object to Object Relationships: 1206
Ability to Get and Hold a Job: 2834
Ability to Identify Positional Relationships of Body Parts: 1206
Ability to Interpret Literary Materials: 1319
Ability to Move Body in Relationship to Objects: 1206
Ability to Move Various Body Parts in Relationship to Each Other: 1206
Ability to Profit from Instruction or Correction: 2924
Ability to Rationalize Dishonesty: 1976
Ability to Read and Comprehend Police Test Material: 734
Ability to Resolve Issues: 1233
Ability to Say Words in Categories: 1058
Ability to Socialize with Co-Workers: 2924
Ability to Swallow Without Food Bolus: 870
Ability to Work Under Pressure: 2605
Ability to Work with Others: 268
Ability Utilization: 1493, 1694, 1695, 1701, 2805
Abjection-Disinterest: 792
Abnormal: 785
Above and Below: 2662
Absence Abuse: 1313
Absence of Bureaucracy: 2587

Absence of Conflict: 1006
Absence of Goals: 1931, 1932
Absorption and Imaginative Involvement: 74
Abstract: 1106, 1214, 2102
Abstract Conceptualization: 64, 1469, 1471
Abstract Fears: 213
Abstract Index: 2431
Abstract Processing: 2236
Abstract Random score: 1132
Abstract Reasoning: 186, 779, 838, 839, 1711, 2000, 2250
Abstract Relations: 2252
Abstract Sequential score: 1132
Abstract Visual Memory: 2701
Abstract-Concrete Content: 2458
Abstract-Concreteness Index: 2661
Abstract-Reasoning vs. Concrete-Reasoning: 2417
Abstract/Visual Reasoning: 2485
Abstracted vs. Grounded: 2417
Abstractedness: 538
Abstraction: 268, 2236, 2402, 2555
Abstraction Quotient: 2402
Absurd Responses: 78
Absurdities: 1370, 2485
Abuse/Neglect Checklist: 2791
Abuse Scale: 448
Abusive Remarks: 1006
Abusive/Secretive/Irresponsible Use: 1729
Abutting Consonants: 468
Abutting Consonants and Vowels/Diphthongs: 468
AC & DC Theory: 924
AC/DC Theory & Schematics & Print Reading: 923
Academic: 930, 1312, 1734, 2358, 2535, 2884
Academic Ability: 180
Academic Achievement: 1161, 1334, 1962, 2793
Academic Activity Climate: 2355
Academic Adjustment: 2525
Academic Advising Needs: 57
Academic Age: 811
Academic Aptitude: 217, 2220, 2221, 2222
Academic Autonomy Task: 2527
Academic Average: 386, 780, 1846
Academic Competence: 2361, 2452
Academic Competence (Efficacy): 1250
Academic Disability: 1522
Academic Drive-Conformity: 2538
Academic Engaged Time: 1275, 2607
Academic Expectations: 1910
Academic Focus: 380
Academic Freedom: 11
Academic Interest and Satisfaction: 844
Academic Interest-Love of Learning: 2538
Academic Learning Time: 907
Academic Performance: 311, 451, 2035, 2537
Academic Problems: 569, 2012
Academic Progress: 874
Academic Satisfaction: 1334
Academic/School-Related Self-Esteem: 746
Academic Self: 2355
Academic Self-Concept: 2321
Academic Self-Concept (Intrinsic Motivation): 1307
Academic Self-Concept-Performance Based: 2313
Academic Self-Concept-Reference Based: 2313
Academic Self Determination: 2534
Academic Skills: 60, 158, 1775, 2322, 2579
Academic Stimulation: 1216
Academic Stress: 2321
Academic Theme: 224
Academic/Work: 2652
Academics: 80, 220
Academics/Cognition: 814
Acceleration: 1921
Accelerational Attempt: 1026
Accent Errors: 1073
Accept Responsibility For Your Actions: 1858
Accept Specific And Difficult Goals: 1858
Acceptability: 1889
Acceptance: 698, 1147, 1216, 1881
Acceptance and Praise: 2355
Acceptance as a Sales Representative: 421
Acceptance by Others: 2751
Acceptance Factors: 2633
Acceptance of Aggression: 1939
Acceptance of Authority: 294, 1396
Acceptance of Child: 1026
Acceptance of Diversity: 2347
Acceptance of Need-Frustration: 2614
Acceptance of Parents' Affection to One Another: 2614
Acceptance of Problem Behavior: 1743
Acceptance of Siblings: 2614
Acceptance of Structure: 2347
Acceptance of Uncertainty: 401
Acceptance of Work Role: 2924
Acceptance or Resignation: 699
Acceptance Skills: 63
Accepting Authority: 40, 2444
Accepting Consequences: 2444
Accepting-Rejecting (AR): 1002
Accepting Responsibility: 2858
Accepting Status: 1689
Access to Emotional/Procedural Supports: 2578
Access to Information and Resources: 14, 2578
Access to People: 14, 2578
Access to Solution: 2578
Access to Support: 14
Access to the Problem: 14, 2578
Access to the Solution: 14
The Accident: 2743
Accident Description: 1978
Accommodating: 412, 485, 1483, 1688, 1711, 1817, 2121, 2756, 2836
Accommodation to Others: 2347
Accommodator: 1469, 1471

Accomplishment: 1276, 1856, 2804, 2922
Account Service: 490
Accountability: 1334, 1545, 1922, 1969, 2347
Accountability Scales: 1744
Accountant: 398, 399, 1790
Accountant/CPA: 380
Accounting: 618, 1794, 2026
Accounting and Finance: 410, 905
Accuracy: 219, 1092, 1231, 1529, 1692, 1765, 1781, 1850, 1930, 1955, 2080, 2667, 2725, 2786
Accuracy of Allegations by the Reporter: 442
Accuracy Score: 2430
Accurate: 618
Achievable Age: 2745
Achievable Health Age: 1499
Achieved Happiness: 2106
Achievement: 35, 68, 401, 820, 908, 1010, 1139, 1150, 1345, 1347, 1493, 1498, 1576, 1628, 1655, 1694, 1695, 1701, 1802, 1862, 1881, 1936, 1957, 1965, 1988, 2265, 2586, 2588, 2803, 2805
Achievement Communication: 36, 1136
Achievement History: 1210
Achievement Investment: 2355
Achievement Motivation: 1620, 1660, 2424, 2647
Achievement Orientation: 421, 480, 1573, 2268
Achievement Scales: 349
Achievement Screener: 822, 2309
Achievement Striving: 1044, 1769, 2218
Achievement Test Information: 2311
Achievement Values: 2346
Achievement via Conformance: 372
Achievement via Independence: 372
Achievements: 140
Achievements: Academic Years: 1566
Achievements at School: 2348
Achiever: 37, 1295
Achieving: 166, 1822
Achieving Approach: 1466, 2540
Achieving Motive: 1466, 2540
Achieving Strategy: 1466, 2540
Acknowledgement: 2804
Acknowledging Others' Efforts: 490
Acknowledging Peer Contributions: 490
Acquiescence: 2417, 2835
Acquire a General Education: 2530
Acquired Knowledge: 813
Acquiring Implicit Awareness of Sound Patterns in Words: 187
Acquiring Knowledge: 1689
Acquisition: 320, 687, 1169, 1644
Acquisition of Technology Knowledge: 2645
Acquisition Recall: 2159
Acquisitive: 1821
Act: 1966
Acting Out: 1960, 2514, 2848
Acting-out/Autonomy-Oriented: 1341
Acting Out Ratio: 1169
Acting Situation: 64
Action Agent Test: 1653
Action Orientation: 1923, 2097
Action Oriented: 1508
Action Program: 295
Action Skill: 1467
Actions: 1313, 1769, 1914, 2218
Actions and Gestures: 1528
Actions with Objects: 1528
Activation: 2017
Active: 695, 980, 1169, 1341, 1822, 2757
Active Body: 892
Active/Competitive: 305
Active/Concrete: 1497
Active Customer Relations: 2386
Active Experimentation: 64, 1469, 1471
Active-Inactive: 1940
Active Involvement: 1881
Active-Passive: 1789
Active Posture: 2308
Active-Recreational: 1010
Active-Recreational Orientation: 480
Active-Social vs. Quiet: 2618
Active with Peers: 1317
Activeness of Home: 1026
Activities: 451, 646, 875, 1790, 2310
Activities and Organizations: 57
Activities of Daily Living: 804, 1808, 2838
Activities with Friends: 1181
Activity: 242, 425, 1494, 1694, 1695, 1701, 1760, 2218, 2346, 2912
Activity Interference Scale: 291
Activity Level: 459, 1066, 1706, 1959
Activity Level and Motor Control: 478
Activity Level/Lability: 2147
Activity of the Beta Cells: 1242
Activity of the Cancer Cells: 1242
Activity of the Pancreas: 1242
Activity of White Blood Cells: 1242
Activity Performance: 2316
Activity Persistence: 320
Activity Preference: 2593
Activity Structure: 707
Activity vs. Lack of Energy: 672, 673
Acts with Integrity: 2101
Actual: 906, 1447, 2133
Actual Age: 1499
Actual Organizational Climate: 1860
Actual Referrals: 184
Actualization: 1558, 1894
Actualization and Self-Expression: 941, 1244, 2273, 2921
Actuary: 1790
Acuity: 2388
Acuity of Biomedical Problems: 2194
Acuity of Psychiatric/Psychological Problems: 2194
Acute Problems: 818

AD/HD Combined: 876
AD/HD Hyperactive-Impulsive: 876
AD/HD Inattentive: 79, 876
Adapt: 1966
Adaptability: 243, 280, 425, 966, 1889, 2776, 2912
Adaptability EQ: 243
Adaptability/Flexibility: 2490
Adaptance: 1984
Adaptation: 1907
Adaptation to Change: 459
Adapted Child: 68
Adapting: 86
Adapting to Change: 2929, 2930
Adapting to Technological Change: 2645
Adaptive: 266, 467, 806, 1086
Adaptive Autonomy: 2136
Adaptive Behavior: 1039, 1300
Adaptive Behavior Composite: 2813
Adaptive Behavior Index: 695
Adaptive Behavior Inventory for Children: 2606
Adaptive Behavior Total: 2204
Adaptive Behaviors: 293, 1194, 2838
Adaptive Functioning: 63, 451
Adaptive Instruction: 1275
Adaptive Motor Functions: 2715
Adaptive Problem-Solving: 467
Adaptive Reaction: 78
Adaptive Reasoning: 570
Adaptive-Reasoning: 2342
Adaptive Regression in the Service of the Ego: 912
Adaptive Skills: 245, 280
Adaptive Thematic: 467
Adaptive Total: 265
Adapts to Cultural Differences: 2101
ADD: 469
Addiction: 999
Addiction Admission Scale (AAS): 1697
Addiction Potential Scale (APS): 1697
Adding and Subtracting Decimals: 1247
Adding and Subtracting Fractions: 1247
Adding and Subtracting Whole Numbers: 1247
Adding Decorations: 726
Addition: 730, 825, 831, 1392, 1738, 2134
Addition and Subtraction: 532
Addition & Subtraction: 1224
Addition and Subtraction Correction: 1405
Addition and Subtraction of Whole Numbers: 171, 1604, 2486
Addition of Whole Numbers: 2486
Addition Sums with Numbers: 254
Addition Sums with Objects: 254
Addition Test: 1405
Additional Advising Information: 57
Additional Behavior Traits: 158
Additional Drug Use Symptoms: 73
Additional Information: 717
Additional Items: 1512
Additional Observations: 276
Additional Questions: 57, 620
Additions: 430, 1073
Additions and Omissions: 1138
Addressing an Envelope: 211
Adequacy of Work Experience: 2348
Adequate/Same-Sex: 2307
ADHD: 469
ADHD Index: 678, 681, 2461
ADHD Quotient: 223
Adjective: 2662
Adjective Pairs: 1197
Adjectives: 430, 1898
Adjectives and Adverbs: 1125, 1248
Adjectives and Attributes: 2215
Adjunctive Techniques and Cognitive Interventions: 310
Adjusted: 86
Adjustment: 19, 690, 1212, 1335, 1962, 2061, 2074
Adjustment Behavior Checklist: 810
Adjustment Disorder: 77, 876, 2107
Adjustment of Home: 1026
Adjustment to School Work: 1716
Adjustment to Stress: 701
Administration: 406, 618, 648, 684, 1551, 1818, 2274, 2424, 2425
Administration and Management: 905, 1044
Administrative: 166
Administrative Ability: 2345
Administrative Assisting: 1794
Administrative/Clerical/Personnel: 179
Administrative Competencies: 1570
Administrative Composite: 1570
Administrative Duties: 989
Administrative Efficiency: 2007
Administrative Index: 401
Administrative Indices: 399
Administrative Issues: 421
Administrative Knowledge: 1032, 2002
Administrative Knowledges: 796
Administrative Scope: 2587
Administrative Support: 1350
Administrative Support/Clerical: 2822
Administrator: 312, 1310
Admission of Problems: 1587
Adolescent Domain: 2510
Adolescent-Parent Relationship Domain: 2510
Adult: 68, 1374, 2280
Adult Development: 380
Adult Distractibility Task: 1099
Adult Interaction: 265
Adult-Motivated: 2181
Adult Needs: 1009, 1264
Adult Personality Inventory: 1568
Adult Problems: 2147
Adult Relations: 2323, 2391
Adult Subsystem: 1565

Adult Vigilance Task: 1099
Adults: 377
Adults and Counselors: 2355
Advanced Planning: 948
Advanced Skills: 1318
Advanced Task Areas: 197
Advanced Vocabulary Test: 1405
Advancement: 1276, 1345, 1493, 1694, 1695, 1701, 2805
Advancement/Mobility: 2584
Advancing: 83
Advantage Index: 1993
Adventure: 1222, 1334
Adventure vs. Security: 865
Adventuring: 380
Adverbials: 1427
Adverbs: 430
Adverbs per T-Unit: 2661
Adverbs/Prepositions: 1739
Adverse Business Conditions: 807
Adverse Effect on Educational Performance: 2669
Advertising: 1364
Advertising Account Executive: 380
Advertising and Design: 1792
Advertising Artist/Writer: 398, 399
Advertising Design: 1794
Advertising Executive: 398, 399, 1790
Advertising/Marketing: 380
Advising: 2876
Advising Information: 57
Advising Response Score: 632
Advisor-Advisee Activity Scales: 8
Aesthetic: 86, 147, 980, 1639, 1724, 1819, 2255, 2539, 2626
Aesthetic Appreciation: 865
Aesthetic-Cultural: 618
Aesthetic Issues: 684
Aesthetic Judgment: 2617
Aesthetic v. Realistic: 417
Aesthetics: 1493, 1769, 2218, 2805
Aesthetics-Arts: 1163
Affect: 158, 1690, 1732, 1734, 2614
Affect Regulation: 2521
Affected by Feelings vs. Emotionally Stable: 477, 888
Affection: 426, 791, 1036, 1169, 1350, 1374, 1594, 2237, 2350
Affectional Expression: 863
Affectionate: 381
Affectionate Toward Parent: 1317
Affectionateness Toward Child: 1026
Affective: 268, 1242, 1355, 1615, 1959, 2001, 2128
Affective Abilities: 1921
Affective Aspects of Reading Instruction: 684
Affective Behavior: 653
Affective Communication: 1582
Affective Component: 1720
Affective Disturbance: 1241, 1587, 1775
Affective Expression: 962, 1008, 1952, 2279
Affective Flattening or Blunting: 2288
Affective Functions: 2647
Affective Inhibition: 1241
Affective Instability: 1959
Affective Language: 1690
Affective Strength: 290
Affects: 793, 824
Affects Balance Index: 791
Affects Expressiveness Index: 791
Affiliation: 68, 467, 495, 908, 1146, 1276, 1347, 1497, 1628, 1655, 1724, 1856, 1936, 1957, 1965, 1988, 2922
Affiliative: 1150, 1243, 1498, 1560, 1575, 1822, 2021, 2022
Affiliative Styles: 1862
Affiliative Tendency: 1627
Affinity for Objects and Things: 1579
Affirmation and Negation: 2215
Affirmative Declarative: 2337
Affixes: 917
Afro-Centric: 2887
After Start: 2475
Afternoon: 1470, 1472, 2069
Agentic Processing (Conventional: 1307
Agents of Change: 684
The Age of Revolutions Continues: 2932
Ages 5-20: 1401
Aggression: 68, 77, 280, 908, 929, 1066, 1169, 1522, 1582, 1706, 1815, 1959, 1965, 1988, 2001, 2242, 2306, 2647, 2716
Aggression and Hostility: 1219
Aggression/Hostility: 1209
Aggression Toward Peers: 2614
Aggressive: 451, 475, 551, 1268, 2841
Aggressive/Acting Out: 281
Aggressive Attitude: 1959
Aggressive Behavior: 424, 451, 2939,
Aggressive Behavior Scale [Externalizers]: 890
Aggressive-Calm: 2446
Aggressive/Defensive: 1150
Aggressive/Defensive Cultures: 1862
Aggressive/Defensive Styles: 1498
Aggressive Interaction: 2447
Aggressive/Rebellious Behavior: 75
Aggressive (Sadistic): 1687
Aggressive/Self-Destructive: 928
Aggressive/Undersocialized: 1341
Aggressiveness: 80, 219, 220, 654, 1821
Aggressivity: 2285
Aggressivity Scale: 2284
Agility/Dynamic Balance: 1062
Agitation: 538, 562, 2216
Agitation-Excitement: 2108, 2109
Agnosias: 987
Agoraphobia: 2448
Agreeable: 1243

Agreeable-Hostile: 2077
Agreeableness: 1044, 1576, 1769, 2218
Agreeing: 1688, 1954
Agreement: 2882
Agreement Between Parent and Evaluator Form: 2791
Agribusiness/Agricultural Production: 905
Agribusiness and Agricultural Production: 410
Agribusiness Manager: 380, 1790
Agricultural Sciences: 905
Agriculture: 399, 411, 618, 905, 1790, 1990, 2026
Agriculture and Life Sciences: 1841
Agriculture/Animals and Forestry: 2822
Agriculture-Forestry-Conservation: 408
Agriculture Mechanics: 1794
Aiming: 644, 1711, 2421
Aiming Accuracy and Speed: 1920
Aimless Actions: 1098
Air Cooled Gas Engine Repair: 1792, 1794
Aircraft Mechanic: 398, 399
Airline Mechanic: 380
Alcohol: 19, 66, 849, 856, 1313, 1335, 1931, 2061, 2285, 2393, 2403, 2554, 2783
Alcohol Abuse: 1661, 2108
Alcohol Abuse and Dependence: 642
Alcohol Addiction Evaluation: 1372, 2550
Alcohol and Drug Use: 1913
Alcohol and Drugs: 2454
Alcohol and Other Drug Abuse: 2604
Alcohol Consumption—Quantity: 1181
Alcohol Consumption—Quantity/Frequency: 1181
Alcohol Dependence: 1687
Alcohol/Drug Problem Acknowledgment: 1698
Alcohol/Drug Problem Proneness: 1698
Alcohol/Drug Use: 1925, 2074
Alcohol History: 1431, 1432
Alcohol Involvement: 136
Alcohol or Drug Abuse: 2305
Alcohol Problem: 1960
Alcohol Problems: 1959
Alcohol Scale: 2284
Alcohol Use: 133, 184, 1207
Alcohol Use Symptoms: 73
Alcohol Withdrawal: 66
Alcoholic Abuse: 2109
Alcoholism: 650, 2107
Alcoholism Severity: 1587
Alertness: 1930
Alertness for Danger/Suspiciousness and Lack of Trust: 1219
Algebra: 444, 570, 621, 622, 684, 947, 1038, 1863, 1997, 2678
Algebra and Functions: 1759
Algebra I: 664
Algebra II: 664
Alienation: 201, 256, 297, 467, 1341, 1698, 1960, 2103, 2115
Alienation-Boredom: 77
Alienation-Depression: 1925
Alienation Index: 1967
Alienation Toward Authority: 2538
Alienation-Self and Others (Si3): 1697
Aligning: 2821
All Fours: 1668
All-Fours: 1258
All Fours Equilibrium: 1668
Allegation Motives: 442
Allergic Inclination: 1686
Allied Health (Dental Services: 410
Alliteration: 1980
Allows for Mutual Influences: 1296
Ally: 1451
Almost Alike Pictures: 987
Alogia: 2288
Alone: 2181, 2607, 2928
Aloneness: 1577, 2874
Aloof-Introverted: 1289
Alphabet: 1534
Alphabet and Dictionary Skills: 299
Alphabet Knowledge: 813, 2682
Alphabet Recognition and Reproduction: 1588
Alphabet-Speech: 2628
Alphabet/Word Knowledge: 821
Alphabetical: 1692
Alphabetizing: 1534, 2054
Alphabetizing & Filing: 2374
Alphabetizing-Filing: 535
Altercentricism: 689
Alternating Consonants: 486
Alternating Half Kneel-Stand: 977
Alternating One Foot Kneel: 977
Alternating Prone Reach: 977
Alternatives: 554
Altruism: 1493, 1769, 2218, 2805, 2915
Altruistic: 1724, 2121
Altruistic Behavior: 2132
Altruistic-Nurturing: 1022, 2704, 2507
AM Composite: 1485
Ambiguous: 950
Ambiguous Sentences: 2693
Ambition: 1212, 1824, 1930, 1955, 2776, 2882
Ambitions Evaluation: 1968
Ambitious: 381, 990
Ambitiousness: 1223
Ambivalent: 1169, 2647
Ambivalent Hostility: 2114
America Becomes a World Power: 145
American Government: 503, 645
American History: 572, 593, 947
American History & Social Studies: 615
American Literature: 504
Amiable: 2453
Amnesia: 2521
Amorality: 1698
Amorality (Ma1): 1697

Amount of Supervision Required: 2924
Amphetamine: 66
Amphetamines: 1931
Amplia Habilidad Cognitiva: 264
Amplia Habilidad Cognitiva-Escala Extendida: 264
Amusement: 1222
Anal Expulsiveness/Retentiveness: 317
Análisis Síntesis: 264
Analog Electronics: 1279, 2643
Analog/Radio: 924
Analogías Verbalis: 264
Analogic Reasoning: 2792
Analogical Reasoning: 1780
Analogies: 125, 388, 899, 1075, 1088, 1800, 2138, 2252, 2324, 2441, 2677
Analysis: 368, 1953, 2346
Analysis of Attributes: 2252
Analysis of Relevant and Irrelevant Information: 2252
Analysis of Response Validity Checklist: 2791
Analysis of Science Materials: 1319
Analysis of Social Studies Materials: 1319
Analysis-Synthesis: 2901
Analyst: 1295
Analytic: 744, 1472, 1658, 2416
Analytic-Autonomizing: 1022, 1704, 2507
Analytical: 618, 1253, 1333, 1954, 1984, 2085, 2453
Analytical Chemistry: 44
Analytical Reasoning: 168, 239, 1115
Analytical Skills: 1467
Analytical Thinking: 166
Analyticity: 367
Analyze: 1966
Analyzing: 380
Analyzing and Interpreting Literature: 505
Analyzing Needs: 490
Analyzing Participants and Situations: 2775
Analyzing Problems Using Mathematical Skills and Concepts: 1094
Analyzing Prospect Needs: 989
Analyzing the Needs and "Entering Behavior" of the Learner: 203
Anatomy: 1214
Anatomy Terminology: 2454
Anergia: 2017
Anger: 77, 78, 439, 690, 847, 1374, 1655, 1698, 1938, 2592
Anger and Aggression: 637, 1141, 2850
Anger (ANG): 1697
Anger Control: 80, 220, 1960, 2496
Anger Control/Hypersensitivity: 1340
Anger Control Problems: 681
Anger-Excitability: 748
Anger Expression: 2496
Anger-Hostility: 2076
Anger/Hostility: 1006
Anger/Hostility Patterns: 1209
Anger-In: 362, 2496
Anger/Irritability: 2782
Anger-Out: 362, 2496
Anglocentric: 2887
Angry: 2647
Angry Hostility: 2218
Angry Reaction: 2496
Angry Temperament: 2496
Angry-Tolerant: 2446
Anhedonia-Asociality: 2288
Animal: 1149, 1214, 2404
Animal Care: 380, 407, 2177
Animal Halves: 2240
Animal Naming: 199
Animal Pegs: 2864
Animal Service: 398, 399
Animals: 684, 1818
Animals and Interests Test: 1085
Animals and Plants: 1285
Anomalous Concept Test: 1257
Anomalous Figure Test: 1257
Anorexia Nervosa: 77, 79, 2107
Answer-Choice: 2733
Answer Choice Frequency: 690
Answering Objections: 490
Answering Questions: 1534
Antecedent Events & Situations: 1732
Antecedents of Substance Abuse: 2551
Anthro-Centric: 2887
Anthropology: 618
Anticipation of Pain vs. Felt-Sensation: 1869
Antiquarianism: 963
Antisocial: 690, 1025, 1335, 1687, 1961, 2061, 2285, 2306, 2393, 2403, 2520
Antisocial-Aggressive: 2322
Antisocial/Aggressive: 2036
Antisocial Attitudes: 1313
Anti-Social Attitudes-Acts: 2108
Antisocial Behavior: 1522, 1963, 2322
Antisocial Behaviors: 1314, 1587, 1959
Antisocial Features: 1959
Antisocial History: 2198
Antisocial Impulses or Acts: 2109
Antisocial Personality: 2107, 2147
Antisocial Personality Disorder: 79
Antisocial Practices (ASP): 1697
Antisocial Reaction: 2615
Antisocial/Risk-Taking: 1207
Anti-Social Tendencies: 374, 427
Antonyms: 2911
Anxiety: 78, 80, 220, 256, 267, 271, 280, 282, 291, 335, 337, 362, 477, 538, 569, 651, 690, 701, 789, 791, 792, 794, 818, 844, 888, 915, 929, 931, 938, 1201, 1214, 1313, 1333, 1455, 1456, 1577, 1626, 1660, 1687, 1698, 1745, 1749, 1779, 1815, 1871, 1925, 1959, 1962, 1991, 2006, 2108, 2109, 2148, 2218, 2242, 2305, 2326, 2367, 2475, 2495, 2602, 2603, 2604, 2615, 2783, 2874

Anxiety (A): 1697
Anxiety About Organization: 1210
Anxiety and Insomnia: 1626
Anxiety and Other Disorders: 2519
Anxiety (ANX): 1697
Anxiety/Depression: 2647
Anxiety Disorder: 73
Anxiety Disorders: 2147
Anxiety Disorders Index: 1730
Anxiety (General): 1481
Anxiety/Insomnia: 1079
Anxiety/Phobic Avoidance: 1207
Anxiety Problems: 2012
Anxiety-Related Disorders: 1959
Anxiety Scale: 2114
Anxiety/Somatic Problems: 2036
Anxiety (Specific): 1481
Anxiety Toward Mathematics: 1599
Anxiety-Withdrawal: 2211
Anxious: 451
Anxious Affect: 1733
Anxious Arousal: 2782
Anxious/Avoidant: 2147
Anxious/Compulsive Behaviors: 1618
Anxious Concern: 136
Anxious Coping Subscale: 1730
Anxious/Depressed: 451, 2939
Anxious Depression: 538, 2120
Anxious-Fearful: 2039
Anxious Feelings: 1685
Anxious/Introspective: 1341
Anxious/Obsessive: 424
Anxious Producer: 1162
Anxious-Relaxed: 218
Anxious-Secure: 2446
Anxious-Shy: 681
Anxious Student: 2530
Apathy: 537, 690
Aphasia: 987
Aphasia Quotient: 2873
Aphasia Screening: 1164
Aphasias: 987
Aphasios: 987
Apologizing: 40
Appearance: 63, 1250, 1941, 1942, 1968, 2369
Appearance and Eating: 63
Appearance and Perception: 1961
Appetite: 1488
Appetite/Willingness to Participate: 870
Appliance Repair: 1792, 1794
Application: 626, 1184, 1601, 1603
Application for Employment: 989
Application for Executive Position: 989
Application for Office Position: 989
Application for Position: 989
Application Forms: 1534
Application in Context: 917
Application in Mechanics: 1094
Application of Rules: 1182
Applications: 369, 370, 1392
Applications Content: 1738
Applied: 2898
Applied Arts: 752, 1790
Applied Chemistry: 1222
Applied Knowledge of Language: 830
Applied Logic: 2019
Applied Math: 618, 1323, 2737, 2738
Applied Mathematics Assessment: 2920
Applied Problems: 2901
Applied Technology: 762
Applied Technology Assessment: 2920
Applying Classroom Facilitation Skills: 2775
Applying Mathematical Skills and Concepts to Solve Problems: 1094
Applying Psychotherapy Theory: 1830
Applying Science Concepts: 1094
Appointment Compliance: 2197
Appraisal of Conflict: 2546
Appraised Age: 2745
Appraised Health Age: 1499
Appraising People and Performance: 1570
Appreciation: 1667
Appreciative: 1222
Appreciative-Depreciative Attitude Toward Medical Students: 1640
Apprehension: 1201, 1321, 1576, 1317
Apprehensive-Avoidant: 1457
Apprehensive vs. Self-Assured: 2417
Apprehensiveness: 538
Approach: 425
Approach-Avoidance Style: 2065
Approach to Data and Information: 1579
Approach to Teacher: 1161
Approachability: 490
Appropriate Behavior: 2763
Appropriate/Compliance: 1006
Appropriate Handling of Sexual Material: 1830
Appropriate/Noncompliance: 1006
Appropriate Physical Interaction: 2450
Appropriateness: 2506
Appropriateness of Personal Relations with Supervisor: 2924
Appropriateness of Topic Sentence: 204
Approval: 1150, 1498, 1655, 1862
Approval of Others: 401
Approval/Reassurance: 716
Approval Seeking: 1294
Approximating: 1826
Apraxia: 562
Apraxias: 987
Apraxic Characteristics Checklist: 164
Aprendizje Visual-Auditivo: 264
Aptitud en Concocimiento: 264
Aptitud en Languaje Escrito: 264

Aptitud en Lectura: 264
Aptitud en Matemáticas: 264
Aptitude Concern: 1163
Aptitude for the Job: 1579
AR Incongruence: 1002
Arbitrative: 1222
Architect: 380, 398, 1790
Architectural Drafting: 1792, 1794
Architecture: 618
Architecture and Environmental Design: 905
Area: 2023
Area/Ethnic Studies: 905
Area of Interest: 392
Areas Needing Attention: 1886
Areas of Emphasis: 1929
Areas of Interest: 391
Arithmetic: 18, 30, 173, 199, 535, 571, 730, 916, 1042, 1043, 1138, 1139, 1167, 1353, 1379, 1524, 1525, 1731, 1802, 1834, 1835, 2220, 2221, 2222, 2387, 2408, 2627, 2665, 2678, 2692, 2795, 2840, 2860, 2862, 2864, 2879
Arithmetic Application: 2736
Arithmetic Aptitude Test: 1405
Arithmetic Attainment: 1786
Arithmetic Computation: 1920, 2795
Arithmetic Computations: 987
Arithmetic Laws and Processes: 348
Arithmetic Perceptions: 120
Arithmetic Problems: 987, 2324
Arithmetic Reasoning: 180, 186, 779, 1430, 2795
Arithmetic Skills: 2736
Arithmetic Subtest: 1382
Arithmetical Problems: 1198
Arm and Leg Extensions: 2141
Arm-Hand Steadiness: 1044, 1711
Arousal: 915, 1647
Arousal-Inducing Parental Attitude: 1630
Arousal Need: 320
Arrangement of Facts: 1364
Arranging Words: 1405
Arrival and Departure: 1220
Arrogant-Calculating: 1289
Arrows: 1771
Art: 406, 618, 635, 1177, 1482, 1790, 2882
Art and Design: 1818
Art/Communications/Design: 993
Art Community: 684
Art: Content Knowledge: 2026
Art: Content/Traditions/Criticism/Aesthetics: 2026
Art Design: 1667
Art/Design: 380
Art Education: 2026
Art History: 91, 118, 684
Art Making: 2026
Art of the Western World: 762
Art or Music: 411
Art Teacher: 1790
Arthritis: 1853
Articles: 430, 1127, 1427, 1898, 2337
Articulation: 124, 866, 2028, 2332, 2470, 2471, 2502, 2706, 2866
Articulation Age: 2866
Articulation and Phonological Skills: 2523
Articulation Development: 761
Articulation Function: 2235
Articulation/Phonology: 653
Articulation Rating: 199
Articulation Survey: 1385
Articulation Total: 1047
Articulatory Agility: 199
Articulatory Competence: 175
Artisan: 1451
Artist: 2825
Artistic: 5, 397, 398, 399, 407, 412, 485, 1074, 1157, 1312, 1395, 1413, 1483, 1711, 1790, 1817, 1822, 1829, 2121, 2257, 2264, 2295, 2360, 2835, 2836
Artistic Interests: 2605
Artistic Performing Abilities: 1238
Artistic Potential: 311, 2537
Artistry: 1396
Arts: 121, 162, 1100, 1285, 1929
The Arts: 749, 1177, 1785
Arts and Crafts: 183
Arts and Entertainment: 2833
Arts & Sciences: 618
Arts/Crafts: 399
Arts-Design: 416
Arts/Literature: 56, 621
Arts-Performing: 416
Arts-Professional: 395, 414, 415, 417, 702, 1541
Arts-Skilled: 395, 414, 415, 417, 702, 1541
As I Would Like It To Be: 2129
As It Is Now: 2129
Ascendancy: 1101, 1158
Asceticism: 893
Ask Trainees to Compliment Each Other: 2923
Ask Trainees to Criticize Each Other: 2923
Ask Trainees to Socialize: 2923
Ask Trainees to Switch Tasks: 2923
Asking and Answering Questions: 2444
Asking for Assistance: 40
Asking for the Order: 490
Asking Questions: 1534
Asocial: 1300
Asocial Index: 1341
Asperger's Disorder: 876
Aspiration: 844, 1163, 2355
Aspiring: 2121
Assemblies: 1911
Assembly: 1042, 1043, 2125, 2774
Asserting: 1688
Assertion: 2452
Assertive: 86, 406, 990, 1205, 1253, 1268, 1334, 1676, 2128

Assertive Behavior Survey Schedule: 1052
Assertive-Directing: 1022, 1704, 2507
Assertive-Nurturing: 1022, 1704, 2507
Assertive Role: 1689
Assertiveness: 37, 185, 243, 490, 654, 1044, 1402, 1440, 1576, 1655, 1721, 1769, 1930, 1955, 2034, 2097, 2218, 2265, 2318, 2347, 2912
Assertiveness Level: 88
Assess: 1966
Assessing Needs and Entering Behavior: 2775
Assessing Progress: 903
Assessment: 684
Assessment/Evaluation/Working with Parents: 684
Assessment in Special Education: 684
Assessment of Behavior Rating Scale: 1909
Assessment of Insight: 434
Assessment Skills: 490
Assessment Validity: 219, 1930, 1955
Assessment Worker's Observation: 184
Assets: 1252
Assets & Strengths: 1732
Assign Challenging Tasks: 138, 139
Assigning Work: 1479, 1480
Assimilator: 1469, 1471
Assistance: 2350
Associate Socially: 138
Associated Factors: 653, 869, 1056
Associated Movements: 1907
Associated Observations: 1907
Associated Observations Selective Attention/Activity: 1907
Association: 1988
Association Index: 320
Association Skill: 1262
Associational Fluency: 1405
Associations: 1424, 2911
Associative Language: 1739
Associative Level: 798
Associative Memory: 239, 644, 1405, 1485
Assuming Responsibility: 40
Assured-Dominant: 1289
Assuring Safety: 2575
Asthma: 1853
Astronomy: 762
Asymmetric Tonic Neck Reflex: 1258
Asymmetrical Tonic Neck Reflex: 1668
Asymmetry: 329
At Breakfast: 2475
At Peak: 2475
At Risk: 2537
Athletic: 1667
Athletic Coach: 380
Athletic Competence: 2369
Athletic Trainer: 380, 398, 399, 1790, 2026
Athletics: 618, 1790, 2882
Athletics/Physical Fitness: 380
Athletics/Sports: 398
The Atmosphere: 684
Atomic Theory: 684
Attachment: 78, 1889, 2525
Attachment/Emotional Functioning: 1265
Attachment-Individuation Balance: 78
Attachment to School: 909
Attempts to Overcome Resistance to Influence: 1402
Attendance: 2311
Attendance and Punctuality: 2824
Attendance/Endurance: 2053, 2826
Attendance/Punctuality: 63
Attending Behavior: 2444
Attending Behaviors and Accuracy Movement: 658
Attending Parent Education/Consultation Meetings: 1884
Attending/Responding: 1868
Attention: 65, 158, 265, 433, 494, 558, 763, 776, 1265, 1292, 1485, 1681, 1722, 1775, 2202, 2288, 2387, 2461
Attention and Listening Skills: 881
Attention and Memory Associate Pairs: 1485
Attention and Response Set: 1771
Attention (Auditory): 778
Attention Checkpoints: 1905, 1908
Attention/Concentration: 476, 566
Attention Control: 235
Attention Control Inventory: 158
Attention Deficit Disorder: 73
Attention-Deficit Hyperactive: 69
Attention-Deficit/Hyperactivity Disorder: 77
Attention/Delinquency: 818
Attention-Demanding: 451
Attention Divided: 1485
Attention-Enhanced: 797, 798
Attention/Executive: 1771
Attention-Focus/Concentration: 224
Attention/Mental Control: 1665
Attention Problems: 158, 245, 280, 424, 451, 2939
Attention Problems-Immaturity: 2211
Attention Problems/Overactive: 2036
Attention Quotient Auditory: 1282
Attention Quotient Full-Scale: 1282
Attention Quotient Visual: 1282
Attention-Reduced: 797, 798
Attention Seeking: 2052
Attention Span: 268, 788, 1066, 1194, 2376
Attention Sustained: 1485
Attention to Detail: 1660, 2346, 2347, 2374
Attention to Details: 490, 781, 782
Attentional: 226, 799
Attentiveness: 679, 731, 732, 1317
Attitude: 152, 288, 1455, 1456, 1941, 1988, 2495, 2618
Attitude Posture: 794
Attitude Scale: 1705
Attitude to Living: 1824
Attitude to Reading: 1232

Attitude to School: 280
Attitude to School Science: 2325
Attitude to Teachers: 280
Attitude Toward Authority: 1926
Attitude Toward Cooperation with Employers: 1926
Attitude Toward Earnings: 2593
Attitude Toward Health: 1926
Attitude Toward Language Arts: 177
Attitude Toward Learning Processes: 177
Attitude Toward Math: 2699
Attitude Toward Mathematics: 177
Attitude Toward Teacher: 177
Attitude Towards Learning Environment: 2526
Attitudes: 715, 793, 1313, 1314, 2333
Attitudes and Behaviors: 2336
Attitudes and Opinions: 1942
Attitudes For Learning: 2614
Attitudes of Others: 1593
Attitudes of Parents and Society: 2625
Attitudes of Peers and Siblings Towards Testee: 242
Attitudes of Teachers-Parents Toward Testee: 242
Attitudes Toward Being a Supervisor: 2104
Attitudes Toward Companies and Business: 2104
Attitudes Toward Creative Behaviors: 725
Attitudes Toward Father: 1005
Attitudes Toward Managers and Executives: 2104
Attitudes Toward Mother: 1005
Attitudes Toward Others: 1961
Attitudes Toward Peers and Associates: 2104
Attitudes Toward Self: 1961
Attitudes Toward Subordinates: 2104
Attitudes Toward Supervision: 2081
Attorney: 380
Attraction to Marriage: 2396
Attractions to Work: 2834
Attributed to You: 1736
Attributes: 397, 1424
Attribution: 1683
Atypical Positions: 2767
Atypical Response: 2782
Atypical Responses: 2242
Atypicality: 280
Audiation/Listening: 1320
Audiation/Reading: 1320
Audiation/Writing: 1320
Audience: 619, 2933
Audio Checking: 1973
Audio-Visual Communications: 1794
Audio Visual Communications Technology: 1792
Audiologist: 1790
Audiology: 2026
Auditing: 38
Auditory: 359, 377, 761, 800, 886, 1073, 1083, 1139, 1164, 1458, 1470, 1472, 1478, 1771, 2219, 2376, 2471, 2596, 2597
Auditory Abilities: 1046
Auditory Ability: 644, 1138
Auditory Acquisition: 320
Auditory Acuity: 2606
Auditory and Vision Testing: 1907, 1909
Auditory and Visual Receptive Functions: 269
Auditory Association: 813, 1240, 2428
Auditory Attention: 1044
Auditory Attention and Memory: 356
Auditory Attention/Vigilance: 356
Auditory-Auditory: 208
Auditory Awareness: 658
Auditory Blending: 1308, 1529
Auditory Closure: 1240, 2628
Auditory Comprehension: 157, 159, 199, 328, 356, 664, 951, 1378, 2045, 2123
Auditory Conceptual Memory: 157
Auditory Decoding: 2426
Auditory Delayed Recall: 1378
Auditory Digit Sequence: 2596
Auditory Discrimination: 157, 346, 552, 565, 827, 1308, 1357, 1529, 2134, 2320, 2469, 2628
Auditory Discrimination and Blending: 1765
Auditory Discrimination and Memory-Recognition of Beginning Sounds: 2434
Auditory Discrimination [nonsense]: 2297
Auditory Discrimination of Sounds: 2428
Auditory Discrimination [real words]: 2297
Auditory Discrimination-Rhyming Words: 2434
Auditory Expressive: 880
Auditory Figure Ground: 2300
Auditory Figure-Ground: 2301
Auditory Hallucinations: 2109
Auditory Interference Task: 1099
Auditory Interpretation of Directions: 2673
Auditory Language: 1475, 1476, 1741
Auditory Language Association: 2628
Auditory Language Classification: 2628
Auditory Letter Span Test: 1405
Auditory Memory: 916, 1224, 1308, 1868
Auditory Memory (Sentences): 2628
Auditory Memory Span: 239
Auditory Motor: 1642
Auditory Number Memory: 2673
Auditory Number Span Test: 1405
Auditory Numeric: 1475
Auditory Numerical: 1476, 1741
Auditory/Olfactory: 1186
Auditory Ordered Recall: 1462
Auditory Perception: 494, 757, 1171, 1194, 2528
Auditory Perception and Discrimination: 1588
Auditory Perception and Recall: 2469
Auditory Perception Skills: 1308
Auditory Preference: 244
Auditory Preferences: 2069
Auditory Processing: 1977, 2236, 2673, 2901
Auditory Processing and Comprehension: 2249
Auditory Processing and Retention: 2251
Auditory Reading: 892

Auditory Recall: 2428, 2471
Auditory Reception: 1240, 1262
Auditory Receptive: 880
Auditory Responsiveness: 193, 2127
Auditory Sentence Memory: 2673
Auditory Sequence Comparison Accuracy: 567
Auditory Sequence Comparison Speed: 567
Auditory Sequence Comparison Thruput: 567
Auditory Sequencing: 813, 1308
Auditory Sequential Memory: 157, 1240, 2134
Auditory Serial Learning: 320
Auditory Seriation: 320
Auditory Short Term Memory: 320
Auditory Skills: 1529, 1707, 2434
Auditory Sounds: 2428
Auditory Strengths: 2181
Auditory Synthesis: 1060
Auditory to Kinesthetic: 2427
Auditory to Visual: 2427
Auditory to Visual-Kinesthetic: 2427
Auditory Unordered Recall: 1462
Auditory Vigilance Task: 1099
Auditory-Visual: 2219
Auditory-Visual Association: 2428, 2628
Auditory-Visual Colors Recognition: 208, 1919
Auditory-Visual Colors Sequence: 1919
Auditory-Visual Colors Sequencing: 208
Auditory-Visual Discrimination: 1751, 2469
Auditory-Visual Recognition: 834
Auditory-Visual-Kinesthetic: 1476
Auditory-Visual-Kinesthetic-Motor: 2219
Auditory-Visual-Kinesthetic Combination: 1741
Auditory Vocal: 1642
Auditory Word Discrimination: 2673
Auditory Word Memory: 2673
Aural and Written Skills: 1120
Aural Cloze with Letter: 1659
Aural Comprehension of Words and Phrases: 1740
Aural Input: 2816
Aural-Oral: 2816
Aural/Oral: 1425
Aural/Oral Communication: 684
Aural-Written: 2816
Author-Journalism: 1334
Author/Writer: 398, 399
Authoritarian: 1655
Authoritarian-Democratic: 1845
Authoritarianism: 2367
Authoritative: 1560, 1575, 1966, 2064
Authority: 391, 392, 1049, 1443, 1493, 1694, 1695, 1701, 1966, 1969, 2020, 2805
Authority Figures: 1689
Authority Figures Present: 1470
Authority-Oriented Learner: 2069
Authority Problems: 1698
Authority Problems (Pd2): 1697
Authorization to Release Information Form: 2791
Autism: 818, 1341
Autism-Optimism: 1721
Autism Quotient: 1091
Autistic Disorder: 876
Auto Diesel Mechanics: 1794
Auto Mechanic: 398, 399, 645, 1790
Auto Mechanics: 2832
Auto Repair: 411
Auto-Shop Information: 180
Autocrat: 1561, 2278
Autocratic: 1419
Autocratic-Aggressive: 1439
Autocratic-Submissive: 1439
Automatic Oral Movements: 164
Automatic Phrase: 1169
Automatic Speech: 199, 207, 356, 987
Automaticity: 320
Automatized Sequences: 199
Automobile Club: 411
Automotive: 2177
Automotive Repair: 411
Automotive Technician: 1792, 1794
Autonomic-Emotional: 950
Autonomic Nervous System Interventions: General: 310
Autonomic Nervous System Interventions: Specific: 310
Autonomic Reactions: 1647
Autonomous Functions: 912
Autonomous Work Environment: 2605
Autonomy: 68, 637, 710, 908, 1294, 1493, 1631, 1694, 1695, 1883, 1930, 1965, 1988, 2256, 2805, 2850, 2917
Autonomy/Independence: 396
Auxilaries/Modals/Copulas: 1898
Availability of Daily Living Assistance: 1743
Availability of Health Services: 1743
Availability of Social-Recreational Activities: 1743
Availability of Strong Support Person: 1795
Available Resources: 1108, 2083
Avenues to Learning: 315
Average: 2414
Average Achiever: 1924
Average Index Score: 1165
Average Intensity: 1291
Average Sentence Length: 251
Avoidance: 291, 1150, 1155, 1292, 1498, 1626, 1655, 2034
Avoidance/Numbing: 766
Avoidance of Peer Interaction: 2447
Avoidance of Punishment: 909
Avoidance of Teacher Interaction: 2447
Avoidance of Use of Grades as a Sanction: 909
Avoidance Scale: 291
Avoidance Style: 1862
Avoidance/Unresponsiveness: 928
Avoidant: 69, 77, 690, 1687, 1961, 2306, 2520

Avoidant Personality: 282
Avoiding: 677, 2149, 2756
Avoiding Jumping to Conclusions: 1780
Avoiding Problems: 2710
Avoiding Risks: 1689
Avolition-Apathy: 2288
Awake-Asleep: 2763
Awareness: 63, 136, 1292, 1705, 1938, 2382
Awareness and Self-Management Skills: 1450
Awareness of Acknowledging Feelings: 1879
Awareness of Adequate Solutions: 1879
Awareness of Communicating in Understandable Terms: 1879
Awareness of Critical Issues: 1879
Awareness of Environmental Influences: 1830
Awareness of Feedback Data: 1879
Awareness of Others: 1396
Awareness of Sales Approach: 2266
Awareness of the Importance of Relevant Aspects of a Child's Past History: 1879
Awareness Score: 685
Away from People (A): 2616

B-expectation: 392
Babbling: 234
Back F (FB): 1697
Back-Up Style-Parent: 1966
Background Information: 620
Background Knowledge: 1588
Background Noise: 1096
Background of the Revolutionary War/the Revolutionary War and Establishing a New Government (1763-1789): 146
Background Record: 1566, 2573
Backing to Velars: 1394
Backward Digit Span Accuracy: 567
Backward Parachute: 1668
Backwards Parachute: 1258
Bad Impression: 86
Balance: 300, 1214, 1282, 1752, 1901, 2706
Balance of World: 162, 1929
Balance/Plateau: 420
Ball Handling Skills: 1225
Ball Skills: 1727
Bank Manager: 380, 398
Bank Teller: 398, 399
Banker: 1790
Banking: 2422, 2443, 2734
Barber/Hairstylist: 398, 399
Barbiturates: 1931
Bargain: 1557
Bargaining: 677, 1222, 1267, 1402
Barrier: 1214
Barriers: 1252, 1754
Barriers to Employee Involvement: 940
Barriers to Employment: 2834
Barron-Welsh Art Scale: 2869
Basal Vocabulary: 769
Based on Body: 2412
Baserunning: 2455
Basic: 1558
Basic AC and DC Theory: 1537
Basic AC/DC Theory: 920, 1279, 2643
Basic Battery: 1657
Basic Biological Problems: 1222
Basic Care: 1009
Basic Checking: 1973, 2087
Basic Chemical Problems: 1222
Basic Concepts: 62, 539, 1392, 1534, 2471
Basic Coping Styles: 1686
Basic Creative Comfort: 1244, 2273
Basic Creature Comfort: 941, 1894
Basic-Creature Comfort: 2921
Basic Dishonest Attitudes: 1976
Basic Earth Materials: 684
Basic Electricity/Electronics: 2884
Basic Facts Screening: 1738
Basic Finance: 684
Basic Grammar: 1997
Basic Honest Attitudes: 1976
Basic Information: 184, 565, 797, 798, 1168
Basic Interest Area Scales: 399
Basic Internet Knowledge: 2645
Basic Level: 2319
Basic Machines: 2884
Basic Math: 2213
Basic Math Computation: 1715
Basic Mathematics Skills: 2901
Basic Motor Generalizations: 657
Basic Neurological Functions/Intactness: 269
Basic Number Skills: 837
Basic Nursing Skills: 1807
Basic Physical Problems: 1222
Basic Physical Properties of Matter and Materials: 2884
Basic Problem Solving and Reading: 1766
Basic Process Scores: 831
Basic Psychological Problems: 1222
Basic Reading: 1194, 1715, 2861
Basic Reading Skills: 2213, 2900, 2901, 2902
Basic Restorative Services: 1807
Basic Senses and Functions: 2838
Basic Services: 1841
Basic Sight Phrases: 917
Basic Sight Words: 917
Basic Skills: 547, 904, 2903
Basic Skills and Concepts: 1067
Basic Skills Certification Reading/Math: 645
Basic Skills Cluster: 2905
Basic Skills Composite Score: 1260
Basic Speech and Hearing Processes: 494
Basic Spelling: 1715
Basic Task Areas: 197
Basic Training Conditions: 1512

Basic Vocabulary and Grammatical Structures: 951
Basic Work Habits: 63
Basic Writing: 2684
Basic Writing Skills: 1606, 2901, 2902
The Basis of Life: 684
Bath and Utility: 661
Bathing and Dressing: 1718
Bathing Skills: 1065
Battery Composite: 353
Batting: 2455
Bead Memory: 2485
Bead Stringing: 2439
Beads in Box: 1919
The Bear Who Liked Hugging People: 2743
Beauty: 1821
Becoming Communicating Partners: 898
Becoming Conversation Partners: 898
Becoming Language Partners: 898
Becoming Play Partners: 898
Becoming Turntaking Partners: 898
Bedroom: 661
Bedtime: 2391
Before Birth: 1887
Beginning Consonants: 1659
Beginning Reading Skill Area: 1659
Beginning Sounds: 1261, 2192
Beginnings and Endings: 2134
Behavior: 124, 478, 674, 814, 965, 1732, 1991, 2046, 2053, 2652, 2826
Behavior Analysis History Questionnaire: 1052
Behavior Change: 1647
Behavior-Disorganized Activity: 224
Behavior Flexibility: 1044
Behavior Observation Web: 2447
Behavior Patterns: 1314
Behavior Potential: 2237
Behavior Problems: 451
Behavior Quotient: 2447
Behavior Rating Card: 1052
Behavior Record Form: 1052
Behavior Regulation: 2316
Behavior Settings: 877
Behavior Status Checklist: 1052
Behavior Style: 2237
Behavior to Child: 1788
Behavior Under Pressure: 2585
Behavioral: 1355, 1770, 1822, 2111, 2321
Behavioral Action: 962, 1952, 2279
Behavioral Characteristics: 276, 2047
Behavioral Control: 2245
Behavioral Disorganization: 2305
Behavioral Distress: 2511
Behavioral Disturbance: 2109
Behavioral/Emotional: 2391
Behavioral Flex: 747
Behavioral Habits: 2789
Behavioral History: 2047
Behavioral Involvement: 1412
Behavioral Irregularities: 2141
Behavioral-Learning Factors: 484
Behavioral Observations of Parent-Child Interaction Form: 2791
Behavioral/Physical Descriptions: 1649
Behavioral Problems Related to Motor Difficulties: 1727
Behavioral Profile: 159
Behavioral Skills: 1467
Behavioral Strengths: 158
Behavioral Symptoms Index: 280
Behaviors You Display: 1736
Behaviour: 1369
Behaviour Composite Score: 1260
Being: 1938
Being a Quick Study: 300
Being Accurate: 2914
Being Alone: 1494
Being Cautious: 262
Being Consistently Punctual: 190
Being Important: 1163
Being Love: 426
Being on Guard: 1163
Being Proud: 1163
Being Results Oriented: 1550
Being Safe: 1163
Being with Other People: 715
Being Yourself: 1163
Belief in Employee Involvement: 940
Belief in Rules: 909
Belief in the Value of Insurance: 421
Belligerence-Negativism: 2108
Belonging: 475, 1163, 1251, 1558, 1894, 1929, 2586
Belonging and Affiliation: 941, 1244, 2273, 2921
Belonging-Social Interest: 262
Belongingness: 1163
Benchwork: 411
Bender: 1337
Bender Visual Motor Gestalt Test: 2606
Benefits: 382
Benefits and Disbenefits to Others: 900
Benefits to Children: 2834
Benefits to Worker: 2834
Benevolence: 2581, 2776
Benevolent: 2800
Benevolent Autocrat: 1561, 2278
Best g Index: 2431
Better Life Style: 2834
Between: 1374
Between Factor Incongruence: 1002
Between the Two Great Wars: 2932
Bias: 2922
Bible Content: 2480
Bibliography: 1491
Big Five Factors: 1576
Bilateral Motor Coordination: 2377

Bilateral Motor Integration: 772
Bilingual: 720
Bilingual Verbal Ability: 309
Bilingualism: 1849
Biochemistry: 45, 1109
Biochemistry/Cell and Molecular Biology: 1124
Biofeedback and Distress: 310
Biological: 42
Biological Science: 618, 645, 2882
Biological Sciences: 1638, 1818
Biologist: 398, 1790
Biology: 92, 118, 141, 386,573, 594, 780, 947, 1044, 1110, 1124, 1846, 1975, 2026, 2530, 2810
Biology and General Science: 2026
Biology E/M [Ecological/Molecular]: 615
Biology-Environmental/Population/Organismic: 618
Biology-Molecular/Cellular/Developmental: 618
Biomechanics and Kinesiology: 684
Bipolar Disorder: 79
Bipolar: Manic: 1687
Birth Control: 2454
Bitch-Nice Guy: 1872
Bizarre: 1169
Bizarre Behavior: 2289
Bizarre Facial & Verbal: 2763
Bizarre Mentation: 1698
Bizarre Mentation (BIZ): 1697
Bizarre Motor Behavior: 2763
Bizarre Sensory Experiences: 1698
Bizarre Sensory Experiences (Sc6): 1697
Black: 1374
Blame Avoidance: 1988
Blaming: 1161
Blaming Self: 291
Blatant Symptoms: 2522
Blending: 827, 917, 1073
Blending and Sequencing: 730
Blending 2/3 Letter Words: 1529
Blends and Digraphs: 861
Blessed Dementia Rating Scale: 434
Blink: 1614
Block Building: 349, 837, 2439
Block Construction: 1771
Block Counting: 1840
Block Design: 268, 2054, 2840, 2859, 2860, 2862, 2864
Block Designs: 1370, 2375
Block Patterns: 2439
Block Printing: 445
Block Spelling: 1740
Blocking: 2290
Blocks: 1323, 1533
Blue-Yellow Deficiency: 1159
Bodily Cues for Tension and Anxiety: 1052
Bodily Pain: 1187, 2397
Body: 63, 133, 1494
Body and Object Use: 234
Body Appearance: 1735
Body Awareness and Control Skills: 2047
Body Composition: 1062
Body Concept: 234
Body Concepts-Awareness: 813
Body Concepts-Use: 813
Body Coordination: 265
Body Denotative: 1258
Body Derotative: 1668
Body Disapproval: 1685
Body Dissatisfaction: 893
Body Functioning: 1735
Body/Health: 439
Body Held Vertical: 1668
Body Image: 157, 793, 1832, 2240, 2380
Body Image and Awareness: 757
Body Image/Self Identification: 2240
Body Lying Prone: 1668
Body Lying Supine: 1668
Body-Part Identification: 199
Body Part Naming: 1771
Body Parts: 987, 2376
Body Pulled Up From Supine: 1668
Body Puzzle: 1865
Body Rotative: 1258, 1668
Body Scheme: 2376
Body Tone: 63
Body Use: 459
Body Weight: 1062
The Body's Defenses: 1242
Boisterous-Quiet: 1964
Bold: 305, 1211
Boldness: 1201, 1930
Bolts: 2057
Bondage and Discipline: 1744
Bonding: 684
Bookkeeper: 380, 398, 399, 1790
Bookkeeping or Office Practices: 411
Borderline: 77, 267, 690, 1687, 1961, 2306, 2520
Borderline Features: 1959
Borderline Tendency: 1685
Boredom and Withdrawal: 538
Boston Naming Test: 434
Botanical: 1149, 2404
Both Eyes: 2852
Both Hands: 1911, 2009, 2125
Both Parents: 810
Boundaries: 1006
Boundary-Breaking Being Fragment-Dependent: 2659
Boy and Girl Relations: 1716
Boy-Girl Relationships: 1492
Boyfriend/Girlfriend: 1496
Brashness: 1963
Breadth of Interest: 1333
Breath Features: 2837
Breathing: 1852
Brickmason/Stonemason/Tile Setting: 410

The Bridge to Modern Times: 2932
Brief IQ: 1485
Bright Lights: 1478
Brings Out the Best in People: 2101
Broad Ability: 2904
Broad Cognitive Ability: 2901
Broad Cognitive Ability-Extended Scale: 2901
Broad English Ability: 2902
Broad External Awareness: 226
Broad Knowledge: 2901
Broad Mathematics: 2901
Broad Reading: 2900, 2901, 2902
Broad View of Control: 1824
Broad View of Job Satisfaction: 1824
Broad View Type A: 1824
Broad Work Adjustment: 275
Broad Written Language: 2901, 2902
Broadcaster: 1790
Brooding: 1698
Brooding (D5): 1697
Buddy: 305
Budgeting: 63, 1923, 2327, 2422, 2443, 2734
Building: 1990
Building a Healthier Company: 2070
Building and Construction: 1044
Building and Home Maintenance Services: 1792
Building and Maintaining Relationships: 903
Building and Mending Relationships: 300
Building Blocks Subscore: 87
Building Construction Occupations: 1792, 1794
Building Friendships: 40
Building Image/Reputation: 1233
Building Maintenance: 2400
Building Memory: 1405
Building Self-Esteem: 40
Building Teams: 1550, 2575
Building Toward Transfer of Training: 2775
Building Trades: 411, 2177
Building Trades Maintenance: 1792, 1794
Building Trust: 490
Builds Tower with Blocks: 345, 347
Bulimarexia: 2107
Bulimia: 893, 2107
Bulimia Nervosa: 77, 79
Bureaucrat: 1561, 2278
Bus Driver: 398, 399
Business: 121, 399, 408, 410, 617, 618, 749, 752, 762, 1100, 1177, 1237, 1334, 1568, 1785, 1789, 1819
Business-Accounting: 618
Business Administration: 2000
Business-Administration: 618
Business and Consumer Law: 684
Business and Economic: 1312
Business and Information Processing: 1794
Business and Office: 2832
Business/Clerical: 2829
Business Club: 411
Business Communications: 684
Business Contact: 2833
Business Contact/Scientific: 387
Business Detail: 412, 485, 1483, 1711, 1817, 2836
Business Education: 2026
Business Education Teacher: 1790
Business-Finance: 416, 618
Business Focus: 1923
Business-General: 618
Business-International: 618
Business Judgment: 361
Business Knowledge: 1923
Business Law: 762
Business Law or Management: 411
Business Letter: 1834
Business Management: 197, 684, 1222, 2424
Business-Management: 416, 618
Business/Management: 905
Business-Marketing: 618
Business Math: 1692
Business Mathematics: 762
Business/Office/Sales: 993
Business Operations: 1831
Business Practice: 533
Business-Professional: 395, 414, 415, 417, 702, 1541
Business-Real Estate: 618
Business Services: 1285
Business-Skilled: 395, 414, 415, 417, 702, 1541
Business Vocabulary: 1692, 2408
Buyer: 1222, 1790, 2825
Buyer/Merchandiser: 398, 399

C-expectation: 392
Cabinet Making: 1794
Cabinetmaking and Millwork: 1792
CAD/CAM: 1794
Cadence Recognition: 1751
Cafeteria Worker: 398, 399
Calculating: 1826, 2054
Calculation: 356, 2901
Calculations: 558, 1667
Calculator: 2023
Calculus: 93, 118, 684
Calculus Readiness: 571
Calculus with Elementary Functions: 506
Calendar Test: 1405
Calm: 381, 2605, 2648
Calming: 2121
Calmness/Anxiousness: 1340
Cam "D" Retarded: 2479
Cam "F" Retarded: 2479
Camera Repair Technician: 398, 399
Campus Perceptions: 121
Cancellation: 2240
Cancer: 1853
The Candidate's Concerns: 421
Candidness Validity Scale: 1972

Candor: 1210
Cannabis Use Symptoms: 73
Cannot Be Scored: 868
Cannot Say (?): 1697, 1698
Capable: 1317
Capacity: 754, 884
Capacity for Intimate Contact: 1939
Capacity for Status: 372
Capitalization: 616, 821, 830, 957, 1248, 1318, 2729
Capitalization and Punctuation: 1125
Capitalization/Punctuation: 2933
Card Catalog: 1491
Card Rotations Test: 1405
Card/Gift Shop Manager: 398, 399
Cardiac: 1853
Cardiovascular/Pulmonary: 1186
Cardiovascular Tendency: 1686
Care: 1819
Care About One Another: 1858
Care for the Environment: 2444
Care Needed: 2120
Care of Living Quarters: 1065
Career: 162, 1494, 1705, 1721, 1929
Career and Achievement: 1824
Career and Life Goals: 57
Career Awareness and Self-Understanding: 341
Career Change Status: 83
Career Choice Anxiety: 409
Career Counseling: 138, 1479, 1480
Career Decision: 404
Career Development: 2346
Career Development and Planning: 684
Career Development Attitudes: 405
Career Development Competency: 1069
Career Development Knowledge and Skills: 405
Career Expectations: 421
Career Experience Summary: 2364
Career Exploration: 405
Career Help: 138, 139
Career Interests: 904
Career/Life-style Scores: 86
Career Maturity: 311
Career Moves: 140
Career Optimism: 1904
Career Path Flexibility: 401
Career Planning: 252, 405, 2357
Career Planning Skills: 1252
Career Planning Subtask: 2527
Career Plans: 401
Career Problems: 569
Career Skills: 2204
Career Strengths and Interests: 2364
Career Worries: 400
Caregiver Assistance: 1906
Caregiver Interactions: 1007
Caregiver Interview and Environmental Observation: 2082
Carelessness: 66
Caretaker: 1452
Caring: 86, 1822
Caring Behaviors: 717
Caring Leadership: 1438
Carpenter: 380, 398, 399, 1790
Carpentry: 398, 399, 410, 1792, 1794, 2400
Carpentry or Home Building: 411
Case Notes Form: 2791
Castration Anxiety/Penis Envy: 317
Castration Seeking: 317
Catastrophizing: 291
Catatonic Behavior: 2109
Categories: 2441
Categories of Good and Bad: 847
Categorization: 1424, 1513
Categorization and Association: 2215
Categorizing: 1472
Category: 1164
Category Flexibility: 1044
Category Naming: 2667
Caterer: 398, 399
Catering/Serving/Smelling/Tasting: 1343, 2925
The Cats: 2743
Cause and Effect: 1182
Causes and Effects: 1188
Causes of Aggression: 1050
Causes of Anxiety: 1050
Causes of Failure: 1050
Causes of Job Turnover: 1050
Causes of Own Aggression: 1049
Causes of Own Anxiety/Fear: 1049
Causes of Own Failure: 1049
Causes of Own Giving Up or Depression: 1049
Causes of Own Guilt: 1049
Causes of Own Inferiority Feelings: 1049
Caution: 2776, 2877
Cautious: 1211, 1253, 2605, 2648
Cautious-Supporting: 1022, 1704, 2507
Cautiousness: 1101
Cell Biology: 1109
Cell Structure and Functions: 684
Cello: 1018
Cellular and Molecular Biology: 1110
Center of Gravity and Gravity: 2884
Central Nervous System Interventions: General: 310
Central Vision and Processing Speed: 2794
Centralization of Influence: Classroom Instruction: 2312
Centralization of Influence: Curriculum and Resources: 2312
CEO/President: 380
Cerebral Mode Dominance: 1197
Certainty: 404, 1453
Certification for Special Education: 2311
Chalk Carving Test: 386
Challenge: 2804

Challenge-Inventiveness: 1143
Challenge Response: 633
Challenger: 727, 1892
Challenging: 1446
Challenging the Process: 1445, 1448, 2635
Challenging Work: 1393
Chance and Data: 622
Chance Game: 1163
Chance Scale: 1183
Change: 68, 544, 908, 1965
Change and Continuity in American Democracy: 1759
Change in Weight: 291
Change Introduction: 2570
Change Management: 1923
Change Orientation: 1948
Change Oriented: 1822
Changes in Personal Life/High-Impact: 2789
Changes in Personal Life/Total: 2789
Changes on the Job/High-Impact: 2789
Changes on the Job/Total: 2789
Changing Role of America in the World: 1759
Characteristics: 821, 1790
Characteristics of the Health Care Technology: 1593
Characterization of Course: 650
Charisma: 490
Charismatic Change: 437
Charts and Graphs Skills: 1247
Cheating Opinions: 646, 660
Check All: 305
Check Scale: 1310
Checking: 30, 754, 1834, 1836, 1973, 2327, 2408
Checking Skills: 964
Cheeks: 276
Chef: 380, 398, 1790
Chemical: 905, 2066
Chemical Abuse: 427
Chemical Dynamics: 43
Chemical Involvement: 201
Chemical Involvement Problem Severity: 1931
Chemical Processes: 1279
Chemical Processes/Instrumentation & Control: 2067
Chemist: 380, 398, 1790
Chemistry: 48, 49, 94, 118, 141, 574, 596, 615, 618, 905, 947, 1044, 1111, 1124, 1975, 2026, 2810
Chemistry/Physics/General Science: 2026
Child: 1374, 2280
Child Abuse: 447
Child Abuse Interview Form: 2791
Child Assessment: 452
Child Behaviors: 864
Child Care: 399, 1237, 1918
Child Care and Family: 2834
Child Care and Guidance: 410, 1792
Child Care Assistant: 398, 399
Child Care Provider: 1790
Child Care Services: 1794
Child Care Skills: 1887
Child Care Worker: 380
Child Description: 454, 872, 2040
Child Development: 380
Child Development/Care/Guidance: 684
Child Domain: 1889
Child Fluency Assessment Digest: 691
Child History Questionnaire: 2791
Child Initiated Behavior: 1788
Child Interview Form: 2791
Child Management: 717
Child Molest: 2393
Child Molest Scale: 1744
Child Moving/Environment Changing: 1727
Child Moving/Environment Stable: 1727
Child Pornography: 1433
Child Relations: 1925
Child Responses to Commands: 864
Child Stationary/Environment Changing: 1727
Child Stationary/Environment Stable: 1727
Child Subsystem: 1565
Child's Adjustment to Home and Community Checklist: 2791
Child's Emotional Needs: 1918
The Child's Psychological Status: 442
The Child's Status: 442
Child-Centeredness of Home: 1026
Childhood: 224
Childhood Abuse: 1685
Childhood and Child Rearing: 1583
Childrearing: 2292
Children: 1495, 1705, 2131, 2869
Children and Parenting: 2034
Children with Special Needs: 684
Children's Behavioral Problems: 1181
Children's Health and Functioning: 1181
Children's Health-Risk Behaviors: 1181
Children's Physical Health Problems: 1181
Children's Psychological Health Problems: 1181
Children's Total Health Problems: 1181
Children's Week: 2611
Chinese: 575, 610, 615
Chiropractor: 398, 399, 1790
Chlorpromazine: 66
Choice: 946
Choice-of-Word Corrections per T-Unit: 2661
Choice Reaction Time for Single Digits: 366
Choleric: 2649
Choose A Picture: 2029
Chooses and Narrows a Topic Appropriately for the Audience and Occasion: 639
Choosing a Path: 1405
Chord Analysis: 1629
Chord Recognition: 1751
Chosen Skill Level: 2882
Chroma Four: 489
Chroma Two: 489
Chronemic: 1284

Chronic Maladjustment: 267
Chronic Stressful Conditions in Personal Life: 2789
Chronic Stressful Conditions on the Job: 2789
Chronic Tension: 1686
Chronicity: 2766
Chronicity of the Fluency Problem: 691
Chronicity Prediction Checklist: 691
Chronological Record of all Case Contacts Form: 2791
Circle: 564
Circumstantiality: 2290
Citizen: 2282
Citizenship: 252, 2204, 2357
Civil: 410, 905
Civil War and Reconstruction: 762
Civilized Disagreement: 2632
Clanging: 2290
Clarification of Goals and Objectives: 490
Clarification/Verification: 87
Clarifies Expectations: 1296
Clarifying and Elaborating: 1147
Clarifying Values: 619
Clarinet: 1280
Clarity: 710, 1283, 1292, 1670, 1860, 2917
Clarity of Communications: 490
Clarity of Goals: 2584
Clarity of Goals and Priorities: 490
Clarity of Mission/Strategic Goals: 490
Clarity of Own Goals: 490
Clarity of Personal Goals: 490
Clarity of Policy: 1026
Clarity of Purpose: 1545, 2423
Clarity of Roles: 2423
Clarity of Rules: 909
Clarity of Your Own Goals: 490
Class Behavior Management: 684
Class Deficiencies: 214
Class Discussion: 948
Class Disrupters: 2875
Class Membership: 2356
Class Participation: 494
Classes: 2518
Classic/Overload Stressor Pattern of Type A Behavior: 1809
Classification: 899, 1224, 1341, 1485, 1873, 1973, 2041, 2487, 2774
Classification and Characteristics of Disorders: 684
Classifying: 2105
Classroom Adaptation: 2122
Classroom Adjustment: 1041
Classroom Arrangement: 452
Classroom Behavior: 258, 2894
Classroom Behaviors: 2323
Classroom Climate: 493
Classroom Communication: 494
Classroom Conformity: 294
Classroom Discussion: 2444
Classroom Environment: 1275
Classroom Focus: 493
Classroom Management: 216, 684
Classroom Orderliness: 909
Classroom Organization/Program Administration/Resources: 684
Classroom Performance: 2351
Classroom Supervision and Organization: 2590
Classroom Volunteering: 1884
Cleanliness: 63
Cleanliness and Health: 1897
Clear and Focused Mission: 2314
Clear Leadership: 1438
Clear Purpose: 2632
Clear Roles and Work Assignments: 2632
Clear Thinking: 551
Clearheaded-Confused: 2077
Clerical: 5, 183, 239, 395, 406, 407, 414, 415, 417, 618, 645, 702, 1044, 1074, 1078, 1157, 1177, 1222, 1413, 1789, 1818, 1841, 2177, 2255, 2257, 2406
Clerical and Language Tests: 839
Clerical Aptitude: 533, 902
Clerical Checking: 2212
Clerical/Clerking: 398, 399
Clerical-Data: 618
Clerical Knowledge: 1692
Clerical Numerical: 2421
Clerical Perception: 168, 2797, 2798, 2799
Clerical Potential: 1212
Clerical/Secretarial/Saleswork Including Business and Some Aspects of Law: 1342
Clerical Services: 411
Clerical Skills Series: 2302
Clerical Speed and Accuracy: 535, 839, 2019
Clerical/Typing/Word Processing: 410
Clerk-Typists: 1692
Clerical Verbal: 2421
Clerical Work: 1990
Client: 716
Client Acceptance: 2096
Client-Centered Change: 437
Client Consultation: 2096
Client History: 279
Client Interview: 2296
Client Preference for Treatment: 184
Client's Assessment of the Fluency Problem: 691
Climate: 1276, 1463, 1494, 1861, 1937, 2133, 2630
Climatic Readiness: 1859
Clinical: 135, 434, 1541
Clinical and Summary Scales: 1525
Clinical Disorders Domain: 77
Clinical Evaluation of Swallowing (Observations): 870
Clinical Impressions: 1242
Clinical Judgment: 1242
Clinical Maladjustment: 280
Clinical Observations/Assessment: 2472
Clinical Personality Patterns: 1687
Clinical Signs: 133

Clinical Status: 2388
Clinical Syndromes: 1685, 1687
Clinician-Administered PTSD Scale for DSM-IV: 1626
Clinician's Assessment of the Fluency Problem: 691
Clock: 1865
Clock Drawing: 545
Clock Reading: 545
Clock Setting: 199, 545
Close Friendships: 2369
Close Relations: 1925
Close Relationships: 2074
Closed-Mindedness: 362
Closed/Open: 1857
Closed Question: 716
Closed System: 1006
Closing Fist and Moving Thumbs: 1653
Closing Skills: 989
Closure Flexibility: 2605
Clothing: 344, 1897
Clothing and Textiles: 684
Clothing and Textiles Management and Production: 1794
Clothing/Apparel/Textiles: 410
Clothing Care: 443
Clothing Management: 2316
Cloze: 986, 2487
Cloze Reading: 1662
Cluster: 570
Cluster Accuracy: 329
Cluster Placement: 329
Cluster Presence: 329
Cluster Simplification: 1394
Clusters: 2651
Co-ordination: 169, 2774
Co-Verbs per T-Unit: 2661
Co-worker Concern: 1163
Co-Workers: 382, 1695, 2915
Co-workers: 648, 1694
Coachability: 219, 1930, 1955
Coaching: 1044, 1560, 1575, 1651, 1923
Coaching and Performance Appraisal Inventory: 1403
Coaching Attitude and Style: 554
Coaching Behavior: 554
Coaching Effectiveness: 554
Coaching Employees: 1479, 1480
Coaching for Teamwork: 490
Coaching Model: 555
Coaching Qualities: 555
Coaching Skills: 490
Coaching Style: 1436
Coaching Techniques: 555
Coalition: 1402
COBOL Programming Proficiency: 2896
Cocaine: 1931, 2554
Coded Information: 964
Coded Instructions: 236
Coding: 535, 1042, 1836, 2105, 2202, 2212, 2302, 2374, 2375, 2408, 2862
Coding Speed: 180
Coerce: 1966
Coercion: 1267
Coercive: 1560, 1575, 2415
Coerciveness of Suggestion: 1026
Coexist: 1557
Cognition: 276, 377, 810, 879, 1388, 1732, 2041, 2459, 2518
Cognition and Communication Screening: 276
Cognition of Figural Classes: 2518
Cognition of Figural Systems: 2518
Cognition of Figural Transformations: 2518
Cognition of Figural Units: 2518
Cognition of Semantic Relations: 2518
Cognition of Semantic Systems: 2518
Cognition of Semantic Units: 2518
Cognition of Symbolic Relations: 2518
Cognition of Symbolic Systems: 2518
Cognitive: 266, 268, 697, 806, 1039, 1044, 1192, 1230, 1355, 1391, 1490, 1959, 2196, 2778
Cognitive Analysis: 962, 1952, 2279
Cognitive and Intellectual Impairment Scale: 2114
Cognitive and Metacognitive Strategies: 1720
Cognitive Aspects: 1978
Cognitive Assessment: 650
Cognitive Avoidance: 699
Cognitive Behavior: 288
Cognitive/Behavioral Tasks Adaptations: 2316
Cognitive/Behavioral Tasks Assistance: 2316
Cognitive Competence: 1881, 1987
Cognitive Competencies: 1570
Cognitive Composite: 1570
Cognitive Control: 2245
Cognitive Correlates: 658
Cognitive Correlates for Manual Communication: 658
Cognitive Deficits: 651
Cognitive Development: 887, 1468, 1918, 1962
Cognitive Development and Intellectual Needs: 976
Cognitive Developmental Skills: 1041
Cognitive Difficulty: 1748
Cognitive Dimension: 1045
Cognitive Disability: 1522
Cognitive Distortion and Immaturity Scale: 1744
Cognitive Disturbance: 1733
Cognitive Efficiency: 1775
Cognitive-Emotional: 41
Cognitive Emphasis: 1275
Cognitive Factor: 2901
Cognitive Flex: 747
Cognitive Functions: 2647
Cognitive Impairment: 1963
Cognitive Independence: 1881
Cognitive/Language: 124
Cognitive Level: 798
Cognitive Maturity: 367

Cognitive Organization: 1984
Cognitive Performance: 2111
Cognitive Problems/Inattention: 681
Cognitive Processes: 269
Cognitive Processes and Specific Concepts: 2838
Cognitive Processing Speed: 320
Cognitive Quotient: 559
Cognitive Restraint of Eating: 894
Cognitive Restructuring: 698
Cognitive (Sc3): 1697
Cognitive Scales: 1728
Cognitive Skills: 275, 547, 904, 1472, 2434
Cognitive Skills Index: 2677
Cognitive Status: 1777
Cognitive Strategies: 2333
Cognitive Structure: 1965
Cognitive Subdomains: 2431
Cognitive Symptoms: 1587
Cognitive System: 2508
Cognitive Thinking: 2043
Cognitive Total: 265
Cognitive-Understanding: 1881
Cognitive Verbal: 2111
Cognitive-Verbal: 653
Cognitive-Worry: 950
Cognitively Directed: 968
Cohabitation and Premarital Sexual Relations: 1583
Cohesion: 480, 544, 1010, 1141, 1743, 2423
Cold-hearted: 1289
Collaborate: 1557
Collaborating: 2756
Collaboration: 436, 1519, 1861, 2133, 2631
Collaboration & Teamwork: 2773
Collaborative Mentoring: 1652
Collaborator: 1892
Collateral Interview Form: 2791
Colleagues: 1565
Collecting and Recording Scientific Data: 1094
Collecting Data: 1281
Collection Management: 684
Collective Bargaining: 684
College Activities: 620
College Algebra: 507
College Algebra-Trigonometry: 508
College Education: 401
The College Environment: 620
College Environment: 57
College Experiences: 57
College Impressions: 57
College-Level French Language: 509
College-Level German Language: 510
College Level Mathematics: 18
College-Level Spanish Language: 511
College Maladjustment (Mt): 1697
College Professor: 312, 1790
College Services: 57
College Services and Characteristics: 57
Collision Repair: 1792, 1794
Color: 1214, 2516, 2517
Color Discrimination: 2297, 2421
Color Form: 1164
Color-Form Scale: 564
Color Identification: 565, 1534
Color Items: 2439
Color Naming: 813
Color-Naming Speed: 2051
Color-Naming Speed With Distraction: 2051
Color Perception: 862, 1614, 2376
Color Recognition: 346, 356, 1357
Color Sort: 2054
Color Vision Deficiency: 2658
Color-Word: 2516, 2517
Color Words: 1224
Colored Block Design: 1513
Colorful: 1211
Colors: 331, 987, 1224
Colour Matching: 2240
Colour Recognition: 1865
Columns: 1364
Combination: 2441
Combinations: 178
Combined: 79
Combined Frequency Index Adaptive Behavior: 890
Combined Frequency Index Maladaptive Behavior: 890
Combined Involvement: 1465
Combined Language Age: 2189
Combined Total: 2402
Combining Objects: 1405
Combining Propositions: 1739
Combustion: 1537
Comfort Reading Level: 832
Command: 2705
Command of Language: 1281
Commands: 199, 1425, 1534
Comments: 917
Comments and Suggestions: 57
Comments by the Respondent and the Interviewer: 642
Commercial: 1724, 1818
Commercial Artist: 380, 1790
Commercial Foods: 1794
Commercial Orientation: 1821
Commercial Sciences: 12
Commercial Sex Experiences: 1433
Commission: 2720
Commissions: 679
Commitment: 379, 490, 1276, 1493, 1757, 1861, 2133, 2282, 2631
Commitment Anxiety: 422
Commitment Ethic: 1948
Commitment Level: 2633
Commitment to Coaching: 490
Commitment to Present Situation: 421
Commitment to Work Force Diversity: 1923

Committing to a Team Approach: 2630
Common Fractions: 1604
Common Objects: 987
Common Sense: 1674
Common Syllables or Phonograms: 827
Common Vision: 1267
Common Words: 835
Commonality: 68, 372, 963
Communicates the Thesis/Specific Purpose in a Manner Appropriate for Audience and Occasion: 639
Communicating: 197, 619, 903, 1281, 1554, 2424
Communicating Effectively: 490
Communicating Effectively Within Teams: 2630
Communicating in Writing: 1551
Communicating Orally: 1551
Communication: 35, 59, 63, 123, 166, 198, 250, 266, 285, 395, 414, 415, 417, 544, 646, 648, 686, 702, 806, 814, 1008, 1067, 1091, 1169, 1194, 1281, 1443, 1541, 1545, 1549, 1591, 1667, 1791, 1855, 1883, 2026, 2034, 2053, 2088, 2096, 2295, 2350, 2385, 2423, 2425, 2459, 2526, 2780, 2813, 2930
Communication Abilities: 2162
Communication Age: 811
Communication and Aids: 1718
Communication and Language: 377, 2778
Communication and Listening Skills: 1492
Communication Arts: 2654
Communication Assessment: 717
Communication Behaviors: 293
Communication Competencies: 1570
Communication Composite: 1570
Communication Difficulties: 537
Communication Effectiveness: 2926
Communication Efficiency Ratio: 209
Communication Expectations: 1583
Communication Expectations-Parent: 1966
Communication Flow: 2587
Communication Inventory: 1403
Communication—Language and Listening Skills: 882
Communication-Oral: 416
Communication/Openness: 2585
Communication Skills: 15, 60, 1233, 2026, 2824, 2826
Communication Style: 1886
Communication Through Gestures: 2052
Communication Through Looking: 2052
Communication Through Manipulation: 2052
Communication Through Pictures or Objects: 2052
Communication Through Pointing: 2052
Communication Through Whole Body Action: 2052
Communication Total: 265
Communication-Written: 416
Communications: 179, 618, 721, 905, 1569, 1841, 1913, 2327, 2605
Communications and Communications Technologies: 410
Communications and Media: 1044
Communications Management: 2098
Communicative: 1334
Communicative Arts: 2137
Communicative Competence: 1041
Communicative Functions: 630, 2024, 2025
Communicative Impact: 164
Communicative Leadership: 1438
Communicative Use of Sounds: 2052
Communicativeness: 1576
Communicator: 1892
Community: 61, 162, 1276, 1861, 1929, 2068, 2131, 2133, 2583, 2605, 2764, 2813
Community Accessibility: 1743
Community and Environmental Health: 684
Community Awareness: 63
Community Leisure: 443
Community Living: 1067
Community Living Skills: 443, 1300
Community Mobility: 1065
Community Participation: 443, 2780
Community Relations: 374
Community Risks and Hazards: 2454
Community Safety: 443
Community Self-Sufficiency: 1, 2
Community Service: 398, 1237, 1493
Community Service Organization Director: 1790
Community Skills: 2195
Community Skills/Safety Skills: 805
Community Spirit: 1926
Community Use: 59, 198
Company Policies: 989, 1694
Company Policies and Practices: 1695, 1701
Comparative: 2337
Comparative/Absolute: 2662
Comparative Government and Politics: 95
Comparing and Contrasting: 647
Comparing Information: 532
Comparison of Partners' Styles of Conflict: 2546
Comparisons: 173, 174, 331
Compassion: 439, 1946
Compassion/Sensitivity: 300
Compatibility: 733, 900
Compatible Values: 490
Compensation: 421, 648, 1494, 1694, 1695, 1701
Compensation Linked to Performance and Skills: 801
Competence: 63, 946, 1098, 1545, 1734, 1735, 1769, 2218, 2521
Competence of the Child as a Witness: 442
Competence of the Child-Observed/Reported: 442
Competence Scales: 451
Competencies Engaged: 900
Competency: 570, 2739
Competency Level: 1624
Competency Modeling: 638
Competent Supervision: 1345
Competing: 2756
Competing Messages: 1046
Competing Sentences: 2301

Competing Words: 2300, 2301
Competing Words Ear Advantage: 2301
Competition: 35, 36, 391, 392, 495, 1136, 1465, 2716, 2793
Competitive: 86, 1150, 1243, 1498, 1822, 1862
Competitive Games: 1689
Competitive Situations: 1689
Competitive Spirit: 1210
Competitiveness: 37, 1576, 1955, 2007, 2265, 2592
Competitiveness Traits: 1955
Complaining: 1688
Complaint Handling by Employees: 640
Completer-Finisher: 296
Completing an Application: 190
Completing Tasks: 2444
Completing Tasks Effectively: 190
Completion Items: 2439
Completions: 2659
Complex Computation: 831
Complex Conceptual Processes: 320
Complex Figure: 1454
Complex Grammatical Structures and Communicating Meaning and Comprehension: 951
Complex Ideational Material: 199
Complex in More Than One Way: 1427
Complex Sentences: 1427
Complex Tasks: 1673
Complexity: 724, 1333, 2201
Complexity Indicator: 2388
Compliance: 788, 1769, 1984, 2218, 2776
Compliance Change: 437
Compliance with Adult Directives and School Rules: 2316
Compliment Trainee's Work: 2923
Component Analysis Rating: 2767
Components: 1042, 1043, 2774
Components of a Balanced Physical Education Program: 684
Comportment: 2387
Composed: 2605, 2648
Composed-Anxious: 2077
Composer: 1667
Composers: 1751
Composing: 1222
Composite: 560, 1039, 1287, 1394, 2056
Composite Index: 2017
Composite Memory Index: 2701
Composite Scales: 1823
Composite Score: 1760, 2898
Composite/Total: 1057
Composite Traits: 1955
Composites: 987
Composition: 97, 98, 617, 971
Composition Knowledge and Skills: 684
Composure: 689, 1930
Compound Series: 1717
Compound Words: 917
Comprehending Dialogues: 1534
Comprehending Statements: 1534
Comprehension: 257, 268, 308, 354, 357, 359, 364, 370, 383, 384, 496, 558, 628, 665, 684, 754, 769, 901, 911, 955, 1072, 1092, 1126, 1131, 1234, 1425, 1529, 1641, 1731, 1765, 1767, 1781, 1873, 2186, 2331, 2338, 2375, 2409, 2427, 2462, 2469, 2481, 2485, 2487, 2667, 2735, 2744, 2840, 2860, 2862, 2864, 2873
Comprehension Ability: 796, 1032, 2002
Comprehension Accuracy: 2174
Comprehension and Fluency and Pronunciation: 951
Comprehension and Interpretation: 2320
Comprehension and Reasoning: 713
Comprehension Auditory: 1282
Comprehension-Knowledge: 2901
Comprehension of Commands: 2331
Comprehension of Essential Ideas: 901
Comprehension of Instructions: 1771
Comprehension of Mechanical Tasks: 1632
Comprehension of Multiple Choice: 987
Comprehension of Oral Spelling: 199
Comprehension of Paragraphs: 356
Comprehension of Points of View: 901
Comprehension of Relations: 10
Comprehension of Sentences: 911, 987
Comprehension of Sequences: 901
Comprehension of Signs and Object-to-Picture Matching: 1064
Comprehension of Singular and Plural: 2215
Comprehension of Three-Word Phrases: 2215
Comprehension of Words and Sentences: 356
Comprehension Problem Profile: 1738
Comprehension Reading Level: 832
Comprehension Scale: 2228
Comprehension Skills: 39
Comprehension Summary: 2725
Comprehension Total: 1047
Comprehension Variance: 1461
Comprehension Visual: 1282
Comprensión Conocimiento: 264
Comprensión de Oraciones: 264
Compromise: 413, 2549, 2638
Compromiser: 1561, 2278
Compromising: 1147, 2149, 2756
Compromising/Negotiating: 40
Compulsions: 876
Compulsive: 136, 1687
Compulsivity: 2006
Computation: 173, 192, 325, 364, 369, 416, 665, 752, 754, 1145, 1601, 1762, 2000, 2105, 2134, 2137, 2383, 2408, 2486, 2699
Computation/Addition: 2089
Computation/Decimals: 2089
Computation/Division: 2089
Computation/Fractions: 2089
Computation/Multiplication: 2089

Computation/Subtraction: 2089
Computation/Whole Numbers: 2089
Computational: 1074, 1413, 2255, 2257
Computational Skill: 1603
Computations: 2774
Computations of Whole Numbers: 343
Computer Activities: 1790
Computer and Data-Processing: 179
Computer and Equipment Use: 2316
Computer and Information Sciences: 410, 905
Computer and PLC: 1279
Computer Applications: 2482
Computer Checking: 236
Computer Club: 411
Computer Literacy: 947
Computer Literacy/Data Processing: 2026
Computer Operator Aptitude: 2895
Computer Programmer: 380, 398, 399, 1790
Computer Programming: 411, 1792, 1794, 2482
Computer Science : 96, 118, 618, 1112, 1124, 1831
Computer Scientist: 398
Computer Systems: 2482
Computer Technology: 1285, 1792, 1794
Computers: 411, 2066
Computers and Electronics: 1044
Computers and PLC: 920, 923, 1537, 2643
Conative (Sc4): 1697
Concealed Words Test: 1405
Concentrates on Task: 2530
Concentration: 1455, 1456, 2236, 2475, 2495
Concentration and Organization: 478
Concentration Impairment and Sublimation: 78
Concentric Square: 1164
Concept Attainment: 63
Concept Formation: 235, 1375, 2901
Concept of the Call: 2751
Concept Production: 320
Concept Recognition: 320
Concept Scores: 831
Concept Synthesis: 320
Concepts: 76, 809, 1278, 1368, 2059, 2137
Concepts and Applications: 364, 2486
Concepts and Directions: 540
Concepts and Knowledge: 2089
Concepts and Problem Solving: 1657
Concepts in Economics: 897
Concepts of Number: 2483
Conceptual: 1822
Conceptual/Analytical: 226
Conceptual Development: 265, 1171
Conceptual Dysfunction: 792
Conceptual Grouping: 1613
Conceptual Knowledge: 1281
Conceptual Level: 215
Conceptual Level Responses: 2892
Conceptual Quotient: 2402
Conceptual Thinking: 1442
Conceptual Understanding: 1759
Conceptualization: 776, 2387, 2555
Conceptualization of Therapy: 1830
Concern: 439
Concern for People: 1655, 2587
Conclusions: 442
Concrete: 2102
Concrete Experience: 64, 1469, 1471
Concrete Random score: 1132
Concrete Sequential score: 1132
Concrete Thinking vs. Abstract Thinking: 477
Concurrent Activities: 2763
Conditions: 1969
Conditions for Instruction: 391
Conditions for Learning: 392
Conduct: 282, 818
Conduct Disorder: 73, 77, 79, 876, 2211
Conduct Problem Scale: 841
Conduct Problems: 280, 469, 681, 1025, 1698, 2012, 2147
Conducting Employee Meetings: 1479, 1480
Conducting Inquiries: 1759
Conducting Performance Appraisals: 1479, 1480
Conducting Selection Interviews: 1479, 1480
Conducting Termination Interviews: 1479, 1480
Confabulation: 329, 2251
Confidence: 80, 220, 367, 698, 1143, 1334, 1830, 1916, 2274
Confidence/Anxiety: 2160
Confident: 1686, 1958
Confident Leadership: 1438
Confident-Unsure: 2077
Configuración de Sonidos: 264
Configural Accuracy: 329
Configural Presence: 329
Configuration: 1610
Confirmative Mentoring: 1652
Confirming Mentoring: 1652
Conflict: 480, 1010, 1149, 1721, 1743, 1757, 2404, 2647, 2652
Conflict Avoidance: 1290
Conflict Management: 717, 1855, 1913, 2425
Conflict over Child Rearing: 1582
Conflict Resolution: 490, 1006, 1440, 2034, 2423, 2521, 2571
Conflict Resolution and Negotiation: 1923
Conflict with Others: 858, 1304, 1305
Conflict with Peers: 1963
Conflicts and Disagreements: 1961
Conformance: 1702, 2869
Conforming: 1685, 1688
Conformity: 1, 2, 1201, 1706, 1881, 2353, 2581, 2784
Conformity/Inquisitiveness: 2160
Conformity/Non-Conformity: 1340
Confrontation: 716
Confrontation Naming: 199, 356
Confronting: 1954

Confronting and Challenging: 556
Confronting Problem Employees: 300
Confrontive: 1205
Confrontive Coping: 2858
Confused/or Opposite Sex: 2307
Confusion: 1374, 1925
Confusion-Bewilderment: 2076
Conjugate Gaze: 1614
Conjunctions: 430, 1427, 1898
Conjunctions and Transition Words: 2727
Conjunctions/Negatives: 1127
Conjunctives: 2233
Connected Discourse: 1534
Connected Speech: 468
Connected Speech Sample: 164
Connection: 2415
Connections Made with Lines: 2659
Connections that Contribute to a Theme: 2659
Conners' ADHD Index: 681
Conners' Global Index: Restless-Impulsive and Emotional Lability: 681
Conscientious: 1294, 1822, 2274
Conscientiousness: 219, 944, 1576, 1769, 1930, 1955, 2218, 2784
Conscientiousness and Reliability: 2420
Conscientiousness/Expediency: 2160
Conscientiousness Index: 2346
Consciousness: 723
Consensual: 1419, 1443
Consensus: 1757
Consensus Decisions: 2632
Consensus Planning: 490
Consensus-Testing: 1147
Consent for Evaluation of Minor(s) Form: 2791
Consent for Psychological Services to Child(ren) Form: 2791
Consequences: 900
Consequences & Purposiveness: 1732
Consequences of HCT Use: 1593
Consequences of Substance Abuse: 2551
Conservation: 2134
Conservation Education: 618
Conservation Officer: 398, 399
Conservatism-Radicalism: 363
Conservative: 1443, 1549
Considerate: 381, 990
Considerateness/Inconsiderateness: 1340
Consideration: 63, 1437, 1444
Consideration of Others: 1449
Consistency: 77, 490, 908, 1133, 1223, 1470, 1688, 2367, 2776
Consistency Auditory: 1282
Consistency Check: 771
Consistency/Long Term: 224
Consistency of Other Information: 442
Consistency of Present Body Description: 795
Consistency of Retrieval: 1058
Consistency Visual: 1282
Consistent-Inconsistent: 1940
Consistent Leadership: 1438
Consistent Use of Noise: 2052
Consolidating: 83
Consolidation Index: 832
Consolidation Values: 2346
Consonant: 2703
Consonant and Vowel Sounds: 1529
Consonant Blends: 827, 2254
Consonant Blends and Digraphs: 1529
Consonant Digraphs: 827, 2254
Consonant Diphthongs: 2180
Consonant Harmony: 1394
Consonant Sequence Reduction: 214
Consonant Singles-Initial and Final: 2651
Consonant Singleton Omissions [Postvocalic]: 214
Consonant Singleton Omissions [Prevocalic]: 214
Consonant Sounds: 740, 1224, 2254
Consonants: 1138
Consonants Composite: 240
Consonants-Blends: 2487
Consonants-Digraphs: 2487
Consonants + Vowels/Diphthongs: 2429
Consonants-Single: 2487
Consonants Total: 2487
Consonants with Alternating Vowels: 486
Construction: 183, 776, 1075, 1818, 2832, 2873
Construction Electricity: 1794
Construction Installation and Distribution: 920
Construction Masonry-Blocklaying: 1794
Construction Masonry-Bricklaying: 1794
Construction Masonry-Stone: 1794
The Construction of Object Relations in Space: 194
Construction Trades: 410, 2000, 2822
Construction/Engineering/Craft: 179
Constructional Ability: 445, 558
Constructional Praxis: 434, 2377
Constructive: 1150, 1565, 2001
Constructive Cultures: 1862
Constructive Styles: 1498
Consultation/Collaboration: 684
Consultative: 1419, 2064
Consulting Skills for Developing Groups and Organizations: 1450
Consulting with Experts: 2070
Consumer Economics: 395, 408, 414, 415, 417, 702, 947, 1541
Consumer Education: 684, 1492
Consumer Health: 1019
Consumer Health and Safety: 684
Contact: 723
Contact and Core Skills: 556
Contact at Work: 1823
Contact with His World: 63
Contact with People: 63
Contact with Teacher: 1884

Contact with Things: 63
Contacts With People: 627
Contemporary Health Problems: 1019
Content: 744, 1094, 1214, 1477, 2470
Content and Style: 2352
Content Area Reading: 1319
Content Area Words: 2487
Content-Bound: 2636
Content Development: 1657
Content Oriented: 1508
Contentment: 791, 1928, 1930
Context Clues: 2180
Contexts: 1284
Contextual: 1276
Contextual Constraints: 1477
Contextual Conventions: 2731
Contextual Decoding: 769
Contextual Language: 2731
Contextual Writing: 2684
Contingent Reward: 1736
Continuations: 2659
Continuing Education: 57
Continuous Quantity: 674
Contract/Procurement Management: 2098
Contradicting Statements: 1780
Contradictions: 430
Contributor: 1892
Contrived Writing: 2731
Control: 35, 401, 475, 480, 849, 920, 1008, 1010, 1036, 1350, 1443, 1545, 1549, 1647, 1682, 1788, 1818, 1878, 1930, 1953, 1966, 2148, 2148, 2917
Control Behavior: 1594
Control Circuits: 1537, 2643
Control Feelings: 1594
Control from Self/Internal: 2759
Control from the Environment: 2759
Control Manager: 312
Control of Details: 490
Control of Hands and Arms: 2052
Control of Incentives/Pay: 490
Control of Speech Musculature: 2052
Control over Self: 2759
Control over the Environment: 2759
Control Precision: 1044
Control Score: 1398
Controlled Associations Test: 1405
Controlled Word Association: 1740
Controlling: 1251, 1688, 1822, 1929, 2621
Controlling Impulsivity: 40
Controls Weak or Absent: 2307
Conventional: 397, 298, 299, 1150, 1205, 1334, 1498, 1655, 1790, 1829, 1862, 2360, 2835
Conventional Mores: 1017
Conventional Scales: 1341
Conventionality: 1927
Conventionalization: 1582
Conventions: 1235
Conventions of Written English: 570, 571
Convergence: 1614
Convergent Production: 1060, 2518
Convergent Production of Figural Units: 2518
Convergent Production of Symbolic Implications: 2518
Convergent Production of Symbolic Systems: 2518
Convergent Production of Symbolic Transformations: 2518
Convergent Production Skills: 1641
Convergent Thinking: 1714
Convergent Thinking: Central Theme: 2297
Converger: 1469, 1471
Conversation: 87, 397, 1064
Conversational Expression: 277
Conversations: 84, 620
Conversing Effectively: 494
Conversion: 1959
Conversion Hysteria (Hy): 1697
Conversion Reaction: 2109
Conversion Reactions: 2615
Converting Statements: 1780
Cooking and Home Management: 63
Cooking or Sewing: 411
Cool Temperature: 1478
Cool vs. Warm: 477
Cooperation: 1443, 1465, 1549, 1655, 1964, 2452, 2716, 2804
Cooperation and Conformity: 2355
Cooperation/Competition: 2585
Cooperational: 2416
Cooperative: 1681, 1686, 1958
Cooperative Education: 2026
Cooperative Involvement: 1465
Cooperativeness: 37, 1223, 1317, 1333, 2265, 2784
Coordinate Geometry: 1997
Coordinated: 618
Coordinating: 197, 2424
Coordination: 224, 445, 1042, 1043, 1044, 1062, 1427, 1673, 2587
Coordination of Household: 1026
Coordinator: 296
Coping: 265, 1263, 1684
Coping Index: 2759
Coping Resource Effectiveness: 698
Coping Scale: 291
Coping Skills: 1733, 2294, 2813, 2814
Coping. Social Support: 1824
Coping Style Profile: 1870
Coping with Anger: 40
Coping with Anxiety: 40
Coping with Conflict: 2444
Coping with Depression: 40
Coping with Difficulties and Emergencies: 1569, 2605
Coping with Environment: 695
Coping with Feelings: 1292
Coping With Pressure: 2425
Coping with Self: 695

Creative Living: 1938
Creative Personality: 68
Creative Potential: 2605
Creative Productive Thinking Abilities: 1921
Creative Representation: 1204
Creative Talent: 1142
Creative Temperament: 372
Creative Thinking Ability: 217
Creative Thinking and Problem-Solving Skills: 1094
Creative Thinking Characteristics: 2622
Creative Thought: 1789
Creative Work: 1345
Creative Writing: 411, 618
Creativity: 311, 727, 966, 1089, 1393, 1493, 1576, 1641, 1655, 1694, 1695, 1701, 1757, 1855, 1861, 1878, 1930, 2000, 2131, 2133, 2295, 2369, 2537, 2679, 2804, 2805, 2915
Creativity and Innovation: 1923
Creativity-Independence: 1163
Credibility Change : 437
Credibility of the Child-Observed/Reported: 442
Credible: 381
Credit Manager: 1790
Cree Questionnaire: 2605
Criminal History: 1766
Criminal Justice: 762
Crippled: 1169
Crises: 1941, 1942
Critical: 1822, 2876
Critical Analysis: 1094
Critical Analysis and Reading Strategies: 2487
Critical-Competitive: 1161
Critical-Complimentary Attitude Toward Medical Schools: 1640
Critical Events Index: 890
Critical Item Endorsement: 77
Critical Items: 1775, 2546
Critical Parent: 68
Critical Pathology Composite: 818
Critical Reasoning: 571
Critical Response Score: 632
Critical Thinking: 186, 621, 17720, 2856, 2857
Critical Thinking Ability: 705, 959
Criticism Tolerance: 2347
Criticize Trainee's Work: 2923
Cross: 564
Cross Modal Efficiency: 320
Cross Out: 2901
Cross Out Letters: 1139
Crosses: 2057
Crossing Feet: 1653
Crossing Out Letters: 1138
Crying: 213, 1488
Crystallization: 83
Crystallized Intelligence: 798
Crystallized Scale: 1378
Cube Comparisons Test: 1405
Cube Copying: 2240
Cube Design: 2792
Cube Tapping: 2439
Cube Test: 1085
Cued List Recall: 1644
Cued Recall: 685
Cued-Recall Intrusions: 375
Cued Recall of Words: 2297
Cued Recall of Words in Discourse: 2297
Cued Speech: 207
Cues for Tension and Anxiety: 1853
Culinary Arts: 380, 1790
Cultural: 147
Cultural Appreciation: 490
Cultural Conformist/Group-Oriented: 1341
Cultural Conformity: 865
Cultural Identifier/Adaptive: 1341
Cultural Identity: 1493, 2805
Cultural Knowledge-Behavior: 747
Cultural Knowledge-General: 747
Cultural Knowledge-Specific: 747
Cultural Leadership: 1438
Cultural Participation Subtask: 2527
Culture: 684, 2585
Curiosity: 724
Current Airway Assessment Information: 2472
Current Behavior/Relationships: 808
Current Chemical/Societal Problems: 684
Current Living Situation: 1649
Current Scales: 748
Current Sexual Allegations/Offenses: 1433
Current Symptom Scales: 362
Current Syndromes: 2305
Curriculum: 452, 648, 684, 843, 1108, 2083
Curriculum and Job Tasks: 648
Curriculum and Teaching Procedure: 1716
Curriculum/Instruction/Assessment: 2026
Curriculum Planning: 638
Custodial Change: 437
Customer and Personal Service: 1044
Customer Focus: 2129, 2385
Customer Motivation: 2713
Customer Relations: 989
Customer Satisfaction: 490
Customer Service: 1177
Customer Service Aptitude Scale: 1972
Customer Service Attitude Scale: 1972
Customer Service Index: 1972
Customer Service Knowledge and Skills: 1900
Customer Service Orientation: 2268
Cutting With Scissors: 1653
CV[CC]: 2175
CVC: 2175
Cylindrical: 1169
Cynicism: 1698
Cynicism (CYN): 1697
Cypher: 1800

D (composite) score: 771
Daddy-Doll: 1872
Daily Activity History: 1431, 1432
Daily Hassles: 1178
Daily Living: 1591, 2296, 2780, 2813
Daily Living Skills: 258, 377, 805, 2579
Daily Routine: 213, 1886
Daily Routine-Leisure Time: 2108
Daily Routine-Leisure Time Impairment: 2109
Daily Routines: 950
Dangerousness: 690
Daring: 381
DASE Word Score: 783
Data: 168, 1478, 2830, 2831
Data Analysis: 1177
Data Analysis/Statistics and Probability: 1759
Data Entry: 1831
Data Entry Operator: 399
Data-Information: 1163
Data Input Operator: 398
Data Management: 1790
Data Orientation: 1163
Data Processing: 410, 1551, 1818, 2026
Data Rational: 1822
Date and Name and Address Checking: 533
Dating: 2454
Dating and Sex: 1942
Dating Experiences: 659
Dating History: 1431, 1432
Datives: 2233
The Day We Cooked Pancakes in School: 2611
Daydreaming: 651
Deaffrication: 1394
Dealing with Ambiguity: 1830
Dealing with Client/Therapist Sexual Feelings: 1830
Dealing with Dependency: 1830
Dealing with Details: 1273
Dealing with Emergencies: 2444
Dealing with Employee Conflicts: 1479, 1480
Dealing with Stress: 40
Dealing with Therapist Identification Issues: 1830
Debasement: 1685, 1687
Deceleration: 83
Deception: 2307
Decide by Rule: 1557
Deciding Situation: 64
Deciding-Influencing: 1163
Decimal Fractions and Per Cent: 1604
Decimals: 172, 343, 831
Decimals and Percentages: 171
Decimals and Percents: 730
Decimals/Ratios/Percents: 1738
Deciphering Languages: 1405
Decision Level/Autonomy: 2585
Decision Making: 40, 252, 405, 717, 1440, 1449, 1545, 1554, 1712, 1948, 2105, 2357, 2571
Decision-Making: 1551
Decision-Making Abilities: 2418
Decision Making Confusion: 422
Decision-Making Opportunities: 648
Decision Making Practices: 2587
Decision Making/Problem Solving: 2423
Decision-Making Problems: 690
Decision-Making Readiness: 2828
Decision Making Speed: 226
Decision-Making Styles: 200
Decision-Making Tasks: 200
Decision Pattern: 1439
Decisions: 1914
Decisions and Planning: 646, 660
Decisive: 1822, 2605, 2648
Decisiveness: 300, 413, 654, 1576, 2588, 2784
Decoding: 867, 2462
Decoding Skills: 39
Decoding Test: 2254
Decorative: 1222
Decroly Matching Game: 1653
Dedicated: 1954
Dedication: 1955
Dedication Traits: 1930, 1955
Deduction: 2856, 2857
Deductive: 2373
Deductive Logic: 703, 704
Deductive Reasoning: 368, 1044, 2252
Deductive Reasoning: Elimination: 2297
Deep-Achieving Approach: 2540
Deep Approach: 1466, 2540
Deep Motive: 1466, 2540
Deep Strategy: 1466, 2540
Defective Color Vision: 1159
Defective Inhibition (Sc5): 1697
Defendence: 1965, 1988
Defending Assertiveness: 1290
Defense: 1239
Defense Mechanisms: 2307
Defensive: 2634
Defensive Abuser vs. Defensive Non-Abuser: 2553
Defensive Avoidance: 2782
Defensive Functions: 912
Defensive Self-enhancement: 1735
Defensive Symptoms: 2522
Defensiveness: 215, 1008, 1209, 1587, 1698, 1729, 1775, 1931, 1933, 1962, 1963, 2115, 2553
Defensiveness and Inconsistency Scores: 1729
Deference: 68, 908, 1988
Deferent: 1243
Defiance: 1749
Defiant: 1317
Deficiency Focusing: 2513
Deficiency Love: 426
Defines Mission: 1276
Definiteness: 2751
Definition: 793
Definitions: 1084, 1378, 2911

Definitions of Set One: 729
Definitions of Set Two: 729
Degree of Ambivalence in Description: 215
Degree of Certainty: 1497
Degree of Comfort or Anxiety with Supervisor: 2924
Degree of Independence/Dependence: 268
Degree of Mastery and Feeling of Competence: 242
Degree of Match: 1593
Degree of Participation: 1945
Degree of Responsibility: 2584
Degree of Satisfaction with Help Received: 1947
Degree to Which a Vocation is Associated with Self Fulfillment: 1497
Dejection: 1223
Delay Avoidance: 2591
Delay of Gratification: 2647
Delay Task: 1099
Delayed: 476, 1644
Delayed List Recall: 1644
Delayed Memory: 2202
Delayed Pairs: 1485
Delayed Presence and Accuracy: 329
Delayed Prose Recall: 1644
Delayed Recall: 470, 685, 1644, 2159, 2227, 2701, 2901
Delayed Recall Index: 2701
Delayed Recall of Word Strings: 2297
Delayed Recognition: 476, 687, 1485, 2909
Delayed Recognition of Pictures: 356
Delayed Recognition of Words: 356
Delayed Response: 2251
Delayed Retention: 329
Delayed Visual Recognition: 1644
Delegating: 197, 1479, 1480, 1550, 1554, 2424, 2571
Delegating Responsibilities: 903
Delegating Style: 1436
Delegation: 1443, 1545, 1549, 2762
Delegation (Permissiveness): 490
Delegative: 2064
Deletion of Final Consonants: 1394
Deletion of Initial Consonants: 1394
Deletions: 2233
Deletions per T-Unit: 2661
Deliberate: 1294
Deliberation: 1769, 2218
Delinquency: 1962, 1963
Delinquency/Antisocial: 2510
Delinquent: 69
Delinquent Behavior: 451, 2939
Delinquent Predisposition: 1685
Delirium: 136
Delivery: 619
Delusional Disorder: 1687
Delusional Thinking: 73
Delusions: 2289
Delusions-Hall-Disorganization: 2305
Delusions-Hallucinations: 2109, 2305
Demand Reconciliation: 1437
Demandingness: 1889
Demands: 1624
Dementia: 562
Democracy of Policy: 1026
Democratic: 1549, 1560, 1575, 1822, 1966
Democratic-Autocratic Attitude Toward Teaching: 1640
Democratic-Cooperative: 1439
Democratic/Humanistic: 1233
Demographic: 434
Demographic and Social History: 484
Demographic Data: 717, 2147
Demographic Information: 291
Demographics: 642, 2311
Demonstrated Abilities: 2555
Demonstrated Community Service: 1795
Demonstrated Trust: 138, 139
Demonstrating a Critical Stance: 1759
Demonstrating Commitment: 1550
Demonstrating Personal Mastery: 1651
Demonstrating Positive Attitudes/Behavior: 190
Demonstrating Professional Commitment: 903
Demonstrative: 2605, 2648
Demonstratives: 430, 1427
Denial: 256, 439, 1169, 1241, 1290, 1341
Denial/Collusion: 1857
Denial of Illness: 2108
Denial of Social Anxiety: 1698
Denial of Social Anxiety (Hy1): 1697
Denial or Illness: 2109
Denial/Refusal: 2251
Dental Assistant: 398, 399, 1790
Dental Assisting: 1794
Dental Hygienist: 398, 399, 1790
Dental Lab Technician: 398
Dental Laboratory Technician: 399
Dentist: 398, 1790
Dentistry: 905
Depalatalization: 2438
Department Profile: 1398
Departmental Procedures: 1108, 2083
Dependability: 490, 942, 1044, 1702, 1964
Dependable: 1333
Dependence: 1169
Dependency: 449, 748, 790, 856, 1290, 1628, 2306
Dependency Feelings: 1012
Dependency Needs: 2615
Dependent: 200, 690, 1150, 1498, 1655, 1687, 1862, 1961, 2306, 2514, 2520
Dependent-Autonomous: 2446
Depersonalization: 690, 1590, 2521
Depersonalization and Derealization: 74
Depersonalization/Derealization: 2216
Depersonalization Disorder: 77
Depersonalized Humans: 847

Depressed: 451, 551
Depressed Affect: 1733
Depressed Mood: 2216
Depressed Mood/Past 12 Months: 1181
Depressed-Optimistic: 218
Depressed/Withdrawn: 424
Depression: 73, 201, 256, 267, 272, 280, 282, 291, 335, 337, 362, 429, 472, 473, 538, 562, 569, 690, 739, 789, 791, 792, 794, 817, 818, 915, 927, 931, 936, 1166, 1213, 1313, 1626, 1628, 1675, 1698, 1745, 1778, 1803, 1871, 1889, 1959, 1962, 1963, 2006, 1017, 2107, 2108, 2218, 2230, 2231, 2232, 2242, 2263, 2326, 2367, 2457, 2602, 2603, 2604, 2615, 2782, 2783, 2865
Depression and Anxiety: 1543
Depression and Calculation and Language: 434
Depression-Anxiety: 748, 2109
Depression (D): 1697
Depression-Dejection: 2076
Depression (DEP): 1697
Depression (General): 1481
Depression/Motivation: 2035
Depression Scale: 2114
Depression Screen: 2554
Depression (Specific): 1481
Depression-Suicide: 2109
Depression/Suicide Potential: 1207, 1208
Depression-Withdrawal: 929, 1815
Depressive: 1687, 1961, 2520
Depressive Affect: 1685
Depressive-Associated Features: 2305
Depressive Features: 1181
Depressive Fluctuations: 1577, 2874
Depressive-Joyful: 2446
Depressive Mood: 2120
Depressive Mood and Ideation: 1181
Depressive Mood/Ideation: 2305
Depressive Reaction: 2447
Depressive Syndrome: 2305
Depressive vs. Light-Hearted: 2618
Depressiveness: 1779
Depth of Knowledge: 1886
Depth Perception: 1044
Depth Visualization: 2889
Derailment: 2290
Derangement of Thought Processes and Peculiar Behavior: 721
Derived Adjectives: 2660
Dermatological: 1186
Describing Objects: 277
Description: 716, 1169
Description Naming: 2667, 2725
Description of Administrative Methods and Personal Characteristics: 1233
Descriptive: 2489
Deserter: 1561, 2278
Design: 1044, 1470, 2069
Design Analogies: 1485
Design-Art-Communications: 408
Design Copying: 1771, 2377
Design Fluency: 1771
Design-Formal/Informal: 2181
Design/Graphics and Communication: 2822
Design-Organization: 2181
Design Reproduction: 797, 798, 1168
Design Sequences: 797, 798, 1168
Designing Instructional Sequences and Learning Materials: 203
Desirability: 219, 1685, 1687, 1965
Desirable Response Inconsistency: 2306
Desire for Responsibility: 752
Desired: 2133
Desires: 1842
Despair: 1631
Destiny Control: 1250
Destructive: 451
Destructive to Property: 2299
Detached: 1243
Detachment: 2306, 2915
Detail: 391, 392
Detail Conscious: 1822
Detail Judgments: 781
Detail Placement: 329
Detail Presence: 329
Detailed Description: 1191
Detailed Personal and Behavioral History: 1972
Detecting Ambiguities: 1780
Detecting Underlying Assumptions: 1780
Detention-Related Technical Knowledges: 796
Determination: 219, 1660, 1821, 1955, 2007
Determining Causes: 2710
Determining Singular and Plural Forms: 1534
Determining Solutions: 2710
Deterministic: 1655
Develop a Life Philosophy: 2530
Develop Creativity: 2530
Develop Human Relations: 2530
Develop Scientific Inquiry Skills: 2530
Developer: 1561, 2278
Developing: 166, 1551
Developing a Resume: 190
Developing and Implementing Technical Ideas: 1569, 2605
Developing Employee Potential: 1569, 2605
Developing Group Cooperation and Teamwork: 2605
Developing Interpretation: 1759
Developing Mature Interpersonal Relationships Task: 2527
Developing New Directions: 807
Developing Others: 1573
Developing Positive Climate: 1233
Developing Staff: 903
Developing Subordinates: 1550
Developing Teamwork: 1569

Developing Within: 802
Development: 420, 1962, 2933
Development of Appreciation for and Creativity in the Arts: 1492
The Development of Democracy: 145
The Development of Imitation: 194
Development of Leisure Skills: 2450
The Development of Means for Obtaining Desired Environmental Events: 194
Development of Multiple Talents: 907
The Development of Operational Causality: 194
Development of Play: 1996
The Development of Schemes for Relating to Objects: 194
Development of Sounds: 2052
The Development of Visual Pursuit and The Permanence of Objects: 194
Development (Social): 454
Developmental: 2111, 1091,
Developmental Assessment Tool: 2082
Developmental Attainment: 1907, 1909
Developmental Biology: 684
Developmental Checklist: 810
Developmental Functions: 158
Developmental History: 1431, 1432, 1886, 2047, 2147
Developmental Phonological Processes: 1394
Developmental-Prescriptive Advising: 8
Developmental Problems: 2147
Developmental Program: 1922
Developmental Quotient: 778
Developmental-Remedial Strategies: 869
Developmental Spelling Ability: 2320
Developmental Stimulation: 1007
Developmentally Related Sexual Behaviors: 457
Deviance: 2306
Deviant Behavior: 1931, 1932, 2195
Deviation: 256
Device: 1593
Dewey Decimal System: 1491
D-expectation: 392
Dexterity: 445, 781, 782, 1323, 1677, 1717, 2515, 2774
Diadochokinesis: 164, 1852
Diadochokinetic Rate: 163
Diagnoses: 1649
Diagnosis for Current Episode: 650
Diagnosis for Lifetime: 650
Diagnostic: 1139, 2306
Diagnostic and Achievement scores for each of the following: Parts of Speech: 1125
Diagnostic and Treatment Services: 410
Diagnostic Comments: 1777
Diagnostic Impression: 434
Diagnostic Interactional Survey: 2082
Diagnostic Number: 2134
Diagnostic Oral Reading: 1738
Diagnostic Reading: 2134
Diagnostic Scales: 349
Diagnostic Skills: 555
Diagrammatic: 128
Diagrammatic Reasoning: 119, 2087, 2641, 2642
Diagrammatic Series: 735
Diagrammatic Thinking: 2641
Diagramming: 119, 670, 2087
Diagramming Relationships: 1405
Diagraphs and the Silent e Rule: 2134
DIAL-3 Total: 809
Diamond: 564
Diastolic Blood Pressure Reading: 2789
Dice: 463, 2023
Dictated Sentences and Handwriting: 2005
Dictation: 786, 835, 2796, 2901, 2902, 2904
Dictation in Spanish: 304
Dictation Spelling: 1606
Dictation/Transcription: 2302
Dictionary Use: 835
Didactic Instruction: 1867
Die Making: 1793
Diesel Engine Mechanics: 1794
Diesel Engine Repair: 1792
Diesel Mechanics: 1792
Diet and Eating Habits: 1791
Dietician: 2825
Dietitian: 398, 1790
Difference: 2448
Difference Between Color-Naming Speed With and Without Distraction: 2051
Difference Between Reading Speed and Color-Naming Speed: 2051
Difference [Conflict]: 2318
Difference Score: 2781
Differences: 1424
Differences Between Behaviors and Perceptions: 2546
Different Letter Groups: 726
Different Uses: 1405
Differentiation: 1254
Differents: 125
Difficult Boss: 807
Difficult Items Correct: 2811
Difficult Items Response Latency: 2811
Difficulties and Strengths: 158
Difficulty: 1128
Difficulty in Making Strategic Transitions: 300
Difficulty in Molding Staff: 300
Diffident: 69
Digit Copying Test: 1390
Digit Span: 1454, 2159, 2202, 2840, 2860, 2862
Digit Symbol: 1731, 2728, 2840
Digit-Symbol: 1840
Digit Symbol-Coding: 2860
Digital & Analog Electronics: 923
Digital and Analog Electronics: 920
Digital Discrimination: 2421
Digital Electronics: 1279, 1537, 2643

Digital Electronics/Computers: 924
Digits Backward: 2701, 2728
Digits Forward: 2701
Diligent: 1211
Dim Lights: 1478
Dimension: 1323, 2583
Dimension Scores: 2278
Dining Skills: 1065
Diphthongs and Combination: 2651
Diphthongs and Vowels Controlled by r: 2254
Diplomacy: 2347
Direct: 1273
Direct Appraisal of Honesty: 2522
Direct Experience: 391, 392
Direct Guidance: 716
Direct Observation: 70
Direct Quotations: 1427
Direct Sales: 752
Direct Trainee to Work Station and Explain Nature of Work: 2923
Direct Trainees to Work Together: 2923
Directing and Delegating: 2575
Directing Style: 1436
Direction: 1169, 1966
Direction of Criticism: 1026
Direction/Position: 331
Directional Errors: 1073
Directionality: 319
Directionality & Spatial Relationships: 1224
Directions (No Cuing): 2376
Directions of Aggression: 2248
Directions-Oral and Written: 2408
Directions (2-Step): 2376
Directive: 1294, 1549, 2121, 2928
Directiveness: 1573
Director: 1915
Disability: 1593
Disagreement About Finances: 1582
Disappointment: 2512
Disassociation: 2109
Discerning: 2121
Discerning Causal Relationships: 1780
Disciplinarian: 1589
Disciplinary: 1222
Disciplinary Contacts: 2311
Disciplinary Friction: 1026
Disciplinary History: 1209
Disciplinary Practices: 2573
Discipline: 213, 836, 1880, 2020, 2570
Discipline Orientation: 1275
Disciplined: 86
Disciplined Imagination: 1396
Disciplining and Counseling: 1570
Disclosure: 442, 1685, 1687
Discomfort: 2115
Discontinuous Quantity: 674
Discord in Home: 1026
Discouragement/Criticism of Pain: 291
Discouragement/Criticism of Wellness: 291
Discourse: 619
Discourse Competence: 2717
Discourse Subscore: 87
Discovery and Creativity: 2355
Discrete Mathematics: 684
Discriminability: 375
Discriminant Function Score: 1241
Discrimination: 1073, 1472, 1868, 1909, 2382
Discrimination and Orientation: 1138, 1139
Discrimination/Matching: 2049
Discrimination of Color/Shape/Size: 2297
Discrimination of Form: 1357
Discrimination of Initial and Final Sounds: 1765
Discrimination of Pictured Objects: 2297
Discrimination Recall: 208
Discrimination Total: 2863
Discussion: 1474
Discussion of Plans: 716
Disease Control: 1019
Disease Conviction: 1241
Disease Dimensions: 1242
Disengagement: 1006
Disengagement Stage: 83
Disinhibition: 894, 2306
Dislike: 1790
Disorganization: 748
Disorganized: 748
Disorientation: 77, 562, 792, 2120
Disorientation Memory: 2109
Disorientation-Memory: 2108
Displacing: 1700
Displaying Good Flow/Logic/Organization: 2775
Disposition: 1649, 1964
Disputatious: 1222
Disregard for Rights: 1290
Disregards Rules vs. Conscientious: 888
Disruption 1: 136
Disruption 2: 136
Disruptive: 1317, 1565
Disruptive Behavior: 2299
Disruptive-Demanding: 2322
Disruptive Social Environment: 1161
Dissatisfaction: 2764
Dissatisfaction with Career: 1209
Dissatisfaction with Children: 1582
Dissatisfaction with Job: 1209
Dissatisfaction with Supervisor: 1209
Dissemblance or Dissimulation: 2887
Disseminating Information: 1884
Dissenting: 1688
Dissimulation: 1963
Dissociation: 2782
Dissociation Summary: 840
Dissociative Amnesia: 74
Dissociative Coping: 847

Dissociative Disorders: 1543
Dissociative Experiences Scale: 1626
Dissociative Psychopathology: 846
Distal Quadrant: 2176
Distance Vision: 1614, 2224
Distancing: 2858
Distant/Near Accommodation: 1614
Distinguishing Between Fact and Opinion: 647
Distinguishing Between Real and Make-Believe: 647
Distinguishing Differences of Kind and Degree: 1780
Distortion: 1226
Distortions: 303
Distractability: 2848
Distractability and Overactivity: 1963
Distractibility: 225, 425, 931
Distractible Speech: 2290
Distraction: 696, 700
Distress: 19, 448, 2061, 2393, 2783
Distressed Mood: 1181
Distribution: 1551
Distributive Studies: 618
District Manager Selection: 2330
Distrust: 1374
Distrust of Others: 1314
Disturbed Peer Relations: 2848
Disturbance-Restless: 1162
Disturbing Interpersonal Behavior: 1, 2
Diurnal Variation: 1488, 2216
Divergent Feeling: 724
Divergent Production: 1060, 2328, 1518
Divergent Production of Figural Units: 2518
Divergent Production of Semantic Units: 2518
Divergent Production of Symbolic Relations: 2518
Divergent Thinking: 724, 1714
Divergent Thinking: Homographs: 2297
Divergent Thinking: Idioms: 2297
Divergent Thinking: Proverbs: 2297
Divergent Thinking: Verbal Absurdities: 2297
Diverger: 1469, 1471
Diversified Occupations: 1794
Diversity Behavior: 975
Divided Attention: 2794
Divided Attention Indicator Alone Premature Responses: 567
Divided Attention Indicator Alone Speed: 567
Divided Attention Indicator Dual Premature Responses: 567
Divided Attention Indicator Dual Speed: 567
Divided Attention Sequence Comparison Accuracy: 567
Divided Attention Sequence Comparison Speed: 567
Divided Attention Sequence Comparison Thruput: 567
Divided Visual Attention: 356
Dividedness: 847
Division: 730, 825, 831, 1392, 1738
Division and Reunion: 145
Division of Home/Child Care/Work Responsibilities: 717
Division of Household Labor and Professional Employment: 1583
Division of Whole Numbers: 1604, 2486
Division Test: 1405
Divorce: 467
Do You Know How To: 1346
Doctor: 2825
Doctor Dissatisfaction: 267
Doctors and Dentists: 213
Document Checking: 1270
Document Literacy: 972
Doesn't Belong: 899
Dogmatic-Inflexible: 1162
Doing Whatever It Takes: 300
Doleful: 1685
Domain Composites: 798
Domain-Specific Sense of Control: 2399
Domestic: 2813
Domestic Activity: 1, 2891
Domestic Behavior: 2127
Domestic Environment: 2117
Domestic/Household Activities: 291
Domestic Satisfaction: 794
Domestic Service: 1222
Domestic Skills: 1718, 2204, 2299
Domestic/Survival Skills: 1066
Domestic Tasks: 1897
Domestic Work: 1990
Domestics: 62
Dominance: 68, 372, 538, 908, 1201, 1289, 1291, 1292, 1660, 1959, 1964, 1984, 1988, 2148, 2353, 2605, 2784
Dominance (Do): 1697
Dominance-Inducing Parental Attitude: 1630
Dominant: 1243, 1253, 1443, 2757
Dominant Hand: 1993, 2009
Dominant Language: 850
Dominant Leadership: 1334
Dominant Style: 400
Dominant vs. Deferential: 2417
Dominant vs. Submissive: 2618
Dominate: 1557
Dominating: 2149
Domination: 490
Don't Like Total: 2869
Dorsiflexion of the Foot: 1258
Dot Locations: 476
Dotting: 1533
Double Meanings: 1378
Double Simultaneous Stimulation of Hand and Cheek: 2141
Doves: 1872
Downward Parachute: 1668
d-Prime: 687
Drafter: 398, 399
Drafting: 410, 2832
Drama: 905, 2882

Dramatic: 1074, 2001
Dramatics: 618, 2295
Dramatizing: 1685
Draw a Boy or Girl: 304
Draw-A-Design: 1613
Draw-a-House: 1865
Draw a Person: 304, 1357
Draw A Person: 346
Draw-a-Person: 1865
Draw-A-Story: 855
Drawing: 2138
Drawing a Clock: 1513
Drawing Conclusions: 1094, 1281
Drawing Conclusions and Making Inferences: 647
Drawing Conclusions Using Mathematical Skills and Concepts: 1094
Drawing from Imagination: 2410
Drawing from Observation: 2410
Drawing to Command: 199
Drawing Up String: 1653
Drawing/Writing: 1278
Dreamer: 727
Dressing: 63, 265, 377, 443, 661, 879, 1041, 1194, 2127, 2299, 2891
Dressing and Simple Hygiene: 2342
Dressing and Undressing: 1907
Dressing/Bathing or Touch: 1265
Dressing Female/Male: 1066
Dressing Skills: 1065
Drill and Recitation: 1474
Drinking Evaluation Category: 1372, 2550
Drinking Habits: 2789
Drinking Problems: 1181
Drive: 219, 793, 1210, 1955, 2605
Drive for Mastery: 285
Drive for Thinness: 893
Drive Strength: 1948
Driven Behavior: 794
Driver: 2453
Driver Education: 2026
Driver Interview: 857
Driver Risk: 856
Drives: 1721
Driving History: 1431, 1432
Driving Violations: 1313
Drug: 19, 856, 2783
Drug Abuse: 2107, 2109
Drug Abuse and Dependence: 642
Drug Abuse Severity: 1587
Drug and Alcohol: 690
Drug and Alcohol Abuse: 762
Drug/Alcohol Abuse: 1209
Drug Attitude: 1967
Drug Avoidance Scale: 1972
Drug Dependence: 1687
Drug History: 1431, 1432
Drug Inquiry Sentence Completion: 2381
Drug Inventory: 434
Drug Problems: 1959
Drug Scale: 2284
Drug Usage: 1499
Drug Use: 1207
Drug Use and Abuse and Dependence: 650
Drug Use Evaluation: 1372, 2550
Drug Use Frequency/Duration/Age of Onset: 1931
Drugs: 849, 1313, 1335, 2061, 2285, 2393, 2403
DSM III-R ADHD: 469
DSM-IV Hyperactive-Impulsive: 681
DSM-IV Hyperactive-Impulsive Symptoms: 678
DSM-IV Inattentive: 681
DSM-IV Inattentive Symptoms: 678
DSM-IV Total: 681
DSM-IV Total ADHD Symptoms: 678
Dual Task Previous Number Alone Accuracy: 567
Dual Task Previous Number Alone Speed: 567
Dual Task Previous Number Alone Thruput: 567
Dual Task Previous Number Dual Accuracy: 567
Dual Task Previous Number Dual Speed: 567
Dual Task Previous Number Dual Thruput: 567
Dual Task Tracking Alone Boundary Hits: 567
Dual Task Tracking Alone Error: 567
Dual Task Tracking Dual Boundary Hits: 567
Dual Task Tracking Dual Error: 567
Due Process: 2534
Dull vs. Bright: 888
Duration: 983, 1753, 1869, 2108, 2543
Duration of Contact with Mother: 1026
Dutiful: 1211
Dutifulness: 1769, 2218
Dyadic Cohesion: 863
Dyadic Consensus: 863
Dyadic Relationships: 1008
Dyadic Satisfaction: 863
Dynamic: 381
Dynamic Flexibility: 1044
Dynamic Strength: 1044
Dynamism: 1223, 2007, 2776
Dyscontrol: 1963
Dyseidesia: 867
Dysfunctional Circularity: 1006
Dysfunctional Sexual Behavior: 2782
Dyslexia: 1083
Dysmenorrhea: 1853
Dysnemkinesia: 867
Dysphasia: 1083
Dysphonesia: 867
Dysphoria: 1745
Dysthymia: 1687
Dysthymic Disorder: 77, 79, 876

The Earliest Civilizations: 2932
Early Academic and Language Skills Composite: 1385
Early Academic Scales: 1385
Early Childhood: 65

Early Childhood Development: 684
Early Childhood Dimensions of Education Rating Scale: 877
Early Childhood Education: 2026
Early Childhood Physical Environment Scales: 877
Early Childhood Programs: 684
Early Childhood Teacher Style Rating Scale: 877
Early Development: 158
Early Developmental History: 808
Early Indicators: 133
Early Learning Composite: 1728
Early Life Problems: 158
Early Morning: 1472
Early Morning Waking: 2216
Early Number Concepts: 349, 837, 2134
Early Words: 1528
Early Years Core Scales: 349
Earner/Consumer: 61
Earnings: 1406
Earth Science: 2026
Earth & Space Sciences: 1759
Earth/Space Science: 1094, 2026
Earth Structure and Geological Processes: 684
Easy Items: 2011
Easy Items Correct: 2811
Easy Items Response Latency: 2811
Eating: 63, 265, 443, 661, 2127, 2891
Eating and Drinking: 1194, 1897, 2316
Eating and Meal Preparation: 2299
Eating Disorder: 73, 1931
Eating Disorders: 642
Eating Dysfunctions: 1685
Eating or Feeding: 1265
Eating/Weight: 2147
Eccentric Perceptions: 2306
Eccentricity: 690
Echolalia: 2290, 2428
Ecology and Conservation: 684
Ecology and Evolution: 1110
Economic: 147, 162, 661, 1639, 1929, 2264, 2442, 2539, 2626
Economic Activity: 1, 2
Economic Activity: 2
Economic and Technological Changes and Their Relation to Society/Ideas/and the Environment: 1759
Economic Evaluation: 1968
Economic Maturity: 421
Economic Motivation: 2007
Economic Resources: 1808
Economic Rewards: 2805
Economic Security: 1716, 2805
Economic-Vocational Activity: 465
Economics: 618, 645, 684, 905, 1113, 1124, 1493, 2026
Economics and Accounting: 1044
Economics and Business: 2675
Economist: 398
Editing: 1606
Editorials: 1364
Educating: 398, 1237
Education: 618, 905, 1177, 1350, 1766, 1818, 1943, 1968
Education Acceptance: 2591
Education and Social Work: 1841
Education and Training: 1044, 1252
Education/Development: 2764
Education-Elementary: 618
Education for Family Living: 1492
Education for Physical and Mental Health: 1492
Education for Wise Use of Leisure Time: 1492
Education of Deaf and Hard of Hearing Students: 2026
Education of Students with Mental Retardation: 2026
Education-Secondary: 618
Education Summary: 2364
Educational Ability: 1760
Educational Activities at Home: 1884
Educational Adjustment Difficulties: 1207, 1208
Educational and Personal Needs: 57
Educational and Social Evaluation: 1968
Educational and Social Services: 1285
Educational Attainments and Intelligence: 235
Educational Environment: 1593
Educational Expectation: 909
Educational Experiences: 57
Educational Finance: 684
Educational Goal: 1593
Educational History: 808, 1431, 1432, 2147
Educational Involvement Subtask: 2527
Educational Leadership: 2026
Educational Level Interest Scale: 618
Educational Orientation: 311, 399, 2537
Educational Outcomes: 57
Educational Plans After High School: 57
Educational Plans and Preferences: 57
Educational Preparation: 57
Educational Psychology: 512
Educational Purpose: 2530
Educational Response: 2529
Educational Roles: 2389
Educational Services: 411
Educational Technology: 1593
Effect of Context: 685
Effective: 2128
Effective Communications/Inarticulateness: 1340
Effective Instructional Leadership: 2314
Effective Test Taking: 1891, 2589
Effective Thinking: 2530
Effectiveness: 1371, 1561, 1667, 1682, 1736, 1737, 2278
Effectiveness in Performance: 1233
Effectiveness in Performing Twenty Specific Administrative Responsibilities Administrative Support: 1233

Effectiveness of Policy: 1026
Effectiveness of the Insulin: 1242
Effectiveness of Treatment: 1242
Effectiveness/Outcomes: 490
Effectiveness/Productivity: 490
Effects Achievement Value and Growth: 1824
Effects from Drug Use: 1931
Effects of Substance Abuse: 938
Effects of Use: 1932
Effects on Patient Functioning: 1777
Effects on the Person: 646, 660
Effects on the Spouse: 646
Efficacy: 790
Efficiency: 66, 158, 268, 379, 654, 1404
Efficiency Under Stress: 2420
Efficient-Inefficient: 1940
Efficient Learning Tools: 1891, 2589
Effort Regulation: 1720
Effort Required: 1542
Effort to Learn: 1163
Egalitarianism: 1881
Ego: 1239
Ego Drive: 654
Ego [Etho]-Defense: 2248
Ego Functioning: 2242
Ego Ideal: 317
Ego Inflation: 1698
Ego Inflation (Ma4): 1697
Ego Integrity: 1631
Ego Status: 1558
Ego-Status: 913, 941, 1244, 1894, 2273, 2921
Ego Strength: 913, 2148
Ego-Strength: 448
Ego Strength (Es): 1697
Egocentric: 1682
Egocentricity: 297, 1959
Egotistic: 1685
Egotistical-Prosocial: 2446
Eights—Challengers/Asserters/Directors: 958
Elaborated Phrases and Sentences: 2657
Elaboration: 724, 1720, 2771
Elaboration Test: 1405
Elaborative Processing: 1307
Elated-Depressed: 2077
Elated Mood: 2109
Elation: 2776
Elation-Grandiosity: 748
Elected Public Official: 398, 1790
Electrical: 1818, 2066, 2152, 2769
Electrical and Electronic: 410
Electrical and Electronic Equipment Repair: 410
Electrical and Power Transmission Installation: 410
Electrical Construction: 1794
Electrical Construction and Maintenance: 1792
Electrical/Electronic: 905, 1818
Electrical/Electronics: 1793
Electrical/Electronics Maintenance: 1793
Electrical Installation: 1792
Electrical Maintenance: 920, 1537, 2643
Electrical Occupations: 1794
Electrician: 380, 398, 399, 1790
Electricity and Magnetism: 684
Electromechanical Technology: 1792
Electromechanics: 2832
Electronic Product Servicing: 1792, 1794
Electronic Technician: 398, 399
Electronic Technology: 1794
Electronics: 398, 399, 1043, 1794, 2832
Electronics Communications: 1792
Electronics Information: 180
Electronics or Electrical Trades: 411
Electronics Technology: 1792
Elementary Algebra: 18, 192, 571, 1997
Elementary Education: 1334, 2026
Elementary School Teacher: 398, 399, 1790
Elements of Music: 684
Elicited Gestures: 159
Elicited Response Errors: 2650
Eliciting Relevant Responses and Testing: 2775
Eliminating Alternatives: 1780
Elimination Problems: 876
Embedded Elements: 1898
Embedded Imperatives: 2233
Embedded Sentence: 2662
The Emergence of Modern America: 146
Emergency Medical Care Knowledge: 1032
Emergency Medical Technician: 380, 398, 399, 1790
Emergency Room Treatment: 1733
Emerging Self: 1041
EMO Questionnaire: 2605
Emotion: 696, 1169, 1927
Emotion and Affect Processing Total: 1690
Emotional: 162, 697, 1333, 1494, 1499, 1620, 1929, 2321, 2508
Emotional Abuse: 442, 460
Emotional Adjustment: 1429, 1618
Emotional Alienation: 1698
Emotional Alienation (Sc2): 1697
Emotional and Physical Neglect and Minimization/Denial of Abuse: 460
Emotional and Sexuality: 2747
Emotional and Social Development: 882
Emotional Autonomy Subtask: 2527
Emotional Awareness and Acceptance: 1499
Emotional Bias: 979
Emotional Control: 219, 294, 1223, 1822, 1955, 2451
Emotional Dimension: 1045
Emotional Discharge: 699
Emotional Distress: 1587
Emotional Disturbance Scale: 841
Emotional Exhaustion: 1590
Emotional Expressivity: 2451
Emotional Functioning: 2030
Emotional Instability: 1321

Emotional Intensity: 654
Emotional Lability: 77, 681, 690
Emotional Makeup: 242
Emotional Management: 1499, 2746, 2747
Emotional Maturity: 944, 1676, 2294, 2537
Emotional Mediating Processes: 320
Emotional Needs: 1895
Emotional Passivity: 320
Emotional Preoccupation: 700
Emotional Problems: 681, 1500
Emotional Profile: 2181
Emotional Psychosocial: 2196
Emotional Ratio: 320
Emotional Resilience: 737, 2007
Emotional Response: 459, 794
Emotional Response to Hearing Impairment: 1190
Emotional Responsiveness: 2605
Emotional Self-Awareness: 243
Emotional Sensitivity: 1577, 2451, 2874
Emotional Social Development: 2319
Emotional Stability: 538, 1057, 1101, 1158, 1201, 1766, 1967, 2007, 2358
Emotional Stability and Control: 871
Emotional Stability vs. Neuroticism: 672, 673
Emotional State: 1649
Emotional Status: 1777
Emotional Style: 186
Emotional Support: 1733, 2793
Emotional Symptoms Index: 280
Emotional Tone: 1006, 1832, 1886
Emotional Vulnerability: 1686
Emotional Well-Being: 2158
Emotionality: 467, 2319, 2656, 2912
Emotionality Toward Child: 1026
Emotionally Mature-Emotionally Immature: 1940
Emotionally Responsive vs. Non-Emotionally Controlled: 2648
Emotionally Stable vs. Reactive: 2417
Emotionally Toned Syllogisms: 979
Emotions: 478, 1941, 1942
Emotions and Feeling States (Affects): 1263
Emotive: 224, 1472
Empathetic: 394, 1253
Empathic: 1819, 2876
Empathic Ability: 845
Empathic Response Score: 632
Empathy: 78, 243, 372, 426, 654, 933, 1333, 1443, 1576, 1948, 2007, 2274, 2347, 2385, 2452, 2912
Empathy Index: 2346
Empathy vs. Egocentrism: 672, 673
Emphasis: 162
Emphasis Dissonance Score: 2571
Emphasis on Basic Skills: 2314
Emphasis on Evaluation: 2412
Emphasizing Facts: 2633
Empirical: 928, 2112
Employability: 2196
Employability Certification: 645
Employability Index: 1972
The Employee Being Trained to Use the Technology: 1593
Employee Commitment: 490
Employee Communication-Motivation: 2573
Employee/Customer Relations Scale: 1972
Employee Involvement: 940
Employee Morale: 2919
Employee Motivation-Labor Relations: 1566
Employee Participation: 801
Employee Relations: 443
Employee Selection-Development: 1566
Employee Training-Evaluation: 2573
Employees/Facilities/Equipment: 1048
Employment: 1766, 1925, 2780
Employment Application: 857
Employment Assistance: 1108, 2083
Employment History: 57, 1431, 1432
Employment History and Experiences: 57
Employment Interview: 1352
Employment Plans: 57
Employment Readiness: 2828
Employment Roles: 2389
Employment Security: 801
Employment Skills: 443
Employment Stability: 2776
Employment Status: 401
Employment Trends: 1406
Employs Reading and Math Skills to Identify and Define a Problem: 2739
Empowered Employees: 2129
Empowered Leadership: 1438
Empowering: 166, 381
Empowerment: 379, 1267
Enabling: 1446
Enabling Behaviors: 559
Enabling Others to Act: 1445, 1448, 2635
Encoding: 867, 2254
Encoding Regular Words: 2254
Encoding Single Consonants: 2254
Encouragement of Maturity: 1216
Encouragement of Participation: 2587
Encouraging: 1147, 1446, 1651
Encouraging Peer Participation: 490
Encouraging the Heart: 1445, 1448, 2635
End Results: 2587
End Sounds: 1261
Ending Consonant: 917
Ending Sounds: 917, 2192
Endocrine: 2508
Endocrine/Hematology: 1186
Endogenous Depression: 1181
Endogenous Features: 2305
Endorse Acts/Opinions: 139
Endorse Acts/Views: 138
Endurance: 68, 908, 1062, 1930, 1965

Enduring: 1251, 1929
Energetic-Tired: 2077
Energies: 2274
Energy: 381, 1914, 2347
Energy/Drive: 2425
Energy/Effort: 2526
Energy/Fatigue: 1187
Energy/Fatigue/Physical Health Composite: 2158
Energy Level: 1333, 2605
Energy Output: 840
Enforcing Work Rules: 2575
Engineer: 398, 1790, 2825
Engineering: 618, 905, 1114, 1124, 1334
Engineering-Aerospace: 618
Engineering and Physical Sciences: 1841
Engineering and Related Technologies (Architectural: 410
Engineering and Technology: 1044
Engineering-Architectural: 618
Engineering-Chemical: 618
Engineering-Civil: 618
Engineering-Design Economics: 618
Engineering-Electrical: 618
Engineering-Mechanical: 618
Engineering/Physical Sciences/Mathematics/Architecture: 2000
Engineering-Physics: 618
Engineering Technology: 1285
English: 56, 97, 98, 160, 165, 570, 597, 850, 918, 992, 1997, 2000, 2530
English Composition: 498, 167
English Composition and English Composition with Essay: 497
English Dominant: 720
English Grammar: 1063
English Language: 348, 576, 1044
English Language and Composition: 118
English-Language Arts: 750
English/Language Arts: 645
English Language/Literature and Composition: 2026
English Language Proficiency: 309, 615
English Literacy Skills: 249
English Literature: 513, 618
English Literature and Composition: 118
English or Foreign Language: 411
English or Literature: 411
English Perceptions: 120, 121
English Teacher: 1790
English Usage: 1760, 1835
English Vocabulary: 304
Enhanced: 136, 799
Enhancing: 1688
Enjoyment of Mathematics: 1599
Enlightenment: 2237
Enmeshment: 1006
Enquiry Index: 2346
Enrichment: 1216, 1921
Enterprising: 86, 381, 397, 398, 399, 1157, 1334, 1790, 1829, 2360, 2835
Entertaining: 381, 1251, 1929, 1964, 2007
Entertainment: 752, 1177
Enthusiasm: 439, 1201, 1867, 2784
Enthusiasm/Depression: 1340
Enthusiastic: 990, 1954
Entitlement: 262, 291, 2306, 2403
Entrepreneur: 312
Entrepreneur (Leader): 2075
Entrepreneurial: 420
Entrepreneurial Creativity: 396
Entry: 420
Environment: 377, 1593, 2483, 2484, 2488, 2508
Environment and Humanity: 762
Environment and Society: 1759
Environment/Behavior Observation Schedule for Early Childhood Environments: 877
Environment Concern: 1163
Environment for Learning: 636, 1108, 2083
Environmental: 1030, 1074, 1169
Environmental Adaptation: 963
Environmental Assessment: 2838
Environmental Behaviors: 2444
Environmental Control: 410
Environmental Design: 618
Environmental Diversity: 1743
Environmental Domain: 1478
Environmental Education: 2026
Environmental Events: 794
Environmental Factors: 267
Environmental Risk Factor: 1931
Environmental Science: 99, 118
Environmental Sensitivity: 1396
Environmental Stimuli: 2181
Environmental Trust: 963
Environmental Wellness: 2746, 2747
Envy: 439
Episodic: 2596
Episodic Memory: 176
EQ Index: 966
Equation Building: 2485
Equations: 2486
Equations & Inequalities: 570
Equilibrium: 684
Equipment Operation: 684
Equivalence: 319
The Era of Political Revolutions: 2932
Eros: 426
Error: 1231, 1703
Error Rate: 769
Error score: 1087
Errors: 268, 2251, 2469
Escape: 1722
Escape-Avoidance: 2858
ESL Certification Applied Performance Test: 645
ESL Certification Listening/Reading: 645

Essay: 1785, 2730
Essay Test: 2655
Essays: 749
Essential Items: 1512
Establishing and Clarifying Purpose Task: 2527
Establishing Performance Standards: 1479, 1480
Establishment Stage: 83
Esteem: 371, 1163
Esthetic: 2800
Esthetic Judgment: 644
Estimate of Gains: 620
Estimate of Intelligence: 1500
Estimated Regularity of Imagery: 1242
Estimated WAIS or WAIS-R IQ: 2402
Estimation: 1392
Estimation of Performance Following Recall: 685
Estimation Skills: 1759
Estrangement in the Home: 1932
Etch A Sketch Maze: 2054
Ethical Behavior: 2444
Ethical Values: 1832
Ethics: 166, 1250, 2148
Ethics and Professionalism: 2424
Ethics in America: 762
Ethics of Technology: 2645
Euphoria: 792
European History: 100, 118, 1117
Evaluated Competition: 2355
Evaluates Outcomes and Effects of Implementing Solutions: 2739
Evaluating Alternatives and Selection of Solutions: 2633
Evaluating Emotional Meanings in Messages: 1505, 2854, 2855
Evaluating Expressions: 570
Evaluating Message Content: 1505, 2854, 2855
Evaluating Performance: 1550, 2575
Evaluating Problems Using Mathematical Skills and Concepts: 1094
Evaluating Team Process and Performance: 2630
Evaluation: 368, 437, 638, 1440, 1441, 1546, 2423, 2518
Evaluation and Acceptance of Feedback: 1292
Evaluation by the Teacher: 2670
Evaluation of Arguments: 2856, 2857
Evaluation of Course Readings: 974
Evaluation of Current Agency: 421
Evaluation of Current Condition: 650
Evaluation of Figural Classes: 2518
Evaluation of Figural Units: 2518
Evaluation of Products: 421
Evaluation of Symbolic Classes: 2518
Evaluation of Symbolic Systems: 2518
Evaluation of the Class: 974
Evaluation of the Syllabus: 974
Evaluative: 1615
Evangelist: 1310
Evangelistic Witness: 2751
Evasion: 78
Even-Tempered: 2605, 2648
Evening: 1472
Evening/Morning: 1470, 2069
Evenness: 2353
Event: 760, 2647
Events Witnessed or Reported by Others: 442
Everyday Math: 1667
Everyday Problem-Solving: 1667
Evidence of Administrative Excellence: 1527
Evidence of Amnesia: 847
Evidence of Examinee Appropriateness: 1527
Evidence of Proper Item Construction: 1527
Evidence of Technical Merit: 1527
Evidence of Thought Disorder: 268
Evidence of Validity: 1527
Evoked Sentences: 1360
Evolution: 684
Exaggerated Problem Presentation: 362
Exaggeration: 654, 1443, 1549, 2011, 2385
Examination Mastery: 707
Examinations: 434, 2541
Examines Situations Using Problem-Solving Techniques: 2739
Examples of the Child's Three Longest Sentences: 1528
Excelling: 1251, 1929
Exceptionality: 475
Excessive Aggressiveness: 355
Excessive Anxiety: 355
Excessive Changes/Crisis Management/Confusion: 1857
Excessive Dependency: 355
Excessive Emotionality: 132, 2874
Excessive Promises: 1857
Excessive Resistance: 355
Excessive Self-Blame: 355
Excessive Sense of Persecution: 355
Excessive Suffering: 355
Excessive Withdrawal: 355
Excitability: 1201
Excitable: 1211
Excitement: 792, 1443, 1549, 2120
Excitement-Seeking: 1769, 1954, 2218
Excusing Attitudes: 1209
Execution: 2210
Executive: 1561, 2278, 2605
Executive Functions: 566, 690
Executive Housekeeper: 398, 399
Executive Index: 2346
Executive or Office Worker: 2825
Executive Planning: 2772
Executive Practices: 1463
Exemption: 1746
Exercise: 1499, 1913
Exercise Physiology: 684

Exercise-Relaxation-Sleep: 1019
Exercising Control: 1545
Exhibiting Good Interpersonal Relations: 190
Exhibition: 68, 908, 1169, 1930, 1965, 1988
Exhibitionism: 2306, 2393
Exhibitionism Scale: 1744
Exhibitionistic: 1243
Existential Vacuum: 2126
Existential Well-Being: 2474
Existentiality: 1939
Existing Culture: 820
Exit Events: 1181
Expansion/War and Reconstruction (1841-1868): 146
Expansion Westward and the Jacksonian Era (1815 thru 1841): 146
Expansive: 1954
Expectancy: 2237
Expectancy Component (Control of Learning Beliefs: 1720
Expectation for Course Grade: 392
Expectation for Cure: 291
Expectations: 907, 1880
Expectations and Attributions: 1275
Expectations and Study Skills: 2530
Expectations for Functioning: 1743
Expectations of Sales Process: 421
Expectations of the Commitment Required: 421
Expedient vs. Conscientious: 477
Experience: 747, 793, 1968, 2830
Experience and Background Inventory: 2605
Experience Profile: 1821
Experience Ratio: 1169
Experience Scores: 1551
Experience with Current Technologies: 1593
Experienced: 381
Experiences: 2831
Experiencing: 716
Experiential: 980
Experiential Acquisition: 1907
Experiential Application: 1909
Experiential Background: 1500
Experiential Training Evaluation: 975
Experimental Psychology: 1122
Experimenting: 1281
Expert: 2415
Expert Orientation Index: 2346
Expertise: 490, 2020, 2804
Expertise Values: 2346
Explain Supervisory Error: 2923
Explaining Inferences: 2710
Explanation: 674
Explanation of Custody Evaluation Procedures for Parents and Attorneys: 2791
Explanations: 87, 348
Explicit: 2898
Explicit Emotional Confusion: 847
Exploitive: 1655
Exploration and Colonization: 145
Exploration of Client Goals: 1830
Exploration of Counselor-Client Relationship: 716
Exploration of Feelings: 1830
Exploration of Issues: 1830
Exploration Stage: 83
Exploration/Trapped: 420
Exploratory: 2001
Explores Beyond Assignments: 2530
Exploring Disagreement: 634
Explosive Strength: 1044
Expository: 2171, 2489
Expository Writing: 1094
Expository Writing Sample: 570
Exposure: 1558, 1559, 1971, 2275, 2634
Exposure to Drugs: 2521
Expressed: 1036
Expressed Concerns: 1685
Expressed Inability: 1162
Expressing: 1251, 1929, 2928
Expressing Feeling: 957
Expressing Feelings: 2444
Expressing Ideas: 956, 957
Expressing Intents: 2693
Expression: 359, 364, 665, 1042, 1043, 1262, 2115, 2463
Expression of Anger: 1290
Expression of Criticism: 226
Expression of Emotion (Communicative): 2052
Expression of Emotion (Non-Communicative): 2052
Expression of Feeling/Affect: 265
Expression of Ideas: 226
Expression of Support: 226
Expression Total: 1319
Expressional Fluency: 1405
Expressive: 265, 266, 305, 377, 987, 1334, 1381, 1667, 1804, 2121, 2335, 2453, 2759, 2813, 2893
Expressive Attention: 763
Expressive Communication: 1065, 2045
Expressive Composite: 2727
Expressive Gesture and Sign Language: 285
Expressive Grammar: 822
Expressive/Imaginative: 1497
Expressive Language: 206, 234, 453, 539, 540, 653, 881, 911, 1041, 1728, 1909, 2043, 2127, 2229, 2243, 2342, 2668, 2680, 2891
Expressive Language Age: 2189
Expressive Language Discrepancy: 2332
Expressive Language Skills: 2055, 2298
Expressive Language/Speech Production: 276
Expressive-Responsive vs. Inhibited: 2618
Expressive Scale: 2228
Expressive Skills: 1385
Expressive Speech: 1524, 1525, 2528
Expressive Verbal Labels: 911
Expressive Verbal Language Development: 1461

Expressive Vocabulary: 76, 655, 656, 822, 1379, 2727
Expressive Writing Ability: 1606
Expressive Writing Development: 1461
Expressiveness: 480, 689, 710, 1010, 1141, 2295
Extended: 199, 1004
Extended Family: 1495, 1496, 2117
Extended Family Relations: 2132
Extended Range Vocabulary Test: 1405
Extending Information: 1623
Extent Flexibility: 1044
Extent Trainee Seeks Assistance from Supervisor: 2924
External: 327, 768, 927
External Adjustment: 2605
External Conflict: 422
External Distractibility: 226
External Focus of World: 162, 1929
External Goals: 421
External Influences: 989
External Relations: 2632
External Stressors: 938
External Support: 2423
Externalized: 1300
Externalized Behavior Measures: 1313
Externalizing: 424, 451, 2452, 2607, 2939
Externalizing Behavior Problems: 931
Externalizing Composite: 818
Externalizing Disorder Factor: 77
Externalizing Problems: 280, 2036, 2446
Extinguishment-Related Technical Knowledge: 1032
Extra Effort: 1736, 1737
Extracted Hamilton: 2305
Extracting Information: 2080
Extraggression: 2248
Extramarital Relations: 2132
Extrapersonal Information: 1468
Extratensive/Intratensive Index: 2759
Extraversing: 1688
Extraversion: 380, 477, 538, 888, 915, 998, 999, 1201, 1366, 1367, 1464, 1660, 1769, 1814, 2218, 2411
Extraversion/Introversion: 1750, 1828
Extraversion vs. Introversion: 672, 673, 1365, 1387, 1755
Extraverted vs. Introverted: 2417
Extrinsic: 1701
Extrinsic Goal Orientation: 1720
Extroversion: 37, 226, 966, 1210, 1576, 2265, 2605
Extroversion/Introversion: 2160
Extroversive/Impulsive vs. Introvertive/Cautious: 2648
Extroverted: 86, 1333, 2411, 2536
Exuberance: 1628
Eye and Hand: 1134
Eye Contact: 63, 2450
Eye-Hand: 1996, 2111
Eye-Hand Accuracy: 535
Eye-Hand Coordination: 816, 1901, 2821, 2889
Eye Tracking: 2141
F Ratio Between C1 and C2 (C3): 2161
F Ratio Between K1 and K2 (K3): 2161
Face Recognition: 1379
Face Valid Alcohol: 2553
Face Valid Other Drug: 2553
Faces: 476, 2193, 2863
Faces and Places: 1379
Facial Expression: 2763
Facial Grimaces: 2543
Facial Memory: 2701
Facilitation: 1284, 2631
Facilitative: 2064
Facilitative Leadership: 2312
Fact Finder: 1411
Fact Retention: 1307
Factor Profile: 467
Factor Scales: 77
Factor Scores: 2648
Factory Work Training: 2400
Facts: 1167, 1182
Factual: 394
Factual Current and Remote Memory: 356
Factual Knowledge: 2903
Factual Recall: 1601, 1603
Faculty: 11
Faculty Concern for Students: 1108, 2083
Faculty Morale: 1003
Faculty Professional Activities: 1108, 2083
Faculty Program Involvement: 1108, 2083
Faculty Research Activities: 1108, 2083
Faculty-Student Acquaintances: 635
Faculty Work Environment: 1108, 2083
Fail: 153, 784
Failed: 868
Failure: 1169
Failure Anxiety: 1161
Failure to Achieve or Persevere: 2510
Failure to Maintain Set: 2892
Fairmindedness: 2776
Fairness: 1912
Fairness in Grading: 836
Fairness of Rules: 909
Faking Good: 2652
False Alarms: 687
False Positives: 375
Fame: 371
Familial: 1030
Familial Acceptance: 2361
Familial Discord: 1698
Familial Discord (Pd1): 1697
Familiar-Trained: 1284
Familiar-Untrained: 1284
Familiarity: 320
Family: 61, 162, 467, 965, 1074, 1683, 1734, 1929, 2371, 2508, 2652, 2783
Family Achievement Expectations: 1210
Family Activities: 1181

Family Activity: 1334
Family Adaptability: 1000, 1014
Family Agreement on Household Tasks: 1181
Family Agreement on Task Sharing: 1181
Family and Consumer Science: 2832
Family and Home: 1941, 1942
Family Arguments: 1181
Family as an Interface With Society: 1918
Family Background and Personal Adjustments: 2348
Family Chemical Dependency: 1931
Family Chemical Use: 201
Family Closeness: 2034
Family Cohesion: 1000, 1014
Family Commitment: 400
Family Companionship: 1216
Family Conflict: 1006
Family Conflicts: 1313
Family Discord: 1685
Family Dysfunction: 267, 1963
Family Estrangement: 201, 1931
Family Flexibility: 2034
Family Functioning: 1832
Family Functioning and Home Environment: 1181
Family Happiness: 1678
Family History: 158, 808, 1431, 1432
Family History of Distress: 1582
Family/Home: 2764
Family Inferiority-Superiority: 1005
Family Influences: 1293, 1983
Family Involvement: 290
Family Level Composite: 1181
Family Life: 1791, 2442
Family Life and Sex Education: 1019
Family Life Situations: 1887
Family Needs-Salary: 1345
Family of Origin: 2147
Family Pathology: 1931
Family Pictures: 476, 2863
Family Problems: 451, 569, 681, 938, 1698
Family Problems (FAM): 1697
Family Relations: 374, 1962
Family Relationships: 684
Family Role Performance: 465
Family Secrets: 2521
Family Social Activities: 1181
Family Stress: 1684
Family Support: 201
Family System Type: 544
Family Task Sharing: 1181
The Family Unit Itself: 1918
Family vs. Controls: 2553
Famous Faces Fluid Scale: 1378
Fantasy: 78, 723, 793, 1769, 2218
Far-Point Copying: 786
Far Vision: 1044
Farm-Agricultural: 1312
Farm/Grounds: 2829
Farm or Ranch: 1222
Farmer: 1723, 1790
Farmer/Rancher: 398, 399
Farming: 752
Farming Club: 411
Farming/Forestry: 380
Farming or Livestock Care: 411
Farpoint: 2852
Farsighted: 381
Fashion: 380
Fashion Designer: 380
Father: 210, 810, 1011, 1049
Father=Ally: 1006
Father/Child Coalition: 1006
Father-Child Relationship: 1297
Father-Mother Attitude Quotient: 1005
Father=Stressor: 1006
Fatigue: 915
Fatigue-Inertia: 2076
Fault Finding: 2641
Favorable Conditions: 1331
Favorable-Unfavorable Attitude Toward Full-Time Teachers: 1640
Fear: 1169, 1522, 1721, 2318, 2636
Fear and Anxiety: 927, 2307
Fear and Worry: 1963
Fear/Anxiety: 1374
Fear Inventory: 1052
Fear of Failure: 1017
Fear of Reinjury: 291
Fear or Nervousness: 459
Fearful: 2647
Fearful/Anxious: 281
Fearfulness: 788, 847
Fears: 213, 424, 1886
Fears (FRS): 1697
Fears of Real Events: 213
Feature Values: 1364
Feedback: 191, 379, 490, 907, 1443, 1545, 1549, 1558, 1559, 1867, 1971, 2275, 2634
Feedback/Communications: 382
Feedback of Results: 1689
Feedback to Peers: 490
Feeding: 63, 377, 879, 1066, 2342
Feeding History: 870
Feeding Problems: 876
Feeding Puff: 2743
Feeding Trial: 870
Feeler: 1331, 1950, 1951
Feeling: 1366, 1688, 1814, 2411, 2536
Feeling for Tonal Center: 1751
Feeling of Anxiety: 2655
Feeling of Belonging: 374
Feeling Reactivity: 1939
Feeling Response: 633
Feelings: 646, 1769, 2218
Feelings About Myself: 1887

Feelings About Parenthood: 1887
Feelings About Studying: 2530
Feelings and Emotions: 1822
Feelings Not Expressed: 2291
Feelings of Alienation: 1963
Feelings of Commitment: 1945
Feelings of Frustration: 1945
Feelings of Guilt: 2216
Feelings of Responsibility: 1945
Feelings of Satisfaction: 1945
Fellow Students: 648
Felt Pain Sensations: 1869
Female: 1374
Female Peers: 210
Female Perception of Father's Ideal: 1535
Female Perception of Ideal Woman: 1535
Female Perception of Man's Ideal Woman: 1535
Female Perception of Mother's Ideal: 1535
Female Self Perception: 1535
Females: 1049
Feminine Attributes: 68
Feminine-Masculinoid: 1940
Femininity: 298, 1222, 2776
Femininity/Masculinity: 372
Femininity-minus-Masculinity Differences: 298
Fetish: 1744
Field: 1819
Field Independence: 1821
Field Office Development: 197, 2424
Fielding Ground Balls: 2455
Fight: 2636
Fight/Flight: 1705
Figural: 2518
Figural Evaluation: 996
Figural Flexibility: 1405
Figural Fluency: 1405
Figural Production: 996
Figural Reasoning: Matrix Analogies: 2297
Figurative Language: 2693
Figurative Usage: 2727
Figure Classifications: 1405
Figure Copy: 2202
Figure Ground: 816, 1485
Figure/Ground: 2376
Figure Ground Discrimination: 1865, 2240
Figure-Ground Perception: 2377
Figure Memory: 763
Figure Recall: 2202
Figure Recognition and Production: 2141
Figure Rotation: 1485, 2304
Figure Series: 1873, 2774
Figure-Structure Preference: 2869
Figures of Speech: 1405
Filing: 532, 1692, 1712, 1834, 1836, 2302, 2408
Filing Names: 2105
Filing Numbers: 2105
Fill the Gaps: 1144
Filtered Words: 2300, 2301
Final Affixes: 861
Final Blends: 2175
Final Consonant Blends: 1529
Final Consonant Blends/Consonant Digraphs/Initial Consonant Blends: 1529
Final Consonant Deletion: 2438
Final Consonants: 468, 486, 827, 1072
Final Devoicing: 1394
Final Digraphs: 2175
Final Examination: 1125
Finance: 618, 1334, 1551
Finances: 1941
Finances-Living Conditions-Employment: 1716
Financial: 1074, 1494, 1495, 1818, 2508, 2803
Financial Accounting: 17, 38
Financial Conditions: 1007
Financial Detail: 407
Financial Freedom: 698
Financial History: 1431, 1432
Financial Management: 2034, 2327
Financial Planner: 380
Financial Planning and Review: 1569, 2605
Financial Responsibility: 2605
Financial Services: 380, 410
Financial Situation: 421, 2208
Financial Skills: 1718
Finding A's Test: 1405
Finding Humor in One's Life: 2369
Finding Main Idea: 647
Finding Relationships: 1315
Finding the Key to a Problem: 174
Finding Word Meaning in Context: 647
Fine: 2813
Fine Artist: 1790
Fine Arts: 410, 411, 905, 1044, 1789, 2530
Fine Arts-B.A. Degree: 618
Fine Arts-B.F.A. Degree: 618
Fine Arts-Mechanical: 399
Fine Arts/Performing Arts: 2000
Fine Finger Dexterity Work Task Unit: 922
Fine Motor: 123, 265, 266, 377, 397, 446, 453, 454, 778, 1192, 1194, 1230, 1259, 1263, 1381, 1610, 1728, 1907, 2049, 2111, 2127, 2342, 2528, 2838, 2881, 2891
Fine-Motor: 1901
Fine Motor Abilities: 2459
Fine Motor-Adaptive: 788
Fine Motor/Adaptive: 2243
Fine Motor Composite: 353
Fine Motor Coordination: 1802
Fine-Motor Development: 757
Fine Motor/Graphomotor Function: 1908
Fine Motor/Graphomotor Functions: 1905
Fine-Motor Skills and Behaviors: 2213
Fine Motor Output: 1909
Fine Motor Regulation: 1282

Fine Motor Skills: 206, 1591, 2299, 2926
Fine Muscle: 265
Fine Tool Dexterity: 1031
Finger Agnosia: 1164
Finger Dexterity: 239, 1031, 1044, 1711, 2421, 2797, 2798, 2799
Finger Discrimination: 1771
Finger Identification: 2377
Finger-Nose-Finger: 1919
Finger Tapping: 1164, 1919
Finger-Tip Number Writing: 1164
Finger-Tip Symbol Writing and Recognition: 1164
Finger to Nose: 2141
Fingertip Tapping: 1771
Finishing Stories: 2029
Fire Attack-Related Technical Knowledge: 1032
Fire Investigation Knowledge: 1032
Firefighter: 398, 399
Firmness: 1928
First Aid: 2327
First and Last Names Test: 1405
First Attempt to Influence: 1402
First Communicative Gestures: 1528
First Pass: 2933
First Semester Examination: 146, 2932
First Semester Test: 145, 1037
First Signs of Understanding: 1528
First Sound Different: 189
First Stop: 563
First Words Comprehension Screen: 1037
First Words Test: 1037
Fitness: 684
Fitness Instructor: 380
Fits and Faints: 1066
Fitting Sixteen Cubes in a Box: 1653
5/5: 1572
5/5 Compromise: 675, 676
Five Items Acquisition: 2159
Five Items Recall: 2159
Five Types of Administrative Responsibilities: 1233
Fives-Observers/Thinkers/Systematizers: 958
Fixation Unity: 2821
Fixed Position-B: 234
Fixed Position-C: 234
Flags: 463
Flexibility: 243, 300, 372, 724, 1062, 1453, 1683, 1860, 1923, 1930, 2425, 2506, 2631, 2751, 2771
Flexibility of Boundaries: 162, 1929
Flexibility of Closure: 644, 1044, 1405
Flexibility of Use: 1405
Flexibility/Openness: 737
Flexible: 381, 695, 2536
Flexible-Cohering: 1022, 1704, 2507
Flight: 2636
Flight Attendant: 1790
Florist: 398, 399, 1790
Fluctuating Income Tolerance: 1821
Fluctuating Salary: 1821
Fluctuations/Language: 847
Fluctuations/Relatedness: 847
Fluency: 159, 199, 250, 251, 653, 724, 1323, 1360, 1568, 1980, 2277, 2470, 2471, 2647, 2706, 2754, 2771, 2833
Fluency of Ideas: 1044
Fluid Intelligence: 798
Fluid Reasoning: 1485, 2901
Flute: 1280
Focus Auditory: 1282
Focus on Making Money: 1821
Focus on Solving the Problem: 72
Focus on the Positive: 72
Focus Visual: 1282
Focused: 1954
Folding Paper: 1653
Follow Directions and Carefulness: 2616
Follow Thru: 1411
Follow-ups and Call-Backs: 989
Following Commands: 338, 1064
Following Diagrammed Instructions: 2421
Following Directions: 781, 782, 1405, 1711, 2183, 2444
Following Instructions: 2641
Following Instructions and Directions: 1505, 2854, 2855
Following Oral Directions: 2105
Following Social Conventions: 2316
Following Through: 2385
Following Written Directions: 2105, 2421
Follows Verbal Directions: 346
Food: 344
Food and Clothing: 343
Food and Nutrition: 684
Food/Beverage Services: 2822
Food/Clothing/Shelter: 1918
Food Preparation: 1065, 1990
Food Production: 1044
Food Production Management and Services: 1794
Food Production/Management/Services: 410
Food Service: 183, 398, 399, 406, 645, 1237, 2177, 2400, 2829, 2832
Food Service Manager: 398, 399, 1790
Foods Selection: 2327
Foot Grasp: 1668
The Foot Grasp: 1258
Foot Operated Hinged Box Work Task Unit: 922
Forceful: 1253, 1685, 1686, 1958
Forcing: 677
Foreign Language: 762, 1044
Foreign Language Pedagogy: 2026
Foreign Language Teacher: 1790
Foreign Languages: 617, 905
Foresight: 2784
Forest Ranger: 398, 399
Forester: 1790

Forestry/Agriculture/Natural Resources: 993
Forestry Products and Processing: 1794
Form: 2470
Form Appropriateness: 1214
Form Assembly: 797
Form Board: 1370, 2375
Form Board Test: 1405
Form Completion: 1485
Form Constancy: 816, 2376
Form Definiteness: 1214
Form Discrimination: 366, 1370, 2439
Form Memory: 1138, 1139
Form Perception: 488, 2421, 2797, 2798, 2799
Form Recognition: 1270
Formación de Conceptos: 264
Formal Design: 1478
Formal Knowledge of Language: 830
Formal Relations: 1293, 1983
Formal Thought Disorder: 2305
Format Checking: 669
Formboard: 2439
Forming Questions and Probes Effectively: 2775
Forms: 343
Forms Checking: 2105
Forms Completion: 1836
Formulae and Valence: 1076
Formulated Sentences: 540
Formulating Labels: 539
Forthright vs. Shrewd: 477, 888
Forward Memory: 1485
Forward Parachute: 1258, 1668
Forward Planning: 1822, 2274
Foundation: 884
Foundation of a Strong Government: 145
Foundations: 1673
Foundations of Education: 762
Foundations of Reading and Basic Instructional Approaches: 684
Four Critical Elements: 202
Four-Letter Words: 1384
Fours-Creators/Expressionists/Individualists: 958
Fractions: 171, 343, 444, 492, 730, 1738
Fractions/Mixed Numbers: 172
Fragmentation: 329
Frames of Reference: 178
Frankness: 1290, 1928
Free Association: 320
Free Child: 68
Free Choice: 1163
Free Choice Play: 1220
Free Expression: 1316
Free-Floating Anxiety: 739
Free Reading Level: 330
Free Recall: 2909
Free-Recall Intrusions: 375
Free-Recall Trial: 375
Free Spelling Error Ratio: 320
Free Writing: 1232, 2691
Freedom: 1393, 1705
Freedom from Disruptive Alcohol and Illegal Drug Use: 944
Freedom from Stress: 382
Freedom of Expression: 2534
Freedom of Movement: 1897
French: 577, 598, 615, 618, 2026
French Aural/Communication: 684
French Comprehension: 1054
French Culture: 684
French Grammar: 684
French Language: 101, 118
French Listening: 578, 599
French Literature: 102, 118
French Reading: 578, 599
French Reading Comprehension: 684
French Vocabulary: 684
Frequency: 1371, 1624, 1651, 1962, 2237, 2542, 2543
Frequency Disfluencies: 691
Frequency of Problems: 1643
Frequent Assessment/Monitoring of Student Achievement: 2314
Freshman College Composition: 514
Friendliness: 1158, 1402
Friendliness/Hostility: 1340
Friendly: 381, 551
Friends: 1495, 1496, 1705, 2131
Friendship: 138, 139, 140, 426, 1946, 2804
Friendship Happiness: 1678
Friendship Self-Concept: 1683
Friendships and Relationships: 1961
Fronting of Velars: 2438
Fruit Distraction Test: 563
Frustration: 257, 683, 1128, 1453, 1611, 1878, 2338, 2462, 2503, 2636
Frustration/Anger Patterns: 1314
Frustration Level: 330, 769, 917
Frustration Problems: 1729
Frustration Reading Grade Level: 758
Frustration Reading Level: 496, 832
Frustration Tolerance: 268, 690, 1207, 1208, 1775, 2347
Fulfillment Orientation: 2355
Full: 1414
Full I Am Test: 2381
Full Incomplete Sentences Test: 2381
Full IQ: 1485
Full Length Alcohol Sentence Completion: 2381
Full-Range Intelligence Quotient: 2431
Full Scale: 2299, 2525
Full Scale IQ: 2792, 2859
Fun Scale: 1655
Function Cues: 1130
Functional: 2001
Functional Academic Skills: 1245
Functional Academic Skills Composite: 1382

Functional Academics: 59, 198
Functional Beliefs: 698
Functional Citizenship: 1492
Functional Communication: 70, 2316
Functional Competence: 2717
Functional Considerations: 332
Functional Expertise: 490
Functional Level: 870
Functional Living Skills Assessment: 1839
Functional Oral Reading: 2249
Functional Performance: 2767
Functional Reading: 2172, 2487
Functional Reading Level: 869
Functional Scanning and Tracking: 356
Functional Short-Term Recognition: 356
Functional Signs: 62, 2422, 2443
Functional Skills: 1906
Functional Skills Subtotal: 1067
Functional Spatial Distribution of Attention: 356
Functional Stress-Child: 1966
Functional Word Recognition: 339, 343
Functional Writing: 356
Functional Writing Skills: 344
Functioning During Past Five Years: 650
Functioning within Social Institutions: 619
Functions: 684
Functions and Graphs: 571
Fundamental Chemical Concepts and Basic Laboratory Tools and Techniques: 684
Fundamental Concepts: 570
Fundamental Visualization: 1485
Fundamentals of College Algebra: 762
Fundamentals of Counseling: 762
Fundamentals-Skills: 174
Fundamentals-Speed: 174
Furnishings and Display for Children: 1264
Further Education/Training: 2780
Future: 1705, 2761
Future Despair: 291, 1686
Future Plans: 1177, 2395
The Future-Vocational and Educational: 1716

G (Group): 1843
Gain Expertise: 2530
Gaining Attention: 2444
Gaining Stature: 1251, 1929
GAMA IQ Score: 1075
Games: 1482, 2001
Games and Routines: 1528
Garage: 2829
Gardener/Groundskeeper: 1790
Gardening: 1222
GAS rating: 2305
GAS [worst period]: 2305
Gastrointestinal: 1186, 1853
Gastrointestinal Somatic Symptoms: 2216
Gastrointestinal Susceptibility: 1686
Gatekeeping: 1147
Gates Matching: 1337
Gathering and Interaction of Peoples/Cultures/and Ideas: 1759
Gathering Information: 1623
GCVR [includes Grammar: 1662
Gender Role: 793
Gender Role-Feminine (GF): 1697
Gender Role-Masculine (GM): 1697
Gender Specific-Female: 805
Gender Specific-Male: 805
General: 42, 464, 895, 900, 927, 1300, 1701
General Abilities-Numerical: 1717
General Abilities-Perceptual: 1717
General Abilities-Verbal: 1717
General Ability: 412, 1816, 1916
General Academic Orientation: 2530
General Achievement Quotient: 1167
General Activities: 2130
General Activity: 1158
General Adaptation: 2446
General Adjustment: 2367, 2605
General Affective Impression: 268
General Aggressiveness-Empirical: 1290
General Aggressiveness-Rational: 1290
General and Outdoor Maintenance: 2400
General and Specific Happiness with the Relationship: 717
General Anthropology: 762
General Anxiety: 1162
General Appraisal: 989
General Aptitude: 2309
General Assertiveness-Empirical: 1290
General Assertiveness-Rational: 1290
General Attitude: 1831
General Babying: 1026
General Background: 627
General Behavior: 757, 1690, 2195
General Behavior and Psychic Integrity Total: 1690
General Biology: 515
General Characteristics of the Imagery: 1242
General Chemical Knowledge: 55
General Chemistry: 46, 47, 386, 516, 780, 1846
General Clerical Ability: 1077
General Clerical Ability Test: 973
General Clerical Skills: 2420
General Cognition: 2431
General Cognitive: 1612
General Cognitive Abilities Tests: 839
General Cognitive Ability: 2899
General Cognitive Functioning: 1665
General Cognitive Proficiency: 1665
General Concepts: 1084
General Counseling: 138
General Culture: 2833
General Development: 453, 1369
General Development Quotient: 806

General Development Score: 872, 2040
General Domain: 2399
General Drafting and Design: 1794
General Drug: 66
General Facts: 657
General Family Responsibility: 2605
General Feeling of Adjustment to the Curriculum: 1492
General Functioning Intelligence: 2420
General Health: 85, 1186, 2397
General Health Perceptions: 2158
General Health Questionnaire: 1626
General Hypochondriasis: 1241
General Impressions: 459
General Incomplete Sentences Test: 2381
General Industrial/Mechanical: 1793
General Information: 10, 779, 1346, 1902, 2159, 2329, 2699
General Information-Intelligence: 2318
General Intellectual Abilities: 1921
General Intelligence/Aptitude Quotient: 2694
General Intelligence Quotient: 1168
General Knowledge: 2026
General Knowledge and Comprehension: 2213
General Labor/Public/Community Service: 2000
General Lifestyle/Importance to Health: 2789
General Lifestyle/Present Effectiveness: 2789
General Logic: 1667
General Mainstreaming: 227
General Maladjustment: 2367
General Managerial Competence: 396
General Marketing: 410
General Mathematics: 55, 570, 2026
General Medicine: 905
General Memory: 476
General Memory Index: 2880
General Mental Ability: 797, 799, 1081
General Mental Ability Composite: 798
General Mental Ability Test: 973
General Mood: 243
General Mood EQ: 243
General Morale: 490, 1223
General Neurological: 85
General Observations: 235
General Pathology Composite: 362
General Philosophy of Life: 2675
General Physical Examination: 1907, 1909
General Protectiveness: 1026
General Psychopathology: 2017
General Questioning Following Recall: 685
General Reactions: 2378
General Reading Quotient: 2409
General Reasoning: 32, 1156, 1383, 1405
General Rights: 2534
General Satisfaction: 1701
General Satisfactoriness: 1702
General-School: 2358
General Science: 180, 2026
General Screening: 2216
General Self: 694, 1250
General-Self: 2358
General Self-Esteem: 746
General Service: 183
General Social: 2148
General Social Skills and Etiquette: 1492
General Somatic Symptoms: 2216
General Style-Practices: 2573
General Teaching/Social Service: 2000
General Technical Skills: 1793
General Test Interpretation: 1830
General Theme: 2615
General Themes: 399
General Visual Perception: 816
General Vocabulary: 87, 2712
General Vocational Development: 2400
General Writing Ability: 2935
Generalist: 420
Generalists: 1692
Generalized Anxiety: 642, 2107
Generalized Anxiety Disorder: 77, 79, 876
Generalized Indecisiveness: 409
Generals: 2694
Generating Alternatives: 2633
Generativity: 1631
Generosity: 1964
Genetics: 684
Genitourinary: 1186
Geographer: 1790
Geographic/Economic/and Cultural Foundations of Society: 1094
Geographical Barriers: 400
Geography: 570, 618, 684, 1044, 1729, 2026
Geologic History: 684
Geological Sciences: 905
Geologist: 1790
Geology: 618, 1116, 1124
Geometric Analogies: 662
Geometric Categories: 662
Geometric Concepts: 2383
Geometric Design: 2864
Geometric Figures: 304
Geometric Forms: 987
Geometric Nonverbal Intelligence Quotient: 662
Geometric Sequence: 1513
Geometric Sequences: 662
Geometrical Calculations: 570
Geometry: 137, 342, 570, 664, 684, 947, 1392, 1604, 1759, 1997
Geometry and Measurement: 2486
Geometry—Angles: 1247
Geometry from a Synthetic Perspective: 684
Geometry from an Algebraic Perspective: 684
Geometry-Measurement: 2736
Geometry—Plane and Solid Figures: 1247

Geometry/Visual: 2678
German: 579, 600, 615, 1761, 2026
German Language: 103, 118
German Listening: 580, 601
German Reading: 580, 601
Gestalt: 169
Gestalt Closure: 1379, 1384
Gestalt Completion: 1370
Gestalt Completion Test: 1405
Gestalt Perception: 356
Gestural: 2008
Gestural Communicative Means: 630
Gesture: 1064
Getting All Learners to Participate: 2775
Getting Better: 2743
Getting Friends: 63
Getting Information: 2425
Getting to the Essence: 634
Getting Unbiased Information: 1570
Getting Your Way: 1273
Gifted Education: 2026
Gifted Program Evaluation: 1090
Give-Up: 1681
Giving: 1251, 1929, 2052
Giving/Accepting Praise or Criticism: 40
Giving Clear Information: 1570
Giving Constructive Feedback: 1651
Giving Directions: 1191, 1255
Giving Feedback and Reinforcement: 2775
Giving Information: 1897
Giving Information or Opinions: 1147
Giving Letter Sounds: 1073
Giving Positive Feedback: 1479, 1480
Giving Talk: 2655
Glare Sensitivity: 1044
Glides: 214
Gliding of Liquid Singletons: 2438
Global: 2358
Global Assessment Scale: 650
Global Depression: 1181
Global Distress: 1582
Global Health Composite: 2158
Global Language: 880
Global Language Rating Scale: 1909
Global Measure of Impairment: 1775
Global Memory: 1462
Global Memory Scale: 1644
Global Pathology Index: 792
Global Psychopathology Scale: 2326
Global Rating: 2290
Global Scale: 2766
Global Self Concept: 1363
Global Self-esteem: 1735
Global Self-Worth: 2369
Global Severity Index: 337, 2602, 2603
Global Stress: 1733
Global Understanding: 1094
Global Writing: 2684
Globalist: 1451
Glottal Replacement: 1394
Gluttony: 439
Goal and Achievement Needs: 2355
Goal Clarity: 2530
Goal Consensus: 2312
Goal-Directedness: 1276
Goal Emphasis: 2587
Goal Integration: 2587
Goal Orientation: 37, 707, 1210, 2265, 2588
Goal-Orientation: 966
Goal-Oriented/Structured: 1233
Goal Pressure: 490
Goal Selection: 403, 413
Goal Setting: 40, 391, 392
Goal Setting and Striving: 913
Goal Setting Skill: 1467
Goal Source [Expectations]: 2530
Goal Source [Self]: 2530
Goal Time Frame [Long-Range]: 2530
Goal Time Frame [Short-Range]: 2530
Goals: 1163, 1494, 1545
Goals and Objectives: 2129
Goals and Responsibilities: 1542
Goals-and-Values: 2131
Goals in Attending College: 2530
Goals of Counseling: 717
Going Along: 262
Good Comprehension: 2589
Good Habits: 1182
Good Impression: 86, 372, 719, 1805
Good Mental Health: 913
Good Skills: 1245
Good Sport: 1964
Goodwill: 2020
Government: 684
Government & Politics-Comparative: 118
Government & Politics-United States: 118
Government/Political Science: 2026
Grade Accuracy: 948
Grade Level: Numbers: 342
Graded Comprehension: 1738
Graded Oral Reading: 1738
Graded Reading Passages: 2503
Graded Spelling: 1765
Graded Words in Context: 2503
Graduate Professional: 1342
Grammar: 87, 430, 494, 628, 830, 971, 1359, 1360, 1425, 1763, 1834, 1836, 2192, 2302, 2668
Grammar and Punctuation: 535
Grammar and Usage: 992
Grammar Comprehension: 455
Grammar Equivalence Judgment: 455
Grammar Formedness Judgment: 455
Grammar Imitation: 455
Grammar Mechanics: 342

Grammar/Usage: 2933
Grammar/Vocabulary/Reading: 985, 986
Grammatic Closure: 1240
Grammatic Competency: 1060
Grammatic Completion: 821, 2695
Grammatic Comprehension: 2694
Grammatic Understanding: 2695
Grammatical Form: 199
Grammatical Morphemes: 2657
Grammatical Punctuation: 2691
Grammatical Structure: 1534
Grandiosity: 1959, 2108, 2109, 2120
Graphesthesia: 2377
Graphic: 2008
Graphic and Clerical Skills: 2420
Graphic and Printing Communications: 410
Graphic Arts: 2832
Graphic Communications Tech: 1794
Graphic Encoding: 2426
Graphic Imaging Technology: 1792
Graphic/Phonemic Cues: 1130
Graphic Relations: 9
Graphicacy: 260
Graphomotor: 1083
Graphomotor Function: 158
Graphs: 444, 1406, 2774
Graphs and Scale Drawings: 1604
Graphs and Tables: 2486
Grasping: 1901
Grasshoppers: 2743
Great Ideas: 2530
Greed: 439
The Greeks: 2932
Greet Each Trainee: 2923
Greeting and Naming: 1064
Greeting Others: 2444
Gregarious: 136
Gregarious-Extraverted: 1289
Gregariousness: 1769, 2218
Grip: 239
Grip Strength: 1164
Grooming: 443, 661, 1194, 2891
Grooming and Personal Hygiene: 2824
Grooming/Eating: 2053, 2826
Gross: 1169, 2813
Gross Body Coordination: 1044
Gross Body Equilibrium: 1044
Gross Motor: 123, 265, 266, 397, 446, 453, 454, 653, 778, 788, 879, 889, 1192, 1194, 1230, 1259, 1263, 1381, 1610, 1907, 1909, 2041, 2046, 2111, 2127, 2243, 2342, 2528, 2838, 2891
Gross-Motor: 1901
Gross Motor Abilities: 2459
Gross Motor/Balance/Coordination Skills: 1041
Gross Motor Composite: 353
Gross-Motor Development: 757
Gross Motor Development Quotient: 2689
Gross Motor Function: 158
Gross Motor Functions: 1905, 1908
Gross Motor Output: 1909
Gross Motor Scale: 1728
Gross Motor Skills: 206, 347, 1707
Gross-Motor Skills: 345, 346, 2299
Gross-Motor Skills and Behaviors: 2213
Gross Motor Skills and Strength: 2926
Gross Speed: 1692
Ground Stroke: 2653
Group: 1478, 2001
Group Achievement Formula: 1924
Group Activities: 2444
Group Assessment of Organization: 1924
Group Behavior: 2035
Group Discussions: 188
Group Functioning: 2587
Group Interaction: 2450, 2526, 2571
Group Involvement and Participation: 2633
Group Learner: 1476, 1741
Group Morale: 1137
Group Performance: 2587
Group Productivity: 1913
Group Rating: 1147
Group Roles: 1440
Group/Team Conflict Situations: 677
Grouping: 1370, 1472
Groups: 1049, 1205
Growth in Skill: 1345
Growth Motivation: 1948
Growth Potential: 1655
Guarded Responses: 1207, 1208
Guardedness: 1313
Guardedness Index: 2604
Guidance: 648, 1746
Guidance Counselor: 380, 398
Guide: 1451
Guidelines for Cardiac Rehabilitation: 1853
Guidelines for Clients: 279
Guiding Mentoring: 1652
Guilt: 791, 915, 1631, 1733, 1748, 2109
Guilt and Fear-of-Failure Daydreaming: 2407
Guilt and Resentment: 538
Guilt and Worry: 136
Guilt Feeling: 317
Guilt/Shame: 1374
Gustatory: 2376

H (Hierarchy): 1843
H-Area: 840
H-P Area: 840
Habits: 478, 1186
Habits and Attitudes: 2541
Hair Stylist: 1790
Haircutting or Styling: 411
Hallucinations: 73, 2108, 2289
Hallucinations and Delusions: 297, 1963

Hallucinogens: 2554
Hand: 133
Hand and Power Tools: 2643
Hand Calculator: 1831
Hand Grasp: 1668
Hand Movements: 1379
Hand-Shaping: 234
Hand Skill: 2141
Hand Strength: 1919
Hand Use: 1901
Handling and Preventing Stress: 1550
Handling Differences: 1292
Handling Emotional Situations: 1479, 1480
Handling Employee Complaints: 1479, 1480
Handling Employee Grievances: 1479, 1480
Handling External Pressure: 807
Handling Frustration: 40
Handling Objections: 989
Handling of Conflicts of Client/Therapist Values: 1830
Handling of Critical Jobs: 300
Handling of Emotions: 1918
Handling Outside Contacts: 1569, 2605
Handling Priorities and Sensitive Situations: 1080
Handling Problems: 63
Hands Closed: 1258
Hands Open: 1258
Hands or Feet: 63
Hands/Tools/Machinery: 1350
Handwriting: 299, 342, 559, 657, 2627, 2901, 2902, 2934
Handwriting Ability: 2320
Hangover: 136
Happiness: 37, 243, 1057, 1374
Happiness and Satisfaction: 1991
Happiness Life-Style: 2106
Happiness/Satisfaction: 1006
Happy: 2647
Happy Attitudes and Values: 2106
Happy Percentage Estimate: 1172
Happy Personality: 2106
Haptic: 1458
Hard: 1563
Hard Driving and Competitive: 1338
Hard Items: 2011
Hard Palate: 1852
Hard Work: 948
Hardware Store Manager: 398, 399
Harm Avoidance: 1730, 1988
Harmavoidance: 1965
Harmonic Readiness: 1176
Harmonious: 1253
Harmonizing: 1147
Harmony: 1752, 1753
Harris-Lingoes Subscales: 1697, 1698
Harshness: 262
Has the Courage to Take Risks: 2101
Hassles: 2512
Have Concern For Measures Of Our Success: 1858
Having A Sense of Quality: 2929
Hawks: 1872
He/I Past Tense (Best/Worst): 1298
He/I Present Tense (Best/Worst): 1298
He or She Is: 2128
He or She Should Be: 2128
Head: 63, 133
Head Movements: 2543
Head Righting: 1668
Headache: 1853
Headlines: 1364
Health: 63, 344, 452, 478, 661, 965, 1252, 1293, 1489, 1716, 1718, 1913, 1968, 1983, 2131, 2348, 2780, 2926
Health and Habits: 1649, 1941, 1942
Health and Health Care: 179
Health and Physical Development: 1716
Health and Physical Education: 2026
Health and Safety: 59, 62, 198, 343, 1246, 2310
Health Assessment: 2511
Health Assisting: 1794
Health Care: 183, 411, 443, 1918, 2422, 2443, 2734
Health-Care History: 1791
Health Care Orientation: 2117
Health Concerns: 1207, 1698, 1959
Health Concerns (HEA): 1697
Health Education: 2026
Health/Education/Social Service: 993
Health Facts: 1188
Health Happiness: 1678
Health History: 124, 1431, 1432, 1886
Health History Inventory: 2606
Health/Hygiene/and Safety: 260
Health in the United States: 684
Health Issues: 2034
Health Knowledge: 1185
Health Maintenance: 1591
Health Occupations: 645
Health Perception: 1187
Health Posture: 794
Health Problem: 1593
Health Problems: 1960
Health Problems or Conditions: 158
Health-Related: 1181
Health-Related Functioning: 1181
Health-Risk Behaviors: 1181
Health Sciences: 905
Health Screening: 184
Health Service: 406
Health Services: 411, 1841, 2822, 2832
Health Symptoms: 1949
Health Technicians: 2822
Health Values: 1733
Health Vigilance: 1733
Healthy: 701
Hearing: 653, 1066, 1591, 2471, 2926

Hearing and Language: 2308
Hearing and Listening: 2052
Hearing and Speech: 1134
Hearing Capacity Level: 496
Hearing for Nonspeech Sounds: 1190
Hearing Loss: 896
Hearing Sensitivity: 1044
Hearing Word Parts: 917
Heat: 684
Heat Treating: 2151
Heating/Air Conditioning/Refrigeration Mechanics: 410
Heating/Ventilation/Air Conditioning & Refrigeration: 1794
Heating/Ventilation/Air Conditioning & Refrigeration (HVAC/R): 1792
Heating/Ventilation & Air Conditioning: 1794
Heating/Ventilation & Air Conditioning (HVAC): 1792
Heavy Activities: 291
Heavy Equipment Maintenance and Repair: 1794
Heavy Equipment Mechanics: 1792
Hedonistic: 1724, 2800
Heel-To-Ear: 1258
Help Before: 136
Help from Friends: 1733
Help Seeking: 1294, 1720
Help-Seeking/Mental Health Professional: 1181
Help-Seeking/Non-Mental Health Professional: 1181
Help Skill: 1467
Helpful: 618
Helpful Customer Relations: 2386
Helping: 380, 1334, 2131
Helping an Employee Make Decisions: 1479, 1480
Helping an Employee Manage Time: 1479, 1480
Helping Others: 2444
Helping Others Excel: 802
Helping People: 1350
Helplessness: 1374, 1655
Hemispatial Neglect: 268
Here's to Your Health: 762
The Heritage of Colonial America: 146
Hero: 479
Hero or Heroine: 2615
Heroin: 1931, 2554
Hesitating: 1688
Heterosexual Socialization: 2614
Heterosexuality: 68, 908
Hidden Figures: 445
Hidden Figures Test: 1405
Hidden Letters: 726
Hidden Patterns Test: 1405
Hidden Pictures: 2441
Hidden Words: 1405
Hiding: 1169
Hierarchical: 2800
High Achiever: 1924
High Anxiety vs. Low Anxiety: 2417
High-Density Lipoprotein (HDL) Level: 2789
High Expectations: 2314
High Frequency Words: 2254
High Level of Responsibility: 807
High/Moderate/Low Drug Involvement: 143
High Origence-High Intellectence: 68
High Origence-Low Intellectence: 68
High Performance Writing: 2589
High-Probability: 199
High Risk: 1890
High School Characteristics: 57
High School Counselor: 1790
High School Environment: 57
High School Experiences: 57
High Stakes: 807
Higher Authority: 1402
Higher Cognitive Deficits: 562
Higher Engineering Trades: 1990
Higher Level Language Skills: 1690
Higher-Order Problem-Solving: 2772
Higher Thought Processes: 493
Hinged Box Work Task Unit: 922
Hiring Talented Staff: 300
Historical: 1789
Historical and Political Bases of Society: 1094
History: 570, 618, 905, 1117, 1124, 1186, 2530
History and Archeology: 1044
History and Observations: 870
History and Observed/Reported Characteristics of the Accused: 442
History and Theory: 1120
History-Behavioral Survey: 2706
History of Delinquency: 1500
History of Learning Disabilities: 1500
History of Onset and Hospitalization: 650
History of Somatic Therapy: 650
History of the United States: 517, 518
History of the Vietnam War: 762
History-Social Science: 750
History/Social Studies: 2026
Histrionic: 690, 1687, 1961, 2306, 2520
Hit Response Time: 679
Hit Response Time Block Change: 679
Hit Response Time Inter-Stimulus Interval Change: 679
Hit Response Time Standard Error: 679
Hit Standard Error Block Change: 679
Hit Standard Error Inter-Stimulus Interval Change: 679
Hits: 679, 687
Hobbies and Interests: 1943
Holding: 83
Holding Back/Withdrawn: 1161
Holistic: 744, 1658
Home: 70, 124, 162, 286, 1929, 1983, 2131, 2318
Home Affective Environment: 1275

Hunter: 1723
Hunting: 1222
Hurtful to Others: 2299
Hurtful to Self: 2299
Husband Abuse: 447
Husband's Marriage Questions: 2885
HVAC: 2152
Hydraulics: 1537, 2644
Hydraulics and Pneumatics: 1637, 2769
Hygiene: 2316, 2327, 2391
Hygiene and Grooming: 2422, 2443
Hyperactive: 451
Hyperactive/Aggression: 1278
Hyperactive-Distractible: 2039
Hyperactive-Impulsive: 79, 81, 221, 282, 873
Hyperactive/Impulsive: 222
Hyperactivity: 4, 65, 80, 220, 223, 225, 245, 280, 469, 681, 931, 1313, 1522, 1962, 2452
Hyperactivity and Distractibility: 1889
Hyperactivity Index: 2673
Hyperactivity-Impulsivity: 67, 65
Hyperactivity/Impulsivity: 65
Hyperactivity/Restlessness: 678
Hyperaffectivity: 2006
Hyperarousal: 766
Hypercaution: 2877
Hypercriticalness: 1223
Hypersensitivity: 1317
Hypertension: 1853
Hypervigilance: 1959
Hypochondriasis: 256, 538, 1698, 1733, 2006, 2216
Hypochondriasis (Hs): 1697
Hypomania: 1698
Hypomania (Ma): 1697
Hypothetical Thought: 467
Hysteria: 701, 739, 1698
Hysteric-Non-Hysteric: 218
Hysterical Behavior: 792
Hysterical Symptoms: 748

I Am: 2128
I/E Ratio: 760
I Want to be Andy: 2743
I Wish I Were: 2128
Iceberg Towing: 2743
Iconic: 391, 392
Idea Fluency: 239
Ideal: 906, 1447
Ideal Body Description: 795
Ideal Concept/Nurse: 2366, 2368
Ideal Concept/Teacher: 2368
Ideal Organizational Climate: 1860
Ideal Self: 68, 1297, 1984, 2368
Idealism: 1832
Idealist: 2675
Idealistic Distortion: 2034
Idealized Influence: 1736
Ideals: 475
Ideaphoria: 239
Ideas: 715, 1769, 2218, 2830, 2831
Ideas-Scientific: 1163
Ideational Fluency: 644, 682, 1405
Ideational Spontaneity: 2605
Identical Pictures Test: 1405
Identicality: 319
Identification: 1534, 2307
Identification and Application of Strategies: 1094
Identification and Case Description: 442
Identification of Body Parts: 565
Identification of Colors and Shapes and Copying Shapes: 1515
Identification of Letters and Writing: 1515
Identification of Numbers and Counting: 1515
Identification of Relationships: 1534
Identification of Self in Mirror: 1653
Identification of Self with Selling Occupation: 2266
Identification Process: 317
Identification Total: 1047
Identification vs. Alienation: 844
Identification With Same-Sex Parent: 2614
Identification with the Company: 989
Identifications: 1084
Identified Program Strengths: 976
Identified Program Weakness: 976
Identifies Body Parts: 345, 346, 347
Identifies Colors: 347
Identifies Objects: 347
Identifies Objects According to Use: 345
Identifies People in Picture by Pointing: 345
Identify Diffusion: 1685
Identify Stress: 78
Identifying and Solving Problems: 1550, 1570
Identifying Author's Purpose: 647
Identifying Good Reasons: 1780
Identifying Important Information: 2495
Identifying Information: 158, 184, 1791, 1978
Identifying Letters: 2320
Identifying Pictured Categories: 2297
Identifying Pictured Category Members: 2297
Identifying Problems: 2633
Identifying Sounds in Words: 861
Identifying Words: 1534
Identity: 1631, 2652
Identity Confusion: 1631
Identity Integration: 1735
Identity Problems: 1959
Identity Scale: 564
Identity Stress: 78
Ideological: 162, 1929
Idioms: 1060
Idiosyncratic Language Ratio: 320
Ignore the Problem: 72
Illness Concerns: 1313
Illogical Errors: 1189

Illogicality: 2290
Imagery: 1732
Imaggression: 2248
Imagination: 724, 1142, 1143, 2647, 2754
Imagination-Playfulness: 2037
Imaginative: 1211, 1954, 2536
Imitated: 2620
Imitated Production: 1126
Imitated Productions: 1127
Imitated Response Errors: 2650
Imitating: 2382
Imitating Hand Positions: 1771
Imitating Other Adult Actions: 1528
Imitation: 459, 2047, 2111, 2705
Immature: 424, 467, 1169
Immature Behavior: 1500
Immature Conformist/Conformist: 1341
Immaturity: 66, 1341, 1522, 1698, 2848
Immediate: 476, 1644
Immediate Auditory Recall of Digits: 356
Immediate Auditory Recall of Digits with Distractions: 356
Immediate Auditory Recall of Functional Information: 356
Immediate-Intrinsic Orientation: 2355
Immediate Memory: 2202, 2249, 2250, 2251
Immediate Memory Span: 470
Immediate Presence and Accuracy: 329
Immediate Prose Recall: 1644
Immediate Recall: 470, 685, 1462, 2227
Immediate Recall of Oral Directions: 2297
Immediate Recall of Word Strings: 2297
Immediate Recognition: 1485, 2909
Immediate Retention: 329
Immediate Visual Recognition: 1644
Immobility: 1482
Immune System: 2508
Impact: 436, 760, 1861, 2068, 2133, 2583
Impact and Influence: 1573, 2268
Impact Management: 1267
Impact of Event Scale: 1626
Impact of Mission: 2585
Impact of Technology: 2645
Impact on Social Relationships: 421
Impaired Concentration: 78, 1647
Impaired Functioning: 2305
Impaired Self-Reference: 2782
Impairment: 1226, 1525
Impairment Due to a Chronic Illness: 1733
Impatience: 2592
Imperative: 2337
Imperception: 1164
Imperialism/Nationalism/and World War I: 2932
Imperturbability: 1698
Imperturbability (Ma3): 1697
Implementation: 83, 1441, 1546, 1564, 1567, 2547, 2548
Implementer: 296
Implementor: 1411
Implications: 2518
Importance: 1651, 2237, 2535
Importance Ratings: 801
Important Activities: 900
Imposing Wishes: 1689
Impotence: 1744
Impoverished Management: 1558, 1571
Impression Management: 1290, 1899, 2417
Impressions: 870
Impressions of This College: 57
Impressions of Your Advisor: 57
Improbable or Absurd Symptoms: 2522
Improve Basic Skills: 2530
Improve Numerical Ability: 2530
Improve Reasoning Skills: 2530
Improve Speaking Skills: 2530
Improvement: 379
Improving Critical Processes: 802
Improving Instruction: 903
Improving Self: 401
Improving Work Procedures and Practices: 1569, 2605
Impulse Action Patterns: 824
Impulse Control: 243, 748, 931, 1832
Impulse Control Disturbance: 2109
Impulse Expression: 256
Impulse Regulation: 893
Impulses: 1239
Impulsive: 2514, 2757
Impulsive-Distractible: 1457
Impulsive Dominating Behaviors: 1618
Impulsive Propensity: 1685
Impulsive-Restrained: 218
Impulsiveness: 690, 840, 1223, 2218, 2403
Impulsivity: 66, 80, 220, 223, 225, 320, 469, 1963, 1965, 2306
Impulsivity and Distractibility: 1963
Impulsivity/Emotional Lability: 678
Impulsivity Errors: 229
Impulsivity-Frustration: 929, 1815
Impulsivity/Hyperactivity: 2461
In and On: 2662
In Seat: 234
Inability to Learn: 2287
Inactivity: 1278
Inadequacy: 66, 467
Inadequate Abilities: 1963
Inanimate: 391, 392, 1149, 1169, 2404
Inappropriate: 2108
Inappropriate Affect: 2289, 2647
Inappropriate Affect-Appearance-Behavior: 2109
Inappropriate Behavior: 2287, 2447, 2763
Inappropriate Behavior Under Normal Circumstances: 283, 928, 2035
Inappropriate Behaviors: 284
Inappropriate Behaviors/Feelings: 817

Inappropriate/Compliance: 1006
Inappropriate/Noncompliance: 1006
Inappropriate Sexual Behaviors: 659
Inappropriate Speech: 4
Inappropriateness: 1778
Inattention: 67, 80, 220, 223, 469, 1161
Inattention-Disorganization: 651
Inattention Errors: 229
Inattention/Memory Problems: 678
Inattentive: 81, 221, 222, 282, 873
Inattentiveness: 1155
Incentive/Motivation: 2585
Incest: 2393
Incident Report Writing: 1763
Incidental Learning: 2159
Inclusion: 945, 1036, 1147, 1350, 2346
Inclusion Behavior: 1594
Inclusion/Exclusion: 1780
Inclusion Feelings: 1594
Inclusive: 2121
Incoherence: 2290
Income: 421
Income Expectations: 421
Income History: 421
Income Management: 2074
Income Needs: 421
Income Needs and Expectations: 421
Incoming Feelings: 1012
Incompetence/Guilt: 2510
Incomplete Man: 1085
Incomplete T-Units per T-Unit: 2661
Incomplete Words: 1405, 2900, 2901
Incompleteness: 1577, 2874
Inconclusive: 868
Incongruence: 1010
Incongruence Between Actual and Ideal Feminine Sex-Role Behaviors (F1): 2161
Incongruence Between Actual and Ideal Masculine Sex-Role Behaviors (M1): 2161
Incongruence Between Present and Ideal Body Description: 795
Incongruence F Ratio: 1002
Inconsequence: 910
Inconsistency: 1002, 1543, 1582, 1729, 1775, 1883, 1959, 1963
Inconsistency F Ratio: 1002
Inconsistency Index: 678, 1730
Inconsistency of Symptoms: 2522
Inconsistency Percentage for Phonemes Tested: 2504
Inconsistency Within the Two Sex-Role Categories (K2): 2161
Inconsistent Responding: 37, 362, 1881, 2265, 2652
Inconsistent Response: 2782
Incontinence: 1066
Increase Self-Understanding: 2530
Increased Knowledge: 948
Increasing Trust: 1550
Increasing Word Length: 163
Indecision: 979
Indecisiveness: 690
Independence: 63, 243, 371, 372, 391, 392, 413, 477, 480, 538, 654, 686, 888, 965, 1010, 1141, 1142, 1201, 1251, 1254, 1334, 1576, 1655, 1660, 1694, 1695, 1701, 1743, 1929, 2053, 2201, 2204, 2349, 2581, 2605, 2776, 2784, 2793, 2804, 2826, 2834, 2915
Independence/Dependence: 36, 1136, 1340
Independence in Relationships: 1682
Independence-Perseverance: 2037
Independence v. Conformity: 417
Independent: 86, 257, 683, 1294, 1611, 1676, 1822, 2338, 2462, 2503
Independent Action: 1689
Independent Authority: 1821
Independent Behavior: 1682
Independent Feelings: 1682
Independent Functioning: 1, 2, 70, 465, 1791
Independent Learning: 1161, 1260
Independent Level: 827
Independent Living: 1801
Independent Play: 234
Independent Player: 420
Independent Reading Grade Level: 758
Independent Reading Level: 496, 917, 1812
Independent Study: 1474
Independent Thoughts: 1682
Independent vs. Accommodating: 2417
Independent Work: 2444
Independent Work Level/Distractibility: 1461
Indeterminable: 720
Index Card Work Task Unit: 922
Index of Overall Adjustment: 2258
Indifference: 1778, 2636
Indifferent: 1790
Indirect: 1273
Indirect Questions: 1427
Individual: 1478, 1823
Individual and Group Assessment: 684
Individual and Paired Sentence Repetition with Pictures: 2331
Individual and Team Development: 1463
Individual and Team Practices: 1463
Individual & Team Relationships: 1545
Individual Behavior Management: 684
Individual Characteristics: 1824
Individual Customer Focus: 2129
Individual Differences and Temperament: 213
Individual Entertainment: 2763
Individual Goals: 379
Individual Growth/Development/Planning: 57
Individual Influences: 1824
Individual Initiation: 2571
Individual Items: 965
Individual Learner: 1476

Individual Learning: 1741
Individual [one-on-one] Conflict Situations: 677
Individual Performance: 1164, 2587
Individual Profile: 1398
Individual Roles: 2508
Individual Sentence Repetition without Pictures: 2331
Individualism: 981, 1465, 2621
Individualist: 1549
Individualistic: 1954
Individuality: 1396
Individualization: 1921
Individualized Consideration: 1736
Individually Structured: 618
Individuating: 1688
Individuation: 78
Indoors: 1478
Induction: 1405
Inductive: 2373
Inductive Reasoning: 168, 239, 368, 644, 1044, 1780
Inductive Reasoning: Analogies: 2297
Inductive Reasoning: Opposites: 2297
Indulgent: 1589
Industrial: 408, 412, 485, 1100, 1483, 1711, 1817, 2836
Industrial Arts: 406, 905
Industrial Electrician: 1792
Industrial Electricity: 1794
Industrial Electronics: 1792, 1794
Industrial Equipment Maintenance and Repair: 410
Industrial Maintenance Mechanic: 1794
Industrial Maintenance Technician: 1793
Industrial Production: 410
Industrial Production Trades: 2822
Industrial Technology: 1792
Industrious: 618
Industriousness: 2784
Industry: 1631, 2803, 2829
Industry Contacts: 421
Industry/Mechanics/Transportation/Construction: 993
Ineffective: 1563
Ineffectiveness: 893
Infant Programs: 452
Infantile Aggression: 1522
Inference: 368, 2856, 2857
Inference Ability: 2690
Inference Test: 1405
Inferences: 356
Inferiority: 1631
Inferiority Avoidance: 1988
Inferiority Feelings: 927
Inflection Production: 455
Inflectional Endings: 917
Influence: 391, 1966, 1984, 2347, 2353
Influence and Control: 2587
Influence Tactic Appropriateness: 2580
Influence Tactic Frequency: 2580
Influence Tactic Skills and Effectiveness: 2580
Influences by Peers or Parents: 777
Influencing: 166, 380, 1253, 1923, 2425, 2928
Influencing Without Authority: 807
Informal: 1374
Informal Design: 1478
Informality: 2632
Informant History: 434
Information: 140, 379, 436, 716, 793, 1412, 1731, 1818, 1914, 2020, 2201, 2415, 2840, 2860, 2862, 2864
Information Access and Checking: 1837
Information Analysis Skill: 1467
Information and Orientation: 2863
Information Collecting: 1551
Information/Data Support: 490
Information Filtering: 490
Information Flow: 1463
Information from Pictures: 565
Information-Gathering Skill: 1467
Information Gathering Style: 768
Information in the Natural Sciences: 2220, 2221, 2222
Information Input: 2016
Information-Intelligence: 1721
Information-Knowledge: 1163
Information Measures: 2000
Information Needs: 1128
Information Ordering: 1044
Information/Orientation: 537
Information Processing: 226, 1455, 1456, 1551, 2250, 2735, 2929
Information Processing Accuracy: 1665
Information Processing Speed: 1665
Information Processing Style: 768
Information Quality: 490
Information Retrieval: 2898
Information Seeking: 1442
Information Sharing: 801
Information Skills: 1467
Information Systems: 38
Information Systems and Computer Applications: 520
Informational Mentoring: 1652
Informational Support: 1733
Informational Text: 1094
Informative: 1759
Informed Feedback: 1275
Infrequency: 77, 86, 1290, 1698, 1932, 1933, 1959, 1965, 2417, 2835
Infrequency (F): 1697
Infrequent Response: 1790
Infrequent Response Patterns: 2490
Infrequent Responses: 1931
Ingenuity: 1042, 1043
Inhalants: 1931, 2554
Inherited Problems: 807
Inhibited: 1243, 1685, 1686, 1958, 1522, 1706
Inhibition of Aggression: 1698
Inhibition of Aggression (Hy5): 1697

Initial Adaptation: 1909
Initial Affixes: 861
Initial Appearance: 2327
Initial Background Information: 158
Initial Blends: 2175
Initial Blends and Digraphs: 917
Initial Consonant Clusters: 917
Initial Consonant Sounds: 917
Initial Consonant Sounds Recognized Auditorily: 827
Initial Consonant Substitution: 827
Initial Consonants: 486, 827, 917, 1072
Initial Digraphs: 2175
Initial Referral Form: 2791
Initial Understanding: 1759, 2487
Initial Voicing: 1394
Initially Correct: 1692
Initially Incorrect: 1692
Initiating: 1147, 2382
Initiating Assertiveness: 1290
Initiating Consonants: 468
Initiation: 1284
Initiation of Structure: 1437
Initiation/Perseveration: 776
Initiative: 37, 942, 1204, 1210, 1350, 1395, 1396,1631, 2268, 2418
Initiative-Cold Calling: 2265
Initiative-General: 2265
Initiative Skill: 1467
Inner Resources: 37
Innovating: 83, 1688
Innovation: 379, 495, 945, 1141, 1333, 2346, 2793, 2917
Innovation/Initiative: 2097
Innovation/Risk: 1545
Innovative: 1443, 1549, 1667, 1681, 1822
Innovativeness: 490
Innovator: 727
Inorganic Chemistry: 50
Input: 1966
Inquiries: 2647
Inquiring: 1334, 1954
Inquiry and Decision Making Using Social Science Tools: 1094
Inquisitiveness: 367, 1396
Insecure Attachment: 297
Insight: 716, 1953, 2385
Insight into Human Nature: 2266
Insight/Unawareness and Indecisiveness: 1340
Insomnia: 2216
Insomnia (Initial): 1488
Insomnia (Late): 1488
Inspection: 1042, 1043, 2066, 2774
Inspirational Motivational: 1736
Inspiring: 1446
Inspiring A Shared Vision: 1445
Inspiring a Shared Vision: 1448, 2635
Inspiring/Instilling Vision: 1651
Installing Flexible Hours: 2070
Institutional/Home Management/Supporting Services: 410
Institutional Ways: 2237
Instructing: 1651
Instructing in Both the Inductive and Deductive Modes: 203
Instruction: 216, 684, 1746, 2804
Instructional: 257, 683, 1611, 2338, 2462, 2503
Instructional Efficiency Index: 2596
Instructional Leadership: 1276
Instructional Level: 769, 827
Instructional Level (Placement): 330
Instructional Management: 648
Instructional Match: 1275
Instructional Methods: 684
Instructional Output: 1909
Instructional Presentation: 1275
Instructional Reading Grade Level: 758
Instructional Reading Level: 496, 832, 917
Instructional Time: 1867
Instructions: 87
Instructor: 391, 392
Instructor Commitment to Student Learning: 2590
Instructor/Facilitator Effectiveness: 975
Instructor Preparation and Enthusiasm: 2590
Instructor's Ability to Keep a Good Balance Between Stimulus-Response-Feedback: 1277
Instructor's Ability to Teach Effectively in Both the Inductive and Deductive Modes: 1277
Instructor's Ability to Teach on "Adult-to-Adult" Basis and not Become Parent: 1277
Instructor's Communication Skills: 2590
Instructor's Effectiveness as a Communicator: 1277
Instructor's Organizational Skills in Pacing and Managing the Instructional Sequence: 1277
Instructor's Role as Catalyst and Facilitator and Mediator of Learning: 1277
Instrument: 1667
Instrument Recognition: 1751
Instrumental: 700, 2416
Instrumental Activity: 2763
Instrumental Determinations: 51
Instrumental Helplessness: 1748, 1749
Instrumentality: 467
Instrumentation: 310
Instrumentation and Control: 1793
Instrumentation and Electrician Technician: 1793
Insurance Agent: 380, 398, 399
Insurance Earnings: 421
Insurance Income: 421
Intake: 2181
Integers: 1605
Integración de Sondidos: 264
Integración Visual: 264
Integrated: 1227, 1721, 2318
Integrated Language Arts: 743

Integrated Mathematics: 743
Integrating: 2149
Integrating Mathematical Concepts and Skills to Solve Problems: 1094
Integration: 1214, 1437, 1938, 2319
Integration-Coping: 1610
Integration of Style and Readiness: 2415
Integrative: 2236, 2636
Integrative Processes: 1405
Integrity: 2347
Integrity Attitude: 2198
Integrity Concerns: 1314
Integrity/Control: 1429
Integrity of Body Image: 1690
Integrity of Gnosis: 1690
Integrity of Praxis: 1690
Intellect: 1821
Intellectance: 1212
Intellective Assessment: 1830
Intellectual: 162, 1499, 1819, 1927, 1929
Intellectual Abilities: 1238
Intellectual Ability: 1089, 2369
Intellectual Ability Tests: 186
Intellectual-Achievement Oriented: 1030
Intellectual and School Status: 1991
Intellectual Concern: 2751
Intellectual Control: 840
Intellectual-Cultural: 1010
Intellectual-Cultural Orientation: 480
Intellectual Deficit: 1522
Intellectual Demands: 945
Intellectual Dependency with Peers: 1161
Intellectual Efficiency: 372, 1429
Intellectual Leadership: 1519
Intellectual Orientation: 2776
Intellectual Performance: 748
Intellectual Processes: 1524, 1525
Intellectual Screening: 1962
Intellectual Skills: 2333
Intellectual Stimulation: 1736
Intellectual Wellness: 2746, 2747
Intellectuality: 1396, 2793
Intelligence: 1153, 1201, 1786, 1964, 2432, 2797, 2798, 2799
Intelligibility: 1056, 2669, 2866
Intelligibility Rating: 783
Intensity: 320, 425, 983, 997, 1133, 1869, 2475, 2595
Intensity of Contact with Mother: 1026
Intensity of Depression: 1488
Inter-Personal Behavior: 1381
Interacting: 452, 234, 653, 661, 875, 1264
Interaction and Conversation: 2024, 2025
Interaction During Supervision: 1830
Interaction Management: 689
Interaction-Orientation: 263
Interaction with Others: 193, 2418
Interaction with Students: 909
Interactional Needs: 1895
Interactions: 2310
Interactive Social: 2308
Interacts About Coursework: 2530
Intercourse: 2454
Interdepartmental Coordination: 1569, 2605
Interest: 397, 412, 723, 731, 732, 1350, 1351, 2256, 2503, 2830
Interest in Firefighting: 733
Interest in Job Content: 1579
Interest in Police Work: 734
Interest in Practical Work/Using Your Hands/Science and Engineering: 1342
Interest in Science: 2325
Interest in Selling: 2266
Interest in Subordinate Growth: 490
Interest in Surroundings: 788
Interest in Working Where You Meet People Including Acting and Writing: 1342
Interest in Working with People in Need: 1342
Interest Inventory: 418, 713, 2000
Interest Level: 1624
Interest Profile: 1821
Interesting Experiences: 371
Interests: 217, 728, 1964, 2831
Interests Summary Sheet: 1820
Interfaces: 191
Interference: 1729
Interference Because of Therapist's Adjustment Problems: 1830
Interference Trial: 470
Intergenerational Issues: 2034
Intergroup: 2149
Intergroup Relationships: 675, 676
Interior Decorator: 1790
Interior Designer: 398, 399
Intermediate Algebra: 571
Intermediate Algebra/Coordinate Geometry: 56
Intermediate Memory: 1525
Internal: 327, 768, 927
Internal Adjustment: 2605
Internal Complaints: 640
Internal Consistency: 224
Internal Distractibility: 226
Internal Focus of World: 162, 1929
Internal Functioning: 728
Internal Goals: 421
Internal Problems: 490
Internal Quality Standards: 490
Internal Scale: 1183
Internal Support: 2423
Internalised Shame Scale: 1626
Internality: 1984, 2030
Internality/Externality: 372
Internalization/Somatic Symptoms: 1962
Internalized: 1300
Internalized Conflict Measures: 1313

Internalizing: 424, 451, 2452, 2607, 2939
Internalizing Behavior Problems: 931
Internalizing Composite: 818
Internalizing Disorder Factor: 77
Internalizing Problems: 245, 280, 2036, 2446
International: 749, 1271, 1785
International Activities: 380
International Affairs: 618
International English Language: 104, 118
International Trade: 897
Internet Information Skills: 2645
Internship/Fieldwork/Clinical Experiences: 1108, 2083
Interoceptive Awareness: 893
Interparental Friction-Harmony: 1005
Interpersonal: 5, 162, 224, 226, 752, 2030, 2269, 2334, 2355, 2667, 2929, 2274
Interpersonal Abuse: 400
Interpersonal Aggression: 1948
Interpersonal and Social Tendencies: 1579
Interpersonal Assertion: 1948
Interpersonal/Assertiveness Difficulties: 1207
Interpersonal Assessment: 2097
Interpersonal Awareness: 1267, 1948
Interpersonal Behavior: 70, 2122, 2824
Interpersonal Behavior and Areas of Conflict: 242
Interpersonal Behaviors: 293, 2444
Interpersonal Classroom Communication: 494
Interpersonal Communication Skills: 1450
Interpersonal Competence: 2587
Interpersonal Competency: 909
Interpersonal Conflict: 467, 938
Interpersonal Conflict Measures: 1313
Interpersonal Conversations: 188
Interpersonal Cooperation: 467
Interpersonal Deference: 1948
Interpersonal Difficulties: 284, 1313
Interpersonal Distrust: 893
Interpersonal-Environmental Context: 1732
Interpersonal EQ: 243
Interpersonal Figures: 1049
Interpersonal Focus (Interpersonal Skills): 1923
Interpersonal Harmony: 962, 1952, 2279
Interpersonal Insight: 2347
Interpersonal Interaction: 2763
Interpersonal Intransitive-Focus on Self: 1298
Interpersonal Involvement: 1294
Interpersonal Pathology: 1932
Interpersonal Problems: 77, 256, 569, 817, 1729
Interpersonal Relations: 197, 252, 275, 280, 283, 824, 928, 1429, 2577, 2886, 2647, 2779, 2874, 2913
Interpersonal Relationship: 243
Interpersonal Relationships: 300, 675, 676, 942, 965, 1194, 1494, 2035, 2357, 2780, 2813, 2814
Interpersonal Sensitivity: 335, 337, 747, 792, 2326, 2602, 2603
Interpersonal Skills: 1467, 2322
Interpersonal Strain: 1825
Interpersonal Strength: 290
Interpersonal Strengths: 37
Interpersonal Stress Assessment: 2511
Interpersonal Style: 186
Interpersonal Style Scores: 86
Interpersonal Support: 1209, 1913
Interpersonal Traits: 1930
Interpersonal Transitive-Focus on Other: 1298
Interpersonal Understanding: 1573, 2268
Interpersonal Values: 2346
Interpersonal Warmth: 654
Interpersonal Ways: 2237
Interpretation: 716, 775, 2487, 2856, 2857
Interpretation of Signs/Symbols: 2376
Interpretations: 348
Interpreting: 1251, 1929
Interpreting Data: 735, 1392
Interpreting Figurative Language: 647
Interpreting Intents: 2693
Interpreting Literature and the Arts: 2742
Interpreting Mathematical Information: 1315
Interpreting Paragraphs: 1203
Interpreting Results: 570
Interpretive: 2898
Interpretive Reasoning: 570
Interrogatives: 1739, 2215
Interruption: 641
Intersensory Integration: 1909, 2816
Interval: 1753
Interval Discrimination: 1751
Interview: 1085
Interview Actions: 1346
Interview Behavior Checklist: 1870
Interview Belligerence-Negativism: 2109
Interview Skills: 2827
Interview With Students/Assessing Attitudes: 207
Interview with the Child: 442
Interviewer Observations: 642
Interviewer Rating: 642
Interviewing: 1830
Interviewing for a Job: 190
Intimacy: 1316, 1631, 1946, 2454, 2804
Intimacy Scale: 2527
Intimate Relationship Happiness: 1678
Intonation: 1753
Intraception: 68, 908
Intraggression: 2248
Intragroup: 2149
Intrapersonal: 243, 1667, 2149
Intrapersonal Behavior: 2122
Intrapersonal EQ: 243
Intrapersonal Information: 1468
Intrapersonal Strength: 290
Intrapsychic: 1683
Intrapsychic Introjection: 1298
Intrapunitive: 78
Intrasensory Integration: 2816

Intrinsic: 1701
Intrinsic and Personality: 1074
Intrinsic Goal Orientation: 1720
Intrinsic Satisfaction: 401
Intrinsic to Job: 1824
Introduce Time Pressure: 2923
Introduction to Biofeedback: 310
Introduction to Biology: 684
Introduction to Business: 762
Introduction to Computing: 762
Introduction to Law Enforcement: 762
Introduction to the Modern Middle East: 762
Introduction to the Teaching of Reading: 2026
Introduction to World Religions: 762
Introductory Business: 2530
Introductory Business Law: 521
Introductory Psychology: 522
Introductory Sociology: 523
Introject: 1298
Introspective/Interactive Stance: 1253
Introversing: 1688
Introversion: 77, 226, 1366, 1464, 1814, 2411, 2784
Introversion-Extraversion: 690
Introversive: 1685, 1686, 1958
Introverted: 2411, 2536
Introverted Personality Style: 1314
Intrusion: 766, 1626
Intrusions: 376
Intrusive: 2939
Intrusive Experiences: 2782
Intuiting: 1688
Intuition: 654, 966, 1366, 2411
Intuitive: 200, 1814
Intuitive Feeling: 1562
Intuitive-Feeling: 1464
Intuitive/Feeling: 1473
Intuitive Thinking: 1562
Intuitive-Thinking: 1464
Intuitive/Thinking: 1473
Intuitor: 1331, 1950, 1951
Invalidity: 909
Invalidity Index: 2306
Inventive: 2121
Inventiveness: 2784
Inventor: 312
Inventory of Articulation Characteristics of Apraxia: 163
Inventory of Oral Reading Skills: 2005
Inventory of Work-Relevant Abilities: 418
Inversión de Numeros: 264
Invest in Close Friends: 72
Investigation: 1254
Investigative: 397, 398, 399, 1790, 1829, 2360, 2835
Investigative Knowledge: 2002
Investigative v. Accepting: 417
Investing in New Equipment: 2070
Investments Manager: 1790
Involuntary Hand-Arm Patterns: 968
Involvement: 413, 495, 637, 710, 909, 1008, 1161, 1216, 1545, 1670, 1824, 1883, 1966, 2587, 2793, 2850, 2917
Involvement in Advocacy Groups: 1884
Involvement in Fund Raising Activities: 1884
Involvement Total: 1884
Involvement with Administration: 1884
Iowa Pressure Articulation Test: 2651
IQ: 1461
IQ Composite: 1380
Irregular: 1427
Irrelevant: 2251
Irrelevant Talk: 1161
Irreproachability: 1251, 1929
Irresponsible/Inattentive: 281
Irritability: 4, 1223, 1241, 1489, 1748, 1959
Is Committed to Making a Difference: 2101
Is Insightful: Sees Things from New Angles: 2101
Is Open to Criticism: 2101
Isolated Functioning: 2706
Isolated-Integrated: 2446
Isolated Sounds in Sequence: 1503
Isolation: 1631, 1963, 2307
Italian: 581, 611, 615, 2026
Item Response Time: 2667, 2725
Items: 2730

Janitor/Janitress: 398, 399
Japanese: 582, 612, 615
Jaw: 1056, 1852
Jittery: 551
Job: 1942, 2196
Job Adaptation Skills: 1252
Job Analysis Rating: 2781
Job Application: 1352
Job Attitude: 1344
Job Behaviors: 197
Job Challenge: 2587
Job Characteristics: 2132, 2585
Job Choices: 1177
Job Clarity: 2587
Job Competence: 2369
Job Context: 2016
Job Descriptions: 1406
Job Difficulties: 1313
Job Dissatisfaction: 267, 2592
Job Experimentation: 401
Job Functions: 2071
Job-Holding Skills: 2081
Job in General: 1348
Job Interest and Challenge: 2584
Job Interest and Satisfaction: 844
Job Involvement: 1338, 2593
Job Itself: 1824
Job Knowledge: 942, 989, 2081
Job Opportunity: 1276

Job Overload: 807
Job Performance and Attitudes: 443
Job Pressure Frequency: 1354
Job Pressure Index: 1354
Job Pressure Severity: 1354
Job Related Behavior: 2443, 2734
Job-Related Behavior: 2422
Job-Related Skills: 2827
Job Review Comparison: 1617
Job Reward: 2587
Job Safety: 443
Job Satisfaction: 400, 909, 1913, 2585, 2776
Job Satisfiers: 2132
Job Search: 443
Job Search Skills: 2422, 2443, 2734
Job Security: 382, 1334, 2584
Job Seeking Skills: 1252
Job-Seeking Skills: 2081, 2327, 2827
Job-Seeking Skills and Knowledge: 341
Job Skill Demand: 1467
Job Skills: 2605
Job Skills: Organization: 2605
Job Stability: 1926, 1968
Job Stress Frequency: 1354
Job Stress Index: 1354
Job Stress Severity: 1354
Job Title/Position: 490
Joining Parts of the Sentence: 1125
Joint Dysfunction: 2766
Journalism: 618
Journalism-Advertising: 618
Journalism-General: 618
Journalism-News Editing: 618
Joviality: 1057
Joy: 791
Judgement and Comprehension: 1042
Judgement/Perception: 1828
Judgement vs. Perception: 1365
Judgemental: 1655
Judging: 1814, 2411
Judging Credibility: 2733
Judging/Perceiving: 1750
Judging vs. Perceiving: 1755
Judgment: 152, 558, 912, 1323, 1568, 1988, 2061, 2393, 2633
Judgment and Comprehension: 1043
Judgment and Comprehension in Practical Nursing Situations: 2220
Judgment and Decision Making: 2605
Judgment and Decision-Making: 1569
Judgment Record: 1566, 2573
Judgments: 2928
Judicious-Competing: 1022, 1704, 2507
Just Before: 2475
Justification: 2733
Justification of Policy: 1026
Justifications Scale: 1744
Juvenility: 218

K-SNAP Composite: 1384
Keep to Self: 72
Keeping Friends: 63
Keeping It Secret: 646, 660
Kendrick Attention and Reasoning Test: 1390
Key Search: 295
Key Words: 1529
Kids Incomplete Sentences Test: 2381
Kindness-Friendliness-Understanding: 836
Kinds of People: 726
Kinesic: 1284
Kinesthesia: 2377
Kinesthetic: 1470, 1478, 1667, 2597
Kinesthetic Competence (Efficacy): 1250
Kinesthetic Preference: 244
Kinesthetic Preferences: 2069, 2181
Kinesthetic Processing: 2236
Kinetic Person Drawing: 268
Kitchen-Cleaning: 661
Kitchen-Cooking: 661
Kitchen Objects: 2884
Kitchen Skills: 1065
Kneel Walk Forward and Back: 977
Knock and Tap: 1771
Knot Tying: 2439
Knowing Science: 1759
Knowledge: 1184, 2901
Knowledge Acquired in a Field: 1795
Knowledge Acquisition Strategies: 2495
Knowledge and Expectations of the Career: 421
Knowledge and Experience of Animals: 2384
Knowledge and Opinions About Sex: 1887
Knowledge and Use of Reference Materials: 2095, 2234
Knowledge of Contractions: 917
Knowledge of Diversity Issues: 975
Knowledge of DSM III: 1830
Knowledge of English Language: 1500
Knowledge of Fire Protection/Prevention Practices: 1032
Knowledge of Inmate Legal Rights: 796
Knowledge of Job: 2425
Knowledge of Personality Theory: 1830
Knowledge of Preferred Occupational Group: 405
Knowledge of Print: 2676
Knowledge of the Behavioral Sciences and Human Relations: 796
Knowledge of the Career: 421
Knowledge Seeking: 980
Known Words/Correct: 322
Knows Use of Objects: 345
Korean: 615

Labeling: 1424
Labels/Nouns and Pronouns: 2215

Labels per T-Unit: 2661
Lability: 320
Labor Management: 1222
Laboratory & Field Work: 570
Laboratory/Field Techniques: 570
Laboratory Studies: 434
Laboratory Technician: 2825
Laboratory Work: 618
Lack Intellectual Independence: 1162
Lack of Assertiveness: 1313
Lack of Competitive Motivation: 1314
Lack of Controlled Drinking: 132, 2874
Lack of Ego Mastery: 1697
Lack of Ego Mastery-Cognitive: 1698
Lack of Ego Mastery-Conative: 1698
Lack of Ego Mastery-Defective Inhibition: 1698
Lack of Emotion: 2109
Lack of Follow-through: 300
Lack of Insight/Candor: 1314
Lack of Medical Comprehensiveness: 291
Lack of Nervous Tendencies: 1926
Lack of Organizational Support Frequency: 1354
Lack of Organizational Support Index: 1354
Lack of Organizational Support Severity: 1354
Lack of Personal Support: 807
Lack of Sensitivity: 1314
Lack of Top Management Support: 807
Lack of Western Ethnocentrism: 747
Lags: 1618
Laissez Faire: 1439
Laissez-Faire: 1736
Landau Response: 1668
Landscape Architect: 380
Language: 5, 33, 82, 97, 165, 234, 259, 268, 319, 364, 383, 384, 389, 446, 454, 547, 558, 559, 566, 619, 761, 778, 788, 800, 804, 809, 810, 812, 879, 886, 904, 1039, 1086, 1094, 1192, 1194, 1202, 1230, 1259, 1318, 1388, 1391, 1490, 1657, 1771, 1789, 1909, 1996, 2111, 2202, 2219, 2387, 2408, 2470, 2484, 2735, 2737, 2738, 2740, 2838
Language Ability: 2345
Language/Abstract Processing Ratio: 320
Language Acquisition Stage: 2139
Language (Afrikaans): 12
Language and Cognition: 889
Language and Educational Skills: 805
Language and General Development: 2319
Language and Literacy: 1204
Language and Reasoning: 1009
Language and Thinking: 478
Language Arts: 342, 684, 742, 2137, 2654
Language Association: 2471
Language Check: 918
Language/Cognition: 916
Language Communication: 1263
Language Complexity Ratio: 320
Language Composite: 1848
Language Comprehension: 315, 453, 1194, 2299, 2801
Language Concepts: 468, 661, 1707, 1801
Language Content and Structure: 494
Language Deficit: 562
Language Development: 1, 2, 465, 887, 1041, 2046
Language Dysfunction: 690
Language/Education: 1369
Language/English: 2483
Language (English): 12
Language Errors: 2429
Language Expression: 315, 359, 383, 384, 628, 2299, 2483, 2801
Language Function: 158, 2235
Language Functions: 1905, 1908
Language Knowledge and Skills: 684
Language Levels: 1579
Language/Literacy: 1658
Language-Literature: 618
Language Mechanics: 383, 384, 2483, 2560, 2654
The Language of Algebra: 1247
Language Processing Total: 1690
Language Proficiency and Intelligibility: 2235
Language Quotient: 241, 2801
Language-Reasoning: 875
Language Sample: 2471
Language Scales: 1385
Language Skills: 359, 1350, 2047, 2105, 2234
Language Stimulation: 1216
Language Total: 1318
Language Usage: 18, 395, 616, 838, 839, 1235, 2293
Language Usage-Sentences: 956
Language Usage (Sentences): 957
Language Usage-Words: 956
Language Usage (Words): 957
Language-Vocabulary: 1139
Large Muscle Coordination: 565
Large Muscle Skills: 2043
Laryngeal: 1056
Larynx: 276
Lassitude-Malaise: 1698
Lassitude-Malaise (Hy3): 1697
Last Sound Different: 189
Lasting Sources of Power: 490
Late Morning: 1470, 1472, 2069
Latency and Utterance Time for Polysyllabic Words: 163
Lateral Dominance: 1164
Lateral Dominance Examination: 1164
Lateralization Key: 1165
Latin: 105, 583, 603, 615, 2026
Latin Literature: 118
Latin-Vergil: 118
Latin (Vergil): 106
Laundering: 212
Laundry: 2327, 2400, 2829
Laundry Service: 2177

Laundry/Serving: 2829
Laundry Skills: 1065
Law: 618, 905, 1334, 1789
Law Enforcement: 618, 1794
Law/Government and Jurisprudence: 1044
Law/Politics: 380, 398, 1790
Law Violations: 1207
Lawyer: 398, 1790, 2825
Lax Control: 1881
Layout/Cutting and Assembly: 2151
Laziness: 439
Lead/Influence: 2836
Lead Maintenance: 1793
Leader: 1317
Leader Control: 1141
Leader Support: 1141
Leadership: 5, 166, 197, 219, 280, 311, 371, 379, 380, 684, 843, 945, 1147, 1157, 1350, 1395, 1641, 1667, 1855, 1926, 1930, 1955, 2295, 2346, 2418, 2537, 2581, 2605
Leadership Abilities: 1921
Leadership Ability: 1089, 2420
Leadership and Initiative: 844
Leadership Avoidance: 1314
Leadership-Coach: 1823
Leadership/Decision Making: 2574
Leadership-Expert: 1823
Leadership-Fighter: 1823
Leadership for Consensus: 490
Leadership for Growth/Productivity: 490
Leadership/Motivation/and Decision-Making Inventory: 1403
Leadership Overall: 1823
Leadership Skill: 1467
Leadership Structure and Consideration: 1711
Leadership Style: 1790
Leadership Style and Practices: 1080
Leadership Styles: 1554
Leadership Success: 2751
Leadership v. Supporting: 417
Leadership Vision: 490
Leading: 407
Leading Employees: 300
Leading Influencing: 485
Leading-Influencing: 412, 1483, 1711, 1817
Learn in Several Ways: 1470
Learned Helplessness: 1748
Learned Skills: 2047
Learning: 283, 476, 928, 1476, 1896, 2053, 2131, 2226, 2236, 2295, 2826
Learning Ability: 32
Learning Activities: 1009, 1264
Learning Alone/Peer Oriented: 1470
Learning Alone/Peer-Oriented Learner: 2069
Learning and Memory: 882
Learning and Retention Processes: 320
Learning and Understanding: 2590
Learning Attitude: 2380
Learning Capability: 227
Learning Characteristics: 2622
Learning/Cognition: 1591
Learning/Cognitive: 1194
Learning/Comprehension Disorder: 928
Learning Disability: 1522
Learning Environment: 1790
Learning Gap: 1467
Learning Index: 2880
Learning Intervention Design and Development: 638
Learning Job Skills: 401
Learning Materials: 1216
Learning Motivation: 1461
Learning Organization: 2773
Learning Outcomes Role-Play: 975
Learning Problems: 280, 284, 1963
Learning Readiness: 2359
Learning Self-Assessment: 975
Learning Set Ratio: 320
Learning Strategies Scales: 1720
Learning/Studying: 2526
Learning Style: 359, 1579
Learning Styles: 1984
Learning Theories: 684
Learning to Learn: 2892
Learning-Verbal: 1775
Learns from Mistakes: 2101
Least Deployed Strengths: 1024, 2014
Least Overdone Strengths: 1023, 2013
Leather-Work: 1990
Lecture: 1474
Lecture Mastery: 707
Lecturing: 391
Left: 1227, 2820
Left Brain: 2545
Left Eye: 2852
Left Frontal: 1525
Left Hand: 2125
Left Hand Dexterity: 2244
Left Hemisphere: 85, 1525
Left Mode Dominance: 1197
Left Parietal-Occipital: 1525
Left-Right Discrimination: 2141
Left Sensorimotor: 1524, 1525
Left Temporal: 1525
Leg Abduction: 1258
Leg Coordination: 1613
Legal: 1177, 1818, 1941
Legal and Ethical Issues in Counseling: 684
Legal and Secretarial: 1551
Legal Assistant: 398, 399
Legal History: 1431, 1432, 2147
Legal Issues: 684, 1649
Legal Knowledge: 2002
Legal Requirements of PL 94-142: 684
Legal Services: 411, 1285, 1841

Legibility: 1283
Legitimate: 2415
Legs: 63
Leisure: 59, 63, 198, 212, 1351, 1493, 1494, 1705, 1818, 1897, 2282
Leisure Activities: 1790, 2034, 2780
Leisure Activity: 2327
Leisure and Social Activities: 1718
Leisure Happiness: 1678
Leisure (Participation): 1493
Leisure Skills: 70, 661, 805, 1065
Leisure Time: 686
Leisure Time Activities: 2130
Leisurely: 1211
Length: 883, 884, 2023
Length of Description: 215
Let's Tell Stories: 2029
Lethargic-Hypoactive: 69
Lethargy: 4
Letter and Word Skills: 1385
Letter Discrimination: 2172
Letter Identification: 1224, 1534, 2905
Letter Knowledge: 2219
Letter Matching: 2691
Letter-Matching: 1529
Letter-Number Sequencing: 2860
Letter-Numbering Sequencing: 2863
Letter Memory: 1138, 1139, 2176
Letter Names in Spoken Words: 861
Letter Names [Lower-Case]: 2175
Letter Names [Upper-Case]: 2175
Letter Naming: 565, 1337, 2172
Letter Perception and Counting: 1920
Letter Recognition: 730, 916, 2134, 2172
Letter Series: 670, 2304
Letter Sets Test: 1405
Letter Sound Relationships: 2175
Letter Sounding: 730
Letter Strings: 835
Letter-Word Identification: 2900, 2901, 2902, 2904
Letter/Word Identification: 2665
Letter Writing: 730, 957, 1224, 2180
Letters: 331, 453, 861, 905, 987, 1802, 2428, 2787
Letters and Letter-Sound Correspondences: 1072
Letters (Auditory): 917
Letters Backward: 2701
Letters Forward: 2701
Letters (Visual): 917
Level and Consistency of Intellectual Response: 459
Level of Activity in Feminine Sex-Role Behaviors (F): 2161
Level of Activity in Masculine Sex-Role Behaviors (M): 2161
Level of Aspiration: 844, 2266
Level of Complexity: 251
Level of Comprehension: 2744
Level of Consciousness: 558
Level of Dissatisfaction: 162, 1929
Level of Functioning Domains: 73
Level of Growth: 162, 1929
Level of Impairment in Functioning: 2018
Level of Insecurity: 162, 1929
Level of Job Stress: 844
Level of Learning: 470
Level of Present Support: 162, 1929
Level of Public Success: 162, 1929
Level of Satisfaction: 162, 1929
Level of Security: 162, 1929
Level of Stress Experienced by the Child: 442
Level of Stress Response: 2605
Level of Work Competency: 2728
Leveling-Sharpening House Test: 563
Levels of English Proficiency: 18
Levels of Projection: 2242
Lexical Decision: 2172
Lexical Discrimination: 366
Liberal Arts Professor: 380
Liberal-Conservative: 1845
Liberal-Traditional Attitude Toward Medical Students: 1640
Librarian: 380, 398, 399, 1790
Library Activities: 635
Library Aide: 2400
Library and Archival Sciences: 905
Library Media Specialist: 2026
Licensed Practical Nurse: 399
Licensing and Certification: 1406
Lie: 77, 1025, 1698, 1962, 2535
Lie (L): 1697
Lie Scale: 1293
Lie Subtest: 746
Life and Career Plans: 2000
Life Change Events: 1181
Life Circumstance Evaluation: 1372, 2550
Life Events: 2512
Life Goals: 57
Life Insurance Agent: 1790
Life-Long Learning: 2929
Life Management Subtask: 2527
Life Restrictions: 2510
Life Satisfaction: 1733
Life Science: 1094, 1334
Life Sciences: 407, 570, 960, 1759
Life Sciences/General Biology: 905
Life Skills: 260, 971
Life Skills Appraisal: 645
Life Skills Certification: 645
Life Stress: 1889
Life Stressor Scales: 1495
Life Stressors: 2510
Life Stressors Scales: 1496
Life Style: 1493, 2805, 2915
Life-Style and Career Planning: 684
Life Style Behaviors: 2074

Life Style Needs: 2586
Life Tasks: 467
Life Threat Reactivity: 1686
Life Transitions: 2034
Lifespan Developmental Psychology: 762
Lifestyle: 396, 749, 1705, 1785
Lifestyle Improvement Suggestions: 1499
Lifestyle Planning Subtask: 2527
Lifetime History: 650
Lifting: 1478
Light: 1470, 2069, 2181
Light Reflex: 1614
Lighting: 1472
Likability: 1735
Like: 1790
Likeability: 1212
Liked By All: 262
Likes: 125
Liking for Lessons: 836
Liking for School: 2753
Liking for Teacher: 836
Liking for Thinking: 865
Limb: 2705
Limb Apraxia and Oral Apraxia: 163
Limbic Mode Dominance: 1197
Limit Setting: 1006, 1316, 1883, 2242
Limited Peer Status: 1963
Limits: 467
Line Orientation: 2202
Linguistic: 21, 23, 25, 799, 1284, 1667, 1907, 2758, 2807
Linguistic Competence: 2717
Linguistic Comprehension: 176
Linguistic Concepts: 539
Linguistic Development: 1171
Linguistic Expression: 176
Linguistic/Human Nonlinguistic/Environmental: 2672
Linguistic Nonverbal: 797
Linguistic Organization: 338
Linguistic Relationships: 2471
Linguistic Verbal: 797
Linguistic vs. Nonlinguistic: 2672
Linking: 1545
Lips: 276, 1056, 1852
Liquid Simplification: 1394
Liquid-l: 214
Liquid-r: 214
List Acquisition: 1644
List Clustering: 1644
List Learning: 1771, 2202
List Recall: 1644, 2202
List Recognition: 1644, 2202
Listener Response: 164
Listener Score: 87
Listening: 84, 165, 233, 257, 339, 340, 392, 541, 575, 576, 597, 602, 610, 612, 645, 666, 684, 821, 822, 971, 985, 1147, 1318, 1459, 1460, 1521, 1651, 1662, 2035, 2462, 2483, 2484, 2632, 2668, 2695
Listening and Language: 1265
Listening and Literature: 1120
Listening and Organizing: 1570
Listening and Talking: 1264
Listening Assessment: 2920
Listening Comprehension: 250, 481, 509, 510, 511, 645, 743, 861, 986, 1224, 1420, 1461, 1534, 1847, 2032, 2093, 2175, 2192, 2339, 2665, 2687, 2861, 2900, 2901, 2902
Listening Comprehension Level: 917
Listening Comprehension: Making Inferences: 2693
Listening Constructively: 634
Listening/Grammar: 2668
Listening Level: 832
Listening Quotient: 2694
Listening Response: 459
Listening Skills: 2709
Listening/Speaking: 1426
Listening to Paragraphs: 540
Listening to Words and Stories: 165, 2484, 2488
Listening Vocabulary: 861, 952, 2487
Listening/Vocabulary: 2668
Literacy: 33, 150, 1826
Literacy and Numeracy: 2926
Literacy Concepts: 1072
Literacy Skill Section: 250
Literacy Skills: 1260
Literal: 199
Literary: 1074, 1157, 1177, 1222, 1413, 2255, 2257
Literary Arts: 407
Literary Knowledge and Skills: 684
Literature: 98, 584, 604, 615, 617, 2882
Literature and Language Studies: 2026
Literature and the Arts: 829
Literature in English: 1118, 1124
Little Pink Tower Test: 1653
Live Work Satisfaction: 2512
Liveliness: 538
Lively vs. Serious: 2417
Living Conditions: 1007
Living Room: 661
Lizards Love Eggs: 2743
Local: 1271
Localization: 1164
Localization of Tactile Stimuli: 2377
Localization Scales: 1525
Locating: 2821
Locating Information Assessment: 2920
Location: 1214, 1533, 2763
Location Concern: 1163
Locations for Sex: 1433
Locations Test: 1405
Locatives: 1427
Locomotion: 265, 377, 1668
Locomotor: 1134, 1901, 2308
Locomotor Function: 133
Locomotor Skills: 2689

Locus of Control: 280, 1683
Logic: 1824
Logic and Mathematics: 1204
Logic and Organization: 1248
Logic and Reasoning: 781, 782
Logic Games: 1667
Logical: 1334
Logical Analysis: 699
Logical/Analytical: 1497
Logical-Mathematical: 1667
Logical Memory: 2863
Logical Persuasion: 1267
Logical Reasoning: 1405
Logical Relationships: 955
Logical Sentences: 2731
Logical Steps: 1378
Logical Thinking: 669
Loneliness: 78, 448
Loner: 1313
Long Delay: 476
Long Term Job Commitment: 944
Long Term Memory Retrieval: 1083
Long Term Recall: 1462
Long Vowel Recognition: 740
Long Vowels: 2180
Long Vowels and Vowel Digraphs: 1529
Long-Delay Cued Recall: 375
Long-Delay Free Recall: 375
Long-Term Perspective: 2097
Long-Term Retrieval: 2901
Looking and Sight: 1265
Looking to Logic: 2412
Lose-Leave: 2549, 2638
Loss of Control: 136, 1931, 1932
Loss of Goal: 2290
Loss of Insight: 2216
Loss of Weight: 2216
Losses Associated with Work: 2834
Lost Child: 479
Loudness: 1753, 2837
Lovability: 1735
Love: 1291, 1938, 2131
Love Behavior: 1679
Love Capacity: 1946
Love Feelings: 1679
Love Motivation: 1679
Love Scale Index: 2291
Love Thoughts: 1679
Low Achiever: 1924
Low Aspirations: 1698
Low Energy: 1749
Low Energy Depression: 538
Low Energy Level: 1748
Low Expectation of Benefit: 362
Low Origence-High Intellectence: 68
Low Origence-Low Intellectence: 68
Low Pass Filtered Speech: 1046
Low Risk: 1890
Low Self-Control: 1321
Low Self-Esteem: 931, 1698, 1748
Low Self-Esteem (LSE): 1697
Low-Probability: 199
Lower Engineering Trades: 1990
Lower Left Quadrant: 1197
Lower Right Quadrant: 1197
Lower Thought Processes: 493
LSD: 66, 1931
Lubrication: 1537, 1637, 2066, 2152, 2644
Lubrication/Bearings/Power Transmission: 2067
Lunchroom Behavior: 2444
Lust: 439

M (meaningless items) score: 771
MacAndrew Alcoholism Scale-Revised: 1698
MacAndrew Alcoholism Scale-Revised (MAC-R): 1697
Machine Design: 1222
Machine Operation: 411, 1222, 1841, 2882
Machine Repair: 1793
Machine Shop Lubrication: 2151
Machine Tools: 2151
Machines/Tools/Equipment: 1637
Machinist: 398, 399
Macroeconomics: 107, 118, 2718
MAE Token Test: 1740
Magazines: 1491
Magic Window: 1379
Magical Transformations: 847
Magician: 1451
Magnification of Symptoms: 2604
Mail Carrier: 398, 399
Main Character: 2647
Maintain: 1557
Maintaining Adult Relationships: 2775
Maintaining Adult-to-Adult (not "Parent-Child") Relationships in Class: 203
Maintaining and Changing Positions: 2316
Maintaining and Controlling Materials and Equipment: 2575
Maintaining Friendships: 40
Maintaining Regular Attendance: 190
Maintaining Supply Lines: 2070
Maintenance: 1793, 2829
Maintenance Behavior: 1147
Maintenance Mechanic: 1793
Maintenance Records: 2769
Maintenance Stage: 83
Maintenance Technician: 1793
Major: 200
Major Admissions of Dishonesty: 1976
Major Depression: 77, 168
Major Depressive Disorder: 79, 876
Major Depressive Episode and Dysthymia: 642
Major Depressive Syndrome: 650

Major-Minor Mode Discrimination: 1751
Major Objectives: 2415
Major Workstyles: 1984
Make Something Out of It: 726
Makes Decisions About Possible Solutions: 2739
Makeup: 1364
Making: 1819
Making a Block Walk: 1653
Making Boxes: 2023
Making Career Decisions: 190
Making Change: 2327
Making Conversation: 2444
Making Decisions: 63, 627, 1550, 2633
Making Decisions and Solving Problems: 903
Making Decisions/Communicating and Having Responsibility: 1343, 2925
Making Decisions/Weighing Risk: 1570
Making Groups: 1405
Making Lengths: 2023
Making Meetings Work: 2630
Making Myself Understood: 634
Making Objects: 726
Making Predictions: 647
Making Presentations to Employees: 1479, 1480
Making Sentences: 84, 1405
Making Team Decisions by Consensus: 2630
Maladaptive Behavior: 2813
Maladaptive Behavior Indexes: 1300
Maladaptive Outcome: 2242
Maladjustive: 1169
Malapropism: 2694
Male: 1374
Male-Female: 2869
Male Peers: 210
Male Perception of Father's Ideal: 1536
Male Perception of Ideal Man: 1536
Male Perception of Mother's Ideal: 1536
Male Perception of Woman's Ideal Man: 1536
Male Self Perception: 1536
Males: 1049
Malevolent: 2800
Malevolent Religiosity: 847
Malingering: 1543, 2011
Man: 854
Man's Ideal Woman: 1535
Man's Perception of Woman's Ideal Man: 1536
Man's Perception of Woman's Ideal Woman: 1535
Man's Self Perception: 1536
Manage Moods: 136
Management: 411, 1177, 1667, 1841, 2882, 2915
Management and Administration: 1285
Management Development: 2424
Management Feedback: 490
Management Focus: 1443, 1549
Management Functions Preference Scores: 1551
Management Information Systems: 762
Management of Content: 1281
Management of Details: 782
Management of Hostility: 721
Management of Numerical Information: 782
Management of Personal Stress: 1830
Management Practices: 640
Management Procedures: 1913
Management Processes: 1824
Management Roles Inventory: 1403
Management Skills Preference Scores: 1551
Management Style/Decision-Making: 1566
Management Style Preference: 1821
Management Style Questionnaire: 2605
Management Support: 490
Management Values: 1861, 2068, 2133, 2583
Management's Credibility: 2584
Management-by-Exception (Active): 1736
Management-by-Exception (Passive): 1736
Management/Supervision: 398
Manager (Administrator): 2075
Manager's Post Training: 975
Managerial: 420, 1030, 1222, 1818, 1984, 2265
Managerial Accounting: 17
Managerial and Professional Job Functions Inventory for Ability: 2605
Managerial Competence: 490
Managerial Credibility: 1861, 2068, 2133, 2583
Managerial Customer Focus: 2129
Managerial Depth: 2585
Managerial/Enterprising: 1497
Managerial Orientation: 2097
Managerial Potential: 372, 1212
Managerial Practices: 1463
Managerial Review: 1937
Managerial Role: 1824
Managerial Style Scores: 1561
Managerial Style Synthesis: 1561
Managerial Traits: 966
Managers/Sales: 1350
Manages Curriculum: 1276
Managing Affective Interference: 351
Managing Business and Fiscal Affairs: 903
Managing Business Diversity: 807
Managing By Fact: 2773
Managing Change: 1479, 1480, 1554
Managing Change Inventory: 1403
Managing Classroom Time Effectively: 2775
Managing Complexities: 490
Managing Conflict: 1080, 1550
Managing Diversity: 490
Managing Home and Transportation: 1246
Managing Money: 1246
Managing Performance: 1545
Managing Risks: 1651
Managing Time: 1554
Mandible: 276
Maneuvering: 1251, 1929
Mania: 73, 77, 1778, 1959, 2107, 2615

Manic: 748
Manic-Depressive Disorder: 2107
Manic Episode: 642
Manic Syndrome: 650, 2305
Manifest Aggression: 1341
Manifest Behavior: 288
Manifestations of Stress: 2321
Manikin: 1653, 2439
Manikin Accuracy: 567
Manikin Speed: 567
Manikin Thruput: 567
Manipulating Sounds Within Words: 187
Manipulation: 1655, 2538
Manipulation Awareness: 1938
Manipulation in Fractions: 831
Manipulation of Emotion: 2052
Manipulation with Movement: 2316
Manipulative: 1472, 2308
Manipulative and Perceptual Skills: 1718
Manipulativeness: 2306
Manipulator/Pragmatist: 1341
Manner: 1968
Manual: 5, 1177
Manual and Tool Skills: 196
Manual Dexterity: 412, 488, 713, 1044, 1711, 1727, 1816, 1901, 2421, 2797, 2798, 2799
Manual Expression: 1240
Manual Form Perception: 2377
Manual Imitation: 2701
Manual Language Expression: 2628
Manual Motor Sequences: 1771
Manual Planning: 488
Manual Skill: 1578
Manual/Skilled Trades: 398, 399
Manual Speed: 1578
Manual Speed and Accuracy: 937
Manual Speed and Dexterity: 395
Manual Speed of Movement: 1920
Manual Training Prerequisites: 658
Manual Work: 1841
Manufacturer's Representative: 380, 398, 399
Manuscript-Cursive Transition: 786
Manuscript Writing: 2213
Many Interests: 1142, 1143, 2037
Map Memory: 1405
Map Orientation: 199
Map Planning Test: 1405
Map Reading: 733, 2234
Mapping and Directions: 2596
Maps and Diagrams: 389, 1318
Marching: 1164
Mare and Foal Picture Completion: 1653
Marijuana: 1931, 2554
Marine Mechanics: 1792, 1794
Marital and Extramarital Sexual Relations: 1583
Marital Conflict: 1006
Marital Conflicts: 2292
Marital Coping: 136
Marital Discord: 1963
Marital Distress Scale (MDS): 1697
Marital History: 1431, 2147
Marital or Living Together Sexual Experiences: 659
Marital Problems: 136, 938
Marital Relations: 2132
Marital Roles: 2389
Marital Satisfaction: 2034
Marital Sex: 646
Market Awareness: 2385
Marketing: 1841, 2026, 2832
Marketing and Distribution: 410
Marketing Director: 380
Marketing/Distribution: 905
Marketing Education: 684, 2026
Marketing Executive: 1790
Marketing Focus: 490
Marketing or Sales: 411
Marketing Planning: 490
Marketing/Sales: 2822
Marketing Support: 1551
Marketplace Awareness: 490
Marriage: 2454
Marriage and Divorce: 1583
Marriage Before the Affair: 646, 660
Marriage Incomplete Sentences Test: 2381
Marriage Satisfaction: 1680
Martyr: 1452
Mascot: 479
Masculine Attributes: 68
Masculine-Aggressive Behavior: 2237
Masculine-Effeminoid: 1940
Masculine/Feminine: 1946
Masculine/Feminine Personal Pronoun: 2662
Masculinity: 298, 1222, 2776
Masculinity-Femininity: 66, 1698, 1706, 2835,
Masculinity/Femininity: 1158
Masculinity-Femininity (Mf): 1697
Masculinity-Femininity of Body: 795
Masonry: 1792
Master Developmental Profile: 2342
Master Machine Repair: 1793
Master-Servant: 1872
Mastery: 1904
Mastery-Competence: 912
Masturbation: 2454
Masturbation Guilt: 317
Masturbation History: 1433
Match Between Person and Technology: 1593
Matches Colors: 347
Matching: 1075, 1485, 2210
Matching Capital and Lower Case Letters: 2434
Matching Colors: 1653
Matching Figures: 1164
Matching Letter-Like Forms: 349, 837
Matching Numbers: 763

Matching Perception: 2044
Matching Pictures: 1164
Matching Tools and Operations: 1632
Matching V's: 1164
Matching-to-Sample Accuracy: 567
Matching-to-Sample Speed: 567
Matching-to-Sample Thruput: 567
Mate: 1494, 2109
Material: 1030
Material Evidence of Affection: 2291
Material Resources: 379
Material Well-Being: 2132
Materialistic: 2121
Materials: 2111, 2875
Materials Handling: 1792, 2177, 2829
Maternal Acceptance: 1987
Maternal Overindulgence: 1012
Maternal Overprotection: 1012
Math: 259, 340, 464, 592, 645, 684, 822, 1194, 1224, 1916, 2138, 2826
Math Ability: 180
Math Accuracy: 567
Math and Concepts: 341
Math Application: 2309
Math Calculation: 821, 822, 2309
Math Computation: 2560, 2735, 2737, 2738
Math Concepts: 1224, 1802
Math Concepts and Problem Solving: 2735
Math Grade Placement: 343
Math Knowledge: 180
Math Problem Solving: 822
Math Reasoning: 821
Math-Related School Subjects Self-Efficacy: 1602
Math Scale: 1972
Math-Science: 1177
Math/Science/Problem-Solving: 895
Math-Science Teacher: 398, 399
Math/Science Teacher: 380
Math Skills: 304, 661
Math Speed: 567
Math Test: 2655
Math Thruput: 567
Math Total: 2735
Math Vocabulary: 343
Mathematical: 2031, 2341
Mathematical Abilities: 2698
Mathematical Applications: 2383
Mathematical Attainment: 1103
Mathematical Calculations: 1460, 2035
Mathematical Capability: 1579
Mathematical Communication: 743
Mathematical Concepts and Operations: 800
Mathematical Content and Concepts: 743
Mathematical Language: 2383
Mathematical Problems: 797
Mathematical Reasoning: 743, 1044
Mathematical Sciences: 12
Mathematical Skills: 1260, 1350
Mathematical Structure: 1604
Mathematician: 398, 1790
Mathematics: 56, 121, 165, 192, 246, 248, 258, 304, 342, 348, 364, 380, 383, 384, 389, 398, 411, 492, 497, 500, 547, 559, 570, 585, 605, 615, 617, 618, 621, 657, 664, 665, 684, 741, 742, 750, 762, 821, 904, 905, 982, 992, 1044, 1094, 1119, 1124, 1202, 1237, 1274, 1279, 1318, 1334, 1386, 1418, 1459, 1657, 1718, 1738, 1759, 1763, 1790, 1790, 1838, 1902, 1997, 2000, 2026, 2090, 2091, 2137, 2241, 2309, 2358, 2484, 2488, 2530, 2560, 2613, 2654, 2666, 2678, 2735, 2740, 2742, 2774, 2901, 2903
Mathematics Achievement: 1249
Mathematics Advanced Skills: 1318
Mathematics and Reasoning: 1043
Mathematics and Science: 411
Mathematics Applications: 1386, 2483
Mathematics Aptitude Test: 1405
Mathematics Club: 411
Mathematics Composite: 1386
Mathematics Computation: 383, 384, 1318, 1386, 2293, 2463, 2483, 2654
Mathematics Concepts: 1318, 2234
Mathematics Concepts and Applications: 364, 383, 384, 665, 2463
Mathematics Concepts and Estimations: 1318
Mathematics Concepts and Operations: 886
Mathematics Inventory: 2005
Mathematics or Science: 411
Mathematics Pedagogy: 2026
Mathematics Perceptions: 120
Mathematics: Problem Solving: 165, 2484
Mathematics Problem Solving: 2234
Mathematics Problem Solving and Data Interpretation: 1318
Mathematics Problems: 1318
Mathematics: Procedures: 165, 2484
Mathematics: Proofs/Models/Problems: 2026
Mathematics Reading: 2861
Mathematics Reasoning: 2861, 2901
Mathematics Skills: 2234
Mathematics Task Self-Efficacy: 1602
Mathematics Teacher: 1790
Mathematics Usage: 1114, 1760
Mathematics Vocabulary: 2712
Maths: 160
Mating: 1721, 2318
Matrices: 349, 837, 1380, 2086, 2485
Matrix Analogies: 1379
Matrix Reasoning: 2859, 2860
Maturity: 1706, 2934
Maturity Fears: 893
Maximum Opportunities for Learning: 2314
Maze Tracing Speed Test: 1405
Mazes: 2212, 2792, 2860, 2862, 2864
Meal Planning and Preparation: 443

Meal Preparation: 212
Meal Time: 1220
Mealtime: 268
Mealtime Behaviors: 1041
Mean Distance: 563
Mean Distress: 1643
Mean Proficiency Score: 87
Meaning: 628
Meaning Cues: 1130
Meaningful Memory: 644
Meaningfulness: 946
Measurable: 2928
Measure: 195
Measurement: 33, 339, 342, 343, 348, 444, 492, 622, 684, 1353, 1392, 1605, 1759, 1921, 2383
Measurement Skills: 1247
Measurements: 62, 1604
Measures: 2089
Measures of Delayed Recall: 1378
Measuring Output: 2070
Mechanical: 183, 407, 412, 485, 905, 1044, 1074, 1100, 1157, 1279, 1312, 1413, 1483, 1711, 1793, 1817, 1818, 2152, 2255, 2257, 2643, 2836
Mechanical Ability: 644, 1717, 1786
Mechanical Activities: 618, 1790
Mechanical and Craft Technology: 1285
Mechanical and Fluid Power Maintenance: 1793
Mechanical Aptitude: 733, 2884
Mechanical Comprehension: 28, 180, 302, 902, 2641, 2642
Mechanical/Construction/Agriculture: 1350
Mechanical Crafts: 380
Mechanical/Craftsmanship Trades: 2822
Mechanical Engineering: 410
Mechanical Equilibrium: 178
Mechanical/Equipment Operation/Hand and Power Tools: 920
Mechanical Familiarity: 1634
Mechanical Familiarity Test: 973
Mechanical/Fixing: 398, 399, 1237
Mechanical Insight: 2774
Mechanical Interests: 2605
Mechanical Interrelationships: 2700
Mechanical Knowledge: 1633, 1635
Mechanical Knowledge Test: 973
Mechanical Maintenance: 924, 1537, 1637, 1793, 2644
Mechanical Maintenance/Tools/Shop Mechanics: 2067
Mechanical Orientation: 963
Mechanical Principles and Repair: 2151
Mechanical Reasoning: 395, 838, 839, 2000
Mechanical/Repairer/Machining: 179
Mechanical Skills: 2420
Mechanical-Technical: 618
Mechanical/Technical/Inventiveness: 895
Mechanical Technology: 1792
Mechanical Tools and Devices: 2700
Mechanical Understanding: 2019
Mechanics: 131, 199, 364, 665, 684, 752, 967, 1042, 1043, 2463, 2882, 2934
Mechanics and Repairers: 410
Mechanics/Industrial Trades: 2000
Media: 1818
Media Executive: 380
Medial Vowels/Diphthongs: 468
Medical: 653, 1237, 1374, 1818, 2255, 2257, 2391, 2834
Medical Assistant: 398, 399
Medical Assisting: 1794
Medical/Biological Sciences: 2000
Medical Care: 63
Medical Conditions: 1181
Medical-Dental: 1177
Medical Facts: 546
Medical History: 133, 484, 2047
Medical History/Health Status: 808
Medical History Inventory: 1052
Medical Illness and Treatment: 1517
Medical Illustrator: 1790
Medical Lab Technician: 398
Medical Laboratory: 905
Medical Laboratory Technician: 399
Medical Laboratory Technologies: 410
Medical Practice: 380
Medical Records Technician: 1790
Medical Researcher: 380
Medical Science: 398, 1790
Medical Sciences: 1285
Medical Self-Care: 2746
Medical Service: 398, 399, 618, 1222, 1334, 1790
Medical Services: 1841
Medical Technician: 618, 1790
Medical Technologist: 1790
Medication Management: 212
Medication Use: 1181
Medications: 63, 484
Medicine: 618
Medicine and Dentistry: 1044
Medium Risk: 1890
Meeting Effectiveness: 1913
Meeting the Child's Basic Needs: 1918
Meetings: 188
Meets Others' Expectations: 1296
Melancholy: 2649
Melodic Line: 199
Melody: 1752
Melody Recognition: 1751
Membership: 1823
Membership and Leadership: 1542
Memoria a Corto Plazo: 264
Memoria Diferida-Aprendizaje Visual Auditivo: 264
Memoria Diferida-Memoria para Nombres: 264
Memoria para Frases: 264
Memoria para Nombres: 264

Memoria para Palabras: 264
Memorization: 1044
Memory: 169, 265, 268, 338, 388, 446, 558, 565, 566, 776, 779, 800, 840, 884, 886, 1042, 1043, 1066, 1164, 1323, 1472, 1524, 1525, 1612, 1641, 1665, 1775, 1837, 190, 2059, 2236, 2250, 2373, 2376, 2387, 2441, 2518, 2677
Memory/Abstractions/Generalizations/Organization: 2035
Memory and Concentration: 690
Memory and Learning: 1771
Memory and Understanding: 2316
Memory Disorder: 562
Memory for Block Designs: 1378
Memory for Digits: 1370, 2375, 2485
Memory for Faces: 1771
Memory for Graphic Elements: 2297
Memory for Location: 2701
Memory for Names: 1771, 2901
Memory for Objects: 2485
Memory for Sentences: 2485, 2900, 2901, 2902
Memory for Stories: 2701
Memory for Words: 2901
Memory for Written/Verbal Instruction: 268
Memory Function: 158
Memory Functions: 1905, 1908
Memory Index: 2159, 2431
Memory of Figural Units: 2518
Memory of Symbolic Implications: 2518
Memory of Symbolic Systems-Auditory: 2518
Memory of Symbolic Systems-Visual: 2518
Memory of Symbolic Units-Auditory: 2518
Memory of Symbolic Units-Visual: 2518
Memory-Orientation: 748
Memory/Orientation: 1246
Memory Process: 1485
Memory Quotient: 2792
Memory/Recall: 1430
Memory Response Sequencing: 320
Memory Screen: 1485
Memory Skills: 359
Memory Span: 644, 1405, 1485, 1840
Men of Science: 1084
Men's Ideal Man: 1536
Menstruation: 2454
Mental: 270
Mental Ability: 537, 714, 1301, 1616
Mental Adaptability: 58
Mental Age Development: 778
Mental Alertness: 10, 58, 186, 1198, 1762, 2758
Mental and Emotional Health: 684
Mental Computation: 1392, 2678
Mental Control: 2863
Mental Dullness: 1698
Mental Dullness (D4): 1697
Mental Health: 1019, 1187, 1449, 1808, 1832, 2397
Mental Health Composite: 2158
Mental Health History: 1431, 1432
Mental Health/Human Services: 410
Mental Health/Social Service Needs: 1807
Mental Health-Illness Rating: 1093
Mental Ill Health: 1824
Mental Improvement: 136
Mental Processes: 2016
Mental Retardation: 2107
Mental Status: 176, 1378, 1649
Mental Toughness: 219, 1955
Mental Toughness vs. Sensitivity: 672, 673
Mentor: 1451
Mentoring: 556
Mentoring Style: 1652
Merchandise Procurement: 2713
Merchandising: 1790
Meta-Achievement: 1655
Meta-Humanistic: 1655
Metacognitive Self-Regulation: 1720
Metal Shop or Woodworking: 411
Metal Testing: 2066
Metals: 2832
Metalworking and Fabrication: 1794
Metalworking Occupations: 1792
Metaphoric: 2112
Metaphorical Language: 356
Meter: 1752
Meter Discrimination: 1751
Method of Evaluation: 1732
Method Used: 2080
Methodical Study: 1307
Methodology: 1966
Methods Dissonance Score: 2571
Metric Measurement: 831
Metrics: 343
Microcomputer Repair: 1792, 1794
Microeconomics: 108, 118, 2718
Microscopic and Submicroscopic Forms of Life: 684
The Middle Ages: 2932
Middle Manager: 2605
Middle of Road: 1563
Middle-of-the-Road Management: 1558, 1571
Middle School English Language Arts: 2026
Middle School Mathematics: 2026
Middle School Science: 2026
Middle School Social Studies: 2026
Middle Sound Different: 189
Middle Sounds: 1261
Military Activities: 618, 1790
Military Enlisted: 398
Military Enlisted Personnel: 1790
Military History: 1431, 2147
Military/Law Enforcement: 380
Military Leadership: 68
Military Officer: 380, 398, 1790
Mineralogy/Petrology and Geochemistry: 1116
Mini-Mental State Exam: 434

Minimal Encourager: 716
Minimal Pairs: 1534
Minimal Sound Pairs: 1420
Minimization of Symptoms: 2604
Minimizing Response Pattern Scales: 1729
Mining and Petroleum: 410
Minister: 1790
Minor Admissions of Dishonesty: 1976
Mirror Tracing: 2728
Miscellaneous: 1271, 1615, 1932, 2109, 2152, 2391, 2884
Miscellaneous Facts: 1076, 1084
Miscellaneous Facts and Scientists: 1082
Miscellaneous Principles: 616
Miscellaneous Psychopathology: 2305
Miscellaneous Services: 410
Mischievous: 1211
Misplacements: 303
Mispronunciations: 1073
Missing Article: 2240
Missing Lines: 2057
Missing Parts: 2375
Missing Premises: 2252
Mission: 1938
Mission Clarity: 379
Missionary: 1561, 2278
Mistrust: 1631, 2306
Mistrust-Trust: 1845
Mistrustful: 1243
Mixed Syllable Sequence: 2706
Mixture Spanish-English: 918
Mobile Equipment: 2769
Mobile Equipment and Rigging: 2867
Mobile Equipment Operation: 2643
Mobility: 686, 1066, 1472, 1482, 1718, 1906, 2181, 2767
Mobility and Travel: 443
Mobility Fears: 213
Mobility/Gross Motor: 1591
Mobility Skills: 1245
Modal Profile: 1717
Modals: 1427
Mode: 991
Mode of Expression Domain: 1478
Mode of Learning: 392
Model: 1896
Modeling: 1216, 1446
Modeling the Way: 1445, 1448, 2635
Modelling: 1551
A Modern America: 145
Modern Concepts: 2736
Modern Hebrew: 586, 606, 615
Modern Physics: 684
Modes: 1284
Modes of Control: 2399
Modes of Instruction: 391
Modest: 1822, 1954
Modesty: 1769, 2218
Modification: 1739
Modification Frequencies: 1906
Modified Premorbid Adjustment Scale: 650
Modified Six Elements: 295
Modifier: 727
Modifiers: 616
Modifying: 1688
Modulation of Anger: 2521
Molecular Biology and Genetics: 1109
Momentum: 178
Monetary: 62
Monetary Concern: 1163
Money: 356, 439, 831, 884, 1705, 1897, 1942, 2127, 2131, 2292, 2915
Money and Banking: 762
Money and Finance: 343, 344
Money and Value: 2299
Money/Banking and Insurance: 897
Money Concepts: 2215
Money Handling: 63
Money Management: 1065, 1409, 2204
Money Management and Shopping: 443
Money/Marketing: 268
Money Measurement: 730
Money-Work-The Future: 1716
Monitor Evaluator: 296
Monitoring: 197, 2424
Monitoring and Assessment: 843
Monitoring and Feedback: 2096
Monitoring and/or Controlling Equipment and/or Processes: 1343, 2925
Monitoring Executive Plans: 490
Monitoring Learning: 2495
Monitoring Personal Output: 490
Monitoring the Team's Work: 490
Monitors Student Progress: 1276
Monosyllabic: 769
Monosyllable Identification: 891
Monroe Visual I Test: 1085
Monroe Visual III Test: 1085
Monthly Global Assessment of Symptoms and Functioning: 1517
Mood: 425, 1889, 1961
Mood Disorders: 2519
Mood Episodes: 2519
Mood Symptoms: 2147
Moodiness/Emotional Lability: 2510
Moods and Management of Personal Life: 717
Moody-Uncooperative: 1457
Moral: 2022, 2652
Moral Development Stages: 1408
Moral Judgment: 2647
Moral Leadership: 1519
Moral Self-approval: 1735
Moral Sense: 1293, 1983
Moral Stage: 1625

Moral Support/Encouragement and Interest: 2291
Moral Type: 1625
Moral Values: 1694, 1695, 1701
Moral-Religious: 1010
Moral-Religious Emphasis: 480
Morale: 909
Moralism: 981
Morality: 2369
Morals and Religion: 1716
More Information Response: 633
Moro Reflex: 1668
Morphemes/Sentence Means: 1427
Morphemes Total: 1427
Morphine: 66
Morphine-Amphetamine: 66
Morpho-Syntax: 2172
Morphological and Syntactic Rules: 241
Morphology: 76, 2886
Morphology Competency: 1060
Mosaic: 2441
Mosaics: 2441
Most Overdone Strengths: 2013
Mother: 210, 810, 1011, 1049, 2825
Mother=Ally: 1006
Mother/Child Coalition: 1006
Mother-Child Relationship: 1297
Mother-Son: 1872
Mother=Stressor: 1006
Mother with Father/Father with Mother Past Tense (Best/Worst): 1298
Mother with Father/Father with Mother Present Tense (Best/Worst): 1298
Motivated/Unmotivated: 2069
Motivating: 197, 1554, 2424
Motivating Goals: 421
Motivation: 37, 242, 1074, 1089, 1455, 1456, 1470, 1545, 1681, 1721, 1968, 2265, 2355, 2356, 2495, 2614
Motivation Assessment of Parents and Children: 1052
Motivation/Compliance: 268
Motivation for Achievement: 37, 1655
Motivation for Change: 279
Motivation for Counseling: 1581
Motivation for Schooling: 2313
Motivation for the Job: 2348
Motivation for Treatment: 1587
Motivation in Mathematics: 1599
Motivation Scales: 1720
Motivation to Complete School Tasks: 1500
Motivational: 2295
Motivational Characteristics: 186, 217, 2622
Motivational Climate: 1913
Motivational Distortion Index: 2346
Motivational Drive: 2776
Motivational Factors: 989
Motivational Needs: 1966
Motivational Strategies: 1275
Motivational Values: 1022, 1704
Motivational Values Systems: 2507
Motor: 124, 266, 270, 661, 761, 800, 809, 810, 812, 815, 1039, 1086, 1139, 1323, 1391, 1490, 1610, 1612, 2376, 2387
Motor Ability: 1138, 1502, 2319
Motor Accuracy: 2377
Motor Behaviors: 315
Motor Control: 924
Motor Coordination: 1375, 1868, 2123, 2421, 2797, 2798, 2799
Motor Co-ordination and Loss of Balance: 1066
Motor Development: 315, 377, 1041, 1194
Motor Discoordination: 1850
Motor-Enhanced: 797, 798
Motor Functions: 1524, 1525
Motor Hyperactivity: 651
Motor Imitation: 2052
Motor Learning: 684
Motor Movements: 63
Motor Organization: 2767
Motor Planning: 1865, 2376
Motor-Reduced: 797, 798
Motor-Reduced Visual Perception: 816
Motor Retardation: 1733
Motor Sequential: 1907
Motor Skills: 1300, 1369, 1791, 2333, 2813
Motor Tempo: 563
Motor Tension-Excess: 2211
Motor Tics: 876
Motor Total: 265
Motor Writing: 1524, 1525
Motorcycle Mechanics: 1792, 1794
Motoric: 799
Motorically Complex Words: 2332
Motors: 920, 1537, 2643
Motors/Regulators/Electronic Equipment/Power Distribution: 923
Mouth/Throat/Nose: 1186
Movement: 63, 1061, 1169, 1214, 1265, 2869, 2926
Movement Around Environment: 2444
Movement of Limbs and Trunk: 1066
Movement of Simple and Complex Objects: 2884
Movement Patterning: 658
Movement Skills—Fine and Gross Motor: 882
Movements of the Extremities: 2543
Multi-Syllabic Words: 2175
Multi-Tasking: 2347
Multifunctional Work Task Unit: 922
Multilimb Coordination: 1044
Multiordinality: 320
Multiple Choice: 209, 591, 614, 2909
Multiple Choice Test: 2655
Multiple Contexts: 2727
Multiple Definitions: 2911
Multiple Directions: 565
Multiple Meanings: 1424

Multiplication: 730, 825, 831, 1392, 1738
Multiplication and Division of Whole Numbers: 171, 2486
Multiplication of Whole Numbers: 1604, 2486
Multiplicity: 847
Multiplying and Dividing Decimals: 1247
Multiplying and Dividing Fractions: 1247
Multiplying and Dividing Whole Numbers: 1247
Multiprocess Reasoning: Analysis: 2297
Multiprocess Reasoning: Task Insight: 2297
Muscle Control: 265
Muscular Bracing: 267
Muscular Discomfort: 291
Muscular System: 2508
Muscular Tension and Anxiety: 1963
Music: 199, 618, 905, 1120, 1124, 1177, 1841, 2882
Music: Analysis: 2026
Music and Movement: 1204
Music and Singing: 2052
Music and Theater: 635
Music Aptitude: 90
Music: Concepts and Processes: 2026
Music: Content Knowledge: 2026
Music/Dramatics: 1790
Music Education: 2026
Music Literacy: 1320
Music Notation: 684
Music or Art: 411
Music/Rhythm: 1194
Music Theory: 109, 118
Musical: 895, 1074, 1222, 1395, 1413, 1667, 2255, 2257, 2295
Musical Aptitude: 1753
Musical/Dramatic: 5
Musical Instrument Repair: 398, 399
Musical Sensitivity: 1752
Musical Style: 1751
Musician: 380, 398, 399, 1310, 1790
Mutilation: 847
My Department: 1398
My Organization: 1398
My Rating: 1147
My Work Group: 1398
Mystery Codes: 1378

Naivete: 1698
Naivete (Pa3): 1697
Name: 1224
Name and Number Checking: 2302
Name Checking: 31
Name Comparison: 1693
Name Finding: 1180
Name Printing: 813
Name Writing: 1164
Names and Sounds of the Alphabet: 1765
Names-Faces: 1644
Names for Stories: 726
Naming: 159, 199, 338, 558, 2873
Naming Body Parts: 987
Naming Capital Letters: 1073, 2254
Naming Common Objects: 2249
Naming Lower Case Letters: 861, 2254
Naming Lower-Case Letters: 1073
Naming Numbers: 254
Naming Objects: 277
Naming Pictures: 2297
Naming Speed: 1980
Naming Vocabulary: 349, 837
Nap Time: 1220
Narcism: 2318
Narcism-Comfort: 1721
Narcissistic: 690, 1687, 1961, 2306, 2520
Narcissistic Love-Object/Anaclitic Love-Object: 317
Narcotics-Drugs: 2108
Narrative: 1759, 2171, 2489
Narrative Memory: 1771
Narrative Text: 1094
Narrative Writing: 199, 1094
Narrow/Focused: 226
Nasals: 214
National: 1271
National Affairs: 749, 1785
National Sciences Reading: 1760
Natural: 1157
Natural Leading: 2751
Natural Science: 618
Natural Sciences: 12, 386, 497, 501, 617, 780, 1846
Natural Sciences and History: 497
Nature: 162, 412, 1789, 1790, 1817, 1929
Nature-Agriculture: 1334
Nature of Man: 1939
Nature/Outdoors: 398, 399, 1237
Navy Enlisted: 399
Near-Point Copying: 786
Near Point Vision: 1614
Near Vision: 1044, 2224
Nearness: 2237
Nearpoint: 2852
Neatness: 329, 1964
Necessary Arithmetic Operations Test: 1405
Necessitating: 2513
Need: 2237
Need for Achievement: 945, 2380
Need for Affection: 1698
Need for Affection (Hy2): 1697
Need for Attention: 865
Need for Career Information: 409
Need for Control: 226, 1655
Need for Diversion: 865
Need for Freedom: 865
Need for Mental Challenge: 2346
Need for Precision: 865
Need for Psychiatric Referral: 1932
Need for Routine: 562

Need for Self-Knowledge: 409
Need for Stability: 2346
Need for Status: 2346
Need for Structure: 2346
Need Privacy: 963
Need Satisfaction: 2052
Needs: 1842
Needs Analysis/Assessment/and Planning: 638
Needs and Preferences: 2052
Needs Mobility: 1470, 2069
Needs Recognition: 2136
Needs-Persistence: 2248
Negation: 1739
Negations: 2233
Negative: 234, 1013, 2001, 2337, 2662, 2728
Negative Affect: 467, 1647, 1960
Negative Affect/General Distress: 1288
Negative Assertive: 2399
Negative Bias: 2882
Negative Child: 1966
Negative Communication: 1705
Negative Emotions: 2074
Negative Feelings: 1161
Negative Health Habits: 1733
Negative Home Environment: 1181
Negative Impression: 1688, 1959
Negative Influence Tactic Frequency: 2580
Negative Interaction: 2052, 2607
Negative Life Change Events: 1181
Negative Life Events: 1495, 1496
Negative Mood: 2512
Negative Mood Scale: 291
Negative Narrative Comments: 2311
Negative Operational: 467
Negative or No Resolution: 1006
Negative Parent: 1966
Negative Peer Relationships: 1025
Negative Preoperational: 467
Negative Program Response: 490
Negative Relationships: 1959
Negative Score Total: 791
Negative Self-Evaluations: 2559
Negative Self-Image: 1931, 1932
Negative Sense of Control: 2399
Negative Situations: 1305
Negative-Social: 224
Negative Social Exchange: 1733
Negative Syndrome: 2017
Negative Temperament: 2306
Negative Total: 1012
Negative Treatment Indicators: 1698
Negative Treatment Indicators (TRT): 1697
Negative Why Questions: 2710
Negative Yielding: 2399
Negatives: 430, 1427, 1898
Neglect: 442, 2521
Neglect/Abandonment: 1006
Negotiating: 1479, 1480
Negotiating/Searching: 401
Negotiating Skills: 490
Negotiation: 1044
Neighborhood: 2131
Neighborhood Observation Behavior Map: 877
Neither X nor Y: 2662
Neologisms: 2290
Neologistic: 199
Nervous Symptoms: 374
Nervous vs. Composed: 2618
Nervous-Obsessive: 451
Nervousness: 1223, 1293, 1983
Nervousness-Calmness: 1964
Net Speed: 1692
Net Strategy: 2877
Network Contacts: 1181
Networking: 197, 2424
Neurological: 434, 1186
Neurological Examination: 1907, 1909
Neuromaturation: 1907
Neuromuscular Intervention: General: 310
Neuromuscular Intervention: Specific: 310
Neuropsychiatric: 2869
Neuropsychological Battery: 434
Neuropsychological Dysfunction: 690, 869
Neuropsychological Impairment: 456
Neuropsychological Symptom Checklist: 1777
Neuropsychology Battery Status: 434
Neurotic: 1341
Neurotic Behavior: 1522
Neurotic Childhood: 748
Neurotic Sensitivity vs. Psychopathic Toughness: 66
Neuroticism: 538, 998, 1146, 1367, 1628, 1779, 2218
Neuroticism or Emotionality: 999
Neutral: 2001, 2647
Neutral Percentage Estimate: 1172
Neutral Syllogisms: 979
New Elements: 2659
New Inventions: 2878
New Pup: 305
New Role Clarity: 2570
New Situation and People: 2834
Newborn Infant Problems: 158
Newcomer Support: 490
News Source: 1364
News Style: 1364
News Values: 1364
Newscast: 84
Newspaper Reporter: 398, 399
Newspaper Writing: 411
Next Career Steps: 2364
Night Vision: 1044
Nightmares and Night Terrors: 213
9/1: 1572
9/1 Win-Lose: 675, 676
9/9: 1572

9/9 Synergistic: 675, 676
Nines-Accepters/Receptionists/Reconcilers: 958
No Code: 2607
No Opinion: 2198
No Response: 234
Nobody: 1011
Nocturnal Waking: 2216
Noise Level: 1470
Nomenclature: 862
Nominals: 1739
Non-Academic: 2358
Nonacademic School Roles: 61
Nonadaptive: 467
Nonadaptive Problem-Solving: 467
Nonadaptive Thematic: 467
Nonauthoritarian Attitude: 909
Non-authority Relationships: 807
Noncommunicative: 234
Noncompliance: 1963
Non-Conforming: 86
Nondevelopmental Phonological Processes: 1394
Nondirected: 2530
Nondominant Hand: 1993
Non-dominant Hand: 2009
Non-Kitchen Objects: 2884
Non-Lifting: 1478
Nonlocomotor: 1901
Non-Marital Intercourse: 659
Nonoccupational: 399
Nonperseverative Errors: 2892
Non-Play: 2001
Nonpreferred Grip: 1164
Non-Preferred Hand: 1911
Non-reiterative Processing: 1307
Non-Sedentary: 1478
Non-Self-Directed: 2759
Nonsense per T-Unit: 2661
Nonsense Syllogisms Test: 1405
Nonsense Words: 835
Nonsupport: 1959
Nonsymbolic Quotient: 2792
Non-TM Disorder: 2766
Non-Transactional Leadership: 1737
Nonverbal: 560, 561, 798, 799, 904, 918, 1171, 1632, 1866, 2123, 2162, 2220, 2221, 2222, 2375, 2701, 2741,
Non-Verbal: 385, 463, 1414, 1673, 1827
Nonverbal Ability: 837
Nonverbal Ability Index: 1756
Nonverbal Behavior: 1417
Nonverbal Communication: 459
Non Verbal Concept: 2236
Non-Verbal Conceptualization: 757
Nonverbal Expressive Skills: 2298
Nonverbal Intelligence: 1152
Nonverbal Intelligence Quotient: 662, 1168
Non-Verbal Language: 2628
Nonverbal Matrices: 763
Nonverbal Memory Index: 2701
Nonverbal Noises: 987
Nonverbal Oral Functions: 2706
Nonverbal Reasoning: 2309
Non-Verbal Reasoning: 2605
Nonverbal Reasoning Ability: 837
Nonverbal Receptive Skills: 2298
Nonverbal Sequence: 2596
Nonverbal Subtest Response Style: 2802
Non-Verbal Symbolic Function: 235
Nonverbal Visual Closure: 663
Nonverbal Visual Reasoning/Memory: 663
Nonviolence Scale: 1972
Non-Word Reading: 1980
Nonwork Goals: 421
Norm Questioning/Norm Favoring: 372
Normal: 701, 785
Normal Color Vision: 1159
Normal Irritability: 1522
Norms and Social Values: 1918
Not Coping: 72
Not Only X But Also Y: 2662
Not Otherwise Specified: 2520
Not Recommended: 2198
Noting Details: 1203
Noun: 2662
Noun Definition: 1534
Noun Modifiers: 1127
Noun Phrase: 1427
Noun Phrase Constituents: 1427
Noun Phrase + Copula + N/Adj: 1427
Noun Phrase + Verb Phrase + [Noun Phrase]: 1427
Noun Plurals: 430
Nouns: 430, 1125, 2487
Novelty-Loving: 1223
NPF: 1323
NPF (emotional stability): 1568
Nuclear: 1004
Nuclear Chemistry: 684
Number: 33, 195, 348, 622, 674, 883, 884, 892, 1405, 2041, 2089, 2711, 2882
Number Ability: 670
Number Addition: 2304
Number and Quantity: 1370
Number Attempted-Speed: 2877
Number Checking: 31, 533
Number Circled-Boldness: 2877
Number Comparison: 1693
Number Comparison Test: 1405
Number Comparisons: 173, 174
Number Concepts: 63, 347, 369, 1357, 1707, 2049, 2134
Number Concepts and Operations: 684
Number Correct Changes: 563
Number Correct Shapes Marked: 563
Number Counting: 813

Number Counting and Perception: 1920
Number Detection: 763
Number Facility: 1044
Number Facts: 343
Number Identification: 1224, 1534
Number Knowledge: 565, 2320
Number Naming: 813
Number/Notation: 2383
Number of Adjectives Checked: 68
Number of Categories Completed: 2892
Number of Close Relationships: 1181
Number of Correct Answers: 1272
Number of Correct Comprehensive Questions: 1272
Number of Correct Responses Obtained with Left Hand: 671
Number of Correct Responses Obtained with Right Hand: 671
Number of Decoding Errors: 1272
Number of Drops: 1135
Number of Favorable Adjectives: 68
Number of Items Checked: 1291
Number of Misarticulations: 2866
Number of Problems Experienced: 1947
Number of Sales: 421
Number of Stressful Events: 1733
Number of Symptoms Endorsed: 2018
Number of Trials Administered: 2892
Number of Unfavorable Adjectives: 68
Number of Words Known: 917
Number of Words Pronounced: 917
Number Operations: 82, 444
Number Perception: 1180
Number Problems: 2375
Number Recall: 1379, 1384
Number Right-Accuracy: 2877
Number Scanning: 1430
Number Screening: 2134
Number Series: 119, 1840, 1873, 2087, 2485
Number Series Completion: 1180
Number Skills: 349, 359, 1066, 1385, 2134
Number Systems and Numeration: 2486
Number Unlocked: 1098
Number Use: 813
Number Writing: 1224
Numbers: 343, 399, 453, 476, 1323, 2127, 2428, 2787
Numbers and Computation: 339
Numbers and Numerals: 730
Numbers and Operations: 1759
Numbers and Time: 1, 2
Numbers/Counting: 331
Numbers/Letters and Words: 1385
Numbers Reversed: 2901
Numeracy: 33, 1826
Numeral Comprehension: 346
Numerals: 987
Numerals in Sequence: 346
Numeration: 325, 1392
Numeric: 391, 392
Numeric Ability: 2345
Numerical: 126, 169, 412, 1078, 1106, 1222, 1370, 1692, 1789, 1819, 1827, 1841, 2121, 2797, 2798, 2799, 2871
Numerical Ability: 186, 395, 644, 839, 937, 960, 961
Numerical Aptitude: 1816
Numerical Awareness: 1712
Numerical Calculation: 1837
Numerical Checking: 1712
Numerical Comprehension: 1973
Numerical Computation: 168, 239, 964, 2019, 2641, 2642
Numerical Concepts: 1065
Numerical Conceptualization: 757
Numerical Critical Reasoning: 119, 1544, 2087
Numerical Estimation: 236, 1712, 1837, 2641
Numerical Fluency: 2373
Numerical/Mathematical: 5
Numerical Memory: 1613
Numerical Operations: 180, 1156, 2861
Numerical Plus Diagrammatic: 129
Numcrical Rcasoning: 168, 239, 356, 838, 937, 1088, 1711, 1973, 2019, 2642
Numerical Skills: 418, 1568, 1836, 2277, 2302, 2374
Numerical Terms: 918
Numerical Test: 736
Numerosity of the Beta Cells: 1242
Numerosity of White Blood Cells: 1242
Nurse: 2825
Nurse Aide: 398, 399
Nurse LPN: 1790
Nurse/LPN: 398
Nurse-Rating Forms: 2368
Nurse-Rating Scale/Patient: 2366
Nurse-Rating Scale/Professionals: 2366
Nurse-Rating Scale/Students: 2366
Nurse RN: 1790
Nurse/RN: 398
Nursing: 618, 905
Nursing Administrator: 380
Nursing and Related Services: 410
Nursing Assisting: 1794
Nursing Care: 63
Nursing Home Administrator: 1790
Nursing Service: 1222
Nursing Status: 2388
Nurturance: 68, 908, 1146, 1289, 1930, 1965, 1988
Nurturant: 1243, 1294
Nurturing: 1688, 1880
Nurturing Parent: 68
Nut and Bolt: 1919
Nutrition: 684, 1019, 1499, 1853, 1913, 2747
Nutrition and Exercise: 2074
Nutritional and Swallowing Status: 2472
Nutritional Assessment: 2511
Nutritional Habits and Awareness/Total: 2789

Nutritional Status: 870
Nystagmus: 1614

O Rings: 2054
Obedient vs. Dominant: 477, 888
Obeying Simple Commands: 1653
Object Assembly: 1731, 2840, 2860, 2862, 2864
Object-Completion: 753
Object Constancy: 1513
Object Control Skills: 2689
Object Identification: 987, 1513
Object Learning Test: 1390
Object Matching: 2240
Object Memory: 2792
Object Nouns: 1127
Object-Number Test: 1405
Object Pronoun: 2337
Object Recall: 2701
Object Recognition: 332, 1308
Object Relations: 297, 912
Object Rotation: 2304
Object Use: 459
Objectivity: 654, 1158, 1660, 1930, 1955
Obliging: 2149
Oboe/English Horn/Bassoon: 1280
Obscene Call: 1744
Observant: 2274
Observation Ability: 1813
Observation/Experimental Design: 570
Observation for Injury: 63
Observational: 41
Observational Ability: 734
Observations: 164
Observations at School: 1884
Observe Trainees Completing the Task Together: 2923
Observe Trainees Working: 2923
Observed Exposure: 755
Observed Feedback: 755
Obsessed: 136
Obsessionality: 739
Obsessions: 876
Obsessions-Compulsions: 2109
Obsessive: 701
Obsessive Compulsive: 690, 2326
Obsessive-Compulsive: 77, 335, 337, 748, 792, 1959, 1961, 2306, 2520, 2602, 2603, 2615
Obsessive Compulsive Disorder: 642
Obsessive-Compulsive Disorder: 77, 2107
Obsessive-Compulsive Symptoms: 2216, 2604
Obsessive Personality: 1313
Obsessive-Guilt-Phobic: 748
Obsessiveness: 1698
Obsessiveness (OBS): 1697
Obstacle-Dominance: 2248
Obstacles: 807
Obtaining a Followership: 1440
Obvious Attributes: 2553
Obvious Conflict: 1006
Occupation: 200, 1088
Occupation/College Variation: 401
Occupational: 1030, 1499, 1943
Occupational Check List: 1943
Occupational Exploration: 1617
Occupational Extroversion-Introversion: 399
Occupational History/Financial Status: 2147
Occupational Information: 403, 413, 1754
Occupational Interest: 1350
Occupational Plans After High School: 57
Occupational Preparation: 57
Occupational Relations: 2132
Occupational Roles Questionnaire: 1825
Occupational Scales: 380, 399, 1984
Occupational Skills: 60
Occupational Strengths: 1984
Occupational Stress Assessment: 2511
Occupational Therapist: 398, 1790
Occupational Therapist Assistant: 399
Occupational Values: 1943
Occupational Wellness: 2746, 2747
Occupations: 1306. 1346, 1790
Ocean Shores and Floors: 684
Ocean Structure: 684
Ocular Alignment/Motility: 1614
Ocular Function: 1614
Ocular-Motor Control: 2715
Odd Movements: 847
Oedipal: 1005
Oedipal Intensity: 317
Office Arithmetic: 534, 1833, 2153, 2408
Office Arithmetic Test: 973
Office Assisting: 1794
Office Checking: 534
Office Equipment: 1818
Office Helper or Assistant: 411
Office Operations: 1177
Office Practices: 380, 398, 399, 1237
Office Services: 1790
Office Supervision and Management: 410
Office Technology: 2026
Office Terms: 1323
Office Visits: 1733
Office Vocabulary: 534
Office Work: 1334, 2882
Officer Control: 1670
Officer Support: 1670
Offspring: 1494
OK Alone: 1705
Olfactory: 2376
Omission: 641, 2720
Omissions: 303, 430, 679, 1073, 2469, 2647
On the Job: 2148
On-Task Behavior: 451, 2444
On-the-Job Social Skills: 2827
One Foot Balance: 977

One-Hand Turning and Placing: 1700
One-on-One Oral Communication: 1480
One-on-One Training: 1479, 1480
One-Order Selling: 1222
One-to-One: 268
1/1: 1572
1/1 Lose-Leave: 675, 676
1/9: 1572
1/9 Yield-Lose: 675, 676
Ones-Perfecters/Quality Performers/Stabilizers: 958
Onlooker: 2001
Onomatopoeia and Images: 2755
Open Communication: 2632
Open Family Communication: 1877
Open Question: 716
Open Syllable Writing: 2180
Open System: 1006
Open to Change vs. Traditional: 2417
Open-Ended Comments: 158
Open-Minded: 990
Open-Mindedness: 367
Opening Doors: 1651
Openness: 401, 1233, 1823, 1912, 2218, 2631
Openness & Trust: 2773
Openness/Honesty and Flexibility: 1417
Openness to Change: 538, 1576
Openness to Experience: 1044, 1769
Openness to Feedback: 1830
Operating Keyboard and Office Equipment: 1343, 2925
Operating Room Technician: 398, 399
Operating Vehicles: 1343, 2925
Operational: 436, 1819
Operational Management and Computer Technology: 684
Operational Results: 490
Operations: 342, 1392
Operations with Decimals and Percents: 2486
Operations with Fractions and Mixed Numbers: 2486
Opiate Withdrawal: 66
Opiates: 1931
Opinions About Children: 1887
Opinions About College: 620
Opinions About Marriage and Having Children: 1887
Opportunistic: 1333
Opportunities: 2274
Opportunities for Advancement: 648
Opportunities for Promotion: 1348
Opportunity for Growth: 490
Opportunity to Learn: 1867
Opposite Sex Peer Relations: 2358
Opposites: 2434
Opposites Test: 1405
Opposition of Thumb and Fingers: 1653
Oppositional: 681, 1150, 1498, 1685, 1862
Oppositional Behavior: 65
Oppositional-Conduct Disorders: 651
Oppositional-Cooperative: 2446
Oppositional Defiant: 69, 79, 282
Oppositional Defiant Disorder: 876
Oppositional-Defiant Disorder: 77
Optician: 1790
Optimal: 797
Optimal Composite: 798
Optimism: 243, 2385
Optimistic: 381, 1676, 1822
Optional Questions: 57
Optional scales: 1524
Optometrist: 1790
Oral: 645, 1145, 1169, 1195, 2688, 2705
Oral and Nasal Hygiene: 1194
Oral Commands: 1060
Oral Communication: 1479, 1923
Oral Communication and Telephone Skill: 343
Oral Composite: 1847
Oral Comprehension: 1044, 2503, 2900
Oral Control: 870
Oral Defense: 1044
Oral Directions: 1353, 1836
Oral Encoding: 2426
Oral Eroticism: 317
Oral Expression: 1044, 1534, 1847, 2816, 2861
Oral Expression: Recreating Speech Acts: 2693
Oral Expressive: 1476, 1478, 1741
Oral Expressiveness: 1475
Oral Fact Finding: 1044
Oral-Gestural Expression: 328
Oral Instructions: 2302
Oral Interview Section: 250
Oral Language: 892, 1336, 2901, 2902, 2904
Oral Language Aptitude: 2901
Oral Language Concepts: 1072
Oral Miscues: 1051
Oral Motor Exam: 164
Oral Motor Examination: 276
Oral-Motor Movement: 2332
Oral Paragraphs: 987
Oral-Peripheral: 2471
Oral-Pharyngeal Dysphagia Symptoms Assessment: 276
Oral Praxis: 2377
Oral Proficiency: 308
Oral Reading: 199, 339, 342, 343, 823, 861, 916, 917, 1272, 1529, 1532, 2433, 2462
Oral Reading Achievement: 2281
Oral Reading and Comprehension: 1802
Oral Reading of Words and Sentences: 356
Oral Reading Quotient: 1131
Oral Reading: Sentences: 2172
Oral Reading: Words: 2172
Oral Sadism: 317
Oral Sentence Reading: 199
Oral Spelling: 1740
Oral State: 276, 870
Oral Vocabulary: 309, 2695, 2900, 2901, 2902

Order: 68, 908, 1163, 1769, 1930, 1965, 1988, 2218
Order and Organization: 495, 637, 710, 1141, 1670, 2793, 2850
Order of Recall: 685
Ordering: 2134
Orderliness: 2588
Orderliness and Responsibility: 2614
Orderliness v. Flexibility: 417
Orderliness vs. Lack of Compulsion: 672, 673
Orderly: 1294
Orderly Work Planning: 490
Ordinality: 2383
Organic: 42
Organic Brain Syndrome: 642, 2107
Organic Chemistry: 52, 684, 780, 1846
Organic Dysfunction-Medical: 1853
Organic Dysfunction-Psychological: 1853
Organic Factors Index: 1226
Organic Reaction: 927
Organicity: 748, 2245
Organisational Ability: 2007
Organisational Design and Structure: 1824
Organisational Forces: 1824
Organisational Processes: 1824
Organisational Structure and Climate: 1824
Organising People: 1551
Organising Things: 1551
Organismal Biology: 1110
Organization: 197, 329, 391, 392, 480, 619, 744, 775, 967, 962, 1010, 1098, 1216, 1333, 1720, 1743, 1997, 2250, 2251, 2297, 2804, 2833
Organization and Format: 2352
Organization Awareness: 490
Organization Climate: 490, 2587
Organization/Coherence: 2933
Organization Identification: 2420
Organization of Effort and Problem Solving: 2675
Organization of Ideas: 348
Organization of Information: 2249
Organization of Language: 494
Organization of the Library: 684
Organization of Time and Materials: 268
Organization of Work: 2587
Organization Skills: 781
Organization Stretch: 490
Organization Structure: 801, 1855
Organization's Complaint Philosophy: 640
Organizational: 5, 1030
Organizational and Job Structure: 1463
Organizational Awareness: 1267, 1573
Organizational Behavior: 762, 1542
Organizational Climate: 2435
Organizational Commitment: 2585
Organizational Congruence: 2585
Organizational Culture: 1276, 1924
Organizational Customer Focus: 2129
Organizational Encouragement of Creativity: 1393
Organizational Impediments: 1393
Organizational Leadership: 1438
Organizational Management: 1790
Organizational Performance: 1913
Organizational Planning: 382
Organizational Practices/Management Control: 1080
Organizational Profile: 1398
Organizational Results: 975
Organizational Role and Work-Setting Patterns: 2419
Organizational Sensitivity: 490
Organizational Strategies: 1657
Organizational Stress Factors: 1913
Organizational Stretch: 490
Organizational Support: 379
Organizational Traits: 1930
Organizational Work Style: 313
Organized: 381, 618, 2536
Organized Play: 2444
Organizing: 380, 1550, 1954, 2571, 1695
Organizing and Activating to Work: 351
Organizing Content Knowledge for Student Learning: 2026
Organizing Information: 1623
Orientation: 413, 558, 1513, 1907, 1938, 2123, 2250, 2297, 2327, 2428, 2761
Orientation and Memory Screen: 73
Orientation/Attention: 338
Orientation for Place: 1513
Orientation for Time: 1513
Orientation of Piece to Recess: 911
Orientation Scales: 380
Orientation to Customers: 2585
Orientation to Employees: 2585
Orientation to Environment: 2249, 2251
Orientation to Factual Memory: 356
Orientation to People: 1579
Orientation to Person/Place/Time: 356
Orientation to Science: 1492
Orientation to Stakeholders: 2585
Orientation to the 16PF Questionnaire: 2419
Orientation Toward Rules and Risk/Impulse Control: 226
Orientational Aids: 1743
Original: 381, 1169
Original Thinking: 1101
Original Writing: 2676
Originality: 644, 682, 724, 1044, 1161, 1162, 1576, 2037, 2754, 2771
Origins: 1494
Ornamentation Test: 1405
Oromotor Sequences: 1771
Orthodontist/Prosthetist: 399
Orthographic Punctuation: 2691
Orthopedic: 1186
Orthotist/Prosthetist: 398
Other: 328, 1061, 1550, 2575
Other Adult/Child Coalition: 1006

Other=Ally: 1006
Other Conflict: 1006
Other Considerations: 2395
Other Current or Past Potential Adult Problems/Stressors: 2147
Other Disorders/Delays: 2147
Other Everyday Objects: 2884
Other Impulse-Related Problems: 1932
Other Information: 2071
Other Job Characteristics: 2016
Other Life Areas: 184
Other Linguistic Structures: 918
Other Minor Neurological Signs: 1907
Other/Mixed: 2554
Other Opioids: 2554
Other Orientation: 2424
Other Physical Findings: 1907
Other Potential Developmental Problems/Stressors: 2147
Other Problems: 646, 660
Other=Stressor: 1006
Other Students: 2875
Others: 1149, 1163, 2404, 2487
Others Finding Out: 646, 660
Others' Perceptions: 2368
Others' Perceptions of Student Self: 2368
Our School Garden: 2611
Out of School/Class Activities: 1921
Out-of-School Referrals: 2311
Outcome: 2614
Outcome Confidence: 2535
Outcomes: 2435
Outcomes of Leadership Styles: 1737
Outdoor: 395, 414, 415, 417, 702, 1074, 1100, 1413, 1541, 2255, 2257, 2264, 2833, 2882
Outdoor-Agribusiness: 416
Outdoor-Nature: 416
Outdoor Play: 452
Outdoors: 406, 618, 1478
Outdoors-Oriented: 618
Outgoing: 1253, 1273, 1443, 1688, 1822, 2385
Outgoing Feelings: 1012
Outlook: 158
Outside Play: 1220
Outside Relationships: 2292
Outside Selling: 1222
Over the Counter Medication: 1733
Overactive: 2514
Overactivity: 69
Overall: 489, 2834
Overall Adjustment: 2776
Overall Competence: 2287
Overall Course Evaluation: 974
Overall CPQ Score: 555
Overall Creative Potential: 728
Overall Desire for Control: 2399
Overall Dimensions: 2016
Overall Effectiveness: 490
Overall Employee Score : 555
Overall Health: 1733
Overall HPW Rating: 801
Overall Influence Assessment: 2580
Overall Instructional Competency: 203
Overall Leadership Effectiveness: 1519
Overall Leadership Style: 1546
Overall Life Enjoyment and Satisfaction: 2130
Overall Measures of Teaching Effectiveness: 1236
Overall "Needs": 1766
Overall Performance: 2096
Overall Prognostic Score: 2504
Overall Quality of Life: 2131
Overall Rating: 2195
Overall Rating Index: 431
Overall Regularity of the Positive Image: 1242
Overall Relationship: 140
Overall Satisfaction: 490
Overall Satisfaction Index: 382
Overall Score of Core Subtests: 2172
Overall Sense of Control: 2399
Overall Severity of Illness: 2108
Overall Skill Level: 258
Overall Strength of Imagery: 1242
Overall Stress Factor: 1949
Overall Writing: 2731
Overcoming Obstacles: 401
Overcontrolled Hostility (O-H): 1697
Overdependence: 300
Overhand Throwing: 2455
Overlapping Figures: 445, 1513
Overload Stressor Pattern: 1809
Overly Specified Symptoms: 2522
Overly Virtuous Self-Views: 362
Overnight Hospital Treatment: 1733
Overprotection: 1779
Overt Anxiety: 1321
Oxidation Reduction and Electrochemistry: 684

P Affiliation: 1215
P Aggression-External: 1215
P Aggression-Home: 1215
P Aggression-Total: 1215
P-Area: 840
P Change: 1215
P (principled moral thinking) score: 771
P (Professional): 1843
P(ress) Achievement: 1215
P Separation: 1215
P Sociability: 1215
P Socioeconomic Status: 1215
P Supervision: 1215
Pacesetting: 1560, 1575
Pacing: 1867
Pacing Activity: 1273
Pain: 1647, 1853, 2158

Pain Beliefs Scale: 291
Pain Complaints: 267
Pain Coping Interview-Research Edition: 1870
Pain Exacerbation: 291
Pain Experience Scale: 1870
Pain History and Status Interview: 1870
Pain Imagery Interview: 1870
Pain Report: 2766
Pain Treatment Responsivity: 1686
Painful Tension: 78
Painter: 398, 399
Painting: 1990
Painting and Decorating: 1792, 1794
Paired Associate Decrement: 320
Paired Associate Index: 320
Paired Associate Learning: 320
Paired Associate Learning Test: 378
Paired Associates: 2909
Paired Recall: 2701
Paired Words Acquisition: 2159
Paired Words Recall: 2159
Palabras Incompletas: 264
Palatal Fronting: 1394
Palate: 162, 1056, 1929
Palliative: 700
Palm Form Recognition: 2141
Palpation Pain: 2766
Panic Disorder: 77, 642, 2107
Panic Disorder Without and With Agoraphobia: 2604
Pantomime: 1064
Paper and Pencil Skills: 1707
Paper and Pencil Test: 1085
Paper Folding: 239, 1485, 2439
Paper Folding and Cutting: 2485
Paper Folding Test: 1405
Paper Form Boards: 2212
Paragraph Comprehension: 180, 2178
Paragraph Construction: 1534
Paragraph-Factual: 2172
Paragraph-Inferential: 2172
Paragraph Learning: 1454
Paragraph Meaning: 348, 2183
Paragraph-Picture: 2172
Paragraph Reading: 2712
Paragraph Recall: 2296
Paragraph Response: 1425
Paragraph Understanding: 1138, 1139
Paragraphing: 1364
Paragraphs: 2373
Paragraphs with Questions: 2487
Paralegal: 1790
Paralinguistic: 1284
Parallel: 2001
Parallel Items Scale: 1744
Parallel Play: 2607
Paranoia: 538, 1488, 1698, 1959, 2006, 2367
Paranoia (Pa): 1697
Paranoia Scale: 2457
Paranoid: 77, 690, 1687, 1961, 2306, 2520
Paranoid Belligerence: 2017
Paranoid Ideation: 335, 337, 792, 2326, 2602, 2603, 2615
Paranoid-Naive: 218
Paranoid Personality: 2615
Paranoid Projection: 2120
Paranoid Schizophrenia: 2615
Paranoid Symptoms: 2216
Paraphasia: 199
Paraphasia in Running Speech: 199
Paraphilias Scales: 1744
Paraprofessional Management: 684
Parasympathetic Nervous System: 2508
Parent: 2109, 2280
Parent & Community-School Relationships: 648
Parent Assessment of Fluency Digest: 691
Parent Behaviors: 864
Parent-Child Conflict: 1963
Parent-Child Friction-Harmony: 1005
Parent-Child Goodness of Fit Observation Form and Checklist: 2791
Parent-Child Interactions: 1007
Parent-Child Relations: 2132
Parent/Community Involvement: 909, 2314
Parent Domain: 1889, 2510
Parent Figure Motivated: 1470
Parent Interview Form: 2791
Parent Involvement: 216, 452, 648, 843
Parent Maladjustment: 1963
Parent Participation: 1275
Parent Questionnaires: 158
Parent Rating Scale: 286
Parent Relations: 2358
Parent Relationships: 2369
Parent Responses to Deviant Child Behaviors: 864
Parent Satisfaction Survey: 649
Parent/School/Community Relations: 1885
Parent Subsystem: 1565
Parent/Teacher: 1039
Parental Attitude: 2380
Parental Concerns: 1791
Parental Custody Index: 41
Parental Education: 909
Parental Health: 1889
Parental/Home-Related Self-Esteem: 746
Parental Involvement: 1316
Parental Qualities: 1005
Parental Reaction Survey Schedule: 1052
Parental Relationships: 1583
Parental Roles: 2389
Parental Strengths and Weaknesses: 213
Parental Stress and Support Checklist: 810
Parental Support: 1883
Parenthood: 2442
Parenting Abilities Checklist: 2791

Parent's Family/Personal History Questionnaire: 2791
Parent's Functioning: 872, 2040
Parent's Questions/Concerns: 872, 2040
Parents: 1496, 1705, 1942, 2355
Parents' and Children's Reinforcement Survey Schedule: 1052
Parents and Community: 648
Parents and Staff: 875
Parents' Functioning: 454
Parents' Questions/Concerns: 454
Parents' School Participation: 1500
Pareo Visual: 264
Park Ranger: 398, 399
Parks and Recreation Coordinator: 1790
Part/Whole Relations: 488
Part-Word Repetitions: 2542
Partially Correct: 2251
Participant Post-Training: 975
Participant Reactions: 975
Participation: 743, 1254, 1493, 1855, 1912, 2129, 2282, 2316, 2607, 2631, 2632
Participation in Group Activities: 268
Participation in the Special Education Process: 1884
Participation in Therapy: 2197
Participation in Treatment: 1065
Participative: 1222
Particles: 1427
Partner Dominance: 2034
Parts: 1323
Parts of a Book: 1491
Parts of Sentence: 1125
Pass: 784
Passage: 1131
Passage Comprehension: 1269, 2901, 2902, 2905
Passed: 868
Passive: 475, 1169, 1268, 2841
Passive Aggressive: 690
Passive-Aggressive: 1961, 2306, 2514, 2520
Passive-Aggressive (Negativistic): 1687
Passive Aggressiveness: 1290
Passive/Assertive/Aggressive Index: 2759
Passive Comprehension: 2900
Passive/Defensive: 1150
Passive/Defensive Cultures: 1862
Passive/Defensive Styles: 1498
Passive Influence: 74
Passive Posture: 2308
Passivity: 2716
Past: 2761
Past and Present Pain History: 484
Past Experience: 1074
Past Family Pathology: 1932
Past History: 650
Past Other than Diagnosis: 2305
Past Participle (irregular): 2337
Past Participle (regular): 2337
Past Scales: 748
Past Symptoms of Affective Disorder: 650
Past Symptoms of Psychosis: 650
Past Tense: 1427
Past Tenses: 2660
Past Treatment: 484
Past Week Functioning: 2305
Pastoralism: 963
Paternal Involvement: 1216
Paternal Overindulgence: 1012
Pathfinder Combined Accuracy: 567
Pathfinder Combined Coordination: 567
Pathfinder Combined Speed: 567
Pathfinder Combined Thruput: 567
Pathfinder Letter Accuracy: 567
Pathfinder Letter Coordination: 567
Pathfinder Letter Speed: 567
Pathfinder Letter Thruput: 567
Pathfinder Number Accuracy: 567
Pathfinder Number Coordination: 567
Pathfinder Number Speed: 567
Pathfinder Number Thruput: 567
Pathognomic Verbalization: 1214
Pathognomonic: 1524, 1525
Pathologic Anatomy Score: 2457
Pathological: 1169
Patience: 37, 1964, 2265
Patience-Impatience: 66
Patient: 1253, 1954, 2577
Patient Care: 2177
Patient Data: 1777
Patient Expectations and Goals: 484
Patient Goals: 2472
Patient Problem Ratings: 484
Patient Reliability: 2245
Patient's Evaluation of Current Functioning: 793
Pattern Analysis: 2485
Pattern Completion: 1607, 1756, 1873, 2375
Pattern Construction: 349, 837
Pattern Matching: 1336
Pattern Memory: 1336
Pattern Misfit: 1931
Pattern Perception: 891
Patterned Exit Interview: 943
Patterned Interview: 989
Patterned Merit Review: 943
Patterns: 1042, 1043, 2441, 2774
Patterns and Functions: 2486
Patterns for Career Activity Interests: 2419
Patterns for Coping with Stressful Conditions: 2419
Patterns of Interpersonal Interaction: 2419
Pay: 382, 1348
Paying Personal Bills: 2327
PCP: 2554
Peaceful: 1821
Peacemaking: 439
Peak: 991
Pedagogy: 2026

Peer: 391, 392, 467
Peer Acceptance: 1987
Peer Affiliation: 2365
Peer Attitude: 2380
Peer Chemical Environment: 1931
Peer Cohesion: 1670, 2917
Peer Conflict Scale: 876
Peer Conversation: 2001
Peer Drug Use: 1932
Peer Equality: 401
Peer Insecurity: 1685
Peer Interaction: 265
Peer Interactions: 2321
Peer Learning: 1720
Peer-Motivated: 2181
Peer Popularity: 2361
Peer Pressure: 2403
Peer Problems: 2012
Peer Rating: 2122
Peer Relations: 61, 449, 2323, 2358, 2391
Peer Relationships: 294, 2294, 2435, 2587
Peer Relationships Subtask: 2527
Peer Social Behavior: 2607
Peer Socialization: 2614
Peer Teaching: 1474
Peers: 286, 377, 2355, 2371
Peers and Play: 478
Peers and Siblings: 2355
Peg Board: 1865
Pegboard Construction: 1513
Pencil Coordination: 892
Pencil Drawing: 2439
Penetration: 1214
Penmanship and Neatness: 1916
Pentobarbital: 66
Pentobarbital-Chlorpromazine-Alcohol: 66
People: 168, 191, 391, 392, 715, 1478, 1549, 2571, 2830, 2831, 2928
People-Business-Influencing: 1163
People Concerns: 1660
People on Your Present Job: 1348
People Orientation: 1163
People Oriented: 1508
People-Pleaser: 1452
People Readiness: 1859
People-Social-Accommodating: 1163
People/Task Orientation: 1253
People You Associate With: 2208
Pep: 1964
Perceived Acceptance: 1292
Perceived Consequences Scale: 291
Perceived Decision Quality: 1945
Perceived Lack of Environmental Support: 362
Perceived Malocclusion: 2766
Perceived Stress: 1733
Perceiving: 966, 1814, 2411
Perceiving Feelings and Listening: 1417
Perceiving Relationships: 1357
Percent: 831
Percent Impaired Score: 1165
Percent Retention: 2863
Percentage Complex: 1427
Percentages: 1605
Percents: 343
Percents Skills: 1247
Perception: 169, 1323, 2111, 2614, 2776
Perception and Discrimination: 2297
Perception of Admirable Character Traits: 334
Perception of Competency: 334
Perception of Follow-Up Consistency: 334
Perception of Objects in Space: 781
Perception of Partner: 1679
Perception of Reality: 2136
Perception of Spatial Perspective: 781
Perception of Supportiveness: 334
Perception of the Mathematics Teacher: 1599
Perceptions in Chemistry: 120
Perceptions in Foreign Languages: 120
Perceptions in History: 120
Perceptions in Language Arts: 120
Perceptions in Physical Education: 120
Perceptions in the Arts: 120
Perceptions in the Social Sciences: 120
Perceptions of Financial Aid Services: 57
Perceptions of Task and Personal Reactions: 900
Perceptual: 126, 412, 812
Perceptual Abilities Tests: 839
Perceptual Ability: 780
Perceptual Ability Test: 386
Perceptual Accuracy: 1711
Perceptual Acuity: 737
Perceptual Age: 1725
Perceptual Aptitude: 1816
Perceptual Development: 377
Perceptual Difference: 2636
Perceptual Discrimination: 265
Perceptual Distortion: 2120
Perceptual/Fine Motor: 879, 2041
Perceptual/Fine Motor Skills: 1041
Perceptual Motor: 265, 653
Perceptual Motor Skills: 359
Perceptual-Motor Skills: 488
Perceptual Organization: 2707
Perceptual Organization Index: 2860
Perceptual-Performance: 1612
Perceptual Processing: 1977
Perceptual Quotient: 1725
Perceptual Reasoning: 2019
Perceptual Responses: 1472
Perceptual Skills: 882
Perceptual Speed: 1044, 1156, 1405
Perceptual Speed and Accuracy: 395, 644, 838
Perceptual Strengths/Preferences: 2181
Perfection: 1655, 1682

Perfectionism: 538, 681, 893, 1576, 2512
Perfectionism Subscale: 1730
Perfectionist: 1452
Perfectionistic: 1150, 1498, 1862
Perfectionistic vs. Tolerates Disorder: 2417
Performance: 152, 268, 379, 1134, 1702, 1731, 1900, 1922, 1840, 2859, 2860, 2862, 2864
Performance and Evaluation: 2547
Performance and Work Habits: 1480
Performance Evaluation: 1564, 1567, 2548, 2571
Performance Fears Subscale: 1730
Performance Goals and Feedback: 1463
Performance Index: 2431
Performance Indicators: 1429
Performance IQ: 2859
Performance Management: 2424
Performance Management-Supervision: 197
Performance (Non-Verbal): 1484
Performance Scale: 798
Performing: 1222
Performing and Visual Arts: 1089
Performing Arts: 380, 1334, 1789, 1841
Performing Before Others: 2444
Performing/Entertaining: 398, 399
Performing Estimating Activities: 1343, 2925
Performing Paced and/or Repetitive Activities: 1343, 2925
Performing Physical Activities: 1343, 2925
Performing Supervisory Duties: 1343, 2925
The Periodic Table: 684
Peripheral Vision: 1044
Permissive-Critical: 1940
Permutations per T-Unit: 2661
Perplexity: 1169
Persecution: 1959
Persecutory Delusions: 2109
Persecutory Ideas: 256, 1698
Persecutory Ideas (Pa1): 1697
Perservation: 329
Perseverance: 267, 490, 1044
Perseverance/Determination: 1497
Perseveration: 2251, 2290
Perseverations: 303, 375, 376
Perseverative Errors: 2892
Perseverative Responses: 2892
Persevering: 2605, 2648
Persistence: 425, 1223, 1928, 1964, 2181, 2784
Persistence Auditory: 1282
Persistence Orientation: 1472
Persistence Visual: 1282
Persistency: 421
Persistent: 1294, 1470, 2069, 2121
Persistent-Sell: 305
Persistent Symptoms: 1978
Persisting: 2929
Persisting While Uncertain: 401
Person: 2351
Person-Person: 1872
Persona: 1946
Personal: 436, 1205, 1983, 2652, 2764, 2813
Personal Accomplishment: 1590
Personal Achievement Formula: 1924
Personal Adequacy: 2776
Personal Adjustment: 1, 2, 68, 280, 874, 930, 1702, 1729, 1926, 2418
Personal Adjustment Index: 973
Personal Adjustment Subscales: 1729
Personal/Affective Development: 40
Personal and Educational Needs: 57
Personal and Social: 1490
Personal and Social Development: 686
Personal Appearance: 288
Personal Appraisal: 2890
Personal Assessment: 2088
Personal Autonomy: 737
Personal Awareness: 490
Personal Behavior: 1381
Personal Behaviors: 293
Personal Care: 1067, 2292, 2327
Personal Care Activities: 291
Personal Care Awareness: 2316
Personal Care Routines: 875, 1264
Personal Care Skills: 1807
Personal/Career Development Profile: 2364
Personal Career Life Summary: 2364
Personal Career Life-Style Effectiveness Considerations: 2419
Personal Characteristics: 1238
Personal Choices: 819
Personal Conduct: 2534
Personal Connections: 490
Personal Consequence: 201
Personal Consequences of Drug Use: 1931
Personal Consequences of Use: 1932
Personal Considerations: 1252
Personal Control: 2065
Personal Conversation: 1191, 1255
Personal Data Response: 346, 347
Personal Development: 1493, 2584, 2805
Personal Development Summary: 2364
Personal Diplomacy: 37, 2265
Personal Effectiveness: 490, 2926
Personal Emotional Adjustment: 2525
Personal Enrichment: 2530
Personal Expectations: 1910
Personal/Family: 2764
Personal Finance: 762
Personal Fitness: 1913
Personal Focus: 1923
Personal Freedom: 1293, 1397, 1983, 2834
Personal Growth: 2074, 2132
Personal Growth/Goal Orientation Dimensions: 495
Personal Happiness: 1678
Personal Health: 1019

Personal Help: 948
Personal History: 1431, 1432
Personal History Review: 943
Personal Hygiene: 377, 805, 1065, 1066, 1718, 1918
Personal Hygiene Activities: 291
Personal Incentive: 1276
Personal Independence: 2030
Personal Information: 159
Personal Information/Family Background: 808
Personal Innovation: 1689
Personal Insight: 2605
Personal Integrity: 1449
Personal Involvement with Chemicals: 1931
Personal Involvement with Drugs: 1932
Personal Issues: 1593
Personal Knowledge: 1065, 1667
Personal Learning Skill: 1467
Personal Living Skills: 443, 1300
Personal Management: 805
Personal Motives: 1821
Personal Opinion of Hearing: 1190
Personal Organization: 2204
Personal Orientation: 675, 676
Personal Orientation Survey: 2364
Personal Power: 1735
Personal Presentation: 2924
Personal Problem Orientation: 637, 710
Personal Problems: 2012
Personal Problems Orientation: 2850
Personal-Psychological Relations: 1716
Personal Qualities: 215
Personal Reactions: 1949
Personal Reflection and Response: 1759
Personal Relations: 1101, 1158
Personal Relationship and Support System: 1766
Personal Relationships: 989, 1824
Personal Requirements: 2071
Personal Resources Questionnaire: 1825
Personal Responsibility: 40, 265
Personal Risk Factor Scales: 1931
Personal Routines: 63
Personal Safety: 1066
Personal Satisfaction: 1163
Personal Security: 909, 2361
Personal Self-Care: 2299
Personal Self-Esteem: 746
Personal Self-Sufficiency: 1, 2
Personal Service: 183, 406, 407, 1074, 1177, 1334, 2177, 2882
Personal Services: 1818, 2822
Personal-Social: 123, 266, 788, 1086, 1134
Personal/Social: 2049
Personal-Social Behavior: 2123
Personal/Social Characteristics: 1593, 2384
Personal/Social Development: 2400
Personal-Social Responsibility: 1, 2
Personal-Social Total: 265
Personal-Social/Self-Help: 2243
Personal Standards: 490
Personal States: 858
Personal Status: 1304, 1670
Personal Strain: 1643
Personal Strain Questionnaire: 1825
Personal Stress Management: 1913
Personal Style: 1579, 1830
Personal Traits: 1579
Personal Values: 490
Personal Warmth: 2346
Personal Welfare: 1194
Personal Work Style: 313
Personalisation: 1254
Personality: 1705, 1716
Personality Changes: 1978
Personality Disorder Domain: 77
Personality Disorder Factor: 77
Personality Disorder Scores: 1961
Personality Evaluation: 1968
Personality Factors: 2266
Personality Functions: 2647
Personality Issues: 2034
Personality Mediators: 794
Personality-Pain Coping Style: 484
Personality Patterns: 1685
Personality Rigidity: 840
Personality Scores: 86
Personality Traits: 966
Personalized: 2021, 2022
Personalized Customer Relations: 2386
Personnel: 2096
Personnel and Human Resources: 1044
Personnel and Training: 1551
Personnel/Human Resource Management: 762
Personnel Management: 1233
Personnel Manager: 398, 399
Personnel or Social Worker: 2825
Personnel Policies: 1345
Personnel Policies and Procedures: 2584
Personnel Practices: 1569, 2605
Personnel Practices for Professional Staff: 684
Perspective: 2659
Perspectives on Technologies: 1593
Persuader: 1295
Persuading: 1551
Persuading/Influencing: 407
Persuading/Influencing Employees: 1479, 1480
Persuasion: 1044, 1667
Persuasive: 5, 381, 406, 1074, 1222, 1413, 1443, 1549, 1759, 1819, 1822, 2121, 2255, 2257, 2274, 2489
Persuasive/Interactive: 305
Persuasive Mentoring: 1652
Persuasiveness: 490, 1437, 1655
Pertinent Personal/Medical History: 1978
Pessimism: 1748, 1749
Pharmacist: 398, 1790

Pharmacy: 618, 905
Pharmacy Technician: 398, 399
Pharyngeal Control: 870
Pharyngeal Stage: 870
Pharyngeal State: 276
Pharynx: 1852
Philosophical: 1222
Philosophy: 437, 618, 1441, 1546, 1564, 1567, 2547, 2548
Philosophy and Religion: 905
Philosophy and Theology: 1044
Phlegmatic: 2648
Phlegmatic vs. Excitable: 477
Phobia: 701, 748, 2109
Phobias: 1959
Phobic Anxiety: 335, 337, 739, 792, 2326, 2602, 2603
Phobic Disorder: 2107
Phobic Disorders: 642
Phobic Feeling: 78
Phobic Personality: 1313
Phonation: 866
Phonemes: 1420
Phonemes in Spoken Words: 861
Phonemic Analysis: 2695
Phonemic Recoding: Bridging to Written Words: 187
Phonetic Analysis: 2487
Phonetic Skills: 1981
Phonetics: 308
Phonic and Visual Skills: 1055
Phonic Blending: 1529
Phonic Patterns: 769
Phonic Recognition: 1529
Phonic Spelling: 1529
Phonic Spelling of Words: 861
Phonic Words: 769
Phonics: 833
Phonics/Sight Ratio: 832
Phonics Written: 833
Phonograms: 861, 917
Phonological Awareness: 2900
Phonological Development: 2144
Phonological Deviancy Score: 214
Phonological Omissions: 214
Phonological Processes: 2429
Phonological Processes Composite: 240
Phonological Processing: 1771
Phonology: 76, 1359, 1360, 1477
Photo Series: 1379
Photographer: 398, 399, 1790
Photography: 411
Photography Club: 411
Photography Knowledge: 1713
Phrase Comprehension: 2178
Phrase Length: 199
Phrase Recall: 2596
Phrases: 1528
Phrases and Sentences: 164
Phrasing: 1752
Physical: 162, 434, 697, 806, 1044, 1499, 1734, 1929, 1943, 1996, 2148, 2196, 2349, 2512, 2652
Physical Abilities: 2358
Physical Abilities Concern: 1163
Physical Ability: 1065
Physical Abuse: 442, 460, 1006, 1931
Physical Abuse Perpetrator: 1932
Physical Activity: 1350, 1493, 2805, 2915
Physical Age: 811
Physical Aggression: 931, 1959
Physical Aggressiveness: 1290
Physical Amenities: 1743
Physical and Life Sciences and Mathematics: 1285
Physical and Mechanical Activities: 627
Physical and Personal Factors: 989
Physical and Psychological Symptom Screens: 2147
Physical and Social Self: 2355
Physical Appearance: 2358
Physical Appearance and Attributes: 1991
Physical Attractiveness: 1743
Physical Behavior: 721
Physical/Behavioral Observations: 442
Physical Chemistry for Life Sciences: 53
Physical Comfort: 1743, 2917
Physical Competence: 1987
Physical Competitiveness: 226
Physical Complaint: 1853
Physical Complaint Survey Schedule: 1052
Physical Complaints: 847
Physical Concomitants (Distracting Sounds): 2543
Physical Coordination: 2420
Physical Danger: 950
Physical Demands: 1350
Physical Development: 1, 2, 63, 684, 887
Physical Dexterity Tasks: 2606
Physical Disabilities: 1744
Physical Disability: 537
Physical Discomfort: 858, 1304, 1305, 2414
Physical Distress: 2511
Physical Domain: 1478, 2766
Physical Education: 618, 905, 2026
Physical Education and Health: 684
Physical Education Teacher: 1790
Physical Effectiveness: 2926
Physical Environment: 1216, 1494, 1825, 1913
Physical Examination Record: 857
Physical Exercise Habits and Awareness: 2789
Physical Factors: 267
Physical/Fear Reaction: 2447
Physical Findings: 1909
Physical Fitness: 439, 698, 1163, 2747
Physical Fitness and Nutrition: 2746
Physical Functioning: 1187, 2158, 2397
Physical Geology: 762
Physical Growth and Development: 684
Physical Harm: 291

Physical Health: 698, 1495, 1496, 1766, 1808, 1918, 2130
Physical Ill Health: 1824
Physical Malfunctioning: 1698
Physical Malfunctioning (D3): 1697
Physical Motor Development: 2319
Physical/Motor Speech and Expressive Language: 653
Physical Performing: 407, 412, 485, 1483, 1711, 1817, 2836
Physical Prowess: 1493, 2805
Physical Readiness: 2475
Physical Record: 989
Physical Recreation: 72
Physical Relations: 9
Physical Science: 618, 645, 762, 1094, 1334, 2026, 2882
Physical Sciences: 407, 570, 905, 960, 1638, 1759, 1818
Physical/Sexual Abuse Victim: 1932
Physical Sexual Problems: 1433
Physical Size: 1500
Physical Skills: 196, 1388
Physical Status: 913, 1777
Physical Strain: 1825
Physical Stress: 1684
Physical Surroundings: 2875
Physical Symptoms: 1181, 1730, 2074
Physical Symptoms/Fears: 283, 284, 817, 928
Physical Symptoms or Fears: 2287
Physical Tasks Adaptations: 2316
Physical Tasks Assistance: 2316
Physical Therapist: 398, 1790
Physical Therapist Assistant: 399
Physical Therapy: 618
Physical Trauma: 2521
Physical Well-Being: 2132
Physically Active: 1317
Physician: 380, 398, 1790
Physician Influence Scale: 291
Physician Qualities Scale: 291
Physicist: 1790
Physics: 110, 118, 587, 607, 615, 618, 905, 947, 1044, 1121, 1124, 1846, 2026
Physics (Electricity and Magnetism): 118
Physics (Mechanics): 118
Physiological: 1959, 2321
Physiological Anxiety: 2214
Physiological Components: 207
Physiological Dependence: 1932
PI: 1958
Piano Technician: 398, 399
Pictorial: 1534
Pictorial Analogies: 662
Pictorial Categories: 662
Pictorial Nonverbal Intelligence Quotient: 662
Pictorial Recognition Memory Test: 378
Pictorial Sequence A: 1513
Pictorial Sequence B: 1513
Pictorial Sequences: 662
Picture Absurdities: 2212
Picture Analogies: 1370
Picture Arrangement: 1731, 2728, 2840, 2860, 2862
Picture Completion: 1731, 2212, 2840, 2860, 2862, 2864
Picture Comprehension: 565
Picture Contact: 1485
Picture Description and Position and Spatial Recognition: 1515
Picture Locations: 476
Picture Matching: 356, 2240
Picture Naming: 1337, 2202
Picture Naming: Categories: 2725
Picture Naming: Nouns: 2667, 2725
Picture Naming: Verbs: 2667, 2725
Picture-Number Test: 1405
Picture Puzzles: 1370
Picture Recall: 2159
Picture Recognition: 2901
Picture Riddles: 1370
Picture Sequence: 2596
Picture Sequence Narration: 1191, 1255
Picture Series: 1370
Picture Similarities: 349, 837
Picture Vocabulary: 309, 345, 346, 347, 2694, 2695, 2901, 2902, 2904
Picture-Word Association: 2178
Pictures: 987, 2705
Pins and Collars: 722
Pipe Assembly: 2054
Pipefitter: 1793
Pipefitter/Plumber: 398, 399
Piping: 1537, 2644
Piping/Pumps: 2067
Pitch: 1154, 1751, 2837
Pitch Discrimination: 1629, 1751
Pitch Recognition: 1751
Place Orientation: 1065
Place-Value and Decimals: 444
Placement Level: 1272
Placement Out of Regular Classroom: 2311
Places: 1163
Placing: 1700
Placing Test: 1696
Plain Block Design: 1513
Plane Geometry: 1997, 1998
Plane Geometry/Trigonometry: 56
Plane Trigonometry: 1999
Planful Problem-Solving: 2858
Planfulness: 1334
Planned Codes: 763
Planned Connections: 763
Planner: 727
Planning: 197, 329, 403, 413, 684, 763, 903, 966, 1043, 1441, 1545, 1546, 1913, 1953, 2265, 2295, 2424, 2571, 2762

Planning and Action: 909
Planning and Decision Making: 1065
Planning and Executing: 1923
Planning and Goal Setting: 1564, 1567, 2547, 2548
Planning and Organization: 37, 989
Planning and Organizing: 2575
Planning and Problem Avoidance: 1545
Planning and Scheduling Work: 1570
Planning Effectively: 1550
Planning for Personal Growth: 490
Planning for Results: 2630
Planning for the Future: 1689
Planning Patterns: 1405
Plant: 296
Plant or Animal Care: 183
Plants: 407, 684, 1818
Plants and Animals: 485, 1483, 1711
Plants/Animals: 2836
Plants/Gardens: 380
Play: 1591, 1878, 1965, 1988, 2001, 2131
Play and Leisure Time: 2813, 2814
Play/Leisure Time: 1791
Play Skills: 2891
Playground Observation Behavior Map: 877
Playing Informally: 2444
Pleasant Emotions: 858, 1304, 1305, 2414
Pleasant Times with Others: 858, 1304, 1305
Pleasant-Unpleasant (PU): 1002
Pleasing Others: 1821
Pleasure: 2804
Pleasure-Inducing Parental Attitude: 1630
Plumber: 1790
Plumbing: 1792, 1794, 2152
Plumbing or Welding: 411
Plumbing/Pipefitting/Steamfitting: 410
Plural: 2337
Plural (irregular): 2337
Pluralism: 1912
Plurals: 347, 1427, 1898, 2660
Plurals and Possessives: 1248
Pneumatics: 1537, 2152, 2644
Pneumatics/Hydraulics: 2067
Poignancy: 1698
Poignancy (Pa2): 1697
Pointing to Objects: 277
Pointing to Parts of a Picture: 277
Points of View: 901
Poise: 1968
Polarities: 1938
Police Officer: 380, 398, 399, 1790
Policies and Operations: 1904
Policies and Procedures: 640
Policy Choice: 1743
Policy Clarity: 1743
Polite Customer Relations: 2386
Political: 1639, 2539, 2626
Political Awareness and Strategic Influence: 2097
Political Behavior: 2132
Political/Economic Structures: 570
Political Science: 618
Political Sciences/Government: 905
Politics: 140
Polydrug Abuse: 2107
Polydrug Use: 1931
Polymer Chemistry: 54
Polysyllabic: 769
Poor Academics: 355
Poor Achievement and Memory: 1963
Poor Anger Control: 355
Poor Attention: 355
Poor Attentional Control: 2407
Poor Coordination: 355
Poor Ego Strength: 355
Poor Impulse Control: 355
Poor Intellectuality: 355
Poor Physical Strength: 355
Poor Planning: 690
Poor Reality Contact: 355
Poor Sense of Identity: 355
Poor Social Conformity: 355
Poor Work Habits: 1162
"Pop" Quiz: 2655
Popliteal Angle: 1258
Popular: 1214
Popularity: 1964, 1991
Popularity/Charisma: 1210
Position: 2763
Position Analysis: 989
Position Familiarity: 421
Position in Space: 816, 883, 1357, 2376
Position of Sound: 2192
Positional Auditory Discrimination: 1534
Positional-Reflexive: 968
Positive: 1013, 2001, 2728
Positive Affect: 467, 1288, 1745
Positive Affect and Sensation Seeking: 1745
Positive Affects Ratio: 791
Positive Assertive: 2399
Positive Attitude Toward Others: 2444
Positive Attitude Toward Self: 2444
Positive Attitudes: 1891, 2589
Positive Bias: 2882
Positive Communication: 1705
Positive-Constructive Daydreaming: 2407
Positive Emotions: 1769, 2218
Positive Formal Thought Disorder: 2289
Positive Health Habits: 1733
Positive Impression: 931, 1688, 1959
Positive Influence Tactic Frequency: 2580
Positive Interaction: 2052, 2316, 2607
Positive Life Change Events: 1181
Positive Life Events: 1495, 1496
Positive Lifestyle Behaviors: 2745
Positive Mood: 1181

Positive Operational: 467
Positive Peer Associations: 909
Positive Preoperational: 467
Positive Program Support: 490
Positive Reappraisal: 699, 2858
Positive Resolution: 1006
Positive School Climate: 2314
Positive Score Total: 791
Positive Self-Concept: 909
Positive Self-Concept or Confidence: 1795
Positive Self-Esteem: 1626
Positive Sense of Control: 2399
Positive Service Attitude: 2347
Positive Situations: 1305
Positive Social Situations: 2414
Positive Symptom Distress Index: 337, 2603
Positive Symptom Total: 337, 2602, 2603
Positive Syndrome: 2017
Positive Temperament: 2306
Positive Total: 1012
Positive Yielding: 2399
Possessive: 2337
Possessive Marker: 1427
Possessive Pronoun: 2337
Possessives: 918, 1898, 2660
Possible Pregnancy Problems: 158
Possible Problems: 454
Possible Problems List: 872, 2040
Post-Evaluating the Participant's Employability Skills: 978
Post-Training Transition: 401
Post-Traumatic Stress: 1543
Post-traumatic Stress Disorder: 690, 1687, 2107
Post-Traumatic Stress Disorder Scales (PK & PS): 1697
Post World War I: 145
Postmodified Subject: 2662
Postmorbid Questions: 2297
Postrotary Nystagmus: 2377
Posttraumatic Stress Disorder: 77, 876
Postural Control: 377, 772
Postural Praxis: 2377
Posture: 1472
The Postwar World: 2932
Potentia: 942
Potential Abilities: 2555
Potential Drawbacks of Career: 421
Potential Estimates: 2605
Potential Level: 827, 2319
Potentiation: 1938
Poverty of Content of Speech: 2290
Poverty of Speech: 2290
Power: 371, 820, 1150, 1250, 1276, 1347, 1498, 1681, 1724, 1823, 1856, 1862, 1936, 1957, 2237, 2753, 2803, 2922
Power Distribution: 1537, 2643
Power Motive: 2021, 2022
Power Seeking: 1222
Power Style: 2021, 2022
Power Supplies: 920, 923, 1279, 1537, 2643
Power Supplies/Power Distribution: 924
Power Transmission: 1537, 1637, 2769
Power Transmissions: 2644
Powerful Others Scale: 1183
Powerlessness: 2636
Practical: 86, 618, 980, 990, 1334, 1822, 1954, 1984, 2255, 2257, 2536
Practical Abilities: 2459
Practical Applications: 570
Practical Arts: 162, 1929
Practical-Female: 1789
Practical Knowledge: 829
Practical-Male: 1789
Practical Mindedness: 2588
Practical Nursing: 1794
Practical Orientation: 637, 710, 2850
Practical Reasoning: 1134, 2081
Practical v. Carefree: 417
Practicality: 1223
Practicalizer: 727
Practice Copy: 2787
Pragmatic Knowledge: 241
Pragmatic Language: 2868
Pragmatics: 76, 628, 2470, 2886
Pragmatist: 2675
Pragnosia: 1778
Praise: 1290
Praise and Recognition: 1345
Praxis: 328, 1513, 2873
Praxis Verbal Command: 2377
Pre-Affair: 660
Pre-Affair Involvement: 646
Pre-Algebra: 1997
Pre-Algebra/Elementary Algebra: 56
Pre-Articulatory and Articulatory Skills: 658
Pre-Elementary and Elementary: 905
Pre-Employment Writing: 341
Pre-Evaluating the Participant's Employability Skills: 978
Pre-Kindergarten Education: 2026
Pre-number: 2134
Pre-reading: 2134
Pre-Reading: 2737
Pre-Speech and Oral Awareness: 658
Pre-Vocational Skills: 2827
Pre-Writing Skills: 968
Preacademic: 804
Preacademic Learning: 1907
Preacher: 1310
Preambulatory Motor Skills and Behaviors: 2213
Precise: 1273
Precise/Administrative: 1497
Precise-Sell: 305
Precise/Systematic: 305

Precision: 1042, 1043, 1323, 2295
Precision Machining: 1792, 1794
Precision Metal Work: 410
Precision Production: 410
Prediction: 685
Prediction of Treatment Response: 1242
Predictive Ability: 2027
Predictive Accuracy: 1437
Predictive Drawing: 2410
Predictor Profile: 2605
Predisposition: 1949
Preference for Drinking over Other Activities: 132, 2874
Preferences: Activities: 1790
Preferences: Work: 1790
Preferred Culture: 820
Preferred Exposure: 755
Preferred Feedback: 755
Preferred Grip: 1164
Preferred Hand: 1911
Preferred Style-Adult: 1966
Preferred Style of Leader-Coach: 1823
Preferred Style of Leader-Expert: 1823
Preferred Style of Leader-Fighter: 1823
Preferred Style of Leader Overall: 1823
Prefers Long-Range Goals to Short-Term or Immediate Needs: 1795
Prefers Reading in Early Afternoon: 2181
Prefers Reading in Late Afternoon: 2181
Prefers Reading in the Evening: 2181
Prefers Reading in the Morning: 2181
Prefers Reading to a Teacher: 2181
Prefixes: 917
Pregnancy and Childbirth: 2454
Pregnancy/Birth/Hospitalization: 653
Prejudice-Acceptance: 1845
Preliminary Estimate of Learning: 2030
Premature Ejaculation: 1744
Premorbid or Intermorbid Personality: 650
Premorbid Pessimism: 1686
Premorbid Questions: 2297
Premorbid Status: 1777
Preoccupation: 1932
Preoccupation with Disease: 1963
Preoccupation with Drugs: 1931
Preoccupation with Sexually Relevant Concepts: 1219
Preparation Style: 1210
Prepare for a Career: 2530
Prepare for Career and/or Graduate Professional School: 2530
Preparing for Clinical Intervention: 310
Preposition: 2337
Prepositional Location Commands: 2215
Prepositions: 430, 918, 1127, 1427
Prepositions and Conjunctions: 1248
Prepositions and Irregular Plural Nouns: 347
Prepositions/Conjunctions/Interjections: 1125
Prepositions per T-Unit: 2661
Prereading: 886, 1657
Prereading Composite: 1659
Prereading Phonics Abilities Inventories: 861
Prerequisites Visual Training: 658
Preschool Delay Task: 1099
Preschool Skills: 488
Preschool Vigilance "0" Task: 1099
Preschool Vigilance "1" Task: 1099
Prescriptive Mentoring: 1652
Presence of a Chronic Illness: 1733
Present: 2761
Present Grade Placement: 1500
Present Health: 2208
Present Level of Academic Achievement: 1500
Present Participle: 2337
Present Progressive Tense: 1427
Present Progressives: 2660
Present Self Concept: 1566
Present Self Concept-Evaluation: 2573
Present Social Orientation: 1566
Present State: 650
Present Tense (third person-irregular): 2337
Present Tense (third person-regular): 2337
Present Tense-3rd Singular: 1427
Present Work and Activities: 2208
Present Work Orientation: 1566
Present Work Values-Orientation: 2573
Presentation Clarity: 948
Presenting Appropriate Appearance: 190
Presenting Benefits: 490
Presenting Complaints: 546
Presenting Information: 808
Presenting Problems: 1649
Preserving: 1688
The Press Test: 2605
Pressure: 490
Pressure of Speech: 2290
Pressure on Peers: 490
Pressure on Team Mates: 490
Pressure Performance: 2605
Pressure Self: 1984
Prestige: 1074, 1493, 2805, 2915
Prestige/Production: 387
Pretend Action: 987
Pretend Gestures: 1528
Pretend To Be a Parent: 1528
Previous Grade Retentions: 1500
Previous Marriages and/or Relationships: 717
Previous Reports and Assessments: 158
Previous Treatment: 184
Prevocational: 686
Prevocational Skills: 1065
Prevocational/Vocational Activity: 1, 2
Price/Income and Personal Growth: 897
Pride in Work: 2256, 2593
Priest: 1310

Primary: 2127
Primary Dimensional Scales: 2326
Primary Dimensions: 792
Primary Relationship: 2442
Primary Scales: 654
Primary Sexual Partners: 1433
Primer-Level Dictation: 199
Primitive and Abnormal Reflexes: 870
Primitive Self: 1946
Principal Leadership: 216
Principal Questionnaire: 649
Principalization: 770
Principles: 626
Principles of Accounting: 524
Principles of Effective Instruction: 684
Principles of Finance: 762
Principles of Financial Accounting: 762
Principles of Macroeconomics: 525
Principles of Management: 526
Principles of Marketing: 527
Principles of Microeconomics: 528
Principles of Physical Science: 762
Principles of Public Speaking: 762
Principles of Statistics: 762
Principles of Supervision: 762
Print Concepts: 800, 887
Print Reading: 1637, 2067, 2151, 2152, 2644, 2769, 2867
Print Shop: 2400
Printed Sentences: 987
Printed Words: 987
Printer: 398, 399
Prints Personal Data: 346
Prior Knowledge: 2503
Priorities: 2762
Priority: 1732
Privacy Rights and Social Needs: 1583
Private Investigator: 398, 399
Private vs. Forthright: 2417
Privateness: 538
Pro-Integration Attitude: 909
Proactivity: 1823
Probability: 178
Probability and Statistics: 195
Probability of Admission: 2388
Problem: 997, 2595
Problem Analysis: 173, 174, 1368, 1837
Problem Areas: 965
Problem Behavior Scale: 2299
Problem Behavior Total: 2036
Problem Behaviors: 1067, 2452
Problem Drinking Indices: 652
Problem Identification: 2242, 2571
Problem Index: 1025
Problem Minimization: 938
Problem-Resolution: 2573
Problem Screens: 1932
Problem Sensitivity: 1044
Problem Severity: 1933
Problem Severity Scales: 1932
Problem Solving: 82, 123, 243, 320, 403, 413, 490, 677, 698, 699, 819, 1094, 1392, 1453, 1705, 1738, 1759, 1861, 1913, 2068, 2105, 2133, 2137, 2250, 2356, 2376, 2486, 2583, 2636, 2710, 2929, 2930
Problem-Solving: 1350, 1551, 1826, 2292, 2358
Problem Solving Ability: 1568, 2277, 2374
Problem-Solving Ability: 394
Problem Solving and Abstract Reasoning: 2249, 2251
Problem Solving and Concrete Reasoning: 2249
Problem Solving and Decision Making: 1923, 2424
Problem-Solving and Decision-Making: 197
Problem Solving-Common Sense: 731, 732
Problem-Solving Communication: 1582
Problem-Solving Confidence: 2065
Problem Solving-Logical Thinking: 731, 732
Problem Solving-Map Reading: 731
Problem Solving-Mechanical: 732
Problem-Solving Patterns: 2419
Problem Solving-Relevancy: 731, 732
Problem Solving/Resourcefulness: 490
Problem-Solving Skills: 15
Problem Solving with Employees: 1479, 1480
Problems: 173, 174, 1368, 1732, 2089
Problems at Home: 419
Problems at School or College: 419
Problems in Applying for a Job or for a Course: 419
Problems in Family Communication: 1877
Problems in Making Decisions: 419
Problems in Obtaining Specific Occupational Information: 419
Problems in Relationship Formation: 362
Problems in Starting Work: 419
Problems of the Current Relationship: 1581
Problems Outside Work: 419
Problems With Child and Self: 448
Problems with Employees: 807
Problems With Family: 448
Problems with Self-Concept: 678
Problems With Others: 448
Procedural: 2121
Procedural Knowledge: 1759
Procedures: 1094, 1281, 1657, 2086
Procesamiento Auditivo: 264
Procesamiento Visual: 264
Process: 831, 1094, 1818
Process-Bound: 2636
Process Control: 1279
Processes: 191, 348
Processing Difference Index: 2596
Processing Efficiency: 1907
Processing in Short Term Memory: 320
Processing/Serving/Dispensing Food: 1048
Processing Speed: 2901
Processing Speed Index: 2860

Processing Written Information: 1343, 2925
Procurement of Supplemental Income: 2327
Producing: 380
Product Presentation: 989
Product Rating: 895
Production: 752, 1443, 1549, 2053, 2100, 2826, 2868
Production Agriculture: 1794
Production and Processing: 1044
Production Emphasis: 1437
Production Operations: 1551
Production Supervision: 1222
Production Welding Calculations: 2867
Productive: 381, 695, 1222, 1681
Productive Attitude: 2347
Productive with Peers: 1161
Productivity: 449, 1283, 1393, 1855, 1972, 2570, 2934, 2935
Productivity-Creativity: 2776
Productivity Index: 2726
Productivity Interference: 291
Professional Advising: 1334
Professional Commitment: 1689
Professional Conduct: 310
Professional Counseling Services: 1583
Professional Development: 909
Professional Help: 1733
Professional Involvement: 421
Professional Knowledge: 2026
Professionalism: 490, 684, 2621
Proficiency Composite: 1570
Proficiency Level: 171, 2178
Profile: 1023, 1024, 2013, 2014
Profile Elevation: 1525
Profile of Conflict Characteristics: 2079
Profile of Group Member Behavior: 2079
Profile of Group Problem Solving: 2079
Profile of Leadership Behavior: 2079
Profile of Organizational Characteristics: 2079
Profile of Own Behavior: 2079
Profile of Personal Interests: 1232
Profit: 371
Prognostic Indices: 1686
Program Awareness: 636
Program Clarity: 637, 2850
Program Leadership/Support: 1233
Program Structure: 875, 1264, 2310
Programmed Instruction: 1474
Programming: 2085
Programming Aptitude: 167, 2897
Progress: 946
Progress Evaluation: 1275
Progress in Therapy: 2197
Progression through Conflict: 1022, 1704
Progressive Figures: 1164
Project Mission: 2096
Project Schedule: 2096
Projected Self: 2371
Projection: 78, 770, 927, 2410
Projection and Introjection: 2307
Projects: 1474
Prolongations: 2542
Promoter: 312, 420
Promotes Department Advancement: 1233
Promotes Instructional Climate: 1276
Promotes Positive Climate: 1233
Promoting Community-Organization Relations: 1569
Promoting Community/Organization Relations: 2605
Promoting Safety Attitudes and Practices: 1569, 2605
Promotional Opportunities: 382
Prompt: 1896
Prompted: 2620
Prompted Production: 1126
Prompted Productions: 1127
Promptness: 40
Prone Equilibrium: 1668
Prone Reach: 977
Pronouns: 430, 1125, 1127, 1248, 1427, 1898
Pronunciation: 84, 87, 250
Proof-Reading: 835, 1144
Proofing: 2901, 2902
Proofreading: 532, 1692
Propaganda: 1222
Properties: 348
Properties and Notations: 570
Property: Own and Others: 2444
Proposals: 155
Propositions: 178
Proprietors/Sales Workers: 2000
Propriety: 2306, 2776
Proprioception: 1865, 2378
Prose Literacy: 972
Prosocial Deficit: 1522
Prosody: 866, 2332
Prosody and Abstract Language: 356
Prospecting: 989
Prospective: 2596
Prosperity and Depression (1920 thru 1940): 146
Prosthetic Aids: 1743
Protect: 138, 139
Protecting: 407
Protection: 140
Protection of the Child: 442
Protective: 412, 485, 1483, 1589, 1711, 1817, 2836
Protective Service: 183, 398, 2882
Protective Services: 410, 905, 1237, 1285, 2822
Protectiveness: 2318
Provide Detailed Instructions: 2923
Provide Vague Instructions: 2923
Provides Appropriate Supporting Material Based on the Audience and Occasion: 639
Providing Feedback: 1545
Providing Help: 1689
Providing Incentives and Recognition: 2070
Proving Yourself: 807

Provision for Privacy: 1743
Provoke: 1966
Proxemic: 1284
Prudence: 1212
Prudent: 980
Psychasthenia: 538, 1698
Psychasthenia (Pt): 1697
Psychedelics: 1931
Psychiatric Problems: 85
Psychiatric Referral: 1931
Psychiatric Symptomatology: 1213
Psychoactive Drug Use: 184
Psychobiological Development: 285
Psychogenic Attitudes: 1686
Psychological: 761, 1494
Psychological Adjustment: 721, 1946
Psychological Benefits of Drug Use: 1931
Psychological Benefits of Use: 1932
Psychological Dependence: 1729
Psychological Discomfort: 1963
Psychological Distress: 2117, 2511
Psychological Disturbance: 1931, 1932
Psychological Factors: 267, 2766
Psychological Functioning: 965
Psychological Harm: 291
Psychological Health: 2916
Psychological Inadequacy: 538
Psychological-Mindedness: 372
Psychological Outlook: 2789
Psychological Readiness: 2415
Psychological Strain: 1825
Psychological Symptoms: 793
Psychological vs. Somatic Perception of Illness: 1241
Psychological Well Being: 2074
Psychologist: 380, 398, 1790
Psychology: 111, 118, 618, 905, 1044, 1122, 1124, 2026, 2530
Psychomotor: 537, 1044
Psychomotor Abilities: 1921
Psychomotor Acceleration: 1698
Psychomotor Acceleration (Ma2): 1697
Psychomotor Behavior: 268
Psychomotor Coordination: 2373
Psychomotor Development: 1278
Psychomotor Retardation: 792, 1698, 2109
Psychomotor Retardation (D2): 1697
Psychomotor Skills: 2030
Psychopathic Deviate: 66, 1698
Psychopathic Deviate (Pd): 1697
Psychopathic Deviation: 538
Psychopathology: 2245
Psychopathy: 1175
Psychosexual Disorders: 2147
Psychosexual Dysfunctions: 642
Psychosexual Stimulation: 2396
Psychosis: 824, 1962
Psychosocial: 1931
Psychosocial Adjustment: 2395
Psychosocial Development: 684
Psychosocial Domain: 2766
Psychosocial Factors: 484
Psychosocial Functioning: 1517
Psychosocial Problem Content Domain: 77
Psychosocial Scales: 1932
Psychosocial Stressors: 73
Psycho-social Substance Use Difficulties: 77
Psychosomapathic-Physical Contentment: 218
Psychosomatic: 681
Psychosomatic Correlates: 1686
Psychosomatic Syndrome: 1963
Psychosomatic Tendencies: 1660
Psychotic Behavior: 1522, 2211
Psychotic Disorders: 2519
Psychotic Disorganization: 2120
Psychotic Experiences: 1959
Psychotic Features: 1960
Psychotic Responses: 218
Psychotic Symptoms: 2147, 2519
Psychotic Syndrome: 650
Psychotic Thinking: 690
Psychoticism: 335, 337, 538, 792, 2326, 2602, 2603
Psychotocism or Tough-Mindedness: 999
PTSD Diagnosis: 2018
PU Incongruence: 1002
Public Administration: 618
Public Administrator: 1790
Public Affairs/Social Work: 905
Public Contact: 1350
Public Relations Director: 380, 1790
Public Relations Person: 312
Public Safety and Security: 1044
Public School Governance and School Community Relations: 684
Public Services: 62
Public Speaking: 188, 380, 398, 618, 1237, 1789, 1790
Pugnacity-Sadism: 1721, 2318
Pull-To-Sitting: 1258
Pulse: 1154
Pumps: 1537, 2644
Pumps and Piping: 1637, 2769
Punctuality: 1223, 1964
Punctuation: 616, 821, 830, 957, 992, 1248, 1283, 1318, 1836, 1997, 2234, 2302, 2729
Punctuation and Capitalization: 955, 956, 2902
Punctuation & Capitalization: 2901
Punitive Control: 1881
Punitive-Permissive: 1845
Purchasing: 1551
Purchasing Agent: 398, 399, 1790
Purchasing Habits: 2422, 2443, 2734
Purchasing/Receiving/Storing Food: 1048
Pure Challenge: 396
Purpose: 191
Purpose and Objectives: 2633

Purpose/Focus: 2933
Pursuit: 1533
Pursuits: 2821
Push/Pressure: 490
Pushy: 305
Putting People at Ease: 300
Pyraphexyl: 66

Quaaludes: 1931
Qualifications Concern: 1163
Qualified: 2198
Qualitative: 329, 391, 392, 2010
Qualitative Indicators: 2647
Qualitative Signs and Referral Indicators: 268
Quality: 1651, 2804, 2837
Quality Centered: 1923
Quality/Continuous Improvement: 1545
Quality Control: 1841
Quality Factors: 2633
Quality Focus: 2385
Quality Is Crucially Important: 1858
Quality Management: 2098
Quality of Conjugal Relationship: 1181
Quality of Effort: 635
Quality of Explanation: 2080
Quality of Relationships: 1006
Quality of Significant Relationship: 1181
Quality of Teaching: 1108, 2083
Quality of the Instructional Program: 636, 1885, 2532, 2623
Quality of Thinking Process: 242
Quality of Work: 942, 2444
Quality of Working Life: 900
Quality Rating: 2767
Quality Ratings: 801
Quality Values: 2129
Quantitative: 21, 23, 25, 385, 547, 560, 561, 664, 1107, 1612, 2020, 2309, 2485, 2758, 2807
Quantitative Ability: 141, 1249, 1975, 2810
Quantitative Concepts: 345, 2901
Quantitative Concepts and Reasoning: 1659
Quantitative Index: 2431
Quantitative Literacy: 972
Quantitative/Mathematics: 1658
Quantitative Reasoning: 349, 780, 1115, 1846, 2000, 2309, 2485
Quantitative Relations: 797
Quantitative Scales: 2647
Quantitative Skill: 1467
Quantitative Skills: 15, 1202
Quantitative Thinking Total: 1319
Quantity: 136, 331
Quantity Food Preparation: 1792
Quantity Foods: 1792
Quantity of Insulin: 1242
Quantity of Suggestion: 1026
Quantity of Work: 942
Quantum Chemistry: 43
Question Answering: 1064
Questioning: 626
Questioning Strategies: 2252
Questionnaire: 2728
Questions: 1054, 1217, 1427, 1898
Quick Functional Screening Test: 1839
Quick-Sell: 305
Quick Start: 1411
Quiet: 1096
Quiet-Withdrawn: 1162

R/L Copying Shapes: 2240
R/L Copying Words: 2240
R/L Discrimination: 2376
Race Horse: 305
Race Relations: 909
Racial Attitudes: 1377
Radio/TV Repair: 398, 399
Radiologic Technician: 398
Radiologic Technologist: 1790
Radiological Technician: 399
Random Answering Pattern: 2553
Random Position-A: 234
Random Position-D: 234
Random Responding: 690
Random Response: 1341
Range of Motion Limitation: 2766
Rank Importance: 1705
Rape Scale: 1744
Rapid/Automatic Naming: 540
Rapid Cognitive Index: 2431
Rapidez en el Procesamiento : 264
Rapidly Reversing Repetitive Hand Movements: 2141
Rapport: 2347
Rapport/Alienation: 1340
Rapport with Child: 1026
Rapport with Teacher: 1162
Rare Deviance: 1522
Rare Symptoms: 2522
Rare Virtues: 2306
Reasons for Leaving This College: 57
Rate: 1056, 1092, 1765, 1850, 2174
Rate Control: 1044
Rate of Intelligible Speech: 209
Rate/Prosody: 2706
Rate/Rhythm: 2837
Rating of Articulation: 1740
Rating of Praxic Features of Writing: 1740
Rating Scales: 341
Ratio: 563
Ratio and Proportion: 444
Ratio of Total Cholesterol to HDL: 2789
Rational: 200, 2112
Rational Cognitive: 1825
Rational Numbers: 1392
Rational-Scientific: 618

Rationality: 1576
Rationalization: 927
Rationalization of Drinking: 132, 2874
Raw Score: 1428
Razonamiento Fluido: 264
Reacting to Stress: 2575
Reaction-Formation: 2307
Reaction Rates: 684
Reaction Time: 1044, 1214, 1665, 1711, 2647
Reaction Time Average: 671
Reaction Time Average for Correct Responses: 671
Reaction Time Average for Incorrect Responses: 671
Reaction Time to Color Stimuli: 2605
Reaction Time to Verbal Stimuli: 2605
Reaction to Stress: 701
Reaction to Supervision: 1830
Reaction to the Affair: 660
Reactions: 2542
Reactions during Assessment: 1909
Reactions of Colleagues and Workmates: 900
Reactions of Superiors: 900
Reactions To Aggression: 1049
Reactions to Authorities: 1050
Reactions to Challenge: 1050
Reactions to Co-Workers: 1050
Reactions to Criticism: 1050
Reactions To Failure: 1049
Reactions To Love and Marriage: 1049
Reactions to Orders: 1050
Reactions To Rejection: 1049
Reactions To Responsibility: 1049, 1050
Reactions To School: 1049
Reactions To Sexual Stimuli: 1049
Reactions Toward Illness: 1853
Reactive: 1655
Reactive Attachment Disorder: 876
Reactive Behavior: 878
Reactivity: 66
Reactivity to Tactile Deep Pressure: 2715
Reactivity to Vestibular Stimulation: 2715
Reacts to Name: 2450
Readability: 2935
Reader's Guide: 1491
Readiness: 339, 340, 342, 1400, 1802, 2213, 2415
Readiness/Academic: 2049
Readiness Auditory: 1282
Readiness Cluster: 2905
Readiness of Criticism: 1026
Readiness of Enforcement: 1026
Readiness of Explanation: 1026
Readiness Skills: 1126
Readiness Style Match Matrix: 2415
Readiness to Compete: 490
Readiness Visual: 1282
Reading: 33, 56, 63, 159, 165, 192, 212, 233, 246, 248, 258, 277, 299, 322, 340, 342, 356, 264, 383, 384, 389, 392, 464, 481, 541, 547, 559, 575, 576, 597, 602, 610, 612, 621, 645, 657, 665, 666, 684, 730, 821, 822, 904, 971, 982, 992, 1061, 1071, 1094, 1138, 1139, 1167, 1202, 1235, 1256, 1261, 1278, 1353, 1386, 1421, 1425, 1426, 1459, 1460, 1521, 1524, 1525, 1738, 1759, 1997, 2001, 2026, 2035, 2127, 2137, 2241, 2293, 1309, 2341. 2358, 2484, 2493, 2556, 2627, 2654, 2668, 2688, 2692, 2711, 2735, 2737, 2738, 2879, 2901, 2902, 2903
Reading a Ruler (Measurement): 2421
Reading Across the Curriculum: 684
Reading Advanced Skills: 1318, 1319
Reading Analytically: 570
Reading and Arithmetic Grade Levels: 1711
Reading & Literature: 570
Reading and Study Skills: 1492
Reading and Writing: 661, 1718, 2873
Reading Aptitude: 2900
Reading Business Tables: 1821
Reading Composite: 1386
Reading Comprehension: 18, 82, 141, 165, 199, 250, 328, 338, 339, 343, 386, 509, 510, 511, 571, 664, 684, 743, 780, 821, 822, 916, 961, 1198, 1249, 1323, 1358, 1386, 1534, 1657, 1762, 1763, 1768, 1836, 1846, 1902, 1975, 2000, 2092, 2094, 2105, 2134, 2175, 2179, 2187, 2221, 2222, 2234, 2309, 2339, 2463, 2483, 2484, 2666, 2676, 2687, 2735, 2795, 2810, 2861, 2900, 2901, 2902
Reading Comprehension and Information-Seeking: 1826
Reading Comprehension and Vocabulary: 2032
Reading Comprehension Cluster: 2905
Reading Comprehension of Functional Paragraphs: 356
Reading Comprehension of Words and Phrases: 1740
Reading Comprehension of Words and Sentences: 356
Reading Comprehension Quotient: 2712
Reading Conventions: 2682
Reading Critically: 570
Reading Decoding: 1386, 1461
Reading/Decoding: 1379
Reading Difficulties: 1262
Reading Efficiency: 2174
Reading Final Score: 1662
Reading for Facts: 901
Reading for Information Assessment: 2920
Reading for Life Skills: 1235
Reading for Literary Experience: 1759
Reading for Meaning: 1232
Reading for Understanding: 1235
Reading Grade-Placement Assessments: 341
Reading/Grammar: 2668
Reading Graphs and Tables: 2234
Reading Instruction Relational Concepts: 1072
Reading Instructions: 211
Reading Knowledge: 1370
Reading/Language: 1418
Reading/Language Arts: 741, 2560
Reading Level: 1272

Reading Level Scores: 2338
Reading/Listening Inventory: 2175
Reading Maps/Graphs/Tables and Diagrams: 2095
Reading/Math: 645
Reading Outcomes: 1534
Reading Perception: 120
Reading Potential: 869
Reading Problems: 651
Reading Quotient: 2676
Reading Rate: 257, 769, 901, 1767, 1768
Reading Readiness: 552
Reading Recognition: 1902, 2666
Reading Retention: 2030
Reading Scores: 257
Reading Screening: 2134
Reading Sentences: 1073
Reading Sentences and Paragraphs: 199
Reading Skill: 960
Reading Skills: 18, 341, 418, 1066, 1838, 2150, 2154, 2157, 2302, 2737
Reading Specialist: 2026
Reading Speed: 2051, 2183
Reading/Spelling: 1916
Reading Study Skills: 2095
Reading Subtest: 1382
Reading the Directions of Schoolwork: 2712
Reading to Gain Information: 1759
Reading to Perform a Task: 1759
Reading Total: 1318, 1319, 2735
Reading Total Score: 2467
Reading/Understanding: 1379
Reading Validity Index: 707
Reading Vocabulary: 165, 1657, 2092, 2094, 2309, 2483, 2484, 2487, 2795, 2900, 2901, 2902
Reading/Vocabulary: 2668
Reading Word Analysis: 663
Reading Words: 1073
Reading-Writing: 2904
Reading/Writing: 250, 620, 2826
Readings: 391
Ready to Learn: 1163
Real Estate: 410
Real Estate Agent: 398, 399
Realism: 981
Realist: 2675
Realistic: 397, 398, 399, 1790, 1829, 2360, 2835
Realistic Self-Appraisal: 1795
Realistic Thinking: 865
Reality Avoidance: 78
Reality Disorientation: 929, 1815
Reality Distortion: 297, 1963
Reality Testing: 243, 297, 748, 912, 2647
Reality Testing Disturbance: 2109
Reality Testing-Social Disturbance: 748
Realtor: 380, 1790
Reason: 1402
Reason for Admission: 2108
Reasoning: 169, 348, 538, 558, 619, 670, 1042, 1270, 1281, 1459, 2105, 2297, 2328, 2329, 2341, 2373, 2577
Reasoning Ability: 734, 1152, 1162
Reasoning About Perception: 2044
Reasoning and Academic Skills: 265
Reasoning and Thinking Style: 1579
Reasoning by Analogy: 1607, 1756
Reasoning/Calculation: 1665
Reasoning Guidance: 1316
Reasoning Quotient: 2792
Reasoning Skills: 1194, 1350
Reasoning with 4-Possibilities Matrix: 1780
Reasoning with Numbers: 532
Reasoning with Relationships: 1780
Reasons for Marrying: 1581
Reassurance: 1317
Rebellious: 1966
Rebus Delayed Recall: 1378
Rebus Learning: 1378
Recall: 320, 626, 1375, 1644, 1886, 2226, 2297
Recall/Closure Composite: 1384
Recall of Designs: 349, 837
Recall of Digits: 837
Recall of Digits Backward: 349
Recall of Digits Forward: 349
Recall of General Information: 2249, 2250, 2251
Recall of Objects: 837
Recall of Objects-Delayed: 349
Recall of Objects-Immediate: 349
Recall of Oral Paragraphs: 2297
Recall Ratio: 320
Recall Score: 685
Recall Total: 2863
Recall Vocabulary: 278
Recalling Facts and Details: 647
Recalling Sentences: 540
Recalling Sentences in Context: 539
Recalls Five Details: 2672
Recalls Five Details With Competing Message: 2672
Recalls Four Critical Elements: 2672
Recalls Two Critical Elements: 2672
Receipt and Propulsion of Objects: 1901
Receiving: 1251, 1929
Receiving Chapter I Services: 2311
Recent Drug Use: 2198
Recent Health: 1733
Recent Memory: 2249, 2250, 2251
Recent Stress: 1686
Reception: 1909
Receptive: 265, 266, 377, 987, 1381, 1804, 2335, 2813, 2893
Receptive Attention: 763
Receptive Awareness: 136
Receptive Communication: 1065
Receptive Composite: 2727
Receptive Gesture and Sign Language: 285

Receptive Grammar: 822
Receptive Language: 206, 234, 276, 539, 540, 881, 1041, 1728, 2127, 2243, 2342, 2668, 2680, 2891
Receptive Language Age: 2189
Receptive Language Dysfunction: 2768
Receptive Language Skills: 2055, 2298
Receptive Prosody: 356
Receptive Skills: 1385
Receptive Speech: 1524, 1525, 2528
Receptive Vocabulary: 76, 655, 656, 822, 1360, 2727
Receptivity: 136
Reciprocity: 630
Recites Alphabet: 346
Reciting: 199
Reciting Numbers: 254
Recognition: 490, 685, 1276, 1694, 1695, 1701, 1724, 1856, 1921, 1930, 2100, 2210, 2226, 2555, 2581, 2586, 2625, 2804, 2922
Recognition Accuracy: 470
Recognition & Reward: 2773
Recognition Drive: 2784
Recognition False Negatives: 2227
Recognition False Positives: 2227
Recognition for Good Performance: 490
Recognition Hits: 375
Recognition Memory: 1485
Recognition Motivation: 654
Recognition of Assumptions: 2856, 2857
Recognition of Capital Letters: 2434
Recognition of Complex Detail: 2889
Recognition of Familiar Faces: 356
Recognition of Good Performance: 490
Recognition of Lower Case Letters: 2434
Recognition of Lowercase Letters: 346
Recognition of Pictures: 349, 837
Recognition/Reinforcement: 490
Recognition/Satisfaction: 490
Recognition of Shape: 911
Recognition of Simple Detail: 2889
Recognition Total: 2863
Recognition Total Correct: 2227
Recognition True Negatives: 2227
Recognition True Positives: 2227
Recognition v. Privacy: 417
Recognition Vocabulary: 2304
Recognizing Abbreviations: 1534
Recognizing and Blending Common Word Parts: 1073
Recognizing Antonyms: 1534
Recognizing Best Habits: 1188
Recognizing Cause and Effect: 647
Recognizing Dubious Authority: 1780
Recognizing Good Performance: 490
Recognizing Homonyms: 1534
Recognizing Improper Questions: 1780
Recognizing Long and Short Vowels: 1534
Recognizing Sentences: 1248
Recognizing Silent Letters: 1534
Recognizing Symmetrical Relationships: 1780
Recognizing Transitive Relationships: 1780
Recognizing Vowels and Consonants: 1534
Recommendation Response: 633
Recommendations: 554, 2472
Recommendations/Plan: 870
Recommended: 2198
Reconocimiento de Dibujos: 264
Recovery: 2129
Recreation: 162, 618, 1825, 1929
Recreation and Leisure Profile: 1839
Recreation/Hobbies: 2764
Recreation/Leisure: 2127
Recreational: 1927
Recreational Movement: 2316
Recreational Reading: 2487
Recreational Use: 1932
Recruiting and Selecting: 2424
Rectitude: 2237
Recuperación a Largo Plazo: 264
The Red Ace of Spades: 2743
Red-Green Deficiency: 1159
Reduced: 799
Reduced Flexibility: 226
Reduces Control: 1296
Reduction: 329
Reduction Decisions: 807
Reduction of/lrw/ Clusters: 2438
Reduction of /s/ Clusters: 2438
Reference Books: 1491
Reference Materials: 1318
Reference Selection and Usage: 684
Reference Skills: 342, 343, 822, 904, 2137
Referent: 2415
Referral and Community Resources: 684
Referral Data: 1777
Refinishing Technology: 1792, 1794
Reflected Self/Classmates: 2368
Reflected Self/Cooperating Teacher: 2368
Reflected Self/Friends: 2368
Reflected Self/Parents: 2368
Reflected Self/Partners: 2368
Reflected Self/Professionals: 2368
Reflected Self/Supervisor: 2368
Reflected Self/Supervisors: 2366
Reflected Self/Teachers: 2368
Reflected Self/Teachers or Professors: 2368
Reflected Teacher Perceptions: 2368
Reflection: 716
Reflection and Rotation: 444
Reflective: 2757
Reflective Observation: 64, 1469, 1471
Reflective Processing (Deep Processing: 1307
Reflex: 1056, 1770
Reflex Integration: 772
Reflexes: 1901
Reform: 712, 1373

Reformer: 1310
Refusal: 467, 2242
Refusals: 1006
Refusing Demands: 1290
Register: 1477
Registered Nurse: 399
Regression: 915, 2307
Regularity of Drinking: 132, 2874
Regulation: 1284
Regulation and Control of Drives: 912
Regulations Enforcement: 1841
Rehabilitation: 712, 1373
Rehabilitation Services: 410
Rehearsal: 1720
Rehearsal Effects: 320
Rehearsal Preparations and Procedures: 684
Reinforcement: 279
Reinforcement Menu: 1052
Reinforcement of Pain: 291
Reinforcement of Self-Concept: 907
Reinforcement of Wellness: 291
Reinforcement Survey Schedules: 1052
Reinforcers for Specific Populations: 279
Reinforces Parent: 1889
Reintegration: 712, 1373
Reject: 1966
Rejecting: 1589
Rejecting Convention: 1931, 1932
Rejection: 78, 1214, 1881, 1988, 2242
Rejection of Child: 1005
Relaciones Especiales: 264
Related Duties: 989
Relatedness of Topic Sentence and Three Other Sentences: 204
Relater: 1915
Relates and Applies Coursework: 2530
Relating: 234, 2111
Relating to and Supporting Staff: 2575
Relating to Others: 40, 166
Relating to People: 459
Relation with Co-workers: 63
Relational Concepts: 813
Relational Terms: 918
Relational Vocabulary: 2695
Relations: 195, 2518
Relations-Peers: 1345
Relations-Subordinates: 1345
Relations-Supervisor: 1345
Relations to People in General: 1716
Relations with Extended Family: 2442
Relations with Parents: 280
Relations With Students: 2351
Relations with Teachers/Peers: 2894
Relationship: 206, 646, 1205, 1477, 2349
Relationship Building: 1267
Relationship Development: 2097
Relationship Dimensions: 495
Relationship Incomplete Sentences Test: 2381
Relationship Problems: 2287
Relationship Skill: 1467
Relationship Stress: 1684
Relationship to an Adult: 285
Relationship to Inanimate Objects (Cognitive): 1263
Relationship to Persons: 1263
Relationship with Co-Workers: 1209
Relationship With Family: 1489
Relationship With Peers: 1489
Relationship with Spouse: 1889
Relationship with Spouse/Partner: 2510
Relationship With Teachers: 1489
Relationship with the Client: 1830
Relationships: 900, 1494, 1545, 1904, 2425, 2647, 2868
Relationships Orientation: 1561, 2278
Relationships to Adults: 1041
Relationships to Children: 1041
Relationships with Children: 2074
Relationships with Colleagues: 1971
Relationships with Employees: 1971
Relationships with Other People: 1824
Relationships with Other Persons: 2016
Relationships with People: 1822
Relationships with Superiors: 1971
Relative and Adverbial Clauses: 2233
Relative Clause: 2662
Relatives: 1427, 2131, 2292
Relaxation Potential: 794
Relaxation Pursuits: 2605
Relaxed: 990, 1822, 2274
Relaxed Style: 37, 2265
Relaxed vs. Tense: 477, 888
Relaying Customer Views: 2385
Relearning: 320
Release: 1557
Relevance: 1861, 2068, 2133, 2583
Relevancy: 1542
Relevancy Scores: 1619
Relevant Means: 1619
Relevant Practice: 1275
Reliability: 1212
Reliance on Others: 2242
Religion: 646, 1705, 1716, 1941, 1942
Religion/Morals/Ethics: 1492
Religious: 1030, 1639, 2539, 2626, 2800
Religious Activities: 380, 398, 399, 618, 1790
Religious Leader: 380, 398
Religious Needs: 1583
Religious Studies: 618
Religious Well-Being: 2474
Religiousness: 1964
Relocation: 401
Remediation: 1746
Remembering Word Pairs: 2693
Reminiscing: 1064

Response to Directions: 304
Response to General Questioning Prior to Recall: 685
Response to Reading: 1281
Response Validity: 546
Responses: 653
Responses to Slips: 2551
Responsibility: 1, 2, 35, 36, 219, 252, 372, 401, 945, 1101, 1136, 1333, 1345, 1694, 1695, 1701, 1825, 1860, 1930, 1955, 1969, 1972, 2181, 2204, 2346, 2355, 2357, 2452, 2776, 2804
Responsibility Implementation: 2423
Responsibility/Irresponsibility: 1340
Responsible: 980, 1470, 1676, 2069
Responsible Behavior: 2444
Responsible Behaviors: 1194
Responsive Naming: 199
Responsive Naming-Nouns: 356
Responsive Naming-Verbs: 356
Responsiveness: 1316, 1823, 1968
Responsiveness to Nonverbal Cues: 1830
Responsiveness to Objects: 193
Responsiveness to the Community: 636
Responsivity: 1216
Restatement: 716
Restaurant Manager: 380, 398, 399, 1790
Restless: 1954
Restless-Impulsive: 681
Restlessness: 2784
Restraint: 712, 1158, 1373, 1443, 1549
Restrictions of Role: 1889
Restrictive-Accepting: 1845
Restrictiveness of Regulation: 1026
Results: 1147, 1969, 2571
Results Focus: 1923
Results of Neuropsychological Testing: 1777
Results Orientation: 2097
Results Oriented: 2274
Retail Commercial Baking: 1792, 1794
Retail Math: 2347
Retail Selling: 1222
Retail Store Manager: 380
Retail Trades: 1792, 1794
Retardation: 2120, 2216
Retardation-Lack of Emotion: 2108, 2109
Retardation-Stubborn: 748
Retention: 2409
Retention of Main Ideals: 901
Retention of Significant Details: 901
Retirement in General: 2208
Retirement Living: 83
Retirement Planning: 83
Retiring: 1688
Retrospective: 2596
Revenge: 1681
Reverie: 2128
Reversal: 770
Reversals: 430, 1138, 2134, 2175, 2469
Reverse Memory: 1485
Reversed Letters: 797, 798
Reversed Similarities: 899
Reversible Active: 2662
Reversible and Nonreversible Passives: 2233
Reversible Passive: 2662
Revised Art Scale: 2869
Revised Manuscript: 2787
Revolutionary America: 145
Revolving Assembly Table Work Task Unit: 922
Reward: 2020, 2415
Reward Sharing: 490
Rewarding: 197, 2424
Rewards: 379, 1163, 1860, 2256
Rewards and Recognition: 1463, 2129
Rewards and Satisfactions: 2584
Rewriting: 1405
Rhetorical: 1667
Rhetorical Skills: 56, 621, 992, 1997
Rhyme: 1980
Rhyming: 740, 1224
Rhyming Words: 2596
Rhythm: 90, 199, 1287, 1524, 1525, 1751, 1753, 2056
Rhythm Concepts: 1320
Rhythm Imagery: 1752
Rhythmic Memory: 1629
Rhythmic Readiness: 1176
Rhythmicity: 425
Riddles: 1379, 2487
Rigging: 1537, 2067, 2151, 2152, 2644, 2769
Right: 1227, 2820
Right and Left: 1085
Right Brain: 2545
Right Eye: 2852
Right Frontal: 1525
Right Hand: 2125
Right Hand Dexterity: 2244
Right Hemisphere: 85, 1525
Right Mode Dominance: 1197
Right Parietal-Occipital: 1525
Right plus Left plus Both Hands: 2125
Right Sensorimotor: 1524, 1525
Right Temporal: 1525
Right-Left: 199
Right-Left Differentiation Subscale Score: 1690
Right/Left Discrimination: 1865
Right-Left Orientation: 1613
Right-Left Preference: 2811
Rigid Type: 1313
Rigid-Flexible: 218
Rigidity: 448, 2621
Rigidity-Dogmatism: 2367
Rigidity/Obsessiveness: 1207
Rise and Fall of the Soviet Union: 762
Risk: 1163, 1493, 2805, 2882
Risk Avoidance: 490
Risk-Avoidance Pattern: 2238

Risk Avoidance Scale: 1972
Risk Factors: 133
Risk Management: 2098
Risk-Neutral Pattern: 2238
Risk-Preference Pattern: 2238
Risk-Taker: 618
Risk Taking: 679, 727, 1333, 1440, 2346, 2425, 2521, 2631
Risk-Taking: 724, 945
Risk Taking/Adventure Style: 1790
Risk-Taking Style: 400
Risk Taking/Uncertainty: 1497
Risk-Taking/Venturesomeness: 490
Risk Tolerance: 966
Risks/Adventure: 380
Road Runner: 305
Road Test in Traffic for Testing/Selecting/Rating/and Training Truck Drivers: 857
Robotics Technology: 1794
ROC Structured: 1513
ROC Unstructured: 1513
Rod "C" Lengthened 1/16 inch: 2479
Rod "E" Shortened 1/16 inch Spring "E" Disconnected at Lever "E": 2479
Role: 191, 820
Role Ambiguity: 1825
Role and Task Definition: 2633
Role Assumptions: 1437
Role Boundary: 1825
Role Clarity: 1913
Role Definition: 794
Role-Emotional: 2397
Role Expectations: 2355
Role Insufficiency: 1825
Role Limitations Due to Emotional Problems: 2158
Role Limitations Due to Physical Health Problems: 2158
Role Limitations-Emotional: 1187
Role Limitations-Physical: 1187
Role Maladaptation: 136
Role Modeling: 1923
Role Orientation: 1582, 1883
Role Overload: 1825
Role Performance: 1008
Role-Physical: 2397
Role Relationship: 2034
Role Strain: 1643
Role Values: 1493
Roles of the Library Media Specialist: 684
Romance: 162, 1929
Romance Languages: 2530
The Romans: 2932
Romantic Love: 1946
Romantic Relationships: 2369
Room Management: 63
Root Words: 1768
Rotation: 329
Rotations: 303
Rote Counting: 346
Route Finding: 1771
Routine Administrative Functions: 1689
Routine/Creative: 387
Routine-Dependence: 1163
Rule Clarity: 495
Rule Conformity: 2315
Rule-Conscious vs. Expedient: 2417
Rule Consciousness: 1576
Rule-Consciousness: 538
Rule Free: 1294
Rule/Group Conformity: 1404
Rule of Silent e: 2254
Rule Shift Card: 295
Rules and Expectations: 2035

Sad: 2647
Sad Mood: 1748, 1749
Sadistic: 690, 2306
Sadness: 1374
Sadness/Depression: 1006
Sado-Masochism: 1744
Safe and Orderly Environment: 2314
Safe Job Performance: 944
Safety: 452, 909, 1558, 1894, 2316, 2327, 2521, 2746
Safety and First Aid: 1019
Safety and Health: 1409
Safety and Order: 941, 1244, 2273, 2921
Safety and Prevention: 1065
Safety/Driver Education: 2026
Safety/Environment: 1788
Safety Features: 1743
Safety Scale: 1972
Safety/Security: 1608
Sage: 1451
SAGES Quotient: 2328
Salary: 1345
Sales: 183, 380, 398, 399, 406, 411, 618, 1177, 1237, 1285, 1334, 1551, 1790, 2882
Sales Ability and Potential: 2269
Sales and Marketing: 1044
Sales Application Verification: 989
Sales Approaches: 989
Sales Aptitude: 2266, 2605
Sales Aptitude Scale: 1972
Sales Aptitude Test: 973
Sales Assistance: 2424
Sales Attitude: 1711
Sales Closing: 2265
Sales Closure: 2713
Sales Complaints: 1222
Sales Comprehension: 2277
Sales Disposition: 2265
Sales Effectiveness: 2271
Sales Focus: 2385
Sales Inventory: 2605

Sales Judgement: 2266
Sales Knowledge: 2713
Sales Motivation: 2277
Sales Orientation: 1948
Sales Potential: 1212
Sales Promotion: 2713
Sales Results: 421
Sales Style Scores: 2278
Sales Style Synthesis: 2278
Sales Terms: 1323
Salesman: 2825
Salesman Performance: 989
Salubrious Lifestyle Scale: 2527
Same/Different: 84, 2192
Same Sex Peer Relations: 2358
Sanctions: 1402
Sanguine: 2649
Satisfaction: 379, 635, 1128, 1276, 1705, 1736, 1737, 2587, 2652
Satisfaction of Individual Motives: 1137
Satisfaction of Interpersonal Relations: 1137
Satisfaction with Experiences at College: 57
Satisfaction With Leadership: 1137
Satisfaction With Parenting: 1883
Satisfaction with Parenting Performance: 1888
Satisfaction with Present Insurance Sales Career: 421
Satisfaction with Spouse/Ex-Spouse Parenting Performance: 1888
Satisfaction with the Parent-Child Relationship: 1888
Satisficing: 490
Savings Ratio: 320
Saxophone and French Horn: 1280
Say What You Hear: 2029
Say Words: 2176
Scale: 1172
Scale for Use With the Blind: 1375
Scale for Use With the Deaf: 1375
Scales: 1042, 1043
Scanning: 1614, 1865, 2487, 2821
Scanning and Tracking: 356
Scanning and Tracking of Single Words: 356
Scapegoat: 479
Scarf Sign: 1258
Scattered Scanning Test: 563
Schedules and Graphs: 343
Scheduling: 452
Schematics and Electrical Print Reading: 920, 1279
Schematics and Print Reading: 1537, 2643
Schematics/Test Instruments: 924
Schizoaffective Disorder: 2107
Schizoid: 690, 1687, 1961, 2306, 2520
Schizoid Personality: 79, 2615
Schizophrenia: 77, 79, 538, 690, 1543, 1698, 1959, 2006, 2107, 2615
Schizophrenia (Sc): 1697
Schizophrenic and Schizophreniform Disorders: 642
Schizophrenic-Objective: 218
Schizotypal: 77, 690, 1687, 1961, 2306, 2520
Scholar: 1310
Scholarly: 618
Scholarly Excellence: 1108, 2083
Scholarly Skills: 707
Scholastic Abilities: 2309
Scholastic Aptitude: 2901
Scholastic Attitude Score: 2670
Scholastic Competence: 2369
School: 286, 451, 467, 478, 1276, 1374, 1496, 1716, 1941, 1942, 2318, 2391
School-Academic: 694
School Achievement: 2605
School Adjustment: 200
School Administrator: 1790
School Administrators: 648
School Affiliation: 2365
School Age Core Scales: 349
School-Acquired Information: 2328
School Attendance: 1500
School Behavior: 777
School Behavior Status Checklist: 1052
School Building/Supplies/Maintenance: 648
School Building/Supplies/Upkeep: 648
School Climate: 216, 843, 2355
School Climate/Environment for Learning: 1885, 2532, 2623
School Climate Survey for Parents: 649
School Climate Survey for Students: 649
School Climate Survey for Teachers: 649
School/Coursework: 2130
School Disturbance Predictor: 1522
School Effort: 909
School Facilities and Programs: 158
School Failure: 2311
School Functioning: 290
School Guidance and Counseling: 2026
School History: 1886
School Information Services: 648
School Interests: 904
School Law: 684
School Leaders Licensure Assessment: 2026
School Library Aide: 411
School Literary Magazine: 411
School Maladjustment: 280
School Math: 1667
School Newspaper: 411
School Officer: 411
School Organization and Administration: 2623
School Perceptions: 120
School Plans: 904
School Play: 411
School Problems: 280, 1698
School Programs and Policies: 216
School Psychologist: 2026
School Questionnaires: 158
School Readiness: 759

School Reinforcement Survey Schedule: 1052
School Relations or Occupational Relations (adult level): 374
School Rewards: 909
School Rules: 2323
School Satisfaction: 1916
School Social Worker: 2026
School Subjects: 1177, 1790
School Success: 1212
School Superintendent: 380
School/Work: 70
Schoolwork: 648
Science: 121, 160, 364, 380, 389, 399, 411, 464, 570, 665, 684, 742, 750, 752, 822, 829, 904, 961, 992, 1094, 1237, 1318, 1418, 1657, 1667, 11759, 1789, 1790, 1838, 2026, 2483, 2484, 2654, 2735, 2740, 2742, 2833, 2901
Science Activities: 635
Science and Mathematics: 617
Science & Technology: 406
Science/Engineering Technicians: 2822
Science Fair: 411
Science-Mathematics-Health: 408
Science-Medical/Life: 416
Science Perceptions: 120
Science-Physical: 416
Science-Professional: 395, 414, 415, 417, 702, 1541
Science Reasoning: 56, 621, 902, 1997
Science-Skilled: 395, 414, 415, 417, 702, 1541
Science Teacher: 1790
Science Vocabulary: 2712
Science Writing: 618
Scientific: 5, 86, 412, 485, 1074, 1157, 1177, 1413, 1483, 1711, 1724, 1817, 1819, 2255, 2257, 2264, 2836
Scientific Attitude: 2325
Scientific Data Processing: 1792
Scientific Research/Development: 398
Scientific/Technical: 1350
Scientific/Technical/Electronic: 179
Scientific/Technical/Health: 993
Scissors: 2439
Scope Management: 2098
Scope of Knowledge: 1886
Scrambled Words: 1405
Screening Composite: 2693
Screening Score: 2239
Screening Test: 2651
Screws: 722
Searching: 2876
Searching Response Score: 632
Seashore Rhythm Test: 1164
Seclusiveness: 2120
Second Order Indices: 2346
Second Pass: 2933
Secondary: 2127
Secondary and Post-Secondary: 905
Secondary Character: 2647
Secondary Traits: 654
Secretarial: 410, 2026
Secretarial-Clerical/Office Workers: 2000
Secretaries: 1692
Secretary: 380, 398, 399, 1790, 2825
Section Index: 2031
Secure: 1676
Security: 371, 1163, 1345, 1694, 1695, 1701, 1724, 2256, 2349, 2586, 2804, 2915
Security and Maintenance: 648
Security/Comfort with Others: 1961
Security Guard: 398, 399
Security/Stability: 396
Sedatives: 2554
Sedentariness: 2882
Sedentary: 1478
Seek Constant Improvement: 1858
Seek Professional Help: 72
Seek Relaxing Diversions: 72
Seek Social Support: 72
Seek Spiritual Support: 72
Seek to Belong: 72
Seeking Alternative Rewards: 699
Seeking Guidance and Support: 699
Seeking Information or Opinions: 1147
Seeking Social Support: 2858
Seeks and Uses Feedback: 2101
Seeks Broad Business Knowledge: 2101
Seeks Company: 2605, 2648
Seeks Opportunities to Learn: 2101
Segmenting Words into Sounds: 187
Seizure: 1853
Selecting and Training: 1554
Selecting Bricks: 254
Selecting/Developing: 2425
Selecting Main Ideas: 1455, 1456
Selection: 1746
Selection and Evaluation Summary: 857, 989
Selection of Jobs Based on Work Preferences: 1617
Selection Test Scores: 627
Selective Analysis of Perception: 2044
Selective Attention: 1020, 1044, 2794
Selective Listening: 1753
Selective Mutism: 876
Selectivity of Symptoms: 2522
Self: 854, 1011, 1443, 1550, 2371, 2575, 2875
Self-Abusive Behavior: 1, 2
Self Acceptance: 2365
Self-Acceptance: 372, 1939
Self Achievement: 1689
Self-Actualization: 243, 1163, 1608, 1655, 2349, 2367
Self-Actualizing: 1150, 1498, 1862
Self-Actualizing Value: 1939
Self-Adequacy: 2355
Self-Administered Questionnaire: 158
Self-Aggrandizing: 1222

Self-Alienation: 1698
Self-Alienation (Pd5): 1697
Self-Appraisal: 403, 413, 2828
Self Assertion: 2365
Self-Assessment: 2632
Self-Assessment of Learning: 975
Self-Assured vs. Apprehensive: 477
Self-Assured vs. Guilt-Prone: 888
Self-Average: 2635
Self-Awareness: 300, 661
Self-Blame: 72
Self Care: 2195
Self-Care: 59, 198, 686, 879, 1409, 1499, 1591, 1825, 1906, 2041, 2296, 2444
Self-Care and Safety: 2747
Self-Care Skills: 60, 1245
Self-Care Social: 2308
Self-Centered Concerns: 1716
Self-Centered/Explosive: 2036
Self Concept: 120, 121, 1734, 2368, 2380, 2894
Self-Concept: 77, 252, 265, 478, 929, 1266, 1276, 1440, 1468, 1586, 1815, 1991, 2354, 2355, 2366, 2371, 2647
Self-Concept in Mathematics: 1599
Self Concept/Nurse: 2368
Self-Concept/Nurse: 2366
Self Concept/Teacher: 2368
Self Confidence: 289
Self-Confidence: 37, 68, 219, 268, 433, 1181, 1290, 1293, 1393, 1396, 1832, 1930, 1955, 1983, 2007, 2034, 2081, 2265, 2535, 2584, 2776, 2784
Self-Confident: 2605, 2648
Self-Confident Scholar: 2530
Self-Consciousness: 2218
Self Control: 1044
Self-Control: 68, 372, 538, 1293, 1294, 1735, 1955, 1983, 2129, 2347, 2452, 2776, 2784, 2835
Self-Control Traits: 1930, 1955
Self-Controlled vs. Unrestrained: 2417
Self-Controlling: 2858
Self-Corrected: 2251
Self-Corrections: 2469
Self Critical: 226
Self-Critical: 37, 2265
Self-Criticism: 790, 2652
Self-Deception: 1932
Self-Deceptive Enhancement: 1899
Self-Defeating: 690, 1687, 2306
Self-Demeaning: 1685
Self Depreciation: 256
Self-Depreciation: 427
Self Description: 819
Self Destructiveness: 2521
Self-Determination: 2780
Self-Determination Characteristics: 2622
Self-Devaluation: 1685
Self-Development: 1923, 2915
Self-Development and Improvement: 1569, 2605
Self Directed: 1966
Self-Directed: 1954, 2759
Self-Directedness: 698
Self-Direction: 1, 2, 59, 198
Self-Direction of Professional Development: 1830
Self-Discipline: 1201, 1769, 2218, 2526, 2762
Self-Disciplined vs. Impulsive: 2618
Self Disclosure: 716
Self-Disclosure: 698, 1292, 1743, 2291
Self-Discovery: 1141
Self-Effacing-Egocentric: 1940
Self-Efficacy: 403, 1307, 1733
Self-Efficacy for Learning and Performance: 1720
Self-Enhancing: 37, 2265
Self Esteem: 226, 2346
Self-Esteem: 280, 289, 1057, 1101, 1276, 1293, 1307, 1608, 1749, 1948, 1983, 2061, 2131, 2362, 2363, 2371, 2403, 2526, 2783
Self-Esteem Problems: 569, 938
Self-Esteem Quotient: 2361
Self Evaluation: 1497, 1830
Self-Evaluation Scale: 1052
Self-Expression: 371, 1292, 1307
Self-Expressions: 63
Self-Focused: 990
Self-Fulfillment: 2751
Self-Harm: 1959, 2306
Self Help: 63, 453, 1194
Self-Help: 454, 1192, 1194, 1259, 1263, 1391, 1733, 1801, 2088, 2528
Self-Help Age: 811
Self-Help Development: 809
Self-Help Scales: 1041
Self-Help Skills: 206, 2043, 2213
Self-Help/Social: 124
Self-Ideal Body Description Difference Score: 795
Self-Identification: 1194
Self Image: 1025, 1618
Self-Image: 1297, 2410, 2535, 2614
Self-Image Problems: 1729
Self Improvement: 2424
Self-Improvement: 1716
Self-Inflicted vs. Other-Inflicted Pain: 1869
Self-Initiated Behavior: 878
Self-Love: 78, 426, 1679
Self-Maintenance: 61, 2763
Self-Management: 2204, 2425
Self-Management Behaviors: 293
Self-Management Skills: 2322
Self Mastery: 707
Self-Medicated Drinking: 75
Self-Motivated: 1954, 2181
Self Nurturing Activity: 2074
Self-Organization: 2776
Self-Orientation: 263
Self-Oriented/Narcissism: 362

Self-Other Comparisons: 401
Self-Other Satisfaction: 2363
Self-Perception Incongruence: 1002
Self Rating: 2122
Self-Rating: 1008
Self-Realization: 372
Self-Reference: 2290
Self Regard: 201
Self-Regard: 243, 1939
Self-Regulation: 1265
Self-Related Behaviors : 2444
Self-Reliance: 280, 374, 538, 1276, 1832, 2347, 2605
Self-Reliance vs. Dependence: 865
Self-Reliant: 2577
Self-Reliant/Self-Oriented vs. Dependent/Group Oriented: 2648
Self-Reliant vs. Group-Oriented: 2417
Self-Respect: 1946
Self Responsibility/Problem Solving: 294
Self Security: 2365
Self-Sentiment: 1721, 2318
Self-/Social Awareness: 331
Self Space: 1494
Self-Strength: 1396
Self-Subordination: 2315
Self Sufficiency: 1044
Self-Sufficiency: 1201, 2007
Self Testing: 1455, 1456
Self-Validation: 467
Self-Willed: 1954
Self-Worth: 294, 1210, 2136, 2371
Selling: 412, 485, 1483, 1711, 1817, 2836
Selling Goods: 1818
Selling Intangibles: 1222
Selling Pressure: 490
Selling Real Estate: 1222
Selling Services: 1818
Semantic: 2518, 2596
Semantic Absurdities: 2911
Semantic Association: 2596
Semantic Categorization: 2172, 2596
Semantic Cluster Ratio: 375
Semantic Clustering: 376
Semantic Evaluation: 996
Semantic Fluency: 2202
Semantic Knowledge: 241
Semantic Production: 996
Semantic Relationships: 540
Semantics: 628, 1359, 2695, 2886
Semantics Quotient: 2694
Semi-Professional: 1342
Semi-Skilled: 1342
Senior Leadership: 2129
Sensate: 1814
Sensation: 1056, 1366
Sensation Seeking: 280, 1745
Sensation vs. Intuition: 1365, 1387
Sense-Making Skill: 1467
Sense of Competence: 1889
Sense of Humor: 1964
Sense of Inadequacy: 280
Sense of Ownership/Sense of Mission: 2097
Sense of Personal Freedom: 374
Sense of Personal Worth: 374
Sense of Reality: 912
Senser: 1331
Sensing: 1688, 2411
Sensing Feeling: 1562
Sensing-Feeling: 1464
Sensing/Feeling: 1473
Sensing/Intuition: 1750, 1828
Sensing Thinking: 1562
Sensing-Thinking: 1464
Sensing/Thinking: 1473
Sensing vs. Intuition: 1755
Sensitive: 1294, 1686, 1958
Sensitive vs. Utilitarian: 2417
Sensitivity: 538, 654, 1201, 1522, 1667, 1946, 2631
Sensitivity/Other Awareness: 1497
Sensitivity to Approval: 1210
Sensitivity to Client Issues: 1830
Sensitivity to Cultural Differences: 1830
Sensitivity to Others: 40
Sensitivity to Rejection: 1627
Sensitivity to Sex-Role Stereotypes: 1830
Sensor: 1950, 1951
Sensorimotor: 1771
Sensorimotor Development: 2778
Sensorimotor Organization: 878
Sensory: 234, 1610, 1615, 1722, 1821, 2111, 2127
Sensory Awareness: 661
Sensory Function: 235
Sensory Imperception: 1164
Sensory Integration: 1868
Sensory Motor: 1801
Sensory Perception: 1194
Sensory Perceptual: 1164
Sensory-Motor: 804
Sensory-Motor Ability: 445
Sensory/Motor Auditory: 1282
Sensory/Motor Visual: 1282
Sensory/Perceptual: 85, 1044
Sensory-Physical Factors: 1732
Sensual: 1169
Sentence Assembly: 540
Sentence Combining: 2694, 2731
Sentence Completion: 821, 1423
Sentence Completion Naming: 2667, 2725
Sentence Complexity: 2458
Sentence Comprehension: 1055, 2178, 2296
Sentence Construction: 744, 2898
Sentence Formation: 1657
Sentence Formulation: 76
Sentence Imitation: 797, 798, 1168, 2695

Sentence Intelligibility: 209
Sentence Length: 2201
Sentence Meaning: 18, 1203, 2183
Sentence Memory: 1337
Sentence Organization: 348
Sentence-Picture: 2172
Sentence Questions: 763
Sentence Reading: 165, 2484, 2488
Sentence Repetition: 763, 1740, 1771
Sentence Response: 1425
Sentence Sequencing: 2712
Sentence Structure: 539, 540, 571, 616, 830, 955, 967, 992, 1248, 1997
Sentence Structure Corrections per T-Unit: 2661
Sentence Structure/Variety: 2933
Sentence-to-Words: 2674
Sentence Variety: 1364
Sentences: 987, 2487, 2864
Sentences and Grammar: 1528
Sentences to Dictation: 199
Sentences Total: 1427
Sentience: 1965, 1988
Sentiment Structures: 1721
Sentimental: 66
Separation: 2521
Separation Anxiety: 79
Separation Anxiety Disorder: 77, 876
Separation Fears: 213
Separation From Mother Figure: 2614
Separation/Panic: 1730
Sequence: 319, 641
Sequence Recognition: 669
Sequenced Functioning: 2706
Sequenced Syllable Rates: 2706
Sequenced Syllables: 2706
Sequenced Vowels: 2706
Sequences: 388, 476, 899, 901, 1075, 2677
Sequences Three Events: 2672
Sequences Three Events With Competing Message: 2672
Sequencing: 445, 831, 1909, 2236, 2434, 2647
Sequencing and Rhythmic Abilities: 235
Sequencing Events [pictured task steps]: 2297
Sequencing Events [recall task steps]: 2297
Sequencing Events [time of year]: 2297
Sequencing Objects [size]: 2297
Sequencing/Pictures: 2240
Sequencing Praxis: 2377
Sequencing Words [alphabetical]: 2297
Sequential: 1907
Sequential and Quantitative Reasoning: 837
Sequential Order: 1485
Sequential Processing: 1472
Sequential Skill: 1262
Sequential Synthesis: 2252
Sequin Form Board: 1653
Serial Clustering: 376
Serial Learning: 320
Serial Pattern Matching: 366
Serial Processing: 1307
Serial Reasoning: 1607, 1756
Serial Writing: 199
Seriation: 320, 2041
Series: 125, 1800, 2240
Series Induction Test: 1257
Serious: 2605, 2648
Seriousness: 1223, 1928
Serve: 2653
Service: 1100, 1157, 1789, 1984, 2264, 2833
Service and Transportation: 179
Service/Dedication to a Cause: 396
Service-Instructional: 416
Service Level Index: 1300
Service Orientation: 1212, 1442, 2490
Service-Professional: 395, 414, 415, 417, 702, 1541
Service-Skilled: 395, 414, 415, 417, 702, 1541
Service-Social: 416
Service to Persons: 2751
Set Terminology: 1604
Setting: 2647
Setting a Developmental Climate: 300
Setting Goals: 1440, 2575
Setting Goals and Objectives: 903, 1550
Setting Goals and Objectives and Planning with Employees: 1480
Setting Goals and Standards: 1570, 2070
Setting Goals/Planning with Employees: 1479
Setting Objectives: 2571
Setting Objectives and Terminal Behavior: 2775
Setting Organizational Objectives: 1569, 2605
Setup and Cleanup: 2316
Sevens-Cheerers/Animators/Cheerleaders: 958
Several Ways: 2069
Severe Clinical Syndromes: 1687
Severe Depression: 1079, 1626
Severe Discrepancy Level: 1461
Severe Personality Pathology: 1687
Severity: 2388
Severity Interval Rating for Phonology: 214
Severity Level: 1522
Severity of Actual Penalties: 1026
Severity of Functional Behavior Problems: 1643
Severity of Symptoms: 2522
Severity Rating: 199
Sex: 646, 1214, 1705, 1716, 1941, 1988
Sex After the Affair: 660
Sex Apprehension/Confidence Scale: 1744
Sex Deviance Scales: 1744
Sex Deviation: 2109
Sex Drive: 2784
Sex Item Truthfulness: 2393
Sex Knowledge and Beliefs Scale: 1744
Sex of Student: 1500
Sex Problems: 927

Sex-Role Preference: 1332
Sex Stereotype: 2882
Sex-Symbol: 2869
Sexual: 1169, 1927
Sexual Abuse: 442, 460, 467, 1006, 1931
Sexual Abuse Perpetrator: 1932
Sexual Abuse Specific Items: 457
Sexual Abuse Survivor's Test: 2381
Sexual Adjustment: 2393
Sexual Assault: 2393
Sexual Behavior: 1, 1522
Sexual Concerns: 1313, 2782
Sexual Discomfort: 1685
Sexual Disorders: 1433
Sexual Dissatisfaction: 1582
Sexual Disturbance: 748
Sexual Dysfunction Scales: 1744
Sexual Dysfunctions: 1433
Sexual Expectations: 2034
Sexual Experiences: 659
Sexual Fantasies: 1433
Sexual History: 1431
Sexual Identification: 2006
Sexual Identity: 2647
Sexual Inadequacies: 1744
Sexual Integrity: 439
Sexual Interaction: 717
Sexual Involvement: 2521
Sexual Maladjustment: 931
Sexual Morality: 2396
Sexual Motivation: 2396
Sexual Obsessions Scale: 1744
Sexual Offenses: 1433, 2395
Sexual Relationship: 2117
Sexual Satisfaction: 793
Sexual Symptoms: 2216
Sexual Trauma: 2521
Sexual Victim History: 1433
Sexuality: 439, 443, 684, 690, 965, 1832
Sexuality and Emotional Awareness: 2746
SFAB Total Score: 2579
Shading: 1214
Shame: 1626
Shame and Doubt: 1631
Shape: 195, 884, 1610, 1919
Shape and Pictorial Representation: 2089
Shape Assembly: 239
Shape Discrimination: 2297
Shape Identification: 565, 1534
Shape Memory Test: 1405
Shape Recognition: 1865, 2297
Shaper: 296
Shapes: 331, 463, 1224, 1717
Shapes Identification: 1513
Shared Attention: 2052
Shared Leadership: 2632
Shares Information: 1296
Sharing: 1953
Sharing Credit: 490
She/I Past Tense (Best/Worst): 1298
She/I Present Tense (Best/Worst): 1298
Sheet Metal: 1792
Sheet Metal Worker: 398, 399
Shepherd: 1723
Shifting Attention Arrow Color Accuracy: 567
Shifting Attention Arrow Color Speed: 567
Shifting Attention Arrow Color Thruput: 567
Shifting Attention Arrow Direction Accuracy: 567
Shifting Attention Arrow Direction Speed: 567
Shifting Attention Arrow Direction Thruput: 567
Shifting Attention Discovery Accuracy: 567
Shifting Attention Discovery Failures to Maintain Set: 567
Shifting Attention Discovery Nonconceptual Responses: 567
Shifting Attention Discovery Perseverative Errors: 567
Shifting Attention Discovery Rule Shifts Completed: 567
Shifting Attention Discovery Speed: 567
Shifting Attention Discovery Thruput: 567
Shifting Attention Instruction Accuracy: 567
Shifting Attention Instruction Speed: 567
Shifting Attention Instruction Thruput: 567
Shifts Attention: 1614
Shocking Things/Earthquakes!: 2743
Shop: 2152
Shop Arithmetic: 1633
Shop Machines/Tools and Equipment: 2644
Shop Machines/Tools/Equipment: 1537
Shoplifting: 2403
Shopping: 63, 212
Shopping and Purchasing: 1065
Short and Long Vowel Sounds: 827, 2254
Short Answers: 1425
Short Blessed Test: 434
Short-Delay Cued Recall: 375
Short Delay Free Recall: 375
Short Incomplete Sentences: 2381
Short Memory: 2202
Short Recognition Memory Test for Faces: 378
Short Recognition Memory Test for Words: 378
Short Story Verbatim: 2159
Short-Term Auditory Memory: 1529
Short-Term Memory: 1644, 1907, 2485, 2901
Short Term Memory Composite: 320
Short Term Memory—Letters: 2180
Short Term Memory Retrieval: 1083
Short Term Memory—Words: 2180
Short Term Recall: 1462
Short-Term Recognition of Pictures: 356
Short-Term Recognition of Words: 356
Short-Term Visual Memory: 261
Short Test: 1753
Short Vowel Sounds: 2254

Show New Way to Work: 2923
Showing Commitment to the Team: 802
Shy vs. Bold: 477
Shy vs. Venturesome: 888
Shyness: 1290, 1628, 1823, 2449
Shyness/Self-Consciousness: 1698
Shyness/Self-Consciousness (Si1): 1697
Sibling=Ally: 1006
Sibling Chemical Use: 1931
Sibling Rivalry: 317
Sibling=Stressor: 1006
Siblings: 1011, 1496, 1500
Sideways Parachute: 1258, 1668
Sight: 832, 833
Sight Vocabulary: 1588, 2134
Sight Word Writing: 2180
Sight Words: 730, 2175
Sight Written: 833
Sign Language: 1194
Significance of U.S. Events: 570
Significance of World Events: 570
Significant Other Drug Problem: 1932
Significant Reading Discrepancy: 869
Signs of Withdrawal: 1729
Silence: 716
Silent Letters: 2175
Silent Reading: 775, 861, 917, 1272, 2462
Silent Reading Comprehension: 823
Silent Reading Paragraphs: 987
Silent Reading Quotient: 1051
Silent Reading Sentences: 987
Silliness: 2109
Similar Meanings: 726
Similarities: 558, 837, 1088, 1424, 1731, 1800, 2375, 2840, 2859, 2860, 2862, 2864, 2878
Similarities and Differences: 2471
Similarity to College Students: 1334
Similarity to Occupational Classifications: 1334
Simon Says: 2029
Simple Blends: 2134
Simple Computation: 831
Simple Figure: 1454
Simple Fractions: 831
Simple Negation: 2052
Simple Phonics: 2180
Simple Questions: 1653
Simple Reaction Time: 366
Simple Responses: 716
Simple Schizophrenia: 2615
Simple Sentence Constructions: 1427
Simple Skills: 987
Simplification: 1226
Simplifying the Work Methods: 2070
Simulation: 1474
Simultaneous: 763
Simultaneous Processing: 798
Sincerity: 2776
Singing: 159, 199
Single Element Core Noun Vocabulary: 2672
Single Word Intelligibility: 209
Single Words: 1126
Singular/Plural Noun Inflection: 2662
Singular/Plural Personal Pronoun: 2662
Sitting: 1258
Sitting and Walking: 1718
Sitting Equilibrium: 1668
Sitting Posture: 1668
Situation Analysis: 2633
Situational: 2508
Situational Discourse: 1191, 1255
Situational/Inhibited: 1341
Situations: 155, 1534, 2441
Situations Involving Other People: 858, 1304
Sixes-Groupists/Relaters/Teamsters: 958
Size: 1610, 1919
Size Discrimination: 2297
Size Errors: 303
Size of Beta Cells: 1242
Size of Network: 1947
Size of the Pancreas: 1242
Size of White Blood Cells: 1242
Size Recognition: 1865, 2240
Sizes: 331
Skateboard News: 2611
Skeptical: 1211
Skepticism-Sincerity: 1845
Ski Instructor: 380
Skill: 570, 2237, 2830
Skill Development: 400
Skill Factors: 2633
Skill in Composing: 1094
Skill Level: 63
Skill Recognition: 2513
Skilled Craft: 1342
Skilled Crafts: 1177
Skilled Personal Services: 1841
Skilled Technician: 1342
Skilled Trades: 1334
Skills: 379, 1163, 1494, 2355, 2831
Skills and Interests: 158
Skills and the Ability to Calculate Intra-Achievement Discrepancies: 2901
Skills Ratings Matrix: 1719
Skimming: 901
Skipping: 1225, 2141
Sleep: 1265, 2764
Sleep and Arousal: 2147
Sleep Disorder: 77
Sleep Disturbance: 792, 1706, 1963
Sleep (General): 1488
Sleep Problems: 451, 876
Sleep-Tension (ST): 1002
Sleepy: 551
Slowing My Thought Processes: 634

Sluggish Tempo: 651
Small Business Owner: 1790
Small Group Relationships: 675, 676
Small Muscle Skills: 2043
Small Parts: 2054
Smoking Symptoms: 1181
Smooth: 1557
Smooth Administration: 909
Smooth Flow: 1850
Smoothing: 677
Snellen Test: 2606
Snowy Pictures: 1405
Sober vs. Enthusiastic: 477, 888
Sociability: 372, 1044, 1057, 1101, 1158, 1212, 1293, 1333, 1482, 1789, 1823, 1930, 1964, 2319, 2346, 2912
Sociability-Group: 1983
Sociability of Family: 1026
Sociability/Poor Peer Relations: 1340
Sociability-Specific Person: 1983
Sociable: 86, 1243, 1294, 1686, 1954, 1958, 2757
Sociable/Communicative Behaviors: 1618
Sociable-Individualistic: 1940
Social: 5, 41, 59, 80, 86, 198, 220, 397, 398, 399, 451, 453, 697, 810, 1177, 1192, 1259, 1639, 1667, 1676, 1734, 1790, 1829, 1927, 1941, 1943, 1983, 1996, 2128, 2360, 2535, 2539, 2626, 2652, 2753, 2835
Social Ability: 1210
Social Acceptability and Moderation of Behavior: 721
Social Acceptance: 2369
Social Acquiescence: 1017
Social Action: 72
Social Activator: 1317
Social Activities: 291
Social Activities with Friends: 1181
Social Activity: 2074, 2195
Social Adaptation: 77, 824
Social Adjustment: 1, 2, 65, 1246, 1618, 2461, 2525, 2605
Social Affect: 653
Social-Affective Behavior: 2459
Social-Affective Signaling: 630
Social Affiliation: 1250
Social Age: 811
Social Aggression/Conduct Disorder: 928
Social Alienation: 1686, 1698, 2510
Social Alienation (Pd4): 1697
Social Alienation (Sc1): 1697
Social Alienation-Personal Disorganization Scale: 2114
Social and Communication Skills: 1245, 1300
Social and Emotional Development: 2213
Social and Friends: 1942
Social and Intellectual Use of Language: 881
Social and Interpersonal: 2926
Social and Leisure Activities: 2442
Social and Personal: 812
Social and Recreational Activities: 1716
Social and Self Help: 234
Social Anxiety: 1341, 1587, 1730
Social Astuteness: 1333
Social Attention: 289
Social Attraction: 289
Social Avoidance: 1698
Social Avoidance (Si2): 1697
Social Awareness: 1067, 2746, 2747
Social Behavior: 1, 2, 288, 653, 657, 1388
Social Behaviour: 1066, 1260
Social Being: 2508
Social/Belonging: 1608
Social Benefits of Drug Use: 1931
Social Benefits of Use: 1932
Social Boldness: 538
Social Change: 2530
Social Comfort: 2347
Social Communication: 2204
Social Communication Skills: 2924
Social/Community Expectations: 2779, 2913
Social Competence: 651, 2322, 2446
Social Concerns/Concentration: 2214
Social Confidence: 1044, 1333, 1489, 1576, 2365
Social-Confidence: 433
Social Conformity: 1044, 1229
Social Conformity vs. Rebelliousness: 672, 673
Social Context: 1861, 2068, 2133, 2583
Social Control: 2451
Social Control/Attention-Seeking: 1340
Social Cooperation: 2036
Social Coping: 2868
Social Desirability: 1008, 1822, 1881, 1883, 1932, 2132, 2274
Social Desirability Bias: 1660, 2490
Social Detachment: 1959
Social Development: 377, 809, 1009, 1041
Social Dimension: 1045
Social Disbelief: 291
Social Discomfort: 1698
Social Discomfort (SOD): 1697
Social Distance: 2006
Social Disturbance: 537
Social Diversion: 696
Social Domain: 1478
Social Domains: 1391
Social Dysfunction: 1079, 1626
Social Ease: 698
Social Education: 63
Social Emotional: 2041, 2528
Social-Emotional: 800, 804, 806, 1039, 1230, 2342, 2767, 2778
Social/Emotional: 879, 1791, 2043
Social-Emotional Development: 887
Social Emotional Response: 2529
Social-Emotional Withdrawal/Depression: 928
Social Engagement: 1, 2, 2607
Social Environment: 2117

Social/Environmental: 1499
Social Etiquette: 1065
Social Evaluation: 950
Social Expectation: 1910
Social Expressivity: 2451
Social/Family Environmental Status: 2194
Social Function: 158, 1906
Social Functioning: 1181, 1187, 1832, 2158, 2305, 2397
Social Functioning and Resources: 1181
Social Group: 1475
Social Impact: 201
Social Imperturbability: 1698
Social Imperturbability (Pd3): 1697
Social Improvement: 136
Social Incompetence: 297, 1962
Social Independence: 2036
Social Individual: 1475
Social Ineptness: 1317
Social Insecurity : 893
Social Insensitivity: 1685
Social Insight: 438
Social Institutions: 1918
Social Integration: 909, 1369
Social Integration in School: 1181
Social Interaction: 443, 813, 1091, 1493, 1868, 2036, 2127, 2296, 2299, 2607, 2805
Social Interaction Scale [Internalizers]: 890
Social Interaction with Training: 2450
Social Interaction Without Communication: 2052
Social Interference: 291
Social-Interpersonal-Heterosexual Roles: 2389
Social Introversion: 256, 1698, 1748, 1749, 1963
Social Introversion (Si): 1697
Social Isolation: 1889, 1931, 1932, 2108, 2109
Social Isolation/Withdrawal: 2510
Social/Leadership: 895
Social Leadership Characteristics: 2622
Social/Legal/Educational: 1350
Social Maladjustment: 789, 1341
Social Manners: 1194
Social Maturity: 63, 2204, 2365
Social Nonconformity: 2115
Social Norms: 1961
Social Orientation: 728, 2763, 2776
Social Outgoingness: 945
Social/Peer-Related Self-Esteem: 746
Social Performance: 279
Social-Personal: 618
Social/Personal Behaviors: 315
Social/Personal Development: 315
Social Phobia: 77, 690, 876, 2448
Social Presence: 372
Social Pressure to Drink: 1304
Social Pressure to Use: 858, 1305
Social Problems: 225, 451, 681
Social Problems at Work: 2414
Social-Psychological Relations: 1716
Social Psychology: 1122
Social Reasoning: 1370
Social Recognition: 1965
Social-Recreational Aids: 1743
Social-Recreational Drug Use: 1931
Social Reform: 2751
Social Relations: 1204, 1493, 2805
Social Relationships: 874, 930, 1397, 2130
Social Resources: 1808
Social Resources Scales: 1495, 1496
Social Responsibility: 243
Social Responsibility (Re): 1697
Social Responsiveness: 285
Social Role: 265
Social Science: 411, 618, 762, 1094, 1334, 2483, 2484, 2882
Social Science Procedures: 570
Social Science Teacher: 1790
Social Science Theory: 684
Social Sciences: 12, 570, 905
Social Sciences and History: 502, 617
Social Self-Peers: 694
Social Sensitivity: 1044, 2451
Social Service: 371, 399, 407, 618, 1074, 1177, 1222, 1334, 1413, 1695, 1701, 1790, 2255, 2257, 2882
Social Services: 1694
Social/Sexual Adjustment: 1207, 1208
Social/Sexual Desirability Scale: 1744
Social-Sexual Relations: 748
Social Situations: 268
Social Skill Deficits: 1963
Social Skills: 60, 65, 280, 374, 1194, 1801, 1918, 1962, 2053, 2452, 2826, 2894, 2924
Social Skills and Social Thinking: 196
Social Skills Total: 2036
Social Smiling: 2450
Social/Solitary: 387
Social Sophistication: 2007
Social Standards: 374
Social Status: 280, 913, 1694, 1695, 1701, 2593
Social Studies: 121, 364, 411, 464, 570, 572, 593, 665, 684, 742, 822, 829, 904, 1318, 1418, 1657, 1838, 2026, 2654, 2735, 2740, 2742, 2901
Social Studies Perceptions: 120
Social Studies Reading: 1760
Social Studies/Sciences: 56, 621
Social Studies Vocabulary: 2712
Social Support: 698, 1825, 2789
Social Symptomatology: 1213
Social Tension: 2414
Social v. Reserved: 417
Social Withdrawal: 1522, 1960, 1963, 2036
Social Work: 1789
Social Worker: 380, 1790, 2825
Socialisation: 2088
Socialization: 1, 2, 372, 443, 465, 538, 814, 929, 1294, 1388, 1815, 2813, 2891

Socialize with Each Trainee: 2923
Socialized: 1334, 2021, 2022
Socialized Aggression: 2211
Socializer: 1915
Socially Appropriate Behavior: 268
Socially Approved Behavior: 2237
Socially Bold vs. Shy: 2417
Socially Confident: 1822
Socially Disapproved Behavior: 2237
Socially Inappropriate Behavior: 1461
Socially Maladjusted: 2287
Socially Mature-Socially Immature: 1940
Socially Offensive Behavior: 2299
Socially Unacceptable Behaviour: 1066
Socially Withdrawn: 281
Society: 749, 1785
Socio-Centric: 2887
Socio-Economic-Environmental Competence: 721
Sociocultural Scales: 2606
Sociodemographic Data: 650
Sociodemographic Factors: 73
Socioeconomic Status: 147
Socioemotional Needs: 976
Sociogram: 286
Sociolinguistic Competence: 2717
Sociological Preferences: 2181
Sociologist: 1790
Sociology: 618, 905, 1124, 2026, 2530
Sociology and Anthropology: 1044
Sociopathic-Empathetic: 218
Sociopathy: 2006
Soft: 1563
Soft C & G: 2175
Soft Palate: 276, 1852
Softness: 262
The Solar System: 684
Solemnity: 2784
Solicitousness for Welfare: 1026
Solid : 153
Solid Geometry: 2456
Solitary: 2001
Solitary Aggressive-Impulsive: 69
Solitary Aggressive-Provocative: 69
Solitary Work: 2420
Solutions: 684
Solving Daily Math Problems: 211
Solving Problems: 619, 1759, 2575
Solving Problems with the Use of Number Sentences: 1604
Solving Team Problems: 2630
Somatic: 78, 690, 927
Somatic Anxiety: 739, 1686, 2216
Somatic Behavior: 1522
Somatic Complaints: 267, 451, 1698, 1733, 1959, 2604, 2939
Somatic Complaints (Hy4): 1697
Somatic Concern: 1962, 1963
Somatic Concern-Functioning: 748
Somatic Concerns: 931, 2108, 2109
Somatic Delusions or Hallucinations: 2109
Somatic Problems: 424, 451
Somatic Symptoms: 1079, 1626
Somatic Symptoms Subscale: 1730
Somatization: 280, 335, 337, 792, 1706, 1871, 1959, 2326, 2602, 2603
Somatization Disorder: 77, 2107
Somatization of Conflict: 362
Somatoform: 1687
Somatoform Disorders: 642
Somatoform Symptoms: 2147
Somesthetic: 1907
Something Wrong: 2475
Sorting: 2134, 2439, 2441
Sorting Shells: 268
Sound: 1472, 2069
Sound Analogies: 2192
Sound and Speech Reception: 285
Sound Blending: 187, 1240, 2900, 2901
Sound Imitation: 1423
Sound-Letter Correspondence: 1659
Sound Localization: 1044
Sound-Music/Talking: 2181
Sound Patterns: 2141, 2901
Sound Production: 2669
Sound-Quiet: 2181
Sound Recognition: 364, 665, 2297
Sound-Symbol Correspondence: 1768
Sound/Symbol Inventory: 2005
Sound Value of Letters: 1529
Sounds: 84
Sounds and Images: 2755
Sounds and Letters: 165, 2484, 2488
Sounds in Isolation: 861
Sounds-in-Sentences: 1095
Sounds-in-Words: 1095
Sounds Within a Syllable Pattern: 1503
Source of Income: 2327
Source of Power: 2580
Sources: 1824
Sources of Information: 389, 1318
Sources of Power Recommendations: 2580
Sources of Stress: 701, 1949
Sources of Support Climate: 2355
Sovereign: 1451
Space: 33, 160, 348, 622, 1214, 2041
Space and Furnishings: 875, 2310
Space and Furnishings for Care and Learning: 1009
Space and Place: 1759
Space Availability: 1743
Space Form: 753
Space Relations: 838, 839, 1633
Space Visualization: 937, 2377
Spanish: 588, 608, 615, 618, 850, 918, 2026
Spanish Dominant: 720

Spanish Grammar: 684
Spanish Language: 112, 118
Spanish Listening: 589, 609
Spanish Literature: 113, 118
Spanish Reading: 589, 609
Spatial: 5, 169, 397, 412, 463, 1472, 1667, 1731, 1827, 2059, 2797, 2798, 2799
Spatial Ability: 644, 837, 2019
Spatial Analysis/Reasoning: 1430
Spatial and Computational: 199
Spatial Aptitude: 1816
Spatial Awareness: 1667
Spatial Distribution of Attention: 356
Spatial Dynamics and Dimensions: 1759
Spatial Localization: 1190
Spatial Memory: 1379, 1485, 2792
Spatial Motor Function: 158
Spatial Neglect: 1865
Spatial Organization: 877, 2596
Spatial Orientation: 1044, 1156, 1405, 2249, 2250, 2251
Spatial Orientation/Memory/Motor: 663
Spatial Orientation/Motor: 663
Spatial Perception: 1151, 1513, 1711, 1786, 2421
Spatial Perception/2-D: 2774
Spatial Perception/3-D: 2774
Spatial Problem-Solving: 1667
Spatial Processing: 1665
Spatial Reasoning: 119, 902, 2641, 2642
Spatial Recognition: 2087, 2642
Spatial Relations: 9, 208, 395, 816, 1357, 1919, 2700, 2901
Spatial Scanning: 1405
Spatial Span: 2863
Spatial Visualization: 168, 733, 1156, 1485, 1607, 1756, 2373
Speaker Score: 87
Speaking: 84, 233, 541, 619, 743, 821, 822, 985, 986, 1061, 1459, 1460, 2035, 2668, 2695
Speaking and Listening Skills: 341, 344
Speaking/Grammar: 2668
Speaking Quotient: 2694
Speaking Rate: 209
Speaking Skills: 2709
Speaking Test: 1662
Speaking/Vocabulary: 2668
Special Activities: 1921
Special Education: 684, 905, 2026
Special Education Teacher: 1790
Special Items: 1618
Special Leading: 2751
Special Letter Combinations: 917
Special Manipulations: 831
Special Needs: 452
Special Personnel: 1921
Special Problems or Handicaps: 2040
Special Report: 1785
Special Scales: 1823
Special Situations: 989
Special Sounds: 730
Specialist: 296, 420
Specialist and Educator: 2351
Specialized Process Scores: 831
Specific Academic Abilities: 1921
Specific Academic Aptitude: 1089
Specific Chemical Knowledge: 55
Specific Computer Skills: 2645
Specific Drives: 2615
Specific Phobia: 876
Specific Processing Skill Deficiencies: 869
Specific Questions: 158
Specific Questions/Clinical Hypotheses: 965
Specification: 83
Specifying Outcomes and "Terminal Behaviors" for a Course: 203
Speculative: 1205
Speech: 339, 340, 377, 494, 657, 1083, 2046, 2470, 2628
Speech and Expressive Language: 653
Speech and Language: 235, 2041, 2308
Speech and Language Production: 1066
Speech and Language Reception: 1066
Speech and Language Skills: 2213
Speech/Auditory: 1278
Speech Clarity: 1044
Speech Communication: 2026
Speech Disorders: 618
Speech Disorganization: 2108, 2109
Speech Distortion: 1190
Speech Disturbance: 2195
Speech Hearing: 1190
Speech Imitation: 234
Speech Intelligibility: 487
Speech-Interview: 1364
Speech-Language Pathology: 2026
Speech Mechanism: 2669
Speech or Debate Team: 411
Speech or Drama: 411
Speech Pathologist: 1790
Speech Rate: 763
Speech Recognition: 1044
Speech Situation Avoidance Reactions: 691
Speech Skills: 2195
Speech-Sounds Perception: 1164
Speech Survey: 2706
Speechreading: 1194
Speed: 354, 1138, 1139, 1270, 1578, 1753, 2659, 2786
Speed and Accuracy: 1835
Speed and Impatience: 1338
Speed and Skill: 1578
Speed Auditory: 1282
Speed DIAL: 809
Speed of Closure: 644, 1044, 1405
Speed of Comprehension: 2744

Speed of Information Processing: 349, 837
Speed of Limb Movement: 1044
Speed of Movement: 63
Speed of Reaction: 2605
Speed Visual: 1282
Speeded Naming: 1771
Spelling: 82, 246, 299, 322, 340, 342, 343, 349, 364, 384, 535, 644, 665, 821, 822, 823, 834, 837, 838, 839, 861, 955, 987, 1073, 1138, 1139, 1232, 1248, 1283, 1318, 1386, 1460, 1524, 1525, 1762, 1802, 1836, 1875, 1902, 2005, 2035, 2220, 2221, 2222, 2234, 2302, 2428,2 463, 2469, 2473, 2483, 2484, 2560, 2627, 2654, 2665, 2666, 2691, 2692, 2731, 2732, 2737, 2796, 2861, 2879, 2901, 2902, 2933
Spelling and Grammar: 1712
Spelling and Punctuation: 348
Spelling/Capitalization: 744
Spelling of Homophones: 2691
Spelling of Regular Single Syllable Words: 1529
Spelling of Short Vowel Words Containing Consonant Blends and Digraphs: 1529
Spelling of 2/3 Letter Words: 1529
Spelling Rules: 830
Spelling to Dictation: 199
Spelling Total Score: 2467
Spelling-Vocabulary: 535
Spiritual: 162, 1499, 1929
Spiritual Beliefs: 2034
Spiritual Guide: 1310
Spiritual Happiness: 1678
Spiritual Help: 1733
Spiritual Isolation: 1931, 1932
Spiritual Love: 1679
Spiritual/Philosophical: 697
Spiritual Values/Religion: 2358
Spirituality: 1946, 2804
Spirituality and Values: 2746, 2747
Spoken: 1534
Spoken Instructions: 445
Spoken Language: 258, 821, 822, 1232, 2123, 2668, 2676, 2695
Spoken Language Quotient: 2676, 2680, 2694
Spondee Identification: 891
Sponsor: 138, 139
Spontaneity: 637, 1939, 2614, 2850
Spontaneous: 768, 990, 1253
Spontaneous Expressive Prosody: 356
Spontaneous Flexibility: 644
Spontaneous Production: 2620
Spontaneous Speech: 207, 2873
Spontaneous Writing: 2731
Spoonerisms: 1980
Sport: 1789
Sports: 1222, 1364
Sports Activity: 2132
Sports and Games Perceptions: 120
Sports and Recreation: 1841
Spouse=Ally: 1006
Spouse/Mate Conflicts: 1313
Spouse or Partner: 1495
Spouse/Partner Influence Scale: 291
Spouse=Stressor: 1006
Spouse's Reaction: 646, 660
Spouse's Relationship with the Lover: 660
Spread Across Functions: 1551
Square: 564
Squares and Counters: 2023
Squat Pick-up: 977
ST Incongruence: 1002
Stability: 654, 945, 1251, 1294, 1660, 1928, 1929, 2767
Stability Index: 2346, 2596
Stabilizing: 83
Stable: 1294, 1676, 2757
Staff: 1276
Staff Communication/Participation: 1566
Staff Conflict: 2312
Staff Control: 637, 710, 2850
Staff Development: 216, 843, 1921, 2310
Staff Facilities: 1743
Staff Functioning: 1743
Staff Resources: 1743
Staffing : 2424
Staffing/Recruiting and Selection: 197
Stagnation: 1631
Stamina: 1044, 1334
Stamina Auditory: 1282
Stamina Visual: 1282
Stand Next to Trainee: 2923
Stand Pat: 305
Standard American English Conventions: 684
Standard Distractibility Test: 1099
Standard or Early Development: 2901
Standard Score: 2296
Standard Setting/Testing: 1147
Standard Vigilance Task: 1099
Standardized Profile Score: 2239
Standards: 1860, 2633
Standards of Excellence: 2584
Standards of Performance: 490
Standing: 1668
Standing and Walking Balance: 2377
Standing Equilibrium: 1668
Standing Height Measurement: 1062
Standing On One Foot: 1653, 1919
Standing on One Leg: 2141
Standing Out from Group: 1689
Standing-Positive Support Reaction: 1258
Standing Up From Supine: 1668
Star: 1164
Staring Episodes: 847
Stars: 684
Starting to Talk: 1528
State Anger: 2496

State Anxiety: 2497, 2498
State Mood-Total: 2499
State-Negative Mood: 2499
State-Positive Mood: 2499
States of Matter: 684
Static and Dynamic Balance: 1727
Static Balance: 1225
Static Strength: 1044
Stating Functions: 1424
Statistical Detail: 1236
Statistical Process Control: 2066
Statistician: 380
Statistics: 114, 118, 684
Statistics and Probability: 684, 2486
Statue: 1771
Status: 945, 1345, 2835
Status-Striving: 2636
Staying Learner-Centered not Information-Centered: 203
Steadiness: 1233, 1928, 2889
Steady: 1273
Steady Worker: 2605, 2648
Steel/ Metals and Materials: 2151
Stenographic Skills: 2501
Stenographic Skills Test: 973
Stereognosis: 2376
Stereognosis and Tactile Discrimination: 445
Stereognosis L: 1865
Stereognosis R: 1865
Stereotyped and Hyperactive Behavior: 1, 2
Stereotyped Behaviors: 1091
Stereotypic Messages: 2672
Stereotypy: 4
Stick Memory: 199
Stilted Speech: 2290
Stimulability: 1095, 2866
Stimulability/Inconsistency Average: 2504
Stimulability Percentage for Phonemes Tested: 2504
Stimulants: 2554
Stimulus Barrier: 912
Stimulus Complexity Ratio: 320
Stimulus Drawing Task: 855
Stimulus Mode: 320
Stimulus Number Sequencing Effects: 320
Stimulus Seeking: 963
Stimulus-Seeking: 1959
Stoichiometry: 684
Stopping of Fricatives and Affricates: 1394
Stopping of Initial Fricatives: 2438
Storage: 1058, 1383
Storage Test: 1405
Store Manager: 1790
Stories: 476, 1054, 2441
Story Completion: 2331
Story Comprehension: 565, 1055, 1659
Story Construction: 798, 2731
Story Memory: 1370, 2202, 2375
Story Problems: 2699
Story Retelling: 1420, 2596
Story Sequences: 797, 798, 1168
Story Structure: 887
Straight Copy: 2787
Straight-Forwardness: 2218
Straight Tower: 1653
Straightforwardness: 1769
Straightforwardness/Composure: 300
Strain Response: 2789
Strange: 451
Stranger Anxiety: 213
Strategic: 1443, 1549, 2385
Strategic Differences with Management: 300
Strategic Focus: 1923
Strategic Goals and Business Objectives: 638
Strategic Inquiry and Proactive Information Gathering: 2097
Strategic Orientation: 1442
Strategic Planning: 490
Strategic Reasoning: 570
Strategic Thinking: 966
Strategies: 1284
Strategist: 420
Strategy: 191, 437, 992, 1997
Strategy Efficiency Index: 2596
Strategy Use: 685
Stratigraphy/Sedimentology/Paleontology/Geomorphology and Hydrology: 1116
Strength: 1276, 1938
Strength/Endurance: 1062
Strength of Cancer Cells: 1242
Strength of Climate: 1276
Strength of Culture: 1276
Strength of Effectiveness Motivation: 910
Strength of Leadership: 490
Strength of Occupational Area: 1984
Strength of the Beta Cells: 1242
Strength of the Pancreas: 1242
Strength of White Blood Cells: 1242
Strength Quotient: 290
Strengths and Weaknesses: 158
Stress: 915, 1655, 1705, 1853, 1959, 2108, 2554, 2766, 2928
Stress Conditions : 1331
Stress Coping: 856
Stress Coping Abilities: 2061, 2284, 2285, 2783
Stress Coping Ability: 849
Stress Effects: 2512
Stress Management: 243, 1948
Stress Management EQ: 243
Stress Monitoring: 698
Stress Patterns: 1209
Stress Symptoms: 1209
Stress Symptoms Checklist: 1870
Stress Tolerance: 243, 1212, 2424
Stress Tolerance Scale: 1972

Stressful Behavior: 1684
Stressful Feelings: 1684
Stressful Thoughts: 1684
Stressors: 2512
Strict Control: 1881
Stride Jump: 1225
Stridency Deletion: 1394
Stridents: 214
String Bass: 1018
Striving for Perfection: 262
Stroke: 1853
Strong Professional Development: 2314
A Strong Set of Shared Values And Beliefs Guide Our Actions: 1858
Structural Analysis: 775
Structural Geology and Geophysics: 1116
Structural Readiness: 1859
Structure: 481, 628, 666, 945, 1444, 1470, 1930, 2069, 2688
Structure and Written Expression: 2032
Structure-Choices: 2181
Structure-Directions: 2181
Structure for Learning: 1275
Structure-Work Checked by Whom: 2181
Structure-Work Checked When: 2181
Structured: 86, 1966
Structured Group Activities: 1220
Structured Role Orientation: 2315
Structured Task or Activity Group: 268
Structured Verbal Group: 268
Structured Work Environment: 401
Structures: 348
Structuring: 698, 1251, 1443, 1549, 1929, 2385
Structuring Comments: 1867
Struggle for Independence: 1005
Stubborn: 1966
Student: 11, 2282
The Student: 1593
Student Academic Orientation: 648
Student Accomplishments: 1108, 2083
Student Activities: 648
Student Activities/Intervention in School: 2532
Student Assessment and Program Evaluation: 684
Student Behavioral Values: 648
Student Characteristics: 684
Student Discipline: 648, 2312
Student Discipline and Behavior: 843
Student Government: 411
Student Influence: 909, 2793
Student Initiative: 289
Student-Instructor Rapport: 948
Student Involvement in Learning: 216
Student Mentors: 1921
Student Observation System: 245
Student Opinions: 493
Student or Trainee: 2109
Student-Peer Relationships: 648
Student Perception of Achievement: 948
Student Perceptions: 2368
Student Personnel Services: 684
Student Rating Scales: 286
Student Ratings of Progress in Specific Objectives: 1236
Student Report Form: 649
Student Responsibility & Discipline: 648
Student Satisfaction Survey: 649
Student Satisfaction with Advising: 8
Student Satisfaction with Program: 1108, 2083
Student Self: 120, 121, 2368
Student Teacher Ratings: 2368
Student Understanding: 1275
Student's Age: 1500
Student's Appraisal: 2351
Student's Attitude About Possible Retention: 1500
Student's Instructional Mastery: 2313
Student's Sense of Control over Performance: 2313
Studio Art: 115
Studio Art (Drawing and General): 118
Study Aids: 1455, 1456
Study and Instructional Preferences: 1472
Study Anxiety: 2538
Study Attitudes: 2591
Study Conditions: 2541
Study Habits: 2591
Study Methods: 2538
Study Skills: 39, 252, 280, 348, 364, 384, 665, 2463, 2483, 2484
Study Time: 1472
Studying: 1493
Stutsman Buttoning Test: 1653
Stutsman Nested Cubes: 1653
Stutsman Picture Formboard: 1653
Stutsman Pyramid Test: 1653
Style: 992, 1752, 1997, 2691, 2731
Style Characteristics: 684
Style-Content: 131
Style Diversity: 2632
Style Effectiveness: 1436
Style Flexibility: 1436
Style of Behavior: 1824
Style/Role and Skill Shifting for Developing Versatility: 1450
Style Scores: 1874
Style/Tone: 2933
Styles of Conflict: 2546
Styles of Doing Things: 1954
Styles of Expressing Emotions: 1954
Styles of Thinking: 1954
Subaphasic: 987
Subcortical/Cerebellar/Spinal: 85
Subject: 2875
Subject and Other Complements: 2233
Subject History: 434
Subject Nouns: 1127

Subject Pronoun: 2337
Subject-Specific Goals: 2530
Subject-Verb Agreement: 1248
Subject/Verb Agreement: 1898
Subjective Depression: 1698
Subjective Depression (D1): 1697
Subjective Distortion Index: 1775
Subjective Distress: 2109
Subjective Feelings: 2130
Subjective Stress: 794
Subjective vs. Objective: 2618
Subjects of Interest: 1306
Sublimation: 78
Submissive: 86, 1243, 1685
Submissiveness: 1223, 1779
Subordinate Development: 2570, 2571
Subordinate Evaluation: 2570
Subordinate Motivation: 2570
Subordinates: 1565
Subordination-Infinitives: 1427
Substance: 674
Substance Abuse: 85, 267, 467, 569. 1006, 1313, 1587, 1729, 1766
Substance Abuse Behavior: 2551
Substance Abuse Control: 1587
Substance Abuse Disorder: 77
Substance Abuse Proneness: 1685
Substance Abuse Subscales: 1729
Substance of Abuse: 1019
Substance Use: 2147
Substance Use and Abuse: 684
Substance Use/Consumption History: 73
Substance Use Disorders: 2519
Substantiation of Allegations: 442
Substitute Uses: 1405
Substitution: 917
Substitutions: 430
Substitutions per T-Unit: 2661
Subtle Attributes: 2553
Subtle Symptoms: 2522
Subtraction: 730, 825, 831, 1392, 2134
Subtraction and Multiplication Test: 1405
Subtraction of Whole Numbers: 2486
Subtraction Sums with Numerals: 254
Subtraction Sums with Objects: 254
Success: 379, 1128
Success/Failure: 289
Success Quotient: 1210
Successful Leadership Experience: 1795
Successive: 763
Successive Processing: 798
Succorance: 68, 908, 1146, 1965, 1988
Succorant: 1243
Sufficiency v. Proliferation of Originality: 1404
Sufficient Resources: 1393
Suffixes: 917, 2175
Suggestions for Improvement: 2745
Suicidal Behavior: 2305
Suicidal Depression: 538
Suicidal Ideation: 569, 1959
Suicidal Ideation/Behavior: 2305
Suicidal Tendency: 1685
Suicidal Thinking: 1960
Suicide: 77, 2216, 2263
Suicide Ideation: 274, 2559
Suicide Orientation: 1311
Suicide Potential: 1931
Suicide Preoccupation: 2521
Suicide Risk: 1932
Suicide-Self Mutilation: 2108, 2109
Suitability for Joint Custody Checklist: 2791
Suitability for Joint Custody Interview: 2791
Sum of Incoming Negative: 1012
Sum of Incoming Positive: 1012
Sum of Negative: 1012
Sum of Negative Mild: 1012
Sum of Negative Strong: 1012
Sum of Outgoing Negative: 1012
Sum of Outgoing Positive: 1012
Sum of Positive: 1012
Sum of Positive Mild: 1012
Sum of Positive Strong: 1012
Summarizing: 647, 1147
Summary: 329, 870, 1372
Summary Judgement: 1233
Summary Risk Rating: 2395
Summary Role: 748, 2109
Summary Score: 2550
Superego: 1239, 1721, 2318
Superego plus Defense: 1239
Superior Orientation: 1437
Superior Relationship: 2570
Superiors: 1565
Superlative: 2337
Supervises Teaching: 1276
Supervision: 380, 382, 1334, 1348, 1818, 1913, 2367, 2424
Supervision and Management: 1542
Supervision Attitudes: 1972
Supervision-Human Relations: 1694, 1695, 1701
Supervision-Technical: 1694, 1695, 1701
Supervisor (Coach): 2075
Supervisor Initiation: 2571
Supervisor Support: 2917
Supervisors and Nonsupervisory Professionals: 2605
Supervisory Ability and Potential: 2572
Supervisory and Managerial Knowledge: 1032, 2002
Supervisory and Managerial Knowledges: 796
Supervisory Competencies: 1570
Supervisory Composite: 1570
Supervisory Encouragement of Creativity: 1393
Supervisory Experience and Ability: 2348
Supervisory Initiative: 1222
Supervisory Job: 1689

Supervisory Leadership: 2435, 2587
Supervisory Practices: 1568, 1569, 2605
Supine Equilibrium: 1668
Supine to Flexion Hold: 977
Supine to Stand: 977
Supplemental Addiction Measure: 2553
Supplementary: 1770
Supplementary Letter Checklist: 2905
Support: 637, 710, 807, 820, 967, 1912, 2581, 2587, 2850
Support-Child: 2242
Support Climate: 2355, 2633
Support/Development: 2933
Support for Innovation: 382
Support for Student Learning: 636, 1885, 2532, 2623
Support-Other: 2242
Support Ratio: 1939
Support Services: 648
Support Structure: 1861, 2068, 2133, 2583
Supporter: 1295
Supporting: 197, 2424
Supporting Style: 1436
Supporting Worker Participation: 2070
Supportive: 1984, 2634
Supportive Boss: 807
Supportive/Social: 1497
Supportive Work Environment: 801
Supports Faculty: 1233
Supports for Parents: 1007
Suppression Index: 320
Suprasegmental Aspects: 486
Supraspan Digit: 1454
Surface Approach: 1466, 2540
Surface Development Test: 1405
Surface Motive: 1466, 2540
Surface Strategy: 1466, 2540
Surroundings: 2915
Survey of Orofacial Structures: 2706
Survey of Phobic or Relationship Reactions: 279
Surveyor: 398, 399
Survival Skills: 1918
Suspicion: 1321
Suspicion-Persecution: 2108
Suspicion-Persecution-Hallucinations: 2109
Suspicious Temperament: 1207
Suspiciousness: 2784
Sustained: 136
Sustaining Attention and Concentration: 351
Sustaining Energy and Effort: 351
Sustentative: 2800
The Swamp-creature: 2743
Sweetheart-Spouse: 1721
Swimming: 1194
Syllabication: 917, 1060, 1073, 1768, 2254
Syllable Reduction: 214, 1394
Syllable Writing: 2180
Syllogisms: 2324
Syllogistic Reasoning: 32
Syllogistic Reasoning (Categorical): 1780
Syllogistic Reasoning (Conditional): 1780
Symbol Digit Coding Accuracy: 567
Symbol Digit Coding Delayed Recall Accuracy: 567
Symbol Digit Coding Immediate Recall Accuracy: 567
Symbol Digit Coding Thruput: 567
Symbol Discrimination: 199, 565
Symbol Number Substitution: 1920
Symbol Recognition: 1357
Symbol Search: 2860, 2862
Symbolic: 2518
Symbolic Behavior: 630
Symbolic Memory: 2792
Symbolic Quotient: 2792
Symbolic Reasoning: 902, 937
Symbolic Relations: 797, 798, 1168
Symbolism: 1242
Symbolization: 2307
Symbolization Versus Realism: 1242
Symbols: 463, 730, 1405, 2373
Symmetric Tonic Neck Reflex: 1668
Sympathetic: 305, 1954
Sympathetic Nervous System: 2508
Sympathetic vs. Indifferent: 2618
Symptom: 2508
Symptom Combinations: 2522
Symptom Dependency: 267
Symptom Intensity Measure: 1775
Symptom Onset and Resolution: 2522
Symptom Screen: 2147
Symptom Severity Rating: 2018
Symptom Severity Score: 2018
Symptoms: 2553
Syndrome Scales: 451
Synergistic: 2549, 2638
Synergistic Integration: 1938
Synergy: 1655, 1939
Synonyms: 821, 2172, 2487, 2727, 2911
Synonyms/Antonyms: 1088
Syntactic Control: 1423
Syntactic Similarities: 2712
Syntax: 628, 901, 1234, 2409, 2471, 2502, 2695, 2886
Syntax and Fluency: 346
Syntax and Sequence: 901
Syntax Matching: 861
Syntax Quotient: 2694
Synthesizer: 727
Synthetic Functions: 912
System Maintenance and Change Dimensions: 495
Systematic: 406, 768, 990, 2274
Systematic Instruction: 2530
Systematic Thinking: 2097
Systematicity: 367
Systematizing: 1688
Systemic Readiness: 1859
Systems: 2518

Systems Analyst: 380
Systems Programming Aptitude: 2609
Systems Thinking: 2929
Systolic Blood Pressure Reading: 2789

T (Task): 1843
Tables: 1042, 1043, 2787
Tachar: 264
Tactfulness: 2346
Tactical: 1443, 1549, 2385
Tactical Orientation: 1821
Tactile: 377, 1164, 1470, 1478, 2376, 2378
Tactile Concrete: 1475
Tactile Finger Recognition: 1164
Tactile Form Recognition: 1164
Tactile Functions: 1524, 1524
Tactile-Kinesthetic Development: 757
Tactile Preference: 244
Tactile Preferences: 2069
Tactile Responsiveness: 193, 2127
Tactual Orientation: 332
Tactual Performance: 1164
Tactual Preferences: 2181
Tailoring: 1990
Taking Action: 2425
Taking Charge: 262
Taking Direction: 63
Taking Disciplinary Action: 1479, 1480
Taking Initiative: 2385
Taking Notes: 2541
Taking Responsibility: 2929
Taking Risks: 401
Talent Areas: 217
Talkative: 2605, 2648
Talkative-Sell: 305
Talking About School: 715
Talking and Listening: 196
Talking Honestly and Openly About Our Relationship: 2381
Tandem Walk: 2141
Tandem Walking: 1225
Tangential: 2251
Tangentiality: 2290
Tangible: 1722
Tangible Support: 1733
Tantrums: 213
Tap Dancer: 1452
Tapping: 1533, 2728
Target: 1164, 1225
Task: 696
Task Accomplishment: 1008, 1545
Task Analysis: 1907, 1909
Task Behavior: 1147
Task Behavior/Completion: 2316
Task Behaviors: 293
Task Completion: 268
Task Environment: 1861, 2068, 2133, 2583
Task Focus: 2347
Task Incompletion: 690
Task Innovation: 1397
Task Management: 1558, 1571
Task Orientation: 294, 495, 1141, 1561, 1867, 2278, 2346, 2356, 2917, 2924
Task-Orientation: 263
Task Oriented: 1317
Task Readiness: 2415
Task-Related Behaviors: 2444
Task Skills: 1065
Task-Specific Observations: 268
Task Strategies: 1824
Task Support: 1397
Task Supports: 2316
Task Value: 1720
Tasks: 2571
Tasks and Projects: 2355
Tasks Performed by Partner: 1181
Tasks Performed by Self: 1181
Taste/Smell/Touch Response and Use: 459
Taxation: 38
Teach Politics: 138, 139
Teach the Job: 138, 139
Teacher: 810, 1310, 2825, 2875
Teacher Affiliation: 2365
Teacher Aide: 398, 399
Teacher Approval: 2591
Teacher Assessment of Fluency Digest: 691
Teacher Attitude: 2621
Teacher Behavior: 843
Teacher Control: 495
Teacher Conversation: 2001
Teacher Expectations: 216, 1275
Teacher Interactions: 2321
Teacher Involvement in Decision Making: 2314
Teacher K-12: 380
Teacher Motivated: 1470
Teacher Perceptions: 2368
Teacher Professionalism: 2026
Teacher Rank: 2890
Teacher Rating Scale: 286
Teacher Report Form: 649
Teacher Satisfaction Survey: 649
Teacher-Student Relationships: 648
Teacher Style and Dimensions of Education Validity Check: 877
Teacher Support: 495
Teacher's Aide: 411
Teachers: 210, 648, 2355, 2753
Teaching: 399, 618, 1128, 1334, 1790
Teaching and Communication: 1449
Teaching Behavior: 2312
Teaching English as a Second Language: 2026
Teaching Games: 1474
Teaching/Learning: 1878
Teaching/Learning Process: 2625

Teaching Methods/Style: 1236
Teaching Service: 1222
Teaching/Social Service: 406
Teaching Speech to Students with Language Impairments: 2026
Teaching Student Learning: 2026
Teaching Students with Emotional Disturbance: 2026
Teaching Students with Learning Disabilities: 2026
Teaching Students with Orthopedic Impairments: 2026
Teaching Students with Special Needs: 684
Teaching Students with Visual Impairments: 2026
Teaching the Child: 1918
Teaching/Training: 1788
Team: 1549, 1823
Team Assessment: 379
Team Atmosphere: 490
Team-Average: 2635
Team Builder: 1563
Team Building: 197, 1479, 1480, 2424, 2571, 2587
Team Commitment: 1860
Team Contributions: 1641
Team Coordination: 379
Team Development: 490
Team Leadership: 1573, 1923
Team Management: 1558, 1571
Team Orientation: 300
Team Orientation Index: 2346
Team Player: 37, 420, 2265, 2385
Team Relations: 2574
Team Unity: 379
Team Work: 1350
Team Worker: 296
Teambuilding: 490
Teaming: 490
Teamwork: 490, 731, 732, 1545, 2924, 2930
Teamwork Assessment: 2920
Teamwork Development: 490
Teamwork/Cooperation: 490
Technical: 305, 1177, 1443, 1549, 1819, 2264, 2385, 2833
Technical Aspects of Counseling: 684
Technical Aspects of Production: 684
Technical Checking: 1712
Technical Competence: 490
Technical Design: 618
Technical Drafting: 1792, 1794
Technical/Functional Competence: 396
Technical/Functional Expertise: 490
Technical Information: 1449
Technical Jobs: 2000
Technical/Mechanical: 5
Technical Police Knowledge: 2002
Technical Services: 1551
Technical Skills: 618
Technical Tasks: 2096
Technical Writer: 1790
Technical Writing: 762, 1334
Technician (Specialist): 2075
Technological: 2121
Technological Literacy: 2930
Technological Readiness: 1859
Technology: 1100
Technology-Civil: 416
Technology Education: 2026, 2832
Technology-Electrical: 416
Technology Management and Application: 1923
Technology-Mechanical: 416
Technology-Professional: 395, 414, 415, 417, 702, 1541
Technology Skill: 1467
Technology-Skilled: 395, 414, 415, 417, 702, 1541
Teenage Sentence Completion: 2381
Teeth: 1852
Telecommunications: 1044
Telephone: 661
Telephone Check: 857
Telephone Check on Executive Applicant: 989
Telephone Repair: 399
Telephone Repair Technician: 398
Telephone Skills: 344
Telephoning: 212
Telling Time: 211, 730
Tells Use of Objects: 347
Temperament: 1593, 2306
Temperament Comparator: 2605
Temperament for the Job: 1579
Temperature: 1470, 1472, 2069, 2181
Temperature and Hypothermia: 1066
Tempo: 1752
Temporal Judgement: 295
Temporal Orientation: 2249, 2250, 2251
Temporal-Sequential Ordering: 158
Temporary Sources of Power: 490
Temptation Situations: 1305
Tendency to Deny Blatant Pathology: 690
Tendency to Look Good or Bad: 690
Tender-Mindedness: 1769, 2218
Tense Symptom Subscale: 1730
Tense vs. Relaxed: 2417
Tension: 538, 1169, 1201, 1321, 2512
Tension-Anxiety: 2076
Tension Control: 698
Tension Index Scores: 1565
Tension Level: 490
Tension/Pressure: 490
Tension Reduction: 72
Tension Reduction Behavior: 2782
Tension Reduction Quotient: 1146
Tension/Stress Level: 490
Tentative Findings: 1777
Tenure: 1900, 1972
Termination: 1284
Terminology: 1364, 1406
Terminology Check: 2454

Test: 1405
Test Administration: 1777
Test Anxiety: 1720, 2656
Test Instruments: 920, 923, 1279, 1537, 2643, 1279
Test Item Truthfulness: 2393
Test Objectivity: 1223
Test of Quantitative Skills: 2898
Test of Verbal Skills: 2898
Test of Written English Score: 666
Test Pilot: 380
Test Strategies: 1455, 1456
Test Taking Attitude: 1372, 1766
Test-Taking Attitude: 2550
Testing and Evaluation: 2590
Testing My Conclusions: 634
Testing Personal Control: 858, 1304, 1305, 2414
Textbook Mastery: 707
Textual Reading: 2487
Texture: 1610, 1751, 1919
Texture/Material: 331
The Technology: 1593
Theater: 618
Theatre: 2026
Thematic Content Area Scores: 1961
Thematic Indicators: 467
Thematic Interpretation: 965
Theme Test: 1405
Theology: 905
Theoretical: 618, 928, 1639, 2539, 2626, 2803
Theoretical Composites: 798
Theoretical Interests: 2605
Theory-S/Theory-T: 2585
Theory Skill: 1467
Theory X-Man is Beast: 2937
Theory X (Reductive Management Beliefs): 1574
Theory X Style (Parent-Child): 1570
Theory Y (Developmental Management Beliefs): 1574
Theory Y-Man is Self-Actualizing: 2937
Theory Y Style (Adult-Adult): 1570
Theory Z-Man is Rational Being: 2937
Therapist's Attitudes to Authority: 1830
Therapy: 646, 660
Therapy and Counseling: 1044
There Must Be Hands-On Management: 1858
Thermochemistry: 684
Thermodynamics: 43
Thing Categories Test: 1405
Things: 168, 715, 1478, 2830, 2831
Things Orientation: 1163
Things/People: 387
Things-Physical: 1163
Thinker: 1331, 1915, 1950, 1951
Thinking: 812, 966, 1366, 1460, 1688, 1814, 2411, 2536
Thinking and Doing: 196
Thinking and Reasoning: 2250, 2673
Thinking Clearly and Analytically: 1570
Thinking Disorder: 256
Thinking/Feeling: 1750, 1828
Thinking Logically: 2914
Thinking Operations: 1513
Thinking Situation: 64
Thinking Style: 186, 1822
Thinking vs. Feeling: 1365, 1387, 1755
Third Pass: 2933
Third-Person Singulars: 2660
13 Scales Aggregated: 2585
Thought/Behavior Disorder: 931
Thought Disorder: 1687, 1959
Thought Disturbance: 427, 2017
Thought Interference: 2655
Thought Problems: 451, 2939
Thought Processes: 912
Thoughtfulness: 1158, 1964
Three Critical Elements: 202
3-Dimensional: 2373, 2398
3-D Blocks: 199
3D Constructions: 445
3D Copying: 2240
Three Element Combination: 2662
Threes-Achievers/Producers/Motivators: 958
Threshold: 425
Thrifty: 381
Throughout the Day: 1220
Throwing a Ball: 1653
Thumb and Finger Circle: 2141
Tic/Elimination/Sleep: 2147
Timbre: 1753
Time: 62, 63, 356, 445, 831, 883, 884, 1231, 1703, 1824, 2897, 2041, 2127, 2367
Time and Money: 1392
Time and Punctuality: 2299
Time and Staffing: 379
Time and Study Environment: 1720
Time Aspect: 1753
Time Concern: 1163
Time Distribution: 2541
Time During the Interview: 1830
Time Effectiveness: 2761
Time Emphasis: 490
Time/Energy: 439
Time for Family: 2834
Time for P.A.I.: 2728
Time-Limit Test: 2655
Time Management: 63, 443, 966, 1455, 1456, 1913, 1923, 1948, 2098, 2425, 2495
Time Management Ability: 1556
Time Management and Prioritizing: 1570
Time Management Inventory: 1403
Time Orientation: 757, 1065, 1938, 1984, 2512
Time Oriented: 1508
Time Pressure: 794
Time Ratio: 1939
Time score: 1087

Time/Sequence: 331
Time Sharing: 1044
Time-Stress Assessment: 2511
Time-Telling: 661
Time to Copy: 2227
Time Together: 1582
Time Urgency: 2592
Time Utilization: 1147
Tinnitus: 1190
Titles: 724
TLC-Expanded Composite: 2693
Tobacco: 2789
Tobacco Use Disorder: 642
Toileting: 63, 265, 377, 443, 661, 879, 1066, 1194, 1220, 2053, 2127, 2299, 2891
Toileting and Hygiene: 1041
Toileting Skills: 1065
Tolerance: 372, 654, 1333, 1928, 2346
Tolerance in Interpersonal Relations: 2420
Tolerance of Diversity: 490
Tolerance of Freedom: 1437
Tolerance of Uncertainty: 1437
Tolerance Subtask: 2527
Tolerances: 2928
Tolerant: 1294
Toleration of Loved Ones' Bothersome Aspects: 2291
Tom Cat: 305
Tonal: 90, 1287, 2056
Tonal Concepts: 1320
Tonal Imagery: 1752
Tonal Memory: 1629, 1751
Tongue: 276, 1056, 1852
Tonic Labyrinthine Prone: 1258
Tonic Labyrinthine Supine: 1258
Tool and Die Maker: 398
Tool and Die Making: 1792
Tool/Die Maker: 399
Toolmaker: 1793
Tools: 62, 1323, 1406, 2057
Tools/Machines/Material and Equipment: 2867
Tools/Material and Equipment: 2151
Tools/Materials and Equipment: 2769
Toothpicks Test: 1405
Top Leadership: 382
Top Management Support: 2096
Top Overdone Strengths: 1023
Top Strengths: 1024, 2014
Top 10 Risks of Death: 1499, 2745
Topic Development: 967
Topical Discourse: 1191, 1255
Topics: 1205
Topics Test: 1405
Topographical Recognition Memory Test: 378
Torture: 847
Total: 308, 701, 707, 793, 979, 1171, 1307, 1374, 1551, 1907, 2122, 2488, 2874
Total Achievement: 821, 822, 829, 2309
Total Adaptive: 1098
Total Adaptive Behavior: 2607
Total Adjustment: 374, 1805
Total Annualized Premiums: 421
Total Anxiety: 1730, 2214
Total Anxiety Sensitivity: 2199
Total-Area: 840
Total Auditory Memory: 1462
Total Autism-Optimism: 2318
Total Child: 1882
Total Cholesterol: 2789
Total Communication: 1877
Total Competence: 451
Total Comprehension: 1269
Total Conflict: 1721, 2318
Total Correct: 671
Total Critical Events: 2607
Total Diagnostic Test: 2651
Total Distance: 563
Total Distress Assessment: 2511
Total Dysfunctional Index: 1006
Total Effort Required: 1542
Total Emotional Behavioral Checklist: 929
Total EQ: 243
Total Error Score: 229, 1286
Total Errors: 231, 842, 1189, 2650
Total Expectation: 392
Total Extroversion: 719
Total Family Satisfaction: 1014
Total Family Violence Score: 1016
Total Fingers: 199
Total General Conceptual Ability: 837
Total Impairment: 2426
Total Incongruence Between Present and Ideal Sex-Role Behavior (C): 2161
Total Integration: 1721, 2318
Total Interaction: 268
Total Intrinsic: 1345
Total Intrusions: 470, 1644
Total Involvement: 1012
Total Items Circled: 1775
Total Items Correct: 2811
Total Language: 540, 628, 830, 2463, 2483, 2861
Total Language Quotient: 2676
Total Language Score: 2045
Total Left: 303
Total Level of Activity (S): 2161
Total Level of Risk: 2552
Total Love Scale: 2291
Total Maladaptive Behavior: 2607
Total Mathematics: 165, 1657, 2463, 2483, 2484, 2737, 2738, 2861
Total Mathematics Self-Efficacy Score: 1602
Total MIRBI Score: 1690
Total Morality Index: 439
Total Motivation: 1721
Total Negative: 1631

Total Negative Behavior: 2607
Total Nonadaptive: 1098
Total Number Correct: 2892
Total Number Correct Score: 2739
Total Number of Errors: 2892
Total Number of Words: 2661
Total Omissions: 2647
Total Parent: 1882
Total Parenting Stress: 2510
Total Pathology: 931
Total Patient Assets: 288
Total Pegs Correctly Placed: 1135
Total Percentile Rank: 81, 222, 873, 874
Total Personal Adjustment: 374
Total Personal Interest: 1721, 2318
Total Physical Child Abuse: 448
Total PMT: 208
Total Positive: 1631
Total Positive Behavior: 2607
Total Positive Self-Perception: 1002
Total Predisposition Score: 2384
Total Problem Performance: 977
Total Psychological Distress: 1733
Total Quality of Life: 2132
Total Quality Performance: 977
Total Readiness: 1977
Total Reading: 165, 1130, 1657, 1902, 2463, 2483, 2484, 2665, 2737, 2861, 2900
Total Reading-Full Scale: 2905
Total Reading-Short Scale: 2905
Total Recall: 685, 1058
Total Rehabilitation: 2196
Total Relationship-Behavior: 2415
Total Relationship Index: 210
Total Relevancy: 1542
Total Resolution: 1631
Total Response: 1790
Total Right: 303
Total Scholastic Aptitude: 838
Total-Self: 2358
Total Self-Concept: 2652
Total Self-Ideal: 1002
Total Self-Image: 1832
Total Self Score: 694
Total Sentences: 2458
Total Sexual Partners: 1433
Total Situational Stress: 2508
Total Social Adjustment: 374
Total Social Support: 1733
Total Spelling Written: 833
Total Spiritual Well-Being: 2474
Total Strategy Score: 685
Total Stress: 794, 2586
Total Suicidal Ideation: 2557
Total Symptoms: 2508
Total Task-Behavior: 2415
Total Team Effectiveness : 2634
Total Test: 1902
Total Test Language Quotient: 1283
Total Time: 842, 1135, 1164, 2647
Total Transformations: 2647
Total Variation in Present Activity Levels (K): 2161
Total Visual Memory: 1462
Total Wellness Assessment: 2511
Total Words: 2458
Total Words Correct: 1105
Total Writing: 1606, 2861
Touch: 1066
Touching/Manipulating Objects: 2450
Tough Job: 140
Tough Mindedness: 538
Tough Mindedness/Benevolence: 2160
Tough Poise: 477, 888, 1201
Tough-Minded: 86, 1822
Tough-Minded vs. Receptive: 2417
Tough-Minded vs. Tender-Minded: 477, 888
Tough-Mindedness: 1930
Toughness: 1821, 2784
Toward Education: 777
Toward People (T): 2616
Toward Teachers: 777
Tower: 1771
Toy Checklist: 1217
Tracing: 1533
Tracking: 1614
Tradition: 1724
Traditional: 1822, 1954
Traditional Limiting Disabilities: 227
Traditional Social Orientation: 2793
Traditional Values: 1333
Traditionalism: 2315
Traffic and Driving Knowledge for Drivers of Motor Trucks: 857
Trail Making: 1164
Trainee Issues: 1830
Trainer: 312
Training: 197, 1351, 1406, 2424
Training and Coaching: 2575
Training and Continuous Learning: 801
Training and Development: 945, 1542
Training and Education: 1463
Training and Support: 421
Training/Coaching/Delegating: 1570
Training Time: 1350
Trait: 2306
Trait Anger: 2496
Trait Anxiety: 1628, 2497, 2498
Trait Arousability: 1628
Trait Dominance-Submissiveness: 1628
Trait Mood-Total: 2499
Trait-Negative Mood: 2499
Trait Pleasure-Displeasure: 1628
Trait-Positive Mood: 2499
Trait Scores: 2648

Tranquility: 1928, 2804
Tranquilizers: 1931, 2554
Transaction Scores: 1565
Transactional Leadership: 1737
Transcribing Machine Operator: 2796
Transcribing Sounds: 1529
Transcription: 209
Transfer of Heat: 2884
Transformational Leadership: 1737
Transformations: 2518, 2647
Transforming: 436
Transforming Leadership Principles: 1450
Transiency: 1500
Transient Dissociative Episodes: 2521
Transition: 2001
Transitions: 807
Translating into Logical Form: 1780
Translating to Symbols: 1315
Translation: 1425
Translator: 1790
Translator/Interpreter: 380
Transport: 1818
Transportation: 63, 183, 212, 411, 1044, 1066, 1884, 2327, 2834
Transportation Aide: 2400
Transportation and Material Moving: 410
Transportation and Telephone: 1409
Transportation/Equipment Operators: 2822
Transportation Skills: 2204
Transpositions: 430, 2332
Transsituational Drug Use: 1931
Transsituational Use: 1932
Trauma/Attitudes and Beliefs Scale: 1626
Trauma Interview Schedule: 1626
Trauma Response Index: 983
Traumatic Stress: 1959, 2604
Travel: 162, 661, 1789, 1929, 2316, 2350, 2926
Travel Agent: 398, 399, 1790
Travel and Transportation: 343, 344
Traveling with Trainer: 2450
Treatment: 650, 1242, 1587
Treatment Assessment Summary: 184
Treatment Attitudes Scale: 1744
Treatment Difficulty Composite: 362
Treatment for Psychiatric Condition: 1517
Treatment Goals & Interventions: 1732
Treatment Issues Scales: 362
Treatment Plan: 184
Treatment Plans: 1830
Treatment Programs: 1313
Treatment Receptiveness: 1932
Treatment Recommendations: 442, 1649, 1777
Treatment Rejection: 1959
Tree: 564
Tremometer: 2728
Trends and Similarities: 2615
Trials to Complete First Category: 2892
Triangle: 564
Triangles: 1379
Triglyceride Level: 2789
Trigonometry: 137, 529, 684
Trombone/Baritone/French Horn: 1280
Trouble-Shooting: 2096
Trouble with the Law and Society: 1313
Truck and Bus Mechanics: 1794
Truck Driver: 398, 399
True Response Inconsistency: 1698, 2306
True Response Inconsistency (TRIN): 1697
Trumpet and Cornet: 1280
Trunk Strength: 1044
Trust: 140, 219, 490, 654, 1631, 1769, 1831, 1930, 1946, 1955, 2218, 2614
Trust in Health Care Personnel: 1733
Trust in Health Care Systems: 1733
Trust in Humanity: 1938
Trust Level: 2633
Trust vs. Defensiveness: 672, 673
Trusting: 381, 1294
Trustworthiness: 1, 2, 944, 1233, 2103, 2490
Trustworthiness Attitude: 1967
Truth: 439
Truth-Seeking: 367
Truthfulness: 19, 849, 856, 1335, 2061, 2285, 2403, 2783
Tuba and Sousaphone: 1280
Turning: 1700
Turning Against Object: 770
Turning Against Self: 770
Turning Test: 1696
Tutoring: 556
24 Hours Before: 2475
2- & 3-Dimensional Figures: 570
Two-Arm Coordination: 1711
Two Critical Elements: 202
2D Construction: 445
2 Dimensional: 2373, 2398
2-Dimensional Space: 674
Two Element Combination: 2662
Two-Hand Coordination: 1711
Two-Hand Turning and Placing: 1700
Twos-Carers/Helpers/Supporters: 958
Type: 430
Type A: 1313, 1338
Type A (TPA): 1697
Type B Behavior Pattern: 1809
Type of Work Wanted: 900
Type-Token Ratio: 2661
Types of Activities Scales: 2530
Types of Aggression: 2248
Types of Emotional Satisfaction: 1251, 1929
Types of People: 1790
Typical: 788
Typical Activities: 1593
Typical Activities/Skills: 2384

Typicalness: 2764
Typing: 1836, 2796
Typing/Keyboarding: 1692
Typing or Office Machines: 411
Typing Skill: 2765
Typing Test: 2302

U (utilizer) score: 771
UCCES Checklist: 2791
UCCES Summary Chart: 2791
Unassuming-Ingenious: 1289
Unassured-Submissive: 1289
Uncaring: 86
Uncertain: 784
Uncertainty: 86, 719, 180, 1828
Uncertainty of Perception: 297
Unclassifiable: 1427
Unclassifiable Constructions: 1427
Uncommitted: 2887
Uncommon Response: 2367
Uncontrolled: 1931, 1932
Unconventionality A-Unconventional Manipulation: 2659
Unconventionality B-Symbolic/Abstract/Fictional: 2659
Unconventionality C-Symbol-Figure-Combinations: 2659
Unconventionality D-Nonstereotypical Utilization of Given Fragments/Figures: 2659
Uncooperative Behavior: 2299
Uncooperative Mood: 1155
Uncooperativeness: 1317
Uncritical: 66
Uncriticalness: 2315
Undemonstrative vs. Excitable: 888
Under: 2928
Underachievement: 2512
Underactivity: 69
Underload Stressor Pattern/Goal-Blocked Type A: 1809
Understand Cultural Diversity: 2530
Understand the World Around Me: 2530
Understanding: 1026, 1061, 1601, 1603, 1965, 1966, 1988, 2382
Understanding and Interpreting Table and Text Material About Firefighting: 733
Understanding and Remembering Information in Lectures: 2854, 2855
Understanding and Remembering Lectures: 1505
Understanding Instructions: 2927
Understanding Literature: 570
Understanding Meaning in Conversations: 1505, 2854, 2855
Understanding Medicine Labels: 211
Understanding-Misunderstanding: 1845
Understanding Numeration Systems: 1604
Understanding of Basic Conceptual Social Science Frameworks: 1094
Understanding of Children: 1887
Understanding of Emotion: 2052
Understanding of Non-Vocal Communication: 2052
Understanding of Usage: 1094
Understanding of Vocalization and Speech: 2052
Understanding Sequence: 647
Understanding Us: 490
Understands and Deals with Racism: 1795
Undisciplined/Poor Self-Control: 1962
Undisciplined Self-Conflict vs. Controlled: 477
Undoing and Ambivalence: 2307
Undressing: 1194
Undue Suspiciousness: 1313
Unfamiliar Responsibilities: 807
Unfamiliar-Trained: 1284
Unfamiliar-Untrained: 1284
Unhappiness: 448
Unhappiness/Depression: 283, 284, 928
Unhappiness or Depression: 2287
Unhappy Percentage Estimate: 1172
Unhealthy: 701
Unilateral/Bilateral Toss: 977
Unintegrated: 1721, 2318
Unintelligible: 234
Uninvested: 467
Union-Financial-Security Skills: 2827
The United States Becomes a World Power (Spanish-American War/World War I/and Settlement 1896–1921): 146
The United States Constitution: 146
United States Government and Politics: 116
United States History: 117, 118, 645, 684, 1117
Units: 2518
Universally Endorsed: 2530
The Universe: 684
Unknown Words/Phonetic Equivalence: 322
Unobtrusiveness/Obtrusiveness: 1340
Unoccupied: 2001
Unpleasant Emotions: 858, 1304, 1305
Unpleasant Emotions/Frustrations: 2414
Unreality: 927
Unreflectiveness: 1161
Unresolved: 467
Unresolved Problems: 2242
Unruly: 1685
Unskilled: 1342
Unskilled Labor: 1222
Unsocialized: 1341
Unsocialized/Passive/Undersocialized Passive: 1341
Unstructured: 1273
Unstructured Group: 268
Untestable: 785
Unusual Experiences/Thoughts: 1313
Unusual or Repetitive Habits: 2299
Unusual Responses: 1006, 1207, 1208
Unusual Thinking: 362
Up/Down Stairs: 2316

Upbeat: 2577
Update: 1785
Updating: 83
Uplifts: 1178
Upper and Lower Case Matching: 1529
Upper Left Quadrant: 1197
Upper Right Quadrant: 1197
Upward Communication: 490
Upward Striving: 2593
Urbanism: 963
Urgent: 1273, 2121
Urges and Temptations: 1304, 2414
Urges and Temptations to Use: 858
Urges/Temptations to Use: 1305
U.S. History: 1759
U.S. Measurement: 831
Usage: 575, 602, 610, 612, 955, 1657, 2234, 2901, 2902
Usage and Expression: 1318
Usage/Mechanics: 56, 621, 992, 1997
Use and Care of Equipment and Materials: 63
Use of Amenities: 1897
Use of Capital Letters: 2234
Use of Communication Through Symbols/Signs or Speech: 2052
Use of Context: 901, 1072
Use of Erotic Materials: 1433
Use of Information: 1897
Use of Language: 1830
Use of Resources: 2423
Use of Sources of Information Composite: 1319
Use of Technology: 2645
Use of Time: 1163
Use of Tools and Materials: 1632
Use of Visual Cues: 2052
Use of Zero: 831
Useful Work Habits: 1891, 2589
Usefulness: 2237
Uses an Organizational Pattern Appropriate to Topic/Audience/Occasion and Purpose: 639
Uses and Application of Principles: 1082
Uses Language That is Appropriate to the Audience/Occasion and Purpose: 639
The Uses of Algebra: 1247
Uses of Objects: 1084
Uses Physical Behaviors that Support the Verbal Message: 639
Uses-Processes-Results: 1076
Uses Pronunciation/Grammar and Articulation Appropriate to the Designated Audience: 639
Uses Vocal Variety in Rate/Pitch and Intensity to Heighten and Maintain Interest: 639
Using a Calendar: 211
Using Appropriate Nonverbal Communication Skills: 494
Using Labor Market Information: 190
Using Language for a Variety of Purposes: 494
Using Machines-Tools-Instruments: 1343, 2925
Using Materials: 2316
Using One's Hands: 715
Using Resources: 2385
Using Science and Technology: 619
Using Statistics: 570
Using Symbols: 1315
Using Tables: 532
Using the Arts: 619
Using the Telephone: 211
Using Time Effectively: 1550
Using Word Families: 1534
Using Words: 2914
Using Your Eyes: 2914
Usual Self: 1984
Utilizing Team Member Abilities: 2630
Utilizing "Working Memory" and Assessing Recall: 351

Vacation Behavior: 2132
Valence: 320
Validity: 1687, 1963
Validity Check: 672, 2109
Validity Scale: 1983
Validity/Truthfulness Scale: 2284
Value: 1679
Value Component: 1720
Value Expectations: 2282
Value Learning for Its Own Sake: 2530
Value of Mathematics in Society: 1599
Value Orientation: 1341
Value/Philosophy: 1886
Values: 478, 1177, 1545, 1769, 2218
Values and Norms: 1008
Values Clarification: 2530
Values Classification: 2136
Values Partner: 1705
Values Self: 1705
Valuing Situation: 64
Vanity: 439
Variability of Interests: 399
Variability of Standard Errors: 679
Variable Response Inconsistency: 1698, 2306
Variable Response Inconsistency (VRIN): 1697
Variation Between Average Levels of Activity in the M and F Scores (K1): 2161
Variation Between Averages for M1 and F1 Differences in Actual and Ideal Behaviors (C1): 2161
Variation Due to Inconsistency Within M1 and F1 Categories (C2): 2161
Variety: 1030, 1216, 1493, 1694, 1695, 1701, 2588, 2804, 2805, 2928
Variety in Sentence Arrangement: 1125
Vectors: 444
Vehicle and Mobile Equipment: 410
Vehicle Safety: 1499
Velar Fronting: 1394

Velar Obstruents: 214
Vendor Evaluation: 975
Venereal Disease: 2454
Ventilation Status: 2472
Venturing: 1954
Verb: 2662
Verb Inflections: 1127
Verb Phrase: 1427
Verb Phrase Constituents: 1427
Verb Phrase + Noun Phrase: 1427
Verb + [that] + Sentence: 1427
Verb Tense: 918
Verb Tenses: 1248
Verbal: 126, 129, 199, 385, 412, 463, 547, 560, 561, 592, 664, 798, 799, 833, 895, 904, 1078, 1106, 1107, 1171, 1274, 1370, 1414, 1484, 1612, 1632, 1673, 1731, 1827, 1866, 1896, 1907, 2008, 2031, 2059, 2123, 2162, 2220, 2221, 2222, 2309, 2358, 2375, 2406, 2701, 2741, 2797, 2798, 2799, 2840, 2859, 2860, 2862, 2864, 2871
Verbal Ability: 141, 180, 644, 837, 960, 961, 1249, 1975, 2810
Verbal Aggression: 931, 1959
Verbal Aggressiveness: 1290
Verbal Agility: 199
Verbal Analogies: 309, 2192, 2901, 2902, 2904
Verbal and Motor Expressive Functions: 269
Verbal and Numeric: 128
Verbal and Quantitative Reasoning: 1873
Verbal Aptitude: 1153, 1816
Verbal Behavior: 288
Verbal Checking: 1712
Verbal Closure: 1405
Verbal Communication: 268, 459, 1383
Verbal Communicative Means: 630
Verbal Comprehension: 32, 169, 186, 349, 837, 937, 1156, 1405, 2019, 2229, 2373, 2616, 2642
Verbal Comprehension Index: 2860
Verbal Concepts: 119, 779, 2087
Verbal-Conceptual: 813
Verbal Critical Reasoning: 119, 1544, 2087
Verbal Delayed: 476
Verbal Emotional Ratio: 320
Verbal Evaluation: 735
Verbal Expression: 356, 1234, 1240
Verbal Expression of Affection: 2291
Verbal Expressive: 1907
Verbal Fluency: 345, 1771, 2007
Verbal Fluency Categories: 434
Verbal Immediate: 476
Verbal Index: 2431
Verbal Information Skills: 2333
Verbal Intelligence Quotient: 1168
Verbal Interaction: 1162
Verbal IQ: 2859
Verbal Labels: 911
Verbal Language Expression: 2628
Verbal Manners: 2824
Verbal Meaning: 670, 1973
Verbal Memory: 1613, 1644
Verbal Memory Index: 2701, 2880
Verbal Negativism: 1162
Verbal-Numerical: 2741
Verbal Oral Functioning: 2706
Verbal Orientation: 2776
Verbal Output: 2382
Verbal Paired Associates: 2863
Verbal Process: 1644
Verbal Processing: 1977, 2236
Verbal Reasoning: 186, 388, 395, 782, 838, 839, 937, 1115, 1638, 1711, 2019, 2309, 2485, 2642, 2677
Verbal Referent: 716
Verbal Relations: 2485
Verbal Repetition: 356
Verbal Response Association: 320
Verbal Risk Orientation: 1472
Verbal Scale: 798
Verbal Sequencing: 2332
Verbal Sequential: 1907
Verbal Similarities: 349
Verbal Skills: 964, 1202
Verbal Span: 1644
Verbal-Spatial: 1472
Verbal-Spatial Relations: 763
Verbal-Spatial-Cognitive: 1610
Verbal Subtest Response Style: 2802
Verbal Test: 736
Verbal Thinking: 657
Verbal Understanding: 397
Verbal Usage: 1973
Verbal Written Association Ratio: 320
Verbs: 430, 1125, 1127, 1739, 1898, 2487
Verbs and Action Commands: 2215
Verification: 1413, 2633
Verification Score: 1984
Versatility: 1395
Versus People (V): 2616
Vertical Communication: 2312
Vertical Expansion: 329
Vertical Line: 564
Vertical Word Processing: 1428
Vestibular: 2378
Veterinarian: 380, 398, 1790
Veterinary Technician: 399
View of Family Role: 2423
Views of Special Figures: 2615
Vigilance: 538
Vigilance Auditory: 1282
Vigilance Decrement: 229
Vigilance "3/5" Task: 1099
Vigilance Visual: 1282
Vigilant vs. Trusting: 2417
Vigor: 791, 1101
Vigor-Activity: 2076

Vigorous vs. Circumspect Individualism: 888
Vigorous vs. Guarded: 477
Viola: 1018
Violence: 19, 849, 1335, 2061, 2285, 2393
Violin: 1018
Visible Number Span Test: 1405
Vision: 377, 653, 1066, 1591, 1923, 1953, 2926
Vision and Looking: 2052
Vision and Strategy: 1463
Vision/Imagination: 490
Visionary: 1451
Visionary Culture Building Scales: 1438
Visionary/Inspirational: 1519
Visionary Leadership: 1438
Visionary Leadership Behavior Scales: 1438
Visionary Leadership Characteristics Scales: 1438
Visiting Erotic Locations: 1433
Visual: 359, 397, 761, 800, 815, 880, 886, 1083, 1139, 1164, 1186, 1278, 1458, 1470, 1472, 1478, 1907, 2049, 2219, 2308, 2376, 2596, 2597
Visual Ability: 1138
Visual Acuity: 663, 2420, 2606
Visual and Coordination Skills: 2420
Visual and Performing Arts: 684, 905, 2026
Visual and Spatial Perception: 1513
Visual Apprehension Span: 320
Visual Art: 1222
Visual Arts: 410, 1841
Visual Association: 1240
Visual Attention: 1771, 2889
Visual Attention and Memory: 356
Visual-Auditory: 208
Visual-Auditory Discrimination: 565
Visual-Auditory Learning: 2901, 2905
Visual Checking: 2927
Visual Closure: 816, 1240, 2628, 2724, 2901
Visual Coding: 1485
Visual Color Discrimination: 1044
Visual Competence: 2544
Visual Copying Far Point: 2428, 2469
Visual Copying Near Point: 2428, 2469
Visual Decoding: 2426
Visual Delayed: 476
Visual Design/Memory/Motor: 663
Visual Design/Motor: 663
Visual Designs Recognition: 208
Visual Designs-Sequencing: 208
Visual Discrimination: 157, 359, 446, 552, 687, 813, 1224, 1308, 1659, 2134, 2320, 2427, 2428, 2469, 2628, 2724, 2817
Visual Discrimination-Forms and Uppercase Letters: 346
Visual Discrimination-Lowercase Letters and Words: 346
Visual Discrimination-Matching Word Forms: 2434
Visual Elements and Principles: 684
Visual Estimation: 2642
Visual Fields: 1614
Visual Figure-Ground: 2628, 2724
Visual-Fine Motor: 1907, 1909
Visual Form Constancy: 2724
Visual Functioning: 663
Visual Functions: 1524, 1525
Visual Hallucinations: 2109
Visual Identification: 2049
Visual Immediate: 476
Visual Input: 2816
Visual Instructions: 445
Visual Judgement: 1837
Visual-Kinesthetic-Motor: 2219
Visual Language: 1475, 1476, 1741
Visual Language Association: 2628
Visual Language Classification: 2628
Visual/Letter Integration: 663
Visual Matching: 2900, 2901
Visual Matrix: 2596
Visual Memory: 813, 1308, 1370, 1405, 1644, 2628, 2724, 2819
Visual Memory Index: 2880
Visual Memory of Words: 861
Visual Memory/Recognition: 1529
Visual Memory/Reproduction: 1529
Visual Motor: 377, 813, 1224, 1642, 2628
Visual-Motor: 2881
Visual-Motor/Adaptive: 889
Visual Motor Coordination: 157, 1357
Visual-Motor Coordination: 552, 565, 1308
Visual-Motor Functioning: 2723
Visual-Motor Integration: 816, 916
Visual-Motor Integration Composite: 2881
Visual Motor Organization: 1513
Visual-Motor Perception: 757
Visual Motor Perception/Fine Motor: 2046
Visual Motor Skills: 347
Visual-Motor Skills: 345, 346
Visual-Motor Speed: 816
Visual Naming: 1740
Visual Numeric: 1475
Visual Numerical: 1476, 1741
Visual-Oral: 2816
Visual Ordered Recall: 1462
Visual Orientation: 332
Visual Perception: 356, 445, 778, 1171, 2134, 2528
Visual Perception and Discrimination: 1588
Visual Perception and Memory to Kinesthetic-Motor: 2427
Visual Perception-Memory: 2427, 2428
Visual Perception Memory for Words: 2469
Visual Perception Memory in Association with Kinesthetic Memory: 2469
Visual Perception-Memory with Kinesthetic Memory: 2428
Visual Perception Skills: 1308
Visual Perception Speed: 2373

Visual-Perceptual-Motor Skills: 2047
Visual-Performing Arts Abilities: 1921
Visual/Performing Arts Aptitude/Talent: 217
Visual Preference: 244
Visual Preferences: 2069
Visual Processes: 566
Visual Processing: 2236, 2901
Visual Processing/Figure-Ground: 663
Visual Processing Functions: 1905, 1908
Visual Processing Total: 1690
Visual Pursuit: 733, 937
Visual Reading: 892
Visual Reception: 1240, 1262, 1728
Visual Recognition: 364, 665, 834
Visual Reproduction: 1644, 2863
Visual Response: 459
Visual Responsiveness: 193, 2127
Visual Scanning: 1690
Visual Selective Attention: 366
Visual Selective Reminding: 2701
Visual Sequence Comparison Accuracy: 567
Visual Sequence Comparison Speed: 567
Visual Sequence Comparison Thruput: 567
Visual Sequential Memory: 157, 1240, 2134, 2701, 2724
Visual Short Term Memory: 320
Visual Skills: 813, 1529, 1707, 2434
Visual Span: 1644
Visual-Spatial: 1370, 2881
Visual/Spatial: 895
Visual-Spatial Relationships: 2724
Visual-Spatial Skills: 338
Visual Speed and Accuracy: 937, 2105
Visual Strengths: 2181
Visual-Tactile Integration: 2715
Visual to Kinesthetic-Motor: 2427
Visual Tracking: 663
Visual Unordered Recall: 1462
Visual-Visual: 208
Visual Vocal: 1642
Visual/Writing Integration: 663
Visual-Written: 2816
Visualization: 1044, 1405, 2000
Visualization and Reasoning: 1485
Visuo Motor Organization: 1336
Visuo-motor Coordination: 2134
Visuo-spatial: 2387
Visuo-Spatial Construction-Clock: 356
Visuo-Spatial Organization for Writing: 356
Visuo-Spatial Skills: 356
Visuomotor Precision: 1771
Visuospatial: 1771
Visuospatial Construction: 176
Visuospatial/Constructional: 2202
Visuosymbolic Processing: 1690
Visuoverbal Processing: 1690
Vitality: 2397
Vividness of Cancer Cells: 1242
Vividness of the Beta Cells: 1242
Vividness of the Insulin: 1242
Vividness of the Pancreas: 1242
Vividness of Treatment: 1242
Vividness of White Blood Cells: 1242
VMI: 815
Vocabulario Oral: 264
Vocabulario Sobre Dibujos: 264
Vocabulary: 82, 84, 168, 202, 239, 304, 342, 352, 364, 370, 383, 384, 389, 494, 535, 565, 665, 684, 775, 782, 901, 955, 957, 1043, 1055, 1072, 1088, 1138, 1198, 1203, 1224, 1234, 1235, 1283, 1318, 1319, 1370, 1380, 1385, 1420, 1425, 1430, 1534, 1731, 1762, 1767, 1836, 2000, 2105, 2186, 2192, 2234, 2236, 2302, 2320, 2324, 2331, 2375, 2402, 2409, 2463, 2471, 2485, 2487, 2560, 2605, 2654, 2657, 2668, 2699, 2731, 2735, 2744, 2774, 2795, 2823, 2840, 2859, 2860, 2862, 2864, 2933
Vocabulary Checklist: 1528
Vocabulary Completion: 1662
Vocabulary Comprehension: 455
Vocabulary/Grammar: 744
Vocabulary in Context: 1235
Vocabulary Inventory: 2605
Vocabulary Knowledge: 1534
Vocabulary Recognition: 1534
Vocabulary Screening: 1358
Vocabulary Skills: 39
Vocabulary Synonym: 1662
Vocabulary Test: 1405
Vocabulary/Word Recognition: 684
Vocal: 1667
Vocal Communicative Means: 630
Vocal Imitation: 2052
Vocal Tics: 876
Vocalization and Expressive Speech: 285
Vocalization of Liquids: 2438
Vocational: 343, 661, 1941, 2127
Vocational Adjustment: 2348
Vocational Adjustment Index: 2220, 2221, 2222
Vocational Agriculture Teacher: 1790
Vocational Assurance: 1223
Vocational Attitudes: 1832
Vocational Behavior: 70
Vocational-Career Abilities: 1921
Vocational Check List: 63
Vocational Environment: 2117
Vocational General Knowledge: 2026
Vocational Goals: 1050
Vocational Home Economics: 410
Vocational Identity: 1754
Vocational Interest Inventory: 2081
Vocational Orientation: 2530
Vocational Orientation and Preparation: 1492
Vocational Satisfaction: 794, 2605
Vocational Skills: 70, 635, 2579

Vocational Strain: 1825
Vocational Vocabulary: 87
Vocational-Technical: 618
Voice: 653, 1360, 2470, 2706
Voice and Speech: 1968
Voice Quality: 2471
Voicing of Initial Voiceless Obstruents: 2438
Volitional Oral Movements-Nonverbal: 164
Volitional Oral Movements-Verbal: 164
Volley: 2653
Volume: 178
Volume and Capacity: 883
Voluntary Movements: 968
Vomiting: 1853
Vowel Digraphs: 1529, 2254
Vowel/Diphthong: 2703
Vowel Diphthongs: 2180
Vowel Diphthongs and Digraphs: 827
Vowel Pronunciation: 917
Vowel Teams: 917
Vowels: 917, 1072, 1073, 1138, 2651
Vowels and Diphthongs: 486, 2332
Vowels-Long: 2487
Vowels-Short: 2487
Vowels Total: 2487
Vowels with R: 827
Voyeurism: 1744
VR Composite: 1485
Vulnerability: 2218, 2508

Wage Earner: 2109
WAI Quotient: 2912
Waiter/Waitress: 398, 399
Waiting: 2450
Walking/Toilet Training: 653
Wallin Peg Boards: 1653
Wanted: 1036
Wanting Recognition: 262
Warehousing Services: 1794
Warm Temperature: 1478
Warm vs. Reserved: 2417
Warm-Agreeable: 1289
Warmth: 538, 1201, 1769, 1959, 2218, 2784
Warning Signs: 2512
Washing: 63
Washing/Grooming: 2127
Washington's Administration Through the War of 1812: 146
Water Retention: 1647
Watts Visuo-Spatial Test: 1390
Wave Motion: 684
Weak: 153
Weak Syllable Deletion: 2438
Weakness: 1938
Wealth: 2237, 2804
Weather: 684
Weekend Activities: 158
Weight: 674, 884
Weight and Shape: 883
Weight by Height: 2606
Weights and Balances: 2616
Welder Maintenance and Operation: 2867
Welding: 1537, 1792, 1794, 2067, 2152, 2644
Welding and Mechanical: 2066
Welding and Rigging: 1637
Welding/Cutting and Arc Air Cutting: 2867
Welfare: 1818
Well-Being: 78, 372, 2237
Wellness and Disease: 684
Western Civilization: 530, 531
Western Europe Since 1945: 762
Westward Expansion: 145
Wh Question: 2337
WH-Questions: 1127
What Happened Last Night: 2611
What to Do With It: 726
What's in the House: 2029
Wheelchair: 1194
White: 1374
Whitely Index of Hypochondriasis: 1241
Whole Brain: 2545
Whole Numbers: 172
Whole Numbers and Money: 492
Whole-Part and Part-Whole Reasoning: 1780
Wide-Range Scale: 2795
Wife Abuse: 447
Wife's and Family's Role: 2348
Wife's Marriage Questions: 2885
Willing/Steady: 305
Willingness: 433
Willingness to Do Common C-Store Tasks: 2347
Willingness to Listen: 490
Win-Lose: 2549, 2638
"Winner's" Image: 1210
Winning: 1251, 1929
WISC-R: 2606
Wishes: 1049
Wishful Thinking: 72
With One Peer: 2181
With Peers: 2181
With Peers and the Teacher: 2181
With Sound: 1478
Withdrawal: 78, 280, 449, 690, 910, 927, 931, 1146, 1169, 1201, 1962, 2716, 2848
Withdrawal and Guarded Accessibility: 1219
Withdrawal-Depression: 1341
Withdrawal or Inattentive Behavior: 2299
Withdrawal-Sociable: 218
Withdrawing Tendencies: 374
Withdrawn: 86, 451, 1966, 2939
Withdrawn-Inattentive: 451
Within: 1374
Within Factor Incongruence: 1002
Within Factor Inconsistency: 1002

Within-School Referrals: 2311
Without Sound: 1478
Witnessing Trauma: 2521
Woman: 854
Woman's Ideal Man: 1536
Woman's Ideal Woman: 1535
Woman's Perception of Man's Ideal Man: 1536
Woman's Perception of Man's Ideal Woman: 1535
Women's Self-Perception: 1535
Wood-Work: 1990
Woodworking: 380, 410
Woordeskat: 2774
Word: 2516
Word Analogies: 713
Word Analysis: 339, 342, 343, 364, 370, 384, 664, 665, 823, 861, 1318, 2560, 2654
Word Analysis Skills: 2175
Word Approximations: 2290
Word Articulation: 2695
Word Association: 239, 1370
Word Associations: 540, 2297
Word Attack: 2463, 2900, 2901, 2905
Word-Attack: 1073
Word Attack Skill Analysis (c-v-c): 832
Word Attack Skill Analysis (c-v/c): 832
Word Attack Skill Analysis (Mix): 832
Word Attack Skill Analysis (Silent e): 832
Word Attack Skill Analysis (Site): 832
Word Attack Skill Analysis (v-l): 832
Word Attack Skill Analysis (v-r): 832
Word Attack Skill Analysis (v-v): 832
Word Attack Skills: 2134
Word-Auditory: 2172
Word Beginnings and Endings Test: 1405
Word Beginnings Test: 1405
Word Choice: 967, 1657
Word Classes: 540
Word Combinations: 1126
Word Completion and Verbal Fluency: 1920
Word Complexity: 2935
Word Comprehension: 1269, 2905
Word Count: 1428
Word Decoding: 2178
Word Definitions: 349, 837, 2727
Word Discrimination: 199, 1138, 1139, 1203, 2695
Word Discrimination Errors: 1139
Word Endings: 1528
Word Endings Test: 1405
Word Finding: 199, 987
Word-Finding Behaviors Index: 2726
Word Finding Profile: 2667, 2725
Word Fluency: 535, 644, 937, 1370, 1405, 2304, 2373, 2605
Word Forms: 1528
Word Generation: 2297
Word Identification: 822, 987, 2134, 2905
Word Identification Test: 891
Word Imitation: 1423
Word Inventory: 240
Word Knowledge: 180, 395, 2898
Word List: 1454
Word List Memory: 434
Word List Recall: 434
Word List Recognition: 434
Word Lists: 476, 2863
Word Matching: 356, 2691
Word Meaning: 348, 823, 1768, 2682
Word Meanings: 1712
Word Morpheme: 1427
Word-Morpheme Index: 1427
Word Opposites: 797, 798, 1168, 2727
Word Order: 1379
Word Ordering: 2694
Word Organization Control: 1423
Word Overlap: 463
Word Pairs: 463, 476, 1454, 2878
Word Parts: 2192, 2487
Word per T-Unit: 2661
Word-Picture Matching: 199
Word Problems: 2383
Word Processing: 1831
Word Processing or Typing: 411
Word Pronunciation: 1532
Word Reading: 165, 199, 349, 837, 2483, 2484, 2487, 2488
Word Reading and Comprehension: 1064
Word Recognition: 199, 342, 357, 496, 684, 823, 861, 916, 1272, 1657, 1802, 2175, 2462, 2481, 2503, 2676, 2910
Word Recognition Grade Placement: 343
Word Recognition in Context: 257, 2338
Word Recognition in Isolation: 257, 2338
Word Recognition [no distraction]: 2297
Word Recognition (Phonetic): 834
Word Recognition (Sight): 834
Word Recognition Skills: 1534
Word Recognition [with distraction]: 2297
Word Repetitions per T-Unit: 2661
Word Retrieval: 2296
Word Selective Reminding: 2701
Word-Semantic: 2172
Word Sequences: 797, 798, 1168
Word Series: 763, 2304
Word Structure: 539, 540
Word Study Skills: 2483, 2484
Word Usage: 957
Word-Visual: 2172
Word Writing: 2180
Words: 164, 628, 987, 2293, 2254
Words and Gestures: 1528
Words and Sentences: 1054, 1528
Words Children Use: 1528
Words-Flash: 1073
Words in Sentences: 2192

Words on Common Signs and Warning Labels: 344
Words per Sentence: 2458
Words/Sentences Means: 1427
Words That Begin Alike: 740
Words-to-Sounds: 2674
Words-to-Syllables: 2674
Words Total: 1427
Words-Untimed: 1073
Work: 59, 198, 1351, 1495, 2130, 2131, 2371, 2442, 2753, 2764
Work Adjustment: 938, 2926
Work Adjustment Difficulties: 1314
Work and Activities: 2216
Work and Leisure: 1409, 1961, 2327
Work Attack: 2902
Work Can Be As Much Fun As Play: 1858
Work Characteristics Domain: 1478
Work Commitment: 2007, 2916
Work Conformance: 2924
Work Driven: 1821
Work Effort Concerns: 1314
Work Environment Risk: 1932
Work Ethic: 945, 2346
Work Ethics: 2930
Work Evaluation: 1968
Work Facilitation: 490, 1545, 2587
Work for Social Causes: 2530
Work Force Focus: 1923
Work Group Profile: 1398
Work Group Supports: 1393
Work Habits: 37, 2294
Work Habits/Attitudes: 275
Work Happiness: 1678
Work Hard and Achieve: 72
Work History: 421, 2198
Work-Hobby: 1789
Work Importance: 2030
Work Interdependence: 2587
Work Interference (WRK): 1697
Work Involvement: 400, 490, 2592
Work Involving Neatness and an Eye for Colour and Shape: 1342
The Work Itself: 382
Work Methods: 2591
Work Motivation: 2490, 2924
Work Motivation Inventory: 1568
Work Motives: 1821
Work on Present Job: 1348
Work or School Behavior: 288
Work Orientation: 372, 728, 1252
Work Output: 2016
Work Performance Skills: 275, 2827
Work Persistence: 2924
Work Pressure: 2917
Work Processes: 1463
Work-Related: 2779
Work Related Behavior: 2913
Work Required: 836
Work/School: 965, 2508
Work/School Self-Concept: 1683
Work Setting: 627
Work Skills: 63, 2299
Work Skills and Concepts: 1067
Work Space: 1494
Work Stress: 1684
Work-Study Skills: 2234
Work Style: 1790, 1904
Work-Team Performance: 1913
Work Together To Get The Job Done: 1858
Work Tolerance: 2924
Work Values Scale: 1972
Workaholic: 1452
Workaholism: 2306
Worker: 2282
Worker Analysis Rating: 2781
Worker-Management Partnerships: 801
Working: 1476, 1493
Working Alone: 1163
Working Conditions: 382, 900, 1345, 1350, 1493, 1694, 1695, 1701, 2805
Working Hard: 401
Working in Teams: 2929
Working Memory for Letters: 320
Working Memory for Words: 320
Working Memory Index: 2860
Working Memory Sequencing Stimulus Number Effects: 320
Working Relationships: 2584
Working Under Hazardous Conditions: 1343, 2925
Working Under Uncomfortable Conditions: 1343, 2925
Working with Aerial and Aquatic Equipment: 1343, 2925
Working With Art-Decor Entertainment: 2925
Working with Art-Decor/Entertainment: 1343
Working With Buyers-Customers-Salespersons: 1343, 2925
Working with Data: 1350
Working with Living Things: 1342
Working With Numbers: 2914, 2927
Working with Objects: 1667
Working with People: 1163, 2350, 1667
Working with the Community: 684
Working with Things: 1350
Working with Your Hands: 1163
Workload Pressure: 1393
Workplace Appraisal: 645
The Workplace Environment: 1593
Workstyle: 186
Workstyle Graph Interpretations: 1984
Workstyle Graphs: 1984
World and U.S. History: 2026
The World Around You: 1163
World Dynamics: 162

World History: 590, 613, 615, 645, 684, 947
World Leadership (1940-Present): 146
World of Work: 260
World-of-Work Information: 405
World Outcomes: 1929
World War II: 2932
Worry: 72, 1025, 2216, 2656
Worry/Anxiety: 1006
Worry/Oversensitivity: 2214
Worrying: 1822
Worst: 1298
Wrist-Finger Speed: 1044, 1711
Write a Story: 1235
Write Your Own Story: 1235
Writer/Editor: 380
Writing: 18, 63, 159, 165, 192, 199, 233, 248, 250, 258, 304, 308, 340, 343, 356, 380, 398, 399, 406, 541, 570, 615, 619, 621, 645, 657, 666, 684, 743, 821, 822, 967, 982, 985, 986, 1064, 1167, 1235, 1237, 1418, 1421, 1425, 1426, 1459, 1460, 1524, 1525, 1662, 1759, 1790, 1826, 1923, 2026, 2035, 2127, 2241, 2309, 2484, 2528, 2668, 2903
Writing a Check and Balancing a Checkbook: 211
Writing a Phone Message: 211
Writing Ability: 1534
Writing Activities: 635
Writing and Alphabetizing: 339
Writing and Drawing Concepts: 800
Writing as a Process: 570
Writing Assessment: 2920
Writing Assignment: 684
Writing Composition: 821, 822, 2309
Writing Concepts: 887
Writing Exercise: 246
Writing Fluency: 1606, 2901, 2902
Writing from Dictation: 987
Writing From Memory: 2676
Writing/Grammar: 2668
Writing Letters: 987
Writing Letters from Dictation: 861
Writing Mechanics: 664, 1657, 2309
Writing Numbers in Sequence: 254
Writing Numbers to Dictation: 254
Writing Numerals: 987, 1357
Writing of Letters: 867
Writing of Numbers: 867
Writing Process: 664, 2933
Writing Quotient: 2676
Writing Reports: 1830
Writing Sample: 591, 614, 1638
Writing Samples: 1606, 2901, 2902
Writing Sentences: 726
Writing Skills: 621, 1066, 1194, 1838, 2031, 2676, 2742
Writing Speaking: 619
Writing Speed: 239, 2373
Writing the Alphabet (Capital): 786
Writing the Alphabet (Lower-Case): 786
Writing to Dictation: 356
Writing/Vocabulary: 2668
Written: 833, 1195, 2813
Written Composition: 2005, 2666
Written Comprehension: 1044
Written Confrontation Naming: 199
Written Directions: 1834
Written Expression: 1044, 1848, 1902, 2729, 2735, 2816, 2861, 2901, 2902
Written Expressive: 1476, 1478, 1741
Written Expressiveness: 1475
Written Instructions: 445, 964
Written Language: 821, 822, 1802, 1902, 2668, 2901, 2902
Written Language Expression: 2628
Written Language Quotient: 2935
Written Language Syntax: 2936
Written/Reading: 1667
Written Spelling: 1740
Written Work: 2316
Wrong Beginning: 1073
Wrong Ending: 1073
Wrong in Several Parts: 1073
Wrong Middle: 1073

X But Not Y: 2662

Yard Care: 661
Yes/No Question: 2337
Yes/No Questions: 356
Yield: 1557
Yield-Lose: 2549, 2638
Yielding: 1688
Yo-Yo: 1225
You Would Object: 2148
Your Effort Counts: 2633

Zoo Map: 295